MODERN FAMILY LAW

MODERN FAMILY LAW

Cases and Materials

Third Edition

D. Kelly Weisberg
Professor of Law
Hastings College of the Law
University of California

Susan Frelich Appleton
Lemma Barkeloo & Phoebe Couzins
Professor of Law
Washington University in St. Louis

ASPEN
PUBLISHERS

76 Ninth Avenue, New York, NY 10011
http://lawschool.aspenpublishers.com

Aspen Publishers
Attn: Permissions Department
76 Ninth Avenue, 7th Floor
New York, NY 10011-5201

Printed in the United States of America.

1 2 3 4 5 6 7 8 9 0

ISBN 0-7355-5610-5

Library of Congress Cataloging-in-Publication Data

Weisberg, D. Kelly.
   Modern family law / D. Kelly Weisberg, Susan Frelich Appleton. — 3rd ed.
    p. cm.
   ISBN 0-7355-5610-5
   1. Domestic relations — United States — Cases. I. Appleton, Susan Frelich, 1948–. II. Title.

KF504.W45 2006
346.7301′5 — dc22

2006019902

About Aspen Publishers

Aspen Publishers, headquartered in New York City, is a leading information provider for attorneys, business professionals, and law students. Written by preeminent authorities, our products consist of analytical and practical information covering both U.S. and international topics. We publish in the full range of formats, including updated manuals, books, periodicals, CDs, and online products.

Our proprietary content is complemented by 2,500 legal databases, containing over 11 million documents, available through our Loislaw division. Aspen Publishers also offers a wide range of topical legal and business databases linked to Loislaw's primary material. Our mission is to provide accurate, timely, and authoritative content in easily accessible formats, supported by unmatched customer care.

To order any Aspen Publishers title, go to *http://lawschool.aspenpublishers.com* or call 1-800-638-8437.

To reinstate your manual update service, call 1-800-638-8437.

For more information on Loislaw products, go to *www.loislaw.com* or call 1-800-364-2512.

For Customer Care issues, e-mail *CustomerCare@aspenpublishers.com*; call 1-800-234-1660; or fax 1-800-901-9075.

Aspen Publishers
a Wolters Kluwer business

Dedicated to

our families

Summary of Contents

Contents		*xi*
Preface		*xxix*
Introduction		*xxxiii*
Acknowledgments		*xxxv*
I.	Private Family Choices: Constitutional Protection for the Family and Its Members	1
II.	Getting Married	111
III.	Being Married: Regulation of the Intact Marriage	229
IV.	Alternative Families	361
V.	Divorce	487
VI.	Financial Consequences of Dissolution	593
VII.	Child Custody	723
VIII.	State Regulation of the Parent-Child Relationship	857
IX.	Adoption and Alternatives to Adoption	1021
Table of Cases		*1149*
Index		*1169*

Contents

Preface	*xxix*
Introduction	*xxxiii*
Acknowledgments	*xxxv*

I. Private Family Choices: Constitutional Protection for the Family and Its Members — **1**

   A. Evolution of the Right to Privacy — 1
      1. The Birth of Privacy — 1
         a. Meanings of Privacy — 1
           Griswold v. Connecticut — *1*
           Michael Grossberg, Governing the Hearth: Law and the Family in Nineteenth-Century America — 5
           Catherine G. Roraback, Griswold v. Connecticut: A Brief Case History — 6
           Notes and Questions — 9
           Eisenstadt v. Baird — *11*
           Notes and Questions — 13
           Problems — 14
         b. Roots of Privacy — 15
           Meyer v. Nebraska — *15*
           Pierce v. Society of Sisters — *16*
           Notes and Questions — 18
      2. The Growth of Privacy — 20
         a. Abortion as a Private Choice — 20

xi

	Roe v. Wade	20
	Sarah Weddington, A Question of Choice	28
	Brief for the Amici Curiae Women Who Have Had Abortions and Friends of Amici Curiae in Support of Appellees, Webster v. Reproductive Health Services	30
	Notes and Questions	31
	Kristin Luker, Abortion and the Politics of Motherhood	35
	Judith Jarvis Thomson, A Defense of Abortion	37
	Sidney Callahan, Abortion and the Sexual Agenda	39
3.	Burdens on Privacy	40
	Stenberg v. Carhart	40
	John Leland, Beyond the Slogans: Inside an Abortion Clinic	45
	Notes and Questions	48
	Problem	56
4.	The Liberation of Privacy	56
	Lawrence v. Texas	56
	Patty Reinert, Pair Proud They Could Get Sodomy Law Thrown Out	64
	Tony Mauro, A "Cultural Milestone" at the High Court: *Lawrence* Gay Attorneys Turned Out in Force to Witness *Lawrence* Arguments	65
	Notes and Questions	66
	Problem	71
B.	When Privacy Rights Conflict	72
1.	Wives and Husbands	72
	Planned Parenthood of Southeastern Pennsylvania v. Casey	72
	Notes and Questions	76
2.	Children and Parents	77
	Planned Parenthood of Northern New England v. Heed	77
	Angela Bonavoglia, Kathy's Day in Court	80
	Notes and Questions	82
	Problem	88
3.	Life and Death	90
	Cruzan v. Director, Missouri Department of Health	90
	Notes and Questions	95
	Note: The Terri Schiavo Case	99
	Problem	100
	In re A.C.	100
	Carol O'Brien, Patient's Lawyer Calls *A.C.* Case Human Sacrifice	105
	Notes and Questions	106
	Problems	108
II.	**Getting Married**	**111**
A.	Introduction: Public versus Private Dimensions of Courtship and Marriage	111

1. Courtship Patterns   111
    John Demos, A Little Commonwealth: Family Life in
        Plymouth Colony   111
    Beth L. Bailey, From Front Porch to Back Seat:
        Courtship in Twentieth-Century America   112
    Jennifer Egan, Love in the Time of No Time   113
2. The Marriage Contract   114
    Maynard v. Hill   *115*
    Henry Maine, Ancient Law   115
    Susan Moller Okin, Justice, Gender, and the Family   116
B. Preparing to Marry: Premarital Controversies   116
    1. Breach of Promise to Marry   116
        Rivkin v. Postal   *116*
        Notes and Questions   119
        Problem   122
    2. Gifts in Contemplation of Marriage   123
        Fowler v. Perry   *123*
        Notes and Questions   125
        Problems   127
C. Premarital Contracts   128
    Simeone v. Simeone   *128*
    Binek v. Binek   *132*
    Notes and Questions   135
    Problem   139
D. Getting Married: Substantive and Procedural Regulations   140
    1. Constitutional Limits on State Regulation of Entry into
        Marriage   140
        Loving v. Virginia   *140*
        Robert A. Pratt, Crossing the Color Line: A Historical
            Assessment and Personal Narrative of Loving v. Virginia   142
        Phyl Newbeck, Virginia Hasn't Always Been for Lovers:
            Interracial Marriage Bans and the Case of Richard and
            Mildred Loving   144
        Zablocki v. Redhail   *145*
        Notes and Questions on *Loving* and *Zablocki*   150
        Problems   154
        Turner v. Safley   *154*
        Sheila Isenberg, Women Who Love Men Who Kill   157
        Notes and Questions   158
        Problems   159
    2. State Regulation of Entry into the Marital Relationship   160
        a. Substantive Restrictions   160
            (i) Capacity to Marry   160
                (1) Same Sex   160
                    Goodridge v. Department of Public Health   *160*
                    David J. Garrow, Toward a More Perfect   169
                        Union
                    Notes and Questions   171
                    Problem   181

Note: Domestic Partnership Legislation 181
(2) Incest 184
In re Adoption of M. 184
Note: Void versus Voidable Distinction 186
Notes and Questions 186
Problem 188
(3) Bigamy 189
State v. Green 189
Jack Anderson, Adventures Among the 193
Polygamists
Notes and Questions 195
Elizabeth Joseph, My Husband's Nine Wives 199
Problem 200
(4) Age 201
Kirkpatrick v. District Court 201
Notes and Questions 203
Problems 207
(ii) State of Mind Restrictions: Fraud and Duress 207
Blair v. Blair 207
Notes and Questions 209
Problem 210
Note: Marriage Fraud in Immigration 211
b. Procedural Restrictions 212
(i) Licensure and Solemnization 212
Carabetta v. Carabetta 212
Harriette Cole, Jumping the Broom:
The African-American Wedding Planner 214
Ginia Bellafante, Even in Gay Circles, the
Women Want the Ring 215
Notes and Questions 215
Problems 218
(ii) Note: Procedural Variations 218
c. Informal Marriages 220
(i) Common Law Marriage 220
Jennings v. Hurt 220
Notes and Questions 223
Problems 226
(ii) The Putative Spouse Doctrine and Other
Curative Devices 227
Problem 228

III. Being Married: Regulation of the Intact Marriage 229

A. Introduction: The Changing Nature of Marriage 229
John W. Blassingame, The Slave Community: Plantation Life
in the Antebellum South 229
Theodore Caplow et al., The Quality of Marriage
in Middletown: 1924-1976 231
Adrienne Rich, Compulsory Heterosexuality and Lesbian
Existence 233

Michael Warner, Beyond Gay Marriage 234
Jessie Bernard, The Future of Marriage 234
Linda J. Waite & Maggie Gallagher, Is Her Marriage Really
  Worse Than His? 236
B. Roles and Responsibilities in Marriage 237
  1. The Common Law View 237
     William Blackstone, Commentaries 237
  2. Marital Property Regimes 238
     a. Introduction 238
     b. Common Law Disabilities 239
     c. Managerial Rules 241
  3. Duty of Support 242
     McGuire v. McGuire 242
     Notes and Questions 244
     Problem 246
     Jessie Bernard, The Good-Provider Role: Its Rise and
       Fall 246
     Note: Constitutional Limits on Sex-Stereotyped Role
       Assignments 248
  4. Names in the Family 250
     Neal v. Neal 250
     Henne v. Wright 252
     Notes and Questions 255
     Problems 258
  5. Employment 259
     Bradwell v. Illinois 259
     Notes and Questions 260
     D. Kelly Weisberg, Barred from the Bar: Women and 260
       Legal Education in the United States 1870-1890
     Note: Married Woman's Domicile 263
     Vaughn v. Lawrenceburg Power System 263
     Notes and Questions 266
     Problems 269
  6. Parenting 270
     a. Pregnancy Leave 270
        Cleveland Board of Education v. Lafleur 270
        Jo Carol Lafleur, "Go Home and Have Your Baby" 274
        California Federal Savings & Loan Association
          v. Guerra 276
        Wendy W. Williams, Equality's Riddle: Pregnancy and
          the Equal Treatment/Special Treatment Debate 279
        Notes and Questions 282
        Problems 285
     b. Balancing Work and Family 285
        Caldwell v. Holland of Texas, Inc. 285
        Family and Medical Leave Act 288
        Notes and Questions 290
        Problems 295
        Martin H. Malin, Fathers and Parental Leave 296

	Dike v. School Board	*298*
	Notes and Questions	300
	Arlie Hochschild & Ann Machung, The Second Shift	302
	Note: Work-Family Conflict Issues	303
	Problem	306
C.	Tort and Criminal Law	307
1.	Tort Actions Against Third Parties: Alienation of Affections and Criminal Conversation	307
	Jones v. Swanson	*307*
	Osborne v. Payne	*311*
	Notes and Questions	312
	Problems	314
2.	Tort Actions Between Spouses	315
a.	Interspousal Immunity Doctrine	315
	G.L. v. M.L.	*315*
	Notes and Questions	317
	Problem	320
b.	Wiretapping	320
	Glazner v. Glazner	*320*
	Notes and Questions	322
	Problems	325
3.	Domestic Violence: Wife Beating	325
a.	Introduction	325
	Richard J. Gelles & Murray A. Straus, Intimate Violence	325
	U.S. Dept. of Justice, Bureau of Justice Statistics, Family Violence Statistics Including Statistics on Strangers and Acquaintances	327
	Beverly Horsburgh, Lifting the Veil of Secrecy: Domestic Violence in the Jewish Community	328
b.	Battered Woman Syndrome	329
	Hawthorne v. State	*329*
	Dr. Lenore Walker, Terrifying Love: Why Battered Women Kill and How Society Responds	331
	Notes and Questions	333
	Problem	338
c.	Duties of Law Enforcement	339
	Town of Castle Rock v. Gonzales	*339*
	Notes and Questions	342
d.	Crimes: Marital Rape	347
	People v. Liberta	*347*
	Notes and Questions	352
	Problems	353
	Note: Property Crimes Between Spouses	354
4.	Evidentiary Privileges Arising from the Marital Relationship	354
	Trammel v. United States	*354*
	Notes and Questions	358
	Problems	359

IV. **Alternative Families**   361

   A. Constitutional Limits on Definitions of "Family"   362
      1. Is a Commune a Family?   362
         U.S. Department of Agriculture v. Moreno   *362*
         Notes and Questions   365
         Problems   368
         Vivian Hamilton, Mistaking Marriage for Social Policy   368
      2. The Extended Family   371
         Moore v. City of East Cleveland   *371*
         Notes and Questions   375
         Problem   377
   B. Cohabitation: Unmarried Couples   377
      1. Introduction   377
         Richard J. Gelles, Contemporary Families: A Sociological
           View   377
      2. Traditional Response: Criminal Sanctions   379
         Lawrence v. Texas   *379*
         Notes and Questions   379
      3. Unmarried Couples' Rights Inter Se   383
         Marvin v. Marvin   *383*
         Notes and Questions   389
         Problems   396
      4. Unmarried Couples, Third Parties, and the State   396
        a. Tort Recovery   396
           Graves v. Estabrook   *396*
           Roy A. Duddy, A Fiancée's Emotional Ordeal   400
           Notes and Questions   401
        b. Employment   405
           Shahar v. Bowers   *405*
           Postscript by Robin Shahar   409
           Notes and Questions   409
           Problem   415
        c. Health   415
           In re Guardianship of Kowalski (Kowalski III)   *415*
           Casey Charles, The Sharon Kowalski Case: Lesbian
             and Gay Rights on Trial   419
           Notes and Questions   419
           Problem   422
        d. Domestic Violence   422
           State v. Yaden   *422*
           Notes and Questions   424
           Problem   426
        e. Familial Benefits: Housing, Inheritance, Adoption   426
           Braschi v. Stahl Associates Co.   *426*
           North Dakota Fair Housing Council v. Peterson   *429*
           Notes and Questions   432
           Problems   437
           Vasquez v. Hawthorne   *438*

		Amy D. Ronner, Homophobia: In the Closet and in the Coffin	440
		Notes and Questions	441
C.		Parents' and Children's Rights in the Nonmarital Family	447
	1.	Support Rights of Nonmarital Children	448
		Clark v. Jeter	*448*
		Notes and Questions	450
		Note on Paternity Establishment	453
		Wallis v. Smith	*456*
		Notes and Questions	458
	2.	Limitations on Unmarried Parents' Rights	460
		Stanley v. Illinois	*460*
		Michael H. v. Gerald D.	*463*
		Notes and Questions	469
		Problems	477
	3.	Extending Paternity Laws to Same-Sex Couples	478
		Elisa B. v. Superior Court	*478*
		Notes and Questions	482

V. Divorce **487**

A.		Introduction	487
	1.	Divorce as a Historical Phenomenon	487
		Lawrence M. Friedman, A History of American Law	487
	2.	Divorce as a Social Phenomenon	490
		Paul Bohannon, The Six Stations of Divorce	490
	3.	Divorce as a Gender-Based Phenomenon	491
		Catherine K. Riessman, Divorce Talk: Women and Men Make Sense of Personal Relationships	492
		E. Mavis Hetherington, Marriage and Divorce American Style	493
B.		Fault-Based Grounds for Divorce	494
	1.	Adultery	494
		Lickle v. Lickle	*494*
		Notes and Questions	496
		Julie H. Hall & Frank D. Fincham, Relationship Dissolution Following Infidelity	499
		Problems	500
	2.	Cruelty	501
		Muhammad v. Muhammad	*501*
		Notes and Questions	503
		Problems	505
	3.	Desertion	505
		Reid v. Reid	*505*
		Notes and Questions	508
		Problem	509
C.		Fault-Based Defenses	510
	1.	Recrimination	510
		Parker v. Parker	*510*
		Notes and Questions	512

		2.	Condonation	512
			Haymes v. Haymes	*512*
			Notes and Questions	514
			Problem	515
			Note: Other Fault-Based Defenses	515
			Problem	516
	D.	No-Fault Divorce		516
		1.	Divorce Reform	516
			Allen M. Parkman, Good Intentions Gone Awry: No-Fault Divorce and the American Family	517
			Lynne Carol Halem, Divorce Reform: Changing Legal and Social Perspectives	519
			California Family Code §§2310, 2311, 2335	520
			Uniform Marriage and Divorce Act §§302, 305	520
			New York Domestic Relations Law §170	521
		2.	Legal Problems Raised by No-Fault Divorce	522
			a. Early Problems of No-Fault	522
			Problems	523
			b. Living Separate and Apart	523
			Bennington v. Bennington	*523*
			Notes and Questions	524
			Note: Abolition of Fault-Based Defenses	526
			c. What Role for Fault?	526
			Feltmeier v. Feltmeier	*526*
			Notes and Questions	530
			Problem	532
		3.	Assessment of the No-Fault "Revolution"	533
			a. Divorce Reform in the United States	533
			Deborah I. Rhode & Martha Minow, Reforming the Questions, Questioning the Reforms: Feminist Perspectives on Divorce Law	533
			b. Divorce Reform: The Comparative-Law Perspective	535
			Naomi Neft & Ann D. Levine, Where Women Stand: An International Report on the Status of Women in 140 Countries	535
			c. Divorce Reform: The Gay Divorce	536
			Kirk Johnson, Gay Divorce: Few Markers in This Realm	536
			Ramona Faith Oswald & Eric Clausell, Same-Sex Relationships and Their Dissolution	536
			Note: The Return of Fault	538
	E.	Access to Divorce		540
		1.	Economic Obstacles	540
			Boddie v. Connecticut	*540*
			Notes and Questions	543
			Problems	544
			Note: Pro Se Divorce	544
			Note: Social and Cultural Obstacles Surrounding Divorce	545

	2.	Access to Alternatives to Divorce	547
		Aflalo v. Aflalo	547
		Notes and Questions	550
F.	The Role of Counsel		552
	1.	Emotional Aspects of Divorce	552
		Andrew Watson, The Lawyer and His Client: The Process of Emotional Involvement	552
		Kenneth Kressel et al., Professional Intervention in Divorce: The Views of Lawyers, Psychotherapists, and Clergy	554
		Moses v. Moses	556
		Notes and Questions	557
	2.	Conflicts of Interest	559
		Florida Bar v. Dunagan	559
		Notes and Questions	561
		Problem	563
		Ethics Committee, Mississippi State Bar Opinion 80	563
		Ethics Committee, State Bar of Montana, Opinion 10	563
		Robert G. Spector, The Do's and Don'ts When One Lawyer Represents Both Parties	564
	3.	Sexual Ethics	566
		In re Tsoutsouris	566
		Notes and Questions	569
		Problems	572
G.	Divorce Jurisdiction		573
	1.	Over the Plaintiff and Defendant	573
		In re Marriage of Kimura	573
		Notes and Questions	578
		Problem	580
		Note: Jurisdiction to Terminate a Same-Sex Marriage or Domestic Partnership	580
	2.	Durational Residency Requirements	582
		Sosna v. Iowa	582
		Notes and Questions	585
	3.	Domestic Relations Exception to Diversity Jurisdiction	586
		Ankenbrandt v. Richards	586
		Notes and Questions	589
		Problems	591

VI.	**Financial Consequences of Dissolution**		**593**
A.	Introduction: The Demise of Fault?		593
B.	Property Distribution: From Title Theory to Contribution		595
	Ferguson v. Ferguson		595
	Uniform Marriage and Divorce Act §307		598
	Stephen D. Sugarman, Dividing Financial Interests on Divorce		598
	American Law Institute, Principles of the Law of Family Dissolution: Analysis and Recommendations §4.12		599

		Notes and Questions on the Theory of Property Division	600
		Problem	605
C.	Spousal Support: Theories of Need, Self-Sufficiency, and Beyond		606
		Mani v. Mani	*606*
		Uniform Marriage and Divorce Act §308	610
		American Law Institute, Principles of the Law of Family Dissolution: Analysis and Recommendations §5.04	610
		Notes and Questions on the Rationales for Postdissolution Support	611
		Problems	617
D.	"Winding Up" a Marriage: Applying Theories of Property and Support		617
	1.	Two Couples' Stories	618
		Michael v. Michael	*618*
		Rosenberg v. Rosenberg	*620*
		Notes and Questions	625
		Problem	628
	2.	Special Problems in Achieving a Fair Dissolution	629
		a. Changing Circumstances	629
		Lucas v. Lucas	*629*
		Notes and Questions	632
		b. Bankruptcy	634
		In re Werthen	*634*
		Notes and Questions	637
		Note: The Family Home	640
		c. Pensions and Employee Benefits	641
		Bender v. Bender	*641*
		Notes and Questions	646
		Problems	649
		Note: Medical Coverage Following Dissolution (COBRA)	650
		d. Investments in a Spouse's Future Success: Degrees, Earning Capacity, and Goodwill	650
		In re Marriage of Roberts	*650*
		Joan Williams, Is Coverture Dead? Beyond a New Theory of Alimony	652
		Notes and Questions	654
		Problems	658
		e. Taxation	659
		Rykiel v. Rykiel	*659*
		Notes and Questions	661
E.	Child Support		666
	1.	Parental Duties	666
		Elisa B. v. Superior Court	*666*
		Notes and Questions	666
	2.	Imposing Support Obligations: From Discretion to Guidelines	668
		Downing v. Downing	*668*

		Notes and Questions	670
		Problem	676
	3.	Postmajority Support	676
		Curtis v. Kline	*676*
		Notes and Questions	678
		Problem	681
	4.	Modification of Child Support	681
		a. Remarriage and New Families	681
		Pohlmann v. Pohlmann	*681*
		Notes and Questions	683
		b. Employment Changes	686
		Olmstead v. Ziegler	*686*
		Notes and Questions	688
		Problems	690
F.	Enforcement		691
	1.	Imprisonment: Criminal Nonsupport and Contempt of Court	691
		State v. Oakley	*691*
		David Ray Papke, State v. Oakley, Deadbeat Dads, and American Poverty	694
		Notes and Questions	695
	2.	The Transformation of Enforcement: From Private to Public Responsibility	698
		a. Traditional Approach	698
		b. Congress Intervenes	699
		c. Evaluation: "Small Change"?	702
	3.	The Challenge of Multistate Cases	703
		a. Jurisdictional Limitations on Establishing Awards	703
		Kulko v. Superior Court	*703*
		Notes and Questions	706
		Problems	708
		b. Modification and Enforcement	709
		Letellier v. Letellier	*709*
		Notes and Questions	712
G.	Separation Agreements		715
	Uniform Marriage and Divorce Act §306		716
	Notes and Questions		716
	Problem		720

VII.	**Child Custody**		**723**
A.	Introduction: Effects of Parental Divorce		723
	Elizabeth Marquardt, Between Two Worlds: The Inner Lives of Children of Divorce		724
B.	Parental Disputes Concerning Child Custody		727
	1.	Standards for Selecting the Custodial Parent: What Should Be the Standard?	727
		a. Presumptions?	727
		Devine v. Devine	*727*
		Notes and Questions	729

b.   Best Interests of the Child?   732
     (i)   Introduction   732
           Robert H. Mnookin, Child-Custody Adjudication:
              Judicial Functions in the Face of Indeterminacy   732
           Uniform Marriage and Divorce Act §402   733
     (ii) Constitutional Factors   734
           (1)   Race   734
                 Palmore v. Sidoti   *734*
                 Notes and Questions   736
                 Problems   737
           (2)   Religion   738
                 Sagar v. Sagar   *738*
                 Notes and Questions   740
                 Problem   743
     (iii) Fitness   743
           (1)   Sexual Orientation   743
                 Fulk v. Fulk   *743*
                 Notes and Questions   746
           (2)   Careers   751
                 Rowe v. Franklin   *751*
                 Notes and Questions   753
                 D. Kelly Weisberg, Professional Women and
                    the Professionalization of Motherhood:
                    Marcia Clark's Double Bind   756
           (3)   Domestic Violence   757
                 Peters-Riemers v. Riemers   *757*
                 Notes and Questions   760
                 Joan S. Meier, Domestic Violence, Child
                    Custody, and Child Protection:
                    Understanding Judicial Resistance and
                    Imagining the Solutions   764
                 Note: Physical Disability   765
c.   Joint-Custody: Presumption, Preference, or Option?   767
     Bell v. Bell   767
     Notes and Questions   769
     Eleanor E. Maccoby & Robert H. Mnookin, Dividing
        the Child: Social and Legal Dilemmas of Custody   774
     Judith G. Greenberg, Domestic Violence and the
        Danger of Joint Custody Presumptions   775
2.   Standards Governing the Noncustodial Parent: Visitation   777
a.   Restrictions on Visitation   777
     Hanke v. Hanke   777
     Notes and Questions   779
     Problems   783
b.   Denial of Visitation   784
     Turner v. Turner   784
     Notes and Questions   786
     Jessica Pearson & Nancy Thoennes, The Denial of
        Visitation Rights: A Preliminary Look at Its
        Incidence, Correlates, Antecedents and
        Consequences   788

3. Standards Governing Parent versus Non-Parent Disputes   789
   Troxel v. Granville   789
   Jones v. Boring Jones   794
   Notes and Questions   795
   Nancy D. Polikoff, This Child Does Have Two Mothers:
      Redefining Parenthood to Meet the Needs of Children
      in Lesbian-Mother and Other Nontraditional Families   806
   Problem   807
4. The Role of Special Participants   808
   a. The Child's Preference   808
      McMillen v. McMillen   808
      Notes and Questions   809
      Problem   812
   b. Representation for the Child   812
      Leary v. Leary   812
      Notes and Questions   814
   c. Role of Experts   817
      In re Rebecca B.   817
      Notes and Questions   819
5. Modification   822
   a. Standard   822
   b. Relocation   823
      Ciesluk v. Ciesluk   823
      Notes and Questions   827
      Problem   832
6. Jurisdiction and Enforcement   833
      In re Forlenza   833
      Notes and Questions on Jurisdiction and
        Enforcement   836
      Problem   843
      Note: International Child Abduction   843
C. What Process Should Govern Custody Disputes?   845
   1. The Adversary System versus Mediation Process
      Elizabeth S. Scott & Robert Emery, Child Custody
         Dispute Resolution: The Adversarial System and
         Divorce Mediation   845
      McLaughlin v. Superior Court   847
      Notes and Questions   850
   2. Coin Flipping   855
      Robert H. Mnookin, Child-Custody Adjudication:
         Judicial Functions in the Face of Indeterminacy   855

VIII. State Regulation of the Parent-Child Relationship   **857**

A. Parental Autonomy: Family Privacy Revisited   857
   1. Constitutional Doctrine and Limitations   857
      Meyer v. Nebraska   857
      Pierce v. Society of Sisters   858
      Prince v. Massachusetts   858

		Wisconsin v. Yoder	*859*
		Troxel v. Granville	*863*
		Notes and Questions	863
		Problems	866
	2.	Procedural Challenges	867
		Parham v. J.R.	*867*
		Planned Parenthood of Northern New England v. Heed	*870*
		Notes and Questions	870
		Problem	873
B.	Child Abuse and Neglect		873
	1.	Introduction	873
		a. The Paradox of Privacy	873
		James Garbarino & Gwen Gilliam, Understanding Abusive Families	873
		b. Child Abuse in Historical Perspective	874
		Peter Stevens & Marian Eide, The First Chapter of Children's Rights	874
		c. The Abusive Parent and the Abused Child	876
		Brandt Steele, Psychodynamic Factors in Child Abuse	876
		Child Maltreatment 2003: Summary of Key Findings	878
	2.	Standards for Intervention in the Family	879
		a. Defining the Threshold	879
		In re Juvenile Appeal	*879*
		Notes and Questions	883
		b. Parental Privilege to Discipline	886
		Newby v. United States	*886*
		Notes and Questions	889
		Problems	894
		c. Neglect	895
		In re A.H.	*895*
		In re Phillip B.	*899*
		Notes and Questions on Neglect	901
		Problem	907
		Note: "Baby Does," Disabled Newborns, and Medical Neglect	907
		d. Emotional Abuse and Neglect	909
		In re Shane T.	*909*
		Notes and Questions	911
		e. Sexual Abuse	914
		M.W. v. Department of Children & Family Services	*914*
		D. Kelly Weisberg, The "Discovery" of Sexual Abuse: Experts' Role in Legal Policy Formulation	917
		Notes and Questions	918
		Problems	923
	3.	Procedures	924
		a. Reporting Requirements	924
		People v. Hodges	*924*
		Notes and Questions	927

	b.	Evidentiary Issues	930
		(i) Syndrome Evidence	930
		Frenzel v. State	*930*
		Notes and Questions	934
		(ii) Privileges	936
		Baltimore City Department of Social Services v. Bouknight	*936*
		Notes and Questions	938
		Problem	940
	c.	Hearsay and the Confrontation Clause	941
		People v. Vigil	*941*
		Notes and Questions	945
4.	Dispositional Alternatives		952
	a.	Temporary Dispositions: Foster Care	952
		Smith v. Organization of Foster Families for Equality and Reform (OFFER)	*952*
		Notes and Questions	960
	b.	Liability for Selection of Disposition	966
		Deshaney v. Winnebago County Department of Social Services	*966*
		Notes and Questions	971
		Problem	972
	c.	Monitoring the Provision of Foster Care	973
		Marisol v. Giuliani	*973*
		Notes and Questions	978
	d.	Permanent Disposition: Termination of Parental Rights	981
		(i) Standard of Proof	981
		Santosky v. Kramer	*981*
		Notes and Questions	986
		Marsha Garrison, Parents' Rights v. Children's Interests: The Case of the Foster Child	988
		(ii) Reasonable Efforts Requirements	
		State ex rel. Children's Services Division v. Brady	*990*
		(iii) The Significance of Emotional Attachment	994
		In re Guardianship of J.C.	*994*
		Notes and Questions on *Brady* and *J.C.*	997
		Problem	999
C.	Children's Autonomy?		1000
1.	Emancipation		1000
	State v. C.R. & R.R.		*1000*
	Notes and Questions		1001
	Problem		1004
2.	When Can Children Sue Their Parents?		1005
	a.	Tortious Injury	1005
		Buono v. Scalia	*1005*
		Notes and Questions	1008
		Note: Childhood Sexual Abuse and Statutes of Limitations	1012
		Problem	1013

		b.	"Divorce" Actions Against Parents	1014
			Ryan v. Ryan	*1014*
			Notes and Questions	1017
			Problem	1020

IX. Adoption and Alternatives to Adoption   **1021**

A.	Background	1022
	Stephen B. Presser, The Historical Background of the	
	American Law of Adoption	1022
B.	Parental Consent to Adoption	1024
	1. Validity and Revocability	1024
	Scarpetta v. Spence-Chapin Adoption Service	*1024*
	Notes and Questions	1026
	2. Unmarried Fathers' Rights	1028
	Adoption of Kelsey S.	*1028*
	Notes and Questions	1032
	Problems	1037
C.	Choosing an Adoptive Family	1038
	1. Placement Criteria	1038
	a. Matching	1038
	In re Baby Boy C.	*1038*
	Elizabeth Bartholet, Where Do Black Children	
	Belong? The Politics of Race Matching in	
	Adoption	1042
	Dorothy Roberts, Shattered Bonds: The Color of	
	Child Welfare	1045
	Notes and Questions	1047
	b. Sexual Orientation	1051
	Lofton v. Secretary of the Department of Children and	
	Family Services	*1051*
	Notes and Questions	1056
	Problems	1059
	2. The Attorney's Role	1060
	Stark County Bar Association v. Hare	*1060*
	Notes and Questions	1063
	Note: Adoption of Children with Special Needs	1066
	3. Equitable Adoption	1067
	Estate of Ford	*1067*
	Notes and Questions	1070
	4. Jurisdiction	1073
	In re Baby Girl Clausen	*1073*
	Notes and Questions	1077
	Problem	1081
	Note: International Adoptions	1082
D.	Consequences of Adoption	1084
	1. Legal Status of the Child	1084
	2. Stepparent and Second-Parent Adoptions	1085
	Adoption of Tammy	*1085*
	Notes and Questions	1087

		3.	Secrecy versus Disclosure	1091
			a. Sealed-Record Laws	1091
			b. Law Reform	1092
			c. "Open Adoption"	1093
			Groves v. Clark	*1093*
			Notes and Questions	1095
		4.	Adoption Failure	1097
			In re Lisa Diane G.	*1097*
			Daniel Golden, When Adoption Doesn't Work . . .	1098
			Notes and Questions	1100
			Problem	1102
	E.	Alternatives to Adoption		1102
		1.	Artificial Insemination	1102
			a. Creating Traditional Families	1103
			In re Adoption of Anonymous	*1103*
			Notes and Questions	1104
			Note: The Rise of Traditional Surrogacy and the *Baby M* Case	1107
			Problems	1110
			b. Creating Nontraditional Families	1110
			Elisa B. v. Superior Court	*1110*
			Gillett-Netting v. Barnhart	*1110*
			Notes and Questions on *Elisa B.* and *Gillett-Netting*	1113
			Problems	1119
		2.	In Vitro Fertilization	1120
			a. Expanding Reproductive Privacy	1120
			Lifchez v. Hartigan	*1120*
			Notes and Questions	1122
			Problems	1127
			b. Deciding the Fate of Frozen Preembryos	1127
			A.Z. v. B.Z.	*1127*
			Notes and Questions	1130
			c. IVF's Progeny: Egg Donation, Gestational Surrogacy, and "Embryo Adoption"	1134
			K.M. v. E.G.	*1134*
			Peggy Orenstein, The Other Mother	1139
			Notes and Questions	1140
			Problems	1146
Table of Cases				*1149*
Index				*1169*

Preface

The theme of this book—the conflict between respect for privacy and deference to state authority—provides a lens for examining family law today. Each chapter of this book uses this lens to explore the actual and appropriate role of the state in family decisionmaking. Chapter I explores the constitutional underpinnings of a right to family privacy. Chapters II and III address the state's regulation of marriage before and after celebration. Chapter IV identifies the extent to which the legal system treats members of alternative families differently from, or similarly to, members of traditional families. Chapters V and VI examine state regulation of divorce, including its financial consequences, and Chapter VII examines the state's role in child custody matters. Chapter VIII explores the limits of family autonomy, emphasizing cases of child abuse and neglect. Chapter IX considers the tension between privacy and state protection arising in adoption and use of new reproductive technologies.

Modern Family Law offers valuable interdisciplinary perspectives. Family law has been heavily influenced by work in the fields of family history, psychology, sociology, social work, medicine, and philosophy. Many of the excerpts, as well as the notes and questions, incorporate these different perspectives in an attempt to shed new light on the nature of legal regulation of the family.

In addition, this book reflects an awareness of the impact that legal rules have on persons' lives. The law affects individuals in profound ways that legal abstractions cannot capture. The book attempts to reveal (through presentation of sociological and psychological research as well as narratives) the subjective experiences of family members when confronted with various socio-legal problems. The book emphasizes that family law is not just analyzed and applied—it is experienced.

Changes in the Third Edition

While preserving the basic organization and overall length of the first two editions, this major revision incorporates new material on virtually every topic previously addressed. It updates earlier developments and includes significant new state and federal legislation and case law. Recent opinions from the United States Supreme Court (Lawrence v. Texas and Castle Rock v. Gonzales) appear as principal cases. Considerable coverage is devoted to the implications of *Lawrence* for many areas of family law (such as same-sex marriage, incest, polygamy, adultery, child custody, adoption, etc.).

Major developments on same-sex marriage and domestic partnerships are incorporated throughout the entire book. The Massachusetts state supreme court case, Goodridge v. Department of Public Health, appears as a principal case. Considerable additional material focuses on the rights (state, federal, international) of same-sex partners in the areas of postdissolution support and property; inheritance law; discrimination in housing, employment, and health benefits; name changes; criminal and tort law; child custody; and regulation of adoption and assisted reproduction. A new section features the "gay divorce" and includes material on conflict-of-laws issues concerning marriage validity, the recognition of domestic partnerships, and dissolution of same-sex relationships. The coverage of same-sex relationships provides a point of departure to explore larger questions about gender roles throughout family law.

Coverage of domestic violence also has been expanded throughout. New material explores developments in tort and criminal law, the effectiveness of restraining orders, judicial responses to "mutual" acts of violence, batterers' treatment programs, supervised visitation programs, the due process implications of rebuttable presumption statutes, failure to protect, the implications of Crawford v. Washington for domestic violence prosecutions, state firearm legislation, specialized domestic violence courts, discrimination against victims of domestic violence (housing, employment), name changes to protect victims, same-sex violence, the relevance of past spousal abuse in custody decisionmaking, and the new provisions of the Violence Against Women Act.

A large number of excerpts have been added to this edition, including those that focus on women's experiences in abortion decisionmaking, the practice of online dating, the motivations of women who marry murderers, gay and lesbian marriage ceremonies, changes in marriage over time, psycho-social benefits of marriage for the individual, same-sex partners' experiences of dissolution and discrimination, the effects of adultery on the decision to divorce and post-divorce adjustment, the role of battering in child custody decisionmaking, the difficulties of enforcing child support obligations in the face of poverty, the effects of divorce on children, and a critical-race perspective on modern adoption policy. Also included are new narratives that provide background on the plaintiffs and attorneys in the landmark cases of *Lawrence* and *Goodridge*. Epilogues to principal cases have been added, updated, and expanded.

This Third Edition continues to emphasize empirical research, and it reflects a sensitivity to the influence of gender, race, and class on family law issues. It incorporates empirical data on abortion; teen pregnancy; marriage (interracial marriage, age at first marriage, rates of remarriage, and covenant marriage); domestic partnerships (reasons for and manner of dissolution, use of written agreements for dissolution and death); divorce; the increase in pro se litigants in family courts; domestic violence (restraining orders, marital rape); developmental outcomes for children of divorce as well as those of same-sex parents; children's custodial preferences; the effects of relocation on children; corporal punishment; foster care; and much more.

Like the earlier edition, this revision gives instructors considerable flexibility in designing family law courses of varying lengths and emphases. The editors have taught two-, three-, and four-unit courses based on these materials. The book can be adapted easily for shorter or longer courses. (The Teacher's Manual accompanying the book provides further pedagogical suggestions and sample syllabi.) For the problem-oriented instructor, the book includes many questions and problems, often derived from actual cases or current events.

Editorial Matters

Cases and excerpts have all been edited, often quite extensively. Most deletions are indicated by ellipses, with some exceptions: Some concurring and dissenting opinions have been eliminated; citations have been modified or eliminated; some footnotes and references have been omitted; and paragraphs have been modified, and sometimes combined, to save space and to make the selections more coherent. Brackets are used at times to indicate substantial deletions. Original footnotes in cases and excerpts are reprinted nonconsecutively throughout the book. The editors' textual footnotes are numbered consecutively and appear in brackets to differentiate them from original footnotes.

We have relied on A Uniform System of Citation (18th ed. 2005), except when that style conflicts with the publisher's style. Statutory citations are to the bound volume and supplement, if possible, rather than to the electronic version.

D. Kelly Weisberg
Susan Frelich Appleton

July 2006

Introduction

Family law explores the legal regulation of the family and its members. These members include husband, wife, parent, and child, as well as unrelated "significant others" who now form alternative families with increasing regularity.

Fundamental to family law today is the tension between respect for family privacy and deference to state authority. This conflict forms the overarching theme of this book. Specifically, the book explores the issue: How does the law allocate responsibility for decisionmaking about private family matters? A respect for privacy gives consideration to individual family members' decisional autonomy on matters that intimately affect them.

Conversely, deference to state authority recognizes that the state has important interests, such as child protection and dispute resolution, that may precipitate intervention in the family. Such concerns necessarily raise questions about the actual, as well as the appropriate, relationship of the state to the family.

Because the state accords legal protection to the family and family members, even basic definitions — what constitutes a "family" and who is a "family member" — are contested. Thus, a central issue explored throughout the book is: Which personal relationships qualify for legal protection and for what purposes?

Family law is a field in transition. Change is apparent in the evolving roles and responsibilities of family members, the definitions of a family, and the nature of legal regulation of the family and its members. The dynamic character of the field results, in part, from societal influences on family law. Over the past several decades, social developments have prompted significant changes in the field, including:

(1) the women's movement, which has led to changes in gender roles as well as public policy;

(2) the children's rights movement, which has recognized children's increased role in decisionmaking;

(3) changing sexual mores, which have resulted in the decreasing influence of morality;

(4) disillusionment with the traditional family, which has contributed to the growth of alternative family forms;

(5) dissatisfaction with traditional dispute resolution processes, which has given rise to alternative forms of dispute resolution;

(6) developments in reproductive technology, which have altered traditional methods of family formation; and

(7) the rise of the "culture wars" in the political arena, where matters of family law have become a key battleground.

All of these developments are challenging established conceptions of the family and parenthood.

Family law also reflects several important legal trends:

(1) the federalization of family law (that is, the increasing congressional role in family policy);

(2) the constitutionalization of family law (that is, the growing recognition of the constitutional dimensions of the regulation of intimate relationships); and

(3) the movement toward uniformity of state law.

These factors partly explain the changing role of the state in the contemporary regulation of the family.

Family law formerly was the exclusive domain of the states. Each state formulated and applied applicable legal rules and procedures. In the past several decades, however, Congress has enacted legislation on many issues of family life —child support, child custody, child abuse and neglect, foster care, adoption, and parental leaves, to name a few. In addition, beginning in the 1960s, the Supreme Court handed down a number of decisions that limit state regulation of the family. One of the most significant developments is the Court's recognition and expansion of the notion of privacy. Today, with the Court's membership in transition, the prospect of a change of course looms large.

Because family law primarily has been a matter of state regulation, considerable variation exists in the legal regulations applicable to the family. In an effort to bring uniformity to the field, the National Conference of Commissioners on Uniform State Laws has promulgated important model statutes (addressing marriage and divorce, premarital agreements, marital property, paternity establishment, child custody jurisdiction, spousal and child support, adoption, and the parentage of children born of new reproductive technologies). Another unifying influence is the American Law Institute (ALI), which now has completed a decade-long project to reconceptualize family law, clarifying the underlying principles and making policy recommendations to guide the states in regulating the dissolution of marriages and nontraditional family relationships.

Today's family law classes offer the challenge and excitement of exploring this rapidly changing legal landscape.

Acknowledgments

The authors would like to thank the many people who contributed to this project. Colleagues at several institutions provided helpful suggestions, including Anita Bernstein, Vivian Hamilton, Dan Keating, Laura Kessler, David Konig, Nancy Polikoff, Dorothy Roberts, Laura Rosenbury, Kate Silbaugh, Nancy Staudt, Peter Wiedenbeck, and Jenny Wriggins. We also gratefully acknowledge the support of Deans Joel Seligman, Kent Syverud, and Academic Dean Shauna Marshall, and the practical insights of Bob Appleton. Several persons skillfully helped with manuscript preparation and administrative tasks, including Stephen Lothrop and Joanne Margherita, assisted by Jo Hobbs, Beverly Owens, and Beverly Taylor.

Dorie Bertram, John Borden, Carolyn Kincaid, Mark Kloempken, and Kathie Molyneaux provided invaluable library assistance. Special thanks for research assistance are merited by Katie Annand, Laura Back, Erin Brown, Molly Kastory Carter, Lynn Combs, Amber Chrystal, Derek Deavenport, Joe Ferrucci, Erin Flynn-Rovak, Claire Hass, Tracy Jacobson, Vlad Kroll, Rosie Lazzaroto, Courtney Nash, Thai Pham, Amanda Pugh, Kate Segal, Janet Simmonds, Lisa Sofio, Sean Tamura-Sato, and Lauren Taub.

Finally, the authors extend their appreciation to Aspen staff, Jessica Barmack and Eric Holt, for their invaluable assistance, and to the anonymous reviewers for their many helpful criticisms and suggestions.

The authors would like to thank the following copyright holders for permission to excerpt their materials:

American Law Institute, Restatement (Second) of Torts (1965), Restatement of the Law of Torts: Liability for Physical Harm (Proposed Final Draft 2005), Restatement (Second) of Conflict of Laws (1971), Principles of the Law of Family Dissolution: Analysis and Recommendations (2002). Copyright © 1965,

Friedman, Lawrence M., A History of American Law, 204-208, 498-504, (1988). Abridged and reprinted with the permission of Simon & Schuster from A History of American Law by Lawrence M. Friedman. Copyright © 1973, 1985, 1988 by Lawrence M. Friedman.

Garbarino, James & Gwen Gilliam, Understanding Abusive Families, 41, 42, 44-46 (1980). Jossey-Bass, Inc., Lexington Books, Simon & Schuster Trade.

Garrison, Marsha, Parents' Rights vs. Children's Interests: The Case of the Foster Child, 22 N.Y.U. Rev. L. & Soc. Change 371, 373-396 (1996). Reprinted with permission from New York University, Review of Law and Social Change.

Garrow, David J., Toward a More Perfect Union, The New York Times Magazine, May 9, 2004 at 52. Copyright © 2004 by The New York Times. Reprinted with permission.

Gelles, Richard J., Contemporary Families, 176-178 (1995). Copyright © 1995 by Sage Publications, Inc. Reprinted by permission of Sage Publications, Inc.

Gelles, Richard J. & Murray A. Straus, Intimate Violence (1988). Reprinted by permission from Intimate Violence, by Richard J. Gelles and Murray A. Straus. Copyright © 1988 by Richard J. Gelles and Murray A. Straus.

Golden, Daniel, When Adoption Doesn't Work . . . ,The Boston Globe, June 11, 1989, Magazine at 16. Copyright © 1989 by Globe Newspaper Company. Reprinted courtesy of The Boston Globe.

Goldstein, Joseph, et al., Before the Best Interests of the Child, 3-13 (1979). Reprinted with the permission of The Free Press, A Division of Simon & Schuster, from Before the Best Interests of the Child by Joseph Goldstein, Anna Freud, Albert J. Solnit. Copyright © 1979 by The Free Press.

Greenberg, Judith G., Domestic Violence and the Danger of Joint Custody Presumptions, 25 N. Ill. U.L. Rev. 403, 407-413 (2005). Reprinted with permission from the author.

Grossberg, Michael, Governing the Hearth: Law and the Family in Nineteenth-Century America. Copyright © 1985 by the University of North Carolina Press. Used by permission of the publisher.

Halem, Lynne Carol, Divorce Reform, 238-254, 269-277 (1980). Reprinted with permission of The Free Press, a Division of Simon & Schuster, from Divorce Reform: Changing Legal and Social Perspectives by Lynne Carol Halem. Copyright © 1980 by The Free Press.

Hall, Julie H. and Frank D. Fincham, Relationship Dissolution Following Infidelity, in Handbook of Divorce and Relationship Dissolution (Mark A. Fine and John H. Harvey, eds. 2006). Copyright © 2006 by Lawrence Erlbaum Associates, Inc., Mahwah, N.J. Reprinted by permission.

Hamilton, Vivian, Mistaking Marriage for Social Policy, 11 Va. J. Soc. Pol'y & L. 207, 355-361, 368-369. Reprinted with permission.

Hetherington, E. Mavis, Marriage and Divorce American Style, The American Prospect Online (April 7, 2002). Reprinted with permission.

Hochschild, Arlie & Ann Machung, The Second Shift, from The Second Shift by Arlie Hochschild and Ann Machung. Copyright © 1989 by Arlie Hochschild. Used by permission of Viking Penguin, a division of Penguin Books USA Inc.

Horsburgh, Beverly, Lifting the Veil of Secrecy: Domestic Violence in the Jewish Community, 18 Harv. Women's L.J. 171-172 (1995). Permission granted by the

Riessman, Catherine K., Divorce Talk: Women and Men Make Sense of Personal Relationships. Copyright © 1990 by Rutgers, The State University. Reprinted by permission of Rutgers University Press.

Roberts, Dorothy, Shattered Bonds: The Color of Child Welfare, 165-172, Basic Books (2002). Reprinted with permission.

Ronner, Amy D., Homophobia: In the Closet and in the Coffin?, 21 Law & Ineq. 65, 8687 (2003). Reprinted with permission.

Roraback, Catherine G., Griswold v. Connecticut: A Brief Case History, 16 Ohio Northern University Law Review 395 (1989). Copyright 1989 by Ohio Northern University Law Review. Reprinted by permission.

Scott, Elizabeth S. & Robert Emery, Child Custody Dispute Resolution, in Psychology and Child Custody Determination: Knowledge, Roles, and Expertise, 23-28, 39-42, 45-51 (Lois A. Weithorn, ed., 1987). Reprinted from Psychology and Child Custody Determinations: Knowledge, Roles, and Expertise, edited by Lois A. Weithorn, by permission of the University of Nebraska Press. Copyright © 1987 by the University of Nebraska Press.

Spector, Robert, The Do's and Don'ts When One Lawyer Represents Both Parties, Family Advocate 16-18 (Spring 1991). Reprinted by permission of ABA Publishing.

Steele, Brandt, Psychodynamic Factors in Child Abuse, in The Battered Child 81, 81-98 (Ray E. Helfer & Ruth S. Kempe, eds., 4th ed., 1987). Reprinted with permission by The University of Chicago Press.

Stevens, Peter & Marian Eide, The First Chapter of Children's Rights, 41 American Heritage 84, 84-91 (1990). Reprinted by permission of American Heritage Magazine, a division of Forbes, Inc. Copyright © 1990 by Forbes, Inc.

Sugarman, Stephen D. & Herma Hill Kay, eds., Divorce Reform at the Crossroads, 117, 130, 139-141, 178-180, 191-199, 209-210 (Yale University Press, 1990). Copyright © 1990 by Yale University. Reprinted by permission of Yale University Press.

Thomson, Judith Jarvis, A Defense of Abortion, 1 Philosophy & Public Affairs 47 (1971). Copyright © 1971 by Princeton University Press. Reprinted by permission of Blackwell Publishing.

Uniform Adoption Act, 9 Uniform Laws Annotated (pt. IA) 11 (1999). Copyright © 1999 by the National Conference of Commissioners on Uniform State Laws and West Group. Reprinted by permission of the National Conference of Commissioners on Uniform State Laws.

Uniform Child Custody Jurisdiction Act, 9 Uniform Laws Annotated (pt. IA) 261 (1999). Copyright © 1999 by the National Conference of Commissioners on Uniform State Laws and West Group. Reprinted by permission of the National Conference of Commissioners on Uniform State Laws.

Uniform Child Custody Jurisdiction and Enforcement Act, 9 Uniform Laws Annotated (pt. IA) 649 (1999). Copyright © 1999 by the National Conference of Commissioners on Uniform State Laws and West Group. Reprinted by permission of the National Conference of Commissioners on Uniform State Laws.

Uniform Marriage and Divorce Act, 9A Uniform Laws Annotated (pt. I) 159, (pt. II) 1 (1998). Copyright © 1998 by the National Conference of Commissioners on Uniform State Laws and West Group. Reprinted by permission of the National Conference of Commissioners on Uniform State Laws.

Uniform Parentage Act, 9B Uniform Laws Annotated 295, 377 (2001) & 452 (Supp. 2005). Copyright © 2005 by the National Conference of Commissioners on Uniform State Laws and West Group. Reprinted by permission of the National Conference of Commissioners on Uniform State Laws.

Uniform Premarital Agreement Act, 9C Uniform Laws Annotated 1 (2001). Copyright © 2001 by the National Conference of Commissioners on Uniform State Laws and West Group. Reprinted by permission of the National Conference of Commissioners on Uniform State Laws.

Waite, Linda & Maggie Gallagher, Is Her Marriage Really Worse Than His?, from The Case for Marriage. Copyright © 2000 by Linda Waite and Maggie Gallagher. Used by permission of Doubleday, a division of Random House, Inc.

Walker, Lenore, Terrifying Love (1989). Copyright © 1990 by Lenore E. Auerbach Walker. Reprinted by permission of HarperCollins Publishers, Inc.

Warner, Michael, Beyond Gay Marriage, in Left Legalism/Left Critique 260 (Wendy Brown & Janey Halley, eds., 2002). Copyright © 2002 by Duke University Press. Reprinted with permission.

Watson, Andrew, The Lawyer and His Client: The Process of Emotional Involvement, Psychiatry for Lawyers (2nd ed. 1978). Reprinted by permission of International Universities Press, Inc.

Weddington, Sarah, A Question of Choice (1992). Copyright © 1992 by Sarah Weddington. Reprinted by permission.

Weisberg, D. Kelly, Barred from the Bar: Women and Legal Education in the United States 1870-1890, 28 J. Legal Educ. 485, 488-493 (1977). Reprinted with permission of Journal of Legal Education, Case Western Reserve University.

Weisberg, D. Kelly, The "Discovery" of Sexual Abuse: Experts' Role in Legal Policy Formulation, 18 U.C. Davis L. Rev. 1 (1984). Copyright © 1984 by The Regents of the University of California. Reprinted with permission.

Weisberg, D. Kelly, Professional Women and the Professionalization of Motherhood: Marcia Clark's Double Bind, 6 Hastings Women's L.J. 295, 312-319, 321-322 (1995). Copyright © 1995 by D. Kelly Weisberg. Reprinted by permission.

Williams, Joan, Is Coverture Dead? Beyond a New Theory of Alimony, 82 Georgetown Law Journal 2227 (1994). Copyright © 1994 by Joan Williams. Reprinted by permission.

Williams, Wendy W., Equality's Riddle: Pregnancy and the Equal Treatment/Special Treatment Debate, 13 N.Y.U. Rev. L. & Soc. Change 325, 333-349 (1984-1985). Reprinted with permission from NYU Review of Law & Social Change, New York University School of Law.

Younger, Judith T., Perspectives on Antenuptial Agreements; An Update, 8 Am. Acad. Matrim. Law 1, 3-4 (1992). Reprinted by permission.

I

Private Family Choices: Constitutional Protection for the Family and Its Members

A. EVOLUTION OF THE RIGHT TO PRIVACY

The Supreme Court has written often that family life belongs in a "private realm" the state cannot enter. What is the source of this limitation on state authority? Whom does it protect — family units or individual family members? What room does it leave for laws governing the family? And what does "family" mean anyhow?

1. The Birth of Privacy

a. Meanings of Privacy

■ **GRISWOLD v. CONNECTICUT**
381 U.S. 479 (1965)

Mr. Justice DOUGLAS delivered the opinion of the Court.

Appellant Griswold is Executive Director of the Planned Parenthood League of Connecticut. Appellant Buxton is a licensed physician and a professor at the Yale Medical School who served as Medical Director for the League at its Center in New Haven. [Appellants were arrested and charged with giving information, instruction, and medical advice to married persons on means of preventing conception.]

The [statute] whose constitutionality is involved . . . provides:

> Any person who uses any drug, medicinal article or instrument for the purpose of preventing conception shall be fined not less than fifty dollars or imprisoned not less than sixty days nor more than one year or be both fined and imprisoned. . . .

1

The appellants were found guilty as accessories and fined $100 each, against the claim that the accessory statute as so applied violated the Fourteenth Amendment. . . . We think that appellants have standing to raise the constitutional rights of the married people with whom they had a professional relationship. . . .

Coming to the merits, we are met with a wide range of questions that implicate the Due Process Clause of the Fourteenth Amendment. Overtones of some arguments suggest that Lochner v. New York, 198 U.S. 45 [(1905)], should be our guide. But we decline that invitation. We do not sit as a super-legislature to determine the wisdom, need, and propriety of laws that touch economic problems, business affairs, or social conditions. This law, however, operates directly on an intimate relation of husband and wife and their physician's role in one aspect of that relation.

The association of people is not mentioned in the Constitution nor in the Bill of Rights. The right to educate a child in a school of the parents' choice — whether public or private or parochial — is also not mentioned. Nor is the right to study any particular subject or any foreign language. Yet the First Amendment has been construed to include certain of those rights.

By Pierce v. Society of Sisters, [268 U.S. 510 (1925)], the right to educate one's children as one chooses is made applicable to the States by the force of the First and Fourteenth Amendments. By Meyer v. Nebraska, [262 U.S. 390 (1923)], the same dignity is given the right to study the German language in a private school. . . .

In NAACP v. Alabama, 357 U.S. 449, 462 [(1958)], we protected the "freedom to associate and privacy in one's associations," noting that freedom of association was a peripheral First Amendment right. . . . In other words, the First Amendment has a penumbra where privacy is protected from governmental intrusion. . . . Association . . . is a form of expression of opinion; and while it is not expressly included in the First Amendment its existence is necessary in making the express guarantees fully meaningful.

The foregoing cases suggest that specific guarantees in the Bill of Rights have penumbras, formed by emanations from those guarantees that help give them life and substance. See Poe v. Ullman, 367 U.S. 497, 516-522 [(1961)] (dissenting opinion). Various guarantees create zones of privacy. The right of association contained in the penumbra of the First Amendment is one, as we have seen. The Third Amendment in its prohibition against the quartering of soldiers "in any house" in time of peace without the consent of the owner is another facet of that privacy. The Fourth Amendment explicitly affirms the "right of the people to be secure in their persons, houses, papers, and effects, against unreasonable searches and seizures." The Fifth Amendment in its Self-Incrimination Clause enables the citizen to create a zone of privacy which government may not force him to surrender to his detriment. The Ninth Amendment provides: "The enumeration in the Constitution, of certain rights, shall not be construed to deny or disparage others retained by the people." . . . We have had many controversies over these penumbral rights of "privacy and repose." See, e.g., Skinner v. Oklahoma, 316 U.S. 535, 541 [(1942)]. . . .

The present case, then, concerns a relationship lying within the zone of privacy created by several fundamental constitutional guarantees. And it concerns a law which, in forbidding the use of contraceptives rather than regulating their manufacture or sale, seeks to achieve its goals by means having a maximum destructive impact upon that relationship. Such a law cannot stand in light of the familiar principle, so often applied by this Court, that a "governmental purpose to control or prevent activities constitutionally subject to state regulation may not be achieved by means which sweep unnecessarily broadly and thereby invade the area of protected freedoms." NAACP v. Alabama, 377 U.S. 288, 307 [(1964)]. Would we allow the police to search the sacred precincts of marital bedrooms for telltale signs of the use of contraceptives? The very idea is repulsive to the notions of privacy surrounding the marriage relationship.

We deal with a right of privacy older than the Bill of Rights — older than our political parties, older than our school system. Marriage is a coming together for better or for worse, hopefully enduring, and intimate to the degree of being sacred. It is an association that promotes a way of life, not causes; a harmony in living, not political faiths; a bilateral loyalty, not commercial or social projects. Yet it is an association for as noble a purpose as any involved in our prior decisions.

Reversed.

Mr. Justice GOLDBERG, whom THE CHIEF JUSTICE and Mr. Justice BRENNAN join, concurring.

I agree with the Court that Connecticut's birth-control law unconstitutionally intrudes upon the right of marital privacy. . . . I add these words to emphasize the relevance of [the Ninth] Amendment to the Court's holding. . . . The Amendment is almost entirely the work of James Madison. . . . It was proffered to quiet expressed fears that a bill of specifically enumerated rights could not be sufficiently broad to cover all essential rights and that the specific mention of certain rights would be interpreted as a denial that others were protected. . . .

. . . To hold that a right so basic and fundamental and so deep-rooted in our society as the right of privacy in marriage may be infringed because that right is not guaranteed in so many words by the first eight amendments to the Constitution is to ignore the Ninth Amendment and to give it no effect whatsoever. [T]he Ninth Amendment simply lends strong support to the view that the "liberty" protected by the Fifth and Fourteenth Amendments from infringement by the Federal Government or the States is not restricted to rights specifically mentioned in the first eight amendments. . . .

Mr. Justice HARLAN, concurring in the judgment. . . .

In my view, the proper constitutional inquiry in this case is whether this Connecticut statute infringes the Due Process Clause of the Fourteenth Amendment because the enactment violates basic values "implicit in the concept of ordered liberty," Palko v. Connecticut, 302 U.S. 319, 325 [(1937)]. For reasons stated at length in my dissenting opinion in Poe v. Ullman, [367 U.S. 497, 522 (1961)], I believe that it does. . . .

. . . Judicial self-restraint will . . . be achieved in this area, as in other constitutional areas, only by continual insistence upon respect for the teachings of history, solid recognition of the basic values that underlie our society, and wise appreciation of the great roles that the doctrines of federalism and separation of powers have played in establishing and preserving American freedoms. . . .

[In a separate concurring opinion, Justice White agrees that the statute violates the liberty protected by the Due Process Clause of the Fourteenth Amendment, questioning how the statutory ban serves the state's asserted interest in deterring illicit sexual relationships.]

Mr. Justice BLACK, with whom Mr. Justice STEWART joins, dissenting. . . .

The Court talks about a constitutional "right of privacy" as though there is some constitutional provision or provisions forbidding any law ever to be passed which might abridge the "privacy" of individuals. But there is not. . . . I like my privacy as well as the next one, but I am nevertheless compelled to admit that government has a right to invade it unless prohibited by some specific constitutional provision. . . .

My Brother Goldberg has adopted the recent discovery[12] that the Ninth Amendment as well as the Due Process Clause can be used by this Court as authority to strike down all state legislation which this Court thinks violates "fundamental principles of liberty and justice," or is contrary to the "traditions and [collective] conscience of our people." He also states, without proof satisfactory to me, that in making decisions on this basis judges will not consider "their personal and private notions." One may ask how they can avoid considering them. Our Court certainly has no machinery with which to take a Gallup Poll. And the scientific miracles of this age have not yet produced a gadget which the Court can use to determine what traditions are rooted in the "[collective] conscience of our people." . . .

Mr. Justice STEWART, whom Mr. Justice BLACK joins, dissenting.

. . . I think this is an uncommonly silly law. As a practical matter, the law is obviously unenforceable, except in the oblique context of the present case. As a philosophical matter, I believe the use of contraceptives in the relationship of marriage should be left to personal and private choice, based upon each individual's moral, ethical, and religious beliefs. As a matter of social policy, I think professional counsel about methods of birth control should be available to all, so that each individual's choice can be meaningfully made. But we are not asked in this case to say whether we think this law is unwise, or even asinine. We are asked to hold that it violates the United States Constitution. And that I cannot do. . . . With all deference, I can find no such general right of privacy in the Bill of Rights, in any other part of the Constitution, or in any case ever before decided by this Court.

At the oral argument in this case we were told that the Connecticut law does not "conform to current community standards." But it is not the function of this Court to decide cases on the basis of community standards. . . . If, as I should surely hope, the law before us does not reflect the standards of the people of Connecticut, the people of Connecticut can freely exercise their true Ninth and Tenth Amendment rights to persuade their elected representatives to repeal it. That is the constitutional way to take this law off the books.

12. See Patterson, The Forgotten Ninth Amendment (1955). . . . In Redlich, Are There "Certain Rights . . . Retained by the People"?, 37 N.Y.U. L. Rev. 787 [(1962)], Professor Redlich, in advocating reliance on the Ninth and Tenth Amendments to invalidate the Connecticut law before us, frankly states:

> But for one who feels that the marriage relationship should be beyond the reach of a state law forbidding the use of contraceptives, the birth control case poses a troublesome and challenging problem of constitutional interpretation. He may find himself saying, "The law is unconstitutional — but why?" There are two possible paths to travel in finding the answer. One is to revert to a frankly flexible due process concept even on matters that do not involve specific constitutional prohibitions. The other is to attempt to evolve a new constitutional framework within which to meet this and similar problems which are likely to arise.

Id., at 798.

■ **MICHAEL GROSSBERG, GOVERNING THE HEARTH:
LAW AND THE FAMILY IN NINETEENTH-CENTURY
AMERICA**
156-157, 175-177, 189-193 (1985)

At the heart of the nineteenth-century controversy over family limitation lay the quiet determination of American mothers and fathers to reduce the number of children they reared. They initiated what historical demographers now designate the "demographic transition": a reduction in family size that characterized most Western nations. In America, white female fertility, the critical measure of family size, declined in each decade of the century, falling from 7.04 in 1800 to 3.56 a hundred years later. . . .

Although the exact sources [of this transition] remain uncertain, some characteristics of the republican household offer clues. . . . These include the child-centered nature of the republican home in which numerous offspring seemed to inhibit proper child care; the rise of what historian Daniel Scott Smith terms "domestic feminism," or the determination of women to assert their individuality and household authority by regulating pregnancy and marital sexuality; the economic incentives of market capitalism in which large families seemed a burden and in which moderation and self-control became prized virtues; the companionate nature of republican matrimony, which fostered the separation of sexual pleasure from protection; and the emerging American insistence on overcoming what had previously been considered natural forces beyond human control. . . .

Though it is difficult to pierce the privacy surrounding family limitation, at the beginning of the nineteenth century, husbands and wives apparently still relied on age-old methods of birth control such as delayed marriage, breast feeding, and abstinence (as well as *coitus interruptus* and other active contraceptive practices). . . .

Although statutes prohibiting various forms of abortion had been on the books since the 1820s, there were few explicit restrictions on contraception until the 1870s. But federal and state acts labeling both abortion and contraception obscene capped the growing determination of family savers to ban all forms of family limitation. [For example, though] he sympathized with women's fears about childbirth and rearing large families, [Augustus] Gardner confidently insisted that efforts made "to avoid propagation, are ten thousand-fold more disastrous to the health and constitution, to say nothing of the demoralization of mind and heart. . . ." Gardner [and his followers] looked to the criminal law for relief.

Self-appointed purity campaigners led the drive against contraception. New Yorkers created the first purity society in 1872, the New York Society for the Suppression of Vice. [T]he society's point man for purity reform was a little known ex-dry goods salesman, Anthony Comstock. The son of devout Connecticut parents, he tried unsuccessfully to make his fortune as a businessman in New York City. The flagrant vices he encountered in the city shocked him into a highly publicized vigilante campaign. It culminated in his appointment as the antivice society's chief agent, thus launching his career as late nineteenth-century America's self-avowed savior of public morals.

Comstock regarded the feeble statutes then on the books as the weakest link in his war on vice. . . . In 1872 he convinced the antivice society to send him to Washington to press for a rigorous national statute. [There] the vice crusader succeeded beyond his wildest expectations. Armed with a display case of vice paraphernalia and vivid tales of his fights with the panderers of obscenity, Comstock enlisted the aid of Vice President Henry Wilson and Supreme Court Justice William Strong to draft a new obscenity law. The bill passed with little debate and became law on 1 March 1873. [It became known as the "Comstock law."]

The act's primary purpose was to ban the circulation and importation of obscene materials through the national mails. Specifically included on the list of banned goods was every article designed, adapted, or intended "for preventing conception or producing abortion, or for indecent or immoral use; and every article, instrument, substance, drug, medicine, or thing which is advertised or described in a manner calculated to lead another to use or apply it for preventing conception or producing abortion, or for any indecent or immoral purpose. . . ." The act set punishment at $5,000 fine, one to ten years at hard labor, or both. . . .

[P]urity crusaders also prodded state legislators into action. Antivice societies, and after 1885 the Social Purity Alliance, succeeded in persuading twenty-two legislatures to enact general obscenity laws and another twenty-four to specifically ban birth control and abortion. [Courts upheld convictions under these laws.]

Let loose by Congress, state legislatures, and the courts, vice hunters prowled the nation sniffing out their prey. Posing as customers or using decoy letters, federal agents and local societies purchased proscribed items and then arrested sellers. . . . Comstock in fact caught his most famous victim with a birth-control ploy. Having been warned not to tangle with the infamous Madame Restell, he took her capture as a personal challenge. In the guise of an impoverished father, Comstock pleaded for contraceptive information because his meager finances could support no more children. When she obliged, he arrested her. Faced with the almost certain prospect of jail at the age of 67, Restell slit her throat with a carving knife. Comstock experienced no remorse: "a bloody end to a bloody life."

. . . Congress strengthened the federal ban in 1908. By the 1930s eight states specifically prohibited the flow of contraceptive information while the rest acted through broadened obscenity laws. Contraception remained a taboo subject, even though, much like prohibition, the statutes expressed a moral standard clearly at odds with actual practices. . . . Birth control, no matter how essential family limitation had become to the republican family, still violated the nation's code of proper domestic behavior. Fears aroused by the immigration of seemingly fecund non-Protestant women, charges of race suicide leveled against non-immigrant mothers who regulated their child bearing, and the ever-present concern over changes in gender responsibilities reinvigorated the stigma attached to the practice.

The constitutionality of the ban was also impenetrable. [Judicial cases] demonstrated the formidable opposition facing birth-control advocates. . . . Birth control continued to be an obscene subject banished from polite society. . . .

■ CATHERINE G. RORABACK, GRISWOLD v. CONNECTICUT: A BRIEF CASE HISTORY
16 Ohio N.U. L. Rev. 395, 395-401 (1989)

The [Connecticut] ban on the use of contraceptives had been on the statute books of this state for some eighty-six years. Many other jurisdictions had similar laws, but by the late 1950's these laws had been either repealed or their impact minimized by judicial interpretation. In 1958 only Connecticut had an absolute ban on contraceptive devices, one without an exception even for situations where the life of the mother might be endangered by a pregnancy. [T]here were regular attempts to obtain legislative repeal of the statute. In each biennial session of the General Assembly a repealer bill was introduced, vociferous and vituperative hearings were held, and the bill was eventually voted down. . . .

[I]t is hard to remember the attitudes toward birth control in the 1950's. The statutory prohibition on the use of contraceptives even by married persons was accepted by many as a legitimate exercise of the police powers of the state. That is not to say that private doctors did not provide such advice and services to their private patients, nor that patients able to afford private medical care did not obtain contraceptive advice. However, even that private care was often circumspect and clandestine, and some private physicians refused to provide these services at all. Certainly these services were not available to unmarried persons.

Although contraceptives were available for purchase in drugstores throughout the state, that availability was usually "under-the-counter." Druggists also sold such items on prescription of a private physician. The activities of the state Planned Parenthood League were limited to educational and legislative programs and a referral service to clinics in neighboring New York and Rhode Island, with transportation furnished by volunteers to enable the women to take advantage of the out-of-state services.

But no medical source of contraceptive advice or services was available in this state to those dependent on publicly provided health care. It was the physicians and medical personnel operating in public clinics who were subjected to public scrutiny and threat of prosecution. And because it was here that these statutes impacted, it was the poor people of this state who were deprived of medically supervised contraceptive advice and services. [After 1940, when nine Planned Parenthood clinics were closed, no public or private facility provided free birth control.]

In 1957, Estelle Griswold, a dynamic, vivacious woman, had only recently become the executive director of the Planned Parenthood League of Connecticut. She found herself frustrated by the legal situation in Connecticut and her inability to organize Planned Parenthood clinics in the state.

In the course of preparations that year for the biennial legislative hearing on repeal of the anti-birth-control statute, she arranged for C. Lee Buxton to testify. Buxton had only recently come to New Haven as professor and chairman of the Department of Obstetrics and Gynecology at the Yale University School of Medicine. . . . He felt deeply that the statute banning the use of contraceptive devices and the accessory statute preventing him from giving what he felt to be the advice and care his patients deserved were gross invasions of his patients' rights, and highly improper impediments on his ability to practice his profession.

It was at this point, as legend has it, that Estelle invited both Lee Buxton and Fowler Harper to her home one day in the fall of 1957 and introduced them over cocktails. Fowler, then a professor at the Yale Law School, taught — among other subjects — family law. He was a social activist, involved in the community, always ready to take on a cause and to use his full energies and legal skills to cure an inequity. . . . He most certainly reacted with verve and gusto as Lee spoke of his frustrations about the Connecticut law banning the use of contraceptives and his inability to properly serve his patients. And, the legend holds, it was from this conversation that the litigation which culminated in *Griswold* originated. . . .

[The chosen strategy was for Dr. Buxton and some of his married patients to seek in state court a declaratory judgment that the statute was unconstitutional or should not apply when pregnancy threatened a woman's life or health.] One of the patients bringing suit was Jane Doe, a young twenty-five year old housewife. . . . While hospitalized [for pregnancy complications] she had suffered a stroke, her pregnancy could not be aborted, and she had had to continue the pregnancy until at term she had a stillbirth. As a result she was permanently paralyzed on her right side, her speech was impaired and she had residual kidney damage. It was Dr. Buxton's opinion that she would not survive another pregnancy.

The other plaintiff-patients were two married couples. One, the Poes, had had three abnormal children, none of whom had survived more than ten weeks. They sought contraceptive advice because they did not feel they could emotionally survive the birth of another such child. The other couple, the Hoes, had conflicting blood groupings and were considered unlikely to have a normal child born to them.

When these suits were begun in May of 1958, there was . . . no discussion of rights of privacy. . . . The due process arguments in the briefs filed in the Connecticut courts stressed rights to life and liberty, to health, to happy marital relationships, free of governmental intrusion. But the obverse of that phrase — privacy — was not used. This is not surprising if one thinks back to the status of privacy law at that time. [The Connecticut Supreme Court of Errors rejected the broad constitutional challenge to the statute and refused to read any exception into it.]

It was in the due process arguments presented on the appeal to the United States Supreme Court in this case that the first specific mention of "privacy" occurred in this litigation. However, the Supreme Court never reached this or any of the other substantive arguments raised on this appeal. Rather, it held [in Poe v. Ullman, 367 U.S. 497 (1961),] that there was no controversy before the Court, that there had been an absence of any prosecutions under the statutes, and that therefore Dr. Buxton and his patients faced no realistic threat of prosecution.

In Connecticut the implications of this disconcerting outcome were pondered. . . . After much consultation and discussion it was finally decided that the Planned Parenthood League of Connecticut would open one facility in New Haven, and that if no prosecution ensued it would expand such services to other cities. Thus on November 1, 1961, the Planned Parenthood League of Connecticut opened the first birth control clinic in [Connecticut] since 1940, with Estelle T. Griswold as its director and C. Lee Buxton was its medical director.

. . . The clinic was in operation only a brief ten days before Mrs. Griswold and Dr. Buxton were arrested on November 10, 1961. Informations charged them with counseling, aiding and abetting certain married women to "use a drug, medicinal article and instrument, for the purpose of preventing contraception." The clinic closed its doors, and the prosecutions proceeded.

From the beginning of this prosecution the defense attacked the statutory contraceptive ban, repeating in depth all of the prior arguments as to the unconstitutionality of the statute but adding now, specifically the infringement which it imposed on the patient's right to privacy. In doing so we drew on the development of that right as it had been expounded at length in the two dissenting opinions in *Poe*. Mr. Justice Douglas's dissent found such a right in "the totality of the constitutional scheme under which we live," [367 U.S. at 521,] while Mr. Justice Harlan found its protection in the due process protections of the fourteenth amendment [id. at 540].

Notes and Questions

1. *Sources.* What are the constitutional sources of the right to privacy, according to *Griswold*? To what alternative sources do the concurring opinions point? Explain the majority's difficulty in identifying the source of this right. On what basis do the dissenters disagree?

2. *State intrusion.* What aspect of the statute disturbs the majority? If Connecticut had sought to prevent use of contraceptives by, say, banning the manufacture or sale of such materials, what result? See The Supreme Court, 1964 Term, 79 Harv. L. Rev. 103, 162 (1965). How significant is the fact that Connecticut prohibited couples' behavior with regard to contraceptive use, as distinguished from some other intimate activity? Compare Stanley v. Georgia, 394 U.S. 557 (1969), with Osborne v. Ohio, 495 U.S. 103 (1990) (both dealing with possession of pornography). See also Williams v. Attorney General, 378 F.3d 1232 (11th Cir. 2004) (finding no fundamental right to, inter alia, use sex toys), *cert. denied sub nom.* Williams v. King, 543 U.S. 1152 (2005).

3. *Role of marriage?* How critical is the marital status of the contraceptive users? To whom does the right to privacy belong, according to *Griswold*? Each spouse? The marital unit? See Martha Albertson Fineman, What Place for Family Privacy?, 67 Geo. Wash. L. Rev. 1207, 1212 (1999) (*Griswold* shows that the "idea of the entity of the family as something 'private' predates, and is analytically separate from, the constitutional idea of individual privacy."). Suppose the spouses disagree. Given *Griswold*, can the state resolve the disagreement in favor of one?

4. *State interests.* Why did Connecticut enact this legislation? What do the excerpts by historian Michael Grossberg and attorney Catherine Roraback (counsel to Planned Parenthood League of Connecticut during *Griswold*) suggest? See also, e.g., Janet Farrell Brodie, Contraception and Abortion in Nineteenth-Century America (1994); John W. Johnson, Griswold v. Connecticut: Birth Control and the Constitutional Right to Privacy (2005); Andrea Tone, Devices and Desires: A History of Contraceptives in America (2001). What role do the state's reasons play in *Griswold*?

5. *Privacy's origins.* In an omitted footnote, Justice Black's dissent claims that the concept of a "right to privacy" originated in an 1890 article by Samuel Warren and his then law partner Louis Brandeis, The Right to Privacy, 4 Harv. L. Rev. 193 (1890). Reportedly written in response to press coverage of the wedding of Warren's socialite daughter, the article sought a legal basis for the protection of privacy. The authors settled on the common law of copyright as a shield against threats posed by new technology, such as "instantaneous photographs" and "mechanical [eavesdropping or broadcasting] devices." Id. at 195. They recommended tort damages for breaches and injunctions in limited cases. As Supreme Court Justice, Brandeis later cited the Constitution for "the right to be let alone." See, e.g., Olmstead v. United States, 277 U.S. 438, 478 (1928) (dissenting opinion) (recognizing Fourth Amendment protection against governmental wiretapping). See also Katz v. United States, 389 U.S. 347, 353 (1967) (adopting Brandeis's reasoning). Goldberg's concurrence in *Griswold* invokes Brandeis's understanding.

How closely does the *Griswold* majority's concept of privacy resemble that of Warren and Brandeis? Does *Griswold*'s notion of privacy protect the right not to have information made public? The right to be let alone? The right to self-determination? For a contemporary analysis, see generally Daniel J. Solove, A Taxonomy of Privacy, 154 U. Pa. L. Rev. 477 (2006).

6. *Privacy and technology.* Given Warren's and Brandeis's fears about new technologies, how should their proposed right to privacy evolve now that sense-enhancing devices can gather information without physical intrusion into constitutionally protected spaces like the home? See Kyllo v. United States, 533 U.S. 27 (2001) (use of thermal imaging technology to detect heat emanating from home constitutes search under Fourth Amendment); Susan Bandes, Power, Privacy, and Thermal Imaging, 86 Minn. L. Rev. 1379 (2002). What new challenges for privacy are posed by the Internet? See, e.g., Anita L. Allen, Gender and Privacy in Cyberspace, 52 Stan. L. Rev. 1175 (2000) (part of symposium on Cyberspace and Privacy: A New Legal Paradigm). By the genomics revolution, initiated by the Human Genome Project? See generally, e.g., Lori B. Andrews, A Conceptual Framework for Genetic Policy: Comparing the Medical, Public Health, and Fundamental Rights Models, 79 Wash. U. L.Q. 221 (2001); Hugh Miller III, DNA Blueprints, Personhood, and Genetic Privacy, 8 Health Matrix 179 (1998). By security measures undertaken in response to the attacks of September 11, 2001? See, e.g., Marc Rotenberg, Privacy and Secrecy After September 11, 86 Minn. L. Rev. 1115 (2002).

7. *Birth control movement.* The radical birth control movement in the United States emerged as part of the Socialist Party's agenda in the early 1900s. Activist Margaret Sanger's role in the movement grew out of her encounter as a visiting nurse with a poor woman who died because she could not avoid another pregnancy. Linda Gordon, The Moral Property of Women: A History of Birth Control Politics in America 144 (2002). But an appreciation of larger issues also motivated Sanger:

> [Sanger recognized] the potential historical and political impact of birth control. Most American socialists at this time, primarily oriented to class relations, saw birth control . . . in terms of economics. They were concerned to help raise the standard of living of workers and thus increase their freedom to take political control over their own lives. Measured against this goal, birth control was at most an ameliorative reform. Seen in terms of sexual politics, however, birth control was revolutionary because it could free women entirely from the major burden that differentiated them from men and made them dependent on men. Sanger gained this perspective in Europe from the sexual liberation theorists such as Havelock Ellis. . . . His idealism about the potential beauty and expressiveness of human sexuality and his rage at the damage caused by sexual repression fired Sanger with a sense of the overwhelming importance, urgency, and profundity of the issue of birth control. . . .

Id. at 145. Sanger founded the American Birth Control League, which later became Planned Parenthood.

8. *Birth control and race.* In contrast to their white counterparts' almost exclusive focus on access to birth control, women of color embraced a more wide-ranging movement that historian Jennifer Nelson claims shaped today's expansive understanding of reproductive freedom. See generally Jennifer Nelson, Women of Color and the Reproductive Rights Movement 186 (2003). For African-American women, this larger agenda for reproductive rights stemmed from a history of sexual

exploitation during slavery[1] and sterilization abuse, as well as societal inattention to high maternal and infant mortality rates. Still, birth control and abortion formed one element of this agenda, despite opposition in the 1970s from Black Nationalist organizations, which condemned such measures as tools for genocide.[2] For other ethnic groups, the particular historical and cultural context also influenced the approach to birth control. For example, Puerto Rican activists, well aware of U.S. sponsored sterilization there and the harm suffered by some Puerto Rican women who participated in tests to develop the birth control pill, broadly advocated women's autonomy and state-supported health care.[3] Similarly, some Native-American women also have worked for birth control as part of a wider mission to improve available health care generally.[4]

■ **EISENSTADT v. BAIRD**
  405 U.S. 438 (1972)

Mr. Justice BRENNAN delivered the opinion of the Court.

Appellee William Baird was convicted at a bench trial in the Massachusetts Superior Court under Massachusetts General Laws Ann., c. 272, §21, first, for exhibiting contraceptive articles in the course of delivering a lecture on contraception to a group of students at Boston University and, second, for giving a young woman a package of Emko vaginal foam at the close of his address. The Massachusetts Supreme Judicial Court unanimously set aside the conviction for exhibiting contraceptives on the ground that it violated Baird's First Amendment rights, but by a four-to-three vote sustained the conviction for giving away the foam. Commonwealth v. Baird, 355 Mass. 746, 247 N.E.2d 574 (1969). . . .

Massachusetts General Laws Ann., c. 272, §21 [provides] a maximum five-year term of imprisonment for "whoever . . . gives away . . . any drug, medicine, instrument or article whatever for the prevention of conception," except as authorized in §21A. . . . As interpreted by the State Supreme Judicial Court, these provisions make it a felony for anyone, other than a registered physician or pharmacist acting in accordance with the terms of §21A, to dispense any article with the intention that it be used for the prevention of conception. [M]arried persons may obtain contraceptives to prevent pregnancy, but only from doctors or druggists on prescription; . . . single persons may not obtain contraceptives from anyone to prevent pregnancy. . . .

The question for our determination in this case is whether there is some ground of difference that rationally explains the different treatment accorded married and unmarried persons under Massachusetts General Laws Ann., c. 272, §§21 and 21A.[7] . . .

[1]. See, e.g., Dorothy Roberts, Killing the Black Body: Race, Reproduction and the Meaning of Liberty 22-55 (1999).

[2]. See Jennifer Nelson, Women of Color and the Reproductive Rights Movement (2003).

[3]. See id. at 19.

[4]. Jael Silliman, et al., Undivided Rights: Women of Color Organize for Reproductive Justice 143 (2004).

7. Of course, if we were to conclude that the Massachusetts statute impinges upon fundamental freedoms under *Griswold*, the statutory classification would have to be not merely *rationally* related to a valid public purpose but *necessary* to the achievement of a *compelling* state interest. E.g., Loving v. Virginia, 388 U.S. 1 (1967). But . . . we do not have to address the statute's validity under that test because the law fails to satisfy even the more lenient equal protection standard.

First. [W]e cannot agree that the deterrence of premarital sex may reasonably be regarded as the purpose of the Massachusetts law.

It would be plainly unreasonable to assume that Massachusetts has prescribed pregnancy and the birth of an unwanted child as punishment for fornication, which is a misdemeanor under Massachusetts General Laws Ann., c. 272, §18. Aside from the scheme of values that assumption would attribute to the State, it is abundantly clear that the effect of the ban on distribution of contraceptives to unmarried persons has at best a marginal relation to the proffered objective. . . . Like Connecticut's laws [in *Griswold*], §§21 and 21A do not at all regulate the distribution of contraceptives when they are to be used to prevent, not pregnancy, but the spread of disease. Nor, in making contraceptives available to married persons without regard to their intended use, does Massachusetts attempt to deter married persons from engaging in illicit sexual relations with unmarried persons. Even on the assumption that the fear of pregnancy operates as a deterrent to fornication, the Massachusetts statute is thus so riddled with exceptions that deterrence of premarital sex cannot reasonably be regarded as its aim. . . .

Second. . . . If health were the rationale of §21A, the statute would be both discriminatory and overbroad. . . . The Court of Appeals [stated]: "If the prohibition [on distribution to unmarried persons] . . . is to be taken to mean that the same physician who can prescribe for married patients does not have sufficient skill to protect the health of patients who lack a marriage certificate, or who may be currently divorced, it is illogical to the point of irrationality." 429 F.2d, at 1401. Furthermore, we must join the Court of Appeals in noting that not all contraceptives are potentially dangerous. . . . "If [health] was the Legislature's goal, §21 is not required" in view of the federal and state laws *already* regulating the distribution of harmful drugs. . . .

Third. If the Massachusetts statute cannot be upheld as a deterrent to fornication or as a health measure, may it, nevertheless, be sustained simply as a prohibition on contraception? . . . We need not and do not, however, decide that important question in this case because, whatever the rights of the individual to access to contraceptives may be, the rights must be the same for the unmarried and the married alike.

If under *Griswold* the distribution of contraceptives to married persons cannot be prohibited, a ban on distribution to unmarried persons would be equally impermissible. It is true that in *Griswold* the right of privacy in question inhered in the marital relationship. Yet the marital couple is not an independent entity with a mind and heart of its own, but an association of two individuals each with a separate intellectual and emotional makeup. If the right of privacy means anything, it is the right of the *individual*, married or single, to be free from unwarranted governmental intrusion into matters so fundamentally affecting a person as the decision whether to bear or beget a child. See Stanley v. Georgia, 394 U.S. 557 (1969). See also Skinner v. Oklahoma ex rel. Williamson, 316 U.S. 535 (1942); Jacobson v. Massachusetts, 197 U.S. 11, 29 (1905).

On the other hand, if *Griswold* is no bar to a prohibition on the distribution of contraceptives, the State could not, consistently with the Equal Protection Clause, outlaw distribution to unmarried but not married persons. In each case the evil, as perceived by the State, would be identical, and the underinclusion would be invidious.

. . . We hold that by providing dissimilar treatment for married and unmarried persons who are similarly situated, Massachusetts General Laws Ann., c. 272, §§21 and 21A, violate the Equal Protection Clause. The judgment of the Court of Appeals is affirmed.

Notes and Questions

1. *Beyond* Griswold. How does *Eisenstadt* resolve the issues left open in *Griswold:* the *distribution* of contraceptives to *unmarried* individuals?

2. *Privacy's meaning.* How does *Eisenstadt* define "privacy"? How does the meaning of "privacy" articulated in *Eisenstadt* differ from that in *Griswold*?

3. *Whose privacy?* Does *Eisenstadt* answer the question whether the right to privacy belongs to the family unit or each member of the family? Does it indicate how to resolve conflicts between family members over intimate matters?

4. *Constitutional basis.* Why does the Court rely on the Equal Protection Clause instead of the parts of the Constitution invoked in *Griswold*? Does *Eisenstadt's* approach provide a firmer basis for the right to privacy?

5. *State interests.* Why did Massachusetts enact the law challenged here? How does the Court address these state interests? In an omitted dissent, Chief Justice Burger writes: "The actual hazards of introducing a particular foreign substance into the human body are frequently controverted, and I cannot believe that unanimity of expert opinion is a prerequisite to a State's exercise of its police power." 405 U.S. at 470 (Burger, C.J., dissenting). Does the majority satisfactorily respond?

6. *Scope of protection.* States routinely create legal distinctions based on marriage. See Baker v. State, 744 A.2d 864 (Vt. 1999) (noting numerous legal benefits state provides only to married couples, in challenge to ineligibility of same-sex couples to marry). How far does *Eisenstadt* go in barring discrimination based on marital status?

7. *Access.* The Court subsequently addressed the substantive issue avoided in *Eisenstadt*. Carey v. Population Services International, 431 U.S. 678 (1977), struck down a statute barring distribution of all contraceptives except by licensed pharmacists. The majority explained that limitations on access to contraceptives impose burdens similar to limitations on use; hence, both must satisfy the compelling state interest test.

8. *Law reform strategies.* Historian David Garrow traces efforts to decriminalize contraception (and later abortion) through both legislative reform and judicial challenges. William Baird, the defendant-appellee in *Eisenstadt*, pursued the latter course, purposefully seeking to be prosecuted for his distribution of Emko vaginal foam at a student gathering at Boston University in 1967. This approach placed Baird in direct conflict with reformers pursuing legislative change:

> [T]he Planned Parenthood League of Massachusetts (PPLM), in its May newsletter to supporters, went out of its way to disassociate itself from both Baird and his court challenge to the existing Massachusetts statute. Baird "is in no way connected with Planned Parenthood. . . . The only way to remove the limitations remaining in the law is through the legislative process."
>
> Baird told two sympathetic journalists who nonetheless characterized him as "a little too intense, a little too filled with the vision of himself as a martyr" that "Planned

Parenthood is a middle class monopoly." [He even picketed its annual dinner once.]
Some years later former PPFA [Planned Parenthood Federation of America] president
Loraine Campbell . . . acerbicly called Baird "a thorn in our flesh for years." . . . On
balance, Campbell said, "Baird did more good than harm," but then, as she memor-
ably declared, "every social change and every forward step in history requires its nuts."

David J. Garrow, Liberty and Sexuality: The Right to Privacy and the Making of
Roe v. Wade 322-323 (updated ed. 1998). What insights about the two avenues for
law reform can be gleaned from Baird's story?

Problems

1. You work on the staff of a state legislator. She seeks your advice on two
different proposed state laws regulating access to contraceptives. One proposal
would require pharmacists to fill all legal prescriptions, including those for contraceptives. The proponents of this bill cite recent cases in which pharmacists refused
on moral grounds to dispense contraceptives even for patients prescribed such
treatment following an unexpected miscarriage or a rape. The other proposal
would enact a "conscience clause" giving pharmacists the right to refuse to fill
prescriptions that conflict with their personal beliefs and values. The proponents
of this bill assert that pharmacists in states without such protections have lost their
jobs for acting in accordance with their religious and moral opposition to contraception, particularly emergency contraception. Which law would you recommend
that the legislator support? On what legal or constitutional grounds? What additional facts would you need to investigate? Is it relevant to your answer whether
emergency contraception (a high dose of ordinary birth control pills taken within
72 hours of unprotected intercourse) disables sperm, prevents ovulation, prevents
fertilization, or prevents implantation? Why? Are there alternative measures that
the legislator ought to consider proposing herself?

For a summary of current state legislative activities on this subject, see National
Conference of State Legislatures, Pharmacist Conscience Clauses: Laws and
Legislation (updated May 2006) (available at http://www.ncsl.org/programs/
health/conscienceclauses.htm). For the standard of review that governs state
restrictions on abortion, see infra p. 48.

2. Suppose an employer provides employees with a comprehensive prescrip-
tion drug plan that includes Viagra, which allows sexual intercourse for some men,
but not contraceptives, which accomplish a similar objective for some women. Has
the employer violated laws that prohibit sex-based discrimination in the workplace
(Title VII and the Pregnancy Discrimination Act)? See In re: Union Pac. R.R.
Employment Practices Litig., 378 F. Supp. 2d 1139 (D. Neb. 2005); Lisa A. Hayden,
Gender Discrimination within the Reproductive Health Care System: Viagra v.
Birth Control, 13 J.L. & Health 171 (1999). If the plan excludes both Viagra
and contraceptives, has the employer eliminated any discrimination? See Erickson v.
Bartell Drug Co., 141 F. Supp. 2d 1266 (W.D. Wash. 2001); Sylvia A. Law, Sex
Discrimination and Insurance for Contraception, 73 Wash. L. Rev. 363 (1998).
Cf. Catholic Charities of Sacramento, Inc. v. Superior Ct., 85 P.3d 67 (Cal.), *cert.
denied*, 543 U.S. 816 (2004) (rejecting employer's Free Exercise and Establishment
Clause challenges); Catholic Charities of the Diocese of Albany v. Senio, 808

N.Y.S. 2d 447 (App. Div. 2006) (rejecting employers' federal and state constitutional challenges).

b. Roots of Privacy

Griswold and *Eisenstadt* break new ground in explicitly recognizing a constitutional right to privacy. Yet some 40 years earlier the Supreme Court expressed an understanding of the family that established a foothold for this right.

■ MEYER v. NEBRASKA
262 U.S. 390 (1923)

Mr. Justice MCREYNOLDS delivered the opinion of the Court.

Plaintiff in error was tried and convicted . . . under an information which charged that on May 25, 1920, while an instructor in Zion Parochial School he unlawfully taught the subject of reading in the German language to Raymond Parpart, a child of 10 years, who had not attained and successfully passed the eighth grade. [A Nebraska statute prohibited any person from teaching languages other than English, except to pupils who had successfully completed the eighth grade, and classified a violation as a misdemeanor, punishable by a fine and/or imprisonment. The state supreme court affirmed the conviction.]

The problem for our determination is whether the statute as construed and applied unreasonably infringes the liberty guaranteed to the plaintiff in error by the Fourteenth Amendment: "No state . . . shall deprive any person of life, liberty or property without due process of law."

While this court has not attempted to define with exactness the liberty thus guaranteed, [w]ithout doubt, it denotes not merely freedom from bodily restraint but also the right of the individual to contract, to engage in any of the common occupations of life, to acquire useful knowledge, to marry, establish a home and bring up children, to worship God according to the dictates of his own conscience, and generally to enjoy those privileges long recognized at common law as essential to the orderly pursuit of happiness by free men. The established doctrine is that this liberty may not be interfered with, under the guise of protecting the public interest, by legislative action which is arbitrary or without reasonable relation to some purpose within the competency of the state to effect. Determination by the Legislature of what constitutes proper exercise of police power is not final or conclusive but is subject to supervision by the courts.

The American people have always regarded education and acquisition of knowledge as matters of supreme importance which should be diligently promoted. . . . Corresponding to the right of control, it is the natural duty of the parent to give his children education suitable to their station in life; and nearly all the states, including Nebraska, enforce this obligation by compulsory laws.

Practically, education of the young is only possible in schools conducted by especially qualified persons who devote themselves thereto. The calling always has been regarded as useful and honorable, essential, indeed, to the public welfare. Mere knowledge of the German language cannot reasonably be regarded as harmful. . . . Plaintiff in error taught this language in school as part of his occupation.

His right thus to teach and the right of parents to engage him so to instruct their children, we think, are within the liberty of the Amendment. ... Evidently the Legislature has attempted materially to interfere with the calling of modern language teachers, with the opportunities of pupils to acquire knowledge, and with the power of parents to control the education of their own.

It is said the purpose of the legislation was to promote civic development by inhibiting training and education of the immature in foreign tongues and ideals before they could learn English and acquire American ideals, and "that the English language should be and become the mother tongue of all children reared in this state." It is also affirmed that the foreign born population is very large, that certain communities commonly use foreign words, follow foreign leaders, move in a foreign atmosphere, and that the children are thereby hindered from becoming citizens of the most useful type and the public safety is imperiled.

That the state may do much, go very far, indeed, in order to improve the quality of its citizens, physically, mentally and morally, is clear; but the individual has certain fundamental rights which must be respected. The protection of the Constitution extends to all, to those who speak other languages as well as to those born with English on the tongue. Perhaps it would be highly advantageous if all had ready understanding of our ordinary speech, but this cannot be coerced by methods which conflict with the Constitution — a desirable end cannot be promoted by prohibited means. ... No emergency has arisen which renders knowledge by a child of some language other than English so clearly harmful as to justify its inhibition with the consequent infringement of rights long freely enjoyed. We are constrained to conclude that the statute as applied is arbitrary and without reasonable relation to any end within the competency of the state.

As the statute undertakes to interfere only with teaching which involves a modern language, leaving complete freedom as to other matters, there seems no adequate foundation for the suggestion that the purpose was to protect the child's health by limiting his mental activities. It is well known that proficiency in a foreign language seldom comes to one not instructed at an early age, and experience shows that this is not injurious to the health, morals or understanding of the ordinary child. [Reversed.]

■ PIERCE v. SOCIETY OF SISTERS
268 U.S. 510 (1925)

Mr. Justice MCREYNOLDS delivered the opinion of the Court.

These appeals are from decrees, based upon undenied allegations, which granted preliminary orders restraining appellants from threatening or attempting to enforce the Compulsory Education Act adopted November 7, 1922. ...

The challenged act, effective September 1, 1926, requires every parent, guardian, or other person having control or charge or custody of a child between 8 and 16 years to send him "to a public school for the period of time a public school shall be held during the current year" in the district where the child resides; and failure so to do is declared a misdemeanor. ... The manifest purpose is to compel general attendance at public schools by normal children, between 8 and 16, who have not completed the eighth grade. And without doubt enforcement of the statute would seriously impair, perhaps destroy, the profitable features of appellees' business and greatly diminish the value of their property.

Appellee, the Society of Sisters, is an Oregon corporation, organized in 1880, with power to care for orphans, educate and instruct the youth, establish and maintain academies or schools, and acquire necessary real and personal property . . . . The Compulsory Education Act of 1922 has already caused the withdrawal from its schools of children who would otherwise continue, and their income has steadily declined. The appellants, public officers, have proclaimed their purpose strictly to enforce the statute.

After setting out the above facts, the Society's bill alleges that the enactment conflicts with the right of parents to choose schools where their children will receive appropriate mental and religious training, the right of the child to influence the parents' choice of a school, the right of schools and teachers therein to engage in a useful business or profession, and is accordingly repugnant to the Constitution and void. And, further, that unless enforcement of the measure is enjoined the corporation's business and property will suffer irreparable injury.

Appellee Hill Military Academy is a private corporation organized in 1908 under the laws of Oregon, engaged in owning, operating, and conducting for profit an elementary, college preparatory, and military training school for boys between the ages of 5 and 21 years. . . . By reason of the statute and threat of enforcement appellee's business is being destroyed and its property depreciated; parents and guardians are refusing to make contracts for the future instruction of their sons, and some are being withdrawn. [The Academy alleges a violation of its Fourteenth Amendment rights and seeks an injunction.]

[The matter was heard] by three judges on motions for preliminary injunctions upon the specifically alleged facts. The court ruled that the Fourteenth Amendment guaranteed appellees against the deprivation of their property without due process of law consequent upon the unlawful interference by appellants with the free choice of patrons, present and prospective. It declared the right to conduct schools was property and that parents and guardians, as a part of their liberty, might direct the education of children by selecting reputable teachers and places. Also, that appellees' schools were not unfit or harmful to the public, and that enforcement of the challenged statute would unlawfully deprive them of patronage and thereby destroy appellees' business and property. . . .

No question is raised concerning the power of the state reasonably to regulate all schools, to inspect, supervise and examine them, their teachers and pupils; to require that all children of proper age attend some school, that teachers shall be of good moral character and patriotic disposition, that certain studies plainly essential to good citizenship must be taught, and that nothing be taught which is manifestly inimical to the public welfare.

The inevitable practical result of enforcing the act under consideration would be destruction of appellees' primary schools, and perhaps all other private primary schools for normal children within the state of Oregon. Appellees are engaged in a kind of undertaking not inherently harmful, but long regarded as useful and meritorious. [T]here are no peculiar circumstances or present emergencies which demand extraordinary measures relative to primary education.

Under the doctrine of Meyer v. Nebraska, 262 U.S. 390 [(1923)], we think it entirely plain that the Act of 1922 unreasonably interferes with the liberty of parents and guardians to direct the upbringing and education of children under their control. As often heretofore pointed out, rights guaranteed by the Constitution may not be abridged by legislation which has no reasonable relation to some purpose within the competency of the state. The fundamental theory of liberty upon which all governments in this Union repose excludes any general power of the state to standardize its children by forcing them to accept instruction from public teachers only. The child is not the mere creature of the state; those who nurture him and direct his destiny have the right, coupled with the high duty, to recognize and prepare him for additional obligations. . . .

The decrees below are affirmed.

Notes and Questions

1. *Substantive due process.* *Meyer* and *Pierce* establish the foundation for the right to privacy. Why? Whose interests does each case vindicate? What is the connection between privacy and the professional and proprietary interests (of teachers and schools) protected by the Court? Note that neither *Meyer* nor *Pierce* mentions "privacy." Nonetheless, *Griswold*, the first case to articulate a constitutional right to privacy, relies on both these precedents.

Despite holdings addressing the economic claims raised by a school teacher and private schools, respectively, *Meyer* and *Pierce* include dicta establishing parental autonomy — the freedom of parents to control the upbringing of their children. Through such dicta, these cases extend substantive due process, found in the constitutional protection of personal "liberty," to limit the authority of government to interfere in certain family matters.

The broad liberal principles of family autonomy in the face of government intervention, found in *Meyer* and *Pierce*, survived the Court's subsequent repudiation of economic substantive due process. See Ferguson v. Skrupa, 372 U.S. 726, 729-730 (1963). Indeed, these cases, along with *Griswold*, form the basis of a revived substantive due process that now protects "a loose amalgam of personal liberties relating to family life." David D. Meyer, Self-Definition in the Constitution of Faith and Family, 86 Minn. L. Rev. 791, 804-805 (2002).

2. *Whose privacy?* Does the nascent interest in privacy recognized in *Meyer* and *Pierce* belong to the family unit or individual family members? Do these precedents help answer similar questions posed about *Griswold* and *Eisenstadt*? What similarities are shared by the two contexts, birth control and childrearing? What distinguishes them?

3. *Slavery, families, and pluralism.* Professor Peggy Davis emphasizes how *Meyer* and *Pierce*, rooted in antislavery traditions that originally produced the Fourteenth Amendment, promote pluralism. Slavery imposed natal alienation on slaves, prohibiting slave parents from teaching chosen moral values to their children. Peggy Cooper Davis, Contested Images of Family Values: The Role of the State, 107 Harv. L. Rev. 1348, 1363 (1994). By contrast, the autonomy recognized by *Meyer* and *Pierce* allows families room to make their own choices and embrace their own values:

> To think of family liberty as a guarantee offered in response to slavery's denials of natal connection is to understand it, not as an end in itself, but as a means to full personhood. People are not meant to be socialized to uniform, externally imposed

values. People are to be able to form families and other intimate communities within which children might be differently socialized and from which adults would bring different values to the democratic process. This reconstructed Constitution gives coherence and legitimacy to the themes of autonomy and social function sounded in *Meyer, Pierce* [and later cases]. The idea of civil freedom that grows out of the history of slavery, antislavery, and Reconstruction entails more than the right to continue one's genetic kind in private. It also entails a right of family that derives from a human right of intellectual and moral autonomy. It entails the right of every individual to affect the culture and embrace, act upon, and advocate privately chosen values. For parents and other guardians, civil freedom brings a right to choose and propagate *values*. For children, civil freedom brings nothing less than the right to grow to moral autonomy, because the child-citizen, like the child-slave, flowers to moral independence only under authority that is flexible in ways that states and masters cannot manage, and temporary in ways that states and masters cannot tolerate.

Id. at 1371-1372.

4. *State interests.* What reasons prompted enactment of the laws struck down in *Meyer* and *Pierce*? What standard of review does the Court use to assess the state interests? Why does the Court find no "emergency" in either case?

5. *History.* Professor Barbara Woodhouse identifies the social and political context in which the cases arose. She explains that the Nebraska law in *Meyer* stemmed from post-World War I anti-German bias. At the time, 16 states had similar English-only laws.

[These language laws were rooted in] the struggle between cultural pluralism and the felt need to articulate a national identity, evident in the long-standing tensions between English-speaking settlers of the Midwest and the large German, Polish, and Scandinavian communities in these states. These immigrant groups often formed isolated cultural enclaves with clubs, parochial schools, ethnic parishes, banks, stores, and insurance companies in which all business was conducted in the language of the home country. To their American-born neighbors, coming from a tradition that mixed the meliorative, unifying strains of populism and progressivism with a nativist distrust for anything foreign, this failure to assimilate seemed at once a threat and a challenge for progressive reform.

Barbara Bennett Woodhouse, "Who Owns the Child?": *Meyer* and *Pierce* and the Child as Property, 33 Wm. & Mary L. Rev. 995, 1004 (1992). By contrast, the Oregon law challenged in *Pierce*, reflecting the movement for universal free public education, was influenced by egalitarian Populist notions common in the 1890s.

The guiding sentiment behind the Oregon law . . . seems to have been an odd commingling of patriotic fervor, blind faith in the cure-all powers of common schooling, anti-Catholic and anti-foreign prejudice, and the conviction that private and parochial schools were breeding grounds of Bolshevism.

Id. at 1017-1018. See also David B. Tyack, The Perils of Pluralism: The Background of the *Pierce* Case, 74 Am. His. Rev. 74 (1968). Contemporary efforts to make English the "official language" of the United States have sparked renewed relevance for *Meyer*. See, e.g., Cal. Educ. Code §305 (West 2002) (eliminating bilingual education in public schools). For further examination of *Meyer* and *Pierce*, see Chapter VIII, section A.

6. *Other sources.* Additional roots of privacy can be found in Skinner v. Oklahoma, 316 U.S. 535 (1942), which invalidated as a denial of equal protection a statute punishing some criminals with sterilization. The Court applied "strict scrutiny" because the statute "involves one of the basic civil rights of man" and inflicts permanent deprivation of "a basic liberty." Id. at 541. This respect for procreative freedom contrasts with the Court's earlier approach in Buck v. Bell, 274 U.S. 200 (1927), upholding compulsory sterilization for an inmate of the State Colony for Epileptics and Feeble Minded, citing protection of the public welfare, and saying "[t]hree generations of imbeciles are enough." Id. at 207.

Does *Buck*'s approach survive *Griswold* and *Eisenstadt*? Does state interference with the ability to procreate implicate the same values and evoke the same analysis as interference with the ability to avoid procreation? In an omitted portion of Justice Goldberg's concurrence in *Griswold*, he observes that the dissenters' refusal to invalidate the birth control prohibition would compel them to uphold "a law requiring compulsory birth control." 381 U.S. at 497. Would it?

Buck, which many regard as the culmination of this country's attraction to the eugenics movement,[5] continues to generate criticism. See, e.g., Dorothy Roberts, Killing the Black Body: Race, Reproduction, and the Meaning of Liberty 69-72 (1999).

The Court also provided an underpinning for the right to privacy in Union Pacific Railway Co. v. Botsford, 141 U.S. 250 (1891). In this personal injury suit, defendant sought to compel plaintiff to submit to a "surgical examination as to the extent of the injury sued for." The Court upheld the refusal below to issue the order, explaining "The right to one's person may be said to be a right of complete immunity: to be let alone." Id. at 251 (quoting Cooley on Torts, 29).

Which approach provides stronger support for the privacy articulated in *Griswold* and *Eisenstadt:* the special concern for control over one's body in *Botsford*? Or the protection for parental autonomy in *Meyer* and *Pierce*?

7. *New applications.* *Meyer* and *Pierce* proved pivotal precedents when the Supreme Court struck down the application of a broad third-party visitation statute in Troxel v. Granville, 530 U.S. 57 (2000) (reprinted in Chapter VII, section B3). Although the case sharply divided the Court, several of the Justices took the opportunity both to reaffirm parents' fundamental liberty interest in childrearing and also to note the changing nature of the American family. 530 U.S. at 63-64, 85, 90, 98 (opinions of O'Connor, Stevens, and Kennedy, JJ.). What is a "family" for purposes of understanding the rights articulated in *Meyer* and *Pierce*? Cf. Chapter IV.

2. The Growth of Privacy

a. Abortion as a Private Choice

■ **ROE v. WADE**
410 U.S. 113 (1973)

Mr. Justice BLACKMUN delivered the opinion of the Court. . . .

The Texas statutes that concern us here . . . make it a crime to "procure an abortion," as therein defined, or to attempt one, except with respect to "an abor-

[5]. Eugenicists sought to improve the human race by curbing reproduction by criminals, the insane, and other "degenerates." See, e.g., Linda Gordon, The Moral Property of Women: A History of Birth Control Politics in America 190-203 (2002).

tion procured or attempted by medical advice for the purpose of saving the life of the mother." Similar statutes are in existence in a majority of the States. . . .

Jane Roe, a single woman who was residing in Dallas County, Texas, instituted this federal action in March 1970 against the District Attorney of the county. She sought a declaratory judgment that the Texas criminal abortion statutes were unconstitutional on their face, and an injunction restraining the defendant from enforcing the statutes.

Roe alleged that she was unmarried and pregnant; that she wished to terminate her pregnancy by an abortion "performed by a competent, licensed physician, under safe, clinical conditions"; that she was unable to get a "legal" abortion in Texas because her life did not appear to be threatened by the continuation of her pregnancy; and that she could not afford to travel to another jurisdiction in order to secure a legal abortion under safe conditions. She claimed that the Texas statutes were unconstitutionally vague and that they abridged her right of personal privacy, protected by the First, Fourth, Fifth, Ninth, and Fourteenth Amendments. By an amendment to her complaint Roe purported to sue "on behalf of herself and all other women" similarly situated. [The district court held that the Ninth and Fourteenth Amendments protected the fundamental right to choose to have children and that the Texas statutes were unconstitutionally vague.]

The principal thrust of appellant's attack on the Texas statutes is that they improperly invade a right, said to be possessed by the pregnant woman, to choose to terminate her pregnancy. Appellant would discover this right in the concept of personal "liberty" embodied in the Fourteenth Amendment's Due Process Clause; or in personal marital, familial, and sexual privacy said to be protected by the Bill of Rights or its penumbras, see Griswold v. Connecticut, 381 U.S. 479 (1965); Eisenstadt v. Baird, 405 U.S. 438 (1972); id., at 460 (White, J., concurring in result); or among those rights reserved to the people by the Ninth Amendment, Griswold v. Connecticut, 381 U.S., at 486 (Goldberg J., concurring). Before addressing this claim, we feel it desirable briefly to survey, in several aspects, the history of abortion, for such insight as that history may afford us, and then to examine the state purposes and interests behind the criminal abortion laws.

VI

It perhaps is not generally appreciated that the restrictive criminal abortion laws in effect in a majority of States today are of relatively recent vintage. Those laws, generally proscribing abortion or its attempt at any time during pregnancy except when necessary to preserve the pregnant woman's life, are not of ancient or even of common-law origin. Instead, they derive from statutory changes effected, for the most part, in the latter half of the 19th century. . . .

[A]t common law, abortion performed before "quickening" — the first recognizable movement of the fetus in utero, appearing usually from the 16th to the 18th week of pregnancy — was not an indictable offense. The absence of a common-law crime for pre-quickening abortion appears to have developed from a confluence of earlier philosophical, theological, and civil and canon law concepts of when life begins. . . .

. . . In a frequently cited passage, Coke took the position that abortion of a woman "quick with childe" is "a great misprision, and no murder." . . . A recent review of the common-law precedents argues, however, that those precedents contradict Coke and that even post-quickening abortion was never established as a common-law crime. This is of some importance because while most American courts ruled, in holding or dictum, that abortion of an unquickened fetus was not criminal under their received common law, others followed Coke in stating that abortion of a quick fetus was a "misprision," a term they translated to mean "misdemeanor." That their reliance on Coke on this aspect of the law was uncritical and, apparently in all the reported cases, dictum (due probably to the paucity of common-law prosecutions for post-quickening abortion), makes it now appear doubtful that abortion was ever firmly established as a common-law crime even with respect to the destruction of a quick fetus.

. . . England's first criminal abortion statute, Lord Ellenborough's Act, 43 Geo. 3, c. 58, came in 1803. It made abortion of a quick fetus, §1, a capital crime, but in §2 it provided lesser penalties for the felony of abortion before quickening, and thus preserved the "quickening" distinction. . . .

. . . In this country, the law in effect in all but a few States until mid-19th century was the pre-existing English common law. Connecticut, the first State to enact abortion legislation, adopted in 1821 that part of Lord Ellenborough's Act that related to a woman "quick with child." The death penalty was not imposed. Abortion before quickening was made a crime in that State only in 1860. In 1828, New York enacted legislation that, in two respects, was to serve as a model for early anti-abortion statutes. First, while barring destruction of an unquickened fetus as well as a quick fetus, it made the former only a misdemeanor, but the latter second-degree manslaughter. Second, it incorporated a concept of therapeutic abortion [necessary to save the life of the woman]. By 1840, when Texas had received the common law, only eight American States had statutes dealing with abortion. . . .

Gradually, in the middle and late 19th century the quickening distinction disappeared from the statutory law of most States and the degree of the offense and the penalties were increased. By the end of the 1950's a large majority of the jurisdictions banned abortion, however and whenever performed, unless done to save or preserve the life of the mother. The exceptions, Alabama and the District of Columbia, permitted abortion to preserve the mother's health. . . . In the past several years, however, a trend toward liberalization of abortion statutes has resulted in adoption, by about one-third of the States, of less stringent laws, most of them patterned after the ALI Model Penal Code, §230.3. . . .

It is thus apparent that at common law, at the time of the adoption of our Constitution, and throughout the major portion of the 19th century, abortion was viewed with less disfavor than under most American statutes currently in effect. Phrasing it another way, a woman enjoyed a substantially broader right to terminate a pregnancy than she does in most States today. [The opinion then noted that the American Medical Association, American Public Health Association, and American Bar Association all supported liberalizing abortion laws.]

VII

Three reasons have been advanced to explain historically the enactment of criminal abortion laws in the 19th century and to justify their continued existence.

It has been argued occasionally that these laws were the product of a Victorian social concern to discourage illicit sexual conduct. Texas, however, does not advance this justification in the present case, and it appears that no court or commentator has taken the argument seriously. . . .

A second reason is concerned with abortion as a medical procedure. When most criminal abortion laws were first enacted, the procedure was a hazardous one for the woman. . . . Thus, it has been argued that a State's real concern in enacting a criminal abortion law was to protect the pregnant woman, that is, to restrain her from submitting to a procedure that placed her life in serious jeopardy.

Modern medical techniques have altered this situation. Appellants and various amici refer to medical data indicating that abortion in early pregnancy, that is, prior to the end of the first trimester, although not without its risk, is now relatively safe. Mortality rates for women undergoing early abortions, where the procedure is legal, appear to be as low as or lower than the rates for normal childbirth. Consequently, any interest of the State in protecting the woman from an inherently hazardous procedure, except when it would be equally dangerous for her to forgo it, has largely disappeared. Of course, important state interests in the areas of health and medical standards do remain. The State has a legitimate interest in seeing to it that abortion, like any other medical procedure, is performed under circumstances that insure maximum safety for the patient. This interest obviously extends at least to the performing physician and his staff, to the facilities involved, to the availability of after-care, and to adequate provision for any complication or emergency that might arise. The prevalence of high mortality rates at illegal "abortion mills" strengthens, rather than weakens, the State's interest in regulating the conditions under which abortions are performed. Moreover, the risk to the woman increases as her pregnancy continues. Thus, the State retains a definite interest in protecting the woman's own health and safety when an abortion is proposed at a late stage of pregnancy.

The third reason is the State's interest — some phrase it in terms of duty — in protecting prenatal life. Some of the argument for this justification rests on the theory that a new human life is present from the moment of conception. The State's interest and general obligation to protect life then extends, it is argued, to prenatal life. Only when the life of the pregnant mother herself is at stake, balanced against the life she carries within her, should the interest of the embryo or fetus not prevail. . . . In assessing the State's interest, recognition may be given to the . . . claim that as long as at least *potential* life is involved, the State may assert interests beyond the protection of the pregnant woman alone.

Parties challenging state abortion laws have sharply disputed in some courts the contention that a purpose of these laws, when enacted, was to protect prenatal life. Pointing to the absence of legislative history to support the contention, they claim that most state laws were designed solely to protect the woman. Proponents of this view point out that in many States, including Texas, by statute or judicial interpretation, the pregnant woman herself could not be prosecuted for self-abortion or for cooperating in an abortion performed upon her by another. They claim that adoption of the "quickening" distinction through received common law and state statutes tacitly recognizes the greater health hazards inherent in late abortion and impliedly repudiates the theory that life begins at conception.

It is with these interests, and the weight to be attached to them, that this case is concerned.

VIII

The Constitution does not explicitly mention any right of privacy. In a line of decisions, however, going back perhaps as far as Union Pacific R. Co. v. Botsford, 141 U.S. 250, 251 (1891), the Court has recognized that a right of personal privacy, or a guarantee of certain areas or zones of privacy, does exist under the Constitution. In varying contexts, the Court or individual Justices have, indeed, found at least the roots of that right in the First Amendment, Stanley v. Georgia, 394 U.S. 557, 564 (1969); in the Fourth and Fifth Amendments; in the penumbras of the Bill of Rights, Griswold v. Connecticut, 381 U.S., at 484-485; in the Ninth Amendment, id., at 486 (Goldberg, J., concurring); or in the concept of liberty guaranteed by the first section of the Fourteenth Amendment, see Meyer v. Nebraska, 262 U.S. 390, 399 (1923). These decisions make it clear that only personal rights that can be deemed "fundamental" or "implicit in the concept of ordered liberty," are included in this guarantee of personal privacy. They also make it clear that the right has some extension to activities relating to marriage, procreation, contraception, family relationships, and child rearing and education [citing *Meyer, Pierce, Eisenstadt, Skinner,* and Loving v. Virginia, 388 U.S. 1 (1967)].

This right of privacy, whether it be founded in the Fourteenth Amendment's concept of personal liberty and restrictions upon state action, as we feel it is, or, as the District Court determined, in the Ninth Amendment's reservation of rights to the people, is broad enough to encompass a woman's decision whether or not to terminate her pregnancy. The detriment that the State would impose upon the pregnant woman by denying this choice altogether is apparent. Specific and direct harm medically diagnosable even in early pregnancy may be involved. Maternity, or additional offspring, may force upon the woman a distressful life and future. Psychological harm may be imminent. Mental and physical health may be taxed by child care. There is also the distress, for all concerned, associated with the unwanted child, and there is the problem of bringing a child into a family already unable, psychologically and otherwise, to care for it. In other cases, as in this one, the additional difficulties and continuing stigma of unwed motherhood may be involved. All these are factors the woman and her responsible physician necessarily will consider in consultation.

On the basis of elements such as these, appellant and some amici argue that the woman's right is absolute and that she is entitled to terminate her pregnancy at whatever time, in whatever way, and for whatever reason she alone chooses. With this we do not agree. Appellant's arguments that Texas either has no valid interest at all in regulating the abortion decision, or no interest strong enough to support any limitation upon the woman's sole determination, are unpersuasive. The Court's decisions recognizing a right of privacy also acknowledge that some state regulation in areas protected by that right is appropriate. As noted above, a State may properly assert important interests in safeguarding health, in maintaining medical standards, and in protecting potential life. At some point in pregnancy, these respective interests become sufficiently compelling to sustain regulation of the factors that govern the abortion decision. The privacy right involved, therefore, cannot be said to be absolute. In fact, it is not clear to us that the claim asserted by some amici that one has an unlimited right to do with one's body as one pleases bears a close relationship to the right of privacy previously articulated in the Court's decisions. The Court has refused to recognize an unlimited right of this kind in the past. Jacobson v. Massachusetts, 197 U.S. 11 (1905) (vaccination); Buck v. Bell, 274 U.S. 200 (1927) (sterilization).

We therefore conclude that the right of personal privacy includes the abortion decision, but that this right is not unqualified and must be considered against important state interests in regulation. . . . Where certain "fundamental rights" are involved, the Court has held that regulation limiting these rights may be justified only by a "compelling state interest," and that legislative enactments must be narrowly drawn to express only the legitimate state interests at stake. . . .

IX . . .

The appellee and certain amici argue that the fetus is a "person" within the language and meaning of the Fourteenth Amendment. In support of this, they outline at length and in detail the well-known facts of fetal development. If this suggestion of personhood is established, the appellant's case, of course, collapses, for the fetus' right to life would then be guaranteed specifically by the Amendment. . . .

The Constitution does not define "person" in so many words. Section 1 of the Fourteenth Amendment contains three references to "person." The first, in defining "citizens," speaks of "persons born or naturalized in the United States." The word also appears both in the Due Process Clause and in the Equal Protection Clause. "Person" is used in other places in the Constitution. . . . But in nearly all these instances, the use of the word is such that it has application only postnatally. None indicates, with any assurance, that it has any possible prenatal application.[54]

All this, together with our observation, supra, that throughout the major portion of the 19th century prevailing legal abortion practices were far freer than they are today, persuades us that the word "person," as used in the Fourteenth Amendment, does not include the unborn. . . .

The pregnant woman cannot be isolated in her privacy. She carries an embryo and, later, a fetus. . . . The situation therefore is inherently different from marital intimacy, or bedroom possession of obscene material, or marriage, or procreation, or education, with which *Eisenstadt* and *Griswold, Stanley, Loving, Skinner* and *Pierce* and *Meyer* were respectively concerned. As we have intimated above, it is reasonable and appropriate for a State to decide that at some point in time another interest, that of health of the mother or that of potential human life, becomes significantly involved. The woman's privacy is no longer sole and any right of privacy she possesses must be measured accordingly.

54. When Texas urges that a fetus is entitled to Fourteenth Amendment protection as a person, it faces a dilemma. Neither in Texas nor in any other State are all abortions prohibited. Despite broad proscription, [a therapeutic] exception always exists. . . . But if the fetus is a person who is not to be deprived of life without due process of law, and if the mother's condition is the sole determinant, does not the Texas exception appear to be out of line with the Amendment's command? There are other inconsistencies between Fourteenth Amendment status and the typical abortion statute. It has already been pointed out that in Texas the woman is not a principal or an accomplice with respect to an abortion upon her. If the fetus is a person, why is the woman not a principal or an accomplice? Further, the penalty for criminal abortion . . . is significantly less than the maximum penalty for murder. . . . If the fetus is a person, may the penalties be different?

Texas urges that, apart from the Fourteenth Amendment, life begins at conception and is present throughout pregnancy, and that, therefore, the State has a compelling interest in protecting that life from and after conception. We need not resolve the difficult question of when life begins. When those trained in the respective disciplines of medicine, philosophy, and theology are unable to arrive at any consensus, the judiciary, at this point in the development of man's knowledge, is not in a position to speculate as to the answer.

It should be sufficient to note briefly the wide divergence of thinking on this most sensitive and difficult question. There has always been strong support for the view that life does not begin until live birth [citing Stoics and Jewish and Protestant communities]. As we have noted, the common law found greater significance in quickening. Physicians and their scientific colleagues have regarded that event with less interest and have tended to focus either upon conception, upon live birth, or upon the interim point at which the fetus becomes "viable," that is, potentially able to live outside the mother's womb, albeit with artificial aid. Viability is usually placed at about seven months (28 weeks) but may occur earlier, even at 24 weeks. [T]he existence of life from the moment of conception [is] the official belief of the Catholic Church. [T]his is a view strongly held by many non-Catholics as well, and by many physicians. Substantial problems for precise definition of this view are posed, however, by new embryological data that purport to indicate that conception is a "process" over time, rather than an event, and by new medical techniques such as menstrual extraction, the "morning-after" pill, implantation of embryos, artificial insemination, and even artificial wombs.

In areas other than criminal abortion, the law has been reluctant to endorse any theory that life, as we recognize it, begins before live birth or to accord legal rights to the unborn except in narrowly defined situations and except when the rights are contingent upon live birth [citing tort and property law]. In short, the unborn have never been recognized in the law as persons in the whole sense.

X

In view of all this, we do not agree that, by adopting one theory of life, Texas may override the rights of the pregnant woman that are at stake. We repeat, however, that the State does have an important and legitimate interest in preserving and protecting the health of the pregnant woman, whether she be a resident of the State or a non-resident who seeks medical consultation and treatment there, and that it has still another important and legitimate interest in protecting the potentiality of human life. These interests are separate and distinct. Each grows in substantiality as the woman approaches term and, at a point during pregnancy, each becomes "compelling."

With respect to the State's important and legitimate interest in the health of the mother, the "compelling" point, in the light of present medical knowledge, is at approximately the end of the first trimester. This is so because of the now-established medical fact . . . that until the end of the first trimester mortality in abortion may be less than mortality in normal childbirth. It follows that, from and after this point, a State may regulate the abortion procedure to the extent that the regulation reasonably relates to the preservation and protection of maternal health. Examples of permissible state regulation in this area are requirements as to the qualifications of the person who is to perform the abortion; as to the licensure of that person; as to the facility in which the procedure is to be performed, that is, whether it must be a hospital or may be a clinic or some other place of less-than-hospital status; as to the licensing of the facility; and the like.

This means, on the other hand, that, for the period of pregnancy prior to this "compelling" point, the attending physician, in consultation with his patient, is free to determine, without regulation by the State, that, in his medical judgment, the patient's pregnancy should be terminated. If that decision is reached, the judgment may be effectuated by an abortion free of interference by the State.

With respect to the State's important and legitimate interest in potential life, the "compelling" point is at viability. This is so because the fetus then presumably has the capability of meaningful life outside the mother's womb. State regulation protective of fetal life after viability thus has both logical and biological justifications. If the State is interested in protecting fetal life after viability, it may go so far as to proscribe abortion during that period, except when it is necessary to preserve the life or health of the mother. . . .

XI

To summarize and to repeat:

1. A state criminal abortion statute of the current Texas type, that excepts from criminality only a *life-saving* procedure on behalf of the mother, without regard to pregnancy stage and without recognition of the other interests involved, is violative of the Due Process Clause of the Fourteenth Amendment.

(a) For the stage prior to approximately the end of the first trimester, the abortion decision and its effectuation must be left to the medical judgment of the pregnant woman's attending physician.

(b) For the stage subsequent to approximately the end of the first trimester, the State, in promoting its interest in the health of the mother, may, if it chooses, regulate the abortion procedure in ways that are reasonably related to maternal health.

(c) For the stage subsequent to viability, the State in promoting its interest in the potentiality of human life may, if it chooses, regulate, and even proscribe, abortion except where it is necessary, in appropriate medical judgment, for the preservation of the life or health of the mother. . . .

This holding, we feel, is consistent with the relative weights of the respective interests involved, with the lessons and examples of medical and legal history, with the lenity of the common law, and with the demands of the profound problems of the present day. The decision leaves the State free to place increasing restrictions on abortion as the period of pregnancy lengthens, so long as those restrictions are tailored to the recognized state interests. The decision vindicates the right of the physician to administer medical treatment according to his professional judgment up to the points where important state interests provide compelling justifications for intervention. Up to those points, the abortion decision in all its aspects is inherently, and primarily, a medical decision, and basic responsibility for it must rest with the physician. . . .

Mr. Justice REHNQUIST, dissenting. . . .

. . . I have difficulty in concluding, as the Court does, that the right of "privacy" is involved in this case. Texas, by the statute here challenged, bars the performance of a medical abortion by a licensed physician on a plaintiff such as Roe. A transaction resulting in an operation such as this is not "private" in the ordinary usage of that word. Nor is the "privacy" that the Court finds here even a distant relative of the freedom from searches and seizures protected by the Fourth Amendment to the Constitution, which the Court has referred to as embodying a right to privacy. Katz v. United States, 389 U.S. 347 (1967).

The fact that a majority of the States reflecting, after all, the majority sentiment in those States, have had restrictions on abortions for at least a century is a strong indication, it seems to me, that the asserted right to an abortion is not "so rooted in the traditions and conscience of our people as to be ranked as fundamental," Snyder v. Massachusetts, 291 U.S. 97, 105 (1934). . . . To reach its result, the Court necessarily has had to find within the scope of the Fourteenth Amendment a right that was apparently completely unknown to the drafters of the Amendment. [T]he drafters did not intend to have the Fourteenth Amendment withdraw from the States the power to legislate with respect to this matter. . . .

■ SARAH WEDDINGTON,[6] A QUESTION OF CHOICE
12-14, 35-38, 44-57 (1992)

My mouth goes dry as I put myself back in those days in Austin [Texas in 1967] when my period was late. I was in my third year of law school, going to school full-time and supporting myself by working several jobs. I was seriously dating Ron Weddington, who was finishing his undergraduate degree after returning from the army; he was planning to start law school the following summer. . . .

[Once pregnancy was confirmed, we] began to go over the possibilities. Abortion was one, but we were worried about the risks of an illegal procedure. . . . If we decided on abortion, the next problem was: Where to go? There were no ads in the phone books or newspapers; this was all undercover. You had to find someone who knew a name, a place — and I refused to tell anyone my situation. . . . Ron heard about a doctor in Piedras Negras, across from Eagle Pass, Texas, who had some medical experience in the United States and who did abortions. Abortion was illegal in Mexico, but the woman Ron spoke to told him [that] several women she knew had been to this doctor, and everything had turned out fine. He charged $400 — cash only. [Ron made the necessary arrangements, obtained a powerful painkiller, and got the name of someone who might help in case of medical trouble.]

I was grateful that at least the inside of the building was clean. I could not read what appeared to be a medical diploma on the wall, but it made me feel better. . . . I was one of the lucky ones. [W]hen I felt the anesthesia taking effect, my last thoughts were: I hope I don't die, and I pray that no one ever finds out about this. . . .

Roe v. Wade started at a garage sale, amid paltry castoffs. [Weddington and her friends were raising money for an abortion referral project.] The referral project volunteers were worried about being involved in covert activity. . . . While we sorted our prized junk at the garage sale, Judy [Smith] posed the primary questions that the volunteers wanted answered: Could they be prosecuted and/or convicted as accomplices to the crime of abortion simply for referring women? Would it

---

[6]. Sarah Weddington is the attorney who represented plaintiff Jane Roe in Roe v. Wade.

make any legal difference if they sent women only to places where abortion was legal? . . . The [Texas] statute made it a crime to "furnish the means for procuring an abortion," but I didn't know whether that applied only to drugs and instruments, not information. I knew Texas also had a general accomplice statute that applied to a variety of crimes.

. . . I began spending time in the [University of Texas] law library, meeting with project volunteers, spending more time in the library, and talking to law professors, law students, and other lawyers. [One day] Judy announced that she wanted a lawsuit filed to challenge the constitutionality of the Texas anti-abortion statute. . . .

[I] had not focused on the possibility of *our* filing a lawsuit. After all, my total legal experience consisted of a few uncontested divorces for friends, ten or twelve uncomplicated wills for people with little property, one adoption for relatives, and a few miscellaneous matters. . . . The idea of challenging the Texas abortion law in federal court was overwhelming [but] I was the best free legal help available [and I wanted to help others avoid what we had gone through]. [P]erhaps my inexperience was a plus. I did not fully appreciate that the odds were stacked against our endeavor. . . .

[Weddington asked former classmate Linda Coffee, who was familiar with federal litigation, to help.] [O]ur constant worry was about the right plaintiffs. . . . Then a woman went to Dallas lawyer Henry McCluskey, a friend of Linda's who knew of the proposed lawsuit. She had had a rough life: She already had one child and did not want another. Her mother had taken her daughter away from her and she seldom got to see her. She had never finished the tenth grade, was working as a waitress, and knew she would lose her job if the pregnancy continued. She could barely support herself, much less a child. . . .

. . . She had found an illegal place in Dallas, she admitted, but she didn't like the looks of it. She had no money to travel to another state. As the conversation continued [in our meeting at a Dallas pizza parlor, this woman] asked if it would help if she had been raped. We said no; the Texas law had no exception for rape. It was just as illegal for a doctor to do an abortion for someone who had been raped as it was in any other situation. I did ask, "Were there any witnesses? Was there a police report? Is there any way that we could prove a rape occurred?" Her answer in each instance was no.

Neither Linda nor I questioned her further about how she had gotten pregnant. I was not going to allege something in the complaint that I could not back up with proof. Also, we did not want the Texas law changed only to allow abortion in cases of rape. We wanted a decision that abortion was covered by the right of privacy. After all, the women coming to the referral project were there as a result of a wide variety of circumstances. . . .

. . . We still had to name our plaintiffs [who would use pseudonyms to protect their privacy]. We picked names that rhymed. I liked "Jane Roe."[7] To me the

---

[7]. Norma McCorvey (who was "Jane Roe" in Roe v. Wade) later announced that she had joined the pro-life movement, saying that she had "always been pro-life [but] just didn't know it" and that she had been exploited by abortion-rights groups. See "Jane Roe" Joins Anti-Abortion Group, N.Y. Times, Aug. 11, 1995, at A12. In McCorvey v. Hill, 385 F.3d 846 (5th Cir. 2004), *cert. denied*, 543 U.S. 1154 (2005), she filed a motion for relief from judgment, seeking to revisit *Roe*. The Fifth Circuit Court of Appeals found that she lacked standing because the case was moot. See also Norma McCorvey with Andy Meister, I am Roe: My Life, Roe v. Wade and Freedom of Choice (1994).

name represented all women, not just one. . . . We were filing . . . against Henry Wade, the elected district attorney of Dallas County, the official responsible for law enforcement in that county. We wanted the court to tell Wade's office to leave doctors alone. [The case] became known as Roe v. Wade. . . .

■ BRIEF FOR THE AMICI CURIAE WOMEN WHO HAVE HAD ABORTIONS AND FRIENDS OF AMICI CURIAE IN SUPPORT OF APPELLEES, WEBSTER v. REPRODUCTIVE HEALTH SERVICES
492 U.S. 490 (1989) (No. 88-605)

FRIENDS LETTER — 172, AT C29-30

When I was six years old, I was forced to endure a 40 mile trip to what was referred to as "Feather Annie's." I stayed in the car with my father and two brothers while my 41 year old mother went inside the private residence. My father's serious attitude instilled fear and insecurity in my older brother and I. When my mother returned to the car she was crying. She repeated the words "I'm afraid I'll die — I'm afraid someone will find out I came here and I'll get her (referring to the woman who performed the abortion) in trouble with the law. I'm glad it's over, but I'm afraid — if I die, what will happen to the children?" It was an awful experience for a child who was too young to understand. All the way home she cried and repeated over and over her fear of dying. I do not remember . . . her expressing any regret, she expressed her relief that it was over. Her fears became contagious and needless to say it was traumatic for me and my older brother (one brother was less than 2 years old). Many years later when my brother and I recalled that day, we agreed that the only crime committed was by a society that forced a woman to have to submit herself to fear and agony of that magnitude. Our mother survived and imbued in us forever was our sympathy for her on that day. After all, she had already born six children, she was in poor health, and my father was unemployed in that year of 1936.

My mother told me that it was a terrible tragedy that the little 2-year old neighbor girl's mother died suddenly. When I became old enough to understand I found out that it was no secret, in the small town we lived in, that the young mother had died from a self induced abortion. As a very young child I was terribly disturbed over the fact that this dear cute little girl had no mother for the reason that her mother had died because she didn't want to have another baby. I felt sad that such a thing could happen, it was hard for me to accept that "Jane's" pretty young mother had to die. I saw sadness in Jane's face and unhappiness was apparent in her father's behavior. I cannot justify a law that allowed such unfortunate circumstances to happen.

In the 1950's my sister lost a good friend who had an illegal abortion. The 28-year old woman who died had five small children. Her unplanned and unwanted pregnancy was more than she was able to handle and her untimely death was the result of not having a choice of a safe and legal abortion. A law with the potential effect of depriving a loving husband and five small children of the presence of a young wife and mother is a disgrace in a compassionate society.

As these excerpts reveal, abortion was a dangerous procedure before legalization. In fact, abortion was the leading cause of maternal deaths in some locales. See generally Ellen Messer & Kathryn E. May, Back Rooms: Voices from the Illegal Abortion Era (1988). See also Laura Kaplan, The Story of Jane: The Legendary Underground Feminist Abortion Service (1995) (account of famous abortion referral-provider service that, in its four-year history, performed 11,000 illegal abortions); Leslie J. Reagan, When Abortion Was a Crime: Women, Medicine, and Law in the United States, 1867-1973 (1997).

Notes and Questions

1. *Roe's right.* What is the nature of the right recognized by Roe v. Wade? Its parameters? Where in the Constitution does *Roe* situate this right? How does this approach compare with that of *Griswold*? Why is the right to terminate a pregnancy not absolute? Why is it "fundamental" (thereby evoking the compelling state interest test)?

2. *Roe's precedents.* Does the protection of childrearing and education in *Meyer* and *Pierce* support *Roe*'s holding? Does the definition of the right to privacy in *Eisenstadt* necessarily include abortion freedom? Constitutional historian David Garrow has documented that Justice Brennan's choice of the "*bear* or beget" language in *Eisenstadt* resulted from Brennan's anticipation of the abortion decision. David J. Garrow, Liberty and Sexuality: The Right to Privacy and the Making of *Roe v. Wade* 541-544 (updated ed. 1998).

3. *Abortion restrictions.* Two types of statutory restrictions were common in the *Roe* era. One type, like the Texas statute, prohibited abortion except to save the life of the mother. A newer type, modeled on the American Law Institute's (ALI) Model Penal Code, permitted abortion if pregnancy would seriously and permanently injure the woman's health; if the fetus suffered from a grave, permanent, and irremediable mental or physical defect; or if the pregnancy resulted from rape. In a companion case to *Roe*, Doe v. Bolton, 410 U.S. 179 (1973), the Court invalidated Georgia's ALI-inspired statute, including its procedural requirements of hospitalization, accreditation, committee approval, two-doctor concurrence, and residency.

4. *Privacy's meanings.* After *Roe*, the Court elaborated on the meaning of "privacy" in Whalen v. Roe, 429 U.S. 589 (1977). Upholding a statute that required recording the identity of those who had obtained certain drugs pursuant to prescription, the Court stated:

> The cases sometimes characterized as protecting "privacy" have in fact involved at least two different kinds of interests. One is the individual interest in avoiding disclosure of personal matters, and another is the interest in independence in making certain kinds of important decisions.

Id. at 598-599. The Court cited *Griswold* twice, for each meaning. Does *Griswold* support both definitions?

5. *Viability.* Why does the state's interest in protecting "potential life" become compelling only after viability? In the balance of competing individual and state

interests, why should the fetus's ability to survive outside the womb determine the woman's rights?[8]

As *Roe* suggests, viability played an important role in prenatal torts. Early cases permitted recovery for prenatal injuries by children subsequently born alive only if the injuries occurred after viability. See, e.g., Bonbrest v. Kotz, 65 F. Supp. 138 (D.D.C. 1946). Yet many cases abandoned the requirement before *Roe*. See, e.g., Hornbuckle v. Plantation Pipe Line Co., 93 S.E.2d 727 (Ga. 1956). Nor is viability currently required in a number of states for the crime of fetal murder. See People v. Davis, 872 P.2d 591 (Cal. 1994) (citing *Roe* to support protection of previable fetus when no conflict with mother's privacy interests).

Many early abortion restrictions disallowed abortions only after quickening (the perception of fetal movement, usually between 16 and 18 weeks of gestation). Though quickening had no biological significance, it may have become important, in the absence of modern pregnancy tests, as the first indication of pregnancy. Without such evidence, prosecutors could not establish the elements of criminal abortion. See James C. Mohr, Abortion in America: The Origins and Evolution of National Policy, 1800-1900, at 4 (1978). Is quickening superior to viability as a benchmark? See Reva Siegel, Reasoning from the Body: A Historical Perspective on Abortion Regulation and Questions of Equal Protection, 44 Stan. L. Rev. 261, 380 (1992) (arguing affirmatively).

6. *Measurement of viability.* In 1973, *Roe* placed viability at approximately 28 weeks. By 1992, the Court placed it at 23 to 24 weeks. Planned Parenthood of Southeastern Pa. v. Casey, 505 U.S. 833, 860 (1992). Current medical literature estimates neonatal survival rates as follows: "1 percent of those born at 22 weeks of gestation, 11 percent at 23 weeks, 26 percent at 24 weeks, and 44 percent at 25 weeks." Betty R. Vohr & Marilee Allen, Extreme Prematurity—The Continuing Dilemma, 352 New Eng. J. Med. 71, 71 (2005) (editorial). What do these figures mean in terms of viability? Suppose technology can advance viability still further? Or make available artificial wombs? See Ainsley Newson, From Foetus to Full Term—Without a Mother's Touch, The Times (London), Aug. 30, 2005, Home News, at 23. See also Akron v. Akron Ctr. for Reprod. Health, 462 U.S. 416, 458 (1983) (O'Connor, J., dissenting) (suggesting this prospect puts *Roe* on a "collision course" with itself). Will the state have the authority to prohibit abortions earlier in pregnancy? Alternatively, might "artificial wombs" or abortion methods compatible with fetal survival give pregnant women *more* freedom to terminate their pregnancies by allowing the state to protect potential life without continued physical imposition on women? Consider here what interest of the pregnant woman *Roe* sought to protect: The freedom to terminate the physical burdens of pregnancy? The freedom to escape reproduction?

7. *Physician's role.* According to *Roe*, to whom does the privacy right belong—the woman or the physician? See Siegel, supra, at 296. Why did the Court choose this approach? This emphasis on the physician receives reinforcement from Doe v. Bolton's broad interpretation of "health," which allows the physician to consider "all factors—physical, emotional, psychological, familial, and the woman's age—relevant to the well-being of the patient." 410 U.S. at 192. See id. at 196-197. What role *should* a physician play in the decision to terminate a pregnancy? In matters of privacy generally?

[8]. On how viability became the compelling point in *Roe*, see Linda Greenhouse, Becoming Justice Blackmun: Harry Blackmun's Supreme Court Journey 96-98 (2005).

8. *Gender equality*. What alternative approaches might the Supreme Court have used? Many feminist commentators prefer an equal protection, over a privacy-based, approach on the theory that abortion freedom is essential for gender equality. For example, Professor Sylvia Law has argued:

> [T]he Court held in Roe v. Wade that the constitutional right to privacy protects the right of women and their physicians to determine whether or not to terminate pregnancy. Nothing the Supreme Court has ever done has been more concretely important for women. Laws denying access to abortion have a sex-specific impact. Although both men and women seek to control reproduction, only women become pregnant. Only women have abortions. Laws restricting access to abortion have a devastating sex-specific impact. Despite the decision's overwhelming importance to women, it was not grounded on the principle of sex equality. . . .
>
> . . . An equality doctrine that ignores the unique quality of [women's reproductive] experiences implicitly says that women can claim equality only insofar as they are like men. Such a doctrine demands that women deny an important aspect of who they are. . . .

Sylvia A. Law, Rethinking Sex and the Constitution, 132 U. Pa. L. Rev. 955, 980-981, 1007 (1984). Proponents of this approach include Justice Ginsburg, who as a litigator persuaded the Supreme Court to apply the Equal Protection Clause to gender discrimination. See, e.g., Ruth Bader Ginsburg, Some Thoughts on Autonomy and Equality in Relation to Roe v. Wade, 63 N.C. L. Rev. 375, 386 (1985). What are the advantages and disadvantages of an equal protection rationale for the right to abortion?

See generally, e.g., Catharine A. MacKinnon, Women's Lives — Men's Laws 127-146 (2005). For elaboration of the gender equality argument and other approaches that the Justices might have used, see What Roe v. Wade Should Have Said: The Nation's Top Legal Experts Rewrite America's Most Controversial Decision (Jack M. Balkin ed., 2005).

9. *Potential life and sex discrimination*. How far should the state go in protecting *potential* life? Professor Frances Olsen ponders this question:

> . . . How would men react to a law that forbad them to ejaculate outside a fertile woman's vagina? While most heterosexual men would probably prefer to ejaculate into a vagina, the idea that they could not ejaculate anywhere else would probably come to seem oppressive and absurd to them. Yet such a law would seem to promote a state interest in *potential life*, as well as a state interest in the life of sperm. To avoid overbreadth, the law could provide that if a man does ejaculate where he is not allowed to, he could avoid criminal liability by collecting as many of the sperm as possible and rushing them to a sperm bank. . . .
>
> Of course, the burden such a law would place upon men is nothing like the burden that antiabortion laws place upon women. Many men would not be affected at all; other men would simply have to make periodic trips to sperm banks. . . . They would disrupt no one's life, disturb no long range plans. The trips would be even less disruptive than a woman's menstrual period, so really no one could properly complain. Perhaps some disgruntled men, whose real complaint might be that they were born male, might object. Their objection, however, should be lodged against mother nature, not against the law — a law reasonably drafted to maximize a man's freedom, consistent with the state's obligation to preserve life.

Many people would consider this example silly, but this putative silliness reflects the value that society places upon men's lives and their freedom. Only convenience prevents us from valuing sperm. In fact, if men rather than women needed sperm to reproduce, some would argue that the state could not constitutionally deny men access to women's sperm.

Frances Olsen, Comment: Unraveling Compromise, 103 Harv. L. Rev. 105, 129-130 (1989). See also Walter Dellinger & Gene B. Sperling, Abortion and the Supreme Court: The Retreat from Roe v. Wade, 138 U. Pa. L. Rev. 83, 106 (1989) (pointing out that, if the state had a sufficiently weighty interest in fetal life, one would expect it to treat the 62 percent of fertilized ova that spontaneously abort as "nothing short of an epidemic or national health crisis").

10. *Reducing abortion.* What other approaches might the state adopt to further the goal of reducing abortion? Olsen suggests social support for pregnant women and children and improved access to contraceptives. She adds that states could "outlaw" the act of impregnating women who do not wish to become pregnant by both requiring a woman's informed consent and imposing a waiting period, before a man could risk impregnating her. Olsen, supra, at 130.

11. *Abortion and motherhood.* Sociologist Kristin Luker attributes the sharp differences concerning abortion to a war over two opposing visions of motherhood. Kristin Luker, Abortion and the Politics of Motherhood (1984). Generally, the pro-choice position embraces feminist and progressive objectives, including equal opportunities for men and women in education and employment, freedom from gender-based assumptions and stereotypes, and the elimination of paternalism. See id. at 118. By contrast, abortion opponents do not regard equality as a primary value because "they believe that men and women are intrinsically different [with] different roles in life" and that "motherhood—the raising of children and families—is the most fulfilling role that women can have." Id. at 159-160. See also Linda Gordon, The Moral Property of Women: A History of Birth Control Politics in America 304-305 (2002) (attributing anti-abortion movement's strength to the view that abortion "represent[s] a multidimensional attack on the 'traditional' family and gender system").

What insights does this analysis provide in evaluating *Roe*? In understanding the controversy that followed *Roe* and persists today? Can one argue that abortion freedom enhances a woman's ability to be a good mother? See Joan C. Williams & Shauna L. Shames, Mothers' Dreams: Abortion and the High Price of Motherhood, 6 U. Pa. J. Const. L. 818, 841 (2004). Does the protection of childrearing in *Meyer* and *Pierce*, supra, support this argument?

12. *Abortion and crime.* Two economists have published empirical evidence suggesting that the legalization of abortion provides a "primary explanation" for large decreases in crime over the preceding decade. John J. Donahue III & Steven D. Levitt, The Impact of Legalized Abortion on Crime, 116 Q.J. Econ. 379, 414 (2001). The authors theorize that abortion prevented the birth of unwanted children who would have grown up to commit crimes. What relevance, if any, do such findings have for the legal and constitutional questions posed by *Roe*?

13. *Comparative law.* Writing in 1987, Professor Mary Ann Glendon claimed that *Roe* put the "United States in a class by itself" among developed nations in the legal treatment of abortion. She reached this conclusion because the United States alone recognized abortion as a right, its policy was not formulated legislatively, it

required neither counseling nor demonstrated reasons for abortion, and it failed to provide significant support for pregnant women and social benefits for mothers.[9]

Today, wide variations in abortion policy exist throughout the world. At the more permissive end of the spectrum, most European Union nations recognize abortion as a "fundamental human right."[10] Liberalization of abortion law has occurred in the last decade in 11 countries — Albania, Benin, Burkina Faso, Cambodia, Chad, Ethiopia, Guinea, Mali, Nepal, South Africa, and Switzerland.[11] Although Russia places no restrictions on first-trimester abortions, it recently reduced to four the number of social circumstances in which abortions up until the 22nd week are permissible: rape, imprisonment of either the wife or husband, the death or severe disability of the husband, and judicial termination of the woman's parental rights.[12] In contrast to the approaches in these countries, tight abortion restrictions govern in Ireland, Malta, Poland, and Portugal.[13] Restrictions in Ireland, which appear in the Irish constitution, have prompted many women to seek abortions abroad, not only in England but also at a reproductive health clinic operated on board a Dutch ship outside Irish territorial waters.[14] To the extent that China's notorious policy of one child per family has resulted in forced abortions and involuntary birth control, as critics claim,[15] it illustrates the different forms that restrictions on reproductive autonomy can take. For wider comparisons, see generally Albin Eser & H.G. Koch, Abortion and the Law: From International Comparison to Legal Policy (Emily Silverman trans., 2005) (survey of abortion policy in 64 countries, including analysis of social conditions, history, and legal regulations); Negotiating Reproductive Rights: Women's Perspectives Across Countries and Cultures (Rosalind P. Petchesky & Karen Judd eds., 1998).

b. Anti-Abortion Laws: Historical and Philosophical Perspectives

■ KRISTIN LUKER, ABORTION AND THE POLITICS OF MOTHERHOOD
20-29 (1984)

In the second half of the nineteenth century abortion began to emerge as a social problem: newspapers began to run accounts of women who had died from "criminal abortions," although whether this fact reflects more abortions, more

[9]. Mary Ann Glendon, Abortion and Divorce in Western Law 22-25 (1987).

[10]. Chad M. Gerson, Development, Toward an International Standard of Abortion Rights: Two Obstacles, 5 Chi. J. Int'l L. 753, 757 (2005).

[11]. Center for Reproductive Rights, Abortion and Law: Ten Years of Reform 2 (Feb. 2005) (briefing paper) (available at http://www.crlp.org/pdf/pub_bp_abortionlaws10.pdf).

[12]. Kelley J. Johnson, "New Thinking About an Old Issue:" The Abortion Controversy Continues in Russia and Ireland — Could Roe v. Wade Have Been the Better Solution?, 15 Ind. Int'l & Comp. L. Rev. 183, 202-208 (2004).

[13]. Center for Reproductive Rights, Reproductive Rights in the European Court of Human Rights (Aug. 2004) (briefing paper) (available at http://www.reproductiverights.org/pdf_bp_RREuropeancourt.pdf). See also Jack Hitt, Pro-Life Nation, N.Y. Times, Apr. 9, 2006, §6 (Magazine), at 40 (reporting on El Salvador's strict anti-abortion regime).

[14]. Johnson, supra note [12], at 194-201; Bryan Mercurio, Abortion in Ireland: An Analysis of the Legal Transformation Resulting from Membership in the European Union, 11 Tul. J. Int'l & Comp. L. 141 (2003).

[15]. See Hannah A. Saona, The Protection of Reproductive Rights Under International Law: The Bush Administration's Policy Shift and China's Family Planning Practices, 13 Pac. Rim L. & Pol'y J. 229 (2004).

lethal abortions, or simply more awareness is not clear. Most prominently, physicians became involved, arguing that abortion was both morally wrong and medically dangerous.

The membership of the American Medical Association (AMA), founded in 1847 to upgrade and protect the interests of the profession, was deeply divided on many issues. But by 1859 it was able to pass a resolution condemning induced abortion and urging state legislatures to pass laws forbidding it; in 1860, Henry Miller, the president-elect of the association, devoted much of his presidential address to attacking abortion. . . . Slowly, physicians responded to the AMA's call and began to lobby in state legislatures for laws forbidding abortion. . . .

Why should nineteenth-century physicians have become so involved with the question of abortion? . . . First, [the physicians themselves] argued, they were compelled to address the abortion question because American women were committing a moral crime based on ignorance about the proper value of embryonic life. According to these physicians, women sought abortions because the doctrine of quickening led them to believe that the embryo was not alive, and therefore aborting it was perfectly proper. Second, they argued, they were obliged to act in order to save women from their own ignorance because only physicians were in possession of new scientific evidence which demonstrated beyond a shadow of a doubt that the embryo was a child from conception onward. . . .

This stand had an important advantage for physicians. It meant that the American women who practiced abortion (and who were generally thought to be members of the "better classes") could be defined as *inadvertent* murderesses. . . . Thus, a physician could condemn the "sin" without the necessity of condemning the "sinner." . . .

[N]either part of the physicians' claim was, strictly speaking, true. Women (and the general public) knew that pregnancy was a *biologically* continuous process from beginning to end, and physicians were not in possession of remarkable new scientific discoveries to use to prove the case. . . . What the anti-abortion physicians achieved, therefore, was a subtle transformation of the grounds of the debate. . . .

[W]hy in the middle of the nineteenth century, did some physicians become anti-abortionists? James Mohr, in a pioneering work on this topic, argues that the proliferation of healers in the nineteenth century created a competition for status and clients. The "regular" physicians, who tended to be both wealthier and better educated than members of other medical sects, therefore sought to distinguish themselves both scientifically and socially from competing practitioners. . . . The abortion issue [gave the "regulars"] a way of demonstrating that they were both more scientifically knowledgeable and more morally rigorous than their competitors.

Mohr suggests that . . . outlawing abortion would remove a lucrative source of income from competitors [whom the "regulars"] called "quacks" and perhaps remove that temptation from the path of the "regulars" as well. In addition, the "regulars" were predominantly white, upper-income, and native-born; as such, they belonged to precisely the same group that was thought to harbor the primary users of abortion. As a result, they were likely to be concerned about the depopulation of their group in the face of mounting immigration (and the higher fertility of immigrants) and about "betrayal" by their own women (because abortion required less male control and approval than the other available forms of birth control). More broadly, Mohr argues that nineteenth-century physicians had a firm ideological belief that abortion was in fact murder. . . .

It is certainly true, as Mohr claims, that the mobilization of American physicians against abortion took place in the context of a profound dilemma within the medical profession, a dilemma produced by the lack of a traditional guild structure, the proliferation of competing medical sects and dissension within the ranks of the regulars themselves. Physicians wanted to upgrade their profession by obtaining licensing laws that would restrict medical practice to only the best and the best-trained among them.

As we know, regular physicians succeeded in their campaign. . . . More than almost any other profession, medicine now rigorously exercises the right to control who shall enter the profession, how they shall practice, and how competitors will be treated; its nineteenth-century stand against abortion contributed substantially to this ultimate success. It is in the context of this drive of professionalization that the political activity of American physicians against abortion must be understood. When examined closely in this context, their actual behavior raises serious doubts about whether they had . . . an unparalleled commitment to the "sanctity of life" of the embryo. . . .

For additional historical accounts, see James C. Mohr, Abortion in America: The Origins and Evolution of National Policy, 1800-1900 (1978); Carroll Smith-Rosenberg, The Abortion Movement and the AMA, 1850-1880, in Carroll Smith-Rosenberg, Disorderly Conduct: Visions of Gender in Victorian America 217 (1985).

■ JUDITH JARVIS THOMSON, A DEFENSE OF ABORTION
1 Phil. & Pub. Aff. 47-63 (1971)

[Assuming we grant that the fetus is a person from the moment of conception, how,] precisely, are we supposed to get from there to the conclusion that abortion is morally impermissible? . . .

[L]et me ask you to imagine this. You wake up in the morning and find yourself back to back in bed with an unconscious violinist. A famous unconscious violinist. He has been found to have a fatal kidney ailment, and the Society of Music Lovers has canvassed all the available medical records and found that you alone have the right blood type to help. They have therefore kidnapped you, and last night the violinist's circulatory system was plugged into yours, so that your kidneys can be used to extract poisons from his blood as well as your own. The director of the hospital now tells you, "Look, we're sorry the Society of Music Lovers did this to you — we would never have permitted it if we had known. But still, they did it and the violinist now is plugged into you. To unplug you would be to kill him. But never mind, it's only for nine months. By then he will have recovered from his ailment, and can safely be unplugged from you." Is it morally incumbent on you to accede to this situation? No doubt it would be very nice of you if you did, a great kindness. But do you *have* to accede to it? . . .

In this case, of course, you were kidnapped; you didn't volunteer for the operation that plugged the violinist into your kidneys. Can those who oppose abortion on the ground I mentioned make an exception for a pregnancy due to rape? Certainly. . . .

[I]t cannot seriously be thought to be murder if the mother performs an abortion on herself to save her life. It cannot seriously be said that she *must* refrain, that she *must* sit passively by and wait for her death. . . . If anything in the world is true, it is that you do not commit murder, you do not do what is impermissible, if you reach around to your back and unplug yourself from that violinist to save your life. . . .

. . . Where the mother's life is not at stake, the argument [based on the fetus's right to life] seems to have a much stronger pull[:] "Everyone has a right to life, so the unborn person has a right to life." And isn't the child's right to life weightier than anything other than the mother's own right to life, which she might put forward as ground for an abortion?

This argument treats the right to life as if it were unproblematic. It is not, and this seems to me to be precisely the source of the mistake. [T]o return to the story I told earlier, the fact that for continued life that violinist needs the continued use of your kidneys does not establish that he has a right to be given the continued use of your kidneys. He certainly has no right against you that *you* should give him continued use of your kidneys. For nobody has any right to use your kidneys unless you give him such a right; and nobody has the right against you that you shall give him this right — if you do allow him to go on using your kidneys, this is a kindness on your part, and not something he can claim from you as his due. Nor has he any right against anybody else that *they* should give him continued use of your kidneys. Certainly he had no right against the Society of Music Lovers that they should plug him into you in the first place. And if you now start to unplug yourself, having learned that you will otherwise have to spend nine years in bed with him, there is nobody in the world who must try to prevent you, in order to see to it that he is given something he has a right to be given. . . .

But it might be argued that there are other ways one can have acquired a right to the use of another person's body than by having been invited to use it by that person. Suppose a woman voluntarily indulges in intercourse, knowing of the chance it will issue in pregnancy, and then she does become pregnant; is she not in part responsible for the presence, in fact the very existence, of the unborn person inside her?

[D]etails make a difference. If the room is stuffy, and I therefore open a window to air it, and a burglar climbs in, it would be absurd to say, "Ah, now he can stay, she's given him a right to the use of her house — for she is partially responsible for his presence there, having voluntarily done what enabled him to get in, in full knowledge that there are such things as burglars, and that burglars burgle." It would be still more absurd to say this if I had had bars installed outside my windows, precisely to prevent burglars from getting in, and a burglar got in only because of a defect in the bars. It remains equally absurd if we imagine it is not a burglar who climbs in, but an innocent person who blunders or falls in. Again, suppose it were like this: people-seeds drift about in the air like pollen, and if you open your windows, one may drift in and take root in your carpets or upholstery. You don't want children, so you fix up your windows with fine mesh screens, the very best you can buy. As can happen, however, and on very, very rare occasions does happen, one of the screens is defective. . . . Someone may argue that you are responsible for its rooting, that it does have a right to your house, because after all you *could* have lived out your life with bare floors and furniture, or with sealed windows and doors.

But this won't do—for by the same token anyone can avoid a pregnancy due to rape by having a hysterectomy, or anyway by never leaving home without a (reliable!) army. . . .

[I]t is worth drawing attention to the fact that in no state in this country is any man compelled by law to be even a Minimally Decent Samaritan to any person. . . . By contrast, in most states in this country women are compelled by law to be not merely Minimally Decent Samaritans, but Good Samaritans to unborn persons inside them. This [at least shows] that there is a gross injustice in the existing state of the law.

For legal analyses based on Thomson's argument, see, e.g., What Roe v. Wade Should Have Said: The Nation's Top Legal Experts Rewrite America's Most Controversial Decision 121-147 (Jack Balkin ed., 2005) (concurring opinion of Robin West); Donald H. Regan, Rewriting Roe v. Wade, 77 Mich. L. Rev. 1569 (1979).

■ SIDNEY CALLAHAN, ABORTION AND THE SEXUAL AGENDA
113 Commonweal 232, 232-236 (1986)

. . . Pro-life feminists, like myself, argue on good feminist principles that women can never achieve the fulfillment of feminist goals in a society permissive toward abortion. . . . The moral right to control one's own body does apply to cases of organ transplants, mastectomies, contraception, and sterilization; but it is not a conceptualization adequate for abortion. The abortion dilemma is caused by the fact that 266 days following a conception in one body, another body will emerge. One's own body no longer exists as a single unit but is engendering another organism's life. . . . Strained philosophical analogies fail to apply: having a baby is not like rescuing a drowning person, being hooked up to a famous violinist's artificial life-support system, donating organs for transplant—or anything else. . . . It does not matter (*The Silent Scream* notwithstanding) whether the fetus being killed is fully conscious or feels pain. . . . Pro-life feminists who defend the fetus empathetically identify with an immature state of growth passed through by themselves, their children, and everyone now alive.

It also seems a travesty of just procedures that a pregnant woman now, in effect, acts as sole judge of her own case, under the most stressful conditions. Yes, one can acknowledge that the pregnant woman will be subject to the potential burdens arising from a pregnancy, but it has never been thought right to have an interested party, especially the more powerful party, decide his or her own case when there may be a conflict of interest. If one considers the matter as a case of a powerful versus a powerless, silenced claimant, the pro-choice feminist argument can rightly be inverted; since hers is the body, hers the risk, and hers the greater burden, then how in fairness can a woman be the sole judge of the fetal right to life? . . .

As the most recent immigrants from non-personhood, feminists have traditionally fought for justice. . . . A woman, involuntarily pregnant, has a moral obligation to the now-existing dependent fetus whether she explicitly consented to its existence or not. . . . The woman's moral obligation arises both from her status as a human being embedded in the interdependent human community and her unique lifegiving female reproductive power. . . .

. . . Pitting women against their own offspring is not only morally offensive, it is psychologically and politically destructive. Women will never climb to equality and social empowerment over mounds of dead fetuses. [Women] stand to gain from the same constellation of attitudes and institutions that will also protect the fetus in the woman's womb — and they stand to lose from the cultural assumptions that support permissive abortion. . . . By pro-choice reasoning, a man who does not want to have a child, or whose contraceptive fails, can be exempted from the responsibilities of fatherhood and child support. . . .

For that matter, why should the state provide a system of day-care or child support, or require workplaces to accommodate women's maternity and the needs of childrearing? Permissive abortion, granted in the name of women's privacy and reproductive freedom, ratifies the view that pregnancies and children are a woman's private individual responsibility. . . .

For additional feminist perspectives challenging the pro-choice position, see generally The Cost of "Choice": Women Evaluate the Impact of Abortion (Erika Bachiochi ed., 2004) (collection of essays).

3. Burdens on Privacy

■ STENBERG v. CARHART
530 U.S. 914 (2000)

Justice BREYER delivered the opinion of the Court.

We again consider the right to an abortion. We understand the controversial nature of the problem. Millions of Americans believe that life begins at conception and consequently that an abortion is akin to causing the death of an innocent child; they recoil at the thought of a law that would permit it. Other millions fear that a law that forbids abortion would condemn many American women to lives that lack dignity, depriving them of equal liberty and leading those with least resources to undergo illegal abortions with the attendant risks of death and suffering. Taking account of these virtually irreconcilable points of view, aware that constitutional law must govern a society whose different members sincerely hold directly opposing views, and considering the matter in light of the Constitution's guarantees of fundamental individual liberty, this Court, in the course of a generation, has determined and then redetermined that the Constitution offers basic protection to the woman's right to choose. Roe v. Wade, 410 U.S. 113 (1973); Planned Parenthood of Southeastern Pa. v. Casey, 505 U.S. 833 (1992). We shall not revisit those legal principles. . . .

. . . We shall set [forth the three controlling principles] in the language of the joint opinion in *Casey*. First, before "viability . . . the woman has a right to choose to terminate her pregnancy." 505 U.S. at 870 (plurality opinion). Second, "a law designed to further the State's interest in fetal life which imposes an undue burden on the woman's decision before fetal viability" is unconstitutional.

[Id.] at 877. An "undue burden is . . . shorthand for the conclusion that a state regulation has the purpose or effect of placing a substantial obstacle in the path of a woman seeking an abortion of a nonviable fetus." Third, "'subsequent to viability, the State in promoting its interest in the potentiality of human life may, if it chooses, regulate, and even proscribe, abortion except where it is necessary, in appropriate medical judgment, for the preservation of the life or health of the mother.'" [Id.] at 879 (quoting Roe v. Wade, 410 U.S. at 164-165).

We apply these principles to a Nebraska law banning "partial birth abortion." The statute reads as follows:

> No partial birth abortion shall be performed in this state, unless such procedure is necessary to save the life of the mother whose life is endangered by a physical disorder, physical illness, or physical injury, including a life-endangering physical condition caused by or arising from the pregnancy itself.

The statute defines "partial birth abortion" as:

> an abortion procedure in which the person performing the abortion partially delivers vaginally a living unborn child before killing the unborn child and completing the delivery.

It further defines "partially delivers vaginally a living unborn child before killing the unborn child" to mean:

> deliberately and intentionally delivering into the vagina a living unborn child, or a substantial portion thereof, for the purpose of performing a procedure that the person performing such procedure knows will kill the unborn child and does kill the unborn child.

The law classifies violation [as a felony carrying a prison term of up to 20 years, a fine of up to $25,000, and automatic revocation of a doctor's license to practice medicine in Nebraska].

I

Dr. Leroy Carhart is a Nebraska physician who performs abortions in a clinical setting. He brought this lawsuit in Federal District Court seeking a declaration that the Nebraska statute violates the Federal Constitution, and asking for an injunction forbidding its enforcement. [After a trial, the District Court held the law unconstitutional, and the Court of Appeals affirmed.]

Because Nebraska law seeks to ban one method of aborting a pregnancy, we must describe and then discuss several different abortion procedures. Considering the fact that those procedures seek to terminate a potential human life, our discussion may seem clinically cold or callous to some, perhaps horrifying to others. There is no alternative way, however, to acquaint the reader with the technical distinctions among different abortion methods and related factual matters, upon which the outcome of this case depends. . . .

1. About 90% of all abortions performed in the United States take place during the first trimester of pregnancy, before 12 weeks of gestational age. During the first

trimester, the predominant abortion method is "vacuum aspiration," which involves insertion of a vacuum tube (cannula) into the uterus to evacuate the contents. Such an abortion is typically performed on an outpatient basis under local anesthesia. Vacuum aspiration is considered particularly safe. . . .

2. Approximately 10% of all abortions are performed during the second trimester of pregnancy (12 to 24 weeks). [At this stage, the] most commonly used procedure is called "dilation and evacuation" (D&E). That procedure (together with a modified form of vacuum aspiration used in the early second trimester) accounts for about 95% of all abortions performed from 12 to 20 weeks of gestational age.

3. [Despite variations, D&E usually] involves (1) dilation of the cervix; (2) removal of at least some fetal tissue using nonvacuum instruments; and (3) (after the 15th week) the potential need for instrumental disarticulation or dismemberment of the fetus or the collapse of fetal parts to facilitate evacuation from the uterus.

4. When instrumental disarticulation incident to D&E is necessary, it typically occurs as the doctor pulls a portion of the fetus through the cervix into the birth canal. . . .

5. The D&E procedure carries certain risks [including perforation and organ damage from sharp instruments and bone fragments and infection from fetal tissue accidentally left behind.] Nonetheless studies show that the risks of mortality and complication that accompany the D&E procedure between the 12th and 20th weeks of gestation are significantly lower than those accompanying induced labor procedures (the next safest midsecond trimester procedure).

6. [A variation of the D&E procedure, "intact D&E," involves removing the fetus from the uterus through the cervix "intact," *i.e.*, in one pass.] It is used after 16 weeks at the earliest, as vacuum aspiration becomes ineffective and the fetal skull becomes too large to pass through the cervix. [If the fetus presents head first, the doctor collapses the skull and then extracts the entire fetus through the cervix. If the fetus presents feet first, the doctor pulls the fetal body through the cervix, collapses the skull, and extracts the fetus through the cervix—a procedure called "dilation and extraction" (D&X).]

8. . . . Despite the technical differences we have just described, intact D&E and D&X are sufficiently similar for us to use the terms interchangeably.

9. Dr. Carhart testified he attempts to use the intact D&E procedure during weeks 16 to 20 because [it reduces various risks, including injury from bone fragments, uterine perforations from instruments, and infection. The District Court concluded] that "the evidence is both clear and convincing that Carhart's D&X procedure is superior to, and safer than, the . . . other abortion procedures used during the relevant gestational period in the 10 to 20 cases a year that present to Dr. Carhart."

10. The materials presented at trial referred to the potential benefits of the D&X procedure in circumstances involving nonviable fetuses, such as fetuses with abnormal fluid accumulation in the brain (hydrocephaly). Others have emphasized its potential for women with prior uterine scars, or for women for whom induction of labor would be particularly dangerous.

11. There are no reliable data on the number of D&X abortions performed annually. Estimates have ranged between 640 and 5,000 per year.

II

[The statute violates the Constitution, as interpreted in *Roe* and *Casey*,] for at least two independent reasons. First, the law lacks any exception "'for the preservation of the . . . health of the mother.'" *Casey*, 505 U.S. at 879 (plurality opinion). Second, it "imposes an undue burden on a woman's ability" to choose a D&E abortion, thereby unduly burdening the right to choose abortion itself. 505 U.S. at 874. . . .

The fact that Nebraska's law applies both pre- and postviability aggravates the [first] constitutional problem presented. The State's interest in regulating abortion previability is considerably weaker than postviability. Since the law requires a health exception in order to validate even a postviability abortion regulation, it at a minimum requires the same in respect to previability regulation.

The quoted standard also depends on the state regulations "promoting [the State's] interest in the potentiality of human life." The Nebraska law, of course, does not directly further an interest "in the potentiality of human life" by saving the fetus in question from destruction, as it regulates only a *method* of performing abortion. Nebraska describes its interests differently. It says the law "'shows concern for the life of the unborn,'" "prevents cruelty to partially born children," and "preserves the integrity of the medical profession." But we cannot see how the interest-related differences could make any difference to the question at hand, namely, the application of the "health" requirement.

Consequently, the governing standard requires [a health exception,] for this Court has made clear that a State may promote but not endanger a woman's health when it regulates the methods of abortion. [The evidence below shows that D&X abortions are safer than other procedures in some cases.]

We find [the state's various] arguments insufficient to demonstrate that Nebraska's law needs no health exception. . . . The D&X is an infrequently used abortion procedure; but the health exception question is whether protecting women's health requires an exception for those infrequent occasions. [T]he State cannot prohibit a person from obtaining treatment simply by pointing out that most people do not need it. . . .

The word "necessary" in *Casey*'s phrase "necessary, in appropriate medical judgment, for the preservation of the life or health of the mother," . . . cannot refer to an absolute necessity or to absolute proof. Medical treatments and procedures are often considered appropriate (or inappropriate) in light of estimated comparative health risks (and health benefits) in particular cases. Neither can that phrase require unanimity of medical opinion. [T]he division of medical opinion about the matter at most means uncertainty, a factor that signals the presence of risk, not its absence. . . .

The Eighth Circuit found the Nebraska statute unconstitutional because, in *Casey*'s words, it has the "effect of placing a substantial obstacle in the path of a woman seeking an abortion of a nonviable fetus." 505 U.S. at 877. It thereby places an "undue burden" upon a woman's right to terminate her pregnancy before viability. Nebraska does not deny that the statute imposes an "undue burden" *if* it applies to the more commonly used D&E procedure as well as to D&X. . . .

. . . We do not understand how one could distinguish, using [the statute's language], between D&E (where a foot or arm is drawn through the cervix) and D&X (where the body up to the head is drawn through the cervix). Evidence before the trial court makes clear that D&E will often involve a physician pulling a "substantial portion" of a still living fetus, say, an arm or leg, into the vagina prior to the death of the fetus. . . .

The Attorney General also points to the Nebraska Legislature's debates, where the term "partial birth abortion" appeared frequently. But those debates hurt his argument more than they help it. . . . The legislature seems to have wanted to avoid more limiting language lest it become too easy to evade the statute's strictures. . . .

In sum, using this law some present prosecutors and future Attorneys General may choose to pursue physicians who use D&E procedures, the most commonly used method for performing previability second trimester abortions. All those who perform abortion procedures using that method must fear prosecution, conviction, and imprisonment. The result is an undue burden upon a woman's right to make an abortion decision. . . .

Justice GINSBURG, with whom Justice STEVENS joins, concurring.
. . . As the Court observes, this law does not save any fetus from destruction, for it targets only "a *method* of performing abortion." . . . Seventh Circuit Chief Judge Posner correspondingly observed, regarding similar bans in Wisconsin and Illinois, that the law . . . prohibits the procedure because the State legislators seek to chip away at the private choice shielded by Roe v. Wade, even as modified by *Casey*. [Hope Clinic v. Ryan, 195 F.3d 857, 880-882 (7th Cir. 1999) (dissenting opinion).] Again as stated by Chief Judge Posner, "if a statute burdens constitutional rights and all that can be said on its behalf is that it is the vehicle that legislators have chosen for expressing their hostility to those rights, the burden is undue."

Justice SCALIA, dissenting.
I am optimistic enough to believe that, one day, Stenberg v. Carhart will be assigned its rightful place in the history of this Court's jurisprudence beside *Korematsu* and *Dred Scott*. The method of killing a human child—one cannot even accurately say an entirely unborn human child—proscribed by this statute is so horrible that the most clinical description of it evokes a shudder of revulsion. And the Court must know (as most state legislatures banning this procedure have concluded) that demanding a "health exception" . . . is to give live-birth abortion free rein. . . .

In my dissent in *Casey*, I wrote that the "undue burden" test made law by the joint opinion created a standard that was "as doubtful in application as it is unprincipled in origin," *Casey*, 505 U.S. at 985; "hopelessly unworkable in practice," 505 U.S. at 986; "ultimately standardless," 505 U.S. at 987. Today's decision is the proof. [I]t is really quite impossible for us dissenters to contend that the majority is *wrong* on the law—any more than it could be said that one is *wrong in law* to support or oppose the death penalty, or to support or oppose mandatory minimum sentences. The most that we can honestly say is that we disagree with the majority on their policy-judgment-couched-as-law. And those who believe that a 5-to-4 vote on a policy matter by unelected lawyers should not overcome the judgment of 30 state legislatures have a problem, not with the *application* of *Casey*, but with its *existence*. *Casey* must be overruled. . . .

Justice KENNEDY, with whom The Chief Justice joins, dissenting. . . .
The Court's failure to accord any weight to Nebraska's interest in prohibiting partial-birth abortion is erroneous and undermines its discussion and holding. . . .

The [medical terminology of the majority shows that it] views the procedures from the perspective of the abortionist, rather than from the perspective of a society shocked when confronted with a new method of ending human life. . . .

Casey is premised on the States having an important constitutional role in defining their interests in the abortion debate. . . . States may take sides in the abortion debate and come down on the side of life, even life in the unborn:

> Even in the earliest stages of pregnancy, the State may enact rules and regulations designed to encourage [a woman] to know that there are philosophic and social arguments of great weight that can be brought to bear in favor of continuing the pregnancy to full term and that there are procedures and institutions to allow adoption of unwanted children as well as a certain degree of state assistance if the mother chooses to raise the child herself. [Casey,] 505 U.S. at 872 (plurality opinion). . . .

Nebraska was entitled to find the existence of a consequential moral difference between [abortion procedures.] The D&X differs from the D&E because in the D&X the fetus is "killed *outside* of the womb" where the fetus has "an autonomy which separates it from the right of the woman to choose treatments for her own body." Witnesses to the procedure relate that the fingers and feet of the fetus are moving prior to the piercing of the skull; when the scissors are inserted in the back of the head, the fetus' body, wholly outside the woman's body and alive, reacts as though startled and goes limp. D&X's stronger resemblance to infanticide means Nebraska could conclude the procedure presents a greater risk of disrespect for life and a consequent greater risk to the profession and society, which depend for their sustenance upon reciprocal recognition of dignity and respect. . . .

In deferring to the physician's judgment [in requiring a health exception], the Court turns back to cases decided in the wake of *Roe*, cases which gave a physician's treatment decisions controlling weight. . . . Rather than exalting the right of a physician to practice medicine with unfettered discretion, *Casey* recognized: "Whatever constitutional status the doctor-patient relation may have as a general matter, in the present context it is derivative of the woman's position." 505 U.S. at 884 (joint opinion of O'CONNOR, KENNEDY, and SOUTER, JJ.). [Justice O'Connor in an omitted concurring opinion] assures the people of Nebraska they are free to redraft the law to include an exception permitting the D&X to be performed when "the procedure, in appropriate medical judgment, is necessary to preserve the health of the mother." The assurance is meaningless. . . . A ban which depends on the "appropriate medical judgment" of Dr. Carhart is no ban at all. . . . This, of course, is the vice of a health exception resting in the physician's discretion. . . .

[In omitted opinions, Justices Stevens and O'Connor concurred, and Chief Justice Rehnquist and Justice Thomas dissented.]

■ JOHN LELAND, BEYOND THE SLOGANS: INSIDE AN ABORTION CLINIC
N.Y. Times, Sept. 18, 2005, §1, at 1

At Little Rock Family Planning Services, the women filed in without making eye contact. [W]omen from as far away as Oklahoma joined the more than one million American women who will probably have abortions this year. Their experiences, at one of only two clinics in the state, offer a ground-level view of abortion in 2005, a landscape altered by shifts in technology, law, demographics and the political climate. . . .

More than 25 million Americans have had abortions since [Roe v. Wade]. Often kept secret, even from close friends or family members, the experience cuts across all income levels, religions, races, lifestyles, political parties and marital circumstances. Though abortion rates have been falling since 1990, to their lowest level since the mid-1970's, abortion remains one of the most common surgical procedures for women in America. More than one in five pregnancies end in abortion.

In the squat, nondescript brick building here, the lofty rhetoric that has billowed through public debate for the last 32 years gave way to the mundane realities of the armed security guard and the metal detector, the surgical table and the settling of the bill before the procedure—$525 to $1,800, cash or credit card only.

While public conversation about abortion is dominated by advocates with all-or-nothing positions—treating the fetus as a complete person, with full rights, or as a nonentity, with none—most patients at the clinic, like most Americans, found themselves on rockier ground, weighing religious, ethical, practical, sentimental and financial imperatives that were often in conflict. Regina cried on the operating table. Kori, 26, who was having her third abortion, asked to watch the procedure on the ultrasound monitor. . . .

The solitary protester outside, Jim Dawson, 74, stood a court-mandated distance from the clinic with a video camera, taping women as they entered, and promising them hellfire if they went through with it—as he has for a decade. . . .

At the clinic, patients . . . spoke only if they could use just their first names. "It's not something I would talk about," said "M," a high school teacher who agreed to be identified only by her middle initial. . . . She said she had never discussed abortion with relatives or colleagues. Only two friends knew she was here. "I'd lose my job," she said. "My family's reputation would be ruined. It makes me nervous even being in the waiting room. You don't want to know who's here, you don't want to be recognized. . . . " Even most staff members at the clinic insisted on using only their first names—"to protect my identity from the anti-choice people," said Lori, a nurse practitioner. . . .

While abortion rates have been falling generally since 1990, the decline has been steepest among teenagers, and rates are lowest among educated, financially secure women. Researchers attribute the drop in teenage abortion to reduced rates of pregnancy, as a result of better access to contraception—including the three-month Depo-Provera injections—and abstinence. Conversely, for poor and low-income women, rates increased during the 1990's, possibly in response to the 1996 welfare overhaul, which reduced support systems for women who carry their fetuses to term. At every income level . . . , African-American women were more likely to terminate their pregnancies than white women.

Leah, 26, said money was a factor in her decision to have an abortion. A former college track athlete, she works in a clothing boutique, a job that she said did not pay enough to support a child. Like many women at the clinic, Leah had conflicted feelings about what she was doing. "I always said I would never, ever have an abortion," she said. "I probably will regret it. I'm pro-choice for cases of incest or rape, but if it's your own fault, you should accept responsibility. And it's my own fault." . . . Karen, 29, who arrived at the clinic 20 weeks pregnant, expressed no qualms about ending her pregnancy. [She did not come in earlier in the pregnancy, she said, because she did not have the money.] Like nearly half of all women who have abortions, she had had one before, when she was 18. She did not look on abortion as shameful, she said, adding, "All of your past goes into making you who you are." She has a 9-year-old son, and she said she felt she could not start again with a newborn child. This, too, is common. More than half of all women having abortions have had children, a percentage that rose in the 1980's but has not changed since 1990, according to the federal Centers for Disease Control and Prevention. . . .

For many women at the clinic, their desire to end their pregnancy clashed with their religious beliefs. Tammy, a Muslim, had her first abortion a year ago, after having three children. She is married and works in a coffee shop in Tennessee. She became pregnant this time after erratically taking her birth control pills. [Similarly, Regina, 28, blamed a faulty contraceptive Depo-Provera shot from an Army nurse in Iraq for her pregnancy. "Every woman has second thoughts, especially because I'm Catholic," she said. She went to confession and met with her priest, she added. "The priest didn't hound me. He said, 'People make mistakes.'" She arrived at the clinic with cuts and bruises sustained after disclosing her pregnancy to her boyfriend, who is now in jail.]

Since 1992, when the Supreme Court recognized states' authority to restrict abortion as long as they did not create an "undue burden," states have enacted 487 laws restricting patients or providers, in many cases calling for mandatory counseling, waiting periods and parental consent for minors. [T]he result is a patchwork of laws and regulations that vary from state to state, some of which may come before the United States Supreme Court. [Arkansas now is one of the most restrictive states], requiring state-scripted counseling at least a day before the procedure [and an offer of ultrasound imaging]. At 20 weeks, doctors are required to tell patients that the fetus feels pain, though this is medically disputed.

At the clinic in Little Rock, patients and staff members said the restrictions were more inconveniences than roadblocks. Patients nodded dutifully as the staff members asked [state-scripted] questions like, "Do you understand that the father of the child must provide financial assistance if you deliver the pregnancy?" . . . For the clinic, the regulations add paperwork and require extra staff members [and impose extra costs that are passed on to the patients]. New licensing laws, enacted in 28 states, require providers to comply with state codes for equipment, record-keeping, building grounds and other areas, which small businesses can find onerous. [Clinics call these] TRAP laws, for targeted regulation of abortion providers. [One physician] likened the regulations to "death by a thousand scratches."

In part because of the legal, financial and emotional pressures, the number of doctors in Arkansas who perform more than occasional abortions has fallen to three, down from six in the late 1990's. The youngest . . . is 59. This reduction mirrors a national trend. Nationally, 1,819 facilities provided abortions in 2000, down from a high of 2,908 in 1982. [Dr. Jerry] Edwards, 63, said he felt an obligation to stay in business. "If we retired, I'm not sure anybody else would come to Arkansas and practice," he said. . . .

Dr. Edwards [and clinic director Ann Osborne] said they felt isolated from the local medical community and the community at large. Even the patients often have a negative view of abortion, [frequently saying] "'I don't believe in this, but my situation is different.'" . . . Though the clinic has developed an equilibrium with its lone demonstrator, Ms. Osborne is wary of any opposition to abortion rights. In 1994, when she was executive director of Preterm Health Services in Brookline,

Mass., an abortion opponent named John C. Salvi III came into the clinic and
started shooting, killing the receptionist. . . .
Copyright © 2005 by The New York Times Co. Reprinted with permission.

Notes and Questions

1. *Continuity or change?* To what extent does *Stenberg* reflect an abortion jurisprudence that follows *Roe*? To what extent does it reveal departures from *Roe*? Does
abortion remain a "fundamental right"? Does it still rest on the right of privacy?
How does the undue burden standard, used by a majority in *Stenberg*, differ from
Roe's strict scrutiny? Would application of the undue burden standard change the
outcome in *Roe*'s companion case, Doe v. Bolton, 410 U.S. 179 (1973), which
invalidated requirements of hospitalization, accreditation, approval by a hospital
committee, the concurrence of two physicians, and state residency? Does the undue
burden standard reach a better accommodation of conflicting individual and state
interests than strict scrutiny? See Michael C. Dorf, Incidental Burdens on Fundamental Rights, 109 Harv. L. Rev. 1175, 1219-1232 (1996); Kathleen M. Sullivan,
The Supreme Court 1991 Term, Foreword: The Justices of Rules and Standards,
106 Harv. L. Rev. 22, 32-34 (1992). Why has the Court retained *Roe*'s controversial
point of viability?

2. *Standard of review.* *Stenberg* relies on Planned Parenthood of Southeastern
Pennsylvania v. Casey, 505 U.S. 833 (1992), a challenge to several provisions of
Pennsylvania's Abortion Control Act. In *Casey*, the sharply divided Court could not
agree on the governing standard of review. The "joint opinion" in *Casey* (presented
by Justices O'Connor, Kennedy, and Souter) embraced *Roe*'s protection for abortion freedom but rejected *Roe*'s trimester framework, announcing the *undue burden
standard* in place of *Roe*'s strict scrutiny. Under this approach, these Justices voted to
uphold several provisions of the Pennsylvania law, including the requirement that
at least 24 hours before the abortion the physician must provide the woman
detailed information about the procedure, its risks, and its alternatives as well as
about the "probable gestational age of the unborn child" and the availability of
printed materials on child support, adoption, and other services.

Four Justices (Chief Justice Rehnquist and Justices White, Scalia, and Thomas),
who would have overruled *Roe* altogether, voted with the joint opinion authors to
uphold these statutory sections under the *rational basis standard*. Two others (Justices Blackmun and Stevens), following *Roe*, would have applied *strict scrutiny*, which
Justice Blackmun said would invalidate all the challenged provisions.

In *Stenberg* a majority embraced the undue burden standard for the first time.
Why does Justice Kennedy refuse to join the majority in *Stenberg*?

3. *Physician's role.* How has the Court's understanding of reproductive autonomy evolved since *Roe*? *Roe*'s emphasis on the physician's role gave way in later
cases to more explicit recognition of the woman's freedom. To what extent does
Stenberg return to the focus on the physician? Justice Kennedy accuses the majority
of using "the perspective of the abortionist." Whose perspective should the Court
use in analyzing abortion restrictions? Other restrictions on private family matters?
To what extent does the required health exception give the physician unlimited
authority?

4. *The road to* Casey *and* Stenberg. After Roe v. Wade and Doe v. Bolton invalidated then-existing abortion laws, state legislatures sought to fill the gap. Several "second-generation challenges" tested the limits of the Court's holdings.

a. *Abortion funding.* In 1977 the Court decided three cases permitting states to refuse Medicaid coverage for nontherapeutic abortions. Beal v. Doe, 432 U.S. 438 (1977); Maher v. Roe, 432 U.S. 464 (1977); Poelker v. Doe, 432 U.S. 519 (1977). Although the government subsidized continued pregnancy and childbirth but not abortion for the indigent, the majority in *Maher* found no "unduly burdensome interference" with the abortion decision, distinguishing the "obstacle" invalidated in *Roe*. The Court treated the refusal to fund abortion as state inaction calling for the rational basis test rather than the strict scrutiny applied in *Roe*. State encouragement of childbirth over abortion, a "value judgment," satisfied this less demanding standard of review.[16]

The Court used a similar analysis to reject challenges to governmental refusals to fund abortions necessary to preserve the woman's health. In Harris v. McRae, 448 U.S. 297 (1980), the Court held that *Roe*'s protection of the right to abortion does not confer an entitlement to funds to realize that right. See also Webster v. Reproductive Health Servs., 492 U.S. 490, 507-513 (1989). How meaningful is the right to abortion without the means to effectuate that right? Does the holding in *McRae* conflict with the importance ascribed to maternal health in *Roe* and *Stenberg*? For a poor woman, is the state's offer of subsidized medical care for childbirth accompanied by its refusal to pay for an abortion an "undue burden"?

See generally Susan Frelich Appleton, Beyond the Limits of Reproductive Choice: The Contributions of the Abortion-Funding Cases to Fundamental-Rights Analysis and to the Welfare-Rights Thesis, 81 Colum. L. Rev. 721 (1981); Michael J. Perry, Why the Supreme Court Was Plainly Wrong in the Hyde Amendment Case: A Brief Comment on Harris v. McRae, 32 Stan. L. Rev. 1113 (1980). See also David Robert Baron, The Racially Disparate Impact of Restrictions on Public-Funding of Abortion: An Analysis of Current Equal Protection Doctrine, 13 B.C. Third World L.J. 1 (1993).

b. *The undue burden standard.* Justice O'Connor was an early critic of *Roe*'s trimester framework. In her dissent in Akron v. Akron Center for Reproductive Health, Inc., 462 U.S. 416, 452-475 (1983), she announced a preference for strict scrutiny review only for "unduly burdensome" abortion restrictions, id. at 461, such as bans or third-party consent, asserting that the state has compelling interests in maternal health and potential life throughout pregnancy. Later, however, she simply labeled the trimester framework "problematic," Webster v. Reprod. Health Servs., 492 U.S. 490, 529 (1989) (O'Connor, J., concurring).

Is the undue burden standard that *Stenberg* takes from *Casey* the same test used in the abortion-funding cases? In Justice O'Connor's earlier opinions? Given her previous position, why in *Casey* did Justice O'Connor adopt viability as the "compelling point"? See generally Peggy Cooper Davis & Carol Gilligan, A Woman Decides: Justice O'Connor and Due Process Rights of Choice, 32 McGeorge L. Rev. 895 (2001); Kenneth L. Karst, Justice O'Connor and the Substance of Equal Citizenship, 2003 Sup. Ct. Rev. 357.

---

[16]. Some challenges brought under state constitutions yielded different results. See, e.g., Simat Corp. v. Arizona Health Care Cost Containment Sys., 56 P.3d 28 (Ariz. 2002); Committee to Defend Reproductive Rights v. Myers, 625 P.2d 779 (Cal. 1981).

Casey's joint opinion expressly permits under the undue burden standard some measures "designed to persuade [the woman] to choose childbirth over abortion." 505 U.S. at 878. What measures does this language allow states to enact? Can you name other protected rights whose exercise the states can try to discourage, with the Supreme Court's blessing?

c. *Informed consent.* Soon after *Roe,* the Court upheld state regulations mandating that the physician obtain the patient's prior written consent, regardless of the stage of pregnancy. Planned Parenthood v. Danforth, 428 U.S. 52 (1976). When states required a detailed list of abortion warnings, however, the Court invalidated these measures because of both their interference with the doctor-patient relationship and their underlying anti-abortion motivation. City of Akron v. Akron Ctr. for Reprod. Health, 462 U.S. 416, 442-449 (1983); Thornburgh v. American College of Obstetricians & Gynecologists, 476 U.S. 747, 759-765 (1986). Why did *Casey* change this result, allowing mandated pre-abortion information and waiting periods?

What is the appropriate role of government in the physician-patient relationship? Beyond providing a forum for malpractice suits, how far can a state go to insure the patient's receipt of information? Does the right to privacy provide an answer? See Susan Frelich Appleton, Doctors, Patients and the Constitution: A Theoretical Analysis of the Physician's Role in "Private" Reproductive Decisions, 63 Wash. U. L.Q. 183, 219-235 (1985). Are detailed informed consent requirements that apply only to abortion paternalistic? Do they discriminate on the basis of sex? Do states enacting such requirements treat abortion patients as "inadvertent murderesses"? Recall Luker, supra, pp. 35-36.

Proposed federal legislation, the "Unborn Child Pain Awareness Act of 2005," includes an informed-consent section that requires abortion providers to tell patients about congressional findings on fetal pain and to offer pre-abortion pain-reducing drugs for the fetus. S. 51, 109th Cong. (2005). What information would you need to evaluate the proposal's constitutionality? See generally Teresa Stanton Collett, Fetal Pain Legislation: Is it Viable?, 30 Pepp. L. Rev. 161 (2003); Note, The Science, Law, and Politics of Fetal Pain Legislation, 115 Harv. L. Rev. 2010 (2002).

Issues of informed consent and abortion funding coalesced in Rust v. Sullivan, 500 U.S. 173 (1991), in which the Court upheld regulations disallowing physicians in federally funded clinics from discussing abortion, despite the patient's request for information, the physician's judgment that patient should consider abortion, the health risks of pregnancy, or state malpractice laws requiring disclosure. To what extent does a physician's state-compelled silence on abortion create an "undue burden"?

d. *Politics and the changing Court.* To what extent is the road from *Roe* to *Casey* and then to *Stenberg* best understood as a reflection of changes in the Supreme Court's composition, in an era when presidential candidates often make explicit campaign promises about how their judicial nominees will address abortion cases? Where should matters of "family values" and morality be decided: in the home, the legislature, or the courts? Or do such labels beg the question? What changes in the Court's abortion jurisprudence will follow from the arrival of Chief Justice Roberts and Justice Alito (in the seats previously held by Chief Justice Rehnquist and Justice O'Connor)? Anticipating a change and seeking to trigger a direct challenge to *Roe,* the South Dakota legislature banned all except life-saving abortions. See, e.g., Monica Davey, Ripples from Law Banning Abortion Spread Through South Dakota, N.Y. Times, Apr. 16, 2006, §1, at 14.

5. *Morality.* Justice Kennedy emphasizes that Nebraska regards D&X abortions as morally different from D&E abortions. To what extent does the disagreement between the majority and Justice Kennedy boil down to conflicting views among the Justices about the appropriate role of morality in constitutional adjudication? Would Justice Kennedy's approach require overturning *Roe* altogether—on the ground that some state legislatures will find all abortions immoral? Or have Justice Kennedy and the other *Stenberg* dissenters persuasively distinguished D&X from other abortions? See Akhil Reed Amar, The Supreme Court, 1999 Term, Foreword: The Document and the Doctrine, 114 Harv. L. Rev. 26, 110 (2000). Is morality distinguishable from religious beliefs? Why would the difference, if any, matter? See, e.g., Michael J. Perry, Religion, Politics, and Abortion, 79 U. Det. Mercy L. Rev. 1 (2001).

6. *Abortion access.* As both the abortion-funding cases and the undue burden standard demonstrate, the Supreme Court has decided that the Constitution does not guarantee easy access to abortion. What access problems can you identify from the data and experiences reported in the *New York Times* story, supra?[17] What has the change in constitutional standard from *Roe* to *Casey* meant in practice? What additional insights does the story provide? Why do you suppose that, despite access problems, African-American women are more likely to terminate their pregnancies than white women? For an historical examination, see Loretta J. Ross, African-American Women and Abortion, in The Abortion Wars: A Half Century of Struggle, 1950-2000, at 161 (Rickie Solinger ed., 1998).

7. *Clinic violence.* Violence creates access problems by dissuading both patients and abortion providers.[18] Courts and legislatures have addressed the issue in several ways.

a. *FACE.* In response to such violence, Congress enacted the Freedom of Access to Clinic Entrances Act of 1994 (FACE), 18 U.S.C. §248 (2000), which bars force, threat of force, or physical obstruction aimed at injuring, intimidating, or interfering with any patients or providers of reproductive health services. Violators face criminal and civil penalties. Federal appellate courts have upheld the constitutionality of FACE against challenges based on the First Amendment, vagueness and overbreadth, equal protection, the Commerce Clause, and the Tenth Amendment. See, e.g., Norton v. Ashcroft, 298 F.3d 547 (6th Cir. 2002), *cert. denied*, 537 U.S. 1172 (2003); American Life League, Inc. v. Reno, 47 F.3d 642 (4th Cir.), *cert. denied*, 516 U.S. 809 (1995). But see United States v. Bird, 401 F.3d 633,

[17]. The situation in Arkansas is not atypical. Only 13 percent of the counties in the United States have an abortion provider. Lawrence B. Finer & Stanley K. Henshaw, The Accessibility of Abortion Services in the United States, 2001, 35 Persp. on Sexual and Reprod. Health 16, 22 (2003). See also, e.g., Evelyn Nieves, S.D. Makes Abortion Rare Through Laws and Stigma; Out-of-State Doctors Come Weekly to 1 Clinic, Wash. Post, Dec. 27, 2005, at A1. Further, physician-abortion rights activists, many of whom were motivated by concern for victims of illegal abortion, are reaching retirement age. See generally Carole Joffe, Doctors of Conscience: The Struggle to Provide Abortion Before and After Roe v. Wade 3-4 (1995).

[18]. Supporters of reproductive choice attribute to anti-abortion violence the deaths of three doctors, two clinic staff members, a clinic escort, and a security guard since 1993; 17 attempted murders since 1991; 4,200 reported acts of violence against abortion providers (i.e., bombings, arsons, death threats, kidnappings, and assaults) since 1977; and more than 92,000 reported acts of disruption (i.e., bomb threats and harassing phone calls) since 1977. NARAL Pro-Choice America Foundation, Clinic Violence and Intimidation 1 (May 3, 2005) (available at http: www.prochoiceamerica.org/issues/abortion/access-to-abortion/clinic-violence.html). Meanwhile, abortions have been declining, with approximately 1,303,000 performed in the United States in 2001. Lawrence B. Finer & Stanley Henshaw, Estimates of U.S. Abortion Incidence in 2001 and 2002 (Alan Guttmacher Institute, May 18, 2005) (available at http://www.guttmacher.org/pubs/2005/05/18/ab_incidence.pdf).

634-637 (5th Cir. 2005) (DeMoss, J., dissenting) (concluding FACE exceeds congressional commerce power, as applied to defendant, who drove a car through a door of a Planned Parenthood facility in Houston).

Applying FACE, Planned Parenthood of the Columbia/Willamette, Inc. v. American Coalition of Life Activists, 290 F.3d 1058 (9th Cir. 2002), *cert. denied*, 539 U.S. 958 (2003), upheld a permanent injunction against the publication of "wanted posters" featuring photographs and addresses of abortion providers. The posters, circulated in hard copy, also appeared on an anti-abortion website called the "Nuremberg Files." The court determined that the posters constituted "true threats" made with the intent to intimidate the providers, given prior incidents, including the murders of some physicians identified on the website. In addition, the court upheld a jury verdict of compensatory damages for the abortion providers, but remanded on the issue of punitive damages. See generally Jennifer Elrod, Note, Expressive Activity, True Threats, and the First Amendment, 36 Conn. L. Rev. 541 (2004).

b. *Other remedies.* The Supreme Court has addressed several controversies between clinics and their supporters, on the one hand, and protestors, on the other. See Scheidler v. National Org. for Women, 537 U.S. 393 (2003) (rejecting RICO claim alleging extortion), 126 S. Ct. 1264 (2006) (applying restrictive interpretation of Hobbs Act); Bray v. Alexandria Women's Health Clinic, 506 U.S. 263 (1993) (rejecting federal cause of action under Ku Klux Klan Act). Compare Hill v. Colorado, 530 U.S. 703 (2000) (upholding statutory "bubble zone"), with Schenck v. Pro-Choice Network, 519 U.S. 357 (1997) (invalidating injunction's "floating buffer zone" but upholding injunction's fixed buffer zone).

8. *Impact on birth control.* To what extent does use of the undue burden test signal not just a retreat from *Roe*, but also a retreat from *Griswold*? What consequences follow for the use of modern methods of birth control? Suppose the IUD and emergency contraception (ordinary birth control pills taken in appropriate doses within 72 hours of intercourse) prevent implantation of fertilized ova? See, e.g., Mitt Romney, Why I Vetoed Contraception Bill, Boston Globe, July 26, 2005, at A17 (Governor's op-ed). Suppose these methods work just as ordinary birth control pills do?

Clashes between women's asserted right to access to birth control, including emergency contraception, and pharmacists' asserted right to decline to fill prescriptions that they find morally objectionable have generated numerous legal actions. See, e.g, Access to Legal Pharmaceuticals Act, S. 809, 109th Cong. (2005) (proposed federal legislation); Gretchen Ruethling, Illinois Pharmacist Sues Over Contraceptive Rule, N.Y. Times, June 10, 2005, A18 (reporting challenge to governor's order "requiring pharmacists to dispense birth control and emergency contraception without delay"). What is the proper balance of these competing interests? Should religious hospitals treating rape victims be required to provide information and/or treatment about emergency contraception? See Brietta Clark, When Free Exercise Exemptions Undermine Religious Liberty and the Liberty of Conscience: A Case Study of the Catholic Hospital Conflict, 82 Or. L. Rev. 625 (2003). Would over-the-counter sales of emergency contraception solve the problem — a step that has long awaited F.D.A. approval and that some states have approached through laws eliminating the need for a physician's prescription? See Monica Davey & Pam Belluck, Pharmacies Balk on After-Sex Pill and Widen Fight, N.Y. Times, April 19, 2005, at A1; Gardiner Harris, Official Quits on Pill Delay at the F.D.A., N.Y. Times, Sept. 1, 2005, at A12.

9. *Medical and technological advances.* What does the undue burden test mean for modern medical advances? Consider RU-486 or mifepristone, the "abortion pill"

developed by French scientists for terminations of early pregnancies and approved in 2000 by the F.D.A. as safe and effective. Under *Stenberg*, can the government ban so-called medical abortions (abortions accomplished through medication, like RU-486) so long as surgical abortions remain available? Must there be a health exception? What must states show to justify applying to medical abortions their restrictions on surgical abortions (e.g., clinic regulations, specified procedures for disposal of fetal remains, and reporting requirements)?

What difference does the availability of an abortion pill make? By making access to abortion more "private," might it eliminate the "public" problems of clinic violence? Does the answer depend upon how states regulate use of RU-486? How have other technological advances, such as the Internet, affected the abortion debate? See Kari Lou Frank, Note, Net Effects: How the Internet Has Changed Abortion Law, Policy, and Process, 8 Wm. & Mary J. Women & L. 311 (2002). What about ultrasound imaging of the fetus? See Neela Banerjee, Church Groups Turn to Sonogram to Turn Women from Abortions, N.Y. Times, Feb. 2, 2005, at A1.

10. *Migratory abortion.* Before *Roe*, abortion restrictions primarily affected poor women because women with means could travel to more permissive jurisdictions.[19] After *Roe*, those seeking postviability abortions traveled to Colorado and Kansas, which permitted them in some conditions.[20] This pattern exemplifies a common phenomenon in family law: crossing state lines to find a more hospitable legal regime. Will the undue burden test exacerbate this phenomenon by providing increased opportunities for state restrictions (for example, waiting periods)? To what extent do such consequences provide support for federal legislation? See generally Seth F. Kreimer, The Law of Choice and Choice of Law: Abortion, the Right to Travel, and Extraterritorial Regulation in American Federalism, 67 N.Y.U. L. Rev. 451 (1992).

11. *Federal ban.* Three years after *Stenberg*, Congress enacted and the President signed the Partial-Birth Abortion Ban Act of 2003, 18 U.S.C.A. §1531 (West Supp. 2004), which makes criminally and civilly liable any physician "who, in or affecting interstate or foreign commerce, knowingly performs a partial-birth abortion." Id. at §1531(a). "Partial-birth abortion" is defined as abortion in which the physician:

> (A) deliberately and intentionally vaginally delivers a living fetus until, in the case of a head-first presentation, the entire fetal head is outside the body of the mother, or, in the case of breech presentation, any part of the fetal trunk past the navel is outside the body of the mother, for the purpose of performing an overt act that the person knows will kill the partially delivered living fetus; and
>
> (B) performs the overt act, other than completion of delivery, that kills the partially delivered living fetus. . . .

Id. at §1531(b)(1). The ban includes an exception when the woman's "life is endangered by a physical disorder, physical illness, or physical injury, including a life-endangering physical condition caused by or arising from the pregnancy

---

[19]. See Sherri Finkbine, The Lesser of Two Evils, in The Case for Legalized Abortion Now 15 (Alan F. Guttmacher ed., 1967) (woman went to Sweden to terminate a pregnancy following use of Thalidomide).

[20]. See Gina Kolata, In Late Abortions, Decisions Are Painful and Options Few, N.Y. Times, Jan. 5, 1992, at A1.

itself. . . . " Id. at §1531(a). The woman herself cannot be prosecuted, but certain relatives of the fetus can sue the physician for damages. Id. at §1531(c) & (e).

How does this statute differ from the Nebraska law invalidated in *Stenberg*? Is there a sufficient health exception? See Michael J. Tierney, Note, Post-Viability Abortion Bans and the Limits of the Health Exception, 80 Notre Dame L. Rev. 465 (2004). Does the description of the proscribed procedure impose an undue burden by leaving open the possibility that the ban applies to other common methods of abortion, as in *Stenberg*? If a Supreme Court without Justice O'Connor decides to uphold this law, is there a basis for distinguishing *Stenberg* or must a majority overrule that precedent? Several lower courts have found the federal statute unconstitutional under *Stenberg*. Carhart v. Gonzales, 413 F.3d 791 (8th Cir. 2005), *cert. granted*, 126 S. Ct. 1314 (2006); Planned Parenthood Fed'n of Am. v. Gonzales, 435 F.3d 1163 (9th Cir. 2006), *cert. granted*, 2006 WL 1167413 (U.S. 2006); National Abortion Fed'n v. Gonzales, 437 F.3d 278 (2d Cir. 2006). See Alex Gordon, Recent Development: The Partial-Birth Abortion Ban Act of 2003, 41 Harv. J. on Legis. 501 (2004).

During the litigation challenging the federal statute, the Justice Department attempted to subpoena individual medical records of patients who had undergone D&X procedures, but these efforts failed, in part because production of such information would invade the patients' privacy. Northwestern Mem'l Hosp. v. Ashcroft, 362 F.3d 923 (7th Cir. 2004); Planned Parenthood Fed'n of Am. v. Ashcroft, 2004 WL 432222 (N.D. Cal. 2004).

Why does the statute exempt the woman from liability? Cf. Leslie Reagan, Victim or Accomplice?: Crime, Medical Malpractice, and the Construction of the Aborting Woman in American Case Law, 1860's-1970, 10 Colum. J. Gender & L. 311 (2001); Suzanne M. Alford, Note, Is Self-Abortion a Fundamental Right?, 52 Duke L.J. 1011 (2003). Do the civil liability provisions present any constitutional problems? See generally A.J. Stone, III, Consti-Tortion: Tort Law as an End-Run Around Abortion Rights After Planned Parenthood v. Casey, 8 Am. U.J. Gender Soc. Pol'y & L. 471 (2000). Could Congress allow the woman (who consented to the procedure) to sue afterwards for wrongful death of the fetus? See Jennifer L. Achilles, Comment, Using Tort Law to Circumvent Roe v. Wade and Other Pesky Due Process Decisions: An Examination of Louisiana's Act 825, 78 Tul. L. Rev. 853 (2004). On what basis does Congress have the authority to ban particular abortion procedures — or to regulate abortion at all? Is abortion interstate commerce? See, e.g., Allan Ides, The Partial-Birth Abortion Ban Act of 2003 and the Commerce Clause, 20 Const. Comment. 441 (2003-2004); Alissa Schecter, Note, Choosing Balance: Congressional Powers and the Partial-Birth Abortion Ban Act of 2003, 73 Fordham L. Rev. 1987 (2005). Cf. United States v. Dinwiddie, 76 F.3d 913, 919-920 (8th Cir.) (upholding Freedom of Access to Clinics Entrances Act against challenge to Congress's authority because abortion patients travel "in interstate commerce"), *cert. denied*, 519 U.S. 1043 (1996).

12. *Fetal protection measures.* Many states have enacted fetal homicide laws, with variations in the stage of fetal development when criminal liability attaches. See Sandra L. Smith, Note, Fetal Homicide: Woman or Fetus as Victim? A Survey of Current State Approaches and Recommendations for Future State Application, 41 Wm. & Mary L. Rev. 1845 (2000) (describing different approaches).

The federal Unborn Victims of Violence Act, 18 U.S.C. §1841 (West Supp. 2005), enacted in 2004, creates a separate criminal offense for killing or injuring an unborn child (at any stage of gestation) during the commission of a federal crime against the pregnant woman. What impact will such legislation have on abortion rights? See, e.g., Amanda K. Bruchs, Note, Clash of Competing Interests: Can the Unborn Victims of Violence Act and Over Thirty Years of Settled Abortion Law Co-Exist Peacefully?, 55 Syracuse L. Rev. 133 (2004).

The federal government also addressed the status of the fetus in revising the State Children's Health Insurance Program (SCHIP), 42 C.F.R. pt. 457 (2005), to include the unborn in the definition of "child." Id. at §457.10. SCHIP provides health insurance coverage for uninsured children in families at the poverty level. Critics see an impact on abortion rights. See Elisabeth H. Sperow, Redefining Child Under the State Children's Health Insurance Program: Capable of Repetition, Yet Evading Results, 12 Am. U.J. Gender Soc. Pol'y & L. 137 (2003). Yet, SCHIP might well provide needed assistance to poor minority women — a view in turn revealing a split between the "mainstream reproductive rights groups" and "many women of color feminists," who emphasize the limits of privacy principles in addressing larger problems of access to health care. Angela Hooton, A Broader Vision of the Reproductive Rights Movement: Fusing Mainstream and Latina Feminism, 13 Am. U.J. Gender Soc. Pol'y & L. 59, 68, 81-82 (2005).

13. *Federalism in family law.* The prospect of federal abortion legislation raises questions of federalism. Traditionally, the "whole subject of the domestic relations of husband and wife, parent and child, belong[ed] to the laws of the States and not to the laws of the United States." In re Burrus, 136 U.S. 586, 593-594 (1890). State control of family law issues was so exclusive that even diversity of citizenship did not give federal courts authority to hear domestic relations cases — a principle known as the "domestic-relations exception" to federal diversity jurisdiction. See Chapter V, section G3.

Griswold changed the traditional approach, signaling that the Constitution limits the states' authority over family law. Also, today the Supreme Court narrowly construes the domestic-relations exception to federal diversity jurisdiction, confining it to divorce, alimony, and custody questions. See Ankenbrandt v. Richards, 504 U.S. 689, 703-704 (1992) (exception inapplicable to tort action, so Missouri mother can sue Louisiana father in federal court on behalf of daughters for damages for alleged abuse).

In recent years, Congress repeatedly has invoked — not always with success — the Commerce Clause and the Fourteenth Amendment to legislate on many family law subjects. E.g., Violence Against Women Act of 1994, 42 U.S.C. §13981 (2000). But see United States v. Morrison, 529 U.S. 598 (2000) (§13981 exceeds Congress's power). Congress has also conditioned the states' use of federal funds on compliance with federal requirements for laws governing the family. E.g., Personal Responsibility and Work Opportunity Reconciliation Act of 1996, Pub. L. 104-193, 110 Stat. 2105 (1996) (codified in scattered sections of, inter alia, 42 U.S.C.).

Should family law reflect national policy or should it vary from state to state? What explains the traditional allocation of authority over questions of family law? The increasing federalization? What impact will the Supreme Court's recent limitations on federal power have on family law? See *Morrison*, supra; United States v. Lopez, 514 U.S. 549 (1995) (Congress lacked authority to enact Gun-Free School Zones Act). Will these limitations also prevent Congress from imposing national standards on family law through its provision of federal funds?

See generally Lynn A. Baker, Conditional Federal Spending After *Lopez*, 95 Colum. L. Rev. 1911 (1995); Naomi R. Cahn, Family Law, Federalism and the

Federal Courts, 79 Iowa L. Rev. 1073 (1994); Anne C. Dailey, Federalism and Families, 143 U. Pa. L. Rev. 1787 (1995); Jill Elaine Hasday, Federalism and the Family Reconstructed, 45 UCLA L. Rev. 1297 (1998); Sylvia Law, Families and Federalism, 4 Wash. U. J.L. & Pol'y 175 (2000); Judith Resnik, Essay, Categorical Federalism: Jurisdiction, Gender, and the Globe, 111 Yale L.J. 619 (2001).

Problem

In an effort to encourage work and "personal responsibility" and to discourage out-of-wedlock births and welfare dependency, New Jersey has adopted a "family cap." Previously, a welfare recipient received an increased allotment of public assistance on the birth of each child. On enactment of the family cap, a welfare recipient gets no such increase regardless of how large her family thereafter becomes. For those newly joining the welfare rolls even after the family cap, however, the allotment is calculated on the basis of actual family size. Hence, for example, the assistance for a family of three children varies, depending on when the children are born (before or after enactment of the family cap) and whether the parent is receiving welfare at the time of the births.

What constitutional challenges might be brought on behalf of those adversely affected by the family cap? Does the law encourage abortion? Given the state's justifications, what result and why? See C.K. v. Shalala, 883 F. Supp. 991 (D.N.J. 1995), aff'd sub nom. C.K. v. New Jersey Dept. of Health & Human Servs., 92 F.3d 171 (3d Cir. 1996). See generally, e.g., Dorothy Roberts, Killing the Black Body: Race, Reproduction, and the Meaning of Liberty 202-245 (1999); Susan Frelich Appleton, When Welfare Reforms Promote Abortion: "Personal Responsibility," "Family Values," and the Right to Choose, 85 Geo. L.J. 155 (1996); Yvette M. Barksdale, And the Poor Have Children: A Harm-Based Analysis of Family Caps and the Hollow Procreative Rights of Welfare Beneficiaries, 14 Law & Ineq. J. 1 (1995); Linda C. McClain, "Irresponsible" Reproduction, 47 Hastings L.J. 339 (1996).

Suppose, alternatively, the state offers $200 to each female current or former drug user who undergoes sterilization or uses long-acting contraceptives? See Zanita Fenton, Project Prevention: Cash for Birth Control, a Solution or a Violation of Rights?, 5 J.L. Soc'y 199 (2003).

4. The Liberation of Privacy

■ LAWRENCE v. TEXAS
539 U.S. 558 (2003)

Justice KENNEDY delivered the opinion of the Court.

Liberty protects the person from unwarranted government intrusions into a dwelling or other private places. In our tradition the State is not omnipresent in the home. And there are other spheres of our lives and existence, outside the home, where the State should not be a dominant presence. Freedom extends beyond spatial bounds. Liberty presumes an autonomy of self that includes freedom of thought, belief, expression, and certain intimate conduct. The instant case involves liberty of the person both in its spatial and more transcendent dimensions.

I

The question before the Court is the validity of a Texas statute making it a crime for two persons of the same sex to engage in certain intimate sexual conduct. In Houston, Texas, officers of the Harris County Police Department were dispatched to a private residence in response to a reported weapons disturbance. They entered an apartment where one of the petitioners, John Geddes Lawrence, resided. . . . The officers observed Lawrence and another man, Tyron Garner, engaging in a sexual act. The two petitioners were arrested, held in custody over night, and charged and convicted before a Justice of the Peace. . . .

. . . The applicable state law is Tex. Penal Code Ann. §21.06(a) (2003). It provides: "A person commits an offense if he engages in deviate sexual intercourse with another individual of the same sex." The statute defines "deviate sexual intercourse" as follows:

"(A) any contact between any part of the genitals of one person and the mouth or anus of another person; or
"(B) the penetration of the genitals or the anus of another person with an object."
§21.01(1). . . .

[P]etitioners were adults at the time of the alleged offense. Their conduct was in private and consensual. [In a trial *de novo*, petitioners raised an unsuccessful equal protection challenge to the law, which criminalizes sexual intimacy by same-sex couples but not identical behavior by different-sex couples. Then, petitioners entered pleas of *nolo contendere*, were each fined $200, and were assessed court costs. On appeal, the court rejected petitioners' equal protection and due process arguments.]

II

We conclude the case should be resolved by determining whether the petitioners were free as adults to engage in the private conduct in the exercise of their liberty under the Due Process Clause of the Fourteenth Amendment to the Constitution. For this inquiry we deem it necessary to reconsider the Court's holding in [Bowers v. Hardwick, 478 U.S. 186 (1986)].

There are broad statements of the substantive reach of liberty under the Due Process Clause in earlier cases [citing *Pierce* and *Meyer*]; but the most pertinent beginning point is our decision in Griswold v. Connecticut, 381 U.S. 479 (1965). [The Court then reviews *Griswold, Eisenstadt, Roe,* and Carey v. Population Services Int'l, 431 U.S. 678 (1977) (invalidating restrictions on minors' contraceptive choices)]. [These subsequent cases] confirmed that the reasoning of *Griswold* could not be confined to the protection of rights of married adults. . . .

The facts in *Bowers* had some similarities to the instant case [including police entry into Hardwick's bedroom while he was engaged in sexual conduct with another male.] One difference between the two cases is that the Georgia statute prohibited the conduct whether or not the participants were of the same sex, while the Texas statute, as we have seen, applies only to participants of the same sex. Hardwick was not prosecuted, but he brought an action in federal court to declare the state statute [unconstitutional.]

The Court began its substantive discussion in *Bowers* as follows: "The issue presented is whether the Federal Constitution confers a fundamental right upon homosexuals to engage in sodomy and hence invalidates the laws of the many States that still make such conduct illegal and have done so for a very long time." Id., at 190. That statement, we now conclude, discloses the Court's own failure to appreciate the extent of the liberty at stake. To say that the issue in *Bowers* was simply the right to engage in certain sexual conduct demeans the claim the individual put forward, just as it would demean a married couple were it to be said marriage is simply about the right to have sexual intercourse. The laws involved in *Bowers* and here are, to be sure, statutes that purport to do no more than prohibit a particular sexual act. Their penalties and purposes, though, have more far-reaching consequences, touching upon the most private human conduct, sexual behavior, and in the most private of places, the home. The statutes do seek to control a personal relationship that, whether or not entitled to formal recognition in the law, is within the liberty of persons to choose without being punished as criminals.

This, as a general rule, should counsel against attempts by the State, or a court, to define the meaning of the relationship or to set its boundaries absent injury to a person or abuse of an institution the law protects. It suffices for us to acknowledge that adults may choose to enter upon this relationship in the confines of their homes and their own private lives and still retain their dignity as free persons. When sexuality finds overt expression in intimate conduct with another person, the conduct can be but one element in a personal bond that is more enduring. The liberty protected by the Constitution allows homosexual persons the right to make this choice.

Having misapprehended the claim of liberty there presented to it, and thus stating the claim to be whether there is a fundamental right to engage in consensual sodomy, the *Bowers* Court said: "Proscriptions against that conduct have ancient roots." Id., at 192. In academic writings, and in many of the scholarly *amicus* briefs filed to assist the Court in this case, there are fundamental criticisms of the historical premises relied upon by the majority and concurring opinions in *Bowers*. . . . At the outset it should be noted that there is no longstanding history in this country of laws directed at homosexual conduct as a distinct matter. Beginning in colonial times there were prohibitions of sodomy derived from the English criminal laws passed in the first instance by the Reformation Parliament of 1533. The English prohibition was understood to include relations between men and women as well as relations between men and men. Nineteenth-century commentators similarly read American sodomy, buggery, and crime-against-nature statutes as criminalizing certain relations between men and women and between men and men. The absence of legal prohibitions focusing on homosexual conduct may be explained in part by noting that according to some scholars the concept of the homosexual as a distinct category of person did not emerge until the late 19th century. . . .

Laws prohibiting sodomy do not seem to have been enforced against consenting adults acting in private. A substantial number of sodomy prosecutions and convictions for which there are surviving records were for predatory acts against those who could not or did not consent, as in the case of a minor or the victim of an assault. . . .

It was not until the 1970's that any State singled out same-sex relations for criminal prosecution, and only nine States have done so. Post-*Bowers* even some of these States did not adhere to the policy of suppressing homosexual conduct. Over the course of the last decades, States with same-sex prohibitions have moved toward abolishing them. In summary, the historical grounds relied upon in *Bowers* are more complex than [Justice White's] majority opinion and the concurring opinion by Chief Justice Burger indicate. Their historical premises are not without doubt and, at the very least, are overstated.

It must be acknowledged, of course, that the Court in *Bowers* was making the broader point that for centuries there have been powerful voices to condemn homosexual conduct as immoral. The condemnation has been shaped by religious beliefs, conceptions of right and acceptable behavior, and respect for the traditional family. For many persons these are not trivial concerns but profound and deep convictions accepted as ethical and moral principles to which they aspire and which thus determine the course of their lives. These considerations do not answer the question before us, however. The issue is whether the majority may use the power of the State to enforce these views on the whole society through operation of the criminal law. "Our obligation is to define the liberty of all, not to mandate our own moral code." Planned Parenthood of Southeastern Pa. v. Casey, 505 U.S. 833, 850 (1992).

[O]ur laws and traditions in the past half century are of most relevance here. These references show an emerging awareness that liberty gives substantial protection to adult persons in deciding how to conduct their private lives in matters pertaining to sex. . . . This emerging recognition should have been apparent when *Bowers* was decided. In 1955 the American Law Institute promulgated the Model Penal Code and made clear that it did not recommend or provide for "criminal penalties for consensual sexual relations conducted in private." ALI, Model Penal Code §213.2, Comment 2, p 372 (1980). It justified its decision on three grounds: (1) The prohibitions undermined respect for the law by penalizing conduct many people engaged in; (2) the statutes regulated private conduct not harmful to others; and (3) the laws were arbitrarily enforced and thus invited the danger of blackmail. ALI, Model Penal Code, Commentary 277-280 (Tent. Draft No. 4, 1955). [Illinois and other states changed their laws accordingly.]

The sweeping references by Chief Justice Burger [concurring] to the history of Western civilization and to Judeo-Christian moral and ethical standards did not take account of other authorities pointing in an opposite direction. A committee advising the British Parliament recommended in 1957 repeal of laws punishing homosexual conduct. The Wolfenden Report: Report of the Committee on Homosexual Offenses and Prostitution (1963). Parliament enacted the substance of those recommendations 10 years later. Sexual Offences Act 1967, §1. Of even more importance, almost five years before *Bowers* was decided the European Court of Human Rights considered a case with parallels to *Bowers* and to today's case. . . . The court held that the laws proscribing the conduct were invalid under the European Convention on Human Rights. Dudgeon v. United Kingdom, 45 Eur. Ct. H. R. (1981) P 52. Authoritative in all countries that are members of the Council of Europe (21 nations then, 45 nations now), the decision is at odds with the premise in *Bowers* that the claim put forward was insubstantial in our Western civilization.

In our own constitutional system the deficiencies in *Bowers* became even more apparent in the years following its announcement. The 25 States with laws prohibiting the relevant conduct referenced in the *Bowers* decision are reduced now to 13, of which 4 enforce their laws only against homosexual conduct. In those States where sodomy is still proscribed, whether for same-sex or heterosexual conduct, there is a pattern of nonenforcement with respect to consenting adults acting in private. The State of Texas admitted in 1994 that as of that date it had not prosecuted anyone under those circumstances. State v. Morales, 869 S.W.2d 941, 943.

Two principal cases decided after *Bowers* cast its holding into even more doubt. In Planned Parenthood of Southeastern Pa. v. Casey, 505 U.S. 833 (1992), the Court reaffirmed the substantive force of the liberty protected by the Due Process Clause. The *Casey* decision again confirmed that our laws and tradition afford constitutional protection to personal decisions relating to marriage, procreation, contraception, family relationships, child rearing, and education. Id., at 851. In explaining the respect the Constitution demands for the autonomy of the person in making these choices, we stated as follows:

> "These matters, involving the most intimate and personal choices a person may make in a lifetime, choices central to personal dignity and autonomy, are central to the liberty protected by the Fourteenth Amendment. At the heart of liberty is the right to define one's own concept of existence, of meaning, of the universe, and of the mystery of human life. Beliefs about these matters could not define the attributes of personhood were they formed under compulsion of the State."

Persons in a homosexual relationship may seek autonomy for these purposes, just as heterosexual persons do. The decision in *Bowers* would deny them this right.

The second post-*Bowers* case of principal relevance is Romer v. Evans, 517 U.S. 620 (1996). There the Court struck down class-based legislation directed at homosexuals as a violation of the Equal Protection Clause. *Romer* invalidated an amendment to Colorado's constitution which named as a solitary class persons who were homosexuals, lesbians, or bisexual either by "orientation, conduct, practices or relationships," id., at 624, and deprived them of protection under state antidiscrimination laws. We concluded that the provision was "born of animosity toward the class of persons affected" and further that it had no rational relation to a legitimate governmental purpose. Id., at 634.

[Although petitioners have a tenable equal protection argument under *Romer*, we must] address whether *Bowers* itself has continuing validity. Were we to hold the statute invalid under the Equal Protection Clause some might question whether a prohibition would be valid if drawn differently, say, to prohibit the conduct both between same-sex and different-sex participants.

Equality of treatment and the due process right to demand respect for conduct protected by the substantive guarantee of liberty are linked in important respects, and a decision on the latter point advances both interests. . . . When homosexual conduct is made criminal by the law of the State, that declaration in and of itself is an invitation to subject homosexual persons to discrimination both in the public and in the private spheres. The central holding of *Bowers* has been brought in question by this case, and it should be addressed. Its continuance as precedent demeans the lives of homosexual persons [by imposing the stigma of a misdemeanor, with resulting sex-offender registration requirements and disclosure requirements for job applications].

The foundations of *Bowers* have sustained serious erosion from our recent decisions in *Casey* and *Romer*. When our precedent has been thus weakened, criticism from other sources is of greater significance [citing commentators, state constitutional decisions, and authorities from other countries that rejected *Bowers*'s reasoning]. The doctrine of *stare decisis* is essential to the respect accorded to the judgments of the Court and to the stability of the law. It is not, however, an inexorable command. . . . *Bowers* was not correct when it was decided, and it is not correct today. It ought not to remain binding precedent. Bowers v. Hardwick should be and now is overruled.

The present case does not involve minors. It does not involve persons who might be injured or coerced or who are situated in relationships where consent might not easily be refused. It does not involve public conduct or prostitution. It does not involve whether the government must give formal recognition to any relationship that homosexual persons seek to enter. The case does involve two adults who, with full and mutual consent from each other, engaged in sexual practices common to a homosexual lifestyle. The petitioners are entitled to respect for their private lives. The State cannot demean their existence or control their destiny by making their private sexual conduct a crime. Their right to liberty under the Due Process Clause gives them the full right to engage in their conduct without intervention of the government. "It is a promise of the Constitution that there is a realm of personal liberty which the government may not enter." *Casey*, supra, at 847. The Texas statute furthers no legitimate state interest which can justify its intrusion into the personal and private life of the individual.

Had those who drew and ratified the Due Process Clauses of the Fifth Amendment or the Fourteenth Amendment known the components of liberty in its manifold possibilities, they might have been more specific. They did not presume to have this insight. They knew times can blind us to certain truths and later generations can see that laws once thought necessary and proper in fact serve only to oppress. As the Constitution endures, persons in every generation can invoke its principles in their own search for greater freedom. [Reversed.]

Justice O'CONNOR, concurring in the judgment. . . .

This case raises a different issue than *Bowers:* whether, under the Equal Protection Clause, moral disapproval is a legitimate state interest to justify by itself a statute that bans homosexual sodomy, but not heterosexual sodomy. It is not. Moral disapproval of this group [homosexuals], like a bare desire to harm the group, is an interest that is insufficient to satisfy rational basis review under the Equal Protection Clause. See, e.g., Department of Agriculture v. Moreno, [413 U.S. 528, 534 (1973)]; Romer v. Evans, 517 U.S., at 634-635. . . . The Texas sodomy law "raises the inevitable inference that the disadvantage imposed is born of animosity toward the class of persons affected." Id., at 634.

. . . While it is true that the law applies only to conduct, the conduct targeted by this law is conduct that is closely correlated with being homosexual. Under such circumstances, Texas' sodomy law is targeted at more than conduct. It is instead directed toward gay persons as a class. [T]he State cannot single out one identifiable class of citizens for punishment that does not apply to everyone else, with moral disapproval as the only asserted state interest for the law. . . .

. . . Texas cannot assert any legitimate state interest here, such as national security or preserving the traditional institution of marriage. Unlike moral disapproval of same-sex relations — the asserted state interest in this case — other reasons exist to promote the institution of marriage beyond mere moral disapproval of an excluded group. A law branding one class of persons as criminal solely based on the State's moral disapproval of that class and the conduct associated with that class runs contrary to the values of the Constitution and the Equal Protection Clause, under any standard of review. . . .

Justice SCALIA, with whom the CHIEF JUSTICE and Justice THOMAS join, dissenting. . . .

I begin with the Court's surprising readiness to reconsider a decision rendered a mere 17 years ago in Bowers v. Hardwick. . . . Today's approach to *stare decisis* invites us to overrule an erroneously decided precedent (including an "intensely divisive" decision) *if:* (1) its foundations have been "eroded" by subsequent decisions; (2) it has been subject to "substantial and continuing" criticism; and (3) it has not induced "individual or societal reliance" that counsels against overturning. The problem is that *Roe* itself—which today's majority surely has no disposition to overrule—satisfies these conditions to at least the same degree as *Bowers*. . . .

[To] distinguish the rock-solid, unamendable disposition of *Roe* from the readily overrulable *Bowers* [we need examine] the third factor. . . . It seems to me that the "societal reliance" on the principles confirmed in *Bowers* and discarded today has been overwhelming. Countless judicial decisions and legislative enactments have relied on the ancient proposition that a governing majority's belief that certain sexual behavior is "immoral and unacceptable" constitutes a rational basis for regulation [citing cases relying on *Bowers*]. State laws against bigamy, same-sex marriage, adult incest, prostitution, masturbation, adultery, fornication, bestiality, and obscenity are likewise sustainable only in light of *Bowers'* validation of laws based on moral choices. Every single one of these laws is called into question by today's decision. . . .

What a massive disruption of the current social order, therefore, the overruling of *Bowers* entails. Not so the overruling of *Roe*, which would simply have restored the regime that existed for centuries before 1973, in which the permissibility of and restrictions upon abortion were determined legislative State-by-State. . . .

[To establish that *Bowers* was wrongly decided, the majority relies on "an] *emerging awareness* that liberty gives substantial protection to adult persons in deciding how to conduct their private lives *in matters pertaining to sex*" (emphasis added). Apart from the fact that such an "emerging awareness" does not establish a "fundamental right," the statement is factually false. States continue to prosecute all sorts of crimes by adults "in matters pertaining to sex": prostitution, adult incest, adultery, obscenity, and child pornography. Sodomy laws, too, have been enforced "in the past half century," in which there have been 134 reported cases involving prosecutions for consensual, adult, homosexual sodomy. [W. Eskridge, Gaylaw: Challenging the Apartheid of the Closet 375 (1999).]

In any event, an "emerging awareness" is by definition not "deeply rooted in this Nation's history and traditions," as we have said "fundamental right" status requires. Constitutional entitlements do not spring into existence because some States choose to lessen or eliminate criminal sanctions on certain behavior. Much less do they spring into existence, as the Court seems to believe, because *foreign nations* decriminalize conduct. . . .

The Texas statute undeniably seeks to further the belief of its citizens that certain forms of sexual behavior are "immoral and unacceptable," *Bowers*, supra, at 196—the same interest furthered by criminal laws against fornication, bigamy, adultery, adult incest, bestiality, and obscenity. *Bowers* held that this *was* a legitimate state interest. The Court today reaches the opposite conclusion. . . . This effectively decrees the end of all morals legislation. If, as the Court asserts, the promotion of majoritarian sexual morality is not even a *legitimate* state interest, none of the above-mentioned laws can survive rational-basis review. . . .

Finally, I turn to petitioners' equal-protection challenge. . . . On its face §21.06(a) applies equally to all persons. . . . To be sure, §21.06 does distinguish between the sexes insofar as concerns the partner with whom the sexual acts are performed: men can violate the law only with other men, and women only with other women. But this cannot itself be a denial of equal protection, since it is precisely the same distinction regarding partner that is drawn in state laws prohibiting marriage with someone of the same sex while permitting marriage with someone of the opposite sex. . . .

[Justice O'Connor's] reasoning leaves on pretty shaky grounds state laws limiting marriage to opposite-sex couples. Justice O'Connor seeks to preserve them by the conclusory statement that "preserving the traditional institution of marriage" is a legitimate state interest. But "preserving the traditional institution of marriage" is just a kinder way of describing the State's *moral disapproval* of same-sex couples. . . .

Today's opinion is the product of a Court, which is the product of a law-profession culture, that has largely signed on to the so-called homosexual agenda, by which I mean the agenda promoted by some homosexual activists directed at eliminating the moral opprobrium that has traditionally attached to homosexual conduct. . . . It is clear from this that the Court has taken sides in the culture war, departing from its role of assuring, as neutral observer, that the democratic rules of engagement are observed. Many Americans do not want persons who openly engage in homosexual conduct as partners in their business, as scoutmasters for their children, as teachers in their children's schools, or as boarders in their home. They view this as protecting themselves and their families from a lifestyle that they believe to be immoral and destructive. The Court views it as "discrimination" which it is the function of our judgments to deter. So imbued is the Court with the law profession's anti-anti-homosexual culture, that it is seemingly unaware that the attitudes of that culture are not obviously "mainstream"; that in most States what the Court calls "discrimination" against those who engage in homosexual acts is perfectly legal; that proposals to ban such "discrimination" under Title VII have repeatedly been rejected by Congress; and that in some cases such "discrimination" is a constitutional right, see Boy Scouts of America v. Dale, 530 U.S. 640 (2000).

Let me be clear that I have nothing against homosexuals, or any other group, promoting their agenda through normal democratic means. Social perceptions of sexual and other morality change over time, and every group has the right to persuade its fellow citizens that its view of such matters is the best. That homosexuals have achieved some success in that enterprise is attested to by the fact that Texas is one of the few remaining States that criminalize private, consensual homosexual acts. But persuading one's fellow citizens is one thing, and imposing one's views in absence of democratic majority will is something else. I would no more *require* a State to criminalize homosexual acts—or, for that matter, display *any* moral disapprobation of them—than I would *forbid* it to do so. . . .

■ **PATTY REINERT, PAIR PROUD THEY COULD GET
SODOMY LAW THROWN OUT**
Hous. Chron., Apr. 25, 2004, at A1

Almost six years after police stormed his apartment and arrested him for having sex with another man, this is what John Lawrence remembers: Harris County Sheriff's Department officers shoving him to the couch, shattering the porcelain birds that were a gift from his mother. The humiliating ride to the station, wearing only handcuffs and underwear. The fingerprinting and mugshot, the bologna sandwich he ate in jail, the jeans another inmate gave him for the ride home, the cabbie who took him, though he had no wallet to pay. And the call to his elderly father to tell him what had happened. . . .

It has been nearly a year since the U.S. Supreme Court used the case of John Lawrence and Tyron Garner to throw out the nation's remaining sodomy laws. . . . In [their first interview] since the case began, Lawrence and Garner said they are proud to have helped defeat an unjust law, overwhelmed by the support they've received and so glad it's over.

"I got a sense of justice for being wronged by the state of Texas," Lawrence said as he sat with Garner in lawyer Mitchell Katine's office. "I feel I've been vindicated." . . . "Would I have done the same thing again? Yes," he said. "When somebody is wronged and they don't stand up for themselves, they're going to get wronged again. I wasn't going to stand for it."

Garner, 36, who sells barbecue from a street stand, agreed. "It was worth it," he said. On Sept. 17, 1998, Garner and his boyfriend, Robert Royce Eubanks, were drinking margaritas and eating dinner at a Mexican restaurant with their friend, Lawrence. . . . Back at [Lawrence's] apartment after dinner, though, Eubanks and Garner argued. Eubanks left angry, saying he was going to buy a soda. Instead, he went to a pay telephone and called the police, reporting that there was a man with a gun in Lawrence's apartment. "I think he was jealous," Garner said.

When two Harris County deputies arrived, the door to the apartment was unlocked. They walked in with Eubanks following and discovered Lawrence and Garner having sex. Lawrence and Garner said they had no idea why they were being arrested. They spent the night in jail.

The charges stemmed from the 1973 Texas Homosexual Conduct Law. . . . At the time, Kansas, Oklahoma and Missouri had similar laws, and nine other states — Louisiana, Mississippi, Alabama, Florida, South Carolina, North Carolina, Virginia, Idaho and Utah — made sodomy a crime for heterosexuals as well as homosexuals. . . . Eubanks was convicted and sentenced to 30 days in jail for filing a false report to a peace officer. Garner forgave him and continued their relationship; Lawrence couldn't. . . .

Immediately after their arrest in 1998, Lawrence and Garner returned to their lives. But Lawrence was stewing. When Katine, a partner at Houston's Williams, Birnberg & Andersen, and the New York-based Lambda Legal Defense and Education Fund offered their services for free, Lawrence decided to fight. Garner was reluctant, but he agreed. "I didn't think we'd win," Garner said. And though his friends and family knew he was gay, he said, "I didn't enjoy being outed with my mugshot on TV. It was degrading to me." . . .

Lawrence, who works nights, set his alarm for 9 a.m. the day the court was expected to rule. He flipped on CNN and heard the announcement. "I bolted out of bed and shouted, 'Thank you, God!'" he said. . . . "I called my brother, and we celebrated with a couple of bottles of champagne," Garner said. By nightfall, hundreds had gathered for a rally at City Hall. Katine, who had spent years shielding his clients from the media, introduced them to the crowd. People stood in line to meet them.

Today, Lawrence and Garner remain friends and date other people. Neither were activists before their case, and they still aren't. . . . Both support the right of gay people to marry but aren't interested themselves. "I'm single and love it," Lawrence said.

Garner is touched by people who recognize him at the grocery store or on the street, and Lawrence loves to tell the story of two burly cops, working security outside a gay nightclub, approaching to give them a hug. Both laugh at the idea of cashing in with a book or a TV movie deal, and they shun comparisons some have made to Jane Roe of abortion rights fame or Rosa Parks, a civil rights icon. "I don't really want to be a hero," Garner said. "But I want to tell other gay people, 'Be who you are, and don't be afraid.'". . . .

■ **TONY MAURO, A "CULTURAL MILESTONE" AT THE HIGH COURT:** *LAWRENCE* **GAY ATTORNEYS TURNED OUT IN FORCE TO WITNESS** *LAWRENCE* **ARGUMENTS**
Tex. Law., Mar. 31, 2004, at 11

Paul Smith brought energy, agility and a full command of the case to the podium when he argued on behalf of the Lambda Legal Defense and Education Fund March 26 in the landmark gay rights case Lawrence v. Texas. He also brought personal experience. Smith, managing partner in Jenner & Block's Washington, D.C., office, is gay, a fact that was not widely talked about. . . .

"I think it gave me a greater comfort level answering questions about homosexuality," says Smith, 48, a veteran of eight U.S. Supreme Court arguments before last week. "And I think there is a symbolic importance to the community that I was up there. . . . " The symbolism was palpable in the courtroom. Dozens of prominent gay lawyers filled the lawyers' section of the gallery. "The most remarkable thing about the argument was the audience," said Walter Dellinger of O'Melveny & Myers, who wrote an amicus curiae brief for several gay and civil rights groups. The presence of so many prominent lawyers who are homosexual was a "cultural milestone," Dellinger said. . . .

Smith's advocacy also marked a milestone for Jenner & Block, which has become well-known as a firm that welcomes gay and lesbian lawyers. . . . He joined the firm 10 years ago "when I was not very 'out' in general, but it has been a very supportive place." Smith also says he has not experienced the kind of discrimination that the clients and other homosexuals face in many parts of the country. "Fortunately, I live in D.C., where there is no law" like the anti-sodomy law at issue in *Lawrence*. . . .

Smith's sexual orientation is notable for another reason: He clerked for the late Justice Lewis Powell in 1981. Five years later, historians have noted that as Powell deliberated in Bowers v. Hardwick, he mused to a law clerk that "I don't believe I've ever met a homosexual." Powell was apparently unaware not only that the clerk he was speaking to was gay, but also that several of his previous clerks were gay.

. . . Smith holds no animosity toward Powell, who was the deciding vote in favor of upholding Georgia's anti-sodomy law. Smith notes that after Powell left the court in 1987, he said he regretted his vote in *Bowers*. "Obviously it was very troubling to him, and he came to believe he had made a mistake," Smith says, "Justice Powell was very much on my mind as I argued."

Notes and Questions

1. *Constitutional basis.* What is the constitutional right protected by *Lawrence*? The majority's opinion begins with the word "liberty" and ends with the word "freedom." Does the Court's opinion reflect a broad libertarian approach under which substantive due process presumptively protects all personal interests? See, e.g., Randy E. Barnett, Justice Kennedy's Libertarian Revolution: Lawrence v. Texas, 2002-2003 Cato Sup. Ct. Rev. 21. To what extent does *Lawrence's* notion of liberty rest on *Griswold's* conception(s) of privacy? Do you agree that "*Lawrence* follows *Griswold* as day follows night"? Matthew Coles, Lawrence v. Texas & the Refinement of Substantive Due Process, 16 Stan. L. & Pol'y Rev. 23, 48 (2005).

2. *Equality.* What role do equality principles play in the majority opinion? How does the majority respond to Justice O'Connor's reliance on the Equal Protection Clause? In Romer v. Evans, 517 U.S. 620 (1996), the Supreme Court used the Equal Protection Clause to invalidate a Colorado state constitutional amendment banning the enactment of laws protecting homosexual orientation, conduct, practices, or relationships. The Court found that the amendment made it more difficult for one group of citizens than for all others to seek aid from the government, and it also raised the inference that the "disadvantage imposed is born of animosity." Id. at 634. Why do you suppose the majority did not use the Equal Protection Clause to decide *Lawrence* as it did *Romer*? What difference would it have made?

Despite the *Lawrence* majority's use of due process, not equal protection, commentators say the opinion synthesizes autonomy and equality principles by rejecting criminal statutes that subordinate a particular group of citizens. See, e.g., Pamela S. Karlan, Foreword: Loving *Lawrence*, 102 Mich. L. Rev. 1447, 1449 (2004) ("*Lawrence* is a case about liberty that has important implications for the jurisprudence of equality."); Laurence H. Tribe, Essay, Lawrence v. Texas: The "Fundamental Right" That Dare Not Speak Its Name, 117 Harv. L. Rev. 1893, 1911 (2004) ("anti-sodomy laws [make outcasts] of homosexuals but not heterosexuals for the obvious reason that heterosexuals have other . . . intimate physical outlets for their lust and their love").

3. *Other constitutional interests.* What other rights and interests does *Lawrence* implicate? Some cite the First Amendment. E.g., Nan D. Hunter, Sexual Orientation and the Paradox of Heightened Scrutiny, 102 Mich. L. Rev. 1528, 1552 (2004) (free expression); Tribe, supra, at 1939-1940 (speech and peaceable assembly). Others discern procedural due process values. See Cass R. Sunstein, What Did *Lawrence* Hold? Of Autonomy, Desuetude, Sexuality, and Marriage, 2003 Sup. Ct. Rev. 27, 28, 73 (citing requirement of fair notice and ban on arbitrary action when enforcement is rare and underlying moral judgments lack public support).

4. Bowers. In Bowers v. Hardwick, 478 U.S. 186 (1986), the Supreme Court held that enforcement of a state sodomy statute did not violate the Constitution. Citing the "ancient roots" of sodomy proscriptions, the majority opinion in *Bowers* found no fundamental right to privacy at stake and saw no connection between "family, marriage, or procreation on the one hand and homosexual activity on the other." Id. at 191. Why did the Supreme Court overturn *Bowers*? How does *Lawrence* explain its overruling of *Bowers*, consistent with the doctrine of *stare decisis*?

5. *Liberty's scope.* Bowers had invoked history and tradition to determine whether an asserted interest merits constitutional protection. What methodology does *Lawrence* use to determine what's "in" and what's "out" of substantive due process? What role do (should) judicial value judgments play? See Sunstein, supra.

What is the scope of the liberty protected in *Lawrence*? Does the majority hew to *Griswold*'s focus on the spatial privacy of the bedroom and the home? What do the "more transcendent dimensions" of "liberty of the person" encompass?

Lawrence quotes language from Planned Parenthood of Southeastern Pennsylvania v. Casey, 505 U.S. 833, 851 (1992), that critics, including Justice Scalia (in an omitted portion of his dissent), call the "sweet-mystery-of-life passage." See 539 U.S. at 588 (Scalia, J., dissenting). Does that language help define the interest at stake? After *Casey*, but before *Lawrence*, the Court apparently repudiated this passage, rejecting a constitutional right to physician-assisted suicide for failure to satisfy two tests: (a) the "Due Process Clause specially protects [only] those fundamental rights and liberties which are, objectively, 'deeply rooted in this Nation's history and tradition,'" and (b) "substantive-due-process cases [require] a 'careful description' of the asserted fundamental liberty interest." Washington v. Glucksberg, 521 U.S. 702, 720-721 (1997). Do these tests remain controlling?

6. *Standard of review.* Bowers, which saw no fundamental right at stake, used the rational basis test. What standard of review does *Lawrence* use? Why?

Professor Mary Anne Case identifies the following as the critical sentence, asserting that the Court's use of the non-restrictive "which" instead of the restrictive "that" reveals the application of rationality review: "The Texas statute furthers no legitimate state interest which can justify its intrusions into the personal and private life of the individual." Mary Anne Case, Of "This" and "That" in Lawrence v. Texas, 2003 Sup. Ct. Rev. 75, 83-84. Matt Coles invokes the same sentence, but emphasizes the word "justify" to find a balancing test that collapses the traditional levels of review. Coles, supra, at 30-31, 37. But see Tribe, supra, at 1917 (strict review).

7. *Morality.* In Bowers, the Supreme Court concluded that Georgia satisfied the rational basis test because its electorate regarded homosexual sodomy as immoral and unacceptable. In *Lawrence*, why do majoritarian moral values fail to justify the Texas statute? Evaluate Justice Scalia's prediction that the *Lawrence* majority's approach dooms "all morals legislation."

Consider philosopher John Stuart Mill's tenet that "the only purpose for which power can be rightfully exercised over any member of a civilised community, against his will, is to prevent harm to others." John Stuart Mill, On Liberty 13 (Gateway ed. 1955) (originally published in 1859). To what extent does Mill satisfactorily resolve the issue in *Lawrence*? Does Mill's "harm principle" preclude legislation based on morality alone?

Even under Mill's harm test, don't moral judgments remain relevant? As Justice Scalia intimates, why can't a legislature regard its disapproval of gay sex as a means of protecting children from the "harm" of exposure "to a lifestyle [believed] to be immoral and destructive" — that is, as a means of sending to children what Professor William Eskridge calls the "no promo homo" message? See William N. Eskridge, Jr., No Promo Homo: The Sedimentation of Antigay Discourse and the Channeling Effect of Judicial Review, 75 N.Y.U. L. Rev. 1327 (2000).

8. *"Moral neutrality" and the culture wars.* Does the *Lawrence* majority opinion reflect a "moral neutrality" necessary in our pluralistic society? Suzanne B. Goldberg, Morals-Based Justifications for Lawmaking: Before and After Lawrence v. Texas, 88 Minn. L. Rev. 1233, 1283 (2004); Louis Michel Seidman, Out of Bounds, 65 Ohio St. L.J. 1329, 1336 (2004). Does the Court's moral neutrality place it on one side of the "culture wars," a term in discourse that encompasses a number of contested family law (and family values) issues, including reproductive rights, gender equality, gay rights, end-of-life decisions, and the legislatures' and courts' roles in such matters? Why has family law, in particular, become the site of such controversy? What role should religion and religious beliefs play in official resolutions of such disputes?

Eskridge sees in *Lawrence* "a jurisprudence of tolerance" designed to manage the culture wars by "lowering the stakes of identity politics"; under this view, the majority's moral judgments cannot support criminal punishment or political exclusion of gays and lesbians but permit discrimination in associations such as the Boy Scouts and activities such as the Boston St. Patrick's Day parade. William N. Eskridge, Jr., *Lawrence*'s Jurisprudence of Tolerance: Judicial Review to Lower the Stakes of Identity Politics, 88 Minn. L. Rev. 1021, 1073-1075 (2004) (citing *Lawrence*, *Romer*, Boy Scouts of America v. Dale, 530 U.S. 640 (2000), and Hurley v. Irish-American Gay, Lesbian, and Bisexual Group, 515 U.S. 557 (1995)).

9. *Foreign law.* What is the appropriate role for foreign legal authorities, such as those cited by the *Lawrence* majority, when battles in the culture wars reach American courts? Note that the Supreme Court recently relied on foreign law to invalidate the juvenile death penalty. Roper v. Simmons, 543 U.S. 551 (2005). See generally Steven G. Calabresi, *Lawrence*, the Fourteenth Amendment, and the Supreme Court's Reliance on Foreign Constitutional Law: An Originalist Reappraisal, 65 Ohio St. L.J. 1097 (2004); Joan L. Larsen, Importing Constitutional Norms from a "Wider Civilization": *Lawrence* and the Rehnquist Court's Use of Foreign and International Law in Domestic Constitutional Interpretation, 65 Ohio St. L.J. 1283 (2004).

10. *Legislative vs. judicial reform.* Justice Scalia's dissent advocates leaving the issue of gay rights to the legislature. An omitted part of this opinion asserts that "the people, unlike judges, need not carry things to their logical conclusion. The people may feel that their disapprobation of homosexual conduct is strong enough to disallow homosexual marriage, but not strong enough to criminalize private homosexual acts — and may legislate accordingly." 539 U.S. at 604. Must courts take matters to their logical conclusions? Do they? What does Justice Scalia's distinction mean in family law, with its many lines drawn for cultural reasons? What is the appropriate role of legislatures and courts, respectively, in the protection of civil liberties for minorities? See Berta E. Hernández-Truyol, Querying *Lawrence*, 65 Ohio St. L.J. 1151, 1225-1226 (2004).

11. *State constitutions.* Judicial reform might come from litigation based on federal or state constitutions. Before *Lawrence*, some courts interpreted state constitutions to grant more protections for private consensual sexual activity than the

federal constitution. See, e.g., Powell v. State, 510 S.E.2d 18 (Ga. 1998) (state right to privacy invalidates Georgia sodomy statute unsuccessfully challenged in *Bowers*). See also In re J.M., 575 S.E.2d 441 (Ga. 2003) (ruling that the state constitution's right of privacy invalidates the criminal fornication statute, as applied to consensual sex in the bedroom of one participant).

12. *The anti-subordination theme.* In an omitted sentence, Justice O'Connor states that the Texas statute violates equal protection because it "threatens the creation of an underclass." The majority, rejecting Texas's argument that the statute simply punishes conduct, condemns the statute for targeting "gay persons as a class." Such language suggests an anti-subordination approach. (The anti-subordination approach to equal protection requires invalidation of laws and legal structures that perpetuate the subordination of disadvantaged groups, such as women or African-Americans.) What groups count for purposes of this anti-subordination analysis? Is Justice Scalia correct that the most salient classification in the Texas law is sex-based, the same classification that restricts access to traditional marriage to one man and one woman? See Chapter II, section D2a(i)(1).

13. *Conduct and identity.* The majority opinion refers to "homosexual conduct," "homosexual persons," and "a homosexual lifestyle." What connection does the majority see among these? Justice O'Connor discerns a close correlation between the prohibited conduct and "being homosexual." Is Justice Scalia correct that one might invoke the same analysis for any criminal law? In an omitted portion of his dissent, he analogizes: "A law against public nudity targets 'the conduct that is closely correlated with being a nudist,' and hence 'is targeted at more than conduct'; it is 'directed toward nudists as a class.'" 539 U.S. at 600. Is the analogy apt?

14. *A relationship test?* The majority envisions sexual intimacy as one part of a more encompassing relationship, criticizing *Bowers* for its assumption that the case concerned "simply the right to engage in certain sexual conduct . . . , just as it would demean a married couple were it to be said marriage is simply about the right to have sexual intercourse." In wake of *Bowers*'s assertion that gay sex has no connection to "family, marriage, or procreation," one gay-rights strategy sought to emphasize the similarities in the day-to-day lives and familial relationships of gay men and lesbians, on the one hand, and their heterosexual counterparts, on the other. See, e.g, Toni M. Massaro, Gay Rights, Thick and Thin, 49 Stan. L. Rev. 45, 104 (1996) ("narratives [about real human beings and their lives] may be the only means of undermining arguments that characterize homosexuality as more like masturbation than like intimacy in heterosexual marriages"). Does *Lawrence* assume a relationship of a particular duration and quality? Would the Court have reached a different outcome or produced a different opinion if it had considered facts revealed in the interview, supra, specifically Garner's ongoing relationship with Eubanks (rather than with Lawrence)?

Alternatively, do all consensual sexual encounters, however fleeting, evoke the protection that *Lawrence* requires? How "discreet" must one keep the relationship? What is the boundary that separates "private" from "public" sex? To what extent does the Court's invocation of sexual privacy come "dangerously close to the bad privacy of the closet"? See Hernández-Truyol, supra, at 1238, 1241. See also Dale Carpenter, The Unknown Past of Lawrence v. Texas, 102 Mich. L. Rev. 1464, 1519 (2004).

Or, is *Lawrence* simply a "sex positive" case, embracing a jurisprudence of sexual pleasure, regardless of the nature of the underlying relationships? Soon after *Bowers*, Sylvia Law linked Georgia's sodomy law with the statutes overturned in *Griswold, Eisenstadt,* and *Roe* by explaining how all these measures burden the capacity to enjoy sexual activity.

> People have a strong affirmative interest in sexual expression and relationships. Through sexual relationships, we experience deep connection with another, vulnerability, playfulness, surcease, connection with birth and with death, and *transcendence*. The power of sexual experience is such that, in every culture, the basic units of human community, nurturing, acculturation, economic sharing, companionship and daily life are built around relationships of sexual expression and taboo.

Sylvia A. Law, Homosexuality and the Social Meaning of Gender, 1988 Wis. L. Rev. 187, 225 (emphasis added). Is this what *Lawrence* had in mind in protecting liberty in its "more transcendent dimensions"? Conflicting interpretations of *Lawrence* figured prominently when a divided U.S. Court of Appeals, rejecting a fundamental right to sexual privacy, upheld a ban on the sale of sex toys, even though restrictions on the ability to purchase such items amount to restrictions on their use. Williams v. Attorney General, 378 F.3d 1232 (11th Cir. 2004), *cert. denied sub nom.* Williams v. King, 543 U.S. 1152 (2005).

15. Lawrence *and other family laws.* What implications does *Lawrence* have for other family law issues? Consider, first, the Court's abortion jurisprudence. Evaluate Justice Scalia's assertion in his dissent in *Lawrence* that *Roe* stands out as a more compelling case for overruling than *Bowers.* Should *Lawrence* have applied the undue burden standard, announced in *Casey* and applied in *Stenberg*? How can you square Justice Kennedy's opinion for the majority in *Lawrence,* with its rejection of the state's reliance on morality, and his dissent in *Stenberg,* which says that "Nebraska was entitled to find the existence of a consequential moral difference between [D&X and D&E abortion procedures]"? *Stenberg,* 530 U.S. at 962.

Justice Scalia contends that *Lawrence* paves the way for constitutional protection of same-sex marriage. On the other hand, the majority disclaims deciding "whether the government must give formal recognition to any relationship that homosexual persons seek to enter." Can you reconcile this limitation with the majority's emphasis on dignity and its repudiation of laws that stigmatize gays as a class? On the impact of *Lawrence* on same-sex marriage, see Chapter II, pp. 170, 173–174. For a discussion of *Lawrence*'s impact on other marriage restrictions, see Chapter II, pp. 197–198 (bigamy).

Does *Lawrence* preclude states from disfavoring gay and lesbian parents in custody decisions or limiting adoptions to heterosexual persons? See Lofton v. Secretary of Dep't of Fam. & Children's Servs., 358 F.3d 804 (11th Cir. 2004), *cert. denied,* 543 U.S. 1081 (2005). See also Chapter VII, section B1b(iii)(1); Chapter IX, section C1b. What implications does *Lawrence* have for domestic violence? According to Professor Marc Spindelman, *Lawrence* erases the problem of sexual violence by assuming men are never victims, treating sex as consensual if not refused, and keeping government intervention at bay. Marc Spindelman, Surviving *Lawrence,* 102 Mich. L. Rev. 1615, 1648, 1649, 1661-1662, 1665 (2004).

16. Lawrence*'s facts.* The interview, supra, offers a glimpse of the facts underlying the case. For a methodical attempt to piece together the factual setting in greater detail, see generally Carpenter, supra. Carpenter's investigation, which produces conflicting stories about the night of the arrest, raises a number of uncertainties not apparent from the Court's statement of facts. For example, he finds

disagreement among witnesses about whether Lawrence and Garner were even in the same room when the police arrived and, if they were, whether the police saw them engaging in sexual activity. See 102 Mich. L. Rev. at 1484, 1513-1514. What reasons might explain the different stories that Carpenter discovers? See also Paris R. Baldacci, Lawrence and Garner: The Love (or at Least Sexual Attraction) That Finally Dared Speak Its Name, 10 Cardozo Women's L.J. 289, 306-307 (2004).

17. *Race, class, and power.* Given its emphasis on *consensual* sex, to what extent should the Court's analysis have paid more attention to race, class, and age — and power disparities? Consider the following facts, not all apparent from the case or the interview: Lawrence was "a fifty-nine-year-old white man who [was] a medical technician . . . working at Bayshore Medical Center" and had a record of previous arrests; Garner, an African-American about twenty years younger than Lawrence, was unemployed at the time of his arrest, had a record of previous arrests, and had a white roommate-boyfriend (Eubanks), who summoned police to Lawrence's residence with a false report of a armed "black man" "going crazy." Hernández-Truyol, supra, at 1234-1237. Both Lawrence and Garner likely had been drinking but were not intoxicated. What perspectives do these facts add to the Court's analysis? See Carpenter, supra, at 1522-1524.

18. *Critiques.* Predictably, *Lawrence* has many critics. Some condemn the "judicial activism" exemplified by majority opinion. E.g., Lino A. Graglia, Lawrence v. Texas: Our Philosopher-Kings Adopt Libertarianism as Our Official National Philosophy and Reject Traditional Morality as a Basis for Law, 65 Ohio St. L.J. 1139, 1141 (2004); Nelson Lund & John O. McGinnis, Lawrence v. Texas and Judicial Hubris, 102 Mich. L. Rev. 1555 (2004). Others take the majority to task primarily for relying on foreign law. E.g., Calabresi, supra.

Some supporters of gay rights also find fault with *Lawrence*. According to Professor Catharine MacKinnon, *Lawrence* reinforces the pervasive problem of gender inequality, "securing for homosexuals heterosexuality's substantive privileges, including its male gendered dominance, by extending rather than dismantling them." Catharine A. MacKinnon, The Road Not Taken: Sex Equality in Lawrence v. Texas, 65 Ohio St. L.J. 1081, 1094 (2004). Spindelman agrees, identifying as the source of the problem *Lawrence*'s "'like-straight' logic," which protects gays and lesbians on the theory that their lives and relationships mirror heterosexuals'. Spindelman, supra, at 1619-1632. This assimilationist approach also has a confining, rather than a liberating effect, according to Professor Katherine Franke, who writes:

> I fear that *Lawrence* and the gay rights organizing that has taken place in and around it have created a path dependency that privileges privatized and domesticated rights and legal liabilities, while rendering less viable projects that advance nonnormative notions of kinship, intimacy, and sexuality.

Katherine M. Franke, The Domesticated Liberty of Lawrence v. Texas, 104 Colum. L. Rev. 1399, 1414 (2004). See also Hunter, supra, at 1549.

Problem

Matthew, who had just turned 18, had consensual oral contact with the genitalia of M.A.R., who turned 15 the month following the incident, while both males were residents at a school for developmentally disabled children. Following his conviction, Matthew was required to register as a sex offender and sentenced to a term of imprisonment 15 times more severe than he would have received for the same conduct if one of the two participants had been female. Under those circumstances, the punishment would have been governed by a special "Romeo and Juliet exception" to the state's unlawful voluntary sexual relations statute, applicable to consensual intercourse, sodomy, or lewd touching when, at the time of he incident, (1) the victim is a child of 14 or 15, (2) the offender is less than 19 years of age and less than 4 years older than the victim, (3) the victim and offender are the only ones involved, and (4) the vicitim and offender are members of the opposite sex. In addition, if the participants had been of different sexes, the offender would not need to register as a sex offender. Following the Supreme Court's ruling in *Lawrence*, Matthew brings a constitutional challenge to his punishment, claiming that the failure to extend the Romeo and Juliet exception to same-sex conduct violates the Equal Protection Clause. Why would Matthew rely on equal protection instead of due process? What interests can the state assert in defending the statutory scheme? What standard of review should the court apply? What result and why? See State v. Limon, 122 P.3d 22 (Kan. 2005).

B. WHEN PRIVACY RIGHTS CONFLICT

1. Wives and Husbands

■ **PLANNED PARENTHOOD OF SOUTHEASTERN PENNSYLVANIA v. CASEY**
505 U.S. 833 (1992)

Justice O'CONNOR, Justice KENNEDY, and Justice SOUTER announced the judgment of the Court and delivered the opinion of the Court [for Part V-C:]

Section 3209 of Pennsylvania's abortion law provides, except in cases of medical emergency, that no physician shall perform an abortion on a married woman without receiving a signed statement from the woman that she has notified her spouse that she is about to undergo an abortion. The woman has the option of providing an alternative signed statement certifying that her husband is not the man who impregnated her; that her husband could not be located; that the pregnancy is the result of spousal sexual assault which she has reported; or that the woman believes that notifying her husband will cause him or someone else to inflict bodily injury upon her. A physician who performs an abortion on a married woman without receiving the appropriate signed statement will have his or her license revoked, and is liable to the husband for damages.

The District Court heard the testimony of numerous expert witnesses, and made detailed findings of fact regarding the effect of this statute. These included:

"273. The vast majority of women consult their husbands prior to deciding to terminate their pregnancy. . . . [. . .]

"281. Studies reveal that family violence occurs in two million families in the United States. This figure, however, is a conservative one that substantially understates (because battering is usually not reported until it reaches life-threatening proportions) the actual number of families affected by domestic violence. In fact, researchers estimate that one of every two women will be battered at some time in their life. . . .

"282. A wife may not elect to notify her husband of her intention to have an abortion for a variety of reasons, including the husband's illness, concern about her own health, the imminent failure of the marriage, or the husband's absolute opposition to the abortion. . . .

"283. The required filing of the spousal consent form would require plaintiff-clinics to change their counseling procedures and force women to reveal their most intimate decision-making on pain of criminal sanctions. The confidentiality of these revelations could not be guaranteed, since the woman's records are not immune from subpoena. . . .

"284. Women of all class levels, educational backgrounds, and racial, ethnic and religious groups are battered. . . .

"285. Wife-battering or abuse can take on many physical and psychological forms. The nature and scope of the battering can cover a broad range of actions and be gruesome and torturous [including murder, rape, child abuse, psychological intimidation, and emotional harm.]

"289. Mere notification of pregnancy is frequently a flashpoint for battering and violence within the family. The number of battering incidents is high during the pregnancy and often the worst abuse can be associated with pregnancy. . . . The battering husband may deny parentage and use the pregnancy as an excuse for abuse. . . .

"290. Secrecy typically shrouds abusive families. . . . Battering husbands often threaten [the wife] or her children with further abuse if she tells an outsider of the violence and tells her that nobody will believe her. A battered woman, therefore, is highly unlikely to disclose the violence against her for fear of retaliation by the abuser. . . . [. . .]"

These findings are supported by studies of domestic violence. . . . In well-functioning marriages, spouses discuss important intimate decisions such as whether to bear a child. But there are millions of women in this country who are the victims of regular physical and psychological abuse at the hands of their husbands. . . . Many may fear devastating forms of psychological abuse from their husbands, including [abuse of their children,] verbal harassment, threats of future violence, the destruction of possessions, physical confinement to the home, the withdrawal of financial support, or the disclosure of the abortion to family and friends. These methods of psychological abuse may act as even more of a deterrent to notification than the possibility of physical violence, but women who are the victims of the abuse are not exempt from §3209's notification requirement. And many women who are pregnant as a result of sexual assaults by their husbands will be unable to avail themselves of the exception for spousal sexual assault, §3209(b)(3), because the exception requires that the woman have notified law enforcement authorities within 90 days of the assault, and her husband will be notified of her report once an investigation begins, §3128(c). If anything in this field is certain, it is that victims of spousal sexual assault are extremely reluctant to report the abuse to the government. . . . We must not blind ourselves to the fact that the significant number of women who fear for their safety and the safety of their children are likely to be deterred from procuring an abortion as surely as if the Commonwealth had outlawed abortion in all cases.

Respondents attempt to avoid the conclusion that §3209 is invalid by pointing out that it imposes almost no burden at all for the vast majority of women seeking abortions. . . . Legislation is measured for consistency with the Constitution by its impact on those whose conduct it affects [, however.] The unfortunate yet persisting conditions we document above will mean that in a large fraction of the cases in which §3209 is relevant, it will operate as a substantial obstacle to a woman's choice to undergo an abortion. It is an undue burden, and therefore invalid. . . .

We recognize that a husband has a "deep and proper concern and interest . . . in his wife's pregnancy and in the growth and development of the fetus she is carrying." [Planned Parenthood of Central Mo. v. Danforth, 428 U.S. 52, 69 (1976).] With regard to the children he has fathered and raised, the Court has recognized his "cognizable and substantial" interest in their custody. Stanley v. Illinois, 405 U.S. 645, 651-652 (1972). . . .

Before birth, however, the issue takes on a very different cast. It is an inescapable biological fact that state regulation with respect to the child a woman is carrying will have a far greater impact on the mother's liberty than on the father's. The effect of state regulation on a woman's protected liberty is doubly deserving of scrutiny in such a case, as the State has touched not only upon the private sphere of the family but upon the very bodily integrity of the pregnant woman. The Court has held that "when the wife and the husband disagree on this decision, the view of only one of the two marriage partners can prevail. Inasmuch as it is the woman who physically bears the child and who is the more directly and immediately affected by the pregnancy, as between the two, the balance weighs in her favor." Danforth, supra, at 71. This conclusion rests upon the basic nature of marriage and the nature of our Constitution: "The marital couple is not an independent entity with a mind and heart of its own, but an association of two individuals each with a separate intellectual and emotional makeup. If the right of privacy means anything, it is the right of the individual, married or single, to be free from unwarranted governmental intrusion into matters so fundamentally affecting a person as the decision whether to bear or beget a child." Eisenstadt v. Baird, 405 U.S. at 453 (emphasis in original). . . .

There was a time, not so long ago, when a different understanding of the family and of the Constitution prevailed. In Bradwell v. State, 83 U.S. (16 Wall.) 130 (1872), three Members of this Court reaffirmed the common-law principle that "a woman had no legal existence separate from her husband, who was regarded as her head and representative in the social state; and, notwithstanding some recent modifications of this civil status, many of the special rules of law flowing from and dependent upon this cardinal principle still exist in full force in most States." Id., at 141 (Bradley, J., joined by Swayne and Field, JJ., concurring in judgment). Only one generation has passed since this Court observed that "woman is still regarded as the center of home and family life," with attendant "special responsibilities" that precluded full and independent legal status under the Constitution. Hoyt v. Florida, 368 U.S. 57, 62 (1961). These views, of course, are no longer consistent with our understanding of the family, the individual, or the Constitution.

[T]he Court held in Danforth that the Constitution does not permit a State to require a married woman to obtain her husband's consent before undergoing an abortion. . . . For the great many women who are victims of abuse inflicted by their husbands, or whose children are the victims of such abuse, a spousal notice requirement enables the husband to wield an effective veto over his wife's decision [contrary to *Danforth*.]

The husband's interest in the life of the child his wife is carrying does not permit the State to empower him with this troubling degree of authority over his wife. . . . A husband has no enforceable right to require a wife to advise him before she exercises her personal choices. If a husband's interest in the potential life of the child outweighs a wife's liberty, the State could require a married woman to notify her husband before she uses a postfertilization contraceptive. Perhaps next in line would be a statute requiring pregnant married women to notify their husbands before engaging in conduct causing risks to the fetus. After all, if the husband's interest in the fetus' safety is a sufficient predicate for state regulation, the State could reasonably conclude that pregnant wives should notify their husbands before drinking alcohol or smoking. Perhaps married women should notify their husbands before using contraceptives or before undergoing any type of surgery that may have complications affecting the husband's interest in his wife's reproductive organs. And if a husband's interest justifies notice in any of these cases, one might reasonably argue that it justifies exactly what the *Danforth* Court held it did not justify — a requirement of the husband's consent as well. A State may not give to a man the kind of dominion over his wife that parents exercise over their children. . . .

Chief Justice REHNQUIST, with whom Justice WHITE, Justice SCALIA, and Justice THOMAS join, . . . dissenting in part . . .

[T]he provision here involves a much less intrusive requirement of spousal notification, not consent. . . . *Danforth* thus does not control our analysis. . . .

The question before us is therefore whether the spousal notification requirement rationally furthers any legitimate state interests. We conclude that it does. First, a husband's interests in procreation within marriage and in the potential life of his unborn child are certainly substantial ones. The State itself has legitimate interests both in protecting these interests of the father and in protecting the potential life of the fetus, and the spousal notification requirement is reasonably related to advancing those state interests. By providing that a husband will usually know of his spouse's intent to have an abortion, the provision makes it more likely that the husband will participate in deciding the fate of his unborn child, a possibility that might otherwise have been denied him. This participation might in some cases result in a decision to proceed with the pregnancy. As Judge Alito observed in his dissent below, "the Pennsylvania legislature could have rationally believed that some married women are initially inclined to obtain an abortion without their husbands' knowledge because of perceived problems — such as economic constraints, future plans, or the husbands' previously expressed opposition — that may be obviated by discussion prior to the abortion." 947 F.2d at 726 (opinion concurring in part and dissenting in part).

The State also has a legitimate interest in promoting "the integrity of the marital relationship." 18 Pa. Cons. Stat. §3209(a) (1990). [T]he spousal notice requirement is a rational attempt by the State to improve truthful communication between spouses and encourage collaborative decisionmaking, and thereby fosters marital integrity. . . .

Notes and Questions

1. *Rationale.* Why did the Court strike down the spousal notification provision? How does a requirement of spousal notification differ from one of spousal consent, which the Court struck down in Planned Parenthood v. Danforth, 428 U.S. 52, 67-72 (1976)? Should one trigger a higher level of scrutiny? Which one? Does the answer depend on the meaning of "privacy"? The standard of review applied?

2. *Undue burden.* Why do Justices O'Connor, Kennedy, and Souter conclude that spousal notification constitutes an undue burden but the 24-hour waiting period does not? See *Casey*, 505 U.S. at 881-887. Realistically, couldn't a woman more easily surmount the former simply by forging her husband's signature? Compare the Court's treatment of the two requirements, considering both the number of women apparently affected and the difficulty of the obstacle created. See Kathleen M. Sullivan, The Supreme Court 1991 Term, Foreword: The Justices of Rules and Standards, 106 Harv. L. Rev. 22, 32-34 (1992). Does the Court's analysis of the spousal notification requirement (emphasizing the "impact on those whose conduct it affects") require consideration of poverty in all applications of the undue burden standard? See Kenneth L. Karst, Poverty and Rights: A Pre-Millennial Triptych, 16 Notre Dame J.L. Ethics & Pub. Pol'y 399 (2002).

3. *Whose privacy?* Does privacy emerge from *Casey* as protection for the individual? The family unit? One approach advocates a constitutional doctrine that favors the "objectively weaker" party in family conflicts. See Jane Rutherford, Beyond Individual Privacy: A New Theory of Family Rights, 39 U. Fla. L. Rev. 627, 652 (1987). Who is "objectively weaker" in reproductive decisionmaking — the woman or the man? What role does privacy doctrine play when the family unit is divided? See David D. Meyer, The Paradox of Family Privacy, 53 Vand. L. Rev. 527, 554-558 (2000) (in "splintered" families, privacy does not keep the state out but locates in the Constitution "a substantive rule for resolving a family's internal conflict").

4. *Who decides?* Who should make the determination when women's and men's rights conflict? Should the state provide pre-abortion hearings at which an impartial arbiter decides? Can you imagine circumstances in which the male should prevail? Suppose that the man seeks to avoid having a child but the woman chooses to carry to term? Must he pay child support under all circumstances? David Shepardson & Eric Lacy, Dads: No Cash for Unwanted Children; In Lawsuit Activists Argue If Women Have Right to Decide Fate of Fetus, Fathers Can Decline Financial Role, The Detroit News, Mar. 9, 2006, at A1 (reporting suit dubbed "Roe v. Wade for Men"). See also Chapter IV, section C1; Chapter IX, section E2b.

5. *Empirical data.* To what extent did the Court rely on empirical data in invalidating the spousal notification requirement? Data from abortion clinics reveal that as many as 86 percent of women inform their male partners about their abortion plans and that married women and single women are equally likely to do so. Marcelle Christian Holmes, Reconsidering a "Woman's Issue:" Psychotherapy and One Man's Postabortion Experiences, 58 Am. J. Psychotherapy 103 (2004). See also Arthur B. Shostak, The Role of Unwed Fathers in the Abortion Decision, in Young Unwed Fathers, Changing Roles in Emerging Policies 288 (Robert L. Lerman & Theodora J. Ooms, eds. 1995) (reporting limited empirical findings). Do such data support or undermine the *Casey* dissent's view of the notification requirement as a valid means of furthering the state's interest in promoting marital

integrity and spousal communication? Domestic violence is explored further in Chapter III, section C3.

6. *Vision of marriage.* What vision of marriage does *Casey* reflect? Does the rejection of traditional gender-based roles provide a better explanation for the outcome than the empirical data? How persuasive is the majority's "parade of horribles" that might follow if the notification requirement were upheld? Do the joint opinion authors have a consistent view of women and their decisionmaking capacity, considering the approach to spousal notification, on the one hand, and the 24-hour waiting period (which they upheld), on the other?

Contrast the majority's reasoning with the assertion that by "isolating" the woman the Court has "endorsed the debasing, sexist notion that reproductive matters are really only women's 'private' concerns" and that "real men do not care about procreation, posterity, and mutuality in procreative and childbearing/rearing responsibilities." Lynn D. Wardle, The Quandary of Pro-Life Free Speech: A Lesson from the Abolitionists, 62 Alb. L. Rev. 853, 948 (1999).

7. *Gender stereotypes. Casey*'s rejection of the traditional concept of marriage, with its subordination of women, complements a line of cases invalidating under the Equal Protection Clause (or other equality principles) laws resting on gender-based stereotypes of males and females. The resulting "gender neutralization" of family law stands out as one of the most transformative developments in the field. See Chapter III, pp. 248-250. To what extent does this egalitarian understanding of family law presuppose a woman's reproductive autonomy, including abortion rights? See generally, e.g., Elizabeth M. Schneider, The Synergy of Equality and Privacy in Women's Rights, 2002 U. Chi. Legal F. 137. According to a biographer of Justice Blackmun, author of *Roe*'s majority opinion, he initially resisted the Court's gender equality rulings but came to understand the link between them and abortion rights, around the time of *Casey*. Linda Greenhouse, Becoming Justice Blackmun: Harry Blackmun's Supreme Court Journey 207-227 (2005).

2. Children and Parents

■ PLANNED PARENTHOOD OF NORTHERN NEW ENGLAND v. HEED

390 F.3d 53 (1st Cir. 2004), **vacated and remanded sub nom.** *Ayotte v. Planned Parenthood of Northern New England, 126 S. Ct. 961 (2006)*

TORRUELLA, Circuit Judge . . .

In June 2003, the New Hampshire legislature passed [an Act prohibiting the performance of an abortion on an unemancipated minor absent written notice to her parents at least 48 hours beforehand, with an exception if the attending abortion provider certifies in the minor's medical record that the abortion is necessary to prevent her death and there is insufficient time to provide the required notice.] If a minor does not want her parent or guardian notified, she may request a state judge, after a hearing, to "authorize an abortion provider to perform the abortion if said judge determines that the pregnant minor is mature and capable of giving informed consent to the proposed abortion," or if the judge determines that "the performance of an abortion upon her without notification of her parent, guardian, or conservator would be in her best interests." [In these "judicial bypass" proceedings, which are confidential and have priority in scheduling, the minor can go forward herself or have a guardian ad litem appointed, and she has a right to appointed counsel. The court must decide in 7 days, with expedited appeals provided.] Access to the trial and appellate courts for the purposes of these petitions "shall be afforded such a pregnant minor 24 hours a day, 7 days a week." Violation of the Act can result in criminal penalties and civil liability [to a person wrongfully denied notification.]

[Plaintiffs-appellees] filed a complaint under 42 U.S.C. §1983, seeking a declaratory judgment that the Act is unconstitutional and [injunctions] to prevent its enforcement once it became effective. [They prevailed in the district court.]

The Attorney General argues that in deciding whether the Act is facially invalid we should apply the "no set of circumstances" standard set forth in United States v. Salerno, 481 U.S. 739 (1987) [(rejecting facial challenge to Bail Reform Act)]. This standard requires plaintiffs challenging a state law as facially invalid to show that "no set of circumstances exists under which the Act would be valid." The Attorney General's argument rests on the premise that the *Salerno* standard is applicable to the Act despite the agreement of a plurality of Justices in Planned Parenthood of Southeastern Pa. v. Casey, 505 U.S. 833, 876-77 (1992), that a law which "has the purpose or effect of placing a substantial obstacle in the path of a woman seeking an abortion of a nonviable fetus" places an unconstitutional "undue burden" on the exercise of her right to choose abortion. A majority of the *Casey* Court applied that standard to determine that an abortion regulation is facially invalid if "in a large fraction of cases in which [the regulation] is relevant, it will operate as a substantial obstacle to a woman's choice to undergo an abortion," thus imposing an "undue burden." Id. at 895 (per Justices O'Connor, Kennedy, and Souter, joined by Justices Stevens and Blackmun). . . .

Despite the Supreme Court's clear application of the undue burden standard in *Casey* and [in Stenberg v. Carhart, 530 U.S. 914 (2000)], it has never explicitly addressed the standard's tension with *Salerno*. [We agree with the district court and six out of seven circuit courts that the undue burden standard] supersedes *Salerno* in the context of abortion regulation.

Complementing the general undue burden standard, the Supreme Court has also identified a specific and independent constitutional requirement that an abortion regulation must contain an exception for the preservation of a pregnant woman's health. See *Stenberg*, 530 U.S. at 929-30. . . . The origin of the health requirement can be traced to *Roe*, which held that "the State, in promoting its interest in the potentiality of human life, may . . . regulate . . . abortion [after fetal viability] *except* where necessary, in appropriate medical judgment, for the preservation of the life or health of the mother." Roe v. Wade, 410 U.S. 113, 164-65 (1973) (emphasis added), *reaff'd Casey*, 505 U.S. at 879 (plurality opinion). . . .

A. HEALTH EXCEPTION

The Attorney General and amici suggest that parental notification laws are shielded from the health exception requirement reiterated in *Stenberg* on account of the interests they aim to protect. Parental notification laws are enacted not only in furtherance of the state's "interest in the potentiality of human life," *Roe*, 410

U.S. at 164, but also in the interest of protecting minors from undertaking the risks of abortion without the advice and support of a parent. [H]owever, the Supreme Court has determined that it "cannot see how the interest-related differences could make any difference to the . . . application of the 'health' requirement." *Stenberg*, 530 U.S. at 931. The Constitution requires a health exception even when the State's interest in regulation is "compelling." See *Roe*, 410 U.S. at 163; see also *Stenberg*, 530 U.S. at 931. Thus, regardless of the interests served by New Hampshire's parental notice statute, it does not escape the Constitution's requirement of a health exception. . . .

Finally, the Attorney General argues that the Act's judicial bypass mechanism allows prompt authorization of a health-related abortion without notice. . . . However, the Act allows courts seven calendar days in which to rule on minors' petitions, and another seven calendar days on appeal. Delays of up to two weeks can therefore occur, during which time a minor's health may be adversely affected. . . . Due to this delay, the Act's bypass provision does not stand in for the constitutionally required health exception. . . .

B. DEATH EXCEPTION

[T]he New Hampshire Act waives its parental notice requirement when a physician can certify that abortion is "necessary to prevent the minor's death and there is insufficient time to provide the required notice." Appellees argue that this death exception is unconstitutionally narrow because (1) it is not possible for a physician to determine with any certainty whether death will occur before the notice provisions could be complied with; (2) it does not allow for circumstances in which abortion is the best, but not the only, option for saving a minor's life; and (3) it does not permit abortion providers to rely on their own good faith judgment about whether an abortion is necessary. . . .

A minimum of forty-eight hours is necessary for compliance with the Act's notification requirement. Dr. Wayne Goldner, a named plaintiff in this case, provided unopposed testimony that physicians cannot predict with adequate precision what course medical complications will take, and thus cannot always determine whether death will occur within this time window.

The Attorney General apparently concedes that an abortion provider must be able to rely on his or her good faith medical judgment in determining whether her patient's life is in danger. [Yet, under the Act,] a physician cannot know whether his or her determination that a minor's life is at risk will be judged according to a standard (e.g., knowingly) that respects her good-faith medical assessment, or by an objective standard (negligently) that would leave the physician's judgment open to *post hoc* second guessing. The resulting uncertainty would, again, impermissibly chill physicians' willingness and ability to provide lifesaving abortions. . . .

C. CONFIDENTIALITY

. . . Appellees argue that the Act does not adequately provide for the confidentiality of [the] judicial bypass procedures. . . . Inadequate confidentiality provisions "raise the specter of public exposure and harassment of women who choose to exercise their personal, intensely private, right, with their physician, to end a pregnancy." [A] lack of confidentiality would also create a significant risk that a minor's parents could learn of her pregnancy and desire for an abortion, resulting in the very harms sought to be avoided by the bypass procedure. Alternatively, a minor might be compelled to delay or decline to seek an abortion out of fear that her parents would find out. Thus, for a large fraction of minors eligible for judicial bypass, inadequate confidentiality would impose an undue burden. . . . Because we have already found the Act in its entirety unconstitutional on other grounds, however, we find it unnecessary to delve further into an evaluation of its confidentiality provisions.

■ ANGELA BONAVOGLIA, KATHY'S DAY IN COURT
Ms., Apr. 1988, at 46-49

On Wednesday, September 23, 1987, at 7:30 A.M., a pregnant 17-year-old we will call "Kathy" — her court-designated name — left her home in a working-class neighborhood of Birmingham, Alabama, and drove alone to the Jefferson County Family Courthouse. Kathy wanted an abortion. But in Alabama, as in 20 other states in the nation, a law exists that forbids a minor (anyone under the age of 18) to give her own consent for an abortion. Alabama's minors must ask one parent for permission, and if they can't do that, they must get a judge's approval before they can have an abortion.

Kathy is a friendly young woman with a big hearty laugh. Her face is round with residues of baby fat, and framed in a mane of blond hair. People tend to describe her as "sensible," which she is, but her sense of competence comes from having had to take care of herself much too early in life. Six years ago her mother remarried, to a man who is an alcoholic. For the last year and a half Kathy has lived mainly on her own, since she doesn't get along with her stepfather. . . .

Waiting for her at the courthouse that September day was the abortion provider Kathy had contacted when she realized she was pregnant [Diane Derzis, the director of Summit Medical Center]. Diane Derzis wanted to find a teenager willing to go to court and take her chances with the ambiguous law. If a judge turned this test case down, she would help the girl appeal, going as far as necessary in the court system to show how punitive the statute is. [Kathy had previously called the Medical Center to arrange an abortion. Her maturity led Derzis to ask her if she would wait five days until the consent law became effective and then go to court to test the new law. In exchange Derzis would arrange for Kathy to have a free abortion.]

"The money was a little bit of why I did it," said Kathy, "but I could have paid." More to the point for Kathy was that "Diane told me it would be a big help to the people who came after me. Everyone thought I was the perfect person to try this out: seventeen, living on my own. And, I thought, with all I've been through, I'm still here, I *know* I can handle this."

Following the instructions set forth in the Alabama law, Derzis had submitted Kathy's request for a judicial hearing to the Jefferson County Family Court. By law, the court had to provide Kathy with free legal representation for her hearing. Her papers were brought by a court officer to a Legal Aid lawyer, J. Wynell (Wendy) Brooks Crew, on September 21. [Judge Charles Nice would be hearing the case two days later.]

But on the day after Crew believed herself to have been appointed as Kathy's attorney, Judge Nice's bailiff approached her and a private attorney, Marcus Jones. According to Crew, the bailiff told Jones *he* had been appointed to represent the minor, and she was to represent the fetus. Wendy Crew said no. She pointed out that she had already talked to Kathy. She also noted that appointing a lawyer for the fetus would be unconstitutional, since, under Roe v. Wade, the fetus cannot be considered a person and does not have a right to representation. . . .

Crew and Jones went into the judge's office. Nice, 68, a slightly built, benevolent-looking man, had in his office pamphlets for Lifeline, an adoption agency run by the virulently anti-choice Sav-A-Life Christian ministry. Hanging on his wall was a photo of some of Lifeline's adoptive parents at their last reunion. Crew told him she wanted to stay on the case. She asked to be appointed Kathy's guardian or to be co-counsel. Judge Nice refused both requests and dismissed Crew.

Now Marcus Jones went into the conference room to meet Kathy. "I was mad," said Kathy. "I felt like I could pull this through with Wendy. Then they bring some man in fifteen minutes before the trial. Men don't really know about this. How is some man gonna stand up there and fight for me when he doesn't even know what's going on? I thought to myself, 'I'm gonna lose.'"

At approximately 9:45 A.M., Kathy and Diane Derzis walked down the hall from the conference room to Judge Nice's courtroom. . . . "I was having heart failure," [Kathy] said. She wanted Derzis to stay, but only court personnel were allowed in the room. That left Kathy in a room with four men — Nice, Jones, the bailiff, and the court officer. . . .

Jones began his questioning. . . . Kathy testified that she would not be 18 until the end of the year, and was therefore still affected by the parental consent law. To establish her maturity, Jones asked her about school. She told him that since she had not graduated, she planned to take the high school equivalency test. She also testified that she had been working full-time and part-time for the last two years and contributed to her own support.

Marcus Jones asked about her family. Kathy testified that her alcoholic stepfather abused her mother and herself. According to Kathy, he beat her so badly one night, she left and moved in with friends. . . . Kathy said she was 10 weeks pregnant. She didn't want to tell her mother about the pregnancy because her mother told her stepfather everything and if he found out about this he might get mad and end by beating her mother.

Kathy testified that she had considered adoption as well as abortion and remembers being surprised when Judge Nice continued to question her about this. . . . After 45 minutes of testimony, Judge Nice left the courtroom to make his decision. . . . Judge Nice returned and read his decision: he would not grant Kathy's request for an abortion; she was not mature enough, it was not in her best interest. The judge told Kathy she should talk to her mother about this decision.

Kathy was stunned. "I was about in tears. How can he say this about me? He didn't feel I was mature enough to make this decision myself? I could feel my eyes start pooling up, and I was going, 'Don't cry, don't cry.'"

"Everyone here at the clinic thinks I'm such a hard bitch," said Diane Derzis, "but I came back the day of that hearing and cried to think of what Kathy went through. I called Wendy and said 'I can't believe we put her through that. Why didn't we just take her to Georgia?'"

But they persevered, filing an appeal of Judge Nice's decision. [Kathy] has never said that she regrets her decision to go to court, but admits that the waiting was terrible: "I kept wishing I had already gotten it over with."

Fourteen days after the hearing, the Alabama Court of Civil Appeals overturned the judge's opinion . . . : "The trial judge in this case abused his discretion by denying the minor's request. . . . More importantly, we can neither discern from the trial court's judgment nor from the record any ground upon which the trial court's conclusion could rest. We can safely say, having considered the record, that, should this minor not meet the criteria for 'maturity' under the statute, it is difficult to imagine one who would." . . .

Notes and Questions

1. *Epilogue*. In a unanimous opinion by Justice O'Connor just before her retirement, the Supreme Court vacated and remanded the *Heed* case for the Court of Appeals to reconsider the remedy. Ayotte v. Planned Parenthood of N. New Eng., 126 S. Ct. 961 (2006). Specifically, without revisiting earlier abortion precedents, the Justices indicated that the court below might prohibit *only* the statute's unconstitutional applications, without "invalidat[ing] the law wholesale." Id. at 969. This narrower remedy, which would leave part of the statute in place, is appropriate only when consistent with legislative intent. Id. at 968. For implications of this remedial approach, see infra pp. 85-86.

2. *Minors' abortion decisionmaking*. The United States Supreme Court interprets the Constitution to permit greater state regulation of minors' abortion rights compared to those of adults. Why? In Bellotti v. Baird, 443 U.S. 622, 634 (1979), a plurality of the Supreme Court invoked the vulnerability of youth; their inability to make mature, informed decisions; and the need to foster the parental role in child-rearing. While these reasons support parental involvement requirements for minors' abortions, *Bellotti* went on to say that states with such laws must also provide an alternative to allow some minors to proceed without their parents. A number of states with abortion restrictions responded, creating procedures for a minor to appear before a judge to "bypass" the parental consent or notification otherwise required (discussed infra pp. 83-85).

a. *Vulnerability*. What does "vulnerability" encompass? *Bellotti* elaborates with references to the Court's holdings protecting minors' constitutional rights. Id. Would a more apt focus consider the emotional effects of abortions on minors? Psychological data fail to show a greater risk of postabortion distress or depression for minors than adult women. See Wendy J. Quinton et al., Adolescents and Adjustment to Abortion: Are Minors at Greater Risk?, 7 Psychol. Pub. Pol'y & L. 491 (2001).

b. *Decisionmaking capacity*. Are adolescents less able to make informed, mature decisions than adults? Studies that have examined the decisionmaking processes of adolescents and adults find few, if any, differences in cognitive abilities, at least for those adolescents who are age 14 and older. See J. Shoshanna Ehrlich, Grounded in the Reality of Their Lives: Listening to Teens Who Make the Abortion Decision Without Involving Their Parents, 18 Berkeley Women's L.J. 61, 150 (2003); Preston A. Britner et al., Psychology and the Law: Evaluating Juveniles' Competence to Make Abortion Decisions: How Social Science Can Inform the Law, 5 U. Chi. L. Sch. Roundtable 35 (1998).

c. *Promoting parental involvement.* Do laws requiring parental consent or notice promote family unity? Parental control? Result in more informed decisions? In actual consultation between parents and their daughters? If the Constitution protects a parent's right to control the upbringing of children under *Meyer* and *Pierce*, supra, why don't parents have absolute authority to prevent a daughter's abortion if they see fit? See Richard F. Storrow & Sandra Martinez, "Special Weight" for Best-Interests Minors in the New Era of Parental Autonomy, 2003 Wis. L. Rev. 789. Or, to direct a teenage daughter to have an abortion despite her wishes to the contrary? See In the Matter of Mary P., 444 N.Y.S.2d 545 (Fam. Ct. 1981).

3. *Parental involvement laws.* Currently, a majority of states require parental involvement in a minor's decision to have an abortion. Twenty-one states require parental consent; 13 states require parental notification. Guttmacher Institute, State Policies in Brief: Parental Involvement in Minors' Abortions (as of Sept. 13, 2005) (available at http:www.guttmacher.org/statecenter/spibs/index.html). Most states require consent or notification of *only one* parent. See id. (only two states require both parents to consent and one state requires both parents to be notified). Six states permit other adult relatives instead of parents to be involved. Id.

4. *Federal proposals and laws. Bellotti*, supra, emphasized the importance of the parental role in minors' decisionmaking. May Congress prohibit other adults from fulfilling this function? Data reveal that virtually all minors consult at least one adult (including relatives, boyfriends' parents, foster parents, or health care professionals). Ehrlich, supra, at 98-100. Proposed federal legislation would subject to both criminal and civil liability anyone, other than a parent, who knowingly transports a minor to a less restrictive state to obtain an abortion; it also would prohibit a physician from performing an abortion on a minor from another state absent parental notification or compliance with a local notification requirement. H.R. 748, 109th Cong. (2005). Proponents call the measure the "Child Interstate Abortion Notification Act"; opponents, conjuring up the image of the supportive grandparent who provides assistance to a teen in trouble, dub it the "Put Granny in Jail Act" or simply the "Teen Endangerment Act." Another federal proposal would require federally funded health clinics to notify parents before providing contraceptives to minors. H.R. 3011, 109th Cong. (2005) ("Parent's Right to Know Act of 2005").

Previously, Congress focused on teen pregnancy in welfare reform. Under the Personal Responsibility and Work Opportunity Act, states can provide assistance only to minor parents who meet specific educational and residential requirements, states can get grants for abstinence education, and states should aggressively enforce statutory rape laws. 42 U.S.C.A. §§602(a)(1)(A)(v), 608(a)(4) & (5), 710, 14016 (West 2003 & Supp. 2005). This last directive stems from empirical evidence showing that adult males father a high proportion of the children born to teen mothers. See Jacqueline E. Darroch et al., Age Difference Between Sexual Partners in the United States, 31 Fam. Plan. Persp. 160 (1999).

5. *Judicial bypass.* Under *Bellotti* and later Supreme Court cases, states with parental involvement laws must provide an alternative procedure allowing the minor to show that she has the maturity to decide independently or, if not, that an abortion would serve her best interests. Currently, 33 of the 34 states requiring parental involvement have a judicial bypass procedure, developed in response to the Court's rulings. See Guttmacher, Parental Involvement, supra (all except Utah).

A judicial bypass has "saved" several different parental involvement laws. See, e.g., Hodgson v. Minnesota, 497 U.S. 417 (1990) (judicial bypass procedure makes two-parent notification requirement constitutional); Lambert v. Wiklund, 520 U.S. 292 (1997) (upholding statute requiring notification of one parent 48 hours before abortion with judicial bypass allowing waiver when notification is not in minor's best interest); Planned Parenthood of Southeastern Pa. v. Casey, 505 U.S. 833, 899-900 (1992) (upholding requirement of "informed parental consent" with bypass). Does the judicial bypass make sense as a means of operationalizing the competing interests at stake? What does *Kathy's Day in Court* suggest?

a. *Rationale?* Why might the Constitution allow state age-based lines for some constitutionally protected activities (for example, the right to marry), but require case-by-case assessments of maturity and best interests when the minor seeks an abortion? See Martin Guggenheim, What's Wrong with Children's Rights 237-244 (2005) (asserting that Court pragmatically responded to social costs of teen pregnancy). Does the bypass regime conflict with criminal prohibitions on consensual sex with minors — that is, statutory-rape and similar provisions that *always* make the minor's own consent legally irrelevant? See Jones v. State, 640 So. 2d 1084 (Fla. 1994). On the other hand, can you square the constitutional framework for minors' abortions with laws treating juvenile offenders as adult criminal defendants? See J. Shoshanna Ehrlich, Shifting Boundaries: Abortion, Criminal Culpability and the Indeterminate Legal Status of Adolescents, 18 Wis. Women's L.J. 77 (2003).

b. *Scope.* Can a state with a parental notice requirement provide for a bypass procedure only for minors with documented experiences of child abuse or neglect? Compare Planned Parenthood v. Miller, 63 F.3d 1452 (8th Cir. 1995) (no), with Planned Parenthood of Blue Ridge v. Camblos, 155 F.3d 352 (4th Cir. 1998) (yes).

c. *Evidentiary standard.* What should be the evidentiary standard for proof of maturity — clear and convincing evidence? A preponderance? See, e.g., In re B.S., 74 P.3d 285 (Ariz. Ct. App. 2003) (holding that minor bears burden of proving entitlement to abortion by clear and convincing evidence).

d. *Judicial role.* Do judges have the requisite expertise to assess maturity and competence? To what extent is the judgment about maturity shaped by the judge's ideology and values? See, e.g., Ex parte Anonymous, 806 So. 2d 1269 (Ala. 2001). Will a judge think it mature or immature for a young woman to become pregnant? Not to want to involve her parents? To choose to assume responsibility herself? What other value judgments may be influential? *Kathy's Day in Court* illustrates one possibility. See also Adam Liptak, On Moral Grounds, Some Judges Are Opting Out of Abortion Cases, N.Y. Times, Sept. 4, 2005, at A1 (reporting recusal of some judges from all bypass proceedings based on moral opposition to abortion); Helena Silverstein & Kathryn Lundwall Alessi, Religious Establishment in Hearings to Waive Parental Consent for Abortion, 7 U. Pa. J. Const. L. 473 (2004). In contrast, one family court judge argues that the minor's very decision to seek an abortion shows deliberation and responsibility and that forcing an unwilling minor to carry to term can never serve her best interests. Nanette Dembitz, The Supreme Court and a Minor's Abortion Decision, 80 Colum. L. Rev. 1251, 1255-1256 (1980).

If the judge decides that a teenager is not mature but that an abortion is nonetheless in her best interests, can the judge still require the minor to consult with her parent(s)? See In re Moe, 423 N.E.2d 1038, 1042 (Mass. App. Ct. 1981) (observing that once the judge decides that an abortion serves the minor's best interests, the judge may not decide it would be "in her even better interest" to consult with one or both parents), *vacated on other grounds*, 523 N.E.2d 794 (Mass. App. Ct. 1988).

e. *Maturity*. The Supreme Court has not clarified the meaning of "maturity." How is a trial court to make such a determination? For example, how relevant is the minor's composure (or lack thereof) during her testimony? See Ex parte Anonymous, 812 So. 2d 1234 (Ala. 2001) (affirming finding of immaturity based on minor's "rehearsed" testimony and lack of emotion). Her academic record? See In re Anonymous, 888 So. 2d 1265, 1271 (Ala. Civ. App. 2004) (rejecting minor's academic standing as basis for finding lack of maturity, but upholding finding based on minor's "demeanor").

f. *Representation*. Does the Constitution require court-appointed counsel for minors in bypass proceedings? See Elizabeth Susan Graybill, Note, Assisting Minors Seeking Abortions in Judicial Bypass Proceedings: A Guardian ad Litem Is No Substitute for an Attorney, 55 Vand. L. Rev. 581 (2002). In some proceedings, judges can appoint guardians ad litem for the fetus, as *Kathy's Day in Court* illustrates. Do such appointments constitute an undue burden on the minor's right to an abortion? See Helena Silverstein, In the Matter of Anonymous, A Minor: Fetal Representation in Hearings to Waive Parental Consent for Abortion, 11 Cornell J.L. & Pub. Pol'y 69 (2001) (no, under *Casey*).

g. *Confidentiality*. *Heed* avoids deciding whether the New Hampshire statute adequately protects confidentiality in bypass proceedings. Given the interests at stake, what guarantees of confidentiality does the Constitution require? Must the state allow the minor to use a fictitious name to protect her anonymity? Must the state restrict the court personnel with access to the records? See Planned Parenthood of S. Ariz. v. Lawall, 307 F.3d 783 (9th Cir. 2002).

6. *Comparing burdens*. Do parental consent requirements impose more onerous burdens than notification requirements? See Planned Parenthood of Cent. N.J. v. Farmer, 762 A.2d 620, 629 (N.J. 2000). What of going to court instead? Is this alternative itself "unduly burdensome"? See id. at 634-638. See generally Martin Guggenheim, Minor Rights: The Adolescent Abortion Cases, 30 Hofstra L. Rev. 589 (2002). Does the undue burden standard apply to such restrictions on minors?

7. *Remedies under the undue burden standard*. *Heed* explains that, in applying the undue burden standard in a facial challenge, most circuit courts have rejected the *Salerno* test, which requires a law's challengers to show no set of facts under which it could operate constitutionally. But see Barnes v. Moore, 970 F.2d 12 (5th Cir.), *cert. denied*, 506 U.S. 1013 (1992). Instead, courts have followed the approach that *Casey*, supra, used to strike down the spousal notification requirement; this approach requires challengers to show a "substantial obstacle" in some fraction of the cases to which the law applies. See, e.g., Fargo Women's Health Org. v. Schafer, 507 U.S. 1013, 1013-1014 (1993) (O'Connor, J., concurring in denial of application for stay and injunction). Does one test or the other make more sense in the particular context of restrictions on abortion? See Michael C. Dorf, Incidental Burdens on Fundamental Rights, 109 Harv. L. Rev. 1175, 1240-1243 (1996). In the even more particular context of parental involvement and judicial bypass requirements for minors' abortions? Do both tests contemplate the introduction of empirical evidence about a law's predicted effect?

In its unanimous opinion in *Ayotte*, supra, the Court did not explicitly choose between the *Salerno* and *Casey* approaches. Rather, it expressed a general preference for enjoining only the unconstitutional applications of a statute while emphasizing the importance of legislative intent: "After finding an application or portion of a statute unconstitutional, we must next ask: Would the legislature have preferred what is left of its statute to no statute at all?" 126 S. Ct. at 968. After noting that "[o]nly a few applications of New Hampshire's parental notification statute would present a constitutional problem," the Court remanded the case for determination whether invalidating only the problematic applications of the statute would comport with legislative intent. Id. at 969. Some observers surmise that the narrow ruling in *Ayotte* maintains a "holding pattern" during the Court's transition; others see in the opinion a new turn in abortion jurisprudence.

What impact would *Ayotte*'s remedial approach have on a challenge to a spousal notification requirement, if the Court revisits that issue, as presented in *Casey*, supra? What impact would it have on a challenge to the federal "Partial Birth Abortion Ban Act," supra pp. 53-54, whose health exception is not as broad as the health exception recognized in *Roe*, supra, and reaffirmed in *Stenberg*, supra? *Ayotte* cites precedents requiring a health exception, with *Stenberg* noticeably absent from the list. 126 S. Ct. at 967. *Ayotte* does, however, discuss the remedy in *Stenberg* (invalidation of the Nebraska statute), observing that the parties there "did not ask for, and we did not contemplate, relief more finely drawn." Id. at 969. Suppose the legislative history of the federal statute shows that Congress intended to challenge *Roe*'s requirement of a broad health exception?

8. *Role of physicians and other professionals*. What role should the physician play in the minor's abortion decision? Should judges delegate the determination of maturity to the physicians who perform the abortions? Would such deference create a conflict of interest?

Should physicians face tort liability for failure to verify the age of the minor? Suppose a minor forges a note of parental permission for abortion or presents false identification. Do parents and/or the minor have a cause of action against the physician who relies on the note? See Pammela S. Quinn, Note, Preserving Minors' Rights After *Casey*: The "New Battlefield" of Negligence and Strict Liability Statutes, 49 Duke L.J. 297 (1999).

In 2005, Missouri, which requires parental consent, enacted legislation subjecting to civil liability any person who "shall intentionally cause, aid, or assist a minor to obtain an abortion" without such consent. Mo. Rev. Stat. §188.250 (S.B.1, 93rd Gen. Assem., 1st Extra. Sess., 2005). The law seeks to stop Missouri minors from traveling to a clinic in nearby Illinois, which does not require parental consent. Can parents sue a Missouri physician, counselor, clergy, or attorney who simply responds to a minor's questions about whether Illinois requires parental consent? What constitutional issues does the law raise?

Under child abuse reporting requirements, can law enforcement officials compel health care professionals to submit medical records of sexually active minors who had abortions as evidence of statutory rape or sexual abuse? See Aid for Women v. Foulston, 441 F.3d 1101 (10th Cir. 2006); Alpha Med. Clinic v. Anderson, 128 P.3d 364 (Kan. 2006).

9. *Medical exceptions*. According to *Roe, Casey*, and *Stenberg*, state regulations must contain adequate provision for abortion in cases of threats to the woman's life or health. Most parental involvement laws make exceptions for medical emergencies. See Guttmacher, Parental Involvement, supra (28 states permit a minor to obtain an abortion in a medical emergency). Evaluate *Heed*'s conclusion that parental involvement laws, similar to other abortion restrictions, must include health and death exceptions of the same scope required for adults. If the state seeks to involve a parent in a daughter's important medical decision (with a judicial bypass

for appropriate cases), why can't the state assume that the parent (or the judge) will protect the minor's health? See also Planned Parenthood of Idaho, Inc. v. Wasden, 376 F.3d 908 (9th Cir. 2004) (invalidating state statute because of impermissibly narrow definition of medical emergency), *cert. denied*, 544 U.S. 948 (2005). Do the legislatures assume that health care providers will be less likely to include parents in their daughters' abortions than in other medical decisions? Or, do the courts assume that parents will exhibit less concern for a daughter's health in the abortion context than they would in connection with any other medical treatment?

10. *Vision of the family.* What is the vision of the family reflected in parental consent and notification statutes? See generally Guggenheim, What's Wrong with Children's Rights?, supra, at 231-244; Anne C. Dailey, Constitutional Privacy and the Just Family, 67 Tul. L. Rev. 955 (1993). Does this vision support (or require) parental involvement laws for minors who want to carry their pregnancies to term? See Emily Buss, The Parental Rights of Minors, 48 Buff. L. Rev. 785 (2000). How is this vision informed by evidence that pregnant teens' parents favor abortion by a four to one ratio? William Saletan, Bearing Right: How Conservatives Won the Abortion War 192 (2003) (citing study).

11. *State constitutions.* Some plaintiffs have had more success in securing abortion rights under state constitutions. See North Fla. Women's Health & Counseling Servs. v. State, 866 So. 2d 612 (Fla. 2003) (holding that parental notification requirement violates the state constitutional right of privacy, given state's disparate treatment of minors for comparable medical procedures); Planned Parenthood of Cent. N.J. v. Farmer, 762 A.2d 620 (N.J. 2000) (holding that requirement of parental notification or bypass violates state constitution's equal protection provision, given absence of corresponding limitation for other medical and surgical care for minor's pregnancy). Florida voters overturned *North Florida Women's Health* in 2004, when they approved an amendment that exempts parental notification for abortion from the state constitutional right to privacy. See Jackie Hallifax, Court Tosses Appeal Over Abortion Measure, Tallahassee Democrat, Jan. 14, 2005, at B2.

12. *Empirical data.* Recall the Court's reliance on empirical data in invalidating the spousal notification requirement in *Casey*, supra. What role should the following data play in the constitutional analysis of restrictions on minors' abortions?

a. *Teen pregnancy.* Although declining, the rates of teen pregnancy and birth in the United States are the highest in the western industrialized world, with 34 percent of young women becoming pregnant at least once before turning 20. The National Campaign to Prevent Teen Pregnancy, General Facts and Stats (May, 2005) (available at http://www.teenpregnancy.org/resources/data/genlfact.asp). The data (and analyses) vary by race. Between 1990 and 2000, the nationwide teen pregnancy rate for African-Americans declined 32 percent; for whites 28 percent; and for Hispanics 15 percent. Alan Guttmacher Institute, U.S. Teenage Pregnancy Statistics: Overall Trends, Trends by Race and Ethnicity and State-by-State Information 2 (Feb. 19, 2004) (summary) (available at http://www.guttmacher.org/pubs/state_pregnancy_trends.pdf). Despite the mainstream view of teen motherhood's devastating consequences (educational, economic, and psychological), some challenge this conventional wisdom for African-American teens, asserting that considerations of health, kinship support, and insurance networks make youthful childbearing rational, as a collective or cultural matter. Arline T. Geronimus, Teenage Childbearing and Social and Reproductive Disadvantage: The Evolution of Complex Questions and the Demise of Simple Answers, 40 Fam. Relations 463 (1991).

b. *Teen abortions.* The abortion rate for teenagers in 2000 was 24.0 per 1,000 young women aged 15-19. Guttmacher, U.S. Teenage Pregnancy, supra. Broken down by race, the rate was 54.9 for African-Americans, 17.9 for whites, and 30.3 for Hispanics.

c. *Reasons for nondisclosure.* For what reasons would a teenager not wish to notify her parents of her pending abortion? Based on in-depth interviews of 26 minors who received judicial authorization for an abortion, Professor Shoshanna Ehrlich found that these teens feared that their parents would be extremely upset or would have a severe adverse reaction (ejecting them from the home, inflicting physical harm or other abuse) or they anticipated parental opposition, pressure to have the baby or get married, or problematic family dynamics. Ehrlich, Grounded in the Reality, supra, at 94-95.

d. *Reasons for choosing abortion.* According to Ehrlich, minors also gave multiple reasons for choosing an abortion, such as: not being ready for motherhood (feelings of insufficient maturity or responsibility); interference with future plans (such as desires to complete education); difficult life circumstances (such as already having a child, not having a place to live, or health problems); concerns about the child's well-being (inability to support the child); and issues related to pregnancy, abortion, and adoption. Id. at 97.

e. *Consequences of parental involvement laws.* What are the consequences of parental involvement laws? Some empirical research finds courts unprepared to handle bypass proceedings. Helena Silverstein & Leanne Speitel, "Honey, I Have No Idea": Court Readiness to Handle Petitions to Waive Parental Consent for Abortion, 88 Iowa L. Rev. 75 (2002). Other data show a negative impact on minors' health resulting from delay, including increased incidence of second-trimester abortions. Jennifer Blasdell, Mother, May I? Ramifications for Parental Involvement Laws for Minors Seeking Abortion Services, 10 Am. U. J. Gender Soc. Pol'y & L. 287, 288-290 (2002) (reviewing data). In *Hodgson,* supra, Minnesota bypass judges testified that the "court experience produced fear, tension, anxiety, and shame among minors, causing some who were mature, and some whose best interests would have been served by an abortion, to 'forego the bypass option and either notify their parents or carry to term.'" 497 U.S. at 441-442. *Hodgson* also indicates that in some states minors' petitions are routinely granted. Id. at 441 (of 3,573 bypass petitions considered between 1981 and 1986, courts granted all but 15). Other research reveals that parental involvement laws lead to a decrease in the number of abortions performed. James L. Rogers et al., Impact of the Minnesota Parental Notification Law on Abortion and Birth, 81 Am. J. Pub. Health 294 (1991) (although minors may be traveling to other states to avoid the requirements). Compare Andrew Lehren & John Leland, Scant Drop Seen in Abortions if Parents Are Told, N.Y. Times, Mar. 6, 2006, at A1, with Associated Press, Study Links Abortion Drop in Texas to Notification, St. Louis Post-Dispatch, Mar. 9, 2006, at A3.

Problem

You are a judge presiding over a judicial bypass proceeding for a 14-year-old petitioner seeking an abortion without parental involvement. The attorney representing the minor elicits the following responses:

Q At the time that the Complaint in this matter was signed, you were pregnant?
A: Yes.

Q: You had consulted with a counselor about that pregnancy?
A: Yeah.
Q: You had determined after talking to the counselor that you felt you should get an abortion?
A: Yes.
Q: You felt that you did not want to notify your parents—
A: Right.
Q: —of that decision? You did not feel for your own reasons that you could discuss it with them?
A: Right.
Q: After discussing the matter with a counselor, you still believed that you should not discuss it with your parents?
A: Right.
Q: And they shouldn't be notified?
A: Right.
Q: After talking the matter over with a counselor, the counselor concurred in your decision that your parents should not be notified?
A: Right.
Q: You were advised that an abortion couldn't be performed without notifying them?
A: Yes.
Q: You then came to me to see about filing a suit?
A: Right.
Q: You and I discussed it as to whether or not you had a right to do what you wanted to do?
A: Yes.
Q: You decided that, after our discussion, you should still proceed with the action to try to obtain an abortion without notifying your parents?
A: Right.
Q: Now, at the time that you signed the Complaint and spoke with the counselor and spoke with me, you were in the first trimester of pregnancy, within your first twelve weeks of pregnancy?
A: Yes.
Q: You feel that, from talking to the counselor and thinking the situation over and discussing it with me, that you could make the decision on your own that you wished to abort the pregnancy?
A: Yes.
Q: You are living at home?
A: Yes.
Q: You still felt, even though you were living at home with your parents that you couldn't discuss the matter with them?
A: Right.

H.L. v. Matheson, 450 U.S. 398, 402-403 n.6 (1981) (quoting transcript). On this evidence, would you grant the petition? If not, as judge, what questions would you pose to obtain the information that you need to decide whether to grant the petition? In particular, what questions would help you determine whether this minor is well informed? Mature? What resolution would serve her best interests?

3. Life and Death

■ CRUZAN v. DIRECTOR, MISSOURI DEPARTMENT OF HEALTH
497 U.S. 261 (1990)

Chief Justice REHNQUIST delivered the opinion of the Court.

. . . On the night of January 11, 1983, Nancy Cruzan lost control of her car as she traveled down Elm Road in Jasper County, Missouri. The vehicle overturned, and Cruzan was discovered lying face down in a ditch without detectable respiratory or cardiac function. Paramedics were able to restore her breathing and heartbeat at the accident site, and she was transported to a hospital in an unconscious state. [P]ermanent brain damage usually results after 6 minutes in an anoxic state; it was estimated that Cruzan was deprived of oxygen from 12 to 14 minutes. She remained in a coma for approximately three weeks and then progressed to an unconscious state in which she was able to orally ingest some nutrition. In order to ease feeding and further the recovery, surgeons implanted a gastrostomy feeding and hydration tube in Cruzan with the consent of her then husband. Subsequent rehabilitative efforts proved unavailing. She now lies in a Missouri state hospital in what is commonly referred to as a persistent vegetative state: generally, a condition in which a person exhibits motor reflexes but evinces no indications of significant cognitive function. The State of Missouri is bearing the cost of her care.

After it had become apparent that Nancy Cruzan had virtually no chance of regaining her mental faculties, her parents asked hospital employees to terminate the artificial nutrition and hydration procedures. All agree that such a removal would cause her death. The employees refused to honor the request without court approval. . . .

We granted certiorari to consider the question of whether Cruzan has a right under the United States Constitution which would require the hospital to withdraw life-sustaining treatment from her under these circumstances.

At common law, even the touching of one person by another without consent and without legal justification was a battery. . . . This notion of bodily integrity has been embodied in the requirement that informed consent is generally required for medical treatment. . . .

The logical corollary of the doctrine of informed consent is that the patient generally possesses the right not to consent, that is, to refuse treatment. Until about 15 years ago and the seminal decision in In re Quinlan, 355 A.2d 647 [(N.J.)], *cert. denied sub nom.* Garger v. New Jersey, 429 U.S. 922 (1976), the number of right-to-refuse-treatment decisions were relatively few. [W]ith the advance of medical technology capable of sustaining life well past the point where natural forces would have brought certain death in earlier times, cases involving the right to refuse life-sustaining treatment have burgeoned.

In the *Quinlan* case, young Karen Quinlan suffered severe brain damage as the result of anoxia, and entered a persistent vegetative state. Karen's father sought judicial approval to disconnect his daughter's respirator. The New Jersey Supreme Court granted the relief, holding that Karen had a right of privacy grounded in the Federal Constitution to terminate treatment. In re Quinlan, 355 A.2d, at 662-664. Recognizing that this right was not absolute, however, the court balanced it against asserted state interests. Noting that the State's interest "weakens and the individual's right to privacy grows as the degree of bodily invasion increases and the prognosis dims," the court concluded that the state interests had to give way in that case. Id., at 664. The court also concluded that the "only practical way" to prevent the loss of Karen's privacy right due to her incompetence was to allow her guardian and family to decide "whether she would exercise it in these circumstances." Ibid.

After *Quinlan*, however, most courts have based a right to refuse treatment either solely on the common law right to informed consent or on both the common law right and a constitutional privacy right. . . . This is the first case in which we have been squarely presented with the issue of whether the United States Constitution grants what is in common parlance referred to as a "right to die." . . .

. . . The principle that a competent person has a constitutionally protected liberty interest in refusing unwanted medical treatment may be inferred from our prior decisions. In Jacobson v. Massachusetts, 197 U.S. 11, 24-30 (1905), for instance, the Court balanced an individual's liberty interest in declining an unwanted smallpox vaccine against the State's interest in preventing disease. . . . But determining that a person has a "liberty interest" under the Due Process Clause does not end the inquiry;[7] "whether respondent's constitutional rights have been violated must be determined by balancing his liberty interests against the relevant state interests." Youngberg v. Romeo, 457 U.S. 307, 321 (1982).

Petitioners insist that under the general holdings of our cases, the forced administration of life-sustaining medical treatment, and even of artificially-delivered food and water essential to life, would implicate a competent person's liberty interest. Although we think the logic of the cases discussed above would embrace such a liberty interest, the dramatic consequences involved in refusal of such treatment would inform the inquiry as to whether the deprivation of that interest is constitutionally permissible. But for purposes of this case, we assume that the United States Constitution would grant a competent person a constitutionally protected right to refuse lifesaving hydration and nutrition.

Petitioners go on to assert that an incompetent person should possess the same right in this respect as is possessed by a competent person. . . . The difficulty with petitioners' claim is that in a sense it begs the question: an incompetent person is not able to make an informed and voluntary choice to exercise a hypothetical right to refuse treatment or any other right. Such a "right" must be exercised for her, if at all, by some sort of surrogate. Here, Missouri has in effect recognized that under certain circumstances a surrogate may act for the patient in electing to have hydration and nutrition withdrawn in such a way as to cause death, but it has established a procedural safeguard to assure that the action of the surrogate conforms as best it may to the wishes expressed by the patient while competent. Missouri requires that evidence of the incompetent's wishes as to the withdrawal of treatment be proved by clear and convincing evidence. The question, then, is whether the United States Constitution forbids the establishment of this procedural requirement by the State. We hold that it does not.

[Missouri asserts] its interest in the protection and preservation of human life, and there can be no gainsaying this interest. [T]he majority of States in this country

---

7. Although many state courts have held that a right to refuse treatment is encompassed by a generalized constitutional right of privacy, we have never so held. We believe this issue is more properly analyzed in terms of a Fourteenth Amendment liberty interest. See Bowers v. Hardwick, 478 U.S. 186, 194-195 (1986).

have laws imposing criminal penalties on one who assists another to commit suicide. We do not think a State is required to remain neutral in the face of an informed and voluntary decision by a physically-able adult to starve to death.

But in the context presented here, a State has more particular interests at stake. The choice between life and death is a deeply personal decision of obvious and overwhelming finality. We believe Missouri may legitimately seek to safeguard the personal element of this choice through the imposition of heightened evidentiary requirements. It cannot be disputed that the Due Process Clause protects an interest in life as well as an interest in refusing life-sustaining medical treatment. Not all incompetent patients will have loved ones available to serve as surrogate decisionmakers. And even where family members are present, "[t]here will, of course, be some unfortunate situations in which family members will not act to protect a patient." In re Jobes, 529 A.2d 434, 477 [(N.J. 1987)]. A State is entitled to guard against potential abuses in such situations. . . .

In our view, Missouri has permissibly sought to advance these interests through the adoption of a "clear and convincing" standard of proof to govern such proceedings. [N]ot only does the standard of proof reflect the importance of a particular adjudication, it also serves as "a societal judgment about how the risk of error should be distributed between the litigants." [Santosky v. Kramer, 455 U.S. 745, 755 (1982).] We believe that Missouri may permissibly place an increased risk of an erroneous decision on those seeking to terminate an incompetent individual's life-sustaining treatment. An erroneous decision not to terminate results in a maintenance of the status quo; the possibility of subsequent developments such as advancements in medical science, the discovery of new evidence regarding the patient's intent, changes in the law, or simply the unexpected death of the patient despite the administration of life-sustaining treatment, at least create the potential that a wrong decision will eventually be corrected or its impact mitigated. An erroneous decision to withdraw life-sustaining treatment, however, is not susceptible of correction. . . .

The Supreme Court of Missouri held that in this case the testimony adduced at trial did not amount to clear and convincing proof of the patient's desire to have hydration and nutrition withdrawn. . . . The testimony adduced at trial consisted primarily of Nancy Cruzan's statements made to a housemate about a year before her accident that she would not want to live should she face life as a "vegetable," and other observations to the same effect. The observations did not deal in terms with withdrawal of medical treatment or of hydration and nutrition. We cannot say that the Supreme Court of Missouri committed constitutional error in reaching the conclusion that it did.

Petitioners alternatively contend that Missouri must accept the "substituted judgment" of close family members even in the absence of substantial proof that their views reflect the views of the patient. They rely primarily upon our decisions in Michael H. v. Gerald D., 491 U.S. 110 (1989), and Parham v. J.R., 442 U.S. 584 (1979). . . . In *Michael H.*, we *upheld* the constitutionality of California's favored treatment of traditional family relationships; such a holding may not be turned around into a constitutional requirement that a State *must* recognize the primacy of those relationships in a situation like this. And in *Parham*, where the patient was a minor, we also *upheld* the constitutionality of a state scheme in which parents made certain decisions for mentally ill minors. Here again petitioners would seek to turn a decision which allowed a State to rely on family decisionmaking into a constitutional requirement that the State recognize such decisionmaking. But constitutional law does not work that way.

No doubt is engendered by anything in this record but that Nancy Cruzan's mother and father are loving and caring parents. If the State were required by the United States Constitution to repose a right of "substituted judgment" with anyone, the Cruzans would surely qualify. But we do not think the Due Process Clause requires the State to repose judgment on these matters with anyone but the patient herself. Close family members may have a strong feeling—a feeling not at all ignoble or unworthy, but not entirely disinterested, either—that they do not wish to witness the continuation of the life of a loved one which they regard as hopeless, meaningless, and even degrading. But there is no automatic assurance that the view of close family members will necessarily be the same as the patient's would have been had she been confronted with the prospect of her situation while competent. All of the reasons previously discussed for allowing Missouri to require clear and convincing evidence of the patient's wishes lead us to conclude that the State may choose to defer only to those wishes, rather than confide the decision to close family members. . . .

Justice O'CONNOR, concurring. . . .

I . . . write separately to emphasize that the Court does not today decide the issue whether a State must also give effect to the decisions of a surrogate decisionmaker. . . . In my view, such a duty may well be constitutionally required to protect the patient's liberty interest in refusing medical treatment. Few individuals provide explicit oral or written instructions regarding their intent to refuse medical treatment should they become incompetent. States which decline to consider any evidence other than such instructions may frequently fail to honor a patient's intent. Such failures might be avoided if the State considered an equally probative source of evidence: the patient's appointment of a proxy to make health care decisions on her behalf. Delegating the authority to make medical decisions to a family member or friend is becoming a common method of planning for the future. Several States have recognized the practical wisdom of such a procedure [by living wills and durable power of attorney statutes for health care decisionmaking]. Moreover, as patients are likely to select a family member as a surrogate, giving effect to a proxy's decisions may also protect the "freedom of personal choice in matters of . . . family life." Cleveland Board of Education v. LaFleur, 414 U.S. 632, 639 (1974).

[N]o national consensus has yet emerged on the best solution for this difficult and sensitive problem. Today we decide only that one State's practice does not violate the Constitution; the more challenging task of crafting appropriate procedures for safeguarding incompetents' liberty interests is entrusted to the "laboratory" of the States. . . .

Justice SCALIA, concurring. . . .

. . . I would have preferred that we announce, clearly and promptly, that the federal courts have no business in this field; that American law has always accorded the State the power to prevent, by force if necessary, suicide—including suicide by refusing to take appropriate measures necessary to preserve one's life; that the point at which life becomes "worthless," and the point at which the means necessary to preserve it become "extraordinary" or "inappropriate," are neither set forth in the Constitution nor known to the nine Justices of this Court any better than they

are known to nine people picked at random from the Kansas City telephone directory; and hence, that even when it is demonstrated by clear and convincing evidence that a patient no longer wishes certain measures to be taken to preserve her
life, it is up to the citizens of Missouri to decide, through their elected representatives, whether that wish will be honored. . . .

The text of the Due Process Clause [protects individuals] against deprivations
of liberty "without due process of law." [N]o "substantive due process" claim can be
maintained unless the claimant demonstrates that the State has deprived him of a
right historically and traditionally protected against state interference. That cannot
possibly be established here.

At common law in England, a suicide — defined as one who "deliberately puts
an end to his own existence, or commits any unlawful malicious act, the consequence
of which is his own death," 4 W. Blackstone, Commentaries *189 — was criminally
liable. Although the States abolished the penalties imposed by the common law (i.e.,
forfeiture and ignominious burial), they did so to spare the innocent family, and not
to legitimize the act. Case law at the time of the Fourteenth Amendment generally
held that assisting suicide was a criminal offense. . . . Thus, "there is no significant
support for the claim that a right to suicide is so rooted in our tradition that it may be
deemed 'fundamental' or 'implicit in the concept of ordered liberty.'" Id., at 100
(quoting Palko v. Connecticut, 302 U.S. 319, 325 (1937)). . . .

. . . Are there, then, no reasonable and humane limits that ought not to be
exceeded in requiring an individual to preserve his own life? There obviously
are, but they are not set forth in the Due Process Clause. . . . Our salvation is the
Equal Protection Clause, which requires the democratic majority to accept for
themselves and their loved ones what they impose on you and me. This Court
need not, and has no authority to, inject itself into every field of human activity
where irrationality and oppression may theoretically occur, and if it tries to do so it
will destroy itself.

Justice BRENNAN, with whom Justice MARSHALL and Justice BLACKMUN join,
dissenting. . . .

[I]f a competent person has a liberty interest to be free of unwanted medical
treatment, as both the majority and Justice O'Connor concede, it must be fundamental. Whatever other liberties protected by the Due Process Clause are fundamental, "those liberties that are 'deeply rooted in this Nation's history and
tradition'" are among them. [T]he State has no legitimate general interest in someone's life, completely abstracted from the interest of the person living that life, that
could outweigh the person's choice to avoid medical treatment. . . .

Moreover, there may be considerable danger that Missouri's rule of decision
would impair rather than serve any interest the State does have in sustaining life. Current medical practice recommends use of heroic measures if there is a scintilla of a
chance that the patient will recover, on the assumption that the measures will be dis-
continued should the patient improve. [Yet, the inability to halt such treatment,
even if it provides little benefit and burdens the patient, might well discourage
starting it.]

Missouri may constitutionally impose only those procedural requirements that
serve to enhance the accuracy of a determination of Nancy Cruzan's wishes or are at
least consistent with an accurate determination. The Missouri "safeguard" that the
Court upholds today does not meet that standard. . . . Missouri's rule of decision
imposes a markedly asymmetrical evidentiary burden. Only evidence of specific

statements of treatment choice made by the patient when competent is admissible to support a finding that the patient, now in a persistent vegetative state, would wish to avoid further medical treatment. Moreover, this evidence must be clear and convincing. No proof is required to support a finding that the incompetent person would wish to continue treatment. [Yet,] from the point of view of the patient, an erroneous decision in either direction is irrevocable. . . .

Even more than its heightened evidentiary standard, the Missouri court's categorical exclusion of relevant evidence dispenses with any semblance of accurate factfinding. . . . While it might be a wise social policy to encourage people to furnish [a living will,] no general conclusion about a patient's choice can be drawn from the absence of formalities. . . .

Finally, I cannot agree with the majority that where it is not possible to determine what choice an incompetent patient would make, a State's role as parens patriae permits the State automatically to make that choice itself. [Even if family members and the patient might have different views, is] there any reason to suppose that a State is *more* likely to make the choice that the patient would have made than someone who knew the patient intimately? To ask this is to answer it. . . .

[Justice Stevens, dissenting, writes that the Constitution requires respect for Nancy Cruzan's "own best interests."]

Notes and Questions

1. *Epilogue.* At a subsequent hearing, a probate court determined that the Cruzans had presented sufficient additional evidence to halt artificial nutrition and hydration. Nancy died 12 days after removal of the feeding tube. The outcome deeply troubled the hospital staff who had cared for her for seven years; they felt "violated and betrayed," observing that "it would be easier for them to cope with the process if Miss Cruzan were allowed to die quickly by lethal injection." Anger in Hospital at Death Order, N.Y. Times, Dec. 16, 1990, §1, at 29. The case took its toll on the Cruzans as well, and Nancy's father committed suicide in 1996.

2. *A constitutional right?* Does the majority recognize a right on the part of *competent* patients to refuse life-sustaining treatment? To the extent that the majority finds such right, what is its constitutional source? Is it "fundamental"? Does it extend to incompetent patients?

3. *Rationale.* How does the rationale of *Cruzan* compare to the privacy-based rationale of In re Quinlan, 355 A.2d 647 (N.J. 1976), cited by the majority? Which rationale is more persuasive? What are the implications of each approach?

4. *History and tradition.* If the Court must look to history and tradition to determine whether an interest merits constitutional protection, then how should the Court resolve evidence of conflicting traditions, for example, the traditional prohibition against suicide (per Justice Scalia) or the tradition of patient self-determination (per Justice Brennan)?

5. *Choice.* The right to die, like the abortion decision, entails making a personal choice. How can such choices be made by incompetent individuals such as Nancy Cruzan? Why wasn't Nancy Cruzan's past expression of her preferences adequate? How can *prior* directives ever express what the patient wants *now*? See Nancy K. Rhoden, Litigating Life and Death, 102 Harv. L. Rev. 375, 410-419 (1988). Should a court simply impute to an incompetent patient, who had not made her wishes known, what most people would prefer? See Norman L. Cantor, *Conroy*, Best Interests and the Handling of Dying Patients, 37 Rutgers L. Rev. 543, 570-577 (1985).

See also Rebecca Dresser, Relitigating Life and Death, 51 Ohio St. L.J. 425 (1990); Nancy K. Rhoden, The Limits of Legal Objectivity, 68 N.C. L. Rev. 845 (1990) (critiques of different standards).

6. *Vision of family.* What vision of the family emerges from the *Cruzan* opinions? Is this vision consistent with the portrayal of the family in the minors' abortion cases? Suppose the family is divided? Compare the "asymmetrical evidentiary burden" approved in *Cruzan* (as characterized by dissenting Justice Brennan) with the asymmetry of requiring bypass proceedings for minors seeking abortions without parental involvement (but not for those carrying a pregnancy to term).

7. *Competing interests.* Should courts be involved routinely in right-to-die cases to ascertain and weigh the competing interests? In situations of doubt, who should have the burden of proof? See Rhoden, Litigating Life and Death, supra (urging presumption of family decisionmaking). On the other hand, *why* would the Constitution disallow a state to "err on the side of life" in response to a given request to withdraw nutrition and hydration from an incompetent patient? What practical effects might follow from *Cruzan*?

8. *Advance directives.* Justice O'Connor urges the use of patient-executed documents to avoid the dilemma in *Cruzan*. If Nancy Cruzan had executed a "living will" directing termination of treatment, would that have changed the result? Missouri law imposes two limitations on such advance directives that would have posed problems in this case. The statute excludes nutrition and hydration from "death prolonging procedures" that one may refuse, and it makes such declaration operative only for patients in a "terminal condition." Mo. Rev. Stat. §§459.010-459.025 (2000). Missouri (like many states), however, authorizes nomination of a surrogate decisionmaker for health care with specific authority to withhold or withdraw artificially supplied nutrition and hydration. Mo. Rev. Stat. §404.820 (2000).

9. *Gender.* Justice Scalia recommends resort to the Equal Protection Clause. How would this approach work? Will it guard against unreasonable impositions of forced medical treatment? Unreasonable abortion restrictions? Do men and women have equal opportunities to exercise the right to die? Consider the following evidence of gender bias:

> Appellate court rulings show four major differences in how courts speak of previously competent women's or men's moral preferences. The first difference is the courts' view that a man's opinions are rational and a woman's remarks are unreflective, emotional, or immature. Second, women's moral agency in relation to medical decisions is often not recognized. Third, courts apply evidentiary standards differently to evidence about men's and women's preferences. Fourth, life-support dependent men are seen as subjected to medical assault; women are seen as vulnerable to medical neglect. Not all of these differences are present in any one case. Each difference (e.g., language describing a woman's reasoning as immature) is present in at least three cases of the gender to which it is attributed and none of the cases of the opposite gender.

Steven H. Miles & Allison August, Courts, Gender and "The Right to Die," 18 Law, Med. & Health Care 85, 87 (1990). But see Susan M. Wolf, Gender, Feminism, and Death: Physician-Assisted Suicide and Euthanasia, in Feminism and Bioethics: Beyond Reproduction 282 (Susan M. Wolf ed., 1996).

10. *Legislation.* The Uniform Health Care Decisions Act allows a competent individual to declare in advance the wish to withhold or withdraw life-sustaining treatment (§§2-4). 9 U.L.A. (pt. IB) 93-110 (2005). The act also allows certain third parties to consent to the withholding or withdrawal of such treatment for incompetent patients who have made no effective declaration — in order of priority: a spouse; an adult child; a parent; an adult sibling (§5). Id. at 111-112. For a tabulation of "right to die" statutes throughout the United States, see Richard A. Leiter, National Survey of State Laws 517 (4th ed. 2003).

The Omnibus Budget Reconciliation Act, 42 U.S.C.A. §1395cc(f) (West Supp. 2005), requires Medicare providers (hospitals, skilled nursing facilities, home health agencies, and hospice programs) to inform adult recipients of the right to refuse treatment.

11. *State experimentation.* Justice O'Connor stresses that these problems belong in the "'laboratory' of the States." What are the likely consequences of this approach? Can a state prevent its domiciliaries from crossing state lines to evade restrictive laws? See In re Christine Busalacchi, 1991 WL 10048 (Mo. Ct. App. 1991) (enjoining father, who desires to remove daughter's feeding tube, from moving her to a more permissive state).

12. *Assisted suicide.* Do *Cruzan* and the abortion cases together establish a foundation for a constitutionally protected right to assisted suicide? Advocates of an expanded right to die that includes physician-assisted suicide claimed to find support in *Casey*'s "sweet-mystery-of-life passage," subsequently invoked in *Lawrence*, supra. See also Ronald Dworkin, Life's Dominion: An Argument About Abortion, Euthanasia, and Individual Freedom (1993). But see, e.g., Susan J. Wolf, Physician-Assisted Suicide, Abortion, and Treatment Refusal: Using Gender to Analyze the Difference, in Physician-Assisted Suicide 167 (Robert F. Weir ed., 1997) (argument ignores role of gender in abortion cases).

Unpersuaded by the proponents' argument, the Supreme Court rejected a substantive due process challenge to Washington's ban on physician-assisted suicide, as applied to the terminally ill. The Court found that the asserted right to die is not objectively rooted in American history and tradition and defies the careful description required for protection as a fundamental right. Washington v. Glucksberg, 521 U.S. 702, 720-721 (1997). The majority emphasized that the assumed right in *Cruzan* was one in avoiding forced treatment, a battery. Id. at 724-725. And, *Casey*'s language was said not to "warrant the sweeping conclusion that any and all important, intimate, and personal decisions are so protected." Id. at 727. The Court held that the state's interests (for example, preserving human life, protecting vulnerable groups, and avoiding the slippery slope to euthanasia) provide a sufficient rational basis for the law. A companion case used similar reasoning to uphold New York's ban against an equal protection challenge based on the different legal consequences of physicians' termination of life-sustaining treatment (as in *Cruzan*) versus their affirmative assistance in hastening death. Vacco v. Quill, 521 U.S. 793 (1997). See generally Symposium, Physician-Assisted Suicide: Facing Death after *Glucksberg* and *Quill*, 82 Minn. L. Rev. 885 (1998) (including contributions by Professors Yale Kamisar, Sylvia Law, Robert Burt, and Susan Wolf).

To what extent does *Lawrence*, supra, challenge the underpinnings of *Glucksberg* and *Quill*? See Dale Carpenter, Is *Lawrence* Libertarian?, 88 Minn. L. Rev. 1140, 1163-1164 (reconciling cases).

13. *"Death with Dignity" in Oregon.* Declining to recognize a constitutional right to assisted suicide, the Court expressly left the issue for democratic resolution. *Glucksberg*, 521 U.S. at 735. Just months after the Supreme Court decisions in 1997, Oregon's Death with Dignity Act, which voters had approved in 1994, became effective. Or. Rev. Stat. §§127.800-127.895 (2003). This legislation allows a competent adult who resides in Oregon, suffers from a terminal disease according to physicians, and voluntarily expresses a wish to die to request and then obtain, after a waiting period, medication "for the purpose of ending his or her life in a humane and dignified manner." Id. at §127.805. During the first two years, 56 individuals received prescriptions under the law, and 42 took the medication and died. See Susan R. Martyn & Henry J. Bourguignon, Now Is the Moment to Reflect: Two Years of Experience with Oregon's Physician-Assisted Suicide Law, 8 Elder L.J. 1, 6-7 (2000).

Does Oregon's law advance autonomy, expanding the "private realm of family life"? Are the restrictions sufficient to protect against involuntary euthanasia? See id. at 53-56 (law "has no teeth" and gives too much authority to physicians). Do such measures pose special risks to undervalued persons, including women and minorities? See Patricia King & Leslie Wolf, Empowering and Protecting Patients: Lessons for Physician-Assisted Suicide from the African-American Experience, 82 Minn. L. Rev. 1015 (1998) (commenting on Supreme Court cases). For a summary of the empirical data, see Brief for the Patient-Respondents at 36-41, Gonzales v. Oregon, No. 04-623 (U.S. July 21, 2005).

14. *The federal response.* Congress responded to Oregon's legislation by prohibiting the use of federal funds for assisted suicide. 42 U.S.C. §§14401-14408 (2000); 42 U.S.C. §238o (2000); 25 U.S.C. §1621x (2000); 38 U.S.C. §1707 (Supp. II 2002). The Drug Enforcement Administration determined that physicians who prescribed medications for suicide assistance violate the federal Controlled Substances Act, but a majority of the Supreme Court invalidated the so-called "Ashcroft Directive" (an interpretive rule named after the then Attorney General), which sought criminal enforcement against conduct specifically authorized by Oregon's Death with Dignity Act. Gonzales v. Oregon, 126 S. Ct. 904 (2006). The majority determined that the interpretive rule violates the federal Controlled Substances Act, contravenes Congress' intent, and oversteps the limits of the Attorney General's authority.

When the Supreme Court in *Glucksberg*, supra, called for the debate about assisted suicide to continue, "as it should in a democratic society," 521 U.S. at 735, did the Justices mean to invite federal action that would trump "experimentation" within the "'laboratory' of the States"? See id. at 788 (Souter, J., concurring); id. at 737 (O'Connor, J., concurring). In deciding *Gonzales*, supra, the majority invoked the ongoing debate about physician-assisted suicide as a reason that "makes the oblique form of the claimed delegation [of medical judgments to the Attorney General] all the more suspect." 126 S. Ct. at 921. See also id. at 911. The *Gonzales* majority also emphasized that, in the absence of clear congressional regulation, the practice of medicine remains a matter of state concern. Id. at 923-925.

For an analysis comparing U.S. law on physician-assisted suicide and euthanasia with that in the Netherlands, which permits such practices, see Kelly Green, Note, Physician-Assisted Suicide and Euthanasia: Safeguarding Against the "Slippery Slope" — the Netherlands versus the United States, 13 Ind. Int'l & Comp. L. Rev. 639 (2003).

Note: The Terri Schiavo Case

Terri Schiavo, age 26, suffered severe brain damage from oxygen deprivation resulting from cardiac arrest of undetermined origin in 1990. After attempted treatments failed to improve her condition, which physicians diagnosed as a persistent vegetative state (PVS), her husband and guardian, Michael Schiavo, sought to withdraw her artificial nutrition and hydration (feeding tube), based on her asserted wishes. Her parents, Robert and Mary Schindler objected, disputing both Michael's claims about Terri's wishes and the PVS diagnosis. In many different lawsuits brought by the parents and/or Florida Governor Jeb Bush, Michael prevailed. E.g., In re Guardianship of Schiavo, 780 So. 2d 176 (Fla. Dist. Ct. App. 2001); In re Schiavo, 851 So. 2d 182 (Fla. Dist. Ct. App. 2003); Bush v. Schiavo, 866 So. 2d 136 (Fla. Dist. Ct. App. 2004).

The case became a cause célèbre in the "culture wars," with "pro-life" and disability-rights advocacy groups actively supporting the Schindlers. When the feeding tube was removed in 2003, the Florida legislature required its reinsertion by adopting a law later ruled unconstitutional. See Bush v. Schiavo, 885 So. 2d 321 (Fla. 2004), *cert. denied*, 543 U.S. 1121 (2005). In 2005, Congress stepped in to support the Schindlers, enacting a special jurisdictional grant for de novo review of the case in federal court. President Bush flew back to Washington before dawn from his Texas ranch to sign the legislation. P.L. 109-3, 119 Stat. 15 (Mar. 21, 2005). Yet, the federal courts also ruled against the Schindlers' claims, including their amended complaint invoking the Americans with Disabilities Act. See Schiavo ex rel. Schindler v. Schiavo, 403 F.3d 1223 (11th Cir.), *stay denied*, 544 U.S. 945 (2005); 403 F.3d 1289 (11th Cir. 2005). See generally, e.g., Samuel R. Bagenstos, Judging the Schiavo Case, 22 Const. Comment. _____ (2005) (forthcoming); Barbara A. Noah, Comment, Politicizing the End of Life: Lessons from the Schiavo Controversy, 59 U. Miami L. Rev. 107 (2004).

Following removal of the feeding tube, Terri Schiavo died March 31, 2005. Although some members of Congress threatened to retaliate against judges who ruled in favor of Michael, most public opinion opposed Congress's intervention altogether. A subsequent autopsy refuted the allegations of the Schindlers and their supporters, who had argued that Michael ended the life of a conscious and alert, although disabled, woman.[21] Florida Governor Jeb Bush's subsequent effort to investigate Michael's possible culpability at the time of Terri's initial collapse produced no evidence. The family battles continued as Michael had Terri's remains cremated and marked her burial site with a stone inscribed to say "I Kept My Promise" and listing the dates February 25, 1990 and March 31, 2005 to memorialize, respectively, when she "departed this earth" and was "at peace."[22]

[21]. See, e.g., Denise Grady, The Hard Facts Behind a Heartbreaking Case, N.Y. Times, June 19, 2005, §4, at 5; Anne E. Kornblut, Debate Over Legislative Actions Is Renewed, N.Y. Times, June 16, 2005, at A24. The autopsy failed to determine the cause of her initial collapse. One theory blamed a potassium deficiency caused by significant weight loss (and possibly bulimia). Although Michael Schiavo won a one million dollar verdict in a malpractice case against Terri's obstetrician for failure to diagnose bulimia (a recovery that some say sparked the disagreements within the family), the autopsy stopped short of reaching any conclusion about the reasons that Terri's heart stopped in the first place. Abby Goodnough, Schiavo Autopsy Say Brain, Withered, Was Untreatable, N.Y. Times, June 16, 2005, at A1.

[22]. Information about Terri Schiavo's death and subsequent events came from the following sources: Carl Hulse & David Kirkpatrick, Even Death Does Not Quiet Harsh Political Fight, N.Y Times, April 1, 2005, at A1; Florida Closes Its Inquiry into Collapse of Schiavo, N.Y. Times, July 8, 2005, at A20; Graham Brink & Jacob Fries, Theresa Marie Schiavo, A Nearby Resting Place, St. Petersburg Times, June 21, 2005, at 1A.

The case arguably upset settled law regarding surrogate decisionmaking, the relevance of the patient's physical condition in treatment termination cases, and the approach to artificial nutrition and hydration. See Lois Shepherd, Terri Schiavo: Unsettling the Settled, 37 Loyola U. Chi. L.J. 297 (2006). Some experts recommend mediation as a better way to resolve such family controversies. See, e.g., Nancy N. Dubler & Carol B. Liebman, Bioethics Mediation: A Guide to Shaping Shared Solutions (2004); I. Glenn Cohen, Negotiating Death: ADR and End of Life Decision-making, 9 Harv. Negot. L. Rev. 253 (2004).

Problem

Jason Hendrix was killed by a roadside bomb while serving in Iraq. For single service personnel, with neither children nor a will but with divorced parents, Pentagon policy gives custody of the remains to the eldest next of kin. In this case, the policy designates Jason's Oklahoma father, age 48, who plans to bury his son in that state. Jason's California mother, age 45, challenges the policy and its application, claiming that her son had told her orally about a year before that he wanted to be buried in California. How should the court decide her challenge? How relevant are the following facts? Although the father was awarded custody of Jason at divorce, Jason stayed in California with his mother during his childhood; later, he moved to Oklahoma to finish high school and live with his father. At death, Jason had an Oklahoma driver's license, he listed Oklahoma as his residence, and some evidence showed he planned to return there after service. See Divorced Father Wins Case Over Son's Remains, N.Y. Times, Nov. 2, 2005, at A18.

■ IN RE A.C.
573 A.2d 1235 (D.C. 1990) (en banc)

TERRY, Associate Judge. . . .

We are confronted here with two profoundly difficult and complex issues. First, we must determine who has the right to decide the course of medical treatment for a patient who, although near death, is pregnant with a viable fetus. Second, we must establish how that decision should be made if the patient cannot make it for herself. . . . We hold that in virtually all cases the question of what is to be done is to be decided by the patient — the pregnant woman — on behalf of herself and the fetus. If the patient is incompetent or otherwise unable to give an informed consent to a proposed course of medical treatment, then her decision must be ascertained through the procedure known as substituted judgment. . . .

This case came before the trial court when George Washington University Hospital petitioned the emergency judge in chambers for declaratory relief as to how it should treat its patient. . . . A.C. was first diagnosed as suffering from cancer at the age of thirteen. In the ensuing years she underwent major surgery several times, together with multiple radiation treatments and chemotherapy. A.C. married when she was twenty-seven, during a period of remission, and soon thereafter she became pregnant. She was excited about her pregnancy and very much wanted the child. . . .

On Tuesday, June 9, 1987, when A.C. was approximately twenty-five weeks pregnant, [doctors diagnosed] an apparently inoperable tumor which nearly filled her right lung. On Thursday, June 11, A.C. was admitted to the hospital as a patient. By Friday her condition had temporarily improved, and when asked if she really wanted to have her baby, she replied that she did.

Over the weekend A.C.'s condition worsened considerably. Accordingly, on Monday, June 15, members of the medical staff treating A.C. assembled, along with her family, in A.C.'s room. The doctors then informed her that her illness was terminal, and A.C. agreed to palliative treatment designed to extend her life until at least her twenty-eighth week of pregnancy. The "potential outcome [for] the fetus," according to the doctors, would be much better at twenty-eight weeks than at twenty-six weeks if it were necessary to "intervene." A.C. knew that the palliative treatment she had chosen presented some increased risk to the fetus, but she opted for this course both to prolong her life for at least another two weeks and to maintain her own comfort. When asked if she still wanted to have the baby, A.C. was somewhat equivocal, saying "something to the effect of 'I don't know, I think so.'" As the day moved toward evening, A.C.'s condition grew still worse, and at about 7:00 or 8:00 P.M. she consented to intubation to facilitate her breathing.

The next morning, June 16, the trial court convened a hearing at the hospital in response to the hospital's request for a declaratory judgment [as to whether it should deliver the fetus via caesarean section]. The court appointed counsel for both A.C. and the fetus, and the District of Columbia was permitted to intervene for the fetus as parens patriae. . . . A neonatologist, Dr. Maureen Edwards, testified that the chances of survival for a twenty-six-week fetus delivered at the hospital might be as high as eighty percent, but that this particular fetus, because of the mother's medical history, had only a fifty to sixty percent chance of survival. Dr. Edwards estimated that the risk of substantial impairment for the fetus, if it were delivered promptly, would be less than twenty percent. However, she noted that the fetus' condition was worsening appreciably at a rapid rate, and another doctor — Dr. Alan Weingold, an obstetrician who was one of A.C.'s treating physicians — stated that any delay in delivering the child by caesarean section lessened its chances of survival.

Regarding A.C.'s ability to respond to questioning and her prognosis, Dr. Louis Hamner, another treating obstetrician, testified that A.C. would probably die within twenty-four hours "if absolutely nothing else is done. . . . As far as her ability to interact, she has been heavily sedated in order to maintain her ventilatory function. She will open her eyes sometimes when you are in the room, but as far as her being able to . . . carry on a meaningful-type conversation . . . at this point, I don't think that is reasonable." . . .

There was no evidence before the court showing that A.C. consented to, or even contemplated, a caesarean section before her twenty-eighth week of pregnancy. There was, in fact, considerable dispute as to whether she would have consented to an immediate caesarean delivery at the time the hearing was held. A.C.'s mother opposed surgical intervention, testifying that A.C. wanted "to live long enough to hold that baby" and that she expected to do so, "even though she knew she was terminal." Dr. Hamner testified that, given A.C.'s medical problems, he did not think she would have chosen to deliver a child with a substantial degree of impairment. Asked whether A.C. had been "confronted with the question of what to do if there were a choice that ultimately had to be made between her own life expectancy and that of her fetus," he replied that the question "was addressed [but] at a later gestational age. We had talked about the possibility at twenty-eight weeks. . . ."

After hearing this testimony and the arguments of counsel, the trial court made oral findings of fact. It found . . . that A.C. would probably die [within a day or two; that the fetus had a 50-60 percent chance of survival]; that because the fetus was viable, "the state has [an] important and legitimate interest in protecting the potentiality of human life"; and . . . that there had been some testimony that the operation "may very well hasten the death of [A.C.]," but that there had also been testimony that delay would greatly increase the risk to the fetus and that "the prognosis is not great for the fetus to be delivered post-mortem. . . ." Most significantly, the court found [that it did not clearly know A.C.'s present views. Relying] on In re Madyun, 114 Daily Wash. L. Rptr. 2233 (D.C. Super. Ct. July 26, 1986), the court ordered that a caesarean section be performed. . . . The operation took place, but the baby lived for only a few hours, and A.C. succumbed to cancer two days later. . . .

A. INFORMED CONSENT and BODILY INTEGRITY

[O]ur analysis of this case begins with the tenet common to all medical treatment cases: that any person has the right to make an informed choice, if competent to do so, to accept or forego medical treatment. . . . In the same vein, courts do not compel one person to permit a significant intrusion upon his or her bodily integrity for the benefit of another person's health. In [McFall v. Shimp, 10 Pa. D.&C.3d 90 (Allegheny County Ct. 1978)], the court refused to order Shimp to donate bone marrow which was necessary to save the life of his cousin. . . . Even though Shimp's refusal would mean death for McFall, the court would not order Shimp to allow his body to be invaded. [McFall also cited the common law, which imposes no duty to rescue another.] It has been suggested that fetal cases are different because a woman who "has chosen to lend her body to bring [a] child into the world" has an enhanced duty to assure the welfare of the fetus, sufficient even to require her to undergo caesarean surgery. Robertson, [Procreative Liberty and the Control of Conception, Pregnancy and Childbirth, 69 Va. L. Rev. 403, 456 (1983)]. Surely, however, a fetus cannot have rights in this respect superior to those of a person who has already been born.[8] . . .

Decisions of the Supreme Court, while not explicitly recognizing a right to bodily integrity, seem to assume that individuals have the right, depending on the circumstances, to accept or refuse medical treatment or other bodily invasion.[9]

8. There are also practical consequences to consider. What if A.C. had refused to comply with a court order that she submit to a caesarean? Under the circumstances, she obviously could not have been held in civil contempt and imprisoned or required to pay a daily fine until compliance. . . . Enforcement could be accomplished only through physical force or its equivalent. A.C. would have to be fastened with restraints to the operating table, or perhaps involuntarily rendered unconscious by forcibly injecting her with an anesthetic, and then subjected to unwanted major surgery. Such actions would surely give one pause in a civilized society. . . .

9. We think it appropriate here to reiterate and emphasize [that this case is not about abortion. The decisional right whether to bear or beget a child] is not at issue here, for the record makes clear that A.C. sought to become pregnant, that she wanted to bear her child as close to term as possible, and that neither she nor anyone associated with her at any time sought to terminate her pregnancy. The issue presented in this case is . . . who should decide how that child should be delivered. That decision involves the right of A.C. (or any woman) to accept or forego medical treatment. The Supreme Court has not yet focused on this question in the context of a pregnancy. . . .

[Yet, the] right is not absolute. . . . In those rare cases in which a patient's right to decide her own course of treatment has been judicially overridden, courts have usually acted to vindicate the state's interest in protecting third parties, even if in fetal state. See Jefferson v. Griffin Spalding County Hospital Authority, [274 S.E.2d 457 (Ga. 1981)] (ordering that caesarean section be performed on a woman in her thirty-ninth week of pregnancy to save both the mother and the fetus). . . .

What we distill from the cases discussed in this section is that every person has the right, under the common law and the Constitution, to accept or refuse medical treatment. This right of bodily integrity belongs equally to persons who are competent and persons who are not. Further, it matters not what the quality of a patient's life may be; the right of bodily integrity is not extinguished simply because someone is ill, or even at death's door. To protect that right against intrusion by others — family members, doctors, hospitals, or anyone else, however well-intentioned — we hold that a court must determine the patient's wishes by any means available, and must abide by those wishes unless there are truly extraordinary or compelling reasons to override them. When the patient is incompetent, or when the court is unable to determine competency, the substituted judgment procedure must be followed.

From the record before us, we simply cannot tell whether A.C. was ever competent, after being sedated, to make an informed decision one way or the other regarding the proposed caesarean section. . . . We think it is incumbent on any trial judge in a case like this, unless it is impossible to do so, to ascertain whether a patient is competent to make her own medical decisions. Whenever possible, the judge should personally attempt to speak with the patient and ascertain her wishes directly, rather than relying exclusively on hearsay evidence, even from doctors. [W]ithout a competent refusal from A.C. to go forward with the surgery, and without a finding through substituted judgment that A.C. would not have consented to the surgery, it was error for the trial court to proceed to a balancing analysis, weighing the rights of A.C. against the interests of the state. . . .

B. SUBSTITUTED JUDGMENT . . .

Under the substituted judgment procedure, the court as decision-maker must "substitute itself as nearly as may be for the incompetent, and . . . act upon the same motives and considerations as would have moved her. . . ." The concept of substituted judgment, which has its roots in English law, was intended to allow courts to make dispositions from the estates of incompetents akin to those that the incompetents would have made if competent. Most [recent] cases involving substituted judgment, however, have arisen in the "right to die" context, and the courts have generally concluded that giving effect to the perceived decision of the incompetent is the proper course, even though doing so will result in the incompetent's death. . . .

We begin with the proposition that the substituted judgment inquiry is primarily a subjective one: as nearly as possible, the court must ascertain what the patient would do if competent. Due process strongly suggests (and may even require) that counsel or a guardian ad litem should be appointed for the patient unless the situation is so urgent that there is no time to do so.

[T]he greatest weight should be given to the previously expressed wishes of the patient. . . . Courts in substituted judgment cases have also acknowledged the importance of probing the patient's value system as an aid in discerning what the patient would choose. . . . Although treating physicians may be an invaluable source of such information about a patient, the family will often be the best source. . . . The court should be mindful, however, that while in the majority of cases family members will have the best interests of the patient in mind, sometimes family members will rely on their own judgments or predilections rather than serving as conduits for expressing the patient's wishes. This is why the court should endeavor, whenever possible, to make an in-person appraisal "of the patient's personal desires and ability for rational choice. . . . "

[If the court remains uncertain, it] may supplement its knowledge about the patient by determining what most persons would likely do in a similar situation. When the patient is pregnant, however, she may not be concerned exclusively with her own welfare. Thus it is proper for the court, in a case such as this, to weigh (along with all the other factors) the mother's prognosis, the viability of the fetus, the probable result of treatment or non-treatment for both mother and fetus, and the mother's likely interest in avoiding impairment for her child together with her own instincts for survival. . . .

[The court set aside the trial court's order because of failure to determine the patient's competence and to follow the substituted judgment procedure.] Having said that, we go no further. We need not decide whether, or in what circumstances, the state's interests can ever prevail over the interests of a pregnant patient. . . . Indeed, some may doubt that there could ever be a situation extraordinary or compelling enough to justify a massive intrusion into a person's body, such as a caesarean section, against that person's will. Whether such a situation may someday present itself is a question that we need not strive to answer here. . . . [23]

BELSON, Associate Judge, concurring in part and dissenting in part. . . .

[T]he already recognized rights and interests [referring to Roe v. Wade and tort protection for postviability injuries] are sufficient to indicate the need for a balancing process in which the rights of the viable unborn child are assigned substantial weight. . . . The balancing test should be applied in instances in which women become pregnant and carry an unborn child to the point of viability. This is not an unreasonable classification because, I submit, a woman who carries a child to viability is in fact a member of a unique category of persons. . . . This is so because she has undertaken to bear another human being, and has carried an unborn child to viability. . . . Also, uniquely, the viable unborn child is literally captive within the mother's body. . . .

. . . The indisputable view that a woman carrying a viable child has an extremely strong interest in her own life, health, bodily integrity, privacy, and religious

---

23. In particular, we stress that nothing in this opinion should be read as either approving or disapproving the holding in In re Madyun, supra. There are substantial factual differences between *Madyun* and the present case. In this case for instance, the medical interests of the mother and the fetus were in sharp conflict; what was good for one would have been harmful to the other. In *Madyun*, however, there was no real conflict between the interests of mother and fetus; on the contrary, there was strong evidence that the proposed caesarean would be beneficial to both. Moreover, in *Madyun* the pregnancy was at full term, and Mrs. Madyun had been in labor for two and a half days; in this case, however, A.C. was barely two-thirds of the way through her pregnancy, and there were no signs of labor. If another *Madyun*-type case ever comes before this court, its result may well depend on facts that we cannot now foresee. For that reason (among others), we defer until another day any discussion of whether *Madyun* was rightly or wrongly decided.

beliefs necessarily requires that her election be given correspondingly great weight in the balancing process. . . . On the other side of the analysis, it is appropriate to look to the relative likelihood of the unborn child's survival. This could range from the situation in *Madyun* where the full-term child's chances for survival were apparently excellent, through a case like the one before us where the unborn child's chances for survival were from fifty to sixty percent. . . . The most important factor on this side of the scale, however, is life itself, because the viable unborn child that dies because of the mother's refusal to have a caesarean delivery is deprived, entirely and irrevocably, of the life on which the child was about to embark. [Applying this balancing test to these facts, Judge Belson would affirm the trial court's order for the caesarean.]

■ **CAROL O'BRIEN, PATIENT'S LAWYER**
CALLS A.C. CASE HUMAN SACRIFICE
Am. Med. News, Mar. 11, 1988, at 18

[On June 16, 1987, lawyer Robert E. Sylvester] got a call seeking legal help for a medical emergency at George Washington U. Hospital. [When] Sylvester learned he would be representing Angela Carder, a 28-year-old office worker who was dying of long-term cancer and who was also carrying a 26-week-old fetus, he came to the hospital, armed with his usual gentle approach and his medical emergency packet — "cases I've collected that lay out common issues."

At the hearing in an administrative room at the hospital, Sylvester for the first time met Carder's parents and her husband. Carder, heavily sedated in her hospital room, was not present. But at the hearing presided over by Judge Emmett G. Sullivan of D.C. Superior Court, "were five or six doctors, a court stenographer, and lawyers hired from a high-powered law firm to represent the fetus and hospital." Sylvester and the ACLU were called to represent Angela.

After talking to her parents, Sylvester learned they had been told the night before their daughter was going to die. [A]fter talking to Carder's parents, her husband, and her physicians, Sylvester, who was unable to interview Angela at the time due to her sedation, believed Angela would not have wanted to submit to caesarian delivery, given the slim chance the baby would survive and be healthy, and the definite possibility the surgery would hasten Carder's imminent death. . . .

" . . . The entire obstetrics department was opposed to it," recalled Sylvester. . . . Later that evening, a baby girl was delivered. The baby lived two hours. No one ever argued that the baby was or could have been viable, Sylvester said. "Strangely, once the baby was born, very little was done to save her . . . because, clearly, this was not a viable fetus."

Sadly, Angela came out of her sedated state briefly, only to learn her baby had died. She cried before slipping back into unconsciousness, and died two days later. "The secondary cause of death was the operation," Sylvester said. . . .

Sylvester gets intensely involved in all his family welfare cases, but the Carder case has had an overwhelming personal impact. A decade ago, Sylvester's first wife died of cancer at age 29 in the same hospital where Carder ultimately succumbed to it at about the same age.

Sylvester spent much of his wife's last eight months with her at George Washington hospital, and he remembers those final days "as the most important in our lives, not the least important. Those days were precious and loving and profound. . . . To say a dying person's last few hours or days doesn't matter is like saying that person's whole life didn't matter." Sylvester's personal tragedy led him to re-evaluate his life, and subsequently nudged him out of a lucrative law practice specializing in international trade law to his current specialty of family welfare and medical emergency law. . . .

Ironically, Sylvester said, the hospital, which sought the court hearing to determine whether a C-section should be done because of liability concerns, could be faced with a potential malpractice or wrongful death suit from Carder's family because of the way the case was handled.

"I think a lawsuit is a distinct possibility," said Sylvester. "This was a human sacrifice case. Can you kill a person for the benefit of a fetus, which under the law is one level away from what we consider a person? There is no Good Samaritan requirement under the law that forces a woman to sacrifice her life for that of her fetus. The irony is Angela all along had a constitutional right to an abortion, but at the end, she had no constitutional right to avoid a life-threatening operation.

"I think gender bias was present in our case, definitely. In a powerful and subliminal way, it's true that many perceive women, especially pregnant women, as second-class citizens, as carriers. What is also compelling about this case is the court was not able to think of this competent individual — and sedation should not be confused with competence — as having vested rights and being capable of exercising them. This case ultimately is about a lack of respect for the individual, and her right to make the medical care decision that is best for herself."

Notes and Questions

1. *The court's reasoning.* The *A.C.* majority stresses that this case does not concern abortion. If so, why is the stage of gestational development relevant? Does this case merely highlight the conflict between the interests of two family members? If so, how and by whom should this conflict be resolved? What light does privacy doctrine or that of liberty interests (under *Cruzan*) shed? To what extent does *A.C.* recall the balance among maternal, fetal, and state interests examined in *Roe* (despite the court's disclaimers)?

How do you explain the outcome reached by the trial court and supported by the *A.C.* dissent? A preference for the interests of the fetus over the mother's? Thinly disguised paternalism? Failure to understand such cases as power struggles over reproduction? See Nancy Ehrenreich, The Colonization of the Womb, 43 Duke L.J. 492 (1993).

What does *A.C.* mean when it holds that the woman's decision must control "in virtually all cases"? How would the majority decide a case like In re Madyun, described in the court's footnote 23?

2. *Vision of family.* What vision of the family emerges from *A.C.*? How does it compare to those in *Casey*, *Heed*, and *Cruzan*?

3. *Race.* The national caesarean rate is 27.6 percent. Stacy Lu, Not-So Special Delivery: State Leads in C-Sections, N.Y. Times, Feb. 20, 2005, NJ Section, at 1. Do all women face an equal risk of court-ordered intervention? One empirical study of 21 court-ordered obstetrical procedures reveals that a disproportionate number

involve minorities and nonnative English speakers. Veronika E. B. Kolder, Janet Gallagher & Michael Parsons, Court-Ordered Obstetrical Interventions, 316 N. Eng. J. Med. 1192, 1195 (1987).

4. *Other cases.* Even when the woman had religious objections to surgery, courts usually ordered a caesarean section before *A.C.* For example, in Jefferson v. Griffin Spalding County Hosp. Auth., 274 S.E.2d 457 (Ga. 1981), the court refused to stay an order giving custody of an almost full-term fetus to the state and requiring the pregnant woman with complete placenta previa to submit to a sonogram and caesarean section, despite her religious objections.

After *A.C.*, George Washington University Medical Center announced a settlement agreeing to accede to the patient's decisions "whenever possible," with judicial intervention "virtually never" appropriate. See Linda Greenhouse, Hospital Policy Sets Out Pregnant Patient Rights, N.Y. Times, Nov. 29, 1990, at A15. Also, in In re Baby Boy Doe, 632 N.E.2d 326 (Ill. App. Ct. 1994), the court rejected a balancing of rights, holding that a competent woman's refusal of treatment (for religious reasons) must be honored despite predicted harm to the fetus. But see Robin Power Morris, Note, The *Corneau* Case, Furthering Trends of Fetal Rights and Religious Freedom, 28 New Eng. J. on Crim. & Civ. Confinement 89 (2002) (noting 2000 case of woman taken into custody for pregnancy's duration because of her opposition to medical care and the death of another child soon after birth).

5. *Medical fallibility.* In cases of court-ordered caesareans, what weight should attach to medical fallibility? For example, in a recent New Jersey case, a doctor insisted on a caesarean, after estimating that the fetus was dangerously large and a labor-inducing drug proved ineffective. At birth, the baby weighed 7 pounds 10 ounces. See Lu, supra. Note that in *A.C.*, the baby died *despite* the caesarean; the placenta blocking the birth canal moved without medical intervention in *Jefferson*, supra; and the mother vaginally delivered an apparently health child in *Baby Boy Doe*, supra. See generally Nancy K. Rhoden, The Judge in the Delivery Room: The Emergence of Court-Ordered Cesareans, 74 Cal. L. Rev. 1951 (1986).

Can medical personnel adequately assess the emotional and cultural impact of intervention? Compare Janet Gallagher, Prenatal Invasions and Interventions: What's Wrong with Fetal Rights, 10 Harv. Women's L.J. 9, 9-10 (1987) (reporting hospital's perception of "happy ending" after forced caesarean over religious objections), with Kolder et al., supra, at 1193 (reporting father's subsequent suicide in same case).

6. *"Maternal-fetal conflicts."* Beyond blood transfusions and caesareans, so-called maternal-fetal conflicts can arise in a number of additional contexts. For example, many states do not honor advance directives (provisions for living wills and the appointment of proxy health care decisionmakers) for incompetent pregnant patients. As a result, the woman can be kept alive until the fetus can mature, despite her expressed wishes to the contrary. See Bretton J. Horttor, A Survey of Living Will and Advanced Health Care Directives, 74 N.D. L. Rev. 233 (1998) (reporting, based on survey, that 36 states prohibit the withdrawal of life support from pregnant women). See also Daniel Sperling, Maternal Brain Death, 30 Am. J.L. & Med. 453 (2004). Similarly, prenatal treatment to prevent transmission of HIV has raised the question of mandatory testing and the administration of medication even to pregnant women who have not consented. Erin Nicholson, Note,

Mandatory HIV Testing of Pregnant Women: Public Health Policy Considerations and Alternatives, 9 Duke J. Gender L. & Pol'y 175 (2002). And nonconsensual drug testing of pregnant women has been rationalized as a means of protecting fetuses from exposure to cocaine. See Ferguson v. City of Charleston, 532 U.S. 67 (2001) (state hospital's action constitutes unreasonable search in violation of Fourth Amendment). See also Dorothy Roberts, Killing the Black Body: Race, Reproduction, and the Meaning of Liberty 150-201 (1999) (noting how such interventions criminalize reproduction for Black and poor women). To compare the U.S. approach with that in England and Canada, see Rosamund Scott, Rights, Duties, and the Body: Law and Ethics of the Maternal-Fetal Conflict (2002).

Would a more helpful analysis present all such situations as "maternal-doctor conflicts," rather than maternal-fetal conflicts, given physicians' "central role in generating and escalating these conflicts"? See Michelle Oberman, Mothers and Doctors' Orders: Unmasking the Doctor's Fiduciary Role in Maternal-Fetal Conflicts, 94 Nw. U. L. Rev. 451, 454, 500 (2000). As larger questions of parental responsibility that include consideration of postnatal obligations? See John A. Robertson, Children of Choice: Freedom and the New Reproductive Technologies 193 (1994) (law does not require parents to donate marrow or organs to children after they are born). As reflections of the subordination of women as a class? See April L. Cherry, The Nonconsensual Medical Treatment of Pregnant Women and Implications for Female Citizenship, 6 U. Pa. J. Const. L. 723, 740-751 (2004).

Problems

1. Nancy Klein, age 32, is 16 weeks pregnant when her husband, Martin Klein, seeks appointment as her guardian so that he can authorize an abortion. Nancy had been comatose for seven weeks following a car accident; physicians had advised Martin that terminating the pregnancy would improve Nancy's chances of recovery. The Kleins have a three-year-old daughter. Nancy's parents support Martin's petition. Abortion at this stage of pregnancy presents some risks (equal to or greater than the risks posed by continued pregnancy, according to some but not all physicians). Abortion will increase the safety of administering medication and permit aggressive rehabilitation should Nancy emerge from her coma, and physicians have little hope that Nancy will recover from her brain damage. Abortion opponents, not related to the family, seek to intervene to prevent the procedure.

Suppose you are the judge on the petition for guardianship. What additional evidence, if any, would you need to decide the case? How would you obtain it? How would you decide the case? See In the Matter of Klein, 538 N.Y.S.2d 274 (App. Div.), *appeal denied*, 536 N.E.2d 627 (N.Y.), *stay denied sub nom.* Short v. Klein, 489 U.S. 1003 (1989).

2. Wife becomes pregnant for the purpose of aborting and donating the fetal tissue to Husband, who suffers from Parkinson's disease, a condition that has been shown to respond favorably to fetal tissue transplantation. See, e.g., The President's Council on Bioethics, Monitoring Stem Cell Research (2004).

All physicians refuse to participate in the plan, however, because of the following state criminal statute:

> 1. No physician shall perform an abortion on a woman if the physician knows that the woman conceived the unborn child for the purpose of providing fetal organs or tissue for medical transplantation to herself or another, and the physician knows that the woman intends to procure the abortion to utilize those organs or tissue for such use for herself or another.
>
> 2. No person shall utilize the fetal organs or tissue resulting from an abortion for medical transplantation, if the person knows that the abortion was procured for the purpose of utilizing those organs or tissue for such use.

Wife and Husband consult you, an attorney, about filing suit to challenge the constitutionality of the statute. How would you proceed? What additional information would you need? If you file suit, assess the chances of success. To what extent would your arguments change if the proposed procedure were sought to benefit the ten-year-old son of Wife and Husband rather than Husband himself? See Mo. Rev. Stat. §188.036 (2000). See also, e.g., S.D. Codified Laws §§34-14-16 to 34-14-20 (Supp. 2003) (prohibiting research that destroys human embryo when research not intended to help preserve life and health of particular embryo); Janet L. Dolgin, Embryonic Discourse: Abortion, Stem Cells, and Cloning, 31 Fla. St. U. L. Rev. 101 (2003).

II

Getting Married

A. INTRODUCTION: PUBLIC VERSUS PRIVATE DIMENSIONS OF COURTSHIP AND MARRIAGE

1. Courtship Patterns

The premarital relationship has become increasingly private. The excerpts below explore the public and private dimensions of courtship over time.

■ JOHN DEMOS, A LITTLE COMMONWEALTH: FAMILY LIFE IN PLYMOUTH COLONY
152, 154-155, 157-162 (2000)

[I]nitial phases of courtship [in colonial Plymouth colony] lacked much formal ceremony (no dating, dances, and so forth). [W]hen a courtship had developed to a certain point of intensity, the parents became directly involved. [The law provided for fines or corporal punishment for any man who proposed marriage to a "daughter or mayde servant" without first securing proper consent but simultaneously placed limits on the power of parents and masters to refuse consent. Appeals, although permitted to local magistrates, were rarely initiated.] Indeed, the reverse situation is what shows up in the Colony records — the situation in which a father sought to forestall an attempt to woo his daughter contrary to his own wishes. . . .

[Following the securing of parental approval, a series of steps remained.] [T]he "betrothal" or "contract" [was] a simple ceremony which bears comparison to our own custody of "engagement." [This] was a very serious undertaking [as] failure to fulfill such a contract would create the likelihood of legal action. [S]exual intimacies between the contracted parties fell into a category all their own [although not official condoned, the usual penalty was relatively. light]

[A]nother formal step became necessary: the "publishing" of the banns [that is, posting notice of the parties' intent to marry for 14 days or making an announcement to this effect three times in a public meeting]. [Still another important matter] was a set of transactions designed to underwrite the economic welfare of the contracted couple. [A] young man would receive the bulk of his portion in the form of land and housing, a woman would be given a variety of domestic furnishings, cattle, and/or money. . . .

[F]ourteen days was the minimum interval allowable between the betrothal ceremony and the wedding itself—between "contract and covenant," in the language of the time. [M]ost couples waited considerably longer: two or three months seems to have been quite customary. [T]radition has it that this was an occasion for sober reflection, and if need be, for reconsideration—before the final step was taken. . . .

■ BETH L. BAILEY, FROM FRONT PORCH TO BACK SEAT: COURTSHIP IN TWENTIETH-CENTURY AMERICA
19-22 (1988)

Between 1890 and 1925, dating—in practice and in name—had gradually, almost imperceptibly, become a universal custom in America. By the 1930s it had transcended its origins. [Dating had its origins in the urban lower classes who lacked the family space (such as the parlor) in which to conduct courtship activities and who took advantage of the excitement and opportunities presented by the urban environment.] The rise of dating was usually explained, quite simply, by the invention of the automobile [but, the automobile] simply accelerat[ed] and extend[ed] a process already well under way. . . .

Dating not only transformed the outward modes and conventions of American courtship, it also changed the distribution of control and power in courtship. One change was generational: the dating system lessened parental control and gave young men and women more freedom. The dating system also shifted power from women to men. [The former courtship practice of "calling" on a woman] gave women a large portion of control. First of all, courtship took place within the girl's home—in women's "sphere," as it was called in the nineteenth century—or at entertainments largely devised and presided over by women. Dating moved courtship out of the home and into man's sphere—the world outside the home. . . .

Second, in the calling system, the woman took the initiative. . . . Contrast these strictures with advice on dating etiquette from the 1940s and 1950s: An advice book for men and women warns that "girls who [try] to usurp the right of boys to choose their own dates" will "ruin a good dating career. . . ." An invitation to go out on a date . . . was an invitation into man's world—not simply because dating took place in the public sphere (commonly defined as belonging to men) [but also] because dating moved courtship into the world of the economy. Money—men's money— was at the center of the dating system. [M]oney shift[ed] control and initiative to men by making them the "hosts," [and] led contemporaries to see dating as a system of exchange. . . .

■ **JENNIFER EGAN, LOVE IN THE TIME OF NO TIME**
N.Y. Times, Nov. 23, 2003, §6 (Magazine), at 66

. . . Online dating is the most lucrative form of legal paid online content. [S]ocietal reasons for this flurry of activity are so profound that it's almost surprising that online dating didn't take off sooner: Americans are marrying later and so are less likely to meet their spouses in high school or college. They spend much of their lives at work, but the rise in sexual harassment suits has made workplace relationships tricky at best. Among a more secular and mobile population, social institutions like churches and clubs have faded in importance. That often leaves little more than the "bar scene" as a source of potential mates. . . .

Improved technology — namely, the proliferation of broadband and the abrupt ubiquity of digital cameras — partly explains online dating's surge in popularity. More critical still is the fact that the first generation of kids to come of age on the Internet are now young adults, still mostly single, and for them, using the Web to find what they need is as natural as using a lung to suck in air. They get jobs and apartments and plane tickets online — why not dates?

Still, a fair number of people continue to feel a stigma about dating online, ranging from the waning belief that it's a dangerous refuge for the desperate and unsavory to the milder but still unappealing notion that it's a public bazaar for the sort of people who thrive on selling themselves. The shopping metaphor is apt; online dating involves browsing and choosing among a seemingly infinite array of possible mates. But those who see a transactional approach to coupling as something new and unseemly would do well to pick up a novel by Jane Austen, where characters are introduced alongside their incomes. There is nothing new about the idea of marriage as a business transaction. . . .

How do [online personals] work and how is the way they work changing the nature of courtship? [F]or the serious online dater, the personal profile — the page allotted to each client on dating Web sites — quickly assumes a pivotal importance. . . . Dating profiles are works in progress, continually edited and tweaked, fortified with newer, more flattering pictures. . . . The exact progression from first contact to in-the-flesh-meeting varies among daters and age groups. For younger people, who grew up with instant-messaging programs, e-mail will often lead to an instant-message exchange (or several), followed by a meeting; those over 30 tend to prefer the phone. . . .

Until the late 1960's, marriage was the best guarantor of regular sex. Thereafter, it was being in a steady relationship. But online dating may be on its way to eliminating that particular incentive for commitment. [O]ne-night stands are commonplace and easy to arrange. . . .

. . . Relationships begun online have a tendency to end there too. This generally happens one of two ways: by e-mail or by no e-mail — i.e., someone disappears. . . . People in fledgling relationships begun online can vanish from one another's lives with the same breathtaking efficiency as a line of text deleted from a word processing document, leaving no hole, no gap in one another's daily lives to mark the fact that they were ever there. For some, an awareness of this exit strategy permeates the enterprise, allowing them to skimp on the niceties they would more or less have to extend toward a person they were likely to meet again. . . .

[E]ven the most jaundiced view of online personals must contend with the fact that people manage to find one another this way — again and again and again. So far in 2003, . . . more than 140,000 Match.com members said they were leaving the site "because they found the person they were seeking there." . . .

Courtship today often includes a stage of cohabitation. The number of unmarried couples has increased dramatically during the past several decades.[1] Currently, over half of first marriages follow a period of cohabitation.[2] A widespread belief is that premarital cohabitation leads to more stable marriages. Surprisingly, available data suggest instead that marriages that follow cohabitation face a higher risk of dissolution.[3] Legal regulation of cohabitation, as an alternative family form, is discussed in Chapter IV, section C.

In addition, the modern family reflects a new development. Many young adults now live with parents for extended periods.[4] Reasons include a desire to delay marriage, or a wish to obtain higher education, and the difficulty of becoming self-supporting (experienced especially by affluent youth who cannot replicate their parents' living standard).[5] Does this development entail a return to more "public" courtship? AIDS also has changed courtship attitudes and behavior (for example, by decreasing sexual experimentation).[6]

2. The Marriage Contract

A classic question asks: Is marriage a contract (a private agreement between two parties) or a status (a public institution regulated by the state)? Or does marriage

---

[1]. The number of unmarried couples increased by over 1100 percent from 1960-2002. Barbara Dafoe Whitehead & David Popenoe, The State of Our Unions: The Social Health of Marriage in America 20 (2004).

[2]. Id. at 20-21. Cohabitation is more common among those who are of lower socioeconomic and educational levels, less religious, and previously divorced, as well as those whose childhood was characterized by parental divorce, absent fathers, or significant parental discord. Id. at 21.

[3]. This finding is controversial, as Whitehead and Popenoe point out, because it is difficult to distinguish between the "selection effect" (i.e., cohabitants may have different characteristics that attract them to unconventional lifestyles) and the effect of the "experience of cohabitation." Id. See also Edward O. Laumann et al., The Social Organization of Sexuality: Sexual Practices in the United States 501 (1994); Helen M. Alvaré, Saying "Yes" Before Saying "I Do": Premarital Sex and Cohabitation as a Piece of the Divorce Puzzle, 18 Notre Dame J.L. Ethics & Pub. Pol'y 7, 26-31 (2004) (both discussing relationship between cohabitation and divorce).

[4]. See U.S. Census Bureau, America's Families and Living Arrangements: 2003, 13 (Nov. 2004) (revealing that 55 percent of men aged 18-24 and 46 percent of women in this age group live at home with one or both parents).

[5]. Martha Farnsworth Riche, Mysterious Young Adults, in Family in Transition 123, 123 (Arlene S. Skolnick & Jerome H. Skolnick eds., 1989).

[6]. See Peter Davis, Exploring the Kingdom of AIDS, in id. at 245, 246-250 (anecdotal evidence that AIDS is decreasing sexual experimentation).

retain features of both? In the following classic case affirming the state's right to regulate marriage and divorce, the Supreme Court addressed these questions.

■ **MAYNARD v. HILL**
   125 U.S. 190 (1887)

Mr. Justice FIELD.

[While] marriage is often termed by text writers and in decisions of courts as a civil contract — generally to indicate that it must be founded upon the agreement of the parties, and does not require any religious ceremony for its solemnization — it is something more than a mere contract. The consent of the parties is of course essential to its existence, but when the contract to marry is executed by the marriage, a relation between the parties is created which they cannot change. Other contracts may be modified, restricted, or enlarged, or entirely released upon the consent of the parties. Not so with marriage. The relation once formed, the law steps in and holds the parties to various obligations and liabilities. It is an institution, in the maintenance of which in its purity the public is deeply interested, for it is the foundation of the family and of society, without which there would be neither civilization nor progress.

[The Supreme Court then cited approvingly a state supreme court's description of marriage as:]

> a social relation like that of parent and child, the obligations of which arise not from the consent of concurrent minds, but are the creation of the law itself, a relation the most important, as affecting the happiness of individuals, the first step from barbarism to incipient civilization, the purest tie of social life, and the true basis of human progress.

[Adams v. Palmer, 51 Me. 481, 484-485 (Me. 1863)]. . . .

■ **HENRY MAINE, ANCIENT LAW**
   163-165 (1963)

The movement of the progressive societies has been uniform in one respect. [I]t has been distinguished by the gradual dissolution of family dependency and the growth of individual obligation in its place. The Individual is steadily substituted for the Family, as the unit of which civil laws take account. The advance has been accomplished at varying rates of celerity, and there are societies not absolutely stationary in which the collapse of the ancient organization can only be perceived by careful study. . . . But, whatever its pace, the change has not been subject to reaction or recoil, and apparent retardations will be found to have been occasioned through the absorption of archaic ideas and customs from some entirely foreign source. Nor is it difficult to see what is the tie between man and man which replaces by degrees those forms of reciprocity in rights and duties which have their origin in the Family. It is Contract. Starting, as from one terminus of history, from a condition of society in which all the relations of Persons are summed up in the relations of Family, we seem to have steadily moved towards a phase of social order in which all these relations arise from the free agreement of individuals. In Western Europe the progress achieved in this direction has been considerable. Thus the status of the Slave has disappeared — it has been superseded by the contractual relation of the servant to his master. The status of the Female under Tutelage, if the tutelage be understood of persons other than her husband, has also ceased to exist; from her coming of age to her marriage all the relations she may form are relations of contract. [W]e may say that the movement of the progressive societies has hitherto been a movement *from Status to Contract*.

■ SUSAN MOLLER OKIN, JUSTICE, GENDER,
    AND THE FAMILY
    122-123 (1989)

[M]arriage itself has long been regarded as a contract, though it is a very peculiar one: it is a contract that does not conform with the *principles* (let alone the counterprinciples) of liberal contract doctrine. It is a preformed status contract, which restricts the parties' freedom to choose their partners (for example, there must be only one partner, and of the opposite sex) and of which they are not free to choose the terms.

The courts' refusal to enforce explicit contracts between husband and wife has been by no means completely attributable to reluctance to intrude into a private community supposedly built upon trust. It has been due at least as much to the fact that the courts have regarded the terms of marriage as already established. When, for example, they have refused to enforce intramarital agreements in which wives have agreed to forgo support for other consideration, and in which husbands have agreed to pay their wives for work done in a family business, they have done so on the grounds that the wife's right to support, in the former case, and her obligation to provide services for her husband, in the latter, are fixed by the marriage contract itself. Likewise, when courts have showed a reluctance to enforce the terms of the preformed contracted itself — for example, refusing to establish a level of adequate support that a wife must receive — it has been on the grounds that, so long as husband and wife cohabit, it is up to him as the family head to determine such matters. Another respect in which marriage is an anomalous contract is that the parties to it are not required to be familiar with the terms of the relationship into which they are entering. . . .

B. PREPARING TO MARRY: PREMARITAL CONTROVERSIES

1. Breach of Promise to Marry

■ RIVKIN v. POSTAL
    2001 WL 1077952 (Tenn. Ct. App. 2001)

Koch, J.

This appeal involves the financial aftermath of a short-lived nonmarital affair that ended badly. . . . David Rivkin and Lori Postal met in April 1994 at a music convention in Memphis. Mr. Rivkin was a successful, award-winning producer. Ms. Postal was a 28-year-old divorcée who was living in Atlanta with her mother and stepfather. She sold bathing suits at wholesale and had also started a record label. Ms. Postal was attending the Memphis convention to obtain a record contract for a singer and a band that she represented. Even though Ms. Postal knew that Mr. Rivkin was married and had three children, she welcomed his romantic advances. Within a short period of time, they began living together at the Peabody Hotel in Memphis and later moved into a house Mr. Rivkin bought in a Memphis suburb.

In early 1995, Ms. Postal discovered she was pregnant with Mr. Rivkin's child. Mr. Rivkin suggested an abortion, but Ms. Postal did not agree. Their child was born in September 1995. Shortly after their child was born, Mr. Rivkin sold the house in Memphis, and the parties moved to Williamson County because they believed that Mr. Rivkin would have greater success as a producer in the Nashville area. Mr. Rivkin was the parties' sole source of support, and he was able to provide an exceptionally affluent lifestyle for Ms. Postal and their child despite his continuing obligations to his wife and children. He purchased a $420,000 home in Williamson County and horses for Ms. Postal. He also hired a nanny for the child. Not surprisingly, Ms. Postal took to this lifestyle. She did not work outside the home but rather spent her time raising the parties' child, training her horses, and entertaining her personal friends and Mr. Rivkin's business associates.

But all was not well with the parties. They entered counseling in an effort to save their relationship. One of their problems stemmed from Ms. Postal's concern that her family knew that she was living with a married man and had given birth to his child. She insisted that Mr. Rivkin buy her an engagement ring to enable her to save face with her family. When Mr. Rivkin did not purchase a ring for her, Ms. Postal ordered a ring herself. Mr. Rivkin eventually paid for the ring after Ms. Postal refused to return it and also permitted her to wear it in front of her family. Ms. Postal told her parents that she and Mr. Rivkin were planning to wed after he was divorced, and Mr. Rivkin did not contradict her. However, the parties themselves never discussed specific wedding plans. . . .

Mr. Rivkin was finally divorced from his wife in March 1997. However, by this time, Mr. Rivkin was no longer living in the parties' house. He saw Ms. Postal on occasion and continued to pay for all her living expenses, the mortgage on the house, the payments on her truck, and all of the child's expenses. [In June 1997], Mr. Rivkin told her that their relationship was over and that he no longer wished to see her.

When it became evident that their relationship had ended, neither party followed Emily Post's sage advice "to take the high road—and move on." In September 1997, Mr. Rivkin filed suit in the Chancery Court for Williamson County seeking a partition of the parties' jointly-owned property and the return of his personal property that was still in Ms. Postal's possession. Ms. Postal responded with a counterclaim seeking damages for breach of promise to marry. . . .

In England, before the founding of this country, questions touching on marriage and breach of a promise of marriage were chiefly the province of the ecclesiastical courts. Those courts, however, lacked power to grant relief in breach of promise to marry cases other than to decree a performance of the marriage on pain of spiritual punishment. Eventually, as marriage began to be viewed as "largely a property transaction, entered into as much for material advantages as for reasons of sentiment," actions for breach of promise to marry found their way into the King's Courts [where the parties obtained damages].

The common-law action for breach of promise to marry made its way to the American colonies along with most of the common law of England. Here, it started out as "popular means of soothing the sufferings of rejected love." In time, however, it became subject to abuse. Borrowing ideas from tort law, the courts began permitting juries to award punitive damages. Most breach of promise to marry actions were brought by women against men, and men's fears of excessive verdicts and their distaste for the scandal surrounding such suits gave women the power to wield the cause of action almost as blackmail.

By the 1930s, newspapers were publishing accounts of "spectacular 'extortion and blackmail rackets'" based on these claims. The publicity of the "unfounded suits, perjury, and excessive verdicts at the hands of . . . seemingly ever gullible . . . [juries] armed with unrestrained discretion" eventually prompted a movement to reform these claims. [William B. Eldridge, Domestic Relations—Breach of Promise Actions, 21 Tenn. L. Rev. 451, 452 (1950)]. Beginning with Indiana in 1935, the states began enacting statutes aimed at ending the perceived abuses associated with breach of promise claims.

Many states abolished the cause of action altogether, prompting courts to jump on a bandwagon of sorts that some thought went too far. It became increasingly evident that the pendulum was swinging too far in the other direction. The barriers erected to correct one evil gave legal protection to another. The courts, perhaps overzealous in their interpretation of legislative intent, construed these statutes as prohibiting tort actions between formerly betrothed parties for fraud and deceit.

Tennessee chose a middle course. Rather than abolish the common-law cause of action for breach of promise to marry, this state chose to rein it in a bit. In 1949, the Tennessee General Assembly passed an act which, according to its caption, was designed "to prevent certain injustices in suits for damages for the breach of promise or contract of marriage." This act circumscribes breach of promise claims in four significant ways. First, Tenn. Code Ann. §36-3-405 provides that these claims could not be joined with other damage claims. Second, Tenn. Code Ann. §36-3-401 requires that promises or contracts of marriage could only be established using either signed, written evidence of the promise or contract or the testimony of at least two disinterested witnesses. Third, Tenn. Code Ann. §36-3-403 requires juries to consider the parties' age and experience in calculating damages. Finally, Tenn. Code Ann. §36-3-404 prohibits awarding punitive damages in cases where the alleged breaching party was over sixty years old. These statutes survive to the present day, and thus this case is governed by their strictures.

. . . To meet [Ms. Postal's] burden of proof in this case, Tenn. Code Ann. §36-3-401 requires her to present either "written evidence of such contract, signed by the party against whom the action is brought" or with the testimony of "at least two disinterested witnesses." . . . We turn first to the "written evidence." In March 1996, one month after he purchased the Williamson County house, Mr. Rivkin executed a quitclaim deed conveying the property to himself and Ms. Postal as joint tenants with right of survivorship. . . .

"It is obvious," as one treatise puts it, "that not only are most engagements to marry arrived at informally and without witnesses or written record, but in many instances there is no explicit exchange of promises at all." 1 Clark §1.2. Accordingly, proof of an engagement would be impossible if the plaintiff were required to produce evidence that at some specific moment the parties formally exchanged promises and reduced these promises to writing. Tenn. Code Ann. §36-3-401 is not intended to go that far. Rather, it calls for signed, written evidence that the parties were, by mutual agreement, on the way to becoming husband and wife. Many kinds of writings would suffice.[10]

Mr. Rivkin testified that he gave Ms. Postal a joint tenant's interest in the Williamson County house as a way of making sure that their child would be provided for should something happen to him. In his words, the quitclaim deed was executed "for the child, in the event something happened to me; [so] that the child would have a house to live in." If we discount this explanation because the trial court stated that it "disbelieve[d] Mr. Rivkin and his denial of any agreement to marry Ms. Postal," we are left with no other direct evidence of Mr. Rivkin's reasons for this conveyance. Ms. Postal herself conceded that Mr. Rivkin never explained to her why he quitclaimed an interest in the Williamson County property to her.

Thus, the only evidence we have regarding the significance of the deed is the deed itself. Nothing within the four corners of the deed alludes to any promise or contract of marriage or to the parties' betrothed status. Executing quitclaim deeds is not only within the province of persons who have agreed or contracted to marry the grantee named in the deed. Quitclaim deeds are commonly used for business transactions between partners, conveyances between family members, cleaning up a title for title insurance purposes, or gifts. Thus, in light of the ubiquitous nature of quitclaim deeds, we decline to hold that an unexplained quitclaim deed between an unmarried man and an unmarried woman, without much, much more, suffices as signed, written evidence of a promise of marriage for the purpose of Tenn. Code Ann. §36-3-401. . . .

Without a writing signed by Mr. Rivkin, Ms. Postal's only remaining avenue for proving that Mr. Rivkin promised to marry her consisted of presenting at least two disinterested witnesses who could substantiate Mr. Rivkin's promise. . . . The only witnesses she called regarding this issue were her parents, Diana Schuyler and Barry Postal. While it is doubtful that a claimant's parent can ever be a disinterested witness in cases of this sort, Ms. Postal's parents are clearly not disinterested witnesses because at the time of trial they were also Ms. Postal's creditors. . . . In summary, we have concluded that Ms. Postal failed to carry the statutory burden of proof placed on persons seeking money damages for a breach of promise or contract of marriage. . . .

Notes and Questions

1. *Majority view.* Most states have abolished the action for breach of promise to marry, as *Rivkin* explains. Only a few jurisdictions still recognize the claim, often with limitations. See, e.g., 740 Ill. Comp. Stat.15/1-4 (2002) (limiting damages and setting forth notice requirements); Md. Code. Ann., Fam. Law §3-102 (2004) (abolishing action unless plaintiff is pregnant); Okla. Stat. tit. 23, §40 (2004) (stating that

---

10. While not intended to be an exhaustive list, the following signed writings might fit the bill: an application for a marriage license, an attested petition to waive the age or waiting requirements for marriage, correspondence between the parties, writing dealing with wedding arrangements, or prenuptial agreements.

damages for the action are at the jury's discretion); Tex. Civ. Prac. & Rem. Code Ann. §16.002 (Vernon 2002) (setting one-year statute of limitations for the action); Folds v. Barber, 597 S.E.2d 409 (Ga. 2004); Sanders v. Gore, 676 So. 2d 866, 869 (La. Ct. App. 1996). Do the limitations in *Rivkin* appropriately "rein in" the cause of action?

2. *Historical background.* The modern action of breach of promise reflects Roman, Germanic, and canon law influences. In early Roman law, the consequences of a broken promise to marry were mild, reflecting a belief in contractual freedom.[7] In contrast, Germanic custom (adopting a moral stance) awarded damages to "punish" the breach.[8] In both traditions, the consequences were more severe if the woman broke the engagement.

The Germanic view of marriage influenced the English and French ecclesiastical courts that enforced the action in the Middle Ages.[9] By 1576, English common law courts also entertained actions for breach of promise.[10] The common law action allowed damages for mental suffering as well as expenses incurred in anticipation of marriage.

Criticisms of the action emerged in the nineteenth century. The House of Commons tried unsuccessfully to limit the action in 1879.[11] Parliament abolished the action in 1970.[12] In America, the controversy culminated in a movement in the 1930s when many states enacted statutes (termed "heart balm" or "anti-heart balm" legislation) to eliminate the action.[13]

3. *Damages.* Breach of promise to marry is a hybrid action, reflecting roots in contract and tort law. A plaintiff may recover the monetary and social value of the marriage (expectation damages), as well as expenses incurred in preparation for the marriage (reliance damages). Damages for mental anguish and humiliation, not normally compensable in contract, may also be recoverable. Punitive damages are sometimes permitted.

Given that marriage has become an emotional commitment rather than a property transaction, should breach-of-promise-to-marry claims provide a cause of action? If so, what damages should be recoverable? Loss of anticipated social and financial position? Compare Stanard v. Bolin, 565 P.2d 94, 97 (Wash. 1977) (such damages "not justified in light of modern society's concept of marriage"), with Bradley v. Somers, 322 S.E.2d 665, 666 (S.C. 1984) (permitting damages for "pecuniary and social advantages").

Should emotional distress be compensated? Should measurement difficulties justify limiting damages to economic loss? Should recovery be limited to reliance damages? See Neil G. Williams, What to Do When There's No "I Do": A Model for Awarding Damages Under Promissory Estoppel, 70 Wash. L. Rev. 1019 (1995)

---

[7]. Patrick Mac Chombaich de Coloquhoun, 1 A Summary of the Roman Civil Law 455 (1988). See also H. F. Jolowicz & Barry Nicholas, Historical Introduction to the Study of Roman Law 233 (3d ed. 1972).

[8]. Rudolf Huebner, A History of Germanic Private Law 601 (1918); Paul Weidenbaum, Breach of Promise in Private International Law, 14 N.Y.U. L.Q. Rev. 451, 452 (1937).

[9]. Jean Brissaud, A History of French Private Law 99 (1912); 3 William Blackstone, Commentaries *92-94.

[10]. The Law Commission, Breach of Promise to Marry 2 n.4 (1969).

[11]. Edwin Hadley, Breach of Promise to Marry, 2 Notre Dame L. Rev. 190, 193 (1927).

[12]. Law Reform (Miscellaneous Provisions) Act, 1970, ch. 33, §1 (Eng.).

[13]. On the abolition movement, see generally James P. Byrnes, The Illinois Anti-Heart Balm Law, 38 Ill. L. Rev. 94 (1943-1944); Nathan P. Feinsinger, Legislative Attack on "Heart Balm," 33 Mich. L. Rev. 980 (1935).

(recommending recovery only for incurred expenditures and forgone economic opportunities). How significant are reliance damages stemming from a broken engagement? Commentators point out that the typical wedding costs $26,000.[14] As the wedding approaches, fewer costs are recoverable in the event of cancellation.

> Engagement rings can usually be returned for a full refund for 60 to 100 days after purchase. But some cities, including New York, allow caterers and hotels to charge for services and rooms that cannot be rebooked when canceled with less than six months notice. Wedding gown makers typically require an initial nonrefundable deposit of half the price of the dress, with the balance on delivery. The week before the wedding, the cake and flowers are delivered. When an engagement is broken the day of the wedding, almost none of the cost can be recovered.[15]

Some companies now offer wedding insurance policies that insure against losses resulting from circumstances out of the control of the bride and groom (but not for the proverbial "cold feet").

4. *Defenses*. Traditional defenses to breach-of-promise claims include physical and mental defects, unchastity of the plaintiff, plaintiff's lack of love for the defendant, and mutuality of the decision to terminate the engagement. Should a plaintiff's obsessive-compulsive disorder excuse a defendant's performance? See Wildey v. Springs, 840 F. Supp. 1259 (N.D. Ill. 1994), *rev'd*, 47 F.3d 1475. (7th Cir. 1995). A defendant's subsequent good faith offer to marry the plaintiff, while not a defense, may mitigate damages. What does this mitigating factor reflect about the nature of the injury?

5. *Seduction*. At common law, and in some states today, tort liability exists for the act of seduction. See L.N.K. ex rel. Kavanaugh v. St. Mary's Med. Ctr., 785 N.E.2d 303 (Ind. Ct. App. 2003). At common law, the tort occurs when an unmarried, previously chaste woman consents to intercourse in reliance on a defendant's false promise to marry. The action was maintainable *not* by the woman, but by one entitled to her services (that is, her father or someone in loco parentis). As the tort gradually became statutorily based, legislatures conferred a right on the woman to sue. Currently, 17 states and the District of Columbia recognize the tort but generally reformulate it as an action for intentional misrepresentation, i.e., false statements that induce a person's acquiescence to sexual relations. Rachel F. Moran, Law and Emotion, Love and Hate, 11 J. Contemp. Legal Issues 747, 774 (2001). On the history of the tort, see Lea Vandervelde, The Legal Ways of Seduction, 48 Stan. L. Rev. 817 (1996). Some states impose criminal liability for the offense. See, e.g., Mich. Comp. Laws §750.532 (2004); Okla. Stat. Ann. tit. 21, §1120 (West 2002). See generally Douglas E. Cressler, An Old Tort with a Unique Hoosier History Finds New Life: Seduction, 47 Res Gestae 26 (June 2004).

Should legislatures abolish all liability (tort and criminal) for seduction, given the fact that a woman's loss of virginity no longer has such a deleterious effect on

[14]. Anya Sostek, Literally Insuring a Good Time: More Brides and Their Families Are Taking Out Insurance to Make Sure Their Special Day's Memories Are Good Ones, Pittsburgh (Pa.) Post-Gazette, June 10, 2005, at E1.

[15]. Keith Bradsher, Ditching Your Betrothed May Cost You: Wedding Rings, Gowns, Cakes and Deposits Add Up, S.F. Chron., Mar. 20, 1990, at B5. Although no actual data are available on the number of broken engagements, Bradsher estimates (based on a comparison of the number of marriage license applications with actual marriages) that approximately 5 percent of engagements in New York City are broken annually.

her marital prospects? See Linda J. Lacey, Introducing Feminist Jurisprudence: An Analysis of Oklahoma's Seduction Statute, 25 Tulsa L.J. 775, 776 (1990) (arguing that penal statutes are "antiquated and unconstitutional"). Or, as one commentator suggests, should legislatures adopt the tort of "sexual fraud" based on a fraudulent misrepresentation of fact, opinion, intention, or law for the purpose of inducing sexual relations that results in serious physical, pecuniary, and emotional loss? See Jane E. Larson, "Women Understand So Little, They Call My Good Nature 'Deceit'": A Feminist Rethinking of Seduction, 93 Colum. L. Rev. 374, 453 (1993).

6. *Online dating.* Fraudulent representations regarding marital status, height, wealth, age, and weight are common in the online dating industry.[16] Should the online dating industry be regulated? If so, how? Although most states have abolished heartbalm actions, should such claims be resurrected to regulate online dating? Cf. Brown v. Strum, 350 F. Supp.2d 346 (D. Conn. 2004) (allegations that defendant committed fraud and intentional infliction of emotional distress by falsely representing himself as divorced on online dating service). See generally David Colker, Cupid Aims for Background Checks, L.A. Times, May 26, 2005 (pointing out that legislators in California, Florida, Michigan, Ohio, and Texas are considering regulatory legislation). See also Carafano v. Metrosplash.com, 339 F.3d 1119 (9th Cir. 2003) (holding that Web service provider was entitled to statutory immunity from tort liability for publicizing a false profile submitted by a non-client third party).

7. *Class and gender.* Historically, most breach-of-promise plaintiffs were women. Damages included: loss of virginity, birth of a non-marital child, and the evaporation of marital prospects. Lawrence M. Friedman, Name Robbers, Privacy, Blackmail, and Assorted Matters in Legal History, 30 Hofstra L. Rev. 1093, 1104-1105 (2002). Ironically, some evidence suggests that today men may be more frequent victims of breach of promise to marry.[17] Friedman also suggests that the decline of breach-of-promise-to-marry claims parallels the decline in the value of middle-class female chastity. Id. at 1123 (explaining that by the time of the 1930s' anti-heartbalm movement, chastity "had lost at least some of its currency"). Although the doctrine was intended to protect middle-class women and families from disgrace, Friedman notes that most plaintiffs, historically were lower-class or working-class women. Id. at 1121.

Problem

Marilyn is dating Donald, a married man, when she discovers that she is pregnant with his child. He promises her that if she has the abortion, he will pay her $75,000 plus medical and legal expenses. He also tells her that he will marry her when his divorce is final and that they will later have a baby together. Marilyn

[16]. Jonathan Sidener, Tall Tales: Fibs about Height, Wealth, Age and Weight Not Uncommon at Online Dating Sites, San Diego Union-Trib., Feb. 9, 2004, at C1 (citing Nielsen research findings that 11 percent of clients at online dating sites are married, and revealing anecdotal evidence about other misrepresentations).

[17]. Mark Coomes, Insurers Eager to Tap Wedding Market as Costs Climb, Times Union (Albany), May 29, 2005, at G8 (reporting data suggesting that men are three times more likely to be left at the altar). See also Runaway Bride Gets Probation, Faces Fine, Akron Beacon J., June 3, 2005, at A4 (recounting a highly publicized case of a bride who was charged with a felony after making false statements to police in which she blamed her cold feet on an abduction).

agrees, has the abortion, and accepts the payment. When they break up, she sues him for intentional and negligent infliction of emotional distress, battery, fraud, and misrepresentation. She alleges that the settlement agreement is unconscionable, against public policy, and was extracted under duress and coercion. Donald moves for summary judgment on the ground that the jurisdiction abrogated claims for breach of promise to marry. What result? See M.N. v. D.S., 616 N.W.2d 284 (Minn. Ct. App. 2000).

2. Gifts in Contemplation of Marriage

■ FOWLER v. PERRY
830 N.E.2d 97 (Ind. Ct. App. 2005)

BAILEY, J.

From June of 1999 to October of 2000, Fowler and Perry lived together in a house in Missouri. During that time, Fowler and Perry had a son. On October 21, 1999, Fowler purchased an engagement ring for Perry for $5,499.00; however, the two were never married. In late October of 2000, Perry and her son moved to Indiana, while Fowler remained in Missouri to finish his education. Once Fowler graduated from college, he planned to move to Indiana to be with Perry and their son. . . .

In April of 2001, Perry informed Fowler that they should stop "seeing each other for a while." Subsequently, Perry attempted to pawn her "engagement ring" because Fowler had not requested it back and she no longer had a use for it. However, at some point during the time that Perry had taken the ring from "jewelry shop to jewelry shop" to pawn it, the ring was stolen from her car. As a result of the theft, Perry received insurance proceeds in the amount of $5,000.00.

On October 25, 2002, Fowler filed a complaint against Perry, seeking, in part, . . . the value of the stolen engagement ring. [After conducting a bench trial, the trial court entered a judgment, in relevant part, in favor of Perry.] On appeal, Fowler argues that the trial court erroneously granted judgment in favor of Perry [on his claim] of entitlement to the purchase price of the stolen engagement ring, which he had given to Perry in contemplation of marriage. . . . In particular, Fowler maintains that [the finding] is clearly erroneous inasmuch as it contains the following language:

> Although the ring has been identified as an engagement ring, the Court was not presented with any evidence of a proposal for marriage, the time, place or exchange of said marital agreement by [Perry.] The mere identification of the ring as an engagement ring, absent other specific facts establishing that same was given in express contemplation of marriage, is insufficient evidence for the Court to order that the value of the same be returned to [Fowler.] The Court must therefore find in favor of [Perry] and against [Fowler] in this request.

We address the propriety of this finding in two parts. First, we examine whether the ring at issue constitutes a gift in contemplation of marriage. In so doing, we note that, at trial, both parties referred to the ring as an engagement ring. An "engagement ring" is defined as "a ring given in token of betrothal."

Webster's Third New International Dictionary 751 (2002). The term "betrothal" refers to "a mutual promise or contract for a future marriage." Id. at 209. In light of the parties' reference to the ring at issue as an engagement ring, the trial court erred when it found that the evidence was insufficient to prove that such ring was given in contemplation of marriage.

Having determined that the engagement ring was given to Perry in contemplation of marriage, we next examine whether, upon the parties' break-up, Fowler was entitled to the return of ring or, in the event that the ring could not be returned, the purchase price of the jewelry. This question is one of first impression in Indiana.

It is undisputed that, at some point, Fowler gave Perry the engagement ring that he purchased for $5,499.00 in cash and trade. That said, we must determine whether the ring was intended as an absolute, or a conditional, gift. In addition to the competency of the donor, a valid inter vivos gift — i.e., an absolute gift — occurs when: (1) the donor intends to make a gift; (2) the gift is completed with nothing left undone; (3) the property is delivered by the donor and accepted by the donee; and (4) the gift is immediate and absolute. Thus, once delivery and acceptance of a gift inter vivos occurs, the gift is irrevocable and a present title vests in the donee. By contrast, a gift is conditional if it is conditioned upon the performance of some act by the donee or the occurrence of an event in the future.

The gift at issue in the present case is an engagement ring. In our society, an engagement ring — i.e., a gift incidental to an engagement — is the symbol and token of a couple's agreement to marry. As such, marriage is an implied condition of the transfer of title to the ring and, thus, the gift does not become absolute until the marriage occurs. Put another way, marriage is a condition precedent before ownership of an engagement ring vests in the donee. Therefore, in the absence of a contrary expression of intent, an engagement ring is a conditional gift given in contemplation of marriage, and not an inter vivos transfer of personal property.[3]

Having concluded that, in most circumstances, an engagement ring is a conditional gift, we next analyze the rightful ownership of the engagement ring when the condition of marriage is never satisfied. The majority of jurisdictions that have considered the ownership of an engagement ring after the engagement was terminated has adopted a "fault-based" approach, wherein the donor is entitled to the return of an engagement ring only if the engagement was broken by mutual agreement or unjustifiably by the donee. See Heiman v. Parrish, 942 P.2d 631, 635 (Kan. 1997); see also [Elaine Marie Tomko, Annotation, Rights in Respect of Engagement and Courtship Presents When Marrying Does Not Ensue, 44 A.L.R.5th 1 (1996)] (providing an extensive summary of the cases arising in this area and the rationales employed to resolve them). The rationale behind the "fault-based" approach is, in large part, as follows:

> On principle, an engagement ring is given, not alone as a symbol of the status of the two persons as engaged, the one to the other, but as a symbol or token of their pledge and agreement to marry. As such pledge or gift, the condition is implied that if both parties abandon the projected marriage, the sole cause of the gift, it should be returned. Similarly, if the woman, who has received the ring in token of her promise, unjustifiably breaks her promise, it should be returned. When the converse situation

---

3. We observe that other types of property may be shown to be conditional gifts given in contemplation of marriage, but such a classification would require specific evidence of such intent, as opposed to a mere showing that the ring was an engagement ring.

occurs, and the giver of the ring, betokening his promise, violates his word, it would seem that a similar result should follow, i.e., he should lose, not gain, rights to the ring. In addition, had he not broken his promise, the marriage would follow and the ring would become the wife's absolutely. The man could not then recover the ring.

44 A.L.R.5th 1 (citing Sloin v. Lavine, 11 N.J. Misc. 899, 168 A. 849 (1933)). Accordingly, under this rationale, the courts should not aid a donor, who has broken his promise of marriage, to regain possession of something that he could not have regained if he had kept his promise.

A minority of jurisdictions has adopted a "no-fault" approach, i.e., the modern trend, holding that once an engagement is broken, the engagement ring should be returned to the donor, regardless of fault. Pursuant to this approach, fault is irrelevant, if ascertainable at all, because ownership of the engagement ring was conditional and the condition of marriage was never fulfilled. [*Heiman*, 942 P.2d at 635] (citing Aronow v. Silver, 223 N.J.Super. 344, 538 A.2d 851 (1987)). Some of these "no-fault" jurisdictions, for example, highlight the fact that the primary purpose behind the engagement period is to allow the couple to test the permanency of their feelings for one another, and with that purpose in mind, it would be irrational to penalize the donor for taking steps to prevent a possibly unhappy marriage. See Fierro v. Hoel, 465 N.W.2d 669 (Iowa Ct. App. 1990). We find this latter approach to be more persuasive.

Indeed, the "no fault" approach is consistent with our "no-fault" system of divorce. See Ind. Code §31-15-1-2 [citing Indiana's no-fault divorce statute]. We do not want to require our judiciary to tackle the seemingly insurmountable task of determining which party was at fault for the termination of an engagement for marriage, as such may force trial courts to sort through volumes of self-serving testimony regarding who-did-what during the engagement.

In adopting the "no-fault" approach, however, we note that, in this modern era, it is not uncommon for both parties to contribute financially to the purchase of an engagement ring. Though not customary, it is also not atypical for the woman, i.e., the donee or recipient, to purchase her own engagement ring. Armed with these realities, we hold that when an engagement ring is purchased in contemplation of marriage and such engagement does not result in marriage, the person who purchased the engagement ring is entitled to its return or, if return of the ring is impossible, to the monetary amount contributed toward the purchase of the ring. [The court notes that the record does not indicate that Perry contributed to the purchase of the ring.]

Here, Fowler's gift to Perry of the engagement ring that he purchased for $5,499.00 was conditioned upon their ensuing marriage. When the promise of marriage was not kept, regardless of fault, the condition was not fulfilled and the ring must be returned to him. Because the ring at issue was stolen, Fowler is entitled to the purchase price of the ring, i.e., $5,499.00. . . .

Notes and Questions

1. *Historical background.* Before the Depression, etiquette did not dictate the gift of a diamond engagement ring. By 1945, however, "the diamond ring rapidly changed from a relatively obscure token of affection to what amounted to an

American tradition." Margaret F. Brinig, Rings and Promises, 6 J.L. Econ. & Org. 203, 204 (1990). Professor Brinig attributes the change to the influence of the diamond industry (through an extensive advertising campaign) and also to the abolition of breach-of-promise-to-marry suits (which resulted, she argues, in the need to give some item as bond or pledge).

2. *Theories of recovery.* The common law treated actions for recovery of gifts given in contemplation of marriage distinctly from breach of promise. As a result, in many jurisdictions anti-heartbalm measures do not bar the former action. Courts generally hold that recovery of such gifts rests on conditional gift theory: property obtained in consideration of marriage is conditioned on the performance of the marriage. If the condition is not met, the transfer has not been completed and the gift is recoverable. The central question, as *Fowler* reveals, is whether the gift was conditioned on the subsequent marriage or was absolute. Courts consider the nature of the gift, surrounding circumstances, and cause of the broken engagement. Other possible theories of recovery include: fraud and unjust enrichment. See Adam D. Glassman, I Do! Or Do I? A Practical Guide to Love, Courtship, and Heartbreak in New York — or — Who Gets the Ring Back Following a Broken Engagement?, 12 Buff. Women's L.J. 47, 56-65 (2004) (explaining theories).

3. *Fault.* At common law, fault barred recovery or retention of the engagement ring. Thus, the man could recover the ring if the woman unjustifiably ended the engagement or if the couple mutually dissolved it, but not if he unjustifiably terminated the engagement. The modernization of divorce law revealed the shortcomings of a fault-based analysis of personal relationships and their dissolution. Hence, the modern trend, as *Fowler* explains, makes fault irrelevant. See also Meyer v. Mitnick, 625 N.W.2d 126 (Mich. Ct. App. 2001); Benassi v. Back and Neck Pain Clinic, 629 N.W.2d 475 (Minn. Ct. App. 2001). But cf. Curtis v. Anderson, 106 S.W.3d 251 (Tex. Ct. App. 2003). What reasons does *Fowler* give for holding fault irrelevant? Are they persuasive? See generally Barbara Frazier, "But I Can't Marry You": Who Is Entitled to the Engagement Ring When the Conditional Performance Falls Short of the Altar?, 17 J. Am. Acad. Matrim. Law. 419 (2001); Rebecca Tushnet, Rules of Engagement, 107 Yale L.J. 2583 (1998).

4. *Other gifts.* Occasionally, suits involve recovery of other objects to either the donee or a third party that were made during the engagement. Should such gifts be treated differently from engagement rings? How does *Fowler* consider this circumstance?

Suppose the man gives the woman other gifts of jewelry. Are such gifts sufficiently distinguishable from an engagement ring to preclude recovery? How does one determine what gifts are "in contemplation of marriage"? Can gifts to a *third party* be in contemplation of marriage? See Cooper v. Smith, 800 N.E.2d 372 (Ohio Ct. App. 2003) (fiancé paid off prospective mother-in-law's car loan and made various improvements to mother-in-law's house).

5. *Married donee.* Should it matter if the donee of the engagement ring is still married to someone else at the time of the engagement? Why? Should the donee's marital status matter in jurisdictions that follow the majority as well as the minority approach?

6. *Gender-based nature of rule.* Given that etiquette and custom dictate that the bride pays for the wedding and the groom for the engagement ring, critics point out that women bear a disproportionate burden for a broken engagement under the prevailing rules. See, e.g., Tushnet, supra (advocating a no-fault rule making

both parties equally liable for money expended in reliance on broken engagements). Until recently, courts failed to consider the gender-based nature of the rule. However, in Albinger v. Harris, 48 P.3d 711 (Mont. 2002), the Montana Supreme Court took this factor into account in reversing a trial court ruling authorizing the return of a $29,000 engagement ring that had been reclaimed several times during a lengthy tumultuous relationship. Rejecting a no-fault conditional gift theory because it "carves an exception in the state's gift law for the benefit of predominately male plaintiffs" (id. at 720), the court elaborated as follows:

> While antenuptial traditions vary by class, ethnicity, age and inclination, women often still assume the bulk of pre-wedding costs, such as non-returnable wedding gowns, moving costs, or non-refundable deposits for caterers, entertainment or reception halls. Consequently, the statutory "anti-heart balm" bar continues to have a disparate impact on women. If this Court were to fashion a special exception for engagement ring actions under gift law theories, we would perpetuate the gender bias attendant upon the Legislature's decision to remove from our courts all actions for breach of antenuptial promises. . . .

Id.

7. *Same-sex couples*. The Restatement (Third) of Property (Wills and Other Donative Transfers) §6.2, cmt. m (2003) provides that engagement rings are conditional gifts that must be returned regardless of fault. The rule is applicable to same-sex couples. Id.

8. *Policy*. Developments in this area raise several policy issues: With the abolition movement regarding actions for breach of promise, should the law also abolish actions for recovery of gifts given in contemplation of marriage and let the loss fall where it lies? Are remedies of the marketplace appropriate for courtship controversies? Should courts refuse to intrude on this private matter?

Problems

1. At an engagement party, Gina Bruno's father gives his daughter and her fiancé $28,000 for the reception and other wedding expenses. The couple receives additional gifts totaling $5,000, which they deposit in a joint savings account. When the fiancé cancels the wedding the night before, Gina and her father (in a class action suit with all other donors at the engagement party) sue to recover the gifts. New York has anti-heart balm legislation. What result? See Bruno v. Guerra, 549 N.Y.S.2d 925 (Sup. Ct. 1990).

2. When plaintiff proposes, he tells defendant that the engagement ring is a gift for her birthday (on December 29th), Christmas, and their engagement. They sign a lease and buy furniture. Plaintiff thereafter confesses that he does not love plaintiff anymore and breaks the engagement. When he arrives to pick up some furniture, defendant asks him to sign a receipt stating that there would be "no future contact between both parties or any request for other belongings." Plaintiff then brings an action to recover $5,490, including the cost of the engagement ring, couch, and television plus interest, first month's rent and security deposit, lost wages, and subway fares associated with the litigation. What result? See Maiorana v. Rojas, 787 N.Y.S.2d 678 (N.Y. City Civ. Ct. 2004).

3. A woman is killed in a plane crash caused by her fiancé's negligence. The fiancé removes her engagement ring at the scene of the accident. The executor of her estate sues to recover the ring or its value. Should the executor prevail? See In re Hahn v. United States, 535 F. Supp. 132 (D.S.D. 1982). See also Matter of Estate of Lowe, 379 N.W.2d 485 (Mich. Ct. App. 1985).

C. PREMARITAL CONTRACTS

■ SIMEONE v. SIMEONE
581 A.2d 162 (Pa. 1990)

FLAHERTY, Justice.

At issue in this appeal is the validity of a prenuptial agreement executed between the appellant, Catherine E. Walsh Simeone, and the appellee, Frederick A. Simeone. At the time of their marriage, in 1975, appellant was a twenty-three-year-old nurse and appellee was a thirty-nine-year-old neurosurgeon. Appellee had an income of approximately $90,000 per year, and appellant was unemployed. Appellee also had assets worth approximately $300,000. On the eve of the parties' wedding, appellee's attorney presented appellant with a prenuptial agreement to be signed. Appellant, without the benefit of counsel, signed the agreement. Appellee's attorney had not advised appellant regarding any legal rights that the agreement surrendered. The parties are in disagreement as to whether appellant knew in advance of that date that such an agreement would be presented for signature. . . .

The agreement limited appellant to support payments of $200 per week in the event of separation or divorce, subject to a maximum total payment of $25,000. The parties separated in 1982, and, in 1984, divorce proceedings were commenced. Between 1982 and 1984 appellee made payments which satisfied the $25,000 limit. In 1985, appellant filed a claim for alimony pendente lite [during the litigation]. [The Superior Court affirmed a special master's denial of her claim, 551 A.2d 219 (Pa. 1988)].

We granted allowance of appeal because uncertainty was expressed by the Superior Court regarding the meaning of our plurality decision in Estate of Geyer, 516 Pa. 492, 533 A.2d 423 (1987). The Superior Court viewed *Geyer* as permitting a prenuptial agreement to be upheld if it either made a reasonable provision for the spouse or was entered after a full and fair disclosure of the general financial positions of the parties and the statutory rights being relinquished. Appellant contends that this interpretation of *Geyer* is in error insofar as it requires disclosure of statutory rights only in cases where there has not been made a reasonable provision for the spouse. Inasmuch as the courts below held that the provision made for appellant was a reasonable one, appellant's efforts to overturn the agreement have focused upon an assertion that there was an inadequate disclosure of statutory rights. Appellant continues to assert, however, that the payments provided in the agreement were less than reasonable.

The statutory rights in question are those relating to alimony pendente lite. . . . The present agreement [expressly stated] that alimony pendente lite was being relinquished. It also recited that appellant "has been informed and understands" that, were it not for the agreement, appellant's obligation to pay alimony pendente lite "might, as a matter of law, exceed the amount provided." Hence, appellant's claim is not that the agreement failed to disclose the particular right affected, but rather that she was not adequately informed with respect to the nature of alimony pendente lite. . . .

There is no longer validity in the implicit presumption that supplied the basis for *Geyer* and similar earlier decisions. Such decisions rested upon a belief that spouses are of unequal status and that women are not knowledgeable enough to understand the nature of contracts that they enter. Society has advanced, however, to the point where women are no longer regarded as the "weaker" party in marriage, or in society generally. Indeed, the stereotype that women serve as homemakers while men work as breadwinners is no longer viable. Quite often today both spouses are income earners. Nor is there viability in the presumption that women are uninformed, uneducated, and readily subjected to unfair advantage in marital agreements. Indeed, women nowadays quite often have substantial education, financial awareness, income, and assets.

Accordingly, the law has advanced to recognize the equal status of men and women in our society. See, e.g., Pa. Const. art. 1, §28 (constitutional prohibition of sex discrimination in laws of the Commonwealth). Paternalistic presumptions and protections that arose to shelter women from the inferiorities and incapacities which they were perceived as having in earlier times have, appropriately, been discarded. It would be inconsistent, therefore, to perpetuate the standards governing prenuptial agreements that were described in *Geyer* and similar decisions, as these reflected a paternalistic approach that is now insupportable.

Further, *Geyer* and its predecessors embodied substantial departures from traditional rules of contract law, to the extent that they allowed consideration of the knowledge of the contracting parties and reasonableness of their bargain as factors governing whether to uphold an agreement. Traditional principles of contract law provide perfectly adequate remedies where contracts are procured through fraud, misrepresentation, or duress. Consideration of other factors, such as the knowledge of the parties and the reasonableness of their bargain, is inappropriate. Prenuptial agreements are contracts, and, as such, should be evaluated under the same criteria as are applicable to other types of contracts. Absent fraud, misrepresentation, or duress, spouses should be bound by the terms of their agreements.

Contracting parties are normally bound by their agreements, without regard to whether the terms thereof were read and fully understood and irrespective of whether the agreements embodied reasonable or good bargains. Based upon these principles, the terms of the present prenuptial agreement must be regarded as binding, without regard to whether the terms were fully understood by appellant. *Ignorantia non excusat.*

Accordingly, we find no merit in a contention raised by appellant that the agreement should be declared void on the ground that she did not consult with independent legal counsel. To impose a per se requirement that parties entering a prenuptial agreement must obtain independent legal counsel would be contrary to traditional principles of contract law, and would constitute a paternalistic and unwarranted interference with the parties' freedom to enter contracts.

Further, the reasonableness of a prenuptial bargain is not a proper subject for judicial review. . . . By invoking inquiries into reasonableness, . . . the functioning and reliability of prenuptial agreements is severely undermined. Parties would not have entered such agreements, and, indeed, might not have entered their marriages, if they did not expect their agreements to be strictly enforced. If parties viewed an agreement as reasonable at the time of its inception, as evidenced by their having signed the agreement, they should be foreclosed from later trying to evade its terms by asserting that it was not in fact reasonable. Pertinently, the present agreement contained a clause reciting that "each of the parties considers this agreement fair, just and reasonable. . . ."

Further, everyone who enters a long-term agreement knows that circumstances can change during its term, so that what initially appeared desirable might prove to be an unfavorable bargain. Such are the risks that contracting parties routinely assume. Certainly, the possibilities of illness, birth of children, reliance upon a spouse, career change, financial gain or loss, and numerous other events that can occur in the course of a marriage cannot be regarded as unforeseeable. If parties choose not to address such matters in their prenuptial agreements, they must be regarded as having contracted to bear the risk of events that alter the value of their bargains.

We are reluctant to interfere with the power of persons contemplating marriage to agree upon, and to act in reliance upon, what they regard as an acceptable distribution scheme for their property. A court should not ignore the parties' expressed intent by proceeding to determine whether a prenuptial agreement was, in the court's view, reasonable at the time of its inception or the time of divorce. These are exactly the sorts of judicial determinations that such agreements are designed to avoid. Rare indeed is the agreement that is beyond possible challenge when reasonableness is placed at issue. Parties can routinely assert some lack of fairness relating to the inception of the agreement, thereby placing the validity of the agreement at risk. And if reasonableness at the time of divorce were to be taken into account an additional problem would arise. Virtually nonexistent is the marriage in which there has been absolutely no change in the circumstances of either spouse during the course of the marriage. Every change in circumstance, foreseeable or not, and substantial or not, might be asserted as a basis for finding that an agreement is no longer reasonable.

In discarding the approach of *Geyer* that permitted examination of the reasonableness of prenuptial agreements and allowed inquiries into whether parties had attained informed understandings of the rights they were surrendering, we do not depart from the longstanding principle that a full and fair disclosure of the financial positions of the parties is required. . . . Parties to these agreements do not quite deal at arm's length, but rather at the time the contract is entered into stand in a relation of mutual confidence and trust that calls for disclosure of their financial resources. It is well settled that this disclosure need not be exact, so long as it is "full and fair." Kaufmann's Estate, 404 Pa. 131, 136 n.8, 171 A.2d 48, 51 n.8 (1961). In essence therefore, the duty of disclosure under these circumstances is consistent with traditional principles of contract law.

If an agreement provides that full disclosure has been made, a presumption of full disclosure arises. . . . The present agreement recited that full disclosure had been made, and included a list of appellee's assets totalling approximately $300,000. Appellant contends that this list understated by roughly $183,000, the value of a classic car collection which appellee had included at a value of $200,000. The master, reviewing the parties' conflicting testimony regarding the value of the car collection, found that appellant failed to prove by clear and convincing evidence that the value of the collection had been understated. . . . Appellant's contention is plainly without merit.

Appellant's final contention is that the agreement was executed under conditions of duress in that it was presented to her at 5 P.M. on the eve of her wedding, a time when she could not seek counsel without the trauma, expense, and embarrassment of postponing the wedding. . . . Although appellant testified that she did not discover until the eve of her wedding that there was going to be a prenuptial agreement, testimony from a number of other witnesses was to the contrary. Appellee testified that, although the final version of the agreement was indeed presented to appellant on the eve of the wedding, he had engaged in several discussions with appellant regarding the contents of the agreement during the six month period preceding that date. Another witness testified that appellant mentioned, approximately two or three weeks before the wedding, that she was going to enter a prenuptial agreement. Yet another witness confirmed that, during the months preceding the wedding, appellant participated in several discussions of prenuptial agreements. And the legal counsel who prepared the agreement for appellee testified that, prior to the eve of the wedding, changes were made in the agreement to increase the sums payable to appellant in the event of separation or divorce. . . . It should be noted, too, that during the months when the agreement was being discussed appellant had more than sufficient time to consult with independent legal counsel if she had so desired. Under these circumstances, there was plainly no error in finding that appellant failed to prove duress.

Hence, the courts below properly held that the present agreement is valid and enforceable. Appellant is barred, therefore, from receiving alimony pendente lite. . . .

McDermott, Justice, dissenting. . . .

I am not willing to believe that our society views marriage as a mere contract for hire. . . . Our courts must seek to protect, and not to undermine, those institutions and interests which are vital to our society. [W]hile I acknowledge the longstanding rule of law that prenuptial agreements are presumptively valid and binding upon the parties, I am unwilling to go as far as the majority to protect the right to contract at the expense of the institution of marriage. Were a contract of marriage, the most intimate relationship between two people, not the surrender of freedom, an offering of self in love, sacrifice, hope for better or for worse, the begetting of children and the offer of effort, labor, precious time and care for the safety and prosperity of their union, then the majority would find me among them. . . .

At the time of dissolution of the marriage, a spouse should be able to avoid the operation of a prenuptial agreement upon clear and convincing proof that, despite the existence of full and fair disclosure at the time of the execution of the agreement, the agreement is nevertheless so inequitable and unfair that it should not be enforced in a court of this state. . . .

[T]he passage of time accompanied by the intervening events of a marriage, may render the terms of the agreement completely unfair and inequitable. While parties to a prenuptial agreement may indeed foresee, generally, the events which may come to pass during their marriage, one spouse should not be made to suffer for failing to foresee all of the surrounding circumstances which may attend the dissolution of the marriage. Although it should not be the role of the courts to void prenuptial agreements merely because one spouse may receive a better result in an action under the Divorce Code to recover alimony or equitable distribution, it should be the role of the courts to guard against the enforcement of prenuptial agreements where such enforcement will bring about only inequity and hardship. It borders on cruelty to accept that after years of living together, yielding their separate opportunities in life to each other, that two individuals emerge the same as the day they began their marriage. . . .

■ BINEK v. BINEK
673 N.W.2d 594 (N.D. 2004)

VANDE WALLE, Chief Justice.

. . . Ruth and Theodore Binek were married on June 21, 1984. At the time of the marriage, Ruth Binek was fifty-two years old and Theodore Binek was sixty-one years old. It was the second marriage for both parties, and both had children from their prior marriages. Theodore Binek's net worth was approximately $600,000 and Ruth Binek's net worth was approximately $30,000. Theodore Binek presented a premarital agreement to Ruth Binek two days before the wedding by leaving it on a table at his home. [The agreement] mutually excluded each party from any property not brought into the marriage by that party, and required Theodore Binek to "provide usual and reasonable maintenance and support" during the marriage. It defined the "interest which each shall have in the estate of the other during the marriage and after the death of either one of them," and stated Ruth Binek would release all rights in Theodore Binek's property or estate which she might have by reason of their marriage. Theodore Binek stated he would not marry Ruth Binek if she did not sign the agreement. . . . Theodore Binek was represented by counsel at the time of the signing, but Ruth Binek was not.

Throughout the marriage, the parties abided by the terms of the agreement. The parties did not commingle their assets. Theodore Binek continued working at the Binek coal mine and Ruth Binek was a homemaker. Theodore Binek paid for most of the living expenses of the parties. In May 2002, Ruth Binek sought a divorce based on irreconcilable differences. At the time of trial, Theodore Binek was eighty-one years old and Ruth Binek was seventy-two years old. Theodore Binek's net worth was approximately $200,000 and Ruth Binek's $30,000 had been depleted as a result of loans made to her relatives, which she claims are not collectible. Ruth Binek is receiving $391 per month in social security and $300 per month in interim spousal support. Theodore Binek is retired and his income consists of approximately $900 per month in social security payments, $1,000 per year from rental property, and $2,000 to $3,000 per year from his photography hobby. [The trial court granted the divorce, enforced the premarital agreement, awarded Ruth the household goods and Theodore all other property.]

The enforceability of the premarital agreement between Ruth Binek and Theodore Binek is governed by common law. Although North Dakota adopted the Uniform Premarital Agreement Act ("UPAA") in 1985, it does not apply to this situation because it was enacted after the parties entered into the agreement and does not contain a provision declaring it applies retroactively. This Court has previously addressed the enforceability of premarital agreements entered into prior to the UPAA in cases involving the rights of a surviving spouse. [Charlson v. Charlson, 197 N.W. 778, 781 (N.D. 1924)] concluded it was proper for the trial court to consider the following when evaluating a premarital agreement:

whether the contract had been entered into with the utmost good faith; whether it was reasonable in its provisions; whether the prospective wife possessed full knowledge of the character and value of her intended husband's property or was chargeable with such knowledge; whether the prospective husband informed his fiancée fully with respect to all facts concerning his property; whether the antenuptial contract provided any reasonable provisions for the support of the wife in case of her survival; whether, upon all of the surrounding circumstances, the provisions made for the wife in the contract were grossly disproportionate to the means of the husband; and whether such inadequacy of provision in the contract was sufficient under all the circumstances to raise a presumption of fraudulent concealment that was not overcome by the proof in the record sufficient to show its absence.

Ruth Binek argues the agreement should not be enforced. She contends she did not enter into it voluntarily, it is unconscionable, and it does not apply to dissolution of the marriage by divorce. In effect, Ruth Binek contends the agreement is unenforceable because it is procedurally and substantively unfair. . . .

Procedurally, Ruth Binek contends she did not enter into the agreement voluntarily because it was presented to her two days before the wedding and Theodore Binek stated he would not marry her if she did not sign it; she was not represented by independent counsel; and she did not receive full financial disclosure. Although it would have been preferable to present the agreement to Ruth Binek more than two days before the wedding, this alone does not render the agreement unenforceable. Nor does the fact Theodore Binek would not have proceeded with the marriage make the agreement procedurally unfair. The purpose of the agreement was to keep the parties' property separate. When, as is the case here, the parties have been previously married and divorced, it is reasonable for one or both of them to seek protection of their property in a subsequent marriage.

The significance of the presentation and signing of the agreement is more relevant in determining whether Ruth Binek understood the agreement and had an opportunity to obtain independent legal advice.

> An agreement to marry can create a fiduciary relationship between individuals if they do not deal at arms length. Persons contracting about marriage are sometimes mismatched in bargaining power and sophistication. Unlike many private contracts, the state has an interest in every marriage contract. We agree with the view that lack of adequate legal advice to a prospective spouse to obtain independent counsel is a significant factual factor in weighing the voluntariness of a premarital agreement. Indeed, adequate legal representation will often be the best evidence that a spouse signed a premarital agreement knowledgeably and voluntarily.

[Lutz v. Lutz, 563 N.W.2d 90 (N.D. 1997) (*Lutz I*)] (citations omitted). However, "the presence of independent counsel is not a prerequisite to enforceability." In re Estate of Lutz, 620 N.W.2d 589 (N.D. 2000) (*Lutz II*). The parties' marriage took place on Thursday, June 21, 1984. Ruth Binek testified Theodore Binek did not do anything to prevent her from consulting an attorney or asking questions prior to signing the agreement. She testified she understood the purpose of the agreement was Theodore Binek's property would remain his and her property would remain hers and, if the parties had gotten divorced after one year, she would have abided by the agreement. Additionally, she testified it was entirely her decision whether to sign the agreement and she voluntarily did so. We conclude Ruth Binek was not deprived of an opportunity to consult independent counsel and understood the effect of the agreement when she signed it.

Ruth Binek contends the agreement should not be enforced because Theodore Binek did not fully disclose the extent of his assets to her before she signed the agreement. The agreement contains a full disclosure clause which states, "each party is possessed of real and personal properties, the nature and extent of which has been fully disclosed by each to the other." In other jurisdictions, a full disclosure clause has been held to create a rebuttable presumption of full disclosure. See Simeone v. Simeone, 525 Pa. 392, 581 A.2d 162, 167 (Pa.1990). In the present case, Ruth Binek testified that before she signed the agreement she knew Theodore Binek owned the Binek coal mine and the equipment thereon, guessed he owned his house, and had been told by her family that he was worth over a million dollars. Further, she testified that Theodore Binek stated he had $600,000; she knew he was worth a substantial amount of money; and she "knew he owned more than [she] did." . . . Based on this testimony, we conclude Ruth Binek was sufficiently aware of Theodore Binek's financial situation when she signed the agreement. Therefore, we hold the premarital agreement was entered into fairly.

Substantively, Ruth Binek contends the agreement is unconscionable because she did not receive full financial disclosure and the effect of enforcing it is to place her on public assistance. Ruth Binek's contention that the agreement is unconscionable because Theodore Binek did not provide a full financial disclosure is not convincing based on our conclusion that Ruth Binek was sufficiently aware of Theodore Binek's financial situation. Unconscionability of a premarital agreement is a matter of law, but it turns on factual findings related to the relative property values, the parties' financial circumstances, and their ongoing need. Under the UPAA, if a premarital agreement causes a party to be eligible for public assistance by eliminating or modifying spousal support, a court may require the other party to provide support to the extent necessary to avoid eligibility of the other for public assistance. . . .

North Dakota case law regarding premarital agreements entered into prior to adoption of the UPAA did not address when unconscionability should be considered. Courts applying the common law have considered unconscionability of a premarital agreement at both the time of execution of the agreement and the time of dissolution of the marriage. . . . This agreement was not unconscionable at the time it was executed. It provided a means for Ruth Binek to keep her own assets and allow them to grow, and Theodore Binek was obligated to support Ruth Binek throughout the marriage. The agreement is not unconscionable at the time of enforcement because it did not govern the parties' rights regarding spousal support. . . . By not addressing spousal support and allowing Ruth Binek to keep her assets separate from Theodore Binek's, the agreement created enough leeway to avoid an unconscionable result based upon the parties' circumstances at the time of dissolution. We hold this premarital agreement is not unconscionable.

Ruth Binek contends the agreement does not apply to a dissolution of the marriage by divorce [but only to death, by providing for the release of all rights in the property or estate of Theodore "by reason of their marriage, whether by way of dower, statutory allowance, widow's allowance, intestate share, or election to take against his will, under the laws of this or any other jurisdiction."] Ruth Binek released all rights she had in Theodore Binek's property which arose out of the marriage. Any rights in the property she would acquire as a result of a property settlement upon divorce would be rights arising out of the marriage. Therefore, the agreement applies to property rights Ruth Binek may have acquired from a divorce decree. . . .

[Finally] Ruth Binek contends the trial court erred by failing to award her spousal support. . . . From this record, we cannot determine whether the trial court denied Ruth Binek spousal support because of the premarital agreement or [state spousal support] guidelines. We conclude the agreement only affects distribution of the couple's property in the form of a property distribution as a result of divorce and does not preclude an award of spousal support. . . . We affirm the trial court's decision enforcing the premarital agreement because it is fair, equitable, reasonable, and just; does not contravene public policy; and was executed fairly. However, because the agreement did not govern the parties' rights to spousal support and the trial court did not sufficiently explain its rationale for denying Ruth Binek spousal support, we reverse and remand for further proceedings in accordance with this opinion.

Notes and Questions

1. *Popularity.* Premarital (also "antenuptial" or "prenuptial") agreements generally limit spousal property rights in the event of dissolution and death. The use of such agreements has risen dramatically in the past few decades. See Donna Beck Weaver, The Collaborative Law Process for Prenuptial Agreements, 4 Pepp. Disp. Resol. L.J. 337, 337 (2004) (citing data revealing that the use of premarital agreements has quintupled in the last 20 years and that 20 percent of remarried couples resort to them). Their increasing popularity stems, in part, from high rates of divorce, remarriage, cohabitation, and also the delayed marriage age. Allison A. Marston, Note, Planning for Love: The Politics of Prenuptial Agreements, 49 Stan. L. Rev. 887, 888 (1997).

2. *Modern view.* The law's treatment of premarital agreements, as *Binek* reveals, combines traditional contract principles respecting private ordering with family law principles of equitable distribution. Prior to the 1970s, courts held these agreements violative of public policy as an inducement to divorce. Courts also feared that a dependent spouse might become a public charge. Contemporary courts regard such agreements more favorably.

3. *Ordinary contracts distinguished.* How do premarital agreements differ from ordinary contracts? Professor Judith Younger notes:

> The first difference is the subject matter. These agreements typically deal with one of, or a combination of, three things: property and support rights during and after marriage; the personal rights and obligations of the spouses during marriage; or the education, care, and rearing of children who may later be born to the marrying couple. These subjects are of greater interest to the state than the subjects of ordinary commercial contract; the state wishes to protect the welfare of the couple and their children during and after marriage, and to preserve the privacy of the family relationship. . . .
>
> The second difference is the relationship of the parties to each other. It is a confidential relationship involving parties who are usually not evenly matched in bargaining power. The possibility, therefore, that one party may overreach the other is greater than in the case of ordinary contracts.

The third difference is the fact that antenuptial agreements are to be performed in the future, in the context of a relationship which the parties have not yet begun and which may continue for many years after the agreement is executed and before it is enforced. The possibility that later events may make it unwise, unfair, or otherwise undesirable to enforce such agreements is also greater than in the case of ordinary contracts.

Judith T. Younger, Perspectives on Antenuptial Agreements: An Update, 8 Am. Acad. Matrim. Law. 1, 3-4 (1992). See also Judith T. Younger, A Minnesota Comparative Family Law Symposium: Antenuptial Agreements, 28 Wm. Mitchell L. Rev. 687 (2001).

4. *Requirements. Simeone* and *Binek* reflect different approaches. *Simeone*, out of deference to private ordering, treats such agreements as ordinary contracts. *Binek* underscores the need for special protection. Further, *Simeone* rejects an examination of substantive fairness whereas *Binek* requires both substantive fairness (at execution of the agreement and dissolution) and procedural fairness (that is, the agreement be entered into voluntarily and with full disclosure).

Some courts adopt yet a third approach. They consider substantive and procedural fairness as alternative requirements, requiring that substantive fairness be present before a court will examine the agreement for procedural fairness. See, e.g., In re Marriage of Spiegel, 553 N.W.2d 309, 315 (Iowa 1996).

Why does *Simeone* reject judicial review of reasonableness? Should intent control? Should a recitation of reasonableness in the agreement serve as a presumption of fairness? Or are premarital agreements "in the nature of contracts of adhesion" (as an omitted concurrence in *Simeone* states)?

Why did the plaintiff in *Binek* contend the prenuptial agreement was invalid? What did the court respond? Why did the court determine that the Bineks' agreement affected the distribution of property but not spousal support? How would the *Simeone* court address this issue?

a. *Unconscionability.* The Uniform Premarital Agreement Act (UPAA), 9C U.L.A. 35 (2001), although requiring both procedural and substantive fairness, sets a higher standard than *Binek* for substantive unfairness. UPAA requires "unconscionability" to invalidate a premarital agreement.

§6. (a) A premarital agreement is not enforceable if the party against whom enforcement is sought proves that:
(1) that party did not execute the agreement voluntarily; or
(2) the agreement was unconscionable when it was executed and, before execution of the agreement, that party:
(i) was not provided a fair and reasonable disclosure of the property or financial obligations of the other party;
(ii) did not voluntarily and expressly waive, in writing, any right to disclosure of the property or financial obligations of the other party beyond the disclosure provided; and
(iii) did not have, or reasonably could not have had, an adequate knowledge of the property or financial obligations of the other party.

b. *ALI Principles.* Under rules approved by the American Law Institute, premarital agreements must meet standards of procedural fairness (i.e., informed consent and disclosure) and substantive fairness. A rebuttable presumption arises that the agreement satisfies the informed consent requirement if (1) it was executed at least 30 days prior to the marriage; (2) both parties had, or were advised to obtain, counsel and had the opportunity to do so; and (3) if one of the parties did not have counsel, the agreement contained understandable information about the parties' rights and the adverse nature of their interests. ALI, Principles of the Law of Family Dissolution: Analysis and Recommendations §7.04 (3)(a)(b) & (c)(2002). Finally, the court must undertake a review of substantive fairness at the time of enforcement, specifically regarding whether enforcement would work a "substantial injustice" based on the passage of time, the presence of children, or changed circumstances that were unanticipated and would have a significant impact on the parties or their children. Id. at §7.05. Which approach do you favor?

5. *Time of determination.* If substantive fairness should be considered, should it be determined as of execution and/or enforcement? Compare the approaches in *Simeone* and *Binek* with those of the UPAA and ALI Principles, supra. The dissent in *Simeone* suggests (in an omitted section) that the following circumstances on dissolution might lead to invalidation of a premarital agreement: (1) a spouse's diminished employment prospects if that spouse remained home due to family responsibilities, such that the spouse would become a public charge or suffer a significantly reduced standard of living; (2) a dependent spouse in a long-term marriage who helped increase the value of the other's property; (3) an unanticipated serious illness rendering the spouse unable to provide self-support. See also Mazzitelli v. Mazzitelli, 2005 WL 221683 (Minn. Ct. App. 2005) (holding that premarital agreement was substantively unfair at time of enforcement because the parties' reasonable expectations did not include wife's absence from work force for almost ten years to raise children while husband amassed substantial assets). Many courts (and the UPAA) provide that a premarital agreement will not be enforced at divorce if it would render one spouse a public charge. See, e.g., Blue v. Blue, 60 S.W.3d 585, 590 (Ky. Ct. App. 2001). For different views regarding the time of the fairness determination, compare Melvin A. Eisenberg, The Limits of Cognition and the Limits of Contract, 47 Stan. L. Rev. 211, 254 (1995) (arguing that the limits of foreseeability provide a strong justification for a fairness review at divorce), with Rebecca Glass, Comment, Trading Up: Postnuptial Agreements, Fairness, and a Principled New Suitor for California, 92 Calif. L. Rev. 215, 251 (2004) (arguing that assessing fairness only at the time of execution encourages both enforceability and predictability).

6. *Relative bargaining power.* Simeone rests, in part, on the rationale that prospective spouses are on equal footing. Did the parties in *Simeone* have equal bargaining power? What relevance should a court attach to such factors as age, financial position, business acumen, obtaining (or rejecting) legal advice, the selection of counsel by the defendant, or previous divorce? Should parties be required to consult independent counsel? Do such inquiries improperly presume that women need special protection? See generally Brian Bix, Premarital Agreements in the ALI Principles of Family Dissolution, 8 Duke J. Gender L. & Pol'y 231, 232 (2001).

One commentator proposes a radical solution to the gendered aspects of premarital contracting. Noting that premarital agreements invariably benefit the party who has more cash, Professor Katharine Silbaugh urges that monetary premarital agreements should not be enforced or, at least, treated with extreme skepticism in order to "properly value unpaid family labor" (i.e., protect the more vulnerable party). Katharine B. Silbaugh, Marriage Contracts and the Family Economy, 93

Nw. U. L. Rev. 65, 142 (1998). What do you think of her suggestion? Compare Howard Fink & June Carbone, Between Private Ordering and Public Fiat: A New Paradigm for Family Law Decision-Making, 5 J. L. & Fam. Stud. 1, 27-28 (2003) (criticizing Silbaugh's argument on three grounds: not applying to all premarital bargains, leading the wealthier party not to marry, and forestalling premarital planning). One commentator goes so far as to suggest that premarital contracts should be mandatory. See Jeffrey Evans Stake, Mandatory Planning for Divorce, 45 Vand. L. Rev. 397 (1992). Do you agree?

7. *Timing of agreement.* The plaintiff in *Simeone* claims duress based on the proximity of the execution of the agreement to the wedding. Should the time period in which a party has to reflect before signing the agreement be relevant? Should statutes require execution of premarital agreements a minimum amount of time before marriage? See, e.g., Minn. Stat. Ann. §519.11 (West 1990 & Supp. 2005) (prior to day of marriage). Is this sound policy? For succession purposes, some jurisdictions hold that those inter vivos conveyances of one spouse that defeat the share of the surviving spouse, if made within a short period before death, are "illusory" and presumptively void. See, e.g., Newman v. Dore, 9 N.E.2d 266 (N.Y. 1937). Should the same presumption apply to set aside premarital agreements executed a short time before marriage?

8. *Disclosure.* What do *Simeone* and *Binek* require in terms of disclosure? Is this synonymous with "detailed" disclosure? Should courts require an attached list of assets? See Cannon v. Cannon, 865 A.2d 563 (Md. 2005) (rejecting idea). Require disclosure of annual income? See Mallen v. Mallen, 622 S.E.2d 812 (Ga. 2005) (rejecting idea).

9. *Confidential relationship.* Many courts take the view that the prospective spouses have a confidential relationship. Compare *Binek* with Pite v. Pite, 2001 WL 238144 (Conn. Super. Ct. 2001) (holding that general knowledge of party's finances is insufficient to satisfy full disclosure necessitated by the confidential relationship between prospective spouses). What difference does it make?

10. *Scope.* UPAA supports a wide latitude regarding prospective spouses' contractual freedom. Among the permissible areas for premarital agreements, UPAA specifies "any other matter, including personal rights and obligations, not in violation of public policy or a statute imposing a criminal penalty." Id. at §3(a). The comment enumerates permissible examples as choice of abode, the freedom to pursue career opportunities, and the upbringing of children. Does this provision interfere with the doctrine of family privacy?

According to the general rule, premarital agreements may not restrict judicial discretion regarding either child custody or child support because of the state's concern with child welfare. One commentator argues that states should permit premarital agreements regarding child custody "so long as the child will not be harmed." Linda Jellum, Parents Know Best: Revising Our Approach to Parental Custody Agreements, 65 Ohio St. L.J. 615, 617 (2004). What do you think of this proposal? See also UPAA §3(b), 9C U.L.A. 43 (2001) (setting forth limitation regarding child support).

Suppose you are about to marry (or to begin a committed relationship). What roles, responsibilities, and other decisions might you want to allocate? Support? Property rights? Names? Employment and its consequences? Domicile? Responsibilities for birth control? Number of children? Parenting responsibilities? Draft an agreement to govern your relationship. Assuming you and your partner reach a satisfactory agreement, should the courts enforce it?

Should the law enforce the following provisions in antenuptial agreements?

a. a parent shall not interfere, in the presence of the children, in punishments by the other parent (e.g., Ball v. Ball, 36 So. 2d 172, 174 (Fla. 1948));

b. children born of the marriage shall attend public school (id.);

c. sexual intercourse shall be limited to only once per week (e.g., Favrot v. Barnes, 332 So. 2d 873, 875 (La. App.), *rev'd on other grounds*, 339 So. 2d 843 (La. 1976);

d. the husband shall reside in a certain locale after the marriage (e.g., Isaacs v. Isaacs, 99 N.W. 268 (Neb. 1904));

e. the husband's mother shall live with the parties (e.g., Koch v. Koch, 232 A.2d 157 (N.J. Super. Ct. App. Div. 1967));

f. the children of the wife's prior marriage shall not live in the household (e.g., Mengal v. Mengal, 103 N.Y.S.2d 992 (Fam. Ct. 1951)).

g. each spouse must undergo counseling before seeking a divorce and, in addition, is precluded from divorce unless fault grounds are present or a two-year separation has occurred (see Chapter V, section D3b, Covenant Marriage);

h. if the husband obtains a no-fault divorce from the wife, he must pay her $15,000/month for five years, but if the husband divorces the wife on fault grounds, she pays him $5,000/month for two years (see Kathleen B. Vetrano, Controlling Behavior Through Divorce Penalties in a Prenuptial?, 15 Fair Share (No. 4) 21 (April 1995));

i. upon divorce, any children) shall spend equal residential time with both parents (e.g., In re Marriage of Littlefield, 940 P.2d 1362 (Wash. 1997) (en banc));

j. the parties shall forgo having children (e.g., Height v. Height, 187 N.Y.S.2d 260 (Sup. Ct. 1959)) (see generally Joline F. Sikaitis, Comment: A New Form of Family Planning? The Enforceability of No-Child Provisions in Prenuptial Agreements, 54 Cath. U.L. Rev. 335 (2004));

k. the wife will receive one half of the husband's property upon divorce only if the parties remain married ten years or more; if the marriage ends sooner, she will receive only 25 percent. See Ray Jordan, People, St. Louis-Post Dispatch, Jan. 21, 2005, at A2 (describing Donald Trump's decision to file for divorce from Marla Maples shortly before their fourth anniversary to evade a similar durational provision in their prenuptial agreement). For another unusual celebrity prenuptial agreement, see Kevin West, Cashing Out: Breaking Up Is Hard to Do, But Splitting the Loot Can Be Even Harder, Money Mag., Dec. 1, 2003 (describing actor Michael Douglas's agreement with Catherine Zeta-Jones, providing that she would receive, upon divorce, one million dollars for each year of the marriage, and a $5 million "bonus" if he had an affair).

Problem

Major league baseball player Barry Bonds meets Susann ("Sun") in Montreal in the summer of 1987 after she emigrates from Sweden. Both are 23 years of age. At the time, Sun is working as a waitress and bartender, training as a beautician and planning a career as a makeup artist for the rich and famous. By January 1988, the two take up residence at Barry's home in Phoenix, Arizona, and decide to marry. Barry is earning $106,000. The day before the wedding, at the offices of Barry's lawyers, the couple signs a premarital contract by which each waives any interest in the earnings and acquisitions obtained by the other during the marriage. Barry's attorneys advise Sun to retain counsel, but she declines. The attorneys read the agreement to her paragraph by paragraph, explaining that she will be waiving her community property rights. After a six-year marriage, Barry petitions for dissolution in California where he now resides. At the time, Barry is earning $8 million annually. Sun, who has custody of the couple's two children, is awarded child support of $10,000 per month per child, and spousal support of $10,000 per month for a four-year period.

Sun argues that the premarital agreement was not executed voluntarily. She claims that she did not understand the terms of the agreement because of her limited English skills. She also asserts that she believed the agreement pertained only to property that was owned prior to the marriage. Barry's attorneys later testify that she understood the agreement and did not appear pressured or confused but rather seemed confident and happy. What result? Is legal counsel essential to the enforceability of premarital contracts? How relevant is a party's waiver of legal counsel? See In re Marriage of Bonds, 5 P.3d 815 (Cal. 2000). Suppose Sun argues that the agreement is unconscionable because of drastically changed circumstances (i.e., Barry's increased wealth). What result? See Blue v. Blue, 60 S.W. 3d 585 (Ky. Ct. App. 2001) (husband's wealth increased from $5 million to $77 million during 11-year marriage).

In response to *Bonds*, supra, the California legislature enacts a statute providing: "Any provision in a premarital agreement regarding spousal support, including, but not limited to, a waiver of it, is not enforceable if the party against whom enforcement of the spousal support provision is sought was not represented by independent counsel at the time the agreement containing the provision was signed, or if the provision regarding spousal support is unconscionable at the time of enforcement." Cal. Fam. Code §1612(c) (West 2004). If this statute had been in effect prior to the *Bonds* case, how would the case have been decided?

D. GETTING MARRIED: SUBSTANTIVE AND PROCEDURAL REGULATIONS

1. Constitutional Limits on State Regulation of Entry into Marriage

■ **LOVING v. VIRGINIA**
388 U.S. 1 (1967)

Mr. Chief Justice WARREN delivered the opinion of the Court.

This case presents a constitutional question never addressed by this Court: whether a statutory scheme adopted by the State of Virginia to prevent marriages between persons solely on the basis of racial classifications violates the Equal Protection and Due Process Clauses of the Fourteenth Amendment. . . .

In June 1958, two residents of Virginia, Mildred Jeter, a Negro woman, and Richard Loving, a white man, were married in the District of Columbia pursuant to its laws. Shortly after their marriage, the Lovings returned to Virginia and established their marital abode in Caroline County. [A] grand jury issued an indictment charging the Lovings with violating Virginia's ban on interracial marriages. [T]he Lovings pleaded guilty to the charge and were sentenced to one year in jail; however, the trial judge suspended the sentence for a period of 25 years on the condition that the Lovings leave the State and not return to Virginia together for 25 years. He stated in an opinion that:

> Almighty God created the races white, black, yellow, malay and red, and he placed them on separate continents. And but for the interference with his arrangement there would be no cause for such marriages. The fact that he separated the races shows that he did not intend for the races to mix. . . .

Virginia is now one of 16 States which prohibit and punish marriages on the basis of racial classifications. Penalties for miscegenation arose as an incident to slavery and have been common in Virginia since the colonial period. The present statutory scheme dates from the adoption of the Racial Integrity Act of 1924, passed during the period of extreme nativism which followed the end of the First World War. The central features of this Act, and current Virginia law, are the absolute prohibition of a "white person" marrying other than another "white person," a prohibition against issuing marriage licenses until the issuing official is satisfied that the applicants' statements as to their race are correct, certificates of "racial composition" to be kept by both local and state registrars [and a penalty of one to five years imprisonment].

In upholding the constitutionality of these provisions in the decision below, the Supreme Court of Appeals of Virginia referred to its 1955 decision in Naim v. Naim, 197 Va. 80, 87 S.E.2d 749, as stating the reasons supporting the validity of these laws. In *Naim*, the state court concluded that the State's legitimate purposes were "to preserve the racial integrity of its citizens," and to prevent "the corruption of blood," "a mongrel breed of citizens," and "the obliteration of racial pride," obviously an endorsement of the doctrine of White Supremacy. The court also reasoned that marriage has traditionally been subject to state regulation without federal intervention, and, consequently, the regulation of marriage should be left to exclusive state control by the Tenth Amendment.

[T]he State contends that, because its miscegenation statutes punish equally both the white and the Negro participants in an interracial marriage, these statutes, despite their reliance on racial classifications do not constitute an invidious discrimination based upon race. The second argument . . . is that, if the Equal Protection Clause does not outlaw miscegenation statutes because of their reliance on racial classifications, the question of constitutionality would thus become whether there was any rational basis for a State to treat interracial marriages differently from other marriages. On this question, the State argues, the scientific evidence is substantially in doubt and, consequently, this Court should defer to the wisdom of the state legislature in adopting its policy of discouraging interracial marriages.

Because we reject the notion that the mere "equal application" of a statute containing racial classifications is enough to remove the classifications from the Fourteenth Amendment's proscription of all invidious racial discriminations, we do not accept the State's contention that these statutes should be upheld if there is any possible basis for concluding that they serve a rational purpose. . . . The clear and central purpose of the Fourteenth Amendment was to eliminate all official state sources of invidious racial discrimination in the States.

There can be no question but that Virginia's miscegenation statutes rest solely upon distinctions drawn according to race. The statutes proscribe generally accepted conduct if engaged in by members of different races. Over the years, this Court has consistently repudiated "(d)istinctions between citizens solely because of their ancestry" as being "odious to a free people whose institutions are founded upon the doctrine of equality." Hirabayashi v. United States, 320 U.S. 81, 100 (1943). At the very least, the Equal Protection Clause demands that racial classifications, especially suspect in criminal statutes, be subjected to the "most rigid scrutiny," Korematsu v. United States, 323 U.S. 214, 216 (1944), and, if they are ever to be upheld, they must be shown to be necessary to the accomplishment of some permissible state objective, independent of the racial discrimination which it was the object of the Fourteenth Amendment to eliminate. . . .

There is patently no legitimate overriding purpose independent of invidious racial discrimination which justifies the classification. The fact that Virginia prohibits only interracial marriages involving white persons demonstrates that the racial classifications must stand on their own justification, as measures designed to maintain White Supremacy. We have consistently denied the constitutionality of measures which restrict the rights of citizens on account of race. There can be no doubt that restricting the freedom to marry solely because of racial classifications violates the central meaning of the Equal Protection Clause.

These statutes also deprive the Lovings of liberty without due process of law in violation of the Due Process Clause of the Fourteenth Amendment. The freedom to marry has long been recognized as one of the vital personal rights essential to the orderly pursuit of happiness by free men.

Marriage is one of the "basic civil rights of man," fundamental to our very existence and survival. Skinner v. State of Oklahoma, 316 U.S. 535, 541 (1942). See also Maynard v. Hill, 125 U.S. 190 (1888). To deny this fundamental freedom on so unsupportable a basis as the racial classifications embodied in these statutes, classifications so directly subversive of the principle of equality at the heart of the Fourteenth Amendment, is surely to deprive all the State's citizens of liberty without due process of law. The Fourteenth Amendment requires that the freedom of choice to marry not be restricted by invidious racial discriminations. Under our Constitution, the freedom to marry or not marry, a person of another race resides with the individual and cannot be infringed by the State.

These convictions must be reversed. . . .

■ **ROBERT A. PRATT, CROSSING THE COLOR LINE: A HISTORICAL ASSESSMENT AND PERSONAL NARRATIVE OF LOVING V. VIRGINIA**
41 How. L.J. 229, 234-244 (1998)

. . . Richard Perry Loving and Mildred Delores Jeter had known each other practically all of their lives, as their families lived just up the road from each other in the rural community of Central Point, Virginia, located in Caroline County. . . . For twenty-three years, Richard's father had defied the racial mores of southern white society by working for Boyd Byrd, one of the wealthiest black farmers in the community. [T]he close-knit nature of their community [led] to an acceptance of personal relationships in a particular setting that would have been anathema elsewhere. So when white Richard Loving, age seventeen, began courting "colored" Mildred Jeter, age eleven, their budding romance drew little attention from either the white or the black communities.

Mildred (part-black and part-Cherokee) had a pretty light-brown complexion accentuated by her slim figure, which was why practically everyone who knew her called her "Stringbean" or "Bean" for short. Richard (part-English and part-Irish) was a bricklayer by trade, but spent much of his spare time drag racing a car that he co-owned with two black friends, Raymond Green (a mechanic) and Percy Fortune (a local merchant). Despite their natural shyness, both Richard and Mildred were well-liked in the community, and the fact that they attended different churches and different schools did not hinder their courtship. When he was twenty-four and she was eighteen, Richard and Mildred decided to legalize their relationship by getting married.

Mildred did not know that interracial marriage was illegal in Virginia, but Richard did. This explains why, on June 2, 1958, he drove them across the Virginia state line to Washington, D.C., to be married. . . . Mr. and Mrs. Loving returned to Central Point to live with Mildred's parents; however, their marital bliss was short-lived. Five weeks later, on July 11, their quiet life was shattered when they were awakened early in the morning as three law officers "acting on an anonymous tip" opened the unlocked door of their home, walked into their bedroom, and shined a flashlight in their faces. Caroline County Sheriff R. Garnett Brooks demanded to know what the two of them were doing in bed together. Mildred answered, "I'm his wife," while Richard pointed to the District of Columbia marriage certificate that hung on their bedroom wall. "That's no good here," Sheriff Brooks replied. He charged the couple with unlawful cohabitation, and then he and his two deputies hauled the Lovings off to a nearby jail in Bowling Green.

[After their conviction and suspended sentences, the Lovings moved to Washington, D.C., where they had three children: Sidney in 1958, Donald in 1959, and Peggy in 1960.] The years in Washington were not happy ones for the couple. Richard struggled to maintain permanent employment while Mildred busied herself tending to the needs of their three children. "I missed being with my family and friends, especially Garnet [her sister]. I wanted my children to grow up in the country, where they could run and play, and where I wouldn't worry about them so much. I never liked much about the city."

Virginia law would not allow Richard and Mildred Loving [to be] in the state at the same time; however, that did not stop them from trying or from succeeding on various occasions. Mildred and the children made frequent visits to Battery, Virginia, the rural black community where her sister and brother-in-law lived. When Mildred would arrive in Battery, some of the neighbors would begin to look at their watches to see how long it would be before Richard's car came cruising through the neighborhood. During those early years, Richard's visits . . . occurred almost exclusively after dark. . . .

The Lovings had not really been that interested in the civil rights movement, nor had they ever given much thought to challenging Virginia's law. But with a major civil rights bill being debated in Congress in 1963, Mildred decided to write to Robert Kennedy, the Attorney General of the United States. The Department of Justice referred the letter to the American Civil Liberties Union. Bernard S. Cohen, a young lawyer doing pro bono work for the ACLU in Alexandria, Virginia, agreed to take the case. He would later be joined by another young attorney, Philip J. Hirschkop. . . .

On December 12, 1966, the U.S. Supreme Court agreed to hear the case. . . . In concluding his oral argument on April 10, 1967, Cohen relayed a message to the Justices from Richard Loving: "Tell the Court I love my wife, and it is just unfair that I can't live with her in Virginia." . . .

Thirty years have passed since the Supreme Court decided to validate Richard Loving's marriage to Mildred Jeter, and social attitudes regarding interracial marriage have undergone a major transformation. . . . But that sentiment is still far from universal. When he was interviewed in 1992 on the twenty-fifth anniversary of the decision, Sheriff Brooks made no apologies for having arrested the Lovings in 1958: "I was acting according to the law at the time, and I still think it should be on the books. I don't think a white person should marry a black person. I'm from the old school. The Lord made sparrows and robins, not to mix with one another." . . .

Mildred Loving, at age 58, remains the same intensely shy woman she has always been. [S]he still sees herself as an ordinary black woman who fell in love with an ordinary white man. . . . Mildred puts it this way:

> We weren't bothering anyone. And if we hurt some people's feelings, that was just too bad. All we ever wanted was to get married, because we loved each other. Some people will never change, but that's their problem, not mine. I married the only man I had ever loved, and I'm happy for the time we had together. For me, that was enough.

■ PHYL NEWBECK, VIRGINIA HASN'T ALWAYS BEEN FOR LOVERS: INTERRACIAL MARRIAGE BANS AND THE CASE OF RICHARD AND MILDRED LOVING
214-220 (2004)

"I feel free now," said Mildred, when told of the Supreme Court decision. [At] the press conference hastily called to celebrate the verdict, Mildred truly looked as though a burden had been lifted. Richard, clad in an open-necked button-down white shirt, looked as though the conference was just one more ordeal that he had to go through. With his ruddy face and crew cut, he appeared profoundly uncomfortable, barely opening his mouth to answer questions. The truth is that left to his own devices, Richard never would have attended the conference, but Mildred had persuaded him to make an appearance after she herself had been convinced by Phil Hirschkop [one of their lawyers] of the importance of the occasion. Grudgingly, Richard told reporters that the hardest thing he had had to endure was leaving his home. In what may have been the only disagreement between the two, Mildred shook her head and said that the hardest part for her had been going to jail. As soon as they could, the couple moved back to Central Point, where Richard built a simple, cinder-block house just up the street from both of their parents, on Passing Road.

It would be gratifying to conclude that Mildred and Richard lived happily ever after, but that was not the case. While the couple was living in neighboring King and Queen County, a cross was burned in the yard of Mildred's mother. Mildred assumes it was meant for her. Another cross burning took place on the couple's lawn shortly after their initial return to Caroline County. The reception in general was not openly hostile, despite a local law enforcement official's belief that public sentiment was opposed to the marriage. The young couple simply blended in with their neighbors and were accepted as such. . . .

Less than a month after the Lovings' fourteenth anniversary and slightly more than eight years after they had earned the right to live as husband and wife in Virginia, Richard was killed. The couple and Mildred's sister Garnet were returning from a visit with friends when their car was broadsided by a drunk driver who had run a stop sign on route 721 in Caroline County, just thirteen miles from their home. Richard, forty-two, died instantly. Mildred lost her right eye, and Garnet suffered minor injuries. There was a tremendous outpouring of sympathy from the community for this woman who, not so long before, had been an exile from the state. . . . Richard is buried in a mostly black graveyard just outside the local Baptist church. Even in death, he refused to be bound by the laws of segregation. . . .

■ ZABLOCKI v. REDHAIL
434 U.S. 374 (1978)

Justice MARSHALL delivered the opinion of the Court.

At issue in this case is the constitutionality of a Wisconsin statute, Wis. Stat. §245.10(1), (4), (5)(1973), which provides that members of a certain class of Wisconsin residents may not marry, within the State or elsewhere, without first obtaining a court order granting permission to marry. The class is defined by the statute to include any "Wisconsin resident having minor issue not in his custody and which he is under obligation to support by any court order or judgment." The statute specifies that court permission cannot be granted unless the marriage applicant submits proof of compliance with the support obligation and, in addition, demonstrates that the children covered by the support order "are not then and are not likely thereafter to become public charges." No marriage license may lawfully be issued in Wisconsin to a person covered by the statute, except upon court order; any marriage entered into without compliance with §245.10 is declared void; and persons acquiring marriage licenses in violation of the section are subject to criminal penalties. . . .

I

Appellee Redhail is a Wisconsin resident who, under the terms of §245.10, is unable to enter into a lawful marriage in Wisconsin or elsewhere so long as he maintains his Wisconsin residency. . . . In January 1972, when appellee was a minor and a high school student, a paternity action was instituted against him in Milwaukee County Court, alleging that he was the father of a baby girl born out of wedlock on July 5, 1971. After he appeared and admitted that he was the child's father, the court [adjudged] appellee the father and ordered him to pay $109 per month as support for the child until she reached 18 years of age. From May 1972 until August 1974, appellee was unemployed and indigent, and consequently was unable to make any support payments.

On September 27, 1974, appellee filed an application for a marriage license with appellant Zablocki, the County Clerk of Milwaukee County, and a few days later the application was denied on the sole ground that appellee had not obtained a court order granting him permission to marry, as required by §245.10. [I]t is stipulated that he would not have been able to satisfy either of the statutory prerequisites for an order granting permission to marry. First, he had not satisfied his support obligations to his illegitimate child, and as of December 1974 there was an arrearage in excess of $3,700. Second, the child had been a public charge since her birth, receiving benefits under the Aid to Families with Dependent Children program. [T]he child's benefit payments were such that she would have been a public charge even if appellee had been current in his support payments.

On December 24, 1974, appellee filed his complaint in the District Court, on behalf of himself and the class of all Wisconsin residents who had been refused a marriage license pursuant to §245.10(1) [claiming violations of equal protection and due process].

II

[The Court turns to the issue of the appropriate level of scrutiny.] Since our past decisions make clear that the right to marry is of fundamental importance, and since the classification at issue here significantly interferes with the exercise of that right, we believe that "critical examination" of the state interests advanced in support of the classification is required.

The leading case of this Court on the right to marry is Loving v. Virginia, 388 U.S. 1 (1967). [*Loving*] could have rested solely on the ground that the statutes discriminated on the basis of race in violation of the Equal Protection Clause. But the Court went on to hold that the laws arbitrarily deprived the couple of a fundamental liberty protected by the Due Process Clause, the freedom to marry. . . . Although *Loving* arose in the context of racial discrimination, prior and subsequent decisions of this Court confirm that the right to marry is of fundamental importance for all individuals. . . .

More recent decisions have established that the right to marry is part of the fundamental "right of privacy" implicit in the Fourteenth Amendment's Due Process Clause. . . . Cases subsequent to *Griswold* and *Loving* have routinely categorized the decision to marry as among the personal decisions protected by the right of privacy. . . .

It is not surprising that the decision to marry has been placed on the same level of importance as decisions relating to procreation, childbirth, child rearing, and family relationships. [I]t would make little sense to recognize a right of privacy with respect to other matters of family life and not with respect to the decision to enter the relationship that is the foundation of the family in our society. The woman whom appellee desired to marry had a fundamental right to seek an abortion of their expected child. . . . Surely, a decision to marry and raise the child in a traditional family setting must receive equivalent protection. And, if appellee's right to procreate means anything at all, it must imply some right to enter the only relationship in which the State of Wisconsin allows sexual relations legally to take place.

By reaffirming the fundamental character of the right to marry, we do not mean to suggest that every state regulation which relates in any way to the incidents of or prerequisites for marriage must be subjected to rigorous scrutiny. To the contrary, reasonable regulations that do not significantly interfere with decisions to enter into the marital relationship may legitimately be imposed. See Califano v. Jobst, 434 U.S. 47 (1977). The statutory classification at issue here, however, clearly does interfere directly and substantially with the right to marry.

Under the challenged statute, no Wisconsin resident in the affected class may marry in Wisconsin or elsewhere without a court order, and marriages contracted in violation of the statute are both void and punishable as criminal offenses. Some of those in the affected class, like appellee, will never be able to obtain the necessary court order, because they either lack the financial means to meet their support obligations or cannot prove that their children will not become public charges. These persons are absolutely prevented from getting married. Many others, able in theory to satisfy the statute's requirements, will be sufficiently burdened by having to do so that they will in effect be coerced into forgoing their right to marry. And even those who can be persuaded to meet the statute's requirements suffer a serious intrusion into their freedom of choice in an area in which we have held such freedom to be fundamental.[12]

III

When a statutory classification significantly interferes with the exercise of a fundamental right, it cannot be upheld unless it is supported by sufficiently important state interests and is closely tailored to effectuate only those interests. Appellant asserts that two interests are served by the challenged statute: the permission-to-marry proceeding furnishes an opportunity to counsel the applicant as to the necessity of fulfilling his prior support obligations; and the welfare of the out-of-custody children is protected. We may accept for present purposes that these are legitimate and substantial interests, but, since the means selected by the State for achieving these interests unnecessarily impinge on the right to marry, the statute cannot be sustained.

There is evidence that the challenged statute, as originally introduced in the Wisconsin Legislature, was intended merely to establish a mechanism whereby persons with support obligations to children from prior marriages could be counseled before they entered into new marital relationships and incurred further support obligations. Court permission to marry was to be required, but apparently permission was automatically to be granted after counseling was completed. The statute actually enacted, however, does not expressly require or provide for any

---

12. The directness and substantiality of the interference with the freedom to marry distinguish the instant case from Califano v. Jobst, 434 U.S. 47 [(1977)]. In *Jobst*, we upheld sections of the Social Security Act providing, inter alia, for termination of a dependent child's benefits upon marriage to an individual not entitled to benefits under the Act. As the opinion for the Court expressly noted, the rule terminating benefits upon marriage was not "an attempt to interfere with the individual's freedom to make a decision as important as marriage." The Social Security provisions placed no direct legal obstacle in the path of persons desiring to get married, and . . . there was no evidence that the laws significantly discouraged, let alone made "practically impossible," any marriages. Indeed, the provisions had not deterred the individual who challenged the statute from getting married, even though he and his wife were both disabled. See Califano v. Jobst. See also id. at 58 n.17 (because of availability of other federal benefits, total payments to the Jobsts after marriage were only $20 per month less than they would have been had Mr. Jobst's child benefits not been terminated).

counseling whatsoever, nor for any automatic granting of permission to marry by the court, and thus it can hardly be justified as a means for ensuring counseling of the persons within its coverage. Even assuming that counseling does take place — a fact as to which there is no evidence in the record — this interest obviously cannot support the withholding of court permission to marry once counseling is completed.

With regard to safeguarding the welfare of the out-of-custody children, appellant's brief does not make clear the connection between the State's interest and the statute's requirements. At argument, appellant's counsel suggested that, since permission to marry cannot be granted unless the applicant shows that he has satisfied his court-determined support obligations to the prior children and that those children will not become public charges, the statute provides incentive for the applicant to make support payments to his children. This "collection device" rationale cannot justify the statute's broad infringement on the right to marry.

First, with respect to individuals who are unable to meet the statutory requirements, the statute merely prevents the applicant from getting married, without delivering any money at all into the hands of the applicant's prior children. More importantly, regardless of the applicant's ability or willingness to meet the statutory requirements, the State already has numerous other means for exacting compliance with support obligations, means that are at least as effective as the instant statute's and yet do not impinge upon the right to marry. . . .

There is also some suggestion that §245.10 protects the ability of marriage applicants to meet support obligations to prior children by preventing the applicants from incurring new support obligations. But the challenged provisions of §245.10 are grossly underinclusive with respect to this purpose, since they do not limit in any way new financial commitments by the applicant other than those arising out of the contemplated marriage. The statutory classification is substantially overinclusive as well: given the possibility that the new spouse will actually better the applicant's financial situation, by contributing income from a job or otherwise, the statute in many cases may prevent affected individuals from improving their ability to satisfy their prior support obligations. And, although it is true that the applicant will incur support obligations to any children born during the contemplated marriage, preventing the marriage may only result in the children being born out of wedlock, as in fact occurred in appellee's case. Since the support obligation is the same whether the child is born in or out of wedlock, the net result of preventing the marriage is simply more illegitimate children.

The statutory classification created by §245.10(1), (4), (5) thus cannot be justified by the interests advanced in support of it. The judgment of the District Court is, accordingly, [a]ffirmed.

Justice STEWART, concurring in the judgment.

I cannot join the opinion of the Court. To hold, as the Court does, that the Wisconsin statute violates the Equal Protection Clause seems to me to misconceive the meaning of that constitutional guarantee. The Equal Protection Clause deals not with substantive rights or freedoms but with invidiously discriminatory classifications. . . . The problem in this case is not one of discriminatory classifications, but of unwarranted encroachment upon a constitutionally protected freedom. I think that the Wisconsin statute is unconstitutional because it exceeds the bounds of permissible state regulation of marriage, and invades the sphere of liberty protected by the Due Process Clause of the Fourteenth Amendment. . . .

The Constitution does not specifically mention freedom to marry, but it is settled that the "liberty" protected by the Due Process Clause of the Fourteenth Amendment embraces more than those freedoms expressly enumerated in the Bill of Rights. And the decisions of this Court have made clear that freedom of personal choice in matters of marriage and family life is one of the liberties so protected. . . . It is evident that the Wisconsin law now before us directly abridges that freedom. The question is whether the state interests that support the abridgement can overcome the substantive protections of the Constitution. . . .

As directed against either the indigent or the delinquent parent, the law is substantially more rational if viewed as a means of assuring the financial viability of future marriages. In this context, it reflects a plausible judgment that those who have not fulfilled their financial obligations and have not kept their children off the welfare rolls in the past are likely to encounter similar difficulties in the future. But the State's legitimate concern with the financial soundness of prospective marriages must stop short of telling people they may not marry because they are too poor or because they might persist in their financial irresponsibility. . . . A legislative judgment so alien to our traditions and so offensive to our shared notions of fairness offends the Due Process Clause of the Fourteenth Amendment. . . .

Justice STEVENS, concurring in the judgment. . . .

A classification based on marital status is fundamentally different from a classification which determines who may lawfully enter into the marriage relationship.[2] The individual's interest in making the marriage decision independently is sufficiently important to merit special constitutional protection. . . .

Under this statute, a person's economic status may determine his eligibility to enter into a lawful marriage. A noncustodial parent whose children are "public charges" may not marry even if he has met his court-ordered obligations. Thus, within the class of parents who have fulfilled their court-ordered obligations, the rich may marry and the poor may not. This type of statutory discrimination is, I believe, totally unprecedented,[3] as well as inconsistent with our tradition of administering justice equally to the rich and to the poor.

The statute appears to reflect a legislative judgment that persons who have demonstrated an inability to support their offspring should not be permitted to marry and thereafter to bring additional children into the world. Even putting to one side the growing number of childless marriages and the burgeoning number of children born out of wedlock, that sort of reasoning cannot justify this deliberate discrimination against the poor.

The statute prevents impoverished parents from marrying even though their intended spouses are economically independent. Presumably, the Wisconsin Legislature assumed (a) that only fathers would be affected by the legislation, and (b) that they would never marry employed women. The first assumption ignores the fact that fathers are sometimes awarded custody, and the second ignores the composition of today's work force. To the extent that the statute denies a hard-pressed parent any opportunity to prove that an intended marriage will ease rather

2. *Jobst* is in the former category; Loving v. Virginia, 388 U.S. 1 [(1967)], is in the latter.

3. The economic aspects of a prospective marriage are unquestionably relevant to almost every individual's marriage decision. But I know of no other state statute that denies the individual marriage partners the right to assess the financial consequences of their decision independently. I seriously question whether any limitation on the right to marry may be predicated on economic status, but that question need not be answered in this case.

than aggravate his financial straits, it not only rests on unreliable premises, but also defeats its own objectives.

These questionable assumptions also explain why this statutory blunderbuss is wide of the target in another respect. The prohibition on marriage applies to the noncustodial parent but allows the parent who has custody to marry without the State's leave. Yet the danger that new children will further strain an inadequate budget is equally great for custodial and non-custodial parents. . . .

. . . Even assuming that the right to marry may sometimes be denied on economic grounds, this clumsy and deliberate legislative discrimination between the rich and the poor is irrational in so many ways that it cannot withstand scrutiny under the Equal Protection Clause of the Fourteenth Amendment.

[Justice Rehnquist, dissenting, would have upheld the statute under the rational basis test as a permissible exercise of the state's power to regulate family life and to assure child support.]

Notes and Questions on *Loving* and *Zablocki*

1. *Historical background.* The statute under which the Lovings were convicted was part of a widespread policy. Antimiscegenation laws (i.e., prohibitions on interracial sexual relations and intermarriage) stemmed from beliefs regarding racial superiority. At one time, 38 states prohibited relationships between Blacks and whites, 14 states banned those between Asians and whites, and 7 states banned those between Native Americans and whites. Even before Virginia enacted its first prohibition in 1662, state officials whipped and publicly humiliated persons who entered into Black-white sexual relationships. Rachel F. Moran, Interracial Intimacy: The Regulation of Race and Romance 17, 19 (2001). Authorities were concerned, in large part, about the status of mulatto offspring in an economy based on slavery.

Concern over miscegenation increased after the Civil War when the emancipation of slaves heightened racial tension. Bolstering this climate was the eugenics movement, which reached its apex during the Progressive Era, and which preached that most maladies were hereditary and that social engineering would improve the human race. This theory led to many state restrictions on marriage. From 1880 to 1920, 20 states and territories revised or added antimiscegenation laws, with interracial marriage singled out for the most stringent regulation. Michael Grossberg, Governing the Hearth: Law and the Family in Nineteenth Century America 136, 138-139 (1985). See also Maria P.P. Root, Love's Revolution: Interracial Marriage (2001); Peter Wallenstein, Tell the Court I Love My Wife: Race, Marriage, and Law—An American History (2002).

2. *Response to* Loving. The *Loving* decision did not evoke the same resistance in the South as Brown v. Board of Education, 347 U.S. 483 (1954) (invalidating segregated schools). Nonetheless, federal courts did intervene occasionally when local authorities refused to issue marriage licenses to interracial couples. In 2000, Alabama became the last state to repeal its antimiscegenation prohibition (based in the state constitution). The closeness of the vote in Alabama reflects the prevalence of negative attitudes in the South toward interracial marriages: 40 percent of Alabamians voted to retain the law. Randall Kennedy, Interracial Intimacies: Sex, Marriage, Identity, and Adoption 279-280 (2004).

3. *Empirical data*. *Loving* marked the beginning of a steady increase in multi-racial marriages. Such marriages have increased tenfold since 1960,[18] and more than tripled between 1980 and 2003.[19] Currently, marriages between African-Americans and whites constitute less than 1 percent of all marriages.[20] The inter-marriage rate involving whites and persons of other races is higher than that of whites and African Americans,[21] leading some commentators to contend that other racial groups are more quickly becoming integrated into American society.[22] Intermarriage rates vary by gender: Black men are more likely to intermarry than Black women, while Asian women are more likely to intermarry than Asian men.[23] Approval of interracial marriage varies by age: for example, the approval rating for Black-white marriages is higher among those persons under 30 years old.[24] Interracial dating is significantly more common than intermarriage.[25]

4. *Marriage evasion acts and lex loci*. Although Virginia's 1924 Racial Purity stat-ute prohibited interracial marriage, the Lovings were convicted for having unknowingly criminalized their valid marriage from the District of Columbia by violating a *different* statute (Va. Code §20-58, enacted in 1878), forbidding residents from leaving the state to marry, with intent to evade the state antimiscegenation law, and then returning to cohabit as husband and wife.

The common law rule of lex loci (the "place of celebration" rule) provides that a marriage valid where performed is valid everywhere. Why wasn't this rule opera-tive in *Loving*? States considered some marriages (e.g., interracial, polygamous, or incestuous unions) exceptions to the rule, on public policy grounds, even without the existence of state bans on marriage evasion. See generally Andrew Koppelman, Interstate Recognition of Same-Sex Marriages and Civil Union: A Handbook for Judges, 153 U. Pa. L. Rev. 2143 (2005) (discussing invocation of public policy exception to marriage validity).

The subject of marriage evasion was addressed by the National Conference of Commissioners on Uniform State Laws (NCCUSL) with the promulgation in 1912 of the Uniform Marriage Evasion Act (UMEA), 9 U.L.A. 225 (1923). UMEA had the following consequences: (1) it declared void all marriages entered into by parties who married in another state for the purpose of evading their home state restric-tions on marriage; (2) it provided that out-of-state residents were permitted to marry only if their marriage was permissible in their home state; (3) it provided that state officers must obtain proof that out-of-state applicants for marriage licenses would be permitted to marry in their home state, and (4) it provided

---

[18]. Tony Pugh, Mixed Marriages Multiplying Tenfold Increase Since 1960 Suggest Softening of Racial Barriers, Pittsburgh Post-Gazette, Mar. 25, 2001, at A11.

[19]. Bureau of the Census, U.S. Dept. of Commerce, Statistical Abstract of the United States 48 (2004-2005) (extrapolation from table 52). Note that, after 2000, the census permits individuals to identify themselves by multiple racial and ethnic affiliations.

[20]. Id. (extrapolation from table 52).

[21]. Kim M. Williams, Multiracialism and the Civil Rights Future, Daedalus, Jan. 1, 2005 (pointing out that higher percentages of both Latinos and Asians marry white spouses).

[22]. See, e.g., Rachel F. Moran, Interracial Intimacy: The Regulation of Race and Romance 174-175 (2001).

[23]. Sharon M. Lee & Barry Edmonston, New Marriages, New Families: U.S. Racial and Hispanic Intermarriage, 60 Population Bull. 1, 4 (June 1, 2005); Moran, supra note [22], at 104, 106.

[24]. Jack Ludwig, Acceptance of Interracial Marriage at Record High, Gallup Poll News Service, June 1, 2004, available at http://gallup.coni/poll/content/print.aspx?ci=11836.

[25]. Alison Stein Wellner, U.S. Attitudes Toward Interracial Dating Are Liberalizing, Population Reference Bureau (reporting the results of a Gallup survey of American teenagers), available at http://www.prb.org (last visited Dec. 6, 2005).

that issuance of a marriage license by a state official in violation of these rules constituted a misdemeanor. UMEA was subsequently withdrawn because few states adopted it; the Uniform Marriage and Divorce Act superseded it in 1970 with a rule (§210) requiring states to recognize marriages provided that they are valid either at the place of celebration or the domicile of the parties.[26]

5. Loving *and precedent.* *Loving* was a landmark discrimination decision. However, antimiscegenation statutes had come before the Court previously. See McLaughlin v. Florida, 379 U.S. 184 (1964) (invalidating a state criminal miscegenation law without expressing any views about interracial marriage); Naim v. Naim, 87 S.E.2d 749 (Va.), *vacated and remanded,* 350 U.S. 891 (1955), *aff'd,* 90 S.E.2d 849 (Va.), *appeal dismissed,* 350 U.S. 985 (1956) (remanded on procedural grounds). The California Supreme Court declared the California antimiscegenation statute unconstitutional in Perez v. Lippold, 198 P.2d 17 (Cal. 1948)—two decades before *Loving*. Why might it have taken the U.S. Supreme Court so long to reach the same result?

Loving cites precedents concerning divorce (Maynard v. Hill), compulsory sterilization (Skinner v. Oklahoma), and, in an omitted section, parental rights (Meyer v. Nebraska). Are the cases apt? Curiously, *Loving* does not cite Griswold v. Connecticut, decided two years earlier. What explains this omission? What contribution might *Griswold* and subsequent privacy cases make to the analysis in *Loving*?

6. Loving's *constitutional basis.* Is *Loving* a case about race or about freedom of choice in marriage? What standard of review does the Court apply? What triggers such review? *Loving* establishes that the right to marry is constitutionally protected. Why should the Constitution protect the right to marry? Where in the Constitution is this right? Does it rest on substantive due process or equal protection? This question plagued commentators until *Zablocki*.

> *Loving* [failed to provide] clear authority for a right to marry that could be characterized as fundamental for purposes of substantive due process or equal protection analysis. . . . [T]he *Loving* opinion stopped short of a clear statement of a right to marry, for the reasoning depended largely on the racial character of the classification. The Court stated two alternative grounds for the decision. The first [was] that the statute was invalid solely because of the racial classification. The second . . . relied on the right to marry, but again the Court referred to the racial nature of the classification, stating, "To deny this fundamental freedom on so insupportable a basis as the racial classifications embodied in these statutes, classifications so directly subversive of the principle of equality at the heart of the Fourteenth Amendment, is surely to deprive all the State's citizens of liberty without due process of law." . . .

Note, The Constitution and the Family, 93 Harv. L. Rev. 1156, 1249 (1980). As a result, some courts restricted *Loving*'s precedential value to the racial discrimination holding. See, e.g., In re Goalen, 512 P.2d 1028 (Utah 1973), *appeal dismissed*

[26]. See Joanna Grossman, Fear and Loathing in Massachusetts: Same-Sex Marriage and Some Lessons from the History of Marriage and Divorce, 14 B.U. Pub. Int. L.J. 87, 103, 113 (2004) (discussing the history of UMEA); Edward Stein, Past and Present Proposed Amendments to the United States Constitution Regarding Marriage, 82 Wash. U. L.Q. 611, 638 (2004) (pointing out that only Vermont, Massachusetts, Louisiana, Illinois, and Wisconsin adopted UMEA in whole or in part).

and cert. denied, 414 U.S. 1148 (1974). What difference does it make if the right derives from the Due Process Clause or the Equal Protection Clause? On which approach did the Court decide *Zablocki*?

7. *Relevance of* Loving *to same-sex marriage.* Advocates of same-sex marriage often equate the ban on same-sex marriage with antimiscegenation laws. For further discussion of this analogy, see infra p.175. On the application of marriage evasion legislation and the rule of lex loci in the context of same-sex marriage, see infra p.171.

8. *Degrees of scrutiny.* *Zablocki* establishes different degrees of scrutiny for regulations infringing the right to marry, that is, rigorous scrutiny for significant interference but minimal scrutiny for "reasonable regulations that do not significantly interfere with decisions to enter into the marital relationship." Justice Powell (in an omitted concurrence) suggests that the Court does not present any means to distinguish between the two types of regulations. Do you agree? What distinguishes the regulation in *Zablocki* from that in Califano v. Jobst, cited in *Zablocki*?

According to *Zablocki*, a significant interference calling for rigorous scrutiny must be "direct" and "substantial." Are these distinct requirements?

> The most common problem in the analysis has been the tendency of the courts to blur the distinction between directness and substantiality. Since recognition of directness requires only an examination of the face of the statute, courts sometimes perform this simple mechanical test and then infer substantiality from directness or insubstantiality from indirectness. The result, of course, is to reduce the test to one of directness. But emphasizing directness to the exclusion of significance creates a danger that the protection of the right to marry will become illusory; only direct interferences will be scrutinized, even though in most cases, the state can achieve a similar interference by indirect means. . . .

Note, The Constitution and the Family, supra, at 1252-1253. What guidelines does *Zablocki* give for identifying a "direct" interference?

9. *Post-Zablocki regulation of the procreation-support link.* The Wisconsin statute invalidated in *Zablocki* was based on the state legislature's concern with the nonpayment of child support by "deadbeat dads." Subsequently, a Wisconsin trial court judge addressed the same problem in a somewhat similar manner by imposing a condition of probation that the defendant avoid having another child unless he proved that he could support that child and current children. See State v. Oakley, 629 N.W.2d 200 (Wis. 2001), *cert. denied*, 537 U.S. 813 (2002) (discussed infra Chapter VI). See also State v. Talty, 814 N.E.2d 1201, 1202 (Ohio 2004) (ordering as a probation condition for nonpayment of child support that the defendant make "all reasonable efforts to avoid conceiving another child" during his probationary period). See also Jim Hannah, Vasectomy Policy Raises Questions, Cincinnati Enquirer, June 27, 2004, at A1 (describing a case in which a judge gave a defendant the choice of a vasectomy as an alternative to jail for nonpayment of child support). See generally Steven M. Berezney, *Zablocki* Reborn?: The Constitutionality of Probation Conditions Prohibiting Deadbeat and Abusive Fathers from Conceiving Children, 5 J. L. Society 255 (2003). On the constitutionality of such child support enforcement mechanisms, see Chapter VI.

Problems

1. Which, if any, of the following statutes or regulations are unconstitutional infringements on the right to marry?

a. a statute preventing any resident who cannot provide a social security number from obtaining a marriage license (Ohio ex rel. Ten Residents of Franklin County v. Belskis, 755 N.E.2d 443 (Ohio Ct. App. 2001));

b. a statute preventing a married woman from adopting her grandson by requiring that her spouse join in the adoption petition (Browder v. Harmeyer, 453 N.E.2d 301 (Ind. Ct. App. 1983));

c. a prohibition on an owner of a horse from having a license because of a spouse's past conviction for possession-sale of a controlled substance (Levinson v. Washington Horse Racing Commn., 740 P.2d 898 (Wash. Ct. App. 1987));

d. a prohibition on married students' participation in athletic programs (Indiana High Sch. Athletic Assn. v. Raike, 329 N.E.2d 66 (Ind. Ct. App. 1975));

e. a harboring and accessory statute that imposes liability for providing shelter, material support, assistance, and comfort to a criminal or fugitive when applied to spouses (U.S. v. Hill, 279 F.3d 731 (9th Cir. 2002));

f. an employment requirement that requires a patrol officer to live within 20 miles from her job and results in her being terminated when she marries a law enforcement officer with a similar residency requirement from a neighboring county (Klatt v. Labor & Indus. Review Bd., 669 N.W.2d 752 (Wis. Ct. App. 2003)).

2. Congress is considering proposed legislation, Personal Responsibility, Work, and Family Promotion Act of 2005, H.R. 240, 109th Cong. (2005). This reauthorization of the 1996 welfare reform legislation would provide $300 million annually for state pro-marriage programs and would require each state to have numerical performance goals for encouraging the "formation and maintenance of healthy 2-parent married families." What programs should the states consider adopting to meet this requirement? Would such programs, as applied to recipients of public assistance, directly and substantially interfere with the right to marry? What policy issues should the implementing states consider? See Angela Onwuachi-Willig, The Return of the Ring: Welfare Reform's Marriage Cure as the Revival of Post-Bellum Control, 93 Cal. L. Rev. 1647 (2005).

■ TURNER v. SAFLEY
482 U.S. 78 (1987)

Justice O'CONNOR delivered the opinion of the Court.

This case requires us to determine the constitutionality of regulations promulgated by the Missouri Division of Corrections relating to inmate marriages. . . . The challenged marriage regulation . . . permits an inmate to marry only with the permission of the superintendent of the prison, and provides that such approval should be given only "when there are compelling reasons to do so." The term "compelling" is not defined, but prison officials testified at trial that generally only a pregnancy or the birth of an illegitimate child would be considered a compelling reason. Prior to the promulgation of this rule, the applicable regulation did not obligate Missouri Division of Corrections officials to assist an inmate who wanted to get married. [Plaintiff inmates brought a class action for injunctive relief and damages.]

In support of the marriage regulation, petitioners first suggest that the rule does not deprive prisoners of a constitutionally protected right. They concede that the decision to marry is a fundamental right under Zablocki v. Redhail, 434 U.S. 374 (1978), and Loving v. Virginia, 388 U.S. 1 (1967), but they imply that a different rule should obtain "in . . . a prison forum." Petitioners then argue that even if the regulation burdens inmates' constitutional rights, the restriction should be tested under a reasonableness standard. They urge that the restriction is reasonably related to legitimate security and rehabilitation concerns.

We disagree with petitioners that Zablocki does not apply to prison inmates. It is settled that a prison inmate "retains those [constitutional] rights that are not inconsistent with his status as a prisoner or with the legitimate penological objectives of the corrections system." Pell v. Procunier, 417 U.S. 817, 822 (1974). The right to marry, like many other rights, is subject to substantial restrictions as a result of incarceration. Many important attributes of marriage remain, however, after taking into account the limitations imposed by prison life. First, inmate marriages, like others, are expressions of emotional support and public commitment. These elements are an important and significant aspect of the marital relationship. In addition, many religions recognize marriage as having spiritual significance; for some inmates and their spouses, therefore, the commitment of marriage may be an exercise of religious faith as well as an expression of personal dedication. Third, most inmates eventually will be released by parole or commutation, and therefore most inmate marriages are formed in the expectation that they ultimately will be fully consummated. Finally, marital status often is a precondition to the receipt of government benefits (e.g., Social Security benefits), property rights (e.g., tenancy by the entirety, inheritance rights), and other, less tangible benefits (e.g., legitimation of children born out of wedlock). These incidents of marriage, like the religious and personal aspects of the marriage commitment, are unaffected by the fact of confinement or the pursuit of legitimate corrections goals.

Taken together, we conclude that these remaining elements are sufficient to form a constitutionally protected marital relationship in the prison context. Our decision in Butler v. Wilson, 415 U.S. 953 (1974), is not to the contrary. That case involved a prohibition on marriage only for inmates sentenced to life imprisonment; and, importantly, denial of the right was part of the punishment for crime.

The Missouri marriage regulation prohibits inmates from marrying unless the prison superintendent has approved the marriage after finding that there are compelling reasons for doing so. . . . In determining whether this regulation impermissibly burdens the right to marry, we note initially that the regulation prohibits marriages between inmates and civilians, as well as marriages between inmates. Although not urged by respondents, this implication of the interests of nonprisoners . . . may entail a "consequential restriction on the [constitutional] rights of those who are not prisoners." See Procunier v. Martinez, [416 U.S. 396, 409 (1974)]. We need not reach this question, however, because even under the reasonable relationship test, the marriage regulation does not withstand scrutiny.

Petitioners have identified both security and rehabilitation concerns in support of the marriage prohibition. The security concern emphasized by petitioners is that "love triangles" might lead to violent confrontations between inmates. With respect to rehabilitation, prison officials testified that female prisoners often were subject to abuse at home or were overly dependent on male figures, and that this dependence or abuse was connected to the crimes they had committed. The [prison] superintendent, petitioner William Turner, testified that in his view, these women prisoners needed to concentrate on developing skills of self-reliance, and that the prohibition on marriage furthered this rehabilitative goal. Petitioners emphasize that the prohibition on marriage should be understood in light of Superintendent Turner's experience with several ill-advised marriage requests from female inmates.

We conclude that on this record, the Missouri prison regulation, as written, is not reasonably related to these penological interests. No doubt legitimate security concerns may require placing reasonable restrictions upon an inmate's right to marry, and may justify requiring approval of the superintendent. The Missouri regulation, however, represents an exaggerated response to such security objectives. . . . Moreover, with respect to the security concern emphasized in petitioners' brief—the creation of "love triangles"—petitioners have pointed to nothing in the record suggesting that the marriage regulation was viewed as preventing such entanglements. Common sense likewise suggests that there is no logical connection between the marriage restriction and the formation of love triangles: surely in prisons housing both male and female prisoners, inmate rivalries are as likely to develop without a formal marriage ceremony as with one. Finally, this is not an instance where the "ripple effect" on the security of fellow inmates and prison staff justifies a broad restriction on inmates' rights. . . .

Nor, on this record, is the marriage restriction reasonably related to the articulated rehabilitation goal. First, in requiring refusal of permission absent a finding of a compelling reason to allow the marriage, the rule sweeps much more broadly than can be explained by petitioners' penological objectives. Missouri prison officials testified that generally they had experienced no problem with the marriage of male inmates, and the District Court found that such marriages had routinely been allowed as a matter of practice at Missouri correctional institutions prior to adoption of the rule. The proffered justification thus does not explain the adoption of a rule banning marriages by these inmates. Nor does it account for the prohibition on inmate marriages to civilians. Missouri prison officials testified that generally they had no objection to inmate-civilian marriages, and Superintendent Turner testified that he usually did not object to the marriage of either male or female prisoners to civilians. The rehabilitation concern appears from the record to have been centered almost exclusively on female inmates marrying other inmates or ex-felons. . . .

Moreover, although not necessary to the disposition of this case, we note that on this record the rehabilitative objective asserted to support the regulation itself is suspect. Of the several female inmates whose marriage requests were discussed by prison officials at trial, only one was refused on the basis of fostering excessive dependency. The District Court found that the Missouri prison system operated on the basis of excessive paternalism in that the proposed marriages of *all* female inmates were scrutinized carefully even before adoption of the current regulation . . . whereas the marriages of male inmates during the same period were routinely approved. That kind of lopsided rehabilitation concern cannot provide a justification for the broad Missouri marriage rule.

. . . On this record . . . the almost complete ban on the decision to marry is not reasonably related to legitimate penological objectives. We conclude, therefore, that the Missouri marriage regulation is facially invalid.

■ SHEILA ISENBERG, WOMEN WHO LOVE MEN WHO KILL
34-35, 223-236 (2000)[*]

Unbelievable as it may seem, there is a population of women who are deeply drawn to men who have murdered. They meet the men while working in prison as nurses, teachers, social workers, or volunteers. Others become pen pals with murderers. Some, who are infatuated, write fan/love letters to celebrity killers such as "Preppie Murderer" Robert Chambers or serial killers such as David Berkowitz, known as Son of Sam. . . . These women want to meet these killers because they are looking for love; some end up marrying these men.

[K]illers seem to have no trouble finding girlfriends and wives. Suspected murderers, indicted murderers, convicted murderers, even serial killers who confess to the most heinous crimes are all able to find love. Once inside prison, a murderer, although usually serving a life sentence, often becomes a magnet for women. . . .

Women who love killers were often little girls lost, reared in dysfunctional families where they were victims of abuse at the hands of harsh, dictatorial fathers aided by passive mothers. A large percentage were raised as Catholics and were severely affected by oppressive church teachings, including sexism, subjugation of women, and repression of sexuality.

Fathers were missing: divorced, dead, always working, drunk, withdrawn. Occasionally, mothers took on fathers' role and behaved like demanding authoritarians. Women who love killers frequently found that their relationships with men mimicked the one they had with their fathers. . . .

As it was between medieval maidens and the courtly knights who protected them, sex and true intimacy between women and the killers they love is usually forbidden by prison systems. These women feel deeply, but what they feel is not mature love or adult sexual passion. It is *romantic* passion—a passion fueled by deprivation and suffering, enhanced by anguish. These women have found the key to never-ending romance: suffering and pain.

Because many women who love killers have real difficulties with intimacy because of the damage done to them in childhood, they have chosen to live a fantasy. The majority of these women don't love real men but an illusion that is based on denial. Each women separates, or compartmentalizes, the murder from the man she loves. She denies his crime.

For women who love serial killers, or other notorious murderers, there is the added thrill of fame. Each serial killer's status gives a woman with low self-esteem a sense of importance; her prestige rises in direct proportion with the heinousness of his crimes.

---

[*] Sheila Isenberg, a journalist, conducted an empirical study of women who love convicted murderers. The author developed a profile of these women based on her interviews with psychiatrists, psychologists, district attorneys, police, and prison officials as well as the couples themselves.

In our patriarchal culture, murderers are often viewed as more than male: the most macho, strong, violent, and brutal of all men. In a majority of movies and television shows, the violent mystique of the murderer — or the cop, spy, under-cover agent, etc. — is the erotic centerpiece. . . . For some women, it *is* thrilling to dance with a master of death. If a woman is seeking excitement, passion, a meaning to life, loving a murderer can make her feel intensely alive. She becomes important, perhaps famous, because she loves a man who has killed. . . .

A murderer is often a con man who wins a woman by manipulation and lying. Some women, gullible, vulnerable, and needy, are ready to believe these charmers. Each woman hears a story that fits her needs: If she needs to believe that he's religious, he'll tell her that. If she wants sweet talk, he'll woo her. If she needs a brilliant existentialist hero, he'll sweep her off her feet with his verbiage. Some murderers are unbelievably charismatic. These men exude self-confidence. The narcissistic and antisocial personalities of these murderers cause them to act as though rules don't apply to them. They act tough and superior. They believe in themselves (or pretend they do) and easily convince susceptible women (literally little girls lost) to believe in them too. But, in truth, these are deeply disturbed men who, by murdering, have irrevocably broken one of our most basic laws. . . .

Notes and Questions

1. *Precedents.* Does *Turner*'s holding follow automatically from *Loving* and *Zablocki*?

2. *Rationale.* What rationale supports depriving life sentence inmates of the right to marry, as the Court previously held in Butler v. Wilson, cited in *Turner*? Does this rationale dictate the automatic dissolution of marriages entered into by life sentence inmates prior to incarceration? Cf. Langone v. Coughlin, 712 F. Supp. 1061 (N.D.N.Y. 1989) (holding unconstitutional a state prohibition on marriage by inmates serving life sentences as not reasonably related to legitimate penological objectives).

3. *Conjugal visits.* Does it follow from *Turner* that a prisoner who marries must be permitted conjugal visits? Ferrin v. Department of Corrections Servs., 517 N.E.2d 1370 (N.Y. 1987), upheld the denial of a life sentence inmate's application to participate in a family reunion program with a woman he married while in prison, on the ground that the marriage was void from inception. Assuming the validity of such restrictions for life sentence inmates, what constitutional arguments would you advance on behalf of Safley (not a life sentence inmate) if she were denied conjugal visits? How meaningful is recognition of the right to marry without conjugal visits?

4. *AIDS-based restrictions.* Should an inmate's right to marry or to have conjugal visitation depend on whether the prisoner has AIDS? In Doe v. Coughlin, 518 N.E.2d 536 (N.Y. 1987), an inmate and his wife challenged prison officials' refusal to allow him to participate in conjugal visits because he had AIDS. The court held that the inmate's condition provided a rational basis for preventing his participation. Did the court use the appropriate level of scrutiny? If the restriction is designed to prevent transmission of disease to the inmate's spouse, does that intrude on the right of marital sexual privacy established by *Griswold*? Does it

intrude on the rights of the inmate's spouse? To what extent should review of inmate restrictions include consideration of the rights of the affected nonprisoners? See generally Ronald G. Turner, Sex in Prison, 36 Tenn. B.J. 12 (2000).

5. *Gender.* Why did the Department of Corrections' policy in *Turner* focus on female inmates? Why did the prison officials conclude that marriage could thwart the rehabilitation of females but not males? Are the problems of abuse and dependency in marriage gender specific? What additional "gendered" insights does Isenberg's excerpt, supra, provide?

Problems

1. Alfie, an indigent prison inmate, is denied a marriage license when he is unable to comply with state law by personally appearing at the county clerk's office. The prison offers two accommodations: transportation by the Sheriff's Office for a fee or application by video conferencing at the prison, subject to judicial approval. However, Alfie does not have the resources to pay the transportation costs, and the court does not have the appropriate equipment to accommodate video conferencing. Does *Turner* require prison officials to facilitate and pay for special procedures to enable prisoners to comply with procedural requirements to marry? See In re Coates, 849 A.2d 254 (Pa. Super. Ct. 2004). See also Toms v. Taft, 338 F.3d 519 (6th Cir. 2003). Must the prison permit solemnization of marriages at the corrections facility? See Lambert v. Myers, 2004 WL 1452423 (N.D. Ill. 2004).

2. Husband, a 41-year-old inmate who is serving a life sentence in state prison, wishes to have a child with Wife, who is 44 years old. Husband learns that the California Department of Corrections (CDC) prohibits family visits for inmates serving life sentences. Given his sentence and Wife's age, Husband requests that (1) a laboratory be permitted to mail him a plastic semen collection container with a prepaid return mailer, (2) he be permitted to ejaculate into the container, and (3) the filled container be returned to the laboratory via overnight mail. Alternatively, he requests that his attorney be permitted to transport the specimen to the laboratory. He and Wife are willing to bear all costs. When the CDC refuses to accommodate Husband's request, he brings an action alleging a violation of his constitutional right to procreate pursuant to 42 U.S.C. §1983 and the Due Process Clause. What result? If the court were to agree that Husband has a constitutional right to procreate noncoitally in this manner, does a female inmate have a corresponding right to be artificially inseminated? See Gerber v. Hickman, 291 F.3d 617 (9th Cir. 2002). See also Goodwin v. Turner, 908 F.2d 1395 (8th Cir. 1990). See generally Rachel Roth, "No New Babies?": Gender Inequality and Reproductive Control in the Criminal Justice and Prison Systems, 12 Am. U.J. Gender Soc. Pol'y & L. 391 (2004).

3. Cipriana Ortiz, a medical benefits administrator for the Los Angeles Police Department, becomes romantically involved with a felon. In requesting personal leave to get married, Cipriana discloses that her boyfriend is an incarcerated felon. Her employer then determines that Cipriana has a conflict of interest because of her access to confidential information about law enforcement personnel. He gives her the choice of ending the relationship or terminating her employment.

She chooses the latter and then files suit alleging that her discharge violates her right to privacy and her right to marry. What result? Ortiz v. Los Angeles Police Relief Ass'n, 120 Cal. Rptr.2d 670 (Ct. App. 2002). See also Keeney v. Heath, 57 F.3d 579 (7th Cir. 1995).

2. State Regulation of Entry into the Marital Relationship

a. Substantive Restrictions

(i) Capacity to Marry

(1) Same Sex

▪ GOODRIDGE v. DEPARTMENT OF PUBLIC HEALTH
798 N.E.2d 941 (Mass. 2003)

MARSHALL, C.J.

. . . The question before us is whether, consistent with the Massachusetts Constitution, the Commonwealth may deny the protections, benefits, and obligations conferred by civil marriage to two individuals of the same sex who wish to marry. We conclude that it may not. The Massachusetts Constitution affirms the dignity and equality of all individuals. It forbids the creation of second-class citizens. In reaching our conclusion we have given full deference to the arguments made by the Commonwealth. But it has failed to identify any constitutionally adequate reason for denying civil marriage to same-sex couples.

We are mindful that our decision marks a change in the history of our marriage law. Many people hold deep-seated religious, moral, and ethical convictions that marriage should be limited to the union of one man and one woman, and that homosexual conduct is immoral. Many hold equally strong religious, moral, and ethical convictions that same-sex couples are entitled to be married, and that homosexual persons should be treated no differently than their heterosexual neighbors. Neither view answers the question before us. Our concern is with the Massachusetts Constitution as a charter of governance for every person properly within its reach. "Our obligation is to define the liberty of all, not to mandate our own moral code." Lawrence v. Texas, 123 S. Ct. 2472, 2480 (2003), quoting Planned Parenthood of Southeastern Pa. v. Casey, 505 U.S. 833, 850 (1992).

Whether the Commonwealth may use its formidable regulatory authority to bar same-sex couples from civil marriage is a question not previously addressed by a Massachusetts appellate court. It is a question the United States Supreme Court left open as a matter of Federal law in *Lawrence*, supra, at 2484, where it was not an issue. There, the Court affirmed that the core concept of common human dignity protected by the Fourteenth Amendment to the United States Constitution precludes government intrusion into the deeply personal realms of consensual adult expressions of intimacy and one's choice of an intimate partner. The Court also reaffirmed the central role that decisions whether to marry or have children bear in shaping one's identity. The Massachusetts Constitution is, if anything, more protective of individual liberty and equality than the Federal Constitution. . . .

[P]laintiffs are fourteen individuals from five Massachusetts counties. [P]lain-
tiffs Gloria Bailey, sixty years old, and Linda Davies, fifty-five years old, [have] been
in a committed relationship for thirty years; the plaintiffs Maureen Brodoff, forty-
nine years old, and Ellen Wade, fifty-two years old, [have] been in a committed
relationship for twenty years and lived with their twelve-year-old daughter; the
plaintiffs Hillary Goodridge, forty-four years old, and Julie Goodridge, forty-
three years old, [have] been in a committed relationship for thirteen years and
lived with their five-year-old daughter; the plaintiffs Gary Chalmers, thirty-five
years old, and Richard Linnell, thirty-seven years old, [have] been in a committed
relationship for thirteen years and lived with their eight-year-old daughter and
Richard's mother; the plaintiffs Heidi Norton, thirty-six years old, and Gina Smith,
thirty-six years old, [have] been in a committed relationship for eleven years and
lived with their two sons, ages five years and one year; the plaintiffs Michael Horgan, forty-one years old, and Edward Balmelli, forty-one years old, [have] been in a
committed relationship for seven years; and the plaintiffs David Wilson, fifty-seven
years old, and Robert Compton, fifty-one years old, [have] been in a committed
relationship for four years and [have] cared for David's mother in their home after a
serious illness until she died.

The plaintiffs include business executives, lawyers, an investment banker, educators, therapists, and a computer engineer. Many are active in church, community,
and school groups. They have employed such legal means as are available to
them—for example, joint adoption, powers of attorney, and joint ownership of
real property—to secure aspects of their relationships. Each plaintiff attests a
desire to marry his or her partner in order to affirm publicly their commitment
to each other and to secure the legal protections and benefits afforded to married
couples and their children. . . .

In March and April, 2001, each of the plaintiff couples [unsuccessfully]
attempted to obtain a marriage license from a city or town clerk's office. [Plaintiffs
filed suit, alleging that denial of a marriage license harms them and their children,[6]
and constitutes a violation of the Massachusetts constitution.[7] Plaintiffs first argue

---

6. The complaint alleged various circumstances in which the absence of the full legal protections of
civil marriage has harmed them and their children. For example, Hillary and Julie Goodridge alleged
that, when Julie gave birth to their daughter (whom Hillary subsequently coadopted) during a delivery
that required the infant's transfer to neonatal intensive care, Hillary "had difficulty gaining access to Julie
and their newborn daughter at the hospital." Gary Chalmers and Richard Linnell alleged that "Gary pays
for a family health insurance policy at work which covers only him and their daughter because Massachusetts law does not consider Rich to be a 'dependent.' This means that their household must purchase a
separate individual policy of health insurance for Rich at considerable expense. . . . Gary has a pension
plan at work, but under state law, because he is a municipal employee, that plan does not allow him the
same range of options in providing for his beneficiary that a married spouse has and thus he cannot
provide the same security to his family that a married person could if he should predecease Rich."

7. Article 1 [provides]: "All people are born free and equal and have certain natural, essential and
unalienable rights; among which may be reckoned the right of enjoying and defending their lives and
liberties; that of acquiring, possessing and protecting property; in fine, that of seeking and obtaining
their safety and happiness. Equality under the law shall not be denied or abridged because of sex, race,
color, creed or national origin."

Article 6 provides: "No man, nor corporation, or association of men, have any other title to obtain
advantages, or particular and exclusive privileges, distinct from those of the community, than what
arises from the consideration of services rendered to the public. . . ."

Article 7 provides: "Government is instituted for the common good; for the protection, safety,
prosperity, and happiness of the people; and not for the profit, honor, or private interest of any one
man, family or class of men: Therefore the people alone have an incontestable, unalienable, and

that because there is no specific prohibition against same-sex marriages in the Massachusetts marriage licensing statutes, G.L. c. 207, the court could interpret the statutes to permit same sex couples to obtain marriage licenses, thereby avoiding the question whether the law is constitutional. Based on the common law and everyday meaning of the term "marriage," the court refuses to construe G.L. c. 207 to permit same-sex couples to marry.]

The larger question is whether, as the department claims, government action that bars same-sex couples from civil marriage constitutes a legitimate exercise of the State's authority to regulate conduct, or whether, as the plaintiffs claim, this categorical marriage exclusion violates the Massachusetts Constitution. We have recognized the long-standing understanding, derived from the common law, that "marriage" means the lawful union of a woman and a man. But that history cannot and does not foreclose the constitutional question.

The plaintiffs' claim that the marriage restriction violates the Massachusetts Constitution can be analyzed in two ways. Does it offend the Constitution's guarantees of equality before the law? Or do the liberty and due process provisions of the Massachusetts Constitution secure the plaintiffs' right to marry their chosen partner? In matters implicating marriage, family life, and the upbringing of children, the two constitutional concepts frequently overlap, as they do here. Much of what we say concerning one standard applies to the other.

We begin by considering the nature of civil marriage itself. . . . Without question, civil marriage enhances the "welfare of the community." It is a "social institution of the highest importance." Civil marriage anchors an ordered society by encourag-ing stable relationships over transient ones. It is central to the way the Commonwealth identifies individuals, provides for the orderly distribution of property, ensures that children and adults are cared for and supported whenever possible from private rather than public funds, and tracks important epidemiological and demographic data.

Marriage also bestows enormous private and social advantages on those who choose to marry. Civil marriage is at once a deeply personal commitment to another human being and a highly public celebration of the ideals of mutuality, companionship, intimacy, fidelity, and family. . . . Because it fulfils yearnings for security, safe haven, and connection that express our common humanity, civil marriage is an esteemed institution, and the decision whether and whom to marry is among life's momentous acts of self-definition.

Tangible as well as intangible benefits flow from marriage. The marriage license grants valuable property rights to those who meet the entry requirements, and who agree to what might otherwise be a burdensome degree of government regulation of their activities. . . . The benefits accessible only by way of a marriage license are enormous, touching nearly every aspect of life and death [e.g., property, taxes, child custody, visitation, support, evidentiary privileges, and health care rights that inure to the parties and their children].

---

indefeasible right to institute government; and to reform, alter, or totally change the same, when their protection, safety, prosperity and happiness require it."

Article 10 provides, in relevant part: "Each individual of the society has a right to be protected by it in the enjoyment of his life, liberty and property, according to standing laws. . . ."

It is undoubtedly for these concrete reasons, as well as for its intimately personal significance, that civil marriage has long been termed a "civil right." The United States Supreme Court has described the right to marry as "of fundamental importance for all individuals" and as "part of the fundamental 'right of privacy' implicit in the Fourteenth Amendment's Due Process Clause" [citing *Loving* and *Zablocki*].

Without the right to marry — or more properly, the right to choose to marry — one is excluded from the full range of human experience and denied full protection of the laws for one's "avowed commitment to an intimate and lasting human relationship." Baker v. State, [744 A.2d 864, 889 (Vt. 1999)]. Because civil marriage is central to the lives of individuals and the welfare of the community, our laws assiduously protect the individual's right to marry against undue government incursion. Laws may not "interfere directly and substantially with the right to marry." Zablocki v. Redhail, [434 U.S. 374, 387].

Unquestionably, the regulatory power of the Commonwealth over civil marriage is broad, as is the Commonwealth's discretion to award public benefits. Individuals who have the choice to marry each other and nevertheless choose not to may properly be denied the legal benefits of marriage. But that same logic cannot hold for a qualified individual who would marry if she or he only could.

For decades, indeed centuries, in much of this country (including Massachusetts) no lawful marriage was possible between white and Black Americans. That long history availed [until] the United States Supreme Court [held] that a statutory bar to interracial marriage violated the Fourteenth Amendment, Loving v. Virginia, 388 U.S. 1 (1967). As both Perez [v. Sharp, 198 P.2d 17 (Cal. 1948) (holding that a state prohibition against interracial marriage violated the due process and equality guarantees of the Fourteenth Amendment)] and *Loving* make clear, the right to marry means little if it does not include the right to marry the person of one's choice. . . . In this case, as in *Perez* and *Loving*, a statute deprives individuals of access to an institution of fundamental legal, personal, and social significance — the institution of marriage — because of a single trait: skin color in *Perez* and *Loving*, sexual orientation here. As it did in *Perez* and *Loving*, history must yield to a more fully developed understanding of the invidious quality of the discrimination.

The Massachusetts Constitution protects matters of personal liberty against government incursion as zealously, and often more so, than does the Federal Constitution, even where both Constitutions employ essentially the same language. . . . The individual liberty and equality safeguards of the Massachusetts Constitution protect both "freedom from" unwarranted government intrusion into protected spheres of life and "freedom to" partake in benefits created by the State for the common good. Both freedoms are involved here. Whether and whom to marry, how to express sexual intimacy, and whether and how to establish a family — these are among the most basic of every individual's liberty and due process rights [citing *Lawrence, Casey, Zablocki, Roe, Eisenstadt*, and *Loving*]. And central to personal freedom and security is the assurance that the laws will apply equally to persons in similar situations. . . . The liberty interest in choosing whether and whom to marry would be hollow if the Commonwealth could, without sufficient justification, foreclose an individual from freely choosing the person with whom to share an exclusive commitment in the unique institution of civil marriage. . . .

[P]laintiffs challenge the marriage statute on both equal protection and due process grounds. . . . Because the statute does not survive rational basis review, we do not consider the plaintiffs' arguments that this case merits strict judicial scrutiny. The department posits three legislative rationales for prohibiting same-sex couples from marrying: (1) providing a "favorable setting for procreation"; (2) ensuring the optimal setting for child rearing, which the department defines as "a two-parent family with one parent of each sex"; and (3) preserving scarce State and private financial resources. We consider each in turn.

The judge in the Superior Court endorsed the first rationale, holding that "the state's interest in regulating marriage is based on the traditional concept that marriage's primary purpose is procreation." This is incorrect. Our laws of civil marriage do not privilege procreative heterosexual intercourse between married people above every other form of adult intimacy and every other means of creating a family. General Laws c. 207 contains no requirement that the applicants for a marriage license attest to their ability or intention to conceive children by coitus. Fertility is not a condition of marriage, nor is it grounds for divorce. People who have never consummated their marriage, and never plan to, may be and stay married. People who cannot stir from their deathbed may marry. While it is certainly true that many, perhaps most, married couples have children together (assisted or unassisted), it is the exclusive and permanent commitment of the marriage partners to one another, not the begetting of children, that is the sine qua non of civil marriage.

Moreover, the Commonwealth affirmatively facilitates bringing children into a family regardless of whether the intended parent is married or unmarried, whether the child is adopted or born into a family, whether assistive technology was used to conceive the child, and whether the parent or her partner is heterosexual, homosexual, or bisexual. If procreation were a necessary component of civil marriage, our statutes would draw a tighter circle around the permissible bounds of nonmarital child bearing and the creation of families by noncoital means. The attempt to isolate procreation as "the source of a fundamental right to marry," [*Goodridge*, 798 N.E.2d at 987] (Cordy, J., dissenting), overlooks the integrated way in which courts have examined the complex and overlapping realms of personal autonomy, marriage, family life, and child rearing. Our jurisprudence recognizes that, in these nuanced and fundamentally private areas of life, such a narrow focus is inappropriate.

The "marriage is procreation" argument singles out the one unbridgeable difference between same-sex and opposite-sex couples, and transforms that difference into the essence of legal marriage. Like "Amendment 2" to the Constitution of Colorado, which effectively denied homosexual persons equality under the law and full access to the political process, the marriage restriction impermissibly "identifies persons by a single trait and then denies them protection across the board." Romer v. Evans, 517 U.S. 620, 633 (1996). In so doing, the State's action confers an official stamp of approval on the destructive stereotype that same-sex relationships are inherently unstable and inferior to opposite-sex relationships and are not worthy of respect.

The department's first stated rationale, equating marriage with unassisted heterosexual procreation, shades imperceptibly into its second: that confining marriage to opposite-sex couples ensures that children are raised in the "optimal" setting. Protecting the welfare of children is a paramount State policy. Restricting marriage to opposite-sex couples, however, cannot plausibly further this policy. "The demographic changes of the past century make it difficult to speak of an average American family. The composition of families varies greatly from household to household." Troxel v. Granville, 530 U.S. 57, 63 (2000). Massachusetts has responded supportively to "the changing realities of the American family," id. at 64, and has moved vigorously to strengthen the modern family in its many variations [citing statutes on paternity and grandparent visitation, and case law on de facto parents and coparent adoption]. Moreover, we have repudiated the common-law power of the State to provide varying levels of protection to children based on the circumstances of birth.

The department has offered no evidence that forbidding marriage to people of the same sex will increase the number of couples choosing to enter into opposite-sex marriages in order to have and raise children. There is thus no rational relationship between the marriage statute and the Commonwealth's proffered goal of protecting the "optimal" child rearing unit. Moreover, the department readily concedes that people in same-sex couples may be "excellent" parents. . . . Given the wide range of public benefits reserved only for married couples, we do not credit the department's contention that the absence of access to civil marriage amounts to little more than an inconvenience to same-sex couples and their children. Excluding same-sex couples from civil marriage will not make children of opposite-sex marriages more secure, but it does prevent children of same-sex couples from enjoying the immeasurable advantages that flow from the assurance of "a stable family structure in which children will be reared, educated, and socialized." [*Goodridge*, 798 N.E.2d 941, 995 (Cordy, J., dissenting).]

In this case, we are confronted with an entire, sizeable class of parents raising children who have absolutely no access to civil marriage and its protections because they are forbidden from procuring a marriage license. It cannot be rational under our laws, and indeed it is not permitted, to penalize children by depriving them of State benefits because the State disapproves of their parents' sexual orientation.

The third rationale advanced by the department is that limiting marriage to opposite-sex couples furthers the Legislature's interest in conserving scarce State and private financial resources. The marriage restriction is rational, it argues, because the General Court logically could assume that same-sex couples are more financially independent than married couples and thus less needy of public marital benefits, such as tax advantages, or private marital benefits, such as employer-financed health plans that include spouses in their coverage.

An absolute statutory ban on same-sex marriage bears no rational relationship to the goal of economy. First, the department's conclusory generalization — that same-sex couples are less financially dependent on each other than opposite-sex couples — ignores that many same-sex couples, such as many of the plaintiffs in this case, have children and other dependents (here, aged parents) in their care. The department does not contend, nor could it, that these dependents are less needy or deserving than the dependents of married couples. Second, Massachusetts marriage laws do not condition receipt of public and private financial benefits to married individuals on a demonstration of financial dependence on each other; the benefits are available to married couples regardless of whether they mingle their finances or actually depend on each other for support.

The department suggests [also] that broadening civil marriage to include same-sex couples will trivialize or destroy the institution of marriage as it has historically been fashioned. Certainly our decision today marks a significant change in the definition of marriage as it has been inherited from the common law, and understood by many societies for centuries. But it does not disturb the fundamental value of marriage in our society.

Here, the plaintiffs seek only to be married, not to undermine the institution of civil marriage. They do not want marriage abolished. They do not attack the binary nature of marriage, the consanguinity provisions, or any of the other gate-keeping provisions of the marriage licensing law. Recognizing the right of an individual to marry a person of the same sex will not diminish the validity or dignity of opposite-sex marriage, any more than recognizing the right of an individual to marry a person of a different race devalues the marriage of a person who marries someone of her own race. If anything, extending civil marriage to same-sex couples reinforces the importance of marriage to individuals and communities. That same-sex couples are willing to embrace marriage's solemn obligations of exclusivity, mutual support, and commitment to one another is a testament to the enduring place of marriage in our laws and in the human spirit.

It has been argued that, due to the State's strong interest in the institution of marriage as a stabilizing social structure, only the Legislature can control and define its boundaries. . . . These arguments miss the point. The Massachusetts Constitution requires that legislation meet certain criteria and not extend beyond certain limits. It is the function of courts to determine whether these criteria are met and whether these limits are exceeded. We owe great deference to the Legislature to decide social and policy issues, but it is the traditional and settled role of courts to decide constitutional issues.

The history of constitutional law "is the story of the extension of constitutional rights and protections to people once ignored or excluded." United States v. Virginia, 518 U.S. 515, 557 (1996) (construing equal protection clause of the Fourteenth Amendment to prohibit categorical exclusion of women from public military institute). This statement is as true in the area of civil marriage as in any other area of civil rights. As a public institution and a right of fundamental importance, civil marriage is an evolving paradigm. The common law was exceptionally harsh toward women who became wives: a woman's legal identity all but evaporated into that of her husband. . . . Alarms about the imminent erosion of the "natural" order of marriage were sounded over the demise of antimiscegenation laws, the expansion of the rights of married women, and the introduction of "no-fault" divorce. Marriage has survived all of these transformations, and we have no doubt that marriage will continue to be a vibrant and revered institution.

We also reject the argument . . . that expanding the institution of civil marriage in Massachusetts to include same-sex couples will lead to interstate conflict. We would not presume to dictate how another State should respond to today's decision. But neither should considerations of comity prevent us from according Massachusetts residents the full measure of protection available under the Massachusetts Constitution. The genius of our Federal system is that each State's Constitution has vitality specific to its own traditions, and that, subject to the minimum requirements of the Fourteenth Amendment, each State is free to address difficult issues of individual liberty in the manner its own Constitution demands. . . .

The marriage ban works a deep and scarring hardship on a very real segment of the community for no rational reason. The absence of any reasonable relationship between, on the one hand, an absolute disqualification of same-sex couples who wish to enter into civil marriage and, on the other, protection of public health, safety, or general welfare, suggests that the marriage restriction is rooted in persistent prejudices against persons who are (or who are believed to be) homosexual. "The Constitution cannot control such prejudices but neither can it tolerate them. Private biases may be outside the reach of the law, but the law cannot, directly or indirectly, give them effect." Palmore v. Sidoti, 466 U.S. 429, 433 (1984) (construing Fourteenth Amendment). Limiting the protections, benefits, and obligations of civil marriage to opposite-sex couples violates the basic premises of individual liberty and equality under law protected by the Massachusetts Constitution. . . .

SPINA, J. (dissenting).

What is at stake in this case is not the unequal treatment of individuals or whether individual rights have been impermissibly burdened, but the power of the Legislature to effectuate social change without interference from the courts, pursuant to art. 30 of the Massachusetts Declaration of Rights. The power to regulate marriage lies with the Legislature, not with the judiciary. Today, the court has transformed its role as protector of individual rights into the role of creator of rights, and I respectfully dissent.

1. *Equal protection.* Although the court did not address the plaintiffs' gender discrimination claim, G.L. c. 207 does not unconstitutionally discriminate on the basis of gender [citing the Massachusetts Equal Rights Amendment that guarantees equality based on (sex, race, color, creed or national origin.)] General Laws c. 207 . . . applies to men and women in precisely the same way. It does not create any disadvantage identified with gender, as both men and women are similarly limited to marrying a person of the opposite sex.

Similarly, the marriage statutes do not discriminate on the basis of sexual orientation. . . . The marriage statutes do not disqualify individuals on the basis of sexual orientation from entering into marriage [a subsequent footnote defines marriage as a civil union between a single man and a single woman *Eds.*]. All individuals, with certain exceptions not relevant here, are free to marry. Whether an individual chooses not to marry because of sexual orientation or any other reason should be of no concern to the court.

The court concludes, however, that G.L. c. 207 unconstitutionally discriminates against the individual plaintiffs because it denies them the "right to marry the person of one's choice" where that person is of the same sex. To reach this result the court relies on Loving v. Virginia, 388 U.S. 1, 12 (1967) [and Perez v. Sharp, 198 P.2d 17 (Cal. 1948) (both holding that the state had no compelling interest in limiting the choice to marry along racial lines)]. Unlike the *Loving* and [*Perez*] cases, the Massachusetts Legislature has erected no barrier to marriage that intentionally discriminates against anyone. . . . In the absence of any discriminatory purpose, the State's marriage statutes do not violate principles of equal protection.

2. *Due process.* The marriage statutes do not impermissibly burden a right protected by our constitutional guarantee of due process implicit in art. 10 of our Declaration of Rights. There is no restriction on the right of any plaintiff to enter into marriage. Each is free to marry a willing person of the opposite sex. . . .

. . . Before applying any level of constitutional analysis there must be a recognized right at stake. Same-sex marriage, or the "right to marry the person of one's choice" as the court today defines that right, does not fall within the fundamental right to marry. Same-sex marriage is not "deeply rooted in this Nation's history," and the court does not suggest that it is. Except for the occasional isolated decision in recent years, see, e.g., Baker v. State, 744 A.2d 864 (Vt. 1999), same-sex marriage is not a right, fundamental or otherwise, recognized in this country. . . .

SOSMAN, J. dissenting.

. . . As a matter of social history, today's opinion may represent a great turning point that many will hail as a tremendous step toward a more just society. As a matter of constitutional jurisprudence, however, the case stands as an aberration. To reach the result it does, the court has tortured the rational basis test beyond recognition. I fully appreciate the strength of the temptation to find this particular law unconstitutional — there is much to be said for the argument that excluding gay and lesbian couples from the benefits of civil marriage is cruelly unfair and hopelessly outdated; the inability to marry has a profound impact on the personal lives of committed gay and lesbian couples (and their children) to whom we are personally close (our friends, neighbors, family members, classmates, and co-workers); and our resolution of this issue takes place under the intense glare of national and international publicity. Speaking metaphorically, these factors have combined to turn the case before us into a "perfect storm" of a constitutional question. In my view, however, such factors make it all the more imperative that we adhere precisely and scrupulously to the established guideposts of our constitutional jurisprudence, a jurisprudence that makes the rational basis test an extremely deferential one that focuses on the rationality, not the persuasiveness, of the potential justifications for the classifications in the legislative scheme. I trust that, once this particular "storm" clears, we will return to the rational basis test as it has always been understood and applied. Applying that deferential test in the manner it is customarily applied, the exclusion of gay and lesbian couples from the institution of civil marriage passes constitutional muster. I respectfully dissent.

CORDY, J. (dissenting, with whom SPINA and SOSMAN, JJ., join). . . .

The marriage statute, which regulates only the act of obtaining a marriage license, does not implicate privacy in the sense that it has found constitutional protection under Massachusetts and Federal law. It does not intrude on any right that the plaintiffs have to privacy in their choices regarding procreation, an intimate partner or sexual relations. The plaintiffs' right to privacy in such matters does not require that the State officially endorse their choices in order for the right to be constitutionally vindicated. . . .

Taking all of [the available social science] information into account, the Legislature could rationally conclude that a family environment with married opposite-sex parents remains the optimal social structure in which to bear children, and that the raising of children by same-sex couples, who by definition cannot be the two sole biological parents of a child and cannot provide children with a parental authority figure of each gender, presents an alternative structure for child rearing that has not yet proved itself beyond reasonable scientific dispute to be as optimal as the biologically based marriage norm. Working from the assumption that a recognition of same-sex marriages will increase the number of children experiencing this alternative, the Legislature could conceivably conclude that declining to recognize same-sex marriages remains prudent until empirical questions about its impact on the upbringing of children are resolved. . . .

■ DAVID J GARROW, TOWARD A MORE PERFECT UNION
N.Y. Times, May 9, 2004, §6 (Magazine), at 52

Mary Bonauto vividly remembers her first day as a lawyer at Gay and Lesbian Advocates and Defenders (GLAD), the small public-interest law office that represents gays and lesbians in the six New England states. "When I came here on March 19, 1990," she recalled not long ago, "one of the things waiting for me on my desk was a request from a lesbian couple in western Massachusetts who wanted to get married." At that time, though, she believed a lawsuit seeking a right to gay marriage had no chance of success in any American appellate court. "It was absolutely the wrong time," she told me, "and I said no."

A generation or two from now, March 19, 1990, may appear in history books the same way that another date appears in accounts of Brown v. Board of Education: Oct. 6, 1936, the day that Thurgood Marshall accepted a full-time job at the N.A.A.C.P. Legal Defense Fund. Marshall, too, said no—for more than a decade—to petitioners who asked him to challenge public-school segregation in the South. Only in 1950, as the legal landscape began to shift, did Marshall finally say yes.

For Bonauto, the wait was shorter but the outcome no less momentous. . . . Bonauto will forever be remembered for [the] landmark decision, Goodridge v. Department of Public Health. . . .

A native of Newburgh, N.Y., Bonauto grew up with her three brothers in what she describes as a "highly Catholic" family. Her father worked as a pharmacist and her mother as a teacher. Bonauto first came to terms with her lesbian identity as an undergraduate at Hamilton College in Clinton, N.Y., but only during her first year of law school at Northeastern University in Boston in 1984-85 did she come out to her parents. When she joined a small law firm in Portland, Me., in 1987, Bonauto was one of only three openly gay lawyers in private practice in the state. In Portland, she also met her life partner, Jennifer Wriggins, now a professor at the University of Maine School of Law.

The late 1980's were an auspicious time for a young lawyer in New England with a commitment to gay equality. In 1989, Massachusetts became the second state, after Wisconsin, to provide anti-discrimination protection to gays in employment, housing and public accommodations. When GLAD advertised for a lawyer to help enforce the new law, Bonauto jumped at the opportunity and moved back to Boston. . . .

[In July 1997 Bonauto filed Baker v. State, 744 A.2d 864, 889 (Vt. 1999), the successful challenge to the constitutionality of Vermont's exclusion of same-sex couples from the right to marry.] Baker v. State was a gay rights landmark, but it nonetheless left the lawyers "crushed," [co-counsel Beth] Robinson remembers, because the high court called for legislative action rather than ordering that marriage licenses be issued to gay couples. "It was a political decision and not a legal decision," Robinson says. When the Vermont Legislature took up the court's invitation, a result was "civil unions," in which the legal benefits of matrimony were extended to gay couples but the all-powerful term—"marriage"—was withheld. The distinction evoked a phrase that Thurgood Marshall knew all too well: "separate but equal," the pre-Brown label for the fictional fairness of segregation.

Bonauto decided to try again, this time in [Goodridge]. . . . When she argued her case to the seven justices, she beseeched them not to dodge the question. Fearful of how Vermont's high court had rendered a decision that allowed for a remedy that stopped short of actual marriage, Bonauto insisted that "civil unions" would not satisfy the requirements of the Massachusetts Constitution. "The Vermont approach is not the best approach for this Court to take," she emphasized, for "when it comes to marriage, there really is no such thing as separating the word 'marriage' from the protections it provides. The reason for that is that one of the most important protections of marriage is the word, because the word is what conveys the status that everyone understands as the ultimate expression of love and commitment." To follow Vermont, she continued, by "creating a separate system, just for gay people, simply perpetuates the stigma of exclusion that we now face because it would essentially be branding gay people and our relationships as unworthy of this civil institution of marriage." . . .

While Bonauto waited for a decision, the legal climate improved [with the U.S. Supreme Court's decision in Lawrence v. Texas, invalidating anti-sodomy laws]. Five months later, the Massachusetts Supreme Judicial Court handed down the ruling for which Bonauto had been waiting: an unparalleled 4-3 decision ending the exclusion of gay couples from marriage. The moral influence of the *Lawrence* decision on the Massachusetts court was made explicit at the very beginning of the *Goodridge* majority opinion, in which Massachusetts Chief Justice Margaret H. Marshall cited *Lawrence* three times in her first three paragraphs. As Matt Coles, head of the American Civil Liberties Union's Lesbian and Gay Rights Project, observes, *Goodridge* "answered that question that *Lawrence* begged." And while "*Goodridge* is the earthquake," Coles says, "*Goodridge* is the earthquake because of *Lawrence*." . . .

But *Goodridge*'s impact was felt not only by gays. Hostile reaction followed . . . including critical words by President Bush in his State of the Union address on January 20. Among those in the audience that evening was the newly elected San Francisco mayor, Gavin Newsom, and Bush's remarks started Newsom thinking. Two weeks later, Newsom instructed his top aides to look into how San Francisco could start issuing marriage licenses to homosexual couples. Newsom's chief of staff, Steve Kawa, phoned Kate Kendell of the San Francisco-based National Center for Lesbian Rights late on the afternoon of Friday, Feb. 6. "The mayor wants to begin issuing marriage licenses to lesbian and gay couples," Kawa told an astounded Kendell. On Monday, Kendell suggested to Newsom's staff that the pioneering lesbian rights activists Phyllis Lyon and Del Martin become the city's first legally wed gay couple. Three days later, on February 14th, Lyon and Martin, ages 79 and 83, were married at City Hall. Literally overnight, Newsom's initiative transformed the gay-marriage story from dry reports of court rulings into vivid pictures of hundreds of homosexual couples standing in line, sometimes in the rain, outside San Francisco City Hall. . . .

When asked to talk about herself, Bonauto insists that "it's totally not about me." Since she and her partner Jennifer Wriggins — and their 2-year-old twin daughters, to whom Bonauto gave birth during the early litigation of *Goodridge* — now live in Maine rather than Boston, Bonauto and Wriggins's desire to marry may fall victim to Massachusetts's nonresident statutory restriction [discussed infra]. Beth Robinson emphasizes Bonauto's "modesty and humility," but insiders who fully appreciate how a very small network of gay lawyers has brought America to the threshold of another civil rights milestone know whom to credit. Disclaiming any desire for an "architect" label, Bonauto says, "I'm happy to be a bricklayer." . . .

Notes and Questions

1. *Epilogue*. Challenges to *Goodridge* materialized in various forms.

a. *Legislature requests judicial clarification*. The Supreme Judicial Court stayed the entry of judgment in *Goodridge* for 180 days to enable the legislature "to take such action as it may deem appropriate in light of this opinion." 798 N.E.2d at 970. In response, the legislature solicited the court's opinion on the constitutionality of proposed legislation that would prohibit same-sex marriage, but allow civil unions providing all the benefits of marriage. Ruling that the bill contained the same defects as the ban on same-sex marriage, the state supreme court condemned the bill's "choice of language that reflects a demonstrable assigning of same-sex, largely homosexual, couples to second-class status." Opinions of the Justices to the Senate, 802 N.E.2d 565, 570 (Mass. 2004). Upon expiration of the stay on May 17, 2004, Massachusetts became the first state to permit same-sex marriage.

b. *Governor's response: enforcing the Marriage Evasion Act*. As the 180-day deadline approached, Massachusetts Governor Mitt Romney restricted the availability of same-sex marriage to *state residents* by requiring proof of residency pursuant to state statutes adopting the Uniform Marriage Evasion Act (Mass. Gen. Laws ch. 207 §§11 & 12). In Cote-Whitacre v. Department of Public Health, 844 N.E.2d 623 (Mass. 2006), 8 nonresident same-sex couples and 13 municipal clerks challenged the constitutionality of the statutory provisions that prohibit contracting marriage by, or issuing marriage licenses to, couples who come to Massachusetts to marry but who plan to return to their home states where same-sex marriages are prohibited. The Supreme Judicial Court ruled that the statutes did not violate the right to due process or equal protection under the state constitution, or the privileges and immunities clause of the federal constitution. The ruling thus prohibits couples from most states from marrying in Massachusetts (because most states have laws or constitutional amendments barring same-sex marriage), but leaves open the possibility that couples from a few states without express prohibitions might marry in Massachusetts. The court remanded the cases of three couples from Rhode Island and New York for a determination whether same-sex marriage is prohibited in those states. See Pam Belluck & Katie Zezima, Massachusetts Court Limits Gay Unions, N.Y. Times, Mar. 31, 2006, at A10. Proposed legislation has been reintroduced in the Massachusetts state legislature to repeal the state marriage evasion statute. Id.

c. *Federal challenge to* Goodridge. A Massachusetts citizen and several state legislators sought an injunction in federal court preventing implementation of *Goodridge*, claiming that the state supreme court had usurped the legislature's authority to define marriage, thereby violating the state constitution's separation of powers. In declining relief, the First Circuit Court of Appeals pointed out that voters and legislators had an alternative method of "preserving the republican government [that] the constitution mandates" by resort to the state constitutional amendment process. Largess v. Mass. Sup. Jud. Ct., 373 F.3d 219, 229 (1st Cir. 2004).

d. *State constitutional amendment*. Following *Goodridge*, the controversy continued in Massachusetts in the form of an attempt to amend the state constitution to define marriage as a heterosexual relationship and to replace same-sex marriage with civil unions. In March 2004, the state legislature passed the proposed amendment by a vote of 105 to 92. According to state law, the legislature had to pass the bill once again in the same form during the next consecutive session before the measure could be placed on the ballot in November 2006. In September 2005, the state legislature *defeated* the proposed constitutional amendment by a vote of 157 to 39. Pam Belluck, Massachusetts Rejects Bill to Eliminate Gay Marriage, N.Y. Times, Sept. 15, 2005, at A12. As a result, same-sex marriages continue to be valid in the state. Opponents of same-sex marriage are mobilizing to place a more restrictive proposed amendment to ban same-sex marriage *without* creating civil unions on the 2008 ballot. Frank Phillips, Senate Boss Plans to Delay Gay Marriage Vote, Boston Globe, Feb. 10, 2005, at B1.

2. *Historical background: Stonewall sets the stage*. The gay liberation movement was triggered by a police raid of a popular Greenwich Village gay bar, the Stonewall Inn, in 1969. The raid and ensuing six days of riots launched an organized gay political movement. See David Carter, Stonewall: The Riots that Sparked the Gay Revolution (2004) (providing an in-depth account of the riots as well as an explanation of the socio-political climate).

3. *The Massachusetts experience with same-sex marriage.* Why was Massachusetts the first state to recognize same-sex marriage? The *Goodridge* plaintiffs' lawyer Mary Bonauto speculates that: (1) the various branches of state government previously expanded gay rights (in the areas of non-discrimination laws, hate crime legislation, foster parenting, and the dissolution of same-sex families); (2) same-sex couples were becoming ubiquitous; (3) the media was offering more coverage to the gay community; (4) attempts to pass state Defense of Marriage legislation (discussed infra) failed; and (5) gay rights advocates concluded that the Massachusetts constitution offered strong protections for individual rights. Mary L. Bonauto, *Goodridge* in Context, 40 Harv. C.R.-C.L. L. Rev. 1, 9-16, 25 (2005).

Boston also has a long history of gay political activism. One of the city's first gay political groups was established in 1969. In 1973, the first national lesbian and gay weekly newspaper began publication there. Massachusetts also elected the country's first openly gay state representative, and the country's first openly gay congressmen. The History Project, Improper Bostonians: Lesbian and Gay History from the Puritans to Playland 198-199 (1998).

Since *Goodridge*, 7,300 same-sex couples have married in Massachusetts. Belluck & Zezima, supra. Public opinion on same-sex marriage has changed significantly in the state. Shortly after *Goodridge*, 53 percent of Massachusetts voters opposed same-sex marriage; by May 2005, only 37 percent of voters voiced opposition. Deb Price, The Sky Didn't Fall in Mass, USA Today, May 17, 2005, at 13A. Cf. Debate on Marriage Fierce 1 Year Later, Iowa City Press-Citizen, May 17, 2005, at 8 (pointing out that a majority of Americans (68 percent) oppose same-sex marriage).

4. *The road to* Goodridge.

a. *Early challenges*: Same-sex couples began challenging the ban on marriage as early as the 1970s, although without success. Early cases held that same-sex marriages were invalid either because of lack of capacity or else relied on dictionary definitions of marriage, thereby avoiding resolution of the constitutional issues. See, e.g., Singer v. Hara, 522 P.2d 1187 (Wash. Ct. App. 1974); Jones v. Hallahan, 501 S.W.2d 588 (Ky. 1973); Baker v. Nelson, 191 N.W.2d 185 (Minn. 1971). Subsequent challenges tried other tactics. See, e.g., Adams v. Howerton, 673 F.2d 1036 (9th Cir. 1982) (refusing to extend the term "spouse," as used in the Immigration and Nationality Act, to include members of same-sex couples); DeSanto v. Barnsley,

476 A.2d 952 (Pa. Super. Ct. 1984) (refusing to recognize a common law marriage for a same-sex couple).

b. *1990s:* Baehr, Brause, *and* Baker. Following the United States Supreme Court's refusal to invalidate criminal sodomy laws in Bowers v. Hardwick, 478 U.S. 186 (1986), plaintiffs began witnessing a more favorable judicial climate in the 1990s on the state level. What explains the resurgence of litigation? Professor William Eskridge attributes the timing to a reduction in employment discrimination against gays and lesbians that freed up activism for other issues; an aging, wealthy gay populace who were desirous of finding long-term partners; and the AIDS epidemic which led to a desire for more serious commitment. See William N. Eskridge, Jr., The Case for Same-Sex Marriage: From Sexual Liberty to Civilized Commitment 58 (1996). See also William N. Eskridge, Jr., Gaylaw: Challenging the Apartheid of the Closet (1999).

In the first judicial ruling favorable to same-sex unions, the Hawaii Supreme Court held that the denial of marriage licenses to same-sex couples implicates the state constitution's Equal Protection Clause, which explicitly bars sex-based discrimination (unlike its federal counterpart). Although refusing to find violations of the right of privacy or due process, the plurality concluded that the decision whether to issue a license to marry a particular person depends on the applicant's sex. Baehr v. Lewin, 852 P.2d 44, 67 (Haw. 1993). On remand, based on a strict-scrutiny standard, the trial court enjoined the denial of marriage licenses after the state failed to establish a compelling state interest to justify the ban. Baehr v. Miike, 1996 WL 694235 (Haw. Cir. Ct. 1996).

An Alaska trial court invalidated that state's prohibition on other constitutional grounds. In Brause v. Bureau of Vital Statistics, 1998 WL 88743 (Alaska Super. Ct. 1998), a trial court held that the privacy and equality provisions of the state constitution prohibited the state from denying marriage to same-sex couples. In both Hawaii and Alaska, however, subsequent state constitutional amendments (e.g., Haw. Const. art. 1, §23; Alaska Const. art 1, §25) nullified those decisions. As a political compromise, the Hawaii legislature enacted the Reciprocal Beneficiaries Act (Haw. Rev. Stat. Ann §§572 (1)-(7) (Michie 1993 & Supp. 2005)). See also Brause v. Alaska, 21 P.3d 357(Alaska 2001) (holding that plaintiffs' constitutional claims were mooted by adoption of the state constitutional amendment); Baehr v. Miike, 994 P.2d 566 (Haw. 1999) (reversing supreme court's original decision as moot).

A favorable judicial ruling in Vermont led to legislative adoption of a form of domestic partnership as an alternative to marriage. In Baker v. State, 744 A.2d 864 (Vt. 1999), the Vermont Supreme Court held that its state constitutional Common Benefits Clause required that same-sex couples be afforded the same benefits as married persons. However, in response to the court's instruction to the legislature to establish a constitutionally acceptable framework to provide those benefits, the state legislature recognized civil unions (Va. Stat. Ann. tit. 15, §§1201-1207 (2002)) (discussed infra). In the first year, the state registered 2,258 civil unions. Fred Bayles, Civil Unions Blur at Vt.'s State Line, USA Today, July 11, 2001, at 3A. The Vermont Supreme Court subsequently rejected a challenge by town clerks claiming that issuance of the marriage licenses violated their religious beliefs. Brady v. Dean, 790 A.2d 428 (Vt. 2001).

c. *The role of* Lawrence. What impact did the Supreme Court's decision in *Lawrence* (Chapter I, p. 56) have on *Goodridge*, according to the principal case and the above excerpts? Does *Lawrence* dictate that the government must give formal recognition to same-sex marriage? Cf. Lewis v. Harris, 875 A.2d 259, 273 (N.J. Super. Ct. App. Div. 2005) (denying plaintiffs' claims to privacy and equal protection, asserting that "there is nothing in *Loving* or *Lawrence* that indicates that the Fourteenth Amendment bars a state from prohibiting marriage between members of the same sex"). An appeal is pending. Evaluate the assertion of Justice Scalia, dissenting in *Lawrence*, that a state interest in preserving traditional marriage is "just a kinder way of describing the State's *moral disapproval* of same-sex couples." 539 U.S. 558, 601 (Scalia, J., dissenting).

5. *The road after* Goodridge. In a move that stunned the nation, San Francisco Mayor Gavin Newsom ordered San Francisco officials to begin issuing marriage licenses to same-sex couples. Beginning on Valentine's Day in 2004, the city issued licenses to more than 4,000 couples before the California Supreme Court enjoined the practice. Bob Egelko, Court Halts Gay Vows Surprise Ruling, S.F. Chron., Mar. 12, 2004, at A1. Subsequently, the California Supreme Court ruled that the mayor overstepped his authority, reasoning that his belief in the unconstitutionality of the marriage licensing law did not justify his actions, and voided the licenses issued by the city. Lockyer v. City & County of San Francisco, 95 P.3d 459 (Cal. 2004).

Gay rights advocates subsequently challenged California's statutory definition of marriage as a heterosexual relationship (Cal. Fam. Code §§300 ("marriage is a personal relationship arising out of a civil contract between a man and a woman"), 308.5 (West 2004) ("only marriage between a man and a woman is valid and recognized in California")). A trial court held the statutes unconstitutional as a violation of the state constitution's Equal Protection Clause but stayed the ruling pending appeal. In re Coordination Proceeding, Special Title [Rule 1550(c)] (Woo v. Lockyer), 2005 WL 583129 (Cal. Super. Ct. 2005). As the appeal was pending, the California legislature narrowly passed a bill that would have made marriage laws gender neutral; however, Governor Arnold Schwarzenegger vetoed the bill.

As this book goes to press, same-sex couples are challenging the validity of marriage bans in several additional states (including Connecticut, Iowa, Maryland, New York, New Jersey, and Washington). See Kerrigan v. Connecticut Dept. of Pub. Health, No. NNH-CV-04-4001813-S (New Haven Super. Ct., filed Sept. 28, 2005); Varnum v. Brien, No. CV5965 (Polk County Dist. Ct., filed Dec. 13, 2005); Deane v. Conway, 2006 WL 148145 (Md. Cir. Ct. 2006) (holding that statute limiting marriage to a man and a woman violates state Equal Rights Amendment); Lewis v. Harris, 875 A.2d 259 (N.J. Super. Ct. App. Div. 2005) (holding that ban on same-sex marriage does not violate equal protection under state constitution); Hernandez v. Robles, 805 N.Y.S.2d 354 (App. Div. 2005) (holding that state ban did not violate due process or equal protection provisions of state constitution); Andersen v. King County, 2004 WL 1738447 (Wash. Super. Ct. 2004) (holding that state ban on same-sex marriage violates privileges and immunities clause and substantive due process rights under state constitution). See also Castle v. State, 2004 WL 1985215 (Wash. Super. Ct. 2004) (holding that state DOMA prohibiting same-sex marriage violates privileges and immunities clause of state constitution).

6. *Level of constitutional scrutiny.* The Supreme Court has adopted different standards of review to evaluate the constitutionality of potentially discriminatory classifications under the Equal Protection Clause. To survive constitutional attack, the classification must be (1) necessary to a compelling state interest (strict scrutiny), or (2) substantially related to an important governmental objective

(intermediate scrutiny), or (3) rationally related to a legitimate government purpose (lowest level of scrutiny). The court evaluates racial classifications under the first test; sex-based classifications are scrutinized under the middle-tier test. What test does the Massachusetts Supreme Judicial Court apply in *Goodridge*? Why?

7. *State interests*. According to the state's arguments in *Goodridge*, what interests justify banning same-sex marriage? Are any of the arguments compelling? Is the potential for procreation essential? See Jamal Greene, Comment, Divorcing Marriage from Procreation, 114 Yale L.J. 1989 (2005). How does the availability of reproductive technology, such as artificial insemination and surrogacy, weaken the case against recognition of same-sex marriage? What other state interests might justify a ban on same-sex marriage? Is a ban necessary to achieve these objectives? See generally George W. Dent, Jr., Traditional Marriage: Still Worth Defending, 18 BYU J. Pub. L. 419 (2004); Stephen C. Whiting, 'Gay Marriage' Is an Oxymoron, 19 Me. B. J. 79 (2004).

8. *Civil marriage*. *Goodridge* emphasizes the focus on the civil, as opposed to religious, nature of marriage. An omitted portion of the majority opinion states:

> [T]he government creates civil marriage. In Massachusetts, civil marriage is, and since pre-Colonial days has been, precisely what its name implies: a wholly secular institution. No religious ceremony has ever been required to validate a Massachusetts marriage. [T]here are three partners to every civil marriage: two willing spouses and an approving State. . . . While only the parties can mutually assent to marriage, the terms of the marriage — who may marry and what obligations, benefits, and liabilities attach to civil marriage — are set by the Commonwealth. . . . Civil marriage is created and regulated through exercise of the police power. . . .

798 N.E.2d at 954. Further, the court asserts that its decision does not mandate access for same-sex couples to religious marriage ceremonies. Id. at 965. Has the court persuasively separated the civil and religious aspects of marriage? Does this approach successfully counter religious-based arguments against same-sex marriage? Could the state, which creates civil marriage, abolish it? Or, does the constitutional right to marry compel the state to establish civil marriage? See Patricia Cain, Imagine There's No Marriage, 16 Quinnipiac L. Rev. 27 (1996).

9. *Civil unions*. How do civil unions differ from marriage? Is recognition of civil unions for same-sex couples (while marriage is reserved for male-female couples) a step forward or backward for gay rights? According to *Goodridge*, civil unions create a "separate but equal" regime. How? Do you agree? Must (may) other states recognize a civil union, such as that contracted in Vermont, for other purposes? See Note: Domestic Partnership Legislation, infra p. 181.

10. *The* Loving *analogy*. What is the role of *Loving* in the court's analysis in *Goodridge* and in the constitutional debate about same-sex marriage? Are antimiscegenation laws analogous to restrictions against same-sex marriage? See Andrew Koppelman, The Gay Rights Question in Contemporary American Law 63, 71 (2002); Andrew Koppelman, Same-Sex Marriage and Public Policy: The Miscegenation Precedents, 16 Quinnipiac L. Rev. 105 (1996). Evaluate Justice Scalia's rejection of the *Loving* analogy in *Lawrence* on the basis that the law in *Loving* "was designed to maintain White Supremacy" but that no discriminatory purpose underlies the sex classifications in Texas's sodomy ban or traditional marriage restrictions. 539 U.S. at 600 (Scalia, J., dissenting).

Goodridge's treatment of the *Loving* analogy reflects factors influencing the life of Chief Justice Margaret Marshall who authored the opinion. As president of the National Union of South African Students in her native South Africa, she opposed apartheid by leading vigils, collecting signatures for petitions, and raising money for families in which a parent had been arrested. For additional background on Justice Marshall, see Emily Bazelon, A Bold Stroke, Legal Aff. 30 (May/June 2004). For other views of the *Loving* analogy, see Susan Frelich Appleton, Missing in Action? Searching for Gender Talk in the Same-Sex Marriage Debate, 16 Stan. L. & Pol'y Rev. 97 (2005); David Orgon Coolidge, Playing the *Loving* Card: Same Sex Marriage and the Politics of Analogy, 12 B.Y.U. J. Pub. L. 201, 235-236 (1998); Edward Stein, Evaluating the Sex Discrimination Argument for Gay and Lesbian Rights, 49 UCLA L. Rev. 471 (2003).

11. *Debate over the importance of marriage for same-sex couples.* What does *Goodridge* say about the benefits of providing same-sex couples with the institution of marriage? Not all gay and lesbian rights activists, however, advocate same-sex marriage. Compare Evan Wolfson, Why Marriage Matters (2004), with Paula L. Ettelbrick, Wedlock Alert: A Comment on Lesbian and Gay Family Recognition, 5 J.L. & Pol'y 107 (1996), and Nancy D. Polikoff, Symposium, We Will Get What We Ask For: Why Legalizing Gay and Lesbian Marriage Will Not "Dismantle the Legal Structure of Gender in Every Marriage," 79 Va. L. Rev. 1535 (1993) (both contending that recognition of same-sex marriage will have many negative consequences, including forced assimilation, undermining the gay liberation movement, and abandonment of efforts of societal transformation of gender-based roles and traditional conceptions of marriage with its ideals of sexual fidelity and procreation). See also William R. Rubenstein, Divided We Litigate: Addressing Disputes Among Group Members and Lawyers in Civil Rights Campaigns, 106 Yale L.J. 1623 (1997).

What legal and social consequences will follow from recognition of same-sex marriage? What will be the impact on our ideas of marriage, relationships, and homosexuality? Would recognition of same-sex marriage lead to a society that does not recognize marriage? See generally Cain, supra; David L. Chambers, What If? The Legal Consequences of Marriage and the Legal Needs of Lesbian and Gay Male Couples, 95 Mich. L. Rev. 447 (1996); Summer L. Nastich, Questioning the Marriage Assumption: The Justifications for "Opposite-Sex Only" Marriage as Support for the Abolition of Marriage, 21 Law & Inequality J. 114 (2003). On the dissolution of same-sex marriage, see Chapter V, p. 536.

12. *Conflict of laws, full faith and credit, and the Defense of Marriage Act.* Now that Massachusetts recognizes same-sex marriage, an important question concerns the recognition of same-sex marriage in other jurisdictions. That is, are other states *required* to recognize marriage licenses issued to same-sex couples in Massachusetts? To illustrate, suppose Julie and Hillary Goodridge, two women who are legally married in Massachusetts, go to Montana. They subsequently ask Montana to recognize their marriage so that they may obtain spousal benefits (health-related, employment-related, etc.). Is Montana required to give effect to their marriage contracted in Massachusetts? Does your answer depend on whether they are Massachusetts domiciliaries who marry in their home state and then visit Montana? Suppose they later move to Montana? Suppose instead that they are Montana domiciliaries who marry in Massachusetts and then return home? Suppose they spend their lives in Massachusetts but a question of intestate succession to property located in Montana arises after one of them dies without a will? See

Andrew S. Koppelman, Interstate Recognition of Same-Sex Marriage and Civil Unions: A Handbook for Judges, 153 U. Pa. L. Rev. 2143, 2144-2146 (2005) (distinguishing evasive marriages, migratory marriages, visitor marriages, and extraterritorial cases).

The analysis to these questions rests on: (a) conflict-of-laws principles, (b) the Full Faith and Credit Clause of the Constitution, and (c) the Defense of Marriage Act.

a. *Choice of law.* Under traditional conflict-of-laws principles, marriage validity is determined by the law of the state where the marriage was celebrated (the rule of lex loci). However, this rule only applies if recognition of the marriage would not offend the forum state's public policy. (Recall *Loving*, in which the couple married in the District of Columbia.) In contrast, the Restatement (Second) of Conflict of Laws §283(1) (1971) has modified the traditional rule as follows:

§283. Validity of Marriage

(1) The validity of a marriage will be determined by the local law of the state which, with respect to the particular issue, has the most significant relationship to the spouses and the marriage. . . .

(2) A marriage which satisfies the requirements of the state where the marriage was contracted will everywhere be recognized as valid unless it violates the strong public policy of another state which had the most significant relationship to the spouses and the marriage at the time of the marriage.

§284. Incidents of Foreign Marriage

A state usually gives the same incidents to a foreign marriage, which is valid under the principles stated in §283, that it gives to a marriage contracted within its territory.

How would Montana resolve the issue of the validity of Julie and Hillary's marriage based on the Restatement?

A few states have marriage evasion statutes that might preclude recognition of a same-sex marriage that was celebrated in Massachusetts to avoid a more restrictive law elsewhere. Such state legislation was modeled on the Uniform Marriage Evasion Act (discussed supra pp. 151–152) that declared void all marriages entered into by parties who married in another state for the purpose of evading their home state restrictions on marriage.

b. *Full faith and credit.* The Full Faith and Credit Clause (art. IV, §1) of the Constitution requires that a state confer full faith and credit on "the public acts, records and judicial proceedings" of sister states. Same-sex marriage poses several issues. First, is marriage a "public act" (for example, similar to legislation), "record," or "judicial proceeding"? "Judicial proceedings" from sister states require the most complete recognition under the Full Faith and Credit Clause, which has been interpreted to foreclose choice-of-law analysis once a court has rendered a final judgment or decree. "Records" have sometimes evoked the same treatment.

By contrast, the Full Faith and Credit Clause has not been read to mandate recognition of the acts of sister states. Rather, the second state can use choice-of-law analysis, including reliance on its own public policy. Thus, Montana might refuse to give full faith and credit to Julie and Hillary's marriage because Montana determines that same-sex marriage violates Montana public policy.

See generally Brian H. Bix, State Interests in Marriage, Interstate Recognition, and the Choice of Law, 38 Creighton L. Rev. 337 (2005); Andrew Koppelman, Interstate Recognition of Same-Sex Civil Unions After Lawrence v. Texas, 65 Ohio St. L.J. 1265 (2004); Linda Silberman, Same-Sex Marriage: Refining the Conflict of Laws Analysis, 153 U. Pa. L. Rev. 2195 (2005); Tobias Barrington Wolff, Interest Analysis in Interjurisdictional Marriage Disputes, 153 U. Pa. L. Rev. 2215 (2005).

c. *Federal and State Defense of Marriage Acts (DOMA's).*

(1) *Federal DOMA.* Congress and a considerable number of states have undermined the movement to recognize same-sex marriage. In October 1996, Congress enacted the Defense of Marriage Act (DOMA), Pub. L. No. 104-199, 110 Stat. 2419 (codified at 1 U.S.C. §7, 28 U.S.C. §1738C (2000)). DOMA has two parts. First, the act provides a federal definition for the terms "marriage" and "spouse" (for purposes of federal benefits) by specifying that marriage is a union of a man and a woman, and the term "spouse" refers only to a person of the opposite sex. 1 U.S.C. §7 (2000). Second, DOMA specifies that states are not required to give effect to same-sex marriage under the Full Faith and Credit Clause. 28 U.S.C. §1738C (2000). DOMA purportedly rests on Congress's power (in art. IV, §1) to implement the Full Faith and Credit Clause. Yet, it represents the first time that Congress has exercised this authority to foster variation rather than promote uniformity among the states. If valid, DOMA leaves a state free to determine whether to recognize same-sex marriages celebrated elsewhere.

Is DOMA unconstitutional under Romer v. Evans, 517 U.S. 620 (1996)? In *Romer*, the Supreme Court invalidated a Colorado constitutional amendment that prohibited a state from singling out gays and lesbians for special civil rights protections. The Court held that discrimination on the basis of sexual orientation, rooted in animosity, violates equal protection. Does DOMA, by singling out same-sex marriage for denial of full faith and credit, violate *Romer*? What impact, if any, does *Lawrence* have on DOMA? Compare Lynn D. Wardle, Non-Recognition of Same-Sex Marriage Judgments under DOMA and the Constitution, 38 Creighton L. Rev. 365 (2005)(arguing that DOMA is constitutional), with Mark P. Strasser, "Defending" Marriage in Light of the *Moreno-Cleburne-Romer-Lawrence* Jurisprudence: Why DOMA Cannot Pass Muster after *Lawrence*, 38 Creighton L. Rev. 421 (2005) (contra).

To date, the federal DOMA has withstood challenges to its constitutionality. See Wilson v. Ake, 354 F. Supp. 2d 1298 (M.D. Fla. 2005) (dismissing a motion for a declaratory judgment by a same-sex couple arguing that their Massachusetts marriage was valid in Florida; holding that DOMA violates neither the Full Faith and Credit Clause nor, based on rational-basis review, due process, or equal protection); In re Kandu, 315 B.R. 123 (W.D. Wash. 2004) (upholding DOMA based on the Tenth Amendment, due process, and equal protection; determining that a lesbian couple, married in Canada, could not file jointly as "spouses" for purposes of bankruptcy protection). See also Smelt v. County of Orange, 2006 WL 1194825 (holding that couple lacked standing to challenge federal DOMA).

Based on concerns about the constitutionality of DOMA, Congress considered legislation, the Marriage Protection Act of 2005 (H.R. 1100, 109th Cong. 1st Sess. (2005)), to amend title 28 of the United States Code to limit federal court jurisdiction over questions regarding the Defense of Marriage Act. The bill passed the House in July 2004 and was reintroduced in 2005. Is such a jurisdiction-stripping measure constitutional? The proposed legislation raises serious questions about the extent to which Congress may curtail federal court jurisdiction. See generally Theodore J. Weiman, Comment, Jurisdiction Stripping, Constitutional Supremacy, and the Implications of Ex Parte Young, 153 U. Pa. L. Rev. 1677 (2005).

(2) *State DOMA's.* Many states have responded to the same-sex marriage debate by enacting state versions of the Defense of Marriage Act (statutes termed "Baby" or "Mini" DOMA's), or by amending their state constitutions to prohibit same-sex marriage, or both. Currently 41 states have statutory DOMA's; 20 states have state constitutional amendments that contain language defining marriage as a relationship between a man and a woman.[27] Other state legislatures are considering the addition of such a ban to their state constitutions.[28] Arguably, such enactments express unequivocally a state's strong public policy, a significant element in traditional choice of law, as explained supra.

Courts are divided on the constitutionality of state DOMA's. Compare Morrison v. Sadler, 821 N.E.2d 15 (Ind. Ct. App. 2005) (holding that Indiana's DOMA does not violate state constitutional guarantees of privacy or equal protection because the ban on same-sex marriage furthered the state's interest in child-rearing); with Castle v. State, 2004 WL 1985215 (Wash. Super. Ct. 2004) (holding that state DOMA violates privileges or immunities clause of state constitution). Courts are also divided on the constitutionality of state constitutional amendments. Compare Citizens for Equal Protection, Inc. v. Bruning, 368 F. Supp.2d 980 (D. Neb. 2005) (ruling that the state constitutional amendment violates the First Amendment and equal protection, and constitutes an unconstitutional bill of attainder), with Li v. Oregon, 110 P.3d 91 (Or. 2005) (upholding the state constitutional amendment defining marriage as a heterosexual relationship, and voiding the 3000 marriage licenses that were issued to same-sex couples, reasoning that the county did not have the authority to issue licenses to same-sex couples).

14. *Proposed federal constitutional amendment.* In February 2004, President Bush called for a federal constitutional amendment defining marriage as a union between a man and a woman. The Federal Marriage Amendment (FMA) (H.J.Res. 56, 108th Cong. (2003)) failed to pass the House of Representatives in September 2004 and was subsequently reintroduced in March 2005 (H.J. Res. 39, 109th Cong. (2005), and June 2006 (S.J. Res. 1, 109th Cong. (2006)). In the latest attempt, the Senate failed (by a vote of 49 to 48) to garner the necessary 60 votes to invoke cloture, a procedure that would limit floor discussion and bring the measure to a vote.

The proposed legislation provides:

SEC. 1. This article may be cited as the "Marriage Protection Amendment."
SEC. 2. Marriage in the United States shall consist only of the union of a man and a woman. Neither the Constitution, nor the constitution of any State, shall be construed to require that marriage or the legal incidents thereof be conferred upon any union other than the union of a man and a woman.

[27]. See National Conference of State Legislatures, Same Sex Marriage, April 2005, available at http://www.ncsl.org/programs/cyf/samesex.htm#DOMA (last visited May 26, 2006); Kavan Peterson, Washington Gay Montage Ruling Looms (Mar. 29, 2006), available at http: //www.stateline.org/live/ViewPage.action?siteNodeId= 136&languageId=1&contentId=20695 (last visited June 10, 2006) (listing states).

[28]. Six states will hold votes on same-sex marriage bans in 2006: Idaho, South Carolina, South Dakota, Tennessee, Virginia, and Wisconsin in November. Similar amendments are pending in a dozen other states. See Peterson, supra note [27] (listing states).

Constitutional amendments require a two-thirds vote in both the House and Senate, and ratification by three-fourths of the states.

15. *Navajo nation and same-sex marriage.* Same-sex marriage spurred a recent controversy in the Navajo nation. In April 2005 the Tribal Council passed the Dine Marriage Act (DMA) banning same-sex marriage on the reservation spanning Utah, Arizona, and New Mexico. ("Dine" is another word for the Navajo people.) After the Nation president vetoed the DMA as discrimination, the Tribal Council voted to override the veto. Sherrick Roanhorse, A Traditional Navajo, The Advocate, Sept. 27, 2005. The Navajo creation story involves *nadleeh*, or caregivers who are part male and part female, leading some to contend that the Navajo nation is inclusive of lesbian, gay, bisexual, and transgender persons.

16. *International developments.* Several countries now recognize same-sex marriage (Netherlands in 2001, Belgium in 2003, and Spain, Canada and South Africa in 2005). The Canadian legislation was prompted by rulings of several provincial appellate courts that the prohibition on same-sex marriage violates the Canadian Charter of Rights and Freedoms. In response, many American same-sex couples have traveled to Canada to marry. See Clifford Krauss, A Wedding in Canada: Gay Couples Follow a Trail North Blazed by Slaves and War Resisters, N.Y. Times, Nov. 23, 2003, at 7; Mar Roman, Spain's Lawmakers OK Same-Sex Marriage, S.F. Chron., July 1, 2005, at A1; Terry Weber, Canada Legalizes Same-Sex Marriage, S.F. Chron., July 21, 2005, at A3. On the Canadian reform movement, see Kevin Alderson & Kathleen A. Lahey, Same-Sex Marriage: The Personal and the Political (2004).

In December 2005, South Africa's highest court (the Constitutional Court) recognized a same-sex marriage between two Pretoria women. Minister of Home Affairs v. Fourie CCT 60/04 (2005). The court held that South Africa's constitution, which prohibits discrimination based on sexual orientation, guarantees the right of same-sex partners to marry. However, the court stayed the ruling for one year to give Parliament time to enact new legislation amending its marriage law. Craig Timberg, S. Africa's Top Court Blesses Gay Marriage, Wash. Post, Dec. 2, 2005, at A16.

17. *Transsexuals and marriage.* Do prohibitions on same-sex marriage have any effect on the marriage of a transsexual (also termed "a trangender person")? Some courts determine marriage validity based on the transsexual's genetic makeup and childbearing capacity (aspects not altered by sexual surgery). Compare In re Marriage of Simmons, 825 N.E.2d 303 (Ill. App. Ct. 2005) and Kantaras v. Kantaras, 884 So.2d 155 (Fla. Dist. Ct. App. 2004) (invalidating marriages between a woman and transsexual who was genetically female), with M.T. v. J.T. 355 A.2d 204 (N.J. Super. Ct. App. Div. 1976) (stating that marriage validity depends on the ability to engage in sexual activity consistent with reconciled anatomy). Should *sexual* capacity be the test for marriage validity?

Some cities and states protect the civil liberties of transgender persons. Minneapolis was the first city to pass such a law in 1975. San Francisco currently protects transgender persons from discrimination in employment, housing, and public accommodations. Carolyn E. Coffey, Battling Gender Orthodox: Prohibiting Discrimination on the Basis of Gender Identity and Expression in the Courts and in the Legislatures, 7 N.Y. City L. Rev. 161,

185 (2004) (pointing out that 74 cities and states have protective ordinances). See also Smith v. City of Salem, 378 F.3d 566 (6th Cir. 2004) (holding that Title VII is applicable to transsexuals who suffer adverse employment decisions due to their non-conforming gender behavior). On legal issues affecting transsexuals, see Michael L. Rosin, Intersexuality and Universal Marriage, 14 Law & Sexuality 51 (2005); Mark Strasser, Marriage, Transsexuals, and the Meaning of Sex, 3 Hous. J. of Health L. & Pol'y 301 (2003). See also Susan Frelich Appleton, Contesting Gender in Popular Culture and Family Law: Middlesex and Other Transgender Tales, 80 Ind. L.J. 391 (2005) (exploring identity conflicts of a famous trangender youth).

Problem

J'Noel was born male, but later has sex reassignment surgery. At her request, the Wisconsin Bureau of Vital Statistics amends her birth certificate to reflect that she is now female. At her place of employment (she is an assistant professor with a Ph.D. in finance), she meets Marshall, a businessman with one adult son Joe from whom he is estranged. While dating, J'Noel informs Marshall of her prior history as a male. They marry, and J'Noel moves to Kansas where Marshall lives. When Marshall dies intestate 11 years later, his son Joe petitions for letters of administration and claims to be the sole beneficiary of his father's estate. Joe alleges that his father's marriage was invalid because J'Noel was born male. What result? See In re Estate of Gardiner, 42 P.3d 120 (Kan. 2002). Does the Kansas court owe full faith and credit to Wisconsin's change in J'Noel's birth certificate? See generally MaryBeth Herald & Julie A. Greenberg, You Can't Take it with You: Constitutional Consequences of Interstate Gender Identity Rulings, 80 Wash. L. Rev. 819 (2005); Mark Strasser, Harvesting the Fruits of *Gardiner:* On Marriage, Public Policy, and Fundamental Interests, 71 Geo. Wash. L. Rev. 179 (2003) (discussing the impact of *Gardiner*).

Note: Domestic Partnership Legislation

Several states have enacted domestic partnership legislation for same-sex couples. Currently, California, Connecticut, the District of Columbia, Hawaii, Maine, New Jersey, and Vermont have benefit schemes ranging from those that offer limited rights to those that confer the same benefits as married couples enjoy.

Some states enacted domestic partnership legislation as a political alternative to the legalization of same-sex marriage. For example, Hawaii became the first state to confer legal rights on domestic partners after voters there passed a constitutional amendment defining marriage as a heterosexual relationship in reaction to Baehr v. Lewin (discussed supra) favoring same-sex marriage. The Reciprocal Partners Benefits Act (Haw. Rev. Stat. Ann. §§572C-1 to 7) offers certain limited rights to members of same-sex couples (designated as *reciprocal beneficiaries*), including: workers compensation benefits (§386-34); property and land ownership benefits (§509-2); some survivorship rights (§560:2-101); family leave (§388-4); and hospital visitation (§323-2). Partners may register if they are at least 18 years old, not married or in another reciprocal beneficiary relationship, and are prohibited from marrying (§572C-4). In addition, parties must sign a declaration indicating their voluntary consent to enter the relationship (id.). Either party may terminate the relationship by filing a notarized declaration, or by getting married (§572C-7).

Both Vermont and Connecticut enacted *civil unions* for same-sex couples. In 2000, the Vermont legislature enacted legislation pursuant to order of the state supreme court in Baker v. State (discussed supra). In April 2005, Connecticut enacted civil unions as a compromise to proposed legislation that would have legalized same-sex marriage. Both states give same-sex couples all of the benefits of marriage except the title "marriage." See An Act Concerning Civil Unions, S.B. No. 963 (eff. Oct. 1, 2005); Vt. St. Ann. Tit. 15, §1204 (2002). Significantly, couples also receive state tax benefits under both state regimes. In order to enter into a valid civil union in either Vermont or Connecticut, parties must not be members of another civil union and must be of the same sex. Furthermore, they may not be blood relatives. Civil unions are terminated in the same manner as marriages.

California's domestic partnership statutes (Cal. Fam. Code §297.5 (West 2004)) became effective on January 1, 2005, and amended the state's existing domestic partnership statute to provide registered domestic partners with the same benefits as married persons. However, California domestic partnerships differ from civil unions in two significant ways: (1) partners may be same-sex couples *or* heterosexual couples where one party is at least 62 years old and eligible for Social Security (§297), and (2) partners are *ineligible* for tax benefits at the state level. The former provision attempts to redress the economic consequences faced by elderly couples whose Social Security benefits would be significantly reduced or eliminated if they married.

In order to register as domestic partners in California, parties must have a common residence, not be married or in another domestic partnership, not related by blood, at least 18 years old, and capable of consenting to the partnership (§297). Domestic partnerships formed in California may be terminated there either via a judicial proceeding or filing a notice of termination with the Secretary of State (§299). Parties may only terminate via notice if they do not share any property interests (other than leases without an option to buy); both parties agree to the dissolution; they have been domestic partners not longer than five years; they agree regarding division of common assets; they have limited assets; and each party waives the right to support from the other (id.).

New Jersey's domestic partnership legislation is more liberal than Hawaii's but not as liberal as Vermont's and Connecticut's. Partners have the right to participate in family insurance plans, hospital visitation, health care decisionmaking for an incapacitated partner, control of the disposition of a partner's remains, exemption from inheritance tax and claiming a partner as a dependent, state pension benefits, and protection against employment discrimination. Parties are eligible if they have a common residence and joint responsibility for the other's welfare; joint ownership (demonstrated by a common bank account, one party designated as the other's primary beneficiary on a will or insurance policy, joint ownership of property, or joint ownership of a car); joint responsibility for basic living expenses; no other marriages or domestic partnerships within the past 180 days; no blood relation; and be at least 18 years old (N.J. Stat. Ann. §26:8A-4 (West Supp. 2005)). As in California, domestic partners may be either a same-sex couple or a heterosexual couple provided one party is at least 62 years old. State law applies at dissolution (§§26:8A-5, 10).

In New Jersey, domestic partners are entitled to limited inheritance tax benefits (§54:34-1-4). They are also afforded visitation rights at hospitals; protection from discrimination (in housing, employment and credit based on their domestic partner status); and partner benefits for state employees (§26:8A-1). However, property acquired by one partner is considered separate property; also domestic partnerships do not affect duties owed by a spouse to children.

Maine also offers limited benefits. In 2004, Maine granted some rights of inheritance to domestic partners (both same sex and heterosexual) who register, are unmarried, and who "are domiciled together under long-term arrangements that evidence a commitment to remain responsible indefinitely for each other's welfare" (Me. Rev. Stat. Tit. 22, §2710). Specifically, the surviving partner is entitled to the same intestate share as a spouse, priority in appointment as administrator of the deceased partner's estate, and the right to determine disposition of the deceased partner's remains.

In April 2006, the District of Columbia passed a bill giving increased rights to domestic partners (defined as same-sex and opposite-sex partners above age 18) in the areas of: intestate succession, alimony and child support, immunity from testifying against a partner in a civil or criminal proceeding, suits for wrongful death, "pre-marital" agreements, durable powers of attorney for health care decisionmaking, and the evidentiary privilege applicable to confidential relationships (involving physicians and religious figures). Joshua Lynsen, Couples Win Expanded D.P. Rights: New Benefits for Gay, Straight D.C. Couples Fall Far Short of Marriage, Wash. Blade, Mar. 31, 2006. The District of Columbia city council first granted rights to domestic partners in 1992, but Congress blocked implementation of the bill for a decade. (Congressional approval is needed for city legislation.) Emily Heil, Gays Face Off in D.C., Advoc., Feb. 14, 2006, at 38.

Note that domestic partnerships are not recognized under federal law for purposes of federal benefits. Nor are their legal protections necessarily transferable to other states. See, e.g., Langan v. Saint Vincent's Hosp., 802 N.Y.S.2d 476 (App. Div. 2005) (holding that a surviving partner of a civil union under Vermont law was not entitled to bring an action under New York law as a "spouse" in a wrongful death claim against a hospital for the death of his male partner). For discussion of the American Law Institute's provisions which provide rights to domestic partners (both same-sex and heterosexual) upon dissolution, see Chapter IV. For discussion of the parental status provisions of domestic partnership legislation, see Chapter VII.

On the international level, the Scandinavian countries have been in the forefront of the movement to recognize same-sex civil unions. The Danish Registered Partnership Act, enacted in 1989, provides same-sex partners the same rights as married couples with the exception of the right to be married in a state church ceremony. Norway, Sweden, Iceland and Finland have enacted similar legislation. In 1999, France introduced a form of civil contract that provides some rights to both same-sex and hetereosexual cohabiting couples. This status does not include such marital rights as tax or inheritance benefits, or the right to adopt. Germany permits same-sex partners to register for "life partnerships" and provides the same inheritance and tenants' rights as those extended to spouses. In 2004, Luxembourg adopted civil partnerships based on the French model. See Associated Press Newsflash, Gay Marriages, Civil Unions Around World, Dec. 5, 2005, available at http://www.mlive.com/ newsflash/international.

Finally, in December 2005, a law went into effect in Great Britain authorizing civil partnerships and extending to registered same-sex couples some of the financial advantages enjoyed by married heterosexual couples, such as tax benefits on inherited real property and pension rights. Alan Cowell, Gay Britains Signing Up as Unions Become Legal, N.Y. Times, Dec. 6, 2005, at A12.

(2) Incest

■ IN RE ADOPTION OF M.
722 A.2d 615 (N.J. Super. Ct. Ch. Div. 1998)

BATTEN, J.S.C.

. . . The undisputed facts are troubling beyond description. [On] January 5, 1991, adoptive parents sought to adopt child M (hereinafter "petitioner"), born November 24, 1975, and voluntarily surrendered by her natural parents to the Division of Youth and Family Services, in May 1989. The adoption was uncontested. Final judgment of adoption entered January 25, 1991 [when] [p]etitioner was then fifteen years old. Two years and ten months later, on November 21, 1993, petitioner attained age eighteen.

At some point in time subsequent to the final judgment of adoption yet prior to September 8, 1997, the marital relationship between the adoptive parents failed. Adoptive mother, on this latter date, filed her complaint for divorce against adoptive father, alleging acts of extreme cruelty. [The adoptive parents actually separated several years prior to the time they filed for divorce.] On November 18, 1997, final judgment of divorce dissolved the marriage of the adoptive parents. On July 29, 1998, petitioner, then twenty-two years of age, gave birth to an infant son. The parties acknowledge that adoptive father is the natural father of the infant.

Poignant realities emerge. First, petitioner and the adoptive father conceived the infant child in or about October 1997, at which time petitioner was twenty-one years of age. Second, conception between petitioner and adoptive father therefore likely occurred *prior* to the November 18, 1997, dissolution of his marriage to adoptive mother. Third, *a fortiori*, adoptive father engaged in a carnal relationship with his adult adoptive daughter while he was yet married to her adoptive mother. Fourth, the foregoing circumstances suggest — and the record stipulated before the court specifically confirms — that the relationship between petitioner and adoptive father had transgressed the parameters of a parent-child relationship well prior to the act of conception. Now the natural parents of the minor child, they desire to marry. Their present legal relationship as adoptive father and adoptive daughter, however, clearly renders the former an "ancestor" of, and the latter a "descendant" to, the other, thereby precluding lawful marriage between them.[6]

___

6. N.J.S.A. 37:1-1 states, in pertinent part, that:

A man shall not marry any of his ancestors or descendants, or his sister, or the daughter of his brother or sister, or the sister of his father or mother, whether such collateral kindred be of the

N.J.S.A. 37:1-1. Hence, petitioner brings this application.

[Although petitioner originally moved to vacate the adoption as to both her adoptive parents, she and her adoptive mother subsequently decided to leave their relationship undisturbed. Petitioner thus sought to vacate the adoption as to her adoptive father only.]

Final judgment of adoption marks a turning point in the status of the natural and adoptive parents. Entry of such a judgment terminates all relationships between the adopted child and his/her natural parents and all of the rights, duties, and obligations of any persons that are founded on such relationships. . . . Subsequent to judgment, the adoptive parents are, as a matter of law, the parents of that child as if the child had been born to the adoptive parents in lawful wedlock.

Under New Jersey law [a] final judgment of adoption "should not be set aside unless it is in the best interest of the child and adoptive parents," and upon the showing of "truly exceptional circumstances" as determined by the particular facts of each case. . . . Indeed, the Legislature has mandated that the Adoption Act of New Jersey "shall be liberally construed to the end that the *best interests of children* be promoted," and "*due regard shall be given to the rights of all persons affected by an adoption.*" N.J.S.A. 9:3-37. [Emphasis added]. . . .

Certainly, the interests of "all persons affected" by this adoption have changed measurably. First, the adoptive child, in whose best interests the adoption occurred, is now, seven years later, (A) twenty-two years of age, (B) a natural mother of a two month old infant son, and (C) intent upon marriage to her son's natural father. The absence of any facts of record which might support a finding of abuse, neglect, domestic violence or other unlawful act suggests a petitioner's conscious decision that her legal relationship with her adoptive father had achieved its purpose and, parent-child status notwithstanding, the complexities and realities of human emotions and relationships warrant transposition of that status from father-daughter co-parents to husband and wife. Through marriage, petitioner legitimizes not only her relationship with her son's father but the status of her infant son as well. . . .

Clearly, the facts here . . . constitute "truly exceptional circumstances" for several reasons. First, all reported cases contemplate an application to vacate a final judgment of adoption at a time during the minority of the adoptive child; here, the petitioner, as adopted child, moves post-emancipation to vacate the judgment of adoption. In this sense, the "best interests" standard of N.J.S.A. 9:2-4 no longer pertains to the adoptive child. Second, the stated purpose of the petition to vacate is eradication of a legal impediment to petitioner's marriage to her adoptive father, a relationship to which petitioner and adoptive father would be entitled absent their present legal status as father-daughter. Third, vacation of the final judgment of adoption would also shed adoptive father of his simultaneous status as natural father and legal grandfather of the minor infant, leaving him the natural father only. Fourth, vacation of the adoption judgment, through its cure of the statutory impediment to marriage, would further legitimize the infant, thereby advancing long-standing policy of this state to protect the status of children. More "truly exceptional circumstances" are difficult to imagine. . . . Petitioner's application

---

whole or half blood. *A woman shall not marry any of her ancestors or descendants*, or her brother, or the son of her brother or sister, or the brother of her father or mother, whether such collateral kindred be of the whole or half blood. *A marriage in violation of any of the foregoing provisions shall be absolutely void.* [Emphasis added].

to vacate the final judgment of adoption as pertains to her adoptive father is — as it must be — granted. . . .

Note: Void versus Voidable Distinction

Statutes and the common law classify invalid marriages as either void or voidable. A void marriage is one that is invalid from inception (void ab initio), that is, it never had legal existence. On the other hand, a voidable marriage is valid until subsequently declared invalid. The distinction becomes important in terms of who may assert the invalidity of a marriage and whether the validity of the marriage may be collaterally attacked.

If a marriage is void, then either party or a third party may challenge the validity of the marriage at any time and in any proceeding. Homer H. Clark, Jr., The Law of Domestic Relations in the United States 93 (2d ed. 1988). See also In re Estate of Santolino, 895 A.2d 506 (N.J. Super. Ct. Ch. Div. 2005) (holding that sister of elderly, ill husband could raise claim posthumously that his marriage was void due to lack of capacity). On the other hand, if a marriage is voidable, its invalidity can only be asserted by one of the parties and only during the marriage (that is, not after death of one of the parties). Further, it cannot be collaterally attacked (that is, in a related proceeding).

The consequences of a particular defect stem from history (ecclesiastical law) as well as public policy (the degree to which the defect offends public policy). Substantive defects (same-sex, bigamous, and incestuous unions) render the marriage void. Less serious substantive defects, such as age, may render the marriage voidable.

Notes and Questions

1. *Historical background.* Virtually all societies have some form of incest taboos. Classic formulations exist in the psychoanalytic, sociological, and anthropological literature. See, e.g., Sigmund Freud, Totem and Taboo (1917); Claude Levi-Strauss, Elementary Structures of Kinship (1967); George Peter Murdock, Social Structure (1949); Talcott Parsons, The Incest Taboo in Relation to Social Structure and the Socialization of the Child, 5 Brit. J. Soc. 101 (1954).

Incest proscriptions can be traced to Leviticus.[29] The Catholic Church also had early proscriptions against incest. Prior to 1215, kinship within the six and seventh degrees (using the canon law method of calculation) rendered a marriage sinful — not null as did impediments within the first five degrees. The Lateran Council of 1215 strengthened the proscriptions: marriages within the fourth degree of consanguinity became null, as did certain affinal (that is, in-law) relationships.[30]

William the Conqueror separated the lay jurisdiction from the ecclesiastical. Ecclesiastical jurisdiction prevailed over marriage. Thus, incest (similar to adultery and bigamy) became ecclesiastic offenses. Between the thirteenth and the sixteenth centuries, prohibitions on incestuous marriages were extensive, but mitigated by dispensations to the wealthy. Incest became a crime in 1650, punishable by

---

[29]. Leviticus 18:6. "None of you shall approach to any that is near of kin to him, to uncover their nakedness."

[30]. 2 Frederick Pollock & Frederic William Maitland, The History of English Law Before the Time of Edward I 387-388 (S. F. C. Milsom ed., 1968) (1898).

death.[31] In 1908, the Punishment of Incest Act, 8 Edw. 7, ch. 45, proscribed three to seven years imprisonment.

2. *Civil and criminal consequences.* Every state specifies the degrees of consanguinity and affinity within which persons may not marry. ("Consanguinity" refers to blood relations, while "affinity" refers to relations by marriage.) Marriage to one's parent, grandparent, brother, or sister is universally prohibited, as is marriage between an aunt and nephew, and between an uncle and niece. Occasionally, states extend the prohibition to marriages between parents and their adopted children, and also to steprelationships. In contrast, most countries and many states permit first cousin marriages.[32]

Most jurisdictions regard incestuous marriages as void ab initio. Incest is also a crime. However, the degrees of relation for marriage restrictions are not necessarily the same as the degrees for criminal liability.

3. *State interests.* According to *Zablocki* (supra p. 145), regulations that substantially and directly interfere with the freedom to marry must receive elevated scrutiny. Do incest laws qualify? What state interests are at stake? Several have been suggested, including the protection of the gene pool from deleterious consequences of inbreeding; protection of persons from exploitation (for example, absence of meaningful consent to marry such as by an older family member compelling a younger); protection of the family from the assumption of incompatible roles by some family members; and protection of societal concepts of decency. Are these state interests "sufficiently important" to justify the restrictions? Note that experts disagree about the harmful consequences of inbreeding.[33] If these state interests are sufficiently important, are the proscriptions sufficiently closely tailored to achieve these goals?

If the goal is prevention of the harmful consequences of procreation, should the state exempt those too old to reproduce? Require genetic testing for marriage licenses? Prohibit marriages involving a partner who carries harmful genetic traits? See, e.g., Ariz. Rev. Stat. Ann. §36-797.42 (West 2003); Ky. Rev. Stat. Ann. §402.310-.340 (Michie 1999) (genetic screening provisions). Require sterilization of such a partner? One commentator suggests more effective and less intrusive means: noncompulsory genetic screening programs, programs regulating known environmental factors that cause birth defects, nutritional programs as well as pre- and post-natal medical care for pregnant women and infants. Carolyn S. Bratt, Incest Statutes and the Fundamental Right of Marriage: Is Oedipus Free to Marry?, 18 Fam. L.Q. 257, 281 (1984). What do you think of these suggestions? Is protection of the gene pool a justifiable function of government? In the interests of privacy, should the decision to perpetuate possibly harmful genetic traits be left to the individual? See also Christine McNiece Meteer, Some "Incest" Is Harmless Incest: Determining the Fundamental Right to Marry of Adults Related by Affinity Without Resorting to State Incest Statutes, 10 Kan. J.L. & Pub. Pol'y 262 (2000).

4. *Privacy.* Do criminal sanctions violate the constitutional right to privacy? In Smith v. State, 6 S.W.2d 512 (Tenn. Crim. App. 1999), appellant was convicted of

---

[31]. 4 William Blackstone, Commentaries *64.

[32]. Joanna Grossman, Should the Law Be Kinder to "Kissin' Cousins"?: A Genetic Report Should Cause a Rethinking of Incest Laws, Apr. 8, 2002, available at http://findlaw.com/grossman/20020408.html (last visited June 26, 2005).

[33]. See Denise Grady, Few Risks Seen to the Children of 1st Cousins, N.Y. Times, Apr. 4, 2002, at A1 (reporting the findings of six studies that discount the harmful genetic consequences of incest).

engaging in an incestuous relationship with her paternal uncle, which had begun when she was a minor. On appeal, she argued that the incest statute violated her right to privacy under the state constitution, i.e., her right to engage in consensual sexual activities in the privacy of the home. Rejecting her argument, the court found that no fundamental right was involved and reasoned that the statute was rationally related to the objective of promoting morality and family stability. *Smith* preceded the U.S. Supreme Court's decision in Lawrence v. Texas by several years. Might a court decide differently after *Lawrence*? See Brett H. McDonnell, Is Incest Next?, 10 Cardozo Women's L.J. 337 (2004) (examining how *Lawrence* affects laws regulating other forms of sexual behavior, focusing on consensual adult incest).

5. *Relatives by adoption. Adoption of M.* addresses prohibitions on marriage of persons related by adoption. What state interest supports such restrictions? How can that interest be served by prohibiting marriage by adoptive siblings who have grown up in separate households? Compare Israel v. Allen, 577 P.2d 762 (Colo. 1978), with In re MEW, 4 Pa. D.&C.3d 51 (1977).

6. *Criminal liability for parties and officials.* Many state statutes not only classify certain marriages as presumptively void but also subject to criminal liability officials who knowingly issue marriage licenses to such couples. The parties themselves, of course, are also subject to criminal penalties — in some jurisdictions rather draconian ones. See, e.g., Cal. Penal Code §285 (West 2004) (previous version of statute authorized up to 50 years imprisonment). Are criminal sanctions appropriate to enforce civil limitations on marriage? Recall the analogous relationship between criminal laws on sodomy and same-sex marriage bans.

7. *Choice of law.* Suppose a couple marries in a state where marriage between first cousins is permitted, but they move to another state where it is prohibited. Which law applies to issues of their marital status? In Cook v. Cook, 104 P.3d 857 (Ariz. App. Div. 2005), Alan marries his first cousin, Peggy, in Virginia where such marriages are valid. They move to Arizona which does not permit such marriages but which follows the rule of lex loci. A few years later, Arizona changes its law, declaring void any out-of-state marriage which would have been prohibited by Arizona's consanguinity statute. When Alan and Peggy seek a divorce in Arizona, should the court refuse on the basis that their marriage was void? Should Virginia or Arizona law apply? Should consanguineous marriages, permitted by and celebrated in one spouse's domicile, receive different treatment from marriages celebrated elsewhere for the sole purpose of evading the domicile's restrictions? See In re May's Estate, 114 N.E.2d 4 (N.Y. 1953).

Problem

Movie director Woody Allen, age 56, has an affair with Soon-Yi Previn, age 22, the adopted daughter of Allen's long-term lover, actress Mia Farrow. (Soon-Yi Previn's adoptive father is Andre Previn, Farrow's former husband.) Although Allen and Farrow had had a biological child together and are the adoptive parents of two other young children, Allen and Farrow never married; in fact, they maintained separate residences.

Should a state legislature criminalize sexual relationships such as Allen's and Soon-Yi Previn's? Preclude the issuance of marriage licenses to such couples? Declare any ensuing marriages void? Consider the following commentary:

Defining the ancient taboo becomes hard in an era of recombinant families created by divorce, remarriage and adoption. The traditional stricture — no carnal relations between parent and child or brother and sister — still holds, but how does it apply in today's blended and extended families, where blood ties are often thin or absent? [Despite, scientific and cultural reasons for the taboo] the most significant damage from incest is psychological. The heart of a family, say experts, is not the bloodline but the emotional connection. "Proper human growth involves gradually separating emotionally from your family so that you can go off and start one of your own," stresses child therapist Carole West of Beverly Hills, California. "Incest disrupts that process." . . .

Anastasia Toufexis, What Is Incest?, Time, Aug. 31, 1992, at 57.[34]

(3) Bigamy

■ **STATE v. GREEN**
99 P.3d 820 (Utah 2004)

criminal bigamy

PARRISH, Justice.
A jury convicted Thomas Green of criminal nonsupport and four counts of bigamy. Green appeals his bigamy convictions. . . .
An avowed polygamist, Green has participated in simultaneous conjugal-type relationships with multiple women. These women all use Green's surname and have borne children who also use the Green surname. Between 1970 and 1996, Green formed relationships with Lynda Penman, Beth Cook, Linda Kunz, Shirley Beagley, June Johnson, LeeAnn Beagley, Cari Bjorkman, Hannah Bjorkman, and Julie Dawn McKinley. Through his relationships with these women, Green has fathered approximately twenty-five children.
Some of the women entered into licensed marriages with Green. The remaining women participated in unlicensed ceremonies, after which they considered themselves married to Green. Green avoided being in more than one licensed marriage at a time by terminating each licensed marriage by divorce prior to obtaining a license for a new marriage. Green then continued his relationships with each of the women he divorced as if no divorce had occurred.
In 1995, Green and his family moved to Juab County, Utah, where they resided together in a collection of shared mobile homes that the family called "Green Haven." Green quartered in one mobile home, while the women and children quartered in others. Some of the mobile home areas were set aside as common dining and laundry areas, and the family shared the bathrooms scattered among the mobile homes. The women spent nights individually with Green in his mobile home on a rotating schedule.
Each of the women shared with Green the duties of raising the children and managing the family by dividing the tasks of cooking for the entire family, doing the family laundry, and home schooling all of the children. In addition, the women assisted with the family business, which consisted of selling magazine subscriptions.

[34]. Technically, incest statutes prohibit sexual conduct between related, consenting adults as well as such conduct between related adults and children. We now more commonly refer to the latter as "sexual abuse of children."

All money earned by the family business was pooled into "the Green Family Household account."

Between 1988 and 2001, Green appeared on various television shows with the women, consistently referring to the women as his wives, and the women likewise acknowledged spousal relationships. In these television appearances, Green acknowledged that his conduct was potentially punishable under Utah criminal statutes. In April 2000, the State filed an information charging Green with, among other things, four counts of bigamy. . . .

[W]e will restrict our review of this case to . . . Green's claims that (1) Utah's bigamy statute violates his federal constitutional right to free exercise of religion; [and] (2) Utah's bigamy statute is unconstitutionally vague in light of Green's conduct. . . .

Utah's bigamy statute provides, in relevant part, as follows:

> A person is guilty of bigamy when, knowing he has a husband or wife or knowing the other person has a husband or wife, the person purports to marry another person or cohabits with another person.

Utah Code Ann. §76-7-101(1) (2003). Green argues that this statute is unconstitutional under the First Amendment to the United States Constitution because it punishes his marital practices in violation of his right to freely exercise his religion. Specifically, Green argues that a law effectively prohibiting religiously motivated bigamy (which we refer to as polygamy) cannot withstand a challenge under the standards articulated by the United States Supreme Court. . . .

First, Green is not the first polygamist to launch an attack on the constitutionality of a law burdening the practice of polygamy. In 1878, polygamist George Reynolds challenged the constitutionality of the Morrill Antibigamy Act, which prohibited bigamy in all territories of the United States. Reynolds v. United States, 98 U.S. 145 (1878). Reynolds argued that he could not be found guilty under the law inasmuch as he believed that marrying more than one woman was his religious duty. The Supreme Court held that the law did not violate the Free Exercise Clause of the First Amendment, finding, in part, that "[l]aws are made for the government of actions, and while they cannot interfere with mere religious belief and opinions, they may with practices." Id. at 166. . . . The Supreme Court reviewed the practice of polygamy, found it to be socially undesirable, and upheld Reynolds' bigamy conviction.

We are cognizant of the fact that *Reynolds* was decided over a century ago and may be antiquated in its wording and analysis. We are similarly cognizant of the fact that its reasoning may not necessarily comport with today's understanding of the language and apparent purpose of the Free Exercise Clause. Nevertheless, the Supreme Court has never explicitly overruled the decision. . . .

We follow the analysis set forth by the Supreme Court in [Employment Div., Dept. of Human Res. v. Smith, 494 U.S. 872 (1990) (holding that state laws penalizing ceremonial ingestion of peyote did not violate the Free Exercise Clause and therefore the state could deny claimants unemployment compensation for work-related misconduct based on use of drug); and Church of the Lukumi Babalu Aye, Inc. v. City of Hialeah, 508 U.S. 520 (1993) (invalidating city ordinances prohibiting ritual slaughter of animals because the regulations were not neutral, not of general applicability, and not justified by a compelling state interest)] and, accordingly, examine Utah's bigamy statute to determine whether it is neutral and of general applicability.

[I]n the case now before us, Green and amici curiae argue that Utah's bigamy statute is not facially neutral. They contend that use of the word "cohabit" in the statute's text amounts to impermissible targeting of the religiously motivated marital practices of polygamists. In furtherance of their contention, Green and amici assert that "cohabit" must be read as plainly referring to polygamists because Utah is the only state that outlaws cohabitation between parties as bigamy and because early federal laws enacted in response to polygamy also made cohabitation an element of the crime of bigamy. We disagree.

. . . Utah's bigamy statute explains what it prohibits in secular terms, without referring to religious practices. The statute does not on its face mention polygamists or their religion. In addition, the word "cohabit" does not have religious origins or connotations; rather, it is a word of secular meaning. Green and amici attempt to infuse the word "cohabit" with religious animus, but in doing so they erroneously circumvent and ignore the word's plain meaning. Utah's bigamy statute is not a statute that "refers to a religious practice without a secular meaning discernable from the language." We accordingly hold that it is facially neutral.

[W]e also must assess the statute's operational neutrality. . . . Utah's bigamy statute does not similarly operate to isolate and punish only that bigamy which results from the religious practices of polygamists. It contains no exemptions that would restrict the practical application of the statute only to polygamists. In fact, the last reported decision of a prosecution under the current bigamy statute in our state courts involved a man who committed bigamy for non-religious reasons. State v. Geer, 765 P.2d 1, 1-2 (Utah Ct. App. 1988). We thus find that Utah's bigamy statute is operationally, as well as facially, neutral. . . .

[W]e move [next] to the second requirement of the Free Exercise Clause — the requirement that "laws burdening religious practice must be of general applicability." . . . As noted above, Utah's bigamy statute does not attempt to target only religiously motivated bigamy. Any individual who violates the statute, whether for religious or secular reasons, is subject to prosecution. . . .

It is true that Utah's bigamy statute has an adverse impact on those wishing to practice polygamy as a tenet of their religion. An adverse impact on religion does not by itself, however, prove impermissible targeting because "a social harm may have been a legitimate concern of government for reasons quite apart from [religious] discrimination." [Church of the Lukumi Babalu Aye, Inc. v. City of Hialeah, 508 U.S. 520, 535 (1993)] (citing *Reynolds*, 98 U.S. 145) (other citations omitted). Indeed, "[i]n many instances, the Congress or state legislatures conclude that the general welfare of society, wholly apart from any religious considerations," demands "regulation of conduct whose reason or effect merely happens to coincide or harmonize with the tenets of some or all religions." McGowan v. Maryland, 366 U.S. 420, 442 (1961).

The Utah legislature has determined that prohibiting bigamy serves this state's best interests. Because Utah's bigamy statute is neutral and of general applicability, the State is not required to show that the interests it serves are compelling or that the statute is narrowly tailored in pursuit of those interests. Instead, the State need show only that the statute is rationally related to a legitimate government end. [W]e assess whether the State has met its burden in this regard. We conclude that Utah's bigamy statute is rationally related to several legitimate government ends.

First, this state has an interest in regulating marriage. . . .

[m]arriage . . . has always been subject to the control of the legislature. That body prescribes the age at which parties may contract to marry, the procedure or form essential to constitute marriage, the duties and obligations it creates, its effects upon the property rights of both, present and prospective, and the acts which may constitute grounds for its dissolution.

Zablocki v. Redhail, 434 U.S. 374, 399 (1978) (Powell, J., concurring in judgment). The State of Utah's interest in regulating marriage has resulted in a network of laws, many of which are premised upon the concept of monogamy. . . .

Beyond the State's interest in regulating marriage as an important social unit, or in maintaining its network of laws, Utah's bigamy statute serves additional legitimate government ends. Specifically, prohibiting bigamy implicates the State's interest in preventing the perpetration of marriage fraud, as well as its interest in preventing the misuse of government benefits associated with marital status.

Most importantly, Utah's bigamy statute serves the State's interest in protecting vulnerable individuals from exploitation and abuse. The practice of polygamy, in particular, often coincides with crimes targeting women and children. Crimes not unusually attendant to the practice of polygamy include incest, sexual assault, statutory rape, and failure to pay child support.[14] Moreover, the closed nature of polygamous communities makes obtaining evidence of and prosecuting these crimes challenging.

All of the foregoing interests are legitimate, if not compelling, interests of the State, and Utah's bigamy statute is rationally related to the furthering of those interests. We therefore hold that Utah's bigamy statute does not violate the Free Exercise Clause of the First Amendment of the United States Constitution. Having so determined, we turn our attention to Green's assertion that Utah's bigamy statute is unconstitutionally vague.

Green argues that Utah's bigamy statute is unconstitutionally vague [because] the statute left him "in a quandary" over how often he could legally reside with and have sexual contact with the women. We disagree and hold that the word "cohabit" is not vague as applied to Green's conjugal-type associations.

The record is clear that Green intended to create and maintain spousal-type relationships with Shirley Beagley, LeeAnn Beagley, Cari Bjorkman, and Hannah Bjorkman. He referred to each of these women as a wife, regardless of whether a licensed marriage existed. The women likewise considered themselves Green's wives and adopted the Green surname. Green spent nights with each woman on a rotating schedule and succeeded in impregnating these four women eighteen times, collectively. . . . Together, Green and the women undertook spousal and parental obligations. . . . With these facts in mind, it is difficult to see how Green

---

14. Green's circumstances illustrate this point. In addition to being convicted of bigamy, Green was also convicted of criminal nonsupport and rape of a child, Linda Kunz, who was thirteen years old at the time of her first sexual association with Green. The potential for conflicts of consanguinity in polygamous associations is illustrated by Green's relationships. Among Green's "wives" are three sets of sisters and three of his own stepdaughters. For another example, see State v. Kingston, 2002 UT App 103, 46 P.3d 761.

could be unsure whether he might be "cohabiting" within the meaning of Utah's bigamy statute. Indeed, Green's conduct produced precisely the situation that bigamy statutes aim to prevent. . . .

[In addition,] Green and amici argue that Utah's bigamy statute affords enforcement officials too much prosecutorial discretion because it does not specifically indicate which of the "myriad of modern living arrangements" should be prosecuted. . . . We find that law enforcement officials encountering Green's circumstances would not be left to pursue their own personal predilections in determining the applicability of Utah's bigamy statute. As we already have discussed, Green's conduct fell unmistakably within the statute's purview. . . . We therefore hold that Green's vagueness challenge fails. . . .

We affirm the district court and hold that (1) Utah's bigamy statute does not violate Green's federal constitutional right to free exercise of religion; [and] (2) Utah's bigamy statute is not unconstitutionally vague as applied to Green's conduct. . . .

■ JACK ANDERSON,[*] ADVENTURES AMONG THE POLYGAMISTS
1 Investigative Rep. Mag. 4-42 (Jan. 1982)

. . . Growing up in a devout Mormon home, I was duly drilled in the subjugation of the flesh and shielded from the lustier chapters of my heritage. But now and again, I picked up a mournful whisper among the adults about some fallen soul who had sunk back into the old ways. I was 18 and a fledgling reporter for The Salt Lake Tribune when whispers of [my second cousin's] relapse made the family rounds. [M]y curiosity was reinforced by the reporter's license to snoop into the hidden and illegal. In due course, I located my second cousin [who led him to the home of an elderly man with a saintly visage, Joseph Musser.]

[Disarmed by the author's youth, Musser began to discuss his religious precepts.] He outlined a "fundamentalist" faith which stressed the traditional doctrines and the old-fashioned virtues. [H]is main theme [was] a review of the moral shambles of modern life [which he traced to monogamy], with its inevitable spawn of divorces and mistresses, unmarried mothers and bachelor fathers, cast-off wives and abandoned children. Did not the rise of abortion and contraception clearly foreshadow its ultimate ends: the destruction of the family? Opposed to this theme of abominations, he said, was the sacred institution of plural marriage, practiced by the Old Testament prophets and rooted in God's great commandment to the human race: "Be fruitful and multiply and replenish the earth." [He said that we] must restore the patriarchal order [and] aspire to stand at the head of a family as numerous as the sands on the seashore. . . . God would provide women in abundance who were prepared to do their duty; we bearers of the seed must extend ourselves to the utmost. . . .

---

[*]Jack Anderson, a Pulitzer Prize–winning journalist, was one of the founders of investigative reporting. He contributed to the exposure of Senator Joseph McCarthy's Communist witch-hunts, and later brought to light the Reagan administration's arms-for-hostages affair with Iran and the secret transcripts of the Nixon-era Watergate hearings. The above excerpt was his first investigative story and was published several decades after he wrote it. He died in December 2005 at the age of 83.

Mormonism [is] a product of the frontier. [Thousands of converts followed founder Joseph Smith to Missouri in the 1830's.] Most of the converts to Mormonism came out of New England. They were a puritanical people, reserved in conduct and strict about sex — attitudes further stiffened by their new faith. [When Smith revealed to the Church leaders the religious basis for polygamy, they quickly divided over the issue.] Even Smith's great disciple, Brigham Young, teetered for a time on the brink of rejection, later saying of his initial reaction: "It was the first time in my life that I desired the grave." But in time, Young not only accepted polygamy but warmed to it and acquired 27 wives.

[T]he Mormons had settled a thousand miles from their nearest neighbors in a land so inhospitable they thought no one else would ever want it, in order to pursue their faith without friction. At last, they felt safe, far from vigilantes, in a territory they controlled. But they underestimated the righteous enmity of the fellow who hears that someone else is savoring a fruit forbidden to him. . . . In 1869, the geographic isolation of the Mormons was broken by the completion of the transcontinental railroad, and they found themselves invaded by miners, railroaders and entrepreneurs, a rowdy bunch not previously noted for their sexual scruples, who set up a great lamentation over Mormon heresies and inequities. It was aimed more at Washington than at heaven, however, for the enterprising Mormons controlled not only the women of Utah, but the land, the commerce and the public offices. [From 1862-1887, Congress enacted several pieces of legislation making bigamy a federal criminal offense and attempting to limit the power of the Mormon Church. In response, the Mormons provided that anyone practicing polygamy would be excommunicated.] So thorough going was the Mormon effort to obliterate all traces of plural marriage that by the time I came along in the third generation, only whispers remained of it. . . .

[The polygamous families that the author met] were generally hardworking and frugal. Although the upwardly mobile polygamist aspired for a separate home for each of his wives and broods, thus to perambulate from one to the other, most had to house their multiple families under one roof. . . . To neighbors, the proliferation of brassieres on clotheslines, or new female faces at the windows or a platoon of strange tots romping in the yard, were explained away as visiting aunts and cousins. . . .

The polygamists also appeared to be a sober people of earnest disposition, who would have been enraged to hear themselves called immoral. . . . Among the men, there was no locker-room hee-hawing and lip-smacking about things sexual. Procreation was seen as the central duty of their lives. . . . Such gratifications, as attended this duty, were to be accepted as the unmentioned rewards of a job well done. [But] I struck up conversations with wives who, once their hair was down, acknowledged it was a problem being forever a regimented and scheduled shareholder in love and home. . . .

[T]he most critical operation in a polygamous society is the selection process by which spouses are distributed. . . . I came quickly to suspect that the prophet Musser was making very liberal interpretations of the Lord's messages. Either that or the Lord had an unerring partiality for old codgers. The choicest girls were going to the leaders themselves or to the wealthier laymen who were the biggest contributors to the cause. . . .

Unknown to me, I was not the only investigator on the beat. [Church elders] hired trusted private investigators to keep an eye on the polygamists. The purpose was to identify any Mormons who might be attracted to the sect and to exert upon them, in quiet confrontation, the Church's powers of persuasion. Those who could not be reclaimed would be excommunicated. [During meetings of polygamists] the investigators would slip among the parked cars outside and copy the license numbers. [T]hus, it was that the license number of my father's old Plymouth, the only wheels available to me, kept appearing in the investigators' reports. In due course, my father was called in by his spiritual superiors for a confrontation that utterly confounded him.

The reader cannot appreciate the depths and nuances of this miscarriage of justice, or the peril of my situation, without knowing something of my father. . . . To say that his Mormon faith was orthodox and unquestioning is to understate its unyielding character. He was a granite block of integrity. [O]ne day I came home to find my father in a towering rage. The unspeakable had been spoken: He had been accused of an undercover flirtation with the polygamists. . . . I was a long time in the doghouse. [S]o ended my first adventures with the polygamists. . . .

Notes and Questions

1. *Epilogue.* Tom Green was convicted of bigamy, criminal nonsupport, and first-degree felony child rape (based on the consummation of his marriage with his 13-year-old "wife"). The Utah Supreme Court upheld his conviction on child rape, ruling that the statute of limitations had not expired (although the 1985 offense was not reported until 1999) because a statutory extension of the limitations period permitted prosecution within four years after a report to law enforcement. The court also ruled that the trial court had jurisdiction, even though the act of consummation (and conception) occurred in Mexico, because the defendant resided in Utah at the time of arrest and because he had committed acts of criminal solicitation and conspiracy in Utah. State v. Green, 108 P.3d 710 (Utah 2005). Green is serving a sentence of five years to life in prison.

In another highly publicized criminal case, a vagrant claiming to be a fundamentalist Mormon preacher, Brian David Mitchell, abducted 14-year-old Elizabeth Smart from her Salt Lake City home and attempted to turn her into a plural wife. See generally John R. Llewellyn, Polygamy Under Attack: From Tom Green to Brian David Mitchell (2004).

2. *Historical background.* Bigamy has a long history. Solomon reportedly had 700 wives and 300 concubines.[35] In medieval England, bigamy was an ecclesiastical offense.[36] Ecclesiastical law also made bigamous marriages void. However, a statute of 1604[37] made bigamy a felony. Bigamy was punishable by death until the reign of William III when the punishment became life imprisonment accompanied by branding of the right hand.[38] An act of George I reduced the punishment to deportation for seven years or imprisonment for two.[39]

---

[35]. 1 Kings 11:3.
[36]. 2 Pollock & Maitland, supra note [30], at 543.
[37]. 1 Jac. 1, ch. 11.
[38]. Bartholomew, The Origin and Development of the Law of Bigamy, 74 Law Q. Rev. 259, 261 (1958).
[39]. Id.

In the United States, polygamy has been associated primarily with the Mormon religion even though the Latter Day Saints repudiated the practice at the time Utah became a state. Law enforcement efforts frequently took the form of prosecutions of polygamists. Short Creek, an isolated community straddling the Arizona-Utah border (now called Colorado City), witnessed the most famous raids. Arizona first raided the community in 1935. In 1944 the Federal Bureau of Investigation raided the community again (as well as several others in Utah, Idaho, and Arizona). Yet another raid, in 1953, resulted in law enforcement officials taking into custody children and mothers and prosecuting the fathers. See In re State ex rel. Black, 283 P.2d 887 (Utah 1955) (upholding a juvenile court ruling declaring children taken in the Short Creek raid as wards of the state despite the parents' claim of freedom of religion.) On the role of polygamy in the Mormon religion, see Sarah Barringer Gordon, The Mormon Question: Polygamy and Constitutional Conflict in Nineteenth Century America (2002); Jon Krakauer, Under the Banner of Heaven: A Story of Violent Faith (2004). For a historical discussion of the role of bigamy in colonial America, see D. Kelly Weisberg, "Under Greet Temptations Heer": Women and Divorce Law in Puritan Massachusetts, 2 Feminist Stud. 183, 188 (1975).

3. *Prevalence*. As *Green* reveals, polygamy continues to flourish in some communities in the United States. One estimate places the number of polygamous households in Utah at 50,000. Michael Janofsky, Young Brides Stir New Outcry on Utah Polygamy, Feb. 28, 2003, at A1. According to another estimate, the number of Utahans living in such households has increased tenfold in the last 50 years and now comprises 2 percent of the state population. James Brooke, Utah Struggles with a Revival of Polygamy, N.Y. Times, Aug. 23, 1998, § 6 (Magazine), at 112. Despite the large number of such families, prosecutions are rare. The prosecution of Tom Green was the first in nearly 50 years. Pamela Manson, The Law Has Been Slow to Step In, Salt Lake Trib., Mar. 14, 2004, at G1.

4. *Civil and criminal consequences*. Bigamy, like incest, has both criminal and civil consequences. Civil restrictions limit an individual's attempt to contract a second marriage (while a valid first marriage exists) by invalidating such marriages. Such a marriage needs no decree to establish its invalidity. (For discussion of the putative spouse doctrine which protects a prior spouse in some cases, see infra p. 227.) States also impose criminal penalties on those who enter into a subsequent marriage when a prior valid marriage exists. However, as discussed in *Green*, Utah's statute (Utah Code Ann. (76-7-101(1) (2003)) extends its prohibition to cover marriage as well as cohabitation in a marriage-like relationship while being legally married to another person. Does the addition of the word "cohabit" in the Utah statute amount to "impermissible targeting of the religiously motivated marital practices of polygamists," as the defendant in *Green* contends? What does the court respond to his argument? Is the response persuasive?

5. *Defenses*. A lack of criminal intent does not necessarily constitute a defense to bigamy. See, e.g., Nev. Rev. Stat. Ann. §201.160 (Michie 2001); Okla. Stat. Ann. tit. 21 §881 (West 2002). Does the First Amendment constitute a defense, according to *Green*? *Green* relies on Reynolds v. United States, 98 U.S. (8 Otto) 145 (1878), which held the offense punishable even when committed under the claim of freedom of religion. Why? (The defendant in *Reynolds*, George Reynolds, was Brigham Young's personal secretary who was requested by Church leaders to marry another wife to test the constitutionality of the law.)

The law does provide a possible defense in the form of "Enoch Arden" statutes. The statutes are named after a sailor in a Tennyson poem who returns home ten years after a shipwreck to find his wife remarried after she suffered years of hardship and loneliness. Under these statutes, a person who remarries after the disappearance of a first spouse, without knowledge that the first spouse is alive, is not guilty of bigamy. The requisite period under English law was seven years; many American jurisdictions reduce the period. See, e.g., Ariz. Rev. Stat. Ann. §13-3606 (West 2001) (five years); Fla. Stat. Ann. §826.02 (West Supp. 2005) (three years).

6. *Constitutional challenges to polygamy laws.*

a. *First Amendment.* Most challenges to polygamy laws have been based on First Amendment claims that such laws infringe on the free exercise of religion. The First Amendment provides that: "Congress shall make no law respecting an establishment of religion, or prohibiting the free exercise thereof." According to *Green*, do polygamy laws also violate the former provision, termed the Establishment Clause? (Under the Establishment Clause, a statute must have a secular legislative purpose; its primary effect must be one that neither advances nor inhibits religion; and it must not foster excessive governmental entanglement with religion.) See generally Stephanie Forbes, Comment, "Why Just Have One?": An Evaluation of the Anti-Polygamy Laws Under the Establishment Clause, 39 Hous. L. Rev. 1517 (2003); Richard A. Vasquez, Note, The Practice of Polygamy: Legitimate Free Exercise of Religion or Legitimate Public Menace? Revisiting *Reynolds* in Light of Modern Constitutional Jurisprudence, 5 N.Y.U.J. Legis. & Pub. Pol'y 225 (2001-2002). Amici in *Green* also raised arguments based on free speech and freedom of association; however, because Green had not briefed these arguments, the court declined to consider them. *Green*, 88 P.3d at 829.

b. *Due Process and* Zablocki. Do polygamy bans violate the right to marry, based on *Zablocki*? To what extent are such prohibitions "direct" and "substantial" interferences with the right to marry? What are the state interests that support the imposition of criminal sanctions and civil restrictions? To what extent are these state interests "sufficiently important" and the means closely tailored to their accomplishment? Does *Zablocki* signify that such restrictions (as well as those for incest) require a heightened standard of review? Or, are these "reasonable regulations that do not significantly interfere with decisions to enter into the marital relationship" which evoke only deferential review?

c. *Due Process and* Lawrence. Does the Supreme Court's decision in Lawrence v. Texas mandate reconsideration of polygamy laws? Justice Scalia, in his dissent in *Lawrence*, (supra p.56) contends:

> State laws against bigamy, same-sex marriage, adult incest, prostitution, masturbation, adultery, fornication, bestiality, and obscenity are likewise sustainable only in light of *Bowers'* validation of laws based on moral choices. Every single one of these laws is called into question by today's decision. . . .

To what extent can (should) the state legislate morality after *Lawrence*? Is "every single one of [the above] laws" called into question by *Lawrence* — or are some of the above types of moral-based laws distinguishable?

In State v. Holm, 2006 WL 1319595 (Utah 2006), the Utah Supreme Court upheld the conviction of a polygamist who challenged the constitutionality of the state bigamy statute. The court rejected defendant's argument that his conduct (i.e., two "spiritual marriages" while he was already legally married) was protected as a fundamental liberty interest based on *Lawrence*. The court distinguished *Lawrence* as follows: (1) the present case implicates the *institution* of marriage (rather than mere private consensual sexual conduct) because the state has an interest in preventing the formation of marital forms it deems harmful, and (2) the present case involves a minor (and sexual conduct involving minors is outside the scope of *Lawrence*). Concurring and dissenting, Chief Justice Durham would have upheld the conviction for unlawful sexual conduct with a minor, but would have overturned the bigamy conviction based on her belief that *Lawrence* protects intimate relationships between consenting adults so long as the participants do not present their relationship as being state-sanctioned and absent fraud or other demonstrable harm. See generally Joseph Bozzuti, Note, The Constitutionality of Polygamy Prohibitions After Lawrence v. Texas: Is Scalia a Punchline or a Prophet?, 43 Cath. Law. 409 (2004).

d. *Same-sex marriage and polygamy.* Opponents of same-sex marriage claim that legalizing same-sex marriage will lead ineluctably to legalization of polygamy. See, e.g., Stanley Kurtz, Beyond Gay Marriage: The Road to Polyamory, Weekly Standard, Aug. 4, 2003, available at 2003 WL 6818991. Are these intimate relationships sufficiently distinguishable to justify legalization of same-sex marriage but not polygamy? See James M. Donovan, Rock-Salting the Slippery Slope: Why Same-Sex Marriage Is Not a Commitment to Polygamous Marriage, 29 N. Ky. L. Rev. 521 (2002).

7. *Other legal consequences of polygamy.* In addition to civil restrictions and criminal sanctions, polygamists may face adverse legal consequences in terms of termination of employment. See, e.g., Potter v. Murray City, 760 F.2d 1065 (10th Cir. 1985) (holding that termination of polygamous police officer does not violate his rights to freedom of religion and privacy); Three Wives and You're Off Bench, Nat'l L.J., Mar. 21, 2005, at 16 (describing the recommendation by the Utah Judicial Conduct Commission that a practicing polygamist be removed from the bench, despite the fact that state attorney general declined to file criminal charges). They may also be characterized as unfit parents in custody and adoption. See, e.g., Shepp v. Shepp, 821 A.2d 635, 637 (Pa. Super. Ct. 2003) (awarding custody to father, who believes in polygamy, provided that he not share his "illegal, immoral, and illogical" beliefs with daughter); Matter of Adoption of W.A.T., 808 P.2d 1083 (Utah 1991) (holding that prospective adoptive parents' practice of polygamy should be only one factor to consider rather than threshold disqualification); Sanderson v. Tryon, 739 P.2d 623 (Utah 1987) (vacating a custody award to father, who no longer practiced polygamy, rather than to the mother, who had entered a new polygamous relationship because morality is only one factor in the consideration of the child's best interests).

Recently, disenchanted wives of polygamists filed suits against family members and church officials, alleging *inter alia* false imprisonment, incest, seduction, physical and sexual abuse, and emotional distress.[40] Officials in Arizona and

---

[40]. Judy Nichols, Wives Suing to Bring End to Abuse Under Polygamy, Ariz. Republic, Oct. 15, 2003, available at www.azcentral.com/specials/specials45/articles/1015polygamywomen.html. See also Andrew Murr & Elise Soukup, A Family's Tangled Ties, Newsweek, Feb. 9, 2004, at 55 (recounting the story of the Kingston family's practice of polygamy).

Utah also are investigating allegations of welfare fraud involving polygamous households.[41]

8. *Utah's Child Bigamy Law.* Among the state interests underlying polygamy prohibitions, as mentioned in *Green*, is the interest in preventing the exploitation which may be associated with polygamous practices. Recall that Green himself was convicted of felony child rape of one of his wives who was thirteen years old when he impregnated her. Should criminal liability attach only in cases involving teenage wives and not in cases involving adult women who freely consent to such relationships? See Maura Strassberg, The Crime of Polygamy, 12 Temp. Pol. & Civ. Rts. L. Rev. 353 (2003) (so arguing).

To address the problem of child sexual exploitation associated with the practice of polygamy, the Utah legislature in 2003 enacted the Child Bigamy Amendment which increases the penalties for bigamy involving teenage brides. Utah Code Annotated §76-7-101.5 (2003) provides that marriage or cohabitation with a person under age 18, while the actor is validly married to another, constitutes a second-degree felony punishable by up to 15 years in prison. (In contrast, adult bigamy is a third-degree felony, pursuant to Utah Code Ann. §76-7-101(2) (2003), punishable by up to five years in prison.) Another criminal provision provides that a parent who knowingly allows a minor to enter into a marriage that is prohibited by law is guilty of a third-degree felony. Utah Code Ann. §30-1-9.1 (2003 & Supp. 2004). The legislature considered, but ultimately rejected, a provision that would have created the crime of inducing a minor to enter into a polygamous relationship, thereby enabling prosecution of church leaders who arrange such marriages. See Recent Developments in Utah Law, 2004 Utah L. Rev. 278; Janofsky, supra.

9. *Conflict of laws.* Suppose a man marries multiple wives in a country where this practice is permitted, such as some Muslim nations. The couple then moves to an American jurisdiction that prohibits such marriages. Should the second jurisdiction recognize the marriages? (Note that the Full Faith and Credit Clause does not apply to the laws of a foreign country.) Should it matter for what purpose the validity is at issue? Compare In re Dalip Singh Bir's Estate, 188 P.2d 499 (Cal. Ct. App. 1948) (holding that deceased Hindu's two wives could share his estate), with Hyde v. Hyde & Woodmansee, L. Rep. 1 P.&D. 130 (1866) (refusing to recognize a polygamous marriage for divorce purposes). Note that current U.S. immigration law denies admission into the United States to persons intending to practice polygamy. 8 U.S.C. §1182(a)(10)(A)(2000).

■ **ELIZABETH JOSEPH, MY HUSBAND'S NINE WIVES**
N.Y. Times, May 23, 1991, at A15

I married a married man. In fact, he had six wives when I married him 17 years ago. Today, he has nine. . . .

---

[41]. Joseph A. Reaves & Mark Shaffer, Polygamist Sect Target of Arizona-Utah Inquiry, Ariz. Republic, Sept. 28, 2003, available at www.azcentral.com/specials/specials45/articles/0928polyg-enforcement-28.html.

... At first blush, [polygamy] sounds like the ideal situation for the man and an oppressive one for the women. For me, the opposite is true. [C]ompelling social reasons make the life style attractive to the modern career woman.

Pick up any women's magazine and you will find article after article about the problems of successfully juggling career, motherhood and marriage. It is a complex act that many women struggle to manage daily. ...

When I leave for the 60-mile commute to court at 7 A.M., my 2-year-old daughter, London, is happily asleep in the bed of my husband's wife, Diane. London adores Diane. When London awakes, about the time I'm arriving at the courthouse, she is surrounded by family members who are as familiar to her as the toys in her nursery. ...

I share a home with Delinda, another wife, who works in town government. [Alex Joseph shares another house with seven other wives and their children.] Most nights, we agree we'll just have a simple dinner with our three kids. ... Mondays, however, are different. That's the night Alex eats with us. ... The same system with some variation governs our private time with him. While spontaneity is by no means ruled out, we basically use an appointment system. ...

Plural marriage is not for everyone. But it is the life style for me. It offers men the chance to escape from the traditional, confining roles that often isolate them from the surrounding world. More important, it enables women, who live in a society full of obstacles, to fully meet their career, mothering and marriage obligations. Polygamy provides a whole solution. I believe American women would have invented it if it didn't already exist.

For other accounts of life in a polygamous family, compare Mary Batchelor et al., Voices in Harmony: Contemporary Women Celebrate Plural Marriage (2000), with Dorothy Allred Solomon, Predators, Prey, and Other Kinfolk: Growing Up in Polygamy (2003).

Problem

Lee (a male) seeks a marriage license to marry J. Bronson (a female). Lee is presently married to Dee (a female) who consents to his second marriage. When Lee reveals to the Salt Lake City county clerk that he is already married and that he wishes to marry another wife, the clerk refuses to issue the marriage license. Lee, Dee, and J. Bronson file suit, asserting that it is their sincere and deeply-held religious belief that the doctrine of plural marriage is ordained by God, and that their belief is analogous to the historical practice of polygamy by the Mormons before Utah became a state. They contend that the clerk's refusal to issue them a marriage license deprives them of their constitutional rights to free exercise of their religious beliefs, right of association, and right to privacy. What result? Does Lawrence provide constitutional protection for such arrangements? See Bronson v. Swensen, 394 F. Supp.2d 1329 (D.Utah 2005).

Scholars have coined the term "polyamory" to describe a variety of consensual non-monogamous intimate relationships. See generally Elizabeth F. Emens, Monogamy's Law: Compulsory Monogamy and Polyamorous Existence, 29

N.Y.U. Rev. L. & Soc. Change 277, 283 (2004) (pointing out that polyamorists share values that challenge the traditional conception of monogamy, including "self-knowledge, radical honesty, consent, self-possession, and privileging love and sex over other emotions and activities such as jealousy"); Maura I. Strassberg, The Challenge of Post-Modern Polygamy: Considering Polyamory, 31 Cap. U. L. Rev. 439 (2003).

(4) Age

■ **KIRKPATRICK v. DISTRICT COURT**
64 P.3d 1056 (Nev. 2003)

SHEARING, J . . .

SierraDawn Kirkpatrick Crow is the daughter of Karen Karay and petitioner Bruce Kirkpatrick. . . . As part of the divorce decree, Karay and Kirkpatrick were awarded joint legal and physical custody of SierraDawn. In 1992, Karay and SierraDawn moved from California to New Mexico. In December 2000, when SierraDawn was fifteen years old, she informed her mother that she desired to marry her guitar teacher, forty-eight-year-old Sauren Crow. SierraDawn's mother approved of the marriage.

However, under New Mexico law, SierraDawn was not permitted to marry. Therefore, SierraDawn, her mother, and Crow traveled to Las Vegas where SierraDawn and Crow could marry, if granted permission by the court. [N.M. Stat. Ann. §§40-1-5, 40-1-6(B) provides that a minor under the age of sixteen is not permitted to marry unless the marriage legitimizes a child born out of wedlock or the minor is pregnant, whereas Nev. Rev. Stat. §122.025 permits a minor under the age of sixteen to marry if she or he secures the consent of one parent and judicial authorization.]

Karay filed a petition with the Clark County district court to obtain judicial authorization for SierraDawn's marriage. With the petition, Karay filed an affidavit consenting to the marriage, in which she stated that she has "seen no other couple so right for each other," that they "have very real life plans at home, in the town in which we all reside," and that "[t]heir partnership and their talents will be most effectively utilized by this marriage." The district court found that good cause existed under Nevada law for the marriage, and ordered that a marriage license be issued to SierraDawn and Crow. On January 3, 2001, SierraDawn and Crow were married in Las Vegas.

When Kirkpatrick first learned of SierraDawn's marriage, he sought an ex parte temporary restraining order in the New Mexico district court. That court granted the temporary restraining order, and awarded Kirkpatrick immediate legal and physical custody of SierraDawn. Four days later, however, the court rescinded its order because it found that SierraDawn's marriage was valid under Nevada law, and that SierraDawn was emancipated as a result of the marriage.[3] . . . Thereafter, Kirkpatrick filed this petition seeking a writ of mandamus to compel the district court to vacate its order authorizing SierraDawn's marriage and to annul the marriage. . . .

___

3. At common law, marriage is generally sufficient to constitute emancipation. . . . It does not appear that judicial action is required for emancipation to occur. . . .

   It is well settled that states have the right and power to establish reasonable limitations on the right to marry. This power is justified as an exercise of the police power, which confers upon the states the ability to enact laws in order to protect the safety, health, morals, and general welfare of society. Pursuant to this power, the Nevada Legislature enacted Nev. Rev. Stat. §122.025 [requiring one-parent consent and judicial authorization for underage marriages].

   Kirkpatrick argues that this statute violates his constitutional interest in the care, custody, and management of his daughter since it neither requires his consent nor gives him an opportunity to be heard on the issue of his daughter's marriage. The United States Supreme Court has held that parents have a fundamental liberty interest in the care, custody, and management of their children. However, the United States Supreme Court has also held that, although these rights are fundamental, they are not absolute. The state also has an interest in the welfare of children and may limit parental authority. The Supreme Court has even held, where justified, that parents can be totally deprived of their children forever. If the state can completely eliminate all parental rights, it can certainly limit some parental rights when the competing rights of the child are implicated.

   The United States Supreme Court has held that the right to marry is a fundamental right [citing *Loving* and *Zablocki*]. . . . The Supreme Court has made it clear that constitutional rights apply to children as well as adults. . . .

   Marriage is the cornerstone of the family and our civilization. As marriage comprises the most sacred of relationships, the decision of whom and when to marry is highly personal, often involving reasons that are complex and vary from individual to individual. The decision to marry should rest primarily in the hands of the individual, with little government interference. As a society, we recognize that reasonable constraints on the right to marry are appropriate, especially when the marriage involves a minor.

   There is no one set of criteria that can be set forth as a litmus test to determine if a marriage will be successful. Neither is there a litmus test to determine whether a person is mature enough to enter a marriage. Age alone is an arbitrary factor. The Nevada Legislature recognized that although most fifteen-year-olds would not be mature enough to enter into a marriage, there are exceptions. Nevada provided for the exceptional case by allowing a fifteen-year-old to marry if one parent consents and the court approves. The statute provides a safeguard against an erroneous marriage decision by the minor and the consenting parent, by giving the district court the discretion to withhold authorization if it finds that there are no extraordinary circumstances and/or the proposed marriage is not in the minor's best interest, regardless of parental consent. The statute strikes a balance between an arbitrary rule of age for marriage and accommodation of individual differences and circumstances.

   Consent of both parents is by no means a constitutional requirement for even the most important of decisions regarding minors [citing Hodgson v. Minnesota, 497 U.S. 417 (1990) (declaring a *two-parent* notification requirement for an abortion unconstitutional in the absence of a judicial bypass).] The *Hodgson* Court went on to hold that two-parent notification "is an oddity among state and federal consent provisions governing the health, welfare, and education of children," such as enlisting in the armed services, obtaining a passport, participating in medical research, or submitting to any surgical or medical procedure. When the state requires the consent of only one parent for significant events in a minor's life, the state implicitly recognizes the common reality of modern families. A significant percentage of children under the age of eighteen live in single-parent households. Furthermore, single-parent consent to a minor's marriage is common throughout the country, and none of these laws has been declared unconstitutional on the basis that the other parent did not consent. Nor have any courts held that a non-consenting parent's due process rights have been violated by failure to notify that parent of a child's desire to marry, with the consent of one parent. Kirkpatrick is making a unique argument without the support of case law.

Kirkpatrick asserts that he has been deprived of his fundamental right to the parent-child relationship, like the parents whose parental rights have been terminated. Contrary to what is apparently Kirkpatrick's view, the parental relationship does not end with the emancipation of a child. The only right that he has lost by his daughter's emancipation is his right to exercise legal control over his daughter during her minority. He still has all the other legal and social attributes of parenthood. Kirkpatrick retains the legal rights of inheritance, as well as all the bonds of love, care, companionship, and influence that any parents have after emancipation of their children. How he chooses to foster those bonds is up to him.

The Supreme Court has held that the usual standard for analyzing a substantive due process challenge to the constitutionality of a state statute that impinges on a fundamental constitutional right is whether the statute is narrowly tailored so as to serve a compelling interest. In family privacy cases involving competing interests within the family, however, the Court has deviated from the usual test. Various child rearing and custody cases demonstrate the Court's application of a more flexible "reasonableness" test, which "implicitly calibrat[es] the level of scrutiny in each case to match the particular degree of intrusion upon the parents' interests."

In this case, we have the interest of the daughter in marriage and the interest of the mother in her daughter's welfare and happiness balanced against the father's interest in the legal control of his daughter for the remainder of her minority. Nev. Rev. Stat. §122.025 strikes an appropriate balance between the various interests. . . .

Notes and Questions

1. *Minimum age.* All states establish a minimum age for marriage. Most jurisdictions set that age at 18. Minors below the statutory minimum age must have parental and/or, in some jurisdictions, judicial consent. See, e.g., Ariz. Rev. Stat. §25-102 (2003) (persons under 18 require parental consent and those under 16 must also have judicial consent). Some states permit pregnant minors to marry at younger ages. See, e.g., N.C. Gen. Stat. Ann. §51-2A (Supp. 2002) (raising minimum age for pregnant minors to marry with judicial consent from 12 to 14, whereas minors from 16 to 18 require parental consent). Why did SierraDawn in the *Kirkpatrick* case decide to marry in Nevada rather than New Mexico? Are minors, such as SierraDawn, capable of informed consent on such "private" matters as marriage and abortion? Should the law treat these issues similarly?

2. *Historical background.* The age of consent for marriage at early common law was 7. Such marriages, however, were voidable as long as either party was too young to consummate the marriage. Several reasons supported the betrothal of children. Children were regarded as property whose marriage assured the

passage of estates and settlement of disputes. Also, fathers took the earliest opportunity of marrying a child so that the right of marriage might not fall to the sovereign.[42] Ultimately, the Church proscribed such betrothals. Parliament passed legislation in 1653 that raised the age of consent to 16 for boys and 14 for girls. For the first time, parental consent was required for the marriage of children below 21.[43] Subsequent legislation declared a marriage void if one party was under 16.[44]

In America, the development of restrictions on youthful marriages reflects an ambivalence concerning respect for family privacy versus deference to state intervention. Historian Michael Grossberg writes:

> Early in the nineteenth century most states resolved [uncertainty about the state's treatment of underage marriage] in favor of a youthful freedom to wed free of public restraints. . . .
> After the nation passed mid-century, however, these lax nuptial policies came under attack. Critics of nuptial mores from the professions, the press, and new reform organizations . . . singled out young brides and grooms as prime sources of marital instability. [M]any lawmakers reacted to the appeals of reformers [by] imposing limits on youthful nuptial rights. A series of acts in the late nineteenth century and early twentieth succeeded in raising the average national statutory age of marriage to sixteen for women and eighteen for men. By 1906 the legal trend had become so commonplace that only seventeen states and territories clung to the old common law standard of twelve and fourteen.
> These nuptial law revisions occurred amidst a broader reassessment of the social and economic place of youth in American life. Persuaded by educators, physicians, and reformers . . . , legislators began legally to segregate youths through compulsory school laws, to provide special courts for them with vast discretionary power over status offenses, as well as to limit nuptial freedom. These statutes used the law to protect a Victorian conception of youth development and marital conduct by prolonging childhood and by saving children from themselves and their misguided parents. . . .

Michael Grossberg, Guarding the Altar: Physiological Restrictions and the Rise of State Intervention in Matrimony, 26 Am. J. Legal Hist. 197, 206-209 (1982). See also Michael Grossberg, Governing the Hearth: Law and Family in Nineteenth-Century America 105-108, 142 (1985).

3. *Empirical data.* Both men and women are marrying later, although men marry even later than women. For example, in 1970, the median age for women's first marriage was 20.8 but 23.2 for men. By 2003, the age had risen to 25.3 for women and 27.1 for men.[45] What factors contribute to this gender-based difference? To delayed marriage? What are the consequences for society of a later first-marriage age? Early marriage correlates with such factors as: a low educational level of a person's parents, many siblings, a non-intact family during early adolescence, religion, race, ethnicity, and geographical region.[46]

[42]. 2 Pollock & Maitland, supra note [30], at 390-391.
[43]. Id. at 389.
[44]. Id. at 390.
[45]. Bureau of the Census, U.S. Dept. of Commerce, Current Population Reports: America's Families and Living Arrangements: Population Characteristics 2003, 12 (2004).
[46]. Laumann, supra note [3], at 478-479 (1994) (explaining that Catholics and African-Americans tend to marry later); Naomi Seiler, Is Teen Marriage a Solution?, Center for Law & Social Policy

4. *Instability.* One rationale for restrictions on underage marriage is that maturity is necessary to ensure stability. Data suggest that early marriages are particularly unstable: almost half of teen marriages end in divorce within 15 years compared to about one-third of marriages for women over twenty.[47] Some states require premarital counseling prior to teen marriages. See, e.g., Cal. Fam. Code §304 (West 2004); Utah Code Ann §30-1-9(3)(b) (Supp. 2000). Is premarital counseling an effective solution? See Wesley Adams, Marriage of Minors: Unsuccessful Attempt to Help Them, 3 Fam. L.Q. 13 (1969) (questioning the effectiveness of counseling). Is a mandatory counseling requirement an invasion of privacy? Are there more effective ways to ensure the stability of underage marriages?

5. *Void-voidable distinction.* State statutes reflect inconsistent treatment of the legal effect of nonage on marriage validity: Some classify such marriages as void, others as voidable. Historically, nonage was classified as a civil, rather than canonical, disability. Civil disabilities rendered marriages void; canonical disabilities made them voidable. See supra p. 186. Suppose Tom marries Jenny when he is 17. The marriage is rocky from inception. Tom, discovering that the statutory minimum age is 18, decides to leave Jenny. Later, he meets and marries Polly, but without securing an annulment of his prior marriage. Tom is prosecuted for bigamy. May he raise the invalidity of his prior marriage in the criminal proceeding? If a statute makes the marriage void, then he may. But, if the statute classifies the marriage as voidable, the marriage remains valid until annulled, thereby precluding collateral attack.

6. *Parental rights.* Parental consent proves important if underage marriages are void and thus vulnerable to third-party attack. Requiring parental consent lessens the likelihood of subsequent parental efforts to invalidate a marriage, such as in *Kirkpatrick*. Why did the court in *Kirkpatrick* refuse to permit SierraDawn's father to annul her marriage? How should a court balance the interests of the child, parents, and state in minors' decision to marry? How should a court balance these interests when parents disagree, as in *Kirkpatrick*? Should the state assure that parents exercise their consent wisely? If so, how? Did SierraDawn's mother exercise her responsibility wisely, in your opinion? See also Berger v. Adornato, 350 N.Y.S.2d 520 (Sup. Ct. 1973) (invalidating nonage statute for its failure to contain guidelines by which parental consent may be withheld). Do you think parents are more likely to withhold parental consent to teen marriages or grant consent too freely? See David A. Gover & Dorothy G. Jones, Requirement of Parental Consent: A Deterrent to Marriage?, 26 J. Marriage & Fam. 205 (1964) (speculating that the latter may be more common).

7. *Minors' rights.* Should parental consent be a necessary and sufficient condition, or should the law require *both* parental consent and judicial authorization for minors to marry? Compare Uniform Marriage and Divorce Act (UMDA) §§203-204, 9A U.L.A. (pt. 1) 179-180 (1998) (minor may marry with either parent's consent or after a finding that the minor is capable of assuming the responsibilities of marriage and that the marriage would be in his best interests), with Cal. Fam. Code §302 (West 2004) (requiring both parental consent and judicial authorization).

Report 3 (Aug. 2002)) (reporting that almost twice as many Latinas aged 18 to 19 marry compared to white women, and that more teens in the South and West marry than in other regions).

[47]. Seiler, supra note [46], at 8-9.

Does an underage minor whose parents refuse consent have adequate recourse? Case law sometimes requires that the parents' refusal not be unreasonable. However, many statutes do not provide for override procedures. Compare Application of Powers, 408 N.Y.S.2d 761 (Fam. Ct. 1978) (even where parental consent unreasonably withheld, court lacked jurisdiction because the statute neither required nor authorized judicial approval), with Iowa Code Ann. §595.2(5) (2001) (where parental consent is unreasonably withheld, the court shall grant approval upon a finding that the underage party is capable of assuming the responsibilities of marriage and that marriage is in the minor's best interest). Should states institute judicial bypass proceedings to parental consent requirements that are similar to those constitutionally required in abortion decisionmaking?

8. *Constitutional challenges.* Are nonage statutes constitutional? Do gender-based age differentials violate equal protection? Compare Phelps v. Bing, 316 N.E.2d 775 (Ill. 1974) and Berger v. Adornato, 350 N.Y.S.2d 520 (Sup. Ct. 1973) (holding that gender-based statutory scheme denied equal protection), with Friedrich v. Katz, 341 N.Y.S.2d 932 (Sup. Ct. 1973) (contra based on state's interest in marriage and role of men as providers). Do nonage statutes violate due process? See Moe v. Dinkins, 533 F. Supp. 623 (S.D.N.Y. 1981) (upholding parental consent requirement on substantive due process grounds, based on rational basis review, because of the state's interest in promoting marriage stability and protecting minors from immature decisionmaking), *aff'd*, 669 F.2d 67 (2d Cir. 1981), *cert. denied*, 459 U.S. 823 (1982).

9. *Teen marriage and welfare reform.* The welfare reform legislation of 1996 (Personal Responsibility and Work Opportunity Reconciliation Act (PRWORA), P.L. 104-193, codified in scattered sections of U.S.C.) contains several provisions intended to promote marriage and reduce nonmarital births. Premised on the belief that marriage reduces poverty, PRWORA includes economic incentives for unwed mothers to marry. A measure to reauthorize PRWORA, proposed in 2005, reflects similar aims. H.R. 240, 109th Cong. (2005). It includes the following congressional finding:

> In 2002, 34 percent of all births in the U.S. were to unmarried women. And, with fewer teens entering marriage, the proportion of births to unmarried teens has increased dramatically (80 percent in 2002 versus 30 percent in 1970). The negative consequences of out-of-wedlock birth on the mother, the child, the family, and society are well documented. These include increased likelihood of welfare dependency, increased risks of low birth weight, poor cognitive development, child abuse and neglect, and teen parenthood, and decreased likelihood of having an intact marriage during adulthood.

Id. at §4(4)(B).

What are the effects of teen marriage? One study highlights the following: (1) teen marriages have a high rate of instability; (2) teens who have a nonmarital birth and subsequently marry but then divorce are worse off economically than those who do not marry; (3) teen mothers are more likely to have a second birth quickly if they marry; (4) teen marriage leads to decreased educational attainment for girls; (5) teen fathers earn less in early adulthood than males who delay parenting until after age 20; and (6) teen marriages often involve high levels of domestic violence. Naomi Seiler, Is Teen Marriage a Solution?, Center for Law & Social Policy Report 7-8 (Aug. 2002). Given the high percentage of babies born to teenagers out-of-wedlock, is it sound governmental policy to encourage teenage girls who become pregnant to marry?

10. *International perspectives.* More than 30 countries allow marriages involving children below the age of 15. The reasons for child marriages are economic (i.e., early marriage relieves parents of economic burdens) as well as the desire to control female sexuality. Elizabeth Warner, Behind the Wedding Veil: Child Marriage as a Form of Trafficking in Girls, 12 Am. U.J. Gender Soc. Pol'y & L. 233, 238 (2004) (pointing out that up to 47 percent of girls are married before age 15 in Bangladesh, and nearly 50 percent of girls before age 18 in Africa). Warner points out that international treaties fail to address the problem adequately. Id. at 236-237.

Problems

1. Seventeen-year-old Jane requests a license to marry Sam. Her parents refuse to give their consent. Jane has previously been married to Tim Brown. That marriage, unlike this one, had her parents' approval. (The prior marriage was subsequently annulled.) The jurisdiction has a statute specifying that the county clerk shall not issue a marriage license if either applicant is under 18 years of age in the absence of parental consent or court order. Should the county clerk issue the marriage license? See Op. Tex. Atty. Gen., No. JM-359 (Oct. 18, 1985); 12 Fam. L. Rep. (BNA) 1022 (Nov. 12, 1985).

2. Crystal meets Matthew when he comes to play video games with her half-brother. When she is 12 and he is 20, they become a couple. A year later, Crystal's mother, who is divorced from her father, petitions for a protective order restraining Matthew from seeing Crystal. Despite the court order, the couple continue to see each other and eventually develop a sexual relationship. When Crystal became pregnant, her mother and Matthew's parents drive the couple to Kansas where persons as young as 12 may marry with parental consent. Nebraska, where the couple resides, prohibits marriages of persons under age 17, and also provides that sexual intercourse between a person who is 19 or older and another person who is younger than age 16 is statutory rape. Should the county clerk grant the marriage license? Should Matthew be charged with statutory rape? How should the state reconcile these two laws? Should the state take any action against Crystal's mother? See Colleen Kenney, Now Wait Begins for Teen Wife, Baby, Lincoln J. Star, Feb. 8, 2006, at A1; Jodi Wilgoren, Rape Charge Follows Marriage to a 14-Year-Old, N.Y. Times, Aug. 30, 2005, at A1.

(ii) State of Mind Restrictions: Fraud and Duress

■ **BLAIR v. BLAIR**
147 S.W.3d 882 (Mo. Ct. App. 2004)

JOSEPH M. ELLIS, Judge.

William Jerry Blair (Husband) appeals from a judgment entered in the Circuit Court of Platte County denying his petition for annulment of his marriage to Nancy Blair. For the following reasons, we affirm.

In July 1976, Husband and Wife had sexual intercourse on one occasion after having worked together for a couple of years. At that time, Wife was married to Jim Farra and was also involved in a long-standing sexual relationship with Sam Kelly. Subsequently, Wife gave birth to a son, Devin, on April 26, 1977. Husband visited Wife in the hospital shortly after Devin's birth, but did not discuss the paternity of the child with her and had no further contact with Wife until 1979.

In January 1979, Wife contacted Husband, told him that he was Devin's father, and asked whether he had any history of disease in his family that might affect Devin later in life. Husband met with Wife and Devin, and he resumed a sexual relationship with Wife a few days later. In March 1979, Wife separated from Mr. Farra and filed a petition for dissolution of that marriage. Subsequently, Wife became pregnant with Husband's child, and on March 13, 1980, Wife gave birth to their daughter, Oralin.

Wife's marriage to Mr. Farra was dissolved in December 1980. Several days after her divorce from Mr. Farra became final, Husband and Wife were married on December 22, 1980. Husband later adopted both Devin and Oralin.

On November 20, 2001, Wife filed a petition for dissolution of her marriage to Husband. . . . . Husband filed an amended answer and cross-petition requesting that the marriage be annulled. In support of his annulment claim, Husband averred that Wife had fraudulently represented to him before their marriage that he was Devin's father and had thereby induced him to marry her. Subsequent testing proved that Husband was indeed not Devin's father and that he was the son of Sam Kelly. . . . .

As grounds for granting an annulment, Husband asserted that Wife perpetrated a fraud upon him regarding Devin's paternity. In order to establish fraud, Husband was required to plead and prove the following elements: (1) a representation by Wife; (2) its falsity; (3) its materiality; (4) Wife's knowledge of its falsity or ignorance of its truth; (5) Wife's intent that the representation be acted upon by Husband; (6) Husband's ignorance of the falsity of the representation; (7) Husband's reliance on the truth of the representation; (8) Husband's right to rely on the representation; and (9) that Husband sustained consequent and proximate injury. . . .

Fraud

Husband notes that he testified at trial that he would not have married Wife if he had known that he was not Devin's father. [T]he trial court was not required to accept Husband's own self-serving testimony that he would not have married Wife but for her representations related to Devin's paternity. Indeed, the overall gist of Husband's testimony appears to have been that he would never have seen Wife again after their one-night-stand if it had not been for her calling and telling him that he had a child and that the marriage was, therefore, the result of that representation. Such testimony does not establish that Husband relied upon the representations regarding Devin's paternity in deciding whether to marry Wife, only that it played a part in his decision to begin a relationship with her.

Sufficient evidence in the record supports the trial court's determination that Husband would have married Wife regardless of the representation as to Devin's paternity. Wife testified that Husband was crazy about her and that she was certain that he would have left his girlfriend and had a relationship with her regardless of Devin's paternity. Husband admitted on cross-examination that, during the two-year courtship the couple had between Wife's initial phone call and their marriage, he fell in love with Wife. In addition, nine months before their marriage, Oralin, who is undisputedly Husband's child, was born. The trial court could reasonably have inferred that Oralin's paternity would have been sufficient to cause Husband to marry Wife. Furthermore, testimony from both Husband and Wife reflects that Husband had questions about Devin's paternity prior to marriage, that he married her anyway, and that he subsequently adopted both children.

Based upon the foregoing testimony, the trial court could more than reasonably have found that Husband would have married Wife regardless of Wife's representations related to Devin's paternity. Such a finding is supported by sufficient evidence and is not against the weight of the evidence. . . . Having determined that this ground for the trial court's denial of Husband's request for an annulment is not erroneous, we need not address Husband's remaining points related to the trial court's other grounds for its decision. . . .

Notes and Questions

1. *Consent requirement.* A marriage may be set aside for lack of consent. Fraud (like duress) vitiates consent and serves as a ground for annulment. Because of the public policy in favor of preserving a marriage whenever possible, many courts apply a strict test for fraud, requiring that the misrepresentation go to the "essentials" to render the marriage voidable. "Essentials" generally includes ability and willingness to engage in sexual relations and childbearing. Given the current ease in obtaining a divorce, does this strict test make sense? Some states (for example, New York) require only that the fraud be material, that is, the plaintiff would not have married defendant but for the fraud. Which test does the court use in *Blair*?

2. *Annulment versus divorce.* An annulment declares that no marriage occurred because some impediment existed at the time of the ceremony. In contrast, divorce terminates a valid marriage, enabling the parties to remarry. Annulments were significant when divorce was difficult to obtain. In England until the Matrimonial Causes Act of 1857, a divorce that enabled the parties to remarry was almost impossible to obtain. Discontented marital partners might, however, secure an annulment for fraud, duress, or nonage. Following divorce reform, however, the importance of annulments decreased.

Different procedural rules govern annulment and divorce. First, annulment jurisdiction exists at either party's domicile, the state where the marriage was celebrated, or any state with personal jurisdiction over the spouses. In contrast, divorce jurisdiction rests on domicile. Second, spousal and child support and division of property did not follow typically from an invalid marriage. Today, many states, by equitable remedies or statute, assimilate the financial consequences of annulment to those of divorce. Third, the "relation back" doctrine is applicable only to annulments. Because a decree of annulment establishes that a marriage never existed, benefits lost by virtue of the marriage may be reinstated. See Haacke v. Glenn, 814 P.2d 1157 (Utah Ct. App. 1991) (granting wife an annulment stemming from husband's concealment of his status as a convicted felon and thereby eliminating wife-attorney's conflict of interest with her employer, Department of Corrections).

Why might the plaintiff in *Blair* have sought an annulment rather than a divorce? Why did the court deny his request?

3. *Consummation.* When considering fraud to annul marriage, courts often distinguish between consummated and unconsummated marriages, sometimes requiring a higher standard for the former. Why? Given current sexual mores, should consummation continue to influence the law of annulment?

4. *Privacy.* Does judicial examination of marriage for purposes of fraud constitute an invasion of privacy?

5. *Tort liability.* Some jurisdictions recognize the tort of fraudulent inducement to marry. See, e.g., Morgan v. Morgan, 388 S.E.2d 2 (Ga. Ct. App. 1989) (permitting recovery to wife for husband's false assertions that he was divorced). However, the quantum of fraud for annulment purposes is considerably less than that required for tort liability. Should a plaintiff be able to secure an annulment as well as tort damages for the same conduct? To recover in tort, must a plaintiff have suffered economic loss to recover for fraudulent inducement to marry? See Miller v. Miller, 956 P.2d 887 (Okla. 1998) (permitting recovery, even without economic loss, to husband for false representations that he fathered wife's child).

6. *Limited purpose marriages.* Prior to the legalization of abortion, couples who conceived a child would agree, sometimes, to marry "in name only" to legitimate the child, and then, after the birth, obtain a divorce. However, the parties agreed that no other marital rights and responsibilities would attach. Many American cases have recognized such "limited purpose" or "sham" marriages, probably to avoid the stigma of illegitimacy. See, e.g., Schibi v. Schibi, 69 A.2d 831 (Conn. 1949); Campbell v. Moore, 1 S.E.2d 784 (S.C. 1939). What purposes are served by failing to recognize such marriages? Are marriages to legitimate a child distinguishable from limited purpose marriages that facilitate an alien's entry into the United States (discussed infra)?

7. *Duress.* Agreements to marry that are procured by force, fear, or coercion are unenforceable. Although duress generally requires physical force or threat of force, lesser forms of duress may suffice if sufficient to overcome plaintiff's free will. Clark, Law of Domestic Relations (2d ed.), supra, at 103. English cases disagree about whether the test should be subjective or objective. Id. at 104.

9. *Forced marriage: international perspective.* Forced arranged marriage is still practiced today in parts of the Middle East, Asia and Africa. An estimated 30,000 forced brides live in Germany and Austria where support groups have flourished to help them find lawyers (to obtain annunments), housing, and new identities (to avoid discovery by their spouses and families). Eric Geiger, Muslim Girls in Austria Fighting Spouses Forced Marriages, S.F. Chron., Dec. 4, 2005, at A15.

Problem

Mr. Patel, an Indian engineer who resides in New Jersey, travels to India to seek a wife of the same caste. A marriage broker arranges a match with Ms. Navitlal. They meet twice to discuss marriage and their respective backgrounds. Ms. Navitlal informs him that her parents are separated and living in different locations. She does not tell him, however, that her mother presently is living with a person of a different caste. The couple is married in a civil ceremony, and the marriage is consummated. Mr. Patel returns to the United States to arrange for his wife to join him. He later returns to India where he undergoes a religious ceremony.

He later testifies that he underwent the Hindu ceremony only because of threats by his wife's brothers. After Ms. Navitlal tires of waiting for her husband to send for her, she travels to the United States. There, she discovers that her husband has no desire to live with her. He asserts that she married him for the sole purpose of gaining entry into the United States. He files for annulment. She counterclaims for divorce. What result? Patel v. Navitlal, 627 A.2d 683 (N.J. Super. Ct. Ch. Div. 1992).

Note: Marriage Fraud in Immigration

Marriage to a U.S. citizen exempts an alien from the quota restrictions of the Immigration and Nationality Act (INA), 8 U.S.C. §1151(a), (b) (2000), thereby avoiding lengthy delays in entering the country. This rule contributes to a strong incentive for aliens to marry citizens. Before 1986, when a citizen petitioned for an adjustment to permanent resident status for an alien spouse, the Immigration and Naturalization Service (INS) would investigate the marriage to determine whether the marriage was genuine.

In 1986, Congress passed the Immigration Marriage Fraud Amendments (IMFA), 8 U.S.C §§1154 (b)(2000), requiring that if the INS finds the marriage genuine, it grants a conditional adjustment of status. The spouse obtains permanent resident status after two years, if the marriage is determined again to be genuine. However, if deportation proceedings have been initiated at any time during the marriage, then §5 requires that the alien spouse leave the United States for two years before any adjustment of status. Justification for this provision rests on the belief that marriage fraud is greater among aliens facing deportation. In Escobar v. INS, 896 F.2d 564 (D.C. Cir. 1990), *withdrawn when reh'g en banc granted*, *appeal dismissed*, 925 F.2d 488 (D.C. Cir. 1991), the U.S. Court of Appeals declared the provision unconstitutional, holding that §5 implicates the *citizen-wife's* right to privacy and due process by forcing her to choose between living without her husband or living outside the United States for two years. The Immigration Act of 1990, 8 U.S.C. §1255(e)(3) (2000), finally changed the law by providing that §5 shall not apply if the alien establishes by clear and convincing evidence that the marriage was entered into in good faith, not for the purpose of procuring the alien's entry, and no consideration was given.

To determine the validity of a marriage between a citizen and an alien, federal investigators often explore such factors as whether the couple is cohabiting, commingling resources, holding property jointly, and has children. Are such investigations violative of the right to privacy and based on stereotypical views of married life?

A mail-order marriage industry has flourished during the past several decades. Evidence suggests that a substantial number of mail-order marriages are fraudulent. See Illegal Immigration and Immigrant Responsibility Act (IIRIRA), (8 U.S.C. §1375(a)(3) (2000)) (reporting congressional findings). The Internet contributed to the rapid growth of the mail-order industry. Until 1996, the mail-order matchmaking industry was largely unregulated. In that year Congress enacted section 652 of the IIRIRA to require the dissemination of information to mail-order brides about the "battered spouse waiver" for conditional permanent residents enacted as part of the Violence Against Women Act of 1994 (8 U.S.C. §1154(a)(1)(A)(iii) (2000)) that allows battered immigrant women to apply for permanent legal residence without their abusive citizen-spouse's participation. (Before VAWA, immigration law required the cooperation of the citizen spouse in order for the alien spouse to obtain lawful status.) The legislation also mandates that the INS publish a report on the mail-order industry, including the extent of fraud and domestic abuse in such marriages, the extent to which abused mail-order spouses self-petition or utilize the remedy of cancellation of deportation (pursuant to 8 U.S.C. §1229(b)(2) (2000)), and the need for further regulation and education regarding the objectives of VAWA and the Immigration Fraud Amendments. 8 U.S.C. §1375(c).

To remedy shortcomings in the legislation, Congress enacted the Battered Immigrant Women Protection Act of 2000 as part of the Victims of Trafficking and Violence Protection Act of 2000, Pub. L. No. 106-386, 114 Stat. 1464 at §§1501-13. This law facilitates self-petitioning by abused spouses, expands the categories of spouses who are eligible for the procedure, and establishes a special visa for those victims of domestic violence who are not eligible for self-petition or cancellation of deportation. The Violence Against Women and Department of Justice Reauthorization Act of 2005, Pub. L. No. 109-162, 119 Stat. 2960, that re-authorized VAWA through 2010, continues to regulate the international marriage broker (IMB) industry. VAWA 2005 prohibits an IMB from providing contact information about minors, requires IMB's to advise foreign clients of the rights and resources available to victims of domestic violence in the United States, requires that the Department of Homeland Security's criminal background checks of clients petitioning for a foreign fiancée or spousal visa be shared with the fiancée or spouse (as well as requiring dissemination of any other background information that the IMB collects), and prohibits American clients from petitioning simultaneously for visas for multiple fiancées.

Recently, a jury awarded $434,000 to Ukrainian immigrant Nataliya Fox in her suit against Encounters International, an Internet matchmaking company. The jury found that the company failed to tell Nataliya about the battered spouse waiver and was negligent in assuring Natiliya that her prospective husband (who had a history of domestic violence) had been carefully screened. This lawsuit was the first of its type to hold an Internet matchmaking service liable. See Daren Briscoe, Mail-Order Misery: Charging Abuse, Imported Brides Are Fighting Back, Newsweek, Feb. 7, 2005, at 54; Dating Service Held Liable in Abuse, S.F. Chron., Nov. 20, 2004, at A2.

b. Procedural Restrictions

(i) Licensure and Solemnization

■ CARABETTA v. CARABETTA
438 A.2d 109 (Conn. 1980)

PETERS, Associate Justice. . . .

The plaintiff and the defendant exchanged marital vows before a priest in the rectory of Our Lady of Mt. Carmel Church of Meriden, on August 25, 1955, according to the rite of the Roman Catholic Church, although they had failed to obtain a marriage license. Thereafter they lived together as husband and wife, raising a family of four children, all of whose birth certificates listed the defendant as their father. Until the present action, the defendant had no memory or recollection of ever having denied that the plaintiff and the defendant were married.

The issue before us is whether, under Connecticut law, despite solemnization according to an appropriate religious ceremony, a marriage is void where there has been noncompliance with the statutory requirement of a marriage. This is a question of first impression in this state. The trial court held that failure to obtain a marriage license was a flaw fatal to the creation of a legally valid marriage and that the court therefore lacked subject matter jurisdiction over an action for dissolution. We disagree with the court's premise and hence with its conclusion.

The determinants for a legally valid marriage are to be found in the provisions of our statutes. . . . The governing statutes at the time of the purported marriage between these parties contained two kinds of regulations concerning the requirements for a legally valid marriage. One kind of regulation concerned substantive requirements determining those eligible to be married. Thus General Statutes (Rev. 1949) §7301 declared the statutorily defined degrees of consanguinity within which a "marriage shall be void." . . . For present purposes, it is enough to observe that, on this appeal, no such substantive defect has been alleged or proven.

The other kind of regulation concerns the formalities prescribed by the state for the effectuation of a legally valid marriage. These required formalities, in turn, are of two sorts: a marriage license and a solemnization. In Hames v. Hames, [316 A.2d 379 (1972)], we interpreted our statutes not to make void a marriage consummated after the issuance of a license but deficient for want of due solemnization. Today we examine the statutes in the reverse case, a marriage duly solemnized but deficient for want of a marriage license.

As to licensing, the governing statute in 1955 was a section entitled "Marriage licenses." It provided, in subsection (a): "No persons shall be joined in marriage until both have joined in an application . . . for a license for such marriage." Its only provision for the consequence of noncompliance with the license requirement was contained in subsection (e): ". . . any person who shall join any persons in marriage without having received such (license) shall be fined not more than one hundred dollars." General Statutes (Rev. 1949) §7302, as amended by §1280b (1951 Supp.) and by §2250c (1953 Supp.). Neither this section, nor any other, described as void a marriage celebrated without license.

As to solemnization, the governing section, entitled "Who may join persons in marriage," [provides that] the celebration of a marriage by a person not authorized by this section to do so, renders a marriage void. We have enforced the plain mandate of this injunction. State ex rel. Felson v. Allen, 129 Conn. 427, 431, 29 A.2d 306 (1942).

In the absence of express language in the governing statute declaring a marriage void for failure to observe a statutory requirement, this court has held in an unbroken line of cases since Gould v. Gould, 78 Conn. 242, 247, 61 A. 604 (1905), that such a marriage, though imperfect, is dissoluble rather than void. . . . Then as now, the legislature had chosen to use the language of voidness selectively, applying it to some but not to all of the statutory requirements for the creation of a legal marriage. Now as then, the legislature has the competence to choose to sanction those who solemnize a marriage without a marriage license rather than those who marry without a marriage license. In sum, we conclude that the legislature's failure expressly to characterize as void a marriage properly celebrated without a license means that such a marriage is not invalid.

The plaintiff argues strenuously that our statutes, far from declaring void a marriage solemnized without a license, in fact validate such a marriage whenever it has been solemnized by a religious ceremony. The plaintiff calls our attention to the language of §7306, as amended, that "all marriages . . . solemnized according to the forms and usages of any religious denomination in this state shall be valid." To the extent that this language suggests greater validity for a marriage solemnized by a religious ceremony than for one solemnized by a civil ceremony, it is inconsistent with other provisions of the statutes with regard to solemnization and licensing. It has long been clear that, under our laws, all authority to join parties in matrimony is basically secular. . . . Whatever may be its antecedents, for present purposes it is sufficient to note that §7306 at the very least reenforces our conclusion that the marriage in the case before us is not void.

The conclusion that a ceremonial marriage contracted without a marriage license is not null and void finds support, furthermore, in the decisions in other jurisdictions. In the majority of states, unless the licensing statute plainly makes an unlicensed marriage invalid, "the cases find the policy favoring valid marriages sufficiently strong to justify upholding the unlicensed ceremony. This seems the correct result. Most such cases arise long after the parties have acted upon the assumption that they are married, and no useful purpose is served by avoiding the long-standing relationship." [Homer Clark, Law of Domestic Relations 41 (1968)].

Since the marriage that the trial court was asked to dissolve was not void, the trial court erred in granting the motion to dismiss. . . .

Wedding ceremonies vary significantly, as the excerpts below demonstrate.

■ HARRIETTE COLE, JUMPING THE BROOM: THE AFRICAN-AMERICAN WEDDING PLANNER
16-18 (1993)

When West Africans were brought forcibly to these shores some four hundred years ago, they were stripped of much of what was theirs. [A]fter the beginning of slavery, Africans were also denied the right to marry in the eyes of the law. Slave-holders apparently thought that their captives were not real people but were, instead, property to be bought and sold. As such, they had no rights. Further, if allowed formally to marry and live together, slaves might find strength in numbers that could lead to revolt. . . .

Yet the enslaved were spiritual people who had been taught rituals that began as early as childhood to prepare them for that big step into family life. . . . Out of their creativity came the tradition of jumping the broom. The broom itself held spiritual significance for many African peoples, representing the beginning of homemaking for a couple. For the Kgatla people of southern Africa, it was custom-ary, for example, on the day after the wedding for the bride to help the other women in the family to sweep the courtyard clean, thereby symbolizing her willingness and obligation to assist in housework at her in-laws' residence until the couple moved to their own home. During slavery . . . a couple would literally jump over a broom into the seat of matrimony. Today, this tradition and many others are finding their way back into the wedding ceremony.

■ GINIA BELLAFANTE, EVEN IN GAY CIRCLES,
THE WOMEN WANT THE RING
N.Y. Times, May 8, 2005, §6 (Magazine), at 91

[T]hree months after the Massachusetts Supreme Judicial Court ruled [in *Goodridge*] that it was unconstitutional to ban gay couples from marrying, a young woman named Bernadette Smith embarked on a [new career as] a wedding planner for gay couples, declaratively naming the new business she created "It's About Time." [O]ne consistent trend has emerged in her operation: most of her clients have been women. [O]f the close to 5,400 couples who have married in Massachusetts since last May, a figure that represents nearly a third of all same-sex partner households in the state identified by the census, almost two-thirds of the couples have been women. . . .

Sociologists and gay-marriage advocates explain the discrepancy largely in terms of the social and economic realities that shape conflicting attitudes about marriage. [T]he statistics in Massachusetts bear out the culturally obvious: that men carry the greater weight of ambivalence on the subjects of marriage and family. On another level the numbers may reflect a wish among women to override the economic vulnerability of living independently. "Women are situated differently in the occupational labor force; there's more value to their marrying," said Christopher Carrington, an anthropologist who has studied gay and lesbian couples. . . .

In many instances, though, there's another force at play: the cultural programming that prompts fantasies of tiered cakes and lilies in 6-year-old girls. For Abby McDonald and Tara Donner, who are to walk down the aisle of the Arlington Street Church in Boston on June 11 in white gowns, accompanied by their fathers, the desire to marry was driven almost entirely by intimate and conformist urges. Ms. Donner, a Wellesley graduate, read Martha Stewart Weddings in college. Neither woman had been in a serious relationship before they came together three and a half years ago, and neither had been particularly interested in a commitment ceremony or civil union, arrangements they say lack marriage's emotional core. [T]hey purchased matching diamond engagement rings, proposed to each other on the Wellesley campus on June 11, and elected to spend a year planning a wedding rather than marry quickly in the flush of last spring's excitement. . . . The couple's reception for 120 guests will be held at the College Club of Boston, paid for in large part by their parents. . . .

In the view of Gary Gates, the senior research fellow at the Charles R. Williams Project on Sexual Orientation Law and Public Policy, at the University of California, Los Angeles, Law School, [the fact] that many gay couples, both female and male, seem inclined toward conventional weddings in Massachusetts reflects the changing demographics of gay life. "For a long time the gay rights movement was about the right to be different; now it's very much about the right to be the same and that's a dramatic change," Dr. Gates said. . . .

Notes and Questions

1. *Licensure requirements*. Statutes in every jurisdiction provide for the manner of issuance of marriage licenses. Yet, the policy favoring marriage validity gives rise to the rule announced in *Carabetta* that a violation of formality requirements, such

as the failure to obtain a marriage license, will not void a marriage. This rule operates unless the jurisdiction has a statute *expressly* making a marriage invalid without a license. See, e.g., Dire v. Dire-Blodgett, 102 P.3d 1096 (Idaho 2004) (pointing out that statute that abolished common law marriage expressly mandates the issuance of a marriage license as a requirement for validity of marriage); Estate of DePasse, 118 Cal. Rptr.2d 143 (Ct. App. 2002) (statutory scheme specifies that obtaining a marriage license is a mandatory requirement for a valid marriage, thereby invalidating deathbed ceremony).

Three justifications exist for licensure statutes: (1) they aid in enforcing marriage laws by requiring persons not qualified to marry for reasons of age, health, or existing marital status to disclose such information; (2) they serve as public health measures by preventing marriages that would be damaging to the health of one spouse or would produce unhealthy children; and (3) licensure serves as proof that the marriage has occurred. Clark, Law of Domestic Relations, supra, at 34.

2. *Solemnization.* In addition to obtaining a license, states also require that the couple have their marriage solemnized by an authorized individual. Those authorized to perform a civil marriage include both religious officials (e.g., clergy) and government officials (judges, etc.). Compare Ranieri v. Ranieri, 539 N.Y.S.2d 381 (App. Div.), *appeal dismissed,* 74 N.Y.2d 792 (1989) (invalidating a marriage performed by a "minister" of the Universal Life Church — a religious corporation not covered by the authorizing statute that permits any individual to become a minister through mail procedure), with Matter of Blackwell, 531 So. 2d 1192 (Miss. 1988) (contra). See also Universal Life Church v. Utah, 189 F. Supp.2d 1302 (D. Utah 2002) (holding that statute prohibiting ordination by mail and the Internet did not violate the Free Exercise Clause or substantive due process, but did violate equal protection by excluding persons who submitted applications by phone, fax, or in person).

3. *Formalities.*

a. *Officials.* Most states provide that marriage licenses will be issued by the county clerk; some states provide for issuance by judges. See, e.g., Ala. Code 1975 §30-1-9 (1998) (probate judges); Kan. Stat. Ann. §23-106 (1995) (clerks or judges).

b. *Where, how long, how much does it cost?* Statutes in approximately half the states require that licenses be procured in the county where one party resides or where the marriage is to be performed. Many statutes provide that the license expires within a short period of time (typically 30 to 60 days). Marriage license fees range from a low of $10 (see, e.g., Ind. Code Ann §33-32-5-1 (West 2004)) to a high of $85 (see, e.g., Minn. Stat. Ann. §517.08 (West 2005) (but providing for reduction in the fee upon participation in premarital counseling). In many states, license fees include a statutorily designated amount for funding domestic violence shelters. See, e.g., Cal. Welf. & Inst. Code §18305 (West 2001); Fla. Stat. Ann. §741.01 (2005).

c. *Waiting periods.* Most states have waiting periods, with some exception for exigent circumstances (such as pregnancy). A majority of jurisdictions require a waiting period (usually 5 days) between the application and issuance of the marriage license; a few states require a waiting period after the issuance of the license but before the ceremony.

4. *Premarital blood tests.*

a. *Health certificate.* Statutes in many states require that, to obtain a marriage license, an applicant must file a health certificate, including certification of blood test results, with the licensing authority stating that the applicant does not have venereal disease or, if infected, is not in a communicable stage. See, e.g., D.C. Code Ann. §30-117 (Michie 2001). Typically, such certificates are confidential; unauthorized disclosure may result in criminal liability. Some states also require tests for German measles. However, rubella tests may be waived for female applicants who are over 50 or sterilized; and lack of immunity does not bar issuance of the license as with venereal disease.

b. *Rationale.* The rationale for the enactment of premarital blood test requirements in the early twentieth century stemmed from concerns about eugenics, urbanization, rising rates of immigration, and the pervasive sexual double standard that reflected fears of the consequences for innocent young women of men's "sowing their wild oats." See generally Allan M. Brandt, No Magic Bullet: A Social History of Venereal Disease in the United States Since 1880 (1987). Do statutes requiring premarital blood tests violate applicants' rights pursuant to the Free Exercise Clause if blood testing violates a precept of their religion? See In re Kilpatrick, 375 S.E.2d 794 (W. Va. 1988).

c. *HIV.* After discovery of the AIDS epidemic, physicians began performing HIV-testing, often without consent, in conjunction with premarital blood tests. See Many AIDS Tests Without Consent, S.F. Chron., Feb. 16, 1990, at A19. In Doe v. Dyer-Goode, 566 A.2d 889 (Pa. Super. Ct. 1989), a trial court refused to impose liability (for invasion of privacy, negligence, battery, intentional infliction of emotional distress) on a physician who tested a patient for AIDS and then incorrectly reported that the patient had tested positive. More than 30 states considered legislation requiring premarital HIV screening; and several states (including Illinois, Louisiana, Missouri, and Texas) enacted such legislation. Michael Closen, Mandatory Premarital HIV Testing: Political Exploitation of the AIDS Epidemic, 69 Tul. L. Rev. 71, 71 (1994). Each of these states subsequently repealed its statute because of concerns about invasion of privacy, the possibility of erroneous results, and costs outweighing benefits (given the small number of HIV infections detected).[48] See also T.E.P. v. Leavitt, 840 F. Supp. 110. (D. Utah 1993) (invalidating statute that prohibited and invalidated marriages involving a person afflicted with AIDS as violative of the Americans with Disabilities Act and Rehabilitation Act).

5. *Effectiveness of procedural requirements.* Do licensure statutes accomplish their purposes? For example, are they effective in protecting couples from sexually transmitted disease? Does the possibility of sanctions deter violations? (A person is guilty of perjury if he or she knowingly makes a false statement to obtain a license.) If the licensing statutes further their ostensible purposes, how can we enforce them if a marriage is held to be valid in the absence of a license? Alternatively, are waiting periods effective or do they represent unnecessary state paternalism? Are waiting periods constitutional? Do they meet the *Zablocki* standard? See Walter E. Harding & Martin R. Levy, Marriage License Fees: Are They Constitutional?, 17 J. Fam. L. 703, 703-707 (1978). Finally, what purpose underlies the solemnization requirement by authorized persons? So long as the parties comply with the state's licensing requirement, why require such strict compliance

---

[48]. Privacy concerns are illustrated by the following account: "In Denver, the state health department has received reports that scores of men named Nancy Reagan are infected with the human immunodeficiency virus. Colorado . . . is discovering that many gay men are edgy about their names being on a master list of the HIV infected. To avoid ending up on the list, they simply write down Nancy Reagan when they are tested, and that's how it gets reported to the state." Randy Shilts, AIDS/The Inside Story, S.F. Chron., Aug. 14, 1989, at A7.

that permits the state to intervene twice in order for the parties to enter a valid marriage?

6. Goodridge *revisited*. Recall that *Goodridge*, supra p. 160, involved a challenge to the limitations of the Massachusetts marriage licensing law, which the court described as "both a gatekeeping and public records statute." 798 N.E.2d at 951. As *Goodridge* illustrates, procedural requirements implement substantive policies. *Goodridge* also emphasizes civil marriage as "a wholly secular institution." Id. at 954. Does the state's authorization of religious officials to perform valid marriages undermine the court's reasoning?

Problems

1. Anna and Dickie are involved in a sexual relationship. Dickie tells Anna that his family believes that he will go to hell if they do not marry. He proposes a "fake" ceremony and she agrees. They have a ceremony, solemnized by a minister, but fail to file the marriage license with the county clerk within 60 days of issuance as required by statute. Instead, Anna burns the license with Dickie's knowledge and consent. They live together for almost two months. Later, Dickie files for divorce and requests a division of property. Anna responds by denying the existence of the marriage or, in the alternative, for an order annuling the marriage on the basis of fraudulent inducement. What result? See Fryar v. Roberts, 57 S.W.2d 727 (Ark. 2001).

2. Husband and Wife participate in a Hindu marriage ceremony in which they exchange rings and vows. They plan to have a subsequent civil ceremony, which never takes place. Presiding over the religious ceremony is an ordained Hindu priest who is not licensed by the city or state of New York to perform marriage ceremonies. Following the ceremony, the parties begin proceedings three times to obtain a marriage license but none is ever secured. Each blames the other for the failure to secure the license. After the ceremony, both parties list themselves as "single" on their tax returns. After seven years' cohabitation (and the birth of a child), Husband brings suit seeking a declaration that the parties were never lawfully married or, in the alternative, a divorce. What result? Persad v. Balram, 724 N.Y.S.2d 560 (Sup. Ct. 2001).

(ii) Note: Procedural Variations

(1) Proxy Marriages

A proxy marriage is one in which at least one party is represented at the ceremony by an agent or proxy. Marriage by proxy was once the exclusive practice of royalty. The practice was valid in England until Parliament enacted legislation in the mid-nineteenth century that required the presence of both parties at the ceremony.[49] Marriage by proxy has been most visible during this century in times of war, frequently to legitimize children. During World War II, proxy marriages were available in Kansas, Oklahoma, and New Jersey for servicemen.[50] Marriages by

[49]. Comment, Persons—Marriage—Validity of Proxy Marriages, 25 S. Cal. L. Rev. 181, 182 (1952).
[50]. W. H. Howery, Marriage by Proxy and Other Informal Marriages, 13 U.K.C. L. Rev. 48, 54 (1944). See also Ernest G. Lorenzen, Marriage by Proxy and the Conflict of Laws, 32 Harv. L. Rev. 473, 479 (1919).

mail, telephone, cable, and radio have occurred. In 2003, as a result of Operation Iraqi Freedom, the California legislature provided statutory authority for proxy marriages for overseas service members who are serving in an armed conflict or war (Cal. Fam. Code §420(b)) (West 2004).

Another use of proxy marriages is to circumvent immigration laws. Prior to 1924 when Congress prohibited the practice, proxy marriages were valid for immigration purposes so long as the marriage was valid in the country where performed.[51] Proxy marriage has also been used to assist political refugees. See, e.g., Apt v. Apt, 1 All. E.R. 620 (1947) (permitting Jewish refugees from Nazi Germany to marry by proxy in Argentina where the husband resided). Yet another group resorting to proxy marriages is prisoners. See, e.g., People v. Tami, 2003 WL 22235337 (Cal. Ct. App. 2003) (concluding that the evidence fails to prove inmate's wife knowingly filed a false marriage license because she cannot be charged with knowledge that a proxy ceremony by telephone was invalid). See also In re Estate of Crockett, 728 N.E.2d 765 (Ill. App. Ct. 2000) (holding that decedent's children had standing to challenge marriage as void ab initio when second wife alone obtained the license and acknowledged vows, where decedent was barely conscious, unable to sign application or certificate, and a representative spoke for him with no evidence of a written proxy).

(2) Confidential Marriages

Some states permit "confidential" or "secret" marriages. See, e.g., Cal. Fam. Code §§500-536 (West 2004); Mich. Comp. Laws Ann. §§551.201 (West 2005). These provisions enable a couple to dispense with some procedural requirements. For example, the California statute, supra, permits unmarried persons, already living together, to marry without procuring a marriage license or filing a health certificate. However, they must participate in a solemnization ceremony by an authorized person and file a marriage certificate which is not open to public inspection except by court order upon a showing of good cause. The purpose of the statute is to encourage cohabitants to legalize their existing relationship by avoiding embarrassment from public disclosure of their belated marriage.

(3) Other Variations

Some states provide for other variations that dispense with traditional licensure or solemnization requirements. A few states permit marriage by declaration (e.g., Mont. Code Ann. §40-1-311 (West 2003); Tex. Fam. Code §§2.401-2.402 (West 1998 & Supp. 2004). Others permit marriage by contracts acknowledged before a judge (e.g., N.Y. Dom. Rel. Law §11(4) (McKinney 1999). Unlike a marriage by declaration, however, the parties to a marriage by contract first must obtain a license. Finally, tribal marriages, contracted according to Native American laws or customs, are also recognized in many jurisdictions. See, e.g., Nev. Rev. Stat. Ann. §122.170 (Michie 2003).

---

[51]. 8 U.S.C. §224(m) (1924) (superseded by 8 U.S.C. §1101(a)(35) (2000) ("the terms "spouse," "wife," or "husband" do not include a spouse, wife, or husband by reason of any marriage ceremony where the contracting parties thereto are not physically present in the presence of each other, unless the marriage shall have been consummated").

c. Informal Marriages

(i) Common Law Marriage

■ JENNINGS v. HURT

N.Y.L.J., Oct. 4, 1989, at 24 (Sup. Ct. N.Y. County), aff'd, *554 N.Y.S.2d 220 (App. Div. 1990),* appeal denied, *568 N.Y.S.2d 347 (N.Y. 1991)*

Justice SILBERMANN.

[Plaintiff Sandra Jennings alleged the existence of a common law marriage. Actor-defendant William Hurt moved to dismiss.]

South Carolina is one of thirteen states (including the District of Columbia) that recognize common-law marriages. South Carolina became a common law state early in the eighteenth century when it adopted the law of common-law marriage which was recognized in the Ecclesiastic Courts in England. . . .

South Carolina law is aptly stated in the case of Fryer v. Fryer, S.C. Eq. 85 (S.C. App. 1832):

> Marriage, with us, so far as the law is concerned has ever been regarded as a mere civil contract. Our law prescribes no ceremony. It required nothing but the agreement of the parties, with an intention that the agreement shall, per se, constitute the marriage. They may express the agreement by parol, they may signify it by whatever ceremony their whim, or their taste, or their religious belief, may select: it is the agreement itself, and not the form in which it is couched, which constitutes the contract. The words used, or the ceremony performed, are mere evidence of a present intention and agreement of the parties. . . .

Although common-law marriages were abolished in New York as of April 29, 1933, New York does give effect to common-law marriages if they are recognized as valid under the law of the state in which it was supposedly contracted.

The sole question to be decided by this court is whether Sandra Jennings is the common-law wife of William Hurt?

Since it is conceded that the parties never had a ceremonial marriage, the answer to that question rests upon certain events that allegedly transpired during the parties' stay in South Carolina and the law of South Carolina. . . .

Jennings and Hurt met in Saratoga, New York in the summer of 1981 while each of them was working there. Shortly thereafter, upon their return to New York City, the parties began living together. [They ceased living together in 1984.] At the time their relationship began, Jennings knew Hurt was still married. The parties had many discussions in which Hurt explained to Jennings his disappointment at his own failure in marriage and his family's history in terms of failed marriages. Hurt frequently discussed his belief that marriage was a promise or a commitment to "God" and that he was experiencing "dismay about having broken that promise." Because of his feelings and pain relating to this subject, Hurt explained that marriage was "not in the cards" for him. This is corroborated by Hurt's conversation with Mary Beth Hurt when he asked for a divorce. Jennings herself stated "he wanted me to know that he did not necessarily mean a marital commitment. . . . "

In the Spring of 1982 Jennings became pregnant. Hurt's counsel began drafting an agreement governing the parties' financial arrangements of living together and for the support of the expected child. The earliest of these agreements is dated May 1982. The pregnancy prompted Hurt to commence divorce proceedings to terminate his marriage to Mary Beth Hurt. In September, 1982, Hurt went to see his former wife to tell her he wanted to finalize the divorce since "Sandy is having a baby."

On October 31, 1982, Jennings joined Hurt in South Carolina where he was already engaged in the filming of the "Big Chill." During their stay in South Carolina from October 31, 1982 to January 10, 1983, the parties lived in the same house and shared a bed. Their social circle consisted of the cast and others connected with the film project. During this period as well as earlier and later times, their relationship was volatile and permeated by arguments.

On December 3, 1982, Hurt's divorce became final. He learned this sometime later from counsel. Jennings testified that she learned of his divorce on December 27, 1982 when he approached her with another version of the "prenuptial agreement" that had been the subject of negotiations between the parties and their counsel. That on that date he said they should sign the agreement, have blood tests and get married. Parenthetically, it is noted that South Carolina does not require blood tests in order to obtain a marriage license. She testified that they then went to a Notary Public to get the agreement signed and returned home. Hurt then spoke to his attorney and after that conversation a fight ensued in which he stated Jennings had tricked him, that the agreement was not valid because she did not have legal counsel. Jennings then allegedly went into the bedroom and started packing to go home to her mother, whereupon Hurt, according to Jennings,

> . . . threw my suitcase on the ground and we had a huge fight and he ended up telling me that it didn't matter because as far as he was concerned we were married in the eyes of God and we had a spiritual marriage and this didn't matter. We were more married than married people.

Jennings' claim to be Hurt's common-law wife is based inter alia, on these events. . . .

Documents admitted in evidence indicate that shortly after December 23, 1982, Hurt received another draft of an agreement the parties had been discussing with each other and with counsel; that on December 27, 1982 Hurt's signature was notarized on the document entitled "Paternity Acknowledgment"; that on December 28, 1982, Jennings' signature was notarized on a sublease for her New York apartment, and that on December 28, 1982, Jennings spoke with someone at her attorneys' telephone number for 17 minutes.

The Notary Public and attorney whose notary appears on both documents, present recollection of having seen the parties only once and yet having witnessed Hurt and Jennings' signature on the "prenuptial agreement" is weakened by these facts. Moreover, the undisputed fact that Hurt signed a paternity acknowledgment on that date is inconsistent with any immediate intention to marry, but is consistent with Hurt's testimony that though his commitment to his child was unequivocal, he had deep reservations about his relationship with Jennings.

The only evidence introduced of a holding forth as husband and wife while the parties were in South Carolina was a conversation with [some persons] in connection with the parties' renting of accommodations for their stay in South Carolina in which Hurt allegedly referred to Jennings as his wife and a telephone call by Hurt to Jennings' obstetrician, Dr. Credle's office, in which he asked about his "wife." The conversation with the [lessors] occurred on October 31, 1982 and thus is irrelevant because it predates the removal of the impediment to marriage. The date of the conversation with Mrs. Credle is unknown but in any event is of little significance.

It is clear from the testimony of [various persons connected with the "Big Chill"] that the community with whom the parties socialized knew Jennings and Hurt were not married. Nor is there a preponderance of credible evidence that the parties held themselves out as husband and wife after December 27, 1982. There is no evidence that Jennings filed tax returns or other forms as married. Significantly, the one document on which Jennings is alleged to have her name "Sandra Cronsberg Hurt" is clearly an altered xerox copy of the original with "Hurt" added afterwards and the document re-xeroxed. Indeed, documents signed by Hurt prior to the commencement of a lawsuit, i.e., will, pension, jury form — all indicated he considered himself single. Hurt's accountant testified that but for one tax return, where by error, the box "married" was checked, all taxes have been filed by Hurt as "single."

The testimony of persons who worked for Jennings for several months, years ago, and who each remember one isolated incident of Hurt referring to Jennings as his "wife" is unbelievable and even if true is barely relevant to prove a holding forth as husband and wife. Scheible, Hurt's employee's testimony is rejected as totally unworthy of belief. She appears as a disgruntled former employee attempting to get even as well as protect her own interests in a lawsuit. . . .

The courts of South Carolina [are] reluctant to declare a common-law marriage unless the proof of such marriage is shown by strong and competent testimony. . . . Jennings's claim that a common-law marriage existed stems, to a large extent, from her present recollection of Hurt's alleged utterance after an argument on December 27, 1983, about seven years ago, that as far as he was concerned they were married in the eyes of God and had a spiritual marriage. To which utterance Jennings says she agreed.

Even were this court to find this testimony credible, the event described by Jennings and the words allegedly spoken do not evince an "intent" to solemnize a marriage but rather the kind of words used by one desiring to continue the parties' present state of living together, i.e., in a relationship short of marriage. . . .

Moreover, where as in this case, the relationship began while one of them was already married, a subsequent divorce does not per se transform this illicit relationship into a common-law marriage. Instead the prior relationship is presumed to continue and the party claiming a common-law marriage must show by a preponderance of the evidence that the relationship underwent some fundamental change following the removal of the impediment. . . .

Accordingly, it would be incumbent on Jennings to show an agreement to enter a common-law marriage after the impediment was removed. . . . The evidence shows a paucity of any "declaration or acknowledgement of the parties" of a marital state. Not one friend of either of the parties testified that the parties held themselves out as married.

Indeed, [a cast member] testified that at his wedding Jennings "wished us luck and that we have a good marriage and expressed the hope that she would be next." This statement belies any change in the relationship of the parties having taken place on December 27 or 28, 1982. It indicates that the prior illicit relationship continued although a hope, at least by one of the parties, to one day marry existed. . . .

. . . For all the foregoing reasons the court finds that Sandra Jennings is not the common-law wife of William Hurt.

Notes and Questions

1. *Epilogue.* Jennings brought the above action as a prelude to seeking an equitable distribution of Hurt's assets, estimated at between $5 and $7 million. Following their separation, Hurt began paying approximately $60,000 annually in child support. (Jennings had requested $192,000, which was denied in an earlier ruling.) In March 1989 Hurt married bandleader Skitch Henderson's daughter Heidi. Subsequently, an appellate court affirmed the judgment in favor of William Hurt. 554 N.Y.S.2d 220, 221 (App. Div. 1990).

2. *Historical background.* American jurisdictions, which adopted common law marriage, followed early English ecclesiastical law. Following the Norman Conquest, when ecclesiastical authorities regulated marriage in England, the Church recognized two types of informal marriage: (1) the exchange of promises to be husband and wife from the present moment; and (2) the exchange of promises to be husband and wife in the future followed by sexual intercourse. Under the second form, the marriage became valid on subsequent consummation. Such marriages were recognized until the enactment of Lord Hardwicke's Act, 26 Geo. II, c. 33, in 1753, which required formalities of church ceremony, publication of banns, and a license. Subsequently, informal marriages continued to be valid only beyond the statute's jurisdiction in Scotland (hence the importance of the first town across the border, Gretna Green) and Ireland.

Professor Lawrence Friedman explains the history of common law marriage in this country:

> [Common-law marriage had a] more solid basis in the social context: the intellectual climate, and the felt needs of the population. [T]here was a shortage of clergymen of every faith in some parts of the United States. Most of the population lived outside the cities; and parts of the country were thinly populated. [M]ore to the point, large numbers of ordinary people owned houses and farms and had a real stake in the economy. There were, apparently, couples who lived together after makeshift ceremonies, or no ceremony at all. These couples raised flocks of children. The doctrine of common-law marriage allowed the law to treat these "marriages" as holy and valid.
>
> [Joel] Bishop, a shrewd observer of law and morals, felt that the early settlers were inclined to make a virtue of necessity, or at least come to terms with it. Despite their "pure morals and stern habits," the settlers could not or would not go along with the strict English marriage laws or their American counterparts. The strict marriage laws of Pennsylvania, for example, were "ill adapted to the habits and customs of society;" a "rigid execution of them," remarked Chief Justice John Bannister Gibson in 1833, "would bastardize a vast majority of the children which have been born within the state for half a century." This was not just a matter of social stigma: It was a question of who got the farm, the house, the country acreage, the lot in town.
>
> Still, there was opposition to common-law marriage. It was, after all, extremely loose. To some people, it seemed a "strange and monstrous crossbreed between concubinage and a marriage." Common-law marriage helped straighten out questions of property rights. But it could also complicate these rights, and it could lead to public scandal.

Lawrence M. Friedman, A History of American Law 141-142 (2005).

Elements √

3. *Requirements.* Common law marriage has four elements: capacity to enter a marital contract, present agreement to be married, cohabitation, and holding out to the community as husband and wife. Only nine states and the District of Columbia currently recognize common law marriage. Andrea Brobeil, Family Law Chapter: Marriage and Divorce, 5 Geo. J. Gender & L. 529, 531 n.4 (2004) (listing Alabama, Colorado, Iowa, Kansas, Montana, Rhode Island, South Carolina, Texas and Utah). Texas continues to recognize the doctrine but limit its application. See Tex. Fam. Code Ann. §2.401 (1998) (requiring a proponent of a common law marriage to file suit to establish the marriage within two years after the parties' separation or else to overcome a rebuttable presumption that no agreement to marry existed). Pennsylvania judicially abolished common law marriage in 2003. See PNC Bank Corp. v. Workers' Comp. Appeal Bd., 831 A.2d 1269, 1282 (Pa. Commw. Ct. 2003) (codified at 23 Pa. Cons. Stat §1103 (West 2001 & Supp 2005) (prospectively abrogating the doctrine for common law marriages formed after January 1, 2005)).

Did Jennings and Hurt hold themselves out as married? What is the evidence pro and con? The main reason for the requirement of a public reputation as man and wife is to prevent fraud. Although an agreement between the parties is necessary, the agreement may be inferred from cohabitation or other circumstantial evidence. In terms of the standard of proof, South Carolina to the contrary, many states require clear and convincing evidence. Clark, Law of Domestic Relations (2d ed.), supra, at 48. See also DeMelo v. Zompa, 844 A.2d 174, 177 (R.I. 2004) (requiring proof of the existence of common law marriage by clear-and-convincing evidence).

Jennings also discusses the problem of an impediment: A valid common law marriage cannot come into existence while a prior marriage exists on the part of one spouse. Why? Many jurisdictions require that the parties must renew their "agreement" and meet the other requirements following the removal of the impediment (in Hurt's case, following his divorce). For a discussion of the split of authority on when and how such relationships ripen into valid common law marriages, see Prevatte v. Prevatte, 377 S.E.2d 114, 117 (S.C. 1989).

4. *Dissolution or death.* Many cases arise on the dissolution of the relationship, as in *Jennings,* or on death when the survivor attempts to claim inheritance or health insurance benefits, workers' compensation, or social security benefits. See, e.g., Thompson v. Barnhart, 2005 WL 23347 (D. Kan. 2005) (ruling that woman could not receive Social Security benefits at man's death because common law marriage was not established due to couple's inconsistent holding themselves out as husband and wife); PNC Bank Corp., supra (affirming recognition of survivor's claim to workers' compensation for spouse's fatal accident based on evidence of affidavit in which couple named woman as "common law spouse" for purposes of man's pension plan). One problem in attempting to establish a common law marriage after the death of one party is the Dead Man's Act. How is a surviving "spouse" to establish a common law marriage in the face of a statute that precludes testimony concerning communications or transactions with a deceased? See Crenshaw v. Bussey, 100 P.3d 568 (Colo. Ct. App. 2004) (holding that a widow who sought appointment as personal representative of spouse's estate could not testify under exception to the dead man's statute to establish status as a common law spouse). Occasionally, claims of common law marriage arise in other contexts. See, e.g., Mesa v. U.S., 875 A.2d 79 (D.C. 2005) (holding that defendant failed

to prove existence of common law marriage, and therefore was unable to invoke marital privilege).

5. *Choice of law.* Can a couple, domiciliaries in a non-common law jurisdiction, obtain marital status by virtue of residing in another jurisdiction that does recognize common law marriage and then returning to the non-common law state? Why did the New York court look to South Carolina law to determine whether the two New Yorkers had entered a common law marriage, given New York's abolition of common law marriage? See also Fritsche v. Vermilion Parish Hosp. Serv. Dist., 893 So. 2d 935 (La. Ct. App. 2005) (holding that, although Louisiana does not recognize common law marriages, the court is obliged to give effect to such marriages validly created in another state). See generally William A. Reppy, Choice of Law Problems Arising When Unmarried Cohabitants Change Domicile, 55 SMU L. Rev. 273 (2002).

A common misconception is that the parties must cohabit for a specified period of time. How long a stay in the nondomiciliary state is sufficient to confer common law marital status? A few days? Compare In re Estate of Bivans, 652 P.2d 744 (N.M. Ct. App. 1982), *cert. quashed*, 652 P.2d 1213 (N.M. 1982), and Kennedy v. Damron, 268 S.W.2d 22 (Ky. 1954) (both holding that mere visits are not enough), with Madewell v. United States, 84 F. Supp. 329 (E.D. Tenn. 1949) (cohabitation for "number of days and nights" sufficient), and Metropolitan Life Ins. Co. v. Holding, 293 F. Supp. 854 (E.D. Va. 1968) (one year sufficient). Courts are influenced by the equities of the situation.

6. *Policy.* Should common law marriage be revived, as some commentators urge? According to one commentator, the doctrine avoids hardship, protects the poor and ignorant, benefits innocent spouses after removal of impediments to a prior formal marriage, and protects children from the stigma of illegitimacy. Walter O. Weyrauch, Informal and Formal Marriage — An Appraisal of the Trend in Family Organization, 28 U. Chi. L. Rev. 88, 101 (1960). Another commentator adds that failure to recognize the doctrine has a significant negative impact on women, especially those who are widowed, abandoned, victims of domestic violence, and minorities and persons of color. Cynthia Grant Bowman, A Feminist Proposal to Bring Back Common Law Marriage, 75 Or. L. Rev. 709, 769-770 (1996). Compare also Marsha Garrison, Is Consent Necessary? An Evaluation of the Emerging Law of Cohabitant Obligation, 52 UCLA L. Rev. 815, 847 (2005) (supporting a narrow doctrine of common law marriage that encompasses only couples who are genuinely committed and have marriage-like relationships), with Maggie Gallagher, Rites, Rights and Social Institutions: Why and How Should the Law Support Marriage?, 18 N.D. J. L. Ethics & Pub. Pol'y 225, 240 (2004) (proposing a revival of common law marriage to strengthen marriage as a social institution).

The arguments against common law marriage include: modern social conditions (urbanization) have eliminated the need for the doctrine, prevention of fraud in the transmission of property, the desire to protect marriage and the family from immoral sexual unions, confusion of the public records, the difficulty of surmounting problems of proof, eliminating evasion of a jurisdiction's statutory requirements, desire to enforce health-related marital requirements through the licensing process, and administrative and judicial efficiency. Bowman, supra. See also Ryan P. Newell, Comment, "To Be Sure He Is My Husband Good Enough," or Is He? An Analysis of Common Law Marriage in Pennsylvania, 109 Penn. St. L. Rev.

337, 354-357 (2004) (discussing arguments for abrogation). Which arguments are more convincing?

In the face of this debate, UMDA takes no position on the validity of common law marriage. The drafters of the act include alternative provisions of §211, preferring to leave the choice to the states. 9A U.L.A. (pt. 1) 195-197 (1998).

7. *Privacy.* To what extent does the constitutional right to privacy limit the state's ability to abolish common law marriage? Does Griswold v. Connecticut, supra Chapter I, imply a concept of marriage that exists independently of state law? See Ellen Kandoian, Cohabitation, Common Law Marriage, and the Possibility of a Shared Moral Life, 75 Geo. L.J. 1829, 1852-1853 (1987). Does the demise of common law marriage signify a trend toward decreased privatization within the family (i.e., less recognition for private ordering)? See Vivian Hamilton, Mistaking Marriage for Social Policy, 11 Va. J. Soc. Pol'y & L. 307, 328 (2004) (arguing that the disappearance of common law marriage in the face of increased institutionalization of matrimony assures that entry into marriage will continue to be a public rather than a private act).

Problems

1. Sandra, a university student, begins dating baseball player Dave Winfield. The couple spends frequent time in California, New Jersey, and Texas. After Sandra becomes pregnant, they discuss marriage. Dave, concerned about his image as fathering a nonmarital child, tells Sandra he wants a private (just the two of them) ceremony. He instructs Sandra to make a reservation at the Amfac Hotel under the name "Mr. & Mrs. David Winfield." After a three-day stay in the honeymoon suite, Sandra tells her mother she and Dave are married. She rents a condo in Houston for them; the name "Winfield" is on the mailbox. Dave pays for rent, food, furniture, medical, and travel expenses. Pursuant to Dave's instructions, Sandra continues to use her surname and signs the baby's birth certificate with her name.

A neighbor, who gave a party in their honor, is prepared to testify that she thought they were married. Further, when the couple vacations in the Bahamas, a local newspaper describes them as husband and wife, as does an announcer at a softball game. Dave does not ask for retractions. Sandra files income tax returns and health insurance forms as single, per Dave's instructions. She does not wear a wedding ring. While living with Sandra, Dave is dating other women, one of whom he eventually marries. Sandra files for divorce, claiming she is his common law wife. Dave testifies that he never agreed to be married, bought the condo to provide for his child and, further, does not recall staying at the Amfac Hotel. Texas recognizes common law marriage, although California and New Jersey do not. What result? Winfield v. Renfro, 821 S.W.2d 640 (Tex. Ct. App. 1991).

2. Maurice and Ann meet at a restaurant where Anne works as a waitress. Soon thereafter, they move into a home purchased by Maurice and titled in his name. Maurice gives Anne an engagement ring and matching wedding band and asks her to marry him (although the wedding never takes place). Anne wears the engagement ring but not the wedding band because she does not believe that she has the right to do so without a formal ceremony. A sign outside their home reads "Hunsakers, Home of the Classics" (referring to the classic car business they operate

together). The telephone answering message states "This is the Hunsaker residence." A grandfather clock, displayed in the living room, has the letters "A," "M," and "H" intertwined. Anne is listed as Maurice's spouse on his insurance policy. They own shares of stock and a time-share condominum as joint tenants. They keep separate bank accounts because Maurice has poor credit; they file income tax returns that list themselves as single. Maurice is listed as Anne's "significant other" on two hospital consent forms that Anne signed. Shortly before his death, Maurice tells his attorney that he wants to leave his entire estate to Anne, whom he refers to as his common law wife. He says that if he does not have a will, his family will "eat [Anne] alive." However, before the will can be drafted, Maurice dies. His surviving sister and brothers claim his estate. Anne claims she was his common law wife based on their ten years' cohabitation. The jurisdiction recognizes common law marriage. What result? In re Estate of Hunsaker, 968 P.2d 281 (Mont. 1998).

(ii) The Putative Spouse Doctrine and Other Curative Devices

Courts and legislatures often strain to recognize marriages that fail to comply with the formal requirements. In so doing, they have developed a variety of curative or mitigative devices — so-called because they cure or mitigate the harsh consequences of invalidity.

The most important of these mitigative devices is the putative spouse doctrine. This doctrine recognizes the marriage of an individual who participated in a marriage ceremony in good faith, in the belief that a valid marriage took place, and in ignorance of an impediment making the marriage void or voidable (for example, a preexisting marriage or a disability such as nonage). Clark, Law of Domestic Relations, supra, at 55. In some situations, a putative marriage will be recognized even in the absence of a ceremony, as when the state allows common law marriage or when the party asserting the doctrine in good faith believed no ceremony was required. See id. at 55 n.64. On later removal of the impediment, the de facto marriage becomes a valid de jure union. Id. at 55.

Section 209 of UMDA, 9A U.L.A. (pt. 1) 192-194 (1998), takes the following approach:

> Any person who has cohabited with another to whom he is not legally married in the good faith belief that he was married to that person is a putative spouse until knowledge of the fact that he is not legally married terminates his status and prevents acquisition of further rights. A putative spouse acquires the rights conferred upon a legal spouse, including the right to maintenance following termination of his status, whether or not the marriage is prohibited (Section 207) or declared invalid (Section 208). If there is a legal spouse or other putative spouses, rights acquired by a putative spouse do not supersede the rights of the legal spouse or those acquired by other putative spouses, but the court shall apportion property, maintenance, and support rights among the claimants as appropriate in the circumstances and in the interests of justice.

In contrast, some states apply the doctrine to property division but not spousal support. See, e.g., Williams v. Williams, 97 P.3d 1124 (Nev. 2004).

In addition, presumptions can sometimes function as curative devices. Rules of evidence in some states raise a presumption of a valid marriage based on a couple's "holding out" as husband and wife, even if the jurisdiction has abolished common law marriage by statute. See e.g., Thompson v. Thompson, 163 S.W.2d 792 (Mo. Ct. App. 1942). Similarly, some states attach a presumption of validity to the later of two (or the latest in a series of) marriages. Thus, for example, if A, who is already married to B, marries C, this second marriage, although bigamous and void, may be presumed valid. To rely on this presumption, one must introduce evidence that the later marriage occurred, and to rebut it one must show "cogent and conclusive" evidence that the earlier marriage continues. Clark, supra, at 72-73. According to Clark, this presumption rests on policies favoring validation of marriages and "the need to make good the parties' expectations." Id. at 71.

Other courts have developed other equitable remedies that, while not creating valid or even de facto marriages, allow some of the incidents of marriage to follow the nonmarital union. See, e.g., Kasey v. Richardson, 331 F. Supp. 580 (W.D. Va. 1971), *aff'd*, 462 F.2d 757 (4th Cir. 1972) (children's insurance benefits under Social Security Act). Some courts have created "marriage by estoppel." For example, in Sutton v. Sutton, 143 S.W.3d 759 (Mo. Ct. App. 2004), the court held that a man, who was already in a common law marriage with another woman when he married his second wife, was precluded by the doctrine of equitable estoppel from questioning the validity of his second marriage. Finally, some courts hold that a common law marriage, even if null and void, will legitimize any issue. See Murphy v. Holland, 377 S.E.2d 363 (Va. 1989).

To what extent should courts apply any of the above devices in cases in which the parties openly cohabit without any belief or reputation that they were married? To what extent should courts apply these remedies to unions ineligible for marriage, such as lesbian or gay cohabitation? See Snetsinger v. Montana Univ. Sys., 104 P.3d 445 (Mont. 2004) (holding that the policy of denying dependent health insurance coverage to same-sex partners of university employees violated the state constitution by conditioning benefits on the relationships of those who had either a solemnized or common law marriage while denying lesbians and gays the right to marry). To what extent do these curative and mitigative devices belong at all today?

Problem

When Dr. Norman J. Lewiston, a renown expert in cystic fibrosis at Stanford University, dies of a heart attack in 1991, three women claim to be his widow. Records reveal that he married Diana Lewiston in 1960 in Connecticut, naming her in a 1966 will as his sole heir. (He suffers his fatal heart attack in the home they share in Palo Alto, California.) They have three children, all now adults. Katy Mayer-Lewiston, who marries him in 1985, attends university events with him. His colleagues believe that she is his wife. The two own a house in a town ten miles away. Robin Phelps of San Diego marries Dr. Lewiston in 1989 during his sabbatical in that city. Believing that he plans to retire soon in San Diego, Robin remains there. See Katherine Bishop, Respected Doctor, Professor and Family Man — 3 Families, in Fact, N.Y. Times, Oct. 23, 1991, at A7. Assume that California's community property law would give half of Dr. Lewiston's property acquired during marriage to the surviving spouse. If all three purported widows seek a share of his estate, to what extent do any of the curative and mitigative devices, discussed above, help resolve their claims? See also In re Estate of Vargas, 111 Cal. Rptr. 779 (Ct. App. 1974).

III

Being Married: Regulation of the Intact Marriage

A. INTRODUCTION: THE CHANGING NATURE OF MARRIAGE

Marriage and the family have evolved over time. Marriage has become more companionate.[1] The family has lost some of its functions.[2] The advent of same-sex marriage has altered radically the traditional definition of marriage and the family. Significantly, these and other changes have contributed to an increase in family privacy[3]—not always with positive consequences. The cases and materials that follow focus on the changing nature of marital rights, roles, and responsibilities.

■ JOHN W. BLASSINGAME, THE SLAVE COMMUNITY: PLANTATION LIFE IN THE ANTEBELLUM SOUTH
171-174, 177 (1979)

[Among slaves in the antebellum South,] many slaves had only one partner. Henry Box Brown, for instance, refused his master's order to take another mate

---

[1]. See Ernest Watson Burgess & Harvey James Locke, The Family: From Institution to Companionship (1953).
[2]. William Fielding Ogburn & Meyer Francis Nimkoff, Technology and the Changing Family (1955).
[3]. For classic historical studies of family privacy, see Philippe Aries, Centuries of Childhood: A Social History of Family Life (1962); David H. Flaherty, Privacy in Colonial New England (1972); Barbara Laslett, The Family as a Public and Private Institution: An Historical Perspective, 35 J. Marriage & Fam. 480 (August 1973).

after his wife was sold because he felt marriage "was a sacred institution binding upon me." Affection was apparently the most important factor which kept partners together. This emerges most clearly in the lamentations and resentments which pervade the autobiographies over the separation of family members. Frequently when their mates were sold, slaves ran away in an effort to find them. . . . Because they were denied all the protection which the law afforded, slaves had an almost mythological respect for legal marriage . . .

[T]he slave faced almost insurmountable odds in his efforts to build a strong stable family. First, and most important of all, his authority was restricted by his master. Any decision of his regarding his family could be countermanded by his master. The master determined when both he and his wife would go to work, when or whether his wife cooked his meals, and was often the final arbiter in family disputes. . . . Some planters punished males by refusing to let them visit their mates when they lived on other plantations. In any event, these slaves could only visit their mates with their master's permission. When the slave lived on the same plantation with his mate, he could rarely escape frequent demonstrations of his powerlessness. The master, and not the slave, furnished the cabin, clothes, and the minimal food for his wife and children. Under such a regime slave fathers often had little or no authority.

The most serious impediment to the man's acquisition of status in his family was his inability to protect his wife from the sexual advances of whites and the physical abuse of his master. Instead, according to Austin Steward, slave husbands had to "submit without a murmur" when their wives were flogged. Sometimes, in spite of the odds, the men tried to protect their mates. . . . Occasionally, slaves killed white men for such acts. Generally, however, the women had no choice but to submit to the sexual advances of white men. . . .

By all odds, the most brutal aspect of slavery was the separation of families. This was a haunting fear which made all of the slave's days miserable. [P]ractically all of the black autobiographers were touched by the tragedy. Death occurred too frequently in the master's house, creditors were too relentless in collecting their debts, the planter's reserves ran out too often, and the master longed too much for expensive items for the slave to escape the clutches of the slave trader. Nothing demonstrated his powerlessness as much as the slave's inability to prevent the forcible sale of his wife and children. . . .

The callous attitudes frequently held by planters toward slave unions are revealed clearly in the statistics: 937 or 34.4 per cent, of the unions were dissolved by masters. An overwhelming majority of the couples were separated before they reached their sixth anniversary. The heartlessness of the planters is revealed more clearly in their separation of slaves who had lived together for decades. . . .

Slave families tended to be characterized also by strong relations with kin and community members, and low birth rates and high infant morality rates because of poor living conditions. For other historical sources on the slave family, see Herbert G. Gutman, The Black Family in Slavery and Freedom, 1750-1925 (1977); Jacqueline Jones, Labor of Love, Labor of Sorrow: Black Women, Work and the Family, From Slavery to the Present (1986); Edmund S. Morgan, American Slavery,

American Freedom (2003); Brenda E. Stevenson, Life in Black and White: Family and Community in the Slave South (1996).

■ THEODORE CAPLOW ET AL., THE QUALITY OF MARRIAGE IN MIDDLETOWN: 1924-1976
in Middletown Families: Fifty Years of Change and Continuity
116-118, 120-121, 124-125, 126, 127, 135 (1982)

[In this excerpt, social scientists assess the quality of marriages in Middletown, a fictional name for a midwestern city, in the 1920s, 1930s, and 1970s.]

MARRIAGE IN THE 1920S

[T]he average marriage in the Middletown of the 1920s was a dreary one, especially for the working class. Marriage for many husbands meant weariness from trying to provide for their families, numerous children, and wives weary from doing other people's washing. For many wives, marriage meant poverty, cruelty, adultery, and abandonment. [M]ost families, although less than happy, were held together by community values discouraging divorce. . . . Married life was disappointing, but the prospect of a divorce was even more painful. . . .

Observations of husbands and wives revealed that most of them developed a relationship with limited companionship. In the social and recreational activities of the 1920s, the sexes were separated more often than not. At dinners, parties, and other social gatherings, men and women seemed to form separate groups so that the men could talk about business, sports and politics and the women could discuss children, dress styles, and local gossip. Men's leisure activities generally excluded women. Business-class husbands played golf or cards at their clubs without their wives. . . . The one recreational activity that husbands and wives shared was card playing with friends in their homes. . . . The limited communication between husbands and wives and the trivial nature of their conversation left many of them isolated in their separate worlds, his pertaining to work and friends and hers to the children and the home. In many marriages, they shared a house, each other's bodies, and little else.

. . . Lack of information about birth control and the prejudice against its use made babies the inevitable consequence of physical intimacy for most working-class couples. The uncertainty of employment often made another child an unwanted burden. The conflict between not wanting more children and needing the physical pleasures of marriage, and the resulting stress placed on the marriage, were evident. [C]omments provide considerable insight into Middletown's working-class marriages of the 1920s. The fact that a wife might not dare ask her husband what he thought about birth control, let alone what he felt about practicing it, shows how shallow some of the relationships were. . . .

MARRIAGE IN THE 1930S

The Great Depression was thought by Middletown people to have mixed effects on marital happiness. On the one hand, they spoke of how married couples spent more time together and became more dependent on each other, and this enforced togetherness was perceived as strengthening the quality of Middletown's marriages. [T]he Depression did increase the amount of time husbands and wives spent together by making outside activities unaffordable. [On the other hand,] [a]lthough couples spent more time together, they often reacted to economic pressures by mutual recrimination. The wives were quick to reproach their husbands for failing to provide for the family's needs, and the husbands were equally quick to defend their wounded egos by lashing out at wives and children. Despite these mounting tensions, the typical marital relationship during the Depression was similar to that of the 1920s. . . .

MARRIAGE IN THE 1970s . . .

[We] have witnessed a major change in the style of communication between husbands and wives. [Women have been encouraged to assert their needs and preferences.] Marriage-enrichment programs . . . have purported to teach thousands of American couples how to communicate with each other more effectively. The women's rights movement [has] fostered a more equal marriage relationship in which the needs and wishes of the wife are considered to be at least as important as those of the husband.

It is difficult to imagine many contemporary wives who would be afraid to discuss birth control with their husbands, particularly after the couple has had several children. The taboo on discussing financial matters observed in the 1920s has almost disappeared, and today nearly all wives play an active role in the management of family finances, especially when they work and contribute to the family income. . . .

Not only are contemporary husbands and wives talking to each other, they are engaging in a great deal of leisure activity together. Shopping; eating out; going for drives and to movies, sporting events, fairs, and musical presentations; and taking part in physical fitness activities are frequently shared by husbands and wives. . . . In contemporary American society, television has become an integral part of daily life, a source of news as well as of recreation. . . .

There is additional evidence suggesting that the quality of the average marital relationship has improved over the past 50 years — the number of wives who mentioned their husbands as a source of strength during difficult times. [W]hen a 1924 sample of Middletown housewives was asked the question "What are the thoughts and plans that give you courage to go on when thoroughly discouraged?" not a single wife mentioned her husband as a source of reassurance. . . . The data suggest again that the marital relationship has deepened since the 1920s and that husbands and wives share each other's burdens and provide emotional support to a greater degree now than then. . . .

All things considered, the quality of marriage seems to have improved substantially in Middletown during the past half a century. Such dismal marriages as the Lynds [the researchers] described as typical in the 1920s are now relatively rare. The overwhelming majority of contemporary husbands and wives say that their marriages are happy and fulfilling.

We do not mean to imply that all marriages in Middletown are happy. The data indicate that most are, but the divorce rate is a reminder that many unhappy marriages occur. Indeed, the high divorce rate is one important reason why contemporary marriages are so happy; most of the unhappy ones have been terminated. . . .

Postscript

In 1999, sociologist Theodore Caplow and associates replicated the landmark study of the typical American community that was conducted in the 1920s by Helen and Robert Lynd. Findings of the recent study include the following: (1) in 1924, married women with children did not work, whereas the great majority of married women (regardless of social class) are employed currently outside the home; (2) in 1924, premarital sexual activity was taboo, although today it is common; (3) cohabitation in 1924 was virtually impossible because of legal sanctions, whereas today, it is quite common; (4) nonmarital births in 1924 were heavily stigmatized (with children being put in orphanages or placed for adoption), but today about 20 percent of white children and the majority of African-American children are nonmarital births; (5) housework in 1924 took up a major fraction of the work day unlike today; and (6) both mothers and fathers are able to spend more time with their children than they did in 1924. See Theodore Caplow et al., The First Measured Century: An Illustrated Guide to Trends in America, 1900-2000 (2000) (known as "Middletown IV" because it followed two earlier replications of the initial study).

On the history of marriage, see also Stephanie Coontz, Marriage, A History: From Obedience to Intimacy, or How Love Conquered Marriage (2005); Nancy F. Cott, Public Vows: A History of Marriage and the Nation (2002); E. J. Graff, What is Marriage For?: The Strange Social History of Our Most Intimate Institution (2004); Hendrik Hartog, Man and Wife in America: A History (2002); John Witte, Jr., From Sacrament to Contract: Marriage, Religion, and Law in the Western Tradition (1997); Marilyn Yalom, A History of the Wife (2002).

■ ADRIENNE RICH, COMPULSORY HETEROSEXUALITY AND LESBIAN EXISTENCE
in Blood, Bread, and Poetry: Selected Prose, 1979-1985, 23, 27, 50-51, 59-60, 63-64, 67 (1986)

. . . A feminist critique of compulsory heterosexual orientation for women is long overdue. . . . The assumption that "most women are innately heterosexual" stands as a theoretical and political stumbling block for feminism. It remains a tenable assumption partly because lesbian existence has been written out of history or catalogued under disease, partly because it has been treated as exceptional rather than intrinsic, partly because to acknowledge that for women heterosexuality may not be a "preference" at all but something that has had to be imposed, managed, organized, propagandized, and maintained by force is an immense step to take if you consider yourself freely and "innately" heterosexual. Yet the failure to examine heterosexuality as an institution is like failing to admit that the economic system called capitalism or the caste system of racism is maintained by a variety of forces, including both physical violence and false consciousness. . . .

. . . Women have married because it was necessary, in order to survive economically, in order to have children who would not suffer economic deprivation or social ostracism, in order to remain respectable, in order to do what was expected of women, because coming out of "abnormal" childhoods they wanted to feel "normal" and because heterosexual romance has been represented as the great female adventure, duty, and fulfillment. . . .

[Within the institution] the absence of choice remains the great unacknowledged reality, and in the absence of choice, women will remain dependent upon the chance or luck of particular relationships and will have no collective power to determine the meaning and place of sexuality in their lives. . . .

■ MICHAEL WARNER, BEYOND GAY MARRIAGE
in Left Legalism/Left Critique 260 (Wendy Brown &
Janet Halley eds., 2002)

Marriage sanctifies some couples at the expense of others. It is selective legitimacy. This is a necessary implication of the institution, and not just the result of bad motives. . . . To a couple that gets married, marriage just looks ennobling. . . . But stand outside it for a second and you see the implication: if you don't have it, you and your relations are less worthy. Without this corollary effect, marriage would not be able to endow anybody's life with significance. The ennobling and the demeaning go together. Marriage does one only by virtue of the other. Marriage, in short, discriminates.

That is one reason why same-sex marriage provokes such powerful outbursts of homophobic feeling in many straight people, when they could just as easily view marriage as the ultimate conformity of gay people to their own norms. They want marriage to remain a privilege, a mark that they are special. Often, they are willing to grant all or nearly all the benefits of marriage to gay people, as long as they don't have to give up the word *marriage*. They need some token, however magical, of superiority. But what about the gay people who want marriage? Would they not in turn derive their sense of pride from the invidious and shaming distinction between the married and the unmarried?

On the exclusionary implications of a heterosexual definition of marriage, see also Judith Butler, Is Kinship Always Already Heterosexual? in Left Legalism/Left Critique, supra, at 229-258; Zachary A. Kramer, Exclusionary Equality and the Case for Same-Sex Families: A Reworking of Martha Fineman's Re-visioned Family Law, 2 Seattle J. Soc. Just. 505 (2004).

■ JESSIE BERNARD, THE FUTURE OF MARRIAGE
16-18, 26-28, 40-41, 49-50 (1982)

There are few findings more consistent, less equivocal, more convincing than the sometimes spectacular and always impressive superiority on almost every index—demographic, psychological, or social—of married over never-married men. Despite all the jokes about marriage in which men indulge, all the complaints they lodge against it, it is one of the greatest boons of their sex. Employers, bankers, and insurance companies have long since known this. And whether they know it or not, men need marriage more than women do. As Samuel Johnson said, marriage is, indeed "the best state for man in general; and every man is a worse man in proportion as he is unfit for the married state."

The research evidence is overwhelmingly convincing. Although the physical health of married men is no better than that of never-married men until middle age, their mental health is far better, fewer show serious symptoms of psychological distress, and fewer of them suffer mental health impairments. [Research has] shown that marriage is an asset in a man's career, including his earning power. The value of marriage for sheer male survival is itself remarkable. It does, indeed, pay men to be married. . . . Men . . . profit greatly from having a wife to help them to take care of their health. . . . In the United States, the suicide rate for single men is almost twice as high as for married men. . . .

The actions of men with respect to marriage speak far louder than words; they speak, in fact, with a deafening roar. Once men have known marriage, they can hardly live without it. Most divorced and widowed men remarry. At every age, the marriage rate for both divorced and widowed men is higher than the rate for single men. Half of all divorced white men who remarry do so within three years after divorce. Indeed, it might not be farfetched to conclude that the verbal assaults on marriage indulged in by men are a kind of compensatory reaction to their dependence on it. . . .

[I]t is hard for us to see how different the wife's marriage really is from the husband's, and how much worse. But, in fact, it is. There is a very considerable research literature reaching back over a generation which shows that: more wives than husbands report marital frustration and dissatisfaction; more report negative feelings; more wives than husbands report marital problems; more wives than husbands consider their marriages unhappy, have considered separation or divorce, have regretted their marriages; and fewer report positive companionship. [Yet it is not] the complaints of wives that demonstrate how bad the wife's marriage is, but rather the poor mental and emotional health of married women as compared not only to married men's but also to unmarried women's.

Although the physical health of married women, as measured by absence of chronic conditions or restricted activity, is as good as, and in the ages beyond sixty-five even better than, that of married men, they suffer far greater mental-health hazards and present a far worse clinical picture. [Research has] found that more married women than married men have felt they were about to have a nervous breakdown; more experience psychological and physical anxiety; more have feelings of inadequacy in their marriages and blame themselves for their own lack of general adjustment. Other studies report that more married women than married men show phobic reactions, depression, and passivity; greater than expected frequency of symptoms of psychological distress; and mental-health impairment. . . .

[W]ives make more of the adjustments called for in marriage than do husbands. . . . One of the most poignant adjustments that wives have to make is in the pattern of emotional expression between themselves and their husbands. Almost invariably, they mind the letdown in emotional expression that comes when the husband's job takes more out of him, or the original warmth subsides. Lee Rainwater found in marriages between men and women in the lower-lower classes that wives tended to adopt their husbands' taciturnity and lack of demonstrativeness rather than insist on winning him over to theirs. . . . The psychological and emotional costs of all these adjustments show up in the increasing unhappiness of wives with the passage of time and in their increasingly negative and passive outlook on life. One measure of these costs can be found in the increasing rate of alcoholism with time. . . .

The problem is not why do young women marry, but why, in the face of all the evidence, do more married than unmarried women report themselves as happy? [One way] to look at the seeming anomaly involved here . . . is that happiness is interpreted in terms of conformity. Wives may, in effect, be judging themselves happy by definition. They are conforming to expectations and are therefore less vulnerable to the strains accompanying nonconformity. The pressures to conform are so great that few young women can resist them. Better, as the radical women put it, dead than unwed. Those who do not marry are made to feel inferior, failures. [S]tereotypes of . . . unmarried women [include] the conventional image of a frustrated, repressed, purse-lipped, unnatural being. . . . Escape from being "an old maid" is one definition of happiness.

Such conformity to the norm of marriage does not have to be imposed from the outside. Women have internalized the norms prescribing marriage so completely that the role of wife seems the only acceptable one. And since marriage is set up as the *summum bonum* of life for women, they interpret their achievement of marriage as happiness, no matter how unhappy the marriage itself may be. They have been told that their happiness depends on marriage, so, even if they are miserable, they *are* married, aren't they? . . .

■ LINDA J. WAITE & MAGGIE GALLAGHER, IS HER MARRIAGE REALLY WORSE THAN HIS?

in The Case for Marriage: Why Married People are Happier, Healthier, and Better Off Financially 162-163 (2001)

[Jessie] Bernard's basic conclusion — marriage is good for men but bad for women — is still widely repeated not only in popular culture but even in college textbooks used in marriage-and-family courses. . . . But is it true? Is his marriage really so different — and better — than hers? The evidence is in, at least for the ways in which marriage is practiced today: Both men and women gain a great deal from marriage. True, marriage does not affect men and women in exactly the same ways. Both men and women live longer, healthier, and wealthier lives when married, but husbands typically get greater health benefits from marriage than do wives. On the other hand, while both men and women get bigger bank accounts and a high standard of living in marriage, wives reap even greater financial advantages than do husbands.

Overall, the portrait of marriage that emerges from two generations of increasingly sophisticated empirical research on actual husbands and wives is not one of gender bias, but one of gender balance: A good marriage enlarges and enriches the lives of both men and women. [Based on their sociological research, the authors conclude that parenting (especially of babies and preschoolers), rather than marriage, is a major contributing factor to women's decreased marital satisfaction.]

See also U.S. Dept. of Health & Human Services, National Center for Health Statistics, Marital Status and Health: United States, 1999-2002 (reporting that married adults were generally found to be healthier than those persons who were widowed, divorced or separated, never married, or living with a partner, and that the differences were not gender-based).

State sanction of same-sex unions also appears to affect the partners' mental health. For recent empirical research, see William N. Eskridge & Darren R. Spedale, Gay Marriage: For Better or for Worse? What We've Learned From the Evidence (2006) (reporting on the societal and personal benefits of state-sanctioned same-sex unions based on Scandinavian data); Gilbert Herdt & Robert M. Kertzner, I Do, But I Can't: The Impact of Marriage Denial on the Mental Health and Sexual Citizenship of Lesbians and Gay Men in the United States, 3 J. Sexuality Res. & Soc. Pol'y 33 (2006) (revealing that bans on same-sex unions cause couples to devalue their relationships, feel discriminated against, and experience high levels of stress).

B. ROLES AND RESPONSIBILITIES IN MARRIAGE

1. The Common Law View

■ 1 WILLIAM BLACKSTONE, COMMENTARIES
442-445

By marriage, the husband and wife are one person in law: that is, the very being or legal existence of the woman is suspended during the marriage, or at least is incorporated and consolidated into that of the husband: under whose wing, protection, and *cover,* she performs everything; and is therefore called in our law-french a *feme-covert;* is said to be *covert-baron,* or under the protection and influence of her husband, her baron, or lord; and her condition during her marriage is called her *coverture.* Upon this principle, of a union of person in husband and wife, depend almost all the legal rights, duties, and disabilities, that either of them acquire by the marriage. . . . For this reason, a man cannot grant anything to his wife, or enter into covenant with her: for the grant would be to suppose her separate existence; and to covenant with her, would be only to covenant with himself: and therefore it is also generally true, that all compacts made between husband and wife, when single, are voided by the intermarriage. . . . The husband is bound to provide his wife with necessities by law, [and] if she contracts debts for them, he is obliged to pay them: but for anything besides necessaries, he is not chargeable. . . . If the wife be indebted before marriage, the husband is bound afterwards to pay the debt; for he has adopted her and her circumstances together. If the wife be injured in her person or her property, she can bring no action for redress without her husband's concurrence, and in his name, as well as her own: neither can she sue or be sued, without making the husband a defendant. . . . In criminal prosecutions, it is true, the wife may be indicted and punished separately; for the union is only a civil union. But, in trials of any sort, they are not allowed to be evidence for, or against, each other: partly because it is impossible their testimony should be indifferent; but principally because of the union of person: and therefore, if they were admitted to be witnesses for each other, they would contradict one maxim of law, ["One ought not be a witness in his own cause"]; and if against each other, they would contradict another maxim, ["No one is bound to accuse himself"]. . . .

But, though our law in general considers man and wife as one person, yet there are some instances in which she is separately considered; as inferior to him, and acting by his compulsion. And therefore all deeds executed, and acts done, by her, during her coverture, are void, or at least voidable; except it be a fine, or the like matter of record, in which case she must be solely and secretly examined, to learn if her act be voluntary. She cannot by will devise lands to her husband, [because] she is supposed to be under his coercion. And in some felonies, and other inferior crimes, committed by her, through constraint of her husband, the law excuses her: but this extends not to treason or murder.

The husband also (by the old law) might give his wife moderate correction. For, as he is to answer for her misbehavior, the law thought it reasonable to entrust him with this power of restraining her, by domestic chastisement, in the same moderation that a man is allowed to correct his servants or children; for whom the master or parent is also liable in some cases to answer. But this power of correction was confined within reasonable bounds; and the husband was prohibited to use any violence to his wife [other than what is reasonably necessary to the discipline and correction of the wife]. . . .

These are the chief legal effects of marriage during the coverture; upon which we may observe, that even the disabilities, which the wife lies under, are for the most part intended for her protection and benefit. So great a favorite is the female sex of the laws of England.

2. Marital Property Regimes

a. Introduction

The state, through its treatment of marital property, regulates certain rights of the spouses upon marriage. According to historian Sir William Holdsworth:

> No legal system which deals merely with human rules of conduct desires to pry too closely into the relationship of husband and wife. Dealings between husband and wife are for the most part privileged. But some rules it must have to regulate the proprietary relationships of the parties. . . . [4]

Two marital property regimes exist in the United States: (1) the common law approach and (2) the community property approach. Each reflects a different philosophy. In the common law system, followed by most jurisdictions, the husband and wife own all property separately. During marriage, property belongs to the spouse who acquired it (traditionally, the wage-earning husband) unless he chooses another form of ownership.

On the other hand, in the community property system, the husband and wife own some property jointly. "Equality is the cardinal precept of the community property system."[5] The community property system is characterized by the

[4]. 3 W. S. Holdsworth, A History of English Law 404 (2d ed. 1909). See also 2 Frederick Pollock & Frederic William Maitland, The History of English Law Before the Time of Edward I 406 (S. F. C. Milsom ed., 1968) (1898).

[5]. William Q. deFuniak & Michael J. Vaughn, Principles of Community Property §1 (2d ed. 1971).

concept of a community of ownership under which the spouses are partners. Each spouse has a present, undivided, one-half interest in all property acquired by the efforts of either spouse during marriage. Unlike the common law system, community property recognizes the contributions, for example, of the homemaker spouse. Moreover, the community property system respects each spouse's separate property. Property that each brought to the marriage remains the property of that spouse. Property acquired by a spouse during the marriage by means of gift or inheritance also constitutes separate property.[6] The community property system is in effect in nine states.[7]

In the Middle Ages the division between the two marital property systems was not clear-cut. Thirteenth-century England adopted a separate property system; France took another path more beneficial to married women.[8] This divergence is all the more remarkable given the countries' many similarities: agrarian, feudal societies, whose clerical and lay elite shared a common language and culture.[9]

b. Common Law Disabilities

The common law and community property systems reflect fundamental differences concerning the position of married women. Until the mid-nineteenth century, Blackstone's famous quotation on coverture, supra, described the status of married women at common law. The common law imposed on a married woman many disabilities, summarized as follows.[10]

(1) *Wife's real property*. The husband acquired an estate in the wife's real property for the duration of the marriage. In the process, the wife lost all power over her real property during the marriage. The husband's interest, termed *jure uxoris*, entitled him to sole possession and control of any real property that the wife owned in fee — whether acquired by her before or after the marriage. If a child was born of the marriage, the husband's rights became a life estate.

Further, the husband could alienate the wife's real property without her consent. She had no similar power. The means of conveyance of real property was the "fine," by which both husband and wife joined in a fictitious lawsuit. A judge secured testimony (in private) of a wife to substantiate the absence of a husband's coercion in her execution of the deed.[11]

[6]. Note, however, that some states' equitable distribution schemes take separate property into account in awarding the marital property. See Chapter VI, section B.

[7]. Five American states (Arizona, California, Louisiana, New Mexico, and Texas) adopted the community property system because of Spanish, Mexican, or French heritage. The four remaining states (Idaho, Nevada, Washington, and Wisconsin) had different reasons. Wisconsin, the latest convert, was influenced by the divorce reform movement and the Uniform Marital Property Act (UMPA), 9A U.L.A. (pt. 1) 97 (1983).

[8]. Pollock & Maitland, supra note [4], at 405, 407; Charles Donahue, Jr., What Causes Fundamental Legal Ideas? Marital Property in England and France in the Thirteenth Century, 78 Mich. L. Rev. 59, 61 (1979).

[9]. Donahue, supra note [8], at 61. Scholars debate the reasons England chose a different property system than France. See Holdsworth, supra note [4], at 408; Pollock & Maitland, supra note [4], at 402 (pointing to the royal courts' surrender of jurisdiction over succession to personal property to the ecclesiastical courts, and upper-class influences). But cf. Donahue, supra note [8], at 83-87 (arguing instead that the family and community were stronger in France than in England, whereas the English monarchy was more powerful than the French).

[10]. Pollock & Maitland, supra note [4], at 403-405.

[11]. Mary Lynn Salmon, Women and the Law of Property in Early America 17 (1986). See also Pollock & Maitland, supra note [4], at 404.

(2) *Dower.* During marriage the wife's primary protection from her husband's conveyances consisted of her right of dower — her life estate of one-third of any land of which the husband was seised in fee at any time during the marriage.[12] The husband could not bar her dower right without her consent. She came into enjoyment of her life estate upon surviving her husband.

(3) *Wife's personal property.* The wife, similarly, had no right to possess personal property. Whatever personal property she owned before marriage, or might acquire thereafter, became her husband's. She also lacked a right of testamentary disposition over any property.[13]

(4) *Wife's lack of rights to husband's personal property.* During the marriage, the husband had the power of disposition (inter vivos or by will) over his personal property. Similarly, all his personal property (including what we might think of as the wife's property) was subject to his creditors. The only exception was the wife's necessary clothes. The husband even could sell or give away his wife's jewels, trinkets, or ornaments (termed her "paraphernalia") during his lifetime.

(5) *Husband's liability.* The husband was liable for the wife's premarital debts, as well as for torts she committed before or during the marriage.

(6) *Wife's contracts.* During the marriage the wife could not enter into contracts except as her husband's agent.[14]

Some New England colonies treated married women even more harshly than England. A few colonies, for example, gave male heads of household considerably more control over family property.[15] This harsh treatment of married women was mitigated somewhat by equitable jurisdiction over women's separate estate. However, the majority of women could not take advantage of such equitable reforms.[16]

The legal status of married women changed little until the mid- to late nineteenth century when many states passed "married women's property acts." This legislation enabled women to own property that they brought to the marriage or acquired thereafter by gift or inheritance. The movement began in Mississippi in 1839 with a statute stipulating that the wife could continue to possess slaves she owned prior to marriage or thereafter acquired (although the husband continued to manage them and reap the profits of their labor).[17] New York legislation, the most progressive, enabled married women to sue and to retain their own earnings.[18] By 1865, 29 states had married women's property acts.[19]

[12]. Dower, not to be confused with dowry, is an inchoate property interest of a married woman that comes into beneficial enjoyment upon widowhood. Dowry refers to goods with which some women, historically, were endowed in anticipation of marriage.

[13]. As Holdsworth points out: "The logical consequence of the views of the common lawyers was the denial to married women of all testamentary capacity, for it is useless to say that a person may make a will if she has nothing to leave." Holdsworth, supra note [4], at 425-426.

[14]. Peggy Rabkin points out these disabilities evolved from a feudal society based on land tenure. Peggy A. Rabkin, The Origins of Law Reform: The Social Significance of the Nineteenth-Century Codification Movement and Its Contribution to the Passage of the Early Married Women's Property Acts, 24 Buff. L. Rev. 683, 689 (1975). See also Peggy A. Rabkin, Fathers to Daughters: The Legal Foundations of Female Emancipation (1980).

[15]. Salmon, supra note [11], at 6.

[16]. Id. at 81. A premarital trust placed funds in the control of a trustee who owed a fiduciary duty (enforceable by the chancery court) to the wife as beneficiary. Most women did not have sufficient property to take advantage of this loophole.

[17]. Norma Basch, In the Eyes of the Law: Women, Marriage and Property in Nineteenth-Century New York 27 (1982).

[18]. Id. at 28.

[19]. Id.

Historians point to several contributing factors to legislative reform:[20] (1) economic antebellum problems contributing to a desire to protect family property by exempting women's property from attachment by husbands' creditors; (2) the codification/law reform; and (3) a desire to improve women's status. Although historians disagree on the primacy of each factor, most concur that the legislation constituted a significant liberalization in the rules to which married women had been subject for centuries.[21]

c. Managerial Rules

The husband as master of the household was an entrenched common law principle. Paradoxically, the community property system also reflected this rule because statutes placed management of community property in the husband's hands.[22] Limited exceptions to male management and control did exist. For example, in many community property states, the wife retained management and control of her earnings. And the joinder requirement for the conveyance or encumbrance of community real property gave the wife some control.[23] The Supreme Court marked the end of such gender-based rules in Kirchberg v. Feenstra, 450 U.S. 455 (1981), which invalidated, on equal protection grounds, a Louisiana statute designating the husband "head and master" of the community.

Three different, facially gender-neutral rules emerged in response to the unconstitutionality of male managerial rules: (1) extension of the separate property philosophy to link management to the source of earnings; (2) joint control (requiring the consent of both spouses for community property transactions); and (3) equal control (either may manage community property regardless of the source of earnings or without securing the other's consent).[24] Most community property jurisdictions follow the last approach.

Reforms have narrowed the gap between the common law and community property systems. Although title theory determines ownership and management in common law states during an intact marriage, many common law states permit spouses who want a more egalitarian ideal to opt for a tenancy by the

[20]. See, e.g., Lawrence M. Friedman, A History of American Law 208-211 (2d ed. 1985); Joan Hoff Wilson, Hidden Riches: Legal Records and Women, 1750-1825, in Woman's Being, Woman's Place: Female Identity and Vocation in American History (Mary Kelley ed., 1979); Richard H. Chused, Married Women's Property Law: 1800-1850, 71 Geo. L.J. 1359 (1983); Rabkin, Origins of Law Reform, supra note [14].

[21]. Buf cf. Lawrence M. Friedman, Law Reform in Historical Perspective, 13 St. Louis U. L.J. 351, 362-363 (1969) (arguing that the legislation worked no significant liberalization because practice had already departed from the common law).

[22]. DeFuniak & Vaughn, supra note [5], at §113. The concept of management and control must be distinguished from ownership. Thus, one spouse may own property that is subject to another spouse's right to management and control of that property. Ownership rights in that property are not relinquished, however, by another spouse's management and control.

[23]. Id. at §115.1.

[24]. Susan Westerberg Prager, The Persistence of Separate Property Concepts in California's Community Property System, 1849-1975, 24 UCLA L. Rev. 1, 70-71 (1976). Despite its facial neutrality, the rule of equal management has been criticized for its gender-based application. See, e.g., Susan Kalinka, Taxation of Community Income, It Is Time for Congress to Override Poe v. Seaborn, 58 La. L. Rev. 73, 85 (1997) (pointing out that, in reality, "equal management statutes generally give management and control over community income to the spouse who earns it").

entireties.[25] In tenancies by the entireties, the spouses share the right of control (i.e., neither spouse can alienate or encumber property without the consent of the other). At divorce, most common law states follow an equitable distribution approach (discussed in Chapter VI). Equitable distribution, which attempts to divide marital property in a fair or equitable manner based on a number of factors, purports to achieve more equal treatment of women.

Another significant modern development, the Uniform Marital Property Act (UMPA) §5, 9A U.L.A. (pt. 1) 103 (1998), imposes a sharing rule from the beginning of the marriage. Under UMPA, absent an agreement, a spouse acting alone can manage and control marital property held in that spouse's name alone, that not held in the name of either spouse, and that held in the name of both spouses in the alternative. Spouses must act together with respect to marital property otherwise held in name of both. The UMPA also allows spouses to enter into marital property agreements with each other regarding the management and control of property during marriage. Id. at §10(c)(2).

3. Duty of Support

■ MCGUIRE v. McGUIRE
59 N.W.2d 336 (Neb. 1953)

MESSMORE, Justice.

The plaintiff, Lydia McGuire, brought this action . . . against Charles W. McGuire, her husband . . . to recover suitable maintenance and support money. [A] decree was rendered in favor of the plaintiff.

The record shows that the plaintiff and defendant were married in Wayne, Nebraska, on August 11, 1919. At the time of the marriage the defendant was a bachelor 46 or 47 years of age and had a reputation for more than ordinary frugality, of which the plaintiff was aware. She had visited in his home and had known him for about 3 years prior to the marriage. [P]laintiff had been previously married. Her first husband . . . died intestate, leaving 80 acres of land in Dixon County. The plaintiff and each of [their two] daughters inherited a one-third interest therein. At the time of the marriage of the plaintiff and defendant the plaintiff's daughters were 9 and 11 years of age. By working and receiving financial assistance from the parties to this action, the daughters received a high school education in Pender. One daughter attended Wayne State Teachers College for 2 years and the other daughter attended a business college in Sioux City, Iowa, for 1 year. [Both] are married and have families of their own. . . .

At the time of trial plaintiff was 66 years of age and the defendant nearly 80 years of age. No children were born to these parties. . . .

The plaintiff testified that she was a dutiful and obedient wife, worked and saved, and cohabited with the defendant until the last 2 or 3 years. She worked

---

[25]. For a discussion of the egalitarian ideal of tenancies by the entireties, see Hanoch Dagan, The Craft of Property, 91 Calif. L. Rev. 1517, 1541-43 (2003) (pointing out that couples can choose the entireties form in 21 states); Carolyn J. Frantz & Hanoch Dagan, The Properties of Marriage, 104 Colum. L. Rev. 75, 124-126 (2005) (explaining property governance during marriage). See also United States v. Craft, 535 U.S. 274 (2002) (holding that husband, as tenant by the entirety under Michigan law, possessed a property interest to which a federal tax lien could attach).

in the fields, did outside chores, cooked, and attended to her household duties such as cleaning the house and doing the washing. For a number of years she raised as high as 300 chickens, sold poultry and eggs, and used the money to buy clothing, things she wanted, and for groceries. She further testified that the defendant was the boss of the house and his word was law; that he would not tolerate any charge accounts and would not inform her as to his finances or business; and that he was a poor companion. . . . On several occasions the plaintiff asked the defendant for money. He would give her very small amounts, and for the last 3 or 4 years he had not given her any money nor provided her with clothing, except a coat about 4 years previous. . . . The defendant had not taken her to a motion picture show during the past 12 years. They did not belong to any organizations or charitable institutions, nor did he give her money to make contributions to any charitable institutions. . . . For the past 4 years or more, the defendant had not given the plaintiff money to purchase furniture or other household necessities. Three years ago he did purchase an electric, wood-and-cob combination stove which was installed in the kitchen, also linoleum floor covering for the kitchen. [T]he house is not equipped with a bathroom, bathing facilities, or inside toilet [or kitchen sink]. Hard and soft water is obtained from a well and cistern. She has a mechanical Servel refrigerator, and the house is equipped with electricity. . . . She had requested a new furnace but the defendant believed the one they had to be satisfactory. She related that the furniture was old and she would like to replenish it, at least to be comparable with some of her neighbors; . . . that one of her daughters was good about furnishing her clothing, at least a dress a year, or sometimes two; that the defendant owns a 1929 Ford coupe equipped with a heater which is not efficient, and on the average of every 2 weeks he drives the plaintiff to Wayne to visit her mother; and that he also owns a 1927 Chevrolet pickup which is used for different purposes on the farm. The plaintiff was privileged to use all of the rent money she wanted to from the 80-acre farm, and when she goes to see her daughters, which is not frequent, she uses part of the rent money for that purpose, the defendant providing no funds for such use. . . . At the present time the plaintiff is not able to raise chickens and sell eggs. [P]laintiff has had three abdominal operations for which the defendant has paid. [P]laintiff further testified that . . . use of the telephone was restricted, indicating that defendant did not desire that she make long distance calls. . . .

It appears that the defendant owns 398 acres of land with 2 acres deeded to a church, the land being of the value of $83,960; that he has bank deposits in the sum of $12,786.81 and government bonds in the amount of $104,500; and that his income, including interest on the bonds and rental for his real estate, is $8,000 or $9,000 a year. . . .

[Defendant appeals, alleging that the decree is not supported by sufficient evidence, and is contrary to law.] The plaintiff relies upon the following cases. [In] Earle v. Earle, 27 Neb. 277, 43 N.W. 118 [(1889)], the plaintiff's petition alleged, in substance, the marriage of the parties, that one child was born of the marriage, and that the defendant sent his wife away from him, did not permit her to return, contributed to her support and maintenance separate and apart from him, and later refused and ceased to provide for her support and the support of his child. The wife instituted a suit in equity against her husband for maintenance and support without a prayer for divorce or from bed and board. The question presented was whether or not the wife should be compelled to resort to a proceeding for a divorce, which she did not desire to do, or from bed and board. On this question, in this state the statutes are substantially silent and at the present time there is no statute governing this matter. The court stated that it was a well-established rule of law that it is the duty of the husband to provide his family with support and means of living — the style of support, requisite lodging, food, clothing, etc., to be such as fit his means, position, and station in life — and for this purpose the wife has generally the right to use his credit for the purchase of necessaries. The court held that if a wife is abandoned by her husband, without means of support, a bill in equity will lie to compel the husband to support the wife without asking for a decree of divorce. . . .

In the case of Brewer v. Brewer, 79 Neb. 726, 113 N.W. 161 [(1907)], the plaintiff lived with her husband and his mother. The mother dominated the household. The plaintiff went to her mother. She stated she would live in the same house with her husband and his mother if she could have control of her part of the house. The defendant did not offer to accede to these conditions. The court held that a wife may bring a suit in equity to secure support and alimony without reference to whether the action is for divorce or not; that every wife is entitled to a home corresponding to the circumstances and condition of her husband over which she may be permitted to preside as mistress; and that she does not forfeit her right to maintenance by refusing to live under the control of the husband's mother. . . .

In the instant case the marital relation has continued for more than 33 years, and the wife has been supported in the same manner during this time without complaint on her part. The parties have not been separated or living apart from each other at any time. In the light of the cited cases it is clear, especially so in this jurisdiction, that to maintain an action such as the one at bar, the parties must be separated or living apart from each other.

The living standards of a family are a matter of concern to the household, and not for the courts to determine, even though the husband's attitude toward his wife, according to his wealth and circumstances, leaves little to be said in his behalf. As long as the home is maintained and the parties are living as husband and wife it may be said that the husband is legally supporting his wife and the purpose of the marriage relation is being carried out. Public policy requires such a holding. It appears that the plaintiff is not devoid of money in her own right. She has a fair-sized bank account and is entitled to use the rent from the 80 acres of land left by her first husband, if she so chooses. . . . Reversed and remanded with directions to dismiss.

Notes and Questions

1. *Doctrines of support and nonintervention.* McGuire illustrates two doctrines. First, *McGuire* reflects the common law duty of support. At common law, a husband had a duty to provide support to his wife; the wife had a correlative duty to render domestic services. Second, the common law *doctrine of nonintervention* specifies that the state rarely will adjudicate spousal responsibilities in an ongoing marriage. Thus, marital support obligations are enforceable only *after* separation or divorce. This principle of family privacy stems from judicial reluctance to disrupt marital harmony or to interfere with the husband's authority. Was there any marital harmony in the McGuire's marriage to disrupt? Should stereotypical rationale trump spousal welfare?

2. *Necessaries doctrine.* The common law *doctrine of necessaries* was the basis of the lower court opinion in Mrs. McGuire's favor. This doctrine imposed liability on a husband to a merchant who supplied necessary goods to a wife. "Necessaries" generally include food, clothing, shelter, and medical care. Many American jurisdictions codified the common law duty of support of dependents via so-called family expense statutes, which render both spouses liable for the support of family members. Such statutes are broader than the common law doctrine (that is, applying to "family expenses" rather than merely "necessaries").

3. *Third-party interests.* Why should the state permit a creditor, but not a spouse, a remedy for support? Professor Shultz argues that "the presence of third party interests, even though minimal compared to the spouses' duties to one another, has been viewed as sufficient to allow disruption of the domestic harmony that could not be disturbed for the sake of resolving the spouses' own problems." Marjorie Maguire Shultz, Contractual Ordering of Marriage: A New Model for State Policy, 70 Cal. L. Rev. 207, 238 (1982). Further, Shultz points out, the necessaries doctrine encourages dealings with a creditor behind the back of the other spouse. Does this approach promote marital harmony?

4. *Criticisms.* Feminist commentators have been especially critical of the doctrine of nonintervention. Professors Nadine Taub and Elizabeth Schneider note:

> The state's failure to regulate the domestic sphere is now often justified on the ground that the law should not interfere with emotional relationships involved in the family realm because it is too heavy-handed. Indeed, the recognition of a familial privacy right in the early twentieth century [Meyer v. Nebraska, 262 U.S. 390 (1923); Pierce v. Society of Sisters, 268 U.S. 510 (1925)] has given this rationale a constitutional dimension. . . .
>
> Isolating women in a sphere divorced from the legal order contributes directly to their inferior status by denying them the legal relief that they seek to improve their situations and by sanctioning conduct of the men who control their lives. . . . But beyond its direct, instrumental impact, the insulation of women's world from the legal order also conveys an important ideological message to the rest of society. Although this need not be the case in all societies, in our society the law's absence devalues women and their functions. . . .

Nadine Taub & Elizabeth M. Schneider, Women's Subordination and the Role of Law, in The Politics of Law: A Progressive Critique 328, 333 (David Kairys ed., 1998).

5. *Equal protection problems.* The gender-based common law necessaries doctrine poses equal protection problems. The issue has arisen, increasingly, when creditor-health care providers attempt to impose liability on a wife for services rendered prior to the husband's death. Courts adopt one of three approaches. First, some abolish the doctrine (thereby holding only the incurring spouse liable for the debt). E.g., Connor v. Southwest Fla. Regional Med. Ctr., 668 So. 2d 175 (Fla. 1995). In response to judicial abolition, some legislatures codified the common law doctrine to impose liability on both spouses. E.g., Va. Code Ann. §55-37 (Michie 1995).

Second, some jurisdictions make the rule gender-neutral (imposing liability equally on both spouses). E.g., St. Luke's Episcopal-Presbyterian Hosp. v. Underwood, 957 S.W.2d 496 (Mo. Ct. App. 1997). Third, other jurisdictions place primary liability on one spouse and secondary liability on the other (requiring the creditor to exhaust the financial resources of one spouse before looking to the other spouse), See, e.g., Cheshire Med. Ctr. v. Rachel R., 663 A.2d 1344 (N.H. 1995). Most jurisdictions that follow this approach impose primary liability on the spouse who incurred the debt. See, e.g., Jersey Shore Med. Ctr.-Fitkin Hosp. v. Estate of Baum, 417 A.2d 1003 (N.J. 1980). Which approach comports with our modern view of marriage? With economic reality? Which better protects women's interests? Is it possible to formulate a gender-neutral rule while, at the same time, to protect dependent or needy spouses?

6. *Definition of "necessary."* Mrs. McGuire's request for attorneys' fees was denied (as not authorized by statute). Should legal fees be considered a "necessary"? See, e.g., Missoula YWCA v. Bard, 983 P.2d 933 (Mont. 1999) (holding that whether an item is a "necessary" depends on case-by-case analysis but finding that a husband may be liable for wife's legal fees to obtain order of protection).

7. *Civil and criminal remedies for non-support.* What additional remedies might Mrs. McGuire have? Civil remedies include suits for separate maintenance based either on statute or equity jurisdiction if the couple is living apart. Criminal remedies also exist: in many states for nonsupport of a child and spouses. What purposes do criminal remedies serve? Would you advise Mrs. McGuire to pursue these?

8. *The good provider role.* One source of marital difficulty in *McGuire* was the husband's neglect of his role of "good provider." How did this gender-linked role develop, and what are its consequences? Consider the excerpt below.

Problem

Husband and Wife marry in 1977. During the course of their marriage, Wife pays for most household expenses, although Husband occasionally contributes to the utility and grocery bills. After 12 years of marriage, Wife informs Husband that she wants a divorce and asks him to leave. She informs him that she is going to, and does, remove him from her health insurance policy. Husband refuses to leave and makes no effort to secure his own coverage. Two years later, in March 1991, Wife files for divorce. On June 3, 1991, they sign an agreement whereby each takes responsibility for his or her own debts. Two days later, Husband is admitted to the hospital with a terminal condition. He submits an outdated insurance card from Wife's policy. Finding it unnecessary to pursue the divorce, Wife instructs her attorney to dismiss the proceedings. Husband dies, leaving a hospital debt of $150,000. The hospital files an action to recover payment from Wife. The jurisdiction has a spousal liability statute providing that both spouses shall be liable "for all debts contracted for necessaries for themselves, one another, or their family during the marriage." What result? Queen's Medical Ctr. v. Kagawa, 967 P.2d 686 (Haw. Ct. App. 1998).

■ JESSIE BERNARD, THE GOOD-PROVIDER ROLE: ITS RISE AND FALL
36 Am. Psychol. 2-10 (Jan. 1981)

. . . Webster's second edition defines the good provider as "one who provides, especially, colloq., one who provides food, clothing, etc. for his family; as, he is a good or an adequate provider." More simply, he could be defined as a man whose wife did not have to enter the labor force. The counterpart to the good provider was the housewife. However the term is defined, the role itself delineated relationships within a marriage and family in a way that added to the legal, religious and other advantages men had over women. . . .

The good provider as a specialized male role seems to have arisen in the transition from subsistence to market — especially money — economies that accelerated with the industrial revolution. The good-provider role for males emerged in this country roughly, say, from the 1830s, when de Tocqueville was observing it, to the late 1970s, when the 1980 census declared that a male was not automatically to be assumed to be head of household. This gives the role a life span of about a century and a half. Although relatively short-lived, while it lasted the role was a seemingly rock-like feature of the national landscape.

As a psychological and sociological phenomenon, the good-provider role had wide ramifications for all of our thinking about families. It marked a new kind of marriage. It did not have good effects on women: The role deprived them of many chips by placing them in a peculiarly vulnerable position. Because she was not reimbursed for her contribution to the family in either products or services, a wife was stripped to a considerable extent of her access to cash-mediated markets. By discouraging labor force participation, it deprived many women, especially affluent ones, of opportunities to achieve strength and competence. It deterred young women from acquiring productive skills. They dedicated themselves instead to winning a good provider who would "take care" of them. . . .

. . . The good-provider role, as it came to be shaped [was] restricted in what it was called upon to provide. Emotional expressivity was not included in that role. One of the things a parent might say about a man to persuade a daughter to marry him, or a daughter might say to explain to her parents why she wanted to, was not that he was a gentle, loving, or tender man but that he was a good provider. He might have many other qualities, good or bad, but if a man was a good provider, everything else was either gravy or the price one had to pay for a good provider. . . . Loving attention and emotional involvement in the family were not part of a woman's implicit bargain with the good provider. . . .

. . . To be a man one had to be not only a provider but a *good* provider. Success in the good-provider role came in time to define masculinity itself. The good provider had to achieve, to win, to succeed, to dominate. He was a bread*winner*. . . . The good provider became a player in the male competitive macho game. What one man provided for his family in the way of luxury and display had to be equaled or topped by what another could provide. . . . The psychic costs could be high. . . .

[I]n an increasing number of cases the wife has begun to share this role. [T]he role-sharing wife now feels justified in making demands on them. The good-provider role with all its prerogatives and perquisites has undergone profound changes. It will never be the same again. Its death knell was sounded when, as noted above, the 1980 census no longer automatically assumed that the male member of the household was its head.

Among the new demands being made on the good-provider role, two deserve special consideration, namely, (1) more intimacy, expressivity, and nurturance — specifications never included in it as it originally took shape — and (2) more sharing of household responsibilities and child care. . . .

Note: Constitutional Limits on Sex-Stereotyped Role Assignments

Marriage has been described as "the vehicle through which the apparatus of state can shape the gender order." Nancy F. Cott, Public Vows: A History of Marriage and the Nation 3 (2000). Constitutional law once reflected the common law's prescription of appropriate gender roles for husbands and wives. In the late nineteenth and early twentieth century, the Supreme Court upheld discrimination against women in employment based on the "separate spheres doctrine" (that is, women occupy the private sphere of home and family while men occupy the public arena of work and politics). Thus, for example, the Court upheld rules barring married women from the practice of law (Bradwell v. Illinois, 83 U.S. (16 Wall.) 130 (1873)) and laws giving working women special legislation to protect them in their childbearing capacity (Muller v. Oregon, 208 U.S. 412 (1908)).

The women's movement in the 1960s triggered major reform in constitutional doctrine. In 1971, the Supreme Court first held that sex discrimination violated the Fourteenth Amendment's Equal Protection Clause. In Reed v. Reed, 404 U.S. 71 (1971), the Court invalidated an Idaho law that gave preference to men over women as administrators of intestate estates. The Court reasoned that the statute, which was based on stereotypical gender roles, lacked a rational basis. *Reed* heralded the beginning of an era of equal protection challenges to sex-based legislation.

The Court announced the applicable level of constitutional scrutiny for gender-based distinctions in 1976. Craig v. Boren, 429 U.S. 190 (1976), challenged the constitutionality of an Oklahoma statute proscribing different ages for men and women to drink beer. The Court applied an intermediate standard of review, maintaining that the classification must serve *important* governmental objectives and must be *substantially* related to achievement of those objectives. This standard, although lower than the strict scrutiny applied to race discrimination ("necessary to a compelling state interest"), was higher than the rational basis test ("rationally related to a legitimate governmental objective") applied to most social legislation. The Supreme Court later elevated the standard of review slightly and now requires an "exceedingly persuasive justification" for gender classifications. United States v. Virginia, 518 U.S. 515 (1996)). See also Nguyen v. INS, 533 U.S. 53, 70 (2001). Note that some states go further, applying strict scrutiny to gender-based classifications (e.g., Sail'er Inn v. Kirby, 485 P.2d 529 (Cal. 1971)). See generally Lee Epstein et al., Constitutional Sex Discrimination, 1 Tenn. J.L. & Pol'y 11 (2004) (empirical analysis comparing standards of review applied to sex discrimination).

Over the years, the Court has wrestled with the meaning of "equal treatment" for men and women in many different contexts. Several cases invalidated gender-based distinctions between widows and widowers in terms of government benefits and, thereby, rejected the gender-based assumption that the husband was the breadwinner and the wife the dependent. See, e.g., Califano v. Goldfarb, 430 U.S. 199 (1977); Weinberger v. Wiesenfeld, 420 U.S. 636 (1975); Frontiero v. Richardson, 411 U.S. 677 (1973). Outside the constitutional context, the Supreme Court has embraced measures designed to dismantle traditional gender stereotypes. For example, reading the Family and Medical Leave Act (discussed infra p. 288) as an anti-discrimination measure, the Court has approved this legislative effort to combat "[s]tereotypes about women's domestic roles [and] parallel stereotypes presuming a lack of domestic responsibilities for men." Nevada Dept. of Human Resources v. Hibbs, 538 U.S. 721, 736 (2003). The Court has had far more difficulty applying equal protection when confronted with classifications that it interpreted to reflect "real" differences, however. See Michael M. v. Superior Court, 450 U.S. 464, 469 (1981) (stating that the Court has upheld gender classifications that "realistically reflect [ ] the fact that the sexes are not similarly situated in certain circumstances").

Our abstract standard of equality, based on the Aristotelian notion, guarantees that likes (that is, "those similarly situated") will be treated alike. But how does one treat women like men in the face of biological differences? And should men provide the norm? Difficulties arose particularly in the Court's treatment of pregnancy (discussed in this chapter). Further, the Court's preference for analyzing cases about reproduction under the Fourteenth Amendment's Due Process Clause ("privacy") left this strand of equal protection doctrine incomplete. See Sylvia A. Law, Rethinking Sex and the Constitution, 132 U. Pa. L. Rev. 955, 1007 (1984). In other cases, the Court treated socially imposed differences (for example, the male as aggressor) as biological differences to justify differential treatment. Thus, despite disclaimers, the Court relied on gender-based stereotypes to exclude women from combat (Rostker v. Goldberg, 453 U.S. 57 (1981)) and certain employment (for example, prison guards) (Dothard v. Rawlinson, 433 U.S. 321 (1977), and to uphold criminal laws applicable to only one sex (for example, statutory rape laws) (Michael M., supra.) See also Orr v. Orr, 440 U.S. 268 (1979), discussed in Chapter VI)). Scholars criticize the consequences of the Court's equality jurisprudence for women. See Feminist Legal Theory: Foundations 211-331 (D. Kelly Weisberg ed., 1993) (essays by Mary Becker, Patricia Cain, Ruth Colker, Christine Littleton, Catharine MacKinnon, Diana Majury, and Martha Minow).

The same-sex marriage debate has prompted renewed examination of the Supreme Court's jurisprudence on gender equality. Some judges have analyzed the exclusion of same-sex couples from marriage as discrimination based on stereotypical understandings of the different roles of men and women in marriage. See Baker v. State, 744 A.2d 864, 907 (Vt. 1999) (Johnson, J., concurring and dissenting). Indeed,

> the anti-stereotyping analysis that animates the Supreme Court's gender discrimination opinions would seem to pose significant challenges for laws that prohibit same-sex couples from marrying. If the Court's precedents stand for the principle that males and females alike must be free to assume various family roles, then by what rationale does a valid marriage require one man and one woman? The male-female requirement rests on stereotypes (whether such stereotypes are invoked to define marriage or to assume its purpose) that limit the role of wife to women and that of husband to men—and in doing so perpetuate the gender hierarchy that the Supreme Court's anti-stereotyping analysis has sought to undo. [M]ore generally, given the face of modern family law, what differentiates the role of a wife from that of a husband—beyond outmoded stereotypes? . . .

Susan Frelich Appleton, Missing in Action? Searching for Gender Talk in the Same-Sex Marriage Debate, 16 Stan. Law & Pol'y Rev. 97, 116 (2005).

Opponents of same-sex marriage increasingly claim that marriage requires "gender complementarity." According to this argument, "marriage should be understood as 'a unique community defined by sexual complementarity — the reality that men and women are "different from, yet designed for" one another.'" David B. Cruz, Disestablishing Sex and Gender, 90 Cal. L. Rev. 997, 1079-1080 (2002) (quoting David Orgon Coolidge, Same Sex Marriage, 38 S. Tex. L. Rev. 1, 29 (1997)). For example, a concurring opinion in a New Jersey case rejecting a constitutional challenge to the exclusion of same-sex couples, invoked authorities that emphasize "the fact of sexual difference" and "the enormous tide of heterosexual desire in human life" to conclude that "[m]arriage's vital purposes is not to mandate procreation but to control or ameliorate its consequences. . . ." Lewis v. Harris, 875 A.2d 259, 276 (N.J. Super. Ct. App. Div. 2005) (appeal pending).

A number of questions follow: Is gender complementarity just another version of the notion that procreation constitutes an essential element of marriage (an argument rejected in *Goodridge,* supra p. 160)? If so, does the argument rest on "real differences"? Or, is the claim that men must pair with women, who can then tame male promiscuity? Cf. William N. Eskridge, The Case for Same-Sex Marriage: From Sexual Liberty to Civilized Commitment 8-13 (1996). Would that rationale reflect an outmoded gender stereotype or a "real difference"? Alternatively, does the gender-complementarity argument, at bottom, focus on parenting — and a vision of male and female parental role models that children need to emulate to behave appropriately themselves as men and women? See Appleton, supra, at 129-132. To what extent are such norms based on stereotypes that the Court has condemned? Consider these questions as you read the materials in the next section.

4. Names in the Family

■ NEAL v. NEAL
941 S.W.2d 501 (Mo. 1997)

Covington, Judge.

Melissa J. Neal appeals the trial court's refusal to restore her maiden name. . . . Melissa J. Neal and Bruce L. Neal were married on September 10, 1994. They separated in February of 1995. Wife was pregnant. She filed a petition for dissolution of marriage in March, in which she requested, inter alia, orders relative to the minor child yet to be born and restoration of her maiden name. Husband answered, denying that the marriage was irretrievably broken and requesting nothing other than a dismissal of Wife's petition. On July 16, 1995, Wife gave birth to the parties' child, a son. On the birth certificate she denominated her maiden name, Gintz, as the child's surname. She did not include the name of Husband on the birth certificate. The parties were divorced by a decree of dissolution filed on September 14, 1995. [After making orders for custody, visitation and support], [t]he court also ordered correction of the Certificate of Live Birth to reflect that Husband is the natural father of the minor child and ordered the surname of the minor child changed to Neal. Wife appealed. . . .

The first issue is Wife's claim of trial court error in refusing to restore her maiden name, Gintz. Matter of Natale, 527 S.W.2d 402 (Mo. App. 1975), controls disposition of the issue. In *Natale,* the Missouri Court of Appeals, Eastern District, provided a thorough summary of the common law and statutory rights to change of name. In that case, Judith Natale, with her husband's consent, petitioned pursuant to section 527.270, RSMo 1969, and Rule 95.01 to have her maiden name restored. She desired to change her name for purposes of professional and personal identity and convenience to her husband and herself in carrying out their professional careers. The trial court denied the petition for change of name. The trial court's refusal was based upon the fact that the petitioner was lawfully married and residing with her legal spouse. Under such circumstances, the trial court reasoned, the granting of the petition could be detrimental to others in the future.

In reversing the judgment, the court of appeals provided historical background of the common law right to change of name, regardless of marital status. The court noted that the common law and statutory methods of changing names coexist for the reason that no constitutional or statutory mandate has invalidated the common law. The court of appeals found that, although it is within the trial court's discretion to find a change of name to be detrimental, the scope of discretion in the trial court to deny a petition for change of name is narrow, even within the marital relationship.

Following the teachings of *Natale,* the court of appeals in Miller v. Miller, 670 S.W.2d 591 (Mo. App. 1984), addressed precisely the issue presented here, a request pursuant to a dissolution proceeding that wife's maiden name be restored. Because there were two children born to Mr. and Mrs. Miller, the trial court refused to change Mrs. Miller's name. As the court of appeals stated in reversing the trial court, no law presumes that it is detrimental for a child to have a name that is different from the parent. Id. at 593. A general concern of possible detriment is insufficient to deny a petition for change of name in light of the obvious legislative intent that such a procedure be available, and by reason of the teachings of *Natale.*

In the present case, the trial court provided no reason for its declination to order restoration of Wife's maiden name. There is no substantial evidence to support the trial court's decision. . . . Under the teachings of *Natale* and *Miller,* the trial court erred in refusing to restore Wife's maiden name. . . .

Wife next contends the trial court erred in granting Husband's request to change the child's name to Neal, Husband's surname. Wife attacks the trial court's decision on abuse of discretion grounds; however, there is a threshold issue that must be decided, and that issue is dispositive. . . .

To hold that the trial court in a dissolution proceeding has authority to change the name of a minor child does not, however, confer upon the trial court authority to change a child's name in the absence of proper procedure. Proper procedure first requires that notice be given by the party seeking to have the child's name changed. Notice is required because in changing a child's name, the trial court's discretion is guided by a determination of what is in the best interests of the child. . . .

In the present case, there was no notice to Wife of Husband's intent to change the name of the minor child. . . . Because the trial court erred in granting Husband's request to change the child's name to Neal for the reasons stated above, it is unnecessary to reach the question of whether there was sufficient evidence in the record to prove that the name change was in the best interest of the child. . . . The judgment of the trial court is reversed and the case is remanded.

Does state regulation of naming children treat men and women differently?

■ HENNE v. WRIGHT
904 F.2d 1208 (8th Cir. 1990), cert. denied, 498 U.S. 1032 (1991)

BRIGHT, Senior Circuit Judge.

. . . Plaintiffs brought this action under 42 U.S.C. §1983 individually and as next friends to their daughters alleging that Neb. Rev. Stat. §71-640.01 (1986) unconstitutionally infringes their fundamental fourteenth amendment right to choose surnames for their daughters. . . .

On April 4, 1985, Debra Henne gave birth to Alicia Renee Henne at a hospital in Lincoln, Nebraska. Following Alicia's birth, Debra completed a birth certificate form at the request of a hospital employee. Debra listed Gary Brinton as the father and entered the name Alicia Renee Brinton in the space provided for the child's name. Brinton, also present at the hospital, completed and signed a paternity form.

At the time of the birth, Debra was still married to Robert Henne. Although Debra and Robert Henne had filed for a divorce prior to Alicia's birth, the decree dissolving the marriage did not become final until after the birth. As a result of her marital status, hospital personnel, acting on instructions from the Department of Health, informed Debra that she could not surname her daughter "Brinton." Debra then filled out a second birth certificate form, entering the child's name as Alicia Renee Henne and leaving blank the space provided for the father's name. Robert Henne has never claimed to be Alicia's father and, pursuant to the divorce decree, pays no child support for her.

[O]n February 4, 1988, Debra Henne went in person to the Bureau of Vital Statistics of the Nebraska Department of Health and requested that Alicia's surname be changed to Brinton and that Gary Brinton be listed on the birth certificate as the father. . . . She also presented a signed acknowledgement of paternity from Gary Brinton and a letter from him requesting that the birth certificate be changed. Personnel at the Bureau of Vital Statistics, acting indirectly at the direction of defendants [Dr. Gregg F. Wright, M.D., Director of the Nebraska Department of Health, and Stanley S. Cooper, Director of the Nebraska Bureau of Vital Statistics], denied Debra's request. . . .

On June 17, 1988, at St. Elizabeth's Hospital in Lincoln, Nebraska, Linda Spidell gave birth to a daughter, Quintessa Martha Spidell. Linda wished to give Quintessa the surname "McKenzie," the same surname as her other two children, who were born in California. Hospital personnel, acting upon instructions from the Department of Health, informed Linda that Quintessa could not be surnamed McKenzie and that if Linda did not complete the birth certificate form the hospital would enter Quintessa's last name as Spidell. Linda completed the form, entering "Spidell" as Quintessa's surname and leaving blank the space provided for the father's name.

Linda surnamed her other children McKenzie simply because she liked that name and not because of any familial connection. For that reason, and because she wishes all three children to share the same name, she wants Quintessa surnamed McKenzie. Linda was not married at the time of Quintessa's birth or at the time of this action and there has been no judicial determination of paternity. At trial, however, both Linda and Ray Duffer, who lives with Linda and her children, testified that Duffer is Quintessa's biological father. . . .

Defendants contend that the district court erred in holding Neb. Rev. Stat. §71-640.01[5] unconstitutional. The district court held that an extension of the fourteenth amendment right of privacy protects a parent's right to name his or her child and that the statute failed to survive even minimal scrutiny. We determine that the fourteenth amendment right of privacy does not protect the specific right at issue here and that the statute rationally furthers legitimate state interests.

This case presents the issue whether a parent has a fundamental right to give a child a surname at birth with which the child has no legally established parental connection. We frame the issue this way because each plaintiff wishes to enter on her daughter's birth certificate a surname proscribed by section 71-640.01. [W]hile section 71-640.01 requires that a child have some legally established parental connection to the surname entered on the birth certificate, it does not prevent either plaintiff from ever giving her daughter the desired surname.[7] The district court overlooked this important distinction. . . .

We now turn to the question whether the right at issue is fundamental. A long line of Supreme Court cases have established that "liberty" under the fourteenth amendment encompasses a right of personal privacy to make certain decisions free from intrusive governmental regulation absent compelling justification [citing Zablocki v. Redhail; Moore v. City of East Cleveland; Roe v. Wade; Loving v. Virginia]. Two of the earliest right to privacy cases, Meyer v. Nebraska, 262 U.S. 390 (1923), and Pierce v. Society of Sisters, 268 U.S. 510 (1925), established the existence of a fundamental right to make child rearing decisions free from unwarranted governmental intrusion. Meyer and Pierce do not, however, establish an absolute parental right to make decisions relating to children free from government regulation.

In determining whether a right not enumerated in the Constitution qualifies as fundamental, we ask whether the right is "deeply rooted in this Nation's history and tradition," Moore v. City of East Cleveland, 431 U.S. at 503. . . . While Meyer and Pierce extended constitutional protection to parental decisions relating to child rearing, the parental rights recognized in those cases centered primarily around

---

5. Section 71-640.01 states: . . . (1) If the mother was married at the time of either conception or birth of the child, or at any time between conception and birth, . . . the surname of the child shall be entered on the certificate as being (a) the same as that of the husband, unless paternity has been determined otherwise by a court of competent jurisdiction, (b) the surname of the mother, (c) the maiden surname of the mother, or (d) the hyphenated surname of both parents; (2) If the mother was not married at the time of either conception or birth of the child, or at any time between conception and birth, the name of the father shall not be entered on the certificate without the written consent of the mother and the person named as the father, in which case and upon the written request of both such parents the surname of the child shall be that of the father or the hyphenated surname of both parents; . . . (4) In all other cases, the surname of the child shall be the legal surname of the mother. . . .

7. Debra Henne could enter the surname Brinton on her daughter's birth certificate by obtaining a judicial determination of paternity on the part of Gary Brinton. Linda Spidell could enter the surname McKenzie on her daughter's birth certificate only by first changing her own surname to McKenzie. Nebraska law provides a procedure, however, whereby either child's name could later be changed. . . .

the training and education of children. . . . By contrast, the parental decision in this case relates to the choice of a child's surname. This subject possesses little, if any, inherent resemblance to the parental rights of training and education recognized by *Meyer* and *Pierce*. Thus, as the district court rightly recognized, constitutional protection for the right to choose a non-parental surname at birth must flow, if at all, from an extension of *Meyer* and *Pierce*. Furthermore, any logical extension of *Meyer* and *Pierce* has to be grounded in the tradition and history of this nation. Given this standard, we necessarily conclude that plaintiffs have presented no fundamental right.

The custom in this country has always been that a child born in lawful wedlock receives the surname of the father at birth, and that a child born out of wedlock receives the surname of the mother at birth. While some married parents now may wish to give their children the surname of the mother or a hyphenated surname consisting of both parents' surname, and some unmarried mothers may wish to give their children the surname of the father, we can find no American tradition to support the extension of the right of privacy to cover the right of a parent to give a child a surname with which that child has no legally recognized parental connection. Plaintiffs therefore have not asserted a right that is fundamental under the fourteenth amendment right of privacy and Neb. Rev. Stat. §71-640.01 need only rationally further legitimate state interests to withstand constitutional scrutiny. . . .

[T]he law rationally furthers at least three legitimate state interests: the state's interest in promoting the welfare of children, the state's interest in insuring that the names of its citizens are not appropriated for improper purposes and the state's interest in inexpensive and efficient record keeping. Specifically, a reasonable legislature could believe that in most cases a child's welfare is served by bearing a surname possessing a connection with at least one legally verifiable parent. Furthermore, the legislature could reasonably perceive that in the absence of a law such as section 71-640.01, the name of a non-parent could be improperly appropriated to achieve a deliberately misleading purpose, such as the creation of a false implication of paternity. Finally, the legislature could reasonably conclude that it is easier and cheaper to verify and index the birth records of a person who has a surname in common with at least one legally verifiable parent. . . . Although the Nebraska legislature could perhaps tailor the statute to more closely serve these purposes, we cannot say that section 71-640.01 bears no rational relationship to the state's legitimate interests. . . .

ARNOLD, Circuit Judge, concurring in part and dissenting in part.

. . . I respectfully dissent. The fundamental right of privacy, in my view, includes the right of parents to name their own children, and the State has shown no interest on the facts of these cases sufficiently compelling to override that right. . . .

Debra Henne wants to give her daughter the surname of the little girl's father. . . . Linda Spidell wants to name her daughter "McKenzie." . . . The government, in the person of the State of Nebraska, says no to both mothers. The most plausible reason it offers is administrative convenience. Records are easier to keep and use if every person has the surname of "at least one legally verifiable parent." This interest is legitimate, and the statute under challenge is rationally related to it. If the appropriate level of constitutional scrutiny were the rational-basis test, I would agree that the law is valid. But if a fundamental right is at stake, the State must show a compelling interest, which it has wholly failed to do. . . .

The real question is . . . how do you tell what [the right of privacy] includes? The limits of the right remain controversial, and no doubt they will continue to be tested by litigation. Precedent tells us at least this much, though: family matters, including decisions relating to child rearing and marriage, are on almost everyone's list of fundamental rights. The right to name one's child seems to me, if anything, more personal and intimate, less likely to affect people outside the family, than the right to send the child to a private school, or to have the child learn German. We know, moreover, from Roe v. Wade, 410 U.S. 113 (1973), that these women had a fundamental right to prevent their children from being born in the first place. It is a bizarre rule of law indeed that says they cannot name the children once they are born. If there was ever a case of the greater including the less, this ought to be it. . . .

Notes and Questions

1. *Name retention.* The feminist movement highlighted the impact of surname changes, upon marriage, on a woman's identity. At common law, adoption of the husband's surname was a custom rather than a legal requirement. In the 1970s and 1980s, litigation focused on married women's right to have their birth name (formerly "maiden name") entered on voting records, automobile registration, or drivers' licenses. See, e.g., Forbush v. Wallace, 341 F. Supp. 217 (D.C. Ala. 1971); State v. Taylor, 415 So. 2d 1043 (Ala. 1982); Davis v. Roos, 326 So. 2d 226 (Fla. Dist. Ct. App. 1976); Traugott v. Petit, 404 A.2d 77 (R.I. 1979); Dunn v. Palermo, 522 S.W.2d 679 (Tenn. 1975). Currently, all states recognize a woman's right to retain her birth name on marriage.

2. *Empirical data.* Since the 1970s, increasing numbers of women have chosen to retain their birth names: 2 percent in 1975 compared to 18.5 percent in 2001. See Claudia Goldin & Maria Shim, Making a Name: Women's Surnames at Marriage and Beyond, 18 J. Eco. Persp. 143, 150 (Spring 2004). According to that study, women who retain their own names are more likely to be highly educated and to have advanced degrees, such as law degrees or Ph.D.'s. Interestingly, women with MBA's, however, are more likely to take their husbands' names. Id. at 156. What are the advantages of changing surnames upon marriage? The disadvantages?

3. *Methods of name change.* Two methods of name change exist: the common law method of consistent, nonfraudulent use and a statutorily prescribed judicial procedure. Most women change their name upon marriage by the first method. Women who elect to change their names upon marriage must change their driver's license, vehicle title, voter registration, passport, bank records, credit cards, medical records, insurance forms, wills, contracts, and Social Security and Internal Revenue Service forms. Id. at 146. Given the difficulty of name change, would a requirement of name retention be less confusing, less onerous, and pose less risk of fraud to creditors?

4. *Post-divorce name resumption.* Statutes often provide for a married woman to resume her birth name upon divorce. See Michael Rosensaft, Comment, The Right of Men to Change Their Names Upon Marriage, 5 U. Pa. J. Const. L.

186, 192 (2002) (noting that 36 states give women this option). As *Neal* illustrates, early cases wrestled with whether the denial of the wife's request could rest on the possibility of detriment to children from having a different last name. Should courts take this factor into account? Cf. Cal. Fam. Code §2081 (2004) (restoration of surname shall not be denied "(a) on the basis that the wife has custody of a minor child who bears a different name, or (b) for any other reason other than fraud"). In *Neal,* the wife failed to secure her husband's consent to restore her surname. Is a wife required to do so? Should judges have discretion to grant or deny a name change? What other difficulties might Mrs. Neal face in attempting to resume her birth name? See Rosensaft, supra, at 193 (explaining that many statutes vest considerable discretion in judges to decide whether to grant a name change).

5. *Men's right to change their surnames upon marriage.* Men occasionally adopt their wives' surnames or, along with their wives, take hyphenated surnames. However, few states provide for a statutory right to men to change their name on marriage; fewer provide for post-divorce name resumption for men. Id. (explaining that five states provide for a statutory right to men to change their names on marriage). But cf. N.C. Gen. Stat. §50-12 (1996).

6. *Same-sex couples.* May members of same-sex couples adopt the same name or choose a hyphenated name? Should it matter if the members of the couple are married or merely domestic partners? Massachusetts, currently the only jurisdiction allowing same-sex marriage, provides by statute that "Each party to a marriage" may take any surname. Mass. Gen. Laws Ann. 47 §1D (West 1998 & Supp. 2005). However, the Massachusetts statute authorizing name resumption upon divorce applies only to women. Mass Gen. Laws Ann. 208 §23 (West 1998 & Supp. 2005). Increasingly, courts are granting name change requests by same-sex couples. See, e.g., In re Application for Change of Name by Bacharach, 780 A.2d 579 (N.J. App. Div. 2001); In re Application of Daniels, 773 N.Y.S.2d 220 (N.Y.C. Civ. Ct. 2003); In re Bicknell, 771 N.E.2d 846 (Ohio 2002); In re Miller, 824 A.2d 1207 (Pa. Super. Ct. 2003).

7. *Name changes: special contexts.*

a. *Transgender persons.* Currently, almost all states permit postoperative transsexuals to change their name and sex on their birth certificate. Generally, states require a court order for the name change; however, a letter from the surgeon who performed the sex-reassignment surgery is necessary to change sex on a birth certificate. Jody Lynee, Comment, Law as a Reflection of Her/His-Story: Current Institutional Perceptions of, and Possibilities for, Protecting Transsexuals' Interests in Legal Determinations of Sex, 5 U. Pa. J. Const. L. 128, 149-150 (2002). If the transsexual is married, should he or she need spousal consent for the name/gender change? See In re Guido, 771 N.Y.S.2d 789 (N.Y. City Civ. Ct. 2003) (holding that a man intending to undergo sex change set forth facts sufficient to warrant grant of application for name change, but since his spouse consented, consent was not at issue).

b. *Victims of domestic violence.* Victims of domestic violence sometimes change their names in an effort to hide from abusers. Some state laws facilitate this effort by providing that records of a name change may be sealed and any publication waived in cases of a threat to safety. See, e.g., N.M. Stat. §40-8-2(B) (1999 & Supp. 2005); N.Y. Civ. Rights Law §64-a (1992 & Supp. 2005); Wash. Rev. Code §4.24.130(5) (2005). Survivors may face more difficulty when seeking to have a child's name changed without notice to, or consultation with, the other parent. But cf. In re M.M., 771 N.Y.S.2d 315 (Sup. Ct. 2003) (finding that court could dispense with notice of name change to father, as well as statutory publication requirement, in light of father's history of domestic violence).

8. *Children's surnames.* Traditionally, children born in wedlock are given their father's name. In response to the women's movement, statutes give parents the right to choose the father's name, the mother's birth name, or a hyphenated name. Nonmarital children, historically, took the mother's name absent the father's consent or a judicial determination of paternity. Parental autonomy regarding naming has special significance in the African-American community, given the history of slavery. See generally Peggy Cooper Davis, Contested Images of Family Values: The Role of the State, 107 Harv. L. Rev. 1348 (1994).

Currently, in name disputes between parents, courts usually one of three standards: a custodial parent presumption, a presumption favoring the status quo, or the best interests of the child test. The best interests approach is followed by a majority of jurisdictions. One court suggests the following guidelines in the best interests determination; the child's preference, the effect of the name change on parent-child relationships, how long the child has had the surname, community respect associated with the name, social difficulties the child might encounter, and the presence of any parental misconduct or neglect. Huffman v. Fisher, 987 S.W.2d 269, 274 (Ark. 1999). Do you agree that these factors are important? What other factors might be relevant?

9. *Paternal bias.* To what extent does *Neal* and the law of surnames reflect Blackstone's regime with its connotation of men's property interests in their wives and children? Some commentators suggest that name-change standards and practices continue to reflect paternal bias. See, e.g., Merle H. Weiner, We Are Family: Valuing Associationalism in Disputes Over Children's Surnames, 75 N.C. L. Rev. 1635, 1753-60 (1997); Jessica R. Powers, Note: An Illegitimate Use of Legislative Power: Mississippi's Inappropriate Child Surname Law in Paternity Proceedings, 8 U.C. Davis J. Juv. L. & Pol'y 153 (criticizing a statute that sets a default practice of changing a nonmarital child's surname to the father's surname following establishment of paternity).

10. *Constitutional issues.* The *Henne* majority determines that the right to choose a child's surname is not "fundamental." Do you agree that this parental decision "possesses little, if any, inherent resemblance to the parental rights of training and education recognized by *Meyer* and *Pierce*"? Does a paternal preference in naming violate the Fourteenth Amendment and/or state equal rights amendments? Cf. Trociuk v. British Columbia (Attorney General), [2003] 1 S.C.R. (holding that the statute conferring upon a mother absolute discretion to refuse to acknowledge a biological father on birth certificate and to refuse to include his surname in child's surname constitutes gender discrimination under the Canadian Charter of Rights and Freedoms (similar to the U.S. Equal Protection Clause)).

11. *International perspectives.* Some countries have quite different customs and regulations about names. For example, Latin American and Spanish custom dictates use of a two-part surname that represents the lineage of both parents. In some countries, parents must secure governmental approval for their choice of a child's first and last names. Recently, France enacted a major reform (C. Civ. art. 311-21), abolishing the paternal preference in naming children and permitting parents to

choose the mother's surname, the father's surname, or a hyphenated name. However, in the event of parental disagreement, the father's choice of name still prevails. Elaine Sciolino, Blow to French Patriarchs: Babies May Get Her Name, N.Y. Times, Jan. 20, 2005, at A3. See also Lizette Alvarez, Jens and Vita, but Molli? Danes Favor Common Names, N.Y. Times, Oct. 8, 2004, at A4 (explaining that the Danish system requires submission of names to two governmental agencies to protect children from ridicule).

Problems

1. Lana and Cara currently are 13 and 16 years old respectively. When their parents divorced ten years ago, the court awarded custody to the mother and visitation to the father. The father has not participated in the girls' lives for the past six years because he chose to avoid conflicts with his ex-wife and not to jeopardize his tenuous bonds with his daughters. He pays child support and provides health insurance benefits. When the girls' mother remarries shortly after the divorce, she and the girls begin using her new husband's name, Kelley. To enable the older daughter to obtain a driver's license, the mother files a petition to change the children's names from that of their biological father (Stratton) to that of Kelley. Their biological father objects, arguing that his surname is the girls' last link to his family and that it should not be severed merely on the grounds of convenience. What result? In re Stratton ex rel. Kelley, 90 P.3d 566 (Okla. Civ. App. 2003).

2. Kevin Matthews and Tara Smith have a nonmarital child Timmy. At Timmy's birth, Tara gives him her married surname (Smith), even though she is separated from her husband, because it is her surname as well as that of her older child. After DNA tests confirm that Kevin is Timmy's father, Kevin files a petition to establish paternity and a request that Timmy carry his surname. Tara objects, contending that it would be confusing for her sons to be raised with different last names. She concedes that she will soon marry Josh Wilson and that she anticipates taking his name. Kevin has provided some child support and has exercised limited visitation rights, subject to Tara's consent. Kevin contends that he wants his son to carry his name, his surname would strengthen the bond between them, and his surname would be less confusing for Timmy because Timmy will know that Kevin is his father. Timmy is now three years old. What result? Matthews v. Smith, 97 S.W.3d 418 (Ark. Ct. App. 2003).

3. A married couple, Barbara and John Smith, who are each the fifth child in their respective families, decide to call their newborn daughter by the name of "5 + 5." They agree to call her "5" for short. When Barbara attempts to enter that name on the birth certificate, hospital personnel (acting on instructions from the Department of Health) inform Barbara that she cannot do so based on a state statute that limits the choice of a child's surname to that of the mother's birth name, father's surname, or a combination of the two. What arguments would you make on Barbara's and John's behalf? See In re Ritchie III, 206 Cal. Rptr. 239 (Ct. App. 1984) (request to change name to "III"); In re Change of Name of Ravitch, 754 A.2d 1287 (Pa. Super. Ct. 2000) (request to change name to the letter "R").

5. Employment

■ **BRADWELL v. ILLINOIS**
83 U.S. (16 Wall.) 130 (1873)

[Mrs. Myra Bradwell, a resident of Illinois, applied to the Illinois State Supreme Court for a license to practice law. Accompanying her petition was the requisite certificate attesting to her good character and qualifications. The Supreme Court of Illinois denied her application. The United States Supreme Court affirmed. Justice Bradley's concurring opinion below is a classic statement of separate spheres ideology.]

Mr. Justice BRADLEY [joined by Justices Swayne and Field], concurring: . . .

. . . The Supreme Court of Illinois denied the application on the ground that [the legislature] had simply provided that no person should be admitted to practice as attorney or counsellor without having previously obtained a license for that purpose from two justices of the Supreme Court, and that no person should receive a license without first obtaining a certificate from the court of some county of his good moral character. In other respects it was left to the discretion of the court to establish the rules by which admission to the profession should be determined. The court, however, regarded itself as bound by at least two limitations. One was that it should establish such terms of admission as would promote the proper administration of justice, and the other that it should not admit any persons, or class of persons, not intended by the legislature to be admitted, even though not expressly excluded by statute. In view of this latter limitation the court felt compelled to deny the application of females to be admitted as members of the bar. Being contrary to the rules of the common law and the usages of Westminster Hall from time immemorial, it could not be supposed that the legislature had intended to adopt any different rule.

The claim . . . under the fourteenth amendment of the Constitution, which declares that no State shall make or enforce any law which shall abridge the privileges and immunities of citizens of the United States . . . assumes that it is one of the privileges and immunities of women as citizens to engage in any and every profession, occupation, or employment in civil life.

It certainly cannot be affirmed, as an historical fact, that this has ever been established as one of the fundamental privileges and immunities of the sex. On the contrary, the civil law, as well as nature herself, has always recognized a wide difference in the respective spheres and destinies of man and woman. Man is, or should be, woman's protector and defender. The natural and proper timidity and delicacy which belongs to the female sex evidently unfits it for many of the occupations of civil life. The constitution of the family organization, which is founded in the divine ordinance, as well as in the nature of things, indicates the domestic sphere as that which properly belongs to the domain and functions of womanhood. The harmony, not to say identity, of interest and views which belong, or should belong, to the family institution is repugnant to the idea of a woman adopting a distinct and independent career from that of her husband. So firmly fixed was this sentiment in the founders of the common law that it became a maxim of that system of jurisprudence that a woman had no legal existence separate from her husband, who was regarded as her head and representative in the social state; and, notwithstanding some recent modifications of this civil status, many of the special rules of law flowing from and dependent upon this cardinal principle still exist in full force in most States. One of these is, that a married woman is incapable, without her husband's consent, of making contracts which shall be binding on her or him. This very incapacity was one circumstance which the Supreme Court of Illinois deemed important in rendering a married woman incompetent fully to perform the duties and trusts that belong to the office of an attorney and counsellor.

It is true that many women are unmarried and not affected by any of the duties, complications, and incapacities arising out of the married state, but these are exceptions to the general rule. The paramount destiny and mission of woman are to fulfill the noble and benign offices of wife and mother. This is the law of the Creator. And the rules of civil society must be adapted to the general constitution of things, and cannot be based upon exceptional cases. . . .

Notes and Questions

1. The Illinois Supreme Court denied Mrs. Bradwell's application to the bar, in part, based on married women's inability to contract. Why, then, could *unmarried* women not practice law?

2. The Supreme Court determined that *admission* to the bar was a matter reserved to the states and not one of the privileges and immunities belonging to citizens. Thus, the Court found inapplicable the privilege and immunities guarantees of both Article IV and the Fourteenth Amendment. In so doing, the Court failed to consider the applicability to women of the Equal Protection Clause. When the Fourteenth Amendment was ratified in 1868, it engrafted the word "male" in the Constitution for the first time, causing considerable concern to nineteenth-century feminists. The Equal Protection Clause was not applied to invalidate gender-based discrimination until Reed v. Reed, 404 U.S. 71 (1971).

3. What authority does Justice Bradley cite in his concurrence to support his recognition of women's separate spheres? What is the danger of relying on history when considering the expansion of constitutional rights? See Aviam Soifer, Complacency and Constitutional Law, 42 Ohio St. L.J. 383, 409 (1981) ("To settle for the constitutionalization of the status quo is to bequeath a petrified forest").

4. For a discussion of Bradwell's role in the founding of the legal newspaper "The Chicago Legal News," see Richard H. Chused, A Brief History of Gender Law Journals: The Heritage of Myra Bradwell's Chicago Legal News, 12 Colum. J. Gender & L. 421 (2003).

Early cases denying women admission to the bar rested on legal and social rationales directed at married women in particular, as the following article reveals.

■ D. KELLY WEISBERG, BARRED FROM THE BAR: WOMEN AND LEGAL EDUCATION IN THE UNITED STATES 1870-1890
28 J. Legal Educ. 485, 488-493 (1977)

One of the paramount concerns of any skilled profession is the regulation of access to the profession. As Chroust has pointed out, in colonial America any person desiring to be admitted to the legal profession had four major avenues of entry.

> He might, by his own efforts and through self-directed reading and study, acquire whatever scraps of legal information were available in books, statutes, or reports; he could work in the clerk's office of some court of record; he could serve as an apprentice or clerk in the law library of a reputable lawyer, preferably one with a law library; or he could enter one of the four Inns of Court in London and receive there the 'call to the bar.'[1]

Chroust's use of the masculine pronoun above is not entirely without significance. "Any" person in colonial America did have four avenues of legal education open to him, provided that that person was male. The first hundred years of American legal education were characterized by a glaring absence of woman lawyers. . . .

The struggle for women to gain entrance to the legal profession began in the late 1860's with Ada Kepley the first woman to graduate from the Union College of Law (now Northwestern) in 1870 and Arabella Mansfield the first woman to be admitted to the bar of any state (Iowa, 1869). However, the battle was by no means over; in reality it had just begun.

Scarcely two months after Arabella Mansfield was admitted to the Iowa bar, Myra Bradwell passed an examination for the Chicago bar, but the Illinois Supreme Court refused to grant her a license to practice law on the grounds of her sex. When the case was taken on a writ of error to the United States Supreme Court, she was once again unsuccessful. In other landmark cases, Lavinia Goodell was refused admission to the Wisconsin bar in 1875 [In re Goodell, 39 Wis. 232 (1875)], Lelia Josephine Robinson was refused admission to the bar of Massachusetts in 1881 [Ex parte Robinson, 131 Mass. 375 (1881)], and Belva Lockwood, although admitted to the District of Columbia bar and admitted to practice before the United States Supreme Court, was still refused admission to the Virginia bar in the 1890's because of her sex [In re Lockwood, 154 U.S. 116 (1893)].

Even after the turn of the century when women were admitted to the bar of almost every state, the battle continued for women's admission to law school. Columbia University first admitted women law students in 1929, Harvard University in 1950 (although women had first applied to Harvard in the 1870's),[8] the University of Notre Dame in 1969, and the last male bastion Washington and Lee University in 1972. . . .

[A] common rationale utilized to bar women from the legal profession was the argument that the impediments growing out of women's legal status at the common law prevented them from gaining access to the profession. [T]he most serious common law disability which would interfere with women practicing law, or so women's opponents maintained, concerned married women's inability to contract.

This legal rationale was based on the fact that married women at this time were disqualified from entering into contracts with third persons without their husband's consent. In both the *Bradwell* and *Lockwood* decisions, it was held that because of this disability at common law, married women could not be permitted to gain admission to the bar.

1. Chroust, The Rise of the Legal Profession in America 173 (1965).
8. When M. Fredrika Perry and Ellen Martin applied to the Harvard Law School in the 1870's, the reason given for denying their applications for admission was that "it was not considered practicable to admit young men and young women to the Law Library at the same time, and it was not considered fair to admit to the Law School without giving the privileges of the Library." Cited in Martin, Admission of Women to the Bar, 1 Chic. L.T. 83 (1886). . . .

However, in some decisions which admitted women to the bar, it was held that married women's inability to contract was not an insurmountable obstacle. In the *Kilgore* decision in Pennsylvania (admitting Mrs. Kilgore), Justice Thayer held that the essential basis of the relationship between lawyer and client was not in contract.

> But what difference does it make if she cannot be sued as upon a contract. There are other adequate remedies for neglect of duty, infidelity, or misbehavior in office, which are provided by law and to which she would undoubtedly be amenable. . . . These laws are an ample security for the client in dealing with an attorney, even if she be a married woman.[18]

[Another] social rationale utilized to bar women from the legal profession centered on woman's traditional role in the family. The professional role of the lawyer was seen to be in direct conflict with the traditional roles of woman as wife and mother. In both the *Bradwell* and *Goodell* decisions, the judges delivered a lengthy discourse on woman's "sphere." The proper sphere for woman, they maintained, citing by way of authority the law of nature and the law of the Creator, was in the home. . . .

Woman's traditional role conflicted with the professional role of lawyer in terms of the divergent sets of priorities of the role sets. The socially approved role for woman as wife and mother had duties associated with it which were expected to be woman's first and primary obligation, superseding any other claim. For the lawyer, obviously, his occupation was intended to be his first priority. Or, as Justice Ryan had asserted in *Goodell*: "The profession enters largely into the well being of society; and to be honorably filled and safely to society, exacts the devotion of life."[34] . . . The requisite personality attributes of the lawyer, moreover, were seen as incompatible with those necessary for the role of wife and mother. The lawyer was supposed to be aggressive — a skilled combatant in the juridical conflicts of the courtroom. Woman was seen as nurturant, gentle, tender. In short, she possessed personality attributes required for the fulfillment of the role of wife and mother. . . .

. . . For the single woman who was not engaged in fulfilling the role of "her destiny," the law was still not to be considered as a possible occupation. The court in *Goodell* had this to say:

> The cruel chances of life sometimes baffle both sexes, and may leave women free from the peculiar duties of their sex. These may need employment. . . . But it is public policy to provide for the sex, not for its superfluous members; and not to tempt women from the proper duties of their sex by opening to them duties peculiar to ours. There are many employments in life not unfit for female character. The profession of law is surely not one of these.[35]

The single woman, thus, was free to enter some other occupation to provide for herself. The legal profession, women's opponents stoutly maintained, should remain forever barred both to her and to her married sisters. . . .

---

18. [14 Wkly. Notes 466 (1883).] Cited in Women as Advocates, 18 Am. L. Rev. 479 (1884).
34. [In re Goodell, 39 Wis. at 244-245.]
35. Id.

Note: Married Woman's Domicile

Domicile is, essentially, a person's legal home. The law of the state of domicile is relevant to determination of marriage validity, the award of a divorce, custody, adoption, tax liability, probate and guardianship, as well as the right to vote, to hold and run for public office, to receive state benefits, or to qualify for tuition benefits at state colleges and universities.

Domicile requires two elements: presence plus intent to remain. A "domicile of choice" is acquired by persons who have legal capacity. A "domicile by operation of law" is assigned to those without legal capacity — traditionally, a category that included married women. At common law, the fiction of marital unity led to the assignment to a married woman of her husband's legal domicile. The Restatement of Conflict of Laws reflected this rule.[26]

The common law rule caused married women considerable hardship and inconvenience. The rule began to change in the 1970s. "The harshness of the common law rule . . . first became apparent in the field of divorce."[27] Constitutional challenges contributed to the rule's demise.[28] Finally, in 1988, the American Law Institute (ALI) revised the Restatement to confer upon married women the ability to acquire a domicile of choice.[29] Case law currently recognizes that neither spouse has a paramount right to select the marital domicile. See Szumanski v. Szumanska, 611 N.Y.S.2d 737 (Sup. Ct. 1994) (wife's refusal to join husband does not constitute abandonment for divorce purposes because a wife should have the same right as husband to choose a domicile).

■ VAUGHN v. LAWRENCEBURG POWER SYSTEM
293 F.3d 703 (6th Cir. 2001)

Boggs, Circuit Judge.

Plaintiffs Keith Vaughn and Jennifer Vaughn, former employees of defendant Lawrenceburg Power System (LPS), filed an action in Tennessee state court alleging that their terminations from LPS in February 1998 violated their rights under the United States Constitution, pursuant to 42 U.S.C. §1983, and under the Tennessee Human Rights Act (THRA), Tenn. Code Ann. §4-21-101 et seq. Specifically, the Vaughns objected to LPS's "anti-nepotism" policy, which requires the resignation of one spouse in the event two employees marry. . . .

Keith Vaughn began work for LPS in 1987, and has worked there in several capacities over a ten-year period. In 1997, he was responsible for maintaining LPS's grounds and buildings. Jennifer Vaughn, née Paige, began working at LPS while in high school, and after her graduation in 1996, started a full-time job as a cashier. During the spring and summer of 1997, Keith and Jennifer became romantically involved. In September 1997, they became engaged.

---

[26]. Restatement of Conflict of Laws §§26, 27, 30, 40 (1934). Only a wife living apart from her husband but *not* guilty of desertion could have a separate domicile. Id. at §38.

[27]. Restatement (Second) of Conflict of Laws §28 cmt. a (Tent. Draft No. 2, 1954).

[28]. See, e.g., Samuel v. University of Pittsburgh, 375 F. Supp. 1119 (W.D. Pa. 1974), *decision to decertify class vacated*, 538 F.2d 991 (3d Cir. 1976) (invalidating, on equal protection grounds, university residency rules that assigned the husband's domicile to the wife for determination of tuition).

[29]. Restatement (Second) of Conflict of Laws §21 (Supp. 1988) ("rules for the acquisition of a domicile of choice are the same for both married and unmarried persons").

Unfortunately for the Vaughns, their marriage was against power system policy. The "employment of relatives" or "anti-nepotism" portion of the LPS manual, which it is undisputed that both Vaughns received, reads as follows:

> It is the policy of the System to employ only one member of a family. No immediate relatives of employees, officers, members of the city governing body, by blood, marriage or adoption, shall be employed for permanent positions at the Lawrenceburg Power System. For purposes of this policy, said relatives are as follows: Spouse, parent, child, brother, sister, grandparent, grandchild, son-in-law, daughter-in-law, father-in-law, mother-in-law, brother-in-law, and sister-in-law.
>
> *When two employees working for the Lawrenceburg Power system are subsequently married, one must terminate employment.*

(Emphasis added.) The Vaughns ran afoul of the second part of this section forbidding marriages within the system, which may be termed LPS's rule of "exogamy."

It soon became common knowledge that the Vaughns were to be married. In late September, LPS Superintendent Ronald Cato met with Keith Vaughn, and pointed out the relevant language just quoted. Over the course of that autumn, Cato met with the Vaughns several times to inform them of the policy and to request that they decide which one of them was going to leave LPS. Cato told them he would need a decision before the marriage took place; he also told them that if they remained unmarried and merely lived together there would be no problem with the exogamy rule. The Vaughns were reluctant to pursue this option, in large part because Jennifer had become pregnant that fall with Keith's son, who was born the following July.

The Vaughns disagreed with the policy's applicability to their situation. Mr. Vaughn knew of three other groups of relatives working at LPS, two brother-in-law/sister-in-law dyads, and a father-in-law/son-in-law pair. Keith Vaughn interpreted the overall anti-nepotism policy as being contravened by the presence of these related co-workers. He states that he so informed Michael Meek, the Administrative Services Manager, who Vaughn claims told him that the other employees were "grandfathered in." . . . Despite urging from Cato, neither of the Vaughns indicated they would resign. Instead, they took their case to a meeting of the Power Board in mid-December 1998, where Keith argued he should be "treated like everybody else." The Power Board was not convinced by the Vaughns' interpretation, apparently distinguishing between the first part of the employment of relatives policy, which does not mandate termination, and the second part, the exogamy rule dealing specifically with employee intermarriage, which does. The Board also refused to change the rule or make an exception, as Cato informed the Vaughns in late December, when he again demanded a decision.

Jennifer and Keith's wedding day was January 16, 1998. Keith had met with Cato the previous day and said "okay" in response to Cato's request for a decision. But Keith did not then tell Cato whether he or Jennifer would leave LPS. When the couple arrived back from their honeymoon, they found a letter suspending both of them for minimum of two weeks, until February 9, 1998 (or until they reached a decision). . . . On February 6, 1998, Keith Vaughn met with Ron Cato and told him the couple planned to have Keith, who was paid more than Jennifer, continue working at LPS while Jennifer resigned. . . . The following Monday, February 9, Keith Vaughn, but not Jennifer Vaughn, arrived at LPS at 8 A.M. to begin work.

Cato called Vaughn [into his office]. Fifteen to thirty minutes later, when Vaughn left Cato's office, he had been fired. . . .

According to Vaughn, Cato asked him for a letter from Jennifer, which Vaughn did not have. Vaughn states that he asked Cato whether he needed the letter "for personal reasons or legal reasons." Cato responded: "I take it you don't fully agree with our policy." Vaughn claims that he responded, "No, sir. I don't fully agree with it, but I accept it because I've got to support — you know, I've got to work and support my family." After this speech, Cato then mentioned the Tennessee right-to-work law [giving the employer the right to terminate an employee for any reason], and fired Keith Vaughn.

Cato's contrasting version is that when told again on February 9 of the couple's decision, he said, "I really need to hear it from her." Vaughn offered to call his wife, but Cato states that he refused to accept this and said, "I'd really rather have a letter." Cato then claims to have asked Vaughn: "Would you consider yourself a disgruntled employee?" Cato states that Vaughn replied in the affirmative. Cato then agrees that he mentioned the right-to-work law. Vaughn supposedly asked if he was fired. Cato states that it was only then that he said: "[I]f you're going to be disgruntled and upset, you are." [A] letter, dated February 9, explained that the Vaughns had not "fully accepted" the policy, and terminated Keith Vaughn for "insubordination." For good measure, it terminated Jennifer for the same reason, Cato writing that because he did not "yet have a written resignation[,] I have no choice[.]"

In January 1999, shortly before their first anniversary, the Vaughns filed a lawsuit against LPS in the Circuit Court for Lawrence County. The complaint alleged violations of 42 U.S.C. §1983 based on "the fundamental right of marriage and freedom of association." . . .

We must first decide at what "level of scrutiny" to evaluate the challenged provision in the LPS manual. In order to trigger heightened constitutional scrutiny, the challenged portion of the anti-nepotism policy, the exogamy rule requiring termination of employment, must be shown to place "a 'direct and substantial' burden on the right of marriage." Our analysis of the case law . . . indicated that we would find direct and substantial burdens only where a large portion of those affected by the rule are absolutely or largely prevented from marrying, or where those affected by the rule are absolutely or largely prevented from marrying a large portion of the otherwise eligible population of spouses.

[T]he essential fact [is] that the policy did not bar Jennifer or Keith from getting married, nor did it prevent them marrying a large portion of population even in Lawrence County. It only made it economically burdensome to marry a small number of those eligible individuals, their fellow employees at LPS. Once Jennifer and Keith decided to marry one another, LPS's policy became onerous for them, but ex ante, it did not greatly restrict their freedom to marry or whom to marry. As a consequence, the exogamy rule in itself must be considered a non-oppressive burden on the right to marry, and so subject only to rational basis review by this court. . . .

. . . LPS asserts that its rule exists to (1) prevent one employee from assuming the role of "spokesperson" for both, (2) to avoid involving or angering a second employee when an employee is reprimanded, (3) and to avoid marital strife or fraternization in the workplace. [A] government employer may have a legitimate concern about the inherent loyalty that one spouse will show to another, making discipline more difficult. Therefore, we conclude LPS has demonstrated its exogamy rule advances a legitimate governmental interest.

The Vaughns claim that the rule, even if advancing a legitimate interest, is an unreasonable means of doing so. They point out that the rule does not affect those willing merely to cohabitate (which in their case would have also involved the bearing of an out-of-wedlock child); the Vaughns note that cohabitating couples may well show a similar degree of loyalty and create the same problems the rule seeks to avoid. . . . There is, no doubt, wide variation in the nature and intensity of the relationships one finds among both married and unmarried couples. Yet there is good reason to believe that the level of commitment signified by marriage — and its attendant legal, moral, and financial obligations — marks those relationships in which, on average, there is likely to be intense loyalty. Whatever the situation may be, de facto, married and unmarried couples are not the same de jure; the law treats them differently, and LPS may do so as well.

The Vaughns raise a better argument by noting again that the consequences to them are inherently more severe than those affecting the couple in [Montgomery v. Carr, 101 F. 3d 1117 (6th Cir. 1996) (finding that a school's antinepotism policy requiring a teacher to transfer if she married another teacher was not a substantial burden on the right to marry).] There, one of the married employees was transferred. Here, both the Vaughns were terminated, and the policy mandated this for, at least, one of them. . . . In response, LPS points out that they simply do not have the option of having a transfer policy, because LPS is an operation of only 50 to 70 employees. . . .

Keith Vaughn claimed to have been terminated in violation of not only his right of freedom of speech under the federal Constitution, but also the Tennessee Human Rights Act. His claim under the THRA is difficult to sustain. . . . An employee-at-will generally may not be discharged for attempting to exercise a statutory or constitutional right or for other reasons that violate a clear public policy evidenced by an unambiguous constitutional, statutory or regulatory provision. [T]he Tennessee Human Rights Act prevents "discrimination because of race, creed, color, religion, sex, age or national origin." Tenn. Code Ann. §4-21-101. The Act also "makes it a discriminatory practice to retaliate against a person because such person has opposed a practice declared discriminatory by" the Act. Tenn. Code Ann. §4-21-301. It is this latter "opposition" provision that has been asserted by the Vaughns. As the defendant points out, however, this provision is integrally connected to the types of discrimination the THRA has specifically forbidden. Tennessee has not included marital status in its list of forbidden employment classifications, and without an unambiguous provision, it is unlikely that a Tennessee court would abrogate its employment-at-will doctrine. . . . Keith Vaughn's claim under THRA was properly dismissed. . . .

Notes and Questions

1. *Historical background.* Derived from the Latin word for "nephew," the word "nepotism" was coined during the Middle Ages to describe Pope Calixtus III's appointment of his unqualified nephews as cardinals.[30] Nepotism often has played

---

[30]. Joan G. Wexler, Husbands and Wives: The Uneasy Case for Antinepotism Rules, 62 B.U. L. Rev. 75, 75 (1982). Some "nephews" may actually have been illegitimate sons. Id. at 75 n.3 (citing W. Durant, The Renaissance 382 (1953)).

a role in politics. President John Kennedy appointed his brother Robert as Attorney General. Congress subsequently enacted an antinepotism statute, 5 U.S.C. §3110 (2000), prohibiting public officials from appointing a relative to a position over which the official exercises jurisdiction. Nonetheless, President Clinton appointed his wife Hillary Rodham Clinton to chair (without pay) the President's Task Force on National Health Care Reform, and a distant cousin to provide travel arrangements for the White House Press Corps.[31]

2. *"No-spouse rules."* Some antinepotism policies limit employment specifically of "spouses"; others limit that of "close relatives." Some prohibit hiring, employment in the same department, or supervision of the other's work. Policies may affect spouses in a number of situations. Commonly, one spouse may seek work from an employer who currently employs the other. Or, employees of the same employer may marry subsequently. The increasing number of women in the work force enhances these possibilities. The problem is acute in small communities and in narrow specialties where the lack of alternatives may make one spouse unemployable. Do female employees disproportionately bear the burden of the no-spouse rule? If so, why?

3. *Business rationale.* Antinepotism policies attempt to ensure that unqualified relatives are not hired. Yet, paradoxically, they ban qualified relatives from being hired as well. The following arguments support antinepotism policies: spouses bring quarrels to work; spouses advance their own interests, leading to complaints of favoritism; employment of spouses promotes dual absenteeism because both partners want the same vacation or shifts; and, such policies prevent the possibility of sexual harassment and workplace violence. Opposing arguments include: the best candidate should not be passed over (or fired) simply because of being married to an employee; willingness to hire couples enables employers to hire a "star"; personnel benefits for employee-spouses are less costly; no-spouse restrictions violate public policy by encouraging cohabitation; and no-spouse policies discriminate against female employees. What do you think of these rationale — both in general and as applied to the plaintiffs in the principal case?

4. *Causes of action.* Both federal and state grounds exist to challenge antinepotism policies.

a. *Constitutional challenges — marriage is a fundamental right.* This cause of action is available only to public employees because constitutional limitations do not apply to private employers. To date, challenges on this ground, such as *Vaughn*, have not been successful. Why? When might a state employer's no-spouse rule "directly and substantially" interfere with the right to marry?

b. *Title VII.* Title VII of the Civil Rights Act of 1964, 42 U.S.C. §2000e-2(a)(1) (2000), a major weapon to combat gender discrimination in the workplace, has provided an important avenue of attack on antinepotism policies. Title VII prohibits discrimination based on race, color, religion, sex, or national origin (but not marital status). Sex discrimination under Title VII may be categorized as either disparate treatment (that is, express classifications) or disparate impact. Most antinepotism litigation under Title VII is based on disparate impact, challenging policies that do not facially distinguish between employees but, in practice, adversely

[31]. The press dubbed this latter appointment "Travelgate." Bill Turque, Judgment Calls, Newsweek, May 31, 1993, at 18-19. Newsweek published a political cartoon with a member of the press quizzically asking the "First Cousin": "You don't have anything without a layover in Arkansas?"

affect a particular class of employees. For example, note that in *Vaughn*, Jennifer planned to resign because Keith earned more money. Given that women earn less than men, no-spouse rules might result in the loss of a wife's job more often than her husband's. To establish disparate impact, however, a plaintiff must demonstrate statistically the adverse effect, which may prove unworkable in firms with small numbers of female employees affected. Even when a plaintiff is able to present the requisite statistical evidence, an employer in a disparate impact action may successfully defend by showing that the policy was justified (by example, by business necessity).

c. *State civil rights statutes*. In contrast to Title VII, some state civil rights statutes prohibit discrimination based on marital status. Why weren't the Vaughns successful under their civil rights statute? Cases often turn on interpretation of the term "marital status"; some courts interpret it broadly to include the identity of the spouse, while others construe it to refer only to the state of being married, single, divorced, or widowed. Cf. Maryland Comm'n on Human Relations v. Baltimore Gas & Elec. Co., 459 A.2d 205 (Md. 1983), with Boaden v. Department of Law Enforcement, 664 N.E.2d 61 (Ill. 1996). This distinction also comes into play in cases in which an employee claims marital status discrimination when terminated because of the employer's hostility toward the employee's spouse. See, e.g., Donato v. AT&T, 767 So. 2d 1146 (Fla. 2000).

5. *Empirical data*. How common is romance in the workplace? One survey found that 58 percent of employees (600 respondents) have had an office romance, of whom 14 percent dated a superior while 19 percent dated a subordinate. Mireya Navarro, Love the Job? What About Your Boss?, N.Y. Times, July 24, 2005, at 91. Only 9 percent of surveyed companies (493 respondents) have formal prohibitions about dating co-workers. Kelli Gavant, HR Gets OK with Romances in Offices, Chi. Daily Herald, Feb. 12, 2005, at 1.

6. *Policy*. Should governmental marriage-promotion initiatives target no-spouse rules? Does it make sense, as a matter of policy, to promote marriage and work as remedies for poverty while allowing employers, like LPS, to terminate employees who marry and to encourage cohabitation instead? Do no-dating policies in the workplace constitute employment discrimination? See New York v. Wal-Mart Stores, 621 N.Y.S.2d 158 (App Div. 1995); McCavitt v. Swiss Reinsurance Am. Corp., 237 F.3d 166 (N.Y. 2001). Should employers be able to impose their morality *outside* the office? Does it change your opinion to note that 21 percent of office romances lead to long-term relationships or marriage? Molly Parker, Cupid Working Overtime, State J.-Reg. (Springfield, Ill.), Apr. 2, 2006, at 41. Should antinepotism policies be limited to employees with supervisory authority? Or, are such policies out of sync with the realities of today's workforce?

7. *Effects of workplace romance*. Can workplace romances create a hostile work environment for *other* employees? In Miller v. Department of Corrections, 30 Cal. Rptr.3d 797, 802 (Cal. 2005), the California supreme court held that pervasive favoritism (accompanying a prison warden's affairs with subordinates) creates a prima facie case of sexual harassment by contributing to a hostile work environment for other employees because it conveys the "demeaning message" that female employees are viewed by management as "sexual playthings" or persons who must engage in sexual conduct "to get ahead in the workplace."

8. *School rules*. Should schools bar teacher-student fraternization? A congressionally-mandated report under the No-Child Left Behind Act, 20 U.S.C.

§§6301-7941 (Supp. 2004) (legislation increasing accountability for student performance by rewarding states and schools for improved achievement) estimates that 4.5 million students are victims of educator sexual misconduct, ranging from jokes to sexual intercourse.[32]

9. *Lawyer-spouses.* Marriage between lawyers poses special ethical problems. Does the possibility of breaches of confidentiality, conflicts of interest, and the appearance of impropriety require a per se rule barring lawyers-spouses from representing clients with adverse interests? If so, should the rule of disqualification extend to other lawyers in their firms? Should the bar extend to lawyers who are living together or dating one another? Formerly, the American Bar Association's Model Rules of Professional Conduct, Rule 1.8(I), provided for a rule of automatic disqualification of lawyer-spouses (as well as other relatives, such as parents, children or siblings), absent consent and disclosure. See also Restatement (Third) of the Law Governing Lawyers §123, cmt. g (2000) requiring informed consent prior to lawyer-spouses' representation of clients with adverse interests.

In 2000, when the ABA Commission on Evaluation of the Rules of Professional Conduct modified the Model Rules, they made several changes in the lawyer-spouse disqualification provision. First, they deleted the automatic spousal/relative disqualification provision from Model Rule 1.8. Second, they added commentary about this issue to revised Model Rule 1.7 ("Conflicts of Interest"), explaining that such representation will ordinarily be considered a conflict of interest; however, because it is characterized as "a *personal interest* conflict," the conflict will not ordinarily be imputed to other members of a firm under Rule 1.10 ("Imputation of Conflicts"), provided that it does not present a "significant risk of materially limiting the representation of the client by the remaining lawyers in the firm." (Rule 1.10(a)). See generally Margaret Colgate Love, ABA Ethics 2000 Commission: Final Report—Summary of Recommendations (June 9, 2001). See also Arizona State Bar Commission on the Rules of Professional Conduct, Op. 2001-10, October 2001 (concluding that the principles governing conflicts of interest for lawyer-spouses should apply also to cohabiting lawyers). On professional responsibility problems facing lawyer-spouses, see generally Thomas K. Byerley, "Til Conflict Do Us Part," 80 Mich. B.J. 68 (May 2001). On the problems of lawyer-judge marriages, see Mark M. Brandsdorfer, Lawyers Married to Judges: A Dilemma Facing State Judiciaries—A Case Study of the State of Texas, 6 Geo. J. Legal Ethics 635 (1993).

Problems

1. Jim and Coleen are state troopers in the same squad in a small Illinois town. Their district is patrolled by three one-person squads (each person patrols in a separate car). The squads rotate every eight hours. Jim and Coleen date and decide to marry. When they notify their supervisor, he informs them of an unwritten policy that prohibits spouses from working on the same shift in the patrol area. Jim and Coleen could remain in the same patrol area on different shifts, or one could transfer to a different patrol area and work the same shift. Jim chooses the latter. After their marriage, they challenge the no-spouse policy under state law, which prohibits employers from discriminating against an employee based on marital

[32]. District Administration, Protecting the Teacher's Pet, Apr. 1, 2005, at 438, 2005 WLNR 6056198 (last visited July 10, 2005).

status (defined as "the legal status of being married, single, separated, divorced, or widowed"). What result? See Boaden v. Department of Law Enforcement, 664 N.E.2d 61 (Ill. 1996).

2. New Jersey law bars judges from political activity. Judge Gaulkin's wife seeks election to the board of education. She asks the New Jersey Supreme Court to change the rule of disqualification that extends to a judge's spouse. The court agrees to reconsider this rule. In doing so, should it lift all restrictions on political activities by a judge's spouse? Or should it permit political activities by a judge's spouse but only with restrictions, such as prohibiting the use of all marital assets for the "political spouse's" campaign as well as the marital home for this spouse's political meetings and fundraisers? See In re Gaulkin, 351 A.2d 740 (N.J. 1976).

6. Parenting

a. Pregnancy Leave

■ CLEVELAND BOARD OF EDUCATION v. LaFLEUR
414 U.S. 632 (1974)

Mr. Justice STEWART delivered the opinion of the Court. . . .

Jo Carol LaFleur and Ann Elizabeth Nelson . . . are junior high school teachers employed by the Board of Education of Cleveland, Ohio. Pursuant to a rule first adopted in 1952, the school board requires every pregnant school teacher to take maternity leave without pay, beginning five months before the expected birth of her child. . . . The teacher on maternity leave is not promised re-employment after the birth of the child; she is merely given priority in reassignment to a position for which she is qualified. Failure to comply with the mandatory maternity leave provisions is ground for dismissal.

Neither Mrs. LaFleur nor Mrs. Nelson wished to take an unpaid maternity leave; each wanted to continue teaching until the end of the school year.[2] Because of the mandatory maternity leave rule, however, each was required to leave her job in March 1971. The two women then filed separate suits. . . .

[Another petitioner] Susan Cohen, was employed by the School Board of Chesterfield County, Virginia. That school board's maternity leave regulation requires that a pregnant teacher leave work at least four months prior to the expected birth of her child. Notice in writing must be given to the school board at least six months prior to the expected birth date. A teacher on maternity leave is declared re-eligible for employment when she submits written notice from a physician that she is physically fit for re-employment, and when she can give assurance that care of the child will cause only minimal interference with her job responsibilities. The teacher is guaranteed re-employment no later than the first day of the school year following the date upon which she is declared re-eligible.

---

2. Mrs. LaFleur's child was born on July 28, 1971; Mrs. Nelson's child was born during August of that year.

Mrs. Cohen informed the Chesterfield County School Board in November 1970, that she was pregnant and expected the birth of her child about April 28, 1971. She initially requested that she be permitted to continue teaching until April 1, 1971. The school board rejected the request, as it did Mrs. Cohen's subsequent suggestion that she be allowed to teach until January 21, 1971, the end of the first school semester. Instead, she was required to leave her teaching job on December 18, 1970. She subsequently filed this suit under 42 U.S.C. §1983. . . .

We granted certiorari in both cases, in order to resolve the conflict between the Courts of Appeals regarding the constitutionality of such mandatory maternity leave rules for public school teachers.[8]

This Court has long recognized that freedom of personal choice in matters of marriage and family life is one of the liberties protected by the Due Process Clause of the Fourteenth Amendment. As we noted in Eisenstadt v. Baird, 405 U.S. 438, 453, there is a right "to be free from unwarranted governmental intrusion into matters so fundamentally affecting a person as the decision whether to bear or beget a child."

By acting to penalize the pregnant teacher for deciding to bear a child, overly restrictive maternity leave regulations can constitute a heavy burden on the exercise of these protected freedoms. Because public school maternity leave rules directly affect "one of the basic civil rights of man," Skinner v. Oklahoma, [316 U.S. 535, 541 (1942)], the Due Process Clause of the Fourteenth Amendment requires that such rules must not needlessly, arbitrarily, or capriciously impinge upon this vital area of a teacher's constitutional liberty. The question before us in these cases is whether the interests advanced in support of the rules of the Cleveland and Chesterfield County School Boards can justify the particular procedures they have adopted.

The school boards in these cases have offered two essentially overlapping explanations for their mandatory maternity leave rules. First, they contend that the firm cutoff dates are necessary to maintain continuity of classroom instruction, since advance knowledge of when a pregnant teacher must leave facilitates the finding and hiring of a qualified substitute. Secondly, the school boards seek to justify their maternity rules by arguing that at least some teachers become physically incapable of adequately performing certain of their duties during the latter part of pregnancy. By keeping the pregnant teacher out of the classroom during these final months, the maternity leave rules are said to protect the health of the teacher and her unborn child, while at the same time assuring that students have a physically capable instructor in the classroom at all times.[9]

8. . . . The practical impact of our decision in the present cases may have been somewhat lessened by several recent developments. At the time that the teachers in these cases were placed on maternity leave, Title VII . . . did not apply to state agencies and educational institutions. On March 24, 1972, however, the Equal Employment Opportunity Act of 1972 amended Title VII to withdraw those exemptions. Shortly thereafter, the Equal Employment Opportunity Commission promulgated guidelines providing that a mandatory leave or termination policy for pregnant women presumptively violates Title VII. While the statutory amendments and the administrative regulations are, of course, inapplicable to the cases now before us, they will affect like suits in the future. . . .

9. The records in these cases suggest that the maternity leave regulations may have originally been inspired by other, less weighty, considerations. For example, Dr. Mark C. Schinnerer, who served as

It cannot be denied that continuity of instruction is a significant and legitimate educational goal. [W]hile the advance-notice provisions in the Cleveland and Chesterfield County rules are wholly rational and may well be necessary to serve the objective of continuity of instruction, the absolute requirements of termination at the end of the fourth or fifth month of pregnancy are not. Were continuity the only goal, cutoff dates much later during pregnancy would serve as well as or better than the challenged rules, providing that ample advance notice requirements were retained. Indeed, continuity would seem just as well attained if the teacher herself were allowed to choose the date upon which to commence her leave, at least so long as the decision were required to be made and notice given of it well in advance of the date selected.

In fact, since the fifth or sixth month of pregnancy will obviously begin at different times in the school year for different teachers, the present Cleveland and Chesterfield County rules may serve to hinder attainment of the very continuity objectives that they are purportedly designed to promote. For example, the beginning of the fifth month of pregnancy for both Mrs. LaFleur and Mrs. Nelson occurred during March of 1971. Both were thus required to leave work with only a few months left in the school year, even though both were fully willing to serve through the end of the term. Similarly, if continuity were the only goal, it seems ironic that the Chesterfield County rule forced Mrs. Cohen to leave work in mid-December 1970 rather than at the end of the semester in January, as she requested.

We thus conclude that the arbitrary cutoff dates embodied in the mandatory leave rules before us have no rational relationship to the valid state interest of preserving continuity of instruction. As long as the teachers are required to give substantial advance notice of their condition, the choice of firm dates later in pregnancy would serve the boards' objectives just as well, while imposing a far lesser burden on the women's exercise of constitutionally protected freedom.

The question remains as to whether the cutoff dates at the beginning of the fifth and sixth months can be justified on the other ground advanced by the school boards — the necessity of keeping physically unfit teachers out of the classroom. There can be no doubt that such an objective is perfectly legitimate, both on educational and safety grounds. . . .

The mandatory termination provisions of the Cleveland and Chesterfield County rules surely operate to insulate the classroom from the presence of potentially incapacitated pregnant teachers. But the question is whether the rules sweep too broadly. That question must be answered in the affirmative, for the provisions amount to a conclusive presumption that every pregnant teacher who reaches the fifth or sixth month of pregnancy is physically incapable of continuing. There is no individualized determination by the teacher's doctor — or the school board's — as to any particular teacher's ability to continue at her job. [T]he Due Process Clause requires a more individualized determination.

Superintendent of Schools in Cleveland at the time the leave rule was adopted, testified in the District Court that the rule had been adopted in part to save pregnant teachers from embarrassment at the hands of giggling schoolchildren; the cutoff date at the end of the fourth month was chosen because this was when the teacher "began to show." Similarly, at least several members of the Chesterfield County School Board thought a mandatory leave rule was justified in order to insulate schoolchildren from the sight of conspicuously pregnant women. . . .

The school boards have not contended in this Court that these considerations can serve as a legitimate basis for a rule requiring pregnant women to leave work; we thus note the comments only to illustrate the possible role of outmoded taboos in the adoption of the rules.

. . . While the medical experts in these cases differed on many points, they unanimously agreed on one — the ability of any particular pregnant woman to continue at work past any fixed time in her pregnancy is very much an individual matter. Even assuming, arguendo, that there are some women who would be physically unable to work past the particular cut-off dates embodied in the challenged rules, it is evident that there are large numbers of teachers who are fully capable of continuing work for longer than the Cleveland and Chesterfield County regulations will allow. Thus, the conclusive presumption embodied in these rules . . . is neither "necessarily (nor) universally true," and is violative of the Due Process Clause.

The school boards have argued that the mandatory termination dates serve the interest of administrative convenience, since there are many instances of teacher pregnancy, and the rules obviate the necessity for case-by-case determinations. Certainly, the boards have an interest in devising prompt and efficient procedures to achieve their legitimate objectives in this area. . . . While it might be easier for the school boards to conclusively presume that all pregnant women are unfit to teach past the fourth or fifth month or even the first month, of pregnancy, administrative convenience alone is insufficient to make valid what otherwise is a violation of due process of law.[13] The Fourteenth Amendment requires the school boards to employ alternative administrative means, which do not so broadly infringe upon basic constitutional liberty, in support of their legitimate goals. . . .

In addition to the mandatory termination provisions, both the Cleveland and Chesterfield County rules contain limitations upon a teacher's eligibility to return to work after giving birth. Again, the school boards offer two justifications for the return rules — continuity of instruction and the desire to be certain that the teacher is physically competent when she returns to work. As is the case with the leave provisions, the question is not whether the school board's goals are legitimate, but rather whether the particular means chosen to achieve those objectives unduly infringe upon the teacher's constitutional liberty. . . .

The respondents . . . do not seriously challenge either the medical requirements of the Cleveland rule or the policy of limiting eligibility to return to the next semester following birth. The provisions concerning a medical certificate or supplemental physical examination are narrowly drawn methods of protecting the school board's interest in teacher fitness; these requirements allow an individualized decision as to the teacher's condition, and thus avoid the pitfalls of the presumptions inherent in the leave rules. Similarly, the provision limiting eligibility to return to the semester following delivery is a precisely drawn means of serving the school board's interest in avoiding unnecessary changes in classroom personnel during any one school term.

The Cleveland rule, however, does not simply contain these reasonable medical and next-semester eligibility provisions. In addition, the school board requires the

---

13. This is not to say that the only means for providing appropriate protection for the rights of pregnant teachers is an individualized determination in each case and in every circumstance. We are not dealing in these cases with maternity leave regulations requiring a termination of employment at some firm date during the last few weeks of pregnancy. We therefore have no occasion to decide whether such regulations might be justified by considerations not presented in these records — for example, widespread medical consensus about the "disabling" effect of pregnancy on a teacher's job performance during these latter days, or evidence showing that such firm cutoffs were the only reasonable method of avoiding the possibility of labor beginning while some teacher was in the classroom, or proof that adequate substitutes could not be procured without at least some minimal lead time and certainty as to the dates upon which their employment was to begin.

mother to wait until her child reaches the age of three months before the return rules begin to operate. The school board has offered no reasonable justification for this supplemental limitation, and we can perceive none. To the extent that the three-month provision reflects the school board's thinking that no mother is fit to return until that point in time, it suffers from the same constitutional deficiencies that plague the irrebuttable presumption in the termination rules. The presumption, moreover, is patently unnecessary, since the requirement of a physician's certificate or a medical examination fully protects the school's interests in this regard. And finally, the three-month provision simply has nothing to do with continuity of instruction, since the precise point at which the child will reach the relevant age will obviously occur at a different point throughout the school year for each teacher.

Thus, we conclude that the Cleveland return rule, insofar as it embodies the three-month age provision, is wholly arbitrary and irrational, and hence violates the Due Process Clause of the Fourteenth Amendment. The age limitation serves no legitimate state interest, and unnecessarily penalizes the female teacher for asserting her right to bear children.

We perceive no such constitutional infirmities in the Chesterfield County rule. In that school system, the teacher becomes eligible for re-employment upon sub-mission of a medical certificate from her physician; return to work is guaranteed no later than the beginning of the next school year following the eligibility determina-tion. The medical certificate is both a reasonable and narrow method of protecting the school board's interest in teacher fitness, while the possible deferring of return until the next school year serves the goal of preserving continuity of instruction. . . .

■ JO CAROL LAFLEUR, "GO HOME AND HAVE YOUR BABY"
in The Courage of Their Convictions 320-328
(Peter Irons ed., 1988)

I learned around January of 1971 that I was pregnant, with the child due to be born around the end of July. Teaching out the school year made perfect sense to me. . . . I thought I was actually contributing, partly by being a good role model [being] a married woman, having a baby, going to a doctor, getting good care. . . . Little did I know that you could not teach in the Cleveland schools past the fourth month of pregnancy.

[The principal, Mr. Wilkins, called Ms. LaFleur to his office about the first of March.] Mr. Wilkins said, I understand you're having a baby in August. . . . You've got to go on maternity leave; you've got to fill out your papers. I said, I don't have to do that, because I'm not leaving. I'm just going to teach until the end of the year. He said, You can't do that; we have rules. I said, My baby isn't scheduled to be born until the summer. I just want to teach school. This class that you just put me in has already lost one teacher. And I teach students who are pregnant. . . . He said, You're a good teacher. I'm not going to fire you, but you've got to take this leave. Mr. Wilkins filled out the maternity leave papers for me, because I wouldn't fill them out. . . . I couldn't believe that anybody would yank from an inner-city school a person who was specially trained to teach there and who *wanted* to teach. . . .

I really thought initially that I could talk Mr. Wilkins out of it, but he would not be moved. [She then asked the teachers' union for help.] The union leader, who was a man said, Oh, Mrs. LaFleur, just go home and have your baby. I said, No! I want to have my baby, but I don't knit, I don't crochet, I don't want to sit home, I just want to teach. It was clear the union had no interest or sympathy whatever. [Later, she called the Women's Equity Action League, who referred her to a constitutional law professor, Jane Picker.] The first time we ever met, Jane said, This child will probably be old enough to read the decision before we ever get a final verdict in this case. No matter the outcome, it's going to end up at the U.S. Supreme Court. . . .

Mr. Wilkins had given me a deadline to leave—near the end of March. . . . Jane tried to get an injunction in the federal court against the schools, to prevent them from barring me from my class. This district court judge, whose name was Connell—elderly, in his seventies—said at the injunction hearing, Mrs. LaFleur will get exactly what she deserves, and she doesn't deserve an injunction. Since we knew he was the trial judge, Jane said, This doesn't bode well. . . .

. . . The school board put on a doctor, a male obstetrician, whose testimony I found really annoying. He was talking about all of the horrible complications that were possible with pregnancy, like placenta previa. There was absolutely *no* data that showed that the act of teaching made it more likely that you would have one of these conditions. In fact, if I were not teaching, I would be home by myself. And if I had a placenta previa and my placenta tore loose, I would much rather be in a school with people who can help me than be in my own home and all of a sudden start hemorrhaging and maybe pass out before I got to a telephone. So if they're worried about your health, putting you in a place of isolation—I remember thinking that their logic didn't make a lot of sense.

It was almost hilarious, in a very pathetic sense, listening to testimony about all of the possible complications of pregnancy. It's a wonder women *ever* have babies, if all of these horrible things happen. . . . The week before my son was born, I played nine holes of golf and I played a set of tennis. The only thing I didn't do was jump the net. . . .

After Judge Connell ruled against me, we filed an appeal with the Sixth Circuit Court of Appeals. . . . Jane had asked me to bring my son, Michael, down to the argument. She said, It can't hurt, if people see that this child is healthy and looks loved. When we got to the courthouse, Michael and I and my husband rode up in the elevator with this older gentleman. He was saying, He's a cute little guy, and I said, He's a sweetheart. When the court comes in, it was Justice Tom Clark of the Supreme Court! I'm going, Oh my gosh. It's a good thing I wasn't yelling at Michael or he wasn't having a tantrum. . . . We won in the court of appeals. . . . The Supreme Court was much iffier. [T]he Court had become much more conservative than in the Earl Warren years. . . .

I remember Justice Blackmun asking the question of Jane Picker, whether she really saw any difference between a man losing his job because he refuses to shave his beard, and a woman losing her job because she's pregnant. And she stood up there, and she put her hands on both hips and she said, Your Honor, that analogy is ludicrous. Simply *ludicrous*. What's the remedy for a man? You shave! For a woman it's abortion, to get rid of the problem. It's a little different, Your Honor. And I could see her husband at counsel table, with his head in his hands—Jane, you shouldn't *say* such things. But Blackmun voted for us. . . .

. . . I remember the day the decision came down. I was teaching a social studies class [with a guest speaker], and we were discussing death and dying. . . . I got called out of the class for a telephone call from a radio station that wanted my opinion on the decision. . . . I called Jane's office. They said, The only thing we know is that you won. . . .

I went running back to my class, doing these *jetes,* these giant leaps down the hall. I went into my class and I calmed down, and I said, Mr. Smith, could I have just one moment? I need to tell the class something. They knew I had been waiting every day. *We won!* Thank you, please resume. He doesn't know what's going on. The kids are screaming, *All right!* . . .

Looking back, I'm not quite sure why I started my case. . . . When I got pregnant, I knew I wasn't sick. I knew I wasn't ill. How could a male-dominated school system say to me, Even though you're not ill, and pregnancy is a perfectly normal condition, you are unfit to teach. The fundamental unfairness of it seemed morally wrong, not just stupid but wrong. . . .

Postscript. Jo Carol LaFleur (now Jo Carol Nesset-Sale) later attended the University of Utah Law School, practiced in the Utah Public Defender's Office, and became counsel for the Utah Bar Association. She is currently teaching at John Marshall Law School, in Atlanta, Georgia. For a recent autobiographical account, see Jo Carol Nesset-Sale, From Sideline to Frontline: The Making of a Civil Rights Plaintiff – A Retrospective By the Plaintiff in Cleveland Board of Education v. LaFleur, A Landmark Pregnancy Discrimination Case, 7 Georgetown J. Gender & Law 1 (2006).

Pregnancy Discrimination Act of 1978. The Pregnancy Discrimination Act of 1978 (PDA) amends, as follows, the definitional section of Title VII of the Civil Rights Act of 1964 that prohibits, inter alia, sex discrimination in employment:

> The terms "because of sex" or "on the basis of sex" include, but are not limited to, because of or on the basis of pregnancy, childbirth, or related medical conditions; and women affected by pregnancy, childbirth, or related medical conditions shall be treated the same for all employment-related purposes, including receipt of benefits under fringe benefit programs, as other persons not so affected but similar in their ability or inability to work. . . .

42 U.S.C. §2000e(k) (2000).

■ CALIFORNIA FEDERAL SAVINGS & LOAN ASSOCIATION v. GUERRA
479 U.S. 272 (1987)

Justice MARSHALL delivered the opinion of the Court.

The question presented is whether Title VII of the Civil Rights Act of 1964, as amended by the Pregnancy Discrimination Act of 1978, preempts a state statute that requires employers to provide leave and reinstatement to employees disabled by pregnancy.

California's Fair Employment and Housing Act (FEHA), Cal. Gov't. Code Ann. §12900 et seq. (West 1980 and Supp. 1986), is a comprehensive statute that prohibits discrimination in employment and housing. In September 1978, California amended the FEHA to proscribe certain forms of employment discrimination on the basis of pregnancy. Subdivision (b)(2) — the provision at issue here — is the only portion of the statute that applies to employers subject to Title VII. It requires these employers to provide female employees an unpaid pregnancy disability leave of up to four months. Respondent Fair Employment and Housing Commission, the state agency authorized to interpret the FEHA, has construed §12945(b)(2) to require California employers to reinstate an employee returning from such pregnancy leave to the job she previously held, unless it is no longer available due to business necessity. In the latter case, the employer must make a reasonable, good faith effort to place the employee in a substantially similar job. The statute does not compel employers to provide paid leave to pregnant employees. Accordingly, the only benefit pregnant workers actually derive from §12945(b)(2) is a qualified right to reinstatement.

Title VII of the Civil Rights Act of 1964, also prohibits various forms of employment discrimination, including discrimination on the basis of sex. However, in General Electric Co. v. Gilbert, 429 U.S. 125 (1976), this Court ruled that discrimination on the basis of pregnancy was not sex discrimination under Title VII. In response to the *Gilbert* decision, Congress passed the Pregnancy Discrimination Act of 1978 (PDA), 42 U.S.C. §2000e(k). The PDA specifies that sex discrimination includes discrimination on the basis of pregnancy.

Petitioner California Federal Savings and Loan Association (Cal. Fed.) is a federally chartered savings and loan association based in Los Angeles; it is an employer covered by both Title VII and §12945(b)(2). Cal. Fed. has a facially neutral leave policy that permits employees who have completed three months of service to take unpaid leaves of absence for a variety of reasons, including disability and pregnancy. Although it is Cal. Fed.'s policy to try to provide an employee taking unpaid leave with a similar position upon returning, Cal. Fed. expressly reserves the right to terminate an employee who has taken a leave of absence if a similar position is not available.

Lillian Garland was employed by Cal. Fed. as a receptionist for several years. In January 1982, she took a pregnancy disability leave. When she was able to return to work in April of that year, Garland notified Cal. Fed., but was informed that her job had been filled and that there were no receptionist or similar positions available. Garland filed a complaint with respondent Department of Fair Employment and Housing. . . . [Prior to the hearing before the Fair Housing and Employment Commission, Cal. Fed. brought this action.] They sought a declaration that §12945(b)(2) is inconsistent with and pre-empted by Title VII and an injunction against enforcement of the section. [The district court granted petitioners' motion for summary judgment; the Ninth Circuit Court of Appeals reversed.] We granted certiorari, and we now affirm.

. . . In order to decide whether the California statute requires or permits employers to violate Title VII, as amended by the PDA, or is inconsistent with the purposes of the statute, we must determine whether the PDA prohibits the States from requiring employers to provide reinstatement to pregnant workers, regardless of their policy for disabled workers generally.

Petitioners argue that the language of the federal statute itself unambiguously rejects California's "special treatment" approach to pregnancy discrimination, thus rendering any resort to the legislative history unnecessary. They contend that the second clause of the PDA forbids an employer to treat pregnant employees any differently than other disabled employees. Because "[t]he purpose of Congress is the ultimate touchstone" of the pre-emption inquiry, however, we must examine the PDA's language against the background of its legislative history and historical context. . . .

It is well established that the PDA was passed in reaction to this Court's decision in General Electric Co. v. Gilbert, 429 U.S. 125 (1976). . . . By adding pregnancy to the definition of sex discrimination prohibited by Title VII, the first clause of the PDA reflects Congress' disapproval of the reasoning in *Gilbert*. Rather than imposing a limitation on the remedial purpose of the PDA, we believe that the second clause was intended to overrule the holding in *Gilbert* and to illustrate how discrimination against pregnancy is to be remedied. Accordingly, subject to certain limitations, we agree with the Court of Appeals' conclusion that Congress intended the PDA to be "a floor beneath which pregnancy disability benefits may not drop — not a ceiling above which they may not rise."

The context in which Congress considered the issue of pregnancy discrimination supports this view of the PDA. Congress had before it extensive evidence of discrimination against pregnancy, particularly in disability and health insurance like those challenged. . . . The reports, debates, and hearings make abundantly clear that Congress intended the PDA to provide relief for working women and to end discrimination against pregnant workers. In contrast to the thorough account of discrimination against pregnant workers, the legislative history is devoid of any discussion of preferential treatment of pregnancy,[20] beyond acknowledgments of the existence of state statutes providing for such preferential treatment. Opposition to the PDA came from those concerned with the cost of including pregnancy in health and disability benefit plans and the application of the bill to abortion, not from those who favored special accommodation of pregnancy.

In support of their argument that the PDA prohibits employment practices that favor pregnant women, petitioners and several amici cite statements in the legislative history to the effect that the PDA does not *require* employers to extend any benefits to pregnant women that they do not already provide to other disabled employees. . . . On the contrary, if Congress had intended to *prohibit* preferential treatment, it would have been the height of understatement to say only that the legislation would not *require* such conduct. It is hardly conceivable that Congress would have extensively discussed only its intent not to require preferential treatment if in fact it had intended to prohibit such treatment.

We also find it significant that Congress was aware of state laws similar to California's but apparently did not consider them inconsistent with the PDA. . . . Title VII, as amended by the PDA, and California's pregnancy disability leave statute share a common goal. The purpose of Title VII is "to achieve equality of employment opportunities and remove barriers that have operated in the past to favor an identifiable group of . . . employees over other employees." Rather than

---

20. The statement of Senator Brooke, quoted in the dissent, merely indicates the Senator's view that the PDA does not itself require special disability benefits for pregnant workers. It in no way supports the conclusion that Congress intended to prohibit the States from providing such benefits for pregnant workers.

limiting existing Title VII principles and objectives, the PDA extends them to cover pregnancy. As Senator Williams, a sponsor of the Act, stated: "The entire thrust . . . behind this legislation is to guarantee women the basic right to participate fully and equally in the workforce, without denying them the fundamental right to full participation in family life." 123 Cong. Rec. 29658 (1977).

Section 12945(b)(2) also promotes equal employment opportunity. By requiring employers to reinstate women after a reasonable pregnancy disability leave, §12945(b)(2) ensures that they will not lose their jobs on account of pregnancy disability. . . . California's pregnancy disability leave statute allows women, as well as men, to have families without losing their jobs.

Thus, petitioners' facial challenge to §12945(b)(2) fails. The statute is not pre-empted by Title VII, as amended by the PDA, because it is not inconsistent with the purposes of the federal statute. . . .

Justice WHITE, with whom THE CHIEF JUSTICE and JUSTICE POWELL join, dissenting. . . .

The second clause [of the PDA] could not be clearer: it mandates that pregnant employees "shall be treated the same for all employment-related purposes" as nonpregnant employees similarly situated with respect to their ability or inability to work. This language leaves no room for preferential treatment of pregnant workers. . . . In sum, preferential treatment of pregnant workers is prohibited by Title VII, as amended by the PDA. Section 12945(b)(2) of the California Gov't. Code, which extends preferential benefits for pregnancy, is therefore pre-empted. . . .

■ **WENDY W. WILLIAMS, EQUALITY'S RIDDLE: PREGNANCY AND THE EQUAL TREATMENT/SPECIAL TREATMENT DEBATE**
13 N.Y.U. Rev. L. & Soc. Change 325, 333-349 (1984-1985)

The treatment of pregnancy and maternity under the law developed in stages. . . .

A. STAGE ONE: 1870 to 1970

[W]omen's "maternal functions" formed the basis of a dual system of law. The system treated women differently than men under the claim that it sought to accommodate to and provide for women's special needs. [Williams first describes the era of protective labor legislation during the late nineteenth and early twentieth centuries.]

[T]here were, beginning in the 1940's, a very few provisions dealing specifically with pregnancy. In the early 1940's, the Women's Bureau of the U.S. Department of Labor recommended that pregnant women not work for six weeks before and two months after delivery. Some states adopted laws prohibiting employers from employing women for a period of time before and after childbirth to protect the health of women and their offspring during that vulnerable time. Where leaves were not accompanied by a guarantee of job security or wage replacement, they "protected" pregnant women right out of their jobs, as the Women's Bureau conceded. At the same time, the unemployment insurance laws of many states rendered otherwise eligible women workers ineligible for unemployment insurance if they were pregnant or had recently given birth. Women unemployed because of state laws or employer policies of mandatory unpaid leave thus were precluded from the resources available to other unemployed workers. Four states, including California, created disability insurance programs to provide partial wage replacement to temporarily disabled workers, but those programs either excluded pregnancy-related disabilities altogether or provided restricted benefits. The absence of legislation concerning pregnancy and employment meant that the issue was left to employers (and, where there were unions, to collective bargaining).

By 1960, the dawn of a new decade that would usher in Title VII, many employers simply fired women who became pregnant. Others provided unpaid maternity leaves of absence, frequently accompanied by loss of seniority and accrued benefits. Few provided job security, much less allowed paid sick leave and vacation time to be used for maternity leave. Payment of disability benefits for childbirth was, at best, restricted, and employer sponsored medical insurance provided, at most, limited coverage of pregnancy-related medical treatment and hospitalization.

Pervasively, pregnancy was treated less favorably than other physical conditions that affected workplace performance. The pattern of rules telegraphed the underlying assumption: a woman's pregnancy signaled her disengagement from the workplace. Implicit was not only a factual but a normative judgment: when wage-earning women became pregnant they did, and should, go home.

B. STAGE TWO: 1970-1976

By 1970, women were in the workforce in unprecedented numbers. Moreover, an increasing number of them were staying after the birth of children.[40] . . . Suits were filed under Title VII and the equal protection clause on the theory that treating pregnancy disabilities differently and less favorably than other disabilities discriminates on the basis of sex. . . .

In 1974, however, the United States Supreme Court eliminated the Equal Protection Clause as a vehicle for an "equal treatment" attack on legislation singling out pregnancy for special treatment. The state statute challenged in Geduldig v. Aiello [417 U.S. 484 (1974)] created a state disability fund, providing temporary, partial wage replacement to private sector workers who became physically unable to work. The statute was liberally interpreted to cover every conceivable work disability, including, according to the record in the case, disability arising from cosmetic surgery, hair transplants, skiing accidents and prostatectomies. It excluded only one type of work disability from coverage — those "arising out of or in connection with" pregnancy. . . .

Justice Stewart, on behalf of a majority of the court, [stated] that the case did not involve discrimination based on gender as such: "The California insurance program does not exclude anyone from benefit eligibility because of gender but merely removes one physical condition — pregnancy — from the list of compensable

40. Between 1950 and 1970, the labor force participation rate for women with children under six years old increased from 12 to 30%. Dept. of Labor, Women's Bureau, Economic Report of the President 93 (1971). By 1979 the rate was 56.1%. U.S. Dept. of Labor, Perspectives on Working Women: A Databook, Table 34, 34 (1980).

disabilities." Translated, this means that the statute bases the exclusion on pregnancy, not on sex itself (a point made evident, the court noted, by the fact that the persons covered by the program — disabled nonpregnant persons — included women). This mechanical parsing was apparently reasoning enough for the Court. . . .

The conclusion that discrimination on the basis of pregnancy was not sex discrimination freed the Court from the obligation to engage in the more activist review it reserves for sex discrimination cases. Indulging the strong presumption of constitutionality appropriate to rational basis review, it concluded that a legislature legitimately could exclude a costly disability. . . . The Court's explanation that exclusion was rational because the "additional" cost of covering pregnancy would upset the pre-established contribution rate or benefit level would apply to any frequent or prolonged disability that had been excluded from the program, however arbitrarily. . . .

Justice Brennan, joined in dissent by Justices Marshall and Douglas, adopted the plaintiffs' position in its entirety. Women disabled by pregnancy-related causes were comparable to other disabled workers for purposes of the California program. . . . Moreover, the exclusion of pregnancy-related disabilities constituted sex discrimination. . . .

[Yet,] when the Court struck down the pregnancy policies in [Cleveland Board of Education v. LaFleur, 414 U.S. 632 (1974)], it invoked not the sex discrimination cases decided under the equal protection clause, but rather, the reproductive choice cases, such as Eisenstadt [v. Baird, 405 U.S. 438 (1972)] and Roe v. Wade [410 U.S. 113 (1973)]. . . . The doctrinal distinction between due process and equal protection analysis of pregnancy issues represented by *LaFleur* and *Geduldig* is in a sense a reiteration of the special treatment/equal treatment dichotomy. To oversimplify, the due process approach is not troubled by and, indeed, invokes a form of special treatment analysis. The liberty interest at stake, defined as the right to choose whether to bear or beget a child without undue state interference, is recognized as "fundamental" precisely because of the central and unique importance to the individual of reproductive choice. The characterization of pregnancy discrimination as sex discrimination, by contrast, requires the comparative analysis of the equal protection mode. Its emphasis is on what is not unique about the reproductive process of women. . . .

C. STAGE THREE: 1976-1978

In General Electric Company v. Gilbert, [429 U.S. 125 (1976)], decided in December of 1976, the Supreme Court dropped the other shoe. Relying heavily on *Geduldig v. Aiello*, it interpreted Title VII as it had the equal protection clause: it held that discrimination on the basis of pregnancy was not sex discrimination. *Gilbert*, on its facts, was very similar to *Geduldig*. It involved a private employer's disability insurance plan almost identical to the California state plan both in its general scope and in its exclusion of pregnancy-related disabilities. . . .

Under Title VII, rules that are "neutral" but have a disproportionate sex-based effect may also violate the Act. However, the particular "neutral" General Electric pregnancy disability rule, said Justice Rehnquist [writing for the majority,] could not even be viewed as having a discriminatory *effect* on women. Men and women, he said, are both covered by the disability program. Moreover, they are covered for the disabilities common to both sexes. Pregnancy disabilities are therefore an "*additional* risk, unique to women." Failure to compensate women for them does not upset the basic sex equality of the program. In a footnote, he drove home the point: Title VII does not require "that 'greater economic benefit[s]' . . . be paid to one sex or the other because of their differing roles in the 'scheme of human existence.'" This conclusion makes breathtakingly explicit the underlying philosophy of the majority of the justices in *Geduldig* and *Gilbert*. Pregnancy, for Rehnquist, is an "extra," an add-on to the basic male model for humanity. Equality does not contemplate handing out benefits for extras—indeed, to do so would be to grant special benefits to women, possibly discriminating against men. The fact that men were compensated under the program for disabilities unique to their sex troubled his analysis not at all.

Justice Brennan, in his dissent in *Geduldig*, almost grasped the essence of the problem when he observed that "the State has created a double standard for disability compensation; a limitation is imposed upon the disabilities for which women workers may recover, while men receive full compensation for all disabilities suffered, including those that affect only or primarily their sex. . . ." What eluded even Justice Brennan was that the statute did not create a "double" standard. Rather, it made man the standard (whatever disabilities men suffer will be compensated) and measured women against that standard (as long as she is compensated for anything he is compensated for, she is treated equally).

For Rehnquist, as long as women are treated in the same way as men in the areas where they are like men—in the disability program this would mean coverage for things like heart attacks, broken bones, appendicitis—that's equality. To the extent the Court will consider the equities with respect to childbearing capacity, it will consider them only in the category where they belong—extra, separate, different. A family, marital or reproductive right—yes, in appropriate circumstances. A public matter of equality and equal protection of women—no. . . .

D. STAGE FOUR: 1978-PRESENT

In reaction to *Gilbert* and [a subsequent case, Nashville Gas Co. v. Satty, 434 U.S. 136 (1977)], Congress in 1978 passed the Pregnancy Discrimination Act (PDA) as an amendment to Title VII, quite plainly requiring that pregnancy be treated under the equality model. [This] equal treatment approach, despite its rocky progress in the Supreme Court, has transformed employer pregnancy policies. . . .[101]

Notes and Questions

1. *Rationale.* LaFleur, decided before the Pregnancy Discrimination Act, was based on due process. Why did the Supreme Court base its decision on due process rather than equal protection?

2. *Antidiscrimination rule.* The PDA does not mandate pregnancy leave. Rather, it is an antidiscrimination rule that requires employers to treat pregnancy the same

---

101. Terminations still occur, no longer on the basis of an overt policy of terminating pregnant women, but in other guises. In such cases, plaintiffs must, like any Title VII plaintiff alleging covert discrimination, demonstrate that the employer intended to discriminate—in these cases because of pregnancy. . . .

as other physical conditions in terms of leave and other employment benefits. How does an employer treat pregnant women *the same as* "other persons not so affected but similar in their ability or inability to work"? Should employers' treatment of pregnant workers be compared to their accommodation of other employees with occupational injuries who are unable to work (the "ability or inability to work" approach) or compared to employers' accommodation of nonpregnant workers injured off the job (the "place of injury" approach that may not lead to as generous accommodations of the employee's disability)? See Jamie L. Clanton, Note, Toward Eradicating Pregnancy Discrimination at Work: Interpreting the PDA to "Mean What It Says," 86 Iowa L. Rev. 703 (2001) (criticizing federal appellate courts' different interpretations).

3. *State protections for pregnant employees.* As *Cal. Fed.* illustrates, some states mandate job-protected unpaid leaves for pregnant employees. See, e.g., Mont. Code Ann. §49-2-310(2)(2003). In addition, some states' temporary disability programs provide partial wage replacement to cover pregnancy. See, e.g., Haw. Rev. Stat. §392-21(a) (1993).

4. *Pregnancy discrimination after the PDA.* Despite the PDA, workers continue to report pregnancy discrimination. Complaints of pregnancy discrimination filed with the Equal Opportunity Employment Commission (the agency charged with administering the PDA) increased 39 percent between 1992 and 2003. Stephanie Armour, Pregnant Workers Report Growing Discrimination, USA Today, Feb. 17, 2005, at B1 (citing a report complied by the National Partnership for Women and Families).

5. *Criticisms of PDA.* Commentators have criticized the PDA for its failure to protect women who suffer discrimination because of pregnancy but who are not fired *during* the pregnancy — i.e., those who are fired because of the pregnancy but *after* their return from leave, or because of employers' fears that the women may become pregnant soon again, or because of gender-based stereotypes about pregnant women's lack of competence in the workplace. Huhta et al., Looking Forward and Back: Using the Pregnancy Discrimination Act and Discriminatory Gender/Pregnancy Stereotyping to Challenge Discrimination Against New Mothers, 7 Employee Rts. & Emp. Pol'y J. 303, 306 (2003). In addition, employers may offer other non-pregnancy reasons (i.e. pretexts) for the discharge or demotion. See, e.g., Groves v. Cost Planning and Mgmt. Int'l, Inc., 372 F.3d 1008 (8th Cir. 2004) (holding that the defendant's down turn in business was a justifiable reason for terminating the pregnant worker even if she had established a prima facie case of discrimination).

6. *Equal treatment versus special treatment.* To what extent does the "special treatment" approach of providing benefits for pregnant workers compromise women's employment opportunities? Might it revitalize early twentieth-century attitudes that women needed protective labor legislation (limiting the hours women could work because of women's childbearing potential)? See Muller v. Oregon, 208 U.S. 412 (1908). On the other hand, without "special treatment," what will happen to the majority of female employees who are likely to require time off from work because of pregnancy? Do non-leave policies have a disproportionate impact on female workers who have children, compared to male workers who have children? Does it follow that the law must require pregnancy-related leaves? See Herma Hill Kay, Equality and Difference: The Case of Pregnancy, 1 Berkeley Women's L.J. 1

(1985). On the equal treatment-special treatment debate, see Feminist Legal Theory: Foundations 121-207 (D. Kelly Weisberg ed., 1993).

7. *Parental leave and the right to privacy.* Do state parental leave statutes violate the right to privacy by compelling men and women to jeopardize job security in order to have children? If so, should these regulations be subject to a higher level of constitutional scrutiny? See Catherine G. Meier, Protecting Parental Leave, A Fundamental Rights Model, 33 Williamette L. Rev. 177 (1997) (so arguing).

8. *Contraception, infertility, and the PDA.* Does the PDA cover an employer's failure to cover prescription contraceptives? See Erickson v. Bartell Drug Company, 141 F. Supp.2d 1266 (W.D. Wash. 2001) (holding that exclusion of prescription contraceptives from comprehensive prescription plan offered by employer discriminated against female employees on basis of sex, and thus violated PDA). See also Brietta R. Clark, Erickson v. Bartell Drug Co.: A Roadmap for Gender Equality in Reproductive Health Care or an Empty Promise?, 23 Law & Ineq. 299 (2005); Julie Manning Magid, Contraception and Contractions: A Divergent Decade Following *Johnson Controls*, 41 Am. Bus. L. J. 115 (2003).

Does the PDA cover discrimination against women who miss work to undergo infertility treatments? See LaPorta v. Wal-Mart Stores, Inc., 163 F.Supp.2d 758 (W.D. Mich. 2001) (holding that plaintiff's alleged disability of infertility did not fall within purview of the PDA). See also Cintra D. Bentley, Note, A Pregnant Pause: Are Women Who Undergo Fertility Treatment to Achieve Pregnancy Within the Scope of Title VII's Pregnancy Discrimination Act?, 73 Chi.-Kent L. Rev. 391 (1998). Do employers violate the PDA if they do not include infertility treatments under employee health insurance programs? See Saks v. Franklin Convoy Co., 316 F.3d 337, 349 (2d Cir. 2003) (holding that the plan did not violate the PDA because it limited infertility treatment coverage for both men and women equally). Is infertility "a pregnancy-related medical condition" covered by Title VII? Or, is infertility distinct from issues of pregnancy?

9. *Fetal protection policies.* Sometimes, pregnancy discrimination derives from an employer's concern about potential liability for harm to the fetus. May an employer refuse to allow women (both pregnant and non-pregnant) to work in an occupation that might pose harm to the (or a potential) fetus? See International Union, UAW v. Johnson Controls, Inc., 499 U.S. 187 (1991) (holding that employer's policy barring all women from jobs involving lead exposure was facially discriminatory because it required only females to prove that they were not capable of reproducing, and that the employer's concerns about protecting the welfare of the next generation did not suffice to establish female sterility as a bona fide occupational qualification). What effect does *Johnson Controls* have on employers' liability to fetuses? See Asad v. Continental Airlines, Inc., 328 F. Supp.2d 772 (N.D. Ohio 2004) (holding that PDA did not preclude employer's potential liability for an infant's injuries for an employer's failure to transfer the pregnant woman from a job with exposure to harmful airplane exhaust fumes).

May an employer lay off a pregnant employee who previously suffered a miscarriage out of fear that she will harm her fetus by continuing to work? Require all pregnant employees to take leaves for the same reason? See Peralta v. Chromium Plating & Polishing Corp., 2000 U.S. Dist. LEXIS 17416 (E.D.N.Y. 2000).

Problems

1. Hunter Tylo is a soap opera star on prime-time television. On "Melrose Place," she plays a happily married woman who suddenly begins an affair. Shortly after she accepts the job, Hunter becomes pregnant. She informs her employer Spelling Entertainment Group. One month later, she is fired. Spelling informs her that they have a contractual right to terminate her if there was a "material change in [her] appearance." Further, Spelling argues that her pregnancy does not conform to the character she portrays. Tylo alleges a violation of the Pregnancy Discrimination Act. What result? See Tylo v. Superior Court, 64 Cal. Rptr.2d 731 (Ct. App. 1997).

2. When a high school honors student becomes pregnant during her senior year, the principal of her public school informs her she can no longer attend class "due to safety concerns," and that she is not permitted to attend commencement or to have her name printed in the graduation program. However, the school permits the baby's father to continue to participate in commencement exercises. The student comes to you for advice. Does she have a claim for pregnancy discrimination? Sex discrimination? See Erica Pippins, Pregnant Student Banned from Graduation Walks Stage Anyway, Montgomery Advertiser, May 18, 2005, at A2; Sally Kalson, Graduation Pregnant with Inequity, Pittsburgh Post-Gazette, May 25, 2005, at A2.

b. Balancing Work and Family

■ **CALDWELL v. HOLLAND OF TEXAS, INC.**
208 F.3d 671 (8th Cir. 2000)

BRIGHT, Circuit Judge.

[Juanita] Caldwell is a single mother, working to support herself and her three-year-old son, Kejuan. Before she was summarily fired, Caldwell worked for Holland, which owns and operates several Kentucky Fried Chicken restaurants in Texarkana, Arkansas. Caldwell worked for Holland for three years, and during that time, she developed an excellent record working at the Kentucky Fried Chicken on Hickory Street.

On Saturday, June 7, 1997, Kejuan awoke with a high fever, pain in his ears, and congestion. Caldwell promptly notified Assistant Manager Loyce, prior to the start of her morning shift, that she would be absent because Kejuan required immediate medical attention. Loyce gave Caldwell permission to miss her shift. That morning, a doctor at an emergency clinic diagnosed Kejuan as having an acute ear infection. During this visit, the doctor prescribed a ten-day course of antibiotics and a two-day decongestant for Kejuan. At the same time, the treating physician informed Caldwell that her son's condition probably would require surgery if her son was to avoid permanent hearing loss, and he recommended that Caldwell schedule a follow-up examination with her son's regular pediatrician, Dr. Mark Wright.

Later that Saturday night, upon the request of an assistant manager, Caldwell worked an evening shift at one of Holland's other restaurant locations. While Caldwell was working, her elderly mother cared for her son and administered his medications. Caldwell did not have any shifts on Sunday. When Caldwell returned to her regular work on Monday morning, June 9, 1997, Mark Monholland, a manager at the Hickory Street restaurant, abruptly fired Caldwell without discussing her absence of June 7, 1997.

The supplemental affidavit of Ms. Caldwell, Kejuan's mother, asserts that Kejuan suffered "incapacity" for more than three consecutive days following his trip to the clinic and recites that Kejuan did not participate in his "normal activities," remained inside the house, and was kept in bed as much as possible. He remained under the care of either his mother or grandmother who administered prescribed medications during "this entire time." During a follow-up visit on July 1, 1997, Dr. Wright prescribed a second ten-day course of antibiotics for Kejuan in an attempt to treat his "persistent ear infection." On July 17, 1997, Kejuan had surgery to remove his adenoids and tonsils and to place tubes in his ears. Following surgery, Kejuan received another course of antibiotics and orders to remain in bed for one week. His mother and grandmother kept him inside following the operation and restricted him from engaging in normal activities.

Caldwell sued and argued that her termination violated the FMLA. . . .

The FMLA allows eligible employees to take up to a total of twelve workweeks of leave per year for, among other things, "serious health conditions" that afflict their immediate family members. See 29 U.S.C. §2612(a)(1)(C) ("to care for the spouse, or son, daughter, or parent, of the employee [who] has a serious health condition"). The employee must show that her family member suffered a serious health condition and that her absence was attributable to the family member's serious health condition.

A "serious health condition" occurs, under the regulations, when the family member suffers an "illness, injury, impairment, or physical or mental condition" that requires "inpatient care" or "continuing treatment" by a health care provider. See 29 C.F.R. §825.114(a). Here, the parties agree that Kejuan never received inpatient care. The pertinent issue is whether Kejuan received continuing treatment. A family member receives continuing treatment if the person experiences "[a] period of *incapacity* . . . of more than three consecutive calendar days" and then receives subsequent treatment, or experiences further incapacity relating to, the same condition. 29 C.F.R. §825.114(a)(2)(i). The subsequent treatment must include, either "[t]reatment two or more times by a health care provider . . . ," or "[t]reatment by a health care provider on at least one occasion which results in a regimen of continuing treatment under the supervision of the health care provider." 29 C.F.R. §825.114(a)(2)(i)(A)-(B). . . .

The applicability of the FMLA, here, turns on whether Caldwell can prove a two-pronged inquiry: first, she must show that Kejuan suffered "a period of incapacity of more than three consecutive calendar days"; second, she must show that Kejuan subsequently received continued, supervised treatment relating to the same condition. . . .

In assessing the first prong of Caldwell's case, we note at the outset that the question of what constitutes incapacity of a three-year-old raises an issue not directly addressed by the regulations. The regulations state that incapacity may be determined based on an individual's "inability to work, attend school or perform other regular daily activities due to the serious health condition, treatment therefor, or recovery therefrom." See 29 C.F.R. §825.114(a)(2)(i). Because most three-year-old children do not work or attend school, the standard offered by the regulations is an insufficient guide. The fact finder must determine whether the child's illness demonstrably affected his normal activity. In making this determination, the fact finder may consider a variety of factors, including but not limited to: whether the child participated in his daily routines or was particularly difficult to care for during that period, and whether a daycare facility would have allowed a child with Kejuan's illness to attend its sessions.

Caldwell avers that Kejuan's ear infection, which was severe enough to warrant emergency treatment, required constant care for a period of more than three days. She states in her supplemental affidavit that Kejuan was incapacitated beginning Saturday, June 7, 1997, for more than three consecutive days. She further states:

> He [Kejuan] remained inside the house and was kept in bed as much as possible. He did not participate in any of his normal activities. He was under the constant care of me (his mother) and his grandmother, and both the prescribed medications and a fever reducer were administered to him during this entire time.

In addition to Caldwell's affidavit, the medical records show that Kejuan's ear infection was a continuing, persistent condition that could only be treated by surgery. Kejuan's period of incapacity, therefore, may be measured over the entire time during which he was suffering from this illness and being treated for it. We note that Kejuan was treated for his condition for ten days following his first visit to the emergency clinic. The medical records state that the condition did not improve, and as a result, Dr. Wright, his regular physician, prescribed another ten-day course of antibiotics. Despite the two medical treatments, Kejuan's condition continued to persist until Dr. Trone, a surgical specialist, performed surgery to remove his tonsils and adenoids on July 17, 1997. This entire period, from June 7-July 17, 1997, may constitute Kejuan's period of incapacity if his illness and these various treatments disrupted his basic daily routines, and if, as the record suggests, his ongoing treatment was not successfully alleviating his condition of disability. . . .

Alternatively, the ten-day period beginning on June 7, 1997 could constitute Kejuan's period of incapacity. As we have noted, his mother's supplemental affidavit refers to constant care and administration of prescribed medications during "this entire time." . . . Even if Kejuan did not sustain "incapacity" under the regulations *prior* to his surgery, the record clearly shows that the inflammation and infection in his ears resulted in a period of incapacity that lasted more than three days once he had the tonsillectomy and adenoidectomy. . . .

FMLA's purpose is to help working men and women balance the conflicting demands of work and personal life. The law requires courts to consider the seriousness of the afflicted individual's condition because the law was designed to prevent individuals like Juanita Caldwell from having to choose between their livelihood and treatment for their own or their family members' serious health conditions. Upon examining the seriousness of Kejuan's ear infection, which required surgery to prevent deafness, we hold that there is at least a question of fact as to whether Kejuan's condition was "serious" under the regulations. . . .

On the second prong of the threshold inquiry, we believe that Caldwell has generated a genuine issue of fact regarding whether Kejuan received "subsequent treatment." Here, after the first ten-day antibiotic treatment, Kejuan was treated by Dr. Wright and later by Dr. Trone in surgery. . . . Furthermore, the record shows at least two post-operative medical visits to monitor Kejuan's condition. . . .

For the reasons stated above, the district court erred in granting a summary judgment of dismissal. Accordingly, we reverse and remand for further proceedings.

■ FAMILY AND MEDICAL LEAVE ACT
29 U.S.C. §§2601, 2611, 2612, 2614 (2000)

§2601. FINDINGS AND PURPOSES

(a) Findings. The Congress finds that

(1) the number of single-parent households and two-parent households in which the single parent or both parents work is increasing significantly; . . .

(3) the lack of employment policies to accommodate working parents can force individuals to choose between job security and parenting; . . .

(5) due to the nature of the roles of men and women in our society, the primary responsibility for family caretaking often falls on women, and such responsibility affects their working lives more than it affects the working lives of men; and

(6) employment standards that apply to one gender only have serious potential for encouraging employers to discriminate against employees and applicants for employment who are of that gender.

(b) Purposes. It is the purpose of this Act

(1) to balance the demands of the workplace with the needs of families, to promote stability and economic security of families, and to promote national interests in preserving family integrity;

(2) to entitle employees to take reasonable leave for medical reasons, for the birth or adoption of a child, and for the care of a child, spouse, or parent who has a serious health condition;

(3) to accomplish such purposes . . . in a manner which accommodates the legitimate interests of employers;

(4) to accomplish such purposes . . . in a manner that, consistent with the Equal Protection Clause of the Fourteenth Amendment, minimizes the potential for discrimination on the basis of sex by ensuring generally that leave is available for eligible medical reasons (including maternity-related disability) and for compelling family reasons, on a gender-neutral basis; and

(5) to promote the goal of equal employment opportunity for women and men, pursuant to such clause.

§2611. DEFINITIONS . . .

(2)(A) "[E]ligible employee" means an employee who has been employed

(i) for at least 12 months by the employer with respect to whom leave is requested under section 2612; and

(ii) for at least 1,250 hours of service with such employer during the previous 12-month period. . . .

(4)(A) "[E]mployer"

(i) means any person engaged in commerce or in any industry or activity affecting commerce who employs 50 or more employees [for each workday, for 20 or more weeks in the current or proceeding year] . . .

(5) "[E]mployment benefits" means all benefits provided or made available to employees by an employer, including group life insurance, health insurance,

disability insurance, sick leave, annual leave, educational benefits, and pensions. . . .

(7) "[P]arent" means the biological parent of an employee or an individual who stood in loco parentis to an employee when the employee was a son or daughter. . . .

(11) "[S]erious health condition" means an illness, injury, impairment, or physical or mental condition that involves

(A) inpatient care in a hospital, hospice, or residential medical care facility; or

(B) continuing treatment by a health care provider.

(12) "[S]on or daughter" means a biological, adopted, or foster child, a step-child, a legal ward, or a child of a person standing in loco parentis, who is [under 18, or mentally or physically disabled].

(13) "[S]pouse" means a husband or wife, as the case may be.

§2612. Leave Requirement

(a) In General.

(1) Entitlement to leave. [A]n eligible employee shall be entitled to a total of 12 workweeks of leave during any 12-month period for one or more of the following:

(A) Because of the birth of a son or daughter of the employee and in order to care for such son or daughter.

(B) Because of the placement of a son or daughter with the employee for adoption or foster care.

(C) In order to care for the spouse, or a son, daughter, or parent, of the employee, if such spouse, son, daughter, or parent has a serious health condition.

(D) Because of a serious health condition that makes the employee unable to perform the functions of the position of such employee. . . .

(b) [Leave generally shall not be taken intermittently.]

(c) Unpaid Leave Permitted. Except as provided in subsection (d), leave granted under subsection (a) may consist of unpaid leave. . . .

(d) Relationship to Paid Leave.

(1) Unpaid leave. If an employer provides paid leave for fewer than 12 work-weeks, the additional weeks of leave necessary to attain the 12 workweeks of leave required under this subchapter may be provided without compensation.

(2) Substitution of paid leave.

[The employee may choose, or the employer may require, accrued paid leave or sick leave be substituted for the unpaid 12-week leave.]

(e) Foreseeable leave

(1) Requirement of notice

[For a foreseeable leave based on a birth or child placement], the employee shall provide the employer with not less than 30 days' notice [except if] the date of the birth or placement requires leave to begin in less than 30 days, the employee shall provide such notice as is practicable.

(2) Duties of employee

[For a foreseeable leave based on planned medical treatment], the employee —

(A) shall make a reasonable effort to schedule the treatment so as not to disrupt unduly the operations of the employer, subject to the approval of the health care provider . . . and

(B) shall provide the employer with not less than 30 days' notice, before the date the leave is to begin, of the employee's intention to take leave [except] that if the date of the treatment requires leave to begin in less than 30 days, the employee shall provide such notice as is practicable.

(f) Spouses Employed by the Same Employer. [If husband and wife] are employed by the same employer, the aggregate number of workweeks of leave to which both may be entitled may be limited to 12 workweeks during any 12-month period. . . .

§2614. Employment and Benefits Protection

(a) Restoration to Position

(1) In general. Except as provided in subsection (b), any eligible employee who takes leave under section 2612 for the intended purpose of the leave shall be entitled, on return from such leave

(A) to be restored by the employer to the position of employment held by the employee when the leave commenced; or

(B) to be restored to an equivalent position with equivalent employment benefits, pay, and other terms and conditions of employment.

[The taking of leave shall not result in the loss of any employment benefit accrued prior to the date on which the leave commenced but the restored employee has no right to the accrual of any seniority benefits during any period of leave.]

(b) Exemption Concerning Certain Highly Compensated Employees.

(1) Denial of restoration. An employer may deny restoration under subsection (a) to any eligible employee described [if]

(A) such denial is necessary to prevent substantial and grievous economic injury to the operations of the employer; . . .

(2) Affected employees. An eligible employee described in paragraph (1) is a salaried eligible employee who is among the highest paid 10 percent of the employees employed by the employer within 75 miles of the facility at which the employee is employed.

(c) [Employer is required to maintain health benefits for the duration of the leave.]

Notes and Questions

1. *Background.* The public outcry for family leave dates from the 1970s. After the women's liberation movement led to expanding employment opportunities for women, the number of mothers who were working outside the home dramatically increased. The largest increase occurred in the numbers of mothers with preschool children.[33] Currently, 70.4 percent of mothers with children under the age of 18 are in the labor force, including 61.8 percent of mothers with children under age 6, and 52.9 percent of mothers with children under one year old.[34]

[33]. "Between 1959 and 1974, the employment rate for mothers with children under three more than doubled, from 15 to 31 percent." Marie Richmond-Abbott, Women Wage Earners, in Feminist Philosophies 135, 136 (Janet A. Kourany et al. eds., 1992).

[34]. Bureau of Labor and Statistics, Employment Characteristics of Families Summary (June 9, 2005), available at http://bls.gov/news.release.famee.nr0.htm.

The FMLA became law after a lengthy battle. First proposed in 1985, the act was twice passed by Congress but vetoed by the first President Bush. President Clinton signed the act in February 1993. According to data compiled by the Department of Labor (DOL) in 2000, more than 35 million employees have taken leave under FMLA since its enactment.[35]

2. *Purposes.* How does the FMLA redress the PDA's shortcomings? Recall the purpose clause of the FMLA. To what extent does the FMLA accomplish these purposes?

3. *Impact on business.* Opponents of the FMLA originally charged that the legislation would have a significant negative impact on industry. Why? According to the DOL report in 2000, 84 percent of employers report that the FMLA has had no effect or a positive effect on productivity, and 90 percent of employers report that the FMLA has had a positive or no effect on profitability and growth.[36] See generally Peter A. Susser, The Employer Perspective on Paid Leave and the FMLA, 15 Wash. U. J.L. & Pol'y 169 (2004).

4. *Criticisms.* The FMLA mandates *unpaid leave* to eligible employees. Are the working poor able to take unpaid leaves? According to DOL statistics, 29 percent of employees who take leave under the FMLA earn less than $30,000 per year; and nearly half of those taking leave earn between $30,000 and $74,000 per year.[37] Significantly, 78 percent of employees who need family leave time do not take it because they cannot afford to miss a paycheck.[38]

Conversely, does the FMLA accommodate the needs of *highly paid* employees? See Saroli v. Automation & Modular Components, Inc., 405 F.3d 446 (6th Cir. 2005). Also, how well does the FMLA address the needs of *single parents*? Of *fathers*? Are employers offering FMLA leaves to fathers on equal terms? Are fathers taking advantage of such leaves? In Knussman v. Maryland, 272 F.3d 625 (4th Cir. 2001), a federal appellate court vacated a $375,0000 verdict to a state trooper whose supervisors refused him FMLA leave to care for his newborn, but affirmed the judgment against a personnel officer on equal protection grounds (for relying on the irrebuttable presumption that only mothers can be primary caregivers). Further, Professor Joanna Grossman criticizes the vision, upon which the FMLA was based, that employers would offer caretaking leaves to men and women on equal terms:

> If only mothers take leave, then the FMLA only accommodates women's caretaking, protection that gives them a measure of job security but at the same time preserves

---

[35]. National Partnership for Women & Families, Highlights of the 2000 U.S. Department of Labor Report, p. 3, available at http://www.nationalpartnershp.org/portals/p3/library/FamilyMedicalLeave/2000DOLLaborReportHighlights.pdf (last visited June 17, 2005). Of those people, 26 percent took time off to care for a new child or for maternity disability reasons; 13 percent to care for a seriously ill parent; 12 percent to care for a seriously ill child and 6 percent to care for a seriously ill spouse.

[36]. Id. at 6.

[37]. Id. at 4.

[38]. National Partnership for Women and Families, State Paid Leave Initiatives in 2004 and Prior State Legislatures: Making Family Leave More Affordable, p. 1, available at http://www.nationalpartnership.org/portalsp3/library/PaidLeave/StateRoundUp2004.pdf (last visited June 17, 2005) (citing Department of Labor's 2000 Balancing the Needs of Families and Employers: Family and Medical Leave Survey). See also Charles L. Baum, Has Family Leave Legislation Increased Leave-Taking?, 15 Wash. U. J.L. & Pol'y 93 (2004) (concluding that enactment of family leave legislation has had minimal effect on actual leavetaking).

employers' incentives to prefer male employees. It also does nothing to equalize the burdens of caretaking themselves.

Joanna L. Grossman, Job Security Without Equality: The Family and Medical Leave Act of 1993, 15 Wash. U. J. L. & Pol'y 17, 18 (2004). See also Heather A. Peterson, Note, The Daddy Track: Locating the Male Employee Within the Family and Medical Leave Act, 15 Wash. U. J.L. & Pol'y 253 (2004).

Does the FMLA go far enough to meet the *full range of needs* of working parents? For example, is the 12-week period of leave sufficient? Given that the period applies both to pregnancy and care of a newborn, might a mother with pregnancy-related complications use all her leave before the birth? See Debbie N. Kaminer, The Work-Family Conflict: Developing a Model of Parental Accommodation in the Workplace, 54 Am. U. L. Rev. 305, 325 (2004) (so contending). Further, does the FMLA provide for a parent's normal childcare obligations, such as taking time off for a child who has a cold, attending school appointments, accommodating school closures for workdays/holidays, or babysitter cancellations? See id. at 308, 326-327 (criticizing the FMLA for its premise of a "medical model" that fails therefore to provide for any non-medical reason). Some countries provide "extended leave" (discussed infra) to accommodate these childrearing responsibilities.

5. *FMLA and nontraditional families.* Does the FMLA limit protection to members of traditional families? For example, how well does the FMLA address the needs of gay and lesbian parents? Of unmarried heterosexual cohabitants who are parents? Only a few jurisdictions provide for family and medical leave for domestic partners. However, because the definition of "domestic partner" generally is limited to same-sex couples, unmarried heterosexual couples with children may not be protected in some cases. See Kimberly Menashe Glassman, Note, Balancing the Demands of the Workplace with the Needs of the Modern Family: Expanding Family and Medical Leave to Protect Domestic Partners, 37 U. Mich. J.L. Reform 837, 840-841, 869-870 (2004). Does a policy that limits family and medical leave to same-sex couples and excludes heterosexual couples violate the Fourteenth Amendment? See id. at 859-966.

6. *Paid leave.* Some states are exploring ways to fund paid family leave programs, such as through use of unemployment insurance programs, temporary disability insurance, or tax incentives. In 2003, California became the first state to enact paid family leave legislation under the temporary disability insurance model, funded through employee contributions. Cal. Unemp. Ins. Code §§3300-3305 (West Supp. 2005). The legislation provides six weeks paid leave (i.e., wage replacement of up to 55 percent of salary and a maximum of $738/week) to employees who take time off to care for a seriously ill child, spouse, parent or domestic partner, or to bond with a minor child after birth or adoption. Id. at §3301(a)(1). Some states are allowing public and private sector employees to use sick time to care for ill family members. Do these policies go far enough? See generally Gillian Lester, A Defense of Paid Family Leave, 28 Harv. J. L. & Gender 1 (2005); Jennifer Thompson, Family and Medical Leave for the 21st Century?, 12 U. Miami Bus. L. Rev. 77, 93 (2004); Anne Wells, Paid Family Leave: Striking the Balance Between The Needs of Employees and Employers, 77 S. Cal. L. Rev. 1067, 1070 (2004).

7. *Serious health condition. Caldwell* is an important case that defines the FMLA requirement of a "serious health condition." See also Rankin v. Seagate Technol-

ogies, Inc., 246 F.3d 1145 (8th Cir. 2001) (holding there was a genuine issue of material fact regarding whether plaintiff could qualify for FMLA leave because of her symptoms of nausea, sleeplessness, coughing, and congestion). What exactly is a "serious health condition," according to the FMLA? Was the toddler's ear infection in *Caldwell* a "serious health condition" under the FMLA? Why or why not? What is a "serious health condition" for a toddler? An infant? Does the definition differ from that of an adult? What qualifies as "subsequent treatment"? Commentators have pointed out that currently courts are broadening the list of "serious health conditions" that qualify for FMLA leave. See, e.g., Paula J. Dehan, Has the FMLA Been Stretched Beyond its Intended Scope?, 29 N. Ky. L. Rev. 629 (2002); Kenza Bemis Nelson, Note, Employer Difficulty in FMLA Implementation: A Look at Eighth Circuit Interpretation of "Serious Health Condition" and "Employee Notice Requirements," 30 J. Corp. L. 609 (2005). Is such a broad reading of the FMLA warranted? See also Katharine B. Silbaugh, Is the Work-Family Conflict Normal or Pathological Under the FMLA? The Potential of the FMLA to Cover Ordinary Work-Family Conflicts, 15 Wash. U. J.L. & Pol'y 193 (2004).

8. *Overlapping rights.* Employees may have overlapping rights to family and medical leave under federal and state law. For example, as *Cal. Fed.* reveals, some states provide maternity, family, or medical leave. Similarly, some employees may have rights under the Americans with Disabilities Act, 42 U.S.C. §§12101-12213 (2000). Does the FMLA preempt these state statutes? Recall *Cal. Fed.*, supra.

9. *Application to state employees.* Until recently, state employees suing under the FMLA in federal courts faced uncertainty created by U.S. Supreme Court decisions barring, under the Eleventh Amendment, claims to recover money damages for the state's failure to comply with some federal statutes. See, e.g., Kimel v. Florida Bd. of Regents, 528 U.S. 62 (2000) (applying to suits based on the American with Disabilities Act); Board of Trustees of the Univ. of Ala. v. Garrett, 531 U.S. 356 (2001) (applying to suits based on the Rehabilitation Act). The Supreme Court resolved this issue regarding the FMLA in Nevada Department of Human Resources v. Hibbs, 538 U.S. 721 (2003), in which a former employee of the state social service department brought suit against his employer for a violation of the FMLA when he sought leave to care for his ill wife. Holding that state employees can sue in federal court to recover money damages from state employers who violate the FMLA, the Court reasoned that the Eleventh Amendment did not bar the claim because Congress made its intention to abrogate Eleventh Amendment immunity clear in the language of the FMLA. See generally Joan C. Williams, *Hibbs* as a Federalism Case; *Hibbs* as a Maternal Wall Case, 73 U. Cin. L. Rev. 365 (2004).

10. *Notice requirement.* The FMLA contains certain notice requirements. What are the employee's duties to notify the employer of the need for a leave? See 29 U.S.C. §2612, supra. Because rights under the FMLA may be co-extensive with rights under state law or under an employer's sick leave policy, must the employee specifically refer to the FMLA to invoke the statute's protection when notifying an employer of the need for a leave? See Ragsdale v. Wolverine World Wide, Inc., 535 U.S. 81 (2002) (holding that a regulation, providing that leave taken by employee does not count against employee's FMLA entitlement if employer does not designate leave as FMLA leave, was contrary to FMLA and beyond authority of Secretary of Labor). See also Rafael Gely & Timothy D. Chandler, Maternity Leave Under the FMLA: An Analysis of the Litigation Experience, 15 Wash. U. J.L. & Pol'y 143, 168

(2004) (reporting research findings that employers use the "legitimate business reasons" defense more frequently than the "notice" defense).

11. *Privacy*. Given that the employer may need to solicit information from an employee's health care providers to ascertain whether the leave qualifies under the FMLA, does such inquiry invade the employee's privacy? See Lisa Bornstein, Inclusion and Exclusion in Work-Family Policy: The Public Values and Moral Code Embedded in the Family and Medical Leave Act, 10 Colum J. Gender & L. 77, 104-105 (2000).

12. *International perspective*. Until the FMLA, the United States was one of two industrialized countries (with South Africa) without national family leave. Even after the FMLA, many countries provide significantly better parental leave policies.

a. *Sweden*. Sweden has long been known for its generous parental leave program. In 1974, Sweden changed its maternity-leave system to a parental-leave system. Since then, the Parental Leave Act (Foraldraledighetslagen,1995:584) has been amended several times. Initially, parents were permitted to take paid leave of six months (divided between them, provided that only one parent took leave at a time). The non-working parent received 90 percent of his or her salary through a public fund financed by payroll taxes. In January 1, 1995, the "daddy month" was introduced, providing a mandatory month's leave for fathers as well as mothers after birth. In January 2002, the "daddy month" was extended to two months. Parental leave currently consists of 480 days (including the mandatory 2 months), of which 390 days are paid at the sick pay rate (80 percent of salary up to a ceiling). Parents each have a right to take 50 percent of the leave, although each parent can transfer some of the leave to the other (except for the mandatory 60 days of leave after the birth). Historically, Swedish mothers take parental leave far more frequently than fathers. For example, in 2001, fathers took only 15.3 percent of all parental leave days. What do such data reveal about the difficulty of changing gender-based assumptions about the sexual division of labor?

In May 2004, the Swedish government established a commission to evaluate the parental leave system. In particular, the commission is exploring: how the system can improve children's access to care by both parents; how the system affects work force participation, what incentives might be used to reduce disparities between the amount of leave taken by mothers and fathers; the effects of the current mandatory 2-month leaves, and whether the current rules are adapted to modern conditions and the modern family. Further changes may result based on the outcome of pending litigation which would give the right to parental leave to any EU citizen who moves to Sweden, after having worked for at least 240 days in any country of the Union. See Stricter Rules Proposed on Swedish Parental Leave, available at http://www.thelocal.se/article.php?ID=1259&date=20050410 (last visited June 24, 2006).

On the Swedish parental leave program, see Eironline (European industrial relations observatory online), Commision to Examine Parental Leave, available at http://www.eiro.eurofound.eu.int/2006/country/sweden.html (last visited June 24, 2006). See also Kathryn Kroggel, Comment, Absent Fathers: National Paid Paternity Leave for the United States — Examination of Foreign and State-Oriented Models, Penn St. Int'l L. Rev. 439, 462 (2004); Martha N. Ozawa, Social Welfare Spending on Family Benefits in the United States and Sweden: A Comparative Study, 53 Fam. Rel. 301 (Apr. 2004), available at 2004 WLNR 17864512.

b. *Other countries' paid leave plans*. Among the 29 advanced industrialized countries which are members of the Organisation for Economic Cooperation and Development (OECD) (of which 18 are members of the European Union), the average parental leave (including paid and unpaid leave) is almost one and a half years; the average duration for the paid portion of the leave is 36 weeks.[39] An emerging trend is for countries to permit parents to take part-time, as well as full-time, leaves and over an *extended period* of time — usually until a child's third, fifth or eighth year. Among the 29 OECD countries, only eight do not offer such extended leave policies. Gillian Lester, A Defense of Paid Family Leave, 28 Harv. J.L. & Gender 1, 64-65 (2005).

What are some of the effects of generous governmental leave policies — on mothers, fathers, and children? One study reports that in countries with supportive parental leave policies, the employment rate of mothers does not diminish as a result of having a child (unlike in the United States). In contrast, in the United States, the addition of one child aged 0-2 reduces the employment rate of mothers by 22 percent.[40]

> These findings suggest that American mothers are unable to continue working because there are inadequate supportive measures such as affordable child care and paid family leave. . . . The inadequate financial supports (public income transfers) are in part responsible for the high poverty rates in the United States . . . Several family researchers found that poverty is the root cause of unfavorable child outcomes [physical, cognitive, emotional development and educational attainment].[41]

Problems

1. Martha and Michael Smith are expecting quadruplets (as a result of fertility treatments). Martha is a schoolteacher; Michael works at a computer company. During the fifth month of Martha's pregnancy, her physician advises complete bedrest. Martha has no difficulty taking time off from work because this is summer vacation. However, she will need someone to take care of her (fix her meals, run errands, and so forth). Michael, as well as her sister Miriam (who works for a brokerage firm), consider taking leave under the FMLA to care for Martha for the remainder of her pregnancy. What advice would you give them about the likelihood that their requests will be granted? See Navarro v. Pfizer Corp., 26 F.3d 90 (1st Cir. 2001).

2. Catherine Marzano is hired by Computer Science Co. (CSC) as a "junior technical recruiter." She is promoted several times. Shortly after her assignment to Mr. Marzi's unit, she learns that she is pregnant. She is reluctant to tell Mr. Marzi because seven employees previously were terminated after taking maternity leave. She does tell him and plans to take leave. However, she notices that Mr. Marzi speaks as "if she wasn't coming back." During her leave, her unit begins experiencing losses (despite the stellar financial performance of CSC). Mr. Marzi eliminates

---

[39]. Sheila Kamerman & Shirley Gatenio, Mother's Day: More than Candy and Flowers, Working Parents Need Paid Time-Off, Clearinghouse on International Developments in Child, Youth and Family Policies: Issue Brief (Spring 2002), available at http://www.childpolicyintl.org/issuebrief/issuebrief5 (last visited July 15, 2005).

[40]. Id. The study also reports research findings regarding European paid parental leave policies, revealing that leaves of short duration (10-20 weeks) increase women's workforce participation without significantly reducing their wages.

[41]. Id.

Catherine's position and nine others. He notifies Catherine by saying that she "would be better off if [she] stays home with the baby and collects unemployment." Catherine alleges pregnancy discrimination and unlawful interference with her rights under the FMLA. What result? Marzano v. Computer Science Corp., 91 F.3d 497 (3d Cir. 1996).

Prior to the FMLA, men occasionally litigated the lack of paternity leave. See, e.g., Danielson v. Board of Higher Educ., 358 F. Supp. 22 (S.D.N.Y. 1972). What barriers prevent fathers from taking family leaves?

■ MARTIN H. MALIN, FATHERS AND PARENTAL LEAVE
72 Tex. L. Rev. 1047, 1049-1052, 1057-1058, 1064, 1072-1075, 1077-1079 (1994)

Largely missing from the debate over maternal work-family conflicts is any discussion of paternal work-family conflicts. The two, however, are linked to a significant extent. Just as the absence of adequate maternal leave policies has been a barrier to women's roles in the workplace, the absence of adequate paternal leave policies has been a barrier to men's roles in the home. Furthermore, as long as parental leave remains de facto maternal leave, work-family conflicts will remain a significant barrier to women's employment and a significant source of discrimination against women. . . .

BARRIERS TO PATERNAL USE OF PARENTAL LEAVE . . .

1. AVAILABILITY . . .

Prior to the FMLA, [the lack of paternal leave policies] posed an absolute barrier for many working men. Employers were much more likely to provide childbirth leave to women than men. . . . Even when leave was made available to employed fathers, pre-FMLA employer policies tended to hide it from them. For example, Catalyst [a research group] found that ninety percent of large companies that offered parental leave for men did so under the rubric of personal leaves of absence and made no attempt to inform their workforce that the leaves were available to new fathers. It was rare for a company expressly to advise male employees of the availability of paternity or parental leave. Consequently, many men failed to take parental leave because they were completely unaware that it was an available option. Instead, fathers tended to create make-shift leaves of short duration by using accrued vacation and personal days. . . .

2. FINANCING PARENTAL LEAVE

Paid paternal leave policies are extremely rare. When parental leave is available to men, it is almost always without pay. Many mothers, on the other hand, are able to take the initial part of a leave following childbirth as disability leave, which often includes full or partial income replacement benefits. The rarity of paid leave for fathers means that almost all working parents face one of two situations: initial paid leave available to the mother coupled with unpaid leave available to the father or unpaid leave available to both parents. In both cases, the absence of pay poses a major barrier to the father's ability to take leave.

When the leave available to the mother is paid and the leave available to the father is not, it sends a signal to the parents that the mother is expected to take leave and the father is not. It becomes easy for the father not to take leave by reasoning that the children will be cared for with little or no drop in household income if only the mother stays home.

When the leave available to both parents is unpaid, the situation is worsened. Because very few families can afford to have no one bringing home a paycheck, unpaid leave forces fathers to compete with mothers for its use. Traditional sex roles that assign primary caregiving responsibilities to mothers and primary bread-winning responsibilities to fathers ensure that when both parents compete for taking leaves, the mother will tend to monopolize the leave. The decision to allocate the unpaid leave to the mother is also economically rational for many couples in which the father earns the higher income.

The birth of a child usually results in an increase in household expenses and is often accompanied by a decrease in maternal contribution to household income. This exacerbates the effects of the lack of adequate funding for paternal parental leaves. . . .

. . . Sweden's experience suggests that funding parental leave greatly increases paternal participation. [T]he history of the Swedish program has been marked by increased use of leave by fathers. Fewer than three percent of Swedish fathers took parental leave in 1974, the first year it was available, as compared with ninety-eight percent of Swedish mothers. In 1975, the amount of paid leave available to be shared by the couple was increased from six to seven months and paternal participation began to increase. By 1977, it had increased to ten percent. . . . In 1989, Sweden increased the almost fully paid leave to twelve months. [F]athers' participation initially jumped to forty-four percent. Another report shows paternal participation at thirty percent. . . . A reasonable conclusion from Sweden's experience is that removal of financial barriers greatly increases fathers' participation in parental leave.

3. WORKPLACE HOSTILITY

Employer sensitivity to the need to accommodate workers' family responsibilities is increasing steadily. Unfortunately, many employers' willingness to make such accommodations is limited to women workers. Men's accommodation requests are often met by, "Your wife should handle it."

The Catalyst survey graphically illustrates the extent of employer hostility to male employees taking parental leave. Large employers are least likely to experience negative financial effects from fathers taking parental leave. Yet, Catalyst found that sixty-three percent of large employers considered it unreasonable for a man to take any parental leave, and another seventeen percent considered paternal leave reasonable only if limited to two weeks or less. Even among large employers providing paternal leave, an amazing forty-one percent considered it unreasonable for a man to actually use it, and another twenty-three percent considered a reasonable leave for a man to be two weeks or less! It appears that many employers extend parental leave to fathers so that they can give the appearance of gender-neutral policies, but never intend for fathers to use it.

The Catalyst survey responses show glaring and pervasive employer hostility toward men taking parental leave. Confirmation of this problem may be found in other sources. For example, when Catalyst interviewed human resource and other managers, it found them quite candid in their assessments that their companies would take a very negative view of fathers who might take leave to care for their children. Another study found executives more likely to accommodate the family needs of women employees than similarly situated men, including being more likely to grant a female accountant's request for a one-month child-care leave than a male's. Fathers who take parental leave justifiably fear for their jobs and their families' financial security.

Employers are not the only source of workplace hostility. Co-worker hostility can generate powerful peer pressure. Such peer pressure can intimidate and deter fathers from taking leave.

Even when leave is available and communicated to employees and financial barriers are removed, workplace hostility can deter many fathers from taking leave. . . .

■ DIKE v. SCHOOL BOARD
650 F.2d 783 (5th Cir. 1981)

GODBOLD, Chief Judge:

Janice Dike, a teacher in the Orange County (Florida) School System, sued the school board and the superintendent of schools under 42 U.S.C. §1983, challenging the board's refusal to permit her to breastfeed her child. . . .

Dike is employed by the school board as a kindergarten teacher at an elementary school. After giving birth to her child she returned to her teaching post. Having chosen to breastfeed her child, Dike wished to feed the child in this manner at all feedings, including the one feeding necessary during the school day. She sought a means of doing so that would not disrupt the education of children attending the school or interfere with her discharge of work responsibilities.

Dike therefore arranged for her husband or her babysitter to bring the child to school during her lunch period, when she was free from any duties. Dike would then nurse the child in privacy in a locked room into which other persons could not see. On occasions when the school asked Dike to perform duties during her lunch period she would hand the infant to her husband or babysitter. She was thus always available for work even during her duty-free hour. She alleges that this routine did not disrupt the educational process at the school or her work performance.

After three months of this routine without disruption or incident the school principal directed Dike to stop nursing her child on campus, citing a school board directive prohibiting teachers from bringing their children to work with them for any reason. The rule's stated rationale is to avoid possible disruptions by the children of teachers and to avoid the possibility of the children having an accident and subjecting the school board to litigation. The principal threatened disciplinary action should Dike continue to nurse the child at school.

Dike heeded these warnings and stopped nursing her child during the school day. But because the child developed an allergic reaction to formula milk, Dike had to artificially extract milk with a breast pump and leave it for the child's mid-day feeding. Dike asserts this new routine caused the child to develop observable psychological changes that also affected her own emotional well-being. She requested permission to resume her earlier procedure, alternatively requesting permission to nurse the child off campus during her non-duty time or to nurse the child in her camper van in the school parking lot. The school board denied these requests, apparently relying on another policy prohibiting teachers from leaving school premises during the school day.

A short time later the infant began refusing to nurse from a bottle. Dike thus had no choice but to breastfeed the child. Because the school board denied her permission to breastfeed on campus or off, Dike was compelled to take an unpaid leave of absence for the remainder of the school term.

Dike sued the board, alleging that it had unduly interfered with a constitutionally protected right to nurture her child by breastfeeding. [The district court, deeming the action frivolous, dismissed her complaint and awarded attorneys' fees to the defendants.]

The Constitution protects from undue state interference citizens' freedom of personal choice in some areas of marriage and family life. These protected interests have been described as rights of personal privacy or as "fundamental" personal liberties. . . . Among these protected liberties are individual decisions respecting marriage [citing *Zablocki* and *Loving*], procreation [citing *LaFleur* and *Skinner*], contraception [citing *Griswold* and *Eisenstadt*], abortion [citing Roe v. Wade], and family relationships. The Supreme Court has long recognized that parents' interest in nurturing and rearing their children deserves special protection against state interference [citing Pierce v. Society of Sisters, and Meyer v. Nebraska].

Breastfeeding is the most elemental form of parental care. It is a communion between mother and child that, like marriage, is "intimate to the degree of being sacred," Griswold v. Connecticut, 381 U.S. at 486. Nourishment is necessary to maintain the child's life, and the parent may choose to believe that breastfeeding will enhance the child's psychological as well as physical health. In light of the spectrum of interests that the Supreme Court has held specially protected, we conclude that the Constitution protects from excessive state interference a woman's decision respecting breastfeeding her child.

Our conclusion that Dike's interest in breastfeeding is a protected liberty interest, however, is the beginning rather than the end of the constitutional inquiry. . . . The Constitution does not prohibit all restrictions of protected liberties, and the school board may establish by appropriate pleading and proof that its regulations prohibiting teachers from leaving campus or bringing children to school, as applied to teachers who wish to breastfeed their children during non-duty time, further sufficiently important state interests and are closely tailored to effectuate only those interests. . . . The school board's interests in avoiding disruption of the educational process, in ensuring that teachers perform their duties without distraction, and in avoiding potential liability for accidents are presumably legitimate. Whether these or other interests are strong enough to justify the school board's regulations, and whether the regulations are sufficiently narrowly drawn, must be determined at trial. . . .

Notes and Questions

1. *Limited protection?* A significant number of mothers choose to breastfeed their babies. See Amy Harmon, 'Lactivists' Take Their Cause, and Their Babies, to the Streets, N.Y. Times, June 7, 2005 at A19 (pointing out that the number of American mothers who choose to breastfeed has reached 70 percent, compared to 50 percent in 1990). However, as *Dike* illustrates, many women must choose annually between breastfeeding and keeping their jobs. See also Henry Wyatt Christrup, Litigating a Breastfeeding and Employment Case in the New Millennium, 12 Yale J.L. & Feminism 263 (2000). Difficulties about accommodations in the workplace also force some mothers to discontinue nursing. Elizabeth L. Graves, Advantages for All, 25 L.A. Law. 21 (Feb. 2003) (citing research revealing that only 18 percent of working mothers still breastfeed their infants at six months, compared to 29 percent of nonworking mothers).

What is the extent of federal protection for breastfeeding? How should *Dike* be decided under the PDA? Under the FMLA? Under Title VII, does breastfeeding discrimination constitute employment discrimination? Under the Americans with Disabilities Act, is breastfeeding a "disability"? For purposes of the PDA and Title VII, how does one equate breastfeeding women to a "similarly situated" class of men? See Maureen E. Eldredge, The Quest for a Lactating Male: Biology, Gender, and Discrimination, 80 Chi.-Kent L. Rev. 875, 875 (2005) (criticizing the PDA and Title VII by saying that courts refuse to recognize discrimination in such cases when biology makes women different from men).

Limited federal legislation permits a woman to breastfeed on any federal property where women and children have a right to be. The Right to Breastfeed Act, Pub. L. No. 106-58 §647; 113 Stat. 430, 478 (1999). In 2005, Congress considered legislation to amend the PDA to prohibit employment discrimination against breastfeeding mothers, offer employers expense credits for providing employees with a place to breastfeed, establish industry standards for breast pumps, and provide tax deductions for breastfeeding equipment and services. H.R. 2122, 109th Cong. (1st Sess. 2005) (last referred to Subcommittee for Employee-Employer Relations on May 31, 2005).

2. *Criticisms of special treatment.* Can an employer grant special treatment for breastfeeding mothers without providing parental leaves to fathers or to non-breastfeeding women? Professor Sylvia Law, who staunchly supports reproductive rights, opposes special treatment for nursing mothers. She elaborates as follows:

> Does the policy have a substantial impact in perpetuating inequality? It seems that it does. Either parent, or a stranger, is biologically capable of caring for a child. Limiting the childrearing to nursing women reinforces the cultural expectation that "the paramount destiny and mission of woman are to full the noble and benign offices of wife and mother" [Bradwell v. Illinois, 83 U.S. (16 Wall.) 130, 141 (1873)]. Such a policy would have to be struck down because it could not withstand strict scrutiny; the state's interest in promoting the physical or psychic benefits of nursing is not sufficiently substantial to justify the burden upon men and women who would choose to take child care leave but who cannot nurse. Also, the oppressive effect upon women who would prefer not to nurse but are compelled to do so in order to qualify for the leave is not justified by the state's interest.

Sylvia A. Law, Rethinking Sex and the Constitution, 132 U. Pa. L. Rev. 855, 1033-1034 (1984). Do you agree?

3. *Limitation on* Dike. *Dike*'s holding that breastfeeding is a constitutional right based on the right of privacy has been narrowed by subsequent case law. See Christrup, supra, at 272 (discussing these developments). The district court dismissed Dike's claim on remand, finding that the school board's policy was narrowly tailored and based on compelling state interests. Shahar v. Bowers (discussed in Chapter IV), overruled *Dike* insofar as it implicated strict scrutiny review of a government employee's freedom of intimate association claim and upheld, instead, use of the balancing-test approach. Finally, Southerland v. Thigpen, 784 F.2d 713 (5th Cir. 1986) narrowed *Dike* by holding it inapplicable to prison inmates.

4. *Different state approaches.* States that provide statutory protection for breastfeeding take various approaches: (a) some exempt breastfeeding from public nudity and other criminal statutes, (b) some provide an affirmative right to breastfeed wherever mothers and babies are otherwise authorized to be present, (c) some protect breastfeeding via civil rights remedies, (d) some mandate or encourage employer accommodation for breastfeeding, and (e) some exempt breastfeeding women from jury duty. Lara M. Gardner, A Step Toward True Equality in the Workplace: Requiring Employer Accommodation for Breastfeeding Women, 17 Wis. Women's L.J. 259, 262-263 (2002). Six states recently passed laws giving a woman the right to breastfeed wherever she "is authorized to be." Harmon, supra.

Florida (site of *Dike*) followed the first two approaches when it became the first state in 1993 to guarantee the right to breastfeed in public. Legislation was introduced by Rep. Miguel de Grandy (R., Miami) (enacted as Fla. Stat. Ann. §§800.02-04 & §847.001 (West 2003)) after a security guard harassed a nursing mother at a shopping center. Cited in Florida Legislature Guarantees Right to Breast-Feed in Public, S.F. Chron., Mar. 4, 1993, at A3. Cf. Derungs v. Wal-Mart Stores, Inc., 374 F.3d 428 (6th Cir. 2004) (holding that employer's prohibition against breastfeeding in a place of public accommodation does not constitutes sex discrimination under state public accommodation statute).

5. *Protection for pumping breast milk?* Is an employer's unfavorable treatment of a nursing mother who has a need or desire to pump breast milk a form of gender discrimination? Does it violate Title VII? The ADA? See Martinez v. NBC, Inc., 49 F. Supp.2d 305 (S.D.N.Y. 1999) (rejecting claims under the ADA and Title VII for an employer's inadequate accommodation of employee's desire to pump breast milk, reasoning that lactation is not a disability within the ADA and that plaintiff is not similarly situated to male employees as required for prima facie case of "sex-plus" discrimination). Should breast pumping be afforded protection in the workplace? If so, how? See Gardner, supra, at 260 (suggesting that employers be required to accommodate breastfeeding women by requiring flexibility in work hours, paid break time and a private sanitary place to breastfeed or pump, and space to store breast milk). See also Cal. Lab. Code §§1030 et seq. (West 2003) (requiring employers to provide break time and space for employees who are nursing mothers to express breast milk). Or, is breastfeeding just a private lifestyle choice that should not merit such protection? See Elissa Aaronson Goodman, Comment, Breastfeeding or Bust: The Need for Legislation to Protect a Mother's Right to Express Breast Milk at Work, 10 Cardozo Women's L.J. 146, 152-154 (2003) (discussing biological-necessity versus cultural-choice theories).

■ ARLIE HOCHSCHILD & ANN MACHUNG, THE SECOND SHIFT
2-10 (1999)

How well do couples [work two full-time jobs and raise young children]? The more women work outside the home, the more central this question. [The author interviewed 50 working couples to determine their allocation of household tasks.]

[I] discovered that women worked roughly fifteen hours longer each week than men. Over a year, they worked an *extra month of twenty-four-hour days a year.* . . . Just as there is a wage gap between men and women in the workplace, there is a "leisure gap" between them at home. Most women work one shift at the office or factory and a "second shift" at home. . . . It was a woman who first proposed to me the metaphor, borrowed from industrial life, of the "second shift." . . . After eight hours of adjusting insurance claims, she came home to put on the rice for dinner, care for her children, and wash laundry. Despite herself, her home life *felt* like a second shift. . . .

Men who share the load at home seemed just as pressed for time as their wives, and as torn between the demands of career and small children. . . . But the majority of men did not share the load at home. Some refused outright. Others refused more passively, often offering a loving shoulder to lean on, an understanding ear as their working wife faced the conflict they both saw as hers. But I came to realize that those husbands who helped very little at home were often indirectly just as deeply affected as their wives by the need to do that work, through the resentment their wives feel toward them. . . .

[E]ven when husbands happily shared the hours of work, their wives felt more *responsible* for home and children. More women kept track of doctors' appointments and arranged for playmates to come over. More mothers than fathers worried about the tail on a child's Halloween costume or a birthday present for a school friend. They were more likely to think about their children while at work and to check in by phone with the baby-sitter.

Partly because of this, more women felt torn between one sense of urgency and another, between the need to soothe a child's fear of being left at day care, and the need to show the boss she's "serious" at work. More women then men questioned how good they were as parents. . . .

As masses of women have moved into the economy, families have been hit by a "speed-up" in work and family life. There is no more time in the day than there was when wives stayed home, but there is twice as much to get done. It is mainly women who absorb this "speed-up." Twenty percent of the men in my study shared housework equally. Seventy percent of men did a substantial amount (less than half but more than a third), and 10 percent did less than a third. Even when couples share more equitably in the work at home, women do two-thirds of the daily jobs at home, like cooking and cleaning up — jobs that fix them into a rigid routine. Most women cook dinner and most men change the oil in the family car. But, as one mother pointed out, dinner needs to be prepared every evening around six o'clock, whereas the car oil needs to be changed every six months. . . . A child needs to be tended daily while the repair of household appliances can often wait. . . .

Another reason women may feel more strained than men is that women more often do two things at once — for example, write checks and return phone calls, vacuum and keep an eye on a three-year-old, fold laundry and think out the shopping list. . . . Beyond doing more at home, women also devote *proportionately more* of their time at home to housework and proportionately less of it to child care. Of all the time men spend working at home, more of it goes to child care. . . . Since most parents prefer to tend to their children rather than clean house, men do more of what they'd rather do. . . . Men also do fewer of the "undesirable" household chores: fewer men than women wash toilets and scrub the bathroom. . . .

All, in all, if in this period of American history, the two-job family is suffering from a speed-up of work and family life, working mothers are its primary victims. It is ironic, then, that often it falls to women to be the "time and motion expert" of family life. Watching inside homes, I noticed it was often the mother who rushed children, saying "Hurry up! It's time to go." . . . Sadly enough, women are more often the lightning rod for family aggressions aroused by the speed-up of work and family life. They are the "villains" in a process by which they are the primary victims. More than the longer hours, the sleeplessness, and feeling torn, this is the saddest cost to women of the extra month a year.

––––––––––––

See generally Cynthia Fuchs Epstein & Arne L. Kalleberg (eds.), Fighting for Time: Shifting Boundaries of Work and Social Life (2004); Arlie Russell Hochschild, The Commercialization of Intimate Life: Notes from Home and Work (2003); Arlie Russell Hochschild, The Time Bind: When Work Becomes Home and Home Becomes Work (2001); Phyllis Moen & Patricia Roehling, The Career Mystique: Cracks in the American Dream (2004); Yun-suk Lee & Linda J. Waite, Husbands' and Wives' Time Spent on Housework, 67 J. Marr. & Fam. 328 (2005).

Note: Work-Family Conflict Issues

1. *Professional women.* How do professional women experience the work-family conflict? Data reveal that most male lawyers are married with children and have non-working wives. In contrast, women lawyers with children constitute a minority of the profession; almost all are married to men who work full-time. Nancy E. Dowd, Resisting Essentialism and Hierarchy: A Critique of Work/Family Strategies for Women Lawyers, 16 Harv. BlackLetter L.J. 185, 198 (2000). In response to the work-family conflict, women lawyers develop three strategies: some forego marriage and children, some choose areas of practice that better accommodate the family, and some follow male models of work and family by pairing with a nurturing male who serves as a full-time caregiver or by hiring caregivers. Id.

For empirical studies of women lawyers' management of the work-family conflict (although now somewhat dated), see Cynthia Fuchs Epstein, Women in Law (1993); Mona Harrington, Women Lawyers: Rewriting the Rules (1995). For a contrasting study of the working poor's experience with the work-family conflict, see Jonathan Kozol, Rachel and Her Children, Homeless Families in America (1988). See generally Sharon Rabin Margalioth, Women, Careers, Babies: An Issue of Time or Timing?, 13 UCLA Women's L.J. 293 (2005).

2. *Restructuring the workplace.* Professor Joan Williams, a prominent feminist legal scholar, argues that the modern workplace is structured around the "ideal worker," a norm that is based on the male model — i.e., persons who have no child

care responsibilities, who are able to work 40 hours per week, and who can work overtime on short notice. Joan Williams, Unbending Gender: Why Family and Work Conflict and What to Do About It 2-3 (2000). This view leads to significant difficulties for mothers in the workplace as they attempt to juggle work and family responsibilities. Frequent suggestions for restructuring the workplace to accommodate parenting obligations focus on part-time employment and child care.

a. *Part-time employment and child care.* One solution is for employers to offer more *part-time employment.* Many parents, especially when their children are young, may choose to work part-time. Yet, part-time employees often do not receive proportionately equal compensation in terms of salary, benefits, and bonuses; may not be taken seriously by employers; and lose opportunities for professional advancement. Debbie N. Kaminer, The Work-Family Conflict: Developing a Model of Parental Accommodation in the Workplace, 54 Am. U. L. Rev. 305, 352-353 (2004). See generally Carroll Seron et al., The Part-Time Paradox: Time Norms, Professional Lives, Family, and Gender (1998); Silvana Sciarra et al., Employment Policy and the Regulation of Part-Time Work in the European Union: A Comparative Analysis (2004).

Another solution is for employers to offer *affordable child care.* Research reveals that mothers are more than twice as likely to quit their jobs when the employer offers inadequate child care or none at all. Mildred Warner et al., Addressing the Affordability Gap: Framing Child Care as Economic Development, 12 J. Affordable Housing & Community Dev. L. 294, 295 (2003) (citing Sandra L. Hofferth & Nancy Collins, Child Care and Employment Turnover, 19 Population Res. & Pol'y Rev. 4, 357-95 (2000)). Further, the government could provide subsidies to families for child care and provide more funding to improve the quality of child care services. For a recent discussion of family-friendly workplace policies and reforms regarding child care, see Anne L. Alstott, No Exit 141-170 (2004).

On the effects of early child care for the child, family, and society, see generally Child Care and Child Development: Results from the NICHD Study of Early Child Care and Youth Development (NICHD Early Child Care Research Network eds., 2005) (comprehensive scientific study of early child care and its relation to child development); Peggie R. Smith, Caring for Paid Caregivers: Linking Quality Child Care with Improved Working Conditions, 73 U. Cin. L. Rev. 399, 401 (2004).

b. *Gender stereotyping.* Mothers in the workplace often face gender stereotypes about their lack of competence and commitment. Such stereotypes are illustrations, according to Professor Joan Williams, of the "maternal wall." According to Williams, many women never get near the glass ceiling because they first confront a maternal wall — i.e., barriers to the work place advancement of family caregivers in the form of the pervasive perception that a devotion to one's family renders one less capable of performing a job. The maternal wall may arise upon pregnancy, motherhood, or working part-time or on a flexible work arrangement. Joan C. Williams & Nancy Segal, Beyond the Maternal Wall: Relief for Family Caregivers Who Are Discriminated Against on the Job, 26 Harv. Women's L.J. 77, 77-79 (2003).

For additional discussion of the maternal wall, see Joan C. Williams, Beyond the Glass Ceiling: The Maternal Wall as a Barrier to Gender Equality, 26 T. Jefferson L. Rev. 1 (2003); Joan C Williams, Litigating the Glass Ceiling and the Maternal Wall, 7 Employee Rts. & Emp. Pol'y J. 287, 288 (2003).

A recent case, Back v. Hastings on Hudson Union Free School Dist., 365 F.3d 107 (2d Cir. 2004), sheds light on the impact of the "maternal wall." A school psychologist who was denied tenure despite outstanding performance reviews sought damages under 42 U.S.C. §1983 (2000), alleging that the termination violated her right to equal protection. She contended that the real reason she was fired was that the defendants presumed that, as a young mother, she would not continue to demonstrate the necessary devotion to her job. The appellate court found that stereotyping about women as caregivers can be evidence of gender discrimination and that a plaintiff need not prove that the defendants treated similarly situated men differently.

3. *The mommy track.* Given the disproportionate impact of the work-family conflict on mothers, one reform might entail separate employment tracks for different women. In a classic article, Felice Schwartz (founder of the nonprofit consulting firm Catalyst) proposes this solution. Her point of departure is that women in management are more costly for the corporation because these women often interrupt their careers for family responsibilities. Felice N. Schwartz, Management Women and the New Facts of Life, 67 Harv. Bus. Rev. 65 (Jan.-Feb. 1989). Schwartz contends that corporations should distinguish between "career-primary" and "career-and-family" women, by identifying the former early, giving them the same opportunities while recognizing that they face sex stereotypes. On the other hand, the corporation should recognize the need to retain "career-and-family" women and provide them with parental leave, support during relocation, flexible benefits, and quality, affordable child care. Professor Karen Czapanskiy addresses some of the implications of the "mommy track" (the name given by the media to Schwartz's proposal) by highlighting its impact on men and children:

> An ideology of unequal labor allocation is not benign for fathers, either. By permitting employers to assume that every male worker has a female partner caring for the home and children, employers are freed to burden workers with schedules and demands that are inconsistent with family responsibilities or enjoyment. Men are denied social support for developing close relationships with their children. In the event of divorce, men may find themselves deprived of a realistic claim to custody because they have not provided daily care for their children nor learned to be fully competent and involved parents.
>
> Children may be victimized the most by gendered parenting and its second shift consequences. First, they experience and learn to replicate exploitative, antidemocratic family lives. [T]hey will learn that boys fulfill a role which includes very little nurturing behavior, and that girls fulfill one loaded with nurturing, but at a high cost when the nurturing is done by one who works for money. [Both boys and girls may] decide not to have children [or] that someone else, either a wife or a day care worker, will have to take care of any children they have. Because their gendered parents have modelled ways to allocate household labor through exploitation, rather than through mutual respect, negotiation, and power sharing, the relationship of the grownup child from the gendered household with a spouse or day care worker is also likely to be unequal and exploitative. . . .

Karen Czapanskiy, Volunteers and Draftees: The Struggle for Parental Equality, 38 UCLA L. Rev. 1415, 1455-1456 (1991). See also Tony Schwartz, Life/Work, Issue 30 (Dec. 1999), at 362 (reminiscing about the death of his mother Felice Schwartz that "she felt so misunderstood by many of the people whose cause she'd championed for so long," and assessing corporate progress on work-family issues since publication of the "mommy track" article).

4. *Race and the work-family conflict.* The work-family conflict has differential effects on those of different races and socioeconomic classes. For example, as discussed earlier, the FMLA's response to the work-family conflict does not impact all families equally. Professor Nancy Dowd observes that current reform efforts, which focus on making leave a *paid* benefit, do not go far enough to address the problems of many families:

> If not done in tandem with making leave a universal benefit, and if not paid at a level sufficient for single parents and low-income parents to take advantage of leave, then those reforms will continue to reproduce race and class hierarchies. To the extent policy presumes the presence of a male breadwinner (or a female breadwinner who has taken on that economic role), it will deliver a double gender disadvantage that is disproportionately distributed by race. . . .

Nancy E. Dowd, Race, Gender, and Work/Family Policy, 15 Wash. U. J.L. & Pol'y 219, 240 (2004).

Professor Dorothy Roberts also addresses the race and class implications of care work. She identifies a dichotomy between "spiritual" and "menial" housework, rooted in the era of slavery and reflected by plantation owners' reliance on "Mammies" to nurture their children. Separate spheres ideology permitted the idealization of women's "spiritual" (moral) role as caregiver and contributed to the separation of the spiritual from the menial aspects of housework. This dichotomy has contemporary ramifications:

> First, women may delegate housework's menial tasks to others while retaining their more valuable spiritual duties. Second, this fragmentation fosters a hierarchy among women because the menial aspects of housework are typically delegated by more privileged women to less privileged ones. At the same time, the availability of a class of menial workers, sustained by race and class subordination, makes this division of women's housework possible. Although women's participation in the market is now widely accepted, the assignment of household work to women and the distinction between spiritual and menial housework both persist. . . .

Dorothy E. Roberts, Spiritual and Menial Housework, 9 Yale J.L. & Feminism 51, 55-56 (1997).

Problem

Diane McCourtney's employer, Seagate Technology, dismisses the accounts clerk for excessive absenteeism. McCourtney's absences stem from her inability to find affordable day care for her infant who suffers frequent respiratory ailments. Following her dismissal, she files a claim for unemployment benefits, which is contested by Seagate and denied by the state Jobs and Training Department. She appeals. Minnesota, similar to many states, requires claimants to show that they are "available" for work, although such availability may be restricted for "good cause." To what extent is McCourtney available for work? Do the restrictions on her availability reflect "good cause"? Should the result depend on the availability for childcare of McCourtney's husband? See McCourtney v. Imprimis Tech., 465

N.W.2d 721 (Minn. Ct. App. 1991). Cf. Phillips v. Martin Marietta Corp., 400 U.S. 542 (1971).

C. TORT AND CRIMINAL LAW

1. Tort Actions Against Third Parties: Alienation of Affections and Criminal Conversation

■ **JONES v. SWANSON**
341 F.3d 723 (8th Cir. 2003)

BYE, Circuit Judge.

A jury awarded Richard M. Jones $450,000 in compensatory damages and $500,000 in punitive damages against Todd V. Swanson in this diversity action for alienation of affection. Todd appeals. . . .

Donna Jones and Todd Swanson grew up in a small rural South Dakota community. They became romantically involved for a short time in 1977 upon Donna graduating from high school. They rekindled the romance in 1978 and again dated for a short time. The relationship ended in 1978, and the two did not see one another for twenty years until 1998.

In the interim, Todd became an orthopaedic surgeon and moved to Las Vegas, Nevada. He married and raised a family. Donna met Richard Jones shortly after the relationship with Todd ended and was married to him in 1981. Donna and Richard have four children and settled in Sioux Falls, South Dakota. Richard worked as a hospital administrator at Sioux Valley Hospital where Donna also worked as a nurse. . . .

On September 23, 1998, Todd's father suffered a heart attack and was taken to Sioux Valley hospital. [Donna ran into Todd when he came to the hospital.] The two struck up a conversation, and Donna mentioned she was having a birthday the next day. Todd asked if he could buy her lunch and Donna agreed. The next day Donna and Todd met at a restaurant. Todd presented her with a birthday card and informed the waiter it was Donna's birthday. Todd also made arrangements for a special birthday dessert. Todd testified Donna talked about her dissatisfaction with her job and marriage during lunch. In particular, she complained she was not getting as much sex from her husband as she wanted. Todd also testified Donna rubbed her leg against his during lunch.

After lunch, Donna and Todd took a walk in a nearby park. As they walked, Todd put his arm around Donna. When they sat down on a bench, Todd put his hand on her knee. Donna again voiced her dissatisfaction with her marriage, saying she "loved Richard as the father of her children but not as a woman loves a man." Donna invited Todd to kiss her and they kissed several times. Todd remarked he had made a "huge mistake" letting Donna go twenty years earlier, and Donna told Todd she had always loved him.

Todd returned to Las Vegas but about a week later the two spoke over the telephone. There was conflicting evidence at trial as to who placed the first call; both said the other called, but it is undisputed over the next several weeks Todd and

Donna spoke hundreds of times.[3] . . . Todd told Donna he was planning to attend a meeting in San Francisco and asked if she could meet him. Donna agreed. . . .

Before leaving for San Francisco, Todd sent Donna a CD and told her to listen to a song entitled "I'll Go On Loving You." When she arrived at the airport, Todd was there to meet her and gave her a bouquet of flowers. . . . Over the course of the weekend, Todd bought Donna a number of gifts and also took her to some of the meetings he attended. At one of the meetings, Donna met Wolfgang Schweizer, the president of Plus Orthopedics. Schweizer and Donna discussed the possibility of her becoming a sales representative for Plus Orthopedics and invited her to visit the company's European headquarters in December.

After San Francisco, Donna and Todd went back to exchanging telephone calls, cards and gifts. During their calls they talked about leaving their respective spouses and making a life together, including where they would live and how their children would react. Among other things, Todd promised Donna a "Brady Bunch" family and future. In cards to Donna, Todd told her how much he cared for and loved her and how much he looked forward to being with her again. He also expressed concern and guilt over the affair. . . .

At about this time, Donna told Richard she had been invited to Europe by Plus Orthopedics to explore the possibility of future employment. In mid-November, she told Richard she was contemplating divorce. Donna denied any involvement with another man and told Richard she was not sure she loved him anymore.

Days later, Donna's sister-in-law and nephew were killed in a car accident. Todd, who was in Sioux Falls for Thanksgiving, attended the funeral. It was then Richard began to suspect something between Todd and Donna. . . . A few days later, Donna admitted to Richard she was having an affair with Todd. . . .

In December 1998, Donna and Todd went to Europe as planned. . . . After their European vacation Todd and Donna began joint and individual counseling sessions to prepare for what lay ahead. In January, Donna moved out of the family home. Todd had encouraged her to get her own place so he could call whenever he wanted. [S]he traveled to California to meet [Todd] at a medical convention where they spent two days and nights together. It was there, for the first time, Todd suggested ending the affair.

Todd testified he began having doubts about the affair and suggested they reconcile with their spouses. Todd testified he told Donna that Richard was a good man and father, and she needed to work on her marriage because their relationship was not going to work out. Todd's, emotions, however, proved fickle. He later sent Donna a Valentine's Day card telling her how much he loved her. . . . In April 1999, Donna moved back home with Richard and they attempted counseling to save the marriage. On July 4, 1999, Richard gave Donna a diamond ring and begged her to stay and work things out. Later that month, when Todd returned to Sioux Falls for his sister's wedding, Donna contacted him and asked to meet. [They had a picnic lunch together and then had sex at Donna's house.]

After Todd's trip to Sioux Falls in July, the relationship continued to cool until November 1999, when Donna flew to Seattle, Washington [to meet Todd]. This was the last time Todd and Donna were intimate together. Afterwards, Todd told

---

3. Telephone records show Donna placed approximately 386 calls and Todd placed 186 calls. Todd gave Donna access to a calling card so the calls would not show up on her bill and she would not have to pay for them.

Donna to go home and reconcile with her husband because it was not going to work out. Instead of flying home, Donna flew to San Diego where she planned to reconnect with Todd who was attending another seminar. . . . When he arrived in San Diego, he left a message telling Donna he would not be able to meet her. Donna was not dissuaded. Instead she waited for Todd at the airport in San Diego because "she wanted [him] to see [her] one more time."

In May 2000, Richard filed suit against Todd for alienation of affection. Donna moved out of the family home permanently in June 2000, and Richard sued for divorce. . . . On appeal, Todd argues 1) there was insufficient evidence to prove the tort of alienation of affection, 2) there was no causal connection between the affair and the breakup of the marriage, [and] 3) the compensatory and punitive damages awards were unwarranted by the evidence and excessive.[5]

. . . The elements of a claim for alienation of affection are 1) wrongful conduct of the defendant, 2) loss of affection or consortium, and 3) a causal connection between the wrongful conduct and the loss of affection or consortium. The essence of the action is malicious interference with the marriage relationship, and a loss of consortium is the actionable consequence of an action for alienation of affection. Consortium is a right growing out of the marital relationship, and includes the right of either spouse to the society, companionship, conjugal affection, and assistance of the other.

> A wife conceivably may transfer her affection from her husband to another because of the latter's kindliness, attractiveness, desirability, financial superiority, or some other reason. Such motivation for transfer of affection may be a substantial factor even though the defendant had nothing to do with it. *The gravamen of an action for alienation of affection [therefore] is enticement. It is based on an intentional tort, not negligence.* The acts which lead to the loss of affection must be wrongful and intentional, calculated to entice the affection of one spouse away from the other. . . . (emphasis added)

[Pankratz v. Miller, 401 N.W.2d 543, 548-549 (S.D. 1987) (quoting Pedersen v. Jirsa, 125 N.W.2d 38, 43 (Minn. 1963))].

. . . Todd argues the evidence showed the marriage between Donna and Richard was over before he arrived on the scene and his actions did not cause the alienation of Donna's affection. In other words, Todd argues his actions were not the proximate cause of Donna's loss of affection for her husband.

There was considerable evidence tending to show the marriage was on precarious footing before Todd arrived on the scene. In the months leading up to the affair, Donna repeatedly expressed dissatisfaction with her marriage and frequently stayed out late drinking with friends. The encounter [at a party when she was drunk and ended up in bed with a man] further illustrates the uncertainty of the marriage's future, and seriously undermines Donna's testimony claiming she loved Richard. Finally, Donna's counselor testified he met with Donna in November 1998, just as the affair was beginning, and Donna was already on her way out of the marriage.

---

5. Todd also complains the tort of alienation of affection is an anachronism and points out its continued viability as a legitimate cause of action has been roundly criticized. The propriety of South Dakota's decision to recognize alienation of affection as a tort claim is not an issue for this court. Despite repeated invitations, the Supreme Court of South Dakota has refused to judicially abolish the cause of action. . . .

There was, however, also evidence suggesting the marriage may have survived or at very least Donna still had affection for Richard. Donna testified the marriage had been near perfect and minimized the problems leading up to the affair. As the affair wound down, Donna moved back home with Richard and started marriage counseling in an attempt to save the relationship. Despite Donna's attempts to reconcile with Richard, Todd continued to pursue the relationship. Clearly Donna was dissatisfied with the marriage, but the evidence was sufficient for the jury to conclude she harbored affection for Richard which was alienated as a result of Todd's involvement.

Todd also argues he was not solely to blame for the affair. Rather, Donna was infatuated with him and pursued the relationship with even greater enthusiasm than he. Richard's cause of action is not dependent upon finding Donna was an unwilling participant in the affair. It could be argued Donna's willingness to become entangled in the affair demonstrates she had no affection for Richard or Todd's conduct was not the proximate cause of her loss of affection. But the jury concluded Donna still loved Richard despite problems in their marriage and would have continued to love him if Todd had not interjected himself. . . .

Along these same lines, Todd argues Donna was infatuated with him and South Dakota law does not allow a recovery for alienation of affection when the loss of affection results from a wife's infatuation. Todd, however, oversimplifies the holding [of prior case law]. [E]vidence of infatuation may be offered to prove the absence of wrongful conduct or to demonstrate a lack of causation, but it does not obviate a defendant's wrongful conduct. Here, the jury was free to conclude Donna was infatuated but left Richard because of Todd's active enticement.

Todd also argues he never intended to harm Richard. The intent to inflict harm, however, is not an element of the tort. . . . Viewing this evidence in the light most favorable to the verdict, it cannot be said there was insufficient evidence to support the jury's verdict. . . .

[Finally, Todd argues the awards of $450,000 in compensatory damages and $500,000 in punitive damages were excessive.] The court found that the evidence of Donna's pre-affair conduct and her dissatisfaction with the marriage undermines Richard's claim for damages. Accordingly, we conclude the evidence does not support the $ 450,000 award of compensatory damages and must be reduced or a new trial ordered.

. . . Todd next argues there was insufficient evidence to justify an award of punitive damages, and alternatively, the award of punitive damages was excessive. . . . Though not overwhelming, we conclude the evidence was sufficient for the jury to reasonably find Todd acted willfully or wantonly and his actions demonstrated a disregard for Richard's rights. [However, the court found that the award of punitive damages was excessive, based on the facts that, although Todd pursued Donna, she was a willing participant and the marriage was in jeopardy before Todd arrived; Todd repeatedly expressed remorse over the affair; and, the punitive damages award represents nearly half of Todd's annual income and nearly 25 percent of his net worth.]

We conditionally affirm the judgment entered on the verdict in favor of Richard, subject to his acceptance of a remittitur judgment in the amount of $150,000 for compensatory damages and a remittitur judgment in the amount of $250,000 for punitive damages. . . .

■ OSBORNE v. PAYNE

31 S.W.3d 911 (Ky. 2000)

WINTERSCHEIMER, Justice.

... Payne and his wife were experiencing marital difficulties and went to Osborne, their parish priest, for counseling. Ultimately, Payne and his wife were divorced following his discovery of a 45-day adulterous relationship between his wife and Osborne. ... Payne sued the former priest for the tort of outrageous conduct and the Diocese of Owensboro under a vicarious liability theory for its alleged negligent training, screening and supervision of Osborne. ... Payne testified that as a result of discovering the adulterous affair, he suffered a nervous breakdown, lost his religion, lost his house and lost his job as well as his wife. ...

Craft v. Rice, 671 S.W.2d 247 (Ky. 1984), is the seminal case involving the tort of intentional infliction of emotional distress or outrageous conduct in Kentucky. In order to establish such a claim, the plaintiff must prove the following elements: The wrongdoer's conduct must be intentional or reckless; the conduct must be outrageous and intolerable in that it offends against the generally accepted standards of decency and morality; there must be a causal connection between the wrongdoer's conduct and the emotional distress and the distress suffered must be severe. [T]he tort is not available for "petty insults, unkind words and minor indignities" [Kroger Company v. Willgruber, 920 S.W.2d 61 (Ky. 1996)]. Rather, it is intended to redress behavior that is truly outrageous, intolerable and which results in bringing one to his knees.

The circuit court summarily dismissed the claim against the former priest for failure to allege misconduct that was sufficient to satisfy the outrageous element of the tort, relying on Whittington v. Whittington, 766 S.W.2d 73 (Ky. Ct. App. 1989). In that case, the claim of the wife was dismissed under CR 12.02 for failure to state a claim upon which relief can be granted; the circuit court concluded that ordinary fraud and adultery can never reach the status of outrageous conduct.

Here, the most important element of the complaint by Payne, as demonstrated by his deposition testimony, is that he was injured as a result of the misconduct of Osborne while in a special relationship as priest and counselor. Moreover, the alleged exploitation of that relationship occurred in a situation when the former priest was aware that the marriage partners were most vulnerable. ... The establishment of the existence of a special relationship between the parties can make conduct outrageous. The use of a confidential relationship between Payne and his priest counselor is the heart of his lawsuit. ... For the purpose of summary judgment, it is evident that the former priest used his relationship with the husband and the wife to obtain a sexual affair with the wife. Conduct and relationship can form the basis for outrageous conduct. [The court held that a genuine issue of material fact existed as to whether the priest's sexual relationship constituted sufficiently outrageous conduct].

The mere fact that in recent years there has been apparently an increasing number of claims against clergy for sexual misconduct does not make the behavior any less outrageous or disgraceful or otherwise actionable. Some jurisdictions have denied relief under a theory of intentional infliction of emotional distress after concluding that the claims were merely an attempt to bring amatory actions which were no longer viable. See Strock v. Pressnell, 38 Ohio St.3d 207, 527 N.E.2d 1235 (1988). However, we are persuaded by the reasoning used in the cases noted by the Court of Appeals including Destefano v. Grabrian, 763 P.2d 275, 285 (Colo. 1988), in which it was stated that: a plaintiff will not be able to mask one of the abolished actions . . . behind a common law label. However, if the essence of the complaint is directed to a cause of action other than one which has been abolished, that claim is legally cognizable.

We note that this Court abolished the action for breach of promise to marry in Gilbert v. Barkes, 987 S.W.2d 772 (Ky. 1999), but stated that it in no way prohibited other remedies, such as claims for breach of contract and intentional infliction of emotional distress, should a party be able to make such a case. It should be emphasized that these claims must be approached on a case-by-case basis, and there is no blanket or automatic imposition of a cause of action in the clergy/counselor relationship.

Payne next argues that Osborne, as a priest, was engaging in an activity sanctioned by the church and ordinarily performed by a priest, that is, marriage counseling. He argues that it was because Osborne was a priest that he was called upon by them; that his help was sought and that he was invited into the home. Payne reasons that the diocese should be vicariously liable for the actions of Osborne. We cannot agree. To accept such a theory would in effect require the diocese to become an absolute insurer for the behavior of anyone who was in the priesthood and would result in strict liability on the part of the diocese for any actionable wrong involving a parishioner. We must conclude that such an argument is absurd. Certainly, the scope of employment of a priest could include marriage counseling, but it clearly does not include adultery. . . .

Here, Payne has failed to present any evidence in the record that Osborne had a history of sexual misconduct involving parishioners or that the diocese had any knowledge that Osborne might conceivably engage in such misconduct. Consequently, we must conclude that the summary judgment granted by the circuit court and affirmed by the Court of Appeals as to the diocese was correct. . . .

Notes and Questions

1. *Elements.* At common law, interference with the marital relationship was remediable by tort actions for *alienation of affections* and *criminal conversation.* Alienation of affections requires: (1) a valid marriage; (2) wrongful conduct by the defendant with the plaintiff's spouse; (3) the loss of affection or consortium; and (4) a causal connection between the defendant's conduct and the deprivation of affection. Restatement (Second) of Torts §683 (1977).

Unlike alienation of affections, criminal conversation requires sexual intercourse. Restatement (Second) of Torts §685 (1977); Dan B. Dobbs, The Law of Torts §442 (2001). Criminal conversation has been called a strict liability tort because the only defenses are the plaintiff's (that is, the injured spouse's) consent and the statute of limitations. The participating spouse's consent is not a defense.

2. *Abolition movement.* After its initial recognition by New York in 1866, the tort of alienation of affections was adopted by virtually every state. Bruce v. Nguyen, Note, Hey, That's My Wife! — The Tort of Alienation of Affection in Missouri, 68 Mo. L. Rev. 241, 241 (2003). Currently, however, most jurisdictions have abolished alienation of affections and criminal conversation either by statute or case law. W. Dudley McCarter, Supreme Court of Missouri Abolishes Alienation of Affection Tort, 59 J. Mo. B. 157, 157 (2003) (pointing out that 34 states abolished the tort by

statute and six by case law). South Dakota (where *Jones* took place) is one of only eight states to recognize alienation of affections. Michele Crissman, Note, Alienation of Affections: An Ancient Tort — But Still Alive in South Dakota, 48 S.D. L. Rev. 518 (2003). See also Helsel v. Noellsch, 107 S.W.3d 231 (Mo. 2003) (abolishing alienation of affections because it is premised on outdated ideas); Smith v. Smith, S.W.3d 660 (Tex. Ct. App. 2004) (holding that legislative abolition of alienation of affections and criminal conversation does not violate the open court's provision of the state constitution).

3. *Rationales.* What are the rationales for retaining tort liability for alienation of affections and criminal conversation? Formerly, liability rested, in part, on the view of the wife as her husband's property. Does the fact that women now are able to litigate these claims militate against abolition? See Hutelmyer v. Cox, 514 S.E.2d 554 (N.C. Ct. App. 1999); Bland v. Hill, 735 So. 2d 414, 421 (Miss. 1999) (dissenting judge so arguing). Does abolition "send the message that we are devaluing the marriage relationship"? Gorman v. McMahon, 792 So. 2d 307 (Miss. Ct. App. 2001). Do the rationales underlying these torts support imposition of liability on a spouse's same-sex lover? See Jones v. Henderson, 2004 WL 1936496 (Tenn. Ct. App. 2004). Do these rationales support imposition of liability for post-separation sexual misconduct? See Misenheimer v. Burris, 610 S.E.2d 271(N.C. Ct. App. 2005). Can meddling in-laws be liable for alienation of affections?

Should divorce provide the sole remedy? Some jurisdictions have abolished criminal conversation while retaining alienation of affections. See, e.g., Saunders v. Alford, 607 So. 2d 1214 (Miss. 1992); Norton v. Macfarlane, 818 P.2d 8 (Utah 1991). Is this approach preferable?

4. *Damages.* In *Jones,* the appellate court found excessive the jury award of $450,000 in compensatory damages and $500,000 in punitive damages. See also Kathryn Quigley, Costly Love Affair for Florida Physician, S.F. Chron., June 9, 2001 (describing a North Carolina award of $910,000 in compensatory damages and $500,000 in punitive damages). Is the harm from adultery alleviated by monetary relief? Do such huge damage awards argue for or against retention of tort liability?

5. *Alternative theories.* As *Osborne* reveals, abolition of alienation of affections and criminal conversation in many jurisdictions left an unanswered question in cases involving marriage counselors: whether spouses could recover based on alternative theories, such as intentional or negligent infliction of emotional distress. Some courts permit such claims despite abolition of the amatory torts. See, e.g., Scamardo v. Dunaway, 650 So. 2d 417 (La. Ct. App. 1995). More often, however, courts hold that the action is barred as a disguised suit for alienation of affections. See, e.g., Jones v. Henderson, supra; McDormott v. Reynolds, 530 S.E.2d 902, 904 (Va. 2000).

How do claims for intentional infliction of emotional distress differ from alienation of affections and criminal conversation? Should a suit based on alienation of affections preclude a suit based on intentional (or negligent) infliction of emotional distress because the suits are based on the same set of facts? See Heiner v. Simpson, 23 P.3d 1041 (Utah 2001) (refusing to preclude plaintiff from bringing several additional actionable claims under the same set of operative facts). Do the causes of action have the same standard of proof? See id. at 1043 (pointing out that alienation cases in Utah are based on the higher clear-and-convincing standard whereas emotional distress cases are based on a preponderance standard).

Do you agree with the court in *Osborne* that extramarital conduct in the context of a fiduciary relationship increases the degree of outrageousness of the conduct to qualify for a claim of intentional infliction of emotional distress? See also Rosenthal v. Erven, 17 P.3d 558, 562 (Or. Ct. App. 2001) (accord). Criticisms of the imposition of liability for intentional infliction claims in the divorce context are discussed in Chapter V.

Some spouses who are injured by counselors' sexual misconduct assert other theories, such as: breach of fiduciary duty (e.g., Cherepski v. Walker, 913 S.W.2d 761 (Ark. 1996) (barring claim)); and health-care-provider malpractice (e.g., Dowling v. Bullen, 94 P.3d 915 (Utah 2004) (rejecting claim because it was based on conduct during treatment of former husband (not wife) as patient). See generally Paul A. Clark, Tort Law: Applying Respondeat Superior to Psychotherapist-Patient Sexual Relationships, 21 Am. J. Trial Advoc. 429 (1997); Robert J. Maurer, Ohio Psychotherapist Civil Liability for Sexual Relations with Former Patients, 26 U. Tol. L. Rev. 547 (1995). Another possible theory of recovery in limited cases is sexual harassment. See Robert Schwaneberg, Love's Wounded Sue for Damages, Star-Ledger (Newark), Feb. 13, 2000, at 1 (describing several such cases). On divorce lawyers' sexual relationships with clients, see Chapter V, section F3.

6. *Loss of consortium.* Early authorities recognized the husband's right to damages for loss of consortium caused by the defendant's wrongful injury to husband's wife. At common law, however, a wife had no cause of action for intentional or negligent injuries to her husband. Hitaffer v. Argonne Co., 183 F.2d 811 (D.C. 1950), was the first court to permit a wife to recover for negligent injuries to her husband. A majority of jurisdictions followed. The claim for loss of consortium encompasses not merely loss of the sexual relationship, but also loss of comfort, affection, and companionship. For a long time, courts had difficulty recognizing the claim by wives because of concerns that the injury to the wife was indirect and the damages too speculative, a damage award would result in double recovery, and the liability might extend too far to other classes of plaintiffs. See Rodriguez v. Bethlehem Steel Corp., 525 P.2d 669 (Cal. 1974) (rejecting these arguments and extending recovery to wife).

Problems

1. In a jurisdiction that recognizes alienation of affections and criminal conversation, a wife in a dissolution proceeding claims a share (as marital property) in the sums recovered by her husband in his claim for alienation of affections and criminal conversation from the man with whom she had been having an affair. Should she prevail? See T.B.G. v C.A.G. (C.A.M.), 772 S.W.2d 653 (Mo. 1989).

2. Keith and Roberta Thornburgh have been married since 1986. In 1997 Keith discovers that Roberta is having an affair with her supervisor, Wade Hunt, at Federal Express ("Fed Ex"). Keith confronts Wade, who breaks up with Roberta. The Thornburghs reconcile. Soon thereafter, several other Fed Ex employees file grievances regarding Wade's sexual misconduct in the workplace, and evidence of Roberta's affair comes to light. Because of Roberta's distress, the employer offers her a transfer to an out-of-state branch. Keith refuses to transfer, so Roberta moves with their two children while Keith is out of town. Keith files suit against Roberta's employer, alleging alienation of affection, negligent infliction of emotional

distress, and intentional infliction of emotional distress. What result? Thornburgh v. Federal Express, Corp., 62 S.W.3d 421 (Mo. Ct. App. 2001).

3. Edna and Robert Destefano, both Catholic, seek marriage counseling from their priest Dennis Grabrian. Grabian, who has previously engaged in sexual relations with other women who came to him for counseling, becomes sexually involved with Edna. Following the Destefanos' divorce, they sue Grabrian (for negligence, intentional infliction of emotional distress, and breach of fiduciary duty) and the diocese (for breach of its duty to supervise). Grabrian counters that the First Amendment precludes tort liability. The jurisdiction has abolished actions for alienation of affections and criminal conversation. What result? Destefano v. Grabrian, 763 P.2d 275 (Colo. 1988). See also Wende C. v. United Methodist Church, 776 N.Y.S.2d 390 (App. Div. 2004). See generally Lindsey Rosen, Constitutional Law — In Bad Faith: Breach of Fiduciary Duty by the Clergy — F.G. v. MacDonell, 696 A.2d 697 (N.J. 1997), 71 Temp. L. Rev. 743, 748-754 (1998) (discussing cases accepting and rejecting claims of clergy malpractice).

4. A father sues Fox Valley Systems and Crown Cork & Seal Co. on behalf of his two children for injuries they suffered stemming from his blindness. The father was injured by an explosion of spray paint allegedly defectively manufactured by defendant. He sues to recover damages to his children from loss of his parental care, love, and guidance. Should the action for loss of consortium extend to a *child* for injury to a parent? See Klaus v. Fox Valley Sys., 912 P.2d 703 (Kan. 1996). Conversely, can *parents* of non-fatally-injured children recover damages for loss of consortium? Reagan v. Vaughn, 804 S.W.2d 463 (Tex. 1990). See generally Benny Agosto, Jr., & Mario A. Rodriguez. What about the Parents?: Can the Parents of a Non-Fatally-Injured Child Recover Damages for Loss of Consortium?, 66 Tex. B.J. 396 (2003).

2. Tort Actions Between Spouses

a. Interspousal Immunity

■ G.L. v. M.L.
550 A.2d 525 (N.J. Super. Ct. Ch. Div. 1988)

KRAFTE, J.S.C.

Do sexual relations between spouses constitute "marital or nuptial privileges" ... thereby entitling any sexual tort committed by one spouse upon the other to interspousal immunity? This court finds that they do not.

The plaintiff in this matter filed for divorce on November 2, 1984. Included in her complaint were four separate counts for personal injury alleging that her husband, the defendant, transmitted genital herpes to her during their marriage. The defendant's insurance carrier, defending against the negligence claim and the defendant's attorney in the matrimonial proceeding defending against the intentional tort claim now join together in bringing a motion for summary judgment dismissing the personal injury counts. . . .

Our highest court examined and incorporated the history and nature of interspousal immunity in Merenoff v. Merenoff, 76 N.J. 535, 539-547, 388 A.2d 951 [N.J. 1978] and abrogated the doctrine regarding tortious conduct stating, ". . . where personal injuries are tortiously inflicted by one spouse upon another, it is just and fair that compensation in appropriate circumstances be afforded the wronged and injured party and, to this end, a suit be allowed to effectuate such recovery." Id. at 557. The *Merenoff* court recognized that there was a range of activity in a marital relationship, characterized as "special matters of privacy and familiarity" beyond the reach of the law of torts because they "fall outside the bounds of a definable and enforceable duty of care" and are encompased [sic] by a marital or nuptial privilege. Id. These areas were not left intact, however, were seen as potential exceptions to the otherwise abrogated doctrine and were to be ultimately defined and developed on a case-by-case basis by future courts. . . .

In the present action, the plaintiff alleges that the defendant continued to have sexual relations with her even after discovering that he had herpes, the result of an extramarital relationship. It is argued by the defendant that sexual intercourse between spouses is by its very nature an act which falls within the scope of a marital or nuptial privilege and therefore his conduct should be shielded from liability. This Court does not agree. It is unconscionable that a person could escape liability for infecting a spouse with genital herpes or other sexually transmitted disease by merely claiming that the transmission occurred during privileged sexual relations of marriage. . . .

Defendant misconstrues the meaning of marital privilege and furthermore destroyed any that may have existed by his own intentional involvement in an extramarital relationship. Defendant cannot simultaneously breach his marital relationship by engaging in extramarital intercourse, and claim nuptial immunity for consequences flowing from his own wilful and intentional conduct. . . .

As to the intentional aspect of the personal injury claim, it is clear that the abolition of the interspousal immunity doctrine pertains to intentional tortious conduct as well as conventional negligence. Plaintiff first observed symptoms of the herpes simplex virus on defendant's body in February 1983, but accepted his explanations to the contrary. Defendant argued that he never intended to inflict the plaintiff with herpes as he was never officially diagnosed until 1987, almost three years after the filing of the complaint. However defendant admitted in his deposition that he told plaintiff of his extramarital affair prior to the couple's separation. It was also stated by the parties' former housekeeper that defendant told plaintiff that he had contracted herpes as a result of this affair and was sorry to have infected her. Defendant has since denied this conversation. Regardless, the intentional act was not that of knowingly transmitting herpes to plaintiff but, rather, it was the act of sexual intercourse with the plaintiff after sexual relations with someone else with whom he carried on a two-year relationship. Such behavior on defendant's part placed plaintiff at risk of physical harm.

There remains a duty of care to one's spouse and the threat of physical harm cannot be excused. "Consent to sexual intercourse vitiated by one partner's fraudulent concealment of the risk of infection with venereal disease is equally applicable today, whether or not partners involved are married to each other." Kathleen K. v. Robert B., 150 Cal. App. 3d 992, 198 Cal. Rptr. 273, 277 (Ct. App. 1984). The Supreme Court of New York has also indicated its willingness to consider a personal injury action for the transmission of genital herpes between spouses. See Maharam v. Maharam, 510 N.Y.S.2d 104, 123 A.D.2d 165 (App. Div. 1986). While allowing that interspousal immunity may exist as a narrow exception in some areas, the [New Jersey] Court was very clear that it ". . . should not be viewed as a catalyst which renders wrongful acts innocuous." *Tevis*, 79 N.J. 422, 429, 400 A.2d 1189 [N.J.

1979], citing Merenoff v. Merenoff, and Long v. Llandy, 35 N.J. 44, 171 A.2d (N.J. 1961). Indeed, at one time, states considered the transmission of syphilis by husband to wife a criminal assault. See State v. Lankford, 29 Del. 1594, 102 A. 63, 64 (Ct. Gen. Sess. 1917). Although a criminal charge is not being addressed, the defendant can not be allowed to hide behind the veil of marital privilege.

This Court holds that the marital privilege of sexual relations does not include immunity to personal injury suits between spouses based upon the transmittal of a sexual disease. Motion for summary judgment is denied. . . .

Notes and Questions

1. *Interspousal immunity.* At common law, the doctrine of interspousal immunity precluded interspousal tort suits. The doctrine was premised on the legal fiction of marital unity (i.e., because husband and wife shared a legal identity, interspousal tort suits were impossible). Passage of the Married Women's Property Acts in the mid-nineteenth century led to recognition of interspousal tort suits regarding women's property. However, the majority of courts continued to adhere to interspousal immunity for personal torts, reasoning that interspousal suits would be fictitious and fraudulent (especially against insurance companies), and that such suits would destroy marital harmony. Abrogation occurred first for intentional acts and, subsequently, for negligent acts. Currently, 46 states have abrogated the doctrine, either fully or partially. Bozman v. Bozman, 830 A.2d 450, 487 (Md. Ct. App. 2003) (abrogating the doctrine and explaining its history). Cf. Gates v. Gates, 587 S.E.2d 32 (Ga. 2003) (confirming that the doctrine still exists in Georgia).

2. *Statute of limitations.* Spouses often pursue interspousal tort litigation at separation or divorce. As a result, statutes of limitations may bar their claims. See, e.g., Dubovsky v. Dubovsky, 725 N.Y.S.2d 832 (N.Y. Sup. Ct. 2001). One commentator points out that short tort statutes of limitation for assault, battery, and other traditional intentional torts (compared to those for negligence or strict liability) "have a powerful impact in limiting [interspousal] claims." Jennifer B. Wriggins, Domestic Violence in the First-Year Torts Curriculum, 54 J. Legal Ed. 511, 513 (2004).

Further, in transmission-of-venereal-disease cases, the infected spouse may be charged with the exercise of reasonable diligence in discovering the nature of the infection (and that knowledge may trigger operation of the statute of limitations). See, e.g., Hamblen v. Davidson, 50 S.W.3d 433 (Tenn. Ct. App. 2000) (holding that a fact issue existed regarding wife's exercise of reasonable diligence). Should a husband's false representation that he is not infected with herpes toll the statute of limitations? See Beller v. Tilbrook, 571 S.E.2d 735 (Ga. 2002). On the problems associated with joinder of the tort action and the divorce action, see Chapter V, pp. 531–532.

3. *Scope of liability.* To what extent should interspousal liability, which first emerged in cases of negligent driving, extend to household accidents? See Brown v. Brown, 409 N.E.2d 717 (Mass. 1980) (wife sustained injuries as a result of husband's allegedly negligent removal of snow). Are there aspects of marital life that should not give rise to liability? Consider the following (posed by the husband's attorney in *Brown*): (1) Wife puts too much salt in meals; Husband gets high blood pressure; (2) Husband wants to have children; Wife does not. She gets pregnant.

(3) Husband normally takes out the garbage. He forgets; Wife lifts the heavy bag and hurts her back. 6 Fam. L. Rep. (BNA) 1162 (Aug. 26, 1980).

4. *Availability of insurance.* Often, the possibility of insurance forms the basis of the interspousal claim. Yet, the ability to file interspousal tort claims is undercut by exclusions in many automobile and homeowners' insurance policies. Most liability policies exclude intentional acts as well as negligent acts if the claimant is a relative of the insured. Such "family member exclusion" clauses similarly limit the availability of relief for domestic violence torts. Wriggins, supra. See also Stearman v. State Farm Mutual Automobile Co., 849 A.2d 539 (Md. 2005) (holding that household exclusion that reduced the limit of liability coverage for bodily injury to the statutory minimum amount was valid in a suit by an insured who was injured as a passenger in a vehicle driven by the spouse).

5. *Privacy.* How persuasive is the rationale for preserving interspousal immunity in cases of sexual torts, according to *G.L.*? Is there more "family privacy" to preserve in this context? See generally Michelle J. Anderson, Marital Immunity, Intimate Relationships, and Improper Inferences: A New Law on Sexual Offenses by Intimates, 54 Hastings L.J. 1465 (2003) (advocating elimination of marital immunity for sexual assaults).

Many feminist legal theorists criticize the interspousal tort immunity doctrine as an example of the lack of legal protection for women in the "private sphere" of family life. For the classic article, see Nadine Taub & Elizabeth M. Schneider, Perspectives on Women's Subordination and the Role of Law, in The Politics of Law: A Progressive Critique 328 (David Kairys ed., 1998). See also Jonathan E.C. May, The Maryland Survey: 2002-2003, 63 Md. L. Rev. 859, 882 (abrogation of interspousal immunity doctrine "removes an arbitrary rule whose effect discriminated against married individuals, and especially married women").

6. *Transmission of venereal disease: background.* Since the early twentieth century, courts have recognized tort liability for transmission of venereal disease. See, e.g. Crowell v. Crowell, 105 S.E. 206 (N.C. 1920). Some early cases, although recognizing the tort of negligent transmission, barred recovery based on interspousal immunity. See, e.g., Bandfield v. Bandfield, 75 N.W. 287 (Mich. 1898). The erosion of the interspousal immunity doctrine permitted litigation of such cases. See *Hamblen*, supra, at 439 ("we join the majority of states [which hold] that an individual who knows or should know he has a venereal disease has a legal duty to use reasonable care in preventing the disease's transmission"). Most courts, similar to *G.L.*, currently extend interspousal liability to cover the transmission of herpes. Common theories of liability in herpes cases include: negligence (and negligence per se), battery, fraudulent misrepresentation, and intentional infliction of emotional distress.

Historically, concern about the impact of venereal disease on the family stemmed in part from several factors, including the influence of the eugenics movement (i.e., the belief that social ills are transmitted through the family by heredity); concerns about immigration (i.e., the belief that immigrants had high rates of infection); worry about industrialization (i.e., a belief in the immorality engendered by city living); and concerns about the sexual double standard (i.e., the belief that dissolute husbands transmitted venereal disease to chaste young women). See generally Allan M. Brandt, No Magic Bullet: A Social History of Venereal Disease in the United States Since 1880 (1987); Sex, Sin and Suffering: Venereal Disease and European Society Since 1870 (Roger Davidson & Lesley A. Hall eds., 2001).

Some states (e.g., California, Florida) have laws that make criminal the transmission of HIV or AIDS. See Sherri Ackerman, AIDS Activist, Patient Gets Real With Teens, Tampa Trib., Apr. 26, 2004, at 1 (relating work of an AIDS activist who won a $5 million tort judgment against his former partner, a San Francisco health commissioner, but whose criminal case was dismissed on grounds of insufficient evidence of intent).

7. *Duty to disclose?* The Restatement of Torts postulates that a spouse has a duty to disclose physical conditions that make cohabitation dangerous. Restatement (Second) of Torts §554 (1977). Does an infected spouse have an affirmative duty to disclose a sexually transmitted condition? See Maharam v. Maharam, 510 N.Y.S.2d 104 (App. Div. 1986) (holding that 31-year marriage gives rise to affirmative duty to disclose herpes). Does the infected spouse's ignorance of his or her disease preclude liability? See McPherson v. McPherson, 712 A.2d 1043 (Me. 1998) (denying recovery because husband, who had an affair, did not know he was infected).

8. *HIV-related status.* Similarly, do spouses have a duty to disclose to each other their HIV- or AIDS-related status? See Doe v. Doe, 519 N.Y.S.2d 595 (Sup. 1987) (holding that wife's allegations for fraud and intentional infliction of emotional distress stemming from husband's failure to disclose past homosexual liaisons, based only on her *possible* exposure to AIDS, were insufficient to state valid causes of action). A case pending in the California Supreme Court explores the extent of the duty to disclose, and also the extent to which the constitutionally protected right of privacy constitutes a limitation on discovery. See John B. v. Superior Court, 18 Cal. Rptr.3d 48 (Ct. App. 2004) (holding that discovery permitted by Court of Appeal of husband's previous sexual partners violated right to privacy; wife was entitled to discover circumstantial evidence that husband knew or should have known he had HIV; wife's inquiries about husband's "lifestyle" were impermissibly intrusive; and husband waived right to privacy of his medical records and results of HIV tests), *review granted sub nom.* John B. v. Bridget B.,100 P. 3d 869 (Cal. 2004). Do children have legal rights against a parent when that parent wrongfully transmits a sexual disease to the other parent? See Josette M. LeDoux, Interspousal Liability and the Wrongful Transmission of HIV-AIDS: Argument for Broadening Legal Avenues for the Injured Spouse and Further Expanding Children's Rights to Sue Their Parents, 34 N. Eng. L. Rev. 392 (2000).

9. *Disclosure by third parties.* How far does the obligation to disclose extend? For example, does the obligation extend to *third parties* to disclose the exposure to an innocent spouse (or sexual partner)? What are the competing policy concerns for mandating such disclosure?

a. Partner notification laws. Many states mandate reporting of communicable diseases, including sexually transmitted diseases, as public health measures dating back to the nineteenth century. Following the onset of the AIDS epidemic in 1981, all states mandated reports by laboratories and physicians of those persons newly diagnosed with AIDS; these reports are then sent to the Centers for Disease Control. Sharron Salmon, Note, The Name Game: Issues Surrounding New York State's HIV Partner Notification Law, 16 N.Y. Sch. J. Hum. Rts. 959, 965 (2000). Currently, 39 states have such laws. Lou Chibbaro, Jr., HIV Names Reporting Gaining in Popularity, Wash. Blade, Dec. 2, 2005, available at http://washblade .com/2005/12-2/news/national (last visited Dec. 8, 2005).

A common component of these laws is a partner notification provision. Some state laws request that the patient contact past and present sex partners. Other provisions place the responsibility for notification on trained health personnel who locate contacts based on information provided by the patient. Still other provisions follow a hybrid model in which health care providers obtain information from the patient about sexual partners but give the patient a period of time to contact partners; failure to do so within the designated time period results in the health care provider informing partners of their exposure while keeping the patient's identify confidential. Salmon, supra, at 968.

b. *Third-party insurance protection for failure to disclose?* Must an insurance company cover a defendant's *family members* in an action for their failure to disclose to a victim that she was exposed to a sexually transmissible disease? In F.S. v. L.D., 827 A.2d 335 (N.J. Super. Ct., 2003), a woman sued a former boyfriend and his adult resident children for negligent infliction of emotional distress in regard to their respective failures to inform her that he was HIV-positive. The insured (boyfriend), together with his adult children, brought a third-party action against their insurance company, alleging that the insurer owed a duty to defend the action under their homeowners' policy. The appellate court ruled that, while the insurer need not indemnify the homeowner in connection with charges that he intentionally refused to tell a girlfriend he was infected with HIV (because of the policy's exclusion of intentional acts), it must cover the homeowner's adult children, who lived in the house and were named defendants in the suit, based on their failure to disclose his infection.

Problem

Wife has an extramarital affair with a doctor. She contracts an unspecified venereal disease from her lover and transmits the disease to Husband. Husband sues Wife, alleging that she was negligent in failing to notify him that she had had an extramarital affair and therefore was at risk of passing a sexually transmissible disease to him. Husband also sues the lover for negligence in failing to notify Wife that he had a sexually transmissible disease and might transmit the disease to her, knowing that Wife was married and at risk of infecting her spouse. The lover defends by asserting that the action is barred by anti-heart balm legislation. How should the court rule on Husband's claim and the lover's defense? See Mussivand v. David, 544 N.E.2d 265 (Ohio 1989).

b. Wiretapping

■ GLAZNER v. GLAZNER
347 F.3d 1212 (11th Cir. 2003)

DUBINA, Circuit Judge:
. . . After being married 19 years, James Glazner filed for divorce against his wife, Elisabeth Glazner. During the divorce proceedings, James put a recording device on a telephone in the marital home. The device recorded a number of conversations between Elisabeth and third parties without the consent of any party to the conversations. Elisabeth discovered the device and filed a complaint in the United States District Court for the Northern District of Alabama against James seeking damages as a result of an alleged violation of Title III, and damages for a number of state law claims.

Elisabeth based her federal claim on the wiretapping provisions of Title III, 18 U.S.C. §§2510-22. Parts of that law prohibit non-consensual recordings of private conversations, subject to certain specified exceptions, and authorize civil remedies on behalf of those who suffer violations of the statutory provisions. During the course of the litigation, James filed a motion for summary judgment. Notwithstanding a finding by the district court that James wiretapped Elisabeth's conversations with third parties, the district court granted James's motion for summary judgment based on [Simpson v. Simpson, 490 F.2d 803 (5th Cir. 1974)], which read an interspousal exemption into the provisions of Title III. . . . Elisabeth filed a timely notice of appeal. . . .

Title III broadly prohibits the interception of wire communications. To determine whether or not James's actions constitute a violation of Title III, we must first look to the language of the statute itself. Title III states:

(1) Except as otherwise specifically provided in this chapter any person who —
(a) intentionally intercepts, endeavors to intercept, or procures any other person to intercept or endeavor to intercept, any wire, oral, or electronic communication . . . shall be punished . . . or shall be subject to suit. . . .

The statute expressly gives "*any* person whose wire, oral, or electronic communication is intercepted, disclosed, or intentionally used in violation of this chapter" the right to bring a civil action against "the person or entity . . . which engaged in that violation." 18 U.S.C. §2520(a) (emphasis added).

In the present case, Elisabeth is "any person" within the meaning of §2520(a). James is "any person" within the meaning of §2511(1)(a). Finally, Elisabeth's conversations that James caused to be intercepted and recorded are any "wire, oral, or electronic communication" within the meaning of §2520(a). The language of Title III is clear and unambiguous. It makes no distinction between married and unmarried persons or between spouses and strangers. It plainly applies to "any person" on both sides of the violation (save only the inapplicable exceptions).

The one circumstance in which a court may properly look beyond the plain language of a statute is where giving effect to the language used by Congress would lead to a truly absurd result. Neither the court in *Simpson* nor any of the parties in this case suggest that the absurdity exception applies to prevent Title III's provisions from governing interspousal behavior. The language of Title III demonstrates that Congress decided that one spouse should not be permitted to record, without consent, electronically transmitted conversations between the other spouse and third parties. This prohibition is not truly absurd.

Equally compelling is the fact that, since the Fifth Circuit decided *Simpson* nearly three decades ago, an overwhelming majority of the federal circuit and district courts, as well as state courts, addressing the issue have refused to imply an exception to Title III liability for interspousal wiretapping. [The court cites twelve cases in support and only three to the contrary.] We are persuaded by the reasoning of all the courts which have refused to find an exception for interspousal wiretapping either explicitly in the text of Title III or implicitly in the legislative history. While we agree with the dissenters that the concept of the rule of law underlying our Constitution requires a substantial measure of continuity, certainty, and respect for precedent, we must follow the Supreme Court's instruction that *stare decisis* should be abandoned where, as here, "a prior judicial ruling should come to be seen so clearly as error that its enforcement was for that very reason doomed." Therefore, we hold that no exception for interspousal wiretapping exists in Title III. . . .

[W]e now turn to the . . . analysis to determine whether the rule overruling *Simpson,* which we announce today, should apply retroactively or prospectively. [W]e examine whether "retrospective operation will further or retard [the rule's] operation." [Chevron Oil Co. v. Huson, 404 U.S. 97, 107 (1971)]. We first note that the purpose of Title III is to "prohibit[ ] all wiretapping and electronic surveillance by persons other than duly authorized law enforcement officials. . . ." 1968 U.S.C.C.A.N. 2112, 2113. Title III partly effectuates this purpose by providing for a civil damages action for victims of illegal wiretapping. 18 U.S.C. §2520. Applying the new *Glazner* rule retroactively would unquestionably further the purpose and operation of Title III by compensating past victims of illegal interspousal wiretapping and, at the same time, deterring those persons who are either currently wiretapping their spouses or planning to do so in the future. Furthermore, we fail to see how applying the statute retroactively would, in any way, retard its operation or purpose. In fact, we see more danger of retarding Title III's operation and purpose by applying it prospectively-only. Therefore, we conclude that the . . . analysis clearly weighs in favor of retroactive application.

We next turn to . . . whether making the rule retroactive would be inequitable. In applying the rule that we announce today retroactively, the primary inequity is the potential for such retroactive application to create liability where none previously existed. If this were truly a situation where the class of persons affected by the new rule would suddenly face a strong likelihood of liability when they faced no possibility of liability before, we would be inclined to view the equities as weighing heavily in favor of pure prospective application. However, such is not the case here. Every state in this circuit has made wiretapping of the sort in which James engaged a crime. . . . Even though retroactive application of the rule we announce today may result in alternative liability in federal court for this class, we conclude that this extension of liability is not sufficiently inequitable to justify prospective-only application given that the class would already be facing felony prosecution, imprisonment, fines, and potential civil liability under state law. . . .

Notes and Questions

1. *Primary issues.* Unauthorized eavesdropping may occur in matrimonial disputes to discover evidence of a spouse's extramarital affair. Among the issues that arise, the first concerns the existence of interspousal civil or criminal liability under federal law. *Glazner* represents the majority rule, finding no interspousal immunity from liability under federal law. The second issue concerns the admissibility of illegally obtained evidence in divorce proceedings. This issue has receded in importance with the advent of no-fault divorce. However, admissibility issues still arise in the custody context. See, e.g., Stinson v. Larson, 893 So. 2d 462 (Ala. Civ. App. 2004) (allowing admission of mother's recordings of conversations between ex-husband and child in custody dispute). See generally Richard C. Turkington, Protection for Invasions of Conversational and Communication Privacy by Electronic Surveillance in Family, Marriage, and Domestic Disputes Under Federal and State Wiretap and Store Communications Acts and the Common Law Privacy

Intrusion Tort, 82 Neb. L. Rev. 693, 700-716 (2004) (addressing current law regarding admissibility in custody disputes).

2. *Federal law.* Title III ("the Wiretap Act") was enacted to protect individuals from nonconsensual interception of wire or oral communications. With certain exceptions (for example, law enforcement officers by court order and agents of the communications common carrier to protect the property rights of the carrier), the act imposes civil and criminal liability by the creation of a new tort, a new crime, and evidentiary rules excluding use of the contents. The act entitles an injured party to recover actual damages of a minimum of $200 per day for each day of violation or $10,000, whichever is greater, plus punitive damages, reasonable attorneys' fees, and litigation costs. 18 U.S.C. §2520(c)(2)(B) (2000).

3. *Trend.* In *Glazner,* the Eleventh Circuit Court of Appeals joined the emerging trend among federal courts (i.e., the 4th, 6th, 8th, 10th, and 11th Circuits) to impose liability for spousal wiretapping in the home under Title III. Only two federal courts of appeal (the 2nd and 5th Circuits) previously found that Congress did *not* intend Title III to apply in this context. However, *Glazner* overruled the decision of its predecessor circuit court (Simpson v. Simpson, 490 F.2d 803 (5th Cir. 1974)), which became binding on the Eleventh Circuit Court of Appeals when the Fifth Circuit was reorganized into two new circuits in 1980.

4. *International protection.* Professor Anita Allen points out that some international guarantees are more explicit than our Constitution about the right to privacy in the home. Anita L. Allen, Uneasy Access: Privacy for Women in a Free Society 59, 191 n.12 (1988). For example, the United Nations Universal Declaration of Human Rights states: "No one shall be subjected to arbitrary interference with his privacy, family home or correspondence, nor to attacks upon his honour and reputation. Everyone has the right to protection of the law against such interference or attacks." Similarly, the European Convention on Human Rights, Article 8, provides: "Everyone has the right to respect for his privacy and family life, his home, and his correspondence."

The Patriot Act ("Uniting and Strengthening America by Providing Appropriate Tools Required to Intercept and Obstruct Terrorism Act"), Pub. L. No.170-56, enacted in October 2001 to give federal authorities wider surveillance powers in the face of terrorism, expands the government's wiretapping ability by permitting "roving surveillance" of cell phones, voice mail, and e-mail. Alison A. Bradley, Extremism in the Defense of Liberty? The Foreign Intelligence Surveillance Act and the Significance of the USA Patriot Act, 77 Tul. L. Rev. 465, 485 (2002).

5. *Rationale.* Why impose liability for interspousal invasions of privacy? To discourage or punish eavesdropping? To penalize revelation to third parties? How are wiretapping and taping different from eavesdropping on an extension phone (which is not prohibited)? Professor Allen describes three forms of domestic privacy: "The first two domestic privacies are inaccessibility of the person in the senses of seclusion and anonymity. . . . The third is inaccessibility of personal information, especially the non-disclosure, through secrecy and confidentiality, of personal facts, opinions, or creative expressions contained in documentary form." Allen, supra, at 60. Does this classification help identify the problem in the wiretapping cases?

Glazner determined that the abolition of the interspousal wiretapping exception applied retroactively to Mr. Glazner. Do you agree that retroactive application would have a deterrent effect — either for those persons who are currently wiretapping their spouses or for those planning to do so in the future?

6. *State protections.* A number of states have passed statutes similar to the federal law. See, e.g., Ohio Rev. Code Ann. §2933.52 (Banks-Baldwin 1997); Va. Code Ann. §§19.2-62, 19.2-69 (Michie 2000). The American Bar Association also has developed a model civil statute that differs from the Wiretap Act in requiring the defendant to know that the surveillance was unlawful; it has no provision for liquidated or punitive damages. ABA Standards for Criminal Justice, Standard 2-6.4 (3d ed. 2001).

Should a spouse be entitled to a "good faith" defense based on the belief that there was nothing illegal about tapping a home phone? Would you recommend adoption of the ABA Standard that would not impose liability in such circumstances? See also Milke v. Milke, 2004 WL 2801585 (D. Minn. 2004) (rejecting husband's "good faith" defense as unsupported by either the law or the facts).

7. *Vicarious consent.* Consent to intercepting the communication precludes the imposition of liability under the federal Wiretap Act. Various federal circuits have wrestled with the issue whether a parent can vicariously consent to the recording of her minor child's phone calls. Should liability arise for interceptions of communications between the other spouse and the couple's children? In Newcomb v. Ingle, 944 F.2d 1534 (10th Cir. 1991), a divorced mother who had custody of two boys recorded her husband's telephone conversations, including one in which the husband instructed the boys as they set fire to the home. The recordings led to the husband's conviction for arson and to juvenile proceedings against the children. On reaching his majority, the older son brought suit. Does he has a cause of action under Title III?

Is spousal wiretapping qualitatively different from parental interceptions? Is a minor's expectation of privacy reduced? Consider the following:

> Once the desire for privacy develops in small children, their parents may justifiably deny them their desired levels of privacy on paternalistic grounds to assure discipline and safety. Teenagers living at home are typically allowed greater privacy than small children. But they may find that their phone calls and visitors are monitored, their bedrooms shared with younger siblings, and their diaries read. In a related vein, they may find that their sexual and reproductive preferences, their "decisional privacy," is effectively pre-empted. . . .

Allen, supra, at 162.

The Sixth Circuit first adopted the vicarious consent doctrine for parental wiretapping in Pollock v. Pollock, 154 F.3d 601 (6th Cir. 1998) (upholding a mother's claim that she acted in child's best interests stemming from her concern that her ex-husband was subjecting the daughter to psychological abuse). See also Stinson v. Larson, 893 S. 2d 462 (Ala. Civ. App. 2004); Apter v. Ross, 781 N.E.2d 744 (Ind. Ct. App. 2003) (both upholding parent's vicarious consent to record child's conversations with other parent). Should parents *always* be entitled to the vicarious consent exemption, or should courts intervene in some cases to protect children's privacy rights? See State v. Christensen, 102 P.3d 789 (Cal. Ct. App. 2004) (holding that state law requires the consent of *all* parties and has no parental exception). See generally Debra Bogosavljevic, Can Parents Vicariously Consent to Recording a Telephone Conversation on Behalf of a Minor Child?: An Examination of the Vicarious Consent Exception Under Title III of the Omnibus Crime Control and Safe Streets Act of 1968, 2000 U. Ill. L. Rev. 321 (2001) (criticizing the exemption on privacy grounds); Turkington, supra, at 710-711 (explaining criticisms of parental exercise of consent).

Problems

1. Attorney William T. Wuliger is retained by David Ricupero to represent him in a divorce. Ricupero records his wife's telephone conversations, including those with her priest, marriage counselor, attorney, and friends. He gives the tapes to Wuliger, informing Wuliger falsely of his wife's knowledge. Wuliger transcribes the tapes and has summaries prepared. Mrs. Ricupero learns of the taping in a hearing on her charges of domestic violence. Wuliger uses the tapes to impeach her, to question her lover (whom she later married), and to examine her about her alleged concealment of marital funds. Mrs. Ricupero charges Wuliger with violations of Title III. What result? Should attorneys receive special treatment under the act? See *United States v. Wuliger*, 981 F.2d 1497 (6th Cir. 1992).

2. After Husband and Wife decide to divorce, Husband begins sleeping in the family's sun room. Wife and the couple's three children continue to use the room regularly because the room contains the family computer and entertainment center. When Wife discovers a letter from Husband's girlfriend in the sun room, she hires an investigator to copy Husband's files from the computer's hard drive. (Husband mistakenly believes that his e-mail cannot be read without his Internet Service Provider password.) In the couple's subsequent custody dispute, Wife seeks to introduce e-mail messages (both received and sent that were saved on Husband's hard drive) between Husband and his girlfriend. Husband argues for suppression of the evidence as a wrongful invasion of his privacy and a violation of the state wiretap act that prohibits a spouse from intercepting the electronic communications of the other without authorization. What result? See *White v. White*, 781 A.2d 85 (N.J. Super. Ct. 2001).

3. Domestic Violence: Wife Beating[*]

a. Introduction

■ **RICHARD J. GELLES & MURRAY A. STRAUS,**
INTIMATE VIOLENCE
84, 88-96 (1988)

. . . The range of homes where wife beating occurs seems to defy categorization. One can pick up a newspaper and read of wife beating in a lower-class neighborhood and then turn the page and read that the wife of a famous rock musician has filed for divorce claiming she was beaten. . . .

---

[*] Although both husbands and wives are victims of domestic violence, the Editors use the term "wife beating" (rather than "spousal abuse") based on the feminist view that gender-neutral terms obscure the nature of this social problem. See Michele Bograd, Feminist Perspectives on Wife Abuse: An Introduction, in Feminist Perspectives on Wife Abuse 13 (Kersti Yllo & Michele Bograd eds., 1988).

The profile of those who engage in violence with their partners is quite similar to the profile of the parents who are abusive toward their children. The greater the stress, the lower the income, the more violence. Also, there is a direct relationship between violence in childhood and the likelihood of becoming a violent adult. Again, we add the caution that although there is a relationship, this does not predetermine that all those who experience violence will grow up to be abusers.

One of the more interesting aspects of the relationship between childhood and adult violence is that *observing* your parents hit one another is a more powerful contributor to the probability of becoming a violent adult than being a victim of violence. The learning experience of seeing your mother and father strike one another is more significant than being hit yourself. Experiencing, and more importantly observing, violence as a child teaches three lessons:

1. Those who love you are also those who hit you, and those you love are people you can hit.
2. Seeing and experiencing violence in your home establishes the moral rightness of hitting those you love.
3. If other means of getting your way, dealing with stress, or expressing yourself do not work, violence is permissible. . . .

Lurking beneath the surface of all intimate violence are confrontations and controversies over power. Our statistical evidence shows that the risk of intimate violence is the greatest when all the decision making in a home is concentrated in the hands of one of the partners. . . .

It goes without saying that intimate violence is most likely to occur in intimate settings. Occasionally couples will strike one another in the car. Husbands sometimes grab their wives at a party or on the street. Husbands or wives rarely slap their partners in public. The majority of domestic combat takes place in private, behind closed doors. . . .

[T]he bedroom is the most lethal room in the house. The criminologist Marvin Wolfgang reported that 20 percent of *all* victims of criminal homicide are killed in the bedroom. The kitchen and dining room are the other frequent scenes of lethal violence between family members.

After 8:00 P.M. the risk for family violence increases. This is almost self-evident, since this is also the time when family members are most likely to be together in the home. . . . The temporal and spatial patterns of intimate violence support our notion that privacy is a key underlying factor that leads to violence. Time and space constrain the options of both the offender and the victim. As the evening wears on, there are fewer places to run to, fewer places to hide. . . .

. . . When we looked at which day of the week violence was most likely to occur, we found that [w]eekends are when families spent the most time together and when the potential for [conflict] is greatest. Not surprisingly, seven out of ten violent episodes we talked about with family members took place on either Saturday or Sunday. Weekends after a payday can be especially violent. . . .

Common sense would not suggest that violence is most likely to erupt at times of the year when families celebrate holidays and the spirit of family togetherness. Yet, contrary to common sense, it is the time from Thanksgiving to New Year's Day and again at Easter that violence in the home peaks. . . .

A number of factors may contribute to the likelihood of domestic violence and abuse during the Christmas season. This is a time when families can assume tremendous financial burdens. Purchasing Christmas gifts can either take a toll on a family's resources or plunge a family into debt. Stress can also come from *not* buying gifts and presents. . . . Holidays also create nonfinancial stress. Christmas and Easter holidays project images of family harmony, love, and togetherness. Songs, advertisements, and television specials all play up the image of the caring, loving, and even affluent family. A family with deep conflict and trouble may see these images in sad and frustrating contrast with their own lives. . . .

Time of day and time of year analysis supports the notion that privacy and stress are important structural components to domestic violence. . . .

■ U.S. DEPT. OF JUSTICE, BUREAU OF JUSTICE STATISTICS, FAMILY VIOLENCE STATISTICS INCLUDING STATISTICS ON STRANGERS AND ACQUAINTANCES
*1-3 (June 2005)**

Family violence accounted for 11% of all reported and unreported violence between 1998 and 2002. Of these roughly 3.5 million violent crimes committed against family members, 49% were crimes against spouses, 22% were sons or daughters victimized by a parent, and 41% were crimes against other family members.

The most frequent type of family violence offense was simple assault. Murder was less than half of 1% of all family violence between 1998 and 2002. About three-fourths of all family violence occurred in or near the victim's residence. Forty percent of family violence victims were injured during the incident. Of the 3.5 million victims of family violence between 1998 and 2002, less than 1% died as a result of the incident.

The majority (73%) of family violence victims were female. Females were 84% of spouse abuse victims and 86% of victims of abuse at the hands of a boyfriend or girlfriend. While about three-fourths of the victims of family violence were female, about three-fourths of the persons who committed family violence were male. Most family violence victims were white (74%), and the majority were between ages 25 and 54 (65.7%). Most family violence offenders were white (70%), and most were age 30 or older (62%).

FATAL FAMILY VIOLENCE

About 22% of murders in 2002 were family murders. Nearly 9% were murders of a spouse, 6% were murders of sons or daughters by a parent, and 7% were murders by other family members. Females were 58% of family murder victims. Of all the murders of females in 2002, family members were responsible for 43%. . . . Eight in ten murderers who killed a family member were male. Males were 83% of spouse murderers and 75% of murderers who killed a boyfriend or

---

* These statistics on family violence are derived from surveys conducted by the Bureau of Justice Statistics (BJS), the BJS database of federal statistics, and two statistical databases maintained by the FBI.

girlfriend. In 2002 family murders were less likely than nonfamily murders to involve a firearm (50% versus 68%). . . .

FAMILY VIOLENCE REPORTED TO POLICE

Approximately 60% of family violence victimizations were reported to police between 1998 and 2002. . . . The most common reason victims of family violence cited for not reporting the crime to police was that the incident was a "private/personal matter" (34%). Another 12% of non-reporting family violence victims did not report the crime in order to "protect the offender."

Among the 2.1 million incidents of family violence reported to police between 1998 and 2002, 36% resulted in an arrest. . . .

FAMILY OFFENDERS IN PRISON

Of the nearly 500,000 men and women in State prisons for a violent crime in 1997, 15% were there for a violent crime against a family member. Nearly half of all the family violence offenders in State prisons were serving a sentence for a sex offense against a family member. . . .

Convicted family violence offenders made up about 22% of the nearly 86,500 convicted violent offenders in local jails in 2002. Most (60%) of these approximately 18.700 jail inmates incarcerated for family violence were in jail for an aggravated assault.

Local jail inmates convicted of family violence reported that—

- their victims were predominantly female (70%)
- nearly 30% of their victims were under age 18.

Among local jail inmates convicted of family violence, 55% injured their victim. . . . Among jail inmates convicted of family violence, 45% had been subject to a restraining order at some point in their life. About 18% were under an active restraining order at the time of admission to jail. . . .

■ BEVERLY HORSBURGH, LIFTING THE VEIL OF SECRECY: DOMESTIC VIOLENCE IN THE JEWISH COMMUNITY
18 Harv. Women's L.J. 171, 172-173 (1995)

. . . You can't know my life. My story would be a bestseller. He hit me before we married—chased me around the room when I refused to marry him. After we married it was much worse. He drank a lot and took drugs. He became even more violent when he was drinking. He was two different people. In public he was the famous doctor, holier than God, loved by all. In private, he was a monster. He controlled absolutely everything. At our home in Miami Beach he wanted the air-conditioning at 72 degrees. If I changed it, he would scream, hit, carry on so. The radio station he liked had to be on in every room. I wasn't allowed to touch it. It was his way or no way. He also beat the children. We have six children. When the children talked in bed past bedtime he would make them do push-ups. Those poor little kids, trying to do push-ups, so young. If they stopped, he would get out the strap or a hanger from the closet. I couldn't interfere. I would get such a smack across the face, my nose would bleed.

I couldn't leave him. It would break my parents' hearts to know that I was unhappy. I had six children. I was not educated. I didn't speak good English. I had no job skills. Where could I go with six kids? I told no one. If I told the rabbi, he would want to talk to my husband and then he would really kill me. I was raised not to complain about your personal problems. You don't hang your dirty laundry outside. It would hurt his practice if I told our friends. Besides, he threatened if I left him he would kill me, himself, and the children. Also, he told me he would disappear and I would never see a cent. Once he showed me a newspaper article about a husband who murdered his wife. He told me he would do this too. . . .

b. Battered Woman Syndrome

■ **HAWTHORNE v. STATE**
408 So. 2d 801 (Fla. Dist. Ct. App. 1982)

PER CURIAM. . . .
This was appellant's second trial for the murder of her husband. Her first conviction, for first degree murder, was reversed by this court in Hawthorne v. State, 377 So. 2d 780 (Fla. 1st DCA 1979). [Defendant's husband was shot to death in the early morning hours of January 28, 1977, in the Hawthorne home by bullets fired from a number of weapons belonging to the deceased.] The last argument by appellant that warrants discussion is that the trial court erred in disallowing the testimony of Dr. Lenore Walker, a clinical psychologist who would have testified as an expert with regard to the battered-woman syndrome. The purpose of such testimony would have been to give the jury a basis for considering whether appellant suffered from the battered-woman syndrome, not in order to establish a novel defense, but as it related to her claim of self-defense. We are aware of the conflicting decisions of various jurisdictions as to the admissibility of this type of expert testimony. See, e.g., Smith v. State, 247 Ga. 612, 277 S.E.2d 678 (1981); State v. Thomas, 66 Ohio St. 2d 518, 423 N.E.2d 137 (1981); Buhrle v. State, 627 P.2d 1378, 1378 (Wyo. 1981); Ibn-Tamas v. United States, 407 A.2d 626 (D.C. App. 1979). The courts that have considered the admissibility of this type of expert testimony have generally analyzed it to see whether it meets three basic criteria: (1) the expert is qualified to give an opinion on the subject matter; (2) the state of the art or scientific knowledge permits a reasonable opinion to be given by the expert; and (3) the subject matter of the expert opinion is so related to some science, profession, business, or occupation as to be beyond the understanding of the average layman. Basically, the same criteria are applicable in the instant case.

The few case authorities which have considered the admissibility of this type of expert testimony disagree primarily with regard to (1) whether the study of the battered-woman syndrome is an area sufficiently developed to permit an expert to assert a reasonable opinion, and (2) whether the battered-woman syndrome is beyond the knowledge and experience of most laymen.

In *Ibn-Tamas* and *Smith*, the courts concluded that the expert testimony should have been allowed, inasmuch as the subject matter was "beyond the ken of the average layman." 277 S.E.2d at 683. "[T]he expert's testimony explaining why a person suffering from battered woman's syndrome would not leave her mate, would not inform police or friends, and would fear increased aggression against herself, would be such conclusions that jurors could not ordinarily draw for themselves." Id. The court in *Ibn-Tamas* also concluded that the expert could provide "an interpretation of the facts which differed from the ordinary lay perception," therefore the subject matter was "beyond the ken of the average layman." 407 A.2d at 635. The *Ibn-Tamas* court determined, however, that the trial court had not ruled on whether the expert, Dr. Lenore Walker, was sufficiently qualified to give an opinion or whether "the state of the pertinent art or scientific knowledge" would permit an expert opinion. 407 A.2d at 635. The court said that this third criterion depended on "whether Dr. Walker's methodology for identifying and studying battered women" was generally accepted. 407 A.2d at 638. The question whether the second and third criteria were satisfied was remanded to the trial court.

In State v. Thomas, the Ohio Supreme Court, determined that expert testimony by a psychiatric social worker was properly excluded because the battered-woman syndrome, was within the jury's understanding and also that the syndrome "is not sufficiently developed, as a matter of commonly accepted scientific knowledge, to warrant testimony under the guise of expertise." 423 N.E.2d at 140.

In Buhrle v. State, the Wyoming Supreme Court, in rejecting Dr. Walker's testimony on the syndrome, said that "we are not saying that this type of expert testimony is not admissible; we are merely holding that the state of the art was not adequately demonstrated to the court, and because of inadequate foundation the proposed opinions would not aid the jury." 627 P.2d at 1378.

We agree with the view expressed by the Georgia Supreme Court in Smith v. State insofar as it concluded that jurors would not ordinarily understand "why a person suffering from battered-woman's syndrome would not leave her mate, would not inform police or friends, and would fear increased aggression against herself. . . ." 277 S.E.2d at 683. In the instant case, however, there has been no determination below as to the adequacy of Dr. Walker's qualifications or the extent to which her methodology is generally accepted indicating that the subject matter can support a reasonable expert opinion. Our determination that this expert testimony would provide the jury with an interpretation of the facts not ordinarily available to them is subject to the trial court determining that Dr. Walker is qualified and that the subject is sufficiently developed and can support an expert opinion.

Appellee argues that to admit this type of expert testimony would violate the rule . . . that "testimony regarding the mental state of a defendant in a criminal case is inadmissible in the absence of a plea of not guilty by reason of insanity," [Zeigler v. State, 402 So. 2d 365, 373 (Fla. 1981)]. In this case, a defective mental state on the part of the accused is not offered as a defense as such. Rather, the specific defense is self-defense which requires a showing that the accused reasonably believed it was necessary to use deadly force to prevent imminent death or great bodily harm to herself or her children. The expert testimony would have been offered in order to aid the jury in interpreting the surrounding circumstances as they affected the reasonableness of her belief. . . . Appellant did not seek to show through the expert testimony that the mental and physical mistreatment of her affected her mental state so that she could not be responsible for her actions;

rather, the testimony would be offered to show that because she suffered from the syndrome, it was reasonable for her to have remained in the home and, at the pertinent time, to have believed that her life and the lives of her children were in imminent danger. It is precisely because a jury would not understand why appellant would remain in the environment that the expert testimony would have aided them in evaluating the case. . . .

Reversed and remanded for a new trial.

■ DR. LENORE WALKER, TERRIFYING LOVE: WHY BATTERED WOMEN KILL AND HOW SOCIETY RESPONDS
23-41 (1989)

I first met Joyce Hawthorne three years after [husband] Aubrey's death.

An ordinary-looking woman of forty, about 5'3" tall, weighing about 150 lbs., she didn't attract much attention. Her smile was rare but sweet; her eyes sparkled when she laughed. She looked just like the church-going mother of five that she was. Judging by her appearance alone, no one would have known that she'd killed a man much larger than herself, firing five guns in the process, even if sometimes her facial expression, at rest, revealed her fear and unhappiness. . . .

Joyce never denied that she'd fired the fatal shots; rather, although she had no memory of it, she claimed that she had been justified in firing them because she had wanted to protect herself and her family from assault, rape, and death. . . . Although she did not remember shooting her husband, she had initially confessed to doing it in order to get the police to release her five children, who were being held for questioning at the time.* [Her prior conviction of first degree murder was reversed because evidence of her husband's alleged abuse toward her and the children was improperly excluded.]

In reversing the judge's previous decision, an appellate court had ruled that evidence about the extensive family abuse in this case could be introduced in the upcoming trial; but nothing had been specifically stated about the permissibility of allowing an expert witness to explain what Joyce's behavior had meant. . . .

Battered Woman Syndrome had not previously been used in the state of Florida to support a self-defense argument (although several other states had, by that time, permitted such testimony in courts of law). Before, it would have been much more common for a woman like Joyce to plead insanity, arguing that her husband's terrible abuse had rendered her temporarily insane. . . . Shortly after Aubrey's death, Joyce Hawthorne had been examined by a psychiatrist, who had found that she knew right from wrong, the legal standard for Florida's insanity plea. I, too, would find that Joyce Hawthorne was legally sane — but terrified that she and her family would be slaughtered, just as Aubrey had threatened. In my opinion, her belief that she and her children were in danger that night had been reasonable, and reasonable perception of imminent physical danger is the legal standard for acting in self-defense.

---

* Two years later, the appellate court ruled that the police should not have promised to release her children in order to force her to give a statement, especially after she and her attorney had already exercised her right not to talk to the detectives. It is never considered a "voluntary" statement when someone is forced to talk under duress. . . .

. . . I agreed with [defense attorney] Leo Thomas that a second jury would have to be carefully educated as to how and why this soft-spoken, church-going mother of five had been able to kill the father of her children. . . . Leo knew that, without understanding the long history of marital abuse Joyce had endured, the average person sitting on a jury could not be expected to comprehend why she had believed her husband would kill her when she refused his sexual advances. . . .

But Battered Woman Syndrome would provide the appropriate explanation; it would delineate the perception of imminency,** and show how that perception was affected by the woman's state of mind. It would make her state of mind comprehensible, because battered women are always afraid of being hurt; any crisis situation may be perceived as a matter of life or death. . . .

Leo Thomas realized that he would have to educate this second jury . . . to make them understand why Joyce hadn't divorced Aubrey despite the daily horror of their marriage; he would have to corroborate Joyce's reports of domestic violence, even if no one else had seen Aubrey beat her; he would have to introduce convincing evidence to demonstrate that Joyce's fear had been reasonable on the night she finally killed him. All this would mean persuading the jury that Aubrey Hawthorne's repeated abuse of his wife had so affected her state of mind that she'd believed she needed to shoot him, to stop him from hurting her — as she perceived him coming toward her, even before he'd actually touched her — on that night in January 1977. Leo would have to help Joyce persuade the jury that her acute state of terror had induced her to use no less than five guns that night, firing at least nine bullets into her husband's body; that, in fact, her behavior had been a demonstration not of anger but of fear. . . .

. . . Most women are at a serious disadvantage when facing an attack from a man who is not only physically stronger but more ready and willing to fight. And battered women who kill are really like battered women who don't kill — they endure the same harassment, the same psychological torture; they experience the same terror — except that they have partners who are ready, able, and willing to kill them. When a battered woman kills her abuser, she has reached the end of the line. She is absolutely desperate, in real despair. She believes, with good reason, that if she does not kill, she will be killed. . . .

After being sworn in, I [found myself] the silent center of a swirling legal argument. . . .

"Dr. Walker is not being presented to testify as to Joyce Hawthorne's mental status," I heard Leo say. "We are not trying to test Florida's insanity standards under the law." . . .

"If Dr. Walker tells the jury what effect the Battered Woman Syndrome had on Joyce Hawthorne's state of mind at the time she killed Aubrey Hawthorne, then she will be testifying as to a mental condition," Ron Johnson countered. "No notice of an insanity plea has been received, and therefore she shouldn't be permitted to testify. The state has the right to examine the defendant if an insanity plea is filed; therefore, we would have been denied that right." . . .

"Judge, this is justifiable homicide we are arguing, not excusable homicide, which would have been a mental health defense. Dr. Walker can testify as to the reasonableness of Joyce Hawthorne's perception that she was in imminent danger

---

** The term *imminent* as it is defined in self-defense statutes usually means "to be on the brink of," not "immediate," as is its more common interpretation.

when she shot her husband. We say she acted in self-defense, not out of a disturbed mental condition." . . .

Ron Johnson assumed a threatening stance. "If you let her testify, Judge, then she takes away the role of the jury to decide if Joyce Hawthorne's perceptions of danger were reasonable. You'll open the door to allow any woman to kill a man she doesn't like, and get away with it!" . . .

"She is a noted feminist," Johnson continued, "she admits to it right here on page 15 of the introduction to her book *The Battered Woman*, so we all know she's biased against men. This woman would have decent people justify the actions of any woman who kills a man, just because he tells her to obey him. It will be open season on killing men, your honor, and you mustn't allow it!" . . .

I knew of no feminists who'd advocated killing men as a way to equalize power. . . . I heard Leo Thomas echo some of my thoughts to the judge.

"Dr. Walker will not be invading the jury's province. The appellate court judges in the case of *Ibn-Tamas vs. the United States* ruled that they needed a psychologist to explain the defendant's state of mind. This is not a feminist issue, your honor. It is about what happens to a woman when she lives with a man whom she loves and who beats her." . . .

Notes and Questions

1. *Epilogue.* Joyce Hawthorne's conviction for first-degree murder was reversed because of, inter alia, the introduction of illegally obtained confessions and the exclusion of testimony about the decedent's violent actions, 377 So. 2d 780 (Fla. Dist. Ct. App. 1979). Her second conviction for second-degree murder was reversed when the appellate court remanded for a determination of the admissibility of BWS evidence (the principal case here). Upon rehearing, the trial court rejected the evidence, reasoning that its scientific basis was not sufficiently accepted. The appellate court affirmed. 470 So. 2d 770 (Fla. Dist. Ct. App. 1985). After Hawthorne was again charged with murder, her attorney successfully argued that a retrial (her fourth) would constitute cruel and unusual punishment.

2. *Common law.* English common law recognized the right of husbands to discipline their wives by use of physical force. Recall Blackstone, supra p. 237. Divorce, rather than criminal sanctions, was considered the appropriate remedy. Further, the interspousal immunity doctrine precluded tort recovery. American common law followed this tradition until the mid-1800s, when courts began to repudiate the right of husbands physically to chastise their wives. During the late nineteenth century, most courts declared wife beating illegal. All jurisdictions currently have a broad range of remedies for spouse abuse, including civil protection orders, civil and criminal liability for assault and battery (attempted murder and murder), and tort liability for intentional infliction of emotional distress. Restraining orders are discussed infra.

On the history of domestic violence legislation, see Linda Gordon, Heroes of Their Own Lives: The Politics and History of Family Violence, Boston, 1880-1960 (2002); Elizabeth Haflin Pleck, Domestic Tyranny: The Making of Social Policy Against Family Violence from Colonial Times to the Present (1989); Elizabeth Schneider, Battered Women and Feminist Lawmaking (2002).

3. *Battered woman's syndrome.* Battered women who kill their husbands often rely on evidence of the battered woman syndrome (BWS), a theory of behavior that characterizes a relationship of physical abuse. BWS derives from the research of psychologist Lenore Walker, who posits: (1) the "cycle theory of violence" and (2) the theory of "learned helplessness." Walker theorizes that abuse occurs within a three-phase cycle: (a) the tension-building phase — a gradual escalation of tension during which the batterer displays hostility and dissatisfaction and the woman attempts to placate him; (b) the acute battering incident in which the batterer explodes into uncontrollable rage (often out of proportion to the situation); and, (c) the contrition phase in which the batterer shows remorse and promises to end the abuse. Despite the promises, the cycle inevitably begins anew.

Walker's theory of "learned helplessness" purports to explain why women stay in a battering relationship even though they could have left their spouses. Relying on the work of by Martin Seligman (Helplessness: On Depression, Development, and Death (1975)) involving shocks to laboratory animals, Walker explains that a battered woman becomes so depressed from the repeated battering that she loses motivation to respond or leave. Lenore Walker, The Battered Woman Syndrome 117-118, 126-127 (2000). BWS is also sometimes analogized to post-traumatic stress disorder (the psychiatric syndrome first diagnosed among veterans of the Vietnam War).

4. *Criticisms.* Walker's theories and BWS have prompted many criticisms. One commentator summarizes the various arguments regarding BWS as follows: (1) it promotes stereotypes of women as helpless, (2) it inaccurately portrays women as mentally ill and hysterical, (3) it fails to explain that victims respond in different ways, (4) it disadvantages minorities, (5) it provides special treatment to defendants in violation of equal treatment and antidiscrimination ideals, and (6) its use as a defense is subject to sexist applications by judges and juries. Sharan K. Suri, Note, A Matter of Principle and Consistency: Understanding the Battered Woman and Cultural Defenses, 7 Mich. J. Gender & L. 107, 126-127 (2000). See also Melanie Randall, Deconstructing the "Image" of the Battered Woman: Domestic Violence and the Construction of "Ideal Victims": Assaulted Women's "Image Problem" in Law, 23 St. Louis U. Pub. L. Rev. 107, 120-121 (2004). For methodological criticisms of Walker's research, see David Faigman, The Battered Woman Syndrome in the Age of Science, 39 Ariz. L. Rev. 67 (1997); David Faigman, Note, the Battered Woman Syndrome and Self-Defense: A Legal and Empirical Dissent, 72 Va. L. Rev. 619, 640-641 (1986).

5. *Defenses.* Expert testimony has been used to support two types of defenses for spousal homicide. Early cases offered syndrome evidence to prove insanity or diminished capacity. Subsequently, BWS was introduced to support a claim of self-defense (as in the principal case). Traditionally, the battered woman who kills her husband faces difficulties in using self-defense because (1) a person must use only proportional force against unlawful armed force; (2) the victim must reasonably fear that she is in imminent danger of bodily harm (and precedents defining "reasonableness" and "imminence" were developed for paradigms such as "the bar room brawl," not intimate violence); (3) the victim cannot have been the aggressor; and (4) in some jurisdictions, the victim must seek to retreat before using deadly defensive force. See Douglas A. Orr, Weiland v. State and Battered Spouse Syndrome: The Toothless Tigress Can Now Roar, 3 Fla. Coastal L.J. 125, 130 (2000) (discussing the "castle doctrine" and noting that Florida joined

the majority of states by deciding that the duty to retreat does not apply when defendant and victim are occupants of the same house). See also Kit Kinports, Deconstructing the "Image" of the Battered Woman: So Much Activity, So Little Change: A Reply to the Critics of Battered Women's Self-Defense, 23 St. Louis U. Pub. L. Rev. 155, 163 (2004) (discussing duty to retreat).

The following problems arise regarding the use of BWS evidence: First, the woman may use lethal force (a gun or knife) against a man who has attacked with his hands. Second, the victim may not pose an immediate threat because he may be incapacitated at the time of the killing (for example, he is asleep or drunk). Third, the woman appears to be the aggressor in the fatal attack. Finally, her husband is a lawful occupant of the dwelling. BWS evidence overcomes these problems by addressing the reasonableness of the perception of the imminence and seriousness of the danger. Applying Walker's theory, the woman experiences the growing tension of phase one and acute battering of phase two. In response, she develops a constant fear of serious bodily harm that she perceives as imminent partially because of the unpredictability of her spouse's rage. Further, the cycle theory of violence also addresses the element of the reasonableness of the amount of force necessary to repel the attack by suggesting that the woman perceives herself trapped in a cycle of potentially deadly violence and feels compelled to use deadly force to preempt the attack of the more powerful, even though perhaps unarmed, aggressor.

6. *Admissibility of evidence:* Frye *and* Daubert. As the principal case reveals, states initially were resistant to the admission of evidence on BWS. However, all 50 states and the District of Columbia now admit such evidence, at least to some degree, either by statute or case law. Janet Parrish, U.S. Dept. of Justice, Trend Analysis: Expert Testimony on Battered and Its Effects on Criminal Cases 12-17 (1996). See also David L. Faigman et al., Modern Scientific Evidence: The Law and Science of Expert Testimony, The Battered Woman Syndrome and Other Psychological Effects of Domestic Violence Against Women (2005) (especially chapter 15 discussing "Scientific Status").

To determine the admissibility of novel scientific evidence, federal courts traditionally relied on the standard set forth in Frye v. United States, 293 F. 1013 (D.C. Cir. 1923): evidence is admissible if it has become generally accepted by scientists in the particular field of study. This classic formulation was superseded by Daubert v. Merrell Dow Pharmaceuticals, Inc., 509 U.S. 579 (1993), which adopted Federal Rule of Evidence 702, and provided that evidence may be admitted if it is helpful to the trier of fact and also, if the methodology is scientifically valid. *Daubert* technically applies to federal courts, but many state courts now adhere to it. Historically, some courts had difficulty finding that BWS met one of these evidentiary standards; however, currently BWS is generally admissible regardless of whether a given jurisdiction follows *Frye* or *Daubert*. Myrna S. Raeder, A Primer on Gender-Related Issues that Affect Female Offenders, 20 Crim. Jus. 4, 11 (2005).

7. *Admissibility for other purposes.* In *Hawthorne,* the issue of admissibility of BWS testimony pertained to the battered woman's claim of self-defense. Courts sometimes have wrestled with the admissibility of BWS testimony for other purposes, such as to bolster the woman's credibility. See, e.g., Minnesota v. Vance, 685 N.W.2d 173 (Minn. Ct. App. 2004) (affirming the admission of BWS testimony to help a jury understand victim's *recantation* of her earlier account in a prosecution

for assault and criminal sexual conduct); People v. White, 780 N.Y.S.2d 727 (N.Y. Dist. Ct. 2004) (denying state's motion to introduce BWS testimony to aid jury understand victim's nine-week *delay in reporting* of assault because testimony would have been more prejudicial than probative).

8. *Implications of* Crawford. Problems sometimes arise for prosecutors because corroboration of battering may be difficult (as the act takes place in private), and victims may not be able to testify (e.g., due to fear, unwillingness, or death). Admission of hearsay evidence in domestic violence cases was fairly common-place before 2004. Tom Lininger, Prosecuting Batterers After *Crawford,* 91 Va. L. Rev. 747, 751 n.21 (2005). In that year, the United States Supreme Court decided Crawford v. Washington, 541 U.S. 36 (2004), a case with significant implications for prosecutions of domestic violence. During investigation of a stabbing, the suspect's wife made a recorded statement that contradicted her husband's claim of self-defense. The state sought to admit her statement that was barred by the husband's assertion of the marital privilege. The court admitted the wife's statement as an exception to the hearsay rule (i.e., an out-of-court statement bearing sufficient indicia of reliability). The U.S. Supreme Court reversed the husband's conviction, holding that the use of the wife's recorded statement violated the Confrontation Clause because the Sixth Amendment requires witness unavailability *and* a prior opportunity for cross-examination when out-of-court testimonial statements are at issue.

Crawford has had a dramatic impact on prosecution of domestic violence by severely limiting the opportunity for admission of victims' and witnesses' out-of-court statements if these persons are unavailable for trial (e.g., afraid to testify), and if their statements are deemed "testimonial" (i.e., made for the purpose of prosecution). As Professor Tom Lininger notes,

> [W]ithin days — even hours — of the *Crawford* decision, prosecutors were dismissing or losing hundreds of domestic violence cases that would have presented little difficulty in the past. For example, during the summer of 2004, half of the domestic violence cases set for trial in Dallas County, Texas, were dismissed because of evidentiary problems under *Crawford.*

Id. at 749-750. In two domestic violence cases, the Supreme Court clarified the meaning of testimonial hearsay. In Davis v. Washington, 2006 WL 1667285 (2006), the Court held that statements to 911 operators are not testimonial and therefore admissible because they are elicited to resolve an emergency. However, in the consolidated case of Hammon v. Indiana, admission of a victim's statement to a responding police officer violates the right to confrontation (absent the opportunity for cross-examination) because the officer was investigating a possible crime.

9. *Federal legislation: VAWA.* In 1994 Congress enacted the Violence Against Women Act (VAWA), Pub. L. No. 103-322, 108 Stat. 1796. Title II, Safe Homes for Women, creates a federal remedy for crossing a state with intent to injury or harass a spouse or intimate partner (18 U.S.C. §2261 (2000) and provides for interstate enforcement of protection orders (18 U.S.C. §2265 (2000)). Title III, which created a federal civil rights remedy for victims of gender-motivated violent crimes (codified at 42 U.S.C. §13981 (1994)), was invalidated by the U.S. Supreme Court in United States v. Morrison, 529 U.S. 498 (2000), as an unconstitutional exercise of congressional power under both Section 5 of the

Fourteenth Amendment and the Commerce Clause. Although Title III no longer provides a federal remedy for victims, some states have enacted civil causes of action similar to those of Title III. Edward S. Snyder & Laura W. Morgan, Domestic Violence Ten Years Later, 19 Am. Acad. Matrimonial Law. 33, 46-47 (2004).

Congress re-authorized VAWA in 2000 as part of the Victims of Trafficking and Violence Protection Act of 2000, 22 U.S.C. §7101-7110 (2000).The legislation provided increased funding for law enforcement activities; shelter services; civil legal services for victims (regarding protection orders, family court matters, housing, immigration); a pilot project for supervised visitation programs for families; programs that address dating violence; the development of policies to address the needs of older and disabled victims; protections for battered immigrant women (see infra); and improved interstate enforcement of protection orders.

On January 5, 2006, President Bush signed the Violence Against Women and Department of Justice Reauthorization Act of 2005, Pub. L. No. 109-162, 119 Stat. 2960, to re-authorize VAWA through 2010. The new legislation expands the scope of VAWA by providing additional funding for training and services to assist elderly victims, women with disabilities, Native-American women, and children exposed to domestic violence; and funding for improved healthcare and legal services for victims. It also expands transitional housing options, protects the confidentiality of homeless victims receiving services, and targets housing discrimination (i.e., denial of applications, eviction, lease termination) against victims of domestic violence.

10. *Battered immigrant women.* VAWA addresses the situation of battered immigrant women. The Immigration and Naturalization Service (INS) formerly required that resident-husbands petition the INS to establish legal residence status for their immigrant wives. Battered wives were at particular risk — alone in a new environment, without family and friends, and with poor language skills. They were often forced to stay with their abusers to avoid deportation and to obtain legal residence. As part of the 2000 re-authorization, VAWA amended the Immigration and Nationality Act to permit and facilitate self-petitioning for battered spouses, and to permit such spouses to apply for suspension of deportation. See Illegal Immigration Reform and Immigrant Responsibility Act of 1996, §204(a)(1), 8 U.S.C.A. §1154 (a)(1)(A)(iii) (West 1999 & Supp. 2005) (self-petitioning); 8 U.S.C.A. §1254(a)(3) (West 1999) (deportation).

VAWA 2005 strengthens the implementation of earlier VAWA provisions that bar the detention and deportation of domestic violence victims; ensures confidential treatment of victims, grants employment authorization to victims who have filed immigration cases, affords access to public benefits to cooperating victim witnesses; permits adjustment of status of battered alien women who enter the country on a fiancé visa but who fail to marry within the 90-day period because of abuse; and allows alien abused children to delay filing petitions for a change of status if abuse caused the delay.

11. *Why didn't she leave?* One of the most difficult issues for jurors to understand is why the battered woman killed her husband instead of merely leaving him. Professor Martha Mahoney attempts to shed light on this issue:

> The "shopworn question" [why didn't she leave?] reveals several assumptions about separation: that the right solution is separation, that it is the woman's responsibility to achieve separation, and that she could have separated. . . .

When we ask the woman, "Exactly what did you do in your search for help?" the answer often turns out to be that she left — at least temporarily. In [one] study, more than seventy percent of the women had left home at some time in response to violence, though only fourteen percent had gone to shelters. Of the women Walker studied, about one quarter left temporarily after each battering incident. . . .

[T]he assumption that the woman's first separation should be permanent ignores the real dangers that the man will seek actively — and sometimes violently — to end the separation. [We ask], "What did he do when you left?" . . . Often, a woman has left several times before she finally ends a marriage. Or, she may have been restrained from leaving by violent or coercive means: by being held prisoner in her home, by being threatened with custody suits, by having her savings taken away before she could depart. [W]e need to reckon with the dangers she faces. . . . The story of the violent pursuit of the separating woman must become part of the way we understand domestic violence to help eliminate the question "Why didn't she leave?" from our common vocabulary.

Martha Mahoney, Legal Images of Battered Women: Redefining the Issue of Separation, 90 Mich. L. Rev. 1, 61-62 (1991).

12. *"Separation assault."* As Professor Mahoney explains, domestic violence survivors are at increased risk of violence when they decide to leave their abusers. See also Deborah M. Goelman, Shelter from the Storm: Using Jurisdictional Statutes to Protect Victims of Domestic Violence After the Violence Against Women Act of 2000, 13 Colum. J. Gender & L. 101, 107 (2004). Professor Mahoney has coined the term "separation assault" to signify the violence that erupts when a victim attempts to leave the batterer. That is, in the batterer's attempt to reassert control, he tries forcefully to prevent the victim from leaving, retaliates against her for leaving, and to compel her to return to him. See also Sarah M. Buel, Access to Meaningful Remedy: Overcoming Doctrinal Obstacles in Tort litigation Against Domestic Violence Offenders, 83 Or. L. Rev. 945, 957 (2004) (referring to the phenomenon as "separation violence"). What are the implications of "separation assault" for legal policy? On battering in same-sex relationships, see infra p. 422.

Problem

Ann and her husband Jeff are having drinks at a bar. When Jeff goes to the bathroom, Greg begins talking to Ann. Jeff returns, becomes jealous and argues with Greg. Jeff leaves with Ann and retrieves two handguns from home. They return to the bar. Greg is shot when he exits. The police charge Jeff with murder. However, the grand jury re-indicts both Ann and Jeff after Ann tells police that she fired the fatal shot accidentally during a struggle between the two men. A jury convicts Ann and Jeff of first degree murder; they are sentenced to life imprisonment. Ann files an application for postconviction relief, alleging that, as a victim of BWS, her husband forced her to relate a false account. She claims that he beat her over an 18-month period whenever she failed to rehearse the story or relate it to his satisfaction. What result? McMaugh v. State, 612 A.2d 725 (R.I. 1992). See generally Alafair S. Burke, Rational Actors, Self-Defense, and Duress: Making Sense, Not Syndromes, Out of the Battered Woman, 81 N.C. L. Rev. 211, 232 (2002).

Historically, law enforcement personnel have been reluctant to interfere in domestic disputes. This reluctance has precipitated a number of civil suits such as the following.

c. Duties of Law Enforcement

■ **TOWN OF CASTLE ROCK v. GONZALES**
125 S. Ct. 2796 (2005)

Justice SCALIA delivered the opinion of the Court.

We decide in this case whether an individual who has obtained a state-law restraining order has a constitutionally protected property interest in having the police enforce the restraining order when they have probable cause to believe it has been violated.

The horrible facts of this case are contained in the complaint that respondent Jessica Gonzales filed in Federal District Court. [At] about 5 or 5:30 P.M. on Tuesday, June 22, 1999, respondent's [ex-]husband took [their] three daughters [ages 10, 9, and 7] while they were playing outside the family home. No advance arrangements had been made for him to see the daughters that evening. When respondent noticed the children were missing, she suspected her husband had taken them. At about 7:30 P.M., she called the Castle Rock Police Department, which dispatched two officers. The complaint continues: "When [the officers] arrived . . . , she showed them a copy of the TRO [that had been issued to her in conjunction with her divorce proceedings that ordered her ex-husband not to "molest or disturb the peace of [respondent] or of any child," and to remain at least 100 yards from the family home at all times.] [She] requested that it be enforced and the three children be returned to her immediately. [The officers] stated that there was nothing they could do about the TRO and suggested that [respondent] call the Police Department again if the three children did not return home by 10:00 P.M."

At approximately 8:30 P.M., respondent talked to her husband on his cellular telephone. He told her "he had the three children [at an] amusement park in Denver." She called the police again and asked them to "have someone check for" her husband or his vehicle at the amusement park and "put out an [all points bulletin]" for her husband, but the officer with whom she spoke "refused to do so," again telling her to "wait until 10:00 P.M., and see if" her husband returned the girls.

At approximately 10:10 P.M., respondent called the police and said her children were still missing, but she was now told to wait until midnight. She called at midnight and told the dispatcher her children were still missing. She went to her husband's apartment and, finding nobody there, called the police at 12:10 A.M., she was told to wait for an officer to arrive. When none came, she went to the police station at 12:50 A.M. and submitted an incident report. The officer who took the report "made no reasonable effort to enforce the TRO or locate the three children. Instead, he went to dinner."

At approximately 3:20 A.M., respondent's husband arrived at the police station and opened fire with a semiautomatic handgun he had purchased earlier that evening. Police shot back, killing him. Inside the cab of his pickup truck, they found the bodies of all three daughters, whom he had already murdered.

[Gonzales brought a civil rights action against the municipality and police officers under 42 U.S.C. §1983, claiming that she had a property interest in enforcement of the restraining order; and that the town deprived her of this property without due process by having a policy that tolerated nonenforcement of restraining orders. The federal district court dismissed the action for failure to state a claim; the Tenth Circuit Court of Appeals reversed. Following a rehearing en banc, the Tenth Circuit reversed the district court opinion and remanded.]

[W]e left a similar question [whether a statute conferred an entitlement to due process protection] unanswered in DeShaney v. Winnebago County Dept. of Social Servs., 489 U.S. 189 (1989), another case with "undeniably tragic" facts: Local child-protection officials had failed to protect a young boy from beatings by his father that left him severely brain damaged. We held that the so-called "substantive" component of the Due Process Clause does not "requir[e] the State to protect the life, liberty, and property of its citizens against invasion by private actors." Id., at 195. We noted, however, that the petitioner had not properly preserved the argument that — and we thus "decline[d] to consider" whether — state "child protection statutes gave [him] an 'entitlement' to receive protective services in accordance with the terms of the statute, an entitlement which would enjoy due process protection."

The procedural component of the Due Process Clause does not protect everything that might be described as a "benefit." . . . Our cases recognize that a benefit is not a protected entitlement if government officials may grant or deny it in their discretion. The Court of Appeals in this case determined that Colorado law created an entitlement to enforcement of the restraining order because the "court-issued restraining order . . . specifically dictated that its terms must be enforced" and a "state statute command[ed]" enforcement of the order when certain objective conditions were met (probable cause to believe that the order had been violated and that the object of the order had received notice of its existence). . . .

The Tenth Circuit's opinion [consisted] primarily of quoting language from the restraining order, the statutory text, and a state-legislative-hearing transcript. . . . The critical language in the restraining order came not from any part of the order itself (which was signed by the state-court trial judge and directed to the restrained party, respondent's husband), but from the preprinted notice to law-enforcement personnel that appeared on the back of the order. That notice effectively restated the statutory provision describing "peace officers' duties" related to the crime of violation of a restraining order [e.g., *A peace officer shall use every reasonable means to enforce a restraining order. . . . A peace officer shall arrest, or, if an arrest would be impractical under the circumstances, seek a warrant for the arrest of a restrained person. . . . A peace officer shall enforce a valid restraining order whether or not there is a record of the restraining order in the registry.*" Colo. Rev. Stat. §18-6-803.5(3) (Lexis 1999) (emphases added).]

The Court of Appeals concluded that this statutory provision [about police officers' duties regarding enforcement of TRO's] — especially taken in conjunction with a statement from its legislative history, and with another statute restricting criminal and civil liability for officers making arrests — established the Colorado Legislature's clear intent "to alter the fact that the police were not enforcing domestic abuse retraining orders," and thus its intent "that the recipient of a domestic abuse restraining order have an entitlement to its enforcement." Any other result, it said, "would render domestic abuse restraining orders utterly valueless."

This last statement is sheer hyperbole. Whether or not respondent had a right to enforce the restraining order, it rendered certain otherwise lawful conduct by her husband both criminal and in contempt of court. The creation of grounds on which he could be arrested, criminally prosecuted, and held in contempt was hardly "valueless" — even if the prospect of those sanctions ultimately failed to prevent him from committing three murders and a suicide.

We do not believe that these provisions of Colorado law truly made enforcement of restraining orders *mandatory*. A well established tradition of police discretion has long coexisted with apparently mandatory arrest statutes [in the criminal law generally]. [A] true mandate of police action would require some stronger indication from the Colorado Legislature than "shall use every reasonable means to enforce a restraining order" (or even "shall arrest . . . or . . . seek a warrant"), §§18-6-803.5(3)(a), (b). That language is not perceptibly more mandatory than the Colorado statute which has long told municipal chiefs of police that they "shall pursue and arrest any person fleeing from justice in any part of the state" and that they "shall apprehend any person in the act of committing any offense . . . and, forthwith and without any warrant, bring such person before a . . . competent authority for examination and trial." Colo. Rev. Stat. §31-4-112 (Lexis 2004). It is hard to imagine that a Colorado peace officer would not have some discretion to determine that — despite probable cause to believe a restraining order has been violated — the circumstances of the violation or the competing duties of that officer or his agency counsel decisively against enforcement in a particular instance. The practical necessity for discretion is particularly apparent in a case such as this one, where the suspected violator is not actually present and his whereabouts are unknown.

The dissent correctly points out that, in the specific context of domestic violence, mandatory-arrest statutes have been found in some States to be more mandatory than traditional mandatory-arrest statutes. . . . Even in the domestic-violence context, however, it is unclear how the mandatory-arrest paradigm applies to cases in which the offender is not present to be arrested. As the dissent explains, much of the impetus for mandatory-arrest statutes and policies derived from the idea that it is better for police officers to arrest the aggressor in a domestic-violence incident than to attempt to mediate the dispute or merely to ask the offender to leave the scene. Those other options are only available, of course, when the offender is present at the scene. . . .

Respondent does not specify the precise means of enforcement that the Colorado restraining-order statute assertedly mandated — whether her interest lay in having police arrest her husband, having them seek a warrant for his arrest, or having them "use every reasonable means, up to and including arrest, to enforce the order's terms," Brief for Respondent 29-30. Such indeterminacy is not the hallmark of a duty that is mandatory. Nor can someone be safely deemed "entitled" to something when the identity of the alleged entitlement is vague. The dissent, after suggesting various formulations of the entitlement in question, ultimately contends that the obligations under the statute were quite precise: either make an arrest or (if that is impractical) seek an arrest warrant. The problem with this is that the seeking of an arrest warrant would be an entitlement to nothing but procedure — which we have held inadequate even to support standing; much less can it be the basis for a property interest. . . .

Even if the statute could be said to have made enforcement of restraining orders "mandatory" because of the domestic-violence context of the underlying statute, that would not necessarily mean that state law gave *respondent* an entitlement to *enforcement* of the mandate. Making the actions of government employees obligatory can serve various legitimate ends other than the conferral of a benefit on a specific class of people. The serving of public rather than private ends is the normal course of the criminal law. . . .

Respondent's alleged interest stems only from a State's *statutory* scheme . . . . She does not assert that she has any common-law or contractual entitlement to enforcement. If she was given a statutory entitlement, we would expect to see some indication of that in the statute itself. . . . The creation of a personal entitlement to something as vague and novel as enforcement of restraining orders cannot "simply g[o] without saying." *Post,* at 2821, n. 16 (Stevens, J., dissenting). We conclude that Colorado has not created such an entitlement.

Even if we were to think otherwise concerning the creation of an entitlement by Colorado, it is by no means clear that an individual entitlement to enforcement of a restraining order could constitute a "property" interest for purposes of the Due Process Clause. Such a right would not, of course, resemble any traditional conception of property. Although that alone does not disqualify it from due process protection . . . , the right to have a restraining order enforced does not "have some ascertainable monetary value." . . . Perhaps most radically, the alleged property interest here arises *incidentally,* not out of some new species of government benefit or service, but out of a function that government actors have always performed — to wit, arresting people who they have probable cause to believe have committed a criminal offense. . . . We conclude, therefore, that respondent did not, for purposes of the Due Process Clause, have a property interest in police enforcement of the restraining order against her husband. . . .

Notes and Questions

1. *Background.* Castle Rock is one of many cases instituted by battered women, beginning in the 1970s, to force local police departments to treat their complaints seriously. Many suits, similar to the suit in *Castle Rock,* were brought under the federal Civil Rights Act, 42 U.S.C. §1983 (2000). Remedies under §1983 require the plaintiff to show a deprivation under color of law of a constitutional right. Generally, no right to police protection exists for private acts of violence, and courts have read inaction to fall short of required "deprivation." Thus, a cause of action arises only if the state discriminates in providing protection to the public in violation of the Equal Protection Clause or if the state has a "special relationship" to an individual such that the state has an affirmative duty to act.

The parameters of the special relationship doctrine as applied to battered spouses were first explored in Balistreri v. Pacifica Police Department, 855 F.2d 1421 (9th Cir. 1988). The Ninth Circuit Court of Appeals affirmed the district court ruling that the battered plaintiff satisfied the special relationship doctrine, thereby imposing a duty of protection on the police, because the police had repeated notice of the husband's assaults and plaintiff had a restraining order. However, after the U.S. Supreme Court severely limited the scope of the special relationship doctrine in DeShaney v. Winnebago County Department of Social Services, 489 U.S. 189

(1989), the Ninth Circuit reheard *Balistreri* and found no substantive due process violation for failure to protect. 901 F.2d 696 (9th Cir. 1990).

2. *The impact of* DeShaney. The Supreme Court in *Castle Rock* cites *DeShaney*, a case based in the context of child abuse which had significant implications for battered women's litigation. *De Shaney* held that, absent a special relationship, the state has no constitutional duty to protect its citizens against deprivation of life, liberty or property committed by private individuals. The U.S. Supreme Court thereby refused to find that state social workers violated a child's *substantive* due process rights by the failure to intervene to protect him from his father's abuse. Post-*DeShaney*, battered plaintiffs were restricted to different theories of liability, by claiming (1) an exception to *DeShaney* (i.e., such as an invocation of the "custodial relationship doctrine" which provides that police have an affirmative duty to protect a victim who in state custody); (2) a violation of procedural, rather than substantive, due process (i.e., the claim of an entitlement to procedural safeguards); (3) a violation of equal protection; and (4) liability under state tort theories. Developments in the Law: Legal Responses to Domestic Violence, Making State Institutions More Responsive, 106 Harv. L. Rev. 1551, 1560 (1993).

Town of Castle Rock eliminated the second theory of liability. Because DeShaney raised the *procedural* due process claim for the first time in his brief before the Court, the *DeShaney* Court had refused to consider that claim. *Castle Rock* addressed that unanswered question by ruling that a constitutional claim for failure to protect did not lie under procedural due process. (Note that the Tenth Circuit Court of Appeals *in Castle Rock,* in the panel decision (307 F.3d 1258 (10th Cir. 2002)), as well as the subsequent rehearing en banc, reached the opposite conclusion because "police never 'heard' nor seriously entertained [Gonzales's] request to enforce and protect her interests in the restraining order." 366 F.3d at 1101 (10th Cir. 2004) (en banc)).

The aforementioned theories present obstacles for battered women's claims. The custodial relationship doctrine does not apply unless a victim is injured while in police custody. The equal protection theory requires actual proof that the non-arrest policy of some police departments denies battered spouses the protection given to victims abused by strangers, and reflects a policy of sex discrimination because women are usually the victims of domestic violence. (The plaintiff in *Balistreri* was permitted to amend her complaint to clarify that the police had violated her right to equal protection because of the particular police officer's dismissive response to the victim's complaint that her husband had assaulted her.) Finally, an action against law enforcement personnel based on negligence may be precluded by sovereign immunity. (In *Castle Rock,* plaintiff's charges against three police officers were dismissed by the Court of Appeals on the basis that they were entitled to qualified immunity. 366 F.3d 1902, 1119 (10th Cir. 2004) (en banc)).

3. Castle Rock: *dissent.* In a sharp dissent in *Castle Rock,* Justice Stevens (joined by Justice Ginsburg) charged that the majority failed to take seriously the following: (1) the purpose and nature of restraining orders, and (2) persuasive authority from other states recognizing that mandatory arrest statutes and restraining orders create an individual right to police action. 125 S. Ct. at 2822. Specifically, the dissent criticized the majority for ignoring legislative history and the intent of the Colorado legislature in enacting their mandatory arrest statute as part of a wave of state laws passed in the 1980s and 1990s that were designed to redress police reluctance to enforce domestic violence restraining orders. According to the

dissent, mandatory arrest statutes "undeniably create an entitlement to police enforcement of restraining orders" (id. at 2819) because, under the statute, "the police were *required* to provide enforcement; they *lacked the discretion to do nothing*" (id. at 2819-2820) (emphasis in the original). The dissent also pointed to decisions of other state courts that recognize that mandatory arrest statutes create rights enforceable against the police under state law. Id. at 2818 (citing, *inter alia*, Nearing v. Weaver, 670 P.2d 137 (Or. 1983)). Finally, the dissent noted that cases have found "property" interests in other state benefits and services (e.g., welfare benefits, disability benefits, etc.) and, therefore, reasoned that police enforcement of a restraining order is "a government service that is no less concrete and no less valuable than other government services, such as education." *Castle Rock,* 125 S. Ct. at 2823 (Justice Stevens, dissenting).

   4. *Police nonintervention.* What explains law enforcement's refusal to intervene to assist Jessica Gonzales in *Castle Rock*? Do you agree that the police were unable to arrest Mr. Gonzales because his whereabouts were "unknown"? Several factors may explain police nonintervention in cases of domestic violence: (1) the police perception that the battered spouse merely wants to scare the abuser, get him out of the house, or obtain transportation to a hospital; (2) the family cannot afford the economic impact of an arrest; (3) the acceptability of the abuse in the spouses' culture; (4) a concern that the abuser may retaliate after the abuse; (5) the fear that criminal justice intervention might lead to the family's dissolution; (6) the concern that prosecutors will not prosecute because of the high attrition rate; and finally (7) the belief that "a man's home is his castle." Raymond I. Parnas, The Police Response to the Domestic Disturbance, 1967 Wis. L. Rev. 914. What role should such concerns play in arrest policies?

   5. *Evidentiary privilege.* Another factor that explains police reluctance to intervene is the difficulty of securing the battered woman's cooperation. Battered women sometimes renege on their request that the batterer be arrested and, subsequently, refuse to testify against him. What role should her decision play in a prosecution? An evidentiary privilege of spousal disqualification prevents a prosecutor from compelling a reluctant spouse to testify against the defendant-spouse. (See discussion of *Trammel,* infra.) Some exceptions to this privilege developed for cases of severe spousal violence. The majority of American jurisdictions, similarly, adopt spousal violence exceptions to the privilege. Malinda L. Seymoure, Isn't It a Crime?: Feminist Perspectives on Spousal Immunity and Spousal Violence, 90 Nw. U. L. Rev. 1032, 1052-1061 (1996) (surveying jurisdictions). See also Kimberly Ann Connor, Note, A Critique of the Marital Privileges: An Examination of the Marital Privileges in the United States Military Through the State and Federal Approaches to the Marital Privileges, 36 Val. U. L. Rev. 119, 147 (2001) (reporting that states are expanding the exception to the privilege for spousal abuse and child abuse).

   Should courts compel a battered spouse to testify on the theory that the dynamics of battering (e.g., fear, self-blame, and so forth) prevent her sound judgment? See generally Cheryl Hanna, No Right to Choose: Mandating Victim Participation in Domestic Violence Prosecutions, 109 Harv. L. Rev. 1850 (1996). Does compelling the victim to testify, despite her objections, signal a policy of disrespect of the woman's wishes? Or, does recognition of spousal immunity in domestic violence cases reflect the antiquated idea that the law does not belong in the private sphere of the family?

6. *Restraining orders: generally.* Civil protection orders ("temporary restraining orders" or TRO's) restrain a respondent from committing further acts of violence or harassment. They may be issued immediately and without notice. They may be temporary or permanent. They may be (but need not be) issued in conjunction with dissolution proceedings. Protective orders may include temporary awards of custody, visitation, and child support, spousal support, as well as attorneys' fees and costs, and possession of the family home. Once served, the adverse party becomes subject to action by local law enforcement upon violation. Does the ex parte nature of these orders deprive a defendant of due process? See State ex rel. Williams v. Marsh, 626 S.W.2d 223 (Mo. 1982) (en banc); State v. Karas, 32 P.3d 1016 (Wash. Ct. App. 2001).

7. *Restraining orders: effectiveness.* How effective are restraining orders — before and after *Castle Rock*? Are they "valueless" or is that "sheer hyperbole"? How likely are victims to continue to seek restraining orders after *Castle Rock*? What legal reforms might make restraining orders more effective?

According to a federally-funded study, a significant percentage (17 percent) of battered women seek and obtain restraining orders. The study notes that victims resort to restraining orders not as a form of early intervention, but rather as an act of desperation. Further, the study confirms that most temporary restraining orders frequently are violated (two-thirds of orders involving rape or stalking compared to one-half of orders involving physical assault). Lynn D. Wardle, Marriage and Domestic Violence in the United States: New Perspectives About Legal Strategies to Combat Domestic Violence, 15 St. Thomas L. Rev. 791, 799 (2003) (reporting findings). Further, a two-year study by a California Task Force on Local Criminal Justice Response to Domestic Violence recently revealed that many state courts are not issuing restraining orders even when required by law; many restraining orders that do get issued are never served; and lax enforcement of restraining orders occurs, especially regarding firearm prohibitions. In response, Attorney General Bill Lockyer sponsored A.B. 1288 to authorize arraignment courts to prohibit domestic violence defendants from possessing firearms and to allow law enforcement personnel to advise a victim if the batterer possesses a firearm, and also S.B. 720 to help ensure that restraining orders are entered into the Department of Justice's database so that the proof of the existence of the order does not rest with victims. Office of the Attorney General, Attorney General Lockyer Report on Domestic Violence Finds Criminal Justice System Is Failing to Protect Victims, Families AG's Task Force Makes 44 Recommendations to Reduce Domestic Violence (press release), July 26, 2005, available at http://ag.ca.gov/newsalerts/release.php?id=1197.

8. *Mandatory arrest.* Mandatory arrest practices are a controversial approach to battering. Over half of the states require mandatory arrest for misdemeanor domestic violence offenses. Leigh Goodmark, Law Is the Answer? Do We Know That for Sure?: Questioning the Efficacy of Legal Interventions for Battered Women, 23 St. Louis U. Pub. L. Rev. 7, 37-38 (2004).

The benefits and detriments of mandatory arrest remain contested. Advocates of mandatory arrest argue that (1) it communicates to offenders that society will not tolerate their behavior; (2) it protects victims more effectively by immediate relief; (3) it empowers the victim to change a situation she may not feel capable of changing herself; (4) it equalizes the position of women; (5) it clarifies the role of police by providing guidelines; (6) it decreases police injuries during domestic disturbances;

and (7) it ensures that all perpetrators are treated similarly. See, e.g., Emily J. Sack, Battered Women and the State: The Struggle for the Future of Domestic Violence Policy, 2004 Wis. L. Rev. 1657, 1677-1678. However, opponents question the effectiveness of such policies, wonder whether arrest is an effective deterrent to abusive behavior, and suggest that mandatory arrest contributes to the escalation of domestic violence. Sack, supra, at 1669, 1678.

Empirical research indicates that mandatory arrest policies serve to reduce recidivism. Early studies by the National Institute of Justice (NIJ) found that arrest in domestic violence cases had a significantly greater effect on reducing recidivism than did mediating the dispute or requiring the offender to leave the home. Subsequent NIJ studies in six cities found that mandatory arrest policies consistently reduced recidivism as compared with alternative responses. Betsy Tsai, Note, The Trend Toward Specialized Domestic Violence Courts: Improvements on an Effective Innovation, 68 Fordham L. Rev. 1285, 1291-1294 (2000). Different measures of recidivism, however, reveal a different level of reduction. See also Arthur L. Rizer III, Mandatory Arrest: Do We Need to Take a Closer Look?, 36 U. West L.A. L. Rev. 1 (2005).

Does the existence of a mandatory arrest policy give rise to a private cause of action against police for failure to protect the victim, according to the Supreme Court in *Castle Rock*? Why or why not? Another legal reform in battering cases that arguably dispenses with discretion is a no-drop policy, requiring the prosecutor to pursue criminal action against the abuser regardless of the victim's wishes. Is a no-drop policy required by the Equal Protection Clause? See Kaylani Robbins, No-Drop Prosecution of Domestic Violence : Just Good Policy, or Equal Protection Mandate?, 52 Stan. L. Rev. 205, 206-208 (1999). Justice Scalia in *Castle Rock* mentions that Jessica Gonzales had another alternative — an action for contempt. Explore the benefits and shortcomings of other legal remedies that were available to Ms. Gonzales: contempt as well as a negligence action against law enforcement. Note that the district court dismissed her claims against the particular law enforcement officers based on qualified immunity. See generally Prentice L. White, Stopping the Chronic Batter Through Legislation: Will It Work This Time?, 31 Pepp. L. Rev. 709, 759-760 (2004) (suggesting alternatives to no-drop policies).

9. *Firearms legislation.* In *Castle Rock,* the husband was able to use a firearm despite the existence of a restraining order. Both federal and state law address the ability of batterers to own firearms. In 1994, Congress enacted legislation in conjunction with VAWA that prohibits those persons from possessing firearms who had protective orders entered against them. Violent Crime Control and Law Enforcement Act of 1994, Pub. L. No. 103-322, §110401, 108 Stat. 2014 (2000). Subsequent legislation imposed firearms restrictions on persons who are convicted of a misdemeanor offense of domestic violence (the "Lautenberg Amendment," Pub. L. No. 104-208, Div. A, sec. 101(f), 58 Tit. VI, (658, enacted as part of the massive Omnibus Consolidated Appropriations Act of 1996) (codified at 18 U.S.C. §§922(g)(8) and 922(g)(9) (2000)). Many states have similar laws. How effective are these laws? See generally Lisa D. May, The Backfiring of the Domestic Violence Firearms Ban, 14 Colum. J. Gender & L. 1 (2005). How might they be made more effective?

10. *Domestic violence courts.* In recent years, several jurisdictions have created special domestic violence courts. The formation of such courts stems from the

following: (1) criticisms of the inability of the traditional system to address domestic violence; (2) recognition of the inadequacy of protective orders to prevent abuse; (3) the inability of the traditional system to identify which batterers are lethal; (4) the cursory treatment of domestic violence in traditional courts; and (5) persistent organizational attitudes of nonintervention. Patricia Tjaden & Nancy Thoennes, Extent, Nature and Consequences of Intimate Partner Violence: Findings from the National Violence Against Women Survey 52-53 (July 2000). The major disadvantage of such courts, of course, is the cost. Would the existence of such a specialized court had led to a different outcome for Jessica Gonzales? Should governmental policy increase funding for these innovative courts?

11. *Privacy.* The seemingly gender-neutral policy of nonintrusion into marital harmony is justified sometimes by the desire to preserve family harmony. Does nonintervention promote family harmony? Does it promote respect for the rights of all family members equally, particularly when one has asked for help? Or does it preserve the freedom of more powerful family members at the expense of weaker members? How much discretion, if any, should law enforcement officials have in battering cases? What light does *Castle Rock* shed on these questions?

d. Crimes: Marital Rape

■ PEOPLE v. LIBERTA
474 N.E.2d 567 (N.Y. 1984), cert. denied,
471 U.S. 1020 (1985)

WACHTLER, Judge.

[Defendant charges that the marital rape exemption in New York's rape and sodomy statutes renders those statutes violative of the Equal Protection Clause.]

I

Defendant Mario Liberta and Denise Liberta were married in 1978. Shortly after the birth of their son, in October of that year, Mario began to beat Denise. In early 1980 Denise brought a proceeding in the Family Court in Erie County seeking protection from the defendant. On April 30, 1980 a temporary order of protection was issued to her by the Family Court. Under this order, the defendant was to move out and remain away from the family home, and stay away from Denise. The order provided that the defendant could visit with his son once each weekend.

On the weekend of March 21, 1981, Mario, who was then living in a motel, did not visit his son. On Tuesday, March 24, 1981 he called Denise to ask if he could visit his son on that day. Denise would not allow the defendant to come to her house, but she did agree to allow him to pick up their son and her and take them both back to his motel after being assured that a friend of his would be with them at all times. The defendant and his friend picked up Denise and their son and the four of them drove to defendant's motel.

When they arrived at the motel the friend left. As soon as only Mario, Denise, and their son were alone in the motel room, Mario attacked Denise, threatened to kill her, and forced her to perform fellatio on him and to engage in sexual intercourse with him. The son was in the room during the entire episode, and the defendant forced Denise to tell their son to watch what the defendant was doing to her.

The defendant allowed Denise and their son to leave shortly after the incident. Denise, after going to her parents' home, went to a hospital to be treated for scratches on her neck and bruises on her head and back, all inflicted by her husband. She also went to the police station, and on the next day she swore out a felony complaint against the defendant. On July 15, 1981 the defendant was indicted for rape in the first degree and sodomy in the first degree.

II

Section 130.35 of the Penal Code provides in relevant part that "A male is guilty of rape in the first degree when he engages in sexual intercourse with a female . . . by forcible compulsion." "Female," for purposes of the rape statute, is defined as "any female person who is not married to the actor" (Penal Law, §130.00, subd. 4). Section 130.50 of the Penal Law provides in relevant part that "a person is guilty of sodomy in the first degree when he engages in deviate sexual intercourse with another person . . . by forcible compulsion." "Deviate sexual intercourse" is defined as "sexual conduct between persons not married to each other consisting of contact between the penis and the anus, the mouth and penis, or the mouth and the vulva" (Penal Law, §130.00, subd. 2). Thus, due to the "not married" language in the definitions of "female" and "deviate sexual intercourse," there is a "marital exemption" for both forcible rape and forcible sodomy. The marital exemption itself, however, has certain exemptions. For purposes of the rape and sodomy statutes, a husband and wife are considered to be "not married" if at the time of the sexual assault they [are living apart pursuant to a court order or a separation agreement].

Defendant moved to dismiss the indictment, asserting that because he and Denise were still married at the time of the incident[1] he came within the "marital exemption" to both rape and sodomy. The People [contended] that the temporary order of protection required Mario and Denise to live apart, and they in fact were living apart, and thus were "not married" for purposes of the statutes. [The trial court dismissed the indictment, holding that the marital exemption applied. The appellate court reversed and remanded, finding that the couple was "not married" for purposes of the statute. The defendant was convicted and appealed. He asserted that both statutes are unconstitutional.]

IV

The defendant's constitutional challenges to the rape and sodomy statutes are premised on his being considered "not married" to Denise and are the same challenges as could be made by any unmarried male convicted under these statutes. The defendant's claim is that both statutes violate equal protection because they are under-inclusive classifications which burden him, but not others similarly situated. . . .

---

1. The defendant and Densie were divorced several months after the assault in the motel room.

A. THE MARITAL EXEMPTION

As noted above, under the Penal Law a married man ordinarily cannot be convicted of forcibly raping or sodomizing his wife. This is the so-called marital exemption for rape. . . . The assumption, even before the marital exemption was codified, that a man could not be guilty of raping his wife, is traceable to a statement made by the 17th century English jurist Lord Hale, who wrote: "[T]he husband cannot be guilty of a rape committed by himself upon his lawful wife, for by their mutual matrimonial consent and contract the wife hath given up herself in this kind unto her husband, which she cannot retract" (1 Hale, History of Pleas of the Crown, p.629). Although Hale cited no authority for his statement it was relied on by State Legislatures which enacted rape statutes with a marital exemption and by courts which established a common-law exemption for husbands. . . .

Presently, over 40 States still retain some form of marital exemption for rape. While the marital exemption is subject to an equal protection challenge, because it classifies unmarried men differently than married men, the equal protection clause does not prohibit a State from making classifications, provided the statute does not arbitrarily burden a particular group of individuals. Where a statute draws a distinction based upon marital status, the classification must be reasonable and must be based upon "some ground of difference that rationally explains the different treatment" (Eisenstadt v. Baird, 405 U.S. 438 [(1972)]).

We find that there is no rational basis for distinguishing between marital rape and nonmarital rape. The various rationales which have been asserted in defense of the exemption are either based upon archaic notions about the consent and property rights incident to marriage or are simply unable to withstand even the slightest scrutiny. . . .

Lord Hale's notion of an irrevocable implied consent by a married woman to sexual intercourse has been cited most frequently in support of the marital exemption. Any argument based on a supposed consent, however, is untenable. Rape is not simply a sexual act to which one party does not consent. Rather, it is a degrading, violent act which violates the bodily integrity of the victim and frequently causes severe, long-lasting physical and psychic harm. To ever imply consent to such an act is irrational and absurd. Other than in the context of rape statutes, marriage has never been viewed as giving a husband the right to coerced intercourse on demand. Certainly, then, a marriage license should not be viewed as a license for a husband to forcibly rape his wife with impunity. A married woman has the same right to control her own body as does an unmarried woman. . . .

The other traditional justifications for the marital exemption were the common-law doctrines that a woman was the property of her husband and that the legal existence of the woman was "incorporated and consolidated into that of the husband" (1 Blackstone's Commentaries [1966 ed.], p.430). . . . Both these doctrines, of course, have long been rejected in this State. . . .

Because the traditional justifications for the marital exemption no longer have any validity, other arguments have been advanced in its defense. The first of these recent rationales, which is stressed by the People in this case, is that the marital exemption protects against governmental intrusion into marital privacy and promotes reconciliation of the spouses, and thus, that elimination of the exemption would be disruptive to marriages. While protecting marital privacy and encouraging reconciliation are legitimate State interests, there is no rational relation between allowing a husband to forcibly rape his wife and these interests. The marital exemption simply does not further marital privacy because this right of privacy protects consensual acts, not violent sexual assaults (see Griswold v. Connecticut, 381 U.S. 479, 485-486 [(1965)]). Just as a husband cannot invoke a right of marital privacy to escape liability for beating his wife, he cannot justifiably rape his wife under the guise of a right to privacy.

Similarly, it is not tenable to argue that elimination of the marital exemption would disrupt marriages because it would discourage reconciliation. [I]f the marriage has already reached the point where intercourse is accomplished by violent assault it is doubtful that there is anything left to reconcile. . . .

Another rationale sometimes advanced in support of the marital exemption is that marital rape would be a difficult crime to prove. A related argument is that allowing such prosecutions could lead to fabricated complaints by "vindictive" wives. The difficulty of proof argument is based on the problem of showing lack of consent. Proving lack of consent, however, is often the most difficult part of any rape prosecution, particularly where the rapist and the victim had a prior relationship. Similarly, the possibility that married women will fabricate complaints would seem to be no greater than the possibility of unmarried women doing so. The criminal justice system, with all of its built-in safeguards, is presumed to be capable of handling any false complaints. Indeed, if the possibility of fabricated complaints were a basis for not criminalizing behavior which would otherwise be sanctioned, virtually all crimes other than homicides would go unpunished.

The final argument in defense of the marital exemption is that marital rape is not as serious an offense as other rape and is thus adequately dealt with by the possibility of prosecution under criminal statutes, such as assault statutes, which provide for less severe punishment. [T]here is no evidence to support the argument that marital rape has less severe consequences than other rape. On the contrary, numerous studies have shown that marital rape is frequently quite violent and generally has *more* severe, traumatic effects on the victim than other rape (see, generally [Diana Russell, Rape in Marriage 190-199 (1982); Martin D. Schwartz, The Spousal Exemption for Criminal Rape Prosecution, 7 Vt. L. Rev. 33, 45-46 (1982); Thomas R. Bearrows, Abolishing the Marital Exemption for Rape: A Statutory Proposal, 1983 U. Ill. L. Rev. 201, 209)].

Among the recent decisions in this country addressing the marital exemption, only one court has concluded that there is a rational basis for it (see People v. Brown, 632 P.2d 1025 (Colo. 1981)). We agree with the other courts which have analyzed the exemption, which have been unable to find any present justification for it [citations omitted]. Justice Holmes wrote: "It is revolting to have no better reason for a rule of law than that so it was laid down in the time of Henry IV. It is still more revolting if the grounds upon which it was laid down have vanished long since, and the rule simply persists from blind imitation of the past" (Holmes, The Path of the Law, 10 Harv. L. Rev. 457, 469 [(1897)]). This statement is an apt characterization of the marital exemption; it lacks a rational basis, and therefore violates the equal protection clauses of both the Federal and State Constitutions. . . .

B. THE EXEMPTION FOR FEMALES

Under the Penal Law only males can be convicted of rape in the first degree.[11] [The court then proceeds to examine the sex-based classification to determine whether it is substantially related to the achievement of an important governmental objective.]

The first argument advanced by the People in support of the exemption for females is that because only females can become pregnant the State may constitutionally differentiate between forcible rapes of females and forcible rapes of males. This court and the United States Supreme Court have upheld statutes which subject males to criminal liability for engaging in sexual intercourse with underage females without the converse being true (Michael M. v. Sonoma County Superior Court, 450 U.S. 464 [(1981)]). The rationale behind these decisions was that the primary purpose of such "statutory rape" laws is to protect against the harm caused by teenage pregnancies, there being no need to provide the same protection to young males.

There is no evidence, however, that preventing pregnancies is a primary purpose of the statute prohibiting forcible rape, nor does such a purpose seem likely. Rather, the very fact that the statute proscribes "forcible compulsion" shows that its overriding purpose is to protect a woman from an unwanted forcible, and often violent sexual intrusion into her body. Thus, due to the different purposes behind forcible rape laws and "statutory" (consensual) rape laws, the cases upholding the gender discrimination in the latter are not decisive with respect to the former, and the People cannot meet their burden here by simply stating that only females can become pregnant.

The People also claim that the discrimination is justified because a female rape victim "faces the probability of medical, sociological, and psychological problems unique to her gender." This same argument, when advanced in support of the discrimination in the statutory rape laws, was rejected by this court [previously], and it is no more convincing in the present case. . . .

Finally, the People suggest that a gender-neutral law for forcible rape is unnecessary, and that therefore the present law is constitutional, because a woman either cannot actually rape a man or such attacks, if possible, are extremely rare. Although the "physiologically impossible" argument has been accepted by several courts, it is simply wrong. The argument is premised on the notion that a man cannot engage in sexual intercourse unless he is sexually aroused, and if he is aroused then he is consenting to intercourse. "Sexual intercourse" however, "occurs upon any penetration, however slight" (Penal Law, §130.00); this degree of contact can be achieved without a male being aroused and thus without his consent.

As to the "infrequency" argument, while forcible sexual assaults by females upon males are undoubtedly less common than those by males upon females this numerical disparity cannot by itself make the gender discrimination constitutional. Women may well be responsible for a far lower number of all serious crimes than are men, but such a disparity would not make it permissible for the State to punish only men who commit, for example, robbery. . . .

---

11. The sodomy statute applies to any "person" and is thus gender neutral. Defendant's gender-based equal protection challenge is therefore addressed only to the rape statute.

[Because a gender-neutral law would better serve the state's objective of deterring and punishing forcible sexual assaults,] we find that section 130.35 of the Penal Law violates equal protection because it exempts females from criminal liability for forcible rape. [I]t is now the law of this State that any person who engages in sexual intercourse or deviate sexual intercourse with any other person by forcible compulsion is guilty of either rape in the first degree or sodomy in the first degree. Because the statutes under which the defendant was convicted are not being struck down, his conviction is affirmed. . . .

Notes and Questions

1. *Trend.* When *Liberta* was decided, most states had statutes exempting husbands from prosecution for rape. Today almost all states have changed their marital rape laws to abolish or limit this exemption. In large part, the movement resulted from feminists' call in the 1970s for reform of rape laws. Michelle J. Anderson, Marital Immunity, Intimate Relationships, and Improper Inferences: A New Law on Sexual Offenses by Intimates, 54 Hastings L.J. 1465, 1465 (2003).

2. *Criticism of reform movement.* Despite the law reform movement, most states retain some form of special treatment for marital rapists. One commentator points out that the majority of states manifest elements of the common law regime by (1) criminalizing a narrower range of offenses if committed within marriage, (2) subjecting marital rape to less serious sanctions, and/or (3) creating special procedural hurdles for marital rape prosecutions (such as reporting requirements to designated professionals or within certain time periods). Jill Elaine Hasday, Contest and Consent: A Legal History of Marital Rape, 88 Calif. L. Rev. 1373, 1375 (2000). She concludes that "the current state of the law represents a confusing mix of victory and defeat for the exemptions' contemporary feminist critics." Id. Do these distinctions survive equal protection challenge?

3. *Living apart.* As *Liberta* reveals, prior to the reform movement, a few states permitted prosecution only if the spouses were living apart at the time of the incident or if one spouse had initiated legal proceedings at the time of the rape. Some states required both conditions. Sarah M. Harless, From the Bedroom to the Courtroom: The Impact of Domestic Violence Law on Marital Rape Victims, 35 Rutgers L. J. 305, 325-330 (2003). Why should it matter whether the husband and wife are living apart? Does this requirement help establish the "legitimacy" of the women as victims? "Legitimacy has to do with whether a victim can successfully persuade the police that she is "deserving" of the status of rape victim." Susan Carol Randall & Vicki McNickle Rose, Barriers to Becoming a "Successful" Rape Victim, in Women and Crime in America 342 (Lee H. Bowker ed., 1981). What additional factors in *Liberta* establish Denise Liberta's legitimacy as a victim?

4. *Privacy.* One of the arguments for the marital rape exemption is its purported protection of the right to privacy. Was the court in *Liberta* focusing on family privacy, marital privacy, or individual privacy? Why does *Liberta* say that the exemption does not further marital privacy? In contrast, one commentator argues that the marital right to privacy should prevail over prosecuting spousal rapists:

> [I]t appears unseemly to permit the public to examine the intimacies of a marital relationship. Allowing the public this examination is to encourage a type of public

voyeurism. Second, one or both of the spouses may feel embarrassed about having the details of their private marital life exposed to the public view. Furthermore, it is questionable whether the complaining spouse alone has the right to waive the marital privacy right of the couple by presenting the matter before the courts and the public. . . .

Michael Gary Hilf, Marital Privacy and Spousal Rape, 16 N. Eng. L. Rev. 31, 34 (1980). Is such reasoning persuasive? Recall Planned Parenthood v. Danforth, discussed in Chapter I. Can the marital right to privacy supersede the individual right to privacy? If so, why?

5. *Empirical evidence.* Marital rape is a form of domestic violence. Studies show that between 10 and 14 percent of married women have been raped by their husbands. David Finkelhor & Kersti Yllo, License to Rape: Sexual Abuse of Wives 222-223 (1985); Diana Russell, Rape in Marriage 89 (2d ed. 1990). Many wives (10 percent) are both battered and raped. Professor Russell suggests that marital rape is frequently quite violent and has more severe and traumatic effects on the victim than nonmarital rape. She found that 52 percent of marital rape victims suffer extreme long-term effects. Russell, supra, at 193. She also noted that 31 percent of the women who had been raped by their husbands were raped over 20 times. Id. at 111. In 91 percent of the cases, the rape occurred in a private setting but in many of these cases it occurred within earshot of others or in front of the children. Id. at 113. See also Lisa R. Eskow, Note, The Ultimate Weapon?: Demythologizing Spousal Rape and Reconceptualizing Its Prosecution, 48 Stan. L. Rev. 677, 684-689 (1996) (discussing the implications of Russell's study).

The above empirical studies, although somewhat outdated, derive from research on the prevalence of marital rape *per se.* More recent data fail to focus on marital rape, being based on a broader definition of violence by *intimate partners.* Jennifer A. Bennice & Patricia A. Resick, Marital Rape: History, Research, and Practice, 4 Trauma, Violence & Abuse 228, 234 (July 2003) (reporting findings of a national study of a sample of 8,000 women, revealing that 7.7 percent of the women had been raped by a current or former spouse, cohabitant, noncohabitant intimate partner, or a date).

6. *Psychological effects.* Why is spousal rape more harmful or traumatic than "stranger rape"? Feelings of betrayal, entrapment, and isolation are common among victims of marital rape and add to the humiliation, physical pain, and guilt that many victims endure. The trauma of marital rape is often more difficult for women to guard against, and thus it severely damages a woman's ability to maintain confidence in forming healthy relationships and trusting intimates. Bennice & Resuick, supra, at 238; Hasday, supra, at 1491-1498 (discussing research).

Problems

1. Mr. and Mrs. Adair have been married for six years. Marital problems arise and result in the wife's sleeping in the basement. One evening, Mrs. Adair is awakened by her husband who sexually assaults her. He is charged with two counts of third degree criminal sexual conduct based on her allegations of digital-anal penetration and digital-oral penetration against her will. Mr. Adair attempts to introduce evidence of specific instances of his wife's subsequent consensual sexual relations with him. The prosecutor seeks to exclude such evidence as barred by a rape-shield statute

that precludes admission of the victim's past sexual conduct "unless material to a fact at issue" and "unless its prejudicial effect is outweighed by its probative value." How should the court rule? See People v. Adair, 550 N.W.2d 505 (Mich. 1996).

2. Husband and Wife have been married for more than twenty years. Before marrying, the parties agreed, in writing, that they will maintain separate residences. The couple agrees to visit each other on weekends in one or the other location according to an agreed-on schedule. After more than 20 years of marriage, Wife files for divorce on the grounds of cruel and inhuman treatment. The court finds sufficient proof that Husband committed marital rape on several occasions. Husband argues that it was impossible for Wife to establish that marital rape constitutes cruel and inhuman treatment because the parties did not cohabit. What result? Why might a court hold that a spouse who has been forced to endure the trauma of a marital rape does not have grounds for divorce? See K v. B., 784 N.Y.S.2d 76 (App. Div. 2004).

Note: Property Crimes Between Spouses

Damage to a spouse's property may be inflicted as part of spousal abuse. Batterers have been known to damage or destroy furniture, windows, skylights, walls, roofs, garages, the other spouse's clothing or car, and items of sentimental value to the spouse. Some batterers injure or kill a family pet, using the animal as a tool to exert control over their victims. See Pam Belluck, Battered Wives' Pets Suffer Abuse Too, N.Y. Times, Apr. 1, 2006, at A10 (citing research noting that 54 percent of battered women in shelters said their abusers harmed or killed their pets). Should animals be included as subjects of domestic violence protection orders? Maine recently was the first state to enact such a law. Id.

A central dilemma concerns whether an abusive spouse can be prosecuted for damaging the victim-spouse's property when that property is jointly owned. In Hughes v. State, 56 P.3d 1088 (Alaska Ct. App. 2002), the defendant broke into his estranged wife's house after learning that she had had an affair. The husband subsequently claimed that he could not be convicted of criminal mischief for his damage to the door because he and his estranged wife were co-owners of the house (so that he did not damage the "property of another"). Rejecting this argument, the court held that a spouse who damages jointly-owned property destroys the other spouse's undivided equal interest in the property.

4. Evidentiary Privileges Arising from the Marital Relationship

■ TRAMMEL v. UNITED STATES
445 U.S. 40 (1980)

Mr. Chief Justice BURGER delivered the opinion of the Court.

We granted certiorari to consider whether an accused may invoke the privilege against adverse spousal testimony so as to exclude the voluntary testimony of his wife. . . .

I

On March 10, 1976, petitioner Otis Trammel was indicted with two others . . . for importing heroin into the United States from Thailand and the Philippine Islands and for conspiracy to import heroin in violation of 21 U.S.C. §§952(a), 962(a), and 963. The indictment also named six unindicted co-conspirators, including petitioner's wife Elizabeth Ann Trammel.

According to the indictment, petitioner and his wife flew from the Philippines to California in August 1975, carrying with them a quantity of heroin. . . . Elizabeth Trammel then traveled to Thailand where she purchased another supply of the drug. On November 3, 1975, with four ounces of heroin on her person, she boarded a plane for the United States. During a routine customs search in Hawaii, she was searched, the heroin was discovered, and she was arrested. After discussions with Drug Enforcement Administration agents, she agreed to cooperate with the Government.

Prior to trial on this indictment, petitioner . . . advised the court that the Government intended to call his wife as an adverse witness and asserted his claim to a privilege to prevent her from testifying against him. At a hearing on the motion, Mrs. Trammel was called as a Government witness under a grant of use immunity. She testified that she and petitioner were married in May 1975 and that they remained married.[1] She explained that her cooperation with the Government was based on assurances that she would be given lenient treatment.[2] She then described, in considerable detail, her role and that of her husband in the heroin distribution conspiracy.

After hearing this testimony, the District Court ruled that Mrs. Trammel could testify in support of the Government's case to any act she observed during the marriage and to any communication "made in the presence of a third person"; however, confidential communications between petitioner and his wife were held to be privileged and inadmissible. . . .

At trial, Elizabeth Trammel testified within the limits of the court's pretrial ruling; her testimony, as the Government concedes, constituted virtually its entire case against petitioner. He was found guilty on both the substantive and conspiracy charges. [On appeal], petitioner's only claim of error was that the admission of the adverse testimony of his wife, over his objection, contravened this Court's teaching in Hawkins v. United States, [358 U.S. 74 (1958)], and therefore constituted reversible error. The Court of Appeals rejected this contention. . . .

II

The privilege claimed by petitioner has ancient roots. Writing in 1628, Lord Coke observed that "it hath beene resolved by the Justices that a wife cannot be produced either against or for her husband." 1 E. Coke, A Commentarie upon Littleton 6b (1628). This spousal disqualification sprang from two canons of medieval jurisprudence: first, the rule that an accused was not permitted to testify in his own behalf because of his interest in the proceeding; second, the concept that

---

1. In response to the question whether divorce was contemplated, Mrs. Trammel testified that her husband had said that "I would go my way and he would go his."

2. The Government represents to the Court that Elizabeth Trammel has not been prosecuted for her role in the conspiracy.

husband and wife were one, and that since the woman had no recognized separate legal existence, the husband was that one. From those two now long-abandoned doctrines, it followed that what was inadmissible from the lips of the defendant-husband was also inadmissible from his wife.

Despite its medieval origins, this rule of spousal disqualification remained intact in most common-law jurisdictions well into the 19th century. . . . Indeed, it was not until 1933, in Funk v. United States, 290 U.S. 371, that this Court abolished the testimonial disqualification in the federal courts, so as to permit the spouse of a defendant to testify in the defendant's behalf. *Funk,* however, left undisturbed the rule that either spouse could prevent the other from giving adverse testimony. The rule thus evolved into one of privilege rather than one of absolute disqualification.

The modern justification for this privilege against adverse spousal testimony is its perceived role in fostering the harmony and sanctity of the marriage relationship. Notwithstanding this benign purpose, the rule was sharply criticized. Professor Wigmore termed it "the merest anachronism in legal theory and an indefensible obstruction to truth in practice." 8 Wigmore §2228, at 221. The Committee on Improvements in the Law of Evidence of the American Bar Association called for its abolition. 63 American Bar Association Reports 594-595 (1938). In its place, Wigmore and others suggested a privilege protecting only private marital communications, modeled on the privilege between priest and penitent, attorney and client, and physician and patient. See 8 Wigmore §2332 et seq.[5]

These criticisms influenced the American Law Institute, which, in its 1942 Model Code of Evidence advocated a privilege for marital confidences, but expressly rejected a rule vesting in the defendant the right to exclude all adverse testimony of his spouse. See American Law Institute, Model Code of Evidence, Rule 215 (1942). In 1953 the Uniform Rules of Evidence, drafted by the National Conference of Commissioners on Uniform State Laws, followed a similar course. . . . Several state legislatures enacted similarly patterned provisions into law. In Hawkins v. United States, 358 U.S. 74 (1958), this Court considered the continued vitality of the privilege against adverse spousal testimony in the federal courts. [*Hawkins*] left the federal privilege for adverse spousal testimony where it found it, continuing "a rule which bars the testimony of one spouse against the other unless both consent." Id., at 78. Accord, Wyatt v. United States, 362 U.S. 525, 528 (1960). . . .

III

[T]he long history of the privilege suggests that it ought not to be casually cast aside. That the privilege is one affecting marriage, home, and family relationships — already subject to much erosion in our day — also counsels caution. At the same time, we cannot escape the reality that the law on occasion adheres to doctrinal concepts long after the reasons which gave them birth have disappeared and after experience suggests the need for change. . . .

---

5. This Court recognized just such a confidential marital communications privilege in Wolfle v. United States, 291 U.S. 7 (1934), and in Blau v. United States, 340 U.S. 332 (1951). In neither case, however, did the Court adopt the Wigmore view that the communications privilege be substituted in place of the privilege against adverse spousal testimony. The privilege as to confidential marital communications is not at issue in the instant case. . . .

Since 1958, when *Hawkins* was decided, support for the privilege against adverse spousal testimony has been eroded further. Thirty-one jurisdictions, including Alaska and Hawaii, then allowed an accused a privilege to prevent adverse spousal testimony. 358 U.S., at 81, n.3 (Stewart, J., concurring). The number has now declined to 24. . . .

[W]e must decide whether the privilege against adverse spousal testimony promotes sufficiently important interests to outweigh the need for probative evidence in the administration of criminal justice.

It is essential to remember that the *Hawkins* privilege is not needed to protect information privately disclosed between husband and wife in the confidence of the marital relationship — once described by this Court as "the best solace of human existence." Stein v. Bowman, 13 Pet., at 223. Those confidences are privileged under the independent rule protecting confidential marital communications. The *Hawkins* privilege is invoked, not to exclude private marital communications, but rather to exclude evidence of criminal acts and of communications made in the presence of third persons.

No other testimonial privilege sweeps so broadly. The privileges between priest and penitent, attorney and client, and physician and patient limit protection to private communications. These privileges are rooted in the imperative need for confidence and trust. . . . The *Hawkins* rule stands in marked contrast to these three privileges. Its protection is not limited to confidential communications; rather it permits an accused to exclude all adverse spousal testimony. As Jeremy Bentham observed more than a century and a half ago, such a privilege goes far beyond making "every man's house his castle," and permits a person to convert his house into "a den of thieves." 5 Rationale of Judicial Evidence 340 (1827). It "secures, to every man, one safe and unquestionable and ever ready accomplice for every imaginable crime." Id., at 338.

The ancient foundations for so sweeping a privilege have long since disappeared. Nowhere in the common-law world — indeed in any modern society — is a woman regarded as chattel or demeaned by denial of a separate legal identity and the dignity associated with recognition as a whole human being. Chip by chip, over the years those archaic notions have been cast aside. . . .

The contemporary justification for affording an accused such a privilege is also unpersuasive. When one spouse is willing to testify against the other in a criminal proceeding — whatever the motivation — their relationship is almost certainly in disrepair; there is probably little in the way of marital harmony for the privilege to preserve. In these circumstances, a rule of evidence that permits an accused to prevent adverse spousal testimony seems far more likely to frustrate justice than to foster family peace. Indeed, there is reason to believe that vesting the privilege in the accused could actually undermine the marital relationship. For example, in a case such as this the Government is unlikely to offer a wife immunity and lenient treatment if it knows that her husband can prevent her from giving adverse testimony. If the Government is dissuaded from making such an offer, the privilege can have the untoward effect of permitting one spouse to escape justice at the expense of the other. It hardly seems conducive to the preservation of the marital relation to place a wife in jeopardy solely by virtue of her husband's control over her testimony.

Our consideration of the foundations for the privilege and its history satisfy us that "reason and experience" no longer justify so sweeping a rule as that found acceptable by the Court in *Hawkins*. Accordingly, we conclude that the existing rule should be modified so that the witness-spouse alone has a privilege to refuse to testify adversely; the witness may be neither compelled to testify nor foreclosed from testifying. This modification — vesting the privilege in the witness-spouse — furthers the important public interest in marital harmony without unduly burdening legitimate law enforcement needs.

Here, petitioner's spouse chose to testify against him. That she did so after a grant of immunity and assurances of lenient treatment does not render her testimony involuntary. [T]he judgment of the Court of Appeals is affirmed.

Notes and Questions

1. *Spousal privileges.* Trammel traces the history of spousal testimonial restrictions. The common law recognized two different privileges. Under the confidential marital communications privilege, private communications between husband and wife are privileged absolutely; either spouse may invoke this privilege. This rule is independent of the privilege at issue in *Trammel:* the ability of a spouse to exclude evidence by the other spouse of criminal acts and of communications in the presence of third parties. *Trammel* left the former privilege untouched in the federal courts. Should courts and legislatures also vest the confidential marital communications privilege in the witness spouse alone? Abolish it? Should the adverse spousal testimonial privilege apply in federal civil, as well as criminal trials? See Katherine O. Eldred, Comment, "Every Spouse's Evidence": Availability of the Adverse Spousal Testimonial Privilege in Federal Civil Trials, 69 U. Chi. L. Rev. 1319 (2002) (so advocating and pointing to a split in the federal courts regarding applicability of the privilege in the civil context).

2. *Impact of* Trammel. *Trammel* had several consequences. First, different rules now apply in the federal (and many state) courts concerning the two different types of spousal communications. Second, at the time *Trammel* was decided, 24 states permitted a spouse to prevent adverse spousal testimony. *Trammel* influenced many states to limit significantly this privilege. Milton C. Regan, Jr., Spousal Privilege and the Meanings of Marriage, 81 Va. L. Rev. 2045, 2060-2061 (1995) (pointing out that fewer states subsequently prevent such testimony).

3. *Exceptions.*

a. *Joint participation.* Should the law recognize an exception for either or both privileges when the spouses have *jointly participated* in the crime? The U.S. Supreme Court did not resolve this issue in *Trammel;* a split exists among the federal appellate courts regarding this issue. Compare United States v. Van Drunen, 501 F. 2d 1393, 1396 (7th Cir. 1974) (holding that the privilege is not available where spouses jointly participate in a criminal act), with Appeal of Maltifano, 633 F.2d 276 (3d Cir. 1980) (holding that the privilege applies regardless of joint participation). See also In re Grand Jury Subpoena, 755 F.2d 1022, 1026 (2d Cir. 1985) (stating that "*Trammel* has some negative implications as regards the joint participation exception"), *vacated,* 475 U.S. 133 (1986) (remanding with instructions to dismiss the cause as moot).

b. *Separated spouses.* Some courts have held that permanent separated status at the time of the communication makes the spousal privilege inapplicable. See, e.g., United States v. Singleton, 260 F.3d 1295, 1299 (11th Cir. 2001).

c. *Familial offenses.* There also exists an exception for offenses committed against a spouse or a child of either spouse. See Kimberly Ann Connor, A Critique of the Marital Privileges: An Examination of the Marital Privileges in the United States Military Through the State and Federal Approaches to the Marital Privileges, 36 Val. U.L. Rev. 119, 142-161 (2001).

4. *Voluntariness.* In vesting the adverse spousal testimony privilege in the witness-spouse, *Trammel* makes much of the fact that Mrs. Trammel gave her testimony voluntarily. The Supreme Court reasons that, because her testimony was voluntary, there was little marital harmony to preserve. Was her testimony in fact voluntary? Is one spouse's willingness to testify against the other an indication that marital harmony is past saving? See generally John William Strong et al., McCormick On Evidence §19 (5th ed. 1999) (discussing the possibility of maintaining marital harmony in cases where one spouse is willing to testify against another).

5. *Images of marriage and family.* What images of marriage and the family does *Trammel* reflect? See Michael W. Mullane, Trammel v. United States: Bad History, Bad Policy, and Bad Law, 47 Me. L. Rev. 105, 147-152 (1995). Further, how does vesting the privilege in the witness-spouse "further the important public interest in marital harmony"? Alternatively, how does vesting it in the defendant-spouse "actually undermine the marital relationship"? Doesn't the rule in *Trammel* put the government in the position of "forc[ing] or encourag[ing] testimony which might alienate husband and wife, or further inflame existing domestic differences" (*Hawkins,* 358 U.S. at 79) (cited in *Trammel*)? Is this an appropriate governmental role? For arguments that *Trammel* encourages the government to turn spouses against each other, see Richard O. Lempert, A Right to Every Woman's Evidence, 66 Iowa L. Rev. 725 (1981); Christopher B. Mueller & Lard C. Kirkpatrick, Evidence: Practice Under the Rules, §5.31, at 555 (1999).

6. *Abolition?* Should the adverse spousal testimony privilege be abolished altogether? Because the privilege is riddled with exceptions, it provides many avenues for appeal. Moreover, whether the privilege furthers its avowed purpose and preserves marital harmony is uncertain. For example, in Vance v. Rice, 524 F. Supp. 1297 (S.D. Iowa 1981), to prevent use of the privilege, a federal court upheld an injunction preventing a couple from marrying despite the woman's pregnancy. Do such results further the rule's objective?

Critics argue that marital privilege does not shape the conduct of the spouse so much as it plays upon certain loyalties to compel the testifying spouse to protect the defendant. For arguments favoring abolition of the rule, see David Medine, The Adverse Testimony Privilege: Time to Dispose of a "Sentimental Relic," 67 Or. L. Rev. 519 (1988); Amanda H. Frost, Updating the Marital Privileges: A Witness-Centered Rationale, 14 Wis. Woman's L.J. 1 (1999).

Problems

1. Kenneth Taylor, a police officer, is charged with aggravated battery of his girlfriend Glenda Richard. The battery consisted of a severe beating with his fists, police flashlight, and service revolver. After Glenda's hospitalization, she agrees to testify against Kenneth and provides a typed statement, an affidavit expressing her desire to prosecute and a video tape affirming that desire. Ten days before the trial, Glenda marries Kenneth. At trial, when the prosecutor calls Glenda as a victim-witness of the assault, she refuses to testify, invoking the spousal privilege for

adverse testimony. Louisiana has no spousal crime exception to the privilege. What arguments would you advance on behalf of Glenda? On behalf of the prosecution? See Louisiana v. Taylor, 642 So. 2d 160 (La. 1994).

2. Former President Bill Clinton is accused of having an extramarital affair with former White House intern Monica Lewinsky and of having committed perjury by denying it before a grand jury investigating his liaison with another woman, Paula Jones. To help build a case against Clinton, independent counsel Kenneth Starr calls Marcia Lewis, the mother of Lewinsky, to testify before a federal grand jury regarding her discussions with her daughter about Lewinsky's relationship with Clinton. The resultant controversy (regarding the wisdom of compelling a mother to testify against her daughter) evokes a demand for an adverse testimonial privilege for parents and children. Do the rationales employed by *Trammel* with respect to the adverse spousal testimonial privilege apply with equal force to parents and children? See Amee A. Shah, The Parent-Child Testimonial Privilege — Has the Time for It Finally Arrived?, 47 Clev. St. L. Rev. 41, 43 & nn.14-15 (1999) (pointing out that nine federal circuits have rejected such a privilege although four states recognize it).

IV

■

Alternative Families

The American family has been experiencing dramatic changes. The traditional nuclear family is on the decline. Currently, less than one in four families fits this family type.[1] In contrast, alternative family forms (such as unmarried heterosexual couples, gay and lesbian couples, and single parents) are proliferating.

This chapter explores the law's response to these alternative family forms. First, the materials focus on the changing legal meaning of "family." To what extent is a "family" limited to ceremonially initiated or biologically based relationships? Does this definition apply for some purposes but not others? Second, the chapter explores the extent to which the legal treatment of these families differs from that of the traditional family. In the cases and materials that follow, consider how the law should treat families that do not conform to heterosexual and marital norms. Should the state define and impose a legal meaning of "family" on all persons without exception? Or should the state honor private choices, so long as a given unit acts like a family and performs familial functions?

Note that this chapter deals with discrimination against non-traditional families in a variety of special contexts (zoning and housing, contract and tort law, employment, health care, domestic violence, inheritance, and adoption). For discussion of same-sex relationships in the context of marriage, see Chapter II; domestic partnerships, see Chapter II; child custody, see Chapter VII; child support, see Chapter VI; and adoption and assisted reproduction, see Chapter IX.

---

[1]. Bureau of the Census, U.S. Dept. of Commerce, Current Population Reports, Family and Living Arrangements: 2003, 2 (2004). In contrast, in 1970, 40 percent of households consisted of married couples with their own children under age 18. Bureau of the Census, U.S. Dept. of Commerce, Current Population Reports, Household and Family Characteristics: March 2000, 3 (2001).

A. CONSTITUTIONAL LIMITS ON DEFINITIONS OF "FAMILY"

1. Is a Commune a Family?

■ U.S. DEPARTMENT OF AGRICULTURE v. MORENO
413 U.S. 528 (1973)

Mr. Justice BRENNAN delivered the opinion of the Court.

This case requires us to consider the constitutionality of §3(e) of the Food Stamp Act of 1964, 7 U.S.C. §2012(e) [established] in 1964 in an effort to alleviate hunger and malnutrition among the more needy segments of our society. Eligibility for participation in the program is determined on a household rather than an individual basis. An eligible household purchases sufficient food stamps to provide that household with a nutritionally adequate diet. The household pays for the stamps at a reduced rate based upon its size and cumulative income. The food stamps are then used to purchase food at retail stores, and the Government redeems the stamps at face value, thereby paying the difference between the actual cost of the food and the amount paid by the household for the stamps.

As initially enacted, §3(e) defined a "household" as "a group of related or non-related individuals, who are not residents of an institution or boarding house, but are living as one economic unit sharing common cooking facilities and for whom food is customarily purchased in common." In January 1971, however Congress redefined the term "household" so as to include only groups of related individuals. Pursuant to this amendment, the Secretary of Agriculture promulgated regulations rendering ineligible for participation in the program any "household" whose members are not "all related to each other."

Appellees in this case consist of several groups of individuals who allege that, although they satisfy the income eligibility requirements for federal food assistance, they have nevertheless been excluded from the program solely because the persons in each group are not "all related to each other." Appellee Jacinta Moreno, for example is a 56-year-old diabetic who lives with Ermina Sanchez and the latter's three children. They share common living expenses, and Mrs. Sanchez helps to care for appellee. Appellee's monthly income, derived from public assistance, is $75; Mrs. Sanchez receives $133 per month from public assistance. The household pays $135 per month for rent, gas and electricity, of which appellee pays $50. Appellee spends $10 per month for transportation to a hospital for regular visits, and $5 per month for laundry. That leaves her $10 per month for food and other necessities. Despite her poverty, appellee has been denied federal food assistance solely because she is unrelated to the other members of her household. Moreover, although Mrs. Sanchez and her three children were permitted to purchase $108 worth of food stamps per month for $18, their participation in the program will be terminated if appellee Moreno continues to live with them.

Appellee Sheilah Hejny is married and has three children. Although the Hejnys are indigent, they took in a 20-year-old girl, who is unrelated to them because "we felt she had emotional problems." The Hejnys receive $144 worth of food stamps each month for $14. If they allow the 20-year-old girl to continue to live with them, they will be denied food stamps by reason of §3(e).

Appellee Victoria Keppler has a daughter with an acute hearing deficiency. The daughter requires special instruction in a school for the deaf. The school is located in an area in which appellee could not ordinarily afford to live. Thus, in order to make the most of her limited resources, appellee agreed to share an apartment near the school with a woman who, like appellee, is on public assistance. Since appellee is not related to the woman, appellee's food stamps have been, and will continue to be, cut off if they continue to live together.

These and two other groups of appellees instituted a class action . . . seeking declaratory and injunctive relief against the enforcement of the 1971 amendment of §3(e) and its implementing regulations. In essence, appellees contend, and the District Court held, that the "unrelated person" provision of §3(e) creates an irrational classification in violation of the equal protection component of the Due Process Clause of the Fifth Amendment. We agree. . . .

The challenged statutory classification (households of related persons versus households containing one or more unrelated persons) is clearly irrelevant to the stated purposes of the Act. As the District Court recognized, "(t)he relationships among persons constituting one economic unit and sharing cooking facilities have nothing to do with their abilities to stimulate the agricultural economy by purchasing farm surpluses, or with their personal nutritional requirements." 345 F. Supp., at 313.

Thus, if it is to be sustained, the challenged classification must rationally further some legitimate governmental interest. . . . Regrettably, there is little legislative history to illuminate the purposes of the 1971 amendment of §3(e). The legislative history that does exist, however, indicates that that amendment was intended to prevent so-called "hippies" and "hippie communes" from participating in the food stamp program. See H.R. Conf. Rep. No. 91-1793, p.8; 116 Cong. Rec. 44439 (1970) (Sen. Holland). The challenged classification clearly cannot be sustained by reference to this congressional purpose. For if the constitutional conception of "equal protection of the laws" means anything, it must at the very least mean that a bare congressional desire to harm a politically unpopular group cannot constitute a legitimate governmental interest. . . .

Although apparently conceding this point, the Government maintains that the challenged classification should nevertheless be upheld as rationally related to the clearly legitimate governmental interest in minimizing fraud in the administration of the food stamp program.[7] In essence, the Government contends that, in adopting the 1971 amendment, Congress might rationally have thought (1) that households with one or more unrelated members are more likely than "fully related" households to contain individuals who abuse the program by fraudulently

---

7. The Government initially argued to the District Court that the challenged classification might be justified as a means to foster "morality." In rejecting that contention, the District Court noted that "interpreting the amendment as an attempt to regulate morality would raise serious constitutional questions." 345 F. Supp. 310, 314. Indeed, citing this Court's decisions [in Griswold v. Connecticut, Stanley v. Georgia, and Eisenstadt v. Baird], the District Court observed that it was doubtful at best, whether Congress, "in the name of morality," could "infringe the rights to privacy and freedom of "association *in the home*." 345 F. Supp., at 314. (Emphasis in original.) Moreover, the court also pointed out that the classification established in §3(e) was not rationally related "to prevailing notions of morality, since it in terms disqualifies all households of unrelated individuals, without reference to whether a particular group contains both sexes." 345 F. Supp., at 315. The Government itself has now abandoned the "morality" argument.

failing to report sources of income or by voluntarily remaining poor; and (2) that such households are "relatively unstable," thereby increasing the difficulty of detecting such abuses. But even if we were to accept as rational the Government's wholly unsubstantiated assumptions concerning the differences between "related" and "unrelated" households we still could not agree with the Government's conclusion that the denial of essential federal food assistance to all otherwise eligible households containing unrelated members constitutes a rational effort to deal with these concerns.

At the outset, it is important to note that the Food Stamp Act itself contains provisions, wholly independent of §3(e), aimed specifically at the problems of fraud. . . . The existence of these provisions necessarily casts considerable doubt upon the proposition that the 1971 amendment could rationally have been intended to prevent those very same abuses.

[I]n practical operation, the 1971 amendment excludes from participation in the food stamp program, not those persons who are "likely to abuse the program," but, rather, only those persons who are so desperately in need of aid that they cannot even afford to alter their living arrangements so as to retain their eligibility. Traditional equal protection analysis does not require that every classification be drawn with precise "mathematical nicety." But the classification here in issue is not only "imprecise," it is wholly without any rational basis. The judgment of the District Court holding the "unrelated person" provision invalid under the Due Process Clause of the Fifth Amendment is therefore affirmed. . . .

Mr. Justice Douglas, concurring. . . .

. . . As the facts of this case show, the poor are congregating in households where they can better meet the adversities of poverty. This banding together is an expression of the right of freedom of association that is very deep in our traditions.

Other like rights have been recognized that are only peripheral First Amendment rights—the right to send one's child to a religious school, the right to study the German language in a private school, the protection of the entire spectrum of learning, teaching, and communicating ideas, the marital right of privacy. As the examples indicate, these peripheral constitutional rights are exercised not necessarily in assemblies that congregate in halls or auditoriums but in discrete individual actions such as parents placing a child in the school of their choice. Taking a person into one's home because he is poor or needs help or brings happiness to the household is of the same dignity.

Congress might choose to deal only with members of a family of one or two or three generations, treating it all as a unit. Congress, however, has not done that here. Concededly an individual living alone is not disqualified from the receipt of food stamp aid, even though there are other members of the family with whom he might theoretically live. Nor are common-law couples disqualified: they, like individuals living alone, may qualify under the Act if they are poor—whether they have abandoned their wives and children and however antifamily their attitudes may be. In other words, the "unrelated" person provision was not aimed at the maintenance of normal family ties. It penalizes persons or families who have brought under their roof an "unrelated" needy person. It penalizes the poorest of the poor for doubling up against the adversities of poverty.

But for the constitutional aspects of the problem, the "unrelated" person provision of the Act might well be sustained as a means to prevent fraud. . . .

I could not say that this "unrelated" person provision has no "rational" relation to control of fraud. We deal here, however, with the right of association, protected by the First Amendment. People who are desperately poor but unrelated come together and join hands with the aim better to combat the crises of poverty. The need of those living together better to meet those crises is denied, while the need of households made up of relatives that is no more acute is serviced. Problems of the fisc, as we stated in Shapiro v. Thompson, 394 U.S. 618, 633 [(1969)], are legitimate concerns of government. But government "may not accomplish such a purpose by invidious distinctions between classes of its citizens." Ibid. . . .

The right of association, the right to invite the stranger into one's home is too basic in our constitutional regime to deal with roughshod. If there are abuses inherent in that pattern of living against which the food stamp program should be protected, the Act must be "narrowly drawn," to meet the precise end. The method adopted and applied to these cases makes §3(e) of the Act unconstitutional by reason of the invidious discrimination between the two classes of needy persons. . . .

Mr. Justice REHNQUIST, with whom THE CHIEF JUSTICE concurs, dissenting.

[O]ur role is limited to the determination of whether there is any rational basis on which Congress could decide that public funds made available under the food stamp program should not go to a household containing an individual who is unrelated to any other member of the household. . . . I do not think it is unreasonable for Congress to conclude that the basic unit which it was willing to support with federal funding through food stamps is some variation on the family as we know it—a household consisting of related individuals. This unit provides a guarantee which is not provided by households containing unrelated individuals that the household exists for some purpose other than to collect federal food stamps. . . .

Notes and Questions

1. *"Family" or "household"?* In *Moreno*, the Supreme Court was willing to include unrelated persons in a definition of "household" for food stamp purposes. Would the Court have reached the same result if the food stamp legislation determined eligibility on a "family" basis, instead of a "household" basis? How do the terms differ? If "family" were defined in terms of "a single housekeeping unit," how would that change the analysis?

In contrast to *Moreno*, consider Village of Belle Terre v. Boraas, 416 U.S. 1 (1974), in which the U.S. Supreme Court upheld a zoning ordinance that restricted land use to "one-family dwellings" and defined a "family" as follows:

(o)ne or more persons related by blood, adoption, or marriage, living and cooking together as a single housekeeping unit, exclusive of household servants. A number of persons but not exceeding (2) living and cooking together as a single housekeeping unit though not related by blood, adoption, or marriage shall be deemed to constitute a family.

In this challenge to a zoning ordinance by a landlord who rented a house to six college students, Justice Douglas, writing for the majority, found no violation of the freedom of association (because a "family" may entertain whomever it pleases) or any other fundamental right. In upholding the ordinance, the Court analogized the group of college students to other "urban problems" such as "[t]he regimes of boarding houses, fraternity houses, and the like . . ." in which "[m]ore people occupy a given space; more cars rather continuously pass by; more cars are parked; noise travels with crowds." Id. at 9. Applying the rational-basis test to the zoning ordinance, the majority saw nothing impermissible in the Village's goal of "lay[ing] out zones where family values, youth values, and the blessings of quiet seclusion and clean air make the area a sanctuary for people." Id.

2. *Views of family.* How do the Court's views of the "families" in *Moreno* and *Belle Terre* differ? For example, *Belle Terre* reveals concerns about transiency, overcrowding, and congestion. Yet, *Moreno* is skeptical about the government's "unsubstantiated assumptions" about the instability of households of unrelated persons. What factors explain the different results? Why might the Court have shown greater deference to the government's interest in *Belle Terre* than in *Moreno*? Why does Justice Douglas concur in *Moreno*, given his majority opinion in *Belle Terre*? Was the outcome different, perhaps, because the *Moreno* plaintiffs conformed more to our concept of the traditional family?

3. *Family values.* What family values do the groups in *Moreno* and *Belle Terre* reflect? Did the group sharing a home in *Belle Terre* pose a greater risk to the "family value" of permanency than the groups excluded by the food stamp restriction that was invalidated in *Moreno*? Cf. Laurence H. Tribe, American Constitutional Law 1403 (2d ed. 1988).

4. *Federal constitutional rights.* Commentators criticize *Moreno* for its unwillingness to address the degree to which the Constitution protects the right to choose with whom to share a home. J. Harvie Wilkinson III & G. Edward White, Constitutional Protection for Personal Lifestyles, 62 Cornell L. Rev. 563, 584 (1977). If *Moreno* and *Belle Terre* raise the right to associate in the home with unrelated individuals, is there a comparable right *not* to associate with relatives? Cf. Robinson v. Block, 869 F.2d 202 (3d Cir. 1989) (co-resident siblings have burden of establishing separateness, under food stamp amendments, to avoid classification as a single household). For a criticism of *Belle Terre*'s assertion that the ordinance implicates no fundamental right, such as association or privacy, see Kenneth L. Karst, The Freedom of Intimate Association, 89 Yale L.J. 624 (1980).

5. *State constitutional rights.* State courts divide on the constitutionality of single-family zoning ordinances as applied to groups. Most follow *Belle Terre*, finding that the ordinances meet the rational basis test. A few, however, decline to adopt *Belle Terre*'s reasoning on the basis of state constitutional rights to either due process or privacy. See Katia Brener, Note, *Belle Terre* and the Single-Family Home Ordinances: Judicial Perceptions of Local Government and the Presumption of Validity, 74 N.Y.U. L. Rev. 447, 456-463 (1999) (discussing cases).

6. *Other group living arrangements.*

a. *Student groups.* After *Belle Terre*, supra, ten college students challenged an ordinance in effect in a New Jersey town that limited occupancy by defining a "family" as:

one or more persons occupying a dwelling unit as a single non-profit housekeeping unit, who are living together as a stable and permanent living unit, being a traditional family unit or the functional equivalency thereof.

Borough of Glassboro v. Vallorosi, 568 A.2d 888, 889 (N.J. 1990). The *Vallorosi* ordinance, similar to that in *Belle Terre*, aimed to preserve stable, permanent housing. Influenced by state precedents equating "single family" with "single housekeeping unit," the New Jersey Supreme Court adopted a functional standard and held that the group complied because they planned to live together for three years, ate together, and shared household tasks and expenses. Is *Vallorosi's* functional standard superior to *Belle Terre's* focus on associational ties?

b. *Unmarried couples.* The Belle Terre zoning ordinance contained an exception permitting two unrelated persons to constitute a family. Plaintiffs argued that the ordinance "reeks with an animosity to unmarried couples," 416 U.S. at 8, and asked why more than two unmarried persons could not constitute a family. How would the Supreme Court respond to an ordinance that excluded unmarried couples? See City of Ladue v. Horn, 720 S.W.2d 745 (Mo. Ct. App. 1986) (rejecting couple's constitutional challenge). See also P.J. Huffstutter, Law Says Unmarried Couple, 3 Kids Can't Cohabit, S.F. Chron., May 23, 2006, at A2 (St. Louis suburb ruled that unmarried couple and their children are violating ban on unrelated persons living together).

c. *Group homes. Belle Terre* (and *Vallorosi,* supra) illustrate the elasticity of the definition of "family" in the use of zoning as an agent of social control. The Supreme Court again examined the issue in City of Cleburne v. Cleburne Living Center, 473 U.S. 432 (1985), in which the city denied an exemption from the local ordinance to a home for the mentally retarded. The group alleged that the ordinance violated equal protection. The Court held the ordinance invalid as applied, reasoning that the denial rested on irrational prejudice. Did the Belle Terre ordinance, as applied, rest on "irrational prejudice" against students? See also City of Edmonds v. Oxford House, 514 U.S. 725 (1995) (challenging land use restriction as applied to group of substance abusers). Is resort to the police power appropriate to exclude "undesirables" from the community?

Congress prohibits discrimination in the sale and rental of real property on the basis of race, color, religion, sex, familial status, national origin, or handicap. Fair Housing Act (FHA), 42 U.S.C. §§3601 et seq (2000). Do group homes qualify for "familial status" treatment for purposes of the FHA's prohibition against housing discrimination (42 U.S.C. §3602(k))? See Keys Youth Services v. City of Olathe, 248 F.3d 1267 (10th Cir. 2001) (holding that denial of special use permit for proposed group home for troubled adolescent males did not violate FHA because employees, who did not reside at home, failed to meet statutory requirement that minors be "domiciled with" their caretakers); Westhab, Inc. v. City of New Rochelle, 2004 WL 1171400 (S.D.N.Y. 2004) (dismissing claim that defendants' application of single-family definition to nonprofit provider of social services for homeless youths discriminated on the basis of familial status in violation of the FHA because none of the staff resides at the home or uses the home for any personal purposes).

d. *Elderly homeowners.* Dutton v. Department of Social Welfare, 721 A.2d 109 (Vt. 1998), addressed whether elderly homeowners and their boarders should be counted as a single household for purposes of state and federal subsidies for energy costs. Is the issue in *Dutton* more closely analogous to that in *Belle Terre* or *Moreno?*

7. *Impact of* Lawrence. Did Lawrence v. Texas set a new due process standard for zoning ordinances, invalidating the principles of *Belle Terre?* A non-profit social services provider for homeless youth raised this issue in *Westhab,* supra. Calling

the plaintiffs' argument "creative" but "erroneous," the court responded that "[z]oning ordinances limiting the number of unrelated persons who can occupy a dwelling have nothing to do with whether sex between consenting adults of the same gender can be criminalized consistent with constitutional guarantees." 2004 WL 1171400 at *9. Do you agree? Suppose the argument had been made in a challenge to an ordinance prohibiting the cohabitation of unmarried couples as in *City of Ladue*, supra? Recall that Justice O'Connor's concurrence in *Lawrence* relies in part on *Moreno*. (Chapter I, supra, p. 56).

Problems

1. A "co-housing movement," originating in Scandinavia, is attracting adherents in California and Washington. Karen and Tom Smith and their two preschoolers move into a development in Seattle that features privately owned homes, common childcare facilities, and a communal dining area and kitchen. Supporters of the co-housing movement claim it responds to contemporary housing needs, specifically, mothers working outside the home and the isolation of the contemporary family. Suppose Seattle attempts to exclude the residents via a zoning ordinance similar to that of *Belle Terre* or *Vallorosi*. Do the residents constitute a "single family"? See generally Charles Durrett & Kataryn McCamant, Co-housing: A Contemporary Approach to Housing Ourselves (2d ed. 1994); Richard Paoli, So Happy Together: Cohousing Developments Offer Residents the Chance to Share Life, S.F. Chron. (Real Estate Section), July 15, 2001, at 1.

2. The Jones family, a polygamous "extended family" claiming to follow early Mormon teachings, desires to move to a community with a zoning ordinance similar to that of *Belle Terre* or *Vallorosi*. How might they fare in a zoning challenge?

Two of the three named family groups in *Moreno* consist of households of single mothers who are caring for dependent adults. A considerable number of persons in the United States today live in single-parent families. In fact, the number of single-parent families has tripled in the last 25 years.[2] African-American single mothers constitute a significant proportion of these families.[3] The article below criticizes American family policy that prioritizes the marital family over other family forms, such as the single-parent family.

■ VIVIAN HAMILTON, MISTAKING MARRIAGE FOR SOCIAL POLICY
11 Va. J. Soc. Pol'y & L. 307, 355-361, 368-369 (2004)

"IN SICKNESS AND IN HEALTH": THE CARETAKING FUNCTION OF MARRIAGE

Society currently designates the nuclear, preferably marital, family as the social structure that supports child caretaking. Yet caretaking benefits not only those for whom care is provided, but also society generally. [For example,] [t]he sick and

[2]. Id. at 7 (reporting longitudinal census data).
[3]. Id. at 9 (reporting current census data).

elderly require care, and we expect that today's young people will provide physical care to us once we are elderly. . . .

Despite the tremendous public interest in dependents' care and upbringing, the state's efforts to directly support dependent caretaking, irrespective of the family structure within which it occurs, have been anemic. The rhetorical importance placed on child caretaking in the U.S. stands in stark contrast to family support policies that are the stingiest in the industrial world. [O]ther countries consistently do more to assist caretakers. France and the Scandinavian countries are among those that have implemented family support policies that directly support caretaking. These policies include subsidized day care, paid parental leave, universal health care, and income supplements to low-earning caretakers. At least in part because of these measures, the child poverty rate in France, for example, is just over five percent, compared to nearly twenty percent in the U.S. . . .

Certainly, some families in the U.S. may receive different types of support, depending on their family and caretaking structures. The state supports some dependents indirectly through the subsidies and supports provided to marital families, support that comes without stigmatization. Married couples receive more protections and benefits than do nonmarital couples — social security, pension, and health insurance benefits are among the measures that assist marital families. While federal income tax laws currently require some two-earner marital families to pay higher taxes than if they were to file singly, they do benefit the family with one primary wage-earner and a stay-at-home dependent spouse (or secondary wage-earner). Thus, while all marital families arguably receive significant net benefits by marrying, the so-called traditional family is rewarded further. Society also privileges and supports marital families in numerous direct and indirect ways.

Across the United States, unmarried men and women who live together are almost as likely to be raising children as are married couples. But because they have chosen not to formalize their relationships, they must manage caretaking without many of the benefits accorded marital families. Also, social support for single-parent families, the vast majority of which are headed by women, can vary dramatically based on the way in which those families were originally formed. Widows, for example, typically received generous and non-stigmatized social security benefits. Divorced and never-married mothers must depend instead on the vicissitudes of the uncertain child support and welfare systems. Not only are these families affected materially, but they also suffer from a social stigma that is reinforced by the existing legal structure.

Some commentators retort that two-parent marital families are best for children, so it is therefore appropriate for the state to subsidize or privilege this family form over others. There are several problems with this argument. [S]ociologist Sara McLanahan has found that data does not support the conclusion that what harms children is the absence of one parent. Instead, McLanahan says, single parenting currently leads to certain types of instability that can harm children. Much of the link between single parenting and negative child outcomes can thus be attributed to low income, less-stable adult presence, and residential mobility after divorce. . . . Other commentators, moreover, have highlighted the danger in isolating a single variable to identify the cause of social phenomena. Single parenthood, for example, is not evenly distributed across society, but instead correlates with other socioeconomic factors. It is therefore difficult to pinpoint the effects of single parenthood on children.

[T]he state should attempt to neutralize any disadvantages of the single-parent household by implementing programs that directly support caretaking efforts. . . . Dependent caretaking is critical to the development of an educated, productive populace. Economic support and well-being is essential to dependent caretaking. The public interest in those functions — as they are performed both within and outside of marriage — therefore compels some degree of government involvement. However, using marriage as a proxy for these two, closely related functions is ham-handed. Regulating marriage means regulating areas in which the state should remain uninvolved — namely, the expressive, companionate, and sexual and procreative aspects of the marital and other intimate relationships. Rather than emphasizing the importance of marriage, government should instead enact more carefully targeted policies to support caretaking and the economic well-being of its citizenry.

What would this look like in practice? First, the state would deemphasize family form. It would eliminate government-sanctioned privileges that currently accompany heterosexual monogamous marriage and that devalue and stigmatize other family structures. It would also introduce programs that directly bolster dependent caretaking and the economic supports that make such caretaking possible. . . . Possible programs could include subsidized or public day care, longer school days and school years, more affordable health care, and workplace protections (including paid family leave policies and flexible schedules. To further ensure the economic security of dependents, the state should also make modifications to the welfare, social security, and tax systems. . . .

Some might suggest that it is incongruous to demand privacy from government intervention in certain aspects of family life but seek its intervention in other aspects. But incongruity appears only if the marital family is viewed as an indivisible unit. Dissecting that unit into its functional parts brings into sharp relief and permits examination of its different components. Once family life has been dissected, the question becomes not how one can justify treating certain aspects of the family differently, but instead how one can justify treating such radically different aspects of the family the same. Why should government privilege marriage as an exclusive instrument of expression (especially when the content of that expression is largely predetermined)? Why should it privilege one form of companionate relationship over others that may serve the same societal functions? Why should sexual and procreative freedom be contingent either upon one's marital or economic status? Why shouldn't the state do more to provide economic support for caretaking — the aspect of family functioning most crucial to its own future well-being?

For other criticisms of governmental policy that prioritizes marriage, see Martha Albertson Fineman, The Neutered Mother, the Sexual Family, and Other Twentieth-Century Tragedies (1995) (revisioning family law by challenging the marital norm to redefine the core family unit as the mother-child dyad); Rachel F. Moran, How Second-Wave Feminism Forgot the Single Woman, 33 Hofstra L. Rev. 223 (2004) (exploring the law's neglect of single women and attributing its cause to a societal tendency to privilege marriage and motherhood); Nancy D. Polikoff, Ending Marriage as We Know It, 32 Hofstra L. Rev. 201 (2003) (book review of a Canadian law reform commission report that recommends the extension of legal protections without regard to whether people are living in traditional conjugal relationships).

For further discussion of the single-parent family, see Part D, infra this chapter, "Parents' and Children's Rights in the Nonmarital Family."

2. The Extended Family

■ MOORE v. CITY OF EAST CLEVELAND
431 U.S. 494 (1977)

Mr. Justice POWELL announced the judgment of the Court, and delivered an opinion in which Mr. Justice BRENNAN, Mr. Justice MARSHALL, and Mr. Justice BLACKMUN joined.

East Cleveland's housing ordinance, like many throughout the country, limits occupancy of a dwelling unit to members of a single family. But the ordinance contains an unusual and complicated definitional section that recognizes as a "family" only a few categories of related individuals, §1341.08.[2] Because her family, living together in her home, fits none of those categories, appellant stands convicted of a criminal offense. The question in this case is whether the ordinance violates the Due Process Clause of the Fourteenth Amendment.

Appellant, Mrs. Inez Moore, lives in her East Cleveland home together with her son, Dale Moore Sr., and her two grandsons, Dale, Jr., and John Moore, Jr. The two boys are first cousins rather than brothers; we are told that John came to live with his grandmother and with the elder and younger Dale Moores (sic) after his mother's death.

In early 1973, Mrs. Moore received a notice of violation from the city, stating that John was an "illegal occupant" and directing her to comply with the ordinance. When she failed to remove him from her home, the city filed a criminal charge. [She claimed that the ordinance was facially unconstitutional. She was convicted and sentenced to 5 days in jail and a $25 fine.]

The city argues that our decision in Village of Belle Terre v. Boraas, 416 U.S. 1 (1974), requires us to sustain the ordinance attacked here. . . . But one overriding factor sets this case apart from *Belle Terre*. The ordinance there affected only *unrelated* individuals. It expressly allowed all who were related by "blood, adoption, or marriage" to live together, and in sustaining the ordinance we were careful to note that it promoted "family needs" and "family values." East Cleveland, in contrast, has chosen to regulate the occupancy of its housing by slicing deeply into the family itself. This is no mere incidental result of the ordinance. On its face it selects certain categories of relatives who may live together and declares that others may not. In particular, it makes a crime of a grandmother's choice to live with her grandson in circumstances like those presented here.

---

2. Section 1341.08 (1966) provides:

"Family" means a number of individuals related to the nominal head of the household or to the spouse of the nominal head of the household living as a single housekeeping unit in a single dwelling unit, [including spouse, parent, or unmarried children, provided the unmarried children have no co-resident children, but] a family may include not more than one dependent married or unmarried child of the nominal head of the household or of the spouse of the nominal head of the household and the spouse and dependent children of such dependent child. . . .

When a city undertakes such intrusive regulation of the family, neither *Belle Terre* nor *Euclid* governs; the usual judicial deference to the legislature is inappropriate. "This Court has long recognized that freedom of personal choice in matters of marriage and family life is one of the liberties protected by the Due Process Clause of the Fourteenth Amendment." Cleveland Board of Education v. LaFleur, 414 U.S. 632, 639-640 (1974). A host of cases, tracing their lineage to Meyer v. Nebraska, 262 U.S. 390, 399-401 (1923), and Pierce v. Society of Sisters, 268 U.S. 510, 534-535 (1925), have consistently acknowledged a "private realm of family life which the state cannot enter." Prince v. Massachusetts, 321 U.S. 158, 166 (1944). Of course, the family is not beyond regulation. See Prince v. Massachusetts, supra, 321 U.S. at 166. But when the government intrudes on choices concerning family living arrangements, this Court must examine carefully the importance of the governmental interests advanced and the extent to which they are served by the challenged regulation.

When thus examined, this ordinance cannot survive. The city seeks to justify it as a means of preventing overcrowding, minimizing traffic and parking congestion, and avoiding an undue financial burden on East Cleveland's school system. Although these are legitimate goals, the ordinance before us serves them marginally, at best. For example, the ordinance permits any family consisting only of husband, wife, and unmarried children to live together, even if the family contains a half dozen licensed drivers, each with his or her own car. At the same time it forbids an adult brother and sister to share a household, even if both faithfully use public transportation. The ordinance would permit a grandmother to live with a single dependent son and children, even if his school-age children number a dozen, yet it forces Mrs. Moore to find another dwelling for her grandson John, simply because of the presence of his uncle and cousin in the same household. . . .

The city would distinguish the cases based on *Meyer* and *Pierce*. It points out that none of them "gives grandmothers any fundamental rights with respect to grandsons," . . . and suggests that any constitutional right to live together as a family extends only to the nuclear family, essentially a couple and their dependent children.

To be sure, these cases did not expressly consider the family relationship presented here. They were immediately concerned with freedom of choice with respect to childbearing, or with the rights of parents to the custody and companionship of their own children, or with traditional parental authority in matters of child rearing and education. But unless we close our eyes to the basic reasons why certain rights associated with the family have been accorded shelter under the Fourteenth Amendment's Due Process Clause, we cannot avoid applying the force and rationale of these precedents to the family choice involved in this case. . . .

Substantive due process has at times been a treacherous field for this Court. There *are* risks when the judicial branch gives enhanced protection to certain substantive liberties without the guidance of the more specific provisions of the Bill of Rights. As the history of the *Lochner* era demonstrates, there is reason for concern lest the only limits to such judicial intervention become the predilections of those who happen at the time to be Members of this Court. That history counsels caution and restraint. But it does not counsel abandonment, nor does it require what the city urges: cutting off any protection of family rights at the first convenient, if arbitrary boundary — the boundary of the nuclear family.

Appropriate limits on substantive due process come not from drawing arbitrary lines but rather from careful "respect for the teachings of history (and), solid recognition of the basic values that underlie our society." Griswold v. Connecticut,

381 U.S., at 501. Our decisions establish that the Constitution protects the sanctity of the family precisely because the institution of the family is deeply rooted in this Nation's history and tradition. It is through the family that we inculcate and pass down many of our most cherished values, moral and cultural.

Ours is by no means a tradition limited to respect for the bonds uniting the members of the nuclear family. The tradition of uncles, aunts, cousins, and especially grandparents sharing a household along with parents and children has roots equally venerable and equally deserving of constitutional recognition. Over the years millions of our citizens have grown up in just such an environment, and most, surely, have profited from it. Even if conditions of modern society have brought about a decline in extended family households, they have not erased the accumulated wisdom of civilization, gained over the centuries and honored throughout our history, that supports a larger conception of the family. Out of choice, necessity, or a sense of family responsibility, it has been common for close relatives to draw together and participate in the duties and the satisfactions of a common home. Decisions concerning child rearing, which *Yoder, Meyer, Pierce* and other cases have recognized as entitled to constitutional protection, long have been shared with grandparents or other relatives who occupy the same household, indeed who may take on major responsibility for the rearing of the children. Especially in times of adversity, such as the death of a spouse or economic need, the broader family has tended to come together for mutual sustenance and to maintain or rebuild a secure home life. This is apparently what happened here.[16]

Whether or not such a household is established because of personal tragedy, the choice of relatives in this degree of kinship to live together may not lightly be denied by the State. [T]he Constitution prevents East Cleveland from standardizing its children and its adults by forcing all to live in certain narrowly defined family patterns. . . .

Mr. Justice BRENNAN, with whom Mr. Justice MARSHALL joins, concurring.

I join the plurality's opinion. . . . I write only to underscore the cultural myopia of the arbitrary boundary drawn by the East Cleveland ordinance in the light of the tradition of the American home that has been a feature of our society since our beginning as a Nation. . . .

. . . The "extended family" that provided generations of early Americans with social services and economic and emotional support in times of hardship, and was the beachhead for successive waves of immigrants who populated our cities, remains not merely still a pervasive living pattern, but under the goad of brutal economic necessity, a prominent pattern virtually a means of survival for large numbers of the poor and deprived minorities of our society. For them compelled pooling of scant resources requires compelled sharing of a household.

The "extended" form is especially familiar among black families.[6] We may suppose that this reflects the truism that black citizens, like generations of white

---

16. We are told that the mother of John Moore, Jr., died when he was less than one year old. He, like uncounted others who have suffered a similar tragedy, then came to live with the grandmother to provide the infant with a substitute for his mother's care and to establish a more normal home environment.

6. B. Yorburg, [The Changing Family 108 (1973)]. The extended family often plays an important role in the rearing of young black children whose parents must work. Many such children frequently "spend all of their growing-up years in the care of extended kin. . . . Often children are 'given' to their grandparents, who rear them to adulthood. . . . Many children normally grow up in a three-generation household and they absorb the influences of grandmother and grandfather as well as mother and father." J. Ladner, Tomorrow's Tomorrow: The Black Woman 60 (1972).

immigrants before them, have been victims of economic and other disadvantages that would worsen if they were compelled to abandon extended, for nuclear, living patterns. . . . In black households whose head is an elderly woman, as in this case, . . . 48% of such black households, compared with 10% of counterpart white households, include related minor children not offspring of the head of the household.[9]

I do not wish to be understood as implying that East Cleveland's enforcement of its ordinance is motivated by a racially discriminatory purpose: The record of this case would not support that implication. But the prominence of other than nuclear families among ethnic and racial minority groups, including our black citizens, surely demonstrates that the "extended family" pattern remains a vital tenet of our society. It suffices that in prohibiting this pattern of family living as a means of achieving its objectives, appellee city has chosen a device that deeply intrudes into family associational rights that historically have been central, and today remain central, to a large proportion of our population. . . .

[The concurring opinion of Justice Stevens, emphasizing Mrs. Moore's right to use her property as she sees fit, has been omitted.]

Mr. Justice STEWART, with whom Mr. Justice REHNQUIST joins, dissenting. . . .

The *Belle Terre* decision . . . disposes of the appellant's contentions to the extent they focus not on her blood relationships with her sons and grandsons but on more general notions about the "privacy of the home." Her suggestion that every person has a constitutional right permanently to share his residence with whomever he pleases, and that such choices are "beyond the province of legitimate governmental intrusion," amounts to the same argument that was made and found unpersuasive in *Belle Terre*. . . .

The appellant is considerably closer to the constitutional mark in asserting that the East Cleveland ordinance intrudes upon "the private realm of family life which the state cannot enter." Prince v. Massachusetts, 321 U.S. 158, 166. Several decisions of the Court have identified specific aspects of what might broadly be termed "private family life" that are constitutionally protected against state interference.

Although the appellant's desire to share a single-dwelling unit also involves "private family life" in a sense, that desire can hardly be equated with any of the interests [which we have previously protected]. The ordinance about which the appellant complains did not impede her choice to have or not to have children, and it did not dictate to her how her own children were to be nurtured and reared. The ordinance clearly does not prevent parents from living together or living with their unemancipated offspring.

But even though the Court's previous cases are not directly in point, the appellant contends that the importance of the "extended family" in American society requires us to hold that her decision to share her residence with her grandsons may not be interfered with by the State. This decision, like the decisions involved in bearing and raising children, is said to be an aspect of "family life" also entitled to substantive protection under the Constitution. Without pausing to inquire how far under this argument an "extended family" might extend, I cannot agree. . . . To equate [Moore's] interest with the fundamental decisions to marry

9. [R. Hill, The Strengths of Black Families 5-6 (1972)].

and to bear and raise children is to extend the limited substantive contours of the Due Process Clause beyond recognition.

The appellant also challenges the single-family occupancy ordinance on equal protection grounds [an issue which the majority did not reach]. Her claim is that the city has drawn an arbitrary and irrational distinction between groups of people who may live together as a "family" and those who may not. . . . I do not think East Cleveland's definition of "family" offends the Constitution. The city has undisputed power to ordain single-family residential occupancy. And that power plainly carries with it the power to say what a "family" is. Here the city has defined "family" to include not only father, mother, and dependent children, but several other close relatives as well. The definition is rationally designed to carry out the legitimate governmental purposes identified in the *Belle Terre* opinion. . . .

Obviously, East Cleveland might have as easily and perhaps as effectively hit upon a different definition of "family." But a line could hardly be drawn that would not sooner or later become the target of a challenge like the appellant's. If "family" included all of the householder's grandchildren there would doubtless be the hard case of an orphaned niece or nephew. If, as the appellant suggests, a "family" must include all blood relatives, what of longtime friends? . . .

Notes and Questions

1. *The tradition of the extended family.* Justice Powell's plurality opinion invalidates the East Cleveland ordinance based on the historical importance of the extended family. In fact, this view is a myth. The Cambridge Group for the History of Population and Social Structure documented, based on computer analysis, that the nuclear (rather than the extended) family predominated before industrialization. See Household and Family in Past Time (Peter Laslett ed., 1972); Peter Laslett, The World We Have Lost Further Explored 97-99 (3d ed. 1984). See also William J. Goode, World Revolution and Family Patterns 6 (1970) (referring to the extended family as the "family form of Western nostalgia"). Would such knowledge have changed the outcome in *Moore?*

2. *Role of race.* Do Justice Powell's plurality opinion and Justice Brennan's concurrence rest on a mythical model of *white* families? Although demographic data support the *mythical* status of the extended family among whites, empirical research support the prevalence of this family form among African-Americans. See Robert Joseph Taylor et al., Developments in Research on Black Families: A Decade Review, in Family in Transition: Rethinking Marriage, Sexuality, Child Rearing, and Family Organization 439, 445-446 (Arlene S. Skolnick & Jerome H. Skolnick eds., 7th ed. 1992). See also Terry Orbuch & Edna Brown, Divorce in the Context of Being African American, in Handbook of Divorce and Relationship Dissolution 481, 491 (Mark A. Fine & John H. Harvey eds., 2006) (documenting the important role of African American grandparents, especially grandmothers, in the lives of their grandchildren). Latino culture encompasses a similar multi-generational view of family. See Ana Novoa, American Family Law: History and Whostory, 19 Chicano-Latino L. Rev. 265, 266-267 (1998).

3. Belle Terre *distinguished.* In applying a stricter standard of review than it used in *Belle Terre,* the Court treats *Moore* as involving not zoning, but rather

family privacy. Why does the Belle Terre ordinance serve "family needs" and "family values" but the East Cleveland ordinance "slic[es] deeply into the family itself"? Is the latter ordinance directed at the same ends (eliminating traffic congestion and overcrowding) or at other family values? Professor Robert Burt responds:

> The plurality did not consider that the purpose of the ordinance was quite straightforward: to exclude from a middle-class, predominantly black community, that saw itself as socially and economically upwardly mobile, other black families most characteristic of lower-class ghetto life.
>
> Perhaps the Court did not see this purpose or, if it did, considered this an "illegitimate goal," though in other cases the Court had been exceedingly solicitous of white middle-class communities' attempts to preserve a common social identity — "zones," as the Court had put the matter [in *Belle Terre*] — "where family values, youth values, and the blessings of the quiet seclusion and clean air make the area a sanctuary for people." . . . I find in [Justice Brennan's] characterization of the East Cleveland ordinance, as "senseless" and "eccentric," precisely what he alleges in it: "a depressing insensitivity toward the economic and emotional needs" of the current majority of residents in East Cleveland.

Robert A. Burt, The Constitution of the Family, 1979 Sup. Ct. Rev. 329, 389.

In an omitted dissent, Justice White disputes the idea that Mrs. Moore's interest in living with her grandchildren is protected by the Due Process Clause. He reasons that the ordinance prevents Mrs. Moore from living only in East Cleveland but that she is free to move elsewhere in Cleveland. Does his suggestion respond to Professor Burt's criticism above?

Justice Brennan, in his concurrence, justifies constitutional protection by noting the devastation that severing an extended family may cause. Might a definition of "family" that prevents unrelated persons from living together have the same consequences?

4. *Criteria for family.* Are blood and legal ties conclusive evidence of a family? Suppose John Moore, Jr. is an adult grandchild who is employed, financially independent, pays rent to his grandmother but seldom interacts with her. Or suppose that Inez Moore takes into her home her neighbor's child when the friend becomes terminally ill. Does a blood relationship merit protection of John Jr.'s residential right but not the child's? What factors, other than consanguinity and marriage, are suggestive of the existence of a family? A parent-child relationship? What problems does this approach perpetuate? See Developments in the Law — The Constitution and the Family, 93 Harv. L. Rev. 1156, 1270-1289 (1980).

5. *Presumption of familial status.* Federal benefit schemes often distinguish among relatives who function as an economic unit. For example, in Lyng v. Castillo, 477 U.S. 635 (1986), the Supreme Court upheld a statute presuming parents, children, and siblings functioned as a single economic unit for food stamp purposes. More distant relatives and unrelated persons were not so presumed, resulting in their larger allotment. Upholding the statute as rational, the Court decided that the distinction did not violate equal protection or burden any fundamental right. Is *Lyng* reconcilable with *Moreno* or *Moore*? See also Bowen v. Gilliard, 483 U.S. 587 (1987).

Problem

States may remove children from parental custody because of abuse or neglect and place them in foster care. State and federal legislation (for example, Title IV-E of the Social Security Act, 42 U.S.C. §§670-676 (1994 & Supp. V 1999)) often provide foster care subsidies. Title IV-E provides funds without regard to whether foster parents are relatives. However, Oregon provides subsidies only to unrelated foster parents for children who are ineligible under Title IV-E. Relatives now wish to care for three Oregon children who were removed from their parents. Sheri Lipscomb's aunt and uncle, who do not have medical coverage for Sheri (who has multiple disabilities) and who do not receive state foster care payments or medical benefits because they are related to her, fear that they will have to give her up. Two other children's foster parents (also relatives) do give them up for lack of state subsidies. The state then places these latter two children with unrelated foster parents and provides benefits. Sheri and the other children challenge the constitutionality of the state's denial of aid to children whose relatives act as foster parents. What result? See Lipscomb v. Simmons, 884 F.2d 1242 (9th Cir. 1989), *reh'g en banc granted*, 907 F.2d 114 (9th Cir. 1990), decided en banc, 962 F.2d 1374 (9th Cir. 1992).[4] See generally Elizabeth Killackey, Kinship Foster Care, 26 Fam. L.Q. 211 (1992); Randi Mandelbaum, Trying to Fit Square Pegs into Round Holes: The Need for a New Funding Scheme for Kinship Caregivers, 22 Fordham Urb. L.J. 907 (1995).

B. COHABITATION: UNMARRIED COUPLES

1. Introduction

■ RICHARD J. GELLES, CONTEMPORARY FAMILIES: A SOCIOLOGICAL VIEW
176-178 (1995)

Cohabitation is the pattern of two unmarried persons of the opposite sex with a romantic interest in each other sharing a residence. It is an increasingly common phenomenon. . . . Thirty years ago, cohabitation as a form of courtship was frowned upon, and participants were subjected to negative social sanctions. Eleanor Macklin, writing about cohabitation in 1972, noted that in 1962 a graduate student at Cornell University was suspended for having a woman living in his apartment. The Cornell University Faculty Council on Student Conduct considered "overnight unchaperoned mixed company" a violation of "sexual morality."

Eight years after Cornell's reprimand to students for cohabitation, there were about 450,000 couples living together in the United States. . . . In 1992, there were 3.3 million unmarried-couple households. . . .

---

[4]. Note that federal welfare reform legislation requires states to "give preference to an adult relative over a non-related caregiver when determining a placement for a child, provided that the relative caregiver meets all relevant State child protection standards." See Personal Responsibility and Work Opportunity Reconciliation Act of 1996, 42 U.S.C. §671 (2000).

There are a number of reasons why cohabitation has become a more popular and socially acceptable form of relationship in the past 30 years. First, evidence from the Scandinavian countries, such as Denmark and Sweden, where cohabitation is much more common suggests that cohabitation does not undermine or destroy the family. . . . Second, modern advances in contraception make it possible for couples to cohabitate without the complications of pregnancy. Changing gender roles and the status of women have somewhat freed woman from the double standard whereby women who cohabitated were seen as immoral and not suitable marriage partners. Colleges, like Cornell, have changed their views, values, and rules regarding student behavior. The concept of *in loco parentis* (in place of the parents) that dominated college rules and regulations in the 1950s and 1960s and that led to curfews, sign-ins, and other regulations has been eliminated. Campuses now have coeducational residence halls, classes on sex education, and dispense birth control pills and condoms (the latter may be more a concession to the threat of AIDS than a change in attitude about premarital sex).

Off college campuses, the increase in the divorce rate has produced a large pool of single individuals of all ages who seek heterosexual relations without immediately committing to a marriage. . . .

Data reveal that unmarried heterosexual couples constitute a small but growing percentage of American couples. In 2003, 4.6 million households were classified as unmarried heterosexual-couple households, representing 9.2 million adults.[5] The proportion of all unmarried heterosexual households has been steadily increasing, from 2.9 percent of all households in 1996 to 4.2 percent in 2003.[6] Moreover, currently, the number of unmarried heterosexual households with children under age 18, approximates that of married-partner households with children (41 percent compared to 45 percent).[7] In general, cohabitants tend to be younger than married persons,[8] and are more likely than married persons to be of different races.[9] Unmarried heterosexual partners with children tend to be less well educated than their married counterparts with children.[10]

Official estimates of the numbers of same-sex couple households also exist, although estimates undoubtedly are low because many gays and lesbians still are reluctant to identify themselves. (The Bureau of the Census first began gathering such information in 1990.) The 2000 census reveals the existence of 594,000 same-sex couples nationwide, and reports that same-sex couple households represent about one in nine of the total of unmarried-partner households.[11] Same-sex

[5]. Bureau of the Census, supra note [1], at 16.
[6]. Id. These data may be low because of the omission of unmarried cohabitants who are not householders and also because of underreporting.
[7]. Id. at 17.
[8]. In 2003, 24 percent of cohabiting women and 16 percent of cohabiting men were under age 25, compared to 4 percent of married women and 2 percent of married men. Id.
[9]. Bureau of the Census, U.S. Dept. of Commerce, Married-Couple and Unmarried-Partner Households: 2000, 11 (Feb. 2003).
[10]. Bureau of the Census, supra note [1], at 17.
[11]. Bureau of the Census, supra note [9], at 1, 4. Data from the 1990 and 2000 censuses are not comparable because of changes in data collection procedures.

unmarried partner households are most likely of all couple-households to be located in cities,[12] and to be in California.[13]

Cohabitation among gays and lesbians, as a visible social phenomenon, may be traced to the emergence of the gay community in New York City between 1890 and World War II.[14] The second wave of gay activism, following the Stonewall rebellion in 1960 in New York City, also led to an increase in the numbers of gay and lesbian cohabitants. The threat of AIDS again spurred an increasing number of gay men to seek long-term monogamous relationships.

2. Traditional Response: Criminal Sanctions

■ LAWRENCE v. TEXAS
539 U.S. 558 (2003)

Review pp. 56-63.

Notes and Questions

1. *Background.* Traditionally, nonmarital fornication and cohabitation were considered deviant behavior and subject to criminal sanctions. See Lawrence M. Friedman, Crime and Punishment in American History (1994). Efforts to revise or repeal these criminal statutes took place against a backdrop of national reforms. The drafters of the Model Penal Code (MPC) first proposed criminalizing cohabitation only if it was "open and notorious." MPC §207.1 (Tent. Draft No. 4, 1955). Subsequently, the ALI Council voted to delete the section because the law was seldom enforced, inconsistent with the widespread policy of nonenforcement of moral standards, without deterrent value, and prone to discriminatory enforcement. Id. at cmt. Many states followed suit. See Margaret M. Mahoney, Forces Shaping the Law of Cohabitation for Opposite Sex Couples, 7 J.L. Fam. Stud. 135, 144-147 (2005) (discussing MPC revision). Only seven states currently retain their criminal cohabitation statutes. Steve Hartsoe, 1805 Law Against Cohabiting Challenged in N. Carolina, Chi. Sun-Times, May 10, 2005, at 34.

The traditional legal response to sexual activity between gays and lesbians, similarly, has been punitive. Criminal prohibitions on sodomy (consensual oral or anal sex) existed in all 50 states before 1961. However, after the MPC recommended decriminalization (MPC §207.5 (Tent. Draft No. 4, 1955); MPC §213.2 (Prop. Off. Draft 1962)), states gradually began abrogating their sodomy laws — beginning with Illinois in 1961. In 1986, 24 states and the District of Columbia had such laws. By 2003, that number had been reduced to 13 jurisdictions — 4 of which enforced their laws only against same-sex sexual conduct. Lawrence v. Texas, 539 U.S. 558, 573 (2003) (explaining history of sodomy laws). See generally Jennifer Naeger, Note, And Then There Were None: The Repeal of Sodomy Laws

---

[12]. Id. at 3.
[13]. Id. at 7. In fact, California has more unmarried-partner households (heterosexual and same-sex couples) than any other state.
[14]. George Chauncey, Gay New York: Gender, Urban Culture, and the Making of a Gay Male World, 1890-1940, at 1 (1994).

After Lawrence v. Texas and its Effect on the Custody and Visitation Rights of Gay and Lesbian Parents, 78 St. John's L. Rev. 397 (2004).

2. *State constitutional challenges.* Prior to *Lawrence*, plaintiffs achieved some success by challenging sodomy laws on state constitutional grounds. See Jegley v. Picado, 80 S.W.3d 332 (Ark. 2002) (same-sex sodomy law violates state constitutional rights of equal protection and privacy); Powell v. State, 510 S.E.2d 18 (Ga. 1998) (sodomy statute violates right of privacy as guaranteed by state constitution due process clause).

3. *Right to privacy.* In Doe v. Duling, 782 F.2d 1202 (4th Cir. 1986), two unmarried adults who maintained separate residences brought suit challenging the constitutionality of Virginia statutes prohibiting fornication and cohabitation. Although neither plaintiff had been arrested, each expressed fears of being prosecuted. Almost twenty years before *Lawrence*, the district court in *Duling* determined that the constitutional right to privacy extends to a single person's right to engage in sexual intercourse; however, the appellate court reversed, holding that plaintiffs lacked standing because they faced only a theoretical threat of prosecution.

4. *Modern applications.* Recently, the Virginia Supreme Court squarely confronted a challenge to the constitutionality of a state fornication statute based on the right to privacy. In Martin v. Ziherl, 607 S.E.2d 367 (Va. 2005), defendant responded to his female sexual partner's claim that he negligently transmitted a venereal disease by contending that she did not state a claim upon which relief could be granted because of her participation in an illegal act of fornication. She countered by challenging the constitutionality of the state fornication statute based on Lawrence v. Texas. Invalidating the statute, the state supreme court reasoned:

> We find no relevant distinction between the circumstances in *Lawrence* and the circumstances in the present case. [D]ecisions by married or unmarried persons regarding their intimate physical relationship are elements of their personal relationships that are entitled to due process protection. . . . We find no principled way to conclude that the specific act of intercourse is not an element of a personal relationship between two unmarried persons or that the Virginia statute criminalizing intercourse between unmarried persons does not improperly abridge a personal relationship that is within the liberty interest of persons to choose. Because Code §18.2-334, like the Texas statute at issue in *Lawrence*, is an attempt by the state to control the liberty interest which is exercised in making these personal decisions, it violates the Due Process Clause of the Fourteenth Amendment. . . .

Id. at 370. See also Mark Strasser, *Lawrence* and Same-Sex Marriage Bans: On Constitutional Interpretation and Sophistical Rhetoric, 69 Brooklyn L. Rev. 1003, 1010 (2004) (presuming that *Lawrence* leads to invalidation of remaining fornication statutes). But cf. John G. Culhane, Writing On, Around, and Through Lawrence v. Texas, 38 Creighton L. Rev. 493, 498 n.35 (2005) (suggesting that, although "courts following *Lawrence* would also strike down laws against cohabitation (or fornication) and adultery" [however] "the Court might distinguish adultery laws from sodomy statutes by emphasizing *Lawrence*'s concern about marriage). See also Hobbs v. Pender County, No. 05 CVS 267 (Pender Cty. Super. Ct., filed Mar. 28, 2005) (challenging the constitutionality of North Carolina cohabitation statute).

Other post-*Lawrence* cases have also wrestled with the limits of the right to privacy that protects consensual sexual conduct. See, e.g., United States v. Marcum, 60 M.J. 198 (2004) (upholding the military's sodomy rule regarding non-forcible sexual acts between a sergeant and a subordinate, reasoning that the acts are not constitutionally protected after *Lawrence* because the difference in rank in the military context signifies a situation where consent might not be freely given). After *Lawrence*, state law enforcement officials have yet to determine if they can prosecute persons for engaging in consensual sexual acts in public places (e.g., parks, sex clubs, or public bathrooms) or for solicitation of sodomy in public places. Lou Chibbaro Jr., Virginia Sodomy Law Down But Not Out, Wash. Blade Online, available at http://www.washblade.com/2003/7-4/news/localnews/soreloser. cfm (last visited July 22, 2005); Matt Chittum, Lexington Man Cleared of Sodomy Charge, Roanoke Times, Feb. 11, 2004, at B1 (explaining that, following *Lawrence*, prosecutors dropped charge of solicitation to commit sodomy against a man who was caught in a raid on an adult bookstore frequented by gay men).

5. *Other constitutional arguments.* The plaintiffs in *Duling* attacked the fornication and cohabitation statutes as violations of their right to privacy as well as their rights to freedom of association and expression. (The district court addressed only the privacy claim, and the court of appeals refused to address any of plaintiffs' constitutional claims.) What is the relationship between the First Amendment and privacy? In an early article, Professor Kenneth Karst argues that "[the intimacies threatened in *Griswold* were another form of expressive conduct, "'the speech of loving.'" Kenneth L. Karst, The Freedom of Intimate Association, 89 Yale L.J. 624, 653 (1980). He contends that *Griswold* established not a right to privacy but a right to intimate association that protects familial-like relationships. He speculates that courts may avoid deciding cases on this ground because "[a]lmost everything we do is expressive one way or another. . . . The First Amendment would, in short, be stretched to cover all our constitutional freedoms." Id. at 654. Similarly, gays and lesbians also argue that governmental restrictions on their conduct implicate the First Amendment's protection of expressive conduct. See James Allon Garland, Breaking the Enigma Code: Why the Law Has Failed to Recognize Sex as Expressive Conduct Under the First Amendment, and Why Sex Between Men Proves That It Should, 12 Law & Sex 159, 164-166 (2003).

Do cohabitation statutes and sodomy statutes violate equal protection? See Martha L. Fineman, Law and Changing Patterns of Behavior: Sanctions on Non-Marital Cohabitation, 1981 Wis. L. Rev. 275, 314-315; H. John Proud, Right Decision, Wrong Constitutional Law: Taking the Better Path with Equal Protection Jurisprudence — Lawrence v. Texas, 29 Dayton L. Rev. 447 (2003) (so arguing).

Some state sodomy statutes provide less severe punishment for sexual acts by persons of the opposite sex (so-called "Romeo and Juliet" statutes) compared to same-sex sexual acts when that activity involves *minors*. State v. Limon, 83 P.3d 229 (Kan. Ct. App. 2004), addressed an 18-years-old male's equal protection challenge to his conviction and sentence (206 months' imprisonment, 60 months' post-release supervision, and mandatory registration for life as a sex offender) pursuant to such a state statute for an act of consensual oral sex with a fourteen-year-old boy. The Kansas court of appeals upheld the statute. The U.S. Supreme Court ordered reconsideration of that ruling in light of Lawrence v. Texas. Limon v. Kansas, 539 U.S. 955 (2003).

Upon reconsideration, the Kansas supreme court ruled that the statute violates equal protection. Applying *Lawrence*, the court found that the state did not have a rational basis for the statuory classification created in the Romeo and Juliet statute because no evidence justified the view that same-sex sexual activity was more harmful to minors than adults, no basis existed to believe that adults who engage in voluntary sex with minors who are of the same sex would have a higher tendency to be more coercive than adults who engaged in voluntary sex with minors of the opposite sex, and no evidence indicated that the prohibited sexual activities would be more likely to transmit disease when engaged in by homosexuals than by heterosexuals. State v. Limon, 122 P.3d 22 (Kan. 2005).

6. *Law and morality*. The relationship between law and morality has prompted considerable philosophical debate. John Stuart Mill, a staunch opponent of state paternalism, asserted that the only rationale for state restrictions on liberty is to prevent harm to others. John Stuart Mill, On Liberty 13 (Gateway ed. 1959). On the other hand, a critic of Mill, Sir Patrick Devlin, counters that society is entitled to prevent harm perpetrated by the "weakness or vice of too many of its members." Patrick Devlin, The Enforcement of Morals 104 (1965). Do bans on cohabitation, fornication, and sodomy safeguard society or are such offenses "victimless crimes"? Is the prevention of such social problems as illegitimacy and/or venereal disease a proper object of legislation? Are these problems sufficiently important to outweigh the right to privacy? Might suppressive measures produce socially undesirable effects? See generally Joel Feinberg, Harmless Wrongdoing, in The Moral Limits of the Criminal Law (1988); Craig L. Carr, Between Virtue and Vice: The Legal Enforcement of Morals, 14 Kan. J.L. & Pub. Pol'y 1 (2004).

7. *Significance of nonenforcement*. In *Duling*, the district court and the court of appeals reached different conclusions on the significance of nonenforcement. How realistic was this threat of prosecution for cohabitation, fornication, or sodomy — before *Lawrence*? One pre-*Lawrence* study reported that situations most likely to prompt prosecution for cohabitation include: (1) welfare fraud; (2) domestic violence complaints; (3) complaints by cohabitants' family members; and (4) investigation of unrelated criminal conduct. Fineman, supra, at 287-293 (study of prosecution rates in Wisconsin during a five-year period in the 1970s). Do these findings support the views of the ALI Council, supra, that these laws result in discriminatory enforcement?

How realistic is the threat of prosecution for cohabitation, fornication, or sodomy — after *Lawrence*? See Duncan Osborne, Illegal Sodomy Prosecutions, Gay City News, Mar. 21-27, 2003, available at http://www.gaycitynews.com/gen212/illegalsodomy.html (pointing out that the Brooklyn DA prosecuted at least 19 persons on sodomy charges after the state's highest court declared the sodomy law unconstitutional).

What is the harm of laws that are rarely enforced? Professor Cass Sunstein suggests that *Lawrence* might be interpreted narrowly as a:

> prohibition on the use of the criminal law in circumstances in which the underlying conduct did not offend citizens' moral commitments, as reflected in a pattern of nonenforcement. In those circumstances, the statutory ban in *Lawrence* was a recipe for arbitrary and even discriminatory action, in a way that does violence to democratic ideals and even the rule of law. . . .

Cass R. Sunstein, The Right to Marry, 26 Cardozo L. Rev. 2081, 2108 (2005). See also Cass R. Sunstein, What Did *Lawrence* Hold?, Of Autonomy, Desuetude, Sexuality, and Marriage, 2003 S. Ct. Rev. 27, 29-30.

8. *New uses for fornication laws*. Prosecutors sometimes bring fornication charges against pregnant teens and their boyfriends in an attempt to deter teen pregnancies. In Idaho, some pregnant girls have been arrested after they applied for state assistance. Is this an appropriate use of such statutes? See Heidi Meinzer, Idaho's Throwback to Elizabethan England: Criminalizing a Civil Proceeding?, 34 Fam. L. Q. 165 (2000); Gregory Hahn, Abortion Consent Bill to Get Vote, Idaho Statesman, Mar. 26, 2005, at 1 (relating account of county prosecutor who won a fornication conviction in a case involving a 14-year-old girl who had sex with an 18-year-old male).

3. Unmarried Couples' Rights Inter Se

■ MARVIN v. MARVIN
557 P.2d 106 (Cal. 1976)

TOBRINER, Justice.

During the past 15 years, there has been a substantial increase in the number of couples living together without marrying. Such nonmarital relationships lead to legal controversy when one partner dies or the couple separates. Courts of Appeal, faced with the task of determining property rights in such cases, have arrived at conflicting positions. . . . We take this opportunity to resolve that controversy and to declare the principles which should govern distribution of property acquired in a nonmarital relationship. . . .

. . . In the instant case plaintiff and defendant lived together for seven years without marrying; all property acquired during this period was taken in defendant's name. When plaintiff sued to enforce a contract under which she was entitled to half the property and to support payments, the trial court granted judgment on the pleadings for defendant, thus leaving him with all property accumulated by the couple during their relationship. . . .

Since the trial court rendered judgment for defendant on the pleadings, we must accept the allegations of plaintiff's complaint as true, determining whether such allegations state, or can be amended to state, a cause of action. We turn therefore to the specific allegations of the complaint.

Plaintiff avers that in October of 1964 she and defendant "entered into an oral agreement" that while "the parties lived together they would combine their efforts and earnings and would share equally any and all property accumulated as a result of their efforts whether individual or combined." Furthermore, they agreed to "hold themselves out to the general public as husband and wife" and that "plaintiff would further render her services as a companion, homemaker, housekeeper and cook to . . . defendant."

Shortly thereafter plaintiff agreed to "give up her lucrative career as an entertainer [and] singer" in order to "devote her full time to defendant . . . as a companion, homemaker, housekeeper and cook"; in return defendant agreed to "provide for all of plaintiff's financial support and needs for the rest of her life."

Plaintiff alleges that she lived with defendant from October of 1964 through May of 1970 and fulfilled her obligations under the agreement. During this period the parties as a result of their efforts and earnings acquired in defendant's name substantial real and personal property, including motion picture rights worth over

$1 million. In May of 1970, however, defendant compelled plaintiff to leave his household. He continued to support plaintiff until November of 1971, but thereafter refused to provide further support. . . .

[D]efendant offers some four theories to sustain the ruling. . . . Defendant first and principally relies on the contention that the alleged contract is so closely related to the supposed "immoral" character of the relationship between plaintiff and himself that the enforcement of the contract would violate public policy.[4] He points to cases asserting that a contract between nonmarital partners is unenforceable if it is "involved in" an illicit relationship. A review of the numerous California decisions concerning contracts between nonmarital partners, however, reveals that the courts have not employed such broad and uncertain standards to strike down contracts. The decisions instead disclose a narrower and more precise standard: a contract between nonmarital partners is unenforceable only *to the extent* that it *explicitly* rests upon the immoral and illicit consideration of meretricious sexual services. . . .

Although the past decisions hover over the issue in the somewhat wispy form of the figures of a Chagall painting, we can abstract from those decisions a clear and simple rule. The fact that a man and woman live together without marriage, and engage in a sexual relationship, does not in itself invalidate agreements between them relating to their earnings, property, or expenses. Neither is such an agreement invalid merely because the parties may have contemplated the creation or continuation of a nonmarital relationship when they entered into it. Agreements between nonmarital partners fail only to the extent that they rest upon a consideration of meretricious sexual services. Thus the rule asserted by defendant, that a contract fails if it is "involved in" or made "in contemplation" of a nonmarital relationship, cannot be reconciled with the decisions. . . .

The principle that a contract between nonmarital partners will be enforced unless expressly and inseparably based upon an illicit consideration of sexual services not only represents the distillation of the decisional law, but also offers a far more precise and workable standard than that advocated by defendant. [A] standard which inquires whether an agreement is "involved" in or "contemplates" a nonmarital relationship is vague and unworkable. Virtually all agreements between nonmarital partners can be said to be "involved" in some sense in the fact of their mutual sexual relationship, or to "contemplate" the existence of that relationship. Thus defendant's proposed standards, if taken literally, might invalidate all agreements between nonmarital partners, a result no one favors. Moreover, those standards offer no basis to distinguish between valid and invalid agreements. By looking not to such uncertain tests, but only to the consideration underlying the agreement, we provide the parties and the courts with a practical guide to determine when an agreement between nonmarital partners should be enforced.

---

4. Defendant also contends that the contract was illegal because it contemplated a violation of former Penal Code section 269a, which prohibited living "in a state of cohabitation and adultery." (§269a was repealed by Stats. 1975, ch. 71, eff. Jan. 1, 1976.) Defendant's standing to raise the issue is questionable because he alone was married and thus guilty of violating section 269a. . . . The numerous cases discussing the contractual rights of unmarried couples have drawn no distinction between illegal relationships and lawful nonmarital relationships. Moreover, even if we were to draw such a distinction . . . plaintiff sought to amend her complaint to assert that the parties reaffirmed their contract after [his] divorce.

Defendant secondly relies upon the ground suggested by the trial court: that the 1964 contract violated public policy because it impaired the community property rights of Betty Marvin, defendant's lawful wife. . . . In the present case Betty Marvin, the aggrieved spouse, had the opportunity to assert her community property rights in the divorce action. The interlocutory and final decrees in that action fix and limit her interest. Enforcement of the contract between plaintiff and defendant against property awarded to defendant by the divorce decree will not impair any right of Betty's, and thus is not on that account violative of public policy.

Defendant's third contention is . . . that enforcement of the oral agreement between plaintiff and himself is barred by Civil Code section 5134, which provides that "All contracts for marriage settlements must be in writing. . . ." A marriage settlement, however, is an agreement in contemplation of marriage. . . . The contract at issue here does not conceivably fall within that definition. [The court also rejected, as a "rather strained contention," defendant's fourth argument that plaintiff was asserting a claim for breach of promise to marry, barred by statute.]

In summary, we base our opinion on the principle that adults who voluntarily live together and engage in sexual relations are nonetheless as competent as any other persons to contract respecting their earnings and property rights. Of course, they cannot lawfully contract to pay for the performance of sexual services, for such a contract is, in essence, an agreement for prostitution and unlawful for that reason. . . . So long as the agreement does not rest upon illicit meretricious consideration, the parties may order their economic affairs as they choose, and no policy precludes the courts from enforcing such agreements.

In the present instance, plaintiff alleges that the parties agreed to pool their earnings, that they contracted to share equally in all property acquired, and that defendant agreed to support plaintiff. The terms of the contract as alleged do not rest upon any unlawful consideration. We therefore conclude that the complaint furnishes a suitable basis upon which the trial court can render declaratory relief. The trial court consequently erred in granting defendant's motion for judgment on the pleadings. . . .

As we have noted, both causes of action in plaintiff's complaint allege an express contract; neither assert any basis for relief independent from the contract. In In re Marriage of Cary, [109 Cal. Rptr. 862 (1973)], however, the Court of Appeal held that, in view of the policy of the Family Law Act, property accumulated by nonmarital partners in an actual family relationship should be divided equally. . . . Although our conclusion that plaintiff's complaint states a cause of action based on an express contract alone compels us to reverse the judgment for defendant, resolution of the *Cary* issue will serve both to guide the parties upon retrial and to resolve a conflict presently manifest in published Court of Appeal decisions.

Both plaintiff and defendant stand in broad agreement that the law should be fashioned to carry out the reasonable expectations of the parties. Plaintiff, however, presents the following contentions: that the decisions prior to *Cary* rest upon implicit and erroneous notions of punishing a party for his or her guilt in entering into a nonmarital relationship, that such decisions result in an inequitable distribution of property accumulated during the relationship, and that *Cary* correctly held that the enactment of the Family Law Act in 1970 overturned those prior decisions. Defendant in response maintains that the prior decisions merely applied common law principles of contract and property to persons who have deliberately elected to remain outside the bounds of the community property system. *Cary*, defendant contends, erred in holding that the Family Law Act vitiated the force of the prior precedents.

[T]he truth lies somewhere between the positions of plaintiff and defendant. The classic opinion on this subject is Vallera v. Vallera, [134 P.2d 761 (Cal. 1943)]. Speaking for a four-member majority, Justice Traynor posed the question: "whether a woman living with a man as his wife but with no genuine belief that she is legally married to him acquires by reason of cohabitation alone the rights of a co-tenant in his earnings and accumulations during the period of their relationship." [T]he majority answered that question "in the negative." *Vallera* explains that "Equitable considerations arising from the reasonable expectation of the continuation of benefits attending the status of marriage entered into in good faith are not present in such a case." (134 P.2d at 763.) In the absence of express contract, *Vallera* concluded, the woman is entitled to share in property jointly accumulated only "in the proportion that her funds contributed toward its acquisition." . . .

The majority opinion in *Vallera* did not expressly bar recovery based upon an implied contract, nor preclude resort to equitable remedies. But *Vallera*'s broad assertion that equitable considerations "are not present" in the case of a nonmarital relationship led the Courts of Appeal to interpret the language to preclude recovery based on such theories. . . .

Consequently, when the issue of the rights of a nonmarital partner reached this court in Keene v. Keene, [371 P.2d 329 (Cal. 1962)], the claimant forwent reliance upon theories of contract implied in law or fact. Asserting that she had worked on her partner's ranch and that her labor had enhanced its value, she confined her cause of action to the claim that the court should impress a resulting trust on the property derived from the sale of the ranch. The court limited its opinion accordingly, rejecting her argument on the ground that the rendition of services gives rise to a resulting trust only when the services aid in acquisition of the property, not in its subsequent improvement. . . .

Thus in summary, the cases prior to *Cary* exhibited a schizophrenic inconsistency. By enforcing an express contract between nonmarital partners unless it rested upon an unlawful consideration, the courts applied a common law principle as to contracts. Yet the courts disregarded the common law principle that holds that implied contracts can arise from the conduct of the parties. Refusing to enforce such contracts, the courts spoke of leaving the parties "in the position in which they had placed themselves," just as if they were guilty parties "in pari delicto."

Justice Curtis noted this inconsistency in his dissenting opinion in *Vallera*, pointing out that "if an express agreement will be enforced, there is no legal or just reason why an implied agreement to share the property cannot be enforced." (134 P.2d at 764; see Bruch, Property Rights of De Facto Spouses Including Thoughts on the Value of Homemakers' Services (1976) 10 Family L.Q. 101, 117-121.) And in Keene v. Keene, [371 P.2d 329 (1962),] Justice Peters observed that if the man and woman "were not illegally living together . . . it would be a plain business relationship and a contract would be implied." [371 P.2d at 338 (diss. opn.).]

Still another inconsistency in the prior cases arises from their treatment of property accumulated through joint effort. To the extent that a partner had contributed *funds* or *property*, the cases held that the partner obtains a proportionate share in the acquisition, despite the lack of legal standing of the relationship. Yet courts have refused to recognize just such an interest based upon the contribution of *services*. As Justice Curtis points out "Unless it can be argued that a woman's services as cook, housekeeper, and homemaker are valueless, it would seem logical that if, when she contributes money to the purchase of property, her interest will be protected, then when she contributes her services in the home, her interest in property accumulated should be protected." (Vallera v. Vallera, 134 P.2d at 764 (diss. opn.).)

Thus as of 1973, the time of the filing of In re Marriage of Cary, the cases apparently held that a nonmarital partner who rendered services in the absence of express contract could assert no right to property acquired during the relationship. The facts of *Cary* demonstrated the unfairness of that rule.

Janet and Paul Cary had lived together, unmarried, for more than eight years. They held themselves out to friends and family as husband and wife, reared four children, purchased a home and other property, obtained credit, filed joint income tax returns, and otherwise conducted themselves as though they were married. Paul worked outside the home, and Janet generally cared for the house and children.

In 1971 Paul petitioned for "nullity of the marriage." Following a hearing on that petition, the trial court awarded Janet half the property acquired during the relationship, although all such property was traceable to Paul's earnings. The Court of Appeal affirmed the award [reasoning that prior cases that denied relief were based] upon a policy of punishing persons guilty of cohabitation without marriage. The Family Law Act, the court observed, aimed to eliminate fault or guilt as a basis for dividing marital property. But once fault or guilt is excluded, the court reasoned, nothing distinguishes the property rights of a nonmarital "spouse" from those of a putative spouse. Since the latter is entitled to half the "quasi marital property" (Civ. Code §4452), the Court of Appeal concluded that, giving effect to the policy of the Family Law Act, a nonmarital cohabitator should also be entitled to half the property accumulated during an "actual family relationship."

Cary met with a mixed reception in other appellate districts. [W]e agree [with the view] that *Cary* distends the act. No language in the Family Law Act addresses the property rights of nonmarital partners, and nothing in the legislative history of the act suggests that the Legislature considered that subject. [A]lthough we reject the reasoning of *Cary* . . . , we share the perception . . . that the application of former precedent in the factual setting of those cases would work an unfair distribution of the property accumulated by the couple. . . .

The principal reason why the pre-*Cary* decisions result in an unfair distribution of property inheres in the court's refusal to permit a nonmarital partner to assert rights based upon accepted principles of implied contract or equity. We have examined the reasons advanced to justify this denial of relief, and find that none have merit.

First, we note that the cases denying relief do not rest their refusal upon any theory of "punishing" a "guilty" partner. Indeed, to the extent that denial of relief "punishes" one partner, it necessarily rewards the other by permitting him to retain a disproportionate amount of the property. Concepts of "guilt" thus cannot justify an unequal division of property between two equally "guilty" persons.

Other reasons advanced in the decisions fare no better. The principal argument seems to be that "[e]quitable considerations arising from the reasonable expectation of . . . benefits attending the status of marriage . . . are not present (in a nonmarital relationship).'' (Vallera v. Vallera, 134 P.2d at 763.) But, although parties to a nonmarital relationship obviously cannot have based any expectations upon the belief that they were married, other expectations and equitable considerations remain. The parties may well expect that property will be divided in accord with the parties' own tacit understanding and that in the absence of such understanding the courts will fairly apportion property accumulated through mutual effort. We need not treat nonmarital partners as putatively married persons in order to apply principles of implied contract, or extend equitable remedies; we need to treat them only as we do any other unmarried persons.

The remaining arguments advanced from time to time to deny remedies to the nonmarital partners are of less moment. There is no more reason to presume that services are contributed as a gift than to presume that funds are contributed as a gift; in any event the better approach is to presume, as Justice Peters suggested, "that the parties intend to deal fairly with each other." [Keene v. Keene, 371 P.2d at 339 (diss. opn.).]

The argument that granting remedies to the nonmarital partners would discourage marriage must fail; as *Cary* pointed out, "with equal or greater force the point might be made that the pre-1970 rule was calculated to cause the income producing partner to avoid marriage and thus retain the benefit of all of his or her accumulated earnings." [109 Cal. Rptr. at 866.] Although we recognize the well-established public policy to foster and promote the institution of marriage, perpetuation of judicial rules which result in an inequitable distribution of property accumulated during a nonmarital relationship is neither a just nor an effective way of carrying out that policy.

In summary, we believe that the prevalence of nonmarital relationships in modern society and the social acceptance of them, marks this as a time when our courts should by no means apply the doctrine of the unlawfulness of the so-called meretricious relationship to the instant case. As we have explained, the nonenforceability of agreements expressly providing for meretricious conduct rested upon the fact that such conduct, as the word suggests, pertained to and encompassed prostitution. To equate the nonmarital relationship of today to such a subject matter is to do violence to an accepted and wholly different practice.

We are aware that many young couples live together without the solemnization of marriage, in order to make sure that they can successfully later undertake marriage. This trial period, preliminary to marriage, serves as some assurance that the marriage will not subsequently end in dissolution to the harm of both parties. We are aware, as we have stated, of the pervasiveness of nonmarital relationships in other situations.

The mores of the society have indeed changed so radically in regard to cohabitation that we cannot impose a standard based on alleged moral considerations that have apparently been so widely abandoned by so many. Lest we be misunderstood, however, we take this occasion to point out that the structure of society itself largely depends upon the institution of marriage, and nothing we have said in this opinion should be taken to derogate from that institution. The joining of the man and woman in marriage is at once the most socially productive and individually fulfilling relationship that one can enjoy in the course of a lifetime.

We conclude that the judicial barriers that may stand in the way of a policy based upon the fulfillment of the reasonable expectations of the parties to a nonmarital relationship should be removed. As we have explained, the courts now hold that express agreements will be enforced unless they rest on an unlawful meretricious consideration. We add that in the absence of an express agreement, the courts may look to a variety of other remedies in order to protect the parties' lawful expectations.[24]

The courts may inquire into the conduct of the parties to determine whether that conduct demonstrates an implied contract or implied agreement of partnership or joint venture, or some other tacit understanding between the parties. The courts may, when appropriate, employ principles of constructive trust. Finally, a nonmarital partner may recover in quantum meruit for the reasonable value of household services rendered less the reasonable value of support received if he can show that he rendered services with the expectation of monetary reward.[25]

Since we have determined that plaintiff's complaint states a cause of action for breach of an express contract, and, as we have explained, can be amended to state a cause of action independent of allegations of express contract,[26] we must conclude that the trial court erred in granting defendant a judgment on the pleadings. [R]eversed and . . . remanded for further proceedings consistent with the views expressed herein.

Notes and Questions

1. *Epilogue.* On remand in *Marvin*, the trial court found: (1) no express contract was negotiated by the parties, and (2) the conduct of the parties did not give rise to an implied contract. Despite these findings, the trial judge awarded the plaintiff $104,000 as "rehabilitative alimony," reasoning:

> The court is aware that Footnote 25 urges the trial court to employ whatever equitable remedy may be proper under the circumstances. The court is also aware of the recent resort of plaintiff to unemployment insurance benefits to support herself and of the fact that a return of plaintiff to a career as a singer is doubtful. Additionally, the court knows that the market value of defendant's property at the time of separation exceeded $1,000,000. In view of these circumstances, the court in equity awards plaintiff $104,000 for rehabilitation purposes so that she may have the economic means to re-educate herself and to learn new, employable skills or to refurbish those utilized, for example, during her most recent employment and so that she may return from her status as companion of a motion picture star to a separate, independent but perhaps more prosaic existence.

5 Fam. L. Rep. (BNA) 3079, 3085 (Apr. 24, 1979). The trial judge arrived at the amount by fixing the award (for a two-year period) at the highest salary plaintiff had earned as a singer prior to the cohabitation.

24. We do not seek to resurrect the doctrine of common law marriage, which was abolished in California by statute in 1895. Thus we do not hold that plaintiff and defendant were "married," nor do we extend to plaintiff the rights which the Family Law Act grants valid or putative spouses; we hold only that she has the same rights to enforce contracts and to assert her equitable interest in property acquired through her effort as does any other unmarried person.

25. Our opinion does not preclude the evolution of additional equitable remedies to protect the expectations of the parties to a nonmarital relationship in cases in which existing remedies prove inadequate; the suitability of such remedies may be determined in later cases in light of the factual setting in which they arise.

26. We do not pass upon the question whether, in the absence of an express or implied contractual obligation, a party to a nonmarital relationship is entitled to support payments from the other party after the relationship terminates.

On appeal, the Court of Appeals deleted the award. The court reasoned that the trial court had merely established plaintiff's need for support and the defendant's ability to pay, but that the award was not supported by law or equity. The court elaborated:

> . . . A court of equity admittedly has broad powers, but it may not create totally new substantive rights under the guise of doing equity. [I]n view of the already-mentioned findings of no damage (but benefit instead), no unjust enrichment and no wrongful act on the part of defendant with respect to either the relationship or its termination, it is clear that no basis whatsoever, either in equity or in law, exists for the challenged rehabilitative award.

176 Cal. Rptr. 555, 559 (Ct. App. 1981).

Soon after separating from Michelle in May 1970, Lee married his childhood sweetheart, Pamela, to whom he remained married until his death in 1987. As a recipient of the Purple Heart for bravery while serving as a Marine in World War II, he is buried in Arlington National Cemetery. Michelle soon began living with actor Dick Van Dyke, with whom she currently resides in Malibu, California. Michelle's attorney, Marvin Mitchelson, was convicted of tax fraud in 1993, released from prison in 1998, readmitted to the California bar in May 2000, and died in September 2004.[15]

2. *State approaches.* Jurisdictions have adopted different approaches to claims by heterosexual former cohabitants. The majority follows *Marvin* in recognizing express and implied agreements as well as equitable remedies. Salzman v. Bachrach, 996 P.2d 1263, 1267-1268 (Colo. 2000) (citing authorities). However, some jurisdictions recognize only express agreement whereas others recognize express and implied agreements (but not equitable remedies). Finally, a few jurisdictions refuse to recognize property rights between cohabitants on public policy grounds (e.g., Hewitt v. Hewitt, discussed infra). For surveys of the different approaches, see Marsha Garrison, Is Consent Necessary? An Evaluation of the Emerging Law of Cohabitant Obligation, 52 UCLA L. Rev. 815, 818 n.4 (2005); Allen M. Parkman, The Contractual Alternative to Marriage, 32 N. Ky. L. Rev. 125, 148-153 (2005).

3. *Empirical research.* How frequently do unmarried couples have written agreements? In a survey of 169 heterosexual and same-sex couples, researchers found that a significant number (71 percent) did not have a written agreement regarding property. Jennifer K. Robbennolt & Monica Kirkpatrick Johnson, Legal Planning for Unmarried Committed Partners: Empirical Lessons for a Preventative and Therapeutic Approach, 41 Ariz. L. Rev. 417, 436 (1999).

---

[15]. Biographical data were compiled from the following sources: Ann Laquer Estin, Ordinary Cohabitation, 76 Notre Dame L. Rev. 1381, 1382 (2001); Randy Kraft, Awesome Arlington Visitors to the National Cemetery Feel the Quiet Weight of History, Morning Call (Allentown, PA), May 25, 2003, at F1; Notable Deaths in 2004, Ft. Worth Star Telegram, Jan. 2, 2005, at A14; Mary Poppins' Cast Relives the Magic and Memories, Courier Mail (Australia), Dec. 3, 2004, at 8; Titbits of Tribute to Hollywood Great—Lee: A Romance by Pamela Marvin (book review), Scotland on Sunday [Scotsman Publication], Sept. 7, 1997, available at 1997 WLNR 2462968.

Those couples (combining heterosexual and same-sex couples) who had written agreements tended to be older, more highly educated, wealthier, had longer relationships and had held a commitment ceremony or exchanged a symbol of the relationship, owned a home jointly, and were less likely to have a child who lived in the household. Same-sex couples were more likely than opposite-sex couples to have executed estate planning documents, such as wills or health care decisionmaking proxies. See also Ellen D.B. Riggle et al., The Execution of Legal Documents by Sexual Minority Individuals, 11 Psychol. Pub. Pol'y & L. 138 (2005) (study of LGBT persons regarding estate planning). Estate planning for same-sex couples is discussed infra this chapter.

4. *Legal significance of* Marvin. *Marvin* permits recovery for cohabitants based on express agreements, and in the absence thereof, implied-in-fact and implied-in-law agreements. Note that *Marvin*'s statements regarding implied agreements are dictum because the plaintiff pleaded an express agreement. Because most agreements between cohabitants are not express, *Marvin*'s importance rests on this dictum and on the suggestion (in footnote 25) of "other equitable remedies." Implied-in-fact remedies are applicable when a court infers contractual intent from the parties' conduct. Implied-in-law remedies are impressed judicially to prevent unjust enrichment, regardless of the parties' intent. Thus, the latter, of course, are not really contracts.

What guidelines does *Marvin* give for determining the existence of implied agreements or the application of additional equitable remedies? Does the court assume that the parties have identical expectations? In reality, don't parties' expectations frequently vary? In addition, the court advocates adherence to a presumption that the parties intend to deal fairly with each other. What facts should raise that presumption? Does this presumption interfere with freedom of contract and constitute impermissible state intervention?

5. *Public policy rationale.* In *Marvin*, the defendant argued that recognition of a contract would violate public policy by impairing the rights of his ex-wife (to whom he was married during part of the cohabitation). Should a cohabitant be disqualified by, preferred to, or share property equally with, a lawful spouse? Does legal recognition of the rights of both women result in equating cohabitation with polygamy? See Ruth Deech, The Case Against Legal Recognition of Cohabitation, in Marriage and Cohabitation 1 Contemporary Societies 300, 306 (John M. Eekelaar & Sanford N. Katz eds., 1980).

6. *Homemaking services.* In *Marvin*, the plaintiff asserts that she provided homemaking services, among other services, in return for the defendant's promise of support. Courts disagree about whether homemaker services are sufficient consideration for an agreement between cohabitants. See Katherine C. Gordon, Note, The Necessity and Enforcement of Cohabitation Agreements: When Strings Will Attach and How to Prevent Them — A State Survey, 37 Brandeis L.J. 245, 247 (1998-1999). Under traditional contract doctrine, domestic services fail to provide such consideration because of the rationales that (1) the woman acted from affection rather than expectation of gain, (2) she intended her actions as a gift, or (3) her services are offset by the man's companionship and services. Should such services constitute consideration? If so, how do we value them? Apportion them?

Does provision of homemaking services fulfill the element of "unjust enrichment" that restitutionary theory requires? Specifically, has the plaintiff conferred a benefit on the defendant at her expense? Was the enrichment "unjust"? Professor Robert C. Casad responds:

... The parties cohabit fully aware of the relevant facts, and the indicia of unjustness found in the fraud, duress, and mistake circumstances are therefore absent. [The parties] probably contemplated that the benefits they would receive — material and non-material — would offset the burdens they undertook. Neither party anticipated paying for the material benefits received from the other except by contributing to the relationship. . . . Under those assumptions, neither party's contributions could unjustly enrich the other. . . .

Robert C. Casad, Unmarried Couples and Unjust Enrichment: From Status to Contract and Back Again, 77 Mich. L. Rev. 47, 55 (1978).

7. *Sexual services*. *Marvin*, interpreting prior case law to stand for the rule that express contracts are enforceable except when founded on sexual services, assumes that the cohabitants' agreement can be separated from the sexual relationship. How does a plaintiff show that the claim is independent from the sexual relationship? Aren't sexual services always an implicit part of an agreement between cohabitants? Or is that confusing the contractual terms with the motive for entering the contract? See Leonard Wagner, Note, Recognizing Contract and Property Rights of Unmarried Cohabitants in Wisconsin: Watts v. Watts, 1988 Wis. L. Rev. 1092, 1113.

By refusing to recognize sexual services as consideration, is a court simply saying that it refuses to confer value on these services for policy reasons? Would recognition of sexual services implicate an invasion of privacy? Professor Fran Olsen counters:

> To make "whisperings across the pillows," sacred, private, and unrepeatable is to support the sexual status quo. . . . Sex is private in part because the state makes it private and because keeping sex private seems to serve the interests of those with power. . . .

Frances E. Olsen, The Myth of State Intervention in the Family, 18 U. Mich. J.L. Reform 835, 857 n.57 (1985). See also David L. Chambers, The "Legalization" of the Family: Toward a Policy of Supportive Neutrality, 18 U. Mich. J.L. Reform 805, 822-825 (1985) (discussing privacy implications of *Marvin*).

8. *Hewitt's hard line*. A few jurisdictions refuse to recognize agreements between cohabitants. See Gordon, supra, at 253 (discussing cases in Georgia, Illinois, and Louisiana). In the classic case of Hewitt v. Hewitt, 394 N.E.2d 1204 (Ill. 1979), the Illinois Supreme Court refused to recognize, on public policy grounds, an agreement between cohabitants. Victoria and Robert Hewitt resided together for 15 years, holding themselves out as husband and wife, and had three children. The couple began living together as college students after the woman became pregnant; the man told her that no formal ceremony was necessary and that the law considered them as husband and wife. At dissolution, the plaintiff alleged that the couple had an express oral agreement to share property equally. In rejecting the woman's claim, the court reasoned that recognition of cohabitants' property rights would equate cohabitation with the abolished doctrine of common law marriage and would undermine marriage. The court deferred to the legislature as a more appropriate body to address the recognition of same-sex relationships.

Hewitt did not signal a total refusal of Illinois courts to recognize cohabitants' claims. In a subsequent case, a court recognized the claim of a cohabitant who furnished almost all the consideration and obtained financing for several vehicles that were purchased during a six-year cohabitation and titled in defendant's name "for insurance purposes." See Spafford v. Coats, 455 N.E.2d 241 (Ill. App. Ct. 1983).

Both *Marvin* and *Hewitt* address the potential impact of cohabitation on the institution of marriage. Which view is more persuasive? Does legal recognition of cohabitants' rights undermine marriage? See Margaret M. Mahoney, Forces Shaping the Law of Cohabitation for Opposite Sex Couples? J.L. & Fam. Stud. 135, 167-176 (2005). Both *Marvin* and *Hewitt* also consider the relationship between cohabitation and common law marriage. How do the legal consequences differ? Both cases implicitly deplore a return to common law marriage. Why? Would resurrection of the doctrine help cohabitants? Support or weaken marriage? See Cynthia Grant Bowman, A Feminist Proposal to Bring Back Common Law Marriage, 75 Or. L. Rev. 709 (1996). Do you agree with *Hewitt* that the legislature is the more appropriate body for law reform?

9. *Gender equality.* Does recognition of cohabitants' rights alleviate gender inequality? Is *Marvin* an advance or a setback for women? What is the effect for women of denying relief? One commentator points out that "courts can justify the failure to enforce cohabitation agreements as mere nonintervention, overlooking the fact that the superior position in which the non-action tends to leave the male partner is at least in part a product of the legal system." Clare Dalton, An Essay in the Deconstruction of Contract Doctrine, 94 Yale L.J. 997, 1107 (1985). On the other hand, some commentators argue that the imposition of remedies undermines gender equality by presuming the woman needs protection. See Deech, supra, at 303. Which view is more persuasive?

10. *Marriage as the standard.* Should the economic consequences of cohabitation imitate the rights and duties of marriage? For example, on remand in *Marvin*, the trial court awarded "rehabilitative alimony," using the traditional factors for spousal support of need versus ability to pay. Should cohabitants be entitled to "spousal support" regardless of contractual intent?

11. *Contract or status principles.* *Marvin* disapproved the status approach of In re Marriage of Cary, 109 Cal. Rptr. 862 (Ct. App. 1973), which treated cohabitants like married persons by granting them half of the accumulated property, based on an extension of no-fault divorce and community property principles. A few community property states currently follow this approach. See Western States Construction v. Michoff, 840 P.2d 1220 (Nev. 1992); Connell v. Francisco, 898 P.2d 831 (Wash. 1995). See also Wilbur v. Delapp, 850 P.2d 1151 (Or. Ct. App. 1993) (extending benefits of state marital property law to unmarried cohabitants). Commentators also have proposed variations of the status-based approach to operate independently of the parties' intentions. For example, Professor Grace Blumberg recommends, for purposes of support and property division, treating cohabitants similarly to married persons if they have remained together for two years. She rejects durational requirements if a child is born to the parties or, for inheritance purposes, if the relationship remains intact until the death of one partner. Grace Ganz Blumberg, Cohabitation Without Marriage: A Different Perspective, 28 UCLA L. Rev. 1125, 1167-1168 (1981). The American Law Institute follows this approach, as discussed infra.

On the other hand, Professor Marsha Garrison favors the contract approach. She reasons that:

[E]vidence shows that married and cohabiting couples tend to behave and view their relationships quite differently: Cohabitants are much less likely than married couples to share or pool resources; cohabitation usually functions as a substitute for being single, not for being married. Cohabitation thus does not imply marital commitment, the accepted basis of marital obligation. Nor, given its typically short duration and limited sharing, is it likely that cohabitation generally induces dependency or leads to unjust enrichment. Because of these differences, it would be unfair to impose marital obligations on cohabitants simply because a relationship has survived for a legislatively determined time period. Individualized inquiry into the nature of a couple's relationship is also undesirable as it is likely to produce uncertain and inconsistent results.

Garrison, supra, at 815. Garrison also recommends honoring cohabitants' commitments by means of reviving common law marriage and providing for "some type of voluntary registration or marriage option for same-sex couples." Id. Which approach do you favor?

12. *Same-sex couples.* By case law, a few American jurisdictions extend recognition of cohabitation contracts to same-sex partners. See, e.g., Gormley v. Robertson, 83 P.3d 1042 (Wash. Ct. App. 2004); Doe v. Burkland, 808 A.2d 1090 (R.I. 2002); Silver v. Starrett, 674 N.Y.S.2d 915 (Sup. Ct. 1998); Posik v. Layton, 695 So. 2d 759 (Fla. 1997). But cf. Mitchell v. Moore, 729 A.2d 1200 (Pa. Super. Ct. 1999) (denying restitution for services during 13-year period that were rendered by former life partner to farm owner, reasoning that defendant was not unjustly enriched).

As evidence of a counter movement, however, the Virginia legislature enacted legislation (effective July 1, 2004) that affirmed the state's refusal to recognize civil unions (including those contracted in another state) and, in addition, voided any contractual arrangements between same-sex couples "purporting to bestow the privileges or obligations of marriage." Va. Code Ann. §20-45.3 (2005). See David Lamb, Virginia Law Ends Same-Sex Partner Contractual Rights, Monterey County (CA) Herald, June 21, 2004, available at 2004 WLNR 4148128 (pointing out fears that the new law could negate partners' powers of attorney, wills, leases, child-custody arrangements, and joint bank accounts).

13. *Canada.* In a landmark case, Canada recognized the property rights of the members of same-sex couples following dissolution. In M. v. H., [1999] 2 S.C.R. 3, two women lived together for ten years (although the duration of the relationship was disputed), owned an advertising business together, and purchased real property together. When the relationship ended, M. sought an order for partition and sale of the house, a share of the business, and a claim for support; and also challenged the constitutionality of the Family Law Act which allowed such financial claims upon dissolution of a unmarried heterosexual relationship, but not that of a same-sex couple. The Canadian Supreme Court concluded that the exclusion of same-sex couples from the definition of "spouse" in the Family Law Act, for purposes of support upon termination of the relationship, violates the Canadian Charter of Rights and Freedoms (similar to our Constitution). The case led to widespread law reform in Canada, prompting some provinces to amend their definition of "spouse" by prohibiting discrimination against gays and lesbians in terms of pensions, benefits, support requirements, and death benefits, and prompting other provinces to permit adoption by same-sex partners. See Gilles

Marchildon, Gay, Lesbian Community Has Reason to Be Shocked, Winnipeg Free Press, June 26, 2001, at A11. Several provinces, by judicial decision, legalized same-sex marriage. In July 2005, the Canadian Parliament legalized same-sex marriage throughout the country.

For further discussion of the dissolution of same-sex marriages as well as civil unions, see Chapter V.

14. *ALI.* The American Law Institute's Principles of the Law of Family Dissolution apply the same rules to the financial claims (property and support) of domestic partners (same-sex or heterosexual) as to marital couples upon dissolution of their relationship. ALI, Principles of the Law of Family Dissolution: Analysis and Recommendations (2002) (Chapter 6: Domestic Partners). To qualify as a domestic partner under ALI §§6.03(3) and (4), two persons must maintain a "common household" by which they share a primary residence only with each other and other family members for a continuous period established by a rule of statewide application. (If unrelated persons are present in the household, the partners must act "jointly . . . with respect of management of the household," according to §6.03(4)). A presumption of a domestic partnership arises if the persons have maintained a common household with their common child for a requisite period or if they have simply maintained the common household for the requisite period. If neither presumption applies, a person may establish that the relationship constitutes a domestic partnership by proof of certain factors (i.e., statements made to each other or jointly to a third party, intermingling finances, economic dependence, emotional or physical intimacy, community reputation as a couple, participation in a commitment ceremony, naming each other as beneficiary of life insurance or of a will, or joint assumption of parenthood). §6.03(7)(a) to (m). (Not surprisingly, these provisions reflect features of Professor Grace Blumberg's status-based approach, supra, because she served as one of the Reporters for the ALI project.) See generally Martha M. Ertman, The ALI Principles' Approach to Domestic Partnership, 8 Duke J. Gender L. & Pol'y 107 (2001).

Note that the ALI Principles regarding premarital, marital, and separation agreements also apply to individuals who are, or plan to become, domestic partners (same-sex and opposite-sex). See ALI Principles, supra, §§7.01, 7.02.

15. *Restatement of Restitution.* The Restatement (Third) of Restitution (in progress) recognizes claims between former cohabitants on the ground of unjust enrichment. According to the new Restatement, if a former cohabitant

> owns a specific asset to which the other has made substantial, uncompensated contributions in the form of property or services, the person making such contributions has a claim in restitution against the other as necessary to prevent unjust enrichment.

Restatement (Third) of Restitution and Unjust Enrichment §28(2) at 24 (Tent. Draft No. 3, 2004). Unlike the status-based approach of the ALI Principles, the Restatement adopts an equitable approach favoring case-by-case determinations. For a critical view of the Restatement's position, see Emily L. Sherwin, Love, Money, and Justice: Restitution Between Cohabitants, 77 U. Colo. L. Rev. 711 (2006) (contending that the Restatement provision disregards traditional rules by endorsing an "expansive reading of the unjust enrichment principle").

Problems

1. Patricia brings an action for breach of contract against her long-term paramour, noted criminal defense attorney Johnnie L. Cochran, Jr. (who successfully defended O.J. Simpson in Simpson's double murder trial). The couple's 17-year relationship began in 1966 when Johnnie was still married to his first wife (whom he divorced in 1978). In 1973, Patricia and Johnnie have a son, and the next year, purchase a house together. Many people believe that the couple is married, especially after Patricia changes her surname to Cochran. Johnnie manages Patricia's finances and, at various times, directs her to quit her jobs and forego her career in order to take care of him and their child. During his first marriage and until 1985 when Johnnie informs Patricia that he is remarrying another woman, he lives with Patricia from 2 to 4 nights per week (staying at his other home the rest of the week). After his remarriage, he never again spends the night at Patricia's, although he visits frequently and takes meals there. Patricia contends that, in 1983, Johnnie orally promised to support her for the rest of her life, and that he did so until 1995 when he became angry after she discussed their relationship on television. Johnnie, citing Marvin v. Marvin, argues that the support agreement is unenforceable because the couple was not living together full-time when the promise was made and also contends that it is violative of public policy because he was married. He characterizes the relationship as little more than "dating." What result? See Cochran v. Cochran, 106 Cal. Rptr.2d 899 (Ct. App. 2001). Cf. Bergen v. Wood, 18 Cal. Rptr.2d 75 (Ct. App. 1993); Levine v. Konvitz, 890 A.2d 354 (N.J. Super.Ct. App. Div. 2006).

2. Anita and Larry begin living together. A few months later, Larry suggests that they jointly build a home. He promises that title will be in joint tenancy with the right of survivorship and that Anita will receive half the equity of the house if the relationship ends. Relying on Larry's promises, Anita obligates herself to pay a $48,000 mortgage. For three years when Larry is unemployed, Anita pays most of the mortgage, taxes, and insurance. When the relationship dissolves ten years later, she discovers that title is in Larry's name. Larry refuses to pay Anita half of the equity in the house. Anita files suit alleging breach of contract and unjust enrichment. Suppose that both *Hewitt* and Spafford v. Coats, supra, are precedents in this jurisdiction. What result? See Ayala v. Fox, 564 N.E.2d 920 (Ill. Ct. App. 1990).

4. Unmarried Couples, Third Parties, and the State

a. Tort Recovery

■ GRAVES v. ESTABROOK
818 A.2d 1255 (N.H. 2003)

Duggan, J.

The plaintiff, Catrina Graves, appeals a ruling [granting] the defendant, Franklin L. Estabrook's, motion to dismiss her complaint for negligent infliction of emotional distress. . . . Graves was engaged to Brett A. Ennis and had lived with him for approximately seven years. On September 23, 2000, Ennis was riding his motorcycle while Graves followed immediately behind him in a car. At an intersection, Estabrook's vehicle failed to yield at a stop sign and collided with Ennis. As Graves looked on, Ennis flipped over the hood of Estabrook's car and landed on the pavement. Graves immediately stopped her car and ran to the aid of her fiancé. She saw blood coming from his mouth and significant trauma to his head. She followed the ambulance that transported her fiancé to the hospital, stayed by his side while he was being treated, and attempted to comfort his parents and son. Ennis died the next day. Graves alleges that as a result of witnessing the collision and death of her fiancé, she suffered shock, severe mental pain and emotional distress.

The issue before us is whether a plaintiff who lived with and was engaged to marry the decedent may recover for negligent infliction of emotional distress. . . .

Many of the first states to recognize bystander liability for negligent infliction of emotional distress limited its scope by applying the "physical impact test," without considering foreseeability. Under the physical impact test, the plaintiff must have sustained a physical impact, no matter how slight, in order to recover. New Hampshire never adopted the physical impact test but instead followed the zone of danger rule. . . . That rule permitted recovery only when the bystander was within a physical zone of danger created by the defendant's negligence. In [Corso v. Merrill, 406 A.2d 300 (N.H. 1979)], however, we rejected the zone of danger rule. Instead, we applied the traditional negligence analysis of foreseeability and concluded that "[a]lthough fear of unlimited liability is a valid concern, we now think that this concern must be weighed against a plaintiff's serious emotional injury that is directly caused by defendant's negligence." [Id. at 304]. . . .

We adopted the test first enunciated in Dillon v. Legg, 441 P.2d 912 (Cal. 1968), in which the California Supreme Court set forth three factors for determining whether a defendant should reasonably foresee injury to a bystander: (1) Whether plaintiff was located near the scene of the accident as contrasted with one who was a distance away from it. (2) Whether the shock resulted from a direct emotional impact upon plaintiff from the sensory and contemporaneous observance of the accident, as contrasted with learning of the accident from others after its occurrence. (3) Whether plaintiff and the victim were closely related, as contrasted with an absence of any relationship or the presence of only a distant relationship. Id. at 920. . . .

This case requires us to examine the scope of *Dillon*'s third factor. The defendant argues that we should continue to follow the California Supreme Court and adopt its subsequent holding in Elden v. Sheldon, 758 P.2d 582 (Cal. 1988). There, the court held that unmarried cohabitants are not "closely related" and cannot recover for negligent infliction of emotional distress. Other courts have adopted the same rule [citing cases in Florida, New Mexico and Texas].

As noted by the New Jersey Supreme Court in Dunphy v. Gregor, 642 A.2d 372, 375 (N.J. 1994), "the [California Supreme Court] in *Elden* was reacting to the experience of the California courts with bystander liability under the *Dillon* standard." After *Dillon*, California courts had significantly expanded the scope of bystander liability [e.g., to eliminate the requirement of visual perception of the injury and to expand the "closely related" factor to include foster parent-child relationships]. Thus, one reason for the holding in *Elden* was a need to rein in the expansion of bystander liability in California. [U]nlike the California Supreme Court, we are not faced with a need to curb bystander liability.

Notwithstanding this difference, the defendant urges us to construe the third factor of *Corso* literally. He argues that we should limit the meaning of "closely related" to a dictionary definition: people "connected by consanguinity," Webster's Third New International Dictionary 1916 (unabridged ed.1961), or "persons connected by kinship, common origin or marriage." American Heritage Dictionary 1473 (4th ed. 2000). . . . The defendant's argument, limiting the analysis to a dictionary definition, amounts to a "dry classification [that] puts the emphasis at the wrong place[ ]." . . . The appropriate analysis is not to resort to a dictionary definition but rather to use our traditional analysis of foreseeability.

In *Elden*, the California Supreme Court rejected a traditional analysis of foreseeability for three policy reasons: first, the State's strong interest in marriage; second, the potential invasion into an unmarried plaintiff's privacy required to prove a close relationship; and third, the need to limit the class of plaintiffs by a bright line rule. *Elden*, 758 P.2d at 586-88. We examine each reason in turn.

First is the State's strong interest in marriage. In *Elden*, the court stated that "to the extent unmarried cohabitants are granted the same rights as married persons, the state's interest in promoting marriage is inhibited." Id. at 586. . . . *Elden* found no convincing reason to permit recovery to couples who bear no legal obligations to each other to the same extent as those who undertake such obligations.

The court in *Elden* apparently relied upon the dubious assumption that the possibility of recovery in tort litigation is an incentive to marry. Rejecting this assumption, the New Jersey Supreme Court observed that "a person who would not otherwise choose to marry would not be persuaded to do so in order to assure his or her legal standing in a future personal injury action should that person have the misfortune of witnessing the serious injury of his or her spouse." *Dunphy*, 642 A.2d at 379. . . . We agree.

The second reason relied upon in *Elden* was the "difficult burden on the courts." *Elden* reasoned that "[a] determination whether a partner in an unmarried cohabitation relationship may recover damages for emotional distress based on such matters as the sexual fidelity of the parties and their emotional and economic ties would require a court to undertake a massive intrusion into the private life of the partners." [*Elden*, 758 P.2d at 587]. Again, we agree with the New Jersey Supreme Court, which noted that "[o]ur courts have shown that the sound assessment of the quality of interpersonal relationships is not beyond a jury's ken and that courts are capable of dealing with the realities, not simply the legalities, of relationships to assure that resulting emotional injury is genuine and deserving of compensation." *Dunphy*, 642 A.2d at 378. . . . Furthermore, the real burden is not on the court but on the plaintiff who chooses to seek recovery for negligent infliction of emotional distress. At the outset, the plaintiff will know that the details of the relationship with the decedent will be examined and that this may involve an intrusion into the plaintiff's private life. The decision to submit to this searching inquiry is the plaintiff's choice and should not be the basis for limiting liability.

Third, the court in *Elden* relied upon [the need to limit the class of plaintiffs by a bright line rule]. The court noted that "[i]t would be an entirely unreasonable burden on all human activity if the defendant who has endangered one man were to be compelled to pay for the lacerated feelings of every other person disturbed by reason of it, including every bystander shocked at an accident, and every distant relative of the person injured, as well as his friends." [*Elden*, 758 P.2d at 588]. The court stated that the absence of a bright line rule "would result in the unreasonable extension of the scope of liability of a negligent actor." Id. While admitting that the "close emotional ties between unrelated or distantly related persons is often strong" and "the result of injury . . . may be as devastating as that suffered by a member of the immediate family," the court concluded that "[t]he problems of multiplication of actions and damages that would result from such an extension of liability would place an intolerable burden on society." Id. (citations and quotations omitted.)

Rejecting the bright line rule in *Elden*, however, does not place an intolerable burden upon society or unfair burden upon a negligent defendant. Rather, it allows recovery for an eminently foreseeable class of plaintiffs. . . . *Elden* argued that "[t]he need to draw a bright line in this area of the law is essential" because there is no "principled distinction between an unmarried cohabitant who claims to have a de facto marriage relationship with his partner and de facto siblings, parents, grandparents or children." *Elden*, 758 P.2d at 588. While this observation is accurate, it fails to consider that there is also no logical distinction between denying recovery to a fiancée who has lived with her betrothed for seven years and allowing recovery to a wife who met and married her husband a week before the accident. See State Dept. of Transp. v. Hill, 963 P.2d 480, 483 (Nev. 1998) (characterizing recovery after the wedding, but not beforehand, as "fallacious"). A bright line rule that includes only individuals related by blood or marriage is

> overinclusive because it permits recovery when the suffering accompanies a legal or biological link between bystander and victim, regardless of whether the relationship between the two is estranged, alienated, or in some other way removed. Conversely, the [rule] is underinclusive because it arbitrarily denies court access to persons with valid claims that they could prove if permitted to do so.

[Note, It's All Relative: A Graphical Reasoning Model for Liberalizing Recovery for Negligent Infliction of Emotional Distress Beyond the Immediate Family, 30 Val. U. L. Rev. 913, 917 (1996)].

More fundamentally, we decline to adopt a bright line rule when a "flexible approach, designed to account for factual nuances" is available. . . . We conclude that "to foreclose [an unmarried cohabitant] from making a claim based upon emotional harm because her relationship with the injured person does not carry a particular label is to work a potential injustice . . . where the emotional injury is genuine and substantial and is based upon a relationship of significant duration that . . . is deep, lasting and genuinely intimate." [*Dunphy*, 642 A.2d at 378]. A number of courts have reached a similar conclusion [citing cases in Hawaii, Nebraska, Ohio, Pennsylvania, Tennessee, West Virginia]. We thus recognize that unmarried cohabitants may have a close relationship, i.e., a "relationship that is stable, enduring, substantial, and mutually supportive . . . cemented by strong emotional bonds and provid[ing] a deep and pervasive emotional security." *Dunphy*, 642 A.2d at 380. In determining whether a relationship meets this standard, a court should

> take into account the duration of the relationship, the degree of mutual dependence, the extent of common contributions to a life together, the extent and quality of shared experience, and . . . whether the plaintiff and the injured person were members of the

same household, their emotional reliance on each other, the particulars of their day to day relationship, and the manner in which they related to each other in attending to life's mundane requirements.

Id. at 378 (quotation omitted).

In this case, the plaintiff alleged in her complaint that she was engaged to the decedent and that they had lived together for seven years immediately preceding the accident. Construing all reasonable inferences in the light most favorable to the plaintiff, we conclude that it is reasonable to infer that in the course of their lengthy cohabitation the plaintiff and her fiancé enjoyed mutual dependence, common contributions to a life together, emotional reliance on each other and attended to life's mundane requirements together. We conclude that the pleadings are reasonably susceptible of a construction that would withstand a motion to dismiss. . . .

The attorney who represented Catrina Graves in Graves v. Estabrook provides the following account of the case.

■ ROY A. DUDDY, A FIANCÉE'S EMOTIONAL ORDEAL,
Trial Mag. (Feb. 2004), at 36, 38-39

[At] Southern New Hampshire Medical Center, [Catrina] stayed at Brett's side for almost 30 hours until he was removed from life support. He had been kept on life support so his organs could be donated and so his son from a former marriage could arrive from Arkansas to say good-bye. Catrina and the Ennis family, who were and remain very close, sought counseling almost immediately after the accident to try to deal with the tragedy. Catrina still sees a psychologist.

About a month after the accident, Catrina and Brett's father came to see me. During our meeting, I saw clearly that Catrina and Brett — along with his family — had a genuine love for one another that had developed over seven years. Catrina saw the Ennis family weekly, and Brett's parents treated her as though she were their own daughter. She called them Mom and Dad.

Catrina also had a good relationship with Brett's son. In fact, she and Mr. Ennis both felt that the son should receive any insurance recovery obtained by Brett's estate. She was more concerned about ensuring that the boy be taken care of than she was about her own future. The family set up a special fund for his benefit, and more than 2,500 attendees at Brett's funeral contributed to it.

This young woman had suffered more egregiously than almost anyone I had met in more than 20 years of law practice. She was completely selfless in her dealings with her fiancé's son and his family. I felt that if ever there were a case to question the state supreme court about whether a bystander — not related by blood or marriage to the decedent yet having deep, familial ties — can recover for negligent infliction of emotional distress, this was it.

But I knew this was going to be difficult. I explained to Catrina and Mr. Ennis that New Hampshire does not recognize common law marriage, so she could not sue for negligent infliction of emotional distress. Also, because the couple were engaged but not married, Catrina was not entitled to participate in the distribution of the estate. Unless the state supreme court changed its position on the claim of negligent infliction of emotional distress [to permit recovery by unmarried cohabitants], she would have no means of recovery. . . .

When I was satisfied that the cause of action stood a viable chance of being allowed by the state supreme court, I filed suit. As expected, defense counsel filed a motion to dismiss, stating that New Hampshire does not allow an unmarried cohabitant to sue for negligent infliction of emotional distress. We began to draft our brief objecting to this motion, knowing it would be the sole basis for the acceptance or denial of an appeal to the state supreme court. [W]ithin a month, the trial court — as expected — dismissed the case.

In April 2002, the state supreme court agreed to hear our appeal. . . . We argued that allowing cohabiting partners to bring emotional distress claims would not be an unlimited expansion of liability, as this demographic included less than 7 percent of all households in New Hampshire. In addition, we contended that societal mores were more accepting of cohabitant relationships. The justices asked probing questions of both me and my opponent, and at the close of the oral argument, I was unsure whether we would prevail.

On March 3, 2003, a divided court issued a 3-2 ruling, holding that Catrina Graves "may recover damages for emotional distress as a result of witnessing the collision." [*Graves*, 818 A.2d at 1257]. The case was reversed and remanded for trial to the superior court. The parties later reached a confidential settlement. . . .

Notes and Questions

1. *Tort recovery generally.* Unmarried cohabitants sometimes try to recover for relationship injuries (such as those resulting from personal injury or death of a partner) through tort actions based on negligent infliction of emotional distress (NIED), loss of consortium, and wrongful death. Unlike claims for NIED and loss of consortium, actions for wrongful death are purely statutory in origin.

2. *Negligent infliction claims.* As *Graves* explains, under the traditional rule, recovery for NIED from witnessing the negligent injury to another was limited to persons who either suffered a physical impact or were in the zone of danger. Currently, more than half the states follow Dillon v. Legg, supra, limiting recovery for emotional distress based on the foreseeability of the trauma to bystanders. Dale Joseph Gilsinger, Annot., Recovery Under State Law for Negligent Infliction of Emotional Distress Under Rule of Dillon v. Legg, or Refinements Thereof, 96 A.L.R.5th 107 (2002 & Supp. 2005). The third prong of *Dillon* focuses on whether the plaintiff and victim had a *sufficiently close relationship* to sustain plaintiff's claim for negligent infliction of emotional distress. As *Graves* explains, courts are split regarding whether to permit such claims for unmarried heterosexual cohabitants. Compare *Graves*, supra (permitting recovery), with Biercevicz v. Liberty Mutual Ins. Co., 865 A.2d 1267 (Conn. Super. Ct. 2004)) (contra).

3. *Rationale.* According to *Graves*, what are the arguments pro and con recognizing cohabitants' claim for NIED? Justice Garibaldi, in a dissent in *Dunphy*, supra, raises additional policy concerns. She protests that exclusion of cohabitants conforms to societal expectations regarding differential treatment of spouses and is less likely to lead to confusion because spouses are treated differently in so many legal contexts (e.g., intestacy, alimony, loss of consortium). 642 A.2d at

381, 382-383. She adds that a policy of exclusion is consistent with non-recognition of common law marriage (which, she asserts, is an ephemeral arrangement that may dissolve at any time). Id. at 382. How persuasive are these arguments? Does the extension of liability advance the objectives of the tort system?

4. *Quality or status?* According to *Graves*, how is a plaintiff to prove the quality of the relationship? What evidence would a defendant introduce to minimize the quality of the relationship? Justice Garibaldi, the dissenting justice in *Dunphy*, supra, points out that the surviving cohabitant has a distinct advantage over the tortfeasor in proving the quality of the relationship because only the survivor (and not the victim) is available to testify regarding details of the relationship. How persuasive is this argument?

How workable is the *Dunphy* standard (adopted by *Graves*) that focuses on the following factors: the duration of the relationship, the degree of mutual dependence, the extent of common contributions to a life together, the extent and quality of shared experience, and membership in the same house? Note that the *Graves* court, rather than conducting a searching inquiry, seems to assume that a seven-year cohabitation plus an engagement automatically engender a sufficiently close relationship. Is this assumption appropriate?

How easy is the *Graves-Dunphy* standard to apply in the following situations: (a) Mary and Joe are engaged when defendant's negligence causes Mary's death. However, the couple is not living together because of opposition from Mary's parents (although the couple spends several nights per week together). They share all assets and expenses. (b) Carol and Paul are living together with their infant for six months before defendant's negligence causes Carol's death. The couple had no plans to marry and kept all accounts separate. Should recovery be allowed in either or both case(s)? Cf. Rosales v. Battle, 7 Cal. Rptr.3d 13 (Ct. App. 2003) (rejecting claim, in the context of wrongful death, of an unmarried cohabitant who was the mother of the victim's four children). Suppose a relationship is not monogamous. Should that preclude recovery? How is "emotional reliance" determined?

5. *Engaged couples.* In *Graves*, the plaintiff and the victim were not merely cohabitants but were engaged to marry. How does this factor strengthen plaintiff's claim? How does a fiancé or fiancée prove the existence of an engagement? Should the length of the engagement matter? Whether the couple has set the date? Exchanged rings? If the accident occurs the day before the wedding? See, e.g., Garrett v. Watson, 2001 WL 238196 (E.D. La. 2001) (granting defendant's motion for summary judgment on a loss of consortium claim because the parties were not married at the time of the accident).

In what ways are cohabitants' claims similar to, and different from, those of engaged persons? Professor Grace Blumberg responds as follows:

> Strictly speaking, a cohabitant's claim is distinguishable. The cohabitant was enjoying consortium at the time of the injury. More importantly, [it] is socially prudent to encourage fiancés and cohabitants to remain with the injured victims of tortfeasors. Denying them loss of consortium recovery on the ground that they were not legally bound to the injured person would seem to sanction and to encourage abandonment of the injured. . . . In this sense, fiancés and cohabitants are similarly situated: neither is bound to be virtuous.

Grace Ganz Blumberg, Cohabitation Without Marriage: A Different Perspective, 28 UCLA L. Rev. 1125, 1138-1139 n.80 (1981).

6. *Loss of consortium*. Most courts deny recovery for loss of consortium to unmarried cohabitants. See, e.g., Fitzsimmons v. Mini Coach of Boston, Inc., 440 N.E.2d 1256 (Mass. 2003) (denying recovery after plaintiff's male partner, with whom she lived for more than 10 years, was injured in a bus accident). Recently, New Mexico became the first jurisdiction to permit a loss of consortium claim by an unmarried cohabitant. Lozoya v. Sanchez, 66 p.3d 948 (N.M. 2003) (extending recovery for loss of consortium to female partner for the injuries sustained in a car accident by her male partner of more than 30 years). See generally Alisha M. Carlile, Note, Like Family: Rights of Nonmarital Cohabitational Partners in Loss of Consortium Actions, 46 B.C.L. Rev. 391 (2005); Gary Johnston, Jr., Comment, Losing the Nuptials in Loss of Consortium; Correcting California's Common Law Claim, U.S.F. L. Rev. 201 (2004); Flynn Sylvest, Note and Comment, New Tort Rules for Unmarried Partners: The Enhanced Potential for Successful Loss of Consortium and NIED Claims by Same Sex Partners in New Mexico After *Lozoya*, 34 N.M. L. Rev. 461 (2004).

7. *Post-marital loss of consortium*. Suppose in *Graves* that Brett Ennis was injured rather than killed. The couple marries after the accident. Should Graves be allowed to recover for the loss of consortium she *subsequently* experiences stemming from the premarital injury? Why? Compare Owens-Illinois, Inc. v. Gianotti, 813 A.2d 280 (Md. Ct. App. 2002) (permitting post-marital recovery), with Zwicker v. Altamont Emergency Room Physicians Med. Group, 118 Cal Rpt.2d 912 (Cal. Ct. App. 2002) (contra).

8. *Wrongful death*. The tort of wrongful death, permitting recovery for fatal injuries, is entirely statutory in origin. Statutory provisions generally limit recovery to legal spouses (although a few statutes permit recovery by a person who is named as a beneficiary in a decedent's will). With regard to recovery by unmarried cohabitants, one commentator notes:

> Because the statutes define the potential beneficiaries with such precision, there are only a few cases in which unmarried cohabitants have even sought recovery for wrongful death, and hints from other cases suggest that they have little reason to be optimistic. In denying recovery to unmarried cohabitants for loss of consortium and negligent infliction of emotional distress, courts often cite the state's refusal to grant similar rights under wrongful death statutes as evidence that state policy disfavors these common-law claims as well.

John G. Culhane, A "Clanging Silence": Same-Sex Couples and Tort Law, 89 Ky. L.J. 911, 957 (2000-2001).

9. *Marvin distinguished*. Has California adopted a paradoxical position toward unmarried couples? Does it make sense to allow recovery by unmarried cohabitants in contract law (*Marvin*) but not tort law (*Elden*)? Does it make sense to allow tort recovery by registered domestic partners but not by *non-registered* partners? See Holguin v. Flores, 18 Cal. Rptr.3d 749 (Ct. App. 2004) (refusing recovery to unmarried male cohabitant for the wrongful death of his female partner, thereby limiting Cal. Civ. Pro. Code §377.60 to registered domestic partners). See generally Michael Jay Gorback, Note, Negligent Infliction of Emotional Distress: Has the Legislative Response to Diane Whipple's Death Rendered the Hard-line Stance of *Elden* and *Thing* Obsolete?, 54 Hastings L.J. 273 (2002).

10. *Demographic data*. To what extent do demographic data (e.g., increases in the numbers of unmarried couples) support arguments for or against legal recog-

nition of the rights of cohabitants? How did Catrina Graves's lawyer use demographic data in support of plaintiff's claim? How did the California Supreme Court in *Marvin* use demographic data in support of plaintiff's claim? Should legal rules mirror social reality, or should other considerations come into play?

11. *Tort recovery by same-sex couples*. If tort recovery is to be permitted to unmarried cohabitants based on a sort of functional equivalency test, should courts permit recovery by members of same-sex couples? What does *Graves* suggest? Does the extension of liability in this case advance the objectives of the tort system? See generally John G. Culhane, Even More Wrongful Death: Statutes Divorced from Reality, 32 Fordham Urb. L.J. 171 (2005); Culhane, A "Clanging Silence," supra; Sylvest, supra.

Some jurisdictions extend *by statute* the right to tort recovery for relationship injuries to *registered* domestic partners based on the broad grant to such couples of all the benefits of marriage. See, e.g., Cal. Fam. Code §297.5 (West 2004); Vt. Stat. Ann. Tit. 15, §1204(e)(2) (2002). Other jurisdictions with domestic partnership laws (i.e., Hawaii and New Jersey) fail to recognize same-sex partners' right to recover for either emotional distress or loss of consortium. However, Hawaii, but not New Jersey, permits recovery by such partners for wrongful death. Culhane, Even More Wrongful Death, supra, at 180, 189. California recently extended that right to some unregistered same-sex partners. See Armijo v. Miles, 26 Cal. Rptr.3d 623 (Ct. App. 2005) (validating amendment to Cal. Code Civ. Proc. §377.60 that grants an unregistered same-sex partner standing for wrongful death purposes if the decedent's death occurred before 2002 and plaintiff can establish the requisite elements of the domestic partnership statute).

Currently, jurisdictions are split on whether to interpret their wrongful death statutes to allow same-sex partners to sue for wrongful death. Compare Langan v. St. Vincent's Hosp., 802 N.Y.S.2d 476 (App. Div. 2005) (holding that surviving partner of civil union under Vermont law was not entitled to bring action under New York law as a "spouse" in a wrongful death claim against hospital for the death of his male partner), with Solomon v. Dist. of Columbia, 21 Fam. L. Rptr. (BNA) 1316 (D.C. Super. Ct. 1995) (permitting a surviving same-sex partner to recover under wrongful death statute as "next of kin"). See also Culhane, Even More Wrongful Death, supra, at 189.

In a famous California case, a trial court extended the right to sue to Sharon Smith for the wrongful death of her same-sex partner of 7 years, Diane Whipple, who was mauled to death by two dogs in the hallway of their San Francisco apartment building. Smith successfully challenged California's law limiting recovery for wrongful death to legal heirs on the grounds of equal protection. See Smith v. Knoller, No. 319532, slip op. (Cal. Super. Ct. Aug. 9, 2001). Smith's testimony before the state legislature generated considerable sympathy for then-pending legislation (A.B. 25) that broadened the rights of same-sex couples to make health care decisions, inherit property, and sue for wrongful death. Kevin Livingston, Bill on Rights of Same-Sex Couples Advances, The (S.F.) Recorder, Mar. 14, 2001, at 3. See also Cal. Civ. Pro. Code §377.60 (West 2004 & Supp. 2005) (giving registered domestic partners standing to sue for wrongful death). See generally Christopher Heredia, Mauled S.F. Woman's Partner Files Wrongful Death Lawsuit, S.F. Chron., Mar. 13, 2001, at A21; Andrew LaMar, Whipple's Death Inspires Legislation, Contra Costa Times, Mar. 8, 2001, at A06; Greg Lucas, Domestic Partners Bill Ok'd By Panel, Mauled Woman's Companion Speaks Up For Rights Legislation, S.F. Chron., Mar. 14, 2001, at A3.

12. *Post-September 11th spousal equivalency legislation.* Following the terrorist attacks on the World Trade Center and the Pentagon on September 11th, 2001, Congress established the Victim Compensation Fund (VCF), as part of the Air Transportation Safety and Stabilization Act, Pub. L. No. 107-42, §§1-601, 115 Stat. 230, to compensate survivors and relatives of victims in exchange for their release of claims against the airline industry. Same-sex partners' eligibility to recover depended upon whether the victim had named the partner as an executor in the decedent's will. However, in cases in which the victim died without a will, eligibility for surviving relatives would be determined by the intestacy laws of the decedent's domicile. This latter provision precluded same-sex partners from recovery because state law makes no provision for intestate inheritance by domestic partners (with the exception of some of the states that recognize domestic partnerships).

Several states (particularly New York, Virginia, and Pennsylvania) that were affected by the terrorist attacks also established programs to accept claims by survivors and family members of victims. In many cases, these programs permitted claims by surviving domestic partners. For example, legislation in New York enabled those New York domestic partners of victims to claim benefits under the federal VCF, provided that the partners filed jointly with the victim's next-of-kin. In addition, the New York Workers' Compensation Law §4 (McKinney 2005), extended workers' compensation benefits to both same-sex and opposite-sex unmarried partners of September 11th victims. Pennsylvania's program permitted "significant others" (including same-sex partners) to recover. However, Virginia's fund did not recognize same-sex partners. See generally Nancy J. Knauer, The September 11 Attacks and Surviving Same-Sex Partners: Defining Family Through Tragedy, 75 Temp. L. Rev. 31 (2002); John O. Enright, Comment, New York's Post-September 11, 2001 Recognition of Same-Sex Relationships: A Victory Suggestive of Future Change, 72 Fordham L. Rev. 2823 (2004); Jane Gross, U.S. Fund for Tower Victims Will Aid Some Gay Partners, N.Y. Times, May 30, 2003, at A1.

Notwithstanding the reforms in New York, domestic partners there continue to face discrimination in terms of achieving spousal equivalency benefits. That is, the post-September 11th reforms were limited in scope, and courts tended to interpret them narrowly. Reforms, therefore, did not lead to widespread recognition of the rights of same-sex partners. See Valentine v. American Airlines, 791 N.Y.S.2d 217 (App. Div. 2005) (upholding denial of workers' compensation benefits to the partner of a flight attendant killed in a plane crash two months after September 11, 2001).

b. Employment

■ **SHAHAR v. BOWERS**
114 F.3d 1097 (11th Cir. 1997)

EDMONDSON, Circuit Judge:

In this government-employment case, Plaintiff-Appellant contends that the Attorney General of the State of Georgia violated her federal constitutional rights by revoking an employment offer because of her purported "marriage" to another woman. . . .

. . . Plaintiff Robin Joy Shahar is a woman who has "married" another woman in a ceremony performed by a rabbi within the Reconstructionist Movement of Judaism. According to Shahar, though the State of Georgia does not recognize her "marriage" and she does not claim that the "marriage" has legal effect, she and her partner consider themselves to be "married."

While a law student, Shahar spent the summer of 1990 as a law clerk with the [office of the state Attorney General, Michael J. Bowers (hereafter "the Department"]. In September 1990, the Attorney General offered Shahar the position of Staff Attorney when she graduated from law school. Shahar accepted the offer and was scheduled to begin work in September 1991.

In the summer of 1990, Shahar began making plans for her "wedding." Her rabbi announced the expected "wedding" to the congregation at Shahar's synagogue in Atlanta. Shahar and her partner invited approximately 250 people, including two Department employees, to the "wedding." The written invitations characterized the ceremony as a "Jewish, lesbian-feminist, outdoor wedding." The ceremony took place in a public park in South Carolina in June 1991.

In November 1990, Shahar filled out the required application for a Staff Attorney position. In response to the question on "marital status," Shahar indicated that she was "engaged." She altered "spouse's name" to read "future spouse's name" and filled in her partner's name: "Francine M. Greenfield." In response to the question "Do any of your relatives work for the State of Georgia?" she filled in the name of her partner as follows: "Francine Greenfield, future spouse."

Sometime in the spring of 1991, Shahar and her partner were working on their "wedding" invitations at an Atlanta restaurant. [While there, they met a paralegal and staff attorney, Susan Rutherford, from the Attorney General's office and mentioned to them the wedding preparations.] In June 1991, Shahar told Deputy Attorney General Robert Coleman that she was getting married at the end of July, changing her last name, taking a trip to Greece and, accordingly, would not be starting work with the Department until mid-to-late September. At this point, Shahar did not say that she was "marrying" another woman. Senior Assistant Attorney General Jeffrey Milsteen, who had been co-chair of the summer clerk committee, was in Coleman's office at the time and heard Coleman congratulate Shahar. Milsteen later mentioned to Rutherford that Shahar was getting married. Rutherford then told Milsteen that Shahar was planning on "marrying" another woman. This revelation caused a stir.

Senior aides to the Attorney General became concerned about what they viewed as potential problems in the office resulting from the Department's employment of a Staff Attorney who purported to be part of a same-sex "marriage." As the Attorney General was out of the office that week, the five aides held several meetings among themselves to discuss the situation.

Upon the Attorney General's return to the office, he was informed of the situation. [He] decided, with the advice of his senior lawyers, to withdraw Shahar's job offer [by stating in writing] that the withdrawal of Shahar's offer:

> has become necessary in light of information which has only recently come to my attention relating to a purported marriage between you and another woman. As chief legal officer of this state, inaction on my part would constitute tacit approval of this purported marriage and jeopardize the proper functioning of this office.

[Shahar instituted suit seeking damages, injunctive relief, and "reinstatement." She argued that revocation of the employment offer violated the rights to free exercise and association, equal protection, and substantive due process. The district court granted the Attorney General's motion for summary judgment.]

Even when we assume, for argument's sake, that either the right to intimate association or the right to expressive association or both are present, we know they are not absolute. Georgia and its elected Attorney General also have rights and duties which must be taken into account. . . . In reviewing Shahar's claim, we stress that this case is about the government acting as employer.

Shahar argues that we must review the withdrawal of her job offer under strict scrutiny. The only precedent to which Shahar refers us for the proposition that strict scrutiny is to be applied to the government as employer is Dike v. School Board, 650 F.2d 783 (5th Cir. 1981). In *Dike*, the Fifth Circuit — our predecessor — implied that a school district's refusal to allow a teacher to breast-feed her child on her lunch hour must withstand strict scrutiny. To the extent that *Dike* might be interpreted as requiring strict scrutiny review of a government employee's freedom of intimate association claim, it misstates the appropriate standard; and we overrule it now. . . . We conclude that the appropriate test for evaluating the constitutional implications of the State of Georgia's decision [is] the same test as the test for evaluating the constitutional implications of a government employer's decision based on an employee's exercise of her right to free speech, that is, the *Pickering* [Pickering v. Board of Ed., 391 U.S. 563 (1968)] balancing test. . . .

. . . To decide this case, we are willing to accord Shahar's claimed associational rights (which we have assumed to exist) substantial weight. But, we know that the weight due intimate associational rights, such as, those involved in even a state-authorized marriage, can be overcome by a government employer's interest in maintaining the effective functioning of his office.

In weighing her interest in her associational rights, Shahar asks us also to consider the "non-employment related context" of her "wedding" and "marriage" and that "[s]he took no action to transform her intimate association into a public or political statement." In addition, Shahar says that we should take into account that she has affirmatively disavowed a right to benefits from the Department based on her "marriage."

To the extent that Shahar disclaims benefits bestowed by the State based on marriage, she is merely acknowledging what is undisputed, that Georgia law does not and has not recognized homosexual marriage. We fail to see how that technical acknowledgment counts for much in the balance.

If Shahar is arguing that she does not hold herself out as "married," the undisputed facts are to the contrary. Department employees, among many others, were invited to a "Jewish, lesbian-feminist, out-door wedding" which included exchanging wedding rings: the wearing of a wedding ring is an outward sign of having entered into marriage. Shahar listed her "marital status" on her employment application as "engaged" and indicated that her future spouse was a woman. She and her partner have both legally changed their family name to Shahar by filing a name change petition with the Fulton County Superior Court. They sought and received the married rate on their insurance. And, they, together, own the house in which they cohabit. These things were not done secretly, but openly. . . .

[T]he Attorney General's worry about his office being involved in litigation in which Shahar's special personal interest might appear to be in conflict with the State's position [is] not unreasonable. In addition, the Department, when the job offer was withdrawn, had already engaged in and won a recent battle [Bowers v. Hardwick, 478 U.S. 186 (1986)] about homosexual sodomy — highly visible litigation in which its lawyers worked to uphold the lawful prohibition of homosexual sodomy. This history makes it particularly reasonable for the Attorney General to worry about the internal consequences for his professional staff (for example, loss of morale, loss of cohesiveness and so forth) of allowing a lawyer, who openly — for instance, on her employment application and in statements to coworkers — represents herself to be "married" to a person of the same sex, to become part of his staff. . . .

Shahar also argues that, at the Department, she would have handled mostly death penalty appeals and that the *Pickering* test requires evidence of potential interference with these particular duties. Even assuming Shahar is correct about her likely assignment within the Department, a particularized showing of interference with the provision of public services is not required. . . . [I]t is not for this court to tie the Department's hands by telling it which Staff Attorneys may be assigned to which cases or duties or to force upon the Attorney General a Staff Attorney of limited utility.

. . . Shahar argues that [the Attorney General] may not justify his decision by reference to perceived public hostility to her "marriage." We have held otherwise about the significance of public perception when law enforcement is involved [citing McMullen v. Carson, 754 F.2d 936, 938 (11th Cir. 1985)]. [A]ssessing what the public perceives about the Attorney General and the Law Department is a judgment for the Attorney General to make in the day-to-day course of filling his proper role as the elected head of the Department, not for the federal judiciary to make with hindsight or from a safe distance away from the distress and disturbance that might result if the decision was mistaken. We must defer to Georgia's Attorney General's judgment about what Georgians might perceive unless his judgment is definitely outside of the broad range of reasonable views. . . .

Shahar says that by taking into account these concerns about public reaction, the Attorney General impermissibly discriminated against homosexuals; and she refers us to the Supreme Court's recent decision in Romer v. Evans, [517 U.S. 620 (1996)]. In *Romer*, the Supreme Court struck down an amendment to a state constitution as irrational because the amendment's sole purpose was to disadvantage a particular class of people (to "den[y] them protection across the board," id. at 633) and because the government engaged in "classification of persons undertaken for its own sake, something the Equal Protection Clause does not permit." Id. at 635.

Romer is about people's condition; this case is about a person's conduct. And, *Romer* is no employment case. Considering (in deciding to revoke a job offer) public reaction to a future Staff Attorney's conduct in taking part in a same-sex "wedding" and subsequent "marriage" is not the same kind of decision as an across-the-board denial of legal protection to a group because of their condition, that is, sexual orientation or preference.

This case is about the powers of government as an employer, powers which are far broader than government's powers as sovereign. In addition, the employment in this case is of a special kind: employment involving access to the employer's confidences, acting as the employer's spokesperson, and helping to make policy. This kind of employment is one in which the employer's interest has been given especially great weight in the past. Furthermore, the employment in this case is employment with responsibilities directly impacting on the enforcement of a state's laws: a kind of employment in which appearances and public perceptions and public confidence count a lot.

Particularly considering this Attorney General's many years of experience and Georgia's recent legal history, we cannot say that he was unreasonable to think that Shahar's acts were likely to cause the public to be confused and to question the Law Department's credibility; to interfere with the Law Department's ability to handle certain controversial matters, including enforcing the law against homosexual sodomy; and to endanger working relationships inside the Department. We also cannot say that the Attorney General was unreasonable to lose confidence in Shahar's ability to make good judgments as a lawyer for the Law Department.

[W]e hold that the Attorney General's interest — that is, the State of Georgia's interest — as an employer in promoting the efficiency of the Law Department's important public service does outweigh Shahar's personal associational interests. . . . Georgia's Attorney General has made a personnel decision which none of the asserted federal constitutional provisions prohibited him from making. . . .

■ POSTSCRIPT BY ROBIN SHAHAR
Personal communication with the authors, August 3, 2005

My professional life has been interesting and enjoyable. I am a Senior Assistant City Attorney for the City of Atlanta Law Department. I began working for the Law Department in 1993 and have handled numerous matters about which I am proud. One of my most meaningful cases was a seven-year suit successfully defending the City's right to offer domestic partnership benefits. This case also opened the door for private employers to offer domestic partnership coverage in Georgia. I have also successfully defended the City against numerous reverse discrimination cases, and was part of a team that successfully defended the City's affirmative action program. I was the city's lead attorney representing Hartsfield Atlanta International Airport for two years, and now serve as the city's attorney representing the Department of Parks, Recreation, and Cultural Affairs.

At the time of this writing, Fran and I are celebrating our 14th anniversary since our commitment ceremony, and 19 years of being together. We have two wonderful children. Although we lost Shahar vs. Bowers and although the en banc decision was profoundly disturbing, we are aware of how the case positively contributes to achieving equal rights for gay men and lesbians. One of the most critical benefits of the case is its educational value. Fran and I were shocked at how many people expressed surprise that gay men and lesbians could be fired simply because of their sexual orientation. In that way, the case helped illustrate the need for legislation protecting gay men and lesbians from discrimination in the workplace. It demonstrated that such legislation is a way of providing gay men and lesbians with equal rights, not "special rights." The case also helped educate the courts about the types of discrimination being faced by gay men and lesbians. It is this type of education, along with the education that goes with gay men and lesbians and their friends and family members coming out and demanding equal rights, that ultimately leads to victories such as Lawrence vs. Texas.

Notes and Questions

1. *Background.* Following the plaintiff's appeal of the summary judgment in favor of the attorney general, the court of appeals initially upheld plaintiff's

intimate association claim under the First Amendment, and ruled that strict scrutiny applied. 70 F.3d 1218 (11th Cir. 1995). However, after granting a rehearing en banc (78 F.3d 499 (11th Cir. 1996)), the court of appeals applied the *Pickering* balancing test to reach the conclusion in the principal case.

One week after the ruling in *Shahar*, former state attorney general Michael Bowers confessed his 15-year-adulterous affair with a former employee. Robin Shahar filed a motion for rehearing, arguing that because Bowers's sexual conduct similarly was prohibited by Georgia law, that undermined the court's conclusion that Bowers did not treat Shahar differently simply because she was a lesbian. The Eleventh Circuit denied her petition, saying that she was not terminated because of her sexual conduct but because of her marriage. Wendy Kaminer, Gay Rights, American Prospect, Feb. 28, 2000, at 67. Shahar later took a job as an attorney with the city of Atlanta, as the above excerpt reveals. See also Joyce Murdoch & Deb Price, Courting Justice: Gay Men and Lesbians v. the Supreme Court 494 (2001). Bowers resigned as state attorney general to run an unsuccessful gubernatorial campaign. He returned to private practice as a partner with the Atlanta firm of Meadows, Ichter and Trigg. Lyle V. Harris, Out of the Wrestling Ring, Into the Courtroom, Atlanta J. & Const., Mar. 3, 2000, at G1.

2. *State interests.* In *Shahar*, plaintiff claims violation of her constitutional rights because she lost her offer of employment at the hands of a state actor. The appellate court relies on the *Pickering* balancing test because the state-employer has special interests. Do you believe that plaintiff's marriage would have interfered with the performance of her daily duties? How many cases involving same-sex unions might be handled regularly by the defendant's office? What role should public perception play in employment decisions involving state actors? See Michele L. Booth, Shahar v. Bowers: Is Public Opinion Transformed into a Legitimate Government Interest When Government Acts as Employer?, 78 B.U. L. Rev. 1235 (1998).

3. *Post-*Lawrence. The *Sharar* court reached its decision six years before the Supreme Court decided Lawrence v. Texas (overturning Bowers v. Hardwick). What effect, if any, might *Lawrence* have on the result in *Shahar*?

4. *Public v. private.* Does *Shahar* imply that plaintiff lost her employment only because she made "public" her relationship? How "private" would plaintiff have had to keep this information to prevent defendant from establishing a sufficiently countervailing state interest? Does *Shahar* suggest that the Constitution affords more protection to those relationships "in the closet"? See also McConnell v. Anderson, 451 F.2d 193, 195 (8th Cir. 1971) (affirming denial of employment to university librarian after employee applied for a marriage license with his same-sex partner because of his "activist role in implementing his unconventional ideas"); Singer v. U.S. Civil Serv. Comm'n, 530 F.2d 247, 249 (9th Cir. 1976), *vacated*, 429 U.S. 1034 (1977) (clerk typist fired for "flaunting" sexual orientation by embracing another male at place of employment). See generally William N. Eskridge, Gaylaw: Challenging the Apartheid of the Closet (2003); Todd Brower, Of Courts and Closets: A Doctrinal and Empirical Analysis of Gay Identity in the Courts, 38 San Diego L. Rev. 565 (2001).

The judicial attitude that penalizes an employee for certain behavior (for example, same-sex marriage, public displays of affection to a member of the same sex, and activism) has prompted one commentator to point out:

what is seen as extravagant flaunting on the part of gay men and lesbians is routine, even expected behavior for heterosexuals in this society. Heterosexuals are free to reveal their status and preferences through public displays of affection as diverse as holding hands and sending out wedding announcements. Conversations among heterosexuals about "the process of forming couples" and one's life with one's partner are "expected and appropriate . . . in social and work settings."

Mary Anne Case, Couples and Coupling in the Public Sphere: A Comment on the Legal History of Litigating for Lesbian and Gay Rights, 79 Va. L. Rev. 1643, 1672 (1993) (quoting Marc A. Fajer, Can Two Real Men Eat Quiche Together? Storytelling, Gender-Role Stereotypes, and Legal Protection for Lesbians and Gay Men, 46 U. Miami L. Rev. 511, 604 (1992)).

5. *Employment discrimination based on sexual orientation.* Although efforts to enact federal legislation barring employment discrimination based on sexual orientation date from 1974, currently no federal law prohibits workplace discrimination in the private sector on this basis.[16] In contrast, women, minorities, persons older than 40, and the disabled all enjoy federal and state protection from employment discrimination. Efforts to pass federal legislation barring employment discrimination based on sexual orientation failed to pass the Senate by one vote in 1996. Proposed legislation, the Employment Nondiscrimination Act (ENDA) of 2001, H.R. 3285, 108th Cong. (2003), prohibits public and private employers, employment agencies, and labor unions from using sexual orientation as a basis in hiring, firing, promotion, or compensation, subject to exemptions for small businesses under 15 employees, religious organizations, and the armed forces.

On the state level, 13 states and the District of Columbia prohibit discrimination based on sexual orientation in private and public employment (but not Georgia, the setting of the principal case). Also, eight states prohibit sexual-orientation discrimination in public employment. Further, at least 124 cities and counties prohibit workplace discrimination based on sexual orientation. See Discrimination Based on Sexual Orientation, available at http://public.findlaw.com (last visited July 27, 2005).

6. *Military discharge.* Gays and lesbians who are members of the armed forces face discharge if they reveal their sexual orientation. The military policy of "Don't Ask, Don't Tell," P.L. 103-160, 10 U.S.C. §654 (2000), prohibits any person who is not heterosexual from disclosing his or her sexual orientation, or from speaking about any homosexual relationships, while serving in the armed forces. According to Servicemembers Legal Defense Network (SLDN) (a non-profit legal services and policy organization dedicated to ending discrimination against gay military personnel), 65,000 active members of the U.S. armed forces are closeted gay men, lesbians and bisexuals; and, about 10,000 have been discharged from the military in the last decade on this ground. See Ann Rostow, PlanetOut Network, July 8, 2005, available at http://news.yahoo.com/s/po/dontaskchallengedinfederalcourt.

---

[16]. However, *federal* government workers are protected from employment discrimination on the basis of sexual orientation. According to 5 U.S.C. §2302(b)(10) (2000), federal government employees are protected from employment discrimination based on "conduct not related to job performance." The EEOC's Office of Personal Management has interpreted this provision to include employment discrimination based on sexual orientation. See http:///www.eeoc.gov/facts/qanda.html (last visited July 30, 2005).

In December 2004, SLDN filed suit in federal district court in Massachusetts on behalf of 12 gay and lesbian former service members challenging the constitutionality of the "Don't Ask, Don't Tell" policy, asserting that the policy denies gay servicepersons the constitutional rights to privacy, equal protection, and freedom of speech. The plaintiffs, service members who were discharged based on the policy, seek reinstatement in the armed forces and an abrogation of the military's ban. Cook v. Rumsfeld, CA No. 04-12546 (D. Mass. filed Dec. 6, 2004), On April 24, 2006, a federal district court in Boston dismissed the lawsuit, reasoning that Congress has authority to establish military policies. Shelley Murphy, Don't Ask, Don't Tell Suit Dismissed, Boston Globe, Apr. 25, 2006, at B1. What is the likely impact of Lawrence v. Texas on the policy? See generally Tobias Barrington Wolff, Political Representation and Accountability Under Don't Ask, Don't Tell, 89 Iowa L. Rev. 1633 (2004) (discussing the policy, its free speech implications, and its future in light of *Lawrence*).

In another lawsuit, Rumsfeld v. Forum for Academic and Institutional Rights (FAIR), 126 S.Ct. 1297 (2006), an association of law schools and law faculty brought suit challenging the constitutionality of the Solomon Amendment requiring the Department of Defense to deny federal funding to institutions of higher education that prohibit access to military recruiters. Upholding the constitutionality of the Amendment, the United States Supreme Court rejected plaintiffs' claims under the First Amendment and the doctrine of unconstitutional conditions (i.e., that the Amendment placed an unconstitutional condition on the receipt of federal funds by forcing plaintiffs to accept government policies with which they disagree).

Also, Congress is presently considering the Military Readiness Enhancement Act of 2005 (MREA), H.R. 1059 (109th Cong., 1st Sess.), introduced in March 2005 by Rep. Marty Meehan (D-MA). The bill would replace the military's "Don't Ask, Don't Tell" ban with a policy of nondiscrimination on the basis of sexual orientation.

In contrast to the policy of the United States, many European nations permit gay servicepersonnel to serve openly in the military. This result stems from a 1999 case of the European Court of Human Rights (applicable to all member states) that invalidated the British ban as a violation of the European Human Rights Convention. See generally Debra A. Luker, The Homosexual Law and Policy in the Military: "Don't Ask, Don't Tell, Don't Pursue, Don't Harass" . . . Don't Be Absurd!, 3 Scholar 267 (2001); Scott Morris, Europe Enters a New Millennium with Gays in the Military While the United States Drowns in Don't Ask, Don't Tell: Twin Decisions by the European Court of Human Rights, 9 Am. U. J. Gender Soc. Pol'y & L. 423 (2001).

7. *Other contexts*. A "Don't Ask, Don't Tell" policy also extends to clergy in some religious denominations. In a widely publicized case, a tribunal of the United Methodist Church removed minister Irene Elizabeth Stroud from her pulpit after she admitted to living in a lesbian relationship. A regional appeals panel reversed the opinion, but the church's highest court, the Judicial Council, defrocked the minister in October 2005. Lesbian Pastor Fired, Int'l Herald Trib., Nov. 2, 2005, at 4.

8. *Employment discrimination based on heterosexual sexual conduct*. Unmarried heterosexual couples also may face adverse employment actions based on their sexual conduct. For example, in Hope International University v. Superior Court, 14 Cal. Rptr.3d 643 (Ct. App. 2004), two professors of a church-affiliated university (who

later married each other) were terminated based on the perception that they had an affair while one of them was still married to another person. The court of appeals held that plaintiffs' claim of marital status discrimination was not viable to the extent such claim was predicated on an allegation that the professors were fired because of the perception that they had an illicit premarital relationship, but that it was viable if predicated on a university policy precluding coworkers from marrying one another. See generally Jason R. Fulmer, Dismissing the "Immoral" Teacher for Conduct Outside the Workplace — Do Current Laws Protect the Interests of Both the School Authorities and Teachers?, 31 J.L. & Educ. 271 (2002); Ralph D. Mawdsley, School Board Control Over Education and a Teacher's Right to Privacy, 23 St. Louis U. Pub. L. Rev. 609, 611-615 (2004). Public employees sometimes also suffer similar problems. See, e.g., Hobbs v. Pender County, No. 05 CVS 267 (Pender Cty. Super. Ct., filed Mar. 28, 2005) (suit on behalf of a sheriff's dispatcher who alleged that she was forced to resign because she was cohabiting in violation of state law). Courts are split regarding whether a public employer may terminate an employee because the latter is cohabiting with an opposite-sex partner. See generally Nonnie L. Shivers, Note, Firing "Immoral" Public Employees: If Article 8 of the European Convention on Human Rights Protects Employee Privacy Rights, Then Why Can't We?, 21 Ariz. J. Int'l & Comp. Law 621 (2004).

Some cases have questioned, in the context of adverse employment decisions affecting persons in non-marital heterosexual relationships, whether the constitutional right to privacy protects the right to participate in an adulterous affair. See, e.g., Sylvester v. Fogley, 383 F. Supp. 2d 1135 (W.D. Ark. 2005) (holding that an adverse employment action stemming from a police officer's off-duty sexual relationship with a principal in an investigation did not violate former's constitutional privacy right based on the public interest of achieving effective law enforcement). Would the outcome be the same based on Lawrence v. Texas?

9. *Empirical data.* Employment discrimination against LGBT persons appears to be a common occurrence. In a national study, the National Gay and Lesbian Task Force reported that 33 percent of its members reported having faced employment discrimination based on sexual orientation. See "The Issues: Non-discrimination," available at http://www.thetaskforce.org/theissues (last visited on July 27, 2005). National polls reveal that, although the public is strongly opposed to same-sex marriage, it strongly supports equal employment opportunities for gays and lesbians. According to Gallup polls conducted in April and May 2005, 56 percent of the public oppose legalizing same-sex marriage and a similar percentage (53 percent) support a proposed constitutional amendment defining marriage as a heterosexual union. Yet, 87 percent of respondents believe that gays and lesbians should have equal opportunities in the workplace. Lydia Saad, Gay Rights Attitudes a Mixed Bag, The Gallup Organization, May 20, 2005, available at http://www.gallup.com/poll/content/default.aspx?ci=16402. An earlier Gallup poll also surveyed American's attitudes about gays and lesbians in military service. Although 40 percent of Americans supported a permissive policy allowing gays to serve openly in the military in 1993 when the "Don't Ask, Don't Tell" policy was implemented, by 2004 that number had increased substantially (to 63 percent). Heather Mason Kiefer, Gays in the Military: Public Says Go Ahead and Tell, The Gallup Poll, Dec. 21, 2004, available at http://www.gallup.com/poll/content/?ci=14419*pg=1. What explains these paradoxical attitudes?

10. *Spousal-equivalency employee benefits.* Increasingly, employers are offering spousal-equivalency employee benefits to same-sex partners. (The range of

benefits include: bereavement leave, family and medical leave, health insurance, COBRA benefits continuation, relocation assistance, adoption assistance, retiree medical coverage, employer-provided life insurance and supplemental life insurance, pension benefits, and employee discounts.) According to data from the Human Rights Campaign (a Washington-based LGBT advocacy organization), by December 31, 2004, a total of 8,250 private employers, state and local governments, government agencies, colleges and universities provided health insurance coverage to employees' domestic partners. Moreover, the number of Fortune 500 companies that offered employer-provided domestic partner health benefits in 2004 was 43 percent, a 9 percent increase from 2003. Daryl Herrschaft, State of the Workplace Report: 2004 (Human Rights Campaign, 2005), at 15 (available at http://www. hrc.org/Template.cfm?Section=Resources1&Template=/ContentManagement/ ContentDisplay.cfm&ContentID=27222).

A university benefits policy recently came under attack in Snetsinger v. Montana University System, 104 P.3d 445 (Mont. 2004). Several university employees and their same-sex partners challenged the university's policy denying health insurance coverage to the employees' partners. The state supreme court held that the policy violated the state constitution's Equal Protection Clause because opposite-sex partners, who were not legally married, were eligible for the benefits. See also Tanner v. Oregon Health Science Univ., 971 P.2d 435 (Or. Ct. App. 1998). But cf. Council of City of New York v. Bloomberg, 791 N.Y.S.2d 107 (App. Div. 2005) (invalidating New York City's law that barred the city from doing business with companies refusing to provide spousal-equivalency benefits to same-sex partners because the law impermissibly ran afoul of the policy underlying the state competitive bidding provisions and was preempted by ERISA). See generally Jonathan A. Hein, Caring for the Evolving American Family: Cohabiting Partners and Employer-Sponsored Health Care, 30 N.M. L. Rev. 19 (2000).

11. *Unemployment compensation.* Unemployment compensation is a federal and state system that aims to alleviate the financial burdens caused by unemployment. Generally, unemployment compensation statutes provide that an employee who voluntarily leaves his or her employment without good cause is not entitled to unemployment compensation benefits. Debra E. Wax, Annot., Eligibility for Unemployment Compensation as Affected by Voluntary Resignation Because of Change of Location of Residence, 21 A.L.R.4th 317, 322 (1983 & Supp. 2005). Cases have wrestled with whether a person who voluntarily resigns because of a change of residence is eligible for benefits. If courts find that the personal reasons for relocation are compelling, they have held that good cause exists. Id. at 322. There is a split of authority as to whether relocation to follow a partner constitutes good cause. See id. at 325-333.

In Norman v. Unemployment Insurance Appeals Board, 663 P.2d 904 (Cal. 1983), the California Supreme Court found that a female claimant who left California to preserve her relationship with her male partner (with whom she was living and to whom she was engaged) when he moved to another state for a job had not established good cause. Yet, in MacGregor v. Unemployment Insurance Appeals Board, 689 P.2d 453 (Cal. 1984), the California Supreme Court found that a female claimant's move to follow her nonmarital male partner of three years, with whom she had a child, to care for his 76-year-old father, had established good cause. Why should the presence of a child distinguish the cases?

Current California legislation permits a registered same-sex partner to relocate with his or her partner without losing unemployment benefits. Cal. Unemp. Ins. Code §1256 (West 1996 & Supp. 2005). Does a policy that protects same-sex registered couples but not some nonmarital heterosexual cohabitants violate equal protection? On the constitutionality of unemployment compensation statutes regarding relocation, see generally Wax, supra, at 344-347.

Problem[17]

Peter, a camera crewman at Onstage Productions, has been living with his partner Austin for 14 years. They jointly own real and personal property and name each other as beneficiaries of their life insurance policies and wills, as well as appointees of each other's health care proxy (conferring medical decision-making power in the event of disability). They participate in a "commitment ceremony" and are open about their relationship. Carolyn, another Onstage employee, lives with her two children and her partner Gordon, for two years. She and Gordon are beneficiaries under each other's life insurance policy and will. Peter asks his benefits manager to consider a welfare and pension benefits policy for employees with same-sex partners. The human resources committee considers two approaches: the "Lotus Alternative," named after a Cambridge, Massachusetts, software firm that was the first private corporation to grant benefits to same-sex partners but not to heterosexual cohabitants; and the "Ben and Jerry" model, named after the Vermont ice cream maker that offers health coverage to the unmarried partners of both heterosexual and homosexual employees. Considering cost, the potential for abuse, and the effects on morale and productivity, what approach should the committee adopt? (Assume that neither approach would violate ERISA.) If a governmental employer (for example, a state university) were exploring similar options, what problems should it consider?

c. Health

■ IN RE GUARDIANSHIP OF KOWALSKI
(KOWALSKI III)
478 N.W.2d 790 (Minn. Ct. App. 1991)

DAVIES, Judge. . . .

Sharon Kowalski is 35 years old. On November 13, 1983, she suffered severe brain injuries in an automobile accident which left her in a wheelchair, impaired her ability to speak, and caused severe loss of short-term memory.

At the time of the accident, Sharon was sharing a home in St. Cloud with her lesbian partner, appellant Karen Thompson. They had exchanged rings, named each other as insurance beneficiaries, and had been living together as a couple for four years. Sharon's parents were not aware of the lesbian relationship at the time of the accident. Sharon's parents and siblings live on the Iron Range, where Sharon was raised.

[17]. This problem is a slightly modified version of the problem in Alice Rickel, Extending Employee Benefits to Domestic Partners: Avoiding Legal Hurdles While Staying in Tune with the Changing Definition of the Family, 16 Whittier L. Rev. 737, 739-742 (1995).

In March of 1984, both Thompson and Sharon's father, Donald Kowalski, cross-petitioned for guardianship. Thompson, expecting that she would have certain visitation rights and input into medical decisions, agreed to the appointment of Mr. Kowalski as Sharon's guardian. The guardianship order, however, gave complete control of visitation to Kowalski, who subsequently received court approval to terminate Thompson's visitation rights on July 25, 1985. Kowalski immediately relocated Sharon from a nursing home in Duluth to one in Hibbing.

In May of 1988, Judge Robert Campbell ordered specialists at Miller-Dwan Medical Center to examine Sharon to determine her level of functioning and whether Sharon could express her wishes on visitation. The doctors concluded that Sharon wished to see Thompson, and the court permitted Thompson to reestablish visitation in January of 1989. The doctors also recommended in 1989 that Sharon be relocated to Trevilla at Robbinsdale, where she currently resides. After Sharon's move, Thompson was permitted to bring Sharon to her St. Cloud home for semi-monthly weekend visits.

In late 1988, Kowalski notified the court that, due to his own medical problems, he wished to be removed as Sharon's guardian. The court granted his request [and] Thompson, on August 7, 1989, filed a petition for appointment as successor guardian of Sharon's person and estate. No competing petition was filed. [At the hearing] Thompson called approximately 16 medical witnesses, [who] had firsthand knowledge of her condition and care. The court also heard testimony from three witnesses in opposition to Thompson's petition: Debra Kowalski, Sharon's sister; Kathy Schroeder, a friend of Sharon and the Kowalskis; and [Karen Tomberlin, a Kowalski family friend]. These witnesses had no medical training, each had visited Sharon infrequently in recent years, and none had accompanied Sharon on any outings from the institution. Sharon's parents chose not to attend the hearing.

[T]he trial court denied Thompson's petition for guardianship and simultaneously appointed Tomberlin as guardian. . . . The only issue on appeal is the court's choice of guardian and its findings and conclusions on the comparative qualifications of Thompson and Tomberlin. [Minn. Stat. §525.551(5) provides that the standard for appointment of a guardian is the best interests of the ward. The statute also enumerates certain criteria, discussed below, relevant in that determination.]

1. THE WARD's EXPRESSED PREFERENCE

The court heard testimony from its appointed evaluation team at Miller-Dwan about Sharon's ability to express a reliable preference as to where and with whom she wanted to be. [T]he doctor overseeing the evaluation submitted the following recommendation to the court:

> We believe Sharon Kowalski has shown areas of potential and ability to make rational choices in many areas of her life and she has consistently indicated a desire to return home. And by that, she means to St. Cloud to live with Karen Thompson again. Whether that is possible is still uncertain as her care will be difficult and burdensome. We think she deserves the opportunity to try.

All the professional witnesses concurred. . . .

The three lay witnesses who opposed Thompson's petition were skeptical that Sharon could reliably express her wishes, saying that Sharon changed her mind too often to believe what she said, given her impaired short-term memory.

Despite the uncontradicted medical testimony about Sharon's capability to make choices in her life, the trial court concluded that Sharon could not express a reliable preference for guardianship. This court finds that, in the absence of contradictory evidence about Sharon's decision-making capacity from a professional or anyone in daily contact with her, the trial court's conclusion was clearly erroneous. . . .

2. PETITIONER's QUALIFICATIONS

The medical professionals were all asked about Thompson's qualifications with respect to the statutory criteria. The testimony was consistent that Thompson: (1) achieves outstanding interaction with Sharon; (2) has extreme interest and commitment in promoting Sharon's welfare; (3) has an exceptional current understanding of Sharon's physical and mental status and needs, including appropriate rehabilitation; and (4) is strongly equipped to attend to Sharon's social and emotional needs.

Sharon's caretakers described how Thompson has been with Sharon three or more days per week, actively working with her in therapy and daily care. They described Thompson's detailed knowledge of Sharon's condition, changes, and needs.

The doctors unanimously testified that their long-term goal for Sharon's recovery is to assist her in returning to life outside an institution. It is undisputed that Thompson is the only person willing or able to care for Sharon outside an institution. In fact, Thompson has built a fully handicap-accessible home near St. Cloud in the hope that Sharon will be able to live there. On the other hand, Sharon's sister testified that none of her relatives is able to care for Sharon at home, and that her parents can no longer take Sharon for overnight visits. Tomberlin testified that she is not willing or able to care for Sharon at home and is in a position only to supervise Sharon's needs in an institution. . . .

The medical witnesses also testified about Thompson's effectiveness with Sharon's rehabilitation. They all agreed that Sharon can be stubborn and will often refuse to cooperate in therapy. They testified, however, that Thompson is best able to get Sharon motivated to work through the sometimes painful therapy. . . .

The trial court concluded that "constant, long-term medical supervision in a neutral setting, such as a nursing home . . . is the ideal for Sharon's *long-term* care," and that "Ms. Thompson is incapable of providing, as a single caretaker, the necessary health care to Sharon at Thompson's home in St. Cloud." (Emphasis in original.) These conclusions are without evidentiary support and clearly erroneous as they are directly contradicted by the testimony of Sharon's doctors and other care providers. . . .

3. THE COURT's CHOICE OF A "NEUTRAL" GUARDIAN

The trial court recognized Thompson and Sharon as a "family of affinity" and acknowledged that Thompson's continued presence in Sharon's life was important. In its guardianship decision, however, the court responded to the

Kowalski family's steadfast opposition to Thompson being named guardian. Debra Kowalski testified that her parents would refuse ever to visit Sharon if Thompson is named guardian. The trial court likened the situation to a "family torn asunder into opposing camps," and concluded that a neutral third party was needed as guardian.

The record does not support the trial court's conclusion that choosing a "neutral" third party is now necessary. Thompson testified that she is committed to reaching an accommodation with the Kowalskis whereby they could visit with Sharon in a neutral setting or in their own home. . . . Thompson's appointment as guardian would not, of itself, result in the family ceasing to visit Sharon. The Kowalskis are free to visit their daughter if they wish. It is not the court's role to accommodate one side's threatened intransigence, where to do so would deprive the ward of an otherwise suitable and preferred guardian.

The court seized upon Tomberlin as a neutral party in this case. This decision, however, is not supported by sufficient evidence in the record as to either Tomberlin's suitability for guardianship or her neutrality. [G]iven that Tomberlin rarely visited Sharon, it is unlikely that [the] witnesses would have been able to comment knowledgeably on Tomberlin's qualifications. . . . There was equally little evidence establishing Tomberlin's neutrality in this case. . . . Tomberlin lives near the Kowalskis and helped facilitate the appearance at the hearing of Schroeder and Debra Kowalski in opposition to Thompson. Both in her deposition and at the hearing, Tomberlin testified that her first and primary goal as guardian was to relocate Sharon to the Iron Range, close to her family. This testimony undermines the one "qualification" relied on by the trial court in appointing Tomberlin — her role as an impartial mediator.

4. COURT-IDENTIFIED DEFICIENCIES IN APPELLANT'S PETITION

. . . The court found fault with Thompson on several issues the court viewed as contrary to Sharon's best interest. [T]he court suggested that Thompson's statement to the family and to the media that she and Sharon are lesbians was an invasion of privacy, perhaps rising to the level of an actionable tort. The court also took issue with Thompson taking Sharon to public events, including some gay and lesbian-oriented gatherings and other community events where Thompson and Sharon were featured guests. Finally, the court concluded that Thompson's solicitation of legal defense funds and her testimony that she had been involved in other relationships since Sharon's accident raised questions of conflicts of interest with Sharon's welfare.

The record does not support the trial court's concern on any of these issues. First, while the extent to which Sharon had publicly acknowledged her sexual preference at the time of the accident is unclear, this is no longer relevant. Since the accident, Sharon's doctors and therapists testified that Sharon has voluntarily told them of her relationship with Thompson. Moreover, Sharon's doctor testified that it was in Sharon's best interest for Thompson to reveal the nature of their relationship promptly after the accident because it is crucial for doctors to understand who their patient was prior to the accident, including that patient's sexuality.

Second, there was no evidence offered at the hearing to suggest that Sharon is harmed or exploited by her attendance at public events. In fact, the court authorized Sharon to travel with Thompson to receive an award at the National

Organization for Women's annual convention. A staff person who accompanied Sharon to one of these events testified that Sharon "had a great time" and interacted well with other people. . . .

Finally, there is no evidence in the record about a conflict of interest over Thompson's collection of defense funds or her other personal relationships. The evidence showed the money was raised in Thompson's own name to help defray the cost of years of litigation and that none of it was used for her personal expenses. Thompson testified that whatever extra money raised was used to purchase special equipment for Sharon, such as her voice machine, motorized wheelchair, hospital bed, and a special lift for transfers. . . .

Appellant also challenges the process by which Tomberlin was named guardian. She points out that Tomberlin never submitted a formal petition and that the court never held a hearing on her qualifications. [T]his court is troubled by the trial court's failure to give notice and its naming of Tomberlin in this manner. . . . While the trial court has wide discretion in guardianship matters, this discretion is not boundless. [I]t appears the trial court clearly abused its discretion in denying Thompson's petition and naming Tomberlin guardian instead. . . . We reverse the trial court and grant Thompson's petition. . . .

In the following excerpt, Karen Thompson describes her painful and frustrating experience when she arrived at St. Cloud Hospital immediately after her partner Sharon Kowalski was seriously injured in a car accident by a drunk driver:

■ CASEY CHARLES, THE SHARON KOWALSKI CASE: LESBIAN AND GAY RIGHTS ON TRIAL
16 (2003)

"Who will I say I am?" [Karen Thompson] asked herself, reading the instructions posed under the intercom [outside the intensive care unit]. Under the push-button intercom system to the left of the entrance, a set of regulations, posted by the hospital for the protection of its severely ill or injured patients, stated that only "family members" were allowed to visit patients. . . .

Trying to ignore the import of the regulations she had just finished reading, Thompson finally mustered enough courage to push the speaker button to ask if Sharon Kowalski was there and what her condition was. "What is your relationship?" a disembodied voice demanded over the intercom. Karen replied that she was a close friend who lived with Sharon. "I'm sorry," the speaker replied. "We can't give out information to anyone except immediate family members." Karen tried to explain, stating that she had come in place of Sharon's parents [who lived farther away], but the voice was adamant. Unsuccessful, Thompson walked in frustration from the intercom to the waiting room. The woman she loved for almost four years was probably less than a hundred feet away from her, but because she was not a family member, she was prevented from knowing whether Sharon was living or dying. . . .

Notes and Questions

1. *Background and epilogue.* Immediately after the accident, relations between Karen and Sharon's parents were cordial. Hostility developed because of Karen's devotion and frequent hospital visits. On a psychologist's advice, Karen disclosed

the women's relationship to the Kowalskis. The family was appalled, denied Sharon's lesbianism, and limited Karen's visitation. Animosity continued as Karen questioned their choice of a nursing home rather than a rehabilitation facility with state-of-the-art brain injury treatment. Sharon's parents moved her to a distant nursing home where she was not permitted an electric wheelchair, typewriter or computer (she could type short sentences); was confined to bed; and was denied visitation by her friends. Contrary to guardianship requirements, her father refused competency testing for three years.

During the eight-year separation from Sharon, Karen fell in love with, and began living with, a teacher. Nonetheless, Karen remained devoted to her ex-partner. After the principal case, Sharon came to live with both women, who care for her in their home. See generally Joyce Murdoch & Deb Price, Courting Justice: Gay Men and Lesbians v. the Supreme Court 260-270 (2001); Karen Thompson & Julie Andrzejewski, Why Can't Sharon Kowalski Come Home? (1988).

2. *Functional versus formalistic definitions.* The principal case, the third litigated dispute between Karen and the Kowalskis, rests on a clash between a functional versus formalistic definition of "family." In *Kowalski I*, 382 N.W.2d 861 (Minn. Ct. App.), *cert. denied*, 475 U.S. 1085 (1986), Karen petitioned for appointment as guardian, arguing that she was best suited based on her intimate relationship and Sharon's preference. Sharon's father, relying on the biological relationship, countered that his "unconditional parental love" supported his appointment.

The trial court, influenced by a formalistic definition of "family," confirmed Sharon's father and gave him power to determine her visitors. At the same time, the court rejected application of the substituted judgment standard, which would have given effect to Sharon's choices and ruled, instead, that the best interests standard should apply (that is, "best interests" as determined by the court). Further, the appellate court determined that Sharon's brain injuries precluded her expression of a reliable preference. The animosity between Karen and the Kowalskis continued. Acting on the advice of Sharon's physician, Mr. Kowalski moved to terminate Karen's visitation. In *Kowalski II*, 392 N.W.2d 310 (Minn. Ct. App. 1986), Karen unsuccessfully petitioned to find Mr. Kowalski in contempt for terminating her visitation and to remove him as guardian.

Both *Kowalski I* and *II* strongly affirm the role of legal family members as guardians with broad powers over incompetents. Moreover, both cases are laden with assumptions and stereotypes about the disabled (for example, reducing Sharon to a child, discounting her preferences, denying her sexuality) and about homosexuals and homosexuality (for example, questioning Sharon's lesbianism, characterizing Karen as sexually abusive and exploitative, stating the need for Sharon to be "protected" from her lover). See Amy L. Brown, Note, Broadening Anachronistic Notions of "Family" in Proxy Decisionmaking for Unmarried Adults, 41 Hastings L.J. 1029, 1059-1062 (1990). How does *Kowalski III*, the principal case, address these issues?

3. *Relevant factors.* In a guardianship conflict between the family and a gay or lesbian partner, what relevance, if any, should attach to:

a. the potential guardian's views of homosexuality? For example, Mr. Kowalski reportedly said, "On the farm and in the Army we called them queers and fruits" and also stated that Karen would never be granted guardianship because "there ain't a law in the United States that allows a lesbian relationship." Nancy Livingston, A Bitter Love Triangle: The Fight Between Family and Lover to Control a Woman's Future, S.F. Chron., Sept. 11, 1988 (This World), at 10.

(b) the manner in which the couple held themselves out? For example, Sharon never told her family of her relationship.

(c) the emotions experienced by the ward following the partner's visits? *Kowalski II* relied in part on Sharon's despondency following visits. Would the battle over guardianship have differed had Kowalski's partner been male?

4. *Hospital visitation.* As the above excerpt reveals, Karen Thompson was unable to visit her partner because hospital policy permitted visitation only by designated "family members." Many gays and lesbians who challenge state marriage restrictions are motivated by medical concerns, such as hospital visitation policies and the right to make health care decisions for partners. For example, in *Goodridge*, Hillary and Julie Goodridge alleged that, when Julie gave birth to their daughter, Hillary had difficulty gaining access to Julie and to their newborn who was placed in the intensive care unit. 798 N.E.2d at 950 n. 6. In another lawsuit challenging Connecticut's marriage restrictions, a plaintiff contends she was unable to visit her partner when the latter underwent major surgery. Tina Susman, 'For Gays, It Happens All the Time: Couples Often Aren't Allowed to Visit Their Partners in a Hospital, Let Alone Make Choices about Loved Ones' Care,' Newsday, Mar. 27, 2005, at A28. Finally, a Baltimore jury rejected a claim by a man who sued the university Trauma Center after it refused to allow him to visit his partner who was dying of AIDS. "By the time he finally got into the hospital room, his partner had lost consciousness and never regained it, and they never had a chance to say goodbye." Id.

Some domestic partnership legislation now explicitly covers the right to hospital visitation. See, e.g., Cal. Health & Safety Code §1261 (2000) (if a domestic partner is hospitalized, the other partner and his or her family, including parents and children, have hospital visitation rights); N.J. Stat. §26:8A-1 (Supp. 2005) (providing visitation rights to a domestic partner of a hospitalized patient); Vt. Stat. Ann. tit. 15, §§1204(e)(10) (2003) (extending legal rights relating to emergency and nonemergency medical care and treatment, hospital visitation and notification).

5. *Medical decisionmaking.* One difficulty faced by Karen Thompson after her partner's accident was her inability to acquire information about Sharon's medical condition and to make medical decisions for her. Thompson & Andrzejewski, supra, at 4. This issue became increasingly serious for same-sex partners after the onset of the AIDS epidemic. What might cohabitants do, prior to incapacity, to ensure they play a role in medical decisionmaking for each other?

Traditionally, the common law included a preference for family members as guardians of incompetents to serve as proxy medical decisionmakers. Statutes and case law contain strict definitions of affinity and consanguinity for such determinations. Many states, however, now broaden common law preferences by permitting an incompetent to designate a proxy decisionmaker by means of a "durable power of attorney for health care decisionmaking." Such a designation is especially important for gay and lesbian couples in light of most states' failure to extend marriage rights to same-sex couples. See generally S. Jeanne Hall, Estate and Tax Planning for Domestic Partners (Same-Sex Partners, POSSLQ's and Other Cohabitants) (ABA, 2005); Catherine A. West, Comment, Gay and Lesbian Partners Are Family Too: Why Wisconsin Should Adopt a Family Consent Law, 19

Wis. Women's L.J. 119 (2004) (discussing health care powers of attorney and the need to include gay and lesbian couples in state family consent laws).

6. *Disposition of the body*. Another medical care-related problem arises after death as to the choice of decisionmaker for the disposition of the body. Because statutes give preference to a deceased's legal spouse (then to children, parents, and siblings), conflicts may arise between the surviving partner and family members. See Jennifer E. Horan, "When Sleep at Last Has Come": Controlling the Disposition of Dead Bodies for Same-Sex Couples, 2 J. Gender, Race & Just. 423 (1999).

7. *Empirical research*. Social scientists recently conducted an online survey of 398 gay, lesbian, bisexual, and transgender persons concerning their execution of five documents: a will, powers of attorney for finances and health care, a living will, and hospital visitation authorization. Findings reveal that nearly 3 out of 5 respondents had executed a will or living trust; over half had executed a power of attorney for health care and a living will; 45 percent had executed a power of attorney for finances; and one third had established a hospital visitation authorization. Ellen D.B. Riggle et al., The Execution of Legal Documents by Sexual Minority Individuals, 11 Psychol. Pub. Pol'y & L. 138, 149 (2005).

Problem

Karen and John live together with Karen's son from a prior marriage. When Karen becomes pregnant, she and John attend a natural childbirth class. They receive permission from Karen's physician for John to be present during labor and delivery. However, Mercy Memorial Hospital (the only hospital in the county equipped to deliver babies) refuses permission because John is not a member of Karen's "immediate family." Hospital policy limits the mother's support personnel to immediate family members. Karen and John allege that the policy violates the state civil rights act prohibiting discrimination in public accommodations and public services because of marital status. What result? See Whitman v. Mercy Mem. Hosp., 339 N.W.2d 730 (Mich. Ct. App. 1983).

d. Domestic Violence

■ STATE v. YADEN
1997 WL 106343 (Ohio Ct. App. 1997)

PAINTER, J.
We are asked to decide whether a person living in a same-sex relationship may be guilty of domestic violence against the other person in violation of R.C. 2919.25. This is an issue of first impression in this district. . . .

In late April 1996, Dave Thompson, Joe Fields, Fields's son, Joe Jr., and defendant-appellant Ronnie Yaden went to a flea market. Fields and Yaden began to argue and the group returned to Fields's apartment. Thompson and Joe Jr. left the apartment temporarily. As the argument became louder, Fields threatened to call the police unless Yaden quieted down. Fields testified that Yaden ripped the phone from the wall and threw it, striking Fields in the forehead. Yaden then allegedly punched Fields in the stomach. . . . Yaden denied hitting Fields either in the head or in the stomach.

Fields and Yaden had been living together as a same-sex couple for approximately four years, but had broken up shortly before this incident. . . . After the breakup, Yaden continued to keep personal belongings in Fields's apartment and would stay with Fields when he had no other place to stay. . . .

[T]he trial court found Yaden guilty of a violation of R.C. 2919.25(A), domestic violence. Yaden has appealed, [arguing] that the trial court erred when it found that a same-sex relationship falls within the statutory definition of "living as a spouse." Yaden asserts that people who are not permitted legally to marry cannot live as though a marriage has occurred.

R.C. 2919.25(A) states that "[n]o person shall knowingly cause or attempt to cause physical harm to a family or household member." R.C. 2919.25(E)(1)(a)(i) defines "family or household member" in pertinent part as "[a] spouse, a person living as a spouse, or a former spouse of the offender." R.C. 2919.25(E)(2) further defines "living as a spouse" as "a person who is living or has lived with the offender in a common law marital relationship, who otherwise is cohabiting with the offender, or who otherwise has cohabited with the offender within one year prior to the date of the alleged commission of the act in question." Thus, Yaden asserts that he and Fields did not "cohabit" when they were living together for the four years prior to the incident, because, in his view, same-sex couples cannot "cohabit."

. . . The definition of "cohabitation" in the context of domestic violence in a same-sex relationship controls our decision on this issue. Jurists across the country have struggled to provide guidance. . . . Each unique set of facts giving rise to each court's focus on certain aspects over other aspects illustrates the complexity, difficulty and danger in creating some all-encompassing definition to describe intimate relationships.

In Alabama, cohabitation means "some permanency of relationship coupled with more than occasional sexual activity between the cohabitants." In California, cohabitation means "an unrelated man and woman living together in a substantial relationship manifested principally by a [sic] permanence, or sexual, or amorous intimacy." In Delaware, the alimony statute defines cohabitation as "regularly residing with an adult of the same or opposite sex, if the parties hold themselves out as a couple, and regardless of whether the relationship confers a financial benefit. . . ." In New Jersey, cohabitation is "generally residing together in a common residence . . . where they generally engage in some, but not necessarily all of the following: meals taken together at the residence; departing from and returning to the residence of the other for employment and/or social purposes; maintaining clothing at the other's residence; sleeping together at the residence, or the residence of the other; and receiving telephone calls at the residence or the residence of the other."

Other definitions include: "living together as husband and wife" (Illinois); "a significant live-together relationship" (Iowa); . . . "living together as husband and wife without a legal marriage having been performed" (Maryland); "living together as man and wife, though not necessarily implying sexual relations" (North Carolina); "living together in the same house" (South Carolina); "dwelling or living together; community of life . . ." (Texas); "doing things ordinarily done by spouses" (Texas); and "liv[ing] together permanently or for an indefinite period and assum[ing] the duties and obligations normally attendant with a marital relationship." (Virginia). [Citations omitted.] . . .

Against this backdrop of definitions, we turn to Ohio jurisprudence in this area. Cohabitation has not been defined by the Ohio Supreme Court. [This court has held] that "cohabitation" is "a man and a woman living together in the same household and behaving as would a husband and wife." But the context of our decision and the decision upon which it was based concerned opposite-sex relationships and did not involve same-sex cohabitation. . . .

The seminal Ohio case with facts describing domestic violence in a same-sex relationship is State v. Hadinger [573 N.E.2d 1191 (Ohio Ct. App. 1991)]. In *Hadinger*, the Tenth District Court of Appeals compiled various definitions given for cohabitation and stated that the only common thread among those definitions was simply "living together in an intimate relationship." The Hamilton County Municipal Court has agreed with *Hadinger* that same-sex couples are subject to the domestic violence statute [State v. Linner, 665 N.E.2d 1180 (Hamilton Cty. Mun. Ct. 1996)]. . . .

In short, definitions of "cohabitation" have two fact-specific prongs: financial support and consortium. Factors that establish financial support include shelter, food, clothing, utilities, and perhaps co-mingled assets. Factors that establish consortium include mutual respect, fidelity, emotional support, affection, society, cooperation, solace, comfort, aid of each other, friendship, conjugal relations and companionship. The facts that rise to the level of "cohabitation" are unique to each case, and can only be sifted on a case-by-case basis by triers of fact.

The *Hadinger* court concluded that, under the language of R.C. 2919.25, the legislature intended the statute to protect persons who are cohabiting, regardless of sex. It is true that same-sex couples are not permitted to be "spouses" with each other. But the definition of "living as a spouse" includes a larger segment of couples — not only "spouses" but also "cohabitors." Opposite-sex couples who "cohabit" are protected. We can see no tangible benefit to withholding this statutory protection from same-sex couples. . . .

Notes and Questions

1. *Legal response.* All states have civil and criminal legislation addressing domestic violence, including provisions for protection orders as well as orders allowing the victim exclusive possession of the home (discussed in Chapter III). Domestic violence statutes generally require that the abuser fall within the designated categories of persons who are either "cohabitants" or "household members" of the victim. Elizabeth Trainor, Annot., "Cohabitation" For Purposes of Domestic Violence Statutes, 71 A.L.R.5th 285, 292 (1999 & Supp. 2005). Determining whether persons are "cohabiting" requires case-by-case analysis of such factors as: sexual relations between the parties at the residence; the sharing of income/ expenses; the joint use/ownership of property; whether the parties hold themselves out as partners; and the continuity and length of the relationship. Id. Why did *Yaden* decide that the victim should be accorded legal protection? As *Yaden* reveals, courts in a few jurisdictions have addressed whether same-sex partners are considered "cohabitants" for purposes of these domestic violence statutes. The few published decisions, like *Yaden*, that address domestic violence in the context of same-sex relationships tend to support expansive interpretations that permit the offender to be charged under applicable domestic violence statutes. Id. at 293. What policy rationale explains such expansive applications of domestic violence statutes?

2. *Comparisons with domestic violence in heterosexual relationships.* How is domestic violence among same-sex couples similar to, and different from, that of heterosexual relationships? A study by the American Bar Association Commission on Domestic Violence (available at http://www.abanet.org/domviol/stats.html (last visited Aug. 1, 2005)) reports that domestic violence among same-sex partners occurs with the same frequency as that among heterosexual relationships and mirrors heterosexual battering (although abusers have an additional 'weapon' of "outing" their partner to family, friends, employers, or community). However, victims of same-sex domestic violence enjoy less protection under state laws and also frequently face denial of shelter services. See also National Coalition of Anti-Violence Programs, Anti-Lesbian, Gay, Bisexual and Transgender Violence in 2005, available at http://www.ncavp.org (last visited June 25, 2006) (surveying various forms of violence in and against the LGBT community). Another study by Lambda (a non-profit agency dedicated to reducing discrimination and homophobia against the LGBT community), finds that domestic violence in same-sex relationships includes the same types of abuse (physical, sexual, emotional) as in heterosexual abuse, occurs in the same cyclical fashion, has the same purpose of maintaining power over one's partner, and similarly results in the victim feeling isolated and believing that the abuse is his or her fault. Yet, same-sex domestic violence has the following distinguishing features: it is more frequently perceived mistakenly as mutual combat, victims face difficulties in utilizing services (especially the worry about "coming out" to service providers), victims fear that others will perceive their relationships as abnormal, victims face a LGBT community that is not supportive because many persons want to maintain the myth that there are no problems in the community, victims face sexism and homophobia, victims have no legal process to untangle the financial incidents of their relationship, and victims fear that their problems will become public because the LGBT community is so small. Lambda, Domestic Violence in Gay, Lesbian, and Bisexual Relationships, available at http://lambda.org/DV_background.htm (last visited June 25, 2006).

3. *Statutory exclusions for same-sex partners.* As *Yaden* reveals, same-sex partners often face difficulties in obtaining protection pursuant to domestic violence statutes. A few state statutes specifically exclude same-sex partners as victims of domestic violence by limiting protection to members of the opposite sex. Ruth Colker, Marriage Mimicry: The Law of Domestic Violence, 47 Wm. & Mary L. Rev. 1841 (2006). Some courts interpret state statutes to include such a limitation even when the statute has no explicit requirement. In the past, some state domestic violence statutes had the same effect by language that precluded gay and lesbian as victims because of the existence of state sodomy statutes. What is the likely impact of Lawrence v. Texas on the legal protections available to victims of same-sex domestic violence? See Tara R. Pfeifer, Comment, Out of the Shadows: The Positive Impact of Lawrence v. Texas on Victims of Same-Sex Domestic Violence, 109 Penn. St. L. Rev. 1251, 1254 (2005) (suggesting that abrogation of sodomy statutes will mean that victims will be more likely to seek legal remedies). Currently, most states incorporate gender-neutral language that renders civil protective orders accessible to both heterosexual and same-sex victims of domestic violence. Id. at 1260.

4. *Application of domestic partnership laws.* Some states' domestic partnership laws explictly offer protections to same-sex partners who are victims of domestic

violence. See, e.g., Haw. Rev. Stat. §586-1(2) (1993 & Supp. 2004); Vt. St. Ann. tit. 15, §1204 (2002). However, note that such statutory protections apply only to *registered* partners. Should the law offer protection from domestic violence based on a "marriage-mimicry" model?

5. *Postscript*. Does a domestic violence statute that applies to "a person living as a spouse" (like the Ohio statute at issue in *Yaden*) violate a state constitutional amendment prohibiting recognition of quasi-marital relationships? Following *Yaden*, Ohio appellate courts disagreed about this issue. Compare State v. Ward, 2006 WL 758540 (Ohio Ct. App. 2006), with State v. Douglas, 2006 WL 1304860 (Ohio Ct. App. 2006). The question of the constitutionality of the statute has been certified to the Ohio Supreme Court for review.

Problem

Mary lives in a small hotel room without kitchen facilities. A friend, Joe, comes to stay during June. In July, Joe rents another motel room, taking his belongings with him. He comes to live with Mary for the last two weeks of August. Joe returns to the hotel room after long days at work only to shower and sleep. Mary and Joe do not cook together and rarely eat together. They have sex occasionally. Mary describes the relationship as that of friends and roommates. Joe admits sleeping in Mary's bed (explaining that there was no other bed) but states that he slept on top of the covers, with his pants on. Joe does not have a key to Mary's room; she leaves the door unlocked. Mary and Joe do not share rent, have a joint bank account, make joint purchases, or hold themselves out as husband and wife. On August 29, Joe beats and terrorizes Mary. He is charged with inflicting corporal injury on a cohabitant under the following penal code provision:

Any person who willfully inflicts upon his or her spouse, or any person who willfully inflicts upon any person of the opposite sex with whom he or she is cohabiting, corporal injury resulting in a traumatic condition, is guilty of a felony, and upon conviction thereof shall be punished by imprisonment in the state prison for 2, 3 or 4 years. . . . (b) Holding oneself out to be the husband or wife of the person with whom one is cohabiting is not necessary to constitute cohabitation as the term is used in this section.

Joe argues that the provision is void for vagueness by not defining "cohabiting." What result? See People v. Holifield, 252 Cal. Rptr. 729 (Ct. App. 1988).

e. Familial Benefits: Housing, Inheritance, Adoption

■ BRASCHI v. STAHL ASSOCIATES CO.
543 N.E.2d 49 (N.Y. 1989)

TITONE, Judge. . . .

Appellant, Miguel Braschi, was living with Leslie Blanchard in a rent-controlled apartment located at 405 East 54th Street from the summer of 1975 until Blanchard's death in September of 1986. [R]espondent, Stahl Associates Company, the owner of the apartment building, served a notice to cure on appellant contending that he was a mere licensee with no right to occupy the apartment since only Blanchard was the tenant of record [and threatened eviction proceedings]. The present dispute arises because the term "family" is not defined in the rent-control code and the legislative history is devoid of any specific reference to the noneviction provision. All that is known is the legislative purpose underlying the enactment of the rent-control laws as a whole.

Rent control was enacted to address a "serious public emergency" created by "an acute shortage in dwellings," which resulted in "speculative, unwarranted and abnormal increases in rents" (L. 1946 ch. 274, codified, as amended, at McKinney's Uncons. Laws of N.Y. §8581 et seq.). These measures were designed to regulate and control the housing market so as to "prevent exactions of unjust, unreasonable and oppressive rents and rental agreements and to forestall profiteering, speculation and other disruptive practices tending to produce threats to the public health [and] to prevent uncertainty, hardship and dislocation" (id.). [The legislation was] initially designed as an emergency measure to alleviate the housing shortage attributable to the end of World War II. . . .

To accomplish its goals, the Legislature recognized that not only would rents have to be controlled, but that evictions would have to be regulated and controlled as well. Hence, section 2204.6 of the New York City Rent and Eviction Regulations, which authorizes the issuance of a certificate for the eviction of persons occupying a rent-controlled apartment after the death of the named tenant, provides, in subdivision (d), noneviction protection to those occupants who are either the "surviving spouse of the deceased tenant or *some other member of the deceased tenant's family who has been living with the tenant* [of record]" (emphasis supplied).

[R]espondent argues that the term "family member" as used in 9 NYCRR 2204.6(d) should be construed, consistent with this State's intestacy laws, to mean relationships of blood, consanguinity and adoption in order to effectuate the over-all goal of orderly succession to real property. Under this interpretation, only those entitled to inherit under the laws of intestacy would be afforded noneviction protection. [R]espondent relies on our decision in Matter of Robert Paul P., 63 N.Y.2d 233, 481 N.Y.S.2d 652, 471 N.E.2d 424 [(1984)], arguing that since the relationship between appellant and Blanchard has not been accorded legal status by the Legislature, it is not entitled to the protections of section 2204.6(d). . . . Finally, respondent contends that our construction of the term "family member" should be guided by the recently enacted noneviction provision of the Rent Stabilization Code (9 NYCRR 2523.5[a], [b][1], [2]) [which includes a precise definition of family members based on the existence of marital or blood ties].

However, as we have continually noted, the rent-stabilization system is different from the rent-control system in that the former is a less onerous burden on the property owner, and thus the provisions of one cannot simply be imported into the other. Respondent's reliance on Matter of Robert Paul P. is also misplaced, since [that case] was based solely on the purposes of the adoption laws and has no bearing on the proper interpretation of a provision in the rent-control laws.

We also reject respondent's argument that the purpose of the noneviction provision of the rent-control laws is to control the orderly succession to real property in a manner similar to that which occurs under our State's intestacy laws. The noneviction provision does not concern succession to real property but rather is a means of protecting a certain class of occupants from the sudden loss of their homes. . . . Moreover, such a construction would be inconsistent with the purposes of the rent-control system as a whole, since it would afford protection to distant blood relatives who actually had but a superficial relationship with the deceased tenant while denying that protection to unmarried lifetime partners. . . .

Contrary to all of these arguments, we conclude that the term family, as used in 9 NYCRR 2204.6(d), should not be rigidly restricted to those people who have formalized their relationship by obtaining, for instance, a marriage certificate or an adoption order. The intended protection against sudden eviction should not rest on fictitious legal distinctions or genetic history, but instead should find its foundation in the reality of family life. In the context of eviction, a more realistic, and certainly equally valid, view of a family includes two adult lifetime partners whose relationship is long term and characterized by an emotional and financial commitment and interdependence. This view comports both with our society's traditional concept of "family" and with the expectations of individuals who live in such nuclear units. In fact, Webster's Dictionary defines "family" first as "a group of people united by certain convictions or common affiliation" (Webster's Ninth New Collegiate Dictionary 448 [1984]). Hence, it is reasonable to conclude that, in using the term "family," the Legislature intended to extend protection to those who reside in households having all of the normal familial characteristics. Appellant Braschi should therefore be afforded the opportunity to prove that he and Blanchard had such a household. . . .

The determination as to whether an individual is entitled to noneviction protection should be based upon an objective examination of the relationship of the parties. In making this assessment, the lower courts of this State have looked to a number of factors, including the exclusivity and longevity of the relationship, the level of emotional and financial commitment, the manner in which the parties have conducted their everyday lives and held themselves out to society, and the reliance placed upon one another for daily family services. These factors are most helpful, although it should be emphasized that the presence or absence of one or more of them is not dispositive since it is the totality of the relationship as evidenced by the dedication, caring and self-sacrifice of the parties which should, in the final analysis, control. Appellant's situation provides an example of how the rule should be applied.

Appellant and Blanchard lived together as permanent life partners for more than 10 years. They regarded one another, and were regarded by friends and family, as spouses. The two men's families were aware of the nature of the relationship, and they regularly visited each other's families and attended family functions together, as a couple. Even today, appellant continues to maintain a relationship with Blanchard's niece, who considers him an uncle.

In addition to their interwoven social lives, appellant clearly considered the apartment his home. He lists the apartment as his address on his driver's license and passport, and receives all his mail at the apartment address. Moreover, appellant's tenancy was known to the building's superintendent and doormen, who viewed the two men as a couple.

Financially, the two men shared all obligations including a household budget. The two were authorized signatories of three safe-deposit boxes, they maintained joint checking and savings accounts, and joint credit cards. In fact, rent was often paid with a check from their joint checking account. Additionally, Blanchard executed a power of attorney in appellant's favor so that appellant could make necessary decisions — financial, medical and personal — for him during his illness.

Finally, appellant was the named beneficiary of Blanchard's life insurance policy, as well as the primary legatee and coexecutor of Blanchard's estate. Hence, a court examining these facts could reasonably conclude that these men were much more than mere roommates. [The court concludes] that appellant has demonstrated a likelihood of success on the merits [and remands the case].

■ NORTH DAKOTA FAIR HOUSING COUNCIL v. PETERSON
625 N.W.2d 551 (N.D. 2001)

SANDSTROM, Justice.

In 1999, an unmarried couple tried to rent from David and Mary Peterson. The Petersons refused because the unmarried couple were seeking to cohabit. The North Dakota Fair Housing Council and Robert and Patricia Kippen—the unmarried couple, who had since married—sued, claiming housing discrimination in violation of the North Dakota Human Rights Act. . . .

[The landlords moved to dismiss the Housing Council on the ground that they lacked standing, and the district court granted the motion. The Housing Council appealed. The district court also granted summary judgment in favor of the Petersons. The Kippens appealed.]

We are asked to decide whether refusing to rent to an unmarried couple because they are seeking to cohabit violates the discriminatory housing practices provision of the North Dakota Human Rights Act, N.D.C.C. §14-02.4-12. The question is one of statutory interpretation. . . . The pertinent human rights statute in effect at the time of the alleged violation, North Dakota Century Code §14-02.4-12 (1995), provided:

> Discriminatory housing practices by owner or agent. It is a discriminatory practice for an owner of rights to housing or real property [to]:
> Refuse to transfer an interest in real property or housing accommodation to a person because of race, color, religion, sex, national origin, age, physical or mental disability, or status with respect to marriage or public assistance . . .

We have not previously addressed the relationship between N.D.C.C. §§12.1-20-10 [the prohibition of cohabitation] and 14-02.4-12 [above]. The issue, however, has been addressed in a formal attorney general's opinion and in two federal district court opinions. We begin with a review of the history of the legislation.

North Dakota has prohibited unlawful cohabitation since statehood. The provision, as codified in 1895, remained essentially unchanged until the 1970s. . . . The 1971 legislative assembly provided for an interim committee to draft a new criminal code. The interim committee considered whether to recommend repeal of the prohibition on unlawful cohabitation. . . . Because sexual offenses were a controversial portion of the proposed new criminal code, alternative provisions were submitted to the 1973 legislature in three separate bills. All three bills contain the same language on unlawful cohabitation [with somewhat different penalties]. The new criminal code [retaining the prohibition] was approved by the 1973 legislature. . . .

The 1983 legislature adopted the North Dakota Human Rights Act. 1983 N.D. Sess. Laws ch. 173. The legislative history reflects no discussion of the cohabitation statute.

The issue of a claimed conflict between the cohabitation statute and the Human Rights Act was presented to the attorney general in 1990. In a formal opinion, the attorney general wrote: . . .

> The North Dakota Supreme Court has not ruled on the apparent conflict between N.D.C.C. §§14-02.4-12's protection of a person's right to housing notwithstanding the person's marital status, and N.D.C.C. §12.1-20-10's prohibition against allowing unmarried couples to live as a married couple. However, there has been similar litigation in other states whose laws prohibit both cohabitation and discriminatory housing practices based on marital statutes. In McFadden v. Elma Country Club, 26 Wash. App. 146 [195], 613 P.2d 146 (1980), the court held that, notwithstanding a statute prohibiting discrimination based upon marital status, a country club could refuse to admit to membership an unmarried woman cohabiting with a man. Id. at 152. The court's holding was based upon the fact the statute prohibiting cohabitation was not repealed when the discrimination statute was enacted. This fact the court said "would vitiate any argument that the legislature intended 'marital status' discrimination to include discrimination on the basis of a couple's unwed cohabitation." Id. at 150.
>
> As in the *McFadden* case, N.D.C.C. §12.1-20-10 was not repealed when N.D.C.C. §14-02.4-12 was enacted. Thus, the continuing existence of the unlawful cohabitation statute after the enactment of N.D.C.C. §14-02.4-12 vitiates "any argument that the legislature intended 'marital status' discrimination to include discrimination on the basis of a couple's unwed cohabitation." *McFadden* at 150. . . .

Attorney General's Opinion 90-12 (1990).

In 1991, House Bill 1403, a measure to repeal the cohabitation statute, was introduced, with the legislator who had requested the 1990 attorney general's opinion as the primary sponsor. . . . The House of Representatives defeated the bill by a vote of 27 yeas and 78 nayes.

In 1999, the United States District Court for North Dakota decided a case involving the alleged conflict between the cohabitation statute and the Human Rights Act and concluded it was not unlawful to refuse to rent to an unmarried couple seeking to cohabit. . . . North Dakota Fair Housing Council, Inc. v. Haider, No. A1-98-077 (D.N.D. 1999). In 2000, the United States District Court for North Dakota decided a suit similar to this one brought by the Housing Council. North Dakota Fair Housing Council v. Woeste, No. A1-99-116 (D.N.D. 2000). The federal court, analyzing North Dakota law and distinguishing federal cases relied on by the Housing Council, concluded the Housing Council lacked standing to sue under the North Dakota Human Rights Act. . . .

With this historical background, we turn to the framework for analyzing statutes and claimed conflicts between statutes. . . . We now consider the meaning of the cohabitation statute and the meaning of the Human Rights Act discriminatory housing practices provision. . . . North Dakota's cohabitation statute, N.D.C.C. §12.1-20-10, states:

> A person is guilty of a class B misdemeanor if he or she lives openly and notoriously with a person of the opposite sex as a married couple without being married to the other person.

The 1973 amendment of the statute removed the language "cohabits as husband or wife" and added "lives openly and notoriously with a person of the opposite sex as a married couple."

Varying definitions of cohabitation exist. The 1996 edition of Merriam Webster's Dictionary of Law defines cohabit as "to live together as a married couple or in the manner of a married couple." The 1999 edition of Black's Law Dictionary, at page 254, defines cohabitation as "[t]he fact or state of living together, esp. as partners in life, usu. with the suggestion of sexual relations." Notorious cohabitation is the "act of a man and a woman openly living together under circumstances that make the arrangement illegal under statutes that are now rarely enforced."[4] Id. The Minnesota Supreme Court has defined "cohabit" as living "together in a sexual relationship when not legally married." State by Cooper v. French, 460 N.W.2d 2, 4 n.1 (Minn. 1990) (citing The American Heritage Dictionary of the English Language 259 (1980) (New College Dictionary)). . . .

The Housing Council asserts that North Dakota has decriminalized all sexual relations among consenting adults. The assertion is contradicted by the cohabitation statute as well as the criminal penalties for adultery, bigamy, prostitution, or incest, notwithstanding the consent of the parties. . . .

At issue is the term "status with respect to marriage," which is undefined under the Human Rights Act. Analyzing other definitions under North Dakota law, the district court concluded the "Legislature intended the phrase to mean being married, single, separated or divorced." The Housing Council and the Kippens argue "status with respect to marriage" is simple: a person is either married or not married. Although it is unlawful to deny housing based solely on whether a person is or is not married, the relevant inquiry is whether a person is divorced, widowed, or separated, rather than simply married or unmarried.

The Petersons argue that although it is true that under the discriminatory housing provision a person cannot be discriminated against because of marital status, the Kippens were denied housing not because they were single, but because they were unmarried and were seeking to live together as if they were married. . . .

Numerous courts have addressed language similar to "status with respect to marriage," the language at issue here. Those courts disagree regarding the appropriate weight to give to words with an import similar to "status with respect to marriage." In McCready v. Hoffius, 222 Mich. App. 210, 564 N.W.2d 493, 495-96 (1997), the court differentiated marital status from conduct by concluding the term "marital status" was legislatively intended to prohibit discrimination "based on *whether* a person is married" (quoting Miller v. C.A. Muer Corp., 420 Mich. 355, 362 N.W.2d 650 (1984)).

The Wisconsin Supreme Court has also concluded refusal to rent to unmarried tenants who choose to live together is based on conduct rather than status. See County of Dane v. Norman, 174 Wis.2d 683, 497 N.W.2d 714 (1993). On the other hand, Alaska, Massachusetts, and California have concluded refusal to rent to unmarried cohabitants is based upon status rather than conduct. [Smith v. Fair Employment & Housing Comm'n, 913 P.2d 909 (Cal. 1996), *cert. denied*, 521 U.S. 1129 (1997); Swanner v. Anchorage Equal Rights Comm'n, 874 P.2d

---

4. Although it is argued cohabitation statutes are rarely enforced, this Court has held the lack of enforcement to be of no significance.

274 (Alaska 1994), *cert. denied*, 513 U.S. 979 (1994); Attorney General v. Desilets, 636 N.E.2d 233 (Mass. 1994)]. . . .

When the legislature enacted the Human Rights Act, it is presumed to have known of the existing criminal cohabitation statute. [B]y suggesting the Human Rights Act requires that housing be provided regardless of compliance with the criminal code, the Housing Council and the Kippens are asking us to repeal or to give new meaning to the cohabitation statute. We are then confronted with the well-established rule precluding amendment or repeal of legislation by implication. . . . The cohabitation statute and the discriminatory housing provision are harmonized by recognizing that the cohabitation statute regulates conduct, not status. The opposite interpretation would render the prohibition against cohabitation meaningless.

Like Michigan, Wisconsin, and Minnesota, we conclude these two provisions may be harmonized while still giving each of them full effect. It is unlawful to openly and notoriously live together as husband and wife without being married. It is unlawful to deny housing based on a person's status with respect to marriage (i.e., married, single, divorced, widowed, or separated). It is not unlawful to deny housing to an unmarried couple seeking to openly and notoriously live together as husband and wife. . . . Under the words of the statute, the rules of statutory construction, and the legislative, administrative, and judicial history, we conclude it is not an unlawful discriminatory practice under N.D.C.C. §14-02.4-12 to refuse to rent to unmarried persons seeking to cohabit. Summary judgment was therefore appropriate. . . .

Notes and Questions

1. *Functional definition. Braschi*, like *Graves* (and *Dunphy* before it), adopts a functional definition of family. The significance of this definition for the recognition of the rights of gay and lesbian partners cannot be underestimated. As one commentator remarks:

> Both *Braschi* and *Dunphy* illustrate the greatest advantage and benefit of pursuing recognition of lesbian and gay families from the functional perspective. These cases promote an examination of the purpose for which the law was adopted and ask whether adhering to formalized definitions of family furthers or obstructs the law's goals. In so doing, the courts paved the way for many types of families to receive long overdue support.

Paula L. Ettelbrick, Wedlock Alert: A Comment on Lesbian and Gay Family Recognition, 5 J.L. & Pol'y 107, 142 (1996).

2. *Familial characteristics. Braschi* states that the legislature intended to protect those who reside in households "having all of the normal familial characteristics." Which "normal familial characteristics" did the Braschi household exhibit? Which did it not? Recall the question posed at the beginning of the chapter: Should the state define and impose a legal meaning of "family" on all persons without exception, or should the law honor private choices, so long as a given unit acts like a family and performs familial functions? See generally Note, Looking for a Family Resemblance: The Limits of the Functional Approach

to the Legal Definition of Family, 104 Harv. L. Rev. 1640 (1991). See also Martha L. Minow, Redefining Families: Who's In and Who's Out?, 62 U. Colo. L. Rev. 269 (1991).

Does *Braschi* sanction legal distinctions between those same-sex couples who do and those who do not fit the traditional family model? For example, suppose one of the partners is not monogamous? See Picon v. O.D.C. Assocs., No. 86-22894 (Sup. Ct. N.Y. Co., Jan. 28, 1991) (minimizing relevance of sexual affair for surviving tenant's occupancy claim because "peccadillos of this nature seem not to be uncommon, even in the marital life of normally married couples"). Suppose the couple keeps their finances separate? See Kath Weston, Families We Choose: Lesbians, Gays, Kinship 113-114 (1991) (reporting empirical findings that lesbian and gay partners tend to manifest more financial independence than do heterosexual couples).

Although many gay and lesbian commentators applaud the result in *Braschi*, some criticize its implications. For example, Professor Mary Ann Case writes:

> In *Braschi*, the court held, in effect, that if you behave like Ozzie and Harriet, or alternatively like Baron and Feme [husband and wife], then you are a couple and can receive the succession rights of family members under the New York rent control laws. The Court of Appeals, in determining whether the household Braschi had shared with his deceased lover . . . focused on things like sexual fidelity, sharing a domicile, and commingling finances as the evidence of commitment it required before recognizing the couple.
>
> Married couples in this society are not required to do the rather conservative things the Court of Appeals required of Braschi and his lover. . . .

Mary Ann Case, Couples and Coupling in the Public Sphere: A Comment on the Legal History of Litigating for Lesbian and Gay Rights, 79 Va. L. Rev. 1643 (1993). Do you agree with Professor Case's criticism that *Braschi* may be "more oppressive for feminists, whatever their sexual preference, than gay marriage would be for anyone"? Id. at 1666. See also Katharine Franke, The Domesticated Liberty of *Lawrence*, 104 Colum. L. Rev. 1399 (2004).

3. *Criticisms of factors.* *Braschi* suggests factors to determine whether an individual qualifies as a family member for noneviction protection. Do you agree with the dissent that these factors "produce[ ] an unworkable test that is subject to abuse" and leads to extended litigation "focusing on such intangibles as the strength and duration of the relationship and the extent of the emotional and financial interdependency"? Does *Braschi*'s necessity of proof of financial interdependence cause more difficulty for low-income cohabitants? One commentator notes that recipients of government benefits programs "often are forced to down play their interconnectedness with a co-occupant in order to maximize their benefit levels." Paris Baldacci, Litigation Succession Rights Cases of Nontraditionally Recognized Families in Rent-Controlled/Stabilized Housing in New York State: Some Evidentiary and Procedural Issues, 242 Practising L. Inst./Est. 89, 117 (Dec. 1995).

4. *Family definition.* Why does the marital couple serve as the model for expanded definitions of "family"? Should the law also recognize nonconjugal relationships when providing familial benefits? What nonconjugal relationships should be covered? For which benefits? See generally Hamilton, Mistaking Marriage for Social Policy, supra this chapter, pp. 368-370.

5. *Landlord-tenant law*. Social forces historically play a role in the development of landlord-tenant law. For example, the civil rights movement and the Vietnam War influenced the "revolution" in tenant rights in the late 1960s and 1970s. Edward H. Rabin, The Revolution in Residential Landlord-Tenant Law: Causes and Consequences, 69 Cornell L. Rev. 517, 546, 550 (1984). What social forces might have played a role in *Braschi?*

6. *Contextual distinctions.* New York distinguishes between "rent control" and "rent stabilization."[18] As *Braschi* reveals, different definitions of "family" apply for rent control versus rent stabilization purposes. The former provides protection against eviction for the co-resident surviving spouse or "some other (co-resident) member of the deceased tenant's family." The latter provision includes a more precise definition, limiting family members to husband, wife, son, daughter, steprelationships, nephew, niece, uncle, aunt, grandparents, grandchildren, and in-law relationships. Further, different definitions apply for inheritance purposes and zoning purposes. How does the *Braschi* majority treat the existence of these conflicting definitions? What is the effect of granting legal recognition for some purposes but not others?

Shortly after *Braschi*, a similar case arose under the rent stabilization legislation. Robert Wells and Stuart Goldstein lived together in a rent stabilized apartment from 1977 to 1987 when Goldstein, the named tenant on the lease, died of AIDS. When the landlord attempted to evict Wells to re-rent at a higher price, Wells argued that *Braschi* applied. The Appellate Division agreed, finding similar purposes behind the two code sections, and ruled that Wells was protected despite the statutory limitations to named family members. The court concluded that the relationship met the *Braschi* standard, noting:

> Both of these individuals demonstrated a high level of emotional commitment to one another and took care of each other's day-to-day needs. They were open about their relationship, and their devotion to one another as life partners was apparent to their family and friends, as is reflected in affidavits by Goldstein's mother and son, who considered Wells to be a part of their family and have characterized the relationship of their son and father and that of a spouse to Wells.

East 10th St. Assocs. v. Estate of Goldstein, 552 N.Y.S.2d 257, 257 (App. Div. 1990).

7. *Braschi*, like *Graves*, presents a dispute not of cohabitants inter se (as *Marvin*), but rather a dispute involving third parties. Does the presence of third parties dictate different treatment of cohabitants in the housing and tort contexts?

Further, how relevant is the fact that *Braschi* did *not* present the court with two openly gay litigants in a contentious dispute? One commentator responds:

> [F]or the equanimity of the New York court's mind . . . , the [*Braschi*] plaintiff was not, after all, in a living gay relation—owing to the death of his life-partner. [C]ourts may give rights to gays by ones, but they will not give rights to gays by twos. . . . So when the courts do on occasion give rights to gays by ones—they do so in spite of rather than

---

[18]. Both rent stabilization and rent control impose ceilings on rent increases, with minor differences. A vacancy in a rent controlled apartment permits a landlord to return the apartment to market rent; a vacancy in a rent stabilized apartment permits a landlord to re-rent at a slightly higher rate. Rent control generally applies to buildings built before 1947. See G. Samuel Zucker, Insurance for Eviction Without Cause: A Middle Path for Tenant Tenure Rights and a New Remedy for Retaliatory Eviction, 28 Urb. Law. 113, 118 n.18 (1996).

because of their gayness. And in giving rights to gays by ones only, the courts, even as they hand out a right, destroy the very basis and idea of gayness, that it is a relation between people.

Richard D. Mohr, Gay Ideas: Outing and Other Controversies 82 (1992). See also William Rubenstein, We Are Family: A Reflection on the Search for Legal Recognition of Lesbian and Gay Relationships, 8 J.L. & Pol'y 89 (1991) (discussing role of stereotypes in *Braschi*).

8. *Epilogue.* In response to *Braschi*, the State Division of Housing and Community Renewal (DHCR) amended administrative regulations to conform the provisions governing lease succession rights and anti-eviction protections. DHCR promulgated an emergency rule broadening the definition of "family" in accordance with *Braschi* and eliminated the distinction between the tenant of record's death and departure. See N.Y. Comp. Codes R. & Regs. tit. 9, §2204.6(d)(3)(i) (Supp. 1996). Landlords' organizations successfully sought to enjoin the rule's implementation. Following *Goldstein*, the Appellate Division of the State Supreme Court vacated the preliminary injunction. Rent Stabilization Assn. v. Higgens, 562 N.Y.S.2d 962 (App. Div. 1990). Subsequently, the Appellate Division reaffirmed the validity of the regulations (592 N.Y.S.2d 255 (App. Div. 1993)) and the Court of Appeals affirmed (608 N.Y.S.2d 930 (1993)).

9. Is housing an appropriate context in which to implement social goals? Is zoning? Recall Moore v. City of East Cleveland and Village of Belle Terre v. Boraas, supra. Are the contexts distinguishable?

10. *Housing discrimination based on marital status.* Peterson reveals that because the federal Fair Housing Act of 1968, amended by the Fair Housing Amendments Act of 1988, 42 U.S.C. §§3601-3619, 3631 (2000), does not prohibit marital status discrimination, unmarried cohabitants generally must resort to state law for protection. Twenty-one states and the District of Columbia have statutory prohibitions against marital status discrimination in housing. Erin P. B. Zasada, Comment, Civil Rights — Rights Protected and Discrimination Prohibited: Living in Sin in North Dakota? Not Under My Lease, North Dakota Fair Housing Council, Inc. v. Peterson, 78 N.D. L. Rev. 539, 549 (2002). Only 3 states (Alaska, California, and Massachusetts), however, provide explicit statutory protection to unmarried couples. Id. Among other states with general prohibitions, jurisdictions are split as to whether the term "marital status" applies to unmarried cohabitants. Id. As a result, courts (like *Peterson*) must turn to legislative history and prior case law.

What is the status/conduct distinction referred to in *Peterson*? Is it a meaningful distinction? See Barbara Endoy, Irreconcilable Cohabitation Statutes and Statutory Proscriptions Against Marital Status Discrimination: McCredy v. Hoffius and the Unworkable Status-Conduct Distinction, 44 Wayne L. Rev. 1809 (1999).

11. *Housing discrimination based on sexual orientation.* Federal law, similarly, does not prohibit housing discrimination based on sexual orientation. The Fair Housing Act, supra, prohibits the refusal to rent or sell a dwelling only on the grounds of race, color, religion, sex, familial status, or national origin. However, a few states have protection against housing discrimination based on sexual orientation. California, Connecticut, the District of Columbia, Massachusetts, Minnesota, New Jersey, Rhode Island, Vermont, and Wisconsin have laws prohibiting discrimination against gays or lesbians; and, Connecticut, Minnesota, and Rhode Island protect transgender persons. Further, several cities make housing

discrimination on the basis of sexual orientation illegal. See Sexual Orientation Discrimination in Rental Housing, available at http://realestate.findlaw.com/ landlord/tenant-fair-housing/tenant-fair-housing-orientation.html (last visited June 25, 2006).

Like *Braschi*, several other classic property law cases involve housing discrimination against gays or lesbians. See, e.g., Hubert v. Williams, 184 Cal. Rptr. 161 (Super. Ct. 1982) (holding that eviction of quadriplegic tenant and his lesbian attendant, allegedly because tenant associated with homosexuals, violated the state Unruh Act prohibiting housing discrimination based on sexual preference); Poff v. Caro, 549 A.2d 900 (N.J. Super. Law Div. 1987) (holding that refusal to rent to homosexuals because of fears that prospective tenants will later acquire AIDS violates state housing discrimination law). See Keith Sealing, Dear Landlord: Please Don't Put a Price on My Soul: Teaching Property Law Students That "Property Rights Serve Human Values," 5 N.Y. City L. Rev. 35, 95-96 (2002) (discussing coverage of sexual orientation in property law casebooks, including these classic cases). See also Levin v. Yeshiva University, 754 N.E.2d 1099 (N.Y. 2001) (holding that university housing policy restricted to legal spouses that excluded lesbian medical students' partners did not on its face discriminate on the basis of marital status, but that complaint was sufficient to allege a disparate impact on basis of sexual orientation in violation of New York City Civil Rights Law).

12. *Freedom of religion defense*. *Peterson* addresses whether landlords' refusal to rent to an unmarried couple violates the housing discrimination prohibition of the North Dakota Human Rights Act. The court wrestled with: (1) whether the statutory protection regarding "status with respect to marriage" included nonmarital cohabitation, and (2) how to resolve the conflict between the state statute prohibiting cohabitation between unmarried persons, and the state anti-housing discrimination provision. How did the court resolve each of those issues? The North Dakota House of Representatives subsequently voted to uphold its prohibition against cohabitation, which had not been enforced since 1938. The vote was necessitated by a need to "send a message" to young people and to counter recent attacks on the "concept of traditional marriage." Brenden Timpe, Cigarettes OK; Shacking Up, No Way: Legislature Deals with Rules for Young Adults, Grand Forks Herald, Jan. 20, 2005, at A2.

Petersen does not elaborate on the landlords' reasons for refusing to rent to the particular unmarried couple. Presumably, the landlords had moral objections. Suppose, however, that a landlord refuses to rent to unmarried couples on religious grounds. Is the First Amendment a defense to the landlord's violation of state housing discrimination provisions? For example, in Smith v. Fair Employment & Housing Commission, 913 P.2d 909 (Cal. 1996), a woman landlord refuses to rent to an unmarried couple because:

> She is a member of Bidwell Presbyterian Church in Chico and has attended there for approximately 25 years. Respondent believes that sex outside of marriage is sinful, and that it is a sin for her to rent her units to people who will engage in nonmarital sex on her property. Respondent believes that God will judge her if she permits people to engage in sex outside of marriage in her rental units and that if she does so, she will be prevented from meeting her deceased husband in the hereafter. . . . Respondent would not rent to anyone who engages in sex outside of marriage, whether they are single, divorced, widowed or married.

Id. at 912.

When the landlord petitions for a writ of mandate to compel the California Commission of Fair Employment and Housing to set aside its decision prohibiting her from discriminating against prospective tenants on the basis of marital status, the California supreme court holds that state law prohibiting discrimination based on "marital status" prohibits the landlord from refusing to rent to prospective tenants because they were not married, and that the prohibition was both generally applicable and neutral toward religion and, therefore, does not violate the land-lord's freedom of religion or "substantially burden" her religious exercise within the meaning of the Religious Freedom Restoration Act (RFRA). What explains the different results in *Peterson* and *Smith*?

See also Swanner v. Anchorage Equal Rights Comm'n, 874 P.2d 274 (Alaska 1994) (holding that enforcement of state statute and municipal code prohibiting landlords from refusing to rent property to unmarried cohabitants because of their marital status did not violate landlords' right to free exercise). Following the U.S. Supreme Court's decision in Boy Scouts of America v. Dale, 530 U.S. 640 (2000) (holding that applying New Jersey's public accommodations law to require the Boy Scouts to admit a gay scoutmaster violated the organization's right of expressive association), a group of landlords unsuccessfully petitioned for reconsideration of *Swanner*. Thomas v. Anchorage Equal Rights Comm'n, 102 P.3d 937 (Alaska 2004).

To date, all cases involving landlords' refusal to rent to unmarried couples on religious grounds involve heterosexual, not same-sex, couples. See Sexual Orientation Discrimination in Rental Housing (findlaw.com), supra (making this observation).

13. How likely are *Braschi* and *Peterson*, respectively, to influence landlords' behavior? Might some landlords use "covert" tactics to give effect to their religious beliefs?

Problems

1. Jay rents a New York City apartment. Ten years later he desires to share his residence with his partner James. Jay receives the landlord's permission to occupy the adjoining apartment as well. Although Jay continues to be the tenant of record on both units, James also lives there and shares rent. After 16 years, the men split up. Jay vacates the apartments. The landlord then serves a "notice of termination of license and/or notice to quit" on James. James refuses to vacate, and the landlord commences eviction proceedings questioning James' right to remain. James asserts as affirmative defenses that the landlord, by accepting his rent, has waived the right to object to James' occupancy and, also, that by virtue of his familial relationship with Jay, James is a legal tenant. What result? Should *Braschi* apply? (Assume that the New York court has not yet ruled on the constitutionality of the administrative regulations that protect family members both on the death or departure of the tenant of record.) See Park Holding Co. v. Power, 554 N.Y.S.2d 861 (App. Div. 1990).

2. Elisha Hack and several other freshman at Yale University in New Haven, Connecticut, bring suit against the institution and its board of trustees challenging a rule that requires all unmarried freshman and sophomores to live in college dormitories. The plaintiffs, all unmarried devout Orthodox Jews, claim that the

university policy requiring residence in the dorms, all of which are co-educational, would conflict with their religious convictions and duties. Plaintiffs make three arguments: (a) Yale University violates plaintiffs' First and Fourteenth Amendment rights because Yale is a state actor or instrumentality based on the state function that it performs; (b) even if it is not clear that Yale is a state actor or instrumentality, plaintiffs are entitled through discovery to explore the interrelationship between the University and the governments of New Haven and Connecticut so that they can make their constitutional claims; and (c) Yale's refusal to exempt religious observers from co-educational housing violates the Fair Housing Act (summarized supra). Are there any additional arguments that plaintiffs should make? How should Yale respond on each argument? How should the court rule on each? See Hack v. President and Fellows of Yale College, 237 F.3d 81 (2d Cir. 2000), cert. denied, 534 U.S. 888 (2001).

■ VASQUEZ v. HAWTHORNE
33 P.3d 735 (Wash. 2001) (en banc)

JOHNSON, J.

[Frank Vasquez and Robert Schwerzler lived together from 1967 to 1995, with the exception of two years during which they lived in different apartments in the same building. When Schwerzler died, he had several assets in his name including: the house he and Vasquez shared, a life insurance policy, two automobiles, and a checking account. Schwerzler died without a will. Vasquez filed a claim against the estate, asserting that he and Schwerzler had been life partners and that he was entitled under case law regulating division of property in meretricious relationships to a share of the community property. Joseph Hawthorne, the appointed personal representative for the estate, denied Vasquez's claim [in order to give the property to Schwerzler's next of kin]. Vasquez filed suit. (These facts are taken from Vasquez v. Hawthorne, 994 P.2d 240 (Wash. Ct. App. 2000).]

The issue in this case is whether the facts were sufficient to grant summary judgment based on the equitable doctrine of meretricious relationship. Granting summary judgment for the plaintiff, the trial court held Frank Vasquez had proved he was involved in a long term, stable, cohabiting relationship with the decedent, Robert Schwerzler. The trial court further found the property acquired during the relationship was the joint property of Vasquez and Schwerzler, and that it passed to Vasquez upon Schwerzler's death and was not part of the estate. Since Schwerzler died without a will, the trial court drew an analogy to community property laws and the probate statute governing intestate distribution in awarding property.

[Vasquez asserted] his claim under several equitable theories. Vasquez made a motion for partial summary judgment requesting relief under the meretricious relationship doctrine. To decide the motion, the trial court considered several conflicting affidavits of the parties. The trial court made two rulings relevant to this case. First, the trial court determined Vasquez and Schwerzler had a meretricious relationship and the property acquired during the course of their relationship was presumed jointly owned. Second, the trial court awarded some of the property to Vasquez by analogizing to our probate laws (i.e., community-like property goes to the survivor). . . . The Court of Appeals reversed [reasoning that because meretricious relationships are marital-like and persons of the same sex cannot be legally married, a meretricious relationship cannot exist between members of the same sex. The Court of Appeals, however,] remanded the case for trial on the theories of implied partnership and equitable trust, which had not been decided by the trial court. We granted Vasquez's petition for review.

A summary judgment motion under CR 56(c) can be granted only if the pleadings, affidavits, depositions, and admissions on file demonstrate no genuine issues of material fact, and that the moving party is entitled to judgment as a matter of law. The court must consider all facts submitted and all reasonable inferences from those facts in the light most favorable to the nonmoving party. The motion should be granted only if, from all the evidence, reasonable persons could reach but one conclusion.

The facts of this case are contested through the affidavits of the parties. First, the nature of the relationship between Vasquez and Schwerzler is disputed. Vasquez presents affidavits asserting he and Schwerzler were a same sex couple. The estate offers affidavits contending Vasquez and Schwerzler were not a same sex couple and did not hold themselves out as such. Vasquez offers as proof of their relationship that he and Schwerzler lived together from April 1967 until October 1995, with the exception of two years in the early 1970s during which they lived in different apartments in the same building. The estate counters that no such relationship existed. Although they lived together, Vasquez and Schwerzler did not travel together on vacation and each had his own bedroom.

Similarly, the nature of Vasquez's and Schwerzler's business relationship is disputed. On the one hand, Vasquez contends the couple made their living recycling boxes and bags. Schwerzler managed their financial affairs and any remuneration Vasquez earned was contributed to their economic community. On the other hand, the estate argues that Schwerzler inherited the bag business from his father and any property he owned was derived from either his inherited wealth or through his separate businesses. Schwerzler placed all property acquired during their 28 years together in his own name, including the house he and Vasquez shared, a life insurance policy, two automobiles, and a checking account. The estate argues Vasquez was merely a handyman and any property found in Schwerzler's home should be included in his estate and pass to his legal heirs.

On review, we conclude the trial court did not have sufficient undisputed factual information to resolve this case on its merits. From the affidavits, the trial court could not determine what type of relationship existed between Vasquez and Schwerzler. Nor could it conclude what property acquired during the course of their relationship could be subject to equitable division. Without proof of the facts asserted, it was not possible for the trial court to know the character of the relationship between Schwerzler and Vasquez, the nature and extent of contribution to any property acquired by the parties, and what equitable theories are most appropriate. Therefore, we must remand this case for the trial court to review under the various theories Vasquez asserts.

Vasquez presented claims for equitable relief under several theories, including meretricious relationship, implied partnership, and equitable trust. When equitable claims are brought, the focus remains on the equities involved between the parties. Equitable claims are not dependent on the "legality" of the relationship between the parties, nor are they limited by the gender or sexual orientation of the parties. For example, the use of the term "marital-like" in prior meretricious relationship cases is a mere analogy because defining these relationships as related to marriage would create a de facto common-law marriage, which this court has refused to do. In re Marriage of Pennington, 14 P.3d 764 (Wash. 2000). Rather than relying on analogy, equitable claims must be analyzed under the specific facts presented in each case. Even when we recognize "factors" to guide the court's determination of the equitable issues presented, these considerations are not exclusive, but are intended to reach all relevant evidence. In a situation where the relationship between the parties is both complicated and contested, the determination of which equitable theories apply should seldom be decided by the court on summary judgment. In this case, the trial court must weigh the evidence to determine whether Vasquez has established his claim for equitable relief.

Because we remand this case for trial, we need not resolve the evidentiary issues raised by the estate concerning the deadman's statute. Any objection to specific testimony will be resolved at trial. We vacate the decision of the Court of Appeals, reverse the trial court's granting of the motion for partial summary judgment, and remand this case for trial. Finally, an award of attorney fees, if any, should be determined at trial.

The following background information was provided by Frank Vasquez's attorney, Terry J. Barnett, of Rumbaugh, Rideout and Barnett, in Tacoma, Washington.

■ AMY D. RONNER, HOMOPHOBIA: IN THE CLOSET AND IN THE COFFIN
21 Law & Ineq. 65, 86-87 (2003)

When [Robert] Schwerzler died, he was seventy-eight years old and Vasquez was sixty-one. It was established in the trial court that Vasquez and Schwerzler had a close personal relationship and held themselves out as a couple. In fact, their circle of friends considered them a couple. Schwerzler gave Vasquez a diamond ring for their seventh anniversary and gave him another one for their twenty-fifth anniversary. Schwerzler had birthday parties for Vasquez and bestowed presents on him for other occasions. He also baked his partner a cake nearly every week throughout their years together. When he was in public, he often referred to Vasquez as "my partner," and said that "he did not know what he would do without him." It was widely acknowledged that Vasquez was completely distraught when his partner of almost three decades died.

There were other interdependencies between the couple that made the loss of his partner devastating for Vasquez, including the fact that Vasquez was illiterate and as a result Schwerzler managed their financial affairs. During the relationship, the title of their acquired property was in Schwerzler's name alone. Throughout their relationship, the men made their living recycling boxes and bags and did this work from home by themselves. It was a business without an overhead that generated a healthy income. Schwerzler, however, had a gambling habit and he squandered much of their earnings in this way. It was also established in the trial court that Schwerzler had announced to others that this income paid for their home and belongings. Unfortunately, when Schwerzler died, the business died with him. Hawthorne, the personal representative of the estate, assigned no value to it.

Aside from the recycling business, the couple had also bought and sold apartment buildings and a house. Vasquez was responsible for tenant relations, rent collection, maintenance, and most of the grounds upkeep. Schwerzler never paid Vasquez for his work in their recycling business, nor for his services in connection with the rental properties. Vasquez presumably did not expect payment "because he and Schwerzler were life partners." Over the years, friends had heard Vasquez tell Schwerzler that he feared "Schwerzler's relatives would put him out on the street" if Schwerzler were the first to die. Schwerzler would allay Vasquez's concerns by telling him that he had made arrangements to provide for Vasquez. Witnesses recalled seeing Schwerzler hug Vasquez as he consoled him.

Schwerzler had several assets in his name when he died, including the house that he and Vasquez shared, a life insurance policy, two automobiles, and a checking account. [N]o will could be found. . . .

Notes and Questions

1. *Inheritance law.* Inheritance law treats unmarried cohabitants (both hetero-sexual and same-sex) differently from legal spouses. According to the general rule, unmarried cohabitants cannot inherit from their partners by intestate succession (i.e., when a person dies without a will). Nor do unmarried cohabitants have the same statutory rights that are guaranteed to legal spouses: the right to a family support allowance during the period of estate administration, protection against unintentional or intentional disinheritance, priority in administration of the decedent's estate, and the right to control the disposition of the decedent's remains. See Mary Louise Fellows et al., Committed Partners and Inheritance: An Empirical Study, 16 Law & Ineq. J. 1, 15 (1998); T.P. Gallanis, Inheritance Rights for Domestic Partners, 79 Tul. L. Rev. 55, 60 (2004); E. Gary Spitko, The Expressive Function of Succession Law and the Merits of Non-Marital Inclusion, 41 Ariz. L. Rev. 1063, 1065 (1999).

What policy arguments exist for and against allowing intestate succession by unmarried cohabitants? Should the rules of intestate succession be applied to support social policy goals (such as the promotion of marriage or family protection of dependents), or should they implement the likely intent of the decedent? See Jennifer Seidman, Comment, Functional Families and Dysfunctional Laws: Committed Partners and Intestate Inheritance, 75 U. Colo. L. Rev. 211 (2004) (arguing that probate laws attempt to honor the presumed intent of the decedent, and urging amendments to the Uniform Probate Code to better achieve this objective with regard to unmarried cohabitants).

2. *Epilogue.* Following the decision in the principal case, attorneys for Mr. Vasquez reached a settlement with Schwerzler's next of kin. Vasquez's attorneys (who had represented him pro bono) agreed to remunerate Schwerzler's family members if they would allow Mr. Vasquez to remain in the home that he had shared with Schwerzler until the latter's death. Until Vasquez's death, Schwerzler's family members would have ownership rights but would acquire exclusive possession at Vasquez's death. See Human Rights Campaign, Settlement Reached in Gay Inheri-tance Lawsuit, July 10, 2002, available at http://www.hrc.org. Do you think the settlement reaches a fair result? What are the implications of *Vasquez* for unmarried heterosexual couples? See Natalie M. Perry, Nine Critical Documents for Every Lesbian and Gay Couple, Mondaq Bus., Briefing, June 11, 2001 (n.p.). See also Daniel B. Kennedy, Til Death Do Us Part, 87 ABA J. 22 (Jan. 2001).

3. *Meretricious relationships in Washington state.* Washington state has been in the forefront of the movement to extend property rights to members of unmarried cohabitants upon dissolution of their intimate relationships. Gavin M. Parr, Note, What Is a "Meretricious Relationship"?: An Analysis of Cohabitant Property Rights Under Connell v. Francisco, 74 Wash. L. Rev. 1243, 1243 (1999). Beginning in 1995, courts in Washington state developed an equitable doctrine that confers legal protection of the property rights of members of an unmarried couple upon dissolution provided that the parties have a "meretricious relationship." That term is defined as a "stable, marital-like relationship where both parties cohabit with knowledge that a lawful marriage between them does not exist." Connell v. Francisco, 898 P.2d 831, 834 (Wash. 1995). Based on *Connell,* courts provide equitable distribution of the property acquired during the relationship by treating it as if it had been the community property of legal spouses. See, e.g., Soltero v. Wimer, 115 P.3d 393 (Wash. Ct. App. 2005) (holding that the trial court did not abuse its discretion by awarding $135,000 as an equitable property distribution to a female cohabitant in a heterosexual relationship). In *Vasquez,* the question was whether a same-sex relationship would qualify under the "meretricious relationship" doctrine.

Justice Alexander in an omitted concurring opinion in *Vasquez* contends that the meretricious relationship doctrine, developed to resolve issues of property distribution upon separation, should not be applied at death. What are the policy arguments in favor of, and against, restricting the doctrine to the dissolution context? Subsequently, in Olver v. Fowler, 126 P.3d 69 (Wash. Ct. App. 2006), the Washington Court of Appeals extended the meretricious relationship doctrine to the context of death, holding that property acquired during a 15-year relationship that would have been community property was subject to equitable division upon the deaths of the man and woman in an automobile accident.

As explained above, Schwerzler's relatives denied that he was gay and insisted that Vasquez served merely as a housekeeper and boarder. Family members' homophobia is one of a number of reasons that cohabitants conceal the nature of their intimate relationships from relatives. Recall *Kowalski,* supra p. 415, in which Sharon Kowalski's relatives similarly denied her sexual orientation. Moreover, even families who are aware of a relative's sexual orientation may be unwilling to acknowledge it publicly. How can a court properly address the evidentiary issues raised by this motivation for "being in the closet" when one party to a relationship can no longer testify on his or her own behalf?

4. *Relevant factors.* The *Vasquez* court, applying Washington's equitable "meretricious relationship" doctrine, criticizes the trial court for granting summary judgment without a detailed inquiry into the specific facts of the case. Washington courts have established several non-exclusive factors for determining whether a "stable, marital-like relationship" exists, including: continuous cohabitation, duration of the relationship, purpose of the relationship, pooling of resources and services for joint projects, and the intent of the parties. *Connell,* supra, at 834. What information would you need to determine if Vasquez and Schwerzler shared this kind of relationship? See Susan N. Gary, Adapting Intestacy Laws to Changing Families, 18 Law & Ineq. 1 (2000) (proposing that states adopt a functional approach to determining family status for purposes of intestate succession); E. Gary Spitko, An Accrual/Multi-Factor Approach to Intestate Inheritance

Rights for Unmarried Committed Partners, 81 Or. L. Rev. 255 (2002) (suggesting 23 factors to consider in determining the status of an unmarried cohabitant).

5. *Same-sex couples and Washington's meretricious-relationship doctrine.* The court of appeals in *Vasquez*, 994 P.2d 240 (Wash. Ct. App. 2000), held that a meretricious relationship cannot exist between members of a same-sex couple because, based on prior case law, the cohabitants must possess the requisite legal ability to wed. Does this reasoning make sense? What policies are supported by recognition of nonmarital cohabitant relationships between persons who could have legally married had they so chosen but not between persons to whom that option was unavailable? In the principal case, the Washington state supreme court permitted same-sex relationships to qualify as meretricious relationships, by saying "[e]qui-table claims are not dependent on the 'legality' of the relationship between the parties, nor are they limited by the gender or sexual orientation of the parties." 33 P.3d at 737.

Following the principal case, in Gormley v. Robertson, 83 P.3d 1042 (Wash. Ct. App. 2004), a court of appeals applied the meretricious-relationship doctrine to divide the property of a lesbian couple upon dissolution of their relationship.

6. *Same-sex marriage in Washington state.* Washington is one of several states with pending cases considering the constitutionality of same-sex marriage. The Washington state supreme court is currently considering two consolidated cases: Andersen v. King County, 2004 WL 1738447 (Wash. Super. Ct. 2004) (hold-ing that state statutes that prohibited same-sex marriage violated the privileges and immunities clause and denied substantive due process rights under the state constitution); and Castle v. State, 2004 WL 1985215 (Wash. Super. Ct. 2004) (hold-ing that state DOMA violated the privileges and immunities clause of the state constitution).

7. *Testate succession.* Unmarried cohabitants may inherit, of course, if their partners include them as beneficiaries in a will. However, even testate succession is not problem-free for gay and lesbian partners. In the classic case of In re Will of Kaufmann, 247 N.Y.S.2d 664 (App. Div. 1964), *aff'd*, 205 N.E.2d 864 (N.Y. 1965), millionaire Robert Kaufmann lived with his partner, lawyer Walter Weiss, for ten years. While Walter managed the household and finances, Robert pursued his interest in painting. In numerous wills, Robert gradually increased Walter's share of his estate. When Robert died, his brother challenged the will on the ground of undue influence. Two juries found undue influence, a finding that was affirmed by the New York Court of Appeals. On the *Kaufmann* case, see Thomas L. Shaffer, Death, Property, and Lawyers: A Behavioral Approach 243-257 (1970); Ray D. Madoff, Unmasking Due Influence, 81 Minn. L. Rev. 571, 592-600 (1997); Jeffrey G. Sherman, Undue Influence and the Homosexual Testator, 42 U. Pitt. L. Rev. 225, 239-248 (1981).

Research leads Professor Jeffrey Sherman to conclude that "the lover-legatee of a homosexual testator faces a more difficult task at probate than does his heterosexual counterpart." Sherman, supra, at 246. Sherman cites the tendency of juries in will contests to return verdicts "more in keeping with their prejudices than with the facts." Id. at 246 n.102. An early empirical study in California determined that the jury finds for the contestant in over 75 percent of will contest cases. Note, Will Contests on Trial, 6 Stan. L. Rev. 91 (1953). Sherman speculates that there would be more litigation involving same-sex partners were it not for the pressure to settle because of the parties' fear of bias against homosexuals. Sherman, supra, at 233 n.43.

8. *Domestic partnership provisions on inheritance.* Only a few states currently have domestic partnership legislation (discussed in Chapter III and Chapter IV). Specific requirements for domestic partnerships vary from jurisdiction to jurisdiction. (Members of same-sex couples in Massachusetts, the only state which recognizes same-sex marriage, are treated as legal spouses.) California, Connecticut, and Vermont grant the most extensive rights to registered same-sex partners, including the right of intestate succession. See, e.g., Cal. Prob. Code §6401(c) (West 1991 & Supp. 2005); S.B. 963, 2005 Gen. Ass., Jan. Sess. (Conn. 2005) (enacted); Vt. Stat. tit. 15 §1204(e)(1) (2002). Laws in Hawaii and Maine also include reciprocal beneficiaries and domestic partners, respectively, as intestate heirs. See Haw. Rev. Stat. §560:2-102 (1993 & Supp. 2004); Me. Rev. Stat. Ann. tit. 18 §2-102 (West 1998 & Supp. 2004). New Jersey's domestic partnership law provides some inheritance tax benefits to domestic partners, but does not confer succession rights as intestate heirs. See N.J. Stat. Ann. §54:34-1 - 4 (West 1996 & Supp. 2005); N.J. Stat. Ann. §§3B:5-3, 4 (West 1983 & Supp. 2005).

An additional question in the probate context is whether states will recognize domestic partnerships created in other states – a problematic issue if a same-sex partner dies owning real property in another state or dies in a different state from the state of registration of the domestic partnership. To date, courts in several jurisdictions refuse to give inter-jurisdictional recognition to domestic partnerships. See, e.g., Rosengarten v. Downes, 806 A.2d 1066 (Conn. 2002); Burns v. Burns, 560 S.E.2d 47 (Ga. Ct. App. 2002); Langan v. St. Vincent's Hospital of New York, 802 N.Y.S.2d 476 (App. Div. 2005). In contrast, a few states with domestic partnership laws (i.e., New Jersey, California) have statutes that provide for recognition of similar relationships that were entered into in other states. Massachusetts also recognizes civil unions entered into in other states. Salucco v. Alldredge, 17 Mass. L. Rep. 498 (Super. Ct. 2004). See Leslie J. Harris, Same-Sex Unions Around the World: Marriage, Civil Unions, Registered Partnerships – What Are the Differences and Why Do They Matter?, 19 Prob. & Prop. 31, 34 (2005); R. Brent Drake, Note: Status of Contract? A Comparative Analysis of Inheritance Rights Under Equitable Adoption and Domestic Partnership Doctrines, 39 Ga. L. Rev. 675 (2005).

9. *Estate planning for gay and lesbian clients. Vasquez* highlights some of the estate planning problems for same-sex partners. Attorney and gay rights activist Roberta Achtenberg identifies additional problems:

> Early in the estate planning process the lawyer should inquire as to the client's concerns about a will contest and should discuss the grounds for such contests and their applicability, if any, to the client's situation. This discussion should serve both to identify potential contestants (if there are any) and in most cases to reduce the client's fears. In this regard it is important to the lawyer to have an accurate picture of the kind of emotional relationship the testator has with her or his biological family. Does the family know the testator is homosexual, or that the testator has a lover or friend whom she or he intends to benefit through the will? Does the testator hold property of such value that a contest by the biological family would be predictable? Is there anything the testator can do during her or his lifetime to minimize the shock which members of the biological family might experience if they were to discover that the bulk of the testator's estate was being left to an "unrelated" person?
>
> [T]he lawyer should not presume that just because a client is a lesbian or gay, she or he does not have a legal spouse from whom she or he was never divorced. . . . Special

caution must be exercised where the client is terminally ill or otherwise in a weakened mental or physical state. Any documents executed under such circumstances will probably be more susceptible to attack than documents executed when the client is healthy and clearly competent. . . .

Sexual Orientation and the Law §4.04 (Roberta Achtenberg ed., 1991).

AIDS raises additional issues, emphasizing the importance of planning for illness, incapacity, and death, including the execution of nominations of conservator (or guardian), powers of attorney to cover asset management and personal care, directives to physicians (for example, living wills), and determinations of eligibility for public benefit programs, that will pay necessary medical, food, and personal support costs. See generally id. at §§13.03[1]-13.04[3]. See also Jennifer Tulin McGrath, The Ethical Responsibilities of Estate Planning Attorneys in the Representation of Non-Traditional Couples, 27 Seattle U. L. Rev. 75 (2003).

10. *Other estate planning vehicles.* Wills provide an important means to ensure that an estate will pass to a loved one. Other alternatives also exist. For example, Bob Schwerzler could have made Frank Vasquez the beneficiary of an inter vivos trust instead of a will. Such instruments, however, are subject to challenges on grounds of undue influence and fraud. See, e.g., Knowles v. Binford, 298 A.2d 862 (Md. 1973) (upholding a finding that aunt was induced by the undue influence of her partner to amend her trust). Schwerzler also might have executed a will contract to devise property to Frank Vasquez (perhaps in exchange for Frank's services during Schwerzler's lifetime). This alternative also presents problems for gay and lesbian partners. See, e.g., Beaumont v. Castator, No. 98, 379 (Okla Civ. App. Feb. 13, 2004), *cert. denied*, 543 U.S. 957 (2004) (rejecting man's claim that he and his deceased partner of 24 years had an oral contract to devise property). See also Camile M. Quinn & Shawna S. Baker, Essential Estate Planning for the Constitutionally Unrecognized Families in Oklahoma: Same-Sex Couples, 40 Tulsa L. Rev. 479, 502-504(2005) (discussing case).

11. *Adult adoption.* Adult adoption is another vehicle that same-sex partners use to create a legally recognized relationship for inheritance purposes. Persons may resort to adult adoption not only to create inheritance rights, but also to obtain decisionmaking authority for a partner in cases of emergency or incapacity, to secure hospital visitation rights, and to obtain benefits under insurance policies or employee benefit packages. Adult adoption generally requires only the consent of the parties (unlike the adoption of a child which is predicated on the best interests of the child).

a. *General rule and exceptions.* Almost all states permit adult adoption. Angie Smolka, Note, That's the Ticket: A New Way of Defining Family, 10 Cornell J.L. & Pub. Pol'y 629, 638-639 (2001) (pointing out that Alabama and Nebraska are exceptions). However, a few states have particular requirements (i.e., co-residence, consanguinity, or age restrictions) that preclude gays or lesbians from adopting their partner. For example, some statutes include requirements that the adoptee be the adoptor's niece, nephew, stepchild, or natural child. E.g., Va. Code Ann §63.1-219.50 (Michie 2002). Other states require that the adoptee's relationship be commenced during the latter's minority. E.g., Idaho Code §16-1501 (Michie 2001 & Supp. 2004). Finally, some states require that the adoptee be some statutorily specified age younger than the adoptor. E.g., Idaho Code §16-1502 (Michie 2001)

(15 years); N.J. Stat. Ann. §2A:22-2 (West 2000) (10 years). See also Joanna Grossman, Adopting Adults: An Estate Planning Device for Gay Partners, available at http://writ.news.findlaw.com/grossman/20010116.html (last visited June 25, 2006) (pointing out that two-thirds of the states allow adult adoption, and one-third permit it with restrictions).

Case law also recognizes same-sex adoption for estate planning purposes. See, e.g., In re Adoption of Swanson, 623 A.2d 1095 (Del. 1993); In re Adoption of Adult Anonymous II, 452 N.Y.S.2d 198 (N.Y. Sup. Ct. 1982); In re Adoption of Adult Anonymous, 106 Misc. 2d 792 (N.Y. Fam. Ct. 1981). But cf. In re Robert Paul P., 471 N.E.2d 424 (N.Y. 1984).

   b. *Setting aside an adoption.* Although adoption may be used as an estate planning tool, it does not ensure inheritance rights because an adoption may still be contested (for example, on grounds of fraud or undue influence) even after the adoptor's death. In Rickard v. McKesson, 774 So.2d 838 (Fla. Ct. App. 2000), a disgruntled niece petitioned to set aside the adoption by her 88-year-old uncle of his 72-year-old gay partner. The uncle (Blackwell) had adopted his life partner in order to permit the latter to inherit Blackwell's interest in a trust that was created by Blackwell's father. (The instrument provided that, if Blackwell died childless, his interest would pass to the niece.) The niece sought to invalidate the adoption because Florida law expressly prohibits a gay or lesbian from adopting either an adult or a child. Fla Stat. Ann. §63.042 (3) (West 2005). (Florida is one of several states with such restrictions.) The Florida Court of Appeals held that the niece's allegations were sufficient to maintain an action to set aside the adoption on the ground of fraud. The Florida statute has withstood constitutional attack on state and federal grounds. See Lofton v. Kearney, 157 F. Supp.2d 1372 (S.D. 2001); Lofton v. Secretary of the Department of Children and Family Services, 358 F.3d 804 (11th Cir. 2004).

   Professor Sherman suggests methods by which a same-sex partner may attempt to insulate an adoption from subsequent attack.

> It might still be advantageous for the homosexual testator to adopt his lover, however, if he promptly informs his prospective heirs of the adoption. A number of states have statutes of limitations requiring that actions to vacate adoption decrees be brought within a certain period of time. [I]f the homosexual adoptor informs his prospective heirs of the adoption as soon as it occurs, it is likely that they will be compelled either to object to the adoption then and there or to acquiesce in it permanently, and they may be most unwilling to challenge the adoptor face to face.

Sherman, supra, at 260-261.

   c. *Other disadvantages of adoption as an estate planning tool.* Other disadvantages also exist if same-sex partners resort to adoption as an estate planning tool. One primary disadvantage is that the adoption relationship cannot be rescinded if the partners later choose to dissolve their relationship. Another disadvantage is that the rights of the adoptee's biological parents terminate upon adoption, thereby severing the adoptee's right to inherit from his or her biological parents or relatives. Maureen B. Cohon, Where the Rainbow Ends: Trying to Find a Pot of Gold for Same-Sex Couples in Pennsylvania, 41 Duq. L. Rev. 495, 499 (2003); Grossman, supra. How will the same-sex marriage movement and the rise of domestic partnership laws affect the use of adult adoption as a planning vehicle for gays and lesbians? See generally Joan M. Burda, Estate Planning for Same-Sex Couples (2004).

C. PARENTS' AND CHILDREN'S RIGHTS IN THE NONMARITAL FAMILY

In recent decades, society has witnessed a steady increase in the number of single-parent families. In fact, single-parent families have more than tripled in the past 25 years.[19] In 2004, of 4 million live births in the United States, 35.7 percent were to single women.[20] Moreover, the birth rate of nonmarital children varies according to race. More than twice as many African-American children compared to white children are born to single mothers.[21]

The dramatic increase in the numbers of single-parent families is attributable in part to the increasing economic independence of women and the decreasing stigma attached to nonmarital births. See Kathryn Edin & Maria Kefalas, Promise I Can Keep: Why Poor Women Put Motherhood Before Marriage 5-6 (2005) (identifying additional factors such as the role of welfare, the declining pool of marriageable men in the inner cities, and pervasive attitudes there toward marriage and childrearing that view marriage as a luxury but children as a necessity).

The single-parent family has its share of problems, usually economic. Because most such families are headed by women, families must survive on the income of only a working mother.[22] Economic difficulties are inevitable, stemming both from gender discrimination (for example, lower salaries for women compared to men) and racial discrimination.[23]

This section explores some of the legal problems faced by single-parent families, in particular, the support rights of nonmarital children and limitations on the rights of parents of nonmarital children. Subsequent chapters address support rights in general (Chapter VI), as well as other problems experienced

[19]. Bureau of the Census, supra note [1], at 7 (the number of female-headed families increased from 3 million in 1970 to 10 million in 2003, compared to the number of male-headed families that increased from less than half a million to 2 million during the same period).

[20]. National Center for Health Statistics, Preliminary Births for 2004, available at http://www.cdc.gov/nchs/products/pubs/pubd/hestats/prelim_births04.htm (last visited Oct. 30, 2005). Childbearing by single women increased 4 percent from 2003. Id. Whereas teenage birth rates declined from 2003 (continuing evidence of a trend beginning in 1991), births to older women (aged 30 and above) increased. Id.

[21]. National Center for Health Statistics, National Vital Statistics Report, vol. 52, no. 10, Dec. 17, 2003, at 49 (Table 13) (reporting that in 2002, 68.2 percent of African-American children were born to unmarried women, compared to 28.5 percent of white children who were born to unmarried women).

[22]. Female-headed families make up 10 million of the 12 million one-parent family groups. Also, female-headed families are more likely than male-headed families to include more than one child and to have family incomes below the poverty level. Bureau of the Census, supra note [1], at 8-9.

[23]. Many single-parent heads-of-household are women of color. For example, in 2003, Black single mothers constituted more than one-third of the number of female-headed families. Id. at 9 (extrapolating from data) (note that data represent "Black only" single mothers, not those of mixed races). Commentators have noted for decades that unmarried women with children comprise one of the truly "hard core poor" groups in the United States. See Nancy Moore Clatworthy, The Non-Traditional Family and the Child, 12 Cap. U. L. Rev. 345, 347 (1983).

by single-parent families, such as custody (Chapter VII), adoption and assisted reproduction (Chapter IX).

1. Support Rights of Nonmarital Children

■ CLARK v. JETER
486 U.S. 456 (1988)

Justice O'CONNOR delivered the opinion of the Court.

Under Pennsylvania law, an illegitimate child must prove paternity before seeking support from his or her father, and a suit to establish paternity ordinarily must be brought within six years of an illegitimate child's birth. By contrast, a legitimate child may seek support from his or her parents at any time. . . .

On September 22, 1983, petitioner Cherlyn Clark filed a support complaint in the Allegheny County Court of Common Pleas on behalf of her minor daughter, Tiffany, who was born out of wedlock on June 11, 1973. Clark named respondent Gene Jeter as Tiffany's father. The court ordered blood tests, which showed a 99.3% probability that Jeter is Tiffany's father.

Jeter moved to dismiss the complaint on the ground that it was barred by the 6-year statute of limitations for paternity actions. In her response, Clark contended that this statute is unconstitutional under the Equal Protection and Due Process Clauses. . . .

[The trial court upheld the statute of limitations and Clark appealed. Before the court decided her case, however, the legislature enacted an 18-year statute of limitations for actions to establish paternity to comply with the federal Child Support Enforcement Amendments of 1984 requiring all states participating in the federal child support program to have procedures to establish the paternity of any child who is less than 18 years old. 42 U.S.C. §666(a)(5) (1982 ed., Supp. IV). The Superior Court concluded that Pennsylvania's new 18-year statute of limitations did not apply retroactively, and it affirmed the trial court's conclusions that the 6-year statute of limitations was constitutional. The Court granted Clark's petition for certiorari.]

In considering whether state legislation violates the Equal Protection Clause of the Fourteenth Amendment, we apply different levels of scrutiny to different types of classifications. . . . Between [the] extremes of rational basis review and strict scrutiny lies a level of intermediate scrutiny, which generally has been applied to discriminatory classifications based on sex or illegitimacy.

To withstand intermediate scrutiny, a statutory classification must be substantially related to an important governmental objective. Consequently we have invalidated classifications that burden illegitimate children for the sake of punishing the illicit relations of their parents, because "visiting this condemnation on the head of an infant is illogical and unjust." Weber v. Aetna Casualty & Surety Co., 406 U.S. 164, 175 (1972). Yet, in the seminal case concerning the child's right to support, this Court acknowledged that it might be appropriate to treat illegitimate children differently in the support context because of "lurking problems with respect to proof of paternity." Gomez v. Perez, 409 U.S. 535, 538 (1973).

This Court has developed a particular framework for evaluating equal protection challenges to statutes of limitations that apply to suits to establish paternity, and thereby limit the ability of illegitimate children to obtain support.

> First, the period for obtaining support . . . must be sufficiently long in duration to present a reasonable opportunity for those with an interest in such children to assert claims on their behalf. Second, any time limitation placed on that opportunity must be substantially related to the State's interest in avoiding the litigation of stale or fraudulent claims.

Mills v. Habluetzel, 456 U.S., at 99-100.

In *Mills*, we held that Texas' 1-year statute of limitations failed both steps of the analysis. We explained that paternity suits typically will be brought by the child's mother, who might not act swiftly amidst the emotional and financial complications of the child's first year. And, it is unlikely that the lapse of a mere 12 months will result in the loss of evidence or appreciably increase the likelihood of fraudulent claims. A concurring opinion in *Mills* explained why statutes of limitations longer than one year also may be unconstitutional. Id., at 102-106 (O'Connor, J., joined by Burger, C.J., and Brennan and Blackmun, JJ., and joined as to Part I by Powell, J., concurring). First, the State has a countervailing interest in ensuring that genuine claims for child support are satisfied. Second, the fact that Texas tolled most other causes of action during a child's minority suggested that proof problems do not become overwhelming during this period. Finally, the practical obstacles to filing a claim for support are likely to continue after the first year of the child's life.

In Pickett v. Brown, 462 U.S. 1 (1983), the Court unanimously struck down Tennessee's 2-year statute of limitations for paternity and child support actions brought on behalf of certain illegitimate children. Adhering to the analysis developed in *Mills*, the Court first considered whether two years afforded a reasonable opportunity to bring such suits. The Tennessee statute was relatively more generous than the Texas statute considered in *Mills* because it did not limit actions against a father who had acknowledged his paternity in writing or by furnishing support; nor did it apply if the child was likely to become a public charge. Nevertheless, the Court concluded that the 2-year period was too short in light of the persisting financial and emotional problems that are likely to afflict the child's mother. Proceeding to the second step of the analysis, the Court decided that the 2-year statute of limitations was not substantially related to Tennessee's asserted interest in preventing stale and fraudulent claims. The period during which suit could be brought was only a year longer than the period considered in *Mills*, and this incremental difference would not create substantially greater proof and fraud problems. . . . Finally, scientific advances in blood testing had alleviated some problems of proof in paternity actions. For these reasons, the Tennessee statute failed to survive heightened scrutiny under the Equal Protection Clause.

In light of this authority, we conclude that Pennsylvania's 6-year statute of limitations violates the Equal Protection Clause. Even six years does not necessarily provide a reasonable opportunity to assert a claim on behalf of an illegitimate child. "The unwillingness of the mother to file a paternity action on behalf of her child, which could stem from her relationship with the natural father or . . . from the emotional strain of having an illegitimate child, or even from the desire to avoid community and family disapproval, may continue years after the child is born.

The problem may be exacerbated if, as often happens, the mother herself is a minor." *Mills,* supra, at 105, n.4 (O'Connor, J., concurring). Not all of these difficulties are likely to abate in six years. A mother might realize only belatedly "a loss of income attributable to the need to care for the child," *Pickett,* supra, at 12. Furthermore, financial difficulties are likely to increase as the child matures and incurs expenses for clothing, school, and medical care. Thus it is questionable whether a State acts reasonably when it requires most paternity and support actions to be brought within six years of an illegitimate child's birth.

We do not rest our decision on this ground, however, for it is not entirely evident that six years would necessarily be an unreasonable limitations period for child support actions involving illegitimate children. We are, however, confident that the 6-year statute of limitations is not substantially related to Pennsylvania's interest in avoiding the litigation of stale or fraudulent claims. In a number of circumstances, Pennsylvania permits the issue of paternity to be litigated more than six years after the birth of an illegitimate child [for example, for intestate succession purposes, in paternity actions initiated by the father, and tolls the limitation during minority in other civil actions as well]. In *Pickett* and *Mills* similar tolling statutes cast doubt on the State's purposed interest in avoiding the litigation or fraudulent claims.

A more recent indication that Pennsylvania does not consider proof problems insurmountable is the enactment by the Pennsylvania Legislature in 1985 of an 18-year statute of limitations for paternity and support actions. 23 Pa. Cons. Stat. §4343(b) (1985). To be sure the legislature did not act spontaneously, but rather under the threat of losing some federal funds. Nevertheless, the new statute is a tacit concession that proof problems are not overwhelming. The legislative history of the federal Child Support Enforcement Amendments explains why Congress thought such statutes of limitations are reasonable. Congress adverted to the problem of stale and fraudulent claims, but recognized that increasingly sophisticated tests for genetic markers permit the exclusion of over 99% of those who might be accused of paternity, regardless of the age of the child. This scientific evidence . . . is an additional reason to doubt that Pennsylvania had a substantial reason for limiting the time within which paternity and support actions could be brought.

We conclude that the Pennsylvania statute does not withstand heightened scrutiny under the Equal Protection Clause. We therefore find it unnecessary to reach Clark's due process claim. . . .

Notes and Questions

1. *Common law rule. Clark* reflects the trend of increasing constitutional protection of the rights of nonmarital children. Traditionally, the law regarded the nonmarital (or "illegitimate") child as *filius nullius* and a bastard. That status affected the child's right to support and inheritance. In many states, only the mother had a common law duty of support for a nonmarital child. The tide turned in Gomez v. Perez, 409 U.S. 535 (1973), in which the United States Supreme Court held that a state cannot grant marital children a statutory right to paternal support while denying this right to nonmarital children. Today, statutes require both parents to support the child regardless of the marital status of the parents. Nonetheless, distinctions still persist in terms of inheritance (explained below).

2. *Statutes of limitations.* At the time of *Clark*, many states had statutes of limitations that restricted the time within which paternity suits could be brought. States justified these short statutory periods to prevent the filing of stale claims and to discourage fraud. Several Supreme Court decisions prior to *Clark* invalidated various short statutes of limitations. E.g., Pickett v. Brown, 462 U.S. 1 (1983) (two-year statute); Mills v. Habluetzel, 456 U.S. 91 (1982) (one-year statute). Thereafter, many states substantially lengthened their statutory periods. Congress also addressed statutes of limitations in paternity establishment, as *Clark* explains. To improve child support enforcement, Congress enacted the Child Support Enforcement Amendments of 1984 requiring states (as a condition for receipt of federal funds) to extend their statutes of limitations to permit paternity establishment for 18 years after birth. 42 U.S.C. §666(a)(5)(A)(ii) (2000).

Subsequently, the Family Support Act (FSA) of 1988, 42 U.S.C. §666(a)(5)(ii) (2000), requires states to permit paternity establishment for children whose paternity actions were dismissed previously under short statutes of limitations. The FSA also requires states to have procedures by which the state can order all parties in a contested case (including the child) to submit to genetic tests. The legislation provides for a limited exception for individuals who can establish good cause for refusing to cooperate. 42 U.S.C. §602(a)(26)(B) (2000).

The FSA also sets performance standards for state programs establishing paternity. States must meet a specified "paternity establishment percentage." 42 U.S.C. §652(g) (2000). See also id. at §654(4)(A). The federal legislation also makes available to state officials seeking to enforce child support obligations the federal "Parent Locator Service," which uses social security numbers to locate absent parents, even in the absence of court-ordered support. Id. at §653(a). A state must make its paternity determination services available, for a fee, to those not receiving public assistance. Id. at §654(6). The Personal Responsibility and Work Opportunity Reconciliation Act (discussed infra p. 455) also addresses paternity establishment.

3. *Constitutional challenges.* The Supreme Court first held discrimination against nonmarital children unconstitutional in the late 1960s. In Levy v. Louisiana, 391 U.S. 68 (1968), the Court ruled that Louisiana's Wrongful Death Act violated the Equal Protection Clause by denying recovery to a nonmarital child for the death of the mother. In Glona v. American Guarantee & Liability Insurance Co., 391 U.S. 73 (1968), the Court reached a similar result, permitting recovery by a mother for the death of her nonmarital child.

In Weber v. Aetna Casualty & Surety Co., 406 U.S. 164 (1972), the Court extended this approach to permit recovery by a nonmarital child for the father's death under a state workers' compensation law. The Court rejected the argument that the denial of recovery would promote the state's interest in "legitimate family relationships." Id. at 173. As the Court explained:

> [I]mposing disabilities on the illegitimate child is contrary to the basic concept of our system that legal burdens should bear some relationship to individual responsibility or wrongdoing. Obviously, no child is responsible for his birth and penalizing the illegitimate child is an ineffectual — as well as an unjust — way of deterring the parent. Courts are powerless to prevent the social opprobrium suffered by these hapless children, but the Equal Protection Clause does enable us to strike down discriminatory

laws relating to status of birth where — as in this case — the classification is justified by
no legitimate state interest, compelling or otherwise.

Id. at 175-176.

4. *Inheritance rights of nonmarital children.* Although the Supreme Court minimized many differences in the legal treatment of nonmarital and marital children,
the Court declined to invalidate all discrimination against nonmarital children,
especially discrimination regarding inheritance rights.

Traditionally, the laws in most states provided that a nonmarital child occupied
the same position as a child born within marriage with regard to inheritance
rights vis-a-vis the child's *mother*. However, while a father always could name a
nonmarital child as a beneficiary in the father's will, the child would receive nothing
if the father died intestate (without a will). The nonmarital child's right to inherit
intestate from the biological father was problematic because of concerns about
proof of paternity.

In the late 1970s, the United States Supreme Court began examining whether
states could impose a higher standard of proof or require particular kinds of proof
in order for nonmarital children to inherit via intestate succession from their
fathers. The Court held that, in order for a nonmarital child to inherit from a
noncustodial biological father, a state could require a higher level of proof in
the form of a judicial declaration of paternity (Lalli v. Lalli, 439 U.S. 259
(1978)), but could not require that the child's parents subsequently marry after
the child's birth (Trimble v. Gordon, 430 U.S. 762 (1977)).

5. *Statutory reform.* Today, an increasing number of jurisdictions recognize the
inheritance rights of nonmarital children. Many states have done so by adopting
the original Uniform Parentage Act (UPA), 9B U.L.A. 377 (2001).

a. *Original UPA.* The movement toward equal rights for nonmarital children,
initiated by a series of Supreme Court decisions beginning with Levy v. Louisiana,
supra, had scholarly roots. In particular, the original UPA, promulgated in 1973,
was influenced by Professor Harry Krause's classic book, *Illegitimacy: Law and Social
Policy* (1971), which called for an end to discrimination against nonmarital children. (Krause became the Reporter for the UPA, drafted by the National Conference of Commissioners on Uniform State Laws.) The original UPA recognized that
according treatment to nonmarital children equal to that enjoyed by their marital
counterparts first requires identifying the fathers of the former. For marital children, the common law (and later many statutes) presumed a woman's husband to be
the father of her children (see infra); to help achieve equal treatment for children
born to unmarried women, the original UPA developed the following network of
presumptions for identifying their fathers:

§4. [Presumptions of Paternity]

(a) A man is presumed to be the natural father of a child if:

(1) he and the child's natural mother are or have been married to each other
and the child is born during the marriage, or within 300 days after the marriage is
terminated by death, annulment, declaration of invalidity, or divorce, or after a decree
of separation is entered by the court;

(2) before the child's birth, he and the child's natural mother have attempted
to marry each other by a marriage solemnized in apparent compliance with the law,
although the attempted marriage is or could be declared invalid, and

       (i) if the attempted marriage could be declared invalid only by a court, the child is born during the attempted marriage, or within 300 days after its termination by death, annulment, declaration of invalidity, or divorce; or

       (ii) if the attempted marriage is invalid without a court order, the child is born within 300 days after the termination of cohabitation;

       (3) after the child's birth, he and the child's natural mother have married, or attempted to marry, each other by a marriage solemnized in apparent compliance with law, although the attempted marriage is or could be declared invalid, and

       (i) he has acknowledged his paternity of the child in writing filed with the [appropriate court or Vital Statistics Bureau];

       (ii) with his consent, he is named as the child's father on the child's birth certificate; or

       (iii) he is obligated to support the child under a written voluntary promise or by court order;

       (4) while the child is under the age of majority, he receives the child into his home and openly holds out the child as his natural child; or

       (5) he acknowledges his paternity of the child in a writing filed with the [appropriate court or Vital Statistics Bureau], which shall promptly inform the mother of the filling of the acknowledgment, and she does not dispute the acknowledgment within a reasonable time after being informed thereof, in a writing filed with the [appropriate court or Vital Statistics Bureau]. If another man is presumed under this section to be the child's father, acknowledgment may be effected only with the written consent of the presumed father or after the presumption has been rebutted.

       (b) A presumption under this section may be rebutted in an appropriate action only by clear and convincing evidence. If two or more presumptions arise which conflict with each other, the presumption which on the facts is founded on the weightier considerations of policy and logic controls. The presumption is rebutted by a court decree establishing paternity of the child by another man.

9B U.L.A. 393-394 (2001). Eighteen states adopted the original UPA. Id. at 377.

    b. *Revised UPA*. In 2000, NCCUSL promulgated a new Uniform Parentage Act, which it revised in 2002. Although the drafters determined that technological advances (including assisted reproductive techniques and increasingly accurate genetic testing) called for an updated statute, the new UPA reaffirms the original policy of equal treatment of children regardless of their parents' marital status. UPA §202, 9B U.L.A. 309 (2001). For additional discussion of the new UPA, see infra pp. 472-474.

Note on Paternity Establishment

    The traditional way to identify the father of a nonmarital child and to impose a support obligation on him was the paternity suit. Proceedings to establish the identity of the biological father are necessary not only for child support purposes but also for inheritance purposes. Paternity actions, rooted in the English bastardy proceeding, historically were quasi-criminal proceedings characterized by short statutes of limitations, proof beyond a reasonable doubt, and trial by jury.

    Increasing public awareness about the problems of child support enforcement on the federal level prompted law reforms (explored below and in Chapter VI), including a reformulation of these elements. As revealed by *Clark*, supra, the

United States Supreme Court invalidated short statutes of limitations in the 1980s. To improve child support enforcement efforts, Congress enacted the Child Support Enforcement Amendments of 1984 requiring states (as a condition for receipt of federal funds) to extend their statutes of limitations to permit paternity establishment for 18 years after birth (a provision that was incorporated subsequently into federal welfare reform legislation in 1996). See 42 U.S.C. §666(a) (5)(A) (West Supp. 2002). Paternity proceedings, now commonly viewed as civil proceedings, raise a number of issues.

a. *Jurisdiction.* To establish the paternity of an out-of-state putative father, a court must obtain personal jurisdiction over him. Traditionally, courts use different theories to extend long-arm bases of jurisdiction: failure to support constitutes the "commission of a tortious act," the breach of a contractual obligaiton within the state, or "doing business" in the state. See, e.g., Jones v. Chandler, 592 So. 2d 966 (Miss. 1991) (finding all three bases of jurisdiction within long-arm statute). See also Unif. Interstate Family Support Act (UIFSA) §201, 9 U.L.A. (pt. 1B) 484 (2005) (providing that a person who has sexual intercourse within the state thereby submits to jurisdiction regarding any ensuing child); Unif. Parentage Act §604(b), 9B U.L.A. 339-340 (2001) (incorporating the UIFSA long-arm provision for establishing personal jurisdiction, now followed by every state). On multistate child support cases, see also Chapter VI, section F3.

b. *Admissible evidence.* Concerns about fraudulent claims of paternity contributed to enactment of short statutes of limitations (discussed supra), as well as rules about the admissibility of evidence. However, such concerns have been eliminated by advances in scientific proof of paternity. Before the development of modern scientific methods, some courts permitted the jury's visual comparison of the baby and the alleged father. See, e.g., Berry v. Chaplin, 169 P.2d 442 (Cal. Dist. Ct. App. 1946). Subsequent medical advances provide increasingly accurate evidence of paternity.

Early testing included the Human Leukocyte Antigens (HLA) blood-testing system which detects markers, or antigens, on white blood cells. When used in combination with red blood cell tests, the HLA test could *exclude* a defendant as the father with a 97.3% percent accuracy rate. Today, scientific advances in DNA testing yield a 99% probability that a given man *is* the child's father. Paula Roberts, Truth and Consequences: Part I, Disestablishing the Paternity of Non-Marital Children, 37 Fam. L.Q. 35, 36 n.5 (2003). DNA tests once required a significant amount of genetic material, often necessitating blood tests. Accurate testing can now be obtained by swiping a cotton swab along the inner cheek. The ease of testing has led to a lucrative business in home paternity tests. Id. at 37 n.16. DNA testing can be performed even after a defendant's death.

c. *Plaintiffs.* Traditionally, paternity actions were brought by the *mother* for support purposes. Gradually, states permitted such actions by the child, the child's representative, and the father. For many decades, *public welfare authorities* brought paternity suits, seeking reimbursement for public funds spent to support the child. This practice stemmed from federal interest in the identification of the father to establish and enforce his child support obligation. Federal provisions in the Aid to Families with Dependent Children (ADDC) program, enacted in 1935 as part of the Social Security Act, required states (as a condition for receipt of federal funds) to undertake paternity establishment procedures (for example, requiring mothers on AFDC to cooperate in paternity establishment and securing support). Welfare reform legislation, (PRWORA), 42 U.S.C. §603 (2000), replaced AFDC with a block grant to the states. PRWORA requires states to adopt new paternity provisions in order to receive federal funds for child support enforcement programs and welfare programs. Under PRWORA, paternity can be established when: *either parent* brings a paternity suit at any time until the child attains age 18 and also when both parents voluntarily acknowledge paternity (discussed below). See Chapter VI for further discussion of child support enforcement.

d. *Submission to genetic testing.* According to PRWORA, upon either parent's request (provided that the request is supported by a sworn statement "establishing a reasonable possibility of the requisite sexual contact between the parties"), a court must order genetic tests. 42 U.S.C. §666(a)(5)(B)(I)(1). However, under the new UPA (§608), courts may deny requests for genetic testing based on estoppel principles "in the interests of preserving a child's ties to the presumed or acknowledged father who openly held himself out as the child's father regardless of whether he is in fact the genetic father." Paternity is established on the basis of such tests. If one party refuses to undergo such tests, a court will establish paternity based on other evidence or by default. Once paternity is established, the court enters an appropriate order that often includes an award of child support. These paternity establishment procedures may create either a rebuttable or conclusive presumption of paternity — at the state's option (id. at §666(a)(5)(G)).

e. *Indigent defendants.* Indigent defendants sometimes lack financial resources to pay for genetic tests that might disprove paternity. In Little v. Streater, 452 U.S. 1 (1981), the U.S. Supreme Court held that the Due Process Clause guarantees the cost of *blood testing* to indigent defendants in paternity actions. However, courts are split regarding whether due process mandates an indigent defendant's *right to counsel* in paternity actions. Compare Ragin v. Lee, 829 A.2d 93, 99 (Conn. Ct. App. 2003) (pointing to prior case law that recognizes the right of indigent parents in paternity cases to be provided counsel at public expense) with Burrell v. Arkansas Dept. of Human Servs., 850 S.W.2d 8 (Ark. Ct. App. 1993) (holding that a putative father did not have a constitutional right to appointed counsel in a paternity proceeding brought by the state, reasoning that no such right attached because father's physical liberty was not in jeopardy).

f. *Jury.* The Supreme Court also has addressed the composition of a jury that is adjudicating a paternity dispute. In J.E.B. v. Alabama ex rel. T.B., 511 U.S. 127 (1994), the Court held that when the state, suing on behalf of the child, uses its peremptory challenges purposely to exclude all men from the jury, it violates the Equal Protection Clause. Most states now provide that the parties in a paternity case are not entitled to a jury.

g. *Standard of proof.* The Supreme Court has held that due process requires only the "preponderance of the evidence" standard of proof in paternity proceedings. In Rivera v. Minnich, 483 U.S. 574 (1987), Jean Marie Minnich, an unmarried woman, filed for child support for her three-week-old son, alleging that Gregory Rivera was the father. Rivera argued that due process required that the standard of proof for paternity establishment be "clear and convincing" evidence, relying on Santosky v. Kramer, 455 U.S. 745 (1982) (mandating the higher standard for termination of parental rights). Rejecting the higher standard, the Court distinguished the state's imposition of parent-child obligations from the termination of those obligations because of the latter's severe consequences (that is, the elimination of preexisting rights). Justice Brennan, dissenting, argued that paternity proceedings result in "the imposition of a lifelong relationship with significant financial, legal, and moral dimensions." 483 U.S. at 583.

h. *Voluntary paternity establishment*. A significant development in paternity establishment is the transformation from judicial proceedings to voluntary affidavits. Beginning in 1992, a few states adopted voluntary programs that targeted mothers at birthing facilities, providing that in-hospital affidavits established a rebuttable presumption of paternity. These programs were so successful that Congress included a requirement in the Omnibus Budget Reconciliation Act of 1993, 42 U.S.C. §666(a)(5)(C)(ii) (2000), for all states to adopt voluntary paternity establishment programs. PRWORA expanded the scope of these programs by providing that (1) a valid, unrescinded, unchallenged acknowledgment of paternity is equivalent to a judicial determination of paternity (rather than merely a presumption of paternity) and is entitled to full faith and credit; (2) parents must be advised of the legal consequences before signing a voluntary acknowledgment; and (3) either parent has the option to rescind within 60 days, but may challenge the voluntary acknowledgment thereafter only judicially and only on limited grounds (fraud, duress, or material mistake of fact). 42 U.S.C. §666(a)(5) (2000). The revised Uniform Parentage Act also complies with the federal mandate by providing for voluntary establishment of paternity and specifies that voluntary affidavits serve as judgments for enforcement purposes. UPA, Art. 3 (cmt) (amended 2002). See generally Jayna Morse Cacioppo, Note, Voluntary Acknowledgments of Paternity: Should Biology Play a Role in Determining Who Can Be a Legal Father?, 38 Ind. L. Rev. 479 (2005).

■ WALLIS v. SMITH
22 P.3d 682 (N.M. Ct. App. 2001)

BOSSON, Judge.

[Peter] Wallis and [Kellie Rae] Smith began an intimate, sexual relationship some time before April 1997. They discussed contraceptive techniques and agreed that Smith would use birth control pills. Wallis and Smith further agreed that their sexual intimacy would last only as long as Smith continued to take birth control pills because Wallis made it clear that he did not want to father a child. Wallis participated in contraception only passively; he relied on Smith to use birth control and took no precautions himself.

As time went by, Smith changed her mind. She chose to stop taking birth control pills, but never informed Wallis of her decision. Wallis continued their intimate relationship, and Smith became pregnant. Smith carried the fetus to term and gave birth to a normal, healthy girl on November 27, 1998. [Wallis sued Smith for money damages, asserting four causes of action — fraud, breach of contract, conversion, and prima facie tort. The district court dismissed for failure to state a claim upon which relief may be granted. Wallis appealed.]

Wallis alleges that he has suffered, and will continue to suffer, substantial economic injury as a proximate result of his unintended fatherhood because New Mexico law requires him to pay child support for the next eighteen years. See NMSA 1978, §40-11-15 (1997). Due to his statutory obligations, Wallis asserts that he has been injured by Smith's conduct, and requests compensatory and punitive damages from her. The district court determined that public policy prohibited the relief sought by Wallis, and dismissed the case with prejudice.

CONTRACEPTIVE FRAUD

. . . At the onset of our discussion it is important to distinguish the factual allegations of this case from other kinds of related lawsuits, and thus underscore the limited reach of this opinion. Wallis's complaint is not about sexually-transmitted disease, e.g., McPherson v. McPherson, 712 A.2d 1043 (Me. 1998), nor does it concern the damages arising from an unwanted pregnancy that led to an abortion, e.g., Alice D. v. William M., 450 N.Y.S.2d 350 (Civ. Ct. 1982), or an undesired pregnancy resulting in medical complications, e.g., Barbara A. v. John G., 193 Cal. Rptr. 422 (Ct. App.1983). This case is not even brought to recover the expense of giving birth. E.g., Chrystal R.M. v. Charlie A.L., 459 S.E.2d 415, 417 (W. Va. 1995); see also §40-11-15(c) (providing recovery for the "reasonable expenses of the mother's pregnancy, birth and confinement"). Wallis's complaint is limited to compensatory damages for the "economic injury" of supporting a normal, healthy child.

Although Wallis insists that he is not attempting to circumvent his child support obligations, we cannot agree. It is self-evident that he seeks to recover for the very financial loss caused him by the statutory obligation to pay child support. At oral argument when pressed by the Court to clarify what damages Wallis was seeking, his counsel stated that Wallis was seeking not punitive, but compensatory damages measured by his "out of pocket loss." Therefore, this case boils down to whether sound public policy would permit our courts to require Smith to indemnify Wallis for child support under the circumstances of this case.

Our legislature has spoken to the public policy that governs the economic consequences of sexual relationships that produce children, and that policy is reflected in New Mexico child support laws. See NMSA 1978, §§40-11-1 to - 23 (1986, as amended through 1997). In 1986, our legislature adopted, with minor revisions, the Uniform Parentage Act (UPA), which outlines the legal procedure to establish a parent-child relationship and the corresponding obligation of child support. See 1986 N.M. Laws, ch. 47, §§1-23; Unif. Parentage Act §§1-30, 9B U.L.A. 287 (West 1987). The UPA imposes a form of strict liability for child support, without regard to which parent bears the greater responsibility for the child's being.

Making each parent financially responsible for the conception and birth of children also illuminates a strong public policy that makes paramount the interests of the child. Our jurisprudence has abandoned the notion that the father of an "illegitimate" child could decline to accept the financial responsibility of raising that child. . . . Placing a duty of support on each parent has the added benefit of insulating the state from the possibility of bearing the financial burden for a child. In our view, it is difficult to harmonize the legislative concern for the child, reflected in the immutable duty of parental support, with Wallis's effort in this lawsuit to shift financial responsibility for his child solely to the mother.

New Mexico is not alone in its view of parental responsibility and the conflict created by lawsuits such as this. To our knowledge, no jurisdiction recognizes contraceptive fraud or breach of promise to practice birth control as a ground for adjusting a natural parent's obligation to pay child support. . . .

Some courts have dismissed contraceptive fraud cases on the ground that the claims reach too far into the realm of an individual's privacy interests. [Stephen K. v. Roni L., 164 Cal. Rptr. 618 (Cal. Ct. App. 1980)]. We agree that individuals are entitled a sphere of privacy into which courts should not tread. A person's choice whether or not to use contraceptives understandably fits into this sphere. We also believe that the "privacy interests involved . . . require a cautious approach," and therefore we elect to rely primarily on the prevailing public policy of child support, while at the same time recognizing the serious privacy concerns implicated and threatened by the underlying lawsuit.

Wallis's attempt to apply traditional contract and tort principles to his contraceptive agreement is unconvincing and, in the end, futile. The contract analogy fails because children, the persons for whose benefit child support guidelines are enacted, have the same needs regardless of whether their conception violated a promise between the parents. Further, a parent being sued for causing the conception and birth of a child is no ordinary tortfeasor; a defendant under these circumstances is legally entitled to collect financial support on behalf of the child. We will not re-enter the jurisprudence of illegitimacy by allowing a parent to opt out of the financial consequences of his or her sexual relationships just because they were unintended. Nor will we recognize a cause of action that trivializes one's personal responsibility in sexual relationships. Indeed, permitting "such actions while simultaneously encouraging paternity actions for support flies in the face of all reason." [Welzenbach v. Powers, 660 A.2d 1133 (N.H. 1995)]. We also observe that if Wallis did not desire children, he was free and able to practice contraceptive techniques on his own.

Wallis tries to make the basis for liability not so much the birth of the child, but the fact that Smith lied, and perpetrated a fraud on him. But not all misrepresentations are actionable. . . . Finally, Wallis argues that our courts have recognized tort claims which measure damages by the economic injury of supporting an unwanted child. See Lovelace Med. Ctr. v. Mendez, 111 N.M. 336, 345, 805 P.2d 603, 612 (1991) [holding that a couple who sought to protect their financial resources by limiting the size of their family through sterilization could sue a negligent physician for economic damages measured by the cost of raising an additional child to the age of majority]. Because *Lovelace* does not speak to the issue of inter-parental liability, which is the crux of Wallis's appeal, it has no bearing on our decision.

Accordingly, we hold that the actions asserted here cannot be used to recoup the financial obligations of raising a child. . . .

Notes and Questions

1. *Basis for child support?* Paternity establishment generally gives rise to a legal obligation to pay child support. Should the child support obligation be based on an adult's biological or social relationship to the child? Should either relationship alone be enough? For example, should a biological father who had sexual intercourse with the child's mother only once and never had any relationship with the child have a legal obligation to support the child? Does a man assume the risk whenever he engages in sexual intercourse?

Should the child support obligation be based on the relationship of the parents, marital or otherwise? Is it more important to identify *a* father than to identify the *"right"* father? See Rivera v. Minnich, 483 U.S. 574 (1987) (upholding preponderance of the evidence standard). See generally Katharine K. Baker, Bargaining or Biology? The History and Future of Paternity Law and Parental Status, 14 Cornell J.L. & Pub. Pol'y 1 (2004); Nandy E. Dowd, From Genes, Marriage and Money to Nurture: Redefining Fatherhood, 10 Cardozo Women's L.J. 132 (2003). For discussion of the child support obligations of same-sex partners, see *Elisa B.* infra this chapter.

2. *Preconception agreements for support.* Suppose Wallis knew that Smith wanted to conceive a child but the two had entered into a written preconception agreement relieving him of support. If a mother chooses not to enforce the support obligation against the father (or her same-sex partner, as the case may be), does that relieve the father (or the same-sex partner) of financial responsibility? Should it matter whether the mother would otherwise require public assistance to support the child? See Budnick v. Silverman, 805 So. 2d 1112 (Fla. Dist. Ct. App. 2002) (refusing to enforce a preconception agreement with which the mother failed to comply, reasoning that the agreement did not reflect the best interests of the child).

3. *Contraceptive fraud.* Should a father's child support obligation be affected by the fact that the mother deceived him about her use of birth control? *Wallis* illustrates the general rule that the mother's contraceptive fraud does not serve as a defense to a father's support obligation. See also L. Pamela P. v. Frank S., 449 N.E.2d 713 (N.Y. Ct. App. 1983). Courts traditionally refuse to grant tort recovery for misrepresentations of contraceptive use unless serious physical injury occurs as the result of the misrepresentation. What explains the court's reluctance? See generally Jane E. Larson, "Women Understand So Little, They Call My Good Nature 'Deceit'": A Feminist Rethinking of Seduction, 93 Colum. L. Rev. 374 (1993) (exploration of sexual fraud).

4. *Other wrongful conduct of mother.* Should the mother's wrongful conduct *ever* relieve the father of liability for child support? That is, should the general rule apply when the woman obtains unauthorized use of "purloined sperm" from (a) a man who is unconscious? See, e.g., S.F. v. State ex rel. T.M., 695 So.2d 1186 (Ala. Civ. App. 1996)); (b) a 15-year-old boy who is a victim of statutory rape? See, e.g., In re Paternity of K.B., 104 P.2d 1132 (Okla. Ct. App. 2004); (c) a fertility clinic from deposited sperm intended for an earlier usage but long after the couple's intimate relationship terminates? See, e.g., In re Parentage of J.M.K., 89 P.3d 309 (Wash. App. Ct. 2004).

See generally Donald C. Hubin, Daddy Dilemmas: Untangling the Puzzles of Paternity, 13 Cornell J.L. & Pub. Pol'y 29, 52-62 (2003) (coining the term "purloined sperm" cases and discussing them); Laura W. Morgan, It's Ten O'Clock: Do You Know Where Your Sperm Are? Toward a Strict Liability Theory of Parentage, 11 Divorce Litig. 1 (1999); Sally Sheldon, "Sperm Bandits," Birth Control Fraud and the Battle of the Sexes, 21 Leg. Stud. 460 (2001); Ellen London, Comment, A Critique of the Strict Liability Standard for Determining Child Support in Cases of Male Victims of Sexual Assault and Statutory Rape, 152 U. Pa. L. Rev. 1957 (2004); Brenda Saiz, Note, Tort Law: Tort Liability When Fraudulent Misrepresentation Regarding Birth Control Results in the Birth of a Healthy Child — Wallis v. Smith, 32 N.M. L. Rev. 549 (2002).

5. *Damages*. Should a parent's support obligations in cases of the other parent's birth-related fraud, if not be dismissed, at least be reduced? To what extent does (should) the mother have a duty to mitigate damages? Would the result change if the alleged father had offered to pay for an abortion? What if the defendant had used birth control that failed? Does any man who engages in sexual intercourse "assume the risk" with all attendant duties? If so, why should actual paternity matter—why not impose shared liability on all men who might have fathered a particular child? See, e.g., State ex rel. Dept. of Soc. Servs. v. Howard, 898 So. 2d 443 (La. Ct. App. 2004) (holding that a husband's status as the legitimate father was not affected by an action to establish biological paternity, and a biological father did not escape his support obligations merely because a legal father could share the responsibility).

6. *Tort claims*. Should a father in Wallis's position be permitted to maintain a tort action for fraud or infliction of emotional distress instead? How much is the emotional harm of unwanted fatherhood worth? See, e.g., Day v. Heller, 653 N.W.2d 475 (Neb. 2002) (rejecting father's suit). In dismissing Wallis's suit, the court did not address his claim of conversion (i.e., use of his "property" in an unauthorized manner). Did Smith "convert" sperm? See Hubin, supra, at 52 (raising the question of what constitutes "authorized use" of sperm and pointing out that if voluntary transfer of a res led to a property right, parking valets would own more, and higher quality, cars). What result if the mother sues for "wrongful conception" of a healthy baby based on the father's false statement that he had a vasectomy? See C.A.M. v. R.A.W., 568 A.2d 556 (N.J. Super. Ct. App. Div. 1990).

7. *Constitutional claims*. Does Wallis have any constitutional claims? Would the right to privacy support or prohibit recognition of tort claims, for example? Does a man have a constitutional right to avoid fatherhood? Is the Fourteenth Amendment violated if the woman has the right to choose parenthood after conception via abortion or adoption but the man has no corresponding right? See Sorrel v. Henson, 1998 WL 886561 (Tenn. Ct. App. 1998).

2. Limitations on Unmarried Parents' Rights

■ **STANLEY v. ILLINOIS**
405 U.S. 645 (1972)

Mr. Justice WHITE delivered the opinion of the Court.

Joan Stanley lived with Peter Stanley intermittently for 18 years during which time they had three children. When Joan Stanley died, Peter Stanley lost not only her but also his children. Under Illinois law the children of unwed fathers become wards of the State upon the death of the mother. Accordingly, upon Joan Stanley's death, in a dependency proceeding instituted by the State of Illinois, Stanley's children were declared wards of the State and placed with court-appointed guardians. Stanley appealed, claiming that he had never been shown to be an unfit parent and that since married fathers and unwed mothers could not be deprived of their children without such a showing, he had been deprived of the equal protection of the laws guaranteed him by the Fourteenth Amendment. . . .

Stanley presses his equal protection claim here. The State continues to respond that unwed fathers are presumed unfit to raise their children. . . . We granted certiorari to determine whether this method of procedure by presumption could be allowed to stand in light of the fact that Illinois allows married fathers — whether divorced, widowed, or separated — and mothers — even if unwed — the benefit of the presumption that they are fit to raise their children.

We must [examine this question]: Is a presumption that distinguishes and burdens all unwed fathers constitutionally repugnant? We conclude that, as a matter of due process of law, Stanley was entitled to a hearing on his fitness as a parent before his children were taken from him and that by denying him a hearing and extending it to all other parents whose custody of their children is challenged, the State denied Stanley the equal protection of the laws guaranteed by the Fourteenth Amendment.

Illinois has two principal methods of removing nondelinquent children from the homes of their parents. In a dependency proceeding it may demonstrate that the children are wards of the State because they have no surviving parent or guardian. Ill. Rev. Stat., c. 37, §§702-1, 702-5. In a neglect proceeding it may show that children should be wards of the State because the present parent(s) or guardian does not provide suitable care. Ill. Rev. Stat., c. 37, §§702-1, 702-4.

The State's right — indeed duty — to protect minor children through a judicial determination of their interests in a neglect proceeding is not challenged here. Rather, we are faced with a dependency statute that empowers state officials to circumvent neglect proceedings on the theory that an unwed father is not a "parent" whose existing relationship with his children must be considered. "Parents," says the State, "means the father and mother of a legitimate child, or the survivor of them, or the natural mother of an illegitimate child, and includes any adoptive parent," Ill. Rev. Stat., c. 37, §701-14, but the term does not include unwed fathers.

Under Illinois law, therefore, while the children of all parents can be taken from them in neglect proceedings, that is only after notice, hearing, and proof of such unfitness as a parent as amounts to neglect, an unwed father is uniquely subject to the more simplistic dependency proceeding. By use of this proceeding, the State, on showing that the father was not married to the mother, need not prove unfitness in fact, because it is presumed at law. Thus, the unwed father's claim of parental qualification is avoided as "irrelevant."

In considering this procedure under the Due Process Clause, we recognize, as we have in other cases, that due process of law does not require a hearing "in every conceivable case of government impairment of private interest." Cafeteria Workers v. McElroy, 367 U.S. 886 (1961). [That case] firmly established that "what procedures due process may require under any given set of circumstances must begin with a determination of the precise nature of the government function involved as well as of the private interest that has been affected by governmental action." . . .

The private interest here, that of a man in the children he has sired and raised, undeniably warrants deference and, absent a powerful countervailing interest, protection. . . . The Court has frequently emphasized the importance of the family. The rights to conceive and to raise one's children have been deemed "essential," Meyer v. Nebraska, 262 U.S. 390, 399 (1923), "basic civil rights of man," Skinner v. Oklahoma, 316 U.S. 535, 541 (1942), and "[r]ights far more precious . . . than property rights," May v. Anderson, 345 U.S. 528, 533 (1953). . . .

Nor has the law refused to recognize those family relationships unlegitimized by a marriage ceremony. The Court has declared unconstitutional a state statute denying natural, but illegitimate, children a wrongful-death action for the death of their mother, emphasizing that such children cannot be denied the right of other children because familial bonds in such cases were often as warm, enduring, and important as those arising within a more formally organized family unit. Levy v. Louisiana, 391 U.S. 68, 71-72 (1968). "To say that the test of equal protection should be the 'legal' rather than the biological relationship is to avoid the issue. For the Equal Protection Clause necessarily limits the authority of a State to draw such 'legal' lines as it chooses." Glona v. American Guarantee Co., 391 U.S. 73, 75-76 (1968). These authorities make it clear that, at the least, Stanley's interest in retaining custody of his children is cognizable and substantial.

For its part, the State has made its interest quite plain: Illinois has declared that the aim of the Juvenile Court Act is to protect "the moral, emotional, mental, and physical welfare of the minor and the best interests of the community" and to "strengthen the minor's family ties whenever possible, removing him from the custody of his parents only when his welfare or safety or the protection of the public cannot be adequately safeguarded without removal . . ." Ill. Rev. Stat., c. 37, §701-2. These are legitimate interests well within the power of the State to implement. We do not question the assertion that neglectful parents may be separated from their children.

But we are here not asked to evaluate the legitimacy of the state ends, rather, to determine whether the means used to achieve these ends are constitutionally defensible. What is the state interest in separating children from fathers without a hearing designed to determine whether the father is unfit in a particular disputed case? We observe that the State registers no gain towards its declared goals when it separates children from the custody of fit parents. Indeed, if Stanley is a fit father, the State spites its own articulated goals when it needlessly separates him from his family. . . .

It may be, as the State insists, that most unmarried fathers are unsuitable and neglectful parents. It may also be that Stanley is such a parent and that his children should be placed in other hands. But all unmarried fathers are not in this category; some are wholly suited to have custody of their children. This much the State readily concedes, and nothing in this record indicates that Stanley is or has been a neglectful father who has not cared for his children. Given the opportunity to make his case, Stanley may have been seen to be deserving of custody of his offspring. Had this been so, the State's statutory policy would have been furthered by leaving custody in him. . . .

It may be argued that unmarried fathers are so seldom fit that Illinois need not undergo the administrative inconvenience of inquiry in any case, including Stanley's. The establishment of prompt efficacious procedures to achieve legitimate state ends is a proper state interest worthy of cognizance in constitutional adjudication. But the Constitution recognizes higher values than speed and efficiency. . . .

Procedure by presumption is always cheaper and easier than individualized determination. But when, as here, the procedure forecloses the determinative issues of competence and care, when it explicitly disdains present realities in deference to past formalities, it needlessly risks running roughshod over the important interests of both parent and child. It therefore cannot stand.

. . . The State's interest in caring for Stanley's children is de minimis if Stanley is shown to be a fit father. It insists on presuming rather than proving Stanley's unfitness solely because it is more convenient to presume than to prove. Under the Due Process Clause that advantage is insufficient to justify refusing a father a hearing when the issue at stake is the dismemberment of his family.

The State of Illinois assumes custody of the children of married parents, divorced parents, and unmarried mothers only after a hearing and proof of neglect. The children of unmarried fathers, however, are declared dependent children without a hearing on parental fitness and without proof of neglect. Stanley's claim in the state courts and here is that failure to afford him a hearing on his parental qualifications while extending it to other parents denied him equal protection of the laws. We have concluded that all Illinois parents are constitutionally entitled to a hearing on their fitness before their children are removed from their custody. It follows that denying such a hearing to Stanley and those like him while granting it to other Illinois parents is inescapably contrary to the Equal Protection Clause. . . .

■ MICHAEL H. v. GERALD D.
491 U.S. 110, reh'g denied, 492 U.S. 937 (1989)

Justice SCALIA announced the judgment of the Court and delivered an opinion, in which THE CHIEF JUSTICE joins, and in all but note 6 of which Justice O'CONNOR and Justice KENNEDY join.

Under California law, a child born to a married woman living with her husband is presumed to be a child of the marriage. Cal. Evid. Code Ann. §621 (West Supp. 1989). The presumption of legitimacy may be rebutted only by the husband or wife, and then only in limited circumstances. The instant appeal presents the claim that this presumption infringes upon the due process rights of a man who wishes to establish his paternity of a child born to the wife of another man, and the claim that it infringes upon the constitutional right of the child to maintain a relationship with her natural father.

The facts of this case are, we must hope, extraordinary. On May 9, 1976, in Las Vegas, Nevada, Carole D., an international model, and Gerald D., a top executive in a French oil company, were married. The couple established a home in Playa del Rey, California, in which they resided as husband and wife when one or the other was not out of the country on business. In the summer of 1978, Carole became involved in an adulterous affair with a neighbor, Michael H. In September 1980, she conceived a child, Victoria D., who was born on May 11, 1981. Gerald was listed as father on the birth certificate and has always held Victoria out to the world as his daughter. Soon after delivery of the child, however, Carole informed Michael that she believed he might be the father.

In the first three years of her life, Victoria remained always with Carole, but found herself within a variety of quasi-family units. In October 1981, Gerald moved to New York City to pursue his business interests, but Carole chose to remain in California. At the end of that month, Carole and Michael had blood tests of themselves and Victoria, which showed a 98.07% probability that Michael was Victoria's father. In January 1982, Carole visited Michael in St. Thomas, where his primary business interests were based. There Michael held Victoria out as his child. In March, however, Carole left Michael and returned to California, where she took up residence with yet another man, Scott K. Later that spring, and again in the summer, Carole and Victoria spent time with Gerald in New York City, as well as on vacation in Europe. In the fall, they returned to Scott in California.

In November 1982, rebuffed in his attempts to visit Victoria, Michael filed a filiation action in California Superior Court to establish his paternity and right to visitation. In March 1983, the court appointed an attorney and guardian ad litem to represent Victoria's interests. Victoria then filed a cross-complaint asserting that if she had more than one psychological or de facto father, she was entitled to maintain her filial relationship, with all of the attendant rights, duties, and obligations, with both. In May 1983, Carole filed a motion for summary judgment. During this period, from March through July 1983, Carole was again living with Gerald in New York. In August, however, she returned to California, became involved once again with Michael, and instructed her attorneys to remove the summary judgment motion from the calendar.

For the ensuing eight months, when Michael was not in St. Thomas he lived with Carole and Victoria in Carole's apartment in Los Angeles and held Victoria out as his daughter. In April 1984, Carole and Michael signed a stipulation that Michael was Victoria's natural father. Carole left Michael the next month, however, and instructed her attorneys not to file the stipulation. In June 1984, Carole reconciled with Gerald and joined him in New York, where they now live with Victoria and two other children since born into the marriage.

In May 1984, Michael and Victoria, through her guardian ad litem, sought visitation rights for Michael *pendente lite*. To assist in determining whether visitation would be in Victoria's best interests, the Superior Court appointed a psychologist to evaluate Victoria, Gerald, Michael, and Carole. The psychologist recommended that Carole retain sole custody, but that Michael be allowed continued contact with Victoria pursuant to a restricted visitation schedule. The court concurred and ordered that Michael be provided with limited visitation privileges *pendente lite*.

On October 19, 1984, Gerald, who had intervened in the action, moved for summary judgment on the ground that under Cal. Evid. Code §621 there were no triable issues of fact as to Victoria's paternity. This law provides that "the issue of a wife cohabiting with her husband, who is not impotent or sterile, is conclusively presumed to be a child of the marriage." The presumption may be rebutted by blood tests, but only if a motion for such tests is made, within two years from the date of the child's birth, either by the husband or, if the natural father has filed an affidavit acknowledging paternity, by the wife.

On January 28, 1985, having found that affidavits submitted by Carole and Gerald sufficed to demonstrate that the two were cohabiting at conception and birth and that Gerald was neither sterile nor impotent, the Superior Court granted Gerald's motion for summary judgment, rejecting Michael's and Victoria's challenges to the constitutionality of §621. The court also denied their motions for continued visitation pending the appeal under Cal. Civ. Code §4601, which provides that a court may, in its discretion, grant "reasonable visitation rights . . . to any . . . person having an interest in the welfare of the child." Cal. Civ. Code Ann. §4601 (West Supp. 1989). It found that allowing such visitation would "violate the

intention of the Legislature by impugning the integrity of the family unit."
[Michael and Victoria appeal.]

Before us, Michael and Victoria both raise equal protection and due process challenges. We do not reach Michael's equal protection claim, however, as it was neither raised nor passed upon below. . . . We address first the [due process] claims of Michael. At the outset, it is necessary to clarify what he sought and what he was denied. California law, like nature itself, makes no provision for dual fatherhood. Michael was seeking to be declared the father of Victoria. The immediate benefit he evidently sought to obtain from that status was visitation rights. But if Michael were successful in being declared the father, other rights would follow — most importantly, the right to be considered as the parent who should have custody. . . . All parental rights, including visitation, were automatically denied by denying Michael status as the father. . . .

Michael contends as a matter of substantive due process that, because he has established a parental relationship with Victoria, protection of Gerald's and Carole's marital union is an insufficient state interest to support termination of that relationship. This argument is, of course, predicated on the assertion that Michael has a constitutionally protected liberty interest in his relationship with Victoria. . . .

In an attempt to limit and guide interpretation of the [Due Process] Clause, we have insisted not merely that the interest denominated as a "liberty" be "fundamental" (a concept that, in isolation, is hard to objectify), but also that it be an interest traditionally protected by our society. . . . This insistence that the asserted liberty interest be rooted in history and tradition is evident, as elsewhere, in our cases according constitutional protection to certain parental rights. Michael reads the landmark case of Stanley v. Illinois, 405 U.S. 645 (1972), and the subsequent cases of Quilloin v. Walcott, 434 U.S. 246 (1978), Caban v. Mohammed, 441 U.S. 380 (1979), and Lehr v. Robertson, 463 U.S. 248 (1983), as establishing that a liberty interest is created by biological fatherhood plus an established parental relationship — factors that exist in the present case as well. We think that distorts the rationale of those cases. As we view them, they rest not upon such isolated factors but upon the historic respect — indeed, sanctity would not be too strong a term — traditionally accorded to the relationships that develop within the unitary family.[3] . . .

Thus, the legal issue in the present case reduces to whether the relationship between persons in the situation of Michael and Victoria has been treated as a protected family unit under the historic practices of our society, or whether on any other basis it has been accorded special protection. We think it impossible to find that it has. In fact, quite to the contrary, our traditions have protected

---

3. Justice Brennan asserts that only "a pinched conception of 'the family'" would exclude Michael, Carole, and Victoria from protection. We disagree. The family unit accorded traditional respect in our society, which we have referred to as the "unitary family," is typified, of course, by the marital family, but also includes the household of unmarried parents and their children. Perhaps the concept can be expanded even beyond this, but it will bear no resemblance to traditionally respected relationships — and will thus cease to have any constitutional significance — if it is stretched so far as to include the relationship established between a married woman, her lover, and their child, during a 3-month sojourn in St. Thomas, or during a subsequent 8-month period when, if he happened to be in Los Angeles, he stayed with her and the child.

the marital family (Gerald, Carole, and the child they acknowledge to be theirs) against the sort of claim Michael asserts.[4]

The presumption of legitimacy was a fundamental principle of the common law. Traditionally, that presumption could be rebutted only by proof that a husband was incapable of procreation or had had no access to his wife during the relevant period. As explained by Blackstone, nonaccess could only be proved "if the husband be out of the kingdom of England (or, as the law somewhat loosely phrases it, *extra quatuor maria* [beyond the four seas]) for above nine months. . . ." 1 Blackstone's Commentaries 456 (J. Chitty ed. 1826). And, under the common law both in England and here, [neither parent could testify to bastardize the child]. The primary policy rationale underlying the common law's severe restrictions on rebuttal of the presumption appears to have been an aversion to declaring children illegitimate, thereby depriving them of rights of inheritance and succession, and likely making them wards of the state. A secondary policy concern was the interest in promoting the "peace and tranquillity of States and families," a goal that is obviously impaired by facilitating suits against husband and wife asserting that their children are illegitimate. . . .

We have found nothing in the older sources, nor in the older cases, addressing specifically the power of the natural father to assert parental rights over a child born into a woman's existing marriage with another man. Since it is Michael's burden to establish that such a power (at least where the natural father has established a relationship with the child) is so deeply embedded within our traditions as to be a fundamental right, the lack of evidence alone might defeat his case. But the evidence shows that even in modern times — when, as we have noted, the rigid protection of the marital family has in other respects been relaxed — the ability of a person in Michael's position to claim paternity has not been generally acknowledged. . . .

Moreover, even if it were clear that one in Michael's position generally possesses, and has generally always possessed, standing to challenge the marital child's legitimacy, that would still not establish Michael's case. As noted earlier, what is at issue here is not entitlement to a state pronouncement that Victoria was begotten by Michael. It is no conceivable denial of constitutional right for a State to decline to declare facts unless some legal consequence hinges upon the requested declaration. What Michael asserts here is a right to have himself declared the natural father and *thereby to obtain parental prerogatives*. What he must establish, therefore, is not that our society has traditionally allowed a natural father in his circumstances to establish paternity, but that it has traditionally accorded such a father parental rights, or at least has not traditionally denied them. . . . What counts is whether the States in fact award substantive parental rights to the natural father of a child conceived within, and born into, an extant

---

4. Justice Brennan insists that in determining whether a liberty interest exists we must look at Michael's relationship with Victoria in isolation, without reference to the circumstance that Victoria's mother was married to someone else when the child was conceived, and that that woman and her husband wish to raise the child as their own. We cannot imagine what compels this strange procedure of looking at the act which is assertedly the subject of a liberty interest in isolation from its effect upon other people — rather like inquiring whether there is a liberty interest in firing a gun where the case at hand happens to involve its discharge into another person's body. The logic of Justice Brennan's position leads to the conclusion that if Michael had begotten Victoria by rape, that fact would in no way affect his possession of a liberty interest in his relationship with her.

marital union that wishes to embrace the child. We are not aware of a single case, old or new, that has done so. This is not the stuff of which fundamental rights qualifying as liberty interests are made.[6] . . .

We do not accept Justice Brennan's criticism that this result "squashes" the liberty that consists of "the freedom not to conform." It seems to us that reflects the erroneous view that there is only one side to this controversy—that one disposition can expand a "liberty" of sorts without contracting an equivalent "liberty" on the other side. Such a happy choice is rarely available. Here, to provide protection to an adulterous natural father is to deny protection to a marital father, and vice versa. If Michael has a "freedom not to conform" (whatever that means), Gerald must equivalently have a "freedom to conform." One of them will pay a price for asserting that "freedom." . . . Our disposition does not choose between these two "freedoms," but leaves that to the people of California. Justice Brennan's approach chooses one of them as the constitutional imperative, on no apparent basis except that the unconventional is to be preferred.

We have never had occasion to decide whether a child has a liberty interest, symmetrical with that of her parent, in maintaining her filial relationship. We need not do so here because, even assuming that such a right exists, Victoria's claim must fail. Victoria's due process challenge is, if anything, weaker than Michael's. Her basic claim is not that California has erred in preventing her from establishing that Michael, not Gerald, should stand as her legal father. Rather, she claims a due process right to maintain filial relationships with both Michael and Gerald. This assertion merits little discussion, for, whatever the merits of the guardian ad litem's belief that such an arrangement can be of great psychological benefit to a child, the claim that a State must recognize multiple fatherhood has no support in the history or traditions of this country. Moreover, even if we were to construe Victoria's argument as forwarding the lesser proposition that, whatever her status vis-à-vis Gerald, she has a liberty interest in maintaining a filial relationship with her natural father, Michael, we find that, at best, her claim is the obverse of Michael's and fails for the same reasons.

Victoria claims in addition that her equal protection rights have been violated because, unlike her mother and presumed father, she had no opportunity to rebut the presumption of her legitimacy. We find this argument wholly without merit. We reject, at the outset, Victoria's suggestion that her equal protection challenge must be assessed under a standard of strict scrutiny because, in denying her the right to maintain a filial relationship with Michael, the State is discriminating against her on the basis of her illegitimacy. See Gomez v. Perez,

6. Justice Brennan criticizes our methodology in using historical traditions specifically relating to the rights of an adulterous natural father, rather than inquiring more generally "whether parenthood is an interest that historically has received our attention and protection." . . .

We do not understand why, having rejected our focus upon the societal tradition regarding the natural father's rights vis-à-vis a child whose mother is married to another man, Justice Brennan would choose to focus instead upon "parenthood." Why should the relevant category not be even more general—perhaps "family relationships"; or "personal relationships"; or even "emotional attachments in general"? Though the dissent has no basis for the level of generality it would select, we do: We refer to the most specific level at which a relevant tradition protecting, or denying protection to, the asserted right can be identified. If, for example, there were no societal tradition, either way, regarding the rights of the natural father of a child adulterously conceived, we would have to consult, and (if possible) reason from, the traditions regarding natural fathers in general. But there is such a more specific tradition, and it unqualifiedly denies protection to such a parent. . . .

409 U.S. 535, 538 (1973). Illegitimacy is a legal construct, not a natural trait. Under California law, Victoria is not illegitimate, and she is treated in the same manner as all other legitimate children: she is entitled to maintain a filial relationship with her legal parents. . . . Since it pursues a legitimate end [protecting the integrity of the marital family] by rational means, California's decision to treat Victoria differently from her parents is not a denial of equal protection. . . .

[In an omitted concurring opinion, Justice O'Connor, joined by Justice Kennedy, objects that the plurality's historical analysis might foreclose the identification of future liberty interests. In a separate concurring opinion, Justice Stevens concludes that the trial court had given Michael H. his constitutionally protected right to be heard.]

Justice BRENNAN, with whom Justice MARSHALL and Justice BLACKMUN join, dissenting. . . .

Today's plurality . . . does not ask whether parenthood is an interest that historically has received our attention and protection; the answer to that question is too clear for dispute. Instead, the plurality asks whether the specific variety of parenthood under consideration—a natural father's relationship with a child whose mother is married to another man—has enjoyed such protection.

If we had looked to tradition with such specificity in past cases, many a decision would have reached a different result. Surely the use of contraceptives by unmarried couples, or even by married couples; the freedom from corporal punishment in schools; . . . and even the right to raise one's natural but illegitimate children, were not "interest[s] traditionally protected by our society" at the time of their consideration by this Court. . . .

In construing the Fourteenth Amendment to offer shelter only to those interests specifically protected by historical practice, moreover, the plurality ignores the kind of society in which our Constitution exists. We are not an assimilative, homogeneous society, but a facilitative, pluralistic one, in which we must be willing to abide someone else's unfamiliar or even repellant practice because the same tolerant impulse protects our own idiosyncracies. Even if we can agree, therefore, that "family" and "parenthood" are part of the good life, it is absurd to assume that we can agree on the content of those terms and destructive to pretend that we do. In a community such as ours, "liberty" must include the freedom not to conform. The plurality today squashes this freedom by requiring specific approval from history before protecting anything in the name of liberty. . . .

. . . This is not a case in which we face a "new" kind of interest, one that requires us to consider for the first time whether the Constitution protects it. On the contrary, we confront an interest—that of a parent and child in their relationship with each other—that was among the first that this Court acknowledged in its cases defining the "liberty" protected by the Constitution [citing Meyer v. Nebraska, Skinner v. Oklahoma, Prince v. Massachusetts].

The evidence is undisputed that Michael, Victoria, and Carole did live together as a family; that is, they shared the same household, Victoria called Michael "Daddy," Michael contributed to Victoria's support, and he is eager to continue his relationship with her. Yet they are not, in the plurality's view, a "unitary family," whereas Gerald, Carole, and Victoria do compose such a family. The only difference between these two sets of relationships, however, is the fact of marriage. . . . However, the very premise of *Stanley* and the cases following it is that marriage is not decisive in answering the question whether the Constitution protects the parental relationship under consideration. . . .

The plurality's exclusive rather than inclusive definition of the "unitary family" is out of step with other decisions as well. This pinched conception of "the family," crucial as it is in rejecting Michael's and Victoria's claims of a liberty interest, is jarring in light of our many cases preventing the States from denying important interests or statuses to those whose situations do not fit the government's narrow view of the family. From Loving v. Virginia, 388 U.S. 1 (1967), to Levy v. Louisiana, 391 U.S. 68 (1968), and Glona v. American Guarantee & Liability Ins. Co., 391 U.S. 73 (1968), and from Gomez v. Perez, 409 U.S. 535 (1973), to Moore v. East Cleveland, 431 U.S. 494 (1977), we have declined to respect a State's notion, as manifested in its allocation of privileges and burdens, of what the family should be. Today's rhapsody on the "unitary family" is out of tune with such decisions. . . .

Notes and Questions

1. *Father's rights.* To what extent does *Stanley* recognize substantive rights for unwed fathers? Whose rights are being vindicated? The father's? The children's? To what extent does *Stanley* accord equal status to unwed fathers and mothers? Is *Stanley* a procedural due process case, dealing with the hearing rights of parents? A substantive due process case, limiting the circumstances when the state may remove children from parents? Or both?

2. *Background.* The Court addressed the constitutional claims of unmarried fathers in three cases decided after *Stanley* but before *Michael H.*:

a. In Quilloin v. Walcott, 434 U.S. 246 (1978), the Court unanimously upheld a Georgia adoption statute requiring only the consent of the mother unless the father had legitimated the child by marriage and acknowledgment or by court order. The mother in *Quilloin*, shortly after her child's birth, married a man who was not the child's father. The mother's new husband petitioned for adoption after the child had lived with him for approximately nine years. The biological father, who had been given notice of the adoption proceeding, responded by requesting that the adoption be denied, that he be declared the child's legitimate father and that he be granted visitation. The natural father, although he never lived with the mother and child and never legitimated the child, had made some support payments and had visited the child on several occasions. The child expressed a desire to be adopted.

The Supreme Court affirmed the stepparent adoption as consistent with the child's best interests. The Court denied the father's procedural due process and equal protection claims. Rejecting the father's argument that due process prohibited termination of his parental rights without a finding of unfitness, the Court noted that the father had received a hearing when he sought to legitimate the child in response to the adoption petition and also distinguished the need for a hearing in this case from the need in *Stanley* because of this father's failure ever to have or seek child custody. The Court also rejected the father's equal protection claim (that is, that the distinction between unmarried and married fathers was unconstitutional) on the ground that his interests were distinguishable from those of a married father because the latter had borne legal responsibility for the rearing of his children. "[L]egal custody of children is, of course, a central aspect of the marital relationship, and even a father whose marriage has broken apart will have borne full responsibility for the rearing of his children during the period of the marriage." Id. at 256.

b. In Caban v. Mohammed, 441 U.S. 380 (1979), an unmarried father brought a successful equal protection challenge to a New York law that permitted the adoption of his children, without his consent, by the husband of the children's mother. Abdiel Caban had lived with Maria Mohammed for five years and had fathered their two children. When the couple separated, the mother began living with another man whom she eventually married. Caban continued to see his children frequently, contributed to their support, and at one point had custody of them. After the mother and her new husband petitioned for adoption, Caban and his new wife cross-petitioned.

The Supreme Court found the statute, which required the consent of only the mother of a nonmarital child, an overbroad gender-based generalization. The Court rejected the state's asserted justifications for the statute: a mother has a closer relationship with her children and the state has an interest in promoting adoption of nonmarital children. The Court pointed out that in this case, both the mother and father had participated in the children's care and support, and also that the state's interest in promoting adoption was not advanced in cases such as this. The Court elaborated:

> In those cases where the father never has come forward to participate in the rearing of his child, nothing in the Equal Protection Clause precludes the State from withholding from him the privilege of vetoing the adoption of that child. . . . But in cases such as this, where the father has established a substantial relationship with the child and has admitted his paternity, a State should have no difficulty in identifying the father even of children born out of wedlock. Thus, no showing has been made that the different treatment afforded unmarried fathers and unmarried mothers under [the statute] bears a substantial relationship to the proclaimed interest of the State in promoting the adoption of illegitimate children.

Id. at 392-393.

c. Finally, in Lehr v. Robertson, 463 U.S. 248 (1983), the Court upheld another New York adoption statute dispensing with notice of adoption proceedings for some fathers of nonmarital children. In *Lehr*, Lorraine Robertson married Richard Robertson eight months after the birth of her nonmarital child. The biological father, Jonathan Lehr, had never contributed to the child's support and had seen her only infrequently. When the child was two, the Robertsons filed an adoption petition. Lehr claimed that the Due Process and Equal Protection Clauses, as interpreted in *Stanley*, gave him a right to notice and an opportunity to be heard. New York law required notice for fathers who had registered with a "putative father registry," as well as those who were adjudicated to be the father, identified on the birth certificate, lived openly with the child and the child's mother, or were married to the mother before the child was six months old. Lehr fit none of these categories. Unanswered by *Quilloin* and *Caban* was the extent of constitutional protection required for a father, such as Lehr, who manifests only a biological relationship with his child. That is, was he entitled to notice and an opportunity to be heard before the child could be adopted?

The Supreme Court rejected both of Lehr's constitutional challenges. The Court concluded that due process does not require notice to a biological father if he has not assumed any responsibility for the care of his child.

> The significance of the biological connection is that it offers the natural father an opportunity that no other male possesses to develop a relationship with his offspring. If he grasps that opportunity and accepts some measure of responsibility for the child's future, he may enjoy the blessings of the parent-child relationship and make uniquely valuable contributions to the child's development. If he fails to do so, the Federal Constitution will not automatically compel a state to listen to his opinion of where the child's best interests lie.

Id. at 262. Further, the Court reasoned that the statute did not constitute a denial of equal protection because it did not distinguish between a mother and father who were similarly situated. Lehr had never established a custodial, personal, or financial relationship with the child. "If one parent has an established custodial relationship with the child and the other parent has either abandoned or never established a relationship, the Equal Protection Clause does not prevent a state from according the two parents different legal rights." Id. at 267-268. The Court distinguished "between the developed parent-child relationship that was implicated in *Stanley* and *Caban*, and the potential relationship involved in *Quilloin* and this case. . . ." Id. at 261.

A troublesome issue, raised by the dissent in *Lehr* but unaddressed by the majority, concerns the degree of constitutional protection to be afforded if the mother actually prevents the father from establishing a relationship with the child. The dissenting opinion in *Lehr* points out that Lehr's efforts to establish a parent-child relationship were thwarted by the mother who concealed her whereabouts from him after the birth (discussed also in Chapter IX).

The *Quilloin-Caban-Lehr* trilogy of cases stand for the principle that an unwed father is entitled to constitutional protection of his parental rights so long as he is willing to accept the responsibilities of parenthood (the "biology plus test"). The extent of this constitutional protection varies according to the degree to which the unwed father manifests a custodial, personal, or financial relationship with the child ("the indicia of parenthood"). To what extent is *Michael H.* consistent with these precedents?

3. *Defining "family"*. Professor Janet L. Dolgin sees familial relationships as the determinative variables in these cases:

> [T]he unwed father cases, from *Stanley* through *Michael H.*, delineate three factors that make an unwed man a father. These are the man's biological relation to the child, his social relation to the child, and his relation to the child's mother. . . . In this regard, *Michael H.* clarifies the earlier cases. A biological father does protect his paternity by developing a social relationship with his child, but this step demands the creation of a family, a step itself depending upon an appropriate relationship between the man and his child's mother.

Janet L. Dolgin, Just A Gene: Judicial Assumptions About Parenthood, 40 UCLA L. Rev. 637, 671 (1993).

4. *Defining "father."* Like Moore v. City of East Cleveland, supra, which overturned the city's definition of "family," both *Stanley* and *Michael H.* test the

government's power to write its own definition of certain terms: "parent" in *Stanley* and "father" in *Michael H.* Can you reconcile *Michael H.* with the two earlier cases? Is footnote 3 in the plurality opinion persuasive?

5. *Presumption of legitimacy.* Professor Michael Grossberg has traced the history of the presumption of legitimacy to the strong reluctance to stigmatize illegitimate children in the post-Revolutionary period. He adds that this reluctance ultimately found expression in the creation of common law marriage, the exclusion of evidence that would bastardize the child of a married woman, the recognition of the offspring of annulled marriages as legitimate, and the adoption of the doctrine of putative marriage. As Grossberg elaborates:

> In the agonizing conflict between a man's right to limit his paternity only to his actual offspring and the right of a child born to a married woman to claim family member-ship, the common law, first in England and then in America, generally made paternal rights defer to the larger goal of preserving family integrity.

Michael Grossberg, Governing the Hearth: Law and the Family in Nineteenth-Century America 201-202 (1985).

6. *Other paternity presumptions.* Given the decreasing stigma of illegitimacy and the increasing accuracy of paternity deerminations, how strong is the case for retention of presumptions?

a. *The original UPA.* The presumption of legitimacy (also known as the marital presumption), which *Michael H.* analyzes, presumptively identifies the legal father only of children born to married women. To extend coverage to children born to *unmarried* women, the original UPA provided for several alternative presumptions, including one based on the *conduct* of a man who "while the child is under the age of majority, . . . receives the child into his home and openly holds out the child as his natural child." (UPA (1973) §4(a)(4), 9B U.L.A. 394 (2001)). When two presumptions conflict, the original UPA directs that "the presumption which on the facts is founded on the weightier considerations of policy and logic controls." §4(b), 9B U.L.A. 394 (2001). See supra pp.452-453 (quoting §4 in its entirety). Does *Michael H.* present a case of conflicting presumptions under this section of the original UPA? If so, which one should control?

b. *The new UPA.* The advent of genetic testing and the rise of assisted repro-ductive technologies prompted the development of a new Uniform Parentage Act in 2000 and some revisions in 2002. This statutory scheme contains the following relevant provisions:

§201. Establishment of Parent-Child Relationship

(a) The mother-child relationship is established between a woman and a child by:
(1) the woman's having given birth to the child [, except as otherwise pro-vided in [Article] 8] [on "gestational agreements" or surrogacy arrangements];
(2) an adjudication of the woman's maternity; [or]
(3) adoption of the child by the woman [; or
(4) an adjudication confirming the woman as a parent of a child born to a gestational mother if the agreement was validated under [Article] 8 or is enforceable under other law].
(b) The father-child relationship is established between a man and a child by:
(1) an unrebutted presumption of the man's paternity of the child under Section 204;

(2) an effective acknowledgment of paternity by the man under [Article] 3, unless the acknowledgment has been rescinded or successfully challenged;

(3) an adjudication of the man's paternity;

(4) adoption of the child by the man; [or]

(5) the man's having consented to assisted reproduction by a woman under [Article] 7 which resulted in the birth of the child [; or

(6) an adjudication confirming the man as a parent of a child born to a gestational mother if the agreement was validated under [Article] 8 or is enforceable under other law].

9B U.L.A. 15 (Supp. 2005).

§204. Presumption of Paternity

(a) A man is presumed to be the father of a child if:

(1) he and the mother of the child are married to each other and the child is born during the marriage;

(2) he and the mother of the child were married to each other and the child is born within 300 days after the marriage is terminated by death, annulment, declaration of invalidity, or divorce [, or after a decree of separation];

(3) before the birth of the child, he and the mother of the child married each other in apparent compliance with law, even if the attempted marriage is or could be declared invalid, and the child is born during the invalid marriage or within 300 days after its termination by death, annulment, declaration of invalidity, or divorce [, or after a decree of separation];

(4) after the birth of the child, he and the mother of the child married each other in apparent compliance with law, whether or not the marriage is or could be declared invalid, and he voluntarily asserted his paternity of the child, and:

(A) the assertion is in a record filed with [state agency maintaining birth records];

(B) he agreed to be and is named as the child's father on the child's birth certificate; or

(C) he promised in a record to support the child as his own.

(5) for the first two years of the child's life, he resided in the same household with the child and openly held out the child as his own.

(b) A presumption of paternity established under this section may be rebutted only by an adjudication under [Article] 6 [on paternity proceedings].

9B U.L.A. 16 (Supp. 2005). Article 6 of the new UPA authorizes paternity proceedings, including genetic testing. For children with no presumed father, a paternity proceeding can be brought at any time. UPA §606 (2000); 9B U.L.A. 30 (Supp. 2005). The following limitations apply to a child with a presumed father:

§607. Limitation: Child Having Presumed Father

(a) Except as otherwise provided in subsection (b), a proceeding brought by a presumed father, the mother, or another individual to adjudicate the parentage of a child having a presumed father must be commenced not later than two years after the birth of the child.

(b) A proceeding seeking to disprove the father-child relationship between a child and the child's presumed father may be maintained at any time if the court determines that:

(1) the presumed father and the mother of the child neither cohabited nor engaged in sexual intercourse with each other during the probable time of conception; and

(2) the presumed father never openly held out the child as his own.

9B U.L.A. 31 (Supp. 2005).

How would a court following the new UPA decide the controversy in the *Michael H.* case? What is the reason for the two-year requirement in §204(a)(5) and the two-year limitation period in §607(a)?

7. *Purpose of presumptions.* What is the purpose of the presumption of legitimacy and the other paternity presumptions? Some commentators contend that such presumptions offered a crude way of determining biological paternity before proof of such facts became scientifically possible. See, e.g., Marjorie McGuire Shultz, Reproductive Technology and Intent-Based Parenthood: An Opportunity for Gender Neutrality, 1990 Wis. L. Rev. 297, 317. *Michael H.* suggests that the presumption was designed to preserve marital harmony and establish the marital family as the norm. See also June Carbone & Naomi Cahn, Which Ties Bind? Redefining the Parent-Child Relationship in an Age of Genetic Certainty, 11 Wm. & Mary Bill Rts. J. 1011 (2003) (suggesting that the presumption facilitates private, rather than public, support for children); Theresa Glennon, Somebody's Child: Evaluating the Erosion of the Marital Presumption of Paternity, 102 W. Va. L. Rev. 547, 590-591 (2000) (suggesting that the presumption reflects a legal consensus that "parenthood within marriage best protects children").

8. *Weight of genetic evidence.* At one time, the presumption of legitimacy was conclusive when the spouses were cohabiting at the time of conception and the husband was neither sterile nor impotent. See, e.g., Kusior v. Silver, 354 P.2d 657, 668 (Cal. 1960); In re Estate of Jones, 8 A.2d 631, 635-636 (Vt. 1939). Today, federal child support legislation gives the states the option of making the presumption rebuttable or conclusive depending on genetic test results indicating a threshold probability that the alleged father is the father of the child. 42 U.S.C.A. §666(5)(G) (West Supp. 2002). Most states now have a rebuttable presumption of legitimacy. Paula Roberts, Truth and Consequences: Part I. Disestablishing the Paternity of Non-Marital Children, 37 Fam. L.Q. 36 n.5 (2003). Given that parenthood currently can be scientifically determined for any child, what role should genetic evidence play? Should genetic evidence always trump presumptions resting on social factors, such as marriage or "holding out" the child as one's own? Should legal paternity rest exclusively on biological paternity? To what extent would a regime of fatherhood resting exclusively on genetics best achieve equal treatment of all children, regardless of the marital status or living arrangements of their mothers? Alternatively, when genetic evidence conflicts with the presumption of legitimacy or one of the other paternity presumptions, should courts consider a child's best interests in resolving the conflict? See, e.g., In re Nicholas H., 46 P.3d 932 (Cal. 2002); Department of Soc. Servs. ex rel. Byer v. Wright, 678 N.W.2d 586 (S.D. 2004). But see B.E.B. v. R.L.B., 979 P.2d 514 (Alaska 1999) (application of paternity by estoppel rests only on risk of financial harm, not emotional harm to child).

9. *Paternity disestablishment.* Increasingly, some jurisdictions are permitting, by case law or statute, the disestablishment of paternity, generally on the basis of paternity fraud. Typically, a former husband or nonmarital father will attempt to invalidate a support obligation after genetic evidence shows that his children are not biologically his offspring. Some states require that the man act within a prescribed time. A few jurisdictions impose criminal penalties for mothers who

intentionally establish paternity for a man who is not the biological father. See generally Paula Roberts, Truth and Consequences: Part III. Who Pays When Paternity Is Disestablished?, 37 Fam. L.Q. 69 (2003). Does disestablishment constitute sound policy? See Melanie B. Jacobs, When Daddy Doesn't Want to Be Daddy Anymore: An Argument Against Paternity Fraud Claims, 16 Yale J. L. & Feminism 193 (2004).

Should a man be permitted to disestablish paternity once he has already assumed the role of the child's father? Courts sometimes deny disestablishment claims based on principles of equitable estoppel. See, e.g., Hubbard v. Hubbard, 44 P.3d 153 (Alaska 2002). Other courts bar paternity disestablishment based on res judicata principles, treating as a final judgment the divorce decree or child support order establishing paternity. See, e.g., State v. R.L.C., 47 P.3d 327 (Colo. 2002); In re Marriage/Children of Betty L.W. v. William E.W., 569 S.E.2d 77, 88 (W.Va. 2002). See also Paula Roberts, Truth and Consequences: Part II. Questioning the Paternity of Marital Children, 37 Fam. L.Q. 55 (2003).

If a would-be father is permitted to disestablish paternity, who becomes responsible for child support? The biological father? Suppose he cannot be found? The state? See *B.E.B.*, supra.

10. *How many fathers? Michael H.* is based on the assumption that a child may have only one father. What is the basis for this assumption? Given modern sexual mores and the high divorce rate, does such an assumption continue to make sense? If the dissenters would afford constitutional protection to Michael's interests because he, Carole, and Victoria lived together as a family for a time, would they afford similar protection to any interests asserted by Scott, another man with whom Carole and Victoria lived? Why or why not?

According to Professor Theresa Glennon, one state (Louisiana) has adopted the concept of dual paternity:

> an alleged biological father may assert his paternity, if done in a timely manner and proven by genetic testing. However, the establishment of the alleged biological father's paternity does not disrupt the rights and responsibilities of the legally presumed father, and the alleged biological father is only permitted visitation with the child if he demonstrates his worthiness to participate in the child's life. If his participation in the child's life does not meet the best interests of the child, the legally recognized biological father retains a support obligation but cannot claim the privilege of parental rights.

Glennon, supra, at 577. For another advocate of dual paternity, see Mary Louise Fellows, A Feminist Determination of the Law and Legitimacy, 7 Tex. J. Women & L. 195, 207 (1998). Is the concept of dual paternity a workable solution to *Michael H.*?

11. *Extant marriage.* How relevant is the fact that when Victoria was born, Carole was apparently *physically* residing with Gerald? Because *Michael H.* was based in large part on judicial reluctance to disrupt an intact marriage, should the traditional presumption of legitimacy be applicable if the married couple has separated or divorced at the time the putative father makes a claim? Compare Brian C. v. Ginger, K., 92 Cal. Rptr.2d 294 (Ct. App. 2000), with Lisa I. v. Superior Court, 3 Cal. Rptr.3rd 927 (Ct. App. 2005). In *Brian C.*, Ginger was separated from her husband when she gave birth to a daughter, the product of an affair with Brian.

Although living with her husband at the time of the affair, Ginger moved out a few months before the birth. She and the baby then lived with Brian for about a year. When Ginger and her husband reconciled, they resisted Brian's attempt to maintain a relationship with the child. After Brian petitioned to establish a parent-child relationship, the court of appeals held that the conclusive presumption of the husband's paternity did not apply. The court ruled that Brian had a constitutionally protected liberty interest in continuation of his relationship with the child, reasoning that (in contrast to the facts in *Michael H.*) this child was not born into "an extant marital family" because Ginger had left her husband and before the birth. Id. at 309.

However, in Lisa I. v. Superior Court, supra, the California court of appeals applied the traditional presumption of legitimacy and rejected the claim of a putative biological father who made a claim for standing to establish paternity of a child who was born six months after the mother's divorce from another man. The child was being raised (in a post-divorce family situation) by the mother and her ex-husband along with their two children. The court held that the application of the statutory paternity presumptions and standing requirements that would deprive the putative father of his opportunity to establish paternity did not violate his constitutionally protected liberty interest because he had only a biological connection but no prior relationship with the child. Pursuant to California Family Code §7611, the mother's ex-husband was the presumed father because the child was born within 300 days after the marriage was terminated by divorce and also because the ex-husband had received the child into his home and openly held out the child as his natural child (in the post-divorce family situation). Are the cases distinguishable? See also Fish v. Behers, 741 A. 721 (Pa. 1999) (holding the presumption of paternity does not apply where husband and wife have divorced, as the underlying policy rationale is not advanced).

12. *Dissent. Michael H.* was decided by a sharply divided court. In an omitted portion of the dissenting opinion, Justice Brennan (joined by Justices Marshall and Blackmun) highlights the divisions, pointing out that five Justices refuse to foreclose the possibility that a natural father in Michael's position might ever have a constitutionally protected interest, four Justices agree that Michael has a liberty interest, and five Justices believe that the flaw is procedural.

13. *Response to* Michael H: *California and elsewhere.* Discomfort with the plurality's decision is evident in legislative and judicial responses to the case. Dissatisfaction with the case led the state legislature in California (the site of *Michael H.*) to amend the conclusive presumption of legitimacy to allow a putative father to move for blood tests within two years of birth in some cases (i.e., if the man who is not the husband has received the child into his home and openly held out the child as his child). Cal. Fam. Code §7541(b) (West 2004 & Supp. 2005), enacted by Stats. 1992, c. 162 (A.B. 2650), §10, amending former Cal. Evid. Code §621. In 2004, the California legislature considered adoption of the revised Uniform Parentage Act (A.B. 2380, introduced by Assemblyman Tom Harman, Feb. 19, 2004). (The bill is currently inactive.)

Six states (Delaware, North Dakota, Texas, Utah, Washington, and Wyoming) have already adopted the new UPA. Uniform Parentage Act: Legislative Fact Sheet, available at nccusl.org (last visited Apr. 21, 2006). The new UPA incorporates California's two-year limitation on the putative father's ability to request blood tests, subject to estoppel principles (regarding the conduct of the parties, the equities of disproving the father-child relationship between the child and the presumed or acknowledged father or the best interests of the child). UPA §608.

As explained above, most states now hold that the common law presumption of legitimacy is rebuttable. Moreover, many states have enacted statutes that permit men like Michael H. to bring actions to establish their paternity to a child born to a married woman. Glennon, supra, at 573.

14. *Nonmarital children and immigration.* The United States Supreme Court decided another case concerning the paternity of nonmarital children in Nguyen v. INS, 200 U.S. 321 (2001). The Supreme Court rejected a claim that different requirements for a nonmarital child's acquisition of citizenship, depending on the gender of the citizen-parent, violate equal protection. According to INS regulations, nonmarital children born abroad to citizen mothers become citizens based on a short residency requirement for the mother. However, additional requirements exist for nonmarital children born abroad to citizen fathers: The father has to act affirmatively to establish paternity before the child reaches the age of 18. The Court reasoned that the distinction satisfied the important governmental interest in assuring that children have a biological and social attachment to their citizen parent: Attachment to the mother is established by the pregnancy and birth, unlike for the father, who has to act affirmatively. The Court was unconvinced by the petitioners' argument that the statutory distinction rested on problems of paternity establishment that were obviated by the reliability of DNA testing. Was the Court's ruling based on stereotypical notions of gender roles? Note that the Court's gender-based stereotypes are belied by the facts: The child's Vietnamese mother abandoned the child soon after birth, whereas the American father brought him to the United States.

See generally Caroline Rogus, Conflating Women's Biological and Social Roles: The Ideal of Motherhood, Equal Protection, and the Implications of the Nguyen v. INS Opinion, 5 U. Pa. J. Const. L. 803 (2003); Laura Weinrib, Protecting Sex: Sexual Disincentives and Sex-Based Discrimination in Nguyen v. INS, 12 Colum. J. Gender & L. 222 (2003).

Problems

1. When Stephanie marries Jeffrey, she is not motivated by love but by a desire to obtain military benefits and to share rent. Thereafter, Stephanie begins an intimate relationship with Paul and bears his child. Before the birth, they move in together. During the two years in which they live together, Paul holds the child out as his son. Subsequently, Stephanie and Paul break up. At that time, Stephanie lies to Paul, telling him that he might not be the father. Paul files suit to establish paternity in California after the legislature has amended the statute (discussed supra) in response to *Michael H.* Stephanie defends, alleging that Jeffrey is the child's father based on the statutory presumption of legitimacy. What result? Comino v. Kelley, 30 Cal. Rptr. 728 (Ct. App. 1994).

2. DeAndre, born out of wedlock, is killed in an auto accident at age 20. Although a judicial proceeding established his biological father's paternity years before, his father never openly acknowledged his son. After DeAndre's death, the young man's mother sues to sever any inheritance rights that his father might claim. State law precludes the father of a nonmarital child from inheriting from

the child if the father either failed or refused to provide support or openly acknowledged the child as his own. The father challenges the statute as an unconstitutional
gender-based classification because unmarried mothers need not meet any
requirements before inheriting from their children. DeAndre's mother and the
state argue that the statute differentiates not on the basis of gender but rather
distinguishes fathers who openly acknowledge their nonmarital children and
those who do not. They also argue that the statute advances the state interest in
encouraging fathers to take responsibility for their nonmarital children by precluding an uninvolved father from profiting from the child's death. What result and
why? See Rainey v. Cheever, 510 S.E.2d 823 (Ga. 1999), *cert. denied*, 527 U.S. 1044
(1999); Eleanor Mixon, Note, Deadbeat Dads: Undeserving of the Right to Inherit
from the Illegitimate Children and Undeserving of Equal Protection, 34 Ga. L.
Rev. 1773, 1775-1776 (2000).

3. Extending Paternity Laws to Same-Sex Couples

The preceding materials focus on statutory and constitutional frameworks to
identify the fathers of nonmarital children. Paternity establishment has long been
necessary to confer rights and obligations on nonmarital children and their parents. Until very recently, the law was not concerned with "maternity establishment"
and its ensuing rights and obligations. Because the woman who gives birth to a
child is easily identifiable, it was not thought necessary to develop a framework to
establish maternity. However, with the advent of reproductive technology and the
increasing recognition of same-sex unions, this issue is arising with greater
frequency.

The following materials focus on these questions: Should paternity laws apply
in a gender-neutral manner to mothers as well as fathers? Put another way, what
role should paternity laws play in the establishment of the rights of children of
lesbian couples and corresponding parental obligations? How should such laws
apply to gay male couples and their children?

■ ELISA B. v. SUPERIOR COURT
117 P.3d 660 (Cal. 2005)

MORENO, J. . . .

On June 7, 2001, the El Dorado County District Attorney filed a complaint in
superior court to establish that Elisa B. is a parent of two-year-old twins Kaia B. and
Ry B., who were born to Emily B., and to order Elisa to pay child support. [Elisa
denied being the twins' parent.] Elisa testified that she entered into a lesbian
relationship with Emily in 1993. They began living together six months later.
Elisa obtained a tattoo that read "Emily, por vida," which in Spanish means
Emily, for life. They introduced each other to friends as their "partner," exchanged
rings, opened a joint bank account, and believed they were in a committed
relationship.

Elisa and Emily discussed having children and decided that they both wished to
give birth. Because Elisa earned more than twice as much money as Emily, they
decided that Emily "would be the stay-at-home mother" and Elisa "would be the

primary breadwinner for the family." At a sperm bank, they chose a donor they both would use so the children would "be biological brothers and sisters." [Each attended the other's insemination procedures, prenatal medical appointments, labor, and delivery.] Elisa gave birth to Chance in November, 1997, and Emily gave birth to Ry and Kaia prematurely in March, 1998. Ry had medical problems; he suffered from Down's Syndrome, and required heart surgery.

They jointly selected the children's names, joining their surnames with a hyphen to form the children's surname. They each breast fed all of the children. Elisa claimed all three children as her dependents on her tax returns and obtained a life insurance policy on herself naming Emily as the beneficiary so that if "anything happened" to her, all three children would be "cared for." Elisa believed the children would be considered both of their children.

Elisa's parents referred to the twins as their grandchildren and her sister referred to the twins as part of their family and referred to Elisa as their mother. Elisa treated all of the children as hers and told a prospective employer that she had triplets. Elisa and Emily identified themselves as coparents of Ry at an organization arranging care for his Down's Syndrome.

Elisa supported the household financially. Emily was not working. Emily testified that she would not have become pregnant if Elisa had not promised to support her financially, but Elisa denied that any financial arrangements were discussed before the birth of the children. Elisa later acknowledged in her testimony, however, that Emily "was going to be an at-home mom for maybe a couple of years and then the kids were going to go into day care and she was going to return to work."

They consulted an attorney regarding adopting "each other's child," but never did so. Nor did they register as domestic partners or execute a written agreement concerning the children. Elisa stated she later reconsidered adoption because she had misgivings about Emily adopting Chance.

Elisa and Emily separated in November, 1999. Elisa promised to support Emily and the twins "as much as I possibly could" and initially paid the mortgage payments [and later the rent for Emily and the twins. Then she stopped providing such support.] At the time of trial, Elisa was earning $95,000 a year.

[The superior court found that Elisa and Emily had rejected the option of using a private sperm donor because "[t]hey wanted the child to be raised *exclusively* by them as a couple"; that they intended to create a child and "acted in all respects as a family"; that Elisa was obligated to support the twins under the doctrine of equitable estoppel. The superior court concluded:] "The need for the application of [equitable estoppel] is underscored by the fact that the decision of Respondent to create a family and desert them has caused the remaining family members to seek county assistance. One child that was created has special needs that will require the remaining parent or the County to be financially responsible of those needs. The child was deprived of the right to have a traditional father to take care of the financial needs of this child. Respondent chose to step in those shoes and assume the role and responsibility of the 'other' parent. This should be her responsibility and not the responsibility of the taxpayer." Elisa was subsequently ordered to pay child support in the amount of $907.50 per child for a total of $1815 per month. . . .

We must determine whether the Court of Appeal erred [in ruling under California's version of the original Uniform Parentage Act (UPA), Cal. Fam. Code §7600 et seq.] that Elisa could not be a parent of the twins born to her lesbian partner, and thus had no obligation to support them. . . . The UPA defines the "'[p]arent and child relationship'" as "the legal relationship existing between a child and the child's natural or adoptive parents. . . . The term includes the mother and child relationship and the father and child relationship." (§7601). One purpose of the UPA was to eliminate distinctions based upon whether a child was born into a marriage, and thus was "legitimate," or was born to unmarried parents, and thus was "illegitimate." Thus, the UPA provides that . . . : "The parent and child relationship extends equally to every child and to every parent, regardless of the marital status of the parents." (§7602.) . . .

Section 7611 provides several circumstances in which "[a] man is presumed to be the natural father of a child," including: if he is the husband of the child's mother, is not impotent or sterile, and was cohabiting with her (§7540); if he signs a voluntary declaration of paternity stating he is the "biological father of the child" (§7574, subd. (b)(6)); and if "[h]e receives the child into his home and openly holds out the child as his natural child" (§7611, subd. (d)). [Although] the UPA contains separate provisions defining who is a mother and who is a father, it expressly provides that in determining the existence of a mother and child relationship, "[i]nsofar as practicable, the provisions of this part applicable to the father and child relationship apply." (§7650.)

The Court of Appeal correctly recognized that, under the UPA, Emily has a parent and child relationship with each of the twins because she gave birth to them. (§7610, subd. (a)). . . . Relying upon our statement in Johnson v. Calvert, [851 P.2d 776 (Cal. 1993)], that "for any child California law recognizes only one natural mother," the Court of Appeal reasoned that Elisa, therefore, could not also be the natural mother of the twins and thus "has no legal maternal relationship with the children under the UPA."

The Attorney General, appearing pursuant to section 17406 to "represent the public interest in establishing, modifying, and enforcing support obligations," argues that the Court of Appeal erred, stating: "*Johnson*'s one-natural-mother comment cannot be thoughtlessly interpreted to deprive the child of same-sex couples the same opportunity as other children to two parents and to two sources of child support when only two parties are eligible for parentage." As we shall explain, the Attorney General is correct that our statement in *Johnson* that a child can have "only one natural mother" does not mean that both Elisa and Emily cannot be parents of the twins [because this case is distinguishable.]

In *Johnson*, [a dispute arising from a gestational surrogacy arrangement], we addressed the situation in which three people claimed to be the child's parents: the husband, who undoubtedly was the child's father, and two women [the biological mother versus surrogate mother], who presented conflicting claims to being the child's mother. We rejected the suggestion of amicus curiae that both the wife and the surrogate could be the child's mother, stating that a child can have only one mother, but what we considered and rejected in *Johnson* was the argument that a child could have three parents: a father and two mothers.[4] . . . The Court of Appeal in the present case erred, therefore, in concluding that our statement in *Johnson* that a child can have only one mother under California law resolved the issue presented in this case. . . .

We perceive no reason why both parents of a child cannot be women. That result now is possible under the current version of the domestic partnership stat-

---

4. We have not yet decided "(whether there exists an overriding legislative policy limiting a child to two parents." [Sharon S. v. Superior Court, 73 P.3d 554, 561 (Cal. 2003)].

utes [providing that: "The rights and obligations of registered domestic partners with respect to a child of either of them shall be the same as those of spouses." Cal. Fam. Code §297.5(d).] Prior to the effective date of the current domestic partnership statutes, we recognized in an adoption case that a child can have two parents, both of whom are women. [Sharon S. v. Superior Court, 73 P.3d 554 (Cal. 2003).] If both parents of an adopted child can be women, we see no reason why the twins in the present case cannot have two parents, both of whom are women.

[W]e proceed to examine the UPA to determine whether Elisa is a parent to the twins in addition to Emily. . . . Subdivision (d) of section 7611 states that a man is presumed to be the natural father of a child if "([h]e receives the child into his home and openly holds out the child as his natural child." The Court of Appeal in [In re Karen C., 124 Cal. Rptr.2d 677 (Ct. App. 2002)], held that subdivision (d) of section 7611 "should apply equally to women." [W]e must determine whether Elisa received the twins into her home and openly held them out as her natural children [pursuant to Cal. Fam. Code §7611]. There is no doubt that Elisa satisfied the first part of this test. . . . Our inquiry focuses, therefore, on whether she openly held out the twins as her natural children.

The circumstance that Elisa has no genetic connection to the twins does not necessarily mean that she did not hold out the twins as her "natural" children under section 7611. We held in [In re Nicholas H., 46 P.3d 932 (Cal. 2002)] that the presumption under section 7611, subdivision (d), that a man who receives a child into his home and openly holds the child out as his natural child is not necessarily rebutted when he admits he is not the child's biological father. The presumed father [Thomas, who was *not* the biological father] in *Nicholas H.*, [was] named as the child's father on his birth certificate and provided a home for the child and his mother for several years [and subsequently sought custody when the child was removed by the court from the mother's care].

We held in *Nicholas H.* that Thomas was presumed to be Nicholas's father despite his admission that he was not Nicholas's biological father. . . . We noted, however, that the UPA does not state that the presumption under section 7611, subdivision (d), *is* rebutted by evidence that the presumed father is not the child's biological father, but rather that it *may* be rebutted in an appropriate action by such evidence. We held that *Nicholas H.* was not an appropriate action in which to rebut the presumption because no one had raised a conflicting claim to being the child's father. Applying the presumption, therefore, would produce the "harsh result" of leaving the child fatherless. . . .

The Court of Appeal in In re Karen C., [124 Cal. Rptr.2d 677 (Ct. App. 2002)], applied the principles discussed in *Nicholas H.* regarding presumed fathers and concluded that a woman with no biological connection to a child [but who had raised a child from birth] could be a presumed mother under section 7611, subdivision (d). . . .

We conclude that the present case, like *Nicholas H* . . . , is not "an appropriate action" in which to rebut the presumption of presumed parenthood with proof that Elisa is not the twins' biological parent. . . . It is undisputed that Elisa actively consented to, and participated in, the artificial insemination of her partner with the understanding that the resulting child or children would be raised by Emily and her as coparents, and they did act as coparents for a substantial period of time. Elisa received the twins into her home and held them out to the world as her natural children. . . .

Declaring that Elisa cannot be the twins' parent and, thus, has no obligation to support them because she is not biologically related to them would produce a result similar to the situation we sought to avoid in *Nicholas H.* of leaving the child father-less. . . . Rebutting the presumption that Elisa is the twin's parent would leave them with only one parent and would deprive them of the support of their second parent. Because Emily is financially unable to support the twins, the financial burden of supporting the twins would be borne by the county, rather than Elisa.

In establishing a system for a voluntary declaration of paternity in section 7570, the Legislature declared: "There is a compelling state interest in establishing pater-nity for all children. Establishing paternity is the first step toward a child support award, which, in turn, provides children with equal rights and access to benefits, including, but not limited to, social security, health insurance, survivors' benefits, military benefits, and inheritance rights. . . ." By recognizing the value of determin-ing paternity, the Legislature implicitly recognized the value of having two parents, rather than one, as a source of both emotional and financial support, especially when the obligation to support the child would otherwise fall to the public. . . .

We observed in dicta in *Nicholas H.* that it would be appropriate to rebut the section 7611 presumption of parentage if "a court decides that the legal rights and obligations of parenthood should devolve upon an unwilling candidate." But we decline to apply our dicta in *Nicholas H.* here, because we did not consider in *Nicholas H.* a situation like that in the present case.

Although Elisa presently is unwilling to accept the obligations of parenthood, this was not always so. . . . We conclude, therefore, that Elisa is a presumed mother of the twins under section 7611, subdivision (d). . . .

Notes and Questions

1. *Rationale.* On what basis does the court determine that Elisa B. is obligated to pay child support? To what extent is the court's recognition of Elisa as a parent of the children born to Emily a prerequisite of her duty of support? In other words, could the court have obligated Elisa to support the twins without recognizing her as their parent?

2. *Benefit.* Who benefits from the court's ruling in *Elisa B.*? Lesbian partners like Elisa B.? Birth mothers like Emily? The children? The state?

3. *UPA.* Which provision(s) of the UPA does the court apply? Why? Is the court's reasoning persuasive that the UPA's paternity provisions should apply to women? Prior to *Elisa B.*, several commentators proposed that states adopt a stat-utory scheme that permits adjudications of maternity in order to treat same-sex partners as legal parents. See, e.g., Melanie B. Jacobs, Micah Has One Mommy and One Legal Stranger: Adjudicating Maternity for Nonbiological Lesbian Co-Parents, 50 Buff. L. Rev. 341 (2002); Margaret S. Osborne, Note, Legalizing Families: Solutions to Adjudicate Parentage for Lesbian Co-Parents, 49 Vill. L. Rev. 363 (2004).

4. *Domestic partnership provisions.* What is the relevance to the ruling in *Elisa B.* of California's adoption of domestic partnership legislation? As the California Supreme Court notes, state domestic partnership legislation would have made both women parents, if they had registered, through a provision that operates in parallel fashion to the presumption of legitimacy. Cal. Fam. Code §297.5(d) (Supp. 2005). See also Vt. Stat. Ann. tit. 15, §1204(f) (2002). To what extent does a system that turns on the formal actions of adults, such as registering as domestic

partners, replicate the inequality problems that the traditional preference for marital children created? See Grace Ganz Blumberg, Legal Recognition of Same-Sex Conjugal Relationships: The 2003 California Domestic Partner Rights and Responsibilities Act in Comparative Civil Rights and Family Law Perspective, 51 UCLA L. Rev. 1555 (2004).

5. *Policy.* Should courts recognize parentage by contract — and its accompanying rights and obligations? Compare In re Parentage of A.B., 818 N.E.2d 126 (Ind. Ct. App. 2004)(holding that agreement makes both women parents), *vacated by* King v. S. B., 837 N. E. 2d 965 (Ind. 2005) (remanding to trial court for determination of child's best interests), with T.F. v. B.L., 813 N.E.2d 1244 (Mass. 2004) (rejecting parentage by contract between former lesbian partners). See also ALI Principles §2.03 (recognizing parents by estoppel in such situations and citing cases). For further discussion of the ALI parentage-by-estoppel provisions, see Chapter VII.

6. *Rebuttal.* If genetic evidence is increasingly permitted to rebut parentage presumptions, what will this development signify for same-sex couples? What limitations on rebuttal does the court's reasoning suggest? Is the case governed by the reasoning in *Nicholas H.*, as the court asserts? Would the analysis of the rebuttal of presumed parentage differ if Elisa and Emily had registered as domestic partners? If genetic evidence controls, what good are parentage presumptions for same-sex couples, who must always use some donated genetic material? What do these questions suggest about rebuttal in more traditional contexts?

7. *Numerical limits.* Does *Elisa B.* suggest that two parents are always better than one? To what extent is *Elisa B.*'s preference for two parents based on economic issues alone? Might more than two parents be better still? Contrast *Michael H.*, supra, which declined to recognize dual paternity, with footnote 4 in *Elisa B.*, where the court cautioned that it had not decided "whether there exists an overriding legislative policy limiting a child to two parents" (citing a case permitting a second-parent adoption by a woman of the biological child of her partner). Should the law fix a specific number of parents as the maximum for all children? See R. Alta Charo, And Baby Makes Three — Or Four, or Five, or Six: Redefining the Family After the Reprotech Revolution, 15 Wis. Women's L.J. 231(2000) (arguing that the preference for heterosexual couples as parents is unwarranted, and the law should recognize same-sex couples and also groups as parents).

8. *Gender neutrality.* Does the court's holding make Elisa the twins' father? Their second mother? Their parent — without any more precise designation? Does it matter? Cf. Michael Levenson, Birth Certificate Policy Draws Fire: Change Affects Same-Sex Couples, Boston Globe, July 22, 2005, at B1 (noting that the governor ordered Massachusetts hospitals to cross out "father" on birth certificates of children born to women in same-sex marriages and replace term with "parent," over the opposition of couples who fear that such altered documents could prove legally questionable). Does the holding in *Elisa B.* follow from the recent move toward eliminating gender-specific role assignments in family law?.

Writing before *Elisa B.*, Professor Susan Dalton criticizes the law for its asymmetrical treatment of parentage for males and females and the underlying incapacity for "imagining a gender-free subject" in this context. Susan E. Dalton, From Presumed Fathers to Lesbian Mothers: Sex Discrimination and Legal Construction of Parenthood, 9 Mich. J. Gender & L. 261, 266 (2003). While the law has accorded a man parental status based on social factors such as marriage to the child's mother or holding out a child as his own, biological ties remained essential for a woman to achieve such status. See id. at 289. To what extent has the California Supreme Court addressed Dalton's critique?

9. *Gay male couples.* How do the doctrines and statutes examined in *Elisa B.* apply to gay male couples? What would Dalton's call for gender neutrality, supra, mean here? In dissenting from the Massachusetts Supreme Judicial Court's conclusion that anything less than marriage would fail to remedy the constitutional violation found in *Goodridge*, Justice Cordy wrote:

> [T]he presumption of paternity . . . reflects reality with respect to an overwhelming majority of those children born of a woman who is married to a man. As to same-sex couples, however, who cannot conceive and bear children without the aid of a third party, the presumption is, in every case, a physical and biological impossibility. It is also expressly gender based: if a married man impregnates a woman who is not his wife, the law contains no presumption that overrides the biological mother's status and presumes the child to be that of the biological father's wife. By comparison, if a married woman becomes impregnated by a man who is not her husband, the presumption makes her husband the legal father of the child, depriving the biological father of what would otherwise be his parental rights [citing, inter alia, *Michael H.*] Applying these concepts to same-sex couples results in some troubling anomalies: applied literally, the presumption would mean very different things based on whether the same-sex couple was comprised of two women as opposed to two men. For the women, despite the necessary involvement of a third party, the law would recognize the rights of the "mother" who bore the child and presume that the mother's female spouse was the child's "father" or legal "parent." For the men, the necessary involvement of a third party would produce the exact opposite result — the biological mother of the child would retain all her rights, while one (but not both) of the male spouses could claim parental rights as the child's father. . . .

Opinion of the Justices to the Senate, 802 N.E.2d 565, 577 n.3 (Mass. 2004) (Cordy, J., dissenting). Is Justice Cordy correct? Does the involvement of a "surrogate mother" for gay male couples require them to adopt the child, preventing them from achieving parentage through a default rule like the presumption of legitimacy? See, e.g., Ginia Bellafante, Surrogate Mothers' New Niche: Bearing Babies for Gay Couples, N.Y. Times, May 27, 2005, at A1.

Assuming that parity with married couples is the goal of those jurisdictions giving same-sex couples access to marriage (or to a similar status with equal rights and benefits), what parentage rules best achieve parity for all couples? See Susan Frelich Appleton, Presuming Women: Revisiting the Presumption of Legitimacy in the Same-Sex Couples Era, 86 B.U. L. Rev. 227 (2006). To what extent would the imposition of greater legal hurdles (such as adoption proceedings) for gay male couples to secure parental status, as compared to their lesbian counterparts, reinforce negative stereotypes about such men? See E. Gary Spitko, From Queer to Paternity: How Primary Gay Fathers Are Changing Fatherhood and Gay Identity, 24 St. Louis U. Pub. L. Rev. 195 (2005). For the law applicable to adoption and surrogacy arrangements, see Chapter IX.

10. *Conflict of laws.* With the states' different positions on same-sex relationships, conflicting approaches to parentage are inevitable. In a recent case, Janet and Lisa, partners who lived together in Virginia, traveled to Vermont to celebrate

a civil union. They then returned to Virginia, where Lisa subsequently gave birth (using donor sperm) to Isabella. Deciding that Vermont would provide a more hospitable environment, the family relocated there. When the women's relationship deteriorated, they completed the papers for dissolution, including a form on which Lisa indicated that Isabella was a child of the civil union. Later, Lisa claimed that she was Isabella's sole parent; however, a Vermont judge rejected that contention and awarded Janet visitation rights. Miller-Jenkins v. Miller-Jenkins, No. 454-11-03, slip op. at 13 & n.6 (Vt. Fam. Ct. Nov. 17, 2004). Lisa then returned to Virginia with Isabelle, where state statutes prohibit same-sex civil unions, voids those unions entered in other states, and makes void any contractual rights created by such unions. Although a Vermont court recognized Janet as a parent of Isabella, a Virginia court held that Lisa is the sole parent. Miller-Jenkins v. Miller-Jenkins, No. CH 04-280, slip op. at 1-2 (Va. Cir. Ct. Oct. 15, 2004) (Final Order of Parentage). The case is currently on appeal in both Vermont and Virginia. Despite state and federal statutes specifying the jurisdictional requirements for deciding child custody and visitation, this case concerns instead the threshold question whether Janet is a parent and also the procedural question whether the Virginia court must give full faith and credit to the parentage determination made by the Vermont court. See Adam Liptak, Custody After Civil Union Puts 2 Rulings in Conflict, N.Y. Times, Sept. 8, 2005, at A18. See also William A. Reppy, Jr., The Framework of Full Faith and Credit and Interstate Recognition of Same-Sex Marriages, 3 Ave Maria L. Rev. 393 (2005) (discussing the case).

11. *Companion cases.* On the same day that it decided *Elisa B.*, the California Supreme Court decided two companion cases resolving custody/visitation/parentage disputes between former lesbian partners. Kristine H. v. Lisa R., 117 P.3d 690 (Cal. 2005); K.M. v. E.G., 117 P.3d 673 (Cal. 2005). For a discussion of these cases, see Chapter VII, p. 803, and Chapter IX, pp. 1134–1144.

V

■

Divorce

A. INTRODUCTION

1. Divorce as a Historical Phenomenon

■ **LAWRENCE M. FRIEDMAN,**
A HISTORY OF AMERICAN LAW
142-144, 378-381 (3d ed., 2005)

England had been a "divorceless society," and remained that way until 1857. Henry VIII had gotten a divorce; but ordinary Englishmen had no such privilege. The very wealthy might squeeze a rare private bill out of Parliament. Between 1800 and 1836 there were, on the average, three of these a year. For the rest, unhappy husbands and wives had to be satisfied with annulment (no easy matter), or divorce from bed and board (*a mensa et thoro*), a form of legal separation, which did not entitle either spouse to marry again. . . . No court before 1857 had authority to grant a divorce. The most common solutions, of course, when a marriage broke down, were adultery and desertion.

In the colonial period, the South was generally faithful to English tradition. . . . In New England, however, courts and legislatures occasionally granted divorce. In Pennsylvania, Penn's laws of 1682 gave spouses the right to a "Bill of Divorcement" if their marriage partner was convicted of adultery. Later, the governor or lieutenant governor was empowered to dissolve marriages, on grounds of incest, adultery, bigamy, or homosexuality. There is no evidence that the governor ever used this power. Still later, the general assembly took divorce into its own hands. The English privy council disapproved of this practice, and in the 1770's disallowed legislative divorces in Pennsylvania, New Jersey, and New Hampshire. The Revolution put an end to the privy council's power.

After Independence, the law and practice of divorce began to change, but regional differences remained quite strong. In the South, divorce continued to be unusual. [L]egislatures dissolved marriages by passing private divorce laws. The Georgia constitution of 1798 allowed legislative divorce, on a two-thirds vote of each branch of the legislature — and after a "fair trial" and a divorce decree in the superior court. . . .

North of the Mason-Dixon line, courtroom divorce became the normal mode rather than legislative divorce. Pennsylvania passed a general divorce law in 1785, Massachusetts one year later. Every New England state had a divorce law before 1800, along with New York, New Jersey, and Tennessee. Grounds for divorce varied somewhat from state to state. New York's law of 1787 permitted absolute divorce only for adultery. Vermont, on the other hand, in 1798 allowed divorce for impotence, adultery, intolerable severity, three years' willful desertion, and long absence with presumption of death. Rhode Island allowed divorce for "gross misbehaviour and wickedness in either of the parties, repugnant to and in violation of the marriage covenant." . . .

The outbreak of divorce laws surely represented a real increase in the demand for legal divorce. More marriages seemed to be cracking under the strains of nineteenth-century life. This increased the demand for divorce — or for legal separation. As the demand for divorce grew, private divorce bills became a nuisance — a pointless drain on the legislature's time. . . .

The rate of divorce in the nineteenth century was the merest trickle compared to rates in later times. But it was noticeable. To many devout and respectable people, it was an alarming fire bell in the night, a symptom of moral dry rot and a cause in itself of further moral decay. [T]he family was changing. There was a slow but real revolution in the way men and women related to each other. William O'Neill put it this way: "when families are large and loose, arouse few expectations, and make few demands, there is no need for divorce." That need arises when "families become the center of social organization." At this point, "their intimacy can become suffocating, their demands unbearable, and their expectations too high to be easily realizable. Divorce then becomes the safety valve that makes the system workable." Moreover, a divorceless state is not a state without adultery, prostitution, fornication. It is certainly not a place where there are no drunken, abusive husbands. What it may be — or rather, what it became later in the century — was a place where the official law and the world of real life were sharply different.

[By 1880, legislative divorce was abolished. From 1850 to 1870, many states adopted highly liberal divorce laws. Divorce was easiest to obtain in western states especially, those least stratified by class.] After 1870, the tide began to turn. Influential moral leaders had never stopped attacking loose divorce laws. Horace Greeley thought that "easy divorce" had made the Roman Empire rot. America could suffer a similar fate. [In 1881, a New England Divorce Reform League was formed which later became the National Divorce Reform League. By 1882, the Connecticut law had been repealed.] Maine's law fell in 1883. A more rigorous divorce law replaced it, with tougher grounds, a six-month wait before divorce decrees became "absolute," and a two-year ban on remarriage of the plaintiff without court permission; the guilty defendant could *never* remarry without leave of the court.

Militant feminists, on the other hand, took up the cudgels for permissive divorce. A furious debate raged in New York. Robert Dale Owen, son of the

Utopian reformer, went into battle against Horace Greeley. [Owen] felt that strict divorce laws, not lax ones, led to adultery. . . .

[A dramatic increase occurred in the divorce rate between 1867-1881 despite the stricter divorce laws.] What accounts for the rising demand for divorce? [A] large number of people simply wanted *formal* acceptance of the fact that their marriages were dead. Just as more of the middle class wanted, and need, their deeds recorded, their wills made out, [and] their marriages solemnized, so they wanted the honesty and convenience of divorce, the right to remarry in bourgeois style, to have legitimate children with their second wife (or husband), and the right to decent, honest disposition of their worldly goods. . . .

"Divorce rings" operated practically in the open. Manufactured adultery was a New York specialty. Henry Zeimer and W. Waldo Mason, arrested in 1900, had lured young secretaries and other enterprising girls for this business. The girls would admit on the witness stand that they knew the plaintiff's husband, then blush, shed a few tears, and leave the rest to the judge. . . . In most states, annulment was rare and hard to get, but not in New York. In New York, they were a prominent loophole in the divorce laws. . . . Friendly divorces were easier in states where "cruelty" was grounds for divorce. . . .

The migratory divorce, for people with money and the urge to travel, was another detour around strict enforcement of divorce law. To attract the "tourist trade," a state needed easy laws and a short residence period. [I]n the twentieth century, Nevada become *the* place. . . . The moral arguments that eventually destroyed the divorce mills in Indiana and the other states had little or no effect in Nevada, a state quite impervious to moral arguments. . . .

The last part of the nineteenth century was an era of national panic over morality, eugenics, the purity of the bloodline, and the future of old-fashioned white America. Whores and divorce had to be constrained. An irresistible force (the demand) met an immovable object (the resistance to divorce). The result was a stalemate. [M]oralists had their symbolic victory, a stringent law strutting proudly on the books. But nobody enforced these laws, least of all the judges. A cynical traffic in runaway and underground divorce flourished in the shadows. Divorce law stood as an egregious example of a branch of law tortured by contradictions in public opinion, [and] in a federal system with freedom of movement back and forth . . . beyond the power and grasp of any single state.

World War II brought higher divorce rates. This consequence stemmed from the effects of wartime separation (such as adultery) and the difficulties of postwar adjustment to married life. Divorce rates stabilized in the 1950s for about ten years.[1] Rates began rising sharply again in the 1960s and 1970s with the advent

[1]. Roderick Phillips, Putting Asunder: A History of Divorce Law in Western Society 557-564 (1988). For other historical studies, see Norma Basch, Declarations of Independence: Women and Divorce in the Early Republic, in Women and the United States Constitution (Sibyl A. Schwarzenback & Patricia Smiths eds., 2003); Norma Basch, Framing American Divorce: From the Revolutionary Generation to the Victorians (2001); Thomas E. Buckley, The Great Catastrophe of My Life: Divorce in the Old Dominion (2002); Lawrence M. Friedman, Private Lives: Families, Individuals, and the Law (2005).

of no-fault divorce.[2] The divorce rate leveled off in the late-1970s and 1980s, and has remained at that level or declined slightly.[3]

Approximately half of all marriages today will end in divorce compared to 10 percent at the beginning of the twentieth century.[4] Currently, one in five adults has been divorced.[5] First marriages that end in divorce last about eight years; remarriages reflect the same dissolution rate and same average duration.[6] The rate of marital disruption (separation or divorce) varies by race, age at first marriage, religion, education, growing up in a two-parent family, and premarital conception.[7]

2. Divorce as a Social Phenomenon

■ PAUL BOHANNON, THE SIX STATIONS OF DIVORCE
in Divorce and After 29-32 (Paul Bohannon ed., 1970)

The complexity of divorce arises because at least six things are happening at once. They may come in a different order and with varying intensities, but there are at least these six difference experiences. . . .

I have called these six overlapping experiences (1) the emotional divorce, which centers around the problem of the deteriorating marriage; (2) the legal divorce, based on grounds [and now, on no fault]; (3) the economic divorce, which deals with money and property; (4) the coparental divorce, which deals with custody, single-parent homes, and visitation; (5) the community divorce, surrounding the changes of friends and community that every divorcee experiences; and (6) the psychic divorce, with the problem of regaining individual autonomy.

[2]. Andrew J. Cherlin, American Marriage in the Early Twenty-First Century, in 15 The Future of Children 33, 36 (2005); U.S. Dept. of Health & Human Servs., Nat'l Center for Health Statistics, Monthly Vital Statistics Report, Divorces and Annulments and Rates, 1940-1990, 1 (1995) (table 1). On the effect of no-fault laws on the divorce rate, compare Ira Mark Ellman, Divorce Rates, Marriage Rates, and the Problematic Persistence of Traditional Marital Roles, 34 Fam. L.Q. 1 (2000) (arguing that the rise in divorce rate predated no fault), with Margaret F. Brinig & F.H. Buckley, No-Fault Laws and At-Fault People, 18 Int'l Rev. L. & Econ. 325 (1998) (presenting data to support theory that no fault resulted in higher divorce rate).

[3]. Bureau of the Census, U.S. Dept. of Commerce, Number, Timing, and Duration of Marriages and Divorces: 2001, 4 (Feb. 2005); Cherlin, supra note [2], at 36.

[4]. Cherlin, supra note [2], at 36.

[5]. Bureau of the Census, Number, Timing, and Duration of Marriages and Divorces, supra note [3], at 1, 6.

[6]. Id. at 9; U.S. Dept. of Health & Human Servs., Nat'l Center for Health Statistics, Vital and Health Statistics: Cohabitation, Marriage, Divorce, and Remarriage in the United States 24 (July 2002) (pointing out that after 5 years, almost 25 percent of remarriages have dissolved compared to 20 percent of first marriages); Bureau of the Census, Number, Timing, and Duration of Marriages and Divorces, supra note [3], at 10 (pointing out the similarity in average duration of marriage and remarriage, but noting that the average duration of remarriages is longer for men (nine years) than for women (eight years)).

[7]. U.S. Dept. of Health & Human Services, Vital and Health Statistics, supra note [6] at 17-18 (reporting that after 10 years, 47 percent of African-American women's marriages ended compared to 20 percent of Asian women's; 48 percent of marriages of young brides (under age 18 at the time of marriage) ended, compared to 24 percent of those who married at age 25 or older; the likelihood of marital disruption varied inversely with the importance attached to religion by the parties; 41 percent of those who grew up in non-intact families faced marital disruption compared to 29 percent of those who grew up in intact families; and, premarital conception led to a higher rate of marital disruption). See also Cherlin, supra note [2], at 38 (pointing out that the divorce rate has fallen for college-educated women).

The first visible stage of a deteriorating marriage is likely to be what psychiatrists call emotional divorce. This occurs when the spouses withhold emotion from their relationship because they dislike the intensity or ambivalence of their feelings. They may continue to work together as a social team, but their attraction and trust for one another have disappeared. [They become] mutually antagonistic and imprisoned, hating the vestiges of their dependence. Two people in emotional divorce grate on each other because each is disappointed. . . .

The economic divorce must occur because in Western countries husband and wife are an economic unit. [T]hey certainly have many of the characteristics of a legal corporation. [A]n economic settlement must be made, separating the assets of the "corporation" into two sets of assets, each belonging to one person. This is the property settlement. . . .

The coparental divorce is necessary if there are children. When the household breaks up, the children have to live somewhere. Taking care of the children requires complex arrangements for carrying out the obligations of parents.

All divorced persons suffer more or less because their community is altered. Friends necessarily take a different view of a person during and after divorce — he ceases to be a part of a couple. . . .

Finally comes the psychic divorce. It is almost always last, and always the most difficult. Indeed, I have not found a word strong or precise enough to describe the difficulty of the process. Each partner to the ex-marriage, either before or after the legal divorce — usually after, and sometimes years after — must turn himself or herself again into an autonomous social individual. People who have been long married tend to have become socially part of a couple or a family; they lose the habit of seeing themselves as individuals. . . .

Divorce is an institution that nobody enters without great trepidation. In the emotional divorce, people are likely to feel hurt and angry. In the legal divorce, people often feel bewildered — they have lost control, and events sweep them along. In the economic divorce, the reassignment of property and the division of money (there is *never* enough) may make them feel cheated. In the parental divorce, they worry about what is going to happen to the children; they feel guilty for what they have done. With the community divorce, they may get angry with their friends and perhaps suffer despair because there seems to be no fidelity in friendship. In the psychic divorce, in which they have become autonomous again, they are probably afraid and are certainly lonely.

However, the resolution of any or all of these various six divorces may provide an elation of victory that comes from having accomplished something that had to be done and having done it well. . . . I know a divorced man who took great comfort in the fact that one of his business associates asked him, when he learned of his divorce, "Do I feel sorry for you or do I congratulate you?" He thought for a moment and said — out of bravado as much as conviction — "Congratulate me." It was, for him, the beginning of the road back.

3. Divorce as a Gender-Based Phenomenon

Men and women experience marriage differently, as we saw in Chapter III. Below, men and women report different experiences of divorce.

■ CATHERINE K. RIESSMAN, DIVORCE TALK:
WOMEN AND MEN MAKE SENSE
OF PERSONAL RELATIONSHIPS
65-72 (1990)

. . . For women, marriage flounders because husbands fail to be emotionally intimate in the ways wives expect them to be. This element of the companionate marriage is the centerpiece in women's accounts, working class and middle class alike. For men, the explanatory schema is very different: particularly for more economically advantaged men, the marriage failed because other relationships — with children, kin, and friends — were not subordinated to it; the marital relationship was not self-contained or was not primary enough to the wife. For both husbands and wives there was a failure in companionship; yet the particular activities women and men wanted to "do together" are strikingly different, especially in working-class marriages. And both women and men lament acts of sexual infidelity and incompatibility, though the interpretations they place on these events are not the same. For women, infidelity is an act of betrayal, living proof the marriage is over. Men have complex and differentiated views of infidelity, even as sex is central to their definition of what a good marriage should provide.

Some might argue that these different constructions arise out of the very different personality structures of women and men. Feminist psychological theory suggests that masculinity becomes defined through separation, whereas femininity becomes defined through relationships.[1] Women and men, in bringing these different orientations into marriage, put severe strains on it. Women define the institution of marriage interpersonally. The relationship with the spouse is one of a series of interpersonal ties that coexist for them — not without conflict, of course. Yet at the same time women want marriage to be emotionally intimate through talking about feelings, problems, and daily experiences, and through understandings that go beyond words. Further, they expect talk to be reciprocal: their husbands will disclose to them at the same time as they share with their husbands. Divorced women's accounts describe men who could not or did not express love in these ways, or whose needs for separation, some might argue, precluded this kind of emotional intimacy.

Men want something very different from marriage. Especially prominent is their desire for the undivided attention of their wives. [Men] want the marital relationship to be exclusive and primary; women in contrast, add it to their other relational investments. Men value the autonomy of the marital pair rather than its interconnectedness. They expect to achieve emotional closeness with their wives through sex and a particular kind of companionship. It is these "doing" aspects of marriage that they emphasize. [T]he masculine style of love emphasizes practical help, shared physical activities, spending time together, and sex — manifestations of love that achieve connection through action rather than talk, just as providing for a family does. This style of love fits well with cultural expectations for men more generally, for achievement, responsibility, instrumentality. . . .

1. See Nancy Chodorow, The Reproduction of Mothering: Psychoanalysis and the Sociology of Gender (Berkeley: University of California Press, 1978); Carol Gilligan, In a Different Voice: Psychological Theory and Women's Development (Cambridge: Harvard University Press, 1982); Jean Baker Miller, Toward a New Psychology of Women (Boston: Beacon Press, 1976).

Neither the women nor the men interviewed, whether working class or middle class, questioned the ideology of the companionate marriage. It was the failure of their particular partners to live up to the ideal that was defined as the problem, not the dream itself. . . .

Below, psychologist E. Mavis Hetherington explains the theory that women's experiences of divorce vary according to *marriage type*.

■ E. MAVIS HETHERINGTON, MARRIAGE AND DIVORCE AMERICAN STYLE
The American Prospect Online, Apr. 7, 2002

GOOD MARRIAGES, BAD MARRIAGES

[In the authors' longterm study of 1,400 divorced families, they identified different types of marriages (described below), ranging from "pursuer-distancer" marriages which are most likely to end in divorce, to traditional marriages which reflect the most stability.]

Pursuer-distancer marriages are those mismatches in which one spouse, usually the wife, wants to confront and discuss problems and feelings and the other, usually the husband, wants to avoid confrontations and either denies problems or withdraws. In disengaged marriages, couples share few interests, activities, or friends. Conflict is low, but so is affection and sexual satisfaction. Operatic marriages involve couples who like to function at a level of extreme emotional arousal. They are intensely attracted, attached, and volatile, given both to frequent fighting and to passionate lovemaking. Cohesive-individuated marriages are the yuppie and feminist ideal, characterized by equity, respect, warmth, and mutual support, but also by both partners retaining the autonomy to pursue their own goals and to have their own friends. Traditional marriages are those in which the husband is the main income producer and the wife's role is one of nurturance, support, and home and child care. These marriages work well as long as both partners continue to share a traditional view of gender roles.

We found that not just the risk of divorce, but also the extent of women's psychological and health troubles, varies according to marriage type — with wives in pursuer-distancer and disengaged marriages experiencing the most problems, those in operatic marriages significantly fewer, and those in cohesive-individuated and traditional marriages the fewest. Like so many other studies, we found that men's responses are less nuanced; the only differentiation among them was that men in pursuer-distancer marriages have more problems than those in the other four types.

The issue is not simply the amount of disagreement in the marriage; disagreements, after all, are endemic in close personal relations. It is how people disagree and solve problems — how they interact — that turns out to be closely associated with both the duration of their marriages and the well-being of wives and, to a lesser extent, husbands. Contempt, hostile criticism, belligerence, denial, and withdrawal erode a marriage. Affection, respect, trust, support, and making the partner feel valued and worthwhile strengthen the relationship.

GOOD DIVORCES, BAD DIVORCES

Divorce experiences also are varied. Initially, especially in marriages involving children, divorce is miserable for most couples. In the early years, ex-spouses typically must cope with lingering attachments; with resentment and anger, self-doubts, guilt, depression, and loneliness; with the stress of separation from children or of raising them alone; and with the loss of social networks and, for women, of economic security. Nonetheless, we found that a gradual recovery usually begins by the end of the second year. And by six years after divorce, 80 percent of both men and women have moved on to build reasonably or exceptionally fulfilling lives.

Indeed, about 20 percent of the women we observed eventually emerged from divorce enhanced and exhibiting competencies they never would have developed in an unhappy or constraining marriage. They had gone back to school or work to ensure the economic stability of their families, they had built new social networks, and they had become involved and effective parents and socially responsible citizens. Often they had happy second marriages. Divorce had offered them an opportunity to build new and more satisfying relationships and the freedom they needed for personal growth. This was especially true for women moving from a pursuer-distancer or disengaged marriage, or from one in which a contemptuous or belligerent husband undermined their self-esteem and child-rearing practices. Divorced men, we found, are less likely to undergo such remarkable personal growth; still, the vast majority of the men in our study did construct reasonably happy new lives for themselves. . . .

———————————

Hetherington and co-author John Kelly also point out that women are more likely than men to initiate divorce and to approach the decision more deliberately. E. Mavis Hetherington & John Kelly, For Better or For Worse: Divorce Reconsidered 40 (2002). They explain that women's motivations for staying in unhappy marriages stem from financial reasons and the concern with raising a male child alone. Men worry about the loss of their children, particularly their sons — leading to the psychologists' finding (confirmed by other studies) that marriages with sons are less likely to break up than those with daughters only. Id. at 41.

B. FAULT-BASED GROUNDS FOR DIVORCE

1. Adultery

■ LICKLE v. LICKLE
52 A.2d 910 (Md. 1947)

DELAPLAINE, Judge.
William F. Lickle, an insurance agent, of Towson, is appealing here from a decree of the Circuit Court for Baltimore County granting his wife, Margaret Lee Lickle, a divorce a vinculo matrimonii. He contends that the evidence fails to support her charge of adultery.

The parties were married in 1917. They had three children, who are now adults. Appellant, a captain in the First World War, is now over 55. The parties have not cohabited as man and wife for many years, although they resided in the same house. In 1937 appellant met A. Gordon Boone, a young Towson lawyer, and his wife, Edith Flint Boone, the co-respondent in this case. Appellant frequently visited their home on Bellona Avenue, went to parties with them, and accompanied them to the races. . . .

In July 1942, Boone received a commission in the United States Navy. . . . During the years when Boone was in the service [overseas], appellant became increasingly intimate with Mrs. Boone. She changed her residence four times during that period. . . . But in each of these homes appellant was a frequent visitor. One of Mrs. Boone's maids testified that he was at the home at Owings Mills "most of the time." Another maid testified that he visited Mrs. Boone in her homes at Riderwood and Ruxton on numerous occasions, staying all night several times a week, and eating many meals there. She also testified that appellant and Mrs. Boone often went motoring together, returning late at night.

Twice during the summer of 1943 appellant and Mrs. Boone vacationed together at Ocean City, Maryland. The first time was early in June, when they stopped at the Delmar Hotel. On that occasion appellant was accompanied by one of his sons, while Mrs. Boone and her elder son, Gordon, Jr., then ten years old, had rooms across the hall. The second trip was entirely different. Appellant and Mrs. Boone, traveling together in an automobile, arrived in Ocean City on July 23. They were unaccompanied. Mrs. Boone had sent her ten-year-old son to camp, and had left her one-year-old son at home with a nurse. Appellant registered at the Ambassador Apartments for both himself and Mrs. Boone, and during the next two weeks they occupied rooms on the third floor of the building. The first night they occupied adjoining rooms with connecting bathroom. After the first night appellant took another room across the hall, but they visited each other's room frequently, sometimes until after midnight. It further appears that in September, 1944, appellant drove Mrs. Boone and her two boys on a trip to Cumberland, and at the Fort Cumberland Hotel, where they spent the night, appellant registered for the party as "William F. Lickle and family."

Boone testified that he had not had sexual relations with his wife since September, 1943. In October, 1943, when he was home on a furlough, she repulsed his advances without any explanation. Three other times — when he returned from Europe in 1944, in June, 1945, and in October, 1945 — she again refused to have relations with him. He then accused her of being fond of another man, and he suspicioned that it was Lickle. In January, 1945, he was ordered to Chicago to act as instructor in amphibious warfare at Northwestern University. He pleaded with her to go with him to Chicago, but she refused even to visit him at any time during the year. . . . He returned home in October, and received his honorable discharge in December, 1945. Several days after Christmas Boone confronted Lickle with the charge that he had committed adultery with Mrs. Boone. Lickle denied that there had been any improper conduct. . . .

In a suit for divorce the burden of proof is on the complainant, but the charge of adultery as a ground for divorce need not be proved beyond a reasonable doubt. . . . However, it is broadly stated that the evidence sufficient to prove the charge of adultery must be so clear, satisfactory and convincing as to lead the unprejudiced mind of a reasonable and prudent man to that conclusion. We have also stated that circumstantial evidence required to prove a charge of adultery in a divorce case must show (1) an opportunity to commit the offense, and (2) a disposition to commit it.

In the instant case appellant and the co-respondent had innumerable opportunities to commit adultery. . . . It is appellant's contention that the evidence fails to show an adulterous disposition. He claims that he cultivated merely a Platonic friendship, which began about ten years ago. He says that he enjoyed talking with Boone's father, and that he helped the family in locating new homes and in various other ways while Boone was overseas. [W]hile opportunity to commit adultery is not in itself sufficient to justify a finding of its commission, in the absence of evidence of a disposition to commit it, such a disposition may be inferred from the conduct of the parties and the surrounding circumstances. . . .

It is our conclusion that the conduct of appellant, a married man, and Mrs. Boone, a married woman, was not consistent with innocence. After carefully considering the evidence, we find no reason to disturb the chancellor's decree. . . .

Notes and Questions

1. *Context.* On what evidence does the court rely to affirm the finding of adultery? Why does Mr. Lickle so strongly contest his wife's charges? Why does the court suggest that Mrs. Boone's status as "a married woman" is relevant? Suppose she had been single?

2. *Definitions.* At common law, the crime of adultery could be committed only with a married woman. For divorce purposes, however, adultery consists of the voluntary sexual intercourse of a married person with someone other than his or her spouse.

Adultery remains a crime in 23 states and the District of Columbia. Melanie C. Falco, Comment, The Road Not Taken: Using the Eighth Amendment to Strike Down Criminal Punishment for Engaging in Consensual Sexual Acts, 82 N.C. L. Rev. 723, 744 (2004). Does Lawrence v. Texas (supra p. 56) raise constitutional questions about such laws? Currently, 29 states make adultery a ground for divorce. National Survey of State Laws 396-411 (Richard A. Leiter, ed., 2003) (extrapolation from survey of divorce grounds in the various states).

3. *Historical background.* Historically, adultery was a common fault-based ground for divorce—but not the most common. See Glenda Riley, Divorce: An American Tradition 124 (1991) (pointing out that from 1887-1906, adultery accounted for 16.3 percent of divorces, cruelty 21.8 percent, and desertion 38.9 percent). What might explain this finding? For another historical study of adultery, see David M. Turner, Fashioning Adultery: Gender, Sex and Civility in England, 1660-1740 (2002) (theorizing the transformation of adultery from sin to breach of good manners). Until the 1970s, adultery was a ground for divorce in all states — in New York the only ground until 1967.

4. *Elements.* Cases are split regarding whether same-sex sexual acts constitute adultery for divorce purposes. Compare S.B. v. S.J.B., 609 A.2d 124 (N.J. Super. Ct. Ch. Div. 1992), with In re Blanchflower, 834 A.2d 1010, 1012 (N.H. 2003). Although case law once required actual intercourse, subsequent decisions appear to follow the English view that considers noncoital acts as adultery. See, e.g., Bonura v. Bonura, 505 So. 2d 143 (La. Ct. App. 1987). But cf. Glaze v. Glaze, 1998 WL 972306 (Va. Cir. Ct.

1998). Note that courts occasionally hold that same-sex sexual acts constitute cruelty for divorce purposes. See, e.g., Morris v. Morris, 783 So. 2d 681 (Miss. 2001).

5. *Corroboration.* In the fault-based era, corroboration was widely required to prove acts of marital misconduct for purposes of divorce. The rationale for the requirement was to prevent collusion. Homer H. Clark, Jr., The Law of Domestic Relations 400, 401 (1968). This requirement necessitated eye-witness testimony (often acquired by private detectives) and contributed to the adversarial nature of divorce proceedings. Despite the traditional requirement of corroboration, courts gradually permitted the introduction of circumstantial evidence to prove adultery. What explains the relaxation of the rule?

A trial court in New York recently recognized the continued importance of the corroboration requirement there by denying a divorce to a wife in a 17-year marriage, based on the absence of corroborating evidence of the husband's adultery. The judge reasoned as follows:

> Adultery cannot be established solely by the admission or confession of the defendant. Rather there must be additional corroborating evidence which supports the finding of adultery. . . . Moreover, merely the general admission by the defendant, that he had an affair with someone other than his wife is not, by itself, an admission that he engaged in adultery within the statutory definition.

Ozkan v. Ozkan, Suffolk Cty. Ct., Aug. 2004. See Chau Lam, Judge Denies Divorce: Adultery Not Enough, Newsday.com, available at http://www.disease.com/news1.htm (last visited Jan. 16, 2006). See also Joanna Grossman, Will New York Finally Adopt True No-Fault Divorce?, Findlaw.com, Oct. 20, 2004, available at http://writ.news.findlaw.com/grossman/20041020. html. (The judge also based his denial on the fact of the wife's resumption of a sexual relationship with the husband after learning of the affair.) Does adherence to the corroboration requirement continue to make sense?

6. *The Internet.* Eavesdropping and wiretapping sometimes provide proof of adultery. Increasingly, spouses are obtaining proof of their partners' adultery from email, pager messages, and records of chat room conversations. A spouse's retrieval of such records, however, may violate the Electronic Communications Privacy Act of 1986 (ECPA), 18 U.S.C. §§2510-2521, 2701-2710, 3117, 3121-3127 (2000), which amended Title III of the Omnibus Crime Control and Safe Street Acts of 1968 by extending the wiretapping proscription to "electronic communications" in addition to wire and oral communications. In cases of violation of the ECPA, the intercepting spouse is subject to civil and criminal penalties if the intercepted spouse has an expectation of privacy in such communications (e.g., if the computer files are password protected). See generally L. Kathryn Hedrick & Mark Gruber, Cybersex and Divorce: Interception of and Access to E-mail and Other Electronic Communications in the Marital Home, 17 J. Am. Acad. Matrim. Law. 1 (2001). See also Jane Gross, When the Computer Opens the Closet, Tennessean-Nashville, Aug. 31, 2004, at 1 (explaining that spouses also are discovering evidence of spouses' *same-sex* affairs via the Internet).

7. *Standard of proof.* The applicable standard of proof may reflect adultery's status as a crime. What standard does *Lickle* follow? See also Hensarling v. Hensarling, 824 So. 2d 583, 594-895 (Miss. 2002); Hughes v. Hughes, 531 S.E.2d 645, 647 (Va. Ct. App. 2000).

8. *Double standard.* A double standard once governed adultery. A wife had to prove that adultery constituted a "course of conduct" to obtain a divorce; a husband could prove a wife's single act. The criminal requirement of a *married* woman's participation reveals a similar bias. A British sociologist suggests two explanations for the gender bias: (1) a married woman was considered her husband's property (that is, adultery was regarded as a form of theft), and (2) adultery of a married woman threatened the lineage. Annette Lawson, Adultery: An Analysis of Love and Betrayal 42 (1988). See also William Corbett, A Somewhat Modest Proposal to Prevent Adultery and Save Families: Two Old Torts Looking for a New Career, 33 Ariz. St. L.J. 895, 1003-1004 (2001) (discussing gender bias).

9. *Adultery in the military.* Although prosecutors rarely bring criminal charges for adultery in the civilian population, the commission of adultery by military service personnel may result in the perpetrator's disciplinary action, discharge, or even court martial. See, e.g., David S. Cloud, Adultery Inquiry Cost General His Command, N.Y. Times, Aug. 11, 2005, at A19 (recounting Army decision to relieve a four-star general of command amidst allegations that he had a consensual extramarital affair with a civilian).

Sources of the military prohibition on adultery include: the Uniform Code of Military Justice, 10 U.S.C. §933 ("conduct unbecoming an officer and a gentleman"); §934 ("disorders and neglects [leading] to the prejudice of good order and discipline in the armed forces"), and the Manual for Courts-Martial, MCM pt. iv P 626 (setting forth requirements for proving adultery, including sexual intercourse and the marital status of the accused or other person as being married to someone else). See C. Quince Hopkins, Rank Matters But Should Marriage?: Adultery, Fraternization, and Honor in the Military, 9 UCLA Women's L.J. 177, 213 (1999). What explains the military's concern with adultery? See id. at 205-209. See generally Martha Chamallas, The New Gender Panic: Reflections on Sex Scandals and the Military, 83 Minn. L. Rev. 305 (1998); Raul V. Esquivel, III, Implications of the Military's Proscription of Adultery Upon Individual Privacy, 47 Loy. L. Rev. 835 (2001).

10. *Policy.* With the evolution of sexual mores and views of marital fault, should adultery be decriminalized? If adultery prohibitions are rarely enforced, why do they remain? See Richard A. Wasserstrom, Is Adultery Immoral? in Today's Moral Problems 209-219 (Richard A. Wasserstrom ed., 3d ed. 1985) (suggesting that prohibitions on adultery rest on public policy supporting promises of sexual exclusivity, condemning deception, and supporting the preservation of nuclear families).

11. *Empirical data: role of gender.* The "Kinsey Report" (based on approximately 18,000 interviews) estimated that half of married men and 26 percent of married women have extramarital affairs. Alfred C. Kinsey et al., Sexual Behavior in the Human Male 585 (1948); Kinsey et al., Sexual Behavior in the Human Female 416 (1953). Subsequent data report that fewer married persons have extramarital affairs and also suggest that the gender gap is closing. The National Health and Social Life Survey, a comprehensive study of 3,432 adults conducted by University of Chicago researchers in the late 1980s, reports that approximately 25 percent of married men and 15 percent of married women have had affairs. Edward O. Laumann et al., The Social Organization of Sexuality: Sexual Practices in the United States 216 (table 5.15) (1994). See also Karen S. Peterson, Affairs Rare

Despite Rumored Popularity, USA Today, Dec. 21, 1998, at D1 (reporting similar gender-based differential in a subsequent study of 5000 men and women conducted by researchers at the University of California, San Francisco).

How does adultery affect the decision to divorce? How does it affect post-divorce adjustment? And, finally, what role does gender play in the decision to divorce in cases of adultery? The following study explores these questions.

■ **JULIE H. HALL & FRANK D. FINCHAM, RELATIONSHIP DISSOLUTION FOLLOWING INFIDELITY**
in Handbook of Divorce and Relationship Dissolution 153, 154, 156, 157-158, 159-160 (Mark A. Fine & John H. Harvey eds., 2006)

Infidelity is the leading cause of divorce. [T]he impact of infidelity differs according to the conditions under which it occurs. . . . The impact of infidelity on a couple's decision to separate depends in large part on the nature of the infidelity and how it was discovered. [F]orms of infidelity evoke different responses. Sexual infidelity is more likely to result in hostile or vengeful, shocked, nauseated or repulsed, humiliated, sexually aroused, or homicidal or suicidal feelings than is emotional infidelity. In contrast, emotional infidelity is more likely to result in undesirable or insecure, depressed, helpless or abandoned, blameworthy, tired, or forgiving emotions than is sexual infidelity. . . .

. . . Catching one's partner red-handed [led] to high rates of relationship dissolution (83.3%), whereas 68% of those who heard of their partner's infidelity from a third party then ended the relationship. Unsolicited disclosure by the unfaithful party was least likely to lead to relationship dissolution. This may be because individuals who voluntarily confess their infidelity to a partner are more committed to repairing the relationship and are willing to make amends. However, it may also be that these individuals provide more mitigating accounts of their infidelity. . . .

[Gender also has been shown to play a role in the relationship between infidelity and relationship dissolution.] [O]verall, women are more likely to report that their divorce was caused by infidelity, specifically their partners' infidelity, than are men. [I]t is evident that men and women react differently to infidelity. [W]omen tend to show a more negative overall emotional reaction to infidelity than do men. Women are more likely than men to feel nauseated or repulsed, depressed, undesirable or insecure, helpless or abandoned, or anxious in reaction to a partner's infidelity. . . .

The association between infidelity and relationship dissolution may also vary depending on the nature or quality of the relationship. [T]he risk of divorce following infidelity appears to decrease with the length of the marriage. Couples who experience infidelity in the early years of marriage are more likely to divorce than those who experience infidelity later in marriage.

The likelihood of relationship termination following infidelity may also depend on the level of satisfaction within the primary relationship. Married or cohabiting partners who break up following infidelity recall lower relationship satisfaction than partners who stay together. . . . Additional negative relationship characteristics are also associated with a higher likelihood of divorce following infidelity. Women involved in high-conflict marriages are more likely to indicate that they would divorce a husband who engaged in a one-night stand or brief affair. . . .

The discovery of a husband's infidelity or divorce following such infidelity is associated with increased risk of a major depressive episode. . . . Although divorce is predictive of depression, it may be that infidelity increases this risk; infidelity-related divorces may be even greater stressors than other divorces, because the heavy emotional and psychological toll associated with adultery is compounded with the distress of divorce. Indeed, individuals who divorce following infidelity are more distressed after the dissolution than those who divorce without infidelity. They are also less well adjusted to the divorce and more attached to the former spouse than are those whose divorce was not related to infidelity. . . .

Problems

1. Diane Goydan, the married mother of two, "meets" Ray on the Internet. Diane and Ray (whose online nickname is "The Weasel") begin a torrid online affair. Diane neglects her job, her husband John, and her children. John notices Diane's long hours online and the increasing monthly charges. He monitors Diane's online conversations and saves them on his hard drive. Eight months after Diane's affair begins, John files for divorce on the ground of adultery. What result? See James Langton, "We Just Clicked" as the Internet Buzzes with On-line Romance, James Langton Offers Some Words of Warning, Sun Telegraph, Mar. 3, 1996, at 5. See also Christina Tavella Hall, Sex Online: Is This Adultery?, 20 Hastings Commun. & Ent. L.J. 201 (1997).

2. Armand and his wife Doris have been married for 28 years. Armand meets a woman at a meeting of Alcoholics Anonymous. Although Doris has no evidence of Armand's infidelity, she confronts him. He confesses. They separate, reconcile briefly, and finally Armand leaves home. During their separation, Doris observes Armand's truck parked in front of the woman's apartment at night. Armand petitions for divorce; Doris counterpetitions on the ground of adultery. The jurisdiction permits divorce on either irreconcilable differences or fault-based grounds (including adultery). According to statute, when alternative grounds exist, a court must determine the "primary cause" of the breakup before awarding the divorce. Armand argues that adultery did not cause the breakdown of the marriage because it began only after his departure and his filing for divorce. What result? See Yergeau v. Yergeau, 569 A.2d 237 (N.H. 1990). See also Barnes v. Barnes, 428 S.E.2d 294 (Va. Ct. App. 1993).

2. Cruelty

■ MUHAMMAD v. MUHAMMAD
622 So. 2d 1239 (Miss. 1993)

BANKS, Justice, for the Court: . . .

Robert J. Muhammad and Debra Muhammad, formerly Robert and Debra Wilson, were married on September 17, 1983, in Flint, Michigan. They resided in Flint until 1987, when they relocated to an Islamic community in French Lick, Jefferson County, Mississippi, known as the University of Islam. . . .

In July 1987, Debra Muhammad and the couple's two month old child, Radeyah, relocated to the University. With the agreement of Debra, Robert remained in Flint for a few more months before permanently relocating to the University himself in October of 1987. Robert sold the couple's house to Debra's father and sold and disposed of some personal property, including a car. A substantial portion of the proceeds was given to the New Nation of Islam.

A second child, Raheem, was born to Robert and Debra Muhammad on August 4, 1988. Robert and Debra lived together with their two children at the University of Islam until October 13, 1989. While Robert was asleep during the late night hours of that date, Debra took the two children and went back to Flint, Michigan. She and the children were transported by Debra's mother, who had come down from Flint, Michigan, to take them back after Debra had communicated to her by phone that Debra was extremely unhappy with life at the University. Robert still resides at the University.

Robert and Debra had been experiencing marital difficulties before moving to the University. Debra indicated to at least one person at the University that she had tried Islam and moved to the University with Robert in an effort to save her marriage. Debra testified that she had been unhappy in the lifestyle at the University from the moment she arrived there.

The University of Islam is comprised of members of the New Nation of Islam [who] practice the "Black Muslim" religion . . . under the leadership of Mr. Marvin Muhammad. To his followers, Marvin Muhammad is . . . accepted as their savior in the sense that he provides them with the spiritual guidance necessary to attaining salvation. The chief earthly mission of the New Nation is to unite peoples of the African diaspora and establish a nation outside the United States that they themselves would govern. . . .

Virtually every aspect of life of the University is impacted by religious doctrine. The social and family structure is strongly paternal. Men are viewed as the maintainers of their wives and children. Women are required to submit to their husbands. The role of the woman is viewed primarily as being the helpmate of her husband. Child care is one of her chief responsibilities. Women make no decisions. They cannot leave the confines of the community without the permission of their husband. Members of the faith are not allowed to ingest alcohol, tobacco, drugs or other intoxicating substances. Neither are they allowed to eat red meat. Although the food supply is adequate in quantity, the diet at the University is fairly limited to beans, broccoli, fish, bread, cauliflower, and sometimes corn. Meals are restricted to one per day for adults. Fasting from these meals periodically occurs. Women are required to breastfeed their children. . . . Mail is subject to being censored. . . .

Robert . . . contends that the trial court erred in granting a divorce to Debra on the ground of "habitual cruel and inhuman treatment." He argues that insufficient evidence was presented at trial. . . . He claims that the chancellor's findings only indicate at best that Debra was unwilling to follow the precepts of the Muslim religion.

The chancellor set forth the following discussion in his opinion with respect to a finding of habitual cruel and inhuman treatment:

> While the most devout and dedicated female followers of Islam apparently do not mind the conditions that exist in the community, the Defendant and Counter-Plaintiff did. She, her husband and two children lived in one room of a small house. There was a lack of privacy. She was unable to go into town or to travel as she pleased. She had no control of personal finances. She had telephone calls withheld from her and her mail was censored. She complained about her diet and the lack of food. Curiously, although the members of the community disdain the government of the United States and its political subdivisions, they allowed the Defendant and Cross-Plaintiff to participate in the WIC Program to secure milk and juice for her children. However, the milk was used in the bakery, and the Defendant had to seek permission from Marvin Muhammad to get diapers for her children. Finally, the Defendant suffered physical abuse at the hands of the Plaintiff. She left Jefferson County in the middle of the night with her children, and the Plaintiff has had very little contact with them since that time.

It is my opinion that these conditions constitute habitual cruel and inhuman treatment. . . . This Court has defined cruel and inhuman treatment in this vein as "conduct endangering life, limb, or health, or creating reasonable apprehension of danger, or unnatural and infamous conduct making the marital relation revolting." . . . Despite the standard's general demand for endangerment to one's health, this Court has held on numerous occasions that the harm . . . need not derive from physical attack by the offending spouse. . . .

[T]he case at bar . . . presents a claim of a nature not squarely confronted by this Court before. The Missouri Court of Appeals decided a similar case in Rogers v. Rogers, 430 S.W.2d 305 (Mo. 1968). In that case, a husband filed for divorce on the ground of "indignities," a statutory ground in that state, after he became deeply dissatisfied with life in a religious community known as the Zion's Order of the Sons of Levi, and his wife preferred to stay in the community. . . . [T]he husband came to resent the authoritarian nature of the organization and objected to the Order's health practices, dietary practices, and policy of arrogating all of the members' work pay into the organization's common fund. The husband eventually left the community and went home. By the time he left, he was very thin and suffered from nervous condition and tularemia. The Missouri Court of Appeals held that the husband was entitled to a divorce [on the ground of general indignities].

[A]s with other cruelty divorce cases, the polestar consideration continues to be the intolerableness of the plight created for the nonoffending spouse. . . . The most common scenario for this type of action is undoubtedly where one spouse engages in overt physical or verbal actions of such a harsh and continuing nature that the other spouse cannot continue to cohabit with the offending spouse without threat of physical or mental harm. In the instant case, Debra Muhammad only testified to one incident where her husband used physical force against her, and that incident was arguably provoked by her. . . .

Nevertheless, Debra's case presents a compelling set of circumstances for a grant of divorce by way of habitual cruel and inhuman treatment. Although Robert himself physically did little to harm Debra, the rules and social order of the University relegated Debra to a status and set of living conditions that would be unbearable to a great many, if not a majority, of the women living in our modern society. Debra's mother indicated that her daughter was on the verge of a nervous breakdown. For Debra, staying in her marital relationship meant continuing to endure the lot which she found oppressive. The only way she could escape these conditions was to leave her marital relationship. Therefore, if a spouse's actions which cause deep personal misery that has no foreseeable end is the gravamen of the action for divorce by reason of habitual cruel and unusual treatment, we cannot say that the chancellor's determination that Debra's case warranted a divorce was "manifestly wrong." . . .

SMITH, Justice, dissenting: . . .

[I]t is clear that it was manifest error to grant the divorce on habitual cruel and inhuman grounds. There is no testimony that indicated Debra was ever in reasonable apprehension of danger to life, limb, or health. Debra's complaints were not with her husband specifically but with the living conditions in the community they chose to live in. These circumstances were not imposed on or directed at her by her husband. [T]he "physical abuse" was one isolated incident in which Debra was not without fault. The chancellor has not set out any conduct by Robert that fits within the criteria required by our law for granting this divorce on habitual, cruel and inhuman treatment. Debra's general dissatisfaction with the community lifestyle is not sufficient. [T]he chancellor should have considered Robert's complaint for divorce on desertion or allowed the parties to consider irreconcilable differences grounds. . . .

Notes and Questions

1. *Elements.* Cruelty, termed "indignities" or "cruel and inhuman treatment," has provided a ground for divorce in most states. Courts generally require a course of conduct of cruel behavior that creates an adverse health effect. What is a "course of conduct"? "Adverse health effect"? The Mississippi court explained:

[T]he charge of cruel and inhuman treatment . . . means something more than unkindness or rudeness or mere incompatibility or want of affection. It has been said that: "The conduct of the offending spouse must be so unkind as to be cruel, that is, so unreasonably harsh and severe as to be inhumane, so lacking in human qualities, so unfeeling or brutal as to endanger, or put one in reasonable apprehension of danger to life, limb, or health. And finally, such conduct must be habitual, that is, done so often, or continued so long, that its recurrence may be reasonably expected whenever occasion or opportunity presents itself."

Kergosien v. Kergosien, 471 So. 2d 1206, 1210 (Miss. 1985) (citing Wires v. Wires, 297 So. 2d 900, 902 (Miss. 1974)). How did the wife in *Muhammad* establish the requisite elements? Was Debra's unhappiness with the religious practices sufficient to establish "habitual cruel and inhuman treatment" by Robert?

Numerous courts maintain that one incident will not satisfy the "course of conduct" requirement. Some courts have ruled, however, that a single incident may suffice if the act is particularly brutal, e.g., Rogers v. Rogers, 2002 WL 1335654 (Ark. Ct. App. 2002) (strangling of spouse); McDowell v. McDowell, 386 S.E.2d 468 (S.C. Ct. App. 1989) (attempt to shoot spouse).

2. *Battered spouses.* In the nineteenth century, divorce on grounds of cruelty was often the only remedy available to battered spouses. See generally Elizabeth Pleck, Domestic Tyranny: The Making of Social Policy Against Family Violence from Colonial Times to the Present (1987).

3. *Mental cruelty.* English ecclesiastical courts required actual or threatened bodily harm. Courts gradually expanded the definition to include mental cruelty. Many jurisdictions require that cruelty be sufficiently severe as to threaten physical or mental health. See David N. Levine, Marital Cruelty: New Wine in Old Bottles, 2 Fam. L.Q. 296, 306 (1968).

What acts establish mental cruelty? Cruel conduct toward a child? See Denisi v. Denisi, 135 N.E.2d 668 (Mass. 1956) (divorce denied despite incest). Unreasonable sexual demands? See Jizmejian v. Jizmejian, 492 P.2d 1208 (Ariz. Ct. App. 1972) (refusal of intercourse); Goldstein v. Goldstein, 235 A.2d 498 (N.J. Super. Ct. Ch. Div. 1967) (insistence on birth control). Does this last present constitutional problems? See also Rocconi v. Rocconi, 2004 WL 2397819 (Ark. Ct. App. 2004) (wife's excessive gambling); Ferro v. Ferro, 871 So. 2d 753 (Miss. Ct. App. 2004) (wife's permitting adult son from previous marriage to live with couple); Richard v. Richard, 711 So. 2d 884 (Miss. 1998) (false accusations of infidelity and incest, watching home shopping network all day, and buying items therefrom instead of paying household bills).

4. *New York law.* New York has particularly strict requirements regarding proof of cruelty for divorce purposes, requiring a "course of conduct"and an adverse effect to physical or mental well-being. See, e.g., Omahen v. Omahen, 735 N.Y.S.2d 236 (App. Div. 2001) (holding that husband's frequent derogatory epithets were insufficient to justify divorce because they posed no danger to wife's health or safety). These requirements reflect a historical concern with preventing easy divorce. Moreover, New York requires a higher degree of proof of cruelty for divorce involving a long-term marriage. See S.C. v. A.C., 798 N.Y.S.2d 348 (Sup. Ct. 2004) (denying divorce in 30-year marriage because husband's obscenities, inappropriate sexual remarks and boorish conduct, when viewed cumulatively, did not sufficiently endanger wife's physical or mental health). What purpose is served by this last rule? Is this rule sound? The New York legislature is presently considering adoption of no-fault divorce.

5. *Trends.* In the nineteenth century, women overwhelming claimed cruelty, desertion, drunkenness, and neglect as the most common grounds for divorce. In contrast, men were more likely to claim adultery. A commentator suggests a possible explanation for this gender-based difference: women value men's roles as providers more than their fidelity. Rachel F. Moran, How Second-Wave Feminists Forgot the Single Woman, 33 Hofstra L. Rev. 223, 250 (2004). In the mid 1960s, the trend shifted to cruelty as the most frequently alleged ground for divorce. Possible reasons include: liberalized interpretation of divorce grounds and acceptance of the idea of the companionate marriage. Jessie Bernard, No News, but New Ideas, in Divorce and After 16-20 (Paul Bohannon ed., 1970). The advent of no-fault divorce and remedies for domestic violence lessened the frequency of cruelty-based divorces. Currently, 27 states provide for cruelty as a ground for

divorce. National Survey of State Laws, supra, at 396-411 (extrapolation from survey of divorce grounds in the various states).

Problems

1. Robert and Olga have been trying for several years to have children. Robert claims that Olga subjected him to verbal abuse over their inability to conceive. Olga claims that Robert finally told her to do "whatever she wanted to do" to become pregnant, at which point she underwent in vitro fertilization procedure. Olga became pregnant by using donor eggs and sperm that had been mixed from donor sperm and Robert's sperm. She forged Robert's signature on the medical consent form. Olga subsequently gives birth to twin girls. Genetic testing determines that Robert is the father. Robert files for divorce on the grounds of cruel and inhuman treatment. What result? See McDonald v. McDonald, 684 N.Y.S.2d 414 (Sup. Ct. 1999).

2. In Shari and Robert's marriage, Robert controls the family finances. He refuses to tell Shari how much he earns and insists that she account for every cent that she spends. He forbids her from writing checks or using credit cards. She must surrender receipts of all of her purchases to him. He criticizes her for the amount that she spends for groceries and gasoline. In addition, he limits her to two baths per week to save money on hot water. He habitually insults and belittles her, refuses to allow her friends to visit, and makes baseless charges that she is unfaithful to him. Shari files for divorce on the ground of cruelty. What result? See Goodfellow v. Goodfellow, 2002 WL 31769028 (Tex. Ct. App. 2002).

3. Desertion

■ REID v. REID

375 S.E.2d 533 (Va. Ct. App. 1989)

KOONTZ, Chief Judge.

[Judith N. Reid sought a divorce on the ground of constructive desertion. Dr. Robert Reid responded seeking a divorce on the ground of desertion. When the commissioner recommended denial of the divorce on fault grounds but the entry of a no-fault divorce decree, both parties filed exceptions and a motion requesting preservation of the issue of fault for appeal. This appeal by Dr. Reid followed.]

The parties were married on June 26, 1965, in Denver, Colorado. Mrs. Reid had obtained a degree in medical technology and was employed at a local hospital. Dr. Reid was in medical school. In 1966, the first of their four children was born. In 1967 the parties moved to New York City where Dr. Reid completed his internship and residency. [Following Dr. Reid's stint in the Navy,] the parties moved to Charlottesville, Virginia, where Dr. Reid obtained a position at the University. He ultimately became tenured, head of his division, and director of the nurse practitioner program. [He subsequently left the university position to establish a medical corporation.]

During the first years of the marriage in which the parties' remaining children were born, Mrs. Reid was a homemaker. In 1980 she began part-time employment with [her husband's corporation] and ultimately became its controller. In 1985 Mrs. Reid and two other individuals, with the concurrence of Dr. Reid, formed King Travel, Inc., a travel agency, [and became president].

In his report, the commissioner reflected: "The testimony of Dr. Reid and Mrs. Reid rarely conflicts. They were talking about two different aspects [perceptions] of what were actually separate lives." The record amply supports the appropriateness of this statement. Mrs. Reid testified in detail as to the gradual breakdown in the marital relationship during this nineteen year marriage. The commissioner concluded that in each specific instance Mrs. Reid identified a marital problem, Dr. Reid did not perceive a problem. In fact, almost to the very end of the marriage, as if they lived separate lives, Dr. Reid considered himself happily married, while Mrs. Reid considered her emotional health endangered.

[Mrs. Reid] does not challenge the chancellor's finding that Dr. Reid did not constructively desert her. [Rather, she asserts she was justified in leaving her husband when she moved out in 1984 because her emotional health was endangered by virtue of the following marital problems]: (1) sexual inactivity, (2) Dr. Reid's excessive work habits, (3) Dr. Reid's failure to assist in the disciplining and rearing of their children, and (4) a lack of "intimacy within the marriage." . . .

It is apparent from the record and particularly Mrs. Reid's testimony that, following the birth of their first child in 1966, the sexual pattern which developed between the couple can best be described as infrequent. While three additional children were conceived and born over the ensuing years, many months passed between acts of sexual intercourse. These periods of abstinence gradually increased until no intercourse occurred for approximately two to three years prior to the final separation. It is also apparent that Dr. Reid suffered periods of sexual impotency, and that the infrequency of intercourse was more a concern to Mrs. Reid than to Dr. Reid.

Compounding this difficult situation, Mrs. Reid described the work pattern of Dr. Reid which she considered excessive. From the beginning of the marriage, Dr. Reid held more than one job. During the Navy years, he worked at night conducting insurance physicals. After accepting the position at the University of Virginia, he worked at night at the emergency room of a nearby hospital, opened a nearby clinic with two other doctors, and ultimately formed Commonwealth Clinical. There is no dispute that these activities severely limited the time available for Dr. Reid to spend at home with his wife and children. . . . Mrs. Reid felt that Dr. Reid was not appropriately supportive of her efforts to discipline [one child in particular] and, rather, conveyed to her the sense that this problem was solely her responsibility.

Mrs. Reid's description of the lack of "intimacy within the marriage," while conceptually understandable, is nebulous at best. On brief, she partially summarizes it as Dr. Reid's refusal "to talk to her about their lives with its joys and its sorrows, about the family and where it was and where it was going, or any other matter not directly related to one of the family financial concerns." . . . It is fair to say that while Dr. Reid was financially supportive, Mrs. Reid bore the major responsibility for raising the children and maintaining the home. In the process she became unhappy and felt unfulfilled. We accept the commissioner's conclusion that this condition was due in major part to Dr. Reid's denial or lack of recognition of the needs and feelings of Mrs. Reid.

While not specifically asserted by Mrs. Reid as a justification for her leaving, it is clear from the evidence that the marital problems of this couple were compounded by the additional responsibilities assumed by Mrs. Reid when she undertook her duties at Commonwealth Systems and eventually King Travel. These activities were encouraged by Dr. Reid, but they did not produce the personal satisfaction or the lessening of Mrs. Reid's frustration as they both apparently had hoped. Finally, the purchase of a large sailing boat and Mrs. Reid's enthusiastic involvement in sailing without Dr. Reid, in turn, merely added more stress to the marriage.

. . . The issue remains, however, whether as a matter of law these circumstances provide a justification for leaving the marriage. In that regard, the additional facts surrounding her leaving become critical.

In April, 1983, in what she describes as an effort to get Dr. Reid's attention, Mrs. Reid informed Dr. Reid that she could no longer endure the stress created by the problems in their marriage. As a result, the parties underwent counseling, which was unsuccessful. Mrs. Reid asserts that at that point she was totally committed to saving the marriage, but that Dr. Reid did not perceive the extent of their problems. The record supports this assertion. Subsequently, in October of that year, Mrs. Reid went on a month long sailing cruise to the Virgin Islands. Upon returning she advised Dr. Reid that she wanted a separation. The separation was delayed because Mrs. Reid underwent a gallbladder operation and she did not want to upset the children at Christmas. . . . Mrs. Reid testified that she eventually made a deposit on an apartment and on a Friday night again discussed the marriage with Dr. Reid. There was no agreement for a mutual separation. She described this conversation as "not being intimate" but rather, "a superficial sort of thing." On the following Monday, without Dr. Reid's knowledge, Mrs. Reid moved to this apartment. She testified that her intent in leaving the marital home was to make Dr. Reid realize that they had a problem, and that she "couldn't go on with it without doing something about it." This separation occurred on April 16, 1984. Mrs. Reid filed her suit for divorce on June 13, 1984. The chancellor sustained the commissioner's finding that as a matter of law Mrs. Reid did not intend to desert the marriage. We disagree. . . .

"Proof of an actual breaking off of matrimonial cohabitation combined with the intent to desert . . . constitutes desertion as grounds for divorce. However, reasons for leaving the marriage other than an intent to desert may justify discontinuance of the relationship without giving rise to grounds for divorce." [Citations omitted.] Under the law existing at the time of the present suit, fault, such as desertion, was a bar to spousal support. . . .

Mrs. Reid's description of her feelings and emotional condition are understandable in terms of human experience. The *cause* of her feelings and emotional condition, however, cannot be attributed factually or legally solely to the conduct of Dr. Reid. Rather, the evidence established that the pattern of conduct, indeed the entire marital relationship, established by both parties in this marriage resulted in her frustration and guided her decision to terminate the marriage. Mrs. Reid's complaints that Dr. Reid absented himself from the home and his proper share of the child discipline while working to provide financially for her and the family cannot serve as the justification for leaving him. Mrs. Reid would have us draw a fine line between where perhaps he excelled in one duty to the family at a sacrifice of another duty. This we cannot do. Her complaint of a "lack of intimacy in the marriage" is, in the final analysis, no more than a reflection of the different personalities of these marital partners and their method of relating to each other. It can be considered no more than a general complaint of unhappiness on the part of one spouse, which is the regrettable risk in all marriages. Finally, her complaint of the infrequency of sexual intercourse was a pattern developed uniquely between them almost from the beginning of the marriage. Moreover, Dr. Reid's periodic impotency was a mutual problem; the solution to which, obviously, was not within his sole control.

Under these circumstances, the most that can be concluded is that there was a gradual breakdown in the marriage relationship. As a result, Mrs. Reid understandably became unhappy and believed her emotional health was endangered. Her response to this problem was to terminate matrimonial cohabitation. The fact that she filed for divorce within two months thereafter belies an intent for a temporary separation. In so doing, she legally deserted the marriage and forfeited her right to spousal support. For these reasons, the commissioner erred in his conclusions of law. . . .

Notes and Questions

1. *Background.* Virginia permits divorce on the no-fault ground of a year's separation as well as on fault-based grounds (adultery, conviction of a felony, cruelty, desertion or abandonment, or causing reasonable apprehension of bodily harm). Va. Code Ann. §20-91 (Michie 2004). If both fault-based and no-fault grounds exist, the judge may use discretion to select the most appropriate ground. Zinkhan v. Zinkhan, 342 S.E.2d 658 (Va. Ct. App. 1986). When *Reid* was filed, proof of fault barred spousal support. Subsequently, the legislature eliminated fault as a bar to spousal support in all cases except adultery. Va. Code Ann. §20-107.1 (Michie 2004).

2. *Epilogue.* Following the principal case, Dr. Reid petitioned for restitution of spousal support paid to Mrs. Reid under the decree that was reversed and set aside on appeal. A panel of the court of appeals affirmed the trial court's denial of the husband's motion. The court of appeals subsequently granted a rehearing en banc and then concluded that restitution could be ordered, remanding for a determination of the amount. On appeal, the Virginia Supreme Court held that the trial court lacked the statutory authority to order restitution of spousal support. Reid v. Reid, 419 S.E.2d 398 (Va. Ct. App. 1992), *rev'd,* 429 S.E.2d 208 (Va. 1993).

3. *Elements.* Desertion constitutes a ground for divorce in 27 jurisdictions. National Survey of State Laws, supra, at 396-422 (extrapolation from survey of divorce grounds in the various states). A spouse's mere departure is not sufficient to prove desertion. Desertion requires a cessation of cohabitation, without cause or consent, but with intent to abandon, continuing for a statutory period.

Although intent to desert, abandon, or terminate the relationship is essential, separation and intent need not occur contemporaneously. Separation without the requisite intent will not constitute desertion; subsequent intent formed after a separation will suffice, however. The desertion, then, dates from the time the intention is formed. Did Mrs. Reid satisfy the requisite elements? Desertion must also occur without justification. Why did the court deem Mrs. Reid's reason(s) unjustified?

Some statutes require that desertion be voluntary. Does desertion caused by imprisonment suffice? See generally Necessity of Voluntariness, 24 Am. Jur.2d Divorce and Separation §65 (1998). Can a spouse who was ordered out of the marital home claim desertion? Cf. Knepp v. Niece, 2003 WL 175192 (Va. Ct. App. 2003) (husband deserted by breaking off marital cohabitation when he ordered wife to leave), with Royer v. Royer, 2004 WL 2093443 (Va. Cir. Ct. 2004) (finding that wife's departure after being told to leave was not desertion for purposes of forfeiting her share in decedent's estate and noting that her action would not constitute desertion for divorce purposes). Must the abandonment be total? See Jeffries v. Jeffries, 138 N.W.2d 882, 884 (Iowa 1965) (husband's regular support barred wife's action for divorce).

Does refusal to engage in sexual relations constitute desertion? See, e.g., Davis v. Davis, 1998 WL 281330 (Va. Ct. App. 1998) (affirming trial court's refusal to find constructive desertion based on wife's refusal of sexual intercourse). Suppose the refusal is "justified" because of health reasons? Religious beliefs? Objections to the other spouse's sexual practices? Would desertion have occurred in *Muhammed*, supra, if Debra had refused to follow Robert to the University of Islam or when she left him there? If so, who would have deserted whom?

4. *Constructive desertion.* Recall that Mrs. Reid filed for divorce on the ground of constructive desertion. Dr. Reid cross-complained for desertion. Constructive desertion constitutes intolerable conduct by one spouse toward an innocent spouse that causes the innocent spouse to leave the marital abode. Thus, if Dr. Reid's conduct gives the plaintiff justification for leaving the home, then Mrs. Reid is not guilty of desertion. Under this ground, a spouse (in this case, Dr. Reid) need not specifically intend that the plaintiff leave. Did Dr. Reid provide just cause for Mrs. Reid to leave?

5. *Gender differences.* To what extent does *Reid* exemplify the thesis of Catherine Riessman and E. Mavis Hetherington, supra pp. 493-494, about gender-based differences in divorce experiences? How does the judge interpret the facts? Compare the court's description of Dr. Reid's work, requiring absence from the home, as "excel[ling] in one duty," with its assessment of Mrs. Reid's work, which the court found "[compounded] the marital problems of this couple."

6. *Statutory period.* Most states require that the desertion continue for at least one year. National Survey of State Laws, supra, at 396-422 (extrapolation from survey of divorce grounds). Why require a statutory period of desertion for divorce? Should parties be able to file once the intent to desert is expressed? Does a statutory period assist courts in determining a party's intent?

7. *Other fault-based grounds.* Additional statutory fault-based grounds include willful nonsupport of wife by husband (e.g., R.I. Gen. Laws §15-5-2 (2002); criminal conviction or imprisonment (e.g., Ala. Code §30-2-1(a)(4) (1999); drunkenness and drug addition (e.g., Tenn. Code Ann. §36-4-101 (2003); impotence (Miss. Code §93-5-1 (2005); and insanity (e.g., Utah Code Ann. §30-3-1(3)(i) (2002)).

Problem

Husband and Wife marry in 1979. In 1997, Husband becomes legally blind. Each weekend, Wife brings Husband to and from his sister's house, allegedly (according to Wife) because his sister wants company. Wife works during the week and sometimes leaves Husband home without food. Wife allows her grandson to live in the marital home for three years, during which time he is often disrespectful of Husband. Husband decides to leave the marital home in 1998 and rents a trailer. Wife does not seek out Husband at his new residence or ask him to return. Husband files for divorce in 2000. Has Husband deserted Wife? Has Wife constructively deserted Husband? See Deen v. Deen, 856 So. 2d 736 (Miss. Ct. App. 2003).

C. FAULT-BASED DEFENSES

1. Recrimination

■ PARKER v. PARKER
519 So. 2d 1232 (Miss. 1988)

LEE, Chief Justice.

[Carolyn Moody Parker appeals the denial of a divorce from James Charles Parker based on recrimination.] The parties were married June 24, 1966, and they lived in Winston County until their separation occurred in February, 1984. No children were born of the marriage. Appellant operated a beauty shop, and appellee operated a garage, both located on three acres of land upon which the parties lived.

. . . Appellant called a number of witnesses [who testified as follows] to establish her ground for divorce of habitual cruel and inhuman treatment. . . .

. . . Charles watched the beauty shop with binoculars while Carolyn was cutting the hair of a male customer. . . . Carolyn arrived home one night to discover Charles and a woman exiting his garage. . . . Charles offered $100.00 to his friend's wife in return for sexual favors. . . . Charles falsely accused Carolyn of "going with" the church song leader and having sex with other men. . . . Charles would check the mileage on Carolyn's car to determine if she had been anywhere while he was gone. . . . Charles had a vision in which the Lord told him that if Carolyn went out on a certain weekend, her face "would not be fit to be seen anymore on the earth . . ." . . . When Charles saw Carolyn dancing with another man at a birthday party, he shoved her into their car, bruising her leg in the process, and called her a "sorry, low-down slut." . . . Charles fired a pistol outside Carolyn's beauty shop. . . . Some of Carolyn's beauty shop customers quit doing business with Carolyn because of her difficulties with Charles. The beauty shop has since gone out of business.

Appellant's physician testified that, at the time of the separation, appellant required hospitalization for "severe anxiety" caused by "family problems" which left her "almost hysterical." She remained hospitalized for four days.

Appellee pled the affirmative defense of recrimination, e.g., that appellant had committed adultery. At the conclusion of the trial, the chancellor remarked . . . :

> The Court finds by clear and convincing evidence that the Plaintiff has been guilty of adultery and that the defense of recrimination does prohibit and preclude the granting of a divorce in this case. . . .

In order for a divorce to be granted on the ground of habitual cruel and inhuman treatment, there must be proof of systematic and continuous behavior on the part of the offending spouse which goes beyond mere incompatibility. . . . We think the evidence fully supported a divorce for appellant on the ground of habitual cruel and inhuman treatment.

. . . The doctrine of recrimination is founded on the basis that the equal guilt of a complainant bars his/her right to divorce, and the principal consideration is that the complainant must come into court with clean hands. The complainant's offense need not be the same offense charged against his spouse, but it must be an offense sufficient to constitute a ground for divorce.

[Professor Marvin Moore states the following reasons for the defense of recrimination:]

> At least four policy-oriented justifications of the doctrine may be found in judicial opinions: (a) By rendering divorces more difficult to procure, recrimination promotes marital stability. (b) The rule tends to deter immorality, since a spouse is less likely to commit adultery (or any other marital offense) if he knows that his misdeed may bar him from obtaining a divorce at some future time. (c) The doctrine serves to protect the wife's economic status. (d) Recrimination prevents persons who are obviously poor marriage risks from being freed to contract — and probably ruin — another marriage.

[Marvin M. Moore, An Examination of the Recrimination Doctrine, 20 S.C. L. Rev. 685, 714-715 (1968).]

These reasons for recrimination offered are impractical and fail with the mores of present times, particularly insofar as they affect the case sub judice. . . . There is no marital stability in the present case, and the marriage has deteriorated to the point where there is no marriage. . . . The record here reflects that the appellant wife did not commit adultery during the time the parties lived together and cohabited as husband and wife, but only after the separation and dissolution of the marriage relationship.

The economic status of the appellant wife here is not protected, but, on the other hand, for practical purposes has been destroyed. The undisputed evidence indicates . . . that appellant's troubles with appellee have adversely affected her business. . . . It is apparent that the public interest in promoting appellant's financial security would be served, not by denying appellant a divorce, but by granting one along with a property settlement sufficient to permit her to resume the operation of her own business.

The State's interest in preventing bad marriages is acknowledged, and it is possible that denial of a divorce in this case will prevent subsequent bad marriages involving these parties. However, it is practically certain that denial of divorce in the present case under these facts would perpetuate an already-existing bad marriage.

While this Court is not suggesting condonation of the conduct of the appellant wife after the separation of the parties, when we balance out the uncontradicted evidence that the conduct of the appellee was responsible for the separation of the parties and the dissolution of their marriage; that the misconduct of the appellant wife occurred after the destruction of the marriage; and that the legislature has, in the least, greatly weakened the defense of recrimination; we are of the opinion that the learned chancellor erred in denying a divorce to appellant. . . .

Notes and Questions

1. *Policy.* Recrimination "prevents the dissolution of those very marriages most appropriate for dissolution." Homer H. Clark, Jr., The Law of Domestic Relations in the United States 527 (2d ed. 1988). Should divorce be granted only to "innocent" parties? Did the *Parker* court abandon the doctrine? If Carolyn had taken a lover upon learning of Charles's adultery, would the result have been the same? How determinative was Charles's cruelty? On the history of the doctrine, see J.G. Beamer, The Doctrine of Recrimination in Divorce, 10 UMKC L. Rev. 213 (1942); J. Herbie DiFonzo, Alternatives to Marital Fault: Legislative and Judicial Experiments in Cultural Change, 34 Idaho L. Rev. 1, 18-19 (1997).

2. *Financial issues.* One commentator points out that the defense of recrimination tended to be raised "as an issue only when one party was dissatisfied with the property arrangements." DiFonzo, supra, at 19. What considerations may have influenced Charles's use of the defense?

Parker cites protection of the wife's economic status as a reason to grant the divorce. If the wife is equally culpable, why should the court concern itself with this issue? In the article cited in *Parker*, Professor Moore asks: "Is it realistic to suppose that a spouse who is induced to commit adultery, cruelty, or some other marital offense is likely to desist out of fear that his actions will enable his mate at some future time to defeat his petition for divorce?" 20 S.C. L. Rev. at 718. What purpose does recrimination serve? If recrimination were abolished as a fault-based defense, should it be retained, nonetheless, to determine alimony? That is, should fault trump financial need?

3. *Modern applications.* Recrimination still surfaces occasionally as a divorce defense. See, e.g., Sproles v. Sproles, 782 So. 2d 742 (Miss. 2001); Edmisten v. Edmisten, 2003 WL 21077990 (Tenn. Ct. App. 2003).

2. Condonation

■ HAYMES v. HAYMES
646 N.Y.S.2d 315 (App. Div. 1996)

MAZZARELLI, Justice. . . .

Gail and Stephen Haymes were married in 1965 and lived together, without interruption, until 1987. They are the parents of two adult children, born in 1967 and 1975. According to plaintiff's allegations, beginning in December 1984, defendant refused to have sexual relations with her, rejecting her repeated overtures. In September 1987, defendant moved out of the couple's home, an act which plaintiff maintains was without her consent and without justification. The plaintiff claimed that defendant engaged in several adulterous relationships with women identified in the complaint. Defendant retained legal counsel, who wrote to plaintiff, suggesting that she retain her own matrimonial lawyer. This action for divorce and related relief was commenced [by wife] in September of 1988. . . .

The couple attempted a reconciliation between November 18, 1988 and January 4, 1989, during which time they resumed residing unhappily together. According to Ms. Haymes, her husband expressed neither remorse for his adultery nor any affection for her during this six-week period. Unable to resolve their problems, Gail and Stephen Haymes returned to living apart and pursuing their respective marital claims. Indeed, in January 1989, defendant asserted his own counterclaim for divorce.

On January 23, 1995, on the eve of the trial herein, defendant moved in open court for dismissal [of wife's causes of action for abandonment and constructive abandonment]. He urged that these claims were precluded because of the wife's admission, during a wholly separate conversion action, that she and the husband resumed living together briefly between November 18, 1988 and January 4, 1989. The wife also conceded that during this time period, while on a family vacation in Vail, Colorado, she and her husband had engaged in sexual relations at least once. According to defendant, upon returning from the family vacation, plaintiff informed him that the attempted reconciliation was a failure and that he was not to come back to the marital home. [T]he parties had later visited Acapulco, Mexico, together in 1990. Plaintiff, in response, argued that a single unsuccessful effort at reconciliation after the matrimonial action had already been commenced is hardly sufficient to defeat, as a matter of law, her claims founded in abandonment. . . .

[T]here is a dearth of current appellate authority in this state directly addressing the legal question presented by this dispute, whether a relatively brief attempt at a reconciliation . . . should require plaintiff to forfeit these otherwise facially valid causes of action for divorce. . . . In our view, common sense teaches that it is consistent with the public policy of this state that couples enduring marital disharmony should be encouraged to attempt reconciliation, particularly when, as here, the marriage is one of long duration. That the courts should, when practicable, encourage the preservation of families, in all their permutations, is so painfully obvious, that the lack of appellate authority so declaring can only be explained by the failure heretofore of anyone to contest such a basic proposition.

The extant case law does not point to a contrary result. . . . Although not exactly on all fours with this case, we find that the authorities relied on by plaintiff, in that they discuss the effect of reconciliation attempts on causes of action other than abandonment, are at least supportive of her position. Moreover, we agree with plaintiff that there is more than an implication in several of the cases that an effort to reconcile is meaningless without a showing that it was made in good faith.

. . . In the case at bar, by granting the motion for summary judgment just prior to opening statements, the trial court prevented plaintiff from endeavoring to prove that defendant did not make a good faith effort to reconcile. The court held plaintiff's abandonment claims were forfeited as a matter of law by the fact she engaged in sexual relations with her husband during the failed reconciliation attempt. However, we view the extant record as ambiguous as to the frequency of those relations and whether they were entered into in good faith by the defendant husband. The prevailing legal authority, even if sparse, seems to hold that cohabitation by itself is insufficient to invalidate a separation agreement or an accrued claim for divorce. . . . Furthermore, in the context of a cruel and inhuman treatment cause of action, it has been held that a short period of cohabitation does not amount to condonation of the cruel and inhuman treatment asserted as the basis of a divorce. [Lowe v. Lowe, 324 N.Y.S.2d 229 (Sup. Ct. 1970), *aff'd*, 322 N.Y.S.2d 975 (App. Div. 1971).]

As long ago as 1928 this court declared, and the Court of Appeals agreed, in the context of a cause of action for cruel and inhuman treatment, that "[w]e are not in accord with defendant's argument that cohabitation after acts of cruelty may be considered as condonation, in the sense in which it would be after an act of adultery. We rule that endurance of unkind treatment in an effort to overcome its practice and continuance of cohabitation does not condone a course of inhuman conduct" [Fisher v. Fisher, 227 N.Y.S. 345 (Sup. Ct. 1928), *aff'd*, 165 N.E. 460 (N.Y. 1929)]. Today, we hold that an estranged couple's attempt at a reconciliation, even where it involves the brief and isolated resumption of cohabitation and/or sexual relations, after a matrimonial action has already been commenced, does not, as a matter of law, preclude an entry of judgment in favor of the spouse who originally had an otherwise valid claim for abandonment. Rather, the trial court should examine the totality of the circumstances surrounding the purported reconciliation, before determining its effect, if any, upon the pending marital proceeding. Among the many factors for the trial court to consider are whether the reconciliation and any cohabitation were entered into in good faith, whether it was at all successful, who initiated it and with what motivation. Although concededly more difficult to apply than a rule which automatically results in the forfeiture of abandonment claims upon the parties making even the most hollow attempt at reconciliation, we conclude that the approach we adopt is not only consonant with human experience and common sense, but with the public policy and law of our State as well. . . .

Notes and Questions

1. *Definition.* Under the principle of condonation, "a spouse who has once condoned a marital transgression by his mate is thereafter barred from using that transgression as grounds for divorce." Marvin M. Moore, An Examination of the Condonation Doctrine, 2 Akron L. Rev. 75 (1969). Grounds that may be condoned include: adultery, cruelty, habitual drunkenness, and, as in *Haymes*, desertion (termed here "abandonment"). However, as *Haymes* explains, some courts limit the application of the condonation defense to adultery.

2. *Requirements.* Does condonation require both forgiveness of marital misconduct and resumption of sexual intercourse? See In re Marriage of Hightower, 830 N.E.2d 862, 867 (Ill. App. Ct. 2005) (condonation is "a question of intent [involving] a combination of factors" and finding that wife condoned husband's infidelity by her ensuing cohabitation); Hoffman v. Hoffman, 762 A.2d 766 (Pa. Super. Ct. 2000) (holding that husband's resumption of sexual relations was evidence of his condonation of wife's infidelity despite his refusal to withdraw the custody action). Is resumption of cohabitation sufficient to establish condonation or must the cohabitation include sexual relations? See Vinson v. Vinson, 880 So. 2d 469 (Ala. Civ. App. 2003) (holding that sexual intercourse may generally be presumed from cohabitation for purposes of condonation); Nemeth v. Nemeth, 481 S.E.2d 181 (S.C. Ct. App. 1997) (finding no condonation because spouses spent two nights together without sexual relations after wife confessed adultery). Does the recurrence of defendant's wrongful conduct (after plaintiff's initial condonation) revive the previous offenses? See Langdon v. Langdon, 854 So. 2d 485 (Miss. Ct. App. 2003). Is it appropriate to assume that the resumption of sexual relations constitutes forgiveness by one party?

3. *Policy.* Does the doctrine raise constitutional issues of family privacy? If so, how? Should condonation serve as grounds for denying divorce, or merely affect the granting of fault-based alimony?

4. *Attorneys' role.* Because of the condonation defense, should divorce attorneys regularly counsel their clients at their first interview and at every opportunity, "Do Not. Under Any Circumstances. Have Sex. With Your Spouse. Again."? See Res Ipsa Loquitur: Condonation, Aug. 12, 2004, available at http://res-ipsa.the-

blinding-white-light.com/archives/002330.html (so suggesting in the context of a discussion of the New York case of Ozkan v. Ozkan, for the reason that some "try to take advantage of that theory by conning the innocent spouse into bed, then using that to leverage a more 'favorable' settlement").

5. *Abolition.* With the advent of no fault (discussed in the next section), many jurisdictions abolished the fault-based defenses. Nonetheless, as *Haymes* reveals, some jurisdictions continue to recognize some or all of these defenses. See Ga. Code Ann. §19-5-4 (2004) (recognizing collusion, connivance, recrimination, and condonation); Edmisten v. Edmisten, 2003 WL 21077990 (Tenn. Ct. App. 2003) (pointing out that the state legislature has limited the defense of recrimination to divorce actions based on adultery). And, a few jurisdictions that have abolished recrimination as a defense still preserve the defense of condonation. See, e.g., 750 Ill. Comp. Stat. Ann. 5/403 (West 2002); Tex. Fam. Code Ann. §6.008 (Vernon 2005). See also the textual Note, Abolition of Fault-Based Defenses, infra p. 526.

6. *Criticisms.* The traditional condonation doctrine was harsh in its application to the forgiving spouse. One commentator notes:

> The practical effect of the rule of condonation is to impose a "do-or-die" decision upon the innocent spouse in the hour of crisis. Confronted suddenly with the knowledge of his partner's infidelity, he must decide promptly whether to pack his suitcase and leave what may have been and could be a very happy home, or to continue marital relations thereby forfeiting the right to dissolve the marriage if it should subsequently cease to be viable. The penalizing effect of the rule is to trap in a cancerous marriage those parties who have made laudable, although unsuccessful, attempts to reconcile.

Arthur L. Fox II, Condonation: An Obstruction to Reconciliation, 2 Fam. L.Q. 259, 259-260 (1969). Is the approach adopted by *Haymes* an improvement?

Problem

Marian and Henry marry in 1964. During the early years of their marriage, they have two sons (both now adults). However, during the past ten years, the parties have engaged in a sexual relationship on only one occasion. At the time they had sexual relations, Henry told Marian that he fantasized about being gay and that she was the only one who could "save" him. Subsequently, Marian finds a hotel receipt that reveals her husband spent the weekend with another man. She also finds letters from a gay pen pal club and pornographic videos and paraphernalia depicting homosexual acts. She files a petition for divorce on the grounds of cruelty. Henry answers, contending that the trial court erred in granting the divorce on the ground of cruelty and that Marian had condoned his homosexual behavior. What result? Thomas v. Thomas, 1996 WL 679985 (Va. Ct. App. 1996).

Note: Other Fault-Based Defenses

In the fault-based era, other common defenses to divorce were connivance and collusion. Connivance constitutes express or implied consent by the plaintiff to the misconduct alleged. 27A C.J.S. Divorce §85 (1986). Courts have offered three reasons why connivance is a defense to divorce: First, according to the Latin maxim *Volenti non fit injuria*, "He who consents cannot receive an injury." Second, a petitioner with unclean hands is not entitled to equitable relief. Third, some states limited divorce to the innocent party, and a conniving spouse was not an innocent party. See Marvin M. Moore, An Analysis of Collusion and Connivance, Bars to Divorce, 36 UMKC L. Rev. 193, 196-197 (1968).

Collusion is an agreement between husband and wife to: (1) commit a marital offense in order to obtain a divorce, (2) introduce false evidence of a transgression not actually committed, or (3) suppress a valid defense. Id. at 194-195. Before no-fault divorce "[t]he collusive divorce, so far from being a rare phenomenon, appears to be the norm." Id. at 226.

Courts sometimes have difficulty distinguishing collusion from connivance. See, e.g., Furst v. Furst, 78 N.Y.S.2d 608 (Sup. Ct. 1948), *modified*, 91 N.Y.S.2d 202 (App. Div. 1949). Professor Moore explains the distinctions:

> Although related in concept and function, collusion and connivance differ in two significant respects: First, connivance requires only the corrupt consent of the plaintiff, while collusion requires that of both spouses; and secondly, connivance cannot occur without the actual commission of a marital offense, while collusion can take place without either party's ever actually giving the other cause for divorce.

Moore, supra, at 195.

Finally, insanity provided a ground for divorce as well as a defense. See Rutherford v. Rutherford, 414 S.E.2d 157 (S.C. 1992). Because divorce required a "guilty" party, mental illness served to relieve the defendant from liability for acts of marital misconduct. See generally DiFonzo, supra; Lawrence M. Friedman, A Dead Language: Divorce Law and Practice Before No-Fault, 86 Va. L. Rev. 1497 (2000) (both providing historical accounts of divorce prior to no fault).

Problem

Mrs. Hollis seeks a divorce on the ground of adultery. Mr. Hollis alleges the defense of connivance. He contends that his wife urged him to date other women. He introduces into evidence a handwritten note to him, stating her hope that he would fall in love with another woman so that Mrs. Hollis could leave the marriage. After the husband began an affair, the wife again wrote to him that she hoped that he and his new love would live together for some time (prior to marriage). Further, the husband testifies that when he and his new woman friend first had sexual relations at a hotel, they received flowers and a card from the wife saying, "My very best wishes to you both today, to your new beginning." What result? See Hollis v. Hollis, 427 S.E.2d 233 (Va. Ct. App. 1993).

D. NO-FAULT DIVORCE

1. Divorce Reform

All states currently offer some form of no-fault divorce. Considerable variation exists, however, as to that form. Two common models, the California Family Law Act and the Uniform Marriage and Divorce Act, are discussed below.

■ ALLEN M. PARKMAN, GOOD INTENTIONS GONE AWRY: NO-FAULT DIVORCE AND THE AMERICAN FAMILY

72-75, 79-81 (2000)

The nation's unequivocal no-fault law became effective in California in 1970. . . . It is impossible to identify exactly when the reform movement began, but the California legislature took its first steps in that direction in 1963. In that year, a House Resolution was passed that initiated a study of the laws on divorce, and an interim committee began the study. . . . Four major themes emerged from the 1964 hearings in the California Assembly which set the agenda for the legislative proposals that followed. There were widespread concerns about:

1. the high divorce rate,
2. the adversary process creating hostility, acrimony, and trauma,
3. a need to recognize the inevitability of divorce for some couples and attempt to make the legal process less destructive for them and their children, and
4. charges made by divorced men that the divorce law and its practitioners worked with divorced women to acquire an unfair advantage over former husbands.

The hearings reached no conclusions, nor was any legislation proposed; the interim committee disbanded. In 1966, Governor Edmund G. Brown, who was enthusiastic about divorce law reform, established a twenty-two member Commission on the Family. This commission consisted of one minister, four legislators, six lawyers, four judges, three psychiatrists, two law professors, one medical doctor, and one member of the State Social Welfare Board. . . .

The commission reviewed the condition of the family and made recommendations in two areas: First, it suggested revisions in the substantive law of divorce. Second, it examined the feasibility of establishing a system of family courts. The commission proposed legislation in the form of a model Family Court Act that would have created a family court, eliminated fault as a ground for divorce, and revised the community property distribution rules. The family court proposal included both the creation of a family court system and the establishment of procedures to encourage the parties to use the court's conciliation and counseling services. The commission also recommended that dissolution should be granted whenever the court found that the legitimate objectives of the marriage had been destroyed and that there was no reasonable likelihood that the marriage could be saved.

[The commission's recommendations served as a working model for subsequent bills.] The major objection raised to these bills was the potentially high cost of the counseling. No definitive action was taken on these bills in 1967, but they were reintroduced in 1968. . . .

James A. Hayes, a member of the Assembly Judiciary Committee, independently put together another proposal that eliminated the major cost-incurring features — a separate family court system and mandatory counseling structure — but kept the marriage-breakdown theory of divorce. [A subsequent bill, drafted by a conference committee of which he was a member, was enacted as the Family Law Act of 1969.]

The new Family Law Act established two grounds for marital dissolution, "irreconcilable differences which have caused the irremediable breakdown of the marriage" and incurable insanity. [The new act had no provision for a family court system or counseling.] Other changes emphasized a new orientation in divorce proceedings. The term *divorce* was replaced by *dissolution of marriage*. A neutral petition form, *In re the Marriage of Mrs. Smith and Mr. Smith*, replaced the adversarial form *Smith v. Smith*. The parties were called "petitioner" and "respondent" rather than "plaintiff" and "defendant," ...

Under the prior law, the property division was unequal when the grounds for divorce were adultery, extreme cruelty, or incurable insanity, with the innocent party allocated a disproportionately large share of the community property. Under the new act, community property usually was to be divided equally, with no regard for fault, unless the division would impair the value of the property, such as a business, or when community funds had been deliberately squandered or misused by one spouse to the extent that an equal division of the remaining assets would no longer be equitable. Alimony was redefined as "support" and was determined by fairness rather than fault. . . .

. . . Often ignored in the histories of no-fault divorce in California was the special interest that Hayes brought to his advocacy of no-fault. James A. Hayes was involved in a bitter divorce action during the evolution of no-fault in the California legislature. [Lawyer Hayes divorced his homemaker wife in 1969, after 25 years of marriage and four children. The final decree was fairly generous to his wife. Three years later, in 1972, Hayes petitioned to end his financial obligations to his wife because he had remarried and assumed new financial obligations.] Hayes's brief in support of his request included a quotation from the 1969 California Assembly Judiciary Committee Report on the new California Family Law Act, which he helped write. Part of the quotation included:

> When our divorce law was originally drawn, woman's role in society was almost totally that of mother and homemaker. She could not even vote. Today, increasing numbers of married women are employed, even in the professions. In addition, they have long been accorded full civil rights. Their approaching equality with the male should be reflected in the law governing marriage dissolution. . . .

When the judge's decision was handed down in March 1973, James Hayes prevailed. Child support was ended, and alimony was gradually reduced to $300 per month [from the previous award of $650]. [A year later Hayes again requested a reduction in alimony. His wife's alimony was further reduced, and the judge told Hayes's 53-year-old ill ex-wife to find employment. That decision was overruled subsequently as an abuse of discretion.]

. . . Hayes was obviously not a casual observer. He was instrumental in enacting no-fault divorce in California; after its passage, in the report that rationalized its passage, he emphasized the equality between men and women. He then used the law and the report to attempt to reduce the financial arrangements to which he had agreed as a condition for his divorce. . . .

In most histories of the passage of the law, James Hayes's role is given only passing notice. If anything, he is pictured as a very active public servant. But the passage of no-fault in California bears witness to the process of legislative self-interest. . . . This is a law that was passed by a legislature dominated by men . . . reenforced by the lobbying efforts of men's interest groups and maneuvered through the California legislature by a man who personally had a great deal to gain from a reduction in the negotiating power of married women. . . .

■ **LYNNE CAROL HALEM, DIVORCE REFORM: CHANGING LEGAL AND SOCIAL PERSPECTIVES**
269-277 (1980)

[THE UNIFORM MARRIAGE AND DIVORCE ACT]

The idea of a national marriage and divorce statute, either in the form of an amendment to the Constitution or a singular law to be adopted by each state, was first proposed in 1884 and continued to spark debates for many years. [T]he Uniform Marriage and Divorce Act [was] ratified by the National Conference of Commissioners on Uniform State Laws in 1970. [The original intent was to remove the concept of fault by substituting the term "irretrievable breakdown" for fault-based grounds and to reject the no-fault ground of separation because it might be construed as a form of punishment.]

The critical blow came from the members of the Family Law Section of the American Bar Association. Whereas in the past, the ABA had been most supportive of the commissioners' bills, this statute proved to be the exception. Without discrediting the concept of no-fault, the Bar attacked the statute on three grounds: the ease and speed with which a divorce could be granted; the absence of conciliation provisions or other brakes on hasty divorce; and the lack of specificity in the regulations governing property division. . . . Using standard conservative arguments, the ABA charged that passage of the act would legalize "easy" or "quickie" divorces. It may be that this position reflected the fear of an insidious plot to minimize the role of legal counsel. . . .

[The commissioners drafted three versions of the statute before they received ABA endorsement in 1974. The 1973 version of the act reintroduced notions of fault.] If the commissioners' capitulation was not total it was, nonetheless, significant. The new statute introduced a clause for the no-fault ground of separation even if the waiting period was abbreviated to 180 days; the term "marital discord" was implicitly linked to the ground of "cruel and inhuman treatment" even if "marital misconduct" was not mentioned; references to reconciliation were more obtrusive even if they were not clearly defined; and the ABA's denouncement of demand divorce received credence through the addition of new safeguards even if they were weak and inoperable.

In other ways, however, the Uniform Marriage and Divorce Act was more progressive than California's law. Issues of marital misconduct were considered irrelevant to custody. [Evidence of fault was relevant to custody in early versions of the California statute but not after 1993.] The effort to discourage spousal maintenance by basing awards on the needs and resources of the parties might eventually prove a more realistic and less acrimonious approach to the problem of post-divorce economics.

Further, incurable insanity and irreconcilable differences did not appear as grounds for dissolution. Whereas the former was largely superfluous in the California act, the latter troubled some purists who objected to the multiplicity of possible translations. Quite obviously the uniform bill had other vagaries. The term "irretrievably broken" was not defined, nor were precise directives furnished

to curtail the discretionary powers of the judiciary. Hence many of the indetermi-
nacies in the California model were duplicated in this statute. But in California the
reformers could predict fairly accurately the court's interpretation would be liberal.
This was not the case with the Uniform Act. . . .

Many states follow the California or UMDA models. Other jurisdictions have
taken different approaches (illustrated below).

■ CALIFORNIA FAMILY CODE §§2310, 2311, 2335
(West 2004) (formerly California Civil Code §§4506,
4507, 4509)

§2310. GROUNDS FOR DISSOLUTION OR LEGAL
SEPARATION

Dissolution of the marriage or legal separation of the parties may be based on
either of the following grounds, which shall be pleaded generally:

    (a) Irreconcilable differences, which have caused the irremediable break-
        down of the marriage.
    (b) Incurable insanity.

§2311. IRRECONCILABLE DIFFERENCES DEFINED

Irreconcilable differences are those grounds which are determined by the court
to be substantial reasons for not continuing the marriage and which make it appear
that the marriage should be dissolved.

§2335. MISCONDUCT; ADMISSIBILITY OF SPECIFIC
ACTS OF MISCONDUCT

Except as otherwise provided by statute, in a pleading or proceeding for dissolution of marriage or legal separation of the parties, including depositions and
discovery proceedings, evidence of specific acts of misconduct is improper and
inadmissible.

■ UNIFORM MARRIAGE AND DIVORCE ACT
§§302, 305
9A U.L.A. (pt. I) 200 (1998)

§302. [DISSOLUTION OF MARRIAGE; LEGAL
SEPARATION]

    (a) The [_____] court shall enter a decree of dissolution of marriage
if: . . .

        (2) the court finds that the marriage is irretrievably broken, if the finding is
supported by evidence that (i) the parties have lived separate and apart for a

period of more than 180 days next preceding the commencement of the proceeding, or (ii) there is serious marital discord adversely affecting the attitude of
one or both of the parties toward the marriage. . . .

§305. [IRRETRIEVABLE BREAKDOWN]

(a) If both of the parties by petition or otherwise have stated under oath or
affirmation that the marriage is irretrievably broken, or one of the parties has so
stated and the other has not denied it, the court, after hearing, shall make a finding
whether the marriage is irretrievably broken.

(b) If one of the parties has denied under oath or affirmation that the marriage
is irretrievably broken, the court shall consider all relevant factors, including the
circumstances that gave rise to filing the petition and the prospect of reconciliation,
and shall:

(1) make a finding whether the marriage is irretrievably broken;
or

(2) continue the matter for further hearing not fewer than 30 nor more than
60 days later, or as soon thereafter as the matter may be reached on the court's
calendar, and may suggest to the parties that they seek counseling. The court, at
the request of either party shall, or on its own motion may, order a conciliation
conference. At the adjourned hearing the court shall make a finding whether the
marriage is irretrievably broken.

(c) A finding of irretrievable breakdown is a determination that there is no
reasonable prospect of reconciliation.

■ NEW YORK DOMESTIC RELATIONS LAW [8]
§170
(McKinney 1999 & Supp. 2005)

An action for divorce may be maintained by a husband or wife to procure a
judgment divorcing the parties and dissolving the marriage on any of the following
grounds:

(1) The cruel and inhuman treatment of the plaintiff by the defendant such that
the conduct of the defendant so endangers the physical or mental well being of the
plaintiff as renders it unsafe or improper for the plaintiff to cohabit with the
defendant.

(2) The abandonment of the plaintiff by the defendant for a period of one or
more years.

(3) The confinement of the defendant in prison for a period of three or more
consecutive years after the marriage of plaintiff and defendant.

(4) The commission of an act of adultery. . . .

(5) The husband and wife have lived apart pursuant to a decree or judgment
of separation for a period of one or more years after the granting of such decree

---

[8]. New York has the strictest divorce law in the country. As the above statute reveals, divorce is
permitted there only on fault-based grounds, or living apart for at least one year pursuant to a decree of
judicial separation or by written agreement. No-fault divorce has been opposed by a coalition consisting
of the Catholic Church and feminist groups. As this book goes to press, however, legislation is being
considered in both the state Assembly and Senate to permit no-fault divorce.

or judgment, and satisfactory proof has been submitted by the plaintiff that he or she has substantially performed all the terms and conditions of such decree or judgment.

(6) The husband and wife have lived separate and apart pursuant to a written agreement of separation, . . . for a period of one or more years after the execution of such agreement and satisfactory proof has been submitted by the plaintiff that he or she has substantially performed all terms and conditions of such agreement. . . .

2. Legal Problems Raised by No-Fault Divorce

a. Early Problems of No-Fault

The advent of no-fault divorce brought its share of legal problems. One problem focused on the method of proof to secure a no-fault divorce, stemming from the concern with making divorce too easily obtainable. Specifically, did a divorce petitioner need to make a personal appearance or would courts permit the petitioner simply to file an affidavit alleging the requisite grounds for a no-fault divorce? In In re Marriage of McKim, 493 P.2d 868 (Cal. 1972), California initially responded to that question by requiring the petitioner (absent exceptional circumstances) to appear personally and to testify at the hearing as to the existence of irreconcilable differences. In requiring a personal appearance, *McKim* ended the practice of permitting divorce by affidavit. California subsequently dispensed with the need for an appearance in all cases. In 1978 the legislature enacted a summary dissolution procedure that permits dissolution in a short period of time upon mutual consent, provided that the parties: (1) have no children, (2) were married less than 5 years, (3) do not own real property, (4) have debts (excluding automobiles) totaling less than $4,000, (5) have no more than $25,000 in community property and separate property, and (6) waive spousal support (Cal. Fam. Code §2400 (West 2004)). Similar summary procedures exist in many jurisdictions.

Another problem concerned discomfort with unilateral divorce, i.e., a divorce desired by only one of the spouses. If only one spouse thought the marriage was "irretrievably broken," was that sufficient to require the court to award a no-fault divorce? See, e.g., In re Marriage of Dunn, 511 P.2d 427, 429 (Or. Ct. App. 1973) (reading a statute patterned on California's to require a difference "that reasonably appears to the court to be in the mind of the petitioner an irreconcilable one [which] need not necessarily be so viewed by both parties"). Yet, other courts resisted no-fault divorce over the objection of one party. For example, in Shearer v. Shearer, 356 F.2d 391 (3d Cir. 1965), *cert. denied*, 384 U.S. 940 (1966), the court reversed a divorce granted to the husband. Despite the couple's constant bickering, their six-year separation initiated by the husband (and his overcoming alcoholism only after the separation), the court concluded that the finding of "incompatibility" was clearly erroneous in light of the wife's interest in continuing the marriage and the couple's ten years cohabitation.

Some states enacted statutes that made divorce more difficult to obtain when only one spouse wanted the divorce. See, e.g., Mo. Rev. Stat. §452.320.2 (2003) (requiring proof of fault or two-year separation in such a case); Nieters v. Nieters, 815 S.W.2d 124 (Mo. Ct. App. 1991) (finding that trial court award of no-fault divorce was erroneous because the evidence did not establish the requisite grounds for divorce when one party denied that the marriage was irretrievably broken). And, in New York, unilateral no-fault divorce is unavailable; even parties who live apart for one year pursuant to a judicial separation often cannot get divorced unless they have reached consensus on all issues. Leslie Eaton, A New Push to Loosen New York's Divorce Law, N.Y. Times, Nov. 30, 2004, at 1 (describing reform efforts).

A number of other problems plagued early no-fault legislation. For example, opponents unsuccessfully challenged early legislation on such constitutional grounds as vagueness, impairment of contract, equal protection, and freedom of religion. See, e.g., In re Walton's Marriage, 104 Cal. Rptr. 472 (Ct. App. 1972); In re Marriage of Franks, 542 P.2d 845 (Colo. 1975). Surprisingly, an occasional constitutional challenge still occurs. See, e.g., Grimm v. Grimm, 844 A.2d 855 (Conn. App. Ct. 2003) (unsuccessful challenge on grounds of freedom of religion); Richter v. Richter, 625 N.W.2d 490 (Minn. Ct. App. 2001) (unsuccessful challenge that dissolution statute interferes with constitutional right to contract).

Problems

1. The jurisdiction of Blackacre has just approved the adoption of domestic partnerships. A Blackacre legislator is proposing the following grounds for termination of a domestic partnership: adultery; willful and continued desertion for at least one year; physical or mental cruelty that endangers the plaintiff's safety or health or makes continued cohabitation unreasonable; separation for at least 18 months with no reasonable prospect of reconciliation; addiction to any narcotic drug; institutionalization for mental illness for two or more years; or imprisonment of the defendant for 18 or more consecutive months after establishment of the domestic partnership. In such proceedings, the court is not required to effectuate an equitable distribution of property. As the legislator's intern, you are asked for your advice on the proposed legislation. See N.J. Stat. §26:8A-10 (2005) (termination of domestic partnerships).

2. Blackacre recently simplified its divorce procedure. A newly enacted statute authorizes divorce-by-mail decrees. Such decrees allow petitioners to divorce without making a personal appearance if: (1) the couple has no minor children and the wife is not pregnant, (2) neither party has real property, (3) neither party desires spousal support, (4) the couple's debts do not exceed $10,000, and (5) the marital property totals less than $15,000. See Ariz. R. Civ. P. Ann. 55(b)(1)(ii) (West 2001). Mary Jones, a Blackacre legislator, is concerned that cutbacks in legal services have resulted in vast numbers of persons whose needs for divorce are not being met. She would like to propose that the simplified procedure be extended. You are her legislative intern. What do you advise?

b. Living Separate and Apart

■ BENNINGTON v. BENNINGTON
381 N.E.2d 1355 (Ohio Ct. App. 1978)

McCORMAC, Judge.
Mary Bennington commenced an action for alimony only, claiming gross neglect of duty and abandonment without just cause as grounds therefor. Larry

Bennington answered, denying grounds for alimony, and counterclaimed for divorce alleging gross neglect of duty and extreme cruelty. His counterclaim was later amended asserting the grounds for divorce of living separate and apart for at least two years without cohabitation. . . .

Plaintiff and defendant were married in 1946. No children have been born to the marriage. In 1963, plaintiff suffered a stroke rendering her permanently and totally disabled and causing her left side to become paralyzed. There have been no sexual relations between the parties since that time.

In 1974, Larry Bennington moved out of the house and into a travel van located adjacent to the house on the same premises. His primary reason for moving into the van was that his wife kept the heat in the house at about 85 to 90 degrees Fahrenheit. He was also irritated about the fact that his wife locked and bolted the door to the house and, when he arrived home from work, it frequently took her fifteen to twenty minutes to come to the door to let him into the house. Her reason for locking the door was apparently for security purposes. There were also other areas of conflict between the parties. However, there was no intention on the part of Larry Bennington to abandon his marital responsibilities when he moved from the house to the van in 1974. On the contrary, he continued to help his disabled wife with household chores, pretty much the same as before moving into the travel van. There was a conflict as to whether he ever slept inside the house again after moving to the van, or whether he used the house otherwise for his comfort and enjoyment. It is clear, however, that he did enter the house regularly to assist his disabled wife.

On November 26, 1976, Larry Bennington finally became thoroughly disenchanted with the entire arrangement and decided to leave home. He went to Arizona for about one month. He then returned, regaining his job. After his return, he lived off of the premises in the van for about three months and then obtained an apartment elsewhere.

R.C. 3105.01(K) provides grounds for divorce ". . . [w]hen husband and wife have, without interruption for two years, lived separate and apart without cohabitation. . . ."

The trial court found that when the husband moved from the house to the van located on the same premises that he was living separate and apart without cohabitation. . . .

The trial court erroneously included the time that the husband lived in the van adjacent to the house as part of the two-year period, as the parties were not living "separate and apart" during that time. During that time there was no cessation of marital duties and relations between the wife and husband. Approximately the same duties were performed by the husband to the wife and by the wife to the husband as prior to the time that the husband moved outside of the house to the van. . . . While the parties were living apart in a limited sense, they were not living separately in a marital sense. . . .

Judgment reversed.

Notes and Questions

1. *Mixed grounds.* With the movement toward no fault, many states merely added no-fault grounds (for example, living separate and apart) to their traditional

fault-based grounds. Thus, a large number of states reflect a "mixed" fault/no-fault regime. This approach contrasts with "pure" no-fault laws in some jurisdictions, such as California.

2. *Statutory variations.* Statutes reflect three types of "living separate and apart" provisions. Clark, Law of Domestic Relations (2d ed), supra, at 518. First, parties must live apart under a judicial decree or separation agreement for a prescribed period. Second, parties must live apart "willingly" or "voluntarily" (that is, by mutual consent). The third, and least restrictive, merely requires proof that the parties lived apart for the statutory period. E.g., UMDA §302(a)(2), 9A U.L.A. (pt. 1) 200 (1998). Which type is the statute in *Bennington*?

3. *Historical background.* Many states had living-apart statutes prior to California's adoption of no fault. DiFonzo, supra, at 39 (citing 23 states). However, such statutes were aimed at forestalling, rather than facilitating, divorce. In addition, the requisite statutory periods were so long (generally five to ten years) that the statutes were seldom utilized. Id. at 42, 44.

4. *Duration.* Durational periods for "living separate and apart" range from six months (for example, UMDA §302(a)(2)) to three years. National Survey of State Laws, supra, at 396-411 (extrapolation from survey of divorce grounds in the various states). In jurisdictions that require lengthy separations before filing for a no-fault divorce, an unhappy spouse must thereby resort to traditional fault-based grounds. What purposes do lengthy separation requirements serve? Do they undermine the purposes of no fault?

5. *Definitions.* Why does the court conclude the parties were not "living separate and apart"? Suppose the van were not adjacent to the house. Down the street? Across town? Is the geographic location determination? Suppose Mr. Bennington obtained an apartment in 1974, yet still returned daily to assist his wife. Is he living separate and apart? May parties who separate to reside in different bedrooms ever establish that they are "living separate and apart"? Compare Jacobi v. Jacobi, 2001 WL 515920 (Va. Cir. Ct. 2001) (denying divorce on ground of living separate and apart because parties continued to reside in marital home in separate bedrooms), with Frey v. Frey, 821 A.2d 623 (Pa. Super. Ct. 2003) (contra).

6. *Outcome.* Did Mrs. Bennington's acts constitute sufficient cruelty for divorce? How did her disability affect the outcome? Were Mr. Bennington's chores in the household after moving to the van "marital duties and relations" or caretaking of a disabled person? Should Mr. Bennington's altruistic behavior preclude his divorce?

7. *Comparison.* How is living separate and apart similar to, and different from, fault-based grounds, particularly desertion? Why is a statutory period required? What difference does it make when it commences? What should toll the statutory period? Suppose the Benningtons were intimate once during the statutory period. Recall the condonation defense. Should fault-based defenses be available?

8. *Economic impact.* Should a party wishing to separate be forced to vacate the marital home, even if not financially able? See Carol Bruch, The Legal Import of Informal Marital Separations: A Survey of California Law and a Call for Change, 65 Cal. L. Rev. 1015 (1977) (requirement causes financial hardship).

9. *Privacy.* One commentator suggests that living-apart statutes spared parties "the intrusion into their privacy which fault divorce proceedings mandated." DiFonzo, supra, at 39. Is this an apt characterization of the proceedings in *Bennington*?

10. *Legal separation distinguished.* Legal separations, constituting an alternative to divorce, were quite common during the fault-based era when divorce was difficult to obtain. Such separations were once called "divorce from bed and board" (from the Latin *divorce a mensa et thoro*) to be distinguished from absolute divorce (or *divorce a vinculo matrimonii* from the bonds of marriage). Decrees of legal separation do not free the parties to remarry but do relieve them from cohabitation. Today, decrees of separation are still necessary in some states to satisfy statutory requirements for the divorce ground of "living separate and apart."

Note: Abolition of Fault-Based Defenses

One important legal issue after the adoption of no fault was the status of fault-based defenses. Many states abolished them legislatively. See, e.g., Colo. Rev. Stat. Ann. §14-10-107(5) (West 2005); Fla. Stat. Ann. §61.044 (West 1997); Minn. Stat. Ann. §518.06 (West 1990); Mont. Code Ann. §40-4-105(4) (2003). Some states abolished them judicially. See Flora v. Flora, 337 N.E.2d 846, 852 (Ind. Ct. App. 1975). On the other hand, some states that added no-fault divorce to their fault grounds still maintain the defenses. See, e.g., Me. Rev. Stat. Ann. tit. 19-A, §902(3) (recrimination), §902(4) (condonation) (West 1998). Fault-based defenses become important in jurisdictions with lengthy separation requirements (which force parties who want a speedier divorce to resort to traditional fault-based grounds) or in those jurisdictions in which fault continues to play a role in spousal support or property division.

c. What Role for Fault?

■ **FELTMEIER v. FELTMEIER**
798 N.E.2d 75 (Ill. 2003)

Justice RARICK delivered the opinion of the court:
Plaintiff, Lynn Feltmeier, and defendant, Robert Feltmeier, were married on October 11, 1986, and divorced on December 16, 1997. [O]n August 25, 1999, Lynn sued Robert for the intentional infliction of emotional distress. . . .
The first matter before us for review is whether Lynn's complaint states a cause of action for intentional infliction of emotional distress. . . . According to the allegations contained in Lynn's complaint, since the parties' marriage in October 1986, and continuing for over a year after the December 1997 dissolution of their marriage:

> "[Robert] entered into a continuous and outrageous course of conduct toward [Lynn] with either the intent to cause emotional distress to [Lynn] or with reckless disregard as to whether such conduct would cause emotional distress to [Lynn], said continuing course of conduct, including but not limited to, the following:
> A. On repeated occasions, [Robert] has battered [Lynn] by striking, kicking, shoving, pulling hair and bending and twisting her limbs and toes. . . .
> B. On repeated occasions, [Robert] has prevented [Lynn] from leaving the house to escape the abuse. . . .

C. On repeated occasions, [Robert] has yelled insulting and demeaning epithets at [Lynn]. Further, [Robert] has engaged in verbal abuse which included threats and constant criticism of [Lynn] in such a way as to demean, humiliate, and degrade [Lynn]. . . .

D. On repeated occasions, [Robert] threw items at [Lynn] with the intent to cause her harm. . . .

E. On repeated occasions, [Robert] attempted to isolate [Lynn] from her family and friends and would get very upset if [Lynn] would show the marks and bruises resulting from [Robert's] abuse to others.

F. On repeated occasions since the divorce, [Robert] has engaged in stalking behavior. . . .

G. On at least one occasion, [Robert] has attempted to interfere with [Lynn's] employment by confiscating her computer. Additionally, [Robert] broke into [Lynn's] locked drug cabinet for work on or about March 23, 1997."

[The court then sets forth the elements for intentional infliction of emotional distress: the conduct must be extreme and outrageous; the actor must either intend that his conduct inflict severe emotional distress, or know that there is at least a high probability that his conduct will cause severe emotional distress; and the conduct must in fact cause *severe* emotional distress.]

In the case at bar, Robert first contends that the allegations of Lynn's complaint do not sufficiently set forth conduct which was extreme and outrageous when considered "[i]n the context of the subjective and fluctuating nature of the marital relationship." In support of this contention, Robert cites several cases from other jurisdictions that have addressed the policy ramifications of allowing a spouse to maintain an action for intentional infliction of emotional distress based upon acts occurring during the marriage. In Pickering v. Pickering, 434 N.W.2d 758, 761 (S.D.1989), the Supreme Court of South Dakota held that the tort of intentional infliction of emotional distress should be unavailable as a matter of public policy when predicated on conduct which leads to the dissolution of a marriage. However, unlike the case at bar, the conduct serving as the basis for the tort in *Pickering* was the wife's extramarital affair, and the court noted that South Dakota law already provided a remedy for this type of claim in the form of an action against the paramour for alienation of affections. Next, Robert cites Hakkila v. Hakkila, 112 N.M. 172, 179, 812 P.2d 1320, 1327 (App. 1991), in which the Court of Appeals of New Mexico found that a husband's insults and occasional violent outbursts over the course of the parties' 10-year marriage were insufficiently outrageous to establish liability for intentional infliction of emotional distress. The *Hakkila* court additionally found insufficient evidence that the alleged wrongful conduct caused severe emotional distress. Notably, while counseling caution, the court did not find that New Mexico's public policy barred recognition of the tort in the marital context.

Finally, Robert cites a Texas case, Villasenor v. Villasenor, 911 S.W.2d 411, 415 n.2 (Tex. Civ. App. 1995), wherein the court, in *dicta*, noted that because the marital relationship "'is highly subjective and constituted by mutual understandings and interchanges which are constantly in flux [,] . . . [f]or purposes of determining outrageous conduct, the insults, indignities, threats, annoyances, petty oppressions, or other trivialities associated with marriage and divorce must be considered upon the individual facts of each case." However, Illinois case law makes clear that under no circumstances would "'mere insults, indignities, threats, annoyances, petty oppressions, or other trivialities'" qualify as outrageous conduct. *McGrath*, 126 Ill.2d at 86, 127 Ill.Dec. 724, 533 N.E.2d 806, quoting Restatement (Second) of Torts §46, Comment *d*, at 73 (1965). Rather, the nature of the defendant's conduct must be so extreme as to go beyond all possible bounds of decency and to be regarded as intolerable in a civilized community. Thus, while we agree that special caution is required in dealing with actions for intentional infliction of emotional distress arising from conduct occurring within the marital setting, our examination of both the law of this state and the most commonly raised policy concerns leads us to conclude that no valid reason exists to restrict such actions or to require a heightened threshold for outrageousness in this context.

One policy concern that has been advanced is the need to recognize the "mutual concessions implicit in marriage," and the desire to preserve marital harmony. See Henriksen v. Cameron, 622 A.2d 1135, 1138-39 (Me. 1993). However, in this case, brought after the parties were divorced, "there is clearly no marital harmony remaining to be preserved." *Henriksen*, 622 A.2d at 1139. Moreover, we agree with the Supreme Judicial Court of Maine that "behavior that is 'utterly intolerable in a civilized society' and is intended to cause severe emotional distress is not behavior that should be protected in order to promote marital harmony and peace." *Henriksen*, 622 A.2d at 1139, quoting Vicnire v. Ford Motor Credit Co., 401 A.2d 148, 154 (Me. 1979). Indeed, the Illinois legislature, in creating the Illinois Domestic Violence Act of 1986 (Act) (750 ILCS 60/101 *et seq.* (West 2002)), has recognized that domestic violence is "a serious crime against the individual and society." . . . Thus, it would seem that the public policy of this state would be furthered by recognition of the action at issue.

A second policy concern is the threat of excessive and frivolous litigation if the tort is extended to acts occurring in the marital setting. Admittedly, the likelihood of vindictive litigation is of particular concern following a dissolution of marriage, because "the events leading to most divorces involve some level of emotional distress." *Henriksen*, 622 A.2d at 1139. However, we believe that the showing required of a plaintiff in order to recover damages for intentional infliction of emotional distress provides a built-in safeguard against excessive and frivolous litigation. . . . Another policy consideration which has been raised is that a tort action for compensation would be redundant. [However,] the laws of this state provide no compensatory relief for injuries sustained [here]. An action for dissolution of marriage also provides no compensatory relief for domestic abuse. In Illinois, as in most other states, courts are not allowed to consider marital misconduct in the distribution of property when dissolving a marriage. See 750 ILCS 5/503(d) (West 2002). After examining case law from courts around the country, we find the majority have recognized that public policy considerations should not bar actions for intentional infliction of emotional distress between spouses or former spouses based on conduct occurring during the marriage.

[W]e now examine the allegations set forth in Lynn's complaint to determine whether Robert's conduct satisfies the "outrageousness" requirement. . . . The issue of whether domestic abuse can be sufficiently outrageous to sustain a cause of action for intentional infliction of emotional distress is apparently one of first impression in Illinois. Other jurisdictions, however, have found similar allegations of recurring cycles of physical and verbal abuse, wherein the conduct went far beyond the "trials of everyday life between two cohabiting people," to be sufficiently outrageous to fall within the parameters of section 46 of the Restatement (Second) of Torts. In the instant case, we must agree with the appellate court that, when the above-summarized allegations of the complaint are viewed in their entirety, they show a type of domestic abuse that is extreme enough to be actionable. . . .

[The court then rejected Robert's contention that Lynn did not suffer severe emotional distress, pointing to her claims of loss of self-esteem, difficulty in forming other relationships, Post Traumatic Stress Disorder, depression, a fear of men, and curtailment of enjoyment of life. Finally, the court considered Robert's argument that Lynn's claim was barred by the applicable statute of limitations.] The ultimate question, however, is when the statute of limitations began to run in the instant case. Generally, a limitations period begins to run when facts exist that authorize one party to maintain an action against another. However, under the "continuing tort" or "continuing violation" rule, "where a tort involves a continuing or repeated injury, the limitations period does not begin to run until the date of the last injury or the date the tortious acts cease." A continuing tort, therefore, does not involve tolling the statute of limitations because of delayed or continuing injuries, but instead involves viewing the defendant's conduct as a continuous whole for prescriptive purposes. . . .

In the instant case, Robert . . . maintains that "each of the alleged acts of abuse inflicted by Robert upon Lynn over a 12-year period are separate and distinct incidents which give rise to separate and distinct causes of action [and therefore, if occurring prior to August 25, 1997, would be time barred], rather than one single, continuous, unbroken, violation or wrong which continued over the entire period of 12 years." We must disagree. While it is true that the conduct set forth in Lynn's complaint could be considered separate acts constituting separate offenses of, *inter alia*, assault, defamation and battery, Lynn has alleged, and we have found, that Robert's conduct *as a whole* states a cause of action for intentional infliction of emotional distress. . . .

We believe the appellate court herein properly applied this reasoning to the facts of this case where:

> "The alleged domestic violence and abuse endured by Lynn . . . spanned the entire 11-year marriage. No one disputes that the allegations set forth the existence of ongoing abusive behavior. Lynn's psychologist, Dr. Michael E. Althoff, found that Lynn suffered from the 'battered wife syndrome.' He described the psychological process as one that unfolds over time. The process by which a spouse exerts coercive control is based upon 'a systematic, repetitive infliction of psychological trauma' designed to 'instill terror and helplessness.' Dr. Althoff indicated that the posttraumatic stress disorder from which Lynn suffered was the result of the entire series of abusive acts, not just the result of one specific incident."

The purpose behind a statute of limitations is to prevent stale claims, not to preclude claims before they are ripe for adjudication, and certainly not to shield a wrongdoer. As the Superior Court of New Jersey stated, in finding that a wife diagnosed with battered woman's syndrome could sue her spouse in tort for physical and emotional injuries sustained by continuous acts of battering during the course of the marriage:

> "It would be contrary to the public policy of this State, not to mention cruel, to limit recovery to only those individual incidents of assault and battery for which the applicable statute of limitations has not yet run. The mate who is responsible for creating the condition suffered by the battered victim must be made to account for his actions—*all* of his actions. Failure to allow affirmative recovery under these

circumstances would be tantamount to the courts condoning the continued abusive treatment of women in the domestic sphere." (Emphasis in original.) Cusseaux v. Pickett, 279 N.J.Super. 335, 345, 652 A.2d 789, 794 (1994).

Therefore, based upon the foregoing reasons, we agree [with] the growing number of jurisdictions that have found that the continuing tort rule should be extended to apply in cases of intentional infliction of emotional distress. . . . Applying the continuing tort rule to the instant case, Lynn's complaint, filed August 25, 1999, was clearly timely and her claims based on conduct prior to August 25, 1997, are not barred by the applicable statute of limitations. . . .

Notes and Questions

1. *Background.* Several factors contribute to applications of tort theories in the divorce context, including the abolition of interspousal immunity, recognition and extension of tort liability for emotional injury, awareness of the problem of domestic violence, and the demise of fault-based divorce. As *Feltmeier* reveals, courts are split over recognition of interspousal suits for emotional distress in the divorce context. See also Linda L. Berger, Lies Between Mommy and Daddy: The Case for Recognizing Spousal Emotional Distress Claims Based on Domestic Deceit that Interferes with Parent-Child Relationships, 33 Loy. L.A. L. Rev. 449, 464-467 (2000). On what basis does *Feltmeier* decide to recognize such suits?

2. *High threshold?* Should courts adopt a high threshold for extreme and outrageous behavior in the marital context? See McCulloh v. Drake, 24 P.3d 1162, 1170 (Wyo. 2001) (setting high standard for recovery "so that the social good which comes from recognizing the tort in a marital setting will not be undermined by an invasive flood of merit-less litigation" [and] to protect defendants from the possibility of long and intrusive trials on frivolous claims"). See also Tiffany Oliver, Intentional Infliction of Emotional Distress Between Spouses: New Mexico's Excessively High Threshold for Outrageous Conduct, 33 N.M. L. Rev. 381 (2003). Should outrageousness be limited to cases in which the spouse's conduct is criminal? See Ira Mark Ellman & Stephen D. Sugarman, Spousal Emotional Abuse as a Tort?, 55 Md. L. Rev. 1268, 1335 (1996).

3. *Policy.* The first issue that *Feltmeier* presents is whether courts should permit interspousal actions for intentional infliction of emotional distress in divorce actions. Do you agree with *Feltmeier*'s resolution of this issue? Does recognition of emotional distress claims in the context of divorce undermine no-fault divorce law? Resurrect the fault-based ground of cruelty? Further or disserve the goals of tort law? Lead to recovery for domestic disputes that are trivial and/or widespread? Lead to double recovery in cases in which fault plays a role in property distribution? Do problems of causation militate against recovery (i.e., the difficulty of proving that the emotional distress was caused by the spouse's conduct and not by the marital difficulties)?

On the policy arguments, compare Ira Mark Ellman, The Place of Fault in a Modern Divorce Law, 28 Ariz. St. L.J. 773 (1996); Ellman & Sugarman, supra; Harry D. Krause, On the Danger of Allowing Marital Fault to Re-Emerge in the Guise of Torts, 73 Notre Dame L. Rev. 1355, 1363-1366 (1998), with Berger, supra; Sarah M. Buel, Access to Meaningful Remedy: Overcoming Doctrinal Obstacles in Tort Litigation Against Domestic Violent Offenders, 83 Or. L. Rev. 945 (2004). See also Chen v. Fisher, 843 N.E.2d 723 (N.Y. 2005)

4. *Special rules?* If tort claims are permitted in the divorce context, should courts limit recognition to interspousal torts that involve injury or physical violence? Should special rules apply to claims of domestic violence? How does *Feltmeier* resolve the issue of whether statutes of limitations should be tolled for victims of spousal abuse who frequently endure years of abuse before filing for divorce? See also Clare Dalton, Domestic Violence, Domestic Torts and Divorce: Constraints and Possibilities, 31 N. Eng. L. Rev. 319, 339-346 (1997); David E. Poplar, Comment, Tolling the Statute of Limitations for Battered Women after Giovine v. Giovine: Creating Equitable Exceptions for Victims of Domestic Abuse, 101 Dick. L. Rev. 161 (1996). Should courts recognize a new tort of domestic violence? See Buel, supra, at 1019-1032.

5. *Privacy.* Should notions of privacy militate against recognition of intentional infliction claims? Cf. Buel, supra, at 976 ("It is ethically questionable for the state to be the sole arbiter of what should remain private and thus within the discretion of the spouses, and what may be considered by the court as within its purview.").

6. *Joinder.* Another issue involving tort liability in the context of divorce is whether courts should *require* joinder of tort claims and divorce claims.

a. *Different views.* Courts that permit interspousal actions for intentional infliction of emotional distress adopt different positions regarding joinder: some prohibit joinder, some mandate joinder, and some adopt a permissive policy of joinder. See Brinkman v. Brinkman, 966 S.W.2d 780, 782 (Tex. Ct. App. 1998) (explaining various positions); Twyman v. Twyman, 855 S.W.2d 619 (Tex. 1995) (adopting permissive joinder). Which approach do you favor? If a court does not permit joinder, is a plaintiff without remedy? May she pursue a separate action? Must she?

b. *Claim preclusion.* If a spouse chooses to pursue a separate tort action postdivorce, can the tortfeasor spouse raise the affirmative defense of res judicata to bar her claim? Professor Sarah Buel charges:

> At first glance it would appear that most states are permissive regarding joinder of tort and divorce actions. However, closer scrutiny reveals that many divorce statutes include specific language that, although joinder is not strictly mandatory, if the subject of the subsequent tort action was at all part of the dissolution, the tort action will be disallowed on grounds of res judicata.

Buel, supra, at 1000-1001. Compare *Chen*, supra; and *Brinkman*, supra (both holding that wife's subsequent tort claims were precluded by res judicata), with Roussel v. Roussel, 2003 WL 22951910 (Va. Cir. Ct. 2003) (holding that wife's assault and battery claims were not barred because neither party chose to address them in the divorce action).

c. *Benefits of joinder.* What benefits follow from joinder? Professor Andrew Schepard responds:

> Divorce litigation comprises a major portion of the caseload of many large state court systems. The policy interest in conserving scarce judicial resources by concentrating all claims between the divorcing couple into a single proceeding is thus great. . . . There is also a related social interest in reducing the private transaction costs (the most significant component of which is legal fees) of settling marital differences. Divorce is generally a zero sum economic transaction: there is not enough money in the marital settlement pot for both spouses to live postdivorce at the same standard of living as before the divorce. Increasing the transaction costs of

the divorce settlement by reopening proceedings reduces further the total resources available for the postdivorce family to live on. . . .

Also weighing in favor of [joinder] is the policy of repose that underlies [res judicata]. Divorce is a wrenching, all-consuming emotional experience. [The husband's and wife's] well-being, and their continued productive functioning as members of society, require that their emotional stability be reestablished quickly and firmly by a final settlement of marital differences.

Andrew Schepard, Divorce, Interspousal Torts, and Res Judicata, 24 Fam. L.Q. 127, 131-132 (1990). See also Oliver, supra, at 392 (arguing that the benefits of joinder outweigh the concerns against joinder).

d. *Distinctions favoring joinder.* Do the different purposes of, or legal theories behind, tort actions and divorce militate in favor of, or against, joinder? Do the different procedural characteristics? For example, if joinder is required, how should a court resolve access to jury trials (normally permitted in tort actions)? See Brennan v. Orban, 678 A.2d 667, 677 (N.J. 1996) (suggesting that certain factors, such as child welfare, may suggest a nonjury trial of a marital tort case but that "society's interest in vindicating a marital tort though the jury process" may dictate otherwise). If a jury trial is ordered, where shall the claim be litigated — in family court or civil court? See id. at 677 (discussing respective advantages and disadvantages of the two fora). How should a court resolve the problem of attorneys' fees (contingent fees are not permitted in divorce actions)?

7. *Economic tort claims.* Not all dissolution-related tort actions involve domestic violence. In Schleuter v. Schleuter, 975 S.W.2d 584 (Tex. 1998), the Texas Supreme Court held that no independent action existed in a divorce proceeding for a spouse's fraudulent depletion of community assets. In so ruling, the court permitted joinder for personal injury claims but not economic torts. Does this rule make sense? See generally Cynthia S. Schiffer, Note, The Allowance of Independent Tort Causes of Action in Divorce Proceedings in Light of Schlueter v. Schlueter, 51 Baylor L. Rev. 1063 (1999). In a similar action involving a husband who created an elaborate scheme to hide his income, another court considered whether a RICO claim could be brought in the context of divorce. See Perlberger v. Perlberger, 1999 WL 79503 (E.D. Pa. 1999), *aff'd*, 242 F.3d 371 (3d Cir. 2000) (holding that wife's RICO claim survived summary judgment). See generally Erin Alexander, Comment, The Honeymoon Is Definitely Over: The Use of Civil RICO in Divorce, 37 San Diego L. Rev. 541 (2000).

Problem

Jane and John Doe have been married for seven years and have a son and twin girls. Unbeknownst to John, his wife had a sexual affair during the marriage with her art professor. John discovers a letter that reveals to him that the children may have been fathered by the professor. DNA testing confirms that John is father of the son but not the twins. The next day John petitions for divorce, alleging adultery, fraud, and intentional infliction of emotional distress. Should he be permitted to bring the tort claim in the divorce proceeding? Should his tort claim be barred by the interspousal immunity doctrine? Does the wife's conduct satisfy the requirements for intentional infliction? See Doe v. Doe, 712 A.2d 132 (Md. Ct. Spec. App. 1998). See generally Linda L. Berger, Lies Between Mommy and Daddy: The Case for Recognizing Emotional Distress Claims Based on Domestic Deceit That Interferes with Parent-Child Relationships, 33 Loy. L.A. L. Rev. 449 (2000).

3. Assessment of the No-Fault "Revolution"

a. Divorce Reform in the United States

■ **DEBORAH L. RHODE & MARTHA MINOW, REFORMING THE QUESTIONS, QUESTIONING THE REFORMS: FEMINIST PERSPECTIVES ON DIVORCE LAW**
in Divorce Reform at the Crossroads 191-199, 209-210
(Stephen D. Sugarman & Herma Hill Kay eds., 1990)

Our central premise is that the legal issues surrounding divorce have been conceived too narrowly. Reform initiatives have too often treated divorce as a largely private dispute and have not adequately addressed its public dimensions. . . .

The leading proponents of initial no-fault reform were lawyers, judges, and law professors. Their primary focus was on the legal grounds for divorce; their primary purposes were to reduce expense, acrimony, and fraud in resolving matters envisioned as essentially private concerns. What is, perhaps, most revealing about these original efforts are the issues that were not on the agenda. Early reform strategies neglected gender equality and public responsibilities.

Although no-fault initiatives coincided with the resurgence of a women's rights movement, proponents of these reforms generally were not seeking to remedy women's disadvantages under traditional family policies. Indeed, to the extent that gender equity appeared at all in discussions among decision makers, the focus involved equity for men. The dominant concern was beleaguered ex-husbands, crippled by excessive alimony burdens, and threats of blackmail. Although this problem was grossly exaggerated, the absence of systematic data allowed policy-makers to rely on anecdotal experiences to formulate the problem they sought to reform.

In part, the absence of women's concerns from the debate reflected the absence of women. Those with greatest influence in policy-making — practicing attorneys, politicians, and family law experts — were overwhelmingly male. The newly emerging women's rights movement was not significantly involved with early divorce reforms, in part because it was understaffed and overextended during this period, but more important, because the implications of such reforms were not yet apparent. Only as the divorce rate escalated and scholars concerned with women's issues began to chronicle its impact did the focus of debate begin to change.

Even when reformers identified gender equality as an objective, they relied almost exclusively on gender-neutral formulations. For example, they succeeded in eliminating explicitly sex-linked provisions (such as those granting alimony only to wives) and in reformulating rules for marital property distribution to require "equal" or "equitable" division of assets. Yet . . . such provisions have secured equality in form, but not equality in fact.

The assumptions underlying early reforms also marginalized the public implications of divorce doctrine. No-fault initiatives began from the premise that decisions involving the termination of marriage should rest with private parties; the public's responsibility was simply to provide efficient legal rules for processing their agreement and resolving any disputes. Within this framework, a couple's allocation of financial and child-rearing obligations appeared to be primarily matters for private ordering. If parties failed to reach agreement, their differences would be resolved under broad discretionary standards mandating equality or equity between the spouses in financial matters and the best interest of the child in custody contests. Public norms about the kinds of resolutions society should endorse receded to the background. As a result, the state was given little responsibility for guiding, enforcing, or supplementing judicial awards.

Paradoxically, this move toward private ordering failed adequately to acknowledge the diversity of private family circumstances. Those who framed and interpreted legal doctrine often overlooked the fact that marriages of different durations, formed during different decades with different expectations, could leave divorcing parties in sharply divergent situations. One single, discretionary standard was thought adequate to deal with circumstances ranging from a couple married for one year while the parties finished college to a couple married for twenty-five years while the woman worked in the home and the husband held paid employment.

Early no-fault reforms gave no special attention to the concerns of particularly vulnerable groups such as displaced homemakers with limited savings, insurance, and employment options; families with inadequate income to support two households (a problem disproportionately experienced by racial minorities); or couples with no children, no significant property, and no need for a formal adjudicative procedure. Nor was child support central to the reform agenda; it appeared only as a side issue, buried within custody and other financial topics.

It bears emphasis what such a limited conception of public responsibility left out. The early reform agenda did not specify clear public norms concerning financial and child-care responsibilities to guide parties' decision making or judicial review. Nor did it mandate effective, affordable enforcement procedures for spousal and child support awards, or state subsidies where private resources were inadequate. Reformers also neglected the impact of postdivorce property divisions — such as the forced sale of the family home — on dependent children. And what was most critical, no-fault initiatives omitted criteria for assessing the outcomes of divorce, outcomes affecting not only the parties and their children but subsequent marriages, stepfamilies, and public welfare responsibilities.

In noting what was absent from the no-fault agenda, we do not mean to devalue its central objective. Reducing the acrimony, expense, and fraud associated with fault-based procedures was a goal worth pursuing on its own right. Given the opposition to liberalizing grounds for divorce, reformers may have been justifiably wary about raising other related issues. But we also believe that the limitations of the original reform movement reflect not only what was politically expedient at that historical moment but also more fundamental conceptual inadequacies. By remaining wedded to traditional public/private distinctions, early divorce reform tended to amplify rather than redress gender inequalities. . . .

. . . Norms governing termination of a marriage should be consistent with the ideal to which marriage aspires — that of equal partnerships between spouses who share resources, responsibilities, and risks. . . . Gender equality and child welfare should become priorities in practice, not just theory, under contemporary divorce law. . . .

b. Divorce Reform: The Comparative-Law Perspective

■ **NAOMI NEFT & ANN D. LEVINE, WHERE WOMEN STAND: AN INTERNATIONAL REPORT ON THE STATUS OF WOMEN IN 140 COUNTRIES**
98 (1997)

Divorce is now legal in nearly every country, and as marriage rates have been declining, divorce rates have been rising, even in some predominantly Roman Catholic countries where divorce has long been a contentious political issue. In Spain divorce was not legalized until 1981. In Brazil, although divorce became legal in 1977, each person was allowed only one divorce during his or her lifetime, a stipulation that was not removed until 1988. In 1995 Ireland became the last major European country to legalize divorce [in situations in which] the couple have been separated for four of the last five years.

The Philippines, also predominantly Roman Catholic, is one of the few countries where divorce is still prohibited. Yet a 1987 law greatly extended the grounds for legal separation and allowed marriages to be easily annulled on psychological grounds. Chile, too, permits legal separation and annulment but not divorce.[9] In both these countries, people who wish to remarry must seek an annulment, and since an annuled marriage never legally existed, the wives in these situations are not legally entitled to alimony or child support from their husbands.

Among developed countries, Russia has the highest divorce rate, for every 100 couples who get married each year, 60 couples get divorced. Other developed countries with high divorce rates include the United States, the Scandinavian countries, and the United Kingdom.

One of the reasons divorce rates are rising around the world is that since the 1970s many countries — among them Argentina, Australia, Canada, India, and Japan — have liberalized their divorce laws to provide divorce by mutual consent or on a no-fault basis. . . .

On comparative divorce rates, see Andrew J. Cherlin, American Marriage in the Early Twenty-First Century, in 15 The Future of Children 33, 45, 46 (2005) (reporting that, among developed countries, the United States' divorce rate is followed by that of Sweden and the other Scandinavian countries, Britain, Canada, France, Germany, and Italy).

See also Mary Ann Glendon, Abortion and Divorce in Western Law 61-81 (1987) (finding that many Western countries that chose to add no-fault grounds

[9]. Chile legalized divorce in 2004 despite longstanding opposition from conservative groups and the Catholic Church. Prior to the new law, couples resorted to annulments often secured by subterfuge — one spouse would testify that the marriage was illegal because of an error on the marriage license (e.g., an incorrect address). Currently, a Chilean divorce requires a one-year separation in cases of mutual consent but three years separation if only one spouse wants the divorce. Couples also must prove that they have tried marriage counseling for at least 60 days. Divorce Finally Legalised, Braz. & S. Cone Rep., Mar. 30, 2004, available at 2004 WLNR 307697. The Philippines still prohibits divorce. Philip Bowring, The Political Legacy of Cardinal Sin, Int'l Herald Trib., June 23, 2005, at 6.

to traditional fault grounds nonetheless provided safeguards by permitting courts to deny no-fault divorces in cases of extreme hardship for nonconsenting innocent spouses); William J. Goode, World Changes in Divorce Patterns (1993) (analyzing world trends in divorce and concluding that increasing divorce rates represent a socioeconomic problem for women and children).

c. Divorce Reform: The Gay Divorce

■ **KIRK JOHNSON, GAY DIVORCE: FEW MARKERS IN THIS REALM**
N.Y. Times, Aug. 12, 1994, at A16

Gay couples who want the right to be legally married make news these days, but consider for a moment the more quietly anguished plight of Bill and Elliott, who only want a divorce. They lived together for 18 years near Kansas City, Mo. They were co-owners of a small business and a home filled with expensive antiques. They wanted a court system that had never legally recognized their union to dissolve it fairly and equitably, amid the bitter storm of recrimination that was sweeping over their lives as their relationship foundered.

"We had a Dickens of a time even getting a judge to listen to us," said Michael J. Albano [who represented one of the men]. Mr. Albano said he had gone through three judges before finding one who would hear the case. And while the fourth judge finally granted a divorce decree, Mr. Albano said the record was sealed. "No one was sure it was legal or appropriate," he added. . . . Just about every gay divorce is like that: loaded with ambiguities and unknowns, conducted in a court system that lawyers and clients say is hostile at worst and indifferent at best. Because gay people cannot be legally married anywhere in the United States [with the current exception of Massachusetts, *Eds.*], there is, for starters, no access to divorce court. . . .

People familiar with family law and gay issues say that the number of homosexuals who seek legal help in dissolving their relationships is unknown, because most such cases are settled quickly out of court. High-profile disputes, like Martina Navratilova's noisy legal separation from her longtime companion, Judy Nelson, remain rare. . . . Some lawyers contend that the complexities of gay divorce will eventually prove the strongest argument yet for gay marriages, since it would establish the right to a fair process when those relationships fall apart. . . .

■ **RAMONA FAITH OSWALD & ERIC CLAUSELL, SAME-SEX RELATIONSHIPS AND THEIR DISSOLUTION**
in Handbook of Divorce and Relationship Dissolution 499, 504-506 (Mark A. Fine & John H. Harvey eds., 2006)

[A] few authors have provided some estimates of relationship dissolution rates [of same-sex couples]. When contacting all couples who had obtained civil unions in Vermont the first year that these became available, Solomon, Rothblum, and Balsam (2004) found that 1% had separated after 1 year. Kurdek (1992) found a 19% dissolution rate during a 4-year study of same-sex cohabiters. [His data] suggest that dissolution for these couples typically occurred after 6-11 years of cohabitation. The longitudinal study by Gartrell (2000) of the transition to lesbian parenthood found that 31% of the coparenting couples had separated by the time their children were 5 years old. They had been together for a mean of 8 years. . . . The findings of Blumstein and Schwartz (1983) suggest that the 10-year mark is significant for relationship longevity: Same-sex couples that had been together for more than 10 years were less likely to break up than those who had been together for 1-10 years. . . .

Virtually everything we know in answer to the question of why and how same-sex couples break up has come from the research program of [Lawrence A. Kurdek]. The top two participant-supplied reasons for ending the relationship were nonresponsiveness (73%; i.e., "there was no communication between us and little support") and partner problems (50%; i.e., "he/she had a drug and alcohol problem"). When presented with a list of reasons for separating and asked to rate how much each one contributed to their breakup, participants agreed on average that the following reasons had contributed to their situation: Frequent absence, sexual incompatibility, and mental cruelty. . . .

In another study focused on adjustment to relationship dissolution, Kurdek (1997) further confirmed the "reasons for leaving" findings by using a comparative sample of 26 gay, 24 lesbian, and 46 heterosexual couples. In this study, no significant differences among gay, lesbian, and heterosexual couples regarding their reasons for ending relationships were found. . . .

In one of his most recent studies comparing heterosexual married partners with same-sex cohabiting couples, Kurdek (1998) again used data collected during a 5-year longitudinal study to assess whether members of married couples differed from those of either gay or lesbian cohabiting couples on five dimensions of relationship quality (intimacy, autonomy, equality, constructive problem solving, and barriers to leaving). [P]artners from both gay and lesbian couples reported higher autonomy and more equality than did partners from heterosexual couples. . . . Heterosexual couples reported significantly more barriers to leaving than did partners in same-sex couples.

In sum, Kurdek's research suggests that same-sex and opposite-sex couples are similar in that partners seem to stay together when they find the relationship rewarding and perceive fewer alternatives to being together. In contrast to heterosexual couples, partners in same-sex couples perceive fewer barriers to leaving, and this is perhaps largely due to their lack of institutionalization. . . .

Courts have been reluctant to address the rights of parties in the "gay divorce." Today, however, Massachusetts (the only state that recognizes same-sex marriage) provides the same divorce procedures to same-sex couples as to heterosexual couples. See Jennifer Peter, First Same-Sex Divorces Now Being Sought, Miami Herald, Dec. 12, 2004, at 16A. Moreover, some states with domestic partnership legislation also permit termination of such relationships by judicial proceedings. See, e.g., An Act Concerning Civil Unions, 2005 Conn. Legis. Serv. Pub. Act No. 05-10 (S.S.B. 963) (eff. Oct, 2005);[10] N.J. Stat. Ann. §26:8A-5, 10 (West Supp.

---

[10]. Litigation is currently pending in Connecticut to recognize same-sex marriage. See Kerrigan v. Connecticut Dept. of Pub. Health, No. NNH-CV-04-4001813-S (New Haven Super. Ct., filed Sept. 28, 2005).

2005); Vt. Stat. Ann. tit. 15, §1207 (2002). California permits a summary procedure for domestic partners in some circumstances (similar to the procedure available to spouses). See Cal. Fam. Code §299(a) (West 2004) (available if the partners do not share any property interests, both agree to the termination, the duration of the domestic partnership is less than five years, both agree on the division of assets, and each partner waives a right to support from the other partner).

California, Connecticut, and Vermont equate same-sex couples to spouses for all purposes, including spousal support and property division at the end of the relationship (although Connecticut and Vermont extend state tax benefits to members of civil unions whereas California does not). See Cal. Fam. Code §297.5(b) (West 2004); An Act Concerning Civil Unions, 2005 Conn. Legis. Serv. Pub. Act No. 05-10 (S.S.B. 963); Vt. St. Ann. tit. 15, §1206 (2002). Reciprocal beneficiaries in Hawaii, however, are able to terminate their relationship without legal consequences. See Haw. Rev. Stat. §572C-7 (Supp. 2004). Similarly, New Jersey law provides that a court is not required to make an equitable distribution of property acquired during the domestic partnership. N.J.S.A. §26:8A-10a.3 (West Supp. 2005). Nor does the legislation provide for support following termination of the domestic partnership, requiring partners to resort to claims for palimony. Jane M. Fearn-Zimmer, Gay 'Marriage' in Transition, 183 N.J. L.J. 96 (Jan. 9, 2006).

For jurisdictional issues involving dissolution of same-sex marriages or domestic partnerships in a different state from the state of creation, see infra this chapter Section G.

Note: The Return of Fault

A movement is afoot to reintroduce fault in the dissolution process. Since 1997, 25 states have considered covenant marriage laws that are designed to preserve the lifelong character of marriage. Such laws have been passed in Louisiana, Arizona, and Arkansas.

Louisiana became the first state in 1997 to allow marriage applicants to choose a "covenant marriage," instead of a traditional marriage. According to Lousiana Revised Statutes Annotated §9:272 (West 2000), couples who choose covenant marriage must sign a declaration of intent that indicates that they have received premarital counseling on the "nature, purpose and responsibilities" of marriage, and that they promise to seek marriage counseling in the event of marital probelms. Divorce is permitted only for adultery, conviction of a felony resulting in death or imprisonment, desertion for at least one year, physical or sexual abuse of a spouse or child, or after a two-year separation without reconciliation. La. Rev. Stat. Ann. §9:307.

Arizona adopted a similar measure in 1998. However, the Arizona statute allows for divorce subject to mutual consent. Ariz. Rev. Stat. Ann. §25-901 (West 2000). The most recent state to pass a covenant marriage statute, Arkansas, did so in 2001. Ark. Code Ann. §§9-11-801 to 9-11-811 (Michie 2002 & Supp. 2003). Proponents of the legislation cited statistics revealing that Arkansas had the third highest divorce rate nationally after Nevada and Tennessee.[11]

---

[11]. Chauncey Brummer, The Shackles of Covenant Marriage: Who Holds the Keys to Wedlock?, 25 U. Ark. Little Rock L. Rev. 261, 277 (2003).

Covenant marriages have not been as popular as supporters originally hoped. In Louisiana, 400 already-married couples signed up for covenant marriages in 1998, but that number dropped to 5 in 1999, and 115 in 2000.[12] A 2003 study found that less than 2 percent of all newly contracted marriages in Louisiana are covenant marriages.[13]

Among state legislatures that considered covenant marriage bills, most adopted less stringent variations, such as reducing marriage license fees for couples who attend premarital counseling.[14] Other proposed legislation would permit divorce only for fraud (California); permit divorce only in the case of adultery (Mississippi); enact lengthy waiting periods before obtaining a no-fault divorce (Missouri and Minnesota); enact strict premarital counseling requirements (Alabama, Nebraska, and Minnesota); and require marital counseling, mediation, and arbitration before permitting a suit for divorce (Colorado).[15]

Supporters of covenant marriage claim that it is preferable to no-fault because divorce negatively affects children's well-being. Their concerns are aimed at making divorce more difficult to obtain and encouraging reconciliation. Additionally, religious groups advocate covenant marriage, alleging that it reaffirms the meaning of marriage.[16] Critics contend, however, that these reforms raise constitutional concerns (placing an undue burden on the right to make decisions regarding family life); conflict-of-laws and choice-of-law questions (possibly forcing non-covenant marriage states to recognize covenant marriages and denying no-fault divorces to spouses who seek them outside of their home state); unauthorized practice of law problems (requiring clergy marriage counselors to counsel couples regarding the "nature and purpose" of marriage); and policy debates (the effect of covenant marriages on preserving the family, protecting women and children, and lowering juvenile crime rates).[17] Furthermore, some worry that covenant marriages may make it more difficult for victims of domestic violence to exit from abusive marriages.[18]

See generally Margaret F. Brinig & Steven L. Nock, What Does Covenant Marriage Mean for Relationships?, 18 N.D. J.L. Ethics & Pub. Pol'y 137 (2004); Peter Hay, The American "Covenant Marriage" in the Conflict of Laws, 64 La. L. Rev. 43 (2003); Daniel W. Olivas, Comment, Tennessee Considers Adopting the Louisiana Covenant Marriage Act: A Law Waiting to Be Ignored, 71 Tenn. L. Rev. 769 (2004); Kristina E. Zurcher, Note, "I Do" or "I Don't"? Covenant Marriage After Six Years, 18 N.D. J.L. Ethics & Pub. Pol'y 273 (2004).

---

[12]. Covenant Marriages on the Decline, Couples Opting for Traditional Unions, Sunday Advocate (Baton Rouge, La.), Feb. 4, 2001, at 23.

[13]. Steven L. Nock et al., Covenant Marriage Turns Five Years Old, 10 Mich. J. Gender & L. 169, 170 (2003). Only 57 licenses for covenant marriages were issued in Arkansas during the first year. Andrew Demillo, Covenant Couples Mean to Stay Wed, Ark. Post-Gazette, Aug. 25, 2002 at A7.

[14]. H. J. Cummins, "I Do" . . . Really; "Super Vows" Aim to Strengthen Marriages, Chi. Sun-Times, Jan. 9, 2000, at 27.

[15]. Lynne Marie Kohm, A Comprehensive Study of Covenant Marriage Proposals in the United States, 12 Regent U. L. Rev. 31, 42-47 (1999).

[16]. Cynthia DeSimone, Comment, Covenant Marriage Legislation: How the Absence of Interfaith Religious Discourse Has Stifled the Effort to Strengthen Marriage, 52 Cath. U.L. Rev. 391, 393-394 (2003).

[17]. Jay Macke, Note, Of Covenants and Conflicts — When "I Do" Means More Than It Used To, But Less Than You Thought, 59 Ohio St. L.J. 1377 (1998).

[18]. Robert M. Gordon, The Limits of Limits on Divorce, 107 Yale L.J. 1435, 1447-1449 (1998).

E. ACCESS TO DIVORCE

1. *Economic Obstacles*

■ **BODDIE v. CONNECTICUT**
401 U.S. 371 (1971)

Mr. Justice HARLAN delivered the opinion of the Court.

Appellants, welfare recipients residing in the State of Connecticut, brought this action in the Federal District Court for the District of Connecticut on behalf of themselves and others similarly situated, challenging, as applied to them, certain state procedures for the commencement of litigation, including requirements for payment of court fees and costs for service of process, that restrict their access to the courts in their effort to bring an action for divorce.

It appears from the briefs and oral argument that the average cost to a litigant for bringing an action for divorce is $60. Section 52-259 of the Connecticut General Statutes provides: "There shall be paid to the clerks of the supreme court or the superior court, for entering each civil cause, forty-five dollars. . . ." An additional $15 is usually required for the service of process by the sheriff, although as much as $40 or $50 may be necessary where notice must be accomplished by publication.

There is no dispute as to the inability of the named appellants in the present case to pay either the court fees required by statute or the cost incurred for the service of process. The affidavits in the record establish that appellants' welfare income in each instance barely suffices to meet the costs of the daily essentials of life and includes no allotment that could be budgeted for the expense to gain access to the courts in order to obtain a divorce. . . .

[Appellants challenged the constitutionality of the statute and sought an injunction to permit them to proceed without payment of fees and costs. A three judge court found the statute constitutional.] We now reverse. Our conclusion is that, given the basic position of the marriage relationship in this society's hierarchy of values and the concomitant state monopolization of the means for legally dissolving this relationship, due process does prohibit a State from denying, solely because of inability to pay, access to its courts to individuals who seek judicial dissolution of their marriages. . . .

. . . Without [the Fifth and Fourteenth Amendments'] guarantee that one may not be deprived of his rights, neither liberty nor property, without due process of law, the State's monopoly over techniques for binding conflict resolution could hardly be said to be acceptable under our scheme of things. . . .

Such [due process] litigation has, however, typically involved rights of defendants — not, as here, persons seeking access to the judicial process in the first instance. This is because our society has been so structured that resort to the courts is not usually the only available, legitimate means of resolving private disputes. . . .

. . . As this Court on more than one occasion has recognized, marriage involves interests of basic importance in our society [citing *Loving, Skinner*, Meyer v. Nebraska]. It is not surprising, then, that the States have seen fit to oversee many aspects of that institution. Without a prior judicial imprimatur, individuals may freely enter into and rescind commercial contracts, for example, but we are unaware of any jurisdiction where private citizens may covenant for or dissolve marriages without state approval. Even where all substantive requirements are concededly met, we know of no instance where two consenting adults may divorce and mutually liberate themselves from the constraints of legal obligations that go with marriage, and more fundamentally the prohibition against remarriage, without invoking the State's judicial machinery.

Thus, although they assert here due process rights as would-be plaintiffs, we think appellants' plight, because resort to the state courts is the only avenue to dissolution of their marriages, is akin to that of defendants faced with exclusion from the only forum effectively empowered to settle their disputes. Resort to the judicial process by these plaintiffs is no more voluntary in a realistic sense than that of the defendant called upon to defend his interests in court. For both groups this process is not only the paramount dispute-settlement technique, but, in fact, the only available one. In this posture we think that this appeal is properly to be resolved in light of the principles enunciated in our due process decisions that delimit rights of defendants compelled to litigate their differences in the judicial forum.

[P]recedent has firmly embedded in our due process jurisprudence two important principles upon whose application we rest our decision in the case before us. [First,] due process requires, at a minimum, that absent a countervailing state interest of overriding significance, persons forced to settle their claims of right and duty through the judicial process must be given a meaningful opportunity to be heard. . . . Our cases further establish that a statute or a rule may be held constitutionally invalid as applied when it operates to deprive an individual of a protected right although its general validity as a measure enacted in the legitimate exercise of state power is beyond question. . . .

No less than these rights, the right to a meaningful opportunity to be heard within the limits of practicality, must be protected against denial by particular laws that operate to jeopardize it for particular individuals. . . . Just as a generally valid notice procedure may fail to satisfy due process because of the circumstances of the defendant, so too a cost requirement, valid on its face, may offend due process because it operates to foreclose a particular party's opportunity to be heard. The State's obligations under the Fourteenth Amendment are not simply generalized ones; rather, the State owes to each individual that process which, in light of the values of a free society, can be characterized as due.

Drawing upon the [these] principles . . . we conclude that the State's refusal to admit these appellants to its courts, the sole means in Connecticut for obtaining a divorce, must be regarded as the equivalent of denying them an opportunity to be heard upon their claimed right to a dissolution of their marriages, and, in the absence of a sufficient countervailing justification for the State's action, a denial of due process.

The arguments for this kind of fee and cost requirement are that the State's interest in the prevention of frivolous litigation is substantial, its use of court fees and process costs to allocate scarce resources is rational, and its balance between the defendant's right to notice and the plaintiff's right to access is reasonable.

In our opinion, none of these considerations is sufficient to override the interest of these plaintiff-appellants in having access to the only avenue open for dissolving their allegedly untenable marriages. Not only is there no necessary connection between a litigant's assets and the seriousness of his motives in bringing suit, but it is here beyond present dispute that appellants bring these actions in good faith. Moreover, other alternatives exist to fees and cost requirements as a means for conserving the time of courts and protecting parties from frivolous litigation, such as penalties for false pleadings or affidavits, and actions for malicious prosecution or abuse of process, to mention only a few. In the same vein we think that reliable alternatives exist to service of process by a state-paid sheriff if the State is unwilling to assume the cost of official service. This is perforce true of service by publication which is the method of notice least calculated to bring to a potential defendant's attention the pendency of judicial proceedings. We think in this case service at defendant's last known address by mail and posted notice is equally effective as publication in a newspaper. . . .

In concluding that the Due Process Clause of the Fourteenth Amendment requires that these appellants be afforded an opportunity to go into court to obtain a divorce, we wish to re-emphasize that we go no further than necessary to dispose of the case before us, a case where the bona fides of both appellants' indigency and desire for divorce are here beyond dispute. We do not decide that access for all individuals to the courts is a right that is, in all circumstances, guaranteed by the Due Process Clause of the Fourteenth Amendment so that its exercise may not be placed beyond the reach of any individual, for, as we have already noted, in the case before us this right is the exclusive precondition to the adjustment of a fundamental human relationship. The requirement that these appellants resort to the judicial process is entirely a state-created matter. Thus we hold only that a State may not, consistent with the obligations imposed on it by the Due Process Clause of the Fourteenth Amendment, pre-empt the right to dissolve this legal relationship without affording all citizens access to the means it has prescribed for doing so. . . .

Mr. Justice DOUGLAS, concurring in the result. . . .

. . . The Court today puts "flesh" upon the Due Process Clause by concluding that marriage and its dissolution are so important that an unhappy couple who are indigent should have access to the divorce courts free of charge. Fishing may be equally important to some communities. May an indigent be excused if he does not obtain a license which requires payment of money that he does not have? How about a requirement of an onerous bond to prevent summary eviction from rented property? The affluent can put up the bond, though the indigent may not be able to do so. Is housing less important to the mucilage holding society together than marriage? The examples could be multiplied. I do not see the length of the road we must follow if we accept my Brother Harlan's invitation. . . .

An invidious discrimination based on poverty is adequate for this case. While Connecticut has provided a procedure for severing the bonds of marriage, a person can meet every requirement save court fees or the cost of service of process and be denied a divorce. Connecticut says in its brief that this is justified because "the State does not favor divorces; and only permits a divorce to be granted when those conditions are found to exist in respect to one or the other of the named parties, which seem to the legislature to make it probable that the interests of society will be better served and that parties will be happier, and so the better citizens, separate, than if compelled to remain together."

Thus, under Connecticut law divorces may be denied or granted solely on the basis of wealth. . . . Affluence does not pass muster under the Equal Protection Clause for determining who must remain married and who shall be allowed to separate.

Notes and Questions

1. *Background.* Some jurisdictions permit indigents to avoid filing fees by proceeding *in forma pauperis.* When *Boddie* was decided, approximately 32 states (excluding Connecticut), as well as the District of Columbia and the federal government, had *in forma pauperis* statutes. Charles Brooks, Note, Boddie v. Connecticut: The Rights of Indigents in a Divorce Action, J. Fam. L. 121, 122 n.5 (1971).

2. *Epilogue.* On remand, the court ordered state officials to waive filing fees. Boddie v. Connecticut, 329 F. Supp. 844 (D. Conn. 1971).

3. *Limitations.* In *Boddie,* Justice Harlan notes, "There is no dispute as to the inability of the named appellants [to pay]" and, later, "it is here beyond present dispute that appellants bring these actions in good faith." Thus, the holding is limited to plaintiffs who make a showing of indigency and who seek a divorce in good faith. How does an indigent demonstrate these requirements?

4. *Premises.* The majority rests its opinion on "the basic position of the marriage relationship in this society's hierarchy of values and the concomitant state monopolization of the means for legally dissolving this relationship." Are both aspects necessary to the result, or are they independent grounds?

5. *Extension to other costs?* If *Boddie* rests on both premises (societal values and monopoly), does an indigency exemption for other divorce expenses (for example, attorneys' fees) follow? Should it matter if the fees are paid to the court or to third parties? How meaningful is a right of access without an attorney? See In re Smiley, 330 N.E.2d 53 (N.Y. 1975). See also Simran Bindra & Pedram Ben-Cohen, Public Civil Defenders: A Right to Counsel for Indigent Civil Defendants, 10 Geo. J. on Poverty L. & Pol'y 1, 28-31 (2003) (discussing *Smiley's* holding in the larger context of access to representation for civil defendants). Do the advent of no-fault divorce and pro se divorce kits alter your views?

6. *Indigents' rights generally.* How far does *Boddie* protect indigents' rights? If *Boddie* rests on a monopoly rationale, then *Boddie* might guarantee access in civil cases generally. But cf. United States v. Kras, 409 U.S. 434 (1973) (no constitutional right to free bankruptcy discharge); Ortwein v. Schwab, 410 U.S. 656 (1973) (no constitutional right to waive filing fees for welfare appeals). How is divorce distinguishable from bankruptcy and welfare? Does *Boddie* mandate waiver of fees in other family law matters (for example, annulment, separation, paternity, custody, and adoption)? Marriage license fees?

7. *State grounds.* Recently, one jurisdiction decided, based on state law rather than constitutional grounds, that an indigent divorce petitioner has the right to appointed counsel. In Sholes v. Sholes, 760 N.E.2d 156 (Ind. 2001), a trial court granted a wife's petition for divorce from her husband who was a life inmate in state prison, awarded her all marital property and the husband's retirement benefits. The husband moved for relief from the default judgment, claiming that he had a right to counsel pursuant to Indiana Code §34-10-1-2 (requiring counsel for civil litigants who are without "sufficient means to prosecute or defend an action"). The state supreme court agreed, finding that the statute imposes a mandatory duty to appoint counsel for indigent civil litigants and also held that such counsel must be compensated.

8. *Alternative rationale.* How sound is *Boddie's* approach? For example, what criteria does the Court suggest for determining which interests are fundamental for due process purposes? Is equal protection a superior approach, as Justice

Douglas suggests (as does Justice Brennan in an omitted concurrence)? See Jeffreys v. Jeffreys, 296 N.Y.S.2d 74 (Sup. Ct. 1968) (state court costs for divorce violate indigents' state and federal rights to equal protection), *rev'd on other grounds*, 300 N.Y.S.2d 550 (App. Div. 1972) (requiring state, but not city, to pay such costs in absence of statutory authorization).

Problems

1. Blackacre has an explicit provision in its state constitution protecting the right to privacy. The Blackacre legislature has just repealed its no-fault laws and reintroduced fault. The Blackacre Family Code permits divorce only for adultery, cruelty, and desertion. John and Jane Doe, a married couple, challenge the statute, alleging that it violates their constitutional right of privacy by disallowing divorce by mutual consent. What result? Does *Boddie* guarantee a constitutional right to divorce, similar to the constitutional right to marry? See Ferrer v. Commonwealth, 4 Fam. L. Rep. (BNA) 2744 (Sept. 26, 1978) (deciding a somewhat similar issue based on Puerto Rican law). See generally Kenneth L. Karst, The Freedom of Intimate Association, 89 Yale L.J. 624, 671-672 (1980).

2. Public interest groups in Arkansas, Arizona, and Louisiana argue that "covenant marriage" laws are unconstitutional in light of *Boddie*. What arguments would they make? See generally David M. Wagner, The Constitution and Covenant Marriage Legislation: Rumors of a Constitutional Right to Divorce Have Been Greatly Exaggerated, 12 Regent U.L. Rev. 53 (1999).

Note: Pro Se Divorce

In the fault-based system, lawyers were essential to prove the existence (or lack) of marital fault. No fault resulted in a diminished role for lawyers and the growth of pro se divorce. Divorce self-help kits and services began proliferating in many states, sparking concerns by the organized bar about the unauthorized practice of law.

Less than a decade after the advent of no fault, researchers conducted studies of the effectiveness of pro se divorce. One study by Yale law students found that most clients, themselves, resolve property, support, and custody issues. The authors questioned whether counsel was necessary for reasons of judicial efficiency or public welfare considerations.[19]

Psychologists, who conducted a subsequent empirical study of pro se divorce funded by the American Bar Association, came to a different conclusion. By comparing a broad sample of self-represented versus attorney-represented cases, these researchers pointed out that pro se divorce has several shortcomings, including that (1) pro se litigants are less satisfied with the terms of their divorces as their cases become more complex, (2) they are less likely to receive tax advice or information about alternative dispute resolution, and (3) many petitioners and respondents encounter difficulties that are never resolved.[20]

[19]. Ralph C. Cavanaugh & Deborah L. Rhode, Project, The Unauthorized Practice of Law and Pro Se Divorce: An Empirical Analysis, 86 Yale L.J. 104, 128-129 (1976).
[20]. Bruce D. Sales et al., Is Self-Representation a Reasonable Alternative to Attorney Representation in Divorce Cases?, 37 St. Louis U. L.J. 553 (1993).

The number of pro se litigants in family law has been steadily increasing. For example, approximately 75 percent of divorces in California currently are brought by pro se litigants, compared to 47 percent two decades ago.[21] Moreover, the number of pro se litigants in family law cases is extraordinarily high. Some commentators estimate that as many as 80 to 90 percent of family law cases involve at least one pro se litigant.[22] Among the reasons for the *generalized* growth in pro se litigation are: an increase in literacy rates, a sense of consumerism, a sense of individualism and belief in one's own abilities; anti-lawyer sentiment and a mistrust of the legal system; the belief that the court will do what is right regardless of the assistance of counsel; a belief that an attorney is unnecessary because the case is simple; and a strategy to gain sympathy or a procedural advantage over represented parties.[23]

This rise in the number of pro se litigants creates considerable difficulty for court personnel — for judges who must determine how to assure a fair trial to pro se litigants without appearing to compromise their own neutrality, and also for court officials who must distinguish between the provision of information versus legal advice.[24] In response to these problems, courts and legal service programs are developing many new forms of assistance. Efforts include simplifying legal forms and instructions, creating self-help centers, developing Internet-based forms of assistance, conducting clinics for litigants, and relying on commercial paralegals and document preparation services to assist litigants.[25]

A particularly innovative self-help center was established in 1995 in Maricopa County, Arizona, funded primarily by the Arizona Supreme Court, State Justice Institute, and local and state bar associations. The center provides educational materials and forms and also furnishes assistance regarding completion of forms. This center has served as a model for other centers in California, Colorado, Florida, and Minnesota.[26]

Note: Social and Cultural Obstacles Surrounding Divorce

Considerable stigma attached to divorce in previous eras. As one commentator explains:

> [Divorce studies] shared a common theme, perhaps best stated by psychiatrist Edmund Bergler:

[21]. Frances L. Harrison et al., Courts Responding to Communities: California's Family Law Facilitator Program: A New Paradigm for the Courts, 2 J. Center Child. & Cts. 61, 61 (2000).

[22]. Drew A. Swank, Note and Comment, The Pro Se Phenomenon, 19 BYU J. Pub. L. 373, 376 (2005). See also Margaret Martin Barry, Accessing Justice: Are Pro Se Clinics a Reasonable Response to the Lack of Pro Bono Legal Services and Should Law School Clinics Conduct Them?, 67 Fordham L. Rev. 1879, 1884 (1999); Steven K. Berenson, A Family Law Residency Program?: A Modest Proposal In Response to the Burdens Created by Self-Represented Litigants in Family Court, 33 Rutgers L.J. 105, 107-112 (2001).

[23]. Swank, supra note [22], at 378.

[24]. Carolyn D. Schwarz, Note, Pro Se Divorce Litigants, 42 Fam. Ct. Rev. 655, 657 (2004).

[25]. Berenson, supra note [22], at 122-131; Jessica Pearson, Court Services: Meeting the Needs of Twenty-First Century Families, 33 Fam. L. Q. 617, 627 (1999). See also Schwarz, supra note [24], at 660-666 (discussing reforms).

[26]. Amy C. Henderson, Meaningful Access to the Courts? Assessing Self-Represented Litigants' Ability to Obtain a Fair, Inexpensive Divorce in Missouri's Court System, 72 UMKC L. Rev. 571, 560-581 (2003).

> Divorce is a neurotic procedure of neurotic people. In the great majority of cases divorce is not a chance occurrence but unconsciously self-provoked, even if only by the choice of a neurotic partner. . . . There is less chance in the choice of marriage partners than is generally assumed. Two neurotics unconsciously seek and find each other. . . .

Augmenting these clinical diagnoses were the data generated by empirical studies on the relationships between mental illness and divorce. Loeb and Price and Blumenthal reported that divorced and separated parents had more emotional disturbances than the nondivorced. Although such studies were not conclusive or unchallenged, the affiliation between psychopathology and divorce was not to be broken. . . .

In many respects it was this prognosis that brought divorce therapy into the arena of marriage counseling. Ostensibly the purpose behind clinical treatment was not chiefly to effect reconciliation but rather to help the divorced or the would-be divorced "to understand the causes of failure, to grow and to mature . . . , and to become potentially better candidates for some marriage in the future."

Lynn Halem, Divorce Reform: Changing Legal and Social Perspectives 181-183 (1980).

In the 1980s many states appointed commissions to study the occurrence of gender bias in the legal system. Nine of those reports found widespread gender bias in the judicial treatment of women at divorce. Lynn Hecht Schafran, Gender and Justice: Florida and the Nation, 42 Fla. L. Rev. 181, 187 (1990); Joan Williams, Is Coverture Dead? Beyond a New Theory of Alimony, 82 Geo. L.J. 2227, 2234 n.30 ((1994).

Case law sometimes reflects gender-based stereotypes in the divorce context. In a classic example, Littlejohn v. Rose, 768 F.2d 765 (6th Cir. 1985), *cert. denied*, 475 U.S. 1045 (1986), an untenured elementary school teacher was not rehired by her school district despite excellent teaching evaluations, allegedly because she was in the midst of a divorce. She filed suit under 42 U.S.C. §1983, seeking reinstatement, back pay, and damages. She argued that her termination was based on her marital status (that is, her impending divorce) in violation of her constitutional rights of privacy and liberty. The Sixth Circuit held that the school board's action violated her right to privacy, reasoning that "[Roe v. Wade] clearly established the existence of a constitutionally protected right to privacy which includes matters relating to procreation and marriage." 768 F.2d at 769.

Although *Littlejohn* involved a public school teacher, anti-divorce policies have surfaced as well in private educational institutions. A religiously-affiliated university recently proposed a policy to terminate employees, and to deny employment to prospective employees, who were either separated or divorced from their spouses for reasons that don't meet "limited scriptural grounds" (i.e., adultery or violence). The university dropped the proposed plan following complaints by employees and alumni. Susan Simpson, University Backs Off Divorce Policy, Daily Oklahoman, Jan. 12, 2006, available at 2006 WLNR 65723.

Gender stereotypes are also present in a highly publicized recent case in which a trial judge denied a divorce to Shawnna Hughes, a 27-year medical assistant, because of her pregnancy. Hughes' abusive husband, who had been served while incarcerated, defaulted. A pro tem commissioner granted the divorce, but before entry of the final order, plaintiff amended her petition to reveal that she was pregnant and that her husband was not the father. Because plaintiff was the recipient of public assistance, the district attorney objected. The judge then vacated the decree, reasoning that plaintiff's failure to give notice of her pregnancy undermined the state's ability to protect the rights either of the child or the state (i.e., to resolve the issue of paternity and seek repayment of welfare money used for child support). On appeal, women's groups and domestic violence organizations filed an amicus brief arguing that the decision violated plaintiff's constitutional rights to equal protection and her right to privacy (regarding marriage, procreation, childbearing, and the decision how to structure her family relationships). Rejecting these arguments, the Washington Court of Appeals affirmed, reasoning that plaintiff's failure to give notice of her pregnancy denigrated important interests of the state and husband. In re Marriage of Hughes, 116 P.3d 1042 (Wash. Ct. App. 2005). Subsequently, a Washington state legislator introduced legislation (H.B. 1171) to prohibit trial courts from using a petitioner's pregnancy as a basis for denying a dissolution. Kelly Kearsley, Bill to Clarify Law: Pregnant Can Divorce, Sponsor Cites Lack of Uniformity in State Decisions, Columbian (Vancouver, WA), Feb. 5, 2005, at C.

See generally Terry Arendell, Gender Bias in Divorce, in Mothers and Divorce: Legal, Economic, and Social Dilemmas (1986); Women and Divorce/Men and Divorce: Gender Differences in Separation, Divorce and Remarriage (Sandra S. Volgy ed., 1991); Penelope E. Bryan, Reasking the Woman Question at Divorce, 75 Chi.-Kent L. Rev. 713 (2000).

2. Access to Alternatives to Divorce

To what extent do religious considerations compel the state to provide access to alternatives to dissolution?

■ AFLALO v. AFLALO
685 A.2d 523 (N.J. Super. Ct. Ch. Div. 1996)

FISHER, J.S.C. . . .

This case requires the court to visit an issue that has previously troubled our courts in matrimonial actions involving Orthodox Jews — a husband's refusal to provide a "get."[1] [T]he parties were married on October 13, 1983 in Ramle, Israel, and have one child, Samantha. Plaintiff Sondra Faye Aflalo has filed a complaint seeking a dissolution of the marriage. . . . Henry does not want a divorce and has taken action with The Union of Orthodox Rabbis of the United States and Canada in New York City (the "Beth Din"[2]) to have a hearing on his attempts at reconciliation. [Sondra did not appear in response to the summons forwarded to her by the Beth Din.]

[At a settlement conference before trial, Henry asserted his refusal to provide Sondra with a "get."] Unlike what the court faced in Segal v. Segal, 278 N.J. Super. 218, 650 A.2d 996 (App. Div. 1994) and Burns v. Burns, 223 N.J. Super. 219, 538 A.2d 438 (Ch. Div. 1987), Henry was not using his refusal to consent to the "get" as

---

1. A "get" is a bill of divorce which the husband gives to his wife to free her to marry again. The word "get" apparently signifies the number 12, the "get" being a twelve-lined instrument. The word is a combination of "gimel" (which has a value of three) together with "tet" (which has a value of nine).

2. The "Beth Din" is a rabbinical tribunal having authority to advise and pass upon matters of traditional Jewish law.

a means of securing a more favorable resolution of the issues before this court. That type of conduct the *Burns* court rightfully labelled "extortion." On the contrary, Henry's position (as conveyed during the settlement conference) was that regardless of what occurs in this court he will not consent to a Jewish divorce.

Henry's position spun off an unexpected problem; it caused his attorney to move to be relieved as counsel. Arguing that since he, too, is a practicing Orthodox Jew, Henry's counsel claims that he would "definitely have a religious problem representing a man who at the conclusion of a divorce proceeding refused, without reason, to give his wife a Get." [His counsel] indicated, upon questioning from the court, that his religious quandary comes not from Henry's use of his consent to a Jewish divorce as leverage in negotiations (which was not occurring), but in the blanket refusal of his client to give a "get" without reason.

Henry opposed his attorney's motion. . . . Henry stated under oath that while he desires a reconciliation he would follow the recommendations of the Beth Din [that is, should reconciliation fail] and give the "get" if that was the end result of those proceedings. The court finds Henry both credible and sincere in this regard; his position clearly eliminates his counsel's stated concerns. . . .

Sondra claims that this court, as part of the judgment of divorce which may eventually be entered in this matter, may and should order Henry to cooperate with the obtaining of a Jewish divorce upon pain of Henry having limited or supervised visitation of Samantha or by any other coercive means. She claims that Minkin v. Minkin, 180 N.J. Super. 260, 434 A.2d 665 (Ch. Div. 1981) authorizes this court to order Henry to consent to the Jewish divorce. . . .

[T]he Free Exercise Clause prohibits governmental regulation of religious beliefs but does not absolutely prohibit religious conduct. Second, to pass constitutional muster, a law must have both a secular purpose and a secular effect. That is, a law must not have a sectarian purpose; it must not be based upon a disagreement with a religious tenet or practice and must not be aimed at impeding religion. Only when state action passes these threshold tests is there a need to balance the competing state and religious interests. . . . Here, the relief Sondra seeks from this court so obviously runs afoul of the threshold tests of the Free Exercise Clause that the court need never reach the delicate balancing normally required in such cases.

The court will first endeavor to describe precisely what it is that Sondra seeks. . . .

"When a man takes a wife and possesses her, if she fails to please him because he finds something obnoxious about her, then he writes her a bill of divorcement, hands it to her, and sends her away from his house." Deuteronomy 24:1-4. From this biblical verse, the Jewish law and tradition that the "power of divorce rests exclusively with the husband" has its genesis. . . . Without such a divorce, the wife remains an "agunah" (a "tied" woman) and may not remarry in the eyes of Jewish law. If she remarries without a "get" she is considered to be an adulteress because she is still halakhically married to her first husband; any subsequent children are considered to be "mamzerim" (illegitimate) and may not marry other Jews.

The court is not unsympathetic to Sondra's desire to have Henry's cooperation in the obtaining of a "get." She, too, is sincere in her religious beliefs. Her religion, at least in terms of divorce, does not profess gender equality. But does that mean that she can obtain the aid of this court of equity to alter this doctrine of her faith? That the question must be answered negatively seems so patently clear that the only surprising aspect of Sondra's argument is that it finds some support in the few cases on the subject.

In *Minkin*, the trial court requested the testimony of several distinguished rabbis. The court viewed the issue as whether a state court could order specific performance of the "ketubah." The "ketubah" is the marriage contract in which the couple is obligated to comply with the laws of Moses and Israel. [It also contains the parties' agreement to recognize the authority of the Beth Din.] In determining that it could specifically enforce the "ketubah," *Minkin* relied on a New York decision [that specific performance would not compel the husband to practice any religion but would merely require him to do what he voluntarily agreed to do]. Analyzing the case against the test used to determine whether state action violates the Establishment Clause . . . , the *Minkin* court said:

> Relying upon credible expert testimony that the acquisition of a get is not a religious act, the court finds that the entry of an order compelling defendant to secure a get would have the clear secular purpose of completing a dissolution of the marriage. Its primary effect neither advances nor inhibits religion since it does not require the husband to participate in a religious ceremony or to do acts contrary to his religious beliefs. Nor would the order be an excessive entanglement with religion.

[180 N.J. Super. at 266, 434 A.2d 665.]

Also, in reliance upon the expert testimony found credible, the *Minkin* court concluded that an order compelling a husband to acquire a "get" is "not a religious act." The court apparently relied on one of the rabbis who testified "that Jewish law cannot be equated with religious law, but instead is comprised of two components—one regulating a man's relationship with God and the other regulating the relationship between man and man. The get, which has no reference to God but which does affect the relationship between two parties, falls into the latter category and is, therefore, civil and not religious in nature." 180 N.J. Super. at 265-266, 434 A.2d 665.

Minkin's approach that the "ketubah" may be specifically enforced without violating the First Amendment is in accord with the decisional law of New York, [Avitzur v. Avitzur, 446 N.E.2d 136 (N.Y. 1983)]; Illinois, [In re Marriage of Goldman, 554 N.E.2d 1016 (Ill. App. Ct. 1990)] and Delaware, Scholl v. Scholl, 621 A.2d 808, 810-812 (Del. Fam. Ct. 1992), and at odds with Arizona, Victor v. Victor, 177 Ariz. 231, 866 P.2d 899, 901-902 (App. 1993) and, now, this court. *Minkin* and its followers (including the New Jersey trial court in *Burns*) are not persuasive for a number of reasons.

First, [*Minkin*] examined the problem against the backdrop of the Establishment Clause and not the Free Exercise Clause. The Establishment Clause prohibits government from placing its support behind a particular religious belief. The Free Exercise Clause, obviously implicated here, prohibits government from interfering or becoming entangled in the practice of religion by its citizens.

Second, the conclusion that an order requiring the husband to provide a "get" is not a religious act nor involves the court in the religious beliefs or practices of the parties is not at all convincing. It is interesting that the court was required to choose between the conflicting testimony of the various rabbis to reach this conclusion. The one way in which a court may become entangled in religious affairs, which the court in *Minkin* did not recognize, was in becoming an arbiter of what is "religious." . . .

Third, the conclusion that its order concerned purely civil issues is equally unconvincing. . . . No matter how one semantically phrases what was done in *Minkin*, the order directly affected the religious beliefs of the parties. By entering the order, the court empowered the wife to remarry in accordance with her religious beliefs and also similarly empowered any children later born to her. . . . Nor is it sound to argue that religion involves only one's relation to the creator and not one's relation to other persons, as may be obligated by religious traditions or teachings. . . . *Minkin* draws too fine a line in its rejection of the latter as an area constituting "religion" to command this court's assent to its holding.

Fourth, *Minkin* fails to recognize that coercing the husband to provide the "get" would not have the effect sought. The "get" must be phrased and formulated in strict compliance with tradition, according to the wording given in the Talmud. The precisely worded "get" states that the husband does "willingly consent, being under no restraint, to release, to set free, and put aside thee, my wife." . . . What value then is a "get" when it is ordered by a civil court and when it places the husband at risk of being held in contempt should he follow his conscience and refuse to comply? . . .

Minkin ultimately conjures the unsettling vision of future enforcement proceedings. Should a civil court fine a husband for every day he does not comply or imprison him for contempt for following his conscience? [S]hould visitation of Samantha be limited pending Henry's cooperation? . . . Should this court enjoin Henry—no matter how imperfect he may be pursuing it [an apparent reference to the fact that Henry has not paid the Beth Din fees]—from moving for reconciliation in that forum and order other relief which the Beth Din apparently cannot give? . . . The spectre of Henry being imprisoned or surrendering his religious freedoms because of action by a civil court is the very image which gave rise to the First Amendment.

It may seem "unfair" that Henry may ultimately refuse to provide a "get." But the unfairness comes from Sondra's own sincerely-held religious beliefs. When she entered into the "ketubah" she agreed to be obligated to the laws of Moses and Israel. Those laws apparently include the tenet that if Henry does not provide her with a "get" she must remain an "agunah." That was Sondra's choice and one which can hardly be remedied by this court. . . .

The First Amendment was designed to protect [against] unwarranted, unwanted and unlawful steps over the "wall of separation between Church and State." This court will not assist Sondra in her attempts to lower that wall. . . .

Notes and Questions

1. *Scope of the problem.* Under traditional Jewish law, only the husband may grant the wife a religious divorce or "get." Commentators estimate that 15,000 Orthodox Jewish women in New York alone are civilly divorced but unable to obtain a religious divorce. Heather Lynn Capell, Comment, After the Glass Has Shattered: A Comparative Analysis of Orthodox Jewish Divorce in the United States and Israel, 33 Tex. Int'l L.J. 331, 337 (1998). The religious doctrine governing the "get" applies to Orthodox and Conservative (but not Reform) Jews.

Dilemmas arise (discussed below) when secular courts are asked to enforce either the religious prenuptial agreement or the decision of a religious tribunal (called a "Beth Din") that orders the husband to grant the wife the religious divorce. On the history and procedure of this religious tribunal, see Ginnine Fried,

Comment, The Collision of Church and State: A Primer to Beth Din Arbitration and the New York Secular Courts, 31 Fordham Urb. L.J. 633, 636-644 (2004).

2. *Motives.* Many husbands use the threat of denying a "get" to extract concessions during divorce. See, e.g., Perl v. Perl, 512 N.Y.S.2d 372, 374 (App. Div. 1987) (husband wanted all jointly owned securities, $65,000, deed to marital home, title to wife's car, and her personal jewelry). Mr. Aflalo has not paid the Beth Din fees (in conjunction with his request for reconciliation) and also is in arrears in his child support obligations. Is it so clear that his motives are "pure"? Should a husband's motives affect the outcome?

3. *Enforceability.* Is the ketubah a valid prenuptial agreement that is enforceable pursuant to contract law or part of a religious marriage ceremony, outside the purview of secular law? Are the court's views in *Aflalo* or *Minkin* (discussed in *Aflalo*) more persuasive? See Michelle Greenberg-Kobrin, Civil Enforceability of Religious Prenuptial Agreements, 32 Colum. J.L. & Soc. Probs. 359, 371 (1999) (arguing that courts should infer a prior contractual commitment on husband's part to give wife a "get" if a ketubah is signed prior to religious ceremony). See also Mayer-Kolker v. Kolker, 819 A.2d 17 (N.J. Super. Ct. App. Div. 2003) (declining to enforce ketubah because the court lacked certainty regarding the translation of the contract; plaintiffs did not present adequate evidence pertaining to its effect; and the court did not have any evidence as to what Mosaic law required in such a situation). Id at 20-21.

4. *Pressures.* Informal and formal pressures exist to make recalcitrant husbands comply with the provision of the religious prenuptial agreement requiring the "get." Some rabbis may apply subtle pressure or the threat of community ostracism. See also Fried, supra, at 651 (discussing Beth's Din's power of ostracism regarding a party who refuses to participate in Beth Din proceedings). The Beth Din, along with the Orthodox Caucus and the Rabbinical Council of America, recently approved a new prenuptial agreement form designed to discourage men from delaying divorce proceedings by requiring a husband who refuses to appear before the Beth Din for divorce proceedings to pay his wife $150 for every day he fails to appear. Some orthodox rabbis refuse to marry a couple who has not signed such an agreement. Holly Lebowitz Rossi, Pact Becomes Marriage Condition, Times Union (Albany, N.Y.), June 21, 2003, at B9.

The Israeli parliament (the Knesset) has enacted a law whereby recalcitrant husbands can be refused employment, a driver's license, or banking privileges. Capell, supra, at 334. In the United States, however, the availability of civil divorce has increased a husband's bargaining power, while at the same time reducing rabbinical leverage.

5. *Legal theories.* Many courts avoid constitutional issues (as *Aflalo* explains) by relying on contract or tort principles. Although most successful cases rely on contract principles, tort remedies are also possible. One commentator suggests the remedy of intentional infliction of emotional distress. Greenberg-Kobrin, supra, at 389. What do you think of her suggestion?

6. *Legislation.* In response to *Avitzur* (the most famous "get" case), New York passed a "get" statute (N.Y. Dom. Rel. Law §253 (McKinney 1999)), providing that no final judgment of divorce may be ordered unless the party who commences the proceeding alleges that he or she has taken or will take (prior to entry of judgment) "all steps" within his or her power to "remove any barrier" to the remarriage of defendant. Would the statute help Mrs. Aflalo, the moving party?

Commentators have questioned the constitutionality of the "get" statute on several grounds. Section 253(7) allows the rabbi who performed the marriage to deny that all barriers had been removed, thus unconstitutionally giving a clerical authority the right to block a civil divorce. The constitutional validity of a statute addressing the problems of a single religion is also questionable. See, e.g., Chambers v. Chambers, 471 N.Y.S.2d 958 (Sup. Ct. 1983) (avoiding due process concerns by deciding the case on narrower contract grounds). The constitutional arguments in *Aflalo* regarding possible Establishment Clause violations apply with equal force to New York's "get" statute because a husband may be compelled to participate in what he considers to be a religious practice to obtain a civil divorce.

Despite widespread doubts as to the statute's constitutionality, the New York legislature extended the application of the statute in 1992. The legislature amended the equitable distribution law to permit a judge to consider the effect of any "barrier to remarriage" in postdivorce decisionmaking regarding property distribution and spousal support. N.Y. Dom. Rel. Law §236B(5)(h) (McKinney 1999). Unlike N.Y. Dom. Rel. §253, this statute takes into account the actions of both spouses in regard to removing barriers to remarriage. Is this sound policy?

7. *Islamic marriage contracts.* Similar legal issues may arise regarding Islamic marriage contracts which make provision for a "mahr" or a sum of money payable by the husband to the wife, part upon the marriage and part upon divorce or the husband's death. Judicial enforcement of these religious marital agreements may violate the Establishment Clause by giving rise to impermissible governmental entanglement in religion. See also Dajani v. Dajani, 204 Cal. App.3d 1387 (Ct. App. 1988) (refusing to enforce a "mahr" on public policy grounds on the basis that it facilitates divorce). See generally Lindsey E. Blenkhorn, Note, Islamic Marriage Contracts in American Courts: Interpreting Mahr Agreements as Prenuptials and their Effects on Muslim Women, 76 S. Cal. L. Rev. 189 (2002); Ghada G. Qaisi, Note, Religious Marriage Contracts: Judicial Enforcement of *Mahr* Agreements in American Courts, 15 J.L. & Religion 67 (2000-2001).

F. THE ROLE OF COUNSEL

1. *Emotional Aspects of Divorce*

■ **ANDREW WATSON, THE LAWYER AND HIS CLIENT: THE PROCESS OF EMOTIONAL INVOLVEMENT**
in Psychiatry for Lawyers 1-36 (2d ed. 1978)

It is often suggested that only trial lawyers or attorneys specializing in Criminal or Domestic Relations Law need know anything of formal psychological theory. Nothing could be further from fact. . . .

Psychoanalytic therapy developed as an offshoot of Sigmund Freud's early exploration of the hypnotic technique. . . . From the time of Freud's collaboration with Breuer in the "Case of Anna," he was aware of the importance of the relationship of patient and doctor as a therapeutic tool as well as hazard. . . . Freud, in his 1910 lecture at Clark University, said, "In every psychoanalytic treatment of a neurotic patient the strange phenomenon that is known as 'transference' makes its appearance. The patient, that is to say, directs towards the physician a degree of affectionate feeling (mingled, often enough, with hostility) which is based on no real relation between them and which — as is shown by every detail of its emergence — can only be traced back to old wishful fantasies of the patient's." From these early beginnings, stems the present concept of transference. . . .

Whenever one makes an acquaintance, there is an immediate flood of perceptions about the newly encountered person. This includes such things as physical characteristics, interests, estimates of various personality traits, and other impressions about his nature. These new, mainly unconscious impressions are associated with many past personal encounters, especially with members of one's immediate family. There is a powerful unconscious tendency to generalize the nature of the new acquaintance so that instead of perceiving a face which is reminiscent of father's face, or a manner of speech which is like brother's, there is the feeling that this new person is *like* father or *like* brother. In other words, from the similarity of a part, the new person is given the whole characteristic of the past figure. Thus, at best, part of the reaction to the new person is inappropriate. While this distortion may be helpful in establishing a close relationship with great rapidity, it can just as likely cause coolness and withdrawal, depending on the nature of the past relationships from which the transference is made. At any rate, the reaction is *not* based on a realistic appraisal of the nature of the new person, and the way is laid open for future problems which can be formidable and difficult to untangle. We must regard this kind of projection as universal and hold it responsible for at least some difficulty in all interpersonal relationships. . . .

The concept of *countertransference* was somewhat later to be discovered, formulated, and understood. . . . Originally, countertransference was defined as the doctor's transference to the patient. In other words, those irrational projections which the patient's character precipitated in the doctor were called countertransference. However, [the term now includes] all of the doctor's reactions and feelings toward his patient and toward all his work with that patient. . . . Transference and countertransference are the two halves in a circle of dynamic interaction between the personalities of the two individuals in the relationship. . . . It is important for professional persons engaged in close personal relationships with clients or patients to understand the nature of this dynamic interaction. . . .

[L]et us turn to some of the specific places in which lawyers might, through a broader understanding of the interview and counseling process, achieve their professional goals more effectively. . . . The question may well be raised as to whether or not it is appropriate or even legitimate for lawyers to embark on the treacherous ground of counseling. However, this is a purely academic question since, for better or for worse, the very nature of a lawyer's activities forces him into this role. . . . For example, a man might arrive in his lawyer's office in a state of marked agitation, demanding that counsel take action to help him gain custody of his three children who "are being ruined by their mother," his former wife. He pours forth his anguished tale about how his oldest son, a boy of superior intelligence with a keen interest in science, is being "allowed to go through school with just passing grades. In addition he spends most of his time sitting around with his friends listening to that deafening rock music crap. She always did want to indulge him and she couldn't care less about whether or not he makes it in this world where a man has to know how to put his best foot forward. She has always acted like success just falls into a person's lap and all you have to do is wait and pick it up." . . .

The traditional response to this kind of request would be for the lawyer to figure out how to make a case for removing the children from the mother, thus satisfying the client's desire to gain custody. Unfortunately, such a course would overlook significant "facts" in the case. [I]t takes counseling skill for a lawyer to help his client bring [the client's] motives into conscious awareness. Counsel must be able to help the father openly evaluate the negative effects of litigation on the children and their parental relationships, as well as the "gains" he is seeking. In place of litigation, alternative routes of problem solving between the parents have to be found and facilitated. All too often counsel's knee-jerk response in matters like this is to reach for the weapon of litigation, a sure route to overkill with no real problem-solving effect. . . .

Let us consider the specific ways in which clients' conscious and unconscious attitudes toward lawyers may impinge upon the professional relationship. First of all, when a client seeks help from a lawyer, he is generally ignorant of the technical aspects of law. His ordinary techniques for judging persons or situations must be suspended, for he has no way of adequately testing the competency of the lawyer he chooses. He may make inquiries about him, and he may be able to investigate past successes and failures; but, generally, he is unable to make any realistic appraisal of skill and trustworthiness. Of necessity, then, he must place himself under the authority and assistance of the lawyer, essentially in blind trust. By virtue of this fact, all the client's previous attitudes toward authority and dependency will be stirred up, usually eliciting a certain amount of irrational fear and concern. He will feel impotent to broach these fears and will conceive of the relationship to his attorney as one of helplessness although, in reality, he is free to procure a new lawyer any time he wishes.

With such an attitude, the client may harbor certain magical expectations, for instance, that the lawyer is able to accomplish any manipulation or transaction that the client desires. Failure to demonstrate such omnipotence generally provokes anger which, since it is irrational and generally unconscious, may only be expressed in distorted ways. A lawyer can deal with this source of trouble more easily by knowing in advance that he is going to be assigned this authority role. . . .

In most law schools there is little opportunity for students to deal directly and consciously with these problems. . . . The law practitioner who takes the time to help his clients disentangle primarily psychological problems is performing as valuable a service as giving legal advice. . . .

■ KENNETH KRESSEL ET AL., PROFESSIONAL INTERVENTION IN DIVORCE: THE VIEWS OF LAWYERS, PSYCHOTHERAPISTS, AND CLERGY
in Divorce and Separation 246, 250-255 (George Levinger & Oliver C. Moles eds., 1979)

Much more frequently than either therapists or clergy, [divorce lawyers in our sample] mentioned sources of stress inherent in the nature of their work. . . . Let us set forth the major sources of role strain reflected in the lawyer interviews.

The *adversary nature of the legal proceedings.* Despite many changes in recent years, divorce remains largely an adversary process in the eyes of the law. [T]he law's formal bias, the availability of legal threats and counter-threats, as well as the emotional agitation of clients, may push even the most cooperative of lawyers toward serious escalation of conflict. (No-fault divorce has not removed the problem; couples still file bitter suits and countersuits over who shall have custody, how much child support shall be paid, etc.)

The one-sidedness of the lawyer's view. The lawyer's objective appraisal of the marital situation is greatly limited by the professional injunction that lawyers deal with only one of the spouses. Our respondents referred frequently to the difficulty of ascertaining the true state of affairs from the perspective provided by their own clients. Hearing only one side, the lawyer is more easily led to over-identify with the client's point of view — and the client may have strong motives, conscious or unconscious, for wishing to use the adversary system as a vehicle for retribution.

The shortage of material resources. Since two households cannot be supported as cheaply as one, it is highly unlikely that both parties to a divorce will be happy with the terms of the economic settlement. The attorney, therefore, is often in the position of being the bearer of bad news. . . .

The economics of the law office. "There are some lawyers who want to litigate, litigate. They get better fees that way — the taxicab with the meter running." How widespread this phenomenon is nobody knows. It represents nonetheless a serious potential conflict of interest between lawyer and client.

Another potential source of conflict stems from the fact that it is generally the husband who pays the wife's legal costs. The lawyer who represents the wife, there-fore, is in the anomalous position of having his fee paid by the opposing side. Unconscious pressures may thus be created for a less than totally effective representation of the wife's interests. The wife herself may have doubts about the degree of allegiance which she can expect from the arrangement.

The non-legal nature of many of the issues. In major areas of their activity, lawyers are operating largely outside the domain of law or legal training. Relatively few of the issues that arise are strictly "issues of law." Moreover, even many legal and financial issues engage psychological judgment and expertise, or personal values (e.g., custody or visitation arrangements that would best meet the emotional needs of both children and parents). Unfortunately, the training of lawyers poorly equips them to understand or handle the psychological and interpersonal issues in divorce, even though such issues may be crucial for creating equitable and workable agreements.

The difficulties in the lawyer-lawyer relationship. Almost universally the lawyers noted that a crucial determinant of divorce outcomes is the relationship between the two opposing attorneys. Indeed, for some respondents a constructive divorce was defined as one in which the two attorneys "come to operate within each other's framework." . . .

[The authors identify six roles that lawyers adopt in response to the problems of divorce practice.]

1. *The Undertaker.* This metaphor (supplied, incidentally, by one of our respondents) rests on two assumptions: that the job is essentially thankless and messy; and that the clients are in a state of emotional "derangement." This stance is also characterized by a general cynicism about human nature and the doubt that good or constructive divorces are ever possible. . . .

2. *The Mechanic.* This is a pragmatic, technically oriented stance. It assumes that clients are basically capable of knowing what they want. The lawyer's task primarily involves ascertaining the legal feasibility of doing what the client wants. . . . A good

outcome lies in producing "results" for the client, "results" usually understood in financial terms. . . .

3. *The Mediator.* This stance is oriented toward negotiated compromise and rational problem solving, with an emphasis on cooperation with the other side and, in particular, the other attorney. . . . Unlike the Undertaker and Mechanic, but like the following three stances, the Mediator tends to downplay the adversary aspect of his role. [A] good outcome is a "fair" negotiated settlement that both parties can "live with" (a frequently used phrase). . . .

4. *The Social Worker.* This stance centers around a concern for the client's post-divorce adjustment and overall social welfare. Regarding women clients in particular, there may be an emphasis on the client's "marketability."

> The main thing is to fully explore her ability to contribute to her own support. I have had agreements where I have been able to get money for college or a business course — or, in one case, a course in cooking.

Even though the attorney represents only one of the parties, there may also be a tendency to consider the interests of the entire family [such as the children]. This stance is also frequently associated with the view that, contrary to many clients' expectations, divorce is not usually an easy solution to marital unhappiness. The involvement of therapists or clergy is welcome. [A] "good" outcome is perceived to be one in which the client achieves social reintegration.

5. *The Therapist.* This stance involves active acceptance of the fact that the client is in a state of emotional turmoil. There is a concomitant assumption that the legal aspects of a divorce situation can be adequately dealt with only if the emotional aspects are engaged by the lawyer. Correspondingly, there is an orientation toward trying to understand the client's motivations. . . . A "good" outcome is conceptualized more or less as it would be in a therapeutically oriented crisis-intervention situation: personal reintegration of the client after a trying, stressful period. Predictably enough, this is also a stance that welcomes involvement of psychotherapists and in which clients may be encouraged to seek such assistance.

6. *The Moral Agent.* In this final stance there is a more or less explicit rejection of neutrality; it is assumed that the lawyer should not hesitate to use his or her sense of "right" and "wrong." This stance appears to be particularly salient when the divorcing couple has children, with the lawyer attempting to serve as a kind of guardian and protector of the children's interests. . . . A constructive outcome is one in which the lawyer's sense of "what is right" is satisfied, not only in relation to the client, but to the other spouse and the children.

We have sought to explain this typology of lawyer stances largely as a product of the role strains characteristic of matrimonial practice. . . .

■ MOSES v. MOSES
1 Fam. L. Rep. (BNA) 2604 (July 22, 1975), **aff'd,** *344 A.2d 912 (Pa. Super. Ct. 1975)*

CERCONE, J.

This appeal has been taken by the husband, Dr. Lawrence Moses, from the lower court's award of attorney's fees and expenses to his wife's counsel. . . .

From December 16, 1968 until February 4, 1969, Mrs. Moses consumed many of the hours for which Mr. Fox billed Dr. Moses in personal and telephonic conversations of staggering numbers. Although the content of those conversations is privileged, there are indications in the record that large parts of the discussions are based upon Mr. Fox's friendship with both Dr. and Mrs. Moses, as well as his professional relationship with Mrs. Moses. Her phone calls to Mr. Fox at all hours of the day and night eventually grew so burdensome that they were apparently the principal case of Mr. Fox's withdrawal from the case in favor of Mr. Robinson.

After his withdrawal, Mr. Fox tendered a bill for $4,842 in counsel fees (121 hours and 5 minutes at $40 per hour) and expenses of $112.10. Only fifty-six days elapsed from the time that Mr. Fox began consulting with Mrs. Moses until he withdrew on February 10, 1969, so that he averaged two hours every day, including weekends and holidays, working on Mrs. Moses' problems. The only tangible result of this labor was the support award for Mrs. Fox and the children of $275 weekly. Indeed, to this day the parties are not divorced. . . .

The difficulty in the instant case is that there can be little doubt that Mr. Moses is able to pay, and Mrs. Moses is unable to pay, the fees charged by Mr. Fox. We also do not dispute the finding by the lower court that Mr. Fox actually spent 121 hours on the case, and that $40 per hour is a fair hourly charge for those services. We do challenge, however, the propriety of Mr. Fox investing so much time in this case. We feel that there is an obligation upon counsel, if he expects his fee to be paid by the other spouse, to control excessive demands upon his time, energy and intellect by the dependent spouse. We find that Mr. Fox failed to exercise such control in the instant case. [C]ase law in other jurisdictions . . . supports our view herein. . . .

Finally, our decision is supported by the American Bar Association's Code of Professional Responsibility, Disciplinary Rule 2-106 (1970), which sets forth the factors that counsel should consider in determining the reasonableness of his fee: "(1) The time and labor required, the novelty and difficulty of the questions involved, and the skill requisite to perform the legal service properly. (2) The likelihood, if apparent to the client, that the acceptance of the particular employment will preclude other employment by the lawyer. (3) The fee customarily charged in the locality for similar legal services. (4) The amount involved and the results obtained. (5) The time limitations imposed by the client or by the circumstances. (6) The nature and length of the professional relationship with the client. (7) The experience, reputation, and ability of the lawyer or lawyers performing the services. (8) Whether the fee is fixed or contingent."

We find that the time and labor required, the results obtained, and the nature and length of Mr. Fox's professional relationship with Mrs. Moses, all militate against the allowance of fees and expenses of roughly $5,000 in the instant case. [T]he allowance for attorney's fees and expenses is reduced to $3,000. . . .

Notes and Questions

1. *Overlapping roles.* *Moses* reveals the overlap between the divorce attorney's role as advocate and psychological counselor. Given the court's advice, how would you recommend that an attorney "control [such] excessive demands upon his time, energy and intellect"?

2. *Marital counseling.* If the divorce attorney believes that a client should consult a trained therapist, should the attorney so suggest? How can the attorney do so in a nonthreatening manner? Might such a suggestion conceivably backfire? If the client refuses to heed the advice, should the attorney withdraw from the case?

Some law firms address this problem by hiring full time mental health professionals (and financial advisors) to assist clients with emotional (and financial) issues that arise during the divorce process. Elizabeth Millard, Continuum of Care: North Carolina Firm Adds Financial and Counseling Professionals to Its Staff, 4 ABA J. E-Report 6 (Apr. 15, 2005).

3. *Empirical data.* Many divorce lawyers provide less emotional support than the attorney in Moses. An empirical study of 40 divorce cases in California and Massachusetts (characterizing representation as a conversational tug-of-war) explains that clients seek to include a "broader picture of their lives, experiences, and needs" (especially regarding the failure of their marriage). Divorce lawyers resist these efforts. "[Lawyers] are interested only in those portions of the client's life that have tactical significance for the prospective terms of the divorce settlement or the conduct of the case." Austin Sarat & William L. F. Felstiner, Divorce Lawyers and Their Clients: Power and Meaning in the Legal Process 144 (1995). Thus, the lawyers "did not act as 'counselors for the situation' nor did they try to provide psychological, emotional, or moral support or guidance for their clients." In fact, lawyers tend to emphasize communicating their legal knowledge in order to move clients toward positions that the lawyers deem reasonable and realistic. Id. at 145.

These findings accord with those of a small-scale empirical study by sociologist Terry Arendell. Arendell reports that 53 (of 60) women had strong complaints about their lawyers. Many complaints focused on the different perceptions of the lawyers' role.

> Most of the women said their attorneys had showed little interest in their present or future problems and had not tried to keep them informed about divorce legalities and the overall legal process. Although they had been sought out as counselors in a personal life crisis, these lawyers soon appeared to be bureaucratic technicians, more concerned with forms, figures, and procedures than with a client's history, fears, or future well-being. . . .
>
> Oversights by attorneys provoked a great deal of anger and frustration. Failure to return phone calls, the most frequent complaint, eroded the attorney-client relationship and increased the woman's sense of stress. . . .

Terry Arendell, Mothers and Divorce: Legal, Economic, and Social Dilemmas 10-11 (1986).[27]

4. *Risks for divorce attorneys.* The emotionally charged divorce context can present danger for attorneys and judges when disgruntled clients occasionally discharge their frustrations by resorting to violence against legal professionals. Lisa Siegel & Keith Griffin, Middletown Shooting an Extreme Example of Risks Routinely Faced by Attorneys for Warring Spouses, Conn. L. Trib., June 21, 2005, at 1. Causes of the violence have been attributed to: (1) no-fault divorce which makes litigants more angry and anxious to lash out at the legal system, and (2) pro se

---

[27]. Of the seven women in Arendell's study who had no complaints, three prepared and filed their own divorce papers, three negotiated a spousal agreement before retaining an attorney, and the remaining woman was a law student!

divorce which eliminates the possibility that a lawyer can help the client understand the process and calm the client. Joan M. Cheever & Joanne Naiman, The Deadly Practice of Divorce, Natl. L.J., Oct. 12, 1992; Siegel & Griffin, supra. Some lawyers suggest that such violence emphasizes the need for greater use of alternative dispute resolution techiques in family law practices. Siegel & Griffin, supra.

2. Conflicts of Interest

■ FLORIDA BAR v. DUNAGAN
731 So. 2d 1237 (Fla. 1999)

PER CURIAM.

. . . After a formal hearing in this matter, the referee found the following facts. In July 1992, [Attorney] Dunagan prepared a bill of sale purporting to transfer certain assets of a restaurant business, "Biscuits 'N' Gravy 'N' More" ("B & G"), to the joint ownership of William and Paula Leucht. Dunagan also prepared the fictitious name filing for this business but, according to a letter sent by him to the Leuchts, inadvertently omitted Paula Leucht's name on the registration form.

Subsequently, a commercial lease dispute arose between B & G and Bay-Walsh Properties (Florida) Inc., d/b/a/ Nova Village Market Partnership ("Bay-Walsh"). The suit filed by Bay-Walsh named B & G, William Leucht, and Paula Leucht as defendants. Dunagan represented B & G and the Leuchts in this action and specifically moved to dismiss Paula Leucht as an improper party to the suit.

Later in 1994, Dunagan was involved in negotiations between the Leuchts and a third party to open another B & G restaurant in Daytona Beach and, in 1994 and 1995, also represented B & G and the Leuchts in an eminent domain suit against the Florida Department of Transportation.

On or about February 23, 1996, Dunagan sent a letter to the Port Orange Police Department and city attorney in which he stated that he represented William Leucht, that William Leucht was the sole owner of B & G, and that although there was a bill of sale which was "considered to put the business in the name of William and Paula Leucht," this "instrument and the legal consequences thereof were duly considered, and it was determined with deliberation that William Leucht would remain the sole owner." The letters further advised that Mr. Leucht intended to fire two employees, after which they would no longer be welcome on the premises of the restaurant, and that if they entered the premises, they would be ejected. The letters purported to notify the police "in order to prevent a breach of the peace from occurring."

Several days after sending these letters, Dunagan filed a petition for dissolution of marriage on behalf of William Leucht against Paula Leucht. A few days later, Paula Leucht called B & G restaurant and was told by an employee that William Leucht was the sole owner and she could not come to the restaurant. Ms. Leucht went to the restaurant anyway and was arrested for disorderly conduct and forcibly removed from the premises. Prior to, during, and after her arrest, Ms. Leucht informed the police that she co-owned the restaurant.

Finally, on May 2, 1996, the judge in the divorce proceeding ordered that William and Paula Leucht were to share equally in the net proceeds from both B & G restaurants, and on October 31, 1996, Dunagan filed a motion to withdraw from representation of William Leucht in the divorce proceeding after Paula

Leucht hired an attorney to file a malpractice lawsuit against him. [Dunagan seeks review of the referee's findings and recommendation.]

Dunagan first argues that the referee erred in finding that his representation of William Leucht in the divorce proceeding after having jointly represented William and Paula Leucht in matters relating to their business presented a conflict of interest. Dunagan argues that the business matters in which he represented the Leuchts were completely unrelated to the dissolution of marriage and that ownership of the business was not a central issue in the divorce; therefore, he reasons, there was no conflict of interest. This argument is without merit.

Rule 4-1.9(a) of the Rules Regulating The Florida Bar prohibits a lawyer who has formerly represented a client from representing another person "in the same or a substantially related matter" where that person's interests are materially adverse to the former client's interests. Whether two legal matters are substantially related depends upon the specific facts of each particular situation or transaction. Further, the comment to rule 4-1.9 states that "[w]hen a lawyer has been directly involved in a specific transaction, subsequent representation of other clients with materially adverse interests clearly is prohibited." . . .

[H]ere Dunagan represented William and Paula Leucht in the formation of their business and, specifically, prepared a bill of sale transferring assets of the business to their joint ownership. Because the business was begun during the marriage, it was a marital asset and as such was inherently an issue in the divorce. Additionally, the petition for dissolution of marriage filed by Dunagan on William Leucht's behalf specifically raised the issue of the ownership of the business and impliedly disputed the validity of the bill of sale prepared by Dunagan in that it alleged that William Leucht "is the sole owner of the restaurant known as 'Biscuits 'N' Gravy 'N' More'." While ownership of the business may not have been a hotly contested issue, it was still an issue involved in the divorce; therefore, at least one prior matter in which Dunagan jointly represented the Leuchts was substantially related to the divorce. . . .

Dunagan next argues that the referee erred in finding that Paula Leucht did not consent to Dunagan's representation of William Leucht in the dissolution of marriage action. Under certain circumstances, a lawyer may be permitted to represent a client despite a conflict of interest, but only if he or she obtains the consent of the appropriate party or parties after consultation. *See* R. Regulating Fla. Bar 4-1.7(a)-(b); 4-1.9(a). Here, the referee found that "no disclosure of the conflict or waiver of same took place, given the uncontested fact that no testimony was provided that the respondent ever consulted with Paula Leucht as to the circumstances which led him to represent William Leucht in the divorce, and to what her position was vis-a-vis his representing William Leucht." This finding is supported by the evidence.

Without consulting with or obtaining Paula Leucht's consent, Dunagan filed a petition for dissolution of marriage against her and on behalf of William Leucht. Shortly thereafter, Paula Leucht arrived home from a trip and discovered that the dissolution petition had been filed. Only then, after first calling Mr. Dunagan's office, did Paula Leucht seek and retain another attorney to represent her in the divorce. Only after she had retained an attorney of her own did Dunagan claim he sought her consent through her attorney.

Dunagan testified that he contacted Ms. Leucht's original and subsequent attorneys who gave their consent as attorneys for her. Ms. Leucht's original attorney, Mr. Beck, submitted an affidavit stating that "pursuant to a conference with my client, Paula K. Leucht, it was agreed that there would be no objection raised to the Respondent, Walter B. Dunagan, Esq., representing William Leucht." Paula Leucht acknowledged that she discussed Dunagan's representation of William Leucht with Beck and he advised her that there were better attorneys to be up against; so, she testified, "we never did say anything about him representing me." However, Ms. Leucht also testified that Beck never clearly advised her of her rights or the possible prejudice Dunagan's representation of her ex-husband presented. Accordingly, Ms. Leucht's and her attorney's failure to affirmatively object cannot be construed as "consent after consultation" as required by the rules.

Dunagan makes much of the fact that he could not personally consult with and obtain Ms. Leucht's consent because she was represented by counsel. However, there was no reason that Dunagan could not have consulted with and attempted to obtain Paula Leucht's consent prior to filing the dissolution petition on behalf of William Leucht and, therefore, prior to the time Paula Leucht retained other counsel to represent her in the divorce. This, in fact, would have been the most appropriate course of action. . . . The rules state that an attorney *shall not represent* conflicting interests unless the client consents. Especially where the conflict exists prior to the beginning of the representation, this can only mean that the necessary consent should be obtained before the attorney agrees to represent the conflicting interest. This was clearly not done in this case. . . .

Dunagan also argues that the referee erred in concluding that his letters to the Port Orange police and city attorney violated rule 4-1.9(b). . . . Rule 4-1.9(b) prohibits a lawyer from using information relating to the representation of a former client to the former client's disadvantage except as permitted by rule 4-1.6 or when the information has become generally known. Dunagan essentially argues that the information in the letter was not used to Paula Leucht's disadvantage because it only addressed who had the right to sole possession of the premises, and Paula Leucht was arrested for disorderly conduct, not trespassing. Therefore, he argues, the letters did not cause her to be arrested.

However, the evidence supports the referee's finding that the letters contributed, at least to some degree, to Ms. Leucht's being arrested and forcibly removed from the premises of the business. Although she was charged with disorderly conduct, the arrest report filled out by the police officer clearly shows that the police officers relied on the letter from Dunagan. [B]ecause Dunagan clearly used information relating to his representation of Paula Leucht to her disadvantage and such disclosures were not permitted under rule 4-1.6, we approve the referee's conclusion that the letters at issue violated rule 4-1.9(b).

Finally, Dunagan argues that the recommended discipline, a ninety-one-day suspension, is too harsh. . . . We find that the recommended suspension is appropriate. [T]he Court has imposed similar suspensions for similar conduct. . . .

Notes and Questions

1. *Epilogue.* After Dunagan's 91-day suspension, he filed a petition for reinstatement to the practice of law. The referee recommended that he not be reinstated for the following reasons: he had remained attorney of record in several cases during

his suspension; he failed to notify an employer (a company for which he lectured) of his suspension; he disagreed with the finding that his representation constituted a conflict of interest; he failed to correct deficiencies in his trust accounting procedures; and he presented no evidence of post-suspension community service. The Florida Supreme Court found the referee's factual findings insufficient to justify denying Dunagan's petition. Florida Bar ex rel. Dunagan, 775 So. 2d 959 (Fla. 2000).

2. *Rationale.* The divorce lawyer may face several ethical problems, including conflicts of interest. In *Dunagan,* what was the nature of the conflict of interest? Why does the court reject Dunagan's arguments that no conflict of interest existed? For example, how were the couple's business matters and divorce related? How were Mr. Leucht's interests materially adverse to his ex-wife's interests?

3. *Scope.* Courts wrestle with the issue how broadly to interpret the term "conflict of interest" for disciplinary or disqualifiation purposes. See, e.g., Ex parte Osbon, 888 So. 2d 1236 (Ala. 2004) (finding a conflict of interest when husband's attorney subpoenaed wife's mental health records and health care provider's attorney, who was partner of husband's attorney, responded to the subpoena); Davis v. Stansbury, 824 S.W.2d 278 (Tex. App. 1992) (finding abuse of discretion in granting husband's motion to disqualify wife's attorney based on latter partner's limited representation of husband in same matter in which unprivileged information had been communicated).

4. *Joint representation.* Is joint representation permissible? If so, when? According to current ethical rules (i.e., Model Code of Professional Responsibility and Model Rules of Professional Conduct), joint representation is permitted if the attorney reasonably believes he or she can adequately represent both clients' interests and if both clients consent after full disclosure of the risks of such representation. The Restatement (Third) of the Law Governing Lawyers §128 (2000) reaffirms this rule.

On the other hand, some states condemn the practice of joint representation via disciplinary rules, case law, or state bar opinions (as illustrated below). See Debra Lyn Bassett, Three's a Crowd: A Proposal to Abolish Joint Representation, 32 Rutgers L.J. 387, 426 & n. 173 (2001). The American Academy of Matrimonial Lawyers (a voluntary association of lawyers and judges that establishes ethical standards for family law practitioners that exceed those of the ABA and most state ethics codes) also admonishes against joint representation, even if clients consent. Which point of view do you find more persuasive?

See also Avi Braz, Note, Out of Joint: Replacing Joint Representation with Lawyer-Mediation in Friendly Divorces, 78 S. Cal. L. Rev. 323 (2004) (arguing that California's malpractice and ethics rules should be interpreted to ban joint representation); Mary E. Chesser, Comment, Joint Representation in a Friendly Divorce: Inherently Unethical?, 27 J. Legal Prof. 155 (2002-2003) (arguing that joint representation is difficult to achieve within the confines of ABA and state standards, and lawyers who chose to represent both parties should proceed cautiously).

5. *Client consent.* Did Mrs. Leucht consent to Mr. Dunagan's representation of her ex-husband in the dissolution action? Why did the Florida supreme court hold that her "failure to affirmatively object" could not be construed as consent pursuant to the state bar rules?

Problem

Wife files a petition for a restraining order for protection against domestic violence from her husband. The court grants her petition, but before the hearing to determine whether the order should be made permanent, Wife files a motion seeking disqualification of her husband's attorney, Charles Esposito. She alleges that she previously consulted Esposito's partner (Davis Upchurch) to ask him to represent her in divorce proceedings; in the course of that one consultation, she claims that she divulged confidential information to Upchurch. Upchurch did not charge her for the consultation; he claims that he was not retained to represent Wife and does not remember anything she told him that might have been confidential. Should Wife's motion be granted? Consider the following: (1) can an attorney-client relationship be established based on one visit?, (2) to fulfill the requirements for disqualification, must the client prove that confidential communications were actually disclosed?, (3) does the existence of the attorney-client privilege depend on whether the client actually hires the attorney?, and (4) were the two proceedings (the restraining order and the dissolution) substantially related, i.e., did the law firm subsequently represent an interest adverse to the former client in a matter that was the same or substantially related to the matter in which it represented the former client? See Metcalf v. Metcalf, 785 So. 2d 747 (Fla. Ct. App. 2001).

■ **ETHICS COMMITTEE, MISSISSIPPI STATE BAR OPINION 80**
Laws. Man. on Prof. Conduct (ABA/BNA) 801:5104
(Mar. 25, 1983)

An attorney may not represent both parties in a no-fault divorce. The interests of the parties are conflicting, inconsistent, diverse, and otherwise discordant, no matter what the parties themselves believe. Serving one client's interest may result in not adequately representing the other client's interest. The lawyer's loyalty will be divided. DRs 5-105(A)(C); ECs 5-14, 5-15.

■ **ETHICS COMMITTEE, STATE BAR OF MONTANA, OPINION 10**
Laws. Man. on Prof. Conduct (ABA/BNA) 801:5401
(Dec. 1980)

A lawyer may represent both spouses in a joint petition for dissolution as a nonadversary procedure. A lawyer may represent both spouses if it is obvious that he can adequately represent the interest of each after each consents to the representation after full disclosure of the possible effect of such representation on the exercise of his independent professional judgment on behalf of each. DRs 5-104; Canon 5.

■ ROBERT G. SPECTOR, THE DO'S AND DON'TS WHEN ONE LAWYER REPRESENTS BOTH PARTIES
Family Advocate, Spring 1991, at 16-18

Representing both parties in an uncontested divorce has traditionally been viewed as an inherent conflict of interest and has been prohibited. However, the past decade has witnessed considerable disagreement over whether it is permissible for a lawyer to perform the role of the intermediary in a "friendly divorce." Many states still view divorce as a real conflict, despite any appearance of harmony [and prohibit joint representation]. Other states have ethics opinions that allow an attorney to represent both husband and wife, albeit under restrictive circumstances. . . .

The perils into which you advance in this situation are quite clear. If something goes wrong with the agreement that has been drafted, it may be set aside. In such a case, you may be sued for malpractice, particularly if the client believes that you truly represented only one of the parties. If that occurs, the existence of the attorney-client relationship may well be a jury question. Or you might be subject to discipline.

Despite all the potential trouble, however, lawyers do take on joint representation and must know how to proceed. In jurisdictions that have adopted the Model Rules of Professional Conduct and that do not otherwise prohibit joint representation, compliance with the strictures of the rule can present problems.

Model Rule 2.2, Intermediary, provides:

> a) A lawyer may act as intermediary between clients if:
> 1) the lawyer consults with each client concerning the implications of the common representation, including the advantages and risks involved, and the effects on the attorney-client privilege, and obtains each client's consent to the common representation;
> 2) the lawyer reasonably believes that the matter can be resolved on terms compatible with the clients' best interests, that each client will be able to make adequately informed decisions in the matter, and that there is little risk of material prejudice to the interests of the clients if the contemplated resolution is unsuccessful; and
> 3) the lawyer reasonably believes that the common representation can be undertaken impartially and without improper effect on other responsibilities the lawyer has to any of the clients.
> b) While acting as intermediary, the lawyer shall consult with each client concerning the decisions to be made and the considerations relevant in making them, so that each client can make adequately informed decisions.
> c) A lawyer shall withdraw as intermediary if any of the clients so requests, or if any of the conditions stated in paragraph (a) is no longer satisfied. Upon withdrawal, the lawyer shall not continue to represent any of the clients in the matter that was the subject of intermediation.

The comment to Rule 2.2 specifically notes that this rule does not apply when you are acting as a mediator or arbitrator—roles the clients may not understand precisely. At the initial interview, you should explain the differences between a mediator, an arbitrator, an intermediary, and an advocate. If one of the clients mistakenly believes that he or she is engaging an advocate, the inevitable result will be an unhappy client and risk for you. . . .

If, in spite of all the warnings, you decide to act as an intermediary, . . . Model Rule 2.2(a)(2), (3) requires that you make three objective determinations: that the matter can be resolved on terms compatible with the clients' best interests with little risk of material prejudice, that the clients are able to make informed decisions, and that the common representation can be undertaken impartially. Once you have made these determinations and have made full disclosure to the clients, you must still obtain each client's consent. Rule 2.2(a)(1). In essence, Rule 2.2(a)(3) requires that you consider whether advocacy will be needed by one of the parties and whether an independent counsel will be required for each party. To determine if that is the case, consider the following factors:

1) The parties' social and economic relationship — When one party dominates another, it is unlikely that the dominated spouse will be able to make an informed decision in his or her best interest. The dominated party needs an independent advocate, not an intermediary.

2) Each party's emotional condition — Most parties to a divorce are under great stress. If either spouse is emotionally disturbed, it will impair his or her ability to make informed decisions. If you believe that this is the case, you should decline intermediary representation.

3) Each party's understanding of divorce law — The parties cannot arrive at an informal decision that is in their best interests unless they know the law that governs their relationship. . . .

4) The extent of disclosure of assets and liabilities — If there has not been full disclosure, an informed decision is impossible. If the parties balk at disclosure, obviously advocacy and independent counsel are needed.

5) The agreement that has been reached — If the parties have reached a general agreement on the various issues of their divorce, you can help them work out the detailed legal problems. However, be sure that the parties have discussed all the issues. If they have not discussed and agreed on most of the issues (you should have a list), contentious negotiations are likely. If this occurs, the spouses need advocates, not an intermediary.

6) The existence of minor children and substantial assets or debts, and the need for alimony or maintenance — The presence of these factors indicates that the divorce is likely to involve complexities. The more complex the divorce, the less likely it is that the parties have adequately discussed the issues. In some states, in fact, the existence of any of the above factors will prohibit your acting as an intermediary.

7) Your relationship with either party — Rule 2.2(a)(3) requires your independent judgment that you can impartially undertake joint representation without its affecting any other responsibilities to the clients. In practice, this means that if you have a close relationship with one of the parties, either personal or professional, you should decline joint representation. A lawyer who has previously represented one of the spouses may have to be disqualified anyway, on the basis of Rule 1.9, Former Client. Even if disqualification under Rule 1.9 would not be required, a lawyer can hardly be thought of as neutral when he or she has benefitted from one of the parties as a client or may do so in the future.

CLIENT CONSENT

Rule 2.2(a)(1) requires that you consult with each client about the implications of common representation and that you get each client's consent to the representation. To obtain consent, follow these guidelines:

1) Get separate consent for each client — Rule 2.2 explicitly requires separate [written] consent from each client. . . .

2) Explain attorney-client privilege in joint representation — Tell clients that the normal attorney-client confidentiality provisions of Rule 1.6 do not apply to jointly represented parties. If you are later forced to withdraw from the case, either party will be able to call you to testify to communications made to you. The comment to Rule 2.2 notes that during common representation, you are still required to keep clients adequately informed and to maintain confidentiality of information. This balance is impossible to maintain. When acting as intermediator, you must maintain full communication with both clients. Rule 2.2(b) requires you to consult with each client concerning the decisions to be made. To ensure that the clients fully understand this point, clearly explain that you will communicate with them only together, never separately.

3) Point out problems of advice — Acknowledge to the clients that an attorney who is not acting as an advocate for either party will not be able to present the best position for either party. This is a point that many clients do not understand. Many of the suits that follow joint representation — either against the lawyer for malpractice or to set aside the agreement — allege that the attorney did not advise the client of the best position to take on certain issues.

4) Explain withdrawal and its problems — Tell the clients that if serious disagreement develops regarding any issue, you will have to withdraw from joint representation. If that occurs, you will not be able to represent either party, and each will have to hire new counsel. It's best to illustrate this with an example — to say, perhaps, that if you discover that one party has not made and does not intend to make full disclosure of assets, you will have to withdraw. . . .

5) Communicate problems of fees — The clients should know that even if you have to withdraw from the case, you will expect to be paid for the time expended. You should also tell them that if you have to withdraw and the clients hire separate counsel, the total fees for the divorce will be higher than if the clients had hired separate counsel at the outset.

6) Explain the benefits of obtaining separate counsel — The difficulties of joint representation are such that some courts have required that you suggest [the possibility and desirability of seeking independent legal advice].

7) Discuss the finality of any agreement — The parties should be informed that any agreement they conclude will likely be as binding as an agreement concluded with independent counsel. Even if a court later decides that the intermediary representation was unwise, the agreement may still be sustained. . . .

3. Sexual Ethics

■ IN RE TSOUTSOURIS
748 N.E.2d 856 (Ind. 2001)

PER CURIAM.

The respondent, James V. Tsoutsouris, engaged in a sexual relationship with his client while he was representing her in a dissolution matter. He claims such a relationship was not improper. Alternatively, he argues that even if it were, it merits only a private reprimand. We disagree. . . .

[A] client hired the respondent [to] represent her in a dissolution action against her second husband [and in a child support action against her first husband]. While the respondent was representing the client in the fall of 1994, the respondent and the client began dating and engaged in consensual sexual relations several times. The respondent did not inform the client how a sexual relationship between them might impact his professional duties to her or otherwise affect their attorney/client relationship.

The respondent ended the sexual relationship a few weeks after it began in 1994. The client hired the respondent for a third legal matter in 1996. In 1997, the client sought psychological treatment. One of the subjects discussed during that treatment was her personal relationship with the respondent three years earlier.

[T]he respondent contends his consensual sexual relationship with his client during his representation of her does not violate the Rules of Professional Conduct. He bases that argument on the lack of evidence establishing that his sexual relationship with the client impaired his ability to represent the client effectively. The respondent contends that a sexual relationship between attorney and client in Indiana is professional misconduct only when it affects the quality of the attorney's representation of the client. The respondent also suggests that Indiana law in 1994 was ambiguous with respect to the impropriety of sexual relations between attorney and client. Therefore, he argues a finding of misconduct would be inappropriate because he was unaware of his obligations to avoid sexual contact with his client at the time of such contact.

Rule 1.7(b) prohibits representation of a client if the representation "may be materially limited . . . by the lawyer's own interests." Although the rule contains general exceptions in instances where the lawyer reasonably believes that the representation will not be adversely affected and the client consents after consultation, these exceptions will not generally avail when the "lawyer's own interests" at issue are those related to a lawyer/client sexual relationship. In effect, the respondent argues that sexual relationships between lawyers and clients ought to be authorized unless there is evidence of impaired representation. We decline to adopt that position.

Twenty-five years ago this Court suspended a lawyer for sexual misconduct with clients and warned of the professional conflicts such intimate associations create. Matter of Wood, 265 Ind. 616, 358 N.E.2d 128 (1976) (finding a violation of Rule 5-101(A) of the Code of Professional Responsibility — the predecessor to Rule 1.7(b) of the Rules of Professional Conduct). In a subsequent case involving the same attorney accused of similar misconduct, this Court ruled that the intermeshing of a lawyer's professional duties with the lawyer's personal sexual interests creates a situation where "the exercise of professional judgment on behalf of a client would be affected by personal interests" in violation of Rule 5-101(A). Matter of Wood, 489 N.E.2d 1189, 1190 (Ind. 1986).

Six years after our second *Wood* decision, the American Bar Association issued an ethics opinion on the subject of sexual relationships between attorneys and clients. ABA Formal Ethics Opinion No. 92-364, Sexual Relations with Clients. The ABA made it clear that attorneys should avoid sexual contact with their clients.[3]

---

3. While the ABA Model Rules of Professional Conduct do not explicitly prohibit a sexual relationship between an attorney and client, we note that such relationships have been unequivocally discouraged, as noted in ABA Ethics Opinion 92-364:

> First, because of the dependence that so often characterizes the attorney-client relationship, there is a significant possibility that the sexual relationship will have resulted from the exploitation of

This position is further bolstered by the recent proposed revisions of the ABA Model Rules of Professional Conduct [that] include a proposed new rule explicitly declaring that "A lawyer shall not have sexual relations with a client unless a consensual sexual relationship existed between them when the client-lawyer relationship commenced." Proposed Model Rule 1.8(j). The proposed rule is further supported by commentary reflecting important policy considerations.[4] . . .

In Matter of Grimm, 674 N.E.2d 551 (Ind. 1996), this Court found an attorney's "sexual relationship with his client during the pendency of dissolution and post-dissolution matters materially limited his representation of her," thereby violating Prof. Cond. R. 1.7(b). *Grimm*, 674 N.E.2d at 554. We explained:

> In their professional capacity, lawyers are expected to provide emotionally detached, objective analysis of legal problems and issues for clients who may be embroiled in sensitive or difficult matters. Clients, especially those who are troubled or emotionally fragile, often place a great deal of trust in the lawyer and rely heavily on his or her agreement to provide professional assistance. Unfortunately, the lawyer's position of trust may provide opportunity to manipulate the client for the lawyer's sexual benefit. Where a lawyer permits or encourages a sexual relationship to form with a client, that trust is betrayed and the stage is set for continued unfair exploitation of the lawyer's fiduciary position. Additionally, the lawyer's ability to represent effectively the client may be impaired. Objective detachment, essential for clear and reasoned analysis of issues and independent professional judgment, may be lost.

Id., 674 N.E.2d at 554.

Grimm is one of several cases decided under the *Rules of Professional Conduct* in which this Court has held that consensual sexual relationships with clients constitute professional misconduct. In Matter of Hawkins, 695 N.E.2d 109 (Ind. 1998), we found a violation of Rule 1.7(b) and held that, by "having sexual relations with his client, the respondent promoted and served his own interests and thereby threatened material limitation of his representation of her." . . . We hold that

---

the lawyer's dominant position and influence and, thus, breached the lawyer's fiduciary obligation to the client. Second, a sexual relationship with a client may affect the independence of the lawyer's judgment. Third, the lawyer's engaging in a sexual relationship with a client may create a prohibited conflict between the interests of the lawyer and those of the client. Fourth, a nonprofessional, yet emotionally charged, relationship between attorney and client may result in confidences being imparted in circumstances where the attorney-client privilege is not available, yet would have been, absent the personal relationship. We believe the better practice is to avoid all sexual contact with clients during the representation.

4. Proposed Comment 17 to Rule 1.8 states:

The relationship between lawyer and client is a fiduciary one in which the lawyer occupies the highest position of trust and confidence. The relationship is almost always unequal; thus, a sexual relationship between lawyer and client can involve unfair exploitation of the lawyer's fiduciary role, in violation of the lawyer's basic ethical obligation not to use the trust of the client to the client's disadvantage. In addition, such a relationship presents a significant danger that, because of the lawyer's emotional involvement, the lawyer will be unable to represent the client without impairment of the exercise of independent professional judgment. Moreover, a blurred line between the professional and personal relationships may make it difficult to predict to what extent client confidences will be protected by the attorney-client evidentiary privilege, since client confidences are protected by privilege only when they are imparted in the context of the client-lawyer relationship. Because of the significant danger of harm to client interests and because the client's own emotional involvement renders it unlikely that the client could give adequate informed consent, this Rule prohibits the lawyer from having sexual relations with a client regardless of whether the relationship is consensual and regardless of the absence of prejudice to the client.

the respondent violated Prof. Cond. R. 1.7(b) and prejudiced the administration of justice in violation of Prof. Cond. R. 8.4(d).

Given our finding of misconduct, we must determine an appropriate sanction. In doing so, we consider the misconduct, the respondent's state of mind underlying the misconduct, the duty of this court to preserve the integrity of the profession, the risk to the public in allowing the respondent to continue in practice, and any mitigating or aggravating factors. As a mitigating factor only, we find no evidence that the respondent's sexual relationship with his client actually impaired his representation of her. In fact, the client hired the respondent to handle another legal matter for her after the sexual relationship ended but before disciplinary charges were filed against the respondent. Moreover, the respondent has not been disciplined previously during his 33 years of practicing law. Given these mitigating factors, we conclude a 30-day suspension from the practice of law is warranted.

Notes and Questions

1. *Trend. Tsoutsouris* and its strong admonishment of attorney-client sexual conduct represented the minority rule until recently. The current trend (influenced by the ABA, discussed infra) has been toward prohibiting sexual relationships between attorneys and clients. Christian F. Southwick, Ardor and Advocacy: Attorney-Client Sexual Relations and the Regulatory Impulse in Texas and Across the Nation, 44 S. Tex. L. Rev. 307, 321 (2002).

2. *ABA.* In 2002, the ABA amended its Model Rules of Professional Conduct to provide that "a lawyer shall not have sexual relations with a client unless a consensual sexual relationship existed between them when the client-lawyer relationship commenced." Model Rules of Prof'l Conduct R. 1.8(j) (2003). As revealed in *Tsoutsouris*, prior to this recent amendment to the Model Rules, an ABA ethics opinion merely *recommended* a ban on sexual relationships between attorneys and clients. See ABA Comm'n on Ethics and Prof'l Responsibility, Formal Op. 92-364 (1992).

Although the Model Rules are not binding, many states have enacted similar ethics rules (some pre-dating the ABA's enactment of 1.8(j)). Does the ABA Model Rule adequately address the issue? See Phillip R. Bower & Tanya E. Stern, Current Development 2002-2003, Conflict of Interest?: The Absolute Ban on Lawyer-Client Sexual Relationships Is Not Absolutely Necessary, 16 Geo. J. Legal Ethics 535 (2003) (discussing the goals of 1.8(j), and arguing that it may be both over- and under-inclusive in terms of achieving its goals).

Indiana (the jurisdiction in *Tsoutsouris*) adopted the ABA Model Rule, effective January 1, 2005, in light of reforms suggested by the Indiana Ethics 2000 Task Force. See Ind. Prof. Cond. R. 1.8(j). See also Donald R. Lundberg & Charles M. Kidd, Survey of the Law of Professional Responsibility, You Say You Want an Evolution?: An Overview of the Ethics 2000 Amendments to the Indiana Rules of Professional Conduct, 38 Ind. L. Rev. 1255, 1266-1267 (2005).

3. *Background.* California was the first state whose bar association approved a rule proscribing attorney-client sexual relationships. California Rules of Professional Conduct 3-120(B) (1995) (effective Sept. 14, 1992) prohibits an attorney from: (1) requiring or demanding sexual relations as a condition of representation,

(2) employing coercion, intimidation, or undue influence in entering into sexual relations, or (3) continuing to represent a client after having sexual relations with that client if the sexual relationship causes the attorney to perform legal services incompetently. The Rule exempts pre-existing sexual relationships and spousal relationships. Id. at 3-120(C). The California state bar rejected an absolute ban based on concerns that a per se rule was not the least restrictive alternative and also would significantly infringe on the freedom of association rights of the attorney and client. Anthony E. Davis & Judith Grimaldi, Sexual Confusion: Attorney-Client Sex and the Need for a Clear Ethical Rule, 7 Notre Dame J.L. Ethics & Pub. Pol'y 57, 91 (1993); Calif. Sex-with-Clients Rule, 7 Laws. Man. on Prof. Conduct (ABA/BNA) 279, 280 (Sept. 11, 1991).

4. *Consensual nature of sexual relationship.* Does the consensual nature of the relationship militate against the imposition of sanctions? Are even apparently consensual attorney-client sexual relationships "dangerous and exploitative" such that regulation is necessary to protect clients and establish public trust in the legal profession? Malinda L. Seymore, Attorney-Client Sex: A Feminist Critique of the Absence of Regulation, 15 Yale J.L. & Feminism 175 (2003) (so arguing). Should it matter if the client, rather than the attorney, initiates the sexual relationship? See Committee on Professional Ethics and Conduct v. Hill, 436 N.W.2d 57 (Iowa 1989) (suspending attorney even though client initiated the sexual relationship, reasoning that attorney should have recognized the potential negative effects on her case). Some commentators argue that attorney-client sex can never be voluntary because of the power imbalance and the client's emotional and financial status. Jennifer Tuggle Crabtree, Does Consent Matter? Relationships Between Divorce Attorneys and Clients, 23 J. Legal Prof. 221, 229-232 (1998). Do you agree?

5. *Harm.* Tsoutsouris argues that his sexual relationship with his client did not impair his ability to represent her. In cases in which no prejudice results to the client's case, what is the harm of attorney-client sexual conduct? To the profession? To the client?

In Guiles v. Simser, 2005 N.Y. Slip Op. 25408 (Sup. Ct. 2005), a New York trial court held that an attorney-client sexual relationship did not give rise to a cause of action even though it violated the state ethical prohibition on sex with clients in domestic relations matters because, even if the lawyer violated his fiduciary duty, the client failed to show any compensable injury (no misuse of information, inadequate legal advice, or detriment to her position). Therefore, the court reasoned that, because the only damage to the client was emotional (and not sufficiently outrageous to establish intentional infliction of emotional distress), allowing the action to proceed would resurrect the repealed tort of seduction. Do you agree that state bar disciplinary action (private censure) is sufficient in such a case and that the client should have no private cause of action because no harm resulted?

What are the dangers inherent in a situation in which the attorney is sexually involved with a client whom he is representing in proceedings involving custody, child support, or property distribution? See, e.g., In re DiSandro, 680 A.2d 73 (R.I. 1996) (calling for withdrawal from representation in such cases). See generally ABA Ethics Opinion, supra (citing harms of: breach of lawyer's fiduciary obligations, negative impact on the independence of the lawyer's judgment, possibility of a conflict of interest, and imparting of confidences in circumstances where the attorney-client privilege is not available); William K. Shirley, Dealing with the

Profession's "Dirty Little Secret": A Proposal for Regulating Attorney-Client Sexual Relations, 13 Geo. J. Legal Ethics 131, 135-148 (1999) (discussing variety of harms). Should special censure be reserved for an attorney's conditioning the exchange of legal services for sexual services? See Attorney Grievance Comm'n of Maryland v. Culver, 849 A.2d 423 (Md. 2004).

Should rules regulating sexual conduct between lawyers and clients have exceptions? Should the rules exempt sexual relationships that predate the professional relationship? See the ABA Model Rule, supra. Do exemptions of preexisting consensual sexual relationships adequately address the issue? See Bower & Stern, supra, at 545 (arguing that sexual relationships that exist prior to the attorney-client relationship may be just as dangerous as those that subsequently arise).

6. *Empirical data.* Although no empirical studies investigate the effects of lawyers' sexual misconduct with clients, the effects of sexual relations between therapists and clients are well documented. For example, 90 percent of patients in one study ($n = 559$) suffered negative effects, including loss of motivation, impaired social adjustment, suicidal feelings or behavior, and increased substance abuse. Jacqueline Bouhoutsos et al., Sexual Intimacy Between Psychotherapists and Patients, 14 Prof. Psychol.: Res. & Prac. 185, 191 (1983). How is the attorney-client relationship similar to, and different from, the psychotherapist-client relationship? See, e.g., Suppressed v. Suppressed, 565 N.E.2d 101, 105 (Ill. App. Ct. 1990) (distinguishing professions), *appeal denied*, 571 N.E.2d 156 (Ill. 1991). Are similar effects to clients likely?

7. *Therapist-client rules.* Regulations currently prohibit sexual conduct between psychotherapists and clients. See, e.g., Cal. Bus. & Prof. Code §726 (West 2003). Some statutes limit prohibitions to conduct within two years of termination of therapy (e.g., Cal. Civil Code §43.93) (West Supp. 2005); other statutes contain absolute prohibitions (e.g., Fla. Stat. Ann. §491.0112) (West 2001). See Kenneth M. Austin et al., Confronting Malpractice: Legal and Ethical Dilemmas in Psychotherapy 145 (1990). One commentator points out that "in stark contrast to lawyers, health care professions confront universal harsh treatment — disciplinary proceedings, civil liability, and criminal liability — for engaging in sexual conduct with their patients." Gretchen M. Staley, Sex and the Divorce Lawyer, 11 J. Contemp. Legal Issues 24, 26 (1999). What might explain the difference in treatment?

8. *Different approaches.* The ABA's recent enactment of Rule 1.8(j) has prompted states to review their policies toward attorney-client sexual relations. Currently, 19 states have some form of prohibition against attorney-client sexual relationships (11 of these states have a per se rule). Jedediah R. Bodger, Revisions to the Rules of Professional Conduct, Nev. Law. 17, 19-20 (Feb. 2004). Many states without a specific ban find attorney-client sexual relations to be professional misconduct under existing rules. Id. at 20. New York limits the ban to domestic relations attorneys. N.Y. Code of Prof. Resp. DR 5-111 (B)(3) (N.Y. Comp. Codes R. & Regs. tit. 22, §1200.29-a(a) (2002). Does this limitation make sense?

See generally Abed Awad, Attorney-Client Sex Should Always Be Off Limits, N.J. L.J., Mar. 13, 2000; Linda Fitts Mischler, Personal Morals Masquerading as Professional Ethics: Regulations Banning Sex Between Domestic Relations Attorneys and Their Clients, 23 Harv. Women's L.J. 1 (2000); Florence Vincent, Comment, Regulating Intimacy of Lawyers: Why Is It Needed and How Should It Be Approached?, 33 U. Tol. L. Rev. 645 (2002).

9. *Other sanctions.* Different types of sanctions might apply to sexual misconduct, such as those for violations of state business and professions codes. Suspensions and disbarrment are possible sanctions. Civil tort remedies, such as intentional infliction of emotional distress or malpractice, might apply (e.g., McDaniel v. Gile, 281 Cal. Rptr. 242 (Ct. App. 1991)). See also Doe v. Roe, 681 N.E.2d 640 (Ill. Ct. App. 1997) (client may pursue claim for breach of fiduciary duty against her divorce lawyer who coerced her into a sexual relationship); Walter v. Stewart, 67 P.3d 1042 (Utah Ct. App. 2003) (reversing summary judgment on plaintiff's claims). Criminal statutes also might be relevant. What approach do you favor?

10. *Privacy.* Does an outright ban on attorney-client sexual relations constitute an unconstitutional intrusion on the attorney's and client's respective right to privacy? In Committee on Professional Ethics and Conduct v. Hill, 436 N.W.2d 57 (Iowa 1989), an attorney had sexual intercourse, purportedly in exchange for money, with a divorce client involved in child custody litigation. The attorney argued that the court's consideration of his conduct violated his right to privacy, protecting private acts between two consenting adults. How should the court rule? See also Linda Fitts Mischler, Reconciling Rapture, Representation, and Responsibility: An Argument Against Per Se Bans on Attorney-Client Sex, 10 Geo. J. Legal Ethics 209, 211 (1997) (suggesting that per se bans intrude on the right to privacy and freedom of intimate association).

11. *Famous cases.* Several famous lawyers' affairs have received publicity. See, e.g., William Vogeler, They Are Trying to Destroy Me, 103 L.A. Daily J., May 2, 1990, at 11 (reporting allegations of sexual misconduct against Marvin Mitchelson). Attorney Melvin Belli went on record saying that sex between a lawyer and client is the "lawyer's prerogative." See Thomas Lyon, Sexual Exploitation of Divorce Clients: The Lawyer's Prerogative?, 10 Harv. Women's L.J. 159 (1987).

12. *Same-sex issues.* Not all sexual misconduct involves a male attorney and female client. After public attention focused on the California state bar rule (discussed supra), the assemblywoman who proposed the legislation began receiving calls from heterosexual men complaining about advances by female attorneys and also from gay men complaining about their male attorneys. Michele Fuetsch, Bar OK's Limits on Lawyer, Client Sex, L.A. Times, Apr. 21, 1991, at A-3.

Problems

1. Recently you receive a telephone call from a former law school friend. He asks for your advice, explaining that he is very attracted to a woman he is representing in a contentious divorce case. Although he is eager to become romantically involved, he would like to know more about potential ethical issues. He confesses that he is so smitten that he has lost his objectivity. Nonetheless, he believes he can continue to represent her effectively even if they begin to see each other romantically.[28] What would you advise?

---

[28]. This problem is posed in Ethics: Affairs of the Heart, ABA J., June, 1990, at 82.

2. Cheryl retains Attorney Drucker to represent her in her divorce. At trial she testifies that during her initial consultation, she discussed her marriage, conjugal relations, and her psychiatric treatment for an anxiety disorder. On her second visit, she alleges that Drucker held her hand, embraced her, and told her of his stressful marriage. When he apologized and offered to refer her to another lawyer, she declined. She was not anxious to retell her personal history. Drucker called her at home that day to tell her he was attracted to her. On three subsequent visits Cheryl alleges that they engaged in sexual activity. Although unable to remember dates, Cheryl pinpoints two of the encounters based on surrounding events (that is, Drucker's daughter was ill, a particular client was in the office). After Drucker ends the relationship, Cheryl's husband discovers her love letters and diary. He confronts her in the presence of their son, who is the subject of a custody dispute. Drucker denies the sexual relationship. The Committee on Professional Conduct files a petition to suspend Drucker from the practice of law. What result? See Drucker's Case, 577 A.2d 1198 (N.H. 1990).

G. Divorce Jurisdiction

1. Over the Plaintiff and Defendant

■ IN RE MARRIAGE OF KIMURA
471 N.W.2d 869 (Iowa 1991)

LAVORATO, Justice. . . .

Ken and Fumi Kimura were married in Japan in 1965. Both are Japanese citizens. They have a daughter and a son. The daughter, Izumi, was twenty-three at the time of the dissolution hearing. The son, Naoki, was twenty-one. Ken and Fumi have lived apart since September 1973.

Ken graduated from Kobe University Medical School in Japan. Currently, he is a pediatric surgeon at the University of Iowa Hospitals and Clinics in Iowa City.

In July 1986 Ken was invited to come to the United States where he took a position at the Long Island Jewish Medical Center in New Hyde Park, New York. When he came to the States, Ken had an H-1 visa. Such a visa is a temporary one, issued to persons with special talents or abilities that may be useful to the United States. [The center filed an application on Ken's behalf for permanent residency status, which he received in October 1987. Subsequently, he was hired at the University of Iowa as an Associate Professor of Medicine.]

In March 1988 Ken filed a divorce mediation proceeding with the family court in Japan. In July he withdrew from the proceeding. Apparently he could not attend that court's reconciliation proceeding between himself and Fumi because of his work.

In December Ken filed a petition for dissolution of marriage in Johnson County District Court. He alleged that he had resided in Iowa for more than one year. He further alleged that his residency was not just for the purpose of obtaining a dissolution. Finally, he alleged a breakdown of the marital relationship.

Because personal service was not possible on Fumi in Iowa, a copy of the petition was mailed to her in Japan. In addition, notice of the petition was published in the Iowa City Press Citizen on December 14, December 21, and December 28.

In February 1989 Fumi filed a preanswer motion in which she contested the district court's subject matter and personal jurisdiction. [Her affidavit pointed out that Ken could not obtain a divorce under Japanese law because his conduct caused the marital problems. At final hearing, Fumi did not personally appear but her attorney did. After testimony about Ken's employment, residence status, and the breakdown of the marriage, the court concluded Ken satisfied residency requirements and dissolved the marriage. Fumi appealed.]

II. THE DUE PROCESS CHALLENGE

Fumi poses the issue this way: "Iowa's assertion of jurisdiction over respondent (who has no contacts with Iowa) or her marriage based solely on petitioner's alleged residence in Iowa violates the due process clauses of the United States and Iowa Constitutions." . . .

Early on, due process required the personal presence of the defendant in the forum state as a condition for rendering a binding personal or in personam judgment against the defendant. Pennoyer v. Neff, 95 U.S. 714, 733 (1878). The rule was expanded in International Shoe Co. v. Washington, 326 U.S. 310 (1945). Now due process does not require such personal presence. Due process only requires that the defendant have certain minimum contacts with the forum state. However, those contacts must be such "that the maintenance of the suit does not offend traditional notions of fair play and substantial justice." *International Shoe*, 326 U.S. at 316. Simply put, there must be a connection among the forum, the litigation, and the defendant.

Fumi relies on [Shaffer v. Heitner, 433 U.S. 186 (1977),] in support of her contention that jurisdiction to grant the dissolution must be tested by the minimum contacts standard of *International Shoe*. A footnote in *Shaffer* suggests her reliance is misplaced. See *Shaffer*, 433 U.S. at 208 n.30. One commentator seems to agree:

> Although the *Shaffer* Court concluded that all assertions of state-court jurisdiction must conform to the standards of *International Shoe* and, thus, be based upon a nexus among the forum, the litigation, and the defendant, the nexus requirement is unlikely to apply to cases in which status provides the basis of the asserted jurisdiction. The power to dissolve the marriage status in an ex parte proceeding normally is thought to stem, at least in part, from the perception of the marriage status as a res, and thus, as a "thing" to which the court's jurisdiction can attach. Despite the obvious analogy between in rem and quasi in rem jurisdiction based on the presence of property and ex parte-divorce jurisdiction based on the presence of a res (marriage status), the Court specifically noted in a footnote [n.30] that it was not suggesting "that jurisdictional doctrines other than those discussed in text, such as the particularized rules governing adjudications of status, are inconsistent with the standard of fairness." The all-inclusive language of the *Shaffer* conclusion, therefore, may not include cases in which status is the basis of the asserted jurisdiction. As far as the *Shaffer* holding is concerned, the forum-litigation-plaintiff nexus recognized as sufficient by the Court in Williams v. North Carolina seems to remain a valid basis of jurisdiction for ex parte divorces.

State-Court Jurisdiction, 63 Iowa L. Rev. at 1005-06 (citations omitted).

In Williams v. North Carolina, 317 U.S. 287 (1942) [hereinafter *Williams I*], the question was whether full faith and credit had to be given to a foreign divorce decree where only one spouse was domiciled in the foreign state and the other spouse had never been there. *Williams I*, 317 U.S. at 298-99. The Supreme Court held that the foreign state's high interest in the marital status of its domiciliaries required that full faith and credit be given such a decree. The Court did require, however, that substituted service on the absent spouse meet due process standards, that is, reasonably calculated to give the absent spouse actual notice and an opportunity to be heard.

In *Williams I* the Court had difficulty classifying dissolution proceedings. Though it did not view such proceedings as in rem actions, neither did it view them as mere in personam actions. According to the Court, domicile of one spouse within the forum state gave that state the power to dissolve the marriage regardless of where the marriage occurred. This court too has deemed domicile as essential to dissolution of marriage jurisdiction.

The cases generally adopt the following explanation of the components for a dissolution of marriage proceeding:

> It is commonly held that an essential element of the judicial power to grant a divorce, or jurisdiction, is domicile. A court must have jurisdiction of the res, or the marriage status, in order that it may grant a divorce. The res or status follows the domiciles of the spouses; and therefore, in order that the res may be found within the state so that the courts of the state may have jurisdiction of it, one of the spouses must have a domicile within the state.

24 Am. Jur. 2d Divorce & Separation §238, at 336 (1983).

Williams v. North Carolina reached the Supreme Court a second time. The Court held that while the finding of domicile by the state that granted the decree is entitled to prima facie weight, it is not conclusive in a sister state but might be relitigated there. Williams v. North Carolina, 325 U.S. 226, 238-39 (1945) [*Williams II*].

The divisible divorce doctrine emerged in Estin v. Estin, 334 U.S. 541, 549 (1948). In *Estin* the Court held that Nevada in an ex parte divorce proceeding could change the marital status of those domiciled within its boundaries. The power to do so stems from Nevada's "considerable interest in preventing bigamous marriages and in protecting the offspring of marriages from being [illegitimate]." *Estin*, 334 U.S. at 546. But Nevada could not wipe out the absent spouse's claim for alimony under a New York judgment in a prior separation proceeding because Nevada had no personal jurisdiction over the absent spouse. So New York did not have to give full faith and credit to that part of the Nevada decree which purported to eliminate the support obligation of its domiciliary. [The Supreme Court reaffirmed *Estin* in Vanderbilt v. Vanderbilt, 354 U.S. 416, 417-418 (1957). *Vanderbilt* differed in the fact that the absent spouse's right to alimony had not been determined before the ex parte divorce in Nevada.]

The divisible divorce doctrine simply recognizes the court's limited power where the court has no personal jurisdiction over the absent spouse. In these circumstances the court has jurisdiction to grant a divorce to one domiciled in the state but no jurisdiction to adjudicate the incidents of the marriage, for example, alimony and property division. In short, the divisible divorce doctrine recognizes both the in rem and in personam nature of claims usually raised in dissolution of marriage proceedings.

We conclude that the all-inclusive language of the *Shaffer* conclusion does not include dissolution of marriage proceedings. In other words, jurisdiction to grant such a dissolution is not to be tested by the minimum contacts standard of *International Shoe*.

We further conclude that domicile continues to be the basis for a court's jurisdiction to grant a dissolution of marriage decree. So the courts of this state have the power to grant dissolution of marriage decrees provided the petitioner is domiciled in this state. Such power exists even though the petitioner's spouse is absent from this state, has never been here, and was constructively rather than personally served. [W]e are left with the question whether Ken established his domicile or residency in this state. . . .

III. CHALLENGE TO DOMICILE OR RESIDENCY

The district court adjudicated only the marital status. And that was done based on Ken being domiciled in this state. None of the incidents of the marriage — for example, alimony and property division — were adjudicated because the court did not have personal jurisdiction over Fumi. . . .

Fumi contends that even if minimum contacts were not the standard, Ken still had to establish that he met the residency requirements of this state before the court could dissolve the marriage. She argues that Ken failed to establish those requirements and so the district court should not have dissolved the marriage. For reasons we discuss, we disagree. . . .

According to [Iowa Code §598.6] Ken had to establish the following: (1) he resided in Iowa for at least one year before the petition was filed; and (2) his residence here was in good faith and not just for the purpose of obtaining a marriage dissolution.

Residence for the purpose of section 598.6 has the same meaning as domicile. To have a residence or domicile within the meaning of this section, "one must have a fixed habitation with no intention of" leaving it.

Once a domicile is established, it continues until a new one is established. A new domicile is established if all of the following things happen: (1) the former domicile is abandoned; (2) there is an actual removal to, and physical presence in the new domicile; and (3) there is a bona fide intention to change and to remain in the new domicile permanently or indefinitely. This intention must be a present and fixed intention and not dependent on some future or contingent event. . . .

We think Ken amply proved that he met the residency requirements of section 598.6. . . . In the affidavit he swore to a number of facts showing that he had abandoned his domicile in Japan in favor of the one here. For example, he swore that he had no other permanent residence other than his residence in Johnson County. In addition, he swore that since moving to Iowa he had obtained an Iowa driver's license and had opened bank accounts at local banks. Finally, he swore that he intends to remain here for an indefinite period so long as his employment at the university is satisfactory to him and the university. . . .

We see nothing in the evidence to support Fumi's contention that Ken's residence here was in bad faith and only for the purpose of obtaining a dissolution of marriage. It may be that one reason Ken came here was — as Fumi suggests — because of our liberal dissolution marriage law as compared to Japan's. But that fact is not sufficient to preclude Ken from establishing a domicile or residence in Iowa, especially in light of his intention to remain here indefinitely.

Nor does Ken's continued Japanese citizenship preclude such a domicile or residence. A foreign citizenship does not — standing alone — bar one from establishing a domicile or residence for dissolution of marriage purposes. . . .

IV. CHALLENGE TO COURT'S RULING REFUSING TO DECLINE JURISDICTION BASED ON FORUM NON CONVENIENS DOCTRINE

[Fumi contends the district court should have declined jurisdiction based on forum non conveniens, arguing] that Japan is the more convenient forum and is the nation with the most significant contacts to the marital status of the parties. . . . Forum non conveniens is a facet of venue. This doctrine presupposes at least two forums in which jurisdiction and venue are proper. Under the doctrine a court may decline to proceed with an action though venue and jurisdiction are proper. The doctrine is a self-imposed limit on jurisdictional power that can be used to avoid unfair, vexatious, oppressive actions in a forum away from the defendant's domicile. . . .

What the moving party must show is that the relative inconveniences are so unbalanced that jurisdiction should be declined on an equitable basis. Factors that bear on this determination include the following: the relative ease of access to sources of proof; the availability of compulsory process for attendance of unwilling, and the cost of obtaining attendance of willing, witnesses; the possibility of view of the premises, if view would be appropriate to the action; the enforceability of the judgment if one is obtained; and all other practical problems that make trial of a case easy, expeditious, and inexpensive. All of these factors pertain to the private interest of the litigant.

Factors of public interest are also considered. They include the administrative difficulties for courts, trial in the forum that is the home of the state law which governs the case, and the burden of jury duty imposed on citizens of a forum with no relation to the litigation. Residency of the plaintiff is also considered but only as one of the many factors in the balancing process.

Whether to apply the doctrine of forum non conveniens lies in the sound discretion of the district court. . . . In deciding whether the district court abused its discretion in this case, we think it would be helpful to look at the divorce process in Japan. Japan has a variety of ways to dissolve a marriage [in contested cases] . . . : divorce through mediation in the family court, divorce by judicial decree in the family court, and divorce by judicial decree in the district court. A person seeking a divorce by judicial decree in the district court must prove fault. . . .

The family court may grant a divorce without proof of such grounds. But a divorce by judicial decree in the family court is rare because if either party objects, the divorce becomes invalid. So a decree of divorce by judicial decision usually issues from the district court.

Before the parties may proceed to the district court they must attempt mediation in the family court. Divorce can be effected without resort to litigation if the parties can agree on terms. If the parties fail to reach agreement, a divorce petition may then be submitted to and processed by the district court. Mediators in family court have no power to arbitrate disputes and are likely to oppose the idea of divorce. As a practical matter, a failure to agree to terms in mediation may mean no divorce in district court.

A divorce in Japan means the severance of all ties between the parties — they virtually become strangers. Usually a lump sum property settlement occurs. Because of enforcement problems, a settlement involving installment payments is rare. Alimony and other postdivorce maintenance payments are not available under Japanese law. Indeed, there is no legal requirement that property be divided or that support be paid. . . .

It has been suggested that divorce in Japan is quick and easy if a party can bribe, coerce, threaten, or persuade the other party to a divorce by mutual consent. A nonconsensual divorce is difficult, if not impossible, to obtain. . . .

For several reasons, the district court here could have determined that Japan is the more convenient forum for the parties. First, Japan has complete jurisdiction over the marital status of the parties and over all the incidents of the marriage. Second, a Japanese court has a societal interest in the marital status of its citizens. Third, given the nature of the divorce proceedings in Japan, Fumi's bargaining power in a family court mediation may be reduced by permitting a dissolution of marriage here. Fourth, Fumi may be at a cultural disadvantage with regard to customs and language in an Iowa proceeding. Last, Iowa is an inconvenient forum in relation to her residence.

On the other hand we think the district court was well within its discretion to deny Fumi's request to decline jurisdiction. Iowa too has an interest in the marital status of its residents. Right or wrong, our legislature has opted for no-fault divorce. One reason, we suspect, was to eliminate the extortion leverage an "innocent" spouse had over a "guilty" spouse. Had the district court honored Fumi's request, Ken — an Iowa resident — would have been denied the protection of Iowa's dissolution law. In short, a ruling in Fumi's favor may have resulted in no dissolution at all for one of this State's residents.

In addition we are impressed with the vigorous representation Fumi enjoyed in the district court and here. We doubt there would be any less representation in a postdissolution action for alimony and property division. . . . Our liberal discovery rules should allow Fumi to discover all of Ken's assets and his income in such an action. This is in contrast to Japan where it is difficult to discover a party's assets in divorce proceedings. Given our liberal rules on alimony and property division, we suspect Fumi might even fare better here than in Japan. . . . The district court did not violate Fumi's rights under either the federal or state constitutions. . . .

Notes and Questions

1. *Special rules. Kimura* reveals that special jurisdictional rules, unlike those in other civil actions, apply to divorce. To terminate a marriage, the plaintiff must be domiciled in the forum state. Personal jurisdiction over the defendant is not required. (Although personal jurisdiction is not required merely to terminate the marriage, it is required to resolve the financial incidents of the marriage.) See also Von Schack v. Von Schack, 893 A.2d 1004 (Me. 2004). However, *notice* to the defendant that complies with due process is required to inform the defendant of the pendency of the action. A divorce without proper notice may be challenged for lack of jurisdiction.

2. *Ex parte divorces.* As *Kimura* indicates, some divorce decrees issued in one state may be collaterally attacked in another state for want of jurisdiction. Williams v. North Carolina, 317 U.S. 287 (1942), established that the domiciliary state of one spouse may grant an ex parte divorce (that is, one in which the forum lacks jurisdiction over the respondent-spouse) entitled to full faith and credit in all other states. Because divorce courts routinely apply local substantive law, the ruling in *Williams I* reinforced the practice of migratory divorce during the fault era, when unhappy spouses often traveled to a new "domicile" to seek a divorce under the forum state's more permissive grounds.

In *Williams II*, however, the Supreme Court limited that holding. Williams v. North Carolina, 325 U.S. 226 (1945). *Williams II* held that, although the full faith and credit obligation assumes the forum has valid jurisdiction as the domicile of the petitioner, a subsequent showing of lack of domicile will allow sister states to refuse to recognize the divorce. The holding thus allowed North Carolina to prosecute for bigamy two North Carolina residents who purported to establish a domicile in Nevada where each got a divorce, married each other, and then immediately returned home.

What rationale underlies the judicial willingness to recognize ex parte divorces? Is the ex parte divorce fair to the "stay-at-home spouse"? To the state whose laws the migratory petitioning-spouse seeks to evade?

3. *Bilateral divorce.* In another line of cases, the Supreme Court has indicated that, when the forum has personal jurisdiction over both spouses in a migratory divorce, the principles of full faith and credit forbid collateral attack. See, e.g., Johnson v. Muelberger, 340 U.S. 581 (1951); Sherrer v. Sherrer, 334 U.S. 343 (1948). If the petitioning spouse has not genuinely established a domicile in the divorce forum (a jurisdictional prerequisite for all divorces, ex parte and bilateral alike), why should personal jurisdiction over the respondent spouse prevent collateral attack, say, by way of a bigamy prosecution? What good is a state's restrictive divorce law if a resident spouse can simply cross state lines, purport to establish a new domicile and — after the personal appearance of the other spouse — obtain a divorce immune from collateral attack?

4. *Transitory presence.* The Supreme Court elaborated the standards for in personam jurisdiction over a defendant in Burnham v. Superior Court, 495 U.S. 604 (1990), which held that a defendant's transitory presence can satisfy due process even when the defendant has no substantial connection to the forum. The Court upheld California's assertion of general jurisdiction over a New Jersey resident who was personally served during a brief trip to conduct business and visit his children in California, his wife's new home. The plurality determined that due process was satisfied because (1) the minimum-contacts/fairness approach to jurisdiction (initiated by *International Shoe*) addresses only absent (not present) defendants, and (2) the long-standing rule conferring jurisdiction upon a defendant personally served in the forum accords with "traditional notions of fair play and substantial justice."

One concurrence (Justice White) rejected the need to entertain individual claims of unfairness for a defendant whose presence in the forum is intentional. Another concurrence (Justices Brennan, Marshall, Blackmun, and O'Connor) insisted on a "fairness" inquiry even for nonresident defendants personally served in the forum, but found such fairness in Mr. Burnham's purposeful, albeit brief, availment of California's benefits (for example, police protection, roads). Then why is it not fair, as Justice Scalia asks in his plurality opinion, to serve a defendant *after* he has left the forum and returned to his home state if receipt of benefits proves determinative?

Note that, as a result of the Court's holding in *Burnham*, the divorce action in *Burnham* becomes a bilateral, rather than an ex parte, proceeding, allowing the forum to resolve the financial incidents of the dissolution.

5. *Foreign country divorces.* In the fault era, disputes arose about divorces obtained in foreign countries by U.S. residents seeking to evade restrictive laws. American courts do not owe full faith and credit to decrees from foreign countries, although they may recognize such divorces under principles of "comity." E.g., Rosenstiel v. Rosenstiel, 209 N.E.2d 709 (N.Y. 1965). Because comity is discretionary, some states refuse to apply the doctrine to recognize foreign divorces. See, e.g., Rahawangi v. Alsamman, 2004 WL 1752957 (Ohio Ct. App. 2004) (refusing to recognize divorce decree obtained in Syria because wife did not receive notice and Syria is not signatory of international treaty applying to child abductions); Jewell v. Jewell, 751 A.2d 735, 739 (R.I. 2000) (holding that a "fly-by-day divorce" obtained in the Dominican Republic where neither party was a resident nor maintained any other connection to the forum was repugnant to state law). For a modern application of comity in the divorce context, see Kalia v. Kalia, 783 N.E.2d 623 (Ohio Ct. App. 2002) (enforcing Indian divorce decree).

6. Has an attorney in a restrictive state violated ethical principles by facilitating the client's out-of-state or foreign-country divorce? See, e.g., In re Donnelly, 470 N.W.2d 305 (Wis. 1991) (suspending an attorney's license for two years for advertising in national publications his arrangement of Dominican Republic divorces, without always cautioning prospective clients about the questionable validity of such decrees).

Problem

A man sends his wife an e-mail via the Internet, informing her that he is divorcing her. The husband relies on Internet notice because he is studying then in a foreign country on a scholarship. Based on that notice, the wife subsequently remarries. After his studies, when the husband returns home, he changes his mind about the divorce and threatens to sue the wife if she will not leave her new husband. The wife requests the court to rule on the sufficiency of the notice. What result? See Egypt Dismisses Net Divorce Case (AP) (visited June 1, 2000) <http://dailynews.yahoo.com/h/ap/20000601/tc/egypt_internet_divorce_1.html>. Would such notice comply with the requirements of due process?

See also Kushnick v. Kushnick, 763 N.Y.S.2d 889 (N.Y.Sup. 2003) (refusing to extend comity to a Mexican divorce that was obtained by Husband over Internet, when Husband never established residency in Mexico, Wife had no notice of divorce action and never executed power of attorney or otherwise consented to submit to jurisdiction).

Note: Jurisdiction to Terminate a Same-Sex Marriage or Domestic Partnership

A same-sex marriage that is validly entered into in Massachusetts by Massachusetts residents may be terminated there on the same basis as a heterosexual marriage. Similarly, a domestic partnership validly entered into in by residents of one state may be terminated in that particular state. However, dissolution of a same-sex marriage or a domestic partnership becomes much more complicated when members of a same-sex couple attempt to dissolve the relationship in a *different* state from the one in which they entered into the union.

States are divided on the issue of whether the second forum has jurisdiction to dissolve the same-sex relationship. Recently, for example, a Connecticut court refused to annul a same-sex marriage entered into in Massachusetts by residents of Connecticut. See Lane v. Albanese, 2005 WL 896129 (Conn. Super. Ct. 2005) (holding that the court lacked subject matter jurisdiction because Connecticut does not recognize same-sex marriage). Similarly, the Connecticut supreme court in Rosengarten v. Downes, 806 A.2d 1066 (Conn. 2002), held that it lacked subject matter jurisdiction to dissolve a Vermont civil union, reasoning that, although the trial court had jurisdiction to dissolve marriages, a civil union did not constitute a marriage. (Note, however, that these rulings occurred before Connecticut's recent adoption of civil unions.)

In contrast, courts in a few other states have determined that they have jurisdiction to dissolve civil unions. See, e.g., Alons v. Iowa Dist. Court for Woodbury County, 698 N.W.2d 858 (Iowa 2005); Salucco v. Alldredge, 2004 WL 864459 (Mass. Super. Ct. 2004). For additional cases, see Barbara J. Cox, Using an "Incidents of Marriage" Analysis When Considering Interstate Recognition of Same-Sex Couples' Marriages, Civil Unions, and Domestic Partnerships, 13 Widener L. Rev. 699, 729-742 (2004) (discussing unpublished Texas case that dissolved a civil union but subsequently vacated the opinion when the state attorney general challenged the court's subject matter jurisdiction, and a West Virginia unpublished case that dissolved a civil union).

Federal and state DOMA's complicate the issue as well. DOMA presents problems specifically for parties who attempt, in a second state, to dissolve a same-sex marriage that was validly entered into in Massachusetts. The federal DOMA permits the second state to refuse to extend recognition to the marriage (and thereby deprives the courts in that second state of jurisdiction to dissolve the relationship). Similarly, if the second state has relevant state statutes or state constitutional amendments, that state enactment might require courts there to deny recognition to the same-sex marriage (and thereby similarly prevent its dissolution).

Not surprisingly, considerable uncertainly exists regarding these jurisdictional issues. For example, even if a civil union were recognized in another state for some purposes, such recognition might not signify that a court in that state would have jurisdiction to grant a dissolution to the couple.

Dissolution of civil unions might be facilitated if the "new" jurisdiction (to which the members of the civil union move) also recognizes a form of domestic partnership. For example, as Professor Herma Hill Kay explains, the California Domestic Partnership Act contains a conflict-of-laws provision that might enable a California court to dissolve a Vermont civil union because California law recognizes domestic partnerships that were validly formed in another jurisdiction regardless of whether the union bears the name "domestic partnership" and also permits a dissolution proceeding even if neither party is a resident of California at the time that the proceeding was filed. Herma Hill Kay, Same-Sex Divorce in the Conflict of Laws, 15 King's College L.J. 63, 83-84 (2004).

Another unknown issue is whether a petitioner must be a resident or a domiciliary of the forum state in order to seek a dissolution of a same-sex relationship when the other partner is absent from that state. As we have seen, jurisdictional rules for ex parte divorces require that at least one spouse be domiciled in the forum state. This result follows because divorce historically has been considered an action *in rem;* thus, subject matter jurisdiction over the marriage (the *res*) is conferred by the domicile of at least one party within the state. Is dissolution of a civil union an action *in rem* that requires domicile? Or, do such unions and domestic partnerships more closely resemble contracts than marriage, so that *in personam* jurisdiction based on the consent of the parties should suffice for dissolution? For example, the California domestic partnership statute indicates that both individuals who enter a domestic partnership there consent to jurisdiction over its dissolution in that state, wherever they might reside at dissolution. Cal. Fam. Code §299(d) (Supp. 2005). See also Kay, supra, at 84 (identifying this issue). Until this issue is resolved, the ability of a member of a civil union to secure a dissolution may depend on whether a state statute in the second state confers dissolution jurisdiction based on the mutual consent of the parties and the implications of such statutes for full faith and credit elsewhere.

See generally Jessica A. Hoogs, Note, Divorce Without Marriage: Establishing a Uniform Dissolution Procedure for Domestic Partners Through a Comparative Analysis of European and American Domestic Partner Laws, 54 Hastings L.J. 707 (2003) (advocating the adoption of a uniform dissolution procedure for same-sex relationships to address support, property division, and child custody/visitation rights, patterned after progressive European partnership legislation); Christopher D. Sawyer, Note, "Practice What You Preach": California's Obligation to Give Full Faith and Credit to the Vermont Civil Union, 54 Hastings L.J. 717 (2003) (exploring recognition of domestic partnerships in jurisdictions other than that of the "home state").

2. Durational Residency Requirements

■ SOSNA v. IOWA
419 U.S. 393 (1975)

Mr. Justice REHNQUIST delivered the opinion of the Court.

Appellant Carol Sosna married Michael Sosna on September 5, 1964, in Michigan. They lived together in New York between October 1967 and August 1971, after which date they separated but continued to live in New York. In August 1972, appellant moved to Iowa with her three children, and the following month she petitioned the District Court of Jackson County, Iowa, for a dissolution of her marriage. Michael Sosna, who had been personally served with notice of the action when he came to Iowa to visit his children, made a special appearance to contest the jurisdiction of the Iowa court. The Iowa court dismissed the petition for lack of jurisdiction, finding that Michael Sosna was not a resident of Iowa and appellant had not been a resident of the State of Iowa for one year preceding the filing of her petition. In so doing the Iowa court applied the provisions of Iowa Code §598.6 (1973) requiring that the petitioner in such an action be "for the last year a resident of the state." . . .

The durational residency requirement under attack in this case is a part of Iowa's comprehensive statutory regulation of domestic relations, an area that has long been regarded as a virtually exclusive province of the States. Cases decided by this Court over a period of more than a century bear witness to this historical fact. ... In Pennoyer v. Neff, 95 U.S. 714, 734-735 (1878), the Court said: "The State ... has absolute right to prescribe the conditions upon which the marriage relation between its own citizens shall be created, and the causes for which it may be dissolved." ...

The imposition of a durational residency requirement for divorce is scarcely unique to Iowa, since 48 States impose such a requirement as a condition for maintaining an action for divorce. As might be expected, the periods vary among the States and range from six weeks to two years. The one-year period selected by Iowa is the most common length of time prescribed.

Appellant contends that the Iowa requirement of one year's residence is unconstitutional for two separate reasons: *first*, because it establishes two classes of persons and discriminates against those who have recently exercised their right to travel to Iowa, thereby contravening the Court's holdings in Shapiro v. Thompson, 394 U.S. 618 (1969); Dunn v. Blumstein, 405 U.S. 330 (1972); and Memorial Hospital v. Maricopa County, 415 U.S. 250 (1974); and, *second*, because it denies a litigant the opportunity to make an individualized showing of bona fide residence and therefore denies such residents access to the only method of legally dissolving their marriage.

State statutes imposing durational residency requirements were, of course, invalidated when imposed by States as a qualification for welfare payments, *Shapiro*, supra; for voting, *Dunn*, supra; and for medical care, *Maricopa County*, supra. But none of those cases intimated that the States might never impose durational residency requirements. ... What those cases had in common was that the durational residency requirements they struck down were justified on the basis of budgetary or recordkeeping considerations which were held insufficient to outweigh the constitutional claims of the individuals. But Iowa's divorce residency requirement is of a different stripe. Appellant was not irretrievably foreclosed from obtaining some part of what she sought, as was the case with the welfare recipients in *Shapiro*, the voters in *Dunn*, or the indigent patient in *Maricopa County*. She would eventually qualify for the same sort of adjudication which she demanded virtually upon her arrival in the State. Iowa's requirement delayed her access to the courts, but, by fulfilling it, she could ultimately have obtained the same opportunity for adjudication which she asserts ought to have been hers at an earlier point in time.

Iowa's residency requirement may reasonably be justified on grounds other than purely budgetary considerations or administrative convenience. A decree of divorce is not a matter in which the only interested parties are the State as a sort of "grantor," and a divorce petitioner such as appellant in the role of "grantee." Both spouses are obviously interested in the proceedings, since it will affect their marital status and very likely their property rights. Where a married couple has minor children, a decree of divorce would usually include provisions for their custody and support. With consequences of such moment riding on a divorce decree issued by its courts, Iowa may insist that one seeking to initiate such a proceeding have the modicum of attachment to the State required here.

Such a requirement additionally furthers the State's parallel interests both in avoiding officious intermeddling in matters in which another State has a paramount interest, and in minimizing the susceptibility of its own divorce decrees to collateral attack. [See Williams v. North Carolina, 325 U.S. 226 (1945).] A State such as Iowa may quite reasonably decide that it does not wish to become a divorce mill for unhappy spouses who have lived there as short a time as appellant had when she commenced her action in the state court after having long resided elsewhere. . . .

Nor are we of the view that the failure to provide an individualized determination of residency violates the Due Process Clause. . . . An individualized determination of physical presence plus the intent to remain, which appellant apparently seeks, would not entitle her to a divorce even if she could have made such a showing. For Iowa requires not merely "domicile" in that sense, but residence in the State for a year in order for its courts to exercise their divorce jurisdiction.

In Boddie v. Connecticut, [401 U.S. 371 (1971)] this Court held that Connecticut might not deny access to divorce courts to those persons who could not afford to pay the required fee. Because of the exclusive role played by the State in the termination of marriages, it was held that indigents could not be denied an opportunity to be heard "absent a countervailing state interest of overriding significance." 401 U.S., at 377. But the gravamen of appellant Sosna's claim is not total deprivation, as in Boddie, but only delay. . . . Affirmed.

Mr. Justice MARSHALL, with whom Mr. Justice BRENNAN joins, dissenting. . . .

The Court omits altogether what should be the first inquiry: whether the right to obtain a divorce is of sufficient importance that its denial to recent immigrants constitutes a penalty on interstate travel. In my view, it clearly meets that standard. The previous decisions of this Court make it plain that the right of marital association is one of the most basic rights conferred on the individual by the State. The interests associated with marriage and divorce have repeatedly been accorded particular deference [citing Loving and Boddie]. . . .

Having determined that the interest in obtaining a divorce is of substantial social importance, I would scrutinize Iowa's durational residency requirement to determine whether it constitutes a reasonable means of furthering important interests asserted by the State. . . .

. . . Iowa's residency requirement, the Court says, merely forestalls access to the courts; applicants seeking welfare payments, medical aid, and the right to vote, on the other hand, suffer unrecoverable losses throughout the waiting period. This analysis, however, ignores the severity of the deprivation suffered by the divorce petitioner who is forced to wait a year for relief. The injury accompanying that delay is not directly measurable in money terms like the loss of welfare benefits, but it cannot reasonably be argued that when the year has elapsed, the petitioner is made whole. The year's wait prevents remarriage and locks both partners into what may be an intolerable, destructive relationship. . . . The Court cannot mean that Mrs. Sosna has not suffered any injury by being foreclosed from seeking a divorce in Iowa for a year. It must instead mean that it does not regard that deprivation as being very severe.

I find the majority's second argument no more persuasive. The Court forgoes reliance on the usual justifications for durational residency requirements — budgetary considerations and administrative convenience. . . . In their place, the majority invokes a more amorphous justification — the magnitude of the interests affected and resolved by a divorce proceeding. Certainly the stakes in a divorce are weighty both for the individuals directly involved in the adjudication and for others immediately affected by it. The critical importance of the divorce process, however, weakens the argument for a long residency requirement rather than strengthens it. . . .

The Court's third justification seems to me the only one that warrants close consideration. Iowa has a legitimate interest in protecting itself against invasion by those seeking quick divorces in a forum with relatively lax divorce laws, and it may have some interest in avoiding collateral attacks on its decrees in other States. These interests, however, would adequately be protected by a simple requirement of domicile — physical presence plus intent to remain — which would remove the rigid one-year barrier while permitting the State to restrict the availability of its divorce process to citizens who are genuinely its own. . . .

Notes and Questions

1. *Residency requirements.* As *Sosna* explains, many states require a divorce petitioner to reside in the forum state for a specified period of time. In some states, residence alone suffices for divorce jurisdiction. Other jurisdictions mandate both durational residence and domicile requirements.[29] Most states' durational residence requirements specify a six-month period; eight states have residency requirements of more than one year; four states require no more than 60 days. Some states have special provisions for members of the military to obtain divorce decrees. Linda D. Elrod & Robert G. Spector, A Review of the Year in Family Law: "Same-Sex" Marriage Issue Dominates Headlines, 38 Fam. L.Q. 777, 812 (Chart 4) (2005). Durational residency requirements may be imposed in lieu of a domiciliary requirement or in addition to that requirement.

2. *Rationale.* Justice Rehnquist distinguishes a one-year delay for permitting dissolution of marriage from a delay for voting, welfare benefits, and medical aid. Is the distinction persuasive? See Shauhin A. Talesh, Note, Welfare Migration to Capture Higher Benefits: Fact or Fiction?, 32 Conn. L. Rev. 675, 683 (2000) (discussing application of residency requirements for different benefits).

In 1999, the United States Supreme Court decided another case addressing durational residency requirements when recent California residents challenged the constitutionality of a state statute limiting new residents, for twelve months, to the level of welfare benefits (under Temporary Assistance to Needy Families) that they would have received in the state of their prior residence. In Saenz v. Roe, 526 U.S. 489, 507 (1999), the Supreme Court held that the state statute violated the Fourteenth Amendment right to travel, and that the federal welfare reform legislation's approval of state durational residency requirements did not "resuscitate the constitutionality" of the state statute because Congress may not authorize the states to violate the Fourteenth Amendment.

3. *Significance of delay.* Justices Rehnquist and Marshall disagree about the significance of delay in petitions for dissolution and the consequences of such delay. Whose argument is more persuasive? Further, Justice Rehnquist distinguishes

---

[29]. However, *Williams*, discussed in *Sosna*, makes clear that domicile is necessary for full faith and credit, regardless of the statutory language. In some instances, durational residency requirements may provide evidence of domicile.

Boddie by claiming the filing fee foreclosed access while the residency requirement in *Sosna* imposes "only delay." Do you agree that indigent plaintiffs have a stronger claim than recent immigrants? Does the decision in *Sosna* neglect the interests of recent immigrants and present hardships for victims of domestic violence? Does the decision reflect discrimination against women who tend to predominate among custodial parents (i.e., moving for jobs, proximity to parents, or a new relationship)?

4. *Divorce mills.* Justice Marshall, dissenting, intimates that the state's real goal is to avoid becoming known as a "divorce mill." During the fault era, because residency requirements for divorce varied from state-to-state, some states with shorter durational requirements and more lenient grounds for divorce (such as Arkansas, Idaho, Florida, Nevada) developed a reputation of divorce mills. Max Rheinstein, Marriage Stability, Divorce, and the Law 76 (1972). Why does such a reputation pose problems? How important are problems of migratory divorce and divorce mills in the no-fault era?

5. *Zablocki's impact.* One student commentator points out that *Sosna* was decided a decade before *Zablocki*. "The case is therefore not indicative either of how the Court would decide the right to divorce issue today nor how it should decide it." She explains further: "[P]etitioners did not raise any challenges on substantive due process grounds or right to privacy grounds." Laura Bradford, Note, The Counterrevolution: A Critique of Recent Proposals to Reform No-Fault Divorce Laws, 49 Stan. L. Rev. 607, 636 n.112 (1997). How do you think *Sosna* would be decided today? Note Justice Marshall's view that the right to divorce is equivalent to the right to marry.

6. *Policy.* In our increasingly mobile society, does it make sense to limit divorce jurisdiction to the state of the parties' domicile? See Rhonda Wasserman, Divorce and Domicile: Time to Sever the Knot, 39 Wm. & Mary L. Rev. 1 (1997) (arguing that the domicile rule fails to preserve state sovereignty or assure the convenience of the parties and that federal legislation would be a better approach to ensure interstate recognition of divorce decrees).

7. *States' rights.* How much deference do the majority and dissent give to the state's exclusive control over family law matters? The parameters of federal versus state authority are reflected in the case below.

3. Domestic Relations Exception to Diversity Jurisdiction

■ ANKENBRANDT v. RICHARDS
504 U.S. 689 (1992)

Justice WHITE delivered the opinion of the Court. . . .

Petitioner Carol Ankenbrandt, a citizen of Missouri, brought this lawsuit . . . on behalf of her daughters L.R. and S.R. against respondents Jon A. Richards and Debra Kesler, citizens of Louisiana, in the United States District Court for the Eastern District of Louisiana. Alleging federal jurisdiction based on the diversity-of-citizenship provision of §1332, Ankenbrandt's complaint sought monetary damages for alleged sexual and physical abuse of the children committed by Richards and Kesler. Richards is the divorced father of the children and Kesler his female companion. [T]he District Court granted respondents' motion to dismiss this lawsuit [concluding] that this case fell within what has become known as the "domestic relations" exception to diversity jurisdiction, and that it lacked jurisdiction over the case. . . .

We granted certiorari limited to the following questions: "(1) Is there a domestic relations exception to federal jurisdiction? (2) If so, does it permit a district court to abstain from exercising diversity jurisdiction over a tort action for damages?" . . . We address each of these issues in turn.

The domestic relations exception upon which the courts below relied to decline jurisdiction has been invoked often by the lower federal courts. The seeming authority for doing so originally stemmed from the announcement in Barber v. Barber, 21 How. 582 (1859), that the federal courts have no jurisdiction over suits for divorce or the allowance of alimony. In that case, the Court heard a suit in equity brought by a wife (by her next friend) in Federal District Court pursuant to diversity jurisdiction against her former husband. She sought to enforce a decree from a New York state court, which had granted a divorce and awarded her alimony. The former husband thereupon moved to Wisconsin to place himself beyond the New York courts' jurisdiction so that the divorce decree there could not be enforced against him; he then sued for divorce in a Wisconsin court, representing to that court that his wife had abandoned him and failing to disclose the existence of the New York decree. In a suit brought by the former wife in Wisconsin Federal District Court, the former husband alleged that the court lacked jurisdiction. The court accepted jurisdiction and gave judgment for the divorced wife.

On appeal [in *Barber*], it was argued that the District Court lacked jurisdiction on two grounds: first, that there was no diversity of citizenship because although divorced, the wife's citizenship necessarily remained that of her former husband; and second, that the whole subject of divorce and alimony, including a suit to enforce an alimony decree, was exclusively ecclesiastical at the time of the adoption of the Constitution and that the Constitution therefore placed the whole subject of divorce and alimony beyond the jurisdiction of the United States courts. Over the dissent of three Justices, the Court rejected both arguments. After an exhaustive survey of the authorities, the Court concluded that a divorced wife could acquire a citizenship separate from that of her former husband and that a suit to enforce an alimony decree rested within the federal courts' equity jurisdiction. The Court reached these conclusions after summarily dismissing the former husband's contention that the case involved a subject matter outside the federal courts' jurisdiction. In so stating, however, the Court also announced the following limitation on federal jurisdiction:

> Our first remark is—and we wish it to be remembered—that this is not a suit asking the court for the allowance of alimony. That has been done by a court of competent jurisdiction. The court in Wisconsin was asked to interfere to prevent that decree from being defeated by fraud.
>
> We disclaim altogether any jurisdiction in the courts of the United States upon the subject of divorce, or for the allowance of alimony, either as an original proceeding in chancery or as an incident to divorce a *vinculo*, or to one from bed and board.

Barber, supra, at 584. . . .

The statements disclaiming jurisdiction over divorce and alimony decree suits, though technically dicta, formed the basis for excluding "domestic relations" cases from the jurisdiction of the lower federal courts, a jurisdictional limitation those courts have recognized ever since. . . . Because we are unwilling to cast aside an understood rule that has been recognized for nearly a century and a half, we feel compelled to explain why we will continue to recognize this limitation on federal jurisdiction.

Counsel argued in *Barber* that the Constitution prohibited federal courts from exercising jurisdiction over domestic relations cases. An examination of Article III, *Barber* itself, and our cases since *Barber* makes clear that the Constitution does not exclude domestic relations cases from the jurisdiction otherwise granted by statute to the federal courts.

Article III, §2, of the Constitution . . . delineates the absolute limits on the federal courts' jurisdiction. But in articulating three different terms to define jurisdiction — "Cases, in Law and Equity," "Cases," and "Controversies" — this provision contains no limitation on subjects of a domestic relations nature. Nor did *Barber* purport to ground the domestic relations exception in these constitutional limits on federal jurisdiction. The Court's discussion of federal judicial power to hear suits of a domestic relations nature contains no mention of the Constitution, and it is logical to presume that the Court based its statement limiting such power on narrower statutory, rather than broader constitutional, grounds. Subsequent decisions confirm that *Barber* was not relying on constitutional limits in justifying the exception. . . .

. . . The dissenters in *Barber* [suggested] that the federal courts had no power over certain domestic relations actions because the court of chancery lacked authority to issue divorce and alimony decrees. . . . We have no occasion here to join the historical debate over whether the English court of chancery had jurisdiction to handle certain domestic relations matters. . . . We thus are content to rest our conclusion that a domestic relations exception exists as a matter of statutory construction not on the accuracy of the historical justifications on which it was seemingly based, but rather on Congress' apparent acceptance of this construction of the diversity jurisdiction provisions in the years prior to 1948, when [Congress last amended the rules applicable to federal diversity jurisdiction]. Considerations of *stare decisis* have particular strength in this context, where "the legislative power is implicated, and Congress remains free to alter what we have done." . . .

In the more than 100 years since this Court laid the seeds for the development of the domestic relations exception, the lower federal courts have applied it in a variety of circumstances. Many of these applications go well beyond the circumscribed situations posed by *Barber* and its progeny. *Barber* itself disclaimed federal jurisdiction over a narrow range of domestic relations issues involving the granting of a divorce and a decree of alimony, and stated the limits on federal-court power to intervene prior to the rendering of such orders:

> It is, that when a court of competent jurisdiction over the subject-matter and the parties decrees a divorce, and alimony to the wife as its incident, and is unable of itself to enforce the decree summarily upon the husband, that courts of equity will interfere to prevent the decree from being defeated by fraud. The interference, however, is limited to cases in which alimony has been decreed; then only to the extent of what is due, and always to cases in which no appeal is pending from the decree for the divorce or for alimony.

Id., at 591.

The *Barber* Court thus did not intend to strip the federal courts of authority to hear cases arising from the domestic relations of persons unless they seek the granting or modification of a divorce or alimony decree. The holding of the case itself sanctioned the exercise of federal jurisdiction over the enforcement of an alimony decree that had been properly obtained in a state court of competent jurisdiction. . . .

Subsequently, this Court expanded the domestic relations exception to include decrees in child custody cases. In a child custody case brought pursuant to a writ of habeas corpus, for instance, the Court held void a writ issued by a Federal District Court to restore a child to the custody of the father. "As to the right to the control and possession of this child, as it is contested by its father and its grandfather, it is one in regard to which neither the Congress of the United States nor any authority of the United States has any special jurisdiction." In re Burrus, [136 U.S. 586, 594 (1890)].

Although In re Burrus technically did not involve a construction of the diversity statute, as we understand *Barber* to have done, its statement that "[t]he whole subject of the domestic relations of husband and wife, parent and child, belongs to the laws of the States and not to the laws of the United States," id., at 593-594, has been interpreted by the federal courts to apply with equal vigor in suits brought pursuant to diversity jurisdiction. This application is consistent with *Barber*'s directive to limit federal courts' exercise of diversity jurisdiction over suits for divorce and alimony decrees. We conclude, therefore, that the domestic relations exception, as articulated by this Court since *Barber*, divests the federal courts of power to issue divorce, alimony, and child custody decrees. Given the long passage of time without any expression of congressional dissatisfaction, we have no trouble today reaffirming the validity of the exception as it pertains to divorce and alimony decrees and child custody orders.

Not only is our conclusion rooted in respect for this long-held understanding, it is also supported by sound policy considerations. Issuance of decrees of this type not infrequently involves retention of jurisdiction by the court and deployment of social workers to monitor compliance. As a matter of judicial economy, state courts are more eminently suited to work of this type than are federal courts, which lack the close association with state and local government organizations dedicated to handling issues that arise out of conflicts over divorce, alimony, and child custody decrees. Moreover, as a matter of judicial expertise, it makes far more sense to retain the rule that federal courts lack power to issue these types of decrees because of the special proficiency developed by state tribunals over the past century and a half in handling issues that arise in the granting of such decrees.

By concluding, as we do, that the domestic relations exception encompasses only cases involving the issuance of a divorce, alimony, or child custody decree, we necessarily find that the Court of Appeals erred by affirming the District Court's invocation of this exception. This lawsuit in no way seeks such a decree; rather, it alleges that respondents Richards and Kesler committed torts against L.R. and S.R., Ankenbrandt's children by Richards. Federal subject-matter jurisdiction pursuant to §1332 thus is proper in this case. . . .

Notes and Questions

1. *Rule and rationale.* Under the "domestic relations exception to federal jurisdiction," federal courts traditionally declined to exercise jurisdiction over

matters of domestic relations even in cases in which plaintiffs could establish the requisite diversity of citizenship and amount in controversy. The rationale was that domestic relations cases involve matters of peculiarly state, rather than federal, law. *Ankenbrandt* narrowed this exception, that is, limiting the types of cases that federal courts could refuse to adjudicate. After *Ankenbrandt*, federal courts could decline jurisdiction only over those cases involving the issuance of divorce decrees and the issuance or modification of child custody or alimony.

2. *Abstention doctrine. Ankenbrandt* left open an alternative means by which federal courts can still "slam shut" the federal courthouse door to some domestic relations matters that do not involve divorce, alimony or custody. In an omitted portion of the opinion, the Court holds that neither the domestic relations exception nor the "abstention doctrine" bars *Ankenbrandt*'s tort claim. The abstention doctrine, delineated in Younger v. Harris, 401 U.S. 37 (1971), and Burford v. Sun Oil Co., 319 U.S. 315 (1943), is founded on principles of federalism. It provides that federal courts may refuse to adjudicate civil proceedings that involve important state interests or substantial policy concerns. *Ankenbrandt* concluded, by way of dicta, that abstention might be proper

> when a case presents "difficult questions of state law bearing on policy problems of substantial public importance whose importance transcends the result in the case then at bar" (citation omitted). Such might well be the case if a federal suit were filed prior to effectuation of a divorce, alimony, or child custody decree, and the suit depended on a determination of the status of the parties.

Ankenbrandt, 504 U.S. 689, 705 (1992).

3. *Advantages?* Why did Carol Ankenbrandt prefer to litigate her tort claim alleging sexual abuse in a federal, rather than state, court? What are the benefits, as well as detriments, that will ensue from *Ankenbrandt* for litigants? Families? Society?

4. *Federalism.* Various considerations have led federal courts to decline jurisdiction over domestic relations issues, including recognition of special state expertise, federal docket congestion, and the ability of state courts to provide local support assuring compliance with decrees. However, critics point out that federal courts are less susceptible to influence and have better evidentiary and discovery processes; state courts have often been criticized for their handling of family law cases, state judges rotate out of family law courts after only one year; the confining authority of local control over family law often restricts the rights of traditionally subordinated groups; distinctions between marital property and marital status are blurry; and federal courts have been willing to intervene in family law cases when constitutional rights were at issue. See Naomi R. Cahn, Family Law, Federalism, and the Federal Courts, 79 Iowa L. Rev. 1073 (1994); Judith Resnik, Categorical Federalism: Jurisdiction, Gender, and the Globe, 111 Yale L.J. 619 (2001).

For example, Professor Anne Dailey, writing in defense of state sovereignty, notes:

> [N]ational authority over family law raises a serious threat of governmental tyranny over the moral identities of developing citizens. To begin with, a politics of the good family life entails a degree of civic engagement and a sense of shared community identity unattainable at the national level. Although family law does not require the

moral homogeneity characteristic of strong communitarian cultures, it does demand a political discourse built upon the normative commitments of a specific historical community. States . . . are far better situated than the national government to develop and sustain a normative political discourse on family. Moreover, regulatory diversity among the fifty states preserves some measure of individual and family choice in matters touching upon the formative conditions of human identity.

Anne C. Dailey, Federalism and Families, 143 U. Pa. L. Rev. 1787, 1791-1792 (1995). See also Brian H. Bix, State of the Union: The States' Interest in the Marital Status of Their Citizens, 55 U. Miami L. Rev. 1, 18-19 (2000) (suggesting that local control of family law matters may also be favored because it allows states to be treated as laboratories, developing a variety of responses to questions of law in the place of a uniform federal response). Professor Naomi Cahn counters:

> Throughout the country, family law has traditionally reflected community norms, [and] the federal courts have attempted to protect the local character of domestic relations law. . . .
> The belief in local control over family law, however, beyond suggesting an inevitability to this means of family regulation, also overlooks the negative aspects of the community. While community can be a powerfully positive force, it can also be an extremely confining form of authority. The courts' examination of whether certain customs are based in community traditions, for instance, may enshrine majoritarian conventions such as a ban on gay marriage or certain consensual sex. Within certain communities, expectations are that women will be confined within traditional roles, thus hindering women's efforts to achieve equality. The many and various state regulations held unconstitutional by the Supreme Court provide yet further examples of the danger of trusting family law to community mores.

Cahn, supra, at 1123.

Problems

1. Jeanne sues in state court, charging that Joseph (the man with whom she has been cohabiting) breached his agreement to provide financial support for the rest of her life. Joseph removes the case to federal court on the basis of diversity. The court raises, on its own motion, the issue whether this "palimony" case falls within the domestic relations exception to federal jurisdiction requiring remand to state court. See Anastasi v. Anastasi, 544 F. Supp. 866 (D.N.J. 1982). How would this case be decided after *Ankenbrandt*? For a post-*Ankenbrandt* case, see Johnson v. Thomas, 808 F. Supp. 1316 (W.D. Mich. 1992).

2. Cometa and Dunn marry in 1989. In September 1994, while Cometa is pursuing a medical residency, Dunn suffers a catastrophic brain injury that leaves him severely disabled. In June 1997, Dunn's father is appointed his conservator and takes him to Georgia to live. Cometa subsequently enters into a liaison with another man; her petition for divorce is granted in December 1998. She is ordered to pay Dunn alimony for five years based on her ability to pay, employment potential, and Dunn's disability. In 1999, Dunn's father, acting on behalf of himself and Dunn, brings an action against Cometa in federal district court in Maine, alleging her mismanagement of Dunn's care, private health insurance, and

property; intentional and negligent infliction of emotional distress by her keeping him in care facilities rather than at home so that she could conduct an affair; breaching a contract with Dunn's father as to payment for construction work on a Georgia house for Dunn; and unjust enrichment for the care provided to Dunn by his father. Cometa moves to dismiss the claims as within the domestic relations exception to federal court jurisdiction. What result? See Dunn v. Cometa, 238 F.3d 38 (1st Cir. 2001).

VI

Financial Consequences
of Dissolution

In the United States, approximately one in five adults has divorced.[1] Their dissolutions often entail a division of property and an award of spousal support (formerly called "alimony" and now often referred to as "maintenance"). In marriages with children, a divorce decree also includes provision for their support.

Termination of marriage thus gives the state significant opportunities for intervention in matters left to private resolution in the intact family. Private choices have a role upon dissolution, however. Increasingly, the law defers to "private ordering"—allowing divorcing parties to negotiate their own financial arrangements in separation agreements and premarital contracts.

This chapter combines theory and practice. It explores traditional and evolving approaches to property division, spousal support, and child support, emphasizing the distinct theoretical bases for each. It also shows that, in practice, different financial issues typically arise together and their resolution often blurs these theoretical distinctions. Finally, it examines the roles of the parties and the state in allocational decisions.

A. INTRODUCTION: THE DEMISE OF FAULT?

Although every state now has some form of no-fault divorce, sharp differences persist about the role of fault in dividing property and determining spousal support.[2]

[1]. Rose M. Kreider, U.S. Census Bureau, Number, Timing, and Duration of Marriages and Divorces: 2001, at 6 (Current Population Reports, Feb., 2005).
[2]. According to a survey by the American Law Institute (ALI), 20 states decide the financial consequences of dissolution without regard to marital misconduct; 5 disregard fault for property division and, as a practical matter, almost always do so for support; 3 almost never consider fault in financial

593

California's early adoption of "pure no-fault"[3] laws prompted a famous study by sociologist Dr. Lenore J. Weitzman.[4]

According to Weitzman's 1985 book, *The Divorce Revolution: The Unexpected Social and Economic Consequences for Women and Children in America*, fault previously played a dual role in determining the economic consequences of divorce. First, marital misconduct provided a rationale for judicial awards and settlements, requiring a "guilty" husband to "pay for his transgressions with alimony" or with an additional portion of marital property.[5] Second, fault offered valuable leverage to an "innocent" spouse who could obtain financial concessions in exchange for cooperation.

Weitzman found that California's transition to a no-fault regime had unexpectedly impoverished women and children because family homes, formerly awarded to "innocent wives," were now being sold (and children displaced) so the proceeds could be divided equally between the spouses. Likewise, support awards were shrinking for women, primarily mothers and homemakers, who were now expected to be self-sufficient. And even a "guilty" spouse could now divorce unilaterally, eliminating the bargaining power of the resisting spouse, often the wife.

Weitzman's empirical study concluded that, just one year after divorce, men were experiencing a 42 percent improvement in their standard of living and women a 73 percent decline.[6] These dramatic figures proved enormously influential, prompting not only a feminist critique of no-fault divorce[7] but also the passage of 14 new laws in California.[8] Subsequent empirical studies have substantiated Weitzman's general finding that men's standard of living rises after divorce, while that of women and children declines,[9] but not her oft-quoted 42/73 percent

---

matters although they could do so under their statutes; 7 disregard fault for property division but consider it in support awards; and 15 states consider misconduct in both areas. American Law Institute, Principles of the Law of Family Dissolution: Analysis and Recommendations 44-47 (2002) (using 1996 survey). See also Linda D. Elrod & Robert G. Spector, A Review of the Year in Family Law: "Same-Sex" Marriage Issue Dominates Headlines, 38 Fam. L.Q. 777, 809 (2005) (listing 26 states that do not consider marital fault in setting alimony); id. at 813 (listing 41 states that consider *economic* misconduct in dividing property).

[3]. The term describes states that, by statute, disregard marital misconduct in deciding both property division and support. See ALI Principles, supra note [2].

[4]. Professors Weitzman and Ruth Dixon studied the social and economic effects of divorce law reform by collecting and analyzing random samples of 2,500 court dockets over a 10-year period and by interviewing 169 family law attorneys, 44 family law judges, and 228 divorced men and women approximately one year after their divorces. Lenore J. Weitzman, The Divorce Revolution: The Unexpected Social and Economic Consequences for Women and Children in America (1985).

[5]. Id. at 12-13.

[6]. Id. at 339.

[7]. See Herma Hill Kay, From the Second Sex to the Joint Venture: An Overview of Women's Rights and Family Law in the United States During the Twentieth Century, 88 Cal. L. Rev. 2017, 2066-2068 (2000).

[8]. Lenore J. Weitzman, The Economic Consequences of Divorce Are Still Unequal: Comment on Peterson, 61 Am. Soc. Rev. 537, 538 (1996). See also Sanford L. Braver, The Gender Gap in Standard of Living After Divorce: Vanishingly Small?, 33 Fam. L.Q. 111, 113 (1999) ("impossible to overestimate how influential Weitzman's" figures were); Fred R. Shapiro, The Most-Cited Legal Books Published Since 1978, 29 J. Legal Stud. 397, 405 (2000) (listing Weitzman's book as the seventh most cited nonlegal book, published since 1978, in legal periodicals).

[9]. See, e.g., Terry Arendell, Mothers and Divorce 37 (1986); Andrea H. Beller & John W. Graham, Small Change: The Economics of Child Support 59 (1993); Eleanor E. Maccoby & Robert H. Mnookin, Dividing the Child: Social and Legal Dilemmas of Custody 128, 259 (1992) (finding also that the economic discrepancy continued in the subsequent three-year period; Liana C. Sayer, Economic Aspects of Divorce and Relationship Dissolution, in Handbook of Divorce and Relationship Dissolution 385 (Mark A. Fine & John H. Harvey eds., 2006) (summarizing research). For an empirical study prior to Weitzman's that reports similar adverse effects, see Karen Seal, A Decade of No-Fault Divorce, 1 Fam.

statistic. Weitzman's work also provoked a spate of criticisms. Some critics question her attempt to generalize from findings based on the California experience.[10] Others find flaws in her data[11] (which Weitzman now concedes[12]) and report a less significant decrease in women's standard of living.[13] Commentators also take Weitzman to task for failing to recognize the extent of adverse economic consequences for women under the fault regime.[14] Weitzman's work has received so much attention that it has become a part of popular culture.[15]

Since California initiated no-fault divorce, attention has focused on three questions about the economic consequences of dissolution: First, what role should fault play? Second, what rationales for dividing property and awarding alimony might take the place of fault? Third, has no-fault divorce financially burdened women (and children) as a class while economically benefiting men? The next two sections address these questions by presenting a variety of materials that examine modern rationales for property division and spousal support awards, respectively.

B. PROPERTY DISTRIBUTION: FROM TITLE THEORY TO CONTRIBUTION

What property can a court allocate between the spouses at dissolution? What theory determines how much to award to each?

■ FERGUSON v. FERGUSON
639 So. 2d 921 (Miss. 1994) (en banc)

PRATHER, Presiding Justice. . . .

[Linda Ferguson, age 44, and Billy Cleveland Ferguson, Sr., age 48, were married in 1967 and separated in 1991. They had two children. During their 24 years of marriage, Linda worked both as a homemaker and as a cosmetologist/beautician. Billy, employed by South Central Bell as a cable repair technician,

---

Advoc. 10 (Spring 1979). Data show that divorce economically harms African-American women even more than white women. Sayer, supra, at 394.

[10]. See, e.g., Marsha Garrison, Good Intentions Gone Awry: The Impact of New York's Equitable Distribution Law on Divorce Outcomes, 57 Brook. L. Rev. 621, 724 (1991) (New York experience); Herbert Jacob, Faulting No-Fault, 1986 Am. B. Found. Res. J. 773.

[11]. Using her data, Richard Peterson was unable to replicate Weitzman's findings. Richard R. Peterson, A Re-Evaluation of the Economic Consequences of Divorce, 61 Am. Soc. Rev. 528 (1996).

[12]. Weitzman, supra note [8].

[13]. See, e.g., Richard R. Peterson, Women, Work, and Divorce 106 (1989) (finding 30-40 percent decrease, which abates over the long term to 5-20 percent); Saul D. Hoffman & Greg J. Duncan, What *Are* the Economic Consequences of Divorce?, 25 Demography 641 (1988) (suggesting that a finding of 33 percent decrease is more realistic); Peterson, supra note [11], at 652 (finding 27 percent decline for women and 10 percent increase for men). See also Richard R. Peterson, Statistical Errors, Faulty Conclusions, Misguided Policy: Reply to Weitzman, 61 Am. Soc. Rec. 539 (1996).

[14]. See, e.g., Stephen D. Sugarman, Dividing Financial Interests on Divorce, in Divorce Reform at the Crossroads 130, 132-135 (Stephen D. Sugarman & Herma Hill Kay eds., 1990); Marygold S. Melli, Constructing a Social Problem: The Post-Divorce Plight of Women and Children, 1986 Am. B. Found. Res. J. 759, 770 (pointing out adverse consequences of fault regime for women and children).

[15]. See Susan Faludi, Backlash: The Undeclared War Against American Women 19 (1991) (accusing Weitzman's work of sending the message that women should remain in bad marriages to avoid the economic consequences of divorce).

installed and maintained local telephone service. Linda filed for divorce, which the chancellor awarded to her on the ground of Billy's adultery. The chancellor also awarded her custody of the 14-year-old son and $300 a month child support as well as the marital home and its contents, four acres of land comprising the homestead, with title to the marital home to be divested from Billy and vested in Linda, debt free; one-half interest in Billy's pension plan, stock ownership plan, and savings and security plan; and periodic alimony in the amount of $400 per month and lump sum alimony in the sum of $30,000 to be paid at the rate of $10,000 annually beginning on January 1, 1992. Billy appeals.]

States have devised various methods to divide marital assets at divorce, and approaches have usually followed one of three systems [separate property, equitable distribution, and community property.] Mississippi, Florida, South Carolina, Virginia, and West Virginia previously followed the separate property system, which was a system that merely determined title to the assets and returned that property to the title-holding spouse.

Our separate property system at times resulted in unjust distributions, especially involving cases of a traditional family where most property was titled in the husband, leaving a traditional housewife and mother with nothing but a claim for alimony, which often proved unenforceable. In a family where both spouses worked, but the husband's resources were devoted to investments while the wife's earnings were devoted to paying the family expenses or vice versa, the same unfair results ensued. The flaw of the separate property system, however, is not merely that it will occasionally ignore the financial contributions of the non-titleholding spouse. The system . . . is also unable to take account of a spouse's non-financial contribution. In the case of many traditional housewives such non-financial contributions are often considerable.[2] Thus, to allow a system of property division to ignore non-financial contributions is to create a likelihood of unjust division of property.

The non-monetary contributions of a traditional housewife have been acknowledged by this Court, and to some extent, case law has helped lessen the unfairness to a traditional housewife in the division of marital property. [T]his Court has allowed lump sum alimony as an adjustment to property division to prevent unfair division. The lump sum award has been described as a method of dividing property under the guise of alimony. . . .

Courts have acknowledged that the power and authority of the chancery court to award alimony and child support have been historically derived from the legal duty of the husband to support the family. As to division of marital assets, it is the broad inherent equity powers of the chancery court that give it the authority to act. General equity principles of fairness undergird this authority. That duty was codified in Miss. Code. Ann. §93-5-23 (Supp. 1993). . . . This Court, therefore, holds that the chancery court is within its authority and power to equitably divide marital assets at divorce. . . .

[T]his Court recognizes the need for guidelines to aid chancellors in their adjudication of marital property division. Therefore, this Court directs the chancery courts to evaluate the division of marital assets by the following guidelines.

---

2. The persistent attempts made to put a monetary value on a homemaker's contribution are likely to undervalue the magnitude of such contributions. Nonetheless, estimates of replacement loss are made as high as $40,000 per year. . . .

[The court lists, inter alia: substantial contribution to the accumulation of the property, the market and emotional value of the assets, tax and other economic consequences of the distribution, the parties' needs, and any other factor that in equity should be considered.]

[F]airness is the prevailing guideline in marital division. . . . All property division, lump sum or periodic alimony payment, and mutual obligations for child support should be considered together. "Alimony and equitable distribution are distinct concepts, but together they command the entire field of financial settlement of divorce. Therefore, where one expands, the other must recede." [LaRue v. LaRue, 304 S.E.2d 312, 334 (W. Va. 1983) (Neely, J., concurring).] Thus, the chancellor may divide marital assets, real and personal, as well as award periodic and/or lump sum alimony, as equity demands. To aid appellate review, findings of fact by the chancellor, together with the legal conclusions drawn from those findings, are required. . . .

. . . Billy contends that he owned all the interest in the pension plan, stock, and savings [obtained through his employer, Bell South], and that it was his separate property. On appeal [of the chancellor's allocation of one-half these asssets to Linda], Billy claims Linda in no way contributed to the acquisition of this property, and nothing was ever issued in her name. . . .

When a couple has been married for twenty-four years, yet the only retirement benefits accumulated throughout the marriage are titled in the name of only one spouse, is it equitable to find only one spouse entitled to financial security upon retirement when both have benefitted from the employer funded plan along the way? When one spouse has contributed directly to the fund, by virtue of his/her labor, while the other has contributed indirectly, by virtue of domestic services and/ or earned income which both parties have enjoyed rather than invested, the spouse without retirement funds in his/her own name could instead have been working outside the home and/or investing his/her wages in preparation for his/her own retirement. . . .

[In addition,] Billy contends the chancellor lacked the authority to order him to convey, free of all encumbrances, his one-half interest in the jointly owned four acres on which the marital home was situated. . . . "A spouse who has made a material contribution toward the acquisition of property which is titled in the name of the other may claim an equitable interest in such jointly accumulated property incident to a divorce proceeding." Jones v. Jones, 532 So. 2d 574, 580 (Miss. 1988) (citing Watts v. Watts, 466 So. 2d 889 (Miss. 1985)). [W]e said that "[i]f 'contribution' toward the acquisition of assets is proven by a divorcing party, then the court has the authority to divide these 'jointly' accumulated assets." Jones, 532 So. 2d at 580. . . .

[There were two mortgages on the marital home.] This Court holds that under existing case law the chancellor was within his authority to order Billy to effect a transfer of title to Linda to the marital home and the surrounding four acres [free and clear of any liens] to accomplish an equitable division. . . . Nonetheless, this issue is remanded for consideration together with the other assets [for equitable] division to be guided by the factors promulgated today. . . .

The chancellor stated on the record that he tended to believe the testimony of [Billy's paramour that he] had withdrawn $30,000.00 from his Bell South Savings and Security Plan and put it where nobody could get to it or find it. He awarded this amount to Linda as lump sum alimony to be paid in three installments. . . . Linda worked and contributed to Billy's financial status, but had no assets of her own; her separate estate pales in comparison to Billy's. This award of lump sum alimony may have been made by the chancellor to give Linda financial security. An explanation of the basis of this award will help this Court determine whether the distribution represents an abuse of discretion or a division supported by the record. Therefore, a remand is warranted on this issue. . . .

■ UNIFORM MARRIAGE AND DIVORCE ACT §307
9A U.L.A. (pt. I) 288 (1998)

[DISPOSITION OF PROPERTY] [ALTERNATIVE A]

(a) [T]he court, without regard to marital misconduct, [in a dissolution] shall, and in a proceeding for legal separation may, finally equitably apportion between the parties the property and assets belonging to either or both however and whenever acquired, and whether the title thereto is in the name of the husband or wife or both. In making apportionment the court shall consider the duration of the marriage, and prior marriage of either party, antenuptial agreement of the parties, the age, health, station, occupation, amount and sources of income, vocational skills, employability, estate, liabilities, and needs of each of the parties, custodial provisions, whether the apportionment is in lieu of or in addition to maintenance, and the opportunity of each for future acquisition of capital assets and income. The court shall also consider the contribution or dissipation of each party in the acquisition, preservation, depreciation, or appreciation in value of the respective estates, and the contribution of a spouse as a homemaker or to the family unit. . . .[16]

■ STEPHEN D. SUGARMAN, DIVIDING FINANCIAL INTERESTS ON DIVORCE
in Divorce Reform at the Crossroads 130, 136-141 (Stephen D. Sugarman & Herma Hill Kay eds., 1990)

[The author attempts to identify a theoretical framework or legal analogy for understanding the financial incidents of divorce. He rejects fault as a suitable principle, given the high social cost imposed. He also rejects the notion of "marriage as contract," in part because modern no-fault, unilateral divorce leaves no room for "the concept of breach and resultant damages." He then considers partnership law.]

Perhaps a better legal analogy to no-fault divorce can be found in partnership law. The idea is that through marriage the man and woman have joined together

---

[16]. Alternative B, designed for community property states, directs the court to assign separate property to the spouse-owner and to effect a "just" division of the community property, without regard to fault and "after considering all relevant factors including" the contribution of each spouse to the acquisition of marital property, including a homemaker's contribution; the value of the property set aside to each; marriage duration; and the economic circumstances of each spouse, including the desirability of awarding the family home to the custodial parent. 9A U.L.A. (pt. I) at 288-289. These two alternatives replaced the original version of §307, reprinted infra p. 601.

(50-50?) in an economic partnership, which, like partnerships generally, can be dissolved by either party. On the ending of the marriage partnership, like other partnerships, there is to be a winding up of the partnership's activities and a distribution of the partnership assets. . . .

Under the partnership analogy all earnings generated by the couple during the marriage would seem to belong to the partnership, as would any things bought with those earnings and any earnings left unspent and saved or invested. . . . In the marriage setting [unlike in traditional financial partnerships], it is as though, as a general rule, all the extra income and asset appreciation of the partnership is simply retained and reinvested in the partnership. . . .

[J]ust as financial partners contribute only some of their property to the typical partnership, certain items of property belonging to the husband and wife could be seen as outside the marital partnership and not subject to division on the marriage's termination. They might include assets the parties bring to the marriage and do not commingle with other marital property, and those gifts and inheritances separately received by either party during the marriage and maintained separately.

If marriage under no-fault is to be seen as a conventional partnership, no formal distinctions would be made between long- and short-duration marriages; to be sure, in long-duration marriages, there might be more assets to distribute. So, too, the family home would not be treated differently from any other asset. The implication of minor children would be ambiguous since there is no obvious counterpart in ordinary partnerships. Does gaining custody mean that you have obtained a partnership asset, or merely that you have assumed a partnership liability for which you should be compensated?

Most important, under the partnership analogy, there would be no spousal support. That is, in the traditional partnership, even though the partners agree to make their earning capacity available to the partnership during its lifetime, they ordinarily just walk away from the dissolved partnership with all their own human capital. This applies both to the human capital they brought to the partnership and to any enhanced human capital they gained during the operation of the partnership. . . .

Traditional financial partners, of course, may anticipate certain problems of partnership breakup and, if they wish, enter into alternative arrangements at the outset. . . . They [even] might agree to be other than 50-50 partners originally. Perhaps married couples could also be encouraged to make specific agreements in advance. . . .

■ AMERICAN LAW INSTITUTE, PRINCIPLES
OF THE LAW OF FAMILY DISSOLUTION:
ANALYSIS AND RECOMMENDATIONS §4.12
(2002)

RECHARACTERIZATION OF SEPARATE PROPERTY AS
MARITAL PROPERTY AT THE DISSOLUTION OF
LONG-TERM MARRIAGES

(1) In marriages that exceed a minimum duration specified in a uniform rule of statewide application, a portion of the separate property that each spouse held at

the time of their marriage should be recharacterized at dissolution as marital property.

(a) The percentage of separate property that is recharacterized as marital property under Paragraph (1) should be determined by the duration of the marriage, according to a formula specified in a rule of statewide application.

(b) The formula should specify a marital duration at which the full value of the separate property held by the spouses at the time of their marriage is recharacterized at dissolution as marital property.

(2) A portion of separate property acquired by each spouse during marriage should be recharacterized at dissolution as marital property if, at the time of dissolution, both the marital duration, and the time since the property's acquisition (the "holding period"), exceed the minimum length specified for each in a rule of statewide application.

(a) The percentage of separate property that is recharacterized as marital property under Paragraph (2) should be determined by a formula, specified in a rule of statewide application, that takes into account both the marital duration and the holding period of the property in question.

(b) The formula should specify a marital duration and holding period at which the full value of the property is recharacterized at dissolution as marital property.

(3) For the purpose of this section, any appreciation in the value of separate property, or income from it, that would otherwise itself be separate property is treated as having been acquired at the same time as the underlying asset, and any asset acquired in exchange for separate property is treated as having been acquired as of the time its predecessor asset was acquired.

(4) A spouse should be able to avoid the application of this section to gifts or inheritances received during marriage by giving written notice of that intention to the other spouse within the time period following the property's receipt that is specified in a rule of statewide application.

(5) The provision of a will or deed of gift specifying that a bequest or gift is not subject to claims under this section should be given effect.

(6) This section should not apply to separate property if, as set forth in written findings of the trial court . . . , preservation of the property's separate character is necessary to avoid substantial injustice.

Notes and Questions on the Theory of Property Division

1. *Development of equitable distribution.* Most American states follow the common law approach to spousal ownership of property during marriage. Eight use a community property approach derived from their French or Spanish heritage; Wisconsin's system is modeled on the Uniform Marital Property Act, 9A U.L.A. (pt. I) 103 (1998). See Chapter III, section B2.

The common law scheme reflects "title theory." Title to property, as evidenced in a deed, for example, determines ownership between the spouses. Property acquired or earned during marriage belongs to the acquiring or earning spouse, unless that spouse acts affirmatively to create joint ownership (for example, buying a house titled jointly in the names of both spouses). Upon divorce, the court assigns property to the owner. In the 1980s, after adopting no-fault grounds and witnessing a rising divorce rate, many states began abandoning the title system in favor of a system of "equitable distribution" applicable at the end of marriage. In *Ferguson*, Mississippi became the last state to abandon the title system. See generally Deborah H. Bell, Family Law at the Turn of the Century, 71 Miss. L.J. 781 (2002) (explaining *Ferguson* and its context).

Before the development of equitable distribution laws, statutes permitting a court to divide property upon divorce were limited, and some states had no such statutes at all. In a few states courts used the doctrine of "special equities" to award a wife who had made substantial contributions a share of her husband's property or applied other equitable remedies, such as resulting trust, constructive trust, or unjust enrichment. See Brett R. Turner, Equitable Distribution of Property §1.02 (2d ed. 1994 & Supp. 2004).

One influential model was the original 1970 version of the Uniform Marriage and Divorce Act (UMDA). Using definitions typical of community property systems, UMDA distinguished separate property from marital property and listed factors courts should consider in making a "just" division of the latter:

§307. [Disposition of Property]

(a) [The court in a dissolution or legal separation proceeding] shall assign each spouse's property to him. It also shall divide the marital property without regard to marital misconduct in just proportions considering all relevant factors including:

(1) contribution of each spouse to acquisition of the marital property, including contribution of a spouse as homemaker;

(2) value of the property set apart to each spouse;

(3) duration of the marriage; and

(4) economic circumstances of each spouse when the division of property is to become effective, including the desirability of awarding the family home or the right to live therein for reasonable periods to the spouse having custody of any children.

(b) For purposes of this Act, "marital property" means all property acquired by either spouse subsequent to the marriage except:

(1) property acquired by gift, bequest, devise, or descent;

(2) property acquired in exchange for property acquired before the marriage or in exchange for property acquired by gift, bequest, devise, or descent;

(3) property acquired by a spouse after a decree of legal separation;

(4) property excluded by valid agreement of the parties; and

(5) the increase in value of property acquired before the marriage.

(c) All property acquired by either spouse after the marriage and before a decree of legal separation is presumed to be marital property, regardless of whether title is held individually or by the spouses in some form of co-ownership such as joint tenancy, tenancy in common, tenancy by the entirety, and community property. The presumption of marital property is overcome by a showing that the property was acquired by a method listed in subsection (b).

9A U.L.A. (pt. I) 289-290 (1998). Laws following this model bring common law states much closer to community property states in the treatment of property after divorce. That is, equitable distribution laws in common law states create a "deferred community property" system, with the concept of marital property becoming effective upon divorce. See Turner, supra, §1.02 n.44.

Although most states adopted equitable distribution by statute (often modeled on UMDA), Mississippi did so by judicial decision in *Ferguson*. What is the source of *Ferguson*'s authority to adopt a new property distribution system? Does the ruling deprive Billy Ferguson of his property without due process? Are the court's "guidelines" really "judicial legislation" in disguise? See *Ferguson*, 639 So. 2d at 940 (Lee, P.J., concurring and dissenting). Does *Ferguson* exemplify "judicial activism"?

2. *Homemaker services.* A significant criticism of the title theory, as *Ferguson* reveals, pertains to its treatment of the traditional homemaker. The long-standing devaluation of homemakers' activities followed from the common law doctrine of coverture, including the wife's duty to perform household services and the husband's rights to her property and earnings. Later, the continuing gender-specific division of labor in the family perpetuated this problem; even in modern families in which women work outside the home, men typically contribute more wages while women contribute more unpaid labor. Katharine B. Silbaugh, Marriage Contracts and the Family Economy, 93 Nw. U. L. Rev. 65, 98 (1998). During the era of divorce reform in the 1970s feminist activists helped secure equitable division laws, designed "to credit the unpaid work that the typical non-employed homemaker put into the partnership," but also benefiting ex-husbands who had depended on their wives' earnings. Nancy Cott, Public Vows: A History of Marriage and the Nation 206 (2000).

UMDA served as an influential catalyst for such reform. How does UMDA treat homemaker services?

3. *Partnership.* Does *Ferguson*'s contribution theory treat marriage as a partnership, the approach examined by Professor Sugarman? What is the difference? Does the partnership analogy, first developed in community property states, provide fair outcomes for homemakers? See Alicia Brokars Kelly, Rehabilitating Partnership Marriage as a Theory of Wealth Distribution at Divorce: In Recognition of a Shared Life, 19 Wis. Women's L.J. 141 (2004). Cf. Carolyn J. Frantz & Hanoch Dagan, Properties of Marriage, 104 Colum. L. Rev. 75, 77 (2004) (theorizing marriage as "an egalitarian liberal community").

Although today property division at divorce reflects the notion of marriage as a partnership based on contribution, this theory has not widely taken hold in default rules governing the distribution of property when one spouse dies. The surviving spouse, more often the wife, is entitled to a smaller share than she might have received if the marriage had ended in divorce. Why does the law not reward the spouse who satisfies the ideal—a marriage that lasts "until death do us part"? See Laura Rosenbury, Two Ways to End a Marriage: Divorce or Death, 2005 Utah L. Rev. 1227.

4. *Marital property versus "hotchpot."* Note how UMDA identifies the property that is subject to division. Alternative A of revised §307 (a model proposed for common law states) gives the court authority to divide the great "hotchpot" of assets owned by either spouse, whenever and however acquired. See Linda D. Elrod & Robert G. Spector, A Review of the Year in Family Law: "Same-Sex" Marriage Issue Dominates Headlines, 38 Fam. L.Q. 777, 813 (2005) (listing 19 states that do not limit property division to marital assets only). Can partnership or contribution theories explain judicial authority to divide property acquired before marriage or received by one spouse as a gift? See, e.g., Baccanti v. Morton, 752 N.E.2d 718, 724-725 (Mass. 2001).

More states, instead, follow the original version of UMDA, directing division of "marital property" only. These statutes define marital property as that acquired by either spouse during the marriage, except when acquired by gift, inheritance, or in exchange for nonmarital or "separate property"; such statutes often presume that all property acquired during the marriage is marital. E.g., Ky. Rev. Stat. Ann. §403.190 (LexisNexis 1999); Mo. Rev. Stat. §452.330 (2000). Why did UMDA's drafters replace the "marital property" with the "hotchpot" approach? See Joan M. Krauskopf, A Theory for "Just" Division of Marital Property in Missouri, 41 Mo. L. Rev. 165, 173-174 (1976) (ABA Family Law Section feared complexity of classifying property as separate or marital). See also Ralph J. Podell, The Case for Revision of the Uniform Marriage and Divorce Act, 7 Fam. L.Q. 169, 175 (1973) (division of all property more equitable).

Under yet another approach, a "hybrid system," the court distributes nonmarital property only after the distribution of marital property, if equity requires. Which approach does *Ferguson* follow? Does the court identify what property is subject to division?

5. *The ALI's approach: recharacterizing separate property.* The American Law Institute's Principles of the Law of Family Dissolution (ALI Principles) seek to guide states in addressing divorce-related questions. The ALI Principles reconceptualize dissolution's financial consequences to enhance consistency among outcomes and to clarify rationales. The ALI Principles propose the use of presumptive formulae ("rules of statewide application") that will allow prediction of judicial outcomes, in turn facilitating settlement at dissolution or encouraging premarital contracts. These presumptive formulae serve as default rules applicable in the absence of agreement by the parties. Courts can depart from the outcomes yielded by the formulae only on written findings that substantial injustice would result.

How does §4.12 of the ALI Principles resemble the "hotchpot" approach? Differ from it? Why should duration of marriage itself transform separate property into marital property (which the ALI Principles subject to presumptively equal division)? Do the ALI Principles provide for greater predictability than laws modeled on UMDA, which make the marriage's length one factor in an equitable division? In addition to promoting predictability, §4.12 claims to reflect the reasonable expectations of spouses. The comments explain:

> After many years of marriage, spouses typically do not think of their separate-property assets as separate, even if they would be so classified under the technical property rules. Both spouses are likely to believe, for example, that such assets will be available to provide for their joint retirement, for a medical crisis of either spouse, or for other personal emergencies. The longer the marriage the more likely it is that the spouses will have made decisions about their employment or the use of their marital assets that are premised in part on such expectations about the separate property of both spouses. If the marriage ends with the death of the wealthier spouse, the common law has traditionally provided the remedy of a forced share for survivors not otherwise provided for. The 1990 revision of the Uniform Probate Code gradually enlarges the spouse's forced share with the duration of the marriage according to a mechanical formula. Section 4.12 of these Principles provides an analogous remedy when the marriage ends with dissolution rather than death.

ALI Principles §4.12 cmt. a. Given that the explanation cites no empirical studies of spousal attitudes about property ownership in long marriages, what is the basis of this approach? Would the same attitudes that the ALI Principles ascribe to spouses also prevail among domestic partners, to whom these rules for family dissolution apply as well? (For the factors triggering recognition of domestic partnerships, see Chapter IV, p. 395)

6. *"Equitable" distribution.* Once a court determines the property subject to division and its value, how does the court determine the amount each party should get? Alternative A of UMDA's revised §307 directs an "equitable" apportionment according to a wide-ranging list of factors of unidentified weight. Other statutes direct the court to divide such property "in just proportions." E.g., 750 Ill. Comp. Stat. §5/503(d) (West Supp. 2005). Are these standards too vague to be helpful?

7. *Debts.* Courts generally allocate debts as well as assets. For example, *Ferguson* addresses responsibility for mortgages. Usually the same principles of classification (that is, separate or marital) govern property and debts, and the same factors guide distribution of both. E.g., Alford v. Alford, 120 S.W.3d 810, 813 (Tenn. 2003) (interpreting "marital debts" to conform to definition of marital property, i.e., "all debts incurred by either or both spouses during the course of the marriage up to the date of the final divorce hearing").

8. *Fault.* Should marital misconduct play a role in the equitable or just division of property? To what extent does the husband's adultery in *Ferguson* explain the court's departure from title theory? Was the court punishing him for his "fault"? Does consideration of fault in dividing property mitigate the harsh effects of no-fault divorce found by Dr. Lenore Weitzman, supra, pp. 594–595? Even if dissolution should be available without regard to fault, does it follow that the law should not impose economic rewards and punishments for behavior during marriage? See, e.g., Singley v. Singley, 846 So. 2d 1004 (Miss. 2002) (court below should have considered wife's extramarital affairs in division of marital property); Williams v. Williams, 55 S.W.3d 405 (Mo. Ct. App. 2001) (uneven allocation of property appropriate in light of wife's abuse of husband); Amsbaugh v. Amsbaugh, 673 N.W.2d 601 (N.D. 2004) (court below properly considered wife's drinking problem in diminishing her share of marital property).

With the advent of equitable distribution, fault considerations (other than financial misconduct) have receded in property division even more rapidly than in alimony awards, discussed infra section C. When published in 2002, the ALI Principles classified 15 states as "full fault," that is, states that consider fault in dividing property and awarding alimony (with 7 additional states considering fault only in awarding alimony). ALI Principles, supra, at 46. What position does UMDA take on the role of fault in property division?

9. *Equal division.* Community property principles, explicitly recognizing marriage as a partnership, give each spouse an undivided one-half interest in property acquired by spousal labor during the marriage. Most, but not all, community property states apply a rule or presumption of equal division at dissolution. Compare Putterman v. Putterman, 939 P.2d 1047 (Nev. 1997) (equal division absent "compelling reasons"), with Wright v. Wright, 65 S.W.3d 715 (Tex. App. 2001) (upholding distribution of 88 percent of community property to wife, based on husband's cruelty). See Kelly, supra, at 158. Equal division contemplates equality in value, not dividing an asset in half.

The ALI Principles dictate a presumption of equal division of marital property in §4.09. This approach disregards fault, in part to achieve predictability and facilitate settlement. Like UMDA, however, the ALI Principles in §4.10 include an exception for financial misconduct with marital assets. Unlike other marital misconduct, financial misconduct can be predictably measured, for example, one spouse's gift of $10,000 in marital property to a lover. Under §4.10, the misconduct must occur within a time period before serving the dissolution petition, specified in a rule of statewide application.

For an equitable distribution, should a court use an equal division as a starting point? Do partnership and contribution rationales presume equal participation by both spouses? See In re Marriage of Massee, 970 P.2d 1203, 1209-1211 (Or. 1999) (analyzing presumption of equal contributions by homemaker and breadwinner).

Does the absence of a presumption of equal division constitute sex discrimination? Will courts disproportionately favor breadwinners over homemakers if given unfettered discretion to achieve an equitable or fair division of property? See Wendt v. Wendt, 757 A.2d 1225, 1241-1245 (Conn. App. Ct. 2000) (rejecting wife's challenge under state ERA).

10. *Need.* Does *Ferguson's* reliance on a contribution rationale leave room to divide property based on need? On what basis did Linda Ferguson "need" the marital home and the other property that was titled to her husband but awarded to her?

Some evidence suggests a "glass ceiling," reflected in decreasing percentage awards for wives as the amount of marital property increases. Professor Mary Moers Wenig discerns in such cases the "enough is enough" principle, based on the notion that need cannot not justify an award above a certain amount. Mary Moers Wenig, The Marital Property Law of Connecticut, Past, Present and Future, 1990 Wis. L. Rev. 807, 873 & n.289. In response, Professor Joan Williams wonders: "In this country we do not ordinarily condition ownership on whether the owners 'need' their property. Why treat wives differently?" Joan Williams, Do Wives Own Half? Winning for Wives After *Wendt*, 32 Conn. L. Rev. 249, 250 (1999).

Can you reconcile need as a factor in property distribution with the egalitarian assumptions of the contribution and partnership rationales? See Martha Albertson Fineman, The Illusion of Equality: The Rhetoric and Reality of Divorce Reform 41-52 (1991). Does consideration of need in property distribution help expose family law's continuing inequalities? Cf. Jill Elaine Hasday, The Canon of Family Law, 57 Stan. L. Rev. 825, 869-870 (2004). Alternatively, does need make more sense as a basis for alimony than for property division? Consider the materials below.

Problem

Rolando and Julieta separate only two years after marrying. During the separation, Rolando sends money to their children (all born before the marriage) and pays for Julieta's surgery. Eight years after separating, they reconcile for four years. In subsequent divorce proceedings, Rolando challenges the court's classification of assets he acquired during the separation as marital property. Assuming the 1970 version of UMDA governs, what result and why? See Rodriguez v. Rodriguez, 908 P.2d 1007 (Alaska 1995). Alternatively, suppose the assets in question had been acquired by Rolando premaritally, while he and Julieta were cohabiting as a prelude to their marriage? See Faulkner v. Goldfuss, 46 P.3d 993, 1002-1003 (Alaska 2002); Tyma v. Tyma, 644 N.W.2d 139 (Neb. 2002); Northrop v. Northrop, 622 N.W.2d 219 (N.D. 2001). See also Loughlin v. Loughlin, 889 A.2d (Conn. App. Ct.), *appeal granted*, 895 A.2d 798 (Conn. 2006).

C. SPOUSAL SUPPORT: THEORIES OF NEED, SELF-SUFFICIENCY, AND BEYOND

The concept of divorce as the dissolution of a partnership leaves unexplained the duty to provide future support for a former spouse. What is the rationale for spousal support? How should the amount be determined? How long should the duty continue?

■ **MANI v. MANI**
   869 A.2d 904 (N.J. 2005)

Justice LONG delivered the opinion of the Court. . . .

. . . Plaintiff, Brenda Mani and defendant, James Mani met in 1970 when she went to work for him in his seasonal amusement business on the Seaside Heights boardwalk. James, a college graduate, was at the time, a half-owner of the board-walk business and a partner in a travel agency in Florida that later failed; Brenda was a college student. Brenda graduated in 1971 and taught preschool for two years while working with James at his business during the summer.

[The couple had no children. During summers they worked together at the boardwalk business 100 hours per week. During winters they vacationed in Florida and Mexico. Brenda received valuable gifts from her father, including $10,000 annually during the early years of the marriage; tax-free bonds; and stock in a family business, Ultimate Corporation, that later traded publicly, split several times, and appreciated considerably. In 1986, using proceeds from Brenda's stock and the first home, the parties built a lavish new home, titled in Brenda's name.]

In 1993, when they were in their 40's, the parties retired from the boardwalk business and lived, in the words of the trial judge, an "extravagant" lifestyle almost exclusively out of Brenda's investment income. Their monthly budgetary expenses ranged from $7,360 [Brenda's estimate] to $13,143 [James' estimate]. Following the conclusion of the boardwalk operation, James, who had obtained a real estate license in Florida, worked briefly for real estate brokers. Although he provided a few referrals, he never showed a property for the firms and earned only about $20,000 in income in all. The couple spent seven years together in retirement before Brenda discovered that her husband was having an affair with a woman with whom the parties socialized. Brenda filed a complaint for divorce alleging adultery and extreme cruelty. . . .

[At trial,] James claimed entitlement to a permanent alimony award of $68,320 per year and Brenda sought to deny alimony altogether. [After allocating the prop-erty,] the judge awarded James [alimony of] $610 per week based "in substantial part on the defendant's economic dependency." In reaching that conclusion, the judge attributed to James the ability to earn a minimum of $25,000 annually and denominated the alimony award as necessary to maintain the marital standard of living. [Both parties appealed.]

[In affirming, the Appellate Division] observed that "the Manis' standard of living was not the result of the parties' joint efforts, but rather solely due to gifts from plaintiff's father." [Also,] James' adultery was significant and "his marital indiscretions warrant consideration in the amount of that award.". . .

James asks us to establish, as a rule of law, that in modern matrimonial practice, fault should play no part in an alimony determination or in an award of counsel fees. . . . Brenda counters that N.J.S.A. 2A:34-23(b) gives courts discretion to "consider any other factors which the court may deem relevant" in arriving at an alimony decision, including marital fault. . . . Amicus Curiae [the New Jersey State Bar Association] urges us to rule that fault should not be a factor in the determination of alimony except in the most egregious circumstances and that the focus of alimony should remain, as is the present practice, on the parties' financial circumstances. . . .

The history of alimony is instructive. In early England, two forms of marital dissolution existed. The most common was an ecclesiastical divorce from bed and board (a mensa et thoro) [or legal separation]. The other form—a civil divorce (a vinculo matrimonii)—which literally means severing the chains of matrimony, although technically available, was extremely rare because it required an act of Parliament. Alimony was granted only in the former class of cases on the theory that husband was obliged to continue to support his wife as long as they remained married. Somehow, with the passage of time, the distinction between true divorce and mere separation was obliterated and alimony began to be awarded in all cases. No rationale was advanced to explain why parties, who were no longer married, remained economically bound to one another.

Divorce based on the English practice was available in the American colonies from the earliest times. The concept of alimony also carried over. Again, as had been the case in England, the reason for alimony, outside the legal separation scenario, remained an enigma. . . . Indeed, many distinct explanations have been advanced for alimony. They include its characterization as damages for breach of the marriage contract; as a share of the benefits of the marriage partnership; as damages for economic dislocation (based on past contributions); as damages for personal dislocation (foregoing the chance to marry another); as compensation for certain specific losses at the time of the dissolution; as deterrence or punishment for marital indiscretion; and as avoidance of a drain on the public fisc. Obviously, some of those purposes favor consideration of fault and some disfavor it. . . .

New Jersey cases have long expressed the view that alimony is neither a punishment for the payor nor a reward for the payee. . . . N.J.S.A. 2A:34-23(b) provides that in all divorce actions "the court may award one or more of the following types of alimony: permanent alimony; rehabilitative alimony; limited duration alimony or reimbursement alimony to either party." When ordering alimony, a "court shall consider" a non-exclusive list of [thirteen] enumerated factors [including the actual need and ability of the parties to pay; the duration of the marriage; the age, physical and emotional health of the parties; the standard of living established in the marriage and the likelihood that each party can maintain a reasonably comparable standard of living; the parties' earning capacities; the equitable distribution of property ordered; and any other factors which the court may deem relevant.]

As is obvious, the words "marital fault" and "responsibility for the breakdown in the marriage" do not appear in the statute, although the so-called "catch all category" arguably permits a court to consider "any other factor" it may "deem relevant." [In addition, N.J.S.A. 2A:34-23(g) provides that, except in divorces based on the ground of separation, "the court *may consider* also *the proofs made* in establishing such ground in determining an amount of alimony or maintenance that is fit, reasonable and just."]

[In 1971, based on the recommendations of its Divorce Law Study Commission, New Jersey reformed its divorce law by adding to the existing fault-based grounds the no-fault ground of separation. The alimony statutes quoted above came word for word from language proposed by the Commission, which explicitly left room for judicial discretion to consider fault in alimony awards. The Commission] concluded that "perhaps the penalty should fit the 'crime,' i.e., the flagrant offender, whether plaintiff or defendant (husband or wife) may be subject to equitable principles when alimony, custody and property rights are determined." The Commission did not, however, further define flagrancy.

[A]lthough our case law has consistently recognized that, under our statutory scheme, fault may be considered in calculating alimony, for over a quarter of a century, courts have declined to place their imprimatur on a wide-ranging use of fault in that context. . . . The thirteen alimony factors listed in N.J.S.A. 2A:34-23(b) clearly center on the economic status of the parties. That is the primary alimony focus. . . .

[O]ur task in this case is to search for a principled approach to the relationship between fault and alimony consistent with legislative intent. [We have scoured the laws of the different states and the commentators' views. They] reflect the full spectrum of approaches. For example, one commentator argues that even in the era of no-fault divorce, there should be consideration of fault in determining alimony to morally coerce better marital conduct. Adrian M. Morse, Jr., Fault: A Viable Means of Re-Injecting Responsibility in Marital Relations, 30 U. Rich. L. Rev. 605, 651 (1996). Another contends that legal recognition of fault may "provide protection and compensation for victims of abuse [of] spousal trust." Barbara Bennett Woodhouse, Sex, Lies and Dissipation: The Discourse of Fault in a No-Fault Era, 82 Geo L.J. 2525, 2529-30 (1994). Other scholars counter that "the potentially valid functions of a fault principle are better served by the tort and criminal law, and attempting to serve them through a fault rule risks serious distortions in the resolution of the dissolution action." [Ira] Mark Ellman, The Place of Fault in a Modern Divorce Law, 28 Ariz. St. L.J. 773, 808-09 (1996). That view aligns with the most recent report of the American Law Institute on Principles of the Law of Family Dissolution: Analysis and Recommendations. That report concluded that economic fault is a valid alimony factor, but that consideration of non-economic fault should be avoided because of its deleterious effect on the dissolution action. More particularly, the ALI report notes that, in a scheme such as ours, in which alimony has economic roots, it will be the unusual case in which the fairness of the result will be improved by a judicial inquiry into the relative virtue of the parties' intimate conduct. . . .

We agree [with this last view] and hold that in cases in which marital fault has negatively affected the economic status of the parties it may be considered in the calculation of alimony. By way of example, if a spouse gambles away all savings and retirement funds, and the assets are inadequate to allow the other spouse to recoup her share, an appropriate savings and retirement component may be included in the alimony award.

[Economic misconduct is relevant to alimony.] The same relevance notion does not apply to the ordinary fault grounds for divorce that lurk in the margins of nearly every case. . . . Moreover, without concomitant benefit, considering non-economic fault can only result in ramping up the emotional content of matrimonial litigation and encouraging the parties to continually replay the details of their failed relationship. Not only is non-economic fault nearly impossible to factor into an alimony computation, but any attempt to do so would have the effect of generating complex legal issues regarding the apportionment of mutual fault, which is present in nearly all cases. That, in turn, would result in the protraction of litigation and the undermining of the goals of no-fault divorce, again without a corresponding benefit.

Thus we hold that to the extent that marital misconduct affects the economic status quo of the parties, it may be taken into consideration in the calculation of alimony. Where marital fault has no residual economic consequences, it may not be considered in an alimony award.

The only exception to that rule is the narrow band of cases involving [egregious fault.] [E]gregious fault is a term of art that requires not simply more, or even more public acts of marital indiscretion, but acts that by their very nature, are different in kind. By way of example but not limitation, California has legislatively barred alimony payments to a dependent spouse who has attempted to murder the supporting spouse. Cal. Fam. Code §4324. Deliberately infecting a spouse with a loathsome disease also comes to mind. Underlying those examples is the concept that some conduct, by its very nature is so outrageous that it can be said to violate the social contract, such that society would not abide continuing the economic bonds between the parties. In the extremely narrow class of cases in which such conduct occurs, it may be considered by the court, not in calculating an alimony award, but in the initial determination of whether alimony should be allowed at all.

In this case, there was no allegation that James' marital fault had any economic consequences or that it was, in any way, egregious. . . . Because the alimony award was a close call, (the Appellate Division stating that it "may be insufficient" to support James in the marital life style), we do not know whether the court would have reached the same conclusion in the absence of the fault consideration. We therefore reverse and remand the case to the Appellate Division for reconsideration of alimony without regard to fault. . . .

One final note on the alimony-fault intersection. This is nothing more than a case involving statutory interpretation. . . . This case codifies what has been the nearly universal practice in our courts. . . . By delimiting the kinds of fault that may be taken into account in an alimony calculus, we have not only created a template for uniformity and predictability in decision-making but have relieved matrimonial litigants and their counsel from the need to act upon the nearly universal and practically irresistible urge for retribution that follows on the heels of a broken marriage. . . .

Justice RIVERA-SOTO, concurring in part and dissenting in part. . . .

[T]he paradigm we adopt today undoubtedly will generate its own flood of litigation because it defies definition. As a result, it takes little imagination to foresee the unending number of claims the standard adopted today — that a party's fault "affected the parties' economic life" — will bring. . . . Similarly, determining what constitutes "fault [that] so violates societal norms that continuing the economic bonds between the parties would confound notions of simple justice" is too subjective a standard, converting the analysis into a simple question of whose personal value system will prevail. It is not a stretch to conclude that having your spouse engage in sexual relations with your friend and yet still demand that you support his lifestyle after divorce at the rate of over $150,000 per year "confounds notions of simple justice." If that is not what this standard means, then it is meaningless. If, on the other hand, that is precisely what this new standard means, then we have created a new and unproven process to achieve a result already reached by tried-and-true methods. . . .

■ UNIFORM MARRIAGE AND DIVORCE ACT §308
9A U.L.A. (pt. I) 446 (1998)

[MAINTENANCE]

(a) [The court in a dissolution or legal separation proceeding] may grant a maintenance order for either spouse only if it finds that the spouse seeking maintenance:

(1) lacks sufficient property to provide for his reasonable needs; and

(2) is unable to support himself through appropriate employment or is the custodian of a child whose condition or circumstances make it appropriate that the custodian not be required to seek employment outside the home.

(b) The maintenance order shall be in amounts and for periods of time the court deems just, without regard to marital misconduct, and after considering all relevant factors including:

(1) the financial resources of the party seeking maintenance, including marital property apportioned to him, his ability to meet his needs independently, and the extent to which a provision for support of a child living with the party includes a sum for that party as custodian;

(2) the time necessary to acquire sufficient education or training to enable the party seeking maintenance to find appropriate employment;

(3) the standard of living established during the marriage;

(4) the duration of the marriage;

(5) the age and the physical and emotional condition of the spouse seeking maintenance; and

(6) the ability of the spouse from whom maintenance is sought to meet his needs while meeting those of the spouse seeking maintenance.

■ AMERICAN LAW INSTITUTE, PRINCIPLES OF THE LAW OF FAMILY DISSOLUTION: ANALYSIS AND RECOMMENDATIONS §5.04
(2002)

COMPENSATION FOR LOSS OF MARITAL LIVING STANDARD

(1) A person married to someone of significantly greater wealth or earning capacity is entitled at dissolution to compensation for a portion of the loss in the standard of living he or she would otherwise experience, when the marriage was of sufficient duration that equity requires the loss be treated as the spouses' joint responsibility.

(2) Entitlement to an award under this section should be determined by a rule of statewide application under which a presumption of entitlement arises in marriages of specified duration and spousal-income disparity.

(3) The value of the award made under this section should be determined by a rule of statewide application that sets a presumptive award of periodic payments calculated by applying a specified percentage to the difference between the incomes the spouses are expected to have after dissolution. This percentage [referred to as the *durational factor*] should increase with the duration of the marriage until it reaches a maximum value set by the rule. . . .

Notes and Questions on the Rationales for Postdissolution Support

1. *A continuing duty?* In its historical review, *Mani* poses the unresolved question "why parties, who [are] no longer married, remain[] economically bound together"? Which of the "distinct explanations" for alimony listed in *Mani* is most persuasive? Even if an economically dependent spouse *needs* support after dissolution, why does a former spouse (rather than parents, children, or the state) bear this responsibility?

2. *Need and gender.* Alimony has its roots in the traditional necessaries doctrine, which imposed on husbands a duty to support their wives during marriage. See McGuire v. McGuire, Chapter III, section B3. See generally Twila L. Perry, The "Essentials of Marriage": Reconsidering the Duty of Support and Services, 15 Yale J. L. & Feminism 1 (2003). The Supreme Court invalidated gender-specific alimony rules in Orr v. Orr, 440 U.S. 268 (1979). Applying intermediate scrutiny to an Alabama statute that allowed courts to require husbands, but not wives, to pay alimony upon divorce, the Court rejected as a legitimate purpose the state's preference for traditional sex-based roles in marriage. It also rejected gender as a proxy for financial need, whether based on a goal of helping needy spouses or compensating women for past discrimination. The Court reasoned that Alabama's individualized judicial hearings to set the amount of an alimony award make reliance on a proxy unnecessary and that a gender-neutral law would achieve the state's ends, while avoiding "the inherent risk of reinforcing stereotypes about the 'proper place' of women and their need for special protection." Id. at 283.

Orr thus suggests that "need" furnishes the underlying rationale for alimony but rejects reliance on gender to determine need. Despite *Orr*, Professor Ira Ellman invokes invokes gendered roles to identify alimony's theoretical basis. He writes:

[Marriage] is a relationship in which the wife makes many initial investments of value only to her husband, investments a self-interested bargainer would make only in return for a long-term commitment. [T]he traditional wife makes her marital investment early in the expectation of a deferred return: sharing in the fruits of her husband's eventual market success. The traditional husband realizes his gains from the marriage in its early years, in the form of increased earning capacity and the production of children; his contribution is deferred until the marriage's later years when he shares the fruits of his enhanced earning capacity with his wife. In any relationship in which the flow of payments and benefits to the parties is not symmetrical over time, there is a great temptation to cheat. The party who has already received a benefit has an incentive to terminate the relationship before the balance of payments shifts. . . .

[Alimony is intended to compensate] the "residual" loss in earning capacity that arises from . . . economically rational marital sharing. . . . This is a residual loss in the sense that it survives the marriage. . . . The function of alimony [is thus] to reallocate the postdivorce financial consequences of marriage in order to prevent distorting incentives. [B]y eliminating any financial incentives or penalties that might otherwise flow from different marital lifestyles, this theory maximizes the parties' freedom to shape their marriage in accordance with their nonfinancial preferences. They can allocate domestic duties according to these preferences without putting one spouse at risk of a much greater financial loss than the other if the marriage fails. . . .

Ira Mark Ellman, The Theory of Alimony, 77 Cal. L. Rev. 1, 42-43, 49-51 (1989). Does this analysis successfully explain why the duty of spousal support continues after divorce?

3. *Need or contract?* Does the marriage contract explain why the duty of spousal support continues after divorce? According to one classic treatment, although "alimony and marriage cannot be separated, [alimony] would seem to be most readily justified on the ground that it places the obligation to support a spouse who is in need upon the party who has undertaken to share the responsibilities and pleasures of such spouse by entering into the solemn compact of marriage, rather than upon the state." 2 Chester G. Vernier, American Family Laws 259, 262 (1932). Does this explanation suggest that part of the marriage contract remains binding after divorce? Or that alimony serves as a remedy for breach of this contract? See Elizabeth S. Scott & Robert E. Scott, Marriage as Relational Contract, 84 Va. L. Rev. 1225, 1309-1310 (1998) (theorizing alimony as legally enforceable insurance payments, under analysis of marriage as long-term relational contract).

Professor Mary Becker writes that need is an unsound basis for alimony, using as an illustration In re Marriage of Otis, 299 N.W.2d 114 (Minn. 1980). Ms. Otis, a skilled executive secretary with a substantial income, had left her job upon marriage. Upon divorce 24 years later, she received rehabilitative maintenance for four years, rather than the permanent alimony she sought.

> Ms. Otis's need — in and of itself — is the weakest imaginable reason for awarding her post-divorce transfer payments. Her current need reflects her investment in her husband's career, an investment from which he will continue to profit. Her need reflects the reliance loss she sustained by not working in order to raise their son and further her husband's career (and in order to avoid embarrassing him by typing). . . . Her needs should be met because a reasonable term of their arrangement, with its traditional division of labor, is that in exchange for her reliance in engaging exclusively in non-wage domestic production and reproduction and contributing to his career rather than her own, she would receive a reasonable share of the profit brought in by her husband's career and a reasonable share of the financial security accumulated for their old age. . . .

Mary E. Becker, Prince Charming: Abstract Equality, 1987 Sup. Ct. Rev. 201, 221. Does Becker's analysis suggest a contractual rationale for alimony? Is this Ellman's approach as well?

4. *"A residual role for fault?"*[17] If alimony provides a remedy in contract, how does a court determine who breached? Does the contractual rationale require consideration of fault? For a feminist dialogue on whether to consider fault in divorce's financial consequences, see Barbara Bennett Woodhouse with Comments

---

[17]. Professor Sugarman poses this question. Sugarman, supra note [14], at 136.

by Katharine T. Bartlett, Sex, Lies, and Dissipation: The Discourse of Fault in a No-Fault Era, 82 Geo. L.J. 2525 (1994). Professor Woodhouse laments:

> The traditional fault paradigm, still dominant in some states, reflected an obsession with controlling women and their sexuality. It had the virtue, however, of protecting (at least in theory) those conventionally "virtuous" spouses who worked hard and kept the promises that their partner failed to keep. By contrast, the new no-fault paradigm tends to reduce marriage to a calculus that considers economic harms, but not violations of physical integrity, intimacy, or trust.

Id. at 2526. See also Katharine B. Silbaugh, Gender and Nonfinancial Matters in the ALI Principles of the Law of Family Dissolution, 8 Duke J. Gender L. & Pol'y 203 (2001).

Why does *Mani* limit consideration of fault in determining alimony? See also Hammer v. Hammer, 139 S.W.3d 239, 244 (Mo. Ct. App. 2004) (maintenance is "not alimony" and "is not about punishing one spouse more than another"). If courts consider fault, must they compare the spouses' respective acts of misconduct? See Congdon v. Congdon, 578 S.E.2d 833 (Va. Ct. App. 2003) (allowing alimony to wife because the court deemed husband's profanity and verbal abuse worse than her adultery). Why does *Mani* create two exceptions to its no-fault approach, economic misconduct and egregious fault? Why should courts consider these exceptions "not in calculating an alimony award, but in the initial determination of whether alimony should be allowed at all"? Why would the New Jersey Bar Association urge a no-fault approach, with an exception for egregious circumstances?

Evaluate the *Mani* dissent's critique of the two exceptions. To what extent does a subjective standard create risks of gender bias? Cf. Hammonds v. Hammonds, 597 So. 2d 653 (Miss. 1992) (adulterous husband to pay only limited alimony to long-term wife because of her adultery); R.G.M. v. D.E.M., 410 S.E.2d 564 (S.C. 1991) (wife's extramarital lesbian activities bar spousal support). How would the *Mani* judges treat domestic violence for purposes of alimony awards? Cf. Cal. Fam. Code §4320 (West 2004) (factors to be considered include history of domestic violence and emotional distress resulting therefrom); id. at §4325 (rebuttable presumption against awarding support to abusive spouse).

An omitted footnote in *Mani* states that, in appropriate cases, tort damages can compensate for harm caused by non-economic fault. Does a tort suit provide a better way to address marital misconduct? See, e.g., Brennan v. Orban, 678 A.2d 667 (N.J. 1996); Ira Mark Ellman, The Place of Fault in a Modern Divorce Law, 28 Ariz. St. L.J. 773, 792-802 (1996). See Chapter V, section D2c.

5. *Standard of living.* What does "need" mean for purposes of computing a support award? Does it refer only to necessities of life? The standard of living during the marriage? See, e.g., In re Marriage of McNaughton, 194 Cal. Rptr. 176 (Ct. App. 1983) (though wife got marital property worth $3 million, court upholds $3,500 per month for support based on lavish lifestyle during 32-year marriage, her needs, and husband's ability to pay); Crews v. Crews, 751 A.2d 524, 527 (N.J. 2000) (standard of living during marriage "serves as the touchstone" for alimony award). Is this what UMDA means by "reasonable needs"? Suppose the family was living beyond its means during the marriage? See In re Marriage of De Guigne, 119 Cal. Rptr.2d 430, 440-441 (Ct. App. 2002). Should the marital

standard of living determine the level of support even after a brief marriage? One tabulation shows that 40 jurisdictions consider the marital standard of living in setting alimony. Elrod & Spector, supra, at 809.

6. *Rehabilitation for self-sufficiency.*

a. *UMDA's influence.* UMDA, promulgated some 30 years before the decision in *Mani*, provided an early model for reform of alimony statutes that were based on fault and gender. Which approach is more "progressive," UMDA's or *Mani's*? How does UMDA frame the parameters of "need"? Note that UMDA makes maintenance a remedy of last resort, to be awarded only when a spouse's "reasonable needs" remain unmet because of the absence of sufficient property or income from appropriate employment. Why did UMDA's drafters make maintenance a disfavored remedy, to be awarded only when equitable distribution of property fails to achieve economic justice? Once this need threshold is satisfied, however, the court has discretion to order support in an amount and duration that is "just," based on all relevant factors.

b. *Purpose.* Jurisdictions following UMDA view self-sufficiency as an important objective, making support a temporary, transitional measure. E.g., In re Marriage of Holden, 81 S.W.3d 217, 226-227 (Mo. Ct. App. 2002).

c. *Duration.* How long should rehabilitation take? Must the recipient have a plan that will lead to greater self-sufficiency? See Weintraub v. Weintraub, 864 So. 2d 22 (Fla. Dist. Ct. App. 2003) (rejecting rehabilitative alimony claim of former trained geneticist for help starting a gourmet dessert business). For what standard of living should rehabilitation aim? What is "appropriate employment" under UMDA? How costly can the rehabilitation training be?

d. *Critique.* Weitzman criticizes UMDA's approach as "unrealistic" in many cases and partly responsible for the economic harm women and children have suffered from no-fault divorce. See Lenore J. Weitzman, Women and Children Last: The Social and Economic Consequences of Divorce Law Reforms, in Feminism, Children, and the New Families 212, 224-229 (Sanford M. Dornbusch & Myra H. Strober eds., 1988).

e. *Gender Stereotypes.* How does the rehabilitation principle change the traditional stereotypes underlying alimony, rejected in *Orr*, supra? What are the purposes of rehabilitative alimony? To spur women to financial independence? To relieve former husbands of long-term support obligations? To foster equality between spouses? As *Mani* illustrates, today courts award alimony to husbands as well as wives.

7. *Types of alimony.* Although UMDA would make all alimony awards serve a rehabilitative purpose, some states have responded by permitting several types of alimony, based on different purposes and rationales. As *Mani* notes, New Jersey explicitly permits permanent, rehabilitative, and limited duration or reimbursement alimony. See also, e.g., Tillman v. Tillman, 791 So. 2d 285, 288 (Miss. Ct. App. 2001) (three types including lump sum, periodic, and rehabilitative alimony); Robertson v. Robertson, 76 S.W.3d 337 (Tenn. 2002) (although rehabilitative alimony preferred, long-term support permissible when rehabilitation of disadvantaged spouse infeasible). What criteria justify permanent alimony? See e.g., Brewer v. Brewer, 846 A.2d 1, 14 (Md. Ct. Spec. App. 2004). Does a disparity in the former spouses' income suffice? Compare, e.g., Rosecan v. Springer, 845 So. 2d 927, 929-930 (Fla. Dist. Ct. App. 2003), with Gates v. Gates, 664 N.W.2d 231, 241-243 (Mich. Ct. App. 2003). See generally Mary Frances Lyle & Jeffrey L. Levy, From Riches to Rags: Does Rehabilitative Alimony Need to be Rehabilitated?, 38 Fam. L.Q. 3 (2004).

8. *Loss compensation.*

a. *Rationale.* Yet another theory of alimony underlies the ALI Principles, for which Professor Ellman served as Chief Reporter. Treating income disparity as a reflection of the economically dependent spouse's loss upon divorce, the ALI Principles invoke Ellman's rationale of loss compensation, supra, as the basis for "compensatory spousal payments." This term covers "residual" financial awards (financial awards other than for child support or property division). See ALI Principles §5.01 cmt. a. The notion of loss compensation also helps explain the gradual recharacterization of separate property as marital property because this process protects a long-term spouse from the unexpected loss of assets. See ALI Principles §4.12, supra. Both mechanisms require that the spouses share the economic losses that divorce would otherwise impose on the dependent spouse alone. Such sharing is accomplished by means of transfer payments from the economically stronger spouse to the economically weaker spouse. Note that the ALI Principles apply to dissolutions of both marriages and domestic partnerships. See supra Chapter IV, p. 395.

b. *The formulaic approach.* How might a legislature draft a law (or a court fashion a rule) based on ALI Principles §5.04? The following illustration is provided:

> A presumption arises that a spouse is entitled to an award under this section whenever that spouse has been married five years or more to a person whose income at dissolution is expected to be at least 25 percent greater than the claimant's. The presumptive award shall equal the difference in the spouses' expected incomes at dissolution, multiplied by the appropriate durational factor. The durational factor is equal to the years of marriage multiplied by .01, but shall in no case exceed .4.

Id. §5.04 cmt. a, illus. 1. The comment continues by explaining:

> Under the illustrative provision, the maximum durational factor would be reached after 40 years of marriage, since .01 × 40 = .4. If at that time Spouse A's expected monthly income were $5,000, and Spouse B's were $3,000, the award would equal .4 × $2,000, or $800 per month, leaving Spouse A with $4,200 monthly and providing Spouse B with $3,800 monthly. If Spouse A earned $3,000 and Spouse B could only be expected to earn $1,000 monthly after dissolution, the award would still equal .4 × $2,000, or $800, leaving A with $2,200 and B with $1,800. These awards would be proportionately less for marriages of shorter duration. . . .

Id.

c. *Justifying compensation.* Is "loss compensation" just another way of saying that marriage is a contract with liquidated damages as the remedy for breach? See Allen M. Parkman, Reforming Divorce Reform, 41 Santa Clara L. Rev. 379, 417 (2001). Does In re Marriage of Otis, as described by Professor Becker, supra, exemplify the rationale for compensatory spousal payments? In what other situations does dissolution impose losses that merit compensation? See ALI Principles §§5.05 (child-care responsibilities), 5.11 (care of certain third parties), and 5.13 (certain losses of premarital living standard after short marriage).

d. *Critiques.* The ALI Principles have sparked a variety of criticisms. See generally, e.g., Silbaugh, supra; Cynthia Lee Starnes, Mothers as Suckers: Pity, Partnership, and Divorce Discourse, 90 Iowa L. Rev. 1513, 1515 (2005) (asserting that the ALI "cast[s] mothers as economic casualties of marriage, sometimes entitled to reparations, but never as equal stakeholders entitled to share in marital profits");

David Westfall, Unprincipled Family Dissolution: The American Law Institute's Recommendations for Spousal Support and Division of Property, 27 Harv. J.L. & Pub. Pol'y 917 (2004) (condemning ALI Principles for internal inconsistencies, failure to curb judicial discretion, and diminution of private ordering).

9. *Equal income sharing.* Professor Jane Rutherford proposes an alternative approach that she calls "income sharing." She would add the incomes of the former couple and divide the total equally among all those to be supported. Jane Rutherford, Duty in Divorce: Shared Income as a Path to Equality, 58 Fordham L. Rev. 539, 578 (1990). Thus, a former husband's annual salary of $100,000 and his former wife's of $50,000 would result in $75,000 for each of them per year. Rutherford explains:

> [T]he theoretical basis for income sharing is quite different from that of alimony. Income sharing is not based on need, pre-divorce standard of living, prior contributions, or fault. Instead, it represents a conscious effort to achieve equality between spouses who have divided their labors during marriage. If spouses have not divided the labor, either because they were not married long enough, or because they did not have children, then income sharing should not apply. . . .

Id. at 578. According to Rutherford, this approach promotes a norm of family sharing and caring, avoids reliance on fault, "empowers the financially disadvantaged who may be economically trapped in destructive relationships," and helps achieve financial equality between spouses. Id. at 578-584. Under such proposals, does alimony become a "lifetime pension" at the level of the marital standard of living? See *Brewer*, 846 A.2d at 14. What are the advantages of Rutherford's proposal over UMDA? Over the ALI Principles? The disadvantages? See also Alicia Brokars Kelly, Rehabilitating Partnership Marriage as Theory of Wealth Distribution at Divorce: In Recognition of a Shared Life, 19 Wis. Women's L.J. 141 (2004).

10. *Alimony, class, and race.* Despite the statutory standards, attempts to maintain the marital standard of living in two postdivorce households usually prove unrealistic except in the wealthiest families. One study finds that income would have to increase by 31 percent for individuals to maintain the same standard of living after dissolution compared with that enjoyed during marriage. See Liana C. Sayer, Economic Aspects of Divorce and Relationship Dissolution, in Handbook of Divorce and Relationship Dissolution 385, 389 (Mark A. Fine & John H. Harvey, eds. 2006). Besides revealing class-based divisions, does the quest for a modern theory of alimony rest on racial stereotypes (that is, an economically powerful husband and a wife who has chosen to give priority to her family over her career) that exclude most African-American marriages? See Twila L. Perry, Alimony: Race, Privilege and Dependency in the Search for Theory, 82 Geo. L.J. 2481, 2493 (1994). Professor Regina Austin points to both evidence that in "some segments of the heterosexual black population, saving and asset accumulation are gender roles assigned to women" and anecdotes that "men [are] the chief cause of black women's asset poverty." Regina Austin, Nest Eggs and Stormy Weather: Law, Culture, and Black Women's Lack of Wealth, in Feminism Confronts Homo Economicus 131, 139 (Martha Albertson Fineman & Terence Dougherty eds., 2005).

How would the law treat postdivorce support if the norm experienced by African-Americans provided the starting point? Does alimony contribute to the racial hierarchy among women and encourage economic dependence by women of privilege? Perry, Alimony, supra, at 2504. See generally June Carbone, Has the Gender Divide Become Unbridgeable? The Implications for Social Equality, 5 J. Gender Race & Just. 31 (2001).

Problems

1. Brian, a 48-year-old commercial pilot, and Ruth, a 47-year-old school-teacher, divorce after 27 years of marriage. They have no children. Brian's annual salary is $75,000; Ruth's is $43,000. The trial court divides the marital property equally and awards Ruth half the difference in their incomes for two years to enable her to obtain additional university credits. All alimony will cease at the end of the two-year period. Ruth appeals, asking for a higher monthly award and alimony for at least 12 years. She claims that even a doctorate degree would not significantly increase her income as a teacher and Brian will continue to have much greater income than she can ever expect. Brian also appeals, arguing that Ruth does not need support and she never expressed interest in additional education before divorce. What result under UMDA and why? Under the illustration showing how §5.05 of the ALI Principles works? Under an income-equalization approach? See Gardner v. Gardner, 881 P.2d 645 (Nev. 1994).

2. John and Connie divorce after six months of marriage. John is a civil engineer earning $40,000 annually. Connie, who has a high school diploma, earns $12,000 as an employee of Citibank. Before marriage Connie earned an additional $400 per month by working the nightshift at Citibank and cleaning houses during the day; at John's urging, upon marriage she switched to the lower paying dayshift and ended her housecleaning job. The court grants Connie a divorce on the basis of John's "extreme mental cruelty" because of his inability to engage in satisfactory inter-course with Connie, John's "homosexual tendencies," and his "incessant and inappropriate passing of gas." The trial court returns the property that each spouse brought into the marriage but orders John to pay Connie's premarital credit card debt of $5,000 and to pay her alimony of $450 monthly for 15 months. John appeals, challenging the allocation of Connie's premarital debt to him and the alimony award. What outcome would be "fair"? Which of the facts should be considered? Excluded from consideration? Which different approaches to property division and support, respectively, would best achieve a fair result? See Osman v. Keating-Osman, 521 N.W.2d 655 (S.D. 1994). Does Lawrence v. Texas, Chapter I, section A4, disallow judicial consideration of John's alleged "homosexual tendencies"?

D. "WINDING UP" A MARRIAGE: APPLYING THEORIES OF PROPERTY AND SUPPORT

Despite the different theoretical bases, courts typically confront property and support questions together, along with related questions such as attorneys' fees, tax liability, and pension rights. The following cases present specific factual contexts for applying the theories explored above while illustrating the interconnections among all of dissolution's financial incidents.

1. Two Couples' Stories

■ MICHAEL v. MICHAEL
791 S.W.2d 772 (Mo. Ct. App. 1990)

PUDLOWSKI, Judge. . . .

[A]ppellant and respondent were married in August 1972 and separated in April 1987. There were no children born of this marriage. . . . Appellant [husband] holds a baccalaureate degree in political science and a master's degree in journalism. Respondent [wife] holds a baccalaureate degree in journalism and a master's degree in public administration.

In 1972, on the day following the parties' marriage, the couple moved to Little Rock, Arkansas where respondent was going to work for Southwestern Bell Corporation. While living in Little Rock, appellant was employed as a reporter for a local newspaper.

In June 1974, respondent received a promotion and was transferred back to St. Louis. In St. Louis, appellant worked for APC Skills Company and then for Maritz, Inc. In 1978, appellant was fired from Maritz, Inc. [T]he couple agreed that appellant would not seek outside employment but instead would devote time to writing fiction. [Respondent then] received another transfer and the couple moved to Oklahoma City.

While living in Oklahoma, appellant continued to pursue a writing career, however, later abandoned this endeavor without ever having written a chapter in a book or a scene in a play. After giving up the attempt at writing, appellant worked briefly in a food store and spent 8-9 months working free-lance public relations. When appellant was not employed outside of the home, the couple agreed that appellant would be responsible for the general upkeep of the house and also for the preparation of the evening meal. Appellant spent several hours a day preparing the couple's dinner. Respondent claimed that appellant's other domestic chores were very lax. For two years while the couple was living in Oklahoma appellant drove respondent to and from work. However, for the rest of the mornings, appellant slept until 10 or 11:00 A.M.

In 1984 respondent was again transferred to St. Louis. After moving to St. Louis, appellant continued to cook the couple's dinner. He also periodically took the respondent to work but did not seek outside employment.

Throughout the marriage, the couple's lifestyle improved and they had a significant amount of disposable income. They were able to purchase homes whenever respondent accepted a job transfer and the couple took many trips including visits to Europe. . . .

At the time of trial, respondent had been working for Southwestern Bell for more than 15 years and was earning over $70,000 per year [and had vested pension benefits equal to $1,169.58 monthly.] Appellant's statement of income and expenses provides that he receives no income from employment, however he receives $75 per month in interest, and his share of the gross income on the previous year's Federal Income Tax Return was $1200.

It is with some interest that we note the gender roles of the parties in this marriage are reversed from the more traditional roles of husband and wife. . . . However, certainly the sex of the parties should have no bearing on the division of marital property or on the allowance or prohibition of maintenance.

The trial court allocated $51,347 or 75.5% of the parties' marital property to respondent and $14,128 or 21.5% to appellant. The court granted appellant no maintenance but allowed appellant $500 for attorney's fees. . . . Appellant claims that the trial court abused its discretion. . . .

Section 452.330 RSMo 1988 directs the trial court to divide the marital property in a just manner, after considering all relevant factors including [each spouse's economic circumstances; the contribution of each to the acquisition of the marital property, including homemaker contributions; the value of the nonmarital property of each; and the conduct during the marriage].

There are two guiding principles inherent in §452.330: "[F]irst property division should reflect the concept of marriage as a shared enterprise similar to a partnership; and, second property division should be utilized as a means of providing future support for an economically dependent spouse." Krauskopf, A Theory for "Just" Division of Marital Property in Missouri, 41 Mo. L. Rev. 165 (1976).

When applying these guiding principles inherent in §452.330 to the present case we find that the trial court abused its discretion in its division of marital property. [First, throughout] the course of the marriage, appellant has become economically dependent on the respondent. At the time of the dissolution of marriage, appellant was unemployed, had not been employed in his chosen field of journalism for fifteen years, and had not been employed full-time since 1978. Conversely, at the time of dissolution of marriage, respondent had elevated herself. . . .

With regard to the second statutory factor [contribution], the trial court found that the respondent, for the greater part of the marriage, had been the sole financial support of the parties and the funds used to acquire the marital property had been earned almost solely by her. Also, the court found that the appellant made no substantial contribution to the marriage as a homemaker because he showed a marked disinclination to undertake the normal domestic duties of a homemaker, engaging only in those duties, such as cooking the evening meal, which he found fulfilling, stimulating and interesting.

Although appellant did not work outside of the home for the majority of the years of the marriage, he did have outside employment for nearly one-third of the marriage. For two additional years appellant drove respondent to work and picked her up from work in the evening. While the appellant's performance of traditional domestic chores was often times lax, he did prepare dinner for himself and respondent throughout the duration of the marriage. We are not finding that appellant's contributions entitled him to an equal division of the marital property, however, we do hold that the trial court's division of property is against the weight of the evidence and therefore an abuse of discretion.

In his second point appellant claims that the trial court erred and abused its discretion in awarding no maintenance to appellant. . . . Appellant does not claim that he is completely unable to support himself. However, due to the extended period of time that appellant has been out of the work force in his field, he requires a period of rehabilitative maintenance during which time he can obtain the necessary education and retraining to allow him to gain satisfactory employment in the field of journalism. Appellant argues that he would require an additional two and one half or three years of education to take course work that would enable him to be self-supporting as a journalist.

We have said that maintenance is awarded when one spouse has detrimentally relied on the other spouse to provide the monetary support during the marriage. If the relying spouse's withdrawal from the marketplace so injures his/her marketable skills that he/she is unable to provide for his/ her reasonable needs maintenance may be awarded. . . . Rehabilitative maintenance is appropriate where there is substantial evidence that the party seeking maintenance will or should become self-supporting. . . .

[The trial court erred.] Appellant's need to acquire fresh skills in order to re-enter the field of journalism is reasonable. Journalism is a competitive field. Every year newly graduated students enter the job market with fine skills. . . . Appellant's plan to return to school in order to increase his marketability as a journalist would ensure that he become self-sufficient. . . .

CRANDALL, Judge, dissenting:

I dissent from that portion of the majority opinion which finds error in the division of the marital property and the denial of maintenance to husband. . . . If we accept the concept of marriage as a shared enterprise similar to a partnership, husband had a negative impact on that partnership. Husband did not sacrifice his career for wife, rather he was a hindrance to her progress. On the issue of maintenance, husband has simply shown that he is unwilling, rather than unable, to support himself through appropriate employment. . . .

■ ROSENBERG v. ROSENBERG
497 A.2d 485 (Md. Ct. Spec. App.), **cert. denied,** *501 A.2d 845 (Md. 1985)*

BELL, J.

Large fortunes beget large problems, which engender predictable issues when the holders of those fortunes enter the domestic relations arena. . . . Eleanor Kantor and Henry A. Rosenberg, Jr., were married on June 22, 1952, in Charleston, West Virginia. Their three sons are all emancipated. On November 1, 1981, Mr. Rosenberg left home with the purpose of ending the marriage. The divorce decree followed a lengthy and highly publicized trial and ended almost thirty-two years of marriage. [The chancellor found, in part, that Mr. Rosenberg had committed adultery on many occasions and Mrs. Rosenberg had done so once, two years after they separated.]

[Henry A. Rosenberg, Jr., was a descendant of the family that in 1931 started the American Trading and Production Corporation (ATAPCO), which was a major shareholder in Crown Central Petroleum Corporation (Crown). He later became chairman of the board and CEO of Crown and a director of most of ATAPCO's subsidiaries.] Crown and ATAPCO prospered through the years and appellant's income soared; his assets swelled, and he adopted and maintained an opulent lifestyle for himself, his wife and his family. In 1983, his cash income exceeded $850,000, and his total annual income including noncash benefits was far more. ATAPCO provided him with free legal, accounting and investment services estimated at more than $50,000 for one year, and Crown supplied a new Cadillac automobile biannually. . . . At the time of the divorce, the chancellor found appellant's net worth was approximately $33 million.

Eleanor Rosenberg, appellee, shared her husband's aspirations and made significant contributions to his success. . . . For instance, in 1955, when the first two of the parties' children were infants, appellant asked appellee to give him "his freedom" to pursue his business career. The witnesses overwhelmingly agreed that she undertook virtually the entire burden of raising the children and of maintaining and managing the family household. Appellant admitted that the single-minded pursuit of his business career led him to neglect his wife and family; he absented himself from the home on weekends and was even late for his 25th wedding anniversary party, a particularly sore point. Witnesses told of leaving the party before appellant's midnight arrival and of appellee's humiliation and embarrassment.

During the marriage, appellee also entertained frequently for her husband's benefit. She routinely invited business associates and community leaders to their home for large parties and intimate dinners. [S]he headed the wives' group [of a large national organization of petroleum refiners] and performed her duties skillfully, diligently and graciously.

The parties owned and occupied a 20-room mansion, maintained by a staff of four, in an exclusive area of Baltimore. Appellant also purchased and furnished two other homes at a combined cost of approximately $550,000. [They vacationed frequently, often traveling in the Crown corporate jet which was at appellant's disposal.]

Appellant's largest asset, and that which experienced the greatest growth, was his ownership interest in ATAPCO. . . .

Over the years, the relationship between appellant and appellee deteriorated. He found interests outside the home, as did she. A substantial difference, however, was that his interests involved, at least in part, other women, while she became prominent in community and charitable enterprises.

In the late 1970's appellee began to abuse alcohol and prescription drugs. Appellant also abused alcohol, but did not suffer the same effects. The situation reached a climax in July 1981, when she admitted herself to Springwood Hospital for drug treatment. He visited his wife at the hospital to announce that he was leaving home and to secure her signature on a separation agreement. She refused and then underwent a brief psychotic episode. As a result, her hospitalization was prolonged by about a month and a half. After her discharge from the hospital, appellant remained in the marital home and continued his efforts to have her sign the separation agreement. He ultimately moved out on November 1, 1981.

[Mrs. Rosenberg filed for dissolution on grounds of adultery, abandonment, and desertion. Mr. Rosenberg's cross-bill alleged a two-year separation as grounds for divorce. The trial lasted four weeks. After the chancellor granted the divorce, Mr. Rosenberg appealed the monetary award, set at $1,520,000 plus any difference between $230,000 and the wife's share of proceeds from the court-ordered sale of the house; the alimony award, set at $275,000 per year; and the award of his wife's expenses and counsel fees, $224,579.95. Mrs. Rosenberg cross-appealed, challenging the failure to classify as marital property the increases in value of her husband's ATAPCO stock.]

MONETARY AWARD

The chancellor meticulously catalogued the assets of the parties, designated the marital property and then valued it. Items of marital property included: (1) an interest-free promissory note from Dorothy Bohny [the new Mrs. Rosenberg]; (2) the interest foregone on that note; and (3) the amount of various cash advances to Dorothy Bohny between June 2, 1982, and April 1, 1984. The chancellor found that these items dissipated the marital property. [Maryland case law regards intentional dissipation as a fraud on marital rights and considers the dissipated property as extant marital property.]

The chancellor in the case sub judice found that appellant had dissipated the marital property by making [a $150,000] loan and cash advances to Dorothy Bohny [after he informed appellee he intended to end the marriage]. We conclude that the evidence supports this finding. [T]he lost interest was also a dissipation of the marital property. . . .

[The chancellor classified the appellant's interests in the family trusts as non-marital assets because they were acquired by gift and accepted the figures of appellee's experts, who valued his interests in the trusts at $28.2 million.]

Following identification of the marital property and its valuation, the statute directs the chancellor to consider nine factors before determining the amount of the monetary award, if any, and the method of payment. . . . A plain reading of the statutory language indicates that the chancellor is not restricted to the categories listed. Rather, he may take into account "[s]uch factors as the court deems necessary or appropriate to consider in order to arrive at a fair and equitable monetary award." Md. Cts. & Jud. Proc. Code Ann., §3-6A-05.

Factors

[Appellant complains here that the chancellor erred in applying several factors listed in the statute, as follows:]

"(1) The contributions, monetary and nonmonetary, of each party to the well-being of the family."

Appellant argues that there was no evidence to support the chancellor's conclusions that: (1) appellee "was forced to accept the full responsibility for the sons' upbringing"; and (2) he "admitted that he neglected his family obligations . . . even to the point of foregoing all but the last hour of his twenty-fifth wedding anniversary. . . ." We disagree. There was such evidence. . . .

"(4) The circumstances and facts which contributed to the estrangement of the parties."

Appellant alleges that there was not a scintilla of evidence presented that he "virtually supported [appellee's] dependency on drugs [and] for at least the last fifteen or so years, [he] maintained liaisons with other women. . . ." Although appellant may not agree with the chancellor's conclusions, there was evidence to that effect. . . .

"(7) How and when specific marital property was acquired, including the effort expended by each party in accumulating the marital property."

The chancellor stated that appellee "contributed, though non-monetarily, substantially more than [appellant] toward the marital property." Appellant complains that the chancellor failed to specify the efforts appellee expended in accumulating the marital property and that the evidence did not indicate any efforts by her. Moreover, he contends that the largest part of the marital property consists of his interests in Crown [pension] benefit plans, and that all of these are attributable to his service as an executive officer of Crown. . . . Appellant declares that "[w]hile [appellee's] effort as the homemaker may have enabled [him] to devote more of his time to earning income, this is not a sufficient basis for a conclusion that [appellee] contributed substantially more than [he] toward the marital property." We simply do not agree.

[T]he basic goal of what has come to be called "The Marital Property Act" is to achieve a fair and equitable distribution. If we were to adopt appellant's legalistic proposition, it would follow that one who does not earn cash can never contribute substantially more than the one who does. This flies in the face of the very purpose of the Act. The conclusion by the chancellor that appellee contributed substantially more toward accumulating the marital property than did appellant, while limited to the unusual situation here presented, is far from clearly erroneous. . . .

One error is apparent, however. [The chancellor had designated the wife's jewelry as gifts but failed to reduce the joint personal property accordingly. This error] should be addressed on remand. . . .

Appellee/Cross-Appellant also seeks review of the monetary award on appeal. [S]he essentially claims only one error—that the chancellor failed to include the increased value of the ATAPCO stock as marital property. She explains that at various times Mr. Rosenberg became the beneficiary of life interests or residuary interests in several trusts [created by his mother and grandmother]. The corpus of the four life interest trusts was comprised largely of ATAPCO stock. ATAPCO, in turn, held about 50% of the voting stock of Crown. It is these four trusts which here concern us. They were all gifts or inheritances and, admittedly, non-marital property at the inception. Through the efforts of appellant, his family and other influences, the value of the trusts grew substantially during the marriage. Hence, appellee claims Mr. Rosenberg's interest in that increased value should have been included as marital property.

Marital property is "all property, however titled, acquired by either or both spouses during their marriage. It does not include property acquired prior to the marriage, property acquired by inheritance or gift from a third party, or property excluded by valid agreement or property directly traceable to any of these sources." Md. Cts. & Jud. Proc. Code Ann., §3-6A-01(e), supra. When property is paid for over a period of time, it is deemed to have been the subject of a continuing acquisition. Thus, if the funds used are partly marital and partly non-marital, the property retains the same character based on the source of those funds, i.e., it is considered partly marital and partly non-marital. . . .

[The chancellor's opinion rejected appellee's argument to include in the marital property the trusts' increased value, finding that she had not proven that appellant's personal efforts at Crown or ATAPCO contributed to this increased value. Rather ATAPCO's worth grew as the result of other factors.]

Appellee . . . claims the facts established that there was a joint venture by the family, and therefore, each was the agent for the other and an increase for one is an increase for all. Although an interesting theory, that is not the test. Appellant only had one voice on these various boards. The chancellor's findings were not clearly erroneous.

ALIMONY

[A]ppellant asserts that "[t]he Chancellor abused his discretion in determining the amount of [the] alimony award and its duration." . . . Under the current statute, the principal function of alimony is rehabilitation. . . . The court may award alimony for an indefinite period of time, however, when it finds that:

> "(i) The party seeking alimony, by reason of age, illness, infirmity, or disability, cannot reasonably be expected to make substantial progress toward becoming self-supporting; or
> "(ii) Even after the receiving party will have made as much progress toward self-support as can reasonably be expected, the respective standards of living of the two parties will be unconscionably disparate."

Md. Code Ann., Art. 16, §1(c)(1), supra.

In the case sub judice the chancellor found that appellant

"will continue as a high level executive at Crown and will most probably become more involved at ATAPCO. He will reap the benefits of his family's history of investment in ATAPCO and Crown for the rest of his life. In all, [appellant's] life will not be financially altered a great deal after his divorce is granted."

He further found that appellee

"is in a totally different situation. She needs money for her everyday living expenses and has been totally dependent upon [appellant] for such funds for almost thirty-two years . . . [She] alone will never become sufficiently self-supporting to allow her to continue the life style she shared with her husband for over thirty years . . . [She] has no specialized skills to enable her to enter the workplace at a level which would allow her to attain her married standard of living, and it is unlikely that she will develop such skills at this stage of her life." . . .

In any event, we hold that the court did not err in awarding appellee indefinite alimony.

Appellant next contends that the court's alimony award to appellee of $275,000 a year is "grossly excessive." In support of this argument, he asserts that during the marriage he provided her with a monthly household allowance of $6,000 per month and that after the separation he "voluntarily increased this amount to $7,000 per month. . . ." He concludes that these amounts reflect the parties' standard of living and, therefore, the court erred in awarding her "as alimony 3.27 times the amount of money she received before the divorce." . . .

In determining the amount and duration of alimony, the court must consider all relevant factors, [including, inter alia, need, contributions, standard of living, and circumstances leading to dissolution]. Md. Code Ann., Art. 16, §1(b), supra. We note at the outset that the record shows appellee estimated her actual monthly expenses for 1984 at $10,088 per month. In addition, she deferred expenses of $7,881, which included contributions, car leasing, furnishings, household maintenance, vacation and travel, furs, insurance, clothing, dental expenses, legal and accounting fees. The amount of alimony sought would have carried an income tax expense of $14,000 a month, making her total expenses $31,969 per month. Appellee was awarded approximately $22,900 per month. Because she was receiving only $7,000 each month from appellant, she borrowed funds to pay some of her expenses, deferred payment on expenses already incurred and delayed incurring any obligation on still others. The fact that appellant was giving her a household allowance during the marriage of $6,000 a month and was paying her $7,000 a month after the separation is in no way indicative of her total needs. . . .

The chancellor reduced the alimony sought by . . . $9,000 a month. He was required to take into account, among other things, her actual expenses and her needs. He was also required specifically to consider any monetary award. . . . As the Court of Appeals noted in McAlear v. McAlear, [469 A.2d 1256, 1259 (Md. 1984)]:

"We recognize . . . that there is an interrelationship between a monetary award . . . and an award of alimony. . . . [I]n determining the amount of a monetary award, equity courts must consider any award of alimony, while in determining the amount of alimony, equity courts must consider any monetary award." . . .

We cannot be positive from the chancellor's opinion whether he considered the income that would accrue from the monetary award. [W]e remand to the chancellor to determine the financial needs and resources of appellee including the effect of the monetary award and all other income. Based on these findings, the chancellor must then review the alimony award.

FEES AND COSTS

The large fortune involved in this case resulted in each issue and potential issue being fought every inch of the way. As a consequence, the lengthy and broad discovery, the long trial and the numerous post-trial hearings generated substantial attorneys' fees and litigation costs for both parties. Over vehement objections, appellee's counsel was awarded $430,390 in attorneys' fees and $224,579 for costs.

Appellant challenges these awards. . . . According to Md. Code Ann., Art. 16, §3, supra, [the court may award a reasonable amount for "reasonable and necessary expenses" after considering the parties' resources and needs.] The award of fees and costs [was] within the "sound discretion of the trial court. . . ." . . .

Notes and Questions

1. *Interwoven analysis.* Questions of property division and spousal support typically arise together in divorce litigation, as *Michael* and *Rosenberg* illustrate. As *Ferguson*, supra, observes: "'Alimony and equitable distribution are distinct concepts, but together they command the entire field of financial settlement of divorce. Therefore, where one expands, the other must recede.'" 639 So. 2d at 929 (quoting LaRue v. LaRue, 304 S.E.2d 312, 334 (W. Va. 1983)). See also Smith v. Smith, 752 A.2d 1023, 1031 (Conn. 1999) (financial orders at dissolution are "entirely interwoven"). Further, while observing the theoretical distinction, a court may award to one spouse the other's separate property (e.g., the residence) as maintenance or support. See, e.g., Smelser v. Smelser, 623 S.E. 2d 480 (Ga. 2005).

The analysis generally addresses property first, considering the following questions: "1. Is it in fact 'property' (the identification question)? 2. Is it marital or nonmarital (the characterization question)? 3. How much is it worth (the valuation question)? 4. How much of it does each spouse get (the distribution question)?" Robert J. Levy, An Introduction to Divorce-Property Issues, 23 Fam. L.Q. 147, 147 (1989).

2. *Classifying property.* On the "characterization question," *Rosenberg* presents the common situation of a spouse working in the family business in which he or she had a premarital ownership interest (thus making it separate property); during the marriage the value of this property increases. Why did *Rosenberg* refuse to classify as divisible marital property the increase in value of appellant's ATAPCO stock? Why wasn't it enough for Mrs. Rosenberg to show her husband's role at Crown and ATAPCO during marriage or her own efforts as hostess and "corporate wife"? What arguments support treating the increases as marital property? As separate

property? Should income from such separate property be treated the same way as appreciation in value?

Most community property jurisdictions classify as separate property appreciation and income from separate property. This approach, the "American rule," traces existing assets to their source: Assets traceable to separate property are treated as separate property, while those traceable to marital funds are treated as marital. The original 1970 version of UMDA §307, supra, reflects this rule. The minority approach, the "Spanish rule," treats as community property any income generated during marriage, even income from separate property.

Equitable distribution states often treat income or appreciation from separate property as marital, based on "marital efforts" or the "contribution" of either spouse. E.g., Payson v. Payson, 552 S.E.2d 839, 841 (Ga. 2001); Warren v. Warren, 866 A.2d 97 (Me. 2005). Did *Rosenberg* reject this approach or simply find no "marital efforts" on the facts? Why is acquisition during marriage, without more, insufficient? Cf. In re Marriage of Massee, 970 P.2d 1203, 1212 (Or. 1999). The classification of income or appreciation from separate property proves particularly important when the breadwinner spouse works in a family or other closely held business and can decide what portion of the business earnings to take as salary (marital property) and what portion to retain or reinvest in the company. See, e.g., Smith v. Smith, 475 S.E.2d 881 (W. Va. 1996). Cf. Anson v. Anson, 772 So. 2d 52, 54-55 (Fla. Dist. Ct. App. 2000), *rev. denied*, 790 So. 2d 1101 (Fla. 2001); Edenfield v. Edenfield, 2005 WL 2860289 (Tenn. Ct. App. 2005).

Similarly, the ALI Principles would classify such income and appreciation as marital property to the extent attributable to spousal labor. ALI Principles, supra, §4.04. In addition, the income and appreciation from separate property recharacterized as marital property under §4.12, supra, is to be divided as marital property.

3. *Dissipation.* The *Rosenberg* court counted as marital property funds that the husband had "intentionally dissipated." Although Mr. Rosenberg's loans and cash advances to his paramour present an easy illustration, what other kinds of expenditures might constitute dissipation? What time period is relevant? Suppose Mr. Rosenberg made the loans years before the marriage ended? Should dissolution trigger an accounting of all losses and unwise expenditures throughout the marriage? See, e.g., Kittredge v. Kittredge, 803 N.E.2d 306, 317 (Mass. 2004) (counting only 10 percent of husband's gambling losses as dissipation of assets because "it was not something that started in response to the breakdown of the marriage or in anticipation of divorce"). Can a court following a strict no-fault approach consider dissipated assets? (Recall that under ALI Principles §4.10, supra, financial misconduct within a specified time period is considered in division of property and that *Mani*, supra, leaves room to consider "economic fault" in determining alimony.)

4. *Equitable distribution.* After valuing the assets, which often requires expert testimony, the court must distribute the property to be divided. To what extent did the statutory factors help determine an equitable award in *Rosenberg*? On what basis did the court decide that Mrs. Rosenberg's contribution exceeded her husband's? Does contribution provide a satisfactory explanation for her property award? In examining another "corporate wife" case, Professor Joan Williams proposes a joint property theory that would equalize the spouses' standards of living and would emphasize family work, instead of contributions to market success. See Joan Williams, Do Wives Own Half? Winning for Wives After *Wendt*, 32 Conn. L. Rev. 249,

267-268 (2000). Would recognition of the value of the corporate wife's services during marriage, through payment or taxation, help achieve justice at divorce? Cf. Marian J. Okada, A Labor of Love: Stories of the American First Lady, a Corporate Wife, and a Military Wife, 9 Cardozo Women's L.J. 527 (2003).

What role does fault play in the property distribution in *Rosenberg*? How much, in terms of property, is adultery worth? Emotional abandonment of one's family? Substance abuse? Is the theory of property division underlying *Rosenberg* the same as that followed in *Michael*? What division of property is "just" in each case? Would the presumption of equal division used in some community property states and in the ALI Principles have provided a better outcome in either?

5. *Support: "just" amounts and durations.* Does *Rosenberg* take a sound approach to issues of support? How does the court arrive at an amount? Why does the Maryland statute make contribution a factor for determining alimony (as well as property division)? What theory of alimony does the opinion reflect? Note how the court requires consideration of property division (the monetary award) in determining alimony.

Why must Mr. Rosenberg make large support payments *indefinitely*? *Rosenberg* demonstrates that, despite the modern emphasis on self-sufficiency, courts still consider this goal inappropriate in some cases. What criteria dictate permanent alimony? Marriage duration? Caring for young children? Fault?

In *Michael*, why is Mr. Michael a candidate for support? For how long? Cf. Or. Rev. Stat. Ann. §107.407 (West Supp. 2005) (after paying support payments for ten years, payor can petition court to set obligation aside if recipient has not made reasonable effort to become self-sufficient). How would the loss-sharing proposal of the ALI's Principles apply in *Michael* and *Rosenberg*? The income-sharing proposal of Professor Rutherford?

6. *Empirical data.* How typical are the applications of the law exemplified in *Michael* and *Rosenberg*? What patterns does the exercise of judicial discretion in divorce cases reveal? In an empirical analysis of alimony awards, Judge Rosalyn Bell (author of *Rosenberg*) found courts are not awarding alimony to men; the husband's income and the duration of the marriage are the most significant factors in alimony awards for wives, followed by the wife's income and occupation; women at fault cannot get court-ordered alimony of any type; and permanent alimony cases usually involve women over 50. Rosalyn B. Bell, Alimony and the Financially Dependent Spouse in Montgomery County, Maryland, 22 Fam. L.Q. 225, 267, 299, 316 (1988). See also Marsha Garrison, How Do Judges Decide Divorce Cases? An Empirical Analysis of Discretionary Decision Making, 74 N.C. L. Rev. 401, 452, 467 (1996) (under New York's equitable distribution statute, judges tend to divide marital property equally, and spousal income and marital duration are best predictors of alimony).

7. *Law and economics.* In economic analysis, legal rules are incentives that influence choices. Thus, the legal rules of divorce may affect future behavior by shaping the expectations of those entering marriage. "A nonpunitive, nonsexist, and nonpaternalistic framework for marriage dissolution, then, should begin with recommendations that encourage sharing behavior during marriage without penalizing such behavior at divorce." Herma Hill Kay, Beyond No-Fault: New Directions in Divorce Reform, in Divorce Reform at the Crossroads 6, 31 (Stephen D. Sugarman & Herma Hill Kay eds., 1990). Do you agree with this goal? What does it mean in practice? Does the outcome in *Rosenberg* help achieve such objectives? Does *Michael*?

Do approaches that acknowledge and compensate women's loss upon divorce encourage women to specialize in domestic matters, "ratify[ing] existing gender inequalities" and "increasing women's economic dependence on their husbands"? June R. Carbone, Economics, Feminism, and the Reinvention of Alimony: A Reply to Ira Ellman, 43 Vand. L. Rev. 1463, 1464-1465 (1990). See also Cynthia Lee Starnes, Victims, Breeders, Joy, and Math: First Thoughts on Compensatory Spousal Payments Under the Principles, 8 Duke J. Gender L. & Pol'y 137 (2001) (ALI approach casts women as victims and favors "breeder" wives).

Does *Rosenberg* support such criticism? What outcome and analysis would have avoided this problem? What impact on future behavior and "gender inequalities" does *Michael* have? Was the determinative factor Mr. Michael's "contribution" or his "need"? To what extent does "fault" play a role in either case? What effect will each court's stance on fault have for the future?

8. *Attorneys' fees and costs.* Courts often require one spouse to pay the other's attorneys' fees and litigation costs. For example, *Michael* (in an omitted section) and *Rosenberg* both affirm such awards. Historically, a gender-based rule premised on the duty to provide necessaries prevailed. Today, many jurisdictions impose responsibility for fees on the spouse in the superior financial position, treating the award as an additional distribution of property or a species of spousal support. See, e.g., 750 Ill. Comp. Stat. 5/508 (West 1999). When the spouses occupy similar financial positions, they now pay their own fees and costs.

The appropriate *amount* of fees often generates dispute, given the emotional climate of divorce proceedings. Most jurisdictions disallow contingent fees in divorce litigation. See, e.g., Amendments to the Rules Regulating the Florida Bar, 763 So. 2d 1002, 1015 (Fla. 2000). But see Alexander v. Inman, 974 S.W.2d 689, 693 (Tenn. 1998) (contingent fees "begrudgingly permitted"). See generally Restatement (Third) of the Law Governing Lawyers §35 cmt. g (2000) (examining underlying policies).

Problem

Judee and Eric, who married in 1986, both came from wealthy families, which provided each of them with sufficient assets so that neither needed to work. They had three children. In 1991, Eric used funds he acquired before the marriage to pay for a home on acreage that the couple used to start a vineyard. Both participated in the vineyard project for the first three years of its existence; later, as it increased in size and the parties separated in 2000, Judee managed the vineyard herself. During the marriage, Eric used his personal assets to pay for the family's living expenses, including a monthly allowance to Judee of $1,000 as well as payment for nannies and other domestic helpers whom Judee hired, trained, and supervised. Based on the couple's informal agreement, Judee used the considerable funds she acquired from her parents as she pleased.

Upon dissolution, Judee (who will have custody of the children) seeks one-half the net value of the home and vineyard and other marital assets, plus maintenance in the amount the family previously spent (to the extent that the child support Eric will pay falls short of this sum), including the monthly allowance of $1,000. Eric makes the following arguments: (a) The home and vineyard are his separate property because he purchased them with separate funds. (b) Although the court should credit Judee's work on the vineyard as a contribution to marital property, it should not recognize additional homemaker contributions because the couple "hired various individuals to help them maintain and run their household" precisely so Judee would not have such responsibilities; hence, she should receive less than half of whatever the court deems to be marital property. (c) Judee should not receive maintenance because she can support herself from trust funds and other assets that her parents had given to her even before the marriage. How should the court resolve Judee's claims and Eric's arguments? Why? See Winkler v. Winkler, 115 P.3d 948 (Or. Ct. App. 2005). See also Zahrigner v. Zahrigner, 815 A.2d 75 (Conn. 2003).

2. Special Problems in Achieving a Fair Dissolution

With courts attempting to divide property "equitably" and to award "just" support, general considerations of fairness often overshadow theoretical distinctions between the two remedies. Given the practice of blurring these lines, what difference does it make whether a particular payment represents property or support? Will the purpose of the payment as property distribution or support always be clear? Should the label used by the court control? If not, what considerations should govern?

a. Changing Circumstances

■ LUCAS v. LUCAS
592 S.E.2d 646 (W. Va. 2003)

ALBRIGHT, Justice. . . .
On March 27, 1997, a divorce was granted to the Appellant and the Appellee. The Appellant was ordered to pay $850.00 monthly in spousal support. On May 10, 2000, the Appellant filed a petition for termination of spousal support alleging that since October 1999, a de facto marriage had existed between the Appellee and a third-party, Mr. David Davis.

[In hearings before the family law master,] the Appellee admitted that she had resided with Mr. Davis in Huntington, West Virginia, for a period of over two years; maintained a conjugal relationship with him; used his residence as her mailing address; shared household duties; and jointly owned several vehicles with Mr. Davis. The Appellee further indicated that she paid Mr. Davis $300.00 monthly toward shared household expenses. [Financial disclosures showed that, since the divorce, the Appellant's gross income had decreased from $128,320 to $116,779.00 and that the Appellee's income in 1999 was $31,000.00. The master found that a de facto marriage, as defined in West Virginia Code §48-5-707 (2001), existed between the Appellee and Mr. Davis and that the evidence justified a reduction of support from $850 monthly to $700 monthly, based on the financial advantages of the de facto marriage; the continuing disparity in the parties' incomes; and the Appellee's stress, thyroid, and stomach ailments. The Family Court judge adopted the master's findings.] The Appellant now appeals to this Court, contending that the lower tribunals erred by failing to completely terminate the Appellant's support obligation. . . .

West Virginia Code §48-5-707(a)(1) provides, in part, as follows: "In the discretion of the court, an award of spousal support may be reduced or terminated upon specific written findings by the court that since the granting of a divorce and the award of spousal support a de facto marriage has existed between the spousal support payee and another person."[4] . . . Prior to the enactment of West Virginia Code §48-5-707, this Court had addressed the question of support reduction based upon the recipient's cohabitation and had formulated express principles controlling the issue. In Wight v. Wight, 284 S.E.2d 625 [W. Va. (1981)], for instance, the appellant argued that the appellee's cohabitation should relieve the appellant from the obligation of continuing to pay support. This Court examined the governing statute at that time, and concluded that the statute "makes no reference to the conduct of the parties after the granting of a divorce. Rather it makes their financial circumstances and needs and the requirements of justice the factors to be considered in determining whether an alimony award should be modified." 284 S.E.2d at 626-27. [Subsequent cases reiterated this rationale.]

Among this Court's general standards regarding modification of spousal support obligations, we have consistently maintained that "the primary standard to determine whether or not a trial court should modify an order awarding alimony is a substantial change of circumstances." This Court has previously noted the difficulty in precisely defining the phrase "substantial change in circumstances" but has recognized that it "most often refers to circumstances which have substantially impacted upon the financial resources and economic needs of the parties subsequent to their divorce." Clay v. Clay, 388 S.E.2d 288, 296 [W. Va. (1989)]. . . .

By adopting West Virginia Code §48-5-707, the legislature has, in practical terms, substantially altered the rules established over many decades by this Court regarding the effect of cohabitation on the issue of continued spousal support. . . . The statute is essentially a unique and particularized form of a modification statute, generally premised upon the change in circumstances occasioned by the de facto marriage. Pursuant to the statute, however, neither reduction nor termination is mandatory. The discretion rests with the court. . . .

[In other jurisdictions, the] specific question of whether a material change in circumstances has been created by a de facto marriage has been extensively

---

4. [The statute provides that the] court should give consideration, without limitation, to circumstances such as the following in determining the relationship of an ex-spouse to another person: [the extent to which the ex-spouse and the other person have held themselves out as a married couple; the duration and circumstances under which the ex-spouse has resided with and maintained a continuing conjugal relationship with the other person; the extent to which the ex-spouse and the other person have exhibited financial interdependence; whether they have worked together to create or enhance anything of value; and whether they have an agreement regarding property sharing or support. The statute continues:]

> (3) On the issue of whether spousal support should be reduced or terminated under this subsection, the burden is on the payor to prove by a preponderance of the evidence that a de facto marriage exists. If the court finds that the payor has failed to meet burden of proof on the issue, the court may award reasonable attorney's fees to a payee who prevails in an action that sought to reduce or terminate spousal support on the ground that a de facto marriage exists. . . .
> (5) An award of rehabilitative spousal support shall not be reduced or terminated because of the existence of a de facto marriage between the spousal support payee and another person.
> (6) An award of spousal support in gross shall not be reduced or terminated because of the existence of a de facto marriage between the spousal support payee and another person. . . .
> (b) Nothing in this subsection shall be construed to abrogate the requirement that every marriage in this state be solemnized under a license or construed to recognize a common law marriage as valid.

examined, premised upon either a guiding statute similar to the West Virginia statute or simply based upon evolving case law. In California, for example, the legislature created a "rebuttable presumption, affecting the burden of proof, of decreased need for spousal support if the supported party is cohabiting with a person of the opposite sex." Cal. Fam. Code §4323(a)(1) (1993). . . . Similarly, a Connecticut statute, General Statutes §46b-86(b) (1991) provides that cohabitation may result in suspension, reduction, or termination of alimony if "living arrangements cause such a change of circumstances as to alter the financial needs of that party." . . .

The Oklahoma legislature, through Okla. St. Ann 43 §134 (1992), provides that cohabitation shall be grounds for reduction or termination of alimony "upon proof of substantial change of circumstances of either party to the divorce relating to need for support or ability to support." The Oklahoma courts have recognized that "the *raison d'etre* of [the statute] is not to regulate morality, but rather to regulate support maintenance when the *need* for continued support has diminished or vanished." Roberts v. Roberts, 657 P.2d 153, 154 (Okla. 1983). The concurring opinion in *Roberts* also addressed the importance of such a statute in domestic relations law, noting that prior to the enactment of the statute, "cohabiting recipients found that it was financially detrimental for them to marry (and thus lose support alimony), while those who married were automatically (with certain exceptions) removed from recipient status." 657 P.2d at 155 (Barnes, C.J., concurring). Subsequent to the enactment of the statute, "the law is equally and equitably applied to both those recipients who marry and those who do not. The law no longer serves as an impetus to discourage or encourage marriage of support recipients, but relies solely, in both cases on true financial need of the parties." Id. . . .

[W]e hold that under West Virginia Code §48-5-707, the essential question is whether the de facto marriage, the circumstances of which having been fully developed through evaluation of the factors enunciated in the statute, warrants the reduction or termination of the ex-spouse payor's financial obligations by creating a substantial change in circumstances altering the recipient's need for spousal support. In assessing this issue, we must remain mindful of the admonition that "the sole purpose of an award of alimony is to provide for the support of a former spouse." *Clay*, 388 S.E.2d at 289.

In fixing the amount of spousal support, if any, to be ordered where modification is requested based upon West Virginia Code §48-5-707, the courts must also be guided by the specific list of [20] factors set forth by the West Virginia Legislature for determining spousal support in the original instance, pursuant to West Virginia Code §48-6-301 (2001). Because of the potentially unstable nature of a de facto marriage, we also recognize that it would rarely be an abuse of discretion for a court to preserve its future options by granting a nominal alimony award. See [Smith v. Mangum, 747 P.2d 606, 611 (Ariz. Ct. App. 1987)] (recognizing that unlike remarriage, cohabitation does not result in the accrual of property rights or legal support obligations). We further hold, consistent with the tenor of the statute, that the burden of proof to establish changed financial circumstances justifying reduction or termination of spousal support under West Virginia Code §48-5-707 remains upon the payor, as the party petitioning for modification. See W. Va. Code §48-5-707(a)(3).

Where a finding of a de facto marriage is made under West Virginia Code §48-5-707, a factual investigation into the financial circumstances, income, and expenses of the support recipient, including contributions in money or in kind by the cohabitant, is necessary in order to determine the recipient's continuing need, if any, for support. Based upon such financial evaluation, a comparison should be made between the financial status and need of the parties to the divorce which originally justified a spousal support award and the financial status and need of those two parties at the time the petition for modification is filed, taking into account the effects of any assistance provided as a consequence of the de facto marriage. The results of that comparison then dictate the issue of reduction or termination of spousal support. . . . Since the record does not disclose that the family law master, family court judge, or circuit court seriously entertained examination of these factors, we deem each of the respective orders to be arbitrary and an abuse of discretion. [Reversed and remanded for further evaluation consistent with the principles in this opinion.]

Notes and Questions

1. *Final versus modifiable?* Distributions of property upon divorce are final, even if the parties' circumstances change significantly after dissolution. By contrast, support awards typically allow modification upon a showing of changed circumstances. UMDA is illustrative:

§316. [Modification and Termination of Provisions for Maintenance, Support, and Property Disposition]

(a) [T]he provisions of any decree respecting maintenance or support may be modified only as to installments accruing subsequent to the motion for modification and only upon a showing of changed circumstances so substantial and continuing as to make the terms unconscionable. The provisions as to property disposition may not be revoked or modified, unless the court finds the existence of conditions that justify the reopening of a judgment under the laws of this state. . . .

(b) Unless otherwise agreed in writing or expressly provided in the decree, the obligation to pay future maintenance is terminated upon the death of either party or the remarriage of the party receiving maintenance. . . .

9A U.L.A. (pt. II) 102 (1998). See also UMDA §307, supra. Which theories of property division and support awards best explain the finality of the former and the modifiability of the latter?

2. *Automatic termination.* Many states have statutes like UMDA, automatically terminating maintenance upon the recipient's remarriage, absent a contrary agreement. E.g., Minn. Stat. Ann. §518.64 subd. 3 (West Supp. 2005). What rationale supports this rule? Is it *always* "unreasonable for a dependent spouse to receive financial support from a former spouse and a present spouse at the same time"? See Amundson v. Amundson, 645 N.W.2d 837, 839 (S.D. 2002). Why? Does the rule reflect outmoded understandings of marriage? Further, if alimony is a transitional remedy, then remarriage may provide the surest path to "self-sufficiency" for divorced women, according to an empirical study by a British scholar:

So for women who have access to a man with reasonable earning capacity, remarriage is a far better economic alternative to increasing hours of paid work. The women who didn't remarry — particularly the urban black women — included many whose earning capacity was steadier than that of any available potential new partners. Compared with welfare, former partner support, or unskilled women's earnings, remarriage to an employed man is an attractive option. It adds a second income to yield a viable household package, presents an opportunity to cut down hours of work, and is now the most usual eventual outcome for American women after divorce. In the UK there is similar evidence of the economic benefits of remarriage. . . .

Mavis Maclean, Surviving Divorce 69, 75-77 (1991). See also Liana C. Sayer, Economic Aspects of Divorce and Relationship Dissolution, in Handbook of Divorce and Relationship Dissolution 385, 392 (Mark A. Fine & John H. Harvey eds., 2006).

3. *Discretionary termination.* Some statutes give the court discretion to decide whether the recipient's remarriage warrants termination. See, e.g., Keller v. O'Brien, 652 N.E.2d 589 (Mass. 1995) (applying Massachusetts statute). But see Cohan v. Feuer, 810 N.E.2d 1222, 1228 (Mass. 2004). What criteria justify continuing maintenance from a prior spouse after the recipient remarries? See, e.g., Taylor v. Taylor, 819 A.2d 684, 688 (Vt. 2002) (absence of "a real, substantial and unanticipated change of circumstances" required for modification). Should the test be whether the new marriage allows continuation of the standard of living enjoyed during the earlier marriage? What answer does *Lucas* suggest? Cf. Mathis v. Mathis, 91 P.3d 662 (Okla. Civ. App. 2004). When *Lucas* asks whether the new marriage creates "a substantial change in circumstances altering the recipient's need for spousal support," how is need determined? How does the type of maintenance or alimony award affect the analysis? Why does the West Virginia statute (quoted in the footnote in *Lucas*) explicitly exclude from such judicial discretion awards of rehabilitative spousal support and spousal support in gross?

4. *Cohabitation and de facto marriage.* Do rules making remarriage an automatic or probable trigger for maintenance termination encourage nonmarital cohabitation? Should cohabitation and remarriage be equated for modification purposes? See Miller v. Miller, 892 A.2d 175 (Vt. 2005). What constitutes cohabitation? Should any sexual relationship of the recipient suffice? How does the West Virginia statute applied in *Lucas* answer these questions? See also, e.g., Snow v. Snow, 750 N.E.2d 1268 (Ill. App. Ct. 2001); In re Marriage of Kopac, 47 P.3d 425 (Kan. Ct. App. 2002); ALI Principles, supra, §5.09. Does West Virginia's approach resurrect common law marriage, despite the statutory disclaimers? To what extent does the required scrutiny of the relationship violate the recipient's right to privacy? Cf., e.g., Moore v. Moore, 817 N.E.2d 111 (Ohio Ct. App. 2004) (rejecting former husband's motion to terminate support, based solely on former wife's sex reassignment surgery and relationship with girlfriend).

5. *Obligor's changed circumstances.* When should changes in the *obligor's* circumstances warrant reduction or termination of spousal support? Suppose the obligor retires? Compare Bogan v. Bogan, 60 S.W.3d 721 (Tenn. 2001), with Jameson v. Jameson, 600 N.W.2d 577 (S.D. 1999). Suffers financial reversals? See Woolf v. Woolf, 901 So. 2d 905 (Fla. Dist. Ct. App. 2005). Cf. Willoughby v. Willoughby, 862 A.2d 654 (Pa. Super. Ct. 2004) (obligor's incarceration). Changes careers? See, e.g., Mizrachi v. Mizrachi, 683 A.2d 137 (D.C. 1996); Gastineau v. Gastineau, 573 N.Y.S.2d 819 (Sup. Ct. 1991). Assumes new family responsibilities through remarriage? Compare, e.g., In re Marriage of Peterka, 675 N.W.2d 353 (Minn. Ct. App. 2004), with In re Marriage of Romero, 122 Cal. Rptr.2d 220 (Ct. App. 2002).

6. *Upward modification.* What occurrences warrant an *increase* in spousal support? The recipient's deteriorating health? See, e.g., Savage v. Savage, 661 N.W.2d 762 (S.D. 2003). A substantial increase in the obligor's ability to pay? Compare, e.g., In re Marriage of Weber, 91 P.3d 706 (Or. 2004), with Crews v. Crews, 751 A.2d 524 (N.J. 2000). See also In re Marriage of Monslow, 912 P.2d 735 (Kan. 1996) (approving inclusion of automatic "escalator clause" in maintenance award to give wife share of anticipated increase in husband's income).

7. *Whose burden?* With the advent of modern short-term maintenance, a recipient who did not achieve self-sufficiency had the burden of seeking modification to extend postdissolution support. Yet in such cases, circumstances had not changed since the initial award, precluding the necessary showing. In response, some states shifted the burden of modification to the obligor by ordering permanent alimony for the recipient. See, e.g., Colucci v. Colucci, 392 So. 2d 577 (Fla. Dist. Ct. App. 1980). See also Cal. Fam. Code §4336(b) (West 2004) (continuing judicial jurisdiction over support after a marriage "of long duration"). But see In re Marriage of Youker, 661 N.W.2d 266 (Minn. Ct. App. 2003).

8. *Nominal support.* Why does *Lucas* suggest preserving nominal support? According to conventional wisdom, an attorney should always ask the court to award at least $1 in support to provide a basis for jurisdiction to modify in the event of future changed circumstances; the absence of a maintenance award was thought to preclude jurisdiction. See, e.g., Longo v. Longo, 663 N.W.2d 604, 610-611 (Neb. 2003). Some modern courts have found the practice an unnecessary formality. See, e.g., Mulling v. Mulling, 912 S.W.2d 934 (Ark. 1996); Saxvik v. Saxvik, 544 N.W.2d 177 (S.D. 1996).

b. Bankruptcy

■ IN RE WERTHEN
329 F.3d 269 (1st Cir. 2003)

BOUDIN, Chief Judge.
Paul Werthen, the debtor in this chapter 7 bankruptcy proceeding, appeals from a judgment of the Bankruptcy Appellate Panel ("BAP") for the First Circuit affirming an order of the bankruptcy court. That order determined that two obligations of Paul to his ex-wife Kathleen Werthen, incurred in their state-court divorce proceeding, were alimony or support rather than property division, and therefore nondischargeable in bankruptcy under 11 U.S.C. §523(a)(5) (2000).[1] We affirm, conceding the case to be a close one under a badly muddled statute.

Paul and Kathleen were married in 1982 and separated in 1995, when Kathleen filed for divorce. During the marriage, Kathleen was the primary

---

1. In relevant part, section 523(a)(5) provides:

    A discharge under . . . this title does not discharge an individual debtor from any debt
    . . .
    (5) to a spouse, former spouse, or child of the debtor, for alimony to, maintenance for, or support of such spouse or child, in connection with a . . . divorce decree . . . but not to the extent that
    . . .
    (B) such debt includes a liability designated as alimony, maintenance, or support, unless such liability is actually in the nature of alimony, maintenance, or support.

caretaker of the home and the couple's four children. Paul was the primary earner, working full time at Whitman Tool & Die Co. ("Whitman"), his family's business in which he held a considerable equity interest. . . .

The picture painted by the state court [, which granted the divorce in 2000,] was not favorable to Paul. He had drinking problems, he physically abused his wife and children during the marriage, and he frustrated Kathleen's efforts to obtain a college degree and a measure of financial independence while strictly limiting her allowance. During the divorce proceedings, he and other family members engaged in obfuscatory tactics or worse, aiming to diminish the award against him. The state court noted these circumstances as supporting a generous award, but they do not by themselves explain which portion of the award was alimony and support.

More pertinent to the level of alimony and support were other findings: that the Werthens were a "middle-to-high income family;" that she would have custody of the children who were still relatively young; that her ability to work was affected by a back injury and limited by her curtailed education; that his past income and the value of his family-company stock were large; and that he had understated income and value to decrease the award. On this last issue, the state court found: "Any which way the Husband could avoid his financial obligations to his wife and children, obfuscate his financial condition, and shrink the marital pool of assets, he tried with all his might."

The final decree awarded Kathleen — under the rubric of "Child Support and Alimony" — one-third of Paul's future bonuses and $450 a week in child support. The former payments are to continue until Paul's death or Kathleen's death or remarriage; and the latter payments are to continue until the youngest child (born in 1989) is emancipated, graduates from college, or reaches the age of twenty-three. . . .

Under the rubric of "Property Division," the state court awarded Kathleen inter alia (1) $222,000, representing 60 percent of the gross bonuses received by Paul in the years 1996-99, reduced to $124,485.84 by amounts in savings accounts already awarded Kathleen (the "past bonus award"); and (2) $611,163.20, representing Kathleen's 40 percent marital share of Paul's 22 percent equity interest in Whitman (the "stock award"). With respect to these two awards, the court structured Paul's payment schedule as yearly installments of $50,000 for nine years beginning in 2000, with the remaining balance due in two separate payments in the tenth and the eleventh years (plus interest on unpaid balances).

[L]ess than 90 days after the final judgment, Paul filed a voluntary petition for chapter 7 bankruptcy. In that proceeding Kathleen successfully sought a ruling that the past bonus and stock awards — largely or entirely yet unpaid — were not subject to discharge [under paragraph (5)]. The bankruptcy court treated the issue as one turning on the intent of, but not necessarily the label employed by, the state court judge in making the awards.

To discern this intent, the bankruptcy court invoked a set of factors set forth in Altavilla v. Altavilla (In re Altavilla), 40 B.R. 938, 941 (Bankr. D. Mass. 1984). In viewing the awards as intended "to provide support" for Kathleen and the children rather than as division of property, the court stressed in its final decision Kathleen's otherwise limited resources and earning capacity, the lengthy pay-out period of the two awards, and several other factors. [The BAP affirmed.]

. . . The issue presented is a recurring one with a long history of case-law and legislative development.[3] Unfortunately, the statutory bifurcation in paragraph (5) rests on an unstable assumption.

Paragraph (5) turns upon a supposed distinction between "support" payments for spouse and children (what the statute calls "alimony to, maintenance for, or support of such spouse or child") and other kinds of divorce awards — for example, a division of jointly owned property. A similar distinction is used to determine the federal tax consequences of such payments and may have other effects under state law.[4] But the concepts are not necessarily identical in each context, and we are concerned here only with the meaning of the terms in section 523(a)(5), which is a matter of federal bankruptcy law.

The underlying concept is easy to grasp: support payments are, roughly speaking, what is given to provide for the upkeep of the recipient spouse and children, while other divisions or payments serve different purposes. The central problem is that the two supposedly separate categories overlap because the need for ongoing support will often depend on how much property the less well-off spouse is given outright. Indeed, under Massachusetts law, courts are authorized expressly to award property "in addition to or *in lieu of* a judgment to pay alimony." Mass. Gen. Laws ch. 208, §34 (2000) (emphasis added).

The federal courts have been unwilling to treat the label applied by the divorce court as controlling for Bankruptcy Code purposes. Nominally, the critical issue is whether the divorce court judge "intended" a particular award to be for support or for something else. In practice, courts look at a range of factors, including the language used by the divorce court and whether the award seems designed to assuage need, as discerned from the structure of the award and the financial circumstances of the recipients.

Here, as usual in cases worth litigating, the factors do not all line up on one side. One of those helpful to Kathleen is that the award of formal alimony and support to her seems quite limited for an upper middle-class household with several children: $450 per week for the four children (roughly $23,400 per year), plus the evanescent obligation that Paul pay Kathleen one-third of his future "bonuses" — a form of compensation that the state court recognized could easily be manipulated downward within a family company. Kathleen did have real earning capacity but it was capped by her frustrated education, childcare obligations and her back injury.

In this situation, it is no great leap to suppose that $50,000 per year for the next decade, representing the structured pay-out of the past bonus and stock awards, was intended in some measure to close the gap. As the bankruptcy court pointed out, the main pay-out period corresponded roughly to the time in which Kathleen would be supporting the children and would be responsible as well, under the

---

3. The alimony exception to bankruptcy discharge originated with Audubon v. Shufeldt, 181 U.S. 575, 577-78 (1901). See also Dunbar v. Dunbar, 190 U.S. 340, 351-52 (1903) (child support). Congress then confirmed the judicially created exception for alimony payments. Act of Feb. 5, 1903, ch. 487, §5, 32 Stat. 797, 798. The distinction between nondischargeable support and dischargeable property division payments developed in case law, e.g., Caldwell v. Armstrong, 342 F.2d 485, 488 n.5 (10th Cir. 1965), and was codified in the 1978 Code. See 11 U.S.C. §523(a)(5); Shine v. Shine, 802 F.2d 583, 586-587 (1st Cir. 1986).

4. In general, alimony is deductible to the payor and taxable to the payee, 26 U.S.C. §§61(a)(8), 62(a)(10) (2000); and in Massachusetts, alimony is modifiable, but property divisions are not, compare Mass. Gen. Laws ch. 208, §37 (2000) (revision of alimony), with Drapek v. Drapek, 503 N.E.2d 946, 949 (Mass. 1987) (no revision of property settlement).

decree, for a portion of their college tuition. That the payment period did not end with anyone's death or exact majority could be a point in Paul's favor, but a payout of fixed property in installments is another way to recognize resources available from the payor in fixing support. . . .

Paul's first argument for an out-and-out discharge is the state court's formal division of its assessments into two boxes; but under paragraph (5), payments intended for the support of spouse and child are not dischargeable and the Massachusetts statute quoted above says that an award of property can be made "in lieu" of alimony. Perhaps a more useful point — which Paul does not stress — is that, although $50,000 a year for alimony might not seem outlandish for a man who averaged roughly $150,000 a year during 1996-99, the final catch-up payments in years 10-11 appear to total over $200,000 apart from accrued interest, which does not sound like annual alimony or support outside the world of the super-rich.

Paul also argues in his brief that a precise calculation of Kathleen's income and needs shows that she was well-off without the disputed awards, but Kathleen's own detailed figures and analysis suggest that she was underfunded. Neither the state court nor the bankruptcy court made a systematic assessment of the numbers in terms of "need." Our own assessment suggests that without the awards, Kathleen would be underfunded at least to some extent in relation to her own description of expenses.

Accordingly, we see no basis to disturb the conclusion of the bankruptcy court. [T]here is substantial reason to believe that the state court in some measure intended the property division to assure adequate support for Kathleen and her children. The raw numbers, the uncertainty of future bonus payments, and the lengthy payout period all support this conclusion. The property-division label applied by the court seems most likely to have reflected no more than the mechanical fact that the payments were to come from identified existing resources.

This could be a different case had Paul argued for a remand. A position neither side has taken is that the two disputed awards were partly intended as support and partly as an equitable division of joint property over and above the amount needed for adequate support. Some allocation of the awards between the two categories might reflect the "right" answer; and some courts have so analyzed such problems. See, e.g., Cummings v. Cummings, 244 F.3d 1263, 1266-67 (11th Cir. 2001); Wright v. Wright (In re Wright), 184 B.R. 318, 319 (Bankr. N.D. Ill. 1995).

But in this case such a division would be very hard to calculate and would consume more time and lawyer expense. . . . Nor is it clear that the result would better correspond to the "intent" of the state judge who was not completing a bankruptcy schedule but trying to solve a down-to-earth problem of allocating assets and income streams in a divorce. . . .

The larger problem remains that the present statute needs revision. It is no accident that the 1970 Commission on the Bankruptcy Laws of the United States recommended that the line-drawing approach between alimony and property division be abandoned. The competing interests are for Congress to sort out; but a more administrable solution is overdue. [Affirmed.]

Notes and Questions

1. *Background.* Under the Bankruptcy Code, when an individual petitions for bankruptcy, the debtor's property becomes part of the bankrupt's "estate," 11

U.S.C. §541 (2000), distributed among creditors. To further bankruptcy's protective policy, the debtor may claim exemption for certain property (for example, a home or car). The Code also allows a debtor spouse to be discharged from certain obligations. The long-standing nondischargeability of spousal support obligations derives from judicial origin (Audubon v. Shufeldt, 181 U.S. 575 (1901)). The rule was subsequently codified and extended to child support in 1903 amendments to the Bankruptcy Act of 1898. Jana B. Singer, Divorce Obligations and Bankruptcy Discharge: Rethinking the Support/Property Distinction, 30 Harv. J. Legis. 43, 47, 53 (1993). By contrast, the debtor could discharge obligations based on property division. What reasons explain the different treatment?

2. *Bankruptcy reform.* The Bankruptcy Reform Act of 1994 (BRA), the applicable statute in *Werthen*, departed from the strict categorical approach embodied in earlier statute. Under §523(a)(15) of the BRA, even if the court had ruled against her by classifying the obligations as property, Kathleen could avoid Paul's attempted discharge by meeting specified procedural requirements, so long as she could establish that the hardship of a discharge outweighed Paul's competing interests. Because *Werthen* classified the obligations in question as alimony or support, the court did not undertake this analysis (as explained in an omitted part of the opinion).

In the Bankruptcy Abuse Prevention and Consumer Protection Act of 2005 (Pub. L. 109-8), Congress partly answered Judge Boudin's call for legislative revision of this "badly muddled statute." The law now applicable to Chapter 7 bankruptcies replaces the complex, double-negative language (quoted in footnote 1 in *Werthen*) with the simple phrase "domestic support obligation." 11 U.S.C.A. §523(a)(5) (West Special Ed. 2005). See also id. at §101(14A) (defining term). In addition, the new statute makes nondischargeable other divorce- or separation-related obligations to a spouse, former spouse, or child — that is, those that are not "domestic support obligations" — thus eliminating the difficulty that bedeviled Judge Boudin and many others. Id. at §523(a)(15). On the other hand, the support/property classification continues to control dischargeability in Chapter 13 bankruptcies.[18] Id. at §1328(a)(2) (excepting from discharge §523(a)(5) obligations but not §523(a)(15) obligations). Further, the new law's means testing for Chapter 7's "unconditional discharges" will probably push more debtors to Chapter 13, which permits only "conditional discharges." See id. at §707.

3. *Policy.* What is the proper balance between bankruptcy law's objective of a "fresh start" for debtors and the fair resolution of the financial incidents of divorce? Why does the new statute continue to allow discharge of property division obligations in Chapter 13 bankruptcies? Cf. Allen M. Parkman, Bringing Consistency to the Financial Arrangements at Divorce, 87 Ky. L.J. 51, 89-91 (1999). When categorizing obligations, how does a bankruptcy judge discern the intent of the parties and the divorce judge? Is *Werthen*'s analysis persuasive? See also, e.g., Cummings v. Cummings, 244 F.3d. 1263 (11th Cir. 2001). Cases under the earlier statutes often revealed judicial efforts to enlarge the definition of "support" and "alimony" to

---

[18]. Chapter 13 bankruptcies provide for debt restructuring by wage earners, while Chapter 7 bankruptcies entail liquidation of "non-exempt equity for the benefit of nonsecured creditors." Shayna M. Steinfeld & Bruce R. Steinfeld, A Brief Overview of Bankruptcy and Alimony/Support Issues, 38 Fam. L.Q. 127, 128 (2004).

thwart the debtor's attempted discharge. See, e.g., Deichert v. Deichert, 587 A.2d 319 (Pa. Super. Ct. 1991) (classifying divorce award to wife of family residence and car as nondischargeable support in the form of shelter and transportation). Does the necessity of choosing the "property" or "support" label give the debtor spouse another chance to reargue issues of fairness and need already lost in the divorce case? See Singer, supra, at 61-64.

4. *Other consequences of classification.* Bankruptcy law makes distinguishing support and property distribution obligations important for several other reasons, beyond dischargeability. For example, the automatic stay of proceedings triggered by a bankruptcy petition does not apply to the collection of domestic support obligations from property not in the bankrupt's estate; similarly, the stay does not apply to the commencement or continuation of proceedings for the establishment or modification of domestic support orders or marriage dissolution, except to the extent the latter proceeding "seeks to determine the division of property that is property of the [bankrupt's] estate." 11 U.S.C.A. §362(b)(2)(A) & (B) (West Special Ed. 2005). Otherwise exempt property of the debtor is liable for domestic support obligations. Id. at §522(c)(1). In addition, unsecured claims for domestic support obligations have first priority. Id. at §507(a)(1)(A).

Tax consequences (discussed infra section D2e) also follow from the classification, as *Werthen* observes. Can a debtor spouse get the best of both worlds, classification as alimony for more favorable tax treatment and as property distribution for dischargeability, to the extent permitted? Cf. In re White, 265 B.R. 547 (Bankr. N.D. Tex. 2001). Further, as shown by *Lucas*, supra, only support obligations are modifiable. Should discharge of the debtor spouse's property obligation permit the divorce court to award the same amount in an upward modification of support? See In re Marriage of Lynn, 123 Cal. Rptr. 2d 611 (Ct. App. 2002). Or, would such modification, in effect, change the division of property, a final award? See In re Trickey, 589 N.W.2d 753 (Iowa Ct. App. 1998).

5. *Debtor's bad faith.* To what extent did the outcome in *Werthen* rest on what the court described as Paul's "obfuscatory tactics or worse"? As one court said in commenting on the BRA's changes, which made some property obligations nondischargeable, "Congress enacted §523(a)(15) because obligors were able to craftily draft settlement agreements to be in property rather than alimony terms and then discharge their marital obligations in bankruptcy." In re Butler, 186 B.R. 371, 372-373 (Bankr. D. Vt. 1995). Does the debtor's bad-faith aim of frustrating the divorce decree justify dismissing the bankruptcy petition altogether? See In re Huckfeldt, 39 F.3d 829 (8th Cir. 1994) (so holding).

6. *Property liens.* One common method of securing an obligation to an exspouse is to impose a lien on the obligor's property in favor of the obligee. In Farrey v. Sanderfoot, 500 U.S. 291 (1991), Gerald Sanderfoot attempted to avoid his ex-wife's judicial lien (imposed to secure his obligation to pay her for her share of the marital assets) against the real estate that the court had allocated to him, by declaring bankruptcy and listing the real estate as exempt homestead property. Although noting that the Bankruptcy Code, 11 U.S.C. §522(f)(1), allows the debtor to avoid the fixing of some judicial liens on exempt property, the Court held that a debtor cannot use this provision to avoid a lien on an interest acquired *after* the lien attached. In other words, to use this provision, the debtor must possess the interest to which the lien fixes, before it fixes. 500 U.S. at 299. Turning to state law (Wisconsin), the Court determined Sanderfoot could not avoid Farrey's lien

because he did not acquire his fee simple interest before Farrey acquired her lien against this interest.

Now, the federal statute provides that a debtor can avoid fixing a judicial lien on exempt property only when the lien does not secure a domestic support obligation. 11 U.S.C.A. §522(f)(1)(A) (West Special Ed. 2005). Further, when state law gives the recipient spouse an ownership interest in property at the time the decree is entered, rather than just imposing a right to payment against the obligor, then the latter's subsequent bankruptcy has no effect — because there is no debt. See In re Nichols, 305 B.R. 418 (Bankr. M.D. Pa. 2004).

7. *Attorneys' fees and costs.* Suppose the divorce court orders one spouse to pay the fees of the attorney who represented the other spouse in the divorce. May debts in the nature of alimony or support (under the earlier statute) or domestic support obligations (under the new statute) go to such third parties directly, or must they go to the family member? Compare 11 U.S.C.A. §101(14A) (West Special Ed. 2005), with In re Maddigan, 312 F.3d 589 (2d Cir. 2002), and Hough v. Hough, 92 P.3d 695 (Okla. 2004).

8. *Bankruptcy data.* Previously, single mothers were no more likely than others to declare bankruptcy; in roughly the last 20 years, however, the numbers have increased by more than 600 percent, with 200,000 single mothers (or one in every 38 and decidedly from the middle class) going bankrupt each year. Elizabeth Warren & Amelia Warren Tyagi, The Two-Income Trap: Why Middle-Class Mothers and Fathers Are Going Broke 105-107 (2003). Such figures reinforce Lenore Weitzman's accusations, supra pp. 594-595, about the impoverishing effect of divorce on women and children. Yet men with alimony and support obligations are also filing for bankruptcy in record numbers, roughly 160,000 annually. Warren & Tyagi, supra, at 120. And more than 300,000 African-American and Hispanic homeowners file for bankruptcy each year. Id. at 159. The three most prevalent reasons for bankruptcies are job loss, family dissolution, and health problems. Id. at 81. Do the 2005 reforms' increased protections for commercial creditors put them in direct competition with women and children trying to collect support obligations? See, e.g., Elizabeth Warren, A Quiet Attack on Women, N.Y. Times, May 20, 2002, at A19.

Note: The Family Home

Frequently, the family home is the most significant marital asset and becomes the focus of the court's effort to effect an equitable distribution of property. Yet this property often serves a support function for the dependent spouse and children.

When one spouse owns the home premaritally as separate property, the other spouse's contributions (financial or homemaking) to its preservation and appreciation can make the increased equity achieved during marriage a divisible asset. See, e.g., Davis v. Davis, 84 S.W.3d 447 (Ark. Ct. App. 2002); Cohen v. Cohen, 937 S.W.2d 823, 833 (Tenn. 1996).

Rules requiring or favoring equal division of marital property often result in the sale of the family home. If the couple has no asset of comparable value to allocate to the spouse not to be awarded the home, the home must be sold so the proceeds can be shared. Dr. Lenore Weitzman helped publicize that such rules disadvantage children. Lenore J. Weitzman, The Divorce Revolution: The Unexpected Social and Economic Consequences of Divorce 384-387 (1985). To remedy this problem, some states allow courts to award the family home, at least temporarily, to the custodial parent, treating use of the residence as a form of child support and reflecting reluctance to uproot the children. See, e.g., Cal. Fam. Code §3802 (West 2004); Mo. Rev. Stat. §452.330.1(1) (2000). See also Nasser-Moghaddassi v. Moghaddassi, 612 S.E.2d 707, 715-718 (S.C. Ct. App. 2005) (distinguishing award of home as marital asset versus as support).

Building on the California statute, the ALI Principles of the Law of Family Dissolution say that child support rules should provide for judicial orders deferring sale of the family residence and that a court may make such order only if it finds that deferral is "economically feasible and would avoid significant detriment to the child." ALI Principles, supra, §3.11. The Principles resolve any conflict between this approach and the presumption of equal division of marital property, supra p. 604, by treating as additional child support "any resulting enhancement in the residential parent's property share" and requiring no adjustment or offset. Id. §4.09(3).

Some commentators would go further. Weitzman, for example, urges legislative directives *requiring* judges to delay the sale of the family residence in the interests of maintaining a stable home for children. Weitzman, supra, at 384-387. See also Martha F. Davis, Comment, The Marital Home: Equal or Equitable Distribution?, 50 U. Chi. L. Rev. 1089 (1983).

When the family home represents a liability (because of a large mortgage), the court can allocate responsibility for the debts. This allocation can occur in the distribution of property. Alternatively, monthly maintenance obligations can include mortgage payments on behalf of a former spouse.

c. Pensions and Employee Benefits

■ BENDER v. BENDER
785 A.2d 197 (Conn. 2001)

BORDEN, J. The principal issue in this certified appeal is whether, in a dissolution action, unvested pension benefits are property subject to equitable distribution. . . . The plaintiff and the defendant, who were married in 1976, have four children, two of whom were minors at the time of trial. . . . The principal cause for the breakdown of the marriage was the fact that nearly all of the defendant's free time was spent in pursuits that did not include the plaintiff or their children, [his] at least one adulterous relationship [, and] some violence on the part of the defendant. Despite the defendant's fairly good income, . . . the parties had acquired virtually no assets and no savings. Furthermore, nearly all of the parties' discretionary income had been expended on the defendant's personal pursuits.

. . . At the time of trial, the defendant had been employed as a firefighter by the city of Meriden for approximately nineteen years. The defendant is entitled to a pension as a firefighter in the event that he reaches twenty-five years of service. His pension, therefore, is unvested, except for purposes of disability. If the defendant were to leave the fire department before twenty-five years of service, other than for a disability, he would receive only his contributions made to the pension, which, at the time of trial, were valued at approximately $27,741.

[The trial court dissolved the marriage, awarded joint custody of the minor children, ordered the defendant to pay child support, issued certain orders of property distribution, and ordered the defendant to pay the plaintiff alimony of $200 per week.] Pursuant to [a] domestic relations order, the trial court ordered "that until such time, if any, as [the] defendant's right to receive retirement benefits from the city of Meriden vests, [the] plaintiff shall be the beneficiary of, and be entitled to receive, the refundable contributions, with accrued interest or yield thereon, if any, made by or on behalf of [the] defendant if such contributions, etc., shall ever become payable by the city of Meriden. And there is hereby entered a [domestic relations order] assigning to [the] plaintiff one half of the disability and/ or retirement benefits earned by [the defendant] from his employment by the city of Meriden for his labors for said city through the date of this decree. (The court is aware that [the] defendant's right to receive retirement benefits has not yet vested.)" [The court made the alimony award modifiable downward in the event plaintiff actually began receiving payments pursuant to the domestic relations order. The defendant appealed.]

I

We distill from the defendant's brief his claim that his unvested pension benefits are not property subject to equitable distribution under §46b-81. The plaintiff claims, to the contrary, that the defendant's interest in his unvested pension benefits is not a mere expectancy, but rather, a presently existing property interest, and, therefore, his unvested pension benefits constitute property subject to equitable distribution. We agree with the plaintiff.

The threshold question of whether unvested pension benefits constitute "property" pursuant to §46b-81 presents a question of statutory interpretation. . . . "The distribution of assets in a dissolution action is governed by §46b-81, which provides in pertinent part that a trial court may assign to either the husband or the wife all or any part of the estate of the other. . . . In fixing the nature and value of *the property*, if any, to be assigned, the court [shall consider a statutory list of factors.] Neither §46b-81 nor any other closely related statute defines property or identifies the types of property interests that are subject to equitable distribution in dissolution proceedings. . . . Black's Law Dictionary (6th Ed. 1990) defines property as the term commonly used to denote everything which is the subject of ownership, corporeal or incorporeal, tangible or intangible, visible or invisible, real or personal; everything that has an exchangeable value or which goes to make up wealth or estate. It extends to every species of valuable right and interest, and includes real and personal property, easements, franchises, and incorporeal hereditaments. . . ."

We repeatedly have stated, and several recent decisions from this court reflect, that trial courts are empowered "to deal broadly with property and its equitable division incident to dissolution proceedings." Although the issue of whether unvested pension benefits are property subject to equitable distribution under §46b-81 is one of first impression for this court, those cases guide our resolution of the present case.

In Thompson v. Thompson, 438 A.2d 839 [(Conn.1981), we considered evidence of the pension benefits but did not treat them as property to be divided.] We reasoned that "[p]ension benefits represent a form of deferred compensation for services rendered. In re Marriage of Brown, 544 P.2d 561 [(Cal. 1976)]. As such they are conceptually similar to wages. . . . " Furthermore, in *Thompson*, we rejected the plaintiff's argument that unvested pension benefits were as speculative as an expected inheritance. Id. [W]e stated: "It is true that the exact amount of the benefits to be received often will depend upon whether the employee survives his retirement age, how long he lives after retirement and what his compensation level is during his remaining years of service. But these contingencies are susceptible to reasonably accurate quantification. . . ." . . .

In Krafick v. Krafick, [663 A.2d 365 (Conn. 1995),] we concluded that *vested* pension benefits constitute property for the purposes of equitable distribution pursuant to §46b-81. In doing so, we emphasized that a broad construction of the term "property" is consistent with the purpose of §46b-81, namely, "to recognize that marriage is, among other things, a shared enterprise or joint undertaking in the nature of a partnership to which both spouses contribute — directly and indirectly, financially and nonfinancially — *the fruits of which* are distributable at divorce." We also recognized, however, that our broad definition of "property," as used in §46b-81, was not without some limitation, and that "§46b-81 applies only to presently existing property interests, not mere expectancies." We thereafter engaged in an analysis whereby we determined that the contingencies to which the vested pension benefits were subject did not render them a mere expectancy because the holder of the benefits had a presently existing interest by way of an enforceable contract right. . . .

[Our] cases reflect a common theme, namely, that in determining whether a certain interest is property subject to equitable distribution under §46b-81, we look to whether a party's expectation of a benefit attached to that interest was too speculative to constitute divisible marital property. . . . In accordance with the purposes of §46b-81, our adherence to that theme has outweighed our adherence to strict contract or property principles in determining whether a certain interest constitutes property for purposes of equitable distribution. Traditional property principles, although relevant[,] are not determinative of whether an interest constitutes property under §46b-81. . . .

In the present case, it is, of course, theoretically possible that the defendant's pension will not vest, whether because of the defendant's resignation, misconduct on his part that results in his dismissal, the defendant's death, or a decision on the part of the municipality to discontinue the pension plan. We conclude, however, that the defendant's expectation in his pension plan, as a practical matter, is sufficiently concrete, reasonable and justifiable as to constitute a presently existing property interest for equitable distribution purposes. Therefore, his unvested pension benefits are not too speculative to be considered property subject to equitable distribution under §46b-81. We believe that any uncertainty regarding vesting is more appropriately handled in the valuation and distribution stages, rather than in the classification stage.

Our conclusion that the defendant's unvested pension benefits are not a mere expectancy is consistent with the nature of retirement benefits, and the fact that employers and employees treat retirement benefits as property in the workplace. We previously have stated [in *Krafick*, supra] that "pension benefits represent a form of deferred compensation for services rendered" because an employee earning pension benefits presumably would receive higher current wages if he or she did not participate in the pension plan. . . .

Furthermore, the theme running through this area of our jurisprudence . . . pays mindful consideration to the equitable purpose of our statutory distribution scheme, rather than to mechanically applied rules of property law. In order to achieve justice, equity looks to substance, and not to mere form. In view of that equitable purpose, the fact remains that nineteen of the twenty-five years necessary for the vesting of the defendant's pension benefits were years in which the parties were partners in marriage. We recognize that retirement benefits, whether vested or unvested, are significant marital assets, and may be, as in the present case, the only significant marital asset. To consider the pension benefits a nondivisible marital asset would be to blink our eyes at reality.

The defendant argues that the portion of his pension benefits that "would result from [his] future labors" is not subject to equitable distribution, and that the only portion subject to equitable distribution is the amount of the contributions in the fund at the time of dissolution. We disagree. The fact that a portion of the pension benefits, once vested, will represent the defendant's service to the fire department after the dissolution does not preclude us from classifying the entire unvested pension as marital property.

We disagree with the dissent that we have, by this analysis, overruled our prior cases. . . . We also reject the dissent's suggestion that the analysis we employ here is inconsistent with our decision in Rubin v. Rubin, [527 A.2d 1184 (Conn. 1987)]. *Rubin* involved a potential inheritance, which, by its nature, is dependent on "the unquantifiable aspects of human nature which often cause wills to be revised." Unvested pension benefits, however, although dependent on certain future contingencies such as length of service and age, are simply not in that same speculative category. Moreover, unlike a potential inheritance, pension benefits represent a trade-off for potentially higher wages not earned during the marriage; they often represent, as in the present case, the only or principal material asset; and they are treated by employers and employees as property in the workplace. Thus, they represent the fruits of the marital partnership in practical and emotional ways not shared by potential inheritances.

II

Having concluded that unvested pension benefits are property for equitable distribution under §46b-81, we next address the methods available to value and distribute such benefits. . . . First, the present value or immediate offset approach "'requires the court to determine the present value of the pension benefits, decide the portion to which the nonemployee spouse is entitled, and award other property to the nonemployee spouse as an offset to the pension benefits to which he or she is otherwise entitled.' . . . '" The present value approach has the advantage of effecting a severance of the parties' economic ties. The present value approach also avoids extended supervision and enforcement by the courts, thereby saving the parties and the courts the time and expense of future litigation.

The major weakness of this approach is that it requires the court to base its division of the unvested pension benefits upon actuarial probabilities rather than actual events. . . . Stated another way, if the present value approach is applied and the pension never vests, the nonowning spouse will have received, at the time of dissolution, other property in return for a share in a pension that never yields an actual benefit. "Further, this method is not feasible when there are insufficient other assets by which to offset the value of the pension. If there are sufficient other assets, however, several courts have favored this approach. . . ." . . .

"The second and third recognized methods for valuing and distributing pensions involve delaying distribution until the pension matures. Under the 'present division' method, the trial court determines at the time of trial, the percentage share of the pension benefits to which the nonemployee spouse is entitled. . . . In other words, the court will declare that, upon maturity, a fixed percentage of the pension be distributed to each spouse. [U]nder the 'reserved jurisdiction' method, . . . the trial court reserves jurisdiction to distribute the pension until benefits have matured. *Once matured*, the trial court will determine the proper share to which each party is entitled and divide the benefits accordingly."

A significant advantage to the deferred distribution approaches is that, because they delay distribution until the pension benefits have vested and matured, they impose equally on the parties the risk of forfeiture. . . . One disadvantage of delaying distribution of the pension benefits is "the cost of prolonging the parties' entanglement with each other. . . ." . . . Although the advantages of the reserved jurisdiction approach are the same as those of the deferred distribution method, there are serious costs and uncertainties that result therefrom: (1) the court must hold a second hearing in order to determine the percentage to which the nonemployee spouse is entitled; and (2) witnesses must testify to events that occurred long ago. [The court concludes that trial judges have discretion on a case-by-case basis to choose the present value method, the present division method of deferred distribution, or any other method that facilitates equitable division; the court, however, expressly rejects the reserved jurisdiction method because the statute bars retained jurisdiction over orders for lump sum alimony or property division.]

ZARELLA, J., dissenting.

The majority overrules a long line of prior decisions that defines the meaning of property for purposes of General Statutes §46b-81. Because I believe that any redefinition is more appropriately the function of the legislature, I respectfully dissent. . . .

The majority correctly recognizes the three part analysis that a trial court must employ when effecting the distribution of property upon dissolution [determining (1) whether the interest is property subject to equitable distribution; (2) whether the interest reasonably could be valued; and, (3) if so, what is the most appropriate method of valuation. The majority, however,] collapses the classification stage of the analysis into the valuation stage, concluding that, if an expectation can be valued, then it is not speculative but, rather, is transformed into property subject to equitable distribution. . . .

Had the court in [Rubin v. Rubin, 527 A.2d 1184 (Conn. 1987),] analyzed the plaintiff's expected inheritance and trust interests according to the majority's test, we would have had to conclude that such interests were property available for distribution pursuant to §46b-81. [I]nasmuch as the majority concludes that the unvested pension benefits are property subject to equitable distribution, it allows for [deferred distribution]. Under the deferred distribution method, the trial court orders a contingent award of expected property, a result that we previously had rejected in *Rubin*. . . .

[A]lthough unvested pension benefits should not be classified as property subject to equitable distribution, §46b-81(c) requires the trial court to *consider* them in fashioning property distribution orders at the time of dissolution. When a pension benefit becomes vested and is in payment status, the trial court may treat this situation as a changed circumstance warranting a modification of an award of periodic alimony under §46b-86. This approach remains faithful to the case law, the language of the relevant statutes and the legislative intent to expand the resources available for equitable distribution. . . .

Notes and Questions

1. *Majority rule.* *Bender* exemplifies the majority rule that nonvested, as well as vested, pensions are marital property subject to division upon dissolution.

2. *Rationale.* What arguments support recognition of vested pensions as marital assets? Nonvested pensions? Are pension benefits "gifts" by the employer? See Daigre v. Daigre, 83 So. 2d 900 (La. 1955). Do they constitute mere expectancies, rather than property interests? How does the *Bender* majority answer this question? The dissent? Should a court consider such contingent interests in determining support rather than property distribution? Does the nonemployee spouse suffer a compensable loss under the ALI Principles, supra, when divorce thwarts the opportunity to enjoy these future benefits?

The landmark case In re Marriage of Brown, 544 P.2d 561 (Cal. 1976), established the majority rule. In *Brown*, a couple divorced after a 24-year marriage, but three years prior to the husband's eligibility for retirement. The husband argued that his nonvested pension rights were not divisible as a community asset. In ruling for the wife, *Brown* overturned a long line of decisions holding nonvested pension rights a "mere expectancy" not subject to division. Justice Tobriner described pension benefits as a form of "deferred compensation" based on the employment contract, a form of property. Id. at 565. *Brown* also noted the unfairness of classifying unvested pensions as separate property. Alimony cannot rectify this unfairness because the spouse "should not be dependent on the discretion of the court . . . to provide her with the equivalent of what should be hers as a matter of absolute right." 544 P.2d at 567.

Courts now use identical analysis to treat unvested stock options as divisible property. See, e.g., Baccanti v. Morton, 752 N.E.2d 718 (Mass. 2001); Fisher v. Fisher, 769 A.2d 1165 (Pa. 2001).

3. *Integrating state and federal law.* Pension plans increasingly play an important role upon dissolution as an asset subject to distribution or as a source of funds for meeting needs and support obligations. Pension benefits (in addition to the marital home) constitute the most significant marital asset for many couples. Nonetheless, courts recognize that equitable division requires considering the speculative and nonmarketable nature of pension rights, regardless of their value. See Blanchard v. Blanchard, 731 So. 2d 175 (La. 1999) (holding inequitable an award of residence to husband and pension rights to wife despite similar value).

a. *Types of plans.* A pension plan is a mechanism by which an employer facilitates an employee's accumulation of savings for retirement. Pension plans may be "qualified" or "nonqualified."[19] Under a qualified plan, the employee defers

---

[19]. The term "qualified plan" simply describes a private plan that qualifies for favorable tax treatment under the Internal Revenue Code, I.R.C. §401(a) (West Supp. 2005). Under such plans, the employer gets an immediate deduction of the employer's contribution, and investments of earnings accumulate tax free.

taxation on the employer's contribution until the funds are distributed during retirement.

Deferred compensation plans may be either defined benefit plans or defined contribution plans. The former provide a fixed dollar amount, usually monthly, payable to the participant upon retirement. The exact benefit is defined by formulae that take into account such factors as age, length of service, and average salary (often the highest average salary for a three- or five-year period).

In contrast, defined contribution plans (of which one popular type is called a "401(k) plan," pursuant to the relevant provision of the Internal Revenue Code), do not provide for payment of a fixed sum upon retirement. Rather, these benefits are based on the employer's (and sometimes the participant's) contributions to the plan. Unlike defined benefit plan funds, defined contribution plan funds are held in a separate account for each participant. The contribution formulae for these plans vary. Some promise a specified annual contribution (for example, a money-purchase plan providing 10 percent of current compensation), while profit-sharing plans may tie the employer's total contribution to current or accumulated profits or may leave the amount to the discretion of the board of directors.

b. *Federal regulation of private pension plans: ERISA.* The Employee Retirement Income Security Act of 1974 (ERISA), 29 U.S.C.A. §§1001 et seq. (West 1999 & Supp. 2005), protects employee retirement benefits through comprehensive federal regulation of private pension plans. The statute expressly preempts state law. With important exceptions for government and church plans, ERISA applies to (1) plans that systematically defer cash compensation until termination of employment or longer ("employee pension benefit plans") and (2) plans providing, inter alia, health care benefits, death and disability benefits, day care centers, and prepaid legal services ("employee welfare benefit plans"). See Peter J. Wiedenbeck, Implementing ERISA: Of Policies and "Plans," 72 Wash. U. L.Q. 559, 564-565 (1994).

c. *REA: QDROs.* Under ERISA, as originally enacted, a nonemployee spouse (for example, the wife of a covered employee) had limited rights to share in the employee's pension upon dissolution,[20] as the result of an "anti-alienation rule" barring assignment or alienation of pension plan benefits (although not welfare plan benefits). See ERISA §206(d)(1), 29 U.S.C. §1056(d)(1) (2000). This protective policy ensures that the participant cannot consume retirement savings before retirement. ERISA made no exceptions for domestic relations claims against an employee's pension plan. In the wake of ERISA, federal and state courts split on whether the anti-alienation rule barred distribution of pension benefits to a non-employee spouse upon divorce.

The Retirement Equity Act of 1984 (REA or REAct) sought to remedy this and other problems experienced particularly by women. REA mandates that ERISA's anti-alienation rule must yield to certain state domestic relations decrees and permits a court to divide pension benefits in the same manner as other marital assets. That is, REA amends ERISA to provide for the enforcement of "qualified domestic relations orders" or QDROs and removes such orders from ERISA's preemption scheme. See ERISA §§206(d)(3), 514(b)(7), 29 U.S.C. §§1056(d)(3), 1144(b)(7)

---

[20]. ERISA, similarly, failed to protect the spouse of a plan participant who died before reaching the plan's retirement age. REA amendments extended protection by providing a "qualified preretirement survivor annuity" or QPSA when the employee spouse had any vested benefits. ERISA §205(a)(2), 29 U.S.C. §1055 (2000 & Supp. II 2002).

(2000). QDROs facilitate the enforcement of awards of spousal support and child support by authorizing retirement plan administrators to make payments directly to a former spouse.

Under the Act, "qualified domestic relations order" means a domestic relations order "which creates or recognizes the existence of an alternate payee's right to, or assigns to an alternate payee the right to, receive all or a portion of the benefits payable with respect to a participant under a plan"; for purposes of this provision, a domestic relations order is a judgment, decree, or order "which relates to the provision of child support, alimony payments, or marital property rights to a spouse, former spouse, child, or other dependent of a participant," made "pursuant to a State domestic relations law (including a community property law)." ERISA §206(d)(3)(B), 29 U.S.C. §1056(d)(3)(B) (2000).

A QDRO thus recognizes the right of another person (the "alternate payee") to receive benefits under a pension plan. That is, the "alternate payee" is treated as a beneficiary under the plan. REA defines an "alternate payee" as "any spouse, former spouse, child, or other dependent of a participant who is recognized by a domestic relations order as having a right to receive all, or a portion of, the benefits payable under a plan with respect to such participant." ERISA §206(d)(3)(K), 29 U.S.C. §1056(d)(3)(K) (2000).

To qualify as a plan beneficiary under a QDRO, the nonemployee spouse must obtain a state court decree (not merely a separation agreement), which specifies the extent to which the plan participant's liability shall be paid from pension assets. Note that pension assets can be distributed under a QDRO not only for property division but also for spousal and child support obligations. Although QDROs facilitate collection of divorce awards by directing retirement plan administrators to make payments directly to the "alternate payee," QDROs have several limitations. The extent of the nonemployee spouse's benefits is governed by those of the employee spouse — that is, the former spouse may not obtain a lump sum distribution, for example, if such an option is not available to the employee spouse. Similarly, if the nonemployee spouse is divorced from an employee whose pension benefits are already subject to a QDRO from a prior divorce, the first ex-spouse will prevail.

d. *Federal pension benefits.* Federal retirement benefit plans cover certain government employees. Both the United States Supreme Court and Congress have addressed the question whether state divorce laws apply to benefits under these plans or whether federal law preempts the field. The Court initially favored federal preemption, with the result that state divorce courts could not award any benefits to the nonemployee spouse. See Hisquierdo v. Hisquierdo, 439 U.S. 572 (1979) (railroad employees' benefits); McCarty v. McCarty, 453 U.S. 210 (1981) (military retirement benefits). Congress, however, later enacted corrective legislation. 45 U.S.C. §231a(c)(4) (2000) (amendments to Railroad Retirement Act extending benefits to divorced spouses married to railroad employee for at least ten years, among other conditions); 10 U.S.C.A. §1408 (West 1998 & Supp. 2005) (Uniformed Services Former Spouses Protection Act overruling retroactively *McCarty* to permit state courts to apply their laws to military retirement benefits upon divorce, with enforcement mechanism available under certain conditions). Feminist commentators have been especially critical of the initial preemption policy. To what extent does this policy reflect gender bias, protecting pensioners (usually husbands) at the expense of needy spouses (usually wives) and reflecting the traditional belief that assets belong only to the spouse who earns them? See, e.g., Sylvia Law, Families and Federalism, 4 Wash. U. J.L. & Pol'y 175, 203 (2000).[21]

As a matter of policy, should military retirement benefits receive different treatment from any other retirement benefits? How does military service differ from other employment? What implications does that difference have for the contributions of the other spouse? Suppose after the judgment dividing the military pension, the military spouse converts the retirement pay to disability pay, which state courts have no authority to divide? See Black v. Black, 842 A.2d 1280 (Me. 2004). Just as Congress changed the initial rule governing certain federal employees (so that now awards to the nonemployee spouse are permitted), should Congress revisit the issue of such military disability pay? The statute that disallows assignment of social security benefits? See 42 U.S.C. §407 (2000). Cf. Neville v. Neville, 791 N.E.2d 434 (Ohio 2003) (although social security benefits are not divisible, a court can consider them as a factor in achieving equitable result).

e. *Pension valuation.* Pension valuation presents complex problems often requiring the assistance of actuarial experts. *Bender* canvasses the available approaches. Do these approaches reveal the speculative nature of unvested pension benefits, as the dissent contends? Which approach best achieves the objectives of equitable division? See generally Brett Turner, Equitable Distribution of Property §6.12 (2d ed. 1994 & Supp. 2004).

Problems

1. Karen and Robert divorced after 26 years of marriage. Karen, a part-time secretary for a church, was earning $645 per month; Robert, an employee of Miller Brewing Co., was earning $2,900 per month. In the division of marital property, Robert got his pension, valued at $11,355, and Karen got other property of roughly the same value (but no interest in Robert's pension). The court ordered Robert to pay Karen $600 per month maintenance. After taking voluntary retirement at age 55, Robert now seeks to terminate maintenance payments, arguing he has no income available. Karen seeks to continue maintenance, arguing that the $2,700 per month Robert gets from his pension is income available for maintenance. What result and why? Is it unfair "double-counting" to consider Robert's pension plan both as an asset in the property division and as income for maintenance payments? See In re Marriage of Olski, 540 N.W.2d 412 (Wis. 1995); In re Marriage of Wettstaedt, 625 N.W.2d 900 (Wis. Ct. App. 2001).

2. David, an employee of the Boeing Corporation in Washington, designated his wife, Donna, as the beneficiary of both a life insurance policy and a pension plan provided by his employer. The couple divorced, and two months later David died intestate in an automobile accident, without ever having changed the beneficiary designation. Under Washington law, however, divorce automatically revokes the designation of a spouse as the beneficiary of a nonprobate asset.

When benefits are paid to Donna under the plans, David's children from a previous marriage sue, invoking the Washington statute and claiming that they

---

[21]. Note that some statutes exempt certain state employees' pensions from classification as marital property, e.g., teachers' pensions. See Woodson v. Woodson, 92 S.W.3d 780, 783 (Mo. 2003); Susan J. Prather, Comment, Characterization, Valuation, and Distribution of Pensions at Divorce, 15 J. Am. Acad. Matrim. Law. 443, 449-451 (1998).

should receive the benefits as David's heirs at law. ERISA governs both of the employee benefit plans in question. ERISA's express preemption clause, which Donna argues applies, says that ERISA "shall supercede any and all State laws insofar as they may now or hereafter relate to any employee benefit plan" covered by ERISA. What result and why? As a matter of policy, is the question one that federal or state legislation should control? On these facts, what role, if any, should the REA's purpose of protecting divorced spouses play? See Egelhoff v. Egelhoff, 532 U.S. 141 (2001). See also Boggs v. Boggs, 520 U.S. 833 (1997).

Note: Medical Coverage Following Dissolution (COBRA)

An important issue for many spouses upon dissolution, especially home-makers, is securing the continuation of medical benefits. Congressional concern about the high cost of medical insurance and its unavailability for dependent ex-spouses resulted in the 1985 enactment of the Consolidated Omnibus Budget Reconciliation Act (COBRA), adding §§601-608 to ERISA and subsequent amend-ments thereto. See 29 U.S.C.A. §§1161-1168 (West 1999 & Supp. 2005).

COBRA requires, inter alia, employers of more than 20 employees to offer continued medical coverage at group rates to "qualified beneficiaries" who would otherwise lose benefits upon the occurrence of certain "qualified events." Qualified beneficiaries (a class including employees and their dependents) may make "elec-tions" for continuation of the same coverage. A "qualified event" includes divorce or legal separation. A spouse is entitled to continued coverage for 36 months following the date of divorce or legal separation. Coverage may not be conditioned on evidence of insurability. The qualified beneficiary must pay the required pre-miums after the COBRA election.

d. Investments in a Spouse's Future Success: Degrees, Earning Capacity, and Goodwill

■ **IN RE MARRIAGE OF ROBERTS**
670 N.E.2d 72 (Ind. Ct. App. 1996)

GARRARD, Judge. . . .

[Matthew and Leigh Anne Roberts] were married on June 24, 1989. In the fall of 1990, Matthew began attending the Valparaiso University Law School as a full-time student. Before law school, Matthew had been employed at Society Bank in South Bend, Indiana and had been earning a salary of $30,000.00 per year at the time he left employment. Matthew and Leigh Anne agreed that Matthew should quit working and attend school full-time while Leigh Anne continued to work to support them. Leigh Anne also assumed primary responsibility for running the household so that Matthew could devote all of his time to his studies.

Two months before Matthew's graduation Leigh Anne learned that she was pregnant, and thereafter the couple separated. Matthew finished third in his grad-uating class and also served as editor-in-chief of the Valparaiso Law Review. After graduation, he took an associate position with a large law firm in Chicago, Illinois. He filed his petition for dissolution of marriage on August 4, 1993.

The major asset of the parties was the marital home, valued at $70,000.00 with a mortgage of $63,245.00. The parties also owned certain personal property and each had 401(k) accounts and IRA accounts. The court determined that Matthew's law degree could not be considered a marital asset subject to distribution. However, the court did include Matthew's student loans, totaling $22,500.00, in valuing the marital estate, and the court found repayment to be the sole responsibility of Matthew. The court determined that, based upon the student loans, the disproportionate earnings history and the earning potential of the parties, the presumption of equal distribution had been rebutted. The court [allocated to Matthew $22,084.96 total assets and $24,500 total debts, resulting in a net debt of $2,415.04; it allocated to Leigh Anne $90,779.98 total assets and $65,245.00 total debts, amounting to net assets of $25,534.98].

Leigh Anne first argues that the trial court should have included Matthew's law degree as a marital asset subject to distribution. . . .

The specific issue of whether a degree obtained during a marriage by one party may be considered marital property upon divorce was addressed in Prenatt v. Stevens, 598 N.E.2d 616 (Ind. Ct. App. 1992), *trans. denied*. In *Prenatt*, the trial court found that the wife's doctoral degree in English, which was obtained during the marriage, was a marital asset. This determination was reversed on appeal, with the court relying upon Wilcox v. Wilcox, 173 Ind. App. 661, 365 N.E.2d 792 (1977) and In re Marriage of McManama, 272 Ind. 483, 399 N.E.2d 371 (1980). In *Wilcox*, the court first noted that any award over and above the assets of the marriage must represent some form of support or maintenance. The court then held that the husband's future earnings could not be considered a marital asset as there was no vested present interest in such income. In *McManama*, the trial court had awarded the wife a lump sum in the amount she had contributed to help her husband obtain his advanced degree on the theory that there had been a dissipation of marital property. Our supreme court reversed, finding that the award was in actuality an award to be paid from the husband's future income. Such an award of future income could only be proper as either support or maintenance, and there was no evidence of any incapacity to support such an award.

Based upon this precedent, *Prenatt* concluded that, despite the legislature's intent for "property" to be interpreted as broadly inclusive, a degree simply does not possess the common characteristics of property:

> A degree is an intangible which is personal to the holder. It is a piece of paper and has no real value except for what the holder chooses to pursue with it. Potential worth is dependent upon choice and availability of work, whether the holder is good at what she does, or a myriad of other potentialities.
>
> Valuation of a degree is fraught with uncertainty because of the personal factors described above. Even if valuation could be made certain, such valuation, whether based on future earning capacity or upon cost of acquisition, would ultimately result in an award beyond the actual physical assets of the marriage. As noted in *Wilcox* and *McManama*, such award is improper.

Prenatt, 598 N.E.2d at 620.

The only statutory exception is I.C. §31-1-11.5-11(d), which states:

> When the court finds there is little or no marital property, it may award either spouse a money judgment not limited to the property existing at the time of final

separation. However, this award may be made only for the financial contribution of one (1) spouse toward tuition, books, and laboratory fees for the higher education of the other spouse.

Thus, a spouse may be reimbursed, even above the assets of the marital estate, but reimbursement is strictly limited.

We agree with the finding in *Prenatt* that a degree does not constitute marital property. While the maintenance statute does not permit any type of "reimbursement maintenance," the enhanced earning ability of a degree-earning spouse may certainly be considered in making a division of the marital assets. See I.C. §31-1-11.5-11(c)(3), (5) (factors which court may consider in rebutting presumption of an equal division of property include the economic circumstances of each spouse and the earnings or earning ability of the parties); see also *Prenatt*, 598 N.E.2d at 622 (Garrard, J., concurring) ("It should be pointed out that the educational achievements and potential earning life referred to by the court in its findings *do* constitute a valid consideration and basis for determining the appropriate disposition of the marital assets. . . .") (emphasis in original).

Therefore, while Indiana does not permit a degree to be included as marital property, and further will not allow an award of future earnings unless the spouse qualifies for maintenance, nevertheless the earning ability of the degree-earning spouse may be considered in determining the distribution of the marital estate. . . .

Leigh Anne also argues that the trial court should have made an award to compensate her for the dissipation of the marital estate by Matthew as a result of the income which the family was deprived of while Matthew attended law school and the contributions Leigh Anne made toward Matthew's education and the household living expenses. [W]e must respond that in employing the term "dissipation," our legislature intended that it carry its common meaning denoting "foolishly" or "aimlessly." Thus, under the circumstances of this case it cannot be said that the money expended in order to secure Matthew's law degree was dissipated, even though Leigh Anne did not receive the benefits she expected therefrom. . . .

Finally, Leigh Anne argues that, if Matthew's law degree is not to be considered a marital asset then, correspondingly, Matthew's student loans should not be considered marital liabilities. We disagree. The student loans were contracted during the marriage and were properly considered as part of the marital estate. Moreover, the court quite properly determined that Matthew should be solely responsible for their repayment. Leigh Anne suffered no harm whatever from their inclusion in the marital pot and the order that Matthew be solely responsible for their repayment. . . .

We affirm the judgment. . . .

■ JOAN WILLIAMS, IS COVERTURE DEAD? BEYOND A NEW THEORY OF ALIMONY
82 Geo. L.J. 2227, 2267-2272, 2274-2275 (1994)

Despite some early support for using the language of property to address the issue of post-divorce impoverishment, it is an article of faith among many family law courts and scholars today that property language is out of place and inherently unconvincing in this context. This dismissal is ironic because . . . conclusions about ownership are inevitable; the only question is whether the family wage will continue to be awarded one-sidely to the husband. The disagreement is not over whether the family wage will be owned, but over who shall own it.

[T]he courts' and commentators' rejection of property language in this context reflects its linkage with arguments of human capital theorists. Such arguments generally have failed to persuade courts, leading many family law scholars to conclude that property rhetoric has failed them. In fact, property rhetoric is not the problem; human capital theory is. . . .

The typical degree case involves a wife who supported her husband through professional school and who claims "property in his degree" when he divorces her shortly after graduation. Courts, with few exceptions, have rejected wives' claims that the degrees are marital property, often using broad language to the effect that human capital does not have the attributes traditionally associated with property. To justify this rejection, courts rely on the traditional Blackstonian image of property rights as the absolute dominion of people over things. This imagery, however, was never an accurate description of property law, and was formally abandoned in the First Restatement of Property in 1936. The 1936 Restatement adopted instead Wesley Hohfeld's view that property rights defined the relationships among people with respect to some valuable interest. The image is not of "absolute" ownership but of an evolving set of claims, in which courts attach the name "property" as a signal they have accepted someone's claim. . . .

[In most degree cases, the] court starts out with a pre-defined notion of what "property" entails. It then inquires whether a degree "fits" that image. Upon deciding that it does not, it concludes that no property right exists in the wife. . . . In contrast to the Hohfeldian view's message that "property" is a word courts use to signal their legal conclusion that someone has an entitlement, the [court's] language sends the message that judges play no active role in determining entitlements. But they do. Conclusions about property are legal conclusions, made in a context where the court has to allocate the asset to someone. . . .

Many modern property rights . . . clash with a model of absolute, alienable, inheritable, and exchangeable entitlements. Examples are pensions and goodwill which are widely recognized as property despite their lack of heritability and their status as income streams provided by "many years of . . . hard work." . . . Courts' refusal to recognize "new property" rights in the context of the family stems not from the logic of property, but from unstated assumptions about who is entitled to what. . . .

If the courts' projected image of property rights is so inaccurate and their property theory half a century out of date, why have the degree cases proved so convincing? . . . Family court judges, almost by definition, are successful lawyers. Most are men who have conformed to an ideal worker pattern in a profession notorious for long hours. This workaholic culture tends to marginalize the ideal workers' wives, as they assume more and more family responsibilities to allow for their husbands' "success." It is also the (upper-middle) class context in which the ideology of gender equality is strongest. In short, the judges in degree cases are heavily invested in the polite fiction — observed in most intact marriages — that the husband's career success and the wife's marginalization both result not from a system that privileges ideal workers who can command a flow of domestic services from women, but from the idiosyncracies of two individuals residing in the republic of choice.[231]

The degree cases also reflect judges' sense that they worked long and hard for their degrees. Their reaction is colored by their struggles in law school and their sense that they have earned everything they have achieved through their own hard work. That degree holders worked long and hard is not the issue. So did their wives, both in the home and (often) at boring, dead-end jobs, passing up opportunities for better positions. The issue is not who worked hard, but whose hard work gives rise to entitlements. . . .

Notes and Questions

1. *Majority rule.* *Roberts* follows the majority of courts in refusing to treat advanced degrees and professional licenses, as well as the enhanced earning capacity therefrom, as property. Hence, the supporting spouse's contribution does not make them divisible assets upon divorce. See, e.g., Stevens v. Stevens, 492 N.E.2d 131 (Ohio 1986); Becker v. Perkins-Becker, 669 A.2d 524 (R.I. 1996). Is Professor Williams's explanation for this rule persuasive? See also Alicia Brokars Kelly, Rehabilitating Partnership Marriage as a Theory of Wealth Distribution at Divorce: In Recognition of a Shared Life, 19 Wis. Women's L.J. 141, 163-166 (2004) (criticizing majority view, which property law does not compel).

Roberts states, however, that Matthew's enhanced earning capacity is a factor in the distribution of property and approves a disproportionate division favoring Leigh Anne. Is this approach fair? Suppose the couple had spent everything on the husband's degree, without accumulating any assets? Does the statute quoted in *Roberts* (now Ind. Code Ann. §31-15-7-6 (West 1999)) solve the problem?

2. *Maintenance as a remedy?* If the couple has no assets to divide, should a court recognize the supporting spouse's contribution by awarding maintenance? Does Leigh Anne *need* support? See also Hodge v. Hodge, 520 A.2d 15, 18 (Pa. 1986) (purpose of alimony is "rehabilitation not reimbursement"). In contrast to *Roberts*, other cases have used maintenance to provide a remedy. E.g., Guy v. Guy, 736 So. 2d 1042 (Miss. 1999) (lump sum alimony); Mahoney v. Mahoney, 453 A.2d 527 (N.J. 1982) ("reimbursement alimony"). See also Meyer v. Meyer, 620 N.W.2d 382 (Wis. 2000) (allowing maintenance remedy when contributions to education occurred to during couple's premarital cohabitation).

3. *A fair result by any means.* Some courts have used a frankly flexible approach, stating that achieving a fair result is more important than whether a traditional "property" or "alimony" label fits. In Washburn v. Washburn, 677 P.2d 152 (Wash. 1984) (en banc), the court declined to identify the husband's veterinary degree as property but went on to say:

> . . . A professional degree confers high earning potential upon the holder. The student spouse should not walk away with this valuable advantage without compensating the person who helped him or her obtain it.

---

231. [See Joan Williams, Gender Wars: Selfless Women in the Republic of Choice, 66 N.Y.U. L. Rev. 1559, 1562-1608 (1991).] The relatively few female judges may be high-human-capital women who may not be sympathetic to the claims of mothers marginalized by motherhood. Id. at 1597-98, 1605-06.

[T]he supporting spouse may be compensated through a division of property and liabilities. In many cases, however, the wealth of the marriage will have been spent toward the cost of the professional degree, leaving few or no assets to divide. Where the assets of the parties are insufficient to permit compensation to be effected entirely through property division, a supplemental award of maintenance is appropriate.

[W]e recognize that the spouse who is capable of supporting someone through school will in most cases also be capable of supporting him or herself after the marriage is dissolved. However, under the extremely flexible provisions of [the statute], a demonstrated capacity of self-support does not automatically preclude an award of maintenance. Indeed, the ability of the spouse seeking maintenance to meet his or her needs independently is only one factor to be considered. . . . Moreover, the factors listed in the statute are not exclusive. . . .

Under our opinion today, Mrs. Washburn may be entitled to an award as compensation for her contribution to her husband's education. Such compensation may be effected through property division, maintenance or a combination of both. . . .

Id. at 158, 161. Despite the Washington Supreme Court's lack of concern about the "label" for Mrs. Washburn's award, what difference will the label make? Suppose Mrs. Washburn remarries. See supra section D2a. Suppose her former husband files for a Chapter 13 bankruptcy. See supra section D2b.

4. *Unjust enrichment?* Does the limited remedy of reimbursement for financial contributions (under the statute quoted in *Roberts*) result in unjust enrichment for the supported spouse? Does an analysis based on unjust enrichment require consideration of fault? Does the supporting spouse deserve compensation not just for financial contributions but also for the loss of a return on the investment in the supported spouse's career? How should a court treat debts from the supported spouse's student loans? See generally Milton C. Regan Jr., Alone Together: Law and the Meanings of Marriage 148-161 (1999); Margaret F. Brinig, Property Distribution Physics: The Talisman of Time and Middle Class Law, 31 Fam. L.Q. 93 (1997); Jana B. Singer, Husbands, Wives and Human Capital: Why the Shoe Won't Fit, 31 Fam. L.Q. 119 (1997).

5. *Valuation.* Under the more flexible approach approved in *Washburn*, supra, how does a judge compute a fair result? One court approved the following approaches: (a) a "cost value approach" by which the court calculates the supporting spouse's contributions (including services) during the marriage; (b) an "opportunity-costs approach" under which the court considers income sacrificed because the student spouse attended school instead of working; (c) a return on investment theory that compensates the supporting spouse according to the present value of the student spouse's enhanced earning capacity; and (d) consideration of the supporting spouse's contribution at one-half of the student spouse's enhanced yearly earning power for the time during which the supporting spouse supported the other spouse. Haugan v. Haugan, 343 N.W.2d 796, 802-803 (Wis. 1984). The concurrence in *Haugan* rejected the third approach because of its reliance on future earning potential. Cf. Katherine Wells Meighan, For Better or For Worse: A Corporate Finance Approach to Valuing Educational Decrees at Divorce, 5 Geo. Mason L. Rev. 193 (1997); Elizabeth S. Scott & Robert E. Scott, Marriage as Relational Contract, 84 Va. L. Rev. 1225, 1275-1277, 1319-1323 (1998).

6. *Attitudes of married professionals.* What remedy would married individuals themselves find fair? According to an empirical study of professional students and their spouses:

> [W]hen a spouse 1) provides monetary support, 2) makes a personal sacrifice, 3) divorces shortly after the spouse attains a degree, leaving few assets to divide, and 4) possesses a lower earning capacity than the professional spouse, participants feel that the supporting spouse deserves recompense. Furthermore, the results show that if some or all of these factors are present in a marriage, *both* spouses think that the supporting spouse should be compensated.

Rebecca Redosh Eisner & Ruth Zimmerman, Note, Individual Entitlement to the Financial Benefits of a Professional Degree: An Empirical Study of the Attitudes and Expectations of Married Professional Students and Their Spouses, 22 U. Mich. J.L. Ref. 333, 363 (1989).

7. *New York's property treatment.* In contrast to the majority approach, New York treats degrees and professional licenses as property subject to equitable division, based on the legislature's definition of marital property. In O'Brien v. O'Brien, 489 N.E.2d 712 (N.Y. 1985), the court explained:

> [The statute] provides that in making an equitable distribution of marital property, "the court shall consider: . . . (6) any equitable claim to, interest in, or direct or indirect contribution made to the acquisition of such marital property by the party not having title, including joint efforts or expenditures and contributions and services as a spouse, parent, wage earner and homemaker, and *to the career or career potential* of the other party [and] . . . (9) the impossibility or difficulty of evaluating any component asset or any interest in a business, corporation or *profession*" (Domestic Relations Law §236[B][5][d][6], [9] [emphasis added]). Where equitable distribution of marital property is appropriate but "the distribution of an interest in a business, corporation or *profession* would be contrary to law" the court shall make a distributive award in lieu of an actual distribution of the property (Domestic Relations Law §236[B][5][e] [emphasis added]). The words mean exactly what they say: that an interest in a profession or professional career potential is marital property which may be represented by direct or indirect contributions of the non-title-holding spouse, including financial contributions and nonfinancial contributions made by caring for the home and family.

Id. at 715-716. Under this approach, the supporting spouse should get an "equitable portion" of this property, based on the present value of "the enhanced earning capacity it affords the holder." Id. at 718. Few other courts define property so expansively. E.g., Postema v. Postema, 471 N.W.2d 912 (Mich. Ct. App. 1991); In re Marriage of Denton, 951 P.2d 693 (Or. 1998). New York has adhered to this approach even when the marriage endures well past the degree date so that both spouses enjoyed the enhanced earning capacity it created. See Holterman v. Holterman, 814 N.E.2d 765, 779-780, 783 (N.Y. 2004) (Smith, J., dissenting). Should courts extend the New York law further to encompass enhanced earning capacity acquired with the help of the other spouse but not based on a degree or license? See Sebastian Weiss, Note, Preventing Inequities in Divorce and Education: The Equitable Distribution of a Career Absent an Advanced Degree or License, 9 Cardozo Women's L.J. 133 (2002).

Property awards are nonmodifiable, and bankruptcy reform makes property division obligations nondischargeable in Chapter 7 proceedings. See supra section D2b. What happens when a professional former spouse, who is ordered to pay under New York law a particular sum as an equitable share of his enhanced earning capacity, suddenly becomes unable to work, say, because of illness?

8. *ALI approach.* Consistent with majority rule, the ALI Principles reject the treatment of earning capacity as divisible property. Instead, they provide for "compensatory spousal payments" to reimburse the supporting spouse for the financial contributions made to the other spouse's education or training. ALI Principles, supra, §§4.07, 5.12. For compensation under §5.12, the education must have been completed in less than a specified number of years (set out in a rule of statewide application) before the filing of the dissolution petition.

The ALI formulation resembles an earlier California statute, which provides for reimbursement of the community "for community contributions to education or training of a party that substantially increases the earning capacity of the party." Cal. Fam. Code §2641(b)(1) (West 2004). This statute contains a rebuttable presumption "that the community has not substantially benefited from community contributions to the education or training made less than 10 years before the commencement of the proceeding, and that the community has substantially benefited from community contributions to the education or training made more than 10 years before the commencement of the proceeding." Id. at §2641(c). This statute provides the exclusive remedy for community contributions to education or training but does not limit consideration of such contributions for purposes of support orders. Id. at §2641(d). For another statutory approach, see, e.g., Iowa Code Ann. §598.21A-1h (West Supp. 2006) (in ordering support, court should consider any mutual agreement made by the parties concerning financial or service contributions "with the expectation of future reciprocation or compensation").

9. *Comparing pensions and goodwill.* The advanced degree cases test the limits of the "new property." See, e.g., Lenore J. Weitzman, The Divorce Revolution: The Unexpected Social and Economic Consequences for Women and Children in America 110-142 (1985). Weitzman's definition of the term includes "tangible and intangible assets that are acquired as part of either spouse's career or career potential," id. at 110, and encompasses pensions and other retirement benefits, the goodwill value of a business or profession, insurance benefits, as well as professional degrees and licenses, id. at 110-142. See Kelly, supra, at 163-164 ("The term 'career asset' and its now popularized synonym human capital was identified by Lenore Weitzman over twenty-five years ago as the major source of wealth for divorcing families."). Given that courts routinely treat pensions and retirement funds as marital property, what explains their reluctance to afford similar treatment to professional degrees and licenses? For example, on what basis would the Connecticut Supreme Court treat unvested pension benefits as divisible property (*Bender*, supra), but not advanced degrees (Simmons v. Simmons, 708 A.2d 949 (Conn. 1998))? Note that some jurisdictions explicitly distinguish between the professional degree (not divisible property) and the professional practice (divisible property). Mace v. Mace, 818 So. 2d 1130 (Miss. 2002). What's the difference?

With respect to professional goodwill, the majority approach regards it as marital property but only if the goodwill exists independently of the professional's reputation. See, e.g., Thompson v. Thompson, 576 So. 2d 267 (Fla. 1991); Dugan v. Dugan, 457 A.2d 1 (N.J. 1983). See also In re Marriage of McTiernan, 35 Cal. Rptr. 3d 287 (Ct. App. 2005). How are such assets valued? Would an award of part of the professional spouse's future income stream provide a sensible remedy? See Alicia Brokars Kelly, Sharing a Piece of the Future Post-Divorce: Toward a More

Equitable Distribution of Professional Goodwill, 51 Rutgers L. Rev. 569 (1999). Cf. Dombrowski v. Noyes-Dombrowski, 869 A.2d 164 (Conn. 2005) (awarding as non-modifiable alimony to husband one-half of wife's future lottery payments, won with a ticket purchased during the marriage).

The ALI Principles in §4.07 follow the majority approach on goodwill while excluding human capital from the definition of property. See Allen M. Parkman, The ALI Principles and Marital Quality, 8 Duke J. Gender L. & Pol'y 157 (2001) (criticizing exclusion).

10. *Awards for lost future earnings.* There is considerable authority for treating as divisible property personal injury awards designed to compensate for lost future earnings. See, e.g., Dalessio v. Dalessio, 570 N.E.2d 139 (Mass. 1991); Wren v. Wren, 785 P.2d 1164 (Wyo. 1990). On what theory?

Professor Grace Blumberg, finding the case law in disarray, proposes an analysis that classifies "awards according to the nature of the assets they replace. Thus, compensation for wages lost during coverture is marital property and compensation for wages lost after marriage is separate property." See Grace Ganz Blumberg, Marital Property Treatment of Pensions, Disability Pay, Workers' Compensation, and Other Wage Substitutes: An Insurance, or Replacement, Analysis, 33 UCLA L. Rev. 1250, 1282 (1986). This analysis can also be applied to life insurance, disability pay, and workers' compensation awards. See generally id. Why isn't a worker's disabled body considered separate property? See In re Marriage of Staton, 624 S.E.2d 548 (W. Va. 2005). Alternatively, why shouldn't the determinative question be whether the benefits in question were acquired through a spouse's labor during marriage? See, e.g., Conner v. Conner, 68 P.3d 1232 (Alaska 2003); Doucette v. Washburn, 766 A.2d 578 (Me. 2001).

Can a court divide a spouse's accrued vacation time or sick leave upon dissolution? See Arnold v. Arnold, 77 P.3d 285 (N.M. Ct. App. 2003). An early retirement incentive package accepted by the employee spouse after divorce? See Olivo v. Olivo, 624 N.E.2d 151 (N.Y. 1993). An attorney's contingent fees for cases started during marriage? See In re Stageberg, 695 N.W.2d 609 (Minn. Ct. App. 2005).

Problems

1. Upon dissolution of the 17-year marriage of New York opera singer Frederica von Stade Elkus, her husband argues that her career and celebrity status constitute marital property subject to equitable distribution. At the time of their marriage in 1973, von Stade had just begun her career and was performing minor roles with the Metropolitan Opera Company. During the marriage, she became a highly successful concert and television performer and international recording artist. Although in the first year of the marriage she earned $2,250, by 1989 she earned $621,878.

During the marriage von Stade's husband served as her voice coach and photographer, traveling with her, critiquing her performance, and photographing her for albums and magazine articles. He claims he sacrificed his own career as an opera teacher and singer to devote himself to her career and to their two children. As a result of his efforts, Elkus contends that he is entitled to equitable distribution of the appreciation of the value of her career and her celebrity status as marital property.

According to New York Domestic Relations Law (see *O'Brien*, supra), marital property is defined as property acquired during the marriage "regardless of the form in which title is held." In enacting the Equitable Distribution Law, the legislature broadly defined the term "marital property" to give effect to the "economic partnership" concept of marriage.

What result and why? See Elkus v. Elkus, 572 N.Y.S.2d 901 (App. Div. 1991). Is celebrity status distinguishable from reputation, which courts in professional goodwill cases have held is not divisible? See also Golub v. Golub, 527 N.Y.S.2d 946 (Sup. Ct. 1988). How should a court rule in a state without New York's expansive definition of property? See Ketterle v. Ketterle, 814 N.E.2d 385, 387 (Mass. App. Ct. 2004) (Nobel Prize-winning husband's status as "superstar in the scientific and academic universe"); Piscopo v. Piscopo, 557 A.2d 1040 (N.J. Super. Ct. App. Div.) (comedian's celebrity goodwill), *cert. denied*, 564 A.2d 875 (N.J. 1989).

2. John and Margaret divorced when he was Manager of Municipal Markets at Merrill Lynch and she was a housewife. The court equally divided their substantial assets and ordered John to pay half his monthly salary as alimony. After John became ill and lost his job, he successfully sought to reduce his alimony obligation, based on the changed circumstances.

Margaret now appeals this modification, contending that the court underestimated John's ability to pay by ignoring his "experience as a savvy investor." She claims that John's "sophisticated investment skills are to him what Luciano Pavarotti's voice is to him: the 'asset' that is capable of earning a significant amount of money." She asks the court to measure John's ability to pay on the basis of the higher yield investments available to him, not his actual income. What result and why? See Miller v. Miller, 734 A.2d 752 (N.J. 1999). But cf. Clark v. Clark, 779 A.2d 42, 47 & n.3 (Vt. 2001).

e. Taxation

The Internal Revenue Code spells out different tax consequences for alimony, property division, and child support. What objectives do these variations in tax treatment achieve? How much room should federal law leave for the parties and/or the divorce court to decide such tax issues? Whom do the rules benefit — and disadvantage? Consider the following materials.

■ RYKIEL v. RYKIEL
838 So. 2d 508 (Fla. 2003)

SHAW, Senior Justice. . . .

Stephen Rykiel ("husband") appealed the final judgment in a divorce proceeding. The Fifth District Court of Appeal (the "Fifth District") reversed, holding as follows:

> Further, an obvious error was made with regard to the alimony award. First, the court ordered that the award of permanent periodic alimony be nontaxable to the receiving party, the former wife. This award cannot stand because there is no legal authority which would permit such a practice. Permanent periodic alimony (i.e., support money) is taxable to the recipient under federal income tax law. 26 U.S.C.A. §71.

Its taxability cannot be changed by a state court order. State law creates legal interests, but federal law determines how those interests shall be taxed.

Rykiel, 795 So. 2d at 92. [On rehearing, the Fifth District added that, under its reading of §71 and temporary Treasury Regulation 26 C.F.R. §1.71-1T, only the parties may agree to make alimony payments nondeductible by the payor and excludable from the payee's gross income and the parties must do so in a written document, or on the record before the trial judge, which would be reduced to judgment.] *Rykiel*, 795 So. 2d at 93 n.1. Karen Rykiel ("wife") sought review [before this court of this pure question of law, which is] subject to de novo review. . . .

This case is governed by the provisions of the Internal Revenue Code and the Code of Federal Regulations governing the Internal Revenue Service, Department of the Treasury. Section 63, Internal Revenue Code (2001), provides as follows in relevant part:

> §63. Taxable income defined
> (a) In general
> Except as provided in subsection (b), for purposes of this subtitle, the term *"taxable income" means gross income*. . . .

I.R.C. §63 (2000) (emphasis added).

Section 71, Internal Revenue Code (2001), provides as follows in relevant part:

> §71. Alimony and separate maintenance payments
> (a) General rule
> *Gross income includes amounts received as alimony* or separate maintenance payments.
> (b) Alimony or separate maintenance payments defined
> For purposes of this section —
> (1) In general
> *The term "alimony* or separate maintenance payment" *means any payment in cash if—*
> (A) such payment is received by (or on behalf of) a spouse under a divorce or separation instrument,
> (B) *the divorce or separation instrument does not designate such payment as a payment which is not includible in gross income under this section and not allowable as a deduction* . . .
> (C) in the case of an individual legally separated from his spouse under a decree of divorce or of separate maintenance, the payee spouse and the payor spouse are not members of the same household at the time such payment is made, and
> (D) there is no liability to make any such payment for any period after the death of the payee spouse and there is no liability to make any payment (in cash or property) as a substitute for such payments after the death of the payee spouse.
> (2) Divorce or separation instrument
> *The term "divorce or separation instrument" means —*
> (A) *a decree of divorce* or separate maintenance or a written instrument incident to such a decree,
> (B) a written separation agreement, or
> (C) a decree (not described in subparagraph (A)) requiring a spouse to make payments for the support or maintenance of the other spouse.
> (c) Payments to support children
> (1) In general
> Subsection (a) shall not apply to that part of any payment which the terms of the divorce or separation instrument fix (in terms of an amount of money or a part of

the payment) as a sum which is payable for the support of children of the payor spouse.

I.R.C. §71 (2000) (emphasis added).

The "question and answer" section in Temporary Treasury Regulation §1.71-1T(b,) Q8 & A8 (2001), addresses this matter further:

> Q. How may spouses designate that payments otherwise qualifying as alimony or separate maintenance payments shall be excludible from the gross income of the payee and non-deductible by the payor?
>
> A. The spouses may designate that payments otherwise qualifying as alimony or separate maintenance payments shall be nondeductible by the payor and excludible from gross income by the payee by so providing in a divorce or separation instrument. . . .

Temp. Treas. Reg. §1.71-1T, Q8 & A8 (2001). . . .

[The Fifth District below] construed the above Code provisions and Treasury regulation to mean that a divorce court does not have the authority to order that "alimony shall be nontaxable to the receiving party." This construction, however, is inconsistent with the above Code provisions and Treasury regulation. Sections 63 and 71 of the Code may be paraphrased as follows:

— Gross income is taxable.
— Gross income includes alimony.
— Alimony includes monetary payments made to a spouse pursuant to a divorce instrument unless that instrument says that the payments are not includible in gross income and not allowable as a deduction.
— If the divorce instrument says that the payments are not includible in gross income and not allowable as a deduction, then the payments are not "alimony," are not included in gross income, and are not taxable.
— A divorce instrument includes a divorce decree.

Under the above provisions, a divorce decree may provide that alimony payments are to be excluded from the gross income of the payee and not deducted by the payor. In such a case, the payments do not constitute "alimony" for tax purposes, are not included in the gross income of the recipient, and are nontaxable to the recipient. Treasury regulation 1.71-1T, which the Fifth District relied on for the proposition that only the parties can agree to such an arrangement, simply states that the parties can agree to such an arrangement; it does not state that a court cannot order such an arrangement. . . . Contrary to the holding of the Fifth District, nothing in the above provisions prevents a court from ordering that alimony payments are to be excluded from the gross income of the payee and not deducted by the payor. . . .

Notes and Questions

1. *Tax consequences.* In reaching a fair and equitable result, courts often take into account the tax consequences of particular distributions of property or awards of support. See, e.g., Solomon v. Solomon, 857 A.2d 1109, 1117 (Md. 2004) (tax liabilities to be considered "other factors" in achieving equitable division when they are "immediate and specific or not speculative").

2. *Spousal support.* As *Rykiel* indicates, the Internal Revenue Code provides that "alimony" is deductible by the payor (or obligor)[22] and included in the gross income of the recipient (or obligee).[23] Hence, the obligee must pay income tax on such payments, just as on salary. States' definitions of maintenance or spousal support vary, but to qualify as "alimony" for federal income tax purposes, the payments must meet the statutory criteria listed in I.R.C. §71(b) (quoted in *Rykiel*).[24] See generally Stephen P. Comeau, An Overview of the Federal Income Tax Provisions Related to Alimony Payments, 38 Fam. L.Q. 111 (2004).

Rykiel also indicates, however, that the law does not require divorcing couples to treat spousal support as alimony under §71. Couples may elect to treat the payments as nondeductible by the obligor and nontaxable to the obligee. Doing so might prove financially advantageous if, given the parties' respective incomes and tax rates, the deduction does not save the obligor as much money as it costs the obligee in taxes. (Use of §71 would have no tax effect if the parties are in the same bracket.). See Melvin B. Frumkes, Alimony Can Be Made Nontaxable, 17 Am. J. Fam. L. 187 (2004). So, for example, in *Rykiel* if Karen's taxable income places her in the 28 percent tax bracket and Stephen's places him in the 25 percent bracket, they would minimize their total income tax liability by making Stephen's spousal support payments to Karen nondeductible by him and nontaxable to her.[25] The Rykiels must indicate this tax treatment in the divorce or separation agreement, and Karen must attach a copy of the instrument to her tax return.

Why did Congress choose the Code's approach to alimony? Should the divorce court as well as the parties be able to choose the tax treatment of spousal support payments? Why?

3. *Transfers of property.* For most transfers of property between spouses or former spouses, if "incident to the divorce," no gain or loss will be recognized.[26] I.R.C. §1041(b) treats the property transferred as a gift to the recipient. As a result,

---

[22]. I.R.C. §62 (West Supp. 2005); I.R.C. §215 (2000). By specifically listing alimony as a deduction used to arrive at "adjusted gross income," §62 allows a dollar-for-dollar deduction from the gross income of the obligor, who can take, in addition, a standard deduction, if beneficial. As a result, the obligor can avoid paying the greater tax rate applicable to the portion of his or her income that would otherwise fall into a higher tax bracket. See I.R.C. §1 (West Supp. 2005).

[23]. I.R.C. §61(a)(2000) (listing "alimony and separate maintenance payments" as one of 15 nonexclusive examples of income).

[24]. Specifically, the payments must be in cash, and they must be received on or behalf of the obligee, according to a divorce or separation instrument (decree or written separation agreement). In addition, in the case of a decree of divorce or separate maintenance, the parties cannot cohabit in the same residence nor file a joint return once payments commence. The obligor's liability for spousal support must terminate on the obligee's death, although the decree or separation agreement may provide that the payments will continue and remain deductible in the event of the obligee's remarriage. I.R.C. §71(b) (2000). See also Treas. Reg. §1.71(b)(2) (1984). Payments of cash to a third party, such as rent, mortgage, or tuition liabilities, may be made if on behalf of the alimony recipient, but any payments to maintain property owned by the obligor, even if used by the recipient, will not qualify. Id.

[25]. According to the table for taxable years beginning in 2005, an unmarried individual with taxable income over $29,700 but not over $71,950 must pay income tax of $4,090 plus 25 percent of the excess over $29,700. For one with a taxable income over $71,950 but not over $150,150, the tax is $14,652.50 plus 28 percent of the excess over $71,950. See I.R.C. §1(c) & Table 1 (West Supp. 2005).

[26]. I.R.C. §1041(a) (2000). See also id. at §1041(e) (rule does not apply to transfers in trusts for the benefit of a spouse when liabilities exceed the basis). Property transfers cannot be "alimony" because they are not cash transfers; a cash transfer will constitute a "property settlement" if it does not meet the other requirements for "alimony" described above. See supra note [24].

At one time, the tax consequences of property transfers varied depending upon state law, either community property or common law, under United States v. Davis, 370 U.S. 65 (1962). According to *Davis*, distributions in community property jurisdictions were nontaxable divisions, simply reflecting

the value of the property is excluded from the recipient's income, under I.R.C. §102(a). Further, the recipient takes the donor's basis in the property. Why did Congress decide to treat property transfers incident to divorce differently from support payments, with respect to taxation?

Suppose, for example, the divorce instrument instructs Stephen to transfer to Karen their home (which Stephen owns), which originally cost $100,000. Currently, the fair market value of the home is $150,000. When Stephen transfers the home to Karen, he will not recognize gain, and Karen will not receive income. Karen will take the property at Stephen's basis ($100,000), rather than the fair market value, deferring recognition of the gain. If Karen subsequently sells this property, the Code allows her to exclude as much as $250,000 gain from her gross income, so long as during the five-year period preceding the sale she or Stephen owned and used the property as a principal residence for periods aggregating two years or more.[27] For §1041 to apply to former spouses, the transfers must occur within one year after the date of the divorce or must be related to the cessation of the marriage.[28] Applicable regulations create a rebuttable presumption that a transfer not pursuant to a divorce or separation instrument and any transfer more than six years after the marriage ends is not "related to the cessation of the marriage."[29] (The same general analysis would apply if Stephen and Karen had owned the home as joint tenants, but then Stephen would only be transferring his one-half to Karen.)

After Stephen transfers the home to Karen, suppose they agree that, while Karen lives in the home, Stephen will pay the mortgage of $1,500 and annual property taxes of $2,000. Whether these expenses qualify as alimony payments on behalf of Karen depends on whether Stephen completely relinquished ownership of the home. By transferring title of the home to Karen, Stephen's payments qualify as deductible alimony made to a third party.[30] If, however, Stephen retains ownership of the home during Karen's occupancy, the identical payments do not qualify as alimony, even if made pursuant to the divorce instrument. In short, alimony payments must be made on behalf of the spouse; if Stephen owns the home, he is paying his own expenses.[31]

4. *Child support.* Unlike alimony, child support payments are nontaxable and nondeductible under I.R.C. §71(c) (quoted in *Rykiel*). What policy considerations does this rule reflect?

5. *"Navigating the system."* The different tax consequences of alimony, property transfers, and child support often determine the most financially advantageous way

---

the preexisting co-ownership of the two spouses, while a distribution in a common law jurisdiction was a taxable transfer in satisfaction of a legal obligation. As a result, in common law states the distribution became the time to tax the transferor spouse on any appreciation that accrued between the initial acquisition of the property and the transfer to the recipient spouse.

[27]. I.R.C. §121 (West Supp. 2005). For purposes of determining the five-year period for Karen, the predivorce period during which Stephen owned the home in which the couple resided is counted. Id. at §121(d)(3)(A). Hence, if the asset in question were, say, shares of stock, rather than a home, and thus ineligible for this special exclusion, the fact that Karen takes Stephen's basis would prove more consequential.

[28]. I.R.C. §1041(c) (2000).

[29]. Treas. Reg. §1.1041-1T(b) (1984).

[30]. Treas. Reg. §1.71-1T(b) (1984).

[31]. See supra note [24]. But then Stephen, rather than Karen, would be entitled to claim the mortgage interest and property tax deductions. I.R.C. §§163(h), 164 (West Supp. 2005).

to "wind up" a marriage. The Code limits the parties' freedom to get the desired tax consequences, however. Consider the following examples:

a. *"Excess alimony payments."* Suppose that Karen's and Stephen's financial circumstances make treatment of transfer payments as alimony more advantageous than treatment as property. If, for example, the parties were attempting to negotiate a settlement and Stephen wanted to treat cash property distribution payments as deductible alimony by making periodic payments that drop substantially within the first three postseparation years, I.R.C. §71(f) provides for recomputation to "recapture" the excess deductions over the amount permitted by the statute. Significantly, it is Stephen's *front-loading* of alimony payments that triggers the recapture of the excess, not his effort to characterize a cash property settlement as alimony. Thus, if Karen were willing to spread out evenly her receipt of the property distribution over the first three postseparation years, Stephen could avoid the recapture by paying Karen her alimony plus one-third of his property obligation during each of these years.

b. *Disguising child support as alimony.* Suppose, now, that Stephen and Karen have three children, ages 10, 15, and 20 and that Stephen wants to deduct as much of his postdivorce payments as possible. If the monthly "alimony" sums that Stephen pays drop each time one of the children reaches age 21, for example, the I.R.S. will treat some of these payments as child support, based on §71(c), which classifies as child support payments "fixed" sums specifically designated by the divorce instrument to be reduced by the happening of a contingency related to the obligor's children, or at a time which is clearly associated with such contingencies. In this illustration, only the portion of these obligations to remain unchanged after the youngest child turns 21 will be treated as alimony. Further, if Stephen pays less each year than the total amount of support specified in the divorce instrument for both Karen and the children, the money received will be regarded as child support first, with only the excess treated as deductible alimony. Careful planning, however, can help the parties structure payments to achieve the desired objective of treating as alimony for tax purposes payments intended as child support.[32]

c. *Critique.* What do these two illustrations reveal? Professor Deborah Geier would discard existing labels and

> explicitly [empower the parties] to determine whether cash transfers—whether denominated alimony, child support, a property settlement, an "equitable distribution" for state law purposes, or otherwise—are includable by the recipient and deductible by the payor, or excludable by the recipient and not deductible by the payor, with simple and clear default rules for taxpayers who fail to make their wishes known in their divorce, separation, or support instrument.

Deborah A. Geier, Simplifying and Rationalizing the Federal Income Tax Law Applicable to Transfers in Divorce, 55 Tax Law. 363, 364 (2002). What advantages does this approach offer?

---

[32]. I.R.C. §71(c)(3) (2000). An attorney might give them the following advice to achieve this goal: First, the divorce instrument should not contain a "fixed" sum payable for the support of the payor's children. Second, the support should not be reduced by any event related to the children (such as attaining majority age or marriage). Third, dates relating to the reduction or termination of child support should not occur within six months before or after any child reaches majority. Treasury Regulation §1.71-aT(c) (1984) treats this period as being "clearly associated with the happening of a contingency relating to a child of the payor."

6. *Other tax considerations.* Divorce entails additional tax consequences because it changes the taxpayer's marital status. The couple can no longer file joint returns, so they must decide to file as either head of household or unmarried.[33] Between the two options, head of household is more advantageous, but it requires that the taxpayer must be unmarried on the last day of the taxable year and maintain as his or her home a household constituting the principal residence for an unmarried descendant or dependent for more than half of the year. Thus, assuming Karen receives custody of the children, she can file as head of household as long as the children live with her for more than half the year.[34] Because Karen and Stephen hypothetically have more than one child, Stephen would benefit if the court awarded him custody of at least one child, so he could also enjoy the preferential status of head of household.

The taxpayer's filing status determines the amount of the standard deduction available under I.R.C. §63(c). The standard deduction is a flat amount provided to all taxpayers of similar status. Deducted from the adjusted gross income, it operates with the personal exemptions (discussed next) to determine taxable income. If Stephen satisfies the head of household requirements, he can take the standard deduction, a figure adjusted annually for cost of living according to §63(c)(4). Conversely, if Karen maintains the household for all three children, Stephen must file as unmarried. This status offers a lower standard deduction, again a figure adjusted annually for cost-of-living adjustments.[35] Thus, the standard deduction illustrates how filing status can directly affect tax liability.

Besides the standard deduction, Karen and Stephen will also be permitted personal exemptions to lower their taxable income. I.R.C. §151 allows an exemption for the taxpayer as well as for any eligible dependents. The dependent must be under 19 years of age, or under 24 years if a student, to be eligible under §151(c). Assuming that Karen's and Stephen's oldest child attends college, they can claim three exemptions in addition to their own. Generally, a taxpayer may claim a dependency exemption if he or she provides over one-half of the dependent's support.[36] However, §152(e) specifically refers to children of divorced parents and treats the custodial parent as providing over one-half of the child's support (regardless of actual contribution). Assuming that Karen retains custody of all three children, Stephen cannot take any additional personal exemptions. Nevertheless, Karen could sign a written declaration releasing her claim to one or more of her dependency deductions, enabling Stephen to take advantage of the available exemptions.[37]

Unlike the standard deduction, §151(d) provides for a "phaseout"[38] of the personal exemptions if the taxpayer's adjusted gross income exceeds a certain

---

[33]. They can file a joint return if they have only a written separation agreement, rather than a decree of divorce or separate maintenance, §6013(d) (West Supp. 2005), but then I.R.C. §71(e) (2000) makes the favorable treatment of alimony unavailable. In addition, unless I.R.C. §7703(b) (West Supp. 2005) applies, they may need to file as married individuals filing separate returns.

[34]. I.R.C. at §2(b) (West Supp. 2005).

[35]. Id. at §63(c)(2), (4).

[36]. Id. at §§151(c), 152(a).

[37]. Id. at §152(e)(2). State courts have split on the question whether they have the power to award the federal exemption to a noncustodial parent. Compare May v. May, 837 A.2d 566 (Pa. Super. Ct. 2003) (allowing award), with Bradley v. Bradley, 512 S.E.2d 248 (Ga. 1999) (disallowing award).

[38]. The impact of the phaseout is reduced for taxable years beginning in 2006 through 2009. I.R.C. §151(d)(3)(E) (West Supp. 2005).

"threshold" amount. As a tax strategy, parties who can reach agreement should allocate the exemptions by comparing their incomes with the threshold amounts. Suppose Karen's high income risks the phaseout of her exemptions. Rather than waste these deductions, she should allocate them to Stephen so all three exemptions are fully utilized.

After tax liability has been determined, additional tax preferences, known as credits, are available to qualifying taxpayers to reduce final tax liability on a dollar-for-dollar basis. Section 24 allows some taxpayers up to $1,000 credit for each child under 17 for whom the taxpayer is entitled to a dependency deduction.[39] Suppose Karen has custody of all three children and works full-time. She would also be entitled to a childcare credit under I.R.C. §21, equal to the applicable percentage of childcare expenses she incurs to remain employed. However, she is only entitled to the expenses she incurs for the care of "qualifying individuals," which §21(b) defines as dependents under the age of 13. Thus, she cannot deduct expenses for the care of her two older children. Because there is only one qualifying individual, §21(c) allows Karen to take a maximum credit of $3,000, subject to certain phaseout limitations.[40]

E. CHILD SUPPORT

1. Parental Duties

■ **ELISA B. v. SUPERIOR COURT**
117 P.3d 660 (Cal. 2005)

Review case, reprinted in Chapter IV, p. 478.

Notes and Questions

1. *Rationale.* Why must Elisa B. pay child support for the twins born to Emily? Could the court have imposed financial resposibility on *Elisa B.* without recognizing her parentage? What reasons support extending paternity statutes, such as the Uniform Parentage Act, to women like *Elisa B.*? What counterarguments might apply?

What theory makes *parents* financially responsible for their children? To the extent that children constitute community assets, the next generation of citizens,

---

[39]. Id. at §24.

[40]. Id. at §21(a)(2). Section 21(a) allows a credit for 35 percent of expenses, reduced (but not below 20 percent) by 1 percent for each $2,000 or fraction thereof by which the taxpayer's adjusted gross income exceeds $15,000. The limit on creditable expenses considered is $3,000 for one qualifying individual and $6,000 for two or more qualifying individuals. For an analysis of feminist perspectives on this credit, see Anne L. Alstott, Tax Policy and Feminism: Competing Goals and Institutional Choices, 96 Colum. L. Rev. 2001, 2056-2059 (1996).

Another credit, the earned income credit, although targeted to low-income individuals, gives a larger credit to those with a qualifying child under the age of 19, or 24 if a student. I.R.C. §32(c)(3) (West Supp. 2005). The statute provides phaseout percentages based on income, increased in stages. Id. at §32(b).

why shouldn't taxpayers assume responsibility — as they do for public education, for example? See, e.g., Scott Altman, A Theory of Child Support, 17 Int'l J. L., Pol'y & Fam. 173 (2003). Note that the litigation in *Elisa B.* began when the state sought to collect private child support so that the twins would not be dependent on public assistance.

2. *Estoppel.* What role, if any, does the doctrine of estoppel play in the court's analysis? What facts give rise to estoppel? In a companion case, Kristine H. v. Lisa R., 117 P.3d 690 (Cal. 2005), the California Supreme Court invoked estoppel more explicitly. Having participated in a prebirth judicial proceeding that stipulated that Kristine and Lisa were both parents of the child whom Kristine, seven months pregnant, was expecting, Kristine was estopped from questioning the stipulation later, after the women's intimate relationship dissolved. The court limited its decision, however, declining to decide the validity of the stipulated judgment for other purposes. Id. at 695.

The American Law Institute's Principles of the Law of Family Dissolution recognize "parents by estoppel." "Parents by estoppel" have the same rights and responsibilities as legal parents, but parental status by estoppel arises only in the context of dissolution of the family relationship. ALI Principles, supra, §2.03. Generally, the status arises when a man has lived with the child for two years (or since birth) and believed that he was the biological father and continued taking parental responsibilities even after the belief no longer existed or, alternatively, when an adult has lived with the child since birth or for two years, accepting full and permanent responsibilities and holding the child out as his or her own, pursuant to a coparenting agreement with the parent or parents, and recognition as a parent would serve the child's best interests. Id. at §2.03(b)(ii)-(iv). On what basis would the ALI Principles recognize Elisa B. as a parent by estoppel? In addition, parentage by estoppel can arise when one is ordered to pay child support. Id. at §203(b)(i). Why should parental status follow from support duties? See Jane Muller-Peterson, Expanding the Definition of Parenthood: Why Equitable Estoppel as Used to Impose a Child Support Obligation on a Lesbian Domestic Partner Isn't Equitable: A Case Study, 4 Geo. J. Gender & L. 781 (2003).

3. *Marital status.* The next section explores the federal framework imposed on the states to assess and collect child support. This framework governs support of both children following dissolution of marriage and also nonmarital children. In fact, Supreme Court rulings giving nonmarital children a right to parental support equal to that of their counterparts born of married parents sparked much of the reform initiated by Congress. See Chapter IV, section C1. Today, states undertake a similar analysis for any child whose parents are not part of an intact family. See, e.g., Jackson v. Proctor, 801 A.2d 1080, 1090 (Md. Ct. Spec. App. 2002) ("[We cannot] sanction a system of calculating support that varies with the parents' prior marital status; to do so would penalize children born out of wedlock."). California law is unusual, however, in that it recognizes that a child's two parents can be women, even in the absence of a same-sex marriage or a registered domestic partnership. See also In re L.B., 122 P.3d 161 (Wash. 2005). Cf. King v. S. B., 837 N.E. 2d 965 (Ind. 2005) (vacating coparentage determination based on intent, but remanding to decide best interests); T.F. v. B.L., 813 N.E.2d 1244 (Mass. 2004) (rejecting contract as a basis for imposing parentage and support duties on mother's former female partner).

4. *Gender.* Should mothers and fathers have identical support duties? In contrast to the norm of equal responsibility now imposed on mothers and fathers to provide child support, Professor Martha Fineman articulates a different vision: The state should provide financial support for mothers so that they can care for their children, because childcare is work that ought to be valued. See generally Martha Albertson Fineman, The Autonomy Myth: A Theory of Dependency (2004). This approach rejects current "welfare reform" measures, included in the federal Personal Responsibility and Work Opportunity Reconcilation Act of 1996, requiring custodial mothers of young children to work outside the home. See 42 U.S.C. §607(b)(5) (2000). Evaluate Fineman's proposal. See generally, e.g., Lee Anne Fennell, Relative Burdens: Family Ties and the Safety Net, 45 Wm. & Mary L. Rev. 1453 (2004); Symposium, The Structures of Care Work, 76 Chi.-Kent L. Rev. 1389-1786 (2001).

Does a father's support duty come from his genetic parentage of the child? Cf. Katharine K. Baker, Bargaining or Biology? The History and Future of Paternity Law and Parental Status, 14 Cornell J.L. & Pub. Pol'y 1 (2004). If so, how do you explain *Elisa B.*, given the absence of a genetic tie?

2. Imposing Support Obligations: From Discretion to Guidelines

A child support award typically requires the periodic transfer of funds from the noncustodial parent to the custodial parent for the benefit of their child. At one time, courts determined child support in the same way they set alimony — using open-ended standards to reach unpredictable results. Now, however, the regime of judicial discretion has given way to a new approach, the use of mathematical formulae called "guidelines." In the following materials, consider what objectives a child support award should seek to achieve and whether the move to guidelines serves these goals.

■ DOWNING v. DOWNING
45 S.W.3d 449 (Ky. Ct. App. 2001)

KNOPF, Judge:

[Donald R. Downing and Sharon A. Downing divorced in 1992. Sharon received sole custody of their two children. In 1998, she filed a motion to increase Donald's child support obligations, based on a substantial increase in his income. The Domestic Relations Commissioner found that Donald's monthly income had increased by $40,000, to $57,000.] In the DRC's recommendations he noted the difficulties in setting child support when the parents' income greatly exceeds the highest level set in the child support guidelines:

> When child support is set outside of the Guidelines, the Court is required to exercise discretion in arriving at a fair and equitable amount of support. . . . A review of the Child Support Guidelines under the column headed for two children indicates that at the high income end, child support increases at the rate of about 4% of combined income. Taking into account the Respondent's income and the Petitioner's income using $57,000.00 per month for the Respondent and $1,500.00 per month for the

Petitioner, and projecting the Guidelines, the base monthly support would calculate to $3,584.00 per month of which the Respondent would have a 97% responsibility. This calculates to $3,475.00 per month[2] [, which I recommend].

The child support guidelines set out in KRS 403.212 serve as a rebuttable presumption for the establishment or modification of the amount of child support. Courts may deviate from the guidelines only upon making a specific finding that application of the guidelines would be unjust or inappropriate. However, KRS 403.211(3)(e) specifically designates that "combined monthly adjusted parental gross income in excess of the Kentucky child support guidelines" is a valid basis for deviating from the child support table. Furthermore, the trial court may use its judicial discretion to determine child support in circumstances where combined adjusted parental gross income exceeds the uppermost level of the guidelines table [$15,000 per month.]

. . . The DRC set out three considerations for his determination of the appropriate level of support: (1) the reasonable needs of the children; (2) the standard of living enjoyed by the parents; and (3) a mathematical projection of the child support guidelines. Donald agrees that the first two criteria are appropriate. [He contends, however, hat the DRC found little evidence on (1) and (2) and relied exclusively on (3).]

[T]he Kentucky Child Support Guidelines are based on the "Income Shares Model." The basic premise of this model is that a child should receive the same proportion of parental income that the child would have received if the parents had not divorced. A review of the Kentucky child support table further shows that it is based upon the assumption that as parental income increases, the proportion of income spent on child support decreases.[14]

---

2. In reaching this calculation, the DRC applied the child support guidelines to the first $15,000.00 of the parties' combined monthly income. The DRC set additional child support by multiplying the excess income by 4%, as follows:

	$58,500.00	combined monthly income of the parties
−	$15,000.00	highest income provided by the Guidelines
	$43,500.00	amount the parents' income exceeds the Guidelines
×	.04	percentage applied to income in excess of the Guidelines
	$1,740.00	projected base monthly support obligation for two children for the amount of income exceeding the Guidelines
+	$1,844.00	base monthly support obligation for two children for parents' combined monthly income of $15,000.00
	$3,584.00	projected base monthly support obligation for two children with combined parental monthly income of $58,500.00
×	.97	Donald's percentage of parents' combined monthly income
	$3,476.48	Donald's projected child support obligation.

14. An examination of the child support table in KRS 403.212 bears out this model. Where the combined monthly adjusted parental gross income is $1,000.00, the base child support for two children is $303.00, or 30.3%; At $5,000.00, the base child support is $1,010.00, or 20.2%; At $10,000.00, the base child support is $1,515.00, or 15.15%; And at the highest income on the chart, $15,000.00 per month, the base child support is $1,844.00, or 12.23%. In this case, the DRC's calculation of the base monthly support works out to approximately 6.1% of Donald and Sharon's combined gross income ($3,584.00/(57,000 + 1,500) = .0612). This percentage of income is about one-half of the percentage used at the highest income level of the child support table.

. . . Sharon takes the position that this Court should adopt a "share the wealth" approach. [Under this approach, while] support must be reasonable under the circumstances, what amount is "reasonable" is defined in relation to a child's "needs" and varies with the circumstances and resources of the parties. The standard of living to which a child is entitled will be measured in terms of the standard of living attainable by the income available to the parents rather than by evidence of the manner in which the parents' income is expended and the parents' resulting lifestyle. . . .

We reject this approach. . . . An increase in child support above the child's reasonable needs primarily accrues to the benefit of the custodial parent rather than the children. In addition, this approach effectively transfers most of the discretionary spending on children to the custodial parent. . . . Beyond a certain point, additional child support serves no purpose but to provide extravagance and an unwarranted transfer of wealth. [C]hild support must be set in an amount which is reasonably and rationally related to the realistic needs of the children. This is sometimes referred to as the "Three Pony Rule." That is, no child, no matter how wealthy the parents, needs to be provided more than three ponies.

We recognize that the DRC did not use a straight-line extrapolation to calculate Donald's child support obligation. . . . Nevertheless, the DRC set child support based almost entirely on the mathematical calculation. In the absence of any other supporting findings or evidence in the record, we must conclude that the amount set by the DRC was arbitrary.

We do not agree with Donald that the highest applicable amount set by the guidelines is the presumptively correct amount of support. To the contrary, once the trial court finds a valid basis under KRS 403.211(3) for deviating from the guidelines chart it has considerable discretion in setting child support above the guidelines . . . based primarily on the child's needs, as set out in specific supporting findings. There was no evidence that the needs of the children [had changed].

Any assessment of the child's reasonable needs should also be based upon the parents' financial ability to meet those needs [and the standard of living during the marriage]. [W]hile a trial court may take a parent's additional resources into account, a large income does not require a noncustodial parent to support a lifestyle for his children of which he does not approve.[24] [Vacated and remanded.]

Notes and Questions

1. *Historical background.* Blackstone described the duty of parents to provide for the support of their children as "a principle of natural law."[41] Traditionally, American divorce laws provided only vague guidance on postdissolution child support, using terms such as "just," "reasonable," or "necessary" to direct courts how to set an award.[42] Later, statutes listed factors to be considered, among others, in the exercise of judicial discretion to determine child support

---

24. Donald claims that the trial court "usurped his parental authority to make lifestyle choices for his children." Yet a child is not expected to live at a minimal level of comfort while the noncustodial parent is living a life of luxury. Moreover, Donald has not provided any evidence that his standard of living has diminished, or what lifestyle he would deem appropriate for his children.

[41]. 1 William Blackstone, Commentaries *447-448.

[42]. 2 Chester G. Vernier, American Family Laws 193 (1932).

obligations,[43] much like the approach many states use for property distribution and spousal support.

Vague standards and judicial discretion resulted in inadequate (or sometimes nonexistent) awards, inconsistency from case to case, disrespect for support orders, and unpredictability, in turn discouraging settlement. Illinois and Maine responded by enacting optional guidelines.[44]

But the difficulties also prompted federal concern as the federal AFDC program (Aid to Families with Dependent Children) faced increasing burdens in meeting the needs of children left unmet by their parents. Seeking to limit these fiscal burdens, in 1984 Congress mandated that by 1987 states use child support guidelines as rebuttable presumptions in so-called Title IV-D cases (in which the state seeks to recover from an absent parent payments made to support a needy child). The guidelines requirement was extended to all cases by the Family Support Act of 1988 (FSA), 42 U.S.C. §667(a)-(b) (2000). Congress imposed these requirements on the states by making compliance a condition for receiving federal AFDC funds. See Jocelyn Elise Crowley, The Politics of Child Support in America 37-38 (2003) (listing major federal child support statutes since 1950).

2. *Objectives.* The unpredictability of a system entrusted entirely to judicial discretion was exacerbated by the absence of any clear theory or objective for child support awards. What purposes should an award seek to achieve? Fairness to the noncustodial parent? Prevention of child poverty? Support to the full extent possible? Continuation of the marital standard of living? Equalization of the standard of living in the custodial and noncustodial households? Then how should child support relate to alimony? In other words, does ensuring a standard of living for the child guarantee the same for the custodial parent? How should in-kind contributions of the custodial parent be evaluated? On the difficulty identifying the goals of the past and current approaches to child support, see generally Marsha Garrison, Autonomy or Community? An Evaluation of Two Models of Parental Obligation, 86 Cal. L. Rev. 41 (1999); Marsha Garrison, The Goals and Limits of Child Support Policy, in Child Support: The Next Frontier 16 (J. Thomas Oldham & Marygold S. Melli eds., 2000).

In contrast to the traditional way of thinking about child support *after* property division and alimony, Professor Mary Ann Glendon proposes a "children first" approach under which property division and spousal support would be addressed only after the children's needs have been met. Mary Ann Glendon, Abortion and Divorce in Western Law 94-95 (1987).

What objectives for child support does *Downing* identify? The federal Advisory Panel on Child Support Guidelines recommended that states should adhere to the following principles in developing guidelines: Both parents should share responsibility for child support; parental subsistence needs should be considered (but child support should virtually never be set at zero); child support should cover a child's basic needs while allowing enjoyment of a parent's higher standard of living;

---

[43]. For example, §309 of the Uniform Marriage and Divorce Act directs courts to set an amount "reasonable or necessary," considering "all relevant factors including: (1) the financial resources of the child; (2) the financial resources of the custodial parent; (3) the standard of living the child would have enjoyed had the marriage not been dissolved; (4) the physical and emotional condition of the child and his educational needs; and (5) the financial resources and needs of the noncustodial parent." 9A U.L.A. (pt. I) 573 (1998).

[44]. Beller & Graham, supra note [9], at 165.

each child has an equal right to share in a parent's income, subject to factors such as age, income, and other dependents; child support determinations should not depend on gender or the marital status of the parents; guidelines should not create economic disincentives for remarriage or work; and guidelines should encourage the involvement of both parents in the child's life. See Laura W. Morgan, Child Support Guidelines: Interpretation and Application §1.02(d) (1996 & Supp. 2004).

The American Law Institute's Principles of the Law of Family Dissolution list nine general objectives, including the child's ability to enjoy both a "minimum decent standard of living" when possible to achieve without impoverishing either parent and a "standard of living not grossly inferior to that of the child's higher income parent," protection of the child from "loss of important life opportunities," fairness to both parents, avoidance of disincentives that discourage parents from working or training for work, as well as fostering cooperation and minimizing parental conflict. ALI Principles, supra, §3.04. See Grace Ganz Blumberg, Balancing the Interests: The American Law Institute's Treatment of Child Support, 33 Fam. L.Q. 39 (1999).

3. *State responses.* Reliance on guidelines achieves uniformity and predictability, as *Downing* suggests, by identifying a precise amount that the court presumptively orders. Jurisdictions have complied with the federal mandate in different ways. Twenty-five jurisdictions adopted guidelines by statute, 8 by administrative regulations, and 18 by court rule or decision. See Morgan, supra, at §1.03.

The income-shares model is the most popular approach, used by 35 states. As *Downing* shows, these states rely on a chart that lists the share of combined parental income allocated for child support at different income levels; parents divide the obligation in proportion to their incomes. Fourteen jurisdictions use, with some variation, the percentage-of-income model, which allocates a fraction of the non-custodial parent's income for child support. Only three states follow Delaware's use of the Melson formula, which prorates between parents the child's support needs based on available net income. See id. For a more detailed summary of each approach, see Robert G. Williams, Implementation of the Child Support Provisions of the Family Support Act: Child Support Guidelines, Updating of Awards, and Routine Income Withholding, in Child Support and Child Well-Being, 93, 96-98 (Irwin Garfinkel et al. eds., 1994).

Building on states' experience under different models, particularly the version of the percentage-of-income approach used in Massachusetts, the ALI Principles have developed a second-generation formula. It starts with marginal expenditure percentages, representing what families spend on their children. It then adjusts the obligation up or down in light of each parent's ability to enjoy basic economic adequacy and each parent's relative ability to support the child. See Blumberg, supra, at 44.

4. *Different models.* What are the advantages and disadvantages of the various approaches?

> The primary advantage of [the percentage-of-income model] is its simplicity. But, its simplicity also forms the basis for criticism because the obligor will pay the same dollar amount whether the custodial parent earns no income or an amount equal to that of the obligor. Advocates have countered that the model contains the implicit assumption that the custodial parent contributes his or her share of financial support directly. . . .

In addition to designating that both parents make a monetary contribution, the [income-shares] model is flexible in allowing for the apportionment between the parents of additional basic expenses such as work-related child care, extraordinary medical expenses, and a variety of custody arrangements. A disadvantage . . . is that it may reduce the incentive for the custodial parent to increase her work effort because the increased income may lower child support payments. Moreover, it can bring about what may seem like perverse changes in the noncustodial parent's contribution. An increase in the noncustodial parent's income could result in a decrease in the amount of child support owed, and a decrease in income could result in an increase in the amount owed. Any version of this model may be criticized for not acknowledging the nonmonetary contribution of the custodial parent in directly caring for the children. [The] Melson model involves the most complex calculations. . . .

Andrea H. Beller & John W. Graham, Small Change: The Economics of Child Support 200-201 (1993). See also Jo Michelle Beld & Len Biernat, Federal Intent for State Child Support Guidelines: Income Shares, Cost Shares, and the Realities of Shared Parenting, 37 Fam. L.Q. 165, 199 (2003) (concluding that income-shares model is most consistent with the federal intent for state guidelines).

The ALI Principles' formula purports to effect the most satisfactory balance of competing interests of the child, the parents, and society. It would probably increase awards, "particularly those involving small families of modest means in which the residential parent, usually the mother, has a lower income than the nonresidential parent." Leslie Joan Harris, The Proposed ALI Child Support Principles, 35 Willamette L. Rev. 717, 718 (1999) (using Oregon as example). Cf. Ira Mark Ellman, Fudging Failure: The Economic Analysis Used to Construct Child Support Guidelines, 2004 U. Chi. Legal F. 167 (questioning coherence of mathematical models and assumptions used to construct all guidelines).

5. *Federal guidelines.* Given the federal goals for child support guidelines, why has Congress not adopted a *national* guideline? Linda Henry Elrod, The Federalization of Child Support Guidelines, 6 J. Am. Acad. Matrim. Law. 103, 128-129 (1990). Advantages of fully federalizing the standards for child support would include eliminating the variability of awards from state to state, improving processing for interstate child support, and ensuring that actual awards meet adequate levels relative to any federally funded child support benefit. See Williams, supra, at 107. What disadvantages would a national guideline pose?

6. *Rebutting the presumption.* Child support guidelines create a rebuttable presumption of the appropriate award. Courts must explicitly justify deviations from the guideline amount. See, e.g., Urquhart v. Urquhart, 533 S.E.2d 80 (Ga. 2000). A frequently litigated issue asks what findings justify rebutting the presumption. See, e.g., Hamiter v. Torrence, 717 N.E.2d 1249 (Ind. Ct. App. 1999). *Downing* addresses a version of this question in determining appropriate child support in high-income families. Why does *Downing* decide that extrapolations from the guidelines do not apply? Should the formula apply in all cases? Does the court's emphasis on "reasonable needs" revive the judicial discretion that guidelines were designed to displace? Given the premise of the income-shares model, why does the court reject the "share the wealth" approach? See also, e.g., Smith v. Smith, 67 P.3d 351 (Okla. Civ. App. 2002). What is the appropriate weight to accord a parent's right to determine the child's lifestyle (footnote 24)?

Empirical evidence suggests a lack of uniformity in judicial application of guidelines in cases of both very high and very low incomes. Most states have responded to the latter by setting floors below which the guidelines do not apply. Beller & Graham, supra, at 202.

7. *Extending the formulaic approach.* Now that guidelines have transformed child support, what explains the absence of similar formulae for property distribution and spousal support? A few jurisdictions have moved in this direction. See, e.g., Mascaro v. Mascaro, 803 A.2d 1186 (Pa. 2002). Indeed, child support guidelines provide the model for the formulaic approach to property distribution and "compensatory spousal payments" proposed by the ALI. See ALI Principles, supra, at 29-30 (explaining "[t]he value of statewide rules establishing presumptive results"). See Ira Mark Ellman, Inventing Family Law, 32 U.C. Davis L. Rev. 855 (1999).

Who will benefit from the trend toward greater consistency and predictability reflected in the adoption of numerical formulae? Cf. Jane C. Murphy, Eroding the Myth of Discretionary Justice in Family Law: The Child Support Experiment, 70 N.C. L. Rev. 209, 218 (1991) (greater tolerance of discretion in family law than in commercial law attributable to gender of parties seeking relief).

8. *Shared custody.* Can mathematical formulae adequately address the variations and complexities of modern allocations of parental responsibility? Increasingly, courts must consider how to apply guidelines to joint custody and other shared parenting arrangements. Do such arrangements justify a deviation from the guidelines? See, e.g., Guillot v. Munn, 756 So. 2d 290 (La. 2000) (stating what obligor must show for deviation). Should each joint custodian be treated as a support obligor for the time the child spends with the other parent? See, e.g., Rogers v. Rogers, 622 N.W.2d 813, 815-816 (Minn. 2001) (so holding except when one parent has sole physical custody and other provides significant physical care). Does joint custody warrant a special formula? See, e.g., Wright v. Osburn, 970 P.2d 1071, 1073-1074 (Nev. 1998) (Springer, C.J., dissenting) (criticizing majority for creating one). See generally Linda D. Elrod & Robert G. Spector, A Review of the Year in Family Law: "Same-Sex" Marriage Issue Dominates Headlines, 38 Fam. L.Q. 777, 811 (2004) (listing 28 states that provide "shared parenting time offset" in computing child support). See also Morgan, supra, at §3.03. Cf. Beld & Biernat, supra, at 200-202 (recommendations).

Should travel expenses for visitation be included in the guidelines amount or ordered as an "add-on" to such award? Or should they be subtracted from the parental income available for child support? See, e.g., Grayson v. Grayson, 103 S.W.3d 559 (Tex. App. 2003). Should employment-related childcare expenses be treated the same way? See Morgan, supra, at §3.02 (treated as an "add-on" or factor for deviating from guidelines).

9. *Family home.* The ALI Principles, supra, §3.05(8), explicitly treat use of the family home by the residential (custodial) parent as a form of additional child support beyond that resulting from the formula, apportioning the costs according to relative parental income and other equities. Under §3.11, an order deferring the sale of the family residence is justified only to avoid "significant detriment to the child" — an assessment based on all relevant factors including, for example, the time the child has lived there, the child's grade in school, and facilitation of the parent's employment. How can you explain the additional benefit the custodial parent will enjoy by living in the family home, given the ALI Principles' strict formulaic approach to property division, compensatory spousal payments, and child support?

10. *Health care coverage*. Federal law now requires state child support guidelines to allocate health care costs (see 42 U.S.C. §652(f) (2000); 45 C.F.R. §302.56 (2005)). Congress also mandates health care coverage for children otherwise ineligible under an employer-sponsored benefit plan (see 42 U.S.C. §1396g-1 (2000)). State responses vary, with some guidelines "ordering one parent to pay for health insurance, and then subtracting the cost from the income of that parent" and others either adding the cost to the child support award and prorating it between the parents or, alternatively, making this expense a factor for deviating from the guidelines. Morgan, supra, at §3.01[a].

11. *Empirical research*. Empirical research has explored the effect of guidelines. Tentative findings from the period when guidelines were first adopted reveal they raise awards as intended — but only for divorced and separated non-Black mothers, not for the never-married and African-American mothers. Economists Beller and Graham speculate that the older guidelines may have had loopholes that resulted in fewer awards for the latter populations. Beller & Graham, supra, at 192, 194.

A subsequent study compares the effects of guidelines in three jurisdictions (Colorado's income-shares, Hawaii's Melson formula, and Illinois's percentage-of-income approaches). This study concludes that the guidelines modestly achieved the congressional objectives of increased award levels, award consistency, and case processing efficiency. No single model produces consistently lower or higher awards, however. Nancy Thoennes et al., The Impact of Child Support Guidelines on Award Adequacy, Award Variability, and Case Processing Efficiency, 25 Fam. L.Q. 325, 345 (1991). Some attribute the modest impact to widespread deviations from the guidelines. Irwin Garfinkel et al., Child Support and Child Well-Being: What Have We Learned, in Child Support and Child Well-Being 1, 9 (Irwin Garfinkel et al. eds., 1994).

Recent analyses reach even more guarded conclusions. The poverty rate for families with a noncustodial parent remains higher than that for other families, and custodial mothers continue to be more likely to be poor than custodial fathers.[45] Under existing guidelines, awards fail to meet the estimated childrearing expenditures calculated by the U.S. Department of Agriculture, a reasonable approximation of actual expenditures on children.[46] Although federal policy on guidelines appears settled (with no changes included in Congress's sweeping 1996 welfare reform), states likely will continue to experiment, using more finely tuned models such as that in the ALI Principles.

[45]. Poverty rates for noncustodial parents decreased between 1993 and 2001 (from 33.3 to 23.4 percent), but in 2001 the poverty rate for custodial-parent families remained roughly four times higher than that for married-couple families with children. In addition, the poverty rate for custodial mothers in 2001, 25 percent, remained significantly higher than that for custodial fathers, 14.7 percent. Timothy S. Grall, U.S. Census Bureau, Custodial Mothers and Fathers and Their Child Support: 2001, at 3 (Current Population Reports, Oct., 2003). See also Irwin Garfinkel et al., A Brief History of Child Support Policies in the United States, in Fathers Under Fire: The Revolution in Child Support Enforcement 22, 24 (Irwin Garfinkel et al. eds., 1998) (describing actual effect of guidelines as modest, despite large potential effects).

[46]. See Laura W. Morgan & Mark C. Lino, A Comparison of Child Support Awards Calculated Under States' Child Support Guidelines with Expenditures on Children Calculated by the U.S. Department of Agriculture, 33 Fam. L.Q. 191, 218 (1999).

Problem

Denise appeals from the trial court's order requiring her former husband, Kevin, to pay $816 monthly child support (instead of the presumptive amount of $1,121 required by the guidelines, based on Kevin's net disposable income). At the time of the order, Kevin was spending only one hour per week with the couple's two young daughters, subject to an order of supervised visitation, stemming from allegations of sexual abuse. In deviating from the guideline, the trial judge explained:

> Presumably the Legislature did not intend to create certain shortfalls in a payor's standard of living solely for the purpose of providing absolute windfalls to the payee parent's and children's standard of living. A child support order of $816 per month will allow Kevin to meet his monthly needs while yet providing Diane and the children with a surplus of $833 over her and the children's stated needs. Such a child support order is in the children's best interest, because to order a guidelines amount providing them with an even larger surplus while leaving Kevin unable to meet his own monthly cost of living would teach them disrespect for the fairness of the legislative and judicial branches of government.

What result when Diane appeals, seeking an award of $1,211 monthly? Was the deviation from the guideline justified? To what extent is the parents' division of time with the children (1 percent for Kevin and 99 percent for Diane) relevant? See In re Marriage of Denise and Kevin C., 67 Cal. Rptr. 2d 508 (Ct. App. 1997).

3. Postmajority Support

■ **CURTIS v. KLINE**
666 A.2d 265 (Pa. 1995)

Justice ZAPPALA. . . .
The issue now before us is whether [Act 62] violates the equal protection clause of the Fourteenth Amendment of the United States Constitution. [This legislation allows a court to order separated, divorced or unmarried parents to provide equitably for educational costs of a child, even after the child has reached 18.]

. . . Appellee filed a petition to terminate his [child] support obligation as to Amber, a student at Kutztown University, and Jason, a student at West Chester University. After Act 62 was promulgated, Appellee was granted leave to include a constitutional challenge to the Act as a basis for seeking relief from post-secondary educational support. . . .

[W]e are satisfied that Act 62 neither implicates a suspect class nor infringes upon a fundamental right. Neither the United States Constitution nor the Pennsylvania Constitution provides an individual right to post-secondary education. . . . Consequently, Act 62 must be upheld if there exists any rational basis for the prescribed classification. . . .

Act 62 classifies young adults according to the marital status of their parents, establishing for one group an action to obtain a benefit enforceable by court order that is not available to the other group. . . . It will not do to argue that this classification is rationally related to the legitimate governmental purpose of obviating difficulties encountered by those in non-intact families who want parental financial assistance for post-secondary education, because such a statement of the governmental purpose assumes the validity of the classification. Recognizing that within the category of young adults in need of financial help to attend college there are some having a parent or parents unwilling to provide such help, the question remains whether the authority of the state may be selectively applied to empower only those from non-intact families to compel such help. We hold that it may not. . . .

It is not inconceivable that in today's society a divorced parent, e.g., a father, could have two children, one born of a first marriage and not residing with him and the other born of a second marriage and still residing with him. Under Act 62, such a father could be required to provide post-secondary educational support for the first child but not the second, even to the extent that the second child would be required to forego a college education. Further, a child over the age of 18, of a woman whose husband had died would have no action against the mother to recover costs of a post-secondary education, but a child over the age of 18, of a woman who never married, who married and divorced, or even who was only separated from her husband when he died would be able to maintain such an action. These are but two examples demonstrating the arbitrariness of the classification adopted in Act 62. . . .

The underlying premise upon which the New Hampshire Supreme Court [in LeClair v. LeClair, 624 A.2d 1350 (N.H. 1993,] undertook its constitutional analysis of the post-secondary educational support scheme was that the legislation created two classifications: married parents and divorced parents. . . . The result is a heightened judicial involvement in the financial and personal lives of divorced families with children that is not necessary with intact families with children. The New Hampshire Supreme Court concluded that because of the unique problems of divorced families, the legislature could rationally conclude that absent judicial involvement, children of divorced families may be less likely than children of intact families to receive post-secondary educational support from both parents.

With all due respect to our sister state, we must reject the New Hampshire Supreme Court's analysis in LeClair. The discriminatory classification adopted by our legislature is not focused on the parents but rather the children. The question is whether similarly situated young adults, i.e., those in need of financial assistance, may be treated differently. [W]e can conceive of no rational reason why those similarly situated with respect to needing funds for college education should be treated unequally. Accordingly, [we] conclude that Act 62 is unconstitutional. . . .

Mr. Justice MONTEMURO [dissenting].

Act 62 . . . operates on the assumption that divorce necessarily involves a disadvantage to the children of broken families, and is intended to assure that children who are thus disadvantaged by the divorce or separation of their parents are not deprived of the opportunity to acquire post secondary school education. In effect, it attempts to maintain the children of divorce in the same position they would have been in had their parents' marriage remained intact. . . .

It would be difficult to argue successfully that the payment of child support is, in general, an obligation freely acknowledged and willingly undertaken by noncustodial parents. The extraordinary amount of time, attention and money devoted by courts, government agencies and legislatures to fashioning and enforcing support orders is testament to the unfortunate fact that the opposite is true. . . .

It has also been widely acknowledged that among the negative effects of divorce on children are those which concern higher education. Courts faced with cases similar to the one at bar have also noted, over and over again, that in divorce, the normative rules of behavior may no longer apply. Ex Parte Bayliss, 550 So. 2d 986 (Ala. 1989); Kujawinski v. Kujawinski, 71 Ill. 2d 563, 376 N.E.2d 1382, 17 Ill. Dec. 801 (1978); Neudecker v. Neudecker, 577 N.E.2d 960 (Indiana 1991); Vrban v. Vrban, 293 N.W.2d 198 (Iowa 1980). Whether because they lose concern for their children's welfare, or out of animosity toward the custodial parent, non-custodial parents frequently become reluctant to provide financial support for any purpose, but are particularly determined to avoid the costs of a college education. . . . Such parents, are, in addition, even less inclined to assist with the educational expenses of daughters than of sons.

The courts addressing the issue have uniformly decided that equal protection is not offended by an attempt to equalize the disparate situation faced by children of divorce. . . . If the Majority's view prevails, there is no recourse for these children, who will be victimized twice, first by the disruptions, both financial and psychological, of their parents' divorce, and again by the system which is theoretically designed to protect them. Moreover, such a course will not benefit the children of intact marriages in which, because of a parental disinterest in education or a view that non-support encourages the work ethic, the parents will also refuse to assist their children. The result will be no improvement for anyone. . . .

Notes and Questions

1. *Historical background.* The problem of parental responsibility for postmajority education arose because of the national trend to lower the age of majority in the wake of the Vietnam War. The trend resulted from widespread public sentiment that youth who could enter combat should be able to drink, vote, and exercise other rights. In response, most statutes lowered the age of majority from 21 to 18. See Kathleen Conrey Horan, Postminority Support for College Education — A Legally Enforceable Obligation in Divorce Proceedings?, 20 Fam. L.Q. 589 (1987). This change jeopardized, however, the ability of many children of divorce to pursue a higher education.

States responded to the ensuing problem of postmajority educational support in a variety of ways. Some legislatures explicitly addressed the question. In some states, courts took the lead by construing existing statutory terms such as "children" and "education" broadly to fashion doctrines of extended dependency and deferred emancipation. See, e.g., Ex parte Bayliss, 550 So. 2d 986 (Ala. 1989). Some used this approach to continue support past minority for high school but not college students. See e.g., Mich. Comp. Laws §552.605b (2005). Others enacted special measures designed to supplement child support under the guidelines with postsecondary education subsidies. See In re Marriage of Mullen-Funderburk, 696 N.W.2d 607 (Iowa 2005). But see In re Donovan, 871 A.2d 30 (N.H. 2005). Most states still do not authorize postmajority educational support. See Laura W. Morgan, Child Support Guidelines: Interpretation and Application §4.05[d] (1996 & Supp. 2004) (state-by-state list). Under §3.12 of the ALI Principles, supra, courts may require parents to provide for a child's "life opportunities." See generally

Carol R. Goforth, The Case for Expanding Child Support Obligations to Cover Post-Secondary Educational Expenses, 56 Ark. L. Rev. 93 (2003).

2. *Applications.* In the states allowing courts to order postmajority support for higher education, reasonable expenses, not the guidelines, determine the amount. Morgan, supra, §4.05[d][2]. Such expenses encompass such education-related costs as: tuition, books, room, and board. In re Gilmore, 803 A.2d 601 (N.H. 2002). Sometimes the obligation also includes continuation of previous child support payments. See Reininger v. Reininger, 871 A.2d 422 (Conn. Super. Ct. 2005). Often, the student must achieve a particular level of academic success and provide the obligor with official documentation. See, e.g., Sebastian v. Sebastian, 798 N.E.2d 224 (Ind. Ct. App. 2003) (C average and enrollment as full-time student); Jansen v. Westrich, 95 S.W.3d 214 (Mo. Ct. App. 2003) (obligor must receive transcript, rather than grades alone). Do such requirements, imposed by statute or court order, unfairly burden the students to whom they apply? Violate their educational privacy rights? See 20 U.S.C.A. §1232g(d) (West 2000 & Supp. 2005).

3. *Equal protection challenges.* Why did *Curtis* focus on the law's classification of children instead of its classification of parents? Does the court's analysis jeopardize laws allowing courts to order divorced parents to pay child support to minors — a protection not provided to minors in intact families? See Stillman v. State, 87 P.3d 200 (Colo. Ct. App. 2003). Must laws providing postmajority educational support for children of divorce also apply to children of never-married parents? See Johnson v. Louis, 654 N.W.2d 886 (Iowa 2002) (no). In contrast to *Curtis*, other courts have examined the different treatment among parents and rejected constitutional challenges. See, e.g., In re Marriage of Kohring, 999 S.W.2d 228 (Mo. 1999) (rejecting equal protection and parental autonomy challenges); In re Marriage of Crocker, 22 P.3d 759 (Or. 2001) (statute survives equal protection review). See also In re Marriage of McGinley, 19 P.3d 954, 960 (Or. Ct. App. 2001) (rejecting argument that divorced parents constitute a suspect class, despite unfavorable depiction in books, movies, and campaigns to collect child support).

What should the legislature do in response to *Curtis*? Must it include intact families in authorizing court-ordered postmajority educational support? Can it? See Chapter VIII, section A.

4. *Reciprocal duties.* At common law the child had a right to support; the parent had a right to the child's services and earnings. See 1 William Blackstone, Commentaries on the Laws of England *453. Although divorce may prevent fulfillment of this reciprocal relationship, the principle that child support is an individual parental responsibility still controls. Professor Harry Krause, however, suggests that family disruption has diminished this reciprocity, with far-reaching consequences:

> . . . When Blackstone formulated the support obligation for the common law world, he was looking at a world that was centered on the ongoing family. Divorce did not exist. . . . Choosing to rest most of his case on natural law and what we now call sociobiology, Blackstone did not say that the support obligation was founded on the reciprocal relationship of parent and child in the ongoing family, but I think it was. This reciprocity had an economic and a social component.
>
> Economically, the support-obligated parent was entitled to the child's earnings until the child reached majority. More important, economic reciprocity extended to the parent's old age. Support received by the young child morally and legally obligated

the adult child to support the aged parent. Thus, before we had Social Security, child support was an "investment" the parent made, to be recovered if needed. . . . Socially, parent and child reciprocity involved an ongoing family life. . . .

The point is that the absent parent may fairly claim that he is not getting his money's worth for the support he is obligated to pay, not on the economic or social level. Today's enlarged child support obligation does not resemble what Blackstone was talking about. . . .

Harry D. Krause, Child Support Reassessed: Limits of Private Responsibility and the Public Interest, in Divorce Reform at the Crossroads 166, 178-180 (Stephen D. Sugarman & Herma Hill Kay eds., 1990). Does increased reliance on public support follow from Krause's analysis? Or unmet needs for children?

5. *Empirical research*. One influential voice in law reform regarding postdivorce postmajority educational support is psychologist Judith Wallerstein. In 2000, Wallerstein published a follow-up study of 49 children of divorce from Marin County, California, as part of her larger longitudinal in-depth study of 131 children and their families. Judith S. Wallerstein et al., The Unexpected Legacy of Divorce: A 25 Year Landmark Study (2000). Confirming her earlier findings, Wallerstein reported that only about 30 percent of children from divorced families receive full or consistent partial college support from one or both parents, compared to almost 90 percent of those children from intact families. See id. at 247-250, 335-336. Wallerstein also found that only about one-third of those fathers who were financially able, in fact, provided financial assistance for their children's college expenses. Judith S. Wallerstein & Sandra Blakeslee, Second Chances: Men, Women and Children a Decade After Divorce 156 (1989). On the basis of her research, Wallerstein recommended the need for legislation mandating postmajority educational support from noncustodial fathers. See, e.g., Richard Morgan, States Split on Asking Divorced Parents to Pay for Children's Tuition, Chron. Higher Educ., Aug. 16, 2002, at A28 (noting Wallerstein's influence on recent Connecticut reforms).

A more recent study criticizes Wallerstein's findings by pointing out that her initial research occurred in the early 1970s before joint custody became widespread and, therefore, questions the relevance of her conclusions for policymaking today. William V. Fabricius et al., Divorced Parents' Financial Support of Their Children's College Expenses, 41 Fam. Ct. Rev. 224 (2003). Fabricius's study, based on a sample of introductory psychology students at Arizona State University, found that fathers with joint custody of their children are more likely to contribute to college expenses than fathers of children in sole maternal custody and that, after controlling for parental income, divorced fathers contribute about the same amount as divorced mothers. The Fabricius research, however, considers the experiences of students from a large public state university, a sample drawn primarily from the surrounding diverse urban environment and characterized by a substantial proportion of students who live at home. As such, this research may not shed much light on the effects of divorce on students (such as those in Wallerstein's sample) drawn primarily from a suburban, higher socioeconomic stratum who attend substantially more costly private or public universities. Moreover, Fabricius bases his analysis on students' perceptions of family incomes and estimates of parental support (arguably imprecise measures) and, more importantly, fails to shed light on the experience of those students unable to attend college at all because of a lack of financial resources.

Problem

Patrick, the son of Cherry and John, was 12 at the time of their divorce. When Patrick turns 18, Cherry (who has custody) files a petition to increase John's child support payments to include $30,000 in combined tuition and expenses at Trinity College, a private college where Patrick has gained admission. Cherry shows that John's net worth exceeds $1 million. Assuming the court has the authority to order postmajority support for education, what result on Cherry's petition and why? What additional evidence, if any, might be relevant in order for the court to decide?

Should the court consider the quality of the relationship between the non-custodial parent and child? See McKay v. McKay, 644 N.E.2d 164 (Ind. Ct. App. 1994); In re Pendergast, 565 N.W.2d 354 (Iowa Ct. App. 1997). Cf. McKay v. McKay, 671 N.E.2d 194 (Ind. Ct. App. 1996). Parental disapproval of the college chosen? Cf. Wineburgh v. Wineburgh, 816 A.2d 1105 (Pa. Super. Ct. 2002). What should be the extent of the noncustodial parent's financial burden — public higher education? Private higher education? Graduate school? What facts must support the determination? Parent(s)' educational background? Academic talent? A wealthy noncustodial parent? See, e.g., Ex parte Bayliss, 550 So. 2d 986 (Ala. 1989), *appeal after remand*, 575 So. 2d 1117 (Ala. Civ. App. 1990).

4. Modification of Child Support

a. Remarriage and New Families

■ **POHLMANN v. POHLMANN**
703 So. 2d 1121 (Fla. Dist. Ct. App. 1997)

Peterson, J. . . . .

[The former husband unsuccessfully petitioned to reduce his child support obligation, alleging that this modification was justified by changed circumstances, including a permanent decrease in his income, his remarriage and his three children from this marriage, and his former wife's remarriage. He appeals.]

We first address the former husband's argument that subsection 61.30(12) is unconstitutional. The subsection provides:

61.30 Child Support Guidelines. — . . .

(12) A parent with a support obligation may have other children living with him or her who were born or adopted after the support obligation arose. The existence of such subsequent children should not as a general rule be considered by the court as a basis for disregarding the amount provided in the guidelines. The parent with a support obligation for subsequent children may raise the existence of such subsequent children as a justification for deviation from the guidelines. However, if the existence of such subsequent children is raised, the income of the other parent of the subsequent children shall be considered by the court in determining whether or not there is a basis for deviation from the guideline amount. *The issue of subsequent children may only be raised in a proceeding for an upward modification of an existing award and may not be applied to justify a decrease in an existing award.*

(Emphasis added). [W]e apply the rational basis standard of review because neither a suspect classification nor a fundamental right is involved. See Feltman v. Feltman, 434 N.W.2d 590 (S.D. 1989). Under the rational basis standard of review, a statute is presumed valid and will be upheld if the classification under the law bears some reasonable relationship to the achievement of a legitimate state purpose. [W]e find that subsection 61.30(12) furthers a legitimate state interest and affirm the trial court's finding of constitutionality. The statute assures that noncustodial parents will continue to contribute to the support of their children from their first marriage notwithstanding their obligation to support children born during a subsequent marriage. Granting priority of child support to children of an earlier first marriage, the *Feltman* court determined that the South Dakota statute provided a fair and logical prioritization of claims against a noncustodial parent's income. *Feltman* at 592. "Without prioritization, the children from the first family might find their standard of living substantially decreased by the voluntary acts of a noncustodial parent. A noncustodial parent who elects to become responsible for supporting the children of a second marriage does so with the knowledge of a continuing responsibility to the children of the first marriage." Id.

We also affirm the trial court's finding that the former husband failed to show a substantial change of circumstances. . . . In an attempt to manufacture a substantial change in circumstances, the former husband and his current wife produced the latter's petition for separate maintenance [and child support] which tellingly was filed only two weeks before trial. The current wife testified that while she filed such petition in order to assure that her three children would be provided for, nothing in their marital relationship has changed. The trial court did not abuse its discretion in finding that the former husband failed to meet his burden of proving a permanent, involuntary, and substantial change in circumstances. . . .

HARRIS, J., dissenting.

The issue in this case, quite simply, is whether it is a "legitimate government interest" for the State, through its legislative process, to prefer certain children over others. . . . It is our obligation, under the constitution of this state, to determine whether the state has the right under any circumstance (even if recommended by a commission) to discriminate between children born to the same parent. There is no doubt that if parents are required to support their children by a second marriage to the same extent that they must support their children from an earlier marriage, the standard of living of all of the children will be affected. But so too will the standard of living of the first-born child in an intact marriage be affected by the birth of the second child. . . . It is not appropriate for the state to punish the children of a second marriage because their parent was involved in a previous divorce.

Although the state should not involve itself with the divorced parent's decision regarding remarriage, our statute is designed to discourage a parent from having a second family unless he or she is willing to support the second family at a lesser standard. . . . At least the parent has assumed the risk of state discrimination. But the children of the later marriage were not aware of the statutory provision nor did they consent to be born into state-mandated poverty. ["Obviously, no child is responsible for his birth and penalizing the . . . child is an ineffectual — as well as unjust — way of deterring the parent." Plyler v. Doe, 457 U.S. 202, 220 (1982).]

[W]e should keep in mind that we are not here dealing with state funds. The state is mandating a disproportionate allocation of the parent's income. . . . The state's current approach is Cinderellian — it makes noncustodial parents appear as wicked stepparents to their own children by requiring them to provide new ball gowns for their first born while supplying hand-me-downs to their later children. . . . The children of the first marriage simply have no more veto power over the noncustodial parent's future reproductive decisions than a child of an intact marriage has over his parents' decision to have additional children. . . . Because the state has no business discriminating between children based solely on the fact of a divorce, there is no legitimate state purpose in requiring a parent to allocate his or her income more to one child than another. . . .

Notes and Questions

1. *Successive families.* A number of factors occurring after dissolution, such as remarriage, may affect a parent's support obligations. The increasing incidence of multiple and "blended" families raises questions about the role subsequent family obligations should play in applying support guidelines to children of a prior marriage. What are the rationale and implications of *Pohlmann*'s approach, sometimes called the "first mortgage" approach? See, e.g., In re Marriage of Ladely, 469 N.W.2d 663 (Iowa 1991); Elizabeth S. Scott & Robert E. Scott, Parents as Fiduciaries, 81 Va. L. Rev. 2401, 2466-2468 (1995). But see Martha Minow, How Should We Think About Child Support Obligations?, in Fathers Under Fire: The Revolution in Child Support Enforcement 302, 313-318 (Irwin Garfinkel et al. eds., 1998) (examining conflicting intuitions on support priorities in successive families).

In applying the rule in *Pohlmann*, should "subsequent" refer to a child's age or the date of a support order? See In re Marriage of Potts, 696 N.E.2d 1263, 1266 (Ill. App. Ct. 1998). Why did the current wife in *Pohlmann* attempt to get a child support order? How should the court calculate the former husband's support obligation to his children with this wife, if they were to divorce? See, e.g., Office of Child Support Enforcement v. Lee, 2005 WL 546445 (Ark. Ct. App. 2005).

Or should obligations to other family members simply constitute a basis for deviating from the guidelines? See Brooks v. Brooks, 622 N.W.2d 670 (Neb. 2001).

2. *Factual variations.* Although *Pohlmann* depicts a common set of facts, there are many variations on this theme. For example, in Gallaher v. Elam, 104 S.W.3d 455 (Tenn. 2003), a married father unsuccessfully attacked the Tennessee guidelines, which the court applied to determine the support of a child conceived as the result of an extramarital affair. The father had challenged the law for failure to take into account his obligations to his older children, born during his extant marriage. And, Buncombe County ex rel. Blair v. Jackson, 531 S.E.2d 240 (N.C. Ct. App. 2000), determined the obligations of one man who had fathered five children with three different women.

Suppose the father in *Pohlmann* had taken a second job so that he could support his new family. Should his now higher income provide a basis to increase his support obligation to the children of his first wife? An amendment to the Florida legislation says: "If such subsequent children exist, the court, when considering an upward modification of an existing award, may disregard the income from secondary employment obtained in addition to the parent's primary employment if the court determines that the employment was obtained primarily to support the subsequent children." Fla. Stat. Ann. §61.30(12)(a) (West 2005).

3. *Different approaches.* When Congress enacted the Family Support Act (FSA) of 1988 (mandating state guidelines), it left to the states the weight to be given to a parent's financial obligations to successive families. See generally Misti Nelc, Inequitable Distribution: The Effect of Minnesota's Child Support Guidelines on Prior and Subsequent Children, 17 Law & Ineq. 97 (1999). In contrast to *Pohlmann*, some courts follow a "second family first" doctrine, deducting the support needed for the second family to determine the parent's available income before applying the guidelines for the first family's support. See Irwin Garfinkel et al., Child Support Orders: A Perspective on Reform, The Future of Children, Spring 1994, at 84, 90. Is this a better approach? Suppose that states following this approach allow the obligor to invoke support of the subsequent family defensively (to show why the court should not increase his present obligation to his prior family), but not offensively (to reduce support to the prior family)? See, e.g., Schuyler v. Briner, 13 P.3d 738 (Alaska 2000). See generally Laura W. Morgan, Positive Parenting and Negative Contributions: Why Payment of Child Support Should Not Be Regarded as Dissipation of Marital Assets, 30 N.M. L. Rev. 1, 6-7 (2000).

4. *Constitutionality.* What constitutional problems does Judge Harris identify in his dissent in *Pohlmann*? Is his analysis persuasive? Does the "second family first" approach have similar flaws because it treats unfairly the earlier children? Should states be required to consider all of an obligor's children, wherever they may be living, and then divide among them the money available for support? Cf. Laura W. Morgan, Child Support Guidelines: Interpretation and Application §2.02 (1996 & Supp. 2004).

Can the law restrict the choice to have a second family as a means of protecting the rights of the first family? Does Zablocki v. Redhail, Chapter II, section D1, apply? As *Pohlmann* illustrates, constitutional challenges to state child support schedules have proven unsuccessful. See, e.g., *Gallaher*, supra (due process, equal protection, and separation of powers challenge); Ward v. McFall, 593 S.E.2d 340 (Ga. 2004) (Supremacy Clause challenge); Georgia Dep't of Hum. Resources v. Sweat, 580 S.E.2d 206 (Ga. 2003) (Takings Clause and other constitutional challenges).

5. *Obligations of stepparents.* What financial responsibilities does the law impose upon stepparents? At common law stepparents had no duty to support their stepchildren either during a marriage or following its dissolution, but courts and legislatures are changing these rules. See generally Margaret M. Mahoney, Stepfamilies and the Law (1994).

Several states have statutes imposing financial responsibility on a stepparent who receives a child into the family, so long as the child remains in the home. E.g., Mo. Rev. Stat. §453.400 (2000). Others simply codify the doctrine of in loco parentis, presuming a stepparent who accepts and supports a child does so as a parent but allowing unilateral termination of that status at any time, e.g., Okla. Stat. Ann. tit. 10, §15 (West 1998) (phrased in terms of husband's support of wife's children by former husband), or look to stepparents only when a child would otherwise become destitute, e.g., Vt. Stat. Ann. tit. 15, §296 (2002). The obligation does not continue, however, upon dissolution of that marriage. See, e.g., Weinand v. Wienand, 616 N.W.2d 1 (Neb. 2000) (ex-stepparent granted visitation not required to pay child support).

The ALI Principles do not recognize a general duty of support by stepparents. One who agrees or undertakes to assume a parental support obligation to a child, however, might later be estopped from denying a parental support obligation. ALI Principles, supra, at §3.03(1)(a). Under such circumstances, a court could impose a child support obligation on the stepparent after the dissolution of the relationship with the child's parent. See id. at cmt. b. An adult obligated to pay child support is a parent by estoppel for purposes of determining custodial and decisionmaking responsibility. Id. at §2.03. See supra p. 667. See also Mary Ann Mason & Nicole Zayac, Rethinking Stepparent Rights: Has the ALI Found a Better Definition?, 36 Fam. L.Q. 227 (2002).

6. *New spouses' and partners' resources.* Should a court, in computing a parent's child support obligation, take into account the income of this parent's new spouse or partner? See, e.g., Department of Revenue v. Mason M., 790 N.E.2d 671 (Mass. 2003); Workman v. Workman, 632 N.W.2d 286 (Neb. 2001). How does the statute quoted in *Pohlmann* address this issue? For an examination of the inconsistencies in the way child support rules treat obligations to prior families and the way the law of property division penalizes such payments, see Morgan, Positive Parenting, supra.

7. *Policy.* Do stepparent obligations make sound policy? Professor David Chambers has observed that empirical studies find stepparents play an important family role:

> Some empirical evidence suggests that when residential stepparents enter children's lives, the children generally see their absent parents less often than they did before. [D]espite the ambiguities of the stepparent relationship, many individual stepparents do form strong emotional bonds with their stepchildren. They are seen by the child as "parent." And, of course, there is ample corresponding evidence that biologic fathers who do not live with their children will not pay child support unless compelled to do so and that they visit their children less and less as time passes, whether or not the mother remarries. In the future, we may come to view residential stepparents as replacing absent parents and assuming some or all of their responsibilities.

David L. Chambers, Stepparents, Biologic Parents, and the Law's Perceptions of "Family" after Divorce, in Divorce Reform at the Crossroads 102, 117 (Stephen D. Sugarman & Herma Hill Kay eds., 1990).

Given these realities, should the law adjust child support obligations whenever remarriage occurs? See id. at 127-128 (rule would risk encouraging remarriage decisions based on economic consequences or spite). Should a stepparent be responsible for continued child support after the breakup of the subsequent marriage? Chambers suggests relevant factors in this determination include the length of time the stepparent lived with the child, the extent of support the stepparent actually provided, and the extent of support the biological parents provided during the marriage. Id. at 128.

8. *Modification.* The issue posed by *Pohlmann* typically arises in litigation seeking to modify an existing child support award, because courts can modify child support awards based upon a showing of changed circumstances. The standards for modifying maintenance and child support are the same under UMDA §316, 9A U.L.A. (pt. II) 102 (1998). See supra p. 632. Should the obligor's acquisition of a second family have the same impact in both contexts?

9. *Retroactive modification.* Most jurisdictions have long disallowed retroactive modification of child support obligations, that is, alterations of payments past due. E.g., Kinsella v. Kinsella, 181 N.W.2d 764 (N.D. 1970). Note that the rule against

retroactive modification places the burden on the obligor to seek modification as soon as circumstances change.

Now, federal legislation requires all states to recognize child support obligations as judgments once due, entitled to full faith and credit, and to disallow retroactive modification. 42 U.S.C. §666(a)(9) (2000). Does this requirement mean that states lose the discretion to forgive arrearages even when equity dictates relief for the obligor or the facts show the obligor's inability to pay during the period in question? See, e.g., State ex rel. Score v. Bidwell, 2004 WL 1318888 (Neb. Ct. App. 2004). But see Department of Human Resources v. Fillingane, 761 So. 2d 869 (Miss. 2000). Cf. Harry D. Krause, Child Support Reassessed: Limits of Private Responsibility and the Public Interest, in Divorce Reform at the Crossroads 166, 175 (Stephen D. Sugarman & Herma Hill Kay eds., 1990) (recommending forgiveness of arrears owed to government when obligor has no hope of repayment).

b. Employment Changes

■ OLMSTEAD v. ZIEGLER
42 P.3d 1102 (Alaska 2002)

FABE, Chief Justice . . .

William Olmstead and Elizabeth Ziegler married in August 1989. Their only child, Lauren, was born in January 1990. They divorced in December 1994. The parties, both of whom are attorneys, entered into a settlement agreement that was incorporated into the divorce decree. The agreement provided for joint legal and physical custody of their daughter and specified that neither party would pay child support to the other. However, Olmstead did agree to pay for their daughter's daycare and education expenses. Their daughter no longer requires constant daycare, and she now attends public schools. Olmstead estimates that he spends approximately $80 per month on child care.

At the time of the divorce, the parties submitted a child support affidavit, as required by Alaska Civil Rule 90.3(3). Olmstead's estimated 1994 annual gross income was $53,000 and Ziegler's was $25,000. Ziegler's estimate proved to be high, as she actually earned $16,753 in 1994. Ziegler was subsequently hired as an attorney with the firm of Baxter, Bruce & Brand in Juneau, where her annual income increased significantly. In 1998, she earned $53,761.

In August 1996 Olmstead's law partner of several years, Patrick Conheady, left the partnership. Conheady claimed that Olmstead was unproductive and frequently played card games on his computer instead of working on his cases. Olmstead became a solo practitioner. While he sought other positions and applied for several state jobs, he was apparently unsuccessful in obtaining other employment. Olmstead's income decreased significantly during this period. In 1996 his income dropped to $10,157. In 1998 he earned $13,075.

In March 1999 Olmstead informed his friends and colleagues in Juneau that he would be leaving the practice of law, as he had decided to go back to school to become a teacher. In order to make ends meet in the meantime, he offered his legal research and writing services to other attorneys. Olmstead has since remarried. Ziegler remains single.

On June 3, 1999, Olmstead filed a motion for an order modifying child support. ... The trial court found that, although their financial situations may have changed, the parties still possessed equal earning capacities. The trial court also reasoned that, although Olmstead was free to change careers, he was not entitled to a modification of child support: "[Olmstead] has elected to learn new things for a while, and perhaps take on a new career. He is free to do so, but under our case law [Ziegler] and the child are not expected to finance these choices." Olmstead appeals. ...

Olmstead claims that the court erred in finding that he was voluntarily underemployed and contends that the court improperly relied upon his decision to change careers in making that finding. Olmstead points out that he did not ask for a modification of child support based upon his income as a student or teacher. Rather, he requested a modification based entirely upon his earnings while he was a practicing attorney. He thus claims that it was improper for the trial court to rely on his career change when he did not make it a basis for his motion. Olmstead adds that he made a mistake by choosing law as a profession, and that he lacks the personality traits necessary for success in the field. ... Ziegler counters that Olmstead's lack of success in law and subsequent move to teaching are the results of his voluntary actions. ...

Voluntarily reducing one's income may not justify a modification of child support. Determining whether or not a parent is voluntarily and unreasonably underemployed is essentially a question of fact. ... A trial court may find that underemployment is voluntary even if the obligor acted in good faith.

We conclude that the trial court did not err in finding that Olmstead was voluntarily and unreasonably underemployed. The evidence before the trial court established that Olmstead took many steps, including closing his office and failing to keep regular business hours, that demonstrated his intent to downsize his practice. He also significantly reduced his workload hoping to obtain a job with the Department of Transportation. In addition, the record contains an affidavit from Olmstead's former partner, Conheady, recounting his difficulties with Olmstead's lack of productivity: Conheady states that he left the partnership because Olmstead was not producing enough billable hours. While Olmstead has repeatedly stated that he was simply a failure at law and was not capable of earning the average lawyer's salary, he has provided scant support for his assertions. In addition, Olmstead's claims that he was unable to make a living practicing law are undermined by the fact that at one time he made over $53,000 a year.

[I]t was permissible for the trial court to consider Olmstead's career change in determining the issue of voluntary and unreasonable underemployment. ... Moreover, ... Civil Rule 90.3 recognizes that "[w]hen a parent makes a career change, this consideration should include the extent to which the children will ultimately benefit from the change." Thus, it is appropriate for the trial court to consider not only the career change, but also its potential impact on the child. Since Olmstead has failed to prove any benefit to the child from his decision to downsize his practice and change careers, the trial court did not err in finding that a modification is not warranted. ...

... Olmstead also claims that the trial court's determination of earning capacity is clearly erroneous and requires reversal. ... Olmstead maintains that there is no evidence to support the trial court's conclusion that his earning capacity was equal to or greater than Ziegler's.

However, the record supports the trial court's view that Olmstead was not working at his full capacity. . . . The trial court based its view of Olmstead's earning capacity on his actual past earnings as well as on other factors discussed above. The trial court had before it ample evidence of Olmstead's work history, qualifications, and job opportunities. Although Olmstead would prefer that the trial court calculate his potential income based only on three years of his earnings of his own choosing, the trial court properly considered Olmstead's qualifications as an attorney with substantial experience. The record also contains evidence that Olmstead at one time made over $50,000 per year while practicing law. Implicit in the trial court's evaluation of Olmstead's earning capacity is its rejection of his claims that he is simply not a successful solo practitioner. Also included in the record are Alaska Department of Labor statistics stating that the average income for male attorneys in Alaska is $65,811. In sum, the trial court's determination that Olmstead had the capacity to earn as much as Ziegler is not clearly erroneous. [Affirmed.]

Notes and Questions

1. *Voluntary reductions.* Courts take different approaches when a parent who decides to change careers or pursue additional education seeks a reduction in child support based on changed circumstances, specifically decreased income. What test does *Olmstead* apply? Is the voluntary nature of the change controlling, or must the court deem the change unreasonable too? What criteria determine unreasonableness? How should courts assess voluntariness? Is the obligor's imprisonment a voluntary or involuntary changes of circumstances? See, e.g., State v. Stoppleworth, 694 N.W.2d 8 (N.D. 2005). What of depression because of a paramour's illness? See Gastineau v. Gastineau, 573 N.Y.S.2d 819 (Sup. Ct. 1991). A decision to go to medical school, if before marriage the parties agreed the father could pursue such training after the mother completed her education? See Harvey v. Robinson, 665 A.2d 215 (Me. 1995). Suppose the obligor must take a lower-paying job because he was fired from his prior job for misconduct? See People ex rel. J.R.T. v. Martinez, 70 P.3d 474 (Colo. 2003).

2. *Other tests.* An alternative approach uses a "good faith" test, disallowing modification only when the change in employment reflects an attempt to evade support obligations. Is this a better standard than that used in *Olmstead*? Who should have the burden of showing the obligor's motive? See Minnear v. Minnear, 814 P.2d 85 (Nev. 1991) (willful underemployment creates presumption of purpose to avoid support obligation and justifies increase in support payments). Another approach employs a "best-interests" standard. See Overbey v. Overbey, 698 So. 2d 811 (Fla. 1997). Finally, some courts use a "balancing test." See Little v. Little, 975 P.2d 108 (Ariz. 1999). See generally Lewis Becker, Spousal and Child Support and the "Voluntary Reduction of Income" Doctrine, 29 Conn. L. Rev. 647 (1997).

3. *Increased income.* If voluntary career changes do not justify reducing child support obligations, how should courts treat changes that increase the obligor's ability to pay? In Smith v. Freeman, 814 A.2d 65 (Md. Ct. Spec. App. 2002), a case about a professional football player whose salary increased significantly under a

new contract, the court emphasized that either a change in the child's needs or a change in parental resources can justify an upward modification. What explains this approach? Would a child presumptively benefit from increased parental income in an intact family? Wouldn't all members in an intact family also experience decreases in income? Why should a child get the benefits but not the burdens of changes in the obligor's fortune? To what extent does dissolution and its financial obligations limit parental freedom to change careers and jobs? Should courts facing these modification issues treat spousal and child support the same? See Graham v. Graham, 597 A.2d 355 (D.C. 1991).

4. *Automatic adjustment.* Frequently, a child support award will become inadequate over time. Does this situation warrant an increase in the award, in contrast to the decreases sought in *Pohlmann* and *Olmstead*? The applicable rule is the same, requiring the party seeking to modify to show sufficiently changed circumstances. This rule, which discourages modification to protect courts from the burden of such proceedings, has "impoverishing effects":

> The prevailing American rule for child support modification in many instances requires the custodial parent, usually the mother, to absorb the effects of inflation, the additional cost of raising older children, and changes in the child's needs, regardless of changes in the obligor's income. To remedy these imbalances, she must bear the cost of pursuing a new action and, in most states, prove that a party's circumstances have substantially changed since the date of the original order. Further, she must make this decision with little guidance as to the likelihood of success: she is generally ignorant of the obligor's true financial situation, and the judge's broad discretion to find that circumstances have or have not substantially changed creates even more uncertainty.

J. Thomas Oldham, Abating the Feminization of Poverty: Changing the Rules Governing Post-Decree Modification of Child Support Obligations, 1994 B.Y.U. L. Rev. 841, 843-844.

Guidelines should make awards easier to update than when they were based on judicial discretion. The Family Support Act of 1988 required state review of the guidelines every four years (42 U.S.C. §667(a) (2000)) as well as administrative review of all awards in Title IV-D cases every three years and all other cases when either parent so requests (id. at §666(a)(10)). Historically, only a small percentage of awards are modified.[47]

The Personal Responsibility and Work Opportunity Reconciliation Act of 1996 (welfare reform legislation) gives states three options for reviewing and adjusting awards: the process required under the Family Support Act, a cost-of-living adjustment (using a consumer price index to update the amount periodically), or an automated adjustment (based on tax or other records). 42 U.S.C. §666(a)(10) (2000). The custodial parent still has the burden of requesting review. Often she will avoid doing so because of unfamiliarity with the process or a desire to avoid antagonizing the obligor. See Paul K. Legler, The Coming Revolution in Child

---

[47]. Robert G. Williams, Implementation of the Child Support Provisions of the Family Support Act: Child Support Guidelines, Updating of Awards, and Routine Income Withholding, in Child Support and Child Well-Being 93, 111-112 (Irwin Garfinkel et al., eds., 1994). One problem may be the difficulty of automatic updating under the income-shares guidelines. Irwin Garfinkel et al., Child Support Orders: A Perspective on Reform, The Future of Children, Spring 1994, at 92. Framing child support awards in terms of a percentage of the obligor's income facilitates automatic adjustment.

Support Policy: Implications of the 1996 Welfare Act, 30 Fam. L.Q. 519, 557-559 (1996); Oldham, supra.

To address such problems, a few states make the passage of time sufficient for modification, by including in awards automatic "escalator clauses" tied to the cost of living or adopting procedures requiring review every three years. See Laura W. Morgan, Child Support Guidelines: Interpretation and Application §5.05 (1996 & Supp. 2004). Should Congress mandate such rules for all states?

Problems

1. At the time of divorce, the court ordered Samih, a chemist earning $46,000 annually in Indiana, to pay $174 per week in child support. When his employer required Samih to relocate to Minnesota, he refused because he wanted to remain close to his children in Indiana. Samih thereupon lost his job and started his own company, Vintage Chemicals. He earned $16,200 the first year and expected to earn $20,000 the following year. He seeks a decrease in his child support obligation based on his reduced income. What result and why? Is Samih's reason for refusing to relocate relevant? See Abouhalkah v. Sharps, 795 N.E.2d 488 (Ind. Ct. App. 2003).

2. Upon divorce, the Missouri court awarded custody of the couple's four children to Linda and ordered Elliot, whose yearly income was $105,000, to pay her $562.50 per month per child. Thereafter, Linda, a physician with an average annual salary of $100,000, remarried and moved with the children to her new husband's home in California. She decided not to resume her medical practice right away, explaining:

> The primary reason, this is really the first opportunity I have had to be home with my children. Moving to a new place there is going to be a lot of adjustments. We felt it was very important for me to be home and helping establish a new routine for everyone. I also do not have a license to practice in California at this point.

Thereafter, the court granted Elliot's petition to reduce his child support payments to $308 per month per child, based on the yearly salary of Linda's new husband ($225,000) and Linda's own earning capacity. In applying the guidelines, the court imputed to Linda income of $100,000 although she presently earns nothing. Linda now appeals contending the court erred in (a) treating her new husband's salary as a sufficient changed circumstance to warrant downward modification and (b) imputing income to a custodial parent who chooses to stay home to care for minor children. What result and why? For (a), would the answer change if she were cohabiting without remarriage? Compare Cook v. Eggers, 593 N.W. 2d 781 (N.D. 1999), with Allred v. Allred, 744 A.2d 70 (Md. Spec. Ct. App. 2000). For (b), should the children's ages matter? See Stanton v. Abbey, 874 S.W.2d 493 (Mo. Ct. App. 1994). See also Bailey v. Bailey, 724 So. 2d 335 (Miss. 1998); Tetreault v. Coon, 708 A.2d 571 (Vt. 1998); ALI Principles, supra, §3.15; Catherine Moseley Clark, Comment, Imputing Parental Income in Child Support Determinations: What Price for a Child's Best Interests? 49 Cath. U. L. Rev. 167 (1999); Karl A. W. DeMarce, Note, Devaluing Caregiving in Child Support Calculations: Imputing

Income to Custodial Parents Who Stay Home with Children: Stanton v. Abbey, 61 Mo. L. Rev. 429 (1996).

F. ENFORCEMENT

Traditionally, enforcement of the financial consequences of divorce was largely a matter of private responsibility. In recent years, however, states and the federal government have assumed a significant role. Although child support enforcement in particular has become a national priority, problems in enforcing property divisions and alimony awards persist as well.

This section examines enforcement mechanisms, including traditional state-created private remedies and modern measures triggered by the "federalization" of this part of family law. Like the recent developments in this area, this section emphasizes enforcement of child support, but it also notes applications to the other financial consequences of dissolution. Throughout this material, consider first how the law should allocate enforcement responsibilities among individual obligees, the states, and the federal government. Further, consider the extent to which the need for effective enforcement mechanisms trumps even fundamental privacy rights and liberty interests, an issue posed by the following case.

1. Imprisonment: Criminal Nonsupport and Contempt of Court

■ **STATE v. OAKLEY**
629 N.W.2d 200 (Wis.), **reconsideration denied & opinion clarified,** *635 N.W.2d 760 (Wis. 2001),* **cert. denied,**
537 U.S. 813 (2002)

JON P. WILCOX, J. . . .
David Oakley (Oakley), the petitioner, was initially charged with intentionally refusing to pay child support for his nine children he has fathered with four different women. The State subsequently charged Oakley with seven counts of intentionally refusing to provide child support as a repeat offender. [D]uring the relevant time period, Oakley had paid no child support and . . . there were arrears in excess of $25,000. [T]he State argued that Oakley should be sentenced to six years in prison. . . .

After taking into account Oakley's ability to work and his consistent disregard of the law and his obligations to his children, Judge Hazlewood observed that . . . "if Mr. Oakley goes to prison, he's not going to be in a position to pay any meaningful support for these children." [The judge imposed a term of probation and] then imposed the condition at issue here: while on probation, Oakley cannot have any more children unless he demonstrates that he had the ability to support them and that he is supporting the children he already had. After sentencing, Oakley filed for postconviction relief contesting this condition. . . .

Refusal to pay child support by so-called "deadbeat parents" has fostered a crisis with devastating implications for our children. Of those single parent households with established child support awards or orders, approximately one-third did not receive any payment while another one-third received only partial payment.[5] For example, in 1997, out of $26,400,000,000 awarded by a court order to custodial mothers, only $15,800,000,000 was actually paid, amounting to a deficit of $10,600,000,000.[6] These figures represent only a portion of the child support obligations that could be collected if every custodial parent had a support order established. Single mothers disproportionately bear the burden of nonpayment as the custodial parent. On top of the stress of being a single parent, the nonpayment of child support frequently presses single mothers below the poverty line. In fact, 32.1% of custodial mothers were below the poverty line in 1997, in comparison to only 10.7% of custodial fathers. Indeed, the payment of child support is widely regarded as an indispensable step in assisting single mothers to scale out of poverty, especially when their welfare benefits have been terminated due to new time limits.

. . . In addition to engendering long-term consequences such as poor health, behavioral problems, delinquency and low educational attainment, inadequate child support is a direct contributor to childhood poverty. . . . Child support — when paid — on average amounts to over one-quarter of a poor child's family income. There is little doubt that the payment of child support benefits poverty-stricken children the most. Enforcing child support orders thus has surfaced as a major policy directive in our society.

In view of the suffering children must endure when their noncustodial parent intentionally refuses to pay child support, it is not surprising that the legislature has attached severe sanctions to this crime. Wis. Stat. §948.22(2). This statute makes it a Class E felony for any person "who intentionally fails for 120 or more consecutive days to provide spousal, grandchild or child support which the person knows or reasonably should know the person is legally obligated to provide. . . ."[19] A Class E felony is punishable with "a fine not to exceed $10,000 or imprisonment not to exceed 2 years, or both." Wis. Stat. §939.50(3)(e). The legislature has amended this statute so that intentionally refusing to pay child support is now punishable by up to five years in prison.

But Wisconsin law is not so rigid as to mandate the severe sanction of incarceration as the only means of addressing a violation of §948.22(2). In sentencing, a Wisconsin judge can take into account a broad array of factors, including the gravity of the offense and need for protection of the public and potential victims. . . . After considering all these factors, a judge may decide to forgo the severe punitive sanction of incarceration and address the violation with the less restrictive alternative of probation coupled with specific conditions. . . . As we have previously observed, "the theory of the probation statute is to rehabilitate the defendant and protect society without placing the defendant in prison." . . .

5. Timothy Grall, Child Support for Custodial Mothers and Fathers, Current Population Reports, United States Census Bureau, 4 (October 2000).
6. United States Census Bureau, U.S. Dep't of Commerce, Current Population Survey, Child Support 1997, Table 1 (1998).
19. In Wisconsin, a circuit court typically orders support payments as a percentage of a parent's income, not as an invariable dollar amount. This means that it is within any parent's ability — regardless of his or her actual income or number of children he or she has — to comply with a child support order.

But Oakley argues that the condition imposed by Judge Hazlewood violates his constitutional right to procreate. This court, in accord with the United States Supreme Court, has previously recognized the fundamental liberty interest of a citizen to choose whether or not to procreate. [Citations omitted.] Accordingly, Oakley argues that the condition here warrants strict scrutiny. That is, it must be narrowly tailored to serve a compelling state interest. Although Oakley concedes, as he must, that the State's interest in requiring parents to support their children is compelling, he argues that the means employed here is not narrowly tailored to serve that compelling interest because Oakley's "right to procreate is not restricted but in fact eliminated." According to Oakley, his right to procreate is eliminated because he "probably never will have the ability to support" his children. Therefore, if he exercises his fundamental right to procreate while on probation, his probation will be revoked and he will face the stayed term of eight years in prison.

. . . We emphatically reject the novel idea that Oakley, who was convicted of intentionally failing to pay child support, has an absolute right to refuse to support his current nine children and any future children that he procreates, thereby adding more child victims to the list. In an analogous case, Oregon upheld a similar probation condition to protect child victims from their father's abusive behavior in State v. Kline, 963 P.2d 697, 699 (Or. Ct. App. 1998). Furthermore, Oakley fails to note that incarceration, by its very nature, deprives a convicted individual of the fundamental right to be free from physical restraint, which in turn encompasses and restricts other fundamental rights, such as the right to procreate. . . .

[The condition of probation is not overly broad. Oakley can satisfy it] by making efforts to support his children as required by law. Judge Hazlewood placed no limit on the number of children Oakley could have. Instead, the requirement is that Oakley acknowledge the requirements of the law and support his present and any future children. If Oakley decides to continue his present course of conduct — intentionally refusing to pay child support — he will face eight years in prison regardless of how many children he has. Furthermore, this condition will expire at the end of his term of probation. He may then decide to have more children, but of course, if he continues to intentionally refuse to support his children, the State could charge him again. . . .

[T]he condition essentially bans Oakley from violating the law again. . . . Accordingly, this condition is reasonably related to his rehabilitation because it will assist Oakley in conforming his conduct to the law. . . .

ANN WALSH BRADLEY, J. [joined by Shirley S. Abrahamson, C.J., and Diane S. Sykes, J.] (dissenting). . . .

. . . Today's decision makes this court the only court in the country to declare constitutional a condition that limits a probationer's right to procreate based on his financial ability to support his children. . . . While on its face the order leaves room for the slight possibility that Oakley may establish the financial means to support his children, the order is essentially a prohibition on the right to have children. Oakley readily admits that unless he wins the lottery, he will likely never be able to establish that ability. . . . In a similar context, the United States Supreme Court has explained that a statutory prohibition on the right to marry, a right closely aligned with the [fundamental] right at issue, was not a justifiable means of advancing the state's interest in providing support for children. Zablocki v. Redhail, 434 U.S. 374,

388-90 (1978). . . . The narrowly drawn means described by the Supreme Court in *Zablocki* still exist today and are appropriate means of advancing the state's interest in a manner that does not impair the fundamental right to procreate. See, e.g., Wis. Stat. §767.265 (garnishment/wage assignment); §767.30 (lien on personal property); §785.03 (civil contempt). These means, as well as other conditions of probation or criminal penalties, are available in the present case. . . .

[U]pholding a term of probation that prohibits a probationer from fathering a child without first establishing the financial wherewithal to support his children [also] carries unacceptable collateral consequences and practical problems. First, prohibiting a person from having children as a condition of probation has been described as "coercive of abortion." . . . Because the condition is triggered only upon the birth of a child [not upon intercourse], the risk of imprisonment creates a strong incentive for a man in Oakley's position to demand from the woman the termination of her pregnancy. It places the woman in an untenable position: have an abortion or be responsible for Oakley going to prison for eight years. . . .

Second, by allowing the right to procreate to be subjected to financial qualifications, the majority imbues a fundamental liberty interest with a sliding scale of wealth. . . . Third, the condition of probation is unworkable. . . . The condition of probation will not be violated until the woman with whom he has sexual relations carries her pregnancy to term. Then, Oakley will be imprisoned, and another child will go unsupported. . . .

I, too, am troubled by the societal problem caused by "deadbeat" parents. . . . Let there be no question that I agree with the majority that David Oakley's conduct cannot be condoned. It is irresponsible and criminal. However, we must keep in mind what is really at stake in this case. The fundamental right to have children, shared by us all, is damaged by today's decision. . . .

■ **DAVID RAY PAPKE, STATE V. OAKLEY, DEADBEAT DADS, AND AMERICAN POVERTY**
26 W. New Eng. L. Rev. 9, 10-15 (2004)

[David Oakley] was born in 1966 in the Taycheedah Correctional Institution, a women's prison in Fond du Lac, Wisconsin. Sharon Oakley, his mother, remained incarcerated until 1974, but authorities, of course, removed Oakley from the prison. After a period in state care, he was raised primarily by his maternal grandparents. Run-ins with law enforcement officials marked his youth, and while in his teens Oakley was sent to Lincoln Hills School, a home for delinquent boys located near Wausau, Wisconsin. . . .

After completing his sentences in juvenile facilities, Oakley lived largely in an area on the western shore of Lake Michigan in central Wisconsin [in rust-belt towns with] significant unemployment [and poverty]. In keeping with national patterns showing that poverty is "particularly rampant among children living in mother-only households," poverty in Manitowoc County is especially pronounced among families with a female family-head and no husband present.

With a limited formal education and virtually no skills, Oakley was unable to find or hold meaningful jobs. . . . As with many of the poor, Oakley's ability to find and get to work was limited by his lack of a motor vehicle. [W]ithout genuine and meaningful work opportunities, [he might well have ceased] to assume work is a regular and regulating factor in [his daily life]. Oakley's lengthy criminal record [for disorderly conduct, receipt of stolen property, illegal firearm possession, and witness intimidation] also without doubt made him less than an ideal hire in the minds of some employers.

The [four] mothers of Oakley's [nine] children, themselves among Manitowoc County's poor, do not unanimously condemn Oakley. . . . Cheri Pasdo, who gave birth to one of Oakley's sons but never married Oakley, considers him dangerously bewitching. "He could talk an Eskimo into buying an ice cube," she said. Jill Cochrane, mother of four of Oakley's children, thinks he never understood the seriousness of parenthood. "He likes having the kids but once they're there to him that's a punishment. He doesn't like them once he's got them," Cochrane said. On the other side, Lucretia Thompson-Smith and Rachel Ward remain sympathetic to Oakley. Thompson-Smith, mother of Oakley's fourteen year-old daughter, does not see much difference between Oakley and the two other fathers of her children when it comes to paying child support faithfully. Even if Oakley had a minimum-wage job, his child support would eat it up. "How could he live?" she asked. . . .

The four women and their children survived on an unpredictable combination of welfare payments, earnings from various jobs, and occasional support from Oakley. Among the poor, income does not necessarily increase annually. Oakley scraped enough together to get by from his off-and-on employment and, to a lesser extent, from criminal activity. The mothers of his children also lived from week to week, trying and sometimes failing to make ends meet.

For what it's worth, Oakley claimed that he paid over seventy percent of his child support to the mothers of his children, and courtroom records confirm that he did at least pay some child support. [Yet] at thirty-four years of age, [Oakley] found himself charged in 1999 with intentional refusal to pay child support in the Manitowoc County Circuit Court, Judge Fred Hazlewood presiding. . . . "If you think I'm trampling over your constitutional rights, so be it," Hazlewood told Oakley at sentencing. The community in general seconded Hazlewood's palpably irritated decision. . . .

Although the specifics of David Oakley's life and the Constitutional issues considered in [*Oakley*] are unique, the ultimate decision in the case and attitudes which buoyed that decision are part of a larger trend. Since at least the mid-1980's, men like Oakley have been demonized [as] "deadbeat dads." . . . The policing and punishing of David Oakley sanctioned by the Wisconsin . . . courts had much the same animus as the national legislative and popular campaigns against "deadbeat dads."

"Enough is enough," the judges and legislators want to shout. But has anything really been accomplished for Oakley, his children, and the mothers of those children? Does the national campaign have the capacity to affect significantly the conduct of transient, uneducated, and impoverished men or to reduce the poverty of their children and their children's mothers?

Notes and Questions

1. *Reconciling* Zablocki. What does *Oakley* hold? Does the majority successfully distinguish this case from *Zablocki*, Chapter II, section D1, and other constitutional

authorities? Does the immediate availability of a prison sentence distinguish these facts from *Zablocki's*? How should a court apply *Zablocki's* "narrow tailoring" requirement to a particular obligor after less onerous means of support enforcement have failed? What result in Oakley's challenge if the order imposing the antiprocreation condition fails explicitly to say that it would terminate upon proof of his support of his children? See State v. Talty, 814 N.E.2d 1201 (Ohio 2004).

2. *Probation conditions.* The majority emphasizes that the defendant could have been incarcerated for the crime of intentional failure to support his children; hence, probation with conditions, however demanding, constitutes a less intrusive alternative. But see *Talty,* supra. Is Judge Hazlewood's approach a welcome innovation designed to address a difficult social problem? Or does it exemplify "unusual, idiosyncratic, and often quite alarming criminal sentences" accomplished through the judicial discretion permitted in fashioning probation conditions? See Andrew Horowitz, Coercion, Pop-psychology, and Judicial Moralizing: Some Proposals for Curbing Judicial Abuse of Probation Conditions, 57 Wash. & Lee L. Rev. 75, 76, 136-141 (2000). Compare, e.g., Kelly R. Skaff, Note, Pay Up or Zip Up: Giving Up the Right to Procreate as a Condition of Probation, 23 St. Louis U. Pub. L. Rev. 399 (2004), with Rebecca L. Miles, Note, Criminal Consequences for Making Babies: Probation Conditions That Restrict Procreation, 59 Wash. & Lee L. Rev. 1545 (2002). See generally Developments in the Law: Alternatives to Incarceration, 111 Harv. L. Rev. 1863 (1998).

3. *Impact on women.* To what extent does the "practical problem" of abortion coercion, which troubles the dissent, undermine the majority's analysis and conclusion? Suppose the defendant had been a "deadbeat mom." Cf. Stacey L. Arthur, The Norplant Prescription: Birth Control, Woman Control, or Crime Control, 40 UCLA L. Rev. 11 (1992) (child abuse); Joan Callahan, Contraception or Incarceration: What's Wrong with This Picture?, 7 Stan. L. & Pol'y Rev. 67 (1996) (same).

All four male members of the Wisconsin Supreme Court joined the majority opinion, and all four females dissented. How do you explain this division, particularly given the data about the disproportionate impact on single mothers of unpaid support obligations? On *Oakley's* implications for women, see Rachel Roth, "No New Babies?": Gender Inequality and Reproductive Control in the Criminal Justice and Prison Systems, 12 Am. U. J. Gender Soc. Pol'y & L. 391 (2004).

4. *Contempt.* Delinquent support obligors also face incarceration (and/or monetary fines) for contempt of court, that is, the failure to comply with a court's order to make payments specified in a divorce, separation, or paternity decree. Courts exercise the contempt power either to punish the contemnor for past misconduct (criminal contempt) or to coerce compliance with a judicial order (civil contempt). Whether the purpose is punitive or remedial determines the criminal versus civil nature and applicable procedural safeguards, such as the standard and burden of proof. Hicks ex rel. Feiock v. Feiock, 485 U.S. 624, 631 (1998) ("substance of proceeding and character of relief" determinative). Because compliance purges civil clear contempt, it is often said that civil contemnors "carry the keys of their prison in their own pockets."

5. *Limitations.*

a. *Inability to pay.* Because civil contempt seeks to coerce compliance, it follows that the obligor's inability to pay precludes use of this remedy to enforce a support award. See, e.g., G.W. v. Sheriff of Jefferson County., 885 So. 2d 807 (Ala. Ct. Civ. App. 2004); Wilson v. Holliday, 774 A.2d 1123 (Md. 2001). Are all of an obligor's resources considered in assessing ability to pay? See Rose v. Rose, 481 U.S. 619 (1987) (upholding contempt of veteran whose sole support derived from disability-related Veterans' Administration benefits); Sibley v. Sibley, 833 So. 2d 847 (Fla. Dist. Ct. App. 2002) (father-contemnor's own father had resources establishing requisite ability to pay), *rev. denied*, 854 So. 2d 660 (Fla. 2003). Present inability to pay also provides a defense to *criminal* contempt.

b. *Burden of proof.* Should the alleged contemnor be required to establish inability to pay, or must the petitioner prove ability to pay? See *Hicks*, 485 U.S. 624. Compare Powers v. Powers, 653 N.E.2d 1154 (N.Y. 1995) (alleged contemnor has burden of going forward but then petitioner must prove ability to pay), with Moss v. Superior Ct., 950 P.2d 59, 78 (Cal. 1998) ("Inability to comply is an affirmative defense which must be proven by a preponderance of the evidence by the alleged contemnor.").

The federal Deadbeat Parents Punishment Act of 1998, 18 U.S.C. §228(a)(3) (2000), which punishes as a felony willful failure to pay a support obligation for a child living in another state if the obligation has remained unpaid for over two years or exceeds $10,000, creates a presumption of willful nonpayment. See Darrell Baugh, Throw the Book at Deadbeat Parents: Criminal Enforcement of Child Support Cases, Fam. Advoc., Fall 2000, at 49, 50-51 (examining Act).

c. *Constitutional limits.* Does imprisonment for failure to pay child support or alimony violate state constitutional prohibitions against imprisonment for debt? See, e.g., Washington ex rel. Daly v. Snyder, 72 P.3d 780 (Wash. Ct. App. 2003), *rev. denied*, 87 P.3d 1184 (Wash. 2004). Does employment under threat of imprisonment for violation of a support order constitute involuntary servitude? See *Moss*, 950 P.2d 59. Given the distinction between civil and criminal contempt as well as the principle of double jeopardy, can an obligor be punished by imprisonment for failure to make the same payments that previously resulted in incarceration for civil contempt? See Dunagan v. Commonwealth, 31 S.W.3d 928 (Ky. 2000).

d. *Right to counsel.* Does the Constitution guarantee obligors who face incarceration for civil contempt a right to counsel? See Anthony v. Council, 316 F.3d 412 (3d Cir. 2003); Mead v. Batchlor, 460 N.W.2d 493 (Mich. 1990) (so holding based on due process, *modifying* Sword v. Sword, 249 N.W.2d 88 (Mich. 1976)).

6. *Empirical research on effectiveness.* How effective is incarceration as an enforcement tool? Professor David Chambers's study of collection rates in Michigan from 1972-1975 "found a close parallel between payments and jailing: the counties that jailed more did in fact collect more." David L. Chambers, Making Fathers Pay: The Enforcement of Child Support 84 (1979). Although he found incarceration (or the threat of it) effective, however, Chambers does not advocate this remedy because he concludes that the probable existence of equally effective but less onerous alternatives makes imprisonment immoral. "It would be immoral in much the same sense that it would be immoral to use a sledgehammer to swat a mosquito on a friend's back. . . ." Id. at 253. Do you agree? See also Drew A. Swank, The National Child Non-Support Epidemic, 2003 Mich. St. DCL L. Rev. 357, 375-378 (citing author's unpublished studies confirming findings that jail is an effective enforcement mechanism).

7. *Reasons for nonsupport. Oakley* cites data demonstrating the enormity of the problem of unmet support obligations. Why do noncustodial parents — generally fathers — fail to pay support? Commentators advance several possible answers:

[M]ost men pay little or no child support because they can get away with it. The gender-based division of labor in the family leads many men to see their children as women's responsibility. . . .

[Fathers often] begin their postdivorce lives with a strong commitment to support their children. Over time, their resolution weakens as relations with their children become emotionally less rewarding or they acquire a new set of family commitments. In effect these men trade in old obligations for new ones. From their point of view, they are not callously disregarding their family responsibilities but rather redefining them as they move from one marriage to the next. . . .

Frank F. Furstenberg, Jr. & Andrew J. Cherlin, Divided Families: What Happens to Children When Parents Part 59-60 (1991). In addition, Chambers points to the anger, confusion, and depression fathers feel upon divorce; their resentment toward relinquishing part of their earnings; their association of money with marital failure; and their weak attachment to their children. Chambers, supra, at 71-75. The increasing use of joint custody might well address the last point. See Margaret F. Brinig & F. H. Buckley, Joint Custody: Bonding and Monitoring Theories, 73 Ind. L.J. 393 (1998) (empirical data suggesting joint custody gives obligor parent greater incentive to pay support because of greater opportunity to monitor how payments are spent).

8. *David Oakley in context.* How does David Oakley's own history, as documented by Professor Papke, supra, affect your understanding of the legal issues presented? Does this history support the hypotheses of Professors Furstenberg and Cherlin, supra? To what extent do enforcement efforts aid those whom the law purports to help? What solution would you propose?

2. The Transformation of Enforcement: From Private to Public Responsibility

a. The Traditional Approach

Oakley exemplifies the increasingly visible role of government in enforcing financial obligations in nonintact families. Although states have long had statutes criminalizing desertion and nonsupport, prosecutors' heavy caseloads, reservations about the propriety and effectiveness of punishment, and limited applications of such laws meant that in the past little help came from direct intervention by the state.

Instead, under the traditional approach to enforcement as a private responsibility, an obligor's failure to comply with a court-ordered transfer of property or an award of spousal or child support left the obligee to initiate judicial proceedings for enforcement, a time-consuming process requiring an attorney. The long-standing state-created remedies available include (in addition to contempt citations) the imposition of a trust on the obligor's property; reducing past-due payments to a money judgment (if accrued installments do not already constitute final judgments), followed by a lien against the obligor's real estate; requiring the obligor to post security or bond; and garnishment or assignment of the obligor's wages or income. See generally Homer H. Clark, Jr., The Law of Domestic Relations in the United States 269-274, 671-682, 739-743 (2d ed. 1988); Paula G. Roberts, Child Support Orders: Problems with Enforcement, The Future of Children, Spring 1994, at 101, 106.

Several practical problems made all these civil remedies inefficient and unpredictable, however. Judicial discretion prevailed and the adversary nature of enforcement proceedings offered a forum unlikely to induce cooperation and compliance. Enforcement of postdivorce obligations to make periodic payments (that is, alimony and child support) proved particularly problematic because they presented such frequent opportunities for noncompliance.

b. Congress Intervenes

The same problems that prompted Congress in the 1980s to direct the states to use child support guidelines had even earlier focused federal attention on support enforcement: Among data showing rising rates of divorce and out-of-wedlock births, an escalating number of female-headed single-parent families, and an increasing "feminization of poverty,"[48] statistics indicated widespread noncompliance with child support awards. The federal AFDC program, as well as state public assistance programs, felt the impact. In several enactments, Congress directed the states to implement new and increasingly aggressive enforcement mechanisms.

Federal involvement began in 1967 when Congress imposed on state welfare agencies responsibility for child support enforcement as a condition for receiving federal funding. Congress entered the field by directing states to comply with specific federal requirements and by adopting a program of federal monitoring. Professor Marsha Garrison continues to trace the history of the federal role under this "carrot and stick" approach:

> Since 1975, through its authority over the Aid for Dependent Children (AFDC) program, Congress has legislated, with bipartisan support, increasingly tough child support requirements. The first congressional enactment established the federal Office of Child Support Enforcement and required each state to establish mechanisms for assisting parents in establishing paternity, obtaining child support awards, and enforcing child support obligations. Although state initiatives in these areas were required for AFDC recipients, they were also made available to families that did not receive welfare benefits. The Child Support Enforcement Amendments of 1984 mandated enhanced state enforcement efforts, including state tax refund interception and automatic wage withholding for overdue payments; the amendments also required the states to develop numerical guidelines that could be used by courts in setting child support awards. . . .

Marsha Garrison, Child Support and Children's Poverty, 28 Fam. L.Q. 475, 476 (1994). See Irwin Garfinkel et al., A Brief History of Child Support Policies in the United States, in Fathers Under Fire: The Revolution in Child Support Enforcement 22 (Irwin Garfinkel et al. eds., 1998).

Initially, such federal involvement was confined to welfare cases. Under the 1975 enactments, creating Title IV-D of the Social Security Act, all AFDC recipients must assign their support rights to the states for collection. Cases in which such support-rights assignments to the state have been made are often denominated

---

[48]. Beller & Graham, supra note [9], at 2-3 (study based on U.S. Census Bureau's Current Population Survey). The data consistently reveal the gendered nature of the problem.

"Title IV-D cases" while all other child-support cases are called "non-Title IV-D" cases.

Significantly, the Family Support Act of 1988 extended this federal involvement to nonwelfare (or non-Title IV-D) cases. See 42 U.S.C. §§651-669 (1994). As noted earlier, this legislation required states to use numerical guidelines as rebuttable presumptions in determining *all* child support awards. It also mandated procedures for establishing paternity of children of unmarried parents. (See Chapter IV, section C1.) Finally, it specified that "each State must have in effect laws requiring the use of the following procedures" for enforcing child support orders: procedures for, inter alia, income withholding, expedited enforcement (administrative processes for establishing and enforcing support obligations), diversion of state income tax refunds, liens against real and personal property for overdue support, posting a bond or giving security for overdue support, and disclosure of overdue support to consumer reporting agencies. These federal directives required each state's law to provide explicitly for such collection devices.

In the Personal Responsibility and Work Opportunity Reconciliation Act of 1996, welfare reform legislation that replaces AFDC with Temporary Assistance for Needy Families (TANF), a block-grant system promising states more authority over their welfare programs, Congress imposed new requirements for child support enforcement. See 42 U.S.C.A. §§651-669a (West 2003 & Supp. 2005). The 1996 law reflects the vision that "support payments should be automatic and inescapable, 'like death or taxes.'" Paul K. Legler, The Impact of Welfare Reform on the Child Support Enforcement System, in Child Support: The Next Frontier 46, 49-50 (J. Thomas Oldham & Marygold S. Melli eds., 2000). All states must now adopt measures that Congress found successful in particular state experiments, detailed below, or risk their eligibility for block grants.

(i) Income Withholding

The Family Support Act of 1988 required states to provide procedures for immediate withholding for *all* child support orders issued on or after January 1, 1994, whether or not the child support obligor had fallen in arrears, unless one party shows good cause or the parties have a written agreement providing an alternative. 42 U.S.C. §666(b) (2000). Under typical statutes implementing this federal directive, an obligor's employer must comply with a court order requiring withholding of up to 50 percent of the obligor's disposable earnings to be paid to the attorney general, court registry, or child support collection office; the employer becomes liable to the obligee for noncompliance and is subject to penalty for discriminatory hiring or discharge based on such order. See, e.g., Tex. Fam. Code Ann. §§158.001-158.405 (Vernon 2002 & Supp. 2004-2005).

The Personal Responsibility and Work Opportunity Reconciliation Act of 1996 strengthens the use of income withholding by establishing a national system to track the employment of delinquent obligors. 42 U.S.C. §653a (2000); see id. at §666(b). Based on an approach pioneered by Washington, all employers in the United States must report new hires to a designated state agency, which will forward the information to a national directory for matching with the Federal Case Registry of Child Support Orders. This reform complements earlier requirements that states obtain each parent's Social Security number upon a child's birth. 42 U.S.C.A. §405(c)(2)(C)(ii) (West Supp. 2005).

*(ii) Tax Refund Interceptions, Automatic Seizures, and
        Administrative Procedures*

In Title IV-D cases, states can notify the Internal Revenue Service of child support delinquencies and the IRS will intercept any tax refund due to the obligor and forward it to the appropriate state agency. See 42 U.S.C. §664 (2000). States must have similar mechanisms in place to seize state tax refunds.

The Personal Responsibility and Work Opportunity Reconciliation Act of 1996 goes farther. States must impose automatic liens on an obligor's assets, similar to the automatic withholding of income. 42 U.S.C. §666(a)(4) (2000). Following a model developed in Massachusetts, states must have administrative procedures for imposing liens. Id. at §666(a)(2), (c).

This development embodies one facet of "mass case processing," which seeks to use computers, databases, bank account records, and the like for handling efficiently the large volume of child support enforcement cases. In addition, states must have central registries of child support orders and centralized units for collection and disbursement.

Administrative liens also exemplify a larger move away from individual, judicial enforcement proceedings in favor of an approach that triggers enforcement automatically, without any initiation by the obligee or court involvement. States must provide certain expedited procedures for routine cases, but nonwelfare obligees can opt out of any of the enforcement measures made available by the Title IV-D agency. See generally Legler, supra.

(iii) License and Passport Suspension

Following successful measures in some states,[49] the Personal Responsibility and Work Opportunity Reconciliation Act of 1996 requires all states to have procedures for withholding, suspending, or restricting licenses (including driver's, professional, occupational, and recreational licenses) of obligors owing overdue support. 42 U.S.C. §666(a)(16) (2000). This legislation mandates the Secretary of State to deny a passport for nonpayment of child support and permits revocation or restriction of one previously issued. Id. at §652(k). Also, states must have procedures for reporting delinquencies to credit bureaus. Id. at §666(a)(7). Similarly, the Fair Credit Reporting Act requires inclusion in consumer reports of failure to pay overdue child support. 15 U.S.C. §1681s-1 (2000).

Some jurisdictions have undertaken new measures, such as "booting" or immobilizing the automobile of a delinquent obligor to induce compliance. While the suspension of a license only sanctions an individual who is caught engaging in the activity, "[b]ooting, like incarceration, a lien on property, or wage garnishment, actually deprives the non-custodial parent of a valued asset."[50] Early studies have shown that such action significantly increases child support payment.[51]

---

[49]. See Margaret Graham Tebo, When Dad Won't Pay, 86 A.B.A. J., Sept. 2000, at 54, 56 (reporting Maryland collected $56.8 million in past-due child support in 1999 by threatening to suspend drivers' licenses).

[50]. Drew A. Swank, Das Boot! A National Survey of Booting Programs' Impact on Child Support Compliance, 4 J.L. Fam. Stud. 265, 267 (2002).

[51]. See Drew A. Swank, The National Child Non-Support Epidemic, 2003 Mich. St. DCL L. Rev. 357, 374.

c. Evaluation: "Small Change"?

Congress's enactment of substantial, new federal requirements as part of welfare reform demonstrates that problems in child support enforcement persist despite 30 years of federally orchestrated efforts. One glimpse of the difficulties emerges in class actions brought by obligees seeking to compel state compliance with federal directives on child support enforcement. Although the Supreme Court has held Title IV-D does not create an enforceable individual federal right to compel compliance with all IV-D requirements, such lawsuits reveal "systemic failures" in some states, including failure to procure wage assignments, failure to disburse support payments in a timely manner, and frequent losses of files. See Blessing v. Freestone, 520 U.S. 329 (1997).

In an influential study conducted prior to the 1996 reforms, economists examined census data to assess the effect of the federal initiatives. Professors Andrea Beller and John Graham found little improvement in child support enforcement despite increased attention to the issue in the 1980s — in short, "small change."[52] Evaluating specific mechanisms, they concluded that income withholding, property liens, bond or security requirements, and criminal penalties have proven most effective.[53] Beller and Graham urged caution, however, in the use of expedited (administrative) processes required by the Family Support Act of 1988 because this enforcement technique appears to produce lower receipt rates for child support. In addition, they encouraged experimentation with innovative techniques such as license seizures.[54] Congress nonetheless included both new administrative processes and license seizures in its 1996 requirements.

More recent assessments remain mixed. One analysis claims that new measures, such as the directory of new hires and license suspensions, helped increase collections significantly.[55] Yet despite ongoing law reform, billions of dollars more could be collected.[56] Oakley, supra, demonstrates that child poverty and collection problems persist,[57] while emphasizing new reliance on criminal sanctions, an avenue Congress pursued in enacting the Deadbeat Parents Punishment Act of 1998, 18 U.S.C. §228(a)(3) (2000), which makes some child support violations federal felonies with enhanced penalties. Further, some data indicate that strict enforcement mechanisms, such as garnishment and income withholding, prove counterproductive because they induce obligors to "go underground," avoiding work in the formal economy so that they can circumvent enforcement.[58]

[52]. Beller & Graham, supra note [9], at 16, 51-52. Only Black mothers and never-married mothers made notable gains. These gains included some increased award and receipt rates but at the same time these mothers received an increasingly smaller proportion of their awards. Id. at 51-52.

[53]. Id. at 2, 255 (recommendations).

[54]. Id. at 256-257.

[55]. The amount rose to $14.3 billion by 1998 (from $1 billion). Marygold S. Melli, Whatever Happened to Divorce?, 2000 Wis. L. Rev. 637, 639-640.

[56]. Of the $34.9 billion in payments due in 2001, custodial parents received approximately $21.9 billion or 62.6 percent. Grall, supra note [45], at 8.

[57]. Census figures show that of about 6.9 million of the custodial parents due child support payments in 2001, "73.9 received at least some payments directly from the noncustodial parent, a proportion unchanged since 1993." Id. at 6. Further, "[w]hile the proportion of custodial parents receiving full payments increased since 1993, the proportion receiving some of the payments due fell from 38.9 percent in 1993 to 28.6 percent in 1999 and was unchanged in 2001." Id.

[58]. Kathryn Edin & Laura Lein, Making Ends Meet: How Single Mothers Survive Welfare and Low Wage Work 187 (1997).

Visions for the future include proposals to create universal assured child support benefits,[59] to locate responsibility for all children outside the private family while providing supports for caregiving,[60] and to make child support enforcement entirely a federal function (for example, by having the IRS enforce all child support orders).[61] Controversy about the "federalization" of family policy likely will persist, given recent decisions curbing Congress's authority over areas traditionally governed by the states.[62]

3. The Challenge of Multistate Cases

A substantial percentage of all child support cases involve parties located in different jurisdictions.[63] Do the special problems raised by these cases, explored below, require federal intervention?

a. Jurisdictional Limitations on Establishing Awards

■ **KULKO v. SUPERIOR COURT**
436 U.S. 84 (1978)

Mr. Justice MARSHALL delivered the opinion of the Court. . . .

Appellant Ezra Kulko married appellee Sharon Kulko Horn in 1959, during appellant's three-day stopover in California en route from a military base in Texas to a tour of duty in Korea. At the time of this marriage, both parties were domiciled in and residents of New York State. Immediately following the marriage, Sharon Kulko returned to New York, as did appellant after his tour of duty. [They lived together in New York for 13 years and then separated. Ezra remained in New York with their children, Darwin and Ilsa, and Sharon moved to California. Sharon returned briefly to sign a separation agreement, which provided that the children would live in New York with their father but spend Christmas, Easter, and summer vacations in California with their mother.] Ezra Kulko agreed to pay his wife $3,000 per year in child support for the periods when the children were in her care, custody, and control. Immediately after execution of the separation agreement, Sharon Kulko flew to Haiti and procured a divorce there; the divorce decree incor-

---

[59]. Irwin Garfinkel, The Limits of Private Child Support and the Role of an Assured Benefit, in Child Support: The Next Frontier 183 (J. Thomas Oldham & Marygold S. Melli eds., 2000).

[60]. Martha Albertson Fineman, Child Support Is Not the Answer: The Nature of Dependencies and Welfare Reform, in Child Support: The Next Frontier 209 (J. Thomas Oldham & Marygold S. Melli eds., 2000).

[61]. See Jonathon S. Jemison, Note, Collecting and Enforcing Child Support Orders with the Internal Revenue Service: An Analysis of a Novel Idea, 20 Women's Rts. L. Rep. 137 (1999).

[62]. Compare United States v. Morrison, 529 U.S. 598 (2000) (invalidating civil damages provision of Violence Against Women Act), with Kansas v. United States, 214 F.3d 1196 (10th Cir.) (upholding 1996 welfare requirements under Congress's spending power), *cert. denied*, 531 U.S. 1035 (2000). See, e.g., Lynn A. Baker, Conditional Federal Spending After *Lopez*, 95 Colum. L. Rev. 1911 (1995); Laura W. Morgan, The Federalization of Child Support, A Shift in the Ruling Paradigm: Child Support as Outside the Contours of "Family Law," 16 J. Am. Acad. Matrim. Law. 195 (1999).

[63]. See John J. Sampson & Paul M. Kurtz, UIFSA: An Interstate Support Act for the 21st Century, 27 Fam. L.Q. 85, 88 (1993) (estimating one-fourth).

porated the terms of the agreement. She then returned to California, where she remarried and took the name Horn.

The children resided with appellant during the school year and with their mother on vacations, as provided by the separation agreement, until December 1973. At this time, just before Ilsa was to leave New York to spend Christmas vacation with her mother, she told her father that she wanted to remain in California after her vacation. Appellant bought his daughter a one-way plane ticket, and Ilsa left, taking her clothing with her. Ilsa then commenced living in California with her mother during the school year and spending vacations with her father. In January 1976, appellant's other child, Darwin, called his mother from New York and advised her that he wanted to live with her in California. Unbeknownst to appellant, appellee Horn sent a plane ticket to her son, which he used to fly to California where he took up residence with his mother and sister.

Less than one month after Darwin's arrival in California, appellee Horn commenced this action against appellant in the California Superior Court. She sought to establish the Haitian divorce decree as a California judgment; to modify the judgment so as to award her full custody of the children; and to increase appellant's child-support obligations. Appellant appeared specially and moved to quash service of the summons on the ground that he was not a resident of California and lacked sufficient "minimum contacts" with the State under International Shoe Co. v. Washington, 326 U.S. 310, 316 (1945), to warrant the State's assertion of personal jurisdiction over him.

[The California Supreme Court upheld the lower courts' denial of appellant's motion to quash. It reasoned that California's long-arm statute was meant to reach all bases of in personam jurisdiction consistent with the Constitution and that jurisdiction over appellant for support of both children was "fair and reasonable" because he purposefully availed himself of the benefits and protections of California law by sending one child, Ilsa, to live there. We reverse.]

The Due Process Clause of the Fourteenth Amendment operates as a limitation on the jurisdiction of state courts to enter judgments affecting rights or interests of nonresident defendants. [T]he constitutional standard for determining whether the State may enter a binding judgment against appellant here is that set forth in this Court's opinion in International Shoe Co. v. Washington, supra: that a defendant "have certain minimum contacts with [the forum State] such that the maintenance of the suit does not offend 'traditional notions of fair play and substantial justice.'" 326 U.S., at 316. [A]n essential criterion in all cases is whether the "quality and nature" of the defendant's activity is such that it is "reasonable" and "fair" to require him to conduct his defense in that State. International Shoe Co. v. Washington, [326 U.S.] at 316-317, 319. . . .

In reaching its result, the California Supreme Court did not rely on appellant's glancing presence in the State some 13 years before the events that led to this controversy, nor could it have. Appellant has been in California on only two occasions, once in 1959 for a three-day military stopover on his way to Korea and again in 1960 for a 24-hour stopover on his return from Korean service. To hold such temporary visits to a State a basis for the assertion of in personam jurisdiction over unrelated actions arising in the future would make a mockery of the limitations on state jurisdiction imposed by the Fourteenth Amendment. Nor did the California court rely on the fact that appellant was actually married in California on one of his two brief visits. We agree that where two New York domiciliaries, for reasons of convenience, marry in the State of California and thereafter spend their entire married life in New York, the fact of their California marriage by itself cannot support a California court's exercise of jurisdiction over a spouse who remains a New York resident in an action relating to child support.

Finally, in holding that personal jurisdiction existed, the court below carefully disclaimed reliance on the fact that appellant had agreed at the time of separation to allow his children to live with their mother three months a year and that he had sent them to California each year pursuant to this agreement. [T]o find personal jurisdiction in a State on this basis, merely because the mother was residing there, would discourage parents from entering into reasonable visitation agreements. Moreover, it could arbitrarily subject one parent to suit in any State of the Union where the other parent chose to spend time while having custody of their offspring pursuant to a separation agreement. As we have emphasized: "The unilateral activity of those who claim some relationship with a nonresident defendant cannot satisfy the requirement of contact with the forum State. [I]t is essential in each case that there be some act by which the defendant purposefully avails him[self] of the privilege of conducting activities within the forum State. . . ." Hanson v. Denckla, [357 U.S. 235, 253 (1958)].

The "purposeful act" that the California Supreme Court believed did warrant the exercise of personal jurisdiction over appellant in California was his "actively and fully consent[ing] to Ilsa living in California for the school year . . . and . . . send[ing] her to California for that purpose." [564 p. 2d 353, 358 (Cal. 1977).] [Yet, a] father who agrees, in the interests of family harmony and his children's preferences, to allow them to spend more time in California than was required under a separation agreement can hardly be said to have "purposefully availed himself" of the "benefits and protections" of California's laws.[7] . . .

The circumstances in this case clearly render "unreasonable" California's assertion of personal jurisdiction. . . . The cause of action herein asserted arises, not from the defendant's commercial transactions in interstate commerce, but rather from his personal, domestic relations. . . . Furthermore, the controversy between the parties arises from a separation that occurred in the State of New York; appellee Horn seeks modification of a contract that was negotiated in New York and that she flew to New York to sign. [T]he instant action involves an agreement that was entered into with virtually no connection with the forum State.

Finally, basic considerations of fairness point decisively in favor of appellant's State of domicile as the proper forum for adjudication of this case, whatever the merits of appellee's underlying claim. It is appellant who has remained in the State of the marital domicile, whereas it is appellee who has moved across the continent. Appellant has at all times resided in New York State, and, until the separation and appellee's move to California, his entire family resided there as well. As noted above, appellant did no more than acquiesce in the stated preference of one of his children to live with her mother in California. This single act is surely not one that a reasonable parent would expect to result in the substantial financial burden

---

7. The court below stated that the presence in California of appellant's daughter gave appellant the benefit of California's "police and fire protection, its school system, its hospital services, its recreational facilities, its libraries and museums. . . ." 564 P.2d, at 356. But, in the circumstances presented here, these services provided by the State were essentially benefits to the child, not the father, and in any event were not benefits that appellant purposefully sought for himself.

and personal strain of litigating a child-support suit in a forum 3,000 miles away, and we therefore see no basis on which it can be said that appellant could reasonably have anticipated being "haled before a [California] court," Shaffer v. Heitner, 433 U.S. [186, 216 (1977)]. To make jurisdiction in a case such as this turn on whether appellant bought his daughter her ticket or instead unsuccessfully sought to prevent her departure would impose an unreasonable burden on family relations, and one wholly unjustified by the "quality and nature" of appellant's activities in or relating to the State of California. International Shoe Co. v. Washington, 326 U.S., at 319.

In seeking to justify the burden that would be imposed on appellant were the exercise of in personam jurisdiction in California sustained, appellee argues that California has substantial interests in protecting the welfare of its minor residents and in promoting to the fullest extent possible a healthy and supportive family environment in which the children of the State are to be raised. These interests are unquestionably important. But while the presence of the children and one parent in California arguably might favor application of California law in a lawsuit in New York, the fact that California may be the "'center of gravity'" for choice-of-law purposes does not mean that California has personal jurisdiction over the defendant. . . .

Notes and Questions

1. *Divisible divorce.* Under the doctrine of divisible divorce, due process requires personal jurisdiction over both spouses to resolve the financial incidents of dissolution, although one can get an ex parte divorce entitled to full faith and credit. E.g., Estin v. Estin, 334 U.S. 541 (1948); Snider v. Snider, 551 S.E.2d 693 (W. Va. 2001). Cf. Abernathy v. Abernathy, 482 S.E.2d 265 (Ga. 1997) (situs of real property has in rem jurisdiction for division at dissolution). Applying this doctrine, *Kulko* finds the father's connections with California insufficient to satisfy due process.

Under this doctrine, Ezra Kulko may remain immune from child-support litigation in California but only until he visits his children there and risks personal service of process. Recall Burnham v. Superior Court (noted Chapter V, pp. 579-580). What impact does this rule have on visitation? Why do benefits provided by California to the children not count as benefits to their father? What alternative jurisdictional rules might avoid these practical and policy-based difficulties? See Monica J. Allen, Child-State Jurisdiction: A Due Process Invitation to Reconsider Some Basic Family Law Assumptions, 26 Fam. L.Q. 293 (1992).

2. *Long-arm statutes.* With the expansion of personal jurisdiction signaled by International Shoe Co. v. Washington, 326 U.S. 310 (1945), states enacted long-arm statutes designed to reach absent defendants. One approach, the "single-act" statute, enumerates specific conduct conferring jurisdiction, such as the commission of a tortious act in the state or the transaction of business there. Some courts have construed these statutes, although enacted with other litigation in mind, to apply in family law cases, reasoning that failure to pay support constitutes a tortious act in the obligee's domicile or that support rights springing from the marriage contract have financial and business implications. See, e.g., Lozinski v. Lozinski, 408 S.E.2d 310 (W. Va. 1991) (haling husband into court in marital domicile after he moved away).

Under this approach, did Ezra Kulko commit a tortious act in California for purposes of justifying jurisdiction? Any assertion of jurisdiction under single-act statutes must satisfy the Due Process Clause's minimum contacts requirement, explained in *Kulko*. As a result, some states have followed a second approach illustrated by California's statute in *Kulko:* legislation that allows courts to assert jurisdiction whenever due process permits, thus encompassing all the single acts usually listed and any additional jurisdictional bases permitted by the Constitution.

3. *Family law long arms.* More recently, states have enacted long-arm statutes explicitly addressing family law cases. For example, Washington's long-arm statute lists several single acts, including "[l]iving in a marital relationship within this state notwithstanding subsquent departure from this state, [as to all proceedings under dissolution of marriage statutes,] so long as the petitioning party has continued to reside in this state. . . . " Wash. Rev. Code Ann §4.28.185(l)(f)(2005). See State ex rel. Mahoney v. St. John, 964 P.2d 1242 (Wyo. 1998) (enforcing, under Full Faith and Credit Clause, Washington support order against absent obligor pursuant to such long-arm jurisdiction).

How should a court construe the marital-relationship language of the Washington statute? Must the defendant conduct "the daily activities of his marital life" in the forum for a particular time? Cf. Panganiban v. Panganiban, 736 A.2d 190, 194 (Conn. Ct. App. 1999). See also Nelson v. Nelson, 891 So. 2d 317 (Ala. Civ. App. 2004); Butler v. Butler, 566 S.E.2d 707 (N.C. Ct. App. 2002). Will a long absence from a state so weaken the contacts with the defendant's previous home that long-arm jurisdiction becomes improper? Cf. Sharp v. Sharp, 765 A.2d 271 (N.J. Super. Ct. App. Div. 2001). Would Washington's statute have helped in *Kulko?*

Should marrying in the state alone suffice? Recall that the Court rejects that basis for California's jurisdiction over Ezra Kulko. In a later child support action, should a court find "purposeful availment" of California's benefits and protections by a parent who had traveled to California to enter a domestic partnership, a legal relationship not availale or recognized where the parent lives? If so, why? should marrying in California be treated differently?

4. *Evolution of UIFSA.* Situations like the one in *Kulko* prompted efforts to design multistate solutions, beginning in 1944 with the proposal by the National Conference of Commissioners on Uniform State Laws (NCCUSL) of the Uniform Support of Dependents Law. Few states enacted this law, and in 1950 NCCUSL promulgated the Uniform Reciprocal Enforcement of Support Act (URESA), enacted in virtually every state and substantially revised in 1968. See 9C U.L.A. 81 (2001). A URESA case required a two-state proceeding, including the filing of a petition in the obligee's state and its transmittal to a court elsewhere with personal jurisdiction over the obligor. The lack of uniformity among the states and the possibility of multiple support orders impaired URESA's success. See generally Tina M. Fielding, Note, The Uniform Interstate Family Support Act: The New URESA, 20 U. Dayton L. Rev. 425 (1994).

The Commissioners replaced the earlier models with the Uniform Interstate Family Support Act (UIFSA), which they approved in 1992, amended in 1996, and amended again in 2001. 9 U.L.A. (pt. IB) 159, 281, 477 (2005). Although based on URESA, UIFSA contains new procedures for establishing, enforcing, and modifying support orders. To assure acceptance by the states, Congress made enactment of UIFSA a condition for federal funding for child support enforcement, under the Personal Responsibility and Work Opportunity Reconciliation Act of 1996. 42 U.S.C. §666(f) (2000). See generally Uniform Interstate Family Support Act (1996) (with More Unofficial Annotations by John J. Sampson), 32 Fam. L.Q. 390 (1998); John J. Sampson with Barry J. Brooks, Uniform Interstate Family Support Act (2001) With Prefatory Note and Comments (With Still More Unofficial Annotations), 36 Fam. L.Q. 329 (2002).

Like its predecessors, UIFSA covers both spousal and child support (but not property distribution), see §101(23), 9 U.L.A. (pt. IB) 177 (2005), and spells out procedures for establishing support orders and enforcing them. UIFSA responds to a number of perceived weaknesses in earlier laws, examined below.

5. *Expanding jurisdiction.* Critics claim that traditional jurisdictional rules still thwart effective support enforcement. As a result, a federal commission exploring law reform initially proposed attacking *Kulko* to allow jurisdiction in most support cases in the state of the child's domicile. This approach, called "child-state jurisdiction," parallels jurisdiction in the child's home state in custody adjudications under the Uniform Child Custody Jurisdiction and Enforcement Act (UCCJEA) and the Parental Kidnapping Prevention Act (PKPA). See Chapter VII, section B6.

In drafting UIFSA, the Commissioners narrowly decided to rely on long-arm statutes instead of the broader "child-state" approach. See Sampson, supra, at 421-422 n.56. UIFSA's eight bases for jurisdiction over absent obligors (set out in §201) include when the individual resided with the child in the state, the child resides in the state "as the result of acts or directives of the individual," the individual engaged in intercourse in the state and the child may have been conceived therefrom, and there is any other basis consistent with the Constitution for the exercise of personal jurisdiction. 9 U.L.A. (pt. IB) 185 (2005). This expanded long-arm jurisdiction facilitates a one-state proceeding, in place of the two-state approach under URESA.

Would UIFSA change the result in *Kulko*? Would the "acts or directives" provision apply? Would its application satisfy due process? Why did the drafters fail to adopt the more expansive "child-state" approach? See generally Allen, supra. Is it time to rethink *Kulko*'s limitations on jurisdiction? See Rosemarie T. Ring, Comment, Personal Jurisdiction and Child Support: Establishing the Parent-Child Relationship as Minimum Contacts, 89 Cal. L. Rev. 1125 (2001) (so arguing). Compare McCaffrey v. Green, 931 P.2d 407 (Alaska 1997), with Taylor v. Jarrett, 959 P.2d 807 (Ariz. Ct. App. 1998).

6. *Choice of law.* What law should govern in a multistate support cases? Note that *Kulko* concedes that California law might govern, even though California lacks jurisdiction. Is it fair to subject Ezra Kulko to California law? Under URESA, the law of any state where the obligor was present when support was sought applies. UIFSA principally applies the forum's procedural and substantive law (§303). 9 U.L.A. (pt. IB) 207 (2005). See also id. at 427 (under §604, law of issuing state governs in enforcement actions).

Problems

1. In *Kulko*, assume that Ezra frequently telephones his children in California, writes to them, provides health insurance for them, pays for their orthodontics, and

furnishes them airline tickets so they can visit him in New York. Suppose that Sharon then files a petition to establish a child support award in California (which, if granted, would be the first child support award for this family). Would California have personal jurisdiction over Ezra to order him to pay child support? Why? See In re Marriage of Crew, 549 N.W.2d 527 (Iowa 1996). See also Blanchard v. Blair, 781 So. 2d 228 (Ala. Civ. App. 2000).

2. Susan and Reginald became common law spouses in Texas. Throughout the marriage, Reginald, a gang member, abused Susan both mentally and physically. When she attempted to leave him, he had a friend stand on her head while he (Reginald) kicked her in the face. He also abused her daughter from a previous relationship and threatened to kill Susan if she reported him. Susan, pregnant, then left and moved to a friend's trailer. When Reginald continued to threaten and harass her, she fled to her father's home in Colorado. Now, after giving birth, she sues Reginald in Colorado for dissolution of marriage and child support. Reginald, who has never visited Colorado, challenges the court's jurisdiction to order child support. What result in Reginald's jurisdictional challenge and why? Does it matter, in applying *Kulko*'s purposeful availment test, that Reginald did not know where Susan was going when she left Texas? See In re Marriage of Malwitz, 99 P.3d 56 (Colo. 2004); Franklin v. Commonwealth, 497 S.E.2d 881 (Va. Ct. App. 1998).

b. Modification and Enforcement

■ LETELLIER v. LETELLIER
40 S.W.3d 490 (Tenn. 2001)

HOLDER, J. . . . .

In May 1989, the Superior Court of the District of Columbia entered an order adjudging Steven G. LeTellier to be the father of Teresa B. LeTellier's child, Nicholas. The court awarded custody of Nicholas to Ms. LeTellier and ordered Mr. LeTellier to pay child support. Ms. LeTellier later moved with Nicholas to Tennessee, and Mr. LeTellier moved to Virginia.

In September 1998, Ms. LeTellier filed petitions in the Juvenile Court of Davidson County, Tennessee, seeking (1) to enroll the District of Columbia order, and (2) to modify the child support award. [A juvenile court granted Mr. LeTellier's motion to dismiss the modification petition on grounds that the Tennessee court lacked subject matter jurisdiction and ordered that the case be transferred to Virginia.]

The Court of Appeals reversed [finding] that the jurisdictional provisions of Tennessee's Uniform Interstate Family Support Act conflict with the Federal Full Faith and Credit for Child Support Orders Act. It held that FFCCSOA preempted UIFSA and conferred jurisdiction upon the Davidson County Juvenile Court. We granted review [and now reverse the Court of Appeals.]

The Uniform Interstate Family Support Act, Tenn. Code Ann. §36-5-2201, et seq., controls the establishment, enforcement, or modification of support orders across state lines. UIFSA is intended to "recognize that only one valid support order may be effective at any one time." Unif. Interstate Family Support Act, U.L.A. (1996) (prefatory notes). Key to promoting UIFSA's intent is the concept of "continuing exclusive jurisdiction." A state that issues a support order has continuing exclusive jurisdiction over that order. No other state may modify that order as long as the issuing state has continuing exclusive jurisdiction.

The issuing state may lose continuing exclusive jurisdiction, however. In this case, the District of Columbia lost continuing exclusive jurisdiction when Mr. LeTellier, Ms. LeTellier, and Nicholas were no longer residents of that state. The District of Columbia "no longer had an appropriate nexus with the parties or the child to justify exercise of jurisdiction to modify." Tenn. Code Ann. §36-5-2205 cmt. . . .

Section 36-5-2611(a) of UIFSA confers subject matter jurisdiction upon Tennessee courts to modify child support orders issued by other states [as follows:]

> (a) After a child support order issued in another state has been registered in this state, the responding tribunal of this state may modify that order only if . . . after notice and hearing it finds that:
>> (1) The following requirements are met:
>>> (i) The child, the individual obligee, and the obligor do not reside in the issuing state;
>>> (ii) *A petitioner who is a nonresident of this state seeks modification;* and
>>> (iii) The respondent is subject to the personal jurisdiction of the tribunal of this state. . . .

Tenn. Code Ann. §36-5-2611(a) (emphasis added).

Because Ms. LeTellier is a resident of Tennessee, she fails to meet [subject-matter jurisdiction] the requirement of §36-5-2611(a)(1)(ii). . . . Ms. LeTellier claims, however, that §36-5-2611(a)(1)(ii) does not preclude the exercise of jurisdiction because §36-5-2201 and §36-5-2202 provide the basis for jurisdiction in this case. Because long-arm jurisdiction was obtained over Mr. LeTellier pursuant to §36-5-2202, [Ms. LeTellier claims this is a one-state proceeding under UIFSA.] The comments to §36-5-2202 . . . describe the one-state proceeding/two-state proceeding dichotomy: "Assertion of long-arm jurisdiction over a nonresident essentially results in a one-state proceeding, notwithstanding the fact that the parties reside in different states."

An effort to establish, enforce, or modify a support decree against an out-of-state resident ordinarily would have an interstate character. An action to establish, enforce, or modify a Tennessee order is transformed into a one-state proceeding when long-arm personal jurisdiction over the out-of-state resident is acquired. . . . Once that is done, the out-of-state resident is no longer out-of-state for purposes of that action, and the action loses its interstate character. [In such one-state cases, the substantive and procedural law of the forum controls. Ms. LeTellier thus argues that the requirements for two-state proceedings, including §35-5-2611(a), do not apply.]

. . . Even assuming [long-arm personal jurisdiction has been satisfied in this case,] the order [Ms. LeTellier] sought to modify was issued by a state other than Tennessee. Tennessee courts lack subject matter jurisdiction to modify out-of-state orders when the provisions of UIFSA are not satisfied. Because this case still retains its interstate character, §36-5-2202 has no application to this case. The remaining provisions of UIFSA, including the subject matter jurisdiction provisions of §36-5-2611(a), still apply. . . .

Moreover, the comments to §36-5-2611 refute any contention that asserting personal jurisdiction over an obligor pursuant to §36-5-2201 is sufficient to confer subject matter jurisdiction to modify an out-of-state decree. The comments also clearly establish that an action to modify an out-of-state support order cannot be brought in the petitioner's home state as Ms. LeTellier attempted:

> ... This restriction attempts to achieve a rough justice between the parties in the majority of cases by preventing a litigant from choosing to seek modification in a local tribunal to the marked disadvantage of the other party. For example, an obligor visiting the children at the residence of the obligee cannot be validly served with citation accompanied by a motion to modify the support order. Even though such personal service of the obligor in the obligee's home State [confers personal jurisdiction], the motion to modify does not fulfill the requirement of being brought by "a [petitioner] who is a nonresident of this State. . . ." In short, the obligee is required to register the existing order and seek modification of that order in a State which has personal jurisdiction over the obligor other than the state of the obligee's residence. Most typically this will be the State of residence of the obligor. . . .

Ms. LeTellier alternatively alleges that the Federal Full Faith and Credit for Child Support Orders Act, 28 U.S.C. §1738B, confers jurisdiction upon the Juvenile Court for Davidson County, Tennessee. FFCCSOA and UIFSA therefore conflict, and FFCCSOA, as federal law, controls. FFCCSOA provides for modification of out-of-state child support orders as follows:

> (e) Authority to modify orders.—A court of a State may modify a child support order issued by a court of another State if—
> (1) the court has jurisdiction to make such a child support order pursuant to subsection (i); and
> (2)(A) the court of the other State no longer has continuing, exclusive jurisdiction of the child support order because that State no longer is the child's State or the residence of any individual contestant. . . .

28 U.S.C. §1738B(e). Subsection (i), regarding jurisdiction, states as follows:

> (i) Registration for modification.—If there is no individual contestant or child residing in the issuing State, the party or support enforcement agency seeking to modify, or to modify and enforce, a child support order issued in another State shall register that order in a State with jurisdiction over the nonmovant for the purpose of modification.

Subsection (i) differs from UIFSA in that it does not contain the non-resident requirement found at §36-5-2611(a)(ii). Ms. LeTellier contends that jurisdiction is proper in the Tennessee court under FFCCSOA in spite of her status as a resident of Tennessee because of the doctrine of federal preemption. We again disagree.

Application of general rules of federal preemption leads us to conclude that FFCCSOA and UIFSA do not conflict. We begin with a presumption that Congress did not intend to preempt UIFSA. . . . In 1988, Congress established the United States Commission on Interstate Child Support ("Commission") to offer recommendations on the resolution of interstate child support problems. As part of its recommendations, the Commission "declared its support for the

Uniform Interstate Family Support Act." H.R. Rep. No. 102-982 (1992). FFCCSOA was signed into law in 1994. From its inception, FFCCSOA was intended to be consistent with UIFSA.

In 1996, Congress enacted a law requiring all fifty states to adopt UIFSA by January 1, 1998. 42 U.S.C. §666(f) (1996). . . . While conflicts between the two laws were recognized, they were characterized as unintentional. Subsequent revisions to FFCCSOA were intended to correct any conflicts and make FFCCSOA consistent with UIFSA. . . .

In the absence of preemption, we apply traditional rules of statutory construction to reconcile both statutes. . . . The word "jurisdiction" as used in FFCCSOA, 28 U.S.C. §1738B(i), is ambiguous. FFCCSOA does not specify whether "jurisdiction" refers to personal jurisdiction alone or to both personal and subject matter jurisdiction. . . .

A consistent reading of UIFSA and FFCCSOA requires only that "jurisdiction" under subsection (i) of FFCCSOA be construed as referring to both personal jurisdiction and subject matter jurisdiction. . . . Accordingly, under FFCCSOA, a state has jurisdiction to modify an out-of-state support order only when the petitioner registers the order in a state having personal and subject matter jurisdiction for the purpose of modification. Since, under §36-5-2611(a) of UIFSA, Tennessee courts do not have subject matter jurisdiction to modify the District of Columbia's order because Ms. LeTellier is a resident of Tennessee, the Juvenile Court for Davidson County did not have "jurisdiction over the nonmovant for the purpose of modification" under FFCCSOA. . . .

Notes and Questions

1. *Enforcement under UIFSA.* UIFSA uses direct enforcement when an order is sent to an obligor's employer in another state, in turn triggering wage withholding (§501), 9 U.L.A. (pt. IB) 232 (2005). Alternatively, UIFSA authorizes direct administrative enforcement of an order issued elsewhere by an agency in the obligor's state (§507), id. at 239. UIFSA includes a registration process (§§601-604), id. at 241-246, allowing courts and agencies in one state to enforce support orders issued in another. UIFSA's requirement that an obligor must contest a foreign order by requesting a hearing within 20 days of notification of the order's registration (§606), id. at 249, has survived due process challenge. Washington v. Thompson, 6 S.W.3d 82 (Ark. 1999). UIFSA explicitly makes visitation irrelevant (§305(d)), 9 U.L.A. (pt. IB) 209-210 (2005). See Clemmons v. Office of Child Support Enforcement, 984 S.W.2d 837 (Ark. 1999) (mother who willfully concealed son, preventing father's visitation, not estopped from recovering support arrearages). Cf. Stanley v. Bouzaglou, 753 N.Y.S.2d 305 (Fam. Ct. 2002) (mother's frustration of father's visitation prevents her from collecting arrearages, but not future child support under UIFSA). See generally Uniform Interstate Family Support Act (1996) (with More Unofficial Annotations by John J. Sampson), 32 Fam. L.Q. 390, 405-406 (1998).

2. *Jurisdiction to modify.* Support awards typically are subject to modification in the rendering state. As a result, some authorities have questioned whether the constitutional full faith and credit requirement applies in such cases or whether other states can refuse to recognize a support award issued elsewhere. Even if the

requirement controls, it would allow a sister state as much room to modify the decree as the rendering state (because "full faith and credit" means that the second forum must treat the decree the same way the rendering state would). In the face of this uncertainty, some jurisdictions based interstate recognition of modifiable support awards on comity. See, e.g., Lowery v. Lowery, 591 A.2d 81 (Vt. 1991). Under URESA (which committed enacting states to rules of reciprocal recognition), enforcement of a support award issued elsewhere often required a cumbersome two-state procedure, involving the courts of both states.

Under URESA, courts took different positions on whether one state could modify another's support decree and on whether the original state must recognize another's modification. Modification outside the issuing state often produced multiple and conflicting support orders.

UIFSA, which has a "One-Order, One-Time" rule, sought to address such problems through modification limitations explained by *LeTellier*. UIFSA's 2001 amendments (§201(b)) clarify the distinction between initial jurisdiction and jurisdiction to modify. 9 U.L.A. (pt. IB) 185 (2005). See John J. Sampson with Barry J. Brooks, Uniform Interstate Family Support Act (2001) With Prefatory Note and Comments (With Still More Unofficial Annotations), 36 Fam. L.Q. 329, 360-361 (2002).

Suppose that one of the LeTelliers had remained in the District of Columbia. Where would jurisdiction to modify lie? On such facts, would jurisdiction depend upon whether Steven or Teresa were seeking the modification? UIFSA provides for continuing and exclusive modification jurisdiction in the state issuing the initial award, so long as the obligor, obligee, or the child lives in the state or, alternatively, the parties consent (§205). 9 U.L.A. (pt. IB) 192 (2005). See, e.g., Teseniar v. Teseniar, 74 P.3d 910 (Alaska 2003); Philipp v. Stahl, 798 A.2d 83 (N.J. 2002). What would UIFSA's approach mean for the facts of *Kulko*, which — despite its significance for jurisdictional rules generally — concerned a petition to modify child support? (To answer this question, do you need to know whether the initial award was the separation agreement in New York or the Haitian divorce decree?)

3. *"Rough justice."* LeTellier explains that (a) UIFSA has different jurisdictional rules for initial jurisdiction and modification jurisdiction and (b) UIFSA has special rules that govern when the issuing state has lost continuing and exclusive jurisdiction to modify (§611). 9 U.L.A. (pt. IB) 254 (2005). How do these latter rules work? See also Walton v. State ex rel. Wood, 50 P.3d 693 (Wyo. 2002) (stating rules and noting that, alternatively, respondent can consent to modification jurisdiction in petitioner's domicile). Do you agree with UIFSA's comments, quoted in *LeTellier*, that the modification rules achieve a "rough justice" between the litigants? See Sampson with Brooks, supra, at 360-361 (approving *LeTellier*'s analysis).

Assuming that the Haitian divorce decree constituted the initial child support award in *Kulko*, would UIFSA's rules disallow Ezra from bringing his modification action in New York, the former marital domicile? Why? Recall the Supreme Court's analysis of fairness in that case. Does the expansion of long-arm jurisdiction for establishing initial awards, plus the requirement of "continuing exclusive jurisdiction" in the issuing state (so long as one party remains there), answer this question? To what extent do UIFSA's limitations address, at least in modification cases, the policy problems posed by rules that subject a parent to personal jurisdiction if service of process is accomplished during a visit with a child who resides out of state?

4. *Enforcement versus modification.* Even if all the parties have left the issuing state, so that state lacks jurisdiction to modify, does the issuing state still retain jurisdiction to enforce its award? Courts have answered this question in the affirmative. E.g., Zaabel v. Konetski, 807 N.E.2d 372 (Ill. 2004); Jurado v. Bradshear, 782 So. 2d 575 (La. 2001). Note that even once the issuing state has lost modification jurisdiction, the original order remains in effect there and in other states in which it had been registered, and it can be registered and enforced even in additional states. See In re Marriage of Metz, 69 P.3d 1128, 1132 (Kan. Ct. App. 2003).

5. *A national standard.* Even before the 1996 welfare reform legislation requiring states to adopt UIFSA, Congress enacted measures to facilitate interstate recognition and enforcement of support orders. The Family Support Act of 1988 required states to adopt procedures insuring finality and full faith and credit for all payments or support obligations once due. 42 U.S.C. §666(a)(9) (2000). This federal legislation prohibits retroactive (as distinguished from prospective) modification everywhere.

As *LeTellier* notes, Congress subsequently enacted the Full Faith and Credit for Child Support Orders Act, 28 U.S.C. §1738B (2000), incorporating many UIFSA concepts. This legislation imposes duties on states to enforce and not modify (except as authorized) child support orders established by other states, consistently with the Act's requirements. It provides for continuing, exclusive jurisdiction by a court that has made an order, so long as the state is the child's state or the residence of any individual contestant, unless a court in another state has modified the order, in accordance with the Act. "Child's state" is defined as "the State in which a child resides." For choice of law, the act generally dictates application of the forum's law, but specifies the law of the issuing state for interpreting orders. In 1996, Congress amended the legislation to make it consistent with UIFSA.

When it required states to adopt UIFSA by 1998 and it amended the full faith and credit statute to achieve consistency with UIFSA, Congress was responding to the 1996 version of UIFSA — before the drafters had finalized the 2001 version. As a result, states have enacted different versions of this "uniform" law. See http://www.nccusl.org/Update/uniformact_factsheets/uniformacts-fs-uifsa.asp (last visited June 14, 2006) (listing 18 states that have enacted 2001 version); Sampson with Brooks, supra, 340-342.

6. *Federal parent locator service.* Special problems arise when the obligor's whereabouts are unknown. Solutions such as those examined in *Kulko* and *LeTellier* assume that obligors can be located, although they might have disappeared to evade support enforcement. Congress responded to this problem by directing the Secretary of Health and Human Services to establish and conduct the "parent locator service." 42 U.S.C.A. §653 (West Supp. 2005). This service relies on Social Security numbers to track absent parents. The Personal Responsibility and Work Opportunity Reconciliation Act of 1996 strengthens this service by incorporating the National Director of New Hires and Federal Case Registry of child support orders. See generally Janet Atkinson, Assisting Children and the Courts: The Federal Parent Locator Service, 83 Judicature 26 (1999).

7. *Federal crimes.* The Child Support Recovery Act (CSRA), 18 U.S.C. §228 (2000), criminalizes the willful failure to pay a past-due support obligation for a child who resides in another state. "Past-due support obligation" means any amount determined by a court order or administrative process to be due for the

support and maintenance of a child, or a child and the parent with whom the child is living, if the amount has remained unpaid for more than a year or exceeds $5,000. The CSRA does not create a private right of action for obligees. See, e.g., Salahuddin v. Alaji, 232 F.3d 305 (2d Cir. 2000).

Congress amended the CSRA in 1998, with the enactment of the Deadbeat Parents Punishment Act, 18 U.S.C. §228(a)(3) (2000), which makes willful failure to pay a support obligation for a child in another state a felony, if the obligation remains unpaid for over two years or exceeds $10,000. Courts have rejected ex post facto challenges to the enhanced penalties for accrued arrearages, reasoning that the amendments cover only postenactment willful failures to pay. See United States v. Wilson, 210 F.3d 230 (4th Cir. 2000); United States v. Russell, 186 F.3d 883 (8th Cir. 1999).

Most courts have upheld the CSRA against challenges that it exceeds Congress's authority under the Commerce Clause and the Tenth Amendment. E.g., United States v. Faasse, 265 F.3d 475 (6th Cir. 2001); United States v. Mussari, 95 F.3d 787 (9th Cir. 1996). These courts have reasoned that the payment of a debt constitutes economic activity and the difference in location of obligor and obligee requires satisfaction of the debt by interstate means. See generally Daniel Robert Zmijewski, The Child Support Recovery Act and Its Constitutionality after US v. Morrison, 12 Kan. J.L. & Pub. Pol'y 289 (2003).

8. *International support enforcement.* Special enforcement problems arise when the obligor flees to another country. Does UIFSA apply? Compare Haker-Volkening v. Haker, 547 S.E.2d 127 (N.C. Ct. App. 2001) (deeming Switzerland not a "state" under UIFSA), with Foreman v. Foreman, 550 S.E.2d 792 (N.C. Ct. App. 2001) (treating England as "state" under UIFSA). The Personal Responsibility and Work Opportunity Reconciliation Act facilitates international support enforcement by establishing procedures for recognition of "foreign reciprocating countries." 42 U.S.C. §659a (2000). The 2001 amendments to UIFSA (§§102(21)), 308(b), 615) expand the definition of "state" to permit enforcement of foreign support orders in the United States and to allow states to arrange with foreign countries for reciprocal child support enforcement. 9 U.L.A. (pt. IB) 177, 215, 263 (2005).

G. SEPARATION AGREEMENTS

Most divorcing parties themselves settle the financial issues incident to dissolution. They then present their agreement to the court for approval.[64] The rules governing property division and spousal and child support thus establish the framework within which such "private ordering" takes place.[65] This section presents the legal principles applicable to separation agreements (also known as property settlement agreements).

---

[64]. See ALI Principles, supra note [2], §7.09 cmt. b, reporter's note ("Studies consistently find that approximately 90 percent of divorces are uncontested.").

[65]. Robert H. Mnookin & Lewis Kornhauser, Bargaining in the Shadow of the Law, 88 Yale L. J. 950, 950-952 (1979).

■ UNIFORM MARRIAGE AND DIVORCE ACT §306
9A U.L.A. (pt. I) 248-249 (1998)

[SEPARATION AGREEMENT]

(a) To promote amicable settlement of disputes between parties to a marriage attendant upon their separation or the dissolution of their marriage, the parties may enter into a written separation agreement containing provisions for disposition of any property owned by either of them, maintenance of either of them, and support, custody, and visitation of their children.

(b) In a proceeding for dissolution of marriage or for legal separation, the terms of the separation agreement, except those providing for the support, custody and visitation of children, are binding upon the court unless it finds, after considering the economic circumstances of the parties and any other relevant evidence produced by the parties, on their own motion or on request of the court, that the separation agreement is unconscionable.

(c) If the court finds the separation agreement unconscionable, it may request the parties to submit a revised separation agreement or may make orders for the disposition of property, maintenance, and support.

(d) If the court finds that the separation agreement is not unconscionable as to disposition of property or maintenance, and not unsatisfactory as to support:

(1) unless the separation agreement provides to the contrary, its terms shall be set forth in the decree of dissolution or legal separation and the parties shall be ordered to perform them, or

(2) if the separation agreement provides that its terms shall not be set forth in the decree, the decree shall identify the separation agreement and state that the court has found the terms not unconscionable.

(e) Terms of the agreement set forth in the decree are enforceable by all remedies available for enforcement of a judgment, including contempt, and are enforceable as contract terms.

(f) Except for terms concerning the support, custody, or visitation of children, the decree may expressly preclude or limit modification of terms set forth in the decree if the separation agreement so provides. Otherwise, terms of a separation agreement set forth in the decree are automatically modified by modification of the decree.

Notes and Questions

1. *Public policy.* At one time, separation agreements were held to violate public policy because they facilitated divorce by removing uncertainty about how a court would resolve the financial incidents. In contrast, UMDA makes the parties' "amicable settlement of disputes" an explicit policy objective.

Why does UMDA reject the traditional disfavor of separation agreements? Does the transition from fault to no-fault divorce explain the change? Does the increasing acceptance of premarital agreements? What are the advantages of "private ordering" over judicial resolution? See Robert H. Mnookin, Divorce Bargaining: The Limits on Private Ordering, 18 U. Mich. J.L. Ref. 1015, 1017-1019 (1985). The disadvantages?

The American Law Institute's Principles of the Law of Family Dissolution also favor private ordering. To encourage settlement, the Principles' formulaic approach to the financial consequences of dissolution is designed to enhance the predictability of the outcome a court would reach. See supra p. 603. Accordingly, the Principles' treatment of agreements sets out the requirements for parties to "opt out" of the default rules that would otherwise govern. See ALI Principles §7.02 cmt. a. Chapter 7 covers premarital agreements, postnuptial agreements, separation agreements, and agreements for domestic partnerships and their dissolution. From a public policy perspective, should the law show more or less deference to separation agreements, compared to premarital agreements? Why? See id. §7.09 cmt. b. Does the psychological stress associated with divorce call for greater legal protection of parties entering separation agreements than premarital agreements? See Mnookin, supra.

2. *Timing.* Does UMDA's "attendant upon" language require that the parties enter the agreement at the time of separation or dissolution or only that the agreement resolve disputes arising then? See, e.g., In re Marriage of Lafaye, 89 P.3d 455 (Colo. Ct. App. 2003) (finding that agreement met timing requirements for neither postnuptial nor separation agreements). In jurisdictions that permit separation agreements but not postnuptial agreements, might strict timing requirements for the former discourage attempted reconciliations? Compare Williams v. Williams, 463 S.E.2d 815 (N.C. Ct. App. 1995), *aff'd*, 469 S.E.2d 553 (N.C. 1996), with Vaccarello v. Vaccarello, 757 A.2d 909 (Pa. 2000).

3. *Unconscionability.* How does a court determine whether an agreement is "unconscionable" under UMDA? Does this standard contemplate a substantive evaluation of fairness or only perfunctory judicial review? See, e.g., In re Marriage of Gundmundson, 955 P.2d 648, 653 (Mont. 1998) (judge makes no inquiry on unconscionability). Some authorities claim that the absence of judicial oversight disproportionately disadvantages women. See, e.g., Penelope Eileen Bryan, The Coercion of Women in Divorce Settlement Negotiations, 74 Denv. U. L. Rev. 931, 937-938 (1997).

The ALI Principles make presumptively unenforceable agreements that would substantially change the property rights or compensatory spousal payments otherwise due, when enforcement would substantially impair the economic well-being of either a party with custody of the children or a party with substantially fewer economic resources than the other party. ALI Principles, supra, §7.09(2). What advantages does this standard have over the "unconscionability" test? What disadvantages? See also id. §7.01 (procedural requirements).

4. *Attorney's role.* Do the policies favoring the settlement of disputes preclude a malpractice judgment against an attorney who advised a client to sign a separation agreement? Does the client's acceptance of the agreement serve as a malpractice defense? See, e.g., Vogel v. Touhey, 828 A.2d 268 (Md. Ct. Spec. App. 2003); Puder v. Buechel, 874 A.2d 534 (N.J. 2005). Does the court's approval of the separation agreement as "not unconscionable"?

Although plaintiffs who show professional negligence causing an economic injury can recover for malpractice, the emotional climate of divorce poses risks for attorneys. What should an attonery do when a client asserts that the highest priority is settling the case quickly and asks the attorney to forego discovery to determine the extent of the marital property? See Baldrige v. Lacks, 883 S.W.2d 947 (Mo. Ct. App. 1994). When policies favoring settlement and mediation clash with "the older, more established value perceived in the resolution of conflict in adversarial proceedings by parties represented by fully independent and empowered attorneys," which should prevail? See Lerner v. Laufer, 819 A.2d 471, 482 (N.J. Super Ct. App. Div. 2003). See generally Lewis Becker, Ethical Concerns in Negotiating Family Law Agreements, 30 Fam. L.Q. 587 (1996); Andrew S. Grossman, Avoiding Legal Malpractice in Family Law Cases: The Dangers of Not Engaging in Financial Discovery, 33 Fam. L.Q. 361 (1999).

5. *The bargaining process.* The conventional wisdom depicts the parties bargaining toward a separation agreement in the "shadow of the law." Under this theory, the outcome the judge would order if the spouses did not settle significantly influences the settlement they will reach. See Robert H. Mnookin & Lewis Kornhauser, Bargaining in the Shadow of the Law: The Case of Divorce, 88 Yale L.J. 950, 951 (1979). In predicting the outcome adjudication would yield, however, attorneys necessarily consider the high proportion of cases that settle. Further, empirical studies show that judicial review operates primarily as a rubber stamp of the parties' agreements and that settlements often reflect not genuine agreement but rather "'the best I can get' solution." Marygold S. Melli et al., The Process of Negotiation: An Exploratory Investigation in the Context of No-Fault Divorce, 40 Rutgers L. Rev. 1133, 1159 (1988). Professor Melli and her co-authors thus conclude that divorce might well represent a system of "adjudication in the shadow of bargaining." Id. at 1147.

6. *Incorporation and merger.* Separation agreements may be "contractual" or "decretal," a distinction with important consequences. Without its incorporation (sometimes called "merger") into a judicial decree, a separation agreement is simply a contract. In one method of incorporation, the judgment recites the essential provisions of the agreement; in the other the judgment refers to the agreement and incorporates its provisions by reference. See Alexander Lindey & Louis I. Parley, 2 Lindey Parley on Separation Agreements and Antenuptial Contracts §83.30 (2d ed. 1998). UMDA §306 creates a presumption of incorporation that parties seeking to avoid must dispel by a clear statement to the contrary.

One consequence that depends on the status of the agreement concerns enforcement. For example, if one party does not perform the terms (say, the obligation to pay support), contempt of court and possible imprisonment provide remedies for noncompliance with a judicial decree. Such remedies are not available for breach of contract. Grace v. Grace, 655 N.W.2d 595, 600 (Mich. Ct. App. 2002). UMDA §306 provides for enforcement remedies for "terms of the agreement set forth in the decree." See also ALI Principles, supra, §7.10.

Similarly, courts can modify some provisions of a judicial decree if circumstances change (that is, support provisions); courts cannot rewrite the terms of a contract no matter how unfair or inadequate they become. See, e.g., Ex parte Owens, 668 So. 2d 545 (Ala. 1995) (court can modify alimony provisions upon changed circumstances when agreement incorporated into decree); Torres v. McClain, 535 S.E.2d 623 (N.C. Ct. App. 2000) (agreement not incorporated into decree raises questions of contract law only). Note that UMDA §306 allows the parties to preclude or limit modification (except for terms concerning children). See also, e.g., Day v. Day, 717 A.2d 914 (Me. 1998).

7. *Tradeoffs.* In reaching a separation agreement, the parties resolve a number of incidents of divorce. The bargaining process may entail purely financial

tradeoffs, for example, decreased alimony for a greater share of the marital property. Alternatively, it may entail negotiation of financial and nonfinancial interests, for example, decreased alimony for sole child custody. See, e.g., Scott Altman, Lurking in the Shadow, 68 S. Cal. L. Rev. 493 (1995) (examining custody-property trades in negotiations); Margaret F. Brinig & Michael V. Alexeev, Trading at Divorce: Preferences, Legal Rules and Transaction Costs, 8 Ohio St. J. Disp. Resol. 279 (1993) (theoretical and empirical investigation).

Some jurisdictions have special rules for "integrated bargains," agreements in which the consideration exchanged between the parties includes both property rights and support payments. For example, support payments in an integrated bargain incorporated into the divorce decree are not modifiable upon a showing of changed circumstances because modification would necessarily alter the property division and upset the parties' carefully crafted quid pro quo. See, e.g., Beasley v. Beasley, 707 So. 2d 1107 (Ala. Civ. App. 1997); Holcomb v. Holcomb, 513 S.E.2d 807 (N.C. Ct. App. 1999). Further, some agreements use terms or a payment structure that leaves unclear whether an obligation represents a division of assets, spousal support, or some of both. See, e.g., Sally Burnett Sharp, Step by Step: The Development of the Distributive Consequences of Divorce in North Carolina, 76 N.C. L. Rev. 2017, 2044-2052 (1998) (discussing lump sum alimony in integrated separation agreements).

8. *Vacating the decree.* Orders dividing property are final in the sense that a court cannot modify them upon changed circumstances (see supra section D2a). Nevertheless, they can be reopened if they form part of an agreement procured by fraud or other improper means. E.g., In re Rossi, 108 Cal. Rptr. 2d 270 (Cal. Ct. App. 2001) (undisclosed lottery jackpot); Shafmaster v. Shafmaster, 642 A.2d 1361 (N.H. 1994) (setting aside property settlement seven years later).

Some courts have vacated divorce judgments based on a stipulated agreement on the ground that the agreement was unconscionable. E.g., Crawford v. Crawford, 524 N.W.2d 833 (N.D. 1994). Should the same standard of unconscionability apply when a party attempts to set aside an agreement after its entry as when the court considers whether to adopt the agreement initially? What does this approach mean for private ordering? Does this view invite "judges to patronizingly and paternalistically meddle in the proposed stipulations of presumptively competent divorcing adults"? *Crawford*, 524 N.W.2d at 837 (Neumann, J., dissenting). See also, e.g., Curtis v, Curtis, 798 N.Y.S.2d 764 (App. Div. 2005).

Some commentators claim that wives are more likely than husbands to enter bad divorce bargains because of factors such as wives' financial dependency, their naive trust of their attorneys and the justice system, their ethic of care, and their greater tendency toward depression. See Penelope Eileen Bryan, Women's Freedom to Contract at Divorce: A Mask for Contextual Coercion, 47 Buff. L. Rev. 1153 (1999). See also Amy L. Wax, Bargaining in the Shadow of the Market: Is There a Future for Egalitarian Marriage?, 84 Va. L. Rev. 509 (1998). Cf. Adams v. Adams, 848 A.2d 991 (Pa. Super. Ct. 2004) (declining to invalidate agreement based on duress, despite wife's assertions of low self-esteem and dominance by abusive husband). Do such generalizations call for standards that give judges more room to vacate divorce decrees based on agreements? Does the perfunctory quality of judicial review at the time of divorce call for more permissive standards in subsequent challenges?

The ALI Principles find a middle ground, affording the parties a short opportunity to challenge the terms after experiencing the agreement's operation, when a court finds that both the agreement is "tainted" by noncompliance with the procedural or substantive requirements of §7.09 and "the challenged terms of the decree were substantially less favorable to the moving party than they would have been without the agreement." ALI Principles, supra, §7.11.

9. *Bargaining with child support.* UMDA §306 treats child support, custody, and visitation specially, making the parties' agreement on these issues not binding on the court and also preserving the possibility of future modification, despite agreement to contrary. Other authorities reflect a similar approach. E.g., Reinsch v. Reinsch, 611 N.W.2d 86 (Neb. 2000); Brescia v. Fitts, 436 N.E.2d 518 (N.Y. 1982); ALI Principles, supra, §§7.06, 7.07, 7.09 & cmt. i.

What explains UMDA's special treatment of provisions concerning children? What is the difference between finding property or maintenance provisions "not unconscionable" and finding (child) support provisions "not unsatisfactory?" Does UMDA allow the parties to leave child support, custody, and visitation as purely matters of contract? Should courts defer to the parties' explicit preclusion of modification of child support in the separation agreement? See Portlock v. Portlock, 518 A.2d 116 (D.C. 1986); Harry D. Krause, Child Support in America: The Legal Perspective 18 (1981); Eleanor E. Maccoby & Robert H. Mnookin, Dividing the Child: Social and Legal Dilemmas of Custody 41 (1992). Should a court be less willing to modify an award of child support based on a separation agreement, in deference to the policy favoring private ordering? Are there reasons a court should be more willing to modify in such cases? Compare Tietig v. Boggs, 602 So. 2d 1250 (Fla. 1992), and Solis v. Tea, 468 A.2d 1276, 1282-1283 (Del. 1983), with Boyd v. Boyd, 343 S.E.2d 581, 584-585 (N.C. Ct. App. 1986).

10. *Predictability?* What impact will federally mandated child support guidelines have on agreements negotiated by parents? If states adopt more predictable rules for property division and alimony, as recommended by the ALI Principles, supra, will settlement increase? Will such reforms enhance autonomy by lessening dependence on experts? The absence of clear rules and the unpredictability of results have been criticized for putting "the disputants at the mercy of legal experts who know the ropes, who control the process (judges and mediators), or who claim special insights into its workings (the lawyers), and so can pressure the parties into accepting solutions that suit the professionals' goals but that often seem unresponsive to the spouses' personal senses of justice and to their self-defined needs." Inga Markovits, Family Traits, 88 Mich. L. Rev. 1734, 1749 (1990).

Problem

In the property settlement agreement judicially ratified, affirmed, and incorporated by reference in the divorce decree, David agrees to relinquish all of his equity in the jointly owned marital home (the couple's only asset) in exchange for Marilyn's promise never to request child support. Their agreement explicitly states that Marilyn "has accepted all of David's equity in lieu of requesting child support" and that "should a court ever grant a child support award against David, Marilyn convenants and agrees to pay directly to David any amount of support that he is directed to pay to any party." Pursuant to the agreement, David conveys to Marilyn his equity in the marital home, valued at $40,000, where she and the children continue to live. Marilyn alone supports the children.

Six years later, David petitions for definite periods of visitation with the children. Marilyn then petitions for David to pay child support. He counters by moving the court to order Marilyn to reimburse him for any amount of child support the court orders. What result? See Kelley v. Kelley, 449 S.E.2d 55 (Va. 1994). See also Ex parte Tabor, 840 So. 2d 115 (Ala. 2002); Esser v. Esser, 586 S.E.2d 627 (Ga. 2003); Savarese v. Corcoran, 709 A.2d 829 (N.J. Super. Ct. Ch. Div. 1997), *aff'd*, 709 A.2d 799 (N.J. Super. Ct. App. Div. 1998); ALI Principles, supra, §3.13.

VII

■

Child Custody

Custody disputes arise in many different settings: divorce, guardianship, child abuse and neglect, and adoption.[1] This chapter focuses primarily on the first of these settings. Post-divorce custody law is characterized by the dual rationale of private dispute resolution and child protection.[2] The resolution of custody disputes thereby reflects the fundamental tension between respect for family autonomy versus the need for state intervention.

When the parents can agree on child custody, the state generally defers to family autonomy. However, in approximately 10 to 20 percent of divorce cases involving children, the parents cannot agree.[3] For these cases, the important question is how these disputes should be resolved. This chapter begins by exploring empirical evidence regarding the effects of divorce on children.

A. INTRODUCTION: EFFECTS OF PARENTAL DIVORCE

The following excerpt sheds light on the experience of divorce from the child's perspective.

---

[1]. On these different "strands" of custody law, see Robert H. Mnookin, Child Custody Adjudication: Judicial Functions in the Face of Indeterminacy, 39 Law & Contemp. Probs. 226, 230-246 (1975). See also Chapter VIII (child abuse) and Chapter IX (adoption and guardianship).

[2]. See Mnookin, supra note [1], at 281.

[3]. Eleanor E. Maccoby & Robert H. Mnookin, Dividing the Child: Social and Legal Dilemmas of Custody 134 (1992).

■ **ELIZABETH MARQUARDT, BETWEEN
TWO WORLDS: THE INNER LIVES OF
CHILDREN OF DIVORCE**
21-22, 30-31 (2005)

Many people imagine that the hardest time for children of divorce is the moment when their parents first part. That moment *is* hard, but it is only the beginning. The division and restructuring of childhood that immediately follow, and which continue up to and beyond the point the child leaves home, throw into question aspects of childhood that were once taken for granted and keep the divorce very much alive for years to come.

[W]e found that almost two-thirds of children of divorce who stay in contact with both parents say they felt like they grew up in two families, not one. Many changes occur in the wake of divorce. But from the child's point of view the essential change is this: The child suddenly inherits two distinct worlds in which to grow up.

Growing up in two worlds creates endless and often painful complications for a child. . . . As children of divorce, we became insiders *and* outsiders in each of our parents' worlds. We were outsiders when we looked or acted like our other parent or when we shared experiences in one world that people in the other knew little or nothing about. [W]e were marked as insiders by whatever traits we shared with the family members in one world — physical characteristics, personality, and name — as well as the experiences we shared with that family. . . . Yet because we grew up living in two worlds we never fully belonged in either place. . . .

To outside observers, the children of divorced parents may look no different than the children of intact parents. We ran on the playground, went to school, argued with our siblings, played with blocks, drew pictures in our bedrooms. But we were also vigilant. When Mom came home we gauged her mood. When we stayed at Dad's we were often quiet and on good behavior. We paid close attention to the different rules at each parent's home and the conflicts in their expectations of us. We wondered if we looked or acted too much like our father and if that made our mother mad at us. We struggled to remember what we were supposed to say, what secrets or information about one parent we should not share with the other. We adjusted ourselves to each of our parents, shaping our habits and beliefs to mimic theirs when we were around them. We often felt like a different person with each of our parents.

Our parents may no longer have been in conflict, but the conflict between their worlds was still alive. Yet instead of being in the open, visible to outsiders, the conflict between their worlds migrated and took root within us. . . .

The author of the above excerpt, together with sociologist Norval D. Glenn, surveyed 1500 adults — those who had experienced a divorce before the age of 14 as well as a comparison group of children from intact families. The researchers found that children of divorce are far more likely than those from intact families to admit that they felt like a different person with each parent, felt like outsiders in their own home, felt more mature than their years, had frequent feelings of being alone, felt more unsafe emotionally, and were less likely to seek comfort from their parents.

What are the *long-term* psychological effects of divorce on children? Several researchers have examined this question. Psychologist Judith Wallerstein conducted a 25-year in-depth study of 60 post-divorce families with 131 children. The sample consisted of families who were referred to her counseling center in the early 1970s. Her original study, Surviving the Breakup: How Children and Parents Cope with Divorce (1980) (co-authored with Joan Kelly) finds that the *immediate* effects of divorce on children vary according to children's gender, age, and developmental stage at the time of divorce: (1) preschoolers manifest regression, aggression, sleep disturbances, and fantasies of abandonment; (2) children aged 5-8 reveal grief, longing for the departed parent, and fantasies of replacement; (3) children aged 8 1/2 to 12 evince anxiety, loneliness, and anger; and (4) adolescents act out, suffer depression, have suicidal thoughts, and express anxiety about having successful marriages.

Wallerstein's 10-year follow-up research, Second Chances: Men, Women, and Children a Decade After Divorce (1989) (co-authored with Sandra Blakeslee), and also her 25-year follow-up study, The Unexpected Legacy of Divorce: The 25 Year Landmark Study (2001), illuminate the continued negative effects of parental divorce. Even years after the divorce, one-third of the children had serious psychological problems (e.g., clinical depression, poor performance in school, difficulty maintaining friendships). She contends that the effects of divorce persist into adulthood: the children of divorce face difficulties in forming and maintaining intimate interpersonal relationships.

Psychologist Mavis Hetherington and journalist John Kelly also conducted a major study of the long-term effects of divorce on children. E. Mavis Hetherington & John Kelly, For Better or For Worse: Divorce Reconsidered (2002). Hetherington and Kelly concur with Wallerstein that divorce is a continuous process that begins long before the actual marital separation and has long-term consequences. However, they reveal more optimism than Wallerstein about the long-term effects and emphasize the resiliency of the children of divorce. Hetherington's longitudinal study of 1400 families and 2500 children (including both divorced and intact families) concludes that the vast majority (75 to 80 percent) of children from divorced homes become well-adjusted adults. Only 20 to 25 percent of the children from divorced families manifest serious social, emotional, or psychological problems (compared to 10 percent of the children from intact families). Id. at 229.

Social psychologist Paul Amato attempts to synthesize the findings of the vast body of research on the effects of divorce on children, and also to reconcile the seemingly divergent findings of Wallerstein and Hetherington. To analyze the results of studies that vary widely in terms of samples, respondents, and methodology, social scientists use the social science technique of meta-analysis (permitting adjustments for variations among studies). Amato's meta-analysis of 93 studies published in the 1960s, 1970s, and 1980s confirms that children of divorce score lower than those of married parents on educational and psychological measures. Paul R. Amato, The Impact of Family Formation Change on the Cognitive, Social, and Emotional Well-Being of the Next Generation, in 15 The Future of Children: Marriage and Child Wellbeing 75, 77 (2005). His *subsequent* meta-analysis conducted during the 1990s, finds that children of divorce again score lower even in an era when divorce was more acceptable and widespread. Id. at 77.

In his attempt to reconcile the findings of Wallerstein with the more opti- mistic long-term findings of Hetherington, Amato confirms that several of Wal- lerstein's claims are consistent with prior research, in particular: (1) children with divorced parents are more likely to experience psychological problems in adulthood (2) they have more problems in forming and maintaining stable inti- mate relationships, and (3) they reach adulthood with weaker ties to parents. Paul R. Amato, Reconciling Divergent Perspectives: Judith Wallerstein, Quanti- tative Family Research, and Children of Divorce, 52 Fam. Relations 334 (2003). Nonetheless, based on his longitudinal research of 671 children of divorce (including a control group of intact families), as well as his meta-analyses above, Amato (like Hetherington and Kelly) concludes that the long-term effects of divorce are *not as pervasive or as severe* as Wallerstein claims. Id. at 336; Amato, Future of Children, supra, at 77. Amato, Reconciling Divergent Perspectives, supra, at 337.[4] Although Wallerstein finds that over one-third of children with divorced parents become psychologically troubled adults, Amato indicates that only 10 percent of children of divorce manifest serious psychological prob- lems in adulthood.

Finally, note that the difficulties that led to the divorce have a significant im- pact on children's post-divorce adjustment, and post-divorce factors also play an important role. Amato finds that evidence about one major post-divorce factor, a parent's or parents' remarriage, is mixed in terms of its effects for children. How- ever, multiple family transitions (involving multiple divorces and remarriages) are more problematic for children than the experience of a single divorce. Id., at 338.[5]

As you read though the materials in this chapter, consider the following ques- tions: What should be the impact on policymakers of the effects of divorce on children? Should governmental policy promote marriage? Discourage divorce? If so, how? Will such policies, without other programmatic interventions, signifi- cantly improve children's well-being? If not, what other interventions should be instituted to improve children's well-being?

[4]. Several researchers attribute Wallerstein's more pessimistic findings to the facts that her respon- dents were clients referred to a counseling center (and thereby may have contained a larger proportion of dysfunctional families); her research was conducted by means of interviews by clinicans (who might have been more likely to identify pathology); and also her early research took place in an era when divorce was less common, leading to the possibility that the children in her sample may have suffered greater stigma which affected their psychological well-being. See Paul R. Amato, Reconciling Divergent Perspectives: Judith Wallerstein, Quantitative Family Research, and Children of Divorce, 52 Fam. Rela- tions 334 (2003); Joan B. Kelly & Robert E. Emery, Children's Adjustment Following Divorce: Risk and Resiliency Perspectives, 52 Fam. Relations 352 (2003).

[5]. For additional research on the effects of divorce on children, see Bonnie L. Barber & David H. Demo, The Kids Are Alright (at Least, Most of Them): Links Between Divorce and Dissolution and Child Well-Being, in Handbook of Divorce and Relationship Dissolution 289 (Mark A. Fine & John H. Harvey, eds. 2006); Robert E. Emery, Marriage, Divorce, and Children's Adjustment (2d. ed. 1999); Robert E. Emery, Postdivorce Family Life for Children: An Overview of Research and Some Implications for Policy, in The Postdivorce Family: Children, Parenting, and Society (Ross A.Thompson & Paul R. Amato, eds. 1999).

B. PARENTAL DISPUTES CONCERNING CHILD CUSTODY

1. Standards for Selecting the Custodial Parent: What Should Be the Standard?

a. Presumptions?

(i) Tender Years Presumption

■ DEVINE v. DEVINE
398 So. 2d 686 (Ala. 1981)

MADDOX, Justice.

[A]ppellant Christopher P. Devine [and] Appellee, Alice Beth Clark Devine were legally and lawfully married on December 17, 1966, . . . and separated in Calhoun County, Alabama, on March 29, 1979. [They have two sons, Matthew, born in 1972, and Timothy, born in 1975.] Since [college] graduation in 1962, Mrs. Devine has taught high school. [I]n 1975 [she] commenced employment with the U.S. Army at Fort McClellan, Alabama, where she was employed continuously through the [trial] as an Educational Specialist. [She] was 38 years of age at the time of [trial]. The Appellant/natural father, Christopher P. Devine [age 41] was a member of the faculty and head of the Guidance and Counseling Department at Jacksonville State University, Jacksonville, Alabama. At the time of the trial, the older son had just completed the first grade at the said University's Elementary Laboratory School and the younger son was enrolled in the said University's Nursery Laboratory School. [The trial court awarded custody of both boys to the mother based on the tender years presumption.]

[T]here exists in Alabama law a presumption that when dealing with children of tender years, the natural mother is presumed, in absence of evidence to the contrary, to be the proper person to be vested with custody of such children. This presumption, while perhaps weaker now than in the past, remains quite viable today. . . .

The sole issue presented for review is whether the trial court's reliance on the tender years presumption deprived the father of his constitutional entitlement to the equal protection of the law. . . .

At common law, it was the father rather than the mother who held a virtual absolute right to the custody of their minor children. This rule of law was fostered, in part, by feudalistic notions concerning the "natural" responsibilities of the husband at common law. The husband was considered the head or master of his family, and, as such, responsible for the care, maintenance, education and religious training of his children. By virtue of these responsibilities, the husband was given a corresponding entitlement to the benefits of his children, i.e., their services and association. It is interesting to note that in many instances these rights and privileges were considered dependent upon the recognized laws of nature and in accordance with the *presumption* that the father could best provide for the necessities of his children. . . .

By contrast, the wife was without any rights to the care and custody of her minor children. By marriage, husband and wife became one person with the legal identity of the woman being totally merged with that of her husband. As a result, her rights were often subordinated to those of her husband and she was laden with numerous marital disabilities. As far as any custodial rights were concerned, Blackstone stated the law to be that the mother was "entitled to no power [over her children], but only to reverence and respect." 1 W. Blackstone, Commentaries on the Law of England 453 (Tucker ed. 1803).

By the middle of the 19th Century, the courts of England began to question and qualify the paternal preference rule. This was due, in part, to the "hardships, not to say cruelty, inflicted upon unoffending mothers by a state of law which took little account of their claims or feelings." W. Forsyth, A Treatise on the Law Relating to the Custody of Infants in Cases of Difference Between Parents or Guardians 66 (1850). Courts reacted by taking a more moderate stance concerning child custody, a stance which conditioned a father's absolute custodial rights upon his fitness as a parent. Ultimately, by a series of statutes culminating with Justice Talfourd's Act, 2 and 3 Vict. c. 54 (1839), Parliament affirmatively extended the rights of mothers, especially as concerned the custody of young children. Justice Talfourd's Act expressly provided that the chancery courts, in cases of divorce and separation, could award the custody of minor children to the mother if the children were less than seven years old. This statute marks the origin of the tender years presumption in England.

In the United States the origin of the tender years presumption is attributed to the 1830 Maryland decision of Helms v. Franciscus, 2 Bl. Ch. (Md.) 544 (1830). In *Helms*, the court, while recognizing the general rights of the father, stated that it would violate the laws of nature to "snatch" an infant from the care of its mother:

> The father is the rightful and legal guardian of all his infant children; and in general, no court can take from him the custody and control of them, thrown upon him by the law, not for his gratification, but on account of his duties, and place them against his will in the hands even of his wife. . . . Yet even a court of common law will not go so far as to hold nature in contempt, and snatch helpless, pulling infancy from the bosom of an affectionate mother, and place it in the coarse hands of the father. The mother is the softest and safest nurse of infancy, and with her it will be left in opposition to this general right of the father.

Thus began a "process of evolution, perhaps reflecting a change in social attitudes, [whereby] the mother came to be the preferred custodian of young children and daughters. . . ." Foster, Life with Father, 11 Fam. L.Q. 327 (1978). . . .

At the present time, the tender years presumption is recognized in Alabama as a rebuttable factual presumption based upon the inherent suitability of the mother to care for and nurture young children. All things being equal, the mother is presumed to be best fitted to guide and care for children of tender years. To rebut this presumption the father must present clear and convincing evidence of the mother's positive unfitness. Thus, the tender years presumption affects the resolution of child custody disputes on both a substantive and procedural level. Substantively, it requires the court to award custody of young children to the mother when the parties, as in the present case, are equally fit parents. Procedurally, it imposes an evidentiary burden on the father to prove the positive unfitness of the mother.

In recent years, the tender years doctrine has been severely criticized by legal commentators as an outmoded means of resolving child custody disputes. . . . In twenty states the doctrine has been expressly abolished by statute or court decision, and in four other states its existence is extremely questionable. . . . In Orr v. Orr, 440 U.S. 268 (1979), the United States Supreme Court held that any statutory scheme which imposes obligations on husbands, but not on wives, establishes a classification based upon sex which is subject to scrutiny under the Fourteenth Amendment. The same must also be true for a legal presumption which imposes evidentiary burdens on fathers, but not on mothers.

[W]e conclude that the tender years presumption represents an unconstitutional gender-based classification which discriminates between fathers and mothers in child custody proceedings solely on the basis of sex.

Notes and Questions

1. *Background.* Beginning in the mid-to late nineteenth century, the tender years presumption applied to custody determinations. The presumption (also called the "maternal preference") provided that the natural mother of a young child was entitled to custody of the child unless she was found unfit. Courts treated the doctrine as: (1) a tie-breaker mandating maternal custody if all other factors are equal, or (2) a rule placing the burden of persuasion on the father to show that paternal custody serves the best interests of the child, or (3) a rule affecting the burden of proof that requires the father, in order to prevail, to prove maternal unfitness. Robert F. Cochran, Jr., The Search for Guidance in Determining the Best Interests of the Child at Divorce: Reconciling the Primary Caretaker and Joint Custody Preferences, 20 U. Rich. L. Rev. 1, 10 (1985). In the 1970s and 1980s, many states (similar to Alabama in *Devine*) declared that the presumption violated the Equal Protection Clause or state equal rights amendments.

The tender years presumption was introduced, as *Devine* suggests, in an influential nineteenth-century American case that carved out an exception to the paternal preference for infants. Social conditions facilitated widespread acceptance of the doctrine. Industrialization, urbanization, and a growing middle class contributed to the increasing privatization of the family, accompanied by a glorification of motherhood and an intense concern with childrearing. See generally Barbara Ehrenreich & Deirdre English, For Her Own Good: 150 Years of the Experts' Advice to Women (1978); Michael Grossberg, Governing the Hearth: Law and the Family in Nineteenth-Century America 234-285 (1985); Richard Sennett, Families Against the Cities: Middle Class Homes of Industrial Chicago, 1872-1890 (1984); Barbara Welter, The Cult of True Womanhood, 1820-1860, 18 Am. Q. 151 (1966).

2. *Presumptions generally.* Consider the advantages and disadvantages of presumptions, generally, in custody decisionmaking. Like all presumptions, the tender years doctrine offers relative certainty and thereby avoids the stress of litigation. However, the presumption clearly puts fathers at a disadvantage because they must prove the mother's unfitness before they can gain custody. But, might a gender-neutral presumption disadvantage the mother? The father?

3. *Best-interests standard.* The tender years presumption has been replaced by the purportedly gender-neutral "best-interests-of-the-child" standard (discussed infra). This highly discretionary standard is based on a list of factors (usually statutory) regarding the child's needs. Some states consider the child's age as one factor in the best-interests analysis. See, e.g., Sockwell v. Sockwell, 822

So. 2d 1219 (Ala. Civ. App. 2001); Steverson v. Steverson, 846 So. 2d 304 (Miss. Ct. App. 2003). For a recent case rejecting a "resurrected" tender years presumption, see Greer v. Greer, 624 S.E. 2d 423 (N.C. Ct. App. 2006) (reversing trial court award to mother based on findings of fact reasoning that a natural bond develops between infants and a breastfeeding mother that were not supported by evidence and not appropriate matters for judicial notice).

4. *ALI Principles*. The American Law Institute's Principles of the Law of Family Dissolution prohibit a court from considering the gender of *either* the parent *or* the child in determining custody arrangements. ALI Principles §2.12(1)(b).

Should the *child's* gender be relevant in custody decisionmaking? That is, should courts award custody of girls to the mother and boys to the father? Most courts award custody irrespective of the child's gender. See, e.g., Giffin v. Crane, 716 A.2d 1029 (Md. Ct. App. 1998) (holding that trial court erred when it assumed that daughter had specific need to be with parent of same gender). But cf. Copeland v. Copeland, 904 So. 2d 1066 (Miss. 2004) (affirming trial court's ruling that gender of son was a factor favoring father's claim to custody). Some evidence suggests, however, that children who are awarded to parents of the same sex are better adjusted and have higher self-esteem. See Robert E. Emery, Marriage, Divorce, and Children's Adjustment 85-86 (1988). Should such data affect custody decision making?

5. *Empirical data*. Although the maternal presumption no longer operates de jure, empirical evidence suggests that most courts continue to award custody to the mother. Eleanor E. Maccoby & Robert H. Mnookin, Dividing the Child: Social and Legal Dilemmas of Custody 112-113 (1992). See also Laura E. Santilli & Michael C. Roberts, Custody Decisions in Alabama Before and After the Abolition of the Tender Years Doctrine, 14 Law & Hum. Behav. 123, 134 (1990) (finding that fathers' minor role in custody decisionmaking pre- and post-*Devine* remained unchanged).

6. *Other presumptions*. States also have abrogated the common-law presumption that custody of a nonmarital child vests in the mother. See, e.g., Rosero v. Blake, 581 S.E.2d 41, 49 (N.C. 2003) (holding that statutory revision regarding custody presumptions abrogated not only the tender years presumption but also the common law presumption vesting custody of an illegitimate child in mother). But cf. Taylor v. Commonwealth, 537 S.E.2d 592 (Va. 2000). On the application of the presumption regarding domestic violence in custody decisionmaking, see infra pp. 757-765.

(ii) Primary Caretaker Presumption

For a brief period, the primary caretaker presumption superseded the tender years presumption in some jurisdictions. According to this presumption, the best interests of the child are served by placing the child with the parent who has taken primary responsibility for the child's care. West Virginia first adopted the presumption in Garska v. McCoy, 278 S.E.2d 357 (W.Va. 1981), and enumerated specific caretaking criteria. Minnesota followed in Pikula v. Pikula, 374 N.W.2d 705 (Minn. 1985), but later abrogated the presumption. Minn. Stat. §518.17(1)(a) (Supp. 2005). West Virginia also subsequently abandoned the presumption. W.Va. Code Ann. §48-11-201 et seq. (2004). Today, primary caretaker status has continued vitality in some jurisdictions only as one factor in the determination of the child's best interests. See, e.g., Kjelland v. Kjelland, 609 N.W.2d 100 (N.D. 2000); Zepeda v. Zepeda, 628 N.W.2d 48 (S.D. 2001).

Commentators have elaborated on the advantages as well as disadvantages of the doctrine. Primary among the advantages are the benefit of a gender-neutral principle (by awarding custody to a parent, irrespective of gender, who has performed more childcare and thereby demonstrated a higher commitment to meeting the child's needs) and the reduction in litigation ensuing from a bright line rule. Among the disadvantages, commentators cite an overemphasis on caretaking tasks and on the importance of attachment by prioritizing the bond to the primary caretaker, a devaluation of the father's role in child development, and a concern with the possibility of an increase in litigation ensuing from such a vague standard. Feminists criticize the manner in which judges apply the doctrine by minimizing women's contributions to childcare (breastfeeding and emotional caretaking) while maximizing men's smaller contributions. See Mary E. Becker, Maternal Feelings: Myth, Taboo, and Child Custody, 1 S. Cal. Rev. L. & Women's Stud. 133 (1992); David L. Chambers, Rethinking the Substantive Rules for Custody Disputes in Divorce, 83 Mich. L. Rev. 477 (1984); Martha L. Fineman & Anne Opie, The Uses of Social Science Data in Legal Policymaking: Custody Determinations at Divorce, 1987 Wis. L. Rev. 107.

When West Virginia rejected the presumption, legislators there replaced it with a version of the American Law Institute's Principles Governing the Allocation of Custodial and Decisionmaking Responsibility for Children that requires the parties to submit a "parenting plan."[6] A parenting plan is a written agreement that specifies authority for caretaking and decisionmaking as well as the manner in which future disputes are to be resolved. About half the states now make some provision for a parenting plan. Some states mandate such plans. Others require them only for joint custody determinations. Still others allow parents to submit them voluntarily or at the order of the judge.[7]

According to the ALI Principles, if the parents agree, the court should enforce their agreement unless the agreement is not voluntary or would be harmful to the child (§2.06(1)(a) & (b)). However, if the parents are unable to agree, the court should award custody based on the allocation of caretaking responsibility prior to the separation (§2.08(1)). The objective is to replicate the division of responsibility that was followed when the family was intact in order to promote stability for the child.[8] In a scheme that favors private ordering, such an allocation of decisionmaking gives deference to the arrangements on which the parties once agreed.

Although some might question whether the ALI recommendation implicitly reinstates the primary caretaker presumption, the ALI provision differs in several

[6]. In 1989, the ALI undertook a decade-long project to reform family law by clarifying its underlying principles and making policy recommendations. The ALI's recommendations reject the "best interests of the child standard" (discussed infra) because of its subjectivity and lack of predictability and favor "private ordering," i.e., parental agreements. See ALI Principles of the Law of Family Dissolution: Analysis and Recommendations §§2.06, 2.11-2.12 (2002) (parenting agreements, and limiting and prohibited factors for such plans) (hereafter ALI Principles).

[7]. Katherine T. Bartlett, U.S. Custody Law and Trends in the Context of the ALI Principles of the Law of Family Dissolution, 10 Va. J. Soc. Pol'y & L. 5, 6-7 (2002). Washington was one of the first states to adopt parenting plan legislation in 1987. Heather Crosby, The Irretrievable Breakdown of the Child: Minnesota's Move Toward Parenting Plans, 21 Hamline J. Pub. L. & Pol'y 489, 509 (2000).

[8]. This "approximation standard" was first formulated by Elizabeth Scott, Pluralism, Parental Preference, and Child Custody, 80 Cal. L. Rev. 615 (1992). See generally Marygold S. Melli, The American Law Institute Principles of Family Dissolution, The Approximation Rule and Shared-Parenting, 25 N. Ill. U. L. Rev. 347 (2005).

ways. Unlike the primary caretaking presumption, the ALI Principles contemplate a spectrum of possibilities. For example, the Principles favor an equal allocation of custodial time if the parents in the intact family had allocated caretaking responsibilities equally. In addition, the ALI rule may be rebutted by specific factors such as a prior parental agreement, the child's preference, the need to keep siblings together, harm to the child's welfare (based on emotional attachment to a parent and the parent's ability/availability to meet the child's needs), avoidance of custodial arrangements that would be impractical or interfere with the child's need for stability, and the need to deal with parental relocation (§2.08(1)(a) to (g)).

b. Best Interests of the Child?

(i) Introduction

■ **ROBERT H. MNOOKIN, CHILD-CUSTODY ADJUDICATION: JUDICIAL FUNCTIONS IN THE FACE OF INDETERMINACY**
39 Law & Contemp. Probs. 226, 233-237, 255-256, 261-264 (1975)

The history of the legal standards governing custody disputes between a child's parents reveals a dramatic movement from rules to a highly discretionary principle. . . . Divorce custody standards now show the overwhelming dominance of the best-interests principle. [My purpose here] is to expose the inherent indeterminacy of the best-interests standard.

. . . An inquiry about what is best for a child often yields indeterminate results because of the problems of having adequate information, making the necessary predictions, and finding an integrated set of values by which to choose. But some custody cases may still be comparatively easy to decide. While there is no consensus about what is best for a child, there is much consensus about what is very bad (e.g., physical abuse); some short-term predictions about human behavior can be reliably made (e.g., chronic alcoholism or psychosis is difficult quickly to modify). Asking which alternative is in the best interests of a child may have a rather clear-cut answer in situations where one claimant exposes the child to substantial risks of immediate harm and the other claimant already has a substantial personal relationship with the child and poses no such risk. [However, most] custody disputes pose difficult choices. [I]n many private disputes, the court must often choose between parties who each offer advantages and disadvantages, knowing that to deprive the child completely of either relationship will be disruptive. . . .

. . . What are some of the implications of the use of indeterminate standards in custody disputes? Would more precise standards that ask an answerable question be better? [T]he use of an indeterminate standard makes the outcome of litigation difficult to predict. This may encourage more litigation than would a standard that made the outcome of more cases predictable. Because each divorcing parent can often make plausible arguments why a child would be better off with him or her, a best-interests standard probably creates a greater incentive to litigate than would a rule that children should go to the parent of the same sex. . . .

Indeterminate standards also pose an obviously greater risk of violating the fundamental precept that like cases should be decided alike. [W]ith an indeterminate standard, the same case presented to different judges may easily result in different decisions. The use of an indeterminate standard means that state officials may decide on the basis of unarticulated (perhaps even unconscious) predictions and preferences that could be questioned if expressed. . . .

. . . While judges may be ill-equipped to develop and evaluate information about the child, having some other state official decide or making various procedural adjustments (such as giving counsel to the child, providing better staff to courts, or making the proceedings more or less formal) will not cure the root problem. The indeterminacy flows from our inability to predict accurately human behavior and from a lack of social consensus about the values that should inform the decision.

[A]djudication by a more determinate rule would confront the fundamental problems posed by an indeterminate principle. But the choice between indeterminate standards and more precise rules poses a profound dilemma. The absence of rules removes the special burdens of justification and formulation of standards characteristic of adjudication. Unfairness and adverse consequences can result. And yet, rules that relate past events or conduct to legal consequences may themselves create substantial difficulties in the custody area. Our inadequate knowledge about human behavior and our inability to generalize confidently about the relationship between past events or conduct and future behavior make the formulation of rules especially problematic. Moreover, the very lack of consensus about values that makes the best-interests standard indeterminate may also make the formulation of rules inappropriate. . . . [9]

■ UNIFORM MARRIAGE AND DIVORCE ACT
9A U.L.A. (pt. II) 282 (1998)

§402 [BEST INTEREST OF CHILD]

The court shall determine custody in accordance with the best interest of the child. The court shall consider all relevant factors including:

(1) the wishes of the child's parent or parents as to his custody;

(2) the wishes of the child as to his custodian;

(3) the interaction and interrelationship of the child with his parent or parents, his siblings, and any other person who may significantly affect the child's best interest;

(4) the child's adjustment to his home, school, and community; and

(5) the mental and physical health of all individuals involved.

The court shall not consider conduct of a proposed custodian that does not affect his relationship to the child.

---

[9]. For additional criticisms of the best interests standard, see Mary E. Becker, Maternal Feelings: Myth, Taboo, and Child Custody, 1 S. Cal. Rev. L. & Women's Stud. 133, 172-183 (1992); Jon Elster, Solomonic Judgments: Against the Best Interests of the Child, 54 U. Chi. L. Rev. 1 (1987).

(ii) Constitutional Factors

(1) Race

■ **PALMORE v. SIDOTI**
466 U.S. 429 (1984)

Chief Justice BURGER delivered the opinion of the Court.

We granted certiorari to review a judgment of a state court divesting a natural mother of the custody of her infant child because of her remarriage to a person of a different race.

When petitioner Linda Sidoti Palmore and respondent Anthony J. Sidoti, both Caucasians, were divorced in May 1980 in Florida, the mother was awarded custody of their three-year-old daughter. In September 1981 the father sought custody of the child by filing a petition to modify the prior judgment because of changed conditions. The change was that the child's mother was then cohabiting with a Negro, Clarence Palmore, Jr., whom she married two months later. Additionally, the father made several allegations of instances in which the mother had not properly cared for the child.

After hearing testimony from both parties and considering a court counselor's investigative report, the court noted that the father had made allegations about the child's care, but the court . . . made a finding that "there is no issue as to either party's devotion to the child, adequacy of housing facilities, or respect[a]bility of the new spouse of either parent."

The court then addressed the recommendations of the court counselor, who had made an earlier report "in [another] case coming out of this circuit also involving the social consequences of an interracial marriage. Niles v. Niles, 299 So. 2d 162." From this vague reference to that earlier case, the court turned to the present case and noted the counselor's recommendation for a change in custody because "[t]he wife [petitioner] has chosen for herself and for her child, a life-style unacceptable to her father *and to society.* . . . The child . . . is, or at school age will be, subject to environmental pressures not of choice."

The court then concluded that the best interests of the child would be served by awarding custody to the father. The court's rationale is contained in the following:

> The father's evident resentment of the mother's choice of a black partner is not sufficient to wrest custody from the mother. It is of some significance, however, that the mother did see fit to bring a man into her home and carry on a sexual relationship with him without being married to him. Such action tended to place gratification of her own desires ahead of her concern for the child's future welfare. *This Court feels that despite the strides that have been made in bettering relations between the races in this country, it is inevitable that Melanie will, if allowed to remain in her present situation and attains school age and thus more vulnerable to peer pressures, suffer from the social stigmatization that is sure to come.*

(Emphasis added.)

The Second District Court of Appeal affirmed without opinion, thus denying the Florida Supreme Court jurisdiction to review the case. We granted certiorari, and we reverse.

The judgment of a state court determining or reviewing a child custody decision is not ordinarily a likely candidate for review by this Court. However, the court's opinion, after stating that the "father's evident resentment of the mother's choice of a black partner is not sufficient" to deprive her of custody, then turns to what it regarded as the damaging impact on the child from remaining in a racially-mixed household. This raises important federal concerns arising from the Constitution's commitment to eradicating discrimination based on race.

The Florida court did not focus directly on the parental qualifications of the natural mother or her present husband, or indeed on the father's qualifications to have custody of the child. The court found that "there is no issue as to either party's devotion to the child, adequacy of housing facilities, or respect[a]bility of the new spouse of either parent." This, taken with the absence of any negative finding as to the quality of the care provided by the mother, constitutes a rejection of any claim of petitioner's unfitness to continue the custody of her child.

The court correctly stated that the child's welfare was the controlling factor. But that court was entirely candid and made no effort to place its holding on any ground other than race. Taking the court's findings and rationale at face value, it is clear that the outcome would have been different had petitioner married a Caucasian male of similar respectability.

A core purpose of the Fourteenth Amendment was to do away with all governmentally-imposed discrimination based on race. Classifying persons according to their race is more likely to reflect racial prejudice than legitimate public concerns; the race, not the person, dictates the category. [T]o pass constitutional muster, [racial classifications] must be justified by a compelling governmental interest. . . .

The State, of course, has a duty of the highest order to protect the interests of minor children, particularly those of tender years. In common with most states, Florida law mandates that custody determinations be made in the best interests of the children involved. Fla. Stat. §61.13(2)(b)(1) (1983). The goal of granting custody based on the best interests of the child is indisputably a substantial governmental interest for purposes of the Equal Protection Clause.

It would ignore reality to suggest that racial and ethnic prejudices do not exist or that all manifestations of those prejudices have been eliminated. There is a risk that a child living with a step-parent of a different race may be subject to a variety of pressures and stresses not present if the child were living with parents of the same racial or ethnic origin.

The question, however, is whether the reality of private biases and the possible injury they might inflict are permissible considerations for removal of an infant child from the custody of its natural mother. We have little difficulty concluding that they are not. The Constitution cannot control such prejudices but neither can it tolerate them. Private biases may be outside the reach of the law, but the law cannot, directly or indirectly, give them effect. . . .

. . . The effects of racial prejudice, however real, cannot justify a racial classification removing an infant child from the custody of its natural mother found to be an appropriate person to have such custody.

The judgment of the District Court of Appeal is reversed.

Notes and Questions

1. *Epilogue.* Following the U.S. Supreme Court's decision above, the mother filed a petition in Texas (where the father and child had moved) for a writ of habeas corpus to recover the child and, in Florida, a motion to compel the return of the child (that was opposed there by the father). The Florida court declined jurisdiction in favor of the Texas court. When the mother appealed that decision, the Florida Court of Appeals affirmed, stating:

> The Supreme Court's decision [in *Palmore*] was that the modification of custody could not be predicated upon the mother's association with a black man. Its opinion did not direct a reinstatement of the original custody decree and the immediate return of the child. The Supreme Court did not say that a Florida court could not defer to a Texas court.

472 So. 2d 843, 846 (Fla. Dist. Ct. App. 1985). The court then determined that it would be in the child's best interests to remain in her father's custody given the passage of time and the "substantial upheavals" in the child's life. Id. at 847.

2. *Different approaches.* Prior to *Palmore*, courts adopted different approaches: (1) race was not relevant to custody; (2) race could be considered as one factor in determining a child's best interests; and (3) race could not be used as the determinative factor. Which view does *Palmore* support? See cases cited in Lee R. Russ, Annotation, Race as Factor in Custody Award or Proceedings, 10 A.L.R.4th 796 (1981 & Supp. 2004).

3. *Pretextual reasoning.* How does an appellate court identify race as the unarticulated rationale of a trial court ruling? Professor Katharine Bartlett notes that, in several cases involving white mothers who lost custody after an affair with an African-American man, the court used different justifications for the custody modification (e.g., the mother lied about the affair, her sexual activity displayed poor judgment). Bartlett explains: "It is difficult to second-guess these cases under a best-interests test because it is not a test that compels transparency." Katharine T. Bartlett, Comparing Race and Sex Discrimination in Custody Cases, 28 Hofstra L. Rev. 877, 884 & n. 35 (2000). See also Dansby v. Dansby, 189 S.W.3d 473 (Ark. Ct. App. 2004) (changing joint custody to an award of sole custody to father, basing the decision not on African-American mother's decision to date only white men, but rather on her entertaining men overnight, smoking marijuana, and speaking disparagingly of the father in the children's presence).

4. *Promoting racial tolerance.* Parents' attitudes sometimes influence judicial decisions. In Tipton v. Aaron, 185 S.W.3d 142 (Ark. Ct. App. 2004), an appellate court reversed a trial court ruling granting a father's request for custody of his Caucasian child. The father, who disapproved of the mother's remarriage to a biracial man and her giving birth to a biracial child, contended that an interracial household would create problems for his son. Reversing, the appellate court reasoned that the mother lived in a diverse community where interracial households were common, the child had a good relationship with the mother's husband, and, finally, the mother's childrearing philosophy promoted racial tolerance while the father's did not.

5. *Fostering racial identity.* Does judicial exclusion of the factor of race operate to promote the best interests of the child or, conversely, work to the child's detriment?

This issue typically arises when a non-white parent contests an award of custody to the Caucasian parent by arguing under the best-interests test, that the former is better qualified to foster the development of the child's racial identity. For example, in Hamilton v. Hamilton, 42 P.3d 1107 (Alaska Ct. App. 2002), an African-American mother appealed a custody award to her children's Caucasian father on this basis. The Alaska Court of Appeals rejected her argument, suggesting that she could foster her children's racial identity during summer vacations when she had custody and pointing out that paternal custody would place the child in a multi-racial home because the father was cohabiting with a Vietnamese woman and her child. Do you find the court's reasoning persuasive?

How much weight should courts attach to the need to promote a child's cultural and racial heritage? See also Warford v. Warford, 2004 WL 2940881 (Minn. Ct. App. 2004) (rejecting father's argument that awarding Caucasian wife sole physical custody would prevent him from sharing with his children his experiences as a racial minority, and finding no evidence that either his wife had prevented him from discussing these issues with the children or that he planned to expose his children to their racial heritage). On the role of race in adoption decisionmaking, see Chapter IX infra.

6. *ALI Principles.* The ALI Principles prohibit courts from considering the race or ethnicity of the child, parent, or other member of the household in determining custody arrangements. ALI Principles §2.12(1)(a) (2002).

Problems

1. Dawn and Kevin and their three children live in South Dakota. Kevin, a member of the Sisseton-Wahpeton Dakota Nation, was adopted at age 7 by a Caucasian couple, the Jones. Dawn, Kevin, and the children live on the Jones's family farm where Kevin is employed. Kevin's adoptive family is extremely close-knit. Dawn, a homemaker, decides to enroll in a nursing program. Kevin's alcoholism (and verbal and physical abuse while intoxicated) contribute to the breakup of the marriage. At trial, a licensed psychologist and a clinical social worker both testify that Dawn should have custody. Nonetheless, the trial court rules that Kevin should have primary physical custody (provided that he remains alcohol-free) because of Kevin's close relationship with the Jones family and also because, as a Native American, Kevin will be better able to deal with the needs of the children. Dawn appeals. What result? See Jones v. Jones, 542 N.W.2d 119 (S.D. 1996). Cf. In re Custody of M.A.L., 457 N.W.2d 723 (Minn. Ct. App. 1990).

2. Teri and Richard, a Caucasian couple, have been married for five years. They have a one-year-old son, Dylan. After Teri files for divorce, both parents seek custody of Dylan. At trial, Richard argues that the court should award him custody because Teri, a nurse, is having a relationship with the African-American doctor for whom she works. A family nurse practitioner testifies, when asked if it would be harmful for Dylan to be raised in this environment, that it would be harmful. She adds that interracial relationships are more acceptable in large cities, but that it may be harmful for a child to be raised in such an environment in a small town such as theirs. The trial court finds both parents fit but awards custody to Richard, stating that extramarital affairs interfere with the well-being of the child. It orders no contact between the child and the doctor (an order Richard did not

even request). Teri appeals. What result? See Parker v. Parker, 986 S.W.2d 557 (Tenn. 1999).

(2) Religion

■ **SAGAR v. SAGAR**
781 N.E.2d 54 (Mass. App. Ct. 2003)

GRASSO, J.

In the course of contentious divorce proceedings between two devout Hindus, the husband moved the court for permission to perform a Hindu religious ritual, Chudakarana,[1] upon the parties' young daughter. After a hearing, a Probate Court judge ordered that, "The religious ceremony known as Chudakarana shall not be performed on the minor child, until the child is of sufficient age to make that determination herself, absent a written agreement between the parties." On appeal from a divorce decree incorporating this order, the father maintains that the order violates his right to free exercise of religion. . . .

Sejal Sagar (wife) and Mahendra Sagar (husband) were married in Baroda, India, in 1990 in a traditional religious ceremony. They had known each other for less than a month; the marriage had been arranged by their respective parents. After marriage, the couple moved to the United States, where their only child, a daughter, was born on June 17, 1998. They separated in November, 1998. [In the divorce proceedings, the trial court awarded joint legal custody and granted physical custody to the wife with liberal visitation to the husband.]

During and after marriage, the parties followed substantially the tenets of the Hindu faith. During the wife's pregnancy and after their daughter's birth, the parties engaged in Hindu ceremonies prescribed to mark various transitions in an infant's life, including a religious baby shower, a homecoming ceremony, a naming ceremony, a first visit to the temple, a ceremony for the child's first solid food, and an ear piercing ceremony. The parties attended temple weekly and even had a temple in their home at which they worshiped on a daily basis.

Their relationship was volatile and marred by numerous instances of the husband's physical and mental abuse of the wife. At various times, the husband threw things at the wife, hit her with a rolling pin, pulled her hair, chased her from their house, and burned her with a cigarette. He tore apart a book given her by her brother. The husband was very controlling. He would allow his wife to telephone her relatives only on birthdays and anniversaries; and the contents of the kitchen cabinets had to be arranged as he specified. He threatened to stop paying tuition for the wife's education should she fail to get straight A's. The husband made questionable transfers of marital assets and refused to comply with a court order to hold certain funds in escrow.

Apart from disagreement over whether the Hindu sacrament of Chudakarana should be performed, the parties are in substantial agreement over the rearing of their daughter, including her religious upbringing. At trial, the husband presented

---

1. On this record, Chudakarana can be described as a ceremony involving tonsure and prayer. While mantras are recited, a priest removes hair from five parts of the child's head, offering some of the hair ritually. The child's entire head is shaved, an auspicious mark is then placed on the child's head, and benedictions are offered.

evidence to support his position that a Hindu may not forgo the ritual of Chudakarana. The ceremony, which is believed to contribute to the child's longevity and ward off illness, should be performed before the child is three years old and is a necessary prerequisite to Hindu marriage. If the ceremony is not performed, an elder (here the father) may atone, allowing the ceremony to be performed at a later date. The wife's position was that Chudakarana is not integral to the Hindu faith. Neither she nor her extended family believe in the efficacy or necessity of the ceremony. She did not participate in the ceremony, nor did her brother or cousins. Prior to marriage, the husband never inquired whether she had participated in Chudakarana; neither did she inform him that she had not.

The father claims that the right to insist upon performance of Chudakarana upon his child is protected under both State and Federal Constitutional provisions respecting free exercise of religion. The [trial] judge's decision appears to conclude that the husband's free exercise claim fails because it is not grounded in a sincerely held religious belief. An essential prerequisite to a free exercise claim is a sincerely held religious belief. A court may not examine the truth behind a person's religious beliefs. However, inquiry into the sincerity of a professed belief is constitutionally appropriate under both the First Amendment; and article 2 of the Massachusetts Constitution.

The judge did not question the husband's general devotion to Hinduism. At the same time, he found that "the husband's reasons for his insistence on having the Chudakarana are not purely religious[,][but] an issue of control." The record supports this determination. We credit, as we must, the judge's finding, based upon his credibility assessment. However, the determination that the husband's motivation is not "purely religious" is different altogether from whether his belief is "sincerely held." We need not, and should not, predicate a decision implicating a parent's free exercise right and his fundamental liberty interest in child rearing upon the tenuous ground that the parents' underlying religious belief is not "sincerely held" because the motivation is not "purely religious."[3]

Although the husband conceptualizes the probate judge's action as a State-imposed limitation on his own free exercise of religion, whether Chudakarana is performed upon the child implicates not only the husband's but also the wife's fundamental rights. These include the right to direct their daughter's upbringing and religious formation.

The due process clause protects certain fundamental rights and liberty interests, including the right of a parent to direct a child's education and upbringing. For the court to issue an order upholding the husband's fundamental right to direct that the ceremony of Chudakarana be performed upon the child would repudiate permanently the wife's corresponding right to direct that the ceremony not be performed. Conversely, to order that the ceremony not be performed, as the wife would have it, would repudiate the husband's fundamental rights.

A court is justifiably loath to order a restriction on either parent's fundamental rights to free exercise of religion and to determine the child's religious upbringing and is constitutionally limited in doing so unless there is a compelling State interest

---

3. We also cannot delve into differences between the parties over whether strict adherence to Hindu religious belief requires that Chudakarana be performed. Resolution of that matter clearly would involve assessment of the religion's doctrine. The First Amendment protects sincerely held religious beliefs even when these differ from the established dogma of a religion or are not accepted as dogma by any religion.

such as preventing demonstrable physical or psychological harm to the child. . . . Here, the husband failed to demonstrate a compelling State interest for performing the ceremony on the child. Evidence was lacking that failure to perform the ceremony would "cause the child significant harm by adversely affecting the child's health, safety, or welfare." Blixt v. Blixt, 774 N.E.2d 1052, 1060 (Mass. 2002). "[H]arm to the child from conflicting religious instructions or practices, which would justify such a limitation [on a parent's right to freedom of religious expression or practice] should not be . . . assumed or surmised; it must be demonstrated in detail." Felton v. Felton, 418 N.E.2d 606, 607 (Mass. 1981). [Conversely, the wife] did not establish that performing the ceremony would subject the child to physical or psychological harm, a compelling State interest that would support an order restricting the husband's fundamental rights. . . .

Here, the evidence did not establish either proposition — that the child would suffer physical or psychological harm by undergoing or by not undergoing the disputed ceremony. . . . [A]bsent proof either way, the order is a narrowly tailored accommodation that "intrudes least on the religious inclinations of either parent and . . . is compatible with the health of the child." [Felton, supra, at 608.] The order neither imposes any limitation upon nor favors either parent's ability to communicate beliefs concerning Chudakarana or to participate in any other beliefs or practices of their shared Hindu faith. The order does not coerce the father to believe as the mother does; nor does it compel him to practice his religion in a particular way. The order leaves open to the parties the opportunity to agree in the future and does not bar future court intervention on this issue should the child be suffering from physical or psychological harm. Finally, the order respects the child's ability to eventually control her own religious destiny while encouraging continued exposure to her parents' religion. . . .

In sum, the evidence as to the impact of performing, or not performing, Chudakarana on the child was insufficient either way to have justified an order restricting either parent's fundamental rights. At such a juncture, the appropriate recourse was an accommodation that intruded least upon both parents' religious inclinations and, at the same time, was compatible with the child's health and well being. The challenged order represents such an accommodation. . . .

Notes and Questions

1. *Different approaches*. In adjudicating custody disputes regarding children's religious upbringing, courts generally take one of three approaches: (1) religion may be one, but not the sole, factor in custody decisionmaking; (2) religion may be considered only to the extent that it affects the child's secular well-being or, (3) religion may be considered only for children with ascertainable religious preferences or for whom religion has become an important part of their identity. Donald I. Beschle, God Bless the Child?: The Use of Religion as a Factor in Child Custody and Adoption Proceedings, 58 Fordham L. Rev. 383, 398-404 (1989).

2. *Constitutional limitations*. The Constitution constrains judicial consideration of religion. According to the First Amendment's Free Exercise Clause, a court may not interfere with a parent's right to practice his or her religion (or not to practice religion). Under the Establishment Clause (requiring separation between church and state and forbidding excessive government entanglement with religion), a

court may not weigh the relative merits of parents' religions or favor an observant parent over a nonreligious one. How can judges adjudicate parental disputes without violating these guarantees? Should courts follow a policy of noninterference? What compelling interest might justify interference?

According to some commentators, courts routinely disregard parents' First Amendment rights by endorsing one parent's religious training over either the other parent's lack of training or the other's religious training. Eugene Volokh, Parent-Child Speech and Child Custody Speech Restrictions, 81 N.Y.U. L. Rev. 631 (2006); Jennifer Ann Drobac, Note, For the Sake of the Children: Court Consideration of Religion in Child Custody Cases, 50 Stan. L. Rev. 1609, 1611 (1998) (surveying more than 50 custody cases).

3. *Adverse effect.* Although courts cannot favor one parent's religion over the other's, courts nonetheless may examine the effect of a religious belief or practice on the child. Most courts permit interference with a parent's religious beliefs or practices only when there is evidence of harm to the child. However, courts adhere to different thresholds of harm — i.e., the effect on the child's secular well-being, serious *threatened* harm to the child's health or safety (the most common approach), or *actual* physical or mental harm to the child. Kent Greenawalt, Child Custody, Religious Practices, and Conscience, 76 U. Colo. L. Rev. 965, 975-976 (2005); Karl A. Menninger, Interference With the Right to Free Exercise of Religion, 63 Am. Jur. Proof of Facts 3d 195 (2005).

What test does *Sagar* follow? What does the court say regarding the presence of harm to the child from the performance of the Hindu ceremony of Chudakarana? Should courts make custody determinations in light of a parent's religious beliefs or practices that are based on the *possibility* of future harm? See Nathaniel Stinnett, Note, Defining Away Religious Freedom in Europe: How Four Democracies Get Away with Discriminating Against Minority Religions, 28 B.C. Int'l & Comp. L. Rev. 429, 440 (2005) (discussing a European Court of Human Rights' ruling that Austria had violated the European Charter of Human Rights by denying custody to an Austrian woman on the ground that her beliefs, as a Jehovah's Witness, might endanger her children's well-being if they ever were to require a blood transfusion).

Does a child's confusion resulting from exposure to different religious beliefs constitute sufficient harm? Compare In re Marriage of Minix, 801 N.E.2d 1201 (Ill. Ct. App. 2003) (refusing to enjoin father from taking child to his religious services because child's resulting confusion failed to rise to requisite level of harm), with Meyer v. Meyer, 789 A.2d 921 (Vt. 2001) (holding that children's confusion and anxiety, severe enough to produce physical symptoms, justified enjoining father's efforts to teach them his religion).

Should courts assume that religious disputes always are harmful for children? See Felton v. Felton, 418 N.E.2d 606, 607-608 (Mass. 1981) (suggesting that "a diversity of religious experience is itself a sound stimulant for a child").

4. *Premarital agreement.* What is the appropriate balance between the parent's constitutional rights and respect for private ordering, for example, when the parents have a premarital agreement regarding children's religious upbringing? In Zummo v. Zummo, 574 A.2d 1130 (Pa. Super. Ct. 1990), the parents (a Jewish mother and Roman Catholic father) orally agreed before their marriage that they would raise their children as Jewish. Upon divorce, the noncustodial father wanted to take the children to Roman Catholic services. Does enforcement of such a

premarital agreement unconstitutionally constrain the father's free exercise of his religion? Does it constitute duress? See Greenawalt, supra, at 984 (discussing these issues). See also Abbo v. Briskin, 660 So. 2d 1157 (Fla. Dist. Ct. App. 1995) (reversing custody order to mother requiring her to raise child as Jewish based on her premarital agreement to convert to Judaism).

5. *First Amendment*. When may a court limit a parent's First Amendment right to express *communications* about religion to his or her child? See, e.g., In re E.L.M.C., 100 P.3d 546, 563 (Colo. Ct. App. 2004) (reversing a trial court order enjoining a parent from teaching a child religious anti-homosexuality views because the other parent was a lesbian); Shepp v. Shepp, 821 A.2d 635 (Pa. Super. Ct. 2003) (denying custody to an excommunicated Mormon father because of his desire to espouse his pro-polygamy views to his children). See also Eugene Volokh, Speech as Conduct: Generally Applicable Laws, Illegal Courses of Conduct, "Situation-Altering Utterances," and the Unchartered Zones, 90 Cornell L. Rev. 1277, 1299-1300 (2005) ("Courts may not diminish the custody rights of a divorced parent because of the supposed harmfulness of the religious doctrine that he is teaching his children, unless the religious teaching is not just against the child's 'best interests' but is actually likely to cause the child significant secular harm.")

6. *Child's religious preference*. What role should the child's own religious preference have in the adjudication of parental disputes? Do you agree that the *Sagar* court appropriately took into consideration the child's preference on the matter of Chudakarana? How should a court evaluate whether the child's preference is genuine or the product of parental pressure? See, e.g., *Zummo*, supra, at 1149 (finding that children's volition was not supported by the evidence, given their ages of 3, 4, and 8, and level of religious training).

7. *Pledge of Allegiance*. In Elk Grove Unified School District v. Newdow, 542 U.S. 1 (2004), Michael Newdow, the atheist father of a public elementary school student, challenged the constitutionality of the school district's policy requiring daily recitation of the Pledge of Allegiance with its phrase "under God." He contended that the policy was indoctrination of his child in violation of the First Amendment. The Ninth Circuit held that Newdow had standing to challenge the practice as an interference with his right to direct the religious education of his daughter and ruled that the school's policy violated the Establishment Clause. Newdow v. U.S. Congress, 292 F.3d 597, 602 (9th Cir. 2002). (The child's mother, who had sole custody and the prerogative of reaching a final decision in the event of parental disagreement on childrearing matters, stated that her daughter had no objection to reciting the Pledge.) On appeal, the U.S. Supreme Court determined, based on state domestic relations law, that a noncustodial father lacks the right to litigate on behalf of his daughter as her next friend. The Court also rejected his argument that the Pledge recitation impaired his right to instruct his daughter on his religious views, noting that he simply did not have the right to "dictate to others what they may and may not say to his child respecting religion." 542 U.S at 2.

Newdow's subsequent challenge on behalf of parents of other children in California school districts was upheld. Denny Walsh, Newdow Files Slogan Suit; Pledge Case Heads to Appeal, Sacramento Bee, Nov. 19, 2005, at A11. Also, he unsuccessfully challenged the motto "In God We Trust" on U.S. currency as a violation of the Establishment Clause. Denny Walsh, Judge Upholds "In God We Trust," Sacramento Bee, June 13, 2006, B1.

8. *ALI Principles*. The ALI Principles prohibit a court from considering the "religious practices" of either the parent or child in custody decisionmaking except in the following situations: (a) if the religious practices present "severe and almost certain harm" to the child (and then a court may limit the religious practices only to the minimum degree necessary to protect the child), or (b) if necessary to protect the child's ability to practice a religion "that has been a significant part of the child's life." ALI Principles §2.12(1)(c).

Problem

When Jeffrey (who is Christian) marries Barbara (who is Jewish), they agree to raise their children as Jews. After the birth of their second child, Jeffrey becomes a member of a fundamentalist Christian faith whose adherents believe that non-members are damned to hell. As a result, Jeffrey makes serious efforts to persuade his children to accept his church's teachings. After the birth of their third child, Barbara adopts Orthodox Judaism and the couple becomes enmeshed in "opposite doctrinal extremes." When the parents file for divorce, both seek custody. Barbara seeks to limit the children's exposure to Jeffrey's religion. The court awards joint legal custody but forbids Jeffrey from exposing the children to religious content that will cause them to feel upset or to worry about themselves or their mother. Barbara appeals the joint custody award, asserting that it is inappropriate because the parents cannot come to any agreement on the children's moral and religious development.

What result? Based on the standard adopted in this jurisdiction, would exposure to the father's religion cause "substantial physical or emotional injury" to the children and have a "similar harmful tendency for the future"? What evidence would suffice to establish substantial harm? Is limiting the children's exposure to Jeffrey's religion appropriate? Does the limitation constitute an invasion of privacy? See Kendall v. Kendall, 687 N.E.2d 1228 (Mass. 1997).

(iii) Fitness

(1) Sexual Orientation

■ **FULK v. FULK**
827 So. 2d 736 (Miss. Ct. App. 2002)

BRIDGES, J., for the court.
This case is before us challenging the [award of] custody of minor child, Jeffery Dustin Fulk, to the biological father, Jeffery A. Fulk. . . . Rhonda and Jeffery were married on September 11, 1999. Their marital bliss ended in separation in September of 2000. One child was born of this union on January 20, 2001. After the birth of the baby, Rhonda briefly returned to the marital home. Further problems ensued, causing Rhonda to take the baby and leave the home permanently on February 1, 2001. On February 6, 2001, Jeffery filed for divorce on the grounds of "cruel and inhumane treatment," adultery and irreconcilable differences. He also was seeking custody of the child. A temporary hearing was held on

February 28, 2001, where Jeffery was granted temporary custody of the child. Rhonda did not appear at this hearing.

On April 5, 2001, Rhonda filed an answer to the divorce complaint admitting irreconcilable differences between the parties [and requesting custody of the child]. Following testimony from the parties and various witnesses, Chancellor Weathersby granted the divorce and awarded sole custody to Jeffery. The chancellor granted Rhonda supervised visitation on Sunday mornings at McDonald's for a minimum of one hour. . . .

Our standard of review is clear. "Chancellors are vested with broad discretion, and this Court will not disturb the chancellor's findings unless the court's actions were manifestly wrong, the court abused its discretion, or the court applied an erroneous legal standard." Mixon v. Mixon, 724 So. 2d 956, 959 (Miss. Ct. App. 1998). "However, where the chancellor improperly considers and applies the [best interests test, applying the factors in Albright v. Albright, 437 So. 2d 1003 (Miss. 1983)], an appellate court is obliged to find the chancellor in error." . . .

The polestar consideration in child custody cases is the best interest and welfare of the child. The *Albright* case provided Mississippi courts with guidelines for determining the best placement of the child after custody disputes. These factors include: (1) age, health and sex of the child; (2) determination of the parent that had the continuity of care prior to the separation; (3) which has the best parenting skills and which has the willingness and capacity to provide primary child care; (4) the employment of the parent and responsibilities of that employment; (5) physical and mental health and age of the parents; (6) emotional ties of parent and child; (7) moral fitness of parents; (8) the home, school and community record of the child; (9) the preference by law; (10) stability of home environment and employment of each parent; and (11) other factors relevant to the parent-child relationship. Marital fault should not be used as a sanction in the custody decision, nor should differences in religion, personal values and lifestyles be the sole basis for custody decisions. . . .

Rhonda asserts that the chancellor erred because she failed to consider each and every *Albright* factor thoroughly. [I]t is our opinion that the chancellor did commit reversible error. The chancellor considered some *Albright* factors but not all. Furthermore, she failed to give sufficient findings as to why she came to the conclusions she did. As Chancellor Weathersby stated, both parties start off "on equal footing." The chancellor's duty was to evaluate each factor and determine which parent would be favored.

The chancellor determined that all of the factors she examined were in favor of the father. Specifically, that the continuity of care factor favored the father, as the baby had been in his care since the enforcement of the temporary custody order. Furthermore, the court ruled that Jeffery had "done a good job with him." Considering parenting skills, the chancellor found that the father has "good skills" but offers no examples. The father's employment weighed in his favor as the mother had no income at the time of the trial. Concerning the health of the child, the court was under the impression that the father has been administering the baby's medicine properly. The court determined that the mother's affair with an emotionally unstable woman did not speak well of the mother's moral fitness and therefore ruled that moral fitness of the home environment would weigh in the father's favor. The chancellor favored the father's stability of the home over that of the mother's but did not offer an explanation of why.

The chancellor did not discuss the factor of the emotional ties between the child and parent and, more importantly, the age and sex of the child. [A]s the child was very young in age, the chancellor did not need to discuss the community and school record of the child but she failed to disclose this on the record. . . . At the time of this trial, the Fulk baby was only two and a half months old. Although the Mississippi Supreme Court, along with this Court, has significantly weakened the once strong presumption of the "tender years doctrine," it is still a viable consideration which should have been discussed. [Sobieske v. Preslar, 755 So. 2d 410, 413 (Miss. 2000).] Furthermore, the chancellor did not offer a valid explanation of how she arrived at the conclusions she did. Simply dictating that the father was favored without explaining *why* he was favored is not enough. Our job, as an appellate court, is to review the chancellor's decision and determine if it was "manifestly erroneous based on a proper analysis of each of the applicable *Albright* factors. This task becomes futile when chancellors fail to consider and discuss each factor when rendering decisions." Powell v. Ayars, 792 So. 2d 240, 244 (Miss. 2001). . . .

Rhonda argues that the chancellor erred by placing too much emphasis on the fact that Rhonda had an adulterous affair with another woman. Jeffery counters that the chancellor was not concerned that the affair was of the lesbian nature but that the person Rhonda had the affair with was a severely emotionally unstable person who testified that she would still be a part of Rhonda's life as a friend and, consequently, be around the baby. Jeffery argues that the chancellor, in determining what was best for the baby, ruled that this unstable person would not be a good influence or provide a good environment for raising a small child.

Albright dictates that "difference in religion, personal values and lifestyles" would not be the sole basis for custody decisions. *Albright*, 437 So. 2d at 1005. Our supreme court addressed a similar issue in 2001 and held that too much weight was placed upon the "moral fitness" factor based upon the mother's homosexual affair and reversed the decision of the chancery court. Hollon v. Hollon, 784 So. 2d 943, 949-50 (Miss. 2001). The chancellor in the case at bar stated that although both Rhonda and her female counterpart in the affair testified that the sexual relationship was over, it was her opinion and that of the court, that the sexual relationship was indeed not over. Furthermore, the chancellor found that it was "unacceptable for any child to be around this type of behavior." Apparently, Chancellor Weathersby forgot that the father was the instigator in the triangle relationship, not the mother. . . . Therefore, it was error for the chancellor to have relied so heavily on the affair, as it was not just Rhonda's affair due to Jeffery's willingness to be an eager participant. . . .

The facts in this case are unusual, as skeletons are in both parties' closets. The record indicates that Rhonda and Jeffery's relationship was unsteady during their entire courtship and marriage. . . . Rhonda is a young mother who does not have a source of income. She lives with her parents and a younger sibling. Both of her parents are unemployed and rely on "checks" as means for survival. As we have previously mentioned, Rhonda and Jeffery had a sexual relationship with one of Rhonda's female friends. Jeffery admits to having used drugs and alcohol heavily, although he claims to have now stopped [although Rhonda disputed this assertion].

Two incidents are very disturbing to this Court in our review of the record. Specifically, the time when Jeffery "forgot" his wife was in his home and padlocked her inside the house since it was his habit to padlock the door. At that time, Rhonda was pregnant and trapped inside the home. Her father had to come and take the door off of the hinges to allow his daughter out of the house. Secondly, we view the domestic disturbance call which ended when the police arrested Jeffery for threatening to kill Rhonda and her family with a claw hammer. Jeffery was charged with resisting arrest and domestic violence. Jeffery proceeded to plead guilty to all charges against him and was sentenced to anger management classes. It is not clear from the chancellor's opinion that she considered these incidents. Her bench ruling states, "I find that the father may have done some things in the past he is not proud of, but the Court thinks that the responsibility of fatherhood has matured him. As the Court said before, I view the marital troubles as being part of his violent temper troubles." We are of the opinion these incidents should have been addressed and considered in making the *Albright* findings. It was error for the chancellor to ignore such matters. . . .

The chancellor granted total custody to Jeffery, the father of the baby. Rhonda was granted a minimum of one hour of visitation at a McDonald's on Sunday mornings beginning at 8:00 A.M. . . . Rhonda claims it was error for this restricted visitation to be imposed as it flies in the face of Mississippi's general visitation guidelines. . . . We agree with Rhonda. . . . By restricting Rhonda's visitation with her child of very tender months, not years, to a public restaurant during the early morning hours on a Sunday, the chancellor abused her discretion and we must reverse. . . . We are reversing for the reasons enumerated in the foregoing opinion and remanding for sufficient findings consistent with this opinion. After appropriate findings are determined, if the chancellor again grants paramount care and custody to the father, it is our opinion that the mother shall be granted overnight and unrestricted visitation, provided no evidence of harm to the child was presented. . . .

Notes and Questions

1. *Epilogue.* Following the principal case, Rhonda and Jeffery entered into a settlement agreement whereby Jeffery retained custody and Rhonda obtained additional visitation. According to Jeffery's attorney, "I see the dad and little boy all the time around town. In fact, I just saw both of them the other day in the hardware store. The little boy is very cute and just as red-headed as his dad who has a pony-tail down to his waist. You know, when the father got temporary custody, that little boy was only about a few weeks old. The judge said to the father, 'Mr. Fulk, how do you know how to take care of such a tiny baby?' The father replied, 'I went to the library, ma'am, and read all about it.'" Personal communication, Boyd Atkinson, Law Offices, Cleveland, Mississippi, February 22, 2006. (Rhonda was represented by Jane E. Tucker, of Phelps Dunbar, Jackson, Mississippi; and Courtney Joslin, National Center for Lesbian Rights, San Francisco.)

2. *Sexual conduct generally.* A threshold consideration in the determination of the child's best interests is parental fitness. The focus on fitness traditionally accorded considerable weight to extramarital sexual conduct. In the fault era, sexual immorality in the form of adultery or cohabitation often resulted in custody denials because courts deemed the "guilty party" unfit. Within the past few decades, dramatic changes in social mores have had an impact on custody law. Under the modern view, influenced by the Uniform Marriage and Divorce Act (UMDA), a parent's sexual conduct is relevant to custody determinations only if

the conduct has an adverse effect on the child (the "nexus test"). See UMDA §402, supra p. 733. Nonetheless, one commentator points out that even in states that have repealed their fornication and cohabitation statutes, heterosexual cohabitation continues to play an important role in custody cases. Margaret M. Mahoney, Forces Shaping the Law of Cohabitation for Opposite Sex Couples, 7 J. L. & Fam. Stud. 135, 154 (2005).

How easy is the nexus test to apply? In Gustaves v. Gustaves, 57 P.3d 775 (Idaho 2002), the Idaho supreme court affirmed a trial court ruling that the mother's adultery had an adverse effect on the child's welfare (i.e., resulting in the child's regressive behavior) based on the open manner in which the mother carried out the affair (i.e., with the knowledge of the father). How does a court separate the effect on the children of the parent's sexual conduct from the effects of the dissolution itself? How would *Fulk* be decided under UMDA?

3. *Gender bias.* In the 1990s, many states and federal courts commissioned studies about gender bias in the legal system. Data from these studies indicate that courts frequently rely on stereotypical views of both men and women in many contexts. See generally Blake D. Morant, Introductory Essay: The Relevance of Gender Bias Studies, 58 Wash. & Lee L. Rev. 1073 (2001); Myra C. Selby, Examining Race and Gender Bias in the Courts: A Legacy of Indifference or Opportunity?, 32 Ind. L. Rev. 1167 (1999).

a. *Gender bias against mothers.* Does judicial consideration of extramarital sexual conduct in custody decisionmaking reflect gender bias against women? In Piatt v. Piatt, 499 S.E.2d 567, 571 (Va. Ct. App. 1998), a couple disagreed about child custody when they separated after five years of marriage. In affirming the trial court's award of primary physical custody to the father, the appellate court rejected the mother's contention that the trial court evaluated her lesbian post-separation conduct more harshly than the father's adulterous heterosexual relationship. In contrast, the dissenting judge agreed with the mother that the trial judge had applied different standards to the parties' sexual conduct, pointing out that the trial judge had found that the mother had behaved promiscuously while finding that the father had not.

Some courts evaluate sexual conduct (especially the mother's) based on whether the parent has legitimized that conduct (that is, by remarriage). See, e.g., In re Marriage of Cripe, 538 N.E.2d 1175 (Ill. App. Ct. 1989). Also, some courts are less tolerant of women in non-monogamous relationships. See, e.g., Boykin v. Boykin, 370 S.E.2d 884, 886 (S.C. Ct. App. 1988) (awarding father custody because mother's relationships with five men during one year were "flagrant promiscuity"). See generally Cynthia A. McNeely, Lagging Behind the Times: Parenthood, Custody, and Gender Bias in the Family Court, 5 Fla. St. U. L. Rev. 891 (1998); Susan Beth Jacobs, Note and Comment, The Hidden Gender Bias Behind "The Best Interest of the Child" Standard in Custody Decisions, 13 Ga. St. U. L. Rev. 845, 893 (1997) ("statistics indicate a strong probability of a gender bias against mothers when judges consider parents' extramarital and postmarital sexual relationships, based to some extent on judges' notions that mothers who engage in extramarital and postmarital sexual relationships are more immoral than fathers").

b. *Gender bias against fathers.* On the other hand, is the legal system biased against fathers? Does the legal system make it difficult, as fathers' rights groups argue, for fathers to obtain sole or joint custody, and thereby "relegat[e] them to the role of economic providers and little else"? Solangel Maldonado, Beyond Economic Fatherhood: Encouraging Divorced Fathers to Parent, 153 U. Pa. L. Rev. 921, 967 (2005) (exploring assertions of male gender bias and concluding that fathers' perception of bias discourages their post-divorce involvement to a greater degree than any actual bias). See also Nancy E. Dowd, Fathers and the Supreme Court: Founding Fathers and Nurturing Fathers, 54 Emory L.J. 1271 (2005) (discussing male gender bias in recent U.S. Supreme Court decisions).

In 2004, an Indiana fathers' rights group filed federal lawsuits in 46 states, seeking class action status and contending that gender bias against men influences custody and child support rulings. The complaints contended that fit parents have a constitutional right to equal custody, but that the child's-best-interest standard often violates that right. Stephanie Francis Ward, Dads Seek Equal Custody Nation-wide, Suits Say 'Child's Best Interest' Violates Parents Rights, 3 ABA J. E-Report 5, Dec. 17, 2004.

A British fathers' rights groups, Fathers 4 Justice, established three years ago to campaign for equality of treatment for fathers in custody decisionmaking, recently disbanded as a consequence of a scandal that followed the discovery of a plot to kidnap Prime Minister Tony Blair's five-year-old son in an effort to bring attention to their cause. Ben Macintyre et al., How Fathers' Fight Set Off the Mother of All Battles; Fathers 4 Justice, Times (U.K.) Jan. 21, 2006, at 34 (explaining that, despite its shock tactics, the radical protest group failed to effectuate reforms). See also Susan Dominus, The Fathers' Crusade, N.Y. Times (Mag.), May 8, 2005, at 26 (describing the fathers' rights movement in England and the United States).

4. *Same-sex sexual conduct: approaches.* Sexual conduct with persons of the same sex is more likely to lead to denial (or changes) of custody. Available data suggest that significant numbers of gays and lesbians are parents.[10] Prior to the 1970s, few gays and lesbians prevailed in custody cases.

Currently, courts take one of three approaches toward same-sex custody disputes: (1) homosexuality constitutes an irrebuttable presumption of unfitness (the per se rule); (2) homosexuality evokes a rebuttable presumption of unfitness and requires that the parent prove the absence of harm (absent such proof, the presumption of unfitness applies); (3) the parent's sexual orientation must have, or will have, an adverse impact on the child in order to lead to a denial of custody (the nexus approach).

At least six states currently follow the per se rule of unfitness. Kate Kendall, Lesbian and Gay Parents in Child Custody and Visitation Disputes, Hum. Rts. Mag., available at http://www.abanet.org/irr/hr/summer03/custody.html (last visited Jan. 26, 2006). For a recent case applying this approach, see Ex parte H.H., 830 So. 2d 21, 26 (Ala. 2002) (Roy Moore, C.J.) (concurring opinion) ("Homosexual

---

[10]. Some studies suggest that as many as ten million children in the U.S. have one or more lesbian, gay, or bisexual parent. Melissa Hart, Meet the "Queerspawn," 12 Gay & Lesbian Rev. 32 (2005) (citing data). See also National Gay and Lesbian Task Force Report, The Issues: Parenting (suggesting estimates of lesbian and gay parents that range from two to eight million), available at http://www.thetaskforce.org/theissues/issue.cfm?issueID=30 (last visited Jan. 26, 2006). The 2000 census found that at least 166,000 children are being raised by gay and lesbian couples (a number undoubtedly low because of underreporting). William Meezan & Jonathan Rauch, Gay Marriage, Same-Sex Parenting and the America's Children, 15 The Future of Children 97, 98 (Fall 2005).

conduct is, and has been, considered abhorrent, immoral, detestable, a crime against nature, and a violation of the laws of nature and of nature's God upon which this Nation and our laws are predicated. Such conduct violates both the criminal and civil laws of this State and is destructive to a basic building block of society — the family").[11]

Most jurisdictions, however, follow the nexus test. Susan M. Moss, Casenote, McGriff v. McGriff: Consideration of a Parent's Sexual Orientation in Child Custody Disputes, 41 Idaho L. Rev. 593, 618-619 (2005).

5. *ALI Principles.* The ALI Principles of the Law of Family Dissolution prohibit a court from considering either the sexual orientation or the extramarital sexual conduct of a parent except upon a showing that such conduct causes harm to the child. ALI Principles §2.12(1)(d) (sexual orientation) & (e) (extramarital sexual conduct). Which of the foregoing three approaches does the ALI Principles follow?

6. *Moral fitness.* Do custody denials to gay and lesbian parents raise constitutional problems? In Lawrence v. Texas, supra Chapter I, the U.S. Supreme Court held that state criminal sodomy laws (that banned same-sex, but not opposite-sex, sodomy) violate the individual's constitutionally protected liberty. The Court rejected moral disapproval as a legitimate interest to justify such differential treatment. What is the likely impact of *Lawrence* on custody decisionmaking? Does *Lawrence* call into question any or all of the foregoing approaches? Does *Lawrence* mandate the view that a parent's sexual conduct or sexual orientation should be irrelevant in the best-interests analysis?

How can an appellate court identify homophobia as the actual rationale of a trial court ruling when that prejudice is unarticulated or when the proffered reasons may be pretextual? See, e.g., Davidson v. Coit, 899 So. 2d 904 (Miss. Ct. App. 2005) (holding that mother's lack of church attendance supported chancellor's decision to change custody from the lesbian mother to the father and rejecting the mother's contention that the court placed improper weight on her sexual orientation).

See generally Nan D. Hunter, Living with *Lawrence,* 88 Minn. L. Rev. 1103 (2004); Matt Larsen, Note, Lawrence v. Texas and Family Law: Gay Parent's Constitutional Rights in Child Custody Proceedings, 60 N.Y.U. Ann. Surv. Am. L. 53 (2004); Jennifer Ellis Lattimore, Note, Life After Lawrence v. Texas: An Examination of the Decision's Impact on a Homosexual Parent's Right to Custody of His/Her Own Children in Virginia, 15 Geo. Mason U. Civ. Rts. L.J. 105 (2004); Jennifer Naeger, Note, And Then There Were None, The Repeal of Sodomy Laws After Lawrence v. Texas and Its Effect on the Custody and Visitation Rights of Gay and Lesbian Parents, 78 St. John's L. Rev. 397 (2004).

7. *Harm.* What showing of harm suffices under the nexus test? Emotional harm? Teasing? See, e.g., Doe v. Doe, 452 N.E.2d 293 (Mass. App. Ct. 1983). Is

---

[11]. Chief Judge Roy Moore subsequently defied a court order by the Eleventh Circuit Court of Appeals to remove a 5000-pound monument to the Ten Commandments (installed in the rotunda of the Judicil Building housing the Alabama Supreme Court) for the reason that it was an unconstitutional endorsement of religion. His defiance led to a judicial ethics complaint that resulted in his suspension and later removal from office. The monument was subsequently removed. See Bill Barrow, Moore Asked for National Guard; [Governor] Riley Says Moore Sought Protection for Monument, Mobile (Ala.) Reg., Dec. 21, 2005, at A5.

potential harm sufficient? Compare Pulliam v. Smith, 501 S.E.2d 898, 904 (N.C. 1998) (finding that father's homosexual activity "will likely create emotional difficulties" for the children), with Berry v. Berry, 2005 WL 1277847 (Tenn. Ct. App. 2005) (noting that trial court's finding of future harm was speculative and not a proper matter for judicial notice), and Taylor v. Taylor, 110 S.W.3d 731 (Ark. 2003) (holding that trial court abused its discretion in modifying custody based on potential for teasing that children might face because their mother's housemate is a lesbian, even though mother denied a sexual relationship). Is harm to the child more likely because a parent is "out" or "in the closet"? See, e.g., Ex Parte J.M.F., 730 So. 2d 1190 (Ala. 1998) (holding that trial court acted within its discretion in modifying custody to husband based on change in wife's lesbian relationship from a discreet affair to a more open relationship).

Does the nexus approach as applied to sexual conduct in general differ from the test as applied to sexual orientation in particular? See Moss, supra, at 619-620 (suggesting that the nexus test in the latter context shifts the focus from the parent's conduct to identity and "makes gay and lesbian parents vulnerable to presumptive findings of harm, resulting from the prevalence of misconceptions about homosexuals and homosexual parenting").

For a discussion of social science research regarding the effects of parents' sexual orientation on children's well-being, see infra this chapter, pp. 805-806.

8. Role of sexual orientation in other custody decisionmaking. Gay and lesbian parents face the possibility of losing custody not only in initial awards but also in child custody modifications and juvenile court neglect determinations. See, e.g., In re E.C., 609 S.E. 2d 381 (Ga. Ct. App. 2004) (reversing a juvenile court finding of neglect that resulted in transfer of custody of children of lesbian mother); L.A.M. v. B.M., 906 So. 2d 942 (Ala. Civ. App. 2004) (holding that the evidence was sufficient to warrant a change of custody to father when mother was engaged in same-sex affair).

Further, gay and lesbian parents face restrictions on, or loss of, their visitation rights. Such restrictions frequently take the form of prohibitions on gay and lesbian parents from associating with a same-sex partner in the presence of the child. Compare McGriff v. McGriff, 99 P.3d 111(Idaho 2004) (affirming trial court order conditioning father's visitation on his not residing in the same house with his male partner), and Davis v. Davis, 2004 WL 2806433 (Ohio Ct. App. 2004) (affirming trial court order prohibiting lesbian mother from having her "female paramour" present during her parenting time), with Downey v. Muffley, 767 N.E.2d 1014 (Ind. Ct. App. 2002) (holding that there was no rational basis for an order prohibiting ex-wife from cohabiting with same-sex partner while living with her children). Do such conditions on custody violate a parent's constitutional rights? Are they unconstitutional after Lawrence v. Texas? Do they implicate the "child protection" and/or "private dispute resolution" strand(s) of custody law? For additional discussion of custody and visitation rights of gay and lesbian parents, see infra this chapter, p. 794, and for a discussion of the role of sexual orientation in adoption, see infra Chapter IX.

(2) Careers

■ **ROWE v. FRANKLIN**
663 N.E.2d 955 (Ohio Ct. App. 1995)

GORMAN, Judge:

Appellant, Kimberly Rowe ("mother"), appeals the trial court's decision designating appellee, Donald J. Franklin ("father"), the residential parent and legal guardian of their then five-year-old son.

[When the parents divorced after four years of marriage, each parent asked for sole custody of the couple's son. While the divorce was pending, the mother moved to Versailles, Kentucky, for her job as a part-time Army pilot. In Kentucky, she applied to law school. She had previously earned a degree in international affairs and business. The father, an ironworker, was unemployed. As part of the divorce proceedings, the trial court ordered that neither parent should remove the child from the state without a court order or parental agreement.]

On September 10, 1993, the mother filed a motion to modify the court's order to allow her to remove the child to Versailles, Kentucky, and to establish his residence there. She had applied to take classes through the University of Kentucky Law School in July and had become pregnant sometime in May by a man whom she had begun seeing in March, and who was married but separated from his wife. In August she enrolled her son in a private school for the times she would attend law school classes. In response to her motion, the father filed an emergency motion for contempt and for return of the child to Ohio. The trial court denied her motion, held the father's contempt motion in abeyance, and allowed the child to remain with the mother until the completion of a previously ordered custody investigation.

Dr. Cynthia Dember completed a psychological evaluation on May 1, 1992. Parenting specialist Jayne Zuberbuhler completed a pre-decree parenting report on February 18, 1993. . . . Dr. Dember and Ms. Zuberbuhler, while finding both parents adequate, ultimately recommended custody of the child be given to the father. [The trial court awarded custody to the father, and the mother appealed.]

In determining which parent should have custody of a minor child in a divorce proceeding, the trial court is bound to consider the best interests of the child. R.C. 3109.04(F). . . . Concern for a child's well-being or best interests does not, however, provide the court carte blanche to judge the rights and lifestyles of parents by nonstatutory codes of moral or social values. Although a court is not obligated to wear blinders as to a parent's lifestyle and/or morals, including sexual conduct, any state interest in competing lifestyles and accompanying moral values which affect child custody would most equitably be served if limited to a determination of the direct or probable effect of parental conduct on the physical, mental, emotional, and social development of the child, as opposed to a determination of which lifestyle choices made by a parent are "correct." In a society as diverse as the one in which we live, a court is ill-equipped to determine which of such choices are "correct." . . .

We first note that the trial court, using the factors enumerated in R.C. 3109.04(F)(1), concluded that both parents had taken a proper parental interest in the child, that the child was very much attached to both parents, that the child interacted appropriately with both parents, that both parents loved and nurtured the child, and that interference with either relationship could hurt the child. The trial court also determined that the child had bonded with his step-brother, had a good relationship with the mother's male companion, and was doing well in the Kentucky school. Even so, the trial court determined that the child should be removed from the mother and custody granted to the father.

The error in the analysis by which the trial court reached its conclusion, however, is apparent from its comparison of the mother's living situation with the father's. The trial court stated that for the first three years of the child's life,

> [u]ntil Dec. 1991, the child lived in the marital residence which is presently occupied by [father]. He is most familiar with the surroundings, the neighborhood, the people in the neighborhood, etc. [The child] has roots in his home in Cincinnati and but for his mother's move to Kentucky, it appears that his home would be one of stability. He has family here both maternal and paternal. He has friends here. He has friends of both parents who care for him here. The only adjustment necessary for [the child] here is that his mother would not be here.

By contrast, the trial court concluded that the mother and the child did not have substantial roots in the Kentucky community, stating it had not been provided with much information regarding that community. The record, however, belies this contention. Uncontested information was available that: the mother had been working in Kentucky for several years, that she had many friends there that she had met at work, that her son was friendly with and associated with her friends' children, that her son had adapted to the school he attended and had friends there, that the child had friends in the neighborhood with whom he played, and that he attended soccer and karate classes in Kentucky.

The trial court then "thoroughly examine[d]" the child's adjustment to his new home. . . . The record does not support the trial court's finding that the home, the mother's work or her school schedule has required "tremendous" adjustment by the child, nor does it indicate what will necessitate future adjustment. . . .

The trial court stated that it had no concerns about either parent's mental health. It found the father to be stable. . . . In contrast it found that the mother made decisions that caused the court to question her stability. Included in these "questionable" decisions were the many moves she made prior to her current situation, the move to Kentucky, and the sudden and complete relationship with her new male companion and the resulting pregnancy. The trial court deemed that these were not decisions in the best interest of the child and concluded that appellant placed her needs before the child's needs.

The trial court failed to recognize that the moves were precipitated by the father refusing, upon advice of counsel, to move from the marital residence, thus forcing the mother to leave the marital residence with the child, if she desired to terminate the marriage, and to live with the child in a variety of makeshift homes for a short transitional period. It entirely discounted how the father's decision subjected the child to changes in the environment. . . .

In examining the parties' commitment to the child, a nonstatutory factor, the trial court concluded that

> [p]ersonal accomplishments and career goals are obviously worthwhile undertakings. To accomplish what Ms. Rowe has as far as academics is concerned is very commendable. However this court perceives that this child has paid a price. The evidence has

shown that Ms. Rowe returned to a full-time law school curriculum when the child was three (3) weeks old. Ms. Rowe returned to her job with the Kentucky National Guard when the child was six (6) weeks old. Ms. Rowe's time to nurture the child has been limited tremendously as she pursues other matters. The Court is cognizant of the time [the child] has spent with babysitters and at child care. In summation, this Court questions the priorities of Ms. Rowe. The *number of poor choices made by Ms. Rowe as to the best interests of [the child] coupled with her personal agenda* indicates to this court that she may not be as committed to [the child's] best interests as she should be.

(Emphasis added.)

The transcript of the mother's law school classes contained in the record indicates that she did not start law school until the fall of 1990 when the child was over two years old. It was at that time that the child received day-care supervision. She had returned to school earlier to continue the coursework necessary to obtain her undergraduate degree the spring semester of 1988 and began taking graduate courses primarily in the evening the following fall. The child was attended to by the parents, family or friends during this period of time. The record shows that the mother did not return to flying until the child was approximately eight months old. . . .

Although pursuing his career and designated as the primary financial support for the family, the father was deemed by the trial court to be dedicated to the well-being of his child and to have a "willingness to be *a good and proper parent.*" (Emphasis added.)

The trial court also considered the mother's relationship with her male companion. [T]he trial court did not like that the mother became sexually involved with a man so soon after the breakup of both of their marriages. . . . There is a total absence of evidence in the record to suggest that the mother's relationship had any unfavorable effect on the child. . . . Although the trial court explicitly stated that the best interest of the child was its primary consideration, the plain meaning of its reasons in reality constitute use of a "reproval of the mother" test. Therefore, we conclude that the trial court abused its discretion by its reliance on an erroneous standard to justify the designation of the residential parent. . . .

Notes and Questions

1. *Career as a factor.* Today, many divorced mothers work outside the home.[12] Maternal employment sometimes plays a role in the application of the best interests standard. In the past, trial courts have denied custody to mothers who were medical students, architects, and nurses, among others. See Burchard v. Garay, 724 P.2d 486 (Cal. 1986); Lewis v. Lewis, 219 N.W.2d 910 (Neb. 1974); Fitzsimmons v. Fitzsimmons, 722 P.2d 671 (N.M. Ct. App. 1986). A number of cases, similar to

---

[12]. Divorced mothers have higher rates of employment than never-married or married mothers. Approximately 77 percent of divorced mothers worked in 1995. Moreover, divorced mothers are more likely to work full-time (83%) than never-married mothers (72%) and married mothers (68%). U.S. Dept. of Health & Human Services, Trends, 1997: Economic Security: Maternal Employment: Percentage of Mothers with Children Under Age 18 Who Are Employed, Full Time and Part Time, http://aspe.hhs.gov/HSP/97trends/Es3-2.htm (last visited Jan. 31, 2006).

Rowe, involve women lawyers. See, e.g., Prost v. Greene, 652 A.2d 621 (D.C. 1995); Young v. Hector, 740 So. 2d 1153 (Fla. Dist. Ct. App. 1998), *rev'd en banc* (1999).

2. *Gender-based role expectations.* What are the conflicting role expectations for working mothers versus working fathers? What gender stereotypes underlie custody determinations involving working mothers? Might the working mother be perceived as a "bad mother"? See Amy D. Ronner, Women Who Dance on the Professional Track: Custody and the Red Shoes, 23 Harv. Women's L.J. 173 (2000). Must working mothers be "supermoms" to prevail in custody disputes? See Lisa Genasci, Working Mothers at Risk in Custody Disputes; Divorce: Scholars Say Courts Often Hold Women to Higher Parenting Standards Than Their Ex-Spouses, L.A. Times, Mar. 5, 1995, at A8. Are mothers who work irregular schedules at a particular disadvantage in custody decisionmaking? See, e.g., Kerkhoff v. Kerkhoff, 400 N.W.2d 752 (Minn. Ct. App. 1987) (awarding custody to father because waitress-mother worked nights and was absent at times to play in traveling band).

3. *Empirical research.* Survey data from the 1980s and 1990s illustrate the nature of the gender stereotypes in judges' attitudes toward working women in custody disputes. One study reports that half of judges express such stereotypical beliefs as "[m]others should be home when their school-age children get home from school"; and, "[a] preschool child is likely to suffer if his/her mother works." Report of the Gender Bias Study of the Supreme Judicial Court, Commonwealth of Massachusetts 63 (1989). More recent research confirms that gender bias continues to pervade custody decisionmaking. A small percentage of female attorneys who were surveyed in a national study of gender bias asserted their belief that custody is "always or usually" denied due to a parent's employment outside the home. Douglas Dotterweich & Michael McKinney, National Attitudes Regarding Gender Bias Child Custody Cases, 38 Fam. & Conciliation Cts. Rev. 208, 214 (2000) (analyzing survey data from approximately 4500 attorneys and judges in four states). See also Joan S. Meier, Domestic Violence, Child Custody, and Child Protection, 11 Am. U.J. Gender Soc. Pol'y & L. 657, 687 (2003) (citing the findings of a recent Massachusetts gender bias study of custody cases).

4. *Day care.* What role should day care arrangements play in custody determinations? How did the trial court in *Rowe* assess this factor?

a. *Gender bias?* What gender stereotypes does a parent's reliance on day care evoke? A recent case held that the trial court abused its discretion by relying on the superiority of a mother's in-home care compared to the *father's* use of day care. In In re Loyd, 131 Cal. Rptr.2d 80 (Ct. App. 2003).

b. *New spouses.* May a court assume that *in-home care* by a stepparent (such as the father's new spouse) is preferable in the best-interests-of-the-child analysis to the caretaking arrangements of the child's working mother? In-home care by a *prospective* new spouse? In West v. West, 21 P.3d 838 (Alaska 2001), the Alaska supreme court held that an award of primary physical custody to the father was improper because it was based on the presumption that the husband's anticipated remarriage and resulting two-parent household was superior to the working mother's caretaking arrangements (i.e., relying on the 16-year-old half-sister as caretaker when the mother started work early). See also Wellman v. Dutch, 604 N.Y.S.2d 381 (App. Div. 1993) (holding that award of custody to father principally because his new spouse would be home to care for child had the impermissible effect of depriving unmarried working mother of her equal right to custody).

c. *Relatives.* Similarly, may a court assume that in-home care by relatives is preferable to the caretaking arrangements of the child's working mother? How should the court weigh the day care contributions of a parent's family members (parent's parents or other relatives) in the best-interests analysis? See, e.g., Ireland v. Smith, 542 N.W.2d 344 (Mich. Ct. App. 1995), *aff'd*, 547 N.W.2d 686 (Mich. 1996) (overturning a custody award to a father that was influenced by his caretaking arrangements, i.e., in-home care by his mother, compared to the caretaking choice of the child's mother, a university student, who relied on day care); Davis v. Davis, 702 N.E.2d 1227 (Ohio Ct. App. 1997) (ruling that award of custody to mother was proper based on the caretaking assistance of her co-resident parents); Spear v. Spear, 506 S.E.2d 820 (W. Va. 1998) (reversing custody award to father because family law master improperly credited father with caretaking tasks performed by his family members or employees).

d. *Statutory preference for parental care.* Some state statutes give a noncustodial parent the opportunity for additional parenting time (similar to a "right of first refusal") when the custodial parent is unavailable and must depend on other childcare providers. Which childcare providers trigger such statutory preferences? See Shelton v. Shelton, 835 N.E.2d 513 (Ind. Ct. App. 2005) (holding that trial court should have given father opportunity for additional parenting time when it became necessary for the child to be cared for by someone other than parent or "family member" because a father takes precedence over a maternal grandmother who is not a "family member" within the meaning of the parenting time statute).

e. *Effects of day care on children.* Controversy about the effects of day care on children dates to the 1970s when an increasing number of mothers entered the work force. Early studies warned of the likelihood of insecure attachment and cognitive deficits in day care children, especially those placed as infants. Subsequent large-scale research from the National Institute of Child Health and Human Development comparing a variety of day care facilities has not substantiated such concerns. See the National Institute of Child Health & Human Development (NICHD) Study of Early Child Care (1997), available at http://secc.rti.org (last visited Feb. 1, 2006); Gwen J. Broude, The Realities of Day Care, Public Interest, Sept. 1, 1996, at 95. See also Susan Faludi, Backlash: The Undeclared War Against American Women 41-45 (1991) (discussing the role of backlash against working women in myths that day care poses high risk of child abuse and developmental problems).

5. *Wealth as a factor.* What weight, if any, should be given to a parent's superior earning capacity? Generally, the relative wealth of the parties is not decisive unless one parent is unable to provide adequately for the child. Thus, for example, in *Wellman*, supra, the appellate court reversed the trial court award of custody to the father based on the relative quality of the father's home environment and his financial ability to support the child. See also *Burchard*, supra (holding that trial court's reliance on the parties' relative economic position was not a proper factor in custody decisionmaking). Although not a decisive factor, should wealth be a relevant factor? See generally Carolyn J. Frantz, Note, Eliminating Consideration of Parental Wealth in Post-Divorce Child Custody Disputes, 99 Mich. L. Rev. 216 (2000).

6. *ALI.* The ALI Principles prohibit the court from considering the parents' relative earning capacities or financial circumstances unless the parents' combined financial resources "set practical limits on the custodial arrangements." ALI Principles §2.12(1)(f). Further, the ALI Principles provide that placement

of the child in day care does not constitute sufficient changed circumstances to warrant custody modification. Id. at §2.15(3)(c).

7. *Time as a factor*. Should the amount of time a parent has available to spend with a child be a relevant factor? Consider the following excerpt.

■ D. KELLY WEISBERG, PROFESSIONAL WOMEN AND THE PROFESSIONALIZATION OF MOTHERHOOD: MARCIA CLARK'S DOUBLE BIND[13]
6 Hastings Women's L.J. 295, 312-319, 321-322 (1995)

In custody determinations, the governing standard is the best interests of the child. . . . Only occasionally is "time" enumerated as a statutory factor. More often, consideration of parental availability enters into the determination implicitly, either because of vague statutory language or because of the tremendous discretion vested by the best interests standard in decisionmakers' determinations of parental fitness.

[There are] several problems . . . in utilizing time as a determinative, or even, [a] relevant, factor. . . . The quantity of time that a parent has available to spend with a child [does not dictate] the quality of that interaction. [Nor, does it guarantee] that the available time [will] be spent with the child. For example, research on mother-child, compared to father-child, relationships reveals that husbands of working wives spend considerably less time than the working mothers in child-care activities. . . . Research has also suggested that, at the time of divorce, fathers often overestimate the time they say they want to spend with their children. . . . Research that documents visitation patterns over time supports this finding. . . .

. . . In addition, a focus on the quantity of time that a child spends with a parent may detract from more important considerations. For example, in Renee B. [v. Michael B., No. V5272186 (N.Y. Fam. Ct. May 8, 1992)], a court-appointed expert determined that the unemployed father would be a better custodian than the mother because of his greater availability. In awarding custody to the father, the appellate court gave little weight to the father's character, which had been described by the trial judge as: "cold, pedantic, and humorless, and above all, with a pervasive quality of controlled anger. [E]ven when directly discussing his daughter, there was little sense of the warmth and empathy for her that the mother displayed" [slip op. at 108]. [And, in Prost v. Greene, 652 A.2d 621 (D.C. App. 1995)], by focusing on [the mother's] availability, the trial court minimized allegations of domestic violence by Prost's husband (which had been serious enough to merit a civil protection order). . . .

[Moreover,] societal views have evolved concerning children's need for quantity time. Sociologist Arlie Hochschild writes that in the second half of the nineteenth century, when a woman's place was in the home, child care experts agreed that the child needed a mother's constant care at home. [However, as] women's roles have changed, so has our concept of children's needs: "Nowadays, a child is

---

[13]. The title refers to the custody dispute of Marcia Clark (the chief prosecutor in the murder trial of O. J. Simpson) in which her husband sought custody of their two sons for the reason that her demanding career rendered him a more fit custodian.

increasingly imagined to need time with other children, to need 'independence-training,' not to need 'quantity time' with a parent but only a small amount of 'quality time.'"

A second problem regarding consideration of time as a factor in custody decision-making is that a reliance on availability "freezes" the status quo. [That is,] it measures the *present time constraints* of one parent against the *present availability* of the other parent to determine fulfillment of the *present time needs* of a child. Yet, any, or all, of these factors may change significantly over time. . . . Consideration of a parent's current career demands assumes that these constraints are reflective of the career as a whole. [And,] in time, [the non-custodial parent] might be promoted into a more demanding position, accept a different job, [and/or] become involved in a new amorous relationship that would take up more of his time. [Further,] children's demands on a parent's time vary as a function of each developmental stage. For example, once children reach school age, they are absent from home for a large portion of the parent's work day. Moreover, school children's after-school lives may quickly fill with extracurricular activities and friendships, thus lessening their need and desire to be with a parent.

A third criticism of reliance on availability as a factor in custody decision-making rests on an unspoken assumption that availability is an objective and easily measurable criteria. [Yet, such assumptions may be] open to challenge. . . . One problem in emphasizing the more visible caretaking activities is that this tends to minimize all the "invisible" work that mothers might perform [e.g.,] arranging for baby-sitting or housekeeper services, scheduling doctors' appointments, scheduling play dates, determining a child's need for new clothes and haircuts, helping with school work, planning domestic chores and events, making grocery lists, paying bills, [and so forth].

. . . A final criticism of reliance on time as a relevant factor in custody decision-making is the subjectivity of the assessment by the parties themselves. Their measurement may be not unbiased, especially given the likelihood of intra-parental conflict and hostility upon divorce. [Sociologist Arlie Hochschild's findings in her book The Second Shift (1989)] suggest that unconscious motivations may also play a role in a parent's measurement of child care contributions. That is, Hochschild suggests that some families participate in "family myths," i.e., delusions that serve some unconscious function. One such myth is that the marriage is egalitarian and that the husband's workload (in terms of housework and child care) is equal to that of the wife. Specifically, Hochschild identifies relationships in which (despite an observable gender-based inequality in the division of labor), *both* the husband and wife refer to the division of labor as "equal" . . . "because equality was so important to [the wife]."

(3) Domestic Violence

■ **PETERS-RIEMERS v. RIEMERS**
644 N.W.2d 197 (N.D. 2002)

NEUMANN, Justice.
. . . Roland met Jenese, a non-U.S. citizen, in Belize in 1995 while vacationing there. . . . In early 1996, at Roland's invitation, Jenese left Belize and moved to

North Dakota. Roland provided her an apartment in Grand Forks and lived with her there. . . . Jenese became pregnant by Roland, and on June 24, 1997 their son, Johnathan, was born. [O]n March 6, 1999 Roland and Jenese were married. . . . After incurring several instances of physical abuse by Roland, Jenese filed a complaint on March 7, 2000 seeking dissolution of the marriage. [T]he court granted Jenese a decree of divorce from Roland on the grounds of adultery, extreme cruelty, and irreconcilable differences. Upon finding Roland had committed domestic violence, the court awarded physical custody of Johnathan to Jenese and provided Roland "closely supervised" visitation with Johnathan. . . . Roland, acting pro se, has appealed and has raised numerous issues on appeal [including that] the trial court failed to make specific findings in concluding that Roland had perpetrated domestic violence. We disagree.

The trial court made the following specific findings regarding Roland committing domestic violence against Jenese, all of which are supported by the evidence:

In the fall of 1996, Jenese became pregnant with the parties' son. A few months later, in February of 1997, Jenese learned of Roland's physical relationship with [another woman]. A physical argument erupted. During the course of such incident, Roland slapped and punched Jenese. He also kicked her in the stomach. Consequently, Jenese suffered vaginal bleeding and obtained medical treatment. . . .

In October of 1999, Jenese heard Johnathan crying outside. She walked out to discover that Johnathan had fallen down the stairs and had hurt himself. Roland was standing a few yards away from Johnathan, talking on his phone instead of tending to his son. Jenese made an angry comment to Roland about his priorities then went back inside. Roland than came into the kitchen and slapped Jenese in the face.

During the marriage, Roland kept pornographic magazines and videos in the marital residence, sometimes in places where Johnathan would encounter them. In January of 2000, Jenese destroyed one of Roland's pornographic videos. When Roland discovered his destroyed tape, he came up behind Jenese as she was making a bed and kicked her in the back.

On March 4, 2000, after a verbal argument, Jenese attempted to leave the marital residence with the parties' son, Johnathan. Roland refused to allow her to leave with Johnathan, but attempted to force her out of her home alone. He pinned her left arm behind her back as she held Johnathan tight in her other arm. Jenese escaped long enough to call 911, but Roland hung up the phone. He then punched her in the face, knocking her to the ground. He broke a finger in the process. Jenese was later diagnosed with a fractured bone in her face.

On March 6, 2000, Jenese obtained a Temporary Protection Order against Roland. On March 7, 2000, Roland was charged with felony assault as a result of striking Jenese. A No Contact Order issued as a condition of Roland's Pretrial Release. After a fully contested hearing, [a]n Adult Abuse Protection Order issued against Roland on March 14, 2000. At all of his appearances in the Protection Order proceeding, and at all times during this divorce, Roland maintained that his striking Jenese on March 4, 2000 was in self-defense. Nevertheless, on October 6, 2000, Roland pled guilty to the reduced charge of misdemeanor assault, admitting that a factual basis existed for that plea.

Roland's argument the court did not make specific findings about Roland's abuse of Jenese is without merit. Roland [also] asserts the trial court erred in finding Roland committed domestic violence but Jenese did not. The trial court made the following specific finding:

Roland committed at least one act of domestic violence which resulted in serious bodily injury to Jenese. During their relationship, there was a pattern of Roland inflicting domestic violence upon Jenese. On occasion, Jenese may have struck, hit or scratched Roland. However, her actions were largely in self-defense and were of a far less serious nature and degree than Roland's domestic violence.

Under N.D.C.C. §14-09-06.2(j) evidence of domestic violence is a specifically enumerated factor for the court to consider in awarding child custody:

j. *Evidence of domestic violence.* In awarding custody or granting rights of visitation, the court shall consider evidence of domestic violence. If the court finds credible evidence that domestic violence has occurred, and there exists one incident of domestic violence which resulted in serious bodily injury or involved the use of a dangerous weapon or there exists a pattern of domestic violence within a reasonable time proximate to the proceeding, this combination creates a rebuttable presumption that a parent who has perpetrated domestic violence may not be awarded sole or joint custody of a child. This presumption may be overcome only by clear and convincing evidence that the best interests of the child require that parent's participation as a custodial parent. The court shall cite specific findings of fact to show that the custody or visitation arrangement best protects the child and the parent or other family or household member who is the victim of domestic violence. If necessary to protect the welfare of the child, custody may be awarded to a suitable third person, provided that the person would not allow access to a violent parent except as ordered by the court. If the court awards custody to a third person, the court shall give priority to the child's nearest suitable adult relative. The fact that the abused parent suffers from the effects of the abuse may not be grounds for denying that parent custody. As used in this subdivision, "domestic violence" means domestic violence as defined in section 14-07.1-01. A court may consider, but is not bound by, a finding of domestic violence in another proceeding under chapter 14-07.1.

Under this statutory provision a single incident of domestic violence which results in serious bodily injury or a pattern of domestic violence creates a presumption that the perpetrator may not be awarded custody. With regard to the domestic violence factor, the trial court made clear and specific findings. The court found Roland had a pattern of inflicting domestic violence upon Jenese and that in at least one instance that violence resulted in serious bodily injury to her. The court found that although Jenese may have at times acted violently toward Roland, her actions were "largely in self-defense." Acts of domestic violence are mitigated when committed in self-defense. The trial court did not find Jenese's conduct toward Roland rose to a level of violence triggering the presumption against her receiving child custody. We conclude the trial court's findings are supported by the evidence and are not clearly erroneous.

Roland asserts the trial court's finding that Roland inflicted extreme cruelty on Jenese is clearly erroneous. Extreme cruelty is defined under N.D.C.C. §14-05-05 as "the infliction by one party to the marriage of grievous bodily injury or grievous mental suffering upon the other." The trial court awarded Jenese a divorce on the grounds of adultery, extreme cruelty, and irreconcilable differences. Considering the physical violence perpetrated against Jenese by Roland and his illicit extramarital affairs, there is substantial evidence to support the trial court's conclusion that extreme cruelty, consisting of both grievous bodily injury and grievous mental suffering, was inflicted by Roland upon Jenese during their marriage. The trial court's underlying findings of extramarital conduct and physical abuse are supported by the evidence and are not clearly erroneous. . . .

Notes and Questions

1. *State approaches.* Virtually all states now require courts to consider domestic violence in custody decisionmaking. Most states include domestic violence as a factor in the best-interests analysis. The emerging trend, however, is to provide that evidence of domestic violence creates a rebuttable presumption against awarding custody to the abusive parent (although states differ on whether the presumption applies only to awards of joint custody or precludes both sole and joint custody). See Annette M. Gonzalez & Linda M. Rio Reichmann, Representing Children in Civil Cases Involving Domestic Violence, 39 Fam. L. Q. 197, 198 (2005) (pointing out that 24 states provide for a rebuttable presumption).

What weight should attach to domestic violence in custody decisions? Do you agree with the suggestion that courts should prefer other alternatives (e.g., supervised visitation and mandated treatment) to rebuttable presumptions against custody awards to batterers? Amy B. Levin, Comment, Child Witnesses of Domestic Violence: How Should Judges Apply the Best Interests of the Child Standard in Custody and Visitation Cases Involving Domestic Violence, 47 UCLA L. Rev. 813, 855 (2000).

2. *Written findings.* A minority of states (like North Dakota in *Peters-Riemers*) require that judges make written findings regarding the existence of domestic violence. Some require findings showing how an award of custody to the perpetrator would serve the child's best interests. Gonzalez & Reichmann, supra, at 213. What is the function of such provisions? Should more states adopt this approach?

3. *Due process.* Do state statutes creating a rebuttable presumption against a custody award to an abusive parent violate that parent's due process rights? If so, how? If not, why not? See Opinion of the Justices to the Senate, 691 N.E.2d 911 (Mass. 1998).

4. *ALI.* The ALI Principles also address the role of domestic violence in custody. According to the Principles, parents and the court share the burden of discovery: Parents must disclose battering in the parenting plan submitted to the court; the court also must have a process to identify abuse. ALI Principles §§2.06, 2.11. Batterers may not receive custodial responsibility unless the court orders appropriate measures to ensure protection of the child and other parent (e.g., by mandated counseling). Id. at §§2.11(2)(I). In addition, the Principles broadly define abuse for purposes of custody determinations (i.e., any physical injury or creation of a reasonable fear thereof on the part of a parent, child, or any member of a household). Id. at §2.03(7). Finally, the Principles suggest that courts be aware that the abuser might try to use custody or visitation rights to harass the victim-spouse. Id. at §2.11(c) cmt. Are these reforms sufficient?

5. *Mutual acts of domestic violence.* How should courts deal with *mutual* acts of domestic violence? How does the court in *Peters-Riemers* address this issue? See generally Joan S. Meier, Domestic Violence, Child Custody, and Child Protection: Understanding Judicial Resistance and Imagining the Solutions, 11 Am. U.J.

Gender Soc. Pol'y & L. 657, 692-696 (2003) (criticizing judicial willingness to attribute mutual blame). See also Monterroso v. Moran, 37 Cal.Rptr.3d 694 (Ct. App. 2006) (holding that trial court acted in excess of its jurisdiction by entering mutual restraining orders without making statutorily-required findings of fact).

According to the ALI Principles, acts of self-defense do not constitute abuse. Rather, if one spouse's act is more extreme or dangerous, "it may be appropriate for the court to impose limits on the primary aggressor but not on the primary victim." ALI Principles §2.11(c) cmt. How does a court determine who is the primary aggressor or primary victim?

6. *Proof.* Statutes addressing the role of domestic violence in custody decision-making differ in regard to the amount of proof that triggers the presumption. Some statutes require one severe incident or a pattern of abuse, whereas other states require a criminal conviction. Kristina C. Evans, Note, Can a Leopard Change His Spots?: Child Custody and Batter's Intervention, 11 Duke J. Gender L. & Pol'y 121, 125-126 (2004). Which policy is preferable? Short of requiring criminal convictions, how might statutes facilitate proof of domestic violence? See, e.g., Ariz. Rev. Stat. Ann. §25-403(B) (West 2000); Cal. Fam. Code §3011 (West 2004) (suggesting police reports, medical records, child protective service records, domestic violence shelter records, school records, and testimony of witnesses).

Statutes also differ regarding the extent to which *past* acts of domestic violence are relevant. In addition, courts have considerable discretion in determining the relevance and the weight to be given to acts of domestic violence in the best-interest analysis. Gonzalez & Reichmann, supra, at 199.

7. *Gender bias?* Gender bias complicates legal responses to domestic violence in custody decision making. Various studies highlight accounts of lawyers and judges who minimize or disbelieve reports of domestic violence. See Jane H. Aiken & Jane C. Murphy, Evidence Issues in Domestic Violence Civil Cases, 34 Fam. L. Q. 43, 44-45 (2000); Martha Albertson Fineman, Domestic Violence, Custody, and Visitation, 36 Fam. L. Q. 211, 217-220 (2002). Given the increased public attention to the problem of domestic violence, what factors explain the continued judicial skepticism about women's credibility? See Meier, supra, at 690-692 (attributing the difficulty in believing battered mothers in part to "demeanor differences between perpetrator and victims"); Erin Street Mateer, Note, Compelling Jekyll to Ditch Hyde: How the Law Ought to Address Batterer Duplicity, 48 How. L.J. 525 (2004) (attributing the denial or sanctioning of domestic violence in part to batterers' duplicitous behavior in concealing and minimizing their violent acts).

8. *Treatment programs.* Some states require that persons convicted of crimes of domestic violence undergo treatment programs. Completion of such programs may be relevant to custody decisionmaking in the following ways: (a) they may be used to rebut the presumption that a batterer should not be given custody of the child; (b) visitation may be conditioned on completion of such a program; (c) treatment may serve as evidence in states without a rebuttable presumption that custody in the batterer serves the best interests of the child. Evans, supra, at 126. What are the advantages and disadvantages of considering completion of treatment programs in determining whether the presumption against custody for batterers has been overcome? How effective are such programs? Should the

focus of treatment programs be on "anger management"? See Lundy Bancroft & Jay G. Silverman, The Batterer as Parent: Addressing the Impact of Domestic Violence on Family Dynamics 14 (2002) (pointing out that many judges overestimate anger, rather than control, as the cause of battering behavior and therefore are likely to refer batterers to "anger management" treatment programs).

See generally Ileana Arias et al., Violence Against Women: The State of Batterer Prevention Programs, 30 J.L. Med. & Ethics 157, 162 (2002) (concluding, based on review of the literature, that "a significant factor for all women is that batterer treatment programs can result in repercussions and in a general worsening of situations for them"); Lisa D. May, The Backfiring of the Domestic Violence Firearms Ban, 14 Colum. J. Gender & L. 1, 3 (2005) (pointing out that recidivism rates for abusers are high, even after an abuser has participated in a batterer treatment program). How does a court determine whether a batterer has "successfully" completed the program? See Evans, supra, at 130.

9. *Lizzie's Law: custody to a batterer who kills.* Is it possible that a batterer who kills his spouse might be a fit parent? See In re H.L.T., 298 S.E.2d 33, 34 (Ga. Ct. App. 1982); In re Lutgen, 532 N.E.2d 976 (Ill. App. Ct. 1988), *appeal denied*, 537 N.E.2d 811 (Ill. 1989). Should legislatures adopt a presumption that a homicidal spouse abuser is not a fit parent absent clear and convincing evidence? In 1997, Massachusetts enacted Mass. Gen. Laws Ann. ch. 209C §3(a) (West 1999), which prohibits a parent convicted of murder of the other parent from visiting the child absent a court order and consent of the child or guardian. The law was nicknamed "Lizzie's Law" after a five-year-old child (Elizabeth Thompson), whose father was convicted of murdering her mother, demanded that the child visit him in prison. New York enacted a broader prohibition on visitation by a person convicted of murder in the first or second degree of a parent, guardian, or sibling. N.Y. Dom. Rel. Law §240 (McKinney 1996) (Lee-Ann Cruz Memorial Act). See generally Holly C. Wallace, Note, Visitation Rights of a Parent Convicted of the First-Degree Murder of the Other Parent: An Analysis of "Lizzie's Law," 37 Brandeis L.J. 233 (1998-1999); Lillian Wan, Note, Parents Killing Parents: Creating a Presumption of Unfitness, 63 Alb. L. Rev. 333 (1999).

Commentators have advocated, and some states have enacted, extensions of such laws to provide for denials of custody as well. See Danice M. Kowalczyk, Note, Lizzie's Law: Healing the Scars of Domestic Murder — an Emerging National Model, 64 Brook. L. Rev. 1241, 1279 (1998); Cal. Fam. Code §3030© (West 1994 & Supp. 2003) (creating a rebuttable presumption that a parent convicted of first degree murder of the other parent is unfit to have custody or unsupervised visitation with the minor "unless the court finds that there is no risk to the child's health, safety and welfare, and states the reasons for its finding in writing or on the record.")

10. *Friendly parent provisions.* Many state statutes have "friendly parent provisions" mandating that courts favor a custody award to the parent most likely to maintain the child's relationship with the other parent. Nancy Ver Steegh, Differentiating Types of Domestic Violence: Implications for Child Custody, 65 La. L. Rev. 1379, 1421 (2005) (noting that 28 states have such provisions). Such statutes were enacted during the 1980s when policy shifts encouraged post-divorce involvement of both parents in children's lives. Id. What problems might these statutes pose for victims of spousal abuse? Because of these problems, should the friendly parent provision be eliminated from child custody practice? See Margaret K. Dore,

The "Friendly Parent" Concept: A Flawed Factor for Child Custody, 6 Loy. J. Pub. Int. L. 41, 42 (2004). Or should there be an exception to such provisions in cases of domestic violence? See id. at 43 (pointing out that Alaska, Oregon, and Vermont have enacted such exceptions). Similar problems are raised by statutes providing for joint custody, see infra p. 768.

11. *Failure to protect*. Should women be deemed unfit parents for allowing themselves to be abused or for failing to protect their children from abuse? In Nicholson v. Scoppetta, 787 N.Y.S.2d 196 (N.Y.2004), several mothers and their children brought a class action pursuant to 28 U.S.C. §1983, challenging the constitutionality of New York City's policy of charging the mothers with neglect and routinely removing children from their mothers' custody on the ground that the mothers — who had not engaged in violence themselves — had failed to protect their children from witnessing domestic violence. A federal district court granted a preliminary injunction, holding that the policy violated the mothers' substantive and procedural due process rights. In re Nicholson, 181 F. Supp. 2d 182, 188 (E.D.N.Y. 2002). The appellate court then certified various questions to the New York Court of Appeals (New York's highest court) regarding the scope of the state statutes under which the city had acted. Nicholson v. Scoppetta, 344 F.3d 154 (2d Cir. 2003). The New York State Court of Appeals ruled that the child's exposure to domestic violence does not presumptively establish neglect and that removal requires additional particularized evidence.

Should state statutes preclude consideration of any effects of domestic violence on the victim in the determination of the child's best interests? See Evans, supra, at 126 n.45 (citing N.D. Cent. Code §14-09-06.2(1)(j) (2002) ('The fact that the abused parent suffers from the effects of the abuse may not be grounds for denying that parent custody.')). See generally Naomi R. Cahn, Battered Women, Child Maltreatment, Prison, and Poverty: Issues for Theory and Practice, 11 Am. U. J. Gender Soc. Pol'y & L. 355 (2003); Beth A. Mandel, Comment, The White Fist of the Child Welfare System: Racism, Patriarchy, and the Presumptive Removal of Children from Victims of Domestic Violence in Nicholson v. Williams, 73 U. Cin. L. Rev. 1131(2003).

12. *Empirical data*. How often do courts grant custody to batterers? Empirical data suggest that trial courts continue to do so with "disturbing" frequency, according to Professor Joan Meier. She notes that several research studies report a significant number of cases in which abusers obtain sole or joint custody even in states with rebuttable presumptions. Meier, supra, at 662. See also id. at n.19 (citing findings of her research revealing that of 38 cases in which mothers alleged abuse and sought to limit fathers' access to children, 36 courts awarded either sole or joint custody to the father).

13. *Bifurcating domestic violence and custody decisionmaking*. Some courts will not consider domestic violence as a factor in custody determinations unless the violence has been directed at the child. See, e.g., Baker v. Baker, 494 N.W.2d 282 (Minn. 1992). Conversely, other courts fail to address custody issues in domestic violence litigation. See, e.g., Sutherlin v. Sutherlin, 843 N.E. 2d 398 (Ill. Ct. App. 2006) (finding that the trial court erred in failing to consider the issue of temporary child custody at a hearing for an order of protection).

Does this bifurcation make sense? What is the relationship between spousal abuse and physical abuse of children? Are batterers more likely to physically abuse children? Considerable research reveals that batterers are several times more likely than nonbattering men to abuse children physically. One large-scale study (n=6000) reports that 49 percent of batterers physically abuse children compared to 7 percent of nonbattering men. Bancroft & Silverman, supra, at 42-43. Subsequent studies confirm these findings, sometimes reporting even higher rates of child victimization among batterers. Id. at 43 (reporting rates from 40 percent to 70 percent of batterers physically abusing children) Moreover, the risk of physical child abuse increases with the severity and frequency of the batterer's violence toward his partner. That is, the most violent batterers are particularly likely to have physically assaulted one or more children. Id. See also id. at 98-129 (especially chapter 5 "Impeding Recovery: The Batterer in Custody and Visitation Disputes").

If the child is not actually abused physically by the batterer, might a child's mere act of *witnessing* domestic violence prove harmful to the child? See generally id. at 37-42; Handbook of Children, Culture, and Violence (Nancy Dowd et al., eds., 2005) (especially the chapter "Child Witnessing of Domestic Violence"); David A. Wolfe et al., The Effects of Children's Exposure to Domestic Violence, 6 Clinical Child & Fam. Psych. Rev. 171, 184 (2003). In response to this concern, many state statutes specify that exposure to domestic violence is a form of child maltreatment. See Lois A. Weithorn, Protecting Children from Exposure to Domestic Violence: The Use and Abuse of Child Maltreatment Statutes, 53 Hastings. L.J. 1 (2001) (examining state statutes). Might the dangers presented by the batterer (to the spouse and the children) persist long after the divorce? See Bancroft & Silverman, supra, at 150-177 (exploring post-separation risks). For further discussion of exposure to domestic violence as a form of child abuse, see also Chapter VIII.

In thinking about the relevance of *past spousal abuse* in the determination of, the best interests of the child in custody decisionmaking, consider the following excerpt.

■ **JOAN S. MEIER, DOMESTIC VIOLENCE, CHILD CUSTODY, AND CHILD PROTECTION: UNDERSTANDING JUDICIAL RESISTANCE AND IMAGINING THE SOLUTIONS**
11 Am. U.J. Gender Soc. Pol'y & L. 657, 705-707 (2003)

[M]any batterers seek custody, not out of a genuine desire to take care of the children, but to retaliate against or further their control of their partner. The persona of many — though not all — batterers, is inconsistent with the qualities needed to make a good parent. People who need to control and abuse their intimate partners are unlikely to be capable of the loving, nurturing and self-disciplined behavior that good parenting requires. By definition, a father who abuses the mother has indicated that he cannot put the children's interests first, since their mother's abuse, by undermining her well-being, is inherently harmful to the children. Many batterers expect children to meet their needs, rather than vice versa; this can lead him to expect children to give up their other interests to spend time with him; to demand quiet to an inappropriate degree; to demand physical affection regardless of their feelings; and to become blaming, tearful, or yelling when they fail to meet his needs.

Batterers are often patriarchal, believing in strict gender roles and subordination of females, and can be controlling or authoritarian toward children of both sexes. Batterers "tend to be rigid, authoritarian parents." They tend to expect their will to be obeyed unquestioningly, or to be inflexible in their arrangements, extremely angry at any sign of non-compliance or disrespect, spank more often and be angry more often than other fathers. In short, they tend to use "power parenting." They are unlikely to possess the empathy that allows parents to treat their children with respect and to validate their feelings, two qualities considered important to raising emotionally healthy, conscientious, caring children.

Many, if not most, batterers both consciously and unconsciously undermine the children's mother and relationships with their mother. Many tell the children that it is their mother's fault that the parents are separated, that they cannot see their father more, that they cannot have certain things, or any other source of sadness in the child's life. Many of my clients' batterers would demean the mother to the children, telling them their mother is a "whore" or "slut," and in at least one case, demanding that the children come out of their rooms to watch him beat her up as punishment for some purported wrong.

Finally, batterers are often manipulative to children as well as partners, denying their own conduct and its effects, blaming the mother, and seeking to persuade the children that they are the "nicer" or "better" parent. Often batterers use the children to further their control over the mother, explicitly or implicitly enlisting the children in his vendetta. . . . In short, it is simply fallacious to assume that past domestic violence is in the past, that it is not directly relevant to future custody, or that it can ever really not impact the children.

Note: Physical Disability

The physical health of the parents is another relevant factor in the best interests determination. All states either permit or mandate consideration of a parent's physical and mental health. Megan Kirshbaum et al., Parents with Disabilities, 4 Center for Families, Child. & Cts. 27, 28 (2003). See also UMDA §402 (5), 9A U.L.A. 561 (1987) (mandating consideration). Formerly, many trial courts assumed that a parent with severe physical disabilities was per se unfit. This presumption manifested itself in different guises according to the disability: "deaf parents are thought to be incapable of effectively stimulating language skills, blind parents cannot provide adequate attention or discipline; and parents with spinal cord injuries cannot adequately supervise their children." Michael Ashley Stein, Mommy Has a Blue Wheelchair: Recognizing the Parental Rights of Individuals with Disabilities, 60 Brook. L. Rev. 1069, 1083 (1994). Courts became concerned especially when the children were not themselves disabled. See id. at 1098.

In the late 1970s, two cases changed the focus from a presumption of unfitness to an emphasis on the *effects* of the parent's disability on the child. In Warnick v. Couey, 359 So. 2d 801 (Ala. Civ. App. 1978), the Alabama Supreme Court refused to change the custodial arrangement of a father when he became partially paralyzed because the child did not appear to be adversely affected. The California Supreme Court echoed this finding in In re Marriage of Carney, 598 P.2d 36 (Cal. 1979), when it refused to change a custody award to a father after he became a quadriplegic as a result of a jeep accident while serving in the military reserves. The California Supreme Court reasoned that the "essence of parenting"

> lies in the ethical, emotional, and intellectual guidance the parent gives to the child throughout his formative years, and often beyond. The source of this guidance is the adult's own experience of life; its motive power is parental love and concern for the child's well-being; and its teachings deal with such fundamental matters as the child's feelings about himself, his relationships with others, his system of values, his standards of conduct, and his goals and priorities in life. Even if it were true, as the court herein asserted, that William cannot do "anything" for his sons except "talk to them and teach them, be a tutor," that would not only be "enough" — contrary to the court's conclusion — it would be the most valuable service a parent can render. Yet his capacity to do so is entirely unrelated to his physical prowess: however limited his bodily strength may be, a handicapped parent is a whole person to the child who needs his affection, sympathy, and wisdom to deal with the problems of growing up. Indeed, in such matters his handicap may well be an asset: few can pass through the crucible of a severe physical disability without learning enduring lessons in patience and tolerance.

598 P.2d at 44. Other courts have permitted parents to retain custody who are paraplegic, quadriplegic, stroke victims, epileptic, and deaf. See Katheryn Katz & Maris Warfman, Custody Disputes Between Parents, in 2 Child Custody and Visitation Law and Practice, §10.11[2][b] (Sandra Morgan Little et al. eds., 2003).

However, courts occasionally presume detriment by imposing restrictions on disabled parents. See, e.g., Clark v. Madden, 725 N.E.2d 100 (Ind. Ct. App. 2000) (reversing a condition that the visually-impaired father employ a housekeeper to assist him in the care of his three-year-old without a specific finding that the child would be endangered absent the restriction). But cf. Arneson v. Arneson, 670 N.W.2d 904 (S.D. 2003) (affirming the denial of physical custody of a three-year-old girl to a father with cerebral palsy who engaged an attendant to help with his daily routines). See also In re Marriage of Heath, 18 Cal. Rptr.3d 760 (Ct. App. 2004) (reversing a presumption of detriment to a younger child based on the older's child's disability).

Commentators criticize that the judiciary ignores the fact that a person's disability, in itself, provides little or no information about parenting abilities. See, e.g., Kirshbaum et al., supra, at 27. Disability rights advocates suggest that courts consider that disabled parents require more time and structural supports, urge elimination of bias in statutes and professional standards, and advocate sensitivity training for legal personnel and custody evaluators. Id. at 41-43; Stein, supra, at 1092-1095, 1098 n. 133.

Until recently, it was thought that the Americans with Disabilities Act of 1996 (ADA), 42 U.S.C. §§12101-12213 (2000) (prohibiting disability-based discrimination in employment, public services, public transportation, public accommodations, and telecommunications) did not apply to child custody. However, in Popovich v. Cuyahoga County Court of Common Pleas, 276 F.3d 808 (6th Cir. 2002), a federal court of appeals ruled that the Eleventh Amendment did not bar the claim under Title II of the ADA of a partially deaf parent who alleged that the family court failed to provide him with hearing assistance in his custody case. Title II protects those with disabilities from being "excluded from participation in [or] denied the benefits of the services, programs, or activities of a public entity." The court ruled that the Eleventh Amendment did not bar disability-based due process claims but only equal protection actions (reasoning that the father's action was based on the due process claim of his fundamental parental rights).

c. Joint-Custody: Presumption, Preference, or Option?

■ **BELL v. BELL**
794 P.2d 97 (Alaska 1990)

MATTHEWS, Chief Justice.

Greg and Debra Bell were married in January 1986. They separated sixteen months later in July 1987. Greg filed for divorce on September 14, 1987. A Partial Decree of Divorce was entered on March 4, 1988, leaving matters related to child custody, child support and property division to be determined by a trial which resulted in this appeal.

On appeal, Greg challenges . . . the trial court's award of legal and physical custody of Scott, the parties' child, to Debra. . . .

Gregory "Scott" Bell was born on August 19, 1986. While married, Greg and Debra shared most child rearing tasks on an equal basis. Since both parents were employed, Sharon Nollman babysat Scott part time beginning about December 1986, and then full time in approximately February 1987. She continued to babysit full time until February 1988, then every other week until the trial.

When Greg and Debra separated, they agreed to share custody of Scott, alternating physical custody every week or so. Both used Nollman to babysit. They accommodated each other's employment, social, and vacation schedules and shared babysitting expenses. A two-day interim custody hearing was held before Master Andrew Brown on October 15-16, 1987. Based upon the recommendations of an Alaska Court Custody Investigator, Master Brown issued a report recommending that Scott remain in the babysitting care of Nollman and that the parties continue their weekly alternating schedule of shared physical custody of Scott. The court approved the Master's report.

Greg and Debra cooperated in the weekly custody exchanges for another ten and one-half months until trial on August 26 and 29, 1988. However, in early 1988, Debra unilaterally began placing Scott at the Saakaaya Daycare Center during the weeks that she had physical custody. Greg continued to use Nollman during the weeks that he had physical custody of Scott.

In March 1988, the parties agreed to bifurcate the proceedings. A Partial Decree of Divorce was entered April 4, 1988. All other issues were reserved for a later adjudication or agreement of the parties.

Greg and Debra continued to accommodate each other's schedules and to share physical custody of Scott on an alternating basis. They also cooperated in making major decisions about Scott's medical care. For example, after Scott was hospitalized with asthma in September 1987, Greg and Debra conferred together with medical specialists and agreed to have tubes implanted in Scott's ears.

At trial, Ardis Cry, Custody Investigator, Alaska Court System, recommended that shared legal custody continue. She further recommended that Scott have a primary home and that Debra be the primary physical custodian.

The trial court awarded legal and physical custody of Scott to Debra. The court also allowed Greg visitation with Scott (1) on alternate weekends from Friday afternoon through Monday morning and on Wednesday evening through Thursday mornings and (2) during four one-week periods spread throughout the year until Scott reaches school age.

Greg contends that the trial court erred by not awarding joint custody to both parents pursuant to AS 25.20.060. AS 25.20.060 states, in part: "The court may award shared custody to both parents if shared custody is determined to be in the best interests of the child." ...

In the present case, the trial court denied joint custody and determined that "the physical and legal custody of [Scott] should be vested with [Debra] subject to [Greg's] rights of visitation. ..." In reviewing the propriety of the trial court's denial of joint custody, we find it necessary to distinguish between two interrelated aspects of a joint custody arrangement. First, an award of joint custody gives both parents "legal custody" of the child. This means that they "share responsibility in the making of major decisions affecting the child's welfare." 17 A.L.R.4th 1015 n.1. Second, an award of joint custody gives both parents "physical custody" of the child. This means that "each is entitled to the companionship of the child over periodic intervals of time." Id.

In an act amending AS 25.20.060, the legislature drew this distinction and expressed a policy favoring the award of joint legal custody, regardless of the physical custody arrangement: The legislature finds that ... it is in the public interest to encourage parents to share the rights and responsibilities of child rearing. While actual physical custody may not be practical or appropriate in all cases, it is the intent of the legislature that both parents have the opportunity to guide and nurture their child and to meet the needs of the child on an equal footing beyond the considerations of support or actual custody. An Act Relating to Child Custody, ch. 88 §1(a), SLA 1982.

In light of this expression of legislative intent, and because the controlling factual finding underlying the trial court's ruling is clearly erroneous, we reverse the award of sole legal custody to Debra.

The trial court's award was apparently based on its finding that Greg and Debra "are incapable of meaningful communication and/or negotiation regarding the matters that relate to the best interests of [Scott]."[1] If this finding is correct, joint custody would be inappropriate because "cooperation between the parents is essential if joint custody is to be in the child's best interest." *Lone Wolf*, 741 P.2d at 1189. Based on our review of the record, however, we hold that this finding is clearly erroneous.

The trial court record and Debra's arguments on appeal indicate only one area of irreconcilable conflict between Greg and Debra — throughout the proceedings below they could not agree on what form of day care would be best for Scott. Greg wanted Scott in Nollman's home, and Debra wanted Scott in Saakaaya Daycare Center.

---

1. The trial court did not isolate any of the other AS 25.20.090 or AS 25.24.150(c) factors as being factually subsidiary to its ruling, other than a finding that Debra is a "much more capable" parent. With respect to denying Greg legal custody, however, the dispositive significance of this finding is undercut by the trial court's finding that "both parties can be classified as fit," and the Greg is a "good parent[ ]." The record amply supports this latter finding. The record reflects, for example, that Greg studied child development and consulted with others about Scott's needs. The child custody investigation found that Greg loves Scott and would provide him with good care. Debra also testified that "Greg is a good parent."

Given the abundance of contrary evidence indicative of their ability to cooperate in Scott's best interest, however, we think that this one conflict does not warrant the trial court's finding of an "inability" to cooperate. Prior to the trial court ruling, Greg and Debra shared custody of Scott for 14 months, alternating physical custody every week or so. This arrangement was initially reached by mutual agreement. Throughout the 14 months, they accommodated each other's employment, social, and vacation schedules, and cooperated in making major decisions about Scott's medical care.

Furthermore, after interviewing Greg and Debra, the custody investigator recommended "joint legal custody" because she found that they had the "ability . . . to deal with each other in a civil and mutual manner" and thought that they demonstrated "potential to facilitate cooperation and compromise." Both Greg and Debra also testified to their ability to work cooperatively in Scott's best interest. Moreover, Debra generally agreed with the investigator's recommendations and was willing to settle the custody issue under the terms the investigator recommended. Thus, at trial, both parties agreed that joint legal custody was appropriate.

In light of such evidence, we are left with a firm conviction that the trial court's finding of an inability to cooperate was erroneous. We realize that the disagreement over daycare relates to a fundamental child care issue. But resolution of this issue did not require denial of that which the Alaska legislature recognizes as the favored course; i.e., joint legal custody. We therefore reverse the trial court's denial of joint legal custody and remand with instructions to enter an award of joint legal custody. Because we cannot ascertain the extent to which the trial court's erroneous finding influenced its decision regarding physical custody, that portion of its judgment is vacated. On remand, the trial court shall reconsider its physical custody/visitation determination, taking new evidence as may be appropriate. . . .

Notes and Questions

1. *Policy.* Joint custody is based on the belief that the child benefits from frequent contact with both parents. The doctrine recognizes that fathers, as well as mothers, have an important role to play in childrearing. A nascent fathers' rights movement spearheaded the passage of joint custody legislation in the late 1970s. See Herbert Jacob, The Silent Revolution: The Transformation of Divorce Law in the United States 136-143 (1988). The doctrine caught on quickly. Virtually all states now permit some form of joint custody.

2. *Definitions.* A custody award resolves the dual issues of "legal custody" and "physical custody." Legal custody confers responsibility for major decisionmaking (that is, the child's upbringing, health, welfare, and education). Physical custody determines the child's residence and confers responsibility for day-to-day decisions regarding physical care. (Compare the ALI Principles' terms of "decisionmaking responsibility" for legal custody and "custodial responsibility" for physical custody.)

In an award of joint legal custody, both parents share responsibility for major childrearing decisions. In such cases, both parents may share physical custody or only one parent may be the actual physical custodian. Thus, joint custody is distinguishable from the traditional award of sole custody, which gave one parent (normally the mother) both legal control and physical custody, while the other parent (normally the father) had visitation rights.

3. *Presumption, preference, or option.* California was the first state to provide for statutory recognition of awards of joint custody in 1980. See Cal. Fam. Code §3080 (West 2004) (formerly Cal. Civ. Code §4600.5(a)). Currently states follow three approaches to joint custody. Some states create a presumption of joint custody (although some of these states require parental agreement as a prerequisite). See Jane C. Murphy, Legal Images of Fatherhood; Welfare Reform, Child Support Enforcement, and Fatherless Children, 81 Notre Dame L. Rev. 325, 337 n.59 (2005) (listing 12 states and the District of Columbia with a presumption of joint custody). Other states, similar to Alaska in *Bell*, have a preference for joint custody. Third, and most common, some states make joint custody one option in the best-interests determination. See generally ALI Principles §2.08 cmt. a (discussing statutory and case law treatment of joint custody).

4. *Constitutional right?* Does a parent have a constitutional right to joint custody? See generally Holly R. Robinson, Joint Custody: Constitutional Imperatives, 54 U. Cin. L. Rev. 27 (1985). See also In re Marriage of Arnold, 679 N.W.2d 296 (Wis. App. 2004) (holding that parents' rights to the care and custody of their children did not mean that they had a fundamental right to equal placement periods after divorce). Does a *child* have a constitutional right to have a court award joint custody? See In re A.R.B., 433 S.E.2d 411 (Ga. Ct. App. 1993).

5. *Goldstein, Freud, and Solnit.* Joint custody signifies a radical departure from conventional psychological wisdom about childrearing. Professors Joseph Goldstein, Anna Freud, and Alfred Solnit propounded the view that stability and minimization of conflict should guide child placement. They said that healthy emotional development requires an "omnipotent" parent on whom the child can rely for all important decisions. To that end, they advocated that custody should be awarded only to one parent who should have power to decide the extent of the other's contact with the child (even prohibiting it). See Joseph Goldstein et al., Beyond the Best Interests of the Child 38 (1973). Do you find their views persuasive?

6. *Parental agreement.* Should parental agreement be a prerequisite to joint custody awards? Many states mandate such agreement. However, other courts award joint custody even if one parent objects. See, e.g., Crider v. Crider, 904 So. 2d 142 (Miss. 2005) (holding that a judge may award joint custody even if parents have not requested it, if in the child's best interests). Is joint custody to unwilling parents likely to succeed? Can the parties to an acrimonious divorce cooperate on childrearing decisions? See Eleanor E. Maccoby & Robert H. Mnookin, Dividing the Child: Social and Legal Dilemmas of Custody 240-242 (1992) (couples who express considerable hostility immediately upon separation continue to manifest significant animosity at a later point in time).

7. *Considerations.* When is an award of joint custody inappropriate? If the parents are geographically separated? How close or far? What constitutes proximity? Might this consideration place the departing partner at a disadvantage?

What kind of time sharing is optimal? Should courts require equal residential time? If courts require equal time, should it be six months with each parent, or nine months with one parent subject to summer vacations with the other, or switching homes every week? Alternating years? See Colvin v. Colvin, 914 So. 2d 662 (La. App. Ct. 2005) (holding that the child's best interests were not met by custody arrangement that provided for child to alternate between his parents in different states on a rotating annual basis). Or should courts order the child(ren) to remain in the family home with the parents alternating periods there (i.e., "the bird's nest" model)? See Michael T. Flannery, Is "Bird Nesting" in the Best Interest of Children?, 57 SMU L. Rev. 295 (2004).

What other considerations should influence awards of joint custody? Should courts consider the effect on the parent of a loss of custody? See Cloutier v. Blowers, 783 A.2d 961 (Vt. 2001) (reversing custody award to mother, finding that the trial court improperly relied on the mother's best interests, rather than the child's, by basing its decision on the fact that the mother had previously experienced the death of a child and would be devastated by losing custody).

8. *Parenting plans.* In a modern statutory development, many states now provide that parents seeking custody must file a parenting plan (i.e., a written agreement specifying the caretaking and decisionmaking authority for their children as well as the manner in which future disputes are to be resolved). Approximately half of the states now provide for such plans. A few states mandate them; some states mandate them only for joint custody; other states give courts discretion to require them. Katherine T. Bartlett, U.S. Custody Law and Trends in the Context of the ALI Principles of the Law of Family Dissolution, 10 Va. J. Soc. Pol'y & L. 5, 6-7 (2002). However, the level of statutorily-required specificity of such plans varies considerably. Id. at 7. What issues should be included in such agreements?

9. *Parental education.* Many states require that divorcing parents participate in parent education (also called "divorce education") programs. Such programs seek to improve post-divorce interactions among family members by educating parents about the negative effects of divorce on children and promoting alternative dispute resolution for post-divorce disputes. As of 2001, a majority of states had legislation or court rules that either mandated or established such programs. Solveig Erickson & Nancy Ver Steegh, Mandatory Divorce Education Classes: What Do the Parents Say?, 28 Wm. Mitchell L. Rev. 889, 895 (2001) (28 states).

Should such programs be "universally implemented and made mandatory"? Lucy S. McGough, Protecting Children in Divorce: Lessons from Caroline Norton, 57 Me. L. Rev. 13, 23 n.52 (2005). Are such programs effective in reducing post-divorce litigation? See id. at 23 n.52. How can such programs protect family members in divorces involving domestic violence? Victoria L. Lutz & Cara E. Grady, Necessary Measures and Logistics to Maximize the Safety of Victims of Domestic Violence Attending Parent Education Programs, 42 Fam. Ct. Rev. 363 (2004).

10. *Joint custody and kidnapping.* Can (should) a parent with joint custody be found guilty of kidnapping? See State v. Froland, 874 A.2d 568 (N.J. Super. Ct. 2005) (answering affirmatively under a kidnapping statute making it unlawful for a person to remove a child with intent to permanently deprive a parent of custody).

11. *Joint custody of pets.* Should pet custody cases be decided in the same way as child custody cases? That is, should divorcing "parents" be awarded joint custody? Or should pets go where the children go? See Gina Spadafori, Joint Custody Not Necessarily the Best Solution for Pets in a Divorce, Sac. Bee, Jan. 15, 2005, at E3; Tracey Tyler, Dogged Man's Lawsuit Thrown Out of Court; Sought Joint Custody of Pet, Toronto Star, Sept. 8, 2005, at B04.

12. *Criticisms of joint custody.* Currently, some states are retreating from joint custody by disavowing joint custody presumptions. James G. Dwyer, A Taxonomy of Children's Existing Rights in State Decision Making about Their Relationships,

11 Wm. & Mary Bill Rts. J. 845, 911 (2003) ("the retreat reflects a growing perception [that joint custody] often is not in the child's best interests, particularly when it is involuntarily imposed on parents and/or when there is a high degree of conflict between the parents"). In contrast, other states are renewing or reconsidering joint custody presumptions. See Lila Shapero, The Case Against a Joint Custody Presumption, 27 Vt. B.J. 37 (opposing Vermont's adoption of a joint custody presumption); Marriage — Presume Joint Custody, LegAlert, 2006 WLNR 1499951, Jan. 26, 2006 (Idaho is considering establishing rebuttable presumption that joint custody is in child's best interests). See also Leslie Eaton, Lawyer Who Fought Pledge Assails Courts on Custody, N.Y. Times, Oct. 23, 2004, at B2 (reporting Michael Newdow's advocacy for a presumption favoring joint custody).

Although originally touted with great enthusiasm, the practice of joint custody has become quite controversial. One commentator identifies several of these criticisms:

> The push by fathers' rights groups for joint custody has been very controversial and has been opposed by women's groups for two reasons: (1) some have seen it as an attempt to reduce the amount of child support by promising a commitment to share the care for the child which is either short-lived or disregarded completely and (2) others have been concerned about the existence of domestic violence.

Marygold S. Melli, The American Law Institute Principles of Family Dissolution, the Approximation Rule and Shared-Parenting, 25 N. Ill. U. L. Rev. 347, 352-353 (2005).

a. *Joint custody of young children.* Some critics question the wisdom of awarding joint custody of infants or toddlers. Most children who experience divorce are quite young. Dana E. Prescott, When Co-Parenting Falters: Parenting Coordinators, Parents-In-Conflict, and the Delegation of Judicial Authority, 20 Me. B.J. 240, 241 (2005) (citing research finding that "[m]ore than half of the children who experience divorce 'do so by age six, and 75 percent of those young children are younger than three years of age'"). How well does joint custody serve the interests of these children? See In re Marriage of Deem, 766 N.E.2d 661 (Ill. App. Ct. 2002) (holding that the trial court erred in awarding custody of a three year old to the mother during the school year and to the father during the summer because of the child's need for greater stability). Should regular overnights be delayed until young children reach the third year of life, as one researcher suggests? See Marsha Kline Pruett et al., Critical Aspects of Parenting Plans for Young Children, 42 Fam. Ct. Rev. 39, 41 (2004) (citing researcher's suggestion).

See generally Michael E. Lamb & Joan B. Kelly, Using the Empirical Literature to Guide the Development of Parenting Plans for Young Children: A Rejoinder to Solomon and Biringen, 39 Fam. Ct. Rev. 365 (2001); Judith Solomon & Zeynep Biringen, Another Look at the Developmental Research, 39 Fam. Ct. Rev. 355 (2001); Judith Solomon & Zeynep Biringen, Another Look at the Developmental Research: Commentary on Kelly and Lamb, 39 Fam. Ct. Rev. 4 (2001); Richard Warshak, Who Will Be There When I Cry in the Night? Revisiting Overnights — A Rejoinder to Biringen et al., 40 Fam. Ct. Rev. 408 (2002); Judith T. Younger, Post-Divorce Visitation for Infants and Young Children — The Myths and the Psychological Unknowns, 36 Fam. L.Q. 195 (2002).

b. *Domestic violence and joint custody.* Another criticism of joint custody concerns its use in cases of domestic violence. Is joint custody, which requires continuing parental communication, appropriate in such cases? Statutes take domestic violence into account in several ways before joint custody can be awarded: Some statutes consider abuse as a factor in joint custody decisions; some create a rebuttable presumption against joint custody when there has been abuse; and some prohibit joint custody if evidence of abuse exists. Naomi R. Cahn, Civil Images of Battered Women: The Impact of Domestic Violence on Child Custody Decisions, 44 Vand. L. Rev. 1041, 1064-1068 (1991). See generally Peter G. Jaffe et al., Child Custody and Domestic Violence: A Call for Safety and Accountability (2003).

A number of influential organizations (including the U.S. House of Representatives, the National Council of Juvenile and Family Court Judges, and the American Bar Association) have passed resolutions finding joint custody inappropriate in cases of domestic violence. Annette M. Gonzalez & Linda M. Rio Reichmann, Representing Children in Civil Cases Involving Domestic Violence, 39 Fam. L.Q. 197, 197 (2005). On the disadvantages of joint custody in the context of domestic violence, consider the excerpt by Judith Greenberg infra. The role of domestic violence in mediation is discussed infra this chapter.

13. *Empirical research.* Joint custody legislation has had a significant impact on custody decisions. Professors Eleanor Maccoby & Robert Mnookin report that in 79 percent of approximately 1000 families in two California counties (in the late 1980s), the divorce decree provided for joint legal custody. This outcome occurred even when one parent opposed joint custody. Maccoby & Mnookin, supra, at 107. This figure represents a significant increase from the 25 percent of judgments providing for joint custody in 1979. Id. at 108.

Does empirical evidence provide support for the policy argument (supra) that joint custody leads to more involvement of both parents in children's lives? Maccoby and Mnookin found that within one year of the court order, children in the vast majority of families tend to reside with their mothers. Id. at 73. That is, irrespective of the legal label attached to custody, most families adopt a maternal residence arrangement within a short period of time after the divorce. Thus, as one commentator concludes: "[R]eforms favoring joint physical custody failed to influence behavior because they were apparently inconsistent with the private preferences of parents regarding custodial arrangements. These laws expressed support for equal sharing of child care responsibility, but the predicted role change has not occurred." Elizabeth S. Scott, Social Norms and the Legal Regulation of Marriage, 86 Va. L. Rev. 1901, 1969 n.190 (2000). See also Shapero, supra, at 37 nn. 9 & 10 (exploring research findings regarding whether joint custody leads to co-parenting as proponents claim). See generally Solangel Maldonado, Beyond Economic Fatherhood: Encouraging Divorce Fathers to Parent, 153 U. Pa. L. Rev. 921 (2005) (exploring fathers' disengagement post-divorce).

How do parents manage the logistics of joint custody? The excerpt below sheds some light on this issue.

■ **ELEANOR E. MACCOBY & ROBERT H. MNOOKIN,**
DIVIDING THE CHILD: SOCIAL AND LEGAL
DILEMMAS OF CUSTODY
212-217, 224-225 (1992)

[C]hildren's age had some bearing on where they would live. The probability was high, and equally high in all age groups, that children would live with their mothers. However, the probabilities of father residence were higher for older children, and the probabilities of dual residence were higher for children between the ages of 3 and 8 than they were for the preteen and teenage children. Thus, in deciding on the initial residential arrangements, parents evidently took the developmental level of the children into account when other circumstances permitted. Some parents told us they did not find dual-residence arrangements workable for infants and toddlers, for whom they felt a single familiar place to sleep was especially important. Others said that teenagers had a greater voice than younger children in decisions about where they were to live and how much they would visit, and that children of this age tended to avoid arrangements in which they would have to sleep in two different houses. . . .

[C]ertain major trends can be seen: first, as might be expected, the parent with whom the child is living takes more responsibility than the non-resident parent for [childcare tasks], and this is true regardless of which parent is reporting. Second, there is a bias toward mothers doing more of the functions when one statistically controls for residence. Thus, mothers do more for children living with their fathers than fathers do for children living with their mothers. . . .

The carry-over of maternal responsibility into the dual-residence situation is pronounced regarding the children's medical regimen. [I]t is usually the parent who has been responsible before the separation — the mother — who continues to arrange for the child's medical regimen. [I]n a substantial number of families it appears that both parents attempt to be involved in managing the child's medical care. We have encountered instances where two parents had different pediatricians (who maintained separate medical records for the child) and where parents did not know whether a treatment (for example, a course of antibiotics for an ear infection) that was supposed to be continued actually was maintained after the child went to the other household. Evidently, this is a function for which coordination is especially important, but for which it does not always occur. . . .

When children were returned from a visit to the other household, parents often wanted to be informed about significant experiences the children might have had during the absence — illnesses, upsetting experiences, and so forth. Many parents commented that the ex-spouse provided little such information upon returning the children, and mothers in particular were concerned about the lack of information. . . .

Does joint legal custody enhance joint decision-making? When California policymakers embodied a preference for joint legal custody in the revised California divorce law, one purpose was to keep non-custodial parents from dropping out of their children's lives. The hope was not only that they would keep up their child support payments more reliably and see the children more often, but that they would involve themselves in decisions concerning the children's lives. [W]hen the children were living with their mothers, a joint legal custody award made essentially no difference in whether the children's contact with their fathers would be maintained. There is a similar result with respect to the involvement of non-residential fathers in decision-making: when factors (such as income) that affect whether a family will be awarded joint legal custody are controlled, non-residential fathers who have joint legal custody are no more likely to be involved in either day-to-day decisions or major decisions.

What are the advantages and disadvantages of joint custody for children, mothers, and fathers? Consider the following excerpt.

■ JUDITH G. GREENBERG, DOMESTIC VIOLENCE AND THE DANGER OF JOINT CUSTODY PRESUMPTIONS
25 N. Ill. U. L. Rev. 403, 407-413 (2005)

Proponents of a presumption in favor of joint custody give several reasons for favoring it. First, they argue that such a presumption would be in the best interests of children. Second, they see joint custody as a means of increasing equality between mothers and fathers and of undermining traditional gender roles. And finally, proponents of joint custody are skeptical of the ability of judges to discern which custodial arrangements will work best in particular situations. A preference for joint custody will minimize judicial intervention in the family, leaving it to the parties to make the shared custodial arrangement work. Although in some settings there may be some truth behind each of these claims, none is sufficiently weighty to support a presumption in favor of joint custody that might inadvertently work to require an abuser and his abused partner to remain in continual contact.

One of the most appealing arguments for joint custody, both legal and physical, is that it is in the best interests of the child. Child psychiatrists have long argued that children benefit from stability. In 1973, Goldstein, Freud and Solnit published their influential *Beyond the Best Interests of the Child* in which they asserted that a single custodial parent should be given as much authority over the child as possible. They thought this would produce stability for the child. More recently, however, commentators have argued that custodial arrangements that mimic the two parent family are the most desirable because they produce stability over time in providing continuing contact with both parents. There have been numerous studies of joint custody arrangements and their effects on children. One concludes bluntly that "children in joint custody are better adjusted, across multiple types of measures, than children in sole . . . custody."

Nevertheless, there is reason to wonder whether joint custody is really as good for children as this assessment implies. The studies' results are sometimes difficult to interpret. Some of the studies consider only joint legal custody, while others lump joint legal and joint physical custody results together. While this may be useful for many purposes, it is problematic for lawyers trying to determine whether a presumption that favors joint physical custody would be in children's best interests. Another problem is that many samples include families that have opted on their own for joint custody in one form or another. The effects of joint custody on children in such families may be radically different from the effects on children whose parents did not agree to the joint custody, but for whom joint custody was ordered by a court. One would expect that families that choose joint custody have parents who get along better than those who prefer sole custody and that this ability to get along pre-divorce would continue postdivorce, producing better outcomes for the children. . . .

Proponents of a presumption in favor of joint custody also argue that it will equalize the positions of men and women and help to undermine traditional gender roles. Sanford Braver argues that awarding sole custody to a mother with visitation to the father leaves men feeling disenfranchised in terms of their children's lives. . . . The argument is that fathers with joint custody, even if only joint legal custody, are able to participate in the lives of their children more equally with their ex-wives. This furthers sexual equality and would be beneficial to everyone. Once again, however, the data on whether joint custody achieves these goals is contradictory. Sanford Braver, in his study of interviews with divorced fathers and mothers, reports that joint legal custody results in higher rates of father-child visitation. This may indicate that fathers are taking on a nurturing role as well as the traditional role of economic bread-winner. However, other studies have had very different findings as to the effect of joint legal custody on role equalization. One large scale review of studies of the impact of fathers' visitation found that fathers' involvement affected the children in varying ways depending on the type of involvement, the mother's acceptance of the father's involvement and the degree of conflict between the parents. This hardly indicates that fathers who have joint custody automatically are perceived as taking on a nurturing role. Furthermore, there is evidence that even if the initial custody order provides for joint physical custody, over time the children are likely to end up living in their mothers' custody. [This] does make it unlikely, however, that awards of shared physical custody are likely to go far toward establishing new, more equal, gender roles. . . .

Various forms of shared or joint custody are bad ideas as custody defaults when the parents do not come to an agreement themselves. Most commentators recognize that where there has been domestic violence, joint custody is inappropriate. . . . Joint custody presumptions have their most powerful effect on cases that are decided by litigation. There, the presumption mandates that the court award joint custody. Unfortunately, cases that get to litigation (or even to judicial intervention short of litigation) are exactly those most likely to involve domestic violence. Recent research shows that approximately seventy five percent of the contested custody cases that require judicial intervention are cases in which there is a history of domestic violence. This means that in situations in which the court sends a case to mediation, orders an evaluation or holds a trial, it is significantly more likely than not that there has been domestic violence. Presumptions in favor of shared custody then do not make sense given that so many of the cases in which the parties cannot resolve the children's custody without judicial intervention are cases involving domestic violence.

Batterers often use any contact afforded them by the court as a means of continuing the abusive relationship with their former partners. Abusive relationships usually involve the batterer establishing control over his victim through a combination of physical, emotional, and financial methods. This is not likely to end with divorce. Indeed, for many targets the abuse becomes worse at separation. Batterers use any opportunity or contact to perpetuate the abuse in an effort to maintain their control. Some use the continuing connection that comes from joint custody or visitation rights to harass or verbally abuse their victims. Others use it as an opportunity to pressure the victim to return to the batterer. Still others continue their physical abuse during these times. . . .

2. Standards Governing the Noncustodial Parent: Visitation

a. Restrictions on Visitation

■ **HANKE v. HANKE**
   615 A.2d 1205 (Md. Ct. Spec. App. 1992)

BELL, Judge.

Appellant, Mary Elizabeth Hanke, brings this appeal, asking us to review an order granting her ex-husband, Dan Wolf Hanke, appellee, overnight visitation with the parties' four-year-old daughter. Ms. Hanke's concern for this child stems, in part, from an incident of sexual abuse by Mr. Hanke of one of Ms. Hanke's daughters (stepchild) from a previous marriage. . . .

On August 1, 1990, Mr. and Ms. Hanke were divorced by a judgment of the Circuit Court for Harford County. Ms. Hanke was granted custody of the parties' child and the issue of Mr. Hanke's visitation privileges was reserved for a later hearing. On March 15, 1991, hearings began to consider visitation. On March 18, 1991, the court ordered unsupervised four-hour visitations on alternate Sunday afternoons from noon until 4:00 P.M. On March 20, 1991, the court ordered Mr. Hanke to submit to a mental health examination by Lawrence Raifman, PhD, J.D. . . . The order of the Harford County judge, who transferred custody to Mr. Hanke, has not been enforced, pending the outcome of the investigation by the Kentucky DSS. [The mother had moved to Kentucky, where her family lived, because she was unable to find employment.]

Mr. Hanke has admitted sexually abusing his 11-year-old stepchild in 1986. This particular instance of sexual abuse was one event, but there is overwhelming evidence that other instances of excessive punishment with sexual overtones had occurred prior to this incident. . . . During a therapy session, Mr. Hanke stated that he was drunk when he sexually molested his stepchild. . . . Mr. Hanke feels that he does not "need any therapy for alcoholism." He did, however, secure therapy for the sexual abuse incident.

At the time of the separation, Ms. Hanke was pregnant with the parties' child who is the subject of this case. The parties separated as soon as Ms. Hanke learned from the 11-year-old child that she had been sexually molested by Mr. Hanke. Criminal charges of sexual molestation were brought against Mr. Hanke for the incident involving his stepchild. As part of the plea bargain entered into by Mr. Hanke for a suspended sentence in the criminal case, he agreed to, among other things, supervised visitation with the parties' child. . . .

The trial judge granted Mr. Hanke unsupervised four-hour weekly visitation periods with the child, beginning in March of 1991. After one of these visits, the parties' child reported to a teenage friend of her stepsister that Mr. Hanke "was touching her where he was not supposed to." Ms. Hanke examined the child and found scarring in the genital area. She immediately reported the matter to the Harford County Department of Social Services (DSS). Based on Ms. Hanke's complaint, DSS had the child examined at Mercy Hospital. The examination was conducted on May 23, 1991 by Dr. Reichel at the Mercy Hospital outpatient clinic. His report states ". . . Prior abuse cannot be excluded." Annetta Bloxham, the DSS caseworker investigating the complaint . . . also testified that she had verified the child's report of sexual molestation . . . by the parents of the teenager, to whom the child had reported the molestation, that the child did indeed report the molestation. This family refused, however, to permit the teenager to testify. . . .

Dr. Raifman, who evaluated Mr. Hanke pursuant to a court order, [concluded] that Mr. Hanke stated that he abused his stepchild to "get at her mother"; that the stepchild had been physically abused by Mr. Hanke for a long time before the incident of sexual abuse; that Mr. Hanke should not be placed in a situation where he is alone with his child; that Mr. Hanke should not continue to use alcohol because he was drunk at the time he sexually abused his stepchild; that Mr. Hanke had not come to terms with his abuse of alcohol as a factor in his abuse of his stepchild. [U]ntil these issues are resolved therapeutically, he is at risk and, therefore, his child is at risk.

Ms. Hanke's attorney, the attorney representing the Harford County DSS, and the attorney representing the child were unanimous in their call for supervised visitation. There was, however, also a small amount of contradictory evidence presented, which the judge seemed to favor, that Ms. Hanke was overreacting to the situation and Mr. Hanke was not a potential danger to their child. On March 18, 1991, the court ordered unsupervised visitation and on August 16, 1991, the court ordered visitation overnight, specifying one of four persons who were close to Mr. Hanke to "be present during visitation periods." The judge refused to protect the child further, and he found that overnight visitation was appropriate.

We have reviewed the findings and holdings in this case, bearing in mind that the ultimate test for custody and visitation is the best interests of the child. In most instances the decision of the trial judge is accorded great deference, unless it is arbitrary or clearly wrong. We hold that, given the circumstances presented in this case, the decision of the trial judge was clearly wrong.

It is obvious that the trial judge was annoyed because Ms. Hanke moved to Kentucky with the child and was unwilling to allow visitation. Even if the judge were correct that Ms. Hanke was not acting in compliance with the judge's orders, his primary responsibility was to protect this minor child, and not to punish Ms. Hanke by ordering overnight visitation. Then, when he could not enforce the overnight visitation order, the judge next removed the child from her custody with no provisions to protect the child. Where the evidence is such that a parent is justified in believing that the other parent is sexually abusing the child, it is inconceivable that that parent will surrender the child to the abusing parent without stringent safeguards. The fact that the judge does not agree with that parent's fear is immaterial. This is not a case in which there is no basis for the mother's belief. Past behavior is the best predictor of future behavior, and Ms. Hanke, while perhaps incorrect, is not unjustified in her belief that there may be some unresolved problems.

Assuming without deciding that the trial judge was correct in ruling that the child was at no or minimal risk in the overnight visitation, he abused his discretion in failing to provide a specific place for the supervised visitation designed to protect the child fully with supervisors satisfactory to all parties. He could do no less. . . .

Notes and Questions

1. *Traditional approach.* Traditionally, a custody award to one parent (typically the mother) was accompanied by an award of visitation rights to the other parent. Some modern custody awards continue to mirror this traditional arrangement. In such cases, the trial judge has considerable discretion to determine the scope of visitation, including placing conditions on visitation by the noncustodial parent. (Conditions on visitation may also occur when the parties have joint custody.) Procedurally, if a parent requests the court to order restrictions on visitation, that parent bears the burden of proof on the need for the restriction.

2. *Constitutional right to visitation?* Is visitation a constitutionally protected right? See Swipies v. Kofka, 419 F.3d 709, 714 (8th Cir. 2005) (holding that a non-custodial father with court-ordered visitation has a liberty interest "at least in some form" that was violated when a sheriff deputy removed his daughter during a court-ordered visitation without a hearing).

3. *Supervised visitation programs.* Many states now provide for supervised visitation programs that furnish services to parents in custody disputes involving various forms of abuse and neglect. Jessica Pearson & Nancy Thoennes, Supervised Visitation: The Families and Their Experiences, 38 Fam. & Conciliation Cts. Rev. 123, 124, 128-129 (2000) (identifying reasons for provision of services, including: substance abuse, sexual abuse, spouse abuse, and neglect). Services range from close supervision by a constant observer to more minimal supervision. Sometimes, supervision takes place only upon transfer of the child. Supervised visits might take place at, or away from, a program center. Nat Stern & Karen Oehme, The Troubling Admission of Supervised Visitation Records in Custody Proceedings, 75 Temp. L. Rev. 271, 272 (2002). What is the purpose of supervised visitation? To evaluate parenting behavior? To reassure the custodial parent? To protect the child's safety? All of these? See Janet R. Johnston & Robert B. Straus, Traumatized Children in Supervised Visitation: What Do They Need?, 37 Fam. & Conciliation Cts. Rev. 135, 135 (1999).

4. *Rebuttable presumption.* Some states create a rebuttable presumption against unsupervised visitation if a parent presents credible evidence of physical or sexual abuse. See, e.g., Tex. Fam. Code §153.004 (Vernon 2004) (providing for a rebuttable presumption "that it is not in the best interests of a child for a parent to have unsupervised visitation if credible evidence is presented of a history or pattern of past or present child neglect or physical or sexual abuse by that parent directed against the other parent, a spouse, or a child"). Should other states follow suit? See Scott A. Young, A Presumption for Supervised Visitation in Texas: Understanding and Strengthening Family Code Section 153.004(E), 37 Tex. Tech L. Rev. 327 (2005) (so arguing).

5. *Considerations.* Based on courts' wide discretion in fashioning visitation orders, courts may specify the time, place, and circumstances of visitation. See generally Roland Fancher, Visitation, in 3 Child Custody and Visitation Law and Practice §16 (Sandra Morgan Little, ed., 2000). Supervised visitation gives rise to a host of difficulties in framing the order. For example, how frequent should

visitation be? Should it include overnights? Who should supervise visitation? A social service worker? A mental health professional? An attorney? A community volunteer? A relative? If the supervisor is a relative, should it be a relative of the abuser? Should it matter if the relative denies that the abuse took place? See Peter Jaffe et al., Parenting Arrangements After Domestic Violence, 6 J. Center for Families, Child. & Cts. 81, 89 (2005) (suggesting that relatives are appropriate as supervisors particularly when the concern is assistance with childcare skills rather than safety).

If payment for the supervisor is required, who should pay? Should the supervisor be someone the child knows? Should the child's feelings about visitation be taken into account? See Carla Garrity & Mitchell A. Baris, Custody and Visitation: Is It Safe?, 17 Fam. Advoc. 40 (1995) (proposing models for supervised visitation, based on the child's age and other factors).

Are the records produced from supervised visitation programs too freely admitted into custody proceedings? See Stern & Oehme, supra, at 280 (pointing out that nearly 80 percent of visitation programs make reports to the court, and nearly 60 percent offer recommendations about parent contact to the court).

6. *Unsupervised visitation.* When should supervised visitation give way to unsupervised visitation? Suppose the parent contends that supervised visitation is interfering with the establishment of a good relationship with the child? See Grant v. Grant, 1995 WL 136775 (Ohio Ct. App. 1995). After a suspension of visitation, should visitation be phased in gradually?

7. *Treatment conditions.* What type of restrictions on visitation are enforceable in cases of physical or sexual abuse? Can a court order an abuser to undergo a psychological examination or treatment program (e.g., for substance abuse, physical abuse, or sexual abuse) as a condition of visitation? See, e.g., Maybin v. Stewart, 885 A.2d 284 (D.C. 2005) (holding that trial court did not abuse its discretion when it ruled that father could exercise supervised visitation rights if he submitted to sexual deviancy examination); Litoff v. Pinter, 670 N.W.2d 860 (N.D. 2005) (evidence supported suspension of father's visitation until he submitted to psychiatric evaluation and assessment for a sexual offender treatment program). Can a court impose a visitation condition requiring a noncustodial parent's attendance at anger management classes — even when that relief is not specifically requested by the opposing party? See Moncher v. Maine, 892 So.2d 1147 (Fla. Ct. App. 2005). Can a court require that visitation be denied until a therapist recommends otherwise? See Carmichael v. Siegel, 754 N.E.2d 619 (Ind. Ct. App. 2001); In re Mark M., 782 A.2d 332 (Md. 2001) (both finding that court order was improper delegation of judicial authority).

Should supervised or unsupervised visitation commence only after a parent *seeks* treatment? See, e.g., Mary D. v. Watt, 438 S.E.2d 521 (W. Va. 1992). Only after a parent *completes* treatment? Who should determine the parent's "successful" completion of the treatment? See Jaffe et al., supra at 89 ("The difficulty arises when it is not clear who bears the responsibility for assessing the perpetrator's progress or compliance with conditions."). Can a court order a parent to comply with a treatment program's requirement of admission of guilt as a condition of visitation? See Wirsching v. Colorado, 360 F.3d 1191, 1205 (10th Cir. 2004) (prison officials did not violate convicted sex offender's rights of familial association and due process by refusing to allow his visitation with his child due to his noncompliance with treat-ment program, nor did requirements violate his right to self-incrimination).

8. *Termination of parental rights.* Some courts may even terminate visitation in cases of severe physical or sexual abuse. Because allegations of abuse introduce criminal elements into a civil proceeding, what standard of proof should be required in termination of parental rights cases to protect the alleged abuser's constitutional rights? See In re A.C., 643 So. 2d 743 (La. 1994); Mullen v. Phelps, 647 A.2d 714 (Vt. 1994) (both requiring clear and convincing evidence). On termination of parental rights generally, see Chapter VIII.

9. *Empirical research.* Research reveals that the majority of children who received supervised visitation are victims of *multiple and severe* trauma (i.e., phys-ical/sexual abuse and neglect, parental substance abuse, and parents' mental illness). Johnston & Straus, supra, at 135. Most visiting parents are fathers (80 percent). Services generally last for 6-7 months. Pearson & Thoennes, supra, at 139-140. Most parents rate the programs more favorably than they rate their interactions with the legal system, although many parents wish that the programs played a more active role, for example, in making assessments about the move to less restrictive visitation. Only about 20 percent of the families leave the program pursuant to court order; another 20 percent exit because the par-ents agree to informal supervision by a friend or relative; other parents simply stop coming (about half of the cases). Id. at 140. Pearson and Thoennes recom-mend that courts "play a more aggressive oversight role" by referring families elsewhere for necessary services and doing more evaluations and more monitor-ing. Id. at 141.

10. *Other conditions.* Other parental conduct may also lead to conditions on visitation, to wit:

a. *Religious exercise.* Disputes concerning the children's religion commonly arise. Because visitation often occurs on weekends, attendance at church or Sunday school may become problematic. Can a parent be required to present children at a particular religious institution during visitation? Conversely, can a court prohibit a parent from exposing the children to one parent's religion during visitation? Do such conditions violate either parent's constitutional rights? See Brown v. Szakal, 514 A.2d 81 (N.J. Super. Ct. Ch. Div. 1986); Zummo v. Zummo, 574 A.2d 1130 (Pa. Super. Ct. 1990). See generally Kent Greenawalt, Child Custody, Religious Practices, and Conscience, 76 U. Colo. L. Rev. 965 (2005); Joanne Ross Wilder, Religion and Best Interests in Custody Cases, 18 J. Am. Acad. Matrim. Law. 211 (2002). See also the discussion of religion in custody decisionmaking, supra this chapter.

b. *Sexual conduct.* Courts may restrict a parent's visitation rights based on the parent's sexual conduct. For example, gay and lesbian parents sometimes experi-ence such restrictions on their visitation rights in the form of conditions disallowing visitation in the presence of that parent's partner or, specifically, overnight visita-tion in the presence of the parent's partner. See, e.g., McGriff v. McGriff, 99 P.3d 111 (Idaho 2004) (holding that trial court did not abuse its discretion by prohibit-ing father from exercising his visitation rights at the home if he were residing in the same house as his partner); Downey v. Muffley, 767 N.E.2d 1014 (Ind. Ct. App. 2002) (reversing trial court order prohibiting mother from cohabiting with her same-sex partner while living with her children). For a case note, see Susan M. Moss, McGriff v McGriff: Consideration of a Parent's Sexual Orientation in

Child Custody Disputes, 41 Idaho L. Rev. 593 (2005). See also Shelley L. Bilbrey, Dancing Nancy: The Harmful and Illogical Dance Among Alabama Courts Over Supervised Visitation Between Gay Parents and Their Children, 26 Law & Psychol. Rev. 177 (2002); Robin Cheryl Miller, Annot., Restrictions on Parent's Child Visitation Rights Based on Parent's Sexual Conduct, 99 A.L.R.5th 475 (1993 & Supp. 2005). See also the discussion of the role of sexual orientation in custody decision-making, infra this chapter, p. 794.

Similar restrictions occur in the context of heterosexual relationships. See, e.g., Camp v. McNair, 2005 WL 3065759 (Ark. Ct. App. 2005) (reversing trial court determination of mother's unfitness and prohibition on overnight visitation because of her cohabitation with a married man).

c. *Substance abuse.* Courts also issue conditions on parents who are substance abusers. A common condition prohibits the parent from using alcohol or drugs during visitation periods. See Cohen v. Cohen, 875 A.2d 814 (Md. App. Ct. 2005) (holding that requirement that husband abstain from alcohol was reasonably related to child's best interest); White v. Nason, 874 A.2d 891 (Me. 2005) (holding that clear and convincing evidence supported the finding that the father was in contempt of a prohibition from possessing or consuming alcohol or other illegal substances while the children were in his care).

d. *Firearms possession.* Occasionally, a court may order a divorcing parent to store firearms safely during visitation periods for a child's protection. In addition to such civil restrictions, some states also have child access prevention (CAP) laws that impose criminal penalties for the negligent storage of a firearm if a child uses the weapon to kill or injure himself or another person. See Andrew J. McClurg, Child Access Prevention Laws: A Common Sense Approach to Gun Control, 18 St. Louis. Pub. L. Rev. 47 (1999). See also Matt Pordum, Lawyer, Court Action Could Have Prevented Boy's Fatal Shooting, Evidence Showed Father Left Guns Throughout Home, Las Vegas Sun., Aug. 29, 2005, at A1 (account of 12-year-old boy who died after father violated custody order to lock up guns).

e. *Criminal convictions.* Parents may be subject to conditions on visitation if they have been convicted of certain crimes (e.g., child abuse, sexual molestation, homicide of the other parent, rape if the child was conceived as a result of the criminal act), or if they are required to register as sex offenders. See generally Dana Lowy & Mary Redfield, Criminal Histories and Parental Custody and Visitation Rights, 26 LA Law. 25 (2003). For a discussion of restrictions applicable to a parent who kills the other parent (Lizzie's Laws), see discussion of domestic violence, supra this chapter, p. 762.

f. *AIDS.* The AIDS epidemic prompted attempts (generally unsuccessful) by custodial parents to restrict children's visitation with HIV-positive parents. See generally Pierce J. Reed & Laura Davis Smith, HIV, Judicial Logic and Medical Science: Toward a Presumption of Noninfection in Child Custody and Visitation Cases, 31 N. Eng. L. Rev. 471 (1997).

g. *Smoking.* Should a parent's smoking lead to conditions on that parent's visitation? See generally Merril Sobie, Second Hand Smoke and Child Custody Determinations — A Relevant Factor or a Smoke Screen?, 18 Pace L. Rev. 41 (1997). Do conditions on smoking violate a parent's right to privacy? See generally Michele L. Tyler, Note, Blowing Smoke: Do Smokers Have a Right? Limiting the Privacy Rights of Cigarette Smokers, 86 Geo. L.J. 783 (1998).

11. *Child's refusal to visit.* Can a court condition a noncustodial parent's visits with a child on the *child's* desire whether or not to see that parent? See In re Marriage of Kimbrell, 119 P.3d 684 (Kan. Ct. App. 2005) (holding such a condition improper because it may deny parenting time in violation of the statutory presumption that a noncustodial parent is entitled to reasonable parenting time in the absence of evidence of endangerment). Cf. In re S.H., 3 Cal. Rptr. 3d 465 (Ct. App. 2003) (similar holding in the context of a dependency hearing). See Judith G. McMullen, "You Can't Make Me!": How Expectations of Parental Control Over Adolescents Influence the Law, 35 Loy. U. Chi. L.J. 603, 606-622 (2004) (reviewing case law). Courts frequently respond to the *child's* refusal to visit by holding the custodial parent in contempt. Is this sound policy?

In one famous case, a trial court held two girls in contempt for refusing to visit their father. The older daughter attributed her refusal to fear of her father (who told her that her mother and grandmother were evil, made her go hunting and kill a bird, gave her a black eye when she tried to prevent him from spanking her sister, and threatened that he would not let her return to her mother). The trial court found the testimony of a psychologist (who recommended against visitation) as "nonsensible" and "less than credible." After finding the children in contempt, the trial judge imposed sanctions to secure the children's compliance with the visitation order. He grounded the younger daughter, prohibiting her from watching television or entertaining friends. In addition, he placed the older daughter in a juvenile detention facility until she complied. The appellate court affirmed the finding that the children were in contempt, but reversed the sanctions because the trial judge did not consider less restrictive alternatives. The appellate court remanded for a new hearing regarding those alternatives. In re Marriage of Marshall, 663 N.E.2d 1113 (Ill. App. Ct. 1996). See generally Janet R. Johnston, Children of Divorce Who Reject a Parent and Refuse Visitation: Recent Research and Social Policy Implications for the Alienated Child, 38 Fam. L.Q. 757 (2005).

12. *Penalty.* What should be the penalty if a parent violates the condition on visitation? Temporary suspension of visitation? Denial of visitation? Contempt? Modification of custody?

Problems

1. When Julie and Randy divorce, the court declares Julie to be the sole custodial parent of their two preschool daughters. The trial court rules that Randy's overnight visitation required the supervision of his parents because of Randy's "penchant for pornography." The court ordered the restriction because Julie presented evidence that Randy liked to view Internet sites exhibiting sexual material and had placed a personal advertisement on an Internet site in an effort to attract females and couples as sexual partners. Randy countered that he looked at the Internet material only late at night after the children were asleep and that he placed the advertisement out of curiosity. Randy contends that the trial court's restriction on his visitation was an abuse of discretion. What result? See Petty v. Petty, 2005 WL 1183149 (Tenn. Ct. App. 2005).

2. Roxie and Jeffrey separate after two years of marriage. Roxie and the couple's baby move in with Roxie's parents. Because Jeffrey performed limited childcare during the marriage and also because of Jeffrey's "unstable lifestyle"

(details unspecified), Roxie requests that Jeffrey's contact be limited to supervised visitation at Roxie's home. Jeffrey does not contest the need for supervised visitation. When Jeffrey moves out-of-state to New Jersey, he requests a different visitation schedule and proposes as "supervisor" his 21-year-old brother and a friend who lives nearby. At the subsequent divorce proceeding, Roxie is awarded custody. The court awards visitation to Jeffrey on "alternative holidays and during the summer vacation provided he gives twenty-four hours notice of his intent to visit [and] that one of the individuals [whom he has suggested] be present during said visitation." Roxie appeals the visitation order, claiming that it is vague and gives no consideration to the qualifications of the visitation supervisors. What result? Would your reasoning change based on the reason for the supervision? Substance abuse? Sexual abuse? Homosexuality? Immaturity? If the court does elaborate further, how should it structure the visitation order (based on each of these possibilities)? See Weber v. Weber, 457 S.E.2d 488 (W. Va. 1995).

b. Denial of Visitation

■ TURNER v. TURNER
919 S.W.2d 340 (Tenn. Ct. App. 1995)

Koch, J.

This appeal involves an acrimonious post-divorce dispute over child support and visitation. . . . This appeal involves the denial of the father's latest petition for modification and the summary suspension of his visitation for not paying child support. . . .

Rebecca Diane Turner (now Turpin) and Charles Daniel Turner were married in September 1984. They had two children before separating in May 1987. After an unsuccessful attempt at reconciliation, Ms. Turner filed for divorce in June 1989. On August 15, 1990, the trial court entered a final order granting Ms. Turner the divorce and awarding her custody of the parties' children. The trial court also granted Mr. Turner visitation rights and ordered him to pay $704.13 per month in child support and to pay for the children's medical insurance. The trial court later denied Mr. Turner's post-trial motion to alter or amend the child support award but granted him additional visitation.

In early November 1990, Ms. Turner sought to have Mr. Turner held in contempt for being $2,166.52 in arrears in his child support. Mr. Turner responded with a petition admitting that he was delinquent in his child support payments and requesting a reduction in his child support because he was financially unable to comply with the August 1990 order. Thereafter, Mr. Turner paid all the child support due through November 30, 1990, and agreed to pay an additional $475 for the children's medical expenses. Following a hearing in January 1991, the trial court entered an order on February 1, 1991, finding Mr. Turner in contempt for failing to pay child support and to obtain medical insurance for his children. The trial court decided not to act on Mr. Turner's petition to modify his child support because "he comes to the Court with unclean hands." In addition, the trial court directed Mr. Turner to begin paying an additional $177 per month to reimburse Ms. Turner for obtaining medical insurance for the children through her group insurance plan at work.

Ms. Turner filed a second petition in May 1991 seeking to hold Mr. Turner in contempt for inappropriate conduct while he was returning her son from visitation. In December 1993, she filed her third contempt petition complaining that Mr. Turner had harassed and abused her and the children and that he was seriously delinquent in his child support obligations. Following an ex parte hearing, the trial court ordered Mr. Turner's arrest and suspended his visitation rights. Mr. Turner responded, as he had in the past, that he was financially unable to meet his child support obligations and again requested the trial court to reduce his child support.

Following a January 1994 hearing, the trial court filed an order on February 14, 1994, finding Mr. Turner in criminal contempt for violating the orders prohibiting him from harassing and abusing Ms. Turner and the children and also finding him in civil contempt for failing to make his child support payments. The trial court sentenced Mr. Turner to ten days for the criminal contempt to be served consecutively with a six-month sentence for civil contempt but determined that Mr. Turner could purge himself of the civil contempt by paying $40,908.86. The trial court also ordered that Mr. Turner's visitation would be summarily suspended if he did not make prompt and timely support payments.

The trial court summarily suspended Mr. Turner's visitation before he was released from jail because he failed to pay his child support. Mr. Turner filed another petition in July 1994 requesting modification of his child support and reinstatement of his visitation. On December 20, 1994, the trial court filed an order denying Mr. Turner's petition. . . .

Mr. Turner . . . takes issue with the trial court's refusal to permit him to visit his children because he is delinquent in paying his child support. While we are not prepared to say that this sanction is never appropriate, we find that the present facts do not warrant suspending Mr. Turner's visitation rights.

Child custody and visitation decisions should be guided by the best interests of the child. They are not intended to be punitive. Pizzillo v. Pizzillo, 884 S.W.2d 749, 757 (Tenn. Ct. App. 1994); Barnhill v. Barnhill, 826 S.W.2d 443, 453 (Tenn. Ct. App. 1991). As a general rule, the most preferable custody arrangement is one which promotes the children's relationships with both the custodial and noncustodial parent.

Ms. Turner argues in her brief that the children are adversely affected by Mr. Turner's failure to support them, and thus their best interests will be served by cutting off their visitation with their father unless he begins supporting them. This assertion would have some merit if the record contained proof to substantiate it. We find no such proof. The record, however, contains some support for concluding that the children are not going without basic necessities because Ms. Turner is presently able to provide for their needs.

The courts may deny or condition continuing visitation on the grounds of parental neglect. See Mimms v. Mimms, 780 S.W.2d 739, 745 (Tenn. Ct. App. 1989) (parental neglect may be considered in relation to the children's best interests). The denial of visitation is warranted, however, only when the noncustodial parent is financially able to support his or her children but refuses to do so. Since the trial court has not conclusively determined that Mr. Turner is at present willfully refusing to support his children even though he is financially able to do so, we have determined that the order curtailing Mr. Turner's visitation rights should likewise be vacated and that this issue should likewise be addressed and definitively decided on remand. Pending the remand hearing, the trial court should enter an interim order permitting Mr. Turner visitation on whatever terms the trial court determines are just and appropriate. . . .

Notes and Questions

1. *Factors*. Because the Constitution protects the parent-child relationship, courts deny visitation reluctantly. What does *Turner* reveal about whether the failure to pay child support justifies a denial of visitation? What other situations justify a ban on visitation? Physical or sexual abuse? See, e.g., Grossman v. Grossman, 772 N.Y.S.2d 559 (App. Div. 2004); Litoff v. Pinter, 670 N.W.2d 860 (N.D. 2003). A parent's incarceration? Compare Laurence v. Nelson, 785 A.2d 519 (R.I. 2001) with Michael M. v. Department of Econ. Sec., 42 P.3d 1163 (Ariz. Ct. App. 2002). See also Rachel D. Costa, Comment, Now I Lay Me Down to Sleep: A Look at Overnight Visitation Rights Available to Incarcerated Mothers, 29 New Eng. J. Crim. & Civ. Confinement 67 (2003); Benjamin Guthrie Stewart, Comment, When Should a Court Order Visitation Between a Child and an Incarcerated Parent?, 9 U. Chi. L. Sch. Roundtable 165 (2002). The risk of child abduction? See, e.g., Damiani v. Damiani, 835 So. 2d 1168 (Fla. Dist. Ct. App. 2002); Moore v. Moore, 2005 WL 1924346 (Ohio Ct. App. 2005). Substance abuse? See, e.g., In re Marriage of DeSantis, 817 P.2d 769 (Or. Ct. App. 1991).

2. *Purpose*. What purpose does denial of visitation serve? Protection? Coercion? Punishment? What does *Turner* respond? Is it ever in the child's best interests to deny all contact with a parent?

3. *Rule and exception*. As *Turner* illustrates, visitation normally will not be conditioned upon payment of child support. Nor may support be withheld because an ex-spouse interferes with visitation. Some courts, however, similar to *Turner*, make an exception for willful and intentional failure to pay child support, which is detrimental to the child. What explains the reluctance to link the two issues?

4. *Defenses*. Should certain actions on the part of the custodial parent that deprive the noncustodial parent of visitation, such as concealment of the child, provide a defense to the noncustodial parent for failure to pay child support during the period of the child's absence (i.e., child support arrearages)? Should it matter if the concealment occurs pre- or post-divorce decree? If the child was a minor or an adult at the time that the claim for payment of support arrearages was brought? See Ira Mark Ellman, Should Visitation Denial Affect the Obligation to Pay Support?, 36 Ariz. St. L.J. 661, 666-683 (2004) (discussion of "arrearage defenses").

5. *Policy*. What are the advantages and disadvantages of disconnecting the issues of support and visitation? Of connecting them? Professor Karen Czapanskiy argues that both approaches limit the custodial parent's need for personal autonomy. She adds that the latter approach invites retaliatory withholding of support payments and limitations on the opportunity to spend time with a child. Karen Czapanskiy, Child Support and Visitation: Rethinking the Connections, 20 Rutgers L.J. 619, 619-620 (1989). She also criticizes the application of both rules because they reflect gender-based parental roles. Id. at 644-658.

Should the usual rule of independence of support and visitation be "applied in a narrower range of cases than it currently is"? See Ellman, supra, at 665 (so arguing). For example, should "divorce decrees make suspension of the support obligation the default result during [ ] concealment periods, subject to the obligee's demonstrating to the court a justification for the concealment"? Id. at 699. If so, what justification would be sufficient? For other commentary on the dependence of visitation and support, compare William V. Fabricius & Sanford L. Braver, Non-Child Support Expenditures on Children by Nonresidential Divorced Fathers, 41 Fam. Ct. Rev. 321 (2003) (advocating reduction of support obligations for non-custodial parents because they incur "appreciable" visitation expenses), with Irwin Garfinkel et al., Visitation and Child Support Guidelines, 42 Fam. Ct. Rev. 342 (2004) (criticizing the methodology and findings of the Fabricius-Braver study).

6. *Remedies.* If interference with visitation is not a defense to nonpayment of support, should the former be grounds for modification of custody? Compare Vernon v. Vernon, 800 N.E.2d 1085 (N.Y. 2003) (modifying custody), with Balius v. Gaines, 914 So. 2d 300 (Miss. Ct. App. 2005) (contra). See also Ellman, supra, at 685-686 (discussing benefits and detriments of imposing a penalty of modification in custodial arrangements).

What other remedies should address a denial of, or interference with, visitation? Some states now provide for "makeup parenting time" for visitation that was allegedly wrongfully denied (i.e., enabling a parent to take parenting time, of the same type and duration, at a later date). See, e.g., Mich. Comp. Laws §552.642 (West 2004). See also In re Kosek, 871 A.2d 1 (N.H. 2005) (finding that increasing husband's visitation time was appropriate sanction for contempt). Other states permit abatement of a noncustodial parent's past or future child support obligation until the custodial parent complies with the visitation order. See Walters v. Walters, 181 S.W.3d 135 (Mo. Ct. App. 2005). Some states order the custodial parent who interferes with visitation to pay the attorneys' fees of the noncustodial parent in any action to enforce visitation. See Kolbet v. Kolbet, 760 N.E.2d 1146 (Ind. Ct. App. 2002). See also Fla. Stat. Ann. §63.13(4)(c) (West 1997 & Supp. 2004) (specifying the following remedies for a custodial parent's refusal to honor a noncustodial parent's visitation rights without proper cause: a requirement that the custodial parent pay the noncustodial parent's court costs and attorneys' fees, a requirement that the custodial parent attend a parenting class, a requirement that the custodial parent do community service, a requirement that the custodial parent pay the costs of a child's visitation, an award of custody to the noncustodial parent if in the child's best interest, any other "reasonable sanction"). On tort remedies for custodial interference, see "Jurisdiction and Enforcement" infra.

7. *Coercion.* Can or should a parent be compelled to exercise visitation rights? See Daniel Pollack & Susan Mason, Mandatory Visitation: In the Best Interest of the Child, 42 Fam. Ct. Rev. 74 (2004). If the noncustodial parent fails to pick up the child at the scheduled time, what remedies should be available to the custodial parent? Suppose the custodial parent had scheduled a business trip or an examination for a time when the child would be visiting the other parent, who fails to come for the child as planned? Can a court order a noncustodial parent who fails to exercise scheduled visitation to pay additional child support? See Lindsay v. Lindsay, 2006 WL 197111 (Tenn. Ct. App. 2006) (holding that the trial court erred when it set a specific dollar penalty if father missed any of his co-parenting time, reasoning that such a penalty is inconsistent with the child support guidelines).

Does empirical research support the rule that the right to visit and duty to support should not be dependent on each other? Consider the excerpt below.

■ **JESSICA PEARSON & NANCY THOENNES,**
THE DENIAL OF VISITATION RIGHTS:
A PRELIMINARY LOOK AT ITS INCIDENCE,
CORRELATES, ANTECEDENTS AND
CONSEQUENCES
10 Law & Pol'y 363, 375-379 (1988)

This paper explores the nature and incidence of the denial of visitation rights and the non-payment of child support. [V]isitation denial is a problem with approximately 22 percent of sample mothers reputedly failing to comply with the visitation terms of their divorce decree. This is consistent with reports of [other studies], however, it should be noted that these levels fall far below the reported levels of non-compliance with child support. Only about half of all custodial parents owed child support receive the full amount of support owed to them in any given year. Even fewer custodians receive all the payments on time.

Estimated levels of visitation denial also fall below levels of non-contact by absent parents noted in previous research. For example, in their longitudinal study of 1,747 households, Furstenburg and North (1983:10) discovered that in cases involving children living in one-parent families where the non-custodian is believed to be alive, "over a third of the children . . . lost contact altogether with the biological parent living outside the home." Hetherington, et al. (1978) report that two years following the divorce, 30 percent of the children saw their fathers about once a month or less. . . .

Clearly, it is inaccurate to assume that all of these are cases in which custodians encourage sporadic visitation or deny the non-custodian regular access to the children. Indeed in her study, Luepnitz notes that:

> In half of the cases when the non-custodial father visits rarely or never, it is because the children dislike him and have decided not to see him. But in many other cases, custodial mothers report that their ex had split the scene "in order to evade child support payments."

(Luepnitz, 1982:34).

Further investigation of visitation non-compliance reveals that it rarely stands alone as a post-divorce problem and that such allegations are accompanied by a host of other visitation-related complaints. Moreover, for most parents visitation difficulties appear to become established fairly early on and fail to deviate over time.

Couples with visitation problems are decidedly more embittered than their compliant counterparts and their lack of cooperation, conflict and anger are apparent at the earliest interview, well before the promulgation of a divorce decree and are corroborated by independent interviewer ratings. Although non-payment of child support cases do not always involve a visitation problem, the two phenomena are related and cases with visitation problems are substantially more likely to involve child support non-payment or disputes over support. Both phenomena appear to stem from conflict patterns between the parents, although we were unable to assess causal order in cases that involved both types of non-compliance. . . .

These findings inspire several policy recommendations. Minimally, there is a need for reliable record keeping of both child support and visitation arrears.

Without reliable record keeping, violations are difficult to prove, make-up policies are impossible to establish or supervise. To date, several states require child support payments to be made through the Clerk of the Court rather than directly to the custodial parent. . . . Objective accounts of visitation denial, however, are harder to come by. One model approach is found in a Michigan law which requires the child support enforcement agency, the Friend of the Court, to keep track of alleged visitation denials (with the custodial parent having an opportunity to contest the allegation) and to supervise make-up visitation orders (Mich. Comp. Laws F25.164 (42)(4)-(5)).

Secondly these findings underscore the importance of interventions with divorcing couples aimed at enhancing their communication skills and reducing levels of anger and hostility. [A] preliminary assessment of relationships between the non-custodial parent and his children reveals that conflict between divorced parents is a good prediction of both child support payment, visitation and other types of involvement (Braver et al., 1985). [I]t appears that neglect of therapeutic elements of the process may vastly diminish its potential effectiveness in reducing post-divorce conflict over visitation and support.

A third conclusion of this research is the need to consider child support and visitation issues concurrently. While there is no evidence to suggest that the two issues should be made contingent upon one another so that the denial of one should be a remedy for the withholding of the other, policy should reflect the fact that they co-occur and that grievances in both areas should be jointly aired. This conclusion runs counter to current practice. To date most court based mediation services deal with the issues of contested child custody and/or visitation only. Child support and the other financial issues of divorce are considered to be beyond the purview of the mediation intervention. In the few settings where child support issues are mediated in court settings, they tend to be handled by a separate staff. . . .

A fourth implication of our research is the need to create and evaluate mechanisms for the enforcement of both child support and visitation orders. As previously noted, Michigan law enables the Friend of the Court in each county to formulate a make-up visitation policy, including compensatory visitation. Other states have explored the use of fines, tort remedies, etc. (See Horowitz and Dodson 1985). Improved visitation enforcement is warranted by the observed incidence of interference, the co-occurrence of visitation and child support problems and equity considerations.

---

3. Standards Governing Parent versus Non-Parent Disputes

■ **TROXEL v. GRANVILLE**
530 U.S. 57 (2000)

Justice O'CONNOR announced the judgment of the Court and delivered an opinion, in which The Chief Justice, Justice GINSBURG, and Justice BREYER join. . . .

Tommie Granville and Brad Troxel shared a relationship that ended in June 1991. The two never married, but they had two daughters, Isabelle and Natalie. Jenifer and Gary Troxel are Brad's parents, and thus the paternal grandparents of Isabelle and Natalie. After Tommie and Brad separated in 1991, Brad lived with his parents and regularly brought his daughters to his parents' home for weekend visitation. Brad committed suicide in May 1993. Although the Troxels at first continued to see Isabelle and Natalie on a regular basis after their son's death, Tommie Granville informed the Troxels in October 1993 that she wished to limit their visitation with her daughters to one short visit per month.

[Two months later, the Troxels filed this petition for visitation.] At trial, the Troxels requested two weekends of overnight visitation per month and two weeks of visitation each summer. Granville did not oppose visitation altogether, but instead asked the court to order one day of visitation per month with no overnight stay. [T]he Superior Court [ordered] visitation one weekend per month, one week during the summer, and four hours on both of the petitioning grandparents' birthdays.

[The Court of Appeals reversed the visitation order based on their statutory interpretation that nonparents lack standing unless a custody action is pending. The state supreme court held that the state statute granting visitation rights to "any parent" at "any time" (Wash. Rev. Code §26.10.160 (3) (1994)) infringed on parents' fundamental right to rear their children. While the appeal was pending, the mother remarried, and her husband adopted the children.]

The demographic changes of the past century make it difficult to speak of an average American family. The composition of families varies greatly from household to household. While many children may have two married parents and grandparents who visit regularly, many other children are raised in single-parent households. In 1996, children living with only one parent accounted for 28 percent of all children under age 18 in the United States. Understandably, in these single-parent households, persons outside the nuclear family are called upon with increasing frequency to assist in the everyday tasks of child rearing. In many cases, grandparents play an important role. For example, in 1998, approximately 4 million children — or 5.6 percent of all children under age 18 — lived in the household of their grandparents.

The nationwide enactment of nonparental visitation statutes is assuredly due, in some part, to the States' recognition of these changing realities of the American family. Because grandparents and other relatives undertake duties of a parental nature in many households, States have sought to ensure the welfare of the children therein by protecting the relationships those children form with such third parties. The States' nonparental visitation statutes are further supported by a recognition, which varies from State to State, that children should have the opportunity to benefit from relationships with statutorily specified persons — for example, their grandparents. The extension of statutory rights in this area to persons other than a child's parents, however, comes with an obvious cost. For example, the State's recognition of an independent third-party interest in a child can place a substantial burden on the traditional parent-child relationship. . . .

The liberty interest at issue in this case — the interest of parents in the care, custody, and control of their children — is perhaps the oldest of the fundamental liberty interests recognized by this Court [citing Meyer v. Nebraska, Pierce v. Soc'y of Sisters, and Prince v. Massachusetts]. In light of this extensive precedent, it cannot now be doubted that the Due Process Clause of the Fourteenth Amendment protects the fundamental right of parents to make decisions concerning the care, custody, and control of their children.

Section 26.10.160(3), as applied to Granville and her family in this case, unconstitutionally infringes on that fundamental parental right. The Washington nonparental visitation statute is breathtakingly broad. According to the statute's text, "*[a]ny person* may petition the court for visitation rights *at any time*," and the court may grant such visitation rights whenever "visitation may serve *the best interest of the child*." §§26.10.160(3) (emphases added). That language effectively permits any third party seeking visitation to subject any decision by a parent concerning visitation of the parent's children to state-court review. Once the visitation petition has been filed in court and the matter is placed before a judge, a parent's decision that visitation would not be in the child's best interest is accorded no deference. Section 26.10.160(3) contains no requirement that a court accord the parent's decision any presumption of validity or any weight whatsoever. Instead, the Washington statute places the best-interest determination solely in the hands of the judge. Should the judge disagree with the parent's estimation of the child's best interests, the judge's view necessarily prevails. Thus, in practical effect, in the State of Washington a court can disregard and overturn any decision by a fit custodial parent concerning visitation whenever a third party affected by the decision files a visitation petition, based solely on the judge's determination of the child's best interests. . . .

Turning to the facts of this case, the record reveals that the Superior Court's order was based on precisely the type of mere disagreement we have just described and nothing more. The Superior Court's order was not founded on any special factors that might justify the State's interference with Granville's fundamental right to make decisions concerning the rearing of her two daughters. [T]he combination of several factors here compels our conclusion that §26.10.160(3), as applied, exceeded the bounds of the Due Process Clause.

First, the Troxels did not allege, and no court has found, that Granville was an unfit parent. That aspect of the case is important, for there is a presumption that fit parents act in the best interests of their children. [S]o long as a parent adequately cares for his or her children (i.e., is fit), there will normally be no reason for the State to inject itself into the private realm of the family to further question the ability of that parent to make the best decisions concerning the rearing of that parent's children.

The problem here is not that the Washington Superior Court intervened, but that when it did so, it gave no special weight at all to Granville's determination of her daughters' best interests. More importantly, it appears that the Superior Court [adopted "a commonsensical approach [that] it is normally in the best interest of the children to spend quality time with the grandparent" and placed] on Granville, the fit custodial parent, the burden of *disproving* that visitation would be in the best interest of her daughters. . . .

The decisional framework employed by the Superior Court directly contravened the traditional presumption that a fit parent will act in the best interest of his or her child. In that respect, the court's presumption failed to provide any protection for Granville's fundamental constitutional right to make decisions concerning the rearing of her own daughters. In an ideal world, parents might always seek to cultivate the bonds between grandparents and their grandchildren. Needless to say, however, our world is far from perfect, and in it the decision whether such an intergenerational relationship would be beneficial in any specific case is for the parent to make in the first instance. And, if a fit parent's decision of the kind at issue here becomes subject to judicial review, the court must accord at least some special weight to the parent's own determination.

Finally, we note that there is no allegation that Granville ever sought to cut off visitation entirely. Rather, the present dispute originated when Granville informed the Troxels that she would prefer to restrict their visitation with Isabelle and Natalie to one short visit per month and special holidays. . . . The Superior Court gave no weight to Granville's having assented to visitation even before the filing of any visitation petition or subsequent court intervention. . . . Significantly, many other States expressly provide by statute that courts may not award visitation unless a parent has denied (or unreasonably denied) visitation to the concerned third party.

Considered together with the Superior Court's reasons for awarding visitation to the Troxels, the combination of these factors demonstrates that the visitation order in this case was an unconstitutional infringement on Granville's fundamental right to make decisions concerning the care, custody, and control of her two daughters. The Washington Superior Court failed to accord the determination of Granville, a fit custodial parent, any material weight. In fact, the Superior Court made only two formal findings in support of its visitation order. First, the Troxels "are part of a large, central, loving family, all located in this area, and the [Troxels] can provide opportunities for the children in the areas of cousins and music." Second, "[t]he children would be benefitted from spending quality time with the [Troxels], provided that that time is balanced with time with the childrens' [sic] nuclear family." These slender findings, in combination with the court's announced presumption in favor of grandparent visitation and its failure to accord significant weight to Granville's already having offered meaningful visitation to the Troxels, show that this case involves nothing more than a simple disagreement between the Washington Superior Court and Granville concerning her children's best interests. The Superior Court's announced reason for ordering one week of visitation in the summer demonstrates our conclusion well: "I look back on some personal experiences. . . . We always spen[t] as kids a week with one set of grandparents and another set of grandparents, [and] it happened to work out in our family that [it] turned out to be an enjoyable experience. Maybe that can, in this family, if that is how it works out." [T]he Due Process Clause does not permit a State to infringe on the fundamental right of parents to make childrearing decisions simply because a state judge believes a "better" decision could be made. [W]e hold that §26.10.160(3), as applied in this case, is unconstitutional. . . .

Because we rest our decision on the sweeping breadth of §26.10.160(3) and the application of that broad, unlimited power in this case, we do not consider the primary constitutional question passed on by the Washington Supreme Court — whether the Due Process Clause requires all nonparental visitation statutes to include a showing of harm or potential harm to the child as a condition precedent to granting visitation. We do not, and need not, define today the precise scope of the parental due process right in the visitation context. [T]he constitutionality of any standard for awarding visitation turns on the specific manner in which that standard is applied. . . . Because much state-court adjudication in this context occurs on a case-by-case basis, we would be hesitant to hold that specific nonparental visitation statutes violate the Due Process Clause as a *per se* matter. . . .

[In separate omitted concurring opinions, Justice Souter upheld the state court's determination of the statute's facial unconstitutionality, and Justice Thomas noted that strict scrutiny ought to apply. In separate omitted dissenting opinions, Justice Scalia declined to recognize unenumerated constitutional rights, and Justice Kennedy reasoned that the best interest doctrine is not always an unconstitutional standard in visitation cases.]

Justice STEVENS, dissenting.

. . . While, as the Court recognizes, the Federal Constitution certainly protects the parent-child relationship from arbitrary impairment by the State, we have never held that the parent's liberty interest in this relationship is so inflexible as to establish a rigid constitutional shield, protecting every arbitrary parental decision from any challenge absent a threshold finding of harm. The presumption that parental decisions generally serve the best interests of their children is sound, and clearly in the normal case the parent's interest is paramount. But even a fit parent is capable of treating a child like a mere possession.

Cases like this do not present a bipolar struggle between the parents and the State over who has final authority to determine what is in a child's best interests. There is at a minimum a third individual, whose interests are implicated in every case to which the statute applies — the child. . . .

[Justice Stevens discusses *Lehr* and *Michael H.* to support his argument that limitations exist to parental liberty interests.] A parent's rights with respect to her child have thus never been regarded as absolute, but rather are limited by the existence of an actual, developed relationship with a child, and are tied to the presence or absence of some embodiment of family. These limitations have arisen, not simply out of the definition of parenthood itself, but because of this Court's assumption that a parent's interests in a child must be balanced against the State's long-recognized interests as parens patriae, and, critically, the child's own complementary interest in preserving relationships that serve her welfare and protection.

While this Court has not yet had occasion to elucidate the nature of a child's liberty interests in preserving established familial or family-like bonds, it seems to me extremely likely that, to the extent parents and families have fundamental liberty interests in preserving such intimate relationships, so, too, do children have these interests, and so, too, must their interests be balanced in the equation. At a minimum, our prior cases recognizing that children are, generally speaking, constitutionally protected actors require that this Court reject any suggestion that when it comes to parental rights, children are so much chattel. The constitutional protection against arbitrary state interference with parental rights should not be extended to prevent the States from protecting children against the arbitrary exercise of parental authority that is not in fact motivated by an interest in the welfare of the child.

This is not, of course, to suggest that a child's liberty interest in maintaining contact with a particular individual is to be treated invariably as on a par with that child's parents' contrary interests. Because our substantive due process case law includes a strong presumption that a parent will act in the best interest of her child, it would be necessary, were the state appellate courts actually to confront a challenge to the statute as applied, to consider whether the trial court's assessment of the "best interest of the child" incorporated that presumption. . . . But presumptions notwithstanding, we should recognize that there may be circumstances in which a child has a stronger interest at stake than mere protection from serious harm caused by the termination of visitation by a "person" other than a parent. The almost infinite variety of family relationships that pervade our ever-changing society strongly counsel against the creation by this Court of a constitutional rule that treats a biological parent's liberty interest in the care and supervision of her child as an isolated right that may be exercised arbitrarily. It is indisputably the business of the States, rather than a federal court employing a national standard, to assess in the first instance the relative importance of the conflicting interests that give rise to disputes such as this. . . .

■ JONES v. BORING JONES
884 A.2d 915 (Pa. Super. Ct. 2005)

KLEIN, J.

The trial judge, the distinguished Susan Devlin Scott, determined by clear and convincing evidence that awarding primary custody to the non-biological parent of a lesbian couple, Patricia Jones ("Jones"), as against the biological mother, Ellen Boring Jones ("Boring"), was in the best interests of the twin children that had been raised by them until the couple parted. [Boring appeals.]

Boring and Jones lived together in a romantic relationship starting in 1988. The two decided to have children by artificial insemination. Boring was impregnated by an anonymous sperm donor, and gave birth to twin boys on December 3, 1996. The parties lived together as a family until January 2001, when Boring left Jones' residence where they all lived, taking the children with her.

Boring does not seriously contest that Jones is in loco parentis, considering the background outlined above and particularly since she filed a support petition against Jones in 2001. Initially, while Judge Scott granted joint legal custody, primary legal custody was in the biological mother, Boring, while Jones had relatively typical partial custody visitation rights. Boring argues that since there was no finding that she, as the biological parent, was unfit, the court applied an incorrect standard or burden of proof. This, however, is not a complete statement of the law.

Initially, the trial judge recognized that there was a presumption that primary custody should go to the biological parent rather than one in loco parentis. It was only after time passed that, based on the record, Judge Scott concluded that Jones had established by clear and convincing evidence that it was in the best interests of the children to transfer primary custody to her. Once it is established that someone who is not the biological parent is in loco parentis, that person does not need to establish that the biological parent is unfit, but instead must establish by clear and convincing evidence that it is in the best interests of the children to maintain that relationship or be with that person. See Kellogg v. Kellogg, 646 A.2d 1246, 1249 (Pa. Super. 1994). . . .

This best-interests analysis, therefore, is weighted in favor of the biological parent. The burden of proof is not evenly balanced, as the parents have a prima facie right to custody, which will be forfeited only if convincing reasons appear that the child's best interest will be served by an award to the third party. This weighted best-interests analysis is based upon a consideration of all factors that legitimately affect the child's physical, intellectual, moral, and spiritual well-being.

. . . While the scale [here] was tipped in favor of Boring, Jones produced clear and convincing reasons to even the scale and then tip it on her side. Jones did not establish that Boring was unfit, and was not required to do so, but Jones did clearly and convincingly establish that the children would be better off with her as the primary custodian and that the children's relationship with both parties would be better fostered if custody were awarded to Jones. . . .

Judge Scott's thoughtful review of the record confirms this. Jones has a strong parental bond with the children and, unlike Boring, never interfered with Boring's role as parent. To the contrary, and as indicated above, the record is replete with evidence that Boring tried in every way possible to sabotage Jones' relationship with the children. Boring tried to relocate out of the area to decrease contact with Jones, although it disrupted the children's schooling. [Boring tried to remove "Jones" from the children's names.] Boring put her own interests ahead of the children's. The custody evaluator determined that Boring suffered from psychological dysfunction that showed Boring's inability to maintain stability in jobs, residence, schooling, or continuity of relationships for her and the children. There also was evidence that Boring had a drinking problem. Further, Boring has a history of ignoring court orders. To the contrary, the evaluator determined that Jones is psychologically healthy and stable.

Judge Scott's considered opinion reflects a painstaking review of the physical, spiritual, moral, and educational issues in the children's lives and a comparison of each party's response to those issues. We have neither the authority nor the inclination to go behind this evaluation.

Jones asserts that the law is changing. As the concept of family evolves, the law will evolve along with it. Jones claims that in the situation presented here, where two people together decide to have a child, although only one is the biological parent, and they both live together and parent the children together following their birth, the standard should be a simple best-interests analysis, and that the law should abandon both the presumption in favor of the biological parent and the "clear and convincing" standard of proof. Since the trial court determined, and we agree, that there was "clear and convincing evidence" in this case, we do not reach that issue today. . . .

Notes and Questions

1. *Common law rule*. At common law, grandparents had no right to visitation with grandchildren in the face of parental objection. All states now have third-party visitation statutes that permit grandparents (and sometimes other persons, as revealed in *Troxel*) to petition for visitation in certain circumstances.

2. *Social factors*. What societal factors explain the expanding legal recognition of grandparents' rights? Professors Andrew Cherlin and Frank Furstenberg point to several factors:

All of these trends taken together — changes in mortality, fertility, transportation, communications, the work day, retirement, Social Security, and standards of living — have transformed grandparenthood from its pre-World War II state. More people are living longer to become grandparents and to enjoy a lengthy period of life as grandparents. They can keep in touch more easily with their grandchildren; they have more time to devote to them; they have more money to spend on them; and they are less likely still to be raising their own children.

Andrew J. Cherlin and Frank Furstenberg, Jr., The Modernization of Grandparenthood, in Arlene S. Skolnick, The Intimate Environment 131 (6th ed. 1989). Custody rights of grandparents take on renewed importance in an era of AIDS, substance abuse, and the feminization of poverty when it is common for biological parents, facing economic or medical difficulties, to ask their own parents for assistance with child care. See generally Karen Czapanskiy, Grandparents, Parents and Grandchildren: Actualizing Interdependency in Law, 26 Conn. L. Rev. 1315 (1994).

3. *Approaches prior to Troxel.* Four types of grandparent visitation statutes existed: (1) those conditioned on the related parent's rights ("derivative rights theory"), (2) those based on family disruption (for example, death of parent or divorce), (3) those based on best interests theory, and (4) those requiring a "substantial relationship" between grandparent and child. Patricia S. Fernandez, Grandparent Access: A Model Statute, 6 Yale L. & Pol'y Rev. 109, 118-124 (1988). Some triggering situations (for example, death or divorce) reflect more than one theory. What type was the Washington statute at issue in *Troxel*?

4. *Natural parent presumption.* A presumption favors natural parents in custody (as opposed to visitation) disputes involving parents versus nonparents. That is, courts apply a rebuttable presumption that custody should be awarded to a natural parent absent evidence of parental unfitness. In a landmark grandparents' rights case, a state supreme court refused to follow that presumption. In Painter v. Bannister, 140 N.W.2d 152 (Iowa 1966), *cert. denied*, 385 U.S. 949 (1966), a father left his young son with the boy's maternal grandparents when the boy's sister and mother died in an automobile accident. When the father remarried and requested the return of his son, the grandparents refused. The father brought a habeas corpus action. Refusing to apply the parental presumption, the court held that the child's best interests would be served by remaining with the stable, church-going Midwestern grandparents rather than the bohemian writer/father. For a discussion of the influence of *Painter* on law reform, see Gilbert A. Holmes, The Tie That Binds: The Constitutional Rights of Children to Maintain Relationships with Parent-Like Individuals, 53 Md. L. Rev. 358, 384 (1994).

For the role of the presumption in another famous grandparents' rights case, see Bottoms v. Bottoms, 457 S.E.2d 102 (Va. 1995) (affirming an award of custody to a maternal grandmother because evidence of the lesbian mother's unfitness was sufficient to rebut the parental presumption).

5. *Right to privacy.* Do grandparents' visitation statutes unconstitutionally infringe on the right to privacy (that is, parents' constitutional right to make decisions regarding their children)? Prior to *Troxel*, courts were split on that question. How does *Troxel* respond? How influential are Meyer v. Nebraska and Pierce v. Society of Sisters in the United States Supreme Court's analysis? Do the plurality and dissent (Justice Stevens) treat these precedents differently?

The Washington state supreme court had interpreted Meyer v. Nebraska and Pierce v. Society of Sisters (see Chapter I) to stand for the principle that the state may only interfere in parental rights to control the upbringing of their children to prevent harm to a child. In re Smith, 969 P.2d 21, 29 (Wash. 1998). Does this comport with your understanding of these cases? The *Troxel* plurality suggests that the burden of litigating a domestic relations proceeding can itself be "so disruptive of the parent-child relationship that the constitutional right of a custodial parent to make certain basic determinations for the child's welfare becomes implicated." Does this burden on a parent's fundamental right to privacy require jurisdictions to impose strict standing requirements (i.e., mandating dismissal of grandparents' petition without an evidentiary hearing if the petitioner fails to make an initial showing of compliance with the statute)? See Conlogue v. Conlogue, 890 A.2d 691 (Me. 2006) (so suggesting).

Why do you suppose that Tommie Granville wanted to limit her daughters' visitation with their deceased father's parents? Should the law be involved in such private dispute resolution? See generally Sandra Day O'Connor, The Supreme Court and the Family, 3 U. Pa. J. Const. L. 573, 577 (2001) (discussing the law's difficulty in the prioritization of interests).

6. *Constitutional issues*. In *Troxel*, the plurality held that the Washington statute, as applied to Tommie Granville, violated the Due Process Clause. In what way(s) was the application defective?

By holding the statute unconstitutional as applied, the Court avoided a ruling that the statute was facially unconstitutional. The Court also evaded identifying the appropriate standard of review. What standard of review should courts apply to nonparental visitation statutes? Should courts be especially protective of parental interests and apply strict scrutiny (as Justice Thomas reasons in an omitted concurrence)? Rational relationship? The undue burden standard (i.e., whether visitation unduly burdens the parents' constitutional rights)? See, e.g., In re Howard, 661 N.W.2d 183 (Iowa 2003); Harrold v. Collier, 836 N.E.2d 1165 (Ohio 2005); In re R.A., 891 A.2d 564 (N.H. 2005) (all applying strict scrutiny to grandparent visitation disputes).

The Justices also disagreed on what the state must show to justify interference with a parent's decision about third-party visitation. What should the test be? The best interests of the child (as Justice Stevens and, in an omitted concurrence, Justice Kennedy believe)? Potential harm to the child if visitation is not granted? What are the advantages and disadvantages of applying each test? Compare In re Parentage of C.A.M.A., 109 P.3d 405 (Wash. 2005) (adopting harm test), with Dodd v. Burleson, 2005 WL 3445612 (Ala. Civ. Ct. App. 2005) (rejecting harm test). If the court requires grandparents to prove that their grandchild would be harmed by denial of visitation, what should be the standard of proof? Compare Roth v. Weston, 789 A.2d 431 (Conn. 2002) (clear and convincing standard), with Moriarty v. Bradt, 827 A.2d 203 (N.J. 2003) and Vibbert v. Vibbert, 144 S.W.3d 292 (Ky. Ct. App. 2004) (both adopting preponderance standard). How substantial must the harm be? See Blixt v. Blixt, 774 N.E.2d 1052, 1060 (Mass. 2002) (requiring significant harm that adversely affects health, safety, or welfare plus a significant preexisting relationship).

7. *Law reform.* In the wake of *Troxel*, state legislatures and courts wrestled with the constitutionality of third-party visitation statutes. Many jurisdictions revised their statutes specifically to limit the number of persons who could seek visitation and to give deference to a fit parent's wishes. Also, some states moved to a more stringent standard than the best interests of the child (i.e., a "harm" test), or alternatively retained the best-interests standard but narrowed it by the inclusion of

particular factors. See Michael K. Goldberg, The New, Narrower Illinois Grand-parent Visitation Statute, 92 Ill. B.J. 578, 581 n.28 (2005) (citing authority); Jen-nifer Kovalcik, Note, Troxel v. Granville: In the Battle Between Grandparent Visitation Statutes and Parental Rights, "The Best Interest of the Child" Standard Needs Reform, 40 Brandeis L.J. 803, 822-825 (2002) (describing reform efforts and advocating uniform application of the best-interests standard with the enumeration of specific factors).

8. *Factors to consider in granting visitation.* If you were a legislator or a judge, what factors would be important to consider in the determination of visitation so as not to infringe on parental rights? For example, in the balance between family privacy and state intervention, should it matter if the dispute involves any of the following?

- an intact family in which both parents object to visitation by the grandpar-ent(s), e.g., Daniels v. Daniels, 885 A.2d 524 (N.J. Super. Ct. 2005) (dismiss-ing grandmother's motion for visitation, holding that the statute could not constitutionally be applied to require parents in an intact family to permit visitation);
- married parents who are not living together, e.g., *Blixt*, supra (reasoning that no state interest is served "by subjecting married parents to visitation complaints merely because they are presently living apart, while exempting all other married parents from the same burden on their fundamental par-ental rights");
- a family disrupted by the death of a parent, e.g., Lamberts v. Lillig, 670 N.W.2d 129 (Iowa 2003) (holding that provision of statute permitting grandparent visitation in the event of the death of the child's parent was unconstitutional, and reconfirming that the parental interest is not lessened by the marital status of a fit parent);
- a family disrupted by divorce but with parents who disagree about the grandparent's visitation, e.g., In re Marriage of Harris, 17 Cal. Rptr. 3d 842 (Cal. 2004) (holding that an order for grandparent visitation that is supported by one of the parents does not infringe upon the other parent's parental rights);
- a child's parents who are not married, e.g., Saul v. Brunetti, 753 So. 2d 26 (Fla. 2000) (holding that the statute giving grandparents of a nonmarital child the right to visitation violated father's right to privacy and that the parents' unmarried status should not affect the analysis);
- a parent (or parents) who agreed to the visitation at one time, e.g., In re M.M.D., 820 N.E.2d 392 (Ill. 2004) (holding that the consent decree entered into by parties, which granted grandparent visitation with child, was valid);
- a grandparent with a significant relationship with the grandchild, e.g., 750 Ill. Comp. Stat. Ann. 5/607(a-5) (West 2005) (specifying *inter alia* such fac-tors as: the length and quality of the relationship between the child and petitioner, whether the child resided with the petitioner for at least six consecutive months, and whether the petitioner had frequent visitation with the child for at least 12 months); or
- the grandparent has been "unreasonably" denied visitation by a parent (see id.).

What light does *Troxel* shed on these situations? See generally Natalie Reed, Note, Third Party Visitation Statutes: Why Are Some Families More Equal Than Others?, 78 S. Cal. L. Rev. 1529 (2005) (advocating protection of childrearing autonomy to single, widowed, separated, and divorced parents).

9. *Role of race.* Should grandparents' rights be accorded more deference among cultural groups in which extended families play an important role? See Reed, supra, at 1567 (citing research showing that African-American children frequently live with their grandmothers who often are single parents).

10. *Pluralism.* Currently, our modern family is characterized by an increasing number of nonparents seeking to continue their relationships with children. How far does *Troxel* go in recognizing the variation in families? How receptive would the Supreme Court be, do you think, in allowing third-party visitation by other members of the extended family? Foster parents? Same-sex former partners? Unrelated caregivers? Might there be risks in an expansive definition of "family"? For example, should visitation be extended to great-grandparents? A parent's boyfriend or girlfriend? Siblings? In Herbst v. Swan, 125 Cal. Rptr. 2d 836 (Ct. App. 2002), a California appellate court examined the constitutionality of a statute permitting sibling visitation upon a finding that one of the parents is deceased and visitation would be in the minor's best interests. When a sister applied for visitation to her unemancipated half-brother (upon the death of both children's father), the court applied *Troxel* to hold the statute unconstitutional as applied because it infringed upon a surviving fit parent's liberty interest to regulate a child's (the half-brother's) associations. See generally Angela Ferraris, Comment, Sibling Visitation as a Fundamental Right in Herbst v. Swan, 39 New Eng. L. Rev. 715 (2004-2005). For a discussion of post-adoption visitation by biological grandparents and siblings, see Chapter IX.

11. *Stepparents' rights.* The sharp rise in divorce has contributed to an increase in the number of blended families that include stepparents. Census data reveal that 5 percent of all children of householders are stepchildren.[14] Should stepparents have custody or visitation rights following dissolution? Traditionally, if a former stepparent sought custody in the face of parental objection, that stepparent had to overcome the biological-parent preference. See David R. Fine & Mark A. Fine, Learning from Social Sciences: A Model for Reformation of the Laws Affecting Stepfamilies, 97 Dick. L. Rev. 49, 56 (1992) (citing survey finding that 38 states have such presumptions). Although stepparents had a legally cognizable relationship with the child during the marriage, they were not entitled to recognition of their parental rights when the marriage terminated. See June Carbone, The Legal Definition of Parenthood: Uncertainty at the Core of Family Identity, 65 Louisiana L. Rev. 1295, 1312 (2005).

Courts have been increasingly willing to grant visitation rights to former stepparents, especially given a long-term relationship with the child. Fine & Fine, supra, at 56. Some states accomplish this result by application of the doctrine of in loco parentis. Carbone, supra, at 1328. Does an award of stepparent visitation infringe on a biological parent's constitutional rights as articulated in *Troxel*? Compare Robinson v. Ford-Robinson, 2005 WL 1041158 (Ark. 2005) (holding that court may award visitation to a stepparent standing in loco parentis over

[14]. Bureau of the Census, U.S. Dept. of Commerce, Adopted Children and Stepchildren: 2000, 3, 6 (Oct. 2003).

the biological parent's objection, reasoning that *Troxel* was distinguishable because petitioner was similar to a noncustodial parent), with In re Marriage of Engelkens, 821 N.E.2d 799 (Ill. Ct. App. 2004) (holding facially unconstitutional a statute allowing reasonable visitation to stepparent if court determines that it is in child's best interests). See generally Paul Amato, The Impact of Family Formation Change on the Cognitive, Social, and Emotional Well-Being of the Next Generation, 15 Future of Children 75, 80 (Fall 2005); John C. Mayoue, Stepping In to Parent, 25 Fam. Advoc. 36 (Fall 2002); Susan L. Pollet, Ozzie and Harriet Reconfigured: Stepparent Rights in the Law, 31 Westchester B.J. 57 (2004).

12. *Psychological parent.* The concept of psychological parent derives from the influential book by Joseph Goldstein et al., Beyond the Best Interests of the Child 17-20 (1973). Based on psychoanalytic theory, Goldstein and his co-authors (Anna Freud and Alfred Solnit) point out:

> Whether any adult becomes the psychological parent of a child is based thus on day-to-day interaction, companionship, and shared experiences. The role can be fulfilled either by a biological parent or by an adoptive parent or by any other caring adult—but never by an absent, interactive adult, whatever his biological or legal relationship to the child may be.

Id. at 19. Goldstein, Freud, and Solnit also advocate the importance of continuity of care. Id. at 31. When asked about the importance courts should attach to the "blood tie," Joseph Goldstein responded:

> The blood tie has become a shorthand, detached over time from its underlying function. It is a nice illustration of how a guideline developed as common law come[s] to be misapplied when the underlying reason for it gets lost. Courts mechanically applied the blood tie notion without taking into account . . . that the reason for it was that the natural parent was expected to be the primary source of care on a continuing basis.

Anne Goldstein, An Interview with Joseph Goldstein, 110 Yale L.J. 925, 930 (2001).

How should courts accommodate the parental preference rule and the best interests standard in disputes involving "psychological parents"? Was Ellen Boring Jones a psychological parent? Consider the following:

> "These judges don't understand what it is to be a mother," Ms. G. [Michelle G., a lesbian co-parent appealing a judge's decision that she has no right to see the children she helped rear] said. "To sit there and say with a straight face that someone who has stayed up all night nursing a child, swabbing her chicken pox, taking joy in her every advancement, picking her up every time she's skinned her knee, or singing her to sleep is not a 'mother' is an absurdity."

Cited in David Margolick, Lesbians' Custody Fight Tests Family Law Frontier, N.Y. Times, July 4, 1990, at A1.

13. *Lesbian mother disputes: traditional approach.* In judicial determinations of custody involving opposite-sex couples, the mother and father begin on equal footing. To prevail in a request for sole custody, the mother and father each strives to satisfy the "best interests of the child" standard. In contrast, in custody disputes involving lesbian couples, the biological mother historically enjoyed a "nearly

insurmountable advantage" over the non-biological mother because of the natural parent presumption that favors a parent over a non-parent. Julie Shapiro, A Lesbian-Centered Critique of Second-Parent Adoptions, 14 Berkeley Women's L.J. 17, 23 (1999).

Two famous cases illustrate the traditional difficulties. In Alison D. v. Virginia M., 572 N.E.2d 27 (N.Y. 1991), Alison and Virginia decided to have a child together after they had lived together for three years. Virginia gave birth to a boy, for whom both parents shared caretaking and provided financial support. When the child was two years old, the women ended their relationship. Initially they agreed to a visitation schedule, but gradually, Virginia restricted Alison's visitation. When the child was six years old, Virginia terminated all contact between Alison and the boy. Alison brought a habeas corpus action to obtain visitation rights. The New York Court of Appeals denied her claim, holding that Alison was not a parent within the meaning of the state visitation statute because she was neither the child's biological nor adoptive parent.

A California court reached a similar result in Nancy S. v. Michele G., 279 Cal. Rptr. 212 (Ct. App. 1991). Nancy gave birth to a girl and later a boy during her relationship with Michele. Shortly after the boy's birth, the women ended their 16-year relationship. After three years of a visitation arrangement, Michele sought to increase her visitation—a move which Nancy opposed. Nancy then sought sole legal and physical custody and a declaration that Michele was not a parent of either child. The court of appeals affirmed the trial court finding for Nancy, holding that: (1) a lesbian partner is not a parent within the meaning of Uniform Parentage Act; (2) custody cannot be awarded to a lesbian partner over the objection of a biological mother absent a finding that parental custody by the biological mother would be detrimental to children; and (3) the claim of de facto parent, or in loco parentis, or equitable estoppel, even if true, would not give a lesbian partner the same rights as a parent in custody dispute. (The case was disapproved by Elisa B. v. Superior Court, 117 P.3d 660 (Cal. 2005), supra Chapter IV).

14. *Functional parenthood: background.* The same court that decided *Alison D.*, supra, also decided Braschi v. Stahl (supra Chapter IV). Recall that *Braschi* was a landmark case adopting a functional definition of the family (conferring protection on a gay relationship under a rent-control ordinance). *Alison D.*, however, refused to apply a functional definition. What might explain the different outcomes? Professor William Rubenstein identifies the following differences in (1) the nature of the parties (landlord-tenant versus parents), (2) the litigants' contemplated future relationships (none, in the one case, versus a continuing relationship in the other), (3) the interests at stake (property versus human relationships), (4) the presence of third-party interests in one case (the child's), (5) the hierarchy of rights (one case involved a potential restriction on a biological parent's constitutional rights), and (6) the role of stereotypes (the speculative harm perpetrated on children by gay and lesbian parents). See William Rubenstein, We Are Family: A Reflection on the Search for Legal Recognition of Lesbian and Gay Relationships, 8 J.L. & Pol'y 89 (1991).

15. *Functional parenthood: limited recognition.* Beginning in the mid to late 1990s, a few courts began applying common law or equitable doctrines of functional parenthood (e.g., psychological parenthood, de facto parenthood, parenthood by estoppel, in loco parentis) to confer rights on lesbian coparents. See, e.g., E.N.O. v. L.M.M., 711 N.E.2d 886 (Mass. 1999) (affirming visitation to a de facto parent who

was a lesbian coparent); V.C. v. M.J.B., 748 A.2d 539 (N.J. 2000) (holding that former partner was entitled to visitation, although not to joint legal custody, based on psychological parent doctrine); T.B. v. L.R.M., 786 A.2d 913 (Pa. 2001) (holding that former partner stood in loco parentis and thus possessed standing to sue for visitation rights); Holtzman v. Knott, 533 N.W.2d 419 (Wis. 1995) (granting visitation rights to psychological parent of nonbiologically related child).

Although such cases "represent positive progress for nonlegal mothers and their children, the results are not fully satisfying," according to one commentator. "The courts have not applied functional parenthood to legalize the parent-child relationship. Rather, the courts have used functional parenthood doctrine merely as a means of preserving a visitation relationship." Melanie B. Jacobs, Applying Intent-Based Parentage Principles to Nonlegal Lesbian Coparents, 25 N. Ill. U. L. Rev. 433, 436 (2005). What do you think of this criticism?

16. *Functional parenthood: factors.* Should courts and legislators adopt a functional (as opposed to a formal) approach that would recognize those who act as parents in non-traditional settings? If so, what factors should be relevant in the determination of a functional "psychological parent"?

Wisconsin was the first jurisdiction to establish a framework for the recognition of second-parent rights. In In re Custody of H.S.H.-K., 533 N.W.2d 419 (Wis. 1995), the Wisconsin Supreme Court held that visitation of a non-biological parent was in the best interest of the child if there is a *parent-like relationship* plus a *significant triggering event* that justified state intervention. The court developed the following test to determine the existence of a parent-like relationship: (1) whether the biological parent "consented to, and fostered, the petitioner's formation and establishment of a parent-like relationship with the child"; (2) whether the petitioner resided together with the child in the same household; (3) whether the petitioner assumed "obligations of parenthood by taking significant responsibility for the child's care, education and development," including contributions to the child's support (which are not required to be monetary), and doing so without any expectation of financial compensation; and (4) whether the petitioner served in the parental role for a sufficient period of time to enable the establishment of a "bonded, dependent" parental relationship with the child. Id at 435-436. The court also defined the "significant triggering event" to evoke state intervention 1) if the custodial parent interfered substantially with the parent-like relationship; and 2) if the parent seeking visitation sought court-ordered visitation within a reasonable time after the custodial parent's interference. Id. at 436.

17. *Biology and parenthood.* The parental preference doctrine assumes that a child may have only one parent of each gender. Can a child have two mothers? Recall the discussion "Extending Paternity Laws to Same-Sex Couples," supra Chapter IV. Until recently, courts rejected this concept, refusing to recognize custodial or visitation rights in cases in which a child would have more than one mother. (In line with such thinking, some courts ruled that it was necessary to terminate one woman's rights in order for the second parent to assert parental rights.) Should the law recognize more than one mother or father? (Recall Michael H. v. Gerald D., supra Chapter IV.)

The "only-one-mother" rule was reflected in Johnson v. Calvert, 851 P.2d 776 (Cal. 1993), in which a gestational surrogate mother (Johnson) refused to give up the child she bore for the Calverts, using their genetic material. The California

Supreme Court ruled that the genetic parents prevailed based on the intent-based parentage approach, reasoning that a woman who intended to bring about the birth of a child that she intended to raise as her own is the natural mother. In so holding, the court stated that a child cannot have two mothers. "[F]or any child California law recognizes only one natural mother, despite advances in reproductive technology rendering a different outcome biologically possible." Id. at 499. This reasoning recently was judicially overruled by K.M. v. E.G., 117 P.3d 673 (Cal. 2005) (discussed in Chapter IX).

As explained above, the second parent's lack of a biological connection to the child traditionally precluded establishment of a legally cognizable parent-child relationship and thereby prevented the second parent from attaining rights to custody and/or visitation. To what extent can (should) risk-averse lesbian co-parents assure their recognition in the event of death or dissolution by the attempt of both parents to establish a biological connection to the child? For example, should they use sperm from a male relative of the co-parent to conceive the child? Or, suppose one woman gestates the child whereas the other woman provides the egg (which is fertilized with donor sperm). Does each mother have a cognizable claim to legal parenthood?

Several recent cases have addressed this latter scenario. Compare K.M. v. E.G., 117 P.3d 673 (Cal. 2005) (holding that both lesbian partners were parents of these children, and that the statute providing that the law treats a sperm donor as if he was not the natural father of a child thus conceived did not apply to this situation) (discussed infra Chapter IX), with In re J.D.M., 2004 WL 2272063 (Ohio Ct. App. 2004) (holding that the trial court was required to make a conclusive finding as to which woman was the child's mother and which partner was assuming parental rights; and to consider whether the shared parenting plan was in the best interest of child).

18. *Resolution of* Jones. *Jones* illustrates a paradigm shift in judicial response to same-sex parent custody disputes. Did *Jones* hold that the nonbiological mother and the biological mother were on equal footing in the custody dispute? For recent cases holding that both partners in a lesbian relationship have parental rights, see Elisa B. v. Superior Court, 117 P.3d 660 (Cal. 2005) (recognizing that both parents of a child can be women, and that the non-biological parent was a parent by virtue of receiving the child into her home and holding the child out as her child) (discussed supra Chapter IV); In re Parentage of L.B., 122 P.3d 161 (Wash. 2005) (holding that a second parent in a lesbian relationship is a de facto parent and stands in legal parity with the other legal parent). Note that the recognition of a lesbian partner as a *parent*, as in *Elisa B.*, eliminates the need to rely on doctrines such as in loco parentis to secure custody or visitation rights.

Do you agree with the resolution of the principal case? How should courts resolve custody disputes between same-sex parents? What is the impact of same-sex marriage, civil unions, or domestic partnerships, where available? See e.g., Cal. Fam. Code §297.5(d) (West 2004 & Supp. 2005). (Note, however, that even in states with domestic partnership legislation, problems may arise if one member of the couple moves to another state that does not recognize domestic partnerships and institutes custody litigation. See, e.g., Miller-Jenkins v. Miller-Jenkins, discussed Chapter IV, p. 484.) Should courts continue to apply the natural parent presumption? Should courts abandon the natural parent presumption and adopt the best interests test, as *Jones* advocates? Should courts recognize the parental status of both parents? If the latter, how should custody disputes be resolved — by means of a presumption of joint custody? By common law claims or equitable claims of de facto or psychological parentage, or the in loco parentis doctrine? Should disputes involving gay male parents be decided the same way as those involving lesbian mothers?

19. *Written agreement*. Should lesbian couples execute written agreements to address issues of custody and visitation? If so, will courts recognize such agreements *during* the relationship? See In re J.D.M., supra. Will courts enforce such agreements *upon dissolution*? Compare Wakeman v. Dixon, 921 So. 2d 669 (Fla. Ct. App. 2006) (holding that coparenting agreements were unenforceable even though non-biological mother had supported and been a de facto parent, based on state constitutional privacy provision that prohibits third party from interfering with parental rights absent demonstrable harm to child), with Rubano v. DiCenzo, 759 A.2d 959 (R.I. 2000) (holding that biological mother was equitably estopped from denying existence of presumption of parental rights on behalf of her partner by the former's conduct permitting partner to assume parental role and by the former's executing agreement conferring visitation rights on partner "because it was in minor's best interest"). Absent a written agreement, can a "course of conduct" establish the parties' agreement to create a parent-child relationship with the child? See In re Custody of H.S.H.-K., 533 N.W.2d 419, 436 n.40 (Wis. 1995) (reasoning that a court could so find).

20. *Law reforms: ALI Principles*. The American Law Institute (ALI) recognizes that biology is not determinative of legal parenthood. In addition to legal parents, the ALI recognizes parents "by estoppel" as well as "de facto" parents (who may be members of opposite-sex or same-sex couples and who may be married or unmarried). A parent by estoppel is a person who acts as a parent in circumstances that would estop the child's legal parent from denying the claimant's parental status. Parent-by-estoppel status may be created when an individual (1) is obligated for child support, or (2) has lived with the child for at least two years and has a reasonable belief that he is the father, or (3) has had an agreement with the child's legal parent since birth (or for at least two years) to serve as a co-parent provided that recognition of parental status would serve the child's best interests. ALI Principles §2.03 (1)(b) (2002).

In contrast, a de facto parent is a person, other than a legal parent or parent by estoppel, who has regularly performed an equal or greater share of caretaking as the parent with whom the child primarily lived, lived with the child for a significant period (not less than two years), and acted as a parent for non-financial reasons (and with the agreement of a legal parent) or as a result of a complete failure or inability of any legal parent to perform caretaking functions. Id. at §2.03 (1)(c).

Both legal parents and parents by estoppel are entitled to presumptive allocations of custodial responsibility (§2.09(1)(a)), joint decisionmaking responsibility (§2.10(b)), and presumptive access to educational and medical records (§2.10(4)). However, the Principles' requirements are more strict regarding de facto parents to avoid inappropriate intrusion into the relationship between the legal parent(s) and children. Thus, a de facto parent is precluded from receiving a majority of custodial responsibility for the child if a legal parent or a parent by estoppel is fit and willing to care for the child (§2.18(1)(a)). Similarly, a de facto parent's rights may be limited or denied if the custodial allocation would be impractical in light of the number of other adults to be allocated custodial responsibility (§2.18(1)(b)).

How well do these provisions address the problems inherent in recognizing third-party rights?

The recently revised Uniform Parentage Act (UPA), similarly, recognizes that biology is not determinative of legal parenthood. See "Extending Paternity to Same-Sex Couples," supra, Chapter IV, p. 478. Does the UPA preclude common law claims of de facto or psychological parentage? See In re Parentage of L.B., 122 P.3d 161, 166 n.5 (Wash. 2005).

21. *Child's interests?* To what extent does the Constitution protect the rights of a child to retain a relationship with a nonparent? Does *Michael H.* (discussed in Chapter IV) shed any light on the matter? In his dissent in *Troxel*, Justice Stevens is alone in urging that children's interests should be taken into consideration in the balancing of interests among parents, grandparents, and state. Moreover, the growing body of case law on second parents' rights to custody and visitation focuses on the parents' right per se. Do children of same-sex couples have an independent right to the maintenance of relationships with both parents upon the dissolution of the parents' relationships? See Nicole M. Onorato, Notes and Comments, The Right to Be Heard: Incorporating the Needs and Interests of Children of Non-marital Families into the Visitation Rights Dialogue, 4 Whittier J. Child & Fam. Advoc. 491 (2005) (so arguing). On the role of children's interests, wishes, and preferences in custody decisionmaking, see infra section B(4).

22. *Role of* Troxel. Does recognition of a second parent's rights infringe on the biological parent's rights, according to *Troxel* and *Jones*? In In re Parentage of L.B., 122 P.3d 161 (Wash. 2005), the Washington Supreme Court addressed this issue, holding that the claim of lesbian mother who qualified as a common law de facto parent did not constitute an unconstitutional infringement on the parental rights of a fit biological parent. The court distinguished *Troxel* by saying: (1) recognition of the common law status of de facto parents places them in parity with biological and adoptive parents, thereby signifying that *both* are parents who have a funda-mental liberty interest in the care, custody, and control of their children; (2) *Troxel* does not address state law determinations of "parents" and "families" and does not place constitutional limitations on the ability of states to define a parent or family. As the court concluded: "Our common law recognition of another class of "parents" eradicates the parent/nonparent dichotomy that was the crux of [*Troxel*]." Id. at 178. See generally Nancy D. Polikoff, The Impact of Troxel v. Granville on Lesbian and Gay Parents, 32 Rutgers L.J. 825 (2001).

23. *Empirical data: children's well-being.* What is the effect of a parent's sexual orientation on children's psychological development? A recent comprehensive review of the literature identifies the following findings: (1) lesbian mothers and gay fathers largely resemble other parents; (2) children of same-sex parents tend not to be confused about their gender identity or more likely to be gay or lesbian; (3) children raised by same-sex parents show no differences (when compared with those children raised by heterosexual parents) in terms of cognitive abilities, behav-ior, self-esteem, depression, or anxiety; and (4) the evidence is mixed on whether the children of same-sex couples are teased by their peers. William Meezan & Jonathan Rauch, Gay Marriage, Same-Sex Parenting, and America's Children, in 15 The Future of Children 97, 103 (Fall 2005). See also Judith Stacey & Timothy Biblarz, (How) Does the Sexual Orientation of Parents Matter?, 66 Am. Soc. Rev. 159 (April 2001) (reviewing the literature on same-sex parenting and finding that children of same-sex parents develop in less gender-stereotypical ways; and

have greater sensitivity, empathy for social diversity and capacity to express feelings).

For a debate in the legal literature on the effect of parents' sexual orientation on children's psychological development, compare Lynn D. Wardle, The Potential Impact of Homosexual Parenting on Children, 1997 U. Ill. L. Rev. 833 (suggesting that parents' sexual orientation may be harmful to children and arguing that the law should reflect a rebuttable presumption that parenting by homosexuals is not in children's best interests) with Carlos A. Ball & Janice Farrell Pea, Warring with Wardle: Morality, Social Science, and Gay and Lesbian Parents, 1998 U. Ill. L. Rev. 253 (contending that Wardle's presumption poses practical, normative, and constitutional problems, and arguing that parenting ability rather than sexual orientation should be determinative in custody decisionmaking).

24. *Governmental policy and children's well-being.* What is the likely effect of the advent of same-sex marriage on the children of same-sex couples? The effect of domestic partnership laws on these children? See generally Jonathan Rauch, Gay Marriage: Why It Is Good for Gays, Good for Straights, and Good for America (2004); Mark Strasser, On Same-Sex Marriage, Civil Unions, and the Rule of Law: Constitutional Interpretation at the Crossroads 39-54 (2002); Evan Wolfson, Why Marriage Matters? America, Equality, and Gay People's Right to Marry 85-103 (2005); Meezan & Rauch, supra, at 108-109. On second-parent adoption for lesbian families, see Chapter IX.

25. *Comparative-law issues.* Several European countries recognize same-sex partnerships but nonetheless disapprove of lesbian and gay parenting. This disapproval is manifest in terms of governmental policy toward custody, adoption, and access to assisted reproduction. For example, Denmark, Norway, Sweden, and France deny custody rights to members of same-sex couples. Developments in the Law — The Law of Marriage and Family, Inching Down the Aisle: Differing Paths Toward the Legalization of Same-Sex Marriage in the United States and Europe, 116 Harv. L. Rev. 2004, 2011-2012 (2003). What explains the different attitudes toward same-sex partnerships versus same-sex parenting? See Nancy D. Polikoff, Recognizing Partners But Not Parents: Gay and Lesbian Family Law in Europe and the United States, 17 N.Y.L. Sch. J. Hum. Rts. 711 (2000).

■ **NANCY D. POLIKOFF, THIS CHILD DOES HAVE TWO MOTHERS: REDEFINING PARENTHOOD TO MEET THE NEEDS OF CHILDREN IN LESBIAN-MOTHER AND OTHER NONTRADITIONAL FAMILIES**
78 Geo. L.J. 459, 474-479, 482 (1990)

Neither biology nor legal adoption is sufficient to establish who is a parent in a complex world affected by cultural norms, technology, and patterns of sexual behavior. Deviation from the one-mother/one-father prescription for parenthood is common. Communal child rearing, surrogacy, open adoption, stepfamilies, and extramarital births all destroy the myth of family homogeneity.

Some cultures have family structures that incorporate many parental figures. In Polynesia, for example, parenting is a collective task. The relative insignificance of biology is exemplified in the language, which generalizes the words for mother, father, and grandparent to all relatives of equivalent age and gender. Children have several houses that they regard as home; the death of a parent is not as acute a crisis as it is in the United States; life transition rituals involve numerous people; and parental rights are not exclusive of other adults.

Parenting is also a community responsibility in certain regions of the United States. Anthropologist Carol Stack [All Our Kin: Strategies for Survival in a Black Community (1974)] documented the assumption of parental rights and responsibilities in The Flats, the poorest section of a black community in a Midwestern city. She described child rearing, or "child-keeping," by relatives and friends that in many circumstances creates parental rights and obligations recognized by the community, even if not by the courts. These parental rights may be coterminous with the rights of the biological mother. They are acquired as a result of joint child rearing or the common knowledge that "[w]hatever happens to me, Ethel be the person to keep my kids." . . .

The prevalence of stepfamilies further dilutes the one-mother/one-father norm. Although not all stepparents function as parents, clearly some do. . . . Open adoption, which has come into existence in recent years, attests to the willingness of some adoptive parents to include and even welcome a child's biological parent into the child's life, yet the law does not easily permit a child to have three legal parents.

The most common challenge to the one-mother/one-father model arises from the ability to determine paternity with a degree of certainty approaching that which exists for maternity. A child may have a biological father and a different functional father, usually the man who is married to that child's mother. The respective rights of these two men have been the subject of a substantial amount of litigation, most of it aimed at identifying one father of the child. In such cases, the state's attempt to reduce all families to the one-mother/one-father model is best exemplified by the presumption, sometimes rebuttable, that the husband of a married woman is the father of her child [citing Michael H. v. Gerald D.].

[C]ourts should protect children's interests within the context of nontraditional families, rather than attempt to eradicate such families by adhering to a fictitious homogenous family model. . . .

Problem

L.M.K.O. is born to Denise and her partner Valerie in Minneapolis. The women chose a known donor, Mark, for medical reasons. Mark signs a donor agreement, waiving parental rights, but later regrets it. So all parties sign an agreement promising him a "significant relationship" with the child. After the birth, Valerie legally adopts the child. At Mark's request, the court grants him parental rights. Simultaneously, the court voids Valerie's adoption on the ground of fraud (asserting she misled the court about the father's existence).

Denise and Valerie separate, and Denise moves with L.M.K.O to Michigan. The court awards visitation rights to both Valerie and Mark. All three have a voice in decisions regarding education, religion, and health. The child visits Valerie and Mark in Minneapolis every other month; they visit her in the off months. When Valerie and Mark complain that the distance is straining their relationship, the court orders Denise to return to Minneapolis as a condition of her retaining sole custody. The three bicker constantly, even about issues such as a flu shot.

Denise now contends that the arrangement is unworkable. "There is neither a legal nor a sociological way to have three parents," she protests. Minn. Stat. §257.022(2)(b) (1998 & Supp. 2001) provides for "reasonable visitation" to persons who have lived in the child's household for two or more years, if the court finds that (1) visitation rights would be in the best interests of the child, (2) the petitioner and child had established emotional ties creating a parent and child relationship, and (3) visitation rights would not interfere with the relationship between the custodial parent and the child. How should the court rule on custody and visitation? See LaChapelle v. Mitten, 607 N.W.2d 151 (Minn. Ct. App. 2000).

See generally Fred Bernstein, This Child Does Have Two Mothers . . . and a Sperm Donor with Visitation, 22 N.Y.U. Rev. L. & Soc. Change (1996); Nancy D. Polikoff, Breaking the Link Between Biology and Parental Rights in Planned Lesbian Families: When Semen Donors are Not Fathers, 2 Georgetown J. Gender & L. 57 (2000). For issues of second parent adoptions and sperm donors' rights, see Chapter IX, section E.

4. The Role of Special Participants

a. The Child's Preference

■ MCMILLEN v. MCMILLEN
602 A.2d 845 (Pa. 1992)

LARSEN, Justice.

Appellant Vaughn S. McMillen (father) appeals from an order of the Superior Court vacating the July 22, 1988 child custody order in his favor and reinstating the order of July 31, 1987, which continued primary custody in appellee Carolyn F. Shemo, formerly Carolyn F. McMillen (mother). We reverse.

[The] parties were married on May 2, 1975 and . . . their son Emmett was born on September 30, 1977. The parties were subsequently divorced in . . . Wyoming on September 25, 1981. At the time of the divorce, the Wyoming court awarded primary custody of Emmett to the mother, subject only to the reasonable visitation of the father.

In March of 1982, the father instituted an action in the Court of Common Pleas of Indiana County, Pennsylvania, seeking partial custody of Emmett. On April 27, 1982, the court awarded general custody of Emmett to the mother with the right of visitation in the father. The court limited the father's visitation to alternating weekends and holidays, one day every other week and two weeks during the summer.

Over the next six years, the father sought modification of the custody order four times and the mother one time. Each time, the Court of Common Pleas significantly expanded the father's visitation rights. From 1986 on, Emmett repeatedly and steadfastly expressed his preference to live with his father. Finally, on July 22, 1988, the Court of Common Pleas awarded general custody of Emmett to the father. . . .

On appeal, the Superior Court vacated the July 22, 1988 custody order and reinstated the previous order of July 31, 1987. In doing so, the Superior Court determined that: 1) the record failed to present any circumstances warranting a change in custody; and 2) the child's best interests would not be served by changing custody merely because the child wished it. . . .

The father argues that the Superior Court, in determining Emmett's best interests, usurped the function of the trial court by ignoring the trial court's factual findings and also failed to give proper weight to Emmett's steadfast desire to live with his father. [A]n appellate court is empowered to determine whether the trial court's incontrovertible factual findings support its factual conclusions, but it may not interfere with those conclusions unless they are unreasonable in view of the trial court's factual findings; and thus, represent a gross abuse of discretion. Having reviewed the previous custody orders in this case, the trial court concluded that both the home of the mother and that of the father were equally acceptable. The trial court, therefore, was forced to look at other factors in making its decision. The only testimony taken at the most recent custody hearing was that of the child, Emmett, who was then almost 11 years old. Emmett testified that he preferred to live with his father.

Although the express wishes of a child are not controlling in custody decisions, such wishes do constitute an important factor that must be carefully considered in determining the child's best interest. The child's preference must be based on good reasons, and the child's maturity and intelligence must be considered. The weight to be given a child's testimony as to his preference can best be determined by the judge before whom the child appears.

Our review of the record shows that Emmett's preference to live with his father is supported by more than sufficient good reasons. Emmett testified that his stepfather frightens, upsets and threatens him, and his mother does nothing to prevent this mistreatment. He testified that he does not get along with either his mother or his stepfather, and that he gets along well with his stepmother. His testimony also revealed that his mother and stepfather leave him alone after school and that, even though his father and stepmother work, he is never left alone when he is at his father's home for the summer. Emmett also stated that his mother interferes with his sporting and farming activities and refuses even to watch him play ball. Thus, we find that Emmett's steadfast wish to live with his father was properly considered, and we find no abuse of discretion in the amount of weight afforded that preference.

Nor do we find an abuse of discretion in the trial court's conclusion that Emmett's best interests would be served more appropriately by placing him in his father's custody. The record supports the trial court's finding that both households were equally suitable. This being so, Emmett's expressed preference to live with his father could not but tip the evidentiary scale in favor of his father. Thus, the trial court's conclusion that it would be in Emmett's best interest to modify the prior custody order by transferring primary custody from the mother to the father is supported by the record, and we find no gross abuse of discretion by the trial court in awarding primary custody to the father.

Notes and Questions

1. *Approaches.* Is it appropriate to consider a child's custodial preference? If so, when? Most states have statutes that call for consideration of the child's wishes,

including (a) those modeled after the Uniform Marriage and Divorce Act, which requires consideration of the child's wishes; (b) those that require consideration of the child's preference after a preliminary finding of maturity; (c) those that require deference to the child's preference for children of a specified age (12 to 14 years); and (d) those that give judges complete discretion as to whether to consider children's wishes. Kathleen Nemechek, Note, Child Preference in Custody Decisions: Where We Have Been, Where We are Now, Where We Should Go, 83 Iowa L. Rev. 437, 445-460 (1998); Randi L. Dulaney, Note, Children Should Be Seen and Heard in Florida Custody Determinations, 25 Nova L. Rev. 815, 819-822 (2001).

2. *Older child's preference*. In general, the older the child, the more likely a court will consider the child's wishes. But cf. Adams v. Adams. 691 N.W.2d 541 (Neb. Ct. App. 2005) (denying wishes of 16-year-old girl to live with her noncustodial mother). How old must the child be? A few states establish a fixed age. Dulaney, supra, at 821-822 (pointing out that statutorily-designated ages range from age 10 in Texas to age 16 in Maryland). Most often, states rely on judicial discretion (sometimes after preliminary findings of maturity or reasoning ability). Compare Thorlaksen v. Thorlaksen, 453 N.W.2d 770 (N.D. 1990) (considering desire of 9- and 11-year-old girls to remain with mother and denying father's motion for modification), with In re Marriage of D.M.B. and R.L.B., 798 S.W.2d 399, 403 (Tex. App. 1990) (affirming exclusion of testimony of eight-year-old girl absent a preliminary finding of maturity).

3. *Empirical research*. Empirical research sheds light on judicial attitudes toward consideration of children's custodial preferences. One study of state court judges (n=48) reports that 80 percent consider the preferences of teenagers age 13 and older to be very or extremely significant; 40 percent give the same weight to the views of children aged 11-13 years. Nonetheless, judges differ considerably in their consideration of preschoolers' preferences: 50 percent believe that the preferences of children aged 3-5 and aged 6-10 were possibly significant, but more than a third responded that they gave no significance to the views of children in those two categories respectively. Most judges agree, however, in terms of according no significance to the preferences of very young children (from infancy to age two). Barbara A. Atwood, The Child's Voice in Custody Litigation: An Empirical Survey and Suggestions for Reform, 45 Ariz. L. Rev. 629, 634-635 (2003).

4. *ALI*. The ALI recommends that courts should depart from a policy of deference to the primary caretaker to accommodate the preference of those children who have attained a specified age (suggesting 11 to 14 years as possible ages for a uniform rule). More weight should be given to the preferences of older children. ALI Principles §2.08, cmt. f (2002). See also Nemechek, supra, at 467 (concluding, based on a study of developmental theory, that statutes should require that judges allow children age 12 and older to make custody decisions). What do you think of these recommendations?

5. *Reasons*. Should the child's reason influence whether the court considers the child's wishes? For example, should a child's testimony be given *more* weight in cases of suspected substance abuse or physical violence? See In re Marriage of Sisson, 665 N.W.2d 441 (Iowa Ct. App. 2003) (holding that evidence supported custody modification in case of physical abuse, despite son's wishes to the contrary). Or if the custodial parent is relocating and the child wants to remain with the noncustodial parent? See Goodhand v. Kildoo, 560 S.W.2d 463 (Va. Ct. App. 2002) (holding that trial court did not ignore child's preference to remain in

state in making best-interest determination). Should the child's testimony be given *less* weight if the court determines that one parent has purposely alienated the child from the other parent? See, e.g., Whiteley v. Leonard, 772 N.Y.S.2d 620 (App. Div. 2004) (after finding a pattern of parental alienation, trial court appropriately discounted child's preference).

6. *Parental unfitness.* Children's preferences are more likely to be considered when both parents are fit (as in *McMillen*) or marginally fit. In such cases, the child's preference may serve as a tie-breaker. Children's preferences may be overridden if the court finds the preferred parent unfit. See, e.g., J.D.V. v. R.M.T., 2004 WL 3245784 (Del. Fam. Ct. 2004) (holding that child's wishes were not relevant when father had criminal record for sexual abuse).

7. *Procedure.* What constitutional concerns are implicated by consideration of a child's custodial preference?

a. *Who?* If it is appropriate to take into account a child's preference, who should do so? The judge? The child's representative? A parent's attorney? A mental health professional?

b. *Where?* By what procedure should the child's preference be taken into account? Should the child testify in open court? Should other witnesses testify in open court about the child's preference? If the parents disagree about whether the child should testify in open court, how should the judge rule? See In re Allen, 97 P.3d 1060 (Kan. Ct. App. 2004) (holding that trial court did not abuse its discretion by refusing mother's request that child be called as a witness).

Should a child discuss his or her custodial preference with a judge in camera (in a private interview)? One study of state court judges reveals judges' reluctance to conduct in camera interviews of children: one-fourth of the respondents report that they never conduct such interviews, and less than one-fifth conduct such interviews on a regular basis. Atwood, supra, at 636. What do you think explains judges' reluctance?

c. *How?* Should counsel (whose?) be present at in camera interviews? See Barrett v. Wright, 897 So. 2d 398 (Ala. Civ. App. 2004) (holding unconstitutional an in camera interview, absent counsel or waiver of presence of counsel). What should be the role of counsel at such interviews? See, e.g., Mo. Rev. Stat. §452.385 (2003) (permitting counsel to participate and to be present). If one parent objects to an in camera interview, can the interview take place? See Kes v. Cat, 107 P.3d 779 (Wyo. 2005) (holding that if one or both parents object(s) to an in camera interview, the court should fashion an alternative procedure). Should these private interviews be recorded? Compare Molloy v. Molloy, 643 N.W.2d 574 (Mich. 2002) (vacating court of appeals decision requiring recording of all future in camera child custody interviews), with Couch v. Couch, 146 S.W.3d (Ky. 2004) (holding that if a trial court relies on a child's statements during an in camera interview, the court must record and disclose the contents of the interview). See also UMDA §404(a), 9A U.L.A. at 380 (providing that the court may interview the child in chambers to ascertain the child's wishes, may permit counsel to be present, and shall record the interview). Should private interviews be limited to a determination of the child's preference or encompass any matter relevant to the custody decision? See Thompson v. Thompson, 683 N.W.2d 250 (Mich. Ct. App. 2004) (holding that trial court did not abuse its discretion by conducting an in camera interview that went beyond a reasonable inquiry into child's parental preference).

Problem

Andrea is the 15-year-old daughter of Jean and David. Andrea's parents have had a marriage marked by a history of domestic violence including severe physical injuries, police intervention, and orders of protection. After a recent physical altercation, Jean commences divorce proceedings and petitions for custody. The father cross-petitions for custody. In an in camera interview, Andrea denies the existence of violence in her parents' marriage and expresses a clear preference for living with her father. Aside from her father's conduct toward her mother, David appears to be a model parent who is involved in Andrea's school work and extracurricular activities and who provides her with many material benefits (television set, clothing, a horse, a trip to Europe). He calls her his "princess," his "best girl." In contrast, Andrea claims that her mother is not significantly involved in her school work or her extracurricular activities and that she does not enjoy her mother's company or their relationship. What result? Wissink v. Wissink, 749 N.Y.S.2d 550 (App. Div. 2002).

b. Representation for the Child

■ **LEARY v. LEARY**
627 A.2d 30 (Md. Ct. Spec. App. 1993)

BELL, Judge.

[Appellant Richard Leary contends that the trial court erred in awarding his ex-wife sole legal custody by failing to instruct the children's counsel as to her duties. He complains that due process requires that the parties know precisely the role of the child's representative.]

When the court appoints an attorney to be a guardian ad litem for a child, the attorney's duty is to make a determination and recommendation after pinpointing what is in the best interests of the child. The attorney who assumes the traditional guardian ad litem role has a responsibility primarily to the court and therefore has absolute immunity for "judicial functions," which include testifying and making reports and recommendations. This more traditional role is defined by the court and the attorney looks to the court for direction and remuneration. . . .

A dichotomy exists between the attorney as guardian and the attorney as advocate, and the lines become very easily blurred. An attorney who has been appointed by the court has to be ever mindful of the Rules of Professional Conduct. In particular, an attorney may run afoul of the dictates of Rule 1.14, which sets forth the guidelines for representation of a client under a disability.[5] The Comment that accompanies Rule 1.14 states in part:

> The normal client-lawyer relationship is based on the assumption that the client, when properly advised and assisted, is capable of making decisions about important matters. When the client is a minor or suffers from a mental disorder or disability,

---

5. Another Rule that must be considered is Rule 1.2, Scope of Representation, which provides: "(a) A lawyer shall abide by a client's decisions concerning the objectives of representation [and] when appropriate, shall consult with the client as to the means by which they are to be pursued. . . ."

however, maintaining the ordinary client-lawyer relationship may not be possible in all respects. In particular, an incapacitated person may have no power to make legally binding decisions. Nevertheless, a client lacking legal competence often has the ability to understand, deliberate upon, and reach conclusions about matters affecting the client's own well-being. Furthermore, to an increasing extent the law recognizes intermediate degrees of competence. For example, children as young as five or six years of age, and certainly those of ten or twelve, are regarded as having opinions that are entitled to weight in legal proceedings concerning their custody.

Perhaps the best example, for purposes of illustration, is when the child expresses an interest in living with one parent, yet the attorney believes that this would not be in the child's "best interests." Does the attorney vigorously advocate the child's position as required by the Rules, or does the attorney make the decision as to what is best for the child and present that to the court? . . .

There appears to be two schools of thought in answering that question: "One school holds that the child's preference is but one fact to be found, while the other maintains that without full advocacy of the preference there would be little reason to have a child's representative at all." Note, Lawyering for the Child: Principles of Representation in Custody and Visitation Disputes Arising from Divorce, 87 Yale L.J. 1126, 1141 (1978). An intermediate view suggests that there should be a "continuum of roles rather than the extremes of advocate and factfinder." Id. at 1141.

In a study of 18 Connecticut attorneys who had received appointments as counsel for children in divorce-related disputes, the researchers observed that some of the attorneys would characterize their role as either advocate or factfinder, yet they would discuss responsibilities that were inconsistent with the characterization. Those attorneys who stated that they served an advocate's role explained that this meant representing the child the way that they would an adult client. These same "advocates," however, also stated that there were instances in which they felt compelled to serve child-protective functions, which included counselling the parents, attending to the child's emotional needs during the litigation, and, in one extreme instance, making a recommendation that was the direct opposite of what the child/client wanted. [Id.]

Recognizing that there is a growing need to define more clearly an attorney's role in custody disputes, the American Bar Association is looking toward drafting standards. Also the bar associations in various states, such as Connecticut, are in the process of drafting their own individual guidelines. . . .

There has been little discussion in Maryland of the role an attorney should play in custody cases. In [Levitt v. Levitt, 556 A.2d 1162 (Md. Ct. Spec. App. 1989)], we established the importance of child counsel in contested custody matters, sending the trial courts a message on "what child counsel's role should be." We do not retreat from that perspective and encourage trial judges to tell their appointed attorneys what [role] they expect. . . .

In the instant case, the trial judge did not enter an order stating the purpose for the appointment. While it would have been preferable for him to have done so, we do not conclude that the omission in this case was fatal. . . .

[Mr. Leary] complains that "Ms. Coates [appointed counsel for the children] clearly perceived her role to be that of 'mouthpiece,' not guardian ad litem or investigator"; her purpose, as she perceived it according to him, was "to simply convey to the Court what the desire of the nine and thirteen year-old boys were. . . ." We do not agree.

[Ms. Coates] described two very intelligent young boys who were outgoing, doing well in school, and able to express their preferences. She was not acting strictly as an advocate of their position, but as a conveyer of their preferences, which she concluded were not improperly motivated. In other words, the circumstances forced her to take the middle ground between advocacy and fact finding.

Ms. Coates investigated what the trial judge wanted to know — namely, the children's preferences — but it was the trial judge, not Ms. Coates, who concluded that joint custody was not to be. In fact, although her recommendations were struck, Ms. Coates concluded that joint custody would be appropriate. We fail to see how the lack of articulated directions by the trial judge, even if preserved, hurt Mr. Leary. . . .

Notes and Questions

1. *Background*. The debate over mandatory representation for children in custody and visitation disputes first surfaced in the 1960s and 1970s. The debate was sparked by the rising divorce rate, concerns about the effects of divorce on children, and recognition of the child's right to counsel in the delinquency context (In re Gault, 387 U.S. 1 (1967)). Should counsel for the child in contested disputes be mandatory? Or at the parents' discretion? See Joseph Goldstein et al., Before the Best Interests of the Child 119 (1979) (so arguing). Does the child have a due process right to counsel in custody decisionmaking?

2. *Discretionary*. Despite considerable support by commentators and practitioners for mandatory counsel, appointment of the child's representative in custody disputes generally remains in the court's discretion. Only two states mandate representation for child in contested custody cases. Wisconsin enacted the first statute requiring guardians ad litem in custody disputes in 1971; New Hampshire became the second state in 1979. See Richard Ducote, Guardians Ad Litem in Private Custody Litigation: The Case for Abolition, 3 Loy. J. Pub. Int. L. 106, 110 (2002). The ABA Family Law Section unsuccessfully proposed an amendment to UMDA in 1972 requiring an attorney for a child in contested custody proceedings. Id.

3. *Special custody contexts*. Some jurisdictions provide for representation in custody cases involving allegations of abuse or neglect. Some courts even find that it is an abuse of discretion to fail to appoint a guardian ad litem in such cases. See, e.g., G.S. v. T.S., 582 A.2d 467 (Conn. App. Ct. 1990). But cf. Schenk v. Schenk, 564 N.E.2d 973 (Ind. Ct. App. 1991). Why is representation necessary in such proceedings? See generally Mary Grams, Guardians Ad Litem and the Cycle of Domestic Violence: How the Recommendations Turn, 22 Law & Ineq. J. 105 (2004); David Peterson, Comment, Judicial Discretion Is Insufficient: Minors' Due Process Right to Participate with Counsel When Divorce Custody Disputes Involve Allegations of Child Abuse, 25 Golden Gate U.L. Rev. 513 (1995). On representation for children in cases of child abuse, see also Chapter VIII, p. 922.

4. *Factors*. When a discretionary standard governs the decision to appoint counsel for children, what factors might influence judicial discretion? See Linda Elrod,

Counsel for the Child in Custody Disputes: The Time is Now, 26 Fam. L. Q. 53, 56 (1992) (identifying the cost factor, concerns about guardian ad litem competence, and the possible redundancy of representation because the parents are represented).

5. *Models of representation*. As *Leary* reveals, considerable debate exists about the appropriate role of the child's representative and the scope of that representation. Although courts and commentators characterize the possible roles differently, several models exist: (1) the court-designated investigator who investigates and makes recommendations to the court, (2) the attorney who represents the child's wishes, (3) the advocate for the "best interests" of the children, (4) the faciltator/mediator, and (5) some combination of the above. Raven C. Lidman & Betsy R. Hollingsworth, The Guardian Ad Litem in Child Custody Cases: The Contours of Our Judicial System Stretched Beyond Recognition, 6 Geo. Mason L. Rev. 255, 256-257 (1998). What roles are most/least invasive of family privacy? If the representative serves as an advocate, should the representative advocate the child's wishes regardless of what the advocate believes is in the child's interests? Should the attorney ever advocate an outcome that conflicts with the client's wishes? If the representative ascertains the child's best interests, does this role usurp the authority of the judge? Is it redundant to represent a position already represented? Does the investigator-neutral factfinder's role conflict with the duty to represent a client zealously (Model Code of Professional Responsibility EC 7-1)? Where does the role of "mouthpiece" (Mr. Leary's term) fit in the continuum? What difficulties does it raise?

Should the representative's role change based on the type of proceeding (e.g., abuse, delinquency, custody)? Based on the child's age or abilities? See Annette R. Appell, Decontextualizing the Child Client: The Efficacy of the Attorney-Client Model for Very Young Children, 64 Fordham L. Rev. 1955 (1996). Professor Martin Guggenheim proposes a rule that an attorney should advocate the child's wishes if the child is at least seven years old. Martin Guggenheim, The Right to Be Represented But Not Heard: Reflections on Legal Representation for Children, 59 N.Y.U. L. Rev. 76, 91 (1978). What are the merits of such a proposal? See also Martin Guggenheim, What's Wrong with Children's Rights (2005) (suggesting that parents, rather than courts and lawyers, should determine what is best for children); Martin Guggenheim, Reconsidering the Need for Counsel for Children in Custody, Visitation and Child Protection Proceedings, 29 Loy. U. Chi. L.J. 299 (1998).

6. *Current state approaches*. Jurisdictions differ on the role of the child's representative. Currently, 23 jurisdictions have a guardian ad litem who generally operates as a best interests attorney; 8 jurisdictions appoint a child's attorney; the remaining 20 jurisdictions appoint either a hybrid (best interests attorney and child's attorney) or a combination of different kinds of representatives depending on the circumstances. Annette M. Gonzalez & Linda M. Rio Reichmann, Representing Children in Civil Cases Involving Domestic Violence, 39 Fam. L.Q. 197, 201-202 (2005) (different approaches in custody cases generally).

7. *Role confusion*. The study cited in *Leary* points out that some attorneys characterize their role as advocate or factfinder but then act inconsistently with those characterizations. Possible factors that might influence an attorney's perception of his or her role include: (a) the state law description, if any, of the role; (b) any

instruction given by, or exceptions of, the appointing judge; (c) the training that the guardian ad litem has received as to his or her role; (d) the age of the child and the guardian's understanding of child development, bonding and attachment, and permanency planning issues. Howard A. Davidson, The Child's Right to Be Heard and Represented in Judicial Proceedings, 18 Pepp. L. Rev. 255, 263 (1991). See also Mary E. Hazlewood, Comment, The New Texas Ad Litem Statute: Is It Really Protecting the Best Interests of Minor Children?, 35 St. Mary's L.J. 1035, 1062-1067 (2004) (analyzing how courts decide which type of advocate to appoint); Diane Somberg, Comment, Defining the Role of Law Guardian in New York State by Statute, Standards and Case Law, 19 Touro L. Rev. 529, 529 (2003) (explaining the confusion caused by the combination of roles to appointed counsel, other attorneys, and even judges).

8. *Attorney as representative?* Few jurisdictions require that the child's representative be an attorney. Lidman & Hollingsworth, supra, at 263. Should a court-appointed representative be an attorney? Guardians ad litem may come from other professions (e.g., social work). What problems ensue from the participation of nonattorney guardians? For example, communications between a child and a nonattorney guardian ad litem are not necessarily privileged. Confidentiality problems may exist even if the court appoints an attorney if the court then denominates the attorney to serve in the role of guardian ad litem. See Bruce A. Green, Lawyers as Nonlawyers in Child-Custody and Visitation Cases: Questions from the "Legal Ethics" Perspective, 73 Ind. L.J. 665 (1998).

9. *Law reform.* Beginning in 2001, several states recommended sweeping changes in the roles of guardians ad litem in custody cases. For example, an Ohio task force recommended statewide standards for GALs regarding qualifications, fees, training, and scope of responsibilities. A Minnesota task force proposed changes in role definition, training, caseload size, supervision, and accountability. Ducote, supra, at 112-116. The primary criticisms include: the GAL role is not subject to consistent definitions, the benefits of GALs are doubtful, GALs undermine fact finding by usurping the judicial role and depriving parents of due process, GALs undermine parental authority and privacy, GALs entail significant costs, GALs are ineffectual in cases of domestic violence, and GALs are unaccountable for their decisions. Id. at 116.

10. *ABA Standards of Practice.* In response to such criticisms, the ABA Section of Family Law formulated Standards of Practice for Lawyers Representing Children in Custody Cases which were approved in August 2003. The ABA Standards abolish the name "guardian ad litem" and provide instead for two types of lawyers for children, each of whom makes evidence-based legal arguments: the Child's Attorney who provides independent legal representation in a traditional attorney-client relationship, and the Best Interests attorney who independently investigates, assesses, and advocates the child's best interests *as a lawyer*. See Standard II(B) ("Definitions" and Cmt.). The Commentary specifies that lawyers appointed in either capacity should not "play any other role in the case, and should not testify, file a report, or make recommendations." See Standard III(B) ("Lawyer's Roles"). The Standards also address the problem of role confusion by providing that a lawyer should accept an appointment only with a full understanding of the functions to be performed. "If the appointed lawyer considers parts of the appointment order confusing or incompatible with his or her ethical duties, the lawyer should (1) decline the appointment, or (2) inform the court of the conflict and ask the

court to clarify or change the terms of the order, or (3) both." See Standards III(A) ("Accepting the Appointment").

11. *AAML Standards.* Prior to the ABA's adoption of Standards, the American Academy of Matrimonial Lawyers (AAML) in 1995 adopted standards of practice for attorneys and guardians ad litem in custody or visitation disputes. These Standards assume that representatives should participate only in cases in which parents request appointment or the court finds appointment necessary. AAML, Representing Children: Standards for Attorneys and Guardians Ad Litem in Custody or Visitation Proceedings, Standard 1.1 & Cmt. (1995) (reprinted at 13 J. Am. Acad. Matrimonial Law. 1, 2-4 (1995)). The Standards suggest that the court should specify in writing the tasks of the representative. Standard 1.3 & Cmt. Further, the Standards address the attorney's role when the court appoints a lawyer as the child's representative, suggesting that the lawyer-representative should advocate the child's wishes for a child who is "unimpaired" (Standards 2.1-2.2). Children under age 12 are rebuttably presumed to be "impaired" (Standard 2.2). The "impaired/unimpaired" distinction parallels that of the ABA Model Rules of Professional Conduct.

c. Role of Experts

■ IN RE REBECCA B.
611 N.Y.S.2d 831 (App. Div.), motion for leave to appeal
denied, *645 N.E.2d 1217 (N.Y. 1994)*

MEMORANDUM DECISION

[In 1986, after Renee B. and Michael B. had been married for five years, Renee filed for divorce and sole custody of their daughter Rebecca. The Family Court granted both motions. In 1992, upon discovering that Michael was sleeping in the same bed as Rebecca, Renee petitioned to eliminate Michael's overnight visitation and to require supervised visitation. Michael cross-petitioned for sole custody. The Family Court denied Michael's cross-petition and affirmed the award of sole custody to the mother. The father appealed.]

[The Family Court] Order, dated May 8, 1992, which, inter alia, denied the motion of appellant father for a transfer of the sole legal custody of his daughter from her mother, to him, [is] unanimously modified on the law and the facts, and in the exercise of discretion, to the extent of granting the transfer of the sole legal custody to appellant, with liberal visitation rights to respondent mother, and otherwise, insofar as consistent with such transfer of sole legal custody to appellant, in all respects [is] otherwise affirmed, without costs or disbursements. It is ordered that any further proceedings in the matter in the Family Court be held before another judge.

The Clinical Director of the Family Court's Mental Health Service was qualified to testify as an expert in clinical psychology. He had met with the child on three occasions for a total of three hours and with her and each parent for about forty minutes. He also had met with each parent separately for about seven hours. He concluded that the child's best interests required the transfer of custody to appellant with liberal visitation for the mother noting that appellant was a much less detrimental influence on the child than was the mother, that he was less likely to cause long-term harm to her than was the mother, that the child perceived him as more loving than her mother, and that she had a more profound bond with him. The child made it clear repeatedly to the Clinical Director that she would prefer to live with her father; the mother's spanking, slapping, and locking of the child in her room was difficult for the child to comprehend.

Another psychiatrist, also recommended a change in custody, for the "main reason" that the mother tried so to exclude appellant from the child's life; he believed that appellant as the custodial parent would give better access to the noncustodial parent. From age seven to eight the child had slept with her father on overnight visits, but there had been no suggestion of any improper action by appellant and the practice had ceased. The psychiatrist had found nothing "intrinsically detrimental" in the arrangement. A supervising social worker employed by the Legal Aid Society, also recommended that custody be transferred to appellant.

A psychiatrist retained by the mother testified that custody should be continued with the mother. However, he had spoken only with the mother and with people to whom he was referred by the mother and not to the child or appellant.

The law guardian, believing that appellant was more likely to foster the noncustodial parent's relationship, concluded that the transfer of custody to him was in the best interest of the child.

The trial court denied appellant's motion to transfer custody to him, terming the testimony of the Clinical Director, the first mentioned psychiatrist and the Social Worker not credible. They were, however, the only experts making a recommendation as to custody who had spoken to all three family members, but the trial court repeatedly described their testimony as "flawed." By discounting the testimony of these three witnesses, the trial court essentially left itself without expert testimony on the child's preferences and the quality of her relationships with her parents. Since the mother's psychiatrist had not interviewed the child or appellant, moreover, little weight should be accorded to his recommendation that custody be awarded to the mother. . . .

A determination had been made by Family Court in 1987 that the mother should have custody. The burden was thus on appellant to demonstrate a substantial change of circumstances to justify a change in custody. He did so in 1991 by showing the preference of the child — then seven years of age — to live with him, by showing the bond which had grown between them, by showing petitioner's rather punitive disciplining of the child, which would over time have a deleterious effect on the child, and especially by his showing of petitioner's efforts to exclude him from the child's life.

We must respect the advantage of the trial judge in observing the witnesses, but the authority of this court in matters of custody is as broad as that of the trial court. It always comes down, however, to the best interests of the child and the ability of the parents "to provide for the child's emotional and intellectual development, the quality of the home environment and the parental guidance provided." The psychiatrist, testifying on behalf of petitioner, said of her: "She is a somewhat temperamental lady who has a temper, and it would be better if she kept her mouth shut more and didn't get into fights with her former husband and her child, but that's normal within the context of this kind of situation." This is not a severe indictment of a person, but it does support other testimony that petitioner tends to be short-tempered and punitive with her daughter and the inference therefrom that the child is being harmed. There has been no showing, on the other hand, that appellant despite his social isolation, tends to be other than helpful, patient, and constructive in his relationship with his daughter.

It has been shown that petitioner attempts to exclude appellant from the child's life. The Clinical Director and the psychiatrist who met with all concerned believe that, if awarded custody, she will continue to do so. Such acts are "so inconsistent with the best interests of the children as to, per se, raise a strong probability that the mother is unfit to act as custodial parent" (Entwistle v. Entwistle, 402 N.Y.S.2d 213, *appeal dismissed,* 44 N.Y.2d 851).

This court finds the testimony of those experts favoring custody of the child to appellant convincing. . . . The trial court's custody award lacked a sound and substantial basis in the record and should not be allowed to stand.

Notes and Questions

1. *Different roles.* Mental health experts play different roles in custody determinations. Frequently, mental health professionals conduct custody evaluations by assessing a parent's strengths and weaknesses, and the children's functioning. They gather data from many different sources (e.g., schools, medical personnel, social service agencies, etc.) and also conduct observations of, and interviews with, the parties. Some evaluators provide the court with assessments of family functioning while others recommend which parent should have custody.

In addition, mental health professionals serve other roles in custody decision-making: expert witnesses educate the court on issues such as the effects of divorce, general psychological principles, or child development; therapists provide supportive therapy to individuals involved in famly court proceedings; psychological evaluators plan therapeutic interventions; mediators facilitate conflict resolution; and special masters monitor the ongoing relationship between the parties. See Janet M. Bowermaster, Legal Presumptions and the Role of Mental Health Professionals in Child Custody Proceedings, 40 Duq. L. Rev. 265, 270-274 (2002) (discussing experts' various roles). See also Marc J. Ackerman, Clinician's Guide to Child Custody Evaluations (2006). Can you identify the various roles of the professionals in *Rebecca B.*?

2. *Backgrounds.* Psychologists, psychiatrists, and social workers are the professionals who most frequently serve in a custody evaluation. How might their different backgrounds and training influence their evaluations? See Melvin G. Goldzband, Custody Cases and Expert Witnesses: A Manual for Attorneys xxi (1980) (noting, for example, that a psychologist, compared to a psychiatrist, "may often depend more upon the tests they perform with the participants than upon clinical or historical criteria"). Should courts limit the number of experts who can participate in a given case? Should there be one court-appointed expert or as many as the parties desire?

3. *Ethical standards.* Professionals in custody determinations must observe professional codes of ethics and standards of practice. For example, psychologists are subject to the American Psychological Association's (APA) Ethical Principles of Psychologists and Code of Conduct (for members of the APA), Specialty Guidelines for Forensic Psychologists, and Guidelines for Child Custody Evaluations in Divorce Proceedings (guidelines applicable to custody evaluators). See American

Psychological Association, Ethical Principles of Psychologists and Code of Conduct, 47 Am. Psychol. 1597 (1992); American Psychological Association, Guidelines for Child Custody Evaluations in Divorce Proceedings, 49 Am. Psychol. 677 (1994); Committee on Ethical Guidelines for Forensic Psychologists, Specialty Guidelines for Forensic Psychologists, 15 Law & Hum. Behav. 655 (1991). See also Marion Gindes, Guidelines for Child Custody Evaluations for Psychologists: An Overview and Commentary, 29 Fam. L.Q. 39 (1995).

4. *Trial court findings*. The appellate court in *Rebecca B.* reversed two prior rulings in favor of the mother (and an 8-year-long custody arrangement) on the basis that the trial judge erred by rejecting much of the expert testimony. In a lengthy opinion (Renee B. v. Michael B., No. V5272186 (N.Y. Fam. Ct. May 8, 1992)), trial judge George L. Jurow (who has a Ph.D. in psychology) explained his reasons for finding certain testimony "not credible" and "flawed":

- the father's expert's objectivity was compromised by his employment as the father's psychiatrist for four years (slip op. at 87); the expert engaged in "collusive interactions" by interviewing the daughter without the mother's knowledge or consent (id. at 88); the expert's conclusion that the mother was alienating the daughter and was responsible for communication difficulties was "factually incorrect and contradicted by other credible evidence" (id. at 89-90) (because the father's confrontations with school officials led them to ban him from the premises, and the father taped all conversations with the wife or daughter); the expert applied a gender-biased standard in recommending paternal custody based on the mother's demanding career as a corporate lawyer (id. at 91-92);
- the supervising social worker (who recommended a custody transfer to the father) adopted "uncritically and without reflection" the opinion of the father's expert without conducting a thorough evaluation (id. at 100);
- the court-appointed expert's evaluation had "important inquiry lapses," (regarding the father's lack of work history and plan to withdraw the daughter from school) (id. at 81); conflicted with that expert's own observations that the father was an "individual who is socially isolated, has no friends, is prone to continued confrontations with people, [and] is 'interpersonally retarded,' . . ." (id. at 82); and, failed to recognize that the daughter's desire to live with her father was the "product of paternal pressure or an excessive degree of overbearing influence" (id. at 83).

Do you agree with the appellate court that the trial court's award "lacked a sound and substantial basis" in the record?

5. *Parental Alienation Syndrome*. The father's expert based his opinion, in part, on evidence of the "Parental Alienation Syndrome," a term that he coined to signify a parent's conscious or subconscious attempts to alienate a client from the other parent. See Richard A. Gardner, The Parental Alienation Syndrome: A Guide for Mental Health and Legal Professionals (1992). Don't many divorcing parents exhibit varying degrees of this syndrome? Although the theory is admissible in court, it has not gained widespread acceptance by professionals. For trenchant critiques, see Carol S. Bruch, Parental Alienation Syndrome and Parental Alienation: Getting It Wrong in Child Custody Cases, 35 Fam. L.Q. 527 (2001); Janet R. Johnston, Children of Divorce Who Reject a Parent and Refuse Visitation:

Recent Research and Social Policy Implications for the Alienated Child, 38 Fam. L.Q. 757 (2005); Alayne Katz, Junk Science v. Novel Scientific Evidence: Parental Alienation Syndrome, 24 Pace L. Rev. 239 (2003); Cheri L. Wood, Note and Comment, The Parental Alienation Syndrome: A Dangerous Aura of Reliability, 27 Loy. L.A. L. Rev. 1367 (1994).

6. *Criticisms*. Are mental health professionals capable of determining custodial arrangements in the best interests of children? Psychologists Lois Weithorn and Thomas Grisso criticize the judicial tendency to allow professionals to play a dispositive role. Arguing that clinical evaluations give a false aura of reliability and convey the impression that psychologists are uniquely qualified to make such decisions, Weithorn and Grisso suggest that expert opinion often results instead from subjective biases and lifestyle preferences. Lois Weithorn & Thomas Grisso, Psychological Evaluations in Divorce Custody: Problems, Principles, and Procedures, in Psychology and Child Custody Determinations 157, 160 (Lois Weithorn ed., 1987). What biases of the mental health profession might be reflected in their recommendations? See Bowermaster, supra, at 291-292 (noting that mental health professionals show a bias toward recommending joint custody and restrictions on relocation). See also Martha Fineman, Dominant Discourse, Professional Language and Legal Change in Child Custody Decisionmaking, 101 Harv. L. Rev. 727, 760-774 (1988) (criticizing the abdication of responsibility to mental health professionals and urging a return of responsibility to the legal profession).

7. *Conflict of interest*. One expert in *Rebecca B.* was the father's treating psychiatrist. This dual role implicates a potential conflict of interest that many professionals regard as an ethical violation. Can a mental health expert who is treating one of the parties be objective? One commentator has argued:

> It would be very difficult, if not impossible, in most cases for a clinician to "set aside" the attitudes and feelings that constitute the "therapeutic orientation" that has been developed with a given individual or family in exchange for the more detached, skeptical, and objective stance that is necessary for the forensic evaluator.

Kirk Heilbrun, Child Custody Evaluation: Critically Assessing Mental Health Experts and Psychological Tests, 29 Fam. L.Q. 63, 70-71 (1995). Recall, too, the excerpt, supra, by Andrew Watson describing countertransference (the therapist's identification with the client). See also Michael R. Freedman, Evaluator Countertransference in Child Custody Evaluations, 7 Am. J. Fam. L. 143 (1993). Is the harm mitigated if the party is a *former* patient? See Heilbrun, supra, at 71 (arguing that the concerns still exist).

8. *Epilogue*. The custody battle cost Renee B. approximately $340,000; the stress resulted in her losing her job.[15] She later filed a motion for leave to appeal, which the New York Court of Appeals denied. 645 N.E.2d 1217 (N.Y. 1994). Subsequently, her husband attempted to hold her in contempt for failure to pay child support. Having difficulty complying with service of process, he decided to have the process server accompany Rebecca on her visitation. Twelve-year-old Rebecca read the legal papers and became distraught at the threat of imprisonment of her mother. On her own initiative, Rebecca contacted her court-appointed guardian

---

[15]. Lisa Genasci, Working Mothers at Risk in Custody Disputes; Divorce: Scholars Say Courts Often Hold Women to Higher Parenting Standards than Their Ex-Spouses, L.A. Times, Mar. 5, 1995, at A8.

and refused to return to her father. In subsequent sessions with her social worker, she described her life with her father as verging on parental abuse: her father prohibited her from calling her mother and required her to disclose all correspondence to prevent her from sending letters to her mother.

In July 1995, Rebecca and her guardian petitioned for a change of custody. The trial court appointed a new expert, awarded the mother temporary custody, and granted the father supervised visitation. On appeal, the temporary award of custody to Renee B. was upheld. The father subsequently moved out of the area. He has had no further contact with the daughter, not even telephone calls on her birthday. Telephone interview with Bernard H. Clair, Attorney for Renee B.; (Clair, Greifer LLP, 555 Madison Avenue, 9th Floor, New York City), Aug. 19, 1997 and June 10, 2006.

5. Modification

a. Standard

The paramount concern with child welfare gives courts continuing power to modify custody orders. The standard for modification is higher than for initial awards of custody in order to ensure stability for the child. The emphasis on stability in child placement decisionmaking is a central tenet of the work by Professors Goldstein, Freud, and Solnit, who strongly oppose alteration in child placement based on the child's need for continuity of care. See Joseph Goldstein et al., Beyond the Best Interests of the Child 37 (1973). Cf. John Batt, Child Custody Disputes and the Beyond the Best Interests Paradigm: A Contemporary Assessment of the Goldstein/Freud/Solnit Position and the Group's Painter v. Bannister Jurisprudence, 16 Nova L. Rev. 621, 643 (1992) (arguing that change is a factor of life and that children are resilient).

Different standards. According to the prevailing standard, the plaintiff has the burden of showing by a preponderance of the evidence that *conditions since the dissolution decree have so materially and substantially changed that the children's best interests require a change of custody.* A few states have adopted a more liberal requirement that modification serve the best interests of the child (regardless of any change in circumstances). Several states have more stringent rules, influenced by UMDA §409(b), 9A U.L.A. 439 (1998), requiring endangerment for nonconsensual changes. Absent serious endangerment, UMDA §409(a) provides for a two-year waiting period following the initial decree.

Do liberal modification standards threaten the constitutionally-based privacy of the postdivorce family unit? See Joan G. Wexler, Rethinking the Modification of Child Custody Decrees, 94 Yale L.J. 757, 803-818 (1985) (so suggesting). Relying on social science evidence that the custodial parent and child require time for postdivorce adjustment, Wexler supports a type of "serious endangerment" standard, under which the noncustodial parent must prove that modification would outweigh any disruption caused by the change. Id. at 783. Further, she argues for a presumption against modification for children under three years of age. Id.

Joint custody. Joint custody awards also may be changed if custody arrangements prove unsuccessful or if circumstances change. Some states ease the traditional rule when sole custody is modified to joint, requiring only that the change to joint custody be in the best interests of the child. See, e.g., Alaska Stat. §25.20.110 (Michie 2004); Mont. Code Ann. §40-4-219 (2003). See also Rehfeld v. Roth, 855 So. 2d 791 (Ala. Civ. App. 2004) (applying best-interests standard when parents have nearly equal time).

ALI. The ALI recommends modification upon a showing of (1) a substantial change in the circumstances (relating to the child or one or both parents) on which the parenting plan was based that makes modification necessary to the child's welfare or (2) harm to the child. ALI Principles §2.15(1) & (2) (2002). Note that the ALI standard "necessary to the child's welfare" is more strict than that in many state approaches. Changed circumstances must be based on facts "that were not known or have arisen since the entry of the prior order and were not anticipated." §2.15(1). Modification based on a more liberal standard is available for consensual changes, changes in the existing arrangements without objection by the parent opposing the modification, minor modifications to the parenting plan, or the attainment of a specified age for a child who expresses a preference for a custodial change. Id., cmt. a. None of the following justifies modification, absent a showing of harm: a parent's loss of income or employment, remarriage or cohabitation, or use of day care. §2.15(3).

In response to the concern that standards facilitating custody modification do not serve the child's interests, one commentator urges that lawyers encourage clients "to try to redraft their parenting plan through mediation, if possible, and discourage clients with minor complaints from continually attempting to relitigate custody." Linda D. Elrod, When Should Custody Orders Be Modified?: Flexibility versus Stability, 26 Fam. Advoc. 40, 41 (2004). Do you agree?

b. Relocation

■ CIESLUK v. CIESLUK
113 P.3d 135 (Colo. 2005)

Justice RICE delivered the Opinion of the Court.

. . . Mother and Father met and married in Nebraska in 1995. One child, Connor, was born to them on February 27, 1997. In September 2002, the parties amicably divorced. Pursuant to the separation agreement incorporated into the decree of dissolution, Mother is the primary residential parent for school residency and other legal residential requirements; Father has parenting time on two weekends and two weekday evenings per month. Mother and Father have joint parental responsibility and decision-making authority.

In February 2003, Mother, a Sprint employee for seven years, was laid off as a result of Sprint's workforce reduction in Colorado. She sought alternative employment in Colorado and in Arizona, where her father, brother, sister-in-law, and nephew reside. Though she was unable to find a comparable job in Colorado, Sprint interviewed her for a position in Arizona. However, Sprint refused to extend her an offer until she committed to relocating to Arizona.

Consequently, in March 2003, Mother filed a motion to modify parenting time pursuant to [Colo. Rev. Stat. §14-10-129] to allow her to relocate. . . . Father opposed the motion and moved for the appointment of a special advocate to determine Connor's best interests. [The special advocate concluded that the father's presence in the child's life would be greatly reduced as a result of the relocation and recommended, therefore, that it was in Connor's best interests to stay in close proximity to both Mother and Father. The trial court denied the mother's motion for modification, stating that "parenthood results in some sacrifice and it is better off for parents to remain in close proximity."] In making this determination, the trial court gave substantial weight to the impact of the move on Connor's relationship with Father and to Mother's failure to establish how the move would "enhance" Connor. Mother appealed.

We first address whether the [test] articulated in [In re Marriage of Francis, 919 P.2d 776 (Colo. 1996)], remains viable in light of the General Assembly's recent amendments to section 14-10-129. [*Francis* established a presumption in favor of the custodial parent. The noncustodial parent could overcome the presumption by establishing by a preponderance of evidence that the negative impact of the move cumulatively outweighed the advantages of remaining with the primary caregiver. In response to dissatisfaction with *Francis*, the General Assembly amended section 14-10-129, to require a court to consider not only the normal best-interest factors, but nine special factors, including: reasons why the party wishes to relocate; reasons why the opposing party is objecting; the history and quality of each party's relationship with the child; the educational opportunities for the child at each location; the presence or absence of extended family at each location; any advantages of the child remaining with the primary caregiver; the anticipated impact of the move on the child; whether the court will be able to fashion a new reasonable parenting time schedule; and any other relevant factors bearing on the best interests of the child.]

Here, the General Assembly's intent to eliminate the *Francis* presumption is readily apparent on the face of the statute. [T]his reading of the statute is equally consistent with the legislative history of the statute, which indicates that legislators proposed the amendments in an effort to eliminate the *Francis* test. See Feb. 12 Hearing (statements of Senator Gordon, Beth Henson, Bill Austin, and Frances Fontana). For example, Senator Gordon, Chairman of the Senate Judiciary Committee and the bill's sponsor, opined that the *Francis* standard was simply too difficult for non-custodial parents to meet. . . .

[W]e turn next to Mother's alternative argument, namely that section 14-10-129, absent a presumption in favor of allowing her to move, discourages her from relocating, and unconstitutionally infringes upon her right to travel. It is well established that a citizen has the right to travel between states. See, e.g., Shapiro v. Thompson, 394 U.S. 618, 629-31 (1969). This right encompasses the right to "migrate, resettle, find a new job, and start a new life." Id. at 629. "[I]t makes no difference that the parent who wishes to relocate is not prohibited outright from doing so; a legal rule that operates to chill the exercise of the right, absent a sufficient state interest to do so, is as impermissible as one that bans exercise of the right altogether." Jaramillo v. Jaramillo, 823 P.2d 299, 306 (N.M. 1991) (citing *Shapiro*, 394 U.S. at 631). Here, though section 14-10-129 does not prohibit outright a majority time parent from relocating, it chills the exercise of that parent's right to travel because, in seeking to relocate, that parent risks losing majority parent status with respect to the minor child.

However, a majority time parent's right to travel is not the sole constitutional right at issue in relocation cases. In addition, a minority time parent has an equally important constitutional right to the care and control of the child [citing *inter alia* Troxel v. Granville.] Though consideration of the parents' competing constitutional interests is important in relocation cases, the conflict is not simply between the parents' needs and desires. Rather, the issue in relocation cases is the extent to which the parents' needs and desires are intertwined with the child's best interests. [Although] most courts that have considered this question have acknowledged that the right to travel is implicated when a child's majority time parent seeks to remove the child from the state, these courts cannot agree on how to balance the right to travel with the rights of the minority time parent in a best interests of the child analysis. Instead, three distinct approaches have developed. The first, Wyoming's, elevates the relocating parent's right to travel over the other competing interests. [Watt v. Watt, 971 P.2d 608 (Wyo. 1999)]. The second approach, adopted in Minnesota, eliminates the need to balance the parents' competing constitutional rights in favor of elevating the child's welfare to a compelling state interest. [LaChapelle v. Mitten, 607 N.W.2d 151 (Minn. Ct. App. 2000)]. The third approach, New Mexico's, treats all the competing interests as equal, holding that both parents' constitutional interests, as well as the best interests of the child, will be best protected if each parent shares equally in the burden of demonstrating how the child's best interests will be impacted by the proposed relocation. [Jaramillo v. Jaramillo, 823 P.2d 299 (N.M. 1991)]. . . . For the reasons set forth below, we adopt the reasoning set forth in *Jaramillo* for relocation disputes in Colorado. . . .

Child parenting disputes present agonizing decisions for trial court judges. [S]uch cases are increasingly common before the courts. According to the U.S. Census Bureau, about 1 in 6 Americans moves each year. Kristin A. Hansen, U.S. Census Bureau, *Geographic Mobility,* (last revised 2001) at http://www.census.gov/population/www/pop-profile/geomob.html (last visited May 24, 2005). . . . Because of the ordinary needs of both parents after a marital dissolution to secure or retain employment, pursue educational or career opportunities, or reside in the same location as a new spouse or other family or friends, it is unrealistic to assume that divorced parents will permanently remain in the same location.

[O]ne of the biggest concerns for the judge is the starting point for analysis. [A] court must begin its analysis with each parent on equal footing; a court may not presume either that a child is better off or disadvantaged by relocating with the majority time parent. Rather, the majority time parent has the duty to present specific, non-speculative information about the child's proposed new living conditions, as well as a concrete plan for modifying parenting time as a result of the move. The minority time parent may choose to contest the relocation in its totality, and thus seek to become the majority time or primary residential parent. Alternatively, the minority time parent may choose not to contest the relocation, but rather object to the revised parenting plan proposed by the majority time parent. In such a circumstance, the minority time parent has the responsibility to propose his or her own parenting plan. Thus, each parent has the burden to persuade the court that the relocation of the child will be in or contrary to the child's best interests, or that the parenting plan he or she proposes should be adopted by the court.

The focus of the court, however, should be the best interests of the child. The court may decide that it is not in the best interests of the child to relocate with the majority time parent. Then, if the majority time parent still wishes to relocate, a new parenting time plan will be necessary. Alternatively, the court may decide that it is in the best interests of the child to relocate with the majority time parent. In that situation, the court must fashion a parenting time plan which protects the constitutional right of the minority time parent to care for and control the child.

In either event, the court must thoroughly disclose the reasons for its decision and make specific findings with respect to each of the statutory factors.

[W]e now address the trial court's application of subsection 14-10-129(2)(c) to the facts of this case. . . . First, the trial court erred when it failed to properly address whether remaining with his primary caregiver would provide Connor any advantages pursuant to subsection 14-10-129(2)(c)(VI). [The court reasonably could have concluded that Connor would benefit directly and indirectly by remaining with Mother if she were to relocate to Arizona. As a direct benefit, Connor would enjoy the stability of remaining with his majority time parent. Connor also would benefit from having day-to-day relationships with his grandfather, uncle, aunt, and nephew. Finally, Mother's increased financial stability and family support would undoubtedly increase her own happiness, which would benefit Connor by giving him a more stable home life. This indirect benefit to Connor is not diminished simply because it primarily benefits Mother. . . .

Having failed to discuss advantages to Connor in relocating with Mother, the trial court then proceeded to relate its concern that Mother:

> "continues to believe that whatever is in her best interest is also in Connor's best interest. The Court notes her reasons to relocate. They are all from her point of view and her benefit, job, help from her family which then, I guess, are indirect benefits to Connor but there was nothing directly about how this would *enhance* Connor." (emphasis added).

[R]equiring a parent to show that a move will "enhance the quality of life for the child" is a remnant of the *Francis* test that the General Assembly did not adopt in amending section 14-10-129. [N]one of the factors listed in subsection 14-10-129(2)(c) requires the majority time parent to establish that the move will directly benefit the child. Most importantly, the trial court did not impose an equal burden on Father to demonstrate the benefits to Connor using the subsection 14-10-129(2)(c) factors. . . . As a result, Mother was required to carry an unequal share of the burden in demonstrating Connor's best interests.

The trial court aggravated these errors in its subsection 14-10-129(2)(c) analysis by relying on a general conclusion that parents should remain in close proximity to the child. In reaching this conclusion, the trial court cited an article from the Journal of Family Psychology [citing Sanford L. Braver et al., Relocation of Children after Divorce and Children's Best Interests: New Evidence and Legal Considerations, J. Fam. Psychol., June 2003, at 206]. Though the article's authors stated, "our data cannot establish with certainty that moves cause children substantial harm," the trial court nevertheless interpreted the article as concluding that "a child is generally not benefited by moving away with the custodial parent from a non-custodial parent." Presumably based upon the Braver's article, the court then concluded that "[p]arenthood results in some sacrifice and it is better off for parents to remain in close proximity." [T]he effect of this generalization was to create a presumption in favor of the minority time parent opposing relocation.

Moreover, Braver's article represents only one of many schools of thought on how parenting time affects children. One theory provides that a child's interests are so aligned with the well-being of the majority time parent that that person's decision on behalf of the child should be honored unless there is proof that the decisions are bad ones. [Judith S. Wallerstein & Tony J. Tanke, To Move or Not to

Move: Psychological and Legal Considerations in the Relocation of Children Following Divorce, 30 Fam. L.Q. 305, 318 (1996) (concluding that "[w]hen a child is de facto in the primary residential or physical custody of one parent, that parent should be able to relocate with the child, except in unusual circumstances")]. Another theory suggests that both parents are entitled to raise the child and that it is extremely important for a child to develop a relationship with both parents. [Joan B. Kelly & Michael E. Lamb, Using Child Development Research to Make Appropriate Custody and Access Decisions For Young Children, 38 Fam. & Conciliation Cts. Rev. 297, 309 (2000) (concluding that "[r]egardless of who has been the primary caretaker . . . children benefit from the extensive contact with both parents that fosters meaningful father-child and mother-child relationships")].

A court's duty is not to determine which of these theories is correct. Rather, a court's sole duty in relocation cases is to determine the best interests of a child based upon the facts of each individual case. . . . The trial court in this case failed to perform its duty in accordance with the statute because it imposed an unequal burden on Mother and created a presumption in favor of Father that was potentially contrary to Connor's best interests. We therefore reverse the court of appeals' holding and remand with instructions to return the case to the trial court for proceedings consistent with this opinion.

Notes and Questions

1. *Frequency of relocation.* Geographic mobility is a fact of life. Within four years after separation or divorce, 75 percent of custodial mothers will relocate at least once, and half of these will relocate again. Sarah L. Gottfried, Note, Virtual Visitation: The New Wave of Communication Between Children and Non-Custodial Parents in Relocation Cases, 9 Cardozo Women's L.J. 567, 568 (2003). Relocation controversies frequently arise in the postdecree period when a parent who has been awarded physical custody decides to relocate for reasons of remarriage, employment or educational opportunities, or the promise of moral or economic support from relatives.

2. *Good faith and motives.* Many courts consider good faith on the part of the custodial parent as a threshold requirement in relocation disputes. See, e.g., Baures v. Lewis, 770 A.2d 214 (N.J. 2001). How does a court determine the existence of good faith? What is the difference between good faith versus motive? Once a parent establishes good faith, should the parent's motive still be relevant? Compare McCoy v. McCoy, 764 A.2d 449, 453 (N.J. Super. Ct. 2001) (citing authority suggesting that good faith should be sufficient), with In re Marriage of LaMusga, 88 P.3d 81 (Cal. 2004) (suggesting that, even if a parent is acting in good faith, the parent's motives remain important). Should the judicial response to a relocation request depend on the petitioner's motive? Respondent's motive? What motives are acceptable? Was Michelle Ciesluk's motive acceptable? Compare O'Bannon v. O'Bannon, 2003 WL 22734673 (Tenn. Ct. App. 2003) (upholding denial of custodial mother's request to move, reasoning that mother's move to accompany new husband did not have a reasonable purpose and was vindictive), and Jones v. Tarnawa, 809 N.Y.S.2d 742 (App. Div. 2006) (affirming determination that mother failed to establish that move would be in children's best interests because

her sole motive was a desire for a "fresh start" in her new marriage), with Dupre v. Dupre, 857 A.2d 242 (R.I. 2004) (holding that mother's request to move to a small South Pacific island to improve her mental state and inspire her artwork should not have been denied, rejecting the need to show a compelling reason for the move).

3. *Procedural posture.* Relocation disputes may arise because a decree, statute, or marital settlement agreement requires a custodial parent to seek permission to leave the jurisdiction. Or, the noncustodial parent may petition to enjoin the move and, sometimes, request a custody modification. Janet M. Bowermaster, Sympathizing with Solomon: Choosing Between Parents in a Mobile Society, 31 J. Fam. L. 791, 796-797 (1992-1993). Absent statutory authority or a settlement agreement, can a trial judge who is making an *initial* custody determination order a parent to live in a specific location? In a post-*Ciesluk* case, the Colorado Supreme Court held that in an initial determination, a court has no statutory authority to order a parent to live in a specific location but must accept the location in which each party intends to live. Spahmer v. Gullette, 113 P.3d 158 (Colo. 2005).

4. *Burden of proof.* In relocation disputes, some courts place the burden of proof on the relocating custodial parent to prove that the move is in the child's best interests. In contrast, other states place the burden of proof on the noncustodial opposing parent to demonstrate the adverse impact of the relocation. Who should bear the burden of proof in relocation cases? What should be the burden of proof? Should the custodial parent have to show that the move is in the best interests of the child, or the noncustodial parent have to show that the move is not? That the move is "necessary"? That there is a "compelling reason" for the move? That there are "exceptional circumstances" justifying the move? See Tropea v. Tropea, 642 N.Y.S.2d 575 (N.Y. 1996) (abandoning the exceptional-circumstances standard which made New York the most restrictive jurisdiction). That the move will prove a real advantage specifically to the child — or to the new family unit? Does a direct benefit in the custodial parent's quality of life translate into a direct benefit to the child? See Hollandsworth v. Knyzewski, 79 S.W.3d 856 (Ark. Ct. App. 2002); In re Marriage of Collingbourne, 791 N.E.2d 532 (Ill. 2003). Or conversely, that the move will result in detriment to the child? Does any interference with the noncustodial parent's visitation constitute a sufficient detriment? Won't there inevitably be an adverse impact on the relationship between the child and noncustodial parent whenever a custodial parent relocates? Should the court consider also the possible detriment from disrupting the child's relationship with the custodial parent? See *LaMusga,* supra, at 379 (Justice Kennard, dissenting).

5. *Modification.* Does relocation automatically constitute a significant change in circumstances that warrants modification of custody (without an additional determination that a change is warranted according to the jurisdiction's modification standard)? Compare *Hollandsworth,* supra (decision to relocate, standing alone, is not a material change in circumstances), with Fowler v. Sowers, 151 S.W.3d 357 (Ky. 2003) (contra). Does a "self-executing change of visitation" order if a parent moves violate public policy? Compare Dellinger v. Dellinger, 278 Ga. 732, 609 S.E.2d 331(Ga. 2004), with Roberts v. Roberts, 64 P.3d 327 (Idaho 2003).

6. *Joint custody.* Many jurisdictions apply more restrictive relocation rules to parents who share joint custody. See, e.g., Potter v. Potter, 119 P.3d 1246 (Nev. 2005) (holding that relocation statute did not govern request to relocate by wife who had joint physical custody). How should courts resolve relocation disputes when parents share joint custody? Compare Maynard v. McNett, 710 N.W.2d

369 (N.D. 2006) (requiring trial court to make an initial determination of primary custody before granting relocation motion of joint custodian), with Fenwick v. Fenwick, 114 S.W.3d 767 (Ky.2003) (holding that, in a joint custody arrangement, when a primary residential custodian gives notice of an intent to relocate, the objecting party has the burden to file for custody modification in order to change the primary residential custodian). In relocation disputes, should courts take into account a parent's actual involvement with a child rather than the legal label? See Kawatra v. Kawatra, 182 S.W.3d 800 (Tenn. 2005).

7. *Trend and counter trend.* Until recently, the trend in relocation cases favored decreasing restrictions on parental moves. However, courts now appear to be moving toward a more fact-specific, case-by-case analysis. Linda D. Elrod & Robert G. Spector, A Review of the Year in Family Law: "Same-Sex" Marriage Issue Dominates Headlines, 38 Fam. L.Q. 777, 792 (2005). The California Supreme Court played a prominent role in the initial trend by recognizing a presumptive right of the custodial parent to relocate in In re Marriage of Burgess, 913 P.2d 473 (Cal. 1996) (adopting a presumption favoring the custodial parent provided that removal would not prejudice the best interests of the child). Courts in a number of other states (including Rhode Island, New Jersey, and Arkansas) adopted this approach. Robert E. Oliphant, Relocation Custody Disputes — A Binuclear Family Centered Three Stage Solution, 25 N. Ill. U. L. Rev. 363, 388 (2005). The California Supreme Court recently weakened *Burgess* significantly in In re Marriage of LaMusga, 88 P.3d 81 (Cal. 2004), which substituted a best-interests analysis, taking into account whether the move would result in detriment to the children's relationship with the noncustodial parent. *Ciesluk* illustrates the counter trend. See also Bodne v. Bodne, 605 S.E.2d 842 (Ga. Ct. App. 2004) (abrogating the presumption favoring the custodial parent in relocation disputes).

8. *Right to travel.* How does *Ciesluk* accommodate the constitutional rights at issue in relocation disputes? Why does it adopt the approach that it does? Which approach do you favor and why? Do relocation restrictions infringe on a parent's right to travel — or only on a parent's right to travel with the child?

The argument that relocation restrictions violate the custodial parent's right to travel was first advanced almost 30 years ago in a classic law review article by a prominent family law professor. Brigitte M. Bodenheimer, Equal Rights, Visitation, and the Right to Move, 1 Fam. Advocate 18 (1978). By inhibiting custodial parents, but not noncustodial parents, from moving, do relocation restrictions violate equal protection? Is requiring a parent to forego moving in order to retain custody an infringement of parental autonomy and family privacy? See, e.g., Taylor v. Taylor, 849 S.W.2d 319, 329-331 (Tenn. 1993).

9. *Parent's consent to restriction.* What effect does a relocation restriction in a *settlement agreement* have on a parent's ability to relocate? See Helton v. Helton, 2004 WL 63487 (Tenn. Ct. App. 2004) (holding that parties' marital dissolution agreement imposing stringent limitations on the custodial parent's right to relocate is unenforceable given applicable statutory standards and judicial authority). On the other hand, suppose the parents agree that the custodial mother can change their child's residence at any time to any place. Is that agreement enforceable? See Delamielleure v. Delamielleure, 704 N.W.2d 746 (Mich. Ct. App. 2005) (holding that blanket consent by father to allow mother to change child's legal residence at any time to any place violates statute).

10. *Gender bias.* Do restrictions on a custodial parent's right to relocate reflect gender bias? See Bowermaster, supra, at 846. Do the restrictions reinforce traditional gender roles? Consider the following:

> [I]t is difficult when reading the cases, to overlook the images of traditional marriage and the corresponding traditional gender roles that are reflected. . . . The standard role pattern in marriage was for the husband to predominate in decision making, including the decision of where the family would live, and to provide for the family's financial support. In exchange for this support, the wife was to care for the household and children and follow the husband in his choice of domicile. [After divorce,] [n]on-custodial parents pay child support, and in return, custodial parents care for the children and keep them available for visitation. . . .
>
> There are obvious problems with this approach. First, in the large number of cases where custodial mothers have remarried and seek to relocate to accompany their spouses, this "child support for child care services" approach creates a paradox. Simply stated, the mother cannot provide services to two husbands at the same time. She cannot fulfill her traditional duty to care for the children and keep them available to both an ex-husband and a present husband when the two have chosen geographically distant domiciles. . . . [Restrictions] only serve to create a domiciliary "squatter's rights." The first husband to choose a domicile for the mother is given tremendous leverage . . . to keep the mother caring for his children within his easy access. . . . Yet the custom for the wife to follow her husband in his choice of marital domicile applies as much to the new spouse as it did to the former spouse.

Id. at 843-845.

11. *Children's interests.* Do courts pay sufficient attention to children's interests in relocation disputes? See Edwin J. Terry et al., Relocation: Moving Forward or Moving Backward?, 31 Tex. Tech. L. Rev. 983, 1023-1025 (2000) (suggesting they do not). Does *Ciesluk* take into account the child's interests and preferences?

12. *Mileage restrictions.* Some jurisdictions have required parents who relocate more than a certain distance from the child's present home to secure court permission. These restrictions sometimes are referred to as "100-mile rules." See, e.g., Mich. Comp. Laws Ann. §722.23 (West 2002); Tenn. Code Ann. §36-6-108 (2001). Is this an appropriate method of accommodating the different interests? See generally Ericka Domarew, Comment, Michigan Keeps It Within Limits: Relocation No More Than "100 Miles," 20 T.M. Cooley L. Rev. 547 (2003).

13. *Intercountry moves.* Should the same rules govern interstate and intercountry moves? See Bednarek v. Velasquez, 830 A.2d 1267 (Pa. Super. Ct. 2003). May a parent restrict the other parent's right to travel with the children to *certain* countries, particularly where a United States court's jurisdiction over child custody may not be enforced? See generally James Grayson, International Relocation, The Right to Travel, and the Hague Convention: Additional Requirements for Custodial Parents, 28 Fam. L.Q. 531 (1994).

14. *Empirical research.* In accommodating interests in relocation disputes, should courts take into account social science research on the effects of relocation on children? Little research has been conducted on this subject, and controversy surrounds existing research findings. How does *Ciesluk* address the role of social science data in relocation disputes?

The controversy focuses on two opposing viewpoints. Psychologist Judith Wallerstein, who filed an extremely influential amicus curiae brief in In re Marriage of Burgess, supra, argues that allowing the custodial parent to relocate with the children promotes the latter's best interests because children's post-divorce adjustment is closely entwined with the well-being of the custodial parent. Wallerstein bases her conclusions primarily on her three-decade-long research on the effects of divorce on children. Judith S. Wallerstein, Brief of Amica Curiae, In re Marriage of Burgess (Sup. Ct. Cal., Dec. 7, 1995) (No. S046116). See also Judith S. Wallerstein & Tony J. Tanke, To Move or Not to Move: Psychological and Legal Considerations in the Relocation of Children Following Divorce, 30 Fam. L.Q. 305, 318 (1996).

Psychologist Richard Warshak and a research study conducted by psychologists Sanford Braver and William V. Fabricius, and law professor Ira Ellman, provide the most prominent opposing view. Warshak's extensive review of the literature emphasizes the importance of the child's relationship with the noncustodial parent in promoting the child's well-being. He charges that Wallerstein's findings rest on only a few cases of relocating parents and also that they derive from an earlier era when divorced fathers saw little of their children. See Richard A. Warshak, Social Science and Children's Best Interests in Relocation Cases: *Burgess* Revisited, 34 Fam. L.Q. 83 (2000).

Braver et al.'s study (cited in *Ciesluk*), based on findings from a questionnaire administered to 600 introductory psychology students about their experiences of divorce, highlights the negative effects of relocation on the children of divorce. On 11 of 14 indicators of well-being, their research reports that children of divorce who move at least one hour away from the noncustodial parent fare worse than those children of divorce whose parents do not move. However, according to prominent social scientist Norval Glenn, the differences between these two groups of children are quite small and, moreover, not significant in terms of the most important areas of psychological well-being (i.e., friendships, dating behavior, substance abuse, and general life satisfaction). Glenn charges that the researchers did not collect sufficient background information on the students to explain the reasons for the differences between the two groups. He elaborates:

> So what is causing these (small) differences in some of these young people's answers to this one Arizona questionnaire? It is how old you were when your parents split up? Is it whether one or both of your parents did, or did not, remarry? Is it the level of child support and alimony your mother received? Is it how much your parents fought and quarreled before the divorce, or how well they cooperated, or failed to cooperate, after the divorce? Or is it whether your mother after the divorce moved an hour or more's drive away from your father? Or is it something else entirely? Again, no one knows for sure, and on the basis of this study, no one could possibly know. To their credit, the researchers acknowledge as much in what amounts to the fine print of the study.

Norval Glenn & David Blankenhorn, Does Moving After Divorce Damage Kids?, available at http://www.thelizlibrary.org/lamusga/glenn.html (last visited Feb. 16, 2006). For another critique, see Carol S. Bruch, Sound Research or Wishful Thinking in Child Custody Cases? Lessons From Relocation Law, 40 Fam. L.Q. (forthcoming 2006.)

Should courts in relocation disputes take into account empirical research that documents the gradual decrease in fathers' visitation patterns? Consider the following:

> [Another] source influencing how children adjust to divorce is open to question: the importance of maintaining ties between the children and their noncustodial parents,

usually the fathers. Although most observers, ourselves included, have believed that continued contact makes a difference in children's adjustment, the evidence in support of that assertion is mixed at best. [S]ome observational studies have reported that children adjust better when they have continuing contact with their noncustodial fathers. But other observational studies and large surveys have found that, other things being equal, the frequency of contact with fathers was not related to children's adjustment. . . .

These negative findings about the importance of contact with the father have surprised and puzzled experts in the field. Perhaps the negative findings result from the low levels of contact that most divorced fathers maintain. . . . Although we still advocate strengthening ties to fathers, we believe that public policy should place lower priority on this objective than on [principles that emphasize promoting the effective functioning of custodial parents in order to improve their children's adjustment and to decrease children's exposure to parental conflict].

Frank F. Furstenberg, Jr. & Andrew J. Cherlin, Divided Families: What Happens to Children When Parents Part 107 (1991).

15. *Law reform.*

a. *ALI standard.* The ALI Principles permit a primary parent to relocate with the child if that parent has been exercising a significant majority of custodial responsibility and has a legitimate reason for moving to a location that is reasonable in light of the purpose. Relocation justifies a custody modification only when it "significantly impairs" either parent's ability to exercise custodial responsibilities. ALI Principles §2.17(1). In this event, the court will revise the parenting plan to accommodate the relocation while maintaining the same proportion of residential responsibility. Valid purposes for the move, according to the ALI Principles, include: the desire to be closer to a support network; a health reason; an employment or educational opportunity; protection of a family member; a desire to accompany a spouse or domestic partner who lives in, or is pursuing educational or employment opportunities in the new location; and to improve quality of life. See generally Katherine T. Bartlett, U.S. Custody Law and Trends in the Context of the ALI Principles of the Law of Family Dissolution, 10 Va. J. Soc. Pol'y & L. 5 (2002).

b. *Mediation.* Some commentators suggest that parents involved in relocation disputes resort to alternative dispute resolution. Should legislatures *mandate* that parents resolve this issue by the use of mediation? See McGough, supra (so suggesting).

c. *Virtual visitation.* At least one commentator advocates expanded use of "virtual visitation." See Gottfried, supra. Some courts are beginning to order divorcing parties to use a website called "Our FamilyWizard.com" to arrange visitation and manage family information (regarding health, extracurricular activities, and childcare). See, e.g., in Rhea v. Rhea, 2005 WL 469189 (Conn. Super. Ct. 2005). But cf. Sullivan v. Knick, 568 S.E.2d 430 (Va. Ct. App. 2002). What do you think of this solution?

Problem

Mother and Father divorce in Vermont when their daughter is two years old. The divorce order, based on the parties' stipulation, provides that Mother will have sole legal custody. For the next few years until the daughter starts school, the parents share her time roughly equally. Thereafter, Father's contact is reduced to one-third when the daughter starts school. Soon thereafter, Mother notifies Father that she and her fiancé intend to move to Maryland for his employment. Mother, who had lost her teaching job because of budget cuts, plans to look for a teaching position in Maryland. Mother files a motion to modify the parent-child contact schedule that was established in final divorce orders, and Father opposes her motion and seeks sole custody. What result? See Hawkes v. Spence, 878 A.2d 273 (Vt. 2005) (adopting ALI relocation standard). See also Hayes v. Gallacher, 972 P.2d 1138 (Nev. 1999) (also adopting ALI standard).

6. *Juridiction and Enforcement*

■ **IN RE FORLENZA**
140 S.W.3d 373 (Tex. 2004)

Justice O'NEILL delivered the opinion of the Court.

. . . Ann Marie and Robert Joseph Forlenza were divorced in Collin County, Texas, on March 1, 1996. [T]he trial court signed an agreed modification order, modifying the original divorce decree, that granted Robert primary custody of their two children, now ten and fourteen years old, and the exclusive right to establish their primary physical residence. That same month, the children moved with Robert to Issaquah, Washington. Over the next five years, Robert moved with the children three more times — on August 30, 1998, they moved to Ohio, on February 19, 1999, they moved to Virginia, and on August 27, 2002, they moved to Colorado where they now reside.[1]

The current dispute arose in 2001 when Robert lost his job in Virginia and was offered a two-year contract job in Taipei, Taiwan. Claiming that she had experienced difficulty in exercising her [visitation] rights, Ann filed this suit on September 10, 2001 [seeking to modify the prior order]. She also requested a restraining order prohibiting Robert from relocating the children outside the United States, which the trial court granted. . . . During a pretrial conference seven days before the scheduled trial date, Robert filed a second motion to dismiss, alleging that the court did not have exclusive continuing jurisdiction under Texas Family Code section 152.202(a) to modify its previous child-custody order. [The trial court denied the motion. The court of appeals reversed.] We granted Ann's petition to determine whether the trial court retained exclusive continuing jurisdiction under the Uniform Child Custody Jurisdiction Enforcement Act (UCCJEA).

Effective September 1, 1999, Texas adopted the UCCJEA, replacing the previous Uniform Child Custody Jurisdiction Act (UCCJA). The UCCJEA was designed, in large part, to clarify and to unify the standards for courts' continuing and modification jurisdiction in interstate child-custody matters. The Act that the UCCJEA replaced, the UCCJA, was drafted in 1968 as a model act designed to prevent repeated custody litigation. But even though all fifty states adopted the UCCJA, some did so with significant departure from the original text. As a result,

---

1. On August 6, 2002, Robert sent Ann notice that he was moving with the children back to Washington where he had a job offer. While visiting his family in Colorado en route to Washington, Robert decided to permanently move to Colorado.

states often interpreted the Act inconsistently and child-custody determinations made in one state were often not accorded full faith and credit in another.

To address some of these problems, in 1980 Congress enacted the Parental Kidnaping Prevention Act (PKPA), which requires states to accord full faith and credit to custody decrees issued by sister states that substantially comply with the PKPA. 28 U.S.C. §1738A (2000). The PKPA authorizes exclusive continuing jurisdiction in the state that issued the original decree as long as one parent or child remains there and that state has exclusive continuing jurisdiction under its own law. Id. §1738A(d). The UCCJA, though, which the states had adopted, does not clearly articulate when a decree-granting state retains exclusive continuing jurisdiction. As states adopted different interpretations of continuing jurisdiction and reached conflicting conclusions about the circumstances under which it endures, the law's uniformity diminished, often resulting in simultaneous proceedings and conflicting custody decrees. The UCCJEA was designed to eliminate inconsistent state interpretations of the UCCJA's jurisdictional aspects and to harmonize the UCCJA with the PKPA.

Article 2 of the UCCJEA specifically grants exclusive continuing jurisdiction over child-custody disputes to the state that made the initial custody determination and provides specific rules on how long this jurisdiction continues. *See* Unif. Child Custody Jur. & Enf. Act §202, 9 U.L.A. 673-674 (Supp. 2004). Rules that prevent another state from modifying a child-custody determination while exclusive continuing jurisdiction remains in the original-decree state complement these provisions. Texas adopted Article 2 without substantial variation from the UCCJEA.

Robert's challenge involves the proper interpretation of [Texas Family Code] section 152.202(a), which governs the duration of the decree-granting state's exclusive continuing jurisdiction. That section provides that a court of this state that has made an initial child-custody determination consistent with section 152.201 has exclusive continuing jurisdiction over the determination until

> (1) a court of this state determines that *neither the child, nor the child and one parent,* nor the child and a person acting as a parent, *have a significant connection with this state and* that *substantial evidence is no longer available in this state* concerning the child's care, protection, training, and personal relationships; or
>
> (2) a court of this state or a court of another state determines that the child, the child's parents, and any person acting as a parent do not presently reside in this state.

Tex. Fam. Code §152.202(a) (emphasis added). Robert does not challenge the prior child-custody order's compliance with section 152.201. And section 152.202(a)(2) does not apply because Ann continues to reside in Texas. Therefore, we must decide whether the trial court properly applied section 152.202(a)(1) in deciding that it had exclusive continuing jurisdiction over these modification proceedings.

Robert's jurisdictional plea contends that Ann failed to establish that a significant connection with Texas exists and that substantial evidence is available here concerning the children's care, protection, training, and personal relationships. . . .

Robert contends that the children no longer have a significant connection with Texas because (1) the children visited here only five times in the four-year period preceding this action, and (2) Ann's residence in Texas is not sufficient, as the commentary to section 152.202 specifically notes that the presence of one parent remaining in the state is not determinative. See Unif. Child Custody Jur. & Enf. Act §152.202 cmt. 1, 9 U.L.A. 674. But Ann does not rely on her mere presence in Texas to establish a significant connection under the statute. Contrary to Robert's briefing, the record indicates that the children actually visited Texas six times in the relevant period. On four of these occasions the children lived with Ann for considerable periods, each lasting approximately one month during the summer. See Fish v. Fish, 596 S.E.2d 654, 656 (Ga. Ct. App.2004) (pointing to extended custodial visitation in state to support court's finding of a significant connection); Ruth v. Ruth, 32 Kan. App.2d 416, 83 P.3d 1248, 1254 (2004) (same). Moreover, we presume that the trial court accepted as true Ann's testimony that more visitation would have occurred in Texas but for Robert's actions and the fact that the children were not allowed to fly to Texas.

Other courts commonly consider visitation within the state as evidence of a significant connection [citations omitted]. In addition, numerous relatives, including Ann's mother and sister and Robert's sister and sister-in-law, live in Texas and maintain a relationship with the children. Moreover, the evidence in this case clearly indicates that Ann maintained a significant relationship with her children. To accommodate the children's schedule over the years, Ann repeatedly flew to Washington, Ohio, and Virginia to see them. Robert admits that Ann made at least fifteen such trips in the four-year period under review. Because the record establishes that the children visited Texas on a number of occasions and maintained a close relationship with their mother and other relatives residing in Texas, all important considerations under the UCCJEA, we hold that the children have a significant connection with Texas sufficient to support the trial court's exclusive continuing jurisdiction over the modification proceedings.

Robert nevertheless claims that the children's contacts with Texas do not rise to the level other Texas courts have required. Specifically, Robert cites In the Interest of Bellamy, 67 S.W.3d 482 (Tex.App.-Texarkana 2002), and In the Interest of C.C.B. & M.J.B., 2002 WL 31727247, at *4 (Tex.App.-El Paso 2002). Those cases, however, do not focus exclusively on the number of times the child has had contact with the state, as Robert suggests. [Rather, the emphasis is on] the nature and quality of the child's relationship with the father and family members who resided in Texas. . . .

Robert claims that no other court has exercised exclusive continuing jurisdiction over children who have resided out of state for more than five years. We disagree. In Fish, the Georgia Court of Appeals determined that the trial court had exclusive continuing jurisdiction pursuant to a prior divorce decree even though the mother and the children had lived in Florida for seven years. 596 S.E.2d 654. Similarly, in Ruth, the Kansas Court of Appeals determined that the trial court had jurisdiction pursuant to a prior divorce decree after the mother and children had lived in Missouri for approximately six years. 83 P.3d at 1254. And in Heath v. Heath, a Connecticut court exercised exclusive continuing jurisdiction even though the children had lived in California for eight years. 2000 WL 1838932, at *2 (Conn. Super. Ct. 2000). Moreover, contrary to Robert's argument, the UCCJEA does not premise the exclusive continuing jurisdiction determination on which state has the *most* significant connection with the child. See In re Dale McCormick, 87 S.W.3d at 750 (stating that "[a]lthough evidence was admitted which establishes that [the child] has significant ties with the state of Kansas, that fact does not necessarily mean that there is no significant connection with Texas or that substantial evidence cannot be found here"). This relative type of inquiry is appropriate under section 152.207, which allows a court with exclusive continuing jurisdiction to decline it in favor of a more convenient forum, but it does not affect the initial section 152.202 jurisdictional analysis. See Tex. Fam.Code. §152.207. Importantly, the only issue before us is whether the Texas court retained jurisdiction; the court could still decline to exercise that jurisdiction if another forum was more convenient. In this case, though, the children's almost continual change of residence supports the trial court's conclusion that the children had a significant connection with Texas based on their visits here and their personal relationships maintained in this state.

Finally, Robert argues that substantial evidence does not exist in Texas regarding the children's care, protection, training, and personal relationships, and section 152.202(a)(1) requires the trial court to find *both* a significant connection with Texas *and* that substantial evidence exists here before it can exercise exclusive continuing jurisdiction. For this proposition, Robert relies upon the court of appeals' statement in *Bellamy* that "Texas retains jurisdiction [under section 152.202(a)] . . . so long as there is still a significant connection with Texas and substantial evidence is still available in Texas." 67 S.W.3d at 484. Robert also cites the commentary to section 152.202, which notes that the original-decree state retains exclusive jurisdiction even if the child has acquired a new home state "so long as the general requisites of the 'substantial connection' jurisdiction provisions of Section 201 are met." Unif. Child Custody Jur. & Enf. Act §202 cmt. 1, 9 U.L.A. 674. Because section 201, which governs the initial custody determination, requires both a significant connection and substantial evidence, Robert concludes that section 202 must as well. We disagree.

Robert's strained construction of the statutory scheme ignores section 152.202(a)(1)'s plain language. That section specifically states that jurisdiction continues until the court determines that there is not a significant connection with Texas *and* that substantial evidence concerning the children's care, protection, training, and personal relationships is no longer available here. Clearly, exclusive jurisdiction continues in the decree-granting state as long as a significant connection exists *or* substantial evidence is present. [The court notes that this interpretation comports with that of other jurisdictions.] Because we conclude that the trial court did not err in concluding that the children had a substantial connection with Texas on September 10, 2001, we need not address whether substantial evidence existed here as well. For the foregoing reasons, we hold that the trial court had exclusive continuing jurisdiction over this modification proceeding. . . .

Notes and Questions on Jurisdiction and Enforcement

1. *UCCJA.* Prior to the late 1960s, a state could assert jurisdiction over child custody if it had a "substantial interest" in the case. See Leonard Ratner, Child Custody in a Federal System, 62 Mich. L. Rev. 795, 808 (1964). This interest might stem from the marital domicile or the current residence of either parent or the child. Such a vague standard often led to concurrent assertions of jurisdiction. In addition, because of judicial willingness to reopen custody decisions

at the behest of a state resident, decrees were freely modifiable in other states. Supreme Court decisions left unclear whether custody decisions were entitled to the protection of the Full Faith and Credit Clause. Id. at 807. The ease with which parents could reopen child custody cases in other states has been described as "a rule of seize-and-run." May v. Anderson, 345 U.S. 528, 542 (1953) (Jackson, J., dissenting).

The Uniform Child Custody Jurisdiction Act (UCCJA) was drafted in 1968 to reduce jurisdictional competition and confusion, as well as to deter parents from forum shopping to religate custody. A version of the UCCJA, which applied to initial custody decisions as well as modifications, was adopted in every state by 1981.

The UCCJA identified four alternate bases of juridiction; sought to locate jurisdiction in the forum with access to the most evidence relevant to the custody decision; attempted to ensure that procedings would occur in one state at a time; and mandated recognition, enforcement, and nonmodification of a decree from another state with jurisdiction under the UCCJA. The four alternate bases for taking jurisdiction included: the child's home state; a significant connection between the state and the parties; emergency jurisdiction when the child is present and the child's welfare is threatened; and, there is no other state that has jurisdiction. "Home state" was defined as the state in which the child lived (immediately preceding the time involved) with a parent or parents for at least six consecutive months.

2. *PKPA.* In 1981, Congress enacted the Parental Kidnapping Prevention Act (PKPA), 28 U.S.C.A. §1738A (2000). Despite its title, the PKPA is also relevant in cases involving jurisdiction over child custody. The PKPA was drafted for several reasons. First, it attempted to provide rules that would apply in all states, even those that might never enact the UCCJA. (By the late 1970s, only about half of the states had enacted the UCCJA.) Second, the UCCJA did not obtain the hoped-for uniformity in the treatment of custody disputes because some state legislatures changed the UCCJA provisions, and some state courts interpreted those provisions in different ways. Russell M. Coombs, Nuts and Bolts of the PKPA, 22 Colo. Law. 2397 (1993).

A principal purpose of the PKPA is to ensure that custody decrees issued by states asserting jurisdiction in conformity with the PKPA receive recognition and enforcement in other states through full faith and credit. The PKPA provides:

§1738A. Full Faith and Credit Given to Child Custody Determinations

(a) The appropriate authorities of every State shall enforce according to its terms, and shall not modify except as provided in subsection (f) of this section [omitted], any child custody determination made consistently with the provisions of this section by a court of another State.

(b) As used in this section, the term— . . .

(4) "home State" means the State in which, immediately preceding the time involved, the child lived with his parents, a parent, or a person acting as a parent, for at least six consecutive months, and in the case of a child less than six months old, the State in which the child lived from birth with any of such persons. Periods of temporary absence of any of such persons are counted as part of the six-month or other period; . . .

(c) A child custody determination made by a court of a State is consistent with the provisions of this section only if —

(1) such court has jurisdiction under the law of such State; and

(2) one of the following conditions is met:

(A) such State (i) is the home State of the child on the date of the commencement of the proceeding, or (ii) had been the child's home State within six months before the date of the commencement of the proceeding and the child is absent from such State because of his removal or retention by a contestant or for other reasons, and a contestant continues to live in such State;

(B)(i) it appears that no other State would have jurisdiction under subparagraph (A), and (ii) it is in the best interest of the child that a court of such State assume jurisdiction because (I) the child and his parents, or the child and at least one contestant, have a significant connection with such State other than mere physical presence in such State and (II) there is available in such State substantial evidence concerning the child's present or future care, protection, training, and personal relationships;

(C) the child is physically present in such State and (i) the child has been abandoned, or (ii) it is necessary in an emergency to protect the child because he has been subjected to or threatened with mistreatment or abuse;

(D)(i) it appears that no other State would have jurisdiction under subparagraph (A), (B), (C), or (E), or another State has declined to exercise jurisdiction on the ground that the State whose jurisdiction is in issue is the more appropriate forum to determine the custody of the child, and (ii) it is in the best interest of the child that such court assume jurisdiction; or

(E) the court has continuing jurisdiction pursuant to subsection (d) of this section.

(d) The jurisdiction of a court of a State which has made a child custody determination consistently with the provisions of this section continues as long as the requirement of subsection (c)(1) of this section continues to be met and such State remains the residence of the child or of any contestant. . . .

The PKPA improved upon the UCCJA in two ways. First, unlike the UCCJA, the PKPA prioritizes the bases of jurisdiction. Specifically, the PKPA gives priority to the "home state" of the child (as defined in (b)(4) above) in determining which state may exercise jurisdiction in a custody dispute. The PKPA and UCCJA also differ on jurisdiction to modify custody. More than one state might have asserted jurisdiction to modify, under the UCCJA's language. The PKPA provides that once a state has exercised jurisdiction, the initial decree-granting state has "*exclusive* continuing jurisdiction" so long as it remains the residence of a child or any contestant.

3. *UCCJEA.* In 1997, the National Conference of Commissioners on Uniform State Laws revised the UCCJA by drafting the Uniform Child Custody Jurisdiction and Enforcement Act (UCCJEA). The new act is intended to harmonize some of the differences between the UCCJA and PKPA. Almost all states now have adopted the UCCJEA.[16]

---

[16]. Based on data provided at the Uniform Law Commissioners' website, 43 states and the District of Columbia have adopted the UCCJEA. Legislative Fact Sheet, available at http://nccusl.org/Update/uniformact_factsheets/uniformacts-fs-uccjea.asp (last visited Feb. 16, 2006).

The UCCJEA differs from its predecessor UCCJA in several ways. Whereas the UCCJA did not prioritize among the four bases of jurisdiction, the UCCJEA follows the PKPA in giving priority to home state jurisdiction. The UCCJEA also goes beyond the PKPA by eliminating the "best interests" language from the second ("significant connection") basis of jurisdiction and, in addition, severely restricts the use of emergency jurisdiction to the issuance of temporary orders. Like the PKPA, the UCCJEA provides strict requirements for modification: The state that makes the initial custody determination has exclusive continuing jurisdiction so long as a child or parent in the original custody determination remains in that state.

The UCCJEA adds definitional clarity to custody decisionmaking. It tracks the PKPA definition of "child-custody determination" to encompass all custody and visitation decrees (temporary, permanent, initial, and modifications) and covers those proceedings related to divorce, separation, neglect, abuse, dependency, guardianship, paternity, termination of parental rights, and protection from domestic violence (but not adoptions).

One other improvement in the UCCJEA concerns the law's response in cases of domestic violence. Under the UCCJA and PKPA, temporary emergency jurisdiction arises in extraordinary circumstances where a child is present in a state and subjected to, or threatened with, mistreatment or abuse. However, the UCCJEA permits a court to exercise emergency jurisdiction to protect the *child, its siblings, or its parents* (not only the particular child in question). See Joan Zorza, The UCCJEA: What Is It and How Does It Affect Battered Women in Child-Custody Disputes, 27 Fordham Urb. L.J. 909, 917 (2000).

The UCCJEA provisions regarding initial jurisdiction, exclusive continuing jurisdiction, and modification are set forth below:

§201. Initial Child-Custody Jurisdiction

(a) Except as otherwise provided in Section 204 [dealing with emergency jurisdiction over abandoned or abused/neglected children], a court of this State has jurisdiction to make an initial child-custody determination only if:

(1) this State is the home state of the child on the date of the commencement of the proceeding, or was the home State of the child within six months before the commencement of the proceeding and the child is absent from this State but a parent or person acting as a parent continues to live in this State;

(2) a court of another State does not have jurisdiction under paragraph (1), or a court of the home State of the child has declined to exercise jurisdiction on the ground that this State is the more appropriate forum . . . and:

(A) the child and the child's parents, or the child and at least one parent or a person acting as a parent, have a significant connection with this State other than mere physical presence; and

(B) substantial evidence is available in this State concerning the child's care, protection, training, and personal relationships;

(3) all courts having jurisdiction under paragraph (1) or (2) have declined to exercise jurisdiction on the ground that a court of this State is the more appropriate forum to determine the custody of the child . . . or

(4) no court of any other State would have jurisdiction under the criteria specified in paragraph (1), (2), or (3).

(b) Subsection (a) is the exclusive jurisdictional basis for making a child-custody determination by a court of this State.

(c) Physical presence of, or personal jurisdiction over, a party or a child is not necessary or sufficient to make a child-custody determination.

§202. Exclusive, Continuing Jurisdiction

(a) Except as otherwise provided in Section 204 [emergency jurisdiction], a court of this State which has made a child-custody determination consistent with Section 201 or 203 has exclusive, continuing jurisdiction over the determination until:

(1) a court of this State determines that neither the child, the child's parents, and any person acting as a parent do not have a significant connection with this State and that substantial evidence is no longer available in this State concerning the child's care, protection, training, and personal relationships; or

(2) a court of this State or a court of another State determines that the child, the child's parents, and any person acting as a parent do not presently reside in this State.

(b) A court of this State which has made a child-custody determination and does not have exclusive, continuing jurisdiction under this section may modify that determination only if it has jurisdiction to make an initial determination under Section 201.

§203. Jurisdiction to Modify Determination.

Except as otherwise provided in Section 204 [emergency jurisdiction], a court of this State may not modify a child-custody determination made by a court of another State unless a court of this State has jurisdiction to make an initial determination under Section 201(a)(1) or (2) and:

(1) the court of the other State determines it no longer has exclusive, continuing jurisdiction under Section 202 or that a court of this State would be a more convenient forum . . . ; or

(2) a court of this State or a court of the other State determines that the child, the child's parents, and any person acting as a parent do not presently reside in the other State.

§204. Temporary Emergency Jurisdiction

(a) A court of this State has temporary emergency jurisdiction if the child is present in this State and the child has been abandoned or it is necessary in an emergency to protect the child because the child, or a sibling or parent of the child, is subjected to or threatened with mistreatment or abuse. . . .

How do these various UCCJEA provisions improve the enforcement of custody decrees? In *Folenza*, the mother sought to modify custody in Texas and the father in Virginia. Was the Texas court correct in its determination of jurisdiction?

4. *Conflicting decrees.*

a. *Extradition*

The United States Supreme Court has twice confronted the problem of conflicting custody decrees, deciding both cases on procedural bases. In California v. Superior Court (*Smolin*), 482 U.S. 400 (1987), Judith Smolin won sole custody of her daughters from a California court when she and Richard Smolin divorced there in 1978. While Judith remarried James Pope and relocated (to Oregon, Texas, and Louisiana) without informing Richard, Richard twice successfully petitioned in California for modifications of the original decree, ultimately winning sole custody himself. Nonetheless, the Popes obtained a decree from a Texas court granting full faith and credit to the original California order of sole custody to Judith. When the Popes failed to comply with the California modification awarding Richard sole custody, Richard and his father engaged in self help, abducting the children from a bus stop in Louisiana and bringing them back to California. Based on Judith's affidavit, Louisiana indicted Richard for kidnapping and attempted to extradite him. Richard attempted to block extradition in California. Ultimately, the United States Supreme Court granted certiorari. In a 7-2 ruling, the Court held that Richard's writ of habeas corpus to block the extradition should be denied because extradition proceedings are not appropriate for entertaining defenses or considering the merits of the charges. Conceding that the California custody decrees established Richard as the lawful custodial under the PKPA, nonetheless, the Supreme Court ruled that the Louisiana courts (rather than the California courts) must determine whether the kidnapping statutes had been violated and whether Richard had any defenses.

Subsequently, a Louisiana court found Richard Smolin not guilty of all charges and dismissed the case. The children remained with their father in California until they reached majority. Telephone interview, Dennis Riordan (attorney for Richard Smolin), Riordan and Horgan, San Francisco, Sept. 30, 1997.

b. *Remedies*

What remedies are available to contestants who might be awarded conflicting decrees by two states? May they seek resolution in federal court? Before 1988, several federal courts of appeal interpreted the PKPA to imply federal jurisdiction. See, e.g., Meade v. Meade, 812 F.2d 1473 (4th Cir. 1987); Flood v. Braaten, 727 F.2d 303 (3d Cir. 1984). The United States Supreme Court finally resolved the issue of federal court jurisdiction in Thompson v. Thompson, 484 U.S. 174 (1988), in which a father sought declaratory and injunctive relief under the PKPA with respect to conflicting state child custody decrees. The United States Supreme Court held that the PKPA did not create an implied cause of action in federal court to determine which of two conflicting state custody decrees is valid, reasoning that the statutory language of the PKPA and its legislative history indicated that Congress did not intend to create a new cause of action and did not intend federal courts "to play the enforcement role." Id. at 184.

5. *Parent locator service.* The PKPA also assists parents in locating an abducting parent by making the federal parent locator service available to state agencies and applying the Fugitive Felon Act to all state felony parental kidnapping cases. The parent locator service was established to assist state welfare departments to locate and force "deadbeat dads" to provide child support. Some proposed to make the service available to private individuals as well as official agencies. However, in the face of resistance by Department of Health and Human Services officials (concerning possible expense and invasions of privacy), the PKPA made the service available only to official agencies. Anne B. Goldstein, The Tragedy of the Interstate Child: A Critical Reexamination of the Uniform Child Custody Jurisdiction Act and Parental Kidnapping Prevention Act, 25 U.C. Davis L. Rev. 845, 918n 335 (1992).

6. *Enforcement remedies generally.* Many remedies exist to enforce custody determinations. Common remedies include civil contempt proceedings and the writ of habeas corpus. Although the latter was originally utilized by prisoners claiming

illegal arrest or unlawful detention, it is increasingly being utilized in child custody cases. See generally Paul J. Buser, Habeas Corpus Litigation in Child Custody Matters: An Historical Mine Field, 11 J. Am. Acad. Matrimonial Law. 1 (1993).

Some states also recognize (either by case law or statute) a tort action for custodial interference. Thus, in some cases, a parent may be liable for abduction or concealment of a child. According to the Restatement (Second) of Torts §700 (1977), the tort of interference with the parent-child relationship requires that: "One who, with knowledge that the parent does not consent, abducts or otherwise compels or induces a minor child to leave a parent legally entitled to its custody or not to return to the parent after it has been left him, is subject to liability to the parent." States also impose criminal liability for custodial interference. See generally Catherine F. Klein et al., Border Crossings: Understanding the Civil, Criminal, and Immigration Implications for Battered Women Fleeing Across State Lines with Their Children, 39 Fam. L.Q. 109 (2005). What is the purpose of civil versus criminal statutes? Are both necessary?

In some states, case law specifies that victims of domestic violence should not be penalized for custodial interference. For example, in Alaska, a court held that a mother's flight with a child to another state did not constitute custodial interference, parental kidnapping or other wrongful conduct that was sufficient to warrant a change in custody. Vachon v. Pugliese, 931 P.2d 371 (Alaska 1996).

7. *Attorney's ethical obligations.* Attorneys who become entangled in clients' self-help efforts potentially face serious consequences. A nonabducting parent generally may resort to two weapons against the abducting parent's attorney who assists the abducting parent by concealing the parent and/or child's whereabouts: to request the court to use its power of contempt to force the attorney to disclose the other parent's (and the children's) whereabouts, and/or to sue the attorney for professional malpractice in some cases. See In re Mendel, 897 P.2d 68 (Alaska 1995); Shehade v. Gerson, 500 N.E.2d 510 (Ill. Ct. App. 1986).

To what extent is an attorney prohibited, permitted, or mandated to disclose information based on the attorney-client privilege? How do the attorney's ethical obligations differ when the client merely is considering an abduction compared to when the client has already abducted the child? See In re Marriage of Decker, 606 N.E.2d 1094 (Ill. 1992). See generally S. Shelton Foss, The Attorney's Dilemma Under Model Rules 1.2 and 1.6: Clients Who Do Not Return Children in Custody Cases, 17 J. Legal Prof. 231 (1992).

Attorneys' ethical obligations are governed by both the attorney-client privilege and state ethics code rules on confidentiality. Under the former, the privilege applies where legal advice is sought from a legal adviser, for communications made in confidence by the client. Communications are permanently protected from disclosure by the client or the legal adviser unless the privilege is waived. Like all privileges, the attorney-client privilege is not absolute. Should the attorney-client privilege yield to the best interests of the child principle? See Bersani v. Bersani, 565 A.2d 1368 (Conn. Super. Ct. 1989).

The attorney also has ethical obligations under state rules of professional responsibility (influenced, in large part, by the ABA's Model Code of Professional Responsibility and the subsequent Model Rules of Professional Conduct). For example, Rule 1.2(d) of the Model Rules of Professional Conduct provides: "A lawyer shall not counsel a client to engage, or assist a client, in conduct that the lawyer knows is criminal or fraudulent." Many of the rules regarding disclosure, generally, pertain to disclosure of a fugitive client's whereabouts. Should such rules be applied to abducting parents?

Only a few jurisdictions have considered the issue whether the attorney-client privilege or the ethical duty of confidentiality protect an attorney from disclosure of a client's whereabouts. One commentator, who surveyed the case law, concludes that courts have not mandated disclosure in those domestic relations cases in which disclosure would threaten the client's safety. Cases that mandate disclosure of a client's whereabouts all involve clients who acted in violation of a court order. Shelly K. Hillyer, Comment, The Attorney-Client Privilege, Ethical Rules of Confidentiality, and Other Arguments Bearing on Disclosure of a Fugitive Client's Whereabouts, 68 Temp. L. Rev. 307, 341, 343 (1995).

Problem

When John and Loree divorce, Loree is awarded temporary physical custody of their daughter Jessica. Loree and Jessica move in with Loree's parents. At the custody hearing, John is awarded permanent physical custody of Jessica. When John attempts to obtain custody of Jessica from Loree, he is denied access by Loree's father, Franklin Rigenhagen. John then obtains a court order and returns to the parents' home. Franklin informs John that Loree and Jessica have left the state. John commences a seven-year search for Jessica. Based on information from the FBI indicating the Rigenhagens might have information about Loree's and Jessica's whereabouts, John files suit against Loree and the Rigenhagens alleging their actions constituted interference with parental custodial rights. John claims damages of over $50,000 in search-related costs, emotional distress, and loss of Jessica's companionship and society. The jurisdiction must decide whether to recognize the tort of custodial interference based on public policy considerations. What result? Larson v. Dunn, 460 N.W.2d 39 (Minn. 1990) (en banc).

Note: International Child Abduction

International child-snatching is a serious problem. Estimates suggest that hundreds of children are abducted either to or from the United States annually.[17] Several factors have contributed to the rise in international abductions, including the ease of international transportation and communication, the increasing number of binational marriages, and the decreasing rigor of passport supervision.[18] In response to this social problem, the Hague Conference on Private International Law adopted the Hague Convention on the Civil Aspects of International Child Abduction in 1980. Seventy-five nations are signatories to this international treaty, including the United States.[19] The United States implemented the Convention by

[17]. Nadine Joy Hazell, New Anti-Abduction Rules on Foreign Travel, Plain Dealer (Cleveland), Aug. 27, 2000, at K4 (reporting that the State Department has approximately 1,000 open international abduction cases at any given time).

[18]. Rania Nanos, Note, The Views of a Child: Emerging Interpretation and Significance of the Child's Objection Defense under the Hague Child Abduction Convention, 22 Brook J. Intl. L. 437, 437 (1996).

[19]. Status Table on the Convention of 25 October 1980 on the Civil Aspects of International Child Abduction, at http://hcch.e-vision.nl/index_en.php?act=conventions.status&cid=24 (last visited Feb. 16, 2006).

enabling legislation, the International Child Abduction Remedies Act (ICARA), 42 U.S.C. §§11601-11610 (2000).

The goal of the Hague Convention is to secure the return of children who are wrongfully removed from or retained in a signatory state and to return them to the country of their "habitual residence" (which must be another contracting nation) where the merits of the custody dispute can be adjudicated. Article 13 of the Convention specifies three affirmative defenses that may be invoked by an abducting parent to defeat the child's return: (1) if the abducting parent establishes that the child's caretaker was not actually exercising custody rights at the time of removal or retention or had consented to removal or retention; (2) if the abducting parent establishes a grave risk that the return would entail physical or psychological harm to the child; and (3) if the court in the forum of the abducting parent finds that the child, who has attained an appropriate age and maturity (based on the court's discretion), objects to the return.[20]

Courts have interpreted various provisions of the Convention, including the meaning of "habitual residence," and the "grave risk of harm" defense. See, e.g., Humphrey v. Humphrey, 434 F.3d 243 (4th Cir. 2006) (holding that father must establish the child's habitual residence by a preponderance of the evidence); Van de Sande v. Van de Sande, 431 F.3d 567 (7th Cir. 2005) (holding that mother satisfied the grave-risk-of-harm defense by establishing the risk of physical abuse by the children's father should they return to Belgium); Gitter v. Gitter, 396 F.3d 124 (2d Cir. 2005) (finding that, in determining a child's "habitual residence," courts should focus on the parents' intent to fix the place of residence and must consider whether the child has becoming acclimatized to the new location). See generally John Crouch, The Hague Convention on Child Abduction, 28 Fam. Advoc. 42 (2005); Deborah M. Zawadzki, Note, The Role of Courts in Preventing International Child Abduction, 13 Cardozo J. Int'l & Comp. L. 353 (2005).

Congress has also addressed international child abduction. In 1993 Congress enacted the International Parental Kidnapping Act (IPKA), 18 U.S.C. §1204 (1994). IPKA (unlike the Hague Convention) imposes criminal sanctions, making it a federal felony for a parent wrongfully to remove or retain a child outside the United States. The IPKA's affirmative defenses differ from those in the Hague Convention: if the defendant has been granted custody or visitation by a court acting pursuant to the UCCJA; is fleeing from domestic violence; or had court-ordered custody and failed to return the child because of circumstances beyond the defendant's control, provided that the defendant made reasonable attempts to notify the other parent.

The National Conference of Commissioners on Uniform State Laws is drafting the Uniform Child Abduction Prevention Act (UCAPA) to address abduction in domestic and international custody disputes. The act authorizes courts to impose "abduction prevention measures" either sua sponte or upon the motion of a parent or child welfare agency. Motions must specify risk factors for abduction (such as a party's prior arrest or conviction for a crime of domestic violence or child abuse).

[20]. Convention on the Civil Aspects of International Child Abduction, Oct. 25, 1980, art. 13, para. 1(a)-(b), T.I.A.S. No. 11,670, at 8, 19 I.L.M. at 1502.

The act also provides for confidentiality if the disclosure of information would put safety at risk.

C. WHAT PROCESS SHOULD GOVERN CUSTODY DISPUTES?

1. *The Adversary System versus Mediation Process*

■ **ELIZABETH S. SCOTT & ROBERT EMERY, CHILD CUSTODY DISPUTE RESOLUTION: THE ADVERSARIAL SYSTEM AND DIVORCE MEDIATION**
in Psychology and Child Custody Determinations: Knowledge, Roles and Expertise 23-27, 39-42, 45-51 (Lois A. Weithorn ed., 1987)

The adversary system has been well established in Anglo-American law for hundreds of years. There are two basic characteristics of this dispute resolution model: the decision maker is a neutral party not involved in the dispute (the judge), and the evidence about the dispute that the judge considers is controlled and developed by the disputing parties themselves. These characteristics have several implications for the process. Each litigant, through an attorney, attempts to present all the evidence favorable to his or her side of the case and unfavorable to the opponent's. . . . Adjudication through this process is designed to produce a "winner" and "a loser." . . .

Few other legal confrontations involve the emotional intensity of a custody dispute. In most litigation the adversaries are strangers, business associates, or acquaintances. The divorcing couple's prior intimate relationship exaggerates from the outset the potential for hostility. Because of the prior relationship, each parent may know particularly hurtful and damaging facts about the other. Further, the subject of the dispute, the custody of their child, may be crucially important to each parent. . . . The nature of the inquiry in custody disputes further heightens the tendency to promote hostility. [C]ustody adjudication focuses on the personal qualities of the parent. Each parent's efforts to persuade the judge that he or she is the better custodian may involve presenting evidence about the character, habits, lifestyle, and moral fitness of the former spouse. While in theory only evidence relating to an individual's capacity as a parent is relevant, any character deficiency or behavior that the judge is likely to view negatively often will be exposed. . . .

DIVORCE MEDIATION

Because of the dissatisfaction with the adversary system, there has been an increased interest in developing alternative methods of resolving child custody disputes. In the past several years, divorce mediation has grown dramatically as the major alternative to either litigation or out-of-court negotiation between attorneys. . . .

In divorce mediation the divorcing parties meet with an impartial third party (or parties) to identify, discuss, and one hopes, settle the disputes that result from marital dissolution. While it shares features with some types of marital and family therapy, mediation can be distinguished from many forms of psychotherapy in that it is short term and problem-focused. The process also requires that the mediator be knowledgeable in the legal and economic as well as the social and psychological consequences of divorce. Further, mediation differs from therapy in its objectives, and the exploration of emotional issues is circumscribed by the goal of negotiating a fair and acceptable agreement. Finally, unlike marital therapy, the goal of mediation is *not* reconciliation.

Divorce mediation embraces a model of dispute resolution considerably different from that characterizing the adversary process. Whereas in mediation the parties give up some procedural control in that the mediator directs much of the process, decisional control is not handed over to a third party as it is in adjudication. That the parents retain decisional control also distinguishes mediation from arbitration. Arbitration, like mediation, may encompass less formal procedures than does litigation, but unlike the mediator, the arbitrator is expected to make a decision for the parties if they do not do so themselves. . . .

Some divorce mediators attempt to settle all four of the major issues that must be decided in a divorce: property division, spousal support, custody and visitation, and child support. Almost all mediators, however, [who] work in public court settings [limit] their practice to the issues of custody and visitation. . . . The process by which decisions are reached and the impact it has on the parents' relationship is critical to the integrative decisions regarding child rearing, since both parents are likely to maintain at least some contact with their children after a divorce. . . .

Proponents have argued that mediation will have benefits in areas that have been termed the "four C's." That is, mediation is said to reduce *conflict*, increase *cooperation*, give people more *control* over important decisions in their lives, and achieve these goals at a reduced public or private *cost*. . . .

[A] number of questions remain about the mediation alternative. . . . These questions encompass debates on whether attorneys or mental health professionals are better trained to conduct mediation, whether mediation should be conducted by teams including one member of each profession, or whether a new, distinct profession must be created. . . .

Another set of questions about mediation concerns who should be included or excluded: whether referrals to court-based mediation programs should be mandatory; whether participation in mediation should be completely voluntary; and whether parents should be referred to mediation at individual judges' discretion. These three options now are variously used in jurisdictions throughout the United States. It has also been asked whether certain cases should automatically be excluded from mediation: for example, cases where there are apparently great discrepancies in the parties' relative bargaining power, as where spouse abuse has occurred, or where independent legal findings on matters such as child abuse or neglect must be made.

A third set of questions pertains to the process of mediation itself. Should children be included in mediation sessions? Should grandparents, stepparents, or other interested relatives have a role? What part should mediators play in deciding the content of the negotiated agreement? Should mediators, for example, work toward negotiating joint custody settlements? Moreover, should mediators refuse to be party to agreements they object to on ethical or psychological grounds? . . .

Finally, a set of questions has been raised about what is to happen once mediation ends. What role should attorneys play in regard to a mediated settlement? Can a single attorney review the agreement, should it be reviewed by two attorneys who hold an adversarial perspective, or need it be reviewed by an attorney at all? Perhaps the most controversial debate about the termination of mediation, however, concerns the mediator's role in any subsequent court hearing. Some have argued that when a court hearing is held after mediation fails to produce an agreement, the mediator *should* make a recommendation to the court.

Proponents of this perspective point to the fact that the mediator is already familiar with the family and that such a recommendation will avoid the duplication of efforts inherent in beginning a new custody investigation. Others argue that strict confidentiality is essential to the mediation process. . . . Practice and judicial policy remain unresolved in regard to the important issue of confidentiality. . . .

The following case wrestles with "the most controversial debate" (according to the above excerpt).

■ McLAUGHLIN v. SUPERIOR COURT
189 Cal. Rptr. 479 (Ct. App. 1983)

RATTIGAN, Associate Justice.

Civil Code section 4607 requires prehearing mediation of child custody and visitation disputes in marital dissolution proceedings conducted pursuant to the Family Law Act. The statute also provides that, if the parties fail to agree in the mediation proceedings, the mediator "may, consistent with local court rules, render a recommendation to the court as to the custody or visitation of the child or children" involved. Pursuant to this provision, respondent superior court has adopted a "local court rule," or policy, which (1) requires the mediator to make a recommendation to the court if the parties fail to agree in the mediation proceedings, but (2) prohibits cross-examination of the mediator by the parties. We hold in this original proceeding that the policy is constitutionally invalid in significant respects. . . .

Petitioner Thomas J. McLaughlin and real party in interest Linda Lee McLaughlin were married in 1969. They have three children, whose ages range between 6 and 13 years. [In May 1982, the husband petitioned for dissolution and custody. In response, the wife requested joint legal custody as well as physical custody. Husband then applied for temporary custody with visitation to the wife. The court issued an order to show cause in which the questions of temporary custody and visitation were set for hearing on June 30. The wife filed a declaration in which she requested temporary custody with visitation to the father.]

[At the hearing on the order to show cause,] petitioner's counsel recited his understanding that the pending issues of temporary custody and visitation were to be "referred for mediation." Counsel also stated his view that "the mediation procedure[,] insofar as it allows the mediator to make a recommendation for the Court, and bars the introduction of any testimony from the mediator about what the parties tell him or her[,] is unconstitutional as a denial of the right to cross-examine." On that ground, counsel in effect moved for a "protective order" which would permit mediation proceedings, but which would provide that if they did not result in agreement by the parties, on the issues of temporary custody and visitation, the mediator would be prohibited from making a recommendation to the court unless petitioner were guaranteed the right to cross-examine the mediator. [T]he court denied the motion on the ground that the "protective order" requested would violate a policy the court had adopted pursuant to Civil Code section 4607, subdivision (e).

[An exchange with counsel] included the only available description of respondent court's policy, which has apparently not been memorialized in a written rule. For these reasons, we quote pertinent passages of the exchange in the margin.[3]

[After the court denied petitioner's motion and request for a stay, he appealed to the California Supreme Court. The Supreme Court stayed the hearing and returned the case to the court of appeals for a hearing on the issue of the constitutionality of the practice of mediator recommendations.]

Civil Code section 4607, subdivision (a), clearly requires prehearing mediation of child custody and visitation disputes in marital dissolution proceedings. Subdivision (e) of the statute is also clear to the effect that the mediator "may, consistent with local court rules," make a recommendation to the court on either issue, or both, if the parties fail to reach agreement in the mediation proceedings. Subdivision (e) does not require or authorize disclosure to the parties of a recommendation made by the mediator to the court, nor of the mediator's reasons; it neither requires nor authorizes cross-examination of the mediator by the parties, which would necessarily require or bring about disclosure of the recommendation and the reasons for it; and the statute's express deference to "local court rules" has the effect of making disclosure and cross-examination matters of local option.

As we have seen, respondent court has exercised this option by adopting a policy which requires that the mediator make a recommendation to the court if the parties have failed to agree on child custody or visitation in the mediation proceedings; requires that the mediator not state his or her reasons for the recommendation; and denies the parties the right to cross-examine the mediator on

3. "The Court [addressing Mr. Brunwasser, petitioner's counsel]: Some counties, as you probably know, do not permit or require a recommendation from the mediator in the event the parties are unable to agree. Some do. This county [i.e., respondent court] does, and therefore, I'm not prepared to give you the protective order you wish. The court feels that in the event the mediator were free to testify as to any of the matters mediated, that is[,] the substance of the matter as gleaned from the mediation session, . . . certainly you would have the right to cross-examine the mediator.

"However, our instructions as a matter of court policy to the mediators are that they are not to state the basis for their . . . recommendation. . . . In short, the recommendation of the mediator is simply . . . a recommendation to the court without any statement of underlying basis. . . . That's the way we do business here. . . .

"Mr. Brunwasser: . . . I have no objection to mediation. What I have an objection to is a procedure which allows the mediator . . . to communicate with the court and not be subject to defend [sic] his or her opinion by cross-examination.

"The Court: I understand that. I hope you equally understand that it is our policy to require a recommendation if the mediation is unsuccessful. It's a starting point which enables the court . . . [,] in the absence of other evidence, to make an interim order based upon the opinion of the trained counselor, and it's a procedure we opted for when this law was enacted. We're satisfied that the law permits that, and so your motion for a protective order is denied."

the ground that the reasons have not been disclosed to the court. Amicus curiae has shown us that one large metropolitan superior court follows an entirely different procedure, and that another has adopted a policy which is essentially similar to respondent court's.[7]

The feature of respondent court's policy which prohibits cross-examination of the mediator is consistent with the provision in subdivision (c) of the statute that the mediation proceedings "shall be confidential." The requirement that the mediator not state to the court his or her reasons for the recommendation is consistent with the provision in subdivision (c) which protects the confidentiality of the parties' "communications" to the mediator by making them "official information within the meaning of Section 1040 of the Evidence Code." The facts remain that the policy permits the court to receive a significant recommendation on contested issues but denies the parties the right to cross-examine its source. This combination cannot constitutionally be enforced. . . .

Respondent court contends that the enforcement of its policy prohibiting cross-examination of a mediator who makes a recommendation to it is constitutionally permissible because only "temporary" child custody and visitation are involved and "due process is not required at every stage of a proceeding." . . . However, the word "temporary" does not appear in Civil Code section 4607. We are not at liberty to interpolate it, by construction. . . . The constitutional infirmities in respondent court's policy are such that it may not be enforced on the theory that only "temporary" custody or visitation are involved. . . .

. . . Our conclusions are consistent with our duty to harmonize the provisions of subdivisions (a) and (e) of the statute without doing violence to its salutary purposes. In addition, it has been shown in the present proceeding that disparities among "local court rules" adopted pursuant to subdivision (e) have had the effect of guaranteeing due process in some superior courts but not in others. Our conclusions will terminate this effect, which the Legislature obviously did not intend.

[The court concluded that the husband was entitled to a writ of mandate which] directs that the court not receive a recommendation from the mediator, as to any contested issue on which agreement is not reached, unless (1) the court has first made a protective order which guarantees the parties the rights to have the mediator testify and to cross-examine him or her concerning the recommendation or (2) the rights have been waived. . . .

---

7. Amicus curiae describes the practice of the Los Angeles County Superior Court . . . : Where prehearing mediation proceedings have been conducted . . . , the court (1) neither receives nor permits a recommendation by the mediator and (2) proceeds to hear and determine the contested issue or issues without referring to the unsuccessful mediation process in any way.

Amicus curiae has filed declarations showing the related practice followed in the Superior Court for the City and County of San Francisco. . . . When the initial hearing is called on the same day [as the mediation session], the parties' attorneys communicate the mediator's recommendation to the court. . . . This (appellate) court interprets the [above declaration] to mean that the mediator's reasons for his or her recommendation are not disclosed to the parties, the attorneys, or the court when the recommendation is made in the first instance. This declaration fairly shows that the court makes the initial order on temporary custody or visitation without permitting cross-examination of the mediator. The declaration does not show whether cross-examination of the mediator is permitted at any later hearing.

Notes and Questions

1. *Benefits*. Mediation is a form of alternative dispute resolution that respects the parties' autonomy in decisionmaking ("private ordering"). In the adversarial system, the judiciary asserts authority over the financial aspects of dissolution and child custody. Mediation, however, confers broad latitude on the divorcing couple to resolve such matters for themselves. Why do Professors Scott and Emery suggest that mediation is better suited to the resolution of custody disputes? What are the benefits and costs of the adversary system? Of the mediation process? See generally Ann L. Diamond & Madeleine Simborg, Divorce Mediation's Weaknesses, Cal. Law., July 1983, at 37; Gary J. Friedman & Margaret L. Anderson, Divorce Mediation's Strengths, Cal. Law., July 1983, at 36; Leonard L. Riskin, Mediation and Lawyers, 43 Ohio State L.J. 29, 33 (1982).

2. *Comparison*. How does mediation differ from other forms of alternative dispute resolution (such as arbitration) and from psychotherapy in terms of objectives, process, and the ultimate decisionmaker? See Joan Kelly, Mediation and Psychotherapy: Distinguishing the Differences, 1 Mediation Q. 33 (1983).

3. *Historical background*. Mediation has long-standing roots in ancient China, Japan, and Africa. In the United States, mediation flourished in the late 1970s, fueled by acceptance of no-fault divorce and dissatisfaction with traditional dispute resolution.

In 1981, California became the first state to require mediation (formerly Cal. Civ. Code §4607, now Cal. Fam. Code §3170 (West 2004)). Mandatory mediation was intended to facilitate parental agreements for joint custody.[21] Before the parties can proceed to a hearing, mediation is required in all cases in which custody and/or visitation is contested. The statute also reformed California's system of Family Conciliation Courts to provide mediation services.

> Court conciliation staffs, particularly in California, were probably the first to offer divorce mediation services as they are now known. California offered court-connected conciliation services as early as 1939. The initial focus of these services was on providing marriage counseling aimed at reconciliation. With the adoption of no-fault divorce and the increase in the divorce rate, the focus of conciliation shifted from reconciliation to divorce counseling and custody mediation. Court mediation services have proliferated in the last few years, with the encouragement (or actual mandate) of legislation. . . .

Jay Folberg, A Mediation Overview: History and Dimensions of Practice, 1 Mediation Q. 3, 6 (1983). Court-ordered mediation services are often limited to a certain number of sessions.

Many state statutes now provide for mediation, either by encouraging the parties to mediate (as an educational tool), providing for discretionary referrals by the court (most common),[22] or, as in California, mandating mediation.[23] Most

---

[21]. Susan Kuhn, Comment, Mandatory Mediation: California Civil Code Section 4607, 33 Emory L.J. 733, 743 (1984).

[22]. Maggie Vincent, Note, Mandatory Mediation of Custody Disputes: Criticism, Legislation, and Support, 20 Vt. L. Rev. 255, 271 (1995).

[23]. Rebecca Hinton, Comment, Giving Children a Right to Be Heard: Suggested Reforms to Provide Louisiana Children a Voice in Child Custody Disputes, 65 La. L. Rev. 1539, 1565 (2005) (pointing out that 13 states now make custody mediation mandatory).

statutes provide for court-connected mediation only of custody (rather than spousal support and property issues). What are the advantages and disadvantages of mandatory, as opposed to voluntary, mediation? See Elliot G. Hicks, Too Much of a Good Thing?, 12 W.V. Law. 4, 14 (1998) (calling mandatory mediation a "serious oxymoron" because it is useful only when parties are willing to work toward settlement); Holly A. Streeter-Schaefer, Note, A Look at Court Mandated Civil Mediation, 49 Drake L. Rev. 367 (2001) (providing a survey of supporting and opposing viewpoints).

4. *Gender differences.* Some critics focus on the shortcomings of mediation for women:

> Increased use of mediation in the courts has caused women's advocates to question whether mediation is serving the needs of women who are undergoing divorces. The concern is that in mediation, the woman, who has traditionally held the less powerful position in society and marriage, will not have the bargaining strength, and negotiating skills necessary to get what she needs out of the mediation, and that in some instances, particularly when the mediation is mandated, the process is so coercive she may be forced to negotiate bad bargains.

Maggie Vincent, Note, Mandatory Mediation of Custody Disputes: Criticism, Legislation, and Support, 20 Vt. L. Rev. 255, 266 (1995). Does the adversarial system or mediation better serve women's interests? Are mediators more likely than courts to engage in gender bias, as another commentator suggests? See Trina Grillo, The Mediation Alternative: Process Dangers for Women, 100 Yale L.J. 1545 (1991); Madeleine B. Simborg & Joan B. Kelly, Beware of Stereotypes in Mediation, 17 Fam. Advoc. 69 (1994). But cf. Joshua D. Rosenberg, In Defense of Mediation, 33 Ariz. L. Rev. 467, 488 (1991) (judges may disguise bias better; bias has more devastating impact in adjudication context).

Would voluntary, rather than mandatory, mediation better serve women's interests? Compare Grillo, supra, at 1610 (advocating voluntary, rather than mandatory, mediation), with Rosenberg, supra, at 503-506 (advocating reform of mandatory mediation to address these shortcomings). Do you agree that many women need the "vindication" that the adversarial process provides rather than the compromise of mediation? See Grillo, supra, at 1560. To better protect women's interests, should property and support issues be settled by the adversary system but custody by mediation? Or should mediation be extended to all issues?

See generally Penelope E. Bryan, Killing Us Softly: Divorce Mediation and the Politics of Power, 40 Buff. L. Rev. 441 (1992); Grillo, supra; Vincent, supra, at 275-282 (exploring methods of improving mediation to address feminist criticisms). See also Rosenberg, supra (criticizing Grillo's views). For an empirical assessment of feminist criticisms, see Jessica Pearson, The Equity of Divorce Mediation Agreements, 9 Mediation Q. 179 (1991); Vincent, supra, at 275-282 (both refuting evidence that women who undergo mediation do not fare as well as those who litigate).

5. *Mediation and domestic violence.* Commentators have long pointed out that mediation poses special dangers for battered women. See Jane Murphy & Robert Rubinson, Domestic Violence and Mediation: Responding to the Challenges of Crafting Effective Screens, 39 Fam. L.Q. 53 (2005). Special concerns include: the increased risk posed to victims before and after mediation sessions; mediated agreements that tend to give abusers more frequent access than litigated outcomes

and thereby provide additional opportunities for abuse; and mediators who are not trained to recognize abusive relationships or to counteract the power imbalance that characterizes the parties' relationship. See Lauri Boxer-Macomber, Revising the Impact of California's Mandatory Custody Mediation Program on Victims of Domestic Violence Through a Feminist Positionality Lens, 15 St. Thomas L. Rev. 883, 886 (2003); Kerry Loomis, Comment, Domestic Violence and Mediation: A Tragic Combination for Victims in California Family Court, 35 Cal. W. L. Rev. 355, 363 (1999).

Several schools of thought exist about the wisdom of mediation in domestic violence cases. Some believe that mediation should never be used in cases of domestic violence; others contend that mediation should be used with adequate safeguards; and still others believe that the choice of mediation should be left to the victim. Murphy & Rubinson, supra, at 53-54. Statutory treatment of mediation in domestic violence cases reveals a similar range of responses: (1) statutory exclusions (e.g., waivers for "good cause" or "extraordinary cause" or if a party will suffer "severe emotional distress"); (2) provisions for separate mediation sessions; and (3) provisions allowing an abused spouse to bring a support person. See Ben Barlow, Divorce Child Custody Mediation: In Order to Form a More Perfect Disunion?, 52 Clev. St. L. Rev. 499, 515-522 (2004-2005) (surveying state statutes). To which view, and to which approach, do you subscribe?

Several organizations have developed rules to regulate the practice of mediation in cases of domestic violence. In 2001, the ABA Section of Family Law and the Association of Family & Conciliation Courts (AFCC) adopted Model Standards of Practice for Family and Divorce Mediation that define domestic violence, require training for mediators and screening by mediators, and provide for safeguards during mediation. See Andrew Schepard, An Introduction to the Model Standards of Practice for Family and Divorce Mediation, 35 Fam. L.Q. 1 (2001). (The ABA Model Standards revise ABA Standards of Practice for Divorce Mediation originally adopted in 1984 that failed to address domestic violence.) The American Law Institute also addresses the issue by requiring courts to develop a screening process to identify cases of domestic violence and then to recommend mediation only when both parties agree. ALI Principles §2.07.

Some commentators criticize existing reforms as ineffective. For example, Murphy & Rubinson, supra, contend that the statutory waivers (e.g., "good cause") include broad and vague standards; statutes often place the burden of identifying abuse on victims who may be particularly reluctant to do so; and court personnel as well as mediators lack the expertise to screen for domestic violence. Id. at 60-64. How can the law more effectively respond to mediation in cases of domestic violence?

6. *Qualifications.* Mediation may be provided by publicly funded court services or by mediators in private practice. Early in the development of mediation, many states failed to specify minimum qualifications for mediators. Now statutes often provide for qualifications for court-connected mediators. However, mediators in the private sector continue to be largely unregulated. In an effort to address this problem, the recently-revised ABA Model Standards of Practice for Family and Divorce Mediation apply to mediators in court-based mediation programs as well as private practice. What should be a mediator's qualifications in terms of education, experience, and specialized training?

7. *Role of the mediator.* Mental health professionals and lawyers constitute the largest percentage of mediators. How might these different orientations affect the role of the mediator and the practice of mediation? One commentator has suggested four conceptual frameworks: (1) the therapeutic framework, with the mediator as healer; (2) the educational framework, with the mediator as teacher; (3) the rational-analytic framework, with the mediator as strategist; and (4) the normative-evaluative framework, with the mediator as judge. See Jane Becker-Haven, Modes of Mediating Child Custody Disputes, Ph.D. Dissertation, Stanford University (1988). Note that the recently-revised ABA Model Standards of Practice for Family and Divorce Mediation apply to all mediators regardless of the mediator's professional orientation. (The 1984 ABA Model Standards applied only to lawyer-mediators.)

8. *Ethical problems.* Ethical problems arose when mediation first became popular. Early questions focused on the proper role of the attorney-mediator. That is, did a lawyer-mediator violate the prohibition on representation of conflicting or potentially differing interests or the prohibition of dual representation (of both husband and wife)? State bar ethics committees ruled that a lawyer-mediator could mediate a dispute for the husband and wife so long as the mediator informs the parties that she or he represents neither and will refrain from representing either if the mediation proves unsuccessful, and advises the parties to seek independent legal counsel to review the agreement. See Linda J. Silberman, Professional Responsibility Problems of Divorce Mediation, 16 Fam. L.Q. 107, 110-119 (1982).

Whether a lawyer-mediator can serve both as a mediator and also as the draftsperson of the parties' written settlement agreement poses a recurring ethical dilemma. When a lawyer-mediator drafts a settlement agreement for divorcing spouses, the mediator is acting as an attorney who is representing opposing litigants. Such representation would violate the ethical ban on representing adverse parties in litigation. (Moreover, many jurisdictions specifically prohibit dual representation in divorce cases.) The Utah State Bar's Board of Bar Commissioners recently issued an opinion prohibiting a lawyer-mediator from representing both spouses in this manner. Utah State Bar Ethics Advisory Op. Comm., Op. 05-03 (2005). See generally Marsha B. Freeman, Divorce Mediation: Sweeping Conflicts Under the Rug, Time to Clean House, 78 U. Det. Mercy L. Rev. 67 (2000); Diana K. Vescovo et al., Ethical Dilemmas in Mediation, 31 U. Mem. L. Rev. 59 (2000).

9. *Role of attorneys.* Attorneys fill a variety of roles in the mediation process. They may serve as mediators, they may also be participant-observers, or reviewers of the mediated agreements. Does the presence of lawyers as participant or reviewer serve to make the system more fair and effective or to undermine the mediation process? See generally Divorce and Family Mediation: Models, Techniques, and Applications (Jay Folberg et al. eds., 2004).

10. *Limitations.* What limitations should exist on private ordering? Should a mediator draft an agreement that the mediator does not believe is "fair" to one or both parties? Should the mediator defer to the parties' sense of fairness? Mediators differ concerning the extent to which a mediator should intervene in dispute resolution. See generally Joseph P. Folger & Sydney E. Bernard, Divorce Mediation: When Mediators Challenge the Divorcing Parties, 10 Mediation Q. 5, 19 (1985) (approximately 25 percent of mediators adopt a highly interventionist stance to achieve fairness and protect weaker parties).

11. *Children's role*. Should children play a role in mediation? What might be the advantages and disadvantages? If children play a role, what should that role consist of? Active participant? Consultant? What factors should influence the nature and extent of children's participation? Note that in England and Wales, since 2004, a nationwide scheme provides that in cases of divorce, children age nine and over are generally expected to attend mediation. N. V. Lowe, The Allocation of Parental Rights and Responsibilities—The Position in England and Wales, 39 Fam. L.Q. 267, 277 (2005). See generally Carol S. Bruch, And How Are the Children? The Effects of Ideology and Mediation on Child Custody Law and Children's Well-Being in the United States, 2 Intl. J.L. & Fam. 106 (1988).

12. *Confidentiality*. Confidentiality is central to the mediation process. As *McLaughlin* explains, some locales permit the mediator to make a recommendation to the court if mediation proves unsuccessful. What is the practical effect?

> The power to make a recommendation to the court gives the mediator considerable authority. Although the court is not bound to follow the mediator's recommendation, such a recommendation will probably influence a judge's decision. The mediator has spent more time with the parties than the judge, and the mediator has seen the parties interact. The mediator may have interviewed the children and other significant people. The mediator's education and experience adds credibility to his or her assessment of the case. Based on the collective weight of these factors, there is a high likelihood that the judge will "rubber stamp" the mediator's recommendation.

Kuhn, supra, at 770-771.

Many commentators criticize this practice. What constitutional concerns are implicated? Are they similar to those posed by the admission of expert testimony (supra)? See also In re Marriage of Gayden, 280 Cal. Rptr. 862 (Ct. App. 1991) (family counselor's recommendation, received orally by telephone because of her unavailability, violated due process).

The statute at issue in *McLaughlin* requires that "[m]ediation proceedings shall be held in private and shall be confidential, and all communications, verbal or written, from the parties to the mediator . . . shall be [privileged]." Once a mediator makes a recommendation and is subject to cross-examination, the mediator may have to divulge confidential communications that were elicited during mediation. Might warning the parties of this possibility interfere with the creation of trust?

McLaughlin requires that the policy of confidentiality yield to due process concerns. Is this an optimum accommodation of these competing interests?

> Permitting the mediator to make a recommendation undermines the neutrality of the mediator's role. The purpose of the mediation is to encourage the parties to create their own agreement. The mediator's opinion should not matter. . . . When the mediator is given the power to choose between the parties, his role is elevated to that of a judge. The best way to guarantee the parties their due process rights and ensure the confidentiality of the mediation sessions is to prohibit the mediator from making a recommendation at all.

Kuhn, supra, at 776. See generally Kent L. Brown, Comment, Confidentiality in Mediation: Status and Implications, 1991 J. Disp. Resol. 307.

McLaughlin also has implications for battered women. The policy of permitting mediators to make recommendations (even if the mediators are subject to cross-examination) permits the disclosure of private information that the victim has chosen to reveal in the mediation. Dunnigan, supra, at 1049.

13. *Collaborative law.* Collaborative law, an innovative form of alternative dispute resolution, was launched in 1990 by Minneapolis family law attorney Stuart Webb. In collaborative law procedures, the parties and their attorneys sign a binding agreement in which they agree to use cooperative techniques without resort to judicial intervention except for court approval of the parties' agreement. Attorneys are prohibited from participating in contested court proceedings for their clients. That is, if the parties are unable to reach an agreement through collaborative law procedures, their attorneys must withdraw from representation.

The attorney's role in collaborative law procedures differs from that of the attorney as mediator. The traditional mediation model involves two parties and the mediator; counsel (if any) provides legal services outside the mediation process. In contrast, collaborative lawyers are advocates for their clients (rather than neutral facilitators). In addition, collaborative lawyers are more directive than traditional mediators in helping their clients realize their goal. Texas became the first state in 2001 to provide, by statute, for resolution of certain family matters by collaborative law procedures. See Tex. Fam. Code §153.0072 (West 2003).

Must an attorney take special care to advise the client about the risks of collaborative law (i.e., if the process fails, the attorneys must withdraw)? See New Jersey Supreme Court Advisory Committee on Professional Ethics, Op. 699 (2006) (concluding that before agreeing to represent a client in a collaborative law process, the lawyer must determine that it will serve the client's interests and alert the client to the risks).

See generally John Lande, The Promise and Perils of Collaborative Law, 12 Disp. Resol. Mag. 29 (Fall 2005); Pauline H. Tesler, Collaborative Family Law, 4 Pepp. Disp. Resol. L.J. 317 (2004); Joshua Isaacs, Note, Current Development, A New Way to Avoid the Courtroom: The Ethical Implications Surrounding Collaborative Law, 18 Geo. J. Legal Ethics 833 (2005).

2. Coin Flipping

■ **ROBERT H. MNOOKIN, CHILD-CUSTODY ADJUDICATION: JUDICIAL FUNCTIONS IN THE FACE OF INDETERMINACY**
39 Law & Contemp. Probs. 226, 289-291 (1975)

RANDOM SELECTION

[Would] a random process of decision be fairer and more efficient than adjudication under a best-interests principle? Individualized adjudication means that the result will often turn on a largely intuitive evaluation based on unspoken values and unproven predictions. We would more frankly acknowledge both our ignorance and the presumed equality of the natural parents were we to flip a coin. Whether one had a separate flip for each child or one flip for all the children, the process would certainly be cheaper and quicker. It would avoid the pain associated with an adversary proceeding that requires an open exploration of the intimate aspects of family life and an ultimate judgment that one parent is preferable to the other. And it might have beneficial effects on private negotiations.

Resolving a custody dispute by state-administered coin-flip would probably be viewed as unacceptable by most in our society. Perhaps this reaction reflects an abiding faith, despite the absence of an empirical basis for it, that letting a judge choose produces better results for the child. Alternatively, flipping a coin might be unacceptable for some because it represents an abdication of the search for wisdom. . . .

[A] coin-flip would be a government affirmation of the equality of the parents. In a custody case, however, a coin-flip also symbolically abdicates government responsibility for the child and symbolically denies the importance of human differences and distinctiveness. Moreover, flipping a coin would deprive the parents of a process and a forum where their anger and aspirations might be expressed. In all, these symbolic and participatory values of adjudication would be lost by a random process. . . .

VIII

State Regulation of the Parent-Child Relationship

Historically, the law regarded children as the property of their parents, particularly of their father.[1] Today, the law increasingly views children as individuals with their own distinct interests. Yet children often are too immature and vulnerable to advance their own interests or exercise their own rights — limitations the law has recognized.[2] Further, the principle of parental autonomy (the freedom to rear children as parents see fit) has long limited state intrusion into the family. Given these starting points, a challenge emerges: how to allocate authority among the parents, the child, and the state to make important decisions affecting the child. The materials that follow explore these issues.

A. PARENTAL AUTONOMY: FAMILY PRIVACY REVISITED

1. Constitutional Doctrine and Limitations

■ MEYER v. NEBRASKA
262 U.S. 390 (1923)

Review case, reprinted in Chapter I, p. 15.

---

[1]. See generally Mary Ann Mason, From Father's Property to Children's Rights: The History of Child Custody in America (1994). See also Barbara Bennett Woodhouse, "Who Owns the Child?": *Meyer* and *Pierce* and the Child as Property, 33 Wm. & Mary L. Rev. 995 (1992).

[2]. See, e.g., Bellotti v. Baird, 443 U.S. 622, 633-637 (1979).

■ PIERCE v. SOCIETY OF SISTERS
268 U.S. 510 (1925)

Review case, reprinted in Chapter I, p. 16.

■ PRINCE v. MASSACHUSETTS
321 U.S. 158 (1944)

Mr. Justice RUTLEDGE delivered the opinion of the Court.

The case brings for review another episode in the conflict between Jehovah's Witnesses and state authority. This time Sarah Prince appeals from convictions for violating Massachusetts' child labor laws, by acts said to be a rightful exercise of her religious convictions. . . .

. . . Mrs. Prince, living in Brockton, is the mother of two young sons. She also has legal custody of Betty Simmons [her niece, age nine] who lives with them. The children too are Jehovah's Witnesses and both Mrs. Prince and Betty testified they were ordained ministers. The former was accustomed to go each week on the streets of Brockton to distribute "Watchtower" and "Consolation," according to the usual plan. She had permitted the children to engage in this activity previously, and had been warned against doing so by the school attendance officer, Mr. Perkins. But, until December 18, 1941, she generally did not take them with her at night.

That evening, as Mrs. Prince was preparing to leave her home, the children asked to go. She at first refused. Childlike, they resorted to tears and, motherlike, she yielded. Arriving downtown, Mrs. Prince permitted the children "to engage in the preaching work with her upon the sidewalks." That is, with specific reference to Betty, she and Mrs. Prince took positions about twenty feet apart near a street intersection. Betty held up in her hand, for passersby to see, copies of "Watch Tower" and "Consolation." From her shoulder hung the usual canvas magazine bag, on which was printed "Watchtower and Consolation 5 cents per copy." No one accepted a copy from Betty that evening and she received no money. Nor did her aunt. But on other occasions, Betty had received funds and given out copies. . . .

[Appellant argues] squarely on freedom of religion under the First Amendment, applied by the Fourteenth to the states. She buttresses this foundation, however, with a claim of parental right as secured by the due process clause of the latter Amendment. Cf. Meyer v. Nebraska, 262 U.S. 390 [(1923)]. Thus, two claimed liberties are at stake. One is the parent's, to bring up the child in the way he should go, which for appellant means to teach him the tenets and the practices of their faith. The other freedom is the child's, to observe these; and among them is "to preach the gospel . . . by public distribution" of "Watchtower" and "Consolation," in conformity with the scripture: "A little child shall lead them." . . .

To make accommodation between these freedoms and an exercise of state authority always is delicate. . . . It is cardinal with us that the custody, care and nurture of the child reside first in the parents, whose primary function and freedom include preparation for obligations the state can neither supply nor hinder [citing *Pierce*]. And it is in recognition of this that these decisions have respected the private realm of family life which the state cannot enter.

But the family itself is not beyond regulation in the public interest, as against a claim of religious liberty. Reynolds v. United States, 98 U.S. 145 [(1878)]; Davis v.

Beason, 133 U.S. 333 [(1890)]. And neither rights of religion nor rights of parenthood are beyond limitation. Acting to guard the general interest in youth's well being, the state as parens patriae may restrict the parent's control by requiring school attendance, regulating or prohibiting the child's labor, and in many other ways. Its authority is not nullified merely because the parent grounds his claim to control the child's course of conduct on religion or conscience. . . .

But it is said the state cannot do so here. . . . The child's presence on the street, with her guardian, distributing or offering to distribute the magazines, it is urged, was in no way harmful to her, nor in any event more so than the presence of many other children at the same time and place, engaged in shopping and other activities not prohibited. . . .

[The] state's authority over children's activities is broader than over like actions of adults. This is peculiarly true of public activities and in matters of employment. A democratic society rests, for its continuance, upon the healthy, well-rounded growth of young people into full maturity as citizens, with all that implies. It may secure this against impeding restraints and dangers, within a broad range of selection. Among evils most appropriate for such action are the crippling effects of child employment, more especially in public places, and the possible harms arising from other activities subject to all the diverse influences of the street. . . .

. . . The case reduces itself therefore to the question whether the presence of the child's guardian puts a limit to the state's power. . . . Parents may be free to become martyrs themselves. But it does not follow they are free, in identical circumstances, to make martyrs of their children before they have reached the age of full and legal discretion when they can make that choice for themselves. Massachusetts has determined that an absolute prohibition, though one limited to streets and public places and to the incidental uses proscribed, is necessary to accomplish its legitimate objectives. . . . The judgment is affirmed.

■ WISCONSIN v. YODER
406 U.S. 205 (1972)

BURGER, C.J., delivered the opinion of the Court. . . .

Respondents Jonas Yoder and Wallace Miller are members of the Old Order Amish religion, and respondent Adin Yutzy is a member of the Conservative Amish Mennonite Church. . . . Wisconsin's compulsory school-attendance law required them to cause their children to attend public or private school until reaching age 16 but the respondents declined to send their children, ages 14 and 15, to public school after they completed the eighth grade. The children were not enrolled in any private school, or within any recognized exception to the compulsory-attendance law, and they are conceded to be subject to the Wisconsin statute.

[R]espondents were charged, tried, and convicted of violating the compulsory-attendance law in Green County Court and were fined the sum of $5 each. Respondents defended on the ground that the application of the compulsory-attendance law violated their rights under the First and Fourteenth Amendments. . . .

[The Amish] object to the high school, and higher education generally, because the values they teach are in marked variance with Amish values and the Amish way of life; they view secondary school education as an impermissible exposure of their children to a "worldly" influence in conflict with their beliefs. The high school tends to emphasize intellectual and scientific accomplishments, self-distinction, competitiveness, worldly success, and social life with other students. Amish society emphasizes informal learning-through-doing; a life of "goodness," rather than a life of intellect; wisdom, rather than technical knowledge; community welfare, rather than competition; and separation from, rather than integration with, contemporary worldly society.

Formal high school education beyond the eighth grade is contrary to Amish beliefs, not only because it places Amish children in an environment hostile to Amish beliefs with increasing emphasis on competition in class work and sports and with pressure to conform to the styles, manners, and ways of the peer group, but also because it takes them away from their community, physically and emotionally, during the crucial and formative adolescent period of life. [H]igh school attendance with teachers who are not of the Amish faith — and may even be hostile to it — interposes a serious barrier to the integration of the Amish child into the Amish religious community. . . .

The Amish do not object to elementary education through the first eight grades as a general proposition because they agree that their children must have basic skills in the "three R's" in order to read the Bible, to be good farmers and citizens, and to be able to deal with non-Amish people when necessary in the course of daily affairs. [However, expert] Dr. Hostetler testified that compulsory high school attendance could not only result in great psychological harm to Amish children, because of the conflicts it would produce, but would also, in his opinion, ultimately result in the destruction of the Old Order Amish church community as it exists in the United States today. . . .

[The Wisconsin Supreme Court reversed the convictions, based on the Free Exercise Clause of the First Amendment. The Supreme Court affirms.]

There is no doubt as to the power of a State, having a high responsibility for education of its citizens, to impose reasonable regulations for the control and duration of basic education. See, e.g., Pierce v. Society of Sisters, 268 U.S. 510, 534 (1925). Providing public schools ranks at the very apex of the function of a State. Yet even this paramount responsibility was, in *Pierce*, made to yield to the right of parents to provide an equivalent education in a privately operated system. [A] State's interest in universal education, however highly we rank it, is not totally free from a balancing process when it impinges on fundamental rights and interests, such as those specifically protected by the Free Exercise Clause of the First Amendment, and the traditional interest of parents with respect to the religious upbringing of their children so long as they, in the words of *Pierce*, "prepare [them] for additional obligations." 268 U.S., at 535. It follows that in order for Wisconsin to compel school attendance beyond the eighth grade against a claim that such attendance interferes with the practice of a legitimate religious belief, it must appear either that the State does not deny the free exercise of religious belief by its requirement, or that there is a state interest of sufficient magnitude to override the interest claiming protection under the Free Exercise Clause. [The Court determines that the Amish objection to school attendance beyond eighth grade is rooted in religious beliefs which directly conflict with the compulsory school attendance law.]

. . . The State advances two primary arguments in support of its system of compulsory education. It notes, as Thomas Jefferson pointed out early in our history, that some degree of education is necessary to prepare citizens to participate effectively and intelligently in our open political system if we are to preserve freedom and independence. Further, education prepares individuals to be self-reliant and self-sufficient participants in society. We accept these propositions.

However, the evidence adduced by the Amish in this case is persuasively to the effect that an additional one or two years of formal high school for Amish children in place of their long-established program of informal vocational education would do little to serve those interests. . . . It is one thing to say that compulsory education for a year or two beyond the eighth grade may be necessary when its goal is the preparation of the child for life in modern society as the majority live, but it is quite another if the goal of education be viewed as the preparation of the child for life in the separated agrarian community that is the keystone of the Amish faith.

The State attacks respondents' position as one fostering "ignorance" from which the child must be protected by the State. No one can question the State's duty to protect children from ignorance but this argument does not square with the facts disclosed in the record. Whatever their idiosyncrasies as seen by the majority, this record strongly shows that the Amish community has been a highly successful social unit within our society, even if apart from the conventional "mainstream." Its members are productive and very law-abiding members of society; they reject public welfare in any of its usual modern forms. . . .

The State, however, supports its interest in providing an additional one or two years of compulsory high school education to Amish children because of the possibility that some such children will choose to leave the Amish community, and that if this occurs they will be ill-equipped for life. . . . However, on this record, that argument is highly speculative. There is no specific evidence of the loss of Amish adherents by attrition, nor is there any showing that upon leaving the Amish community Amish children, with their practical agricultural training and habits of industry and self-reliance, would become burdens on society because of educational shortcomings. . . .

The requirement for compulsory education beyond the eighth grade is a relatively recent development in our history. Less than 60 years ago, the educational requirements of almost all of the States were satisfied by completion of the elementary grades, at least where the child was regularly and lawfully employed. . . . We should also note that compulsory education and child labor laws find their historical origin in common humanitarian instincts, and that the age limits of both laws have been coordinated to achieve their related objectives. . . . The requirement of compulsory schooling to age 16 must therefore be viewed as aimed not merely at providing educational opportunities for children, but as an alternative to the equally undesirable consequence of unhealthful child labor displacing adult workers, or, on the other hand, forced idleness. . . .

In these terms, Wisconsin's interest in compelling the school attendance of Amish children to age 16 emerges as somewhat less substantial than requiring such attendance for children generally. . . . There is no intimation that the Amish employment of their children on family farms is in any way deleterious to their health or that Amish parents exploit children at tender years. . . .

Finally, the State, on authority of Prince v. Massachusetts, [321 U.S. 158 (1944),] argues that a decision exempting Amish children from the State's requirement fails to recognize the substantive right of the Amish child to a secondary education, and fails to give due regard to the power of the State as parens patriae to extend the benefit of secondary education to children regardless of the wishes of their parents. Taken at its broadest sweep, the Court's language in *Prince*, might be read to give support to the State's position. However, the Court was not confronted in *Prince* with a situation comparable to that of the Amish as revealed in this record. . . .

Our holding in no way determines the proper resolution of possible competing interests of parents, children, and the State in an appropriate state court proceeding in which the power of the State is asserted on the theory that Amish parents are preventing their minor children from attending high school despite their expressed desires to the contrary. Recognition of the claim of the State in such a proceeding would, of course, call into question traditional concepts of parental control over the religious upbringing and education of their minor children recognized in this Court's past decisions. It is clear that such an intrusion by a State into family decisions in the area of religious training would give rise to grave questions of religious freedom comparable to those raised here and those presented in [*Pierce*]. On this record we neither reach nor decide those issues. . . .

Indeed it seems clear that if the State is empowered, as parens patriae, to "save" a child from himself or his Amish parents by requiring an additional two years of compulsory formal high school education, the State will in large measure influence, if not determine, the religious future of the child. Even more markedly than in *Prince*, therefore, this case involves the fundamental interest of parents, as contrasted with that of the State, to guide the religious future and education of their children. . . .

Mr. Justice DOUGLAS, dissenting in part.
. . . The Court's analysis assumes that the only interests at stake in the case are those of the Amish parents on the one hand, and those of the State on the other. The difficulty with this approach is that, despite the Court's claim, the parents are seeking to vindicate not only their own free exercise claims, but also those of their high-school-age children. . . . If the parents in this case are allowed a religious exemption, the inevitable effect is to impose the parents' notions of religious duty upon their children. Where the child is mature enough to express potentially conflicting desires, it would be an invasion of the child's rights to permit such an imposition without canvassing his views. . . . And, if an Amish child desires to attend high school, and is mature enough to have that desire respected, the State may well be able to override the parents' religiously motivated objections. . . .

[T]he children should be entitled to be heard. While the parents, absent dissent, normally speak for the entire family, the education of the child is a matter on which the child will often have decided views. He may want to be a pianist or an astronaut or an oceanographer. To do so he will have to break from the Amish tradition.[2]

It is the future of the student, not the future of the parents, that is imperiled by today's decision. If a parent keeps his child out of school beyond the grade school, then the child will be forever barred from entry into the new and amazing world of diversity that we have today. The child may decide that that is the preferred course,

---

2. A significant number of Amish children do leave the Old Order. Professor Hostetler notes that "the loss of members is very limited in some Amish districts and considerable in others." J. Hostetler, Amish Society 226 (1968). In one Pennsylvania church, he observed a defection rate of 30%. Rates up to 50% have been reported by others. Casad, Compulsory High School Attendance and the Old Order Amish: A Commentary on State v. Garber, 16 Kan. L. Rev. 423, 434 n.51 (1968).

or he may rebel. It is the student's judgment, not his parents', that is essential if we are to give full meaning to what we have said about the Bill of Rights and of the right of students to be masters of their own destiny.[3] . . . The views of the two children in question were not canvassed by the Wisconsin courts. [N]ew hearings [should] be held on remand of the case. . . .

■ **TROXEL v. GRANVILLE**
530 U.S. 57 (2000)

Review case, reprinted in Chapter VII, p. 789.

Notes and Questions

1. *Parental autonomy.* *Meyer* and *Pierce* establish the foundation for the right to privacy. See Chapter I, section A1b. They include within the protection of liberty in the Due Process Clause parental autonomy, the right to rear a child as the parent sees fit.

2. *Children as property.* Although revered as "liberal icons" that protect privacy and promote pluralism, *Meyer* and *Pierce* express a conservative attachment to the patriarchal family and a view of children as property owned by their parents, according to Professor Barbara Bennett Woodhouse in "Who Owns the Child?": *Meyer* and *Pierce* and the Child as Property, 33 Wm. & Mary L. Rev. 995, 996 (1992). After examining the historical context of the cases, she concludes:

> . . . By constitutionalizing a patriarchal notion of parental rights, *Meyer* and *Pierce* interrupted the trend of family law moving toward children's rights and revitalized the notion of rights of possession. . . . Patriarchal notions of ownership do not lend themselves to a child-centered theory of custody or parenthood. . . .
>
> [O]ur legal system fails to respect children. Children are often used as instruments, as in *Meyer* and *Pierce*. The child is denied her own voice and identity and becomes a conduit for the parents' religious expression, cultural identity, and class aspirations. The parents' authority to speak for and through the child is explicit in *Meyer*'s "right of control" and *Pierce*'s "high duty" of the parent to direct his child's destiny. . . .

Id. at 1113-1114. If property ownership provides the wrong legal model for the parent-child relationship, what alternatives might prove more helpful? See, e.g., Merry Jean Chan, Note, The Authorial Parent: An Intellectual Property Model of Parental Rights, 78 N.Y.U. L. Rev. 1186 (2003) (positing parenting as a form of creative expression, protected by the First Amendment); Anne C. Dailey,

---

3. The court below brushed aside the students' interests with the offhand comment that "when a child reaches the age of judgment, he can choose for himself his religion. 182 N.W.2d 539, 543 [(Wis. 1971)]. But there is nothing in this record to indicate that the moral and intellectual judgment demanded of the student by the question in this case is beyond his capacity. Children far younger than the 14- and 15-year-olds involved here are regularly permitted to testify in custody and other proceedings. Indeed, the failure to call the affected child in a custody hearing is often reversible error. Moreover, there is substantial agreement among child psychologists and sociologists that the moral and intellectual maturity of the 14-year-old approaches that of the adult. See, e.g., J. Piaget, The Moral Judgment of the Child (1948); D. Elkind, Children and Adolescents 75-80 (1970). . . .

Developing Citizens, 91 Iowa L. Rev. 431 (2006) (examining developmental approach, with focus on caregiving as precondition for preparing children for democratic citizenship); Elizabeth S. Scott & Robert E. Scott, Parents as Fiduciaries, 81 Va. L. Rev. 2401 (1995). More recently, Woodhouse writes that the conventional focus on parental rights versus state intervention overlooks realities, such as modern mass-market culture, which require an "environmental" or contextual approach to childhood. Barbara Bennett Woodhouse, Reframing the Debate about the Socialization of Children: An Environmental Paradigm, 2004 U. Chi. Legal F. 85.

3. Prince *and its precedents.* Based on *Meyer* and *Pierce*, how should the Court have decided *Prince*? Is *Prince* a stronger or weaker case for parental autonomy than *Meyer* or *Pierce*, given that Sarah Prince's parental autonomy claim rested more squarely on her asserted freedom of religion and Betty's own beliefs were put in evidence? In light of the outcome in *Prince*, what does the Court mean by "a private realm of family life which the state cannot enter"?

4. *Harm? Prince* reveals that the state's interest (as parens patriae) in protecting children from harm limits parental autonomy. What harm threatened nine-year-old Betty? Was she actually harmed or merely exposed to the risk of harm? Should the mere risk of harm justify state intervention in the family? Who decides what constitutes harm to a child? Does *Prince* identify the scope of state power to restrict parental freedom in the interest of child protection?

To what extent does *Troxel* depart from *Prince*'s harm standard? What do the different Justices say about this standard in *Troxel*? Do the *Troxel* opinions go beyond the context of third-party visitation to open the door for other state incursions on parental autonomy that cannot be justified as necessary to protect a child from harm or potential harm?

5. Yoder *and its precedents.* Do *Meyer* and *Pierce* dictate the outcome in *Yoder*? Or should *Prince* control? Under *Prince*'s test, is there sufficient harm or risk of harm in *Yoder* to justify state intervention? Are the *Yoder* parents making "martyrs" of their children, despite *Prince*'s admonition?

As the Court explains in *Yoder*, compulsory school attendance laws grew out of the same concerns that produced the child labor restrictions in *Prince*. What distinguishes work on the family farm for Amish children from other child labor? What of the risk of harm to the Amish child who later chooses to leave the fold but has never completed high school?

6. *Standard of review. Yoder* claims to use a "balancing process." What level of judicial scrutiny did the Court in fact employ? Compare City of Boerne v. Flores, 521 U.S. 507, 544 (1997) (O'Connor, J., dissenting) (*Yoder* used compelling state interest test), with Immediato v. Rye Neck School Dist., 73 F.3d 454, 461 (2d Cir.) (*Yoder* used rational basis test), *cert. denied*, 519 U.S. 813 (1996). What does the discussion of harm in the *Troxel* opinions signal about the standard of review that applies to state infringements on parental autonomy? See Stephen G. Gilles, Parental (and Grandparental) Rights After Troxel v. Granville, 9 Sup. Ct. Econ. Rev. 69, 116-138 (2001).

7. Yoder's *factual basis.* What facts prove determinative to *Yoder*'s outcome? Specifically, how much weight did the majority accord to the Amish opposition to exposure to worldly activities, the law-abiding nature of the Amish population, and the farmwork to be undertaken in place of continued schooling? Recent publicity raises questions about the Court's premises. In some parts of the country,

when Amish children turn 16, they are free to enjoy "rumspringa" (or "running around") until making a conscious choice to join the church; this interval can last for years and often includes listening to rock music, driving cars, and experimenting with drugs and alcohol. See Christopher Isenberg, Lives: Running Free, N.Y. Times, May 26, 2002, §6 (Magazine), at 58; Beth Pinsker, The Dangers of a Date with the Outside World, N.Y. Times, May 26, 2002, §2, at 18. In addition, Amish youth are increasingly working in sawmills and woodworking shops instead of on the family farm, in turn prompting efforts to secure an exemption to federal child labor laws that prevent proximity to dangerous machinery. Steven Greenhouse, Foes of Idle Hands, Amish Seek an Exemption From a Child Labor Law, N.Y. Times, Oct. 18, 2003, at A9. Would such evidence have changed the outcome in *Yoder*?

8. *Other schooling choices.* How far can one generalize from *Yoder*'s holding?

a. *Home schooling.* Does *Yoder* protect a parent's choice of home schooling?[3] See, e.g., Clonlara v. Runkel, 722 F. Supp. 1442 (E.D. Mich. 1989). If *Yoder* protects home schooling, does it undervalue the state's interest in exposing minors to relationships with diverse peers? See Emily Buss, The Adolescent's Stake in the Allocation of Educational Control Between Parent and State, 67 U. Chi. L. Rev. 1233 (2000).

b. *Vouchers.* In Zelman v. Simmons-Harris, 536 U.S. 639 (2002), the Court upheld an Ohio school voucher program that included parochial schools against a challenge claiming a violation of the First Amendment's Establishment Clause. The majority emphasized that the program did not have the prohibited effect of advancing religion because individual parental choices about how to use the state assistance, not government action itself, directed the funds to religious schools. Would vouchers make available the private school option protected in *Pierce*, regardless of a family's economic status? Does *Troxel* guarantee greater school choice for parents? See Ira Bloom, The New Parental Rights Challenge to School Control: Has the Supreme Court Mandated School Choice? 32 J.L. & Educ. 139 (2003). Note that many state constitutions would prohibit use of vouchers at parochial schools. See, e.g., William G. Ross, The Contemporary Significance of *Meyer* and *Pierce* for Parental Rights Issues Involving Education, 34 Akron L. Rev. 177, 201-202 (2000).

9. *Common law parental autonomy.* Long-standing common law principles of family privacy and parental authority reinforce the constitutional analysis in *Meyer*, *Pierce*, *Yoder*, and *Troxel*. For example, in Roe v. Doe, 272 N.E.2d 567 (N.Y. 1971), the court applied to the parent-child relationship in the intact family the same rule of nonintervention that McGuire v. McGuire (see Chapter III, section B3) invoked for married couples. Declining to allow judicial interference with a father's decision to withhold support from his daughter unless she lived in a college dormitory instead of an apartment, the court said:

> The father has the right, in the absence of caprice, misconduct or neglect, to require that the daughter conform to his reasonable demands. Should she disagree, and at her age [20, when the age of majority was 21] that is surely her prerogative, she may elect not to comply; but in so doing, she subjects herself to her father's lawful wrath. Where, as here, she abandons her home, she forfeits her right to support.

---

[3]. All 50 states permit home schooling. Ralph D. Mawdsley, Home Schools and the Law, 137 Educ. L. Rep. 1 (1999). Most states have specific legal requirements that home school programs must meet. See National Survey of State Laws 231-246 (Richard A. Leiter ed., 4th ed. 2003).

Id. at 570. Does the court suggest that it would reach a different result had it deemed the father's demands "unreasonable"? Who decides reasonableness? Does this standard sufficiently protect the family from state intervention? See id. at 571 (Jasen, J., concurring). *Roe* also exemplifies the traditional view treating as reciprocal the parent's duty of support and the child's duty of obedience. See Katharine T. Bartlett, Re-Expressing Parenthood, 98 Yale L.J. 293, 297-298 (1988).

10. *The children's rights? Yoder* avoided deciding whether Amish children have their own right to a secondary education. Can the interests of parents and their children be separated? Compare the majority opinion with that of Justice Douglas. What weight should the Court accord to the social science data in Douglas's footnote 3? If the children have separate interests, can the state speak for the children more effectively than their parents can?

If the children have independent interests, how should they be considered? See generally Dena S. Davis, The Child's Right to an Open Future: *Yoder* and Beyond, 26 Cap. U. L. Rev. 93 (1997). See also Emily Buss, What Does Frieda Yoder Believe?, 2 U. Pa. J. Const. L. 53, 68-70 (1999) (hypothesizing Frieda Yoder's disagreement with her parents). In an omitted footnote, Justice Douglas suggests canvassing the small number of Amish school children. If an Amish child expressed a preference for secondary school, would he or she continue to live at home? Receive parental support? What other consequences might follow? Alternatively, should the issue be what serves the children's own best interests, rather than what the children say they want? If so, does that simply return the analysis to the question whether parents or the state can better serve such interests? Compare, e.g., Martin Guggenheim, What's Wrong with Children's Rights (2005), and Emily Buss, Essay, "Parental" Rights, 88 Va. L. Rev. 635 (2002) (preferring parents), with James G. Dwyer, Religious Schools v. Children's Rights (1998) (preferring state).

Suppose in *Pierce* the child did not want to go to private school? See Stephen L. Carter, Parents, Religion, and Schools: Reflections on *Pierce*, 70 Years Later, 27 Seton Hall L. Rev. 1194, 1220-1223 (1997). What difference should the child's own wishes make in addressing third-party visitation disputes, the issue in *Troxel*? See Chapter VII, section B3.

Problems

1. The school board in New York City adopts a condom distribution program for high school students. Designed to curb both the increasing rate of adolescent HIV-infection and the rising number of teenage pregnancies, the program allows any high school student who so wishes to obtain condoms without parental notification or consent. Parents challenge the program, claiming it infringes their due process rights to rear their children as they see fit. They assert that the Constitution requires that the program have a parental "opt-out" provision, to honor their freedom to promote the value of sexual abstinence to their children. The school board asserts that such a provision would leave the children of parents who "opt out" vulnerable to HIV and pregnancy, if those children were sexually active without parental knowledge.

What result and why? Compare Alfonso v. Fernandez, 606 N.Y.S.2d 259 (App. Div. 1993), *appeal dismissed*, 637 N.E.2d 279 (N.Y. 1994), with Curtis v. School

Comm. of Falmouth, 652 N.E.2d 580 (Mass. 1995), *cert. denied*, 516 U.S. 1067 (1996). See Miranda Perry, Comment, Kids and Condoms: Parental Involvement in School Condom-Distribution Programs, 63 U. Chi. L. Rev. 727 (1996); Pilar S. Ramos, Comment, The Condom Controversy in the Public Schools: Respecting a Minor's Right of Privacy, 145 U. Pa. L. Rev. 149 (1996). Is the dispute one between parents and the school board alone? What interests do the students have at stake? How should such interests be taken into account?

2. The American Association of Nude Recreation (AANR), a national social nudism organization, opens a week-long juvenile nudist summer camp in Virginia. In addition to traditional camp activities, including arts and crafts, the agenda includes an educational component designed to teach the values associated with social nudism, including sessions devoted to topics like "Nudity and the Law," "Overcoming the Clothing Experience," and "Nudism and Faith." After several "naturalist" parents enroll their children in the program but before the camp session begins, Virginia amends its licensing statute for juvenile camps, imposing for nudist camps a categorical requirement that a parent or guardian must register and to "be present with" the juvenile during camp. What constitutional challenges might the affected parents have against the Virginia statutory amendment? What challenges might their children have? Does AANR have standing to raise these challenges? What result on the merits and why? See White Tail Park, Inc. v. Stroube, 413 F.3d 451 (4th Cir. 2005); Central Tex. Nudists v. Travis County, 2000 WL 1784344 (Tex. App. 2000), *cert. denied*, 534 U.S. 952 (2001).

2. *Procedural Challenges*

■ **PARHAM v. J.R.**
442 U.S. 584 (1979)

BURGER, C.J., delivered the opinion of the Court.

The question presented in this appeal is what process is constitutionally due a minor child whose parents or guardian seek state administered institutional mental health care for the child and specifically whether an adversary proceeding is required prior to or after the commitment.

(a) Appellee J.R., a child being treated in a Georgia state mental hospital, was a plaintiff in this class action based on 42 U.S.C. §1983, in the District Court for the Middle District of Georgia. Appellants are the State's Commissioner of the Department of Human Resources, the Director of the Mental Health Division of the Department of Human Resources, and the Chief Medical Officer at the hospital where appellee was being treated. Appellee sought a declaratory judgment that Georgia's voluntary commitment procedures for children under the age of 18, Ga. Code §§88-503.1, 88-503.2 (1975), violated the Due Process Clause of the Fourteenth Amendment and requested an injunction against their future enforcement. [Two other named plaintiffs are J.L., whose mother requested his indefinite commitment at the hospital and whose parents subsequently relinquished their parental rights, and J.R., a neglected child whom the state removed from his parents and placed in seven different foster homes before successfully seeking his admission to the hospital.]

(d) Georgia Code §88-503.1 (1975) provides for the voluntary admission to a state regional hospital of children such as J.L. and J.R. Under that provision, admission begins with an application for hospitalization signed by a "parent or guardian." Upon application, the superintendent of each hospital is given the power to admit temporarily any child for "observation and diagnosis." If, after observation, the superintendent finds "evidence of mental illness" and that the child is "suitable for treatment" in the hospital, then the child may be admitted "for such period and under such conditions as may be authorized by law."

. . . Any child who has been hospitalized for more than five days may be discharged at the request of a parent or guardian. §88-503.3(a) (1975). Even without a request for discharge, however, the superintendent of each regional hospital has an affirmative duty to release any child "who has recovered from his mental illness or who has sufficiently improved that the superintendent determines that hospitalization of the patient is no longer desirable." §88-503.2 (1975). . . .

[The District Court held that the Georgia statute violates due process because civil commitment constitutes a severe deprivation of a child's liberty (both freedom from bodily restraint and freedom from emotional harm) requiring notice and a hearing. Although the court recognized that public hospitals make available care similar to that offered at private facilities and that most parents seek such commitment in good faith, the court relied on a witness] who expressed an opinion that "some still look upon mental hospitals as a 'dumping ground.'" . . . The District Court also rejected the argument that review by the superintendents of the hospitals and their staffs was sufficient to protect the child's liberty interest. The court held that the inexactness of psychiatry, coupled with the possibility that the sources of information used to make the commitment decision may not always be reliable, made the superintendent's decision too arbitrary to satisfy due process. . . .

. . . Assuming the existence of a protectible property or liberty interest, the Court has required a balancing of a number of factors. [W]e must consider first the child's interest in not being committed. Normally, however, since this interest is inextricably linked with the parents' interest in and obligation for the welfare and health of the child, the private interest at stake is a combination of the child's and parents' concerns. Next, we must examine the State's interest in the procedures it has adopted for commitment and treatment of children. Finally, we must consider how well Georgia's procedures protect against arbitrariness in the decision to commit a child to a state mental hospital.

(a) It is not disputed that a child, in common with adults, has a substantial liberty interest in not being confined unnecessarily for medical treatment and that the state's involvement in the commitment decision constitutes state action under the Fourteenth Amendment. For purposes of this decision, we assume that a child has a protectible interest not only in being free of unnecessary bodily restraints but also in not being labeled erroneously by some persons because of an improper decision by the state hospital superintendent.

(b) . . . Appellees argue that the constitutional rights of the child are of such magnitude and the likelihood of parental abuse is so great that the parents' traditional interests in and responsibility for the upbringing of their child must be subordinated at least to the extent of providing a formal adversary hearing prior to a voluntary commitment.

Our jurisprudence historically has reflected Western civilization concepts of the family as a unit with broad parental authority over minor children. . . . Surely, this [authority] includes a "high duty" to recognize symptoms of illness and to seek and follow medical advice. The law's concept of the family rests on a presumption that parents possess what a child lacks in maturity, experience, and capacity for judgment required for making life's difficult decisions. More important, histori- cally it has recognized that natural bonds of affection lead parents to act in the best interests of their children. 1 W. Blackstone, Commentaries *447; 2 J. Kent, Commentaries on American Law *190. . . .

Nonetheless, we have recognized that a state is not without constitutional control over parental discretion in dealing with children when their physical or mental health is jeopardized. [Yet simply] because the decision of a parent is not agreeable to a child or because it involves risks does not automatically transfer the power to make that decision from the parents to some agency or officer of the state. The same characterizations can be made for a tonsillectomy, appen- dectomy, or other medical procedure. Most children, even in adolescence, sim- ply are not able to make sound judgments concerning many decisions, including their need for medical care or treatment. Parents can and must make those judgments. Here, there is no finding by the District Court of even a single instance of bad faith by any parent of any member of appellees' class. We cannot assume that the result in [*Meyer* and *Pierce*] would have been different if the children there had announced a preference to learn only English or a prefer- ence to go to a public, rather than a church, school. The fact that a child may balk at hospitalization or complain about a parental refusal to provide cosmetic surgery does not diminish the parents' authority to decide what is best for the child. Neither state officials nor federal courts are equipped to review such parental decisions. . . .

(c) The State obviously has a significant interest in confining the use of its costly mental health facilities to cases of genuine need. . . . The State in performing its voluntarily assumed mission also has a significant interest in not imposing un- necessary procedural obstacles that may discourage the mentally ill or their families from seeking needed psychiatric assistance. The parens patriae interest in helping parents care for the mental health of their children cannot be fulfilled if the parents are unwilling to take advantage of the opportunities because the admission process is too onerous, too embarrassing, or too contentious [as a result of adversary proceedings].

(d) [T]he risk of error inherent in the parental decision to have a child insti- tutionalized for mental health care is sufficiently great that some kind of inquiry should be made by a "neutral factfinder" to determine whether the statutory requirements for admission are satisfied. . . . Due process has never been thought to require that the neutral and detached trier of fact be law trained or a judicial or administrative officer. Surely, this is the case as to medical decisions, for "neither judges nor administrative hearing officers are better qualified than psychiatrists to render psychiatric judgments." In re Roger S., 19 Cal. 3d 921, 942, 569 P.2d 1286, 1299 (1977) (Clark, J., dissenting). Thus, a staff physician will suffice, so long as he or she is free to evaluate independently the child's mental and emotional condition and need for treatment. [Moreover, a formalized adversary hearing would signifi- cantly intrude on the parent-child relationship and risks exacerbating existing tensions between parent and child.]

It has been suggested that a hearing conducted by someone other than the admitting physician is necessary in order to detect instances where parents are "guilty of railroading their children into asylums" or are using "voluntary commitment procedures in order to sanction behavior of which they [disapprove]." Ellis, Volunteering Children: Parental Commitment of Minors to Mental Institutions, 62 Calif. L. Rev. 840, 850-851 (1974). [Yet it] is unrealistic to believe that trained psychiatrists . . . will often be deceived about the family situation surrounding a child's emotional disturbance. Surely a lay, or even law-trained, factfinder would be no more skilled in this process than the professional. . . .

(e) Georgia's statute envisions a careful diagnostic medical inquiry to be conducted by the admitting physician at each regional hospital, [periodic reviews, and an] affirmative statutory duty to discharge any child who is no longer mentally ill or in need of therapy. [T]he periodic reviews described in the record reduce the risk of error in the initial admission and thus they are necessary. Whether they are sufficient to justify continuing a voluntary commitment is an issue for the District Court on remand. [For wards of the state, who often have no adults who know them well and care about them, the Court suggests that, on remand, the District Court consider the need for more rigorous review procedures, to prevent such children from "getting lost in the shuffle."]

On this record, we are satisfied that Georgia's medical factfinding processes are reasonable and consistent with constitutional guarantees. . . . The judgment is therefore reversed, and the case is remanded to the District Court for further proceedings consistent with this opinion. . . .

■ PLANNED PARENTHOOD OF NORTHERN NEW ENGLAND v. HEED
390 F.3d 53 (1st Cir. 2004), **vacated and remanded sub nom.**
Ayotte v. Planned Parenthood of Northern New England, 126 S. Ct. 961 (2006)

Review the case, reprinted in Chapter I, p. 77.

Notes and Questions

1. *Fair procedures?* *Yoder* demonstrates that constitutional law generally gives parents authority to make important decisions for their children. It does not expressly address, however, whether children have a right to fair *procedures* to ensure that parents are acting to promote their welfare. How does *Parham* answer this question?

2. *Voluntary treatment.* If the children in *Parham* opposed the commitments, why were they nonetheless classified as *voluntary* commitments (rather than involuntary commitments, which are governed by elaborate procedural protections, including judicial determinations)? Would the district court's approach have implications for all medical treatments parents choose for unwilling children? Should the Court have consulted empirical data about minors' decisionmaking capacities and the possible effects of mental illness? See, e.g., Rhonda Gay Hartman, Coming of Age: Devising Legislation for Adolescent Medical Decision-Making, 28 Am. J.L. & Med. 409 (2002); Frances J. Lexcen & N. Dickon Reppucci, Effects of Psychopathology on Adolescent Medical Decision-Making, 5 U. Chi. L. Sch. Roundtable 63 (1998).

3. *Parham's premises.* Critics contend that *Parham* rests on myths about the family and about mental hospitals. See Gary B. Melton et al., No Place to Go:

The Civil Commitment of Minors 127-138 (1998). Do the changing realities of children's lives — evident in today's variety of family structures and a society that expects children to dress and behave like adults — require rethinking *Parham*'s assumptions about family decisionmaking? See Janet L. Dolgin, The Fate of Child-hood: Legal Models of Children and the Parent-Child Relationship, 61 Alb. L. Rev. 345, 347-350 (1997).

Based on assumptions about how commitment decisions are reached, the majority concluded that Georgia's procedures adequately address the risk that parents will erroneously commit healthy children. What of the risk that children with serious emotional and mental problems will be committed even though they could receive adequate treatment in less drastic settings than a state institution? See James W. Ellis, Some Observations on the Juvenile Commitment Cases: Reconceptualizing What the Child Has at Stake, 31 Loy. L.A. L. Rev. 929, 930 (1998). See also Miye A. Goishi, Unlocking the Closet Door: Protecting Children from Involuntary Civil Commitment Because of Their Sexual Orientation, 48 Hastings L.J. 1137 (1997) (lack of clear admission criteria creates risk of commitment for gay youth); Alexander V. Tsesis, Protecting Children Against Unnecessary Institutionalization, 39 S. Tex. L. Rev. 995, 1005 (1998) (citing findings that most juvenile patients today have eating disorders, problems in school, or disagreements with parents).

4. *Different approaches.* Not all courts have reached *Parham*'s result. In re Roger S., 569 P.2d 1286 (Cal. 1977), held that, for a child's voluntary commitment to a mental institution, both federal and state constitutions require an administrative hearing, an opportunity to present evidence, an opportunity to cross-examine adverse witnesses, and appointment of counsel for minors not greatly disabled nor dangerous. The court also held parents could not institutionalize minors over 13 under the voluntary commitment statute. The court relied on an article arguing due process requires procedural safeguards to protect against parents' unfettered discretion to institutionalize their children. Id. at 1296 n.9. See James W. Ellis, Volunteering Children: Parental Commitment of Minors to Mental Institutions, 62 Cal. L. Rev. 840 (1974).

Which approach, that in *Parham* or that in *Roger S.*, is more sound? See Jan C. Costello, Essay, Why Have Hearings for Kids if You're not Going to Listen?: A Therapeutic Jurisprudence Approach to Mental Disability Proceedings for Minors, 71 U. Cin. L. Rev. 19, 23-24 (2002) (noting factual distinctions between the cases).

5. *Impact of safeguards.* Would enhanced procedural safeguards dissuade parents from seeking psychiatric help for their children, as the *Parham* majority fears? In omitted footnote 18 the Court observes that "a state may elect to provide such adversary hearings [when] parents and a child may be at odds, but nothing in the Constitution compels such procedures." When a state requires adversary hearings before a child's commitment, does the state unconstitutionally infringe parental autonomy? See State ex rel. T.B. v. CPC Fairfax Hosp., 918 P.2d 497 (Wash. 1996) (describing Washington's procedures).

6. *Private facilities.* Can parents avoid all issues of "due process" by choosing the more costly option of a private facility? Compare R.J.D. v. The Vaughan Clinic, 572 So. 2d 1225 (Ala. 1990) (no state action to invoke federal protection of civil rights), with *T.B.*, 918 P.2d 497 (relying on statutory protections).

California law now requires postadmission independent clinical reviews for minors committed to private mental health facilities. In these procedures, within five days of a child's request, a mental health professional with no direct financial relationship with the facility or treating physician hears testimony, interviews the child, and determines whether continued hospitalization is appropriate. Costello, supra, at 29-30.

7. *Proposed reforms.* The number of "troubled and troublesome youth" is growing while parents increasingly face difficulties in obtaining mental health services for these children. See Lois A. Weithorn, Envisioning Second-Order Change in America's Responses to Troubled and Troublesome Youth, 33 Hofstra L. Rev. 1305 (2005). Some parents who cannot afford mental health treatment must relinquish the child to foster care, to trigger eligibility for government-sponsored services available to wards of the state. See, e.g., Dennis E. Cichon, The Ignored Population: Children in the Mental Health System, 17 T.M. Cooley L. Rev. 9 (2000). Reformers suggest looking beyond the fragmented and overlapping services provided by schools, health care systems, the child welfare system, and the juvenile justice system to develop " 'metasystem' capabilities." Weithorn, supra, at 1311, 1474. See also Patrick Geary, Note, Juvenile Mental Health Courts and Therapeutic Jurisprudence: Facing the Challenges Posed by Youth with Mental Disabilities in the Juvenile Justice System, 5 Yale J. Health Pol'y L. & Ethics 671 (2005) (suggesting specialized mental health courts).

8. *Other applications.* What does *Parham* mean for efforts to subject to judicial review parental decisionmaking in other contexts?

a. *Visitation.* Does the analysis in *Parham* help explain why *Troxel* rejected Washington's attempt to let a court decide whether parental denials of third-party visitation frustrate the child's best interests? In *Troxel*, the plurality opinion and Justice Stevens's dissent both cite *Parham* for the principle that the law presumes fit parents act in their child's best interests. 530 U.S. at 66; id. at 86. See also id. at 77 (Souter, J., concurring). See David D. Meyer, The Modest Promise of Children's Relationship Rights, 11 Wm. & Mary Bill Rts. J. 1117 (2003).

b. *Abortion.* Why has the Court departed from *Parham*'s approach in abortion cases? Omitted sections of *Parham* compare commitment to a mental institution with abortion. The Court has held that states seeking to compel parental involvement in abortion decisions must provide an alternative allowing a minor to prove she is sufficiently mature to make her own choice or establish that her best interests favor abortion, see Chapter I, section B2. In such cases, the Court has relied on procedure to protect the minor's own rights—a court proceeding (called a "judicial bypass") facilitates the necessary exceptions to state rules that parents should make abortion choices for their minor daughters or should receive advance notice.

What distinctions in the two contexts prompted the Court to require judicial review when the state allows a parent to veto a daughter's abortion but to defer to parental autonomy in civil commitments of minors? Note that a physician plays a key role in both contexts. See Dolgin, supra, at 391-392 (*Parham*'s analysis relied on adult authority, not just parental authority).

c. *Sterilization.* What procedural safeguards, if any, does due process require when parents of an adult child with developmental disabilities seek to have her sterilized, as recommended by physicians, before she moves to a group home? See, e.g., In re Wirsing, 573 N.W.2d 51 (Mich. 1998); In re Grady, 426 A.2d 467 (N.J.

1981). See generally Norman L. Cantor, Making Medical Decisions for the Profoundly Mentally Disabled (2005). Is the surgery "voluntary" because parents have requested it?

Problem

Zach, age 16, recently told his parents that he is gay. In response, his parents enrolled him in a fundamentalist Christian "boot camp" program promising "reparative therapy" to make him straight. See Alex Williams, Gay Teenager Stirs a Storm, N.Y. Times, July 17, 2005, §9, at 1 (reporting story of Zach and describing program of "Love in Action"). If Zach, depressed and anxious, opposes his parents' decision, what procedural or substantive recourse does he have? See John Alan Cohan, Parental Duties and the Right of Homosexual Minors to Refuse "Reparative" Therapy, 11 Buff. Women's L.J. 67 (2002/2003). If Zach's public school, rather than Zach himself, had disclosed his sexual orientation to his parents, would the school have violated his right to privacy? See C.N. v. Wolf, 410 F.Supp. 2d 894 (C.D. Cal. 2005). (On the question whether "reparative therapy" constitutes child abuse, see infra pp. 913-914.)

B. CHILD ABUSE AND NEGLECT

Despite the principle of parental autonomy, child abuse and neglect provide a compelling reason for state intervention in the family. In fact, states have elaborate child-protection systems to address such situations. This section explores the extent to which the state can intervene in the family in the interest of child protection. In the materials that follow, consider when the state can invoke its authority and, also, how well the child-protection system achieves its goals.

1. Introduction

a. The Paradox of Privacy

■ JAMES GARBARINO & GWEN GILLIAM, UNDERSTANDING ABUSIVE FAMILIES
41, 42, 44-46 (1980)

To most Americans, the value of privacy is unquestioned. . . . Although privacy may be valuable, it does not come without costs to the individual and to the community; some are paid by children in the form of abuse and neglect. . . .

. . . Families have become less and less dominated by kinship and neighborhood relationships, and more and more by individual privacy. . . . Americans place a high value on owning a single-family home, on the freedom a car brings, and on being independent of all regulations. It is as if we were trying to make every man (and woman) an island. Opportunities for privacy have increased markedly in recent decades. . . .

[Yet,] [s]ocial connectedness provides access to social and economic resources that can aid the family in times of stress. Such involvement provides personalized observation of the family. It combats family climates that induce depression, anger, helplessness, loss of control, and violence. Without privacy it is unlikely that a pattern of maltreatment can be established and maintained. Abuse or neglect generally will be inhibited or at least identified at an early stage when families are involved in an active exchange network with prosocial friends, neighbors, and relatives. . . .

The allure of privacy is great. It permits individualism to flourish and insulates the family against external meddling by persons who may have their own interests to advance. . . . Privacy provides the potential for a quiet atmosphere, whereas kinship intrusion is psychologically noisy. Despite this, privacy may be damaging or even lethal for children when combined with the factors that elicit abusive behavior.

Privacy alone is not, of course, sufficient to produce abuse and neglect. [H]owever, there are circumstances in which parent-child relations are placed in special jeopardy by privacy. . . . When families are exposed to loss of income, excessive work schedules (too much or too little), or other conditions that lead to frustration and tension, the probability of maltreatment is markedly increased. These social conditions interact with the parenting style of the child's caregivers. When the parent is deficient in the ability to empathize with the child, the potential for abuse is heightened. . . . For a child in a stable and psychologically healthy family, isolation is a limiting factor on development. For a child in a family plagued by stress and parental instability, isolation is dangerous and can be lethal. . . .

b. Child Abuse in Historical Perspective

■ **PETER STEVENS & MARIAN EIDE, THE FIRST CHAPTER OF CHILDREN'S RIGHTS**
41 Am. Heritage 84, 84-91 (1990)

In the quiet New York courtroom, the little girl began to speak. "My name is Mary Ellen McCormack. I don't know how old I am. . . . I have never had but one pair of shoes, but can't recollect when that was. . . . My bed at night is only a piece of carpet, stretched on the floor underneath a window, and I sleep in my little undergarment, with a quilt over me. I am never allowed to play with any children or have any company whatever. Mamma has been in the habit of whipping and beating me almost every day. She used to whip me with a twisted whip, a raw hide. The whip always left black and blue marks on my body. I have now on my head two black and blue marks which were made by mamma with the whip, and a cut on the left side of my forehead which was made by a pair of scissors in mamma's hand. . . . I have no recollection of ever having been kissed. . . . I have never been taken on my mamma's lap, or caressed or petted. I never dared to speak to anybody, because if I did I would get whipped. . . . Whenever mamma went out I was locked up in the bedroom. . . . I have no recollection of ever being in the street in my life."

At the beginning of 1874 there were no legal means in the United States to save a child from abuse. Mary Ellen's eloquent testimony changed that, changed our legal system's view of the rights of the child. . . .

When Mary Ellen's mother, Frances Connor, immigrated to the United States from England in 1858, she took a job at the St. Nicholas Hotel in New York City as a laundress. There she met an Irishman named Thomas Wilson who worked in the hotel kitchen shucking oysters. They were married in April 1862, shortly after Wilson had been drafted into the 69th New York, a regiment in the famous Irish Brigade. Early in 1864 she gave birth to their daughter, whom she named Mary after her mother and Ellen after her sister.

The birth of her daughter seems to have heralded the beginning of Frances Wilson's own decline. Her husband was killed that same year. . . . In May 1864, unable to pay someone to watch the baby while she was at work, she gave Mary Ellen over to the care of a woman named Mary Score for two dollars a week, the whole of her widow's pension. [When Frances Wilson was unable to pay for the upkeep of her child, Mary Score took Mary Ellen to the Department of Charities.] The little girl — whose mother was never to see her again — was sent to Blackwells Island in July 1865. . . .

[A couple named Thomas and Mary McCormack had lost their three children to disease.] [T]he McCormacks went to the Department of Charities. . . . The child they chose as their own was Mary Ellen Wilson. . . . Shortly after bringing the child home, Thomas McCormack died, and his widow married a man named Francis Connolly. Little more than that is known of the early childhood of Mary Ellen. . . .

Late in 1873 Etta Angell Wheeler, a Methodist caseworker serving in the tenements of New York City, received a disturbing report [of child abuse from a landlord]. Though social workers often witnessed scenes of cruelty, poverty, and grief, Wheeler found Mary Ellen's plight especially horrifying. She went first to the police; they told her she must be able to furnish proof of assault in order for them to act. Charitable institutions she approached offered to care for the child, but first she must be brought to them through legal means. There were none. Every effort Wheeler made proved fruitless. Though there were laws to protect children — laws, in fact, to prevent assault and battery to any person — there were no means available for intervention in a child's home.

Finally Wheeler's niece had an idea. The child, she said, was a member of the animal kingdom; surely Henry Bergh, the founder of the American Society for the Prevention of Cruelty to Animals, who was famous for his dramatic rescue of mistreated horses in the streets of New York, might be willing to intervene. Within the hour Wheeler had arranged a meeting with Bergh. [On the basis of observations of a detective hired by Bergh and Etta Wheeler's testimony, Bergh's lawyers, Elbridge T. Gerry and Ambrose Monell, presented a petition on behalf of Mary Ellen to the New York Supreme Court.] They showed that Mary Ellen was held illegally by the Connollys, who were neither her natural parents nor her lawful custodians, and went on to describe the physical abuse Mary Ellen endured, the marks and bruises on her body, and the general state of deprivation that characterized her existence. . . . The lawyers requested that a warrant be issued, the child removed from her home and placed in protective custody, and her parents brought to trial. . . .

Mary Ellen was turned over to the temporary custody of the matron of police headquarters. [I]ndictments were brought against Connolly, the first for her assault on the child with scissors on April 7, the second for the continual assaults inflicted on the child throughout the years 1873 and 1874. After twenty minutes of deliberation the jury returned a verdict of guilty of assault and battery. Connolly was sentenced to one year of hard labor in the city penitentiary, then known as the Tombs. In handing down this sentence, the judge defined it not only as a punishment to Connolly but also as a statement of precedence in child abuse cases. . . .

[In 1874, Henry Bergh founded the New York Society for the Prevention of Cruelty to Children. Mary Ellen was raised by Etta Wheeler's sister. She married a widower and had two girls, one of whom she named after Etta Wheeler.]

———————————

On the history of the Mary Ellen case, see Stephen S. Zawistowski, The Mary Ellen Wilson Child Abuse Case and the Beginning of Children's Rights in 19th Century America (2005). On the history of child abuse, see Lloyd deMause, The History of Childhood (1995); Philip J. Greven, Spare the Child: The Religious Roots of Punishment and the Psychological Impact of Physical Abuse (1992); Murray A. Straus, Beating the Devil Out of Them: Corporal Punishment in American Families and Its Effect on Children (2001).

c. The Abusive Parent and the Abused Child

■ **BRANDT STEELE, PSYCHODYNAMIC FACTORS IN CHILD ABUSE**
in The Battered Child 81, 81-84, 89-90 (Ray E. Helfer &
Ruth S. Kempe eds., 4th ed. 1987)

The term *child abuse* [covers the] whole spectrum of maltreatment of children. [It] involves children of all ages, from infancy through adolescence, and caretakers of both sexes, all ages, and with various kinds of relationships to the child. . . .

[I]t is common for abusive or neglectful caretakers to give a history of having experienced some significant degree of neglect, with or without accompanying physical abuse. [I]t is quite rare to see an abuser who does not relate this history if questioned appropriately. [Several persons,] during evaluation for maltreatment of their children, stoutly denied having been mistreated themselves as children. Upon further questioning as to who did the disciplining in the family and what disciplinary measures were used, they freely described being whipped or beaten to the point of lacerations or bruising, but in no way did they consider this abuse, because the discipline was "appropriate punishment for misbehavior." Others will, for some time, maintain a denial of having been abused because of a persistent fear that, even though they are now adults, their parents might again attack them if they complain or criticize parental actions. Others hesitate to give a true history, lest the family be brought into some sort of difficulty or be disgraced in the community. More rarely, there is a genuine amnesia for the unpleasant events of childhood as a result of unusually strong repression. . . . There are others who, although they actually remember maltreatment, find it too painful to deal with and comfort themselves by maintaining a fantasy that their parents really were good to them. . . .

Physical abuse is usually not a constant or daily occurrence. There are often many days, weeks, or even months between attacks. To be sure, there may be almost daily emotional abuse in the form of yelling and verbal castigation, belittlement, and criticism, as well as disregard and lack of attention. But it is the physical attacks occurring intermittently in discrete episodes which give us the clearest picture of the abusive phenomenon. There are four conditions which seem necessary for abuse to occur:

1. A caretaker who has the predisposition for abuse related to the psychological residues of neglect or abuse in his or her own early life.
2. A crisis of some sort placing extra stress on the caretaker.
3. Lack of lifelines or sources of help for the caretaker, because either he or she is unable to reach out or the facilities are not available.
4. A child who is perceived as being in some way unsatisfactory.

These four factors interact in a mutually reinforcing way. Abusive parents live in a state of precarious balance between emotional supply and demand. They are more needy because of their low self-esteem, but less able to reach out for pleasure and support, and so turn with increased need to those who are least able to provide full satisfaction, their infants. Any crisis, even a small one . . . becomes unmanageable because of the parent's poor coping techniques and inability or reluctance to seek help. Financial and housing crises are very upsetting, but most devastating are emotional crises related to loss or abandonment by important persons or the emotional desertion of a spouse after marital conflict. It is the infant's disturbing behavior during ordinary caretaking, excessive crying, or his errors during toilet training which are the common stimuli to parental turmoil that culminates in the abusive act. . . .

In 1974 Congress enacted the Child Abuse Prevention and Treatment Act (CAPTA), 42 U.S.C. §§5101-5119 (2000 & Supp. 2005), to provide funding for state child protective services. In order to qualify for federal funds, states must adopt procedures for reporting and investigating abuse (including specified definitions of child maltreatment), provide immunity from prosecution to persons who make good-faith reports, provide for confidentiality of records, and provide for the appointment of a guardian ad litem (who is not required to be an attorney) to represent children in judicial proceedings. The act also establishes the National Center on Child Abuse and Neglect (NCCAN), to gather statistical data.[4] The act was amended and reauthorized by the Keeping Children and Families Safe Act of 2003, Pub. L. No. 108-36, 117 Stat. 800 (2003). Recent amendments mandate that states require health care providers to report infants who are prenatally exposed to drug abuse to child protective services, disclose confidential information to governmental agencies if necessary for the purpose of child protection, promptly inform perpetrators of allegations of maltreatment, develop background checks of adults in prospective adoptive and foster care homes, and adopt procedures to improve the training and supervision of caseworkers. (Specific provisions of CAPTA are discussed throughout this chapter.)

[4]. The National Center on Child Abuse and Neglect conducted several national incidence studies (referred to as NIS) to collect and analyze data regarding child maltreatment. The first NIS was published in 1981, the second in 1988, and the third in 1996. See Andrea J. Sedlak & Diane D. Broadhurst, U.S. Dept. of Health & Human Servs., Nat'l Center on Child Abuse and Neglect, Third National Incidence Study of Child Abuse and Neglect: Final Report (Sept. 1996) [hereafter NIS-3]. For a summary of these findings, see Executive Summary of the Third National Incidence Study of Child Abuse and Neglect (Sept. 1996) [hereafter NIS-3 Executive Summary]. Completion of NIS-4 is scheduled for February 2008.

■ CHILD MALTREATMENT 2003: SUMMARY OF KEY FINDINGS (APRIL 2005)

U.S. Dept. of Health & Human Services, Administration of Children, Youth and Families, available at http://nccanch.acf.hhs.gov

• Victims

An estimated 906,000 children were determined to be victims of child abuse or neglect in 2003. The rate of victimization per 1,000 children in the national population has dropped from 13.4 children in 1990 to 12.4 children in 2003.

More than 60 percent of child victims experienced neglect. Almost 19 percent were physically abused, 10 percent were sexually abused, and 5 percent were emotionally maltreated. In addition, 17 percent were associated with "other" types of maltreatment, based on specific state laws and policies. [Numbers sum to more than 100 percent because some children were victims of more than one type of maltreatment.]

Children [from] birth to 3 years had the highest rates of victimization at 16.4 per 1,000 children of the same age group. Girls were slightly more likely to be victims than boys.

Pacific Islander, American Indian or Alaska Native, and African-American children had the highest rates of victimization when compared to their national population. While the rate of white victims of child abuse or neglect was 11.0 per 1,000 children of the same race, the rate for Pacific Islanders was 21.4 per 1,000 children, the rate for American Indian or Alaska Natives was 21.3 per 1,000 children, and the rate for African-Americans was 20.4 per 1,000 children.

• Reports of Child Abuse and Neglect

In 2003, an estimated 2.9 referrals concerning the welfare of approximately 5.5 million children were made to CPS agencies throughout the United States. Of these, approximately two-thirds (an estimated 1.9 million) were accepted for investigation or assessment; one-third were not accepted.

More than one-half (57 percent) of all reports that alleged child abuse or neglect were made by such professionals as educators, law enforcement and legal personnel, social services personnel, medical personnel, mental health personnel, child daycare providers, and foster care providers. Such nonprofessionals as friends, neighbors, and relatives submitted approximately 43 percent of reports.

Approximately 30 percent of the reports that were investigated included at least one child who was found to be a victim of abuse or neglect. Fifty-eight percent of the reports were found to be unsubstantiated (including those that were intentionally false); the remaining reports were closed for additional reasons.

• Fatalities

Child fatalities are the most tragic consequence of maltreatment. For 2003, an estimated 1,500 children died due to abuse or neglect. More than three-quarters (79 percent) of children who were killed were younger than 4 years old; 10 percent were 4 to 7 years old; 5 percent were 8 to 11 years old; and 6 percent were 12 to 17 years old.

Infant boys (younger than 1 year) had highest rate of fatalities, with nearly 18 deaths per 100,000 boys of the same age in the national population. Infant girls (younger than 1 year) had a rate of 14 deaths per 100,000. The overall rate of child fatalities was 2 deaths per 100,000 children. . . .

• Perpetrators

Approximately 80 percent of perpetrators were parents. Other relatives accounted for 6 percent, and unmarried partners of parents accounted for 4 percent of perpetrators. The remaining perpetrators included persons with other (camp counselor, school employee, etc.) or unknown relationships to the child victims.

Female perpetrators, who were mostly mothers, were typically younger than male perpetrators, who were mostly fathers. Women also comprised a larger percentage of all perpetrators than men: 58 percent compared to 42 percent. . . .

2. Standards for Intervention in the Family

a. Defining the Threshold

■ IN RE JUVENILE APPEAL (83-CD)
455 A.2d 1313 (Conn. 1983)

SPEZIALE, Chief Justice.

This is an appeal by the defendant, mother of five children, from the order of the Superior Court for juvenile matters granting temporary custody of her children to the plaintiff commissioner of the department of children and youth services [DCYS].

The defendant and her six children lived in a small apartment in New Haven. They had been receiving services from [DCYS] as a protective service family[1] since 1976, and were supported by the Aid to Families with Dependent Children program. Michelle Spicknall, a DCYS caseworker, was assigned to the defendant's case in January 1979. In the next nine months she visited the defendant's home twenty-seven times. She considered the family situation "marginal," but noted that the children were "not abused [or] neglected." It was Spicknall's opinion that the children were very happy and active, and that they had a "very warm" relationship with their mother.

During the night of September 4-5, 1979, the defendant's youngest child, nine-month-old Christopher, died. The child was brought by ambulance to Yale-New Haven Medical Center where resuscitation was unsuccessfully attempted by his pediatrician, Dr. Robert Murphy. No cause of death could be determined at that time, but the pediatrician noticed some unexplained superficial marks on Christopher's body.

Because of Christopher's unexplained death, the plaintiff commissioner of children and youth services seized custody of the defendant's five remaining children on September 5, 1979, under authority of the "96-hour hold" provision of General Statutes §17-38a(e), which permits summary seizure [of the child and "any other children similarly situated"] if the commissioner has probable cause to believe that a child is "suffering from serious physical illness or serious physical injury or is in immediate physical danger from his surroundings, and that immediate

---

1. A protective services family is one which has come to the attention of DGYS as having a potential for abuse, neglect, abandonment, or sexual exploitation. DCYS then investigates the family and, where appropriate, provides "support systems to bolster family functioning."

removal from such surroundings is *necessary to insure the child's safety. . . .* " (Emphasis added.)

On September 7, 1979, in the Juvenile Court for New Haven, DCYS filed petitions of neglect . . . for each of the defendant's children. Accompanying each petition was an affidavit for orders of temporary custody asking that the court issue temporary ex parte orders to keep the five children in DCYS custody under authority of §46b-129(b)(2).[5] The petitions alleged, in addition to Christopher's unexplained death, that the defendant's apartment was dirty, that numerous roaches could be found there, that beer cans were to be found in the apartment, that the defendant had been observed drinking beer, that on one occasion the defendant may have been drunk, that a neighbor reported that the children once had been left alone all night, and that the two older children had occasionally come to school without having eaten breakfast. On the basis of these allegations, on September 7, 1979, the court granted, ex parte, temporary custody to the commissioner pending a noticed hearing on temporary custody set for September 14, 1979, within ten days of the ex parte order as required. . . .

At the September 14 temporary custody hearing, DCYS presented testimony of Spicknall confirming and elaborating on the conditions of the defendant's home and on the defendant's beer drinking. Christopher's pediatrician testified concerning Christopher's treatment and physical appearance when the child was brought to the hospital on September 5. The doctor also testified that, although the pathologist's report on the autopsy was not complete, the external marks on Christopher's body were not a cause of death, that no internal injuries were found, and that the child had had a viral lung infection. He also explained, on cross-examination, the term "sudden infant death syndrome" and its pathology. At the conclusion of the state's case, the court found "probable cause" and ordered temporary custody of the children to remain with the plaintiff commissioner of children and youth services.

The defendant appealed to this court claiming that General Statutes §46b-129(b) violates the due process clause of the fourteenth amendment both because it is an impermissible infringement on her right to family integrity, and because the statute is unconstitutionally vague. . . .

A. FAMILY INTEGRITY

The Connecticut legislature has declared: "The public policy of this state is: To protect children whose health and welfare may be adversely affected through injury and neglect; to strengthen the family and to make the home safe for children by enhancing the parental capacity for good child care; to provide a temporary or permanent nurturing and safe environment for children when necessary; and for these purposes to require the reporting of suspected child abuse, investigation of

---

5. General Statutes §46b-129(b) provides: "If it appears from the allegations of the petition . . . , that there is reasonable cause to find that the [child's] condition or the circumstances surrounding his care require that his custody be immediately assumed to safeguard his welfare, the court shall either (1) issue an order to the parents or other person having responsibility for the care of [the child] to show cause at such time as the court may designate why the court shall not vest in some suitable agency or person the [child's] temporary care and custody pending a hearing on the petition, or (2) vest in some suitable agency or person [the child's] temporary care and custody pending a hearing upon the petition which shall be held within ten days from the issuance of such order on the need for such temporary care and custody. . . .

such reports by a social agency, and provision of services, where needed, to such child and family." General Statutes §17-38a(a).

In administering this policy, courts and state agencies must keep in mind the constitutional limitations imposed on a state which undertakes any form of coercive intervention in family affairs. The United States Supreme Court has frequently emphasized the constitutional importance of family integrity. "The rights to conceive and to raise one's children have been deemed 'essential,' 'basic civil rights of man,' and '[r]ights far more precious . . . than property rights.' " "It is cardinal with us that the custody, care and nurture of the child reside first in the parents, whose primary function and freedom include preparation for obligations the state can neither supply nor hinder." The integrity of the family unit has found protection in the Due Process Clause of the Fourteenth Amendment, the Equal Protection Clause of the Fourteenth Amendment, and the Ninth Amendment. [The right to family integrity includes "the most essential and basic aspect of familial privacy — the right of the family to remain together without the coercive interference of the awesome power of the state." [Citations omitted.]

B. CRITERIA FOR COERCIVE INTERVENTION BY THE STATE

Where fundamental rights are concerned we have a two-part test: "[1] regulations limiting these rights may be justified only by a 'compelling state interest,' and . . . [2] legislative enactments must be narrowly drawn to express only the legitimate state interests at stake." The state has a substantial interest in protecting minor children [citing Prince v. Massachusetts]; intervention in family matters by the state is justified, however, only when such intervention is actually "in the best interests of the child," a standard long used in this state.

Studies indicate that the best interests of the child are usually served by keeping the child in the home with his or her parents. "Virtually all experts, from many different professional disciplines, agree that children need and benefit from continuous, stable home environments." Institute of Judicial Administration — American Bar Association, Juvenile Justice Standards Project, Standards Relating to Abuse and Neglect, p.45 (Tentative draft, 1977). The love and attention not only of parents, but also of siblings, which is available in the home environment, cannot be provided by the state. Unfortunately, an order of temporary custody often results in the children of one family being separated and scattered to different foster homes with little opportunity to see each other. Even where the parent-child relationship is "marginal," it is usually in the best interests of the child to remain at home and still benefit from a family environment.

The defendants' challenge to the temporary custody statute, §46b-129(b), must be addressed in light of the foregoing considerations. The defendant contends that only when the child is "at risk of harm" does the state's interest become a compelling one, justifying even temporary removal of the child from the home. We agree.

[A]ny criteria used to determine when intervention is permissible must take into account the competing interests involved. The parent has only one interest, that of family integrity; and the state has only one compelling interest, that of protecting minor children. The child, however, has two distinct and often contradictory interests. The first is a basic interest in safety; the second is the important interest, discussed above, in having a stable family environment. Connecticut's child welfare statutes recognize both the conflicting interests and the constitutional limitations involved in any intervention situation. . . .

The language of [summary seizure provision] §17-38a(e) clearly limits the scope of intervention to cases where the state interest is compelling. . . . Intervention is permitted only where "serious physical illness or serious physical injury" is found or where "immediate physical danger" is present. It is at this point that the child's interest no longer coincides with that of the parent, thereby diminishing the magnitude of the parent's right to family integrity; and therefore the state's intervention as parens patriae to protect the child becomes so necessary that it can be considered paramount. A determination that the state interest is compelling does not alone affirm the constitutionality of the statute. More is needed. The second part of the due process analysis . . . requires that statutes affecting fundamental rights be "narrowly drawn to express only the legitimate state interests at stake." General Statutes §17-38a(e) meets this part of the test by requiring, in addition to the compelling need to protect the child, that the assumption of temporary custody by the commissioner be immediately "necessary to insure the child's safety." This phrase requires that various steps short of removal from the home be used when possible in preference to disturbing the integrity of the family. The statute itself mentions supervised in-home custody, but a wide range of other programs short of removal are a part of existing DCYS procedure.

The challenged [temporary custody] statute, §46b-129(b), does not contain the "serious physical illness or serious physical injury" or "immediate physical danger" language of §17-38a(e). We note, however, [that] statutes on a particular subject be "considered as a whole, with a view toward reconciling their separate parts in order to render a reasonable overall interpretation. . . ." This is no less true when the legislature has chosen to place related laws in different parts of the General Statutes. Therefore, the language limiting coercive intervention [in §17-38a] must be read as applying equally to such intervention [in §46b-129]. Because we hold that General Statutes §46b-129(b) may be applied only on the basis of the criteria enunciated in §17-38a, we reject the defendant's claim that §46b-129(b) is unconstitutional.

In the instant case, no substantial showing was made at the temporary custody hearing that the defendant's five children were suffering from either serious physical illness or serious physical injury, or that they would be in immediate physical danger if they were returned to the defendant's home. The DCYS caseworker admitted at trial, as did the state's counsel at argument before this court, that without the unexplained death of Christopher there was no reason for DCYS to have custody of the other children. The medical evidence at the hearing indicated no connection between Christopher's death and either the defendant or the conditions in her home. . . . There was, therefore, no evidence before the court to indicate whether his death was from natural causes or was the result of abuse. Yet with nothing before it but subjective suspicion, the court granted the commissioner custody of the defendant's other children. It was error for the court to grant to the commissioner temporary custody when no immediate risk of danger to the children was shown. . . .

Petitions for neglect and for temporary custody orders, like the petitions to terminate parental rights . . . , "are particularly vulnerable to the risk that judges or social workers will be tempted, consciously or unconsciously, to compare unfavorably the material advantages of the child's natural parents with those of prospective adoptive parents [or foster parents]." [In re Juvenile Appeal (Anonymous), 420 A.2d 875 (1979).]

This case clearly shows that these dangers do exist; it is shocking that the defendant's children have been in "temporary" custody for more than three years. This is a tragic and deplorable situation, and DCYS must bear full responsibility for this unwarranted and inexcusable delay. . . . The failure of DCYS properly to administer §46b-129 does not, however, affect its constitutionality. . . .

Notes and Questions

1. *Stages of intervention. Juvenile Appeal* reveals that state intervention must be necessary to protect the child from real, immediate physical harm, given the constitutional right to family integrity. Initial intervention may take one of two forms: summary seizure or temporary custody. At the former hearing (which is ex parte), the court determines if an emergency exists, that is, if the child is in such immediate danger that the child's welfare dictates summary removal from the home. A finding of the need for summary seizure results in deferring the temporary custody determination for a short statutorily designated period of time (for example, 96 hours in *Juvenile Appeal*).

At the adversarial hearing on temporary custody, the court determines whether requisite facts exist to find a child within the statutory definition of "abused," "neglected," "dependent," or "in need of care." This proceeding is referred to as a "jurisdictional," "adjudicatory," or "factfinding" hearing. After making such a determination, the court conducts the next "dispositional" phase. The court chooses among various dispositions: conditions on custody, family preservation services, foster care, or termination of parental rights.

2. *Concurrent jurisdiction.* Concurrent civil and criminal jurisdiction sometimes exist. In addition to civil proceedings in a juvenile or family court to declare the child a ward of the court, the state may also initiate criminal proceedings against a parent. Occasionally, the child (or the child's representative) may also initiate a tort claim against the caretaker. What are the consequences for the child, the abuser, and the family based on civil versus criminal processing?

What factors dictate the nature of the proceeding? One judge, with experience in both juvenile and criminal courts, remarks that the processing of abuse cases often reveals the arbitrary nature of state intervention. Judge Leonard P. Edwards, Corporal Punishment and the Legal System, 36 Santa Clara L. Rev. 983, 1006 (1996). Might civil proceedings sometimes be preferable to criminal proceedings? When? Should one court process both criminal and related civil proceedings in child abuse cases, as one commentator urges? Judith D. Moran, Fragmented Courts and Child Protection Cases: A Model Proposal for Reform, 40 Fam. Ct. Rev. 488, 491-495 (2002).

3. *Identification.* Abused and neglected children come to the attention of state child protective agencies in several ways: (a) mandatory referrals by professionals under state reporting laws (discussed infra this chapter); (b) referrals by friends, relatives, neighbors, and other observers who suspect child abuse; and (c) referrals from criminal justice personnel following a parent's arrest. See Mark I. Soler et al., Representing the Child Client ¶¶4.01, 4.02 (1994).

4. *The policy of minimal intervention*. As *Juvenile Appeal* illustrates, state intervention in the family sometimes is unnecessary and, in fact, harmful. In the late 1970s, mental health professionals Joseph Goldstein, Anna Freud, and Albert J. Solnit propounded a policy of "minimum intervention" and the adoption of a "least detrimental alternative standard" in child welfare decisionmaking. In their book, Before the Best Interests of the Child, they contend:

> [W]e believe that a child's need for continuity of care by autonomous parents requires acknowledging that parents should generally be entitled to raise their children as they think best, free of state interference. This conviction finds expression in our preference for *minimum state intervention* and prompts restraint in defining justifications for coercively intruding on family relationships. . . . So long as a child is a member of a functioning family, his paramount interest lies in the preservation of his family. . . .
>
> [C]omplex and vital developments require the privacy of family life under guardianship by parents who are autonomous. The younger the child, the greater is his need for them. When family integrity is broken or weakened by state intrusion, his needs are thwarted and his belief that his parents are omniscient and all-powerful is shaken prematurely. The effect on the child's developmental progress is invariably detrimental. The child's need for safety within the confines of the family must be met by law through its recognition of family privacy as the barrier to state intrusion upon parental autonomy in child rearing. These rights—parental autonomy, a child's entitlement to autonomous parents, and privacy—are essential ingredients of "family integrity." . . .
>
> [T]here is a further justification for a policy of minimum state intervention. It is that the law does not have the capacity to supervise the fragile, complex interpersonal bonds between child and parent. As parens patriae the state is too crude an instrument to become an adequate substitute for flesh and blood parents. The legal system has neither the resources nor the sensitivity to respond to a growing child's ever-changing needs and demands. It does not have the capacity to deal on an individual basis with the consequences of its decisions, or to act with the deliberate speed that is required by a child's sense of time. . . .
>
> To recognize how critical are the developmental stages and how essential are autonomous parents for the protection of their children is also to recognize that [some parents] may fail to protect their child from unwarranted risk. . . . Yet, to acknowledge that some parents, whether biological, adoptive, or longtime foster, may threaten the well-being of their children is not to suggest that state legislatures, courts, or administrative agencies can always offer such children something better. . . .

Joseph Goldstein et al., Before the Best Interests of the Child 4-5, 9, 11-13 (1979). See also Joseph Goldstein et al., Beyond the Best Interests of the Child (1973); Joseph Goldstein et al., The Best Interests of the Child: The Least Detrimental Alternative, 91-92 (1996).

Goldstein, Freud, and Solnit's views (cited in an omitted footnote in *Juvenile Appeal*) supported efforts to narrow the bases on which courts could assert jurisdiction over abused or neglected children. Very narrow standards were formulated in model legislation; however, the standards were never approved by the ABA nor adopted by state legislators. See IJA-ABA, Juvenile Justice Standards Relating to Abuse and Neglect, Standard 2.1 (Final Draft 1980) (cited in *Juvenile Appeal*). For another (not as extreme) noninterventionist stance, see Michael Wald, State

Intervention on Behalf of "Neglected" Children: A Search for Realistic Standards, 27 Stan. L. Rev. 985 (1975); Michael Wald, State Intervention on Behalf of "Neglected" Children: Standards for Removal of Children from Their Homes, Monitoring the Status of Children in Foster Care, and Termination of Parental Rights, 28 Stan. L. Rev. 623 (1976); Michael Wald, Thinking about Public Policy Toward Abuse and Neglect of Children, 78 Mich. L. Rev. 645 (1980) (reviewing *Before the Best Interests of the Child*).

The work of Goldstein, Freud, and Solnit received its share of criticisms. See Marsha Garrison, Child Welfare Decisionmaking: In Search of the Least Drastic Alternative, 75 Geo. L.J. 1745, 1762-1765 (1987) (criticizing the lack of empirical basis, overoptimism, neglect of social context in which problems emerge and in which proposed standards would be administered, and failure to address parents' voluntary placement of children in state care).

What are the advantages and disadvantages of narrow versus broad definitions of abuse and neglect? On what grounds *should* legislatures permit intervention into the private family? How should statutes balance the interests in family privacy and child protection?

5. *Vagueness.* Broad definitions of abuse and neglect in both summary seizure and temporary custody provisions pose constitutional shortcomings. For example, in an omitted portion of *Juvenile Appeal*, the court declines to decide whether Connecticut's statutory definition of neglect is unconstitutionally vague. That statute defines the terms "dependent," "neglected," and "uncared for" as follows:

> [A] child or youth may be found "dependent" whose home is a suitable one for him, save for the financial inability of his parents, parent, guardian or other person maintaining such home, to provide the specialized care his condition requires.
>
> [A] child or youth may be found "neglected" who (A) has been abandoned or (B) is being denied proper care and attention, physically, educationally, emotionally or morally or (C) is being permitted to live under conditions, circumstances or associations injurious to his well-being or (D) has been abused. . . .
>
> [A] child or youth may be found "uncared for" who is homeless or whose home cannot provide the specialized care which his physical, emotional or mental condition requires. . . .

Conn. Gen. Stat. Ann. §46b-120 (West 2004 & Supp.2005). Do the terms "dependent," "neglected," "proper care and attention," or "uncared for" provide parents with adequate warning that their acts may lead to state intervention? Despite numerous constitutional challenges on grounds of vagueness, courts generally have upheld statutes with broad definitions of abuse and neglect. But cf. Roe v. Conn, 417 F. Supp. 769, 779-780 (M.D. Ala. 1979) (holding Alabama's child neglect statute unconstitutional in the case of a "neglected" Caucasian child who was summarily removed from his home, and his mother's parental rights terminated, on the ground that the mother was socializing with African-American males and residing in an African-American neighborhood).

6. *Threshold.* Was the necessary threshold for intervention met in *Juvenile Appeal*? Did the state intervene because of one child's death or the condition of the home? Would either, alone, have proved sufficient? *Juvenile Appeal* also asks whether harm to one child justifies intervention on behalf of other unharmed siblings. On prospective abuse, see page 920.

b. Parental Privilege to Discipline

∎ NEWBY v. UNITED STATES
797 A.2d 1233 (D.C. Ct. App. 2002)

GLICKMAN, Associate Judge.

. . . On a warm Monday afternoon in September, appellant brought her children to a park in southwest Washington, D.C., for a family outing. Before long a commotion broke out, attracting the attention of witnesses who were picnicking nearby. These witnesses watched as appellant, screaming obscenities, pummeled and kicked her six-year-old daughter, who was crying and trying to run away. Dismayed and alarmed, the witnesses summoned the police. Appellant was arrested and charged with second degree cruelty to children, a ten-year felony. The government later dropped that charge, choosing instead to prosecute appellant on one count of simple assault, a 180-day misdemeanor. . . .

Three eyewitnesses called by the government testified that appellant struck her daughter some ten to fifteen times on her head, neck and shoulders, and kicked her with a shod foot in the middle of her back. The beating continued after appellant knocked her daughter to the ground. The witnesses particularly remembered seeing appellant smack her daughter's face with the back of her hand, on which appellant was wearing several prominent rings.

Testifying in her own defense, appellant explained that her daughter had been misbehaving all afternoon and was especially wild and overexcited at the picnic area. Appellant feared that the child, who was running around in a "rage," would fall in the Potomac River, burn herself on a hot barbecue grill, or run in the path of a car. After exhausting non-violent efforts to distract and quiet her daughter, appellant said, she grabbed and hit the child. Appellant also kicked her in the back of her leg, in order, she said, to stop her from running away toward the river. Appellant admitted that she was angry and had lost control of the situation. She insisted, however, that she never intended to hurt her daughter, but only to discipline her for her own good. Appellant testified, without contradiction, that the child suffered no physical injuries.

[Appellant was charged with simple assault, pursuant to D.C. Code §22-404a, providing "[w]hoever unlawfully assaults, or threatens another in a menacing manner, shall be fined not more than $1,000 or be imprisoned not more than 180 days, or both." The statute permits a common law parental privilege defense.]

We turn to appellant's argument that her assault conviction must be reversed because the government did not prove that she acted out of malice when she punished her daughter. By the term "malice" in this context, appellant means the state of mind that this court described when it construed the offense of cruelty to children in Carson v. United States, 556 A.2d 1076, 1079 (D.C. 1989): "a parent acts with malice when a parent acts out of a *desire to inflict pain* rather than out of genuine effort to correct the child, or when the parent, in a genuine effort to correct the child, acts with a *conscious disregard* that serious harm will result." (Emphasis supplied.). . . . Appellant argues, however, that the government was obliged to prove malice to overcome her affirmative defense, the so-called parental discipline defense.

A parent's privilege to use reasonable force to discipline her minor child without being subjected to criminal liability for battery or assault is rooted in the common law, where it has a long pedigree. Blackstone, for example, deemed it settled that "battery is, in some cases, justifiable or lawful; as where one who hath authority, a parent or a master, gives moderate correction to his child, his scholar, or his apprentice." 2 William Blackstone, Commentaries *120. The privilege is recognized throughout the United States. Although some jurisdictions have embodied the parental discipline defense in statutes, often with refinements, it remains a common law defense in the District of Columbia. . . .

The precise contours of the parental discipline defense have not been articulated fully in the case law of this jurisdiction. [Our prior cases], summary though they are, emphasize not the non-malicious state of mind of the parent, but rather the purpose and the reasonableness of the force used. The widely accepted Criminal Jury Instructions [(No. 4.06 (4th ed., 1966 Supp.)] likewise states that "[t]o be justified, the force must have been used for the purpose of exercising parental discipline and must be reasonable."

This basic conception of the parental discipline defense is reinforced by decisions construing the common law of Maryland, to which we look for guidance when our own precedent is not dispositive. . . . The first limitation "is that the force truly be used in the exercise of domestic authority by way of punishing or disciplining the child — for the betterment of the child or promotion of the child's welfare — and not be a gratuitous attack." [Anderson v. State, 487 A.2d 294, 298 (Md. Ct. Spec. App. 1985)]. The second limitation "is that the amount of force used be moderate and reasonable." Id. "The use of immoderate force is the thing that defeats the parental privilege, even where otherwise applicable." Id. at 299.

The District of Columbia and Maryland cases do not support appellant's contention that under the common law, "the government [is required] to prove malice before a parent, in a parental discipline case, could be found guilty of assault and battery." Much less do the cases support appellant's extravagant assertion that "what constitutes 'reasonable' parental discipline in our jurisdiction is therefore defined solely with reference to the parent's state of mind." Rather, the government could "defeat" the parental discipline defense by proving either that the parent did not have a genuine disciplinary purpose or that the force used was immoderate or unreasonable. This "reasonable force" standard for genuine parental discipline appears to be the common law rule in the majority of jurisdictions.

We recognize that not all jurisdictions employ the reasonable force standard. In the common law of some jurisdictions, the parental discipline privilege is based on a malice standard along the lines that appellant proposes. [W]e would not choose to follow the minority of courts that "hold that in the absence of malice, parents [have] almost unfettered discretion to physically dominate their children." [Kandice K. Johnson, Crime or Punishment: The Parental Corporal Punishment Defense — Reasonable and Necessary, or Excused Abuse?, 1998 U. Ill. L. Rev. 413, 435.] As Johnson reports, replacing the reasonable force standard with a malice standard would reduce the level of protection that the criminal law affords children:

> In jurisdictions using the malice standard or variations thereof, great deference is given to the authority of parents to raise children as they see fit. Parental authority

dominates the concern for the physical well-being of the child. As such, in all but the worst cases of abuse, when the child is subjected to conduct that could or does result in death, serious injury, or disfigurement, a parent's right to discipline is given priority over the consequences to the child. . . .

Johnson, *supra,* at 436 (footnotes omitted). A malice standard for the parental discipline defense also would run counter to the public policy reflected in the child neglect and abuse law of the District. That law states that a child whose parent inflicts, or fails to make reasonable efforts to prevent the infliction of, "excessive corporal punishment" is an "abused" child entitled to legal protection. D.C. Code §16-2301(23) (2001). Under this provision, we have stated, "a parent's right to manage a child has its limits," and corporal punishment "must be reasonable under the facts and circumstances of the case." In re L.D.H., 776 A.2d 570, 575 (D.C. 2001) (citations omitted). The test is an "objective" one that does not turn on the existence of parental malice. Parental good intentions do not excuse physical abuse.

Appellant nonetheless urges adoption of a malice standard in criminal prosecutions on the ground that "a general intent mens rea in parental discipline cases would not adequately safeguard a parent's constitutional right to decide how best to raise her child without undue interference from the government." This argument is flawed in that it ignores the availability of the parental discipline defense based on a reasonableness standard and assumes that nothing less than a malice standard will do to protect the due process "right of parents to make decisions concerning the care, custody and control of their children." Troxel v. Granville, 530 U.S. 57, 66 (2000) (citations omitted). But as the opinion in *Troxel* is careful to point out, the constitutional presumption against state intervention exists only "so long as a parent adequately cares for his or her children." Id. at 68. The "state has a wide range of power for limiting parental freedom and authority in things affecting the child's welfare." Prince v. Massachusetts, 321 U.S. 158, 167 (1944). Constitutionally protected parental prerogatives are sufficiently respected in a criminal assault prosecution by requiring the government to overcome the parental discipline defense beyond a reasonable doubt — by proving either that the punishment was unreasonable or that it was not genuinely disciplinary — without also requiring the government to prove that the parent acted with malice toward her child.

To say that much is not to say that the common law reasonableness standard is necessarily beyond criticism. One arguable shortcoming is that "[w]ith 'reasonableness' as their only guide, parents have little guidance as to the limits of a lawful physical interaction with their children, and fact finders are left to define the privilege on a case-by-case basis." Johnson, *supra,* at 467. . . . Perhaps the criminal sanction should be reserved for the most egregious cases, [as Professor Monrad Paulsen opines below[15]], or should entail a heightened *mens rea* requirement — if not malice, then perhaps a lesser degree of recklessness. Refinements to the common law reasonableness standard implicate policy issues that are mainly for the legislative branch rather than the courts, however. . . .

---

15. In Paulsen's view, "[t]he harsh remedies of the criminal law are appropriate only in severe cases, cases which indicate that further harm may be done to others, cases which call for vengeance (if that call should ever be heeded), or cases which so disturb the community's sense of security that the events cannot go unremarked." [Monrad G. Paulsen, The Legal Framework for Child Protection, 66 Colum. L. Rev. 679, 692 (1966)].

We hold that the government was not required to prove malice in order to rebut appellant's assertion of the parental discipline defense. We therefore reject appellant's argument that her conviction must be overturned because there was insufficient evidence of malice. For the foregoing reasons, appellant's conviction of simple assault is affirmed.

Notes and Questions

1. *Battered child syndrome.* One of the most common manifestations of child abuse is "the battered child syndrome." Radiologists played a prominent role in recognition of this problem.[5] In a classic article, Dr. C. Henry Kempe (the principal author) coined the term and speculated that some unexplained traumatic injuries to children may have been inflicted intentionally by parents.[6] The term, now widely accepted in medical literature and case law, signifies a child who manifests multiple fractures in different parts of the body that are in various stages of healing; parental explanations are at odds with clinical findings. Many courts, including the Supreme Court, accept battered child syndrome evidence in criminal cases. See Estelle v. McGuire, 502 U.S. 62 (1991).

2. *Age of victims.* In *Newby*, the victim was 6 years old. The largest category of child maltreatment victims are young children, typically under age three.[7] How appropriate is corporal punishment of infants or young children? Of teenagers? If appropriate, what form should it take? Among infants and young children, head injuries are especially common, leading to recognition of the "shaken baby syndrome" by which severe, repetitive shaking may result in brain damage, paralysis, eye injury, seizures, developmental delays, and death.[8] The victim in the principal case was female. Why do you suppose that boys are likely to be more severely injured?[9]

3. *Perpetrators.* The abuser in the case was the child's mother. Biological parents are the perpetrators of most physical abuse, followed by stepparents and other parent substitutes.[10] Children are more likely to be neglected by female perpetrators but more likely to be seriously abused by males.[11] Do such gender-based findings "demonstrate a serious need for rethinking the design of prevention and treatment strategies that now focus primarily on females."[12] If so, how?

[5]. See Stephen Pfohl, The Discovery of Child Abuse, 24 Soc. Probs. 310 (1977).

[6]. C. Henry Kempe et al., The Battered Child Syndrome, 181 JAMA 17 (1962). Although Kempe and his colleagues are credited with the discovery of abuse, another pediatric radiologist, John Caffey, first noticed the phenomenon. See John Caffey, Multiple Fractures in the Long Bones of Infants Suffering from Chronic Subdural Hematoma. 56 Am.J.Roentgenology 163 (1946).

[7]. See U.S. Dept. of Health & Human Servs., Administration on Children, Youth and Families: Child Maltreatment: 2003.

[8]. See U.S. Dept. of Health & Human Servs., A Nation's Shame: Fatal Child Abuse and Neglect in the United States 15 (1995) (reporting that shaken baby syndrome results in 10 to 12 percent of deaths). See also Stephan Lazoritz & Vincent J Palusci, Shaken Baby Syndrome: A Multidisciplinary Approach (2002).

[9]. Child Maltreatment: 2003, supra note [7].

[10]. NIS-3, supra note [4], at 6 (birth parents are the perpetrators in 72 percent of the cases of physical abuse, followed by other parent and parent substitutes in 21 percent of the cases).

[11]. Id. at 13 (87 percent of the children were neglected by females versus 43 percent by males); A Nation's Shame, supra note [8], at 13 (men inflict more fatal injuries).

[12]. A Nation's Shame, supra note [8], at 14.

4. *Munchausen's Syndrome by Proxy.* Mothers are more likely to be the perpetrators of one particular form of abuse, "Munchausen's Syndrome by Proxy." In the condition, named after the famous storyteller-soldier Baron Von Munchausen, the parent induces illness, often by poison or medication overdose, in a child (the "proxy"). Sometimes, the illness or injury is fabricated. Abuse stems from the *parent*'s craving for attention. Several jurisdictions have ruled that evidence of Munchausen Syndrome by Proxy is admissible in child abuse prosecutions. See, e.g., In re K.T., 836 N.E.2d 769 (Ill. App. Ct. 2005); State v. Hocevar, 7. P.3d 329 (Mont. 2000). See generally Julie Gregory & Marc D. Feldman, Sickened: The Memoir of a Munchausen by Proxy Childhood (2003); Melissa A. Prentice, Note, Prosecuting Mothers Who Maim and Kill: The Profile of Munchausen Syndrome by Proxy Litigation in the Late 1990s, 28 Am. J. Crim. L. 373 (2001).

5. *Physical abuse or discipline?* A threshold issue in many cases is whether the injury resulted from abuse or discipline. As *Meyer* and *Pierce*, supra, established, parents have a constitutionally protected right to raise their children as they see fit, including the privilege to administer *reasonable* discipline. What distinguishes abuse from discipline? Must the punishment result in bodily harm? See State v. Lefevre, 117 P.3d 980 (N.M. 2005) (reversing father's conviction for battery by finding that his grabbing his daughter's hand was an isolated act of punishment that constituted reasonable force resulting in temporary bruises).

When does spanking become child abuse? Some jurisdictions exempt spanking from the definition of child abuse in civil or criminal statutes. See Cal. Welf. & Inst. Code §300(a) (West 1998 & Supp. 2001) (exempting from abuse "reasonable and age-appropriate spanking to buttocks where there is no evidence of serious physical injury"); Okla. Stat. Ann. tit. 21, §844 (West 2002) (exempting from criminal liability "spanking, switching or paddling" accompanied by ordinary force). How helpful are such definitions in the determination of excessive discipline? See generally Kandice K. Johnson, Crime or Punishment: The Parental Corporal Punishment Defense — Reasonable and Necessary or Excused Abuse?, 1998 U. Ill. L. Rev. 413 (1998).

6. *Empirical data.* Sixty-five percent of Americans approve of spanking children, according to a recent ABC News Poll (n=1,015). Among parents with minor children at home, 50 percent report that they "sometimes" spank their child. This percentage is consistent with data reported in a Gallup poll a decade ago. Julie Crandall, Support for Spanking; Most Americans Think Corporal Punishment Is OK, available at http://abcnews.go.com/sections/us/DailyNews/spanking_poll021108.html (last visited Feb. 20, 2006). See also Deana Pollard, Banning Child Corporal Punishment, 77 Tul. L. Rev. 575, 581-583 (2003).

7. *Statutory formulations.* According to the majority rule, a parent is not criminally liable if the assault to the child constitutes "reasonable force" and is administered as a means of discipline. Approximately half of the states recognize a parental privilege for corporal punishment by statute, whereas the remaining states resort to case law. Tamar Ezer, A Positive Right to Protection for Children, 7 Yale Hum. Rts. & Dev. L.J. 1, 17 (2004).

According to the Restatement (Second) of Torts §147(1) (1965), the generally accepted standard for the limits of parental discipline is:

> A parent is privileged to apply such reasonable force or to impose such reasonable confinement upon his child as he reasonably believes to be necessary for its proper control training, or education.

Factors in the determination of reasonableness include age, sex, physical and mental condition of the child; nature of child's offense and apparent motive; influence of child's example on other children of the same family or group; whether the force or confinement is reasonably necessary and appropriate to compel obedience to a proper command; and whether it is disproportionate to the offense, unnecessarily degrading, or likely to cause serious or permanent harm. Restatement (Second) of Torts §150 (1965).

Similarly, the ALI Model Penal Code §3.08 defines the parent's use of force as "justifiable" if the force is used to "promot[e] the welfare of the minor, including the prevention or punishment of his misconduct; and, [if] the force . . . is not designed to cause or known to create a substantial risk of causing death, serious bodily harm, disfigurement, extreme pain or mental distress or gross degradation." The privilege to discipline is delegable by the parent, such as to a teacher or to some other person in loco parentis. See Restatement (Second) of Torts §147(2) (1965); ALI Model Penal Code §3.08(2). See also State v. West, 515 N.W.2d 484 (Wis. Ct. App. 1994) (extending privilege to foster parents). But cf. Teresa Mosher Boyd, Corporal Punishment and the Legal System, 11 J. Contemp. Legal Issues 491, 494 (2000) (stating that some states, such as California, prohibit foster parents from using corporal punishment).

8. *Provocation.* Might a child's acts be sufficient provocation to render punishment "reasonable"? See State v. Brunner, 1985 WL 8658 (Ohio Ct. App. 1985) (beating five-year-old with belt for foul language that led to threat of eviction was disciplinary and not excessive).

9. *Reasonableness.* Should the law take into account differences in the perception of reasonableness? For example, one commentator points to the controversy about whether spanking constitutes abuse or discipline. "Therapists are more inclined to believe that it is abusive, possibly leading to negative, long-term sequelae for the child, whereas CPS workers [child protective service] are less prone to see it as actionable." Murray Levine & Howard J. Doueck, The Impact of Mandated Reporting on the Therapeutic Process: Picking Up the Pieces 140 (1995).

Similarly, should the law take into account *cultural* differences in evaluating reasonableness? See In re D.L.W., 589 N.E.2d 970, 972 (Ill. App. Ct. 1992) (terminating father's parental rights and disregarding father's justification for spanking with wooden board and banging son's head against wall). See generally Jill E. Korbin, Culture and Child Maltreatment, in The Battered Child, supra, at 29; Michael Futterman, Comment, Seeking a Standard: Reconciling Child Abuse and Condoned Child Rearing Practices Among Different Cultures, 34 U. Miami Inter-Am. L. Rev. 491 (2003); Michele Wen Chen Wu, Note, Culture Is No Defense for Infanticide, 11 Am. U.J. Gender Soc. Pol'y & L. 975 (2003).

10. *Parental tort immunity.* The parent-child immunity doctrine prevents an unemancipated child from suing a parent in tort. The doctrine originated in a trilogy of cases beginning at the end of the nineteenth century. See Hewellette v. George, 9 So. 885 (Miss. 1891) (refusing a claim of false imprisonment by an unemancipated daughter against her mother for maliciously committing her to an insane asylum); McKelvey v. McKelvey, 77 S.W. 664 (Tenn. 1903) (denying liability in suit by daughter for cruel and inhumane treatment by her father and stepmother); Roller v. Roller, 79 P. 788 (Wash. 1905) (denying liability in a civil suit by a minor against father for rape). The primary rationale for the doctrine was the

promotion of family harmony. By the 1950s, almost all states had adopted the doctrine, applying it to negligent as well as intentional torts.

Wisconsin started the trend toward abrogation in Goller v. White, 122 N.W.2d 193 (Wis. 1963) (permitting a foster son to sue his foster father for injuries sustained while riding on the drawbar of a tractor). As other states followed suit, two primary approaches emerged. California replaced the doctrine in Gibson v. Gibson, 479 P.2d 648 (Cal. 1971), with the "reasonable parent standard" that permitted recovery if a parent fails to meet the standard of care required by a "reasonable and prudent parent." New York substituted a general duty of care standard. Holodook v. Spencer, 324 N.E.2d 338 (N.Y. 1974).

Virtually all jurisdictions now have either abrogated the doctrine or limited it substantially. Among the latter, some states permit suits on a case-by-case basis, such as motor vehicle accidents, sexual abuse, intentional torts, or the conduct of a family business. See, e.g., Newman v. Cole, 872 So. 2d 138 (Ala. 2003) (recognizing exception to parent-child immunity doctrine in wrongful death action when parent's intentional injury caused child's death). See generally Dan B. Dobbs & Paul T. Hayden, Torts and Compensation: Personal Accountability and Social Responsibility for Injury 388 (4th ed. 2001); Joseph J. Basgier, Comment, Children's Rights: A Renewed Call for the End of Parental Immunity in Alabama and Arguments for the Further Expansion of a Child's Right to Sue, 26 Law & Psychol. Rev. 123, 124-131 (2002). Is tort law an effective means of protecting children from physical abuse?

11. *Intergenerational transmission.* Evidence suggests that abuse is "transmissible" intergenerationally. That is, maltreated children are likely, as adults, to choose abusive partners and to become abusive or neglectful parents. Even childhood *exposure* to domestic violence increases the likelihood that a boy will become a batterer upon adolescence or adulthood, and that a girl will become a victim of abuse upon reaching adulthood.[13] Scholars have proposed different explanations for the "violence begets violence" theory. Some support a social learning perspective (children learn the appropriateness of aggression). Others advance psychologically based attachment theory (early experiences with abusive parents are repeated when not well-integrated into the personality).[14]

Evidence similarly suggests the "intergenerational transmission of violence." That is, childhood maltreatment increases the possibility that the victim will commit future delinquent and criminal acts. Specifically, abused and neglected children are more likely to have subsequent juvenile and adult arrest records, have a first arrest at a young age, commit several offenses, and commit more violent acts.[15]

12. *Witnessing abuse.* Sometimes, siblings witness a parent's abuse of another child. Should this form of exposure to domestic violence constitute child abuse and neglect? Evidence suggests that a child's exposure to violence *between* parents leads to severe physical and psychological effects (such as aggressiveness, behavior

[13]. See Lundy Bancroft & Jay G. Silverman, The Batterer as Parent: Addressing the Impact of Domestic Violence on Family Dynamics 48 (2002); Brandt F. Steele, Psychodynamic and Biological Factors in Child Maltreatment, in The Battered Child 73, 74 (Mary Edna Helfer et al. eds., 5th ed., 1997).

[14]. Joan Kaufman & Edward Zigler, The Intergenerational Transmission of Abuse, in Child Maltreatment: Theory and Research on the Causes and Consequences of Child Abuse and Neglect 136-137 (Dante Cicchetti & Vicki Carlson eds. 1989).

[15]. Office of Juvenile Justice and Delinquency Prevention, Juvenile Offenders and Victims: A National Report 42 (1995); Jennifer Langhinrichsen-Rohling et al., The Relationship Behavior Networks of Young Adults: A Test of the Intergenerational Transmission of Violence Hypothesis, 19 J. Fam. Violence 139 (2004).

problems, hyperactivity, anxiety, withdrawal, and learning difficulties). Might exposure to a parent's abuse of a *sibling* have the same effects? See Lundy Bancroft & Jay G. Silverman, The Batterer as Parent: Addressing the Impact of Domestic Violence on Family Dynamics 37-42 (2002); Brooke Kintner, Note, The "Other" Victims: Can We Hold Parents Liable for Failing to Protect Their Children From Harms of Domestic Violence?, 31 New Eng. J. Crim. & Civ. Confinement 271, 276-282 (2005). States are responding to this problem by incorporating "childhood exposure to domestic violence" into their statutory definitions of child abuse and neglect. See Lois A. Weithorn, Protecting Children From Exposure to Domestic Violence: The Use and Abuse of Child Maltreatment Statutes, 53 Hastings L.J. 1 (2001) (reviewing research, analyzing recent statutory approaches, and suggesting reforms).

What are the difficulties of interpreting existing child abuse and neglect statutes to incorporate childhood exposure to domestic violence? See id. at 26-41. See also Alan J. Tomkins et al., The Plight of Children Who Witness Women Battering: Psychological Knowledge and Policy Implications, 18 Law & Psychol. Rev. 137 (1994). Note that the National Center for Child Abuse and Neglect and its National Incidence Study of Child Abuse and Neglect defines as emotional neglect "chronic or extreme spouse abuse or *other domestic violence* in the child's presence (emphasis added)."[16]

13. *Cross-cultural perspectives.*

a. *Swedish ban.* In 1979 Sweden became the first country to prohibit corporal punishment by parents. The ban on physical punishment or "humiliating treatment" in the Swedish Parenthood and Guardianship Code followed considerable public concern over the rising incidence of abuse. The ban was actually the third stage of legislative reform. The first reform occurred in 1957 when the Swedish Parliament eliminated the parental privilege from the Penal Code—i.e., removing parental physical punishment as a defense to criminal assault. In the second stage, the Swedish Parliament in 1966 removed references to even mild forms of corporal punishment from the Parents' Code. See generally Joan E. Durrant, The Swedish Ban on Corporal Punishment: Its History and Effects, in Family Violence Against Children: A Challenge for Society 23-24 (Detlev Frehsee et al. eds., 1996); Dennis Alan Olson, Comment, The Swedish Ban of Corporal Punishment, 1984 B.Y.U. L. Rev. 447. Several Swedish parents unsuccessfully challenged the ban as a violation of their rights to family privacy and freedom of religion under the European Convention for the Protection of Human Rights and Fundamental Freedoms. X, Y and Z v. Sweden, 5 EHRR 147 (1983).

The Swedish ban significantly changed attitudes toward corporal punishment in Sweden and abroad. Before the ban, 54 percent of all adult Swedes considered corporal punishment necessary occasionally. By 1996 only 11 percent of respondents indicated that they were positively inclined to use even mild forms of punishment. Durant, supra, at 152.

The Swedish ban also initiated a worldwide trend. Ten other nations followed Sweden's example (Austria, Croatia, Cyprus, Denmark, Finland, Germany, Iceland, Israel, Latvia, and Norway). Joan E. Durrant, Legal Reform and Attitudes Toward Physical Punishment in Sweden, 11 Int'l J. Children's Rts. (No. 1) 147, 168

[16]. NIS-3, supra note [4], at 2.10.

(2003). The Swedish ban also influenced international human rights law. Article 19 of the 1989 United Nations Convention on the Rights of the Child (which imposes human rights obligations on signatory nations) requires governments to protect children from all forms of maltreatment, and Article 37 provides that no child shall be subject to cruel, inhuman, or degrading punishment. Although the Convention does not contain an explicit prohibition of "physical punishment," the international committee that interprets the Convention has emphasized that "corporal punishment of children is incompatible with the Convention" and recommends that "the physical punishment of children in families be prohibited." Cited in Linda Rose-Krasnor et al., Physical Punishment and the U.N. Convention on the Rights of the Child, Int'l Soc. Study of Behav. Dev. Newsletter, No. 2, Serial No. 38 (2001), at 9.

b. *Britain.* In 1998 the European Court of Human Rights held in A. v. United Kingdom, 27 EHRR 611 (1998), that a stepfather's beating of a nine-year-old boy with a bamboo garden stake violated the boy's human rights, even though a British court earlier deemed the punishment "reasonable chastisement" pursuant to British law. Sarah Lyall, European Court Rebukes Britain in Case of Stepfather Beating Son, Plain Dealer (Cleveland), Sept. 24, 1998, at A6. In response, the British government promised to amend the law. In 2002, when no legislation was yet forthcoming, a United Nations committee criticized the British law of "reasonable chastisement" as incompatible with the nation's obligations under the Convention on the Rights of the Child. In 2004, Parliament considered but rejected a total ban on corporal punishment and decided instead to limit the scope of reasonable chastisement. Alan Cowell, The House of Lords Restrains the Hand That Hits the Child, N.Y. Times, July 6, 2004, at A4. The new law allows "mild smacking" of children but prohibits any physical punishment that causes visible bruising. Simon Baker, Call for All-Out Ban on Smacking, Commissioners in Appeal for Free Vote, Daily Post (Liverpool, UK), Jan. 23, 2006, at 4.

c. *Canada.* In January 2004, in response to a challenge by a Toronto-based children's advocacy group (the Canadian Foundation for Children, Youth and the Law), the Canadian Supreme Court upheld Section 43 of the Canadian Criminal Code (Canada's so-called "spanking law") which permits the use of reasonable force to discipline children. However, the Court set new guidelines defining the limits of "reasonable force," specifically providing that corporal punishment for children under age two and for teenagers was unreasonable, as was corporal punishment using implements or directed at the child's face or head. The Court also distinguished between corporal punishment by parents and teachers, ruling that the latter was unacceptable. Teachers can use limited force to restrain unruly students (i.e., to remove them from a classroom or to break up a fight), but cannot resort to corporal punishment. See Jim Brown, Spanking Law Upheld, http://www.fathers.ca/news_reports_on_spanking.htm (last visited Feb. 20, 2006).

Problems

1. When Mrs. Jones picks up 11-year-old Bobby after school, he hands his mother a detention slip from a teacher. The detention slip is based on an event that happened six months before. Mrs. Jones requests an explanation from the teacher, who indicates that the note attached to the detention slip was missing. That same

night, Mr. and Mrs. Jones discover another disciplinary note from a different teacher in Bobby's backpack; that note has been marked over with black magic marker.

Bobby denies stealing the first note and defacing the second. His parents are particularly distressed at his dishonesty, which has been a disciplinary issue for some time. Mr. Jones tells Bobby, "I don't believe you," and hits Bobby twice on the buttocks. The father then leaves, telling Bobby that his mother will mete out the rest of his punishment. Mrs. Jones orders Bobby to his room to think over his misdeeds. When she enters his room to ask if he is ready to "tell the truth," he insists that his teacher is lying. Mrs. Jones then spanks Bobby several times with a belt, telling him, "I'm going to have to make this hurt for a time." A short time later, Bobby confesses.

That night, when the parents are retiring for bed, they notice Bobby trying to make a quantity of toilet paper go down the shower drain. Mrs. Jones previously had disciplined Bobby's sister for placing wads of toilet paper in the shower. Mrs. Jones demands to know who perpetrated the act. When both children deny their role, Mrs. Jones requires them to do exercises — pushups or squats for a certain length of time. If they are "out of form," they are "swatted with a belt to correct that form." Ultimately, Bobby's sister confesses, and Mrs. Jones then spanks her daughter three times with her belt.

The following day, a school official notices bruises, marks, and welts on both children. Bobby's shoulders and back are almost completely covered by bruises, and his legs are bruised to some extent. The school official reports Mrs. Jones to the authorities. Both children are examined by a physician but require no treatment. Mrs. Jones appeals her conviction of several counts of child abuse. What result? See State v. Jones, 747 N.E.2d 891 (Ohio Ct. App. 2000).

2. Tom, a 12-year-old boy with Attention Deficit-Hyperactivity Disorder and Tourette's Syndrome, is defiant on the day that his family moves into their new house. He refuses to help with the move. His mother asks Tom repeatedly to retrieve the trash can from the old house which is located a block away. He finally obeys, but, in the process, strews trash all over the kitchen floor. When he denies the act, while crying and screaming, his stepfather determines that Tom is "out of control." The stepfather leads him to his bedroom and spanks him eight to ten times with a belt. His sister tells their biological father who reports the act to authorities. After finding bruises on the boy's shins, thigh, posterior, belt line and arms, the social services department files a petition alleging that Tom is an abused child. What result? See In re T.A., 663 N.W.2d 225 (S.D. 2003).

c. Neglect

(i) Physical Neglect

■ IN RE A.H.
842 A.2d 674 (D.C. 2004)

GLICKMAN, Associate Judge.

D.H. asks us to reverse the judgment of the trial court that she neglected her five small children. . . . The five respondents in this case were between seven months and seven years of age when the Child and Family Services Agency (CFSA) removed them from the care of their mother, appellant D.H., and petitioned the Superior Court Family Division to find them neglected. The children had been residing with D.H. and their maternal grandmother J.H. in a two-story townhouse apartment in East Capitol Dwelling, a public housing project operated by the District of Columbia Housing Authority. . . .

[T]he trial court received testimony from four witnesses in the following order: Vivian Norris, the East Capitol Dwelling property manager who referred the H. family to CFSA in June of 2000; Ms. Kellerhouse, the petitioning social worker; Metropolitan Police Officer McKoy Perry, who assisted in the emergency removal of the children from the home; and D.H. The respondents' grandmother J.H. was present during the proceeding but was not called as a witness.

Vivian Norris testified that she first came in contact with the H. family when she participated in a required property inspection in January 2000. Ms. Norris stated that when she entered the H. home, she smelled a "foul odor" from feces and waste and saw "trash all over the floor." The children were running about, naked or minimally clothed, and visibly dirty (though they did not appear to be ill or disabled). In the kitchen, Ms. Norris noticed that the gas oven was on, the oven door was open, and the burners on the stove were lit. Because the children were playing in the kitchen, Ms. Norris turned the oven and burners off and told D.H. "that wasn't safe with them running around and having the door all the way down and the oven on." D.H. responded that she needed the oven to provide heat because her furnace had stopped working. D.H. had never complained about the lack of heat or reported that the furnace was broken.

Ms. Norris stated that the kitchen was in "deplorable" condition. "[T]here was some meat out on the table that looked as if it was just sitting there to be cooked 'cause it was raw meat. But it had roaches crawling on it. She had other types of open' food on the counter and dirty dishes and stuff like that with roaches crawling all around, the table and counter top areas." The rooms upstairs were in no better shape. "The bedrooms had clothes and trash all on the floors, I mean to the point where you would have to kick through it to get into that space. And that's in every room." The bathroom was "filthy," and Ms. Norris found feces in the "baby pot" and the bathtub. D.H. told her that the family had been using the bathtub as a toilet because the toilet was "stopped up." As in the case of the furnace, D.H. had never reported this problem.

Following this inspection, Ms. Norris arranged for repairs and maintenance to be performed in the townhouse, including a roach extermination. . . . Ms. Norris reinspected the apartment the following week and again in May 2000. On each occasion, Ms. Norris testified, the unit was still fetid and filthy as before. . . . During her last visit, in May, Ms. Norris told D.H. and J.H. that she would notify the CFSA because the children never had clothes on and were not in a clean environment, and D.H. and J.H. were doing nothing about it. According to Ms. Norris, D.H. was "nonchalant," saying that she had cleaned the house and acting as if "she didn't see anything wrong with that situation."

Kimberly Kellerhouse became involved with the H. family after the CFSA was notified. Ms. Kellerhouse testified that she worked with Families Together, a crisis intervention program run jointly by the CFSA and a private social services agency to help families with abused or neglected children remain intact and avoid removal of the children to foster care. Ms. Kellerhouse and an assistant met the H. family for the first time on June 19, 2000, when they visited the home to begin a week-long suitability assessment. [She testified] that the hot water heater and the heating system in the apartment were broken and there had been no heat all winter. The refrigerator had also been broken for some time. . . .

Ms. Kellerhouse interviewed D.H. as part of her initial assessment. D.H. told her that she could not get up early enough in the morning to hold a job, though she had worked in a summer job when she was in high school. [Ms.] Kellerhouse told D.H. that the apartment was not a fit place to live and that she would investigate alternatives. In response, and throughout the interview, D.H. was notably passive and seemingly acquiescent in the deleterious conditions in which she and her children were living. Ms. Kellerhouse "didn't get a sense of urgency. . . . [She] got, really, a sense of apathy." Ms. Kellerhouse ascertained that D.H. had never been assessed for clinical depression or other mental health issues.

Ms. Kellerhouse returned to the H. residence four days later, on June 23, 2000. Conditions in the home were, if anything, worse. . . . Ms. Kellerhouse visited the H. family again on June 27, 2000. The apartment was still filthy and roach-infested. . . . Ms. Kellerhouse and her supervisors became convinced that the Families Together Program would not be able to help the H. family and that the children needed to be removed for their own safety. In part this was because Ms. Kellerhouse developed concerns about D.H.'s parenting; she described, for example, seeing D.H. ignore her baby's cries during one visit and threaten her children with a belt on another occasion. D.H. told Ms. Kellerhouse that she administered "whoopings" if the children went too close to the stove or misbehaved.[9] More important to Ms. Kellerhouse, though, was the "level of desensitization" that D.H. and the H. family displayed with respect to the deplorable surroundings in which they were living. . . . On June 29, 2000, Ms. Kellerhouse and the CFSA case worker removed the H. children from the home. The following day they filed a neglect petition in Superior Court.

The police officer who assisted in the removal of the children on June 29 was Officer McCoy Perry. Officer Perry's observations that day matched those of Ms. Norris and Ms. Kellerhouse. . . .

The only other witness at the fact finding hearing was D.H. herself. D.H. testified that she was twenty-two years old and had completed the eleventh grade in high school. . . . D.H. emphatically denied that the conditions in the apartment were as bad as the other witnesses had described them. She accused each of the other witnesses of exaggerating and outright lying. . . . D.H. testified that she washed dishes daily, did major cleaning every Sunday, and did the laundry every two weeks. She claimed that she kept fresh food in the house, despite the lack of a working refrigerator, by going shopping every day. D.H. said that all her children were healthy and that her older children were doing well in school. She did not think the lack of heat was a problem for the children or that she was irresponsible in keeping them in an unheated apartment through the winter, because they had enough blankets and they never said they were cold. D.H. testified that the children were never left alone in the kitchen when the oven

---

9. Ms. Kellerhouse did not witness D.H. abuse her children, however, nor did she observe any signs of physical mistreatment. She testified that the H. children did not appear sick or malnourished; they had the required immunizations; they had clothing to wear; and the two children of school age were attending school.

door was open—which, she said, was mainly during the night, when the family was asleep.[11]

Regarding her financial resources, D.H. testified that she had not worked since high school. She had not been able to get a job, she said, because she did not have a high school diploma or a G.E.D. Her mother J.H. also was unemployed. In 2000, when her children were living with her, D.H. received $400 a month in TANF (Temporary Assistance for Needy Families) benefits. The rent on the East Capitol Dwelling apartment, which D.H. paid, was around $100 each month.

[R]elying most heavily on the testimony of Ms. Kellerhouse and Officer Perry while giving less weight to the testimony of Ms. Norris and D.H., the judge entered findings of neglect. The judge concluded that D.H. and J.H. bore at least some of the responsibility for allowing the children to live in deleterious conditions and that this was not due to their lack of financial means. Reviewing D.H.'s testimony, the judge found that she "appeared either unaware, uncaring, or both regarding the deplorable conditions in which she and her children were living." The judge did not arrive at this conclusion lightly; he was both troubled and perplexed by the "strange nonchalance" that D.H. displayed when confronted about the unsafe and unsanitary environment in the home. . . .

D.H. contends that insufficient evidence was presented in the fact finding hearing to sustain the judge's ruling that her children were neglected. . . . D.H. finds support for her arguments in In re T.G., 684 A.2d 786 (D.C. 1996), the only previous published decision of this court to consider a neglect petition predicated on the existence of deplorable living conditions comparable to those in this case. . . .

A child is neglected within the meaning of former D.C. Code §16-2301(9)(B) if the child is "without proper parental care or control, subsistence, education as required by law, or other care or control necessary for his or her physical, mental, or emotional health, and the deprivation is not due to the lack of financial means of his or her parent, guardian, or other custodian." Where such deprivation is established, this definition does not require proof that the child has already sustained actual injury as a result. . . .

. . . The majority in T.G. did not dispute that "constant exposure to filthy living conditions creates the risk of physical deterioration" and that "we don't need to leave children in deplorable conditions until they get hurt. . . ." 684 A.2d at 789 & 789 n. 5. The T.G. majority simply was troubled by the fact that the neglect petitions before it were predicated on nothing more than a single snapshot of the family's existence—the deplorable living conditions at issue in the case had been observed on only one, possibly uncharacteristic, day, and there was no evidence (or so the majority concluded) that those conditions were other than temporary or that the parents tolerated them. . . .

The focus in the instant case was not so narrow. The allegations of neglect were not based in this case on a mere snapshot. The District presented credible evidence that deplorably unsanitary and unsafe living conditions were allowed to persist in the H. home over a period of several months at least. . . .

---

11. After the children were removed from D.H.'s home, they went to live with her sister. D.H. maintained regular contact with the children and attended to their medical care, schooling, and similar matters. The children were in good health, doing well in school, and evidently having their needs met.

That brings us to the remaining issue — whether there was sufficient proof that the deprivations in this case were not due to D.H.'s lack of financial resources. The statutory requirement that the government prove that "the deprivation is not due to the lack of financial means" of the parent, guardian or custodian has proved to be nettlesome in both theory and practice. . . . When a case, like this one, presents multiple deprivations, some due to lack of financial means and some due to other factors, the statute requires that the neglect determination be based on the factors not attributable to the lack of financial means. . . .

[T]he purpose of the financial means proviso is obscure. . . . Clear answers [are] not to be found, so far as we are aware, in the legislative history of the law or past opinions of this court. The premise seems to be, though, that when it is poverty alone that causes an otherwise fit parent to be unable to care for her child, adequate public or private benefits should and will be made available to the family — benefits that the parent can be counted on to put to good use to remedy the child's deprivation, thereby rendering a formal neglect proceeding unnecessary. . . .

. . . Like the trial judge, we are not blind to the role that poverty and forces beyond D.H.'s control played in her family's life. Nevertheless, we are persuaded that unlike in *T.G.*, the judge here did have a substantial evidentiary basis for his finding that the principal unsafe and unsanitary conditions in the H. family home were not due to a parental lack of the financial means to remedy them. . . . D.H. did not present any evidence to rebut the inference that the public assistance she received was adequate. To the contrary, she claimed to be able to support her family — to clean, to do laundry, to buy food, to pay her rent, and so forth. And there was no evidence that her children were malnourished or unhealthy (though there were indications that they were ill-clothed).

. . . We will not pretend to think this was an easy case for the trial judge to decide, but his judgments were supported by the evidence and we see no reason to reverse them. . . .

(ii) Medical Neglect

■ IN RE PHILLIP B.
156 Cal. Rptr. 48 (Ct. App. 1979)

CALDECOTT, Presiding Justice.

A petition was filed by the juvenile probation department in the juvenile court, alleging that Phillip B., a minor, came within the provision of [California] Welfare and Institutions Code section 300, subdivision (b), because he was not provided with the "necessities of life."

The petition requested that Phillip be declared a dependent child of the court for the special purpose of ensuring that he receive cardiac surgery for a congenital heart defect. Phillip's parents had refused to consent to the surgery. The juvenile court dismissed the petition. The appeal is from the order.

Phillip is a 12-year-old boy suffering from Down's Syndrome. At birth his parents decided he should live in a residential care facility. Phillip suffers from a congenital heart defect — a ventricular septal defect that results in elevated pulmonary blood pressure. Due to the defect, Phillip's heart must work three times harder than normal to supply blood to his body. When he overexerts, unoxygenated blood travels the wrong way through the septal hole reaching his circulation, rather than the lungs.

If the congenital heart defect is not corrected, damage to the lungs will increase to the point where his lungs will be unable to carry and oxygenate any blood. As a result, death follows. During the deterioration of the lungs, Phillip will suffer from a progressive loss of energy and vitality until he is forced to lead a bed-to-chair existence.

Phillip's heart condition has been known since 1973. At that time Dr. Gathman, a pediatric cardiologist, examined Phillip and recommended cardiac catheterization to further define the anatomy and dynamics of Phillip's condition. Phillip's parents refused.

In 1977, Dr. Gathman again recommended catheterization and this time Phillip's parents consented. The catheterization revealed the extensive nature of Phillip's septal defect, thus it was Dr. Gathman's recommendation that surgery be performed.

Dr. Gathman referred Phillip to a second pediatric cardiologist, Dr. William French of Stanford Medical Center. Dr. French estimates the surgical mortality rate to be five to ten percent, and notes that Down's Syndrome children face a higher than average risk of postoperative complications. Dr. French found that Phillip's pulmonary vessels have already undergone some change from high pulmonary artery pressure. Without the operation, Phillip will begin to function less physically until he will be severely incapacitated. Dr. French agrees with Dr. Gathman that Phillip will enjoy a significant expansion of his life span if his defect is surgically corrected. Without the surgery, Phillip may live at the outside 20 more years. Dr. French's opinion on the advisability of surgery was not asked.

It is fundamental that parental autonomy is constitutionally protected. The United States Supreme Court has articulated the concept of personal liberty found in the Fourteenth Amendment as a right of privacy which extends to certain aspects of a family relationship. "It is cardinal with us that the custody, care and nurture of the child reside first in the parents, whose primary function and freedom include preparation for obligations the state can neither supply nor hinder." (Prince v. Massachusetts (1944) 321 U.S. 158, 166.) . . .

Parental autonomy, however, is not absolute. The state is the guardian of society's basic values. Under the doctrine of parens patriae, the state has a right, indeed, a duty, to protect children. (See, e.g., Prince v. Massachusetts, supra, 321 U.S. 158 at p.166.) State officials may interfere in family matters to safeguard the child's health, educational development and emotional well-being.

One of the most basic values protected by the state is the sanctity of human life. (U.S. Const., 14th Amend., §1.) Where parents fail to provide their children with adequate medical care, the state is justified to intervene. However, since the state should usually defer to the wishes of the parents, it has a serious burden of justification before abridging parental autonomy by substituting its judgment for that of the parents.

Several relevant factors must be taken into consideration before a state insists upon medical treatment rejected by the parents. The state should examine the seriousness of the harm the child is suffering or the substantial likelihood that he will suffer serious harm; the evaluation for the treatment by the medical profession; the risks involved in medically treating the child; and the expressed preferences of the child. Of course, the underlying consideration is the child's welfare and whether his best interests will be served by the medical treatment.

Section 300, subdivision (b), permits a court to adjudge a child under the age of 18 years a dependent of the court if the child is not provided with the "necessities of life."

The trial judge dismissed the petition on the ground that there was "no clear and convincing evidence to sustain this petition." The rule is clear that the power of the appellate court begins and ends with a determination as to whether there is any substantial evidence, contradicted or uncontradicted, which will support the conclusion reached by the trier of fact. . . .

Turning to the facts of this case, one expert witness testified that Phillip's case was more risky than the average for two reasons. One, he has pulmonary vascular changes and statistically this would make the operation more risky in that he would be subject to more complications than if he did not have these changes. Two, children with Down's Syndrome have more problems in the postoperative period. This witness put the mortality rate at five to ten percent, and the morbidity would be somewhat higher. When asked if he knew of a case in which this type of operation had been performed on a Down's Syndrome child, the witness replied that he did, but could not remember a case involving a child who had the degree of pulmonary vascular change that Phillip had. Another expert witness testified that one of the risks of surgery to correct a ventricular septal defect was damage to the nerve that controls the heart beat as the nerve is in the same area as the defect. When this occurs a pacemaker would be required.

The trial judge, in announcing his decision, cited the inconclusiveness of the evidence to support the petition.

On reading the record we can see the trial court's attempt to balance the possible benefits to be gained from the operation against the risks involved. The court had before it a child suffering not only from a ventricular septal defect but also from Down's Syndrome, with its higher than average morbidity, and the presence of pulmonary vascular changes. In light of these facts, we cannot say as a matter of law that there was no substantial evidence to support the decision of the trial court. . . .

Notes and Questions on Neglect

1. *Epilogue.* Following In re Phillip B., the appellants' petition for a rehearing was denied; the California Supreme Court also denied appellants' petition for a hearing. Professor Martha Minow relates the sequel:

> Two volunteers, a married couple named Heath, befriended Phillip at the institution and started to bring him home for holiday visits, with his parents' consent. The Heaths grew frustrated when the Beckers continued to refuse treatment for Phillip's heart and when they also successfully defended against a dependency proceeding brought by the state charging them with neglect. [The Beckers' refusal of treatment stemmed from their worry that Phillip might outlive them and be a burden to his brothers.] The Heaths then initiated their own legal proceedings seeking to become Phillip's guardians and seeking authority to approve surgery to repair Phillip's heart. It was an unusual legal strategy, orchestrated by lawyer Jay Spears and law professor

Robert Mnookin. The lawyers, on behalf of the Heaths, converted the earlier legal question of whether the parents had fallen so low in their conduct to justify state intrusion in the private family into a contested custody case between two plausible sets of parents or guardians. Not only did this reworking of the case suggest an easier standard to justify governmental intervention, it also offered a real, long-term option for Phillip beyond approval of heart surgery.

After a twelve-day trial, Judge William Fernandez issued an extensive and unusually candid and expressive opinion. He began by asking, "Who speaks for the child?" He considered Phillip's parents, his friends, and his institutional caretakers. The judge compared the conceptions of Phillip held by his parents and by his friends, the Heaths. According to the court, the Beckers held onto the picture of Phillip they acquired when he was born and their physician had advised institutional care. The Beckers viewed Phillip as an unskilled and devalued person, incapable of loving others. The Heaths, in contrast, pictured Phillip as an educable and valuable person, capable of loving others. The judge found the Heaths' conception more persuasive and likely to provide a less detrimental alternative, but the judge also decided that Phillip's own rights had to be explored before resolving the guardianship issue.

Nothing in the law governing guardianship specified rights for a child or incompetent person like Phillip. Nonetheless, Judge Fernandez noted an emerging constitutional right to "habilitation," a right for persons with mental disabilities to acquire and maintain skills to cope and lead more useful and meaningful lives. Similarly, the judge found California law protections against unfair stigma for persons with mental retardation and minors with grave disabilities. From these principles, the judge inferred that fourteen-year-old Phillip had a right to express his preference regarding his placement.

This was an innovation, as the judge acknowledged, and it created a practical difficulty: how could the preference of a mentally disabled teenager be discerned and respected? For Judge Fernandez, Phillip's own views could no more be ignored that they could themselves be determinative. The judge turned to the doctrine of "substituted judgment" which obliges a court to discern "as nearly as possible the incompetent person's 'actual interests and preferences.'" Judge Fernandez then adopted an unusual method to derive this substituted judgment, a "platonic dialogue with the court posing the choices to Phillip and Phillip's preference being ascertain [sic] from the more logical choice." In the dialogue, the judge again focused on the alternate pictures the Beckers and the Heaths held of Phillip, and what those alternatives implied for his future. The court also credited the apparent psychological closeness between Phillip and the Heaths. The judge in conclusion granted guardianship to the Heaths without terminating the Beckers' parental rights. His decision was affirmed a year and a half later by the appellate court.[17]

Martha Minow, Guardianship of Phillip Becker, 74 Tex. L. Rev. 1257, 1257-1258 (1996).

[17]. Guardianship of Phillip B., 188 Cal. Rptr. 781 (Ct. App. 1983). Phillip's heart surgery was successful. In a subsequent settlement, the Heaths assumed all responsibility for Phillip, while the Beckers ended judicial proceedings and received visitation at least two days per year. When Phillip turned 18, the Heaths adopted him. See Robert H. Mnookin, The Guardianship of Phillip B.: Jay Spears' Achievement, 40 Stan. L. Rev. 841, 853-854 (1988).

Phillip Becker-Heath recently turned 39 years old. After two years' residence in a group home, he returned to the Heaths' home following the death of his girlfriend of 20 years. Phillip's biggest problem now, according to Pat Heath, "is finding decent work—because of all the government cutbacks." He still participates in the Special Olympics in bowling, basketball, and golf. No one from Phillip's biological family has contacted him since one week after his heart surgery in 1983. Mr. Becker passed away from cancer in 1995. "They don't know what they missed," Pat Heath says. "He's absolutely been the joy of my life." Personal communication with Pat Heath, Jan. 4, 2005.

2. *What constitutes neglect?* Civil and criminal neglect law constitute a constraint on parental rights. Neglect includes the failure to provide adequate food, clothing, shelter, supervision, education, or medical care. See James M. Gaudin, Jr., Effective Intervention with Neglectful Families, 20 Crim. Just. & Behav. 66, 67 (1993) (defining neglect). Definitional problems abound, however. Broad-based neglect statutes typically confer considerable discretion on the state to intervene. Did the court correctly assert jurisdiction in *A.H.?*

3. *Role of poverty.* When is court intervention appropriate in cases of physical neglect? Were the children in *A.H.* removed because of neglect or because of poverty? How does the court in *A.H.* address this issue? Was there evidence that the children were suffering adverse health effects? Without such a showing, should the state be allowed to remove children from parental custody? Is the *risk* of harm sufficient to justify intervention? If so, when?

Child protective services have long been criticized as being class biased.[18] Vague and broad juvenile court standards allow child protective service workers and judges to impart middle-class biases and personal values into the decisionmaking process. Should removal from the home be permitted when the children can be protected by alternative means, such as the provision of housekeeping services?

In the case of In re N.M.W., 461 N.W.2d 478 (Iowa Ct. App. 1990), an appellate court affirmed the removal of a five-year-old girl from a home with unsanitary conditions. In response, Judge Sackett (dissenting) offers the following criticisms:

> I agree with the majority it would be in the child's best interests to live in a cleaner house. However, the house could have been cleaned without taking the child from her mother. I do not, however, feel removal from the parental home was in the child's best interests and feel the matter should be remanded to direct reasonable efforts be utilized to allow the child to return home. Houses can be cleaned, but the trauma a child experiences when he or she is removed from the only parental home he or she has ever known can cause emotional scars that can last a lifetime . . . .
>
> The majority decision also concerns me because it may be interpreted as setting standards for housekeeping that need to be met before we allow parents to keep their children. If I were convinced: (1) only people with clean houses were good parents, (2) for a child to be healthy it is necessary for him or her to be raised in a sanitary house, and (3) a child suffers less by being removed from his or her parents than from growing up in a dirty house, I could agree with the majority. I am not convinced of these things . . . .

Id. at 482-483. Do you agree?

4. *Incidence of neglect.* Although more attention is devoted to the battered child, neglect is a far more common form of child maltreatment. More than 60 percent of child victims experience neglect compared to 19 percent who are physically abused, 10 percent who are sexually abused, and 5 percent who are emotionally maltreated.[19]

---

[18]. See Daan Braveman & Sarah Ramsey, When Welfare Ends: Removing Children from the Home for Poverty Alone, 70 Temple L. Rev. 447 (1997); James Garbarino, The Role of Economic Deprivation in Child Maltreatment, in The Battered Child, supra note [13], at 49; Andrea Charlow, Race, Poverty, and Neglect, 28 Wm. Mitchell L. Rev. 763 (2001); Candra Bullock, Comment, Low-Income Parents Victimized by Child Protective Services, 11 Am. U. J. Gender Soc. Pol'y & L. 1023 (2003).

[19]. Child Maltreatment: 2003, supra note [7].

5. *Failure to thrive*. One common form of neglect in young children is "failure to thrive" (FTT), a condition of severe developmental delays and malnutrition. No consensus exists about its characterization; FTT has been characterized as abuse, neglect, and emotional maltreatment. See Ann Haralambie, Handling Child Custody, Abuse and Adoption Cases 290 (1993) (categorizing it as neglect); Leonard Karp & Cheryl Karp, Domestic Torts 61 (Supp. 1994) (categorizing it as abuse but mentioning that mental health officials often categorize it as neglect).

The term originated in the post-World War II period to describe children living in institutions where mortality was high. Physicians subsequently reported the condition in children living at home. Ruth S. Kempe & Richard B. Goldbloom, Malnutrition and Growth Retardation ("Failure to Thrive") in the Context of Child Abuse and Neglect, in The Battered Child, supra, at 312, 313. Failure to thrive is difficult to treat. "Although the cause of the malnutrition is lack of adequate calories, the problem usually occurs in a context of a moderately or severely disturbed parent-child relationship and is not readily cured by simple re-education of the parents about better feeding." Id. at 331.

Court sometimes consider a child's weight gain and general improvement while in state custody as evidence of parental neglect in failure-to-thrive cases. See, e.g., In re Kayla C., 797 N.Y.S.2d 559 (App. Div. 2005); In re Goff, 2003 WL 1793063 (Ohio Ct. App. 2003). See generally R. Kim Oates & Ruth S. Kempe, Growth Failure in Infants, in The Battered Child, supra, at 374.

6. *Exposure to battering as neglect?* Do statutory definitions of "neglect" include instances in which a parent "allows" a child to witness domestic abuse? Nicholson v. Scoppetta, 820 N.E.2d 840 (N.Y. 2004), involved a federal class action on behalf of mothers and their children who were removed from the home pursuant to New York's statutory scheme on the ground that the children were neglected because the mother had suffered domestic violence to which the children were exposed. When the mothers and their children challenged the constitutionality of the city's policy based on 42 U.S.C. §1983, the New York Court of Appeals held that evidence that a caretaker allowed a child to witness domestic abuse against that caretaker was insufficient, without more, to satisfy the statutory definition of a "neglected child." On the problem of failure to protect, see also infra p. 912.

7. *Homelessness.* Should homelessness constitute per se neglect? See In re Ivey, 576 S.E.2d 386 (N.C. Ct. App. 2003) (holding that neither homelessness nor joblessness will per se support a finding of abuse or neglect).

8. *Child abandonment.* One extreme form of neglect is child abandonment. What parental acts constitute abandonment? Incarceration? See Michael J. v. Arizona Dept. of Econ. Sec., 995 P.2d 682 (Ariz. 2000). Failure to contact children who are in foster care? See N.A. v. J.H., 571 So. 2d 1130, 1133 (Ala. Civ. App. 1990). Failure to pay child support? See In re S.J., 849 S.W.2d 608 (Mo. Ct. App. 1993). A child is considered abandoned when a parent has not provided support or maintained contact for a statutory period of time, when the parent cannot be found, or when the parent has left the child in circumstances that cause him or her harm.[20]

---

[20]. National Clearinghouse on Child Abuse and Neglect, Definitions of Child Abuse and Neglect: Summary of State Laws (2005), available at http://nccanch.scf.hhs.gov/general/legal.statutes/define.pdf.

See also G.C. v. Alaska Dept. of Health & Soc. Servs., 67 P.3d 648 (Alaska 2003) (adopting a two-part test, finding abandonment if "the parent's conduct evidenced a disregard for his or her parental obligations" and "that disregard led to the destruction of the parent-child relationship").

The growing number of newborn abandonments has prompted legislative action. Many states have enacted legislation (called "Baby Moses" laws or "Safe Haven" laws) to allow mothers who have given birth to surrender their newborns to a hospital employee anonymously and with impunity. Such legislation, addressed primarily to pregnant teenagers who abandon their newborns because of shame or fear, is intended to prevent the discarding of babies in trash bins or other isolated places. Considerable variation exists among the statutes concerning the definition of children who may be left (i.e., younger than three or thirty days, abused children), the location where children may be left (i.e., hospitals only, or also police or fire stations), the identity of the persons who may leave children (i.e., biological parent only, or any person with lawful custody), and the procedures for accepting children (i.e., anonymity always, or whether questions may be asked by the recipients). Jeffery A. Parness, Deserting Mothers, Abandoned Babies, Lost Fathers: Dangers in Safe Havens, 24 Quinnipiac L. Rev. 335, 345 (2006).

Do you think the legislation is an adequate solution to the problem? See Carol A. Duncan, She Could Have Safely and Anonymously Surrendered Her Newborn Infant Under California Law — Did She Know That?, 4 J. Legal Advoc. & Prac. 15 (2002) (advocating the need for publicizing such laws); Stephanie E. Dreyer, Note, Texas' Safe Haven Legislation: Is Anonymous, Legalized Abandonment a Viable Solution to Newborn Discardment and Death?, 12 Tex. J. Women & L. 167 (2002) (discussing criticisms); Ana L. Parid, Note, The Case for "Safe Haven" Laws: Choosing the Lesser of Two Evils in a Disposable Society, 28 New Eng. J. Crim. & Civ. Confinement 61 (2002) (suggesting an effective safe haven statute).

Do safe haven laws adequately protect the rights of fathers? Thirty of the 42 states with safe haven laws do not require notice to the father before terminating parental rights. Are such provisions constitutional? See Dayna R. Cooper, Note, Fathers Are Parents Too: Challenging Safe Haven Laws with Procedural Due Process?, 31 Hofstra L. Rev. 877 (2003). See also Parness, supra (suggesting that safe haven laws violate fathers' rights to equal protection).

9. *Vehicular neglect.* Should individuals be subject to liability for abuse and neglect for leaving a child unattended in a vehicle? In the last two decades, approximately 178 heat-related deaths of children have occurred in automobiles. Stephanie Armagost, An Innocent Mistake or Criminal Conduct: Children Dying of Hyperthermia in Hot Vehicles, 23 Hamline J. Pub. L. & Pol'y 109, 111 (2001). The death rate is high because the internal temperature of a vehicle increases very quickly, and small children's under-developed body cooling system makes them particularly susceptible to heat stroke. Ironically, most states have laws against leaving animals, but not children, unattended in cars. Id. at 115. Should states enact legislation that imposes criminal liability on parents who leave children unattended in vehicles, or should law enforcement resort instead to traditional laws, such as manslaughter, child endangerment, neglect or maltreatment? See id. at 117-119. See People v. Maynor, 683 N.W.2d 565 (Mich. 2004); Kelly v. Commonwealth, 592 S.E.2d 353 (Va. Ct. App. 2004). Courts are less willing to convict when the children are older and suffer no harm. See, e.g., State v. Sammons, 889 So. 2d 857 (Fla. Ct. App. 2004); State v. Tice, 686 N.W.2d 351 (Minn. Ct. App. 2004).

10. *Cultural defense*. Should courts take into account cultural differences when evaluating whether the lack of traditional medical treatment constitutes neglect? See In re Jertrude O., 466 A.2d 885 (Md. Ct. Spec. App. 1983) (affirming finding that child was "in need of assistance" based on evidence that scars resulted from "cupping," an African custom in which a cow horn is heated and pressed against the body to withdraw sickness). See also Susan Hall Dudley, Note, Medical Treatment for Asian Immigrant Children — Does Mother Know Best?, 92 Geo. L.J. 1287 (2004).

11. *Religious beliefs as defense to neglect*. Some parents' refusal to consent to medical treatment for their child is premised on religious beliefs. The ensuing conflict pits the state's interest in child protection against the parent's First Amendment rights. Cases often arise when state officials petition the juvenile or family court to assume jurisdiction (based on neglect) and request the court to order the necessary medical treatment. In re L.S., 87 P.3d 521 (Nev. 2004).

Many states exempt faith healing from the definitions of child abuse and neglect. Zaven T. Saroyan, Spiritual Healing and the Free Exercise Clause: An Argument for the Use of Strict Scrutiny, 12 B.U. Pub. Int. L.J. 363, 367 (2003). See also National Clearinghouse on Child Abuse and Neglect Information, Reporting Laws: Religious Exemptions (2003), available at http://www.abuse .com/child_abuse/religious_exemptions.pdf. Notwithstanding such exemptions in their child abuse statutes, some jurisdictions prosecute parents under their criminal statutes, reasoning that child neglect and manslaughter statutes govern different situations (protection versus punishment), and that the legislature never intended that neglect statutes would immunize a parent from manslaughter liability. Does this paradoxical situation (when one statute gives permission to act according to one's religion, but the state permits subsequent prosecution for that same conduct) violate due process for lack of notice? See Saroyan, supra, at 368 (so arguing).

The federal response to spiritual treatment exemptions has vacillated. Although the Child Abuse Prevention and Treatment Act (CAPTA), 42 U.S.C. §§5101-5105 (2000), originally did not include spiritual treatment exemptions, regulations of the Department of Health, Education and Welfare (which were promulgated pursuant to the act) required states to include such exemptions. Subsequent Department of Health and Human Services regulations excluded the spiritual treatment exemption. See Elizabeth A. Lingle, Treating Children by Faith: Colliding Constitutional Issues, 17 J. Legal Med. 301, 307 (1996).

Even so, most states did not repeal their religious exemptions statutes in response. Misty Boyer, Note, Death by Religious Exemption: Parents Refusing Their Child Necessary Medical Treatments Based Upon Their Own Religious Beliefs — Should States Endorse a System that Denies Necessary Medical Treatment to Children?, 4 Whittier J. Child & Fam. Advoc. 147 (2004).

See generally James G. Dwyer, Spiritual Treatment Exemptions to Child Medical Neglect Laws: What We Outsiders Should Think, 76 Notre Dame L. Rev. 147 (2000); Janna C. Merrick, Spiritual Healing, Sick Kids and the Law: Inequities in the American Healthcare System, 29 Am. J.L. & Med. 269 (2003); David E. Steinberg, Children and Spiritual Healing: Having Faith in Free Exercise, 76 Notre Dame L. Rev. 179 (2000).

Problem

Margaret is a single parent raising David (age 12) and Amy (age 17). To support the family, Margaret works two jobs, 60 hours per week. Her son David is the target of frequent bullying at school because of his short stature and studious demeanor. In response, David often misses school. He also has personal hygiene problems. Margaret repeatedly requests that the school district move David to a different school because of the bullying. In the course of an investigation of David's truancy, the Department of Children and Families (DCF) visits the home. They find clothes and articles piled high and completely covering the floors, kitchen surfaces, table tops, chairs, and other furniture. The toilet, sink, and bathtub are dirty. Believing that children need to do chores and shoulder responsibility, Margaret refuses to clean the apartment. A few days after DCF's visit, David attempts suicide. When DCF learns of David's suicide attempt, they charge Margaret with felony child neglect.

The relevant statute provides: "Any person who willfully or unlawfully causes or permits any child under the age of sixteen years to be placed in such a situation that the physical or mental health of such child is likely to be injured shall be guilty of felony child neglect." What result? If David did commit suicide, who (if anyone) would be liable? See State v. Scruggs, 2004 WL 1245557 (Conn. Super. Ct. 2004). See generally Avi Salzman, Woman is Spared Prison in Case Tied to Son's Suicide, N.Y. Times, May 15, 2004, at A14; Marc Santora, After Son's Suicide, Mother is Convicted Over Unsafe Home, N.Y. Times, Oct. 7. 2003, at A27.

Note: "Baby Does," Disabled Newborns, and Medical Neglect

Parents may refuse medical care for their child because the seriousness of the child's condition leads the parents to believe that treatment would be futile or that death may be a more humane outcome than survival. Do such parental acts constitute neglect? Over a decade ago, this question swirled at the heart of a nationwide controversy. Two legal cases, in Indiana and New York (referred to as the "Baby Doe Cases"), precipitated federal legislative efforts addressing the withholding of medical attention from disabled newborns.

Initially, the federal response viewed medical nontreatment of newborns as a form of discrimination against the disabled. Baby Doe was born in 1982 in Indiana with Down's Syndrome and suffering from an esophageal obstruction. Surgery could correct the digestive tract ailment. However, the infant's Down's Syndrome (a genetic condition that results in mental retardation) could not be remedied. Without surgery, the baby would die from starvation. Because of the baby's Down's Syndrome, the parents decided to withhold both their consent to surgery and all food and water. The juvenile court refused the hospital's request to assert jurisdiction. The Indiana Court of Appeals, likewise, refused to order treatment. In re Infant Doe, No. GU 8204-004A (Monroe County Cir. Ct., Apr. 12, 1982). The Indiana Supreme Court rejected a petition for a writ of mandamus. State ex rel. Infant Doe v. Baker, No. 482 S 140 (Ind. May 27, 1982). In Infant Doe v. Bloomington Hospital, 464 U.S. 961 (1983), the Supreme Court denied certiorari. Baby Doe died six days after birth.

Baby Doe's death precipitated the formulation of a new policy by the Department of Health and Human Services (DHHS) warning hospitals that the withholding of food and medical care from seriously ill newborns might possibly result in the providers' loss of federal funding under §504 of the Rehabilitation Act of 1973, 29 U.S.C. §794(e) (1994) (prohibiting discrimination against the disabled by federally funded programs). The failure to treat seriously disabled infants would constitute "discrimination against the handicapped" under the act. Discriminating Against the Handicapped by Withholding Treatment of Nourishment; Notice to Health Care Providers, 47 Fed. Reg. 26,027 (1982). DHHS subsequently published an Interim Final Rule requiring hospitals to post a notice that such discrimination was a violation of federal law. Nondiscrimination on the Basis of Handicap, 48 Fed. Reg. 9630 (1983) (codified at 45 C.F.R. §84.61 (2000)).

Medical groups challenged the regulations. American Academy of Pediatrics v. Heckler, 561 F. Supp. 395 (D.D.C. 1983), invalidated the regulations on procedural grounds (that is, the failure to comply with the public comment requirements of the Administrative Procedure Act). In response, DHHS again promulgated regulations, this time complying with the requisite procedures. DHHS's final regulations in 1984 differed only slightly from the interim regulations.

A second Baby Doe was born while the final federal regulations were being formulated. Baby Jane Doe, born in New York State in 1983, suffered from spina bifida, microcephaly, and hydrocephalus. The baby's condition was not as life threatening as Indiana's Baby Doe. However, even with corrective surgery, the baby risked retardation and impaired physical functioning. Without surgery, the baby risked death within two weeks to two years. The baby's parents eventually decided to withhold their consent to surgery, while consenting to antibiotic and palliative treatment.

Thereupon, a private attorney, representing the "right to life" movement, filed an unsuccessful suit to compel the surgery. Weber v. Stony Brook Hosp., 469 N.Y.S.2d 63 (App. Div. 1983) (per curiam). The Baby Jane Doe case prompted DHHS again to act. Eight days after the baby's birth, DHHS received a complaint that the hospital was engaged in discrimination against the disabled. DHHS sought the baby's medical records. The parents and hospital refused. When DHHS sought to compel the release of the records, a district court found no evidence of a §504 violation nor any basis to order such disclosure. The Second Circuit affirmed. United States v. University Hosp., 729 F.2d 144 (2d Cir. 1984).

Ultimately, medical groups (including the American Medical Association and the American Hospital Association) challenged the validity of the DHHS final regulations. In Bowen v. American Hospital Association, 476 U.S. 610 (1986), the Supreme Court held that parental withholding of consent does not constitute discriminatory nontreatment by the hospital, and also that the promulgation of the federal regulations exceeded DHHS's statutory authority.

In response, the federal government adopted a radically different approach: classifying medical nontreatment as a form of child abuse and neglect. The Child Abuse Amendments of 1984, amending CAPTA, 42 U.S.C. §§5101-5107 (2000), incorporated a new provision stating that the withholding of medically indicated treatment, with certain exceptions, constitutes a form of child neglect.[21] 42 U.S.C.

---

[21]. 42 U.S.C. §5106(g) (2000) defines "withholding of medically indicated treatment" as follows:

failure to respond to the infant's life-threatening conditions by providing treatment (including appropriate nutrition, hydration and medication) . . . except that the term does not

§5106 (2000). States failing to include this new definition of neglect faced the loss of federal funds. "Although commentators have questioned their impact and effectiveness, the Child Abuse Amendments remain in place today as the legislation most directly affecting medical decisions for newborns with disabilities."[22]

d. Emotional Abuse and Neglect

■ IN RE SHANE T.
453 N.Y.S.2d 590 (Fam. Ct. 1982)

LEDDY, Jr., Judge. . . .

Shane is the natural child of the respondents and presently resides with his mother and two sisters. His father is a construction worker who has been separated from his wife for some time, although they continue to see each other. [Shane is 14 years old.]

Over the course of the last several years, Shane has been subjected to an unrelenting torrent of verbal abuse by his father directed at his sexual identity. Specifically, he has been regularly called a "fag," "faggot," and "queer." In desperation, the boy pleaded with his mother to intervene on his behalf and prevail upon his father to cease making these accusations. However, the mother's efforts were abortive, resulting only in a repetition of the taunts by the father with the added assertion that they were true.

Nor were these accusations limited to the home. On one particular occasion, the respondent father humiliated the boy by calling him a "fag" while they were shopping in a store.

[Family Court Act] Section 1012(e)(i) defines an "abused child" as one

> Less than eighteen years of age whose parent or other person legally responsible
> for his care . . . inflicts or allows to be inflicted upon such child physical injury by other
> than accidental means which causes or creates a substantial risk of death, or serious or
> protracted disfigurement, or protracted impairment of physical or emotional health
> or protracted loss or impairment of the function of any bodily organ. . . .

As defined in the Penal Law [which uses similar wording], "physical injury means impairment of physical condition or *substantial pain*." Penal Law Section 10.00(9) (emphasis supplied). Whether "substantial pain" has been established is ordinarily a question for the trier of fact. . . . In deciding whether Shane has experienced "substantial pain," the Court initially considers the observation of Chief Judge Cooke: "Pain is, by definition, a subjective concept and cannot be quantified or expressed with precision. Knowledge of the circumstances and the

---

include the failure to provide treatment (other than appropriate nutrition, hydration, or medication) to an infant when, in the treating physician's or physicians' reasonable medical judgment, (A) the infant is chronically and irreversibly comatose; (B) the provision of such treatment would (i) merely prolong dying, (ii) not be effective in ameliorating or correcting all of the infant's life-threatening conditions, or (iii) otherwise be futile in terms of the survival of the infant; or (C) the provision of such treatment would be virtually futile in terms of the survival of the infant and the treatment itself under such circumstances would be inhumane.

[22]. Mary Crossley, Infants with Anencephaly, the ADA, and the Child Abuse Amendments, 11 Issues L. & Med. 379, 383 (1996).

description of the sensation accompanying the use of force, however, provide a ready basis for measuring, within one's own experience, the degree of pain felt by another." Matter of Philip A. [,49 N.Y.2d 198,] 202, 424 N.Y.S.2d 418, 400 N.E.2d 358 (Cooke, J. dissenting).

It must be immediately observed that there is no specific requirement of the use of force in the definition of an abused child. Thus, Judge Cooke's statement relating to "the use of force" is specifically referenced to the assault statute that was under consideration in Matter of Philip A. (supra). In fact, while Section 1012(e)(i) of the Family Court Act is derived from Section 10.00(10) of the Penal Law, there are substantial differences between the statutes. Thus, it is sufficient for a finding of abuse that there be protracted impairment of emotional health or a substantial risk thereof. It is clear, therefore, that it is the actual or potential impact on the child, as opposed to the per se seriousness of the injury, that forms the predicate for abuse. In this regard, the Family Court Act provision differs markedly from the Penal Law definition of "serious physical injury." Furthermore, while section 1012(e)(i) of the Family Court Act makes specific reference to "emotional health," section 10.00(10) of the Penal Law refers merely to "health."

The foregoing is consistent with the fact that Article 10 of the Family Court Act is a civil proceeding "designed to establish procedures to help protect children from injury or mistreatment and to help safeguard their physical, mental and *emotional well-being*." FCA Section 1011 (emphasis supplied). Therefore, this Court concludes that the "physical injury" referred to in Section 1012(e)(i) of the Family Court Act need not be inflicted by physical force. Rather, to constitute abuse, mere words are sufficient provided that their effect on the child falls within the language of the statute. . . .

As he testified, Shane repeatedly tried to forestall tears, but they beseiged (sic) his eyes, nonetheless. He told the Court how he would cry and his stomach would twist when his father called him a "fag." At one point, he was asked whether he was beginning to believe that he was a homosexual. He clenched his hands, sat forward, and cried out "No!". His demeanor strongly suggested, however, that he would like someone, anyone to reassure him.

It should be noted that, in addition to the verbal indignities to which he was subjected, Shane was frequently forced to remove his father's shoes and massage his feet. The boy complied without protest since he was constantly in fear of his father. This fear was well-founded since the father has a history of assaultive behavior in the home. Against this background, it is hardly surprising that Shane is now in therapy. . . .

To fail to acknowledge this boy's plight would be an affront to the clear legislative intent of Article 10 of the Family Court Act; to fail to label the father's actions as child abuse would strip the phrase of all meaning; to fail to warn other parents against this insidious type of abuse would perpetuate the suffering of countless other defenseless children.

The respondent father seeks to justify his verbal abuse of Shane as a form of legitimate parental discipline designed to cure the child of certain unspecified "girlie" behavior. He stated that it would be embarrasing (sic) to him if Shane were "queer." . . . While a parent's right to raise his or her child remains fundamental, it is equally fundamental that children have constitutional rights which must be respected by all, including their parents. In re Gault, 387 U.S. 1, and its progeny leave no doubt that the bill of rights is not for adults alone. Time and again, courts have reiterated the validity of state interference in the parental-child relationship when necessary to protect the child's health and welfare. . . .

The behavior of this respondent father is as serious a form of abuse as if he had plunged a knife into the stomach of this child. In fact, it's probably worse since the agony and heartache suffered by Shane has already assailed him for several years and constitutes a grave and imminent threat to his future psychological development. . . .

Therefore, on the entire record it is ordered that Shane T. be . . . declared to be an abused child by both respondents, [be] remanded to the Commissioner of Social Services, [and] that the Family Court Clinic be . . . directed to perform an immediate psychiatric and psychological evaluation of Shane on an emergency basis.

Notes and Questions

1. *Scope of the problem.* Emotional maltreatment accounts for a small, but significant, proportion of reported cases of abuse and neglect.[23] Courts and commentators have been slow to recognize emotional maltreatment as child abuse, in part because emotional maltreatment (unlike physical maltreatment) leaves no visible marks. Early statutory definitions of "abuse" emphasized serious *physical* injuries. See generally Sana Loue, Redefining the Emotional and Psychological Abuse and Maltreatment of Children, 26 J. Legal Med. 311 (2005).

2. *Definitional problems.* What was the definitional problem posed by the statute in *Shane*? Shane's father attempted to justify his behavior as a "legitimate form of discipline." When does "discipline" become emotional abuse? See In re S.M.B., 597 So. 2d 848 (Fla. Dist. Ct. App. 1992). Part of the difficulty of defining emotional abuse stems from the various purposes for which the term is used, that is, research, program eligibility, legal jurisdiction, or medical intervention. See Bruce Fisher & Jane Berdie, Adolescent Abuse and Neglect: Issues of Incidence, Intervention and Service Delivery, 2 Child Abuse & Neglect 173, 177 (1978). Other problems include: some definitions focus on the response of the child while others focus on behavior of the abuser, disagreement exists with respect to the classification scheme and the conduct encompassed within each category, and many definitions are silent with respect to the intent of the caregiver. Loue, supra, at 317. How helpful is the following definition of "child abuse" and "neglect" in CAPTA?

> the physical or *mental injury*, sexual abuse or exploitation, negligent treatment, or maltreatment of a child under the age of eighteen, or the age specified by the child protection law of the State, by a person including any employee of a residential facility or any staff person providing out of home care who is responsible for the child's welfare under circumstances indicating harm or threatened harm to the child's health

[23]. Data from the third National Incidence Study reveal that emotionally abused children represent 18 percent of all abused children; emotionally neglected children represent 24 percent of all neglected children. NIS-3, supra note [4], at 3.3 (extrapolated from Table 3-1), 3.6, 3.7. Some researchers suggest, however, that psychological maltreatment may be more common than other forms of maltreatment because it is so often unreported and appears in combination with other forms of abuse and neglect. Marla R. Brassard & David B. Hardy, Psychological Maltreatment in The Battered Child, supra note [13], at 397.

or welfare. The term encompasses both acts and omissions on the part of a reasonable person. [45 C.F.S. §1340.2(d) (2003) (originally codified at 42 U.S.C. §5106(g)) (emphasis added).]

The third NIS defines emotional abuse as close confinement (tying, binding, and other inappropriate confinement or physical restriction); verbal or emotional assaults (belittling, denigrating, scapegoating, or other rejecting treatment as well as threats of abandonment, beatings, or sexual assault); other abusive, exploitative or punitive behaviors where physical contact did not occur (for example, intentional withholding of food, shelter, sleep, or other necessities or excessive demands).[24] Emotional neglect is "inadequate nurturance or affection, chronic or extreme domestic violence in the child's presence, knowingly permitting drug or alcohol abuse or other maladaptive behavior, failure (or refusal) to seek needed treatment for an emotional or behavioral problem, and other inattention of the child's developmental or emotional needs."[25]

3. *Physical manifestation.* What is the rationale of requiring a physical manifestation of psychological abuse, as in *Shane*? Should physical manifestations be a prerequisite for intervention? How might this requirement pose problems for a child who is more "hardy" than Shane? Suppose the emotional abuse has *not yet* resulted in injury or impairment? Do physical manifestations of a child's psychological problems always justify state intervention? Should statutes confer jurisdiction, for example, in the case of an underweight adolescent who has symptoms of an eating disorder such as anorexia nervosa?

4. *Form of intervention.* Should intervention differ for victims of emotional versus physical abuse? Is psychological abuse always present in physical and sexual abuse? What intervention did *Shane* order? Was it appropriate? Can you think of alternatives? Should a tort action lie for infliction of emotional distress?

5. *Failure to protect.* In *Shane*, the child's mother fails to report the allegations to police and child protective services. Considerable controversy exists about the extent of liability if a mother fails to protect a child from an abuser. Why might a mother fail to act? If she does fail to act, should she be liable for neglect or "passive" abuse? If she is a victim of abuse herself, should she be able to introduce expert testimony on battered woman syndrome? What should be the disposition in such cases?

Should the child be removed from the mother's custody because of her failure to protect the child? See Nicholson v. Scoppetta, 820 N.E.2d 840 (N.Y. 2004) (avoiding constitutional issues by finding that, based on state law, witnessing abuse does not, by itself, presumptively establish neglect and also that removal requires additional particularized evidence). Should the mother's parental rights be terminated? See In re Kibby, 2006 WL 198421 (Mich. Ct. App. 2006); Wimmer v. Roanoke City Dept. of Soc. Servs., 2006 WL 88477 (Va. Ct. App. 2006) (terminating parental rights for failure to protect, among other reasons). See generally Justine A. Dunlap, Sometimes I Feel Like a Motherless Child: The Error of Pursuing Battered Mothers for Failure to Protect, 50 Loy. L. Rev. 565 (2004); Evan Stark, A Failure to Protect: Unravelling "The Battered Mother's Dilemma," 27 W. St. U. L. Rev. 29 (1999-2000).

[24]. NIS-3, supra note [4], at 3.6.
[25]. Id. at 3.9.

6. *Adolescent abuse*. Should the form of intervention differ according to the age of the victim? Adolescents predominate as victims of emotional abuse. Physical abuse of adolescents often tends to be severe, as parents feel that more "routine" punishments (for example, spanking) are less effective with older children. Despite the frequency and severity of adolescent abuse, adolescent abuse is often unreported.[26]

7. *Consequences of abuse*. Child maltreatment contributes to a wide range of longterm emotional problems, many of which are not evident until late adolescence. These effects include: depression, substance abuse, social impairment, low self-esteem, suicidal behavior, as well as psychiatric diagnoses and hospitalizations.[27] Researchers report that a history of physical abuse increases the incidence of a suicide attempt by almost 5 times, while a history of emotional abuse increases the rate by more than 12 times.[28] Adolescent abuse is also a contributing factor to runaway behavior and adolescent prostitution.[29]

8. *Abuse of gay and lesbian youth*. Gay and lesbian youth are particularly susceptible to emotional abuse and neglect by parents.[30] One reason is parents' difficulty accepting youth's sexual orientation. As one commentator explains:

> The disclosure of one's homosexual orientation to parents, that is, the "coming out" process, is often fraught with trauma for both the child and the parents. Parental response to the disclosure often centers on a preoccupation that they will be socially stigmatized as having been inadequate parents or for having a deviant child, the attribution of blame to the other parent or to themselves for having produced a deviant child, or the loss of their own expectations for their child, such as the production of grandchildren. Many parents also may feel isolated or alienated from their child, who now claims an identity that is foreign to them. Although some parents remain loving and open when confronted with the knowledge of their child's sexual orientation, many others prohibit any overt acknowledgment of the child's sexual orientation or become resentful or hostile . . . . Some parents may respond to their child's disclosure and/or the child's crisis by attempting to "fix" the child through counseling or other treatment, such as hormone therapies or institutionalization. Others may eject the children from their homes, leaving them essentially homeless.[31]

---

[26]. Brassard & Hardy, in The Battered Child, supra note [17], at 396; Sandra J. Kaplan et al., Child and Adolescent Abuse and Neglect Research: A Review of the Past 10 Years. Part I: Physical and Emotional Abuse and Neglect, 38 J. Am. Academy of Child & Adolescent Psych. 1214 (1999); Pamela D. Mayhall & Katherine Eastlack Norgard, Child Abuse and Neglect: Sharing Responsibility 65 (1986).

[27]. Ruth S. Kempe, A Developmental Approach to the Treatment of Abused Children, in The Battered Child, supra note [17], at 543, 545; Murray A. Straus & Glenda Kaufman Kantor, Corporal Punishment of Adolescents by Parents: A Risk Factor in the Epidemiology of Depression, Suicide, Alcohol Abuse, Child Abuse, and Wife Beating, 29 Adolescence 543, 550 (1994).

[28]. Kaplan et al., supra note [26] at 1217.

[29]. Sana Loue, Redefining the Emotional and Psychological Abuse and Maltreatment of Children, 26 J. Legal Med. 311, 329 (2005).

[30]. Id. at 319. An early study conducted by the National Gay Task Force reveals that 33 percent of gay and lesbian youth report emotional abuse by family members. Cited in Paul Gibson, Gay Male and Lesbian Youth Suicide, in U.S. Dept. of Health & Human Servs. Youth Suicide Report 110, 127 (1989).

[31]. Loue, supra note [29], at 325-326. According to research conducted by the U.S. Department of Health and Human Services, 26 percent of gay youth were forced to leave home because of family conflicts stemming from disclosure of their sexual orientation. LGBT Youth Risk Data, available at www.lambdalegal.org/cgi-bin/iowa/news/resources.html?record=1662 (last visited Mar. 17, 2006).

Emotional abuse contributes to the disproportionate number of suicide attempts by gay and lesbian youths.[32]

Parental attempts to change their child's sexual orientation is known as "reparative therapy" (also called "conversion therapy" and "reorientation therapy"). Does such "therapy" constitute child abuse? Compare Karolyn Ann Hicks, "Reparative" Therapy: Whether Parental Attempts To Change a Child's Sexual Orientation Can Legally Constitute Child Abuse, 49 Am. U. L. Rev. 505 (1999) (arguing that it does), with Sean Young, Note, Does "Reparative" Therapy Really Constitute Abuse?: A Closer Look, 6 Yale J. Health Pol'y, L. & Ethics 163 (2006) (contra).

9. *Parricide.* Should child abuse serve as an affirmative defense to parricide? Although murders of parents are the most infrequent form of intrafamilial homicide, an estimated 200 to 400 juvenile and adult children kill their parents or stepparents every year. Kathleen M. Heide et al., Battered Child Syndrome: An Overview of Case Law and Legislation, 41 Crim. Law Bulletin 219 (2005). Parricide offenders generally suffer longterm physical, emotional, or sexual abuse; witness the abuse of other family members; attempt unsuccessfully to get help from others; and finally resort to violence as a mechanism to escape the abuse. Id. at 220-221. Because these murders generally occur in non-confrontational situations, the youthful perpetrators cannot meet the traditional requirements of self defense. See generally Alan Dershowitz, Abuse Excuse (1994); Jessica L. Hart & Jeffrey L. Helms, Factors of Parricide: Allowance of the Use of Battered Child Syndrome as a Defense, 8 Aggression & Violent Behavior 671 (2003).

e. Sexual Abuse

■ M.W. v. DEPARTMENT OF CHILDREN & FAMILY SERVICES
881 So. 2d 734 (Fla. Ct. App. 2004)

COPE, J.

M.W. appeals an order adjudicating his three natural daughters dependent. [O]n July 1, 2001, M.W. was arrested for sexual battery on his stepdaughter, J.G. The petition alleges that M.W. had sexual intercourse with his stepdaughter over a three-year period, beginning when the child was ten years old. As to the criminal charges, M.W. was released on bail and the criminal charges remain pending.

The Department filed a petition for dependency as to the stepdaughter J.G. and M.W.'s natural daughters, J.W. 1, J.W. 2, and J.W. 3. With regard to the stepdaughter, M.W. entered a consent plea to the dependency petition. Pursuant to this consent, the stepdaughter was adjudicated dependent as to M.W.

Four days later, the trial court conducted an adjudicatory hearing on the petition for dependency as to M.W.'s natural daughters. They were eight, seven, and three years old at the time of the dependency hearing. M.W. was present at the hearing and represented by counsel, but did not testify.

---

[32]. Id. at 328. These youth are two to three times more likely to attempt suicide than other youth and constitute 30 percent of completed suicides. Gibson, supra note [30], at 110. Some researchers suggest that LGBT youth of color who are abused may suffer particularly severe psychological consequences. Rich C. Savin-Williams & R.G. Roderiquez, A Developmental, Clinical Perspective on Lesbian, Gay Male, and Bisexual Youths, in Adolescent Sexuality: Advances in Adolescent Development 77, 94 (T. P. Gullotta et al. eds., 1993).

The trial court received testimony from a psychologist who had evaluated M.W., and took judicial notice of the consent order relating to the stepdaughter. The court entered an order adjudicating the natural daughters dependent as to M.W. The order states, in part:

> . . . 4b. Dr. Schzechowicz testified that there would be a high risk of sexual abuse re-occurring if [M.W.] had access to the Child [J.G.]. As such, no contact with [J.G.] was recommended. Dr. Schzechowicz further recommended that [M.W.] be ordered to attend and successfully complete the Mentally Disordered Sex Offender (MDSO) Program.
>
> 4c. Dr. Schzechowicz testified that even though according to the testing [M.W.] had exhibited a low risk of recidivism [as to the natural daughters], there were concerns regarding his psychological functioning and he presented as a psychological[ly] maladjusted individual. [M.W.] showed no remorse and blamed the victim-child for any alleged misconduct. Hence, the risk to the Children [the natural daughters] according to Dr. Schzechowicz, was increased by [M.W.'s] commission of a similar act on another Child, to-wit: [J.G.], the Children's half-sister.
>
> . . . 6. The Court finds, that based on the totality of the circumstances, and after reviewing the documents admitted into evidence as well as hearing expert testimony on the matter, the risk of imminent sexual abuse to the above captioned Children [the natural daughters] is increased by the Father commission of a similar act on another Child, to-wit, the Children's half-sibling, [J.G.], his lack of remorse and his psychological functioning.
>
> It is hereby ordered and adjudged that the above captioned Children be adjudicated dependent within the meaning and intent of Florida Statutes Chapter 39.

[On appeal] M.W. argues that the evidence was legally insufficient to support the dependency order. He argues that his sexual abuse of his stepdaughter is insufficient to support a dependency adjudication as to his natural daughters. He contends that the psychologist's testimony defeats the Department's petition. We disagree.

The Florida Supreme Court has said, "The purpose of a dependency proceeding is not to punish the offending parent but to protect and care for a child who has been neglected, abandoned, or abused." M.F. v. Florida Department of Children and Families, 770 So. 2d 1189, 1193 (Fla. 2000).

In administering the child protection system, "The health and safety of the children served shall be of paramount concern." Fla. Stat. §39.001(1)(b)1. (2002).

Under the statute, a dependent child includes one who is "at substantial risk of imminent abuse, abandonment, or neglect by the parent or parents or legal custodians." Id. §39.01(14)(f). In making that determination, the trial court is to look at the totality of the circumstances.

M.W. relies on the M.F. decision, but that reliance is misplaced. In M.F., the father had sexually abused one of his children, K.F. The father was convicted of sexual battery and imprisoned for fifteen years. K.F. was adjudicated dependent as to the father.

In further proceedings, the trial court found M.F.'s other children dependent, on the theory that the other children were at risk of prospective abuse. Rejecting that rationale for the dependency order, the Florida Supreme Court reasoned that since the father was imprisoned for fifteen years and presumably would have no contact with the children, it would follow that there was no risk of prospective abuse.

The present case differs from *M.F.* In the present case the father is at liberty on bail and there is thus no physical impediment to his having contact with the children. The remaining children are all younger daughters, who are plainly not old enough to protect themselves.

The *M.F.* court ruled that an adjudication of dependency based on the fact that a parent has sexually abused one child is a factor which can be considered in deciding whether the remaining children are at prospective risk. Id. The father has admitted to having repeated sexual intercourse with his stepdaughter and an adjudication of dependency as to that child has been entered.

M.W. argues, however, that the following testimony of the psychologist supports his position that the instant order should be reversed:

Q: Do you have an opinion regarding whether M.W. is at high risk to re-engage in sexually illegal behavior in the future?

A: If you're talking about M.W., and I'm going to make an assumption here that he did engage in the behavior he's charged with, if he actually did this, then if you were to give him unfettered access to the alleged victim in this case, then my opinion is there would be a very high risk to his stepdaughter. If we're talking about the other children, the signs would indicate that he is not a high risk and if these are his natural children. Based on both the Static Actuarial and Dynamic Risk Factors.

Q: Just so that we can be clear. Supposing, let's assume that M.W. is found guilty of this offense that he was arrested and charged with. Is there an increased risk for his natural children?

A: Of course, ma'am. Any time someone engages in sexually inappropriate behavior, the likelihood of future behavior increases. The results of the testing would indicate that the likelihood in terms of his sexually abusing his natural children *is below base rates, but it's not zero, by any means*.

Transcript, March 27, 2003, at 19-20 (emphasis added).

M.W. argues that since the psychologist said M.W. is not a high risk to his natural children, it follows that the legal standard for a dependency order has not been satisfied. We disagree. In deciding whether there is a substantial risk of imminent abuse, the trial court is to examine all of the circumstances. This includes the severity of potential harm as well as the likelihood it will occur. In this case the risk to be protected against is sexual abuse of minor children. It is among the greatest of harms that can be inflicted on children. It is physical harm which is serious criminal conduct. Because the nature of the harm is so great, it is intolerable to allow even a low probability that M.W. will sexually abuse the other children. The psychologist here testified that while the danger to the natural children was below base rates, "*it's not zero, by any means*." (Emphasis added).

As we interpret M.W.'s position, he wants us to rule that the trial court cannot order protective services unless there is reason to believe that, more probably than not, he will sexually abuse his other children. The contention apparently is that if the likelihood is below fifty percent, then the young children must be left to fend for themselves. That analysis is incorrect under the statute and under the *M.F.* decision. Quite apart from the psychological evaluation results, in M.W.'s own statements to the psychologist, he denied responsibility and blamed the victim. Further, at the time of the proceeding below, treatment in the MDSO program had been recommended, but it is not clear whether treatment had begun. In any event, M.W. had completed no such program. These factors, too, support the conclusion that M.W. cannot be left to his own devices. The trial court applied the correct legal standard and the dependency order is fully supported by the evidence.

■ **D. KELLY WEISBERG, THE "DISCOVERY" OF SEXUAL ABUSE: EXPERTS' ROLE IN LEGAL POLICY FORMULATION**
18 U.C. Davis L. Rev. 1, 1-2, 5-8, 18-19, 25-28, 31 (1984)

Despite evidence of sexual abuse of children throughout history, the labeling of this phenomenon as a pervasive social problem is relatively recent. The phenomenon has received so much attention that it has been labeled several times in the past half century. . . .

Legal policy directed at sexual abuse of children has undergone several successive reformulations in the past half century. In each stage, a new definition of criminal behavior and proscribed sanctions were enacted into law. Different participants were involved in each successive stage of the labeling process. . . .

I. ERA OF THE SEXUAL PSYCHOPATH: FROM "BADNESS TO SICKNESS"[15]

The first comprehensive legal labeling of child molestation appeared in the 1930's. [P]sychiatrists were the first experts relied upon to define the problem. Their initial reaction was to label such sexual crimes as indicative of an "illness," one they were uniquely qualified to treat. The impetus for the labeling came from several sexually-motivated murders of children in the late 1930's. . . . The incomprehensibility of sexual crimes involving children spurred the call for experts — qualified to understand and assess the situation, to study the problem, and to make recommendations for its solution.

[P]sychiatrists diagnosed child molestation as a form of mental illness, terming the illness "sexual psychopathy." They suggested a treatment for the patient: the patient should be hospitalized until "well" or normal again. . . . Statutes utilized medical terminology and labeled the offender with psychiatric nomenclature. . . .

[T]he call for these experts came at a time when the public was increasingly aware of the promise of psychiatry. . . . Freud's writings in the early twentieth century stimulated interest in the use of psychiatry to explain the irrational. World War I increased public awareness of psychiatry's value in treating war casualties. The Leopold-Loeb[16] trial revealed that psychiatry could have specific application to criminal law. These factors contributed to the emergence of psychiatrists in legal policymaking. . . .

---

15. The term was coined by two sociologists in their social historical analysis of the transformation from religious and criminal to medical designations of deviance. See generally P. Conrad & J. Schneider, Deviance and Medicalization: From Badness to Sickness (1980).

16. This trial in 1924 of two middle-class youths for murder was the first time psychiatrists testified as expert witnesses to explain criminal behavior. See Note, The Leopold-Loeb Case, 97 Cent. L.J. 327 (1924).

II. THE FIRST RELABELING: THE 1950'S

Legislation in the 1950's reflects the reconstruction and relabeling of child molestation. . . . Several states repealed or amended their sexual psychopath statutes and enacted different legislation dealing with sex offenses. [The sexual psychopath became the "mentally disordered sex offender" or "sexually dangerous person."] One trend was evident: [m]edical nomenclature was deemphasized, and criminal terminology became more prominent. . . .

Several factors explain the relabeling of this social problem in the 1950's. [S]ocietal recognition of psychiatry's shortcomings may [provide one explanation]. [L]egislation of the 1950's reflected a more realistic appraisal of the answers psychiatry could and could not supply. . . . The acute shortage of psychiatric personnel in public institutions after World War II frustrated hopes of treatment for sex offenders. . . . Another explanation for the relabeling process may be found in sexual behavior research. An important influence on policymakers was Alfred Kinsey [who] helped dispel certain widespread beliefs about sex offenders [i.e., that sex criminals progressed from minor to major sex crimes, and that sex crimes were increasing].

III. THE THIRD LABEL — POLICYMAKING IN THE 1970'S

In the early 1970's child molestation received yet another label: "sexual abuse," or "child sexual abuse." The new label appeared in both federal and state legislation. The federal Child Abuse Prevention and Treatment Act, enacted in 1974, required each state to adopt a uniform definition of abuse that included "physical or mental injury, sexual abuse or exploitation, negligent treatment, or maltreatment" in order to qualify for federal monies for the prevention and treatment of abuse. . . .

New experts played a role in the labeling process: psychologists and social workers became preeminent in this period. These experts focused on the familial offender — the father or stepfather molester. Instead of hospitalization or civil commitment for the patient, the recommended treatment was family counseling. The experts viewed the entire family, rather than merely the perpetrator, as the source of the problem. For the first time attention was also focused on the child victim, for whom counseling was also recommended. . . .

Notes and Questions

1. *Empirical data.* Sexual abuse constitutes the third most common type of child maltreatment (after neglect and then physical abuse).[33] How does sexual abuse by family members differ from molestation by strangers? In contrast to common belief, most offenders are known to the child, as in *M.W.* A classic study reveals that 27 percent of offenders are parents, stepparents, or mother's boyfriends (including 13 percent natural fathers compared to 14 percent stepfathers or

---

[33]. Based on 2003 data, victims of neglect account for 60 percent of all child victims of maltreatment, victims of physical abuse for 19 percent, and victims of sexual abuse for 10 percent. Child Maltreatment: 2003, supra note [7].

residential paramours). Only 25 percent are strangers (the remainder were nonresidential relatives or acquaintances).[34] Most sexual abuse occurs in the child's own home. Often, the child is subjected to repeated offenses prior to discovery.

Research reports many negative long-term effects suffered by the victims of sexual abuse, including truancy, delinquency, running away, promiscuity and prostitution, sexual disturbances, depression, suicide, and revictimization. See Susan K. Reichert, Medical Evaluation of the Sexually Abused Child, in The Battered Child, supra, at 313, 315.

2. *Legal responses.* As *M.W.* illustrates, legal responses to familial sexual abuse may encompass civil proceedings, conferring jurisdiction over the victim by the juvenile court, as well as criminal proceedings against the perpetrator. Some childhood victims when they become adults also initiate tort claims to recover damages from the perpetrator.

3. *Victim characteristics.* The girls in *M.W.* were prepubescent. Although the median age of sexual abuse victims is 11, children as young as infants may be sexually abused. Girls are sexually abused more often than boys. Reichert, supra, at 313. How might the consequences of sexual abuse differ based on the victim's age? Gender? See generally Michel Dorais, Don't Tell: The Sexual Abuse of Boys (2002); Judith Lewis Herman, Father-Daughter Incest (2d ed., 2000).

4. *Continuum.* Sexual abuse constitutes a continuum, ranging from indecent exposure and fondling, to sodomy and intercourse. Should the legal consequences (civil versus criminal) differ depending on the type of abuse? The extent of coercion? Consider that in 60 percent of cases, the child was coerced by force or threat of harm; in 15 percent by bribes; and in 25 percent, the "lure was more subtle and was based on the child's natural loyalty and affection." Vincent De Francis, Protecting the Child Victim of Sex Crimes Committed by Adults vii (American Humane Assoc., 2d ed., 1981).

5. *Discovery.* Unlike physical abuse, sexual abuse rarely reveals physical manifestations, although pregnancy and venereal disease do occur. Reichert, supra, at 314. More commonly, behavioral indicators are present, such as unusually sophisticated sexual knowledge, infantile behavior, appearing withdrawn, poor peer relationships, unwillingness to participate in physical activities, delinquent acts, or running away. David P. H. Jones, Assessment of Suspected Child Sexual Abuse, in The Battered Child, supra, at 297-298; Reichert, supra, at 315. This lack of physical manifestations presents evidentiary problems (discussed infra this chapter).

Many sexually abused children first come to attention when they, in turn, abuse other children. Jones, supra, at 298. How should the courts and child protective services deal with sexually abused children who in turn abuse other children? Data suggest that child molesters often have been sexually abused as children.

---

[34]. Vincent De Francis, Protecting the Child Victim of Sex Crimes Committed by Adults vii, 40-41 (American Humane Assoc., 2d ed. 1981). Researchers who conducted the national incidence studies categorize perpetrator relationships differently than De Francis in his classic study. For example, NIS data for 1994 reveals that more than one-fourth of sexually abused children were abused by a biological parent; 25 percent were sexually abused by "other parents or parent-substitutes, such as step-parents, fathers' girlfriends," and less than one half were abused by someone other than the above perpetrators. NIS-3, supra note [4], at 6.5.

Brandt F. Steele, Psychodynamic and Biological Factors in Child Maltreatment, in The Battered Child, supra, at 83, 84.

6. *Parent-child affection.* In another family court case adjudicating children dependent because of the father's sexual abuse, the father's expert testified as to the warm relationship between the father and his two daughters. In re Jaclyn P., 578 N.Y.S.2d 252, 255 (App. Div. 1992). Is a close parent-child relationship inconsistent with the existence of sexual abuse? See also Marcia Sheinberg & Peter Fraenkel, The Relational Trauma of Incest: A Family-Based Approach to Treatment 32-33 (2001) (describing a victim's warm feelings about her stepfather-abuser).

7. *Prospective abuse.* Child protective service workers often are concerned about the possibility of prospective abuse, as *M.W.* reveals. On what basis does *M.W.* conclude that the defendant's biological daughters (who were not sexually abused) should be declared wards of the court? Do you agree? Compare In re M.F., 770 So. 2d 1189 (Fla. 2000). Early researchers noted a pattern of sequential sexual abuse: When one abused child is removed from the home, a younger sibling is likely to become the next victim. See Judith Lewis Herman, Father-Daughter Incest 94 (1981). Does such evidence have any relevance to the court's assertion of jurisdiction in a situation similar to *M.W.*? See generally Robin Fretwell Wilson, The Cradle of Abuse: Evaluating the Danger Posed by a Sexually Predator Parent to the Victim's Siblings, 51 Emory L.J. 241 (2002).

8. *Policy rationale.* Given that sexual abuse rarely leaves physical manifestations, does sexual abuse evoke intervention merely because of the ensuing emotional harm? Does it present an arguably weaker case for intervention than physical abuse? Some commentators would permit intervention only if a parent has been *convicted* of a sexual offense. See Joseph Goldstein et al., Before the Best Interests of the Child 62 (1979). They explain this controversial recommendation as follows:

> Sexual relations between parent and child tend to remain well-guarded family secrets. When suspicion is aroused, the harm done by inquiry may be more than that caused by not intruding. The harm already inflicted on the child — and it may be difficult to learn its extent — is aggravated by violations of family integrity, particularly by the investigation that is triggered. Further, since no consensus exists about the proper treatment or about what disposition would be less harmful, there is no justification from the child's point of view for dragging the matter into the open by invoking the child's placement process. For these reasons, justification for separating the child and offending parent seems best left to the criminal law. [W]e know enough to declare that a child is harmed even by a parent's nonviolent sexual abuse, but not enough to know that state intervention can offer something less detrimental. Thus, the authority to assume the risks of intervention, including the termination of parental rights, arises only after the parent-child relationship has been severed by the criminal process.

Id. at 64-65. Is this view persuasive?

9. *Children's fabrications and suggestibility.* How likely are children to fabricate sexual abuse? Some prominent researchers conclude that children are unlikely to do so. See, e.g., Gail S. Goodman & Alison Clarke-Stewart, Suggestibility in Children's Testimony: Implications for Sexual Abuse Prosecutions, in The Suggestibility of Children's Recollections: Implications for Eyewitness Testimony 92, 98-99

(John Doris ed., 1991). A considerable body of research conducted in the 1980s reports a low incidence of false allegations by children.[35]

How susceptible are children to the suggestion of others (such as caretakers, interviewers, and so forth) that abuse took place? Can these suggestions distort the child's recollection of events? Psychological studies report that older children (i.e., older than age 10) are not more suggestible than adults, although pre-school children are more capable of being influenced. Research also reveals that children tend to be more suggestible about peripheral details (that is, time, place of abuse), rather than salient issues (that is, occurrence of abuse, type of touching). See John E. B. Myers et al., Psychological Research on Children as Witnesses: Practical Implications for Forensic Interviews and Courtroom Testimony, 28 Pac. L.J. 3, 27-29 (1996); John E. B. Myers, 1 Evidence in Child, Domestic and Elder Abuse Cases 25-28 (3d ed. 2005); Lucy S. McGough, Child Witnesses: Fragile Voices in the American Legal System 67-69 (1994). But cf. Stephen J. Ceci & Richard D. Friedman, The Suggestibility of Children: Scientific Research and Legal Implications, 86 Cornell L. Rev. 33 (2000).

Should judges compel psychiatric examinations for child victims of sexual offense to assess their credibility? Judges in some jurisdictions do so. See Jane Dever Prince, Note, Competency and Credibility: Double Trouble for Child Victims of Sexual Offenses, 9 Suffolk J. Trial & App. Advoc. 113 (2004).

Some courts have adopted pretrial "taint hearings" to determine whether the child's statements have been so tainted by suggestive interrogation techniques that the statements should be excluded. See, e.g., State v. Michaels, 642 A.2d 1372 (N.J. 1994). Are such hearings sound policy? Compare John E. B. Myers, Taint Hearings for Child Witnesses? A Step in the Wrong Direction, 46 Baylor L. Rev. 873 (1994), with Clayton Gillette, Comment, Appointing Special Masters to Evaluate the Suggestiveness of a Child-Witness Interview: A Simple Solution to a Complex Problem, 49 St. Louis U. L.J. 499 (2005).

10. *Parental allegations of abuse.* Sometimes, sexual abuse allegations arise in the context of child custody proceedings. One empirical study found that such allegations occur in approximately 2 percent of custody disputes. See Kathleen Coulborn Faller, Child Maltreatment and Endangerment in the Context of Divorce, 22 U. Ark. Little Rock L. Rev. 429, 430 (2000) (citing study of 9,000 cases). Some commentators vehemently criticize "the persistent belief among judges and evaluators that child sexual abuse is frequently fabricated." Joan S. Meier, Domestic Violence, Child Custody, and Child Protection: Understanding Judicial Resistance and Imagining the Solutions, 11 Am. U.J. Gender Soc. Poly & L. 657, 683 (2003). See also Faller, supra, at 430. Many judges consider mothers who make such allegations as "hysterical" and motivated solely by the desire to influence the outcome in the custody battle. Nat Stern & Karen Oehme, The Troubling Admission of Supervised Visitation Records in Custody Proceedings, 75 Temp. L. Rev. 271, 286 (2002).

Some state legislatures have responded to concerns about parental fabrications of sexual abuse allegations. See, e.g., Cal. Fam. Code §3027.1 (2004) (authorizing a court to grant monetary sanctions if it finds that a parent knowingly makes a false

[35]. See, e.g., Mark D. Everson & Barbara W. Boat, False Allegations of Sexual Abuse by Children and Adolescents, 28 J. Am. Acad. Child & Adolescent Psychiatry 230 (1989); Kathleen C. Faller, Child Sexual Abuse: An Interdisciplinary Manual for Diagnosis, Case Management, and Treatment 22, 126 (1988). See also John E.B. Myers, 1 Evidence in Child, Domestic and Elder Abuse Cases 364 (3d ed. 2005) (existing research suggests that "[f]abricated allegations of sexual abuse appear to be uncommon").

allegation of sexual abuse). Nonetheless, some commentators point out that the skepticism about the veracity of sexual abuse allegations is "not supported by either the literature or clinical experience." Stern & Oehme, supra, at 287. For empirical research, see Janet R. Johnston et al., Allegations and Substantiations of Abuse in Custody-Disputing Families, 43 Fam. Ct. Rev. 283 (2005); Nancy Thoennes & Patricia G. Tjaden, The Extent, Nature, and Validity of Sexual Abuse Allegations in Custody/Visitation Disputes, 14 Child Abuse & Neglect 151 (1998).

11. *Counsel for the abused child*. Does a child have a constitutional right to counsel in child abuse and neglect proceedings? See Barbara Ann Atwood, Representing Children: The Ongoing Search for Clear and Workable Standards, 19 J. Am. Acad. Matrim. Law. 183, 187 (2005) (pointing out that some courts so hold). See also Kenny A. ex rel. Winn v. Perdue, 356 F. Supp. 2d 1353 (N.D. Ga. 2005) (holding that foster children have a right to counsel in all deprivation proceedings, including but not limited to termination of parental rights proceedings, pursuant to state constitution and state statute). In contrast to the widespread discretionary policy on representation for the child in custody proceedings, many jurisdictions now provide for mandatory appointment of counsel in those custody cases that involve allegations of abuse or neglect. Why might representation in these proceedings be advisable? What should be the role of the child's representative in these proceedings? See Donald N. Duquette, Legal Representation for Children in Protection Proceedings: Two Distinct Lawyer Roles Are Required, 34 Fam. L.Q. 441 (2000).

a. *CAPTA and the GAL*. Federal legislation spurred the adoption of guardian ad litem (GAL) programs for abused and neglected children. The Child Abuse Prevention and Treatment Act (CAPTA) of 1974, 42 U.S.C. §§5101-5707 (2000), requires that for states to qualify for federal funds for the prevention and treatment of abuse

> in every case involving an abused or neglected child which results in a judicial proceeding, a guardian ad litem, who has received training appropriate to the role, and who may be an attorney or a court appointed special advocate who has received training appropriate to that role (or both), shall be appointed to represent the child.

42 U.S.C. §5106a(b)(2)(A)(xiii). Despite CAPTA's requirement, however, states are not required to appoint attorneys as guardians ad litem. (Guardians ad litem may come from many professions, such as law, social work, psychology, etc.) Only about half of the states require guardians to be attorneys. Randi Mandelbaum, Revisiting the Question of Whether Young Children in Child Protection Proceedings Should be Represented by Lawyers, 32 Loy. U. Chi. L.J. 1, 23 (2000). Some jurisdictions rely on a court-appointed special advocate (termed CASA's), i.e., trained community volunteers who are appointed to represent abused and neglected children. Should the child's representative be an attorney? Is there a great, lesser, or the same need for legal representation for children in abuse or neglect proceedings compared to custody proceedings?

b. *ABA Standards of Practice*. The ABA approved Standards of Practice for Lawyers Who Represent Children in Abuse and Neglect Cases in 1996. See Standards of Practice for Lawyers Who Represent Children in Abuse and Neglect Cases (reprinted in 29 Fam. L. Q. 375 (1995)). The Standards apply in cases of: (1) petitions filed for the protection of a child; (2) petitions to change legal custody, visitation, or guardianship involving allegations of abuse or neglect; or (3) actions to terminate parental rights.

The Standards provide that the child's attorney should represent the child's expressed preferences. If the attorney believes that the child's preference would be seriously injurious to the child, the lawyer may request appointment of a separate guardian ad litem—while continuing to represent the child's expressed preference "unless the child's position is prohibited by law or without any factual foundation." Standard B-4(3). According to the Standards, the attorney shall not reveal to the judge the basis of the attorney's request for appointment of a guardian ad litem which would compromise the child's position. See generally Jean Koh Peters, Representing Children in Child Protective Proceedings: Ethical and Practical Dimensions (2d ed. 2001); David R. Katner, Coming to Praise, Not to Bury, the New ABA Standards of Practice for Lawyers Who Represent Children in Abuse and Neglect Cases, 14 Geo. J. Legal Ethics 103 (2000).

Problems

1. At Angela's first visit to Dr. Smith for prenatal care, he orders blood tests that confirm his suspicion that she is using cocaine. Dr. Smith reports his concerns to Child Protective Services (CPS). CPS files a motion to take Angela's 36-week fetus into immediate protective custody pursuant to a statute that requires a showing "that the welfare of the child demands the child's immediate removal from his or her present custody."

The juvenile court issues an order for summary removal directing that "petitioner's unborn child shall be detained [pursuant to statute] by the sheriff's department and transported to County Memorial Hospital for inpatient treatment and protection. Such detention will by necessity result in the detention of the unborn child's mother." Before the order is executed, Angela appears voluntarily at an inpatient drug treatment facility. The juvenile court then amends its order to provide that detention will be at that facility but if Angela attempts to leave or fails to participate, both she and her fetus are to be detained and transported to County Memorial Hospital. Following issuance of the summary removal order, CPS files another petition under the state Children in Need of Supervision (CHINS) statute that provides that the juvenile court has jurisdiction if the "parent, guardian or legal custodian neglects, refuses or is unable for reasons other than poverty to provide necessary care, food, clothing, medical or dental care or shelter so as to seriously endanger the physical health of the child." For the designation of birth date, the petition states "Due Date 10/4/95" and for the sex of the child, the petition states "Unknown."

Angela seeks a supervisory writ to prohibit the court from continuing to exercise jurisdiction in the CHINS proceeding. She asserts that the relevant statutes do not vest the juvenile court with jurisdiction over her or her fetus. Alternatively, if the statute does grant authority, she claims that it violates procedural and substantive due process and equal protection. What result? See Angela M.W. v. Kruzicki, 561 N.W.2d 729 (Wis. 1997). Cf. State v. McKnight, 576 S.E.2d 168 (S.C. 2003).

Do drug tests on urine samples of maternity patients who are suspected of using cocaine violate the Fourth Amendment? See Ferguson v. City of Charleston, 532 U.S. 67 (2001).

Suppose that Angela is HIV-positive. Her physician prescribes medication to reduce the risk of transferring the virus to the fetus, but she refuses to take the medication. Does her refusal constitute abuse or neglect of her unborn child? See New Jersey Div. of Youth and Family Servs. v. L.V., 889 A.2d 1153 (N.J. Super Ct. Ch. Div. 2005).

2. Denise Perrigo, a 29-year-old single mother, is breast-feeding her two-year-old daughter, Cherlyn. Curious about whether it is normal to feel sexually aroused while nursing, Denise calls a community volunteer center to find the number for La Leche League, a breast-feeding support group. She is mistakenly referred to the Rape Crisis Center where a volunteer interprets her question as evidence of sexual abuse and reports it to the child abuse hotline. After an investigation, including a five-hour police interrogation, Denise spends the night in jail. Criminal charges are dismissed subsequently, but social workers summarily remove Cherlyn from Denise's custody and petition the local juvenile court to assert jurisdiction over Cherlyn as an abused or neglected child. The juvenile court awards temporary custody to the state social services department and places the child in foster care. Denise appeals. What result? See Lisa Levitt Ryckman, A Simple Question Leads Mom to Jail, Chi. Trib., Feb. 9, 1992, at 16.

3. John, the stepfather of a 15-year-old girl, is a nudist who likes to walk around the house nude. He has a habit of walking in on his stepdaughter while she is in the bathtub and asking her sexually explicit questions, such as whether she wants to show him her genitals or whether she would like help learning how to kiss. He tells her that she is free to say no. His stepdaughter feels uncomfortable with her stepfather's nudity, his embarrassing questions, and his violations of her privacy. She says he often says "weird" things to her. John is charged with sexual abuse. He claims that he has never actually touched his stepdaughter in an inappropriate way, and argues that oral conversations, without any evidence of physical or emotional abuse, do not constitute sexual abuse. What result? See John D. v. Department of Soc. Servs., 744 N.E.2d 659 (Mass. App. Ct. 2001).

3. Procedures

a. Reporting Requirements

■ PEOPLE v. HODGES
13 Cal. Rptr. 2d 412 (App. Dept. Super. Ct. 1992)

Moon, Acting Presiding Judge.

In what appears to be a case of first impression, we are asked to determine whether appellants, a pastor and assistant pastor of the South Bay United Pentecostal Church, who are also the president and principal of the South Bay Christian Academy, were properly convicted of violating the Child Abuse and Neglect Reporting Act, Penal Code, section 11166, subdivision (a). The statute provides . . . "[A]ny child care custodian . . . who has knowledge of or observes a child in his or her professional capacity or within the scope of his or her employment whom he or she knows or reasonably suspects has been the victim of child abuse shall report the known or suspected instance of child abuse to a child protective agency immediately or as soon as practically possible. . . ." . . .

At trial, the victim, 20-year-old Christine G., testified that she had attended South Bay Christian Academy. [W]hen she was 17 years old (in March 1988) she decided to seek help from appellant Hodges [president of the school and pastor of the church] by telling him her stepfather, Lyn M., a minister in the church, had been molesting her for many years. Christine testified she confided in a classroom teacher who, in turn, made an appointment with Mr. Hodges during the schoolday. [Mr. Hodges then informed her stepfather of the allegations.] Christine testified she met with Mr. Hodges the day after he spoke with her stepfather. He told her that her stepfather confessed to everything and that he would be handling the situation. Mr. Hodges told Christine not to tell anyone about what her stepfather had done to her.

A few days later Mr. Hodges called Christine back into his office. He told her he had sent her stepfather to a retreat. Mr. Hodges handed her a letter of apology from her stepfather. This was approximately two weeks after their initial meeting.

Mr. Hodges wanted Christine's mother and stepfather to come into the office after she read the letter. . . . Christine told Mr. Hodges she did not want to talk to her parents. He insisted, and they came into the office and spoke with her. Christine pleaded with Mr. Hodges not to make her go home with them because she was afraid of her stepfather. Mr. Hodges arranged to have her parents pick her up from school the next day and bring her home. Instead, Christine ran away. She also told others about the situation even though Mr. Hodges told her not to.

After running away, Christine received instructions to return to see Mr. Hodges. She went to his office during school hours. Appellant Nobbs was also there. Mr. Hodges told her unless she returned home she would not be allowed to return to school and she would not graduate. This meeting was held approximately a week and a half after Christine was given the letter. Christine returned home and left immediately after graduation. . . .

[During a subsequent investigation by a child abuse detective for the police department, Mr. Hodges was asked why he did not report the information to the police or child protective services or if he knew he was mandated to report.] Mr. Hodges told the officer he knew of the reporting laws, and he understood he was a mandated reporter. Mr. Hodges told the officer he wanted to take care of the matter within the church. Mr. Hodges stated he disciplined the stepfather by having him write a letter of apology to the victim and by having the stepfather confess in front of the entire congregation. Additionally, Mr. Hodges took away his ministerial license. [Nobbs had a similar interview with the detective.]

Mr. Hodges testified [that] he did not contact the police because he believed that his role in the matter was a pastoral one, specifically dealing with Christine's inability to forgive her stepfather. He did not believe the incidents described by Christine were "sexual abuse"; he believed they were sins. He stated he had to follow the Scriptures concerning disciplining a Christian. [Mr. Nobbs testified that he believed] that when he received information concerning what had taken place between Christine and her stepfather, he was acting in a pastoral capacity as assistant pastor.

[The jury found both appellants guilty.] Appellants first contend they were not acting as "child care custodians" within the meaning of the statute. According to appellants, Mr. Hodges was counseling Christine, a member of the church with a spiritual problem, as the pastor of the church. Appellants argue most of the meetings were not during school hours. They also argue Mr. Nobbs was not acting as a child custodian, but rather was called to be informed that Christine's stepfather would be relieved of his ministerial duties and Mr. Nobbs would have to assume them.

The jury was instructed on the definition of a child care custodian pursuant to section 11165.7: "'[C]hild care custodian' means a teacher; . . . administrative officer, supervisor of child welfare and attendance . . . of any public or private school." . . . The record reflects substantial evidence to support the jury's finding that appellants were child care custodians. The school attended by the victim, South Bay Christian Academy, was operated by South Bay United Pentecostal Church. . . . Religious and academic classes were taught. Appellants were involved in running the school as president and principal (as well as holding pastoral positions with the church). Appellant Nobbs took care of the day-to-day management of the school while appellant Hodges had overall responsibility for decisions concerning the school. . . . Christine testified she sought Hodges's help because he was in charge of the school. . . .

Appellants next contend the statute [§11166(a)] violates due process as applied to them, as it fails to give adequate notice of the obligation to report. . . . As respondent notes, the terms "child," "child abuse," and "child protective agency" are all defined in the Reporting Act, as is "child care custodian." . . . The intent of the Reporting Act, as stated by the Legislature, is to protect children from abuse, including neglect, willful cruelty, or unjustifiable punishment and unlawful corporal punishment or injury. The Legislature has been sufficiently definite in drafting the Reporting Act to give the constitutionally required degree of notice to those subject to its requirements.

Appellants also contend the statute as applied in this case is insufficiently specific given its impact on activities potentially subject to First Amendment protection. . . . Appellants argue they were obligated by the dictates of their faith and precepts stemming therefrom not to disclose to the community the contents of pastoral communications with Christine. . . . The issue becomes whether appellants' failing to report known child abuse as required by the statute and instead choosing to handle the problem within the church, even if motivated by sincere religious beliefs, is protected religious activity under the First Amendment. . . . Here, if appellants are held to be exempt from the mandatory requirements of the Reporting Act, the act's purpose would be severely undermined. There is no indication teachers and administrators of religious schools would voluntarily report known or suspected child abuse. Children in those schools would not be protected. The protection of all children cannot be achieved in any other way. . . .

Appellants argue the Reporting Act constitutes excessive governmental entanglement with religion [in violation of the First Amendment's establishment clause]. . . . The court, in effect, has barred a pastor from religious counseling of suspected child abuse among the members of his or her congregation, thus interfering substantially with the pastoral role of its ministers.

The comprehensive reporting requirement is designed to ensure the health and safety of children and fulfills a vital and appropriate secular purpose. In Prince v.

Massachusetts (1944) 321 U.S. 158, 166-167, the court stated, "The right to practice religion freely does not include liberty to expose the community or the child to communicable diseases or the latter to ill health or death." . . . The compelling state interest furthered by the act justifies the interference with appellants' religious practices when appellants are acting in the capacity of child care custodians within the meaning of the statute. . . .

Notes and Questions

1. *Background.* All states currently require certain professionals to report suspected child abuse and neglect. Reporting statutes were enacted during a period of unprecedented legislative activity in the mid-1960's. Several organizations (for example, the Children's Bureau of the National Center on Child Abuse and Neglect, American Medical Association, and Program of State Governments) proposed model legislation. A central purpose of these statutes was to encourage reporting by physicians who might treat a victim. Subsequent revisions expanded the mandated reporters (to include schoolteachers, social workers, psychologists, nurses, dentists, opthamologists, coroners, psychiatrists, and in some cases, "any" person), and the types of reportable maltreatment (to include sexual and emotional abuse, and eliminating the requirement for "serious" physical injury).

On the history of reporting statutes, see Allan H. McCoid, The Battered Child and Other Assaults Upon the Family: Part One, 50 Minn. L. Rev. 1 (1965-1966); Monrad G. Paulsen, Child Abuse Reporting Laws: The Shape of the Legislation, 67 Colum. L. Rev. 1 (1967); Stephen Pfohl, The Discovery of Child Abuse, 24 Soc. Probs. 310 (1977).

2. *Purposes.* Reporting laws have the following purposes: to facilitate identification of abused children, designate agencies to receive and investigate child maltreatment, and provide services to families to prevent re-abuse. Seth C. Kalichman, Mandated Reporting of Suspected Child Abuse: Ethics, Law, & Policy 13 (1993). Does the legislation accomplish its purposes? Does the dramatic increase in cases of abuse and neglect[36] prove that the legislation serves its purposes?

3. *Standard.* Does a mandated reporter have a responsibility to investigate the alleged abuse, as Mr. Hodges did, or merely to report it? How certain must a professional be before making a report? How certain was Mr. Hodges? Does a "reasonable suspicion" suffice? What constitutes "reasonable suspicion"? Does the objective "reasonable suspicion" standard improve enforcement? Ensure overreporting?

4. *Designated professionals.* What problems ensue from the imposition of liability on the following professionals?

a. *Clergy.* The pastor-defendants in *Hodges* were convicted as child-care providers. Many states now mandate reporting of abuse by clergy. Does mandatory reporting of abuse by clergy violate the First Amendment according to *Hodges*?

Traditionally, most jurisdictions had a privilege (termed the "priest-penitent" or "clergy-communicant" privilege) that allowed clergy to keep confidential

---

[36]. The incidence of reported cases of child abuse and neglect increased from 150,000 in 1963 to 3 million in 1995. Victor I. Vieth, Passover in Minnesota: Mandated Reporting and the Unequal Protection of Children, 24 Wm. Mitchell L. Rev. 131, 135 (1998) (citing research).

parishioners' communications (such as those involving child abuse). In the wake of the Catholic Church sex abuse scandal, an increasing number of state legislatures abrogated or weakened the penitential communications privilege. In 2002, law enforcement authorities in Boston, Massachusetts, revealed that more than 700 children had been victims of sexual abuse by Catholic priests over the past sixty years. Church officials in the Boston Archdiocese, although aware of the abuse (including the case of one priest who molested 130 children), chose to keep the matter secret. See generally Susan Vivian Mangold, Reforming Child Protection in Response to the Catholic Church Child Sexual Abuse Scandal, 1. 14 U. Fla. J.L. & Pub. Pol'y 155 (2003).

Criticisms of clergy privilege also surface regarding Jehovah's Witnesses whose religious practices discourage reporting abuse to secular authorities. See Berry v. Watchtower Bible and Tract Soc'y., 879 A.2d 1124 (N.H. 2005). See generally Andrew A. Beerworth, Treating Spiritual and Legal Counselors Differently: Mandatory Reporting Laws and the Limitations of Current Free Exercise Doctrine, 10 Roger Williams U. L. Rev. 73 (2004); Caroline E. Law Miller, Comment, Holding Clergy Accountable: Maryland Should Require Clergy to Report Suspected Child Abuse, 34 U. Balt. L. Rev. 337 (2005).

b. *Attorneys*. Some states mandate reporting by attorneys. Among these states, some require an attorney to report only information that was obtained *outside* the attorney-client relationship. In contrast, a few states require attorneys to report abuse even if the information was obtained during the attorney-client relationship. Camile Glasscock Dubose & Cathy O. Morris, The Attorney as Mandatory Reporter, 68 Tex. B.J. 208, 210 (2005).

The ABA Model Rules of Professional Conduct (2003) do not specify the reporting of abuse as an exception to the rules of confidentiality. However, the ALI's Restatement (Third) of the Law Governing Lawyers, Comment h, does permit the attorney to report child sexual abuse without violating the attorney-client privilege. The American Academy of Matrimonial Lawyers Standards of Conduct (2.26) (1991) includes perhaps the strongest admonition ("An attorney should disclose evidence of a substantial risk of physical or sexual abuse of a child by the attorney's client"). See Lisa Hansen, Comment, Attorneys' Duty to Report Child Abuse, 19 J. Am. Acad. Matrim. Law. 59, 65 (2004) (discussing the various rules).

c. *Psychotherapists*. Most states require reporting by mental health professionals. How does the police function inherent in the reporting laws comport with the therapeutic role? With ethical standards for confidentiality? See generally Christopher Bollas & David Sundelson, The New Informants: The Betrayal of Confidentiality in Psychoanalysis and Psychotherapy (1995); Ralph Slovenko, Psychotherapy and Confidentiality: Testimonial Privileged Communication, Breach of Confidentiality, and Reporting Duties (1998). Should legislators create an exemption for psychotherapists, similar to that for clergy in some jurisdictions?

d. *Educators*. Early versions of child abuse reporting laws designated teachers as mandatory reporters. Subsequent amendments added other school personnel, such as administrators, counselors, school psychologists, school nurses, and day care providers. See generally Eric A. Hamilon, Note, Kentucky Law Issue: Commonwealth v. Allen: An Eye-Opener for Kentucky's Teachers, 27 N. Ky. L. Rev. 447 (2000).

5. *Comparison*. Are laws that were intended to increase reporting of *physical* abuse, primarily by emergency room *physicians*, well-tailored to encourage

reporting of other forms of abuse by other professionals? See Kalichman, supra, at 12 (noting that "a single standard that assumed homogeneity in professional training, circumstances of practice, and conditions under which suspicions of maltreatment occur" ignores particular aspects of various professional contexts).

6. *Professionals' liability for failure to report.* Most states impose misdemeanor liability on professionals who fail to report. What purposes of the criminal law are served by the imposition of sanctions against these professionals? Additional civil sanctions may be imposed, including the suspension or revocation of professional licenses.

A majority of jurisdictions refuse to recognize a private cause of action that would allow the child to recover damages for the professional's failure to report. See, e.g., Fulton-DeKalb Hosp. Auth. v. Reliance Trust Co., 608 S.E.2d 272 (Ga. Ct. App. 2004), Doe 1 ex rel. Tanya S. v. North Cent. Behavioral Health Systems, Inc., 816 N.E.2d 4 (Ill. App. Ct. 2004); Doe v. Marion, 605 S.E.2d 556 (S.C. Ct. App. 2004). But cf. Landeros v. Flood, 551 P.2d. 389 (Cal. 1976); Ham v. Hospital of Morristown, 917 F. Supp. 531 (E.D. Tenn. 1995).

7. *Government liability.* Does a reporting statute give rise to a duty on the part of the state to protect the child who is the subject of that report? As a general rule, the government is not required to protect individuals against private violence ("the public duty rule") unless the state actor owes the plaintiff a duty different from that owed to the general public. Normally, the existence of a statute is not sufficient to create that special duty. Restatement (Second) of Torts §315 (1965). However, a number of jurisdictions have recently held that their reporting statutes impliedly give rise to a civil duty on the part of social service agencies to investigate reports of child abuse and that breach of that duty can result in tort liability (pursuant to a state tort claims act or wrongful death act). See Horridge v. St. Mary's County Dept. of Soc. Servs., 854 A.2d 1232 (Md. 2004); Radke v. County of Freeborn, 694 N.W.2d 788 (Minn. 2005). On the constitutional right to state protection in cases of child abuse, see DeShaney v. Winnebago, infra this chapter.

8. *Immunity.* All jurisdictions grant immunity to those persons *making* a report that later is determined erroneous. Some states grant absolute immunity; others provide immunity only for reports made with "reasonable cause" or in good faith. Are there disadvantages to granting immunity? See Diana Kerckhoff March, Over-Extension of Immunity in the Child Abuse and Neglect Reporting Act, 26 Beverly Hills Bar Assn. J., Winter 1992, at 9 (immunity protects negligent or malicious reports).

9. *Central register.* Many statutes require that state agencies maintain a register of all reported cases of suspected abuse and neglect. Originally, registries were designed to ascertain the incidence of abuse and to assist professionals keep track of parents suspected of abuse. Subsequently, social service agencies and some employers rely on the registries to preclude child abusers from child care employment. Such registries often contain a high number of unsubstantiated reports of abuse.

Do these registries violate the due process rights of alleged abusers? In the classic case of Valmonte v. Bane, 18 F.3d 992 (2d Cir. 1994), plaintiff was reported by a school official after she slapped her preteen as punishment for stealing. Although the subsequent proceedings were dismissed, plaintiff's name remained in the state register. Plaintiff argued that the procedures violated her due process rights because she would be harmed if she applied for a position in her chosen field of child care. The court found that the procedures implicated plaintiff's liberty interest (because of the mandatory requirement for employer verification) and failed to protect plaintiff's due process rights.

Many states provides for expungement procedures. Criticisms of such procedures include (1) the ability to request expungement may lapse after a short period; (2) the agency's burden of proof is slight; (3) statutes often are silent on the right to counsel and to cross-examine witnesses; (4) some statutes prevent disclosure of accusers' identities; and (5) statutes do not require a neutral hearing officer. Michael R. Phillips, Note, The Constitutionality of Employer-Accessible Child Abuse Registries: Due Process Implications of Governmental Occupational Blacklisting, 92 Mich. L. Rev. 139, 143-144 (1993). How might such statutes' shortcomings be addressed? See also Lyon v. Department of Children & Family Servs., 807 N.E.2d 423 (Ill. 2004) (holding that use of credible-evidence standard in an expungement proceeding is not an automatic deprivation of due process because the more stringent preponderance standard is used in the subsequent stage of the proceeding).

10. *Empirical research.* What are the effects of reporting laws for the therapeutic relationship? One study reports that more than one-fourth of abusive parent-clients terminated treatment following a report. Murray Levine & Howard J. Doueck, The Impact of Mandated Reporting on the Therapeutic Process: Picking Up the Pieces 133 (1995). Other possible negative effects include client anger, distrust and sense of betrayal, and increased resistance to treatment. Id. at 133-134. Some research suggests that reporting might have positive effects on the therapeutic relationship, especially if the abuser is not the client. See Kalichman, supra, at 53-54. Levine & Doueck, supra, at 131-133 (noting increased trust and self-disclosure).

11. *Family privacy.* Some commentators criticize reporting laws for their cultural bias, ensuing burden on the social welfare system, negative effects on families, high proportion of false reports, and questionable effectiveness in protecting children. See, e.g., Douglas J. Besharov, Limiting Abuse Reporting Laws: Should Current Reporting Laws Regarding Sexual and Physical Abuse of Children Be Sharply Limited to Discourage Overreporting? Yes, in Debating Children's Lives: Current Controversies on Children and Adolescents 287 (Mary Ann Mason & E. Gambrill eds., 1994); Joseph Goldstein et al., In the Best Interests of the Child (1986); E. D. Hutchinson, Mandatory Reporting Laws: Child Protective Case Finding Gone Awry?, 38 Social Work 56 (1993). Given these criticisms, do reporting laws justify the considerable intrusion on family privacy?

b. Evidentiary Issues

(i) Syndrome Evidence

■ **FRENZEL v. STATE**
849 P.2d 741 (1993), aff'd, *938 P.2d 867 (Wyo. 1997),*
cert. denied, *522 U.S. 959 (1997)*

CARDINE, Justice . . .

[Appellant was charged with seven acts of first degree sexual assault on his 17-year-old daughter (D-2). Each assault involved forced penetration either orally or vaginally with the appellant's penis or another object. Appellant challenges the admission of expert testimony concerning the Child Sexual Abuse Accommodation Syndrome (CSAAS) as violative of Wyoming Rule of Evidence 702 (which permits admission of expert testimony only if it will assist the trier of fact) on the basis that CSAAS is not generally recognized in the field of psychology and thus is not sufficiently reliable to assist the jury.]

In order to properly address these issues, it is necessary to understand the content of the expert's testimony. Dr. Ned Tranel was qualified as an expert in child psychology and child sexual psychopathology. The relevant testimony developed as follows:

* * *

[Dr. Tranel]: There is — when one encounters a condition of child sexual psychology — a child sexual abuse accommodation syndrome. [A] syndrome refers to a pattern of behaviors which are called symptoms, and in order for this syndrome to exist, then we look at the presence of or question whether . . . there is evidence of certain characteristics or symptoms, and there are five of these.

[Prosecutor]: Could you list those?

[Dr. Tranel]: [F]irst, is secrecy. . . . The second one is a sense of helplessness, and the reason that's relevant is because there is usually a child involved and usually the perpetrator is an adult. . . . The third characteristic is a pattern of accommodation, . . . which enables the person to survive over a long period of time. . . . The fourth characteristic is delayed reporting. Sometimes disclosure is used instead of reporting, and reporting is delayed and conflicted, and the reason for this, and in this case there is a classic pattern here. . . . The last characteristic we find in this syndrome is retraction or sometimes called recanting or taking back the disclosure of the sexual abuse. . . .

[Prosecutor]: [W]hat patterns of behavior manifested by [the victim] and the testing results indicated whether or not she may fit within that particular syndrome?

[Dr. Tranel]: . . . There was evidence that this was, I use the term classic pattern, there was, first of all, the secrecy that I mentioned, and that was re-enforced by the abortive attempt that she made early on to disclose the pattern of abuse. She first attempted to report this to her grandmother who didn't believe her and called her a liar. She made another abortive attempt to report this to her uncle, . . . who believed her but then also participated in the abusive pattern, and there were other abortive attempts during her academic career but none of them were followed through on with any length of time because, mainly because of the frequent and sudden moves that characterized her life throughout her academic career. So the secrecy was sustained until, I have it in my note, I don't recall the exact date, it was returning from California to Wyoming with the Sheriff or Deputy [after her arrest on a charge of writing bad checks], and that finally led to disclosure, which was pursued more diligently. The second feature I mentioned was the helplessness, and that was part of the environment in which she lived as well as the relationship between her and the abusers, those including her father, her grandfather, and her uncle. All of them, of course, older and bigger, plus she was experiencing the helplessness associated with a pattern of extreme poverty and cultural deprivation and academic failure, and she had no opportunity to overcome that and feel good about herself.

... Then the third thing was the entrapment or the accommodation where she eventually learned techniques for surviving or living with this continuing pattern, and one of the techniques she used or typically was to react initially with aggression and fighting and succumb and adapt and assume a passive stance as things continued on. [T]he next thing was the delayed disclosure, and I already mentioned the attempts at disclosure which were not fruitful, and the last one, and I have no evidence of this from anywhere, that there was ever an occasion of recantation or taking back what she said. That apparently did not ever occur as far as I know.

[Prosecutor]: How does the absence of recantation fit into your evaluation of her as it pertains to that syndrome?

[Dr. Tranel]: That's not surprising in view of her age. Recantation is a common part of this syndrome among younger children at early ages, particularly, and I am talking about four to eight years on, recanting is common. Among older adults it's less common. It's not surprising we don't see recantation here at the level of eighteen or nineteen years old. . . .

[Prosecutor]: Can you summarize for us, Dr. Tranel, your opinion as to whether or not the character and personality type of [the victim], based upon your testing of her and evaluation, is consistent with the behavior pattern of other adolescents who have been victims or manifested symptoms of child sexual psychopathology? . . .

[Dr. Tranel]: My opinion is that this is a classic pattern of a long history of child sexual abuse. The symptoms evident today are consistent with a pattern of sexual abuse. The behavior is consistent with a pattern of sexual abuse. The cognitive and the academic functioning is also consistent with a pattern of prolonged severe sexual abuse. . . .

ADMISSIBILITY OF CSAAS EVIDENCE

. . . Appellant argues that CSAAS is not a recognized diagnosis within the field of psychology, and therefore was inappropriately offered to assist the trier of fact. This argument is couched in terms of United States Supreme Court precedent, Frye v. United States, 293 F. 1013 (D.C. Cir. 1923). . . .

Previously, we used three criteria in assessing the admissibility of scientific expert witness testimony. First, the subject matter of the expert testimony must be beyond the understanding of laypersons and be distinctly related to some science. Second, the expert must possess sufficient skill, experience, or knowledge within the science to raise the inference that the expert's testimony will assist the trier of fact. Third, the scientific basis of the expert testimony must be in such a state of development so as to permit the expert to make a reasonable opinion.

[T]his court has not yet faced the admissibility of CSAAS evidence. We will here flesh out the basic purpose of CSAAS and examine how other jurisdictions have dealt with it. The purpose of CSAAS is to define a "common language" for clinical psychologists dealing with child sexual abuse and to assist them in providing therapy and treatment. CSAAS is not intended as a means of detecting the existence of abuse. . . . Because CSAAS is not diagnostic, the majority of courts dealing with CSAAS testimony have limited its admissibility. Some jurisdictions require a limiting instruction when CSAAS evidence is offered. Other courts will not admit testimony concerning CSAAS if offered to prove abuse occurred. Several jurisdictions admit CSAAS testimony solely to rehabilitate the victim's credibility. A few jurisdictions never admit CSAAS because it has not attained scientific acceptance [citations omitted].

CSAAS testimony is restricted because it offers no help to the jury of proof that abuse occurred. There is general agreement on the notion that CSAAS is unreliable for determining whether abuse actually occurred. The evidence is unreliable because there is considerable controversy and dispute over the inclusive traits. The list of symptoms associated with child sexual abuse includes behaviors which might also be manifest in a child who was not sexually abused but has been subject to some other childhood stress. . . . When CSAAS evidence is freely admitted without limitation, the danger of misleading the jury becomes significant.

Today, we adopt, generally, the view taken by [several other jurisdictions to admit CSAAS evidence with certain limitations (discussed below)]. We do so because we find that CSAAS evidence has yet to reach the stage of development which would permit an expert to reasonably conclude, on the basis of CSAAS alone, that abuse occurred. Therefore, CSAAS does not assist the trier of fact on the issue of whether abuse actually occurred. Additionally, we believe that admission of CSAAS evidence, without limitation, would run too high a risk of misleading the jury and therefore be more prejudicial than probative under W.R.E. 403. . . .

Qualified experts on child sexual abuse may, therefore, use evidence of CSAAS characteristics of sexually abused children for the sole purpose of explaining a victim's specific behavior which might be incorrectly construed as inconsistent with an abuse victim or to rebut an attack on the victim's credibility. For example, if the facts of a particular case show that the victim delayed reporting the abuse, recanted the allegations, kept the abuse secretive, or was accommodating to the abuse, then testimony about that particular characteristic of CSAAS would be admissible to dispel any myths the jury may hold concerning that behavior. . . . However, expert testimony of CSAAS cannot be used for the purpose of proving whether the victim's claim of abuse is true.

Having determined the general parameters for admitting CSAAS testimony, we must now discern whether Dr. Tranel's testimony, concerning CSAAS, was proper. . . . Throughout Dr. Tranel's testimony, he never directly states that, because D-2 represents a classic case of CSAAS, she was abused. Instead he explains in detail each specific CSAAS characteristic and how it applies in D-2's case. The majority of this testimony appeared to explain D-2's behavior, which included delayed reporting, accommodation, secrecy and helplessness. Therefore, it was appropriate for the State to explain some of these inconsistencies through Dr. Tranel's CSAAS testimony.

Dr. Tranel, however, also described the fifth trait of CSAAS, recantation, which he explained was inapplicable to D-2. Since D-2 never recanted, the explanation of that particular type of behavior was unnecessary, and Dr. Tranel's CSAAS testimony exceeded its admissible purpose. We cannot say, however, that Dr. Tranel's impermissible comments regarding recantation adversely affected the appellant's substantial rights.

Although Dr. Tranel's testimony references CSAAS often, CSAAS is not the sole basis for his ultimate conclusion that D-2's case represents "a classic pattern of a long history of child sexual abuse." Dr. Tranel performed a battery of psychological and intelligence tests when he examined D-2. In fact, as evidenced by the prosecutor's questions, Dr. Tranel's ultimate conclusion appears to be grounded in the totality of his examination not solely on his CSAAS analysis. Therefore, . . . sufficient admissible bases exist to support Dr. Tranel's testimony. . . .

In reaching our decision today, we acknowledge the inherent difficulties of proving sexual abuse. Usually, only two eye witnesses exist, the victim and the accused, thus putting a premium on credibility. It is, therefore, often necessary for the prosecution to enlist the services of an expert to explain the victim's unusual behavior in delayed reporting, accommodation and like aberrations. However, we cannot abrogate time-tested and fundamental tenets of evidence because child sexual abuse is an increasingly prevalent problem. Rule 702, W.R.E. requires that expert evidence assist the trier of fact in order to be relevant and admissible. The determination of whether the evidence assists the trier of fact is premised on the reliability of that evidence. CSAAS evidence has not yet reached the stage of development to make it, alone, a reliable indicator of the existence of sexual abuse. . . .

Notes and Questions

1. *Syndrome evidence.* The Supreme Court first addressed the admissibility of syndrome evidence in child abuse cases in Estelle v. McGuire, 502 U.S. 62 (1991). A defendant, who was found guilty of second degree murder of his infant, challenged the admission of evidence of prior injuries revealing that the infant was a victim of "battered child syndrome." The Court held that the admission of such evidence did not violate his due process rights.

2. *Approaches.* Child Sexual Abuse Accommodation Syndrome (CSAAS) is a term coined by psychiatrist Dr. Roland Summit to show that certain behavior is characteristic of sexually abused children. See Roland C. Summit, The Child Sexual Abuse Accommodation Syndrome, 7 Child Abuse & Neglect 177 (1983). In judicial proceedings, CSAAS is useful to explain reasons for certain behavior exhibited by sexually abused children (i.e., delay in reporting, half-truths, and recantations) that might lead jurors to question victims' truthfulness. Although many jurisdictions currently admit evidence of the battered child syndrome, admissibility of the child sexual abuse accommodation syndrome (CSAAS) is more controversial. Why? See Mary Ellen Reilly, Note, Expert Testimony on Sexually Abused Child Syndrome in a Child Protective Proceeding: More Hurtful Than Helpful, 3 Cardozo Pub. L. Pol'y & Ethics J. 419 (2005).

Frenzel reveals that jurisdictions take different approaches to the admissibility of CSAAS evidence. Some courts exclude behavioral science testimony regarding child sexual abuse because such evidence has not attained scientific acceptance. Among the jurisdictions that admit syndrome evidence in child sexual abuse cases, most (like *Frenzel*) limit its admissibility. What was the limitation adopted by the Wyoming Supreme Court in *Frenzel*? See generally Dyane L. Noonan, Note, Where Do We Go From Here? A Modern Jurisdictional Analysis of Behavioral Expert Testimony in Child Sexual Abuse Prosecutions, 38 Suffolk U. L. Rev. 493, 501-509 (2005) (survey).

3. *Adequacy.* Are the limitations imposed by some states adequate? That is, are jurors able to understand that CSAAS testimony is offered only to assist in evaluating credibility rather than to prove abuse? Or is the limitation too restrictive? See

Rosemary L. Flint, Note, Child Sexual Abuse Accommodation Syndrome: Admissibility Requirements, 23 Am. J. Crim. L. 171, 173 (1995) (criticizing the rule that forbids introduction of CSAAS unless the defense has expressly raised issues of the victim's credibility because often contradictions are merely implied, with the result that CSAAS testimony is not permitted).

4. *Frye test.* The traditional *Frye* test for the admissibility of novel scientific evidence, named after Frye v. United States, 293 F. 1013 (D.C. Cir. 1923), permits admission of novel scientific evidence if it has attained "general acceptance in the particular field in which it belongs." Id. at 1014. In Daubert v. Merrell Dow Pharmaceuticals, 509 U.S. 579 (1993), the Supreme Court held that Federal Rule of Evidence 702 superseded *Frye.* In so doing, the Court liberalized rules for both the admission of expert testimony and scientific evidence from a focus on "general acceptance" to relevance-plus-reliability. The Supreme Court suggested courts consider the factors of falsifiability, peer review and publication, known or potential error rate, as well as general acceptance.

Although *Daubert* applies in federal courts, many state courts continue to follow *Frye.* How should courts decide on the applicability of the *Frye* test and *Daubert* to CSAAS? Compare Irving v. State, 705 So. 2d 1021 (Fla. Ct. App. 1998) (holding that CSAAS evidence would not pass the *Frye* test) with State v. Edelman, 593 N.W.2d 419 (S.D. 1999) (holding that CSAAS evidence was admissible under *Daubert*).

5. *Other syndromes.* CSAAS (like many other syndromes such as the battered woman syndrome, the post-traumatic stress disorder syndrome, and the rape trauma syndrome) focuses on the victim. Should syndrome evidence that focuses on the abuser (for example, the battering parent syndrome, the sex abuser profile) be admissible? Are evidentiary concerns regarding admissibility similar or different? For example, Underwood v. State, 425 S.E.2d 20 (S.C. 1992), admitted evidence of a sex abuser profile as analogous to the battered child syndrome. Is this an apt analogy? On the battering parent syndrome, see Hoosier v. State, 612 So. 2d 1352 (Ala. Crim. App. 1992); Commonwealth v. Day, 569 N.E.2d 397, 399-400 (Mass. 1991).

Should a parent be entitled to admission of expert testimony indicating that he does *not* fit a battering parent profile? See generally Myrna S. Raeder, The Better Way: The Role of Batterers' Profiles and Expert "Social Framework" Background in Cases Implicating Domestic Violence, 68 U. Colo. L. Rev. 147 (1997). Alternatively, should evidence that a parent was an abused child be admissible to establish that the parent is *likely* to abuse? Compare Tucker v. Shelby County Dept. of Pub. Welfare, 578 N.E. 2d 774 (Ind. Ct. App. 1991) (admitting such evidence), with State v. Pulizzano, 456 N.W.2d 325 (Wis. 1990) (rejecting it).

6. *Other evidentiary issues.*

a. *Prior acts by the abuser.* To admit evidence of prior incidents of child abuse, courts usually require that the prior incident be "substantially similar." In a famous case, Dr. Elizabeth Morgan alleged that her ex-husband Dr. Eric Foretich sexually abused their daughter Hilary. Morgan went to jail for contempt rather than reveal the daughter's whereabouts. In an action for damages for the abuse brought by Morgan and Hilary, the court of appeals held that the trial judge erred in excluding evidence of prior sexual abuse by Foretich of Hilary's half sister. The court stated that the evidence tended to identify Foretich as the perpetrator because he had access to both girls and also that the relevance of such evidence outweighed its possible prejudicial effect. Morgan v. Foretich, 846 F.2d 941, 944-945 (4th Cir. 1988). For additional discussion of this case, see infra p. 939. The Federal Rules of Evidence were amended in 1994 to permit the admission of evidence of similar crimes in criminal prosecutions for molestation. Fed. R. Evid. 414(a).

b. *Unusually sophisticated sexual knowledge.* In many courts, the extent of young children's sexual knowledge is one method of determining whether a child's allegations of sexual abuse are credible. See, e.g., State v. Pulizzano, supra, at 334-335. Is a child's sexual *knowledge* an appropriate means of testing the child's *experience*? Are there alternative ways that a child may acquire such knowledge?

c. *Anatomically correct dolls.* Determinations of child sexual abuse increasingly rely on the use of anatomically correct dolls because many victims are young and unable to testify about incidents of abuse. Dolls may be used either to help children communicate better during an interview or to supply a mental health professional with information from which inferences of sexual abuse may be drawn.

Although early cases wrestled with the admissibility of such evidence, a growing number of jurisdictions now admit such evidence. See, e.g., Commonwealth v. Trowbridge, 647 N.E.2d 413 (Mass. 1995); State v. Waddell, 504 S.E.2d 84 (N.C. Ct. App. 1998). Further, the Child Victims' and Child Witnesses' Rights Act, 18 U.S.C. §3509(L) (2000 & Supp. 2005), applicable to the federal courts, allows the use of anatomical dolls to assist the child in testifying. Despite the trend favoring admissibility, some commentators warn that therapists misuse the dolls, their testimony conveys an aura of infallibility, and the dolls themselves elicit sexual play.[37] Empirical research, however, fails to support the last concern. Comparing sexually abused children with a control group reveals that the nonabused children (unlike the abused children) rarely engage in sexual play with the dolls or demonstrate sexual intercourse and show a pervasive lack of interest in the dolls.[38]

(ii) Privileges

■ BALTIMORE CITY DEPARTMENT OF SOCIAL SERVICES v. BOUKNIGHT
493 U.S. 549 (1990)

Justice O'CONNOR delivered the opinion of the Court.

In this action, we must decide whether a mother, the custodian of a child pursuant to a court order, may invoke the Fifth Amendment privilege against self-incrimination to resist an order of the juvenile court to produce the child. We hold that she may not.

Petitioner Maurice M. is an abused child. When he was three months old, he was hospitalized with a fractured left femur, and examination revealed several

---

[37]. See Stephen J. Ceci & Maggie Bruck, Jeopardy in the Courtroom: A Scientific Analysis of Children's Testimony 161-186 (1995); Andrea Weinerman, Note, The Use and Misuse of Anatomically Correct Dolls in Child Sexual Abuse Evaluations: Uncovering Fact . . . Or Fantasy?, 16 Women's Rts. L. Rep. 347 (1995).

[38]. See Danya Glaser & Carole Collins, The Response of Young, Non-Sexually Abused Children to Anatomically Correct Dolls, 30 J. Child Psychol. & Psychiatry 547 (1989); Lois Jampole & M. Kathie Weber, An Assessment of the Behavior of Sexually Abused and Nonsexually Abused Children with Anatomically Correct Dolls, 11 Child Abuse & Neglect 187 (1987); Abigail B. Sivan et al., Interaction of Normal Children with Anatomical Dolls, 12 Child Abuse & Neglect 295 (1988).

partially healed bone fractures and other indications of severe physical abuse. In the hospital, respondent Bouknight, Maurice's mother, was observed shaking Maurice, dropping him in his crib despite his spica cast, and otherwise handling him in a manner inconsistent with his recovery and continued health. Hospital personnel notified Baltimore City Department of Social Services (BCDSS) of suspected child abuse. In February 1987, BCDSS secured a court order removing Maurice from Bouknight's control and placing him in shelter care. [Following a subsequent hearing, the juvenile court asserted jurisdiction over Maurice and returned him to Bouknight's custody subject to conditions, such as her completion of a parenting course.]

Eight months later, fearing for Maurice's safety, BCDSS returned to juvenile court. BCDSS caseworkers related that Bouknight would not cooperate with them and had in nearly every respect violated the terms of the protective order. BCDSS stated that Maurice's father had recently died in a shooting incident and that Bouknight, in light of the results of a psychological examination and her history of drug use, could not provide adequate care for the child. On April 20, 1988, the court granted BCDSS' petition to remove Maurice from Bouknight's control for placement in foster care. BCDSS officials also petitioned for judicial relief from Bouknight's failure to produce Maurice or reveal where he could be found. [She had failed to reveal his whereabouts to BCDSS officials visiting her home, and relatives had not seen the child recently.] Also on April 20, the juvenile court, upon a hearing on the petition, cited Bouknight for violating the protective custody order and for failing to appear at the hearing. Bouknight had indicated to her attorney that she would appear with the child, but also expressed fear that if she appeared the State would "'snatch the child.'"

The court issued an order to show cause why Bouknight should not be held in civil contempt for failure to produce the child. Expressing concern that Maurice was endangered or perhaps dead, the court issued a bench warrant for Bouknight's appearance. [Following a contempt citation for failure to produce the child, the] court directed that Bouknight be imprisoned until she "purge[d] herself of contempt by either producing [Maurice] before the court or revealing to the court his exact whereabouts." The juvenile court rejected Bouknight's subsequent claim that the contempt order violated the Fifth Amendment's guarantee against self-incrimination. . . .

The Fifth Amendment provides that "No person . . . shall be compelled in any criminal case to be a witness against himself." The Fifth Amendment's protection "applies only when the accused is compelled to make a testimonial communication that is incriminating." . . . Bouknight claims the benefit of the privilege because the act of production would amount to testimony regarding her control over, and possession of, Maurice [thereby aiding the state in prosecuting her].

The possibility that a production order will compel testimonial assertions that may prove incriminating does not, in all contexts, justify invoking the privilege to resist production. Even assuming that this limited testimonial assertion is sufficiently incriminating and "sufficiently testimonial for purposes of the privilege," [Fisher v. United States, 425 U.S. 391, 411 (1976),] Bouknight may not invoke the privilege to resist the production order because she has assumed custodial duties related to production and because production is required as part of a noncriminal regulatory regime.

The Court has on several occasions recognized that the Fifth Amendment privilege may not be invoked to resist compliance with a regulatory regime constructed to effect the State's public purposes unrelated to the enforcement of its criminal laws. [The Court then discusses Shapiro v. United States, 335 U.S. 1 (1948) (holding that no Fifth Amendment protection attaches to protection of business records that were required to be available for public inspection) and California v. Byers, 402 U.S. 424 (1971) (holding that the Fifth Amendment was not implicated by the statutory requirement that drivers must give identifying information after accident).]

These principles readily apply to this case. Once Maurice was adjudicated a child in need of assistance, his care and safety became the particular object of the State's regulatory interests. . . . By accepting care of Maurice subject to the custodial order's conditions (including requirements that she cooperate with BCDSS, follow a prescribed training regime, and be subject to further court orders), Bouknight submitted to the routine operation of the regulatory system and agreed to hold Maurice in a manner consonant with the State's regulatory interests and subject to inspection by BCDSS. In assuming the obligations attending custody, Bouknight "has accepted the incident obligation to permit inspection." Wilson, 221 U.S. at 382. The State imposes and enforces that obligation as part of a broadly directed, noncriminal regulatory regime governing children cared for pursuant to custodial orders. . . .

. . . Many [custodial] orders will arise in circumstances entirely devoid of criminal conduct. Even when criminal conduct may exist, the court may properly request production and return of the child, and enforce that request through exercise of the contempt power, for reasons related entirely to the child's well-being and through measures unrelated to criminal law enforcement or investigation. This case provides an illustration: concern for the child's safety underlay the efforts to gain access to and then compel production of Maurice. Finally, production in the vast majority of cases will embody no incriminating testimony, even if in particular cases the act of production may incriminate the custodian through an assertion of possession or the existence, or the identity, of the child. . . . In these circumstances, Bouknight cannot invoke the privilege to resist the order to produce Maurice.

We are not called upon to define the precise limitations that may exist upon the State's ability to use the testimonial aspects of Bouknight's act of production in subsequent criminal proceedings. But we note that imposition of such limitations is not foreclosed. . . .

Notes and Questions

1. *Policy rationale.* Bouknight illustrates a conflict between the state's interest in child protection and the individual's constitutional protection against self-incrimination. Does child protection justify this exception to the privilege against self-incrimination? If the Court had recognized Bouknight's Fifth Amendment right, what would be the implication for child protection? See Lisa J. Jacobs, Comment, Baltimore City Department of Social Services v. Bouknight: Limiting a Mother's Right to Invoke the Fifth Amendment, 17 New Eng. J. Crim. & Civ.

Confinement 423, 438 (1991) (suggesting that social workers would be more reluctant to return abused children if supervision of a family had proved difficult).

2. *Epilogue.* Following the Supreme Court opinion, the juvenile court held a new hearing at which Ms. Bouknight again refused to answer questions about Maurice's disappearance. She continued her incarceration for contempt. In 1993, Ms. Bouknight's lawyers moved for her release. She then admitted, for the first time, that Maurice was residing with a friend (whom she would not name). In 1995, at another hearing, Bouknight named a friend with whom she had grown up. Police detectives could not verify the friend's existence.

Court-appointed lawyers for the child continued to believe that Maurice was dead. They stated, in a confidential report to the court, that they believed Ms. Bouknight was capable of fabricating the story based on prior evidence of her deception (that is, her theft in 1988 from her physician-employer to purchase a life insurance policy for Maurice). In 1995 her attorneys again petitioned for her release, arguing that it was unlikely that her continued confinement would induce compliance. She was released after seven years. See Kate Shatzkin, Bouknight Is Released After Seven Years in Jail, Baltimore Sun, Nov. 1, 1995, at A1. See also Carolyn Kennedy, In Our Defense 169-179 (1991).

3. *Immunity.* In *Bouknight*, the Court did not decide whether Bouknight's testimony could be used against her in subsequent criminal proceedings. Should Bouknight have been granted immunity from prosecution?

4. *Anology. Bouknight* analogizes a custodian of a child to a custodian of business records, asserting that both are appropriate for governmental regulation requiring incidental self-incrimination. Is the analogy apt?

5. *Tightening the privilege.* The Supreme Court recently made it more difficult to invoke the privilege against self-incrimination. In Hiibel v. Sixth Judicial Dist. Court of Nev., 542 U.S. 177 (2004), the Court held that a defendant's conviction for refusal to identify himself (for informal questioning pursuant to a stop-and-identify statute in a non-traffic stop situation) did not violate his right against self-incrimination. One commentator highlights the implications of *Hiibel* for prosecutions involving domestic violence and sexual assault:

> Victims of domestic violence and sexual assault sometimes wish to "take the Fifth" for a variety of reasons: They fear that their inconsistent statements over time may subject them to prosecution for perjury; they fear that their own violence against their assailants may amount to criminal conduct; or they have no valid basis for the privilege and are simply seeking to avoid testifying on a particular issue. [T]he Supreme Court tightened the test for determining whether statements are truly self-incriminating. The new test requires a closer nexus between the statement and the potential criminal liability of the speaker. [T]he privilege against self-incrimination currently offers less solace to victims than it has in the past.

Tom Lininger, Bearing the Cross, 74 Fordham L. Rev. 1353, 1371-1372 (2005).

6. *Similar cases.*

a. Morgan v. Foretich. In a case with striking parallels to *Bouknight*, plastic surgeon Elizabeth Morgan was cited for contempt for failure to disclose the whereabouts of her young daughter Hilary. Morgan v. Foretich, 546 A.2d 407 (D.C. 1988). Following divorce from dentist Eric Foretich, Morgan refused to permit Foretich visitation on the grounds that he had sexually abused the child. Finding that Morgan had failed to prove the abuse charges, the superior court found her in contempt and ordered a resumption of visitation (first supervised visitation, later unsupervised). Morgan appealed the visitation order, hid the child, and refused to disclose her whereabouts. The judge sentenced her to two years for contempt. Public outcry, particularly by feminists, resulted in the District of Columbia Civil Contempt Imprisonment Limitation Act of 1989, D.C. Code Ann. §11-741 (1995) (referred to as the Elizabeth Morgan Act), limiting incarceration in the District for civil contempt in a custody proceeding to 12 months. Morgan eventually joined her daughter and the child's grandparents in New Zealand (where the child had been hidden), and both later returned to Washington, D.C., where her daughter attended American University.

Foretich subsequently challenged the constitutionality of the legislation, claiming that its enactment violated the constitutional prohibition against bills of attainder (pursuant to Article III) by singling him out for legislative punishment. The U.S. Court of Appeals for the District of Columbia agreed, reasoning that the reputational injury arising from the existence of the legislation, which implicitly branded Foretich as an abuser, was sufficient to confer Article III standing. Foretich v. United States, 351 F.3d 1198 (D.C. Cir. 2003). Morgan recently left her practice in Washington, D.C., to accompany her daughter (now called Ellen Morgan), now 24, to Los Angeles where she plans to start an acting career. Amy Argetsinger & Roxanne Roberts, Reliable Source: Notes on Newsmakers, Wash. Post, Nov. 10, 2005 (available at 2005 WLNR 18136877). Is contempt an appropriate sanction in *Bouknight* and Morgan v. Foretich? What might explain the lengthy confinement for both Morgan and Bouknight? See Melinda L. Mosely, Comment, Civil Contempt and Child Sexual Abuse Allegations: A Modern Solomon's Choice, 40 Emory L.J. 203, 240 n. 130 (1991) (suggesting the possibility of bias against women who make allegations of abuse during divorce).

b. *Rilya Wilson case*. In another case with eerily similar facts, the Florida Department of Children and Families (DCF) removed five-year-old Rilya Wilson from the custody of her drug-addict mother and placed her in foster care with Pamela Graham. Despite DCF's responsibility to make a home visit once per month, the agency failed to visit for more than a year. When DCF finally inquired about the child's welfare, Graham was unable to produce the child. She falsely claimed that someone from DCF had taken the child and subsequently contended that her roommate either killed the child or gave her away to "an unknown 'Spanish lady.'" DCF also learned that Graham and her roommate allegedly beat the child with a switch, locked her in a laundry room for days, burned her with an iron, tied her to the bed at night, and deprived her of food. Dana Canedy, Miami 5-Year-Old Missing for Year Before Fact Noted, N.Y. Times, May 1, 2002, at A16. See also Sara J. Klein, Protecting the Rights of Foster Children: Suing Under §1983 to Enforce Federal Child Welfare Law, 26 Cardozo L. Rev. 2611, 2611-2612 (2005) (discussing case).

Problem

A juvenile court declares Ariel, the nine-year-old son of Teresa, to be a Child in Need of Assistance and commits him to foster care. When he disappears from his foster home, police reach the conclusion that his mother absconded with him.

Teresa is charged with kidnapping. While the criminal case is pending, Teresa is brought before the juvenile court and questioned about Ariel's whereabouts and where she was when she last saw the child. When she refuses to answer either question, she is found guilty of contempt and incarcerated. She appeals the finding of contempt after the child is located. What result? See In re Ariel G., 858 A.2d 1007 (Md. Ct. Spec. App. 2003). See also Kristine H. Rea, Note, Recent Development: In re Ariel G., 35 U. Balt. L.F. 159 (2005).

c. Hearsay and the Confrontation Clause

Many provocative procedural issues emerge during the prosecution of sexual child abuse cases. These issues arise from the desire to protect a child victim from the trauma of the judicial process while at the same time safeguarding the defendant's constitutional rights. The following materials explore these conflicting interests.

■ PEOPLE v. VIGIL
127 P.3d 916 (Colo. 2006)

RICE, Justice.

Joe E. Vigil was convicted of sexual assault on a child . . . Defendant Vigil and John Kohl were visiting the home of Brett Brown. All the men were drinking alcohol. While Brown and Kohl were on the Internet, Vigil sat in another room and played a game with Brown's seven-year-old son, JW, the victim in this case. [The father testified at trial that he went to check on his child.] When the father attempted to open the bedroom door, he encountered resistance. The father pushed his head into the room and saw Vigil positioned over the child. Vigil and the child both were partially undressed, and the father saw "skin to skin" contact. While the father comforted his child, Vigil fled the house. The child, who had tears in eyes and appeared scared and confused, told his father that Vigil "stuck his winkie in his butt" and that his "butt hurt."

Upon hearing this, the father ran outside after Vigil and watched Vigil run down the street, simultaneously pulling up his pants. Next, the child's father called 911. While the father was on the phone, Kohl, the father's friend, observed the child curled up, crying, and shaking. The father's friend asked the child if he were hurt. Two or three times the child told the father's friend that his "butt hurt."

A police officer responding to the father's call saw Vigil walking on the sidewalk near the father's home. When the police officer stepped out of his car, Vigil pulled out a knife and held it to his own throat. When the officer asked Vigil what he was doing, Vigil responded, "I done bad." Then Vigil stabbed himself in the throat and chest. At the hospital, Vigil told emergency room personnel that he wanted to die and that he "did a bad thing."

Later, the child and his mother went to the hospital with another police officer. Around 3:00 A.M. the police officer asked a doctor to perform a victim sexual assault kit. Before examining the child, the doctor spoke with the police officer to learn why the child was at the hospital and how law enforcement was involved. Next, the doctor performed a forensic sexual abuse examination on the child. When the doctor asked the child whether anyone had hurt him, the child said that someone had hurt him. When the doctor asked if the child felt pain, the child said, "It felt like a poop." During the examination, the doctor found bruising around the child's anus, and he took an anal swab. A forensic scientist analyzed the swab and discovered the presence of semen but did not identify the source of the semen. A few days after the alleged assault, a police officer conducted a videotaped interview of the child.

[Vigil was subsequently charged with one count of sexual assault on a child. A jury found him guilty. At trial, the judge ruled that the child was unavailable to testify.] On appeal Vigil argued that the trial court violated his constitutional right of confrontation by admitting . . . the child's statements to his father and his father's friend, and the child's statements to the doctor. . . .

In Crawford v. Washington, [541 U.S. 36 (2004)], the United States Supreme Court held that admitting testimonial hearsay at trial, absent the unavailability of the declarant and a prior opportunity for cross-examination by the defendant, violates the accused's confrontation right under the Sixth Amendment to the United States Constitution. The *Crawford* majority did not adopt a precise definition of the term "testimonial." The Court, however, did provide some guidance. Specifically, *Crawford* held that, at a minimum, statements are testimonial if the declarant made them at a "preliminary hearing, before a grand jury, or at a former trial; and [in] police interrogations." [Id. at 68.] Beyond this explicit guidance, the Supreme Court discussed three formulations of statements that might qualify as testimonial, namely: 1) "ex parte in-court testimony or its functional equivalent — that is, material such as affidavits, custodial examinations, prior testimony that the defendant was unable to cross-examine, or similar pretrial statements that declarants would reasonably expect to be used presecutorially"; 2) "extrajudicial statements . . . contained in formalized testimonial materials, such as affidavits, depositions, prior testimony or confessions"; and 3) "statements that were made under circumstances which would lead an objective witness reasonably to believe that the statement would be available for use at a later trial." [Id. at 51-52.]

We start our analysis by determining whether the child's statements to the doctor are testimonial in nature, and specifically, whether the statements fit into any of the clearly proscribed areas of testimonial evidence, as delineated by *Crawford*. Clearly, the child did not make his statements in the course of a preliminary hearing, in front of a grand jury, or at a prior trial; therefore, these formulations of testimonial evidence are not at issue. However, the defendant contends that the child made his statement in the course of a police interrogation, the fourth clearly defined area of testimonial evidence in *Crawford*, and therefore the statements are testimonial in nature.

Ordinarily, if a law enforcement official is involved during the course of questioning, such questioning would be considered a "police interrogation." Because the questioning in this case was done by a doctor as part of a sexual assault examination, we must decide whether this questioning constituted police interrogation . . . . In light of the concerns stated in *Crawford*, we examine first, whether and to what extent government officials were involved in producing the statements and second, whether their purpose was to develop testimony for trial. Courts from other jurisdictions which have considered this issue are divided in their conclusions. The supreme courts in Oregon and Maryland [State v. Mack, 101 P.3d 349 (Or. 2004); State v. Snowden, 867 A.2d 314 (Md. 2005)] have analyzed this issue and determined that questioning by social workers, at the behest of the police, constitutes police interrogation and that, therefore, the Confrontation Clause bars the testimony. In addition, courts which have analyzed the police interrogation issue in terms of questioning by doctors have reached the opposite conclusion, reasoning that a doctor is questioning the child for the purpose of providing a diagnosis and treatment, rather than eliciting the child's testimony for trial.

Although each factual situation must be judged on its own merits, the facts of this case are more like those in the cases where courts found a child's statement to a doctor to be non-testimonial. As the doctor testified at trial, his purpose in questioning the child was to determine whether the child would "say something that could help [the medical personnel] understand what the potential injuries were." The child's responses helped the doctor develop his opinion regarding whether a sexual assault had occurred and how best to treat the child. Thus, rather than being an agent of the police, the doctor's job involved identifying and treating sexual abuse. The fact that the doctor was a member of a child protection team does not, in and of itself, make him a government official absent a more direct and controlling police presence . . . In fact, the police officer in the instant case testified that she was not involved in the medical examination or in the room when the doctor performed the examination . . . Accordingly, we conclude that, under *Crawford*'s explicit guidance, the child's statements to the doctor are not testimonial evidence . . .

Even though the child's statements were not the product of police interrogation and therefore are not clearly testimonial according to *Crawford*, we must also determine whether the child's statements fall into one of the three formulations of the "core class" of testimonial statements at which the Confrontation Clause was directed and are therefore testimonial. *Crawford*, 541 U.S. 36, 52-52. In this regard, Vigil argues that these statements are testimonial because the child made the statements to the doctor under circumstances which would have led an objective witness reasonably to believe that the statements would be available for use at a later trial. In addition, Vigil argues that the phrase "objective witness" must be defined as an objectively reasonable adult observer educated in the law. The People disagree with this construction and argue that the phrase "objective witness" should be defined as an objectively reasonable person in the position of the declarant.

Based on our reading of *Crawford* and our review of other courts deciding this issue, we hold that the "objective witness" language in *Crawford* refers to an objectively reasonable person in the declarant's position. Applying this test to the instant case, we determine that an objectively reasonable person in the declarant's position would not have believed that his statements to the doctor would be available for use at a later trial. [N]o objective witness in the position of the child would believe that his statements to the doctor would be used at trial. Rather, an objective seven-year-old child would reasonably be interested in feeling better and would intend his statements to describe the source of his pain and his symptoms. In addition, an objectively reasonable seven-year-old child would expect that a doctor would use his statements to make him feel better and to formulate a medical diagnosis. He would not foresee the statements being used in a later trial.

Thus, from the perspective of an objective witness in the child's position, it would be reasonable to assume that this examination was only for the purpose of medical diagnosis, and not related to the criminal prosecution. No police officer was present at the time of the examination, nor was the examination conducted at the police department. The child, the doctor, and the child's mother were present in the examination room. Accordingly, we reverse the court of appeals and conclude that the child's statements to the doctor were not testimonial . . . .

Since we find that the child's statements to the doctor are non-testimonial, we must next [analyze the constitutionality of non-testimonial statements under the federal confrontation clause as set forth in Ohio v. Roberts, 448 U.S. 56 (1980)]. To satisfy the *Roberts* test, the child's statement must bear sufficient indicia of reliability by falling within a "firmly rooted hearsay exception" or bearing "particularized guarantees of trustworthiness." A statement made for the purpose of medical diagnosis or treatment qualifies as a firmly rooted exception to the hearsay rule. Where a firmly rooted hearsay exception is at issue, reliability is implied and it is not necessary for the declarant to be unavailable.

Vigil argues that the prosecution failed to meet its burden of proving that the child's statements to the doctor satisfied the hearsay exception for statements made for purposes of medical diagnosis or treatment. Specifically, Vigil implies that the prosecution had a burden to support the child's statement to the doctor through some independent demonstration of trustworthiness. We conclude otherwise.

Colorado Rule of Evidence 803(4) excepts from the hearsay rule "statements made for purposes of medical diagnosis or treatment and describing medical history, or past or present symptoms, pain, or sensations, or the inception or general character of the cause or external source thereof insofar as reasonably pertinent to diagnosis or treatment." CRE 803(4) (2005). [O]nce the proponent establishes that the statements were made to a physician for the purposes of diagnosis or treatment, that the statements were reasonably pertinent to diagnosis or treatment, and that the physician relied on the statements in reaching an expert opinion, then the statements qualify for admission without regard to an independent demonstration of trustworthiness.

In its written order, the trial court found all the facts necessary to admit the child's statement to the doctor as statements made for purposes of medical diagnosis or treatment. [T]he child's mother and the police officer took the child to the doctor so that he could offer a diagnosis regarding whether the child was sexually assaulted; the statements regarding the history as to where the child was hurt were reasonably pertinent to diagnosing the cause of the child's bruising and redness; the doctor relied on the statements in reaching the opinion that the child had been hurt by a penis. Therefore, the trial court properly found that the history the doctor elicited from the child was admissible under CRE 803(4) and that the People provided an adequate foundation. Accordingly, we conclude that the child's statements for purposes of medical diagnosis and treatment bore sufficient indicia of reliability. Admission of these statements did not violate Vigil's federal constitutional right to confront the witnesses against him . . . .

[Additionally,] Vigil argues that the child's statements to his father and his father's friend are testimonial and, therefore, the trial court violated his federal constitutional right to confrontation because he did not have a prior opportunity to cross-examine the child. To address this argument, we must determine whether the child's excited utterances to the father and the father's friend are testimonial statements.

Under the explicit guidance of Crawford v. Washington, the child's statements to his father and his father's friend do not constitute testimonial evidence because the child did not make the statements at a preliminary hearing, before a grand jury, at a former trial, or during a police interrogation. The facts do not suggest that any government officials were involved when the child made the statements to his father and his father's friend; thus, we need not further examine whether the situation presented the dangers of police interrogation. . . . Finally we analyze [these] statements . . . to determine whether an objectively reasonable witness in the child's position would believe that his statement would be used at a later trial. When the child made these statements, he was at home speaking informally to his father and his father's friend. An objectively reasonable seven-year-old boy would make statements expressing pain and explaining what had happened with an interest in seeking comfort and help. The facts do not indicate the child was making these statements in an attempt to develop testimony for trial . . . .

Because the child's statements to his father and his father's friend are non-testimonial, we must assess whether the statements bear sufficient indicia of reliability to satisfy the federal Confrontation Clause. As discussed above, a hearsay statement that falls within a firmly rooted exception satisfies this test. An excited utterance is a firmly rooted hearsay exception. Where an excited utterance is at issue, reliability is implied and it is not necessary for the declarant to be unavailable. . . . Therefore, we conclude that the child's excited utterances bore sufficient indicia of reliability and that admission of these statements did not violate Vigil's federal constitutional right to confront the witnesses against him. . . .

Notes and Questions

1. *Constitutional issues*. Two primary constitutional issues arise in regard to the admission of a child abuse victim's testimony. *Vigil* addresses the admissibility of the victim's *out-of-court statements* about abuse. In addition, federal and state courts have addressed the constitutionality of *in-court procedures* involving child abuse victims. Both types of cases implicate the defendant's right of confrontation under the Sixth Amendment.

2. *Child's out-of-court statements*. Reports of child abuse frequently come from teachers, law enforcement, social services personnel, family members, and friends. When the out-of-court statement of a child ("a declarant") to such a person is offered at trial in order to establish the fact of the abuse ("the proof of the matter asserted"), the statement is termed "hearsay." Hearsay is generally not admissible because of its lack of reliability, although there are many exceptions to the hearsay rule.

a. *Impact of* Crawford. *Vigil* raises the issue of the constitutionality of the admission of a child's hearsay evidence under the Confrontation Clause. Hearsay evidence is particularly useful in child abuse prosecutions because the child victim may be unavailable to testify. Why might such victims be unavailable to testify? *Vigil* explains and applies the rule announced by the Supreme Court in Crawford v. Washington, 541 U.S. 36 (2004), a case that has created a "paradigm shift in confrontation clause analysis." Rene L. Valladares & Franny Forsman, Crawford v. Washington: The Confrontation Clause Gets Teeth, 12 Nev. Law. 12 (2004). In *Crawford*, the defendant's wife made a recorded statement during a police investigation that contradicted her husband's subsequent claim of self-defense. The trial court admitted the wife's recorded statement (her in-court testimony was barred by the marital privilege) as an exception to the hearsay rule, reasoning that the statement bore sufficient indicia of reliability. Reversing, the United States Supreme Court held that the use of her statement violated the Confrontation Clause because a defendant must have a prior opportunity for cross-examination when out-of-court testimonial statements are at issue. *Crawford* has had a dramatic impact on prosecution of battering and child abuse by severely limiting the admission of victims' and witnesses' out-of-court statements. Tom Lininger, Prosecuting Batterers After *Crawford*, 91 Va. L. Rev. 747 (2005); Myrna Raeder, Remember the Ladies and the Children Too, *Crawford*'s Impact on Domestic Violence and Child Abuse Cases, 71 Brook. L. Rev. 311 (2005).

b. *Testimonial vs. nontestimonial.* After *Crawford*, the admissibility of hearsay evidence now depends on whether the out-of-court statement is deemed "testimonial." Testimonial statements will not be admitted unless the declarant is *available* for cross-examination at trial or, *if the declarant is unavailable, the statement was previously subject to cross-examination.* Should the determination of whether a statement is "testimonial" depend on the *recipient* of the statement? If so, are statements to a police officer always testimonial? See Wilson v. State, 151 S.W.3d 694, 698 (Tex. App. 2004). Statements that are part of informal questioning rather than formal interrogations? See People v. Bradley, 799 N.Y.S.2d 472 (App. Div. 2005). Are statements to non-government officials nontestimonial? See State v. Geno, 683 N.W.2d 687 (Mich. Ct. App. 2004). Statements to family members? Compare State v. Brigman, 615 S.E.2d 21 (N.C. Ct. App. 2005), with In re E.H., 823 N.E.2d 1029 (Ill. Ct. App. 2005). Are statements to 911 operators testimonial?

The Supreme Court recently decided two consolidated cases to address gaps left by *Crawford* concerning the meaning of "testimonial hearsay." Both cases involve the admissibility of domestic violence victims' statements. In Davis v. Washington, 2006 WL 1667285 (2006), the Court held that statements to 911 operators are not testimonial and therefore admissible because they are elicited to resolve an emergency. However, in Hammon v. Indiana, the Court ruled that admission of a victim's statement to a responding police officer violates the defendant's right to confrontation (absent the opportunity for cross-examination) because the officer was investigating a possible crime. Although neither case involves children's hearsay, the decision will have significant implications for child abuse prosecutions.

c. *A special test for children's testimonial statements?* As *Vigil* explains, *Crawford* asserted that the determination of a statement as "testimonial" depends, in part, on whether the statement was made under circumstances which would lead a witness to believe that the statement would be available for use at a later trial. Should the admissibility of a child's out-of-court statement depend on whether *the child* reasonably believed that the statement could be used later for trial? How does *Vigil* respond to this issue? Why did the court determine that all of the child's statements were nontestimonial and therefore should have been admissible?

One commentator has proposed a special test for determining whether a child's statement is testimonial: From the child-declarant's perspective, a statement is testimonial not only if the child understood its potential for formal prosecutorial use, but also "if the child understood that she was reporting wrongdoing and that some adverse consequences — including that Mommy would get mad — would be visited on the wrongdoer." Daniel E. Monnat, The Kid Gloves Are Off: Child Hearsay After Crawford v. Washington, 30 Champion 18, 20 (Jan/Feb. 2006) (citing view of Professor Richard D. Friedman). What do you think of such a test?

If a child makes a statement about the abuse to a person who is a state-designated reporter (i.e., physician, teacher, or social worker), does the child's statement thereby become testimonial because of the nature of the government involvement (i.e., the statutory duty to report)? See Raeder, supra, at 377 ("mandatory reporting arguably makes any reporter a government proxy, virtually excluding all hearsay of unavailable children").

3. *Exceptions to the hearsay rule.* Beginning in the 1980s, many states responded to the problem of child sexual abuse by expanding exceptions to the hearsay rule: codifying "tender years" hearsay exceptions, expanding two "firmly rooted" hearsay exceptions (the excited utterance and the medical diagnosis-treatment exception), and increasing the use of residual or catch-all hearsay exceptions (which are admissible if the statements have sufficient indicia of trustworthiness). The Federal Rules of Evidence, enacted in 1975, codify many of the preceding hearsay exceptions.

a. *Tender years hearsay statutes.* Many states created special "tender years" hearsay exceptions that permit the admission of a sexually abused child's previous out-of-court statements (e.g., to a parent, friend, therapist). Approximately 40 states enacted tender years hearsay statutes. Kevin R. O'Neil, Navigating the Confrontation Clause Waters After Crawford v. Washington; Where Have We Gone and Where Are We Headed?, 51 Naval L. Rev. 175, 206 (2005). State legislatures enacted these statutes because of the failure of traditional hearsay exceptions to permit admission of children's statements. Robert G. Marks, Should We Believe the People Who Believe the Children?: The Need for a New Sexual Abuse Tender Years Hearsay Exception Statute, 32 Harv. J. on Legis. 207, 221 (1995). Most of these statutes require that if the child is unavailable, there must be corroborating evidence. Some statutes require that if the child is unavailable at trial, the child must have been cross-examined when the statement was made. Other statutes admit hearsay provided that, if the child is unavailable, the court determines that the statements are trustworthy. Id. at 238-240.

b. *Excited utterances or spontaneous declaration.* In another exception to the hearsay rule, an out-of-court statement is admissible provided that it was spontaneous and made under circumstances of shock or excitement. See Fed. R. Evid. 803(2). The rationale for this exception is that statements made while the declarant is in the throes of excitement are less likely to be fabricated. Many courts have expanded this exception for child sexual abuse victims to permit admission of a child's statement even if considerable time has elapsed between the abuse and the statement because children often delay reporting due to "fear, loyalty or lack of comprehension." Melissa Lloyd, Comment, Juridical Hubris: A Comment on Baugh v. State of Florida, 5 Barry L. Rev. 129, 135 (2005).

c. *Medical diagnosis and treatment.* A statement is admissible under the medical diagnosis or treatment exception if the statement describes a medical condition and is pertinent to diagnosis or treatment. See Fed. R. Evid. 803(4). The rationale for this exception is that patients are likely to provide truthful information to health care providers because they know that false statements will affect their treatment. (Note that general statements about the abuse are admissible under this exception but not those relating to the identity of the perpetrator.) Marks, supra, at 230-231.

In response to the difficulties of prosecuting child sexual abuse, states have expanded the medical diagnosis and treatment exception.

d. *Residual hearsay exception.* Finally, a residual hearsay exception is sometimes used in child sexual abuse cases to admit statements that are not covered by another rule, provided that such statements have equivalent guarantees of trustworthiness. See Fed. R. Evid. 803(24) (for a declarant regardless of availability), 804(b)(5) (for a declarant who is unavailable).

Both excited utterance and medical diagnosis exceptions are considered "firmly rooted" hearsay exceptions. The residual exception and tender years statutory exception are not so considered. Marks, supra, at 219. What is the likely impact of *Crawford* on these various hearsay exceptions? See Robert P. Mosteller, Crawford v. Washington: Encouraging and Ensuring the Confrontation of Witnesses, 39 U. Rich. L. Rev. 511, 518 (2005) (pointing out that *Crawford's* impact on these types of hearsay "is particularly uncertain"). For an in-depth discussion of the hearsay rule and its exceptions in child abuse litigation, see John E. B. Myers, 2 Evidence in Child, Domestic and Elder Abuse Cases 473-660 (3d ed. 2005).

4. *The Supreme Court: children's statements to physicians.* The United States Supreme Court has decided two cases concerning the admissibility of a child's out-of-court statement to a physician. In Idaho v. Wright, 497 U.S. 805 (1990), a defendant was convicted of molesting his five-year-old and two-year-old daughters based on the younger child's statements to a pediatrician. The statements were admitted under the state's "residual exception." (Resort to this exception was necessitated, rather than the exception for medical diagnosis and treatment, because the child incriminated her father as her *sister's* abuser.) Under the residual exception, to satisfy the Confrontation Clause, the prosecution has to produce the victim or, if she is unavailable, the statement has to manifest sufficient guarantees of reliability. Reversing the defendant's conviction, the Supreme Court held inadmissible the child's statements to her pediatrician because they lacked the requisite guarantees of trustworthiness for the reasons that the interview was conducted without procedural safeguards, contained leading questions, and was based on the doctor's preconceived ideas.

A subsequent case, White v. Illinois, 502 U.S. 346 (1992), also challenged the admissibility of statements about a sexual assault made by a four-year-old girl to her mother, baby-sitter, police officer, emergency room nurse, and physician. The Supreme Court held that these statements were admissible (and that the prosecution was not required to produce the young victim at trial) under the spontaneous declaration and medical examination exceptions to the hearsay rule. Note that in *Crawford*, the Supreme Court admits that "Although our analysis in this case [*Crawford*] casts doubt on that holding [*White*], we need not definitively resolve whether it survives our decision today. . . ." *Crawford*, 541 U.S. at 60.

5. *Special testimonial procedures: background.* Many states have enacted legislation providing for special testimonial procedures to protect child abuse victims as witnesses. The United States Supreme Court first examined the issue of whether a special testimonial procedure violated the defendant's Sixth Amendment right to confrontation in Coy v. Iowa, 487 U.S. 1012 (1988), in which the defendant was charged with sexually assaulting two 13-year-old neighbors. Iowa law permitted a complaining witness to testify either via one-way closed-circuit television or behind a screen. The Supreme Court, emphasizing the importance of a defendant's face-to-face meeting with witnesses, held that use of the screen procedure violated the

defendant's right to confrontation. (In dicta, the Court stated that exceptions would be allowed when necessary to further an important public policy. Id. at 1021.)

In Maryland v. Craig, 497 U.S. 836 (1990), involving a prosecution of a pre-school director for child abuse and sexual abuse, the Supreme Court held that the right to confrontation does not prohibit a procedure by which a child victim testifies via one-way closed-circuit television. Despite the procedure preventing the child from seeing the accused, the Court reasoned that the existence of other requisites of confrontation preserved the defendant's rights: the establishment of the child's competence; testimony under oath; cross-examination; and the witness's visibility to the judge, jury, and defendant. The majority also determined that the state's interest in the well-being of abuse victims "may be sufficiently important to out-weigh, at least in some cases, a defendant's right to face his or her accusers in court." Id. at 853. The Supreme Court drew support from literature documenting the psychological trauma of child victim witnesses and the number of states with special protective procedures.

6. *Determination of necessity. Coy,* supra, ruled unconstitutional a statute incor-porating a *legislatively imposed* presumption of trauma and suggested the need for *individualized hearings* to support testimonial protection. How should the trial judge determine "necessity" to find a child "unavailable" for testifying? Should the trial judge personally interview the victim? See U.S. v. Rouse, 111 F.3d 561 (8th Cir. 1997) (holding that a judge may make a finding based on personal observations and questioning). Should the judge admit expert testimony? See Lomholt v. Iowa, 327 F.3d 748 (8th Cir. 2003) (finding that expert testimony by a sexual abuse counselor, based on her observations of children's behavior during counseling session when defendant's name was mentioned, was sufficient to establish case-specific findings to allow closed-circuit television). What should be the standard of proof for necessity? See, e.g., Cal. Penal Code §1347(b)(2) (West 2004) (clear and convincing evidence of trauma). What relevance, if any, should the following factors play in the determination of necessity: the child's age, gender, severity and frequency of the abuse, threats?

In the determination of necessity, to what extent is a court's reliance on *pre-dictive* evidence by expert witnesses justified? What are the psychological effects of testifying on children? Might the experience of testifying actually have beneficial effects for child victims? Existing research fails to state conclusively whether testify-ing is harmful or beneficial to sexually abused children. Most children are appre-hensive about the prospect of testifying. However, in the long-term, sexually abused children who testify are just as well adjusted as sexually abused children who do not take the stand. See John E.B. Myers, 1 Evidence in Child, Domestic and Elder Abuse 134-141 (3d ed. 2005); Gail Goodman et al., Innovations for Child Witnesses: A National Survey, 5 Psychol. Pub. Pol'y & L. 255, 258 (1999) (summarizing data).

Vigil, Craig, Coy, and *White* involve molestation by an unrelated adult. Most sexual abuse is perpetrated by family members rather than strangers. In the deter-mination of "necessity" for child victims to qualify for special protective proce-dures, would victims of familial abuse be likely to suffer more or less trauma from testifying than other victims?

7. *Law Reform.*

a. *Federal legislation.* In response to *Craig,* supra, Congress enacted the Child Victims' and Child Witnesses' Rights Act (CVCWR), 18 U.S.C. §3509 (2000 & Supp. 2005). The Act provides, as an alternative to children's courtroom testimony, that a child witness may testify by means of two-way closed-circuit television or by videotaped depositions provided that: (1) the child is unable to testify because of fear; (2) there is a substantial likelihood (established by expert testimony) that the child will suffer emotional trauma from testifying, (3) the child suffers a mental or other infirmity, and (4) conduct by the defendant or defense counsel causes the child to be unable to continue testifying.

CVCWR goes further than *Craig* by permitting testimony via two-way closed circuit television (in contrast to the one-way closed circuit procedure authorized by statute in *Craig*). CVCWR also provides such other protections as: requiring that competency exams be appropriate in light of the child's age and development, protecting confidentiality, requiring the use of multi-disciplinary child abuse teams, permitting the appointment of a guardian ad litem and the use of an adult support person, and allowing the use of testimonial aids, such as anatomical dolls. Janet Leach Richards, Protecting the Child Victim in Abuse Cases, 34 Fam. L.Q. 393, 400-401 (2000). Several federal courts have upheld the constitutionality of CVCWR. See, e.g., United States v. Etimani, 328 F.3d 493 (9th Cir. 2003); United States v. Carrier, 9 F.3d 867 (10th Cir. 1993).

b. *Uniform Law.* The Uniform Law Commissioners approved the Uniform Child Witness Testimony by Alternative Methods Act (UCWTAMA) in 2002. The Act gives authority to civil and criminal judges to order a hearing to determine whether good cause exists to allow a child to testify by an alternative method. The Act has been approved by three states. See Uniform Child Witness Testimony by Alternative Methods Act, Legislative Fact Sheet, available at http://nccusl.org/ Update/uniformact_factsheets/uniformacts-fs-ucwtbama.asp (last visited Mar. 15, 2006). Some commentators criticize the Act, claiming (1) it violates the federal Confrontation Clause, as interpreted by *Craig*, by encompassing *any* shielding procedure, by failing to limit the considerations by which judges permit shielding, and by not limiting the types of cases in which shielding is permissible; (2) it violates many state constitutional provisions requiring face-to-face confrontation; and (3) it has negative consequences from a public policy perspective by diminishing the presumption of innocence. See Katherine Grearson, Note, Proposed Uniform Child Witness Testimony Act: An Impermissible Abridgement of Criminal Defendants' Rights, 45 B.C. L. Rev. 467, 491-496 (2004) (discussing criticisms).

8. *Constitutionality of other protective procedures.* States legislatures have enacted a number of protective mechanisms for child victims of sexual abuse.

a. *Videotaping.* Many states authorize preservation of a child's testimony on videotape for later presentation at trial as a substitute for the presence of the child. Some videotaping statutes require that the defendant be present and cross-examination allowed at the videotaping session. Other statutes permit the videotape to be used subject to an opportunity for subsequent cross-examination at a judicial hearing. Are these statutes constitutional after *Crawford*? Must a defendant have an opportunity for cross-examination any time that a child's videotaped testimony is introduced at trial? Should it matter who conducted the videotaped session (i.e., a social worker, law enforcement)?

b. *Courtroom closure.* Despite the Sixth Amendment guarantee of a "public trial" in criminal prosecutions, trial judges have the discretion to close the courtroom to spectators and the press to lessen trauma to victims and witnesses. The Supreme Court examined the constitutionality of one closure statute in Globe Newspaper v.

Superior Court, 457 U.S. 596 (1982), and permitted closure subject to a particularized finding that takes into account the victim's age, maturity and understanding, the nature of the crime, desires of the victims, and the interests of parents and relatives. Note that the Child Victims' and Child Witnesses' Rights Act, supra, permits judges to close their courtrooms, at the judge's discretion, when child victims testify. See 18 U.S.C. §3509(e) (2000).

9. *Other protective mechanisms*. States have developed additional protective evidentiary rules.

a. *Abrogation of marital privilege*. Some states have statutory provisions eliminating the marital disqualification privilege (disqualifying a spouse as a witness against the other spouse) in cases of child sexual abuse. See, e.g., Mass. Gen. Laws, ch. 233, §20 (West 2004).

b. *Extensions of the statute of limitations; delayed discovery rules.* Many states have adopted delayed discovery rules that extend the statute of limitations for tort recovery in child sexual abuse cases because victims may repress memories of the abuse for years afterward. See generally Elizabeth A. Wilson, Suing for Lost Childhood: Child Sexual Abuse, the Delayed Discovery Rule, and the Problem of Finding Justice for Adult-Survivors of Child Abuse, 12 UCLA Women's L.J. 145 (2003). See also Stogner v. California, 539 U.S. 607 (2003) (holding unconstitutional, as a violation of the Ex Post Facto Clause, the application of a state law extending the criminal statute of limitations in a case of sexual child abuse to revive a prosecution that was time-barred at the time of enactment of the amendment). On the controversy about the admissibility of evidence based on repressed memories, see generally Lynn Holdsworth, Is It Repressed Memory with Delayed Recall or Is It False Memory Syndrome? The Controversy and its Potential Legal Implications, 22 L. & Psychol. Rev. 103 (1998); Camille L. Fletcher, Note, Repressed Memories: Do Triggering Methods Contribute to Witness Testimony Reliability?, 13 Wash. U. J.L. & Pol'y 335 (2003).

Following the clergy sexual abuse scandal, some states extended their statutes of limitations. For example, the Massachusetts legislature extended the statute of limitations so that it began to run three years after a minor reaches majority, and even further for victims of repressed memories. See Peter E. Smith, The Massachusetts Discovery Rule and Its Application to Non-Perpetrators in "Repressed Memory" Child Sexual Abuse Cases, 30 New Eng. J. on Crim. & Civ. Confinement 179 (2004) (citing Mass. Gen. Laws ch. 260, §4C).

10. *Policy*. Are these protections necessary for child victims of sexual abuse? Should child witnesses be treated differently from adults? How far should courts extend the rationale for special protective procedures for child victim witnesses? To child *eyewitnesses*? See Marx v. State, 987 S.W.2d 577 (Tex. Crim. App. 1999). To child victims of crimes of a *nonsexual nature*? See Ex parte Taylor, 957 S.W.2d 43 (Tex. Ct. App. 1997). See also Barbara Gilleran-Johnson & Timothy R. Evans, The Criminal Courtroom: Is It Child Proof?, 26 Loy. U. Chi. L.J. 681, 697 (1995) (arguing that testifying in such crimes as aggravated battery, kidnaping, cruelty to children, and domestic battery, can be just as damaging to the child). Should other special protective procedures that are applicable to adult victims of sexual assault be extended to children—such as rape shield laws which preclude the admissibility of prior sexual conduct evidence? See Churchfield v. State, 769 A.2d 313 (Md. Ct. App. 2001).

11. *Competency.* Competency rules provide an additional judicial check on the reliability of child witnesses. How does a court determine a child's competency to testify? At early common law, children under age 14 were presumed to be incompetent as witnesses. Case law gradually liberalized this rule, holding that capacity is determined not by age, but rather by the ability to differentiate truth from falsehood and an understanding of the duty to tell the truth. See Rex v. Brasier, 168 Eng. Rep. 202 (1770); Wheeler v. United States, 159 U.S. 523 (1895). The Federal Rules of Evidence bolstered the movement to abolish the presumption of incompetence for young children. Eliminating the distinctions between child and adult witnesses, Fed. R. Evid. 601 provides that "[e]very person is competent to be a witness except as otherwise provided in these rules." In response to the adoption of the Federal Rules in 1975, many states liberalized their competency requirements for child witnesses. Further, some state statutes have special competency rules for child victims and child eyewitnesses in child abuse litigation. Myers, 1 Evidence in Child Abuse, supra, at 77-81.

4. Dispositional Alternatives

a. Temporary Dispositions: Foster Care

Once the state establishes that grounds exist for intervention, the state must determine a placement for the child. This section explores various dispositional alternatives.

■ SMITH v. ORGANIZATION OF FOSTER FAMILIES FOR EQUALITY AND REFORM (OFFER)
431 U.S. 816 (1977)

Mr. Justice BRENNAN delivered the opinion of the Court.

Appellees, individual foster parents[1] and an organization of foster parents, brought this civil rights class action pursuant to 42 U.S.C. §1983 . . . on their own behalf and on behalf of children for whom they have provided homes for a year or more. They sought declaratory and injunctive relief [alleging] that the

---

1. Appellee Madeleine Smith is the foster parent with whom Eric and Danielle Gandy have been placed since 1970. The Gandy children, who are now 12 and 9 years old respectively, were voluntarily placed in foster care by their natural mother in 1968, and have had no contact with her at least since being placed with Mrs. Smith. The foster-care agency has sought to remove the children from Mrs. Smith's care because her arthritis, in the agency's judgment, makes it difficult for her to continue to provide adequate care. . . .

Appellees Ralph and Christiane Goldberg were the foster parents of Rafael Serrano, now 14. His parents placed him in foster care voluntarily in 1969 after an abuse complaint was filed against them. [The Goldbergs eventually separated, placing Rafael in residential care].

Appellees Walter and Dorothy Lhoton were foster parents of the Wallace sisters, who are voluntarily placed in foster care by their mother in 1970. The two older girls were placed with the Lhotons in that year, their two younger sisters in 1972. In June 1974, the Lhotons were informed that the agency had decided to return the two younger girls to their mother and transfer the two older girls to another foster home. The agency apparently felt that the Lhotons were too emotionally involved with the girls and were damaging the agency's efforts to prepare them to return to their mother. [The children eventually were returned to their mother.]

procedures governing the removal of foster children from foster homes [N.Y. Soc. Serv. Law §§383(2), 400, and 18 N.Y.C.R.R. §450.14] violated the Due Process and Equal Protection Clauses. . . . A group of natural mothers of children in foster care[5] were granted leave to intervene on behalf of themselves and others similarly situated. [The district court determined that the preremoval procedures were an unconstitutional deprivation of due process by denying the foster child a hearing before transfer to another foster home or return to the natural parents. 418 F. Supp. 277, 282 (S.D.N.Y. 1976).]

The expressed central policy of the New York system is that "it is generally desirable for the child to remain with or be returned to the natural parent because the child's need for a normal family life will usually best be met in the natural home, and . . . parents are entitled to bring up their own children unless the best interests of the child would be thereby endangered," Soc. Serv. Law §384-b(1)(a)(ii). But the State has opted for foster care as one response to those situations where the natural parents are unable to provide the "positive, nurturing family relationships" and "normal family life in a permanent home" that offer "the best opportunity for children to develop and thrive." §§384-b(1)(b), (1)(a)(i). [T]he distinctive features of foster care are, first, "that it is care in a *family*, it is noninstitutional substitute care," and, second, "that it is for a *planned* period — either temporary or extended. This is unlike adoptive placement, which implies a *permanent* substitution of one home for another."

Under the New York scheme children may be placed in foster care either by voluntary placement or by court order. Most foster care placements are voluntary. They occur when physical or mental illness, economic problems, or other family crises make it impossible for natural parents, particularly single parents, to provide a stable home life for their children for some limited period. [Under voluntary placements, a written agreement between the parent and agency may provide for the child's return at a specified date, but if not, the child must be returned within 20 days of notice from the parent.]

The agency . . . commonly acts under its authority to "place out and board out" children in foster homes. Foster parents, who are licensed by the State or an authorized foster-care agency, provide care under a contractual arrangement with the agency, and are compensated for their services. The typical contract expressly reserves the right of the agency to remove the child on request. . . .

The New York system divides parental functions among agency, foster parents, and natural parents, and the definitions of the respective roles are often complex and often unclear. The law transfers "care and custody" to the agency, but day-to-day supervision of the child and his activities, and most of the functions ordinarily associated with legal custody, are the responsibility of the foster parent. Nevertheless, agency supervision of the performance of the foster parents takes forms indicating that the foster parent does not have the full authority of a legal custodian. Moreover, the natural parent's placement of the child with the agency does not surrender legal guardianship; the parent retains authority to act with respect to the child in certain circumstances [e.g. consent to surgery, etc.]. The

---

5. Intervenor Naomi Rodriguez, who is blind, placed her newborn son Edwin in foster care in 1973 because of marital difficulties. When Mrs. Rodriguez separated from her husband three months later, she sought return of her child. Her efforts over the next nine months to obtain return of the child were resisted by the agency, apparently because it felt her handicap prevented her from providing adequate care. [She] finally prevailed, three years after she first sought return of the child. . . .

natural parent has not only the right but the obligation to visit the foster child and plan for his future; failure of a parent with capacity to fulfill the obligation for more than a year can result in a court order terminating the parent's rights on the ground of neglect.

Children may also enter foster care by court order. . . . The consequences of foster-care placement by court order do not differ substantially from those for children voluntarily placed, except that the parent is not entitled to return of the child on demand . . . ; termination of foster care must then be consented to by the court.

The provisions of the scheme specifically at issue in this litigation come into play when the agency having legal custody determines to remove the foster child from the foster home, either because it has determined that it would be in the child's best interests to transfer him to some other foster home, or to return the child to his natural parents in accordance with the statute or placement agreement. Most children are removed in order to be transferred to another foster home. The procedures by which foster parents may challenge a removal made for that purpose differ somewhat from those where the removal is made to return the child to his natural parent.

Section 383(2), n.3, supra, provides that the "authorized agency placing out or boarding (a foster) child . . . may in its discretion remove such child from the home where placed or boarded." Administrative regulations implement this provision. The agency is required, except in emergencies, to notify the foster parents in writing 10 days in advance of any removal. The notice advises the foster parents that if they object to the child's removal, they may request a "conference" with the Social Services Department. The department schedules requested conferences within 10 days of the receipt of the request. The foster parent may appear with counsel at the conference, where he will "be advised of the reasons (for the removal of the child), and be afforded an opportunity to submit reasons why the child should not be removed." §450.10(a). The official must render a decision in writing within five days after the close of the conference, and send notice of his decision to the foster parents and the agency. The proposed removal is stayed pending the outcome of the conference.

If the child is removed after the conference, the foster parent may appeal to the Department of Social Services for a [full adversary administrative hearing which is subject to judicial review]; however, the removal is not automatically stayed pending the hearing and judicial review.

This statutory and regulatory scheme applies statewide.[28] In addition, regulations [applicable to New York City] provide even greater procedural safeguards [in the form of a *preremoval* trial, upon request of the foster parents, if a child is being transferred to another foster home]. One further preremoval procedural safeguard is available. [Soc. Serv. Law §392] provides a mechanism whereby a foster parent may obtain preremoval judicial review of an agency's decision to remove a child who has been in foster care for 18 months or more.

----

28. There is some dispute whether the procedures set out in 18 N.Y.C.R.R. §450.10 and Soc. Serv. Law §400 apply in the case of a foster child being removed from his foster home to be returned to his natural parents. [N]othing in either the statute or the regulations limits the availability of these procedures to transfers within the foster-care system. Each refers to the decision to remove a child from the foster family home, and thus on its face each would seem to cover removal for the purpose of returning the child to its parents. . . .

Foster care of children is a sensitive and emotion-laden subject, and foster-care programs consequently stir strong controversy. [F]oster care has been condemned as a class-based intrusion into the family life of the poor. See, e.g., Jenkins, Child Welfare as a Class System, in Children and Decent People 3 (A. Schorr ed. 1974). It is certainly true that the poor resort to foster care more often than other citizens. . . .

The extent to which supposedly "voluntary" placements are in fact voluntary has been questioned on other grounds as well. For example, it has been said that many "voluntary" placements are in fact coerced by threat of neglect proceedings and are not in fact voluntary in the sense of the product of an informed consent. Mnookin, [Foster Care In Whose Best Interests?, 43 Harv. Educ. Rev. 599, 601 (1973)]. Studies also suggest that social workers of middle-class backgrounds, perhaps unconsciously, incline to favor continued placement in foster care with a generally higher-status family rather than return the child to his natural family, thus reflecting a bias that treats the natural parents' poverty and lifestyle as prejudicial to the best interests of the child. This accounts, it has been said, for the hostility of agencies to the efforts of natural parents to obtain the return of their children.

Appellee foster parents as well as natural parents [note] that children often stay in "temporary" foster care for much longer than contemplated by the theory of the system. The District Court found as a fact that the median time spent in foster care in New York was over four years. Indeed, many children apparently remain in this "limbo" indefinitely. Mnookin, [Child-Custody Adjudication: Judicial Functions in the Face of Indeterminacy, 39 Law & Contemp. Probs. 226, 273 (1975)]. The District Court also found that the longer a child remains in foster care, the more likely it is that he will never leave. . . . It is not surprising then that many children, particularly those that enter foster care at a very early age and have little or no contact with their natural parents during extended stays in foster care, often develop deep emotional ties with their foster parents.[40]

Yet such ties do not seem to be regarded as obstacles to transfer of the child from one foster placement to another. The record in this case indicates that nearly 60% of the children in foster care in New York City have experienced more than one placement, and about 28% have experienced three or more. [E]ven when it is clear that a foster child will not be returned to his natural parents, it is rare that he achieves a stable home life through final termination of parental ties and adoption into a new permanent family.

[W]e present this summary in the view that some understanding of those criticisms is necessary for a full appreciation of the complex and controversial system with which this lawsuit is concerned. [But, our] task is only to determine whether the District Court correctly held that the present procedures preceding the removal from a foster home of children resident there a year or more are constitutionally inadequate. . . .

---

40. The development of such ties points up an intrinsic ambiguity of foster care that is central to this case. The warmer and more homelike environment of foster care is intended to be its main advantage over institutional child care, yet because in theory foster care is intended to be only temporary, foster parents are urged not to become too attached to the children in their care. Mnookin, [43 Harv. Educ. Rev.,] at 613. Indeed, the New York courts have upheld removal from a foster home for the very reason that the foster parents had become too emotionally involved with the child. In re Jewish Child Care Assn. (Sanders), 5 N.Y.2d 222, 183 N.Y.S.2d 65, 156 N.E.2d 700 (1959). See also the case of the Lhotans, named appellees in this case. . . .

Our first inquiry is whether appellees have asserted interests within the Four-teenth Amendment's protection of "liberty." . . . The appellees' basic contention is that when a child has lived in a foster home for a year or more, a psychological tie is created between the child and the foster parents which constitutes the foster family the true "psychological family" of the child. That family, they argue, has a "liberty interest" in its survival as a family protected by the Fourteenth Amendment. Upon this premise they conclude that the foster child cannot be removed without a prior hearing satisfying due process. Appointed counsel for the children, . . . however, disagrees, and has consistently argued that the foster parents have no such liberty interest independent of the interests of the foster children, and that the best inter-ests of the children would not be served by procedural protections beyond those already provided by New York law. The intervening natural parents of children in foster care, . . . also oppose the foster parents, arguing that recognition of the procedural right claimed would undercut both the substantive family law of New York, which favors the return of children to their natural parents as expeditiously as possible, and their constitutionally protected right of family privacy, by forcing them to submit to a hearing and defend their rights to their children before the children could be returned to them.

[We] turn to appellees' assertion that they have a constitutionally protected liberty interest . . . in the integrity of their family unit. This assertion clearly presents difficulties. . . . There does exist a "private realm of family life which the state cannot enter," Prince v. Massachusetts, 321 U.S. 158, 166 (1944), that has been afforded both substantive and procedural protection. But is the relation of foster parent to foster child sufficiently akin to the concept of "family" recognized in our precedents to merit similar protection? [W]e are not without guides to some of the elements that define the concept of "family" and contribute to its place in our society.

First, the usual understanding of "family" implies biological relationships, and most decisions treating the relation between parent and child have stressed this element. Stanley v. Illinois, 405 U.S. 645, 651 (1972), for example, spoke of "(t)he rights to conceive and to raise one's children" as essential rights. . . . A biological relationship is not present in the case of the usual foster family. But biological relationships are not exclusive determination of the existence of a family. . . . No one would seriously dispute that a deeply loving and interdepen-dent relationship between an adult and a child in his or her care may exist even in the absence of blood relationship. At least where a child has been placed in foster care as an infant, has never known his natural parents, and has remained continuously for several years in the care of the same foster parents, it is natural that the foster family should hold the same place in the emotional life of the foster child, and fulfill the same socializing functions, as a natural family. For this reason, we cannot dismiss the foster family as a mere collection of unrelated individuals.

But there are also important distinctions between the foster family and the natural family. First, unlike the earlier cases recognizing a right to family privacy, the State here seeks to interfere, not with a relationship having its origins entirely apart from the power of the State, but rather with a foster family which has its source in state law and contractual arrangements. . . . Here, however, whatever emotional ties may develop between foster parent and foster child have their origins in an arrangement in which the State has been a partner from the outset. . . .

A second consideration related to this is that ordinarily procedural protection may be afforded to a liberty interest of one person without derogating from the substantive liberty of another. Here, however, such a tension is virtually unavoidable. Under New York law, the natural parent of a foster child in voluntary placement has an absolute right to the return of his child in the absence of a court order obtainable only upon compliance with rigorous substantive and procedural standards, which reflect the constitutional protection accorded the natural family. Moreover, the natural parent initially gave up his child to the State only on the express understanding that the child would be returned in those circumstances. These rights are difficult to reconcile with the liberty interest in the foster family relationship claimed by appellees. It is one thing to say that individuals may acquire a liberty interest against arbitrary governmental interference in the family-like associations into which they have freely entered, even in the absence of biological connection or state-law recognition of the relationship. It is quite another to say that one may acquire such an interest in the face of another's constitutionally recognized liberty interest that derives from blood relationship, state-law sanction, and basic human right an interest the foster parent has recognized by contract from the outset. Whatever liberty interest might otherwise exist in the foster family as an institution, that interest must be substantially attenuated where the proposed removal from the foster family is to return the child to his natural parents.

As this discussion suggests, appellees' claim to a constitutionally protected liberty interest raises complex and novel questions. It is unnecessary for us to resolve those questions definitively in this case, however, for like the District Court, we conclude that "narrower grounds exist to support" our reversal. We are persuaded that, even on the assumption that appellees have a protected "liberty interest," the District Court erred in holding that the preremoval procedures presently employed by the State are constitutionally defective.

Where procedural due process must be afforded because a "liberty" or "property" interest is within the Fourteenth Amendment's protection, there must be determined "what process is due" in the particular context. . . . Consideration of the procedures employed by the City and State of New York [in light of the factors in Mathews v. Eldridge, 414 U.S. 319 (1976), i.e., the private interest affected; the risk of an erroneous deprivation of such interest by the procedures; and, the government's interest, including fiscal or administrative burdens, that additional or substitute procedural requirements would entail] requires the conclusion that those procedures satisfy constitutional standards.

Turning first to the procedure applicable in New York City, [SSC Procedure No. 5] provides that before a child is removed from a foster home for transfer to another foster home, the foster parents may request an "independent review." . . . Such a procedure would appear to give a more elaborate trial-type hearing to foster families than this Court has found required in other contexts of administrative determinations. The District Court found the procedure inadequate on four grounds, none of which we find sufficient to justify the holding that the procedure violates due process.

First, the court held that the "independent review" administrative proceeding was insufficient because it was only available on the request of the foster parents. [That is,] the proceeding should be provided as a matter of course, because the interests of the foster parents and those of the child would not necessarily be coextensive, and it could not be assumed that the foster parents would invoke the hearing procedure in every case in which it was in the child's interest to have a hearing. . . . We disagree. As previously noted, the constitutional liberty, if any, sought to be protected by the New York procedures is a right of *family* privacy or autonomy, and the basis for recognition of any such interest in the foster family must be that close emotional ties analogous to those between parent and child are established when a child resides for a lengthy period with a foster family. If this is so, necessarily we should expect that the foster parents will seek to continue the relationship to preserve the stability of the family; if they do not request a hearing, it is difficult to see what right or interest of the foster child is protected by holding a hearing. [C]onsideration of the interest to be protected and the likelihood of erroneous deprivations . . . do not support the District Court's imposition of [automatic hearings]. Moreover, automatic provision of hearings [would impose] a substantial additional administrative burden on the State. . . .

Second, the District Court faulted the city procedure on the ground that participation is limited to the foster parents and the agency and the natural parent and the child are not made parties to the hearing. This is not fatal in light of the nature of the alleged constitutional interests at stake. When the child's transfer from one foster home to another is pending, the interest arguably requiring protection is that of the foster family, not that of the natural parents. Moreover, the natural parent can generally add little to the accuracy of factfinding concerning the wisdom of such a transfer. . . . Much the same can be said in response to the District Court's statement [that it would sometimes be advisable to appoint a representative for the child]. But nothing in the New York City procedure prevents consultation of the child's wishes. . . . Such consultation, however, does not require that the child or an appointed representative must be a party with full adversary powers in all preremoval hearings.

The other two defects in the city procedure found by the District Court must also be rejected. One is that the procedure does not extend to the removal of a child from foster care to be returned to his natural parent. But as we have already held, whatever liberty interest may be argued to exist in the foster family is significantly weaker in the case of removals preceding return to the natural parent, and the balance of due process interests must accordingly be different. . . . Similarly, the District Court pointed out that the New York City procedure coincided with the informal "conference" and postremoval hearings provided as a matter of state law. This overlap in procedures may be unnecessary or even to some degree unwise, but a State does not violate the Due Process Clause by providing alternative or additional procedures beyond what the Constitution requires.

Outside New York City, where only the statewide procedures apply, foster parents are provided not only with the procedures of a preremoval conference and postremoval hearing provided by 18 N.Y.C.R.R. §450.10 and Soc. Serv. Law §400, but also with the preremoval *judicial* hearing available on request to foster parents who have in their care children who have been in foster care for 18 months or more, Soc. Serv. Law §392. [A] foster parent in such case may obtain an order that the child remain in his care.

The District Court found three defects in this full judicial process. First, a §392 proceeding is available only to those foster children who have been in foster care for 18 months or more. . . . We do not think that the 18-month limitation [renders] the New York scheme constitutionally inadequate. The assumed liberty interest to be protected in this case is one rooted in the emotional attachments that develop over time between a child and the adults who care for him. But there is no reason to assume that those attachments ripen at less than 18 months or indeed at any precise point. . . .

The District Court's other two findings of infirmity in the §392 procedure have already been considered and held to be without merit. . . . Finally, the §392 hearing is available to foster parents, both in and outside New York City, even where the removal sought is for the purpose of returning the child to his natural parents. Since this remedy provides a sufficient constitutional preremoval hearing to protect whatever liberty interest might exist in the continued existence of the foster family when the State seeks to transfer the child to another foster home, a fortiori the procedure is adequate to protect the lesser interest of the foster family in remaining together at the expense of the disruption of the natural family.

. . . Since we hold that the procedures provided by New York State in §392 and by New York City's SSC Procedure No. 5 are adequate to protect whatever liberty interest appellees may have, the judgment of the District Court is reversed.

Mr. Justice STEWART, with whom THE CHIEF JUSTICE and Mr. Justice REHNQUIST join, concurring in the judgment.

. . . I cannot understand why the Court thinks itself obliged to decide these cases on the assumption that either foster parents or foster children in New York have some sort of "liberty" interest in the continuation of their relationship. Rather than tiptoeing around this central issue, I would squarely hold that the interests asserted by the appellees are not of a kind that the Due Process Clause of the Fourteenth Amendment protects.

[T]he predicate for invoking the Due Process Clause — the existence of state-created liberty or property — [is] missing here. New York confers no right on foster families to remain intact, defeasible only upon proof of specific acts or circumstances. Similarly, New York law provides no basis for a justifiable expectation on the part of foster families that their relationship will continue indefinitely. . . .

What remains of the appellees' argument is the theory that the relation of the foster parent to the foster child may generate emotional attachments similar to those found in natural families. The Court surmises that foster families who share these attachments might enjoy the same constitutional interest in "family privacy" as natural families. . . .

But under New York's foster-care laws, any case where the foster parents had assumed the emotional role of the child's natural parents would represent not a triumph of the system, to be constitutionally safeguarded from state intrusion, but a failure. The goal of foster care, at least in New York, is not to provide a permanent substitute for the natural or adoptive home, but to prepare the child for his return to his real parents or placement in a permanent adoptive home by giving him temporary shelter in a family setting. . . . Perhaps it is to be expected that children who spend unduly long stays in what should have been temporary foster care will develop strong emotional ties with their foster parents. But this does not mean, and I cannot believe, that such breakdowns of the New York system must be protected or forever frozen in their existence by the Due Process Clause of the Fourteenth Amendment.

One of the liberties protected by the Due Process Clause, the Court has held, is the freedom to "establish a home and bring up children." Meyer v. Nebraska, supra, 262 U.S., at 399. . . . But this constitutional concept is simply not in point when we deal with foster families as New York law has defined them. The family life upon which the State "intrudes" is simply a temporary status which the State itself has created. It is a "family life" defined and controlled by the law of New York, for which New York pays, and the goals of which New York is entitled to and does set for itself.

Notes and Questions

1. *Holding.* OFFER held that the preremoval hearing regulations afforded by New York City and the state accorded sufficient due process protection to foster parents. *Must* such a hearing be provided before removal, or can a social services agency rely on less formal interviews? In other words, how should the Court decide the substantive issue that Justice Stewart accuses the majority of "tiptoeing around"?

2. *Majority view.* In the wake of *OFFER*, most courts refuse to recognize the liberty interests of foster parents. See Terese B. v. Commissioner of Children & Families, 789 A.2d 1114 (Conn. Ct. App. 2001); In re C.M., 86 P.3d 1025 (Kan. Ct. App. 2004); In re McDaniel, 2004 WL 1144390 (Ohio Ct. App. 2004). However, some courts have recognized long-term foster relationships and the rights of foster parents in other limited situations. See, e.g., Rodriquez v. McLoughlin, 49 F. Supp. 2d 186 (S.D.N.Y. 1999) (holding that a foster parent, who has cared for a child for four years and initiated adoption proceedings, has a constitutionally protected liberty interest in the foster parent-child relationship).

3. *Kinship care.* Should courts treat foster parents who are relatives differently from those non-relatives in terms of recognition of foster parents' rights? See Gabrielle A. Paupeck, Note, When Grandma Becomes Mom: The Liberty Interests of Kinship Foster Parents, 70 Fordham L. Rev. 527 (2001) (arguing that kinship foster parents and their foster children should enjoy a due process right of family association).

Like the children in *OFFER*, most children in foster care are placed in foster family homes. However, an increasing number of children are placed with close relatives (a practice that is known as "kinship care"). A disproportionate number of these children are African-American and cared for by grandparents.[39] Among the benefits of kinship care are: family continuity and the reduced trauma that comes from separation from biological parents. However, children in kinship care are more likely to live in poverty; and also to have caregivers who are older, less financially stable, less well educated and with more health problems than non-kin caregivers. In addition, the child's parents are more likely to have access to a child in kinship care — a situation which is particularly problematic when removal results from parental abuse. See Cynthia G. Hawkins-Leon & Carla Bradley, Race

[39]. U.S. Census Bureau, Grandparents Living With Grandchildren: 2000. Almost 6 million people aged 30 and over were coresident grandparents, of whom 42 percent are primary caregivers. Forty percent of African-Americans, Native Americans and Pacific Islands grandparent caregivers have been responsible for their grandchildren for 5 years or more.

and Transnational Adoption: The Answer is Neither Simply Black of White Nor Right or Wrong, 51 Cath. U.L. Rev. 1227, 1278 (2002). See generally Margaret F. Brinig & Steven L. Nock, How Much Does Legal Status Matter? Race, Kinship Care and Adoption, 36 Fam. L.Q. 449 (2002); Sonia Gipson Rankin, Note, Why They Won't Take the Money: Black Grandparents and the Success of Informal Kinship Care, 10 Elder L.J. 153 (2002).

Should kinship foster parents' rights be recognized via guardianship proceedings? What are the advantages and disadvantages of this approach? See Susan L. Brooks et al., A Better Option?, 42 Tenn. B.J. 16 (2005) (advocating federally subsidized guardianships); CASA v. Department of Servs. for Children, Youth & Families, 834 A.2d 63 (Del. Ct. 2003) (affirming order granting legal guardianship of two minor children to non-relative foster parents).

4. *Historical background.* The modern foster care system has its roots in a nineteenth-century social movement. Charles Loring Brace (founder of the New York Children's Aid Society in 1853) sent poor children from large East Coast urban areas by "orphan trains" to live and work in Midwest farm families instead of in almshouses or other institutional settings. Despite its nomenclature, the practice was not limited to orphans. Although Brace's supporters lauded his child protection motives, critics claimed that the shipment of child labor westward constituted exploitation, removed children from parental care without valid consent, and disregarded the best-interests-of-the-child principle. See generally Stephen O'Connor, Orphan Trains: The Story of Charles Loring Brace and the Children He Saved and Failed (2001).

5. *Voluntary surrender.* As *OFFER* explains, a parent (rather than the state) often initiates foster placement. What does *OFFER* reveal about the problems posed by such voluntary surrenders? See, e.g., Young v. County of Fulton, 160 F.3d 899 (2d Cir. 1998) (mother who voluntarily placed sons in foster care brought §1983 action against social services department for denying her right to visit her sons without a prior hearing and conspiring to take her sons permanently in violation of her custodial rights).

6. *Psychological parent doctrine.* The concept of the "psychological parent" was formulated by Joseph Goldstein, Anna Freud and Alfred Solnit in Beyond the Best Interests of the Child (1973). The theory suggests that psychological parent-child relationships may develop when children are placed in the care of unrelated adults such as foster parents. Moreover, the authors argue that disrupting a stable relationship with psychological parents, even if the latter are temporary non-relative caregivers, is traumatic. Does *OFFER* adequately protect the "psychological parent-child" relationship?

Does a foster child have an independent, constitutionally protected liberty interest to maintain contact with a foster-psychological parent? See Harriet II v. Alex LL, 740 N.Y.S.2d 162 (App. Div. 2002) (holding that the Family Court lacked jurisdiction to order a standing hearing to determine if the child had a parent-like relationship with his former foster mother). See also Stephanie Moes, Note, Being Seen and Heard: Webster v. Ryan's Constitutional Protection for Children's Right to Maintain Contact with Foster Parents, 71 U. Cin. L. Rev. 331(2002).

7. *Foster parents' liability.* An omitted section of footnote 40 in *OFFER* makes the point that foster parents sometimes provide inadequate care, even abusing and neglecting foster children.[40] Are foster parents liable for injuries that occur in

[40]. According to national data, .5 percent of the perpetrators of abuse or neglect are foster parents. Child Maltreatment: 2003, supra note [7] (Figure 5-2, Perpetrators by Relationship to Victims,

foster care? Does the parent-child immunity doctrine preclude liability? Compare Nichol v. Stass, 735 N.E.2d 582 (Ill. 2000) (recognizing limited grant of parental liability for toddler's death by drowning), with Wallace v. Smyth, 786 N.E.2d 980 (Ill. 2002) (finding that parental immunity is not available to foster parents.)

Similarly, does the sovereign immunity doctrine insulate foster parents from liability? See Smith v. Four Corners Mental Health Ctr., Inc., 70 P.3d 904 (Utah 2003) (holding that an issue of fact existed as to whether foster parents were governmental employees who would be entitled to governmental immunity or independent contractors who would not). Should foster parents be immune from liability for injuries to foster children?

Since 1997, federal law requires foster parents to undergo criminal background checks. See 42 U.S.C. §671(a)(20) (2000). Does this legislation provide an adequate safeguard? On the issue of whether children have a constitutional right to be free from harm inflicted by governmental caregivers, see DeShaney v. Winnebago, infra this chapter. See generally Carolyn A. Kubitschek, Government Liability for Abuse of Children in Foster Care, 2 Ann. 2005 ATLA-CLE 1743 (2005); Lynn D. Wardle, Liability of State Child Placement Agencies and Personnel When Children Are Victims of Molestation in Foster Care and Adoption Placements, 6 J. L. Fam. Stud. 59, 72-74 (2004).

8. *Foster care population.*

a. *Entry into foster care.* When *OFFER* was decided, the typical parent who placed a child in foster care was a divorced spouse with financial problems, an unwed mother, or a mother on welfare who was unable temporarily to care for a child because of illness or financial problems. A leading authority suggests that family disruption, financial difficulties, and medical reasons were the primary factors for placement.[41] Neglect, abuse, and abandonment also accounted for many children's entry into foster care. Beginning in the mid 1980s, significant changes occurred in the numbers of children in foster care, their characteristics, and the reasons for their entrance into care. In 1980 approximately 300,000 children were in foster care. That number practically doubled by 1998.[42] More African-American, Hispanic children, and Native American children entered foster care, and more sibling groups needed to be placed together. A considerable number of children entered foster care because their families lacked adequate housing. Substance abuse was another contributing factor — the increasing use of crack cocaine led to more infants being placed in foster care due to drug toxicity at birth, substance-related abandonment or inadequate parenting. In addition, children with HIV or whose parents died of AIDS added to the problem. As a result of these factors, many children entered foster care with special needs.

b. *Current characteristics.* As of 2003, an estimated 523,000 children were in foster care. Of these children, 46 percent were in nonrelative foster family homes, 23 percent were in relative foster homes, 19 percent were in group

---

2003), available at http://www.acf.hhs.gov/programs/cb/pubs/cm03/figure5_2.htm. See also Randi Mandelbaum, Are Abused and Neglect Children in New Jersey Faring Any Better Since the Tragedies of 2003?, 236 N.J. Law. 9 n. 9 (2005) (citing estimates that one in ten abused children who are removed from their parents are re-abused while in foster care).

[41]. Alfred Kadushin, Child Welfare Services 366 (1967).

[42]. Sandra Bass et al., Children, Families, and Foster Care: Analysis and Recommendations, in 14 The Future of Children 5, 8 (2004) (pointing out that the number of children entering foster care climbed to 568,000 in 1998 and noting reasons for the increase).

homes or institutions, 5 percent were in pre-adoptive homes, and 7 percent were in other types of placements. The median age of children in foster care was 10.9 years. In terms of racial characteristics, 39 percent of children in foster care were white/non-Hispanic, 35 percent were Black/non-Hispanic, 17 percent were Hispanic, and 9 percent were children of other racial/ethnic origins. Slightly more than half of the children in foster care were male. The average time spent in foster care was 11 months; however, half of those who left foster care had been in care for more than 2 years, and 9 percent had been in care for 5 or more years. Of 281,000 children who exited foster care in 2003, 55 percent were reunited with parent(s) or primary caretakers(s), 18 percent were adopted, 15 percent went to live with a relative or guardian, and 8 percent were emancipated.[43]

9. *Epilogue*. Although the Supreme Court reversed the district court's finding of unconstitutionality in *OFFER*, the case had an impact. First, the Gandy children (see footnote 1 supra) were permitted to remain with their foster mother Mrs. Smith. Eventually, she adopted them. Second, the litigation put on notice those states without any preremoval conferences that their procedures might be constitutionally flawed. Third, the litigation resulted in new procedural protections in New York City (although not state-wide) regarding the formal hearings prior to intra-foster care transfers. Foster parents (who must request these hearings) may appear with counsel; witnesses are sworn and subject to cross-examination; and expert testimony is often taken. Although only a small number of such hearings are held, the reversal rate for these contested decisions is quite high. David L. Chambers & Michael S. Wald, Smith v. OFFER, in In the Interest of Children: Advocacy, Law Reform, and Public Policy 114-116 (Robert H. Mnookin ed. 1985).

10. *Foster care reform.*

a. *Adoption Assistance and Child Welfare Act.* Foster care was envisioned as a temporary solution to family disfunction or disruption. However, in the 1970s, public attention began focusing on the problem of "foster care drift." The term signifies the experience of foster care children who undergo multiple foster care placements, moving endlessly from foster home to foster home without any hope of family reunification or adoption. Many commentators criticized the practice and highlighted its psychological harm to children.[44] The United States Supreme Court added fuel to the debate with its criticism of foster care drift in Smith v. OFFER, supra.

Concern about the "limbo" of foster care motivated legislative reform on the federal and state levels. In 1980 Congress enacted the Adoption Assistance and Child Welfare Act (AACWA), 42 U.S.C. §§620-28, 670-79(a) (2000 & Supp. 2005). The primary objective of the AACWA was to facilitate finding permanent homes for children (by preventing the need for removal, returning children to their families, or placing them for adoption). The AACWA provides federal matching funds to states for administering foster care and adoption services (emphasizing preventive and rehabilitative services) subject to certain requirements.

To qualify for federal funding, AACWA requires that (1) states must formulate case plans ("permanency planning") that are designed to achieve placement in the least possible restrictive setting and that focus on family reunification, (2) states

---

[43]. U.S. Dept. of Health & Human Servs., Administration for Children & Families, Foster Care: Numbers and Trends (2005).

[44]. See, e.g., Joseph Goldstein et al., Beyond the Best Interests of the Child (1973); Robert H. Mnookin, Foster Care — In Whose Best Interest?, 43 Harv. Educ. Rev. 599 (1973); Michael S. Wald, State Intervention on Behalf of "Neglected" Children, 28 Stan. L. Rev. 623 (1976).

must conduct periodic case reviews (case files must be reviewed by agencies and courts every 6 months with dispositional hearings held after 18 months), and (3) states must make "reasonable efforts" (id. at §671(a)(15)) to prevent the need to remove a child from the home and to facilitate the child's return as soon as possible. (On the meaning of "reasonable efforts" and whether a private right of action exists to enforce the AACWA to ensure that states make "reasonable efforts," see infra p. 990.) Even before Congress passed the AACWA, individual states were acting independently to adopt legislation that pointed in the same direction. After 1980, states adopted legislation to conform to the minimum requirements for federal funding set out by the AACWA.

b. *Adoption and Safe Families Act.* Following federal legislative reform, several problems remained. In 1997, Congress enacted the Adoption and Safe Families Act (ASFA), 42 U.S.C. §675(5) (2000), as a response to the concerns of legislators and child welfare agencies that AACWA's policy of preservation and reunification of families was exposing children to unnecessary risks. One of ASFA's most important reforms is to clarify the meaning of the AACWA's "reasonable efforts" standard. Under AACWA, states had to make reasonable efforts to prevent the need for foster care and to reunify families after placement. However, AACWA failed to specify the extent of the efforts that were required.

In contrast, ASFA recognizes that reunification is not possible or advisable in all cases. Rather than emphasizing AACWA's policy of family preservation and reunification, ASFA emphasizes the child's best interest by providing for speedier termination of parental rights. Thus, ASFA eliminates the reasonable efforts requirement in the AACWA for the most severe cases (i.e., torture, sexual abuse, a parent murders another child, or a parent loses parental rights to a sibling) (42 U.S.C. §675(a)(15)(D)). In addition, ASFA aims to facilitate adoption by reducing the amount of time that children spend in foster care. ASFA shortens the period triggering permanency hearings to no later than 12 months after the child's entry into foster care and also requires states to seek termination of parental rights for children who have been in foster care for 15 of the last 22 months (42 U.S.C. §675(5)(E)). States need not file such petitions if (1) a relative cares for the child, (2) a state agency believes that termination would not be in the best interests of the child, or (3) a state agency has failed to provide the family with reunification services.

Does ASFA's fast-track parental rights termination assume that all children who are available for adoption will be adopted? Is termination of parental rights in the best interest of the child, even in cases where he or she does not have a new permanent home? Compare Hawkins-Leon & Bradley, supra, at 1246-1247; with Dorothy E. Roberts, Is There Justice in Children's Rights?: The Critique of Federal Family Preservation Policy, 2 U. Pa. J. Const. L. 112, 118-138 (1999).

11. *LGBT issues in foster care.*

a. *Eligibility requirements for foster parents.* Because federal law fails to prohibit discrimination in foster care based on sexual orientation, some states have restrictions on the placement of children with LGBT foster parents. For example, Connecticut law provides that state agencies may consider sexual orientation in placing a child in foster care. Conn. Gen. Stat. Ann §45a-726a (West 2003). Utah restricts eligibility of LGBT foster parents by banning placement of children with cohabiting couples while at the same time outlawing same-sex marriage. Utah Code Ann. §78-30-1(3)(b); §78-30-1-2(5); §624-4a-602(5)(b) (2004). A proposed amendment to a Texas foster care bill (S.B.6), authored by Rep. Robert Talton (called the "Talton Amendment"), prohibits the placement of children with a gay or lesbian foster parent and also "allow[ing] a child to remain in foster care" with a foster parent who is "homosexual or bisexual." In 2004, a similar Arkansas policy providing that no person could serve as a foster parent "if any adult member of that person's household is a homosexual" was invalidated in Howard v. Child Welfare Agency Review Board, Case No. CV 1999-9881 (Ark. Cir. Ct., 6th Div., December 29, 2004). See Dennis Coleman, Lambda Legal's Letter of Opposition to Talton Amendment to Texas S.B. 6, Foster Care Project, April 27, 2005, available at http://www.lambdalegal.org/cgi-bin/iowa/cases/documents .html?record=1693.

b. *Safety and services for youth.* LGBT children also experience bias from foster care agencies and foster families.[45] In Joel A. v. Giuliani, 218 F.3d 132 (2d Cir. 2000), gay and lesbian foster children in New York City brought a class action seeking to set aside a settlement of a prior class action suit involving New York City's child welfare system (see Marison v. Giuliani, infra p. 973), alleging that the failure to provide them with appropriate services and safe conditions of care deprived them of their federal and state statutory and constitutional rights. Affirming the earlier *Marisol* settlement, the Second Circuit Court of Appeals determined that the system-wide benefits of the settlement would inure to all members of the class, including the *Joel A.* plaintiffs, by redressing the inadequacies of the city's foster care system. See generally Gerald P. Mallon, We Don't Exactly Get the Welcome Wagon: The Experiences of Gay and Lesbian Adolescents in Child Welfare Systems (1998); Katrina Greiner, Gay, Lesbian, Bisexual and Transgendered Youth in Foster Care, 5 Geo. J. Gender & L. 502 (2004).

12. *Aging out of foster care.* Many foster children, particularly those who are not adopted or reunified with their families, exit foster care at the age of 18. Approximately 20,000 teens leave foster care each year because they have reached the age of majority.[46] These children "age out," i.e., they are no longer eligible for foster care benefits regardless of whether they have sufficient skills or resources to live on their own. Many of these youths face unemployment, homelessness, incarceration, and pregnancy. In the mid 1980s, federal legislation first recognized the needs of older foster care children. As a result, in 1986, Congress enacted the Independent Living Initiative (ILI), 42 U.S.C. §677 (2000), requiring specific planning to help these youth before they exit foster care. The ILI required states to provide services to foster care children to prepare them for independent living. In 1999 Congress amended the ILI by enactment of the Foster Care Independence Act (FCIA), 42 U.S.C. §677 (2000), to provide additional funding for improved services to older youths. Specifically, FCIA offers programs in education, training or post-secondary

---

[45]. For a study of the extent of the problem in 14 states plus recommendations for reform, see Lambda Legal, Youth in the Margins: A Report on the Unmet Needs of Lesbian, Gay, Bisexual, and Transgender Adolescents in Foster Care Including a Survey of Fourteen States and Proposals for Reform (2001), available at http://www.lambdalegal.org/cgi-bin/iowa/news/publications.html?record=899 (last visited Mar. 17, 2006). The recommendations include: states should provide group facilities specifically for LGBT youth, offer LGBT youth services, offer sensitivity training on LGBT issues to foster care personnel, and ensure that LGBT youth receive sexuality education that covers HIV-prevention information.

[46]. Susan Vivian Mangold, Extending Non-Exclusive Parenting and the Right to Protection for Older Foster Children: Creating Third Options in Permanency Planning, 48 Buff. L. Rev. 835, 863 (2000) (citing congressional findings, H.R. 3443, 106th Cong. 1999).

education, employment, and financial support that may continue until youth reach age 21 if necessary. FCIA allows Medicaid coverage to youths between the ages of 18 and 21 who were in foster care on their eighteenth birthday. FCIA also authorizes additional funding to assist states to find permanent homes for foster care youths.

See generally Michele Benedetto, An Ounce of Prevention: A Foster Youth's Substantive Due Process Right to Proper Preparation for Emancipation, 9 U.C. Davis J. Juv. L. & Pol'y 381 (2005); Betsy Krebs & Paul Pitcoff, Reversing the Failure of the Foster Care System, 27 Harv. Women's L.J. 357 (2004) (criticizing FCIA).

b. Liability for Selection of Disposition

■ **DESHANEY v. WINNEBAGO COUNTY DEPARTMENT OF SOCIAL SERVICES**
489 U.S. 189 (1989)

Chief Justice REHNQUIST delivered the opinion of the Court. . . .

The facts of this case are undeniably tragic. Petitioner Joshua DeShaney was born in 1979. In 1980, a Wyoming court granted his parents a divorce and awarded custody of Joshua to his father, Randy DeShaney. The father shortly thereafter moved to Neenah, a city located in Winnebago County, Wisconsin, taking the infant Joshua with him. There he entered into a second marriage, which also ended in divorce.

The Winnebago County authorities first learned that Joshua DeShaney might be a victim of child abuse in January 1982, when his father's second wife complained to the police, at the time of their divorce, that he had previously "hit the boy causing marks and [was] a prime case for child abuse." The Winnebago County Department of Social Services (DSS) interviewed the father, but he denied the accusations, and DSS did not pursue them further. In January 1983, Joshua was admitted to a local hospital with multiple bruises and abrasions. The examining physician suspected child abuse and notified DSS, which immediately obtained an order from a Wisconsin juvenile court placing Joshua in the temporary custody of the hospital. Three days later, the county convened an ad hoc "Child Protection Team" — consisting of a pediatrician, a psychologist, a police detective, the county's lawyer, several DSS caseworkers, and various hospital personnel — to consider Joshua's situation. At this meeting, the Team decided that there was insufficient evidence of child abuse to retain Joshua in the custody of the court. The Team did, however, decide to recommend several measures to protect Joshua, including enrolling him in a preschool program, providing his father with certain counselling services, and encouraging his father's girlfriend to move out of the home. Randy DeShaney entered into a voluntary agreement with DSS in which he promised to cooperate with them in accomplishing these goals.

Based on the recommendation of the Child Protection Team, the juvenile court dismissed the child protection case and returned Joshua to the custody of his father. A month later, emergency room personnel called the DSS caseworker handling Joshua's case to report that he had once again been treated for suspicious injuries. The caseworker concluded that there was no basis for action. For the next six months, the caseworker made monthly visits to the DeShaney home, during which she observed a number of suspicious injuries on Joshua's head; she also noticed that he had not been enrolled in school and that the girlfriend had not moved out. The caseworker dutifully recorded these incidents in her files, along with her continuing suspicions that someone in the DeShaney household was physically abusing Joshua, but she did nothing more. In November 1983, the emergency room notified DSS that Joshua had been treated once again for injuries that they believed to be caused by child abuse. On the caseworker's next two visits to the DeShaney home, she was told that Joshua was too ill to see her. Still DSS took no action.

In March 1984, Randy DeShaney beat 4-year-old Joshua so severely that he fell into a life-threatening coma. Emergency brain surgery revealed a series of hemorrhages caused by traumatic injuries to the head inflicted over a long period of time. Joshua did not die, but he suffered brain damage so severe that he is expected to spend the rest of his life confined to an institution for the profoundly retarded. Randy DeShaney was subsequently tried and convicted of child abuse.

[Joshua and his mother brought this action under 42 U.S.C. §1983 alleging that respondents deprived Joshua of his liberty without due process of law by failing to intervene to protect him. The district court granted summary judgment for respondents and the court of appeals affirmed, 812 F.2d 298 (7th Cir. 1987)].

The Due Process Clause of the Fourteenth Amendment provides that "[n]o State shall . . . deprive any person of life, liberty, or property, without due process of law." . . . But nothing in the language of the Due Process Clause itself requires the State to protect the life, liberty, and property of its citizens against invasion by private actors. The Clause is phrased as a limitation on the State's power to act, not as a guarantee of certain minimal levels of safety and security. It forbids the State itself to deprive individuals of life, liberty, or property without "due process of law," but its language cannot fairly be extended to impose an affirmative obligation on the State to ensure that those interests do not come to harm through other means. Nor does history support such an expansive reading of the constitutional text. . . . Its purpose was to protect the people from the State, not to ensure that the State protected them from each other. The Framers were content to leave the extent of governmental obligation in the latter area to the democratic political processes.

. . . Petitioners contend, however, that even if the Due Process Clause imposes no affirmative obligation on the State to provide the general public with adequate protective services, such a duty may arise out of certain "special relationships" created or assumed by the State with respect to particular individuals. Petitioners argue that such a "special relationship" existed here because the State knew that Joshua faced a special danger of abuse at his father's hands, and specifically proclaimed, by word and by deed, its intention to protect him against that danger. Having actually undertaken to protect Joshua from this danger — which petitioners concede the State played no part in creating — the State acquired an affirmative "duty," enforceable through the Due Process Clause, to do so in a reasonably competent fashion. Its failure to discharge that duty, so the argument goes, was an abuse of governmental power that so "shocks the conscience," Rochin v. California, 342 U.S. 165, 172 (1952), as to constitute a substantive due process violation.

We reject this argument. [The Court distinguished the state's affirmative duty to provide medical care for incarcerated prisoners under the Eighth Amendment's prohibition against cruel and unusual punishment, citing Estelle v. Gamble, 429 U.S. 97 (1976).] In Youngberg v. Romeo, 457 U.S. 307 (1982), we extended this analysis beyond the Eighth Amendment setting, holding that the substantive component of the Fourteenth Amendment's Due Process Clause requires the State to provide involuntarily committed mental patients with such services as are necessary to ensure their "reasonable safety" from themselves and others. . . .

But these cases afford petitioners no help. Taken together, they stand only for the proposition that when the State takes a person into its custody and holds him there against his will, the Constitution imposes upon it a corresponding duty to assume some responsibility for his safety and general well-being. The rationale for this principle is simple enough: when the State by the affirmative exercise of its power so restrains an individual's liberty that it renders him unable to care for himself, and at the same time fails to provide for his basic human needs — e.g., food, clothing, shelter, medical care, and reasonable safety — it transgresses the substantive limits on state action set by the Eighth Amendment and the Due Process Clause. The affirmative duty to protect arises not from the State's knowledge of the individual's predicament or from its expressions of intent to help him, but from the limitation which it has imposed on his freedom to act on his own behalf. In the substantive due process analysis, it is the State's affirmative act of restraining the individual's freedom to act on his own behalf — through incarceration, institution-alization, or other similar restraint of personal liberty — which is the "deprivation of liberty" triggering the protections of the Due Process Clause, not its failure to act to protect his liberty interests against harms inflicted by other means.

The *Estelle-Youngberg* analysis simply has no applicability in the present case. Petitioners concede that the harms Joshua suffered did not occur while he was in the State's custody, but while he was in the custody of his natural father, who was in no sense a state actor.[9] While the State may have been aware of the dangers that Joshua faced in the free world, it played no part in their creation, nor did it do anything to render him any more vulnerable to them. That the State once took temporary custody of Joshua does not alter the analysis, for when it returned him to his father's custody, it placed him in no worse position than that in which he would have been had it not acted at all; the State does not become the permanent guar-antor of an individual's safety by having once offered him shelter. Under these circumstances, the State had no constitutional duty to protect Joshua. . . .

The most that can be said of the state functionaries in this case is that they stood by and did nothing when suspicious circumstances dictated a more active role for them. In defense of them it must also be said that had they moved too soon to take custody of the son away from the father, they would likely have been met with

_____

9. Had the State by the affirmative exercise of its power removed Joshua from free society and placed him in a foster home operated by its agents, we might have a situation sufficiently analogous to incarceration or institutionalization to give rise to an affirmative duty to protect. Indeed, several Courts of Appeals have held, by analogy to *Estelle* and *Youngberg*, that the State may be held liable under the Due Process Clause for failing to protect children in foster homes from mistreatment at the hands of their foster parents. See Doe v. New York City Dept. of Social Services, 649 F.2d 134, 141-142 (CA2 1981), after remand, 709 F.2d 782, *cert. denied sub nom.* Catholic Home Bureau v. Doe, 464 U.S. 864 (1983); Taylor ex rel. Walker v. Ledbetter, 818 F.2d 791, 794-797 (CA11 1987) (en banc), *cert. pending sub nom.* Ledbetter v. Taylor, No. 87-521. We express no view on the validity of this analogy, however, as it is not before us in the present case.

charges of improperly intruding into the parent-child relationship, charges based on the same Due Process Clause that forms the basis for the present charge of failure to provide adequate protection.

The people of Wisconsin may well prefer a system of liability which would place upon the State and its officials the responsibility for failure to act in situations such as the present one. They may create such a system, if they do not have it already, by changing the tort law of the State in accordance with the regular law-making process. But they should not have it thrust upon them by this Court's expansion of the Due Process Clause of the Fourteenth Amendment.

Justice BRENNAN, with whom Justice MARSHALL and Justice BLACKMUN join, dissenting. . . .

I cannot agree that respondents had no constitutional duty to help Joshua DeShaney. . . . In a constitutional setting that distinguishes sharply between action and inaction, one's characterization of the misconduct alleged under §1983 may effectively decide the case. Thus, by leading off with a discussion (and rejection) of the idea that the Constitution imposes on the States an affirmative duty to take basic care of their citizens, the Court foreshadows — perhaps even preordains — its conclusion that no duty existed even on the specific facts before us. This initial discussion establishes the baseline from which the Court assesses the DeShaneys' claim that, when a State has — "by word and by deed," — announced an intention to protect a certain class of citizens and has before it facts that would trigger that protection under the applicable state law, the Constitution imposes upon the State an affirmative duty of protection.

The Court's baseline is the absence of positive rights in the Constitution and a concomitant suspicion of any claim that seems to depend on such rights. From this perspective, the DeShaneys' claim is first and foremost about inaction (the failure, here, of respondents to take steps to protect Joshua), and only tangentially about action (the establishment of a state program specifically designed to help children like Joshua). And from this perspective, holding these Wisconsin officials liable — where the only difference between this case and one involving a general claim to protective services is Wisconsin's establishment and operation of a program to protect children — would seem to punish an effort that we should seek to promote.

I would begin from the opposite direction. I would focus first on the action that Wisconsin has taken with respect to Joshua and children like him, rather than on the actions that the State failed to take. . . .

Because of the Court's initial fixation on the general principle that the Constitution does not establish positive rights, it is unable to appreciate our recognition in *Estelle* and *Youngberg* that this principle does not hold true in all circumstances. . . . In striking down a filing fee as applied to divorce cases brought by indigents, see Boddie v. Connecticut, 401 U.S. 371 (1971) . . . , we have acknowledged that a State's actions — such as the monopolization of a particular path of relief — may impose upon the State certain positive duties. . . .

Wisconsin has established a child-welfare system specifically designed to help children like Joshua. Wisconsin law places upon the local departments of social services such as respondent (DSS or Department) a duty to investigate reported instances of child abuse. While other governmental bodies and private persons are largely responsible for the reporting of possible cases of child abuse, Wisconsin law channels all such reports to the local departments of social services for evaluation and, if necessary, further action. Even when it is the sheriff's office or police department that receives a report of suspected child abuse, that report is referred to local social services departments for action; the only exception to this occurs when the reporter fears for the child's immediate safety. In this way, Wisconsin law invites — indeed, directs — citizens and other governmental entities to depend on local departments of social services such as respondent to protect children from abuse.

The specific facts before us bear out this view of Wisconsin's system of protecting children. Each time someone voiced a suspicion that Joshua was being abused, that information was relayed to the Department for investigation and possible action. . . . Even more telling . . . is the Department's control over the decision whether to take steps to protect a particular child from suspected abuse. While many different people contributed information and advice to this decision, it was up to the people at DSS to make the ultimate decision (subject to the approval of the local government's Corporation Counsel) whether to disturb the family's current arrangements. . . .

In these circumstances, a private citizen, or even a person working in a government agency other than DSS, would doubtless feel that her job was done as soon as she had reported her suspicions of child abuse to DSS. Through its child-welfare program, in other words, the State of Wisconsin has relieved ordinary citizens and governmental bodies other than the Department of any sense of obligation to do anything more than report their suspicions of child abuse to DSS. If DSS ignores or dismisses these suspicions, no one will step in to fill the gap. . . . Conceivably, then, children like Joshua are made worse off by the existence of this program when the persons and entities charged with carrying it out fail to do their jobs.

It simply belies reality, therefore, to contend that the State "stood by and did nothing" with respect to Joshua. Through its child-protection program, the State actively intervened in Joshua's life and, by virtue of this intervention, acquired ever more certain knowledge that Joshua was in grave danger. These circumstances, in my view, plant this case solidly within the tradition of cases like *Youngberg* and *Estelle*. . . .

I would allow Joshua and his mother the opportunity to show that respondents' failure to help him arose, not out of the sound exercise of professional judgement that we recognized in *Youngberg* as sufficient to preclude liability, but from the kind of arbitrariness that we have in the past condemned. . . .

Justice BLACKMUN, dissenting. . . .

Poor Joshua! Victim of repeated attacks by an irresponsible, bullying, cowardly, and intemperate father, and abandoned by respondents who placed him in a dangerous predicament and who knew or learned what was going on, and yet did essentially nothing except, as the Court revealingly observes, "dutifully recorded these incidents in [their] files." It is a sad commentary upon American life, and constitutional principles — so full of late of patriotic fervor and proud proclamations about "liberty and justice for all," that this child, Joshua DeShaney, now is assigned to live out the remainder of his life profoundly retarded. Joshua and his mother, as petitioners here, deserve — but now are denied by this Court — the opportunity to have the facts of their case considered in the light of the constitutional protection that 42 U.S.C. §1983 is meant to provide.

Notes and Questions

1. *Rule and exceptions. DeShaney* holds that the government has no affirmative duty to protect a child from harm by private persons, even if the state is aware of that danger. Federal courts recognize two exceptions to *DeShaney*'s "no affirmative duty" rule.

a. *State-created danger. DeShaney* rejects the imposition of liability in part because the state played no part in the creation of the danger faced by Joshua DeShaney. Is the Court's rationale persuasive? Several federal courts have imposed liability based on a "state-created danger" exception, i.e., the state has placed the individual in a position of enhanced danger that he or she would not have faced. See, e.g., Currier v. Doran, 242 F.3d 905 (10th Cir. 2001); Omar v. Lindsey, 328 F. Supp. 2d 1287 (M.D. Fla. 2004).

b. *Custodial relationship. DeShaney* also contemplates another exception by recognizing that liability might attach "when the State takes a person into its custody and holds him there against his will." What examples does the Court provide of such custodial relationships? Why should liability be imposed for harm inflicted by private actors in these situations, according to the Court?

2. *Foster care relationship.* Do youth in foster care have a substantive due process right to be free from physical and emotional harm? According to *DeShaney*, the state owes a duty only to a child in state custody. Does *DeShaney* recognize the possibility that foster care might give rise to the state's affirmative duty to protect? In what ways does foster care constitute the requisite type of "custodial relationship"? How is it analogous to "incarceration, institutionalization or other similar restraints on personal liberty"? How is it distinguishable? See Michele Benedetto, An Ounce of Prevention: A Foster Youth's Substantive Due Process Right to Proper Preparation for Emancipation, 9 U.C. Davis J. Juv. L. & Pol'y 381, 402-403 (2005) (discussing meaning of "custodial" relationship for foster youth). Several federal circuits have recognized foster children's constitutional right to be protected by their foster caregivers. See Sharon Balmer, Comment, From Poverty to Abuse and Back Again: The Failure of the Legal and Social Services Communities to Protect Foster Children, 32 Fordham Urb. L.J. 935, 949 (2005) (citing the Second, Third, Fifth, Sixth, Seventh, Eighth, Tenth, Eleventh, and District of Columbia Circuits).

Should liability depend on whether the state has licensed the foster care facility or merely given the youth permission to remain in an informal foster care relationship with an unrelated family who agreed to care for him? See Nicini v. Morra, 212 F.3d 798 (3d Cir. 2000).

Courts are split as to the standard of liability to apply to such claims by foster children. Some courts apply a "deliberate indifference standard" (a gross negligence standard), while others apply a "professional judgment standard" (requiring a substantial departure from accepted professional standards). What should be the standard of liability when a foster care agency fails to protect a foster child from abuse? Which standard best protects children's interests without unduly burdening social services? See Laura A. Harper, Note, The State's Duty to Children in Foster Care — Bearing the Burden of Protecting Children, 51 Drake L. Rev. 793 (2003).

3. *School relationships.* Should the state be liable to protect a child from harm by private actors in educational settings? In what ways is the school context analogous to "incarceration, institutionalization or other similar restraints on personal

liberty"? In what ways is it distinguishable? Do compulsory attendance laws create the requisite custodial relationship?

4. *Voluntary v. nonvoluntary.* *DeShaney* contemplated a custodial relationship characterized by coercive restraint. Foster children may be placed in foster care pursuant to either a voluntary-placement agreement (by parental consent) or a court order. Should the state's liability to a foster child depend on the voluntary versus non-voluntary nature of the child's entry into foster care? See, e.g., Miracle v. Spooner, 978 F. Supp. 1161, 1169 (N.D. Ga. 1997) ("foster care will always constitute involuntary custody because the state does not give the child an alternative"). See generally Erwin Chemerinsky, Government Duty to Protect: Post-*DeShaney* Developments, 19 Touro L. Rev. 679 (2003); Michele Miller, Note, Revisiting Poor Joshua: State-Created Danger Theory in the Foster Care Context, 11 Hastings Women's L.J. 243 (2000).

5. *Privacy.* The *DeShaney* majority observes that the Due Process Clause invoked by plaintiffs to compel intrusion protects the family from unwarranted intervention. See also Joseph Goldstein et al., Before the Best Interests of the Child (1979) ("Too Early, Too Late, Too Much, or Too Little"). What is the proper constitutional balance between excessive and insufficient state intrusion, according to the majority? The dissent?

6. *Removal versus return.* Should governmental liability for a child's subsequently inflicted injuries depend on the agency's decision to *return* an abused child to the same home where the initial abuse occurred or to *transfer* the child to another placement (where the subsequently inflicted injury occurs)? See, e.g., S.S. ex rel. Jervis v. McMullen, 225 F.3d 960 (8th Cir. 2000) (en banc) (rejecting liability for state officials' return of abused child to her father's custody, knowing that he associated with a convicted pedophile who subsequently sexually assaulted her). See generally Bryan R. Berry, Note, Crime of Dispassion: Eighth Circuit (Mis)Applies *DeShaney* in Failing to Hold State Employees Accountable to the Children They Protect, 66 Mo. L. Rev. 881 (2001); Recent Case, Eighth Circuit Denies Liability for Returning Child in State Custody to Parent Despite Known Potential For Abuse, 114 Harv. L. Rev. 1653 (2001).

7. *Policy.* What should be the extent of social service workers' liability in child abuse cases? Should they be immune from suit? If so, in all case? Some? What are the advantages and disadvantages of conferring immunity?

Problem

An infant is taken into custody by the Virginia Department of Social Services after discovery by medical personnel that he and his older siblings are suffering from severe malnutrition. After the mother moves to Pennsylvania, a Virginia court returns custody of the boy to her, subject to supervision of the Philadelphia Department of Social Services. Nearly two years later, the four-year old (who weighs 13 pounds) is found to have suffered irreversible brain damage. The child, through a guardian ad litem, sues the Philadelphia authorities for damages allegedly caused by their failure to protect him from his mother. Did the Virginia agency's actions impose duties on the Philadelphia Department of Social Services that established a "special relationship" between the latter agency and the child? See McComb v. Wambaugh, 934 F.2d 474 (3d Cir. 1991).

c. Monitoring the Provision of Foster Care

■ MARISOL v. GIULIANI
929 F. Supp. 662 (S.D.N.Y. 1996)

Robert J. WARD, District Judge. . . .

Plaintiffs are eleven children all of whom have suffered, and some of whom continue to be at risk of, severe abuse and neglect. These children allege that defendants, who are officials with responsibility for the Child Welfare Administration of the City of New York (CWA) now renamed the New York City Administration for Children's Services (ACS), mishandled plaintiffs' cases and, through defendants' actions or inactions, deprived plaintiffs of their [rights under the state and federal constitutions], as well as under numerous federal and state statutes.

The factual allegations of the complaint portray a child welfare program in crisis and collectively suggest systemic deficiencies of gross proportions. . . .

Marisol A. is a five-year old who was born two days after her mother, Ms. A., was arrested on charges of dealing drugs. CWA placed Marisol with Ms. C. during and subsequent to Ms. A.'s incarceration but, in 1994, CWA restored Marisol to her mother's custody despite her criminal history and reports that she was abusing Marisol during visitations. CWA failed to assess properly the appropriateness of this placement and took no steps to supervise or monitor Ms. A.'s home. Upon regaining custody, Ms. A. confined Marisol to a closet for several months, deprived her of sustenance resulting in her eating her own feces and plastic garbage bags to survive, and both physically and sexually abused her to the point of injury. During this period, Ms. A.'s sister and Ms. C. filed multiple reports of abuse with CWA to no avail. . . . Despite Ms. C.'s eagerness to adopt Marisol, CWA has not begun the process of terminating Ms. A.'s parental rights and has not provided Marisol with counseling or support services.

Lawrence B. died on February 18, 1996 of AIDS-related illness at the age of nineteen. Lawrence's mother died of AIDS in or around 1985 leaving him an orphan and he entered the foster care system in 1995, at age seventeen, pursuant to a voluntary agreement signed by his aunt who could no longer care for him. After taking custody, CWA failed to assess Lawrence's medical condition for almost two months and then shuttled him from one inappropriate placement to another. . . .

Thomas C. is a fifteen-year old who has been in foster care since he was seven. In those eight years, Thomas endured numerous placements including a hospital, a diagnostic center, and a residential treatment center (RTC). In 1993, without adequate investigation, CWA approved Thomas' placement with Rev. D., a minister [who] sexually abused Thomas. He has since attempted suicide twice and has run away from the RTC only to return after facing hardship and abuse on the streets. CWA has failed to determine the appropriateness of the RTC placement, to pursue the possibility of adoption, or to provide Thomas with counseling. . . .

Ozzie E. is a fourteen-year old who suffers from seizure disorder, brain lesions, and behavioral problems. In 1995, Ozzie's father placed him in foster care after finding himself unable to care for Ozzie. Although Ozzie and his mother, Ms. E., both want to be reunited, he remains in a group home because CWA has failed to provide any family preservation services to enable Ms. E. to care for him. . . .

Brandon H. is a seven-year old who was placed in foster care at birth because his mother was twelve at the time and in foster care herself. In early 1992, CWA placed Brandon with Ms. W. but did not file a petition seeking termination of parental rights until later that year. The court terminated those rights in 1994 but, despite Ms. W.'s willingness to adopt him, CWA still has not even taken steps to transfer Brandon's case to the agency's adoption division. CWA thus allows Brandon to remain in foster care without addressing his need for permanency.

Steven I. is a sixteen-year old who has developed severe psychiatric and emotional problems after spending his entire life in foster care. Steven exhibits violent behavior and, by age twelve, Steven had attempted to rape a nine-year-old girl, had stabbed other children with pencils, and had lit several fires. After CWA ignored a recommendation that Steven receive long-term residential treatment, his behavior deteriorated to the point that, at age fifteen, he was committed to New York Hospital as a "sexual predator." Upon his release, CWA placed him in an inappropriate group home from which he ran away in 1994. He now lives on the streets and CWA has failed to locate him or to provide him with any treatment.

In support of their claims, plaintiffs specifically allege that defendants fail to: (1) appropriately accept reports of abuse and neglect for investigation; (2) investigate those reports in the time and manner required by law; (3) provide mandated preplacement preventive services to enable children to remain at home whenever possible; (4) provide the least restrictive, most family-like placement to meet children's individual needs; (5) provide services to ensure that children do not deteriorate physically, psychologically, educationally, or otherwise while in CWA custody; (6) provide children with disabilities, including HIV/AIDS, with appropriate placements; (7) provide appropriate case management or plans that enable children to return home or be discharged to permanent placements as quickly as possible; (8) provide services to assist children who are appropriate for adoption in getting out of foster care; (9) provide teenagers adequate services to prepare them to live independently once they leave the system; (10) provide the administrative, judicial, or dispositional reviews to which children are entitled; (11) provide caseworkers with training, support, or supervision; and; (12) maintain adequate systems to monitor, track, and plan for children.

[Plaintiffs bring this action pursuant to 42 U.S.C. §1983 seeking injunctive or declaratory relief and alleging violations of the Constitution, the Adoption Assistance and Child Welfare Act, Child Abuse Prevention and Treatment Act (CAPTA), and Americans with Disabilities Act.]

A. PLAINTIFFS' FEDERAL CONSTITUTIONAL CLAIMS . . .

Initially, the court agrees with defendants that those abused and neglected children not actually in ACS "custody" have no substantive due process right to be protected from harm under *DeShaney*.] The following analysis of plaintiffs' substantive due process claims, therefore, applies only to custodial plaintiffs. The issue facing this Court with respect to custodial plaintiffs [is not] whether they are entitled to protection from harm but, rather, how broad that protection must be. The Supreme Court has held that the right to be free from harm encompasses the right to essentials of care including adequate food, shelter, clothing, and medical attention. [Youngberg v. Romeo, 457 U.S. 307, 324 (1982).] Additionally, the state must provide reasonably safe conditions of confinement. Custodial plaintiffs, however, ask this Court to take an expansive view and recognize a substantive due process right to be free not only from physical harm but also from psychological, emotional, and developmental harm. Defendants, on the other hand, urge this Court to take a narrower approach to custodial plaintiffs' substantive due process claims.

The Court is inclined, at this juncture, to take a broad view of the concept of harm in the context of plaintiffs' substantive due process claims. Clearly, the state is required to protect children in its custody from physical injury. This Court further finds that custodial plaintiffs have a substantive due process right to be free from unreasonable and unnecessary intrusions into their emotional well-being. . . .

As a key element of their substantive due process claims, plaintiffs allege that defendants have violated "their right to be housed in the least restrictive, most appropriate and family-like placement." In support of their motions to dismiss, however, defendants argue that custodial plaintiffs do not have a Fourteenth Amendment due process right to the least restrictive, optimal level of care or placement and, therefore, that children who are kept in foster care longer than necessary or who are denied services to enable them to reunite with their families fail to state a claim.

Courts generally agree that the Fourteenth Amendment does not require the state to provide children in foster care with an optimal level of care or treatment. Thus, to the extent that custodial plaintiffs allege a substantive due process right to a least restrictive, optimal placement, their claims must be dismissed.

Individuals in state custody, however, do have a constitutional right to conditions of confinement which bear a reasonable relationship to the purpose of their custody. Courts have extended this right to the child welfare context. Doe v. New York City Dept. of Social Servs., 670 F. Supp. 1145, 1174 (S.D.N.Y. 1987). The goal of the child welfare system is "to further the best interest of children by helping to create nurturing family environments without infringing on parental rights." Id. Plaintiffs thus are entitled to conditions and duration of foster care which are reasonably related to this goal. . . .

This Court is satisfied that the right to be free from harm encompasses the right alleged by plaintiffs to appropriate conditions and duration of foster care. Indeed, the crux of plaintiffs' latter claim is that defendants' failure to provide safe and appropriate placements has caused them to suffer impermissible harm. Custodial plaintiffs have alleged sufficient facts to support the claim that they have been deprived of even adequate or appropriate conditions of foster care including certain basic necessities which defendants are obligated to provide. Thus, to the extent that custodial plaintiffs can establish that the conditions and duration of foster care are so inadequate as to violate plaintiffs' Fourteenth Amendment due process right to be free from harm, they are entitled to do so and defendants' motions to dismiss are denied.

Another key element of plaintiffs' substantive due process claims is the allegation that defendants have violated "their right not to be deprived of a family relationship absent compelling reasons." . . . The right to family integrity is derived both from the First Amendment's broad right of association and the Fourteenth Amendment's general substantive due process protections. . . . Although the Supreme Court has held the parent-child relationship to be constitutionally protected, courts nevertheless have been loathe to impose a constitutional obligation on the state to ensure a particular type of family life [for example, adoptive placement].

Plaintiffs in the instant case [challenge] defendants' general failure to provide services that function to preserve the family unit. Courts have held, however, that plaintiffs "do not have a constitutional right to rely on an agency to strengthen and reunite their families even if that agency has a statutory duty to do so." Dixey v. Jewish Child Care Assoc., 522 F. Supp. 913, 916 (S.D.N.Y. 1981) (citing Child v. Beame, 412 F. Supp. 593 (S.D.N.Y. 1976)). Thus, plaintiffs cannot argue that defendants have violated their right to family integrity and, to the extent that custodial plaintiffs allege a substantive due process right to associate with their biological family members, their claims must be dismissed.

Nevertheless, plaintiffs do have a constitutional right to protection from harm as noted above. Plaintiffs' family integrity claims are closely related to those pertaining to the duration of foster care and, by extension, fall within the concept of harm for substantive due process purposes. Indeed, plaintiffs suggest that defendants unnecessarily place children in foster care and allow children properly in foster care to languish without taking steps to reunite them with their biological family where appropriate. Once again, this Court is persuaded that plaintiffs have stated facts sufficient to support a claim. . . .

B. PLAINTIFFS' FEDERAL STATUTORY CLAIMS . . .

[Defendants request dismissal of plaintiffs' causes of action brought pursuant to various provisions of the Adoption Assistance Act, Multiethnic Placement Act, and CAPTA on the ground that these provisions do not provide for a private right of action.]

When deciding whether a private right of action exists to enforce a federal funding statute, courts are bound by any expression of clear intent on the part of Congress to create such a right. Where no unambiguous statement of intent exists, courts must determine if the statute creates enforceable rights, privileges, or immunities. [The Supreme Court has set forth factors for courts to consider: (1) whether the provision in question was intended to benefit plaintiff; (2) whether the provision "reflects merely a 'congressional preference' for a certain kind of conduct rather than a binding obligation on the governmental unit"; and (3) whether the asserted interest is so vague and amorphous as to be beyond the competence of the judiciary to enforce. Wilder v. Virginia Hosp. Assoc., 496 U.S. 498, 509 (1990).] Once these three factors have been met, the burden shifts to the state actor to show Congressional intent to [foreclose such private enforcement].

. . . Whether a private right exists to enforce provisions of the Adoption Assistance Act has been the subject of recent debate in both the judicial and legislative branches of government. In 1992, the Supreme Court considered whether a private individual could bring a §1983 claim to enforce §671(a)(15) of the Adoption Assistance Act. [In Suter v. Artist M., 503 U.S. 347, 364 (1992)], the Court held that §671(a)(15) [the "reasonable efforts requirement"] was too vague and amorphous to provide a cause of action under §1983 and that Congress did not intend "to create the private remedy sought by plaintiffs.". . . .

In 1994, however, Congress expressed its disapproval of the Supreme Court's decision in *Suter* and amended the [Social Security Act or SSA]. See 42 U.S.C. §§1320a-2 (1994) [hereinafter "Amendment"]. The Amendment states:

> In an action brought to enforce a provision of this chapter, such provision is not to be deemed unenforceable because of its inclusion in a section of this chapter requiring a State plan or specifying the required contents of a State plan. This section is not intended to limit or expand the grounds for determining the availability of private actions to enforce State plan requirements other than by overturning any such grounds applied in Suter v. Artist M., but not applied in prior Supreme Court decisions respecting such enforceability; provided, however, that this section is not intended to alter the holding in Suter v. Artist M. that section 671(a)(15) of this title is not enforceable in a private right of action.

Id. Plaintiffs argue that this Amendment is a clear expression of Congress' intent to create a private right of action to enforce provisions of the Adoption Assistance Act other than §671(a)(15). In the alternative, plaintiffs argue that the Amendment shows Congress' intent to reject the Supreme Court's reasoning in *Suter* and to require courts to return to the pre-*Suter* approach when deciding whether to recognize a private right of action to enforce provisions other than §671(a)(15). Defendants, however, stand by their reading of the import of *Suter*. They argue that not only did Congress preclude any private right to enforce §671(a)(15) but also that it left open to judicial construction whether plaintiffs can rely on §1983 to enforce the other provisions of the Adoption Assistance Act. Defendants urge this Court to apply the reasoning in *Suter* to plaintiffs' claims.

This Court does not read the Amendment as a clear expression of Congress' intent to create a private right of enforcement. Rather, this Court is persuaded that Congress has expressed its intent to require courts to apply pre-*Suter* case law to determine the private enforceability of SSA provisions other than §671(a)(15). Courts that recently have considered this issue have adopted this approach. . . . The Court must now apply the factors set forth in *Wilder* to decide whether plaintiffs are entitled to pursue their claims under §1983.

Plaintiffs allege violations of §622(b)(9) and of §627(a) and (b) of subchapter IV-B of the SSA. The Multiethnic Placement Act, §622(b)(9), sets forth as part of the requirements for federal funding that a state plan for child welfare services "provide for the diligent recruitment" of potential foster and adoptive parents who are racially and ethnically diverse. Of the other provisions relied upon by plaintiffs, §627(a) describes the foster care protections that the state must offer in order to gain additional payments and §627(b) outlines the further requirements the state must meet to avoid a reduction of its allotment. With respect to the first *Wilder* factor, both §§622 and 627 are intended to benefit the members of the proposed class of plaintiffs. Further, the language of these provisions is mandatory and sets forth the requirements that the state must meet to be eligible for funding, to gain additional funding, and to avoid a reduction in funding. The second *Wilder* factor thus is met. Finally, determining state compliance with these provisions is well within the abilities of the Court. None of these provisions is so vague or amorphous as to be beyond the competence of the Court to enforce.

[The court then held that plaintiffs alleged sufficient facts to support claims under SSA §671(a), subchapter IV-E, setting forth the requisite elements of a state foster care plan to qualify for federal funding.]

Plaintiffs further allege violations of two provisions of CAPTA which govern federal grants to states for child abuse and neglect prevention and treatment programs. The first, 42 U.S.C. §5106a(b)(2), requires a state, as a condition of federal funding, to initiate a prompt investigation into all reports of abuse or neglect and to take immediate steps to protect children whom the state believes have suffered or are at risk of suffering abuse or neglect. The second, 42 U.S.C. §5106a(b)(3), requires a state to have in effect administrative procedures, personnel, training procedures, facilities, and related programs and services "to ensure that the State will deal effectively with child abuse and neglect cases" in order to be eligible for federal funds.

Defendants again ask this Court to dismiss these claims on the ground that plaintiffs have no private right of action to enforce these statutes. Courts have differed in their interpretation of whether CAPTA creates rights enforceable by private individuals pursuant to §1983. Plaintiffs do not argue, as they did with respect to the Adoption Assistance Act, that there exists a well-established private right to enforce CAPTA. At the same time, defendants do not argue that Congress has expressed its intent to preclude private enforcement of the statute. Rather, the parties expect this Court to undertake a traditional *Wilder* analysis to determine whether plaintiffs are entitled to pursue these claims.

As to the first prong of *Wilder*, there is no dispute that the members of the proposed class of plaintiffs are the intended beneficiaries of the CAPTA provisions at issue. Moving to the second inquiry, [t]he statute sets forth clear conditions which the state must meet to qualify for a federal grant and does so through the use of mandatory and not precatory language. The sole area of contention is whether these CAPTA provisions meet the third *Wilder* prong or whether they are so vague and amorphous as to be beyond the enforcement power of the Court. . . .

Defendants argue that the language in §5106a(b)(2) requiring the state to conduct prompt investigations and to take immediate steps to protect children at risk is too ambiguous and that the Court, therefore, is not qualified to assess compliance. To the contrary, this Court certainly is competent to determine whether the state has made any efforts to comply with this provision. Further, the Court can look to professional standards to determine whether an investigation was properly and promptly initiated and whether the protective steps taken were appropriate. This provision, therefore, is not so vague as to be beyond the enforcement power of the Court. With respect to §5106a(b)(3), defendants do not cite any language from this provision as being too ambiguous to be enforced judicially. Accordingly, §5106a(b)(3) likewise survives the third prong of *Wilder*. Finally, defendants have not argued that Congress has precluded expressly private plaintiffs from pursuing §1983 claims alleging violations of CAPTA. [The court also held that plaintiffs alleged sufficient facts to support claims under the ADA and the Rehabilitation Act.]

Notes and Questions

1. *Epilogue.* A settlement was eventually reached in the *Marisol* litigation. The settlement required: (1) a two-year study of city and state child welfare systems by a national panel of experts who would provide recommendations for reform, (2) the establishment of a regional office of the Office of Children and Family Services in New York City to supervise child welfare services and file all fatality reports in a timely manner, (3) the implementation of a statewide computer

system to collect child welfare data, and (4) a review of state Central Register policies regarding screening of hotline calls. See Marisol v. Giuliani, 185 F.R.D. 152 (S.D.N.Y. 1999).

By the time the panel of experts (funded by the Annie E. Casey Foundation, a well-respected organization with expertise in the provision of foster care services) completed its work in 2000,

> the number of children in foster care had decreased by 18 percent over two years, and the number of newly admitted children had decreased nearly 24 percent. More families accused of abuse or neglect were being referred by ACS workers to preventive programs like counseling and drug treatment. And more kids were getting foster placements in their own neighborhoods, increasing the chances that they would stay in the same school and continue to see their families. At the same time, the panel found that the reforms hadn't helped reunify children with their families more quickly and that changes like better contracts between the city and private foster care agencies had yet to translate into improved casework.

Daphne Eviatar, Deep Impact: Lawyers Bent on Reforming Child Welfare Agencies Learn to Love their Inner Bureaucrat, 2004 Legal Aff. 51, 54 (Jan./Feb. 2004).

2. *AACWA*. Following federal reform efforts to enact the AACWA in 1980, many states received federal funds but without complying with federal requirements. Several class action suits were brought by foster children against state and local governments to enforce the act. This effort began with Lynch v. King, 550 F. Supp. 325 (D. Mass. 1982), *aff'd sub nom.* Lynch v. Dukakis, 719 F.2d 504 (1st Cir. 1983), in which a federal court for the first time recognized a private right of action against a state agency for the failure to comply with federal foster care requirements.

3. Suter *preclusion*. The Supreme Court brought a temporary halt to this promising avenue of enforcement in Suter v. Artist M., 503 U.S. 347 (1992) (holding that Congress did not confer a private right of enforcement requiring the state to make "reasonable efforts" to prevent a child from being removed from the home and to reunify the child with his family). Efforts continued, as *Marisol* reveals, to find other theories to reform the child welfare system. See generally Barbara L. Atwell, "A Lost Generation": The Battle for Private Enforcement of the Adoption Assistance and Child Welfare Act of 1980, 60 U. Cin. L. Rev. 593 (1992); Jim Moye, City Hall Can Be Beaten: Litigation Strategies for Child and Family Advocates Under the Adoption and Safe Families Act of 1997, 4 J.L. Fam. Stud. 303 (2002).

4. *Other reform litigation*. Reformers attempted to remedy many state child welfare systems. See Timothy Arcaro, Florida's Foster Care System Fails Its Children, 25 Nova L. Rev. 642, 682 (2001) (noting that "There are at least twenty-seven states and many more localities presently ordered by a court to improve child welfare services"). Child welfare reformers often avoid *Suter* preclusion by instituting suits under other federal and state constitution grounds, other federal statutory causes of action, state statutes, and local regulations. See, e.g., Ocean v. Kearney, 123 F. Supp.2d 618 (S.D. Fla. 2000) (recognizing a private cause of action under a different AACWA provision, §671(a)(16)); K.J. v. Division of Youth & Family Serv., 363 F. Supp.2d 728 (D.N.J. 2005) (denying defendants' motion to dismiss claims under §1983, the state child welfare statute, and the state tort claims act). See generally Sara J. Klein, Note, Protecting the Rights of Foster Children: Suing Under §1983 to Enforce Federal Child Welfare Law, 26 Cardozo L. Rev. 2611 (2005).

5. *Assessment of "impact litigation." Marisol* was the most significant of the child welfare class action lawsuits. Does impact litigation, such as *Marisol*, hinder reform efforts in any way? What are the benefits and shortcomings of shifting control over the child welfare system from elected government officials to judges? See Ross Sandler & David Schoenbrod, Democracy by Decree: What Happens When Courts Run Government? (2004); Anthony M. Bertelli & Laurence E. Lynn, Jr., A Precept of Managering Responsibility: Securing Collective Justice in Institutional Reform Litigation, 29 Fordham Urb. L.J. 317 (2001) (arguing that federal courts should abstain from institutional reform cases "when the institutional defendant is governed by a precept of managerial responsibility").

In contrast to the approach in many child welfare reform lawsuits (for example, in Washington, D.C., Connecticut, and Kansas City, Mo.), the *Marisol* settlement did not call for federal court oversight. Rather, the settlement provided that the plaintiffs would not reinstate their lawsuit if the state child welfare agency made "good faith efforts" at reform. What do you think of such an approach? When should federal courts get involved in public agency reform? When should they allow public administrators to manage their own agencies, as Bertelli & Lynn, supra, suggest? In *Marisol*, the plaintiffs also requested that the court order the state child welfare system into receivership. Is this private-sector creditor's remedy appropriate? What problems does it pose?

Further, foster care systems historically have been managed by the government using public funds. There has been a recent trend, however, to privatize certain functions that were formerly performed by government. Might foster care systems be more effectively administered by private companies? What problems might ensue from this approach? See generally Martha Minow, Public Values in an Era of Privatization: Public and Private Partnerships: Accounting for the New Religion, 116 Harv. L.Rev. 1229 (2003). See generally Sarah Hultman Dunn, The Marisol A. v. Giuliani Settlement: "Innovative Resolution" Or "All-Out Disaster?," 35 Colum. J.L. & Soc. Probs. 275 (2002).

6. *Abstention*. Reformers in Florida filed a class action suit in federal court alleging that state authorities violated the constitutional rights of foster children due to the welfare system's widespread shortcomings. Bonnie L. ex rel. Hadsock v. Bush, 180 F. Supp. 2d 1321 (S.D. Fla. 2001). The court dismissed the case based on the abstention doctrine, reasoning that the federal litigation would have interfered with an ongoing state court proceeding in which the plaintiffs would have the opportunity to raise their claims. When is abstention appropriate? Inappropriate? Is it sound policy? See Nora Meltzer, Note, Dismissing the Foster Children: The Eleventh Circuit's Misapplication and Improper Expansion of the *Younger* Abstention Doctrine in Bonnie L. v. Bush, 70 Brooklyn L. Rev. 635 (2004).

7. *Pew Commission*. In May 2004, the Pew Commission (a national nonpartisan panel funded by the Pew Charitable Trusts) issued a report on foster care reform. Among its recommendations, the report emphasized the need to improve (1) judicial processing of child welfare cases by adopting court performance measures to improve tracking and analyzing caseloads and to identify procedural problems such as inadequate representation that result in frequent delays in case processing, and (2) the federally mandated self-assessment review (Child and Family Service Reviews) process that assesses states' compliance with federal requirements (e.g., by the use of more comprehensive measures to evaluate the

well-being of children receiving in-home services and foster care). See generally Sarah Ramsey, Fixing Foster Care or Reducing Child Poverty: The Pew Commission Recommendations and the Transracial Adoption Debate, 66 Mont. L. Rev. 21 (2005).

8. *Recent issues*. Recent litigation focuses on remedying the abuse suffered by foster children as well as the number of placements they experience. See, e.g., Joel A. v. Giuliani, 218 F.3d 132 (2d Cir. 2000) (class action suit seeking relief for bias-related victimization); Braam v. State, 81 P.3d 851 (Wash. 2002) (class action suit to reduce number of placements for foster children). What are various ways of addressing these problems?

9. *The* Wilder *Litigation*. In the book, The Lost Children of Wilder: The Epic Struggle to Change Foster Care (2001), journalist Nina Bernstein explores the shortcomings of New York City's foster care system through a presentation of the life stories of Shirley Wilder and her son. Wilder was a 13-year-old abused, runaway, African-American plaintiff in a class action suit, initiated in 1973, that challenged the constitutionality of the religious matching provision that resulted in preferential foster care placements for Jewish and Catholic children. See Wilder v. Bernstein, 645 F. Supp. 1292 (S.D.N.Y. 1986) (approving consent decree), *aff'd*, 848 F.2d 1338 (2d Cir. 1988).

The settlement in Marisol v. Giuliani (the principal case herein) also ended the *Wilder* lawsuit (securing equal access to foster care placement), and incorporated some of the *Wilder* requirements. On the same day of the *Wilder* settlement and in the same courthouse, another class action suit (Reynolds v. Giuliani, 118 F. Supp. 2d 352 (S.D.N.Y. 2000)) was filed that challenged some of the city's newly implemented welfare practices. Ironically, and unbeknownst to the plaintiff's attorneys, the plaintiff in that suit was Shirley Wilder's grandson.

d. Permanent Disposition: Termination of Parental Rights

(i) Standard of Proof

■ SANTOSKY v. KRAMER
455 U.S. 745 (1982)

Justice BLACKMUN delivered the opinion of the Court. . . .

Under New York law, the State may terminate, over parental objection, the rights of parents in their natural child upon a finding that the child is "permanently neglected." The New York Family Court Act §622 requires that only a "fair preponderance of the evidence" support that finding. Thus, in New York, the factual certainty required to extinguish the parent-child relationship is no greater than that necessary to award money damages in an ordinary civil action. . . . The question here is whether New York's "fair preponderance of the evidence" standard is constitutionally sufficient.

Petitioners John Santosky II and Annie Santosky are the natural parents of Tina and John III. In November 1973, after incidents reflecting parental neglect, respondent Kramer, Commissioner of the Ulster County Department of Social Services, initiated a neglect proceeding under Fam. Ct. Act §1022 and removed

Tina from her natural home. About 10 months later, he removed John III and placed him with foster parents. On the day John was taken, Annie Santosky gave birth to a third child, Jed. When Jed was only three days old, respondent transferred him to a foster home on the ground that immediate removal was necessary to avoid imminent danger to his life or health.

In October 1978, respondent petitioned the Ulster County Family Court to terminate petitioners' parental rights in the three children. [When petitioners challenged the "preponderance" standard,] [t]he Family Court Judge rejected this constitutional challenge, and weighed the evidence under the statutory standard. While acknowledging that the Santoskys had maintained contact with their children, the judge found those visits "at best superficial and devoid of any real emotional content." After deciding that the agency had made "'diligent efforts' to encourage and strengthen the parental relationship," he concluded that the Santoskys were incapable, even with public assistance, of planning for the future of their children. The judge later held a dispositional hearing and ruled that the best interests of the three children required permanent termination of the Santoskys' custody. [Petitioners unsuccessfully appealed.]

Last Term in Lassiter v. Department of Social Services, 452 U.S. 18 (1981), this Court [held] that the Fourteenth Amendment's Due Process Clause does not require the appointment of counsel for indigent parents in every parental status termination proceeding. The case casts light, however, on the two central questions here — whether process is constitutionally due a natural parent at a State's parental rights termination proceeding, and, if so, what process is due. . . .

The fundamental liberty interest of natural parents in the care, custody, and management of their child does not evaporate simply because they have not been model parents or have lost temporary custody of their child to the State. Even when blood relationships are strained, parents retain a vital interest in preventing the irretrievable destruction of their family life. If anything, persons faced with forced dissolution of their parental rights have a more critical need for procedural protections than do those resisting state intervention into ongoing family affairs. When the State moves to destroy weakened familial bonds, it must provide the parents with fundamentally fair procedures.

In *Lassiter*, the Court and three dissenters agreed that the nature of the process due in parental rights termination proceedings turns on a balancing of the "three distinct factors" specified in Mathews v. Eldridge, 424 U.S. 319, 335 (1976): the private interests affected by the proceeding; the risk of error created by the State's chosen procedure; and the countervailing governmental interest supporting use of the challenged procedure. . . . Evaluation of the three *Eldridge* factors compels the conclusion that use of a "fair preponderance of the evidence" standard in [termination] proceedings is inconsistent with due process.

"The extent to which procedural due process must be afforded the recipient is influenced by the extent to which he may be 'condemned to suffer grievous loss.'" Whether the loss threatened by a particular type of proceeding is sufficiently grave to warrant more than average certainty on the part of the factfinder turns on both the nature of the private interest threatened and the permanency of the threatened loss.

Lassiter declared it "plain beyond the need for multiple citation" that a natural parent's "desire for and right to 'the companionship, care, custody, and management of his or her children'" is an interest far more precious than any property right. 452 U.S., at 27 quoting Stanley v. Illinois, 405 U.S., at 651. When the State initiates a parental rights termination proceeding, it seeks not merely to infringe that fundamental liberty interest, but to end it. . . . Thus, the first *Eldridge* factor — the private interest affected—weighs heavily against use of the preponderance standard at a state-initiated permanent neglect proceeding. . . .

[T]the factfinding hearing pits the State directly against the parents. The State alleges that the natural parents are at fault. The questions disputed and decided are what the State did—"made diligent efforts,"—and what the natural parents did not do—"maintain contact with or plan for the future of the child." The State marshals an array of public resources to prove its case and disprove the parents' case. Victory by the State not only makes termination of parental rights possible; it entails a judicial determination that the parents are unfit to raise their own children.[10]

[U]ntil the State proves parental unfitness, the child and his parents share a vital interest in preventing erroneous termination of their natural relationship. Thus, at the factfinding, the interests of the child and his natural parents coincide to favor use of error-reducing procedures. . . .

Under Mathews v. Eldridge, we next must consider both the risk of erroneous deprivation of private interests resulting from use of a "fair preponderance" standard and the likelihood that a higher evidentiary standard would reduce that risk. . . . In New York, the factfinding stage of a state-initiated permanent neglect proceeding bears many of the indicia of a criminal trial. . . . The State, the parents, and the child are all represented by counsel. The State seeks to establish a series of historical facts about the intensity of its agency's efforts to reunite the family, the infrequency and insubstantiality of the parents' contacts with their child, and the parents' inability or unwillingness to formulate a plan for the child's future. The attorneys submit documentary evidence, and call witnesses who are subject to cross-examination. [T]he judge then determines whether the State has proved the statutory elements of permanent neglect by a fair preponderance of the evidence.

At such a proceeding, numerous factors combine to magnify the risk of erroneous factfinding. Permanent neglect proceedings employ imprecise substantive standards that leave determinations unusually open to the subjective values of the judge. [T]he court possesses unusual discretion to underweigh probative facts that might favor the parent. Because parents subject to termination proceedings are often poor, uneducated, or members of minority groups, such proceedings are often vulnerable to judgments based on cultural or class bias.

The State's ability to assemble its case almost inevitably dwarfs the parents' ability to mount a defense. No predetermined limits restrict the sums an agency may spend in prosecuting a given termination proceeding. The State's attorney usually will be expert on the issues contested and the procedures employed at the

---

10. The Family Court judge in the present case expressly refused to terminate petitioners' parental rights on a "non-statutory, no-fault basis." Nor is it clear that the State constitutionally could terminate a parent's rights *without* showing parental unfitness. See Quilloin v. Walcott, 434 U.S. 246, 255 (1978) ("We have little doubt that the Due Process Clause would be offended '[i]f a State were to attempt to force the breakup of a natural family, over the objections of the parents and their children, without some showing of unfitness and for the sole reason that to do so was thought to be in the children's best interest,'" quoting Smith v. Organization of Foster Families, 431 U.S. 816, 862-863 (1977) (Stewart, J., concurring in judgment)).

factfinding hearing, and enjoys full access to all public records concerning the family. The State may call on experts in family relations, psychology, and medicine to bolster its case. Furthermore, the primary witnesses at the hearing will be the agency's own professional caseworkers whom the State has empowered both to investigate the family situation and to testify against the parents. Indeed, because the child is already in agency custody, the State even has the power to shape the historical events that form the basis for termination.[13]

The disparity between the adversaries' litigation resources is matched by a striking asymmetry in their litigation options. Unlike criminal defendants, natural parents have no "double jeopardy" defense against repeated state termination efforts. If the State initially fails to win termination, as New York did here, it always can try once again to cut off the parents' rights after gathering more or better evidence. Yet even when the parents have attained the level of fitness required by the State, they have no similar means by which they can forestall future termination efforts.

Coupled with a "fair preponderance of the evidence" standard, these factors create a significant prospect of erroneous termination. A standard of proof that by its very terms demands consideration of the quantity, rather than the quality, of the evidence may misdirect the factfinder in the marginal case. . . .

Raising the standard of proof would have both practical and symbolic consequences. . . . An elevated standard of proof in a parental rights termination proceeding would alleviate "the possible risk that a factfinder might decide to [deprive] an individual based solely on a few isolated instances of unusual conduct [or] . . . idiosyncratic behavior." Addington v. Texas, 441 U.S., at 427. "Increasing the burden of proof is one way to impress the factfinder with the importance of the decision and thereby perhaps to reduce the chances that inappropriate" terminations will be ordered. Ibid.

The Appellate Division approved New York's preponderance standard on the ground that it properly "balanced rights possessed by the child . . . with those of the natural parents. . . ." 427 N.Y.S.2d, at 320. By so saying, the court suggested that a preponderance standard properly allocates the risk of error *between* the parents and the child. That view is fundamentally mistaken.

The court's theory assumes that termination of the natural parents' rights invariably will benefit the child.[15] Yet we have noted above that the parents and the child share an interest in avoiding erroneous termination. Even accepting the court's assumption, we cannot agree with its conclusion that a preponderance standard fairly distributes the risk of error between parent and child. Use of that standard reflects the judgment that society is nearly neutral between

---

13. In this case, for example, the parents claim that the State sought court orders denying them the right to visit their children, which would have prevented them from maintaining the contact required by Fam. Ct. Act §614.1.(d). The parents further claim that the State cited their rejection of social services they found offensive or superfluous as proof of the agency's "diligent efforts" and their own "failure to plan" for the children's future. . . .

15. This is a hazardous assumption at best. Even when a child's natural home is imperfect, permanent removal from that home will not necessarily improve his welfare. See, e.g., Wald, State Intervention on Behalf of "Neglected" Children: A Search for Realistic Standards, 27 Stan. L. Rev. 985, 993 (1975) ("In fact, under current practice, coercive intervention frequently results in placing a child in a more detrimental situation than he would be in without intervention").

Nor does termination of parental rights necessarily ensure adoption. Even when a child eventually finds an adoptive family, he may spend years moving between state institutions and "temporary" foster placements after his ties to his natural parents have been severed.

erroneous termination of parental rights and erroneous failure to terminate those rights. For the child, the likely consequence of an erroneous failure to terminate is preservation of an uneasy status quo. For the natural parents, however, the consequence of an erroneous termination is the unnecessary destruction of their natural family. A standard that allocates the risk of error nearly equally between those two outcomes does not reflect properly their relative severity.

Two state interests are at stake in parental rights termination proceedings — a parens patriae interest in preserving and promoting the welfare of the child and a fiscal and administrative interest in reducing the cost and burden of such proceedings. A standard of proof more strict than preponderance of the evidence is consistent with both interests.

. . . As parens patriae, the State's goal is to provide the child with a permanent home. Yet while there is still reason to believe that positive, nurturing parent-child relationships exist, the parens patriae interest favors preservation, not severance, of natural familial bonds. . . . We cannot believe that it would burden the State unduly to require that its factfinders have the same factual certainty when terminating the parent-child relationship as they must have to suspend a driver's license. [Without deciding the outcome under a constitutionally proper standard], we vacate the judgment of the Appellate Division and remand the case for further proceedings not inconsistent with this opinion. . . .

Justice REHNQUIST, with whom THE CHIEF JUSTICE, Justice WHITE, and Justice O'CONNOR join, dissenting.

. . . New York has created an exhaustive program to assist parents in regaining the custody of their children and to protect parents from the unfair deprivation of their parental rights. And yet the majority's myopic scrutiny of the standard of proof blinds it to the very considerations and procedures which make the New York scheme "fundamentally fair." . . .

The three children to which this case relates were removed from petitioners' custody [pursuant to New York's procedures] and in response to what can only be described as shockingly abusive treatment.[10]

[P]etitioners received training by a mother's aide, a nutritional aide, and a public health nurse, and counseling at a family planning clinic. In addition, the plan provided psychiatric treatment and vocational training for the father, and counseling at a family service center for the mother. Between early 1976 and the final termination decision in April 1979, the State spent more than $15,000 in these efforts to rehabilitate petitioners as parents.

Petitioners' response to the State's effort was marginal at best. They wholly disregarded some of the available services and participated only sporadically in

---

10. Tina Apel, the oldest of petitioners' five children, was removed from their custody by court order in November 1973 when she was two years old. Removal proceedings were commenced in response to complaints by neighbors and reports from a local hospital that Tina had suffered injuries in petitioners' home including a fractured left femur, treated with a home-made splint; bruises on the upper arms, forehead, flank, and spine; and abrasions of the upper leg. The following summer, John Santosky III, petitioners' second oldest child, was also removed from petitioner's custody. John, who was less than one year old at the time, was admitted to the hospital suffering malnutrition, bruises on the eye and forehead, cuts on the foot, blisters on the hand, and multiple pin pricks on the back. Jed Santosky, the third oldest of petitioners' children, was removed from his parents' custody when only three days old as a result of the abusive treatment of the two older children.

the others. As a result, and out of growing concern over the length of the children's stay in foster care, the Department petitioned in September 1976 for permanent termination of petitioners' parental rights so that the children could be adopted by other families. Although the Family Court recognized that petitioners' reaction to the State's efforts was generally "non-responsive, even hostile," the fact that they were "at least superficially cooperative" led it to conclude that there was yet hope of further improvement and an eventual reuniting of the family. Accordingly, the petition for permanent termination was dismissed. [In October 1978, the agency again filed a termination proceeding because petitioners had made few efforts to take advantage of social services or to visit their children.]

[T]he State's extraordinary 4-year effort to reunite petitioners' family was not just unsuccessful, it was altogether rebuffed by parents unwilling to improve their circumstances sufficiently to permit a return of their children. At every step of this protracted process petitioners were accorded those procedures and protections which traditionally have been required by due process of law. . . . It is inconceivable to me that these procedures were "fundamentally unfair" to petitioners. . . . The interests at stake in this case demonstrate that New York has selected a constitutionally permissible standard of proof.

On one side is the interest of parents in a continuation of the family unit and the raising of their own children. The importance of this interest cannot easily be overstated. Few consequences of judicial action are so grave as the severance of natural family ties. . . . On the other side of the termination proceeding are the often countervailing interests of the child. A stable, loving homelife is essential to a child's physical, emotional, and spiritual well-being. . . .

In addition to the child's interest in a normal homelife, "the State has an urgent interest in the welfare of the child." Lassiter v. Department of Social Services, 452 U.S., at 27. Few could doubt that the most valuable resource of a self-governing society is its population of children who will one day become adults and themselves assume the responsibility of self-governance. . . .

When, in the context of a permanent neglect termination proceeding, the interests of the child and the State in a stable, nurturing homelife are balanced against the interests of the parents in the rearing of their child, it cannot be said that either set of interests is so clearly paramount as to require that the risk of error be allocated to one side or the other. Accordingly, a State constitutionally may conclude that the risk of error should be borne in roughly equal fashion by use of the preponderance-of-the-evidence standard of proof. . . .

Notes and Questions

1. *Standard.* According to *Santosky*, the minimum standard of proof in termination cases is clear and convincing evidence. States may require a higher standard. See generally Linda Lee Reimer Stevenson, Comment, Fair Play or a Stacked Deck?: In Search of a Proper Standard of Proof in Juvenile Dependency Hearings, 26 Pepp. L. Rev. 613 (1999). Should they do so?

2. *Criticisms.* Does the clear-and-convincing standard adequately protect the rights of abused children? Adequately protect family autonomy? Ensure that children spend lengthy periods in foster care? See Sharon B. Hershkowitz, Due Process and the Termination of Parental Rights, 19 Fam. L.Q. 245, 292-295 (1985).

3. *Scope.* How far does the *Santosky* standard extend? To restrictions on parental rights that fall short of complete termination? See In re R.W., 10 P.3d 1271 (Colo. 2000) (requiring only preponderance standard when parental rights were limited by guardianship. To a termination hearing following a parent's voluntary relinquishment of a child? See Coleman v. Smallwood, 800 S.W.2d 353, 356 (Tex. Ct. App. 1990) (requiring clear and convincing evidence).

4. *Stages.* Termination of parental rights proceedings generally involve two stages: an initial stage at which the court makes a determination of unfitness (the "unfitness stage") and a subsequent stage at which the court determines whether termination would be in the child's best interests (sometimes called "the best interests stage"). (*Santosky* refers somewhat differently to the stages of a child neglect proceeding, pursuant to New York statute, as "the fact-finding hearing" at which the state is required to prove permanent neglect and "the dispositional hearing" at which the court determines which placement is in the child's best interests.) These stages may occur in a single hearing.

Although *Santosky* requires the clear-and-convincing standard before termination of parental rights, many states reason that *Santosky* applies only to the initial determination of unfitness and therefore adopt different standards of proof for the best interests stage. Brian C. Hill, Comment, The State's Burden of Proof at the Best Interests Stage of a Termination of Parental Rights, 2004 U. Chi. Legal F. 557, 559 (2004). Is a heightened standard appropriate at this subsequent stage? See, e.g., In re D.T., 818 N.E.2d 1214 (Ill. 2004) (adopting preponderance-of-the-evidence standard for best interests stage). What light does *Santosky* shed on this question?

5. *Presumptions.* In response to ASFA's emphasis on speedier termination of parental rights, many states adopted statutes providing that a parent is presumed unfit following a conviction for aggravated battery or attempted murder of *any* child (including a sibling). Do these statutory presumptions raise constitutional concerns? See Florida Dept. of Children & Families v. F.L., 880 So. 2d 602 (Fla. 2004) (holding that statutory rebuttable presumption terminating parental rights when rights to a sibling have been terminated impermissibly shifts burden of proof to show a lack of substantial risk of harm to current child); In re D.W., 827 N.E.2d 466 (Ill. 2005) (application of mandatory conclusive presumption of unfitness violates equal protection).

6. *Parent's right to counsel.* The Supreme Court examined the parent's right to counsel in termination of parental rights proceedings in Lassiter v. Department of Social Services, 452 U.S. 18 (1981). The Court rejected the argument that procedural due process requires the appointment of counsel for indigent parents. Applying a case-by-case balancing test, the Court weighed (1) the state's and parent's shared interest in the accuracy of the decision; (2) the cost of providing indigent parents with counsel; (3) the state's interest in informal procedures; (4) the complexity of the issues; (5) the incapacity of the indigent parent; and (6) the risk of error. The Court held that, although petitioner had not made a sufficient showing of these factors, in a case in which the parent's interests were especially high and the state's interests were particularly low, due process might require the appointment of counsel. Is *Santosky* consistent with *Lassiter*?

Despite the Supreme Court's holding in *Lassiter*, many states guarantee indigent parents the right to counsel in parental termination proceedings. Trisha M. Anklam, The Price of Justice: In Light of *LaVallee*, What Should Massachusetts

Courts Do When Attorneys Are Not Available to Represent Indigent Parents Involved in Care and Protection Matters?, 32 N. Eng. J. on Crim. & Civ. Confinement 111, 112 (2006). Are indigent parents' due process rights violated by the lengthy delays that often ensue when attorneys are not appointed promptly after the initiation of a termination of parental rights proceeding? See In re M.J.M.L., 31 S.W.3d 347 (Tex. Ct. App. 2000) (holding that mother's due process rights were not violated by the failure to appoint an attorney until six months after the suit was filed).

_____

Child welfare reform in the 1970s revolved around concerns with "foster care drift," that is, children who were removed from their biological parents but who remained in foster care for years. Reformers' efforts culminated in 1980 in the AACWA (p. 979) with its twin goals of family reunification or, alternatively, more x-ref rapid termination of parental rights to free children for adoption. However, commentators are raising provocative questions about the wisdom of severance of the parent-child tie, as the following excerpt reveals.

■ MARSHA GARRISON, PARENTS' RIGHTS v. CHILDREN'S INTERESTS: THE CASE OF THE FOSTER CHILD
22 N.Y.U. Rev. L. & Soc. Change 371, 373-374, 379, 384, 394-395 (1996)

The perception that parents do make "uniquely valuable contributions" to their child's development has led children's advocates to favor retention of traditional parental prerogatives in most contexts. [In contrast, in the case of foster care], advocates have here argued in favor of faster and easier termination of the parent-child relationship. A comparison of the divorce and foster care literature illustrates the difference in approach: In divorce, the child's relationship with a noncustodial parent is almost invariably described as a positive factor in her development that should be encouraged and facilitated; termination of the parental relationship is approved only in extreme cases where the parent threatens the child's health or safety. In foster care, however, the noncustodial parent is typically seen as a threat to the child's relationship with her foster parent or her opportunity to obtain adoptive parents; termination of parental rights is urged whenever the child's return home cannot be accomplished quickly.

[F]rom the child's perspective, divorce and long-term foster care placement are not obviously different. In both contexts, the child's relationship with a noncustodial parent is maintained through visitation and sporadic contact rather than a day-to-day relationship. In both contexts, the child has another parent, or parent-figure, who provides day-to-day care and to whom the child is likely to be deeply attached. In both contexts, the day-to-day parent and the noncustodial parent may cooperate or, alternatively, express hostility and compete for the child's love.

Parents whose children enter foster care are less likely to exhibit capable parenting than those who divorce, but the available evidence does not suggest that parental capacity affects the strength of the parent-child relationship. As John Bowlby, one of our foremost developmental psychologists, has put it, "[t]he attachment of children to parents who by all ordinary standards are very bad parents is a never-ceasing source of wonder to those who seek to help them."

[W]hile foster care and divorce are clearly different and we lack research providing direct comparisons, there is much to suggest that, from the perspective of the child, these two situations present more similarities than differences. In each case, a parental attachment must be maintained through visitation rather than day-to-day contact. . . .

Decades of research have also established that a child's ties to his parents do not lose their importance simply as a result of separation or loss of day-to-day contact. "The parent-child tie . . . can be greatly distorted [but it] is not to be expunged by mere physical separation." . . . An absent parent remains important to the child because the parental relationship is a primary source of the child's identity and self-esteem. . . . The parent also represents the child's history and his unique biological inheritance. Even children adopted at birth often wish to learn about their biological parents. . . .

Rather than resolving the child's relationship with a parent from whom the child is separated, loss of contact thus has the potential consequence of making such a resolution far more difficult. Parental absence may enhance the child's tendency toward self-blame or exaggeration; the child may idealize the absent parent, blame herself for disruption in the relationship, or exaggerate the parent's flaws. Such extreme responses impede the child's ability to effectively mourn her loss and maintain her self-esteem. Loss of contact may also inhibit the child's ability to form a realistic assessment of her situation and current, realistic relationships. . . .

[Garrison proposes an alternative to traditional adoption: preservation of parental visitation postadoption.] Adoption's powerful symbolism not only obscures the very real benefits that this solution confers on the taxpayer, but it imposes direct costs on the children we intend to help. The positive future symbolized by an adoption order inexorably darkens the past and stigmatizes both the child's former parents and identity. Her acceptance of a new family implies abandonment of her biological family and the death of her old self. . . . Many older foster children cannot face such a loss, and even those who are willing to do so pay a heavy price: The past can be buried, but it cannot be erased. The attempt to wipe away the past may also cause more harm than good. . . . The price of adoption's symbolic benefits is neglect of the child's real emotional needs. . . .

Divorce law today potentially affects all children while child welfare law is reserved for those who are poor. The result is a class-based divide — in advocacy, theory, and law — that assumes real differences in children's pain based essentially on the receipt of public benefits. We have expected poor children, and only poor children, to gratefully sacrifice their past lives in order to obtain the benefits it suits us to provide. In the process, we have further stigmatized the lives of the children for whom foster placement will be inevitable, and subjected many of them to the further impermanence of "revolving door" care.

But the emotional lives of poor children are not different from those of the more fortunate. Their parents are equally significant. Their need for evidence of parental love and for opportunities for reconciliation are just as great. For most, loving foster or adoptive parents will not, any more than stepparents, erase the ties that bind parent and child. . . .

(ii) Reasonable Efforts Requirements

■ STATE EX REL. CHILDREN'S SERVICES DIVISION v. BRADY
899 P.2d 691 (Or. Ct. App. 1995)

HASELTON, Judge.

Michelle Brady appeals from a judgment terminating her parental rights to her daughter.[1] We review de novo, and reverse.

The issue here is whether a mentally impaired mother lacks the capacity to care for her special needs child. [Michelle's daughter] was born two months prematurely on April 21, 1993. She weighed only two-and-a-half pounds at birth and suffered from life-threatening medical conditions, including severe heart and lung problems. Because of those conditions, child spent the first 15 weeks of her life in the neonatal intensive care unit. . . .

Mother was 18 when child was born. She was, and is, a person of low average intelligence, who exhibits certain mental and psychological difficulties. . . . She was a runaway in her early teens, dropped out of school in the eleventh grade, and experienced a series of abusive relationships, including, most recently, with father. Mother met father in 1990, when she was homeless, and their relationship was volatile and periodically violent.

Despite the instability in her life, mother visited child at the hospital daily, spending hours with her. Mother met with the nursing staff to discuss child's special needs, and expressed her commitment and determination to learn and to be a good parent. Nonetheless, following an altercation between mother and father, which required the intervention of hospital security, hospital staff became concerned that the parents might be incapable of meeting child's needs and, consequently, contacted [Children's Services Division or CSD].

[W]hen child was six weeks old, a CSD intake investigator contacted mother and father to determine if they could care for child on her release from the hospital. After the initial interview, the investigator recommended that the couple attend psychological evaluations and CSD-sponsored men's and women's domestic violence groups. CSD did not offer mother any other assistance or training in parenting a special needs child.[3]

At CSD's insistence, Dr. James Ewell conducted a psychological examination of mother. [He] learned that she had sustained substantial head injuries, including a contusion to the front part of her brain, in an automobile collision when she was 14. Immediately after that collision, mother had experienced a seizure in the emergency room and had been hospitalized for 11 days. After being released from the hospital, she had continued to experience seizures and was placed on appropriate medication. Nonetheless, mother had continuing problems with concentration, memory, and vision, and had experienced blackouts and anxiety attacks.

Ewell also administered several diagnostic tests, which indicated that mother had low average intelligence and impaired empathy, problem solving, and psychological sensitivity. Based on those results and the interview, Ewell concluded that

---

1. The judgment also terminated the parental rights of child's father. He does not appeal.
3. Mother attended the CSD women's violence group between September 1993, and August 1994, but her participation was sporadic.

mother has an irreversible condition known as organic personality syndrome with passive-aggressive features. . . . Ewell concluded that mother lacked the skills to care for child on her release from the hospital:

> . . . I do not believe [mother's] current psychological condition would allow her to commit to taking adequate care of her daughter. I do not believe she would be able to adequately assess [child's] needs, or respond appropriately in times of emergency. Her learning ability and follow through seem to be impaired. I also doubt that [mother] would be able to adequately manage her anger so that [child] would not be exposed to domestic violence. At the time of this assessment, [mother] had not yet demonstrated an ability to maintain a home setting that would be adequate for her daughter's specialized care.
>
> In many ways, [mother] must be seen as an adolescent who herself is still in need of parenting. Her problem-solving abilities, "common sense," and psychological sensitivities are impaired. She will probably require extended assistance and guidance in establishing herself as an adult. Her ability to parent a "fragile infant, who will require very specialized care" would seem to be severely lacking. I therefore could not recommend that [child] be sent to live with [mother] once the child is released from the hospital.
>
> *Prior to [mother] assuming responsibility for her daughter, I believe she will need to complete anger management classes, parenting classes and additional educational programs designed to increase her skills and abilities. She may also need to live with [child] in a foster home-like setting, wherein an experienced and responsible adult caregiver can provide constant supervision/ guidance.* Long-term psychotherapy for [mother] would also be indicated at this time.

(Emphasis supplied.)

[Following Ewell's evaluation, CSD petitioned the circuit court to assume jurisdiction. The court did so and placed the child in the care of Erika Hatzel, a foster parent with experience in caring for medically needy infants.] After child was placed in foster care, mother's access and interaction was limited to two one-hour supervised visits per week at CSD's offices. Mother attended all visitations on time, without fail, and made up the ones that were canceled because of child's periodic health problems. While there, mother used all of the available time to play with child, and child appeared to enjoy being with mother.

In October 1993, CSD requested that Margaret Veltman of the BASE program assess the parents' skills and abilities. [Veltman] concluded: "[Mother and father] are young parents who show an obvious interest in parenting their infant, but who, despite their efforts, are currently unable to meet her needs for interaction. The [child] is a medically fragile, premature infant who will require very specialized care if she is expected to thrive and reach normalcy." Veltman did not, however, specifically assess mother's "task solving" ability to discern and respond to child's special needs.

[After] receiving Veltman's report, CSD decided to petition for termination of the parents' rights. At that time, child was eight months old. Once CSD made that decision, it offered neither parent any further assistance or support in acquiring the skills needed to care for their special needs child. In particular, CSD never offered the educational and training assistance identified in Ewell's report. As the CSD caseworker explained, CSD "did not feel the parents were capable with their limitations to parent this child in the foreseeable future and, therefore, we did not offer further services at that point."

. . . Despite CSD's lack of assistance — or perhaps because of it — mother, on her own initiative, undertook a variety of "self-help" efforts to improve her life generally and her capability as a parent, particularly. Mother (1) contacted the Young Parents Program (administered by a local church) and began individual counseling, as well as parenting classes that included infant CPR; (2) took substantial steps to terminate her relationship with father, including obtaining a restraining order against him; (3) pursued a course of study towards attaining a general equivalency diploma; and (4) provided volunteer services at a senior center.

The termination hearing was held in October 1994. At that time, child was 18 months old. Her medical condition had improved, but her coloration, chest, and breathing still needed to be checked three to four times a day. Child walked with difficulty and still did not speak in any identifiable fashion. She continued to be an "extremely fussy" child who woke up several times each night, was uncomfortable with strangers and was extremely sensitive to noise.

[F]ive aspects of the termination hearing are especially pertinent: First, CSD relied almost exclusively on the Ewell and Veltman evaluations to establish mother's present and future incapacity to care for child. Ewell's report had been generated 16 months earlier; Veltman's, 10 months earlier. Although Ewell defended his original diagnosis, Veltman conceded that she was not capable of rendering an informed opinion as to mother's ability to care for child at the time of the hearing or in the foreseeable future.

Second, Robert Carter, [mother's counselor at the Young Parents Program,] disputed Ewell's diagnosis of an organic personality syndrome. . . . In Carter's view, mother's stress disorder was amenable to treatment. Although Carter testified that it would take mother at least two years to overcome her condition, he believed that she had made substantial progress in handling stress, managing her anger, and developing self worth, and that, with continued treatment, the likelihood of overcoming the effects of her stress syndrome would improve "immeasurably."

With particular reference to mother's ability to care for child, Carter acknowledged that mother had poor organizational skills, which could materially impair her ability to care for a child with diverse special needs. However, Carter testified that mother's organizational deficits were related to her post-traumatic stress disorder and that, as the symptoms of that disorder abated through treatment, mother's organizational skills were improving and would continue to improve.

Third, child's pediatrician, Michael Eustis, testified as to her current medical condition. Eustis stated that, although child's heart and lung problems were "by and large resolving," they would still require careful monitoring, which could not be reduced to a "checklist" form. Eustis observed that, although child's medical problems were decreasing, her developmental needs would increase in the future. He was, however, unable to describe those future needs with particularity. . . .

Fourth, mother testified simply, but cogently, about child's special needs and her ability to meet those needs. Under searching cross-examination, her responses were clear, direct, and thoughtful.

Fifth, and finally, CSD did not present any evidence of an imminent, compelling need to terminate mother's rights, rather than maintaining the status quo, including continuing foster care. There was no evidence that child was immediately adoptable, or that her prospects for adoption would be materially prejudiced if mother's rights were not immediately terminated. Indeed, Eustis testified that, on a one to ten scale of adoptability, with ten being highly adoptable, child is a "two." The CSD case worker concurred that she "would have to really do some recruiting" to find a suitable adoptive family. . . .

The trial court granted CSD's petition [basing] termination on a variety of alternative grounds, including not only mother's inability to provide care because of her mental deficiency, but also mother's "lack of effort . . . to make return of the child possible"; mother's failure to provide, or attempt to provide, "care, attention, and love"; mother's failure to pay a reasonable portion of child's medical care and foster care; and mother's "failure to implement a plan designed to lead to the integration of the child into the parent's home."

[W]e disagree. . . . Our disposition rests, ultimately, on the conjunctive character of the state's burden under ORS 419B.504. The state must prove, by clear and convincing evidence, that a parent is presently unable to meet a child's needs, and that "integration of the child into the home of the parent . . . is improbable in the foreseeable future due to conduct or conditions not likely to change."

Here, the question of mother's present ability to meet child's needs is close and difficult. . . . However, regardless of mother's present capabilities, the state failed to prove by clear and convincing evidence that child's integration into mother's home is "improbable in the foreseeable future due to . . . conditions . . . not likely to change." ORS 419B.504.

Mother has never had a meaningful opportunity to develop and demonstrate parenting skills. Child remained in the hospital after birth and was placed directly in foster care. Thereafter, mother's contact with her was limited. . . .

CSD's principal evaluator, Ewell, acknowledged that, with appropriate guidance and training, mother might ultimately assume primary responsibility for child. Nonetheless, except for referring mother to the women's violence group, CSD never provided such assistance. . . . Mother's circumstances are analogous to those in State ex rel. Juv. Dept. v. Chapman, 631 P.2d 831 (1981), which reversed a termination order because, in part, "CSD had offered no services, suggestions, encouragement, training, or any advice of any kind to the parents to enable them to develop skills to care for the child properly." Indeed, mother's position is more compelling than that of the parents in *Chapman*, because here CSD's retained expert, Ewell, recommended that mother be given such assistance, and CSD disregarded that recommendation.

Given those circumstances, mother's commitment to child, and her undeniable determination to be a good parent, we are not "'independently satisfied that the conduct and conditions of the mother are not likely to change.'" *Pennington*, 799 P.2d 694 (Or. Ct. App. 1990) (quoting State ex rel. Juv. Dept. v. Wyatt, 34 Or. App. 793, 798, 579 P.2d 889, rev. den., 283 Or. 503 (1978)). In both *Pennington* and *Wyatt*, we granted parents "second chances" by reversing termination orders, because the parents had begun to make progress and were "entitled to a chance to show it is permanent." Here, mother has never been given even a first chance. She deserves that opportunity. . . .

(iii) The Significance of Emotional Attachment

■ IN RE GUARDIANSHIP OF J.C.
608 A.2d 1312 (N.J. 1992)

HANDLER, J. . . .

A.C., who was born in Colombia and came to this country as a teenager, is the natural mother of three children. Two girls, J.C. and J.M.C., were born in July 1983 and in January 1985, respectively, and J.C., a boy, was born in August 1986. A.C. voluntarily placed her two girls in foster care with the Division of Youth and Family Services (DYFS) in August 1985. The children were returned to her after three months. Almost a year later, in October 1986, A.C. again placed the two girls, along with her new child, J.C., in foster care, where they have remained for the past five and a half years.

A.C. began unsupervised weekend visits with her children soon after their placement in foster care, seeing them regularly twice a month during the following year. Although DYFS had intended to reunite the family, in November 1987 the agency stopped unsupervised visits out of concern that the children were not being properly cared for. DYFS also came to believe that A.C. was addicted to drugs and was being abused by her husband (who, she claims, was not the father of any of the children). However, bi-monthly visits at the DYFS office continued. In April of the following year, A.C. entered drug treatment. By November 1988 the agency concluded that the children could not be returned successfully and that preparation should be initiated for their permanent placement and adoption.

[The agency filed a petition seeking termination of A.C.'s parental rights. The court concluded that termination was in the best interests of the children, even though A.C. had not, as a matter of law, abandoned the children. A.C. appealed.]

[A] trial court should make [specific findings] before it terminates parental rights. The first finding is that the child's health and development have been or will be seriously impaired by the parental relationship. Secondly, the court must conclude that the parents are unable or unwilling to eliminate the harm and that a delay in permanent placement will add to the harm. Third, the court should be convinced that alternatives to terminating parental rights have been thoroughly explored and exhausted, including sufficient efforts made to help the parents cure the problems that led to the placement. Fourth, all of those considerations must inform the determination that termination of parental rights will not do more harm than good. . . .

When the child's biological parents resist the termination of their parental rights, the court's function will ordinarily be to decide whether the parents can raise their children without causing them further harm. In most cases proofs will focus on past abuse and neglect and on the likelihood of it continuing. However, the cornerstone of the inquiry is not whether the biological parents are fit but whether they can cease causing their child harm. The analysis of harm entails strict standards to protect the statutory and constitutional rights of the natural parents. The burden falls on the State to demonstrate by clear and convincing evidence that the natural parent has not cured the initial cause of harm and will continue to cause serious and lasting harm to the child. . . .

[T]he bulk of the evidence addressed the issue of harm to the children emanating from the prospect of their being removed from their respective foster parents and returned to their mother. Most of the evidence related to the older girl, J.C.

The DYFS social workers and the psychologist who evaluated J.C. concurred that she was a child with serious emotional problems and potentially-significant learning disabilities. Nonetheless, Ms. Rodriguez testified that J.C. "[was] doing very well [in a new home, that of Mr. and Mrs. D., her foster parents] since July of this year. She [was] well adjusted. She has done remarkably well, especially in school where she has been so behind." Referring to the report of Dr. Paul Kennedy, a child psychiatrist, the witness stated, "[J.C.] is able to attach and trust someone again. And she is very bonded to this new caretaker." . . .

John Frederickson, [the guardian ad litem] submitted a report in which he "found that [J.C.] is very attached to Mr. & Mrs. [D.] as well as Nicole [Mr. D.'s daughter by an earlier marriage]." He noted further, "J.C. indicated that she is very happy here and wished Mr. & Mrs. [D.] to be 'her mommy and daddy' and wants very much to live with them and have Nicole as her sister." . . .

After receiving Mr. Frederickson's report, the court requested a "bonding evaluation between the children and their respective foster parents" from a court psychologist, Regina Johnson. With respect to J.C., Ms. Johnson concluded:

> [J.C.] is most definitely bonded with the [D] family. She is expressive and stated, "I love them a lot, I want to stay with them — they are nice to me." [S]eparation from the [D's] would be detrimental to this child's emotional and physical well-being. . . . Further separation will leave permanent scars.

The evidence relating to the younger child, J.M.C., was not as extensive [but it indicated bonding with her foster family as well]. [The court psychologist] recommended expressly that there be a "termination of parental rights." . . .

[On remand,] the parties stipulated to several facts about A.C.'s rehabilitation. With respect to her housing situation, they agreed that she was living in the same apartment in which she had been living since December 1989. Concerning her work, they agreed that she had a steady job, that she had been working there for the previous two years, and that there was on-site after school child care at her workplace. Finally the parties "stipulated" that A.C. asserted that she was drug and alcohol free and that DYFS had no evidence to suggest otherwise. . . .

Dr. Matthew Johnson testified on behalf of A.C. He found a strong and enduring bonded relationship between J.C. and A.C. He believed "erasing" the biological mother from the child's life would cause the child serious emotional harm, particularly regarding the child's identity and development in adolescence. . . . There was much less focus during the second trial on the younger child, J.M.C. Dr. Johnson found that she had significant relationships with both her foster mother and her natural mother. However, he was not able to say conclusively that there was bonding in either case. . . .

The critical question is whether termination of parental rights is justified under the broad statutory standard of section 15(c) and section 20 predicated on the best interests of the child. [W]e are compelled by the record as it currently stands to conclude that there is not clear and convincing evidence to support the findings necessary to terminate parental rights. . . .

As the contrasting opinions of the experts in this case illustrate, there are competing psychological theories of the effects of parental bonding. In large measure, the variances in their recommendations derive from different assumptions concerning the fragility versus resiliency of the child psyche. Those who . . . urge the wider use of psychological parenting theory see children as highly vulnerable and fragile. Their psyches are easily injured by traumatic events and those injuries can adversely shape their subsequent development. See Goldstein, Freud & Solnit, [Beyond the Best Interests of the Child 33 (1973)]. In contrast, others, presumably like Dr. Johnson, posit more flexibility in children, arguing that attachments "support the development of independence." Change under the right circumstances can play a positive role in children's development. Indeed, a good deal of recent literature on the subject argues that psychological parenting theory overestimates the importance of continuity in care in relation to other factors that affect child development, such as the quality of care children receive. See Marsha Garrison, Why Terminate Parental Rights?, 35 Stan. L. Rev. 423, 458-59 (1983). In addition, experts and commentators differ over the importance of ongoing relationships between children and their natural parents. Although natural parents can be a disruptive influence for children who have been adopted, some commentators and psychologists believe that trying to eliminate the natural parents from the children's lives and memory is impossible, and therefore wrong.

Moreover, there are the grave pitfalls that may be encountered in the application of otherwise sound psychological parenting and bonding theories. Scholars and some courts suggest that theories of parental bonding may be relied on too often to keep children in foster care rather than return them to their parents.

In addition, the uncritical use of bonding theory can increase the risk of institutional bias. That risk may be reflected in attitudes that tilt the process in favor of the agency and its social workers and foster parents. The theories of bonding also may be misused to determine only which set of parents is optimum or even "better" in some vague social sense, rather than capable of rearing the child without serious harm.

Further, to keep termination proceedings based on bonding theory focused on whether the children have a reasonable opportunity for stable and continuous development may be difficult. Termination of parental rights does not always result in permanent placement of the child. . . .

The tangles and snares that surround bonding theory are evident in this case. Important testimony was presented by DYFS employees and valuable information by the guardian. They furnished probative evidence establishing empirically the affection and strength of the relationship of the children with their respective foster parents. However, they were not qualified to express opinions concerning psychological bonding and the harmful consequences to the children from its disruption. . . . The primary support for the trial court's decision came from Ms. Regina Johnson. [H]er testimony revealed that she had little or no formal training in conducting bonding evaluations or comprehensive knowledge of the relevant scientific literature. Nor did she have an opportunity to evaluate A.C. or her relationship with the children. . . .

A.C.'s expert, Dr. Johnson was qualified. His testimony in part supported the conclusion that a strong bond existed between the children and their respective adoptive parents. . . . Nevertheless, we are unable to say here that Dr. Johnson's conclusion that there was a strong relationship between the children and their adoptive parents demonstrated that serious harm would ensue if the children were returned to their mother. . . . Weighing the potential harm that terminating J.C.'s relationship with her mother against that which might come from removing her from her foster home is painfully difficult, but it is a decision that necessarily requires expert inquiry specifically directed to the strength of each relationship.

We thus conclude that there is not clear and convincing evidence to support the determination to terminate A.C.'s parental rights. That does not mean, however, that termination may not be an appropriate resolution. [W]e remand to the trial court in order that additional evidence may be adduced directly addressing whether the two children have bonded with their foster parents and if so whether breaking such bonds would cause the children serious psychological or emotional harm. . . . A.C. should be allowed visitation with the children sufficient to enable the experts to consider those relationships. . . .

Notes and Questions on *Brady* and *J.C.*

1. *Federal mandate.* Every state has statutory provisions authorizing the permanent removal of an endangered child from the home. Before termination of parental rights, however, the state must provide rehabilitation services, including reunification efforts. Federal legislation (AACWA) mandates the provision of these services. 42 U.S.C. §§620 et seq., 670 et seq. (2000). Some state statutes contained "reasonable efforts requirements" prior to the enactment of the AACWA, but the AACWA triggered widespread adoption of these requirements.

2. *Approaches.* States adopt different approaches to the "reasonable efforts" requirement. Some states expressly require the child welfare agency to prove that it has made reasonable efforts to rehabilitate the parent as a condition precedent to termination of parent rights. Other states hold that "reasonable efforts" is a factor to be considered in termination determinations. David J. Herring, Inclusion of the Reasonable Efforts Requirements in Termination of Parental Rights Statutes: Punishing the Child for the Failure of the State Child Welfare System, 54 U. Pitt. L. Rev. 139, 172-175 (1992). Significantly, if a given statute requires rehabilitation services, a parent may interpose the defense that the state failed to fulfill its statutory mandate prior to termination of parental rights. Is the "reasonable efforts" requirement constitutionally compelled?

3. *"Reasonable efforts" defined.* What constitutes "reasonable efforts"? Because neither the AACWA nor many state statutes define the term, courts interpret whether the provision of certain services satisfies the requirement. Cases have held that reasonable efforts have been satisfied by housing assistance; the provision of day care, medical or legal services; treatment for substance abuse or domestic violence; and counseling. See, e.g., Dvorak v. S.H., 624 N.W.2d 678 (N.D. 2001); In re Rysene W., 2001 WL 861923 (Conn. Super. Ct. 2001).

4. *Exceptions.* Are "reasonable efforts" required when they are likely to be futile? ASFA removed the "reasonable efforts" requirement in cases in which (1) the child has been the victim of aggravated circumstances, such as torture, abandonment, or sexual abuse; (2) the parent has killed another child or attempted to do so; or (3) the state has terminated the parent's rights with respect to a sibling. 42 U.S.C.

§§671(a)(15)(D)(I), (ii), (iii) (2000). Are there any other circumstances when the provision of "reasonable efforts" would be likely to be futile?

5. *Special contexts.* What services did the state offer in *Brady*? Did those services constitute "reasonable efforts"? In *Brady*, the state's attempt to provide reasonable efforts was complicated by the mother's mental disability. What does "reasonable efforts" mean in the context of mentally disability? See also In re Welfare of Children of A.O., 2006 WL 619109 (Minn. Ct. App. 2006); In re Christopher B., 823 A.2d 301 (R.I. 2003). See also Susan Kerr, The Application of the Americans with Disabilities Act to the Termination of Parental Rights of Individuals with Mental Disabilities, 16 J. Contemp. Health L. & Pol'y 387 (2000).

6. *Time-limited services.* How much time must the state devote to providing "reasonable efforts" before terminating parental rights? ASFA currently emphasizes the time-limited nature of rehabilitation services, restricting services to those provided within a 15-month period following placement of a child into foster care. 42 U.S.C. §629a(b) (2000). Is this period sufficient to provide meaningful services? See Will L. Crossby, Defining Reasonable Efforts: Demystifying the State's Burden Under Federal Child Protection Legislation, 12 B.U. Pub. Int'l L.J. 259, 292 (2003).

7. *Duration in foster care.* ASFA requires that states must seek termination of parental rights for any child who has been in foster care for 15 of the last 22 months. 42 U.S.C. §675(5)(c)(2000). This "15/22 provision" is subject to three exceptions: if a child is living in kinship foster care, if a state agency has determined that termination would not be in the child's best interests, and if a state agency has failed to provide family reunification services.

Does the time spent in foster care justify a reduction in, or elimination of, the state's requirement to use "reasonable efforts"? See, e.g., In re S.J.J., 104 P.3d 74 (Wyo. 2005) (state need not meet "reasonable efforts" requirement in termination proceedings based on child's duration in foster care). Is a child's stay in foster care an appropriate indicator of parental unfitness? Does such a statutory presumption violate a parent's right to due process? See In re Ty M., 655 N.W.2d 672 (Neb. 2003). Should the time period differ for younger versus older children? See Joseph Goldstein et al., Before the Best Interests of the Child 46 (1979) (advocating a shorter period for children under age three).

8. *Policy.* Does termination of parental rights provide the optimum way to achieve permanence for those children in long-term foster care with no immediate prospect of returning to parents? What alternatives ought to be considered to serve the best interests of such children? Do you agree with Professor Marsha Garrison, supra p. 988, that states should allow continued visitation by biological parents? Does inclusion of "reasonable efforts" requirements before termination inflict harm on children by creating insurmountable obstacles to the termination of parental rights, as some commentators argue? Compare Elizabeth Bartholet, Nobody's Children: Abuse and Neglect, Foster Drift, and Adoption Alternative (1999) (arguing that the state should be more aggressive in removing children from their biological families and placing them for adoption), with Martin Guggenheim, Somebody's Children: Sustaining the Family's Place in Child Welfare Policy, 113 Harv. L. Rev. 1716 (1999) (book review rebutting Bartholet's assumptions and conclusions).

9. *Parental substance abuse.* As illustrated in *J.C.*, mothers whose babies are born with symptoms of drug addiction may experience difficulty regaining custody, even after the mothers stop using drugs. Why? Does ASFA provide enough help for drug-addicted parents? What does "reasonable efforts" mean in the context of parental substance abuse? See generally Maxine Eichner, Children, Parents, and the State: Rethinking Relationships in the Child Welfare System, 12 Va. J. Soc. Pol'y & L. 448, 468-469 (2005); Sharon G. Elstein, Children Exposed to Parental Substance Abuse: The Impact, 34 Colo. Law. 29 (2005); Mary O'Flynn, Comment, The Adoption and Safe Families Act of 1997: Changing Child Welfare Policy Without Addressing Parental Substance Abuse, 16 J. Contemp. Health L. & Pol'y 243, 260-261 (1999).

10. *Emotional attachment.* Can a child's attachment to foster parents alone be a sufficient ground for termination of a biological parent's rights? See Frank J. Dyer, Termination of Parental Rights in Light of Attachment Theory: The Case of Kaylee, 10 Psychol. Pub. Pol'y & L. 5 (2004) (advocating adoption by long-term caretakers even though birth parents may have been rehabilitated). Would such an approach be constitutional? What does *Santosky* suggest? If a child's emotional attachment to foster parents is not a sufficient ground for termination, may it at least provide a reason to limit the "reasonable efforts" requirement? See In re E.R., 688 N.W.2d 384 (N.D. 2004).

Problem

Bobby B. is removed from home and placed in foster care when he is two years old during a crack-cocaine binge of his single mother. Several months later, Bobby's HIV-infected mother decides that she wants his return so that she can spend her remaining time with him. To achieve this goal, she completes parenting classes and a drug rehabilitation program, as ordered by the Juvenile Court. She has not yet found employment, as directed by the court, because she is participating in a job-training program to achieve that goal.

The year is 2020; Congress has repealed the Adoption Assistance and Child Welfare Act, which required states to seek family preservation and reunification when possible and to hold "permanency planning" hearings within 18 months of children's removal. The governing statute merely requires "reasonable efforts" to unite biological families. As a court-appointed guardian ad litem, you have learned that, although Bobby had regular supervised visits with his mother, he has bonded with his foster mother and father and regards them as his psychological parents. The foster parents have asked to adopt Bobby, an outcome supported by the state Department of Family Welfare because of Bobby's mother's prognosis. In deciding how to handle Bobby's case, you must address the following questions posed by the judge: Should a child in a loving foster home be put through a wrenching separation when the parent seeking return is likely to die or become seriously ill? Alternatively, is time with a parent so important to a child's identity that it should override other considerations? What result? See Felicia R. Lee, Difficult Custody Decisions Being Complicated by AIDS, N.Y. Times, Mar. 4, 1995, at 1, 16.

C. CHILDREN'S AUTONOMY?

The parental autonomy principle entitles parents to speak for children. In child abuse and neglect proceedings, the state as parens patriae asserts its interest on behalf of children. When can children speak for themselves?

1. Emancipation

■ STATE v. C.R. & R.R.
797 P.2d 459 (Utah Ct. App. 1990)

JACKSON, J. . . . .

In October 1984, R.R., nearly fifteen, left his parents' home and lived with various relatives. In the spring of 1985, a petition was filed with the juvenile court alleging that R.R. was a dependent child. See Utah Code Ann. §78-3a-16(1)(c) (1987); Utah Code Ann. §78-3a-2(20) (1987). When R.R.'s mother admitted the allegations in July 1985, the juvenile court found R.R. to be dependent within the meaning of the statute and temporarily awarded legal custody of R.R. to the Utah Department of Family Services (DFS). . . . In October 1986, the temporary order terminated and custody of R.R. was awarded to his parents, to be supervised by DFS until June 1987.

The State filed a petition against R.R.'s parents in the fall of 1988 . . . , seeking reimbursement of $1,159.06 in support for R.R. expended by the State during the period of January 1985 through October 10, 1986. Relying on the common law doctrine of emancipation, R.R.'s parents contested the petition and claimed that their duty to support R.R. was terminated in October 1984 when he voluntarily left their home to live elsewhere and live a lifestyle of which they disapproved. According to the parents' unrefuted testimony, they never ordered R.R. to leave. They were willing to support him in their own home along with his younger siblings if he would agree to abide by their rules. R.R. left to reside elsewhere, they testified, because he refused to accept their condition that he give up his homosexual lifestyle. In response, the State argued that R.R.'s parents had not met their burden of proving emancipation because there was no evidence R.R. was financially independent or that he was able to provide his own residence. The State also argued that R.R. had not left home voluntarily because his parents had forced him to leave the household.

[In this case and another, the juvenile court declined to apply the doctrine of emancipation.] The basic issue presented in these appeals is whether the juvenile court erroneously concluded that the doctrine of emancipation is not a part of the law in Utah. This ruling involves a question of law . . .

In American law, judicial emancipation refers to the nonstatutory termination of certain rights and obligations of the parent-child relationship during the child's minority. Katz, Schroeder & Sidman, Emancipating Our Children — Coming of Legal Age in America, 7 Fam. L.Q. 211, 214 (1973) (hereinafter Katz).

As a result of statutory and common law developments, the American parent is generally held responsible for his child's financial support, health, education, morality, and for instilling in him respect for people and authority. To facilitate the performance of these obligations, the parent is vested with the custody and control of the child, including the requisite disciplinary authority. And, under a heritage of the past, the parent is also entitled to the child's services, and, by derivation, to his or her earnings. When a child is adjudicated a fully emancipated minor, these reciprocal rights and responsibilities are extinguished and are no longer legally enforceable: the emancipated child is thus legally treated as an adult. Although apparently undeveloped at English common law, the doctrine of emancipation has been described as a "basic tenet of family law" in this country, applied by American courts since the early nineteenth century. . . . In several nineteenth century decisions, the fact that a minor voluntarily abandoned the parent's home to pursue a life free from parental control was alone considered sufficient to support a finding of emancipation that terminated the parent's duty of support. As a result, third parties who subsequently furnished necessaries to the minor could not recover from the parent, even in the absence of evidence that the minor was either capable of self-support or had actually supported himself.

[T]he doctrine of emancipation continues to be an accepted part of the common law in this country. [On remand, the trial court should articulate the factors relevant to showing emancipation, determine whether the parents established that their sons were emancipated, and decide whether application of the doctrine would conflict with any Utah law, such as those providing parental support duties.]

Notes and Questions

1. *Common law emancipation.* The doctrine of emancipation ends certain disabilities of minority even before the age of majority. Correlatively, it releases parents from certain obligations to their minor children. Thus it allows minors to free themselves from parental control before adulthood. See generally Sanford N. Katz et al., Emancipating Our Children — Coming of Legal Age in America, 7 Fam. L.Q. 211 (1973). Such issues often arise in postdivorce litigation because, absent an agreement or decree to the contrary, emancipation generally ends child support. See, e.g., Garrison v. Garrison, 147 S.W.3d 925 (Mo. Ct. App. 2004). Even parental agreements might not prove conclusive here, however, because parents cannot bargain away their children's support rights. E.g., Patetta v. Patetta, 817 A.2d 327, 330 (N.J. Super. Ct. App. Div. 2003); Riggins v. O'Brien, 559 S.E.2d 673, 675 (Va. 2002).

2. *Case law criteria.* What factors should a court use to determine emancipation? Courts often consider financial independence; living away, especially with parental consent; and creation of new relationships inconsistent with a subordinate role in the parents' family, such as marriage. See, e.g., Young v. Young, 654 N.E.2d 880 (Ind. Ct. App. 1995). Compare Purdy v. Purdy, 578 S.E.2d 30 (S. C. Ct. App. 2003) (pregnancy, cohabitation, and employment insufficient if minor not self-supporting), with Caldwell v. Caldwell, 823 So. 2d 1216, 1221 (Miss. Ct. App. 2002) (child's "adult decisions," such as becoming pregnant, help show emancipation). Traditionally, enlistment in the military triggered emancipation. Today, courts hold enrollment in a military service academy meets the test because the program is inconsistent with parental control. E.g., Bishop v. Bishop, 671 A.2d 644 (N.J. Super. Ct. Ch. Div. 1995).

3. *Statutory criteria.* Some states have codified the criteria for emancipation. For example, under California's Emancipation of Minors Act, marriage, active duty in the armed forces, or a judicial declaration emancipates a person under 18. Cal.

Fam. Code §7002 (West 2004). To obtain a judicial declaration of emancipation, a minor must petition the court, setting forth that he or she is at least 14 years old, willingly living apart from parents with their acquiescence, managing his or her own financial affairs (shown by an attached declaration of income and expenses), and has no income derived from criminal activity. Id. at §7120(b). The Court must grant the petition if it finds the minor has met these requirements "and that emancipation would not be contrary to the minor's best interest." Id. at §7122(a). Why does California specify the age of 14? Cf., e.g., Kan. Stat. Ann. §§38-108 through 38-109 (2000) (no age specified); Va. Code Ann. §16.1-331 (2003) (16th birthday). For the history of California's legislation, see Carol Sanger & Eleanor Willemsen, Minor Changes: Emancipating Children in Modern Times, 25 U. Mich. J.L. Reform, 239, 250-263 (1992).

4. *Consequences.* Emancipation confers adult status for many legal purposes, such as parental support; control over earnings; and the capacity to enter into a binding contract, make a will, establish a residence, and enroll in school. See Cal. Fam. Code §7050 (West 2004). See also, e.g., Va. Code Ann. §16.1-334 (2003). Notwithstanding emancipation, however, some prerogatives (for example, driver's license, voting) come only with the attainment of a certain age. Why?

5. *Parental role.* Who must initiate the child's departure from home for emancipation to occur? In some states, the child must initiate the departure because otherwise parents could "'divorce their children' and avoid paying child support simply by sending their children away to live with a third party or, worse yet, just throwing the child out of the house." Dunson v. Dunson, 769 N.E.2d 1120, 1124 (Ind. 2002). Some authorities, however, say that the parent's intent controls. E.g., Randolph v. Randolph, 8 S.W.3d 160, 164 (Mo. Ct. App. 1999); Foxvog v. Foxvog, 578 N.W.2d 916, 919 (Neb. Ct. App. 1998). Yet disobeying parental authority, without good cause, triggers emancipation. Compare Commissioner of Soc. Servs. v. Jones-Gamble, 643 N.Y.S.2d 182 (App. Div. 1996), with Weigert v. Weigert, 699 N.Y.S.2d 597 (App. Div. 1999). Who decides whether parent or child caused the "breakdown"? See also Roe v. Doe, 272 N.E.2d 567 (N.Y. 1971). On remand in *C.R.*, must the court determine whether R.R. or his parents initiated his departure from home? The principal case, in reviewing early precedents, refers to the minor's "voluntarily" leaving the parental home.

California's statute, supra, contemplates "the consent or acquiescence of the minor's parents or legal guardians." Cal. Fam. Code §7120(b)(2) (West 2004). In a study based on interviews with 18 minors in the San Francisco Bay Area, Professors Carol Sanger and Eleanor Willemsen found "an unexpected level of adult participation in almost all aspects of the decision-making process," although the California statute contemplates a child-initiated process. Sanger & Willemsen, supra, at 271. They concluded that, in most cases, adults initiated and influenced the child's decision to become emancipated; the quick and simple process "involves no significant investigation of the minors' living circumstances or best interests"; most minors and their parents experience significant conflict before emancipation; and, for the minors, "[l]ife after emancipation is often precarious and lonely, and the decision to become emancipated is regarded with ambivalence." Id. at 297.

6. *Gay youth.* Of what relevance to the question of R.R.'s emancipation is the family disagreement about his "homosexual lifestyle"? The family conflict precipitating R.R.'s departure from home is not uncommon. Empirical studies show a substantial number of gay youths running away or otherwise becoming homeless.

See Gabe Kruks, Gay and Lesbian Homeless/Street Youth: Special Issues and Concerns, 12 J. Adolescent Health 515 (1991); Gary Remafedi, Adolescent Homosexuality: Psychosocial and Medical Implications, 79 Pediatrics 331 (1987). See also Sonia Renee Martin, A Child's Right to be Gay: Addressing the Emotional Maltreatment of Queer Youth, 48 Hastings L.J. 167, 176-177 (1996).

7. *Public assistance.* The juvenile court found R.R. "dependent" (statutorily defined to include "a minor who is homeless or without proper care through no fault of [the minor's] parent, guardian, or custodian," Utah Code Ann. §78-3a-103 (Supp. 2005)). Does this designation and the award of temporary custody to the Department of Family Services preclude a finding of emancipation on remand? Suppose R.R. left home but relied on public assistance for support? Does the availability of public assistance undermine parental autonomy by allowing a child to become "emancipated" from parental control without becoming self-supporting? Compare, e.g., Dowell v. Dowell, 73 S.W.3d 709 (Mo. Ct. App. 2002), with Oneida County Comm'r of Soc. Servs., 659 N.Y.S.2d 606 (App. Div. 1997).

8. *Teen parents.* At common law, becoming a parent emancipates a minor. Should states establish a minimum age for parenting or otherwise regulate parenting by minors? Why? See Emily Buss, The Parental Rights of Minors, 48 Buff. L. Rev. 785 (2000). See also Harry Willekens, Rights and Duties of Underage Parents: A Comparative Approach, 18 Int'l. J.L. Pol'y & Fam. 355 (2004).

Teenage parents must live with their parents or in other adult-supervised settings to qualify for assistance under the Personal Responsibility and Work Opportunity Reconciliation Act of 1996, 42 U.S.C. §608(a)(5) (2000). Another provision, designed to deter teen pregnancy, gives the states the option of enforcing support orders against the grandparents of children whose parents are minors receiving welfare; the provision explicitly refers to the "parents of the noncustodial parent." Id. at §666(a)(18). What impact will this requirement have on parental autonomy? On the ability of children to escape parental authority? On the rise of grandparents' rearing of their teens' children and the implications, see generally Jami L. Crews, When Mommy's a Minor: Balancing the Rights of Grandparents Raising Grandchildren Against Minors' Parental Rights, 28 Law & Psychol. Rev. 133 (2004).

9. *Duration.* Once achieved, does emancipation last forever? Most authorities have answered in the negative. Thus, for example, if the marriage that emancipated a child is annulled, the emancipation terminates. See, e.g., Crimmins v. Crimmins, 745 N.Y.S.2d 686 (Fam. Ct. 2002); Berks County Children & Youth Servs. v. Rowan, 631 A.2d 615 (Pa. Super. Ct. 1993). But see Rennie v. Rennie, 718 So. 2d 1091 (Miss. 1998); State ex rel. Dep't of Health & Human Resources v. Farmer, 523 S.E.2d 840 (W. Va. 1999). Note that R.R.'s emancipation was only temporary.

10. *Partial emancipation?* Is emancipation "all or nothing"? The maturity deemed necessary for different adult activities may vary. Should the law therefore recognize partial or limited emancipation? See, e.g., Mitchell v. Mitchell, 963 S.W.2d 222 (Ky. Ct. App. 1998) (married emancipated minor cannot settle personal injury claim). Cf. Hillary Rodham, Children Under the Law, 43 Harv. Educ. Rev. 487, 507 (1973) (advocating "abolition of the general status of minority and adoption of an area-by-area approach (as has already been done . . . in the motor vehicle statutes)").

11. *The mature minor rule*. The mature minor rule, followed in many jurisdictions, is a species of limited or partial emancipation. Under this exception to the common law rule requiring parental consent for medical treatment of a minor, a child close to majority can give effective consent if capable of appreciating the nature, extent, and consequences of the treatment. See, e.g., Cardwell v. Bechtol, 724 S.W.2d 739 (Tenn. 1987); Cara D. Watts, Asking Adolescents: Does a Mature Minor Have a Right to Participate in Health Care Decisions?, 16 Hastings Women's L.J. 221 (2005). See also Barbara L. Atwell, The Modern Age of Informed Consent, 40 U. Rich. L. Rev. 591, 592 (2006) (examining convergence of medical innovations and delay in "fully realized adulthood"). If the parent nonetheless remains financially responsible for the medical treatment in question, does the rule undermine parental autonomy and control?

Some states statutorily adopted a mature minor rule specifically for medical care related to drug abuse, venereal disease, and pregnancy, excluding abortion. See, e.g., 410 Ill. Comp. Stat. Ann. 210/4 (West 2005); Mo. Rev. Stat. §431.061(4) (2000). But see Rhonda Gay Hartman, AIDS and Adolescents, 7 J. Health Care L. & Pol'y 280 (2004). Why do such statutes cover these particular situations? Is a lesser degree of maturity necessary for the medical care specified by these statutes than for other treatment? Or do such statutes reflect altogether different concerns? See Martin Guggenheim, What's Wrong with Children's Rights 236 (2005) (all agree that treatment is the only appropriate result). What explains the requirement of parental or judicial involvement for abortion and the absence of similar requirements for medical treatment incident to childbirth? See Planned Parenthood of Cent. N.J. v. Farmer, 762 A.2d 620 (N.J. 2000); Richard F. Storrow & Sandra Martinez, "Special Weight" for Best-Interests Minors in the New Era of Parental Autonomy, 2003 Wis. L. Rev. 789, 797-801.

Should mature minors be able to refuse life-sustaining treatment? Compare In re E.G., 549 N.E.2d 322 (Ill. 1989), with O.G. v. Baum, 790 S.W.2d 839, 842 (Tex. Ct. App. 1990). See Commonwealth v. Nixon, 761 A.2d 1151 (Pa. 2000); Ann Eileen Driggs, Note, The Mature Minor Doctrine: Do Adolescents Have the Right to Die?, 11 Health Matrix 687 (2001).

Problem

Five-year-old Elian Gonzalez used an inner tube to survive a hazardous boat trip from Cuba to Florida, although his mother and others who were attempting to come to the United States perished. In Miami, Elian was placed temporarily in the custody of his great uncle, Lazaro Gonzalez, and his family. Elian's father, who had separated from his mother several years before but had maintained an ongoing relationship with the boy, asked the Miami relatives to return him to Cuba, where Elian would live with his father, his wife, and their child. The Miami relatives decline and now file a petition for asylum on behalf of Elian. Assuming that the federal asylum statute applies to a child, who should decide whether Elian applies for asylum or returns to Cuba? Elian? His father? The Miami relatives who now have custody? The Immigration and Naturalization Service? A family court? If so, should the decision be made in Miami or Cuba? Of what relevance is the fact that Elian's custodial parent, his mother, had decided to move with him to the United States? Of what relevance are arguments that Elian's father might have asked for the boy's return because of pressure from the Cuban government? See Gonzalez v. Reno, 212 F.3d 1338 (11th Cir.), *cert. denied*, 530 U.S. 1270 (2000). Cf. Reno v. Flores, 507 U.S. 292, 302-303 (1993). See generally, e.g., David B. Thronson, Kids Will Be Kids? Reconsidering Conceptions of Children's Rights Underlying Immigration Law, 63 Ohio St. L.J. 979 (2002).

Assume instead now that Elian arrived in the United States at age 12, not 5. He firmly expressed his desire to stay with his Miami relatives instead of returning to Cuba to live with his father, stepmother, and half brother. Six months after Elian's arrival, his father seeks the assistance of the family court in Miami in returning Elian to his custody; the Department of Children and Family Services asks this court to adjudge Elian a minor in need of supervision and a ward of the state (so that he can remain in the United States); and Elian seeks a declaration of emancipation. What result and why?

This latter scenario is based on the case of Walter Polovchak, who came to the United States with his parents from the then Ukrainian Soviet Socialist Republic and refused to accompany them when they returned. See In re Polovchak, 454 N.E.2d 258 (Ill. 1983), *cert. denied*, 465 U.S. 1065 (1984). See also Polovchak v. Meese, 774 F.2d 731 (7th Cir. 1985); Leslie A. Fithian, Note, Forcible Repatriation of Minors: The Competing Rights of Parent and Child, 37 Stan. L. Rev. 187 (1984). Walter tells his own story in Walter Polovchak & Kevin Klose, Freedom's Child (1988).

2. When Can Children Sue Their Parents?

a. Tortious injury

■ **BUONO v. SCALIA**
843 A.2d 1120 (N.J. 2004)

JUSTICE VERNIERO delivered the opinion of the Court.

This appeal implicates the doctrine of parental immunity articulated in Foldi v. Jeffries, 461 A.2d 1145 [(N.J.1983)]. At midday on June 17, 2000, the residents of a local street in Bayonne were hosting a block party. [P]arked cars were removed from the street, which was closed to traffic. Within the enclosed area, about fourteen adults had gathered and several children were riding their bicycles, including Michael Scalia who was five-and-a-half years old. Michael had learned to ride his two-wheel bike, without its training wheels, approximately two months earlier. Alphonse Scalia, the boy's father, was watching his son from an approximate distance of five to eight feet. Michael's mother was at the family home preparing food for the party. While Michael rode, another resident, Diane Buono, was standing "within arm[']s length" of her daughter, Kathryn, who was then sixteen-months old. As Michael approached Kathryn's position, his father yelled to him, "watch out." Unfortunately, Michael did not respond and struck Kathryn with the bike, causing both children to fall to the ground. Engaged in conversation, Diane Buono neither witnessed the accident nor heard Alphonse Scalia shout the warning. As a result of the mishap, Kathryn required an unspecified number of stitches.

[Suing on behalf of himself and his daughter, Vincent Buono] asserted that Michael negligently had ridden his bike, that the Scalias negligently had supervised their son, and that such negligence had caused Kathryn's injuries. [The trial court] concluded that plaintiff had not overcome the rebuttable presumption that the child, Michael, was incapable of negligence. Relying on *Foldi*, supra, the trial court also concluded that the doctrine of parental immunity barred plaintiff's claims against Michael's parents because there was no willful or wanton misconduct attributable to either of them. Plaintiff appealed only the parental immunity issue, arguing that immunity did not apply because the injured child is not a child of a defendant parent, but rather a third party. . . .

. . . Historically, courts did not recognize the parental immunity doctrine. One of the earliest reported decisions involving the doctrine is Hewlett v. George, 9 So. 885 (Miss. 1891), *overruled by* Glaskox v. Glaskox, 614 So. 2d 906 (Miss. 1992). In *Hewlett*, the court held that an unemancipated child could not sue her parents for personal injuries. The court grounded its conclusion on the public policy favoring family tranquility. Numerous states then adopted the parental immunity doctrine and "applied it to both negligent and intentional torts." . . .

Thirty-five years [after adopting parental immunity to protect family tranquility in 1935,] this Court curbed the doctrine significantly [in an automobile accident case in which we rejected a father's immunity defense.] Although we noted that academic writers "have condemned parent-child immunity[,]" we recognized that there "may be areas involving the exercise of parental authority . . . which should not be justiciable in a court of law."

We more fully explained that narrow concept of immunity in *Foldi*, supra. There, the Court held that the parental immunity doctrine would "preclude liability in cases of negligent supervision, but not for a parent's willful or wanton failure to supervise his or her children." Further, the Court stated that the doctrine would be applicable only in "special situations that involve the exercise of parental authority and customary child care." The Court reached its determination by evaluating two competing principles, still relevant today. The first tenet is "that liability ordinarily should be imposed upon those who wrongfully injure others." The second is that parents have a right to raise their children in accordance with their own beliefs without undue interference from the courts. In a lengthy but critical passage, the Court observed:

> There are certain areas of activities within the family sphere involving parental discipline, care, and control that should and must remain free from judicial intrusion. Parents should be free to determine how the physical, moral, emotional, and intellectual growth of their children can best be promoted. . . . Indeed, every parent has a unique philosophy of the rearing of children. . . .
>
> There is no recognized correct theory on how much freedom a parent should allow his or her children. . . . As each parent is different, so is each child. There is no one ideal "formula" for how much supervision a child should receive at a given age. . . . The parent is clearly in the best position to know the limitations and capabilities of his or her own children. These intangibles cannot be adequately conveyed within the formal atmosphere of a courtroom. Nor do we believe that a court or a jury can evaluate these highly subjective factors without somehow supplanting the parent's own individual philosophy. [461 A.2d at 1152.] . . .

Although the case law focuses on suits brought by children against their parents for bodily injury, some of the prior decisions have involved claims by other defendants against the injured child's parents for contribution. *Foldi* itself touched on such a claim against the parents of the child in that case. After a neighbor's dog bit the child, we barred the child's claim against her parents and also barred the neighbor's third-party claim against the parents for indemnity. [We stated that, for policy reasons, we would remove from immunity only intentional torts and willful and wanton supervisory misconduct, so that third-party claims may properly be brought against parents in appropriately severe lack-of-supervision cases.]

We hold that application of the above tenets should result in parental immunity on the narrow facts before us. [A]lthough this might be the first instance of applying the doctrine to a situation involving a third-party claim (other than a claim from a joint tortfeasor), such application flows naturally from *Foldi*'s existing policy rationale. . . .

Unlike driving a motor vehicle or crossing a street, the conduct here falls within the purview of parental philosophy involving a child's upbringing, entitling defendant to immunity as a matter of law. Alphonse Scalia determined that his five-and-a-half-year-old child could ride a bike within the confines of a neighborhood block party, in the presence of Scalia himself, and in the presence of other parents presumably supervising their own children. That was a valid exercise of parental decision-making entitled to judicial deference. [T]here is no reasonable suggestion that Michael's father acted willfully, wantonly, or recklessly as those terms are described in this opinion. The inattention, if any, of Alphonse Scalia was brief, making him at worst merely negligent. Under those circumstances, the trial court did not err in granting defendant's motion.

A contrary holding would lead to the incongruent result that *Foldi* would prevent suit against Kathryn's mother but not against Michael's father, although both parents appear to have been exercising the same degree of supervision over their respective children. In that regard, the trial court stated that "[Kathryn's] mother obviously wasn't watching her daughter enough to even see the accident take place, despite the fact that she indicates that she was an arm[']s length away from her daughter." . . .

There are many places, such as playgrounds, picnic areas, and local parks, where parents watch over their children in seemingly safe environments, but unfortunately where mishaps and accidents do occur. If we were to force parents to defend against their negligent but otherwise honest errors of judgment in those settings, then we would risk opening the floodgates of intrusive litigation in precisely the manner that *Foldi* sought to avoid. . . .

[We embrace] a judicial policy that seeks merely to define the limited circumstances under which parents can rear their children free "from scrutiny by judge or jury." [F]orcing these parties to defend against claims and counterclaims would consume not only their own resources but society's as well. We are not as convinced as the dissenters that incurring such costs to adjudicate child-rearing decisions by Michael's father or Kathryn's mother — decisions that were neither willful nor reckless — reflects a proper balancing of interests. . . . The judgment of the Appellate Division is affirmed. . . .

Notes and Questions

1. *Parental immunity.* The majority holds that whether Buono can recover against Scalia for negligent supervision depends upon whether young Michael Scalia could recover on such claim against his own father. How does the court resolve this threshold issue? Alternatively, suppose Kathryn Buono had sued her mother to recover damages for negligent supervision. Should a jury decide whether each parent acted reasonably? Or should parents be immune from such suits? *Buono* traces the history of parental immunity, which recently has fallen out of favor among courts and scholars alike. According to the Arkansas Supreme Court, 11 states have abrogated the doctrine altogether, 4 states and the District of Columbia never adopted the doctrine, 21 states have abrogated the doctrine for the negligent operation of a motor vehicle when liability insurance coverage provides funds for recovery, and 8 states apply the doctrine even when such insurance coverage obtains. Verdier v. Verdier, 2005 WL 3217092 (Ark. 2005) (declining to abolish immunity in toto and distinguishing homeowner's insurance from automobile insurance.)

Courts have recognized immunity for noncustodial parents, Ascuitto v. Farricielli, 711 A.2d 708 (Conn. 1998), and foster parents, Nichol v. Stass, 735 N.E.2d 582 (Ill. 2000), but not residential care facilities, Wallace v. Smyth, 786 N.E.2d 980 (Ill. 2002). Should immunity apply to a stepparent who acts as a parent and whom the child regards as a parent? See C.M.L. v. Republic Servs., 800 N.E.2d 200, 206-207 (Ind. Ct. App. 2003). Courts have more readily abrogated immunity for intentional torts, compared to negligence. E.g., Newman v. Cole, 872 So. 2d 138 (Ala. 2003) (willful and intentional infliction of injury causing death); Herzfeld v. Herzfeld, 781 So. 2d 1070 (Fla. 2001) (sexual abuse).

2. *Rationale.* Historically, the underlying justifications for parental immunity included "family harmony, deterrence of fraud and collusion, and protection of the family's coffers." *Buono*, 843 A.2d at 1131 (Long, J., concurring and dissenting). What explains the continuing vitality of the parental immunity doctrine in some jurisdictions? Consider the analysis of the Connecticut Supreme Court in rejecting an approach that would make insurance coverage determinative:

> We . . . note that the "unseemly discord" engendered by intrafamily lawsuits is not solely financial in origin. "The prospect of greeting an adolescent judgment creditor at the dinner table each day would likely strain the familial relationship even for the most saintly of parents." Dzenutis v. Dzenutis, [512 A.2d 130, 134 (Conn. 1986).] Although we have noted that this discord may be lessened by the presence of insurance, the manner in which an adverse judgment is satisfied is not the sole, or even the primary, threat to family harmony that results when an unemancipated child brings an action against a parent.[9] Additionally, we recognize that attorneys frequently advise their clients not to communicate personally with opposing parties. The practical difficulties in maintaining this confidentiality between a parent and child would seem almost insurmountable. . . .

---

9. . . . A negligence action for personal injury uniquely implicates the parent's authority to care for his or her child in a way that is not inherently present in a property dispute. A negligence action is, therefore, especially likely to be disruptive of family harmony.

Ascuitto, 711 A.2d at 716-717. Do similar policy concerns support immunity when the parent is the plaintiff and the child the tortfeasor? See, e.g., Bushey v. Northern Assur. Corp. of Am., 766 A.2d 598, 607-611 (Md. 2001).

3. *Privacy. Buono* explains that New Jersey retains immunity for negligence in some circumstances. Why? Given the reasoning in *Buono*, do the pluralism and family privacy protected in *Meyer* and *Pierce*, Chapter I, section A1b, require such immunity? Does *Buono*'s approach address the concerns raised in *Ascuitto*, supra?

4. *Alternative approaches.* Does *Buono* clearly identify the situations in which parental immunity applies? What constitutes "customary child-care activities or a legitimate exercise of parental authority"? Does this categorical approach give parents "carte blanche" to act negligently in such situations? See Gibson v. Gibson, 479 P.2d 648, 653 (Cal. 1971). Because of such concerns, some courts have abolished immunity in toto in favor of *a reasonable parent* standard. E.g., Hartman v. Hartman, 821 S.W.2d 852 (Mo. 1991). Some states use this standard even in cases of negligent supervision. Broadbent v. Broadbent, 907 P.2d 43 (Ariz. 1995). Does it follow that every child injured as a result of parental conduct gets to ask a jury to decide reasonableness? What problems does this conclusion pose?

New revisions to the Restatement of Torts do not expressly include the parent-child relationship in the list of relationships that impose a duty of reasonable care "for risks that arise within the scope of the relationship." Restatement (Third) of the Law of Torts: Liability for Physical Harm §40 (Proposed Final Draft No. 1 2005). What might explain this omission? See id. at §40 cmt. o (explaining nonexclusivity of current list to allow developments recognizing additional affirmative duties) & Reporters' Notes on cmt. o (discussing parental immunity and negligent supervision).

5. *Apportionment.* How should a jurisdiction that has abolished immunity apportion liability for a child's injuries between one parent who actively inflicts abuse and the other who passively allows the abuse to occur? See Comment, Speaking Out Against Passive Parent Child Abuse: The Time Has Come to Hold Parents Liable for Failing to Protect Their Children, 37 Hous. L. Rev. 253 (2000)? Between a babysitter who intentionally abuses the child and the parents who negligently fail to detect the signs of danger? See Glomb v. Glomb, 530 A.2d 1362 (Pa. Super. Ct. 1987). See also Rider v. Speaker, 692 N.Y.S.2d 920 (Sup. Ct. 1999) (holding babysitter but not parents liable for negligent supervision).

6. *Parental accountability for harm to third parties.* According to *Buono*, precisely what is the connection between parental immunity, on the one hand, and the responsibility of parents for injuries caused by their children to third parties, on the other? Should the same standards govern in both contexts? Concurring and dissenting in *Buono*, Justice Long, who would have followed the trend and abrogated parental immunity altogether, wrote:

> The exercise of parental autonomy should, at most, insulate parents from suit by their own children but should not allow them to escape liability when an improper choice is made and a third-party suffers harm. Whatever the balance of interests may be in a case between parent and child, it is clear that when parental autonomy is balanced against the right of an innocent third-party victim to redress, that autonomy must yield.

843 A.2d at 1131. Do you agree? The Restatement (Second) of Torts (1965) addresses accountability to third parties as follows:

§316. Duty of Parent to Control Conduct of a Child

A parent is under a duty to exercise reasonable care so to control his minor child as to prevent it from intentionally harming others or from so conducting itself as to create an unreasonable risk of bodily harm to them, if the parent

(a) knows or has reason to know that he has the ability to control his child, and

(b) knows or should know of the necessity and opportunity for exercising such control.

By contrast, the proposed final draft of the revised Restatement recognizes the relationship of a parent and dependent children as a "special relationship" and provides that "[a]n actor in a special relationship with another owes a duty of reasonable care to third persons with regard to risks posed by the other that arise within the scope of the relationship." Restatement (Third) of the Law of Torts: Liability for Physical Harm §41 (Proposed Final Draft No. 1 2005). As applied to the Scalias' liabilty for Kathryn Buono's injuries, what consequences follow from the two different Restatement formulations?

Laws holding parents responsible for the wrongs of their children have received renewed attention in the wake of school shootings. See, e.g., Rhonda V. Magee Andrews, The Justice of Parental Accountability: Hypothetical Disinterested Citizens and Real Victims' Voices in the Debate Over Expanded Parental Liability, 75 Temp. L. Rev. 375 (2002); Andrew C. Gratz, Comment, Increasing the Price of Parenthood: When Should Parents Be Held Civilly Liable for the Torts of Their Children?, 39 Hous. L. Rev. 169 (2002); Amy L. Tomaszewski, Note, From Columbine to Kazaa: Parental Liability in a New World, 2005 U. Ill. L. Rev. 573. Should the parents' homeowners insurance policies cover such liability? See Hazel Glenn Beh, Tort Liability for Intentional Acts of Family Members: Will Your Insurer Stand By You?, 68 Tenn. L. Rev. 1 (2000).

Criminal responsibility for a child's crimes requires a showing that the parent committed a prohibited act or omission with the requisite mens rea; parental status alone does not suffice. See generally John Kip Cornwell, Preventing Kids from Killing, 37 Hous. L. Rev. 21, 54-59 (2000). Parental liability laws also have been used to prosecute parents for allowing their children to engage in sexual activities. See People v. Maness, 732 N.E.2d 545 (Ill. 2000) (holding unconstitutionally vague prohibition on parent's knowingly permitting sexual abuse of minor); Susan S. Kuo, A Little Privacy, Please: Should We Punish Parents for Teenage Sex?, 89 Ky. L.J. 135 (2000/2001).

Will parental liability laws help curb youth violence and sex? Will they invite intrusion into minors' privacy? See, e.g., Alison S. Aaronson, Notes & Comments, Changing with the Times: Why Rampant School Violence Warrants Legalization of Parental Wiretapping to Monitor Children's Activities, 9 J. L. & Pol'y 785 (2001). Can you square such laws with the growing practice of trying juvenile offenders as adult criminal defendants? See generally Elizabeth S. Scott & Laurence Steinberg, Essay, Blaming Youth, 81 Tex. L. Rev. 799 (2003).

To what extent does the notion of parental responsibility follow from the basic principle of parental autonomy, which lets parents make decisions and speak for their children? Notwithstanding parental autonomy, do parental liability laws assume knowledge, supervision, and control that many parents realistically cannot exercise? See generally Andrews, supra; James Herbie DiFonzo, Parental

Responsibility for Juvenile Crime, 80 Or. L. Rev. 1, 38-49 (2001); Judith G. McMullen, "You Can't Make Me!": How Expectations of Parental Control over Adolescents Influence the Law, 35 Loy. U. Chi. L.J. 603 (2004) (examining visitation and truancy contexts). Consider, for example, the work requirements that the Personal Responsibility and Work Opportunity Reconciliation Act imposes on parents of even young children. 42 U.S.C. §607 (2000). What's a "reasonable parent" to do?

7. *Emotional injuries.* Should courts allow children to recover damages for emotional harm intentionally inflicted by their parents? This question divided the court in Burnette v. Wahl, 588 P.2d 1105 (Or. 1978), a suit by five children in state custody whose mothers abandoned them, depriving them of support and nurture and causing psychological damage. The majority affirmed dismissal of the case, on the theory that such litigation would undermine child welfare laws and the state policy favoring family reunification. One dissent, citing the psychological harm resulting from the separation of mother and child (and its costs to society), would find such harm compensable, with defendants shouldering so much of the financial burden as possible. Id. at 1112-1115 (Lent, J., concurring and dissenting in part). A second dissent would also allow the case to proceed, finding support for this new tort in the state's child protection laws and its criminal prohibitions punishing child abandonment as a felony. Id. at 1115-1119 (Linde, J., dissenting).

Which analysis is most persuasive? Why would the majority conclude civil liability threatens family unity more than criminal liability? Than juvenile court intervention? Would the approach used in *Buono* allow recovery, at least in cases of willful abandonment? Would the reasonable parent standard?

8. *Extensions?* How far would the dissenters in *Burnette*, supra, extend parental liability for emotional harm? Should parents be liable for the emotional harm and resulting costs of therapy caused by the physical abuse a stepparent inflicts on the child's mother while the child watches? See Courtney v. Courtney, 413 S.E.2d 418 (W. Va. 1991) (recognizing the cause of action), *after remand*, 437 S.E.2d 436 (W. Va. 1993) (specifying applicable statute of limitations). For the damage caused by child neglect? See Janet Weinstein & Ricardo Weinstein, Before It's Too Late: Neuropsychological Consequences of Child Neglect and Their Implications for Law and Social Policy, 33 U. Mich. J.L. Reform 561 (2000) (harm to brain development); Andrew J. Walker, Quit Neglecting Me or I'm Going to Sue You: An Unconventional Look at Child Neglect, 17 Am. J. Fam. L. 11 (2003). By the parents' divorce? See Judith S. Wallerstein et al., The Unexpected Legacy of Divorce: A 25 Year Landmark Study (2000) (finding lifelong emotional scars from parental divorce). Parental pressure to attend law school despite the child's wish to become a musician? See Hansen v. Hansen, 608 P.2d 364 (Colo. Ct. App. 1979) (unsuccessful "parental malpractice" case). Parental refusal to accept their child's homosexuality? Cf. *C.R.*, supra section C1. See generally G. Steven Neeley, The Psychological and Emotional Abuse of Children: Suing Parents in Tort for the Infliction of Emotional Distress, 27 N. Ky. L. Rev. 689 (2000).

9. *Other family torts.* Jurisdictions divide on whether children can sue tortfeasors for causing loss of parental consortium, that is, the loss of parental care, guidance, and nurturance as the result of injuries suffered by the parent. Compare, e.g., Rolf v. Tri State Motor Transit Co., 745 N.E.2d 424 (Ohio 2001) (recognizing cause of action even for emancipated children), with, e.g., Taylor v. Beard, 104 S.W.3d 507 (Tenn. 2003) (declining to recognize cause of action). To what extent do precedents permitting the child's recovery for such losses support recovery for similar losses

occasioned by willful parental abandonment, as in *Burnette*, supra? Jurisdictions also split on whether parents can cover for loss of filial consortium, caused by a tortfeasor's nonfatal injuries to a child. Compare, e.g., Frank v. Superior Ct., 722 P.2d 955 (Ariz. 1986) (recognizing cause of action), with, e.g., Vitro v. Mihelcic, 806 N.E.2d 632 (Ill. 2004) (declining to recognize cause of action). Can you reconcile decisions permitting children to sue for loss of parental consortium with those rejecting parental suits for loss of filial consortium? See Roberts v. Williamson, 111 S.W.3d 113 (Tex. 2003). And vice versa? See *Frank*, 722 P.2d at 959-960 (explaining old master-servant basis of parent's interest).

Note: Childhood Sexual Abuse and Statutes of Limitations

Although many jurisdictions have readily abandoned parental immunity in cases of alleged childhood sexual abuse, sometimes plaintiffs fail to sue for damages in a timely manner because they claim to suffer from "traumatic amnesia," which temporarily repressed their memories of the abuse and which dissipated only after psychotherapy triggered "recovered memories." See, e.g., Hearndon v. Graham, 767 So. 2d 1179 (Fla. 2000). Generally, a child's minority tolls the statute of limitations, which begins to run only once an individual reaches majority. The cases of repressed and recovered memories raise the issue whether these plaintiffs should have additional time to sue.

Controversy in the scientific and academic communities has complicated the law's response. See First Report of the American Psychological Association Working Group on Investigation of Memories of Childhood Abuse, 4 Psychol. Pub. Pol'y & L. 931 (1998). Some scientists challenge the very existence of recovered memory, demonstrating how therapists can produce "memories" in their patients. See Elizabeth Loftus & Katherine Ketcham, The Myth of Repressed Memory: False Memories and Allegations of Sexual Abuse (1994). See also, e.g., Richard A. Leo, The Social and Legal Construction of Repressed Memory, 22 Law & Soc. Inquiry 653 (1997). Nonetheless, individuals claim to have experienced sexual abuse and recovered memories, and this school of thought finds supporters as well. See, e.g., Marilyn Van Derbur, Miss America by Day: Lessons Learned from Ultimate Betrayals and Unconditional Love (2003) (memoir); Lynne Henderson, Suppressing Memory, 22 Law & Soc. Inquiry 695 (1997); Jocelyn B. Lamm, Easing Access to the Courts for Incest Victims: Toward an Equitable Application of the Delayed Discovery Rule, 100 Yale L.J. 2189 (1991).

Some jurisdictions now toll the statute of limitation until well past the victim's adulthood in such cases. See, e.g., Conn. Gen. Stat. Ann. §52-577d (West Supp. 2005) (departing from general limit of 3 years after tort occurred to allow sexually abused minors to sue within 30 years after reaching majority). Others adopt a delayed discovery approach, so that "a cause of action does not accrue until the plaintiff either knows or reasonably should know of the tortious act. . . ." *Hearndon*, 767 So. 2d at 1184. See also, e.g., id. at 1185-1186 (citing cases from other states); Or. Rev. Stat. §12.117 (West 2003) (three years after injury or causal connection between abuse and injury discovered). Some authorities distinguish between "type 1 claims," in which the plaintiff asserts ongoing recollections of the abuse but fails to connect the abuse to severe psychological problems until recent therapeutic intervention, and "type 2 claims," in which the plaintiff asserts that memories remained completely repressed until just before the lawsuit, extending the time for suit in the latter but not the former. See, e.g., Messina v. Bonner, 813 F. Supp. 346 (E.D. Pa. 1993); Clay v. Kuhl, 727 N.E.2d 217 (Ill. 2000). Such extensions of the time to sue cannot revive already time-barred claims, however. See Stogner v. California, 539 U.S. 607 (2003).

Several jurisdictions, however, continue to reject arguments for lengthening the time in which adult survivors of childhood sexual abuse can bring civil suits. See, e.g., Lemmerman v. Fealk, 534 N.W.2d 695 (Mich. 1995); Dalrymple v. Brown, 701 A.2d 164 (Pa. 1997). Further, the use of recovered memory therapy has produced a backlash. For example, in one highly publicized case, a jury awarded a father $500,000 against two therapists whom he claimed planted false memories of child sexual abuse in his daughter's mind. Ramona v. Ramona, No. 61898 (Super. Ct. Napa County Cal.) (cited in Ramona v. Superior Ct., 66 Cal. Rptr. 2d 766, 770 n.5 (Ct. App. 1997)). See also Johnson v. Rogers Mem'l Hosp., Inc., 627 N.W.2d 890 (Wis. 2001) (allowing parents' claim against daughter's therapist to proceed for fuller development of record). But see Trear v. Sills, 82 Cal. Rptr. 2d 281 (Ct. App. 1999) (rejecting liability because therapist owes no duty to patient's parents); Cynthia Grant Bowman & Elizabeth Mertz, A Dangerous Direction: Legal Intervention in Sexual Abuse Survivor Therapy, 109 Harv. L. Rev. 549 (1996) (arguing against therapists' liability to third parties). This backlash, in turn, raises questions about whether attorneys should be liable for filing suits based on claims later determined to be false. See Cynthia Grant Bowman & Elizabeth Mertz, Attorneys as Gatekeepers to the Court: The Potential Liability of Attorneys Bringing Suits Based on Recovered Memories of Childhood Sexual Abuse, 27 Hofstra L. Rev. 223 (1998).

The controversy reaches beyond civil actions against parents and stepparents, with implications for similar claims against other authority figures, such as clergy and teachers. See, e.g., Powel v. Chaminade Coll. Prep., Inc., 2006 WL 1605006 (Mo. 2006); William A. Gray, Note, A Proposal for Change in Statutes of Limitations in Childhood Sexual Abuse Cases, 43 Brandeis L.J. 493 (2005). In addition, some advocate applying the special timing rules developed by some jurisdictions to *all* forms of maltreatment suffered during childhood (not just sexual abuse). See Elizabeth A. Wilson, Suing for Lost Childhood: Child Sexual Abuse, the Delayed Discovery Rule, and the Problem of Finding Justice for Adult-Survivors of Child Abuse, 12 UCLA Women's L.J. 145 (2003).

Problem

Lindsay sues her mother for injuries suffered as the result of a car accident caused by her mother when Lindsay was a five-month fetus. Assume that this state has created exceptions to the parental immunity doctrine to permit direct suits for personal injuries from motor torts and also has case law allowing suits against third parties for prenatal and preconception torts. E.g., Renslow v. Mennonite Hospital, 367 N.E.2d 1250 (Ill. 1977).

Should the court submit to the jury the question whether the mother negligently inflicted Lindsay's prenatal injuries? Why? Compare Stallman v. Youngquist, 531 N.E.2d 355 (Ill. 1988), and Remy v. MacDonald, 801 N.E.2d 260 (Mass. 2004), with Bonte v. Bonte, 616 A.2d 464 (N.H. 1992). Should the answer change if Lindsay were suing her mother for prenatal injuries caused by her mother's employment in a hazardous workplace? Cf. International Union, UAW v. Johnson Controls, Inc., 499 U.S. 187 (1991). For fetal alcohol syndrome caused by her mother's drinking during pregnancy or for the effects of her mother's illegal drug use? See Chenault v. Huie, 989 S.W.2d 474 (Tex. App. 1999). See also Barbara Katz Rothman, Recreating Motherhood 109-110 (2000); Moses Cook, From Conception Until Birth: Exploring the Maternal Duty to Protect Fetal Health, 80 Wash. U. L.Q. 1307 (2002).

Finally, can Lindsay sue her mother for "wrongful life" for choosing to have Lindsay born with impairments, rather than terminating the pregnancy once she learned of Lindsay's injuries (or a genetic disease)? See Lois Shepherd, Protecting Parents' Freedom to Have Children with Genetic Differences, 1995 U. Ill. L. Rev. 761. Cf. generally Mark Strasser, Wrongful Life, Wrongful Birth, Wrongful Death, and the Right to Refuse Treatment: Can Reasonable Jurisdictions Recognize All But One?, 64 Mo. L. Rev. 29 (1999).

Do such suits call for the development of a "reasonable pregnant woman" standard? What are the implications for parental autonomy? For the right to privacy?

b. "Divorce" Actions Against Parents

■ RYAN V. RYAN
677 N.W.2d 899 (Mich. Ct. App.), **appeal denied,**
690 N.W.2d 98 (Mich. 2004)

KELLY, J. . . .

Defendants Timothy and Chris Ryan and their four children lead an upper middle class lifestyle [in Grand Rapids, Michigan] with the children attending private schools. Plaintiff Claire Ryan, the oldest child, was a few months shy of her seventeenth birthday at the time of the events giving rise to this action. In 2001, the relationship between plaintiff and defendants deteriorated. According to defendants, plaintiff began dating Ryan McGinn in early 2000. Although defendants were initially supportive of this relationship, viewing it as "normal dating," they became concerned when plaintiff reported excessive drinking at McGinn's house, that McGinn's mother, Adele McGinn-Loomis, did not like plaintiff, and that McGinn complained of problems with his parents.

On July 5, 2001, Timothy Ryan found plaintiff packing her bags and threatening to run away. [He stopped her and sought counseling.] According to the counselor, plaintiff suffered from a depressive disorder and borderline personality features. On September 10, 2001, plaintiff packed her bags and left the house to stay with family friends. Defendants decided to allow plaintiff to stay at the friends' home for a few days, presumably as a "cooling off" period. But because plaintiff had not returned by the end of the week, Timothy Ryan called the friends, suggesting that they tell plaintiff she was no longer welcome at the friends' home. Plaintiff subsequently moved to McGinn-Loomis's home, although defendants did not approve of this living arrangement. . . .

Timothy Ryan called the police on September 17, 2001, and reported that plaintiff had run away from home and was at McGinn-Loomis's house. When the police arrived at McGinn-Loomis's house, plaintiff told the police that she would not go with her father and that, if she were forced to, she would run away again. . . . That evening, defendants decided to send plaintiff to Cross Creek Manor, a private boarding school in Utah. That same evening, plaintiff called McGinn-Loomis twice, stating that she was being sent to a boarding school that she did not want to attend and "begging" McGinn-Loomis to come and get her. The following day, plaintiff was flown to Utah and was no longer in the trial court's jurisdiction.

[On September 19, 2001, the trial court entered an ex parte order stating that any police department having proper jurisdiction is authorized to detain the plaintiff and return her to Grand Rapids immediately; that the minor child be placed at the Bridge in Grand Rapids for a period of 2 weeks and pending a hearing; and that the circuit court will immediately schedule a hearing regarding the plaintiff's complaint.] At the time the order was entered, no complaint [had been filed] and plaintiff was already residing in Utah. . . . Rather, there were two telephone calls between the trial court [at the judge's home], McGinn-Loomis [who is a deputy clerk in the trial court], and the purported attorney[6] for plaintiff, Mary L. Benedict.

The following day, Benedict filed a "Complaint for Return and Divorce from Parents." The complaint, based primarily on defendants' choice of school for plaintiff, requested that plaintiff be divorced from her parents because she is an adult able to make her own decisions. [Subsequently,] Benedict filed a motion for the appointment of a guardian ad litem, release of records, and temporary placement. Benedict also filed a motion for an amended ex parte order for the return of plaintiff to Grand Rapids [and] requested that plaintiff be allowed to live with a family friend during the pendency of this matter, or, if that option was unavailable, that plaintiff be permitted to choose an alternative living situation. [Defendants contended that the order was invalid because it was issued ex parte; that the motion for the appointment of a guardian was not supported by a required affidavit; that an action for children to divorce their parents does not exist in Michigan; and that plaintiff lacked capacity to contract with Benedict for representation.]

Before the motion was heard, Benedict filed an "amended complaint" [unsupported by required affidavits and documents,] which essentially consisted of a petition for emancipation and a petition alleging abuse and neglect. It is uncontested that plaintiff, who was still in Utah, had no contact with Benedict before the "amended complaint" was filed. . . .

On October 9, 2001, the trial court entered an order appointing Judy Ostrander guardian ad litem for plaintiff. [At a subsequent hearing, Benedict argued] that in this case the fundamental rights of the child and the parents conflict. She further argued that plaintiff's best interests were at issue and that the school in Utah was not in her best interests, but rather, was emotionally harmful. [The trial court dismissed the original "divorce" complaint but accepted an amended complaint seeking emancipation and a third-party guardianship. In the ensuing months, the trial court ordered that the defendants receive counseling; it placed plaintiff, who had returned to Michigan, in foster care, pursuant to the guardian ad litem's recommendation; it issued an order permitting plaintiff contact with McGinn and McGinn-Loomis while severely curtailing] defendants' contact with plaintiff.

---

6. We use the term "purported attorney" because, as a minor, plaintiff did not have the capacity to retain an attorney.

Yet defendants continued to pay for plaintiff's support, private school tuition at West Catholic High School, medical insurance, and other expenses. . . .

On March 22, 2002, the trial court heard defendants' motion for summary disposition of the petition for emancipation and the petition alleging abuse and neglect. At that time, Benedict declared that she filed a motion to dismiss both petitions and the other requests for declaratory relief without prejudice. [The trial court granted this motion, entered an order denying defendants' motion to have the orders declared void ab initio, and entered an order dismissing the case without prejudice. We reverse and remand.]

The trial court's September 19, 2001, ex parte order and the order appointing the guardian ad litem, entered pursuant to plaintiff's complaint for divorce, are void because the trial court lacked subject-matter jurisdiction over an action for "divorce from parents," a claim unrecognized in Michigan. The circuit court's jurisdiction over divorce cases is strictly statutory. [The divorce statutes pertain only to a marriage between a man and a woman. Thus,] while the family division of the circuit court has subject-matter jurisdiction over married couples seeking a divorce, it is without jurisdiction over claims filed by children to divorce their parents. [For similar reasons, plaintiff] also lacked standing to file the "complaint for divorce from parents." . . .

We also find without merit the premise on which the "complaint for divorce from parents" was based, i.e., that plaintiff objected to her parents' decision to send her to a private boarding school in Utah. Historically, Michigan has recognized the right of parents to manage their children without state interference, absent compelling circumstances that threaten a child's safety and welfare. Michigan laws and procedural rules, in keeping with the United States Constitution, "protect[] the sanctity of the family precisely because the institution of the family is deeply rooted in this Nation's history and tradition." Moore v City of East Cleveland, 431 U.S. 494, 503 (1977). The Fourteenth Amendment's Due Process Clause provides heightened protection against governmental interference with the fundamental liberty interest of parents to make decisions concerning the care, custody, and control of their children. This includes the right of parents to control their children's education. Troxel v. Granville, 530 U.S. 57, 68 (2000); Meyer v. Nebraska, 262 U.S. 390, 401 (1923).

. . . Here, the trial court wrongfully interfered in the Ryan family's life on the basis of an unrecognized claim brought by an attorney without authority to act on plaintiff's behalf. Not only did the trial court fail to give special weight to defendants' decision to send plaintiff to a private boarding school specializing in troubled teenage girls, but also gave no weight to the presumption that defendants were fit parents. Instead, the trial court, without holding any hearing whatsoever, substituted its judgment for that of parents who had never been determined unfit. . . .

The filing of this action calls into question the good faith and competence of plaintiff's purported attorney. . . . Clearly Benedict failed to make any inquiry into or analysis of the factual or legal elements of the problem. Instead, Benedict presented the court with an unverified, legally unsupported complaint for a claim that has never existed in Michigan. For these reasons, the ex parte order for the return of plaintiff and the order appointing a guardian ad litem entered pursuant to plaintiff's complaint for divorce are void. . . .

The trial court erred in denying defendants' motion for summary disposition of plaintiff's petition for emancipation because it was defective on its face and lacked factual support. [T]he trial court should have granted defendants' motion for summary disposition and dismissed the petition with prejudice. . . .

Defendants also argue that the trial court improperly exercised its jurisdiction by ordering the temporary placement of plaintiff. We agree. . . . Because the amended complaint requested suitable placement, termination of defendants' parental rights, and removal of plaintiff from defendants' custody, the trial court was required to conduct a preliminary hearing to determine whether probable cause existed to substantiate that the facts alleged in the petition were true and fell within [the statute.] Yet, without conducting the required hearing, the trial court in essence took custody of plaintiff by removing her from defendants' care and custody and placing plaintiff in foster care. . . . Child protective proceedings protect children, but the procedural rules are also designed to protect parents from the risk of an erroneous deprivation of the parents' liberty interest in the management of their children. . . .

We are deeply troubled that this matter was allowed to proceed in the trial court for as long as it did and in the manner in which it did. On the basis of improperly filed documents that were filed by an attorney without authority to act on plaintiff's behalf, the trial court, in a fundamental misunderstanding or disregard of its proper role, stripped defendants of their basic constitutional rights to manage and care for their child without state interference. The trial court completely ignored the principle that, absent a showing of parental unfitness, the state may not interfere with an intact family. We reverse and remand this case to the trial court with the direction to enter an order of dismissal with prejudice in favor of defendants and vacate all previous orders. . . .

Notes and Questions

1. *Rationale.* Why does the court rule that Claire Ryan's suit must be dismissed with prejudice? Was the problem procedural or substantive? To what extent does the problem lie in her attempt to seek relief under Michigan's divorce statute? Or, would the case have failed on the merits under any theory? Would Claire have presented a more compelling case for relief if she had been living in foster care for an extended period?

2. *Background.*

a. *"Gregory K."* The idea of a child's suit to "divorce" his or her parents entered the public consciousness in the 1990s when a Florida youth, "Gregory K.," age 11, claimed to bring such action to terminate his mother's parental rights based on abandonment and neglect so that his foster parents could adopt him. He prevailed in the trial court, which recognized a child's "constitutional right to terminate his relationship with his biological parents on the basis of their neglect and abuse." Jerri A. Blair, *Gregory K. and Emerging Children's Rights*, Trial, June 1993, at 22. The court of appeal ruled that the trial court had erred in allowing Gregory to proceed in his own name, because he lacked legal capacity (a remediable, procedural problem), but concluded that the error was harmless, given the separate TPR petitions filed by the foster father (an attorney), the foster mother, the guardian ad litem, and the Department of Health and Rehabilitative Services. The court allowed the adoption by the foster parents to stand. Kingsley v. Kingsley, 623 So. 2d 780 (Fla. Dist. Ct. App. 1993). Dissenting in part, Chief Judge Harris emphasized that termination of parental rights must rest on parental misconduct (rather than a "no-fault" basis) and that a child has "no right to change parents simply because the child finds substitutes that he or she likes better. . . ." Id. at 790.

The case sparked a lively debate about the implications for family privacy, parental autonomy, children's rights, and the child welfare system. See generally, e.g., Theresa Glennon & Robert G. Schwartz, Looking Back, Looking Ahead: The Evolution of Children's Rights, 68 Temp. L. Rev. 1557 (1995); Jamie D. Manasco, Parent-Child Relationships: The Impetus Behind the Gregory K. Decision, 17 Law & Psychol. Rev. 243 (1993); George H. Russ, Through the Eyes of a Child, "Gregory K.": A Child's Right to Be Heard, 27 Fam. L.Q. 365 (1993) (written by Gregory's adoptive father).

b. *Children's rights generally.* The 1960s witnessed a number of landmark decisions recognizing constitutional rights for children, apart from the interests of parents or the state. E.g., In re Gault, 387 U.S. 1 (1967) (procedural due process guarantees juvenile delinquent notice and counsel); Tinker v. Des Moines Indep. Community Sch. Dist., 393 U.S. 503 (1969) (recognizing First Amendment right of student to wear black arm band). Subsequent decisions including *Yoder* and *Parham,* supra, however, reflected greater deference to state authority and parental prerogatives. E.g., McKeiver v. Pennsylvania, 403 U.S. 528 (1971) (procedural due process does not guarantee juvenile delinquent a jury trial); Hazelwood Sch. Dist. v. Kuhlmeier, 484 U.S. 260 (1988) (upholding school control of student newspaper, over First Amendment challenge). What explains the retreat from "children's liberation"? See Martha Minow, What Ever Happened to Children's Rights?, 80 Minn. L. Rev. 267 (1995). See generally Martin Guggenheim, What's Wrong with Children's Rights 1-16 (2005).

On children's rights as part of the international human rights movement, see generally, e.g., John Quigley, United States and its Participation in the Convention on the Rights of the Child: U.S. Ratification of the Convention of the Rights of the Child, 22 St. Louis U. Pub. L. Rev. 401 (2003); Lauren M. Spitz, Note, Implementing the U.N. Convention on the Rights of the Child: Children's Rights Under the 1996 South African Constitution, 38 Vand. J. Transnat'l. L. 853 (2005).

3. *Children in the "private" family.* To what extent does family privacy preclude all relief for minors like Claire Ryan? Does Claire meet the requirements, as you understand them, for emancipation (assuming she had complied with procedural requirements, such as filing affidavits)? See supra section C1.

a. *"Relationship rights?"* Professor David Meyer writes that the recognition of some children's rights against the state becomes problematic when the issue concerns children's asserted "constitutional rights of privacy or autonomy *within* the family. . . ." David D. Meyer, The Modest Promise of Children's Relationship Rights, 11 Wm. & Mary Bill of Rts. J. 1117, 1118 (2003) (emphasis added). He notes, however, that the dissenting opinions of Justices Stevens and Scalia in Troxel v. Granville (Chapter VII, section B3) suggest an openness to addressing such questions, particularly when children have developed relationships with individuals whom the law does not formally recognized as parents. 11 Wm. & Mary Bill of Rts. J. at 1119-1120.

Are such "relationship rights" advanced — or undermined — by the Adoption and Safe Families Act (ASFA), which requires states receiving federal funds for their adoption and foster care programs to petition for termination of parental rights for any child in foster care under state responsibility for 15 of the last 22 months, as well as in cases in which the parent has committed certain violent crimes against a child? See 42 U.S.C. §675(5) (2000). Why? For critical reviews, compare Dorothy Roberts, Shattered Bonds: The Color of Child Welfare 104-133 (2001), with Elizabeth Bartholet, Nobody's Children: Abuse and Neglect, Foster Drift, and the Adoption Alternative 158-159 (1999). See supra section B4a.

b. *Right to counsel? Ryan* says that Claire, a minor, lacked the capacity to contract for legal representation. Under common law children have no freedom of contract, and they can later disaffirm agreements they made while minors. See, e.g., David S. Tanenhaus, Between Dependency and Liberty: The Conundrum of Children's Rights in the Gilded Age, 23 Law & Hist. Rev. 351, 363 (2005). Should children have at least the freedom to seek legal advice to determine whether they have more substantive rights at stake? Under what circumstances should courts impose or accept representation of children without parental consent? Cf., e.g., Joseph Goldstein et al., Before the Best Interests of the Child 111-129 (1979); Emily Buss, "You're My What?" The Problems of Children's Misperceptions of Their Lawyers' Roles, 64 Fordham L. Rev. 1699 (1996); Jacob Ethan Smiles, A Child's Due Process Right to Legal Counsel in Abuse and Neglect Dependency Proceedings, 37 Fam. L.Q. 485 (2003). For additional exploration of such questions, see Chapter VII, section B4b (in child custody proceedings) and supra pp. 922-923 (in abuse and neglect proceedings).

c. *"Exit rights."* A recent case makes clear what some children have at stake in their attempts to end their relationship with a parent. Patrick Holland, a Massachusetts youth, sued to "divorce" his father, who was serving a life term for murdering Patrick's mother; under a settlement, the father relinquished his parental rights. Peter DeMarco, Killer Gives Up Parental Rights after Son Seeks "Divorce," Boston Globe, July 27, 2004, at A1; Megan Tench, Boy Who Divorced Parent Is Adopted, Boston Globe, March 25, 2005, at B2.

To what extent does privacy for the family entity require "a right of exit" for children, comparable to spouses' right to divorce? Professor Barbara Bennett Woodhouse observes:

> Most fictive entities recognized by the state, from corporations to marriages, are created through voluntary acts and offer various rights of participation as well as a right of exit. The caretaking unit, composed . . . by persons who are inherently and essentially in positions of inequality, is uniquely dangerous and more open, rather than less open, to abuse if completely privatized. This is especially true because children have few, if any, exit options. The right of exit was integral to the message of *McGuire* [in Chapter III, section B3]. Compare the situation of children whose parents fail to live up to their duties. Children have limited exit options, they cannot file for divorce, no matter how badly their parent has treated them.

Barbara Bennett Woodhouse, The Dark Side of Family Privacy, 67 Geo. Wash. L. Rev. 1247, 1253 (1999). See also Laura M. Purdy, Boundaries of Authority: Should Children Be Able to Divorce Their Parents?, in Having and Raising Children: Unconventional Families, Hard Choices, and the Social Good 153, 155 (Uma Narayan & Julia J. Bartkowiak eds., 1999).

Children have standing in some states to initiate TPR proceedings. See In re Appeal in Pima County Juvenile Severance Action No. S-113432, 872 P.2d 1240 (Ariz. Ct. App. 1993); Ann M. Haralambie, Handling Child Custody, Abuse and Adoption Cases §13.04 (1993) (discussing statutes allowing individuals to initiate termination proceedings). Even if children have no right to initiate TPR proceedings, should they have the opportunity to consent or to withhold consent when the state seeks to terminate their parents' rights? See, e.g., In re Adoption/Guardianship Nos. T00130003, 805 A.2d 254 (Md. 2002) (applying statutory requirement).

d. *Dispute Resolution.* Many states permit parents to seek court supervision of children or adolescents deemed ungovernable or beyond parental control — juvenile court intervention based on so-called status offenses. E.g., 705 Ill. Comp. Stat. Ann. 405/3-3 (West 1999). If parents can obtain state assistance in disputes with their children, should the law authorize the child to do so as well? See, e.g., In re Sumey, 621 P.2d 108 (Wash. 1980). One proposal would allow either parents or the teen to initiate a purely civil action seeking individualized court resolution of parent-adolescent disagreement. Randy Frances Kandel & Anne Griffiths, Reconfiguring Personhood: From Ungovernability to Parent Adolescent Autonomy Conflict Actions, 53 Syracuse L. Rev. 995, 1060 (2003). What are the advantages and disadvantages of this approach?

Problem

Ernest and Regina Twigg sought discovery to determine the paternity of Kimberly Mays. They alleged that Kimberly, who was reared by Robert Mays and his wife (now deceased), was actually the Twiggs' daughter, who had been switched at birth at the hospital. (The daughter reared by the Twiggs, born on the same date at the same hospital, had died of a heart ailment; during the course of her medical treatment, the Twiggs first learned that she was not their biological daughter.) After stipulated blood tests corroborated the Twiggs' claim and the Twiggs sued for custody, Kimberly (age 15) sues for termination of their parental rights so that she can remain with Mays. What result and why? See Twigg v. Mays, 1993 WL 330624 (Fla. Cir. Ct. 1993). Alternatively, suppose Kimberly sues to terminate Robert Mays's parental rights because she prefers to live with the Twiggs? See Kim Mays Happy with Family, St. Petersburg Times, Nov. 15, 1994, at 5B. See generally Cynthia R. Mabry, The Tragic and Chaotic Aftermath of a Baby Switch: Should Policy and Common Law, Blood Ties, or Psychological Bonds Prevail?, 6 Wm. & Mary J. Women & L. 1 (1999).

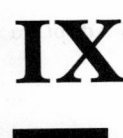

IX

Adoption and Alternatives to Adoption

Adoption law traditionally has focused on the placement of children with biologically unrelated adults, with "best interests" as the guiding principle. Recently, however, the focus of adoption law has expanded beyond child welfare. High divorce and remarriage rates as well as the emergence of nontraditional family forms have brought increasing attention to such variations as stepparent adoptions, second-parent adoptions, and adult adoptions. The setting of adoption law also has changed as the number of white infants available for placement shrinks, the number of children with special needs awaiting homes grows, and new medical procedures offer the infertile alternatives to adoption.

Two themes stand out in this chapter. First, the ensuing materials highlight the conflict between the right to privacy and the state's authority to intervene in family decisionmaking in the context of adoption and its alternatives. Second, as these materials show, both adoption and the parentage rules applied to assisted reproduction accord official recognition to certain relationships, while making other relationships legally irrelevant. Throughout this chapter, consider how the law responds when interests in reproductive self-determination, family integrity, and confidentiality clash with the state's interest in the welfare of children (or children-to-be). Consider too how legally constructed connections shape society's understanding of the family.

A. BACKGROUND

■ STEPHEN B. PRESSER, THE HISTORICAL BACKGROUND OF THE AMERICAN LAW OF ADOPTION
11 J. Fam. L. 443, 446-489 (1971)

We can document the practice of adoption among the ancient Babylonians, Egyptians, and Hebrews, as well as the Greeks, but the most advanced early law on adoption which we have is from the Romans. In contrast with current adoption law, which has as its purpose the "best interests" of the child, it appears that ancient adoption law, and particularly the Roman example, was clearly designed to benefit the *adopter*, and any benefits to the adoptee were secondary. There were two broad purposes that Roman adoption law served: (1) to avoid extinction of the family, and (2) to perpetuate rites of family religious worship . . . .

[Adoption was not known at common law.] The usual explanation for the absence of a legal recognition of adoption in the English common law is the inordinately high regard for blood lineage of the English. [Another possible reason was xenophobia.]

The purpose of the American adoption statutes passed in the middle of the nineteenth century was to provide for the welfare of dependent children, a purpose quite different from that of the old Roman laws. [On the other hand, in England] there were mechanisms for the care of children, dependent and otherwise, that made adoption for social welfare purposes unnecessary. These mechanisms, which were instituted early and which were very well developed by the seventeenth century, were the institutions of "putting out" and "apprenticeship." In a very real sense these institutions were a form of "adoption," although the purpose was neither inheritance nor the perpetuation of the adopter's family, but the temporary training of the child. [T]he customs of "apprenticeship" and "service" were brought to America by the New England Puritans . . . .

The first comprehensive adoption statute was passed in 1851 in Massachusetts. Among its key provisions were requirements 1) that written consent be given by the natural parents . . . ; 2) that the child himself must consent if he is fourteen years of age or older; 3) that the adopter's [spouse] must join in the petition for adoption; 4) that the probate judge . . . must be satisfied that the petitioner(s) were "of sufficient ability to bring up the child . . . and that it is fit and proper that such adoption should take effect" . . . ; 5) that once the adoption was approved by the probate court, the adopted child would become "to all intents and purposes" the legal child of the petitioner(s); [and] 6) that the natural parents would be deprived by the decree of adoption of all legal rights and obligations respecting the adopted child. . . .

[The purpose of the Massachusetts law and others like it remains unclear. One theory says that an increase in adoptions arranged by foundling societies prompted these statutes.] It is naive to attribute the passage of adoption statutes in so many states solely to the activities of "foundling societies." The activities of these societies is demonstrative of a larger movement for child welfare of which the passage of the adoption statutes also represents a part. This movement came about as a result of the economic changes which made the stop-gap institutions of apprenticeship, service, and indenture quite unable to cope with the great numbers of children who had been neglected by their families and also were neglected, until about the middle of the nineteenth century in most cases, by the society and the state. In order to understand better the motives that lay behind the passage of the adoption statutes, it is important to understand some of these other developments in child welfare work. . . .

[F]rom philanthropic motives most probably inspired by the continuing plight of dependent children in the hands of public authorities, private agencies for the care of such children were founded. . . . In the first half of the nineteenth century, at least seventy-seven such agencies were founded. . . . After 1850 the increase in the number of such agencies was even more rapid. . . . Before 1850, the private agencies sought to teach their charges to read and write. . . . Prior to the establishment of the public school systems and compulsory attendance, the agencies felt their primary service should be to give to their children the rudiments of an education before they were placed out in indenture or service.

Around 1850, however, private agencies began to be founded with the avowed purpose of placing younger children in a suitable family atmosphere. The work of some of the "infant's hospitals," "foundling asylums," and "maternity hospitals" in New York and Boston stands out in this regard, as does the work of the Children's Aid Societies started in those cities in 1853 and 1865, respectively. . . . The Children's Aid Societies made efforts to place children in suitable homes, usually homes far from the city, in the expanding states and territories of the West. [T]he Children's Aid Society of New York [ ] placed over twenty thousand children in homes out of New York City in the twenty years after it was founded. . . .

[Many of] the children placed by such agencies as the New York Children's Aid Society found themselves in situations which not only resembled "adoption" as we know it today but which was called by the same name. As the phenomenon of children in adopted homes became more common, there was increased pressure not only to pass laws regulating and insuring the legal relations between adopted children and their natural and adoptive parents, but to guarantee that some benefits of heirship were conferred on the adopted child. This pressure, which originated with the activities of the charitable associations working in child welfare, led to passage of the general adoption statutes in the third quarter of the nineteenth century. . . .

On the Massachusetts adoption statute, see Jamil S. Zainaldin, The Emergence of a Modern American Family Law: Child Custody, Adoption, and the Courts, 1796-1851, 73 Nw. U. L. Rev. 1038 (1979). On the history of American adoption generally, see Michael Grossberg, Governing the Hearth: Law and Family in Nineteenth-Century America 271-280 (1985); Naomi Cahn, Perfect Substitutes or the Real Thing?, 52 Duke L.J. 1077 (2003); Chris Guthrie & Joanna L. Grossman, Adoption in the Progressive Era: Preserving, Creating, and Re-Creating Families, 43 Am. J. Legal Hist. 235 (1999).

B. PARENTAL CONSENT TO ADOPTION

1. Validity and Revocability

■ **SCARPETTA v. SPENCE-CHAPIN
ADOPTION SERVICE**
269 N.E.2d 787 (N.Y. 1971)

JASEN, J.

This appeal involves the return of an out-of-wedlock infant to its natural mother after she had executed a purported surrender of the child to an authorized adoption agency. . . .

The infant child was born on May 18, 1970, to Olga Scarpetta, who was unmarried and 32 years old. She had become pregnant in her native Colombia by a married Colombian in the summer of 1969. Seeking to minimize the shame of an out-of-wedlock child to herself and her family, Miss Scarpetta came to New York for the purpose of having her child. She was well acquainted with this country and its language. She had had her early schooling in New Jersey and her college education in California. Indeed, she had been trained in the social sciences.

Four days after the birth of the child, she placed the infant for boarding care with Spence-Chapin Adoption Service, an agency authorized by statute to receive children for adoption. Ten days later, a surrender document was executed by Miss Scarpetta to the agency, and on June 18, 1970, the baby was placed with a family for adoption. Five days later, on June 23, 1970, the mother repented her actions and requested that the child be returned to her.

After several unsuccessful attempts to regain her child from the agency, the mother commenced this habeas corpus proceeding. Before the surrender, the mother had had a number of interviews with representatives of the adoption agency. On the other hand, shortly before or after the birth of the child, her family in Colombia, well-to-do, and devout in their religion, were shocked that she should put out her child for adoption by strangers. They assured her of their support and backing and urged her to raise her own child. [The courts below ruled in favor of Scarpetta. This court affirms.]

The resolution of the issue of whether or not a mother, who has surrendered her child to an authorized adoption agency, may regain the child's custody, has received various treatment by the legislatures and courts in the United States. At one extreme, several jurisdictions adhere to the rule that the parent has an absolute right to regain custody of her child prior to the final adoption decree. On the other hand, some jurisdictions adhere to the rule that the parent's surrender is final, absent fraud or duress. The majority of the jurisdictions, however, place the parent's right to regain custody within the discretion of the court — the position which, of course, our Legislature has taken. The discretionary rule allows the court leeway to approve a revocation of the surrender when the facts of the individual case warrant it and avoids the obvious dangers posed by the rigidity of the extreme positions.

In New York, a surrender executed by a mother, in which she voluntarily consents to a change of guardianship and custody to an authorized agency for the purpose of adoption, is expressly sanctioned by law. (Social Services Law,

§384.) The statute nowhere endows a surrender with irrevocability foreclosing a mother from applying to the court to restore custody of the child to her. In fact, the legislation is clear that, until there has been an actual adoption, or the agency has met the requirements of the Social Services Law [requiring agency or court approval of surrender following notice], the surrender remains under, and subject to, judicial supervision.

Inherent to judicial supervision of surrenders is the recognition that documents of surrender are unilateral, not contracts or deeds, and are almost always executed under circumstances which may cast doubt upon their voluntariness or on understanding of the consequences of their execution. . . . Of necessity, therefore, there is always an issue about the fact of surrender, document or no document. On the other hand, the courts have the strongest obligation not to permit surrenders to be undone except for the weightiest reasons. . . .

Having the power to direct a change of custody from the agency back to the natural parent, notwithstanding the document of surrender, the court should exercise it only when it determines "that the interest of such child will be promoted thereby and that such parent is fit, competent and able to duly maintain, support and educate such child." (Social Services Law, §383, subd. 1.) . . . It has repeatedly been determined, insofar as the best interests of the child are concerned, that "[the] mother or father has a right to the care and custody of a child, superior to that of all others, unless he or she has abandoned that right or is proved unfit to assume the duties and privileges of parenthood." [Citations omitted.]

The primacy of status thus accorded the natural parent is not materially altered or diminished by the mere fact of surrender under the statute, although it is a factor to be considered by the court. To hold, as the agency suggests — that a surrender to an authorized adoption agency constitutes, as a matter of law, an abandonment — would frustrate the policy underlying our legislation, which allows a mother to regain custody of her child, notwithstanding the surrender to the agency, provided, of course, that there is some showing of improvidence in the making of the surrender, that the interest of such child will be promoted and "that such parent is fit, competent and able to duly maintain, support and educate such child." . . .

In no case, however, may a contest between a parent and nonparent resolve itself into a simple factual issue as to which affords the better surroundings, or as to which party is better equipped to raise the child. It may well be that the prospective adoptive parents would afford a child some material advantages over and beyond what the natural mother may be able to furnish, but these advantages, passing and transient as they are, cannot outweigh a mother's tender care and love unless it is clearly established that she is unfit to assume the duties and privileges of parenthood.

We conclude that the record before us supports the finding by the courts below that the surrender was improvident and that the child's best interests — moral and temporal — will be best served by its return to the natural mother.

Within 23 days after the child had been given over to the agency, and only 5 days after the prospective adoptive parents had gained provisional custody of the child, the mother sought its return. If the matter had been resolved at that time, much heartache and distress would have been avoided. . . .

[The court rejects the prospective adoptive parents' petition to intervene on the ground that intervention would necessarily lead to disclosure of the names of the natural parents and prospective adoptive parents to each other in violation of the policy of secrecy, which relies on the adoption agency to serve as intermediary.] Similarly, we find no merit to the contention that the failure to allow the prospective adoptive parents to intervene in the instant proceeding deprived them of due process of law so as to render the court's determination awarding custody of the child to the mother, constitutionally invalid. The prospective adoptive parents do not have legal custody of the baby. Spence-Chapin, the adoption agency, by virtue of the mother's surrender, was vested with legal custody. The agency, in turn, had placed the baby with the prospective adoptive parents pursuant to an arrangement reached between them, for the purpose of prospective adoption of the child. This arrangement is, of course, subject to our adoption statutes, and in no way conveys any vested rights in the child to the prospective adoptive parents. . . .

Notes and Questions

1. *Epilogue*. After the court's decision, the adoptive family (the DiMartinos) fled with "Baby Lenore" to Florida. Scarpetta filed a habeas corpus action there, claiming full faith and credit for the New York decision. The DiMartinos successfully argued that they should not be bound by litigation in which they were not permitted to participate. At the ensuing trial, the court focused on the child's best interests. Experts testified on her development with the DiMartinos and the trauma separation would cause. The Florida court ruled the DiMartinos should retain custody. Henry H. Foster, Jr., Adoption and Child Custody: Best Interests of the Child?, 22 Buff. L. Rev. 1, 8 (1972). The U.S. Supreme Court denied certiorari, DiMartino v. Scarpetta, 404 U.S. 805 (1971).

In response to the case, New York amended the statute. It now provides that in contested revocation cases parents who consented "have no right to the custody of the child superior to that of the adoptive parents" and custody "shall be awarded solely on the basis of the best interests of the child," with no presumption favoring any particular disposition. N.Y. Dom. Rel. Law §115-b(6)(d)(v) (McKinney Supp. 2005).

2. *Agency placement*. The adoption process often begins, as *Scarpetta* illustrates, when the birth parent voluntarily relinquishes (or "surrenders") the child to a state-licensed or state-operated agency. The agency takes legal custody and selects an adoptive family. After a residential period under the agency's supervision, a court issues an adoption decree. Traditionally, neither the birth parents nor the adopters learn the others' identities. Moreover, if the placement fails during the trial period, the child returns to the agency's care, not to the birth parent whose rights are terminated by the relinquishment. Advocates claim that only agency adoptions serve the birth parents' needs for counseling and support, the child's needs for placement with capable and prepared adopters, and the adopters' needs for a full range of services. See L. Jean Emery, Agency Versus Independent Adoption: The Case for Agency Adoption, The Future of Children, Spring 1993, at 139, 140-142; Susan A. Munson, Comment, Independent Adoption: In Whose Best Interest?, 26 Seton Hall L. Rev. 803, 804-809 (1996). Today, most agency placements involve older children who spent time in foster care. Ruth-Arlene W. Howe, Adoption Laws and Practices in 2000: Serving Whose Interests?, 33 Fam. L.Q. 677, 681-683 (1999).

3. *The relinquishment experience.* According to the principal case, why did Olga Scarpetta relinquish her child? Why did she change her mind?

Consider the thesis of historian Rickie Solinger, developed from communications with birth mothers:

> Based on what I've learned about the experiences of birthmothers in the United States, I want to suggest that the conventional understanding of adoption should be turned on its head. Almost everybody believes that on some level, birthmothers *make a choice to give their babies away*. . . . I argue that adoption is rarely about mothers' choices; it is, instead, about the abject choicelessness of some resourceless women.

Rickie Solinger, Beggars and Choosers: How the Politics of Choice Shapes Adoption, Abortion, and Welfare in the United States 67 (2001). For example, following World War II, white unmarried mothers faced enormous pressure to relinquish because adoption practice treated them as deviant and unfit to parent, yet able to provide valuable resources (babies) to married infertile couples. See id. at 69-70. How have these social constraints evolved over time?

In balancing the competing interests in a case like *Scarpetta*, what weight should be accorded to the emotional experiences of birth parents in relinquishment? See Holli Ann Askren & Kathaleen C. Bloom, Postadoptive Reactions of the Relinquishing Mother: A Review, JOGNN, July/Aug. 1999, at 395 ("at risk for long-term physical, psychologic, and social repercussions"). Advocates of reform have questioned the traditional postrelinquishment goal of encouraging the birth mother to "reconstitute her life quickly by bolstering the defenses of denial and repression at the cost of other emotional needs." Eva Y. Deykin et al., The Postadoption Experience of Surrendering Parents, 54 Am. J. Orthopsychiatry 271, 272 (1984). See Ann Fessler, The Girls Who Went Away: The Hidden History of Women Who Surrendered Children for Adoption in the Decade Before Roe v. Wade (2006).

4. *Revocation of consent. Scarpetta* surveys different approaches to revocation. Which is most sound? What can states do to improve the consent process and minimize attempted revocations? See Elizabeth J. Samuels, Time to Decide? The Laws Governing Mothers' Consents to the Adoption of Their Newborn Infants, 72 Tenn. L. Rev. 509 (2005); Karen D. Laverdiere, Note and Comment, Content Over Form: The Shifting of Adoption Consent Laws, 25 Whittier L. Rev. 599 (2004). Jurisdictions recognize several bases for revoking consent to adoption:

a. *Time period.* One approach makes determinative the timing of consent or revocation. For example, under the Uniform Adoption Act (UAA) §§2-408, 2-409, a parent can revoke relinquishment of consent within 192 hours (8 days) of the child's birth. 9 U.L.A. (pt. IA) 60-63 (1999). See also, e.g., In re Adoption of Baby Girls Mandell, 572 N.E.2d 359 (Ill. App. Ct. 1991) (12-month limit). An alternative approach makes voidable consents executed less than a certain number of days after birth. See In re Baby Girl T., 21 P.3d 581 (Kan. Ct. App. 2001) (upholding statute's 12-hour period). Finally, some jurisdictions allow withdrawal of consent anytime before the final decree of termination of parental rights or adoption. E.g., 25 U.S.C. §1913(c) (2000) (Indian Child Welfare Act). How much time for revocation ought to be allowed?

b. *Fraud, duress or immaturity.* Many states invalidate consent procured by fraud or coercion. E.g., Ariz. Rev. Stat. Ann. §8-106(D) (Supp. 2005); Va. Code Ann. §63.1-219.12 (2002); Gruett v. Nesbit, 17 P.3d 1090, *reconsideration denied,*

21 P.3d 168 (Or. Ct. App. 2001) (setting aside adoption because of agency's misrepresentation of birth father's lack of interest); Gunderman v. Helms, 68 P.3d 1021 (Utah Ct. App. 2003) (remanding to determine birth mother's claim of duress).

Can minors validly consent to adoption? See T.R. v. Adoption Servs., Inc., 724 So. 2d 1235 (Fla. Dist. Ct. App. 1999) (youth and poverty do not constitute duress); In re Adoption of D.N.T., 843 So. 2d 690, 708-710 (Miss. 2003). Some jurisdictions address this problem by requiring the consent of the minor birth parent's parents. See, e.g., Minn. Stat. Ann. §259.24(2) (West Supp. 2006). But see Mo. Rev. Stat. §453.050 (2000) (waiver of consent valid even if parent is under age 18). Can a minor birth parent who subsequently seeks to revoke consent be bound by her own parents' consent?

5. *Consent substitutes.* Can a state constitutionally grant an adoption *without* valid parental consent? Involuntary termination of parental rights comporting with all procedural and substantive requirements dispenses with the need for parental consent. (See Chapter VIII, section B4d.) Can a state replace consent or the usual grounds for termination of parental rights with a showing that adoption serves the child's best interests? See, e.g., Mass. Gen. Laws Ann. ch. 210, §3(a)(ii) (West Supp. 2005) (so permitting); In re W.E.T., 793 A.2d 471 (D.C. 2002); Gray v. Bourne, 614 S.E.2d 661 (Va. Ct. App. 2005). What considerations should a best-interests analysis include? See In re Adoption of Victor A., 872 A.2d 662 (Md. 2005) (not availability of adoptive homes). Will a statutory time period in foster care meet the constitutional test? Compare In re H.G., 757 N.E.2d 864 (Ill. 2001), with Doe v. Roe, 578 S.E.2d 733 (S.C. Ct. App. 2003).

If the state can dispense with parental consent, can it do so in a way that treats birth fathers and mothers differently? The next case explores this question.

2. Unmarried Fathers' Rights

■ **ADOPTION OF KELSEY S.**
823 P.2d 1216 (Cal. 1992)

BAXTER, J.

The primary question in this case is whether the father of a child born out of wedlock may properly be denied the right to withhold his consent to his child's adoption by third parties despite his diligent and legal attempts to obtain custody of his child and to rear it himself, and absent any showing of the father's unfitness as a parent. . . .

Kari S. gave birth to Kelsey, a boy, on May 18, 1988. The child's undisputed natural father is petitioner Rickie M. He and Kari S. were not married to one another. At that time, he was married to another woman but was separated from her and apparently was in divorce proceedings. He was aware that Kari planned to place their child for adoption, and he objected to her decision because he wanted to rear the child.

Two days after the child's birth, petitioner filed an action in superior court under Civil Code section 7006 to establish his parental relationship with the child and to obtain custody of the child. [The court awarded petitioner temporary custody, stayed all adoption proceedings, and prohibited contact with the prospective adopters.] On May 24, 1988, Steven and Suzanne A., the prospective adoptive parents, filed an adoption petition under Civil Code section 226 [, alleging] that only the mother's consent to the adoption was required because there was no presumed father under section 7004, subdivision (a). [The court modified its order and awarded the birth mother temporary custody.] The court ordered the mother to live with the child in a shelter for unwed mothers. [T]he trial court prohibited visitation by either the prospective adoptive parents or petitioner. [The prospective adopters then petitioned under §7017 to terminate petitioner's parental rights.] The superior court consolidated that proceeding with the adoption proceeding. The court allowed petitioner to have supervised visitation with the child at the women's shelter where the child was living with his mother. The court also allowed the prospective adoptive parents to have unsupervised visitation at the shelter.

[Despite a stipulation of petitioner's biological paternity, the court below held that he was not a "presumed father" under the controlling statute. After four days of hearings, including arguments by the child's attorney that petitioner should retain parental rights, the court held that the child's best interests required termination of his parental rights, by a bare preponderance of the evidence.] Petitioner appealed. He contended the superior court erred by: (1) concluding that he was not the child's presumed father; (2) not granting him a parental placement preference; and (3) applying a preponderance-of-the-evidence standard of proof. The Court of Appeal rejected each of his contentions. . . .

Section 7004 states, "A man is presumed to be the natural father of a child . . ." if the man meets any of several conditions set forth in the statute. Whether a biological father is a "presumed father" under section 7004 is critical to his parental rights. If the mother of a child . . . consents to the child's adoption, [t]he child's best interest is the sole criterion where there is no presumed father. As in the present case, the trial court's determination is frequently that the child's interests are better served by a third party adoption than by granting custody to the unwed natural father.[1]

Mothers and presumed fathers have far greater rights. [A] mother or a presumed father must consent to an adoption absent a showing by clear and convincing evidence of that parent's unfitness. . . .

A man becomes a "presumed father" under section 7004, subdivision (a)(4) if *"[h]e receives the child into his home* and openly holds out the child as his natural child." (Italics added.) It is undisputed in this case that petitioner openly held out the child as being his own. Petitioner, however, did not physically receive the child into his home. He was prevented from doing so by the mother, by court order, and allegedly also by the prospective adoptive parents. . . .

There remains . . . the question of whether a natural father's federal constitutional rights are violated if his child's mother is allowed to unilaterally preclude him from obtaining the same legal right as a presumed father to withhold his consent to his child's adoption by third parties. [This question] has not been addressed by the United States Supreme Court. We are guided, however, by a series of high court decisions dealing with the rights of unwed fathers. [The Court then analyzed three

---

[1]. The relevant statutes are now Cal. Fam. Code §§7611, 7611.5, & 7612 (West 2004 & West Supp. 2006).–Eds.

Supreme Court precedents: Stanley v. Illinois, 405 U.S. 645 (1972); Quilloin v. Walcott, 434 U.S. 246 (1978); and Caban v. Mohammed, 441 U.S. 380 (1979). These cases are examined in Chapter IV, section C2].

The high court again considered the rights of biological fathers only four years later in Lehr v. Robertson (1983) 463 U.S. 248. The father and mother lived together before the child's birth, and he visited the child in the hospital when the child was born. He did not, however, live with either the mother or child after its birth, and he did not provide them with any financial support. Nor did he offer to marry the mother. Eight months after the child's birth, the mother married another man. When the child was two years old, the mother and her new husband began adoption proceedings. One month later, the biological father filed an action seeking a determination of his paternity, an order of support, and visitation with the child. Shortly thereafter, the biological father learned of the pending adoption proceeding, and almost immediately he sought to have it stayed pending the determination of his paternity petition. The state court informed him that it had already signed the adoption order earlier that day, and then dismissed his paternity action. . . . The Lehr court, held that, "because appellant, like the father in Quilloin, has never established a substantial relationship with his daughter . . . the New York statutes at issue in this case did not operate to deny appellant equal protection [in treating him differently from other fathers]."

[Lehr] did not purport to decide the legal question in the present case, that is, whether the mother may constitutionally prevent the father from establishing the relationship that gives rise to his right to equal protection. The Lehr court, however, recognized the uniqueness of the biological connection between parent and child. "The significance of the biological connection is that it offers the natural father an opportunity that no other male possesses to develop a relationship with his off-spring. If he grasps that opportunity and accepts some measure of responsibility for the child's future, he may enjoy the blessings of the parent-child relationship and make uniquely valuable contributions to the child's development." (Id., at p.262.) Lehr can fairly be read to mean that a father need only make a reasonable and meaningful attempt to establish a relationship, not that he must be successful against all obstacles. [The court then considered Michael H. v. Gerald D., 491 U.S. 110 (1989), reprinted in Chapter IV, section C2.]

[O]ne unifying and transcendent theme emerges. The biological connection between father and child is unique and worthy of constitutional protection if the father grasps the opportunity to develop that biological connection into a full and enduring relationship. . . .

Petitioner asserts a violation of equal protection and due process under the federal Constitution; more specifically, that he should not be treated differently from his child's mother. . . . Respondents do not adequately explain how an unwed mother's control over a biological father's rights [substantially furthers the state's important] interest in the well-being of the child. The linchpin of their position, however, is clear although largely implicit: Allowing the biological father to have the same rights as the mother would make adoptions more difficult because the consent of both parents is more difficult to obtain than the consent of the mother alone. This reasoning is flawed in several respects.

A. Respondents' view too narrowly assumes that the proper governmental objective is adoption. [T]he constitutionally valid objective is the protection of the child's well-being. . . . If the possible benefit of adoption were by itself sufficient to justify terminating a parent's rights, the state could terminate an unwed mother's parental rights based on nothing more than a showing that her child's best interest would be served by adoption. . . .

B. Nor is there evidence before us that the statutory provisions allowing the mother to determine the father's rights are, in general, substantially related to protecting the child's best interest. [Respondent] assumes an unwed mother's decision to permit an immediate adoption of her newborn is always preferable to custody by the natural father, even when he is a demonstrably fit parent. . . .

C. The lack of any substantial relationship between the state's interest in protecting a child and allowing the mother sole control over its destiny is best demonstrated by the results that can arise when a mother prevents the father from obtaining presumed status under section 7004, subdivision (a). . . . Under the statute, the father has basically two ways in which to achieve that status: he can either marry the mother, or he can receive the child into his home and hold it out as his natural child. Of course, the first alternative is entirely within the mother's control. . . . The system also leads to irrational distinctions between fathers. Based solely on the mother's wishes, a model father can be denied presumed father status, whereas a father of dubious ability and intent can achieve such status by the fortuitous circumstance of the mother allowing him to come into her home, even if only briefly — perhaps a single day. . . .

D. We must not lose sight of the way in which the present case and others like it come before the courts. A mother's decision to place her newborn child for adoption may be excruciating and altogether altruistic. Doing so may reflect the extreme of selflessness and maternal love. As a legal matter, however, the mother seeks to sever all ties with her child. [Yet even if] the mother somehow has a greater connection than the father with their child and thus should have greater rights in the child, the same result need not obtain when she seeks to relinquish custody and to sever her legal ties with the child and the father seeks to assume his legal burdens. . . .

E. In summary, we hold that section 7004, subdivision (a) and the related statutory scheme [are unconstitutional]. If an unwed father promptly comes forward and demonstrates a full commitment to his parental responsibilities — emotional, financial, and otherwise — his federal constitutional right to due process prohibits the termination of his parental relationship absent a showing of his unfitness as a parent. Absent such a showing, the child's well-being is presumptively best served by continuation of the father's parental relationship. Similarly, when the father has come forward to grasp his parental responsibilities, his parental rights are entitled to equal protection as those of the mother.

A court should consider all factors relevant to that determination. The father's conduct both before and after the child's birth must be considered. Once he knows or reasonably should know of the pregnancy, he must promptly attempt to assume his parental responsibilities as fully as the mother will allow and his circumstances permit. In particular, the father must demonstrate "a willingness himself to assume full custody of the child — not merely to block adoption by others." [In Matter of Raquel Marie, 559 N.E.2d 418, 428 (N.Y. 1990).] A court should also consider the father's public acknowledgement of paternity, payment of pregnancy and birth expenses commensurate with his ability to do so, and prompt legal action to seek custody of the child. . . .

[I]f (but only if) the trial court finds petitioner demonstrated the necessary commitment to his parental responsibilities, there will arise the further question of whether he can be deprived of the right to withhold his consent to the adoption. . . . For purposes of remand, . . . any finding of petitioner's unfitness must be supported by clear and convincing evidence. Absent such evidence, he shall be permitted to withhold his consent to the adoption.

[If] the trial court concludes that petitioner has a right to withhold consent, that decision will bear only on the question of whether the adoption will proceed. Even if petitioner has a right to withhold his consent (and chooses to prevent the adoption), there will remain the question of the child's custody. That question is not before us, and we express no view on it. . . .

Notes and Questions

1. *Independent placement.* The independent adoption in *Kelsey S.* contrasts with the agency placement in *Scarpetta*. Generally, in independent adoptions the birth parents select the adopters themselves, often with the assistance of an intermediary such as an attorney, and place the child directly with the adopters, pending the issuance of a final adoption decree. The UAA has several distinct provisions for "direct" and agency placements (for example, §§2-102, 2-103). 9 U.L.A. (pt. IA) 30-33 (1999). A few states prohibit or strictly limit independent placements. See Elizabeth J. Samuels, Time to Decide? The Laws Governing Mothers' Consents to the Adoption of Their Newborn Infants, 72 Tenn. L. Rev. 509, 519 n.68 (2005).

Critics claim independent adoptions primarily help adults seeking a child to adopt, at the expense of child welfare. L. Jean Emery, Agency Versus Independent Adoption: The Case for Agency Adoption, The Future of Children, Spring 1993, at 139, 143. Supporters assert: (a) birth parents prefer independent adoption because it allows them to select the adopters; (b) adopters avoid long waiting lists and play an active role in the process; and (c) children avoid the necessity of spending a transitional period in foster care. Mark T. McDermott, Agency Versus Independent Adoption: The Case for Independent Adoption, The Future of Children, Spring 1993, at 146, 147. Because adoptive parents often pay birth parents' expenses in independent placements, some call these "gray market" adoptions. See generally Madelyn Freundlich, The Market Forces in Adoption (2000).

2. *Thwarted fathers. Kelsey S.* considers the rights of a "thwarted father" to veto an infant's adoption planned by the birth mother. In deciding in favor of the father, how accurate is the court's analysis of the Supreme Court's precedents? See Lehr v. Robertson, 463 U.S. 248, 268-269 (1983) (White, J., dissenting). Justice White describes how Lehr and the mother had cohabited, how he had visited her and the infant in the hospital upon birth, and how later he "never ceased his efforts to locate" them (even hiring a detective), despite the mother's efforts to conceal their whereabouts. Lehr also offered financial support. If Justice White's recitation of the facts in *Lehr* is accurate, then the Supreme Court had already rejected the equal protection claims of a father who tried to maintain a relationship with his child but was thwarted by the mother's unilateral actions. Do the two cases warrant different approaches because *Lehr*, unlike *Kelsey S.*, concerned a stepparent adoption in which the birth mother would continue to rear the child?

Are there constitutionally acceptable reasons for giving biological mothers greater authority than fathers to determine placement of a nonmarital child? See generally Mary L. Shanley, Unwed Fathers' Rights, Adoption, and Sex Equality: Gender-Neutrality and the Preservation of Patriarchy, 95 Colum. L. Rev. 60 (1995).

3. *Competing interpretations.* Professor David Meyer identifies two different ways to interpret the Supreme Court precedents. Under the "child centered" view, only an actual parent-child relationship matters, not the efforts of a father whom the mother successfully thwarts. David D. Meyer, Family Ties: Solving the Constitutional Dilemma of the Faultless Father, 41 Ariz. L. Rev. 753, 764 (1999). Under a second reading, "the Supreme Court is concerned not simply with the existence or non-existence of a meaningful father-child relationship, but ultimately also with the strength of the father's moral claim [, that is,] whether the claimant has acted in a way deserving of protection." Id. Which view do you discern in the Supreme Court cases, including the opinions in *Michael H.* (see Chapter IV, section C2)? In *Kelsey S.?*

Under the second view, how does a father show he is deserving? Should sending one holiday card prevent a finding of abandonment? See In re Peshek, 759 N.E.2d 411 (Ohio Ct. App. 2001). Does an *offer* to provide support for the mother suffice? See In re Adoption of Anderson, 624 S.E.2d 626 (N.C. 2006). See also Escobedo v. Nickita, 2006 WL 563600 (Ark. 2006). Can the father's prebirth conduct toward the mother be determinative? Compare In re Adoption of Baby E.A.W., 658 So. 2d 961 (Fla. 1995) (father's prebirth "abandonment" of mother suffices to free child for adoption), with Ex parte F.P., 857 So. 2d 125 (Ala. 2003) (limiting application of prebirth abandonment statute). If there are several possible fathers, must they all take affirmative steps before birth to preserve their rights? See In re Adoption of D.M.M., 955 P.2d 618 (Kan. Ct. App. 1997) (yes). Does the father's criminal conduct prevent a finding that he is deserving, for purposes of halting an adoption? Compare In re C.D.M., 39 P.3d 802 (Okla. 2001) (stalker-father could not invoke protective order, which prohibited contact with child, as excuse for abandonment), with In re Adoption of TLC, 46 P.3d 863 (Wyo. 2002) (rejecting reliance on father's incarceration to show willful failure to support). If the child is conceived as the result of a sexual assault, is the biological father's consent required? An omitted footnote in *Kelsey S.* states that the constitutional protections do not apply in such circumstances. 823 P.2d at 1237 n.14. See also In re Adoption of A.F.M., 15 P.3d 258 (Alaska 2001). But see In re Kyle F., 5 Cal. Rptr. 3d 190 (Ct. App. 2003) (distinguishing statutory rape from forcible rape to allow father to demonstrate right to withhold consent to adoption).

4. *Maternal deception.* Suppose the mother purposely misidentifies the father when relinquishing the child. Later, she marries the biological father and joins with him to halt adoption proceedings. Should the pair regain custody? See In the Interest of B.G.C., 496 N.W.2d 239 (Iowa 1992) ("Baby Jessica" case). Will recognition of the biological father's rights raise the "specter of newly named genetic fathers, upsetting adoptions, perhaps years later"? Id. at 247 (Snell, J., dissenting). Should (could) a state require a woman to identify the father correctly or to notify him of her pregnancy as a precondition to adoption? Cf. In re Termination of Parental Rights of Biological Parents of Baby Boy W., 988 P.2d 1270 (Okla. 1999).

Consider the highly publicized "Baby Richard" case, in which the mother falsely told the father the newborn had died. Later they married and sought the child's return. The court held the father had shown sufficient interest in the child to preclude termination of his rights based solely on the child's best interests. It invalidated the adoption, removing the child from his family of four years. In re Petition of John Doe, 638 N.E.2d 181 (Ill.), *cert. denied*, 513 U.S. 994 (1994). The birth father then successfully sought a writ of habeas corpus, requiring the child's transfer to his custody. In re Petition of Kirchner, 649 N.E.2d 324 (Ill.), *stay denied sub nom.* O'Connell v. Kirchner, 513 U.S. 1138 (1995). Later the birth parents separated, leaving the child in the birth mother's custody. Dirk Johnson, Father Who Won Custody Case Over Adopted Boy Moves Out, N.Y. Times, Jan. 22, 1997, at A10.

5. *The child's rights.* How should a court balance the rights of biological parents against the child's liberty interest in remaining with a "psychological family"? In Baby Richard's case and similar controversies, courts have declined to allow a child's best interests to trump a thwarted father's rights. See *John Doe*, 638 N.E.2d 181; *B.G.C.*, 496 N.W.2d 239. Do you agree with this approach? For another account of a child returned to his birth mother after his birth father challenged his adoption, see Caught in Tangle of Adoption Laws, Children Suffer, USA Today, Jan. 24, 2005, at 10A (Evan Scott case).

If a court makes the child's best interests determinative, should it focus on short-term or long-term interests? What weight should a court accord to potential trauma from separation from the psychological family? According to psychological theory, disrupted early attachment jeopardizes the formation of later intimate relationships. See Marcus T. Boccaccini & Eleanor Willemsen, Contested Adoption and the Liberty Interest of the Child, 10 St. Thomas L. Rev. 211, 291 (1998). Media reports claim that Baby Jessica and Baby Richard have fared well despite their traumatic removal from long-term adoptive placements and the subsequent dissolutions of their birth parents' relationships. See Leonard Greene, Heartbreak Kids Enjoy Normal Childhoods, N.Y. Post, Mar. 9, 2001, at 19; Gregory A. Kelson, In the Best Interest of the Child: What Have We Learned from Baby Jessica and Baby Richard?, 33 J. Marshall L. Rev. 353, 362, 370-371 (2000). See also infra p.1077.

6. *Statutory reforms.*

a. *Expanded definitions.* In the wake of high-profile challenges to adoptive placements by the thwarted fathers of Baby Jessica and Baby Richard, several states expanded the grounds for terminating parental rights, broadening definitions of "abandonment" and "unfitness." Most of these laws, however, have not been interpreted to allow "no-fault" terminations. See Meyer, supra, at 770-792.

b. *Registries.* Several states use "putative father registries," which eliminate the need for adoption notification or consent for a man who failed to take the initiative by registering. See id. at 756-757. The Supreme Court approved reliance on a registry system in *Lehr*, supra. The Uniform Parentage Act, revised in 2000, follows this approach to facilitate and expedite infant adoptions, where "time is of the essence," while requiring notification to fathers of older children and exempting fathers of infants who initiate timely proceedings to establish paternity. 9B U.L.A. 24 (Supp. 2005) (cmt. on Art. 4). See also 9B U.L.A 322 (2001) (§402 requires registration no later than 30 days after birth or commencement of paternity proceedings before termination of his parental rights). What information must the risk-averse man provide if he registers before he knows of a pregnancy? What problems do you see in this approach? See Tamar Lewin, Unwed Fathers Fight for Babies Placed for Adoption by Mothers, N.Y. Times, March 19, 2006, §1, at 1. See generally Laurence C. Nolan, Preventing Fatherlessness Through Adoption While Protecting the Parental Rights of Unwed Fathers: How Effective Are Paternity Registries?, 4 Whittier J. Child & Fam. Advoc. 289 (2005).

c. *Publication.* Another approach requires notifying unidentified fathers by posting or publication. See, e.g., Uniform Putative and Unknown Fathers Act, 9C U.L.A. 63, 67-68 (2001) (§3 allows court to order publication or posting of notice if likely to lead to actual notice of father). How well will these methods achieve actual notification if they exclude the mother's name to protect her privacy? See Jones v. South Carolina Dept. of Soc. Servs., 534 S.E.2d 713 (S.C. Ct. App. 2000).

Florida enacted a controversial approach designed to enhance actual notification of an unknown father, requiring preadoption publication to include the minor's birth name, each city in which conception might have occurred, and the name of the mother and any man she reasonably believes might be the father. Does the measure violate the right to privacy by interfering with both a woman's autonomy in choosing adoption and her interest in protecting intimate personal information from disclosure, without satisfying strict scrutiny? G.P. v. State, 842 So. 2d 1059 (Fla. Dist. Ct. App. 2003) (holding statutory requirements violate state constitutional right to privacy). See Alison S. Pally, Father by Newspaper Ad: The Impact of In re the Adoption of a Minor Child on the Definition of Fatherhood, 13 Colum. J. Gender & L. 169 (2004) (critiquing Florida's "biology only" test for fathers); Claire L. McKenna, Note, To Unknown Male: Notice of Plan for Adoption in the Florida 2001 Adoption Act, 79 Notre Dame L. Rev. 789 (2004) (analyzing of Florida requirements under compelled speech doctrine).

d. *Presumed paternity.* In revising the original Uniform Parentage Act (UPA) in 2000, the drafters initially eliminated the presumption at issue in *Kelsey S.*, reasoning that increasingly accurate genetic tests make conduct-based presumptions obsolete. Two years later, however, the drafters reconsidered and included a limited "holding out" rule: In order for such conduct to create a presumption of paternity, "for the first two years of the child's life, [the man must have] resided in the same household with the child and openly held out the child as his own." What explains the reconsideration? Is it relevant that the drafters had retained the traditional marital presumption (discussed in Chapter IV, section C2)? See Unif. Parentage Act §204(a)(5) & cmts. to 2002 version, 9B U.L.A. 16-17 (Supp. 2005). Does the new UPA's approach address the problem of the "thwarted father" in adoption cases? Why must the necessary conduct occur during the first two years of the child's life?

e. *Uniform Adoption Act.* The UAA, §3-504(c)-(d), allows termination of the rights of a birth father who has not demonstrated an interest in parenting his child unless he can show a "compelling reason" for his failure to do so. 9 U.L.A. (pt. IA) 86-87 (1999). Even so, the court can nevertheless terminate his rights if it finds evidence that failure to terminate will be "detrimental" to the child or granting custody to him would pose a risk of "substantial harm" to the child's well-being. Id. Although the act protects a birth mother's right to remain silent about the birth father, it requires advising her that her choice may delay the adoption or subject it to challenge, that the lack of information about the father's medical and genetic history may be detrimental to the adoptee, and that she faces a civil penalty for knowingly misidentifying the father. UAA §3-404, id. at 79-80.

7. *Adoption versus custody. Kelsey S.* explicitly distinguishes adoption from custody, stating that even if the biological father can block the adoption, custody remains a separate issue. Does the court suggest that the prospective adoptive parents might retain custody even without an adoption decree? See also In re Adoption of Daniele G., 105 Cal. Rptr. 2d 341 (Ct. App. 2001) (applying *Kelsey S.* to award guardianship to would-be adopters because removal would be detrimental); People ex rel. A.J.C., 88 P.3d 599 (Colo. 2004) (ruling child's best interests determine custody after failed adoption). Cf. In re Baby Girl L., 51 P.3d 544 (Okla. 2002) (interpreting "best interests" to require showing of severe psychological harm to justify continued custody with would-be adopters). Yet if custody might remain with the adopters, why does the court say that to prevail in blocking an adoption a birth father must demonstrate a willingness to assume *full custody*? The UAA §3-506 follows the court's approach, allowing a court that denies an adoption petition to determine the child's legal custody. 9 U.L.A. (pt. IA) 90 (1999). See Meyer, supra, at 792-812 (critiquing Illinois and other laws allowing custody without adoption, in response to Baby Richard case). Professor Meyer proposes instead adoption with visitation rights for biological parents, in other words, "non-consensual open adoption." Id. at 833-845. Evaluate this proposal.

8. *Estoppel.* In a concurring and dissenting opinion in *Kelsey S.*, Justice Mosk would have reached the same result based on equitable estoppel: the conduct of the biological mother and adoptive parents, thwarting the father's efforts, should equitably estop them from challenging his status as a presumed father. Mosk claims this approach would avoid an unnecessary declaration of unconstitutionality and "needless uncertainty in the application of statutory categories that have been consistently employed for almost 20 years," to the detriment of all parties, "especially the child." 823 P.2d at 1239. Is this approach preferable?

Can a putative father be estopped from *preventing* an adoption? See In re Adoption of S.A.J., 838 A.2d 616 (Pa. 2003) (father's denial of paternity estops him from subsequently claiming paternity to prevent stepparent adoption). Can estoppel *create* parental rights requiring termination before others can adopt the child? Suppose a birth mother and her partner obtain a prebirth decree recognizing both as parents. See Kristine H. v. Lisa R., 117 P.3d 690 (Cal. 2005); American Law Institute, Principles of the Law of Family Dissolution §§2.03, 3.03 (2002). See also infra pp.1072-1073.

9. *Empirical evidence.* An early classic study reveals that surrender of a child for adoption long remains an emotional issue. Eva Y. Deykin et al., Fathers of Adopted Children: A Study of the Impact of Child Surrender on Birthfathers, 58 Am. J. Orthopsychiatry 240, 246-247 (1988). This survey of self-identified birth fathers reports that most had negative views of the surrender and some felt obsessed with finding the child. Id. at 244, 246. Despite such data, other studies reveal that many birth mothers, adoptive parents, and adoptees hold negative attitudes about birth fathers, associating them with desertion and failure to take responsibility. Most respondents did not support the release of identifying information on adoptees to birth fathers even when supporting the same for birth mothers. Paul Sachdev, The Birth Father: A Neglected Element in the Adoption Equation, 72 Fam. in Soc'y: J. Contemp. Hum. Servs. 131 (1991). Compare Elizabeth S. Cole & Kathryn S. Donley, History, Values, and Placement Policy Issues in Adoption, in The Psychology of Adoption 273, 285 (David M. Brodzinsky & Marshall D. Schecter eds., 1990) (research fails to justify negative views of birth fathers), with

Anne B. Brodzinsky, Surrendering an Infant for Adoption: The Birthmother Experience, in The Psychology of Adoption, supra, at 295, 315 ("interested, committed birthfathers remain in the minority").

Problems

1. Mark (then 20) asks Stephanie (then 15) to marry after a short acquaintance. She declines. A few months later they learn Stephanie is pregnant. They decide on adoption. Stephanie then leaves Arizona to visit California. After meeting John and Margaret there, she chooses them to adopt the baby.

On her return to Arizona, Stephanie's relationship with Mark deteriorates. Stephanie excludes him from birthing classes. Following two violent outbursts, Mark attempts suicide and enters drug rehabilitation therapy. He then informs Stephanie he no longer favors adoption.

Stephanie returns to California, gives birth, places the child with John and Margaret, and consents to their adoption. Mark, when he learns of the birth a week later, immediately consults an attorney, sends out birth announcements, and purchases baby supplies. Thereafter, he consistently expresses his desire to take full parental responsibilities.

John and Margaret seek to terminate Mark's parental rights in California. They claim that *Kelsey S.* gives Mark no veto over the adoption because he failed to demonstrate full commitment to parental responsibilities throughout the pregnancy. Mark also invokes *Kelsey S.*, counterarguing that he attempted to maintain a relationship with Stephanie during the pregnancy and that since birth he has done everything possible to assume full parental responsibility. He also claims that John and Margaret's interpretation of *Kelsey S.* discriminates by allowing mothers to decide after birth to withhold consent for adoption while requiring fathers to decide early in the pregnancy.

What result and why? What policy issues does each reading of *Kelsey S.* raise? See Adoption of Michael H., 898 P.2d 891 (Cal. 1995); Carol A. Gorenberg, Fathers' Rights vs. Children's Best Interests: Establishing a Predictable Standard for California Adoption Disputes, 31 Fam. L.Q. 169 (1997).

2. T.W. gives birth to twin daughters in Missouri. While the premature twins are hospitalized, T.W. brings them breast milk. Because T.W. is rearing three other children, she explores the possibility of placing the twins for adoption. Seeking an open adoption (which Missouri does not permit), she chooses a California couple whom she finds with help from an adoption professional and the Internet. Later, she reclaims the twins, within the permissible time period for revocation, because she concludes that the couple would not respect her preference for continuing contact. Next, she chooses a British couple, and an Arkansas court issues the adoption decrees. After British social service workers find this couple unfit and the Arkansas adoption is set aside for lack of jurisdiction, the twins are placed in foster care in Missouri. T.W., who by then changes her mind about adoption, seeks the twins' return to her custody.

The family court terminates T.W.'s parental rights on the ground that she abandoned the twins and emotionally abused them by relinquishing them twice for adoption. T.W. appeals, contending that she neither abandoned nor abused the twins and asserting that no other permissible basis for termination exists. What result and why? See In re K.A.W., 133 S.W.3d 1 (Mo. 2004); Robert Patrick, Mom Set to See 'Net Twins,' Now 5, St. Louis Post-Dispatch, March 21, 2006, at A1. Cf. In re Adoption of D.N.T., 843 So. 2d 690, 706-707 (Miss. 2003). Of what relevance is T.W.'s use of the Internet to find a placement? If the foster parents now wish to adopt the children, *should* the court resolve the dispute by deciding whether adoption or their return to T.W. will serve their best interests? See Moore v. Asente, 110 S.W.3d 336 (Ky. 2003). *Can* the court decide on the basis of the twins' best interests? Cf. In re R.C., 745 N.E.2d 1233 (Ill. 2001).

C. CHOOSING AN ADOPTIVE FAMILY

1. *Placement Criteria*

a. Matching

■ **IN RE BABY BOY C.**
805 N.Y.S.2d 313 (App. Div. 2005)

GONZALEZ, J. . . .

[Baby Boy C. was born in California on March 22, 2004, to Rita C. and her boyfriend Justin W. Rita is one-half Native American Indian and is a registered member of the Tohono O'odham Nation tribe.] Justin is Caucasian and Jewish. On April 13, 2004, Rita and Justin executed extrajudicial consents in Arizona to the termination of their parental rights and the adoption of the child by petitioners Jeffrey A. and Joshua A., who have been certified as qualified adoptive parents in New York. Included in Rita's executed consent were representations that she was a member of the Tribe, that the child may be an "Indian child" under [the Indian Child Welfare Act (ICWA), 25 U.S.C. §1901 et. seq.,] and that she was aware of the placement preferences in ICWA but desired that they be waived, and that a finding of good cause [be] entered to permit the child's adoption by petitioners. [An Arizona court accepted the consents and terminated the birth parents' rights. The Tribe received notice but did not appear. Meanwhile, petitioners took custody of the child, returned to New York, and commenced this adoption proceeding in April 2004. Over petitioners' opposition, the Tribe moved to intervene in the adoption proceeding.]

[After a hearing], Family Court found that ICWA did not apply since the Tribe failed to meet its burden of proving that the subject child was part of an "existing Indian family." The court found that Rita's ties to the Tribe were mainly in her childhood and adolescence, but that as an adult she had "divorced herself from the community affairs, politics and social and religious life of the Tribe," thereby demonstrating a "rejection of her Indian heritage." [Rita had also testified that neither of her other children was being reared in an Indian setting and she had no interest in having this child reared in the tribal culture.] Rita's rejection of her own Indian heritage, in turn, "has acted to break the link between the Tribe and Rita's nuclear family." [After a subsequent best-interests hearing, the court decided the proposed adoption should go forward. The Tribe appeals.]

ICWA was enacted by Congress in 1978 as a product of the rising concern in the mid-1970s over the effect on Indian children, families and tribes of abusive welfare practices that separated large numbers of Indian children from their families and tribes through adoption or foster care placement in non-Indian homes (Mississippi Choctaw Indians Band v Holyfield, 490 U.S. 30, 32 [1989]). ICWA's stated purpose is "to protect the best interests of Indian children and to promote the stability and security of Indian tribes and families by the establishment of minimum Federal standards for the removal of Indian children from their families and the placement of such children in foster or adoptive homes which will reflect the unique values of Indian culture" (25 USC §1902). . . . ICWA seeks to achieve this goal by establishing "a Federal policy that, where possible, an Indian child should remain in the Indian community" and ensuring that Indian child welfare determinations are not based on "a white, middle-class standard which, in many cases, forecloses placement with [an] Indian family" [citing legislative history].

[T]he plain language of ICWA makes the act applicable to this adoption proceeding. As noted, ICWA applies to any "child custody proceeding" involving an "Indian child" (25 USC §1903[1], [4]. [P]etitioners' argument that ICWA is inapplicable rests entirely on its claim that the ["existing Indian family" (EIF)] exception removes this proceeding from the Act. . . . The EIF exception was first articulated by the Supreme Court of Kansas in Matter of Adoption of Baby Boy L. (643 P.2d 168 [1982]). [In finding the ICWA inapplicable, the court said:]

> "[T]he overriding concern of Congress and the proponents of the Act was the maintenance of the family and tribal relationships existing in Indian homes and to set minimum standards for the removal of Indian children from their existing Indian environment. It was not to dictate that an illegitimate infant who has never been a member of an Indian home or culture, and probably never would be, should be removed from its primary cultural heritage and placed in an Indian environment over the express objections of its non-Indian mother." (Id. at 205-206.) . . .

The common rationale behind [*Baby Boy L.* and similar decisions from other states] was that because Congress's primary goal in passing ICWA was to prevent the removal of Indian children from Indian families, that purpose would not be served by applying the Act to children who had never been a part of an existing Indian family.

The legal landscape surrounding the EIF exception changed in 1989, when the United States Supreme Court decided [*Holyfield*]. *Holyfield* involved twin babies born out of wedlock to parents who were both enrolled members of the petitioner tribe. Although both parents lived on the reservation, they traveled 200 miles away from the reservation for the birth [and consented to adoption by a specific non-Indian couple whom they had selected. The Court held that] under federal domicile law, the children were domiciled on the reservation within the meaning of ICWA's exclusive tribal court jurisdiction provision, even though the children had never been physically present on the reservation. . . . In rejecting the notion that ICWA could be avoided by the fact that the parents had "voluntarily surrendered" the child, the *Holyfield* court stated that tribal jurisdiction was not meant to be defeated by the actions of individual tribe members or parents, "for Congress was concerned not solely about the interests of Indian children and families, *but also about the impact on the tribes themselves of the large number of Indian children adopted by non-Indians"* ([490 U.S.] at 49 [emphasis added], citing 25 USC §1901[3] ["there is no resource that is more vital to the continued existence and integrity of Indian tribes than their children"]).

The *Holyfield* Court also emphasized that a major concern of Congress was the "detrimental impact" on the Indian children themselves of being placed outside their culture in non-Indian homes. To this end, Congress made ICWA's jurisdictional and placement provisions applicable not only to involuntary removals of Indian children, but also to voluntary adoptions involving placement with non-Indian families "because of concerns going beyond the wishes of individual parents."

In the wake of *Holyfield*, many state courts rejected the EIF exception. . . . Notwithstanding *Holyfield*, two districts of the California Court of Appeals not only adopted the EIF exception to ICWA, but also held that ICWA was unconstitutional absent the EIF exception. [In In re Bridget R., 49 Cal. Rptr. 2d 507 (Ct. App. 1996),] the court held that ICWA does not apply to a voluntary termination of parental rights proceeding respecting an Indian child who is not domiciled on an Indian reservation unless the parents are of American Indian descent and "maintain a significant social, cultural or political relationship with their tribe." Otherwise, the *Bridget R.* court held, ICWA would violate the child's constitutional rights. . . .

[*Bridget R.*] found that a child had a fundamental right to placement in a stable and permanent home, thereby triggering strict scrutiny, which requires that the legislation serve a compelling governmental interest and be actually necessary and effective in accomplishing that purpose. Although the court found that the compelling interest prong had been met, it held that ICWA's purpose of preserving American Indian culture would not be served by applying it to children whose biological parents did not have a significant relationship with an Indian community. Applying ICWA to remove such a child from a home in which he or she had formed familial bonds, the *Bridget R.* court determined, would violate the child's substantive due process rights.

[*Bridget R.*] also found that ICWA violated the child's equal protection rights because it required different treatment of Indian and non-Indian children who were similarly situated. It reasoned that although disparate treatment was not constitutionally offensive when it was based on the social, cultural and political relationships between Indian children and their tribes, where such "relationships do not exist or are very attenuated, the only remaining basis for applying ICWA rather than state law in proceedings affecting an Indian child's custody is the child's genetic heritage in other words, race." . . .

Having considered the various arguments and authorities for and against the acceptance of the EIF exception, we reject it as fundamentally inconsistent with both the plain language of ICWA and one of its core purpose of preserving and protecting the interests of Indian tribes in their children. We also conclude that, contrary to Family Court's holding, ICWA is constitutional because it is rationally related to fulfilling this expressed purpose.

[As a matter of statutory interpretation, because] Congress has clearly delineated the nature of the relationship between an Indian child and tribe necessary to trigger application of the Act, judicial insertion of an additional criteria for applicability is plainly beyond the intent of Congress and must be rejected. Another

1041

problem with the EIF exception is that its acceptance would undermine the significant tribal interests recognized by the Supreme Court in *Holyfield.* . . . If the EIF exception were applied in this instance, Rita would have succeeded in nullifying ICWA's purpose at the expense of the interests of the Tribe. . . . Where, as here, Rita has rejected Indian life and culture and, then, voluntarily relinquished her newborn Indian child to be adopted by a non-Indian couple, the detriment to the Tribe is quite significant — the loss of two generations of Indian children instead of just one.

The EIF exception also conflicts with the Congressional policy underlying ICWA that certain child custody determinations be made in accordance with Indian cultural or community standards. The EIF exception is clearly at odds with this policy because it requires state courts to make the inherently subjective factual determination as to the "Indianness" of a particular Indian child or parent, a determination that state courts "are ill-equipped to make." . . .

We also find that ICWA is not constitutionally infirm absent the EIF exception. . . . The decisions finding ICWA unconstitutional without the EIF exception, such as *Bridget R.,* are premised on the existence of a fundamental right or suspect classification. [A child has no fundamental right to adoption, which is strictly a creature of statute.] [With regard to the equal protection claim, courts] have consistently held that federal laws that treat Indians differently from non-Indians do not derive from race, but rather from the political status of the parents or children and the quasi-sovereign nature of the tribe [citations omitted]. [With neither a fundamental right nor a suspect classification implicated, the court applies the rational basis test, finding ICWA reasonably related to the protection of Indian tribes and families and to the fulfillment of Congress's unique guardianship obligation toward Indians.]

Perhaps the most fundamental flaw in the reasoning of the courts that have accepted the EIF exception is the failure to give adequate consideration to the statutory "good cause" exception in 25 USC §1915, which permits state courts to depart from the placement preferences upon a showing of good cause. . . . Although ICWA does not define "good cause," regulations promulgated by the Bureau of Indian Affairs provide that good cause must be based on one or more of the following considerations: (1) the request of the biological parents or the child when of sufficient age; (2) the extraordinary physical or emotional needs of the child as established by testimony of a qualified expert witness; and (3) the unavailability of suitable Indian families for placement (see 44 Fed. Reg. 67,584; 67,594 f.3 [1979]).

The EIF exception loses much of its force when viewed in light of the "good cause" exception, since that provision already provides state courts with the flexibility to deviate from the placement preferences in circumstances where the interests of the parent or child outweigh the tribe's interest in the strict application of those preferences. Here, had Family Court found ICWA applicable and held a placement preference/good cause hearing, it may well have reached the same result of permitting the adoption to proceed without having to rely on a judicially created exception to ICWA that is inconsistent with its language and purpose. [The court also decides that ICWA does not grant the Tribe intervention as a matter of right in adoption proceedings but that New York's civil practice rules permit tribal intervention on remand here.]

■ ELIZABETH BARTHOLET, WHERE DO BLACK CHILDREN BELONG? THE POLITICS OF RACE MATCHING IN ADOPTION

139 U. Pa. L. Rev. 1163, 1164-1188, 1237 (1991)

When I first walked into the world of adoption, I was stunned at the dominant role race played. . . . Early in the process of exploring how I might adopt, I discovered that the first order of business for the agencies responsible for matching children waiting for homes with prospective parents is to sort and allocate by race. The public and most of the traditional private adoption agencies would not consider assigning a waiting minority child to me, a white person, except as a last resort, and perhaps not even then. The organizations and individual entrepreneurs that arrange independent adoptions, while more willing to place across racial lines, also sorted children by race. In this part of the adoption world, minority children might actually be easier for the white prospective parent to find than a white child, and they were often available for a lesser fee. . . .

The familiar refrain that there are no children available for adoption is a reflection of the racial policies of many adoption agencies and the racial preferences of many adoptive parents. The reality is that there are very few *white* children by comparison to the large pool of would-be white adopters. But there are many *non-white* children available to this pool, both through independent adoption in this country and through international adoption. And there are many non-white children waiting in foster care who are unavailable solely because of adoption agency insistence that they not be placed transracially.

Racial thinking dominates the world of international adoption as well. [Bartholet, a single mother of one child from an early marriage, adopted two children from Peru.] I discovered during my two adoption trips to Peru something about how children may be rated in racial terms in their own country as well as here. Most of the children available for adoption in Peru are of mixed indian and spanish heritage. But there is tremendous variety in ethnic features and skin color. For my second adoption I was offered by the government adoption agency an unusually white, one-month-old baby. My initial reaction upon meeting him was disappointment that he did not look like my first child from Peru. Christopher's brown-skinned face with its indian features had become the quintessence of what a child—my child—should look like. But I decided that it was foolish to look for another baby-Christopher, as I had decided years earlier that it would be foolish to look in adoption for a clone of my biological son. I took this baby home and named him Michael. Within twenty-four hours I found myself tearing through the streets in a taxi, mopping his feverish body with a wet cloth, and terrified, as I saw his eyes lose contact with mine and begin to stare off into the middle distance, that he would die in my arms before we got to the hospital emergency room. . . . Sometime during that taxi ride, or in the hospital room, I became hopelessly attached.

Several weeks later I sat with a blanketed Michael in my arms in the office of one of Lima's fanciest pediatricians. Michael had recovered from the fever but had been suffering from nausea and diarrhea almost ever since. . . . I had been to three different doctors. . . . I told this new doctor the story of Michael's troubles, trying with my words and tone to convey my sense of desperation—to make him understand that if he didn't help us Michael might die. The doctor sat impassively, interrupting me only when my three-year old Christopher wandered over to the bookshelves. Pointing with apparent disgust, as if some small and dirty animal had invaded his office, the doctor asked, "What is he?" I thought the question truly peculiar and the answer rather obvious, but explained that this was my son (perhaps he thought it was the child of the Peruvian nanny who was with me?). At the end of my story the doctor, who had still made no move to look at Michael, assured himself that the nanny spoke no English, and he then proceeded to tell me that he could get me another child, in a way that would avoid all the troublesome procedures of a Peruvian adoption. Women were giving birth in his hospital all the time who would not keep their babies. He could have the birth certificate for one of these babies made out showing me as the mother and the baby would be mine.

When I finally realized that this hospital baby was being suggested as a substitute for the one on my lap, I said in what I hoped was a polite but firm tone that I planned to keep this child and that I was here because I was afraid the child was seriously ill. I asked if the doctor could please now examine the child. . . . I put Michael on the table and started to undress him, and for the first time the doctor looked at him. . . . It was overwhelmingly clear that Michael's value had been transformed in the doctor's eyes by his whiteness. Whiteness made it comprehensible that someone would want to cure and keep this child rather than discard him. . . .

I learned more about my own feelings about race as I puzzled through the process of creating my adoptive family. Adoption compels this kind of learning. You don't just get at the end of one general child line when you're doing adoption. There are a lot of lines, each identified by the race, disabilities, and age of the children available, together with the length of wait and the difficulty and cost of adoption. In choosing which line to join, I had to think about race, and to think on a level that was new to me. I had to try to confront without distortion the reality of parenting someone of another race — since the child and I would have to live that reality. . . . I had to think about whether it would be racist to look for a same-race child or racist to look for a child of another race. . . .

[O]ne day, when he is three and one-half, Christopher says to me across the kitchen table at dinner, "I wish you looked like me." . . . I am left to puzzle at the meaning of this pain. . . . Is it, as the opponents of transracial adoption would have us believe, a piece of a permanent anguish at the sense that he does not truly belong in the place where he should most surely belong — his family? Or should I simply take it as a signal that living as a part of a multi-racial, multi-ethnic, multi-cultural family will force us to confront the meaning of racial and other differences on a regular basis?

This child is as inside my skin as any child could be. It feels entirely right that he should be there. Yet the powers that be in today's adoption world proclaim with near unanimity that race-mixing in the context of adoption should be avoided if at all possible, at least where black or brown-skinned American children are involved. . . .

[C]urrent racial matching policies represent a coming together of powerful and related ideologies — old fashioned white racism, modern-day black nationalism, and what I will call "biologism" — the idea that what is "natural" in the context of the biological family is what is normal and desirable in the context of adoption. Biological families have same-race parents and children. The laws and policies surrounding adoption in this country have generally structured adoption in imitation of biology, giving the adopted child a new birth certificate as if the child had been born to the adoptive parents, sealing off the birth parents as if they had never existed, and attempting to match adoptive parents and children with respect to looks, intellect and religion. The implicit goal has been to create an adoptive family which will resemble as much as possible "the real thing" — the "natural" or biological family that is not. . . .

But the question is . . . whether today's powerful racial matching policies make sense from the viewpoint of either the minority children involved or the larger society. . . . Minority children are pouring, in increasing numbers, into the already overburdened foster care system, and current policies stand in the way of placing these children with available adoptive families. . . .

The controversy over transracial adoption that has arisen in recent decades has primarily involved the placement of children generally identified as black with white families. . . . Through the middle of this century there were near-absolute barriers to transracial adoption posed by adoption agency practice, by social attitudes, and by the law. As adoption agencies gained increasing power in the late nineteenth and early twentieth centuries to screen prospective parents and to assign waiting children to particular homes, they helped to institutionalize the racial barriers. Agencies adopted a powerful "matching" philosophy. Prospective parents were ideally to be matched with children who were physically and mentally as close a match as possible to the biological children they might have produced. This kind of matching was thought to maximize the chances for a successful bonding and nurturing relationship between parent and child. . . .

The 1960s represented a period of relative openness to transracial adoption. Foreign adoptions helped pave the way. In the aftermath of the Korean War, South Korea made many of its abandoned and orphaned children available for adoption. Large numbers of these were mixed race children who had been fathered by black American soldiers stationed in Korea. . . . The civil rights movement in this country brought increasing attention to the plight of the minority children who had languished in the foster care systems over the years. This movement's integrationist ideology made transracial adoption a sympathetic idea to many adoption workers and prospective parents. Transracial adoption also served the needs of the waiting white parents, for whom there were not enough color-matched children available, as well as the interests of the agencies in putting together adoptive families and reducing the foster care population. And so agencies began to place waiting black children with white parents when there were no black parents apparently available. The reported number of transracial placements rose gradually to 733 in 1968, and it more than tripled in the next three years to reach a peak of 2574 in 1971. . . .

In 1972 this brief era of relative openness to transracial adoption came to an abrupt end. That year an organization called the National Association of Black Social Workers (NABSW) issued a position statement against transracial adoption [calling it a form of "genocide"]. It stated:

> Black children should be placed only with Black families whether in foster care or for adoption. Black children belong, physically, psychologically and culturally in Black families in order that they receive the total sense of themselves and develop a sound projection of their future. Human beings are products of their environment and develop their sense of values, attitudes and self concept within their family structures.

Black children in white homes are cut off from the healthy development of themselves as Black people. . . .

Others joined in the attack on transracial adoption, arguing with the NABSW that transracial adoption constituted an attack upon the black community and that it harmed black children by denying them their black heritage and the survival skills needed for life in a racist society.

The attack on transracial adoption appeared to have an immediate and significant impact. The numbers fell from a peak of 2574 in 1971 [to 831 in 1975]. [The Child Welfare League and adoption] agency bureaucrats moved swiftly to accommodate the position taken by the NABSW. . . . A parallel development occurred with respect to the adoptive placement of Native American children. [My own] investigation has made clear to me that race is used as the basis for official decision-making in adoption in a way that is unparalleled in a society that has generally endorsed an anti-discrimination and pro-integration ideology. . . .

This matching scheme confronts a major problem in the fact that the numbers of children falling into the black and the white pools do not "fit," proportionately, with the number of prospective parents falling into their own black and white pools. In 1987, 37.1% of the children in out-of-home placement were black as compared with 46.1% white. Although no good statistics are available, the general understanding is that a very high percentage of the waiting adoptive parent pool is white. . . .

The matching process surfaces, to a degree, in written rules and documented cases. But it is the unwritten and generally invisible rules that are central to understanding the nature of current policies. . . . The rules generally make race not simply "a factor," but an overwhelmingly important factor in the placement process. . . .

[A]doption is not supposed to be about parent or community rights and interests, but rather about serving the best interests of children. Adoption laws throughout this country provide that agencies are to make children's interests paramount in placement decisions. Arguments can be made that black children in general will benefit from efforts to strengthen the black community, and that racial matching policies represent one such effort. The problem is that . . . racial matching policies seem contrary to the immediate and long-term interests of the specific black children waiting for homes. . . .

■ **DOROTHY ROBERTS, SHATTERED BONDS:
THE COLOR OF CHILD WELFARE**
165-172 (2002)

The shift in federal policy from family preservation toward adoption [exemplified by the Adoption and Safe Families Act of 1997 (ASFA)[2]] corresponded with the change in the federal position on transracial adoption. The relationship

[2]. ASFA requires states to seek terminations of parental rights after a limited period of foster care (42 U.S.C. §675(5) (2000)) and provides financial incentives for states to increase adoptions of children in foster care (42 U.S.C.A. §673b (West Supp. 2005)). For discussion of ASFA, see Chapter VIII, p.964. – Eds.

between these two trends was more than a coincidence of timing. The new adoption law was tied to the growing movement to remove barriers to adoption of Black children by white middle-class couples. White adoptive families are seen as a major source for reducing the large numbers of Black children in foster care. At the same time, family preservation policies are seen as a hindrance to while families' ability to adopt them. Although the federal adoption law is racially neutral on its face, its connection to transracial adoption reveals the racial politics that undergirds its popularity. Most of the biological families whose bonds the law disparages are Black, whereas most of the adoptive families whom the law favors are white.

For decades, the federal government permitted public adoption agencies to enforce race-matching policies that sought to place Black children exclusively with Black adoptive families. But in the 1990s, after aggressive lobbying by supporters of transracial adoption, Congress took steps to remove barriers to whites willing to adopt children of other races. Transracial adoption was championed as a critical step in increasing the numbers of adoptions of Black children, the population with the lowest rate of exit from foster care. Advocates argued that race-matching policies forced Black children to languish in foster care awaiting scarce Black adoptive parents when they could have been adopted. . . .

Adoption policy has historically tracked the market for children, serving the interests of adults seeking to adopt more than the interests of children needing stable homes. Foster care and adoption have a supply and demand relationship. While the foster care system provides a source of children for adopters, adoption provides a source of homes for children in foster care. For example, in the early 1900s, child welfare officials softened the child rescue philosophy of the nineteenth century and refrained from terminating parental rights when the supply of newborns available for adoption exceeded demand. In more recent decades, however, the growing demand for adoptable older children as babies became scarce helped to generate policies that free children for adoption by terminating parental rights quickly. . . . Roe v. Wade's protection of women's rights to abortion and the diminished social stigma attached to single motherhood have drastically cut the numbers of white women who give up their babies for adoption, creating what has been called the "White Baby Famine." Until recently, the number of adoptions in the United States steadily declined since reaching a peak of 175,000 in 1970.

All of the literature advocating the elimination of racial considerations in child placements focuses on making it easier for white people to adopt Black children. . . . Transracial adoption advocates don't mention the possibility of Blacks adopting white children. Nor do they acknowledge that most race-matching in adoption involves matching white adoptive parents with white children. Child welfare agencies routinely allow whites to choose the white foster children they prefer. . . .

[Congressional and media] rhetoric supporting ASFA praised reforms in federal child welfare policy for removing the twin barriers to adoption — race-matching restrictions and prolonged family preservation efforts. Terminating parents' rights faster and abolishing race-matching policies were linked as a strategy for increasing adoptions of Black children by white families. Connecting these two issues — family preservation and transracial adoption — allowed commentators to claim that the foster care problems could be solved by moving more Black children from their families into white adoptive homes. . . .

Transracial adoption becomes especially explosive in the context of terminating parental rights to free children for adoption. . . . These contests bring to the surface a theme that runs more subtly through some of the discourse supporting transracial adoption — the belief that Black children fare better if raised by white adoptive families than if returned home. Advocates of transracial adoption frequently assert the benefits of racial assimilation that Black children and white parents experience by living together. . . . As in the rhetoric promoting ASFA, the rhetoric promoting transracial adoption supports the dissolution of poor Black families by depicting adoptive homes as superior to children's existing family relationships.

The picture painted by the media and advocates of transracial adoption as a panacea for the foster care crisis bears little connection to the real world adoption market. The transracial adoption issue is a red herring. It diverts attention from the main harms the child welfare system inflicts on Black families. The white couples the public envisions as adoptive parents are typically not interested in the poor Black children who make up the bulk of the foster care population. The vast majority of white adoptive parents are only willing to take a white child. . . .

Even when they adopt outside their race, whites generally prefer non-Black children of Asian or Latin American heritage. . . . The notion that state agencies are turning away thousands of white parents anxious to adopt Black foster children is ludicrous. Yet this mirage is held out as a reason for opposing policies that preserve Black families. . . .

Notes and Questions

1. *The debate.* What role should race play in choosing an adoptive family? Ethnic and cultural background? Why does the law prefer the placement of Native American children with Native American families, according to *Baby Boy C.?* Do similar reasons justify race matching in adoption? To what extent can or should the law specify such placement preferences for minority children without doing the same for white children? Whose analysis do you find more persuasive, Professor Bartholet's or Professor Roberts's? See also Hawley Fogg-Davis, The Ethics of Transracial Adoption (2002); Randall Kennedy, Interracial Intimacies: Sex, Marriage, Identity, and Adoption 402-446; 480-518 (2003) (opposing race matching and ICWA's preferences); Rachel F. Moran, Interracial Intimacy: The Regulation of Race and Romance 127-153 (2001) (emphasizing complexities of determining proper role of race and background); Twila L. Perry, The Transracial Adoption Controversy: An Analysis of Discourse and Subordination, 21 N.Y.U. Rev. L. & Soc. Change 33 (1993-1994) (critiquing political agenda underlying transracial adoption and the emotional strains placed on adoptees). What does the debate about transracial adoption say about mothering, hierarchy, and other themes emphasized in feminist analysis? See Twila L. Perry, Transracial and International Adoption: Mothers, Hierarchy, Race, and Feminist Legal Theory, 10 Yale J.L. & Feminism 101 (1998).

2. *Constitutional limits.* In challenges to some of the restrictive policies described by Professor Bartholet, usually by white adults seeking to adopt African-American children, courts early on held unconstitutional absolute prohibitions on transracial adoptions. Compos v. McKeithen, 341 F. Supp. 264 (E.D. La. 1972); In re Adoption of Gomez, 424 S.W.2d 656 (Tex. Ct. App. 1967). Can race constitute *one* factor in

state in state placement decisions? See In re Petition of R.M.G., 454 A.2d 776 (D.C. 1982). Some cases limiting the use of race in adoption rely on Palmore v. Sidoti, 466 U.S. 429 (1984), reprinted Chapter VII, B1b(ii)(1). See, e.g., In re D.L., 479 N.W.2d 408 (Minn. Ct. App. 1991). Does *Palmore* apply to adoptions? What factors differentiate postdissolution custody adjudications from adoption? If *Palmore* applies, does it foreclose the possibility that race matching might satisfy strict scrutiny? See *R.M.G.*, supra.

3. *Relative preferences.* To what extent can states promote race matching, while avoiding constitutional problems, by promulgating preferences for adoptive placements with relatives? See, e.g., *D.L.*, supra; Moran, supra, at 131. What considerations support such preferences? What difficulties do they pose? State statutes and practices vary. Compare In re Adoption of B.C.S., 793 N.E.2d 1054 (Ind. Ct. App. 2003) (statute contains no preference for relatives), and In re Adoption of D.M., 710 N.W.2d 441 (S.D. 2006) (no statutory right of relatives to intervene), with Baker v. Webb, 127 S.W.3d 622 (Ky. 2004) (setting aside adoption to allow second cousins to intervene), and State ex rel. D.B. v. M.O. 870 So. 2d 1143 (La. Ct. App. 2004) (applying statutory preference for adoption by relatives). Does the Constitution give relatives a right to adopt over strangers? Do their biological connections to the child require the same analysis applicable to unmarried fathers? Why? See Mullins v. Oregon, 57 P.3d 789 (9th Cir. 1995). As noted below, the ICWA contains a relative preference for Native American children. Does equal protection require extending this preference to all children?

4. *Empirical data.* According to data from 2000, 15 percent of all adoptions from foster care are transracial (defined as one in which the child's race differs from at least one adoptive parent). Madalyn Freundlich, Transracial & Transcultural Adoptions, 27 Fam. Advoc. 40, 40 (2004). Empirical studies support transracial adoption as a "basically positive" alternative to long-term foster care. Rita J. Simon et al., The Case for Transracial Adoption 74, 155 (1994) (20-year study of 83 families). In 1991, approximately 108 transracial adoptees, then young adults, were asked whether they wished they had had a same-race placement. Seven percent answered affirmatively, 67 percent answered negatively, 4 percent were not sure, and 22 percent did not reply. Rita J. Simon & Rhonda M. Roorda, In Their Own Voices: Transracial Adoptees Tell Their Stories 21, 25 (2000). Increasingly, the literature includes memoirs reflecting personal experiences with transracial adoption. E.g., Barbara Katz Rothman, Weaving a Family: Untangling Race and Adoption (2005) (adoptive parent's perspective); Susan R. Harris, Race, Search, and My Baby-Self: Reflections of a Transracial Adoptee, 9 Yale J.L. & Feminism 5 (1997); Andrew Morrison, Transracial Adoption: The Pros and Cons and the Parents' Perspective, 20 Harv. BlackLetter L.J. 127 (2004) (adoptive sibling's view). See Kennedy, supra, at 447-479 (summarizing such literature).

5. *Federal statutes.*

a. *"Barriers to interethnic adoption."* As Professor Roberts indicates in the excerpt above, Congress has legislated the "removal of barriers to interethnic adoption" by providing that no state nor other entity in a state receiving federal funds can "deny to any individual the opportunity to become an adoptive or a foster parent, on the basis of the race, color, or national original of the individual, or of the child, involved." 42 U.S.C. §1996b (2000) (amending the earlier, and less restrictive, federal Multi-Ethnic Placement Act). Does this statute limit only the practices of adoption agencies, or does it bind judges as well? See In re Adoption of Vito, 712

N.E.2d 1188, 1196 (Mass. Ct. App. 1999) (federal law does not constrain judge in "crafting an order she determines to be in the child's best interests"), *vacated and remanded*, 728 N.E.2d 292, 305 n.27 (Mass. 2000) (avoiding this issue).

b. *ASFA.* Congress enacted the Adoption and Safe Families Act 1997 to promote adoption by, inter alia, requiring states to seek terminations of parental rights after a limited period of foster care (42 U.S.C. §675(5) (2000)) and providing financial incentives for states to increase adoptions of children in foster care (42 U.S.C.A. §673b (West Supp. 2005)). To what extent do these measures encourage transfer of African-American children to white families — serving the needs of adopters rather than children, as Roberts contends? What reforms would address these problems?

c. *ICWA.* As *Baby Boy C.* illustrates, the Indian Child Welfare Act gives Native American background a prominent, if not decisive, role, with preference accorded (absent good cause) to placement with: (1) a member of the child's extended family, (2) other members of the Indian child's tribe, or (3) other Indian families. 25 U.S.C. §1915(a) (2000). In removing "barriers to interethnic adoption," Congress explicitly left intact the ICWA's placement preferences. 42 U.S.C. §1996b(3) (2000). Why? Do the frequent analyses of the ICWA's preferences as race-matching measures expose a fundamental misunderstanding about Indian identity? See Barbara Ann Atwood, Flashpoints Under the Indian Child Welfare Act: Toward a New Understanding of State Court Resistance, 51 Emory L.J. 587 (2002); Carole Goldberg, Critical Race Studies: Descent Into Race, 49 UCLA L. Rev. 1373 (2002).

Given the interpretation of the ICWA in *Baby Boy C.*, what constitutes good cause to depart from the Act's preferences? Do "the prevailing social or cultural standards of the [parent's or extended family's] community," which apply to meeting the ICWA's preference requirements (25 U.S.C. §1915 (2000)), also govern the determination of good cause? See In re Adoption of Sara J., 123 P.3d 1017 (Alaska 2005)? Did the court correctly reject the EIF exception? Most courts have done so. See *Baby Boy C.*, 805 N.Y.S. 2d at 322 n.4 (listing states). Why do some courts reason that, without the exception, the ICWA would be unconstitutional? Compare In re Santos Y., 112 Cal. Rptr. 2d 692 (Ct. App. 2001), with Hoots v. K.B., 663 N.W.2d 625 (N.D. 2003). For critiques of the judge-made EIF exception, see, e.g., Atwood, supra; Goldberg, supra, at 1380-1388.

6. *Classifying: criticisms.* The controversy over the EIF reveals a larger problem about classifications in adoptive placement. The ICWA defines "Indian child" as "any unmarried person who is under age eighteen and is either (a) a member of an Indian tribe or (b) is eligible for membership in an Indian tribe and is the biological child of a member of an Indian tribe." 25 U.S.C. §1903(4) (2000). Does this definition promote the ICWA's goals? Optimize child placements? To the extent that race plays a role in adoptive placements, what families provide a good "match" for children of mixed race? See Moran, supra, at 139-140; Jane Maslow Cohen, Race-Based Adoption in a Post-*Loving* Frame, 6 B.U. Pub. Int. L.J. 653 (1997); Jennifer L. Rosato, "A Color of Their Own": Multiracial Children and the Family, 36 Brandeis J. Fam. L. 41 (1997-98). Professor Ruth-Arlene W. Howe predicts that eliminating consideration of race will actually increase discrimination:

> Elimination of race from all placement decision-making sets the stage for reinforcing old prejudices and discriminatory practices toward African Americans and for anachronistic recommodification of *young* African American children, without

providing any strong assurance that the needs of such children will be met appropriately. Instead, white adults seeking healthy infants now have an opportunity to "garner the market" on the only expanding "crop" of healthy newborns — voluntarily relinquished biracial nonmarital infants (many with one black and one white parent). Prior to Interethnic Adoption Provisions, these babies would be considered black under the customary "one-drop" rule for determining race.

Ruth-Arlene W. Howe, Adoption Laws and Practices in 2000: Serving Whose Interests?, 33 Fam. L.Q. 677, 684-685 (1999). See also Stephanie R. Richardson, Note, Strict Scrutiny, Biracial Children, and Adoption, 12 B.U. Pub. Int. L.J. 203 (2002); Jennifer Swize, Note, Transracial Adoption and the Unblinkable Difference: Racial Dissimilarity Serving the Interests of Adopted Children, 88 Va. L. Rev. 1079 (2002).

Case law raises numerous questions about the factors that agencies and the state can (and cannot) consider in choosing an adoptive placement. See, e.g., Adoption of Richardson, 59 Cal. Rptr. 323 (Ct. App. 1967) (adopters' deafness); Crump v. Montgomery, 154 A.2d 802 (Md. 1959) (intelligence); McClement v. Beaudoin, 700 N.Y.S.2d 570 (App. Div. 1999) (adopters' age); Depew v. Depew, 42 P.3d 873 (Okla. Civ. App. 2001) (couple's divorce). Today, scholars challenge attempts to create "the 'as if' family" through adoption, emphasizing how a family functions, rather than how it looks. E.g., Mary Lyndon Shanley, Making Babies, Making Families: What Matters Most in an Age of Reproductive Technologies, Surrogacy, Adoption, and Same-Sex and Unwed Parents 15-20 (2001).

7. *Religious matching.* How should the law classify children for purposes of religious matching? What problems does this practice pose? New York law includes a preference for placing children with caregivers of the same religion. N.Y. Soc. Servs. Law §373 (McKinney 2003). In *Baby Boy C.*, the lower court noted the Tribe's argument that Jewish law would not recognize the child as Jewish, despite his Jewish birth father, given the mother's identity. 784 N.Y.S.2d 334, 337 (Fam. Ct. 2004).

8. *Parental autonomy.* What weight should the law give to birth parents' preferences in adoptive placements? For example, in *Baby Boy C.*, the birth mother consented to the child's adoption by Joshua and Jeffrey, stating "I . . . approve and agree that the child be brought in the Jewish faith." 784 N.Y.S.2d at 336. See also Ark. Code Ann. §9-9-102 (2002) (directing courts to honor genetic parents' religious preferences for placement, if possible); Mass. Gen. Laws Ann. ch. 210, §5B (West 1998) (directing courts to honor parents' religious designation of child, unless inconsistent with best interests). What constitutional issues do these laws raise?

Should the policies of the ICWA give way to birth parents' autonomy? How does Mississippi Band of Choctaw Indians v. Holyfield, 490 U.S. 30 (1989), summarized in *Baby Boy C.*, resolve this issue? See also Perry, Transracial and International Adoption, supra, at 150-151 (feminists must address conflict between parental autonomy and argument for deference to ethnic groups' desires for intra-ethnic placement).

Professor Richard Banks argues that, even without state race-matching policies, accommodating adoptive parents' race-based preferences makes the state complicit in discrimination. R. Richard Banks, The Color of Desire: Fulfilling Adoptive Parents' Racial Preferences through Discriminatory State Action, 107

Yale L.J. 875 (1998). Cf. Fogg-Davis, supra, at 74-92. Should (must?) the state ignore such preferences when placing children?

9. *Whose benefit?* Although adoption's history in the United States has emphasized child welfare objectives, the practice long has served adults' interests as well. Adoption's antecedents, "placing out" and apprenticeship, provided care for children while also advancing the economic needs of adults, as noted by Professor Presser, supra, p.1022. Later, as the childsaving movement and the children's aid societies that it developed sought families for children in need, advocates learned to appeal to adults' emotional vulnerabilities. From 1907-1911, the *Delineator*, a popular women's magazine, secured over 2,000 placements by publishing advertisements of (white) children and appealing to women's rescue impulses and maternal longings. Julie Berebitsky, Like Our Very Own: Adoption and the Changing Culture of Motherhood, 1851-1950 at 51-74 (2000). The shift in focus from child welfare to adult interests began in earnest after World War II, an era of "compulsory parenthood" that saw adoption as a service for the infertile. Elaine Tyler May, Barren in the Promised Land: Childless Americans and the Pursuit of Happiness 141 (1997). At this time, adoption agencies sought both to "match" children and adopters on many characteristics so that adoption might "imitate nature" and to use adoption to construct model families that others might follow. See id. at 137-142. See also Berebitsky, supra, at 6, 103. Who benefits from matching? When this practice produces so-called "baby shortages," what do such market analyses reveal about adoption's objectives, given the availability of many older children, children with disabilities, and children of color? See, e.g., Susan Frelich Appleton, Adoption in the Age of Reproductive Technology, 2004 U. Chi. Legal F. 393, 402-405.

b. Sexual Orientation

■ LOFTON v. SECRETARY OF THE DEPARTMENT OF CHILDREN AND FAMILY SERVICES
358 F.3d 804 (11th Cir. 2004), cert. denied, *543 U.S. 1081 (2005)*

BIRCH, Circuit Judge

In this appeal, we decide the states' rights issue of whether Florida Statute §63.042(3), which prevents adoption by practicing homosexuals, is constitutional . . . For purposes of this statute, Florida courts have defined the term "homosexual" as being "limited to applicants who are known to engage in current, voluntary homosexual activity," thus drawing "a distinction between homosexual orientation and homosexual activity." During the past twelve years, several legislative bills [and court challenges have failed to overturn the provision, which was enacted in 1977.]

Six plaintiffs-appellants bring this case. The first, Steven Lofton, is a registered pediatric nurse who has raised from infancy three Florida foster children, each of whom tested positive for HIV at birth. By all accounts, Lofton's efforts in caring for these children have been exemplary, and his story has been chronicled in dozens of news stories and editorials as well as on national television. . . .

John Doe, also named as a plaintiff-appellant in this litigation, was born on 29 April 1991. Testing positive at birth for HIV and cocaine, Doe immediately entered the Florida foster care system. Shortly thereafter, Children's Home Society, a private agency, placed Doe in foster care with Lofton, who has extensive experience treating HIV patients. At eighteen months, Doe sero-reverted and has since tested HIV negative. In September of 1994, Lofton filed an application to adopt Doe but refused to answer the application's inquiry about his sexual preference and also failed to disclose Roger Croteau, his cohabitating partner, as a member of his household. After Lofton refused requests from the Department of Children and Families ("DCF") to supply the missing information, his application was rejected pursuant to the homosexual adoption provision. [In 1997,] in light of the length of Doe's stay in Lofton's household, DCF offered Lofton the compromise of becoming Doe's legal guardian. This arrangement would have allowed Doe to leave the foster care system and DCF supervision. However, because it would have cost Lofton over $300 a month in lost foster care subsidies and would have jeopardized Doe's Medicaid coverage, Lofton declined the guardianship option unless it was an interim stage toward adoption. Under Florida law, DCF could not accommodate this condition, and the present [constitutional challenge] ensued. . . .

B. Florida's Adoption Scheme

. . . Under Florida law, "adoption is not a right; it is a statutory privilege." Unlike biological parentage, which precedes and transcends formal recognition by the state, adoption is wholly a creature of the state.

In formulating its adoption policies and procedures, the State of Florida acts in the protective and provisional role of *in loco parentis* for those children who, because of various circumstances, have become wards of the state. Thus, adoption law is unlike criminal law, for example, where the paramount substantive concern is not intruding on individuals' liberty interests, see, e.g., [Lawrence v. Texas, 539 U.S. 558 (2003)]; Roe v. Wade, 410 U.S. 113 (1973), and the paramount procedural imperative is ensuring due process and fairness. . . . Because of the primacy of the welfare of the child, the state can make classifications for adoption purposes that would be constitutionally suspect in many other arenas. For example, [in] screening adoption applicants, Florida considers such factors as physical and mental health, income and financial status, duration of marriage, housing, and neighborhood, among others. . . .

The decision to adopt a child is not a private one, but a public act. [A] person who seeks to adopt is asking the state to conduct an examination into his or her background and to make a determination as to the best interests of a child in need of adoption. In doing so, the state's overriding interest is not providing individuals the opportunity to become parents, but rather identifying those individuals whom it deems most capable of parenting adoptive children and providing them with a secure family environment. . . .

C. Appellants' Due Process Challenges

1. Fundamental Right to "Family Integrity"

Neither party disputes that there is no fundamental right to adopt, nor any fundamental right to be adopted. . . . Nevertheless, appellants argue that, by prohibiting homosexual adoption, the state is refusing to recognize and protect constitutionally protected parent-child relationships between Lofton and Doe. . . . Only by being given the opportunity to adopt, appellants assert, will they be able to protect their alleged right to "family integrity."

[Appellants] seize on a few lines of dicta from [Smith v. Organization of Foster Families for Equality and Reform, 431 U.S. 816 (1977),] in which the Court acknowledged that "biological relationships are not [the] exclusive determination of the existence of a family," [id. at 842,] and noted that "adoption, for instance, is recognized as the legal equivalent of biological parenthood," id. at 844 n.51. Extrapolating from *Smith*, appellants argue that parental and familial rights should be extended to individuals such as foster parents and legal guardians and that the touchstone of this liberty interest is not biological ties or official legal recognition, but the emotional bond that develops between and among individuals as a result of shared daily life.

We do not read *Smith* so broadly. . . . The emotional connections between Lofton and his foster child . . . originate in arrangements that have been subject to state oversight from the outset. We conclude that Lofton [and the other appellants] could have no justifiable expectation of permanency in their relationships. Nor could [they] have developed expectations that they would be allowed to adopt, in light of the adoption provision itself. . . .

2. Fundamental Right to "Private Sexual Intimacy"

. . . Appellants argue that the Supreme Court's recent decision in Lawrence v. Texas, 539 U.S. 558 (2003), which struck down Texas's sodomy statute, identified a hitherto unarticulated fundamental right to private sexual intimacy. They contend that the Florida statute, by disallowing adoption to any individual who chooses to engage in homosexual conduct, impermissibly burdens the exercise of this right.

. . . *Lawrence*'s holding was that substantive due process does not permit a state to impose a criminal prohibition on private consensual homosexual conduct. The effect of this holding was to establish a greater respect than previously existed in the law for the right of consenting adults to engage in private sexual conduct. Nowhere, however, did the Court characterize this right as "fundamental" [or apply strict scrutiny.] We are particularly hesitant to infer a new fundamental liberty interest from an opinion whose language and reasoning are inconsistent with standard fundamental-rights analysis. [The court also distinguishes *Lawrence* because adoption involves minors and entails official recognition, not private conduct.]

D. Appellants' Equal Protection Challenge

[Finding neither a fundamental right nor a suspect class,] we review the Florida statute under the rational-basis standard. . . . Florida contends that the statute is only one aspect of its broader adoption policy, which is designed to create adoptive homes that resemble the nuclear family as closely as possible. Florida argues that the statute is rationally related to Florida's interest in furthering the best interests of adopted children by placing them in families with married mothers and fathers. Such homes, Florida asserts, provide the stability that marriage affords and the presence of both male and female authority figures, which it considers critical to optimal childhood development and socialization. In particular, Florida emphasizes a vital role that dual-gender parenting plays in shaping sexual and gender identity and in providing heterosexual role modeling. Florida argues that disallowing adoption into homosexual households, which are necessarily motherless or fatherless and lack the stability that comes with marriage, is a rational means of furthering Florida's interest in promoting adoption by marital families.

Florida clearly has a legitimate interest in encouraging a stable and nurturing environment for the education and socialization of its adopted children. It is chiefly from parental figures that children learn about the world and their place in it, and the formative influence of parents extends well beyond the years spent under their roof, shaping their children's psychology, character, and personality for years to come. . . . The adage that "the hand that rocks the cradle rules the world" hardly overstates the ripple effect that parents have on the public good by virtue of their role in raising their children. . . .

. . . Florida argues that its preference for adoptive marital families is based on the premise that the marital family structure is more stable than other household arrangements and that children benefit from the presence of both a father and mother in the home. Given that appellants have offered no competent evidence to the contrary, we find this premise to be one of those "unprovable assumptions" that nevertheless can provide a legitimate basis for legislative action. Paris Adult Theatre I v. Slaton, 413 U.S. 49, 62-63 (1973). Although social theorists from Plato to Simone de Beauvoir have proposed alternative child-rearing arrangements, none has proven as enduring as the marital family structure, nor has the accumulated wisdom of several millennia of human experience discovered a superior model. See, e.g., Plato, The Republic, Bk. V, 459d-461e; Simone de Beauvoir, The Second Sex (H. M. Parshley trans., Vintage Books 1989) (1949). Against this "sum of experience," it is rational for Florida to conclude that it is in the best interests of adoptive children, many of whom come from troubled and unstable backgrounds, to be placed in a home anchored by both a father and a mother.

. . . Arguing that the statute is both overinclusive and underinclusive, appellants contend that the real motivation behind the statute cannot be the best interest of adoptive children. . . . Appellants note that Florida law permits adoption by unmarried individuals and that, among children coming out [of] the Florida foster care system, 25% of adoptions are to parents who are currently single. Their argument is that homosexual persons are similarly situated to unmarried persons with regard to Florida's asserted interest in promoting married-couple adoption. . . .

. . . The Florida legislature could rationally conclude that homosexuals and heterosexual singles are not "similarly situated in relevant respects." It is not irrational to think that heterosexual singles have a markedly greater probability of eventually establishing a married household and, thus, providing their adopted children with a stable, dual-gender parenting environment. Moreover, as the state noted, the legislature could rationally act on the theory that heterosexual singles, even if they never marry, are better positioned than homosexual individuals to provide adopted children with education and guidance relative to their sexual development throughout pubescence and adolescence. . . . "It could be that the assumptions underlying these rationales are erroneous, but the very fact that they are arguable is sufficient, on rational-basis review, to immunize the legislative choice from constitutional challenge." [Heller v. Doe, 509 U.S. 312, 333 (1993).]

Appellants make much of the fact that Florida has over three thousand children who are currently in foster care and, consequently, have not been placed with permanent adoptive families. According to appellants, because excluding homosexuals from the pool of prospective adoptive parents will not create more eligible married couples to reduce the backlog, it is impossible for the legislature to believe that the statute advances the state's interest in placing children with married couples.

. . . Appellants misconstrue Florida's interest, which is not simply to place children in a permanent home as quickly as possible, but, when placing them, to do so in an optimal home, i.e., one in which there is a heterosexual couple or the potential for one. According to appellants' logic, every restriction on adoptive-parent candidates, such as income, instate residency, and criminal record — none of which creates more available married couples — are likewise constitutionally suspect as long as Florida has a backlog of unadopted foster children. The best interests of children, however, are not automatically served by adoption into *any* available home merely because it is permanent. . . .

Noting that Florida law permits homosexuals to become foster parents and permanent guardians, appellants contend that this fact demonstrates that Florida must not truly believe that placement in a homosexual household is not in a child's best interests. . . . We have not located and appellants have not cited any precedent indicating that a disparity between a law and its enforcement is a relevant consideration on rational-basis review, which only asks whether the legislature could have reasonably thought that the challenged law would further a legitimate state interest. . . . Foster care and legal guardianship are designed to address a different situation than permanent adoption, and "the legislature must be allowed leeway to approach a perceived problem incrementally." . . .

Appellants cite recent social science research and the opinion of mental health professionals and child welfare organizations as evidence that there is no child welfare basis for excluding homosexuals from adopting.[23] . . . In considering appellants' argument, we must ask not whether the latest in social science research and professional opinion *support* the decision of the Florida legislature, but whether that evidence is so well established and so far beyond dispute that it would be irrational for the Florida legislature to believe that the interests of its children are best served by not permitting homosexual adoption. Also, we must credit any conceivable rational reason that the legislature might have for choosing not to alter its statutory scheme in response to this recent social science research. We must assume, for example, that the legislature might be aware of the critiques of the studies cited by appellants — critiques that have highlighted significant flaws in the studies' methodologies and conclusions, such as the use of small, self-selected samples; reliance on self-report instruments; politically driven hypotheses; and the use of unrepresentative study populations consisting of disproportionately affluent, educated parents.[24] Alternatively, the legislature might consider and credit other studies that have found that children raised in homosexual households fare differently on a number of measures, doing worse on some of them, than

---

23. For the sake of simplicity, our discussion here will attribute to appellants not only their own arguments but also the arguments made in the amicus brief filed jointly on their behalf by the Child Welfare League of America, Children's Rights, Inc., the Evan B. Donaldson Adoption Institute, and the National Center for Youth Law.

24. See e.g., D. Baumrind, Commentary on Sexual Orientation: Research and Social Policy Implications, 31 Developmental Psychol. 130 (No. 1, 1995) (reviewing various studies and questioning them on "theoretical and empirical grounds" because of flaws such as small sample sizes, reliance on self-report instruments, and self-selected, unrepresentative study populations); R. Lerner & A.K. Nagai, No Basis: What the Studies Don't Tell Us About Same-Sex Parenting, Marriage Law Project (Jan. 2001) (reviewing forty-nine studies on same-sex parenting and finding recurring methodological flaws, including failure to use testable hypotheses, lack of control methods, unrepresentative study populations, self-selected sample groups, and use of negative hypotheses); J. Stacey & T. Biblarz, (How) Does the Sexual Orientation of Parents Matter, 66 Am. Soc. Rev. 159, 166 (2001) (reviewing 21 studies and finding various methodological flaws, leading authors to conclude that "there are no studies of child development based on random, representative samples" of same-sex households).

children raised in similarly situated heterosexual households.[25] Or the legislature might consider, and even credit, the research cited by appellants, but find it premature to rely on a very recent and still developing body of research, particularly in light of the absence of longitudinal studies following child subjects into adulthood and of studies of adopted, rather than natural, children of homosexual parents.[26]

We do not find any of these possible legislative responses to be irrational. Openly homosexual households represent a very recent phenomenon, and sufficient time has not yet passed to permit any scientific study of how children raised in those households fare as adults. [I]t is hardly surprising that the question of the effects of homosexual parenting on childhood development is one on which even experts of good faith reasonably disagree. Given this state of affairs, it is not irrational for the Florida legislature to credit one side of the debate over the other. Nor is it irrational for the legislature to proceed with deliberate caution. . . .

III. Conclusion

. . . The State of Florida has made the determination that it is not in the best interests of its displaced children to be adopted by individuals who "engage in current, voluntary homosexual activity," [Department of Health & Rehab. Servs. v. Cox, 627 So. 2d 1210, 1215 (Fla. Dist. Ct. App. 1993)], and we have found nothing in the Constitution that forbids this policy judgment. Thus, any argument that the Florida legislature was misguided in its decision is one of legislative policy, not constitutional law. The legislature is the proper forum for this debate, and we do not sit as a superlegislature "to award by judicial decree what was not achievable by political consensus" . . .

Notes and Questions

1. *Background.* Lofton, Croteau, and their five foster children now live in Portland, Oregon. All five tested HIV-positive at the time of placement, as did another child who died of AIDS complications. The three eldest children remain under the supervision of Florida, which made the initial foster placements and which requested Lofton quit his job to stay home with the children. (He did so.) The dispute in the principal case arose when Bert ("John Doe") seroconverted to HIV-negative, in turn becoming "adoptable." Florida continues to look for an adoptive home for Bert, who has lived with Lofton and Croteau since placement as an infant in 1991. See Fred A. Bernstein, Married or Not, It's a Full House, N.Y. Times, Nov. 20, 2003, §F, at 1; The Lofton-Croteau Family (available at http://www.lethimstay.com/loftons.html) (last visited Mar. 15, 2006).

25. See, e.g., K. Cameron & P. Cameron, Homosexual Parents, 31 Adolescence 757, 770-774 (1996) (reporting study findings that children raised by homosexual parents suffer from disproportionately high incidence of emotional disturbance and sexual victimization); Stacey & Biblarz, supra, at 170 (concluding, based on study results, that "parental sexual orientation is positively associated with the possibility that children will attain a similar orientation, and theory and common sense also support such a view").

26. We also note Justice Cordy's extensive, and persuasive, discussion of the currently available body of research on the question of homosexual parenting in his dissenting opinion in Goodridge v. Dep't of Health, 798 N.E.2d 941 (Mass. Nov. 18. 2003). . . .

2. *State restrictions.* Adoption by gays and lesbians has emerged as "a second front in the culture wars." Andrea Stone, Drives to Ban Gay Adoption Heat Up; In 16 States Laws or Ballot Votes Proposed, USA Today, Feb. 21, 2006, at 1A. Although several states explicitly permit adoptions without regard to sexual orientation (as shown by the authorization of second-parent adoptions, examined infra section D2), Florida is not alone in maintaining restrictions. See, e.g., Conn. Gen. Stat. Ann. §45a-726a (West 2004) (expressly allowing consideration of sexual orientation in foster care and adoptive placements); Okla. Stat. Ann. tit. 10 §7502-1.4(A.) (West Supp. 2006) (declining recognition of adoptions from other jurisdictions "by more than one individual of the same sex"); Utah Code Ann. §78-30-1 (2002) (prohibiting adoption by person cohabiting with another but not in valid marriage). By early 2006, 16 states had taken steps to impose restrictions on adoptions by gays and lesbians through legislation or ballot initiatives. Stone, supra.

3. *Lofton's precedents.* In upholding Florida's ban on adoptions by gay men and lesbians, *Lofton* dismisses arguments based on the Supreme Court ruling in Lawrence v. Texas, reprinted Chapter I, section A4. On what bases is *Lawrence* distinguishable? Indistinguishable? According to *Lofton*, the Florida adoption statute, as interpreted by the state courts, "draw[s] a distinction between homosexual orientation and homosexual conduct." Recall the *Lawrence* majority's observation that laws targeting the sexual conduct of gay men and lesbians create a stigma and invite status-based discrimination. Does the Florida adoption statute, as interpreted by state courts, avoid this problematic effect? Does *Lofton's* critique of *Lawrence's* standard of review mean that *Lawrence* has no precedential value at all? In an omitted section, *Lofton* also distinguishes Romer v. Evans, 517 U.S. 620 (1996).

See generally, e.g., Christopher D. Jozwiak, Lofton v. Secretary of the Department of Children & Family Services: Florida's Gay Adoption Ban Under Irrational Equal Protection Analysis, 23 Law & Ineq. 407 (2005); Benjamin C. Morgan, Comment, Adopting *Lawrence*: Lawrence v. Texas and Discriminatory Adoption Laws, 53 Emory L.J. 1491 (2004); Note, Unfixing *Lawrence*, 118 Harv. L. Rev. 2858, 2868-2869 (2005). For a defense of *Lofton*, see Lynn D. Wardle, Preference for Marital Couple Adoption—Constitutional and Policy Reflections, 5 J.L. Fam. Stud. 345 (2003).

4. *Constitutional protections in adoption.* A number of authorities, like *Lofton*, disclaim the existence of a right to adopt. See, e.g., Griffith v. Johnston, 899 F.2d 1427, 1437 (5th Cir. 1990); Ruth-Arlene W. Howe, Adoption Laws and Practices in 2000: Serving Whose Interests?, 33 Fam. L.Q. 677, 678-679 (1999). What consequences follow from this principle? Can state actors reject adoption applications for *any* reason? Do applicants have a right to a statement of reasons for rejection or fair procedures? Does the reasoning in *Lofton* leave room for race-based matching and other placement criteria designed to find the "best" adoptive home for a child?

5. *Placement preferences.* The UAA §2-104 lists in order of preference factors an *agency* should consider in determining a child's best interests in the selection of adoptive parents: the previous adoption of a sibling, characteristics requested by the minor's birth parent or guardian, custody of the minor for 6 months within the preceding 24 months or half the child's life, and status as relative with whom the child has established a positive emotional relationship by one who makes a written adoption request. After considering these possibilities, the agency can consider

other individuals. 9 U.L.A. (pt. IA) 33-34 (1999). Alternatively, the child's parent or guardian can select an adoptive family and place the child directly. UAA §2-102, id. at 12. Under the Act, most adopters must have a favorable preplacement evaluation. UAA §§2-102, 2-104, 7-101, id. at 30-31, 33-34, 124. All placements require an evaluation before the adoption becomes final. UAA §§3-601 through 3-603, id. at 91-92. Does a critical analysis of *Lofton* raise questions about all bases for attempting to optimize adoptive placement, including the factors specified by the UAA?

6. *Adoption versus foster care.* While refusing to allow gays and lesbians to adopt, Florida permits them to serve as foster parents, even on a long-term basis. Why? How does the court address the apparent inconsistencies in the Florida system? See John A. Robertson, Gay and Lesbian Access to Assisted Reproductive Technology, 55 Case W. Res. L. Rev. 323, 338-339 (2004). Does the Florida restriction contravene the "best-interests" standard? See Lauren Schwartzreich, Restructuring the Framework for Legal Analyses of Gay Parenting, 21 Harv. BlackLetter J. 109 (2005). On the other hand, given the ongoing de facto relationship of Lofton and his children, what would be the advantages of adoption versus foster care? Recall that Florida continues to search for adoptive parents for Bert. See also Margaret F. Brinig & Steven L. Nock, How Much Does Legal Status Matter? Adoptions by Kin Caregivers, 36 Fam. L.Q. 449, 462 (2002) (finding "foster care does not compare favorably with adoption for any children").

Data show that adoptions by gay men and lesbians will significantly increase the number of homes for parentless children. See Evan B. Donaldson Adoption Institute, Adoption by Lesbians and Gays: A National Survey of Adoption Agency Policies, Practices, and Attitudes (Oct. 29, 2003) (available online at <http://www.adoptioninstitute.org/whowe/Gay%20and%20Lesbian%20Adoption1.html>) (last visited Nov. 22, 2005). Without such adoptions, some of these children will have no parents at all. Allen P. Fisher, Still "Not Quite as Good as Having Your Own"? Toward a Sociology of Adoption, 29 Ann. Rev. Soc. 335, 349 (2003). One reason might be that adoption remains socially devalued among all prospective parents except gays, lesbians, and single persons. Id. at 356.

6. *Religious objections.* The advent of same-sex marriage in Massachusetts, the state's anti-discrimination laws, the license requirement for all adoption agencies, and the Catholic Church's opposition to adoptions by gays and lesbians (labeled "a form of violence against children") have combined to spark a crisis. Mary Szaniszlo, Holy Wars: State, Agency Mum on Church Gay-Adopt Stance, The Boston Herald, Dec. 8, 2005, news section, at 5. In 2005, Catholic Charities managed 41 adoption cases (700 since 1987), mostly of children with special needs; to remain licensed, however, the agency cannot discriminate against gays and lesbians. John Garvey, State Putting Church Out of Adoption Business, Boston Globe, March 14, 2006, at A15 (op-ed). Should the legislature create a special exemption from the anti-discrimination laws for such religious adoption agencies? See Scott Helman, Romney Shifts Tone on Gay Adoption, Boston Globe, March 14, 2006, at A1 (Governor's proposal).

7. *Social science evidence.* Evaluate *Lofton*'s consideration of empirical studies under the rational basis test. Should the court have noted that the studies were not undertaken in the context of adoption? Even if all the existing studies find no difference in the outcomes of children reared by gay and lesbian parents and those raised by heterosexual parents, would the court have reached the same result? What does the court's analysis of the evidence say about the court's (and

legislature's) understanding of the "cause" of one's sexual orientation? Does the court's analysis of the evidence assume that all children themselves are heterosexual? For reviews of the social science literature, see Carlos A. Ball, Lesbian and Gay Families: Gender Nonconformity and the Implications of Difference, 31 Cap. U. L. Rev. 691 (2003) (analyzing report of American Academy of Pediatrics finding no meaningful difference for children based on parents' orientation and essay of sociologists Stacey and Biblarz finding evidence of some differences); Fisher, supra, at 348-349 (concluding that evidence does not show harm to children of gay and lesbian parents); Charlotte Patterson, Children of Lesbian and Gay Parents: Summary of Research Findings, in Same-Sex Marriage: Pro and Con: A Reader 246 (Andrew Sullivan ed., rev. ed. 2004) (finding no appreciable difference in terms of children's gender identity, gender-role behavior, and sexual identity). For discussion of such studies in the context of child custody decisions see Chapter VII, section B1b(iii)(1).

Does the court's concept of "harm" to children living in nontraditional family settings rest on assumptions about gender performance and role modeling? Do these assumptions, in turn, presume distinct behavior and roles for males and females? Some data assert that daughters reared by lesbian mothers are more "masculine" than those raised by heterosexual parents. See Philip A. Belcastro et al., A Review of Data Based Studies Addressing the Effects of Homosexual Parenting on Children's Sexual and Social Functioning, in Same-Sex Marriage, supra, at 250, 250. See also David K. Flaks et al., Lesbians Choosing Motherhood: A Comparative Study of Lesbian and Heterosexual Parents and Their Children, in Same-Sex Marriage, supra, at 246, 248 (noting more effective parenting skills in lesbian couples, compared to other families, probably because of gender differences, rather then sexual orientation). Can this basis for prohibiting adoptions by gays and lesbians survive challenge under the Supreme Court precedents that find equal protection violations in official role assignments resting on gender stereotypes? See Chapter III, pp. 248-250. See also Kari E. Hong, Parens Patriarchy: Adoption, Eugenics, and Same-Sex Couples, 40 Cal. W. L. Rev. 1 (2003). For a gay adoptive father's account of how he addressed some "role model" questions raised by his young son, see Dan Savage, The Commitment: Love, Sex, Marriage, and My Family 236-241 (2005).

Problems

1. Christine knowingly relinquished her baby for adoption by a same-sex couple. Under state statutes, the biological parent can select the adoptive parents so long as a court determines the placement serves the child's best interests. During the adoption proceedings, Christine's parents (with whom she and the baby lived for four months after the birth) submit a competing petition to adopt the child. They argue that, despite a favorable home study for the placement Christine chose, adoption by homosexuals is not in the child's best interests. They also attack the constitutionality of the adoption statutes, arguing that (a) the Constitution requires a preference for placement with relatives, particularly those who have established a relationship with the child; (b) the absence of a statutory preference for placement with relatives in the adoption statute violates equal protection, given the relative preference in the foster care statute; and (c) the adoption statutes are

unconstitutional because they permit the biological parent to select a placement to the exclusion of other biological relatives, to the detriment of the child. Are these arguments persuasive? See In re Adoption of M.J.S., 44 S.W.3d 41 (Tenn. Ct. App. 2000). See also In re Petition to Adopt T.L.A., 677 N.W.2d 428 (Minn. Ct. App. 2004). Cf. In re G.C.B., 870 P.2d 1037 (Wash. Ct. App. 1994).

2. Scholars propose that states screen and license *all* parents, not only those who take children into their homes through adoption and foster care. They claim that parenting entails responsibilities at least as significant as operating a motor vehicle, which requires a driver's license. See, e.g., Hugh LaFollette, Licensing Parents, 9 Phil. & Pub. Aff. 182 (1980). With the development of long-term contraceptives for women, the means of implementing a parental licensing program exist. Would this program be desirable? Constitutional? If neither, what justifies parental screening and state approval for adoption? For literature supporting the idea, see Roger W. McIntire, Parenthood Training or Mandatory Birth Control: Take Your Choice, Psychology Today, Oct. 1973, at 34; Claudia Pap Mangel, Licensing Parents: How Feasible?, 22 Fam. L.Q. 17 (1988). For a counterargument, see Lawrence E. Frisch, On Licentious Licensing: A Reply to Hugh LaFollette, 11 Phil. & Pub. Aff. 173 (1982).

2. The Attorney's Role

■ STARK COUNTY BAR ASSOCIATION v. HARE
791 N.E.2d 966 (Ohio 2003)

PER CURIAM. . . .

In April 2000, respondent [David B. Hare, an attorney since 1989] attempted to arrange an adoption for the first time. The birth mother, whom respondent had represented in a divorce and who still owed him $2,300 in legal fees, was pregnant with twins. Respondent learned of the pregnancy at a debtor's exam in March 2000, at which time he also learned that the birth mother was unemployed and unmarried and did not intend to marry the biological father. They discussed adoption, and he advised that he would be willing to help with the arrangements.

. . . Although respondent had never done an adoption before, she testified that he said he had handled "a lot" of adoptions. She also testified that respondent offered to pay her for her time off work during pregnancy and for six to eight weeks after the twins' delivery, her medical bills and other expenses, and "anything" else she needed. . . .

The birth mother, who was scheduled to deliver in June 2000, agreed to have respondent arrange the adoption of her unborn children. Between April and June of that year, respondent issued eight checks totaling $2,889 for the birth mother's use [which she applied] to rental payments, a motor vehicle inspection, a daughter's trip to Washington, D.C., and [other] expenses. . . . Respondent disputed the birth mother's testimony, insisting that as far as he knew all of these checks had been issued to the birth mother to pay for medical expenses. . . .

On April 28, 2000, respondent interviewed a couple who wanted to adopt the twins. He demanded a $1,500 nonrefundable retainer to pay for their interview and advised that the twins' adoptions would cost $50,000. Respondent decided to charge this amount because he knew parents who had adopted one child from a foreign country, and they had paid $25,000 in legal fees. The couple agreed to proceed, and respondent interviewed them about their background. Three days later, respondent selected the couple as the prospective adoptive parents.

Respondent told the prospective adoptive parents that in addition to the $50,000 legal fee, they would also have to pay $10,000 for the birth mother's medical expenses before the births. In total, the couple paid respondent $61,500: $1,500 for the interview, $20,000 on May 12, 2000, and $40,000 on June 19, 2000. Respondent picked up the $40,000 check himself at the couple's home, explaining that he needed the money to finish paying the bills for the adoptions.

Between April and June 2000, the birth mother, biological father, and prospective adoptive parents completed preliminary adoption requirements. During those proceedings, respondent assured the adoptive mother that although the court had concerns about her previous divorces, they would be able to complete the adoption because he was a friend of the probate judge. At some point, respondent also told the birth mother that he could no longer represent her in the adoption because of a conflict of interest [and] arranged for her representation by another attorney, telling the other attorney first that his fee would be either $134 or $143 and later that his representation would have to be on a pro bono basis . . . because the birth mother did not have any money.

The birth mother delivered the twins on June 22, 2000. On June 27, 2000, respondent filed preliminary estimated accountings in probate court that were required to disclose any disbursements of value in connection with the adoptions. Respondent, who had paid living expenses to the birth mother and had received over $60,000 from the prospective adoptive parents, represented in those filings that no such disbursements had been made. . . .

Also on June 27, 2000, respondent appeared on the adoptive parents' behalf in probate court, along with the birth mother and her counsel and the birth father, for the initial consent hearing. The court awarded temporary custody of the twins to the adoptive parents subject to a final consent hearing six months later.

Prior to the June 2000 hearing, respondent had permitted the birth mother to use a 1993 Oldsmobile that he said was worth $6,000. In July 2000, after the birth mother gave her initial consent to the adoptions, respondent transferred title of the vehicle to her. Respondent also filed a notice of satisfaction of the $2,300 judgment he had against the birth mother. The birth mother testified that respondent told her, "I let you go" on the judgment amount, which he quoted as $2,700. Respondent denied this and testified that he declared the judgment satisfied because he knew the birth mother had no assets. Thereafter, respondent stopped assisting the birth mother financially [including refusing to pay the medical bills that she submitted].

In anticipation of the final consent hearing, respondent forwarded for the birth parents' signature the final accountings for the twins' adoptions. Again, these documents did not list any disbursements for medical expenses or attorney fees. The adoptive mother asked respondent why he had omitted the $50,000 in legal fees and $10,000 in medical expenses they had paid. Respondent explained that "in a private adoption, the monies involved do not need to be disclosed." . . . The adoptive parents signed the accounts, and respondent filed them with the probate court on November 20, 2000. . . .

On December 28, 2000, at what was to be the final adoption hearing, the birth mother withdrew her consent to the adoption, citing her unpaid medical bills. She testified that she no longer trusted respondent's representations about the twins' placement. At the same hearing, the birth mother's attorney asserted a conflict of interest and withdrew.

Thereafter, the birth mother retained a third attorney, who also eventually represented the birth father. The new attorney arranged for the birth mother to become more familiar with the adoptive parents. At the birth mother's request and with the adoptive parents' consent, respondent subsequently withdrew from representing the adoptive parents. Notwithstanding this withdrawal, respondent advised the adoptive parents prior to a meeting with the birth mother and her new attorney "not to discuss money whatsoever because money in a private adoption is private."

[With a new attorney, the birth parents consented again; the adoptive parents disclosed to the court their payment to Hare; and the twins, who had been removed from the adoptive parents and placed in foster care, were returned to them. They recouped some of their money and completed the adoption requirements again.] The probate court approved the twins' adoptions in July 2002.

The panel found that by charging the adoptive parents a $50,000 legal fee in these adoptions, respondent clearly violated DR 2-106(A) (charging or collecting a clearly excessive fee). The panel cited evidence indicating that local adoption lawyers charged hourly rates of $125 to $150 for customary total fees of $2,000 to $3,000 and the fact that respondent had formally accounted for only a few hours of work.

The panel also found respondent in violation of DR 5-101(A)(1) (accepting employment in a conflict of interest without a client's consent after full disclosure) because he had acquired an interest in these adoptions through improper payments to the birth mother and also had not disclosed these payments to the adoptive parents. The panel further found violations of DR 5-103(A) (acquiring an improper proprietary interest in a client's case) and (B) (providing improper financial assistance to a client) because respondent had paid the birth mother's personal expenses and given her a car, neither of which was a permissible advance of court costs or other litigation expenses.

The panel additionally found respondent in violation of DR 7-102(A)(3) (knowingly failing to disclose that which an attorney is required by law to reveal [i.e., the fees and payments]), (4) (knowingly using perjured or false evidence), (5) (making a false statement of law or fact), (6) (creating or preserving evidence the attorney knows or should know is false), and (7) (counseling a client in conduct the attorney knows is illegal or fraudulent). . . . Finally, the panel found that respondent violated DR 9-102(A) (failing to keep client's funds in a separate and identifiable trust account) by depositing into his personal accounts all the money paid to him by the adoptive parents, which included unearned and unapproved attorney fees as well as funds intended to be used for the birth mother's medical expenses. . . .

. . . The panel concluded that respondent had dishonestly and selfishly attempted to conceal the exorbitant fee he charged for these adoptions. [R]espondent has attempted to evade responsibility for and conceal evidence of his shameful betrayal of his clients' interests and professional oath. Disbarment is the only appropriate sanction. . . .

Notes and Questions

1. *Attorneys in private placements.* Private adoptions present a host of challenges for the attorney. Beyond the ethical violations cited in the principal case, consider the following: On what basis did Hare select the adoptive parents? What obligation, if any, does he have to ensure their suitability as parents? What difficulties does his representation of both the birth mother and the adopters, even temporarily, pose?

2. *"Baby broker" laws.* Statutes in many states impose tight restrictions on child placement. For example, New York prohibits all placements except those by "an authorized agency" or "a parent, legal guardian or relative with the second degree." N.Y. Soc. Serv. Law §374(2) (McKinney 2003). The statute defines the prohibited conduct, "plac[ing] out," as arranging for the child's free care in a family other than that of a relative, "for the purpose of adoption or for the purpose of providing care." N.Y. Soc. Serv. Law §371(12) (McKinney Supp. 2005). See also, e.g., Ala. Code §26-10A-33 (LexisNexis 1992); Del. Code Ann. tit. 13, §904 (Supp. 2004); Mass. Gen. Laws ch. 210, §11A (1998).

Such "baby broker" laws were enacted both to prevent commercial trafficking in babies ("baby selling") and to prevent placement by the untrained. See In re Preadoption Certificate Concerning Carballo, 521 N.Y.S.2d 375 (Fam. Ct. 1987). Given the latter goal, what activities do such statutes prohibit? Why do such laws exempt parents and some relatives? To what extent can attorneys or other third parties serve as intermediaries under the New York statute? For what can attorneys receive fees? See also Galison v. District of Columbia, 402 A.2d 1263 (D.C. 1979); People v. Schwartz, 356 N.E.2d 8 (Ill. 1976).

3. *Fees and expenses.* Despite the usual exemption for parents in placement restrictions, of course, even parents cannot "sell" their children. See Maryland v. Runkles, 605 A.2d 111 (Md. Ct. App. 1992). On the other hand, payment of the birth mother's medical expenses by the adoptive parents has long been permissible. See, e.g., Or. Rev. Stat. Ann. §163.537 (West 2003); In re Baby Boy P., 700 N.Y.S.2d 792 (Fam. Ct. 1999). What costs can be reimbursed? See N.Y. Soc. Serv. Law §374(6) (McKinney 2003) (listing reimbursable expenses); In re D.S.D., 19 P.3d 204 (Kan. Ct. App. 2001) (adopters may pay indigent biological father's attorneys fees); In re Adoption No. 9979, 591 A.2d 468 (Md. Ct. App. 1991) (not maternity clothes); In re Baby Girl D., 517 A.2d 925 (Pa. 1986) (no reimbursement for counseling, housing, medical expenses not directly beneficial to the child, including Lamaze classes and sonograms). See generally U.S. Department of Health and Human Servs., Administration for Children and Families, Administration on Children, Youth and Families, Children's Bureau, National Adoption Information Clearinghouse, State Regulation of Adoption Expenses (State Statute Series 2005) (available at http://naic.acf.hhs.gov/general/legal/statutes/expenses.pdf).

The UAA, §7-102, prohibits payments for placement, parental consent, or relinquishment, subject to a civil penalty. 9 U.L.A. (pt. IA) 125 (1999). The UAA, §7-103, permits, however, payment for the services of an agency, advertising, medical and travel expenses, counseling, living expenses for the birth mother for a reasonable period, disclosure of the child's medical and psychological history, legal services and court costs, evaluations of the adopters, and any other service the court finds reasonably necessary. Such payments cannot be made contingent on placement, relinquishment, or consent to adoption. Id. at 126.

4. *Ethical challenges.* May an attorney ethically keep a file of adults interested in adopting and then select one over the others when a birth parent seeks help in placement? See In re Petrie, 742 P.2d 796 (Ariz. 1987). Does the birth mother's attorney, who facilitates her plan to relinquish her newborn for adoption, have any obligation to the birth father and his parents, who want to rear the child? Does the duty to the birth mother require the attorney to assist in thwarting the father's effort to establish a relationship with the child? Does the father have any remedies against the attorney? See Sprouse v. Eisenman, 2005 WL 289460 (Ohio Ct. App. 2005). In a malpractice action against an attorney who negligently advised birth parents that they could revoke their consent, what damages should they recover for loss of exclusive care of the child? See Collins v. Missouri Bar Plan, 157 S.W.3d 726 (Mo. Ct. App. 2005).

5. *Multiple clients.* Under what circumstances can one attorney represent both the adoptive parents, whom the attorney has selected, and the birth mother or father? Do such parties always have adverse interests? According to *Petrie*, supra, having such multiple clients is permissible only if it is obvious that the attorney can adequately represent the interests of each and if each consents after full disclosure of the possible effects. The Model Rules of Professional Conduct, addressing attorneys as intermediaries, requires full disclosure of the implications of common representation, client consent thereto, full explanations of each decision to be made, and withdrawal from the matter upon request or dissatisfaction. Further, the attorney must reasonably believe that the matter can be resolved impartially and consistent with the clients' best interests. Model Rules Prof'l Conduct R. 2.2 (2004). Does this *general* rule provide appropriate regulation of adoption intermediaries *in particular*?

Although the American Bar Association has stated expressly that "a lawyer may not ethically represent both the adoptive and biological parents in a private adoption proceeding," it recognizes that "some authorities have held otherwise." ABA Comm. on Ethics and Prof'l Responsibility, Informal Op. 1523 (1987). See also, e.g., In re Adoption of Gustavo G., 776 N.Y.S.2d 15 (App. Div. 2004) (rejecting per se disqualification of adopter's attorney, which previously represented placing foster care agency); Restatement (Third) of the Law Governing Lawyers §130 (2000) (requiring consent for multiple representation in nonlitigated matter if substantial risk of material and adverse effect on one client's interests). For example, California treats as unethical joint representation in independent adoptions absent both parties' written consent. The consent must include, inter alia, notice to the birth parents of the right to independent counsel with reasonable attorneys' fees assumed by the adoptive parents, waiver by the birth parents of independent representation, and an agreement that the attorney for the adoptive parents will represent the birth parents. Cal. Fam. Code §8800 (West 2004). See also Debra Lyn Bassett, Three's A Crowd: A Proposal to Abolish Joint Representation, 32 Rutgers L.J. 387 (2001).

6. *Adoption facilitators.* When only parents and licensed agencies can place children, what services can nonagency intermediaries provide to assist a parent in selecting a placement? According to the Nevada Attorney General, a lawyer who merely sends video or audio tapes, letters, resumes, or other information describing prospective adoptive parents to the birth mother violates a statute prohibiting

adoptive placement by a person not licensed to place children. Nev. Rev. Stat. Ann. §127.310 (West Supp. 2005) makes it a misdemeanor for any unlicensed person or organization to place, arrange the placement of, or assist in placing or arranging the placement of any child for adoption. This statute defines "[a]rrange the placement of a child" as "to make preparations for or bring about any agreement or understanding concerning the adoption of a child." Id. at §127.220.

How would the sending of tapes, letters, and resumes fare under the following statute?

> The selection of a prospective adoptive parent or parents shall be personally made by the child's birth parent or parents and may not be delegated to an agent. The act of selection by the birth parent or parents shall be based upon his, her, or their personal knowledge of the prospective adoptive parent or parents.

Cal. Fam. Code §8801(a) (West 2004). The statute then lists specific information required to satisfy "personal knowledge." Id. at §8801(b). But see also id. at §8637 (attorneys as adoption facilitators).

7. *The commodification controversy.* Despite the prohibition on buying and selling children, most authorities agree that today's practice of independent adoption often entails the payment of money, particularly for white infants. See Madelyn Freundlich, The Market Forces in Adoption 11-13 (2000); Adam Pertman, Adoption Nation: How the Adoption Revolution Is Transforming America 185-203 (2000). But see Martha M. Ertman, What's Wrong With a Parenthood Market? A New and Improved Theory of Commodification, 82 N.C. L. Rev. 1 (2003); Amanda C. Pustilnik, Note, Private Ordering, Legal Ordering, and the Getting of Children: A Counterhistory of Adoption Law, 20 Yale L. & Pol'y Rev. 263 (2002).

Birth parents often have the opportunity to choose from several competing prospective adopters, as dramatized on a prime-time televised broadcast that tracked a young woman's interviews with five couples seeking to adopt her baby and her ultimate selection of one. ABC News, 20/20, Be My Baby, Apr. 30, 2004 (available on LEXIS). Sometimes, the birth mother lives temporarily with the prospective adopters to assess personally their parenting styles and interactions with the child. See, e.g., In re Adoption of E.H., 103 P.3d 177 (Utah Ct. App. 2004), *remanded,* 2006 WL 1528603 (Utah 2006). What are the advantages and disadvantages of this selection process?

Why not legitimize baby selling, given the existence of a market and controversy about matching and other placement practices? A provocative article contends that an adopter's willingness to pay ensures the child will be well cared for. Elisabeth M. Landes & Richard A. Posner, The Economics of the Baby Shortage, 7 J. Legal Stud. 323 (1978). The authors attribute discomfort with the idea to concerns about overreaching, racial ranking, and the spectre of baby breeding. Nonetheless, citing the current availability of abortion and the decreased stigma of rearing nonmarital children, they ask: "[W]hat social purposes are served by encouraging these alternatives to the baby sale?" Id. at 346. Is this analysis persuasive? Judge Posner advocates removing the "price ceiling" for independent adoptions, given the decreasing supply of available children. Richard A. Posner, Sex and Reason 409-416 (1992).

Note: Adoption of Children with Special Needs

Children in foster care with histories of abuse and neglect and ensuing psychological problems are often called "children with special needs" or "hard-to-place children." These terms also include all children over four years of age, children of color, sibling groups, and children with handicaps, including HIV infection.[3]

To encourage adoptions of such children, state and federal programs provide financial assistance. See generally Seth A. Grob, Adoption Subsidies: Advocating for Children with Special Needs, 7 U.C. Davis J. Juv. L. & Pol'y 83 (2003). Tax law offers incentives, including some credits and exclusions. See I.R.C. §§23, 137 (LexisNexis 2006). The UAA, §2-105, requires agencies receiving federal funds to make diligent efforts to recruit adopters for these children. 9 U.L.A. (pt. IA) 35-36 (1999).

Adoptions of children with special needs have risen to constitute almost half of all domestic adoptions by nonrelatives.[4] Although about 75 percent of adopters of children with special needs report satisfaction with these placements, about 10 to 15 percent end before the final decree is issued. Most of these disrupted adoptions involve older children, while placements of younger children with disabilities and serious medical problems produce higher success rates. Like age, emotional and behavioral problems (including a past history of physical and sexual abuse) are predictors of disruption. Adopters' unrealistic expectations and their rigidity in family interactions also tend to correlate with poor outcomes.[5]

According to some critics, existing governmental support is inadequate. Adoptive families complain about the state's failure to disclose the full extent of the problems experienced by some children in subsidized adoption programs, preventing appropriate treatment; they also contend that more services are necessary to make such placements work. See Griffith v. Johnston, 899 F.2d 1427 (5th Cir. 1990). Child welfare advocates recommend improved efforts to recruit adopters, the removal of barriers to nontraditional families, acceleration of the process by which children removed from parental custody become available for adoption, and provision of postadoption services.[6] Because children of color are usually included in the definition of children with special needs, the debate about transracial adoption inevitably surfaces in these calls for reform. See, e.g., Sarah Ramsey, Fixing Foster Care or Reducing Child Poverty: The Pew Commission Recommendations and the Transracial Adoption Debate, 66 Mont. L. Rev. 21 (2005).

Other critics, like Professor Roberts, supra, pp. 1045-1047, condemn legislation like the Adoption and Safe Families Act (ASFA) for favoring adoptive homes over birth families and for failing to encourage systemic reform. See also, e.g., Amy Wilkinson-Hagen,

---

[3]. See Judith K. McKenzie, Adoption of Children with Special Needs, The Future of Children, Spring 1993, at 62, 63. On September 30, 2003, 523,085 children were in foster care, with 118,761 awaiting adoption. The largest fraction of the waiting children, 40 percent, were classified as "Black Non-Hispanic." During 2003, 281,472 children exited foster care, but only 18 percent left for adoption. U.S. Dept. of Health and Human Servs., Administration for Children and Families, Administration on Children, Youth and Families, Children's Bureau, The AFCARS Report, Preliminary FY 2003 Estimates as of April 2005 (10) (available at http://www.acf.hhs.gov/programs/cb/publications/afcars/report10.pdf).

[4]. National Council for Adoption, Adoption Factbook III 27 (1999) (48.5 percent in 1996, up from 26.5 percent in 1986).

[5]. These figures and conclusions are reported in James A. Rosenthal, Outcomes of Adoption of Children with Special Needs, The Future of Children, Spring 1993, at 77, 79-81.

[6]. See McKenzie, supra note [3], at 73-75; Rosenthal, supra note [5], at 84-86.

Note, The Adoption and Safe Families Act of 1997: A Collision of Parens Patriae and Parents' Constitutional Rights, 11 Geo. J. on Poverty L. & Pol'y 137, 138 (2004) (critiquing goal of "permanency at any cost — even the cost of unnecessary state termination proceedings"). But see Elizabeth Bartholet, Nobody's Children: Abuse and Neglect, Foster Drift, and the Adoption Alternative 188-189 (1999). Preliminary empirical evidence associates ASFA with an increase in adoptions of young children, a possible shift to adoption from reunification with birth parents, and an increase in older children with no legal parents because adoption often does not follow the termination of parental rights. Richard P. Barth et. al., From Anticipation to Evidence: Research on the Adoption and Safe Families Act, 12 Va. J. Soc. Pol'y & L. 371, 381-383, 392-395 (2005).

3. Equitable Adoption

■ **ESTATE OF FORD**
   82 P.3d 747 (Cal. 2004)

WERDEGAR, J.

Terrold Bean claims the right to inherit the intestate estate of Arthur Patrick Ford as Ford's equitably adopted son. . . . Born in 1953, Bean was declared a ward of the court and placed in the home of Ford and his wife, Kathleen Ford, as a foster child in 1955. Bean never knew his natural father, whose identity is uncertain, and he was declared free of his mother's control in 1958, at the age of four. Bean lived continuously with Mr. and Mrs. Ford and their natural daughter, Mary Catherine, for about 18 years, until Mrs. Ford's death in 1973, then with Ford and Mary Catherine for another two years, until 1975.

During part of the time Bean lived with the Fords, they cared for other foster children and received a county stipend for doing so. Although the Fords stopped taking in foster children after Mrs. Ford became ill with cancer, they retained custody of Bean. The last two other foster children left the home around the time of Mrs. Ford's death, but Bean, who at 18 years of age could have left, stayed with Ford and Mary Catherine.

Bean knew the Fords were not his natural parents, but as a child he called them "Mommy" and "Daddy," and later "Mom" and "Dad." Joan Malpassi, Mary Catherine's friend since childhood and later administrator of Ford's estate, testified that Bean's relationship with Mary Catherine was "as two siblings" and that the Fords treated Bean "more like Mary rather than a foster son, like a real son was my observation." Mary Catherine later listed Bean as her brother on a life insurance application.

Bean remained involved with Ford and Mary Catherine even after leaving the Ford home and marrying. Ford loaned Bean money to help furnish his new household and later forgave the unpaid part of the debt when Bean's marriage was dissolved. Bean visited Ford and Mary Catherine several times per year both during his marriage and after his divorce. When Ford suffered a disabling stroke in 1989, Mary Catherine conferred with Bean and Malpassi over Ford's care; Ford was placed in a board and care facility, where Bean continued to visit him regularly until his death in 2000.

Mary Catherine died in 1999. Bean and Malpassi arranged her funeral. Bean petitioned for Malpassi to be appointed Ford's conservator, and with Malpassi's agreement Bean obtained a power of attorney to take care of Ford's affairs pending establishment of the conservatorship. Bean also administered Mary Catherine's estate, which was distributed to the Ford conservatorship. When a decision was needed as to whether Ford should receive medical life support, Malpassi consulted with Bean in deciding he should. When Ford died, Bean and Malpassi arranged the funeral.

The Fords never petitioned to adopt Bean. Mrs. Ford told Barbara Carter, a family friend, that "they wanted to adopt Terry," but she was "under the impression that she could not put in for adoption while he was in the home." She worried that if Bean was removed during the adoption process he might be put in "a foster home that wasn't safe."

Ford's nearest relatives at the time of his death were the two children of his predeceased brother, nephew John J. Ford III and niece Veronica Newbeck. Neither had any contact with Ford for about 15 years before his death, and neither attended his funeral. John J. Ford III filed a petition to determine entitlement to distribution (Prob. Code, §11700), listing both himself and Newbeck as heirs. Bean filed a statement of interest claiming entitlement to Ford's entire estate under [Probate Code §6455 (equitable adoption). After trial, the court ruled against Bean because it found no clear and convincing evidence of "an intent to adopt." Bean appealed.]

I. Criteria for Equitable Adoption

[The judicial doctrine] of equitable adoption allows a person who was accepted and treated as a natural or adopted child, and as to whom adoption typically was promised or contemplated but never performed, to share in inheritance of the foster parents' property. . . . [2] California decisions have explained equitable adoption as the specific enforcement of a contract to adopt. Yet it has long been clear that the doctrine, even in California, rested less on ordinary rules of contract law than on considerations of fairness and intent for, as Justice Schauer put it [in his dissenting opinion in Estate of Radovich, 308 P.2d 14, 24 (Cal. 1957)], the child "should have been" adopted and would have been but for the decedent's "inadvertence or fault." [M]oreover, the contracts purportedly being enforced were made between foster parents and their minor charges, yet neither court addressed the children's capacity to contract, suggesting, again, that the contract served mainly as evidence of the parties' intent, rather than as an enforceable legal basis for transmission of property.

Bean urges that equitable adoption be viewed not as specific enforcement of a contract to adopt, but as application of an equitable restitutionary remedy he has identified as quasi-contract or, as his counsel emphasized at oral argument, as an application of equitable estoppel principles. While we have found no decisions articulating a quasi-contract theory, courts in several states have, instead of or in addition to the contract rationale, analyzed equitable adoption as arising from "a broader and vaguer equitable principle of estoppel." (Clark, The Law of Domestic

---

2. In California, at least, adoption itself is "purely statutory in origin and nature." (Estate of Radovich [, 308 P.2d 14 (Cal. 1957)] (dis. opn. of Schauer, J.).) The effect of an equitable adoption finding, therefore, is limited to the child's inheritance rights and does not in other respects equate the child's rights with those of a statutorily adopted child.

Relations in the United States, [926 (2d ed. 1988)]). Bean argues Mr. Ford's conduct toward him during their long and close relationship estops Ford's estate or heirs at law from denying his status as an equitably adopted child.

For several reasons, we conclude the California law of equitable adoption, which has rested on contract principles, does not recognize an estoppel arising merely from the existence of a familial relationship between the decedent and the claimant. The law of intestate succession is intended to carry out [the decedent's likely intent]. The existence of a mutually affectionate relationship, without any direct expression by the decedent of an intent to adopt the child or to have him or her treated as a legally adopted child, sheds little light on the decedent's likely intent regarding distribution of property. [E]quitable adoption in California is neither a means of compensating the child for services rendered to the parent nor a device to avoid the unjust enrichment of other, more distant relatives who will succeed to the estate under the intestacy statutes. Absent proof of an intent to adopt, we must follow the statutory law of intestate succession.

In addition, a rule looking to the parties' overall relationship in order to do equity in a given case, rather than to particular expressions of intent to adopt, would necessarily be a vague and subjective one, inconsistently applied, in an area of law where "consistent, bright-line rules" are greatly needed. Such a broad scope for equitable adoption would leave open to competing claims the estate of *any* foster parent or stepparent who treats a foster child or stepchild lovingly and on an equal basis with his or her natural or legally adopted children. . . .

While a California equitable adoption claimant need not prove all the elements of an enforceable contract to adopt, therefore, we conclude the claimant must demonstrate the existence of some direct expression, on the decedent's part, of an intent to adopt the claimant. [I]n addition to a contract or other direct evidence of the intent to adopt, the evidence must show "objective conduct indicating mutual recognition of an adoptive parent and child relationship to such an extent that in equity and good conscience an adoption should be deemed to have taken place."

II. Standard of Proof of Equitable Adoption

. . . Several good reasons support the rule [requiring clear and convincing evidence, the standard used by the court below.] First, the claimant in an equitable adoption case is seeking inheritance outside the ordinary statutory course of intestate succession and without the formalities required by the adoption statutes. . . . Second, the claim involves a relationship with persons who have died and who can, therefore, no longer testify to their intent. Finally, too relaxed a standard could create the danger that "a person could not help out a needy child without having a de facto adoption foisted upon him after death." [Jan Ellen Rein, Relatives by Blood, Adoption, and Association: Who Should Get What and Why, 37 Vand. L. Rev. 711, 782 (1984).]

Although the evidence showed the Fords and Bean enjoyed a close and enduring familial relationship, evidence was totally lacking that the Fords ever made an attempt to adopt Bean or promised or stated their intent to do so; they neither held Bean out to the world as their natural or adopted child (Bean, for example, did not take the Ford name) nor represented to Bean that he was their child. Mrs. Ford's single statement to Barbara Carter was not clear and convincing evidence that Mr. Ford intended Bean to be, or be treated as, his adopted son. [Affirmed.]

Notes and Questions

1. *Background.* Equitable adoption is a judicially created doctrine. The majority of courts (among those that have considered the issue) recognize the doctrine. See R. Brent Drake, Note, Status or Contract? A Comparative Analysis of Inheritance Rights Under Equitable Adoption and Domestic Partnership Doctrines, 39 Ga. L. Rev. 675, 681 (2005) (27 jurisdictions recognize the doctrine by case law). The practice traces back to the era when "orphan trains" brought indigent children from urban centers to families in the west. See Johnson v. Johnson, 617 N.W.2d 97, 101-102 (N.D. 2000). See also Hendrik Hartog, Someday All This Will Be Yours: Inheritance, Adoption, and Obligation in Capitalist America, 79 Ind. L.J. 345 (2004).

2. *Theories.* Jurisdictions rely on one of two theories to establish equitable adoption: implied contract or equitable estoppel. Under the former, a court enforces a foster parent's *implied promise* to adopt a child. Under the latter, a court considers the child's performance of filial services to protect the child from the adoptive parents' *neglect to finalize* the adoption. Drake, supra, at 684. In contrast, many jurisdictions refuse to recognize the doctrine because adoption is purely statutory in origin, so a court may not grant an adoption absent compliance with the statutory formalities. See generally Tracy Bateman Farrell, Annot., Modern Status of Law as to Equitable Adoption or Adoption by Estoppel, 122 A.L.R.5th 205 (2004) (citing authority).

3. *Criticisms.* Each of the theoretical bases has shortcomings. The implied contract approach suffers because of conceptual difficulties in applying specific performance (e.g., enforcement after the death of a party, a reluctance to enforce personal service contracts, the lack of a meeting of the minds). Estoppel raises questions about the child's detrimental reliance on the contract, especially a child who is too young to understand the contract and who lacks meaningful alternatives. See Jan Ellen Rein, Relatives by Blood, Adoption, and Association: Who Should Get What and Why?, 37 Vand. L. Rev. 711, 774-777 (1984) (discussing these and other criticisms).

Under either theory, courts usually condition relief on a showing of some agreement between the foster parents and the biological parent(s). E.g., Hulsey v. Carter, 588 S.E.2d 717 (Ga. 2003). Did any such agreement exist in Terry Bean's case? Why or why not? Can the requisite agreement ever arise when foster parents take custody of a child through a court's assertion of its dependency jurisdiction?

4. *Intent to Adopt.* Although *Ford* adheres strictly to the requirement of an intent to adopt, other courts adopt a more liberal approach. For example, the court in Smalley v. Parks, 108 S.W.3d 138, 141 (Mo. Ct. App. 2003), reasons that the requisite agreement may be shown by "acts, conduct, and admissions of the adopting parent." Would Terry Bean have been more successful under this approach? What possible reasons might explain Mrs. Ford's reluctance to formally adopt Terry? Might agency policy have played a role (i.e., the discouragement of the formation of ties between foster parents and foster children, in turn leading to Mrs. Ford's fear that Terry might be removed from their home)?

5. *Status-based approach*. Many commentators criticize reliance on the contract theory and advocate instead a status-based approach. See Drake, supra, at 684, 712. To date, West Virginia alone follows this approach:

> While the existence of an express contract of adoption is very convincing evidence, an implied contract of adoption is an unnecessary fiction created by courts as a protection from fraudulent claims. We find that if a claimant can, by clear, cogent and convincing evidence, prove sufficient facts to convince the trier of fact that his status is identical to that of a formally adopted child, except only for the absence of a formal order of adoption, a finding of an equitable adoption is proper without proof of an adoption contract.

Wheeling Dollar Savings & Trust Co. v. Singer, 250 S.E.2d 369, 374 (W. Va. 1978). Under the status-based approach, what criteria should be used to determine whether a child has been equitably adopted? Does Braschi v. Stahl (Chapter IV, Section B4e) provide any guidance? According to *Wheeling*, supra, the claimant must prove by clear and convincing evidence that she or he was treated the same, from a young age, as a formally adopted child. Relevant circumstances include love and affection, filial obedience, reliance, representation that the child is a natural or adopted child, an invalid or ineffectual adoption proceeding, and the birth parent's surrender of ties. 250 S.E.2d at 373-374. How would Terry Bean fare under this approach?

Should application of the equitable adoption doctrine depend on the adoptee's good faith belief that he or she was a legally adopted child or a biological child? Did Terry Bean have such a belief? Should application of the doctrine require severance of the child's ties to the biological parents? For example, *Hulsey*, supra, held that a stepchild failed to establish equitable adoption because, in part, she continued to have contact with her biological father and his extended family. Does this rationale hark back to the traditional notion that a child can have only one set of parents?

6. *Legal obstacle*. In a common scenario in equitable adoption cases, an impediment prevents the foster parents from finalizing the adoption. For example, in the classic case of Estate of Wilson, 168 Cal. Rptr. 533 (Ct. App. 1980), a child's adoption failed when the birth mother could not be found to provide consent. As an adult, the petitioner discovered only after the foster parents' deaths that he had not been adopted. When he sought recognition as their heir, the court applied equitable adoption, citing the requisite agreement to adopt and continuation of the parent-child relationship during their joint lifetimes.

The *Wilson* holding was codified in California Probate Code §6454, which permits the establishment of a parent-child relationship in the context of both foster parenthood and stepparenthood. Specifically, the statute requires a personal relationship between the claimant and the decedent that began during the child's minority and continued for their joint lifetimes and also a legal barrier but for which the foster parent would have adopted the child. Terry Bean originally brought claims under this statutory provision as well as the equitable adoption doctrine. Why was this former statute inapplicable in *Ford*?

Under this test and several others, the relationship and/or agreement to adopt must occur during the child's minority. See, e.g., Samek v. Sanders, 788 So. 2d 872 (Ala. 2000). Why?

7. *Scope.* Should the doctrine of equitable adoption apply only to inheritance questions? Traditionally, the doctrine has had this narrow scope. Recall footnote 2 in *Ford*. See also Jolley v. Seamco Labs., Inc., 828 So. 2d 1050 (Fla. Dist. Ct. App. 2002) (child cannot recover for equitable adopter's wrongful death); In re M.L.P.J., 16 S.W.3d 45 (Tex. App. 2000) (doctrine inapplicable to claims for child support and health insurance). Even then, some courts recognize the equitably adopted child's right to inherit only *from* the would-be adopter. E.g., Estate of Furia, 126 Cal. Rptr. 2d 384 (Ct. App. 2002); see also Sanderson v. Bathrick, 76 P.3d 1236 (Wyo. 2003) (doctrine inapplicable to anti-lapse statute, when would-be adopter dies testate). What explains this narrow scope? Should the doctrine apply in other contexts? Which ones?

8. *Equitable parent doctrine.* Despite the traditionally narrow scope, courts increasingly are recognizing a broader modern variation of equitable adoption, often called the "equitable parent doctrine." In one prevalent fact pattern, some states recognize as an equitable parent a man who first learns upon divorce that his wife's child (whom he had treated as his own) is not his biological offspring. In these cases, the doctrine allows the man parental custodial or visitation rights, or it may result in support duties. See, e.g., In re Marriage of Gallagher, 539 N.W.2d 479 (Iowa 1995) (recognizing husband as equitable parent based on estoppel against mother, with remand to determine child's best interests); Atkinson v. Atkinson, 408 N.W.2d 516, 519 (Mich. Ct. App. 1987) (requiring mutual acknowledgment as father and child or cooperation of the mother in the development of the relationship, husband's desire to have parental rights, and his willingness to pay child support); *Johnson*, supra (holding equitable adoption applicable to postdissolution child support). Nonetheless, some courts limit or reject the equitable parent approach in such cases. See, e.g., Van v. Zahorik, 597 N.W.2d 15 (Mich. 1999) (refusing to extend doctrine to man who met functional criteria but had not married the mother); D.G. v. D.M.K., 557 N.W.2d 235 (S.D. 1996) (rejecting doctrine for man who knew all along that he was not child's father).

In a second increasingly common fact pattern, a lesbian couple who agreed to rear children together become involved in a custody, visitation, or child-support dispute after their relationship dissolves. Initially, courts recognized only the biological or adoptive mother as a parent in such disputes, giving her exclusive authority to control access to the child (and the exclusive responsibility for support), regardless of her former partner's participation in childrearing or the child's attachment. E.g., Alison D. v. Virginia M., 572 N.E.2d 27 (N.Y. 1991). More recently, courts have accorded parental prerogatives based on estoppel or other equitable principles. See Kristine H. v. Lisa R., 117 P.3d 690 (Cal. 2005) (estoppel based on prebirth stipulation of parentage); In re L.B., 122 P.3d 161 (Wash. 2005) (recognizing common law de facto parentage under court's equitable authority), *cert. denied*, 126 S. Ct. 2021 (2006). See also American Law Institute, Principles of the Law of Family Dissolution: Analysis and Recommendations §§2.03, 3.03 (2002) (recognizing parents by estoppel and de facto parents). Some courts bypass an estoppel-based analysis, instead expansively construing "parent" in the state's parentage statutes. E.g., Elisa B. v. Superior Ct. (reprinted

Chapter IV, section C3). Cf. In re A.B., 837 N.E.2d 965 (Ind. 2005), *vacating and remanding* 818 N.E.2d 126 (Ind. Ct. App. 2004)). (Chapter VII, section B3, also examines these issues.)

Given these more recent decisions, in which everyone knows that the mother's former partner is not the child's biological parent, why do some courts declare that a man can achieve recognition as an equitable parent only if he mistakenly believed that he was the child's biological father, as in *D.G.*, supra? Should the method of conception, donor insemination versus sexual intercourse, matter? See infra section E1b. Should it matter whether the would-be equitable parent is seeking recognition (as in a custody and visitation dispute) or disclaiming recognition (as in a child-support dispute)? Compare, e.g., *A.B.*, supra, with *Elisa B.*, supra.

4. Jurisdiction

■ IN RE BABY GIRL CLAUSEN
502 N.W.2d 649 (Mich. 1993)

PER CURIAM. . . .

[O]n February 8, 1991, Cara Clausen gave birth to a baby girl in Iowa. . . . On February 10, 1991, Clausen signed a release of custody form, relinquishing her parental rights to the child. Clausen, who was unmarried at the time of the birth, had named Scott Seefeldt as the father. On February 14, 1991, he executed a release of custody form.

[On February 25, 1991, petitioners Roberta and Jan DeBoer, Michigan residents, petitioned a juvenile court in Iowa to adopt the child. At a hearing held the same day,] the parental rights of Cara Clausen and Seefeldt were terminated, and petitioners were granted custody of the child during the pendency of the proceeding. The DeBoers returned to Michigan with the child, and she has lived with them in Michigan continuously since then.

However, the prospective adoption never took place. On March 6, 1991, nine days after the filing of the adoption petition, Cara Clausen filed a motion in the Iowa Juvenile Court to revoke her release of custody. In an affidavit accompanying the request, Clausen stated that she had lied when she named Seefeldt as the father of the child, and that the child's father actually was Daniel Schmidt. Schmidt filed an affidavit of paternity on March 12, 1991, and on March 27, 1991, he filed a petition in the Iowa district court, seeking to intervene in the adoption proceeding initiated by the DeBoers. [He and Clausen married in April, 1992.]

[The Iowa district court found that Schmidt was the biological father and that the DeBoers failed to establish either that Schmidt had abandoned the child or that his rights should be terminated. It determined that a best interests of the child analysis becomes appropriate only after a showing of abandonment.] On the basis of these findings, the court concluded that the termination proceeding was void with respect to Schmidt, and that the DeBoers' petition to adopt the child must be denied. Those decisions have been affirmed by the Iowa appellate courts. [In re BGC, 496 N.W.2d 239 (Iowa, 1992). On remand, the Iowa district terminated the DeBoers' rights as temporary guardians and custodians.]

On the same day their rights were terminated in Iowa, the DeBoers filed a petition in Washtenaw Circuit Court [in Michigan], asking the court to assume jurisdiction under the UCCJA. The petition requested that the court enjoin enforcement of the Iowa custody order and find that it was not enforceable, or, in the alternative, to modify it to give custody to the DeBoers. [The Michigan court] entered an ex parte temporary restraining order, which directed that the child remain in the custody of the DeBoers, and ordered Schmidt not to remove the child from Washtenaw County.

[The Michigan court] found that it had jurisdiction to determine the best interests of the child. It denied Schmidt's motion for summary judgment [to dissolve the preliminary injunction and enforce the Iowa judgment], and directed that the child remain with the DeBoers until further order of the court.[9] [The court of appeals reversed, concluding Michigan lacked jurisdiction under the UCCJA and the DeBoers lacked standing. Following a petition for declaratory and injunctive relief by the child's guardian ad litem, the circuit court entered an order temporarily continuing the status quo. This court granted the DeBoers' application to appeal, limited to issues of jurisdiction and standing, and the Schmidts' application to appeal, limited to the question whether the complaint should be dismissed for failure to state a claim.]

Interstate enforcement of child custody orders has long presented vexing problems. This arose principally from uncertainties about the applicability of the Full Faith and Credit Clause of the United States Constitution. Because custody decrees were generally regarded as subject to modification, states had traditionally felt free to modify another state's prior order.

The initial attempt to deal with these jurisdictional problems was the drafting of the Uniform Child Custody Jurisdiction Act, promulgated by the National Conference of Commissioners on Uniform State Laws in 1968. That uniform act has now been enacted, in some form, in all fifty states, the District of Columbia, and the U.S. Virgin Islands. . . . In 1980, Congress [enacted] the Parental Kidnapping Prevention Act, 28 U.S.C. §1738A. The PKPA "imposes a duty on the States to enforce a child custody determination entered by a court of a sister State if the determination is consistent with the provisions of the Act." Thompson v. Thompson, 484 U.S. 174, 175-176 (1988). The PKPA includes provisions similar to the UCCJA, and emphatically imposes the requirement that sister-state custody orders be given effect. . . .

In its March 29, 1993, opinion, the Court of Appeals agreed with Daniel Schmidt that the Washtenaw Circuit Court lacked jurisdiction to modify the Iowa custody orders and was instead required to enforce them. [It explained that adoption proceedings are custody proceedings under the UCCJA; that the custody matter was still pending in Iowa, where further proceedings had been scheduled; and that Iowa did not fail to conform to the UCCJA when it did not determine the best interests of the child.]

---

9. [P]roceedings have continued in Iowa. On January 27, 1993, the Iowa district court held the DeBoers in contempt of court, and issued bench warrants for their arrest. The Iowa juvenile court entered an order on February 17, 1993, restoring Cara (Clausen) Schmidt's parental rights.

A best interests of the child determination hearing began in Washtenaw Circuit Court on January 29, 1993, and continued for eight days. In a decision rendered from the bench on February 12, 1993, the Washtenaw Circuit Court found that it was in the best interests of the child for her to remain with the DeBoers. That decision is not at issue in the instant appeal.

The congressionally declared purpose of the PKPA is to deal with inconsistent and conflicting laws and practices by which courts determine their jurisdiction to decide disputes between persons claiming rights of custody. Inconsistency in the determination by courts of their jurisdiction to decide custody disputes contributes to "the disregard of court orders, excessive relitigation of cases, [and] obtaining of conflicting orders by the courts of various jurisdictions. . . ." For these reasons, among others, Congress declared that the best interests of the child required the establishment of a uniform system for the assumption of jurisdiction. . . .

The [DeBoers' argument] that in this context the best interests purpose of the PKPA mandates a best interests analysis in Iowa, failing which the Iowa decision is not entitled to full faith and credit, would permit the forum state's view of the merits of the case to govern the assumption of jurisdiction to modify the foreign decree. . . .

It has been aptly noted that the vulnerability of a custody decree to an out-of-state modification presented the greatest need of all for the reform effort of the PKPA. . . . Certainty and stability are given priority under the PKPA, which gives the home state exclusive continuing jurisdiction. Thus, the PKPA expressly provides that if a custody determination is made consistently with its provisions, "the appropriate authorities of every State *shall* enforce [it] according to its terms, and *shall not* modify" that custody decision. 28 U.S.C. §1738A(a) (emphasis added). . . . At the time of commencement of both the termination and adoption proceedings, Iowa unquestionably had jurisdiction under its own laws and Iowa was unquestionably the home state of the child. . . .

Where the custody determination is made consistently with the provisions of the PKPA, the jurisdiction of the court that made the decision is exclusive and continuing as long as that state "remains the residence of the child or of any contestant," and it still has jurisdiction under its own laws. 28 U.S.C. §1738A(d). Unquestionably, Daniel Schmidt continues to reside in Iowa. Furthermore, Iowa law provides for continuing jurisdiction in custody matters. . . . The courts of this state may only modify Iowa's order if Iowa has declined to exercise its jurisdiction to modify it. 28 U.S.C. §1738A(f). Iowa has not declined to exercise its jurisdiction to modify its custody order; it has simply declined to order the relief sought by the DeBoers. . . .

The DeBoers advance a variety of arguments in support of their claim that they have standing to litigate regarding the custody of the child. [Yet] when the temporary custody order was rescinded, they became third parties to the child and no longer had a basis on which to claim a substantive right of custody. . . .

[T]he next friend for the child argues that we should recognize the right of a minor child to bring a Child Custody Act action and obtain a best interests of the child hearing regarding her custody. . . . We do not believe that the Child Custody Act can be read as authorizing such an action. The act's consistent distinction between the "parties" and the "child" makes clear that the act is intended to resolve disputes among adults seeking custody of the child.

It is true that children, as well as their parents, have a due process liberty interest in their family life. However, in our view those interests are not independent of the child's parents. [T]he natural parent's right to custody is not to be disturbed [absent a showing of unfitness], sometimes despite the preferences of the child. [The court rejected the due process and equal protection arguments raised on the child's behalf.] In the Iowa proceedings, a challenge to Daniel Schmidt's fitness was vigorously prosecuted by the DeBoers, and they failed to prove that he was unfit. . . . [48] . . .

We direct the Washtenaw Circuit Court to enter an order enforcing the custody orders entered by the Iowa courts. In consultation with counsel for the Schmidts and the DeBoers, the circuit court shall promptly establish a plan for the transfer of custody [within 31 days]. It is now time for the adults to move beyond saying that their only concern is the welfare of the child and to put those words into action by assuring that the transfer of custody is accomplished promptly with minimum disruption of the life of the child.

LEVIN, J. (dissenting).

I would agree with the majority's analysis if the DeBoers had gone to Iowa, purchased a carload of hay from Cara Clausen, and then found themselves in litigation in Iowa with Daniel Schmidt, who also claimed an interest in the hay. It could then properly be said that the DeBoers "must be taken to have known" that, rightly or wrongly, the Iowa courts might rule against them, and they should, as gracefully as possible, accept an adverse decision of the Iowa courts. Michigan would then have had no interest in the outcome, and would routinely enforce a decree of the Iowa courts against the DeBoers. But this is not a lawsuit concerning the ownership, the legal title, to a bale of hay. . . .

The PKPA was enacted to protect the child. . . . Congress enacted the PKPA, not because of an abstract concern about "interstate controversies over child custody," but rather "in the interest of greater stability of home environment and of secure *family relationships* for the child." . . . Congress identified the "home state" of the child as the "state which can best decide the case in the interest of the child." "Home state" is defined as the "State in which, immediately preceding the time involved, the child lived with his parents, a parent, *or a person acting as a parent, for at least six consecutive months*, and in the case of a child less than six months old, the State in which the child lived from birth with any of such persons." (Emphasis added.) . . .

Michigan is the child's home state because she has lived in Michigan with the DeBoers, persons "acting as a parent," for at least six consecutive months — actually for over two years. Michigan, the home state, would also qualify as the state having jurisdiction under the PKPA pursuant to the alternative "significant connection" test for a case where no state is the home state. . . . There is more substantial evidence concerning the child's present or future care, protection, training and personal relationships in Michigan than in Iowa. . . . There was no contact between Daniel Schmidt and the child in Iowa, minimum contact between Cara Schmidt and the child in Iowa, and maximum contact between the child and the DeBoers in Michigan. . . . Assuming that the PKPA applies to adoption proceedings, and that is the assumption on which the majority opinion is predicated, the underlying themes of the act must be observed. . . .

Professor Clark wrote that subject matter jurisdiction in adoption should be given to the home state of the child. . . . As Professor Clark explains, the only issues

---

48. Even if we were to conclude that the child has [constitutional] interests that were not adequately represented in the previous Iowa proceedings, the PKPA would require that any new action on her behalf be brought in Iowa, which has continuing exclusive jurisdiction. . . .

in an adoption proceeding with respect to the natural parents, are "whether the consent is genuine, or whether the alleged abandonment or neglect did occur. These resemble *the issues in the ordinary transitory lawsuit,* and there is thus no need for any requirements of domicile or residence on the part of the natural parents."[53]

But, suggests Professor Clark, "since adoption consists of matching a child with a new parent or set of parents," there is a need for a "thorough opportunity to study the child and his background. To give the court this opportunity, the child must be present and available in the jurisdiction."[54] He concludes . . . that that subject matter jurisdiction in adoption should be where the adoptive parents reside and the child is physically present. . . .

A decree rendered by a state other than the home state is not a determination made "consistent with the provisions" of the PKPA. A decree rendered without consideration of the child's best interests is not a decree that the Congress intended that all other states must enforce. [Michigan law would require a best interests hearing.]

The sympathetic portrayal of the Schmidts in the majority opinion ignores that it was Cara Schmidt's fraud on the Iowa court and on Daniel Schmidt that is at the root of this controversy. . . . To fault the DeBoers is unwarranted. [They left Iowa with the child in good faith.] Why should they have believed that Cara Schmidt was telling the truth when she said she had fraudulently named the other man as the father? The DeBoers discovered that Schmidt had a dismal record as a father. . . . The Iowa courts thought there was sufficient merit in the DeBoers' claims that they maintained custody of the child with the DeBoers until after the Iowa Supreme Court ruled. One [dissenting] justice agreed with the DeBoers. . . .

If the danger confronting this child were physical injury, no one would question her right to invoke judicial process to protect herself against such injury. There is little difference, when viewed from the child's frame of reference, between a physical assault and a psychological assault. . . . It is only because this child cannot speak for herself that adults can avert their eyes from the pain that she will suffer.

Notes and Questions

1. *Epilogue.* The United States Supreme Court refused to stay the order entered pursuant to the Michigan Supreme Court's opinion. 509 U.S. 1301 (1993). After the transfer, Baby Jessica became Anna Schmidt. Although Anna's home life has been marked by parental unemployment and divorce, she has fared well by all accounts, despite the emotional trauma predicted when she left the DeBoers' custody. See Brian Dickerson, A Child's Life Shows Folly of Adults, Media, Detroit Free Press, Feb. 24, 2003, at 1B. The DeBoers adopted again, then divorced, but later reconciled and remarried. Pair Who Fought for Baby Jessica Plan to Remarry, Atlanta J. & Atlanta Const., Feb. 4, 2001, at A6; Milestones, Time Magazine, June 20, 1994, at 23.

2. *Governing statutes.* How sound is the majority's premise that statutes governing multijurisdictional *custody* disputes (the Uniform Child Custody Jurisdiction

53. [2 Clark, Domestic Relations, 2d ed., §21.3,] p.595. (Emphasis added.)
54. Id., §21.3, p.596.

Act (UCCJA) and the Parental Kidnapping Prevention Act (PKPA)) control in termination and adoption proceedings as well? Several courts have applied these statutes to such cases. See, e.g., In re Adoption of Asente, 734 N.E.2d 1224, 1231 (Ohio 2000) (majority of jurisdictions apply UCCJA and PKPA to adoptions). See also People ex rel. A.J.C., 88 P.3d 599 (Colo. 2004) (applying UCCJA and PKPA to custody battle after failed adoption); In re D.N.T., 843 So. 2d 690, 704-705 (Miss. 2003) (UCCJA applies to custody issues in contested adoption); In re Adoption of H.L.C., 706 N.W.2d 90 (S.D. 2005) (UCCJA applies to termination proceedings to free child for adoption and yields same result dictated by PKPA).

Do custody and adoption proceedings differ in ways that call for different jurisdictional rules? See generally Bernadette W. Hartfield, The Uniform Child Custody Jurisdiction Act and the Problem of Interstate Adoption: An Easy Fix?, 43 Okla. L. Rev. 621 (1990); Herma Hill Kay, Adoption in the Conflict of Laws: The UAA, Not the UCCJA, Is the Answer, 84 Cal. L. Rev. 703, 712-728 (1996).

3. *Applying the statutes.* Assuming that the UCCJA and the PKPA apply, which analysis is more convincing, the majority's or the dissent's? Did Iowa satisfy the requirements for "home state" or any other jurisdictional basis? Do the statutes require a best interests inquiry? Will the majority's reasoning invite fraudulent identification of a child's father (as the dissent predicts)? Will the dissent's approach encourage prospective adopters to delay returning a child, despite an impediment to adoption in the state where the child was relinquished, in hopes of obtaining in their domicile a more favorable outcome based on a best-interests analysis (as the majority fears)?

Where is a child's home state when a pregnant woman flees Illinois, for fear that the state will take custody of her expected infant, and gives birth in Indiana en route to Tennessee, where some of her other children live? See In re D.S., 840 N.E.2d 1216 (Ill. 2005) (Illinois, even though the child has never been present there, under UCCJEA (discussed infra)). Is the presence of the adoption agency in a state sufficient to make it the "home state"? See Adoption House, Inc. v. A.R., 820 A.2d 402 (Del. Fam. Ct. 2003) (no, under UCCJEA (discussed infra)). Regarding the need for a "best-interests" determination, see *A.J.C.*, supra (UCCJA does not require full faith and credit in absence of best-interests determination, when failed adopters seek custody).

4. *Nexus to forum.* If the UCCJA and the PKPA do not apply, what connections with the forum state confer adoption jurisdiction? Considerable authority uses as an alternative domicile, traditionally that of the child, or according to some modern courts, that of the adoptive parent. Eugene F. Scoles et al., Conflict of Laws §16.5 (3d ed. 2000); see Homer H. Clark, The Law of Domestic Relations in the United States 870-872 (2d ed. 1988); Restatement (Second) of Conflict of Laws §78 (1971). Is domicile preferable to the bases used under the UCCJA and the PKPA? Where is an infant domiciled? See Mississippi Band of Choctaw Indians v. Holyfield, 490 U.S. 30, 47-48 (1989) (common law assigns illegitimate children their mother's domicile; hence, a child's domicile of origin may be a place where child has never been).

Must a court at the child's or adopter's domicile have personal jurisdiction over the child's birth parents, absent a previous termination of parental rights?

Cf. Armstrong v. Manzo, 380 U.S. 545 (1965). Would this requirement remain controlling if the UCCJA and the PKPA govern adoptions? See Chapter VII, section B6.

In Division of Youth & Family Services v. M.Y.J.P., 823 A.2d 817 (N.J. Super. Ct. App. Div. 2003), a mother who remained in Haiti after the father took their son to live in New Jersey challenged that state's jurisdiction to terminate her parental rights. In New Jersey, the child had been removed from the father and placed with foster parents, who wished to adopt him. The lower court decided it had jurisdiction, based on its parens patriae authority to serve the child's best interests. On appeal, court affirmed, invoking both the "status exception" to the minimum-contacts requirement and the mother's purposeful availment of New Jersey's benefits when she acceded to the care of her son by state child welfare authorities. Do you agree with the outcome? Which rationale works best — parens patriae, the status exception, or purposeful availment? Why?

5. *Interstate compact.* The widely enacted Interstate Compact on the Placement of Children (ICPC) also governs multistate adoptions. See, e.g., Mo. Ann. Stat. §210.620 (Vernon 2004) (with note listing complementary laws in 50 other jurisdictions). The statute specifies procedural requirements for transferring the custody of a child to adoptive parents from another state but does not establish jurisdiction. *Asente*, 734 N.E.2d at 1230-1231. See also Alternative Options & Servs. for Children v. Chapman, 106 P.3d 744 (Utah Ct. App. 2004) (holding statute inapplicable when out-of-state pregnant women travel to Utah to give birth and relinquish children there). Courts have cited failure to comply with the ICPC as a reason to allow revocation of parental consent to adoption. See, e.g., In re Adoption of A.M.M., 949 P.2d 1155 (Kan. Ct. App. 1997).

6. *Law reform.* Drafted in the wake of the Baby Jessica case, the UAA modifies the UCCJA to account for the distinctive features of adoption proceedings, in which there is often no "home state." Under §3-101,

> (a) Except as otherwise provided . . . , a court of this State has jurisdiction over a proceeding for the adoption of a minor commenced under this [Act] if:
>
> (1) immediately before commencement of the proceeding, the minor lived in this State with a parent, a guardian, a prospective adoptive parent, or another person acting as parent, for at least six consecutive months, excluding periods of temporary absence, or, in the case of a minor under six months of age, lived in this State from soon after birth with any of those individuals and there is available in this State substantial evidence concerning the minor's present or future care;
>
> (2) immediately before commencement of the proceeding, the prospective adoptive parent lived in this State for at least six consecutive months, excluding periods of temporary absence, and there is available in this State substantial evidence concerning the minor's present or future care;
>
> (3) the agency that placed the minor for adoption is located in this State and it is in the best interest of the minor that a court of this State assume jurisdiction because:
>
> (i) the minor and the minor's parents, or the minor and the prospective adoptive parent, have a significant connection with this State; and
>
> (ii) there is available in this State substantial evidence concerning the minor's present or future care;

(4) the minor and the prospective adoptive parent are physically present in this State and the minor has been abandoned or it is necessary in an emergency to protect the minor because the minor has been subjected to or threatened with mistreatment or abuse or is otherwise neglected; or

(5) it appears that no other State would have jurisdiction under prerequisites substantially in accordance with paragraphs (1) through (4), or another State has declined to exercise jurisdiction on the ground that this State is the more appropriate forum to hear a petition for adoption of the minor, and it is in the best interest of the minor that a court of this State assume jurisdiction. . . .

U.L.A. (pt. IA) 67-68 (1999). The section goes on to disallow a state from exercising jurisdiction if a proceeding is pending in another state (with jurisdiction under the Act) or another state has issued a decree, unless that state no longer has jurisdiction. This legislation would not displace the ICPC, supra; rather, once a court assumes jurisdiction under the UAA, it considers whether the parties complied with the ICPC. See Joan Heifetz Hollinger, The Uniform Adoption Act: Reporter's Ruminations, 30 Fam. L.Q. 345, 368 (1996).

How would the UAA apply in Baby Jessica's case? See Joan Heifetz Hollinger, Adoption and Aspiration: The Uniform Adoption Act, the DeBoer-Schmidt Cases, and the American Quest for the Ideal Family, 2 Duke J. Gender L. & Poly. 15 (1995); Kay, supra. Only Vermont has enacted the UAA. See 9 U.L.A. (pt. IA) 2 (Supp. 2005).

To eliminate any confusion, the Uniform Child Custody Jurisdiction and Enforcement Act (UCCJEA), which revises the UCCJA to make it more consistent with the PKPA, explicitly states in §103 that it does not apply to adoption proceedings. The comment explains that the UAA governs adoption jurisdiction. 9 U.L.A. (pt. IA) 660-661 (1999). See, e.g., White v. Adoption of Baby Boy D., 10 P.3d 212 (Okla. 2000). How likely is this approach to eliminate jurisdictional conflicts and achieve uniformity, given that only one state (Vermont) has enacted the UAA? See http://www.nccusl.org/Update/uniformact_factsheets/ uniformacts-fs-aa94.asp (last visited June 15, 2006). By contrast, 45 jurisdiction have enacted the UCCJEA, with the legislation pending in 5 more, including Vermont. See http://www.nccusl.org/Update/uniformact_factsheets/uniformacts-fs-uccjea.asp (last visited June 15, 2006). What jurisdictional principles govern adoption in these states?

Specifically, does the UCCJEA preclude a state's jurisdiction despite proceedings pending elsewhere, given the statute's disclaimer of its application to adoption? In *A.J.C.*, supra, the Colorado Supreme Court concluded that Colorado could assert jurisdiction to decide whether a couple there could retain custody of a child following a failed adoption in Missouri—the state where the child was born and initially relinquished, where the Colorado couple had filed their adoption petition, where the birth mother withdrew her consent, and where the court then halted the adoption proceedings. With the UCCJEA (enacted in Colorado) inapplicable to adoptions, the supreme court concluded that the failure to consider the child's best interests in Missouri (where the earlier UCCJA remains in force) amounts to a declination of jurisdiction, leaving room for Colorado courts to decide custody.

See 88 P.3d at 611. Has the Colorado Supreme Court forgotten the history of the UCCJA, PKPA, and the UCCJEA? See Chapter VII, section B6. Assess the dissenting judge's concerns for "the jurisdictional free-for-all that will surely result from the majority's approach and the harm done to children who will be forced to suffer under conflicting custody orders and perpetual jurisdictional disputes." 88 P.3d at 614 (Coats, J., dissenting).

Problem

Camille, age 16, who had been living with her father, Curt, for five months in Texas, gave birth to Diane there. The birth father, Dan, also lived in Texas. When the baby was about two months old, Camille and Diane moved back to Camille's previous residence, the house of her mother, Sally, in Arizona. With Camille's agreement, Sally filed papers in an Arizona court to be named Diane's guardian, so that a responsible adult would have authority over Diane and the child could receive health coverage under Sally's insurance. Soon thereafter, Camille and Diane visited Mississippi, where Curt had moved, because Camille wanted Diane and the child's grandfather to get to know one another. Although Camille intended to return to Arizona with Diane, about a week after arriving in Mississippi she met Rick and Carol, whose mother lived with Curt (although he was still married to Sally). Camille and Diane moved into the home of Rick and Carol, in response to their invitation. Carol cared for Diane and supported both Camille and Diane for several months; during most of this period, Camille was present at the home during the day but spent many nights elsewhere with a new boyfriend, Calvin. Carol and Rick discussed adopting Diane with Camille; without consulting Sally or obtaining any independent counsel, Camille agreed and signed a letter asking the Arizona court to terminate Sally's guardianship there.

About three months after Camille and Diane arrived in Mississippi, the Arizona guardianship was terminated, and Carol and Rick submitted in a Mississippi court a sworn complaint for adoption, which Camille signed under oath, again without consulting Sally or counsel. Just two weeks later, however, Camille filed an objection to the proceedings, asking the court to nullify any documents she had signed in anticipation of the adoption matter. Nevertheless, the Mississippi court awarded temporary custody of Diane to Carol and Rick, who required Camille to leave their home and denied Camille the opportunity to see Diane.

Camille, now joined by Sally in Mississippi, immediately seeks to revoke any consent to adoption and asks for custody. (a) When Camille and Sally assert that Mississippi lacks jurisdiction over the adoption that Carol and Rick are pursuing, who should prevail and why? (b) Should the same jurisdictional rules govern consensual adoptions and contested adoptions, like the present one? Why? (c) Is Sally a necessary party to the adoption proceeding? What would you need to know to determine whether, Dan, the birth father, is a necessary party or must have notice of the proceedings? (d) Will Camille and Sally prevail when they argue that Camille was not competent to consent to adoption because of her age, relying by analogy to abortion statutes which require parental involvement or a judicial bypass for minors? Why? See Chapter I, section B2. (e) Of what relevance is the following statement by the court? "The record is replete with bad decisions Camille has made her entire life. She has proven herself immature beyond understanding, as evidenced adequately by her own testimony of leaving Diane with almost strangers (Rick and Carol) while she spent the nights at her new boyfriend's house having sex and smoking marihuana with him." (f) Of what relevance is the following information? Carol and Rick had desperately wanted to adopt. Carol's mother suggested that Carol and Rick take in Camille and Diane, once they arrived in Mississippi. Carol often came to Camille crying about her inability to have children or adopt. Carol and Rick gave Camille spending money and encouraged her to spend time with friends while they cared for Diane. The attorney for Carol and Rick drafted the paperwork for terminating the Arizona guardianship and providing consent to adoption, which Camille signed after she was promised she would have six months to change her mind. When Camille summoned Sally to Mississippi and then told Carol and Rick she had changed her mind, Carol cried, and Rick "told Camille 'to get the f— out of his house' and that 'no one was going to take this baby from them — that he would hurt anyone that tried.'" For judicial answers to these questions, see In re D.N.T., 843 So. 2d 690 (Miss. 2003); id. at 712 (Cobb, J., concurring); id. at 716 (McRae, J., dissenting).

Note: International Adoptions

The shortage of "highly desirable" adoptees, as well as agency restrictions on adopters, have led some Americans to seek children from abroad. Out of almost 2,100,000 adopted children in the United States in 2000, about 12.5 percent were foreign born.[7] The highly publicized cases of Baby Richard (supra pp.1033-1034) and Baby Jessica, which returned children to biological parents after lengthy periods with adoptive families, reportedly sparked increased interest in transnational adoptions, believed by many to be less vulnerable to such disruptions. See, e.g., Alison Fleisher, Note, The Decline of Domestic Adoption: Intercountry Adoption as a Response to Local Adoption Laws and Proposals to Foster Domestic Adoption, 13 S. Cal. Rev. L. & Women's Stud. 171 (2003).

Several bodies of law apply to international adoptions: federal immigration laws, state adoption standards, and the foreign country's relinquishment requirements. Often a child must be adopted in the country of origin in order to be able to travel to the United States and then again in the state where the adoptive parents live, because decrees from foreign countries are not entitled to full faith and credit.

Some long-standing barriers have begun to change. For example, federal law, which limits entry to foreign adoptees who are "orphans," has been relaxed through an expanded definition. The term now includes not only children whose parents both have died but also those whose parents both have disappeared,

---

[7]. Census data from 2000 show 257,792 foreign-born adopted children compared to 1,801,123 native-born adopted children. Rose Kreider, Adopted and Stepchildren 2000 at 12 (October 2003). See also Adoption Factbook III, supra note [3], at 27 (placing international adoptions at 17.2 percent of all nonrelative adoptions in U.S., based on 1996 figures).

abandoned or deserted them, or become separated or lost from them. 8 U.S.C.A. §1101(b)(1)(F) (West 2006).

In 2000, the United States enacted implementing legislation for the Hague Convention on Protection of Children and Cooperation in Respect of Intercountry Adoption. 42 U.S.C.A. §§14901-14954 (West 2005). This Convention, which applies only when both countries involved are Convention parties, is designed to regularize international adoptions by requiring a finding that the child is adoptable and a determination that the adoption would serve the child's best interests. The Convention also establishes supervisory Central Authorities to impose minimum norms and procedures and mandate recognition of such adoptions elsewhere. For the final rules under the Convention and the statute, see Department of State, Hague Convention on Intercountry Adoption: Intercountry Adoption Act of 2000, 70 Fed. Reg. 8064-8161 (Feb. 15, 2006) (rules on accreditation of agencies and approval of persons, to be codified at 22 CFR pt. 96); id. at 8161-8164 (rules on preservation of records, to be codified at 22 CFR pts. 97, 98). For critical analyses, see Amy Grillo Kales, Note, The Intercountry Adoption Act of 2000: Are Its Laudable Goals Worth Its Potential Impact on Small Adoption Agencies, Independent Intercounty Adoptions, and Ethical Independent Adoption Professionals?, 36 Geo. Wash. Int'l L. Rev. 177 (2004) (analyzing law and its impact on adoption agencies); Caeli Elizabeth Kimball, Barriers to the Successful Implementation of the Hague Convention on Protection of Children and Co-operation in Respect of Intercountry Adoption, 33 Denv. J. Int'l L. & Pol'y 561 (2005) (criticizing U.S. delay in effectuating regulations, required for full ratification and implementation of Hague Convention).

In addition, states no longer require a full state proceeding if a foreign adoption has been completed. See, e.g., In re Adoption of W.J., 942 P.2d 37 (Kan. 1997). Finally, federal legislation now provides that, when certain statutory conditions are met, children adopted from abroad by U.S. citizens automatically become U.S. citizens. 8 U.S.C. §1413(b) (2000). See 8 U.S.C.A. §1101(b)(1)(F) (West 2006) (immediate relative classification for such children).

Like transracial adoption, international adoption provokes controversy. Supporters insist that international adoptions provide opportunities for growth, love, and well-being that would otherwise elude certain children, while also demonstrating the importance of common humanity. E.g., Elizabeth Bartholet, International Adoption: Current Status and Future Prospects, The Future of Children, Spring 1993, at 89, 90. Critics point out the similarity to baby selling, given the predominance of market behavior. Jacqueline Bhabha, Moving Babies: Globalization, Markets, and Transnational Adoption, 28-Sum. Fletcher F. World Aff. 181 (2004); David M. Smolin, Intercountry Adoption as Child Trafficking, 39 Val. U. L. Rev. 281 (2004). See also Sara Corbett, Where Do Babies Come From?, N.Y. Times, June 16, 2002, §6 (Magazine), at 42 (cover story examining "baby laundering" and the "mysterious origins of Cambodian 'orphans' — and the complex ethics for Americans adopting them"). These critics see privileged Americans satisfying their own needs by exploiting poor children, separating them from their families and culture, and effacing birth parents. According to historian Rickie Solinger, "the incidence of adoption, that is, the transfer of babies from women of one social classification to women in a higher social classification or group (within the same country or transnationally), may be a very accurate index of the vulnerable status of women in the country of the birth mother." Rickie Solinger, Beggars and Choosers:

How the Politics of Choice Shapes Adoption, Abortion, and Welfare in the United States 67 (2001). See also id. at 28. Some countries that previously permitted adoptions by Americans have recently tightened restrictions, revoking the accreditation of U.S. adoption agencies and imposing new rules for adopters. See, e.g., Vanessa Hua, Russian Adoptions Held Up by Red Tape; Agencies Lose Accreditation Under Tighter Controls, S.F. Chron., Feb. 23, 2006, at B4.

For other perspectives, see generally, e.g., Sara Dillon, Making Legal Regimes for Intercountry Adoption Reflect Human Rights Principles: Transforming the United Nations Convention on the Rights of the Child with the Hague Convention on Intercountry Adoption, 21 B.U. Int'l L.J. 179 (2003); Bernie D. Jones, International and Transracial Adoptions: Toward a Global Critical Race Feminist Practice?, 10 Race & Ethnic Anc. L.J. 43 (2004); Barbara Stark, Baby Girls from China in New York: A Thrice-Told Tale, 2003 Utah L. Rev. 1231.

D. CONSEQUENCES OF ADOPTION

1. Legal Status of the Child

An adoption decree terminates the legal relationship between the adoptee and all biological relatives and replaces it with new ties to the adoptive family. This principle treats the adoptee as a legitimate blood descendant of the adopter for all purposes.[8] Certain consequences regarding inheritance law follow: Many courts hold that adopted children inherit by intestate succession from their adoptive, but not from their biological, parents. E.g., In re Estate of Shehady, 491 P.2d 528 (N.M. 1971). See also Pyles v. Russell, 36 S.W.3d 365 (Ky. 2000). Similarly, some courts have construed the term "issue" in wills or trusts to exclude (from testate succession or as trust beneficiaries) those biological children adopted out of the decedent's family, unless a contrary intent plainly appears. E.g., Crumpton v. Mitchell, 281 S.E.2d 1 (N.C. 1981).

Moreover, modern law largely has replaced the "stranger-to-the-adoption" doctrine (which excludes the adoptee from class-gift language[9] in a will or trust when the testator or settlor was not the adoptive parent) with a presumption that inclusion is intended, unless the document expressly excludes adoptees. See Unif. Probate Code §2-611, 8 U.L.A. (pt. I) 434 (1998) (Prior Art. II); In re Estate of Jenkins, 904 P.2d 1316 (Colo. 1995). Cf. Watson v. Baker, 829 N.E.2d 648 (Mass. 2005) (applying prior statute).

---

[8]. The 1969 version of the UAA was written in these terms. Unif. Adoption Act §14, 9 U.L.A. (pt. IA) 198-199 (1999). The drafters' comment explains:

> The termination of relationship of parent and child between the adopted person and his natural parents and the family of the natural parents follows the trend of modern statutes and is desirable for many reasons. It eases the transition from old family to new family by providing for a clean final "cutoff" of legal relationships with the old family. It also preserves the secrecy of adoption proceedings . . . by reducing the selfish reasons an individual might have to discover his antecedents.

Id. at 199.

[9]. Examples of class-gift language are "children," "issue," and "heirs."

The general rule that adoption creates new relationships in place of biological ties raises questions other than inheritance. For example, does the preference for placing siblings together still apply once one sibling has been adopted? See In re Shanee Carol B., 550 S.E.2d 636 (W. Va. 2001). Should laws barring marriages between close relatives (incest restrictions) apply to relationships by adoption? Compare Israel v. Allen, 577 P.2d 762 (Colo. 1978), with In re MEW, 4 Pa. D.&C.3d 51 (C.P. Allegheny 1977). See also State v. Hall, 48 P.3d 350 (Wash. 2002) (biological father guilty of incest despite daughter's adoption).

Contemporary authorities show increasing flexibility about whether the consequences of adoption must be "all or nothing." The new UAA, while adhering to the general rule severing legal ties with the biological family, §§1-104, 1-105, provides that adoption does not terminate a former parent's duty to pay arrearages for child support, §1-105. 9 U.L.A. (pt. IA) 23-24 (1999). Similarly, some statutes provide for inheritance by adopted children from their biological parents. See, e.g., Tex. Fam. Code Ann. §161.206 (Vernon Supp. 2005).

2. Stepparent and Second-Parent Adoptions

■ ADOPTION OF TAMMY
619 N.E.2d 315 (Mass. 1993)

GREANEY, J.

In this case, two unmarried women, Susan and Helen, filed a joint petition in the Probate and Family Court Department under G.L. c. 210, §1 (1992 ed.) to adopt as their child Tammy, a minor, who is Susan's biological daughter. . . . Based on [a] finding that Helen and Susan "are each functioning, separately and together, as the custodial and psychological parents of [Tammy]," and that "it is the best interest of said [Tammy] that she be adopted by both," the judge entered a decree allowing the adoption. Simultaneously, the [Probate and Family Court] judge reserved and reported to the Appeals Court the evidence and all questions of law, in an effort to "secure [the] decree from any attack in the future on jurisdictional grounds." We transferred the case to this court on our own motion. We conclude that the adoption was properly allowed under G.L. c. 210.

. . . Helen and Susan have lived together in a committed relationship, which they consider to be permanent, for more than ten years. In June, 1983, they jointly purchased a house in Cambridge. Both women are physicians specializing in surgery. At the time the petition was filed, Helen maintained a private practice in general surgery at Mount Auburn Hospital and Susan, a nationally recognized expert in the field of breast cancer, was director of the Faulkner Breast Center and a surgical oncologist at the Dana Farber Cancer Institute. Both women also held positions on the faculty of Harvard Medical School.

For several years prior to the birth of Tammy, Helen and Susan planned to have a child, biologically related to both of them, whom they would jointly parent. Helen first attempted to conceive a child through artificial insemination by Susan's brother. When those efforts failed, Susan successfully conceived a child through artificial insemination by Helen's biological cousin, Francis. The women attended childbirth classes together and Helen was present when Susan gave birth to Tammy on April 30, 1988. Although Tammy's birth certificate reflects Francis as her biological father, she was given a hyphenated surname using Susan and Helen's last names.

Since her birth, Tammy has lived with, and been raised and supported by, Helen and Susan. Tammy views both women as her parents, calling Helen "mama" and Susan "mommy." Tammy has strong emotional and psychological bonds with both Helen and Susan. Together, Helen and Susan have provided Tammy with a comfortable home, and have created a warm and stable environment which is supportive of Tammy's growth and over-all well being. Both women jointly and equally participate in parenting Tammy, and both have a strong financial commitment to her. . . . Francis does not participate in parenting Tammy and does not support her. His intention was to assist Helen and Susan in having a child, and he does not intend to be involved with Tammy, except as a distant relative. Francis signed an adoption surrender and supports the joint adoption by both women.

Helen and Susan, recognizing that the laws of the Commonwealth do not permit them to enter into a legally cognizable marriage, believe that the best interests of Tammy require legal recognition of her identical emotional relationship to both women. Susan expressed her understanding that it may not be in her own long-term interest to permit Helen to adopt Tammy because, in the event that Helen and Susan separate, Helen would have equal rights to primary custody. Susan indicated, however, that she has no reservation about allowing Helen to adopt. Apart from the emotional security and current practical ramifications which legal recognition of the reality of her parental relationships will provide Tammy, Susan indicated that the adoption is important for Tammy in terms of potential inheritance from Helen. Helen and her living issue are the beneficiaries of three irrevocable family trusts. Unless Tammy is adopted, Helen's share of the trusts may pass to others. . . .

Over a dozen witnesses, including mental health professionals, teachers, colleagues, neighbors, blood relatives and a priest and nun, testified to the fact that Helen and Susan participate equally in raising Tammy, that Tammy relates to both women as her parents, and that the three form a healthy, happy, and stable family unit. [Both extended families unreservedly endorsed the adoption. The home study conducted by the Department of Social Services, the psychiatrist appointed as Tammy's guardian ad litem, and the attorney appointed to represent her interests all supported the adoption for her best interests.]

1. The initial question is whether the Probate Court judge had jurisdiction under G.L. c. 210 to enter a judgment on a joint petition for adoption brought by two unmarried cohabitants in the petitioners' circumstances. We answer this question in the affirmative.

There is nothing on the face of the statute which precludes the joint adoption of a child by two unmarried cohabitants such as the petitioners. Chapter 210, §1, provides that "[a] person of full age may petition the probate court in the county where he resides for leave to adopt as his child another person younger than himself, unless such other person is his or her wife or husband, or brother, sister, uncle or aunt, of the whole or half blood." Other than requiring that a spouse join in the petition, if the petitioner is married and the spouse is competent to join therein, the statute does not expressly prohibit or require joinder by any person. [I]t is apparent from the first sentence of G.L. c. 210, §1, that the Legislature considered and defined those combinations of persons which would lead to adoptions in violation of public policy. Clearly absent is any prohibition of adoption by two unmarried individuals like the petitioners. . . .

In this case all requirements in [the statute] are met, and there is no question that the judge's findings demonstrate that the directives [in the statute,] and in case law, have been satisfied. Adoption will not result in any tangible change in Tammy's daily life; it will, however, serve to provide her with a significant legal relationship which may be important in her future. At the most practical level, adoption will entitle Tammy to inherit from Helen's family trusts and from Helen and her family under the law of intestate succession, to receive support from Helen, who will be legally obligated to provide such support, to be eligible for coverage under Helen's health insurance policies, and to be eligible for social security benefits in the event of Helen's disability or death. Of equal, if not greater significance, adoption will enable Tammy to preserve her unique filial ties to Helen in the event that Helen and Susan separate, or Susan predeceases Helen. . . . The conclusion that the adoption is in the best interests of Tammy is also well warranted.

2. The judge also posed the question whether, pursuant to G.L. c. 210, §6 (1992 ed.), Susan's legal relationship to Tammy must be terminated if Tammy is adopted. Section 6 provides that, on entry of an adoption decree, "all rights, duties and other legal consequences of the natural relation of child and parent shall . . . except as regards marriage, incest or cohabitation, terminate between the child so adopted and his natural parents and kindred." Although G.L. c. 210, §2, clearly permits a child's natural parent to be an adoptive parent, §6 does not contain any express exceptions to its termination provision. The Legislature obviously did not intend that a natural parent's legal relationship to its child be terminated when the natural parent is a party to the adoption petition.

Section 6 clearly is directed to the more usual circumstances of adoption, where the child is adopted by persons who are not the child's natural parents (either because the natural parents have elected to relinquish the child for adoption or their parental rights have been involuntarily terminated). The purpose of the termination provision is to protect the security of the child's newly-created family unit by eliminating involvement with the child's natural parents. . . . Reading the adoption statute as a whole, we conclude that the termination provision contained in §6 was intended to apply only when the natural parents (or parent) are not parties to the adoption petition. . . .

Notes and Questions

1. *Stepparent adoptions*. Today, stepparent adoptions are estimated to comprise half of all adoptions. Typically, the adopter is the spouse of one biological parent. See Unif. Adoption Act, 9 U.L.A. (pt. IA) 103-104 (1999) (cmt. on Art. 4). Under the UAA, §4-103, stepparent adoptions do not affect:

> (1) the relationship between the adoptee and the adoptee's parent who is the adoptive stepparent's spouse or deceased spouse;
> (2) an existing order for visitation or communication with a minor adoptee by an individual related to the adoptee through the parent who is the adoptive stepparent's spouse or deceased spouse;
> (3) the right of the adoptee or a descendant of the adoptee to inheritance or intestate succession through or from the adoptee's former parent; or

(4) a court order or agreement for visitation or communication with a minor adoptee which is approved by the court. . . .

Id. at 106.

Such statutory protections raise the possibility of dual inheritance, affording adoptees an advantage denied to biological children. The Uniform Probate Code's general rule against dual inheritance (§2-113) does not explicitly prevent an adoptee from inheriting from biological and adoptive relatives. 8 U.L.A. (pt. I) 91 (1998) (Rev. Art. II). Indeed, this Code (§2-114(b)) creates an exception to the general rule in stepparent adoptions, providing that the adoptee and his or her descendants continue to inherit from and through the biological noncustodial parent in cases of intestate succession. Id.

Why permit dual inheritance in these cases? See e.g., Raley v. Spikes, 614 So. 2d 1017 (Ala. 1993). Note that, without such provisions, courts might deny stepparent adoptions because the loss of intestate inheritance from the biological parent would prevent the adoption from serving the child's best interest. See Matter of Gerald G.G., 403 N.Y.S.2d 57 (App. Div. 1978).

2. *Second-parent adoption. Tammy* permits a practice called second-parent adoption. See, e.g., Jane S. Schacter, Constructing Families in a Democracy: Courts, Legislatures, and Second-Parent Adoption, 75 Chi.-Kent L. Rev. 933 (2000). Some states now have statutes explicitly permitting the practice under some circumstances. E.g., Cal. Fam. Code §9000(b) (West Supp. 2006) (for domestic partners); Conn. Gen. Stat. Ann. §45a-724(a)(3) (West 2004) (for one who shares parental responsibility). In the absence of such clear statutory authority, as in *Tammy*, does second-parent adoption conflict with the usual requirements for adoption? How? How did the court in *Tammy* address these issues?

a. *Statutory construction.* On what basis does the majority decide that the Massachusetts adoption statute permits Susan and Helen to adopt Tammy jointly? An omitted dissent rejects this conclusion, despite deciding that Helen can adopt Tammy while Susan retains her parental rights (the majority's second approach). Which presents the more persuasive statutory interpretation regarding joint adoption, the majority or the dissent? If Susan and Helen can jointly adopt Susan's biological child, would they be able to adopt jointly a child not related to either of them? See In re Infant Girl W., 845 N.E.2d 229 (Ind. Ct. App. 2006). In re Adoption of Carolyn B., 774 N.Y.S.2d 227 (App. Div. 2004) (permitting the joint adoption). What of two adults not in a committed cohabiting relationship? See Angela Mae Kupenda, Two Parents Are Better Than None: Whether Two Single African American Adults—Who Are Not in a Traditional Marriage or a Romantic or Sexual Relationship with Each Other—Should Be Allowed to Jointly Adopt and Co-Parent African American Children, 35 U. Louisville J. Fam. L. 703 (1996-97).

Alternatively, consider the second approach, reading the statute to permit Helen to adopt while Susan retains parental rights. Courts divide on this issue. Compare In re Adoption of Luke, 640 N.W.2d 374 (Neb. 2002) (finding child ineligible for adoption under statute without relinquishment by birth mother), with In re Adoption by R.B.F., 803 A.2d 1195 (Pa. 2002) (construing statutory amendment to permit adoption without termination of parental rights for good cause shown). See also Sharon S. v. Superior Ct., 73 P.3d 554 (Cal. 2003) (permitting second-parent adoption before effective date of California's domestic partnership legislation).

Should the special treatment of stepparent adoptions, which allows one birth parent to retain parental rights, control here? Before Vermont permitted same-sex couples to enter civil unions, see Chapter II, p. 173, its supreme court allowed second-parent adoptions to come within the statutory exception for stepparents. In re Adoptions of B.L.V.B. & E.L.V.B., 628 A.2d 1271 (Vt. 1993). The legislature later codified this holding. Vt. Stat. Ann., tit. 15A, §1-102(b) (2002). The UAA follows this approach, indicating in comments that the provisions on stepparent adoptions should apply. 9 U.L.A. (pt. IA) 105 (1999) (cmts. to §4-102). Will courts necessarily construe "stepparent" to cover someone like Helen in *Tammy*? Compare, e.g., *Luke*, supra, with In re Adoption of K.S.P., 804 N.E.2d 1253 (Ind. Ct. App. 2004).

b. *Policy considerations.* The division of authority on second-parent adoptions highlights the tension between two oft-stated principles: that adoption law is purely statutory and that adoption law should serve a child's best interests. See, e.g., Mark Strasser, Courts, Legislatures, and Second-Parent Adoptions: On Judicial Deference, Specious Reasoning, and the Best Interests of the Child, 66 Tenn. L. Rev. 1019 (1999); Amanda C. Pustilnik, Note, Private Ordering, Legal Ordering, and the Getting of Children: A Counterhistory of Adoption Law, 20 Yale L. & Pol'y Rev. 263, 291-295 (2002).

Considering the child's best interests, what are the advantages to Tammy of the second-parent adoption? First, second-parent adoptions ensure that Tammy will be able to maintain her ties with Helen even if the relationship between Helen and Susan dissolves. Without such official recognition, some courts have denied standing to coparents and permitted the biological mother to foreclose visitation. E.g., Alison D. v. Virginia M., 572 N.E.2d 27 (N.Y. 1991). Such adoptions can also ensure postdissolution support for the child and resolve disputes about the child between a coparent and a deceased biological mother's relatives. E.g., Mariga v. Flint, 822 N.E.2d 620 (Ind. Ct. App. 2005) (allowing biological mother to sue adoptive mother for child support after relationship ended); Clifford K. v. Paul S. ex rel. Z.B.S., 619 S.E.2d 138 (W. Va. 2005) (granting custody to coparent in litigation with deceased mother's father). Second, such adoptions provide benefits while the couple's relationship remains intact, for example, permitting the coparent to consent to medical treatment for the child, to have access to school records, or to obtain insurance coverage for the child through an employer. See In re Adoption of Evan, 583 N.Y.S.2d 997, 998-999 (Surr. Ct. 1992); American Bar Association, House of Delegates, Report 112A (Aug. 11-12, 2003) (report supporting resolution in favor of joint adoptions and second-parent adoptions) (available at http://www.abanet.org/leadership/2003/journal/112.pdf). Do these benefits also support "third-parent adoptions," for example, in cases in which a lesbian couple uses a known semen donor and all three adults plan to have a role in the child's upbringing? See Pamela Gatos, Note, Third-Parent Adoption in Lesbian and Gay Families, 26 Vt. L. Rev. 195 (2001).

Emphasizing the benefits to children, the American Academy of Pediatrics supports second-parent adoption. See Erica Goode, Group Wants Gays to Have Right to Adopt a Partner's Child, N.Y. Times, Feb. 4, 2002, at A17. Are there child welfare reasons to disallow such adoptions? See, e.g., William C. Duncan, In Whose Best Interests: Sexual Orientation and Adoption Law, 31 Cap. U. L.

Rev. 787, 798-802 (2003). Cf. *Clifford K.*, 619 S.E.2d at 161 (Maynard, J., dissenting in part).

3. *Same-sex marriage*. If Susan and Helen could have married (which Massachusetts would now permit), would the second-parent adoption become unnecessary?[10] Beyond making statutory provisions on stepparent adoptions expressly applicable, would the automatic rules of parentage for a mother's spouse obviate the need for Helen to go to court to formalize her relationship with Tammy? See Chapter IV, section C3. To what extent should the availability of same-sex marriage and second-parent adoption diminish the availability of equitable remedies designed to fill gaps in the law that nontraditional families have faced? See, e.g., Titchenal v. Dexter, 693 A.2d 682 (Vt. 1997). See also Julie Shapiro, A Lesbian-Centered Critique of Second-Parent Adoptions, 14 Berkeley Women's L.J. 17, 32-25 (1999) (using *Titchenal*, supra, to illustrate problems posed for lesbians by second-parent adoptions).

Does the ruling in *Tammy* compel recognition of same-sex marriage? Once a state permits second-parent adoptions, what reason supports restricting marriage to heterosexual couples? Are children who are the subject of such second-parent adoptions disadvantaged compared to children of married parents? In holding that the Massachusetts constitution prohibits denying same-sex couples access to the benefits of marriage, the court relied on *Tammy* to reject the state's arguments identifying procreation as the essential element of marriage and supporting marriage restrictions as a means to ensure an optimal setting for childrearing. Goodridge v. Department of Pub. Health, 798 N.E.2d 941, 962 n.24, 963, 966 n.30 (Mass. 2003). But see id. at 1000 (Cordy, J., disssenting). On the clash between Massachusetts law and the Catholic Church's opposition to adoptions by gays and lesbians, see supra p.1058.

4. *Interstate recognition*. Do the Full Faith and Credit Clause (U.S. Const. art. IV) and the federal statute implementing it (28 U.S.C. §1738 (2000)) require a state that does not permit second-parent adoption to recognize one granted in another state? Does the Defense of Marriage Act (DOMA) apply here, to the extent that it relieves states from the obligation "to give effect to any public act, record, or judicial proceeding of any other State, territory, possession, or tribe respecting a relationship between persons of the same sex that is treated as a marriage under the laws of such other State, territory, possession, or tribe, or a right or claim arising from such relationship"? 28 U.S.C. §1738C (2000). Suppose a state statute specifically prohibits recognition of "an adoption by more than one individual of the same sex from any other state or foreign jurisdiction"? Okla. Stat. Ann. tit. 10 §7502-1.4(A.) (West Supp. 2006).

Note that the obligation to recognize another state's judicial decrees is much more demanding than that required for another state's public acts, but requires the court issuing the decree to have had jurisdiction. See Russell v. Bridgens, 647 N.W.2d 56 (Neb. 2002) (reversing summary judgment and remanding, with burden on challenger of second-parent adoption to show absence of jurisdiction). Compare Chapter II, pp. 177-179 (marriage licenses, which are public acts), with Chapter V, p. 579 (divorce decrees). This rule makes particularly salient the

---

[10]. In fact, the couple (who had moved to Los Angeles) married in San Francisco when same-sex weddings were being performed there and before the judicial invalidation of such marriages. Helen Cooksey, Susan Love, N.Y. Times, Feb. 22, 2004, §9, at 12 (weddings and celebrations).

available bases for adoption jurisdiction, supra section C4, including the PKPA. See Ralph U. Whitten, Choice of Law, Jurisdiction, and Judgment Issues in Interstate Adoption Cases, 31 Cap. U. L. Rev. 803 (2003). Several scholars argue that full faith and credit requires interstate recognition of second-parent adoptions. E.g., Barbara J. Cox, Adoptions by Lesbian and Gay Parents Must Be Recognized by Sister States Under the Full Faith and Credit Clause Despite Anti-Marriage Statutes that Discriminate against Same-Sex Couples, 31 Cap. U. L. Rev. 751 (2003); Robert G. Spector, The Unconstitutionality of Oklahoma's Statute Denying Recognition to Adoptions by Same-Sex Couples from Other States, 40 Tulsa L. Rev. 467 (2005); Whitten, supra. See also Finstuen v. Edmondson, 2006 WL 1445354 (W.D. Okla. 2006). But see Lynn D. Wardle, A Critical Analysis of Interstate Recognition of Lesbigay Adoptions, 3 Ave Maria L. Rev. 561 (2005) (examining six reasons justifying refusals to recognize such adoptions from other states).

Even without reaching the question of full faith and credit, a majority of the Virginia Supreme Court ruled that statutes require changing birth certificates to show both parents following the second-parent adoptions of Virginia children decreed in other states. Davenport v. Little-Bowser, 611 S.E.2d 366 (Va. 2005). Should the court have considered the public policy expressed in Virginia's own failure to authorize second-parent adoption and its "mini DOMA," which makes void in Virginia a same-sex marriage celebrated elsewhere and "any contractual rights created by such marriage" (Va. Code Ann. §20-45.2 (2004))? See Davenport, 611 S.E.2d at 374-375 (Hassell, C.J., dissenting). See also Va. Code Ann. §20-45.3 (2004).

3. Secrecy versus Disclosure

a. Sealed-Record Laws

Since World War II, secrecy shrouded the adoption process in most states. The reasons included the stigma associated with illegitimate births, the fear that birth parents would intrude in adoptive families, and the belief that adoptive families should imitate biological families. To maintain this secrecy, statutes provide for the issuance of a new birth certificate when a child is adopted, changing the name of the adoptee to that of the adoptive parents. (The original birth certificate is then sealed.)

Courts have rejected adult adoptees' constitutional challenges to sealed-record laws, concluding that the right to privacy does not include a fundamental "right to know" one's biological parents and that adoptees do not constitute a suspect class for equal protection purposes. The laws survive rational basis review as protection for the interests of all parties. See, e.g., In re Roger B., 418 N.E.2d 751 (Ill.), appeal dismissed sub nom. Barth v. Finley, 454 U.S. 806 (1981). Commentators suggest that, today, courts would reach different results for adult adoptees, given the recognized importance of identity interests and other developments in family law, including challenges to the traditional unitary family. Naomi Cahn & Jana Singer, Adoption, Identity, and the Constitution: The Case for Opening Closed Records, 2 U. Pa. J. Const. L. 150 (1999); Jennifer R. Racine, Comment, A Fundamental Rights Debate: Should Wisconsin Allow Adult Adoptees Unconditional Access to Adoption Records and Original Birth Certificates?, 2002 Wis. L.

Rev. 1435. But see In re Adoption S.J.D., 641 N.W.2d 794 (Iowa 2002) (rejecting adoptee's First Amendment challenge to sealed birth records).

Most sealed-record statutes permit disclosure on a showing of good cause. E.g., Ga. Code Ann. §19-8-23(a) (2004). Courts have been more willing to find good cause for medical (such as for diagnosis of genetic disease) than psychological reasons. Compare, e.g., Doe v. Ward Law Firm, P.A., 579 S.E.2d 303 (S.C. 2003) (child's health problems constitute good cause), with In re Philip S., 881 A.2d 931 (R.I. 2005) (rejecting asserted religious basis for good cause). Although courts have declined to treat a psychological "need to know" as good cause, in a concurring opinion in In Application of Maples, 563 S.W.2d 760 (Mo. 1978), Judge Seiler explained the need adoptees have for finding their origins: "All of us need to know our past, not only for a sense of lineage and heritage, but for a fundamental and crucial sense of our very selves: our identity is incomplete and our sense of self retarded without a real personal historical connection. . . ." Id. at 767. Experts in other fields view adoptees' searches as a helpful response to the psychological problems caused by secrecy.[11]

Sealed records can create special problems for adoptive parents of "special needs" children whose medical histories might yield important information about their current problems. Some states now routinely authorize release of the child's medical history (and that of the parents and grandparents) to adoptive parents. See Okla. Stat. Ann. tit. 10, §7504-1.1 (West 1998). Further, without health information about their birth families, adult adoptees have trouble providing for their children's medical care. See Carol Barbieri, Your Mother Would Know, N.Y. Times, Nov. 29, 2005, at A1 (op-ed).

b. Law Reform

Two states, Alaska and Kansas, have long allowed adult adoptees to view their birth records. Alaska Stat. §18.50.500 (2004); Kan. Stat. Ann. §65-2423 (2002). The modern wave of legislative reform elsewhere includes different approaches. (1) Some states have created voluntary registries that will provide information when both parties, e.g., birth family member and adoptee, have registered. E.g., Ark. Code Ann. §9-9-503 (2002). Voluntary matching over the Internet, without state assistance, has made such laws obsolete. Adam Pertman, Adoption Nation: How the Adoption Revolution Is Transforming America 32 (2000). (2) Some states have statutes under which an intermediary will contact one party to obtain consent to release information once the other party has registered. E.g., Ind. Code Ann. §31-19-25-8 (West 1999). (3) Some states have enacted laws honoring a party's request for information in the absence of a veto registered by the other party. E.g., Mich. Comp. Laws Ann. §710.68(7) (West 2002). See generally Caroline B. Fleming, Note, The Open-Records Debate: Balancing the Interests of Birth Parents and Adult Adoptees, 11 Wm. & Mary J. Women & L. 461, 474-475 (2005) (examining reforms).

---

[11]. See, e.g., Robert S. Andersen, Why Adoptees Search: Motives and More, 67 Child Welfare 15, 18 (1988). See also Annette Baran & Reuben Pannor, Open Adoption, in The Psychology of Adoption 316, 318 (David M. Brodzinky & Marshall D. Schechter eds., 1990).

More recently, some states have gone further. For example, Tennessee enacted both a disclosure provision opening adoption records and a "contact veto" to be exercised if one party does not want communication from the other. Tenn. Code Ann. §§36-1-127; 36-1-128 (2005). An initiative in Oregon, Measure 58, gave adult adoptees access to their birth records. See Or. Rev. Stat. Ann. §432.240 (West 2003). These laws have been challenged by birth mothers who relinquished children under promises of confidentiality along with opponents who claim the reforms will encourage abortion and discourage adoption. Both state and federal courts have rejected arguments that these reforms unconstitutionally impair vested rights and the obligation of contracts and violate the rights of reproductive privacy and nondisclosure. See Doe v. Sundquist, 106 F.3d 702 (6th Cir.), *cert. denied,* 522 U.S. 810 (1997); Doe 1 v. State, 993 P.2d 822 (Or. Ct. App. 1999), *rev. denied,* 6 P.3d 1098 (Or.), *stay denied,* 530 U.S. 1228 (2000); Doe v. Sundquist, 2 S.W.3d 919 (Tenn. 1999). See generally Pertman, supra; Cahn & Singer, supra; Fleming, supra; Elizabeth J. Samuels, The Idea of Adoption: An Inquiry into the History of Adult Adoptee Access to Birth Records, 53 Rutgers L. Rev. 367 (2001). For a review of recent reforms here and abroad, see D. Marianne Brower Blair, The Impact of Family Paradigms, Domestic Constitutions, and International Conventions on Disclosure of an Adopted Person's Identities and Heritage: A Comparative Examination, 22 Mich. J. Int'l L. 587 (2001).

c. "Open Adoption"

The movement to open adoption records has focused on adoptees who have reached adulthood. In addition, the asserted "need to know" and the belief that secrecy can result in psychological difficulties for all parties have prompted a new approach, "open adoption," that focuses on young adoptees.[12]

■ GROVES v. CLARK
982 P.2d 446 (Mont. 1999)

Justice WILLIAM E. HUNT, SR. delivered the Opinion of the Court. . . .

This is the second appeal filed in this case concerning post-adoption visitation between Groves and L.C. A more detailed account of the facts of this case can be found in Groves v. Clark, 920 P.2d 981 [(Mont. 1996)]. To summarize, in January 1994, when L.C. was three years old, Groves signed a document terminating her parental rights to L.C., relinquishing custody of L.C. to Lutheran Social Services (LSS), and consenting to adoption. Groves and the Clarks signed a written visitation agreement which provided the following: Groves would have unrestricted visitation with L.C. so long as she gave the Clarks two days notice; Groves would have unrestricted telephone contact with L.C.; and Groves would have the right to take L.C. out of school in the event she had to "go to Butte for some emergency."

---

[12]. Open adoption was introduced in the literature in 1976 in an article noting the absence of secrecy in adoption in traditional Hawaiian culture. Annette Baran et al., Open Adoption, 21 Soc. Work 97 (1976). See Reuben Pannor & Annette Baran, Open Adoption as Standard Practice, 63 Child Welfare 245 (1984).

This agreement was drafted by the LSS and neither party consulted an attorney before signing it. In February 1994, the District Court entered an order terminating Groves' parental rights to L.C. and awarding custody of L.C. to LSS. In September 1994, the Clarks legally adopted L.C.

Groves and the Clarks abided by the terms of the visitation agreement until June 5, 1995, when Groves notified the Clarks that she wanted to take L.C. to Butte for the weekend and the Clarks refused. The Clarks told Groves that she was welcome to visit L.C. in their home, but could not take L.C. on extended out-of-town trips. [Groves then sought specific performance of the visitation agreement, and the Clarks objected, moving for summary judgment. The District Court denied Groves' petition for specific performance on the ground that the post-adoption visitation agreement was void and unenforceable. Groves appealed to this Court, which reversed, holding:]

> Birth parents and prospective adoptive parents are free to contract for post-adoption visitation and . . . trial courts must give effect to such contracts when continued visitation is in the best interest of the child.

We remanded the case to the District Court for a hearing on whether enforcement of the parties' visitation agreement would be in the best interest of L.C.

Based on the evidence produced at trial, the [District Court] found that a bond existed between Groves and L.C. and that it was highly likely L.C. would suffer from issues of abandonment, identity, and grieving unless appropriate visitation with Groves was granted. Ultimately, the court found that continued visitation between Groves and L.C. was in L.C.'s best interest. . . . Specifically, the court granted Groves unsupervised monthly weekend visitation with L.C. and required the parties to share equally in the transportation costs. Additionally, the court granted Groves telephone contact with L.C. at least once per week. The court recommended that the parties seek adoption counseling and attempt to agree upon future visitation modifications that may be appropriate as L.C. matures.

[On appeal,] the Clarks assert that the adoptive parents' wishes are paramount in deciding whether a post-adoption visitation agreement should be enforced. The Clarks cite several cases from other jurisdictions purportedly holding that adoptive parents have the right to determine whether it is in the best interest of the adopted child to maintain contact with the birth mother. [Citations omitted.] The Clarks also cite cases from other jurisdictions purportedly holding that the mere fact that the adoptive parents oppose visitation provides a sufficient basis for finding that visitation is not in the best interest of the child. [Citations omitted.]

We reject the Clarks' assertions. . . . The law in Montana, which also happens to be the law of this case, is clear: whether a post-adoption visitation agreement is enforceable shall be decided by the District Court pursuant to a "best interests" analysis. The adoptive parents' wishes is but one factor among many to be considered by the District Court.

Next, the Clarks argue that the court did not adequately consider and evaluate the evidence when applying the "best interests" standard. [The Clarks] testified that visitation adversely affected L.C. in that afterward she would evidence insecurity about her adoption status, would be moody and difficult to discipline. On the other hand, the court heard the testimony of the [Groves'] experts including

Kathy Gerhke [an adoptive parenting instructor] and Debbie O'Brien [a family counselor] which explained this as a normal occurrence. Based on their testimony, this court finds that it is highly likely L.C. will suffer from issues of abandonment, identity, and grieving unless appropriate visitation is granted. L.C. lived with her mother for over three years. The evidence, including from a visitation facilitator, was that visitation was a happy experience for L.C. . . .

[T]he Clarks assert that visitation with Groves is not in L.C.'s best interests because the Clarks do not know the details of the visitation such as where L.C. will be, what L.C. will be doing, and with whom L.C. will be associating. The Clarks have expressed concern over L.C.'s sleeping arrangements at Groves' residence. The Clarks disapprove of L.C. snowmobiling and riding in a car without wearing a seatbelt. . . . These concerns were not presented to the District Court at trial. . . .

[W]e determine that the court's finding that visitation between Groves and L.C. was in the best interest of L.C. was not clearly erroneous. The finding was supported by substantial evidence, the court did not misapprehend the effect of the evidence, and we do not believe a mistake was committed. . . . We [also] agree with the District Court that modification of the parties' original visitation agreement was within its discretion in accordance with determining the best interests of L.C. The policy of this state is that "in matters relating to children, the best interests of the children are paramount." [F]ailure to apply this rule to disputes involving post-adoption visitation agreements could potentially lead to absurd results. It would be incongruous for a court to hold that visitation is in the best interest of a child and then enforce a visitation agreement that was not in the best interest of the child. For these reasons, we determine that the District Court did not abuse its discretion in modifying the parties' post-adoption visitation agreement. . . .

Notes and Questions

1. *Background.* The rise of open or cooperative adoption emerged from several developments: First, an increasing number of older children, with established bonds to their birth families, have been freed for adoption. Second, because of the decreased availability of the most sought-after infants for adoption following the legalization of abortion, birth parents can demand enhanced conditions in placement, including open-adoption arrangements. Finally, experts claim that an open system avoids the damaging psychological effects of anonymity for adoptees, birth parents, and adopters. See, e.g., Annette Ruth Appell, The Move Toward Legally Sanctioned Cooperative Adoption: Can It Survive the Uniform Adoption Act?, 30 Fam. L.Q. 483, 483 (1996). See also Adam Pertman, Adoption Nation: How the Adoption Revolution Is Transforming America 47 (2000); U.S. Department of Health and Human Services, Administration for Children and Families, Administration on Children, Youth and Families, Children's Bureau, Cooperative Adoption: Contact Between Adoptive and Birth Families After Finalization (2003 Adoption State Statute Series Ready Reference) (available at http://naic.acf.hhs.gov/general/legal/statutes/cooperative.pdf).

With the prevalence of both adoptions by stepparents and relatives and also adoptions of foster children, most adoptions today are not anonymous.

2. *Enforcement.* Several states allow voluntary open adoption but permit the adoptive parents to determine whether to abide by such agreements. *Groves* cites cases from Arizona, Colorado, Maryland, and Pennsylvania taking this

position. Alternatively, some states authorize judicial approval of such agreements upon a finding of best interests and then enforcement of agreements so approved. See, e.g., Minn. Stat. Ann. §259.58 (West 2003); Birth Mother v. Adoptive Parents, 59 P.3d 1233, 1236 (Nev. 2002) (rejecting enforcement "if the agreement is not incorporated in the adoption decree").

The UAA, §4-113, expressly provides for judicial enforcement of visitation agreements in stepparent adoptions. 9 U.L.A. (pt. IA) 110-112 (1999). Otherwise, however, it permits "mutually agreed-upon communication between birth and adoptive families" without making such agreements enforceable. See id. at 15 (Prefatory Note ¶9). The UAA's failure to dictate enforceability has evoked criticism from proponents of open adoption. See, e.g., Appell, supra.

3. *Parental rights.* Why does *Groves* go beyond all of these approaches, allowing courts to fashion arrangements that the parties have not chosen? Does *Groves* make adoptive parents "second class" parents? Should adoptive parents have the same rights as other parents to determine the extent of their children's visitation, if any, with legal strangers? See Troxel v. Granville, Chapter VII, section B3. In *Groves*, who should resolve the asserted disputes about snowmobiling and seatbelts? Does open adoption conflict with the very concept of adoption, as some older cases have held? E.g., Hill v. Moorman, 525 So. 2d 681 (La. Ct. App. 1988); Cage v. Harrisonburg Dept. of Soc. Servs., 410 S.E.2d 405 (Va. Ct. App. 1991). Evaluate Professor Meyer's proposal for non-consensual open adoptions to solve the legal problem posed by birth parents' flawed consent in cases such as Baby Jessica and Baby Richard. See David D. Meyer, Family Ties: Solving the Constitutional Dilemma of the Faultless Father, 41 Ariz. L. Rev. 753, 833-846 (1999).

4. *Grandparent visitation.* Some states have special rules authorizing postadoption visitation by grandparents. E.g., Tex. Fam. Code §161.206(c) (Vernon Supp. 2005). Why not rely on the general best-interests test for such cases? To what extent does *Troxel* make these laws constitutionally vulnerable? Compare Ex Parte D.W., 835 So. 2d 186 (Ala. 2002) (distinguishing *Troxel* to uphold authorization of visitation by "natural grandparents" after intrafamily adoption), with Visitation of Cathy L.(R.)M. v. Mark Brent R., 617 S.E.2d 866 (W. Va. 2005) (*Troxel* requires giving adoptive parents special weight in deciding whether biological grandparents can visit, even in intrafamily adoptions).

5. *Sibling visitation.* Are special rules warranted for postadoption visitation by biological siblings? Why? Compare In re Adoption of Anthony, 448 N.Y.S.2d 377 (Fam. Ct. 1982) (ordering visitation in child's best interests), and Cocose v. Diane B., 803 N.Y.S.2d 17 (Fam. Ct. 2005) (refusing to dismiss petition for sibling visitation, despite adoptive parents' argument based on *Troxel*), with In re Adoption of T.J.F., 798 N.E.2d 867 (Ind. Ct. App. 2003) (using adopted child's best interests to halt visitation with biological sibling), and Adoption of Pierce, 790 N.E.2d 680 (Mass. App. Ct.) (upholding dismissal of sister's claim for visitation with her adopted brother). Should preservation of a child's relationship with a biological sibling operate as a reason to reject adoption as the best permanency plan for the child? Should the court consider the impact on both siblings or only the child to be adopted? See In re Celine R., 71 P.3d 787 (Cal. 2003). See generally William Wesley Patton, The Status of Siblings' Rights: A View Into the New Millennium, 151 DePaul L. Rev. 1 (2001); Angela Ferraris, Comment, Sibling Visitation as a Fundamental Right in Herbst v. Swan, 39 New Eng. L. Rev. 715 (2005); Meghann M.

Seifert, Note, Sibling Visitation after Adoption: The Implications of the Massachusetts Sibling Visitation Statute, 84 B.U. L. Rev. 1467 (2004).

6. *Guardianship.* Open adoption forms part of a larger debate about whether the parent-child relationship must be complete and exclusive or whether the law ought to recognize a child's connections with multiple parental figures. See, e.g., Katharine T. Bartlett, Rethinking Parenthood as an Exclusive Status: The Need for Legal Alternatives When the Premise of the Nuclear Family Has Failed, 70 Va. L. Rev. 879 (1984). Professor Brigitte Bodenheimer pioneered this approach, suggesting as a "compromise" in contested adoption cases naming a guardian without terminating biological parents' rights. Brigitte M. Bodenheimer, New Trends and Requirements in Adoption Law and Proposals for Legislative Change, 49 S. Cal. L. Rev. 10, 41 (1975).

Traditionally, parents serve as a child's "natural guardians," but courts appoint a guardian for a minor (or incompetent) when parental care is unavailable or inadequate to serve a particular need of the child. See, e.g., Cotton v. Wise, 977 S.W.2d 263 (Mo. 1998). Cf. Freeman v. Rushton, 2005 WL 174760 (Ark. 2005) (statutory preference for fit parent as guardian does not require his selection). Recall that in *Lofton*, supra, the state allowed the petitioner to become the child's guardian but not his adoptive parent. Most courts defer to parental autonomy in the appointment of a minor's guardian even after the parent's death. See, e.g., Bristol v. Brundage, 589 A.2d 1 (Conn. App. Ct. 1991). But see In re Joshua S., 796 A.2d 1141 (Conn. 2002) (distinguishing cases in which state has filed neglect petition). For illustrations of the use of guardianship law, see In re Guardianship of Kowalski, Chapter IV, Section B4c; Guardianship of Phillip B., Chapter VIII, section B2c).

The HIV/AIDS epidemic prompted the development of a new type of guardianship, standby guardianship, enabling parents suffering from terminal illness to plan for the future of their children before death or incapacitation. This approach responds to the particular needs of ill single mothers by allowing for a "backup" guardian without requiring the mother to relinquish parental rights. See, e.g., Va. Code Ann. §§16.1-349 to -355 (2003). Likewise, absence for military service might prompt a parent to name a guardian. E.g., Lebo v. Lebo, 886 So. 2d 491 (La. Ct. App. 2004). Finally, reforms aimed at meeting the needs of the numerous children in foster care include proposals for subsidized guardianships. See Sarah Ramsey, Fixing Foster Care or Reducing Child Poverty: The Pew Commission Recommendations and the Transracial Adoption Debate, 66 Mont. L. Rev. 21, 46-48 (2005); Mark F. Testa, The Quality of Permanence — Lasting or Binding? Subsidized Guardianship and Kinship Foster Care as Alternatives to Adoption, 12 Va. J. Soc. Pol'y & L. 499 (2005).

4. Adoption Failure

■ IN RE LISA DIANE G.
537 A.2d 131 (R.I. 1988)

KELLEHER, J.

The single but significant issue presented by this controversy is whether a Family Court justice can grant relief to the plaintiffs, the adoptive parents of a daughter who was eight years old in 1983 when the decree of adoption was entered in the Family Court. The gist of the parents' complaint is that the adoption decree was procured by the fraudulent conduct or misrepresentations of certain representatives of the Department of Children and Their Families (DCF). The parents contend that DCF never informed them that the staff at Bradley Hospital, an institution noted for its treatment of the emotionally disturbed, had informed DCF that the eight-year-old, because of her behavioral problems, should not be placed for adoption. In the Family Court the parents sought nullification of the adoption decree and compensation for the expenses they incurred in caring for the child. . . .

[W]e have ruled that a natural mother who has consented to have her child placed for adoption but subsequently seeks to vacate the adoption decree must prove her claim to relief by clear and convincing evidence. We believe that the same standard should be satisfied in situations in which, as here, the adopting parents are the ones seeking to invalidate the adoption decree. . . .

The Legislature has seen fit to vest exclusive jurisdiction in the area of adoptions in the Family Court. If the adoptive parents are to prevail on their claim of fraud or misrepresentation that has been perpetrated on them, the fraud or the misrepresentation has also been perpetrated on the Family Court. In these circumstances [of asserted fraud] we are of the belief that the Family Court, because of its exclusive jurisdiction in the subject matter of adoption, has the inherent power to adjudicate the claim now put forth by the adoptive parents.

. . . Any determination of the plaintiff's claim in the Family Court will necessarily involve a consideration of the child's best interest. However, this consideration must be balanced against the harm suffered by the adoptive parents as a result of the alleged conduct of DCF.

Accordingly the adoptive parents' appeal is sustained, and the dismissal order is vacated. The case is remanded to the Family Court for a trial and adjudication of the plaintiffs' claim.

The following excerpt amplifies the facts of In re Lisa Diane G.

■ **DANIEL GOLDEN, WHEN ADOPTION DOESN'T WORK...**
Boston Globe, June 11, 1989, Magazine Section, at 16

For years after Sheila was born in 1968, Bob and Joan Gordon wanted another child, but the timing never seemed right. Even with two incomes—he was a mechanic, she a lab technician—they barely scraped by. They couldn't afford for Joan to take a maternity leave, never mind paying for day care.

[In 1981,] Joan heard that Rhode Island, like other states, was offering older children for adoption. Here, she thought, was a practical alternative. She would not have to quit her job, and Sheila's longing for a younger sister might be fulfilled at last.

The Gordons, whose names have been changed in this story to protect their privacy, were very specific when social workers from the Rhode Island Department of Children and Their Families visited their suburban home. They wanted a girl between the ages of 6 and 10 who would be in school while they worked. She could have a physical disability, they said, but not an emotional one. The Gordons knew their limits: A troubled girl would need more care than they felt ready to give. . . .

When Joan saw blond, blue-eyed Lisa, the hard-headed attitude she had maintained throughout the adoption process yielded to her heart. "Something instinctively told me to go with this child," she says. "Her background was so traumatic. You wanted to just reach out and love this little girl."

Only 6 years old, Lisa had suffered a lifetime's worth of pain and separation. She never knew her father, and her mother abused her. Covered with bites and bruises, she was placed in a foster home. She was adored there, but her stay ended abruptly when her foster father died of a heart attack. She was removed from her next foster home after the family accused her of killing its cat and trying to smother a baby. She was then sent to a state-supervised group home. Along the way, she lost contact with her older brother and sister, who had been adopted.

Lisa's social worker assured the Gordons that Lisa had emerged from these upheavals emotionally intact. . . . "We were led to believe that once she was part of a good, secure home, she would be fine, and her problems would disappear," Joan says. Assuming they had been told all, the Gordons never asked to read Lisa's file. . . .

Adoption is supposed to last a lifetime. Like marriage, it is meant to be an unswerving commitment, for better or for worse. Yet, while adoption has a far higher success rate than marriage, it too is plagued by divorce. Today, an increasing number of adoptive parents are relinquishing their children to the state, or even going to court to nullify the adoption. Most of these "disruptions," as they are termed, involve adoptions of older children with physical or emotional problems stemming from abuse by their natural parents. Infant adoptions are less prone to break up. . . . Beset by lawsuits from disenchanted parents, adoption agencies are reassessing their credo that all children can be adopted. . . .

The main reason for the surge in disruptions is a shift in the type of children being adopted. Until the 1970s, only infants were considered adoptable. Then an increase in abortions, coupled with greater social acceptance of single mothers, reduced the pool of available infants. At the same time, the number of abused and neglected older children was on the rise. Advocacy groups argued that these children, who were often warehoused in institutions or shunted from one foster home to another, needed adoptive homes. In 1980, a federal law enshrined "permanency planning" as a goal for children in state care; the law also expanded subsidies for adoptive parents. Like the deinstitutionalization of mental patients in the same era, this policy was both humanely intended and inexpensive, but it had the consequence of dumping some difficult people into a society that was not equipped to handle them. . . .

Once Lisa Gordon's adoption was finalized in 1983, the Department of Children and Their Families closed her case. Soon afterward, Joan Gordon decided that her daughter needed psychotherapy, and she asked the department to pay for it. . . . Late in 1984, Joan finally obtained medical insurance that covered therapy, and the family began seeing a psychologist. Instead of helping, Joan says, "the therapy was a catalyst for her to get worse." [For example, Lisa, who disliked the chore of fetching wood from the backyard, set fire to the wood pile.]

By 1985, the Gordons' house simmered with antagonism. Sensing the tension, Sheila's friends stopped coming over. . . . Bob's relationship with Lisa was, by turns, more antagonistic and more affectionate than Joan's. Lisa could goad her father into angry outbursts one minute and cuddle up to him the next. So Joan was not surprised one morning in April 1986 when Lisa . . . volunteered to fix the soup that Bob, as was his custom, would take to work. When Lisa gave him the thermos on his way out the door, he opened the lid and smelled something unusual. It was the disinfectant Lysol. . . .

It took one more incident for Joan to make up her mind. [Lisa told the school nurse her father had hit her with a board.] Obeying the law, the nurse reported the allegation to the state. After an investigation, the charges were dropped, and Joan went to the office of the state Department of Children and Their Families, saying she wouldn't leave until Lisa was removed from her house. State officials gave in and arranged for Lisa to be evaluated at Bradley Hospital, a psychiatric facility for children in Rhode Island.

Three members of the hospital's staff listened to Lisa describe the Lysol episode in a passionless monotone. One of them asked, "Did you want to kill him?" She said, simply, "Yes." She was admitted to the hospital immediately. . . .

Notes and Questions

1. *Epilogue.* On remand, the court revoked the adoption. Lisa was institutionalized. The adoptive parents, who had also sought damages, withdrew that request. Subsequently, they dissolved their marriage, in part because of the stress Lisa had created. Telephone interview with Stephen E. Cicilline, attorney for plaintiffs (July 23, 1997).

2. *Failures.* Adoption failure occurs either when the child is removed before the adoption is final (disruption) or when a final adoption is abrogated or annulled (dissolution). See Kathy S. Stolley, Statistics on Adoption in the United States, The Future of Children, Spring 1993, at 26, 31. The adoption failure rate is increasing because of the growing number of placements of special needs children (including older children) and children with previous foster care. About 10-14 percent of adoptions of special needs children "disrupt"; children placed between ages 10 and 14 have a disruption rate of 21 percent, with 35 percent for those over 15. Richard P. Barth, Risks and Rates of Adoption Disruption, in National Council for Adoption, Adoption Factbook III 381, 382 (1999).

3. *Standards.* Must the agency that placed the child consent to abrogation? Must the adopters have a reasonable basis for seeking to relinquish parental rights? See In re J.F., 862 A.2d 1258 (Pa. Super. Ct. 2004). When, if ever, should a court set aside an adoption? Suppose an adoptive father alleges that he relied on fraudulent assurances that the child, born to a married woman, was his biological son? See McAdams v. McAdams, 109 S.W.3d 649 (Ark. 2003) (holding suit time-barred). Does abrogation ever serve the child's best interests? See In re Adoption of B.J.H., 564 N.W.2d 387, 392-393 (Iowa 1997); In re Adoption of Hemmer, 619 N.W.2d 848 (Neb. 2000).

Should cases be decided by courts based on equitable discretion or legislative criteria? See, e.g., Cal. Fam. Code §9100 (West 2004) (developmental disability or mental illness arising from conditions prior to adoption); Ky. Rev. Stat. Ann. §199.540(1) (LexisNexis 1998) (different racial heritage). Who may petition for abrogation? What time limits, if any, should control? See, e.g., Mich. Comp. Laws Ann. §710.64(1) (West 2002) (21 days); Neb. Rev. Stat. §43-116 (2004) (2 years). Does abrogation infringe the adoptee's constitutional rights? See In re Adoption of Kay C., 278 Cal. Rptr. 907 (Ct. App. 1991) (no).

4. *Wrongful adoption.* As an alternative to abrogation, some parents have successfully sued adoption agencies for fraud or the tort of "wrongful adoption," based on the defendant's concealment of the child's medical condition. See, e.g., Jackson v. State, 956 P.2d 35 (Mont. 1998); Mallette v. Children's Friend & Serv., 661 A.2d 67 (R.I. 1995). What public policy issues do such negligence suits raise? Compare Richard P. v. Vista Del Mar Child Care Serv., 165 Cal. Rptr. 370, 374 (Ct. App. 1980), with M.H. v. Caritas Fam. Servs., 488 N.W.2d 282, 288 (Minn. 1992).

Must plaintiffs prove they would not have adopted but for the misrepresentation? See McKinney v. State, 950 P.2d 461 (Wash. 1998) (jury must find proximate cause). Can plaintiffs recover punitive damages? See Ross v. Louise Wise Servs., Inc., 777 N.Y.S.2d 618 (Sup. Ct. 2004) (claim can proceed). Can they recover for emotional distress? Compare Price v. State, 57 P.3d 639 (Wash. 2002) (permitting recovery), with Rowey v. Children's Friend & Servs., 2003 WL 23196347 (R.I. Super. 2003) (only when supported by medical evidence). Can agencies obtain valid waivers of disclosure? See Ferenc v. World Child, Inc., 977 F. Supp. 56 (D.D.C. 1997), aff'd, 172 F.3d 919 (D.C. Cir. 1998) (yes). Does the adopted child have a claim? See Dresser v. Cradle of Hope Adoption Ctr., Inc., 358 F. Supp. 2d 620, 640-642 (E.D. Mich. 2005) (agency owes duty to child to provide medical information so adopters can obtain proper treatment). But see *Rowey*, supra. Should governmental immunity protect state placement agencies from such claims? Compare Young v. Van Duyne, 92 P.3d 1269 (N. Mex. Ct. App. 2004), with Eischen v. Stark County Bd. of Comm'rs., 2002 WL 31831395 (Ohio Ct. App. 2002). Apart from a negligence claim, does the placement agency have a fiduciary responsibility to provide information about family health history to adoptive parents? See Dahlin v. Evangelical Child & Fam. Agency, 252 F. Supp. 2d 666 (N.D. Ill. 2002) (plaintiffs must prove at trial). In the adoptive parents' suit for damages, can a court compel an adult adoptee to release his or her medical treatment records? See Sirca v. Medina County Dep't of Human Servs., 762 N.E.2d 407 (Ohio Ct. App. 2001). Can the adoptive parents' other children recover damages for the harms that they suffered from the wrongful adoption? See Roe v. Jewish Children's Bureau of Chicago, 790 N.E.2d 882 (Ill. App. Ct. 2003).

5. *Disclosure laws.* Several modern statutes require full disclosure to prospective adoptive parents of the child's medical history, e.g., Ariz. Rev. Stat. Ann. §8-129(A) (West 1999); Cal. Fam. Code §8706 (West 2004).

The UAA, §2-106, contains a detailed list of background information that must be disclosed to prospective adopters before they accept physical custody of the child. The list includes current medical and psychological history (including prenatal care), genetic diseases or drug addictions by the genetic parent, performance in school, and allegations of parental abuse or neglect. 9 U.L.A. (pt. IA) 36-37 (1999). How readily can such information be obtained? For exploration of this question, see Marianne Brower Blair, The Uniform Adoption Act's Health Disclosure Provisions: A Model That Should Not Be Overlooked, 30 Fam. L.Q. 427 (1996). Should preadoptive genetic testing become a part of the placement process? Would such tests violate privacy rights? See Jessica Ann Schlee, Notes & Comments, Genetic Testing: Technology That Is Changing the Adoption Process, 18 N.Y.L. Sch. J. Hum. Rts. 133 (2001).

6. *Policy.* To what extent do sealed-record laws, supra pp. 1091-1092, facilitate fraud by adoption agencies? Do biological parents have a duty of full disclosure in

relinquishing their children? To the extent that such laws impose disclosure duties on birth parents upon relinquishment, should these duties include updating the information in the event of subsequent familial health problems? See R. Scott Smith, Disclosure of Post-Adoption Family Medical Information: A Continuing Birth Parent Duty, 35 Fam. L.Q. 553 (2001). Will subsidized adoption of children with special needs reduce the incidence of fraud? Do you agree with the call for "consumer protection" laws for adopters who obtain children abroad, many of whom have spent time in institutional settings? See Donovan M. Steltzner, Note, Intercountry Adoption: Toward a Regime That Recognizes the "Best Interests" of Adoptive Parents, 35 Case W. Res. J. Int'l L. 113 (2003).

Problem

Barbara gives birth to a child and relinquishes him to the Children's Home Society (CHS), a state-licensed private adoption agency, which places the baby in an adoptive family. As part of the relinquishment process, CHS provides counseling for Barbara. It also obtains detailed health and background information from her. Ten years later Barbara marries and has two children, a daughter and a son. When this son dies in infancy, Barbara learns she carries a genetic defect that afflicts male offspring. Barbara contacts CHS to determine the health of her first son and learns from CHS that he, too, suffers from the genetic disease.

Barbara sues CHS for wrongful death, negligent and intentional infliction of emotional distress, and fraud. In essence, she claims CHS had a duty to inform her of the genetic disease of the son she relinquished, to enable her to make informed choices about future childbearing. What result? See Olson v. Children's Home Soc'y, 252 Cal. Rptr. 11 (Ct. App. 1988). But cf. Molloy v. Meier, 679 N.W.2d 711 (Minn. 2004).

E. ALTERNATIVES TO ADOPTION

1. Artificial Insemination

To the extent that adoption provides a way for childless adults to construct a family, medicine and technology now offer alternatives. Assisted reproductive technologies or ARTs range from the very simple artificial (or donor) insemination, which has been practiced the longest,[13] to much more advanced interventions.

---

[13]. Well over 100,000 women undergo artificial insemination in the United States each year. In 1987, the number was 172,000. Congress of the United States, Office of Technology Assessment, Artificial Insemination in the United States: Summary of a 1987 Survey — Background Paper 3 (1988). Some authorities now prefer the term "alternative insemination" to "artificial insemination." See Mary Lyndon Shanley, Making Babies, Making Families: What Matters Most in an Age of Reproductive Technologies, Surrogacy, Adoption, and Same-Sex and Unwed Parents 80 (2001).

a. Creating Traditional Families

■ **IN RE ADOPTION OF ANONYMOUS**
345 N.Y.S.2d 430 (Sur. Ct. 1973)

SOBEL, Surrogate. . . .

As a preliminary, there are two types of artificial insemination. Homologous insemination is the process by which the wife is artificially impregnated with the semen of her husband [(AIH).] Heterologous insemination is the artificial insemination of the wife by the semen of a third-party donor [(AID).] The utilization of AID procedures is bound to increase because of the unavailability — no doubt due to the "pill" and liberalized abortion laws — of adoptive children. Relatively recent too is the practice of AID where the husband's family has a history of hereditary disease or where RH incompatibility has led to repeated stillbirths. . . .

The facts in this proceeding are briefly stated. During the marriage the child was born of consensual AID. The husband was listed as the father on the birth certificate. Later the couple separated and the separation was followed by a divorce. Both the separation agreement and the divorce decree declare the child to be the "daughter" and "child" of the couple. The wife was granted support and the husband visitation rights. He has faithfully visited and performed all the support conditions of the decree. The wife later remarried and her new husband is petitioning to adopt the child. The first husband has refused his consent. Confronted with that legal impediment, the petitioner has suggested that the first husband's consent is not required since he is not the "parent" of the child. . . . If the husband is the "parent" of a child born of consensual AID, in the absence of his consent to the adoption, the petition must be dismissed. . . .

The leading case . . . is People v. Sorensen [, 68 Cal. 2d 680 (1968)]. *Sorensen* was a criminal prosecution on complaint of the welfare authorities against the husband for failure to support a minor child born during the marriage of consensual AID. The California Supreme Court without dissent held: the defendant is the lawful father of a dependent child born of consensual AID; that the term "father" as used in the penal statute is not limited to a biologic or natural father; the determinative factor is whether the legal relationship of father and child exists. The court reasoned that a child conceived through AID does not have a "natural" father; that the anonymous donor is not the "natural" father; that he does have a "lawful" father and the intent of the Legislature was to include a lawful father in the penal sanctions; further, that "In light of these principles of statutory construction, a reasonable man who, because of his inability to procreate, actively participates and consents to his wife's artificial insemination in the hope that a child will be produced whom they will treat as their own, knows that such behavior carries with it the legal responsibilities of fatherhood and criminal liability for nonsupport. . . ." This is the principle of equitable estoppel found in several other cases. . . .

[Gursky v. Gursky, 242 N.Y.S.2d 406 (Sup. Ct. 1963), the leading New York case,] is not persuasive. It is the only published decision which flatly holds that AID children are illegitimate. It has been criticized. (Note, 1968 U. of Ill. L. Forum 203, 208.) The "historical concept" and the statutory definition of "a child born out of wedlock" upon which it relies were developed and enacted long before the advent of the practice of artificial insemination. The birth of AID children was not then contemplated. An AID child is not "begotten" by a father who is not the husband;

the donor is anonymous; the wife does not have sexual intercourse or commit adultery with him; if there is any "begetting" it is by the doctor who in this specialty is often a woman. The suggestion that the husband might not regard the child as his own has been dispelled by our gratifying experience with adoptive parents. Since there is consent by the husband, there is no marital infidelity. The child is not born "out of wedlock" but in and during wedlock. And finally legislative inaction is an unsound basis for any inferences favorable or unfavorable. . . .

Basically the problem of the status of AID children vis-à-vis the "father" is one of policy. . . . New York has a strong policy in favor of legitimacy [so] it would seem absurd to hold illegitimate a child born during a valid marriage, of parents desiring but unable to conceive a child, and both consenting and agreeing to the impregnation of the mother by a carefully and medically selected anonymous donor. [O]ur liberal policy is for the protection of the child, not the parents. It serves no purpose whatsoever to stigmatize the AID child; or to compel the parents formally to adopt in order to confer upon the AID child the status and rights of a naturally conceived child.

[A] child born of consensual AID during a valid marriage is a legitimate child entitled to the rights and privileges of a naturally conceived child of the same marriage. The father of such child is therefore the "parent" (Domestic Relations Law, §111) whose consent is required to the adoption of such child by another. . . .

Notes and Questions

1. *Infertility.* Statistics show that approximately 6 million women and approximately 2 million couples in the United States suffer impaired ability to have children.[14] Worldwide, 8 to 12 percent of couples experience some infertility.[15] Use of AIH as a medical response to male infertility reportedly began in the 1790s and AID in 1884. See Lee M. Silver, Remaking Eden: How Genetic Engineering and Cloning Will Transform the American Family 178-179 (1998). The popularity of AID (or donor insemination) grew over the years, especially during the "baby boom" following World War II. See Elaine Tyler May, Barren in the Promised Land: Childless Americans and the Pursuit of Happiness 75-78, 147-149 (1997).

2. *Statutory responses.* Many jurisdictions now address by statute the issue presented in *Anonymous.* Eighteen have followed the 1973 Uniform Parentage Act, whose §5 recognizes as the father the husband who consents in writing to AID performed by a licensed physician and states that the "donor of semen provided to a licensed physician for artificial insemination of a woman other than the donor's wife is treated in law as if he were not the natural father. . . ." 9B U.L.A. 377, 407-408 (2001). The new Uniform Parentage Act (new UPA), first promulgated in 2000 and revised in 2002, reaches the same result in §§702 and 704, providing that the husband's failure to consent to assisted reproduction does not preclude his recognition as father, if the man and woman during the first two years

[14]. Centers for Disease Control, National Center for Health Statistics, Fast Stats, Infertility (available at http://www.cdc.gov/nchs/fastats/fertile.htm) (visited Dec. 25, 2006).
[15]. Marcia C. Inhorn, Global Infertility and the Globalization of New Reproductive Technologies: Illustrations from Egypt, 56 Soc. Sci. & Med. 1837, 1839 (2003).

of the child's life reside in the same household with the child and openly hold the child as their own. 9B U.L.A. 355-356 (2001); id. at 39-41 (Supp. 2005). See also ALI Principles §§2.03, 3.03 (estoppel).

3. *The adoption analogy.* Anonymous examines Gursky v. Gursky, 242 N.Y.S.2d 406 (Sup. Ct. 1963), in which the husband's duty to support an AID child rested on his implied promise and equitable estoppel. Does this approach apply the principle of equitable adoption or equitable parenthood to consensual artificial insemination? See generally Bridget R. Penick, Note, Give the Child a Legal Father: A Plea for Iowa to Adopt a Statute Regulating Artificial Insemination by Anonymous Donor, 83 Iowa L. Rev. 633 (1998).

What other principles from adoption law should apply to artificial insemination cases? Should the husband of a woman who uses AID undertake a stepparent adoption of the child? See Welborn v. Doe, 394 S.E.2d 732 (Va. Ct. App. 1990).

4. *Anonymity versus disclosure.* The 1973 UPA (§5) explicitly provided for sealed records concerning donor insemination. 9B U.L.A. 407-408 (2001). Even while litigation and legislative reform began to give adult adoptees access to information about their birth parents (see supra pp.1092-1093), a norm of secrecy prevailed for donor insemination. Why? What similarities between an adoptee and an individual conceived by donor insemination are relevant to an asserted "right to know"? What dissimilarities? See generally Mary Lyndon Shanley, Collaboration and Commodification in Assisted Procreation: Reflections on an Open Market and Anonymous Donation in Human Sperm and Eggs, 36 Law & Soc'y Rev. 257 (2002); Elizabeth Siberry Chestney, Note, The Right to Know One's Genetic Origin: Can, Should, or Must a State That Extends This Right to Adoptees Extend an Analogous Right to Children Conceived with Donor Gametes?, 80 Tex. L. Rev. 365 (2001); Lucy R. Dollens, Note, Artificial Insemination: Right of Privacy and the Difficulty in Maintaining Donor Anonymity, 35 Ind. L. Rev. 213 (2001).

Recent developments have brought significant changes in policy and practice. Some foreign countries, including the United Kingdom, now make information available. See R. v. Secretary of State for Health, (2002) EWHC 1593 (Q.B. Admin.) Eng. 28 (recognizing right to personal identity in family life, which allows children of donor insemination to seek information and requires balancing against other interests); Heather Timmons, World Briefing Europe: Britain: Sperm Donors to Lose Anonymity, N.Y. Times, Jan. 22, 2004, at A12. Today, parents often openly discuss their children's origins, sperm banks facilitate donor-child meetings when the donor has agreed to such contact, and children can register on a website designed introduce them to others conceived by the same donor. See Amy Harmon, Hello, I'm Your Sister. Our Father Is Donor 150, N.Y. Times, Nov. 20, 2005, §1, at 1; Linda Villarosa, Once-Invisible Sperm Donors Get to Meet the Family, N.Y. Times, May 21, 2002, §F, at 5. Yet fertility clinics fear that they will lose donors without promises of anonymity. See Amy Harmon, Are You My Sperm Donor? Few Clinics Will Say, N.Y. Times, Jan. 20, 2006, at A1.

5. *Policy issues.*

a. *Eugenics.* Assisted reproduction allows recipients to select genetic material. Sperm banks provide elaborate profiles of donors' characteristics, including physical characteristics, educational backgrounds, skills, interests, and talents. See, e.g., The Sperm Bank of California, Donor Catalogue and Profiles (available at http://www.thespermbankofca.org/dcp.html) (visited Dec. 26, 2005). The Repository of Germinal Choice, established in 1980 by a wealthy Californian, promised to provide the sperm of Nobel Prize winners. For a journalist's investigation and profiles of some of the donors and resulting children, see David Plotz, The Genius Factory: The Curious History of the Nobel Prize Sperm Bank (2005). Why shouldn't those using donor insemination be informed and demanding consumers? Instead, should medical personnel make the selection?

b. Fraud. The practice of artificial insemination resulted in a famous case of fraud. In 1992, Dr. Cecil Jacobson was convicted on 52 counts of fraud and perjury for telling his patients he used semen from anonymous donors for artificial insemination when in fact he used his own. For federal prosecutors, the case posed unique questions about privacy rights versus law enforcement: On the one hand, the patients had a right to know about their physician's alleged fraud, and genetic testing of the children would be necessary to prove the case. On the other hand, suppose the family members would prefer not to know. How should the prosecutors proceed? See Sabra Chartrand, Parents Recall Ordeal of Prosecuting in Artificial-Insemination Fraud Case, N.Y. Times, Mar. 15, 1992, §1, at 16. The DNA tests ultimately revealed that Jacobson had fathered 15 children in the seven families participating in the case until conclusion. Id. Jacobson was sentenced to five years in prison and ordered to pay fines and restitution exceeding $116,000. See United States v. Jacobson, 4 F.3d 987, 1993 WL 343172 (4th Cir. 1993) (unpublished opinion upholding convictions on appeal), *cert. denied*, 511 U.S. 1069 (1994). See generally Cyrene Grothaus-Day, Criminal Conception: Behind the White Coat, 39 Fam. L.Q. 707, 712-716 (2005) (calling Jacobson's crime "genetic rape").

6. *Medical regulation.* What role should the state play in screening and checking the medical histories of semen donors? What records should be kept? What risks follow from inadequate donor screening and record-keeping?

The practice of donor insemination long remained unregulated, with wide variations in screening performed by physicians providing such treatment. See Congress of the United States, Office of Technology Assessment, Artificial Insemination Practice in the United States: Summary of a 1987 Survey — Background Paper (1988). But see N.H. Rev. Stat. Ann. §§168-B:10, 168-B:12 (2002) (medical evaluation of sperm donors and recipients required since 1990). Occasional litigation highlights the risks of improper screening. See Johnson v. Superior Ct., 95 Cal. Rptr. 2d 864 (Ct. App. 2000) (allowing plaintiff family to compel anonymous donor's deposition in negligence action against sperm bank for using semen with family history of kidney disease).

The F.D.A. first took steps to regulate donated reproductive tissue in rules that became effective in May, 2005. See U.S. Food and Drug Administration, FDA News: FDA Finalizes New Rule on Donor Eligibility for Human Tissue and Cells (May 20, 2004) (available at http://www.fda.gov/bbs/topics/news/2004/NEW01070.html). These donor eligibility rules require testing for specific diseases, including HIV and hepatitis. 21 CFR §§127.45-127.90 (2005). In accompanying non-binding recommendations, the F.D.A. now classifies as "high risk" and ineligible any man who has had sex with another man in the preceding five years — effectively precluding gay men from donating semen. U.S. Department of Health and Human Services, Food and Drug Administration, Center for Biologics and Research, Guidance for Industry: Eligibility Determination for Donors of Human Cells, Tissues, and Cellular and Tissue-Based Products (HCT/Ps) (May 2004) (available at www.fda.gov/cber/gdlns/tissdonor.pdf.).

7. *AIH. Anonymous* distinguishes AID from AIH, a practice sometimes used when the husband's fertility problems consist of a low sperm count or decreased motility. Families might also use AIH when the husband (or other prospective father) faces a life- or health-threatening situation, such as war or illness. Semen stored in advance can be used even after the man's death. See infra section E1b.

In several publicized cases, mix-ups have occurred, resulting in the use of the wrong man's semen — often a man of a different race. E.g., Sara Lyall, British Judge Rules Sperm Donor Is Legal Father in Mix-Up Case, N.Y. Times, Feb. 27, 2003, at A1 (court recognizes Black donor as father of children born, following clinic error, to white couple, who are permitted to retain custody); Avi Salzman, Looking for Answers After a Mistake At the Start of Life, N.Y. Times, July 25, 2004, §14CN, at 1 (reporting African-American woman's decision not to use emergency contraception after physician discovered using wrong semen (probably of a white man) immediately after insemination). How do you explain the frequency of racial differences in the reported mix-ups? See Dorothy Roberts, Killing the Black Body: Race Reproduction, and the Meaning of Liberty 251-252 (1999). See also Leslie Bender, Genes, Parents, and Assisted Reproductive Technologies: ARTs, Mistakes, Sex, Race & Law, 12 Colum. J. Gender & L. 1 (2003); Raizel Liebler, Are You My Parent? Are You My Child? The Role of Genetics and Race in Defining Relationships After Reproductive Technological Mistakes, 5 DePaul J. Health Care L. 15 (2002).

Note: The Rise of Traditional Surrogacy and the *Baby M* Case

In the 1970s, some couples unable to procreate because of the *wife's* infertility, her genetic disease, or her disability also began to turn to artificial insemination. These couples arranged to use the husband's semen to inseminate a willing woman who, following conception and in exchange for compensation, would carry her pregnancy to term for the couple. Then, she would terminate her parental rights to the resulting child so that the biological father's wife could complete adoption proceedings. Pioneered by Michigan attorney Noel Keane, who drafted the first such formal agreement in 1976, these arrangements became known as "surrogate-mother arrangements" or simply "surrogacy arrangements." See generally Lori B. Andrews, Between Strangers: Surrogate Mothers, Expectant Fathers and Brave New Babies (1989).

Surrogacy commanded the national limelight in 1986 when one "surrogate mother," Mary Beth Whitehead, gave birth to a baby girl but refused to relinquish her to the commissioning couple, William and Elizabeth Stern, who had agreed to pay $10,000 to her and $7,500 to the Infertility Center of New York (ICNY), one of Keane's agencies. Although the Sterns prevailed in the trial court, they lost their suit to enforce the surrogacy contract before New Jersey Supreme Court in the famous case In re Baby M, 537 A.2d 1227 (N.J. 1988). Specifically, the state supreme court held that the "surrogacy contract conflicts with: (1) laws prohibiting the use of money in connection with adoptions; (2) laws requiring proof of parental unfitness or abandonment before termination of parental rights is ordered or an adoption is granted; and (3) laws that make surrender of custody and consent to adoption revocable in private placement adoptions." Id. at 1240. The court also emphasized the agreement's inconsistency with public policies that attempt to keep together children and "both of their natural parents." Id. at 1247. While leaving room for unpaid surrogacy by willing parties, the court refused to terminate Whitehead's parental rights over her objection; it recognized William Stern (not Whitehead's husband) as the child's father; and it found that nonenforcement of the contract worked no violation of the Sterns' constitutional rights. Based on the testimony of 11 experts, the court determined that custody with the Sterns would serve the child's best interests. Although the relationship between Whitehead and the Sterns stemmed solely from the agreement they signed at the ICNY, they would henceforth share the rearing of a daughter because, on remand, Whitehead won a gradually increasing visitation schedule. See 14 Fam. L. Rep. (BNA) 1276 (Apr. 12, 1988).

While data showed that the parties perform most surrogacy contracts without resort to litigation, the failed surrogacy arrangement in *Baby M* sparked enormous controversy. Feminists divided, with some advocating a complete ban on surrogacy on the grounds that it commodifies and exploits women and children,[16] reduces women to "baby machines,"[17] subjects them to the patriarchal control of the medical profession,[18] and resembles slavery[19] and prostitution.[20] These critics questioned the very term "surrogate mother," arguing that a woman who gestates a pregnancy and gives birth is simply a mother, without qualification.[21] Others condemned surrogacy's underlying racist and eugenic motivations, pursued at the expense of existing children who need homes.[22] Still others, however, argued that surrogacy restrictions constitute unwarranted intrusion into reproductive autonomy, reflecting gender stereotypes and paternalism.[23] In particular, Professor Marjorie Shultz, urging deference to the intent of the parties, saw in surrogacy a unique opportunity for gender-neutral parentage laws:

> . . . To say that the factual issues are "the same" as if Whitehead and William Stern had simply had a child out of wedlock, ignores the centrally important fact that modern reproductive techniques allow the separation of personal and sexual intimacy from procreation. . . . It ignores that the father here differs in important ways from

[16]. See, e.g., Anita L. Allen, Privacy, Surrogacy, and the *Baby M Case*, 76 Geo. L.J. 1759, 1783, 1791 (1988); Cass R. Sunstein, Neutrality in Constitutional Law (With Special Reference to Pornography, Abortion, and Surrogacy), 92 Colum. L. Rev. 1, 47 (1992).

[17]. See, e.g., Gena Corea, Junk Liberty, in Reconstructing Babylon: Essays on Women and Technology 142, 153-156 (H. Patricia Hynes ed., 1991). See also Robyn Rowland, Living Laboratories: Women and Reproductive Technologies 198 (1992) (use of brain-dead "surrogates" as "female incubators").

[18]. See, e.g., Gena Corea, The Mother Machine: Reproductive Technologies from Artificial Insemination to Artificial Wombs (1985).

[19]. Professor Allen observes that slavery "had the effect of causing black women to become surrogate mothers on behalf of slave owners." Anita L. Allen, Surrogacy, Slavery and the Ownership of Life, 13 Harv. J.L. & Pub. Poly. 132, 140 (1990).

[20]. E.G., Carole Pateman, The Sexual Contract 209-218 (1988); Margaret Jane Radin, Contested Commodities 131-153 (1996).

[21]. E.g., Barbara Katz Rothman, Recreating Motherhood 168-172 (2000).

[22]. Elizabeth S. Anderson, Is Women's Labor a Commodity?, 19 Phil. & Pub. Affairs 71, 91 (1990).

[23]. See, e.g., Debra Satz, Markets in Women's Reproductive Labor, 21 Phil. & Pub. Affairs 107, 117 (1992) ("dilemma for those who wish to use the mother-fetus bond to condemn [surrogacy] contracts while endorsing [privacy] right to choose abortion"); Carmel Shalev, Birth Power 9-10 (1989) ("[A]mid the serious debate on the morality of [all varieties of] medical reproduction, only surrogacy has been addressed in terms of criminal norms. It occurred to me that the reason for this was the untraditional role that women play in these arrangements.").

stereotypical unwed fathers. In particular, it ignores that the child in question exists only because of its progenitors' individual intentions, their reciprocal decisions, and their behavior and expectations in the wake of such decisions. . . .

. . . Unlike biologically-based variables, the capacity to form and express intentions is gender-neutral. [H]aving rejected any role for intention, the court fell back on gender stereotypes to resolve the issues. . . . The court's decision reinforced stereotypes regarding the desirability of segregating women from the market, the unpredictability of women's intentions and decisions, and the givenness of women's biological destiny. Perhaps worst of all, it acted to lock in existing gender-based spheres of influence in our society, refusing to recognize fragile, emergent male efforts to claim a meaningful role in access to and nurture of children. . . .

Marjorie Maguire Shultz, Reproductive Technology and Intent-Based Parethood: An Opportunity for Gender-Neutrality, 1990 Wis. L. Rev. 297, 376-379. But see Pamela Laufer-Ukeles, Essay, Approaching Surrogate Motherhood: Reconsidering Difference, 26 Vt. L. Rev. 407, 436 (2002) (arguing that surrogacy reveals the need for "an asymmetrical notion of [gender] equality").

Consistent with the *Baby M* opinion, many lawmakers and commentators called for legislation — despite deep disagreement about whether such enactments should criminalize, regulate, or protect surrogacy and whether the law of adoption, artificial insemination, or reproductive privacy should provide the governing principles. Even efforts to enact a uniform law in the United States, the Uniform Status of Children of Assisted Conception Act (USCACA), produced two alternatives, with one framework banning surrogacy and the other regulating it. See 9C U.L.A. 383 (2001). About half the states enacted surrogacy statutes. Some outlaw the practice. E.g., N.Y. Dom. Rel. Law §§121-123 (McKinney 1999). Others permit but regulate it. E.g., Fla. Stat. Ann. §63.213 (West 2005) (allowing "preplanned adoption agreement" but not for valuable consideration beyond expenses and with opportunity for mother to rescind within seven days of birth). Others take a permissive stance: For example, Arkansas recognizes the intended parents (including the biological father only if unmarried). Ark. Code Ann. §9-10-201 (2002). And Nevada exempts surrogacy agreements from the ban on payment in adoptive placements. Nev. Rev. Stat. Ann. §127.287(5) (2000).

Other countries also developed legal responses, such as England's Surrogacy Arrangements Act of 1985 and its Human Fertilisation and Embryology Act of 1990. The legal variations, both at home and abroad, raise many classic conflict of laws issues when "surrogates," commissioning couples, and brokers seek hospitable regimes. See, e.g., Hodas v. Morin, 814 N.E.2d 320 (Mass. 2004); Susan Frelich Appleton, Surrogacy Arrangements and the Conflict of Laws, 1990 Wis. L. Rev. 399.

Today, the "traditional surrogacy arrangement" exemplified in *Baby M*, in which the "surrogate mother" provides both genes and gestation, has given way to more technologically sophisticated collaborations made possible by in vitro fertilization (IVF). "Gestational surrogacy arrangements" use ova removed from the intended mother (i.e., Elizabeth Stern in *Baby M*) or from a donor, but not from the woman who will gestate the pregnancy. Although more costly than traditional surrogacy, gestational surrogacy evokes a more favorable legal response in some jurisdictions. As a result, infertility clinics now routinely use gestational surrogacy. See 9B U.L.A. 361 (2001) (prefatory cmt. to Art. 8 of new Uniform Parentage Act). Responding to these developments, a new Uniform Parentage Act (UPA) was drafted to supercede USCACA, supra. See 9B U.L.A. 5-6 (Supp. 2005) (prefatory Note to UPA). For examination of gestational surrogacy and other arrangements employing IVF, including the new UPA's provisions and Israel's approach, see infra section E2c.

Problems

1. Marcia wants to have children but her husband Eric does not. Marcia decides to pursue AID. Although Eric voices his objection, Marcia proceeds. She later gives birth to a son, whom blood tests show cannot be Eric's biological child. In divorce proceedings that begin before the baby's birth, Marcia seeks child support from Eric. She argues the child has a right to support. In claiming that he has no duty to pay, Eric invokes a state statute like the provision of the 1973 Uniform Parentage Act expressly referring to the husband's consent. What result? See In re Marriage of Witbeck-Wildhagen, 667 N.E.2d 122 (Ill. App. Ct. 1996). Cf. K.S. v. G.S., 440 A.2d 64 (N.J. Super. Ct. Ch. Div. 1981); Lane v. Lane, 912 P.2d 290 (N. Mex. Ct. App. 1996). If the family had remained intact until after the child's birth, would the husband's behavior prove relevant? See Brown v. Brown, 125 S.W.3d 840 (Ark. Ct. App. 2003); R.S. v. R.S., 670 P.2d 923 (Kan. Ct. App. 1983); see also §705 Unif. Parentage Act, 9B U.L.A. 41 (Supp. 2005).

Who has the burden of proof on the consent issue? See Jackson v. Jackson, 739 N.E.2d 1203 (Ohio Ct. App. 2000); In re Marriage of M.C., 65 S.W.3d 188 (Tex. App. 2001). Can Eric recover in tort from the physician? Cf. Shin v. Kong, 95 Cal. Rptr. 2d 304 (Ct. App. 2000). See generally Karen DeHaan, Note, Whose Child Am I? A Look at How Consent Affects a Husband's Obligation to Support a Child Conceived Through Heterologous Artificial Insemination, 37 Brandeis L.J. 809 (1998-1999).

2. Suppose the *Baby M* court awards custody to Mary Beth Whitehead. Should it now order William Stern to pay child support? What precedents would compel this result? Alternatively, what risks would such support duties create? What should the legislature say on this subject? See Martha A. Field, Surrogate Motherhood 98-101 (1988). See also J.F. v. D.B. 2006 WL 630009 (Ohio Ct. App. 2006).

b. Creating Nontraditional Families

■ **ELISA B. v. SUPERIOR COURT**
117 P.3d 660 (Cal. 2005)

Review case, reprinted in Chapter IV, p. 478.

■ **GILLETT-NETTING v. BARNHART**
371 F.3d 593 (9th Cir. 2004)

BETTY FLETCHER, Circuit Judge.
Plaintiff-Appellant Rhonda Gillett-Netting, on her own behalf and on behalf of her minor children Juliet O. Netting and Piers W. Netting, appeals the district

court's grant of summary judgment for the Commissioner of Social Security [denying the children's claim for insurance benefits based on the earnings of their deceased father, Robert Netting.][4]

In December 1994, Netting was diagnosed with cancer. At the time, he and his wife, Gillett-Netting, were trying to have a baby together, but Gillett-Netting suffered from fertility problems that had caused her to miscarry twice. Because doctors advised Netting that chemotherapy might render him sterile, he delayed the start of his treatment for several days so that he could deposit his semen at the University of Arizona Health Sciences Center, where it was frozen and stored for later use by his wife. Netting quickly lost his battle with cancer. He died on February 4, 1995, before his wife was able to conceive. Earlier, Netting confirmed that he wanted Gillett-Netting to have their child after his death using his frozen sperm. In-vitro fertilization of Gillett-Netting's eggs with Netting's sperm was undertaken successfully on December 19, 1995. . . . Juliet and Piers Netting were born on August 6, 1996.

On August 19, 1996, Gillett-Netting filed an application on behalf of Juliet and Piers for Social Security child's insurance benefits based on Netting's earnings. [The Social Security Administration (SSA) and later an Administrative Law judge denied the application on the ground the twins were not dependent on Netting at the time he died].

Under the [Social Security] Act, every child is entitled to benefits if the claimant is the child, as defined in 42 U.S.C. §416(e), of an individual who dies fully or currently insured; the child or the child's representative files an application for benefits; the child is unmarried and a minor (or meets disability requirements) at the time of application; and the child was dependent on the insured wage earner at the time of his death. 42 U.S.C. §402(d)(1). It is undisputed that Netting was fully insured under the Act when he died, that Juliet and Piers are his biological children and are unmarried minors, and that Gillett-Netting filed an application for child's insurance benefits on their behalf. . . .

The Act defines "child" broadly to include any "child or legally adopted child of an individual," as well as a stepchild who was the insured person's stepchild for at least nine months before the insured person died, and a grandchild or stepgrandchild of the insured person under certain circumstances. See 42 U.S.C. §416(e). Courts and the SSA have interpreted the word "child" used in the definition of "child" to mean the natural, or biological, child of the insured.

The Commissioner argues and the district court held that "child" is further defined by 42 U.S.C. §§416(h)(2), (3). . . . Under the current version of §416(h), a claimant whose parentage is disputed is deemed to be the child of an insured individual if: (1) the child would be entitled to take an intestate share of the individual's property under the laws of the state in which the individual resided at death; (2) the child's parents went through a marriage ceremony resulting in a purported marriage between them that, but for a legal impediment unknown to them at the time, would have been a valid marriage; (3) the deceased wage earner acknowledged the claimant as his or her child in writing; (4) the deceased wage

---

4. Gillett-Netting also argues that applying the Act to preclude the award of child's insurance benefits to posthumously conceived children violates the children's right to equal protection of the laws. Because we conclude that Juliet and Piers are entitled to benefits under the Act, we do not reach Gillett-Netting's equal protection claim.

earner, before dying, had been decreed by a court to be the parent of the claimant; (5) the deceased wage earner, before dying, had been ordered by a court to contribute to the support of the claimant because the claimant was his or her child; or (6) the insured individual is shown by evidence satisfactory to the Commissioner to have been the parent of the claimant and to have been living with or contributing to the support of the claimant at the time that he died. See U.S.C. §§416 (h)(2), (3).

Although these provisions offer means of "determining whether an applicant is the child . . . of a fully or currently insured individual," id. at §416(h)(2)(A), when parentage is disputed, nothing in the statute suggests that a child must prove parentage under §416(h) if it is not disputed. We conclude that these provisions do not come into play for the purposes of determining whether a claimant is the "child" of a deceased wage earner unless parentage is disputed. In this case, the Commissioner concedes that Juliet and Piers are Netting's biological children. Therefore, we conclude that the district court erred by holding that Juliet and Piers are not Netting's children for the purposes of the Act.

. . . The only remaining issue is whether Juliet and Piers, the undisputed biological children of a deceased, insured individual, are statutorily deemed dependent on Netting without proof of actual dependency. Under the Act, a claimant must show dependency on an insured wage earner in order to be entitled to child's insurance benefits. 42 U.S.C. §402(d)(1). However, the Act statutorily deems broad categories of children to have been dependent on a deceased, insured parent without demonstrating actual dependency. It is well-settled that all legitimate children automatically are considered to have been dependent on the insured individual, absent narrow circumstances not present in this case. Similarly, "illegitimate" children who prove parentage under 42 U.S.C. §§416(h)(2), (3) are "deemed to be the legitimate child of such individual" and, therefore, are deemed to have been dependent on the insured wage earner. 42 U.S.C. §402(d)(3). Thus, the provisions of §416(h) described above typically come into play to prove dependency rather than parentage. . . .

Juliet and Piers are indisputably Netting's legitimate children under the law of the state in which they reside. "Arizona has eliminated the status of illegitimacy[.]" State v. Mejia, 399 P.2d 116 [(Ariz.1965)]. In Arizona, "[e]very child is the legitimate child of its natural parents and is entitled to support and education as if born in lawful wedlock." Ariz. Rev. Stat. §8-601. . . . Under Arizona law, Netting would be treated as the natural parent of Juliet and Piers and would have a legal obligation to support them if he were alive, although they were conceived using in-vitro fertilization, because he is their biological father and was married to the mother of the children. See Ariz. Rev. Stat. §25-501 (providing that children have a right to support from their natural parents; the biological father of a child born using artificial insemination is considered a natural parent if the father is married to the mother). Although Arizona law does not deal specifically with posthumously-conceived children, *every* child in Arizona, which necessarily includes Juliet and Piers, is the legitimate child of her or his natural parents.[7]

---

7. This is not to say that every posthumously-conceived child in Arizona would be eligible for survivorship benefits on the basis of the earnings of the deceased sperm donor. If the sperm donor had not been married to the mother, Arizona would not treat him as the child's natural parent, and he likely would have no obligation to support the child if he were alive. In such circumstances, no eligibility for benefits would exist unless the Commissioner made a determination that the claimant was the

The Commissioner nevertheless argues that Juliet and Piers do not satisfy the "legitimate child" requirement, and therefore cannot be deemed dependent under §402(d)(3), unless they also are able to inherit from Netting under state intestacy laws or meet one of the other provisions of §416(h). This is not the case. Legitimacy in §402(d)(3) is determined in accordance with state law. See Jimenez v. Weinberger, 417 U.S. 628, 635-36 (1974) (noting that children who are considered legitimate under state law are entitled to child's insurance benefits without proving dependency). While §416(h) provides alternative avenues for children to be deemed legitimate, nothing in the Act suggests that a child who is legitimate under state law separately must prove legitimacy under the Act. It would make little sense to require a child whose parents were married to demonstrate legitimacy by showing she meets a test set forth in §416(h), for example by showing that her parent acknowledged her in writing or that a court determined her parentage prior to the parent's death.[8]

Because Juliet and Piers are Netting's legitimate children under Arizona law, they are deemed dependent under §402(d)(3), and need not demonstrate actual dependency nor deemed dependency under the provisions of §416(h). As Netting's legitimate children, Juliet and Piers are conclusively deemed dependent on Netting under the Act and are entitled to child's insurance benefits based on his earnings. . . .

Notes and Questions on *Elisa B.* and *Gillett-Netting*

1. *Unmarried women and AID.* When an unmarried woman uses artificial insemination, does the resulting child have no father on the theory that the law does not recognize semen donors as fathers? If the donor is known, should the law recognize him as the child's father? Note that the term "unmarried women" applies to single women, women in a relationship with a significant other who is not a legal spouse (as in *Elisa B.*), and widows (as in *Gillett-Netting*).

a. *Single women.* Today, a significant number of "single mothers by choice" achieve their goal of having children via donor insemination. See, e.g., Amy Harmon, First Comes the Baby Carriage, N.Y. Times, Oct. 13, 2005, at G1 (reporting support group with 4,000 members); Jennifer Egan, Wanted: A Few Good Sperm, N.Y. Times, Mar. 19, 2006, §6 (Magazine), at 46. Professor Marsha Garrison criticizes as anomalous rules declaring that such children have no legal father because "outside the AID context, our legal system grants no parent, male or female, the right to be a sole parent." Marsha Garrison, Law Making for Baby Making: An Interpretive Approach to the Determination of Legal Parentage, 113 Harv. L. Rev. 835, 906 (2000). Some cases involving known donors have reached results consistent with Garrison's view, invoking the child's best interests.

---

dependent child of the deceased wage earner for purposes of the Act by virtue of satisfying one of the requirements in §416(h).

8. Because Juliet and Piers are Netting's legitimate children under Arizona state law, we need not consider whether they could be deemed dependent for another reason, such as their ability to inherit property from their deceased father under Arizona intestacy laws. See generally Woodward [v. Commission of Soc. Security 760 N.E.2d 257 (Mass. 2002)]. As a practical matter, in most cases legitimate children would be able to inherit under state intestacy laws, but they need not demonstrate their ability to do so in order to be entitled to child's insurance benefits.

See, e.g., C.M. v. C.C., 407 A.2d 849 (N.J. Juv. & Dom. Rel. Ct., Cumberland County 1979) (recognizing donor as father); Ferguson v. McKiernan, 855 A.2d 121 (Pa. Super. Ct. 2004) (requiring known donor to contribute child support because parents cannot bargain away children's rights), *appeal granted*, 868 A.2d 378 (Pa. 2005); In re Sullivan, 157 S.W.3d 911 (Tex. App. 2005) (recognizing donor's standing to establish parentage under UPA). But see Lamaritata v. Lucas, 823 So. 2d 316 (Fla. Dist. Ct. App. 2002). Under California law, a woman can foreclose a known donor's parental status so long as a licensed physician performs the insemination. Compare Steven S. v. Deborah D., 25 Cal. Rptr. 3d 482 (Ct. App. 2005), with Jhordan C. v. Mary K., 224 Cal. Rptr. 530 (Ct. App. 1986).

b. *Women in nonmarital relationships.* How does the reasoning in *Elisa B.* resemble that in In re Adoption of Anonymous, supra? How does it differ? To what extent does the court in *Elisa B.* rely on the parties' relationship? On specific conduct by Elisa? Does such reasoning obviate the need for second-parent adoption, as in Adoption of Tammy, supra, or even same-sex marriage (or domestic partnerships) to secure parental rights?

Courts have relied on conduct to recognize the mother's partner as the parent of a child conceived by donor insemination in several other cases involving both heterosexual and same-sex relationships. See, e.g., In re M.J., 787 N.E.2d 144 (Ill. 2003) (allowing mother to proceed on promissory estoppel claim against male former paramour, who did not provide semen); C.E.W. v. D.E.W., 845 A.2d 1146 (Me. 2004) (recognizing mother's former partner as de facto parent with standing to seek award of parental rights); T.B. v. L.R.M., 786 A.2d 913 (Pa. 2001) (recognizing standing for mother's former partner, in loco parentis), *after remand*, 874 A.2d 34 (Pa. 2005); Tripp v. Hinckley, 736 N.Y.S.2d 506 (App. Div. 2002) (allowing known donor expanded visitation after mother's same-sex relationship ended); In re L.B., 122 P.3d 161 (Wash. 2005) (recognizing mother's former partner as de facto parent); In re Parentage of J.M.K., 119 P.3d 840 (Wash. 2005) (recognizing as father former partner who provided semen used for in vitro fertilization). See also In re Guardianship of I.H., 834 A.2d 922 (Me. 2003) (no notice required for anonymous donor in guardianship proceeding by mother's same-sex partner). Despite the variations, might one read these cases to suggest that the law prefers *two parents* (as Garrison argues) but has become increasingly indifferent about not only the second parent's absence of genetic contribution but also his or her gender? But see Anonymous v. Anonymous, 754 N.Y.S.2d 559 (App. Div. 2003) (rejecting legal status for donor-fiancé); Thomas S. v. Robin Y., 618 N.Y.S.2d 356 (App. Div. 1994) (authorizing filiation order for semen donor, already involved in life of child being reared by two lesbian co-parents); LaChapelle v. Mitten, 607 N.W.2d 151 (Minn. Ct. App. 2000) (approving joint custody to mother and former partner, while recognizing some parental rights for known donor).

c. *Posthumous conception.* To what extent does the law's preference for two parents explain *Gillett-Netting*? Why is the twins' mother not estopped from seeking government benefits for children whom she knew in advance would not have a second parent's support? On what basis did the court find the twins dependent on a father who died before they were conceived? Children born after a parent's death raise several legal issues, as noted below:

2. *Background.* A posthumous child is a child who was conceived before a parent's death but born thereafter. A common law presumption, now codified in

many states, legitimates a child born within nine months after the death of the mother's husband. Reproductive technologies, including cryopreservation of genetic material, have made possible the birth of an increasing number of children who are *conceived* posthumously. The occurrence of posthumous conception is likely to increase during wartime because soldiers often freeze semen before deployment. Finally, physicians can now extract semen from men after death. See Lori B. Andrews, The Clone Age: Adventures in the New World of Reproductive Technology 222-236 (2000) ("the sperminator"); Robert Salladay, Advancing the Issue: Reproduction and the Law; Controversy Continues to Dog a Procedure That Allows Human Embryos to Be Frozen for Use at a Later Date: "Dead Dads" Create Legal Issues, Daily Press, June 16, 2004, at A3 (describing case of daughter born four years after postmortem sperm extraction).

a. *Federal benefits.* Social Security survivors' benefits are available to "dependents" of a deceased wage earner. To qualify for survivors' benefits under the Social Security Act, a child must prove "dependency" on the deceased parent. Legitimate children are presumed dependent, but many states follow the common law approach noted above, which excludes children *conceived after* the parent's death. How does *Gillett-Netting* address this problem?

Gillett-Netting is the culmination of a lengthy battle to secure Social Security survivors' benefits for posthumously conceived children. For earlier cases, see, e.g., In re Estate of Kolacy, 753 A.2d 1257 (N.J. Super. Ch. Div. 2000); Woodward v. Commissioner of Social Sec., 760 N.E.2d 257 (Mass. 2002); see Michael K. Elliott, Tales of Parenthood from the Crypt: The Predicament of the Posthumously Conceived Child, 39 Real Prop. Prob. & Tr. J. 47, 60-62 (2004) (discussing 1991 case, Hart v. Chater).

b. *Inheritance rights.* Only a few states address the issue of the inheritance rights of posthumously conceived children. Some statutes grant rights to such children if the deceased parent gave consent during his lifetime. However, the nature of that consent varies. Compare La. Rev. Stat. Ann. §9:391.1(A) (West Supp. 2006) (requiring the deceased's authorization that his spouse use his gametes), with Tex. Fam. Code Ann. §160.707 (Vernon 2002) (requiring that the deceased spouse "consented in a record that if assisted reproduction were to occur after death the deceased spouse would be a parent of the child"). See also Human Fertilisation and Embryology (Deceased Fathers) Act 2003, Ch. 24 s. 1 (Eng.) (recognizing decedent as father if he previously consented in writing, the woman elects within 42 days of the birth for the decedent to be treated as the father, and no other person is to be treated as the father).

What should the law require for a posthumously conceived child to inherit from this parent's intestate estate? *Woodward*, supra, requires the surviving parent to establish in a timely manner the deceased's genetic relationship and affirmative consent to conceive posthumously and to support the child. 760 N.E.2d at 269. How should the parent manifest consent? Should a presumption of a child's entitlement arise merely from the existence of a parent's cryopreserved reproductive material? See Elliott, supra, at 58. Some states refuse to permit a posthumously conceived child to inherit unless the deceased's will provided for the child. See Fla. Stat. Ann. §742.17(4) (West 2005).

Given that genetic material can be frozen and brought to term years after the deaths of both biological parents, should states require children's claims for inheritance or benefits to commence within a certain time after the parent's death? What period of time would you propose? See Ronald Chester, Posthumously Conceived Heirs under a Revised Uniform Probate Code, 38 Real Prop. Prob. & Tr. J. 727, 736-738 (2004) (proposing a three-year limitation on actions to determine whether posthumous conceived children are "descendants"). See also La. Rev. Stat. Ann. §9:391.1(A) (West Supp. 2006) (requiring that the child be born within three years of the decedent's death).

See generally Charles P. Kindregan & Maureen McBrien, Posthumous Repro-duction, 39 Fam. L.Q. 579 (2005); Julie E. Goodwin, Not All Children are Created Equal: A Proposal to Address Equal Protection Inheritance Rights of Posthumously Conceived Children, 4 Conn. Pub. Int. L.J. 234 (2005); Kristine S. Knaplund, Postmortem Conception and a Father's Last Will, 46 Ariz. L. Rev. 91 (2004); Kayla VanCannon, Note, Fathering a Child from the Grave: What Are the Inheri-tance Rights of Children Born Through New Technology After the Death of a Parent?, 52 Drake L. Rev. 331 (2004).

3. *Genetic connection?* Although the father in *Gillett-Netting* supplied the genetic material, should a biological relationship be essential to the child's status and rights? Should a posthumously conceived child qualify as a dependent for the purpose of federal benefits or inheritance rights if the husband, prior to his death, consented to the wife's use of donor insemination? The new Uniform Par-entage Act (§707) provides:

> If an individual who consented in a record to be a parent by assisted reproduction dies before placement of eggs, sperm, or embryos, the deceased individual is not a parent of the resulting child unless the deceased spouse consented in a record that if assisted reproduction were to occur after death, the deceased individual would be a parent of the child.

9B U.L.A. 43 (Supp. 2005). The comment to this section assumes the use of the deceased's genetic material. Does §707's text clearly impose this requirement? How well does this model provision address the questions raised by posthumous conception?

4. *Property rights.* Posthumous insemination and conception also raise questions about the nature and "ownership" of genetic material. Does one have a right to bequeath such material for use in posthumous reproduction?

Hecht v. Superior Court, 20 Cal. Rptr. 2d 275 (Ct. App. 1993), addressed this question in a will contest between Deborah Hecht, the girlfriend of decedent William Kane, and Kane's adult children from a prior marriage. Before committing suicide, Kane deposited semen in a sperm bank and willed the semen to Hecht. Kane's children urged destruction of the semen, to prevent the birth of children outside "a traditional family" and to protect existing family members from finan-cial and emotional distress. Id. at 279.

The court concluded that "at the time of his death, decedent had an interest, in the nature of ownership, to the extent that he had decisionmaking authority as to the use of his sperm for reproduction. Such interest is sufficient to constitute 'property' within the meaning of [the] Probate Code." Id. at 283. According to the court, California case law and statutes fail to support a public policy against insemination of unmarried women, and Kane's children failed to persuade the court initially that it would be better for a posthumously conceived child not to be born, sufficient to overcome the decedent's decision. The court subsequently ordered release of the sperm to Hecht without deciding whether any resulting child could inherit as Kane's heir. 59 Cal. Rptr. 2d 222, 228 (Ct. App. 1996). See also Hall v. Fertility Inst. of New Orleans, 647 So. 2d 1348 (La. Ct. App. 1994). Cf. Kurchner v. State Farm Fire & Cas. Co., 858 So. 2d 1220 (Fla. Ct. App. 2003) (treating frozen semen as personal property, so that destruction not covered by insurance policy for bodily injury).

5. *"Lifestyle" screening versus access rights.* Should states restrict artificial insemination to traditional families? Some statutes provide that practitioners can perform insemination "only at the request and with the written consent of the husband and wife." See Okla. Stat. Ann. tit. 10 §553 (West 1998). Should recipients receive the same screening and state approval (through judicial proceedings) as adoptive parents?

Do you agree that "lesbians and/or single women are entitled to the full range of reproductive technologies that married couples enjoy access to"? Justyn Lezin, (Mis)Conceptions: Unjust Limitations on Legally Unmarried Women's Access to Reproductive Technology and Their Use of Known Donors,14 Hastings Women's L.J. 185, 189 (2003). Assuming state action, what particular constitutional rights are at stake? See generally Catherine DeLair, Ethical, Moral, Economic and Legal Barriers to Assisted Reproductive Technologies Employed by Gay Men and Lesbian Women, 4 DePaul J. Health Care L. 147 (2000). To what extent is posthumous conception a protected right of the deceased, assuming he chose to father a child after his death? See John A. Robertson, Posthumous Reproduction, 69 Ind. L.J. 1027 (1994). Do the children-to-be have rights or interests at stake justifying state restrictions on access to assisted reproduction? See Helen M. Alvaré, The Turn Toward the Self in the Law of Marriage & Family: Same-Sex Marriage & its Predecessors, 16 Stan. L. & Pol'y Rev. 135, 158-162 (2005). But see John A. Robertson, Gay and Lesbian Access to Assisted Reproductive Technology, 55 Case W. Res. L. Rev. 323, 347 (2004) (noting "non-identity problem" in attempts to justify restrictions to protect children because "the children sought to be protected by banning . . . access to ARTs will not then be born").

May health care professionals not employed by the state decline to perform insemination based on the patient's marital status or sexual orientation? See Holly J. Harlow, Paternalism Without Paternity: Discrimination Against Single Women Seeking Artificial Insemination by Donor, 6 S. Cal. Rev. L. & Women's Stud. 173 (1996); Robertson, Gay and Lesbian Access, supra, at 353-355. Suppose the health care provider asserts a religious belief? In North Coast Women's Care Med. Group, Inc. v. Benitez, 37 Cal. Rptr. 3d 20 (Ct. App. 2005), Guadalupe Benitez sued a medical group and two of its physicians after they declined to perform the interuterine insemination (IUI) that she sought. A lesbian with a domestic partner, Benitez claimed discrimination based on her sexual orientation, which California civil rights statutes make illegal. The evidence showed that the doctors provided other infertility treatment for Benitez and that the physicians might have refused to perform IUI because of her unmarried status (a basis for discrimination now, but not then, prohibited by state civil rights statutes). Despite physicians' affirmative defense invoking the free exercise of religion, Benitez prevailed on her motion for summary adjudication. On appeal, the court directed the lower court to vacate its order and to allow the defendants to present evidence that their religious beliefs prohibited them from performing IUI on *any* unmarried woman, regardless of sexual orientation. Assuming a more fully developed factual record, how would you resolve the competing individual interests?

6. *Implications and policy questions.*

a. *Self-insemination.* Women have long performed insemination themselves, without medical assistance. See, e.g., Francie Hornstein, Children by Donor Insemination: A New Choice for Lesbians, in Rita Arditti, et al., Test-Tube Women: What Future for Motherhood 373, 375 (1984) (citing turkey basters as "now synonymous with self-help insemination"). What are the consequences for attempts to regulate the practice? Note that California law, however, protects the woman from the assertion of parental rights by a known donor only if a physician has performed the procedure. See *Jhordan C.*, supra. Nonetheless, a woman can perform self-insemination with semen from an anonymous donor obtained from a sperm bank. See *North Coast Women's Care Med. Group, Inc.*, supra.

b. *Gender.* What are the implications for gender roles and the traditional family? Judge Posner writes:

> Artificial insemination . . . is rich with social implications. [A]s a practical matter, it places lesbian custody of children beyond the reach of governmental regulation. Beyond that, it allows women to escape having to share parental rights with men, since the sperm donor, whether provided through the woman's physician or through a sperm bank, is anonymous. It therefore accelerates the shift of economic power from men to women. . . .

Richard A. Posner, Sex and Reason 421 (1992). See also Amy Agigian, Baby Steps: How Lesbian Alternative Insemination Is Changing the World (2004).

c. *Commodification.* According to Professor Martha Ertman, sperm banks pay donors about $60 per donation; recipients pay sperm banks between $120 and $275 per vial of semen; once shipping costs and doctor's visits are added, "alternative insemination can cost between $500 and $1,000 for the first insemination and between $300 and $700 for each subsequent insemination"; and most women become pregnant within six attempts. Martha M. Ertman, What's Wrong with a Parenthood Market? A New and Improved Theory of Commodification, 82 N.C.L. Rev. 1, 14-16 (2003). She continues:

> . . . AI is a literal market and a relatively free, open market. . . . Markets, by definition, exist where supply and demand determine prices for the transfer of goods and services. Banks and recipients demand sperm, and donors and banks supply it. Suppliers (donors and sperm banks) transfer sperm on the condition of donor anonymity and indemnity for any injury or illness. Buyers (sperm banks and prospective mothers), in turn, demand medical and social information about the donor, further protections against disease transmission, and anonymity. . . . Moreover, lack of regulation and a relatively low price for the gametes means that it is both an open market in which a large number of people can participate, and a free market that flourishes because of its comparative freedom from regulation. . . .
>
> Alternative insemination generally involves at least two separate transactions. The sperm bank first purchases sperm from a donor and subsequently sells the sperm to a woman who uses it to become a mother. . . . While the transactions differ in important respects, both transactions commodify gametes, and in doing so commodify parental rights and responsibilities. . . .

Id. at 16. Ertman proceeds to highlight both the negative implications of such commodification as well as its benefits, including the facilitation of new family forms. Id. at 26-42. How should the law respond?

d. *Comparison to adoption.* For those considering adoption and donor insemination (e.g., a heterosexual couple with male factor infertility, a single woman, or a lesbian couple), how might the law's approach influence preferences? How do the two ways to become parents compare in terms of cost, state regulation, and risks? What other factors should enter the comparison? The scant empirical data on the preferences of infertile couples reveal adoption as a last resort. Why? See Susan Frelich Appleton, Adoption in the Age of Reproductive Technology, 2004 U. Chi. Legal F. 393, 426-433. The data also show gender differences, including a preference for assisted reproduction with donors over adoption among females and vice versa among males. Id. at 431. For a critique of the status quo and recommendations for law reform, see Elizabeth Bartholet, Family Bonds: Adoption, Infertility, and the New World of Child Production (1999).

Problems

1. Ellen and Lee, cohabiting in an intimate relationship, agreed in writing that Lee would have parental rights to and parental responsibilities for the child that Ellen planned to conceive using semen from an anonymous donor. After the child was born and the adults' relationship deteriorated, Lee unsuccessfully sued for recognition as a parent. Lee now commences a separate suit, seeking enforcement of the agreement or, alternatively, damages for its breach. What result and why? Would the result vary depending upon whether Lee is male or female? Suppose instead that Ellen is the plaintiff, seeking support from Lee for the child? If both Ellen and Lee are women, does the state's law on same-sex relationships affect the result? Why? Compare Dunkin v. Boskey, 98 Cal. Rptr. 2d 44 (Ct. App. 2000), with T.F. v. B.L., 813 N.E.2d 1244 (Mass. 2004), and Wakeman v. Dixon, 921 So. 2d 669 (Fla. Dist. Ct. App. 2006).

2. Lisa and Janet, a lesbian couple living in Virginia, traveled to Vermont, where they celebrated a civil union. After returning to Virginia, they decided to have a child, for whom they would jointly have rearing and financial responsibilities. After Lisa gave birth in Virginia to Isabella (conceived by AID, performed in Virginia) and Virginia enacted several laws limiting the rights of same-sex couples, Lisa, Janet, and the baby all moved to Vermont, in search of a more hospitable environment for their nontraditional family. Subsequently, the adults' relationship deteriorated, and Lisa returned to Virginia with Isabella. Vermont's civil union law, if applicable, would make Janet a second parent of Isabella, just as a husband would be recognized as the legal parent of a child born to his wife. Vt. Stat. Ann. tit. 15, §1204(f) (2002). Virginia law expressly prohibits civil unions, however. Va. Code Ann. §20-45.3 (2004). Janet now seeks visitation with Isabella, over Lisa's objections. Which state should decide this issue? Why? If Janet seeks recognition of her parentage rights in Vermont, who will prevail? If both women dissolved their civil union in a Vermont court, which recognized Janet as a legal parent, must a Virginia court respect that ruling, despite its contrary law and public policy? For the unpublished rulings in this case, see Miller-Jenkins v. Miller-Jenkins, No. 454-11-03 (Fam. Ct. Vt., Nov. 17, 2004); Miller-Jenkins v. Miller-Jenkins,

No. CH04-280 (Ch. Va., Oct. 15, 2004); 32 Fam. L. Rep. (BNA) 1261 (Apr. 11, 2006). See also, e.g., Susan Frelich Appleton, Presuming Women: Revisiting the Presumption of Legitimacy in the Same-Sex Couples Era, 86 B.U. L. Rev. 227 (2006); Helene S. Shapo, Essay, Assisted Reproduction and the Law: Disharmony on a Divisive Social Issue, 100 Nw. U. L. Rev. 465, 473-474 (2006).

2. In Vitro Fertilization

Advances in medicine offer new responses to infertility that go well beyond artificial insemination and traditional surrogacy. Many of these ARTs use or build on in vitro fertilization (literally, fertilization in glass), first successfully used to produce a human birth in 1978. The law has lagged behind medicine, however, leaving important questions unanswered.

a. Expanding Reproductive Privacy

■ **LIFCHEZ v. HARTIGAN**
735 F. Supp. 1361 (N.D. Ill. 1990)

WILLIAMS, Judge.
Dr. Lifchez represents a class of plaintiff physicians who specialize in reproductive endocrinology and fertility counselling. . . . Dr. Lifchez is suing the Illinois Attorney General and the Cook County State's Attorney, seeking a declaratory judgment that [§6(7)] of the Illinois Abortion Law is unconstitutional. . . .

VAGUENESS

Section 6(7) of the Illinois Abortion Law provides as follows:

> No person shall sell or experiment upon a fetus produced by the fertilization of a human ovum by a human sperm unless such experimentation is therapeutic to the fetus thereby produced. Intentional violation of this section is a Class A misdemeanor. Nothing in this subsection (7) is intended to prohibit the performance of in vitro fertilization.

Ill. Rev. Stat., Ch. 38 para. 81-26, §6(7) (1989). Dr. Lifchez claims that the Illinois legislature's failure to define the terms "experimentation" and "therapeutic" renders the statute vague, thus violating his due process rights under the Fourteenth Amendment. . . .

One of the more common procedures performed by reproductive endocrinologists is amniocentesis. Amniocentesis involves withdrawing a portion of the amniotic fluid in order to test it for genetic anomalies. It is performed on women considered to be at risk for bearing children with serious defects. The purpose of the procedure is to provide information about the developing fetus; this information is often used by women in deciding whether or not to have an abortion. Although now routinely performed, amniocentesis could be considered experimental under at least two of Dr. Lifchez' [proposed] definitions: it could be classified as pure research, since there is no benefit to the fetus, the subject being "experimented" on; it could also be experimental . . . if the particular practitioner or clinic were doing it for the first time.

Amniocentesis illustrates well the problem of deciding at what point a procedure graduates from "experimental" to routine. . . . Dr. Lifchez can hardly be expected to know which of his medical activities would be illegal now if he were to look back on the quick evolution of amniocentesis from (very likely) illegal experiment in 1975 to explicitly endorsed "process" in 1985. [B]ecause of the meteoric growth in reproductive endocrinology, any classification of a particular procedure as either "experimental" or "routine" could easily be out-of-date within six months. . . . A statute is unconstitutionally vague if the mere passage of time can transform conduct from being unlawful to lawful. . . .

Many other procedures that Dr. Lifchez performs on his patients could fall within the ambit of §6(7). Among these are in vitro fertilization and the many techniques spawned through research into in vitro fertilization. The difficulty posed by these procedures is not just whether or not they are "experimental," but whether they are "therapeutic to the fetus." . . . In vitro fertilization itself is explicitly permitted by the statute. Related reproductive technologies are less certain. Embryo transfer, for example, involves removal of an embryo from one woman's uterus and placing it in the uterus of a second woman. The variations on this basic technique are considerable. A donated egg could be fertilized in vitro (with a partner's or a donor's sperm), be placed in a second woman's uterus to gestate for five days, and then be flushed out for implantation in the woman trying to get pregnant. That this procedure is experimental is undisputed. Whether it is "therapeutic to the fetus" (actually, embryo . . .) is more complicated. . . . Removing an embryo from one woman's uterus, where it is gestating, for implantation in another woman, may be therapeutic for the woman trying to get pregnant, but it is not necessarily therapeutic for that embryo. . . .

[The court concluded that the scienter requirement in §6(7) did not save it from being unconstitutionally vague.]

REPRODUCTIVE PRIVACY

Section 6(7) of the Illinois Abortion Law is also unconstitutional because it impermissibly restricts a woman's fundamental right of privacy, in particular, her right to make reproductive choices free of governmental interference with those choices. Various aspects of this reproductive privacy right have been articulated in a number of landmark Supreme Court cases [citing *Griswold*, *Eisenstadt*, and *Roe*, all included in Chapter I, section A].

Section 6(7) intrudes upon this "cluster of constitutionally protected choices." Embryo transfer and chorionic villi sampling [a method of prenatal testing for birth defects] are illustrative. Both procedures are "experimental" by most definitions of that term. Both are performed directly, and intentionally, on the fetus. Neither procedure is necessarily therapeutic to the fetus. . . .

Both procedures, however, fall within a woman's zone of privacy as recognized in Roe v. Wade, Carey v. Population Services International, [431 U.S. 678 (1977),] and their progeny. Embryo transfer is a procedure designed to enable an infertile woman to bear her own child. It takes no great leap of logic to see that within the cluster of constitutionally protected choices that includes the right to have access to contraceptives, there must be included within that cluster the right to submit to a medical procedure that may bring about, rather than prevent, pregnancy. Chorionic villi sampling is similarly protected. The cluster of constitutional choices that includes the right to abort a fetus within the first trimester must also include the right to submit to a procedure designed to give information about that fetus which can then lead to a decision to abort. Since there is no compelling state interest sufficient to prevent a woman from terminating her pregnancy during the first trimester, there can be no such interest sufficient to intrude upon these other protected activities during the first trimester. By encroaching upon this protected zone of privacy, §6(7) is unconstitutional. . . .

Notes and Questions

1. *Procreative liberty.* *Lifchez* relies on Roe v. Wade, Chapter I, section A2, to conclude that the right to privacy protects use of and access to reproductive technologies. The leading proponent of this position, Professor John Robertson, has written that "procreative liberty is a deeply held moral and legal value that deserves a strong measure of respect in all reproductive activities [to be] equally honored when reproduction requires technological assistance." John A. Robertson, Children of Choice: Freedom and The New Reproductive Technologies 4 (1994). Robertson's book goes on to advocate reproductive autonomy for seven major reproductive technologies, including in vitro fertilization (IVF) and forms of collaborative reproduction, that is, procreation that requires contribution from parties other than the intended parents.

2. *Abortion underpinnings.* *Lifchez* relies in part on Roe v. Wade to recognize a right to productive privacy. To what extent does the legal status of IVF depend on the continued vitality of *Roe*? Some states are now outlawing all but life-saving abortions to challenge the Supreme Court to overrule *Roe*. See Monica Davey, South Dakota Bans Abortion, Setting Up a Battle, N.Y. Times, March 7, 2006, A1. The new South Dakota ban, for example, finds that "each human being is totally unique immediately at fertilization" and seeks to protect "unborn human beings." H.B. 1215, 81st Leg. Ass., 2006 Reg. Session (S.D. 2006) (signed by Gov. March 6, 2006, and to be classified as S.D. Laws Chap. 22-17). What are the implications for IVF?

3. *Moral and ethical objections.* Assuming a constitutional right to use reproductive technologies like IVF exists, what state interests justify its infringement? Does the goal of bringing as least some IVF-created embryos to term make inapplicable the asserted state interests behind the South Dakota abortion ban, supra?

Feminist Gena Corea raises moral and ethical objections to IVF, claiming that it exploits women. See Gena Corea, The Mother Machine: Reproductive Technologies from Artificial Insemination to Artificial Wombs 100-134 (1985). The Catholic Church has found IVF morally illicit because it deprives the child *"of being the result and fruit of a conjugal act* in which spouses can become 'cooperators with God for giving life to a new person.'" Congregation for the Doctrine of the Faith, Instruction on Respect for Human Life in its Origin and on the Dignity of Procreation: Replies to Certain Questions of the Day 29-31 (1987). On the other hand, a British commission concluded the practice is ethically acceptable. Department of Health & Social Security, Report of the Committee of Inquiry into Human Fertilisation and Embryology 31-34 (Chairman: Dame Mary Warnock DBE) (Presented to Parliament by Command of Her Majesty, July 1984). Can moral and ethical objections to IVF support state prohibitions? Cf. Stenberg v. Carhart (Chapter I, section A3, and Lawrence v. Texas, Chapter I, section A4.

4. *Health and safety.* Could IVF be banned or restricted to protect the health of the children-to-be? How does one assess harm to a not-yet-conceived individual who would not exist without the technology? See Philip G. Peters, Jr., How Safe Is Safe Enough?: Obligations to the Children of Reproductive Technology (2004). Hormones used to induce superovulation can produce dangerous multifetal pregnancies requiring "selective abortion" (killing some fetuses to improve the chances for others) or creating significant risks of premature birth and neurological problems, in addition to health dangers for the mother. See, e.g., Lars Noah, Assisted Reproductive Technologies and the Pitfalls of Unregulated Biomedical Innovation, 55 Fla. L. Rev. 603 (2003).

In addition, some data indicate that children of IVF suffer a disproportionate incidence of birth defects. See Robin Fretwell Wilson, Uncovering the Rationale for Requiring Infertility in Surrogacy Arrangements, 29 Am. J.L. & Med. 337, 343-347 (2003). Particular concerns have been prompted by intracytoplasmic sperm injection (ICSI), which entails the injection of a single sperm into the center of an ovum and allows, for example, a man with a very low sperm count to become a genetic father. The process may allow fertilization (in vitro) with unsuitable sperm and risks transmission of genetic abnormalities causing the underlying infertility. ICSI has flourished in the absence of any longitudinal studies about its safety. The President's Council on Bioethics, Reproduction and Responsibility: The Regulation of New Biotechnologies 39-40 (2004).

5. *Prenatal testing. Lifchez* observes that prenatal testing, like other reproductive technologies, is not beneficial to the embryo or fetus. Do parents have a right to such tests to enable them to select the characteristics of their children (or to terminate pregnancies when gestating a fetus with undesired problems)? Today, preimplantation genetic diagnosis (PGD) of embryos created in vitro together with new information from the Human Genome Project are increasing such choices. See, e.g., Lee M. Silver, Remaking Eden: How Genetic Engineering and Cloning Will Transform the American Family 266-280 (1998) ("the designer child"); Maxwell J. Mehlman, The Law of Above Averages: Leveling the New Genetic Enhancement Playing Field, 85 Iowa L. Rev. 517 (2000). See also Michael J. Sandel, The Case Against Perfection, The Atlantic, Apr. 2004, at 50; Kelly M. Plummer, Comment, Ending Parents' Unlimited Power to Choose: Legislation Is Necessary to Prohibit Parents' Selection of Their Children's Sex and Characteristics, 47 St. Louis U. L.J. 517 (2003). Does the Americans with Disabilities Act restrict physicians' discretion to turn away ARTs patients with disabilities in order to prevent the birth of children with disabilities? See Carl H. Coleman, Conceiving Harm: Disability Discrimination in Assisted Reproductive Technologies, 50 UCLA L. Rev. 17, 60-67 (2002).

Prenatal testing, including amniocentesis and chorionic villi sampling, began to flourish after *Roe*'s legalization of abortion. Such testing and the larger practice of genetic counseling became a form of defensive medicine as families successfully sued for "wrongful birth," claiming that professional negligence resulted in the birth of a child with handicaps whom the parents, if properly informed, would have aborted. E.g., Bader v. Johnson, 732 N.E.2d 1212 (Ind. 2000); Berman v. Allan, 404 A.2d 8 (N.J. 1979). Courts have been less hospitable to "wrongful life" claims brought on behalf of the afflicted child. Compare, e.g., Hester v. Dwivedi,

733 N.E.2d 1161 (Ohio 2000), with Procanik v. Cillo, 478 A.2d 755 (N.J. 1984). See generally Elizabeth Weil, A Wrongful Birth?, N.Y. Times, March 12, 2006, §6 (Magazine), at 48. To whom do health professionals performing genetic testing and counseling owe a duty of care? All the members of the patient's family who might carry or pass on the gene or chromosomal abnormality? See Molloy v. Meier, 679 N.W.2d 711 (Minn. 2004).

Lifchez treats these technologies as a positive development, enhancing reproductive autonomy. Are there negative consequences for pregnant women, who are asked "to accept their pregnancies and their babies . . . and yet be willing to abort the genetically damaged fetus"? Barbara Katz Rothman, The Tentative Pregnancy: How Amniocentesis Changes the Experience of Motherhood 6 (1993).

6. *Feminist perspectives.* Some feminists condemn IVF. Professor Dorothy Roberts observes that "new reproductive technologies, such as in vitro fertilization and surrogacy, function primarily to fulfill men's desires for genetically related offspring." Dorothy E. Roberts, The Genetic Tie, 62 U. Chi. L. Rev. 209, 239 (1995). See also, e.g., Elizabeth Bartholet, Family Bonds: Adoption and the Politics of Parenting 187-229 (1999); Corea, supra; Robyn Rowland, Living Laboratories: Women and Reproductive Technologies (1992). Reports from Egypt substantiate this hypothesis. There, infertile husbands, whose wives could have conceived while young but became too old to bear children, are leaving these wives and remarrying women of reproductive age with whom they can use ICSI to father biological children. Marcia C. Inhorn, Global Infertility and the Globalization of New Reproductive Technologies: Illustrations from Egypt, 56 Soc. Sci. & Med. 1837, 1846 (2003).

What legal conclusions for IVF follow from feminist critiques? A ban on these procedures? Government intervention through mandated warnings to ensure "informed" consent, as some states require for abortions? If the state can outlaw surrogacy in part to protect even those women who want to participate (see supra p.1109), can it not outlaw IVF despite the wishes of otherwise infertile women? Could women bring a successful sex discrimination challenge to such laws? Or do technologies such as IVF, in contrast to abortion, perpetuate a stereotypical view of women? Suppose some women yearn to contribute to this stereotype?

7. *Infertility and gender.* Both women and men react to infertility with strong emotions. But data suggest gender differences:

> Although men considered childlessness as a painful experience, it did not preclude a full and enjoyable life. . . . Wives spoke of enjoying their quality of life, but described something as missing. [For women, infertility] overtook other aspects of life. It was a continuous, biopsychosocial, spiritual struggle; a loss; a feeling of being passed by; and a feeling of incompleteness or emptiness. . . .

Su An Arnn Phipps, A Phenomenological Study of Couples' Infertility: Gender Influence, 7 Holistic Nurse Prac. 44, 46-47 (1993). See also Judith Daniluk & Joss Hurtig-Mitchell, Themes of Hope and Healing: Infertile Couples' Experiences of Adoption, 81 J. Counseling & Dev. 389, 392 (2003); Laurie Tarkan, Fertility Clinics Begin to Address Mental Health, N.Y. Times, Oct. 8, 2002, at F5. For an historical examination, see generally Elaine Tyler May, Barren in the Promised Land: Childless Americans in Pursuit of Happiness (1995).

Are women to blame for their own infertility? Pointing to inadequate leave policies, childcare, and shared parenting by men, sociologist Barbara Katz Rothman writes:

> Shall we blame the woman for putting off childbearing while she became a lawyer, art historian, physician, set designer, or engineer? Or shall we blame the system that makes it so very difficult for young lawyers, art historians, physicians, set designers, and engineers to have children without wives to care for them? Men did not have to delay entry into parenthood for nearly as many years in the pursuit of their careers as women do now. It is easier to blame the individual woman than to understand the political and economic context in which she must act, but it does not make for good social policy.

Barbara Katz Rothman, Recreating Motherhood 98 (2000). See also Chapter III, section B6b.

7. *The regulatory scheme.*

a. *Laissez-faire approach.* Whatever the concerns prompted by IVF, a laissez-faire approach to assisted reproduction prevails in the United States, with any limits left up to the market — health care providers, fertility clinics, and patients desperate to explore every possible route to procreation. See Susan Frelich Appleton, Adoption in the Age of Reproductive Technology, 2004 U. Chi. Legal F. 393, 421-426. In the one notable exception to this self-regulation, federal legislation (designed in part to develop "informed consumers") requires ARTs programs to report their pregnancy rates to the Department of Health and Human Services for annual publication and distribution to the public. 42 U.S.C. §§263a-1 to 263a-7 (2000). See U.S. Department of Health and Human Services, Centers for Disease Control and Prevention, Assisted Reproductive Technology Success Rates, 2003 National Summary and Fertility Clinic Reports (December 2005). The required information now includes the number of singleton (as distinguished from multiple) pregnancies and births. Lyria Bennett Moses, Understanding Legal Responses to Technological Change: The Example of In Vitro Fertilization, 6 Minn. J. L. Sci. & Tech. 505, 590 (2005). For a summary of the patchwork of state regulations, including, for example, New Hampshire's time limits on embryo storage and Pennsylvania's reporting requirements, see id. at 537-538.

b. *Other countries.* Once a country famous for reproductive innovation, Italy now takes a much more restrictive approach, with laws prohibiting the freezing and testing of embryos and limiting the number of harvested eggs to three. Elisabeth Rosenthal & Elisabetta Povoledo, Vote on Fertility Law Fires Passions in Italy, N.Y. Times, June 11, 2005, at A7. A referendum to repeal the law failed because 50 percent of the eligible voters declined to participate after the Vatican urged a boycott. See Ian Fisher, Italian Vote to Ease Fertility Law Fails for Want of Voters, N.Y. Times, June 14, 2005, at A11.

In examining the specific issue of regulation designed to address the problem of multifetal pregnancies, one writer has identified the following approaches among common law countries: "professional guidelines supplemented by government intervention (United States [which requires information disclosure, noted supra]), professional guidelines with strong incentives to comply (New South Wales), professional guidelines with mandated compliance (Victoria), and regulation by a government authority using a clear rule (United Kingdom)." Moses, supra, at 603-604. Several European countries (Austria, Germany, Ireland, and Switzerland) ban PGD while others (Belgium, Greece, Holland, Italy, Norway, and the United Kingdom) restrict it to medical uses. Bratislav Stankovic, "It's a Designer Baby!": Opinions on Regulation of Preimplantation Genetic Diagnosis, 2005 UCLA J.L. Tech. 3, 50 (2005). See generally David Adamson, Regulation of Assisted Reproductive Technologies in the United States, 39 Fam. L.Q. 727, 739-742 (2005) (international comparisons); Erik Parens & Lori P. Knowles, Reprogenetics and Public Policy: Reflections and Recommendations, Hastings Center Report Supp. S15-S17 (July–Aug. 2003) (examining regulations in United Kingdom and Canada). Worldwide, the differences in laws as well as costs have prompted the rise of "reproductive tourism." See, e.g., Felicia R. Lee, Driven by Costs, Fertility Clients Head Overseas, N.Y. Times, Jan. 25, 2005, at A1; Debora Spar, Perspective: Reproductive Tourism and the Regulatory Map, 352 New Eng. J. Med. 531 (2005).

c. *Recommendations.* The President's Council on Bioethics proposes federally funded data collection to assess the effects of IVF and related procedures on women and the resulting children. The President's Council on Bioethics, supra, at 39-44, 195-198, 210-212. Professor Jennifer Rosato recommends a two-tiered approach under which states would adopt restrictions designed to address the greatest hazards (e.g., limiting the number of embryos implanted to no more than three per cycle), complemented by federal oversight. Jennifer Rosato, The Children of ART (Assisted Reproductive Technology): Should the Law Protect Them From Harm?, 2004 Utah L. Rev. 57.

8. *Paying for IVF.* Is infertility an "illness" and IVF a "treatment" therefor? The issue arises in determining whether the procedure is covered by medical insurance that reimburses only treatment of illness. See Egert v. Connecticut General Life Ins. Co., 900 F.2d 1032 (7th Cir. 1990). Some successful challenges to restrictive insurance coverage have been brought under the Americans with Disabilities Act. See, e.g., Pacourek v. Inland Steel Co., 858 F. Supp. 1393 (N.D. Ill. 1994); 916 F. Supp. 797 (N.D. Ill. 1996). See also Bragdon v. Abbott, 524 U.S. 624 (1998). But see Krauel v. Iowa Methodist Med. Ctr., 95 F.3d 674 (8th Cir. 1996). See generally Karen L. Goldstein & Caryn H. Okinaga, Assisted Reproductive Technology, 3 Geo. J. Gender & L. 409, 432-437 (2002) (summarizing pertinent statutes and cases). A Connecticut statute, effective in 2005, requires insurance coverage for two cycles of IVF (with no more than two preembryos implanted per cycle) but only for women no older 40 years of age. Conn. Gen. Stat. §38a-509 (available on Westlaw, 2006). What reasons explain this particular legislative response? What concerns does it raise? See Bartholet, supra, at 213-214 (criticizing move toward mandated insurance coverage for IVF, because it "would simply stack the deck even more in favor of procreation," rather than adoption).

Beyond questions of insurance, can patients deduct the costs of infertility treatment as medical expenses on their tax returns? See Katherine T. Pratt, Inconceivable? Deducting the Costs of Fertility Treatment, 89 Cornell L. Rev. 1121 (2004); Anna L. Benjamin, The Implications of Using the Medical Expense Deduction of I.R.C. §213 to Subsidize Assisted Reproductive Technology, 79 Notre Dame L. Rev. 1117 (2004).

Should Medicaid provide assistance for poor persons seeking fertility treatments? What consequences follow from the prevailing approach, under which Medicaid benefits do not cover IVF and most private physicians are unwilling to serve Medicaid recipients? See Dorothy Roberts, Killing the Black Body: Race, Reproduction, and the Meaning of Liberty 253 (1999) (most Blacks excluded from access).

Problems

1. Melinda's employer, a state university, fires her because she used so many of her available sick leave and vacation days, usually in half-day increments, to undergo (so far unsuccessful) fertility treatments. Melinda sues the university, claiming that her termination violates the Pregnancy Discrimination Act. The university moves to dismiss, arguing the PDA does not apply. What result? Would the Family and Medical Leave Act provide protection for Melinda's job? (For the PDA and FMLA, see Chapter III, section B6.) See Erickson v. Board of Governors, 911 F. Supp. 316 (N.D. Ill. 1995), *rev'd on other grounds*, 207 F.3d 945 (7th Cir. 2000), *cert. denied sub nom.* United States v. Board of Governors, 531 U.S. 1190 (2001). But see Saks v. Franklin Covey Co., 316 F.3d 337 (2d Cir. 2003).

2. You work in the general counsel's office of a large university, whose medical school has a successful program offering patients assisted reproductive technologies, including IVF. The program's directors consult your office about whether they may decline to provide services to HIV-positive women. What reasons, if any, would justify the exclusion of HIV-positive women? What legal and ethical considerations would enter your analysis? What advice would you give? See Nanette R. Elster, HIV and ART: Reproductive Choices and Challenges, 19 J. Contemp. Health L. & Pol'y 415 (2003).

b. Deciding the Fate of Frozen Preembryos

■ **A.Z. v. B.Z.**
725 N.E.2d 1051 (Mass. 2000)

COWIN, J.

We . . . consider for the first time the effect of a consent form between a married couple and an in vitro fertilization (IVF) clinic (clinic) concerning the disposition of frozen preembryos [at the time of the couple's divorce.] The husband [A.Z.] and wife [B.Z.] were married in 1977. For the first two years of their marriage they resided in Virginia, where they both served in the armed forces. [They moved to Maryland and later to Massachusetts. They experienced fertility problems, including failure to achieve pregnancy with medical assistance, ectopic pregnancies, and removal of wife's fallopian tubes, before they turned to IVF, using wife's ova and husband's sperm.] They underwent IVF treatment from 1988 through 1991. As a result of the 1991 treatment, the wife conceived and gave birth to twin daughters in 1992. During the 1991 IVF treatment, more preembryos were formed than were necessary for immediate implantation, and two vials of preembryos were frozen for possible future implantation.

In the spring of 1995, before the couple separated, the wife desired more children and had one of the remaining vials of preembryos thawed and one preembryo was implanted. [No pregnancy resulted. The husband first learned of this attempt] when he received a notice from his insurance company regarding the procedure. During this period relations between the husband and wife deteriorated. The wife sought and received a protective order against the husband. . . .

Ultimately, they separated and the husband filed for divorce [while] one vial containing four frozen preembryos remained in storage at the clinic. . . .

In order to participate in fertility treatment, including . . . IVF, the clinic required egg and sperm donors (donors) to sign certain consent forms for the relevant procedures. . . . The only forms that both the husband and the wife were required to sign were those entitled "Consent Form for Freezing (Cyropreservation) of Embryos" (consent form), one of which is the form at issue here.

Each consent form explains the general nature of the IVF procedure and outlines the freezing process, including the financial cost and the potential benefits and risks of that process. The consent form also requires the donors to decide the disposition of the frozen preembryos on certain listed contingencies: "wife or donor" reaching normal menopause or age forty-five years; preembryos no longer being healthy; "one of us dying"; "should we become separated"; "should we both die." Under each contingency the consent form provides the following as options for disposition of the preembryos: "donated or destroyed — choose one or both." A blank line beneath these choices permits the donors to write in additional alternatives not listed as options on the form, and the form notifies the donors that they may do so. The consent form also informs the donors that they may change their minds as to any disposition, provided that both donors convey that fact in writing to the clinic. . . .

. . . Every time before eggs were retrieved from the wife and combined with sperm from the husband, they each signed a consent form. The husband was present when the first form was completed by the wife in October, 1988. They both signed that consent form after it was finished. The form, as filled out by the wife, stated, inter alia, that if they "should become separated, [they] both agree[d] to have the embryo(s) . . . return[ed] to [the] wife for implant." The husband and wife thereafter underwent six additional egg retrievals for freezing and signed six additional consent forms. . . .

Each time after signing the first consent form in October, 1988, the husband always signed a blank consent form. . . . Each time, after the husband signed the form, the wife filled in the disposition and other information, and then signed the form herself. . . . In each instance the wife specified in the option for "should we become separated," that the preembryos were to be returned to the wife for implantation. . . .

. . . The probate judge [below] determined that the "best solution" was to balance the wife's interest in procreation against the husband's interest in avoiding procreation. Based on his findings, the judge determined that the husband's interest in avoiding procreation outweighed the wife's interest in having additional children and granted the permanent injunction in favor of the husband.

. . . While IVF has been available for over two decades and has been the focus of much academic commentary, there is little law on the enforceability of agreements concerning the disposition of frozen preembryos. Only three States have enacted legislation addressing the issue [citing statutes from Florida, New Hampshire, and Louisiana]. Two State courts of last resort, the Supreme Court of Tennessee and the Court of Appeals of New York, have dealt with the enforceability [after divorce] of agreements between donors regarding the disposition of preembryos and have concluded that such agreements should ordinarily be enforced. [I]n Davis v. Davis 842 S.W.2d 588 (Tenn. 1992), *cert. denied sub nom.* Stowe v. Davis, 507 U.S. 911, (1993), [the] wife sought to donate the preembryos at issue to another couple for implantation. The court stated that agreements between donors regarding disposition of the preembryos "should be presumed valid and should be enforced." 842 S.W.2d at 597. In that case, because there was no agreement between the donors regarding disposition of the preembryos, the court balanced the equitable interests of the two parties and concluded that the husband's interest in avoiding parenthood outweighed the wife's interest in donating the preembryos to another couple for implantation. Id. at 603.

The Court of Appeals of New York, in Kass v. Kass, [696 N.E.2d 174 (N.Y. 1998,] agreed with the Tennessee court's view that courts should enforce agreements where potential parents provide for the disposition of frozen preembryos. . . . The wife sought custody of the preembryos for implantation. According to the New York court, agreements "should generally be presumed valid and binding, and enforced in any dispute between [the donors]." . . . Therefore the court enforced the agreement that provided that the frozen preembryos be donated to the IVF clinic.

. . . This is the first reported case involving the disposition of frozen preembryos in which a consent form signed between the donors on the one hand and the clinic on the other provided that, on the donors' separation, the preembryos were to be given to one of the donors for implantation. In view of the purpose of the form (drafted by and to give assistance to the clinic) and the circumstances of execution, we are dubious at best that it represents the intent of the husband and the wife regarding disposition of the preembryos in the case of a dispute between them. In any event, for several independent reasons, we conclude that the form should not be enforced in the circumstances of this case.

First, the consent form's primary purpose is to explain to the donors the benefits and risks of freezing, and to record the donors' desires for disposition of the frozen preembryos at the time the form is executed in order to provide the clinic with guidance if the donors (as a unit) no longer wish to use the frozen preembryos. The form does not state, and the record does not indicate, that the husband and wife intended the consent form to act as a binding agreement between them should they later disagree as to the disposition. . . .

Second, the consent form does not contain a duration provision. . . . Third, the form uses the term "should we become separated" in referring to the disposition of the frozen preembryos without defining "become separated." Because this dispute arose in the context of a divorce, we cannot conclude that the consent form was intended to govern in these circumstances. Separation and divorce have distinct legal meanings. . . .

The donors' conduct in connection with the execution of the consent forms also creates doubt whether the consent form at issue here represents the clear intentions of both donors. . . . A clinic representative told her that "she could cross out any of the language on the form and fill in her own [language] to fit [the wife's] wishes." Further, although the wife used language in each subsequent form similar to the language used in the first form that she and her husband signed together, the consent form at issue here was signed in blank by the husband, before the wife filled in the language indicating that she would use the preembryos for implantation on separation. . . . Finally, the consent form is not a separation agreement that is binding on the couple in a divorce proceeding pursuant to G. L. c. 208, §34. The consent form does not contain provisions for custody, support, and maintenance, in the event that the wife conceives and gives birth to a child.

With this said, we conclude that, even had the husband and the wife entered into an unambiguous agreement between themselves regarding the disposition of the frozen preembryos, we would not enforce an agreement that would compel one donor to become a parent against his or her will.[22] As a matter of public policy, we conclude that forced procreation is not an area amenable to judicial enforcement. It is well-established that courts will not enforce contracts that violate public policy. . . .

The Legislature has already determined by statute that individuals should not be bound by certain agreements binding them to enter or not enter into familial relationships. [T]he Legislature abolished the cause of action for the breach of a promise to marry [and] provided that no mother may agree to surrender her child "sooner than the fourth calendar day after the date of birth of the child to be adopted" regardless of any prior agreement. . . . In our decisions, we have also indicated a reluctance to enforce prior agreements that bind individuals to future family relationships. In R. R. v. M. H., 689 N.E.2d 790 (1998), we held that a surrogacy agreement in which the surrogate mother agreed to give up the child on its birth is unenforceable unless the agreement contained, inter alia, a "reasonable" waiting period during which the mother could change her mind. . . .

We glean from these statutes and judicial decisions that prior agreements to enter into familial relationships (marriage or parenthood) should not be enforced against individuals who subsequently reconsider their decisions. This enhances the "freedom of personal choice in matters of marriage and family life." Moore v. East Cleveland, 431 U.S. 494, 499 (1977), quoting Cleveland Bd. of Educ. v. LaFleur, 414 U.S. 632, 639-640 (1974). . . .

In this case, we are asked to decide whether the law of the Commonwealth may compel an individual to become a parent over his or her contemporaneous objection. . . . Enforcing the [1991 consent form against the husband] would require him to become a parent over his present objection to such an undertaking. We decline to do so. . . .

Notes and Questions

1. *Cryopreservation.* Despite the disputes it can produce, cryopreservation of preembryos offers several advantages. It allows a woman to attempt to achieve pregnancy on several successive occasions without repeating surgery to remove ova. This process also allows for the possibility of replacing preembryos during a spontaneous ovulatory cycle and avoids the risk of multiple pregnancy that inheres in the simultaneous use of numerous preembryos. The Ethics Committee of the American Fertility Society, Ethical Considerations of the New Reproductive Technologies, 53 Fertility and Sterility 58S (Supp. 2 1990). Finally, the process allows for posthumous reproduction by women. See Anne Reichman Schiff, Arising from the Dead: Challenges of Posthumous Procreation, 75 N.C. L. Rev. 901 (1997).

22. . . . We express no view regarding whether an unambiguous agreement between two donors concerning the disposition of frozen preembryos could be enforced over the contemporaneous objection of one of the donors, when such agreement contemplated destruction or donation of the preembryos either for research or implantation in a surrogate. . . .

2. *Classifying embryos.* Early disputes sought to classify frozen preembroyos. In Del Zio v. Presbyterian Hospital, 1978 U.S. Dist. LEXIS 14450 (S.D. N.Y. 1978), a couple won $50,000 for the deliberate destruction of a culture containing their eggs and sperm by health care providers who questioned the safety of this then-untried procedure. The jury based its award on plaintiffs' claims for emotional distress, while rejecting their claims for conversion of property. Are embryos property? Compare York v. Jones, 717 F. Supp. 421 (E.D. Va. 1989) (property), with Davis v. Davis, 842 S.W.2d 588, 594-597 (Tenn. 1992) (interim category between "persons" and "property"). Should frozen embryos and frozen sperm be classified the same way? See Hecht v. Superior Ct., 20 Cal. Rptr. 2d 275, 283 (Ct. App. 1993) (relying on *Davis* to conclude that decedent had ownership interest in his frozen sperm at the time of his death sufficient to constitute "property" within Probate Code). See generally Katheleen R. Guzman, Property, Progeny, Body Part: Assisted Reproduction and the Transfer of Wealth, 31 U.C. Davis L. Rev. 193 (1997); Kermit Roosevelt III, The Newest Property: Reproductive Technologies and the Concept of Parenthood, 39 Santa Clara L. Rev. 79 (1998).

Louisiana has a statutory scheme defining the "in vitro fertilized human ovum" as both a "juridical person" until implanted and a "biological human being" and entitling "such ovum to sue or be sued." La. Rev. Stat. Ann. §§9:121-9:124 (2000). The law prohibits intentional destruction of "viable" fertilized ova, explaining that "[a]n in vitro fertilized human ovum that fails to develop further over a thirty-six hour period except when the embryo is in a state of cryopreservation, is considered non-viable and is not a juridical person." Id. at §9:129. The statute makes available for "adoptive implantation" those fertilized ova for which the IVF patients have renounced their own parental rights for in utero implantation. Id. at §9:130. The law precludes inheritance rights for an ovum unless live birth occurs. Id. at §9:133. Louisiana applies the "best interest of the in vitro fertilized ovum" test in any disputes. Id. at §9:131. Does this test mean that the party seeking implantation must prevail? The trial court in *Davis* so ruled. See 842 S.W.2d at 594. See Diane K. Yang, Note, What's Mine Is Mine, but What's Yours Should Also Be Mine: An Analysis of State Statutes That Mandate the Implantation of Frozen Preembryos, 10 J.L. & Pol'y 587 (2002).

3. *Precommitment strategies versus contemporaneous consent.* Before A.Z., most authorities assumed that agreements and consent forms signed by the "progenitors" would determine the disposition of frozen embryos. A.Z. reviews the case law that led many IVF clinics to obtain agreements designed to prevent future disputes about disposition. Why does A.Z. decline to follow the statement on the consent form? More generally, why does A.Z. say that courts should not enforce precommitment strategies, that is, advance directives, to determine the disposition of embryos? The approach adopted by A.Z., requiring contemporaneous mutual consent, derives from an analysis by Professor Carl Coleman. Carl H. Coleman, Procreative Liberty and Contemporaneous Choice: An Inalienable Rights Approach to Frozen Embryo Disputes, 84 Minn. L. Rev. 55 (1999). See also, e.g., In re Marriage of Witten, 672 N.W.2d 768 (Iowa 2003). What implications does this approach have for the trend toward "private ordering" in family law?

Do you agree with A.Z.'s statement that contemporaneous mutual consent safeguards reproductive autonomy ("freedom of personal choice in matters of marriage and family life")? Criticizing A.Z., Professor John Robertson asserts that "a main argument for enforcing precommitments for disposition of frozen embryos is the importance of the freedom that it provides individuals at Time A to control or restrain future reproductive choices at Time B." John A. Robertson, Precommitment Strategies for Disposition of Frozen Embryos, 50 Emory L.J. 989, 1038-1039 (2001). In addition, enforcement promotes efficiency, relieving courts of the burden of resolving such disputes. Id. at 1039. Texas follows this approach. Roman v. Roman, 2006 WL 304922 (Tex. App. 2006). See also Cahill v. Cahill, 757 So. 2d 465 (Ala. Civ. Ct. App. 2000) (upholding form agreement giving physicians control over embryos). For additional support of a contractual approach, see Sara D. Petersen, Comment, Dealing with Cryopreserved Embryos Upon Divorce: A Contractual Approach Aimed at Preserving Party Expectations, 50 UCLA L. Rev. 1065 (2003); Karissa Hostrup Windsor, Note, Disposition of Cryopreserved Embryos After Divorce, 88 Iowa L. Rev. 1001 (2003). Under a contractual approach, should courts recognize implied agreements? Contract defenses? See Windsor, supra, at 1025-1027. See also Marysol Rosado, Note, Sign on the Dotted Line: Enforceability of Signed Agreements, upon Divorce of the Married Couple, Concerning the Disposition of Their Frozen Embryos, 36 New Eng. L. Rev. 1041 (2002).

4. *Alternative approaches.*

a. *Balancing.* Without a controlling agreement, courts have balanced the progenitors' competing interests. When such disagreements arise in the abortion context, the Supreme Court has said the woman's decision prevails. See Planned Parenthood of Southeastern Pa. v. Casey, Chapter I, section B1. On what basis might one argue that a woman's interest in implanting frozen embryos should trump a man's in avoiding parenthood? See, e.g., Kass v. Kass, 1995 WL 110368 (N.Y. Sup. Ct. 1995), *rev'd*, 633 N.Y.S.2d 581 (App. Div. 1997), *aff'd*, 696 N.E.2d 174 (N.Y. 1998); Ruth Colker, Pregnant Men Revisited or Sperm Is Cheap, Eggs Are Not, 47 Hastings L.J. 1063 (1996); Tracey S. Pachman, Disputes Over Frozen Preembryos & the "Right Not to be a Parent," 12 Colum. J. Gender & L. 128 (2003).

b. *Forced parenthood.* Although *A.Z.* does not expressly use a balancing approach, it suggests that one former spouse's interest in avoiding parenthood outweighs the other's interest in implantation. Several other courts facing such disputes articulate a principle against forcing parenthood on an unwilling party. J.B. v. M.B., 783 A.2d 707 (N.J. 2001); Davis v. Davis, 842 S.W.2d 588, 604 (Tenn. 1992). What, precisely, does the notion of "forced parenthood" entail? Would an agreement to relieve the unwilling party of parental duties address the problem? Would such agreements be enforceable? What insights do the data on postdissolution parental support contribute to these questions? (See Chapter VI, section F.) If the unwilling party's interest lies in avoiding genetic reproduction, can you reconcile these cases with those that impose responsibility on fathers who conceived as the result of birth-control fraud? (See Chapter IV, section C1.) Don't support obligations in such cases impose "forced parenthood"? Cf. Shanna Flowers, Deadbeat Dads Don't Need More Excuses, Roanoke Times, March 14, 2006, at B1 (reporting suit dubbed "Roe v. Wade for Men" to allow unwilling men to opt out of fatherhood). See generally Susan B. Apel, Cryopreserved Embryos: A Response to "Forced Parenthood" and the Role of Intent, 39 Fam. L.Q. 663 (2005); Ellen Waldman, The Parent Trap: Uncovering the Myth of "Coerced Parenthood" in Frozen Embryo Disputes, 53 Am. U.L. Rev. 1021 (2004). See also Robertson, supra, at 1032-1038. To what extent did Roe v. Wade, Chapter I, section A2, address the burdens of unwanted genetic parenthood, apart from the burdens of unwanted pregnancy?

c. *Last procreative chance.* In balancing the competing interests or requiring mutual contemporaneous consent, some courts have also considered whether the party seeking implantation has or will have other procreative opportunities. See, e.g., *J.B.*, 783 A.2d at 716-717. Professor Robertson points out the significance of this exception because, "[a]lthough there will be few men who will become infertile during the IVF and embryo storage process, many women might," as their age advances. Robertson, supra, at 1014. In a well-known Israeli case, Nachmani v. Nachmani, F.H. 2401/95, several of the justices noted that the preembryos represented the only chance for the estranged wife (who sought to implant them) to become a genetic mother. See Helene S. Shapo, Frozen Pre-Embryos and the Right to Change One's Mind, 12 Duke J. Comp. & Int'l L. 75, 79 (2002). Another approach favoring the party seeking parenthood emphasizes the teleology of the parties' earlier agreement: their purpose to develop a parent-child relationship, which in turn undermines subsequent autonomy-based claims. Olivia Lin, Note, Rehabilitating Bioethics: Recontextualizing In Vitro Fertilization Outside Contractual Autonomy, 54 Duke L.J. 485 (2004). See also D. Kelly Weisberg, The Birth of Surrogacy in Israel 86 (2005) (noting that justices in *Nachmani,* supra, invoked such reasoning).

d. *Legislative responses.* A few jurisdictions provide statutorily for the disposition of preembryos. For example, Louisiana law, examined supra, limits destruction. Florida, on the other hand, calls for written agreements between the commissioning couple and the treating physician and spells out default rules for particular situations. Fla. Stat. Ann. §742.17 (West 2005). The European Court of Human Rights, applying British legislation, has upheld the requirement that both parties contemporaneously consent to implanation. Evans v. United Kingdom, no. 6339/05, ECHR, 2006 (available at http://www.echr.coe.int.eng). For suggestions of what the U.S. could learn from the regulatory schemes in effect in other countries, see Christina C. Lawrence, Note, Procreative Liberty and the Preembryo Problem: Developing a Medical and Legal Framework to Settle the Disposition of Frozen Preembryos, 52 Case W. Res. L. Rev. 721, 745-750 (2002).

5. *Destruction.* What legal rules should govern the storage of the growing number of unused cryopreserved preembryos? British law has a five-year limit, amended to allow additional time if both progenitors consent. See §14 Human Fertilisation and Embryology Act of 1990, ch. 37; Human Fertilisation and Embryology Regulations 1996, SI 1996 No 375, reg 2, Schedule. Six to ten thousand preembryos were destroyed August 1, 1996, pursuant to the law. See Youssef M. Ibrahim, Ethical Furor Erupts in Britain: Should Embryos Be Destroyed?, N.Y. Times, Aug. 1, 1996, at A1. What approach should the United States follow? In 2001, President George W. Bush denied federal funding for stem cell research that would have destroyed frozen preembryos donated for research, while allowing support on cell lines already established from such sources. See Doe v. Shalala, 122 Fed. Appx. 600 (4th Cir. 2004) (describing policy and affirming dismissal of embryos' challenge to previous policy). The debate over use of such embryos for research continues, with a number of states committing to support such science and a few private ventures moving forward without federal assistance. See, e.g., David Chen, New Jersey Awards $5 Million in Grants for Stem Cell Research,

N.Y. Times, Dec. 17, 2005, at B2; Gina Kolata, Embryonic Cells, No Embryo Needed: Hunting for Ways Out of an Impasse, N.Y. Times, Oct. 11, 2005, at F1.

6. *The biological connection?* How important are physical connections, genetic or otherwise, in *A.Z.* and other judicial analyses of disposition disputes? Suppose, for example, the embryos had been created from donated eggs? Would the fact that the former wife did not endure superovulation and ovum retrieval diminish her interest? Does the forced-parenthood rationale apply to a commissioning adult who used another's genetic material? Suppose she does not plan to gestate herself preembryos conceived from donor eggs but intends to parent the resulting child? See Litowitz v. Litowitz, 48 P.3d 261 (Wash. 2002); Lainie M. C. Dillon, Comment, Conundrums with Penumbras: The Right to Privacy Encompasses Non-Gamete Providers Who Create Embryos with the Intent to Become Parents, 78 Wash. L. Rev. 625 (2003).

IVF's capacity to split once unitary concepts of parentage prompts questions not only about control of frozen preembryos but also about the rights to and responsibilities for resulting children, as the following materials demonstrate.

c. IVF's Progeny: Egg Donation, Gestational Surrogacy, and "Embryo Adoption"

■ K.M. v. E.G.
117 P.3d 673 (Cal. 2005)

MORENO, J. . . .

[W]e must decide whether a woman who provided ova to her lesbian partner so that the partner could bear children by means of in vitro fertilization is a parent of those children. . . . On March 6, 2001, petitioner K.M. filed a petition to establish a parental relationship with twin five-year-old girls born to respondent E.G., her former lesbian partner. [At a subsequent hearing on K.M.'s motion for custody and visitation,] E.G. testified that she first considered raising a child before she met K.M., at a time when she did not have a partner. She met K.M. in October, 1992 and they became romantically involved in June 1993. E.G. told K.M. that she planned to adopt a baby as a single mother. E.G. applied for adoption in November, 1993. K.M. and E.G. began living together in March, 1994, and registered as domestic partners in San Francisco.

[Later, E.G., usually along with K.M., visited several fertility clinics and attempted artificial insemination.] K.M. testified that she and E.G. planned to raise the child together, while E.G. insisted that, although K.M. was very supportive, E.G. made it clear that her intention was to become "a single parent." [E.G. then unsuccessfully attempted IVF.]

In January, 1995, [Dr. Mary Martin at the fertility practice of the University of California at San Francisco Medical Center (UCSF)] suggested using K.M.'s ova. E.G. then asked K.M. to donate her ova, explaining that she would accept the ova only if K.M. "would really be a donor" and E.G. would "be the mother of any child," adding that she would not even consider permitting K.M. to adopt the child "for at least five years until [she] felt the relationship was stable and would endure." E.G. told K.M. that she "had seen too many lesbian relationships end quickly, and [she] did not want to be in a custody battle." E.G. and K.M. agreed they would not tell anyone that K.M. was the ova donor.

K.M. acknowledged that she agreed not to disclose to anyone that she was the ova donor, but insisted that she only agreed to provide her ova because she and E.G. had agreed to raise the child together. K.M. and E.G. selected the sperm donor together. K.M. denied that E.G. had said she wanted to be a single parent and insisted that she would not have donated her ova had she known E.G. intended to be the sole parent.

On March 8, 1995, K.M. signed a four-page form on UCSF letterhead entitled "Consent Form for Ovum Donor (Known)." The form states that K.M. agrees "to have eggs taken from my ovaries, in order that they may be donated to another woman." [The form included a waiver of any claim to the donated eggs or any parental rights to the resulting child.] E.G. signed a form entitled "Consent Form for Ovum Recipient" that stated, in part: "I acknowledge that the child or children produced by the IVF procedure is and shall be my own legitimate child or children and the heir or heirs of my body with all rights and privileges accompanying such status." [The parties disagree about their expectations in signing these forms.]

Ova were withdrawn from K.M., and embryos were then created in vitro and implanted in E.G. on April 13, 1995. K.M. and E.G. told K.M.'s father about the resulting pregnancy by announcing that he was going to be a grandfather. The twins were born on December 7, 1995. The twins' birth certificates listed E.G. as their mother and did not reflect a father's name. As they had agreed, neither E.G. nor K.M. told anyone K.M. had donated the ova, including their friends, family and the twins' pediatrician. Soon after the twins were born, E.G. asked K.M. to marry her, and on Christmas Day, the couple exchanged rings.

Within a month of their birth, E.G. added the twins to her health insurance policy, named them as her beneficiary for all employment benefits, and increased her life insurance with the twins as the beneficiary. K.M. did not do the same. E.G. referred to her mother, as well as K.M.'s parents, as the twins' grandparents and referred to K.M.'s sister and brother as the twins' aunt and uncle, and K.M.'s nieces as their cousins. Two school forms listed both K.M. and respondent as the twins' parents. The children's nanny testified that both K.M. and E.G. "were the babies' mother."

The relationship between K.M. and E.G. ended in March, 2001 and K.M. filed the present action. In September, 2001, E.G. and the twins moved to Massachusetts to live with E.G.'s mother. [The courts below rejected K.M.'s claims.]

K.M. asserts that she is a parent of the twins because she supplied the ova that were fertilized in vitro and implanted in her lesbian partner, resulting in the birth of the twins. . . . The Court of Appeal in the present case concluded, however, that K.M. was not a parent of the twins, despite her genetic relationship to them, because she had the same status as a sperm donor. . . . In [Johnson v. Calvert, 851 P.2d 776 (Cal. 1993),] we considered the predecessor statute to [Family Code] section 7613(b), former Civil Code section 7005. We did not discuss whether this statute applied to a woman who provides ova used to impregnate another woman, but we observed that "in a true 'egg donation' situation, where a woman gestates and gives birth to a child formed from the egg of another woman with the intent to raise the child as her own, the birth mother is the natural mother under California law." We held that the statute did not apply under the circumstances in *Johnson* [a gestational surrogacy case], because the husband and wife in *Johnson* did not intend to "donate" their sperm and ova to the surrogate mother, but rather "intended to procreate a child genetically related to them by the only available means."

The circumstances of the present case are not identical to those in *Johnson*, but they are similar in a crucial respect; both the couple in *Johnson* and the couple in the present case intended to produce a child that would be raised in their own home. [Thus, this is not a "true 'egg donation'" case.]

Although the predecessor to section 7613 was based upon the Model [Uniform Parentage Act (UPA)], the California Legislature made one significant change; it expanded the reach of the provision to apply to both married and unmarried women. "[T]he California Legislature has afforded unmarried as well as married women a statutory vehicle for obtaining semen for artificial insemination without fear that the donor may claim paternity, and has likewise provided men with a statutory vehicle for donating semen to married and unmarried women alike without fear of liability for child support." (Jhordan C. v. Mary K., [224 Cal. Rptr. 530 (Ct. App. 1986).] . . . But there is nothing to indicate that California intended to expand the reach of this provision so far that it would apply if a man provided semen to be used to impregnate his unmarried partner in order to produce a child that would be raised in their joint home. It would be surprising, to say the least, to conclude that the Legislature intended such a result. The Colorado Supreme Court considered a related issue and reached a similar conclusion [in In Interest of R.C., 775 P.2d 27, 29 (Colo. 1989), a case about] the parental rights, if any, of a man who provided semen to a physician that was used to impregnate an unmarried friend of the man. . . . [Here,] K.M. and E.G. were more than "friends" when K.M. provided her ova, through a physician, to be used to impregnate E.G.; they lived together and were registered domestic partners. Although the parties dispute whether both women were intended to be parents of the resulting child, it is undisputed that they intended that the resulting child would be raised in their joint home. Neither the Model UPA, nor section 7613(b) was intended to apply under such circumstances.

. . . K.M.'s genetic relationship with the twins constitutes evidence of a mother and child relationship under the UPA and, as explained above, section 7613(b) does not apply to exclude K.M. as a parent of the twins. The circumstance that E.G. gave birth to the twins also constitutes evidence of a mother and child relationship. Thus, both K.M. and E.G. are mothers of the twins under the UPA.[6] It is true we said in *Johnson* that "for any child California law recognizes only one natural mother." But as we explain in the companion case of Elisa B. v. Superior Court [Chapter IV, section C3], this statement in *Johnson* must be understood in light of the issue presented in that case; "our decision in *Johnson* does not preclude a child from having two parents both of whom are women."

Justice Werdegar's dissent argues that we should determine whether K.M. is a parent using the "intent test" [, which we applied to choose between two women when each adduced evidence of maternity, giving birth and genetic relationship]. It would be unwise to expand application of the *Johnson* intent test as suggested by Justice Werdegar's dissent beyond the circumstances presented in *Johnson*.

---

6. Contrary to the suggestion in Justice Werdegar's dissent [, we do not use a best-interests standard]. We simply follow the dictates of the UPA.

Usually, whether there is evidence of a parent and child relationship under the UPA does not depend upon the intent of the parent. For example, a man who engages in sexual intercourse with a woman who assures him, falsely, that she is incapable of conceiving children is the father of a resulting child, despite his lack of intent to become a father. Justice Werdegar's dissent states that predictability in this area is important, but relying upon a later judicial determination of the intent of the parties, as the dissent suggests, would not provide such predictability. The present case is a good example.

The superior court in the present case found that K.M. signed a waiver form, thereby "relinquishing and waiving all rights to claim legal parentage of any children who might result." But such a waiver does not affect our determination of parentage. Section 7632 provides: "Regardless of its terms, an agreement between an alleged or presumed father and the mother or child does not bar an action under this chapter." A woman who supplies ova to be used to impregnate her lesbian partner, with the understanding that the resulting child will be raised in their joint home, cannot waive her responsibility to support that child. Nor can such a purported waiver effectively cause that woman to relinquish her parental rights.

In light of our conclusion that section 7613(b) does not apply and that K.M. is the twins' parent (together with E.G.), based upon K.M.'s genetic relationship to the twins, we need not, and do not, consider whether K.M. is presumed to be a parent of the twins under section 7611, subdivision (d), which provides that a man is presumed to be a child's father if "[h]e receives the child into his home and openly holds out the child as his natural child." [Reversed.]

KENNARD, J., dissenting.

. . . Because K.M. donated her ova for physician-assisted artificial insemination and implantation in another woman, and knowingly and voluntarily signed a document declaring her intention *not* to become a parent of any resulting children, she is not a parent of the twins. . . . In the 12 years since this court's decision in *Johnson*, an unknown number of Californians have made procreative choices in reliance on it. For example, in the companion case of Kristine H. v. Lisa R. [117 P.3d 690 (Cal. 2005),] a lesbian couple obtained a prebirth stipulated judgment declaring them to be "the joint *intended legal parents*" of the child born to one of them (italics added), language they presumably used in order to bring themselves within *Johnson* where the preconception intent to become a parent is the determinative inquiry. We do know that prebirth judgments of parentage on behalf of the nonbiologically related partner of a child's biological parent have been entered in this state, and that such judgments were touted to same-sex couples as less expensive and time consuming than second parent adoption. How will today's majority holding affect the validity of the various procreative choices made in reliance on *Johnson*? . . .

. . . The majority amends the sperm-donor statute by inserting a new provision making a sperm donor the legal father of a child born to a woman artificially inseminated with his sperm whenever the sperm donor and the birth mother "*intended that the resulting child would be raised in their joint home*," even though both the donor and birth mother also intended that the donor *not* be the child's father. Finding nothing in the statutory language or history to support this construction, I reject it. . . .

WERDEGAR, J., dissenting. . . .

. . . Precisely because predictability in this area is so important, I cannot agree with the majority that the children in this case do in fact have two mothers. Until today, when one woman has provided the ova and another has given birth, the established rule for determining disputed claims to motherhood was clear: we looked to the intent of the parties. Indeed, we have no other test sufficient to the task. Furthermore, to apply *Johnson*'s intent test to the facts of this case necessarily leads to the conclusion that E.G. is a mother and K.M. is not.

. . . The majority criticizes the [intent] test as basing "the determination of parentage upon a later judicial determination of intent made years after the birth of the child." But the task of determining the intent of persons who have undertaken assisted reproduction is not fundamentally different than the task of determining intent in the context of disputes involving contract, tort or criminal law, something courts have done satisfactorily for centuries. . . . [When two women divide] the genetic and gestational components of motherhood, only an examination of their intent permits us to determine whether we are dealing with an ovum donation agreement, a gestational surrogacy agreement, or neither. If courts can perform one of these tasks acceptably, they can also perform the other.

No more persuasive is the majority's suggestion that to respect the formally expressed intent of the parties to an ovum donation agreement is prohibited by the rule that parental obligations may not be waived by contract. . . . Certainly parental obligations may not be waived by contract. But *Johnson*'s intent test does not *enforce* ovum donation and gestational surrogacy agreements; it merely directs courts to consider such documents, along with all other relevant evidence, in determining preconception intent.

As a final reason for rejecting the intent test, the majority suggests that to apply the test outside the context of *Johnson* might shield from the obligations of fatherhood, contrary to existing law, a man who, lacking the intent to become a father, "engages in sexual intercourse with a woman who assures him, falsely, that she is incapable of conceiving children . . . ." But no one, to my knowledge, proposes to apply the intent test to determine the parentage of children conceived through ordinary sexual reproduction. . . .

The new rule the majority substitutes for the intent test entails serious problems. First, the rule inappropriately confers rights and imposes disabilities on persons because of their sexual orientation. In a standard ovum donation agreement, such as the agreement between K.M. and E.G., the donor confirms her intention to assist another woman to become a parent without the donor becoming a parent herself. The majority's rule vitiates such agreements when its conditions are satisfied—conditions that include the fact the parties to the agreement are lesbian. Although the majority denies that its rule depends on sexual orientation, the opinion speaks for itself. The majority has chosen to use the term "lesbian" no less than six times in articulating its holding. Moreover, the majority prevents future courts from applying its holding automatically to persons other than lesbians by stating that it "decide[s] only the case before us, which involves a lesbian couple who registered as domestic partners." . . . Why should a lesbian not have the same right as other women to donate ova without becoming a mother, or to accept a donation of ova without accepting the donor as a coparent, even if the donor and recipient live together and both plan to help raise the child? [This approach, in turn, requires a formal definition of "lesbian."]

Other problems arise from the majority's attempt to limit its holding to cases in which the ovum donor and birth mother intend to raise the children together. Except in the context of the majority's new rule, a person's preconception intent to participate in *raising* a child has no relevance to the determination of natural parentage. The duty to raise children (by personal care or through payment of child support) is imposed by law regardless of the parents' intent or wishes. Many persons who become parents do not intend to raise children (e.g., casual inseminators and parents who abandon their babies) and, conversely, many people intend to raise children without becoming parents (e.g., nannies and some stepparents and grandparents). . . . Perhaps the most serious problem with the majority's new rule is that it threatens to destabilize ovum donation and gestational surrogacy agreements. One important function of *Johnson*'s intent test was to permit persons who made use of reproductive technology to create, before conception, settled and enforceable expectations about who would and would not become parents. *Johnson*, supra, thus gave E.G. a right at the time she conceived to expect that she alone would be the parent of her children — a right the majority now retrospectively abrogates. E.G.'s expectation has a constitutional dimension. (See Troxel v. Granville [, 530 U.S. 57, 65 (2000) (due process clause protects a parent's fundamental right to make decisions concerning the care, custody and control of her children)]. We cannot recognize K.M. as a parent without diminishing E.G.'s existing parental rights. . . .

The following excerpt describes K.M.'s situation before her victory in the California Supreme Court:

■ PEGGY ORENSTEIN, THE OTHER MOTHER
N.Y. Times, July 25, 2004, 6§ (Magazine), at 24

[K.] hadn't seen the twins, who were living [with her former partner, E., in Massachusetts after their break-up] in a month, and then only for eight hours. For her, the issue was simple: she wanted her daughters back. . . .

[Recalling the form she signed before the first administration of hormones to stimulate superovulation,] K. says it seemed obvious that the form was meant for anonymous donors, not for a live-in lover. (The clinic later stopped requiring lesbian couples to sign it.) One section included the phrase "I agree not to attempt to discover the identity of the recipient." Could K. have challenged the language? Could she have crossed sections out? If so, it didn't occur to her at the time. "I believed I had to sign the form to do the procedure," she says now. "It was something for the clinic — it wasn't anything between my partner and me. We were having a family. I look back on that now, and I think, Oh, my God." . . .

[Although California cases have relied on intent to determine parentage, the] trouble is that, as with K. and E., by the time a couple gets to court, acrimony and regret can obscure intent. In that way, K. and E.'s case is like those of hundreds of gay couples who did not or could not pursue second-parent adoption. Typically, however, only one partner is the biological (or adoptive) parent; the other relies on the evolving notion of "psychological parenthood." Some states, like New Jersey, recognize a second mom or dad who wiped runny noses and helped with homework — who had a clear parental role regardless of the actual legal relationships.

In those places, K. might have had an easy case. Other states, like New York, side with birth mothers regardless of what a gay couple's intent may have been. . . .

Everything reminds her of the girls. She pulls out another picture, this one shot on a recent getaway, of two Adirondack chairs overlooking a wine-country valley. "This is where my girls would hang out if they had been there," she says. Nor does she find relief at night: in her dreams she searches for her daughters, trying to swim through turbid water or to run to them on legs that won't obey. She wakes up gasping.

A child's voice floats in through an open window. . . . K. winces. "Sometimes I have to turn on some music so I won't hear that baby," she says.

It is, of course, the children's voices that are missing from this debate. What are their wishes, their feelings, their needs? As with heterosexual couples, gay partners in a hostile split will say and do hurtful things. They will use children as weapons. With no legal recognition of their families, however, without the possibility of marriage or, in some states, second-parent adoption, doing so is just that much easier. Ultimately, it is the children who suffer. . . .

Notes and Questions

1. *Collaborative reproduction.* IVF makes possible several forms of "collaborative reproduction." For example, an intended mother can gestate a fetus conceived with a donor's egg and the sperm of her husband/partner. See, e.g., In re C.K.G., 173 S.W.3d 714 (Tenn. 2005). Or, the intended parents can hire a "gestational surrogate" after creating a preembryo with their own genetic material. See, e.g., Johnson v. Calvert, 851 P.2d 776 (Cal. 1993); Culliton v. Beth Israel Deaconess Med. Ctr., 756 N.E.2d 1133 (Mass. 2001). Sometimes, a gestational surrogate carries donated genetic material (a donated embryo or an embryo created with a donor egg or donor sperm or both) so that one or both intended parents has no biological tie to the resulting child. See, e.g., In re Marriage of Buzzanca, 72 Cal. Rptr. 2d 280 (Ct. App. 1998); Litowitz v. Litowitz, 48 P.3d 261 (Wash. 2002). And, as in *K.M.*, lesbian couples can divide genetic and gestational contributions, giving each woman a biological tie to the child. See, e.g., In re J.D.M., 2004 WL 2272063 (Ohio Ct. App. 2004).

2. *Intent-based parentage.* Dissenting in *K.M.*, Justice Werdegar urges reliance on the parties' intent. Under this approach, as originally advocated by Professor Marjorie Shultz, "[w]ithin the context of artificial reproductive techniques, intentions that are voluntarily chosen, deliberate, express and bargained-for ought presumptively to determine legal parenthood." Marjorie Maguire Shultz, Reproductive Technology and Intent-Based Parenthood: An Opportunity for Gender Neutrality, 1990 Wis. L. Rev. 297, 323. The California Supreme Court first applied the test in *Johnson*, supra, to recognize as parents the commissioning couple who provided the genetic material and intended to rear the child, rather than the gestational surrogate who decided during the pregnancy not to relinquish the child upon birth. Given the conflicting indicia of maternity under California parentage statutes (gestation and genetics), the court broke the "tie" based on the parties' intent and causation (but for the agreement, the child would not exist). Thereafter, *Buzzanca*, supra, invoked intent to rule that divorcing spouses were both the legal parents of a child who was created from a frozen embryo that

they obtained from a fertility clinic and who was born to a gestational surrogate whom they hired; as a result, John Buzzanca could not avoid paying child support. Despite these precedents, California courts have not used intent to resolve disputes in "traditional surrogacy" cases (in which the gestational surrogate bears her genetic child, as in *Baby M*, supra, pp.1107-1110). See In re Marriage of Moschetta, 30 Cal. Rptr. 2d 893 (Ct. App. 1994).

What are the advantages of intent-based parentage? The disadvantages? How should a court determine the parties' intent when they offer conflicting testimony, as in *K.M.*?

3. *Alternatives to intent.*

a. *Uniform Parentage Act of 1973.* The 1973 version of the Uniform Parentage Act, which California enacted, indicates that genetic parentage establishes legal parentage (§11). 9B U.L.A. 445 (2001) (blood tests). See also *Culliton*, supra. As applied in an egg-donation case, however, this principle would require issuance of a birth certificate identifying the genetic mother as the legal mother and a subsequent adoption by the intended mother. Given the legal treatment of AID, does this approach violate equal protection? See Soos v. Superior Ct., 897 P.2d 1356 (Ariz. Ct. App. 1994). As a practical matter, would the state require genetic testing of each child at birth to determine parentage?

b. *New Uniform Parentage Act.* Because of technological advances in genetics and reproductive medicine, the National Conference of Commissioners on Uniform State Laws promulgated a new UPA in 2000 and revised it in 2002. This model statute generally treats egg donors as sperm donors, with no legal status (§702), and makes the intended mother the legal mother without government intervention. 9B U.L.A. 355 (2001). More broadly, this model always recognizes as the legal mother the woman giving birth (§201(a)), with her husband as the presumed father. 9B U.L.A. 15 (Supp. 2005). See also, e.g., *C.K.G.*, supra (recognizing gestational, intended mother). The Act, however, goes on to provide for "gestational agreements," as follows:

Section 801. Gestational Agreement Authorized

(a) A prospective gestational mother, her husband if she is married, a donor or the donors, and the intended parents may enter into a written agreement providing that:

(1) the prospective gestational mother agrees to pregnancy by means of assisted reproduction;

(2) the prospective gestational mother, her husband if she is married, and the donors relinquish all rights and duties as the parents of a child conceived through assisted reproduction; and

(3) the intended parents become the parents of the child.

(b) The man and the woman who are the intended parents must both be parties to the gestational agreement.

(c) A gestational agreement is enforceable only if validated as provided in Section 803.

(d) A gestational agreement does not apply to the birth of a child conceived by means of sexual intercourse.

(e) A gestational agreement may provide for payment of consideration.

(f) A gestational agreement may not limit the right of the gestational mother to make decisions to safeguard her health or that of the embryos or fetus.

9B U.L.A. 45 (Supp. 2005). Validation of a gestational agreement requires procedures tantamount to a preconception adoption, including a home study and judicial approval (§803), and makes the intended parents the child's legal parents (§807). Id. at 47; 9B U.L.A. 368 (2001). The parties can terminate a validated gestational agreement only before the pregnancy begins, or a court can do so for good cause (§806). Id. at 367. A gestational agreement without validation is not enforceable, but the intended parents may be liable for support (§809). Id. at 369.

Seven states have enacted the new UPA (Delaware, North Dakota, Oklahoma, Texas, Utah, Washington, and Wyoming), and it is pending in several other state legislatures. See http://www.nccusl.org/Update/uniformact_factsheets/unifor macts-fs-upa.asp (last visited June 15, 2006). For a summary of other state legislative schemes, see Amanda Mechell Holliday, Comment, Who's Your Daddy (and Mommy)? Creating Certainty for Texas Couples Entering into Surrogacy Contracts, 34 Tex. Tech. L. Rev. 1101 (2003). See generally Amy M. Larkey, Note, Redefining Motherhood: Determining Legal Maternity in Gestational Surrogacy Arrangements, 51 Drake L. Rev. 605 (2003) (surveying approaches and urging enactment of new UPA); Adam P. Plant, Commentary, With a Little Help from My Friends: The Intersection of the Gestational Carrier Surrogacy Agreement, Legislative Inaction, and Medical Advancement, 54 Ala. L. Rev. 639 (2003).

c. An "interpretive approach." Professor Marsha Garrison proposes an "interpretive approach" that would apply to children conceived with technological assistance the same legal principles that govern parentage of other children. Marsha Garrison, Law Making for Baby Making: An Interpretive Approach to the Determination of Legal Parentage, 1113 Harv. L. Rev. 835 (2000). Under this approach, which relies on analogy and "fairness," the court properly classified Baby M, supra, pp. 1107-1110, as an adoption case because one woman intended to rear the child of another. 13 Harv. L. Rev. at 882, 898. This approach also leads Garrison to conclude that the law should treat semen donors as fathers when unmarried women use AID (because, outside this context, the law always recognizes two parents). Id. at 903-912. Considering the closest analogies, she goes on to recommend that the law treat egg donors as semen donors, recognize the genetic mother in gestational surrogacy cases, and require adoption proceedings in cases like Buzzanca, supra. Id. at 897-898, 912-920. Do you agree?

d. Functional approaches. Several contemporary authorities emphasize conduct and lived familial relationships in determining parentage. E.g., Nancy E. Dowd, From Genes, Marriage and Money to Nurture: Redefining Fatherhood, 10 Cardozo Women's L.J. 132 (2003); E. Gary Spitko, The Constitutional Function of Biological Paternity: Evidence of the Biological Mother's Consent to the Biological Father's Co-Parenting of her Child 48 Ariz. L. Rev. 97 (2006). See also ALI Principles §2.03 (recognizing parents by estoppel and de facto parents). To what extent does intent-based parentage resemble the functional approach? See Richard F. Storrow, Parenthood by Pure Intention: Reproduction and the Functional Approach to Assisted Parentage, 53 Hastings L.J. 597 (2002). Does the majority in K.M. simply re-examine the parties' original intent in light of their conduct, by which both K.M. and E.G. functioned as the twins' parents? See Melanie B. Jacobs, Applying Intent-Based Parentage Principles to Nonlegal Lesbian

Coparents, 25 N. Ill. U. L. Rev. 433 (2005). What does the news story about K.M. add to the analysis?

4. *Default rules and departures.* Most of the rules surveyed above attempt to articulate default rules that determine parentage in the absence of affirmative steps to achieve a different allocation of rights and responsibilities, for example, a termination of parental rights and adoption, steps which entail considerable state intervention. Even with a rule based on intent, however, must the parties take action to memorialize their plans and prevent future challenges?

a. *Adoption.* When should the law make adoption necessary? Why does California require adoption by the intended mother in traditional surrogacy cases while allowing intent to control in gestational surrogacy cases? See, e.g., Janet L. Dolgin, An Emerging Consensus: Reproductive Technology and the Law, 23 Vt. L. Rev. 225 (1998). In recognizing the commissioning couple as the parents in *Buzzanca*, supra, the court expressly rejected an "adoption default" model for most collaborative reproductive arrangements. 72 Cal. Rptr. 2d at 289. On what basis should couples like the Buzzancas be able to avoid adoption procedures in order to become the parents of a child with no genetic nor gestational tie to either of them? Evaluate the approach of the new UPA, supra, which requires, in effect, a pre-implantation adoption whenever the intended mother is not the woman giving birth.

The pitfalls of an adoption requirement for the intended parents (as illustrated in *Baby M*, supra, pp. 1107-1110) have prompted fertility clinics to avoid traditional surrogacy arrangements; even when the intended mother can supply neither ova nor gestational capacity, the preferred approach now combines the use of ova from one woman and the gestational services of another—an arrangement more likely to evoke recognition of the intended parents by default. 9B U.L.A. 361 (2001) (prefatory cmt. to Art. 8). See, e.g., *Litowitz*, supra.

b. *Birth certificates.* Default rules also determine the parentage information entered on the child's birth certificate. In some cases, however, the parties have gone to court before the child is born to litigate the content of the anticipated birth certificate. In *Culliton*, supra, a gestational surrogacy case, the genetic and intended parents successfully petitioned to be named as parents on the original birth certificate. In other gestational surrogacy cases, courts have reached a similar result, contrary to the new UPA. E.g., Belsito v. Clark, 644 N.E.2d 760 (Ohio Com. Pleas 1994); Doe v. N.Y. City Bd. of Health, 782 N.Y.S.2d 180 (Sup. Ct. 2004) (ordering two sets of birth certificates, with the first (naming the gestational mother) to be sealed).

c. *Prebirth stipulations and judgments.* Justice Kennard's dissenting opinion in *K.M.* notes the increasingly common California practice of obtaining prebirth stipulated judgments of parentage for children of assisted reproduction. Same-sex couples have used this procedure more often than others. Howard Fink & June Carbone, Between Private Ordering and Public Fiat: A New Paradigm for Family Law Decision-making, 5 J.L. Fam. Stud. 1, 45 (2003). To what extent does *K.M.* jeopardize this practice? Does a prebirth judgment foreclose a later change of mind? If not, what good is it? If so, what limits should apply? Should courts in states hospitable to this practice enter a prebirth judgment when the only connection to the jurisdiction is the child's birth there, arranged solely for the purpose of obtaining the judgment? See Hodas v. Morin, 814 N.E.2d 320 (Mass. 2004). Must other states recognize the judgment? Although obtaining a prebirth judgment represents a departure from default parentage rules, the procedure arguably produces fewer opportunities for judicial disapproval than with conventional adoptions. Fink & Carbone, supra, at 47. (Recall *Lofton*, supra.) Should an adoption follow after the child is born? See id. at 50. See also Steven H. Snyder & Mary Patricia Byrn, The Use of Prebirth Parentage Orders in Surrogacy Proceedings, 39 Fam. L.Q. 633 (2005) (exploring utility of prebirth orders in various states). Are there default rules, requiring no judicial intervention, that would allow gay male couples to become the legal parents of a child born pursuant to surrogacy arrangements? See Susan Frelich Appleton, Presuming Women: Revisiting the Presumption of Legitimacy in the Same-Sex Couples Era, 86 B.U. L. Rev. 227 (2006).

d. *Other consequences.* Fixing parental status before or at the time of birth (either through a default rule or a prebirth judgment) can have other important consequences, such as eligibility for authority to consent to the infant's medical care and insurance coverage for neonatal intensive care. See Mid-South Ins. Co. v. Doe, 274 F. Supp. 2d 757 (D.S.C. 2003).

5. *"Embryo adoption."* In *Buzzanca*, supra, the intended parents' commissioned a surrogate to gestate donated genetic material. Professor Elizabeth Bartholet calls these "technological adoptions." Elizabeth Bartholet, Family Bonds: Adoption and the Politics of Parenting 219 (revised ed. 1999). Abortion opponents use the term "embryo adoption" for what others call "embryo donation." E.g., Sarah Blustain, Embryo Adoption, N.Y. Times, Dec. 11, 2005, §6 (Magazine), at 67. How does the terminology affect our understanding of adoption, with its traditional emphasis on child welfare? Should the law attempt to encourage or discourage such advances? Congress has authorized funding to promote the practice. See Paula J. Manning, Baby Needs a New Set of Rules: Using Adoption Doctrine to Regulate Embryo Donation, 5 Geo. J. Gender & L. 677, 678 (2004). What effect would Professor Garrison's recommended adoption procedures for such cases, supra, have? See Garrison, supra, at 917-920. Would additional restrictions on the use of such reproductive technologies prompt more adoptions of already-born children awaiting placements? On the other hand, "why do why infertile couples alone and not all persons who reproduce have the obligation to adopt kids in need of parents"? John A. Robertson, Children of Choice: Freedom and the New Reproductive Technologies 277 (1993).

To what extent does a preference for white babies explain why the infertile might choose "embryo adoption" over conventional adoption? Alternatively, does the use of the term "adoption" in this new context reinforce adoption's stigma by suggesting "there is something deeply suspect" about parenting someone else's child? Bartholet, supra, at 69. Cf. Matter of Doe, 793 N.Y.S.2d 878 (Sur. Ct. 2005) (applying adoption exclusion in settlor's trust to his daughter's twins, born to gestational surrogate with donor ova). See generally Susan Frelich Appleton, Adoption in the Age of Reproductive Technology, 2004 U. Chi. Legal F. 393, 438-442; Katheryn D. Katz, Snowflake Adoptions and Orphan Embyos: The Legal Implications of Embryo Donations, 18 Wis. Women's L.J. 179 (2003); Charles P. Kindregan & Maureen McBrien, Embryo Donation: Unresolved Legal Issues in the Transfer of Surplus Cryopreserved Embryos, 49 Vill. L. Rev. 169 (2004). For additional legislative proposals, see Becky A. Ray, Embryo Adoptions: Thawing Inactive Legislatures with a Proposed Uniform Law, 28 S. Ill. U. L.J. 423 (2004).

6. *Race and class.* In *Johnson*, supra, the gestational surrogate was part African-American; the genetic, intended mother was Filipina; and the genetic, intended father was white. Janet L. Dolgin, Just a Gene: Judicial Assumptions About Parenthood, 40 UCLA L. Rev. 637, 687 (1993). To what extent did the race of the parties influence the determination of parentage? See April L. Cherry, Nurturing in the Service of White Culture: Racial Subordination, Gestational Surrogacy, and the Ideology of Motherhood, 10 Tex. J. Women & L. 83 (2001). Will gestational surrogacy produce a new class of poor and minority women who provide care for the children of wealthy whites — prenatally? See, e.g., Dorothy E. Roberts, Spiritual and Menial Housework, 9 Yale J.L. & Feminism 51 (1997); Angie Godwin McEwen, Note, So You're Having Another Woman's Baby: Economics and Exploitation in Gestational Surrogacy, 32 Vand. J. Transnat'l L. 271 (1999).

7. *Limitations.*

a. *Egg selling.* What limits would you recommend on payment for egg donation? Many college newspapers publish advertisements for young, white donors, with high SAT scores. See Kenneth Baum, Golden Eggs: Towards the Rational Regulation of Oocyte Donation, 2001 B.Y.U. L. Rev. 107; Julia D. Mahoney, The Market for Human Tissue, 86 Va. L. Rev. 163 (2000). Some fertility clinics have oocyte sharing programs, allowing patients to receive treatment for reduced fees in exchange for donating some of their eggs to other patients. What is the proper way to balance autonomy, protection from exploitation, and fair compensation for hormonal therapy and surgery that entail some risks? See The Ethics Committee of the American Society for Reproductive Medicine, Financial Incentives in Recruitment of Oocyte Donors, 74 Fertility & Sterility 216 (2000) (more than $5,000 requires justification, more than $10,000 is inappropriate, and sharing programs need clear and fair policies).

With respect to rules allowing or prohibiting payments, should the law treat sperm, eggs, and embryos alike? Why? See generally Martha M. Ertman, What's Wrong with a Parenthood Market? A New and Improved Theory of Commodification, 82 N.C. L. Rev. 1, 14-16 (2003). While conceding existing commerce in sperm and eggs, the President's Council on Bioethics has called for interim legislation prohibiting the purchase and sale of human embryos. Why? See The President's Council on Bioethics, Reproduction and Responsibility: The Regulation of New Biotechnologies 226-227 (2004).

b. *Screening.* Should the state screen intended parents who use assisted reproduction as adoption law requires? What limits ought to govern? Should the law condition surrogacy on the intended mother's infertility? See Robin Fretwell Wilson, Uncovering the Rationale for Requiring Infertility in Surrogacy Arrangements, 29 Am. J.L. & Med. 337 (2003).

What limits, if any, on family form should control? If single women can have children by donor insemination, see supra section E1b, can single men become fathers via surrogacy? Gay male couples? Cf. J.F. v. D.B., 2004 WL 1570142 (Pa. Ct. Com. Pleas 2004) (holding surrogacy contract void because it failed to provide for an intended mother), 2006 WL 1047113 (Pa. Super. Ct. 2006) (vacating trial court and denying standing to "surrogate"); Rice v. Flynn, 2005 WL 2140576 (Ohio Ct. App. 2005) (proceeding in same case).

c. *Age.* In response to pregnancies achieved by postmenopausal women using donor eggs, France enacted legislation restricting infertility procedures to living heterosexual couples of childbearing age. Sherri A. Jayson, Comment, "Loving

Infertile Couple Seeks Woman Age 18-31 to Help Have Baby. $6,500 Plus Expenses and a Gift": Should We Regulate the Use of Assisted Reproductive Technologies by Older Women?, 11 Alb. L.J. Sci. & Tech. 287, 325-327 (2001). See also Terry Wilkinson, Fertility Law Divides Italians, L.A. Times, June 11, 2005, at A3 (attributing support for Italy's new restrictions, in part, to past "granny births"). Would similar legislation in the United States survive constitutional challenge? Does "old" parenthood pose harm to children? Parents? Society? Should similar restrictions apply to artificial insemination to deter old fatherhood? Such questions followed reports of the birth of a daughter to a 63-year-old California woman, who used a donor egg. See Gina Kolata, Childbirth at 63 Says What About Life?, N.Y. Times, Apr. 27, 1997, §1, at 20.

8. *The Israeli approach.* Surrogacy was legalized in Israel in 1996 with the passage of the Surrogate Motherhood Agreements Law, 1996 S.H. 1577. As of March 2004, 78 children have been born there by surrogacy. No birth mothers have attempted to breach the agreement. The legislation permits only gestational surrogacy in which the surrogate has no genetic connection to the child. A governmental committee must approve all surrogate agreements. Many of the legal requirements for surrogacy are based on religious ("halachic") considerations: the surrogate must be unmarried, a nonrelative of the commissioning parents, and a member of the same religion as the intended mother; the sperm must be that of the intended father (although egg donation is permitted). In addition, all parties must be adults and residents of Israel. Government protocols specify that surrogates must not undergo more than seven implantation attempts during an 18-month period; prohibit surrogacy by birth mothers who are older than forty, who have more than five previous births, and who have undergone two previous caesarean sections; the intended mother must be age 48 or younger, and the intended father must be 59 or younger. The intended mother must document her infertility or her inability to carry a child to term. Payments are permitted to cover actual costs, compensation for inactivity, suffering, lost income, or temporary loss of earning ability, or any other reasonable compensation. See D. Kelly Weisberg, The Birth of Surrogacy in Israel 197-200 (2005). For other international perspectives on surrogacy, see Surrogate Motherhood: International Perspectives (Rachel Cook & Shelley Day Sclater eds., 2003); Vanessa S. Browne-Barbour, Bartering For Babies: Are Preconception Agreements in the Best Interests of Children?, 26 Whittier L. Rev. 429, 460-467 (2004).

Problems

1. Robert and his wife, Denise, arranged to have a Denise bear a child conceived from embryos created for them with Robert's sperm and eggs from an anonymous donor. Clinic doctors transferred some of the embryos not only to Denise but also to Susan, an unmarried woman who arranged to become a single mother with an embryo from anonymous donors. Denise gave birth to a girl and Susan a boy — genetic siblings. After the clinic disclosed the error, Robert and Denise sue for parental rights to the boy while Susan asserts that she is his sole legal parent. Whom should the court recognize as the parents? Why? Can intent-based parentage resolve this dispute? Should the court give both families some access to the child? See Robert B. v. Susan B., 135 Cal. Rptr. 2d 785 (Ct. App. 2003);

Marjorie M. Shultz, Taking Account of ARTs in Determining Parenthood: A Troubling Dispute in California, 19 Wash. U. J.L. & Pol'y 77 (2005).

If the mix-up had resulted in one woman giving birth to twin boys, one of whom was genetically hers and her husband's and the other the genetic child of a second married couple, would your answers change? Suppose the error were disclosed before the twins' birth? Suppose the second couple's own efforts to have a child had failed — so the twin in question was their only chance for offspring? Suppose the first couple and their genetic son is Caucasian and the second couple and the second twin are African-American? See Perry-Rogers v. Fasano, 715 N.Y.S.2d 19 (App. Div. 2000); Leslie Bender, Genes, Parents, and Assisted Reproductive Technologies: ARTs, Mistakes, Sex, Race, & Law, 12 Colum. J. Gender & L. 1 (2003). Suppose the mix-up in either case resulted not from negligence but from the clinic's deliberate misuse of genetic material that came to light several years after the children were born? See Prato-Morrison v. Doe, 126 Cal. Rptr. 2d 509 (Ct. App. 2002); Alice M. Noble-Allgire, Switched at the Fertility Clinic: Determining Maternal Rights When a Child Is Born from Stolen or Misdelivered Genetic Material, 64 Mo. L. Rev. 517 (1999).

2. Jim and Tom, a gay couple, live in a state that has neither same-sex marriage nor legally recognized domestic partnerships but has enacted the new UPA, as amended in 2002. They locate a woman willing to serve as a commercial surrogate for them. The court refuses to grant the necessary preconception adoption, however, because the legislation (§801(b)) specifically refers to "[t]he man and the woman who are the intended parents." 9B U.L.A. 45 (Supp. 2005). On what basis can Jim and Tom challenge this restriction? Will they succeed? How would their challenge fare if they were attacking instead the 2000 version of the UPA, which specified that the intended parents must be a married couple? 9B U.L.A. 362 (2001). See Brooke Dianah Rodgers-Miller, Adam and Steve and Eve: Why Sexuality Segregation in Assisted Reproduction in Virginia Is No Longer Acceptable, 11 Wm. & Mary J. Women & L. 293 (2005). In each scenario, how would the recognition of same-sex marriage or domestic partnerships change the result? Is a surrogacy agreement void if it fails to provide for a legal mother for the child-to-be? Cf. J.F. v. D.B., 2004 WL 1570142 (Pa. Ct. Com. Pleas 2004). See generally Marla J. Hollandworth, Gay Men Creating Families Through Surro-Gay Arrangements: A Paradigm for Reproductive Freedom, 3 Am. U.J. Gender & L. 183 (1995); Ann MacLean Massie, Restricting Surrogacy to Married Couples: A Constitutional Problem? The Married-Parent Requirement in the Uniform Status of Children of Assisted Conception Act, 18 Hastings Con. L.Q. 487 (1991).

Anecdotal evidence indicates that many surrogates prefer to work with male couples like Jim and Tom. See, e.g., Ginia Bellafante, Surrogate Mothers' New Niche: Bearing Babies for Gay Couples, N.Y. Times, May 27, 2005, at A1. What reasons might explain this preference?

3. Ruth and Rob have discovered that he is infertile. They wish to have a child, but they find abhorrent the thought of using a third party's genetic material, as AID would require. They are interested in the possibilities presented by cloning, which would allow them to have a child genetically related only to one of them. Their state, however, is one of several banning human reproductive cloning. E.g., Cal. Health & Safety Code §24185 (West Supp. 2006); R.I. Gen. Laws §23-16.4-2 (2001). What constitutional challenges can they raise against the state ban? Do their reasons for pursuing cloning matter? Will their challenge succeed? See Yuriko

Mary Shikai, Don't Be Swept Away by Mass Hysteria: The Benefits of Human Reproductive Cloning and its Future, 33 Sw. U. L. Rev. 259 (2004); Evelyne Shuster, Human Cloning: Category, Dignity, and the Role of Bioethics, 17 Bioethics 518 (2003); Cass R. Sunstein, Is There a Constitutional Right to Clone?, 53 Hastings L.J. 987 (2002) (part of symposium "Conceiving a Code for Creation: The Legal Debate Surrounding Human Cloning"). Cf. Kerry Lynn Macintosh, Illegal Beings: Human Clones and the Law (2005). Note that one variant on cloning techniques can allow the creation of a child with two genetic mothers — an option that might hold particular interest for lesbian couples. See Lee M. Silver, Remaking Eden: How Genetic Engineering and Cloning Will Transform the American Family 206-222 (1998). Would a lesbian couple have a stronger or weaker constitutional case against the cloning ban than Ruth and Rob?

Table of Cases

Principal cases appear in italics.

A. v. United Kingdom, 894
A.B., In re, 1073
Abbo v. Briskin, 742
Abernathy v. Abernathy, 706
Abouhalkah v. Sharps, 690
A.C., In re, 100, 106, 107, 781
Adair, People v., 354
Adams v. Adams, 719, 810
Adams v. Howerton, 172
Adoption House, Inc. v. A.R., 1078
Adoption No. 9979, In re, 1063
Adoption of _____. *See* party name
Adoption/Guardianship Nos. T00130003,
    In re, 1020
Adult Anonymous, In re Adoption of, 446
Adult Anonymous II, In re Adoption of,
    446
Aflalo v. Aflalo, 547, 551, 552
A.F.M., In re Adoption of, 1033
A.H., In re, 895, 903
Aid for Women v. Foulston, 86
A.J.C., People ex rel., 1036, 1078, 1080,
    1081
Akron v. Akron Ctr. for Reprod. Health,
    32, 50
Albinger v. Harris, 127
Alexander v. Inman, 628
Alfonso v. Fernandez, 866

Alford v. Alford, 604
Alison D. v. Virginia M., 801, 1072, 1089
Allen, In re, 811
Allred v. Allred, 690
Alons v. Iowa District Court for Woodbury
    County, 581
Alternative Options & Servs. for Children
    v. Chapman, 1079
American Academy of Pediatrics v.
    Heckler, 908
American Life League, Inc. v. Reno, 51
A.M.M., In re Adoption of, 1079
Amsbaugh v. Amsbaugh, 604
Amundson v. Amundson, 632
Anastasi v. Anastasi, 591
Andersen v. King County, 174, 443
Anderson, In re Adoption of, 1033
Ankenbrandt v. Richards, 55, *586*, 590, 591
Anonymous, Ex parte, 84, 85
Anonymous, In re Adoption of, 1103, 1105,
    1114
Anonymous v. Anonymous, 1114
Anson v. Anson, 626
Anthony, In re Adoption of, 1096
Anthony v. Council, 697
Appeal in Pima County Juvenile Severance
    Action, In re, 1020
Appeal of Maltifano, 358

1149

Application for Change of Name of
 Bacharach, In re, 256
Application of Daniels, In re, 256
Apt v. Apt, 219
Apter v. Ross, 324
A.R.B., In re, 770
Ariel G., In re, 941
Armijo v. Miles, 404
Armstrong v. Manzo, 1079
Arneson v. Arneson, 766
Arnold, In re Marriage of, 770
Arnold v. Arnold, 658
Asad v. Continental Airlines, Inc., 284
Ascuitto v. Farricielli, 1008
Asente, In re Adoption of, 1078
Atkinson v. Atkinson, 1072
Audubon v. Shufeldt, 638
Avitzur v. Avitzur, 551
Ayala v. Fox, 396
Ayotte v. Planned Parenthood of Northern
 New England, 82, 85, 86
A.Z. v. B.Z., 1127, 1131, 1132

Baby Boy C., In re, 1038, 1047, 1049, 1050
Baby Boy Doe, In re, 107
Baby Boy P., In re, 1063
Baby Boy W., In re Termination of
 Parental Rights of Biological Parents
 of, 1033
Baby E.A.W., In re Adoption of, 1033
Baby Girl Clausen, In re, 1073, 1077
Baby Girl D., In re, 1063
Baby Girl L. In re, 1036
Baby Girl T., In re, 1027
Baby Girls Mandell, In re Adoption of,
 1027
Baby Jessica case, 1033, 1034, 1079, 1082,
 1096
Baby M, 1107-1110, 1141, 1142, 1143
Baby Richard case, 1033-1034, 1036, 1082,
 1096
Baccanti v. Morton, 602, 646
Back v. Hastings on Hudson Union Free
 Sch. Dist., 304
Bader v. Johnson, 1123
Baehr v. Lewin, 173, 181
Baehr v. Miike, 173
Bailey v. Bailey, 690
Baker v. Baker, 763
Baker v. Nelson, 172
Baker v. State, 13, 169, 173, 175, 182, 249
Baker v. Webb, 1048

Baldrige v. Lacks, 717
Balistreri v. Pacifica Police Dept., 342, 343
Balius v. Gaines, 787
Ball v. Ball, 139
*Baltimore City Dept. of Soc. Servs. v.
 Bouknight, 936*, 938, 939, 940
Bandfield v. Bandfield, 318
Barnes v. Barnes, 500
Barnes v. Moore, 85
Barrett v. Wright, 811
Barth v. Finley, 1091
Baures v. Lewis, 827
Bayliss, Ex parte, 678, 681
B.C.S., Adoption of, 1048
Beal v. Doe, 49
Beasley v. Beasley, 719
Beaumont v. Castator, 445
B.E.B. v. R.L.B., 474, 475
Becker v. Perkins-Becker, 654
Bednarek v. Velasquez, 830
Bell v. Bell, 767, 770
Beller v. Tilbrook, 317
Bellotti v. Baird, 82, 83
Belsito v. Clark, 1143
Benassi v. Back & Neck Pain Clinic, 126
Bender v. Bender, 641, 646, 649, 657
Bennington v. Bennington, 523, 525
Bergen v. Wood, 396
Berger v. Adornato, 205, 206
Berks County Children & Youth Servs. v.
 Rowan, 1003
Berman v. Allan, 1123
Berry v. Berry, 750
Berry v. Chaplin, 454
Berry v. Watchtower Bible & Tract Soc'y of
 New York, Inc., 928
Bersani v. Bersani, 842
B.G.C., In the Interest of, 1033, 1034
Bicknell, In re, 256
Biercevicz v. Liberty Mutual Ins. Co., 401
Binek v. Binek, 132, 135, 136, 137, 138
Birth Mother v. Adoptive Parents, 1096
Bishop v. Bishop, 1001
Bivans, In re Estate of, 225
B.J.H., In re Adoption of, 1100
Black v. Black, 649
Blackwell, Matter of, 216
Blair v. Blair, 207, 209
Blanchard v. Blair, 709
Blanchard v. Blanchard, 646
Blanchflower, In re, 496
Bland v. Hill, 313
Blessing v. Freestone, 702

Blixt v. Blixt, 797, 798
Blue v. Blue, 137, 140
B.L.V.B. v. E.L.V.B., 1089
Boaden v. Department of Law
    Enforcement, 268, 270
Board of Governors, United States v., 1127
Board of Trustees of the Univ. of Alabama
    v. Garrett, 293
Boddie v. Connecticut, 540, 543, 544, 586
Bodne v. Bodne, 829
Boerne v. Flores, 864
Bogan v. Bogan, 633
Boggs v. Boggs, 650
Bonbrest v. Kotz, 32
Bonnie L. ex rel. Hadsock v. Bush, 980
Bonte v. Bonte, 1013
Bonura v. Bonura, 496
Borough of Glassboro v. Vallorosi, 367,
    368
Bottoms v. Bottoms, 796
Bowen v. American Hosp. Assn, 908
Bowen v. Gilliard, 376
Bowers v. Hardwick, 65, 66, 67, 69, 173,
    197, 404
Boy Scouts of America v. Dale, 437
Boyd v. Boyd, 720
Boykin v. Boykin, 747
Bozman v. Bozman, 317
Braam v. State, 981
Bradley, People v., 946
Bradley v. Bradley, 665
Bradley v. Somers, 120
Bradwell v. Illinois, 248, 259, 260, 261, 262,
    300
Brady v. Dean, 173
Bragdon v. Abbott, 1126
Braschi v. Stahl Assoc. Co., 426, 432, 433,
    434, 435, 436, 437, 801, 1071
Brause v. Alaska, 173
Brause v. Bureau of Vital Statistics, 173
Bray v. Alexandria Women's Health Clinic,
    52
Brennan v. Orban, 532, 613
Brescia v. Fitts, 720
Brewer v. Brewer, 614, 616
Brian C. v. Ginger K., 475
Brigman, State v., 946
Brinkman v. Brinkman, 531
Bristol v. Brundage, 1097
Broadbent v. Broadbent, 1009
Bronson v. Swensen, 200
Brooks v. Brooks, 683
Browder v. Harmeyer, 154

Brown, In re Marriage of, 646
Brown, People v., 350
Brown v. Board of Educ., 150, 169
Brown v. Brown, 317, 1110
Brown v. Strum, 122
Brown v. Szakal, 781
Brunner, State v., 891
Bruno v. Guerra, 127
B.S., In re, 84
Buck v. Bell, 20
Budnick v. Silverman, 459
Buncombe Cty. ex rel. Blair v. Jackson, 683
Buono v. Scalia, 1005, 1008, 1009, 1011
Burchard v. Garay, 753, 755
Burford v. Sun Oil Co., 590
Burgess, In re Marriage of, 829
Burnette v. Wahl, 1011
Burnham v. Superior Court, 579, 580, 706
Burns v. Burns, 444
Burrell v. Arkansas Dept. of Human Servs.,
    455
Burrus, In re, 55
Bush v. Schiavo, 99
Bushey v. Northern Assurance Corp. of
    Am., 1009
Butler, In re, 639
Butler v. Butler, 707
Butler v. Wilson, 158
Buzzanca, In re Marriage of, 1140, 1141,
    1143

Caban v. Mohammed, 470, 471
Cage v. Harrisonburg Dept. of Soc. Servs.,
    1096
Cahill v. Cahill, 1132
Caldwell v. Caldwell, 1001
Caldwell v. Holland of Texas, Inc., 285, 292,
    293
Califano v. Goldfarb, 248
*California Federal Savings & Loan Associa-
    tion v. Guerra, 276*
C.A.M. v. R.A.W., 460
Camp v. McNair, 782
Campbell v. Moore, 210
Cannon v. Cannon, 138
Carabetta v. Carabetta, 212, 215
Carafano v. Metrosplash.com, 122
Carballo, In re Preadoption Certificate
    Concerning, 1063
Cardwell v. Bechtol, 1004
Carey v. Population Servs. Int'l, 13
Carhart v. Gonzales, 54

Carmichael v. Siegel, 780

Carney, In re Marriage of, 765

Carolyn B., In re Adoption of, 1088

Cary, In re Marriage of, 385, 386, 387, 388, 393

CASA v. Dept. of Servs. for Children, Youth & Families, 961

Castle v. State, 174, 179, 443

Castle Rock, town of v. Gonzales, 339, 343, 344, 345, 346, 347

Catholic Charities of the Diocese of Albany v. Senio, 14

Catholic Charities of Sacramento, Inc. v. Superior Court, 14

Cathy L. (R.) M., Visitation of, v. Mark Brent R., 1096

C.D.M., In re, 1033

Celine R., In re Adoption of, 1096

Central Texas Nudists v. Travis County, 867

C.E.W. v. D.E.W., 1114

Chambers v. Chambers, 552

Change of Name of Ravitch, In re, 258

Chen v. Fisher, 530, 531

Chenault v. Huie, 1014

Cherepski v. Walker, 314

Cheshire Med. Ctr. v. Rachel R., 246

Christensen, State v., 324

Christine Busalacchi, In re, 97

Christopher B., In re, 998

Churchfield v. State, 951

Ciesluk v. Ciesluk, 823, 828, 829, 830, 831

Citizens for Equal Protection, Inc. v. Bruning, 179

City of Cleburne v. Cleburne Living Ctr., 367

City of Edmonds v. Oxford House, 367

City of Ladue v. Horn, 367, 368

C.K. v. New Jersey Dep't of Health & Human Servs., 56

C.K. v. Shalala, 56

C.K.G., In re, 1140, 1141

Clark v. Clark, 659

Clark v. Jeter, 448, 450, 451, 453

Clark v. Madden, 766

Clay v. Kuhl, 1013

Clemmons v. Office of Child Support Enforcement, 712

Cleveland Board of Education v. LaFleur, 270, 281, 282, 299

Clifford K. v. Paul S. ex rel. Z.B.S., 1089, 1090

Clonlara v. Runkel, 865

Cloutier v. Blowers, 771

C.M., In re, 960

C.M. v. C.C., 1113, 1114

C.M.L. v. Republic Servs., 1008

C.N. v. Wolf, 873

Coates, In re, 159

Cochran v. Cochran, 396

Cocose v. Diane B., 1096

Cohan v. Feuer, 633

Cohen v. Cohen, 640, 782

Coleman v. Smallwood, 987

Collingbourne, In re Marriage of, 828

Collins v. Missouri Bar Plan, 1064

Colucci v. Colucci, 634

Colvin v. Colvin, 770

Comino v. Kelley, 477

Commissioner of Soc. Servs. v. Jones-Gamble, 1002

Committee on Prof'l Ethics & Conduct v. Hill, 570, 572

Committee to Defend Reprod. Rights v. Meyer, 49

Commonwealth v. Day, 935

Commonwealth v. Nixon, 1004

Commonwealth v. Trowbridge, 936

Compos v. McKeithen, 1047

Congdon v. Congdon, 613

Conlogue v. Conlogue, 797

Connell v. Francisco, 393, 442

Conner v. Conner, 658

Connor v. Southwest Florida Regional Med. Ctr., 245

Cook v. Cook, 188

Cook v. Eggers, 690

Cook v. Rumsfeld, 412

Cooper v. Smith, 126

Coordination Proceeding, Special Title, In re, 174

Copeland v. Copeland, 730

Cote-Whitacre v. Department of Pub. Health, 171

Cotton v. Wise, 1097

Couch v. Couch, 811

Council of City of New York v. Bloomberg, 414

Courtney v. Courtney, 1011

Coy v. Iowa, 948

C.R. & R.R., State v., 1000

Craig v. Boren, 248

Crawford v. Crawford, 719

Crawford v. Washington, 336, 945

Crenshaw v. Bussey, 224

Crew, In re Marriage of, 709

Crews v. Crews, 613, 634

Crider v. Crider, 770

Crimmins v. Crimmins, 1003
Cripe, In re Marriage of, 747
Crocker, In re Marriage of, 679
Crockett, In re Estate of, 219
Crump v. Montgomery, 1050
Crumpton v. Mitchell, 1084
Cruzan v. Director, Missouri Dept. of Health,
  90, 95, 96, 97, 106
Culliton v. Beth Israel Deaconess Med.
  Ctr., 1140
Cummings v. Cummings, 638
Currier v. Doran, 971
Curtis v. Anderson, 126
Curtis v. Kline, 676, 679
Curtis v. School Comm'n of Falmouth, 866
Custody of H.S.H.-K., In re, 802, 804
Custody of M.A.L., In re, 737

Dahlin v. Evangelical Child & Family
  Agency, 1101
Daigre v. Daigre, 646
Dajani v. Dajani, 552
Dalessio v. Dalessio, 658
Dalip Singh Bir's Estate, In re, 199
Dalrymple v. Brown, 1013
Damiani v. Damiani, 786
Daniele G., In re Adoption of, 1036
Daniels v. Daniels, 798
Danielson v. Board of Higher Educ., 296
Dansby v. Dansby, 736
Daubert v. Merrell Dow Pharm., Inc., 335,
  935
Davenport v. Little-Bowser, 1091
Davidson v. Coit, 749
Davis, People v., 32
Davis v. Davis, 509, 640, 750, 755, 1131,
  1132
Davis v. Roos, 255
Davis v. Stansbury, 562
Davis v. Washington, 336, 946
Day v. Day, 718
Day v. Heller, 460
D.B. v. M.O., State ex rel., 1048
Deane v. Conway, 174
Decker, In re Marriage of, 842
Deem, In re Marriage of, 772
Deen v. Deen, 510
DeGuigne, In re Marriage of, 613
Deichert v. Deichert, 639
Delameilleure v. Delameilleure, 829
Dellinger v. Dellinger, 828
DelZio v. Presbyterian Hosp., 1131

Dematteo v. Dematteo, 138
Denise & Kevin C., In re Marriage of,
  676
Denisi v. Denisi, 504
Denton, In re Marriage of, 656
Department of Human Resources v.
  Fillingane, 686
Department of Revenue v. Mason, 685
Department of Soc. Servs. ex rel. Byer v.
  Wright, 474
Depasse, Estate of, 216
Depew v. Depew, 1050
Derungs v. Wal-Mart Stores, Inc., 301
DeSantis, In re Marriage of, 786
DeSanto v. Barnsley, 172
DeShaney v. Winnebago County Dept. of Soc.
  Serv. 340, 342, 343, 929, 962, *966*, 971,
  972, 974
Destefano v. Grabrian, 312, 315
Devine v. Devine, 727, 729
D.G. v. D.M., 1072, 1073
Dike v. School Board, 298, 300, 301
Dillon v. Legg, 397, 401
DiMartino v. Scarpetta, 1026
Dire v. Dire-Blodgett, 216
DiSandro, In re, 570
Division of Youth & Family Servs. v.
  M.Y.J.P., 1079
D.L., In re, 1048
D.L.W., In re, 891
D.M., In re Adoption of, 1048
D.M.B. and R.L.B., In re Marriage of, 810
D.M.M., In re Adoption of, 1033
D.N.T., In re Adoption of, 1028, 1038,
  1078, 1081-1082
Dodd v. Burleson, 797
Doe, Matter of, 1144
Doe v. Baker, 907
Doe v. Bloomington Hosp., 907
Doe v. Bolton, 31, 32, 48, 49
Doe v. Burkland, 394
Doe v. Coughlin, 158
Doe v. Doe, 319, 532, 749
Doe v. Duling, 380, 381, 382
Doe v. Marion, 929
Doe v. New York City Bd. of Health, 1143
Doe v. Roe, 1028
Doe v. Shalala, 1133
Doe v. Sundquist, 1093
Doe v. Ward Law Firm, P.A., 1092
Doe 1 ex rel. Tanya S. v. North Cent.
  Behavioral Health Systems, Inc., 929
Doe 1 v. State, 1093

Dombrowski v. Noyes-Dombrowski, 658
Donato v. AT&T, 268
Donnelly, In re, 580
Dothard v. Rawlinson, 249
Doucette v. Washburn, 658
Dowell v. Dowell, 1003
Dowling v. Bullen, 314
Downey v. Muffley, 750, 781
Downing v. Downing, *668*, 671, 672
Dresser v. Cradle of Hope Adoption Ctr.,
　　Inc., 1101
D.S., In re, 1078
D.S.D., In re, 1063
D.T., In re, 987
Dubovsky v. Dubovsky, 317
Dugan v. Dugan, 657
Dunagan v. Commonwealth, 697
Dunkin v. Boskey, 1118
Dunn, In re Marriage of, 522
Dunn v. Cometa, 592
Dunn v. Palermo, 255
Dunphy v. Gregor, 397, 401, 402, 432
Dunson v. Dunson, 1002
Dupre v. Dupre, 828
Dutton v. Department of Soc. Welfare,
　　367
Dvorak v. S.H., 997
D.W., Ex parte, 1096

East 10th St. Assocs. v. Estate of Goldstein,
　　434, 435
E.C. & S.C. Children, In re, 750
Edelman, State v., 935
Edenfield v. Edenfield, 626
Edmisten v. Edmisten, 512, 515
E.G., In re, 1004
E.H., In re, 946
E.H., In re Adoption of, 1065
Eisenstadt v. Baird, *11*, 13, 15, 20, 31, 70,
　　271, 281, 299, 349
Eischen v. Stark County Bd. of Comm'rs,
　　1101
Elisa B. v. Superior Court, 459, *478*, 482,
　　483, 484, 485, *666*, 667, 668, 801, 803,
　　1073, 1110, 1113, 1114
Elk Grove Unified Sch. Dist. v. Newdow,
　　742
Elkus v. Elkus, 659
E.L.M.C., In re, 742
Engelkens, In re Marriage of, 800
E.N.O. v. L.M.M., 801

E.R., In re, 999
Erickson v. Bartell Drug Co., 14, 284
Erickson v. Board of Governors, 1127
Escobar v. INS, 211
Escobedo v. Nickita, 1033
Esser v. Esser, 721
Estate of _____. *See* party name
Estelle v. McGuire, 889, 934
Estin v. Estin, 706
Evan, In re Adoption of, 1089
Ex parte _____. *See* party name

Fargo Women's Health Org. v. Schafer, 85
Farrey v. Sanderfoot, 639
Faulkner v. Goldfuss, 605
Favrot v. Barnes, 139
Feltmeier v. Feltmeier, *526*, 530, 531
Felton v. Felton, 741
Fenwick v. Fenwick, 829
Ferenc v. World Child, Inc., 1101
Ferguson v. City of Charleston, 108, 923,
　　924
Ferguson v. Ferguson, *595*, 601, 602, 603,
　　604, 605, 625
Ferguson v. McKiernan, 1114
Ferguson v. Skrupa, 18
Ferrer v. Commonwealth, 544
Ferrin v. Department of Corrections Servs.,
　　158
Ferro v. Ferro, 504
Finstuen v. Edmonson, 1091
Fish v. Behers, 476
Fisher v. Fisher, 646
Fitzsimmons v. Fitzsimmons, 753
Fitzsimmons v. Mini Coach of Boston, Inc.,
　　403
Flood v. Braaten, 841
Flora v. Flora, 526
Florida Bar ex rel. Dunagan, 562
Florida Bar v. Dunagan, *559*, 562
Florida Dept. of Children & Families v.
　　F.L., 987
Folds v. Barber, 120
Forbush v. Wallace, 255
Ford, Estate of, *1067*, 1070, 1071, 1072
Foreman v. Foreman, 715
Foretich v. United States, 940
Forlenza, In re, *833*
Fowler v. Perry, *123*, 126
Fowler v. Sowers, 828
Foxvog v. Foxvog, 1002
F.P., Ex parte, 1033

Frank v. Superior Ct., 1012
Franklin v. Commonwealth, 709
Franks, In re Marriage of, 523
Freeman v. Rushton, 1097
Frenzel v. State, 930, 934
Frey v. Frey, 525
Friedrich v. Katz, 206
Fritsche v. Vermilion Parish Hosp. Serv.
    Dist., 225
Froland, State v., 771
Frontiero v. Richardson, 248
Fryar v. Roberts, 218
Frye v. United States, 935
F.S. v. L.D., 320
Fulk v. Fulk, 743, 747
Fulton-De Kalb Hosp. Auth. v. Reliance
    Trust Co., 929
Furia, Estate of, 1072
Furst v. Furst, 516

Galison v. District of Columbia, 1063
Gallagher, In re Marriage, of, 1072
Gallaher v. Elam, 683, 684
Gardiner, Estate of, In re, 181
Gardner v. Gardner, 617
Garrett v. Watson, 402
Garrison v. Garrison, 1001
Garska v. McCoy, 730
Gastineau v. Gastineau, 633, 688
Gates v. Gates, 317
Gaulkin, In re, 270
Gault, In re, 814, 1018
Gayden, In re Marriage of, 854
G.C. v. Alaska Dept. of Health & Soc.
    Servs., 905
G.C.B., In re, 1060
Geduldig v. Aiello, 280, 281, 282
General Electric Co. v. Gilbert, 277, 278,
    281, 282
Geno, State v., 946
Gerald G.G., Matter of, 1088
Gerber v. Hickman, 159
Gibson v. Gibson, 892, 1009
Giffen v. Crane, 730
Gillett-Netting v. Barnhart, 1110, 1113,
    1114, 1115, 1116
Gillmore, In re, 679
Gitter v. Gitter, 844
G.L. v. M.L., 315, 318
Glaze v. Glaze, 496
Glazner v. Glazner, 320, 322, 323
Globe Newspaper v. Superior Court, 950

Glomb v. Glomb, 1009
Glona v. American Guarantee & Liab. Ins.
    Co., 451, 462, 469
Goalen, In re, 152
Goff, In re, 904
Goldstein v. Goldstein, 504
Goller v. White, 892
Golub v. Golub, 659
Gomez, In re Adoption of, 1047
Gomez v. Perez, 450, 467, 469
Gonzales v. Oregon, 98
Gonzales v. Reno, 1005
Goodell, In re, 261, 262
Goodfellow v. Goodfellow, 505
Goodhand v. Kildoo, 810
Goodridge v. Department of Pub. Health, 160,
    169, 170, 171, 172, 173, 174, 175, 176,
    215, 218, 1090
Goodwin v. Turner, 159
Gorman v. McMahon, 313
Gormley v. Robertson, 394, 443
G.P. v. State, 1035
Grace v. Grace, 718
Grady, In re, 872
Graham v. Graham, 689
Grand Jury Subpoena, In re, 358
Grant v. Grant, 780
Graves v. Estabrook, 396, 401, 402, 403, 404,
    432, 434
Gray v. Bourne, 1028
Grayson v. Grayson, 674
Green, State v., 189, 195, 196, 197, 199
Greer v. Greer, 730
Griffith v. Johnston, 1057, 1066
Grimm v. Grimm, 523
Griswold v. Connecticut, 1, 6, 10, 13, 15, 18,
    20, 31, 52, 55, 67, 70, 146, 152, 158,
    226, 299, 350
Grossman v. Grossman, 786
Groves v. Clark, 1093, 1096
Groves v. Cost Planning & Management
    Int'l, Inc., 283
Gruett v. Nesbit, 1027, 1028
G.S. v. T.S., 814
Guardianship of _____. *See* party
    name
Guido, In re, 256
Guiles v. Simser, 570
Guillot v. Munn, 674
Gunderman v. Helms, 1028
Gundmundson, In re Marriage of,
    717
Gursky v. Gursky, 1105

Gustaves v. Gustaves, 747
Gustavo G., In re Adoption of, 1064
Guy v. Guy, 654
G.W. v. Sheriff of Jefferson County, 696

Haacke v. Glenn, 209
Hack v. President & Fellows of Yale
   College, 438
Haker-Volkening v. Haker, 715
Hall, State v., 1085
Hall v. Fertility Inst. of New Orleans,
   1117
Ham v. Hospital of Morristown, 929
Hamblen v. Davidson, 317, 318
Hamilton v. Hamilton, 737
Hamiter v. Torrence, 673
Hammer v. Hammer, 613
Hammon v. Indiana, 336, 746
Hammonds v. Hammonds, 613
Hanke v. Hanke, 777
Hansen v. Hansen, 1011
Harris, In re Marriage of, 798
Harris v. McRae, 49
Harrold v. Collier, 797
Hartman v. Hartman, 1009
Harvey v. Robinson, 688
Haugan v. Haugan, 655
Hawkes v. Spence, 833
Hawthorne v. State, 329, 333, 335
Hayes v. Gallacher, 833
Haymes v. Haymes, 512, 514, 515
Hazlewood Sch. Dist. v. Kuhlmeier, 1018
Hearndon v. Graham, 1012
Heath, In re Marriage of, 766
Hecht v. Superior Court, 1116-1117, 1131
Height v. Height, 139
Heiner v. Simpson, 313
Helsel v. Noellsch, 313
Helton v. Helton, 829
Hemmer, In re Adoption of, 1100
Henne v. Wright, 252, 257
Hensarling v. Hensarling, 497
Herbst v. Swan, 799
Hernandez v. Robles, 174
Herzfeld v. Herzfeld, 1008
Hester v. Dwivedi, 1123, 1124
Hewellette v. George, 891
Hewitt v. Hewitt, 390, 392, 393, 396
H.G., In re, 1028
H.H., Ex parte, 748
Hicks ex rel. Feiock v. Feiock, 696
Hightower, In re Marriage of, 514

Hiibel v. Sixth Judicial Dist. Court of Nev.,
   938
Hill v. Colorado, 52
Hill v. Moorman, 1096
Hisquierdo v. Hisquierdo, 648
Hitaffer v. Argonne Co., 314
H.L. v. Matheson, 89
H.L.C., In re Adoption of, 1078
H.L.T., In re, 762
Hobbs v. Pender County, 380, 413
Hocevar, State v., 890
Hodas v. Morin, 1109, 1143
Hodge v. Hodge, 654
Hodges, People v., 924, 927
Hodgson v. Minnesota, 83, 88
Hoffman v. Hoffman, 514
Holcomb v. Holcomb, 719
Holden, In re Marriage of, 614
Holguin v. Flores, 403
Holifield, People v., 426
Hollandsworth v. Knyzewski, 828
Hollis v. Hollis, 516
Holm, State v., 197
Holodook v. Spencer, 892
Holterman v. Holterman, 656
Holtzman v. Knott, 802
Hoosier v. State, 935
Hoots v. K.B., 1049
Hope Int'l Univ. v. Superior Court, 412
Hornbuckle v. Plantation Pipe Line Co., 32
Horridge v. St. Mary's County Dept. of
   Soc. Servs., 929
Hough v. Hough, 640
Howard, In re, 797
Howard v. Child Welfare Agency Review
   Board, 965
Hubbard v. Hubbard, 475
Hubert v. Williams, 436
Huckfeldt, In re, 639
Huffman v. Fisher, 257
Hughes, In re Marriage of, 547
Hughes v. Hughes, 497
Hughes v. State, 354
Hulsey v. Carter, 1070
Humphrey v. Humphrey, 844
Hunsaker, In re Estate of, 227
Hutelmyer v. Cox, 313
Hyde v. Hyde & Woodmansee, 199

Idaho v. Wright, 948
I.H., In re Guardianship of, 1114
Immediato v. Rye Neck Sch. Dist., 864

In re _____. *See* party name
Indiana High Sch. Athletic Assn v. Raike, 154
Infant Doe, In re, 907
International Shoe Co. v. Washington, 706
International Union, UAW v. Johnson
    Controls, Inc., 284
Ireland v. Smith, 755
Irving v. State, 935
Isaacs v. Isaacs, 139
Israel v. Allen, 188, 1085
Ivey, In re, 904

Jackson v. Jackson, 1110
Jackson v. Proctor, 667
Jackson v. State, 1101
Jaclyn, In re, 920
Jacobi v. Jacobi, 525
Jacobson, United States v., 1106
Jameson v. Jameson, 633
Jansen v. Westrich, 679
J.B. v. M.B., 1132, 1133
J.C., In re Guardianship of, 994, 997, 999
J.D.M., In re, 803, 804
J.D.V. v. R.M.T., 811
J.E.B. v. Alabama ex rel. T.B., 455
Jefferson v. Griffin Spalding County Hosp.
    Auth., 107
Jeffries v. Jeffries, 509
Jeffrys v. Jeffrys, 544
Jegley v. Picado, 380
Jenkins, In re Estate of, 1084
Jennings v. Hurt, 220, 223, 224
Jersey Shore Med. Ctr.-Fitkin Hosp. v.
    Estate of Baum, 246
Jertrude O., In re, 906
Jewell v. Jewell, 580
J.F., In re, 1100
J.F. v. D.B., 1145, 1147
Jhordan C. v. Mary K., 1114
Jizmejian v. Jizmejian, 504
J.M., In re, 69
J.M.F., Ex parte, 750
J.M.K., In re Parentage of, 1114
Joel A. v. Giuliani, 965, 981
John B. v. Bridget B., 319
John B. v. Superior Court, 319
John D. v. Department of Soc. Servs., 924
John Doe, In re Petition of, 1034
Johnson v. Calvert, 1140, 1145
Johnson v. Johnson, 1070
Johnson v. Lewis, 679
Johnson v. Muelberger, 579

Johnson v. Rogers Mem'l Hosp., Inc., 1013
Johnson v. Superior Court, 1106
Johnson v. Thomas, 591
Jolley v. Seamco Labs., Inc., 1072
Jones, In re Estate of, 474
Jones, State v., 895
Jones v. Boring Jones, 794, 803, 805
Jones v. Chandler, 454
Jones v. Hallahan, 172
Jones v. Henderson, 313
Jones v. Jones, 737
Jones v. South Carolina Dept. of Soc.
    Servs., 1035
Jones v. State, 84
Jones v. Swanson, 307, 313
Jones v. Tarnawa, 827
Joshua S., In re, 1097
Jurado v. Bradshear, 714
Juvenile Appeal (83-CD), In re, 879, 883,
    884, 885

K. v. B., 354
Kalia v. Kalia, 580
Kandu, In re, 178
Kansas v. United States, 703
Kantaras v. Kantaras, 180
Karas, State v., 345
Kasey v. Richardson, 228
Kass v. Kass, 1132
Katz v. United States, 9
K.A.W., In re, 1038-1039
Kawatra v. Kawatra, 829
Kay C., In re Adoption of, 1100
Kayla, In re, 904
Keeney v. Heath, 160
Keller v. O'Brien, 633
Kelley v. Commonwealth, 905
Kelley v. Kelley, 721
Kelsey S., Adoption of, 1028, 1032, 1033,
    1035, 1036, 1037
Kendall v. Kendall, 743
Kennedy v. Damron, 225
Kergosien v. Kergosien, 503
Kerkhoff v. Kerkhoff, 754
Kerrigan v. Connecticut Dept. of Pub.
    Health, 174, 537
Kes v. Cat, 811
Ketterle v. Ketterle, 659
Keys Youth Servs. v. City of Olathe, 367
Kibby, In re, 912
Kilpatrick, In re, 217
Kimbrell, In re Marriage of, 783

Kimel v. Florida Bd. of Regents, 293
Kimura, In re Marriage of, 573, 578, 579
King v. S.B., 483, 667
Kingsley v. Kingsley, 1018
Kinsella v. Kinsella, 685
Kirchberg v. Feenstra, 241
Kirchner, In re Petition of, 1034
Kirkpatrick v. District Court, 200, 203, 205
Kittredge v. Kittredge, 626
K.J. v. Division of Youth & Family Serv., 979
Kjelland v. Kjelland, 731
Klatt v. Labor & Indus. Review Bd., 154
Klaus v. Fox Valley Sys., 315
Klein, In the Matter of, 108
K.M. v. E.G., 1134, 803, 1139, 1140, 1142
Knepp v. Niece, 509
Knowles v. Binford, 445
Koch v. Koch, 139
Kohring, In re Marriage of, 679
Kolacy, In re Estate of, 1115
Kolbet v. Kolbet, 787
Kopac, In re Marriage of, 633
Kosek, In re Marriage of, 787
Kowalski, In re Guardianship of, 415, 420, 421, 442, 1097
Krauel v. Iowa Methodist Med. Ctr., 1126
Kristine H. v. Lisa R., 485, 667, 1036, 1072
K.S. v. G.S., 1110
K.S.P., In re Adoption of, 1089
K.T., In re, 890
Kujawinski v. Kujawinski, 678
Kulko v. Superior Court, 703, 706, 707, 708, 709, 713, 714
Kurchner v. State Farm Fire & Cas. Co., 1117
Kushnick v. Kushnick, 580
Kusior v. Silver, 474
Kyle F., In re, 1033
Kyllo v. United States, 10

LaChapelle v. Mitten, 808, 825, 1114
Ladely, In re Marriage of, 683
Lafaye, In re Marriage of, 717
Lalli v. Lalli, 452
L.A.M. v. B.M., 750
Lamaritata v. Lucas, 1114
Lambert v. Myers, 159
Lambert v. Wiklund, 84
Lamberts v. Lillig, 798
LaMusga, In re Marriage of, 827, 828, 829
Landeros v. Flood, 929

Lane v. Albanese, 581
Lane v. Lane, 1110
Langan v. Saint Vincent's Hosp., 183, 404, 444
Langdon v. Langdon, 514
Langone v. Coughlin, 158
LaPorta v. Wal-Mart Stores, Inc., 284
Largess v. Massachusetts Supreme Judicial Court, 171
Larson v. Dunn, 843
LaRue v. LaRue, 625
Lassiter v. Department of Soc. Servs., 987
Laurence v. Nelson, 786
Lawrence v. Texas, 56, 65, 66, 67, 68, 69, 70, 71, 97, 170, 174, 197, 367, 368, *379,* 380, 381, 382, 409, 410, 412, 413, 425, 617, 749, 750, 1057, 1123
L.B., In re, 667, 1072, 1114
Leary v. Leary, 812, 815
Lebo v. Lebo, 1097
Lefevre, State v., 890
Lehr v. Robertson, 470, 471, 1032, 1034
Lemmerman v. Fealk, 1013
Lerner v. Laufer, 718
LeTellier v. LeTellier, 709, 713, 714
Levin v. Yeshiva Univ., 436
Levine v. Konvitz, 396
Levinson v. Washington Horse Racing Comm'n, 154
Levy v. Louisiana, 451, 452, 462, 469
Lewis v. Harris, 174, 250
Lewis v. Lewis, 753
Li v. Oregon, 179
Liberta, People v., 347, 352
Lickle v. Lickle, 494, 497
Lifchez v. Hartigan, 1120, 1122, 1124
Limon, State v., 72, 381, 382
Limon v. Kansas, 381
Lindsay v. Lindsay, 787
Lindsey v. Lindsey, 514
Lipscomb v. Simmons, 377
Lisa Diane G., In re, 1097, 1098, 1099, 1100
Lisa I. v. Superior Court, 475, 476
Litoff v. Pinter, 780, 786
Litowitz v. Litowitz, 1134, 1140
Little v. Little, 688
Little v. Streater, 455
Littlefield, In re Marriage of, 139
Littlejohn v. Rose, 546
L.N.K. ex rel. Kavanaugh v. St. Mary's Med. Ctr., 121
Lockwood, In re, 261

Lockyer v. City & County of San
  Francisco, 174
Lofton v. Kearney, 446
Lofton v. Secretary of Dept. of Children &
  Family Servs., 70, 446, *1051*, 1056,
  1057, 1058, 1059, 1097
Lomholt v. Iowa, 949
Longo v. Longo, 634
Louisiana v. Taylor, 360
Loving v. Virginia, 140, 150, 151, 152, 153,
  155, 158, 163, 167, 174, 175, 176, 177,
  202
Lowe, Estate of, Matter of, 128
Lowery v. Lowery, 713
Loyd, In re, 754
Lozinski v. Lozinski, 706
Lozoya v. Sanchez, 403
L. Pamela P. v. Frank S., 459
L.S., In re, 906
Lucas v. Lucas, 629, 633, 634, 639
Luke, Adoption of, 1088, 1089
Lutgen, In re, 762
Lynch v. Dukakis, 979
Lynch v. King, 979
Lyng v. Castillo, 376
Lynn, In re Marriage of, 639
Lyon v. Department of Children & Family
  Servs., 930

M., In re Adoption of, 184, 188
M. v. H., 394
Mace v. Mace, 657
MacGregor v. Unemployment Ins. Appeals
  Bd., 414
Madewell v. United States, 225
Madigan, In re, 640
Madyun, In re, 106
Maharam v. Maharam, 316, 319
Mahoney v. Mahoney, 654
Maiorana v. Rojas, 127
Mallen v. Mallen, 138
Mallette v. Children's Friend & Serv., 1101
Malwitz, In re Marriage of, 709
Maness, People v., 1010
Mani v. Mani, 606, 611, 613, 614, 626
Maples, Application of, 1092
Marcum, United States v., 380
Mariga v. Flint, 1089
Marisol v. Giuliani, 965, 973, 978, 979, 980,
  981
Mark M., In re, 780
Marriage of _____. *See* party name

Marriage/Children of Betty L.W. v.
  William E.W., In re, 475
Marshall, In re Marriage of, 783
Martin v. Ziherl, 380
Martinez v. NBC, Inc., 301
Marvin v. Marvin, 383, 389, 390, 391, 392,
  393, 396, 403, 404, 434
Marx v. State, 951
Mary D. v. Watt, 780
Maryland v. Craig, 949
Maryland v. Culver, 571
Maryland v. Runkles, 1063
Maryland Comm'n on Human Relations v.
  Baltimore Gas & Elec. Co., 268
Marzano v. Computer Science Corp., 296
Mascaro v. Mascaro, 674
Massee, In re Marriage of, 605, 626
Mathis v. Mathis, 633
Matter of _____. *See* party name
Matthews v. Smith, 258
May v. Anderson, 837
May v. May, 665
Maybin v. Stewart, 780
Mayer-Kolker v. Kolker, 551
Maynard v. Hill, 115, 142, 152
Maynard v. McNett, 828
Maynor, People v., 905
May's Estate, In re, 188
Mazzitelli v. Mazzitelli, 137
M.C., In re Marriage of, 1110
McAdams v. McAdams, 1100
McCaffrey v. Green, 707
McCarty v. McCarty, 648
McCavitt v. Swiss Reinsurance Am. Corp.,
  268
McClement v. Beaudoin, 1050
McComb v. Wambaugh, 972
McConnell v. Anderson, 410
McCorvey v. Hill, 29
McCourtney v. Imprimis Tech., 306
McCoy v. McCoy, 827
McCulloh v. Drake, 530
McDaniel, In re, 960
McDaniel v. Gile, 572
McDonald v. McDonald, 505
McDormott v. Reynolds, 313
McDowell v. McDowell, 504
McGinley, In re Marriage of, 679
McGriff v. McGriff, 750, 781
McGuire v. McGuire, 242, 244, 245, 246,
  611, 865
McKay v. McKay, 681
McKeiver v. Pennsylvania, 1018

McKelvey v. McKelvey, 891

McKim, In re Marriage of, 522

McKinney v. State, 1101

McKnight, State v., 923, 924

McLaughlin v. Florida, 152

McLaughlin v. Superior Court, 847, 853, 854

McMillan v. McMillan, 808, 811

McNaughton, In re Marriage of, 613

McPherson v. McPherson, 319

McTiernan, In re Marriage of, 657

Mead v. Batchlor, 697

Meade v. Meade, 841

Mendel, In re, 842

Mengal v. Mengal, 139

Mesa v. U.S., 224

Messina v. Bonner, 1013

Metcalf v. Metcalf, 563

Metropolitan Life Ins. Co. v. Holding, 225

Metz, In re Marriage of, 714

M.E.W., In re, 188, 1085

Meyer v. Meyer, 654, 741

Meyer v. Mitnick, 126

Meyer v. Nebraska, 15, 18, 19, 20, 31, 34, 83, 152, 245, 796, *857*, 858, 863, 864, 865, 869, 890, 960, 1009, 1016, 1018

M.F., In re, 920

M.H. v. Caritas Fam. Servs., 1101

Michael v. Michael, 618, 625, 627, 628

Michael H., Adoption of, 1037

Michael H. v. Gerald D., 463, 469, 471, 472, 474, 475, 476, 477, 483, 484, 802, 805, 807, 1033

Michael J. v. Arizona Dept. of Econ. Sec., 904

Michael M. v. Department of Econ. Sec., 786

Michael M. v. Superior Court, 249

Michaels, State v., 921

Mid-South Ins. Co. v. Doe, 1144

Milke v. Milke, 324

Miller, In re, 256

Miller v. Department of Corrections, 268

Miller v. Miller, 210, 251, 633, 659

Miller-Jenkins v. Miller-Jenkins, 485, 803, 1119, 1120

Mills v. Habluetzel, 451

Minister of Home Affairs v. Fourie CCT, 180

Minix, In re Marriage of, 741

Minkin v. Minkin, 551

Minnear v. Minnear, 688

Minnesota v. Vance, 335

Miracle v. Spooner, 972

Misenheimer v. Burris, 313

Mississippi Band of Choctaw Indians v. Holyfield, 1050, 1078

Missoula YWCA v. Bard, 246

Mitchell v. Mitchell, 1003

Mitchell v. Moore, 394

Mizrachi v. Mizrachi, 633

M.J., In re, 1114

M.J.M.L., In re, 988

M.J.S., In re Adoption of, 1060

M.L.P.J., In re, 1072

M.M., In re, 257

M.M.D., In re, 798

M.N. v. D.S., 123

Moe, In re, 84

Moe v. Dinkins, 206

Molloy v. Meier, 1102, 1124

Molloy v. Molloy, 811

Moncher v. Maine, 780

Monslow, In re Marriage of, 634

Monterroso v. Moran, 761

Moore v. Asente, 1038

Moore v. City of East Cleveland, 371, 375, 376, 471

Moore v. Moore, 633, 786

Morgan v. Foretich, 935, 938

Morgan v. Morgan, 210

Moriarty v. Bradt, 797

Morris v. Morris, 497

Morrison v. Sadler, 179

Moschetta, In re Marriage of, 1141

Moses v. Moses, 556, 557

Moss v. Superior Court, 697

M.T. v. J.T., 180

Muhammad v. Muhammad, 501, 503

Mullen v. Phelps, 781

Mullen-Funderberk, In re Marriage of, 678

Muller v. Oregon, 248, 283

Mulling v. Mulling, 634

Mullins v. Oregon, 1048

Murphy v. Holland, 228

Mussivand v. David, 320

M.W. v. Department of Children & Family Servs., 914, 918, 919, 920

M.W. v. Kruzicki, 923

N.A. v. J.H., 904

Nachmani v. Nachmani, 1133

Naim v. Naim, 141, 152

Nancy S. v. Michele G., 801

Nashville Gas Co. v. Satty, 282

Nasser-Moghaddassi v. Moghaddassi, 641

Navarro v. Pfizer Corp., 295

Neal v. Neal, 250, 256, 257
Nearing v. Weaver, 344
Nelson v. Nelson, 707
Nemeth v. Nemeth, 514
Neudecker v. Neudecker, 678
Nevada Dept. of Human Resources v.
    Hibbs, 249, 293
Neville v. Neville, 649
New Jersey Div. of Youth & Family Servs.
    v. L.V., 924
New York v. Wal-Mart Stores, 268
Newby v. United States, 886
Newcomb v. Ingle, 324
Newdow v. U.S. Congress, 742
Newman v. Cole, 892, 1008
Newman v. Dore, 138
Nguyen v. INS, 248, 477
Nichol v. Stass, 962, 1008
Nicholas H., In re, 474, 483
Nichols, In re, 640
Nicholson, In re, 763
Nicholson v. Scoppetta, 763, 904, 912
Nicholson v. Williams, 763
Nicini v. Morra, 971
Nieters v. Nieters, 522
N.M.W., In re, 903
Norman v. Unemployment Ins. Appeals
    Bd., 414
North Coast Women's Care Med. Group,
    Inc. v. Benitez, 1117, 1118
North Dakota Fair Housing Council v.
    Peterson, 429, 435, 436, 437
North Florida Women's Health & Coun-
    seling Servs. v. State, 87
Northrop v. Northrop, 605
Northwestern Mem'l Hosp. v. Ashcroft, 54
Norton v. Ashcroft, 51
Norton v. Macfarlane, 313

Oakley, State v., 153, *691,* 695, 696, 697,
    698, 702
O'Bannon v. O'Bannon, 827
O'Brien v. O'Brien, 656, 659
Occean v. Kearney, 979
O'Connell v. Kirchner, 1034
Office of Child Support Enforcement v.
    Lee, 683
O.G. v. Baum, 1004
Ohio ex rel. Ten Residents of Franklin
    County v. Belskis, 154
Olivo v. Olivo, 658
Olmstead v. United States, 9

Olmstead v. Ziegler, 686, 688, 698
Olski, In re Marriage of, 649
Olson v. Children's Home Soc'y, 1102
Olver v. Fowler, 442
Omahen v. Omahen, 504
Omar v. Lindsey, 971
Opinion Texas Gen., 207
Orr v. Orr, 249, 611, 614
Ortiz v. Los Angeles Police Relief Ass'n,
    160
Ortwein v. Schwab, 543
Osbon, Ex parte, 562
Osborne v. Ohio, 9
Osborne v. Payne, 311, 313, 314
Osman v. Keating-Osman, 617
Otis, In re Marriage of, 612, 615
Overbey v. Overbey, 688
Owens, Ex parte, 718
Owens-Illinois, Inc. v. Gianotti, 403
Ozkan v. Ozkan, 497, 515

Pacourek v. Inland Steel Co., 1126
Painter v. Bannister, 796, 822
Palmore v. Sidoti, 734, 736
Panganiban v. Panganiban, 707
Parentage of A.B., In re, 483
Parentage of C.A.M.A., In re, 797
Parentage of J.M.K., In re, 459
Parentage of L.B., In re, 803, 805
Parham v. J.R., 867, 870, 871, 872, 1018
Park Holding Co. v. Power, 437
Parker v. Parker, 510, 512, 738
Patel v. Navitlal, 211
Paternity of K.B., In re, 459
Patetta v. Patetta, 1001
Payson v. Payson, 626
Pendergast, In re, 681
People v. _____. *See* party name
People ex rel. J.R.T. v. Martinez, 688
Peralta v. Chromium Plating & Polishing
    Corp., 284
Perez v. Lippold, 152
Perl v. Perl, 551
Perlberger v. Perlberger, 532
Perry-Rogers v. Fasano, 1147
Persad v. Balram, 218
Peshek, In re, 1033
Peterka, In re Marriage of, 633
Peters-Riemers v. Riemers, 757, 760
Petrie, In re, 1063
Petty v. Petty, 783
Phelps v. Bing, 206

Philip S., In re, 1092

Philipp v. Stahl, 713

Phillip B., In re, 109, 899, 901

Phillips v. Martin Marietta Corp., 307

Piatt v. Piatt, 747

Pickett v. Brown, 451

Picon v. O.D.C. Assocs., 433

Pierce, In re Adoption of, 1096

Pierce v. Society of Sisters, 16, 18, 19, 20, 34, 83, 245, 796, 857, *858,* 863, 864, 866, 869, 890, 1009

Pikula v. Pikula, 730

Piscopo v. Piscopo, 659

Pite v. Pite, 138

Planned Parenthood v. Danforth, 50, 76

Planned Parenthood v. Miller, 84

Planned Parenthood Fed'n of Am. v. Ashcroft, 54

Planned Parenthood Fed'n of Am. v. Gonzales, 54

Planned Parenthood of Blue Ridge v. Camblos, 84

Planned Parenthood of Central New Jersey v. Farmer, 85, 87, 1004

Planned Parenthood of Idaho v. Wasden, 87

Planned Parenthood of Northern New England v. Heed, 77, 82, 85, 86, 106, *870*

Planned Parenthood of Southern Arizona v. Lawall, 85

Planned Parenthood of Southeastern Pennsylvania v. Casey, 32, 48, 49, 50, 51, 54, 67, 72, 76, 77, 84, 85, 86, 97, 106, 1132

PNC Bank Corp. v. Workers' Comp. Appeal Bd., 224

Poe v. Ullman, 8

Poelker v. Doe, 49

Poff v. Caro, 436

Pohlmann v. Pohlmann, 681, 683, 684, 685, 689

Pollock v. Pollock, 324

Polovchak, In re, 1005

Polovchak v. Meese, 1005

Popovich v. Cuyahoga County Court of Common Pleas, 766

Portlock v. Portlock, 720

Posik v. Layton, 394

Postema v. Postema, 656

Potter v. Murray City, 198

Potter v. Potter, 828

Potts, In re Marriage of, 683

Powel v. Chaminade Coll. Prep., Inc., 1013

Powell v. State, 69, 380

Powers v. Powers, 697

Prato-Morrison v. Doe, 1147

Prevatte v. Prevatte, 224

Price v. State, 1101

Prince v. Massachusetts, 858, 864, 881

Procanik v. Cillo, 1124

Prost v. Greene, 754, 756

Pulizzano, State v., 935, 936

Pulliam v. Smith, 750

Purdy v. Purdy, 1001

Putterman v. Putterman, 604

Pyles v. Russell, 1084

Queen's Medical Ctr. v. Kagawa, 246

Quilloin v. Walcott, 469, 470, 471

Quinlan, In re, 95

R. v. Secretary of State for Health, 1105

R.A., In re, 797

Radke v. County of Freeborn, 929

Ragin v. Lee, 455

Ragsdale v. Wolverine World Wide, Inc., 293

Rahawangi v. Alsamman, 580

Rainey v. Cheever, 478

Raley v. Spikes, 1088

Ramona v. Ramona, 1013

Ramona v. Superior Court, 1013

Randolph v. Randolph, 1002

Ranieri v. Ranieri, 216

Rankin v. Seagate Technologies, Inc., 292

R.B.F., In re Adoption by, 1088

R.C., In re, 1038

Reagan v. Vaughn, 315

Rebecca B., In re, 817, 819, 820, 821

Reed v. Reed, 248, 260

Rehfeld v. Roth, 823

Reid v. Reid, 505, 508, 509

Reininger v. Reininger, 679

Reinsch v. Reinsch, 720

Remy v. MacDonald, 1013

Renee B. v. Michael B., 756, 820

Rennie v. Rennie, 1003

Reno v. Flores, 1005

Renslow v. Mennonite Hosp., 1013

Rent Stabilization Assn v. Higgens, 435

Resources v. Sweat, 684

Rex v. Brasier, 952

Reynolds v. Giuliani, 981

Reynolds v. United States, 196, 197

R.G.M. v. D.E.M., 613

Rhea v. Rhea, 832
Rice v. Flynn, 1145
Richard v. Richard, 504
Richard P. v. Vista Del Mar Child Care
    Serv., 1101
Richardson, Adoption of, 1050
Richter v. Richter, 523
Rickard v. McKesson, 446
Rider v. Speaker, 1009
Riggins v. O'Brien, 1001
Ritchie III, In re, 258
Rivera v. Minnich, 455, 459
Rivkin v. Postal, 116, 119, 120
R.J.D. v. Vaughan Clinic, 871
R.L.C., State v., 475
R.M.G., In re Petition of, 1048
Robert B. v. Susan B., 1146
Robert Paul P., In re, 446
Roberts, In re Marriage of, 650, 654, 655
Roberts v. Roberts, 828
Roberts v. Williamson, 1012
Robertson v. Robertson, 614
Robinson, Ex parte, 261
Robinson v. Block, 366
Robinson v. Ford-Robinson, 799
Rocconi v. Rocconi, 504
Rodriguez v. Bethlehem Steel Corp., 314
Rodriguez v. McLoughlin, 960
Rodriguez v. Rodriguez, 605
Roe v. Conn, 885
Roe v. Doe, 865, 1002
Roe v. Jewish Children's Bureau of
    Chicago, 1101
Roe v. Wade, 20, 29, 30, 31, 32, 33, 34, 35,
    39, 48, 49, 50, 51, 52, 53, 54, 70, 77, 81,
    86, 106, 163, 253, 255, 281, 299, 1122,
    1133
Roger B., In re, 1091
Roger S., In re, 871
Rogers v. Rogers, 504, 674
Rolf v. Tri State Motor Transit Co., 1011
Roller v. Roller, 891
Roman v. Roman, 1132
Romer v. Evans, 66, 68, 164, 178, 1057
Romero, In re Marriage of, 633
Roper v. Simmons, 68
Rosales v. Battle, 402
Rose v. Rose, 697
Rosecan v. Rosecan, 614
Rosenberg v. Rosenberg, 620, 625, 626, 627,
    628
Rosengarten v. Downes, 444, 581
Rosenstiel v. Rosenstiel, 580

Rosenthal v. Erven, 314
Rosero v. Blake, 730
Ross v. Louise Wise Servs., 1101
Rossi, In re, 719
Rostker v. Goldberg, 249
Roth v. Weston, 797
Roussel v. Roussel, 531
Rowe v. Franklin, 751, 754
Rowey v. Children's Friend & Servs., 1101
Royer v. Royer, 509
R.S. v. R.S., 1110
Rubano v. DiCenzo, 804
Rumsfeld v. Forum for Academic & Inst'l
    Rights, 412
Russell v. Bridgens, 1090
Rutherford v. Rutherford, 516
R.W., In re, 987
Ryan v. Ryan, 1014, 1019
Rykiel v. Rykiel, 659, 663
Rysene W., In re, 997

Saenz v. Roe, 585
Sagar v. Sagar, 738, 741, 742
Sail'er Inn v. Kirby, 248
S.A.J., In re Adoption of, 1036
Saks v. Franklin Convoy Co., 284, 1127
Salahuddin v. Alaji, 715
Salucco v. Alldredge, 444, 581
Salzman v. Bachrach, 390
Sanders v. Gore, 120
Sanderson v. Bathrick, 1072
Sanderson v. Tryon, 198
Santolina, In re Estate of, 186
Santos Y., In re, 1049
Santosky v. Kramer, 455, 981, 986, 987, 999
Sammons, State v., 905
Sara J., In re Adoption of, 1049
Saul v. Brunetti, 798
Saunders v. Alford, 313
Savage v. Savage, 634
Savorese v. Corcoran, 721
Saxvik v. Saxvik, 634
S.B. v. S.J.B., 496
S.C. v. A.C., 504
Scamardo v. Dunaway, 313
*Scarpetta v. Spence-Chapin Adoption Serv.,
    1024*, 1026, 1027, 1032
Scheidler v. National Org. for Women, 52
Schenck v. Pro-Choice Network, 52
Schenk v. Schenk, 814
Schiavo, In re Guardianship of, 99
Schiavo ex rel. Schindler v. Schiavo, 99

Schibi v. Schibi, 210
Schleuter v. Schleuter, 532
Schuyler v. Briner, 684
Schwartz, People v., 1063
Scruggs, State v., 907
Sebastian v. Sebastian, 679
S.F. v. State ex rel. T.M., 459
S.H., In re, 783
Shafmaster v. Shafmaster, 719
Shahar v. Bowers, 301, *405*, 409, 410
Shane Carole B., In re, 1085
Shane T., In re, 909
Sharon S. v. Superior Court, 1088, 1089
Sharp v. Sharp, 707
Shearer v. Shearer, 522
Shehade v. Gerson, 842
Shehady, In re Estate of, 1084
Shelton v. Shelton, 755
Shepp v. Shepp, 198, 742
Sherrer v. Sherrer, 579
Shin v. Kong, 1110
Sholes v. Sholes, 543
Short v. Klein, 108
Sibley v. Sibley, 697
Simat Corp. v. Arizona Health Care Cost
    Containment Sys., 49
Simeone v. Simeone, 128, 134, 136, 137,
    138
Simmons, In re Marriage of, 180
Simmons v. Simmons, 657
Simpson v. Simpson, 321, 322, 323
Singer v. Hara, 172
Singer v. U.S. Civil Serv. Comm'n, 410
Singley v. Singley, 604
Sirca v. Medina County Dept. of Human
    Servs., 1101
Sisson, In re Marriage of, 810
S.J., In re, 904
S.J.D., In re Adoption of, 1091, 1092
S.J.J., In re, 998
Skinner v. Oklahoma, 20, 152
Smalley v. Parks, 1070
S.M.B., In re, 911
Smelser v. Smelser, 625
Smiley, In re, 543
Smith, In re, 797
Smith v. City of Salem, 181
Smith v. Fair Employment & Housing
    Comm'n, 431, 436, 437
Smith v. Four Corners Mental Health Ctr.,
    Inc., 962
Smith v. Freeman, 688
Smith v. Knoller, 404

*Smith v. Organization of Foster Families for
    Equality and Reform, 952*, 963
Smith v. Smith, 313, 625, 626, 673
Smith v. State, 187, 188, 329, 330
Snetsinger v. Montana Univ. Sys., 228, 414
Snider v. Snider, 706
Snow v. Snow, 633
Sockwell v. Sockwell, 729
Solis v. Tea, 720
Solomon v. Dist. of Columbia, 404
Solomon v. Solomon, 661
Soltero v. Wimer, 442
Soos v. Superior Court, 1141
Sorrel v. Henson, 460
Sosna v. Iowa, 582, 585, 586
Spafford v. Coats, 393, 396
Spahmer v. Gullette, 828
Spear v. Spear, 755
Spiegel, In re Marriage of, 136
Sprouse v. Eisenman, 1064
S.S. ex rel. Jervis v. McMullen, 972
St. Luke's Episcopal-Presbyterian Hosp. v.
    Underwood, 245
Stageberg, In re, 658
Stallman v. Youngquist, 1013
Stanard v. Bolin, 120
Stanley v. Bouzaglou, 712
Stanley v. Georgia, 9
Stanley v. Illinois, 460, 469, 470,
    471, 472
Stanton v. Abbey, 690
Stark County Bar Ass'n v. Hare, 1060, 1063
State ex rel. Black, In re, 196
*State ex rel. Children's Services Division v.
    Brady, 990*, 998
State ex rel. Dept. of Health & Human
    Servs. v. Farmer, 1003
State ex rel. Dept. of Soc. Servs. v. Howard,
    460
State ex rel. Mahoney v. St. John, 707
State ex rel. Score v. Bidwell, 686
State ex rel. T.B. v. CPC Fairfax Hosp.,
    871
State ex rel. Williams v. Marsh, 345
State v. _____. *See* party name
Staton, In re Marriage of, 658
Stearman v. State Farm Mutual Auto. Co.,
    318
Stenberg v. Carhart, 40, 48, 49, 50, 51, 53,
    54, 86, 1123
Steven S. v. Deborah D., 1114
Stevens v. Stevens, 654
Steverson v. Steverson, 730

Stillman, State v., 679
Stinson v. Larson, 322, 324
Stogner v. California, 951, 1013
Stoppleworth, State v., 688
Stratton ex rel. Kelley, In re, 258
Sullivan, In re, 1114
Sullivan v. Knick, 832
Sumey, In re, 1020
Suppressed v. Suppressed, 571
Suter v. Artist M., 979
Sutherlin v. Sutherlin, 763
Sutton v. Sutton, 228
Swanner v. Anchorage Equal Rights
    Comm'n, 31, 437
Swanson, In re Adoption of, 446
Swipies v. Kofka, 779
Sword v. Sword, 697
Sylvester v. Fogley, 413
Szumanski v. Szumanska, 263

T.A., In re, 895
Tabor, Ex parte, 721
Talty, State v., 153, 696
Tami, People v., 219
Tammy, Adoption of, 1085, 1088, 1089,
    1090, 1114
Tanner v. Oregon Health Science Univ.,
    414
Taylor, Ex parte, 951
Taylor, State v., 255
Taylor v. Beard, 1011
Taylor v. Commonwealth, 730
Taylor v. Jarrett, 708
Taylor v. Taylor, 633, 750, 829
T.B. v. L.R.M., 802, 1114
T.B.G. v. C.A.G., 314
T.E.P. v. Leavitt, 217
Terese B. v. Comm'r of Children &
    Families, 960
Teseniar v. Teseniar, 713
Tetreault v. Coon, 690
T.F. v. B.L., 483, 667, 1119
Thomas v. Anchorage Equal Rights
    Comm'n, 437
Thomas v. Thomas, 515
Thomas S. v. Robin Y., 1114
Thompson v. Barnhart, 224
Thompson v. Thompson, 227, 657, 811,
    841
Thorlaksen v. Thorlaksen, 810
Thornburgh v. American College of Ob-
    stetricians & Gynecologists, 50

Thornburgh v. Federal Express Corp., 315
Tice, State v., 905
Tietig v. Boggs, 720
Tillman v. Tillman, 614
Tinker v. Des Moines Indep. Community
    Sch. Dist., 1018
Tipton v. Aaron, 736
Titchenal v. Dexter, 1090
T.J.F., In re Adoption of, 1096
T.L.A., In re Petition to Adopt, 1060
TLC, Adoption of, 1033
Toms v. Taft, 159
Torres v. McClain, 718
Town of Castle Rock v. Gonzales, 339, 343,
    344, 345, 346, 347
T.R. v. Adoption Servs., Inc., 1028
Trammel v. United States, 344, 354, 358,
    359, 360
Traugott v. Petit, 255
Trear v. Sills, 1013
Trickey, In re, 639
Trimble v. Gordon, 452
Tripp v. Hinckley, 1114
Trociuk v. British Columbia (Attorney
    General), 257
Tropea v. Tropea, 828
Troxel v. Granville, 20, 789, 795, 796, 797,
    799, 800, 805, *863*, 864, 865, 866, 872,
    1018
Tsoutsouris, In re, 566, 569, 570
Tucker v. Shelby County Dept. of Pub.
    Welfare, 935
Turner v. Safley, 154, 158, 159
Turner v. Turner, 784, 786
Twigg v. Mays, 1020
Twyman v. Twyman, 531
Tylo v. Superior Court, 285
Ty M., In re, 998
Tyma v. Tyma, 605

UAW v. Johnson Controls, Inc., 1014
Underwood v. State, 935
Union Pac. R.R. Employment Practices
    Litig., In re, 14
Union Pacific Ry. Co. v. Botsford, 20
United States v. Bird, 51
United States v. Carrier, 950
United States v. Craft, 242
United States v. Davis, 662
United States v. Etimani, 950
United States v. Faasse, 715
United States v. Frye, 335

United States v. Hahn, In re, 128
United States v. Hawkins, 359
United States v. Hill, 154
United States v. Kras, 543
United States v. Lopez, 55
United States v. Morrison, 55, 336, 703
United States v. Mussari, 715
United States v. Rouse, 949
United States v. Russell, 715
United States v. Singleton, 358
United States v. University Hosp., 908
United States v. Van Drunen, 358
United States v. Virginia, 248
United States v. Wilson, 715
United States v. Wuliger, 325
Universal Life Church v. Utah, 216
Urquhart v. Urquhart, 673
U.S. Dept. of Agriculture v. Moreno, 362,
    365, 366, 367, 368, 376

Vaccarello v. Vaccarello, 717
Vacco v. Quill, 97
Vachon v. Pugliese, 842
Valentine v. American Airlines, 405
Valmonte v. Bane, 929
Van v. Zahorik, 1072
Van de Snade v. Van de Snade, 844
Vance v. Rice, 359
Vargas, In re Estate of, 228
Varnum v. Brien, 174
Vasquez v. Hawthorne, 438, 441, 442, 443, 444
Vaughn v. Lawrenceburg Power System, 263,
    267, 268
V.C. v. M.J.B., 802
Verdier v. Verdier, 1008
Vernon v. Vernon, 787
Vibbert v. Vibbert, 797
Victor A., In re Adoption of, 1028
Vigil, People v., 941, 945, 946, 949
Village of Belle Terre v. Boraas, 365, 366,
    367, 368, 371, 372, 374, 375, 376, 435
Vinson v. Vinson, 514
Visitation of _____. *See* party name
Vito, In re Adoption of, 1049, 1050
Vitro v. Mihelcic, 1012
Vogel v. Touhey, 717
Von Schack v. Von Schack, 578
Vrban v. Vrban, 678

Waddell, State v., 936
Wakeman v. Dixon, 804, 1119

Wallace v. Smythe, 962, 1008
Wallis v. Smith, 456, 459
Walter v. Stewart, 572
Walters v. Walters, 787
Walton v. State ex rel. Wood, 713
Walton's Marriage, In re, 523
Ward v. McFall, 684
Warford v. Warford, 737
Warnick v. Couey, 765
Warren v. Warren, 626
Washburn v. Washburn, 654, 655
Washington ex rel. Daly v. Snyder, 697
Washington v. Glucksberg, 67, 97, 98
Washington v. Thompson, 712
Watson v. Baker, 1084
Weber v. Aetna Cas. & Sur. Co., 448, 451
Weber v. Stony Brook Hosp., 908
Weber v. Weber, 634, 784
Webster v. Reproductive Health Servs., 30,
    49
Weigart v. Weigart, 1002
Weinand v. Weinand, 684
Weinberger v. Wiesenfeld, 248
Weintraub v. Weintraub, 614
Welborn v. Doe, 1105
Welfare of Children of A.O., In re, 998
Wellman v. Dutch, 754, 755
Wende C. v. United Methodist Church,
    315
Wendt v. Wendt, 605
Werthen, In re Marriage of, 634, 638, 639
West, State v., 891
West v. West, 754
Western States Construction v. Michoff,
    393
Westhab, Inc. v. City of New Rochelle, 367
W.E.T., In re, 1028
Wettstaedt, In re Marriage of, 649
Whalen v. Roe, 31
Wheeler v. United States, 952
Wheeling Dollar Savings & Trust Co. v.
    Singer, 1071
White, In re, 639
White, People v., 336
White v. Adoption of Baby Boy D., 1080
White v. Illinois, 948
White v. Nason, 782
White v. White, 325
White Tail Park, Inc. v. Stroube, 867
Whitely v. Leonard, 811
Whitman v. Mercy Mem'l Hosp., 422
Wilbur v. Delapp, 393
Wilder v. Bernstein, 981

Wildey v. Springs, 121
Will of Kaufmann, In re, 443
Williams v. Attorney General, 9, 70
Williams v. King, 9, 70
Williams v. North Carolina, 579, 584, 585
Williams v. Williams, 227, 604, 717
Willoughby v. Willoughby, 633
Wilson, Estate of, 1071, 1072
Wilson v. Ake, 178
Wilson v. Holliday, 696
Wilson v. State, 946
Wimmer v. Roanoke City Dept. of Soc.
    Servs., 912
Wineburgh v. Wineburgh, 681
Winfield v. Renfro, 226
Winkler v. Winkler, 629
Winn v. Perdue, 922
Wirsching v. Colorado, 780
Wirsing, In re, 872
Wisconsin v. Yoder, 859, 864, 865, 866, 870,
    1018
Wissink v. Wissink, 812
Witbeck-Wildhagen, In re Marriage of,
    1110
Witten, In re Marriage of, 1131
W.J., In re Adoption of, 1083
Woo v. Lockyer, 174
Woodson v. Woodson, 649
Woodward v. Commissioner of Soc. Sec.,
    1115
Woolf v. Woolf, 633

Workman v. Workman, 685
Wren v. Wren, 658
Wright v. Osburn, 674
Wright v. Wright, 604, 637

X, Y, & Z v. Sweden, 893

Yaden, State v., 422, 424, 425
Yergeau v. Yergeau, 500
Young v. County of Fulton, 961
Young v. Hector, 754
York v. Jones, 1131
Youker, In re Marriage of, 634
Young v. Van Duyne, 1101
Young v. Young, 1001
Younger v. Harris, 590

Zaabel v. Konetski, 714
Zablocki v. Redhail, 145, 150, 152, 153, 155,
    158, 163, 187, 192, 197, 202, 217, 684,
    695, 696
Zahrigner v. Zahrigner, 629
Zelman v. Simmons-Harris, 865
Zepeda v. Zepeda, 731
Zinkhan v. Zinkhan, 508
Zummo v. Zummo, 741, 742, 781
Zwicker v. Altamont Emergency Room
    Physicians Med. Group, 403

Index

ABA
  Ethics Commission on the Evaluation of the
      Rules of Professional Conduct, 269
  Family Law Section, 519, 814
  Juvenile Justice Standards, 881, 884
  Model Rules of Professional Conduct, 563,
      567n, 568-71, 817, 842, 928
  Model Rules of Professional Responsibility,
      842
  Standards for Criminal Justice, 324
  Standards of Practice for Family and Divorce
      Mediation, 852-853
  Standards of Practice for Lawyer Mediators in
      Family Disputes, 853
  Standards of Practice for Lawyers Who
      Represent Children in Abuse and
      Neglect Cases, 922-923
  Standards of Practice for Lawyers Who
      Represent Children in Custody Cases,
      816
Abandonment
  as factor in emotional abuse, 912-913, 1011
  as ground for divorce, 263, 508-509, 513-514,
      521-545
  as ground for termination of parental rights,
      471, 962, 994, 1017, 1025, 1034, 1037
  as neglect, 904-905
  "Baby Moses" laws, 905
  liability for, 244, 1011
Abduction of children
  attorney's ethical obligations to disclose
      whereabouts, 842-843
  criminal extradition as remedy, 840-841
  international child abduction, 843-844
    Hague Convention on Civil Aspects of
      International Child Abduction, 843-844
    International Child Abduction Remedies Act
      (ICARA), 844
    International Parental Kidnapping Act
      (IPKA), 844,
    statistics on, 843
  Parental Kidnapping Prevention Act (PKPA),
      834, 837-839, 841
  tort of custodial interference, 843
Abortion. *See also* Fetus; Pregnancy
  abortion pill (RU-486), 52-53
  access, 33, 51, 53
  adolescents and, 77-89
  as crime, 20-22, 28-30, 32, 35-37
  as medical procedure, 23-24, 30
  bypass proceedings, 77-80, 82-88
  Catholic Church and, 26
  common law, on 21-22
  comparative law and, 34-35
  consent requirements, 50
  constitutional guarantee, 20-28, 31-35, 40-63,
      76-77
  D & E, D & X procedures, 42-45, 51
  definition for criminal liability, 20-22
  dilation procedures, 42-45
  effect on crime rate, 34
  empirical evidence, 34, 76-77, 83
  equal protection and, 33
  family cap and, 56

Abortion (*Cont.*):
  fathers and, 72-77
  feminist views of, 33, 37-40
  fetal tissue and, 108-109
  fundamental right, 25, 28, 31, 48
  funding for, 49, 50
  gender discrimination and, 33
  health exception, 43-45, 48, 53, 54, 78-79
  history, 21-22, 35-37
  husbands and, 72-77
  informed consent requirement, 48, 50, 77
  maternal health and, 8, 22, 26-27
  "mature minor" concept, 77-78, 82, 1004
  Medicaid payment for, 49
  minors' rights to, 77-89
  morality of, 51
  notification requirement, 72-77
  parental consent requirement, 77-89
    judicial bypass, 80, 82-88
  parental notification requirement, 78
  partial-birth abortion, 40-45, 53-54
  philosophical views on, 37-40
  physicians' role, 32, 48, 86
  poverty, 55, 76
  psychological data on adolescents'
    decisionmaking, 82
  quickening distinction, 21-23, 26, 32, 36
  religion and, 26
  reproductive technology, 1107-1120
  response to *Roe*, 31-35
  right to privacy, 20-28, 31
  RU-486, 52-53
  Samaritan duty and, 37-39
  spousal consent, 72-77
  spousal notification, 76
  state constitutions and, 49n
  statistics on, 87
  technology and, 32
  theological issues, 26-27
  travel for purposes of, 53
  trimester framework, 26-27, 31-32, 48
  undue burden standard, 40-44, 47, 48, 49-54,
    70, 74, 76-80
  viability, 26-27, 31-32
  violence and, 51
  waiting periods, 53, 76, 77
  welfare recipients and, 56, 83
Abuse. *See* Child abuse and neglect
Acquired Immune Deficiency Syndrome (AIDS)
  adoption and, 1097
  blood tests and marriage, 216-217
  cause of children in foster care, 1064
  conjugal prison visits and, 158
  disclosure, 319
  estate-planning, 391, 444-445
  grandparents' custody, factor in, 796
  influence of, on courtship/marriage, 114
  phobia, 319

  premarital testing, 216-217
  prenatal treatment to prevent, 107
  privacy-related concerns, 217
  reunification of child with HIV-infected
    mother, 999
  spousal duty of disclosure, 319
  "standby" guardianship, 1097
Adolescents
  abortion rights, 72-89
  bypass proceedings, 77-80, 82-88
  condom availability programs, 866-867
  emancipation and, 1105-1111
  homosexuality and, 1000-1005
  marriage, 201-207, 1110
  "mature minor" concept, 77-78, 82, 1004
  medical treatment, 1004
  mental hospitalization, 867-870
  parental consent
    regarding abortion, 77-89, 971
    regarding commitment to mental hospital,
      867-870
    regarding marriage, 201-207
    regarding medical care, 1004
  parental notification
    regarding abortion, 72-77
  pregnancy, 87
  premarital counseling requirement, 205
  public assistance, 1003. *See also* Personal
    Responsibility and Work Opportunity
    Reconciliation Act
  sexual activity, 87
  sexual orientation and, 913-914, 1002-1003,
    1011
  statutory rape, 83, 84, 86, 192, 207, 249, 351,
    459, 913-914
Adoption
  abrogation, 1100-1101
  access to information about origins, 1092, 1105
  adult adoption, 445-447
  agency adoptions, 1024-1026, 1032
  attorney's role, 1060-1065
  baby selling, 1063-1065
  best interests test, 1021, 1029, 1072-1085
  biological parents' attitudes toward
    relinquishment, 1036
  child support arrearages, 1085
  confidentiality concerns, 1091-1092
  consent, 1024-1028
    pre-birth consent, 1024-1027
    revocation of consent, 1024-1028
  custody distinguished, 1036
  embryo, 1134, 1144
  empirical evidence, 1036, 1067
  equitable adoption, 1067-1073, 1214
  ethical issues, 1064
  failure, 1097-1102
  grandparent visitation postadoption, 1096
  "gray market", 1032

historical background, 1022-1023
identification of biological father, 1035
independent adoption, 1032, 1063, 1064
Indian Child Welfare Act, 1038
inheritance, 444-446, 1068-1073, 1084-1088,
    1115-1116, 1181
intermediaries, 1063-1064
international adoption, 1082-1084
Internet, 1037-1038, 1092
jurisdiction, 1073-1082
law reform, 1034-1035, 1079-1081
legal consequences of adoption, 1084-1085
matching, 1038-1051
National Association of Black Social Workers'
    policy statement, 1044-1045
notice to biological father, 1035
open adoption, 1093-1097
parental "licensing," 1060
placement criteria
  relevance of age in placement, 1050
  relevance of disability, 1050
  relevance of ethnic identity in placement,
      1038-1041, 1042-1051
  relevance of intelligence, 1050
  relevance of marital status, 1050
  relevance of race in placement,
      1038-1051
  relevance of religion in placement, 1050
  relevance of sexual orientation, 1051-1060
polygamy and, 198
putative father registries, 1034-1035
records, access to, 1063, 1091-1092
relinquishment, 1026, 1027, 1064
second-parent adoption, 1085-1091
sexual orientation, role of, 1051-1060
special needs children, 1066-1067, 1092
state-subsidized, 1066, 1102
stepparent adoption, 1085-1091
surrogacy and, 1107-1110
termination of parental rights, as dispensing
    with consent, 1029
transracial adoption, 1042-1051, 1066
Uniform Adoption Act, 1027, 1032, 1035,
    1036, 1057-1058, 1063, 1066, 1078-
    1080, 1080, 1084n, 1087-1089, 1095,
    1096, 1101
Uniform Parentage Act, 1034
Uniform Putative and Unknown Fathers' Act,
    1035
unmarried father's rights, 1028-1038
  consent, 1028-1038, 1082
  due process, 1030
  equal protection, 1030-1032
  notice, 1035
  opportunity to develop relationship, 1032,
      1037
  pre-birth conduct, 1032
  standard to terminate, 1034-1035

statutory protection for rights of,
    1034-1035
thwarted by mother, 1032-1035
wrongful adoption, 1101
Adoption and Safe Families Act, 964, 987,
    979, 997-999, 1018, 1045-1049,
    1066-1067
Adoption Assistance and Child Welfare Act,
    963-964, 999, 979, 988
  goals, 963
  permanency planning requirements, 963
  private right of action, 964, 976
  reasonable efforts requirement, 964, 976
Adultery
  artificial insemination constituting, 1104
  corroboration, 497
  criminal consequences, 431
  disclosure, 499
  double standard, 498
  during marital separation, 500
  elements of, 496
  empirical data on, 498
  frequency, 498
  gender-based, commission of, 494-500
  grounds for divorce, 494-500
  military, 498
  morality of, 498, 500
  on-line conduct as, 497
  privacy concerns, 498
  same-sex acts as constituting, 496
  spousal support and, 512
  standard of proof, 497
AFDC. *See* Aid to Families with Dependent
    Children
Affinity relationships, 187. *See also* Incest
African-Americans
  abortion and, 46, 51
  adolescent pregnancy, 87
  adoption, 1042-1051, 1066
  antimiscegenation laws, 150-153, 166, 175
  birth control movement, 10-11
  child support, 616-617
  common law marriage, 225
  domestic violence, 328-329
  extended families, 87, 375
  forced caesarean sections, 106-107
  foster children, 1064
  grandparents' custody rights, 799
  marriage, age at, 204n
  marriage customs, 214
  right to die, 98
  slavery, 11, 141, 150, 214
  slave marriages, 229-231
  single parents, 447
  spousal support, 616
AID. *See* Artificial insemination
Aid to Families with Dependent Children,
    454-455, 671, 699, 700

AIDS. *See* Acquired Immune Deficiency
        Syndrome
Agreements to marry. *See* Marriage
ALI
   Family Dissolution, Principles of
      child support, 615, 641, 667,
         672-675, 684-685
      "compensatory spousal payments," 615,
         628, 657, 674, 717
      custody
         approximation standard, 731
         child's preferences, 808-812
         "custodial responsibility," 769
         custody modification, 823
         day care, as a factor, 754
         "decisionmaking responsibility," 769
         de facto parent, 804-805
         domestic violence, as a factor, 757-765
         gender, as a factor, 729
         modification, 823
         parent by estoppel, 804-805
         parenting plans, 730-731
         race, as a factor, 734-737
         relative earning capacity, 755-756
         religion as a factor, 743
         relocation, 832
         sexual conduct, as a factor, 749
         sexual orientation, as a factor, 749
      de facto parent generally, 804-805
      degrees and licenses, 657
      domestic partners, 395
      family home, 641, 674
      goodwill, 658
      loss compensation rules, 610
      marital misconduct, 594n
      parent by estoppel generally, 804-805,
         1036, 1068-1069, 1070, 1072
      premarital contracts, 136-137
      Principles, background, 731n
      property division, 599-605, 615, 674
      recharacterization of separate property,
         599-605
      separation agreements, 786, 789-794
      spousal support, 610, 615
   Model Penal Code
      on abortion, 22, 31
      on cohabitation, 379
      on justifiable force, 891
      on sodomy, 379
Alienation of affections, 307-312
Alimony. *See* Spousal support
Alternative dispute resolution. *See also* Child
        custody mediation
   arbitration, 846
   collaborative law, 855
   conciliation, 850
   mediation, 845-855

   mandatory, 846
   therapy distinguished, 846
Alternative families. *See* Cohabitation;
        Communes; Extended families;
        Sexual orientation
AMA, 36-37
American Academy of Matrimonial Lawyers,
        620, 817
American Bar Association. *See* ABA
American Indian. *See* Native American, Indian
        Child Welfare Act
American Law Institute. *See* ALI
American Medical Association. *See* AMA
American Psychological Association. *See* APA
Americans with Disabilities Act, 99, 217, 293,
        300, 766, 974, 1123, 1126
Amish, 859-863
Annulment. *See also* Fraud
   divorce distinguished, 99
   duress as ground for, 210
   fraud as ground for, 207-209
   grounds for, 209
   historical background, 209
   immigration fraud, 210-212
   "relation back" doctrine, 209
   spousal/child support following, 209
   standard for consummated marriages, 210
APA Guidelines for Child Custody Evaluations in
        Divorce Proceedings, 819
Artificial insemination, 1102-1120. *See also* In
        Vitro Fertilization; Surrogacy
   access to, 1117
   child support, 1110
   custody and visitation rights of same-sex
        partners, 794-795, 800-801,
        1114-1117
   disclosure 1105
   donor screening, 1106
   father's consent
      to insemination, 1105, 1110
      required for adoption, 1103-1104
   father's legal obligations, 1104
   fraud, 1106
   legitimacy of offspring, 1104, 1112-1115,
        1119-1120
   posthumous, 1110-1117, 1130
   same-sex partners, 1114, 1117
   sperm donor, parental status of, 1105,
        1110-1117, 1141
   statutory responses, 1105
   types of, 1102
Uniform Parentage Act, 1034, 1104
Uniform Putative and Unknown Fathers Act,
        1035
Uniform Status of Children of Assisted
        Conception Act, 1109
   unmarried mothers and, 1117-1118

Assisted reproduction. *See* Artificial
    Insemination; Egg Donation; In vitro
    fertilization; Surrogacy
Assisted suicide, 67, 97-98
Attorney
    adoption and, 1032, 1060-1065
    attorney-client privilege, 563, 842-843
    child abuse reporting, 928
    children, attorneys for
        abuse proceedings, 922
        custody proceedings, 812-817
        delinquency proceedings, 815
        guardians ad litem, 813-817, 817
        guidelines, 815
        roles of, 815
    confidentiality, 563, 817, 842-843
    conflicts of interest, 559-566
    counseling role, 552-573
    disclosure rules, 562, 563
    discretionary vs. mandatory, 815
    divorce, right to, 543
    dual representation, 562-566
    empirical research, 558, 571
    ethical obligations, 552-573
    fees in divorce cases, 556-558
    joint representation, 562, 564, 565, 566
    Model Rules of Professional Conduct, 562,
        564, 567n, 569
    privacy concerns, 815
    relocation disputes, 823-833
    risks to divorce attorneys, 558-559
    roles of divorce attorneys, typology, 552-573
    role strain, 554-556
    same-sex marriage litigation, 169-170
    separation agreements, 715-721
    sexual relations with client, 566-573
    surrogacy arrangements, 1107
    transference, 552-554

Baby selling. *See* Adoption; Surrogacy
Baird, William, 11, 13-14
Bankruptcy, 634-641
    attorneys fees, dischargeability of, 640
    Bankruptcy Reform Act, 638
    child support obligations, dischargeability of,
        640
    difficulties caused for women creditors, 640
    liens to secure obligation, 639-640
    pensions and, 641
    policy of, 638-639
    property division, dischargeability of, 638-640
    spousal support obligations, dischargeability
        of, 640
Bankruptcy Reform Act, 638
Battered child. *See* Child abuse and neglect
Battered spouses. *See* Domestic violence
Battered Women Immigrant Protection Act, 212
Best interests of the child. *See* Adoption;
    Custody; Guardianship

Bigamy. *See* Polygamy
Biological fathers' rights. *See* Unmarried Parents
Birth control. *See* Abortion; Contraception;
    Pregnancy
Blackstone, William
    on duty of child support, 744, 670, 679
    on parents' right to children's earnings, 94,
        679
    on suicide, 94
    on wife beating, 238
    on wife's common law disabilities, 237-238,
        239
    on nonaccess, 466
Bradwell, Myra, 284, 259-262, 300
Brandeis, Louis, 9-10
Breach of promise to marry, 116-123
Breastfeeding, legal regulation of, 298-301, 730-
    731,

Canadian Charter of Rights and Freedom, 180,
    257, 394
Cesarean section, forced, 100-109
Central registry for reports of child abuse. *See*
    Child abuse and neglect
Child abuse and neglect
    adolescent abuse, 913
    allegations of, in custody proceedings,
    Baby Does, 907-909
    battered child syndrome, 889
    causes, 877
    Child Sexual Abuse Accommodation
        Syndrome, 934-936
    child-victim as witness, 941-952
    civil procedures, 883
    concurrent jurisdiction, 883
    Confrontation Clause, 941-952
    corporal punishment as, 888-889
    criminal procedures, 883-919
    cross-cultural perspectives, 893-894
    cultural defense, 906
    defined, 904, 912
    discipline, distinguished, 886-895, 912
    disposition alternatives. *See also* Foster care;
        Termination of Parental Rights
        foster care, 952-966, 973-981
        liability for selection of disposition, 966-972
        summary seizure, 879-885
        termination of parental rights, 981-999
    effects, 919
    empirical data, 890-891, 1049
    emotional abuse, 918-919, 930, 909-911
    emotional neglect, 911
    evidentiary problems, 930-941
        anatomically-correct dolls, 936
        battered child syndrome, 889
        competency, 950, 952
        hearsay and Confrontation Clause,
            941-952
        privileges, 936-941

Child abuse and neglect (*Cont.*):
    repressed memories, 951
    statutes of limitation, 951, 1012-1013
    syndrome issues, 930-934
  exposure to domestic violence, 892
  fabricating abuse, 920-921
  failure to protect, 912
  failure to thrive, 904
  fetal abuse, 923-924
  foster care. *See* Foster care
  gay and lesbian youth, 913-914, 1002-1003
  guardian ad litem, 922
  historical perspective, 874-876, 961,
      1006, 1008, 1016
  homelessness as neglect, 904
  incidence, 877, 889, 904, 911, 919
  indicia of abuse, 890
  intergenerational transmission of abuse, 892
  international perspectives, 893-894
  Juvenile Justice Standards Relating to Abuse
      and Neglect, 881, 884
  medical neglect, 899-901, 907-909
  Munchausen's Syndrome by Proxy, 890
  National Center on Child Abuse and Neglect,
      877n, 919n
  National Incidence Studies, 877, 904, 911, 919
  nomenclature "sexual abuse," 917-918
  parental immunity doctrine, 891-892
  parental liability for child's suicide, 907
  parental privilege to discipline, 886-895
  parricide, 914
  physical neglect, 895-899
  prenatal abuse, 923-924
  privacy, 873
  procedures for removal from home
    stages of intervention, 883
    summary seizure, 879-885
    termination of parental rights, 883,
      920, 922, 955, 981-999
  prospective abuse, 915, 920
  psychodynamic factors, 876-877
  reasonable parent standard, 892, 1009, 1011
  registry, 929
  religious beliefs as basis for neglect, 906
  reporting laws, 924-930
    civil liability, 929
    criminal liability, 929-930
    duty to report, 927-930
    effects on therapeutic relationship, 930
    empirical research, 930
    immunity, 939
    purposes of, 927
    sanctions for failure to report, 929
  repressed memories of child sexual abuse, 951
  right to counsel, 922
  sexual abuse, 914-924
  shaken baby syndrome, 889
  statutes of limitations, 951, 1012-1013

  summary seizure, 879-882
  termination of parental rights. *See*
      Termination of parental rights
  tort suits for, 883, 891-892, 912, 929, 951
  transmission of abuse, 892, 819
  transmission of violence, 892
  trauma of testifying, 949
  vague statutory standards, 885
  vehicular neglect, 950
  videotaped testimony, 950
  witnessing abuse, effects of, 892-893
Child Abuse Prevention and Treatment Act
    (CAPTA), 877, 922
Child custody
  Acquired Immune Deficiency Syndrome as
    factor, 782
  adoption distinguished,
  ALI Principles. *See* ALI
  attorney for child
    discretionary vs. mandatory, 814
    ethical obligations, 815
    guidelines for, 815, 922
    in cases of abuse, 922
    role of, 815
  best interests standard, 729, 732-733
    criticisms of, 732-733
  career as factor, 751-755
  child's preference, 808-812
  cohabitation of parent as factor, 746
  custodial interference, 787, 842
  day care, role of, 754
  defined, 769
  disability, role of, 764-765
  domestic violence as factor, 757-765
  effects of divorce on children, 723-726
  enforcement remedies, 841-842
  equitable parent, 1072-1073
  experts' role, 817-822
  failure to protect, 763
  fathers' rights groups, 747-748
  fitness, 743-750
  friendly-parent provision, 762-763
  functional definition of family, 801
  geographic restrictions on travel, 821,
    823-833
  gender-based criticisms of standards,
    729-732
  gender bias, 754, 761, 830, 851
  grandparents' rights, 789-799, 805-807
  guardian ad litem, 812
  historical background, 850
  international enforcement of custody rights,
    843-844
  joint custody
    benefits of, 775-777
    child support, 674
    criticisms of, 771, 775-777
    defined, 769

domestic violence and, 773, 760, 775-777
effect of parental agreement, 770
empirical research, 773, 763
factors affecting awards, 736, 770
historical background, 769
influence of fathers' rights groups, 747-748
modification, 822-833
parental agreement required, 770
presumption, preference, or option,
  767-775
jurisdiction, 833-845
  extradition, 840-841
  full faith and credit clause, applicability of,
    837
  federal court jurisdiction, 841
  Hague Convention on Civil Aspects of
    International Child Abduction, 843
  International Child Abduction Remedies
    Act, 844
  International Parental Kidnapping Act, 844
  Parental Kidnapping Prevention Act,
    837-839
  Uniform Child Abduction Prevention Act,
    844
  Uniform Child Custody Jurisdiction Act,
    836-837
  Uniform Child Custody Jurisdiction and
    Enforcement Act, 838-840, 1080-1081
maternal deference standard, 729
maternal preference, 729
mediation, 933-949. *See also* Alternative
    dispute resolution; Child custody
    mediation.
modification of custody, 820
  child's preference, 808-811
  joint custody, 814
  Parental Kidnapping Prevention Act,
    837-839
  standards, 899
  Uniform Marriage and Divorce Act, 733
  Uniform Child Custody Jurisdiction Act,
    836-837
  Uniform Child Custody Jurisdiction and
    Enforcement Act, 838-840
natural parent presumption, 796
nexus test, 747
parent vs. non-parent disputes, 789-808
parent locator service, 714, 841
parental alienation syndrome, 820-821
Parental Kidnapping Prevention Act,
    837-839
parental preference, 800, 802, 811
parenting plans, 771
paternal preference, 728-729
physical disability as factor, 765-767
primary-caretaker presumption, 730-732
psychological parent, 800-801
race as factor, 734-738

religion as factor, 738-743
relocation disputes, 823-833
representation, 812-817
separating siblings, 732
sexual conduct generally, as factor, 746-747
sexual orientation as factor, 743-750
smoking as factor, 782
statistics on, 723
stepparents' rights, 799
tender years' presumption, 727-732
time as factor, 756
tort of custodial interference, 843
Uniform Child Custody Jurisdiction Act
    (UCCJA), 833-836
Uniform Child Custody Jurisdiction and
    Enforcement Act (UCCJEA), 833-834,
    838-840
Uniform Marriage and Divorce Act (UMDA),
    733, 746, 810
unmarried fathers, visitation rights of,
    463-478
visitation. *See* Visitation
wealth as a factor, 755
Child custody mediation, 845-856. *See also*
    Alternative dispute resolution
  benefits, 846-847
  children's role, 854
  confidentiality, 842, 845, 854
  criticisms of adversary system, 845-847
  definition, 850
  disadvantages, 851, 853
  domestic violence and, 851-852
  due process concerns, 849, 854
  ethical issues, 853
  feminist concerns regarding, 851
  mandatory vs. voluntary, 846
  qualifications of mediators. 852
  role of attorney, 853
  role of mediator, 853
  roots of, 850-851
  standards of practice, 852
Child labor, 858-865, 961
Child neglect. *See* Child abuse and neglect
Child placement. *See* Adoption; Foster care
Child support. *See also* Enforcement of support
  adoption, terminating arrearages, 1085
  ALI, Family Dissolution, Principles of,
    667, 672-675
  artificial insemination, 1110
  automatic adjustment, 689
  bankruptcy, effect of, 640
  choice of law, 708
  common law duty, 679
  discretion, role of, 668
  educational expenses, 678-679
  effects of guidelines, 672
  emancipation and, 1001
  empirical research, 673

Child placement (*Cont.*):
  enforcement of, 691-715. *See also* Enforcement
      of support
  failure to pay, 699-715
  Fair Credit Reporting Act, 701
  family home and, 640-641, 674
  Family Support Act, 671, 672, 689, 700, 702,
      708, 709, 712-714
  Federal Case Registry of Child Support
      Orders, 700
  Full Faith and Credit for Child Support
  Orders Act, 709
  grandparents' responsibility for, 1003
  guidelines for determining, 668-676, 689
  health care costs, 675
  income-shares model, 669, 672
  increase in income as changed circumstance,
      668-670
  joint custody, in cases of, 674
  jurisdiction
      for postmajority support cases, 678
      full faith and credit clause, applicability of,
          707, 737
      interstate enforcement, 703-709
  Melson formula, 672-675
  modification of, 681, 685-689 *See also*
      Modification of support
  nonmarital children, 448-450, 454
  objectives of, 668, 671-672
  Parent Locator Service, 714
  passport revocation, 701
  percentage-of-income standard, 672
  postmajority support, 676-681
  remarriage effect on, 681-686
  separation agreements and, 720
  stepchildren, support of, 683-685
  taxation, 659
  Uniform Interstate Family Support Act. *See*
      Uniform Interstate Family Support Act
  Uniform Reciprocal Enforcement of Support
      Act. *See* Uniform Reciprocal
      Enforcement of Support Act
  unmarried fathers, obligations of, 448-450,
      454
  visitation, relationship to support, 783,
      784-787
Child Support Enforcement Amendments,
    448-454, 699
Child Support Recovery Act, 714, 715
Child welfare agencies. *See* Child abuse and
    neglect
Choice of law. *See* Conflict of laws
Civil unions. *See also* Domestic partnerships;
    Same-sex marriage;
    Sexual orientation
  benefits, 182-183
  dissolution, 182, 580-582
  eligibility, 182
  international developments, 180

interstate recognition, 151, 176, 177
  requirements, 444
Clergy malpractice, 311-315
Clergy sex abuse scandal, 951
Cloning, 1147-1148
Cohabitation
  ALI Principles, 393, 395
  as stage of courtship, 114, 377, 388
  Canadian law, 370-371
  child custody/visitation, effect on, 746
  common law marriage distinguished, 224,
      386n, 392-394, 400
  criminal laws, 379-383
  cross-cultural perspectives, 368, 394-395
  domestic partnership ordinances, 444
  domestic violence and, 422-426
  due process, 363-366, 371-375
  effects on institution of marriage, 388, 392
  empirical research, 390
  employment discrimination, 412-413
  equal protection and, 381
  freedom of expression, 381
  freedom-of-religion defense to housing
      discrimination, 436
  functional vs. formalistic definition of family,
      366-367, 420
  gender equality, 393, 447
  historical background, 379-380
  homemaking services, 391
  housing discrimination and, 426-440
  morality, 388, 392
  polygamy and, 391
  premarital, 114, 388
  presumptions of marriage, 227-228
  privacy concerns, 380
  putative spouse doctrine distinguished,
      227-228
  restitutionary remedies, 391, 394, 395
  rights of unmarried cohabitants,
      adoption, 445-447
      contract generally, 383-396, 403
      custody, 746
      disposition of body, 422
      employment, 405-415
      government benefits, 414
      health benefits, 415-419
      housing, 426-440
      inheritance, 441
      medical decisionmaking, 415-419
      pensions, 414, 415
      property rights, 383-396
      "spousal" support, 383-396, 538
      tort, 396-405
      unemployment benefits, 389
  same-sex partners, 378-379, 380-381, 390,
      394-395, 403-425, 433, 441-447
  Scandinavian laws, 378
  spousal equivalency legislation, 405
  spousal support, effect on, 383-396, 538

Cohabitation (*Cont.*):
  statistics on, 361, 377-378, 390, 438
  status-based approach, 387-388, 393, 395, 402
  tort law, 396-404
Co-housing movement, 363
Commitment of minors to mental hospital. *See*
      Mental hospitals
Common law marriage
  arguments for/against, 225-226
  choice of law, 225
  duration of residence, 225
  historical background, 223-224
  impediments to marriage, 224
  inheritance, 224
  legitimacy of issue, 228
  privacy right and, 226
  requirements, 224
  Uniform Marriage and Divorce Act, 152
  validity, 220-228
Communes, 362-371
  food stamp eligibility, 363-367
  zoning ordinances, 368
Community property, 596, 598, 601-604,
      626-627, 648
Compulsory school attendance. *See* Education
Comstock, Anthony, 5-6
Comstock laws, 5-6
Conflict of laws
  abortion, 53
  breach-of-promise suits, 116
  child support, 708
  common law marriage, 225
  covenant marriage, 538-539
  divorce, 573-592
  polygamy, 199
  property division, 706
  right to die, 97
  same-sex marriages, validity, 176-177
  support, 707
  surrogacy, 1109
  validity of marriage in general, 177
Consanguinity, 166, 187, 213.
      See also Incest Consent
  abortion and, 77-89
  adoption and, 1024-1028
  AIDS testing, 217
  artificial insemination, 1102-1104
  competence of minors to give, 82
  disabled infant, care of, 907-909
  emancipated minors' ability to give, 1001
  "informed consent," 48, 50, 77
  "mature minor," 77-78, 82
  medical treatment, 1004
  parental
    for minor's abortion, 77-89
    for minor's marriage, 201-207
    for minor's medical treatment, 1004
  spousal consent to abortion, 72-77
  spousal consent to insemination, 1105

Consolidated Omnibus Budget Reconciliation
      Act, 650
Contempt proceedings
  nonpayment of support, 691-715
  civil vs. criminal contempt, 700
Contraception
  beliefs about harm, 5
  birth control movement, history of, 5-9, 13
  compulsory, 20
  condom distribution in schools, 866
  efficacy of laws, 5-9
  emergency, 14, 52
  fraudulent misrepresentation regarding, 459
  obscenity and, 5-6
  privacy issues, 1-9, 13-14
  race and, 10-11
  refusal to dispense, 14, 52
  sex discrimination and, 14
  sterilization, 20, 872
  welfare recipients and, 7, 56
Corporal punishment. *See* Child abuse and neglect
Courtship, 111-114
Covenant marriage, 538-539, 544
Criminal conversation, 307-315
Cruelty. *See* Child abuse and neglect; Divorce;
      Domestic violence

Daycare, 302, 305, 306
  role in custody proceedings, 753
Deadbeat Parents Punishment Act, 697, 702, 715
Death with Dignity Act, 98
Defense of Marriage Act (DOMA), 174, 176-179,
      443, 581, 1090, 1091
Dependent children.
      See Child abuse and neglect
Desertion, 503-509
  as ground for divorce, 508
  elements of, 509
  constructive desertion distinguished, 509
Disabled newborns, 907-908
Discrimination
  age-related, 206
  disability-related, 293, 300, 765-767,
      907-909
  employment, 270-295
  gender-related, 129-167, 279-285, 293-327,
      330-331, 907-908
  homosexuality. *See* Sexual Orientation
  housing, 426-438
  marital status, 285-293, 487, 1218
  poverty, 55, 76, 149-150
  pregnancy, 270-285
  race, 106-107, 141-142, 146-148, 152-153
  sexual orientation, 169-181
  transsexuals, 181
Divorce
  abolition of fault-based defenses, 515, 526
  access to divorce, 536-583, 540-552
  adultery as grounds for, 494-500

Divorce (*Cont.*):
  alternative dispute resolution. *See* Alternative
    dispute resolution
  annulment distinguished, 209
  attorney, role of. *See* Attorney
  as a process, 490-491
  bankruptcy. *See* Bankruptcy
  bilateral divorce, 579
  California law reform movement, 520
  child support. *See* Child support
  child's suit to divorce parents, 1014-1020
  collusion as defense to, 515-516
  comity, 580
  comparative-law perspective, 535
  condonation as a defense to, 512-515, 525,
    526, 580
  conflicts of interest, 559-566
  connivance as a defense to, 515-516
  constitutional issues involved in, 523, 540-542,
    547-552, 573-591
  constructive desertion, 505-508
  conviction of felony, as grounds for, 508
  costs and fees, 540-542
  covenant marriage, 544
  cruelty as ground for, 501-505
  custody. *See* Child custody
  desertion as ground for, 505-510
  divisible divorce doctrine, 575, 706
  divorce mill states, 586
  domicile, 576-577
  dual representation, 562-566
  effects on children, 723-726
  empirical research, 544, 558, 571
  ex parte divorce, 579, 775
  fault, return-to-movement, 538-539
  fault-based defenses generally, 510-516, 580
  fault-based grounds generally, 494-510
  foreign divorces, validity of, 580-715
  full faith and credit, 579
  gay divorce, 536-537
  gender-based differences in divorce
    experience, 491-493, 546, 556, 601
  "get," 602-607, 547-550
  historical background, 486-490, 496,
    517-519, 550, 564-568
  impotence as ground for, 488, 509
  incompatibility as ground for, 492, 522
  indigents' right to, 543
  insanity, 516, 520, 546, 568, 569
  Internet, 580, 782
  jurisdiction, 573-592
  legal separation, 520, 526, 598
  living separate and apart, 523-226
  no fault
    assessments of, 533-534
    gender-equality and, 533-534
    irreconcilable differences, 500, 503, 519,
      520, 522
  irretrievable breakdown, 519, 521-523
  legal problems raised by, 522-533
  procedures, 522, 523, 545
  notice, 578-582
  privacy and, 525
  property division. *See* Property division
  pro se divorce, 544-545
  rate of, 489-490, 517, 593
  recrimination as defense to, 510-512, 526
  religious divorce, 550
  remarriage, 681-686
  residency, durational requirements, 582-586
  right to counsel, 543, 596
  separation distinguished, 526
  sexual ethics, 566-573
  socio-cultural obstacles, 545-547
  stages of, 490-491
  statistics on, 489-490
  stigma, 545-547
  summary dissolution, 522
  spousal support. *See* Spousal support
  tax consequences, 659-666
  tort suits, 526-532
  Uniform Marriage and Divorce Act. *See*
    Uniform Marriage and Divorce Act
  unilateral divorce, 522-523
  violence, 333, 558-559
  waiting periods, 525, 539
  willful nonsupport as grounds for, 509
Domestic partnership. *See also* Civil Unions;
    Same-sex marriage,
    Sexual orientation
  benefits, 182-183, 426-444
  dissolution, 182, 580-582
  domestic violence, 424
  eligibility, 182
  international developments, 180
  interstate recognition, 151, 176, 177
  requirements, 444
Domestic relations exception to federal diversity
    jurisdiction, 55-56, 586-592
Domestic violence. *See also* Child abuse and
    neglect; Torts
  battered woman syndrome, 329-339
  Blackstone on, 333
  child's custodial preference, 812
  civil/criminal remedies, 335-336
  cruelty as ground for divorce, 501-505
  custody and, 757-764
  discrimination (work, housing) 337
  duress as defense, 338
  duties of law enforcement, 339-347
  effects on child of witnessing, 326
  evidentiary issues, 354
  failure to protect, 763
  federal legislation on, 336-337
  firearms legislation, 346
  friendly parent provision, 762

historical background, 333
immigrant women, 337
interspousal tort liability for, 333
joinder, 531
joint custody, 773
Lizzie's law, 762-763
mandatory arrest policy, 341-342, 345-346
marital rape, 347-354
mutual acts, 760-761
name changes for victims, 256-257
privacy, 347, 352-353
profile of abusers, 326
property crimes involved, 354
restraining orders, 201, 339-346
same-sex partners, 422-426
sex discrimination, 339-347
spatial patterns, 326-327
special relationship doctrine, 342-343
specialized courts, 346-347
stalking, 345
statistics on, 327-328, 345, 346, 353
stereotypes, 334
temporal patterns, 326-327
tort law, 530-532
treatment programs, 761-762
Violence Against Women Act, 211-212, 336
Don't Ask, Don't Tell policy, 411-412, 413

Earnings
parent's common law right to minor's, 679-680
women's right to earnings. 240
Education
Amish, 859-866
compulsory education statutes, 16-18
family privacy concept, 16-18
foreign language teaching, 15, 19
parental authority regarding, 16-20
postmajority support, 676-680
public vs. private, 16-18
religious beliefs and, 17
Egg donation, 1134-1148. *See also* Embryos
Emancipation. *See also* Adolescents
adult- vs. child-initiated, 1001
California law regarding, 1002
common law, 1001
defined, 1000, 1002
effect on parental rights/duties, 1001-1002
marriage, effect of, 1001
mature minor rule of limited emancipation, 1004-1005
military service, effect of, 1001-1002
parental consent to emancipation, 1005
statutory criteria, 1001-1002
Embryos. *See also* In vitro fertilization; Surrogacy
adoption, 1134, 1141-1144
as persons, 1131
as property, 1131
disputes involving, 1127-1148

frozen, 1131-1132
inheritance and, 1067-1073
legal status of, 1127-1148
matching, 1038-1059
misappropriated, 1146-1147
records, 1091-1093
selection of, 1122-1124
surrogacy and, 1107-1110, 1130, 1136
transfers, 1144-1145
unused, 1133-1134
Employee Retirement Income Security Act (ERISA), 414, 647
Employment
breastfeeding and legal regulation of, 298-301
equal protection challenges. 280-281
equal treatment/special treatment debate, 283-284, 300-301
family leave, 285-295
comparative-law perspective, 535
Family and Medical Leave Act, 248-250, 286-296, 1127
fetal-protection policy, 284
lawyer marriages and professional responsibility, 260-270
mandatory maternity leaves, 270-274
married women's disabilities, at common law, 259-263, 285-293
"mommy track," 305-306
nepotism rules, 263-293
new mom discrimination, 283
paternity leave, 294-296, 320-323
pregnancy discrimination, 276-296, 293-310,
Pregnancy Discrimination Act, 274-279, 282-285, 1127
privacy-related concerns, 284
protective labor legislation, 279-285
sexual fraternization rules, 265-266
spousal identity rules, 268
statistics, 291
Title VII, 267-284, 289-290, 300, 325
work-family conflict, 325-331, 292-298, 302-306
voluntary change in, 686-688
Enforcement of support
administrative proceedings, 707-708
bankruptcy. *See* Bankruptcy
contempt proceedings, 655-657
civil vs. criminal contempt, 697
due process requirements, 712-721, 760-767
Deadbeat Parents Punishment Act, 702, 715
defenses to nonpayment
inability to pay, 696-697
visitation rights, connection to, 784-786
empirical research, 786-787
Family Support Act, 684, 700
federal role in, 698-703
Full Faith and Credit for Child Support Orders Act, 709-715

Enforcement of support (*Cont.*):
  incarceration and, 695-696, 697
  income withholding, 700
  international enforcement, 715
  interstate enforcement
    civil enforcement, 700, 701, 718
    criminal enforcement, 696-698, 702
    federal role, 697, 706-708
    full faith and credit clause, applicability of,
      714
    jurisdiction, 704, 706-708
    parent locator service, 714-715
    procreation, restrictions on, 684
    Revised Uniform Reciprocal Enforcement of
      Support Act, 707
    Social Security Act, 699
    Uniform Interstate Family Support Act,
      707-713
    Uniform Reciprocal Enforcement of Support
      Act, 707-708
    wage-withholding, 702
  license suspensions, 702
  liens, 700-702
  passport suspensions, 701
  right to counsel, 697
  tax refund interceptions, 701
  welfare agencies' role, 699
Engagement rings. *See* Gifts in Contemplation of
  marriage
Enoch Arden statutes, 197 *See also* Polygamy
Equitable distribution. *See* Property division
Eugenics movement, 6, 20, 150, 217
Euthanasia. *See* Disabled newborns; Right to die.
Extended family, 371-376

Fair Credit Reporting Act, 701
Family and Medical Leave Act,
  288-294
Family home, deferred sale after divorce,
  640-641
Family privacy. *See also* Privacy
  abortion and, 20-28, 31-35
  as fundamental right, 2-3
  contraception and, 1-4, 9, 13
  education and, 16-18
  historical background, 245n, 229n
  premarital agreements, 138
  same-sex relationships, 57
  sterilization, 872
  summary seizure, 879-885
Family Support Act, 451, 671-672, 784, 789,
  700-702
Family Violence Prevention and Services Act,
  370, 336
Fathers. *See also* Adoption; Paternity; Visitation
  abortion-related rights, 72-77
  adoption consent, 1127-1128
  paternal preference, 728-729
  unmarried fathers' rights

adoption, 1028-1038
  custody, 1028-1038
  fitness, 1028-1032
  visitation, 1029-1036
Federal role in family law, 55-56, 645-651, 756,
  763-769
Fetus. *See also* Abortion; Pregnancy
  as "person," 22-25
  criminal responsibility for fetal injury, 22-25
  father's interest, 72-77
  fetal tissue, 108-109
  fetal murder, 32
  prenatal abuse and neglect, 1121-1123
  quickening distinction, 21-22
  tort liability for injury to, 32
  viability
    defined, 26-27
    medical technology and, 31-32, 52-53
    state's "compelling" interest after, 26-27,
      31-32
Firearms
  custody and, 782
  domestic violence regulations, 345, 346
Fitness. *See* Child custody
Food stamp program, 363-365
Fornication laws, 383
Foster care
  abuse by foster parents, 878
  aging out of care, 965-966
  contributing factors to rising incidence, 962-963
  defined, 953
  District of Columbia litigation,
  extended, 988
    effect on child, 988-989, 1091-1092
  foster care population, 962-963
  foster care reform, 963-964
  foster parents' rights, 960-961
    due process, 966
    liberty interest, 956-961, 982-983
  gay/lesbian youth, 965
  governmental-subsidized, 961
  historical background, 961
  kinship care, 377, 960-961
  New York system critique, 953, 959
  permanency planning, 963, 1099
  pre-removal hearings, 959-960
  "psychological" parent, 961, 996
  reasonable efforts requirements, 964,
    997-999
  rehabilitation services, 997-998
  remedies to system-wide problems
    legislative reform, 978, 988, 996
    judicial reform, 973-981
  removal of children from foster family,
    953-963
  reunification efforts, 963-964, 997-999
  special needs children, 990-992
  "temporary" placement, 1015-1017
  "voluntary" placement, 885, 953-957

Foster Care Independence Act, 965
  aging out of care, 965-966
  gay/lesbian youth, 965
Fraud
  adoption-related, 1027-1028
  for annulment, 207-209
  contraceptive, 456-460
  Internet, 211-212
  marriage fraud in immigration, 211
  regarding artificial insemination, 106
  regarding contraception, 512-515
Freedom of Access to Clinic Entrances Act
      (FACE), 54
Freedom of religion. *See* Religion
Fugitive Felon Act, 841
Full faith and credit
  child custody decree, applicability to, 836-837
  child support decrees, applicability to, 714
  divorce decrees, applicability to, 578-579, 638-
      639
  same-sex partners, applicability to, 176-177
Full Faith and Credit for Child Support Orders
      Act, 709-714

Gestational surrogacy. *See* Surrogacy
Gifts in contemplation of marriage, 123-128
Goldstein, Joseph, Anna Freud & Alfred J. Solnit,
      theories, 770, 800, 822, 884-885
Grandparents
  custody rights, 796
  support duties of grandparents, 1110, 1003
  visitation rights, 789-794, 795-799, 1096
Guardianship
  best interests test, 736-737
  for health care decisionmaking, 99, 108, 421
  of minors, 1097, 1204-1205
  "standby" guardianship, 1205
Guardians ad litem, 814-817
  in child abuse proceedings, 814, 1122
  in custody proceedings, 817
Guidelines. *See* Child support
Gun Free school Zones Act, 55

Hague Convention on the Civil Aspects of Int'l
      Child Abduction, 931-932, 843-845
Hague Convention on Protection of Children and
      Cooperation in Respect of Intercountry
      Adoption, 1083-1084
Hart, H.L.A., 454
Health care. *See* Abortion; Contraception;
      Medical Care
HIV. *See* Acquired Immune Deficiency
      Syndrome
Homelessness, 904, 965, 966, 1064
Homemaker services, 602. *See also* Property
      division; Spousal support
Homicide. *See* Child abuse; Domestic violence
Homosexuality. *See* Same-sex marriage; Sexual
      Orientation

Immigration
  adoption and, 1082-1084
  asylum, 1004-1005
  emancipation and, 1005
  Illegal Immigration Reform and Immigration
      Responsibility Act, 337
  Immigration and Nationality Act, 211
  Immigration and Naturalization Service,
      211, 337, 1004
  Immigration Fraud Amendments, 212
  marriage, 211-212
  privacy, 211
Illegal aliens, 211
Illegitimate children. *See* Nonmarital children
Incest, 184-189
  affinity, 187
  adopted relatives and, 184-186, 188
  civil consequences, 187
  consanguinity, 187
  constitutional issues, 187, 188
  criminal consequences, 187, 188
  historical background, 186-187
  legal effect, 187-188
  policy, 187
  privacy, 187-188
  taboos, reasons for, 189
Indian Child Welfare Act, 1049
Indigents
  abortion, 55, 76
  contraception, 7, 56
  defense of inability to pay, child support,
      696-697
  family cap, 56
  paternity establishment, due process rights,
      455-456
  right to marry, 145-150
  right to divorce, 540-544, 585-586
  welfare reform. *See* Welfare
Infants
  abandoned, 904-905, 1150
  child abuse of, 889
  disabled, 907-909
  Baby Jane Doe case, 907-909
  federal legislation, 907-909
  Infant Doe case, 907
  withholding treatment
    as discrimination, 907
    as neglect, 908-909
Infertility. *See* Artificial insemination; In vitro
      fertilization; Surrogacy.
Informed consent. *See* Consent
Inheritance
  adoption and, 1084, 1088
  common law marriage, 225
  dower, 239-241
  embryos, 1131
  equitable adoption and, 1069, 1070
  estate planning, 444-445
  genetic material, 1116-1118, 1131

Inheritance *(Cont.)*:
 intestate succession rights, cohabitants',
  438-440, 441-443
 living wills, 92, 107
 nonmarital children's rights, 450-453
 posthumous reproduction, 1116-1119, 1131,
  1145-1146
 premarital contracts regarding, 135
 same-sex partners' rights, 438-440,
  441-443
 stepparents, 1087-1088
 Uniform Probate Code, 1087
 will, women's common law disabilities
  regarding, 240
Insurance
 child support, 674
 division of property, 657
 for in vitro fertilization, 1126
 medical, postdivorce, 650
 tort liability, 1009
Internal Revenue Code. *See* Taxation
Internet
 adoption, 1027
 adultery, 500, 497
 assisted conception, 1147
 dating, 113
 divorce, 580, 782
 legislation regulating, 497
 marriage, 211
 virtual visitation, 832
Interspousal immunity. *See* Marriage
Interstate Compact on the Placement of
  Children, 1079, 1080
Intestacy. *See* Inheritance
International Parental Kidnapping Act, 844
In vitro fertilization. *See also* Egg donation;
  Embryo transfers; Surrogacy
 as medical experimentation, 1120-1127
 disputes involving embryos, 1127-1134
 ethical issues, 1121
 insurance for, 1126
 legal issues, 1120-1148
 legislation regulating, 1120
 Medicaid assistance for, 1125-1126
 objections to, 1125
 protected by right to privacy, 1121-1122
Jehovah's Witnesses, 858-859
Joint custody. *See* Child custody
Jurisdiction
 abortion restrictions, 31-35, 53
 adoption jurisdiction, 1078-1079
 annulment jurisdiction, 209
 child custody jurisdiction. *See* Child custody
 child support, jurisdiction
  interstate enforcement. *See* Enforcement of
   support divorce jurisdiction
 comity, 580
 divorce, 573-592. *See also* Divorce

 domestic relations exception to diversity
  jurisdiction, 586-592
 enforcement of support. *See* Enforcement of
  support
 full faith and credit clause
  child custody decrees, applicability to, 700, 714
  child support decrees, applicability to, 714,
   784
  divorce decrees, applicability to, 578-579
  same-sex partners, applicability to, 176-177
 international enforcement of support, 714-715
 interstate enforcement of support. *See*
  Enforcement of support
 paternity establishment, 453-454
 property division. *See* Property division
 spousal support. *See* Spousal support

Juvenile courts. *See* Child abuse and neglect;
  Emancipation
Juvenile Justice Standards. *See* ABA

Lawyers. *See* Attorney
Legitimacy. *See* Nonmarital children; Paternity
Lex loci, rule of, 151
Liens, as enforcement of support obligation,
  639, 698, 702
Life-support, termination of, 90-100. *See also*
  Right to die
Living wills, 92, 107

Maintenance. *See* Spousal support
Marital property. *See also* Property division
  common law property regime, 238, 600
 community property regime, 238, 600
 historical background, 238-242
 managerial rules, 241
 married-women's common law disabilities, 239
 necessaries doctrine, 245
 title theory, 600
 Uniform Marital Property Act (UMPA), 242
Marriage
 age of consent for, 203-207
 antimiscegenation laws, 150-154, 166, 175
 as contract, 114-116
 as status, 115-116
 authorizing officials, 214, 216, 218
 blood tests, 216-218
 breach of promise, 116-123
 ceremonies, 214-215
 changing nature of, 229-235
 common law, 220-227
 confidential marriages, 219
 conflict of laws, 176-177, 263
 constitutional limits on regulation of entry into,
  140-160
 covenant marriage, 538-539, 544
 cross-cultural perspectives, 214
 doctrine of non-intervention, 244-245

domicile, 263
duress, 210
duty of support, 242-250
duty to disclose STD's, 319
employment, 259-270. *See also* Employment
empirical research, 236
evidentiary privileges arising from, 354-360
federal legislation, 154
fraud, 192-193
gender-based roles, 248-250, 378, 477, 493
gender-specific effects, 234-237
gifts in contemplation of, 123-128
good provider role, 246-250
health certificate, 216
HIV-testing, 217
immigration fraud, 212
inmate marriage, 154-156
Internet, 211
interracial marriage, 140-145, 150-154
    attitudes toward, 144
    statistics on, 144-145
interspousal immunity, 315-318, 322, 333,
        530, 532
legal disabilities of married women, 239
    common law, 239
license fees, 216-217
licensure generally, 212-217
limited purpose marriage, 210
managerial rules, 241
marital property regimes, 238, 600. *See also*
        Property division
marital rape, 348-354
marital status discrimination, 412-413, 430, 435
marriage by estoppel, 228
names
    children's surnames, 251-255, 258-261
    married women's, 250-251, 255-258
    same-sex partners, 256
necessaries doctrine, 245
parental consent, 202, 203-204, 205-206
premarital contracts, 128-140. *See also*
        Premarital Contracts
premarital controversies, 116-123
presumptions of marriage validity, 205
procedural restrictions on, 212-228
pro-marriage policies, 154
proxy marriage, 218-219
putative spouse doctrine, 227-228
remarriage
    child support, effect on, 685-686
    restraints on, 684
    spousal support, effect on, 632-633
same sex. *See* Civil unions; Sexual Orientation
slave marriages, 229-231
solemnization, 212, 216
state regulation of entry into, 160-228
statistics on, 236-237
substantive restrictions on, 160-207

age, 201-207
bigamy/polygamy, 189-201
incest, 184-189
poverty-related, 145-157
race, 140-145
same-sex, 160-184
teen marriages, 205-207
torts, interspousal, 315-325
tort actions vs. third parties for interference
        with marriage, 307-315
tribal marriages, 219
void/voidable distinction, 205
waiting periods, 216
welfare reform, 154, 206
work-family conflict, 290-296, 298-301
wiretapping, 320-322
Marriage agreements. *See* Premarital contracts;
        Separation agreements
"Mature minor" rule, generally, 77-78, 82,
        1104-1105. *See also* Abortion;
        Emancipation
Marriage Protection Act, 178-179
Mediation. *See* Alternative dispute resolution;
        Child custody mediation
Medicaid
    funding for abortion, 49
    funding for IVF, 1126
Marriage Protection Act, 178-178
Medical decisionmaking
    cohabitants, 415-422
    consent requirements for abortion
        parental, 77-89
        spousal, 72-77
    disabled newborns, 907-909
    durable powers of attorney for health care
        decisionmaking, 93
    living wills, 92, 107
    mature minor, 77-78, 82
    mental commitment of child, 870-873
    refusal of treatment, 901
    religious beliefs and, 107
    right to die, 90-100
Melson Formula. *See* Child support
Mental health
    as factor in custody decisionmaking, 819
    as factor in termination of parental rights, 998
Mental hospitals
    institutionalization of juveniles, 867-873
    procedural safeguards, 867-871
    statistics on, 872
    "voluntary" commitment, 871
Military
    adultery, 498
    discrimination against gays/lesbians, 411-412
    Don't Ask, Don't Tell, 411-412, 413
Mill, John Stuart, 67, 382
Minors. *See* Adolescents; Children
Miscegenation statutes. *See* Marriage

Model Penal Code. *See* ALI
Modification
  child support, 685-690
    employment changes, 686-690
    remarriage, 685-686
    retroactive, 686
  custody and visitation, 822-833. *See also* Child
    Custody
    standards, 822-823
    relocation, 823-833
  jurisdiction. *See also* Jurisdiction
    full faith and credit clause, application of, 707
    Uniform Interstate Family Support Act,
      707-709, 712
  separation agreements, 715
  spousal support
    career changes, effect of, 686-691
    changes in circumstances, 669-674
    cohabitation of former spouse, effect of, 674
    cost of living adjustments, automatic, 673
    decrease in income as basis, 673
    increase in income as basis, 673
  Uniform Marriage and Divorce Act, 519,
    598-601
"Mommy track," 305-306. *See also*
    Employment
Mormonism, 193-201. *See also* Polygamy
Multiethnic Placement Act, 976-977

Names
  children's surnames, 251-255, 258-261
  domestic violence victims, 256-257
  married women's, 250-251, 255-258
  men's surnames, 257
  transgender persons, 256
Native American
  adoption, 1045
  common law marriage and, 219-220
  custody, 1049-1050
  freedom of religion, 219
  same-sex relationships, 180
  tribal marriage, 219
Necessaries doctrine, 245
Neglect. *See* Child abuse
Nepotism. *See* Employment
Newborns. *See* Infants
Nonmarital children. *See* Paternity; Unmarried
    Parents
  custody issues, 458-478
  due process rights, 455, 463, 469-471
  equal protection, 460-463, 465-469
  historical background, 447
  immigration, 477
  inheritance rights, 452-456
  jurisdiction, 454-455
  legal disabilities, 451-456
  paternity establishment, 448-456
  qualification for AFDC, 455-456

  statutes of limitations for paternity
    establishment, 448-451
  support rights of, 448-460
  visitation by father, 460-478
  Uniform Parentage Act, 452
Nonpayment of support. *See* Enforcement of
    support
Notice
  biological father's right to, in adoption
    decisionmaking, 469-470
  ex parte divorce and, 574-575, 579
  foster parents' right to, removal context, 963
  parental right to, in abortion decisionmaking,
    78
  spousal right to, in abortion decisionmaking, 76

Obscenity
  Comstock laws, 5-6
  historical background, 5-6
  relationship to laws on contraception, 5-9
Omnibus Budget Reconciliation Act, 97
Orphan train, 961, 1070

Parental kidnapping. *See* Abduction
Parental Kidnapping Prevention Act, 708,
    837-841, 1074, 1078
Parental termination. *See* Termination of
    parental rights
Parent-child disputes
  abortion-related, 77-89
  education-related, 16-20
  emancipation, 1014-1018
  guardianship, 867-870
  medical care, 867-870, 1004
  reasonable parent standard, 892, 1009-1011
  testimonial privilege, 360
  wiretapping, 1010
Parent locator service, 451, 714, 841
Parental "licensing," 1060
Paternalism, legal
  regarding abortion, 34, 50, 106
  regarding cohabitation/fornication laws, 382
  regarding marriage, 129, 156, 217
  regarding medical decisionmaking, 106, 1004
Paternity. *See also* Legitimacy; Nonmarital children
  admissible evidence, 454
  artificial insemination, 1134-1136
    sperm donors, parental status, 1128,
      1135-1137, 1141
  blood tests to establish, 448, 454, 463-464
  disestablishment of, 474-475
  "good cause" refusal to identify, 1041
  indigent defendants, 455
  jurisdiction to establish, 453-454
  jury composition, 455
  misrepresentation as defense to support, 456-459
  nonmarital child's inheritance claims,
    450-453

presumption of legitimacy, 472-477, 484, 1120, 1144
presumption of paternity, 473-476
privacy, 459
probability of paternity, 454
problems of proof, 454-456
purpose of establishing, 450
putative father registry, 527, 1147
same-sex couples and, 478-485
standard of proof, 455-456
statutes of limitation, 447-451
voluntary establishment of, 456
Uniform Interstate Family Support Act, 454
Uniform Parentage Act, 476, 479
Patriot Act, 323
Pension benefits. *See* Property division;
  Retirement benefits
Personal Responsibility and Work
  Opportunity Reconciliation Act, 55, 83, 206,
    377, 451, 689, 700-701, 708, 714-715,
    1003, 1011
Physicians
  duty to report abuse, 924-930
  role in maternal-fetal conflicts, 32, 48, 86
Polyamory, 200-201
Polygamy, 189-201
  adoption and, 199
  child bigamy laws, 199
  civil consequences, 197
  conflict of laws, 199
  constitutional issues, 198
  criminal consequences, 197
  custody, 199
  Enoch Arden statutes, 197
  exploitation of women, 199
  feminism and, 199-201
  freedom of religion, 197
  historical background, 197-201
  policy reasons to regulate, 198
  privacy-related concerns, 198
  statistics on, 197, 201
  validity of, 189, 198
  zoning, 391
Pregnancy. *See also* Abortion; Contraception
  adolescent, 80-89
  Cesarean section forced, 104
  discrimination, 270-285
  fetal-protection policy, 284
  living wills and, 92, 107
  prenatal torts, 32
  refusal of treatment during, 104
  substance abuse during, 999-1000
  surgical intervention, 104
  terminal illness and, 90-100
Pregnancy Discrimination Act (PDA), 14,
    276-285
Premarital contracts, 128-140
  confidential relationship and, 138

contractual freedom regarding, 138
defined, 135
difference from ordinary contracts, 136
disclosure, 136-138
divorce, as inducing, 135
divorce bonuses, 139
duress in execution, 138-139
enforcement, time of, 138
fairness requirements, 135-137
gender issues, 137
inheritance, 138
policy underlying, 136
privacy, 138
representation, 138-140
Uniform Premarital Agreement Act, 132, 136
unconscionability, 136
voluntary requirements, 138, 140
Premartial controversies. *See also* Premartial
    contracts
  breach of promise, 116-123, 126, 127
  gifts in contemplation of marriage, 123-128
Principles of the Law of Family Dissolution.
    See ALI
Privacy
  abortion and, 20-28, 31, 72-77
  adoption records and, 1093
  adultery, 497
  AIDS and, 107-108
  attorneys' sexual misconduct, 572
  breastfeeding, 299
  "closet," 69, 410, 440, 750
  cohabitation/fornication laws, 379-383
  common law marriage and, 220
  communes and, 363
  conflict of wives and husbands' rights, 72-77
  conflict of parent-child rights, 77-89
  contraceptives and, 1-9, 13-14
  courtship, 111-114
  divorce and, 580, 596-597, 645
  domestic violence, 380, 387
  duty to disclose STD's, 319
  family leave and, 295
  family privacy distinguished, 1-4, 13-14,
    18, 76
  First Amendment and, 422-423
  grandparents' visitation statutes, 796
  immigration fraud and, 212
  individual right to privacy distinguished, 13-5
  international protections, 356
  marital rape, 353
  marital right distinguished, 1-4, 74
  meanings of, 1-15
  military, 380-381, 412
  minors' rights, 76
  modification, custody, 829
  nonmarital children, 474
  parental leaves, 297, 300
  parental liability laws, 1010

Privacy (*Cont.*):
  polygamy and, 191
  premarital agreements, 135
  right to die, 90-100
  right to marry, 146-158, 163
  right to use reproductive technologies, 1122
  roots of constitutional doctrine, 1-15, 20
  sexual orientation and, 57-66, *See also* sexual
    orientation
  state constitutions and, 49n, 68-69, 422
Procreation. *See* Abortion; Contraception;
  Privacy
Professional responsibility. *See* Attorney
Property division
  ALI, Family Dissolution, Principles of. *See* ALI
  bankruptcy. *See* Bankruptcy
  celebrity status, 658
  characterization of property, 600, 662, 691
  choice of law, 708
  common law property regimes, 600
  community property regimes, 600, 603-605
  contribution theory, 604-605
    homemaking as contribution, 604
  debt, allocation of, 604
  disability pay, 649, 658
  dissipation, 626, 652
  earning capacity, 654-657
  equitable distribution, 600-604
  fault, role in, 593, 627, 654, 692
  goodwill value of business, 657
  guidelines, 737
  home, ownership of, 754, 757
  homemaker services, 604
  hotchpot approach, 602-603
  insurance, 657-658
  intangible assets, 657
  jurisdiction. *See* Jurisdiction
  liens, 639, 701
  lost future earnings, 658
  marital misconduct as factor, 604
  marital property systems generally, 600
  medical coverage, 650
  need-based theory, 605-606
  "new" property, 653
  no-fault, 597-599
  partnership theory, 600, 602
  pension benefits, 641-649, 657
  personal injury awards, 658
  professional degrees and licenses, 650-657
  retirement benefits, 642-649
  separate property, 657
  separate vs. marital property,
    characterization, 620-625
  sex discrimination, 605
  taxation, 659-663
  title theory, 595-695
  Uniform Marital Property Act, 600
  Uniform Marriage and Divorce Act, 519,
    598-603

  valuation, 655
  workers' compensation, 658
Pro se divorce. *See* divorce
Proxy marriages. *See* Marriage
Punishment. *See* Child abuse and neglect;
  Domestic violence
Putative spouse doctrine, 227-228. *See also*
  Marriage

Qualified domestic relations orders, (QDRO's),
  647-648. *See also* Property division;
  Retirement benefits

Race
  adoption, factor in, 1038-1051
  custody, factor in, 734-737
  contraception and, 10-11
  domestic violence, 328-329, 337
  foster care, 1046-1051
  marriage, 140-145, 150-153
  obstetrical intervention, 106-107
  spousal support and, 616
  surrogacy and, 1145
Rape
  marital, 347-350, 352-354
  reform legislation, 352
  statutory, 83-84, 86, 207, 351, 459
Reciprocal Beneficiaries Act, 173. *See also*
  Marriage; Sexual orientation
Religion, role of
  adoption, 1050-1051
  bigamy, 190
  child abuse reporting, 926
  child custody, 777-783
  child labor, 859-862
  divorce 547-552
  education, 863-866
  housing discrimination, 429
  neglect, factor in, 906
Relocation controversies. *See* Child custody
Remarriage. *See* Marriage
Removal of children from home. *See* Child abuse
  and neglect; Foster care; Termination of
  parental rights
Reproductive control. *See* Abortion;
  Contraception; Pregnancy; Sterilization
Reproductive technologies, 1102-1147. *See also*
  Artificial insemination; Egg donation; In
  vitro fertilization; Surrogacy
Restatement of Conflict of Laws, 263
Restatement of Restitution, 395
Restatement (Second) of Conflict of Laws, 177,
  263, 1078
Restatement (Second) of Torts, 312, 528,
  890-891, 1009
Restatement (Third) of Law Governing Lawyers,
  562, 628, 928, 1064
Restrictions on marriage, 160-207
  age, 201-207

bigamy, 189-201
conflict of laws. *See* Conflict of laws
constitutional issues, 140-207
incest statutes, 184-189
poverty-related, 145-157
procedural, 212-228
race, 140-145
same-sex marriages, 160-184
state-of-mind, 205-207
substantive, 140-207
Retirement Equity Act, 647
Retirement benefits, 642-649
bankruptcy and, 649
division of, 644-649
Employee Retirement Income Security Act,
646-650
federal regulation of private pension plans,
646-648
military retirement benefits, 647
qualified domestic relations orders, 646-647
railroad employees' benefits, 647
Retirement Equity Act, 646
types of pension plans, 645-646
Uniformed Services Former Spouses
Protection Act, 648
valuation issues, 648
vested vs. unvested, 644-645
Revised Uniform Reciprocal Enforcement of
Support Act, 707, 708
Right to die, 90-100
Romeo and Juliet statutes, 72, 381

Same-sex marriage. *See also* Civil unions;
Domestic partnerships; Sexual
orientation
adoption, 1051-1660
analogy to racial discrimination, 146
assisted conception, 1147
child support, 478-485
commitment ceremonies, 395
constitutional amendments,
federal, 179
state, 171, 172, 173, 178, 179
custody-related issues, 806-806
Defense of Marriage Act, 174, 176-179,
443, 581, 1090, 1091
dissolution, 536-538, 580-582
domestic violence, 422-424
empirical research, 237
employment discrimination, 405, 409,
411, 412
estate planning issues, 444-445
gifts in contemplation of marriage, 123-128
inheritance issues, 438-447
international developments, 180
jurisdictional issues, 580-582
Massachusetts experience, 172
names, 256

Navajo nation, 180
pending litigation, 174, 443, 537n
privacy-related issues 173-174, 179
property-related issues, 538
sodomy laws, 170
spousal support, 538
statistics, 237
tort law, 404
transgender persons, 180-181
validity, 174, 177
Sanger, Margaret, 10
Schiavo, Terri, 99-100
Schools. *See* Education
Separation agreements
ALI, Family Dissolution, Principles of,
603-608
attorneys' role, 791
children's rights regarding, 703-705
divorce decrees based on, 15, 717-720
fraud, 719
impact of federal guidelines on, 720
incorporation, 718
integrated bargain, 718-719
modification, 719, 720, 721
policy favoring settlement, 717, 718
support provisions, 720-721
unconscionability, 717, 720, 721
Uniform Marriage and Divorce Act, 716, 717,
718, 719
Sex education, 378, 866-867
Sexual abuse. *See* Child abuse and neglect
Sexual child abuse. *See* Child abuse
and neglect
Sexual orientation. *See also* Civil Unions;
Domestic partnerships
adolescents, 965, 1002-1003
adoption by same-sex partners, 446
analogy to race, 175-176
as factor in custody dispute, 743-750,
800-805
bias concerning, 748-749
constitutional issues, 749
judicial approaches, 748-749
nexus test, 749-750
restrictions on visitation, 781-782
civil unions, 151, 160-184, 215, 237, 394, 395,
404, 444, 485, 536-538, 581-582, 803,
806, 1089, 1119
"closet," 69, 173, 410-411, 440, 442,
497, 750, 871
domestic violence, 425-426
emancipation and, 1002-1003
empirical research, children's development,
805-806
employment discrimination, 405-415
equal protection, 171, 173-174,
178-179
gay liberation movement, 172, 176

Sexual orientation (*Cont.*):
  housing discrimination, 426-438
  inheritance rights, 438-440, 441-447
  medical decisionmaking for partner, 415-419
  military, 411-412
  privacy right, 57-66, 173
  property rights of cohabitants at dissolution, 394
  same-sex marriage, validity of, 160-181
    conflict of laws, 176-179
    debate within gay community, 176
  sodomy laws and, 57-66, 381-382
  statistics, 361, 378
  surrogacy and, 1147
  transgender persons, 180-181
  transsexuals, 180-181
Single-parent families, 368-370, 447, 699. *See also* Child support; Nonmarital children; Unmarried parents
Social Security Act, 699
Sodomy laws. *See* Sexual orientation
Spousal abuse. *See* Domestic Violence
Spousal consent. *See* Consent
Sperm donors, parental status of, 1105, 1141
Spousal support, 605-666
  ALI, Family Dissolution, Principles of. *See* ALI
  attorneys' fees, 628
  bankruptcy, effect of, 634-640
  cohabitation of former spouse, effect, 633
  "compensatory spousal payments," 610-611
  determination of need, 605, 610-612
  doctrine of nonintervention (during marriage), 242-246
  duration of support, 612, 626
  empirical research, 656
  enforcement. *See* Enforcement of support
  fault, role in, 508-509, 611-612
  feminist concerns, 612, 616, 628
  guidelines for, 656
  historical background, 593-594
  income sharing, 616-617
  jurisdiction. *See* Jurisdiction
  loss compensation, 615-616
  modification of, 632-633
  need-based theory, 611-612
  no-fault divorce and, 613
  pension benefits, 657
  professional licenses and degrees, 650-659
  racial stereotypes, 616
  rehabilitation theory, 614
  remarriage, effect of, 632-633
  standard of living, 613-614
  taxation, 659
  termination 630-633
  theories of, 612-617
  Uniform Marriage and Divorce Act, 602-605, 610

Stepparents
  adoption, 1087-1089
  child support obligations, 684
  custody rights, 799
  visitation rights, 799
Sterilization, 20, 872. *See also* Contraception
Substance abuse
  as factor in abuse and neglect, 877, 923, 994, 999
  as grounds for divorce, 509
  as grounds for termination of parental rights, 994, 999
  during pregnancy, 923-924
Summary seizure, 872-883. *See also* Child abuse and neglect
Surrogacy. *See also* Embryo transfers; In vitro fertilization
  adoption and, 1107-1109
  artificial insemination, 1109
  as alternative to adoption, 1107
  as babyselling, 1107
  breach of contract
    by sperm donor and wife, 1107
    by surrogate, 1107
  child support and, 1110
  conflict of laws issues, 1109
  constitutional issues, 1108
  custody, 1107-1110
  enforcement of contract, 1107
  exploitation aspects, 1108
  feminist views, 1108
  gestation, 1109
  Israeli law, 1146
  legislative responses to, 1109
  obstacles to paternity establishment by sperm donor, 1108
  public policy concerns, 1109
  relevance of race, 1108
  same-sex couples, use of, 1114, 1117
  sperm donor's rights, 1108
  traditional, 1107-1110
  Uniform Parentage Act, 1109, 1136
  Uniform Status of Children of Assisted Conception Act, 1147
  validity of surrogacy agreement, 1107-1108

Taxation
  adoption credit, 1066
  child support, 663, 666
  dependency exemptions, 663
  property division, 662-663
  spousal support, 661
Technology
  abortion and, 32
  new reproductive technologies, 1113-1139
  privacy, 10
Tender years presumption. *See* Child custody

Termination of parental rights, 981-999
  abandonment, as factor in, 1034, 1035
  child-initiated, 1014-1020
  dispensing with need for adoption
    consent, 1034-1035
  biological fathers' rights, 1028-1037
  procedures, 981-999
  right to counsel, 987-988
  standard of proof, 981-988
  substance abuse, 999
  unfitness, as factor in, 460-463
  unknown father's rights, 1035-1036
  vague statutory standards, 885
Thompson, Judith Jarvis, 37-39
Title II, 336, 766
Title III, 320-325, 336-337, 497
Title IV-D, 671, 689, 702
Title IV-E, 377
Tide VII, 14, 63, 181, 267, 268, 271, 276-282,
    300-301, 289-290, 304-307, 309, 325
Torts
  alienation of affections, 307-315
  criminal conversation, 307-315
  custodial interference, 842
  intentional infliction of emotional
    distress, 315
  intraspousal immunity, 315-320
  intraspousal torts, 315-320
  loss of consortium, 314-315
  parental liability, 1010-1011
  parent-child immunity, 1005-1014
  prenatal torts, 1013-1014
  procedure, joinder, 524-532
  reasonable parent standard, 1005-1007, 1009
  Restatement (Second) of Torts
    duty to disclose sexually transmitted disease, 319
    justifiable use of force, 890-891
  sexual misconduct, 572
  sexual torts, 315-320
  wrongful adoption, 1100
  wrongful life, 1014, 1123
Transsexuals. *See* Sexual Orientation
Transgender. *See* Sexual Orientation.

Unemployment compensation
  cohabitant's right to. *See* Employment
Uniform Adoption Act (UAA), 1027, 1035, 1080,
    1095, 1101
Uniform Child Abduction Prevention Act,
    844-845
Uniform Child Custody Jurisdiction Act
    (UCCJA), 833, 837, 841, 1074, 1078
Uniform Child Custody Jurisdiction and
    Enforcement Act (UCCJEA), 833, 838,
    1080
Uniform Child Witness Testimony by Alternative
    Methods Act, 950
Uniform Interstate Family Support Act (UIFSA),
    707-709, 712-713

Uniform Marital Property Act (UMPA),
    239n,242, 600
Uniform Marriage and Divorce Act (UMDA)
  best interests of the child, 733
  common law marriage, 226
  custody, 685, 733
  background, formation, 567-568, 519-520
  grounds for dissolution, 520-521
  homemaker services, 602
  minor's marriage, 207
  modification of child support, 685
  modification of custody, 822
  modification of spousal support, 632-633, 685
  property division, 598, 601, 602, 603, 604,
    605, 626, 632
  putative spouse doctrine, 227
  rejection of fault, 519-520
  separation agreements, 716, 717, 718-719,
    720
  sexual conduct, relevance of, 746
  spousal support, 610, 614, 616, 632,
    634, 685
  tribal marriages, 219
Uniform Marriage Evasion Act, 151
Uniform Parentage Act (UPA), 452, 453, 456,
    457, 472, 476, 479, 666, 801, 805, 1034,
    1035, 1104, 1109, 1110, 1136, 1141
  artificial insemination, 1104, 1106
  nonmarital children, 452
  paternity, establishment, 453, 473-474,
    1034-1035
Uniform Premarital Agreement Act, 132, 136
Uniform Probate Code, 441, 603, 1088, 1116
Uniform Putative and Unknown Fathers Act, 1035
Uniform Reciprocal Enforcement of Support Act
    (URESA), 707
Uniform Status of Children of Assisted
    Conception Act, 1109, 1147
Uniform Support of Dependents Law, 707
United Nations Universal Declaration of Human
    Rights, 323
Unmarried couples. *See* Cohabitation; Sexual
    orientation
Unmarried parents. *See also* Nonmarital children
  adoption and, 469-470
  child support obligations, 448-452
  constitutional rights, 460-473
  custodial rights of unmarried mothers, 469
  custodial rights of unmarried fathers,
    460-473, 1028-1038
  due process protection, 455, 469
  equal protection, 448-450, 452, 469
  inheritance rights of children, 450,
    451, 452
  legal parenthood, criteria for, 469-471
  paternity suits. *See* Paternity
  presumed fathers, parental rights of,
    453, 473-474
  statistics, 447

Unmarried parents (*Cont.*):
  Uniform Parentage Act (UPA), 453
  visitation rights of unwed fathers, 463-469
Unwed fathers. *See* Unmarried parents

Venereal disease, 216-218. *See also* Acquired
        Immune Deficiency Syndrome
Viability. *See* Abortion; Fetus; Pregnancy
Victims of Trafficking and Violence Protection
        Act, 212, 337
Violence. *See* Child abuse and neglect; Domestic
        violence
Violence Against Women Act (VAWA), 55,
Violence Against Women Reauthorization Act,
        212, 337
Visitation. *See also* Adoption; Custody
  Acquired Immune Deficiency Syndrome as
        factor, 782
  biological parents' right, 1095, 1096
  child's refusal to visit, 783
  child support, relationship to, 784-789
  conditions on
      regarding homosexual parents, 781, 791-808,
      regarding religion, 781
      regarding sexual abuse, 777-783
      regarding sexual conduct, 781
      regarding smoking, 782
      relocation, 827-833
  custodial interference with, 842
  denial of, 784-787
  grandparents' rights, 789-794, 795-799, 1096
  hospital visitation, 182, 421-422, 445

interference with, 784-789, 929
judicial discretion in fashioning,
        779-780
Lizzie's Law, 762
postadoption visitation rights, 797,
        1095, 1096
privacy-related concerns, 797
siblings' rights, postadoption, 1096
statistics on, 788-789
supervised visitation, 777-782
stepparents' visitation rights, 1095, 1096
unsupervised visitation, 762, 777-780

Walker, Lenore, 329-331, 334,
Weitzman, Lenore, 604-640, 657
Welfare, 46, 56, 83, 149, 154, 199, 206, 294, 344,
        367, 377n,382, 454-455, 532, 540-542,
        547, 583-585, 633, 647, 689-695, 699,
        702n,703n,841, 899, 903n,906, 973-
        981, 1019, 1027, 1038, 1045-1051,
        1055n,739, 754, 765, 766, 767, 784,
        785, 1109-1110, 1245. *See also* Personal
        Responsibility and Work Opportunity
        Reconciliation Act.
Wills, 92, 107. *See also* Inheritance, living wills.
Wiretapping, 9, 320-324, 497, 1010
Work-family conflict, 303-306
Wrongful adoption, 1101
Wrongful birth, recovery for, 1014, 1023
Wrongful life, 1014, 1123

Zoning, 361, 365-368, 375, 434